Introducing

the
Prentice Hall Library

featuring the
Penguin Literature Library

Hundreds of titles from
the world's foremost publisher
of classic and contemporary
favorites, from
Beowulf to *Black Hawk Down*

CALIFORNIA TEACHER'S EDITION

PRENTICE HALL LITERATURE

Timeless Voices, Timeless Themes

GOLD LEVEL

ISBN 0-13-054812-X

2 3 4 5 6 7 8 9 10   05 04 03 02

Prentice Hall

Upper Saddle River, New Jersey
Glenview, Illinois
Needham, Massachusetts

Comprehensive standards-based reading support

The interactive student text features:

- *Reading and literary analysis support before, during, and after every selection*
- *A clean, one-column design that mirrors the format of a novel*
- *Point-of-use reading and literary analysis questions that ensure reading mastery*
- *Easy-to-find definitions of key vocabulary*
- *Built-in comprehension checks*
- *Background information at point of use*

Before

Introduce strategies and increase comprehension through consistent instruction and strategies that precede each selection: preview, literary analysis, and reading strategy.

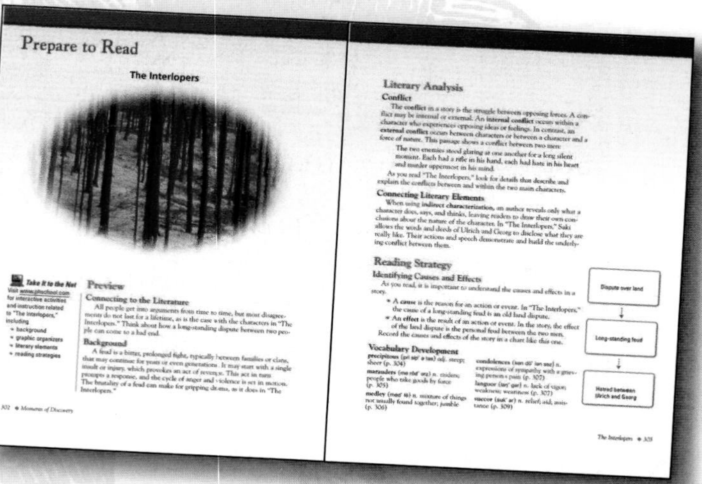

Prepare to Read

The Interlopers

Take It to the Net Visit www.phschool.com for interactive activities and instruction related to "The Interlopers," including
- background
- graphic organizers
- literary elements
- reading strategies

Preview

Connecting to the Literature

All people get into arguments from time to time, but most disagreements do not last for a lifetime, as is the case with the characters in "The Interlopers." Think about how a long-standing dispute between two people can come to a bad end.

Background

A feud is a bitter, prolonged fight, typically between families or clans, that may continue for years or even generations. It may start with a single insult or injury, which provokes an act of revenge. This act in turn prompts a response, and the cycle of anger and violence is set in motion. The brutality of a feud can make for gripping drama, as it does in "The Interlopers."

302 ◆ Moments of Discovery

Literary Analysis

Conflict

The **conflict** in a story is the struggle between opposing forces. A conflict may be internal or external. An **internal conflict** occurs within a character who experiences opposing ideas or feelings. In contrast, an **external conflict** occurs between characters or between a character and a force of nature. This passage shows a conflict between two men:

The two enemies stood glaring at one another for a long silent moment. Each had a rifle in his hand, each had hate in his heart and murder uppermost in his mind.

As you read "The Interlopers," look for details that describe and explain the conflicts between and within the two main characters.

Connecting Literary Elements

When using **indirect characterization**, an author reveals only what a character does, says, and thinks, leaving readers to draw their own conclusions about the nature of the character. In "The Interlopers," Saki allows the words and deeds of Ulrich and Georg to disclose what they are really like. Their actions and speech demonstrate and build the underlying conflict between them.

Reading Strategy

Identifying Causes and Effects

As you read, it is important to understand the causes and effects in a story.

- A **cause** is the reason for an action or event. In "The Interlopers," the cause of a long-standing feud is an old land dispute.
- An **effect** is the result of an action or event. In the story, the effect of the land dispute is the personal feud between the two men.

Record the causes and effects of the story in a chart like this one.

Dispute over land → Long-standing feud → Hatred between Ulrich and Georg

Vocabulary Development

precipitous (prē sip′ ə təs) *adj.* steep; sheer (p. 304)

marauders (mə rôd′ ərz) *n.* raiders; people who take goods by force (p. 305)

medley (med′ lē) *n.* mixture of things not usually found together; jumble (p. 306)

condolences (kən dō′ lən səz) *n.* expressions of sympathy with a grieving person's pain (p. 307)

languor (laŋ′ gər) *n.* lack of vigor; weakness; weariness (p. 307)

succor (suk′ ər) *n.* relief; aid; assistance (p. 309)

The Interlopers ◆ 303

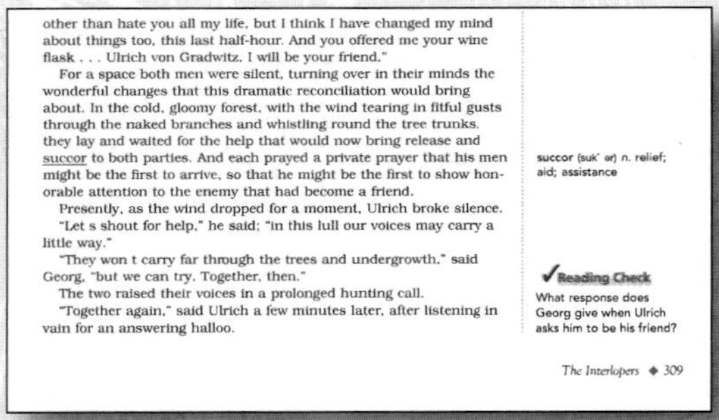

other than hate you all my life, but I think I have changed my mind about things too, this last half-hour. And you offered me your wine flask . . . Ulrich von Gradwitz, I will be your friend."

For a space both men were silent, turning over in their minds the wonderful changes that this dramatic reconciliation would bring about. In the cold, gloomy forest, with the wind tearing in fitful gusts through the naked branches and whistling round the tree trunks, they lay and waited for the help that would now bring release and succor to both parties. And each prayed a private prayer that his men might be the first to arrive, so that he might be the first to show honorable attention to the enemy that had become a friend.

Presently, as the wind dropped for a moment, Ulrich broke silence. "Let s shout for help," he said; "in this lull our voices may carry a little way."

"They won t carry far through the trees and undergrowth," said Georg, "but we can try. Together, then."

The two raised their voices in a prolonged hunting call.

"Together again," said Ulrich a few minutes later, after listening in vain for an answering halloo.

succor (suk′ ər) n. relief; aid; assistance

✓**Reading Check**

What response does Georg give when Ulrich asks him to be his friend?

The Interlopers ◆ 309

During

Reinforce the literary analysis and reading strategies introduced in the Prepare to Read section through point-of-use annotations in the side column of each selection.

After

Review and assess comprehension of reading selection by reviewing, applying, and extending the literary analysis and reading strategies that accompany the selection.

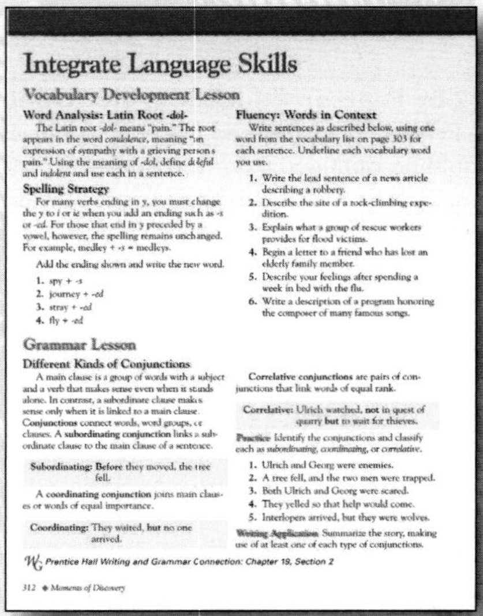

Integrate Language Skills

Vocabulary Development Lesson

Word Analysis: Latin Root -dol-

The Latin root *-dol-* means "pain." The root appears in the word *condolence*, meaning "an expression of sympathy with a grieving person s pain." Using the meaning of *-dol*, define *doleful* and *indolent* and use each in a sentence.

Spelling Strategy

For many verbs ending in y, you must change the y to *i* or *ie* when you add an ending such as *-s* or *-ed*. For those that end in y preceded by a vowel, however, the spelling remains unchanged. For example, medley + *-s* = medleys.

Add the ending shown and write the new word.

1. spy + *-s*
2. journey + *-ed*
3. stray + *-ed*
4. fly + *-ed*

Fluency: Words in Context

Write sentences as described below, using one word from the vocabulary list on page 303 for each sentence. Underline each vocabulary word you use.

1. Write the lead sentence of a news article describing a robbery.
2. Describe the site of a rock-climbing expedition.
3. Explain what a group of rescue workers provides for flood victims.
4. Begin a letter to a friend who has lost an elderly family member.
5. Describe your feelings after spending a week in bed with the flu.
6. Write a description of a program honoring the composer of many famous songs.

Grammar Lesson

Different Kinds of Conjunctions

A main clause is a group of words with a subject and a verb that makes sense even when it stands alone. In contrast, a subordinate clause makes sense only when it is linked to a main clause. **Conjunctions** connect words, word groups, or clauses. A **subordinating conjunction** links a subordinate clause to the main clause of a sentence.

Subordinating: Before they moved, the tree fell.

A **coordinating conjunction** joins main clauses or words of equal importance.

Coordinating: They waited, **but** no one arrived.

Correlative conjunctions are pairs of conjunctions that link words of equal rank.

Correlative: Ulrich watched, **not** in quest of quarry **but** to wait for thieves.

Practice Identify the conjunctions and classify each as *subordinating, coordinating,* or *correlative*.

1. Ulrich and Georg were enemies.
2. A tree fell, and the two men were trapped.
3. Both Ulrich and Georg were scared.
4. They yelled so that help would come.
5. Interlopers arrived, but they were wolves.

Writing Application Summarize the story, making use of at least one of each type of conjunctions.

Prentice Hall Writing and Grammar Connection: Chapter 19, Section 2

312 ◆ Moments of Discovery

Manage teacher resources effectively

Teacher's Edition

The California Teacher's Edition provides

- Direct instruction and customization notes for varying levels of learners
- Complete lesson planners for every unit
- An integrated components guide for every selection
- Complete correlation to the California standards

Resource Pro® CD-ROM with Planning Express Software

This CD-ROM provides electronic access to all selection-specific print materials. Create customized lesson plans and download California standards from the web with the Local Objectives Editor.

Time and Resource Manager

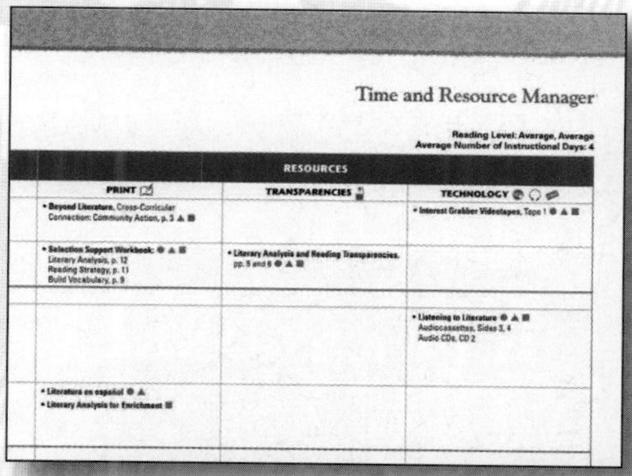

Save time with this unique planning tool that precedes *every* selection and provides a components guide with page references and suggestions for block scheduling.

California Language Arts Standards and Framework Handbook

Created especially for California teachers, this handbook demonstrates where the California standards are presented within the student text and highlights how the program will support teachers in meeting the California Standards and Framework. The Handbook includes

- Research-Based Help for the Teaching of Reading
- California Standards: Progression and Background
- California High School Exit Exam correlation

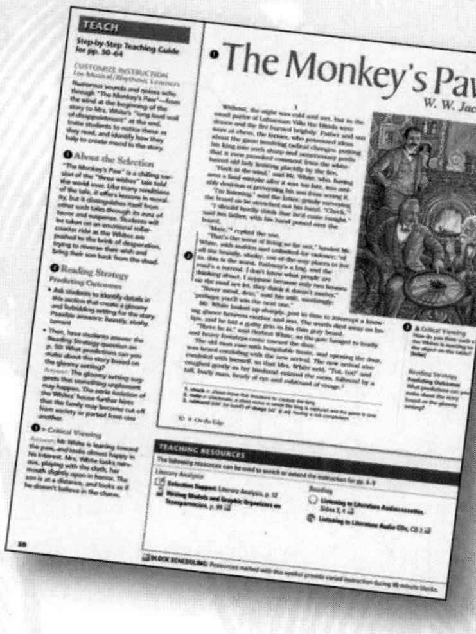

Step-by-Step Teaching Guide

Organize your lessons with this detailed guide that includes lesson objectives, strategies for monitoring student progress, instruction for reteaching key skills, and a suggested pacing guide for every selection. Step-by-step instruction, correlated to the California standards, is provided in the Teacher's Edition column notes within each selection.

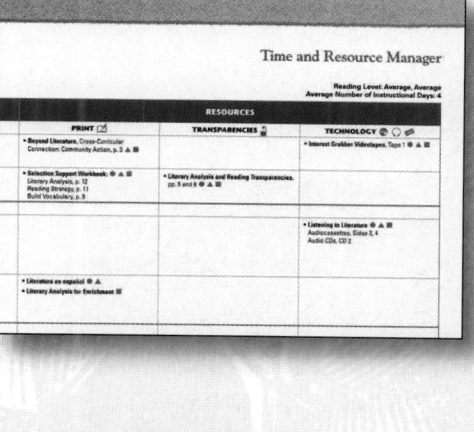

Unmatched reading instruction and practice for every level of learner

The Reading Achievement System provides comprehensive support for all levels of readers.

Teaching Guidebook for Universal Access

Identify issues affecting struggling readers, English-language learners, and special education students.

Reading Diagnostic and Improvement Plan

Assess students' mastery of reading skills, identify areas of weakness, and prescribe an improvement plan based on diagnostic test results. Skills support and lessons are provided in Basic Reading Skills: Comprehensive Lessons for Improvement.

Basic Reading Skills: Comprehensive Lessons for Improvement

Reveal the wonder of literature to *all* your students! Lesson plans, practice sheets, and transparencies help you meet the specific needs of struggling readers and English-language learners.

Reader's Companion

Review and reinforce key literary skills with this consumable interactive student workbook that provides

- Reproductions of selections from the Student Edition
- Write-on lines in the margins so students can take notes at point of use
- Critical thinking and comprehension questions throughout and after each selection
- Pronunciation guides and definitions of key vocabulary words

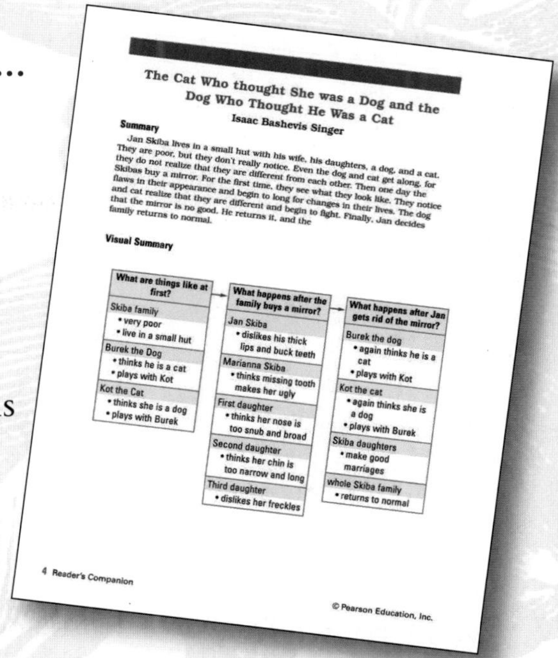

The Cat Who thought She was a Dog and the Dog Who Thought He Was a Cat

Isaac Bashevis Singer

Summary

Jan Skiba lives in a small hut with his wife, his daughters, a dog, and a cat. They are poor, but they don't really notice. Even the dog and cat get along, for they do not realize that they are different from each other. Then one day the Skibas buy a mirror. For the first time, they see what they look like. They notice flaws in their appearance and begin to long for changes in their lives. The dog and cat realize that they are different and begin to fight. Finally, Jan decides that the mirror is no good. He returns it, and the family returns to normal.

Visual Summary

What are things like at first?

Skiba family
- very poor
- live in a small hut

Burek the Dog
- thinks he is a cat
- plays with Kot

Kot the Cat
- thinks she is a dog
- plays with Burek

What happens after the family buys a mirror?

Jan Skiba
- dislikes his thick lips and buck teeth

Marianna Skiba
- thinks missing tooth makes her ugly

First daughter
- thinks her nose is too snub and broad

Second daughter
- thinks her chin is too narrow and long

Third daughter
- dislikes her freckles

What happens after Jan gets rid of the mirror?

Burek the dog
- again thinks he is a cat
- plays with Kot

Kot the cat
- again thinks she is a dog
- plays with Burek

Skiba daughters
- make good marriages

whole Skiba family
- returns to normal

4 Reader's Companion

© Pearson Education, Inc.

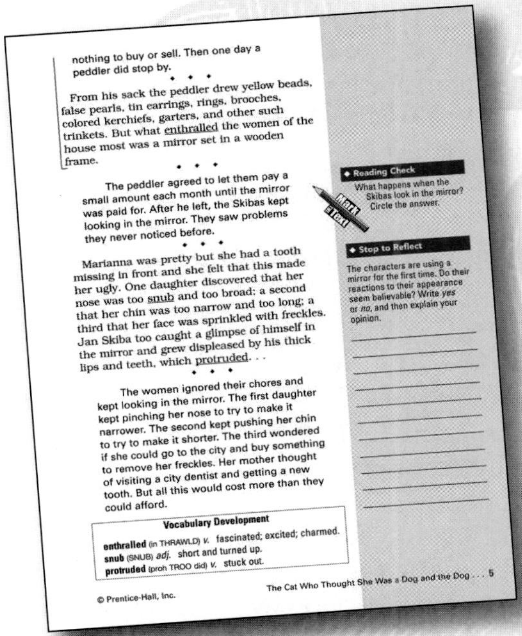

nothing to buy or sell. Then one day a peddler did stop by.

• • •

From his sack the peddler drew yellow beads, false pearls, tin earrings, rings, brooches, colored kerchiefs, garters, and other such trinkets. But what enthralled the women of the house most was a mirror set in a wooden frame.

• • •

The peddler agreed to let them pay a small amount each month until the mirror was paid for. After he left, the Skibas kept looking in the mirror. They saw problems they never noticed before.

• • •

Marianna was pretty but she had a tooth missing in front and she felt that this made her ugly. One daughter discovered that her nose was too snub and too broad; a second that her chin was too narrow and too long; a third that her face was sprinkled with freckles. Jan Skiba too caught a glimpse of himself in the mirror and grew displeased by his thick lips and teeth, which protruded. . .

• • •

The women ignored their chores and kept looking in the mirror. The first daughter kept pinching her nose to try to make it narrower. The second kept pushing her chin to try to make it shorter. The third wondered if she could go to the city and buy something to remove her freckles. Her mother thought of visiting a city dentist and getting a new tooth. But all this would cost more than they could afford.

◆ Reading Check

What happens when the Skibas look in the mirror? Circle the answer.

Mark the Text

◆ Stop to Reflect

The characters are using a mirror for the first time. Do their reactions to their appearance seem believable? Write *yes* or *no*, and then explain your opinion.

Vocabulary Development

enthralled (in THRAWLD) *v.* fascinated; excited; charmed.
snub (SNUB) *adj.* short and turned up.
protruded (proh TROO did) *v.* stuck out.

© Prentice-Hall, Inc.

The Cat Who Thought She Was a Dog and the Dog . . . 5

Adapted Reader's Companion

Using the same format and featuring the same selections as the *Reader's Companion*, this consumable student workbook is designed to help struggling readers by providing

- Larger font for easier reading
- Unique adaptations of selections, featuring passages of authentic text
- Built-in reading comprehension strategies in the margin, especially for struggling readers and special education students

English Learner's Companion

This consumable student workbook contains the same abridged selections and features as the *Adapted Reader's Companion*. The questions and support features are specifically designed to provide additional support for English Language Learners, including

- Vocabulary and pronunciation guides
- English language development strategies, including idioms and colloquialisms
- Culture notes providing background information for relevance

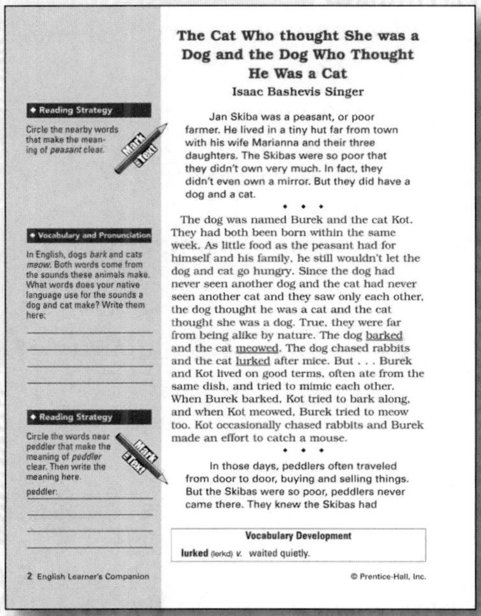

The Cat Who thought She was a Dog and the Dog Who Thought He Was a Cat

Isaac Bashevis Singer

◆ Reading Strategy

Circle the nearby words that make the meaning of *peasant* clear.

Mark the Text

Jan Skiba was a peasant, or poor farmer. He lived in a tiny hut far from town with his wife Marianna and their three daughters. The Skibas were so poor that they didn't own very much. In fact, they didn't even own a mirror. But they did have a dog and a cat.

• • •

The dog was named Burek and the cat Kot. They had both been born within the same week. As little food as the peasant had for himself and his family, he still wouldn't let the dog and cat go hungry. Since the dog had never seen another dog and the cat had never seen another cat and they saw only each other, the dog thought he was a cat and the cat thought she was a dog. True, they were far from being alike by nature. The dog barked and the cat meowed. The dog chased rabbits and the cat lurked after mice. But . . . Burek and Kot lived on good terms, often ate from the same dish, and tried to mimic each other. When Burek barked, Kot tried to bark along, and when Kot meowed, Burek tried to meow too. Kot occasionally chased rabbits and Burek made an effort to catch a mouse.

• • •

In those days, peddlers often traveled from door to door, buying and selling things. But the Skibas were so poor, peddlers never came there. They knew the Skibas had

◆ Vocabulary and Pronunciation

In English, dogs *bark* and cats *meow*. Both words come from the sounds these animals make. What words does your native language use for the sounds a dog and cat make? Write them here:

◆ Reading Strategy

Circle the words near peddler that make the meaning of *peddler* clear. Then write the meaning here.

peddler:

Mark the Text

Vocabulary Development

lurked (lerkd) *v.* waited quietly.

2 English Learner's Companion

© Prentice-Hall, Inc.

Complete program components

Student Edition

Teacher's Edition

Core Resources:

- Program Overview
- Professional Development
- Daily Language Practice
- Formal Assessment
- Open Book Tests
- Selection Support Skills Development Workbook TE
- Vocabulary and Spelling Practice Book TE
- Performance Assessment and Portfolio Management

Reading and Skills Support

- Beyond Literature
- Literatura en español
- Literary Analysis for Enrichment
- Resources for Teaching Novels, Plays, and Literature Collections
- Selection Support: Skills Development Workbook
- Vocabulary and Spelling Practice Book

Reading Achievement System

- Teaching Guidebook for Universal Access
- Reading Diagnostic and Improvement Plan
- Basic Reading Skills: Comprehensive Lessons for Improvement
- Reader's Companion
- Adapted Reader's Companion
- English Learner's Companion

Prentice Hall Reading Intervention Kit

- Reading Skills Diagnostic
- Basic Reading Skills Intervention Lessons
- Writing and Language Skills Diagnostic
- Basic Writing and Language Skills Intervention Lessons

Prentice Hall Assessment System

- California Diagnostic Tests
- California Assessment Workbook
- Review and Remediation Skill Book
- Skills Practice Answers and Explanations on Transparencies

Transparencies

- Fine Art Transparencies Volume I
- Fine Art Transparencies Volume II
- Literary Analysis and Reading Transparencies
- Writing Models and Graphic Organizers on Transparencies
- Daily Language Practice Transparencies

Technology

- Resource Pro® CD-ROM
- Listening to Literature: Book on Audiocassette or CD
- Spanish Readings on CD
- Spanish/English Summaries on CD
- Test Preparation CD-ROM
- Interest Grabber Videos
- Got It! Assessment Videos
- Listening to Music CDs
- Writing and Grammar I-text
- Literature in Performance Videos

California Reading/Language Arts Standards Handbook

California High School Exit Exam Correlation T8

These pages identify the selected California Language Arts Standards that are present on the California High School Exit Exam. These standards are from grades eight, nine, and ten and represent three Language Arts Domains: Reading, Writing, and Written and Oral English Language Conventions.

California Standards Correlation T12

This chart directs you to pages on which the skills in the California standards are taught.

California High School Exit Exam

The California High School Exit Exam consists of selected Language Arts standards from grades eight, nine, and ten. This chart identifies the pages in the literature book where those standards appear. All standards in red will be present on the High School Exit Exam.

	Standards	Pages
	READING DOMAIN (Grades Nine and Ten with two standards from Grade Eight as noted)**	
1.0	**Word Analysis, Fluency, and Systematic Vocabulary Development**	
1.1	Identify and use the literal and figurative meanings of words and understand word derivations.	38, 84, 118, 138, 145, 160, 174, 184, 194, 210, 224, 254, 274, 288, 312, 322, 354, 364, 392, 416, 452, 464, 478, 500, 510, 532, 550, 566, 586, 604, 622, 642, 670, 692, 706, 720, 793, 817, 859, 876, 922, 936, 948, 962, 1062
1.2	Distinguish between the denotative and connotative meanings of words and interpret the connotative power of words.	128, 234, 300, 332, 378, 727, 818, 910
1.3	Identify Greek, Roman, and Norse mythology and use the knowledge to understand the origin and meaning of new words (e.g., the word *narcissistic* drawn from the myth of Narcissus and Echo).	843, 1019
2.0	**Reading Comprehension (Focus on Informational Materials)**	
****8.2.1**	Compare and contrast the features and elements of consumer materials to gain meaning from documents (e.g., warranties, contracts, product information, instruction manuals).	*TVTT Silver Level pages* 112, 326, 488, 662, 861
2.1	Analyze the structure and format of functional workplace documents, including the graphics and headers, and explain how authors use the features to achieve their purposes.	131, 196, 197, 198, 199, 394, 395, 396, 397, 535, 536, 537, 538, 880, 881, 882, 883
2.2	Prepare a bibliography of reference materials for a report using a variety of consumer, workplace, and public documents.	1070, 1071, 1072, 1073, 1074, 1075
2.3	Generate relevant questions about readings on issues that can be researched.	187
2.4	Synthesize the content from several sources or works by a single author dealing with a single issue; paraphrase the ideas and connect them to other sources and related topics to demonstrate comprehension.	909
2.5	Extend ideas presented in primary or secondary sources through original analysis, evaluation, and elaboration.	276
2.6	Demonstrate the use of sophisticated learning tools by following technical directions (e.g., those found with graphic calculators and specialized software programs and in access guides to World Wide Web sites on the Internet).	480, 481, 482, 483
2.7	Critique the logic of functional documents by examining the sequence of information and procedures in anticipation of possible reader misunderstandings.	483
2.8	Evaluate the credibility of an author's argument or defense of a claim by critiquing the relationship between generalizations and evidence, the comprehensiveness of evidence, and the way in which the author's intent affects the structure and tone of the text (e.g., in professional journals, editorials, political speeches, primary source material).	90, 91, 92, 93, 131, 163, 247, 256, 257, 258, 259, 445, 517, 629, 964, 965, 966, 967, 1066, 1067, 1068, 1069
3.0	**Literary Response and Analysis Structural Features of Literature**	
[illegible]	Articulate the relationship between the expressed purposes and characteristics of different forms of dramatic literature (e.g., comedy, tragedy, drama, dramatic monologue).	733, 769, 792, 860

	Standards	Pages
	READING DOMAIN (Grades Nine and Ten with two standards from Grade Eight as noted), continued**	
3.2	Compare or contrast the presentation of a similar theme or topic across genres to explain how the selection of genre shapes the theme or topic.	589, 607, 649, 673, 955, 1051
3.3	Analyze interactions between main and subordinate characters in a literary text (e.g., internal and external conflicts, motivations, relationships, influences) and explain the way those interactions affect the plot.	95, 213, 261, 303, 979
3.4	Determine characters' traits by what the characters say about themselves in narration, dialogue, dramatic monologue, and soliloquy.	177, 213, 261, 303, 315, 357, 419, 533, 553, 569, 860, 1049
3.5	Compare works that express a universal theme and provide evidence to support the ideas expressed in each work.	95, 187, 227, 281, 291, 325, 367, 455, 471, 709, 939, 955
3.6	Analyze and trace an author's development of time and sequence, including the use of complex literary devices.	17, 49, 439, 539
3.7	Recognize and understand the significance of various literary devices, including figurative language, imagery, allegory, and symbolism, and explain their appeal.	41, 121, 177, 187, 201, 247, 291, 411, 589, 635, 895, 903, 913, 925, 1020
3.8	Interpret and evaluate the impact of ambiguities, subtleties, contradictions, ironies, and incongruities in a text.	95, 281, 325, 339, 357, 385, 399, 419, 844
3.9	Explain how voice, persona, and the choice of a narrator affect characterization and the tone, plot, and credibility of a text.	151, 163, 345, 503, 523, 533
3.10	Identify and describe the function of dialogue, scene designs, soliloquies, asides, and character foils in dramatic literature.	732a
****8.3.7**	Analyze a work of literature, showing how it reflects the heritage, traditions, attitudes, and beliefs of its author. (Biographical approach) May be present on the High School Exit Exam.	*TVTT Silver Level pages* 142, 340, 532, 612, 872, 909, 928
3.11	Evaluate the aesthetic qualities of style, including the impact of diction and figurative language on tone, mood, and theme, using the terminology of literary criticism. (Aesthetic approach) May be present on the High School Exit Exam.	5, 121
3.12	Analyze the way in which a work of literature is related to the themes and issues of its historical period. (Historical approach) May be present on the High School Exit Exam.	164, 168, 297, 904
	WRITING DOMAIN (Grades Nine and Ten)	
1.0	**Writing Strategies**	
1.1	Establish a controlling impression or coherent thesis that conveys a clear and distinctive perspective on the subject and maintain a consistent tone and focus throughout the piece of writing.	85, 211, 275, 453, 587, 671, 693, 817
1.2	Use precise language, action verbs, sensory details, appropriate modifiers, and the active rather than the passive voice.	47, 409, 479, 643, 721, 763, 859, 901, 911, 949, 963
1.3	Use clear research questions and suitable research methods (e.g., library, electronic media, personal interview) to elicit and present evidence from primary and secondary sources.	85, 129, 175, 185, 195, 255, 323, 333, 393, 409, 433, 587, 671, 693, 901, 923, 937, 1049
1.4	Develop the main idea within the body of the composition through supporting evidence (e.g., scenarios, commonly held beliefs, hypotheses, definitions).	721
1.5	Synthesize information from multiple sources and identify complexities and discrepancies in the information and the different perspectives found in each medium (e.g., almanac, microfiche, new sources, in-depth field studies, speeches, journals, technical documents).	39, 47, 119, 139, 211, 235, 301, 355, 365, 379, 417, 453, 511, 533, 551, 605, 643, 949
1.6	Integrate quotations and citations into a written text while maintaining the flow of ideas.	911, 963

	Standards	Pages
	WRITING DOMAIN (Grades Nine and Ten), continued	
1.7	Use appropriate conventions for the documentation in the text, notes, and bibliographies by adhering to those in style manuals (e.g., Modern Language Association Handbook, The Chicago Manual of Style).	444a, 379, 1070
1.8	Design and publish documents by using advanced publishing software and graphic programs.	15, 161, 225, 235, 313, 465, 567, 623, 707, 721, 877, 1063
1.9	Revise writing to improve the logic and coherence of the organization and controlling perspective, the precision of word choice, and the tone by taking into consideration the audience, purpose, and formality of the context.	290a, 314a, 324a, 384a, 418a, 606a, 894a, 912a, 924a, 301, 323, 333, 393, 433, 623, 721, 901, 923, 937
2.0	**Writing Applications (Genres and their Characteristics)**	
2.1	Write biographical or autobiographical narratives or short stories: a. Relate a sequence of events and communicate the significance of the events to the audience. b. Locate scenes and incidents in specific places. c. Describe with concrete sensory details the sights, sounds, and smells of a scene and the specific actions, movements, gestures, and feelings of the characters; use interior monologue to depict the characters' feelings. d. Pace the presentation of actions to accommodate changes in time and mood. e. Make effective use of descriptions of appearance, images, shifting perspectives, and sensory details.	140, 141, 142, 143, 379, 417, 465, 567, 624, 625, 626, 627
2.2	Write responses to literature: a. Demonstrate a comprehensive grasp of the significant ideas of literary works. b. Support important ideas and viewpoints through accurate and detailed references to the text or to other works. c. Demonstrate awareness of the author's use of stylistic devices and an appreciation of the effects created. d. Identify and assess the impact of perceived ambiguities, nuances, and complexities within the text.	195, 289, 313, 433, 533, 551, 605, 707, 884, 885, 886, 887, 889, 911, 1049
2.3	Write expository compositions, including analytical essays and research reports: a. Marshal evidence in support of a thesis and related claims, including information on all relevant perspectives. b. Convey information and ideas from primary and secondary sources. c. Make distinctions between the relative value and significance of specific data, facts and ideas. d. Include visual aids by employing appropriate technology to organize and record information on charts, maps, and graphs. e. Anticipate and address readers' potential misunderstandings, biases, and expectations. f. Use technical terms and notations accurately.	129, 139, 434, 435, 436, 437, 501, 707, 843, 968, 969, 970, 971, 1019, 1070, 1071, 1072, 1073, 1074, 1075

	Standards	Pages
	WRITING DOMAIN (Grades Nine and Ten), continued	
2.4	Write persuasive compositions: a. Structure ideas and arguments in a sustained and logical fashion. b. Use specific rhetorical devices to support assertions (e.g., appeal to logic through reasoning; appeal to emotion or ethical belief; relate a personal anecdote, case study, or analogy). c. Clarify and defend positions with precise and relevant evidence, including facts, expert opinions, quotations, and expressions of commonly accepted beliefs and logical reasoning. d. Address readers' concerns, counterclaims, biases, and expectations.	175, 185, 211, 225, 235, 301, 334, 335, 336, 365, 511, 877, 1063
2.5	Write business letters: a. Provide clear and purposeful information and address the intended audience appropriately. b. Use appropriate vocabulary, tone, and style to take into account the nature of the relationship with, and the knowledge and interests of, the recipients. c. Highlight central ideas or images. d. Follow a conventional style with page formats, fonts, and spacing that contribute to the document's readability and impact.	236, 237, 238, 239, 323, 793
2.6	Write technical documents (e.g., a manual on rules of behavior for conflict resolution, procedures for conducting a meeting, minutes of a meeting): a. Report information and convey ideas logically and correctly. b. Offer detailed and accurate specifications. c. Include scenarios, definitions, and examples to aid comprehension (e.g., troubleshooting guide). d. Anticipate readers' problems, mistakes, and misunderstandings.	39, 255, 501, 512, 513, 514, 515
	WRITTEN AND ORAL ENGLISH LANGUAGE CONVENTIONS DOMAIN (Grades Nine and Ten)	
1.0	**Written and Oral English Language Conventions**	
1.1	Identify and correctly use clauses (e.g., main and subordinate), phrases (e.g., gerund, infinitive, and participial), and mechanics of punctuation (e.g., semicolons, colons, ellipses, hyphens).	300, 464, 478, 532, 550, 566, 586, 604, 900, 910, 922, 936, 948, 962, 1077
1.2	Understand sentence construction (e.g., parallel structure, subordination, proper placement of modifiers) and proper English usage (e.g., consistency of verb tenses).	174, 194, 354, 364, 378, 452, 500, 510, 622, 762, 793, 817, 876
1.3	Demonstrate an understanding of proper English usage and control of grammar, paragraph and sentence structure, diction, and syntax.	14, 38, 46, 84, 128, 138, 160, 184, 210, 254, 274, 288, 312, 322, 392, 408, 416, 432, 642, 670, 692, 706, 720, 843, 859, 1019, 1048, 1062, 1077
1.4	Produce legible work that shows accurate spelling and correct use of the conventions of punctuation and capitalization.	184, 194, 622, 936
1.5	Reflect appropriate manuscript requirements, including title page presentation, pagination, spacing and margins, and integration of source and support material (e.g., in-text citation, use of direct quotations, paraphrasing) with appropriate citations.	1070

California Grade 9 Standards Correlation

This correlation identifies the pages on which the California Standards appear in this book. With the help of this chart, you will know exactly where to find solid, fully developed instruction on any standard.

Standards		Pages
	READING DOMAIN	
1.0	**Word Analysis, Fluency and Systematic Vocabulary Development**	
	Vocabulary and Concept Development	
1.1	Identify and use the literal and figurative meanings of words and understand word derivations.	38, 84, 118, 138, 145, 160, 174, 184, 194, 210, 224, 254, 274, 288, 312, 322, 354, 364, 392, 416, 452, 464, 478, 500, 510, 532, 550, 566, 586, 604, 622, 642, 670, 692, 706, 720, 793, 817, 859, 876, 922, 936, 948, 962, 973, 1062
1.2	Distinguish between the denotative and connotative meanings of words and interpret the connotative power of words.	128, 234, 300, 332, 378, 727, 818, 910
1.3	Identify Greek, Roman, and Norse mythology and use the knowledge to understand the origin and meaning of new words (e.g., the word *narcissistic* drawn from the myth of Narcissus and Echo).	843, 1019
2.0	**Reading Comprehension (Focus on Informational Materials)**	
	Structural Features of Informational Materials	
2.1	Analyze the structure and format of functional workplace documents, including the graphics and headers, and explain how authors use the features to achieve their purposes.	131, 196, 197, 198, 199, 394, 395, 396, 397, 535, 536, 537, 538, 880, 881, 882, 883
2.2	Prepare a bibliography of reference materials for a report using a variety of consumer, workplace, and public documents.	1070, 1071, 1072, 1073, 1074, 1075
	Comprehension and Analysis of Grade-Level-Appropriate Text	
2.3	Generate relevant questions about readings on issues that can be researched.	187
2.4	Synthesize the content from several sources or works by a single author dealing with a single issue; paraphrase the ideas and connect them to other sources and related topics to demonstrate comprehension.	909
2.5	Extend ideas presented in primary or secondary sources through original analysis, evaluation, and elaboration.	276
2.6	Demonstrate the use of sophisticated learning tools by following technical directions (e.g., those found with graphic calculators and specialized software programs and in access guides to World Wide Web sites on the Internet).	480, 481, 482, 483
	Expository Critique	
2.7	Critique the logic of functional documents by examining the sequence of information and procedures in anticipation of possible reader misunderstanding.	483
2.8	Evaluate the credibility of an author's argument or defense of a claim by critiquing the relationship between generalizations and evidence, the comprehensiveness of evidence, and the way in which the author's intent affects the structure and tone of the text (e.g., in professional journals, editorials, political speeches, primary source material).	90, 91, 92, 93, 131, 163, 241, 247, 256, 257, 258, 259, 445, 517, 629, 964, 965, 966, 967, 1066, 1067, 1068, 1069
3.0	**Literary Response and Analysis Structural Features of Literature**	
3.1	Articulate the relationship between the expressed purposes and characteristics of different forms of dramatic literature (e.g., comedy, tragedy, drama, dramatic monologue).	733, 769, 792, 860
3.2	Compare or contrast the presentation of a similar theme or topic across genres to explain how the selection of genre shapes the theme or topic.	589, 607, 649, 673, 1051

	Standards	Pages
	READING DOMAIN, continued	
	Narrative Analysis of Grade-Level-Appropriate Text	
3.3	Analyze interactions between main and subordinate characters in a literary text (e.g., internal and external conflicts, motivations, relationships, influences) and explain the way those interactions affect the plot.	95, 213, 261, 303, 979
3.4	Determine characters' traits by what the characters say about themselves in narration, dialogue, dramatic monologue, and soliloquy.	177, 213, 261, 303, 315, 357, 419, 533, 553, 569, 763, 860, 1049
3.5	Compare works that express a universal theme and provide evidence to support the ideas expressed in each work.	95, 187, 227, 281, 291, 325, 367, 455, 471, 709, 939, 955
3.6	Analyze and trace an author's development of time and sequence, including the use of complex literary devices (e.g., foreshadowing, flashbacks).	17, 49, 439, 539
3.7	Recognize and understand the significance of various literary devices, including figurative language, imagery, allegory, and symbolism, and explain their appeal.	41, 121, 177, 187, 201, 247, 291, 411, 589, 635, 895, 913, 925, 1020
3.8	Interpret and evaluate the impact of ambiguities, subtleties, contradictions, ironies, and incongruities in a text.	95, 281, 325, 339, 357, 385, 399, 419, 844
3.9	Explain how voice, persona, and the choice of a narrator affect characterization and the tone, plot, and credibility of a text.	151, 163, 345, 503, 523, 533
3.10	Identify and describe the function of dialogue, scene designs, soliloquies, asides, and character foils in dramatic literature.	732a
	Literary Criticism	
3.11	Evaluate the aesthetic qualities of style, including the impact of diction and figurative language on tone, mood, and theme, using the terminology of literary criticism. (Aesthetic approach)	120a, 5, 121
3.12	Analyze the way in which a work of literature is related to the themes and issues of its historical period. (Historical approach)	164, 168, 297, 902, 904
	WRITING DOMAIN	
1.0	**Writing Strategies**	
	Organization and Focus	
1.1	Establish a controlling impression or coherent thesis that conveys a clear and distinctive perspective on the subject and maintain a consistent tone and focus throughout the piece of writing.	85, 211, 275, 453, 587, 671, 693, 817
1.2	Use precise language, action verbs, sensory details, appropriate modifiers, and the active rather than the passive voice.	47, 409, 479, 643, 721, 763, 859, 901, 911, 949, 963
	Research and Technology	
1.3	Use clear research questions and suitable research methods (e.g., library, electronic media, personal interview) to elicit and present evidence from primary and secondary sources.	85, 129, 175, 185, 195, 255, 323, 333, 393, 409, 433, 587, 671, 693, 901, 923, 937, 1049
1.4	Develop the main idea within the body of the composition through supporting evidence (e.g., scenarios, commonly held beliefs, hypotheses, definitions).	721
1.5	Synthesize information from multiple sources and identify complexities and discrepancies in the information and the different perspectives found in each medium (e.g., almanac, microfiche, new sources, in-depth field studies, speeches, journals, technical documents).	47, 119, 139, 211, 235, 301, 355, 365, 379, 417, 453, 511, 533, 551, 605, 643, 949
1.6	Integrate quotations and citations into a written text while maintaining the flow of ideas.	911, 963

	Standards	Pages
	WRITING DOMAIN, continued	
1.7	Use appropriate conventions for the documentation in the text, notes, and bibliographies by adhering to those in style manuals (e.g., Modern Language Association Handbook, The Chicago Manual of Style).	365, 379, 1070
1.8	Design and publish documents by using advanced publishing software and graphic programs.	15, 161, 225, 235, 289, 313, 465, 479, 567, 623, 707, 721, 763, 877, 1063
	Evaluation and Revision	
1.9	Revise writing to improve the logic and coherence of the organization and controlling perspective, the precision of word choice, and the tone by taking into consideration the audience, purpose, and formality of the context.	301, 323, 333, 393, 433, 623, 721, 901, 923, 937
2.0	**Writing Applications (Genres and their Characteristics)**	
2.1	Write biographical or autobiographical narratives or short stories a) Relate a sequence of events and communicate the significance of the events to the audience. b) Locate scenes and incidents in specific places. c) Describe with concrete sensory details the sights, sounds, and smells of a scene and the specific actions, movements, gestures, and feelings of the characters; use interior monologue to depict the characters' feelings. d) Pace the presentation of actions to accommodate changes in time and mood. e) Make effective use of descriptions of appearance, images, shifting perspectives, and sensory details.	15, 119, 140, 141, 142, 143, 161, 355, 379, 417, 465, 567, 624, 625, 626, 627
2.2	Write responses to literature:a) Demonstrate a comprehensive grasp of the significant ideas of literary works. b) Support important ideas and viewpoints through accurate and detailed references to the text or to other works. c) Demonstrate awareness of the author's use of stylistic devices and an appreciation of the effects created. d) Identify and assess the impact of perceived ambiguities, nuances, and complexities within the text.	195, 289, 313, 433, 533, 551, 605, 707, 884, 885, 886, 887, 889, 911, 1049
2.3	Write expository compositions, including analytical essays and research reports: a) Marshal evidence in support of a thesis and related claims, including information on all relevant perspectives. b) Convey information and ideas from primary and secondary sources. c) Make distinctions between the relative value and significance of specific data, facts and ideas. d) Include visual aids by employing appropriate technology to organize and record information on charts, maps, and graphs. e) Anticipate and address readers' potential misunderstandings, biases, and expectations. f) Use technical terms and notations accurately.	129, 139, 434, 435, 436, 437, 501, 707, 843, 968, 969, 970, 971, 1019, 1070, 1071, 1072, 1073, 1074, 1075
2.4	Write persuasive compositions: a) Structure ideas and arguments in a sustained and logical fashion. b) Use specific rhetorical devices to support assertions (e.g., appeal to logic through reasoning; appeal to emotion or ethical belief; relate a personal anecdote, case study, or analogy). c) Clarify and defend positions with precise and relevant evidence, including facts, expert opinions, quotations, and expressions of commonly accepted beliefs and logical reasoning. d) Address readers' concerns, counterclaims, biases, and expectations.	175, 185, 211, 225, 235, 301, 334, 335, 336, 365, 511, 877, 1063
2.5	Write business letters: a) Provide clear and purposeful information and address the intended audience appropriately. b) Use appropriate vocabulary, tone, and style to take into account the nature of the relationship with, and the knowledge and interests of, the recipients. c) Highlight central ideas or images. d) Follow a conventional style with page formats, fonts, and spacing that contribute to the document's readability and impact.	236, 237, 238, 239, 323, 793
2.6	Write technical documents (e.g., a manual on rules of behavior for conflict resolution, procedures for conducting a meeting, minutes of a meeting): a) Report information and convey ideas logically and correctly. b) Offer detailed and accurate specifications. c) Include scenarios, definitions, and examples to aid comprehension (e.g., troubleshooting guide). d) Anticipate readers' problems, mistakes, and misunderstandings.	39, 255, 501, 512, 513, 514, 515

	Standards	Pages
	WRITTEN AND ORAL ENGLISH LANGUAGE CONVENTIONS DOMAIN	
1.0	**Written and Oral English Language Conventions**	
	Grammar and Mechanics of Writing	
1.1	Identify and correctly use clauses (e.g., main and subordinate), phrases (e.g., gerund, infinitive, and participial), and mechanics of punctuation (e.g., semicolons, colons, ellipses, hyphens).	274, 288, 300, 464, 478, 532, 550, 566, 586, 604, 900, 910, 922, 936, 948, 962, 1077
1.2	Understand sentence construction (e.g., parallel structure, subordination, proper placement of modifiers) and proper English usage (e.g., consistency of verb tenses).	118, 174, 194, 332, 354, 364, 378, 452, 500, 510, 622, 762, 793, 817, 876
1.3	Demonstrate an understanding of proper English usage and control of grammar, paragraph and sentence structure, diction, and syntax.	14, 38, 46, 84, 128, 138, 160, 184, 210, 254, 274, 288, 312, 322, 392, 408, 416, 432, 642, 670, 692, 706, 720, 843, 859, 1019, 1048, 1062, 1077
	Manuscript Form	
1.4	Produce legible work that shows accurate spelling and correct use of the conventions of punctuation and capitalization.	184, 194, 622, 936
1.5	Reflect appropriate manuscript requirements, including title page presentation, pagination, spacing and margins, and integration of source and support material (e.g., in-text citation, use of direct quotations, paraphrasing) with appropriate citations.	1070
	LISTENING AND SPEAKING DOMAIN	
1.0	**Listening and Speaking Strategies**	
	Comprehension	
1.1	Formulate judgments about the ideas under discussion and support those judgments with convincing evidence.	161, 301, 1063
1.2	Compare and contrast the ways in which media genres (e.g., televised news, news magazines, documentaries, online information) cover the same event.	972
	Organization and Delivery of Oral Communication	
1.3	Choose logical patterns of organization (e.g., chronological, topical, cause and effect) to inform and to persuade, by soliciting agreement or action, or to unite audiences behind a common belief or cause.	255, 911
1.4	Choose appropriate techniques for developing the introduction and conclusion (e.g., by using literary quotations, anecdotes, references to authoritative sources).	175, 225, 379, 693
1.5	Recognize and use elements of classical speech forms (e.g., introduction, first and second transitions, body, conclusion) in formulating rational arguments and applying the art of persuasion and debate.	313, 501, 817
1.6	Present and advance a clear thesis statement and choose appropriate types of proof (e.g., statistics, testimony, specific instances) that meet standard tests for evidence, including credibility, validity, and relevance.	1076
1.7	Use props, visual aids, graphs, and electronic media to enhance the appeal and accuracy of presentations.	39, 139, 323, 453, 465, 643, 707, 763, 859, 923, 963
1.8	Produce concise notes for extemporaneous delivery.	85, 235, 289, 393, 417, 511, 671, 843, 949, 1049

	Standards	Pages
	LISTENING AND SPEAKING DOMAIN, continued	
1.9	Analyze the occasion and the interests of the audience and choose effective verbal and nonverbal techniques (e.g., voice, gestures, eye contact) for presentations.	15, 47, 119, 129, 185, 195, 211, 323, 355, 365, 409, 479, 533, 587, 605, 623, 937
	Analysis and Evaluation of Oral and Media Communications	
1.10	Analyze historically significant speeches (e.g., Abraham Lincoln's "Gettysburg Address," Martin Luther King, Jr.'s "I Have a Dream") to find the rhetorical devices and features that make them memorable.	644, 645, 646, 647
1.11	Assess how language and delivery affect the mood and tone of the oral communication and make an impact on the audience.	333, 726, 793, 1019
1.12	Evaluate the clarity, quality, effectiveness, and general coherence of a speaker's important points, arguments, evidence, organization of ideas, delivery, diction, and syntax.	516, 726
1.13	Analyze the types of arguments used by the speaker, including argument by causation, analogy, authority, emotion, and logic.	338, 726
1.14	Identify the aesthetic effects of a media presentation and evaluate the techniques used to create them (e.g., compare Shakespeare's *Henry V* with Kenneth Branagh's 1990 film version).	628
2.0	**Speaking Applications (Genres and their Characteristics)**	
2.1	Deliver narrative presentations: a) Narrate a sequence of events and communicate their significance to the audience. b) Locate scenes and incidents in specific places. c) Describe with concrete sensory details the sights, sounds, and smells of a scene and the specific actions, movements, gestures, and feelings of the characters. d) Pace the presentation of actions to accommodate time and mood changes.	144, 275, 433
2.2	Deliver expository presentations: a) Marshal evidence in support of a thesis and related claims, including information on all relevant perspectives. b) Convey information and ideas from primary and secondary sources accurately and coherently. c) Make distinctions between the relative value and significance of specific data, facts, and ideas. d) Include visual aids by employing appropriate technology to organize and display information on charts, maps, and graphs. e) Anticipate and address the listener's potential misunderstandings, biases, and expectations. f) Use technical terms and notations accurately.	567, 1076
2.3	Apply appropriate interviewing techniques: a) Prepare and ask relevant questions. b) Make notes of responses. c) Use language that conveys maturity, sensitivity, and respect. d) Respond correctly and effectively to questions. e) Demonstrate knowledge of the subject or organization. f) Compile and report responses. g) Evaluate the effectiveness of the interview.	47, 240, 551
2.4	Deliver oral responses to literature: a) Advance a judgment demonstrating a comprehensive grasp of the significant ideas of works or passages (i.e., make and support warranted assertions about the text). b) Support important ideas and viewpoints through accurate and detailed references to the text or to other works. c) Demonstrate awareness of the author's use of stylistic devices and an appreciation of the effects created. d) Identify and assess the impact of perceived ambiguities, nuances, and complexities within the text.	888
2.5	Deliver persuasive arguments (including evaluation and analysis of problems and solutions and causes and effects): a) Structure ideas and arguments in a coherent, logical fashion. b) Use rhetorical devices to support assertions (e.g., appeal to logic through reasoning; appeal to emotion or ethical belief; by use of personal anecdote, case study, or analogy). c) Clarify and defend positions with precise and relevant evidence, including facts, expert opinions, quotations, expressions of commonly accepted beliefs, and logical reasoning. d) Anticipate and address the listener's concerns and counterarguments.	722, 723, 724, 725, 877
2.6	Deliver descriptive presentations: a) Establish clearly the speaker's point of view on the subject of the presentation. b) Establish clearly the speaker's relationship with that subject (e.g., dispassionate observation, personal involvement). c) Use effective, factual descriptions of appearance, concrete images, shifting perspectives and vantage points, and sensory details.	438

PRENTICE HALL LITERATURE

Timeless Voices, Timeless Themes

GOLD LEVEL

Prentice Hall

Upper Saddle River, New Jersey
Glenview, Illinois
Needham, Massachusetts

ISBN 0-13-054805-7

2 3 4 5 6 7 8 9 10 05 04 03 02

Prentice Hall

PRENTICE HALL LITERATURE

Timeless Voices, Timeless Themes

Copper
Bronze
Silver
Gold
Platinum
The American Experience
The British Tradition

ACKNOWLEDGMENTS

Grateful acknowledgment is made to the following for copyrighted material:

The Estate of Margaret Walker Alexander "Memory" from *For My People* by Margaret Walker. Copyright 1942 Yale University Press.

American Library Association From "Books and Bytes: Digital Connections. Passing Time in Times Past" by Virginia A. Walker, from *Book Links (Connecting Books, Libraries, and Classrooms),* May 1999, Volume 8, No. 5. Copyright © 1999 by the American Library Association.

Arcade Publishing, Inc. Reprinted from *Haiku: This Other World,* by Richard Wright. Published by Arcade Publishing, New York, New York. Copyright © 1998 by Ellen Wright. Used by permission.

Arte Público Press "The Harvest" by Tomás Rivera is reprinted with permission from the publisher of *La Cosecha* (Houston: Arte Público Press—University of Houston, 1989).

Bantam Books, A Division of Random House, Inc. "One Ordinary Day, With Peanuts," excerpts from *Just an Ordinary Day: The Uncollected Stories* by Shirley Jackson. Copyright © 1997 by The Estate of Shirley Jackson. Used by permission of Bantam Books, a division of Random House, Inc.

Susan Bergholz Literary Services From "A Celebration of Grandfathers." Copyright © 1983 by Rudolfo Anaya. First published in *New Mexico Magazine,* March 1983. "Julia Alvarez's Aha Moment" by Julia Alvarez. Copyright © 2000 by Julia Alvarez. First published in *O, The Oprah Magazine* 1, No. 5 (November 2000). Reprinted by permission of Susan Bergholz Literary Services, New York. All rights reserved. "Woman's Work" by Julia Alvarez, published in *The New York Times*, September 5, 1994. Copyright © 1994 by The New York Times Co.

Brandt & Hochman Literary Agents, Inc. "The Most Dangerous Game" by Richard Connell. Copyright, 1924 by Richard Connell. Copyright renewed © 1952 by Louise Fox Connell. "Sonata for Harp and Bicycle" from *The Green Flash* by Joan Aiken. Copyright © 1957, 1958, 1959, 1960, 1965, 1968, 1969, 1971 by Joan Aiken. Reprinted by permission of Brandt & Hochman Literary Agents, Inc.

(Acknowledgments continue on page R43, which constitutes an extension of this copyright page.)

CONTRIBUTING AUTHORS

The contributing authors guided the direction and philosophy of *Prentice Hall Literature: Timeless Voices, Timeless Themes*. Working with the development team, they helped to build the pedagogical integrity of the program and to ensure its relevance for today's teachers and students.

Kate Kinsella

Kate Kinsella, Ed.D., is a faculty member in the Department of Secondary Education at San Francisco State University. A specialist in second-language acquisition and adolescent reading and writing, she teaches coursework addressing language and literacy development across the secondary curricula. She has taught high-school ESL and directed SFSU's *Intensive English Program* for first-generation bilingual college students. She maintains secondary classroom involvement by teaching an academic literacy class for second-language learners through the University's *Step to College* partnership program. A former Fulbright lecturer and perennial institute leader for TESOL, the California Reading Association, and the California League of Middle Schools, Dr. Kinsella provides professional development nationally on topics ranging from learning-style enhancement to second-language reading. Her scholarship has been published in journals such as the *TESOL Journal,* the *CATESOL Journal,* and the *Social Studies Review.* Dr. Kinsella earned her M.A. in TESOL from San Francisco State University and her Ed.D. in Second Language Acquisition from the University of San Francisco.

Kevin Feldman

Kevin Feldman, Ed.D., is the Director of Reading and Early Intervention with the Sonoma County Office of Education (SCOE). His career in education spans thirty-one years. As the Director of Reading and Early Intervention for SCOE, he develops, organizes, and monitors programs related to K–12 literacy and prevention of reading difficulties. He also serves as a Leadership Team Consultant to the California Reading and Literature Project and assists in the development and implementation of K–12 programs throughout California. Dr. Feldman earned his undergraduate degree in Psychology from Washington State University and has a Master's degree in Special Education, Learning Disabilities, and Instructional Design from U.C. Riverside. He earned his Ed.D. in Curriculum and Instruction from the University of San Francisco.

Colleen Shea Stump

Colleen Shea Stump, Ph.D., is a Special Education supervisor in the area of Resource and Inclusion for Seattle Public Schools. She served as a professor and chairperson for the Department of Special Education at San Francisco State University. She continues as a lead consultant in the area of collaboration for the California State Improvement Grant and travels the state of California providing professional development training in the areas of collaboration, content literacy instruction, and inclusive instruction. Dr. Stump earned her doctorate at the University of Washington, her M.A. in Special Education from the University of New Mexico, and her B.S. in Elementary Education from the University of Wisconsin–Eau Claire.

Joyce Armstrong Carroll

In her forty-year career, Joyce Armstrong Carroll, Ed.D., has taught on every grade level from primary to graduate school. In the past twenty years, she has trained teachers in the teaching of writing. A nationally known consultant, she has served as president of TCTE and on NCTE's Commission on Composition. More than fifty of her articles have appeared in journals such as *Curriculum Review, English Journal, Media & Methods, Southwest Philosophical Studies, English in Texas,* and the *Florida English Journal.* With Edward E. Wilson, Dr. Carroll co-authored *Acts of Teaching: How to Teach Writing* and co-edited *Poetry After Lunch: Poetry to Read Aloud.* She co-directs the New Jersey Writing Project in Texas.

Edward E. Wilson

A former editor of *English in Texas,* Edward E. Wilson has served as a high-school English teacher and a writing consultant in school districts nationwide. Wilson has served on both the Texas Teacher Professional Practices Commission and NCTE's Commission on Composition. Wilson's poetry appears in Paul Janeczko's anthology *The Music of What Happens.* With Dr. Carroll, he co-wrote *Acts of Teaching: How to Teach Writing* and co-edited *Poetry After Lunch: Poetry to Read Aloud.* Wilson co-directs the New Jersey Writing Project in Texas.

CALIFORNIA PROGRAM ADVISORS

The California program advisors provided ongoing input throughout the development of *Prentice Hall Literature: Timeless Voices, Timeless Themes.* Their valuable insights ensure that the perspectives of the teachers throughout California are represented within this literature series.

Dawn Akuna
Teacher of Reading
Harriet Eddy Middle School
Elk Grove, CA

Kathy Allen
English Language Arts Teacher
Palos Verdes Intermediate School
Palos Verdes, CA

Maxine K. Bigler
Associate Director, Region II, Migrant Education, Butte County Office of Education
Chico, CA

Cathy Cirimele
Teacher of English
Bullard High School
Fresno, CA

Jesse L. Culbert
English Teacher
Willowbrook Middle School
Compton, CA

Terry Day
English and Speech Teacher
Downey High School
Modesto, CA

Yvonne Divans-Hutchinson
Language Arts Teacher
King/Drew Magnet High School of Medicine and Science
Los Angeles, CA

Diane Erickson
Teacher of English
Oxford Academy
Cypress, CA

Cynthia Hardy Gayle
Assistant Principal
Rancho del Rey Middle School
Chula Vista, CA

Joe Glover
Language Arts/ELD Teacher
Mesa Intermediate School
Palmdale, CA

Jeannette Hampton
Literacy Coordinator for Sacramento City USD, Retired
Fern Bacon Basic Middle School
Sacramento, CA

Carleen Hemric
Language Arts Teacher
Pershing Middle School
San Diego, CA

Kimberly Wise Johnson, M.Ed.
English Teacher
Arcade Fundamental Middle School
Sacramento, CA

Keith R. Jones
English/Social Studies Teacher
Elmhurst Middle School
Oakland, CA

Karen Kessinger
Teacher of English
San Bernardino High School
San Bernardino, CA

Gail Catherine Kidd
Language Arts Teacher
Center Middle School
Azusa, CA

Alan J. Leonard
English Instructor, Retired
Anaheim, CA

Catherine C. Linn, Ph.D.
Teacher of Literature and Writing
Palm Springs High School
Palm Springs, CA

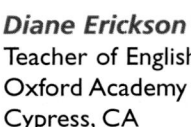

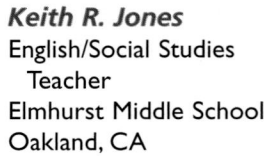

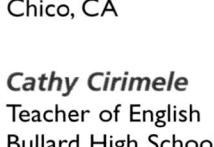

Karen Lopez
English Teacher
William S. Hart High School
Newhall, CA

Robert Lopez
ELL Instructor
Gage Middle School
Huntington Park, CA

Celia Monge Mana
Language Arts Teacher
Horace Mann Middle School
San Francisco, CA

Kathleen Marshall
English Teacher
Stagg High School
Stockton, CA

Peggy P. Moore
Middle School Educator, Retired
Bayshore School District
Daly City, CA

Akiko Morimoto
Language Arts Teacher
Washington Middle School
Vista, CA

Dewhanne Nyivih
Former English Teacher
Marshall Fundamental High School
Pasadena, CA

Judith L. O'Brien
Language Arts Instructor
Walter Stiern Middle School
Bakersfield, CA

Ann Okamura
Teacher of English
Laguna Creek High School
Elk Grove, CA

Judy Plouff
Language Arts/Social Studies Teacher
Sherman Oaks Center for Enriched Studies
Reseda, CA

Jan Reed
English Curriculum Specialist, Retired
Garden Grove USD
Garden Grove, CA

Marian Reimann
Assistant Principal, Curriculum and Instruction
Sutter Middle School
Winnetka, CA

Lynne Richter
Teacher of English
Fulton Middle School
Van Nuys, CA

Maureen Rippee
English Instructor
Wilson High School
Long Beach, CA

Meredith Ritner
Language Arts Teacher
Alieso Viejo Middle School
Alieso Viejo, CA

Sharon Schiesl
Language Arts Teacher
Mendez Fundamental Intermediate School
Santa Ana, CA

Carol J. Schowalter
Language Arts Teacher
El Roble Middle School
Claremont, CA

Cheryl Spivak
Language Arts/Reading Intervention Teacher
Portola Middle School
Tarzana, CA

Peggy Todd Stover
Teacher of English
Independence High School
San Jose, CA

Michael C. Sullivan
Language Arts Teacher
Pacifica High School
Garden Grove, CA

Sandra Sullivan
Language Arts Teacher
Garden Grove High School
Garden Grove, CA

Vanna Turner
Language Arts Teacher
Albert Einstein Middle School
Sacramento, CA

Linda Valdez
English Teacher
Camarillo High School
Camarillo, CA

Sonia Wilson
English Teacher
Steve Garvey Junior High School
Lindsay, CA

Mary Jo Wynne
Language Arts/Social Studies Teacher
Assumption of the Blessed Virgin Mary School
Pasadena, CA

California Grade 9 Language Arts Standards

Here is a complete list of the Standards so that you can know what you're expected to learn this year.

READING

1.0 Word Analysis, Fluency, and Systematic Vocabulary Development: In this strand of standards, you will use your prior knowledge of word origins to learn the meanings of new words and to use these words correctly.

Vocabulary and Concept Development

1.1 Identify and use the literal and figurative meanings of words and understand word derivations.

Many English words have both literal and figurative meanings. In the 9th grade, you will learn to recognize both kinds of meanings and use them appropriately. You will also develop a deeper understanding of language by learning about the sources, or derivations, of words.

Example: **Figurative meaning**
"What did we say to each other
that now we are as the deer
who walk in single file . . ."
—from "Simile," by N. Scott Momaday

1.2 Distinguish between the denotative and connotative meanings of words and interpret the connotative power of words.

Each word has an explicit definition, or denotation; the connotation of a word suggests other, less explicit meanings, or ideas that are associated with the word. You will recognize denotations and connotations, and understand how connotations add to language.

Example: **Connotative meaning**
"We do not ride on the railroad; it rides upon us."
—from *Walden*, by Henry David Thoreau

1.3 Identify Greek, Roman, and Norse mythology and use the knowledge to understand the origin and meaning of new words (e.g., the word *narcissistic* drawn from the myth of Narcissus and Echo).

Many English words have their origins in classical and other ancient languages. Knowing this mythology can help us understand where the new English words we encounter come from and what they mean.

Example: **Greek mythology**
Music: Drawn from the myth of the Muses, literally "the art of the Muse"

2.0 READING COMPREHENSION (FOCUS ON INFORMATIONAL MATERIALS): In this strand, you will study grade-level materials and examine the positions they take on various issues, the arguments they present, and the different ways they are organized. You will also begin working towards the goal of reading two million words a year from a variety of sources.

Structural Features of Informational Materials

2.1 Analyze the structure and format of functional workplace documents, including the graphics and headers, and explain how authors use the features to achieve their purposes.

You will study the kinds of documents used in the workplace, such as reports and memoranda. You will learn why these documents are written and how they use such features as graphics and headers, or labels that tell the reader about the purpose of a block of text.

2.2 Prepare a bibliography of reference materials for a report using a variety of consumer, workplace, and public documents.

A bibliography is a list of information about the sources you use for references in an essay or report. You will prepare and write a bibliography for a report using consumer, workplace, and public documents as sources.

Example: **Automobile safety**
Network of Employers for Traffic Safety. "Road readiness: NETS 1998 planner." Washington: The Network, 1997.

Comprehension and Analysis of Grade-Level-Appropriate Text

2.3 Generate relevant questions about readings on issues that can be researched.

When you research an issue, you can get more out of readings by asking questions about how the text relates to the issue. You will learn how to think of relevant questions to ask yourself as you research.

Example:
How have United States companies worked with the government to improve automobile safety?

2.4 Synthesize the content from several sources or works by a single author dealing with a single issue; paraphrase the ideas and connect them to other sources and related topics to demonstrate comprehension.

Another important research skill is synthesizing, or bringing together ideas from a number of different sources. You will synthesize ideas from different texts by the same author by paraphrasing the ideas and connecting them to similar topics.

Example:
"Overcrowded schools undermine student performance."
—from "Standing in the Way," by Bob Herbert
". . . class size reduction in the early grades has many benefits, including higher pupil achievement . . ."
—from "Fewer Students, Greater Gains," by Bob Herbert
Synthesis: Smaller classes would improve student performance.

2.5 **Extend ideas presented in primary or secondary sources through original analysis, evaluation, and elaboration.**

You will learn how to take the ideas you find in primary and secondary sources and develop them further on your own by examining them, deciding how valuable they are, and working out their details.

Example:
"Let every man make known what kind of government would command his respect, and that will be one step toward obtaining it."
—from "Civil Disobedience," by Henry David Thoreau

Thoreau wrote in 1849 that all citizens should speak out about what they think government should be, which is the first step in making government better.

2.6 **Demonstrate use of sophisticated learning tools by following technical directions (e.g., those found with graphic calculators and specialized software programs and in access guides to World Wide Web sites on the Internet).**

Technical direction—such as the instruction manuals included with graphic calculators or computer software, or the access guides you might find on the Internet—are a sophisticated type of writing that you will show you can understand and use.

Expository Critique

2.7 **Critique the logic of functional documents by examining the sequence of information and procedures in anticipation of possible reader misunderstandings.**

In documents that present a sequence of instructions or steps, the order in which the information appears can be very confusing to a reader. You will examine these functional documents and decide if the information is presented in a logical order.

Example: **Illogical order**
1. Turn the main switch to the "on" position to start the projector.
2. Thread the film through the lamp housing to the take-up reel before starting the projector.

2.8 **Evaluate the credibility of an author's argument or defense of a claim by critiquing the relationship between generalizations and evidence, the comprehensiveness of evidence, and the way in which the author's intent affects the structure and tone of the text (e.g., in professional journals, editorials, political speeches, primary source material).**

In many informational texts, authors make claims or arguments. You will decide how credible or convincing these arguments are by examining the generalizations the authors make and the evidence used to support them, as well as the way the text has been shaped by the author's purpose.

Example:
"The prime myth about the British monarchy is that it is not political. It is intensely and variously political, a huge political fact, . . . a definer of the national image, a load on the national psyche, the focus of feeling and opinion that is itself politically potent."
—from "Blair and the Queen," by Hugo Young, *The Guardian*

3.0 LITERARY RESPONSE AND ANALYSIS: In this group of standards, you will read important literary works that are connected to the subjects you will study in history and social science classes. You will respond to these works and examine them in detail, looking for themes and patterns that appear in many different literary works.

Structural Features of Literature

3.1 **Articulate the relationship between the expressed purposes and the characteristics of different forms of dramatic literature (e.g., comedy, tragedy, drama, dramatic monologue).**

One of the focuses of your reading in the 9th grade will be dramatic literature, such as comedies, tragedies, dramas, and monologues or long speeches. You will explain how the different types of dramatic literature are shaped by their purposes.

***Example:* Comedy**
purpose: to entertain via humor
TONY: What was it about [me] that first took your girlish heart?
ALICE: The back of your head.
—from *You Can't Take it with You,*
Moss Hart and George S. Kaufman

3.2 **Compare and contrast the presentation of a similar theme or topic across genres to explain how the selection of genre shapes the theme or topic.**

A genre is any particular type of literature. You will follow one theme or topic through literary works from different genres, and explain how the theme or topic is affected by each genre.

Narrative Analysis of Grade-Level-Appropriate Text

3.3 **Analyze interactions between main and subordinate characters in a literary text (e.g., internal and external conflicts, motivations, relationships, influences) and explain the way those interactions affect the plot.**

The plot of a literary work is often affected by the way the main characters interact with less important characters. You will examine those interactions—including conflicts between and within characters, the motives behind characters' actions, and the relationships between characters—and explain how they affect the plot.

***Example:* External conflict**
"Imagine my surprise, nay, my consternation, when, without moving from his privacy, Bartleby, in a singularly mild, firm voice, replied, 'I would prefer not to.' "
—from "Bartleby, The Scrivener,"
by Herman Melville

3.4 **Determine characters' traits by what the characters say about themselves in narration, dialogue, dramatic monologue, and soliloquy.**

Sometimes, literary characters talk about themselves as they narrate stories, speak to other characters, or—in dramatic literature—speak directly to the audience. From these examples, you will learn about the qualities characters have.

***Example:* Dialogue**
WILLY: I know it when I walk in. They seem to laugh at me.
LINDA: Why? Why would they laugh at you? Don't talk that way, Willy.
—from *Death of a Salesman,*
by Arthur Miller

3.5 Compare works that express a universal theme and provide evidence to support the ideas expressed in each work.

A universal theme is a central message or idea about life that is expressed by works of literature from many different times and cultures. You will compare different literary works that express the same universal theme, and find examples in each work to support this theme.

Example: **Peace**
"Peace is not an absence of war, it is a virtue, a state of mind, a disposition for benevolence . . ."
—Baruch Spinoza
"Is life so dear, or peace so sweet, as to be purchased at the price of chains of slavery?"
—from "Speech in the Virginia Convention," by Patrick Henry

3.6 Analyze and trace an author's development of time and sequence, including the use of complex literary devices (e.g., foreshadowing, flashbacks).

You will study how an author creates a sense of the past and the future, and of time passing, in a literary work. The literary devices authors use to achieve this include foreshadowing and flashbacks.

Example: **Flashback**
"The rest of our family, however, felt the full impact of Hitler's anti-Jewish laws [in 1938], so life was filled with anxiety."
—from *The Diary of a Young Girl*, by Anne Frank

3.7 Recognize and understand the significance of various literary devices, including figurative language, imagery, allegory, and symbolism, and explain their appeal.

Literary devices are special ways that authors use language to create effects and convey meaning. You will learn about such devices—including figurative or non-literal language, the use of images that appeal to the senses, and the use of elements of a story to symbolize themes or ideas—and explain how they affect a reader.

Example: **Figurative language**
"The story of Wing Biddlebaum is a story of hands. Their restless activity, like unto the beating of the wings of an imprisoned bird, had given him his name."
—from "Hands," by Sherwood Anderson

3.8 Interpret and evaluate the impact of ambiguities, subtleties, contradictions, ironies, and incongruities in a text.

Not all works of literature are simple and straightforward. Many have ambiguous or uncertain meanings. They may be very subtle; their elements may seem to contradict one another; their conflicts might be resolved in ironic ways; or they may contain moments that seem puzzling and out of place.

3.9 Explain how voice, persona, and the choice of a narrator affect characterization and the tone, plot, and credibility of a text.

A narrator is the person who tells the story of a literary work; persona and voice describe the qualities of the narrator's voice. You will explain how the decisions an author makes about voice, persona, and narrator affect the tone and plot and credibility of a work.

Example:
"We did not say she was crazy then. We believed she had to do that."
—from "A Rose for Emily," by William Faulkner

3.10 Identify and describe the function of dialogue, scene designs, soliloquies, asides, and character foils in dramatic literature.

Dramatic literature includes special types of language, including dialogue between characters, soliloquies a main character might deliver, or asides a character might make to the audience. Drama also features secondary characters who serve as foils for the main characters, as well as set designs.

Example: **Soliloquy**
"Oh, that this too too solid flesh would melt,
Thaw, and resolve itself into a dew!"
—from *Hamlet*, by William Shakespeare

Literary Criticism

3.11 Evaluate the aesthetic qualities of style, including the impact of diction and figurative language on tone, mood, and theme, using the terminology of literary criticism. (Aesthetic approach)

In the aesthetic approach to literature, you will use appropriate language to evaluate the style of literary works—including how the choice of words and use of figurative language in a work affect its tone, mood, and themes.

Example:
"No, no, go not to Lethe, neither twist / Wolf's-bane tight-rooted, for its poisonous wine."
—from "Ode on Melancholy," by John Keats

3.12 Analyze the way in which a work of literature is related to the themes and issues of its historical period. (Historical approach)

In the historical approach to literature, you will look closely at a literary work and figure out how its themes and the issues it addresses are connected to the historical period in which it was written.

Example:
"The problem of the twentieth century is the problem of the color line."
—from "To the Nations of the World," by W.E.B. Du Bois

WRITING

1.0 WRITING STRATEGIES: In this set of standards, you will write essays that present clear and understandable perspectives and well-constructed, tightly reasoned arguments. Your essays will hold together, stay focused on their topics, and show that you understand your readers and your purpose. You will move through the different steps of the writing process at an appropriate pace.

Organization and Focus

1.1 Establish a controlling impression or coherent thesis that conveys a clear and distinctive perspective on the subject and maintain a consistent tone and focus throughout the piece of writing.

The writing you will do in the 9th grade will establish an impression of the subject or a thesis that clearly presents your original perspective. Your writing will stay focused on the impression or thesis and keep the same tone from beginning to end.

Example: **Thesis**
High schools should expand varsity sports programs because sports are an important part of the educational experience.

1.2 **Use precise language, action verbs, sensory details, appropriate modifiers, and the active rather than the passive voice.**

In your writing, you will use language that is clear and specific, including verbs that describe actions and the active instead of the passive voice, and details that appeal to the senses.

Example: **Sensory details**
"The play area was bordered by wood-slat benches where old-country people sat cracking roasted watermelon seeds . . ."
—from *The Joy Luck CLub,* by Amy Tan

Research and Technology

1.3 **Use clear research questions and suitable research methods (e.g., library, electronic media, personal interview) to elicit and present evidence from primary and secondary sources.**

To find evidence in primary and secondary sources, you will use clear research questions and such research methods as library research, electronic media, and personal interviews.

Example: **Research question**
How did the lives of women in the western United States in the nineteenth century differ from the lives of women who lived in the East in the same time period?

1.4 **Develop the main ideas within the body of the composition through supporting evidence (e.g., scenarios, commonly held beliefs, hypotheses, definitions).**

Your essays will have main ideas that you will develop by supporting them with such evidence as scenarios, beliefs that many people share, hypotheses or theories, and definitions of important terms and concepts.

Example: **Commonly held belief**
The common agreement that education is the key to a better life reaches as far back as Aristotle, who wrote, "Education is the best provision for old age."

1.5 **Synthesize information from multiple sources and identify complexities and discrepancies in the information and the different perspectives found in each medium (e.g., almanacs, microfiche, news sources, in-depth field studies, speeches, journals, technical documents).**

As you conduct your research, you will find information in many different sources, including almanacs, microfiche, news sources, in-depth field studies, journals, and technical documents. To get a full understanding of the topic, you will combine all of the information, taking note of different perspectives they offer.

1.6 **Integrate quotations and citations into a written text while maintaining the flow of ideas.**

In your research essays, you will fully integrate exact quotes into your writing and include the correct citations, while keeping your essay's ideas flowing smoothly.

Example:
"Kate Chopin, *The Atlantic* concluded, was 'a genuine and delightful addition to the ranks of our storytellers.' "
—from *Kate Chopin,* by Emily Toth

1.7 **Use appropriate conventions for documentation in the text, notes, and bibliographies by adhering to those in style manuals (e.g., Modern Language Association Handbook, The Chicago Manual of Style).**

It is very important to document the information you borrow from your sources. The correct methods of documentation of all types can be found in style manuals, like *The Modern Language Association Handbook* and the *Chicago Manual of Style*.

Example: **Bibliography (MLA style)**
Mount, Charles Merrill. *Monet: A Biography*. New York: Simon and Schuster, 1966.

1.8 **Design and publish documents by using advanced publishing software and graphic programs.**

You will use advanced computer desktop publishing programs for creating graphics to design and create—or publish—documents.

Evaluation and Revision

1.9 **Revise writing to improve the logic and coherence of the organization and controlling perspective, the precision of word choice, and the tone by taking into consideration the audience, purpose, and formality of the context.**

Revising is an important part of the writing process. As you revise, strengthen the organization and overall perspective of your writing by improving logic and coherence. You will also make your word choice more precise and make your tone more appropriate for your audience, purpose, and context.

Example: **Precision of word choice, formality**
Original: Back in the 1850's and later, things changed a lot for lots of women, especially in New England.
Revised: During the second half of the nineteenth century, the lives of many New England women changed dramatically.

2.0 WRITING APPLICATIONS (GENRES AND THEIR CHARACTERISTICS): In this string of standards, you will combine what you have learned writing narratives, expository essays, persuasive essays, and descriptive texts, and use this knowledge to write texts of at least 1,500 words each. Your writing will show that you have mastered standard American English as well as the research, organization, and drafting skills and strategies taught in the previous strand of 9th grade standards.

2.1 **Write biographical or autobiographical narratives or short stories: a) Relate a sequence of events and communicate the significance of the events to the audience; b) Locate scenes and incidents in specific places; c) Describe with concrete sensory details the sights, sounds, and smells of a scene and the specific actions, movements, gestures, and feelings of the characters; use interior monologue to depict the characters' feelings; d) Pace the presentation of actions to accommodate changes in time and mood; e) Make effective use of descriptions of appearance, images, shifting perspectives, and sensory details.**

In the 9th grade, you will master the writing of biographical or autobiographical narratives or short stories. You will demonstrate the skills of: sequencing events; describing details of place, characterization, and mood; pacing; and shifting perspectives within your narrative.

***Example:* Autobiographical narrative**
"That is why, walking across a school campus on this particular December morning, I keep searching the sky. As if I expected to see, rather like hearts, a lost pair of kites hurrying toward heaven."
—from "A Christmas Memory," by Truman Capote

2.2 **Write responses to literature: a) Demonstrate a comprehensive grasp of the significant ideas of literary works; b) Support important ideas and viewpoints through accurate and detailed references to the text or to other works; c) Demonstrate awareness of the author's use of stylistic devices and an appreciation of the effects created; d) Identify and assess the impact of perceived ambiguities, nuances, and complexities within the text.**

Effective responses to literature show that you understand the important ideas of the literary works you read; support your ideas with accurate and detailed references to literary works; acknowledge the effects the author achieves with stylistic devices; and critique the works' ambiguities, nuances, and complexities.

***Example:* Response to literature**
"*Hamlet,* like the sonnets, is full of some stuff that the writer could not drag to light, contemplate, or manipulate into art. And when we search for this feeling, we find it, as in the sonnets, very difficult to localize."
—from "Hamlet," by T. S. Eliot

2.3 **Write expository compositions, including analytical essays and research reports: a) Marshal evidence in support of a thesis and related claims, including information on all relevant perspectives; b) Convey information and ideas from primary and secondary sources accurately and coherently; c) Make distinctions between the relative value and significance of specific data, facts, and ideas; d) Include visual aids by employing appropriate technology to organize and record information on charts, maps, and graphs; e) Anticipate and address readers' potential misunderstandings, biases, and expectations; f) Use technical terms and notations accurately.**

In expository compositions, including analytical essays and research reports, you will support your theses and claims with relevant, accurate information; show an understanding of the value of each fact and idea; and strive for clarity by using charts, graphs, and correct terms and notations.

2.4 **Write persuasive compositions: a) Structure ideas and arguments in a sustained and logical fashion; b) Use specific rhetorical devices to support assertions (e.g., appeal to logic through reasoning; appeal to emotion or ethical belief; relate a personal anecdote, case study, or analogy); c) Clarify and defend positions with precise and relevant evidence, including facts, expert opinions, quotations, and expressions of commonly accepted beliefs and logical reasoning; d) Address readers' concerns, counterclaims, biases, and expectations.**

Persuasive compositions feature logically structured ideas and arguments. You will support your argument with rhetorical devices that persuade your readers by appealing to their logic, emotions, and beliefs; defend your position clearly with logical reasoning and precise, relevant evidence; and address expectations or disagreements your readers might have.

Example:
"One may well ask: 'How can you advocate breaking some laws and obeying others?' The answer lies in the fact that there are two types of laws: just and unjust."
—from "Letter from Birmingham Jail," by Martin Luther King, Jr.

2.5 **Write business letters: a) Provide clear and purposeful information and address the intended audience appropriately; b) Use appropriate vocabulary, tone, and style to take into account the nature of the relationship with, and the knowledge and interests of, the recipients; c) Highlight central ideas or images; d) Follow a conventional style with page formats, fonts, and spacing that contribute to the documents' readability and impact.**

You will learn how to write business letters that provide clear, purposeful information and appropriately address your intended audience. Your writing will reflect suitable vocabulary and tone, focus on a central idea, and follow a standard business style for readability.

Example: Application
I am writing to apply for an internship with your company. My resume and two letters of recommendation are enclosed.

2.6 **Write technical documents (e.g., a manual on rules of behavior for conflict resolution, procedures for conducting a meeting, minutes of a meeting): a) Report information and convey ideas logically and correctly; b) Offer detailed and accurate specifications; c) Include scenarios, definitions, and examples to aid comprehension (e.g., troubleshooting guide); d) Anticipate readers' problems, mistakes, and misunderstandings.**

In 9th grade, you will write technical documents, like minutes of meetings, that report accurate information and ideas, include definitions and examples, and anticipate any problems readers may encounter.

***Example:* Minutes of a meeting**

Old Business

- October Meeting Minutes: Minutes of last month's meeting were read.

WRITTEN AND ORAL ENGLISH LANGUAGE CONVENTIONS

1.0 WRITTEN AND ORAL ENGLISH LANGUAGE CONVENTIONS: In this strand of standards, you will master the conventions of standard English for writing and speaking.

Grammar and Mechanics of Writing

1.1 Identify and correctly use clauses (e.g., main and subordinate), phrases (e.g., gerund, infinitive, and participial), and mechanics of punctuation (e.g., semicolons, colons, ellipses, hyphens).

In the 9th grade, you will show that you recognize and can correctly use clauses and the different types of phrases, as well as such punctuation marks as semicolons, colons, ellipses, and hyphens.

Example: **Clauses**
"The translucent walls of childhood no longer close them in, for suddenly they discover the wide gateways and the gates ready to swing open at a touch of a hand."
—from *Family,* by Margaret Mead

1.2 Understand sentence construction (e.g., parallel structure, subordination, proper placement of modifiers) and proper English usage (e.g., consistency of verb tenses).

Sentences can be put together using several different strategies, including parallel structure and subordination. You will master these aspects of sentence construction, the proper placement of modifiers, and such English usage conventions as consistent verb tenses.

Example: **Parallel structure, consistency of verb tenses**
". . . we shall fight in the fields and in the streets, we shall fight in the hills; we shall never surrender."
—from "Speech on Dunkirk," by Winston Churchill

1.3 Demonstrate an understanding of proper English usage and control of grammar, paragraph and sentence structure, diction, and syntax.

You will also show that you understand English usage, grammar, diction, and syntax, as well as effective sentence and paragraph structures.

Manuscript Form

1.4 Produce legible work that shows accurate spelling and correct use of the conventions of punctuation and capitalization.

At this grade level, the written work you present in class should be legible, including accurate spelling and correct punctuation and grammar.

1.5 Reflect appropriate manuscript requirements, including title page presentation, pagination, spacing and margins, and integration of source and support material (e.g., in-text citation, use of direct quotations, paraphrasing) with appropriate citations.

Your work should also follow appropriate rules for manuscripts, which may include requirements for a title page, page numbering and margins, line spacing, and the use and citing of material borrowed from sources.

Example: **Integration of source (MLA)**
In "Barn Burning," an illiterate boy reads the labels of cans with "his stomach . . . from the scarlet devils and the silver curve of fish" (Faulkner 3).

LISTENING AND SPEAKING

1.0 LISTENING AND SPEAKING STRATEGIES: In this group of standards, you will make skillful decisions about speaking, such as tailoring your gestures, tone, and vocabulary to suit your audience. Also, you will deliver focused and coherent presentations that clearly convey solid reasoning and your own perspective on the topic.

Comprehension

1.1 Formulate judgments about the ideas under discussion and support those judgments with convincing evidence.

In the 9th grade, you will show that you understand ideas being discussed by forming judgments about them and supporting your judgments with convincing evidence.

Example: **Forming judgments**
"[*The Jungle*] is remembered as a stomach-turning exposé of unsanitary conditions and deceitful practices in the meat-packing industry . . . and it contributed enormously to the landmark passage of the Pure Food and Drug Act of 1906."
—from "Introduction to *The Jungle*," by Morris Dickstein

1.2 Compare and contrast the ways in which media genres (e.g., televised news, newsmagazines, documentaries, online information) cover the same event.

You will also demonstrate your comprehension of news coverage by comparing and contrasting the way different news media—including television news, newsmagazines, documentaries, and online news sources—report on the same event.

Organization and Delivery of Oral Communication

1.3 Choose logical patterns of organization (e.g., chronological, topical, cause and effect) to inform and to persuade, by soliciting agreement or action, or to unite audiences behind a common belief or cause.

At this grade level, you will make oral presentations that inform, persuade, or unite your audience behind one cause or belief. Your presentations will be logically organized, using chronological, topical, and cause-and-effect patterns.

Example: **Speech to unite**
"I shall see our young braves and our chiefs sitting in the houses of law and government, ruling and being ruled by the knowledge and freedoms of *our* great land."
—from "There Is a Longing," by Chief Dan George

1.4 Choose appropriate techniques for developing the introduction and conclusion (e.g., by using literary quotations, anecdotes, and references to authoritative sources).

You will develop the introductions and conclusions of your presentations by using appropriate strategies, such as literary quotations, anecdotes, and references to sources.

Example: **Conclusion**
Therefore, if anyone suggests it is a bad idea to get involved in local government, remember Walt Whitman's words: "Political democracy . . . supplies a training school for making first-class men."

1.5 **Recognize and use elements of classical speech forms (e.g., introduction, first and second transitions, body, conclusion) in formulating rational arguments and applying the art of persuasion and debate.**

Classical speech form includes such elements as the introduction, transitions, the body, and the conclusion. You will recognize these elements, use them to develop rational arguments, and apply them persuasively in debate.

Example: **Introduction**
". . . now standing upon the soil which once was, and now ought to be, the property of this tribe, . . . I would shake you by the hand, and ask you to listen, for a little while, to what I have to say."
—from "Quinney's Speech," by John Wannuaucon Quinney

1.6 **Present and advance a clear thesis statement and choose appropriate types of proof (e.g., statistics, testimony, specific instances) that meet standard tests for evidence, including credibility, validity, and relevance.**

Your presentations will present clear thesis statements and support them with credible, valid, relevant types of proof, including statistics, testimony from experts, and specific examples.

Example: **Thesis**
"The history of the present king of Great Britain is a history of repeated injuries . . . To prove this, let facts be submitted to a candid world."
—from The Declaration of Independence, by Thomas Jefferson

1.7 **Use props, visual aids, graphs, and electronic media to enhance the appeal and accuracy of presentations.**

You will make your presentations more appealing and accurate by using props, visual aids like graphs, and electronic media.

Example: **Graphs**

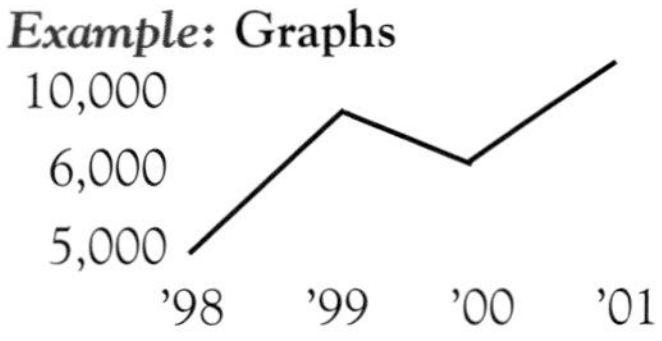

1.8 **Produce concise notes for extemporaneous delivery.**

At this grade level, you will be expected to deliver oral communications without preparation. You will learn to take concise notes that will help you make these extemporaneous presentations.

Example: **Notes**
1) Introduce topic: Causes of the Civil War
2) List major causes
   A) Conflict over slavery
   B) Industrial North vs. Agricultural South

1.9 **Analyze the occasion and the interests of the audience and choose effective verbal and nonverbal techniques (e.g., voice, gestures, eye contact) for presentations.**

To make your presentations more effective, you will use techniques—including voice, gestures, and eye contact—that are appropriate for the occasion and your audience.

Example:
For her Speech to the Commonwealth, Britain's Queen Elizabeth elected to wear her formal robes and crown of state to commemorate the annual occasion and the dignitaries in attendance.

Analysis and Evaluation of Oral and Media Communications

1.10 Analyze historically significant speeches (e.g., Abraham Lincoln's "Gettysburg Address," Martin Luther King, Jr.'s "I Have a Dream") to find the rhetorical devices and features that make them memorable.

At this grade level, you will examine and evaluate historic speeches such as Abraham Lincoln's "Gettysburg Address" and Martin Luther King, Jr.'s "I Have a Dream," in order to find out what makes them memorable.

Example: **Rhetorical device: repetition**
". . . that the government of the people, by the people, for the people, shall not perish from the earth."
—from "The Gettysburg Address," by Abraham Lincoln

1.11 Assess how language and delivery affect the mood and tone of the oral communication and make an impact on the audience.

You will also consider the language and delivery of oral communication, evaluating how they make an impact on the audience by affecting mood and tone.

1.12 Evaluate the clarity, quality, effectiveness, and general coherence of a speaker's important points, arguments, evidence, organization of ideas, delivery, diction, and syntax.

You will listen closely to a speaker's argument and evaluate its clarity, quality, effectiveness, and general coherence, paying close attention to the organization of ideas, major points, evidence, delivery, diction, and syntax.

Example: **Clarity of important points**
"If a free society cannot help the many who are poor, it cannot save the few who are rich."
—from "Inaugural Address," by John F. Kennedy

1.13 Analyze the types of arguments used by the speaker, including argument by causation, analogy, authority, emotion, and logic.

You will also analyze the types of argument the speaker uses, including such strategies as cause and effect, making analogies, relying on authorities, appealing to emotions, and the use of logic.

Example: **Argument by emotion**
"I see one-third of a nation ill-housed, ill-clad, ill-nourished."
—from "Second Inaugural Address," by Franklin D. Roosevelt

1.14 Identify the aesthetic effects of a media presentation and evaluate the techniques used to create them (e.g., compare Shakespeare's Henry V with Kenneth Branagh's 1990 film version).

Finally, you will study and evaluate the aesthetic effects media can achieve by comparing how the same presentation changes in different media—for example, by evaluating the effects the medium of film has on a play.

2.0 SPEAKING APPLICATIONS (GENRES AND THEIR CHARACTERISTICS): In this set of standards, you will focus on delivering both formal, planned presentations and on-the-spot, unprepared presentations that use traditional rhetorical strategies, such as narration, exposition, persuasion, and description. You will speak with a mastery of standard American English, making use of the skills mastered in the previous group of standards.

2.1 Deliver narrative presentations: a) Narrate a sequence of events and communicate their significance to the audience; b) Locate scenes and incidents in specific places; c) Describe with concrete sensory details the sights, sounds, and smells of a scene and the specific actions, movements, gestures, and feelings of characters; d) Pace the presentation of actions to accommodate time or mood changes.

In grade 9, you will master the narrative presentation, both fictional and autobiographical. You will add in such elements as a standard plot line, character development, concrete details that appeal to the senses, pacing that changes with the time and mood of your narrative, and other elements of story-writing.

***Example*: Feelings of a character**
"I hoped then that life might offer me the opportunity to serve my people and make my own humble contribution to their freedom struggle."
—from "I Am Prepared to Die," by Nelson Mandela

2.2 Deliver expository presentations: a) Marshal evidence in support of a thesis and related claims, including information on all relevant perspectives; b) Convey information and ideas from primary and secondary sources accurately and coherently; c) Make distinctions between the relative value and significance of specific data, facts, and ideas; d) Include visual aids by employing appropriate technology to organize and display information on charts, maps, and graphs; e) Anticipate and address the listener's potential misunderstandings, biases, and expectations; f) Use technical terms and notations accurately.

At this grade level, you will deliver expository presentations that present clear theses that are supported with well-organized evidence drawn from every relevant perspective. In addition, you will include informative visual aids, address any problems or expectations your listeners might have, and use all terms correctly.

***Example*: Marshalling evidence**
Carbon dioxide is a major contributor to global warming trends. Michael D. Lemonick states, in his article "Life in the Greenhouse," that "humans have increased the concentration of carbon dioxide, the most abundant heat-trapping gas in the atmosphere, to 30% above the pre-industrial levels . . ."

2.3 Apply appropriate interviewing techniques: a) Prepare and ask relevant questions; b) Make notes of responses; c) Use language that conveys maturity, sensitivity, and respect; d) Respond correctly and effectively to questions; e) Demonstrate knowledge of the subject or organization; f) Compile and report responses; g) Evaluate the effectiveness of the interview.

In grade 9, you will learn how to conduct interviews appropriately. You will prepare relevant questions that demonstrate your knowledge of the subject and ask them using mature, sensitive, and respectful language. You will learn how to effectively use your notes to report on the responses and evaluate the interview.

***Example*: Ask relevant questions**
"A character in *Things Fall Apart* remarks that the white man 'has put a knife on the things that held us together, and we have fallen apart.' Are those things still severed, or have the wounds begun to heal?"
—from "An African Voice: Interview with Chinua Achebe," by Katie Bacon

2.4 Deliver oral responses to literature: a) Advance a judgment demonstrating a comprehensive grasp of the significant ideas of works or passages (i.e., make and support warranted assertions about the text); b) Support important ideas and viewpoints through accurate and detailed references to the text or to other works; c) Demonstrate awareness of the author's use of stylistic devices and an appreciation of the effects created; d) Identify and assess the impact of perceived ambiguities, nuances, and complexities within the text.

In grade 9, you will learn how to state clearly your thoughts and opinions on a literary work, and support them with the best possible evidence from the text and other texts that deal with your thesis. You will show that you understand the effects the author achieves with stylistic devices; you will also identify and evaluate the works' ambiguities, nuances, and complexities.

Example: **Reference to literary work**
"I am thinking now of what I rate the best one [literary work from the late 1950s]: Salinger's *Catcher in the Rye*, perhaps because this one expresses so completely what I have tried to say: a youth, father to what will, must someday be a man . . ."

—from *Faulkner in the University*, by William Faulkner

2.5 Deliver persuasive arguments (including evaluation and analysis of problems and solutions and causes and effects): a) Structure ideas and arguments in a coherent, logical fashion. b) Use rhetorical devices to support assertions (e.g., by appeal to logic through reasoning; by appeal to emotion or ethical belief; by use of personal anecdote, case study, or analogy). c) Clarify and defend positions with precise and relevant evidence, including facts, expert opinions, quotations, expressions of commonly accepted beliefs, and logical reasoning. d) Anticipate and address the listener's concerns and counterarguments.

In grade 9, you will learn how to construct oral presentations that will help you convince an audience of your position. You will learn how to support your assertions with the best possible evidence, and use verbal and nonverbal strategies to emphasize your message. You will learn how to defend your position clearly with logical reasoning and precise, relevant evidence.

Example: **Rhetorical devices, logic**
"We aren't engaged in any negative protest and in any negative argument with anybody. We are saying that we are determined to be men. We are determined to be people."

—from "I've Been to the Mountaintop," by Martin Luther King, Jr.

2.6 Deliver descriptive presentations: a) Establish clearly the speaker's point of view on the subject of the presentation; b) Establish clearly the speaker's relationship with that subject (e.g., dispassionate observation, personal involvement); c) Use effective, factual descriptions of appearance, concrete images, shifting perspectives and vantage points, and sensory details.

Finally, you will deliver descriptive presentations in which you establish a clear point of view on the subject, clarifying how close to or distant from it you are, describing images and appearances, and shifting perspectives and points of view.

Example: **Description, sensory details**
". . . on a little hill, in a lonely cabin, overspread by the forest oak, I first drew my breath . . ."

—from "An Address to the Whites," by Elias Boudinot

Contents in Brief

UNIT 1

THEME: *Spine Tinglers*

SKILLS WORKSHOPS

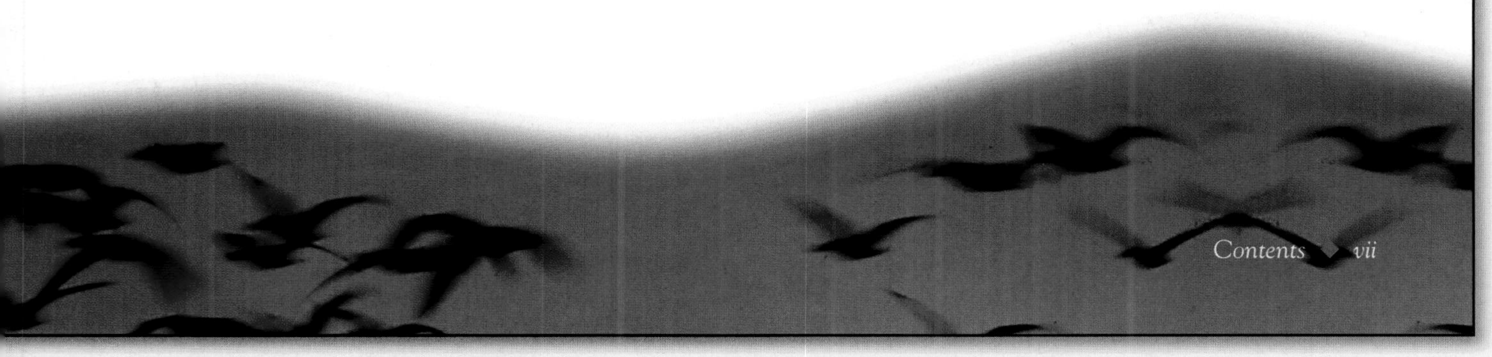

UNIT 2

THEME: *Challenges and Choices*

SKILLS WORKSHOPS

UNIT 3

THEME: *Moments of Discovery*

UNIT 4

THEME: *The Lighter Side*

SKILLS WORKSHOPS

UNIT 5

THEME: *Visions of the Future*

UNIT 6 GENRE: *Short Stories*

SKILLS WORKSHOPS

UNIT 7

GENRE: *Nonfiction*

SKILLS WORKSHOPS

UNIT 8

GENRE: *Drama*

SKILLS WORKSHOPS

UNIT 9

GENRE: *Poetry*

Comparing Literary Works

Comparing Literary Works

Comparing Literary Works

(Continued on page xvi.)

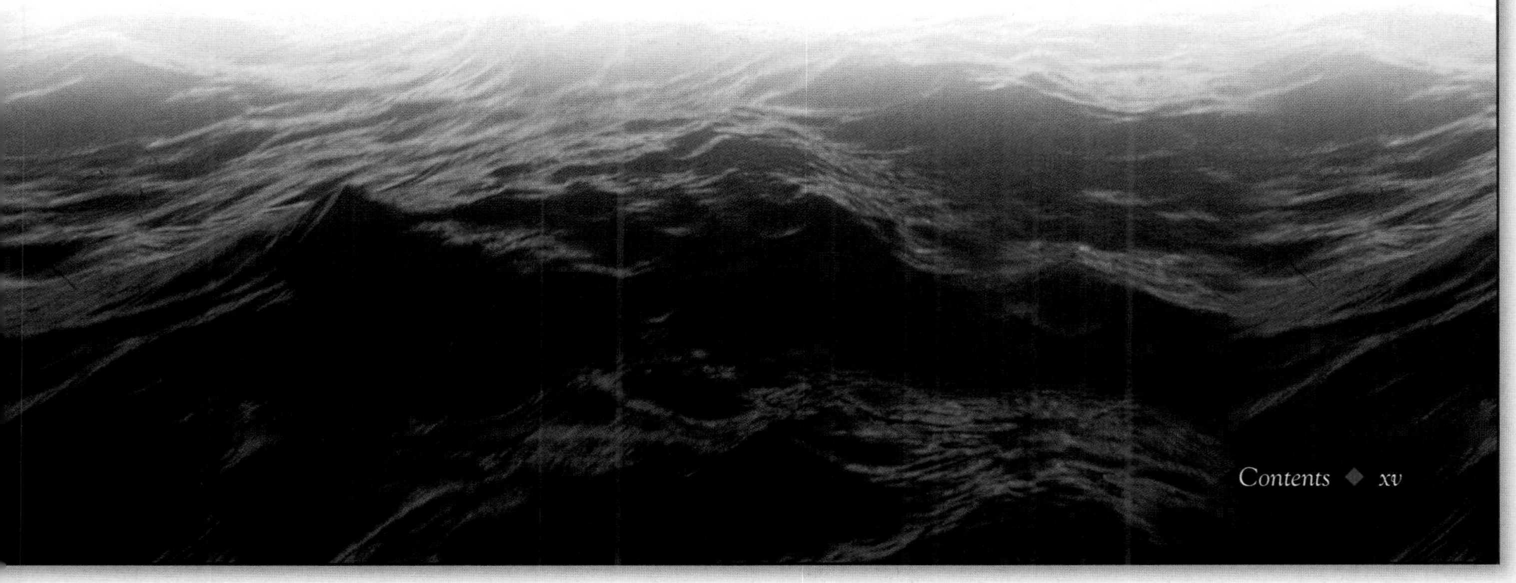

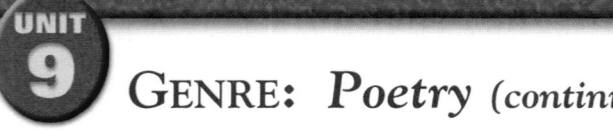

UNIT 9 GENRE: *Poetry* (continued)

Comparing Literary Works

Comparing Literary Works

SKILLS WORKSHOPS

UNIT 10

GENRE: *The Epic*

Complete Contents by Genre

Short Stories

POETRY

Comparing Literary Works

Reading Informational Materials

Connections

How to Read Literature

Writing Workshops

Listening and Speaking Workshops

Assessment Workshops

Objectives

1. To identify the purposes and characteristics of the major literary genres
2. To apply an in-depth understanding of genre as an aid to reading comprehension

How to Use Learn About Literature

"Learn About Literature" pages help students become better readers by acquainting them with the conventions of the major literary genres. Each page contains definitions, sample passages, and comprehension questions about the major genres. These elements will help students build an in-depth understanding of genre that will improve their reading comprehension skills.

Literary Genres

Short Story and Nonfiction

- Have students read the definition of a short story and the accompanying excerpt. Then, ask them to respond to the question.
  Answer: The character's conflict arises from the facts that she is fully equipped to lead a life of wealth and privilege—but she happens to be poor.
- Then, have students read the definition of nonfiction and respond to the question that follows.
  Answer: Students may say that the author's comic tone and references to dodging Chevrolets while playing football demonstrate that his purpose is to entertain and amuse his readers.

Learn About Literature

Forms of Literature

Short Story • Nonfiction • Drama • Poetry • Folk Literature

Just as there are different styles of music, such as classical or rock, so too are there different forms of literature. Each is called a genre and has its own distinct characteristics. These pages present a brief explanation and an example of each genre. They will help you understand and appreciate the literature when you read these various works in their entirety.

Short Story

A **short story** is a brief work of fiction. In most short stories, one main character faces a conflict that is resolved in the plot. In addition, a short story usually conveys a theme, or message about life. Good craftsmanship goes into the writing of a good story, which must accomplish its purpose in relatively few words.

What do you learn about a character's conflict in this story's opening?

She was one of those pretty, charming young women who are born, as if by an error of Fate, into a petty official's family. She had no dowry, no hopes, not the slightest chance of being appreciated, understood, loved, and married by a rich and distinguished man; so she slipped into marriage with a minor civil servant at the Ministry of Education.

FROM "THE NECKLACE," GUY DE MAUPASSANT, P. 608

Nonfiction

Nonfiction is writing that tells about real people, places, objects, events, and ideas. Many of the nonfiction articles in this book are either essays or biographical or autobiographical sketches. All discuss the real world as opposed to an imaginary one. The author of a nonfiction article may wish to convey and explain information, convince readers to accept a particular idea or opinion, or simply entertain and amuse readers.

Based on its opening, what do you sense is the author's purpose in this nonfiction article?

The essence of childhood, of course, is play, which my friends and I did endlessly on streets that we reluctantly shared with traffic. As a daring receiver in touch football, I spent many happy years running up and down those asphalt fields, hoping that a football would hit me before a Chevrolet did.

FROM "GO DEEP TO THE SEWER," BILL COSBY, P. 368

ENRICHMENT: Literature Library

To extend students' understanding of different genres, use titles in the **Prentice Hall Literature Library.** This collection includes novels, plays, and special literature anthologies, each with its own study guide.

Novels
Canyons
Great Expectations
The Master Puppeteer
The Odyssey
The Old Man and the Sea
The Strange Case of Dr. Jekyll and Mr. Hyde
A Tale of Two Cities
To Kill a Mockingbird
When Legends Die

Play
A Midsummer Night's Dream

Special Anthologies
Authors In Depth, Platinum Level
Today's Nonfiction
Workplace Writing

"In the midst of any adventure, a born writer has a desire to hurry home and put it into words."

—Maxine Hong Kingston

Drama

Drama is written to be performed by actors. The script is made up of dialogue and monologue—the words the actors say—and stage directions, which comment on how and where the action occurs.

How does the appearance of this dramatic text differ from the appearance of a short story?

> **HORACE.** That's a pretty piece.
> **MARY CATHERINE.** Yes, it is.
> [*A pause. They dance again.* HORACE *stops.*]
> **HORACE.** I'm ready to go if you are, Mary Catherine.
> **MARY CATHERINE.** I'm ready. [*They start out.*] Scared?
>
> FROM "THE DANCERS," HORTON FOOTE, P. 734

Poetry

Poetry is literature that appears in verse form. It often has a regular rhythm and, sometimes, a rhyme scheme. Some poems tell a story, while other poems present a single image or express a single emotion or thought. Most poems use concise, musical, and emotionally charged language to convey an idea.

How do the lines of poetry below differ in form from the prose paragraphs on the facing page?

> Some say the world will end in fire,
> Some say in ice.
> From what I've tasted of desire
> I hold with those who favor fire.
>
> FROM "FIRE AND ICE," ROBERT FROST, P. 472

Folk Literature

Folk literature is the unwritten lore of a specific people or culture, passed down through the generations by word of mouth until, at some point, it is put into writing. Folk literature includes myths, folk tales, fairy tales, legends, and fables. Such stories express the hopes, fears, loves, dreams, and values of the people who tell them and pass them on.

What does the beginning of this myth indicate about the values of people in ancient Greece?

> King Acrisius of Argos had only one child, a daughter, Danaë. She was beautiful above all the other women of the land, but this was small comfort to the King for not having a son.
>
> FROM "PERSEUS," EDITH HAMILTON, P. 214

CUSTOMIZE INSTRUCTION FOR UNIVERSAL ACCESS

For Less Proficient Readers	For English Learners	For Advanced Readers
Ask students to find in this book an example of folk literature, a short story, a nonfiction article, and a poem. Then, have them point out the structural elements of each selection that reveal its genre.	Ask students to bring to class examples of each genre that they have encountered in their home language. Have them point out the key genre characteristics of each.	Have students read the first two pages of "The Necklace," pp. 608–609, to add more details to what they know about the story's characters, setting, and plot.

Discuss the Quotation

- Born in Stockton, California, Maxine Hong Kingston grew up among immigrants from her father's village in China; her first language was a dialect of Cantonese. The storytelling she absorbed in her childhood has infused her writing ever since.
- Have students read Kingston's quotation. Ask them whether they have ever, in the midst of an "adventure," wished they could tell someone about it, even while the event was still going on. Something of that impulse is at the core of a writer's motive.

Literary Genres

Dramatic Literature, Poetry, and Folk Literature

- Draw students' attention to the definition of dramatic literature, and have students respond to the accompanying question.
  Answer: Students may point out differences in format. Speakers' names appear in bold type; actions—stage directions—are printed in italic and bracketed.
- Next, have students read the definition of poetry, and ask them to respond to the question.
  Answer: Students may note that the words are laid out in rhythmic lines; certain words at the ends of lines rhyme ("fire," "desire"). Some students may sense that words themselves are used differently than in the passages on p. xxvi; the language is figurative rather than literal.
- Finally, have students read the definition of folk literature and answer the question.
  Answer: Students may note that one cultural value of ancient Greece was to esteem male children rather than daughters.

Short Stories

- Have a volunteer read aloud the introduction to short stories. Then, ask students to explain how short stories allow them to "travel" to different worlds
  Possible response: Short stories provide encounters with people and places readers might not otherwise get to know or visit.
- Have students work in pairs to write definitions of plot, characters, setting, point of view, and theme based on their prior knowledge. Then, as they read, have students compare their own definitions to those given in the book.

Elements of a Short Story
Plot

- Read the definition of plot. Then, have students copy the plot diagram into their notebooks. As a class, annotate the diagram by writing a short definition of each plot element.
- Have students answer the question about "The Red-Headed League," and then discuss their answers.
  Answer: The opening introduces a red-headed man; based on the title of the story, the reader infers his involvement in a "league."

Elements of a Short Story
Characters

- After students read the definition of characters, have them describe examples of the three methods of characterization from stories they have read in the past.
- Then, have students answer the question about Nat from "The Birds."
  Answer: Though a husband and a father, Nat is something of a loner; he enjoys doing solitary work in the outdoors, where he has opportunity to birdwatch.

Short Stories

Plot • Characters • Setting • Point of View • Theme

Short stories invite you to travel to fictional places, meet interesting and unusual people, and get involved with the problems they face. This book presents a variety of short stories. No two are exactly the same, although all the stories share certain characteristics and follow a prescribed structure.

Plot

The **plot** of a short story is its sequence of events. It involves both characters and a problem, or conflict. The plot begins with an exposition that introduces the characters, setting, and basic story. The action rises as characters try to resolve the problem. Tension increases as events lead to a climax, or high point of interest or suspense. The climax is followed by falling action, leading to the resolution of the conflict.

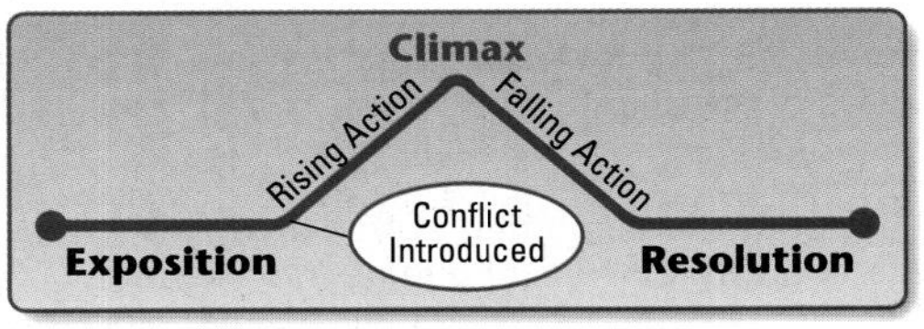

Which plot details do you learn from the opening sentence of this short story?

> I had called upon my friend, Mr. Sherlock Holmes, one day in the autumn of last year and found him in deep conversation with a very stout, florid-faced, elderly gentleman with fiery red hair.
>
> FROM "THE RED-HEADED LEAGUE," SIR ARTHUR CONAN DOYLE, P. 96

Characters

The **characters** in a short story are the people or animals who participate in the action. Writers can develop characters in a variety of ways. Details about characters are revealed through their physical description and their words and actions. In addition, writers reveal characters through their interaction with other characters in the story.

What do the details in the following passage tell you about Nat's character?

> Nat Hocken, because of a wartime disability, had a pension and did not work full-time at the farm. He worked three days a week, and they gave him the lighter jobs: hedging, thatching, repairs to the farm buildings.
>
> Although he was married, with children, his was a solitary disposition; he liked best to work alone. It pleased him when he was given a bank to build up, or a gate to mend at the far end of the peninsula, where the sea surrounded the farmland on either side. Then, at midday, he would pause and eat the pasty that his wife had baked for him, and, sitting on the cliff's edge, watch the birds.
>
> FROM "THE BIRDS," DAPHNE DU MAURIER, P. 50

"They ghosted you up a swell story . . ." —*Langston Hughes*

Setting

The **setting** of a story is the time and place of the action. Time can include not only the historical period—past, present, or future—but also a specific year, season, or time of day. Place may involve not only the geographical place—a region, country, state, or town—but also the social, economic, or cultural environment.

In some stories, setting serves as a decorative but nonessential background. In contrast, the setting of other stories may drive the action by providing a problem that the characters must face and overcome.

Which details in this passage help you to identify the setting of the story?

> I belong in Cleveland, Ohio. One winter's night, two years ago, I reached home just after dark, in a driving snowstorm, and the first thing I heard when I entered the house was that my dearest boyhood friend and schoolmate, John B. Hackett, had died the day before, and that his last utterance had been a desire that I would take his remains home to his poor old father and mother in Wisconsin. I was greatly shocked and grieved, but there was no time to waste in emotions; I must start at once.
>
> FROM "THE INVALID'S STORY," MARK TWAIN, P. 596

Point of View

The **point of view** in a story is the vantage point from which the story is told. In *first-person narration*, the storyteller is a character in the action. In *third-person narration*, the storyteller reports events, taking no direct part in the action.

Which clues in this sentence indicate the point of view of this short story?

> I was six when my mother taught me the art of invisible strength.
>
> FROM "RULES OF THE GAME," AMY TAN, P. 262

Theme

The **theme** of a short story is the central message or insight into life revealed through the work. In some stories, the theme may be stated directly. In most stories, however, the theme is only implied. You must use the story's events to help you draw conclusions about its theme.

Based on the following passage, what might be the theme of this story?

> He also felt the warmth of the earth. He sensed he was inside someone. Then he understood what Don Trine was doing. He was not crazy, he simply liked to feel the earth when it was sleeping.
>
> FROM "THE HARVEST," TOMÁS RIVERA, P. 616

CUSTOMIZE INSTRUCTION FOR UNIVERSAL ACCESS

For Special Needs Students	For Gifted/Talented Students	For Advanced Readers
To help students follow a story's plot as they read, use the Story Map transparency on p. 83 of **Writing Models and Graphic Organizers on Transparencies.**	Ask students to rewrite a scene from a short story from the point of view of a different character. Then, have them explain how the story differs when told from this point of view.	Have students work in small groups to determine the implied theme of a movie they've all seen. Remind them to consider the title, the main character's actions, and important dialogue near the movie's end.

Discuss the Quotation

- Tell students that though Langston Hughes is known primarily as a poet, he published in all the major genres. In his prolific lifetime he produced sixteen books of poetry, two novels, three collections of stories, four collections of nonfiction, and twenty plays.
- Have students read the quotation and ask them to react to Hughes's choice of verb.
  Answer: Students may know that a "ghostwriter" is paid to write for someone else, who then takes credit for authorship. Ask students whether Hughes is playing with this sense of "ghosted" or intends another meaning.

Elements of a Short Story

Setting

- Have students read the definition of setting. Then, have them read the passage from "The Invalid's Story" and answer the question.
  Answer: The references to Cleveland, dark, and a driving snowstorm indicated that the setting is a winter evening in the Midwest.

Elements of a Short Story

Point of View

- Discuss with students the different vantage points from which a story can be told and how pronouns can be key indicators. Then, choose a story the class has read. Have students identify its point of view and explain how it would differ if told from another vantage point.
- Ask the question about point of view in "Rules of the Game."
  Answer: The use of the pronouns "I" and "my" indicate that the story is told in the first-person point of view.

Elements of a Short Story

Theme

- After students read the definition of theme, ask them why it is important to understand the theme of a story they are reading.
  Possible response: The theme makes a fictional story relevant by connecting it to issues of real life.
- Discuss with students the answer to the question about "The Harvest."
  Possible response: Students may agree that the implied theme is the importance of making a connection with the earth.

Nonfiction

- Read the introduction to nonfiction to students, and then ask them which forms of nonfiction they read most frequently and why they do so.
- If possible, bring to class an assortment of articles, essays, journals, and biographical and autobiographical specimens. Have students work in small groups to categorize each item according to its form.

Forms of Nonfiction
Autobiography

- Have a volunteer read the definition of an autobiography, and then ask students to give examples of autobiographies they have read.
- Ask students to read the passage from *Rosa Parks: My Story* and respond to the accompanying question.
  Answer: Students may agree that Rosa Parks's purpose is to explain the values that motivated her actions.

Forms of Nonfiction
Biography

- Have students read the definition of biography. In distinguishing between biography and autobiography, students might find it helpful to invoke personal pronouns: An autobiography is an "I" account; a biography is a "he" or "she" account of a person's life.
- Ask students to read the passage from "Arthur Ashe Remembered" and answer the accompanying question.
  Possible response: Students may perceive that the author included these details about Ashe's mother to show a significant childhood event that shaped Ashe's life. These details also underscore the paradox of Ashe's statement that his life was "a succession of fortunate circumstances."

Nonfiction

Autobiography • Biography • Essay • Informational Text

Nonfiction is prose writing that presents and explains ideas or that tells about real people. Among nonfiction forms are essays, newspaper and magazine articles, journals, travelogues, biographies, and autobiographies. In this book, you will read several kinds of nonfiction and have the opportunity to explore the similarities and differences among them.

Autobiography

An **autobiography** is a form of nonfiction in which a person relates his or her own life story. It may tell about the person's whole life or only part of it. The author's purpose may be to explain his or her values, to teach lessons about life, to entertain or amuse readers, or any combination of these.

What does this passage from Rosa Parks's autobiography suggest about her purpose for writing?

As I sat there, I tried not to think about what might happen. I knew that anything was possible. I could be manhandled or beaten. I could be arrested. People have asked me if it occurred to me then that I could be the test case the NAACP had been looking for. I did not think about that at all. In fact if I had let myself think too deeply about what might happen to me, I might have gotten off the bus. But I chose to remain.

FROM ROSA PARKS: MY STORY, ROSA PARKS, P. 168

Biography

A **biography** is a form of nonfiction in which a writer tells the life story of another person. Biographies have been written about many famous people, historical and contemporary, but they can also be written about "ordinary" people. As with an autobiography, a biography is factual and may be written to express a person's values, to teach lessons about life, or to entertain or inspire readers. A biography usually emphasizes the causes and effects of a person's actions.

Why might a writer have included the information presented here in a biography of Arthur Ashe?

He once described his life as "a succession of fortunate circumstances." He was in his twenties then. More than half of his life was behind him. His memory of his mother was confined to a single image: in a blue corduroy bathrobe she stood in a doorway looking out on the courts and playing fields surrounding their house, which stood in the center of a Richmond playground. Weakened by illness, she was taken to a hospital that day, and died at the age of twenty-seven. He was six.

FROM "ARTHUR ASHE REMEMBERED," JOHN MCPHEE, P. 682

"It has always seemed to me that truth is not just 'stranger than fiction,' but also more interesting."
—Jim Haskins

Essay

An **essay** is a short nonfiction work about a particular subject. It presents a main idea and supports it with examples, facts, statistics, or anecdotes.

- A *narrative essay* tells a true story.
- An *expository essay* gives information, discusses ideas, or explains a process.
- A *persuasive essay* tries to convince readers to do something or to accept the writer's point of view.
- A *reflective essay* presents the writer's reflections or thoughts on a topic of personal importance.

What does this opening from an essay suggest about its main idea?

It has taken me a good number of years to come to any measure of respect for summer. I was, being May-born, literally an "infant of the spring" and, during the later childhood years, tended, for some reason or other, to rather worship the cold aloofness of winter. . . . For the longest kind of time I simply thought that *summer* was a mistake.
FROM "ON SUMMER," LORRAINE HANSBERRY, P. 656

Informational Text

Informational text is writing that provides the knowledge to guide and educate you. Informational texts include magazine and newspaper articles on current topics, as well as instructional manuals and textbooks.

Based on this lead paragraph from a newspaper article, how might you expect the text to educate or enlighten you?

San Francisco—In dim light they appear to be sleeping, but they've been dead up to 4,000 years: more than 100 astoundingly well-preserved mummies unearthed in a Chinese desert, whose inexplicably blond hair and white skin could topple dogmas about early human history.
FROM "CAUCASIAN MUMMIES MYSTIFY CHINESE," KEAY DAVIDSON, P. 132

Discuss the Quotation

- Tell students that Jim Haskins is a titan of the nonfiction genre, having written more than one hundred books. Many of his titles are biographies or autobiographical collaborations with prominent African Americans such as Rosa Parks, Coretta Scott King, and Andrew Young.
- Discuss the quotation with students, asking them to cite recent "true events" that struck them as odd, strange, or "more interesting" than fiction.

Forms of Nonfiction
Essays

- Read the definition of essay with students. Ask students which types of essays they have read. Which types have they written themselves?
- Have students read the passage from "On Summer" and answer the accompanying question.
  Answer: The opening suggests that Hansberry's main idea will be her developing respect for the season of summer.

Forms of Nonfiction
Informational Texts

- After students read the definition of informational texts, have them take an inventory of the books they have in their lockers and book bags, and on their desks. Which of them are *not* informational texts?
- Ask students to read the passage on mummies and answer the question.
  Answer: Students may surmise that the article will answer questions about the unusual characteristics of these mummies and their unexpected presence in a Chinese desert.

Drama

- Read the introduction to dramatic literature to students, emphasizing the importance of imagining a performance rather than simply reading a text.
- Ask students to share any experiences they have had in seeing a play performed or participating in a production.

Elements of Drama

Types of Plays

- Have a volunteer read the descriptions of the various types of plays, and then ask students to give examples of comedies, tragedies, and dramas they have read or seen.
- Ask students to read the passage from *The Tragedy of Romeo and Juliet* and respond to the accompanying question.
  Answer: The title is a giveaway, of course, but the high body count of these few lines also indicates that *Romeo and Juliet* is a tragedy.

Elements of Drama

Dialogue and Monologue

- Have students read the definitions of dialogue and monologue.
- Ask students to read the passage from *The Dancers* and answer the accompanying question.
  Possible response: Students may infer that Horace is shy and lacks confidence in his dancing skills. Mary Catherine loves to dance and is eager to persuade Horace to do so.

Drama

Types of Plays • Dialogue and Monologue • Stage Directions • Plot and Conflict

Drama consists of writing that is intended to be performed by actors for an audience. The script combines dialogue—the words the actors say—with stage directions—the author's comments on how and where the actors should move and speak. As you read drama, you "set the stage" in your own mind, using your imagination to visualize the scenery, lighting, costumes, and actors.

Types of Plays

Not all plays are the same in their tone, style, or message. A **comedy** is a humorous play with a happy ending. A **tragedy** is a play in which a hero suffers a major downfall. A **drama** is a serious play, although the consequences are not necessarily as dire as those in a tragedy.

From what type of play do you think the following passage comes? Why?

BENVOLIO.
O noble Prince, I can discover all
The unlucky manage of this fatal brawl.
There lies the man, slain by young Romeo,
That slew thy kinsman, brave Mercutio.

FROM THE TRAGEDY OF ROMEO AND JULIET, WILLIAM SHAKESPEARE, P. 770

Dialogue and Monologue

The action of a play is conveyed mainly through **dialogue**—the conversations between two or more characters. A **monologue** is a lengthy speech that one character addresses to others on stage. Both dialogue and monologue reveal character traits and advance the story action in drama.

What do you learn about the speakers in this brief piece of dialogue?

MARY CATHERINE. I love to dance.
HORACE. Well . . . I don't dance too well.
MARY CATHERINE. There's nothing to it but confidence.
HORACE. That's what my sister says. . . .
MARY CATHERINE. I didn't learn for the longest kind of time for lack of confidence and then Emily gave me a long lecture about it and I got confidence and went ahead and learned. Would you like to come in for a while?
HORACE. Well . . . if it's all right with you. . . .
MARY CATHERINE. I'd be glad to have you.
HORACE. Thank you.

FROM THE DANCERS, HORTON FOOTE, P. 734

> "The play's the thing . . ." —William Shakespeare

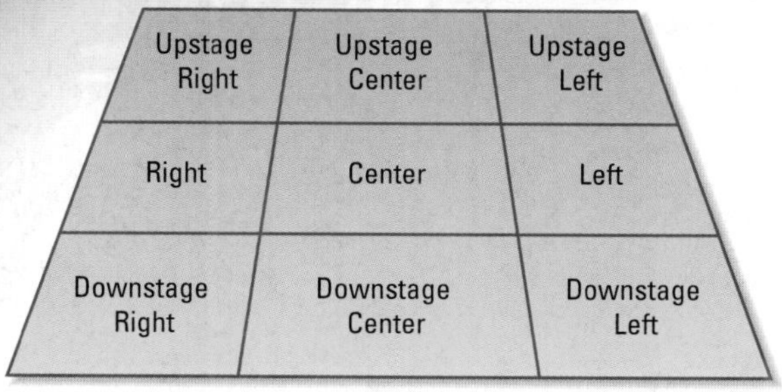

Stage Directions

Stage directions are the instructions for performing the play and the descriptions of settings, characters, and actions. When you read dramatic literature, the stage directions can help you visualize the play. Using a staging chart like the one shown above, you can imagine where the scenery is and how the actors move by following the indications of downstage, upstage, left, and right.

What information in these stage directions helps you visualize the setting of the play?

> [*Scene: The stage is divided into four acting areas: downstage left is the living room of* INEZ *and* HERMAN STANLEY. *Downstage right is part of a small-town drugstore. Upstage right is the living room of* ELIZABETH CREWS. *Upstage left, the yard and living room of* MARY CATHERINE DAVIS.]
>
> FROM THE DANCERS, HORTON FOOTE, P. 734

Plot and Conflict

A play, much like a short story, contains a **plot,** or series of events, involving a **conflict,** or problem, that one or more characters face. The conflict is introduced early in the play, perhaps in its opening scene. Tension builds to the climax, and by the final scene of the play, the conflict has been resolved, either happily or unhappily, for the main characters.

What kind of conflict is indicated in this dialogue?

> **EMILY.** I don't feel good . . . . [*She begins to cry.*] Oh, Mother, I don't want to go to the dance tonight. Please, ma'm, don't make me. I'll do anything in this world for you if you promise me . . .
>
> **ELIZABETH.** Emily. This is all settled. You are going to that dance. Do you understand me? You are going to that dance. That sweet, nice brother of Inez Stanley's will be here any minute. . . .
>
> FROM THE DANCERS, HORTON FOOTE, P. 734

Discuss the Quotation

- Tell students that Shakespeare frequently included scenes from plays and discussions about the craft of acting within the context of his plays. For example, this quotation is from *Hamlet,* from a scene in which Prince Hamlet plans to put on a play that will reenact the murder of his father and, he hopes, startle the murderer—the current king—into betraying his guilt.
- Discuss the quotation with students. Point out that the quotation concludes " . . . Wherein I'll catch the conscience of the king." Have students brainstorm for new endings for this quotation that reflect the power and the potential of dramatic literature.

Elements of Dramatic Literature

Stage Directions

- Read the explanation of stage directions. Demonstrate downstage and upstage by moving about the front of the classroom as if it were a stage.
- Have students read the passage from *The Dancers.* Work as a class to answer the question by using the chalkboard to sketch the scene described in the stage directions.

Elements of Dramatic Literature

Plot and Conflict

- After students read the definitions of plot and conflict, note that they should be familiar with these concepts from their experiences with short stories.
- Ask students to read the passage from *The Dancers* and answer the question.
  Answer: Students should recognize that Emily's weepy refusals and Elizabeth's grim imperatives indicate an unhappy conflict over an arranged date.

Learn About Literature
continued

Poetry

- Read the introduction to poetry to students, emphasizing the importance of the sound and structure of language.
- To give students a sense of the essential characteristics of poetry, read a lyric poem of your own choosing to the class or play a poem selected from the **Listening to Literature** Audiocassettes or Audio CDs in the Teaching Resources.

Elements of Poetry
Types of Poetry

- Have students read the definitions of the different types of poetry, and then ask them to give examples of narrative, lyric, and dramatic poems they have read.
- Ask students to read the passage from "Summer" and respond to the accompanying question. **Answer:** The speaker's expression of emotion and the alliterative music of his language will help students identify "Summer" as a lyric poem.

Elements of Poetry
Poetic Form

- Have students read the definition of poetic form. If possible, bring to class examples of some of the various forms poems can take.
- Ask students to read the passage from "Dream Deferred" and answer the accompanying question. **Possible response:** Students may note that the poet achieves a strong dramatic emphasis by setting the last lines of the poem apart.

Poetry

Types of Poetry • Poetic Form • Figurative Language • Rhyme and Rhythm

Poetry is writing that combines language, images, and sounds to create a special emotional effect. A poem's sound and structure are different from those of prose, the writing you find in short stories and nonfiction. Poetry is arranged in lines and stanzas, and its language is more visual and musical than prose. A story speaks to readers, but a poem sings to them.

Types of Poetry

There are many different types of poems. A **narrative poem,** like a short story, tells a story that includes a plot, characters, and a setting. A **lyric poem** expresses the observations and feelings of a speaker in a musical way. A **dramatic poem** uses the techniques of drama in the form of a monologue for one speaker or dramatic dialogue for two or more speakers.

Which details in this passage help you to recognize it comes from a lyric poem?

I like hot days, hot days
Sweat is what you got days
Bugs buzzin from cousin to cousin
Juices dripping
Running and ripping
Catch the one you love days

FROM "SUMMER," WALTER DEAN MYERS, P. 927

Poetic Form

Poetic form refers to the way the lines of a poem are shaped and arranged. Often, a poet groups lines into formal units called *stanzas.* A stanza may have any number of lines. Poetic form affects the way the poem is read aloud and, to a degree, the message that the poem conveys.

Why do you think the last lines of this poem have been set apart?

Harlem

What happens to a dream deferred?

Does it dry up
like a raisin in the sun?
Or fester like a sore——
And then run?
Does it stink like rotten meat?
Or crust and sugar over——
like a syrupy sweet?

Maybe it just sags
like a heavy load.

Or does it explode?

"DREAM DEFERRED," LANGSTON HUGHES, P. 904

"To have great poetry, there must be great audiences, too."
—Walt Whitman

Figurative Language

Figurative language is writing or speech that is not meant to be taken literally. It is often used to create vivid impressions by setting up fresh comparisons between dissimilar things.

In a **simile,** *like* or *as* is used to compare two basically different things. For example, the simile "I wandered lonely as a cloud" compares the speaker to a cloud and emphasizes the speaker's aimlessness.

In contrast to a simile, a **metaphor** states a comparison of two things directly. In the metaphor "if dreams die / Life is a broken-winged bird," the poet compares life to an injured bird and shows the effect of losing hope.

In **personification,** a nonhuman subject is given human characteristics. In the lines "Let the rain kiss you. / Let the rain sing you a lullaby," the poet personifies the rain, making it seem vital and alive.

What comparisons do you find in these lines of poetry?

> Continuous as the stars that shine
> And twinkle on the milky way,
> They stretched in never-ending line
> Along the margin of a bay:
> Ten thousand saw I at a glance,
> Tossing their heads in sprightly dance.
> FROM "I WANDERED LONELY AS A CLOUD," WILLIAM WORDSWORTH, P. 896

Rhythm and Rhyme

In addition to poetic conventions like figurative language and stanza structure, the elements of rhythm and rhyme give poetry its musical qualities.

Rhythm in a poem is the pattern of stressed (´) and unstressed (˘) syllables in each line. Notice the regular rhythm in this line:

´ ˘ ´ ˘ ´ ˘ ´ ˘
Once upon a midnight dreary . . .

Rhyme in a poem is the repetition of sounds at the ends of words. For example:

Once upon a midnight dreary,
While I pondered, weak and weary . . .

What rhythm and rhyme do you find in these lines of poetry?

> Two roads diverged in a yellow wood,
> And sorry I could not travel both
> And be one traveler, long I stood
> And looked down one as far as I could
> To where it bent in the undergrowth;
> FROM "THE ROAD NOT TAKEN," ROBERT FROST, P. 188

Discuss the Quotation

- Tell students that Walt Whitman knew from personal experience the importance of a "great audience": in his lifetime he never had one. Whitman's robust, sprawling free verse was despised by most literary critics of his day. Only in relatively recent times has a "great audience" recognized Whitman as the father of modern poetry in America.
- Discuss the quotation with students, asking them to consider the possible ways in which an audience—or an individual reader—contributes to the success of a poem.

Elements of Poetry
Figurative Language

- After students read the definitions of similes, metaphors and personification, ask them to devise an example of each on their own. Have volunteers share their examples with the class.
- Ask students to read the passage from "I Wandered Lonely as a Cloud" and answer the accompanying question.
  Answer: Students may recognize that flowers are compared to stars; the word "as" marks this comparison as a simile. Point out that by describing the flowers' "tossing their heads in sprightly dance," the poet is using personification.

Elements of Poetry
Rhythm and Rhyme

- Read the definitions of rhythm and rhyme with the class. Have students read the example lines aloud several times; you may wish to augment these with other lines of your own choosing.
- Have students read the passage from "The Road Not Taken" and answer the accompanying question.
  Answer: Students should discern the rhymes *wood, stood, could* and *both, undergrowth.* (The rhyme scheme is *abaab.*) Each line consists of nine syllables, with the stress usually on the second syllable of a pair. To help students hear the rhythm of the lines, read the poem aloud as a class and have students clap on the stressed syllable.

Learn About Literature
continued

Folk Literature

- Read the introduction to folk literature to students, and then ask them to list examples of various types of folk literature they have read.
- Point out to students that one of the incidental characteristics of folk literature is the lack of identifiable authors. Usually, the author is unknown. When authors are attributed to works of folk literature, they may be simply the first to write down works that had long existed in oral tradition.

Forms of Folk Literature

Myth

- Have a volunteer read the definition of myth, and then ask students to give examples of myths with which they are familiar.
- Ask students to read the passage from "Perseus" and respond to the accompanying question. **Answer:** The king's inquiry of a god and the priestess's prophecy are details suggestive of myth.

Forms of Folk Literature

Folk Tale

- Read the definition of folk tale with students. Ask them to mention some examples of folk tales they read or heard when they were children.
- Have students read the passage from "Talk" and answer the accompanying question. **Possible response:** Students may find that the talking yam and its specific complaints to the country man are amusing.

Folk Literature

Myth • Folk Tale • Tall Tale • Epic

Not all stories were written down when they were first told. Folk literature comes from generations of peoples or cultures that passed down their favorite tales orally before ever recording them. Folk literature includes myths, folk tales, tall tales, and epics. Like a favorite family recipe, folk literature holds special enjoyment for all those who know it and pass it on.

Myth

A **myth** is a fictional tale that explains the actions of gods or the causes of natural phenomena. It involves supernatural elements and has little historical truth to it. Among the most familiar myths today are those of the ancient Greeks and Romans.

Myths have several purposes. They serve as a cultural history, explaining natural phenomena such as oceans and mountains. They also reinforce a culture's values. Finally, they are a source of entertainment.

Which details in this passage indicate that it is from a myth?

King Acrisius of Argos had only one child, a daughter, Danaë. She was beautiful above all the other women of the land, but this was small comfort to the King for not having a son. He journeyed to Delphi to ask the god if there was any hope that some day he would be the father of a boy. The priestess told him no, and added what was far worse: that his daughter would have a son who would kill him.

FROM "PERSEUS," EDITH HAMILTON, P. 214

Folk Tale

A **folk tale** is a story composed orally and then passed from person to person by word of mouth. As part of an oral tradition, folk tales originated among people who could neither read nor write. They entertained one another by telling stories aloud, often about heroes, adventure, magic, or romance. Like mythology, folk tales also help reinforce a culture's values and explain the natural world.

This passage comes from an African folk tale. Which elements make it an appealing story to hear?

Once, not far from the city of Accra on the Gulf of Guinea, a country man went out to his garden to dig up some yams to take to market. While he was digging, one of the yams said to him, "Well, at last you're here. You never weeded me, but now you come around with your digging stick. Go away and leave me alone!"

FROM "TALK," HAROLD COURLANDER AND GEORGE HERZOG, P. 412

> *"I speak to the black experience, but I am always talking about the human condition."*
> —*Maya Angelou*

Tall Tale

A **tall tale** is a kind of humorous story in which characters possess superhuman abilities and impossible happenings occur. Tall tales were common on the American frontier, when characters like Paul Bunyan and Febold Feboldson were favorites. Tall tales are told in common, everyday speech and employ some realistic detail in addition to exaggeration.

Which details from this passage indicate that it is from a tall tale?

> . . . The sun shone on his cornfield until the corn began to pop, while the rain washed the syrup out of his sugar cane.
>
> Now the cane field was on a hill and the cornfield was in a valley. The syrup flowed downhill into the popped corn and rolled it into great balls. Bergstrom says some of them were hundreds of feet high and looked like big tennis balls from a distance. You never see any of them now, because the grasshoppers ate them all up in one day, July 21, 1874.
>
> FROM "FEBOLD FEBOLDSON," PAUL R. BEATH, IN WRITERS OF THE AMERICAN MIDWEST, PRENTICE HALL LITERATURE LIBRARY, P. 23

Epic

An **epic** is a long narrative poem about the deeds of gods or heroes in war or travel. An epic is written in ornate, poetic language. It incorporates myth, legend, and history and often includes the intervention of the gods in human affairs.

In an epic, the poet begins by announcing the subject and asking a Muse, one of the nine goddesses of the arts, literature, and sciences, to help.

Homer's epic *Odyssey* (p. 980) tells the story of the Greek hero Odysseus, the king of Ithaca.

Which characteristics of an epic do you find in this opening verse of Homer's *Odyssey*?

> Sing in me, Muse, and through me
> tell the story
> of that man skilled in the ways of
> contending,
> the wanderer, harried for years on end,
> after he plundered the stronghold
> of the proud height of Troy.
>
> FROM THE ODYSSEY, HOMER, P. 980

CUSTOMIZE INSTRUCTION FOR UNIVERSAL ACCESS

For English Learners	For Less Proficient Readers
Have students think of tall tales, myths, or folk tales from their home cultures. Ask them to describe the plot and characters to the class. Then, have the class seek parallels to tall tales, myths, or folk tales that they know about. Discuss with students why folk stories from around the world share common elements.	To help students identify the setting of a tall tale, myth, or folk tale, have them keep a list of details related to time, place, and culture as they read. Pause frequently to allow students to share the details they have found. Then, discuss what these details reveal about the time and place in which the story occurs.

Discuss the Quotation

- Tell students that Maya Angelou is best known for her autobiography *I Know Why the Caged Bird Sings,* the title of which is derived from a poem by Paul Laurence Dunbar (cited on p. 292).
- Discuss the quotation with students, pointing out that all folk literature emerges from the experiences of a particular culture, yet such literature endures because it speaks about "the human condition."

Forms of Folk Literature
Tall Tale

- Have students read the definition of the tall tale and ask them to list any they recall reading. (Students may mention tall tales involving Paul Bunyan, Pecos Bill, Davy Crockett, and John Henry, among others.)
- Ask students to read the passage from "Febold Feboldson" and answer the accompanying question.
  Possible response: The sun pops corn in the field while simultaneously rain washes syrup out of the cane to create giant popcorn balls—these unlikely events identify the passage as part of a tall tale.

Forms of Folk Literature
Epic

- After students read the definition of an epic, have them name an epic that they have read or know about.
- Ask students to read the passage from the *Odyssey* and answer the question.
  Answer: Students may cite the fact the the speaker invokes the aid of the Muse to tell the story of his hero's long journey.

Unit Objectives

1. To read selections in different genres that develop the theme "Spine Tinglers"
2. To apply a variety of reading strategies, particularly literal comprehension strategies, appropriate for reading these selections
3. To analyze literary elements
4. To use a variety of strategies to build vocabulary
5. To learn elements of grammar, usage, and style
6. To use recursive writing processes to write in a variety of forms
7. To develop listening and speaking skills
8. To express and support responses to various types of texts
9. To prepare, organize, and present literary interpretations

Meeting the Objectives

With each selection, you will find instructional materials through which students can meet these objectives. Further, you will find additional practice pages for reading strategies, literary analysis, vocabulary, and grammar in the **Selection Support: Skills Development Workbook** in your **Teaching Resources.**

Background

Art

The Storm, by Edvard Munch

Edvard Munch (1863–1944) was a painter and graphic artist who studied in Paris as well as in his native Norway. Munch's work reflects his obsession with depression, fear, and death. Ask students the following question about the painting:

What emotions do you think the people are feeling and why?
Answer: The postures of the people suggest that they are paralyzed with fear. The dark surroundings and the title of the painting suggest that a dangerous storm is brewing. The woman in white probably feels isolated. The artist highlights her separation by contrasting her bright clothing to the dark landscape and muted colors worn by the other people.

UNIT 1 Spine Tinglers

The Storm, 1893, Edvard Munch, ©1997 The Museum of Modern Art, New York

UNIT FEATURES

Connections	Reading Informational Material
Every unit contains a feature that connects literature to a related topic, such as art, science, or history. In this unit, the excerpt from Sebastian Junger's *The Perfect Storm* on pp. 86–89 offers a study of nature's fury. Use the information and questions on the Connections pages to enrich students' understanding of the selections presented within the unit.	These selections will help students learn to analyze and evaluate informational texts, such as workplace documents, technical directions, and consumer materials. They will expose students to the organization and features unique to nonnarrative texts. In this unit, students learn the form and purpose of a movie review.

Exploring the Theme

Turn the page to enter a world of suspense and mystery. Here, extraordinary events are commonplace, and desperate acts or unexplained phenomena can change the course of a life forever. Experience these stories, poems, and essays—if you dare! Your heart will race, your fists will clench, and your spine will tingle.

In "The Cask of Amontillado," a man is driven to cold-blooded, methodical murder for reasons known only to himself. Follow the condemned man as he is unknowingly led to a terrifying end. Scream out a warning to him if you choose, but he is not likely to hear you. His fate has already been decided by others more powerful.

▲ **Critical Viewing** Which details in this painting create a sense of mystery or suspense? **[Analyze]**

ASSESSMENT RESOURCES

- **Selection Support: Skills Development Workbook**
- **Formal Assessment**
- **Open Book Tests**
- **Performance Assessment and Portfolio Management**
- **Extension Activities**

Assessing Student Progress

Listed below are tools that are available to measure the degree to which students meet the unit objectives.

Informal Assessment

The questions in the Review and Assess sections are a first-level response to the concepts and skills presented with the selections. Students' responses provide a brief, informal measure of their grasp of the material. These responses can indicate where further instruction and practice are needed. Follow up with the practice pages in **Selection Support: Skills Development Workbook.**

Formal Assessment

The **Formal Assessment** booklet contains the Selection Tests and Unit Tests.

- Selection Tests measure comprehension and skills acquisition for each selection or group of selections.
- Each Unit Test provides students with thirty multiple-choice questions and five essay questions designed to assess students' knowledge of the literature and skills taught in the unit.

The **Open Book Tests** ask students to demonstrate their ability to synthesize and communicate information from selections or groups of selections.

To assess student writing, you will find rubrics and scoring models in the **Performance Assessment and Portfolio Management** booklet. In this booklet, you will also find scoring rubrics for listening and speaking activities.

Alternative Assessment

The **Extension Activities** booklet contains writing activities, listening and speaking activities, and research and technology activities that are appropriate for students with different ability levels. You may also use these activities as an alternative measure of students' growth.

▶Critical Viewing

Answer: The use of muted colors, the position of the figures, and the overall lack of detail in the painting all create a sense of mystery and suspense.

Why Read Literature?

The "Why Read Literature?" page in each unit presents a list of possible purposes for reading. Each purpose for reading is connected to one or more of the selections in the unit. Good readers set a purpose before reading to help them read actively and focus on meaningful details.

Unit 1 introduces three purposes for reading. "Read for the Love of Literature" encourages students to give themselves a good scare. "Read to be Entertained" persuades students to confront the unexpected while reading. "Read for Information" encourages students to learn more about an archaeological mystery.

How to Use This Page

- Tell students that before reading each selection in this unit, they should set a purpose for reading. This will help them read in a more active and focused manner.
- Explain that they can increase their love of literature by reading about the horror of being buried alive in "The Cask of Amontillado," or being hunted by a madman in "The Most Dangerous Game."
- A reader will be more entertained when he or she pays careful attention to the characters, details, and situations in a selection. In "The Listeners," students can take note of the mysterious sounds and images to increase their enjoyment of this poem. The drama of a baseball game is captured in "Casey at the Bat."
- Reading to obtain information is another valuable purpose for reading. Students should focus on the specific type of information they want to learn. In "Caucasian Mummies Mystify Chinese," students can read to learn more about how these unusual mummies were discovered in a remote region of China.

Why Read Literature?

Whenever you read a work of suspense, you have a purpose, or reason. You might just want to experience the feeling of a good scare, but you may have other reasons for reading as well. Preview these three purposes you might set before reading works in this unit.

1 Read for the Love of Literature

Edgar Allan Poe was obsessed with the fear of being buried alive. Poe conveyed this horror so imaginatively in his stories that he inspired one Russian reader to patent his own device. The mechanism enabled the "deceased" to signal those above ground that they had acted a little too hastily. You may understand why someone would go to such lengths when you read **"The Cask of Amontillado,"** page 6.

What happens when the hunter becomes the hunted? That is the ominous question Richard Connell seeks to answer in a frightening story about a different kind of hunt. You may not be able to resist rushing to the end to learn what happens in **"The Most Dangerous Game,"** page 18.

2 Read to Be Entertained

Sometimes the most unexpected events happen at the end of a close contest when the entire game is on the line. Find out what happens when it all comes down to the final man in Ernest Thayer's **"Casey at the Bat,"** page 42.

If you have ever heard footsteps echoing loudly on an empty street at night or imagined a lurking shadow behind every tree, you will sympathize with the spooked horseman in Walter de la Mare's **"The Listeners,"** page 122.

3 Read for Information

The discovery of 100 Caucasian mummies in a remote region of China challenges established beliefs about ancient Chinese history. Learn more about these mysterious mummies by reading Keay Davidson's article **"Caucasian Mummies Mystify Chinese,"** page 132.

Take It to the Net

Visit the Web site for online instruction and activities related to each selection in this unit.
www.phschool.com

ENRICHMENT: Further Reading

Have students choose one or more of the works below to extend the unit theme "Spine Tinglers" or to read more by the unit authors.

The Maltese Falcon by Dashiell Hammett
In this novel, Sam Spade, Hammett's tough detective, becomes caught up in a mystery centered on a valuable gold statue of a falcon.

The Strange Case of Dr. Jekyll and Mr. Hyde by Robert Louis Stevenson
The classic story of the double life of a respectable doctor who unlocks the door to his terrible alter-ego can be found in the **Prentice Hall Literature Library.**

Rebecca by Daphne du Maurier
In this novel, Du Maurier, author of "The Birds," weaves a chilling tale of suspense and mystery.

How to Read Literature

Use Literal Comprehension Strategies

Your first goal in reading is to understand what the writer is saying. This task becomes more difficult when writers use unfamiliar words or construct sentences that do not make sense when you first read them. You can use the following literal comprehension strategies to help clear up confusion.

1. Break down long sentences.

- Read sentences in meaningful groups of words, not word by word.
- Figure out the subject of the sentence. Then, determine what the sentence is saying about that subject.
- Rearrange the sentence if you are confused by word order, as the example at right demonstrates.

Breaking Down Sentences

Poe's sentence: The thousand injuries of Fortunato I had borne as best I could, but when he ventured upon insult I vowed revenge.

Rearranged sentence: I had borne the thousand injuries of Fortunato as best I could, but I vowed revenge when he ventured upon insult.

2. Use context clues.

Context refers to the words, phrases, sentences, and ideas that surround a word. Use clues contained in the context to help determine the meaning of unfamiliar words or phrases. Look at this sample passage:

> "I wanted the ideal animal to hunt," explained the general. "So I said: 'What are the attributes of an ideal *quarry*?' "
>
> —*from* "The Most Dangerous Game"

If the word *quarry* is unfamiliar, you could determine its meaning by looking at the previous sentence and noticing how the word *ideal* is repeated. The general is looking for the *ideal* animal to hunt, so you can conclude that *quarry* probably means a hunted animal.

3. Summarize.

Summarizing involves picking out key events, describing them briefly in your own words, and then placing them in order of occurrence to concisely report the action or main idea of a selection. Prepare a summary to serve these purposes:

- Make sure you understand what happens in a story as you read.
- Remind yourself of basic plot events later on.

4. Predict.

Predicting, or making guesses about what will happen later in a selection, keeps you actively involved in a story. Use prediction to avoid missing important details and to check your understanding of what you have read.

As you read this unit's selections, apply these strategies to increase your understanding of the text.

How to Read Literature

The "How to Read Literature" page in each unit presents a set of strategies to help readers understand authors' words and ideas. Each reading strategy is taught in conjunction with one or more of the selections within the unit. Good readers develop a bank of strategies from which they can draw as needed.

Unit 1 introduces four literal comprehension strategies. To understand a selection fully, students must make sense of the words on the page as well as the author's ideas. The strategies on this page help readers go beyond a simple scan of a text.

How to Use This Page

Introduce the strategies for literal comprehension, presenting each as a tool for developing understanding when reading the selections in this unit.

- As they read "The Cask of Amontillado" (p. 6), students will break down long sentences into meaningful groups of words.
- As they read "The Most Dangerous Game" (p. 18), students will use context clues to determine the meanings of unfamiliar words.
- As they read "Casey at the Bat" (p. 42), students will learn how to summarize sections of the poem to help them better understand what they are reading.
- As they read "The Birds" (p. 50), students will learn how predicting future events can help them check their understanding of a story.

MODEL A READING STRATEGY

Explain to students that summarizing sections of a selection can help them better understand what they are reading by helping them to focus on the main points and details.

Show students how to summarize a stanza of a poem by modeling a summary of the first stanza of "Casey at the Bat":

> The Mudville team was losing the game by two runs. There were two outs with one inning left to play, and the fans were very disappointed.

You may want to point out to students that a summary contains only the most important details, stated in their own words.

The Cask of Amontillado

Lesson Objectives and CA Correlations

1. **To analyze and respond to literary elements**
   - Literary Analysis: Mood **R 3.6**
   - Connecting Literary Elements: Description
2. **To read, comprehend, analyze, and critique a short story**
   - Reading Strategy: Breaking Down Confusing Sentences
   - Reading Check questions
   - Review and Assess questions
   - Assessment Practice (ATE)
3. **To develop word analysis skills, fluency, and systematic vocabulary**
   - Vocabulary Development Lesson: Latin Prefixes: *pre-* **R 1.1**
4. **To understand and apply written and oral language conventions**
   - Spelling Strategy
   - Grammar Lesson: Common and Proper Nouns **LC 1.3**
5. **To understand and apply appropriate writing and research strategies**
   - Writing Lesson: Description of a Set **W 2.1**
   - Extension Activity: Storyboard **W 1.8**
6. **To understand and apply listening and speaking strategies**
   - Extension Activity: Retelling **LS 1.9**

STEP-BY-STEP TEACHING GUIDE	PACING GUIDE
PRETEACH	
Motivate Students and Provide Background	
Use the Motivation activity (ATE p. 4)	5 min.
Read and discuss the Preview material and Background information (SE/ATE p. 4) [A]	5 min.
Introduce the Concepts	
Introduce the Literary Analysis and Reading Strategy (SE/ATE p. 5) [A]	15 min.
Pronounce the vocabulary words and read their definitions (SE p. 5)	5 min.
TEACH	
Monitor Comprehension	
Informally monitor comprehension by circulating while students read independently or in groups [A]	30 min.
Monitor students' comprehension with the Reading Check notes (SE/ATE pp. 7, 9, 11)	as students read
Develop vocabulary with Vocabulary notes (SE pp. 7, 9, 10, 11; ATE p. 7)	as students read
Develop Understanding	
Develop students' understanding of mood with the Literary Analysis annotations (SE p. 8; ATE pp. 7, 8, 9, 11) [A]	10 min.
Develop students' ability to break down confusing sentences with the Reading Strategy annotations (SE p. 10; ATE pp. 8,10)	10 min.
ASSESS	
Assess Mastery	
Assess students' mastery of the Reading Strategy and Literary Analysis by having them answer the Review and Assess questions (SE/ATE p. 13)	20 min.
Use one or more of the print and media Assessment Resources (ATE p. 15) [A]	up to 45 min.
EXTEND	
Apply Understanding	
Have students complete the Vocabulary Development Lesson and the Grammar Lesson (SE p. 14) [A]	20 min.
Apply students' ability to select precise details using the Writing Lesson (SE/ATE p. 15) [A]	45 min.
Apply students' understanding using one or more of the Extension Activities (SE p. 15)	20–90 min.

[A] **ACCELERATED INSTRUCTION:** Use the strategies and activities identified with an [A].

UNIVERSAL ACCESS
● = Below Level Students
▲ = On-Level Students
■ = Above Level Students

Time and Resource Manager

Reading Level: Challenging
Average Number of Instructional Days: 4

RESOURCES			
	PRINT	TRANSPARENCIES	TECHNOLOGY
	• **Beyond Literature,** Humanities Connection: Coats of Arms, p. 1 ▲ ■		• **Interest Grabber Video,** Tape 1 ● ▲ ■
	• **Selection Support Workbook:** ● ▲ ■ Literary Analysis, p. 4 Reading Strategy, p. 3 Build Vocabulary, p. 1	• **Literary Analysis and Reading Transparencies,** pp. 1 and 2 ● ▲ ■	
	• **Adapted Reader's Companion** ● • **Reader's Companion** ●		• **Listening to Literature** ● ▲ ■ Audiocassettes, Side 1 Audio CDs, CD 1
	• **English Learner's Companion** ● ▲ • **Literatura en español** ● ▲ • **Literary Analysis for Enrichment** ■		
	• **Formal Assessment:** Selection Test, pp. 1–3 ● ▲ ■ • **Open Book Test,** pp. 1–3 ● ▲ ■ • **Performance Assessment and Portfolio Management,** p. 18 ● ▲ ■ • PRENTICE HALL ASSESSMENT SYSTEM ● ▲ ■	• PRENTICE HALL ASSESSMENT SYSTEM ● ▲ ■ Skills Practice Answers and Explanations on Transparencies	• **Test Bank Software** ● ▲ ■ • **Got It! Assessment Videotapes,** Tape 1 ● ▲
	• **Selection Support Workbook:** ● ▲ ■ Build Grammar Skills, p. 2 • **Writing and Grammar,** Gold Level ● ▲ ■ • **Extension Activities,** p. 1 ● ▲ ■	• **Daily Language Practice Transparencies** ● ▲ • **Writing Models and Graphic Organizers on Transparencies** ● ▲ ■	• **Writing and Grammar iText CD-ROM** ● ▲ ■ ***Take It to the Net*** www.phschool.com

BLOCK SCHEDULING: Use one 90-minute class period to preteach the selection and have students read it. Use a second 90-minute class period to assess students' mastery of skills and have them complete one of the Extension Activities.

PRETEACH

Step-by-Step Teaching Guide for pp. 4–5

Motivation

Students will discover that this horrifying tale of revenge is as gripping as any horror movie they've seen. To entice an audience to see a new horror movie, a movie studio creates a trailer that shows glimpses of the film. Give students a verbal "trailer" of "The Cask of Amontillado" by writing the following excerpts on the chalkboard:

> *We . . . stood together upon the damp ground of the catacombs of the Montresors."*
>
> *We had passed through long walls of piled skeletons, with casks and puncheons intermingling, into the inmost recesses. . . ."*

Have students discuss these images. What do they think will happen in the catacombs?

Interest Grabber Video

As an alternative, play "Mardi Gras" on Tape 1 to engage student interest.

1 Background

Social Studies

During the Middle Ages, both religious orders and families buried their dead in charnels—long arcaded galleries bordering a church courtyard. By the fourteenth century, charnels were so full that people began digging up the old bones to make room for new ones. Old bones remained in the charnel, piled up where they were out of the way. They were often left in the open. As late as the eighteenth century, a visitor to the Franciscan monastery in Toulouse, France, saw a charnel of mummies—bodies that had been preserved for centuries and were lined up in rows in the charnel and catacombs.

Prepare to Read

The Cask of Amontillado

Take It to the Net

Visit www.phschool.com for interactive activities and instruction related to "The Cask of Amontillado," including

- background
- graphic organizers
- literary elements
- reading strategies

Preview

Connecting to the Literature

Often, it does not take much to spark a desire for revenge. It can start with a simple insult or an unresolved dispute. You encounter these situations in books, movies, television shows, and in real life. Sometimes, as in this story, a quest for revenge can get out of hand.

1 Background

Much of the action in this story takes place in catacombs. These long passageways and side tunnels stretch out like cities of the dead. In past centuries, many wealthy European families held funerals in catacombs beneath the family manor. The dead were then laid to rest, surrounded by the bones of their ancestors. The most extensive known catacombs are found outside Rome.

TEACHING RESOURCES

The following resources can be used to enrich or extend the instruction for pp. 4–5.

Motivation

Interest Grabber Video, Tape 1

Background

Beyond Literature, p. 1

Take It to the Net

Visit www.phschool.com for background and hotlinks for "The Cask of Amontillado."

Literary Analysis

Literary Analysis and Reading Transparencies, Mood, p. 1

Reading

Selection Support: Reading Strategy, p. 3; Build Vocabulary, p. 1

Literary Analysis and Reading Transparencies, Break Down Confusing Sentences, p. 2

BLOCK SCHEDULING: Resources marked with this symbol provide varied instruction during 90-minute blocks.

❷ Literary Analysis

Mood

The **mood** of a work of literature is the primary feeling that the reader experiences while reading it. In "The Cask of Amontillado," Edgar Allan Poe carefully chooses words and details to create a mood of eerie suspense. In this example, notice how the italicized words affect the mood.

> We passed through a *range of low arches*, *descended*, passed on, and *descending* again, arrived at a *deep crypt*, in which the *foulness* of the air caused our flambeaux rather to *glow* than flame.

As the story unfolds, see how quickly the mood changes.

Connecting Literary Elements

A **description** is a portrait painted in words of a person, place, or object. In "The Cask of Amontillado," description creates the eerie mood. For example, details such as *drops of moisture* that *trickle among the bones* help readers picture the scene and sense the mood. Take note of dark descriptions that contribute to the mood.

❸ Reading Strategy

Breaking Down Confusing Sentences

When you approach Poe's writing, you may need to **break down confusing sentences**. To do this:

- Read sentences in meaningful sections, not word by word.
- Figure out the subject—who or what the sentence is about. Then, determine what the sentence is saying about that subject.
- Rearrange, change, or take out words to make the sentence clearer.

If you come to a difficult sentence while you are reading, use a chart like this one to break the sentence into sections and clarify information about the subjects. The example on the right breaks down the first sentence in the story.

Subject	Information About the Subject
I (narrator)	had borne the thousand injuries of Fortunato
he (Fortunato)	ventured upon insult
I (narrator)	vowed revenge

Vocabulary Development

precluded (prē klo͞od′ id) *v.* prevented; made impossible in advance (p. 7)

retribution (re′ trə byo͞o′ shən) *n.* payback; punishment for a misdeed (p. 7)

accosted (ə kôst′ id) *v.* greeted, especially in an aggressive way (p. 7)

afflicted (ə flikt′ id) *v.* suffering or sickened (p. 8)

explicit (eks plis′ it) *adj.* clearly stated (p. 8)

recoiling (ri koil′ iŋ) *v.* staggering back (p. 10)

termination (tʉr′ mə nā′ shən) *n.* end (p. 10)

subsided (səb sīd′ id) *v.* settled down; became less active or intense (p. 11)

CUSTOMIZE INSTRUCTION FOR UNIVERSAL ACCESS

For Special Needs Students	For Less Proficient Readers	For English Learners
Have students read the adapted version of "The Cask of Amontillado" in the **Adapted Reader's Companion.** This version provides basic-level instruction in an interactive format with questions and write-on lines. Completing the adapted version will prepare students to read the selection in the Student Edition.	Have students read the selection in the **Reader's Companion.** This version provides basic-level instruction in an interactive format with questions and write-on lines. After students finish the selection in **Reader's Companion,** have them complete the questions and activities in the Student Edition.	Have students read the adapted version of the selection in the **English Learner's Companion.** This version provides basic-level instruction in an interactive format with questions and write-on lines. Completing the adapted version will prepare students to read the selection in the Student Edition.

❷ Literary Analysis

Mood

- Write the word *mood* on the chalkboard. Ask students what this word means to them. Explain that the mood of a story is the feeling it arouses in the reader. Have a volunteer read the quotation at the left aloud. Ask students what mood it creates.
- Explain that Poe is famous for his attempt to achieve a single effect in each story. The effect of "The Tell-Tale Heart," for example, is fear or horror. As students read, have them consider the effect Poe creates.
- Have students think about the effect of the descriptive details. Poe creates a mood by giving details that appeal to all five senses. Have students watch for details as they read, and think about how descriptive details draw them into the story.

❸ Reading Strategy

Breaking Down Confusing Sentences

- Explain that when sentences contain many clauses and details, readers can lose track of what the writer is saying. Have students look at the quotation under Literary Analysis: Mood. This sentence contains several clauses and descriptive details that may confuse readers' understanding of the main point.
- Challenge students to identify the main subject of the sentence *(we)* and the main actions taken by the subject *(passed, descended, arrived)*. Once they have established the main idea of the sentence, students can then examine the details that give them further description and information.
- Encourage students to practice this strategy as they come across confusing sentences in "The Cask of Amontillado."

Vocabulary Development

- Pronounce each vocabulary word for students and read the definitions as a class. Have students identify any words with which they are already familiar.

E-Teach

Visit E-Teach at www.phschool.com for teachers' essays on how to teach, with questions and answers.

TEACH

Step-by-Step Teaching Guide for pp. 6–12

CUSTOMIZE INSTRUCTION
For Musical/Rhythmic Learners

Have students note the many sound effects and sound-imitating words Poe uses in his description of the events that take place in the catacombs. How does he use words to create sounds? How does he help readers hear the scene? What do the sound effects add to the story's mood? Which verbs and adjectives recreate sounds for the reader?

❶ About the Selection

This story illustrates how a person can become so obsessed with revenge that he or she can descend into madness and commit unspeakable acts. The main character, Montresor, has vowed to avenge the unnamed insults of Fortunato, an old acquaintance. With a mix of flattery and reverse psychology, Montresor lures and traps Fortunato in the catacombs below his house.

❷ Background

Art

The Court Jester, 1875, by William Merritt Chase

American artist William Merritt Chase studied in New York with painter Joseph O. Eaton and at the National Academy of Design. *The Court Jester* won the Medal of Honor at the 1876 Centennial Exhibition in Philadelphia.

1. How does this painting help you understand the story?
   Answer: It shows how Fortunato was dressed. It adds details about the carnival.
2. Is the man in the painting on the alert or unsuspecting?
   Answer: He is preoccupied and seems unaware of his surroundings.

❸ ▶Critical Viewing

Answer: The costume in the painting matches the verbal description of Fortunato's costume.

❶

The Cask of Amontillado[1]

Edgar Allan Poe

The Court Jester, 1875 (detail), William Merritt Chase, Pennsylvania Academy of the Fine Arts, Philadelphia

❷

❸ ▲ **Critical Viewing** How does this costume compare with your image of the costume worn by Fortunato? **[Compare and Contrast]**

TEACHING RESOURCES

The following resources can be used to enrich or extend the instruction for pp. 6–12.

Literary Analysis

- **Selection Support:** Literary Analysis, p. 5

Reading

- **Reader's Companion**
- **English Learner's Companion**
- **Listening to Literature Audiocassettes,** Side 1 ■
- **Listening to Literature Audio CDs,** CD 1 ■

■ **BLOCK SCHEDULING:** Resources marked with this symbol provide varied instruction during 90-minute blocks.

5 The thousand injuries of Fortunato I had borne as I best could, but when he ventured upon insult I vowed revenge. You, who so well know the nature of my soul, will not suppose, however, that I gave utterance to a threat. At *length* I would be avenged; this was a point definitely settled—but the very definitiveness with which it was resolved precluded the idea of risk. I must not only punish but punish with impunity.[2] A wrong is unredressed when retribution overtakes its redresser. It is equally unredressed when the avenger fails to make himself felt as such to him who has done the wrong.

It must be understood that neither by word nor deed had I given Fortunato cause to doubt my good will. I continued, as was my wont, to smile in his face, and he did not perceive that my smile *now* was at the thought of his immolation.[3]

He had a weak point—this Fortunato—although in other regards he was a man to be respected and even feared. He prided himself on his connoisseurship[4] in wine. Few Italians have the true virtuoso[5] spirit. For the most part their enthusiasm is adopted to suit the time and opportunity, to practice imposture upon the British and Austrian millionaires. In painting and gemmary, Fortunato, like his countrymen, was a quack, but in the matter of old wines he was sincere. In this respect I did not differ from him materially; I was skillful in the Italian vintages myself, and bought largely whenever I could.

It was about dusk, one evening during the supreme madness of the carnival season, that I encountered my friend. He accosted me with excessive warmth, for he had been drinking much. The man wore motley.[6] He had on a tight-fitting parti-striped dress, and his head was surmounted by the conical cap and bells. I was so pleased to see him that I thought I should never have done wringing his hand.

I said to him, "My dear Fortunato, you are luckily met. How remarkably well you are looking today. But I have received a pipe[7] of what passes for Amontillado, and I have my doubts."

"How?" said he. "Amontillado? A pipe? Impossible! And in the middle of the carnival!"

"I have my doubts," I replied: "and I was silly enough to pay the full Amontillado price without consulting you in the matter. You were not to be found, and I was fearful of losing a bargain."

"Amontillado!"

"I have my doubts."

"Amontillado!"

"And I must satisfy them."

"Amontillado!"

precluded (prē klo͞od′ id) *v.* prevented; made impossible in advance

retribution (re trə byo͞o′ shən) *n.* payback; punishment for a misdeed

accosted (ə kôst′ id) *v.* greeted, especially in a forward or aggressive way

6 ✓ **Reading Check**

Why does the speaker vow revenge on Fortunato?

1. **Amontillado** (ə män′ tə ya′ dō) *n.* a pale, dry sherry.
2. **impunity** (im pyo͞o′ ni tē′) *n.* freedom from consequences.
3. **immolation** (im′ ə lā′ shən) *n.* destruction.
4. **connoisseurship** (kän′ ə sʉr′ ship) *n.* expert judgment.
5. **virtuoso** (vʉr′ cho͞o ō′ sō) *adj.* masterly skill in a particular field.
6. **motley** (mät′ lē) *n.* a clown's multicolored costume.
7. **pipe** (pīp) *n.* large barrel, holding approximately 126 gallons.

4 Literary Analysis

Mood

- Have a volunteer read the first sentence aloud. Ask students which they think is worse: insult or injury? Point out that the narrator gives no information about the injuries and insults. Ask how this affects the story's mood.
  Possible responses: It makes the reader sympathetic toward Fortunato. It adds to the suspense since information is withheld.
- Ask students to define the mood created by the first two paragraphs. Which specific details create this mood?
  Possible response: The mood is creepy and spine-tingling. The reader knows that the narrator is bent on a cruel revenge. The narrator's false friendliness toward Fortunato shows that he is very calm and controlled, which suggests that he'll succeed.

5 Vocabulary Development

The Latin Prefix *pre-*

- Call students' attention to the word *precluded* and its definition. Note to students that the Latin prefix *pre-* means "before" or "in advance."
- Have students suggest other words that contain this prefix and list them on the chalkboard.
  Possible Responses: prepare, predict, prevent.
- Finally, have students define the listed words, using a dictionary to check their definitions.

6 ✓ Reading Check

Answer: Montresor believes that Fortunato has not only injured but insulted him.

CUSTOMIZE INSTRUCTION FOR UNIVERSAL ACCESS

For Special Needs Students	For Gifted/Talented Students	For Advanced Readers
Read aloud the first two paragraphs of the story. Have students identify details that show Montresor's mental state. As students read independently, they should continue to note actions that reveal Montresor's condition.	Suggest that students use details from the story and from the painting on p. 6 to draw, paint, or describe costumes and props they would use in a dramatized version of the story.	Paraphrasing can help draw attention to elements of Poe's style. Have students paraphrase selected passages, then contrast their work with the original. What new aspects of Poe's style are evident?

7 Literary Analysis

Mood

- Have two volunteers read this conversation aloud. How does the conversation affect the story's mood? **Answer:** Most readers will be frightened for Fortunato. The suspense mounts as Fortunato falls into the narrator's trap. Montresor's false friendliness and concern add to the horror.
- Ask the Literary Analysis question on p. 8: How does Fortunato's cough add to the eerie mood? **Answer:** The cough suggests illness and may foreshadow Fortunato's death. The sound of the cough echoes off the damp walls, adding to the suspense and tension the reader feels.

8 Reading Strategy

Breaking Down Confusing Sentences

- Copy this sentence on the chalkboard. Ask volunteers to identify the subject and the verb. If they have trouble, help them. **Answer:** subject: *orders,* verb: *were*
- Have students rephrase the sentence more simply. **Possible response:** I knew my orders would make them leave the house as soon as I turned my back.
- Ask students why they think Poe wrote the sentence as he did. **Possible answers:** He wants to give the story a romantic flavor. He wants the story to seem timeless, not modern. He wants to achieve a dramatic effect.

9 Critical Thinking

Analyze

- Ask two volunteers to read this dialogue aloud. Have students give their impressions of the two characters.
- Point out that Montresor's words don't accurately reflect his thoughts and intentions. How does that affect students' impressions of his character? **Possible answers:** It shows that he is very self-controlled. It shows that he finds it easy to lie and act a part. It shows that he is not impulsive; he doesn't speak without thinking.

"As you are engaged, I am on my way to Luchesi. If any one has a critical turn it is he. He will tell me—"

"Luchesi cannot tell Amontillado from sherry."

"And yet some fools will have it that his taste is a match for your own."

"Come, let us go."

"Whither?"

"To your vaults."

"My friend, no; I will not impose upon your good nature. I perceive you have an engagement. Luchesi—"

7 "I have no engagement—come."

"My friend, no. It is not the engagement, but the severe cold with which I perceive you are afflicted. The vaults are insufferably damp. They are encrusted with niter."

"Let us go, nevertheless. The cold is merely nothing. Amontillado! You have been imposed upon. And as for Luchesi, he cannot distinguish sherry from Amontillado."

Thus speaking, Fortunato possessed himself of my arm; and putting on a mask of black silk and drawing a *roquelaure*[8] closely about my person, I suffered him to hurry me to my palazzo.

8 There were no attendants at home; they had absconded to make merry in honor of the time. I had told them that I should not return until the morning, and had given them explicit orders not to stir from the house. These orders were sufficient, I well knew, to insure their immediate disappearance, one and all, as soon as my back was turned.

I took from their sconces two flambeaux, and giving one to Fortunato, bowed him through several suites of rooms to the archway that led into the vaults. I passed down a long and winding staircase, requesting him to be cautious as he followed. We came at length to the foot of the descent, and stood together upon the damp ground of the catacombs of the Montresors.

The gait of my friend was unsteady, and the bells upon his cap jingled as he strode.

"The pipe," he said.

"It is farther on," said I; "but observe the white webwork which gleams from these cavern walls."

He turned towards me, and looked into my eyes with two filmy orbs that distilled the rheum of intoxication.

9 "Niter?" he asked, at length.

"Niter," I replied. "How long have you had that cough?"

"Ugh! ugh! ugh!—ugh! ugh! ugh!—ugh! ugh! ugh!—ugh! ugh! ugh!—ugh! ugh! ugh!"

My poor friend found it impossible to reply for many minutes.

"It is nothing," he said, at last.

"Come," I said, with decision, "we will go back; your health is precious. You are rich, respected, admired, beloved; you are happy, as once I was.

afflicted (ə flikt´ id) *v.* suffering or sickened

explicit (eks plis´ it) *adj.* clearly stated

Literary Analysis
Mood How does Fortunato's cough add to the eerie mood?

8. ***roquelaure*** (räk´ ə lôr) *n.* knee-length cloak.

ENRICHMENT: Social Studies Connection

Carnival

Carnival is a period of midwinter that culminates in Mardi Gras (literally "Fat Tuesday")—the day before Ash Wednesday, which begins the Christian festival of Lent. The word *carnival* is from two Latin words. *Carne* means *flesh* or *meat* and *vale* means *farewell.* Carnival gets its name from the fact that Mardi Gras is a literal farewell to meat—the final day for feasting and merrymaking before the fasting and self-denial of Lent.

Because Lent lasts for 40 days, people traditionally indulge themselves to excess during carnival. Carnival is a time for costume parties, balls, parades, and pranks—the more outrageous the better. Poe's story evokes the annual carnival in Venice, Italy, one of the world's oldest and most brilliant carnival celebrations.

You are a man to be missed. For me it is no matter. We will go back; you will be ill, and I cannot be responsible. Besides, there is Luchesi—"

"Enough," he said; "the cough is a mere nothing; it will not kill me. I shall not die of a cough."

"True—true," I replied; "and, indeed, I had no intention of alarming you unnecessarily—but you should use all proper caution. A draft of this Medoc will defend us from the damps."

Here I knocked off the neck of a bottle which I drew from a long row of its fellows that lay upon the mold.

"Drink," I said, presenting him the wine.

He raised it to his lips with a leer. He paused and nodded to me familiarly, while his bells jingled.

"I drink," he said "to the buried that repose around us."

"And I to your long life."

He again took my arm, and we proceeded.

"These vaults," he said, "are extensive."

"The Montresors," I replied, "were a great and numerous family."

"I forget your arms."

"A huge human foot d'or, in a field azure; the foot crushes a serpent rampant whose fangs are imbedded in the heel."

"And the motto?"

"Nemo me impune lacessit."[9]

"Good!" he said.

11 The wine sparkled in his eyes and the bells jingled. My own fancy grew warm with the Medoc. We had passed through long walls of piled skeletons, with casks and puncheons[10] intermingling, into the inmost recesses of the catacombs. I paused again, and this time I made bold to seize Fortunato by an arm above the elbow.

"The niter!" I said; "see, it increases. It hangs like moss upon the vaults. We are below the river's bed. The drops of moisture trickle among the bones. Come, we will go back ere it is too late. Your cough—"

"It is nothing," he said; "let us go on. But first, another draft of the Medoc."

I broke and reached him a flagon of De Grâve. He emptied it at a breath. His eyes flashed with a fierce light. He laughed and threw the bottle upwards with a gesticulation I did not understand.

I looked at him in surprise. He repeated the movement—a grotesque one.

10 ▲ Critical Viewing
Which details of this photograph reflect the mood of the story? **[Connect]**

12 ✓ Reading Check
Where is Montresor bringing Fortunato?

9. ***Nemo me impune lacessit*** Latin for "No one attacks me with impunity."
10. **puncheons** (pun´ chənz) *n.* large barrels.

10 ▶ Critical Viewing

Answer: The walls are close together; the passageway is empty and descends into darkness. The photograph reflects the sense of danger in the story.

11 Literary Analysis

Description and Mood

- Ask students to summarize this description of the scene.
  Answer: The passage is damp and deep underground. Montresor and Fortunato are surrounded by skeletons and barrels of wine.
- Ask how these descriptive details affect the story's mood.
  Answer: The dampness is uncomfortable. Being enclosed underground among skeletons is claustrophobic and frightening. The niter growing on the walls makes the catacombs and vaults seem alive. These descriptive details add to the mood of horror.

12 ✓ Reading Check

Answer: Montresor is bringing Fortunato to the deepest and farthest part of the catacombs, where some of the wine is stored.

13 Reading Strategy

Breaking Down Confusing Sentences

- Have partners work together to break down each of these three sentences. Tell them to look first for the subject and verb, and then to deal with each detail.
- Have students rephrase each sentence as concisely and simply as possible without leaving out important information. Use the Reading Strategy question on p. 10 as an example.
  Possible responses: Because the bones had been moved, we could see within the wall a space about four feet deep, three feet wide, and six or seven feet high. Montresor describes a small recess or niche in the wall, large enough to hold the body of a man.

Monitor Progress Have students rephrase the other two sentences in this section on their own.
Possible response: Bones that had once lined the fourth wall now lay in a pile on the floor. The niche had not been specially built; it was just a space between two supporting columns and its back wall was granite.

- Have students compare and contrast their versions of these sentences with Poe's. How would their versions affect the impression Montresor makes on the reader?
  Possible response: Poe's language is mysterious and descriptive. This language shows that Montresor enjoys dwelling on the details of his planned crime and that he is not a direct and straightforward person.

"You do not comprehend?" he said.

"Not I," I replied.

"Then you are not of the brotherhood."

"How?"

"You are not of the masons."[11]

"Yes, yes," I said; "yes, yes."

"You? Impossible! A mason?"

"A mason," I replied.

"A sign," he said, "a sign."

"It is this," I answered, producing from beneath the folds of my *roquelaure* a trowel.

"You jest," he exclaimed, recoiling a few paces. "But let us proceed to the Amontillado."

"Be it so," I said, replacing the tool beneath the cloak and again offering him my arm. He leaned upon it heavily. We continued our route in search of the Amontillado. We passed through a range of low arches, descended, passed on, and descending again, arrived at a deep crypt, in which the foulness of the air caused our flambeaux rather to glow than flame.

At the most remote end of the crypt there appeared another less spacious. Its walls had been lined with human remains, piled to the vault overhead, in the fashion of the great catacombs of Paris. Three sides of this interior crypt were still ornamented in this manner. From the fourth side the bones had been thrown down, and lay promiscuously upon the earth, forming at one point a mound of some size. 13 Within the wall thus exposed by the displacing of the bones, we perceived a still interior crypt or recess, in depth about four feet, in width three, in height six or seven. It seemed to have been constructed for no especial use within itself, but formed merely the *interval* between two of the colossal supports of the roof of the catacombs, and was backed by one of their circumscribing walls of solid granite.

It was in vain that Fortunato, uplifting his dull torch, endeavored to pry into the depth of the recess. Its termination the feeble light did not enable us to see.

"Proceed," I said: "herein is the Amontillado. As for Luchesi—"

"He is an ignoramus," interrupted my friend, as he stepped unsteadily forward, while I followed immediately at his heels. In an instant he had reached the extremity of the niche, and finding his progress arrested by the rock, stood stupidly bewildered. A moment more and I had fettered him to the granite. In its surface were two iron staples, distant from each other about two feet, horizontally. From one of these depended a short chain, from the other a padlock. Throwing the links about his waist, it was but the work of a few seconds to secure it. He was too much astounded to resist. Withdrawing the key I stepped back from the recess.

"Pass your hand," I said, "over the wall; you cannot help feeling the

recoiling (ri koil′ iŋ) *v.* staggering back

Reading Strategy
Breaking Down Confusing Sentences
Restate the sentence starting "Within the wall . . ." What is the narrator describing?

termination (tʉr mə nā′ shən) *n.* end

---

11. masons the Freemasons, an international secret society.

niter. Indeed, it is *very* damp. Once more let me *implore* you to return. No? Then I must positively leave you. But I must first render you all the little attentions in my power."

"The Amontillado!" ejaculated my friend, not yet recovered from his astonishment.

"True," I replied; "the Amontillado."

As I said these words I busied myself among the pile of bones of which I have before spoken. Throwing them aside, I soon uncovered a quantity of building stone and mortar. With these materials and with the aid of my trowel, I began vigorously to wall up the entrance of the niche.

I had scarcely laid the first tier of the masonry when I discovered that the intoxication of Fortunato had in a great measure worn off. The earliest indication I had of this was a low moaning cry from the depth of the recess. It was *not* the cry of a drunken man. There was then a long and obstinate silence. I laid the second tier, and the third, and the fourth; and then I heard the furious vibrations of the chain. The noise lasted for several minutes, during which, that I might hearken to it with the more satisfaction, I ceased
14 my labors and sat down upon the bones. When at last the clanking subsided, I resumed the trowel, and finished without interruption the fifth, the sixth, and the seventh tier. The wall was now nearly upon a level with my breast. I again paused, and holding the flambeaux over the masonwork, threw a few feeble rays upon the figure within.

A succession of loud and shrill screams, bursting suddenly from the throat of the chained form, seemed to thrust me violently back. For a brief moment I hesitated, I trembled. Unsheathing my rapier, I began to grope with it about the recess; but the thought of an instant reassured me. I placed my hand upon the solid fabric of the catacombs, and felt satisfied. I reapproached the wall; I replied to the yells of him who clamored. I reechoed, I aided, I surpassed them in volume and in strength. I did this, and the clamorer grew still.

It was now midnight, and my task was drawing to a close. I had completed the eighth, the ninth, and the tenth tier. I had finished a portion of the last and the eleventh; there remained but a single stone to be fitted and plastered in. I struggled with its weight; I placed it partially in its destined position. But now there came from out the niche a low laugh that erected the hairs upon my head. It was succeeded by a sad voice, which I had difficulty in recognizing as that of the noble Fortunato. The voice said—

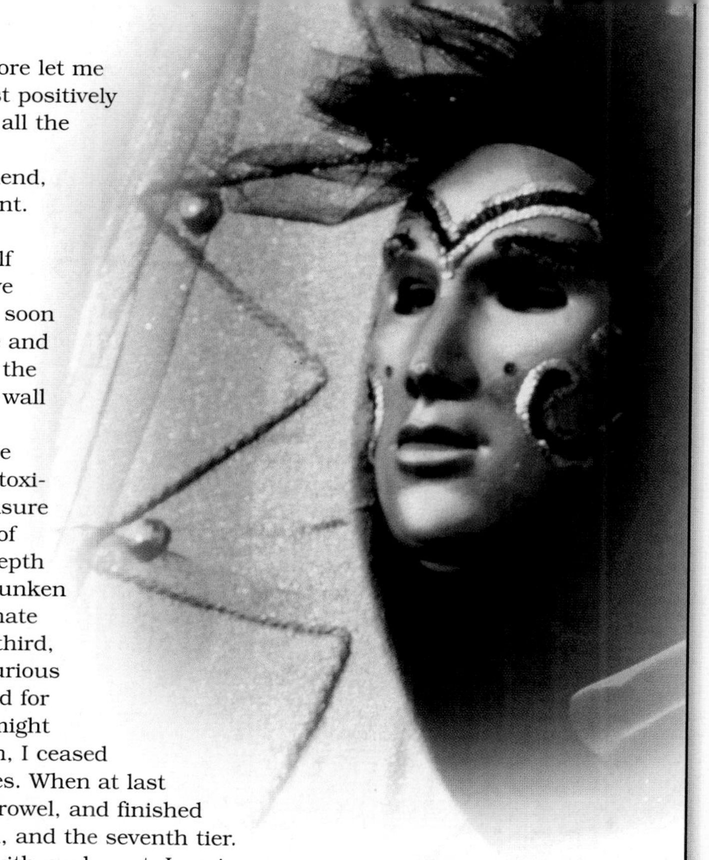

15 ▲ Critical Viewing Explain how the context of a story might make a festive mask such as this one appear sinister. **[Interpret]**

subsided (səb sīd′ id) *v.* settled down; became less active or intense

16 ✓ Reading Check What has Montresor done to Fortunato?

14 Literary Analysis

Description and Mood

- Have students read these two paragraphs silently. Ask which of the five senses Poe's language appeals to.
  Answer: hearing
- Ask why students think Poe uses so many sound effects in this description. What aspect of the setting makes Montresor so aware of the sounds he hears?
  Answer: Montresor can't see Fortunato on the other side of the wall he's building. In the deep silence of the crypt, he is only aware of the sounds Fortunato makes.

Monitor Progress Ask students how the sound effects in the passage affect the mood Poe creates in the reader.
Answer: The screams, moans, and yells would be frightening in any setting, but they are more so in the dark underground tunnels. The screams make the reader feel Fortunato's desperation and terror. Even Montresor hesitates for a moment at these sounds.

15 ▶ Critical Viewing

Answer: A mask can't change its expression, and it has no eyes, only holes for the wearer's eyes. Lack of expression can make any face seem sinister, because the person's actions are hard to predict.

16 ✓ Reading Check

Answer: Montresor has entombed Fortunato alive.

CUSTOMIZE INSTRUCTION FOR UNIVERSAL ACCESS

For Gifted/Talented Students	For Advanced Readers
Have students create a soundtrack for "The Cask of Amontillado." Suggest that they first select music that reflects the moods of the story, from the carnival mood of the beginning to the eeriness of the crypt. They may wish to add sound effects: the jingling of Fortunato's bells, the clank of chains, the scraping of trowel on stone.	Have students form a small reading group in which to read Poe's short story "The Masque of the Red Death." After reading the story, students can gather to discuss it and compare and contrast it to "The Cask of Amontillado." What themes and motifs do the two stories have in common? How does the difference in narrative point of view change the effect on the reader? Which story is more horrifying and why?

ASSESS

Answers for p. 12

Review and Assess

1. Possible answers: Montresor may be most disturbing when he kindly urges Fortunato to leave the catacombs, knowing all along that he will never let him go.
2. **(a)** Montresor describes Fortunato as vain about his expertise in wines, and not perceptive enough to see that Montresor is his enemy, an enemy worthy of respect and even fear. Fortunato seems insensitive to Montresor's pride and self-respect. **(b)** Fortunato's belief that he knows all about wines, and his desire to be respected for that belief, make him receptive to Montresor's flattery. Fortunato also trusts Montresor as an old acquaintance.
3. **(a)** Montresor puts on a mask and cloak so that no one will recognize him with Fortunato. He makes sure his servants are all out of the house. He remembers to bring a trowel. He entombs Fortunato deep within the crypts, where no one will find him by accident. **(b)** He knows that the more he urges a return, the more a vain Fortunato will insist on proceeding.
4. **(a)** Fortunato has injured and insulted him; Poe doesn't give the reader any details of these injuries and insults. **(b)** Montresor feels that revenge counts for nothing unless the victim knows the avenger did it himself.
5. Possible answers: Yes, because some unjust actions are beyond the reach of the law. No, because laws exist to protect everyone and attempts at private revenge will ultimately damage society.

"Ha! ha! ha!—he! he! he!—a very good joke, indeed—an excellent jest. We will have many a rich laugh about it at the palazzo—he! he! he!—over our wine—he! he! he!"

"The Amontillado!" I said.

"He! he! he!—he! he! he!—yes, the Amontillado. But is it not getting late? Will not they be awaiting us at the palazzo, the Lady Fortunato and the rest? Let us be gone."

"Yes," I said, "let us be gone."

"*For the love of God, Montresor!*"

"Yes," I said, "for the love of God!"

But to these words I hearkened in vain for a reply. I grew impatient. I called aloud—

"Fortunato!"

No answer. I called again—

"Fortunato!"

No answer still. I thrust a torch through the remaining aperture and let it fall within. There came forth in return only a jingling of the bells. My heart grew sick; it was the dampness of the catacombs that made it so. I hastened to make an end of my labor. I forced the last stone into its position; I plastered it up. Against the new masonry I reerected the old rampart of bones. For the half of a century no mortal has disturbed them. *In pace requiescat!*[12]

---

12. ***In pace requiescat!*** Latin for "May he rest in peace!"

Edgar Allan Poe

(1809–1849)

One of the first great American storytellers, Edgar Allan Poe blazed the trail for writers like Stephen King.

Poe's amazing but dark imagination may have had its roots in his troubled childhood, for he was orphaned by the age of three. Trouble plagued Poe in his adult life, too. He had to leave the University of Virginia when John Allan, his foster father, refused to pay the gambling debts that Poe had amassed. Later, Poe's dismissal from West Point caused Allan to disown him.

Poe found some happiness when he married Virginia Clemm. After she died of tuberculosis in 1847, however, Poe became increasingly antisocial. In 1849, he was discovered in a delirious condition in a Baltimore street. Three days later, he was dead at the age of forty.

Review and Assess

Thinking About the Selection

1. **Respond:** At what point in the story do you find Montresor most disturbing? Explain.
2. (a) **Recall:** How does Montresor describe Fortunato's actions and attitudes early in the story? (b) **Analyze Causes and Effects:** Which character traits make Fortunato such an easy prey for Montresor?
3. (a) **Recall:** What specific steps does Montresor take to ensure that his plan works? (b) **Interpret:** Why does Montresor keep urging Fortunato to turn back?
4. (a) **Recall:** Why does Montresor hate Fortunato? (b) **Support:** Why does Montresor feel he has the right to take justice into his own hands?
5. **Evaluate:** Montresor acts as judge and executioner in this story. Explain whether you think individuals are ever justified in taking justice into their own hands.

ASSESSMENT PRACTICE: Reading Comprehension

Vocabulary **(For more practice, see Test Preparation Workbook, p. 1.)**

Many assessment tests specify that students will use a knowledge of the meanings of prefixes and suffixes to determine word meanings. Use the following sample test item to show students how to use their knowledge of the Latin prefix *pre-* to determine the meanings of words.

If Montresor had committed an act of spontaneous rage, the effect on the reader would be vastly different. The act is more chilling because it is premeditated.

In this passage, the word premeditated means—

A cruel
B planned
C secret
D vengeful

By recalling that the Latin prefix *pre-* means "before" and combining that knowledge with their understanding of the word *meditation,* students should be able to see that *B* is the correct answer.

Review and Assess

Literary Analysis

Mood

1. Name at least three images that contribute to the story's eerie **mood**.
2. (a) Describe the mood of the scene in which Montresor first tells Fortunato about the Amontillado. (b) How does the mood change as the story unfolds?
3. How does Montresor's response to Fortunato's screams add to the mood as the story reaches its high point?

Connecting Literary Elements

4. Which **descriptions** of Fortunato shape your impression of him the most? Explain.
5. Using a chart like the one below, show how the descriptions of the catacombs contribute to the mood.

Description of Catacomb	Mood Created

Reading Strategy

Breaking Down Confusing Sentences

6. To **break down** the following sentence, make a flowchart like the one below to show the three things that Montresor does after Fortunato grabs his arm.

"Thus speaking, Fortunato possessed himself of my arm; and putting on a mask of black silk and drawing a *roquelaure* closely about my person, I suffered him to hurry me to my palazzo."

Fortunato grabs Montresor's arm.	→		→		→	

7. Break down this sentence to explain what has happened: "A moment more and I had fettered him to the granite."

Extend Understanding

8. **Career Connection:** If you were a lawyer, what evidence would you use to prove Montresor's guilt?

Quick Review

Mood is the feeling that a piece of literature creates in the reader.

A **description** is a portrait in words of a person, place, or object.

To **break down** a confusing sentence, rearrange, change, or take out words in order to identify its subject and what is being said about that subject.

Take It to the Net

www.phschool.com

Take the interactive self-test online to check your understanding of the selection.

ENRICHMENT: Further Reading

Other Works by Edgar Allan Poe

"The Black Cat"
"The Masque of the Red Death"
"Murders in the Rue Morgue"
"The Tell-Tale Heart"

Take It to the Net

Visit www.phschool.com for more information on Edgar Allan Poe.

Answers for p. 13

Review and Assess

1. Possible answers: Montresor's black mask and cloak; the long, winding staircase; the dark recesses of the crypt; many images of skeletons, niter, and dampness.
2. **(a)** The carnival atmosphere and Fortunato's costume create a festive mood. **(b)** As the story unfolds, the mood grows more and more frightening.
3. Montresor has planned his revenge carefully and intends to go through with it, but even he is horrified by Fortunato's screams. Montresor's response contributes to the frightening mood.
4. Fortunato is dressed as a fool and is tipsy. He isn't perceptive enough to realize that Montresor hates him. He's too vain to agree that the vaults are too damp for him with his cough.
5. Charts should be similar to the following:

Description	Mood
long, dark passages	danger; gloom
niter growing on walls	eeriness
skeletons and piles of bones	horror and doom

6. Montresor puts on a black silk mask. Montresor pulls a cloak around his body. Montresor lets Fortunato lead him to his own palazzo.
7. The subject is *I;* the verb is *had fettered.* Montresor has quickly chained Fortunato to the granite wall.
8. Evidence might include witnesses who saw Montresor and Fortunato together at the carnival or knew that Montresor hated Fortunato. Since there were no witnesses to the crime, proving guilt would be difficult.

EXTEND

Answers for p. 14

1 Vocabulary Development

Word Analysis

1. preview
2. prejudice
3. precaution

Spelling Strategy

1. smiling
2. jingled
3. believable
4. facing

Concept Development: Antonyms

1. b	3. b	5. c	7. c
2. a	4. a	6. b	8. b

2 Grammar Lesson

1. Edgar Allan Poe wrote the story.
2. A modern writer might set the story in New Orleans.
3. Mardi Gras, held in February or March, is a wild celebration.
4. Montresor led him through the catacombs.
5. It would be difficult to find Montresor in the French Quarter.

Writing Application

Have students exchange papers, underline the common nouns, and double-underline the proper nouns. Partners can go over the work together.

Integrate Language Skills

1 Vocabulary Development Lesson

Word Analysis: Latin Prefix *pre-*

The Latin prefix *pre-*, as found in *precluded*, means "before" or "in advance." Identify the word from the list below that best fits each definition.

preview precaution prejudice

1. To see in advance
2. Judgment without sufficient facts
3. Care taken in advance

Spelling Strategy

When you add an ending that begins with a vowel to a word that ends in a silent *e*, the *e* is usually dropped. For example, when adding *-ing* to the word *subside*, drop the silent *e* to form *subsiding*. Write the word formed by adding the ending to each word below.

1. smile + *-ing*
2. jingle + *-ed*
3. believe + *-able*
4. face + *-ing*

Concept Development: Antonyms

Identify the antonym, or opposite, of the first word.

1. precluded: (a) prevented, (b) aided, (c) started
2. retribution: (a) reward, (b) disaster, (c) assignment
3. accosted: (a) sought, (b) retreated, (c) discovered
4. subsided: (a) increased, (b) created, (c) challenged
5. afflicted: (a) weary, (b) skeptical, (c) blessed
6. explicit: (a) unnecessary, (b) vague, (c) impatient
7. recoiling: (a) unfastening, (b) releasing, (c) advancing
8. termination: (a) height, (b) beginning, (c) extension

2 Grammar Lesson

Common Nouns and Proper Nouns

A **common noun** names any one of a class of people, places, or things—for example, *man*, *city*, or *month*. A **proper noun** names a specific person, place, or thing and always begins with a capital letter—for example, *William*, *Los Angeles*, or *September*.

In the following excerpt from "The Cask of Amontillado," the common nouns are underlined, and the proper noun is in boldface.

Example: I paused again, and this time I made bold to seize **Fortunato** by an arm above the elbow.

Practice Copy each sentence below. Draw one line under each common noun and two lines under each proper noun.

1. Edgar Allan Poe wrote the story.
2. A modern writer might set the story in New Orleans.
3. Mardi Gras, held in February or March, is a wild celebration.
4. Montresor led him through the catacombs.
5. It would be difficult to find Montresor in the French Quarter.

Writing Application Write a paragraph about a scene from the story. Use at least three common nouns and three proper nouns.

WG *Prentice Hall Writing and Grammar Connection: Chapter 16, Section 1*

TEACHING RESOURCES

The following resources can be used to enrich or extend the instructions for pp. 14–15.

Vocabulary

- **Selection Support:** Build Vocabulary, p. 1
- **Vocabulary and Spelling Practice Book** (Use this booklet for skills enrichment.)

Grammar

- **Selection Support:** Build Grammar Skills, p. 2
- **Writing and Grammar,** Gold Level, p. 342 ■
- **Daily Language Practice Transparencies**

Writing

- **Writing and Grammar,** Gold Level, p. 106
- **Writing and Grammar iText CD-ROM** ■
- **Writing Models and Graphic Organizers on Transparencies,** p. 17

■ **BLOCK SCHEDULING:** Resources marked with this symbol provide varied instruction during 90-minute blocks.

❸ Writing Lesson

Description of a Set

Imagine that "The Cask of Amontillado" is being made into a movie. Choose a scene from the story. Use your imagination to expand upon Poe's description as you prepare a vivid, precise description of a set design for that scene.

Prewriting Review the scene you have chosen and picture it in your mind. Jot down precise details of sight, sound, smell, taste, and texture.

Model: Gathering Precise Details

Scene: Montresor meets Fortunato.
Poe: "It was about dusk, one evening during the supreme madness of the carnival season, . . ."
Set Details: rough cobblestone street, lit by flickering torches distant sound of singing; people in costumes

Precise details, such as *rough cobblestones* and *flickering torches*, will help the audience "see" the scene.

Drafting Organize your set description by describing it spatially, moving from left to right or from the foreground to the background. Refer to your notes, and include the specific elements of the set.

Revising Read your draft aloud to a classmate. Add or change any details that you feel will help readers see your set more clearly.

WG *Prentice Hall Writing and Grammar Connection: Chapter 6, Section 2*

❹ Extension Activities

Listening and Speaking Retell part of "The Cask of Amontillado" from Fortunato's perspective. Include the following in your **retelling:**

- Fortunato's thoughts about Montresor in the beginning and at the end of the story
- Fortunato's feelings about the situation

Present your retelling to your class, using tones and gestures you think Fortunato would use. After your retelling, ask your classmates for feedback.

Research and Technology In a group, create a **storyboard** outlining the main events of the plot for a movie version of "The Cask of Amontillado." Draw each important scene in comic-book style. For each frame, write a brief description of the action. Include Poe's main events and any important events that you add. Use graphics software to help create the storyboard scenes. **[Group Activity]**

Take It to the Net www.phschool.com
Go online for an additional research activity using the Internet.

ASSESSMENT RESOURCES

The following resources can be used to assess students' knowledge and skills.

Selection Assessment

- **Formal Assessment,** pp. 1–3
- **Open Book Test,** pp. 1–3
- **Got It! Assessment Videotapes,** Tape 1
- **Test Bank Software**

Take It to the Net
Visit www.phschool.com for self-tests and additional questions on "The Cask of Amontillado."

Writing Rubric

- **Performance Assess. and Portfolio Mgmt.,** p. 18

PRENTICE HALL ASSESSMENT SYSTEM

- **Workbook**
- **Skill Book**
- **Transparencies**
- **CD-ROM**

❸ Writing Lesson

- Go over the model on the page with students. Explain that they are meant to produce a verbal description of a set, not a drawing. As Poe did in his story, they must create a sensory impression in words.
- Have students decide which setting they will describe—the carnival, the passages in the catacombs, or the niche in which Fortunato is entombed. Students can look back through the story and jot down details of these settings.
- Use the Description rubric in **Performance Assessment and Portfolio Management,** p. 18, to evaluate students' descriptions.

❹ Extension Activity

Research and Technology

- Review the main elements of plot with students. Have them identify the exposition, rising action, climax, and resolution of the story.
- Remind students that dramatic adaptations of literary works often include events beyond the ones described by the writer. Students may want to consider including a scene in which Fortunato insults Montresor, for instance, or they may want to show Montresor, fifty years after the murder, sitting down and telling a friend about it as Poe indicates in the opening sentences.
- Students may want to work with partners. Partners should decide together which scenes to include and what will happen in them. One partner can draw the scenes and the other can write the descriptions.

CUSTOMIZE INSTRUCTION For Universal Access

To address different learning styles, use the following activities suggested in the **Extension Activities** booklet, p. 1.

- For Verbal/Linguistic Learners, use Activity 5.
- For Interpersonal and Musical/Rhythmic Learners, use Activity 6.

The Most Dangerous Game

Lesson Objectives and CA Correlations

1. **To analyze and respond to literary elements**
   - Literary Analysis: Suspense **R 3.6**
   - Connecting Literary Elements: Conflict
2. **To read, comprehend, analyze, and critique a short story**
   - Reading Strategy: Using Context Clues
   - Reading Check questions
   - Review and Assess questions
   - Assessment Practice (ATE)
3. **To develop word analysis skills, fluency, and systematic vocabulary**
   - Vocabulary Development Lesson: Related Words: Forms of *scruples* **R 1.1**
4. **To understand and apply written and oral language conventions**
   - Spelling Strategy
   - Grammar Lesson: Pronouns and Antecedents **LC 1.3**
5. **To understand and apply appropriate writing and research strategies**
   - Writing Lesson: Survival Manual **W 2.6**
   - Extension Activity: Database **W 1.5**
6. **To understand and apply listening and speaking strategies**
   - Extension Activity: Video Trial **LS 1.7**

STEP-BY-STEP TEACHING GUIDE	PACING GUIDE
PRETEACH	
Motivate Students and Provide Background	
Use the Motivation activity (ATE p. 16)	5 min.
Read and discuss the Preview material and Background information (SE/ATE p. 16) [A]	10 min.
Introduce the Concepts	
Introduce the Literary Analysis and Reading Strategy (SE/ATE p. 17) [A]	15 min.
Pronounce the vocabulary words and read their definitions (SE p. 17)	5 min.
TEACH	
Monitor Comprehension	
Informally monitor comprehension by circulating while students read independently or in groups [A]	15 min.
Monitor students' comprehension with the Reading Check notes (SE/ATE pp. 19, 21, 23, 25, 27, 29, 31, 33, 35)	as students read
Develop vocabulary with Vocabulary notes (SE pp. 19, 20, 23, 27, 28, 29, 31; ATE p. 27)	as students read
Develop Understanding	
Develop students' understanding of suspense with Literary Analysis annotations (SE pp. 20, 22, 24, 25, 26, 32, 34, 35; ATE pp. 22, 24, 25, 26, 30, 32, 34, 35) [A]	5 min.
Develop students' understanding of using context clues with Reading Strategy annotations (SE pp. 23, 24; ATE pp. 21, 23, 24, 29, 31)	5 min.
ASSESS	
Assess Mastery	
Assess students' mastery of the Reading Strategy and Literary Analysis by having them answer the Review and Assess questions (SE/ATE p. 37)	20 min.
Use one or more of the print and media Assessment Resources (ATE p. 39) [A]	up to 50 min.
EXTEND	
Apply Understanding	
Have students complete the Vocabulary Development Lesson and the Grammar Lesson (SE p. 38) [A]	20 min.
Apply students' ability to anticipate readers' questions using the Writing Lesson (SE/ATE p. 39) [A]	45 min.
Apply students' understanding using one or more of the Extension Activities (SE p. 39)	20–90 min.

[A] ACCELERATED INSTRUCTION:
Use the strategies and activities identified with an [A].

UNIVERSAL ACCESS
● = Below-Level Students
▲ = On-Level Students
■ = Above-Level Students

Time and Resource Manager

Reading Level: Average
Average Number of Instructional Days: 5

RESOURCES		
PRINT	**TRANSPARENCIES**	**TECHNOLOGY**
• **Beyond Literature,** Workplace Skills Connection: Dealing with Competition, p. 2 ▲ ■		• **Interest Grabber Video,** Tape 1 ● ▲ ■
• **Selection Support Workbook:** ● ▲ ■ Literary Analysis, p. 8 Reading Strategy, p. 7 Build Vocabulary, p. 5	• **Literary Analysis and Reading Transparencies,** pp. 3 and 4 ● ▲ ■	
• **Adapted Reader's Companion** ● • **Reader's Companion** ●		• **Listening to Literature** ● ▲ ■ Audiocassettes, Sides 1 and 2 Audio CDs, CDs 1 and 2
• **English Learner's Companion** ● ▲ • **Literatura en español** ● ▲ • **Literary Analysis for Enrichment** ■		
• **Formal Assessment:** Selection Test, pp. 4–6 ● ▲ ■ • **Open Book Test,** pp. 4–6 ● ▲ ■ • PRENTICE HALL ASSESSMENT SYSTEM ● ▲ ■	• PRENTICE HALL ASSESSMENT SYSTEM ● ▲ ■ Skills Practice Answers and Explanations on Transparencies	• **Test Bank Software** ● ▲ ■ • **Got It! Assessment Videotapes,** Tape 1 ● ▲
• **Selection Support Workbook:** ● ▲ ■ Build Grammar Skills, p. 6 • **Writing and Grammar,** Gold Level ● ▲ ■ • **Extension Activities,** p. 2 ● ▲ ■	• **Daily Language Practice Transparencies** ● ▲	• **Writing and Grammar iText CD-ROM** ● ▲ ■ ***Take It to the Net*** www.phschool.com

BLOCK SCHEDULING: Use one 90-minute class period to preteach the selection and have students read it. Use a second 90-minute class period to assess students' mastery of skills and have them complete one of the Extension Activities.

PRETEACH

Step-by-Step Teaching Guide for pp. 16–17

Motivation

Have students predict what this story is about based on the following clues: the story's title and the photos and illustrations. Encourage students to make their predictions as detailed as possible. Write students' predictions on the chalkboard. When students have finished reading the story, review the predictions.

Interest Grabber Video

As an alternative, play "Hunting for Survival" on Tape 1 to engage student interest.

❶ Background

One of the best-known of all big-game hunters was Theodore Roosevelt (1858–1919), president of the United States from 1901 to 1909. Though sickly as a child, Roosevelt became a vigorous outdoorsman. He traveled the world to hunt big game: on one year-long African safari, he shot nine lions, eight elephants, and thirteen rhinos. Nowadays governments carefully limit hunting to preserve game populations and protect habitats. Roosevelt himself played a huge role in America's conservation movement. As president, he set aside 125 million acres in the United States as protected land, doubled the number of national parks, and founded 51 wildlife reserves.

Prepare to Read

The Most Dangerous Game

Take It to the Net

Visit www.phschool.com for interactive activities and instruction related to "The Most Dangerous Game," including

- background
- graphic organizers
- literary elements
- reading strategies

Preview

Connecting to the Literature

Some competitions can be friendly, while others can be fierce. If one side takes the competition more seriously than the other, the situation can become unpleasant, or even dangerous. In "The Most Dangerous Game," a competition becomes a life-or-death situation.

❶ Background

The main characters in this story enjoy hunting big game—large animals, such as lions or bears—for sport. For hunting enthusiasts, big-game hunting is the ultimate test of skill. In recent times, however, this sport has become controversial as populations of big-game animals have dwindled or have even become endangered.

TEACHING RESOURCES

The following resources can be used to enrich or extend the instruction for pp. 16–17.

Motivation

Interest Grabber Video, Tape 1: Hunting for Survival

Background

Beyond Literature, p. 2

Take It to the Net

Visit www.phschool.com for background and hotlinks for "The Most Dangerous Game."

Literary Analysis

Literary Analysis and Reading Transparencies, Suspense, p. 3

Reading

Selection Support: Reading Strategy, p. 7; Build Vocabulary, p. 5

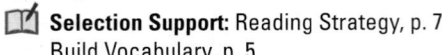

Literary Analysis and Reading Transparencies, Using Context Clues, p. 4

BLOCK SCHEDULING: Resources marked with this symbol provide varied instruction during 90-minute blocks.

❷ Literary Analysis

Suspense

Suspense is the reader's feeling of curiosity, uncertainty, or even anxiety about the outcome of events in a story. Writers can create suspense by putting characters into tense or risky situations. In this example from the story, the uncertainty of the situation helps to create suspense.

> For a seemingly endless time he fought the sea. He began to count his strokes; he could do possibly a hundred more and then—

As you read, pay attention to events and details that create suspense.

Connecting Literary Elements

Conflict plays a key role in establishing suspense. A **conflict** is a struggle between opposing forces, setting one character against another character, a character against nature, or a character against himself or herself. In "The Most Dangerous Game," suspense grows as the conflict between the story's two main characters intensifies.

❸ Reading Strategy

Using Context Clues

As you read, use **context clues** to figure out the approximate meaning of an unfamiliar word.

- Look at the words, phrases, and sentences that surround the unfamiliar word. These "surroundings" are the context. In particular, look for words or details that might describe or rename the word.
- Once you find clue words, create a definition that makes sense to you. Reread your sentence using your new definition in place of the difficult word to see whether the sentence now makes more sense.

Use a chart like this to gather context clues and figure out meanings.

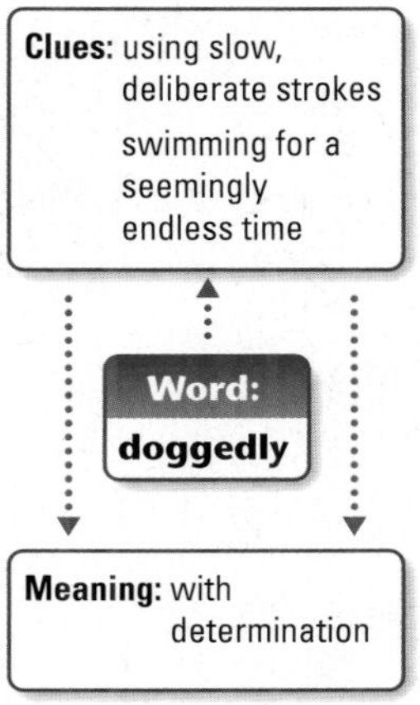

Vocabulary Development

palpable (pal′ pə bəl) *adj.* able to be touched or felt (p. 19)

indolently (in′ də lənt lē) *adv.* lazily; idly (p. 20)

bizarre (bi zär′) *adj.* odd in appearance (p. 23)

naive (nä ēv′) *adj.* unsophisticated (p. 27)

scruples (scro͞o′ pəlz) *n.* misgivings about something one feels is wrong (p. 27)

blandly (bland′ lē) *adv.* in a mild and soothing manner (p. 28)

grotesque (grō tesk′) *adj.* having a strange, bizarre design (p. 29)

futile (fyo͞ot′ ’l) *adj.* hopeless (p. 31)

❷ Literary Analysis

Suspense

- In literature, *suspense* is the emotion readers feel when the writer leaves them hanging—not knowing the outcome of a dangerous or emotional situation in a story.
- Point out the word *dangerous* in the story's title. This word creates a mood of suspense even before the story begins. It is already clear that this story will include fear and excitement.
- As students read "The Most Dangerous Game," have them look for especially suspenseful moments. When does the writer hint at dangerous situations?

❸ Reading Strategy

Using Context Clues

- Remind students that a word's *context* is its setting—the words and phrases that surround it. These surrounding words and phrases often give clues to the meanings of unfamiliar words.
- Write the following quotation from the story on the chalkboard:

  Sometimes I think evil is a tangible thing—with wave lengths, just as sound and light have.

- Point out to students that the sentence suggests that evil has physical, measurable qualities. How does this context clue reveal the meaning of *tangible*?
  Answer: The clue suggests a meaning of "real or actual."
- Have students look up *tangible* in a dictionary. They will see that its specific meaning is "something that can be touched."

Vocabulary Development

- Pronounce each vocabulary word for students, and read the definitions as a class. Have students identify any words with which they are already familiar.

CUSTOMIZE INSTRUCTION FOR UNIVERSAL ACCESS

For Special Needs Students	For Less Proficient Readers	For English Learners
Have students read the adapted version of "The Most Dangerous Game" in the **Adapted Reader's Companion.** This version provides basic-level instruction in an interactive format with questions and write-on lines. Completing the adapted version will prepare students to read the selection in the Student Edition.	Have students read the selection in the **Reader's Companion.** This version provides basic-level instruction in an interactive format with questions and write-on lines. After students finish the selection in **Reader's Companion,** have them complete the questions and activities in the Student Edition.	Have students read the adapted version of the selection in the **English Learner's Companion.** This version provides basic-level instruction in an interactive format with questions and write-on lines. Completing the adapted version will prepare students to read the selection in the Student Edition.

E-Teach

Visit E-Teach at www.phschool.com for teachers' essays on how to teach, with questions and answers.

TEACH

Step-by-Step Teaching Guide for pp. 18–36

CUSTOMIZE INSTRUCTION
For Bodily-Kinesthetic Learners

"The chase"—one person pursuing another—is the basis for many active games, from tag and hide-and-seek to paintball wars and capture-the-flag. Ask students who have played such games whether it is more exciting to chase or be chased. After a group discussion, students can write brief journal entries about how they felt during games of pursuit. They can apply this knowledge as they read the story of the "game" Zaroff forces Rainsford to play.

❶ About the Selection

In addition to keeping readers on the edge of their seats, "The Most Dangerous Game" asks an important question about human nature: Are human beings really civilized? The author contrasts Zaroff, whose style of living reflects highly cultured tastes but who hunts other human beings for sport, with Rainsford, who is horrified at the idea of taking a human life. However, when Rainsford is forced into the role of a "beast at bay," the primitive side of his nature emerges.

❷ Background

Art

Peering Through the Jungle, by Larry Noble

Commercial artist Larry Noble creates book and magazine covers, movie posters, and advertising art. The painting shown here appeared on the cover of a book called *Life During Wartime*.

1. Use the illustration to predict what the story will be about.
   Possible answers: It will be about an escaped prisoner or someone hiding in the jungle.
2. How do you think the person in the painting feels? Why do you think so?
   Answer: Since the person is hiding, he or she must be frightened.

❸ ▶Critical Viewing

The viewer wonders to whom the eye belongs, and whether the person is hiding or spying.

❸ ▲ Critical Viewing How does this painting create a feeling of suspense? **[Analyze]**

TEACHING RESOURCES

The following resources can be used to enrich or extend the instruction for pp. 18–36.

Literary Analysis

- **Selection Support:** Literary Analysis, p. 8

Reading

- **Reader's Companion**
- **English Learner's Companion**
- **Listening to Literature Audiocassettes,** Sides 1 and 2 ■
- **Listening to Literature Audio CDs,** CDs 1 and 2 ■

■ **BLOCK SCHEDULING:** Resources marked with this symbol provide varied instruction during 90-minute blocks.

1

The Most Dangerous Game

Richard Connell

4 "Off there to the right—somewhere—is a large island," said Whitney. "It's rather a mystery—"

"What island is it?" Rainsford asked.

"The old charts call it 'Ship-Trap Island,' " Whitney replied. "A suggestive name, isn't it? Sailors have a curious dread of the place. I don't know why. Some superstition—"

"Can't see it," remarked Rainsford, trying to peer through the dank tropical night that was palpable as it pressed its thick warm blackness in upon the yacht.

"You've good eyes," said Whitney, with a laugh, "and I've seen you pick off a moose moving in the brown fall bush at four hundred yards, but even you can't see four miles or so through a moonless Caribbean[1] night."

"Not four yards," admitted Rainsford. "Ugh! It's like moist black velvet."

"It will be light in Rio," promised Whitney. "We should make it in a few days. I hope the jaguar guns have come from Purdey's. We should have some good hunting up the Amazon.[2] Great sport, hunting."

"The best sport in the world," agreed Rainsford.

"For the hunter," amended Whitney. "Not for the jaguar."

"Don't talk rot, Whitney," said Rainsford. "You're a big-game hunter, not a philosopher. Who cares how a jaguar feels?"

palpable (pal′ pə bəl) *adj.* able to be touched or felt

5 **Reading Check**

How do sailors feel about the mysterious "ship-trap island"?

1. **Caribbean** (kar′ ə bē′ ən) the Caribbean Sea, a part of the Atlantic Ocean, bounded by South America, Central America, and the West Indies.
2. **Amazon** (am′ ə zän′) large river in South America.

Peering Through the Jungle, Larry Noble, Sal Barracca & Associates

2

4 Critical Thinking

Infer

- Remind students that writers don't tell readers everything straight out, More often, they imply aspects of character, theme, and plot. Readers draw inferences from these hints and implications.
- Ask students what they can infer about Ship-Trap Island. Point out that hints about it include its name and the things Whitney says about it.
  Answer: Its name suggests that ships have often been wrecked trying to reach it. Since Whitney isn't well-informed about it, he has probably never been there or known anyone who was there. The superstition suggests that sailors avoid the island.
- Have students read on up to "I think I'll turn in now, Rainsford" on p. 20. Ask them what else they can infer about the island, and what they base their inferences on.
  Answer: No one likes to go near the island. Whitney says it is God-forsaken, which suggests that no one lives there. The sailors' superstition must be based on something concrete; perhaps ships have been lost near the island, or the place is prone to storms and bad weather.

5 Reading Check

Answer: The sailors dread the island. It frightens them.

CUSTOMIZE INSTRUCTION FOR UNIVERSAL ACCESS

For Special Needs Students	For English Learners	For Advanced Readers
Have students choose partners with whom to read the story's dialogue aloud. One student can play Rainsford, the other can play both Whitney and Zaroff. Reading the dialogue aloud will help students comprehend the conflicts and plot.	Have students write down the names of each animal mentioned in the story—jaguar, snake, and so on. Have students draw each animal on one side of a flash card and write its name on the back. Students can use the cards to enlarge their vocabularies.	Have students write brief essays examining the effect of Rainsford's and Zaroff's character on the conflict between them. How would the conflict have changed if their personalities had been different? How might Whitney, for example, have acted in Rainsford's place?

6 Critical Thinking

Infer

- Ask students what they can infer about Rainsford based on his and Whitney's conversation about hunting. Have them explain their reasoning.
  Answer: Rainsford is unimaginative; he can't see any point of view except his own. Since he is sure he'll never be a hunter's prey, he assumes the prey has no feelings.
- What can students infer about Whitney? Does he enjoy hunting as much as Rainsford? Why or why not?
  Answer: He probably doesn't enjoy it quite as much. He realizes that hunting is no fun for the animals being hunted, and this bothers his conscience a little.

7 Literary Analysis

Suspense

- Ask the Literary Analysis question on p. 20: What effect does Rainsford's response have on the reader?
  Answer: Readers may believe that something frightening will confront Rainsford unexpectedly. Because he is not sensitive to the atmosphere of the place, he is the most likely one to come face to face with a threat.
- Ask students how the sound of the shot adds to the suspense.
  Answer: The island is supposed to be deserted, but the shot must have come from there. The story has already been full of references to the violent sport of hunting, but the actual firing of a gun brings the violence center stage.
- What about this paragraph makes the reader want to turn the page and continue?
  Answer: The reader wants to know who fired the shot and at what or whom the person was shooting.

"Perhaps the jaguar does," observed Whitney.

"Bah! They've no understanding."

6 "Even so, I rather think they understand one thing—fear. The fear of pain and the fear of death."

"Nonsense," laughed Rainsford. "This hot weather is making you soft, Whitney. Be a realist. The world is made up of two classes—the hunters and the huntees. Luckily, you and I are the hunters. Do you think we've passed that island yet?"

"I can't tell in the dark. I hope so."

"Why?" asked Rainsford.

"The place has a reputation—a bad one."

"Cannibals?" suggested Rainsford.

"Hardly. Even cannibals wouldn't live in such a God-forsaken place. But it's gotten into sailor lore, somehow. Didn't you notice that the crew's nerves seemed a bit jumpy today?"

"They were a bit strange, now you mention it. Even Captain Nielsen—"

"Yes, even that tough-minded old Swede, who'd go up to the devil himself and ask him for a light. Those fishy blue eyes held a look I never saw there before. All I could get out of him was: 'This place has an evil name among sea-faring men, sir.' Then he said to me, very gravely: 'Don't you feel anything?'—as if the air about us was actually poisonous. Now, you mustn't laugh when I tell you this —I did feel something like a sudden chill.

"There was no breeze. The sea was as flat as a plate-glass window. We were drawing near the island then. What I felt was a—a mental chill; a sort of sudden dread."

"Pure imagination," said Rainsford. "One superstitious sailor can taint the whole ship's company with his fear."

Literary Analysis
Suspense What effect does Rainsford's response have on the reader?

"Maybe. But sometimes I think sailors have an extra sense that tells them when they are in danger. Sometimes I think evil is a tangible thing—with wave lengths, just as sound and light have. An evil place can, so to speak, broadcast vibrations of evil. Anyhow, I'm glad we're getting out of this zone. Well, I think I'll turn in now, Rainsford."

"I'm not sleepy," said Rainsford. "I'm going to smoke another pipe on the afterdeck."

"Good night, then, Rainsford. See you at breakfast."

"Right. Good night, Whitney."

There was no sound in the night as Rainsford sat there, but the muffled throb of the engine that drove the yacht swiftly through the darkness, and the swish and ripple of the wash of the propeller.

Rainsford, reclining in a steamer chair, indolently puffed on his favorite brier. The sensuous drowsiness of the night was on him. "It's so dark," he thought, "that I could sleep without closing my eyes; the night would be my eyelids—"

indolently (in′ də lənt lē) *adv.* lazily; idly

7 An abrupt sound startled him. Off to the right he heard it, and his ears, expert in such matters, could not be mistaken. Again he heard the sound, and again. Somewhere, off in the blackness, someone had fired a gun three times.

ENRICHMENT: Social Studies Connection

Faraway Places

The Caribbean, Rio, the Amazon, Malacca—all these exotic names evoke thoughts of faraway, fabulous places. You may want to share these facts with students:

- The Caribbean Sea is enclosed on three sides by South and Central America and the West Indies, a chain of lush tropical islands of which Cuba is the largest. The Caribbean empties into the Atlantic Ocean.
- The Amazon River, 4,000 miles long, flows eastward across Brazil from the Andes Mountains of Peru to the Atlantic Ocean. Rio de Janeiro is a Brazilian city of over 5 million people.
- Malacca is a province of Malaysia, which occupies territory on the Malay Peninsula and the island of Borneo in the south Pacific. When this story was written, Malaysia was called Malaya and was a British protectorate.

Rainsford sprang up and moved quickly to the rail, mystified. He strained his eyes in the direction from which the reports had come, but it was like trying to see through a blanket. He leaped upon the rail and balanced himself there, to get greater elevation; his pipe, striking a rope, was knocked from his mouth. He lunged for it; a short, hoarse cry came from his lips as he realized he had reached too far and had lost his balance. The cry was pinched off short as the blood-warm waters of the Caribbean Sea closed over his head.

He struggled up to the surface and tried to cry out, but the wash from the speeding yacht slapped him in the face and the salt water in his open mouth made him gag and strangle. Desperately he struck out with strong strokes after the receding lights of the yacht, but he stopped before he had swum fifty feet. A certain cool-headedness had come to him; it was not the first time he had been in a tight place. There was a chance that his cries could be heard by someone aboard the yacht, but that chance was slender, and grew more slender as the yacht raced on. He wrestled himself out of his clothes, and shouted with all his power. The lights of the yacht became faint and ever-vanishing fireflies; then they were blotted out entirely by the night.

Hat, Knife, and Gun in Woods, David Mann, Sal Barracca & Associates

8 ▲ **Critical Viewing** Based on this painting, predict what might happen in the story. **[Predict]**

Rainsford remembered the shots. They had come from the right, and doggedly he swam in that direction, swimming with slow, deliberate strokes, conserving his strength. For a seemingly endless time he fought the sea. He began to count his strokes; he could do possibly a hundred more and then—

Rainsford heard a sound. It came out of the darkness, a high screaming sound, the sound of an animal in an extremity of anguish and terror.

He did not recognize the animal that made the sound; he did not try to; with fresh vitality he swam toward the sound. He heard it again; then it was cut short by another noise, crisp, staccato.

"Pistol shot," muttered Rainsford, swimming on.

9 Ten minutes of determined effort brought another sound to his ears—the most welcome he had ever heard—the muttering and growling of the sea breaking on a rocky shore. He was almost on the rocks before he saw them; on a night less calm he would have been shattered against them. With his remaining strength he dragged himself from the swirling waters. Jagged crags appeared to jut into the opaqueness, he forced

10 ✔ **Reading Check**

What happens to Rainsford after he hears a gunshot while on the ship?

8 ▶ Critical Viewing

Possible responses: The story will involve hunting. Someone will be killed.

9 Reading Strategy

Using Context Clues

- Have students use context clues to define the word *crags.* Have them identify the clues they used.
  Answer: *Crags* is a plural noun. The paragraph says that the shore line is rocky and that the rocks would have killed Rainsford if the waves had thrown him against them. This suggests that the rocks are jagged. Therefore, *crags* must be a synonym for rocks.
- Have students use context clues to define *opaqueness.*
  Answer: *Opaqueness* is a noun. The first three pages of the story stressed how dark the night was, and that the characters couldn't see very far through the darkness. *Opaqueness* means "darkness" or "dimness."

10 ✔ Reading Check

Answer: Rainsford accidentally falls overboard, swims to shore, and hauls himself out of the water.

11 Literary Analysis

Conflict and Suspense

- Ask the Literary Analysis question on p. 22: Which details of Rainsford's struggle build suspense?
  Answer: Rainford's difficult swim to an unknown shore is followed by a desperate climb and a plunge into dense jungle. His hunger adds a new suspense: What will he eat?
- Have students describe the conflict facing Rainsford since falling overboard.
  Answer: Rainsford is alone in a conflict with nature. He is now in a jungle with no resources beyond his own strength, intelligence, and instincts.

12 ▶Critical Viewing

Answer: The picture suggests that Rainsford is both strong and fortunate to have pulled himself to shore.

13 Literary Analysis

Conflict and Suspense

- Remind students that suspense is the result of a reader wanting to know the outcome of a conflict. Ask students what details make them want to read on.
  Answer: Readers want to find out who lives in the house. They want to know why anyone would build such a huge house on a deserted island.
- Ask students whether they can make any educated guesses about the occupant(s) of the house. Which clues in the text suggested these guesses to them?
  Answer: The size of the building indicates wealth. It must be the house of the person who fired the shots Rainsford heard. The person who lives there is an exceptionally skilled and daring hunter according to Rainsford's analysis of the kill site.

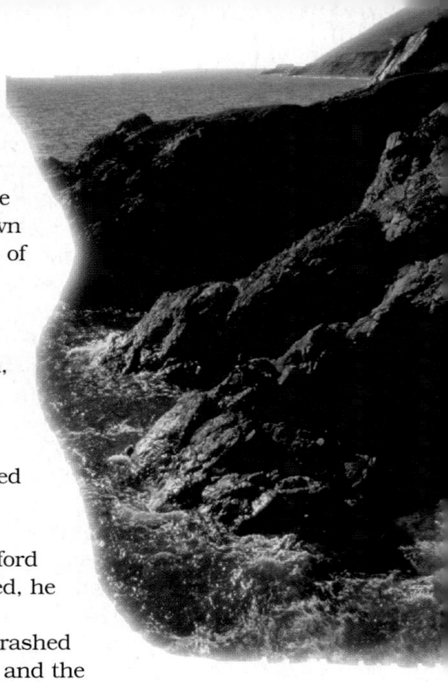

11 himself upward, hand over hand. Gasping, his hands raw, he reached a flat place at the top. Dense jungle came down to the very edge of the cliffs. What perils that tangle of trees and underbrush might hold for him did not concern Rainsford just then. All he knew was that he was safe from his enemy, the sea, and that utter weariness was on him. He flung himself down at the jungle edge and tumbled headlong into the deepest sleep of his life.

When he opened his eyes he knew from the position of the sun that it was late in the afternoon. Sleep had given him new vigor; a sharp hunger was picking at him. He looked about him, almost cheerfully.

"Where there are pistol shots, there are men. Where there are men, there is food," he thought. But what kind of men, he wondered, in so forbidding a place? An unbroken front of snarled and ragged jungle fringed the shore.

He saw no sign of a trail through the closely knit web of weeds and trees; it was easier to go along the shore, and Rainsford floundered along by the water. Not far from where he had landed, he stopped.

Some wounded thing, by the evidence a large animal, had thrashed about in the underbrush; the jungle weeds were crushed down and the moss was lacerated; one patch of weeds was stained crimson. A small, glittering object not far away caught Rainsford's eye and he picked it up. It was an empty cartridge.

"A twenty-two," he remarked. "That's odd. It must have been a fairly large animal too. The hunter had his nerve with him to tackle it with a light gun. It's clear that the brute put up a fight. I suppose the first three shots I heard was when the hunter flushed his quarry[3] and wounded it. The last shot was when he trailed it here and finished it."

He examined the ground closely and found what he had hoped to find—the print of hunting boots. They pointed along the cliff in the direction he had been going. Eagerly he hurried along, now slipping on a rotten log or a loose stone, but making headway; night was beginning to settle down on the island.

13 Bleak darkness was blacking out the sea and jungle when Rainsford sighted the lights. He came upon them as he turned a crook in the coast line, and his first thought was that he had come upon a village, for there were many lights. But as he forged along he saw to his great astonishment that all the lights were in one enormous building—a lofty structure with pointed towers plunging upward into the gloom. His eyes made out the shadowy outlines of a palatial château;[4] it was set on a high bluff, and on three sides of it cliffs dived down to where the sea licked greedy lips in the shadows.

"Mirage," thought Rainsford. But it was no mirage, he found, when he

12 ▲ Critical Viewing What does this picture suggest about Rainsford's struggle to climb out of the water and on to land? **[Analyze]**

Literary Analysis
Conflict and Suspense Which details of Rainsford's struggle build suspense?

3. **flushed his quarry** (kwôr′ ē) drove his prey into the open.
4. **palatial château** (pə lā′ shəl sha tō′) a mansion as luxurious as a palace.

opened the tall spiked iron gate. The stone steps were real enough; the massive door with a leering gargoyle[5] for a knocker was real enough; yet about it all hung an air of unreality.

14 He lifted the knocker, and it creaked up stiffly, as if it had never before been used. He let it fall, and it startled him with its booming loudness. He thought he heard steps within; the door remained closed. Again Rainsford lifted the heavy knocker, and let it fall. The door opened then, opened as suddenly as if it were on a spring, and Rainsford stood blinking in the river of glaring gold light that poured out. The first thing Rainsford's eyes discerned was the largest man Rainsford had ever seen—a gigantic creature, solidly made and black-bearded to the waist. In his hand the man held a long-barreled revolver, and he was pointing it straight at Rainsford's heart.

Out of the snarl of beard two small eyes regarded Rainsford.

"Don't be alarmed," said Rainsford, with a smile which he hoped was disarming. "I'm no robber. I fell off a yacht. My name is Sanger Rainsford of New York City."

The menacing look in the eyes did not change. The revolver pointed as rigidly as if the giant were a statue. He gave no sign that he understood Rainsford's words, or that he had even heard them. He was dressed in uniform, a black uniform trimmed with gray astrakhan.[6]

"I'm Sanger Rainsford of New York," Rainsford began again. "I fell off a yacht. I am hungry."

The man's only answer was to raise with his thumb the hammer of his revolver. Then Rainsford saw the man's free hand go to his forehead in a military salute, and he saw him click his heels together and stand at attention. Another man was coming down the broad marble steps, an erect, slender man in evening clothes. He advanced to Rainsford and held out his hand.

In a cultivated voice marked by a slight accent that gave it added precision and deliberateness, he said: "It is a very great pleasure and honor to welcome Mr. Sanger Rainsford, the celebrated hunter, to my home."

Automatically Rainsford shook the man's hand.

"I've read your book about hunting snow leopards in Tibet, you see," explained the man. "I am General Zaroff."

Rainsford's first impression was that the man was singularly handsome; his second was that there was an original, almost bizarre quality about the general's face. He was a tall man past middle age, for his hair was a vivid white; but his thick eyebrows and pointed military mustache were as black as the night from which Rainsford had come. His eyes, too, were black and very bright. He had high cheek bones, a sharp-cut nose, a spare, dark face, the face of a man used to giving orders, the face of an aristocrat. Turning to the giant in uniform, the general made a sign. The giant put away his pistol, saluted, withdrew.

"Ivan is an incredibly strong fellow," remarked the general, "but he

Reading Strategy
Using Context Clues
Which context clues can you use to determine the meaning of *discerned*?

bizarre (bi zär′) *adj.* odd in appearance

15 **Reading Check**
What does Rainsford find when he finally makes it to the island?

5. **gargoyle** (gär′ goil) *n.* strange and distorted animal form projecting from a building.
6. **astrakhan** (as′ trə kan′) *n.* loosely curled fur made from the skins of young lambs.

14 Reading Strategy
Using Context Clues

- Ask the Reading Strategy question on p. 23: Which context clues can you use to determine the meaning of *discerned?*
  Answer: The *-ed* ending suggests that it's a verb. It is an action taken by the eyes. Rainsford's eyes are adjusting to the change in light. Therefore, *discerned* must mean "perceived," or "saw."
- Challenge students to continue using context clues to figure out the meanings of unfamiliar words as they read the story.

15 Reading Check

Answer: Rainsford finds a palatial house in which live a huge bearded man who threatens to shoot him and an elegantly dressed man, General Zaroff, who welcomes him.

CUSTOMIZE INSTRUCTION FOR UNIVERSAL ACCESS

For English-Language Learners	For Gifted/Talented Students
Have students list the place names mentioned in the story, such as Rio and the Amazon on p. 19. Have students identify these places in their own languages, then find out where they are and learn one or two facts about them. Have students work together to make a set of flash cards that give clues to each place on the front and identify it on the back. Students can use the cards to learn the place names.	Have students work together to make two classroom maps of Rainsford's adventures. The first map should be a long-distance view of the area where Rainsford falls overboard; the second, a close-up map of the island, showing Death Swamp (p. 31), Zaroff's chateau, and other important locations. Students can search the story for geographical clues and use an atlas to help them with the first map.

16 Literary Analysis

Suspense

- Ask the Literary Analysis question on p. 24: What is your impression of the general? Can he be trusted?
  Answer: The general seems commanding, friendly, and concerned for Rainsford's welfare. It's early to tell whether he's trustworthy, but the fact that his servant seems violent is cause for doubt.
- Ask students what seems strange or unusual about the general. What questions about him would they like to have answered? Do their questions add to the story's suspense?
  Possible answers: Students may cite certain physical qualities as strange: the black eyebrows and moustache, black eyes, red lips, and pointed teeth. Questions might include: Why is the general living on a remote island? What does he find to hunt on the island? Why is he staring at Rainsford in an odd way? How can he afford all the luxurious goods in the house?

17 Reading Strategy

Using Context Clues

- Ask the Reading Strategy question on p. 24: Which context clues suggest the approximate meaning of *amenities?*
  Answer: It is a plural noun. Since it refers to items from civilization, it evidently refers to the food, crystal, linen, and other objects in the room. *Amenities* means "pleasant or agreeable things."

Monitor Progress Have students use context clues to define *appraising.* Ask them to identify the clues they used to determine the meaning.
Answer: It is a verb. The general's stare is what makes Rainsford uncomfortable. The word is used as a synonym for "studying," so it must mean something like "looking closely to find something out."

has the misfortune to be deaf and dumb. A simple fellow, but, I'm afraid, like all his race, a bit of a savage."

"Is he Russian?"

16 "He is a Cossack,"[7] said the general, and his smile showed red lips and pointed teeth. "So am I."

"Come," he said, "we shouldn't be chatting here. We can talk later. Now you want clothes, food, rest. You shall have them. This is a most restful spot."

Ivan had reappeared, and the general spoke to him with lips that moved but gave forth no sound.

"Follow Ivan, if you please, Mr. Rainsford," said the general. "I was about to have my dinner when you came. I'll wait for you. You'll find that my clothes will fit you, I think."

It was to a huge, beam-ceilinged bedroom with a canopied bed big enough for six men that Rainsford followed the silent giant. Ivan laid out an evening suit, and Rainsford, as he put it on, noticed that it came from a London tailor who ordinarily cut and sewed for none below the rank of duke.

The dining room to which Ivan conducted him was in many ways remarkable. There was a medieval magnificence about it; it suggested a baronial hall of feudal times with its oaken panels, its high ceiling, its vast refectory table where twoscore men could sit down to eat. About the hall were the mounted heads of many animals—lions, tigers, elephants, moose, bears; larger or more perfect specimens Rainsford had never seen. At the great table the general was sitting, alone.

"You'll have a cocktail, Mr. Rainsford," he suggested. The cocktail was surpassingly good; and, Rainsford noted, the table appointments were of the finest—the linen, the crystal, the silver, the china.

They were eating *borsch*, the rich, red soup with whipped cream so dear to Russian palates. Half apologetically General Zaroff said: "We do our best to preserve the amenities of civilization here. Please forgive any lapses. We are well off the beaten track, you know. Do you think the champagne has suffered from its long ocean trip?"

"Not in the least," declared Rainsford. He was finding the general a most thoughtful and affable host, a true cosmopolite.[8] But there was one small trait of the general's that made Rainsford uncomfortable. 17 Whenever he looked up from his plate he found the general studying him, appraising him narrowly.

"Perhaps," said General Zaroff, "you were surprised that I recognized your name. You see, I read all books on hunting published in English, French, and Russian. I have but one passion in my life, Mr. Rainsford, and it is the hunt."

"You have some wonderful heads here," said Rainsford as he ate a particularly well cooked filet mignon. "That Cape buffalo is the largest I ever saw."

"Oh, that fellow. Yes, he was a monster."

Literary Analysis
Suspense What is your impression of the general? Can he be trusted?

Reading Strategy
Using Context Clues Which context clues suggest the approximate meaning of *amenities*?

7. **Cossack** (käs´ ak) member of a people from southern Russia, famous for their fierceness.
8. **cosmopolite** (käz mäp´ ə līt´) *n.* person at home in all parts of the world.

"Did he charge you?"

"Hurled me against a tree," said the general. "Fractured my skull. But I got the brute."

"I've always thought," said Rainsford, "that the Cape buffalo is the most dangerous of all big game."

For a moment the general did not reply; he was smiling his curious red-lipped smile. Then he said slowly: "No. You are wrong, sir. The Cape buffalo is not the most dangerous big game." He sipped his wine. "Here in my preserve on this island," he said in the same slow tone, "I hunt more dangerous game."

Rainsford expressed his surprise. "Is there big game on this island?"

The general nodded. "The biggest."

"Really?"

18 "Oh, it isn't here naturally, of course. I have to stock the island."

"What have you imported, general?" Rainsford asked. "Tigers?"

The general smiled. "No," he said. "Hunting tigers ceased to interest me some years ago. I exhausted their possibilities, you see. No thrill left in tigers, no real danger. I live for danger, Mr. Rainsford."

The general took from his pocket a gold cigarette case and offered his guest a long black cigarette with a silver tip; it was perfumed and gave off a smell like incense.

"We will have some capital hunting, you and I," said the general. "I shall be most glad to have your society."

"But what game—" began Rainsford.

"I'll tell you," said the general. "You will be amused, I know. I think I may say, in all modesty, that I have done a rare thing. I have invented a new sensation. May I pour you another glass of port, Mr. Rainsford?"

"Thank you, general."

The general filled both glasses, and said: "God makes some men poets. Some He makes kings, some beggars. Me He made a hunter. My hand was made for the trigger, my father said. He was a very rich man with a quarter of a million acres in the Crimea,[9] and he was an ardent sportsman. When I was only five years old he gave me a little gun, specially made in Moscow for me, to shoot sparrows with. When I shot some of his prize turkeys with it, he did not punish me; he complimented me on my marksmanship. I killed my first bear in the Caucasus[10] when I was ten. My whole life has been one prolonged hunt. I went into the army—it was expected of noblemen's sons—and for a time commanded a division of Cossack cavalry, but my real interest was always the hunt. I have hunted every kind of game in every land. It would be impossible for me to tell you how many animals I have killed."

The general puffed at his cigarette.

"After the debacle[11] in Russia I left the country, for it was imprudent for an officer of the Czar to stay there. Many noble Russians lost

Literary Analysis
Suspense How does this discussion about the biggest game create suspense?

19 **Reading Check**
Why has Zaroff lost interest in hunting tigers?

9. **Crimea** (krī mē´ ə) region in southwestern Russia on the Black Sea.
10. **Caucasus** (kô´ kə səs) mountain range in southern Russia.
11. **debacle** (di bäk´ əl) *n.* bad defeat—Zaroff is referring to the Russian Revolution of 1917, a defeat for upper-class Russians like himself.

18 Literary Analysis

Suspense

- Remind students that by hinting at information or only disclosing a portion of the full picture, an author can generate suspense.
- Ask the Literary Analysis question on p. 25: How does this discussion about the biggest game create suspense?
  Answer: The author is withholding information from the reader—the general does not say what animal challenges him more than a tiger or a Cape buffalo.

19 Reading Check

Answer: The general is such a skilled hunter and so much smarter than a tiger that he finds no risk and therefore no zest in hunting it.

ENRICHMENT: Social Studies Connection

The Russian Revolution

On p. 25, Zaroff refers to "the debacle in Russia." He is speaking of the Bolshevik Revolution that ended the Russian monarchy and gave birth to the Soviet Union.

From the 1500s until 1917, Russia was ruled by monarchs called czars. The word czar is derived from Caesar, the first emperor of Rome. For most of the time, the Romanov family ruled the country. In 1905, a rebellion robbed the czar, Nicholas II, of much of his absolute power, making him a constitutional monarch.

In March 1917, a moderate socialist government came to power. The radical Bolsheviks, however, were not satisfied, and in October they seized power and established a communist government that would last until 1991. Zaroff's comment that "it was imprudent for an officer of the Czar to stay" in Russia was quite true; many Russian aristocrats became refugees.

20 Background

History

Cossack comes from a Turkish word meaning "adventurer" or "free man." Early Cossacks included Tartar nomads and runaway serfs; they established several independent strongholds within Russia. Gradually, Cossacks allied themselves to the Russian czar and joined Russian armies as elite cavalry units. Cossacks became famous for their skill as horsemen, for their loyalty to the czar, and for their ferocity in battle.

21 Literary Analysis

Suspense

- Point out to students how the author builds up suspense in this scene. At the top of p. 25, the general referred to hunting the most dangerous of all animals. The conversation goes on at length, and neither Rainsford nor the reader yet has any idea of this animal's identity. Not until halfway down p. 27 does Zaroff reveal that the animal is man.
- Ask the Literary Analysis question on p. 26: What do you think Zaroff is going to identify as the "most dangerous game"?
  Answer: Zaroff wants to hunt an animal that can reason. The only animal that can reason is a human being.

everything. I, luckily, had invested heavily in American securities, so I shall never have to open a tea room in Monte Carlo or drive a taxi in Paris. Naturally, I continued to hunt—grizzlies in your Rockies, crocodiles in the Ganges, rhinoceroses in East Africa. It was in Africa that the Cape buffalo hit me and laid me up for six months. As soon as I recovered I started for the Amazon to hunt jaguars, for I had heard they were unusually cunning. They weren't." The Cossack♦ sighed. "They were no match at all for a hunter with his wits about him, and a high-powered rifle. I was bitterly disappointed. I was lying in my tent with a splitting headache one night when a terrible thought pushed its way into my mind. Hunting was beginning to bore me! And hunting, remember, had been my life. I have heard that in America business men often go to pieces when they give up the business that has been their life."

"Yes, that's so," said Rainsford.

The general smiled. "I had no wish to go to pieces," he said. "I must do something. Now, mine is an analytical mind, Mr. Rainsford. Doubtless that is why I enjoy the problems of the chase."

"No doubt, General Zaroff."

"So," continued the general, "I asked myself why the hunt no longer fascinated me. You are much younger than I am, Mr. Rainsford, and have not hunted as much, but you perhaps can guess the answer."

"What was it?"

"Simply this: hunting had ceased to be what you call 'a sporting proposition.' It had become too easy. I always got my
21 quarry. Always. There is no greater bore than perfection."

The general lit a fresh cigarette.

"No animal had a chance with me any more. That is no boast; it is a mathematical certainty. The animal had nothing but his legs and his instinct. Instinct is no match for reason. When I thought of this it was a tragic moment for me, I can tell you."

Rainsford leaned across the table, absorbed in what his host was saying.

"It came to me as an inspiration what I must do," the general went on.

"And that was?"

The general smiled the quiet smile of one who has faced an obstacle and surmounted it with success. "I had to invent a new animal to hunt," he said.

"A new animal? You're joking."

"Not at all," said the general. "I never joke about hunting. I needed a new animal. I found one. So I bought this island, built this house, and here I do my hunting. The island is perfect for my purpose—there are jungles with a maze of trails in them, hills, swamps—"

Literature in context 20 — History Connection

♦ Cossack

Zaroff was a Cossack, a member of a special Russian military unit that enjoyed an elite and privileged status. As a result, these soldiers were fiercely independent. When the czar—the ruler of Russia—was overthrown in the Russian Revolution of 1917, Cossacks like Zaroff were banished, executed, or forced into exile. As a Cossack, Zaroff is unwilling to acknowledge that the rules of ordinary people apply to him.

Czar Nicholas II, overthrown in the Russian Revolution of 1917

Literary Analysis

Suspense What do you think Zaroff is going to identify as the "most dangerous game"? Explain.

ENRICHMENT: Social Studies Connection

Hunting and Gathering

Human beings have hunted for their food for more than half a million years. Only in the most recent 1 percent of human history have people farmed the land and grown crops. Anthropologists think hunting may have encouraged many common human traits, such as cooperation with one another, organization, and aggression. There are few hunting and gathering societies left in the world, although many people still hunt for sport and often eat the deer and other game they shoot. The only people who still exist solely by hunting are the Mbuti Pygmies of the Central African rain forest and the disappearing Bushmen of the Kalahari in Southern Africa. Societies that combine hunting with other means of sustenance include some Native North and South American tribes and the Aborigines of Australia.

"But the animal, General Zaroff?"

"Oh," said the general, "it supplies me with the most exciting hunting in the world. No other hunting compares with it for an instant. Every day I hunt, and I never grow bored now, for I have a quarry with which I can match my wits."

Rainsford's bewilderment showed in his face.

"I wanted the ideal animal to hunt," explained the general. "So I said: 'What are the attributes of an ideal quarry?' And the answer was, of course: 'It must have courage, cunning, and, above all, it must be able to reason.' "

"But no animal can reason," objected Rainsford.

"My dear fellow," said the general, "there is one that can."

"But you can't mean—" gasped Rainsford.

"And why not?"

"I can't believe you are serious, General Zaroff. This is a grisly joke."

"Why should I not be serious? I am speaking of hunting."

"Hunting? General Zaroff, what you speak of is murder."

The general laughed with entire good nature. He regarded Rainsford quizzically. "I refuse to believe that so modern and civilized a young man as you seem to be harbors romantic ideas about the value of human life. Surely your experiences in the war—"

"Did not make me condone cold-blooded murder," finished Rainsford stiffly.

Laughter shook the general. "How extraordinarily droll you are!" he said. "One does not expect nowadays to find a young man of the educated class, even in America, with such a naive, and, if I may say so, mid-Victorian point of view.[12] It's like finding a snuff-box in a limousine. Ah, well, doubtless you had Puritan ancestors. So many Americans appear to have had. I'll wager you'll forget your notions when you go hunting with me. You've a genuine new thrill in store for you, Mr. Rainsford."

naive (nä ēv´) *adj.* unsophisticated

"Thank you, I'm a hunter, not a murderer."

22 "Dear me," said the general, quite unruffled, "again that unpleasant word. But I think I can show you that your scruples are quite ill founded."

scruples (scroo´ pəlz) *n.* misgivings about something one feels is wrong

"Yes?"

23 "Life is for the strong, to be lived by the strong, and, if need be, taken by the strong. The weak of the world were put here to give the strong pleasure. I am strong. Why should I not use my gift? If I wish to hunt, why should I not? I hunt the scum of the earth—sailors from tramp ships—lascars,[13] blacks, Chinese, whites, mongrels—a thoroughbred horse or hound is worth more than a score of them."

"But they are men," said Rainsford hotly.

"Precisely," said the general. "That is why I use them. It gives me pleasure. They can reason, after a fashion. So they are dangerous."

"But where do you get them?"

24 **Reading Check**

What kind of animal does Zaroff hunt?

12. **mid-Victorian point of view** a point of view emphasizing proper behavior and associated with the time of Queen Victoria of England (1819–1901).
13. **lascars** (las´ kərz) *n.* Oriental sailors, especially natives of India.

22 Vocabulary Development

Scruples

- Tell students that *scruple* is derived from the Latin for "pebble" and originally referred to a tiny unit of weight.
- Speculate with students how the meaning of *scruple* might have developed its current sense of "moral concern or caution."
  Answer: A tiny unit of weight may be associated with preciseness and carefulness. Over time this meaning came to include a sense of moral carefulness, of carefully "weighing" the consequences of actions.

23 Critical Thinking

Compare and Contrast

- Remind students that comparing means finding common characteristics and contrasting means finding unique ones.
- Have students compare and contrast Zaroff's speech to the one Rainsford made to Whitney at the top of p. 20.
  Answers: Rainsford claimed that there were two classes—the hunters and the huntees. Zaroff divides the world into the strong and the weak. So far, the two men agree completely. However, Rainsford finds it easy to kill jaguars because "they've no understanding"—they can't reason. He doesn't apply this to human beings. Zaroff sees no difference between a human being and any other animal.

24 Reading Check

Answer: Zaroff hunts human beings.

25 ▶ **Critical Viewing**

Answer: Hunting would be difficult. The undergrowth is so dense that it would be hard to follow a trail. It might be hard to see, because the trees block sunlight. There are many places an animal can hide.

26 Critical Thinking

Evaluate

- Ask students to evaluate Zaroff's assertion that what he does is a game. If so, how is it like a game? If not, how is it different? **Answer:** It may be a game for Zaroff, because it is a test of his skill and he enjoys it. He considers it a sport. It is not a game for the other participants, who have to choose between "hunting" and torture at Ivan's hands. They are participating by force and it is no fun for them. It results in death for them.

25 ▲ **Critical Viewing** What might it be like to hunt in an environment such as the one pictured here? **[Speculate]**

The general's left eyelid fluttered down in a wink. "This island is called Ship-Trap," he answered. "Sometimes an angry god of the high seas sends them to me. Sometimes, when Providence is not so kind, I help Providence a bit. Come to the window with me."

Rainsford went to the window and looked out toward the sea.

"Watch! Out there!" exclaimed the general, pointing into the night. Rainsford's eyes saw only blackness, and then, as the general pressed a button, far out to sea Rainsford saw the flash of lights.

The general chuckled. "They indicate a channel," he said, "where there's none: giant rocks with razor edges crouch like a sea monster with wide-open jaws. They can crush a ship as easily as I crush this nut." He dropped a walnut on the hardwood floor and brought his heel grinding down on it. "Oh, yes," he said, casually, as if in answer to a question, "I have electricity. We try to be civilized here."

"Civilized? And you shoot down men?"

A trace of anger was in the general's black eyes, but it was there for but a second, and he said, in his most pleasant manner: "Dear me, what a righteous young man you are! I assure you I do not do the thing you suggest. That would be barbarous. I treat these visitors with every consideration. They get plenty of good food and exercise. They get into splendid physical condition. You shall see for yourself tomorrow."

"What do you mean?"

"We'll visit my training school," smiled the general. "It's in the cellar. I have about a dozen pupils down there now. They're from the Spanish bark San Lucar that had the bad luck to go on the rocks out there. A very inferior lot, I regret to say. Poor specimens and more accustomed to the deck than to the jungle."

He raised his hand, and Ivan, who served as waiter, brought thick Turkish coffee. Rainsford, with an effort, held his tongue in check.

26 "It's a game, you see," pursued the general blandly. "I suggest to one of them that we go hunting. I give him a supply of food and an excellent hunting knife. I give him three hours' start. I am to follow, armed only with a pistol of the smallest caliber and range. If my quarry eludes me for three whole days, he wins the game. If I find him"—the general smiled—"he loses."

"Suppose he refuses to be hunted?"

"Oh," said the general, "I give him his option, of course. He need not play the game if he doesn't wish to. If he does not wish to hunt, I turn

blandly (bland´ lē) *adv.* in a mild and soothing manner him over to Ivan. Ivan once had the honor of serving as official knouter[14] to the Great White Czar, and he has his own ideas of sport. Invariably, Mr. Rainsford, invariably they choose the hunt."

"And if they win?"

The smile on the general's face widened. "To date I have not lost," he said.

Then he added, hastily: "I don't wish you to think me a braggart, Mr. Rainsford. Many of them afford only the most elementary sort of problem. Occasionally I strike a tartar.[15] One almost did win. I eventually had to use the dogs."

"The dogs?"

"This way, please. I'll show you."

The general steered Rainsford to a window. The lights from the windows sent a flickering illumination that made grotesque patterns on the courtyard below, and Rainsford could see moving about there a dozen or so huge black shapes; as they turned toward him, their eyes glittered greenly.

grotesque (grō tesk´) *adj.* having a strange, bizarre design

"A rather good lot, I think," observed the general. "They are let out at seven every night. If anyone should try to get into my house—or out of it—something extremely regrettable would occur to him." He hummed a snatch of song from the Folies Bergère.[16]

"And now," said the general, "I want to show you my new collection of heads. Will you come with me to the library?"

"I hope," said Rainsford, "that you will excuse me tonight, General Zaroff. I'm really not feeling at all well."

"Ah, indeed?" the general inquired solicitously. "Well, I suppose that's only natural, after your long swim. You need a good, restful night's sleep. Tomorrow you'll feel like a new man, I'll wager. Then we'll hunt, eh? I've one rather promising prospect—"

Rainsford was hurrying from the room.

27 "Sorry you can't go with me tonight," called the general. "I expect rather fair sport—a big, strong black. He looks resourceful—Well good night, Mr. Rainsford; I hope you have a good night's rest."

The bed was good, and the pajamas of the softest silk, and he was tired in every fiber of his being, but nevertheless Rainsford could not quiet his brain with the opiate of sleep. He lay, eyes wide open. Once he thought he heard stealthy steps in the corridor outside his room. He sought to throw open the door; it would not open. He went to the window and looked out. His room was high up in one of the towers. The lights of the château were out now, and it was dark and silent, but there was a fragment of sallow moon, and by its wan light he could see, dimly, the courtyard; there, weaving in and out in the pattern of shadow, were black, noiseless forms; the hounds heard him at the window and looked up, expectantly, with their green eyes. Rainsford went back to the bed

28 **Reading Check**

Explain the game that Zaroff plays.

14. **knouter** (nout´ ər) *n.* someone who beats criminals with a leather whip, or knout.
15. **tartar** (tär´ tər) *n.* stubborn, violent person.
16. **Folies Bergère** (fô´ lē ber zher´) musical theater in Paris.

27 Reading Strategy

Using Context Clues

- Have students use context clues to define the word *solicitously* and make a short list of synonyms for it.
  Answers: *Solicitously* is an adverb describing the way the general speaks to Rainsford. Since he is wishing him a good night's rest, the word must mean something like "considerately" or "with concern." Synonyms include *considerately, anxiously, attentively.*
- Have students use context clues to define the word *opiate.*
  Answer: *Opiate* is something that can be obtained from sleeping, something that can "quiet the brain." This suggests that *opiate* is a medicinal substance that brings calm. Rainsford is very disturbed, and wants to escape his thoughts temporarily. *Opiate* must mean "forgetfulness."

28 Reading Check

Answer: Zaroff captures men from passing ships and gives them a choice: to submit to torture or to "hunt" with him. He gives each man food, a knife, and three hours' start. Then, he chases the man. If Zaroff hasn't caught him in three days, the hunted man wins the game. To date Zaroff has always caught and killed his prey.

CUSTOMIZE INSTRUCTION FOR UNIVERSAL ACCESS

For Less Proficient Readers

In 1932, RKO Studios in Hollywood began work on two films: *The Most Dangerous Game* and the more famous *King Kong.* Since the films were being shot at the same time, the studio saved money by using the same jungle sets and several of the same actors for both films. Have students gather for a screening of *The Most Dangerous Game.* Seeing the story brought to life on screen will help students follow the story's plot and themes. After seeing the film, have students compare and contrast it with the story. What are the obvious differences? Why do students think the filmmakers made these changes? Was the story or the film more exciting? more dramatic? more believable? Students can address these questions in a group discussion.

29 ▶ **Critical Viewing**

Answer: Because Rainsford is at the top of a tower, he can't get out the window and escape from the island. He is forced to submit to Zaroff's game.

30 Literary Analysis

Suspense and Conflict

- Ask students to explain the source of the conflict between Zaroff and Rainsford. Can this conflict be resolved?
  Answer: They don't agree about the appropriateness of hunting men. Rainsford makes a moral judgment about Zaroff. The conflict can't be resolved; they will never agree.
- Then, ask the Literary Analysis question on p. 30: Why does this conflict between Rainsford and Zaroff escalate the suspense?
  Answer: It makes it clear to the reader that Zaroff intends to kill Rainsford if he can.

and lay down. By many methods he tried to put himself to sleep. He had achieved a doze when, just as morning began to come, he heard, far off in the jungle, the faint report of a pistol.

General Zaroff did not appear until luncheon. He was dressed faultlessly in the tweeds of a country squire. He was solicitous about the state of Rainsford's health.

"As for me," sighed the general, "I do not feel so well. I am worried, Mr. Rainsford. Last night I detected traces of my old complaint."

To Rainsford's questioning glance the general said: "Ennui. Boredom."

Then, taking a second helping of crêpes suzette, the general explained: "The hunting was not good last night. The fellow lost his head. He made a straight trail that offered no problems at all. That's the trouble with these sailors; they have dull brains to begin with, and they do not know how to get about in the woods. They do excessively stupid and obvious things. It's most annoying. Will you have another glass of Chablis, Mr. Rainsford?"

"General," said Rainsford firmly, "I wish to leave this island at once."

The general raised his thickets of eyebrows; he seemed hurt. "But, my dear fellow," the general protested, "you've only just come. You've had no hunting—"

"I wish to go today," said Rainsford. He saw the dead black eyes of the general on him, studying him. General Zaroff's face suddenly brightened.

He filled Rainsford's glass with venerable Chablis from a dusty bottle.

30 "Tonight," said the general, "we will hunt—you and I."

Rainsford shook his head. "No, general," he said. "I will not hunt."

The general shrugged his shoulders and delicately ate a hothouse grape. "As you wish, my friend," he said. "The choice rests entirely with you. But may I not venture to suggest that you will find my idea of sport more diverting than Ivan's?"

He nodded toward the corner to where the giant stood, scowling, his thick arms crossed on his hogshead of chest.

"You don't mean—" cried Rainsford.

"My dear fellow," said the general, "have I not told you I always mean what I say about hunting? This is really an inspiration. I drink to a foeman worthy of my steel—at last."

The general raised his glass, but Rainsford sat staring at him.

"You'll find this game worth playing," the general said enthusiastically. "Your brain against mine. Your woodcraft against mine. Your strength and stamina against mine. Outdoor chess! And the stake is not without value, eh?"

"And if I win—" began Rainsford huskily.

"I'll cheerfully acknowledge myself defeated if I do not find you by midnight of the third day," said General Zaroff. "My sloop will place you on the mainland near a town."

The general read what Rainsford was thinking.

"Oh, you can trust me," said the Cossack. "I will give you my word as

29 ▲ **Critical Viewing**
How does Rainsford's room, high in a tower, add to the suspense of the story? **[Connect]**

Literary Analysis
Suspense and Conflict
Why does this conflict between Rainsford and Zaroff escalate the suspense?

a gentleman and a sportsman. Of course you, in turn, must agree to say nothing of your visit here."

"I'll agree to nothing of the kind," said Rainsford.

"Oh," said the general, "in that case— But why discuss that now? Three days hence we can discuss it over a bottle of Veuve Cliquot, unless—"

The general sipped his wine.

31 Then a businesslike air animated him. "Ivan," he said to Rainsford, "will supply you with hunting clothes, food, a knife. I suggest you wear moccasins; they leave a poorer trail. I suggest too that you avoid the big swamp in the southeast corner of the island. We call it Death Swamp. There's quicksand there. One foolish fellow tried it. The deplorable part of it was that Lazarus followed him. You can imagine my feelings, Mr. Rainsford. I loved Lazarus; he was the finest hound in my pack. Well, I must beg you to excuse me now. I always take a siesta after lunch. You'll hardly have time for a nap, I fear. You'll want to start, no doubt. I shall not follow till dusk. Hunting at night is so much more exciting than by day, don't you think? Au revoir,[17] Mr. Rainsford, au revoir."

General Zaroff, with a deep, courtly bow, strolled from the room.

From another door came Ivan. Under one arm he carried khaki hunting clothes, a haversack of food, a leather sheath containing a long-bladed hunting knife; his right hand rested on a cocked revolver thrust in the crimson sash about his waist. . . .

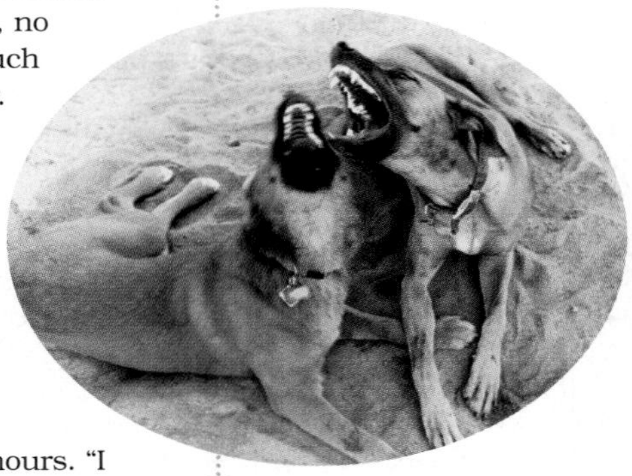

Rainsford had fought his way through the bush for two hours. "I must keep my nerve. I must keep my nerve," he said through tight teeth.

He had not been entirely clear-headed when the château gates snapped shut behind him.

His whole idea at first was to put distance between himself and General Zaroff, and, to this end, he had plunged along, spurred on by the sharp rowels of something very like panic. Now he had got a grip on himself, had stopped, and was taking stock of himself and the situation.

He saw that straight flight was futile; inevitably it would bring him face to face with the sea. He was in a picture with a frame of water, and his operations, clearly, must take place within that frame.

"I'll give him a trail to follow," muttered Rainsford, and he struck off from the rude paths he had been following into the trackless wilderness. He executed a series of intricate loops; he doubled on his trail again and again, recalling all the lore of the fox hunt, and all the dodges of the fox. Night found him leg-weary, with his hands and face lashed by the branches, on a thickly wooded ridge. He knew it would be insane to blunder on through the dark, even if he had the strength. His need for rest was imperative and he thought: "I have played the fox, now I must

17. au revoir (ō´ rə vwär´) French for "until we meet again."

Reading Strategy
Using Context Clues
Which clues help you determine the meaning of *hence*?

32 ▲ Critical Viewing
Based on this photograph, what adjective might best describe Zaroff's dogs?
[Analyze]

futile (fyōōt´ əl) *adj.* useless; hopeless

33 ✓ Reading Check
What is Rainsford's initial strategy?

31 Reading Strategy
Using Context Clues

- Ask the Reading Strategy question on p. 31: What clues help you determine the meaning of *hence?* **Answer:** Since the game will be over in three days, *hence* must mean "from now."
- Have students use context clues to determine the meaning of *deplorable.* Then, have them check the dictionary definition. **Answer:** *Deplorable* describes the general's feeling about losing his best dog. It must mean something like "regrettable" or "unfortunate." The dictionary definition is "lamentable, sad, grievous."

32 ▶ Critical Viewing

Answer: Students may say that the dogs are large, fierce, frightening, strong, or powerful.

33 ✓ Reading Check

Answer: Rainsford decides to get as far away from Zaroff as possible.

34 Literary Analysis

Suspense and Conflict

- Read aloud the bracketed passage to students. Ask students to describe the mood of this passage using details from the text.
- Then ask the first Literary Analysis questions on p. 32: Which words in this paragraph help create suspense?
  Answers: Words that increase the suspense include *apprehensive, wounded, dead,* and *startled.* Conflict and suspense are intensified because the reader and Rainsford know that the general is an excellent hunter; Rainsford will have difficulty escaping.

35 Literary Analysis

Suspense and Conflict

- Point out that since p. 31, Rainsford has kept repeating "I will not lose my nerve."
- Then, ask students the second Literary Analysis question on p. 32: How are the conflict and suspense intensified at this point?
  Answer: Because the general has a pistol, the reader knows Rainsford may be shot and killed here. Rainsford can do nothing but keep still and silent and wait. Because the general takes his time, Rainsford and the reader get more and more tense, waiting for him to take action. Suspense is intensified because the general deliberately prolongs the chase.

play the cat of the fable." A big tree with a thick trunk and outspread branches was nearby, and, taking care to leave not the slightest mark, he climbed up into the crotch, and stretching out on one of the broad limbs, after a fashion, rested. Rest brought him new confidence and almost a feeling of security. Even so zealous a hunter as General Zaroff could not trace him there, he told himself; only the devil himself could follow that complicated trail through the jungle after dark. But, perhaps, the general was a devil—

34 An apprehensive night crawled slowly by like a wounded snake, and sleep did not visit Rainsford, although the silence of a dead world was on the jungle. Toward morning when a dingy gray was varnishing the sky, the cry of some startled bird focused Rainsford's attention in that direction. Something was coming through the bush, coming slowly, carefully, coming by the same winding way Rainsford had come. He flattened himself down on the limb, and through a screen of leaves almost as thick as tapestry, he watched. The thing that was approaching was a man.

It was General Zaroff. He made his way along with his eyes fixed in utmost concentration on the ground before him. He paused, almost beneath the tree, dropped to his knees and studied the ground. Rainsford's impulse was to hurl himself down like a panther, but he saw the general's right hand held something metallic—a small automatic pistol.

The hunter shook his head several times, as if he were puzzled. Then he straightened up and took from his case one of his black cigarettes; its pungent incense-like smoke floated up to Rainsford's nostrils.

Rainsford held his breath. The general's eyes had left the ground and were traveling inch by inch up the tree. Rainsford froze there, every muscle tensed for a spring. But the sharp eyes of the hunter stopped before they reached the limb where Rainsford lay; a smile spread over his brown face. Very deliberately he blew a smoke ring into the air; then he turned his back on the tree and walked carelessly away, back along the trail he had come. The swish of the underbrush against his hunting boots grew fainter and fainter.

35 The pent-up air burst hotly from Rainsford's lungs. His first thought made him feel sick and numb. The general could follow a trail through the woods at night; he could follow an extremely difficult trail; he must have uncanny powers; only by the merest chance had the Cossack failed to see his quarry.

Rainsford's second thought was even more terrible. It sent a shudder of cold horror through his whole being. Why had the general smiled? Why had he turned back?

Rainsford did not want to believe what his reason told him was true, but the truth was as evident as the sun that had by now pushed through the morning mists. The general was playing with him! The general was saving him for another day's sport! The Cossack was the cat; he was the mouse. Then it was that Rainsford knew the full meaning of terror.

"I will not lose my nerve. I will not."

Literary Analysis
Suspense Which words in this paragraph help create suspense?

Literary Analysis
Suspense and Conflict How are the conflict and suspense intensified at this point?

He slid down from the tree, and struck off again into the woods. His face was set and he forced the machinery of his mind to function. Three hundred yards from his hiding place he stopped where a huge dead tree leaned precariously on a smaller, living one. Throwing off his sack of food, Rainsford took his knife from its sheath and began to work with all his energy.

The job was finished at last, and he threw himself down behind a fallen log a hundred feet away. He did not have to wait long. The cat was coming again to play with the mouse.

Following the trail with the sureness of a bloodhound, came General Zaroff. Nothing escaped those searching black eyes, no crushed blade of grass, no bent twig, no mark, no matter how faint, in the moss. So intent was the Cossack on his stalking that he was upon the thing Rainsford had made
36 before he saw it. His foot touched the protruding bough that was the trigger. Even as he touched it, the general sensed his danger and leaped back with the agility of an ape. But he was not quite quick enough; the dead tree, delicately adjusted to rest on the cut living one, crashed down and struck the general a glancing blow on the shoulder as it fell; but for his alertness, he must have been smashed beneath it. He staggered, but he did not fall; nor did he drop his revolver. He stood there, rubbing his injured shoulder, and Rainsford, with fear again gripping his heart, heard the general's mocking laugh ring through the jungle.

"Rainsford," called the general, "if you are within the sound of my voice, as I suppose you are, let me congratulate you. Not many men know how to make a Malay mancatcher. Luckily, for me, I too have hunted in Malacca. You are proving interesting, Mr. Rainsford. I am going now to have my wound dressed; it's only a slight one. But I shall be back. I shall be back."

When the general, nursing his bruised shoulder, had gone, Rainsford took up his flight again. It was flight now, a desperate, hopeless flight, that carried him on for some hours. Dusk came, then darkness, and still he pressed on. The ground grew softer under his moccasins; the vegetation grew ranker, denser; insects bit him savagely. Then, as he stepped forward, his foot sank into the ooze. He tried to wrench it back, but the muck sucked viciously at his foot as if it were a giant leech. With a violent effort, he tore his foot loose. He knew where he was now. Death Swamp and its quicksand.

His hands were tight closed as if his nerve were something tangible that someone in the darkness was trying to tear from his grip. The softness of the earth had given him an idea. He stepped back from the quicksand a dozen feet or so, and, like some huge prehistoric beaver, he began to dig.

Rainsford had dug himself in in France♦ when a second's delay meant death. That had been a placid pastime compared to his digging now.

Literature 37 in context Social Studies Connection

♦ *WWI Trenches*

When Rainsford "digs himself in," he is drawing on his experience as a soldier. In World War I, soldiers protected themselves from their enemies by digging deep trenches. The soldiers then lived in the trenches and took turns charging the enemy's trenches in the face of machine-gun fire. Imagine the fear Rainsford must feel if his experience as a soldier is considered "a placid pastime compared to his digging now."

Canadian Troops Leave the Trenches, World War I

38 ✓Reading Check

What does Rainsford build in an effort to save himself?

36 Critical Thinking

Compare and Contrast

- On p. 30, the general called his hunt with Rainsford "outdoor chess." Ask students who are familiar with chess to describe the game to the class.
- Have students compare and contrast what happens here with a chess game.

  Answer: In chess, each player tries to checkmate, or trap, the opposing king to win the game. Like the hunt, chess involves strategy and offensive and defensive maneuvers. Like the hunt, it is a contest of one person's intelligence and strategic skills against another's. A chess game, however, is played at a table on a board; it does not involve physical danger to the players. In chess, the players begin at equal strength; in this hunt, Zaroff has the advantage because he has a gun, he is familiar with the terrain, and he is the hunter.

37 Background

Social Studies

Modern artillery, machine guns, and barbed wire drastically changed the face of combat in World War I—but generals were slow to change their tactics. Massive assaults by hundreds of thousands of soldiers produced horrific casualties, but little or no gain on the battlefield. On the first day of the Battle of the Somme, for example, more than 57,000 British soldiers were killed or wounded. That Rainsford was able to survive trench warfare may help explain his abilities in his combat with Zaroff.

38 ✓Reading Check

Answer: Rainsford builds a Malay mancatcher—a booby-trap that would have killed Zaroff if he hadn't jumped back in time.

CUSTOMIZE INSTRUCTION FOR UNIVERSAL ACCESS

For Less Proficient Readers	For Advanced Readers
To help students visualize the Malay mancatcher that Rainsford makes, send a volunteer to the chalkboard to sketch a diagram based on details in the story. You may wish to follow the same procedure for the two other traps Rainsford will make in the story. Interested students may wish to create models of these traps.	Point out Zaroff's emphasis on being civilized—he is always polite and well-dressed and has surrounded himself with luxuries. Have students consider what they think it means to be civilized. Ask whether, by their definitions, animals are not much more civilized than human beings (they don't kill for sport, they don't fight wars, they don't destroy the environment). Students can choose sides for a debate on the issue.

39 Literary Analysis

Suspense and Conflict

- Discuss the ways the author has built up suspense throughout the story. Ask students whether they feel they have yet reached the story's climax, or moment of greatest suspense and excitement.
  Answer: The climax won't come as long as the conflict between Rainsford and the general continues.
- Ask students who seems to be winning the conflict—Rainsford or the general? What qualities of the man make him victorious in the conflict?
  Answer: The general won the first round because he found Rainsford, but decided to let him go. Rainsford won the next two rounds, because he escaped detection, injured the general, and killed the dog. Both men do well in the game because they are experienced hunters, and they don't lose their courage.
- Ask the Literary Analysis question on p. 34: How does Rainsford feel after his efforts? How does this passage make you, the reader, feel?
  Answer: Rainsford is anxious to know whether his trap will work; he "lived a year in a minute." The reader is also eager to see what will happen next.

40 ▶ Critical Viewing

Answer: Rainsford might be dashed to death on the rocks; he might be able to swim to safety.

The pit grew deeper; when it was above his shoulders, he climbed out and from some hard saplings cut stakes and sharpened them to a fine point. These stakes he planted in the bottom of the pit with the points sticking up. With flying fingers he wove a rough carpet of weeds and branches and with it he covered the mouth of the pit. Then, wet with sweat and aching with tiredness, he crouched behind the stump of a lightning-charred tree.

He knew his pursuer was coming; he heard the padding sound of feet on the soft earth, and the night breeze brought him the perfume of the general's cigarette. It seemed to Rainsford that the general was coming with unusual swiftness; he was not feeling his way along, foot by foot. Rainsford, crouching there, could not see the general, nor could he see
39 the pit. He lived a year in a minute. Then he felt an impulse to cry aloud with joy, for he heard the sharp crackle of the breaking branches as the cover of the pit gave way; he heard the sharp scream of pain as the pointed stakes found their mark. He leaped up from his place of concealment. Then he cowered back. Three feet from the pit a man was standing, with an electric torch in his hand.

"You've done well, Rainsford," the voice of the general called. "Your Burmese tiger pit has claimed one of my best dogs. Again you score. I think, Mr. Rainsford, I'll see what you can do against my whole pack. I'm going home for a rest now. Thank you for a most amusing evening."

At daybreak Rainsford, lying near the swamp, was awakened by a sound that made him know that he had new things to learn about fear.

Literary Analysis
Suspense How does Rainsford feel after his efforts? How does this passage make you, the reader, feel?

40
◀ **Critical Viewing** Imagine Rainsford at the edge of the cliff. What would result from his leaping into the crashing waves? **[Speculate]**

It was a distant sound, faint and wavering, but he knew it. It was the baying of a pack of hounds.

Rainsford knew he could do one of two things. He could stay where he was and wait. That was suicide. He could flee. That was postponing the inevitable. For a moment he stood there, thinking. An idea that held a wild chance came to him, and, tightening his belt, he headed away from the swamp.

The baying of the hounds drew nearer, then still nearer, nearer, ever nearer. On a ridge Rainsford climbed a tree. Down a watercourse, not a quarter of a mile away, he could see the bush moving. Straining his eyes, he saw the lean figure of General Zaroff; just ahead of him Rainsford made out another figure whose wide shoulders surged through the tall jungle weeds; it was the giant Ivan, and he seemed pulled forward by some unseen force; Rainsford knew that Ivan must be holding the pack in leash.

They would be on him any minute now. His mind worked frantically. He thought of a native trick he had learned in Uganda. He slid down the tree. He caught hold of a springy young sapling and to it he fastened his hunting knife, with the blade pointing down the trail; with a bit of wild grapevine he tied back the sapling. Then he ran for his life. The hounds raised their voices as they hit the fresh scent. Rainsford knew now how an animal at bay feels.

He had to stop to get his breath. The baying of the hounds stopped abruptly, and Rainsford's heart stopped too. They must have reached the knife.

He shinnied excitedly up a tree and looked back. His pursuers had stopped. But the hope that was in Rainsford's brain when he climbed
41 died, for he saw in the shallow valley that General Zaroff was still on his feet. But Ivan was not. The knife, driven by the recoil of the springing tree, had not wholly failed.

"Nerve, nerve, nerve!" he panted, as he dashed along. A blue gap showed between the trees dead ahead. Ever nearer drew the hounds. Rainsford forced himself on toward that gap. He reached it. It was the shore of the sea. Across a cove he could see the gloomy gray stone of the
42 château. Twenty feet below him the sea rumbled and hissed. Rainsford hesitated. He heard the hounds. Then he leaped far out into the sea. . . .

When the general and his pack reached the place by the sea, the Cossack stopped. For some minutes he stood regarding the blue-green expanse of water. He shrugged his shoulders. Then he sat down, took a drink of brandy from a silver flask, lit a perfumed cigarette, and hummed a bit from *Madame Butterfly.*[18]

General Zaroff had an exceedingly good dinner in his great paneled dining hall that evening. With it he had a bottle of Pol Roger and half a bottle of Chambertin. Two slight annoyances kept him from perfect enjoyment. One was the thought that it would be difficult to replace Ivan; the other was that his quarry had escaped him; of course the

18. ***Madame Butterfly*** an opera by Giacomo Puccini.

Literary Analysis
Suspense How does this peaceful scene add to the suspense?

43 **Reading Check**
What happens to Ivan during the hunt?

41 Critical Thinking
Compare and Contrast

- Have students contrast Rainsford's present feelings about animals at bay to his earlier statement to Whitney about jaguars. What has changed Rainsford's attitude?
  Answer: Rainsford believed that jaguars felt nothing; now he knows exactly how frightened and outraged creatures are when they are at bay because he is now at bay himself.
- Then, have students contrast the horror Rainsford expressed about hunting men to his reaction to having killed Ivan. Has Rainsford changed his attitude?
  Answer: Rainsford shows no horror at Ivan's death, but this doesn't mean he thinks hunting men is acceptable. He is fighting for his life and is entitled to defend himself.

42 Literary Analysis
Suspense

- Ask students to point out words and phrases in this paragraph that heighten their desire to know the outcome.
  Answer: *They would be on him any minute; his mind worked frantically; he ran for his life; the hounds raised their voices; Rainsford's heart stopped.*
- Then, ask students the Literary Analysis question on p. 35: How does this peaceful scene add to the suspense?
  Answer: Although the scene is peaceful, the reader doesn't know if Rainsford is alive or dead. Note that the story is now being told from Zaroff's perspective. By making this shift, the author maintains suspense until the very last line of the story.

43 Reading Check
Answer: Ivan is killed when he trips Rainsford's spring-knife trap.

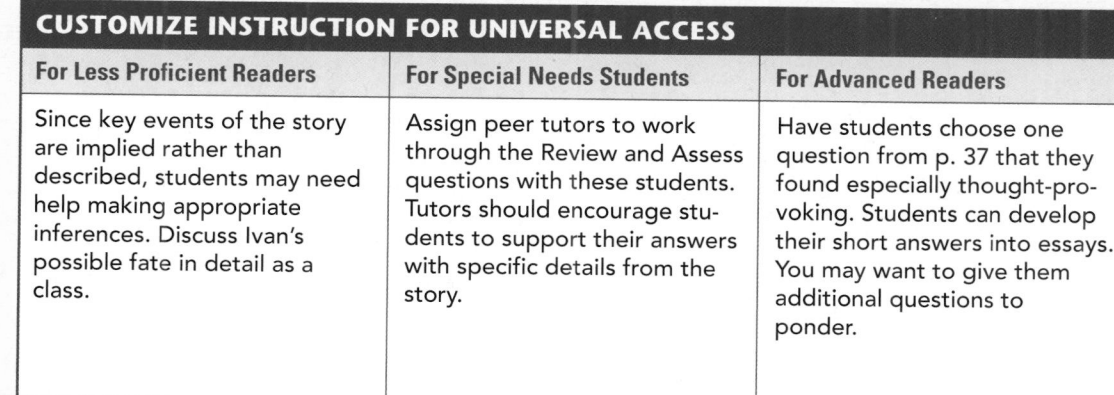

CUSTOMIZE INSTRUCTION FOR UNIVERSAL ACCESS

For Less Proficient Readers	For Special Needs Students	For Advanced Readers
Since key events of the story are implied rather than described, students may need help making appropriate inferences. Discuss Ivan's possible fate in detail as a class.	Assign peer tutors to work through the Review and Assess questions with these students. Tutors should encourage students to support their answers with specific details from the story.	Have students choose one question from p. 37 that they found especially thought-provoking. Students can develop their short answers into essays. You may want to give them additional questions to ponder.

ASSESS

Answers for p. 36

Review and Assess

1. Students will probably admire Rainsford's courage, intelligence, and ability to keep calm in emergencies. They will probably dislike his attitude about hunting big game.
2. **(a)** Zaroff believes that human beings are the most dangerous game. **(b)** Since he is a deliberate sadist and murderer, students will probably not find Zaroff civilized.
3. **(a)** Rainsford enjoys hunting big game and believes animals have no understanding of fear or death. **(b)** Both enjoy the challenge of hunting big game, but Zaroff has become bored with this and is stalking human beings. Rainsford is horrified at the idea of hunting people.
4. **(a)** Rainsford and Zaroff fight and Rainsford kills Zaroff. **(b)** Rainsford knows that the "game" can only end in death—his, or Zaroff's. His statement expresses his intention to fight to the death.
5. Rainsford will probably never hunt again, because now he knows what hunted animals experience.
6. **(a)** Possible answers: cruel, heartless, insane. **(b)** Students may draw parallels between Zaroff and historical mass murderers, serial killers, and others who disregard the value of human life.

American hadn't played the game—so thought the general as he tasted his after-dinner liqueur. In his library he read, to soothe himself, from the works of Marcus Aurelius.[19] At ten he went up to his bedroom. He was deliciously tired, he said to himself, as he locked himself in. There was a little moonlight, so, before turning on his light, he went to the window and looked down at the courtyard. He could see the great hounds, and he called: "Better luck another time," to them. Then he switched on the light.

A man, who had been hiding in the curtain of the bed, was standing there.

"Rainsford!" screamed the general. "How in God's name did you get here?"

"Swam," said Rainsford. "I found it quicker than walking through the jungle."

The general sucked in his breath and smiled. "I congratulate you," he said. "You have won the game."

Rainsford did not smile. "I am still a beast at bay," he said, in a low, hoarse voice. "Get ready, General Zaroff."

The general made one of his deepest bows. "I see," he said. "Splendid! One of us is to furnish a repast for the hounds. The other will sleep in this very excellent bed. On guard, Rainsford. . . ."

He had never slept in a better bed, Rainsford decided.

---

19. Marcus Aurelius (ô rē´ lē əs) Roman emperor and philosopher (A.D. 121–180).

Review and Assess

Thinking About the Selection

1. **Respond:** What do you admire or dislike about Rainsford?
2. **(a) Recall:** What, according to Zaroff, is the most dangerous game? **(b) Analyze:** Based on his attitude, would you call Zaroff "civilized"? Why or why not?
3. **(a) Recall:** Early in the story, what do you learn about Rainsford's views on hunting? **(b) Compare and Contrast:** How does Rainsford's attitude toward hunting compare with Zaroff's?
4. **(a) Recall:** What happens at the end of the story? **(b) Infer:** In the last scene of the story, why does Rainsford say "I am still a beast at bay"?
5. **Draw Conclusions:** How do you think the hunting experience with Zaroff changed Rainsford?
6. **(a) Analyze:** What words would you use to describe Zaroff's character? **(b) Apply:** Do you think people like Zaroff exist in real life? Explain.

Richard Connell

(1893–1949)

Richard Connell seemed destined to become a writer: He was a sports reporter at the age of ten! By the time he was sixteen, Connell was editing his father's newspaper in Poughkeepsie, New York. He stayed involved in journalism at Harvard University, where he was an editor for the *Daily Crimson*. During World War I, Connell edited his division's newspaper and reported on wartime events.

In 1924, Connell published the story you have just read. A year later, he settled in Beverly Hills, California. The film version of "The Most Dangerous Game" was released in 1932 and has inspired many other adventure movies. Connell's success as a movie screenwriter continued for the rest of his life, and he received two Academy Award nominations for his work.

ASSESSMENT PRACTICE: Reading Comprehension

Context **(For more practice, see Test Preparation Workbook, p. 2.)**

Many assessment tests specify that students will use context such as explanations, examples, and definitions to determine the meanings of words in a variety of written texts. To demonstrate how to use context clues to determine word meanings, write this text from the selection on the chalkboard:

> But it was no mirage, he found. . . . The stone steps were real enough; yet all about it hung an air of unreality.

In this passage, the word mirage means—

- **A** miracle
- **B** nightmare
- **C** illusion
- **D** futuristic

Ask students to look for words in the text that are clues to the meaning of *mirage*. Since the reality of the steps proves that they are no mirage, *mirage* must mean "the opposite of reality," or illusion. The correct answer is *C*.

Review and Assess

Literary Analysis

Suspense

1. (a) Find three details that provide early clues about Zaroff's hobby. (b) How do these clues create **suspense**?
2. Using a chart like the one below, show how the details of Rainsford's first night build a sense of dread.

Details	How They Build a Sense of Dread

3. In your opinion, what are the three most suspenseful events in the story? Why?

Connecting Literary Elements

4. Early in the story, Rainsford says, "The world is made up of two classes—the hunters and the huntees." How does his **conflict** with Zaroff help Rainsford understand this expression in a new way?
5. In addition to conflicts between characters, stories may include conflicts between a character and nature and internal conflicts within a character. Use a chart like this one to explain each conflict.

Rainsford vs. Nature	Rainsford vs. a person	Rainsford vs. himself

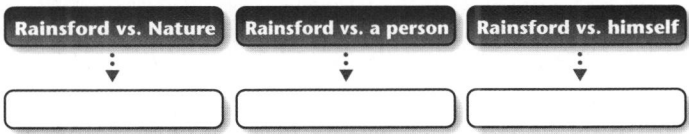

Reading Strategy

Using Context Clues

6. For each passage from the story, give an approximate meaning for the italicized word and explain which **context clues** helped you.
(a) He heard [the sound] again; then it was cut short by another noise, crisp, *staccato*. "Pistol shot," muttered Rainsford, swimming on. (b) To Rainsford's questioning glance the general said: "*Ennui*. Boredom."

Extend Understanding

7. **Career Connection:** What careers, other than hunter, would be suited to someone with Rainsford's skills and attitudes? Why?

Quick Review

Suspense is the reader's feeling of curiosity, uncertainty, even anxiety about the outcome of events in a story.

A **conflict** is a struggle between opposing forces.

Context clues—hints in surrounding words, phrases, and sentences—can help you to figure out the approximate meaning of an unfamiliar word.

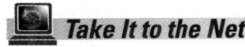

Take It to the Net

www.phschool.com

Take the interactive self-test online to check your understanding of the selection.

Review and Assess

1. **(a)** Clues include the terrified screams of an animal Rainsford can't identify; the pistol shot that cuts off the screams; and the evidence Rainsford finds at the place Zaroff killed his prey. **(b)** These clues make the reader curious to find out what is happening on the island, and hint at danger and violence.
2.

Details	Sense of Dread
"spurred on by panic"	shows that Rainsford is frightened and vulnerable
"night crawled by a wounded snake"	shows that Rainsford can't relax because of fear of being caught
Zaroff has a pistol	makes danger concrete and immediate
Zaroff lets Rainsford escape	tells reader that Rainsford's ordeal will continue and that Zaroff is very skilled

3. Students might select Rainsford's struggle in the sea, the sinister dinner conversation about "the most dangerous game," or the final confrontation in Zaroff's room as the most suspenseful events in the story.
4. Rainsford now knows that anyone can become a "huntee." Being hunted simply means to be afraid, to be less powerful than a predator.
5. Conflicts include Rainsford against the sea for Rainsford's life; Rainsford against Zaroff for Rainsford's life; and Rainsford's struggle with his own fear and panic.
6. **(a)** *Staccato* means short and sharp. This is how a pistol sounds. **(b)** *Ennui* means boredom, since these two words are used as synonyms.

continued

Answers continued

7. Rainsford's skills include the ability to use weapons, the ability to survive in the wild, and the ability to keep his wits about him in emergencies. The armed forces, espionage, and police work are examples of jobs for which he might be suited.

EXTEND

Answers for p. 38

❶ Vocabulary Development

Word Analysis

Possible responses: I felt some scruples about taking advantage of the situation. However, I soon realized that my opponent was unscrupulous enough to use any advantage she could. I decided there was no point in being scrupulous with her.

Spelling Strategy

1. terrible
2. correct
3. regrettable
4. impossible

Fluency: Clarify Word Meaning

1. naive
2. futile
3. palpable
4. indolently
5. bizarre
6. grotesque
7. blandly
8. scruples

❷ Grammar Lesson

1. P: his; A: sailor
2. P: they; A: shots
3. P: you; A: Rainsford
4. P: I, my; A: general
5. P: he; A: Rainsford

Writing Application

Sample answers:

1. Rainsford could not believe his ears when the general spoke of hunting human beings.
2. Rainsford could find his way around in the jungle by keeping track of its paths.
3. Zaroff raised his champagne glass and rose to make a toast.
4. Rainsford wished he had never come to the island after he learned its secret.

Integrate Language Skills

❶ Vocabulary Development Lesson

Word Analysis: Forms of *scruples*

The noun *scruples* refers to the uncomfortable feeling one has about doing something one thinks is wrong. By adding the suffix *-ous*, you form *scrupulous*, which means "having scruples."

Use *scruples*, *scrupulous*, and *unscrupulous* in a paragraph.

Spelling Strategy

The suffixes *-able* and *-ible* have the same meaning but slightly different spellings. The suffix *-able*, as in *palpable*, is more common, but *-ible*, as in *tangible*, sometimes applies.

Review each item below. Write *Correct* if the spelling is correct. If the spelling is incorrect, write the correct spelling.

1. terrable
2. unquenchable
3. regrettible
4. impossable

Fluency: Clarify Word Meaning

Complete each item with a vocabulary word from the list on page 17.

1. The farmer was ___?___ about city life.
2. "Surrender now," commanded the conqueror. "Resistance is ___?___."
3. The silence was so ___?___ that you could cut it with a knife.
4. He lounged on the couch ___?___.
5. They met under rather ___?___ circumstances: a camel auction.
6. With its fans and twisted features, the mask was amazingly ___?___.
7. The officer phrased his sentences ___?___ to avoid making people angry.
8. She had her ___?___ and would not give in to peer pressure.

❷ Grammar Lesson

Pronouns and Antecedents

Pronouns are words that stand for nouns or for words that take the place of nouns. **Antecedents** are the words for which pronouns stand. Some of the most common pronouns are *I/me/my/mine*, *you/your/yours*, *he/him/his*, *she/her/hers*, *we/us/our/ours*, and *they/them/their/theirs*.

In these examples, the pronouns are set in italics; the antecedents are underlined.

Examples: Rainsford feared for *his* life.

Zaroff's dogs used *their* sense of smell.

The jungle is a unique place with *its* wild animals and dense trees.

Practice Copy these sentences. Underline each pronoun and circle its antecedent.

1. One superstitious sailor can taint the whole company with his fear.
2. Rainsford remembered the shots. They had come from the right.
3. Follow Ivan, if you please, Mr. Rainsford. . . .
4. The general said, "I was about to have my dinner."
5. He had never slept better, Rainsford decided.

Writing Application Write sentences that include pronouns by using *Rainsford* and *jungle* as the antecedents.

WG Prentice Hall Writing and Grammar Connection: Chapter 16, Section 2

TEACHING RESOURCES

The following resources can be used to enrich or extend the instructions for pp. 38–39.

Vocabulary

Selection Support: Build Vocabulary, p. 5

Vocabulary and Spelling Practice Book (Use this booklet for skills enrichment.)

Grammar

Selection Support: Build Grammar Skills, p. 6

Writing and Grammar, Gold Level, p. 346

Daily Language Practice Transparencies

Writing

Writing and Grammar, Gold Level, p. 232

Writing and Grammar iText CD-ROM

BLOCK SCHEDULING: Resources marked with this symbol provide varied instruction during 90-minute blocks.

❸ Writing Lesson

Survival Manual

Rainsford triumphs because he has the knowledge he needs to survive. Think about Rainsford's situation, and create a set of detailed instructions on how to survive a ruthless pursuer that you think Rainsford would write.

Prewriting Review the story and note the techniques Rainsford uses. Make a list of questions readers might have about techniques. Then, arrange your notes into a logical order.

Model: Anticipating Readers' Questions

What materials would I need if I were building a trap?
Could I build a trap if I didn't have tools? How?
How large or deep should the trap be?

A list of potential trouble spots can help a writer plan an effective guide.

Drafting Using your questions and answers, write a first draft of Rainsford's survival manual. Give precise measurements or other specifications, define terms, and provide examples when necessary.

Revising To improve your draft, try to follow the instructions. For example, if you have described how to create a trap, try drawing the trap based on your instructions. Add any details necessary to ensure that your readers can follow the directions.

WG *Prentice Hall Writing and Grammar Connection: Chapter 11, Section 2*

❹ Extension Activities

Listening and Speaking With a group of classmates, put Rainsford on trial for killing Zaroff. These tips will help you plan a **video trial:**

- Plan arguments for both the prosecution and the defense.
- Have the two sides use props or diagrams to make their arguments accurate and persuasive.

Videotape your trial and show it to the rest of your class. After classmates see the video, discuss the effect of this form of media on viewers' perceptions of the trial. **[Group Activity]**

Research and Technology Hunting has threatened the population of many big-game species. Create a **database** of information about two or three big-game species, such as moose, jaguar, lion, tiger, elephant, crocodile, grizzly bear, or Cape buffalo. Use the database to help prepare a presentation about these species and their status today.

Take It to the Net www.phschool.com

Go online for an additional research activity using the Internet.

❸ Writing Lesson

- Go over the model with students. They may wish to base their manuals on Rainsford's situation, using details from the story. Alternatively, they may want to make up different scenarios in settings with which they are more familiar.
- Students can work with partners on the manuals. During the drafting process, pairs can exchange manuals and point out any areas that need clarification.

❹ Extension Activities

Listening and Speaking

- Meet with interested students to plan this activity. Students can volunteer for the roles they would like to play—Rainsford, his lawyer, the prosecuting attorney, the judge, and the jury members. Students should not write out their testimony and questions beforehand but should improvise based on preparatory discussions.
- If video equipment is not available, students can stage the trial live in class.

CUSTOMIZE INSTRUCTION For Universal Access

To address different learning styles, use the following activities suggested in the **Extension Activities** booklet, p. 2.

- For Musical/Rhythmic Learners, use Activity 5.
- For Verbal/Linguistic Learners, use Activity 6.
- For Visual/Spatial Learners, use Activity 7.

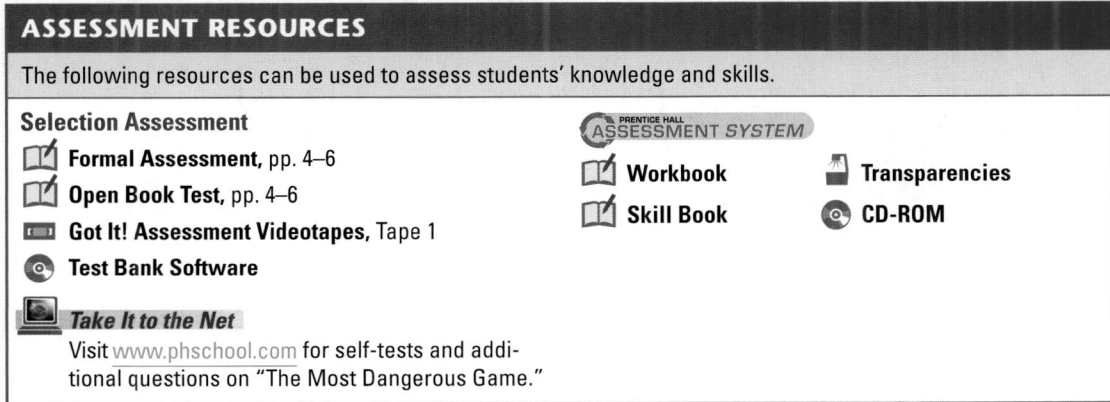

ASSESSMENT RESOURCES

The following resources can be used to assess students' knowledge and skills.

Selection Assessment

- **Formal Assessment,** pp. 4–6
- **Open Book Test,** pp. 4–6
- **Got It! Assessment Videotapes,** Tape 1
- **Test Bank Software**

Take It to the Net

Visit www.phschool.com for self-tests and additional questions on "The Most Dangerous Game."

PRENTICE HALL ASSESSMENT SYSTEM

- **Workbook**
- **Skill Book**
- **Transparencies**
- **CD-ROM**

Casey at the Bat

Lesson Objectives and CA Correlations

1. **To analyze and respond to literary elements**
   - Literary Analysis: Climax and Anticlimax **R 3.7**
   - Connecting Literary Elements: Narrative Poem
2. **To read, comprehend, analyze, and critique a poem**
   - Reading Strategy: Summarizing
   - Reading Check questions
   - Review and Assess questions
   - Assessment Practice (ATE)
3. **To develop word analysis skills, fluency, and systematic vocabulary**
   - Vocabulary Development Lesson: Word Analysis: Forms of *tumult* **R 1.1**
4. **To understand and apply written and oral language conventions**
   - Spelling Strategy
   - Grammar Lesson: Possessive Nouns **LC 1.3**
5. **To understand and apply appropriate writing and research strategies**
   - Writing Lesson: Sportscast **W 2.3**
   - Extension Activity: Research Report **W 1.5**
6. **To understand and apply listening and speaking strategies**
   - Extension Activity: Sports Interview **LS 1.9, 2.3**

STEP-BY-STEP TEACHING GUIDE	PACING GUIDE
PRETEACH	
Motivate Students and Provide Background	
Use the Motivation activity (ATE p. 40)	5 min.
Read and discuss the Preview material and Background information (SE/ATE p. 40) [A]	5 min.
Introduce the Concepts	
Introduce the Literary Analysis and Reading Strategy (SE/ATE p. 41) [A]	15 min.
Pronounce the vocabulary words and read their definitions (SE p. 41)	5 min.
TEACH	
Monitor Comprehension	
Informally monitor comprehension by circulating while students read independently or in groups [A]	10 min.
Monitor students' comprehension with the Reading Check note (SE/ATE p. 43)	as students read
Develop vocabulary with Vocabulary notes (SE pp. 43, 44)	as students read
Develop Understanding	
Develop students' understanding of climax and anticlimax with the Literary Analysis annotations (SE/ATE p. 43) [A]	10 min.
Develop students' understanding of summarizing with the Reading Strategy annotations (SE/ATE p. 44)	5 min.
ASSESS	
Assess Mastery	
Assess students' mastery of the Reading Strategy and Literary Analysis by having them answer the Review and Assess questions (SE/ATE p. 45)	15 min.
Use one or more of the print and media Assessment Resources (ATE p. 47) [A]	up to 45 min.
EXTEND	
Apply Understanding	
Have students complete the Vocabulary Development Lesson and the Grammar Lesson (SE p. 46) [A]	20 min.
Apply students' knowledge of vivid verbs using the Writing Lesson (SE/ATE p. 47) [A]	45 min.
Apply students' understanding of the poem using one or more of the Extension Activities (SE p. 47)	20–40 min.

[A] **ACCELERATED INSTRUCTION:**
Use the strategies and activities identified with an [A].

UNIVERSAL ACCESS
● = Below-Level Students
▲ = On-Level Students
■ = Above-Level Students

Time and Resource Manager

Reading Level: Easy
Average Number of Instructional Days: 3

RESOURCES		
PRINT	**TRANSPARENCIES**	**TECHNOLOGY**
		• **Interest Grabber Video,** Tape 1 ● ▲ ■
• **Selection Support Workbook:** ● ▲ ■ Literary Analysis, p. 12 Reading Strategy, p. 11 Build Vocabulary, p. 9	• **Literary Analysis and Reading Transparencies,** pp. 5 and 6 ● ▲ ■	
• **Adapted Reader's Companion** ● • **Reader's Companion** ●		• **Listening to Literature** ● ▲ ■ Audiocassettes, Side 3 Audio CDs, CD 2
• **English Learner's Companion** ● ▲ • **Literatura en español** ● ▲ • **Literary Analysis for Enrichment** ■		
• **Formal Assessment:** Selection Test, pp. 7–9 ● ▲ ■ • **Open Book Test,** pp. 7–9 ● ▲ ■ • **Performance Assessment and Portfolio Management,** p. 18 ● ▲ ■ • PRENTICE HALL ASSESSMENT SYSTEM ● ▲ ■	• PRENTICE HALL ASSESSMENT SYSTEM ● ▲ ■ Skills Practice Answers and Explanations on Transparencies	• **Test Bank Software** ● ▲ ■ • **Got It! Assessment Videotapes,** Tape 1 ● ▲
• **Selection Support Workbook:** ● ▲ ■ Build Grammar Skills, p. 10 • **Writing and Grammar,** Gold Level ● ▲ ■ • **Extension Activities,** p. 3 ● ▲ ■	• **Daily Language Practice Transparencies** ● ▲ • **Writing Models and Graphic Organizers on Transparencies** ● ▲ ■	• **Writing and Grammar iText CD-ROM** ● ▲ ■ ***Take It to the Net*** www.phschool.com

BLOCK SCHEDULING: Use one 90-minute class period to preteach the selection and have students read it. Use a second 90-minute class period to assess students' mastery of skills and have them complete one of the Extension Activities.

PREACH

Step-by-Step Teaching Guide for pp. 40–41

Motivation

When someone asked 1920s baseball star Babe Ruth if he knew that he made more money than President Herbert Hoover, Ruth replied, "I had a better year than he did!" Today, many major-league salaries are more than double that of the President of the United States, and stars earn many millions each year. Ask students why society rewards baseball stars so magnificently. Go around the room and have students share thrilling moments they have seen in baseball, from watching Mark McGwire hit his record-breaking home run to cheering a great play in a local game. Tell students they are going to read a poem about a great sports hero.

Interest Grabber Video

As an alternative, play "A Dramatization" on Tape 1 to engage student interest.

❶ Background

Physical Education

A major-league baseball game lasts for nine innings. The visiting team always receives the courtesy of batting first, which means that the home team always has a last chance to win the game. A game is finished after nine innings if one team is ahead. If the score is tied after the end of the ninth inning, play continues until someone wins—no matter how many more innings it takes. If the visiting team scores in the top of an inning, the home team always gets a chance to tie or win in the bottom of the inning.

Prepare to Read

Casey at the Bat

Baseball Players Practicing, 1875, Thomas Eakins Museum of Art, Rhode Island School of Design

Take It to the Net

Visit www.phschool.com for interactive activities and instruction related to "Casey at the Bat," including
- background
- graphic organizers
- literary elements
- reading strategies

Preview

Connecting to the Literature

Sporting events can really keep you on the edge of your seat! An athlete can break a world record, or a losing team can charge to victory at the last minute. This poem may remind you of nail-biting moments you have experienced while either watching or playing a sport.

❶ Background

In most cases, a baseball game does not end until all innings have been played and one team has scored the most runs. As a result, a team that is behind always has the chance for a comeback as long as players keep getting base hits and avoid making the final out. "Casey at the Bat" captures the hopes of a team that is behind by two runs as they go to bat for a final time.

TEACHING RESOURCES

The following resources can be used to enrich or extend the instruction for pp. 40–41.

Motivation

Interest Grabber Video, Tape 1

Background

Beyond Literature, p. 3 ■

Take It to the Net

Visit www.phschool.com for background and hotlinks for "Casey at the Bat."

Literary Analysis

Literary Analysis and Reading Transparencies, Climax and Anticlimax, p. 5 ■

Reading

Selection Support: Reading Strategy, p. 11; Build Vocabulary, p. 9

Literary Analysis and Reading Transparencies, Summarizing, p. 6

■ **BLOCK SCHEDULING:** Resources marked with this symbol provide varied instruction during 90-minute blocks.

❷ Literary Analysis

Climax and Anticlimax

The **climax** of a story, or any type of narrative, is its biggest moment. During the climax, you can expect the following:

- The action of the story is at its peak.
- The feelings of the readers are at their most intense.

At the climax, you know that you are about to discover how the story's main problem or struggle will turn out.

If the action starts in a grand manner but the outcome is trivial or disappointing, the story has an anticlimax, too. An **anticlimax** is the point at which you learn that the story has not turned out the way you had expected. As you read "Casey at the Bat," notice how the story builds to its climax, and decide whether or not the story has an anticlimax.

Connecting Literary Elements

The climax is a key element in a story—whether that story is told in a movie, a novel, a short story, or a narrative poem. "Casey at the Bat" is an example of a **narrative poem,** a poem that tells a story. Like other stories, a narrative poem has a sequence of events and characters whose lives are set in a specific time and place.

❸ Reading Strategy

Summarizing

Summarizing sections of a poem or story can help you better understand what you are reading. Follow these steps as you summarize:

- State the main points and details of a passage briefly and in your own words.
- Notice important story details and fit them into your picture of what is happening.
- Use your own language and style to express that information.

Use a chart like the one shown here to help you summarize.

Main Points
- a baseball game - one team is losing - fans are watching
Details
Mudville: the home-team fans are worried
Summary
"In the last inning of its game, Mudville is losing. There are two outs against them, and the fans are worried."

Vocabulary Development

pallor (pal′ ər) *n.* paleness (p. 43)

wreathed (rēthd) *v.* curled around (p. 43)

writhing (rīth′ iŋ) *v.* twisting; turning (p. 43)

tumult (to͞o′ mult) *n.* noisy commotion (p. 44)

❷ Literary Analysis

Climax and Anticlimax

- Tell students that *climax* was originally a Greek word meaning "staircase" or "ladder." Draw a simple diagram of a stepladder on the chalkboard and mark the top step with an asterisk. Explain that in terms of a story's plot, the climax is the top step of the ladder—the moment of greatest excitement or suspense. Just as each rung of a ladder brings a person closer to the top step, each event in a plot builds toward the climax.
- Write the word *anticlimax* on the chalkboard and underline the prefix *anti.* Remind them that the prefix *anti* means *not.* Ask students what they think an anticlimax is.
  Answer: The anticlimax is the opposite of a climax—it is not a high point of interest, but a letdown.

❸ Reading Strategy

Summarizing

- Read to the class a news article on a recent baseball game from a local newspaper. Note that the article is a *summary* or brief description that tells who won the game and how and when the teams scored. (A box score includes additional individual and team statistics.)
- Ask students why summaries are helpful to readers.
  Answer: Summaries provide all the essential information in a form that is easy to read and easier to remember.
- As students read "Casey at the Bat," they may want to pause along the way and summarize the action up to that point. This will help them keep track of the plot.

Vocabulary Development

- Pronounce each vocabulary word for students, and read the definitions as a class. Have students identify any words with which they are already familiar.

E-Teach

Visit E-Teach at www.phschool.com for teachers' essays on how to teach, with questions and answers.

CUSTOMIZE INSTRUCTION FOR UNIVERSAL ACCESS

For Special Needs Students	For Less Proficient Readers	For English Learners
Have students read the adapted version of "Casey at the Bat" in the **Adapted Reader's Companion.** This version provides basic-level instruction in an interactive format with questions and write-on lines. Completing the adapted version will prepare students to read the selection in the Student Edition.	Have students read the selection in the **Reader's Companion.** This version provides basic-level instruction in an interactive format with questions and write-on lines. After students finish the selection in **Reader's Companion,** have them complete the questions and activities in the Student Edition.	Have students read the adapted version of the selection in the **English Learner's Companion.** This version provides basic-level instruction in an interactive format with questions and write-on lines. Completing the adapted version will prepare students to read the selection in the Student Edition.

TEACH

Step-by-Step Teaching Guide for pp. 42–44

CUSTOMIZE INSTRUCTION
For Musical/Rhythmic Learners

The strong rhythm and regular rhyme scheme of "Casey at the Bat" have made it a favorite read-aloud for over a century. Have a group of interested students collaborate on a recitation of the poem. One student can read the narration, others can take the roles of Casey and the umpire, and the rest can be the fans, cheering and booing where the poem indicates. Work with students to help them decide on sound effects. After planning and rehearsing, students can perform their recitation for the class.

❶ About the Selection

"Casey at the Bat" is a narrative poem that uses vivid words and dramatic details to create suspense leading to an anticlimax. It is the ninth inning and Mudville is down by two runs with two out. When two men reach base safely, Casey strides to the plate. He strikes out with a wild swing at the third pitch, the game is over, and the Mudville fans are inconsolable.

❷ Background

Art

Baseball Players Practicing, by Thomas Eakins

Philadelphia native Thomas Eakins (1844–1916) is considered, along with Winslow Homer, the greatest American realist painter of the nineteenth century. Eakins was also a great teacher of painting.

1. How does this painting help you appreciate the poem?
   Answer: It illustrates the way players dressed and looked at the time the poem was written.
2. What does the painting show about the continuity of baseball?
   Answer: Baseball hasn't changed much, though batters and catchers now wear protective equipment and adopt different postures at the plate.

❸ ▶Critical Viewing

Answer: The batter in the painting seems poised and relaxed. Casey is haughty and scornful, then enraged.

❶ Casey at the Bat

Ernest Lawrence Thayer

❷ 

Baseball Players Practicing, 1875, Thomas Eakins Museum of Art, Rhode Island School of Design

❸ ▲ Critical Viewing Compare and contrast the stance and attitude of the batter in this painting with Casey's stance and attitude. **[Compare and Contrast]**

TEACHING RESOURCES

The following resources can be used to enrich or extend the instruction for pp. 42–44.

Literary Analysis

- **Selection Support:** Literary Analysis, p. 4

Reading

- **Reader's Companion**
- **English Learner's Companion**
- **Listening to Literature Audiocassettes,** Side 3
- **Listening to Literature Audio CD,** CD 3

BLOCK SCHEDULING: Resources marked with this symbol provide varied instruction during 90-minute blocks.

It looked extremely rocky for the Mudville nine that day;
The score stood two to four, with but an inning left to play.
So, when Cooney died at second, and Burrows did the same,
A pallor wreathed the features of the patrons of the game.

A straggling few got up to go, leaving there the rest,
With that hope which springs eternal within the human breast.
For they thought: "If only Casey would get a whack at that,"
They'd put even money now, with Casey at the bat.

4

But Flynn preceded Casey, and likewise so did Blake,
And the former was a pudd'n, and the latter was a fake.
So on that stricken multitude a deathlike silence sat;
For there seemed but little chance of Casey's getting to the bat.

But Flynn let drive a "single," to the wonderment of all.
And the much-despised Blakey "tore the cover off the ball."
And when the dust had lifted, and they saw what had occurred,
There was Blakey safe at second, and Flynn a-huggin' third.

Then from the gladdened multitude went up a joyous yell—
It rumbled in the mountaintops, it rattled in the dell;[1]
It struck upon the hillside and rebounded on the flat;
For Casey, mighty Casey, was advancing to the bat.

There was ease in Casey's manner as he stepped into his place,
There was pride in Casey's bearing and a smile on Casey's face;
And when responding to the cheers he lightly doffed[2] his hat,
No stranger in the crowd could doubt 'twas Casey at the bat.

Ten thousand eyes were on him as he rubbed his hands with dirt,
Five thousand tongues applauded when he wiped them on his shirt;
Then when the writhing pitcher ground the ball into his hip,
Defiance glanced in Casey's eye, a sneer curled Casey's lip.

And now the leather-covered sphere came hurtling through the air,
And Casey stood a-watching it in haughty grandeur there.
Close by the sturdy batsman the ball unheeded sped;
"That ain't my style," said Casey. "Strike one," the umpire said.

5

From the benches, black with people, there went up a muffled roar,
Like the beating of the storm waves on the stern and distant shore.
"Kill him! kill the umpire!" shouted someone on the stand;
And it's likely they'd have killed him had not Casey raised his hand.

1. **dell** (del) *n.* small, secluded valley.
2. **doffed** (däft) *v.* lifted.

pallor (pal′ ər) *n.* paleness

wreathed (rēthd) *v.* curled around

Literary Analysis
Climax and Anticlimax
What expectation for Casey do the successes of Flynn and Blake create?

writhing (rīth′ iŋ) *v.* twisting; turning

6 **Reading Check**
What happens when the first ball is thrown to Casey?

4 Literary Analysis
Climax and Anticlimax

- Have a volunteer read aloud the first two stanzas of the bracketed passage. Ask students to predict what will happen when Casey comes to bat.
  Answer: The fans will rejoice at the prospect of winning the game.
- Ask the Literary Analysis question on p. 43: What expectation for Casey do the successes of Flynn and Blake create?
  Answer: Since Flynn and Blake both hit safely and Casey is the team's best hitter, the reader expects that Casey will also get a hit.

5 Critical Thinking
Infer

- Ask students what they can infer from the fans' reaction to the called strike.
  Answer: The fans are intensely involved in the game and believe the umpire erred in his call.
- Ask students if they find the fans' reaction realistic.
  Answer: Students may agree that today's fans get just as upset when calls go against their team, and that they care just as much about their team's success.

6 Reading Check

Answer: Casey doesn't swing at the pitch and the umpire calls it a strike.

CUSTOMIZE INSTRUCTION FOR UNIVERSAL ACCESS

For Less Proficient Readers	For Gifted/Talented Students
Encourage students to summarize the action as they read the poem. After every two or three stanzas, they can stop and sum up what has happened so far. Remind students to include only the main ideas and most important details. Partners can check each other's summaries to see if they are accurate and concise.	Ask students to translate the events of "Casey at the Bat" to another sport, such as basketball, football, or soccer. They may tell the story in prose or poetry, but they should focus on one hero and deliver an anticlimactic ending.

ASSESS

7 Reading Strategy

Summarizing

- Ask students why Thayer chose to summarize the rest of the game but to describe Casey's at-bat in detail.
  Answer: Casey's at-bat is the most important one in the game. It deserves a detailed description.
- Ask students the Reading Strategy question on p. 44: State the main points and details of these two stanzas briefly and in your own words.
  Answer: Casey strikes out on the third pitch, and the fans are heart-broken.

Answers for p. 44

Review and Assess

1. Students will probably say no, because readers don't expect heroes to fail.
2. **(a)** Cooney and Burrows are both thrown out at second base. The fans begin to leave, convinced that the game is lost. **(b)** The reader wants to know how the game will come out. When two men reach base safely and the power hitter comes up, there's a good chance that Mudville will win.
3. **(a)** Casey is strong, fearless, and proud. **(b)** Students may describe Casey as a star athlete, utterly confident in his abilities.
4. **(a)** He is furious. **(b)** He might have been too angry to judge the pitch accurately.
5. **(a)** He strikes out swinging. **(b)** Casey may have been shocked by his unexpected failure and sorry for disappointing the fans.
6. **(a)** All baseball fans identify with this dramatic description of the turning point of a game, because most games have crucial moments like this. **(b)** Yes, because it is suspenseful, entertaining and captures a dramatic moment in sport.

With a smile of Christian charity great Casey's visage[3] shone;
He stilled the rising tumult, he made the game go on;
He signaled to the pitcher, and once more the spheroid flew;
But Casey still ignored it, and the umpire said, "Strike two."

"Fraud!" cried the maddened thousands, and the echo answered
 "Fraud!"
But one scornful look from Casey and the audience was awed;
They saw his face grow stern and cold, they saw his muscles strain,
And they knew that Casey wouldn't let the ball go by again.

7

The sneer is gone from Casey's lips, his teeth are clenched in hate.
He pounds with cruel vengeance his bat upon the plate:
And now the pitcher holds the ball, and now he lets it go,
And now the air is shattered by the force of Casey's blow.

Oh, somewhere in this favored land the sun is shining bright,
The band is playing somewhere, and somewhere hearts are light:
And somewhere men are laughing, and somewhere children shout,
But there is no joy in Mudville: Mighty Casey has struck out.

tumult (to͞o´ mult) *n.* noisy commotion

Reading Strategy
Summarizing State the main points and details of these two stanzas briefly and in your own words.

3. **visage** (viz´ ij) *n.* face.

Review and Assess

Thinking About the Selection

1. **Respond:** Did you expect the poem to end the way it did? Why or why not?
2. (a) **Recall:** What happens in the first two stanzas? (b) **Analyze Causes and Effects:** How does the first part of the poem make you want to keep reading?
3. (a) **Recall:** Describe Casey, citing details of his appearance and actions. (b) **Infer:** What type of player would you say Casey is? Why?
4. (a) **Recall:** How is Casey described before the last pitch? (b) **Draw Conclusions:** How might Casey's attitude have affected his game?
5. (a) **Recall:** What is the outcome of Casey's turn at bat? (b) **Speculate:** Based on what you know about Casey, what do you think was his reaction? Why?
6. (a) **Analyze:** Why do you think this poem—written more than a century ago—has remained one of the most popular sports poems to this day? (b) **Evaluate:** Do you think the poem deserves this status? Why or why not?

Ernest Lawrence Thayer

(1863–1940)

It is not surprising that "Casey at the Bat" reads like a sports story in verse. The poet, Ernest Lawrence Thayer, spent many years working as a newspaper reporter. Thayer began his reporting career working on *The Lampoon*, Harvard University's humor magazine. He later worked at newspapers in New York and California.

"Casey at the Bat" first appeared in the *San Francisco Examiner* on June 3, 1888, under Thayer's pen name, Phin. The poem became such a favorite that in 1953 it inspired an operetta called *The Mighty Casey*.

ASSESSMENT PRACTICE: Reading Comprehension

Context Clues (For more practice, see Test Preparation Workbook, p. 3.)

Many assessment tests require students to select a word with nearly the same meaning as a specified word. Demonstrate how to use context clues to respond successfully, even when the prompt word is unfamiliar. Write the following example on the chalkboard:

The tired sailor was buoyed by the cheerful news that the ship would be in port for a week of rest and relaxation.

The word buoyed most nearly means ______

A floating
B encouraged
C heartsick
D worsened

The context shows that being *buoyed* is a result of cheerful news and the anticipation of rest and relaxation. This shows that *B*, *encouraged,* makes the most sense.

Review and Assess

Literary Analysis

Climax and Anticlimax

1. What problem or struggle sets the stage for the **climax**?
2. Which lines of the poem present the climax itself? Explain.
3. Is the outcome of the poem an **anticlimax**? Why or why not?

Connecting Literary Elements

4. Complete a chart like this one to show that "Casey at the Bat" has the three major elements of a **narrative poem**.

Characters	Time and Place	Sequence of Events

5. To which elements in the chart did Thayer give the most attention? Explain.
6. (a) How would "Casey at the Bat" be different if it were written as a short story or play? (b) Would the story be as effective if it were not told in the form of a poem?

Reading Strategy

Summarizing

7. What information is left out of the following summary of lines 5–8? "Some fans left, but most stayed because they were hopeful."
8. Use a chart like this one to explain what happened at the beginning, middle, and end of the poem. Then, in three sentences, summarize the entire poem.

Beginning	Middle	End
Summary:		

Extend Understanding

9. **Sports Connection:** How might defeat add to a player's popularity?

Quick Review

The **climax** of a narrative is its moment of peak action and greatest intensity.
An **anticlimax** occurs when the outcome is trivial or disappointing when compared to the reader's expectations.

A **narrative poem** is a poem that tells a story.

When you **summarize** a passage, you briefly state its main points and details in your own words.

Take It to the Net
www.phschool.com
Take the interactive self-test online to check your understanding of the selection.

Answers for p. 45

Review and Assess

1. With two out and two men on in the ninth inning and his team down by two runs, the star hitter comes to the plate.
2. Lines 47 and 48 present the climax. The poem has built to Casey's last swing at the ball.
3. Yes; the outcome was the opposite of the one the fans and probably many readers expected.
4. Chart should include the following:

Characters	Mudville players, opposing pitcher, the umpire, the fans, Casey
Setting	the Mudville baseball diamond
Events	Down 2–4 with two out in the ninth inning, Flynn hits a single. Blake hits a double. Casey strikes out.

5. Thayer gave the most attention to the plot. Casey is the only character described in any detail, and readers have to infer most of the information about the setting.
6. **(a)** A play would have more dialogue. A story would have more description and might let the reader learn what the characters are thinking. **(b)** It might be equally effective, but it would lack the poem's rhythm and intense emotional focus.
7. The summary omits the fans' hope that Casey would come to bat.
8. Beginning: With their team down by two with two out in the ninth inning, Flynn hits a single and Blake hits a double.
Middle: Casey steps up to the plate and takes two called strikes.
End: Casey swings and misses at the third pitch and loses the game.
9. Fans might sympathize more with an athlete who fails.

EXTEND

Answers for p. 46

❶ Vocabulary Development

Word Analysis

1. tumultuous
2. tumult
3. tumultuously

Fluency: Sentences

Sample answers:

1. A tumult resulted when armed policemen halted protesters marching down Broad Street.
2. At first I thought the branch was writhing, but I soon perceived that a snake was slithering along it toward the trunk.
3. I think Bobby is ill; I don't like the pallor of his face.
4. The porch columns of the old house had almost disappeared under the climbing ivy that wreathed them all the way to the roof.

Spelling Strategy

1. glorious
2. tempestuous
3. religious

❷ Grammar Lesson

1. Casey's face
2. fans' eyes
3. pitcher's head
4. outfielder's glove
5. moment's work

Writing Application

Sample answers:

1. The catcher's mitt protects his hands from injury.
2. The coach's fury erupted when the runner took off for second base against orders.
3. The first baseman asked the young fan's name as he autographed her ticket stub.

Integrate Language Skills

❶ Vocabulary Development Lesson

Word Analysis: Forms of *tumult*

Learning other forms of a word can expand your vocabulary. *Tumult*, a noun, is changed into an adjective, *tumultuous*, by adding the suffix *-ous*. You may already know that the adjective *tumultuous* means "wild and noisy." If so, when you come across the noun *tumult* in "Casey at the Bat," you will be able to figure out that it means "a noisy commotion."

On your paper, complete each sentence with one of the following words.

tumult   tumultuous   tumultuously

1. Her supporters gave the senator a __?__ greeting following her speech.
2. An explosion caused a __?__ downtown.
3. The crowd responded __?__ when he struck out.

Fluency: Words in Sentences

For each item below, write a sentence that uses a word from the vocabulary list on page 41.

1. Write the first sentence of a news article describing a noisy demonstration in the city.
2. Describe the way a snake moves.
3. Explain why you think that your friend may not be feeling well today.
4. Tell about an old house that has ivy growing around its pillars.

Spelling Strategy

When you add the suffix *-ous* to a word, you may need to make additional spelling changes. For example, when you add *-ous* to *tumult*, you add a *u* before the suffix to form *tumultuous*.

Write the adjective form of each noun below.

1. glory   2. tempest   3. religion

❷ Grammar Lesson

Possessive Nouns

A **possessive noun** is used to show ownership. It serves as an adjective by modifying another noun.

In these lines, the possessive nouns are set in italics. Notice that, in the first example, the underlined word that is "owned" is not a physical object but an aspect of Casey's personality.

Examples: There was ease in *Casey's* manner as he stepped into his place, . . .

The *team's* defeat was discouraging.

The *player's* fans roared loudly.

Practice List the five possessive nouns in the following paragraph, as well as the word that is "owned" by each one.

Casey's face broke into a grin when he connected with the ball. Every fan's eyes followed the ball as it flew over the pitcher's head. The ball reached the top of its arc and then fell—right toward an outfielder's glove. It took only a moment's work to catch the ball and declare Casey "out."

Writing Application For each noun below, write a sentence using it as a possessive noun.

1. catcher   2. coach   3. fan

WG Prentice Hall Writing and Grammar Connection: Chapter 29, Section 6

TEACHING RESOURCES

The following resources can be used to enrich or extend the instructions for pp. 46–47.

Vocabulary

- **Selection Support:** Build Vocabulary, p. 9
- **Vocabulary and Spelling Practice Book** (Use this booklet for skills enrichment.)

Grammar

- **Selection Support:** Build Grammar Skills, p. 10
- **Writing and Grammar,** Gold Level, p. 712
- **Daily Language Practice Transparencies**

Writing

- **Writing and Grammar,** Gold Level, p. 63
- **Writing and Grammar iText CD-ROM**
- **Writing Models and Graphic Organizers on Transparencies,** p. 17

BLOCK SCHEDULING: Resources marked with this symbol provide varied instruction during 90-minute blocks.

❸ Writing Lesson

Sportscast

Like "Casey at the Bat," a good sportscast uses vivid and lively language. Vivid language captures the thrills and disappointments of a sports event. Write a sportscast about Casey's experience that hooks your audience and tells a good story.

Prewriting Create a list of the vivid verbs—action words with a punch—that describe Casey's experience. For example, list ways that Casey might swing the bat or ways the pitcher might throw the ball to Casey.

Drafting As you draft, picture the game in your mind. Make sure the verbs you choose are appropriate for describing a baseball game.

Revising Reread your draft. Using this model as an example, circle the verbs in your draft and decide whether more lively action words would make your writing sparkle.

Model: Revising to Include Vivid Verbs

Ana Moreno ~~ran~~ *raced* down the court, the Panthers in hot pursuit. She ~~saw~~ *spotted* a teammate's signal and ~~gave~~ *slipped* Keisha Washington the ball. Washington's play ~~got~~ *bagged* the victory.

Vivid verbs make the action in these sentences more exciting and easier to visualize.

WG *Prentice Hall Writing and Grammar Connection: Chapter 4, Section 4*

❹ Extension Activities

Listening and Speaking With a partner, role-play a **sports interview** with Casey. Follow these suggestions as you plan:

- Identify your audience and list the questions that would interest them.
- Practice verbal strategies, such as changing the pitch and tone of your voice. For example, if Casey is upset about the recent loss, he should sound disappointed or angry.

Role-play your interview in front of your class, and ask classmates to evaluate your work. **[Group Activity]**

Research and Technology In "Casey at the Bat," the fans have very high expectations of Casey, Mudville's famous player. Write a **research report** comparing a famous baseball player in history to a famous present-day baseball player. Use library resources such as the Internet, newspapers, and books to research the experiences of each player. In your report, compare their lifestyles and successes.

Take It to the Net www.phschool.com
Go online for an additional research activity using the Internet.

ASSESSMENT RESOURCES

The following resources can be used to assess students' knowledge and skills.

Selection Assessment

- **Formal Assessment,** pp. 7–9
- **Open Book Test,** pp. 7–9
- **Got It! Assessment Videotapes,** Tape 1
- **Test Bank Software**

Take It to the Net
Visit www.phschool.com for self-tests and additional questions on "Casey at the Bat."

Writing Rubric

- **Performance Assess. and Portfolio Mgmt.,** p. 18

PRENTICE HALL ASSESSMENT SYSTEM

- **Workbook**
- **Skill Book**
- **Transparencies**
- **CD-ROM**

❸ Writing Lesson

- Have students look back through "Casey at the Bat" for examples of vivid verbs and images that appeal to the five senses and bring the game to life. For example, "Cooney *died* at second" shows not only that he was thrown out, but that the team's hopes were deflated.
- Remind students that listeners to a radio sportscast can't see the action. For this reason, radio sportscasters have to include much more description and lively language than television sportscasters.
- Use the Description rubric in **Performance Assessment and Portfolio Management,** p. 18, to evaluate students' sportscasts.

❹ Extension Activity

Research and Technology

- Introduce students to *The Baseball Encyclopedia,* a one-volume encyclopedia containing career statistics for every major league player in history. The annual *World Almanac* also includes several pages of baseball records past and present.
- You might want to suggest the following past/present pairs of players to students who have trouble finding topics:
  - Lou Gehrig and Cal Ripken, Jr., owners of the two longest consecutive-game streaks in history
  - Babe Ruth and Mark McGwire, two star home-run hitters
  - Willie Mays and Andruw Jones, two spectacular center fielders

CUSTOMIZE INSTRUCTION
For Universal Access

To address different learning styles, use the following activities suggested in the **Extension Activities** booklet, p. 3.

- For Musical/Rhythmic and Interpersonal Learners, use Activity 4.
- For Linguistic/Interpersonal Learners, use Activity 5.
- For Verbal/Linguistic Learners, use Activity 6.

The Birds

Lesson Objectives and CA Correlations

1. **To analyze and respond to literary elements**
   - Literary Analysis: Foreshadowing **R 3.6**
   - Connecting Literary Elements: Imagery
2. **To read, comprehend, analyze, and critique a story**
   - Reading Strategy: Predicting **R 3.6**
   - Reading Check questions
   - Review and Assess questions
   - Assessment Practice (ATE)
3. **To develop word analysis skills, fluency, and systematic vocabulary**
   - Vocabulary Development Lesson: Anglo-Saxon Suffix: *-ful* **R 1.1**
4. **To understand and apply written and oral language conventions**
   - Spelling Strategy
   - Grammar Lesson: Reflexive and Intensive Pronouns **LC 1.3**
5. **To understand and apply appropriate writing and research strategies**
   - Writing Lesson: Bird's-Eye View of a Place **W 1.1**
   - Extension Activity: Multimedia Presentation **W 1.3**
6. **To understand and apply listening and speaking strategies**
   - Extension Activity: Panel Discussion **LS 1.8**

STEP-BY-STEP TEACHING GUIDE	PACING GUIDE
PRETEACH	
Motivate Students and Provide Background	
Use the Motivation activity (ATE p. 48)	5 min.
Read and discuss the Preview material and Background information (SE/ATE p. 48) A	5 min.
Introduce the Concepts	
Introduce the Literary Analysis and Reading Strategy (SE/ATE p. 49) A	15 min.
Pronounce the vocabulary words and read their definitions (SE p. 49)	5 min.
TEACH	
Monitor Comprehension	
Informally monitor comprehension by circulating while students read independently or in groups A	50 min.
Monitor students' comprehension with the Reading Check notes (SE/ATE pp. 51, 53, 55, 57, 59, 61, 63, 65, 67, 69, 71, 73, 75, 77, 79, 81)	as students read
Develop vocabulary with Vocabulary notes (SE pp. 51, 54, 61 62, 67, 69, 70, 77; ATE p. 57)	as students read
Develop Understanding	
Develop students' understanding of foreshadowing with the Literary Analysis annotations (SE/ATE pp. 52, 54, 55, 58, 60, 62, 66, 67, 70, 71, 74, 78, 79, 80) A	5 min.
Develop students' understanding of predicting with the Reading Strategy annotations (SE /ATE pp. 51, 53, 59, 61, 63, 64, 66, 70, 74, 75, 81)	5 min.
ASSESS	
Assess Mastery	
Assess students' mastery of the Reading Strategy and Literary Analysis by having them answer the Review and Assess questions (SE/ATE p. 83)	15 min.
Use one or more of the print and media Assessment Resources (ATE p. 85) A	up to 45 min.
EXTEND	
Apply Understanding	
Have students complete the Vocabulary Development Lesson and the Grammar Lesson (SE p. 84) A	20 min.
Apply students' knowledge of consistent viewpoint using the Writing Lesson (SE/ATE p. 85) A	45 min.
Apply students' understanding of the story using one or more of the Extension Activities (SE p. 85)	20–90 min.

A ACCELERATED INSTRUCTION:
Use the strategies and activities identified with an A.

UNIVERSAL ACCESS
● = Below Level Students
▲ = On-Level Students
■ = Above Level Students

Time and Resource Manager

Reading Level: Average
Average Number of Instructional Days: 4

RESOURCES		
PRINT	**TRANSPARENCIES**	**TECHNOLOGY**
• **Beyond Literature,** Cross-Curricular Connection: Science, p. 4 ▲ ■		• **Interest Grabber Video,** Tape 1 ● ▲ ■
• **Selection Support Workbook:** ● ▲ ■ Literary Analysis, p. 16 Reading Strategy, p. 15 Build Vocabulary, p. 13	• **Literary Analysis and Reading Transparencies,** pp. 7 and 8 ● ▲ ■	
		• **Listening to Literature** ● ▲ ■ Audiocassettes, Sides 3 and 4 Audio CDs, CDs 3 and 4
• **Literatura en español** ● ▲ • **Literary Analysis for Enrichment** ■		
• **Formal Assessment:** Selection Test, pp. 10–12 ● ▲ ■ • **Open Book Test,** pp. 10–12 ● ▲ ■ • **Performance Assessment and Portfolio Management,** p. 18 ● ▲ ■ • Prentice Hall Assessment System ● ▲ ■	• Prentice Hall Assessment System ● ▲ ■ Skills Practice Answers and Explanations on Transparencies	• **Test Bank Software** ● ▲ ■ • **Got It! Assessment Videotapes,** Tape 1 ● ▲
• **Selection Support Workbook:** ● ▲ ■ Build Grammar Skills, p. 14 • **Writing and Grammar,** Gold Level ● ▲ ■ • **Extension Activities,** p. 4 ● ▲ ■	• **Daily Language Practice Transparencies** ● ▲ • **Writing Models and Graphic Organizers on Transparencies** ● ▲ ■	• **Writing and Grammar iText CD-ROM** ● ▲ ■ ***Take It to the Net*** www.phschool.com

BLOCK SCHEDULING: Use one 90-minute class period to preteach the selection and have students read it. Use a second 90-minute class period to assess students' mastery of skills and have them complete one of the Extension Activities.

PRETEACH

Step-by-Step Teaching Guide for pp. 48–49

Motivation

This story grips readers' attention by describing a series of attacks on people by huge flocks of birds. Underlying the suspenseful events of the plot is an important message—human inability to predict or control forces of nature. Have students discuss why it is impossible for people to predict outcomes in conflicts with the forces of nature.

Interest Grabber Video

As an alternative, play "Facts about Birds" on Tape 1 to engage student interest.

1 Background

Film

The film version of *The Birds* was released in 1963 when Alfred Hitchcock was at the height of his popularity. Born in London in 1899, Hitchcock had directed several British films before venturing across the Atlantic to Hollywood in 1940. Perhaps in deference to American audiences, Hitchcock changed the setting of *The Birds* from England to California. He also altered the characters' names and relationships and some details of the story, but the attacks of the birds follow DuMaurier's descriptions faithfully. A great number and variety of real birds, specially trained, were used in the film. The live birds and the number of special effects and trick shots required to film the attacks meant that the film took three years of preparation and shooting before its release. Critics were unimpressed with the writing and acting, but the birds, the real stars of the film, terrified audiences and critics alike.

Prepare to Read

The Birds

Take It to the Net

Visit www.phschool.com for interactive activities and instruction related to "The Birds," including
- background
- graphic organizers
- literary elements
- reading strategies

Preview

Connecting to the Literature

You step outside and the sky is dark and threatening. Low rumbles of thunder are becoming louder. You look at the threatening scene and fear makes your blood run cold. Daphne du Maurier's "The Birds" will probably evoke these same eerie feelings as you read about nature itself brooding and eventually striking out.

1 Background

Imagine sitting in a dark movie theater, watching images of flocks of birds descending upon average people in an unsuspecting town. This is what it was like to see *The Birds*, which filmmaker Alfred Hitchcock adapted from this story. After reading "The Birds," you will probably see why Hitchcock decided to adapt the story into his frightening film.

TEACHING RESOURCES

The following resources can be used to enrich or extend the instruction for pp. 48–49.

Motivation

Interest Grabber Video, Tape 1: Facts about Birds

Background

Beyond Literature, p. 4

Take It to the Net

Visit www.phschool.com for background and hotlinks for "The Birds."

Literary Analysis

Literary Analysis and Reading Transparencies, Foreshadowing, p. 7

Reading

Selection Support: Reading Strategy, p. 15; Build Vocabulary, p. 13

Literary Analysis and Reading Transparencies, Predicting, p. 8

BLOCK SCHEDULING: Resources marked with this symbol provide varied instruction during 90-minute blocks.

❷ Literary Analysis

Foreshadowing

As its name suggests, **foreshadowing** is the author's use of clues to hint at future events. In this passage from "The Birds," for instance, du Maurier hints at danger to come.

> The birds had been more restless than ever this fall of the year.

Keep an eye out for other examples of foreshadowing as you read; in particular, watch for details that seem unusual or disturbing.

Connecting Literary Elements

Imagery is language that a writer uses to create word pictures for the reader. These pictures, or images, are created by details of sight, sound, taste, touch, smell, or movement. In "The Birds," vivid images help bring the scenes to life. They also call attention to details—and help you discover the foreshadowing clues that du Maurier provides.

❸ Reading Strategy

Predicting

Predicting, or making guesses about what will happen before a story ends, can often help you check your understanding of a story.

- To make a prediction, start by looking for small but unusual details. These details might be minor events that catch your attention but that the characters in the story seem to ignore.
- Ask yourself what would happen if the detail were to become more important. In "The Birds," for example, think about what would happen if a disturbing detail were multiplied many times.
- Note your predictions, but be prepared to revise your guesses as the story develops.

Use a chart to help you record your predictions. The chart shown here presents a small but unusual detail from "The Birds."

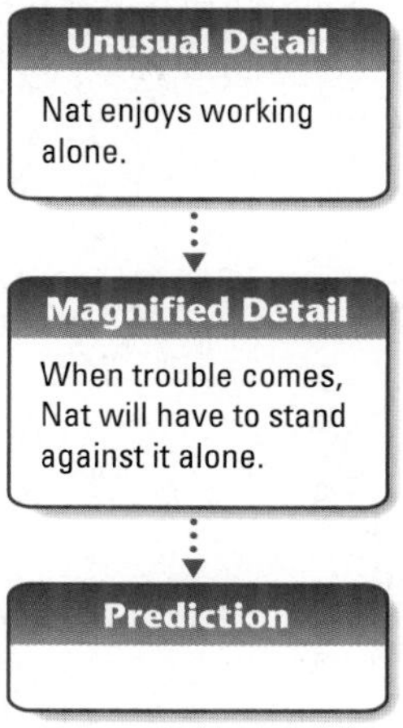

Unusual Detail
Nat enjoys working alone.
Magnified Detail
When trouble comes, Nat will have to stand against it alone.
Prediction

Vocabulary Development

placid (plas´ id) *adj.* calm (p. 51)

garish (gar´ ish) *adj.* too bright (p. 54)

recounted (ri kount´ ed) *v.* told in detail; narrated (p. 61)

sullen (sul´ ən) *adj.* gloomy (p. 62)

furtively (fur´ tiv lē) *adv.* stealthily, so as to avoid being heard (p. 67)

imperative (im per´ ə tiv) *adj.* urgent; absolutely necessary (p. 69)

reconnaissance (ri kän´ ə səns) *adj.* exploratory in nature, as when observing to seek information (p. 70)

fretful (fret´ fəl) *adj.* irritable and discontented (p. 77)

❷ Literary Analysis

Foreshadowing

- Tell students that *foreshadowing* is a writer's use of clues or hints to suggest future events. By using foreshadowing, a writer can create suspense for readers and prepare them for surprising or unlikely outcomes.
- Have students review "The Cask of Amontillado" for examples of foreshadowing. For instance, Montresor carries a trowel with him to the vaults. This suggests that he will use it in his revenge against Fortunato.
- As students read "The Birds," have them note details that seem to alert them to strange or unusual events that lie ahead. When strange, surprising, or horrifying things happen, students should look back to see which details foreshadowed these incidents.

❸ Reading Strategy

Predicting

- Write the word *predict* on the chalkboard, drawing a vertical line between the prefix *pre-* and the root *dict.* Explain that *predict* comes from two Latin words and literally means "say before."
- Make sure students understand that a prediction is not a wild guess; it is based on details already known.
- Challenge students to pause at the end of every page or two of "The Birds" to predict what may come next for Nat and his family.

Vocabulary Development

- Pronounce each vocabulary word for students, and read the definitions as a class. Have students identify any words with which they are already familiar.

CUSTOMIZE INSTRUCTION FOR UNIVERSAL ACCESS

For Less Proficient Readers	For English Learners	For Advanced Readers
Have students familiarize themselves with the vocabulary words on p. 49 before they begin reading. As students read, they can list other unfamiliar words. After reading, partners can compare lists, teach each other as many words as they can, and work together to define the rest.	This story is full of British idioms that may not be familiar to students. Point out that many of these are defined in the footnotes. Encourage students to use these notes, context clues, and common sense to define these terms before checking a dictionary.	As students read, have them consider DuMaurier's vocabulary. How do her characters speak? How does the diction of this story compare with that of the other stories in this unit? What effect does diction have on this story?

E-Teach

Visit E-Teach at www.phschool.com for teachers' essays on how to teach, with questions and answers.

TEACH

Step-by-Step Teaching Guide for pp. 50–82

CUSTOMIZE INSTRUCTION for Visual/Spatial Learners

Have students note Du Maurier's use of color words throughout the story. On the first page, for instance, winter has banished the autumn colors, and the black and white birds cloud the sky. What colors does Du Maurier associate with the birds? With the winter landscape? Have students write about how Du Maurier uses color words and images to appeal to readers' sense of sight and what effect this use of colors has on the impact of the story.

❶ About the Selection

Nat, a part-time handyman, is shocked when a flock of small songbirds flies into the open window of his children's bedroom and attacks them. Later, as the radio announces a state of emergency because birds are attacking all over England, Nat boards up the house. On a trip to find food at the farm, Nat finds that birds have slaughtered his employers. The radio ceases to broadcast. The family gathers supplies and food from the farm and begins waiting the night out in the kitchen, aware that the birds have broken in upstairs.

❷ Background

Art

Attack of the Birds, by Lev Tabenkin

Russian painter Lev Tabenkin graduated from the Moscow Polygraphic Institute during the Soviet era. His paintings often include unusual images of animals—exaggerated in size or threatening in aspect.

1. What is your immediate reaction to this image? Explain.
   Answer: Students may find the violence or the woman's helplessness horrifying or disturbing.
2. Why do you think the birds are attacking the woman?
   Possible answers: The birds may be defending their nests or seeking food.

❸ ▶Critical Viewing

Answer: Birds might attack people.

❶ The Birds

Daphne du Maurier

Attack of the Birds, 1994, Lev Tabenkin, Maya Polsky Gallery

❷

❸ ▲**Critical Viewing** Based on this painting, what do you think might happen in this story? **[Predict]**

TEACHING RESOURCES

The following resources can be used to enrich or extend the instruction for pp. 50–82.

Literary Analysis

- **Writing Models and Graphic Organizers on Transparencies,** p. 64 ■
- **Selection Support:** Literary Analysis, p. 16

Reading

- **Listening to Literature Audiocassettes,** Sides 3 and 4 ■
- **Listening to Literature Audio CDs,** CDs 3 and 4 ■

■ **BLOCK SCHEDULING:** Resources marked with this symbol provide varied instruction during 90-minute blocks.

On December the third the wind changed overnight and it was winter. Until then the autumn had been mellow, soft. The leaves had lingered on the trees, golden-red, and the hedgerows were still green. The earth was rich where the plow had turned it.

Nat Hocken, because of a wartime disability, had a pension and did not work full-time at the farm. He worked three days a week, and they gave him the lighter jobs: hedging, thatching, repairs to the farm buildings.

Although he was married, with children, his was a solitary disposition; he liked best to work alone. It pleased him when he was given a bank to build up, or a gate to mend at the far end of the peninsula, where the sea surrounded the farmland on either side. Then, at midday, he would pause and eat the pasty[1] that his wife had baked for him, and, sitting on the cliff's edge, watch the birds. Autumn was best for this, better than spring. In spring the birds flew inland, purposeful, intent; they knew where they were bound; the rhythm and ritual of their life brooked no delay. In autumn those that had not migrated overseas but remained to pass the winter were caught up in the same driving urge, but because migration was denied them followed a pattern of their own. Great flocks of them came to the peninsula, restless, uneasy, spending themselves in motion; now wheeling, circling in the sky, now settling to feed on the rich new-turned soil, but even when they fed it was as though they did so without hunger, without desire. Restlessness drove them to the skies again.

4 Black and white, jackdaw and gull, mingled in strange partnership, seeking some sort of liberation, never satisfied, never still. Flocks of starlings, rustling like silk, flew to fresh pasture, driven by the same necessity of movement, and the smaller birds, the finches and the larks, scattered from tree to hedge as if compelled.

Nat watched them, and he watched the sea birds too. Down in the bay they waited for the tide. They had more patience. Oyster catchers, redshank, sanderling, and curlew watched by the water's edge; as the slow sea sucked at the shore and then withdrew, leaving the strip of seaweed bare and the shingle churned, the sea birds raced and ran upon the beaches. Then that same impulse to flight seized upon them too. Crying, whistling, calling, they skimmed the placid sea and left the shore. Make haste, make speed, hurry and begone; yet where, and to what purpose? The restless urge of autumn, unsatisfying, sad, had put a spell upon them and they must flock, and wheel, and cry; they must spill themselves of motion before winter came.

"Perhaps," thought Nat, munching his pasty by the cliff's edge, "a message comes to the birds in autumn, like a warning. Winter is coming. Many of them perish. And like the people who, apprehensive of death before their time, drive themselves to work or folly, the birds do likewise."

1. **pasty** (pas´ tē) *n.* a meat pie.

Reading Strategy
Predicting How could this scene of "strange partnership" hint at a danger later on?

placid (plas´ id) *adj.* calm

5 **Reading Check**
What happens to the birds that do not migrate?

4 Reading Strategy
Predicting

- Remind students that they should be prepared to revise their predictions as they read. Sometimes they may find out that their initial predictions were wrong. Other times they may learn new information that may affect their original predictions.
- Ask the Reading Strategy question on p. 51: How could this scene of "strange partnership" hint at a danger later on?
Answer: If these birds are not usually seen together, the reader wonders why. This unnatural behavior creates a sense of unease.

5 Reading Check

Answer: The birds stay in the area, flying or feeding restlessly.

CUSTOMIZE INSTRUCTION FOR UNIVERSAL ACCESS

For Less Proficient Readers	For Special Needs Students	For Advanced Readers
The story's many long complex-compound sentences may make reading difficult for students. Encourage them to read these sentences carefully to find the main subject and verb, then to read each clause and determine how it relates to the sentence's main idea.	Have students use the Sunburst graphic organizer in **Writing Process Models and Graphic Organizers on Transparencies,** p. 64, to record main idea and supporting details. Students can pause at the end of each page or so and note its main ideas and details.	Have students examine Nat's thoughts in the final paragraph on p. 51. What do they think he means? Do they think his musings make sense, or are they fantastical and unrealistic? Students can return to this passage and discuss it again after they finish the story.

6 Literary Analysis

Foreshadowing

- Point out this detail in the first paragraph at the right: *The whole machine and the man upon it would be lost momentarily in the great cloud of wheeling, crying birds.* What might this detail foreshadow?
  Answer: There are many more birds than there are people. This detail suggests that, in a conflict between birds and people, birds would win.
- Ask students the first Literary Analysis question on p. 52: What might the birds' restlessness and large numbers foreshadow?
  Answer: These details might foreshadow trouble of some sort. The birds seem unsettled, and Nat finds them disturbing.

7 Literary Analysis

Foreshadowing and Imagery

- Remind students that imagery is language that appeals to one or more of the five senses. To which of the five senses does DuMaurier appeal in these two paragraphs?
  Answer: The descriptions appeal to the sense of sight. The cold, the wind, and the stab to Nat's hand appeal to the sense of touch. The roaring sea and tapping birds appeal to the sense of hearing.
- Ask the second Literary Analysis question on p. 52: What image of the wind does this description generate and what might it foreshadow about the next day?
  Answer: The wind invades the house; it gets in through the cracks and under the doors. This may foreshadow another "invasion" of the house.
- Suggest that students use charts to keep track of examples of imagery throughout the story. Students can note phrases or sentences in one column and the sense(s) to which they appeal in the other.

6 The birds had been more restless than ever this fall of the year, the agitation more marked because the days were still. As the tractor traced its path up and down the western hills, the figure of the farmer silhouetted on the driving seat, the whole machine and the man upon it would be lost momentarily in the great cloud of wheeling, crying birds. There were many more than usual; Nat was sure of this.

Always, in autumn, they followed the plow, but not in great flocks like these, nor with such clamor.

Nat remarked upon it when hedging was finished for the day. "Yes," said the farmer, "there are more birds about than usual; I've noticed it too. And daring, some of them, taking no notice of the tractor. One or two gulls came so close to my head this afternoon I thought they'd knock my cap off! As it was, I could scarcely see what I was doing, when they were overhead and I had the sun in my eyes. I have a notion the weather will change. It will be a hard winter. That's why the birds are restless."

7 Nat, tramping home across the fields and down the lane to his cottage, saw the birds still flocking over the western hills, in the last glow of the sun. No wind, and the gray sea calm and full. Campion in bloom yet in the hedges, and the air mild. The farmer was right, though, and it was that night the weather turned. Nat's bedroom faced east. He woke just after two and heard the wind in the chimney. Not the storm and bluster of a sou' westerly gale, bringing the rain, but east wind, cold and dry. It sounded hollow in the chimney, and a loose slate rattled on the roof. Nat listened, and he could hear the sea roaring in the bay. Even the air in the small bedroom had turned chill: a draft came under the skirting of the door, blowing upon the bed. Nat drew the blanket round him, leaned closer to the back of his sleeping wife, and stayed wakeful, watchful, aware of misgiving without cause.

Then he heard the tapping on the window. There was no creeper on the cottage walls to break loose and scratch upon the pane. He listened, and the tapping continued until, irritated by the sound, Nat got out of bed and went to the window. He opened it, and as he did so something brushed his hand, jabbing at his knuckles, grazing the skin. Then he saw the flutter of the wings and it was gone, over the roof, behind the cottage.

It was a bird; what kind of bird he could not tell. The wind must have driven it to shelter on the sill.

He shut the window and went back to bed, but, feeling his knuckles wet, put his mouth to the scratch. The bird had drawn blood. Frightened, he supposed, and bewildered, the bird, seeking shelter, had stabbed at him in the darkness. Once more he settled himself to sleep.

Literary Analysis

Foreshadowing What might the birds' restlessness and large numbers foreshadow?

Literary Analysis

Foreshadowing and Imagery What image of the wind does this description generate, and what might it foreshadow about the next day?

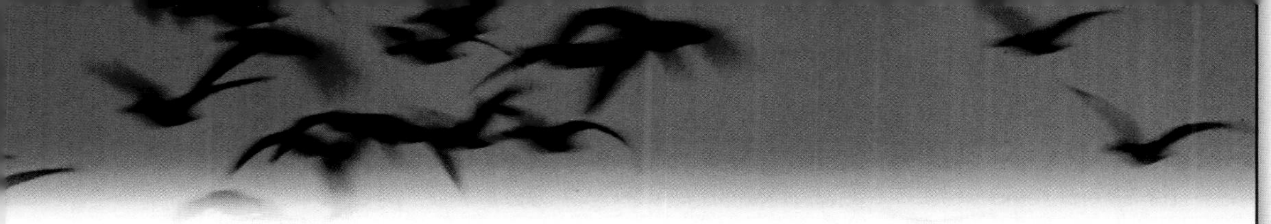

Presently the tapping came again, this time more forceful, more insistent, and now his wife woke at the sound and, turning in the bed, said to him, "See to the window, Nat, it's rattling."

"I've already seen to it," he told her; "there's some bird there trying to get in. Can't you hear the wind? It's blowing from the east, driving the birds to shelter."

"Send them away," she said, "I can't sleep with that noise."

He went to the window for the second time, and now when he opened it there was not one bird upon the sill but half a dozen; they flew straight into his face, attacking him.

He shouted, striking out at them with his arms, scattering them; like the first one, they flew over the roof and disappeared. Quickly he let the window fall and latched it.

"Did you hear that?" he said. "They went for me. Tried to peck my
8 eyes." He stood by the window, peering into the darkness, and could see nothing. His wife, heavy with sleep, murmured from the bed.

"I'm not making it up," he said, angry at her suggestion. "I tell you the birds were on the sill, trying to get into the room."

Suddenly a frightened cry came from the room across the passage where the children slept.

"It's Jill," said his wife, roused at the sound, sitting up in bed. "Go to her, see what's the matter."

Nat lit the candle, but when he opened the bedroom door to cross the passage the draft blew out the flame.

There came a second cry of terror, this time from both children, and stumbling into their room, he felt the beating of wings about him in the darkness. The window was wide open. Through it came the birds, hitting first the ceiling and the walls, then swerving in mid-flight, turning to the children in their beds.

"It's all right, I'm here," shouted Nat, and the children flung themselves, screaming, upon him, while in the darkness the birds rose and dived and came for him again.

"What is it, Nat, what's happened?" his wife called from the further bedroom, and swiftly he pushed the children through the door to the passage and shut it upon them, so that he was alone now in their bedroom with the birds.

He seized a blanket from the nearest bed and, using it as a weapon, flung it to right and left about him in the air. He felt the thud of bodies, heard the fluttering of wings, but they were not yet defeated, for again and again they returned to the assault, jabbing his hands, his head, the little stabbing beaks sharp as pointed forks. The blanket became a weapon of defense; he wound it about his

Reading Strategy
Predicting Based on this detail and others, predict what will happen in the children's room.

9 **Reading Check**
What happens in the children's room?

CUSTOMIZE INSTRUCTION FOR UNIVERSAL ACCESS

For Advanced Readers

The events of this story might be described as a plague of birds. Students may have heard about plagues of locusts or grasshoppers. These insects swarm to a given place, drop from the sky, and literally eat everything in sight, stripping the fields bare. Students can read effective descriptions of plagues of locusts in chapters 25, 26, and 32 of Laura Ingalls Wilder's *On the Banks of Plum Creek;* in Chapter 10 of the biblical Book of Exodus; and in Doris Lessing's short story "A Mild Attack of Locusts." Wilder describes a locust attack on a Minnesota farm in 1877; Exodus tells of a plague of locusts in Egypt, about 1400 B.C; Lessing recounts an attack on a South African farm during the mid-20th century. Have students read one or more of these descriptions and compare and contrast them with the attacks of the birds in this story. Which is more frightening? Why?

8 Reading Strategy

Predicting

- Ask students whether they anticipated that the birds would attack a person. If anyone did, have him or her point out specific details that led to this prediction.
- Ask the Reading Strategy question on p. 53: Based on this detail and others, predict what will happen in the children's room. **Possible responses:** Birds tried to get into Nat's room and attack. The scream suggests that perhaps the same thing has happened in the children's room.

9 Reading Check

Answer: Several birds fly in through the open window and attack the children.

⑩ Literary Analysis

Foreshadowing and Imagery

- Point out the statement that these different types of birds don't usually flock together. Ask whether students remember any detail in the story that foreshadows that they would do this.
  Answer: On p. 51, the story referred to the jackdaws and gulls as "a strange partnership." This foreshadows the different songbirds collaborating in an attack on the family.
- Ask the Literary Analysis question on p. 54: What might the imagery of this description foreshadow?
  Answer: It suggests that there may be a desperate battle between the birds and the human beings. It suggests that the birds intend to kill the human beings.

head, and then in greater darkness beat at the birds with his bare hands. He dared not stumble to the door and open it, lest in doing so the birds should follow him.

How long he fought with them in the darkness he could not tell, but at last the beating of the wings about him lessened and then withdrew, and through the density of the blanket he was aware of light. He waited, listened; there was no sound except the fretful crying of one of the children from the bedroom beyond. The fluttering, the whirring of the wings had ceased.

He took the blanket from his head and stared about him. The cold gray morning light exposed the room. Dawn and the open window had called the living birds; the dead lay on the floor. Nat gazed at the little corpses, shocked and horrified. They were all small birds, none of any size; there must have been fifty of them lying there upon the floor. There were robins, finches, sparrows, blue tits, larks, and ⑩ bramblings, birds that by nature's law kept to their own flock and their own territory, and now, joining one with another in their urge for battle, had destroyed themselves against the bedroom walls or in the strife had been destroyed by him. Some had lost feathers in the fight; others had blood, his blood, upon their beaks.

Literary Analysis Foreshadowing and Imagery What might the imagery of this description foreshadow?

Sickened, Nat went to the window and stared out across his patch of garden to the fields.

It was bitter cold, and the ground had all the hard black look of frost. Not white frost, to shine in the morning sun, but the black frost that the east wind brings. The sea, fiercer now with the turning tide, white-capped and steep, broke harshly in the bay. Of the birds there was no sign. Not a sparrow chattered in the hedge beyond the garden gate, no early missel-thrush or blackbird pecked on the grass for worms. There was no sound at all but the east wind and the sea.

Nat shut the window and the door of the small bedroom, and went back across the passage to his own. His wife sat up in bed, one child asleep beside her, the smaller in her arms, his face bandaged. The curtains were tightly drawn across the window, the candles lit. Her face looked garish in the yellow light. She shook her head for silence.

garish (gar´ ish) *adj.* too bright

"He's sleeping now," she whispered, "but only just. Something must have cut him, there was blood at the corner of his eyes. Jill said it was the birds. She said she woke up, and the birds were in the room."

His wife looked up at Nat, searching his face for confirmation. She looked terrified, bewildered, and he did not want her to know that he was also shaken, dazed almost, by the events of the past few hours.

"There are birds in there," he said, "dead birds, nearly fifty of them. Robins, wrens, all the little birds from hereabouts. It's as though a madness seized them, with the east wind." He sat down on the bed beside his wife and held her hand. "It's the weather," he said, "it must be that, it's the hard weather. They aren't the birds, maybe, from here around. They've been driven down from upcountry."

"But, Nat," whispered his wife, "it's only this night that the weather

CUSTOMIZE INSTRUCTION FOR UNIVERSAL ACCESS

For Less Proficient Readers	For Advanced Readers
Ask each student to find a descriptive paragraph that seems particularly effective, or one that gave them special reading challenges. Make sure they choose lengthy paragraphs. Have each student summarize his or her paragraph briefly, then reread it at least twice, slowly and carefully, making sure that they understand each detail. Students can analyze what made the paragraph effective. Encourage them to discuss specific images.	As students read, have them think about the birds as characters in the story. Do they exist as individual personalities, or only as a group? How would students describe this group personality? What details convey this impression? What about these birds, other than their attacks on people, is different from the way birds normally behave? Have students analyze the birds' character or characters in brief essays after they finish reading.

turned. There's been no snow to drive them. And they can't be hungry yet. There's food for them out there in the fields."

"It's the weather," repeated Nat. "I tell you, it's the weather."

His face, too, was drawn and tired, like hers. They stared at one another for a while without speaking.

"I'll go downstairs and make a cup of tea," he said.

The sight of the kitchen reassured him. The cups and saucers, neatly stacked upon the dresser, the table and chairs, his wife's roll of knitting on her basket chair, the children's toys in a corner cupboard.

He knelt down, raked out the old embers, and relit the fire. The glowing sticks brought normality, the steaming kettle and the brown teapot comfort and security. He drank his tea, carried a cup up to his wife. Then he washed in the scullery,[2] and, putting on his boots, opened the back door.

11 The sky was hard and leaden, and the brown hills that had gleamed in the sun the day before looked dark and bare. The east wind, like a razor, stripped the trees, and the leaves, crackling and dry, shivered and scattered with the wind's blast. Nat stubbed the earth with his boot. It was frozen hard. He had never known a change so swift and sudden. Black winter had descended in a single night.

The children were awake now. Jill was chattering upstairs and young Johnny crying once again. Nat heard his wife's voice, soothing, comforting. Presently they came down. He had breakfast ready for them, and the routine of the day began.

"Did you drive away the birds?" asked Jill, restored to calm because of the kitchen fire, because of day, because of breakfast.

"Yes, they've all gone now," said Nat. "It was the east wind brought them in. They were frightened and lost, they wanted shelter."

"They tried to peck us," said Jill. "They went for Johnny's eyes."

"Fright made them do that," said Nat. "They didn't know where they were in the dark bedroom."

"I hope they won't come again," said Jill. "Perhaps if we put bread for them outside the window they will eat that and fly away."

She finished her breakfast and then went for her coat and hood, her schoolbooks and her satchel. Nat said nothing, but his wife looked at him across the table. A silent message passed between them.

"I'll walk with her to the bus," he said. "I don't go to the farm today."

And while the child was washing in the scullery he said to his wife, "Keep all the windows closed, and the doors too. Just to be on the safe side. I'll go to the farm. Find out if they heard anything in the night." Then he walked with his small daughter up the lane. She seemed to have forgotten her experience of the night before. She danced ahead of him, chasing the leaves, her face whipped with the cold and rosy under the pixie hood.

"Is it going to snow, Dad?" she said. "It's cold enough."

He glanced up at the bleak sky, felt the wind tear at his shoulders.

---

2. **scullery** (skul′ ər ē) *n.* a room next to the kitchen where pots and pans are washed and stored.

Literary Analysis
Foreshadowing
Overnight, "black winter" has taken hold of the countryside. What might the suddenness of this change foreshadow?

12 ✓ **Reading Check**
What does Nat ask his wife to do before he leaves the house?

11 Literary Analysis

Foreshadowing and Imagery

- Ask a volunteer to read this paragraph aloud. Have students discuss the imagery. To which senses to the details appeal? What is the effect?
  Answer: The color words appeal to the sense of sight. "Like a razor," "dry," and "frozen hard" appeal to the sense of touch. "Crackling" appeals to the sense of hearing. The effect is bleak, depressing, and scary.
- Remind students that good predictions are based on close attention to details in a story. Ask students to identify details in the story that foreshadow this change in the weather.
  Answer: Details include the story's first sentence saying that "the wind changed overnight"; the farmer's prediction on p. 52 that the weather would change and the winter would be hard; the description of the dry east wind from p. 52.
- Ask the Literary Analysis question on p. 55: Overnight, "black winter" has taken hold of the countryside. What might the suddenness of this change foreshadow?
  Answer: Winter often symbolizes death, because it is the time of year when many plants die or "sleep" until spring. The sudden coming of winter suggests that death is coming.

12 ✓ Reading Check

Answer: Nat asks his wife to keep the windows and doors shut while he's out.

13 Critical Thinking

Inferring

- After students read this description of Jill, ask them what they can infer about her silence about the birds.
  Answer: She seems cheerful, so she may have recovered from the attack. However, she may feel the attack was too strange to discuss outside the family.
- What can students infer about Nat from Jim's opinion of him? What can they infer about Jim?
  Answer: Nat is thoughtful and intelligent. He is unlike the people around him. Jim is unimaginative, since he never reads. He may be insecure, since he faults Nat for being "superior."

14 ▶Critical Viewing

Answer: The landscape around the bird is barren. The sky is blue, but the mirror reflects a red sky. Nothing looks the way it should. The mood of the painting is unsettling and strange, comparable to the eerie mood of the story.

"No," he said, "it's not going to snow. This is a black winter, not a white one."

All the while he searched the hedgerows for the birds, glanced over the top of them to the fields beyond, looked to the small wood above the farm where the rooks and jackdaws gathered. He saw none.

The other children waited by the bus stop, muffled, hooded like Jill, the faces white and pinched with cold.

Jill ran to them, waving. "My dad says it won't snow," she called, "it's going to be a black winter."

She said nothing of the birds. She began to push and struggle with another little girl. The bus came ambling up the hill. Nat saw her on to it, then turned and walked back towards the farm. It was not his day for work, but he wanted to satisfy himself that all was well. Jim, the cowman, was
13 clattering in the yard.

"Boss around?" asked Nat.

"Gone to market," said Jim. "It's Tuesday, isn't it?"

He clumped off round the corner of a shed. He had no time for Nat. Nat was said to be superior. Read books, and the like. Nat had forgotten it was Tuesday. This showed how the events of the preceding night had shaken him. He went to the back door of the farmhouse and heard Mrs. Trigg singing in the kitchen, the wireless[3] making a background to her song.

"Are you there, missus?" called out Nat.

She came to the door, beaming, broad, a good-tempered woman.

"Hullo, Mr. Hocken," she said. "Can you tell me where this cold is coming from? Is it Russia? I've never seen such a change. And it's going on, the wireless says. Something to do with the Arctic Circle."

"We didn't turn on the wireless this morning," said Nat. "Fact is, we had trouble in the night."

"Kiddies poorly?"

"No . . ." He hardly knew how to explain it. Now, in daylight, the battle of the birds would sound absurd.

He tried to tell Mrs. Trigg what had happened, but he could see from her eyes that she thought his story was the result of a nightmare.

"Sure they were real birds," she said, smiling, "with proper feathers and all? Not the funny-shaped kind that the men see after closing hours on a Saturday night?"

"Mrs. Trigg," he said, "there are fifty dead birds, robins, wrens, and such, lying low on the floor of the children's bedroom. They went for me; they tried to go for young Johnny's eyes."

14 ▲ **Critical Viewing** Compare and contrast the mood of the painting with the mood of the story so far. **[Compare and Contrast]**

3. **wireless** (wir′ lis) *n.* radio.

Landscape From a Dream, 1936–38, Paul Nash, Tate Gallery, London

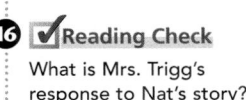

Mrs. Trigg stared at him doubtfully.

"Well there, now," she answered, "I suppose the weather brought them. Once in the bedroom, they wouldn't know where they were to. Foreign birds maybe, from that Arctic Circle."

"No," said Nat, "they were the birds you see about here every day."

"Funny thing," said Mrs. Trigg, "no explaining it, really. You ought to write up and ask the *Guardian.* They'd have some answer for it. Well, I must be getting on."

She nodded, smiled, and went back into the kitchen.

16 **Reading Check**

What is Mrs. Trigg's response to Nat's story?

15 Background

Art

Landscape from a Dream 1936–1938, by Paul Nash

Paul Nash (1889–1946) was an English painter who lived through two world wars. He enlisted in the army in 1914 and was appointed an official war artist. He was reappointed in 1940 when England declared war on Hitler's Germany. Most of Nash's paintings from the mid-1930s are surrealist landscapes.

1. What impression of nature does this painting convey? Is this the same impression the story conveys?
   Answer: The painting suggests that nature is harsh and threatening.
2. Point out some elements that the painting has in common with the story.
   Answer: The painting shows a powerful, threatening bird. The oddness of mirrors on a beach and their strange reflections create a sense of disturbance similar to that of the story.

16 **Reading Check**

Answer: Mrs. Trigg does not take Nat's concerns seriously.

⓱ Background

World History

Germans hoped to bomb the English into surrender with their months-long Blitz, but they never came close to breaking the British spirit. Civilians coped bravely with casualties, lost homes and businesses, blackouts, and bomb shelters. While cities were being pounded, the RAF recovered its full strength. The Blitz ended in failure. See Enrichment below for more details.

⓲ Literary Analysis

Foreshadowing

- Have students read the bracketed passage to themselves. Tell students that, as they read, they should pay attention to the details about the weather.
- Ask students the Literary Analysis question on p. 58: What might the "unnatural" weather foreshadow? **Answer:** The strange weather suggests that something has gone wrong with nature and that other odd events may occur.

Nat, dissatisfied, turned to the farm gate. Had it not been for those corpses on the bedroom floor, which he must now collect and bury somewhere, he would have considered the tale exaggeration too.

Jim was standing by the gate.

"Had any trouble with the birds?" asked Nat.

"Birds? What birds?"

"We got them up our place last night. Scores of them, came in the children's bedroom. Quite savage they were."

"Oh?" It took time for anything to penetrate Jim's head. "Never heard of birds acting savage," he said at length. "They get tame, like, sometimes. I've seen them come to the windows for crumbs."

"These birds last night weren't tame."

"No? Cold, maybe. Hungry. You put out some crumbs."

Jim was no more interested than Mrs. Trigg had been. It was, Nat thought, like air raids in the war.♦ No one down this end of the country knew what the Plymouth folk had seen and suffered. You had to endure something yourself before it touched you. He walked back along the lane and crossed the stile to his cottage. He found his wife in the kitchen with young Johnny.

"See anyone?" she asked.

"Mrs. Trigg and Jim," he answered. "I don't think they believed me. Anyway, nothing wrong up there."

"You might take the birds away," she said. "I daren't go into the room to make the beds until you do. I'm scared."

"Nothing to scare you now," said Nat. "They're dead, aren't they?"

⓲ He went up with a sack and dropped the stiff bodies into it, one by one. Yes, there were fifty of them, all told. Just the ordinary, common birds of the hedgerow, nothing as large even as a thrush. It must have been fright that made them act the way they did. Blue tits, wrens—it was incredible to think of the power of their small beaks jabbing at his face and hands the night before. He took the sack out into the garden and was faced now with a fresh problem. The ground was too hard to dig. It was frozen solid, yet no snow had fallen, nothing had happened in the past hours but the coming of the east wind. It was unnatural, queer. The weather prophets must be right. The change was something connected with the Arctic Circle.

The wind seemed to cut him to the bone as he stood there uncertainly, holding the sack. He could see the white-capped seas breaking down under in the bay. He decided to take the birds to the shore and bury them.

Literature in context ⓱ World History Connection

♦ *Preparing for the Blitz*

As he prepares for the birds' attack, Nat again draws a parallel between this situation and World War II. After striking British Royal Air Force (RAF) bases in August and September of 1940, German forces believed that they had destroyed the RAF. They then began to bomb civilian targets in what was called the *Blitz* (the German word for "lightning"). The Blitz continued until May of 1941, with raids almost every night. Blackout boards and shelters became a familiar part of British life during that difficult time.

A World War II Bomb Shelter

Literary Analysis
Foreshadowing What might the "unnatural" weather foreshadow?

ENRICHMENT: History Connection

The Blitz

German bombs struck Buckingham Palace and destroyed the House of Commons. Entire neighborhoods of London were devastated. Miraculously, St. Paul's Cathedral remained unscathed; it was by far the largest building in its central London neighborhood, and its great dome had formed a tempting target for the German bombers because of its importance as an architectural masterpiece.

German bombers did not confine their attacks to London. They also attacked the town of Coventry, destroying its cathedral; a memorial now stands on the site, and a new cathedral was built after the war.

Many of Germany's cultural treasures were also destroyed by Allied bombs. An attack on the city of Dresden late in the war reduced it to rubble and killed thousands of civilians.

When he reached the beach below the headland he could scarcely stand, the force of the east wind was so strong. It hurt to draw breath, and his bare hands were blue. Never had he known such cold, not in all the bad winters he could remember. It was low tide. He crunched his way over the shingle[4] to the softer sand and then, his back to the wind, ground a pit in the sand with his heel. He meant to drop the birds into it, but as he opened up the sack the force of the wind carried them, lifted them, as though in flight again, and they were blown away from him along the beach, tossed like feathers, spread and scattered, the bodies of the fifty frozen birds. There was something ugly in the sight. He did not like it. The dead birds were swept away from him by the wind.

"The tide will take them when it turns," he said to himself.

He looked out to sea and watched the crested breakers, combing green. They rose stiffly, curled, and broke again, and because it was ebb tide the roar was distant, more remote, lacking the sound and thunder of the flood.

Then he saw them. The gulls. Out there, riding the seas.

What he had thought at first to be the whitecaps of the waves were gulls. Hundreds, thousands, tens of thousands . . . They rose and fell in the trough of the seas, heads to the wind, like a mighty fleet at anchor, waiting on the tide. To eastward, and to the west, the gulls were there. They stretched as far as his eye could reach, in close formation, line upon line. Had the sea been still they would have covered the bay like a white cloud, head to head, body packed to body. Only the east wind, whipping the sea to breakers, hid them from the shore.

19 Nat turned and, leaving the beach, climbed the steep path home. Someone should know of this. Someone should be told. Something was happening, because of the east wind and the weather, that he did not understand. He wondered if he should go to the call box by the bus stop and ring up the police. Yet what could they do? What could anyone do? Tens of thousands of gulls riding the sea there in the bay because of storm, because of hunger. The police would think him mad, or drunk, or take the statement from him with great calm. "Thank you. Yes, the matter has already been reported. The hard weather is driving the birds inland in great numbers." Nat looked about him. Still no sign of any other bird. Perhaps the cold had sent them all from upcountry? As he drew near to the cottage his wife came to meet him at the door. She called to him, excited. "Nat," she said, "it's on the wireless. They've just read out a special news bulletin. I've written it down."

"What's on the wireless?" he said.

"About the birds," she said. "It's not only here, it's everywhere. In London, all over the country. Something has happened to the birds."

Together they went into the kitchen. He read the piece of paper lying on the table.

"Statement from the Home Office at 11 A.M. today. Reports from all over the country are coming in hourly about the vast quantity of birds

Reading Strategy
Predicting Do you think Nat will call the police? Why?

20 **Reading Check**
What does Nat see riding the seas?

4. **shingle** *n.* area of beach covered with waterworn gravel.

19 Reading Strategy

Predicting

- Ask students to consider the relationship between predicting and foreshadowing. How can a writer's use of foreshadowing help readers make predictions as they read?
  Answer: Foreshadowing is a writer's use of clues to hint at future events in a story. These hints can help readers make predictions about what may happen.
- Ask the Reading Strategy question on p. 59: Do you think Nat will call the police? Why?
  Answer: Since Nat expects the police will be skeptical and there is little to be done about the birds in any case, it is unlikely he will call.

20 Reading Check

Answer: He sees thousands of gulls.

21 Literary Analysis

Imagery and Foreshadowing

- Have a volunteer read aloud the bracketed passage to the class.
- Ask the Literary Analysis question on p. 60: Which details found in Nat's description foreshadow unusual events to come?
  Answer: Nat says that the gulls are "waiting." He thinks they may be waiting for the time to attack the house and the Triggs' farm.

22 Critical Thinking

Compare and Contrast

- Explain to students that, once again, Nat compares the country's present situation to the situation in World War II.
- "Blackout boards" and curtains were used in the war to seal windows so no light escaped at night to guide enemy bombers. Strict "blackout rules" prohibited the use of headlights and streetlights during the war. How is Nat's current situation similar to that during the war? How is it different?
  Answer: Alike: People are having to build barricades to protect their homes from air attacks. People rely on the radio for information. Different: The war involved enemy bombers, not birds; people knew why the enemy was attacking, but the birds' attacks seem motiveless; bombs can do more damage more quickly than flocks of birds.
- What do these memories of war suggest about Nat's situation?
  Possible response: These war thoughts hint that Nat is becoming aware that birds are at war with humans and that the results might be catastrophic.

flocking above towns, villages, and outlying districts, causing obstruction and damage and even attacking individuals. It is thought that the Arctic airstream, at present covering the British Isles, is causing birds to migrate south in immense numbers, and that intense hunger may drive these birds to attack human beings. Householders are warned to see to their windows, doors, and chimneys, and to take reasonable precautions for the safety of their children. A further statement will be issued later."

A kind of excitement seized Nat; he looked at his wife in triumph.

21 "There you are," he said. "Let's hope they'll hear that at the farm. Mrs. Trigg will know it wasn't any story. It's true. All over the country. I've been telling myself all morning there's something wrong. And just now, down on the beach, I looked out to sea and there are gulls, thousands of them, tens of thousands—you couldn't put a pin between their heads—and they're all out there, riding on the sea, waiting."

"What are they waiting for, Nat?" she asked.

He stared at her, then looked down again at the piece of paper.

"I don't know," he said slowly. "It says here the birds are hungry."

He went over to the drawer where he kept his hammer and tools.

"What are you going to do, Nat?"

"See to the windows and the chimneys too, like they tell you."

"You think they would break in, with the windows shut? Those sparrows and robins and such? Why, how could they?"

He did not answer. He was not thinking of the robins and the sparrows. He was thinking of the gulls . . .

22 He went upstairs and worked there the rest of the morning, boarding the windows of the bedrooms, filling up the chimney bases. Good job it was his free day and he was not working at the farm. It reminded him of the old days, at the beginning of the war. He was not married then, and he had made all the black-out boards for his mother's house in Plymouth. Made the shelter too. Not that it had been of any use when the moment came. He wondered if they would take these precautions up at the farm. He doubted it. Too easygoing, Harry Trigg and his missus. Maybe they'd laugh at the whole thing. Go off to a dance or a whist drive.[5]

"Dinner's ready." She called him, from the kitchen.

"All right. Coming down."

He was pleased with his handiwork. The frames fitted nicely over the little panes and at the bases of the chimneys.

When dinner was over and his wife was washing up, Nat switched on the one o'clock news. The same announcement was repeated, the one which she had taken down during the morning, but the news bulletin enlarged upon it. "The flocks of birds have caused dislocation in all areas," read the announcer, "and in London the sky was so dense at ten

5. **whist drive** *n.* a card game organized for a group.

Literary Analysis
Imagery and Foreshadowing Which details found in Nat's description foreshadow unusual events to come?

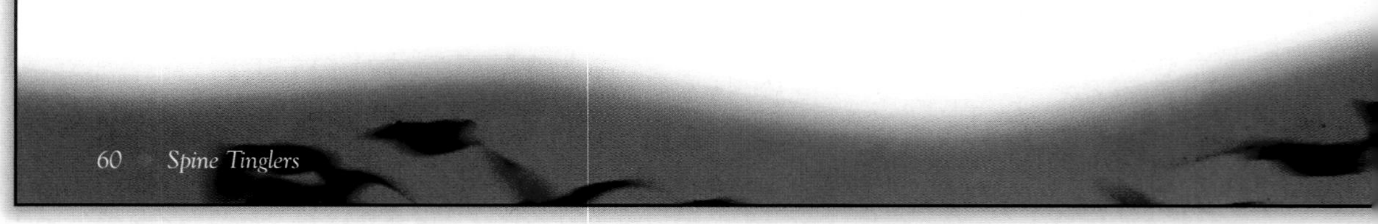

ENRICHMENT: Science Connection

The Wireless

On p. 59, Nat's wife listens to the wireless and takes down an important message. Throughout the story, Nat relies on the wireless as a central source of information—until it ceases to function.

At the time of this story, shortly after World War II, Britain was not highly technological. Private homes did not have television sets, and many people in rural areas, Nat's family included, did not have their own telephones. The Internet was far in the future. People relied on the wireless, or radio, as a source of news, music, and entertainment.

Public radio service began in Britain in 1922. Five years later the British Broadcasting Corporation was organized. The BBC was the only radio broadcaster in Britain until 1973.

o'clock this morning that it seemed as if the city was covered by a vast black cloud.

23 "The birds settled on rooftops, on window ledges, and on chimneys. The species included blackbird, thrush, the common house sparrow, and, as might be expected in the metropolis, a vast quantity of pigeons and starlings, and that frequenter of the London river, the black-headed gull. The sight has been so unusual that traffic came to a standstill in many thoroughfares, work was abandoned in shops and offices, and the streets and pavements were crowded with people standing about to watch the birds."

Various incidents were recounted, the suspected reason of cold and hunger stated again, and warnings to householders repeated. The announcer's voice was smooth and suave. Nat had the impression that this man, in particular, treated the whole business as he would an elaborate joke. There would be others like him, hundreds of them, who did not know what it was to struggle in darkness with a flock of birds. There would be parties tonight in London, like the ones they gave on election nights. People standing about, shouting and laughing . . . "Come and watch the birds!"

Nat switched off the wireless. He got up and started work on the kitchen windows. His wife watched him, young Johnny at her heels.

"What, boards for down here too?" she said. "Why, I'll have to light up before three o'clock. I see no call for boards down here."

"Better be sure than sorry," answered Nat. "I'm not going to take any chances."

"What they ought to do," she said, "is to call the Army out and shoot the birds. That would soon scare them off."

"Let them try," said Nat. "How'd they set about it?"

"They have the Army to the docks," she answered, "when the dockers strike. The soldiers go down and unload the ships."

"Yes," said Nat, "and the population of London is eight million or more. Think of all the buildings, all the flats and houses. Do you think they've enough soldiers to go around shooting birds from every roof?"

"I don't know. But something should be done. They ought to do something."

Nat thought to himself that "they" were no doubt considering the problem at that very moment, but whatever "they" decided to do in London and the big cities would not help the people here, three hundred miles away. Each householder must look after his own.

"How are we off for food?" he said.

"Now, Nat, whatever next?"

"Never mind. What have you got in the larder?"[6]

"It's shopping day tomorrow, you know that. I don't keep uncooked

6. larder (lärd´ ər) *n.* place where food is kept; pantry.

Reading Strategy
Predicting Based on the reaction to the birds, predict what you think might happen.

recounted (ri kount´ ed) *v.* told in detail; narrated

24 **Reading Check**
What steps does Nat take to protect his family and his home?

23 Reading Strategy

Predicting

- Read aloud the bracketed passage to students. Have students pay careful attention to people's reactions to the birds.
- Ask the Reading Strategy question on p. 61: Based on the reaction to the birds, predict what you think might happen.
  Answer: These people don't seem to be alarmed; they are only surprised and interested to see so many birds. This means they will be vulnerable if an attack comes.

24 Reading Check

Answer: Nat nails boards over all the windows and fills up the chimney bases so that the birds can't get in.

25 Literary Analysis

Foreshadowing

- Ask students the Literary Analysis question on p. 62: What might the circling gulls foreshadow?
Answer: They seem to be preparing for an attack.
- Ask students whether any details earlier in the story foreshadowed the events described in this paragraph. If so, what are they?
Answer: No specific detail suggested that the gulls would move with the turn of the tide. However, the story suggests that everything in nature is collaborating against man. The wind brings the change in the weather and seems to direct the birds' movements. The tide is also a force of nature, and it is not surprising that it should trigger the attack on man.

food hanging about, it goes off. Butcher doesn't call till the day after. But I can bring back something when I go in tomorrow."

Nat did not want to scare her. He thought it possible that she might not go to town tomorrow. He looked in the larder for himself, and in the cupboard where she kept her tins. They would do for a couple of days. Bread was low.

"What about the baker?"

"He comes tomorrow too."

He saw she had flour. If the baker did not call she had enough to bake one loaf.

"We'd be better off in the old days," he said, "when the women baked twice a week, and had pilchards[7] salted, and there was food for a family to last a siege, if need be."

"I've tried the children with tinned fish, they don't like it," she said.

Nat went on hammering the boards across the kitchen windows. Candles. They were low in candles too. That must be another thing she meant to buy tomorrow. Well, it could not be helped. They must go early to bed tonight. That was, if . . .

He got up and went out of the back door and stood in the garden, looking down toward the sea. There had been no sun all day, and now, at barely three o'clock, a kind of darkness had already come, the sky sullen, heavy, colorless like salt. He could hear the vicious sea drumming on the rocks. He walked down the path, halfway to the beach. And then he stopped. He could see the tide had turned. The rock that had shown in midmorning was now covered, but it was not the sea that held his eyes. The gulls had risen. They were circling, hundreds of them, thousands of them, lifting their wings against the wind. It was the gulls

25 that made the darkening of the sky. And they were silent. They made not a sound. They just went on soaring and circling, rising, falling, trying their strength against the wind.

Nat turned. He ran up the path, back to the cottage.

"I'm going for Jill," he said. "I'll wait for her at the bus stop."

"What's the matter?" asked his wife. "You've gone quite white."

"Keep Johnny inside," he said. "Keep the door shut. Light up now, and draw the curtains."

"It's only just gone three," she said.

"Never mind. Do what I tell you."

He looked inside the tool shed outside the back door. Nothing there of much use. A spade was too heavy, and a fork no good. He took the hoe. It was the only possible tool, and light enough to carry.

He started walking up the lane to the bus stop, and now and again glanced back over his shoulder.

The gulls had risen higher now, their circles were broader, wider, they were spreading out in huge formation across the sky.

He hurried on; although he knew the bus would not come to the top of the hill before four o'clock he had to hurry. He passed no one on the

sullen (sul′ ən) *adj.* gloomy

Literary Analysis
Foreshadowing What might the circling gulls foreshadow?

7. **pilchards** (pil′ chərdz) *n.* small fish similar to sardines.

way. He was glad of this. No time to stop and chatter.

At the top of the hill he waited. He was much too soon. There was half an hour still to go. The east wind came whipping across the fields from the higher ground. He stamped his feet and blew upon his hands. In the distance he could see the clay hills, white and clean, against the heavy pallor of the sky. Something black rose from behind them, like a smudge at first, then widening, becoming deeper, and the smudge became a cloud, and the cloud divided again into five other clouds, spreading north, east, south, and west, and they were not clouds at all; (26) they were birds. He watched them travel across the sky, and as one section passed overhead, within two or three hundred feet of him, he knew, from their speed, they were bound inland, upcountry; they had no business with the people here on the peninsula. They were rooks, crows, jackdaws, magpies, jays, all birds that usually preyed upon the smaller species; but this afternoon they were bound on some other mission.

"They've been given the towns," thought Nat; "they know what they have to do. We don't matter so much here. The gulls will serve for us. The others go to the towns."

He went to the call box, stepped inside, and lifted the receiver. The exchange would do. They would pass the message on.

"I'm speaking from Highway," he said, "by the bus stop. I want to report large formations of birds traveling upcountry. The gulls are also forming in the bay."

"All right," answered the voice, laconic, weary.

"You'll be sure and pass this message on to the proper quarter?"

"Yes . . . yes . . ." Impatient now, fed-up. The buzzing note resumed.

"She's another," thought Nat, "she doesn't care. Maybe she's had to answer calls all day. She hopes to go to the pictures tonight. She'll squeeze some fellow's hand and point up at the sky and say 'Look at all them birds!' She doesn't care."

The bus came lumbering up the hill. Jill climbed out, and three or four other children. The bus went on towards the town.

"What's the hoe for, Dad?"

They crowded around him, laughing, pointing.

"I just brought it along," he said. "Come on now, let's get home. It's cold, no hanging about. Here, you. I'll watch you across the fields, see how fast you can run."

He was speaking to Jill's companions, who came from different families, living in the council houses.[8] A short cut would take them to the cottages.

"We want to play a bit in the lane," said one of them.

"No, you don't. You go off home or I'll tell your Mammy."

They whispered to one another, round-eyed, then scuttled off across the fields. Jill stared at her father, her mouth sullen.

"We always play in the lane," she said.

"Not tonight, you don't," he said. "Come on now, no dawdling."

8. **council houses** *n.* housing units built by the government.

Reading Strategy

Predicting What might happen if these details about the birds were multiplied many times?

(27) **Reading Check**

What important message is Nat trying to report when he goes to the call box?

(26) Reading Strategy

Predicting

- Ask the Reading Strategy question on p. 63: What might happen if these details about the birds were multiplied many times?
  Answer: A multiplication of these events would suggest that the bird attacks were global. Tell students to watch for other clues in the story suggesting the attacks are occurring elsewhere in the world.
- Have students predict where these birds are going. Have them explain their predictions.
  Answer: The birds are probably in search of more human prey; there are far more of them than are needed to attack the few people in the area.

(27) Reading Check

Answer: Nat is trying to report his sighting of large flocks of birds flying inland toward the urban areas.

CUSTOMIZE INSTRUCTION FOR UNIVERSAL ACCESS

For English Learners

This story provides a good opportunity for students to learn the names of many species of birds, such as those listed in the first full paragraph above. Have students note down all the bird names they find as they go through the story. Their lists may include jackdaw, gull, starling, finch, lark, oyster catcher, redshank, sanderling, curlew, robin, sparrow, brambling, thrush, blackbird, wren, pigeon, rook, crow, magpie, jay, gannet, woodpecker, hawk, buzzard, kestral, and falcon. They can look them up in nature guides or encyclopedias that will show the birds' pictures as well as giving indications of their size, habitat, and diet. Students can work together on a poster or bulletin board showing drawings or photocopies of the various birds, with their names and a few facts about them written under each bird's picture.

28 Reading Strategy

Predicting

- Ask students the Reading Strategy question on p. 64: What do you predict will happen if Nat and Jill do not move along more quickly?
  Answer: The gulls may attack them.

29 Vocabulary Development

Anglo-Saxon Suffix *-ful*

- Point out the word *cheerful* in this paragraph. Have students define it and explain how they know what it means.
  Answer: It means "full of cheer" because *-ful* means "full of."
- Have students add *-ful* to the words *hope, fear,* and *dread.* Then, ask them to use these words to describe events on this page.
  Possible responses: Nat was hopeful Jill would get home safely. Trigg was not at all fearful about a bird attack. The huge flocks of birds create a dreadful pattern in the sky.

He could see the gulls now, circling the fields, coming in toward the land. Still silent. Still no sound.

"Look, Dad, look over there, look at all the gulls."

"Yes. Hurry, now."

"Where are they flying to? Where are they going?"

"Upcountry, I dare say. Where it's warmer."

He seized her hand and dragged her after him along the lane.

"Don't go so fast. I can't keep up."

The gulls were copying the rooks and crows. They were spreading out in formation across the sky. They headed, in bands of thousands, to the four compass points.

"Dad, what is it? What are the gulls doing?"

They were not intent upon their flight, as the crows, as the jackdaws had been. They still circled overhead. Nor did they fly so high. It was as though they waited upon some signal. As though some decision had yet to be given. The order was not clear.

"Do you want me to carry you, Jill? Here, come pick-a-back."

28 This way he might put on speed; but he was wrong. Jill was heavy. She kept slipping. And was crying too. His sense of urgency, of fear, had communicated itself to the child.

"I wish the gulls would go away. I don't like them. They're coming closer to the lane."

He put her down again. He started running, swinging Jill after him. As they went past the farm turning he saw the farmer backing his car out of the garage. Nat called to him.

"Can you give us a lift?" he said.

"What's that?"

29 Mr. Trigg turned in the driving seat and stared at them. Then a smile came to his cheerful, rubicund face.

"It looks as though we're in for some fun," he said. "Have you seen the gulls? Jim and I are going to take a crack at them. Everyone's gone bird-crazy, talking of nothing else. I hear you were troubled in the night. Want a gun?"

Nat shook his head.

The small car was packed. There was just room for Jill, if she crouched on top of petrol tins on the back seat.

"I don't want a gun," said Nat, "but I'd be obliged if you'd run Jill home. She's scared of the birds."

He spoke briefly. He did not want to talk in front of Jill.

"O.K.," said the farmer, "I'll take her home. Why don't you stop behind and join the shooting match? We'll make the feathers fly."

Jill climbed in, and turning the car, the driver sped up the lane. Nat followed after. Trigg must be crazy. What use was a gun against a sky of birds?

Now Nat was not responsible for Jill, he had time to look about him. The birds were circling still above the fields. Mostly herring gull, but the black-backed gull amongst them. Usually they kept apart. Now they were united. Some bond had brought them together. It was the black-

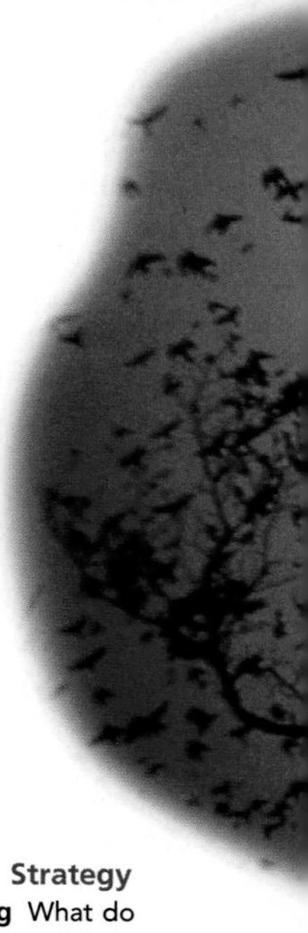

Reading Strategy
Predicting What do you predict will happen if Nat and Jill do not move along more quickly?

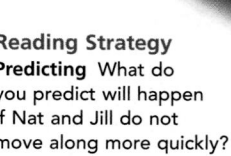

31 backed gull that attacked the smaller birds, and even newborn lambs, so he'd heard. He'd never seen it done. He remembered this now, though, looking above him in the sky. They were coming in towards the farm. They were circling lower in the sky, and the black-backed gulls were to the front, the black-backed gulls were leading. The farm, then, was their target. They were making for the farm.

Nat increased his pace toward his own cottage. He saw the farmer's car turn and come back along the lane. It drew up beside him with a jerk.

"The kid has run inside," said the farmer. "Your wife was watching for her. Well, what do you make of it? They're saying in town the Russians have done it. The Russians have poisoned the birds."

"How could they do that?" asked Nat.

"Don't ask me. You know how stories get around. Will you join my shooting match?"

"No, I'll get along home. The wife will be worried else."

30 ▲ **Critical Viewing**
What do the scraggly tree and the scores of birds in the photograph convey about the setting of this story? **[Infer]**

32 ✔ **Reading Check**
Why does Nat ask Mr. Trigg to take Jill home?

30 ▶ **Critical Viewing**

Answer: The picture shows a bleak, hostile setting overrun with birds as the darkness falls.

31 Literary Analysis

Foreshadowing

- Point out that the black-backed gulls are joining forces with smaller birds on which they would usually prey. Ask students where DuMaurier foreshadowed this ominous detail.
  Answer: On the first page of the story, Nat noticed the "strange partnership" of jackdaws and gulls. When Nat repulsed the attack on the children's bedroom, he noticed that different species of birds, which would not normally mix with one another, had collaborated on the attack.
- Ask students what effect the repetition of this detail has on the story.
  Possible response: It makes the story even more eerie, because the birds are acting against their natures. It makes the family's situation seem even more dangerous.

32 ✔ **Reading Check**

Answer: Jill will be safer at home than she is out in the open, and Nat wants to stay outdoors to check on the birds.

CUSTOMIZE INSTRUCTION FOR UNIVERSAL ACCESS

For Less Proficient Readers	For Advanced Readers
Have students create graphic organizers on which to outline the story's basic plot, main characters, setting, and major themes. Have partners compare organizers to see whether they agree on the main points. If they disagree, have them go back to the story to resolve the difference of opinion. Ask students which of these four elements is most important to the story's overall effect, and have them explain why they think so.	As students read the central section of the story, have them pay special attention to the characters. Point out that they are all ordinary people leading ordinary lives, going about their business of work, school, and play, when the bizarre events of the story disrupt their comfortable routines. Have students compare and contrast the ordinariness of the characters with the extraordinary situation in which they find themselves.

33 Reading Strategy

Predicting

- Ask students to describe Trigg in one word.
  Possible answers: *careless, smug, overconfident, complacent, foolish*
- Ask students the Reading Strategy question on p. 66: Based on this conversation, what do you think will happen to the farmer?
  Answer: Since he doesn't believe the stories about the attacks, Trigg won't board up his house as Nat did, or prepare in any way. The birds will get him and possibly his wife.

34 Literary Analysis

Foreshadowing

- Pause after students have read this paragraph and lead a discussion on DuMaurier's use of foreshadowing throughout the story. Point out that as early as p. 52, she introduced the idea of birds attacking human beings with the image of the man on the tractor "lost momentarily in a great cloud of birds." Have students identify details that foreshadowed this direct attack on Nat. Ask how the story would have been different if the attack had not been foreshadowed, but had simply happened out of the blue.
  Possible answer: By skillful foreshadowing, DuMaurier helps the reader accept the fantastic event of a bird attack.
- Ask the Literary Analysis question on p. 66: What future events might the words *with each attack, they become bolder* foreshadow?
  Answer: These words suggest that the attacks will continue and become more devastating.

"My missus says if you could eat gull there'd be some sense in it," said Trigg. "We'd have roast gull, baked gull, and pickle 'em into the bargain. You wait until I let off a few barrels into the brutes. That'll scare 'em."

"Have you boarded your windows?" asked Nat.

"No. Lot of nonsense. They like to scare you on the wireless. I've had more to do today than to go round boarding up my windows."

33 "I'd board them now, if I were you."

"Garn. You're windy. Like to come to our place to sleep?"

"No, thanks all the same."

"All right. See you in the morning. Give you a gull breakfast."

The farmer grinned and turned his car to the farm entrance.

Nat hurried on. Past the little wood, past the old barn, and then across the stile to the remaining field.

As he jumped the stile he heard the whir of wings. A black-backed gull dived down at him from the sky, missed, swerved in flight, and rose to dive again. In a moment it was joined by others, six, seven, a dozen, black-backed and herring mixed. Nat dropped his hoe. The hoe was useless. Covering his head with his arms, he ran toward the cottage. They kept coming at him from the air, silent save for the beating wings. The terrible, fluttering wings. He could feel the blood on his
34 hands, his wrists, his neck. Each stab of a swooping beak tore his flesh. If only he could keep them from his eyes. Nothing else mattered. He must keep them from his eyes. They had not learned yet how to cling to a shoulder, how to rip clothing, how to dive in mass upon the head, upon the body. But with each dive, with each attack, they became bolder. And they had no thought for themselves. When they dived low and missed, they crashed, bruised and broken, on the ground. As Nat ran he stumbled, kicking their spent bodies in front of him.

He found the door; he hammered upon it with his bleeding hands. Because of the boarded windows no light shone. Everything was dark.

"Let me in," he shouted, "it's Nat. Let me in."

He shouted loud to make himself heard above the whir of the gulls' wings.

Then he saw the gannet, poised for the dive, above him in the sky. The gulls circled, retired, soared, one after another, against the wind. Only the gannet remained. One single gannet above him in the sky. The wings folded suddenly to its body. It dropped like a stone. Nat screamed, and the door opened. He stumbled across the threshold, and his wife threw her weight against the door.

They heard the thud of the gannet as it fell.

His wife dressed his wounds. They were not deep. The backs of his hands had suffered most, and his wrists. Had he not worn a cap they would have reached his head. As to the gannet . . . the gannet could have split his skull.

The children were crying, of course. They had seen the blood on their father's hands.

"It's all right now," he told them. "I'm not hurt. Just a few scratches.

Reading Strategy
Predicting Based on this conversation, what do you think will happen to the farmer? Explain your prediction.

Literary Analysis
Foreshadowing What future events might the words *with each attack, they became bolder* foreshadow?

You play with Johnny, Jill. Mammy will wash these cuts."

He half shut the door to the scullery so that they could not see. His wife was ashen. She began running water from the sink.

"I saw them overhead," she whispered. "They began collecting just as Jill ran in with Mr. Trigg. I shut the door fast, and it jammed. That's why I couldn't open it at once when you came."

"Thank God they waited for me," he said. "Jill would have fallen at once. One bird alone would have done it."

Furtively, so as not to alarm the children, they whispered together as she bandaged his hands and the back of his neck.

furtively (fur´ tiv lē) *adv.* stealthily, so as to avoid being heard

"They're flying inland," he said, "thousands of them. Rooks, crows, all the bigger birds. I saw them from the bus stop. They're making for the towns."

"But what can they do, Nat?"

"They'll attack. Go for everyone out in the streets. Then they'll try the windows, the chimneys."

"Why don't the authorities do something? Why don't they get the Army, get machine guns, anything?"

"There's been no time. Nobody's prepared. We'll hear what they have to say on the six o'clock news."

Nat went back into the kitchen, followed by his wife. Johnny was playing quietly on the floor. Only Jill looked anxious.

"I can hear the birds," she said. "Listen, Dad."

Nat listened. Muffled sounds came from the windows, from the door. Wings brushing the surface, sliding, scraping, seeking a way of entry. The sound of many bodies, pressed together, shuffling on the sills. Now and again came a thud, a crash, as some bird dived and fell. "Some of them will kill themselves that way," he thought, "but not enough. Never enough."

"All right," he said aloud. "I've got boards over the windows, Jill. The birds can't get in."

35 He went and examined all the windows. His work had been thorough. Every gap was closed. He would make extra certain, however. He found wedges, pieces of old tin, strips of wood and metal, and fastened them at the sides to reinforce the boards. His hammering helped to deafen the sound of the birds, the shuffling, the tapping, and more ominous—he did not want his wife or the children to hear it—the splinter of cracked glass.

Literary Analysis
Foreshadowing Think about what Nat has done to get his house ready for this attack. What might the cracked glass foreshadow, and why?

"Turn on the wireless," he said, "let's have the wireless."

This would drown the sound also. He went upstairs to the bedrooms and reinforced the windows there. Now he could hear the birds on the roof, the scraping of claws, a sliding, jostling sound.

He decided they must sleep in the kitchen, keep up the fire, bring down the mattresses, and lay them out on the floor. He was afraid of the bedroom chimneys. The boards he had placed at the chimney bases might give way. In the kitchen they would be safe because of the fire. He would have to make a joke of it. Pretend to the children they were playing at camp. If the worst happened, and the birds forced an entry down

36 ✓ **Reading Check**
What steps does Nat take to prepare his house against the birds?

35 Literary Analysis
Foreshadowing

- Have a volunteer read this paragraph aloud while students listen. Ask which details in the story foreshadowed Nat's preparations and the damage done to the glass.
  Answer: The comparisons to the World War II bomb shelters foreshadowed the importance of establishing a safe area. The warnings on the radio suggested boarding up windows and building up defenses. The statement that the birds grew bolder with every attack shows that they won't be contented with just tapping on the glass as they were the previous night; they are trying to break in.
- Ask the Literary Analysis question on p. 67: What might the cracked glass foreshadow, and why?
  Answer: The cracked glass shows that the house isn't strong or solid enough to keep the birds out. It also suggests that the birds might be able to crack through the boards with their strong beaks.

36 ✓ Reading Check

Answer: Nat reinforces the boards over the windows with strips of tin, wood, and other metals.

CUSTOMIZE INSTRUCTION FOR UNIVERSAL ACCESS
For Gifted/Talented Students

Nat's wife wonders why the authorities don't do something to stop the birds. On p. 71, Nat imagines scientists and naturalists finding a solution to the situation. Challenge students to come up with a way for the country to win the conflict with the birds. As students will read on p. 69, the birds are attacking all over the country and a national emergency is declared; this means there are no limits to the money or resources students can call on to stop the attacks. Have students discuss their ideas in a group. In what ways are the birds vulnerable? What advantages do human beings possess in a struggle against birds? What advantages do the birds have, and how might human beings compensate for those advantages?

37 Literary Analysis

Foreshadowing

- Ask students which details in the story foreshadowed this unusual change in the wireless programming.
  Answer: When Nat and his wife listened to the wireless earlier, they heard stories of huge flocks of birds flying to the towns and cities and roosting there while people stared at them. Details of attacks on Nat's house suggest that the birds in the cities also attacked.
- What might the change in programming foreshadow?
  Answer: It might foreshadow that devastating attacks have been made on London, where the broadcast originates. Nat says that a change in programming usually means a national crisis or special circumstance.

38 ▶Critical Viewing

Answer: Students may find the dark sky and the huge birds menacing. The darkness in the sky suggests that a storm is coming.

the bedroom chimneys, it would be hours, days perhaps, before they could break down the doors. The birds would be imprisoned in the bedrooms. They could do no harm there. Crowded together, they would stifle and die.

He began to bring the mattresses downstairs. At sight of them his wife's eyes widened in apprehension. She thought the birds had already broken in upstairs.

"All right," he said cheerfully, "we'll all sleep together in the kitchen tonight. More cozy here by the fire. Then we shan't be worried by those silly old birds tapping at the windows."

He made the children help him rearrange the furniture, and he took the precaution of moving the dresser, with his wife's help, across the window. It fitted well. It was an added safeguard. The mattresses could now be laid, one beside the other, against the wall where the dresser had stood.

"We're safe enough now," he thought. "We're snug and tight, like an air-raid shelter. We can hold out. It's just the food that worries me. Food, and coal for the fire. We've enough for two or three days, not more. By that time . . ."

37 No use thinking ahead as far as that. And they'd be giving directions on the wireless. People would be told what to do. And now, in the midst of many problems, he realized that it was dance music only coming over the air. Not Children's Hour, as it should have been. He glanced at the dial. Yes, they were on the Home Service all right. Dance records. He switched to the Light program. He knew the reason. The usual programs had been abandoned. This only happened at exceptional times. Elections and such. He tried to remember if it had happened in the war, during the heavy raids on London. But of course. The B.B.C.[9] was not stationed in London during the war. The programs were broadcast from other, temporary quarters. "We're better off here," he thought; "we're better off here in the kitchen, with the windows and the doors boarded, than they are up in the towns. Thank God we're not in the towns."

At six o'clock the records ceased. The time signal was given. No matter if it scared the children, he must hear the news. There was a pause after the pips.[10] Then the announcer spoke. His voice was solemn, grave. Quite different from midday.

"This is London," he said. "A National Emergency was proclaimed at four o'clock this afternoon. Measures are being taken to safeguard the lives and property of the population, but it must be understood that these are not easy to effect immediately, owing to the unforeseen and unparalleled nature of the present crisis. Every householder must take

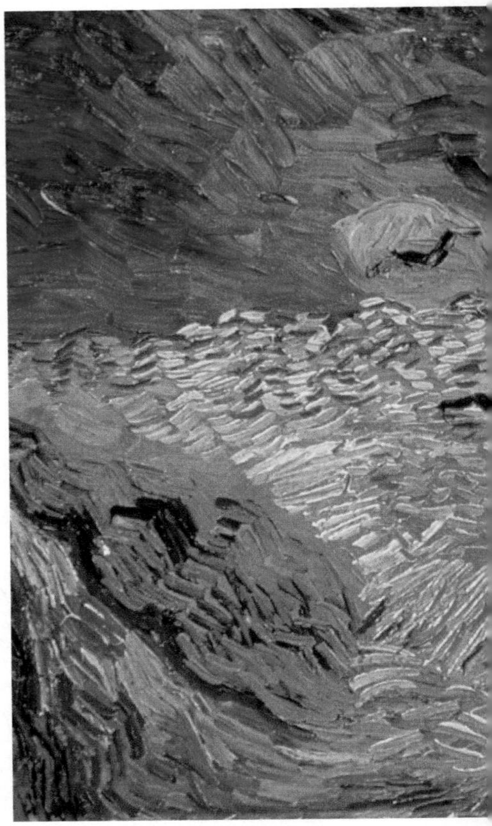

38 ▲ **Critical Viewing** What feelings conveyed through this painting might be similar to those conveyed through the story? **[Describe]**

9. B.B.C. British Broadcasting Corporation.
10. pips *n.* beeping sounds that indicate the time.

CUSTOMIZE INSTRUCTION FOR UNIVERSAL ACCESS

For Advanced Readers

Point out that the birds are attacking all over England. Ask students why they think DuMaurier chose to set her story on the shores of the Channel in an isolated area, rather than in a big city like London or Manchester. Have students consider what changes the story would undergo if the setting were changed. Would the characters be different types of people? Would there be more characters? After students have read the description of the family's night barricaded in the kitchen on pp. 71–75, ask how people under attack in a city or town would have spent the night under the same circumstances. After some discussion, students can agree on a new setting and write an outline describing the major changes this new setting would involve, and why these changes are required.

Wheatfield With Crows, Vincent van Gogh, Van Gogh Museum, Amsterdam, The Netherlands

precautions to his own building, and where several people live together, as in flats and apartments, they must unite to do the utmost they can to prevent entry. It is absolutely imperative that every individual stay indoors tonight and that no one at all remain on the streets, or roads, or anywhere withoutdoors.[11] The birds, in vast numbers, are attacking anyone on sight, and have already begun an assault upon buildings; but these, with due care, should be impenetrable. The population is asked to remain calm and not to panic. Owing to the exceptional nature of the emergency, there will be no further transmission from any broadcasting station until 7 A.M. tomorrow."

They played the National Anthem. Nothing more happened. Nat switched off the set. He looked at his wife. She stared back at him.

"What's it mean?" said Jill. "What did the news say?"

"There won't be any more programs tonight," said Nat. "There's been a breakdown at the B.B.C."

imperative (im per´ ə tiv) *adj.* urgent; absolutely necessary

40 **Reading Check**

What important news is revealed through the broadcast?

---

11. withoutdoors *adv.* old-fashioned variation of "outdoors."

39 Background

Art

Wheatfield With Crows, Vincent van Gogh

Vincent van Gogh (1853–1890) was born in Holland and spent most of his brief career in France.

Van Gogh painted landscapes and portraits. His style was so new and unique that collectors and other painters did not know what to think of it; Van Gogh sold only one painting in his lifetime. However, his brilliant colors and the energy and passion of his brush strokes have since won him the admiration and adulation of millions of art lovers and critics.

1. Sum up the mood of this painting in one word. Which details create this mood?
   Possible answers: Students may use words such as *threatening, violent, harsh, dramatic.* The brush strokes convey a sense of movement to the field and sky as well as the flock of crows. The sky looks as if a storm is about to break.
2. How might Nat respond to this scene?
   Possible answer: Attuned to weather and the behavior of birds, Nat might find this scene threatening.

40 Reading Check

Answer: The birds are attacking people and towns all over England.

41 Literary Analysis

Imagery and Foreshadowing

- Have students identify all the words that relate to sound in this passage.
  Answer: *shuffling, beating, sweeping, whistling, singing, clatter, tapping, jostling, droning*
- What does DuMaurier accomplish with this use of sensory language?
  Answer: DuMaurier uses words as if they were sound effects. She enables the reader to hear the noises made by the birds and by Nat.
- Ask students the Literary Analysis question on p. 70: What might this quiet moment foreshadow?
  Answer: It might symbolize the calm before a storm. It suggests that the birds are regrouping for another attack.

42 Reading Strategy

Predicting

- Ask students the Reading Strategy question on p. 70. Point out that Nat's wife and Jill predict that the planes will kill the birds and rescue them. Do students agree? Does Nat agree?
  Answer: Jill and her mother may be wrong. If birds fly into the propellers, the planes could be knocked out of the sky.
- Do you think it's possible for birds to destroy planes?
  Answer: Students may cite actual examples of planes—even large airliners—being brought down by collisions with flocks of birds.

"Is it the birds?" asked Jill. "Have the birds done it?"

"No," said Nat, "it's just that everyone's very busy, and then of course they have to get rid of the birds, messing everything up, in the towns. Well, we can manage without the wireless for one evening."

"I wish we had a gramophone,"[12] said Jill, "that would be better than nothing."

She had her face turned to the dresser backed against the windows. Try as they did to ignore it, they were all aware of the shuffling, the stabbing, the persistent beating and sweeping of wings.

"We'll have supper early," suggested Nat, "something for a treat. Ask Mammy. Toasted cheese, eh? Something we all like?"

He winked and nodded at his wife. He wanted the look of dread, of apprehension, to go from Jill's face.

41 He helped with the supper, whistling, singing, making as much clatter as he could, and it seemed to him that the shuffling and the tapping were not so intense as they had been at first. Presently he went up to the bedrooms and listened, and he no longer heard the jostling for place upon the roof.

"They've got reasoning powers," he thought; "they know it's hard to break in here. They'll try elsewhere. They won't waste their time with us."

Supper passed without incident, and then, when they were clearing away, they heard a new sound, droning, familiar, a sound they all knew and understood.

Literary Analysis
Foreshadowing What might this quiet moment foreshadow?

42 His wife looked up at him, her face alight. "It's planes," she said; "they're sending out planes after the birds. That's what I said they ought to do all along. That will get them. Isn't that gunfire? Can't you hear guns?"

Reading Strategy
Predicting What do you predict will happen to the planes?

It might be gunfire out at sea. Nat could not tell. Big naval guns might have an effect upon the gulls out at sea, but the gulls were inland now. The guns couldn't shell the shore because of the population.

"It's good, isn't it," said his wife, "to hear the planes?" And Jill, catching her enthusiasm, jumped up and down with Johnny. "The planes will get the birds. The planes will shoot them."

Just then they heard a crash about two miles distant, followed by a second, then a third. The droning became more distant, passed away out to sea.

"What was that?" asked his wife. "Were they dropping bombs on the birds?"

"I don't know," answered Nat. "I don't think so."

He did not want to tell her that the sound they had heard was the crashing of aircraft. It was, he had no doubt, a venture on the part of the authorities to send out reconnaissance forces, but they might have known the venture was suicidal. What could aircraft do against birds that flung themselves to death against propeller and fuselage, but hurtle to the ground themselves? This was being tried now, he supposed, over

reconnaissance (ri kän´ ə səns) *adj.* exploratory in nature, as when observing to seek information

12. **gramophone** (gram´ ə fōn´) *n.* phonograph; record player.

the whole country. And at a cost. Someone high up had lost his head.

"Where have the planes gone, Dad?" asked Jill.

"Back to base," he said. "Come on, now, time to tuck down for bed."

It kept his wife occupied, undressing the children before the fire, seeing to the bedding, one thing and another, while he went round the cottage again, making sure that nothing had worked loose. There was no further drone of aircraft, and the naval guns had ceased. "Waste of life and effort," Nat said to himself. "We can't destroy enough of them that way. Cost too heavy. There's always gas. Maybe they'll try spraying with gas, mustard gas. We'll be warned first, of course, if they do. There's one thing, the best brains of the country will be on to it tonight."

43 Somehow the thought reassured him. He had a picture of scientists, naturalists, technicians, and all those chaps they called the back-room boys, summoned to a council; they'd be working on the problem now. This was not a job for the government, for the chiefs of staff—they would merely carry out the orders of the scientists.

"They'll have to be ruthless," he thought. "Where the trouble's worst they'll have to risk more lives, if they use gas. All the livestock, too, and the soil—all contaminated. As long as everyone doesn't panic. That's the trouble. People panicking, losing their heads. The B.B.C. was right to warn us of that."

Upstairs in the bedrooms all was quiet. No further scraping and stabbing at the windows. A lull in battle. Forces regrouping. Wasn't that what they called it in the old wartime bulletins? The wind hadn't dropped, though. He could still hear it roaring in the chimneys. And the sea breaking down on the shore. Then he remembered the tide. The tide would be on the turn. Maybe the lull in battle was because of the tide. There was some law the birds obeyed, and it was all to do with the east wind and the tide.

He glanced at his watch. Nearly eight o'clock. It must have gone high water an hour ago. That explained the lull: the birds attacked with the flood tide. It might not work that way inland, upcountry, but it seemed as if it was so this way on the coast. He reckoned the time limit in his head. They had six hours to go without attack. When the tide turned again, around one-twenty in the morning, the birds would come back . . .

There were two things he could do. The first to rest, with his wife and the children, and all of them snatch what sleep they could, until the small hours. The second to go out, see how they were faring at the farm, see if the telephone was still working there, so that they might get news from the exchange.

He called softly to his wife, who had just settled the children. She came halfway up the stairs and he whispered to her.

"You're not to go," she said at once, "you're not to go and leave me alone with the children. I can't stand it."

Her voice rose hysterically. He hushed her, calmed her.

"All right," he said, "all right. I'll wait till morning. And we'll get the wireless bulletin then too, at seven. But in the morning, when the tide

Literary Analysis
Foreshadowing and Imagery In what ways does this image of experts gathering add to the tension of the story?

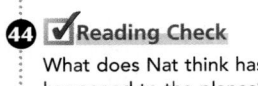

44 **Reading Check**
What does Nat think has happened to the planes?

43 Literary Analysis
Foreshadowing and Imagery

- Ask students the Literary Analysis question on p. 71: In what ways does this image of experts gathering add to the tension of the story?
  Answer: If so many experts are gathering, the situation is clearly very serious all over the country. The thought of experts gathering also lends a note of hope to the story; it makes the reader want to see if the experts solve the situation.
- Then, ask students which earlier details foreshadowed Nat's theory that the birds obey the forces of the tides and the east wind.
  Answer: Throughout the story, there have been references to the wind bringing a change in the weather and affecting the behavior of the birds. On p. 62, Nat observes that the birds have begun moving as the tide turns.

44 Reading Check
Answer: Nat believes that the planes all crashed due to collisions with masses of birds.

CUSTOMIZE INSTRUCTION FOR UNIVERSAL ACCESS
For Less Proficient Readers

Have students gather for a screening of Alfred Hitchcock's film version of *The Birds* (1963). Share the Background information on p. 48 with students before they see the film. After the film, students can have a group discussion of it. What were the major differences between story and film? Was the film more or less horrifying than the story? How and why? What effect did the change in time and place have? Why do students think Hitchcock decided to change the setting? Did his changes to the characters and the story make it more or less gripping and fascinating? What importance did the presence of the caged lovebirds have? Have students explain their answers.

45 Critical Thinking

Speculate

- Point out that Nat thinks the cows will be waiting in the yard—outdoors. Evidently, Nat thinks it will be safe for the cows to stay in the open; they won't be attacked. Have students speculate about why Nat thinks this.
  Possible response: The birds are out to destroy human beings, not animals.
- Invite students to speculate about the motive behind the attacks. Ask students whether the story provides any evidence for a motive. Does the apparent safety of the cows versus the peril of the humans suggest a motive?
  Possible response: The fact that the birds would not be interested in the "easy meal" of the unprotected cows suggests that they are not motivated by hunger. The birds are activated by hatred for humans.

45 ebbs again, I'll try for the farm, and they may let us have bread and potatoes, and milk too."

His mind was busy again, planning against emergency. They would not have milked, of course, this evening. The cows would be standing by the gate, waiting in the yard, with the household inside, battened behind boards, as they were here at the cottage. That is, if they had time to take precautions. He thought of the farmer, Trigg, smiling at him from the car. There would have been no shooting party, not tonight.

The children were asleep. His wife, still clothed, was sitting on her mattress. She watched him, her eyes nervous.

"What are you going to do?" she whispered.

He shook his head for silence. Softly, stealthily, he opened the back door and looked outside.

It was pitch dark. The wind was blowing harder than ever, coming in steady gusts, icy, from the sea. He kicked at the step outside the door. It was heaped with birds. There were dead birds everywhere. Under the windows, against the walls. These were the suicides, the divers, the ones with broken necks. Wherever he looked he saw dead birds. No trace of the living. The living had flown seaward with the turn of the tide. The gulls would be riding the seas now, as they had done in the forenoon.

In the far distance, on the hill where the tractor had been two days before, something was burning. One of the aircraft that had crashed; the fire, fanned by the wind, had set light to a stack.

He looked at the bodies of the birds, and he had a notion that if he heaped them, one upon the other, on the windowsills they would make added protection for the next attack. Not much, perhaps, but

something. The bodies would have to be clawed at, pecked, and dragged aside before the living birds could gain purchase on the sills and attack the panes. He set to work in the darkness. It was queer; he hated touching them. The bodies were still warm and bloody. The blood matted their feathers. He felt his stomach turn, but he went on with his work. He noticed grimly that every windowpane was shattered. Only the boards had kept the birds from breaking in. He stuffed the cracked panes with the bleeding bodies of the birds.

When he had finished he went back into the cottage. He barricaded the kitchen door, made it doubly secure. He took off his bandages, sticky with the birds' blood, not with his own cuts, and put on a fresh bandage.

His wife had made him cocoa and he drank it thirstily. He was very tired.

"All right," he said, smiling, "don't worry. We'll get through."

He lay down on his mattress and closed his eyes. He slept at once. He dreamt uneasily, because through his dreams there ran a thread of something forgotten. Some piece of work, neglected, that he should have done. Some precaution that he had known well but had not taken, and he could not put a name to it in his dreams. It was connected in some way with the burning aircraft and the stack upon the hill. He went on sleeping, though; he did not awake. It was his wife shaking his shoulder that awoke him finally.

"They've begun," she sobbed, "they've started this last hour. I can't listen to it any longer alone. There's something smelling bad too, something burning."

46 ▲ Critical Viewing
Which images found in this picture foreshadow danger? **[Describe]**

47 Reading Check
Briefly describe what Nat finds when he steps outside the cottage.

46 ▶ Critical Viewing

Answer: The dark, threatening clouds and the red color of the picture suggest danger.

47 Reading Check

Answer: Nat finds the dead bodies of the birds. He sees dead birds everywhere he looks.

Reading Strategy

Predicting

After students have read this page (up to "awoke him finally"), have them predict what Nat forgot to do. Ask them which details support their predictions. Then have them read on to see whether their predictions were correct.

Answer: Since his worry is connected with fire, he must have forgotten to bring in firewood or fuel, or to block the fireplaces properly so that birds can't come down the chimneys.

ENRICHMENT: Cultural Collection

Science Fiction Films

Beginning with Japan's *Godzilla* (1954), filmmakers began making monster films featuring giant creatures that destroy cities, overpower armies, and threaten civilization. Various films have featured giant creatures of all kinds: insects and spiders, scorpions, frogs—even giant rabbits *(Night of the Lepus,* 1972).

These films began appearing in the early years of the Atomic Age, and the bizarre size and raging behavior of the creatures are usually attributed to atomic weapons or radiation leaks. (In more recent films, pollution is often the culprit.) These movies express a clear moral: humans are being punished for violating nature or seeking to know too much. There is often an anti-science attitude in these films, though it is usually a young scientist who finally figures out how to save the world.

48 Reading Strategy

Predicting

Ask the Reading Strategy question on p. 74: What will happen next inside the house? Which details led you to this prediction?

Answer: Birds will come down the chimney, since there is nothing to stop them; Nat's only way to scare them off is to light the fire.

Literary Analysis

Foreshadowing

Ask the Literary Analysis question on p. 74: What effect does the sound of the clock have on the story?

Answer: It serves as a reminder that high tide will occur in a little more than four hours. The birds will begin another attack with the arrival of high tide.

Then he remembered. He had forgotten to make up the fire. It was smoldering, nearly out. He got up swiftly and lit the lamp. The hammering had started at the windows and the doors, but it was not that he minded now. It was the smell of singed feathers. The smell filled the kitchen. He knew at once what it was. The birds were coming down the chimney, squeezing their way down to the kitchen range. (48)

He got sticks and paper and put them on the embers, then reached for the can of paraffin.[13]

"Stand back," he shouted to his wife. "We've got to risk this."

He threw the paraffin onto the fire. The flame roared up the pipe, and down upon the fire fell the scorched, blackened bodies of the birds.

The children woke, crying. "What is it?" said Jill. "What's happened?"

Nat had no time to answer. He was raking the bodies from the chimney, clawing them out onto the floor. The flames still roared, and the danger of the chimney catching fire was one he had to take. The flames would send away the living birds from the chimney top. The lower joint was the difficulty, though. This was choked with the smoldering, helpless bodies of the birds caught by fire. He scarcely heeded the attack on the windows and the door: let them beat their wings, break their beaks, lose their lives, in the attempt to force an entry into his home. They would not break in. He thanked God he had one of the old cottages, with small windows, stout walls. Not like the new council houses. Heaven help them up the lane in the new council houses.

"Stop crying," he called to the children. "There's nothing to be afraid of, stop crying."

He went on raking at the burning, smoldering bodies as they fell into the fire.

"This'll fetch them," he said to himself, "the draft and the flames together. We're all right, as long as the chimney doesn't catch. I ought to be shot for this. It's all my fault. Last thing, I should have made up the fire. I knew there was something."

Amid the scratching and tearing at the window boards came the sudden homely striking of the kitchen clock. Three A.M. A little more than four hours yet to go. He could not be sure of the exact time of high water. He reckoned it would not turn much before half-past seven, twenty to eight.

"Light up the Primus,"[14] he said to his wife. "Make us some tea, and the kids some cocoa. No use sitting around doing nothing."

That was the line. Keep her busy, and the children too. Move about, eat, drink; always best to be on the go.

He waited by the range. The flames were dying. But no more blackened bodies fell from the chimney. He thrust his poker up as far as it could go and found nothing. It was clear. The chimney was clear. He wiped the sweat from his forehead.

"Come on now, Jill," he said, "bring me some more sticks. We'll have

Reading Strategy
Predicting What do you predict will happen next inside the house? Which details led you to this prediction?

Literary Analysis
Foreshadowing What effect does the sound of the clock have on the story? Explain.

13. **paraffin** (par´ ə fin) *n.* kerosene.
14. **Primus** (prī´ məs) *n.* small, portable stove.

CUSTOMIZE INSTRUCTION FOR UNIVERSAL ACCESS

For Gifted/Talented Students	For Advanced Readers
Ask students to imagine that their own community was under attack from birds. How would they create a bird-proof shelter in their own home or school? How might they be able to improve upon Nat's efforts? Students might draw a detailed plan or create a model of an ideal shelter.	Note to students that the weapons of the air force and the navy had little impact on the birds. Ask students to suggest other weapons or strategies that might be used in stopping the birds. Remind students that their plans must avoid harm to human populations.

a good fire going directly." She wouldn't come near him, though. She was staring at the heaped singed bodies of the birds.

"Never mind them," he said. "We'll put those in the passage when I've got the fire steady."

The danger of the chimney was over. It could not happen again, not if the fire was kept burning day and night.

"I'll have to get more fuel from the farm tomorrow," he thought. "This will never last. I'll manage, though. I can do all that with the ebb tide. It can be worked, fetching what we need, when the tide's turned. We've just got to adapt ourselves, that's all."

They drank tea and cocoa and ate slices of bread and Bovril.[15] Only half a loaf left, Nat noticed. Never mind though, they'd get by.

"Stop it," said young Johnny, pointing to the windows with his spoon, "stop it, you old birds."

"That's right," said Nat, smiling, "we don't want the old beggars, do we? Had enough of 'em."

49 They began to cheer when they heard the thud of the suicide birds.

"There's another, Dad," cried Jill, "he's done for."

"He's had it," said Nat. "There he goes, the blighter."

This was the way to face up to it. This was the spirit. If they could keep this up, hang on like this until seven, when the first news bulletin came through, they would not have done too badly.

"Give us a cigarette," he said to his wife. "A bit of a smoke will clear away the smell of the scorched feathers."

"There's only two left in the packet," she said. "I was going to buy you some from the Co-op."

"I'll have one," he said, "t'other will keep for a rainy day."

No sense trying to make the children rest. There was no rest to be got while the tapping and the scratching went on at the windows. He sat with one arm round his wife and the other round Jill, with Johnny on his mother's lap and the blankets heaped about them on the mattress.

"You can't help admiring the beggars," he said; "they've got persistence. You'd think they'd tire of the game, but not a bit of it."

Admiration was hard to sustain. The tapping went on and on and a new rasping note struck Nat's ear, as though a sharper beak than any hitherto had come to take over from its fellows. He tried to remember the names of birds; he tried to think which species would go for this particular job. It was not the tap of the woodpecker. That would be light and frequent. This was more serious, because if it continued long the wood would splinter as the glass had done. Then he remembered the hawks. Could the hawks have taken over from the gulls? Were there buzzards now upon the sills, using talons as well as beaks? Hawks, buzzards, kestrels, falcons—he had forgotten the birds of prey. He had forgotten the gripping power of the birds of prey. Three hours to go, and while they waited, the sound of the splintering wood, the talons tearing at the wood.

15. **Bovril** (bō´ vril) *n.* thick beef-flavored liquid used to make broth.

Reading Strategy

Predicting Based on the spirit Nat and his family are showing, what do you predict will happen?

50 **Reading Check**

How do the birds get into the house?

49 Reading Strategy

Predicting

- Ask the Reading Strategy question on p. 75: Based on the spirit Nat and his family are showing, what do you predict will happen?
  Answer: They will not give up or give in. They will hold out against the birds for as long as they can. They may turn out to be strong enough to defeat or outlast the birds.
- Ask which aspects of the situation favor the human beings, and which ones favor the birds.
  Answer: The human beings are smarter; Nat has already figured out when it will be safe to go outdoors and he has planned how to make the best use of the time he has. The birds are more numerous and therefore physically stronger. Nat and his family are isolated.

50 Reading Check

Answer: The birds come down the chimneys.

⑤① Background

Art

Over and Above #13, by Clarence Carter

Clarence H. Carter was born in Portsmouth, Ohio in 1904. He studied at the Cleveland School of Art. Today, many of his paintings hang in American museums. Carter has also taught in various fine arts programs throughout the country.

1. How does this illustration help you appreciate the helpless feelings of the family?
   Answer: The bird's beak is extremely sharp. Its eyes look narrow and intimidating; its stare is fixed. It doesn't look vulnerable in any way, but it looks like it could inflict serious injury with its sharp beak.
2. How does the artist make the bird look frightening?
   Answer: The close-up view makes the bird look gigantic. The fact that it is looking down from above makes it look strong and powerful. The stark white color and the vivid eyes are frightening.

⑤② ▶Critical Viewing

Answer: This bird looks threatening, like those in the story. It is a white bird, like many of the birds described in the story.

⑤①

Over and Above #13, 1964, Clarence H. Carter

Nat looked about him, seeing what furniture he could destroy to fortify the door. The windows were safe because of the dresser. He was not certain of the door. He went upstairs, but when he reached the landing he paused and listened. There was a soft patter on the floor of the children's bedroom. The birds had broken through . . . He put his ear to the door. No mistake. He could hear the rustle of wings and the light patter as they searched the floor. The other bedroom was still clear. He went into it and began bringing out the furniture, to pile at the head of the stairs should the door of the children's bedroom go. It was a preparation. It might never be needed. He could not stack the furniture against the door, because it opened inward. The only possible thing was to have it at the top of the stairs.

"Come down. Nat, what are you doing?" called his wife.

"I won't be long," he shouted. "Just making everything shipshape up here."

He did not want her to come; he did not want her to hear the

⑤② ▲ **Critical Viewing** Would you expect a bird in this story to look like the bird in this picture? Explain. **[Describe]**

ENRICHMENT: Science Connection

Birds of Prey

Birds of prey include several species of large birds, such as those Nat mentions. Eagles and owls are also birds of prey. These birds hunt by soaring through the air looking for small animals in the open. They have exceptionally keen vision, so they need not soar too close to the earth. They are equipped with needle-sharp talons to grip their prey and hooked beaks to tear the prey apart.

Human hunters nearly wiped out many species of birds of prey, but today people are working to help these birds make a comeback. Some birds of prey have even adapted to life in cities. Because hawks and falcons like to build nests in high places, they have found city bridges and skyscrapers to their liking, and they find plenty of pigeons and rats to eat.

pattering of the feet in the children's bedroom, the brushing of those wings against the door.

53 At five-thirty he suggested breakfast, bacon and fried bread, if only to stop the growing look of panic in his wife's eyes and to calm the fretful children. She did not know about the birds upstairs. The bedroom, luckily, was not over the kitchen. Had it been so, she could not have failed to hear the sound of them up there, tapping the boards. And the silly, senseless thud of the suicide birds, the death and glory boys, who flew into the bedroom, smashing their heads against the walls. He knew them of old, the herring gulls. They had no brains. The black-backs were different; they knew what they were doing. So did the buzzards, the hawks . . .

He found himself watching the clock, gazing at the hands that went so slowly round the dial. If his theory was not correct, if the attack did not cease with the turn of the tide, he knew they were beaten. They could not continue through the long day without air, without rest, without more fuel, without . . . His mind raced. He knew there were so many things they needed to withstand siege. They were not fully prepared. They were not ready. It might be that it would be safer in the towns after all. If he could get a message through on the farm telephone to his cousin, only a short journey by train upcountry, they might be able to hire a car. That would be quicker—hire a car between tides . . .

His wife's voice, calling his name, drove away the sudden, desperate desire for sleep.

"What is it? What now?" he said sharply.

"The wireless," said his wife. "I've been watching the clock. It's nearly seven."

"Don't twist the knob," he said, impatient for the first time. "It's on the Home where it is. They'll speak from the Home."

They waited. The kitchen clock struck seven. There was no sound. No chimes, no music. They waited until a quarter past, switching to the Light. The result was the same. No news bulletin came through.

"We've heard wrong," he said. "They won't be broadcasting until eight o'clock."

They left it switched on, and Nat thought of the battery, wondered how much power was left in it. It was generally recharged when his wife went shopping in the town. If the battery failed they would not hear the instructions.

"It's getting light," whispered his wife. "I can't see it, but I can feel it. And the birds aren't hammering so loud."

She was right. The rasping, tearing sound grew fainter every moment. So did the shuffling, the jostling for place upon the step, upon the sills. The tide was on the turn. By eight there was no sound at all. Only the wind. The children, lulled at last by the stillness, fell asleep. At half-past eight Nat switched the wireless off.

"What are you doing? We'll miss the news," said his wife.

"There isn't going to be any news," said Nat. "We've got to depend upon ourselves."

fretful (fret′ fəl) *adj.* irritable and discontented

54 Reading Check

Why does Nat put the furniture at the top of the stairs?

53 Literary Analysis

Imagery

- Have students list words in this passage that appeal to the sense of hearing. What effect does this have on Nat's mood? on the reader's?
  Answer: Words include *pattering, brushing, tapping, thud, smashing.* The sounds make Nat feel tense and anxious; they may have a similar effect on the reader.
- Point out that in spite of the many sound effects DuMaurier uses in this story, no birds have sung, cried, or called to another since p. 52. Ask students what effect this silence has on the reader.
  Answer: It adds to the sense of unreality and makes the situation even more bizarre. Normally, birds sing and they call to one another. It adds to DuMaurier's suggestion that all nature is disturbed.

54 Reading Check

Answer: Nat knows that the furniture will be a barrier between the birds upstairs and the family in the kitchen.

55 Literary Analysis

Foreshadowing and Imagery

- Read this paragraph aloud while students listen. Ask students how birds usually behave. Do they sit absolutely still? What do they do? Answer: Usually birds fly and flutter around, or they hop along the ground looking for food. Often they sing and chirp while they are doing these things.
- What effect does this change from normal bird behavior have on the characters and on the reader? Answer: It frightens everyone. The birds no longer seem safe and predictable.
- Ask the Literary Analysis question on p. 78: Do you think this image of the birds waiting and watching foreshadows an end to danger? Answer: No, because Nat saw them waiting and watching the day before; they were only waiting for night to attack. If the danger were over, they would fly away, not sit and wait.

56 Literary Analysis

Foreshadowing

- Point out to students that the sheep and cows are unharmed, even though they were out in the open all night. Ask students which detail foreshadowed their safety. Answer: During the night, Nat thought about the cows, but showed no sign of concern for them. Since Nat's predictions and deductions have been correct so far, the reader may surmise that the cows would be safe.
- The birds do not harm the farm animals. What does this suggest about the birds' real purpose? Answer: This suggests that the birds' main motive is not hunger but rather malice toward humans.

He went to the door and slowly pulled away the barricades. He drew the bolts and, kicking the bodies from the step outside the door, breathed the cold air. He had six working hours before him, and he knew he must reserve his strength for the right things, not waste it in any way. Food, and light, and fuel; these were the necessary things. If he could get them in sufficiency, they could endure another night.

55 He stepped into the garden, and as he did so he saw the living birds. The gulls had gone to ride the sea, as they had done before; they sought sea food, and the buoyancy of the tide, before they returned to the attack. Not so the land birds. They waited and watched. Nat saw them, on the hedgerows, on the soil, crowded in the trees, outside in the field, line upon line of birds, all still, doing nothing.

He went to the end of his small garden. The birds did not move. They went on watching him.

"I've got to get food," said Nat to himself. "I've got to go to the farm to find food."

He went back to the cottage. He saw to the windows and the doors. He went upstairs and opened the children's bedroom. It was empty, except for the dead birds on the floor. The living were out there, in the garden, in the fields. He went downstairs.

"I'm going to the farm," he said.

His wife clung to him. She had seen the living birds from the open door.

"Take us with you," she begged. "We can't stay here alone. I'd rather die than stay here alone."

He considered the matter. He nodded.

"Come on, then," he said. "Bring baskets, and Johnny's pram.[16] We can load up the pram."

They dressed against the biting wind, wore gloves and scarves. His wife put Johnny in the pram. Nat took Jill's hand.

"The birds," she whimpered, "they're all out there in the fields."

"They won't hurt us," he said, "not in the light."

They started walking across the field towards the stile, and the birds did not move. They waited, their heads turned to the wind.

When they reached the turning to the farm, Nat stopped and told his wife to wait in the shelter of the hedge with the two children.

"But I want to see Mrs. Trigg," she protested. "There are lots of things we can borrow if they went to market yesterday; not only bread, and . . ."

"Wait here," Nat interrupted. "I'll be back in a moment."

56 The cows were lowing, moving restlessly in the yard, and he could see a gap in the fence where the sheep had knocked their way through, to roam unchecked in the front garden before the farmhouse. No smoke came from the chimneys. He was filled with misgiving. He did not want his wife or the children to go down to the farm.

"Don't gib[17] now," said Nat, harshly, "do what I say."

---

16. **pram** *n.* baby carriage.
17. **gib** (jib) *v.* hesitate.

Literary Analysis
Foreshadowing and Imagery Do you think the image of the birds waiting and watching foreshadows an end to danger?

CUSTOMIZE INSTRUCTION FOR UNIVERSAL ACCESS

For Gifted/Talented Students

After students have finished reading, have them review the story for especially memorable images. Have them use these images to design book jackets for "The Birds." Remind students that book jackets should capture central events of the plot or major themes of the story, without giving away too much information. Students should look through the story to see how the birds are described, which colors DuMaurier constantly refers to, how the overall setting looks, and so on. Students can work with colored pencils, markers, paints, pen and ink, or any media they like. Post their completed work in the classroom.

She withdrew with the pram into the hedge, screening herself and the children from the wind.

He went down alone to the farm. He pushed his way through the herd of bellowing cows, which turned this way and that, distressed, their udders full. He saw the car standing by the gate, not put away in the garage. The windows of the farmhouse were smashed. There were many dead gulls lying in the yard and around the house. The living birds perched on the group of trees behind the farm and on the roof of the house. They were quite still. They watched him.

57 Jim's body lay in the yard . . . what was left of it. When the birds had finished, the cows had trampled him. His gun was beside him. The door of the house was shut and bolted, but as the windows were smashed it was easy to lift them and climb through. Trigg's body was close to the telephone. He must have been trying to get through to the exchange when the birds came for him. The receiver was hanging loose, the instrument torn from the wall. No sign of Mrs. Trigg. She would be upstairs. Was it any use going up? Sickened, Nat knew what he would find.

"Thank God," he said to himself, "there were no children."

He forced himself to climb the stairs, but halfway he turned and descended again. He could see her legs protruding from the open bedroom door. Beside her were the bodies of the black-backed gulls, and an umbrella, broken.

"It's no use," thought Nat, "doing anything. I've only got five hours, less than that. The Triggs would understand. I must load up with what I can find."

He tramped back to his wife and children.

"I'm going to fill up the car with stuff," he said. "I'll put coal in it, and paraffin for the Primus. We'll take it home and return for a fresh load."

"What about the Triggs?" asked his wife.

"They must have gone to friends," he said.

"Shall I come and help you, then?"

"No; there's a mess down there. Cows and sheep all over the place. Wait, I'll get the car. You can sit in it."

Clumsily he backed the car out of the yard and into the lane. His wife and the children could not see Jim's body from there.

"Stay here," he said, "never mind the pram. The pram can be fetched later. I'm going to load the car."

Her eyes watched his all the time. He believed she understood, otherwise she would have suggested helping him to find the bread and groceries.

They made three journeys altogether, backwards and forwards between their cottage and the farm, before he was satisfied they had everything they needed. It was surprising, once he started thinking, how many things were necessary. Almost the most important of all was planking for the windows. He had to go round searching for timber. He wanted to renew the boards on all the windows at the cottage.

Literary Analysis
Foreshadowing Do you think that the deaths of everyone at the farm foreshadow a similar fate for Nat and his family? Why or why not?

58 **Reading Check**
What does Nat find at the Triggs' farm?

CUSTOMIZE INSTRUCTION FOR UNIVERSAL ACCESS

For Gifted/Talented Students	For Advanced Readers
The silence of the radio means that Nat's family faces the end completely alone. Ask students to devise a scenario in which Nat could be rescued. What forces might still exist to combat the birds? How might they reach Nat's family?	Have students analyze Nat's character. What do they think of him? Is he heroic, or is he too much of an ordinary man to be considered a hero? Which aspects of Nat's character help him survive the conflict when everyone else in the area is killed? Do students think Nat will be able to triumph over the birds in the end? Have them write brief essays about Nat. Students might want to compare or contrast Nat to heroes from other stories, or from movies or television shows.

57 Literary Analysis

Foreshadowing

- Ask students which details foreshadowed the deaths of Jim and the Triggs.
  Answer: They didn't believe Nat's story of the attack on his house or the radio warnings. Mr. Trigg said that he didn't intend to board up his windows. Jim thought Nat was imagining things when Nat warned him about the birds.
- Ask the Literary Analysis question on p. 79: Do you think that the deaths of everyone at the farm foreshadow a similar fate for Nat and his family? Why or why not?
  Possible responses: No, because the Triggs didn't take any precautions against the birds. Yes, because Nat and his family can't do enough to protect themselves; the birds are too strong for them.

58 Reading Check

Answer: Nat discovers that the cows haven't been milked, that the building is surrounded by dead birds, and that Jim and the Triggs are dead.

59 Literary Analysis

Foreshadowing

- Ask students which details foreshadowed Nat's failure to get the exchange on the telephone. **Answer:** The lack of any news broadcasts suggested a general breakdown in communications.
- Ask the Literary Analysis question on p. 80: What might the dead phone line foreshadow? **Answer:** It suggests that Nat's family will be completely alone in its struggle against the birds.

Candles, paraffin, nails, tinned stuff; the list was endless. Besides all that, he milked three of the cows. The rest, poor brutes, would have to go on bellowing.

59 On the final journey he drove the car to the bus stop, got out, and went to the telephone box. He waited a few minutes, jangling the receiver. No good, though. The line was dead. He climbed on to a bank and looked over the countryside, but there was no sign of life at all, nothing in the fields but the waiting, watching birds. Some of them slept—he could see the beaks tucked into the feathers.

"You'd think they'd be feeding," he said to himself, "not just standing in that way."

Then he remembered. They were gorged with food. They had eaten their fill during the night. That was why they did not move this morning . . .

No smoke came from the chimneys of the council houses. He thought of the children who had run across the fields the night before.

"I should have known," he thought; "I ought to have taken them home with me."

He lifted his face to the sky. It was colorless and gray. The bare trees on the landscape looked bent and blackened by the east wind. The cold did not affect the living birds waiting out there in the fields.

"This is the time they ought to get them," said Nat; "they're a sitting target now. They must be doing this all over the country. Why don't our aircraft take off now and spray them with mustard gas? What are all our chaps doing? They must know, they must see for themselves."

He went back to the car and got into the driver's seat.

"Go quickly past that second gate," whispered his wife. "The postman's lying there. I don't want Jill to see."

He accelerated. The little Morris bumped and rattled along the lane. The children shrieked with laughter.

"Up-a-down, up-a-down," shouted young Johnny.

It was a quarter to one by the time they reached the cottage. Only an hour to go.

"Better have cold dinner," said Nat. "Hot up something for yourself and the children, some of that soup. I've no time to eat now. I've got to unload all this stuff."

He got everything inside the cottage. It could be sorted later. Give them all something to do during the long hours ahead. First he must see to the windows and the doors.

He went round the cottage methodically, testing every window, every door. He climbed on to the roof also, and fixed boards across every chimney, except the kitchen. The cold was so intense he could hardly bear it, but the job had to be done. Now and again he would look up, searching the sky for aircraft. None came. As he worked he cursed the inefficiency of the authorities.

Literary Analysis
Foreshadowing What might the dead phone line foreshadow?

"It's always the same," he muttered. "They always let us down. Muddle, muddle, from the start. No plan, no real organization. And we don't matter down here. That's what it is. The people upcountry have priority. They're using gas up there, no doubt, and all the aircraft. We've got to wait and take what comes."

He paused, his work on the bedroom chimney finished, and looked out to sea. Something was moving out there. Something gray and white amongst the breakers.

"Good old Navy," he said, "they never let us down. They're coming down-channel, they're turning in the bay."

60 He waited, straining his eyes, watering in the wind, towards the sea. He was wrong, though. It was not ships. The Navy was not there. The gulls were rising from the sea. The massed flocks in the fields, with ruffled feathers, rose in formation from the ground and, wing to wing, soared upwards to the sky.

The tide had turned again.

Nat climbed down the ladder and went inside the kitchen. The family were at dinner. It was a little after two. He bolted the door, put up the barricade, and lit the lamp.

"It's nighttime," said young Johnny.

His wife had switched on the wireless once again, but no sound came from it.

"I've been all round the dial," she said, "foreign stations, and that lot. I can't get anything."

"Maybe they have the same trouble," he said, "maybe it's the same right through Europe."

She poured out a plateful of the Triggs' soup, cut him a large slice of the Triggs' bread, and spread their dripping upon it.

They ate in silence. A piece of the dripping ran down young Johnny's chin and fell on to the table.

"Manners, Johnny," said Jill, "you should learn to wipe your mouth."

The tapping began at the windows, at the door. The rustling, the jostling, the pushing for position on the sills. The first thud of the suicide gulls upon the step.

"Won't America do something?" said his wife. "They've always been our allies, haven't they? Surely America will do something?"

Nat did not answer. The boards were strong against the windows, and on the chimneys too. The cottage was filled with stores, with fuel, with all they needed for the next few days. When he had finished dinner he would put the stuff away, stack it neatly, get everything shipshape, handy-like. His wife could help him, and the children too. They'd tire themselves out, between now and a quarter to nine, when the tide would ebb; then he'd tuck them down on their mattresses, see that they slept good and sound until three in the morning.

He had a new scheme for the windows, which was to fix barbed

Reading Strategy
Predicting What do you think will happen next?

61 **✓Reading Check**
What theory does Nat develop to explain why the birds do not move in the morning?

60 Reading Strategy

Predicting

- Ask students the Reading Strategy question on p. 81: What do you think will happen next?
  Answer: The birds will attack the house again and no military force will come to the rescue.
- Have students give reasons for their predictions.
  Answer: The birds have evidently killed everyone else in the area; the Triggs, Jim, and the postman are all dead, and Nat saw no signs of life at the council houses. The birds will attack Nat's house because Nat and his family may be the only ones left.
- Challenge students to predict how the story will end. Have them give reasons for their predictions.

61 ✓Reading Check

Answer: The birds haven't moved because they aren't hungry; also, they are waiting for the tide to turn.

CUSTOMIZE INSTRUCTION FOR UNIVERSAL ACCESS

For Advanced Readers

Have students read and think about the next-to-last paragraph of the story (p. 82). In this paragraph, Nat hints at a motivation for the attacks of the birds. Why does he think they are attacking? Do students agree with his theory? Why or why not? You may wish to share the information about science fiction films in the Enrichment note on p. 73. These films usually provide a clear cause for creature attacks. Note that DuMaurier only hints at possible reasons for the birds' behavior. Does this lack of explanation make "The Birds" less realistic—or more eerie and mysterious? Ask students to express their opinion in a brief essay.

ASSESS

Answers for p. 82

Review and Assess

1. Students will probably say yes, because they always wanted to know what would happen next.
2. **(a)** Nat works part-time at a nearby farm. He likes working alone. **(b)** Yes. Nat enjoys watching birds during his breaks from work. He likes working outdoors, especially near the sea.
3. **(a)** They are more restless than usual, and there are many more of them. **(b)** Since there are more birds, there is less food to go around; this might explain their attacks.
4. **(a)** He blames it on the weather. **(b)** He doesn't really believe it. He repeats it as though he's trying to convince himself. He is badly frightened.
5. **(a)** Possible answers: Some students may repeat the story's speculations about hunger or changing weather; others may suggest the birds are seeking revenge or are being controlled by aliens. **(b)** Yes, because people have been the enemies of many species of animals for centuries. No, because usually an animal won't kill unless it needs food or its territory or offspring are threatened. **(c)** The story suggests that nature can be a more powerful, dangerous, and mysterious force than people think.
6. **(a)** Possible answer: Most readers may expect that the characters are doomed. **(b)** The point of the story is that the threat of nature always exists and people will never be able to control it; DuMaurier doesn't resolve the situation because the struggle of humans with nature is not resolved.

wire in front of the boards. He had brought a great roll of it from the farm. The nuisance was, he'd have to work at this in the dark, when the lull came between nine and three. Pity he had not thought of it before. Still, as long as the wife slept, and the kids, that was the main thing.

The smaller birds were at the window now. He recognized the light tap-tapping of their beaks and the soft brush of their wings. The hawks ignored the windows. They concentrated their attack upon the door. Nat listened to the tearing sound of splintering wood, and wondered how many million years of memory were stored in those little brains, behind the stabbing beaks, the piercing eyes, now giving them this instinct to destroy mankind with all the deft precision of machines.

"I'll smoke that last cigarette," he said to his wife. "Stupid of me, it was the one thing I forgot to bring back from the farm."

He reached for it, switched on the silent wireless. He threw the empty packet on the fire, and watched it burn.

Review and Assess

Thinking About the Selection

1. **Respond:** Did you find "The Birds" suspenseful? Explain.
2. (a) **Recall:** In the beginning of the story, what does the narrator say about Nat and how he spends his days? (b) **Analyze:** Do his actions suggest that Nat is sensitive to the natural world? Why or why not?
3. (a) **Recall:** According to Nat, what is different about the birds this fall? (b) **Analyze:** How might this new difference in the birds contribute to their destructive nature?
4. (a) **Recall:** When Nat cleans up after the first attack, how does he explain the birds' behavior? (b) **Evaluate:** How strongly do you think he believes his own explanation?
5. (a) **Draw Conclusions:** Why do you think the birds have begun attacking and trying to kill people? (b) **Connect:** Do you think that an animal population could suddenly turn against people? Why? (c) **Generalize:** What message do you think the story conveys about the relationship between humans and the natural world?
6. (a) **Connect:** What ending do you think most readers expect? (b) **Evaluate:** Why might this story have an inconclusive ending?

Daphne du Maurier

(1907–1989)

Du Maurier was born in London into a family of actors, artists, and writers. Her father was an actor and theater manager who specialized in playing criminals on the stage, and her grandfather was a novelist who illustrated his own writing.

The Loving Spirit (1931), du Maurier's first novel, became a bestseller, propelling her into a lifelong career as a writer. She followed with a series of romantic novels that were tinged with mystery and suspense.

Du Maurier's stories caught the attention of director Alfred Hitchcock, who specialized in suspenseful films. In addition to *The Birds*, Hitchcock made two other films based on du Maurier's tales, including *Rebecca*, which won the Academy Award for Best Picture in 1940.

ASSESSMENT PRACTICE: Reading Comprehension

Anglo-Saxon Suffix *-ful* (For more practice, see Test Preparation Workbook, p. 4.)

Many assessment tests specify that students will use prefixes and suffixes to determine the meanings of words in a variety of written texts. To demonstrate how to use the suffix *-ful* to determine word meanings, write this text from the selection on the chalkboard:

> He suggested breakfast, bacon and fried bread, if only to stop the growing look of panic in his wife's eyes and to calm the fretful children.

In this passage, the word fretful means—

A full of wonder
B irritable
C without care
D unaware

Students should know that "to fret" means "to worry or complain." The correct answer is choice *B*.

Review and Assess

Literary Analysis

Foreshadowing

1. How does Nat's sighting of masses of gulls riding the sea **foreshadow** possible disaster?
2. What does the BBC announcement of a national emergency foreshadow?
3. Using a chart like this one, explain what you think the scene at Triggs' farm at the end of the story foreshadows for Nat's family.

Scene at Triggs' Farm	Possible Outcomes

Connecting Literary Elements

4. (a) Reread the description of the children's bedroom after Nat has fought off the birds in the dark of the night (p. 53). Use a chart like the one shown here to record the **imagery** in that description. (b) Explain the effect that you think each image is meant to have.

Image	Explanation of Effect

5. (a) Review the last three paragraphs of the story, and find at least two vivid details. (b) How do these details add to the suspense?

Reading Strategy

Predicting

6. What were the first hints that led you to **predict** the outcome?
7. Review the predictions you made as you read. (a) Identify one prediction that was accurate and one that you later revised. (b) For each, explain how details later in the story supported or contradicted your prediction.

Extend Understanding

8. **Science Connection:** What questions about the bird invasion might a scientist raise to help understand the events of the story?

Quick Review

Foreshadowing is the author's use of clues that hint at events to come.

Imagery is the use of language to create word pictures in a reader's mind.

When you **predict,** use details to make educated guesses about what will happen later in the story.

Take It to the Net

www.phschool.com

Take the interactive self-test online to check your understanding of the selection.

Answers for p. 83

Review and Assess

1. There are too many gulls; this suggests that they are waiting for darkness to attack.
2. The announcement makes it clear that birds are attacking all over the country, and it foreshadows disaster for people throughout the country.
3. The Triggs' dead bodies suggest that Nat and his family may be killed. However, since the Triggs did nothing to protect themselves and Nat took many precautions, Nat and his family may survive.
4. Images: the sounds of the birds moving and falling to the floor; the feel of their soft feathers and sharp beaks; the sight of their corpses on the floor. Effects: horror, fear, bewilderment because the attack seems random
5. **(a)** Possible details: the sounds of the birds upstairs and the silence of the radio. **(b)** The details remind the reader and the characters that the birds are close and no help is coming.
6. Possible response: The silence of the radio, the destruction of the airplanes, and the absence of any successful organized defense strongly suggest that Nat's family will not be rescued.
7. Answers will vary depending on students' predictions. Make sure they point to details in the story that support or contradict their predictions.
8. Possible questions: Why did the birds attack? What influence did the wind and the tides have on the birds? How can the birds' violence be controlled?

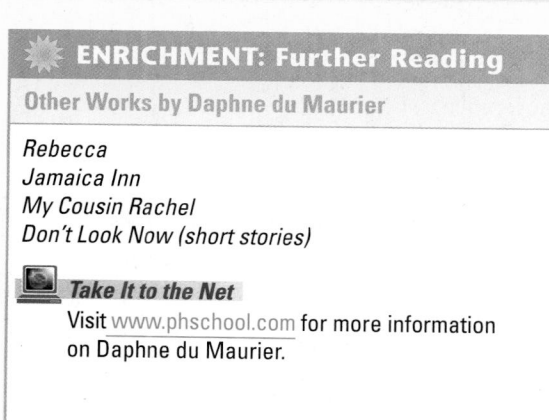

ENRICHMENT: Further Reading

Other Works by Daphne du Maurier

Rebecca
Jamaica Inn
My Cousin Rachel
Don't Look Now (short stories)

Take It to the Net

Visit www.phschool.com for more information on Daphne du Maurier.

EXTEND

Answers for p. 84

1 Vocabulary Development

Word Analysis

1. sorrowful; unhappy
2. teaspoonful; one-third of a tablespoon
3. helpful; of use
4. regretful; wishing something hadn't happened
5. spiteful; hurtful or malicious
6. restful; calming or quiet

Fluency: Clarify Word Meaning

1. c **3.** d **5.** f **7.** h
2. e **4.** a **6.** b **8.** g

Spelling Strategy

1. securely
2. houseful
3. discouragement

2 Grammar Lesson

1. reflexive
2. intensive
3. intensive
4. intensive
5. reflexive

Writing Application

Sample answers:

1. Nat asked himself why the birds attacked.
2. We completed the job ourselves.

Integrate Language Skills

1 Vocabulary Development Lesson

Word Analysis: Anglo-Saxon Suffix *-ful*

In "The Birds," the children are described as *fretful* about the frightening situation they face. The word *fretful* contains the Anglo-Saxon suffix *-ful*. The suffix means "having the quality of," as in *forgetful*; "having the quality that would fill," as in *handful*; or "full of," as in *fretful*. Therefore, *fretful* literally means "full of fret or worry," and it is no surprise that a fretful person is irritable or discontented.

Add the suffix *-ful* to these words. Then, using your knowledge of the suffix *-ful*, provide a definition for each of the words you generate.

1. sorrow
2. teaspoon
3. help
4. regret
5. spite
6. rest

Fluency: Clarify Word Meaning

Match each vocabulary word with its synonym.

1. placid	a. gloomy
2. garish	b. urgent
3. reconnaissance	c. calm
4. sullen	d. exploratory
5. furtively	e. gaudy
6. imperative	f. stealthily
7. recounted	g. irritable
8. fretful	h. narrated

Spelling Strategy

Most words ending in silent *e* keep the *e* before a suffix beginning with a consonant. For example, *grace* + *-ful* = *graceful*. Write the correct spelling of each word below.

1. securly 2. housful 3. discouragment

2 Grammar Lesson

Reflexive and Intensive Pronouns

A **reflexive pronoun** ends in *-self* or *-selves* and indicates that someone or something performs an action to, for, or upon itself. Reflexive pronouns point back to a noun or pronoun that appears earlier in the sentence. They are essential to the meaning of a sentence. In contrast, an **intensive pronoun** also ends in *-self* or *-selves* but simply adds emphasis to a noun or pronoun in the same sentence.

Reflexive: "Once more he settled *himself* to sleep."

Intensive: "You had to endure something *yourself* before it touched you."

Practice Identify whether each underlined pronoun below is reflexive or intensive.

1. Jill read herself a story after supper.
2. Her parents themselves had encouraged her.
3. They said, "If you children want to play, you will have to see to it yourselves."
4. Nat whispered, "I will go outside and take a look around myself."
5. He convinced himself they were safe.

Writing Application Write two sentences that include these pronouns, used as indicated.

1. himself (reflexive)
2. ourselves (intensive)

WG *Prentice Hall Writing and Grammar Connection: Chapter 16, Section 2*

TEACHING RESOURCES

The following resources can be used to enrich or extend the instruction for pp. 84–85.

Vocabulary

Selection Support: Build Vocabulary, p. 13

Grammar

Selection Support: Build Grammar Skills, p. 14

Writing and Grammar, Gold Level, p. 349

Daily Language Practice Transparencies

Writing

Writing and Grammar, Gold Level, p. 112

Writing and Grammar iText CD-ROM

Writing Models and Graphic Organizers on Transparencies, p. 17

BLOCK SCHEDULING: Resources marked with this symbol provide varied instruction during 90-minute blocks.

❸ Writing Lesson

Bird's-Eye View of a Place

Imagine how different "The Birds" would be if it were told from the point of view of one of the birds. The action would be described from above rather than below. Write a description of a scene in the story as it would look to a bird flying overhead.

Prewriting To see the scene from above, make a blueprint of the scene by drawing what you have chosen to describe. Label the key places.

Drafting Refer to your sketch as you draft your bird's point of view. Include details that indicate a downward-looking perspective. For example, a bird in the sky would be able to see Nat's entire house, but it would not, for example, see the color of Nat's eyes.

Revising Reread your description, checking for inconsistencies in viewpoint. Correct any passages that describe something from the ground up.

Model: Revising to Maintain a Consistent Viewpoint

The shingled roof of the library peeked through the ~~oak~~ trees. ~~A look through the windows showed that it was a busy place today.~~

To keep this viewpoint consistent, details that could be seen only from ground level are eliminated.

WG *Prentice Hall Writing and Grammar Connection: Chapter 6, Section 4*

❹ Extension Activities

Listening and Speaking In "The Birds," people try to protect themselves from birds. In real life, birds often need protection from people. In a small group, hold a **panel discussion** in which you answer the following questions:

- What dangers do humans pose to bird populations?
- What can be done to protect birds and their habitats?

Each participant should research the topic and prepare a set of concise notes for easy reference during the discussion. **[Group Activity]**

Research and Technology Prepare a research report and give a **presentation** on any four of the birds mentioned in this story. For each bird, research size, distinguishing features, natural habitats, and behaviors. Use the Internet or the CD-ROM edition of an encyclopedia to locate photographs and factual information.

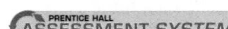

Take It to the Net www.phschool.com

Go online for an additional research activity using the Internet.

- Remind students that birds won't see things from a human perspective. Since birds are small, things that look small to a person might look enormous to a bird.
- Use the Description rubric in **Performance Assessment and Portfolio Management,** p. 18 to evaluate students' scenes.

❹ Extension Activities

Research and Technology

- Suggest that students confine their research to the types of birds mentioned in the story.
- Group discussion can be held in front of the rest of the class so that everyone can learn from the research.

CUSTOMIZE INSTRUCTION
For Universal Access

To address different learning styles, use the following activities suggested in the **Extension Activities** booklet, p. 4.

- For Verbal/Linguistic Learners, use Activities 4 and 6.
- For Interpersonal and Bodily/Kinesthetic Learners, use Activity 5.

ASSESSMENT RESOURCES

The following resources can be used to assess students' knowledge and skills.

Selection Assessment

- **Formal Assessment,** pp. 10–12
- **Open Book Test,** pp. 10–12
- **Got It! Assessment Videotapes,** Tape 1
- **Test Bank Software**

Take It to the Net

Visit www.phschool.com for self-tests and additional questions on "The Birds."

Writing Rubric

- **Performance Assess. and Portfolio Mgmt.,** p. 18

PRENTICE HALL ASSESSMENT SYSTEM

- **Workbook**
- **Skill Book**
- **Transparencies**
- **CD-ROM**

Lesson Objectives

1. To understand the connection between past and present depictions of nature's wrath and fury and human beings' responses to natural disasters
2. To explore the power that natural disasters have on the human imagination

Connections

Both Daphne du Maurier's story "The Birds" and Sebastian Junger's *The Perfect Storm* convey important messages about the unpredictability of nature and people's inability to control the forces of nature. Have students reread "The Birds" on pp. 50–82 after they have read the excerpt from *The Perfect Storm*. What similarities and differences can students identify in the ways in which the people in both stories cope with danger and risk?

Nature's Fury

- Explain to students that Junger's book is a work of nonfiction. It tells the story of the crew of a small fishing boat (the *Andrea Gail*) in Gloucester, Massachusetts, and their fate in October 1991 after encountering a powerful storm at sea.
- The natural setting for this story is a "nor'easter," a particularly strong type of storm that can occur in the northeastern United States. The particular storm detailed in Junger's book was referred to as "the perfect storm" because of the rare combination of meteorological factors that created it.
- Point out to students that both du Maurier's "The Birds" and Junger's *The Perfect Storm* are works that focus on the more sinister aspects of the natural world and derive their power from the unexpected danger of this seemingly harmless world.

CONNECTIONS
Literature Past and Present
Nature's Fury

from
The Perfect Storm
Sebastian Junger

"The Birds" draws its power from the transformation of a common, harmless animal into something dark and sinister.

Other authors tap the same power to transform the ordinary in nature into the extraordinary. In his 1997 book "The Perfect Storm," Sebastian Junger uses the true story of boats caught in a major storm to demonstrate the power extreme weather has on our imagination. He shows how extreme weather can transform familiar landscapes, like a gently rolling sea, into territory that is suddenly alien and hostile. In the following excerpt, people are exposed to the furious side of nature, providing insight into the different ways that people cope with danger and risk.

2:30 AM—s/v [sailing vessel] is running out of fuel, recommend we try to keep Falcon o/s [on-scene] until Tamaroa arrives.
5:29 AM—Falcon has lost comms [communication] with vessel, vessel is low on battery power and taking on water. Pumps are keeping up but are run by ele [electric].
7:07 AM—Falcon o/s, vessel has been located. Six hours fuel left. People on board are scared.

The H-3 arrives on scene around 6:30 and spends half an hour just trying to locate the *Satori*. The conditions are so bad that she's vanished from the Falcon's radar, and the H-3 pilot is almost on top of her before spotting her in the foam-streaked seas. The Falcon circles off to the southwest to prepare a life-raft drop while the H-3 takes up a hover directly over the boat. In these conditions the Falcon pilot could never line up on something as small as a sailboat, so the H-3 acts as a stand-in. The Falcon comes back at 140 knots, radar locked onto the helicopter, and at the last moment the H-3 falls away and the jet makes the drop. The pilot comes screaming over the *Satori*'s mast and the copilot pushes two life-raft packages out a hatch in the floorboards. The rafts are linked by a long nylon tether, and as they fall they

ENRICHMENT: Science Connection

Nor'easters

Similar to a cyclone, a nor'easter is a storm system that circulates in a counterclockwise motion. This motion results in strong northeast winds, hence the name "nor'easter." Nor'easters occur most often in the late fall and early winter. These storms are spawned when the jet stream dips farther south than usual, drawing cold arctic air down from the north and bringing up warmer air from the south. The warm air rises over the cold air, creating instability.

The nor'easter that sank the *Andrea Gail* was the result of the coming together of astonishing meteorological conditions. Late October 1991, a cyclone formed along a cold front off the northeast coast of the United States. At the same time, Hurricane Grace, which had formed a day earlier, was moving up the eastern seaboard. This hurricane was absorbed by the storm, strengthening its already dramatic force.

cartwheel apart, splashing down well to either side of the *Satori.* The tether, released at two hundred feet into a hurricane-force wind, drops right into Bylander's hand.

The H-3 hovers overhead while the *Satori* crew haul in the packages, but both rafts have exploded on impact. There's nothing at either end of the line. The *Tamaroa* is still five hours away and the storm has retrograded[1] to within a couple of hundred miles of the coast; over the next twenty-four hours it will pass directly over the *Satori.* A daylight rescue in these conditions is difficult, and a nighttime rescue is out of the question. If the *Satori* crew is not taken off in the next few hours, there's a good chance they won't be taken off at all. Late that morning the second H-3 arrives and the pilot, Lieutenant Klosson, explains the situation to Ray Leonard. Leonard radios back that he's not leaving the boat.

It's unclear whether Leonard is serious or just trying to save face. Either way, the Coast Guard is having none of it. Two helicopters, two Falcon jets, a medium-range cutter, and a hundred air- and seamen have already been committed to the rescue; the *Satori* crew are coming off now. *"Owner refuses to leave and says he's sailed through hurricanes before,"* the Comcen[2] incident log records at 12:24 that afternoon. *"Tamaroa wants manifestly unsafe voyage so that o/o [owner-operator] can be forced off."*

A "manifestly unsafe voyage" means that the vessel has been deemed an unacceptable risk to her crew or others, and the Coast Guard has the legal authority to order everyone off. Commander Brudnicki gets on the radio with District One and requests a manifestly unsafe designation for the *Satori,* and at 12:47 it is granted. The *Tamaroa* is just a couple of miles away now, within VHF[3] range of the *Satori,* and Brudnicki raises Leonard on the radio and tells him he has no choice in the matter. Everyone is leaving the boat. At 12:57 in the afternoon, thirteen hours after weighing anchor, the *Tamaroa* plunges into view.

There's a lot of hardware circling the *Satori.* There's the Falcon, the H-3, the *Tamaroa,* and the freighter *Gold Bond Conveyor,* which has been cutting circles around the *Satori* since the first mayday call. Hardware is not the problem, though; it's time. Dark is only three hours away, and the departing H-3 pilot doesn't think the *Satori* will survive another night. She'll run out of fuel, start getting knocked down, and eventually break apart. The crew will be cast into the sea, and the helicopter pilot will refuse to drop his rescue swimmer because he can't be sure of getting him back. It would be up to the *Tamaroa* to maneuver alongside the swimmers and pull them on board, and in these seas it would be almost impossible. It's now or never.

The only way to take them off, Brudnicki decides, is to shuttle them back to the *Tamaroa* in one of the little Avons. The Avons are twenty-one-foot inflatable rafts with rigid hulls and outboard engines;

1. **retrograded** (reʹtrə grādʹ ed) *v.* moved backward.
2. **Comcen** (kämʹ sen) *abbrev.* Coast Guard abbreviation for the Command Center, which keeps track of rescue operations.
3. **VHF** *abbrev.* Very High Frequency; radio frequency used by ships for communication.

tether (te*th*ʹ ər) *n.* rope or chain attached to an object.

mayday (mā́ dā́) radio distress signal used for ships in trouble.

Thematic Connection
What steps do the rescue crew take to battle nature?

✓ Reading Check
Why is it critical to save the *Satori* crew before nightfall?

Background
Nautical Knots

This nautical measure of speed dates back to the early days of sailing. To estimate a ship's speed, a sailor would throw a float overboard. This float was attached to a piece of rope with knots tied in it; each knot was a specific distance apart. The sailor then counted the number of knots that slipped through his hands in a fixed period of time and reported the speed of the ship in "knots."

Background
"Mayday"

This distress signal is derived from the French term *M'aider,* which means "Help me!" The term was made official by an international telecommunications conference in 1948.

✓ Reading Check

Answer: The people trying to rescue the crew of the *Satori* don't think the ship will make it through another night. It is running out of fuel and will eventually break apart in the high winds and damaging waves.

CUSTOMIZE INSTRUCTION FOR UNIVERSAL ACCESS

For Less Proficient Readers	For English Learners
To aid student comprehension, have students create timelines based on the information in this selection. Students can then refer to the information in their timelines to help them keep track of the events described.	Students may have difficulty with the technical language in this selection. Review with students the vocabulary words and footnotes before they read, making sure they can properly pronounce each word and understand its definition.

▶Critical Viewing

Answer: Students may cite such dangers as snapping or tangled cables and straps; loss of control of the helicopter; and people being battered by wind and waves.

one of them could make a run to the *Satori*, drop off survival suits, and then come back again to pick up the three crew. If anyone wound up in the water, at least they'd be insulated and afloat. It's not a particularly complicated maneuver, but no one has done it in conditions like this before. No one has even *seen* conditions like this before. At 1:23 PM the *Tamaroa* crew gathers at the port davits,[4] three men climb aboard the Avon, and they lower away.

It goes badly from the start. What passes for a lull between waves is in fact a crest-to-trough change of thirty to forty feet. Chief bosun[5] Thomas Amidon lowers the Avon halfway down, gets lifted up by the next wave, can't keep up with the trough and freefalls to the bottom of the cable. The lifting eye gets ripped out of its mount and Amidon almost pitches overboard. He struggles back into position, finishes lowering the boat, and makes way from the *Tamaroa*.

The seas are twice the size of the Avon raft. With excruciating slowness it fights its way to the *Satori*, comes up bow-to-stern,[6] and a crew member flings the three survival suits on deck. Stimpson grabs them and hands them out, but Amidon doesn't back out in time. The sailboat rides up a sea, comes down on the Avon, and punctures one of her air bladders. Things start to happen very fast now: the Avon's bow collapses, a wave swamps her to the gunwales,[7] the engine dies, and she falls away astern. Amidon tries desperately to get the engine going again and finally manages to, but they're up to their waists in water and the raft is crippled. There's no way they can even get themselves back onto the *Tamaroa*, much less save the crew of the *Satori*. Six people, not just three, now need to be rescued.

The H-3 crew watches all this incredulously. They're in a two o'clock hover with their jump door open, just over the tops of the waves. They can see the raft dragging heavily through the seas, and the *Tamaroa* heaving through ninety-degree rolls. Pilot Claude Hessel finally gets on the radio and tells Brudnicki and Amidon that he may have another way of doing this. He can't hoist[8] the *Satori* crew directly off their deck, he says, because the mast is flailing too wildly and might entangle the hoist. That would drag the H-3 right down on top of the boat. But he could drop his rescue swimmer, who would take the people off the boat one at a time and bring them up on the hoist. It's the best chance they've got, and Brudnicki knows it. He consults with District One and then gives the okay.

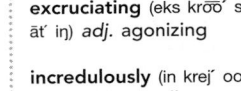

▲ Critical Viewing What dangers does a rescue like the one shown here present? **[Analyze]**

excruciating (eks kro͞o´ shē āt´ iŋ) *adj.* agonizing

incredulously (in krej´ oo ləs lē) *adv.* unwilling or unable to believe

flailing (flāl´ iŋ) *v.* swinging freely

4. **port davits** (dā´ vits) *n.* cranes used to raise and lower inflatable rafts, located on the left side of a ship.
5. **Chief bosun** (bō´ sən) *n.* officer in charge of the ship's crew and equipment; also spelled boatswain.
6. **bow-to-stern** (bou to͞o stʉrn) *nautical term.* from the front of a ship (*bow*) to its rear (*stern*).
7. **gunwales** (gun´ əls) *n.* upper edge of the side of a boat or ship.
8. **hoist** *v.* lift by means of a special apparatus.

The rescue swimmer on Hessel's helicopter is Dave Moore, a three-year veteran who has never been on a major rescue. ("The good cases don't come along too often—usually someone beats you to them," he says. "If a sailboat gets in trouble far out we usually get a rescue, but otherwise it's just a lot of little stuff.") Moore is handsome in a baby-faced sort of way—square-jawed, blue-eyed, and a big open smile. He has a dense, compact body that is more seallike than athletic. His profession of rescue swimmer came about when a tanker went down off New York in the mid-1980s. A Coast Guard helicopter was hovering overhead, but it was winter and the tanker crew were too hypothermic to get into the lift basket. They all drowned. Congress decided they wanted something done, and the Coast Guard adopted the Navy rescue program. Moore is twenty-five years old, born the year Karen Stimpson graduated from high school.

Moore is already wearing a neoprene wetsuit. He puts on socks and hood, straps on swim fins, pulls a mask and snorkel down over his head, and then struggles into his neoprene gloves. He buckles on a life vest and then signals to flight engineer Vriesman that he's ready. Vriesman, who has one arm extended, gatelike, across the jump door, steps aside and allows Moore to crouch by the edge. That means that they're at "ten and ten"—a ten-foot hover at ten knots. Moore, who's no longer plugged into the intercom, signals final corrections to Vriesman with his hands, who relays them to the pilot. This is it; Moore has trained three years for this moment. An hour ago he was in the lunch line back on base. Now he's about to drop into the maelstrom.

Hessel holds a low hover with the boat at his two o'clock. Moore can see the crew clustered together on deck and the *Satori* making slow, plunging headway into the seas. Vriesman is seated next to Moore at the hoist controls, and avionicsman[9] Ayres is behind the copilot with the radio and search gear. Both wear flightsuits and crash helmets and are plugged into the internal communication system in the wall. The time is 2:07 PM. Moore picks a spot between waves, takes a deep breath, and jumps.

hypothermic (hī´ pō thur´ mik) *adj.* having a dangerously low body temperature

maelstrom (māl´ strəm) *n.* violent or turbulent whirl of air and water

9. **avionicsman** (ā´ vē än´ iks man) *n.* crew member in charge of electronic equipment.

Connecting Literature Past and Present

1. How do characters in both this excerpt from *The Perfect Storm* and "The Birds" employ science and technology to deal with a natural threat?
2. (a) How are the two stories similar in their portrayal of human beings facing natural disasters? (b) Does the fact that "The Birds" is fiction affect the way you feel about the characters? Why or why not?
3. Explain the similarities and differences in the ways that characters in each selection face danger.

Sebastian Junger

(b. 1962)

The widespread popularity of *The Perfect Storm* surprised even its author, Sebastian Junger. Though *The Perfect Storm* was his first book, Junger has written many articles for *Outside*, *Men's Journal*, and *The New York Times Magazine*.

Junger is drawn to the subject of ordinary people performing dangerous work. He might feel a connection to them because he has participated in dangerous work himself. His past jobs have included a freelance writing assignment in war-torn Bosnia and work as a climber for a tree removal service.

Answers

Connecting Literature Past and Present

1. In *The Perfect Storm,* characters employ science and technology as ways of rescuing a stranded ship in a storm. In "The Birds," characters use science and technology in an attempt to understand why the birds are behaving as they are and to eliminate their threat.
2. **(a)** Students should say that both stories portray human beings who are very determined to overcome the threats posed by the natural disasters.
(b) Students may say that the fact that "The Birds" is fictional does not affect the ways readers feel about the characters. The story is so powerful and gripping that its being fiction does not diminish its power.
3. Students may mention that the characters in both stories show great courage and determination to triumph over the dangers they face. However, the characters in "The Birds" are faced with birds that violently attack and seem to want to kill them. In *The Perfect Storm,* characters face the hazards of a storm, just as dangerous, though not as strange, as killer birds.

Lesson Objectives

1. To identify the support a writer uses to back up opinions expressed in a film review
2. To distinguish between fact and opinion in a film review
3. To analyze the reviewer's argument and evaluate the persuasive language he or she uses

About Movie Reviews

- Have students read "About Movie Reviews." Review the three bulleted points to help students focus attention on the importance of critically reading film reviews.
- Ask students to discuss the kinds of information they usually find in a film review. Students may mention information about the film's production, a plot synopsis, and the reviewer's opinions about the movie.
- Have students discuss their experiences with movie reviews in the past. Do students regularly read movie reviews before they go to see a film? To what extent do they base their decisions on whether or not to see a movie on the reviews?

Reading Strategy

Identifying Support for Response

- Review with students the difference between a fact and an opinion. Remind students that a fact can be proved; an opinion cannot. Write the following two statements on the chalkboard:

  Alfred Hitchcock directed *The Birds*. *The Birds* is a very scary movie.

  Ask students to identify the fact and the opinion. Lead students to see that the first statement is a fact and the second, an opinion.
- Explain to students that their task as a reader is to pay careful attention to the persuasive language used in a review. Students must not only distinguish between the facts and opinions expressed by the reviewer, but also look for evidence that supports the opinions.

READING INFORMATIONAL MATERIALS

Movie Reviews

About Movie Reviews

Reviews of new films are published in most newspapers on the day they open. In addition, reviews can be found in many magazines, as well as on the Internet, radio, and TV. Writers of movie reviews usually summarize the film's plot and comment on whether they feel the film is worth seeing. Movie critics support their opinions by analyzing the plot, acting, visual appeal, and other elements of the film. Before you allow a review to influence your opinion, follow these steps:

- Distinguish between fact and opinion in the review.
- Analyze the critic's arguments.
- Evaluate the persuasive language the critic uses.

Reading Strategy

Identifying Support for Response

Reviewers know that in order to sway readers, they need to defend their views with convincing reasons. To persuade readers that their opinions are valid, film critics respond to particular elements of a film, providing examples that support their response.

For example, the author of this review of Alfred Hitchcock's *The Birds* finds the movie frightening. As you read the review, look for details he provides to support his response. Use a chart like the one below to jot down the reviewer's responses to particular elements of the film. Identify his support of those responses through his examples and explanations.

Element	Reviewer's Opinion	Support
Special Effects: Bird swooping down on townspeople in scene with gas station explosion	". . . special effects in *The Birds* provide believable and extraordinary horror . . ."	Special effects experts handled bird scenes so well that moviegoers exiting the theater would probably glance up at the sky fearfully.

The Birds

DeWitt Bodeen

[In his film, Hitchcock] has the cinematic advantage [over du Maurier's short story] of being able to show the birds graphically, as they gather and wait like [an evil] army and then swoop in to destroy and kill. In one scene, for example, a bird authority named Mrs. Bundy (Ethel Griffies) sits in a restaurant assuring her listeners that there are many varieties of birds, all of which stick to their own kind, making it impossible for them to unite for any form of attack. As she speaks, however, the birds outside gather and then inexplicably dive down upon the people, seemingly at random. Hitchcock has a special photographic adviser named Ub Iwerks, who, with the aid of special effects expert Laurence A. Hampton, handled the bird scenes in such an effective way that anyone coming out of a theater where *The Birds* had been screened as a matinee attraction was likely to glance up to the sky warily. *The Birds* was nominated for a special effects Academy Award in 1963, but lost to *Cleopatra* for no apparent reason, a fact that upset many critics, since the special effects in *The Birds* provide believable and extraordinary horror and are uncannily executed.

Hitchcock begins his story in San Francisco, where a bachelor attorney, Mitch Brenner (Rod Taylor), meets a wealthy, cool blonde named Melanie Daniels (Tippi Hedren). The two flirt and tease each other, and Melanie is especially taken with Mitch. She impulsively decides to visit Brenner at his home in Bodega Bay, a little north of the city, where he spends weekends with his sister Cathy (Veronica Cartwright) and mother (Jessica Tandy). Brenner's former girlfriend, Annie Hayworth (Suzanne Pleshette), also lives there, teaching at an elementary school a little apart from the main village center.

When Melanie arrives, bringing a cage with two lovebirds which she has bought for Mitch as a joke, the townspeople eye her ominously, for the birds in the area are already gathering around the town, behaving queerly and

The reviewer provides a summary of the film's plot in paragraphs 2, 3, and 4.

The writer identifies actors and actresses by name.

The first part of this sentence presents a fact, while the second part offers an opinion.

The Birds

- Explain to students that they will encounter movie reviews in newspapers, magazines, and journals, as well as on television and the Internet.
- Have students read the review and the notes that identify its main elements.
- Call students' attention to the first note on this page. Have students identify the persuasive language the reviewer uses when describing the special effects. Lead students to see that *believable* and *extraordinary horror* are persuasive words that the reviewer uses to express an opinion.
- Explain to students that movie reviews often provide a summary of the film's plot. Ask students why they think this information is included in a film review.
  Answer: Students should say that the plot summary gives details about the story events, characters, and genre. People use this information to decide if the movie has something of interest for them. It helps them decide whether or not to see the movie.

CUSTOMIZE INSTRUCTION FOR UNIVERSAL ACCESS

For Special Needs Students	For Advanced Readers
To help students distinguish between fact and opinion, ask them to name one of their favorite movies. Begin by asking factual questions about the movie, such as: Who directed it? When was it made? Who stars in the movie? Then, ask students questions designed to elicit opinions about the movie. Lead students to see the difference between these statements of fact and opinion.	Have students locate a current review in a newspaper or magazine for a movie they have seen. Ask them to write a brief essay that evaluates the reviewer's opinions of the movie and how well he or she supports these opinions. If students disagree with the opinions expressed in the review, encourage them to offer their own opinions. Remind them to support their opinions when necessary.

The Birds

- Have students continue reading the review and the notes that identify some of its main elements.
- When students have finished reading the review, ask them to summarize the reviewer's main points.
- Then, have students identify the reviewer's opinions of the movie, both positive and negative. Encourage students to determine if the reviewer has adequately supported these opinions in the review.
- Finally, ask students to evaluate the persuasiveness of this review. Do students think it is a strongly persuasive review? Why or why not? Would they go see this movie based on this review?

The Birds

setting the people on edge. Melanie decides to rent a boat, take the birds across the bay to Mitch's house, give them to Cathy, then quietly return and wait for Mitch's reaction. When they do meet again he begins to like her more, and they fall in love, against his mother's wishes.

After these events, the birds begin more attacks. In one instance they swoop down on a service station, where an attendant is frightened and drops the gasoline line, allowing a spill to spread over the area. A driver watching the birds moving in to attack absentmindedly lights his cigarette and drops the lighted match in the path of the gasoline. There is a huge explosion, and that whole area of the town square is set afire. The camera pulls back for a full overhead shot of the disaster, while the birds sweep through the sky overhead and screech in triumph.

. . .

Hitchcock puts this dark, bizarre, frightening fairy tale before the camera with rare skill. The birds in all their terror and power were manipulated by a trainer named Ray Berwick; without him and the special effects crew, the film would not have been so believable. The picture is handsomely photographed in Technicolor by Robert Burks, and Hitchcock intensifies the spellbound, eerie atmosphere of his story by having no musical background score. Instead, he uses an electronic sound device called a Trautonium, designed by Oskar Sala, and upon this device a toneless, monotonous, but frightening and otherworldly composition by Remi Gassman is played. The advance publicity campaign for the film was expertly handled; on billboards all over numerous cities as well as in the newspapers there appeared the warning message "The Birds Is Coming," piqueing interest in the story.

. . .

There is . . . much more to the film than merely birds. There are some seeming inconsistencies in the plot, and allusions which were criticized by contemporary reviewers are now analyzed at great length. As with all Hitchcock films there is more than a mere story; the complexities of this film are perhaps more difficult to decipher than most. It is never really clear in the film why the birds are attacking, or what, if anything, Melanie's love birds have to do with their behavior. The birds may be avenging something, but there is no evidence of what that something is. The children who are attacked are certainly innocent of any wrongdoing, and in some cases the people killed inadvertently cause their own deaths by panicking.

. . .

The true meaning of the film . . . cannot be pinpointed. This perhaps illustrates one of the greatest aspects of Hitchcock's films: so many questions are left unanswered that they can reveal new insights and nuances of meaning even after repeated viewings.

After a summary, the reviewer offers his opinion. Here, he offers praise.

The reviewer uses specific descriptive words to illustrate his opinion of film elements such as cinematography and music.

Check Your Comprehension

1. According to the reviewer, what advantage does the filmmaker have over the short story writer?
2. What did Ub Iwerks, Laurence A. Hampton, Ray Berwick, Robert Burks, Oskar Sala, and Remi Gassman contribute to the film?
3. (a) According to the reviewer, what are some of the unanswered questions raised by the film? (b) What is the reviewer's opinion of these questions?
4. How did those in charge of publicity do a good job?

Applying the Reading Strategy

Identifying Support for Response

5. Cite three examples DeWitt Bodeen gives to support his opinion that the movie is made "with rare skill."
6. Bodeen finds parts of the film "difficult to decipher," yet he does not think that this is a flaw. How does he defend this response?
7. Complete your own evaluation of the ideas in Bodeen's review. View Alfred Hitchcock's *The Birds*, and then write a brief summary comparing your response to the reviewer's.

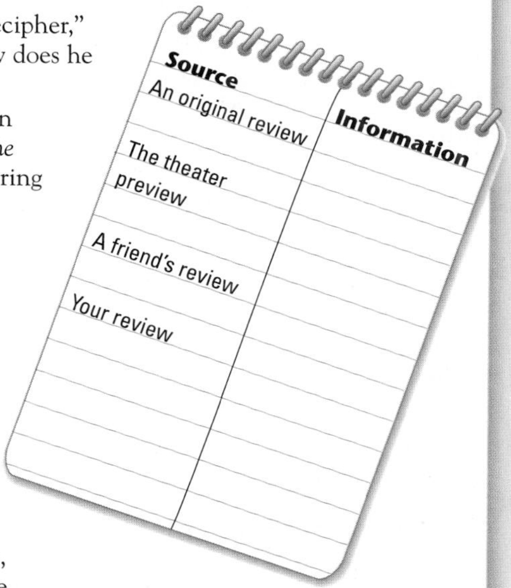

Activity

Evaluating Movie Reviews

Choose a film currently showing in theaters. Using a chart like the one shown, record review information from a variety of sources. Then, see the film and write your own review, providing reasons for your opinion.

Compare your findings to decide which sources gave accurate, convincing, or reliable reviews and whether you agreed with the opinions stated. Then, summarize what you have learned from this exercise.

Contrasting Informational Materials

Movie Reviews and Advertisements

1. Find several movie advertisements and review them to determine the key characteristics of this form of informational material.
2. (a) What do reviews and advertisements have in common? (b) How are they different?
3. Which form do you find more reliable? Explain.

Answers for p. 93

Check Your Comprehension

1. The filmmaker has the advantage of showing the birds graphically.
2. Ub Iwerks was a special photographic advisor, Laurence A. Hampton provided expert support for special effects, Ray Berwick was an animal trainer who handled the live birds, Robert Burke was the photographer, Oskar Sala designed a special electronic sound device used in the movie, and Remi Gassman played this sound device.
3. **(a)** Some of the unanswered questions include: What do Melanie's love birds have to do with the birds' vicious behavior? Why are the children attacked? What is the true meaning of the film? **(b)** The reviewer appreciates the fact that the film leaves questions unanswered because it allows for new insights and interpretations each time the movie is viewed.
4. The publicity campaign for the film stimulated a great deal of curiosity.

Applying the Reading Strategy

5. Possible response: Bodeen cites the behavior of the trained birds, the special effects, and the background score.
6. Bodeen defends this response by saying that he enjoys the fact that new insights and nuances are revealed after repeated viewings.
7. Students' essays should offer opinions about the movie. Remind students that they should support these opinions with details and examples from the movie whenever possible.

Activity

Suggest that students choose a movie they have not seen. This way, the information they choose to gather may not be swayed by their own preconceived opinions of the movie. Students should clearly identify the information provided by each of the sources. You may wish to have students present short oral reports on their findings.

continued

Answers continued

Contrasting Informational Materials

Make sure that students understand that advertisements are used for publicity purposes. This will greatly affect the information provided. While both movie reviews and advertisements are based on films, their differing purposes make their content different. Have students keep these contrasting purposes in mind as they respond to the questions.

The Red-headed League

Lesson Objectives and CA Correlations

1. **To analyze and respond to literary elements**
   - Literary Analysis: The Mystery **R 3.3**
   - Connecting Literary Elements: Characterization
2. **To read, comprehend, analyze, and critique a story**
   - Reading Strategy: Finding Key Details **R 3.8**
   - Reading Check questions
   - Review and Assess questions
   - Assessment Practice (ATE)
3. **To develop word analysis skills, fluency, and systematic vocabulary**
   - Vocabulary Development Lesson: Latin Word Root: *-spec* **R 1.1**
4. **To understand and apply written and oral language conventions**
   - Spelling Strategy
   - Grammar Lesson: Coordinate Adjectives **LC 1.2, 1.3**
5. **To understand and apply appropriate writing and research strategies**
   - Writing Lesson: Detective Story **W 2.1**
   - Extension Activity: The Science of Detective Work **W 2.1**
6. **To understand and apply listening and speaking strategies**
   - Extension Activity: Role-play an Interrogation **LS 1.9**

STEP-BY-STEP TEACHING GUIDE	PACING GUIDE
PRETEACH	
Motivate Students and Provide Background	
Use the Motivation activity (ATE p. 94)	5 min.
Read and discuss the Preview material and Background information (SE/ATE p. 94) [A]	10 min.
Introduce the Concepts	
Introduce the Literary Analysis and Reading Strategy (SE/ATE p. 95) [A]	15 min.
Pronounce the vocabulary words and read their definitions (SE p. 95)	5 min.
TEACH	
Monitor Comprehension	
Informally monitor comprehension by circulating while students read independently or in groups [A]	50 min.
Monitor students' comprehension with the Reading Check notes (SE/ATE pp. 97, 99, 101, 103, 105, 107, 109, 111, 113, 115)	as students read
Develop vocabulary with Vocabulary notes (SE pp. 97, 103, 107, 108; ATE pp. 107, 112)	as students read
Develop Understanding	
Develop students' understanding of mystery with Literary Analysis annotations (SE/ATE pp. 97, 98, 101, 102, 103, 105, 106, 108, 111, 112, 113, 114) [A]	10 min.
Develop students' understanding of finding key details with Reading Strategy annotations (SE/ ATE pp. 98, 100, 102, 104, 107, 110, 115)	10 min.
ASSESS	
Assess Mastery	
Assess students' mastery of the Reading Strategy and Literary Analysis by having them answer the Review and Assess questions (SE/ATE p. 117)	15 min.
Use one or more of the print and media Assessment Resources (ATE p. 119) [A]	up to 50 min.
EXTEND	
Apply Understanding	
Have students complete the Vocabulary Development Lesson and the Grammar Lesson (SE p. 118) [A]	20 min.
Apply students' knowledge of elaboration using the Writing Lesson (SE/ATE p. 119) [A]	45 min.
Apply students' understanding of the story using one or more of the Extension Activities (SE p. 119)	20–90 min.

A **ACCELERATED INSTRUCTION:**
Use the strategies and activities identified with an [A].

UNIVERSAL ACCESS
● = Below Level Students
▲ = On-Level Students
■ = Above Level Students

Time and Resource Manager

Reading Level: Challenging
Average Number of Instructional Days: 5

RESOURCES		
PRINT	**TRANSPARENCIES**	**TECHNOLOGY**
• **Beyond Literature,** Career Connection: Detective, p. 5 ▲ ■		• **Interest Grabber Video,** Tape 1 ● ▲ ■
• **Selection Support Workbook:** ● ▲ ■ Literary Analysis, p. 20 Reading Strategy, p. 19 Build Vocabulary, p. 17	• **Literary Analysis and Reading Transparencies,** pp. 9 and10 ● ▲ ■	
• **Authors In Depth,** Gold Level, p. 2 ■		• **Listening to Literature** ● ▲ ■ Audiocassettes, Side 5 Audio CDs, CD 5
• **Literatura en español** ● ▲ • **Literary Analysis for Enrichment**		
• **Formal Assessment:** Selection Test, pp. 13–15 ● ▲ ■ • **Open Book Test,** pp. 13–15 ● ▲ ■ • **Performance Assessment and Portfolio Management,** p. 13 ● ▲ ■ • PRENTICE HALL ASSESSMENT SYSTEM ● ▲ ■	• PRENTICE HALL ASSESSMENT SYSTEM ● ▲ ■ Skills Practice Answers and Explanations on Transparencies	• **Test Bank Software** ● ▲ ■ • **Got It! Assessment Videotapes,** Tape 1 ● ▲
• **Selection Support Workbook:** ● ▲ ■ Build Grammar Skills, p. 18 • **Writing and Grammar,** Gold Level ● ▲ ■ • **Extension Activities,** p. 5 ● ▲ ■	• **Daily Language Practice Transparencies** ● ▲	• **Writing and Grammar iText CD-ROM** ● ▲ ■ ***Take It to the Net*** www.phschool.com

BLOCK SCHEDULING: Use one 90-minute class period to preteach the selection and have students read it. Use a second 90-minute class period to assess students' mastery of skills and have them complete one of the Extension Activities.

PRETEACH

Step-by-Step Teaching Guide for pp. 94–95

Motivation

Test students' powers of observation by asking them a few questions such as: How many steps are there at the entrance to the school building? What is pictured on the back of a nickel? Which color stripe is at the top of the American flag—red or white? Students will be surprised at the difficulty they have answering these questions correctly. Point out that these are objects they see every day, yet they haven't really paid attention to them. This is the difference between seeing and observing. Tell them that they are about to read a story of a man who not only sees, but observes every small detail of his surroundings.

Interest Grabber Video

As an alternative, you may wish to play "What Makes a Good Mystery?" on Tape 1 to engage students' interest.

1 Background

Literary History

London's popular *Strand* magazine commissioned a series of six Sherlock Holmes stories from Doyle in 1891. Readers went wild for Holmes after the first story appeared, and Doyle was able to nearly double his fee for another six stories. Doyle's final Holmes story appeared in 1927, but the detective is as popular today as he was when his creator was alive. Holmes has been the subject of scholarly biographies, fans have founded numerous societies and reading clubs, and writers such as Laurie King continue to publish new Holmes adventures. Doyle created one of the most beloved literary characters of all time in his keen-eyed, sharp-witted consulting detective.

Prepare to Read

The Red-headed League

Take It to the Net

Visit www.phschool.com for interactive activities and instruction related to "The Red-headed League," including

- background
- graphic organizers
- literary elements
- reading strategies

Preview

Connecting to the Literature

Just a quick glance at a person can give you clues to his personality. This sizing up of people is part of the unpaid detective work of everyday life. As you read "The Red-headed League," notice how the brilliant detective Sherlock Holmes uses the technique of keen observation to solve a mystery.

1 Background

This story is one of many tales about the exploits of the world's most famous fictional detective, Sherlock Holmes. Often shown wearing a cape and deerstalker cap, Holmes is recognized even by people who have never read a Sherlock Holmes mystery.

TEACHING RESOURCES

The following resources can be used to enrich or extend the instruction for pp. 94–95.

Motivation

Interest Grabber Video, Tape 1

Background

Beyond Literature, p.5

Take It to the Net

Visit www.phschool.com for background and hotlinks for "The Red-headed League."

Literary Analysis

Literary Analysis and Reading Transparencies, Mystery, p. 9

Reading

Selection Support: Reading Strategy, p. 19; Vocabulary, p. 17

Literary Analysis and Reading Transparencies, Finding Key Details, p. 10

BLOCK SCHEDULING: Resources marked with this symbol provide varied instruction during 90-minute blocks.

❷ Literary Analysis

The Mystery

A **mystery** is a story of suspense that usually contains a crime, a crime-solver, a criminal, suspects, and key details such as clues, alibis, and characters' possible reasons for committing a crime. When you read a line like the following from "The Red-headed League," you know that you are embarking on detective work and there is a mystery to solve.

> ". . . I want to find out about them, and who they are, and what their object was in playing this prank—if it was a prank—upon me. It was a pretty expensive joke for them, for it cost them two and thirty pounds."

Read "The Red-headed League" carefully to find details the writer has provided to help you solve the mystery.

Connecting Literary Elements

In "The Red-headed League," **characterization**, the way in which characters are developed, provides vital clues to solving the mystery. Writers reveal characters through a variety of techniques, including direct statements, descriptions, and characters' words, thoughts, and actions. Notice how each character in the story is developed and which details are clues to solving the mystery.

❸ Reading Strategy

Finding Key Details

Readers of mysteries try to solve the crime along with—or even before—the detective. This is done by noting **key details**, pieces of information that have a bearing on the crime. These key details are often clues to the mystery. For example, subtleties in a character's actions may reveal something significant. Use a chart like the one shown to record the key details that you find as you read. For each detail, note its possible importance to the case.

Key Detail

Wilson's assistant is willing to work for half wages.

↓

Importance

It's odd that someone volunteers for less pay.

Vocabulary Development

singular (siŋ′ gyə lər) *adj.* rare; extraordinary (p. 97)

avail (ə vāl′) *v.* be of help (p. 103)

hoax (hōks) *n.* deceitful trick (p. 104)

introspective (in′ trə spek′ tiv) *adj.* causing one to look into one's own thoughts and feelings (p. 107)

vex (veks) *v.* annoy (p. 108)

conundrums (kə nun′ drəmz) *n.* puzzling questions or problems (p. 108)

astuteness (ə sto͞ot′ nis) *n.* shrewdness (p. 108)

formidable (fôr′ mə də bəl) *adj.* awe-inspiring (p. 108)

CUSTOMIZE INSTRUCTION FOR UNIVERSAL ACCESS

For Less Proficient Readers	For English Learners	For Advanced Readers
Have students choose partners with whom to read the story. Partners can pause at the end of every two pages and compare ideas. What clues to the mystery have they found? Where do these clues seem to lead?	Students may have difficulty with Doyle's old-fashioned British English. As they read, students can note phrases that puzzle them. Assign peer tutors to help them "translate" these phrases into modern speech.	As students read, have them pretend they are Holmes. Have them observe every small detail, note every clue, and think along with the main character. Students can try to solve the mystery before Holmes does.

❷ Literary Analysis

The Mystery

- Ask students what they think of when they hear the word *mystery*. Explain that mystery fiction is a literary form that gives its characters (and the reader) a puzzle to solve. A mystery usually describes a crime and shows the characters solving *who* committed the crime, *how* they did it, and *why* they did it.
- As students read "The Red-headed League," have them watch for clues to the mystery. Have them pay attention to the ways in which Doyle reveals clues about the mystery.
- Have a volunteer read the Connecting Literary Elements passage. Remind students that an author can develop a character through physical description; through the character's own speech, thoughts, and dialogue; through other characters' speech, thoughts, and dialogue about the character; and the narrator's direct comments about the character.

❸ Reading Strategy

Finding Key Details

- Explain that part of the enjoyment of reading mysteries is trying to solve the puzzle. Readers are provided the same clues and evidence as the fictional detectives.
- The most important part of solving the crime in question is paying attention to details. The author will often provide important clues in ways that make them seem unimportant.
- Students can use a graphic organizer like the one shown on p. 95 to record the key details they find as they read.

Vocabulary Development

- Pronounce each vocabulary word for students, and read the definitions as a class. Have students identify any words with which they are already familiar.

E-Teach

Visit E-Teach at www.phschool.com for teachers' essays on how to teach, with questions and answers.

TEACH

Step-by-Step Teaching Guide for pp. 96–116

CUSTOMIZE INSTRUCTION
Visual/Spatial Learners

Students should enjoy the illustrations that accompany this selection. Share the information in the Background note below. As students read the story, have them study the details of the illustrations and find the passage in the story that each one depicts.

❶ About the Selection

Pawnbroker Jabez Wilson comes to consulting detective Sherlock Holmes with a tale of a mysterious "Red-headed League" that offered him employment for several weeks and then disappeared. Holmes soon discovers that master criminals invented the League to lure Wilson from his pawnshop so that they could dig a tunnel from his cellar into the vaults of a nearby bank.

❷ Background

Art

Illustrations for "The Red-headed League," by Sidney Paget

Englishman Sidney Paget (1860–1908) had a successful career as a painter and illustrator. He is best remembered for his original illustrations for the Holmes stories, which first appeared in the popular *Strand* magazine.

1. How do these illustrations help you appreciate the story?
Answer: They show the styles of hair and clothing worn at the time. They depict various dramatic moments in the action.
2. Challenge students to identify the characters and scenes shown in each illustration.
Answer: On p. 96, Ross shakes Wilson's hand; on p. 100, Spaulding speaks to Wilson; on p. 104, Wilson finds that the League is dissolved; on p. 106, Holmes sits in an armchair; on p. 110, Merryweather lights the way for Holmes, Watson, and Jones; on p. 114, Holmes seizes Clay.

❶

The Red-headed League

Sir Arthur Conan Doyle

❷

TEACHING RESOURCES

The following resources can be used to enrich or extend the instruction for pp. 96–116.

Literary Analysis

Selection Support: Literary Analysis, p. 20

Reading

Listening to Literature Audiocassettes, Side 5 ▪

Listening to Literature Audio CDs, CD 5 ▪

Extension

Authors In Depth, Gold Level
(This collection includes additional selections by Sir Arthur Conan Doyle for extended reading.)

▪ **BLOCK SCHEDULING:** Resources marked with this symbol provide varied instruction during 90-minute blocks.

I had called upon my friend, Mr. Sherlock Holmes, one day in the autumn of last year and found him in deep conversation with a very stout, florid-faced, elderly gentleman with fiery red hair. With an apology for my intrusion, I was about to withdraw when Holmes pulled me abruptly into the room and closed the door behind me.

"You could not possibly have come at a better time, my dear Watson," he said cordially.

"I was afraid that you were engaged."

"So I am. Very much so."

"Then I can wait in the next room."

"Not at all. This gentleman, Mr. Wilson, has been my partner and helper in many of my most successful cases, and I have no doubt that he will be of the utmost use to me in yours also."

The stout gentleman half rose from his chair and gave a bob of greeting, with a quick little questioning glance from his small, fat-encircled eyes.

3 "Try the settee,"[1] said Holmes, relapsing into his armchair and putting his finger tips together, as was his custom when in judicial moods. "I know, my dear Watson, that you share my love of all that is bizarre and outside the conventions and humdrum routine of everyday life. You have shown your relish for it by the enthusiasm which has prompted you to chronicle, and, if you will excuse my saying so, somewhat to embellish so many of my own little adventures.

"Your cases have indeed been of the greatest interest to me," I observed.

"You will remember that I remarked the other day, just before we went into the very simple problem presented by Miss Mary Sutherland, that for strange effects and extraordinary combinations we must go to life itself, which is always far more daring than any effort of the imagination."

"A proposition which I took the liberty of doubting."

"You did, Doctor, but none the less you must come round to my view, for otherwise I shall keep on piling fact upon fact on you until your reason breaks down under them and acknowledges me to be right. Now, Mr. Jabez Wilson here has been good enough to call upon me this morning, and to begin a narrative which promises to be one of the most singular which I have listened to for some time. You have heard me remark that the strangest and most unique things are very often connected not with the larger but with the smaller crimes, and occasionally, indeed, where there is room for doubt whether any positive crime has

Literary Analysis
The Mystery What does Holmes's comment about Watson indicate about the crime-solver in this mystery?

singular (siŋ′ gyə lər) *adj.* rare; extraordinary

4 **✓ Reading Check**
Who has helped Holmes in many of his cases?

1. **settee** (se tē′) *n.* small sofa.

3 Literary Analysis

The Mystery and Characterization

- Point out that in the first few paragraphs, readers already know that this is a mystery story. It is clear that Holmes solves problems for people, and that he is good at this work.
- Ask students to share their first impressions of Holmes. Which specific details give them this impression?
  Possible responses: He enjoys solving problems. He is interested in anything unusual: "my love of all that is bizarre." He is energetic and alert: he pulls Watson "abruptly" into the room, and he is clearly very interested in Wilson's problem.
- Ask students the Literary Analysis question on p. 97: What does Holmes's comment about Watson indicate about the crime-solver in this mystery?
  Answer: It shows that Holmes is the crime-solver and that Watson is his partner and assistant. Holmes' mention of successful cases suggests that he is good at his work.

4 ✓ Reading Check

Answer: Dr. Watson has helped him.

CUSTOMIZE INSTRUCTION FOR UNIVERSAL ACCESS

For Special Needs Students	For Gifted/Talented Students	For Advanced Readers
As students read, they can fill out graphic organizers noting the plot, characters, setting, and theme of this story. Afterwards, they can use these notes to briefly retell the story. Listeners should be sure students' stories are accurate in detail.	Have students pretend that they are editors to whom this story has been submitted for publication. Have them write reviews discussing plot, characters, setting, and theme. Reviews should use details from the story to make a strong case for or against publication.	Have students gather in a small group to debate which of the four short-story elements is most important to "The Red-headed League." Could the same story have worked in a different setting? How much do the personalities add to the reader's enjoyment of the story?

5 Reading Strategy

Finding Key Details

- Ask the Reading Strategy question on p. 98: Which details of Wilson's appearance does Watson seem to regard as most important?
  Answer: Watson notices Wilson's weight, his sloppy clothing, his fiery red hair, and his discontented expression.

Monitor Progress Have students try Watson's inspection. Which details about Holmes, Watson, and Wilson do they think are the most important? What do these details tell them?
Answers: Holmes's dialogue shows that he is intelligent and precise; also, he is usually right and Watson wrong. However, Holmes values Watson's assistance. Since Watson chronicles Holmes' adventures and even embellishes them, he clearly admires Holmes and wishes he were like him. Wilson's sloppy appearance suggests that he is very much upset and probably not well-off.

6 Literary Analysis

The Mystery

- Point out to students that although Watson can see the details Holmes mentions, the reader cannot. Doyle presents this item not as a puzzle for the reader to solve, but as an example of Holmes' power of observation and deduction. Since readers now know that Holmes is very shrewd and observant, they believe that he can solve the mystery.
- Ask students the Literary Analysis question on p. 98: Why are Holmes's observations of Wilson more meaningful than Watson's?
  Answer: The details Holmes sees tell him something about Wilson's background and experiences.

been committed. As far as I have heard it is impossible for me to say whether the present case is an instance of crime or not, but the course of events is certainly among the most singular that I have ever listened to. Perhaps, Mr. Wilson, you would have the great kindness to recommence your narrative. I ask you not merely because my friend Dr. Watson has not heard the opening part but also because the peculiar nature of the story makes me anxious to have every possible detail from your lips. As a rule, when I have heard some slight indication of the course of events, I am able to guide myself by the thousands of other similar cases which occur to my memory. In the present instance I am forced to admit that the facts are, to the best of my belief, unique."

The portly client puffed out his chest with an appearance of some little pride and pulled a dirty and wrinkled newspaper from the inside pocket of his great coat. As he glanced down the advertisement column, with his head thrust forward and the paper flattened out upon his knee, I took a good look at the man and endeavored, after the fashion of my companion, to read the indications which might be presented by his dress or appearance.

5 I did not gain very much, however, by my inspection. Our visitor bore every mark of being an average commonplace British tradesman, obese, pompous, and slow. He wore rather baggy gray shepherd's check trousers, a not over-clean black frock coat, unbuttoned in the front, and a drab waistcoat with a heavy brassy Albert chain, and a square pierced bit of metal dangling down as an ornament. A frayed top hat and a faded brown overcoat with a wrinkled velvet collar lay upon a chair beside him. Altogether, look as I would, there was nothing remarkable about the man save his blazing red head, and the expression of extreme chagrin and discontent upon his features.

Reading Strategy
Finding Key Details Which details of Wilson's appearance does Watson seem to regard as most important?

6 Sherlock Holmes's quick eye took in my occupation, and he shook his head with a smile as he noticed my questioning glances. "Beyond the obvious facts that he has at some time done manual labor, that he takes snuff,[2] that he is a Freemason,[3] that he has been in China, and that he has done a considerable amount of writing lately, I can deduce nothing else."

Mr. Jabez Wilson started up in his chair, with his forefinger upon the paper, but his eyes upon my companion.

"How, in the name of good fortune, did you know all that, Mr. Holmes?" he asked. "How did you know, for example, that I did manual labor? It's as true as gospel, for I began as a ship's carpenter."

"Your hands, my dear sir. Your right hand is quite a size larger than your left. You have worked with it, and the muscles are more developed."

"Well, the snuff, then, and the Freemasonry?"

"I won't insult your intelligence by telling you how I read that, especially as, rather against the strict rules of your order, you use an arc-and-compass breastpin."

Literary Analysis
The Mystery Why are Holmes's observations of Wilson more meaningful than Watson's?

2. **snuff** powdered tobacco.
3. **Freemason** member of a secret society.

ENRICHMENT: LITERATURE CONNECTION

Whodunit?

Edgar Allan Poe is credited as the inventor of the detective story. "The Murders in the Rue Morgue" (1841) is the first appearance of several staple features of the genre: an amateur detective not associated with the police; the friend or assistant who is also the first-person narrator; the presentation of clues to the reader; and the solving of the crime by logical deduction. Writers who followed in Poe's footsteps include Frenchman Emile Gaboriau and Englishmen Wilkie Collins and his close friend Charles Dickens. The Holmes stories, of course, became the most popular of all. A heterogeneous assortment of detectives have followed in Holmes's wake—men and women, aristocratic and common, professional police and amateurs. The genre is extraordinarily popular all over the world.

"Ah, of course, I forgot that. But the writing?"

"What else can be indicated by that right cuff so very shiny for five inches, and the left one with the smooth patch near the elbow where you rest it upon the desk?"

"Well, but China?"

"The fish that you have tattooed immediately above your right wrist could only have been done in China. I have made a small study of tattoo marks and have even contributed to the literature of the subject. That trick of staining the fishes' scales of a delicate pink is quite peculiar to China. When, in addition, I see a Chinese coin hanging from your watch-chain, the matter becomes even more simple."

Mr. Jabez Wilson laughed heavily. "Well, I never!" said he. "I thought at first that you had done something clever, but I see that there was nothing in it, after all."

"I begin to think, Watson," said Holmes, "that I make a mistake in explaining. *'Omne ignotum pro magnifico,'*[4] you know, and my poor little reputation, such as it is, will suffer shipwreck if I am so candid. Can you not find the advertisement, Mr. Wilson?"

"Yes, I have got it now," he answered with his thick red finger planted halfway down the column. "Here it is. This is what began it all. You just read it for yourself, sir."

I took the paper from him and read as follows:

> To THE RED-HEADED LEAGUE:
>
> 7 On account of the bequest of the late Ezekiah Hopkins, of Lebanon, Pennsylvania, U. S. A., there is now another vacancy open which entitles a member of the League to a salary of £4♦ a week for purely nominal services. All red-headed men who are sound in body and mind, and above the age of twenty-one years, are eligible. Apply in person on Monday, at eleven o'clock, to Duncan Ross, at the offices of the League, 7 Pope's Court, Fleet Street.

"What on earth does this mean?" I ejaculated after I had twice read over the extraordinary announcement.

Holmes chuckled and wriggled in his chair, as was his habit when in high spirits. "It is a little off the beaten track, isn't it?" said he. "And now, Mr. Wilson, off you go at scratch and tell us all about yourself, your household, and the effect which this advertisement had upon your fortunes. You will first make a note, Doctor, of the paper and the date."

"It is *The Morning Chronicle* of April 27, 1890. Just two months ago."

"Very good. Now, Mr. Wilson?"

"Well, it is just as I have been telling you, Mr. Sherlock Holmes," said Jabez Wilson, mopping his forehead; "I have a small pawnbroker's business at Coburg Square, near the City. It's not a very large

4. ***Omne ignotum pro magnifico*** (äm′ nā ig nō′ təm prō mag nē′ fē kō) Latin for "Whatever is unknown is magnified."

Literature in context — Math Connection

♦ *Pound Conversions*

The advertisement announces a League salary of four pounds a week. The pound is the monetary unit of Great Britain. Its equivalency in American dollars fluctuates, depending on current economic conditions. At the time Doyle wrote the story, one British pound equaled about $4.85, so four pounds would have equaled about $19.40. This was considered a large amount at the time in which the story is set, particularly for such simple work.

8 Reading Check

Who is eligible for the position posted in the advertisement?

7 Background

Math

When this story was written, British money was divided into pounds, shillings, and pence. Twelve pence (pennies) made a shilling, and 20 shillings made a pound. Other coins included the crown (worth 5 shillings), the sovereign (worth one pound), the half-crown, the half-sovereign, and the florin (worth 2 shillings). Late in the twentieth century, England shifted to a decimal monetary system in which 100 pence made one pound. The old shillings and florins were replaced with coins such as twopence, fivepence, tenpence, and so on.

8 Reading Check

Answer: Red-haired men over the age of twenty-one are eligible.

CUSTOMIZE INSTRUCTION FOR UNIVERSAL ACCESS

For English Learners	For Gifted/Talented Students
Have partners work together to make illustrated dictionaries of unfamiliar terms in the story. Examples include *settee, frock coat, Albert chain, crib,* and so on. Encourage students to use context clues, the illustrations, and other aids to help them figure out precisely what the words and phrases mean. They should check their definitions in dictionaries or encyclopedias.	Challenge a small group of students to dramatize the story. They can perform it as a dramatic reading, a radio play, a pantomime, or a fully staged presentation. Encourage them to use their creativity and imagination to entertain the class. Students can work together on the script, divide up the roles, choose a director, and locate all necessary props and costumes.

❾ Reading Strategy

Finding Key Details

- Ask the Reading Strategy question on p. 100: Which details about Vincent Spaulding are unusual enough to interest Sherlock Holmes?
  Answer: Spaulding's willingness to work for half the normal salary surprises Holmes.
- Have students speculate on why Spaulding is willing to work for half wages. Point out that a boy or very young man might accept low wages as an apprenticeship, but Spaulding is a full-grown man. Also, Spaulding is clearly very smart and capable.
  Answers: Spaulding has some ulterior motive for wanting to work for Wilson. Spaulding may intend to take advantage of him in some way.
- Ask students what Spaulding might be doing in the cellar. Do they think he is really a photographer? Why or why not?
  Possible responses: If he really is a photographer, he might be running some kind of business relating to his photography and it's convenient for him to be Wilson's assistant as a cover. If he isn't really a photographer, he is working in the cellar on some other project that Wilson doesn't know about.

affair, and of late years it has not done more than just give me a living. I used to be able to keep two assistants, but now I only keep one; and I would have a job to pay him but that he is willing to come for half wages so as to learn the business."

"What is the name of this obliging youth?" asked Sherlock Holmes.

"His name is Vincent Spaulding, and he's not such a youth, either. It's hard to say his age. I should not wish a smarter assistant, Mr. Holmes; and I know very well that he could better himself and earn twice what I am able to give him. But, after all, if he is satisfied, why
❾ should I put ideas in his head?"

"Why, indeed? You seem most fortunate in having an employee who comes under the full market price. It is not a common experience among employers in this age. I don't know that your assistant is not as remarkable as your advertisement."

"Oh, he has his faults, too," said Mr. Wilson. "Never was such a fellow for photography. Snapping away with a camera when he ought to be improving his mind, and then diving down into the cellar like a rabbit into its hole to develop his pictures. That is his main fault, but on the whole he's a good worker. There's no vice in him."

"He is still with you, I presume?"

"Yes, sir. He and a girl of fourteen, who does a bit of simple cooking and keeps the place clean—that's all I have in the house, for I am a widower and never had any family. We live very quietly, sir, the three of us; and we keep a roof over our heads and pay our debts, if we do nothing more.

"The first thing that put us out was that advertisement. Spaulding, he came down into the office just this day eight weeks, with this very paper in his hand, and he says:

" 'I wish to the Lord, Mr. Wilson, that I was a red-headed man.'

" 'Why that?' I asks.

" 'Why,' says he, 'here's another vacancy on the League of the Red-headed Men. It's worth quite a little fortune to any man who gets it, and I understand that there are more vacancies than there are men, so that the trustees are at their wits' end what to do with the money. If my hair would only change color, here's a nice little crib all ready for me to step into.'

" 'Why, what is it, then?' I asked. You see, Mr. Holmes, I am a very stay-at-home man,

Reading Strategy
Finding Key Details
Which details about Vincent Spaulding are unusual enough to interest Sherlock Holmes?

ENRICHMENT: SOCIAL STUDIES CONNECTION

City of London

When Jabez Wilson says that his pawnshop is "near the City," the capital C shows that he is referring to a neighborhood within London and not to the entire city. The City (short for "City of London") is one of the oldest parts of London and has been a commercial and financial center since before the Norman Conquest of England, nearly 1,000 years ago. City of London landmarks include St. Paul's Cathedral, the Central Criminal Court at the Old Bailey, and the Bank of England. The neighborhood's main street is the Strand, which becomes Fleet Street when it crosses Chancery Lane. Much of the original City of London was destroyed in the Great Fire of 1666; a tall stone column stands atop a hill in the City as a monument to the fire.

and as my business came to me instead of my having to go to it, I was often weeks on end without putting my foot over the doormat. In that way I didn't know much of what was going on outside, and I was always glad of a bit of news.

" 'Have you never heard of the League of the Red-headed Men?' he asked with his eyes open.

" 'Never.'

" 'Why, I wonder at that, for you are eligible yourself for one of the vacancies.'

" 'And what are they worth?' I asked.

" 'Oh, merely a couple of hundred a year, but the work is slight, and it need not interfere very much with one's other occupations.'

"Well, you can easily think that that made me prick up my ears, for the business has not been over-good for some years, and an extra couple of hundred would have been very handy.

" 'Tell me all about it,' said I.

" 'Well,' said he, showing me the advertisement, 'you can see for yourself that the League has a vacancy, and there is the address where you should apply for particulars. As far as I can make out, the League was
10 founded by an American millionaire, Ezekiah Hopkins, who was very peculiar in his ways. He was himself red-headed, and he had a great sympathy for all red-headed men; so when he died it was found that he had left his enormous fortune in the hands of trustees, with instructions to apply the interest to the providing of easy berths to men whose hair is of that color. From all I hear it is splendid pay and very little to do.

" 'But,' said I, 'there would be millions of red-headed men who would apply.'

" 'Not so many as you might think,' he answered. 'You see it is really confined to Londoners, and to grown men. This American had started from London when he was young, and he wanted to do the old town a good turn. Then, again, I have heard it is no use your applying if your hair is light red, or dark red, or anything but real bright, blazing, fiery red. Now, if you cared to apply, Mr. Wilson, you would just walk in; but perhaps it would hardly be worth your while to put yourself out of the way for the sake of a few hundred pounds.'

"Now, it is a fact, gentlemen, as you may see for yourselves, that my hair is of a very full and rich tint, so that it seemed to me that if there was to be any competition in the matter I stood as good a chance as any man that I had ever met. Vincent Spaulding seemed to know so much about it that I thought he might prove useful so I just ordered him to put up the shutters for the day and to come right away with me. He was very willing to have a holiday,[5] so we shut the business up and started off for the address that was given us in the advertisement.

"I never hope to see such a sight as that again, Mr. Holmes. From north, south, east, and west every man who had a shade of red in his hair had tramped into the city to answer the advertisement. Fleet

5. **holiday** a day off from work; a vacation.

Literary Analysis

The Mystery The Red-headed League seems too good to be true. What appears most suspicious about this club?

11 **Reading Check**

Why did Wilson believe he had a good chance of being chosen for the position?

10 Literary Analysis

The Mystery

- Pause at this point and ask students if any part of Wilson's story has aroused their suspicions. Have them explain their answers.
  Answers: Spaulding's eagerness for Wilson to answer the advertisement is suspicious. So is his willingness to work for half the usual salary and his detailed knowledge of the Red-headed League. Spaulding is probably involved in some plot to trick Wilson.
- Have students compare the wording of the advertisement (on p. 99) with the information Spaulding gives Wilson. What does Spaulding's knowledge add to the mystery?
  Answer: He knows much more than the newspaper says. Holmes, Watson, and Wilson, who all live in London, have never heard of the League. This suggests that Spaulding may have been behind the advertisement and that it's a trick of some sort.
- Ask students the Literary Analysis question on p. 101: The Red-headed League seems too good to be true. What appears most suspicious about this club?
  Answer: The club offers a substantial amount of money to red-headed men in exchange for very easy work. The club seems especially interested in men with Wilson's shade of red hair.

11 Reading Check

Answer: Wilson knew his hair was a fiery red and that this was unusual.

CUSTOMIZE INSTRUCTION FOR UNIVERSAL ACCESS

For Less Proficient Readers	For Special Needs Students	For Advanced Readers
Have students consider this story as a series of causes and effects. They can note each interesting or surprising detail, such as Spaulding's willingness to work for half wages, in one column of a chart. In the other column, they can note possible causes for this effect.	Have students choose partners with whom to read the story. Each partner should read on his or her own, and then pause every one or two pages to summarize the story up to that point. Each partner should make sure that the other's summary is accurate. Students can try predicting what may come in the next page or two.	After students have read the story, challenge them to retell it from Holmes's point of view. Their versions will be much shorter than the original; they need not repeat Wilson's story, for instance. Have students consider the tone Holmes would use and how he would reveal his solution to the crime.

12 Reading Strategy

Finding Key Details

- Ask students to describe the role that Spaulding plays in this scene. Which details of his behavior seem suspicious?
  Answer: He urges Wilson not to give up. He pushes and shoves until Wilson is at the head of the line. It seems very important to him that Wilson get the job. Since he only recently began working for Wilson, it seems strange that he should be so eager to see him get the job with the League.
- Then, ask the Reading Strategy question on p. 102: What do you notice about how the League interviewer receives Wilson?
  Answer: He treats him differently from the other applicants. He shuts the door so that they can speak privately.

13 Literary Analysis

The Mystery

- Read aloud the bracketed passage to the class.
- Ask students whether they think the red-headed man at the table seems honest and straightforward or untrustworthy. Have them give reasons to support their responses.
  Answer: His red hair suggests that the league may be genuine. His immediate choice of Wilson as the right man for the vacancy is suspicious.
- Then, ask students the Literary Analysis question on p. 102: What is suspicious about the way in which the vacancy was filled?
  Answer: No questions are asked about Wilson's background or his interest in the position. No other applicants were given any kind of interview.

Street was choked with red-headed folk, and Pope's Court looked like a coster's orange barrow.[6] I should not have thought there were so many in the whole country as were brought together by that single advertisement. Every shade of color they were—straw, lemon, orange, brick, Irish-setter, liver, clay: but, as Spaulding said, there were not 12 many who had the real vivid flame-colored tint. When I saw how many were waiting, I would have given it up in despair: but Spaulding would not hear of it. How he did it I could not imagine, but he pushed and pulled and butted until he got me through the crowd, and right up to the steps which led to the office. There was a double stream upon the stair, some going up in hope, and some coming back dejected: but we wedged in as well as we could and soon found ourselves in the office."

"Your experience has been a most entertaining one," remarked Holmes as his client paused and refreshed his memory with a huge pinch of snuff. "Pray continue your very interesting statement."

"There was nothing in the office but a couple of wooden chairs and a deal table, behind which sat a small man with a head that was even redder than mine. He said a few words to each candidate as he came up, and then he always managed to find some fault in them which would disqualify them. Getting a vacancy did not seem to be such a very easy matter, after all. However, when our turn came the little man was much more favorable to me than to any of the others, and he closed the door as we entered, so that he might have a private word with us.

" 'This is Mr. Jabez Wilson,' said my assistant, 'and he is willing to fill a vacancy in the League.'

" 'And he is admirably suited for it,' the other answered. 'He has every requirement. I cannot recall when I have seen anything so fine.' He took a step backward, cocked his head on one side, and gazed at my hair until I felt quite bashful. Then suddenly he plunged forward, 13 wrung my hand, and congratulated me warmly on my success.

" 'It would be injustice to hesitate, said he. 'You will, however, I am sure, excuse me for taking an obvious precaution.' With that he seized my hair in both his hands, and tugged until I yelled with the pain. 'There is water in your eyes,' said he as he released me. 'I perceive that all is as it should be. But we have to be careful, for we have twice been deceived by wigs and once by paint. I could tell you tales of cobbler's wax which would disgust you with human nature.' He stepped over to the window and shouted through it at the top of his voice that the vacancy was filled. A groan of disappointment came up from below, and the folk all trooped away in different directions until there was not a red head to be seen except my own and that of the manager.

" 'My name,' said he, 'is Mr. Duncan Ross, and I am myself one of the pensioners upon the fund left by our noble benefactor. Are you a married man, Mr. Wilson? Have you a family?'

Reading Strategy
Finding Key Details What do you notice about how the League interviewer receives Wilson?

Literary Analysis
The Mystery What is suspicious about the way in which the vacancy was filled?

6. **coster's orange barrow** pushcart of a seller of oranges.

ENRICHMENT: SOCIAL STUDIES CONNECTION

London

In Sherlock Holmes's day, Great Britain was the center of a powerful empire on which, in a popular phrase, "the sun never set"—meaning that Britain ruled countries all across the globe. London, the capital city of England, was the largest city in the world. It was an international capital of art, science, manufacturing, finance, and trade. It was also a port that carried people and goods to and from such faraway places as Australia, Hong Kong, and India.

The Industrial Revolution began in the late 1700s. Because it gave rise to so many new jobs in the city, thousands of people migrated there from the countryside. In Sherlock Holmes's day, London was home to more people of more diverse backgrounds and classes than ever before.

"I answered that I had not.

"His face fell immediately.

" 'Dear me!' he said gravely, 'that is very serious indeed! I am sorry to hear you say that. The fund was, of course, for the propagation and spread of the red-heads as well as for their maintenance. It is exceedingly unfortunate that you should be a bachelor.'

"My face lengthened at this, Mr. Holmes, for I thought that I was not to have the vacancy after all: but after thinking it over for a few minutes he said that it would be all right.

" 'In the case of another,' said he, 'the objection might be fatal, but we must stretch a point in favor of a man with such a head of hair as yours. When shall you be able to enter upon your new duties?

" 'Well, it is a little awkward, for I have a business already,' said I.

" 'Oh, never mind about that, Mr. Wilson!' said Vincent Spaulding. 'I should be able to look after that for you.'

" 'What would be the hours?' I asked.

" 'Ten to two.'

"Now a pawnbroker's business is mostly done of an evening, Mr. Holmes, especially Thursday and Friday evening, which is just before pay-day: so it would suit me very well to earn a little in the mornings. Besides, I knew that my assistant was a good man, and that he would see to anything that turned up.

" 'That would suit me very well,' said I. 'And the pay?'

" 'Is £4 a week.'

14 " 'And the work?'

" 'Is purely nominal.'

" 'What do you call purely nominal?'

" 'Well, you have to be in the office, or at least in the building, the whole time. If you leave, you forfeit your whole position forever. The will is very clear upon that point. You don't comply with the conditions if you budge from the office during that time.'

" 'It's only four hours a day, and I should not think of leaving,' said I.

" 'No excuse will avail,' said Mr. Duncan Ross: 'neither sickness nor business nor anything else. There you must stay, or you lose your billet.'[7]

" 'And the work?'

" 'Is to copy out the Encyclopedia Britannica. There is the first volume of it in that press. You must find your own ink, pens, and blotting-paper, but we provide this table and chair. Will you be ready tomorrow?'

" 'Certainly,' I answered.

" 'Then, good-bye, Mr. Jabez Wilson, and let me congratulate you once more on the important position which you have been fortunate enough to gain.' He bowed me out of the room, and I went home with my assistant, hardly knowing what to say or do, I was so pleased at my own good fortune.

7. **billet** (bil' it) *n.* position; job.

avail (ə vāl') *v.* be of help

Literary Analysis
The Mystery What is it about the nature of Wilson's job that sounds suspicious?

15 **Reading Check**
Who offered to look after Wilson's pawnbroker business while he was at his other job?

14 Literary Analysis
The Mystery

- Ask students what Wilson's acceptance of the conditions means for his pawnshop.
  Answer: He will be away from it for four hours a day; Spaulding will be in charge.
- Ask students why Spaulding might want to get Wilson out of the pawnshop for four hours a day at a time when the shop won't be busy.
  Answer: He might be running his own business out of the shop. He might be scheming to steal from Wilson. He may want a private place where he can meet with associates without being interrupted.
- Ask the Literary Analysis question on p. 103: What is it about the nature of Wilson's job that sounds suspicious?
  Answer: He is not allowed to leave the building in which he'll be working. He is asked to copy a book by hand, a job that serves no purpose at all.

15 Reading Check
Answer: Vincent Spaulding, his assistant, offered to look after the business.

16 Critical Thinking

Drawing Conclusions

- Explain to students that a character or reader can look at a number of statements or pieces of information to see what they mean when taken together, whether they form a pattern, or indicate a next step. This process is called *drawing a conclusion.*
- Have students read the first paragraph on p. 104. What conclusion does Wilson draw about his day's experiences? Why does he draw this conclusion?
  Answer: He concludes that the Red-headed League is a fraud, because it seems to good to be true.
- Ask students to draw conclusions about Duncan Ross's frequent appearances in Wilson's writing room. What conclusion can they draw when he stops coming?
  Possible answers: At first, Ross wants to be sure Wilson is copying out the Encyclopedia; later, he trusts him and doesn't check on him so often. Once assured that Wilson doesn't leave the building, Ross stops checking on Wilson.
- Then, ask students what conclusions the reader can draw about Wilson at this point in the story. Have students explain their answers.
  Answer: He isn't very smart. He knows the Red-headed League is too good to be true, but he goes along with the deal anyway. He trusts everything Spaulding says to him and never questions why Spaulding is willing to work for half the usual salary. He trusts Spaulding to look after the pawnshop even though he's only known him for a month.

"Well, I thought over the matter all day, and by evening I was in low spirits again: for I had quite persuaded myself that the whole affair must be some great hoax or fraud, though what its object might be I could not imagine. It seemed altogether past belief that anyone could make such a will, or that they would pay such a sum for doing anything so simple as copying out the Encyclopedia Britannica. Vincent Spaulding did what he could to cheer me up, but by bedtime I had reasoned myself out of the whole thing. However, in the morning I determined to have a look at it anyhow, so I bought a penny bottle of ink, and with a quill-pen, and seven sheets of foolscap paper,[8] I started off for Pope's Court.

hoax (hōks) *n.* deceitful trick

"Well, to my surprise and delight, everything was as right as possible. The table was set out ready for me, and Mr. Duncan Ross was there to see that I got fairly to work. He started me off upon the letter A, and then he left me; but he would drop in from time to time to see 16 that all was right with me. At two o'clock he bade me good-day, complimented me upon the amount that I had written, and locked the door of the office after me.

"This went on day after day, Mr. Holmes, and on Saturday the manager came in and planked down four golden sovereigns for my week's work. It was the same next week, and the same the week after. Every morning I was there at ten, and every afternoon I left at two. By degrees Mr. Duncan Ross took to coming in only once of a morning, and then, after a time, he did not come in at all. Still, of course, I never dared to leave the room for an instant, for I was not sure when he might come, and the billet was such a good one, and suited me so well, that I would not risk the loss of it.

"Eight weeks passed away like this, and I had written about Abbots and Archery and Armor and Architecture and Attica, and hoped with diligence that I might get on to the B's before very long. It cost me something in foolscap,and I had pretty nearly filled a shelf with my writings. And then suddenly the whole business came to an end."

"To an end?"

"Yes, sir. And no later than this morning. I went to my work as usual at ten o'clock, but the door was shut and locked, with a little square of cardboard hammered on to the middle of the panel with a tack. Here it is, and you can read for yourself."

8. **foolscap paper** writing paper.

He held up a piece of white cardboard about the size of a sheet of notepaper. It read in this fashion:

THE RED-HEADED LEAGUE
IS
DISSOLVED.
October 9, 1890.

Sherlock Holmes and I surveyed this curt announcement and the rueful face behind it, until the comical side of the affair so completely overtopped every other consideration that we both burst out into a roar of laughter.

"I cannot see that there is anything very funny," cried our client, flushing up to the roots of his flaming head. "If you can do nothing better than laugh at me, I can go elsewhere."

"No, no," cried Holmes, shoving him back into the chair from which he had half risen. "I really wouldn't miss your case for the world. It is most refreshingly unusual. But there is, if you will excuse my saying so, something just a little funny about it. Pray what steps did you take when you found the card upon the door?"

"I was staggered, sir. I did not know what to do. Then I called at the offices round, but none of them seemed to know anything about it. Finally, I went to the landlord, who is an accountant living on the ground floor, and I asked him if he could tell me what had become of the Red-headed League. He said that he had never heard of any such body. Then I asked him who Mr. Duncan Ross was. He answered that the name was new to him.

" 'Well,' said I, 'the gentleman at No. 4.'

" 'What, the red-headed man?'

17 " 'Yes.'

" 'Oh,' said he, 'his name was William Morris. He was a solicitor[9] and was using my room as a temporary convenience until his new premises were ready. He moved out yesterday.'

" 'Where could I find him?'

" 'Oh, at his new offices. He did tell me the address. Yes, 17 King Edward Street, near St. Paul's.'

"I started off, Mr. Holmes, but when I got to that address it was a manufactory of artificial kneecaps, and no one in it had ever heard of either Mr. William Morris or Mr. Duncan Ross."

"And what did you do then?" asked Holmes.

"I went home to Saxe-Coburg Square, and I took the advice of my assistant. But he could not help me in any way. He could only say that if I waited I should hear by post. But that was not quite good enough, Mr. Holmes. I did not wish to lose such a place without a struggle, so, as I had heard that you were good enough to give advice to poor folk who were in need of it, I came right away to you."

"And you did very wisely," said Holmes. "Your case is an exceedingly remarkable one, and I shall be happy to look into it. From what

9. **solicitor** member of the legal profession.

Literary Analysis
The Mystery At this point, another suspect enters the picture. Which clues point toward this character as a suspect?

18 **Reading Check**
After eight weeks at his new job, what does Wilson find posted on the door?

17 Literary Analysis

The Mystery

- Have a volunteer read aloud the bracketed passage. Then ask students the Literary Analysis question on p. 105: At this point, another suspect enters the picture. Which clues point toward this character as a suspect?
  Answer: The character uses two different names. He lies about his reason for renting the room at No. 4.
- Ask students whether they now have definite evidence that Spaulding and Ross/Morris are friends, and what that evidence is.
  Answer: Since Spaulding knew all about the League and it is now clear that the League never existed, it is evident that Spaulding and Ross are working together.

Monitor Progress Ask students why they think Ross/Morris and Spaulding set up the Red-headed League. Have them defend their answers with evidence from the story.
Possible answers: They wanted to play a practical joke on Wilson. They wanted Wilson out of the pawnbroker's shop for four hours every day so they could use it for some purpose of their own. Perhaps they wanted to take over the pawnbroker's business.

18 Reading Check

Answer: He finds a card telling him that the Red-headed League has been dissolved.

CUSTOMIZE INSTRUCTION FOR UNIVERSAL ACCESS

For Gifted/Talented Students

Have students choose partners with whom to do some research on any aspect of Victorian London that interests them. They might investigate the early history of the London police department, study forms of transportation such as the hansom cab and the Underground, investigate the popularity of the Holmes stories in their own day, or discuss the position of women in society. Students can give class presentations on their research. They might want to dress up as Holmes and Watson and present it in character, write newspaper articles on their topic, or any other format that appeals to them. Encourage creativity and imagination. Have students clear their topics with you before they begin writing.

19 Literary Analysis

The Mystery and Characterization

- Pause at this point and have students give their impressions of Holmes and Watson. Ask students to identify how they formed these impressions.
  Answer: So far, Watson has had little to say or do. He is clearly not as observant as Holmes. Holmes is alert, intelligent, and enjoys exercising his wits on puzzles.
- Ask the Literary Analysis question on p. 106: Explain what is revealed in this passage about Holmes as a crime-solver.
  Answer: Holmes is a good listener. He remembers what Wilson has told him and he asks about the key details of the story. He apparently recognizes Spaulding, which shows that he has experience with criminals. He believes he can solve the crime in a day or two, so he has confidence in himself.
- Ask students to make the connection between Holmes's personality and his success as a detective.
  Answer: Holmes is smart, observant, self-confident, and knowledgeable about the criminal world. These are all excellent qualities in a detective.

you have told me I think that it is possible that graver issues hang from it than might at first sight appear."

"Grave enough!" said Mr. Jabez Wilson. "Why, I have lost four pound a week."

"As far as you are personally concerned," remarked Holmes, "I do not see that you have any grievance against this extraordinary league. On the contrary, you are, as I understand, richer by some £30, to say nothing of the minute knowledge which you have gained on every subject which comes under the letter A. You have lost nothing by them."

"No, sir. But I want to find out about them, and who they are, and what their object was in playing this prank—if it was a prank—upon me. It was a pretty expensive joke for them, for it cost them two and thirty pounds."

"We shall endeavor to clear up these points for you. And, first, one or two questions, Mr. Wilson. This assistant of yours who first called your attention to the advertisement—how long had he been with you?"

"About a month then."

"How did he come?"

"In answer to an advertisement."

"Was he the only applicant?"

"No, I had a dozen."

19 "Why did you pick him?"

"Because he was handy and would come cheap."

"At half-wages, in fact."

"Yes."

"What is he like, this Vincent Spaulding?"

"Small, stout-built, very quick in his ways. No hair on his face, though he's not short of thirty. Has a white splash of acid upon his forehead."

Holmes sat up in his chair in considerable excitement. "I thought as much," said he. "Have you ever observed that his ears are pierced for earrings?"

"Yes, sir. He told me that a gypsy had done it for him when he was a lad."

"Hum!" said Holmes, sinking back in deep thought. "He is still with you?"

"Oh, yes, sir; I have only just left him."

"And has your business been attended to in your absence?"

"Nothing to complain of, sir. There's never very much to do of a morning."

"That will do, Mr. Wilson. I shall be happy to give you an opinion upon the subject in the course of a day or two. Today is Saturday, and I hope that by Monday we may come to a conclusion."

"Well, Watson," said Holmes when our visitor had left us, "what do

Literary Analysis
The Mystery and Characterization Explain what is revealed in this passage about Holmes as a crime-solver.

ENRICHMENT: LITERATURE CONNECTION

Holmes and Watson

Sherlock Holmes and Dr. Watson first met in Doyle's 1887 novel *A Study in Scarlet.* Watson, an army doctor, had been wounded and sent home; he and Holmes were both looking for someone with whom to share a flat. Homes' first words to Watson were "You have been in Afghanistan, I perceive." Watson is astonished, and Holmes explains which details in his new acquaintance's appearance showed that he had been in the army in Afghanistan. The two men moved into 221 Baker Street, and Watson soon began writing up the stories of Holmes's cases for publication. In the second Holmes novel, *The Sign of the Four*, Watson marries and leaves Baker Street for his own home. However, he continues assisting Holmes on various cases until the late 1920s; the two men remain the closest of friends in spite of strong differences in character.

you make of it all?"

"I make nothing of it," I answered frankly. "It is a most mysterious business."

"As a rule," said Holmes, "the more bizarre a thing is the less mysterious it proves to be. It is your commonplace, featureless crimes which are really puzzling, just as a commonplace face is the most difficult to identify. But I must be prompt over this matter."

"What are you going to do, then?" I asked.

"To smoke," he answered. "It is quite a three pipe problem, and I beg that you won't speak to me for fifty minutes." He curled himself up in his chair, with his thin knees drawn up to his hawk-like nose, and there he sat with his eyes closed and his black clay pipe thrusting out like the bill of some strange bird. I had come to the conclusion that he had dropped asleep, and indeed was nodding myself, when he suddenly sprang out of his chair with the gesture of a man who has made up his mind and put his pipe down upon the mantelpiece.

"Sarasate[10] plays at the St. James's Hall this afternoon," he remarked. "What do you think, Watson? Could your patients spare you for a few hours?"

"I have nothing to do today. My practice is never very absorbing."

20 "Then put on your hat and come. I am going through the City first, and we can have some lunch on the way. I observe that there is a good deal of German music on the program, which is rather more to my taste than Italian or French. It is introspective, and I want to introspect. Come along!"

introspective (in´ trə spek´ tiv) *adj.* causing one to look into one's own thoughts and feelings

21 We traveled by the Underground as far as Aldersgate; and a short walk took us to Saxe-Coburg Square, the scene of the singular story which we had listened to in the morning. It was a poky, little, shabby-genteel place, where four lines of dingy two-storied brick houses looked out into a small railed–in enclosure, where a lawn of weedy grass and a few clumps of faded laurel bushes made a hard fight against a smoke-laden and uncongenial atmosphere. Three gilt balls and a brown board with "JABEZ WILSON" in white letters, upon a corner house, announced the place where our red-headed client carried on his business. Sherlock Holmes stopped in front of it with his head on one side and looked it all over, with his eyes shining brightly between puckered lids. Then he walked slowly up the street, and then down again to the corner, still looking keenly at the houses. Finally he returned to the pawnbroker's, and, having thumped vigorously upon the pavement with his stick two or three times, he went up to the door and knocked. It was instantly opened by a bright-looking, clean-shaven young fellow, who asked him to step in.

Reading Strategy
Finding Key Details
Which key details in this passage seem to be clues that help Holmes solve the crime?

"Thank you," said Holmes, "I only wished to ask you how you would go from here to the Strand."

"Third right, fourth left," answered the assistant promptly, closing the door.

22 **Reading Check**
What reasons does Mr. Wilson give for hiring Vincent Spaulding?

10. Sarasate (sä rä sä´ tā) Spanish violinist and composer.

20 Vocabulary Development
Latin Root *-spec-*

- Read aloud the next-to-last sentence of this paragraph. Point out the definition of *introspective* in the margin. Write the word on the chalkboard and break it up into its prefix, root, and suffix. Students should easily understand that *intro-* means "into, inside, inward." If you or any student in the class wears eyeglasses, point them out and tell the class that eyeglasses are also called *spectacles*. This clue will help students remember that *-spec-* has to do with looking or seeing.
- Challenge students to list and define other words based on the root *-spec-*.
  Answer: Possible words include *respect, prospect, aspect, inspect, spectator, spectacular, specter, spectrum,* and other forms of these words.

21 Reading Strategy
Finding Key Details

- Before students read this paragraph, ask what they think Holmes might learn from this visit to the pawnshop.
  Answer: He might ask Spaulding some questions. He might explore the shop for signs of what Spaulding has been up to.
- Then, ask the Reading Strategy question on p. 107: Which key details in this passage seem to be clues that help Holmes solve the crime?
  Answer: Holmes bangs his stick on the sidewalk to find out something. He may be listening for a hollow sound. He needs to get a look at Spaulding.

22 Reading Check

Answer: Spaulding was willing to work for half the salary and was a good worker.

23 Literary Analysis

The Mystery

- Ask students what they think Holmes has learned on his visit to Saxe-Coburg Square.
  Answer: He learned something from the knees of Spaulding's trousers—they may have been stained or torn in a way that showed Holmes he had knelt in a particular place to do some work. He learned something from beating the pavement—he may have heard a hollow sound.
- Ask students why they think Holmes doesn't share what he learns with Watson.
  Answer: Holmes may not want to say anything until he has solved the whole puzzle. Holmes may enjoy teasing Watson, who isn't as observant as he is himself. The author may be withholding this information to give the reader a chance to solve the puzzle.
- Ask the Literary Analysis question on p. 108. What might be Holmes's motive for familiarizing himself with the order of the buildings behind Saxe-Coburg Square?
  Answer: He may think this has something to do with the Wilson case.

24 Literary Analysis

Characterization

- Have students read the paragraph beginning "My friend was an enthusiastic musician" that begins on p. 108. Ask students to summarize Watson's statement about the two sides of Holmes's personality.
  Answer: One side is energetic and physically active; the other side is thoughtful and quiet.
- Ask students to speculate on how these two sides of Holmes's character work together to form a complete whole.
  Answer: When Holmes is between cases, he enjoys music and daydreams. He rests during these periods, so that when a case comes, he is eager and fit for the work and the activity. Tracking down criminals and solving problems refreshes his brain, and he relaxes once again with his music.

"Smart fellow, that," observed Holmes as we walked away. "He is, in my judgment, the fourth smartest man in London, and for daring I am not sure that he has not a claim to be third. I have known something of him before."

"Evidently," said I, "Mr. Wilson's assistant counts for a good deal in this mystery of the Red-headed League. I am sure that you inquired your way merely in order that you might see him."

"Not him."

"What then?"

"The knees of his trousers."

"And what did you see?"

"What I expected to see."

"Why did you beat the pavement?"

"My dear doctor, this is a time for observation, not for talk. We are spies in an enemy's country. We know something of Saxe-Coburg Square. Let us now explore the parts which lie behind it."

23 The road in which we found ourselves as we turned round the corner from the retired Saxe-Coburg Square presented as great a contrast to it as the front of a picture does to the back. It was one of the main arteries which conveyed the traffic of the City to the north and west. The roadway was blocked with the immense stream of commerce flowing in a double tide inward and outward, while the footpaths were black with the hurrying swarm of pedestrians. It was difficult to realize as we looked at the line of fine shops and stately business premises that they really abutted on the other side upon the faded and stagnant square which we had just quitted.

"Let me see," said Holmes, standing at the corner and glancing along the line, "I should like just to remember the order of the houses here. It is a hobby of mine to have an exact knowledge of London. There is Mortimer's, the tobacconist, the little newspaper shop, the Coburg branch of the City and Suburban Bank, the Vegetarian Restaurant, and McFarlane's carriage-building depot. That carries us right on to the other block. And now, Doctor, we've done our work, so it's time we had some play. A sandwich and a cup of coffee, and then off to violin land, where all is sweetness and delicacy and harmony, and there are no red-headed clients to vex us with their conundrums."

24 My friend was an enthusiastic musician, being himself not only a very capable performer but a composer of no ordinary merit. All the afternoon he sat in the stalls wrapped in the most perfect happiness, gently waving his long, thin fingers in time to the music, while his gently smiling face and his languid, dreamy eyes were as unlike those of Holmes, the sleuthhound, Holmes the relentless, keen-witted, ready-handed criminal agent, as it was possible to conceive. In his singular character the dual nature alternately asserted itself, and his extreme exactness and astuteness represented, as I have often thought, the reaction against the poetic and contemplative mood which occasionally predominated in him. The swing of his nature took him from extreme languor to devouring energy; and, as I knew

Literary Analysis
The Mystery What might be Holmes's motive for familiarizing himself with the order of the buildings behind Saxe-Coburg Square?

vex (veks) *v.* annoy

conundrums (kə nun′ drəmz) *n.* puzzling questions or problems

astuteness (ə sto͞ot′ nis) *n.* shrewdness

formidable (fôr′ mə də bəl) *adj.* awe-inspiring

CUSTOMIZE INSTRUCTION FOR UNIVERSAL ACCESS

For Advanced Readers

Explain to students that Holmes and Watson are a much-beloved pair of literary characters. Why do students think they continue to be so popular? Challenge students to locate and read another Holmes story. You might suggest "The Adventure of Charles Augustus Milverton," "The Adventure of the Missing Three-Quarter," or "The Adventure of the Empty House." "The Final Problem" can be found in **Authors In Depth,** Gold Level. Using clues from "The Red-headed League" and the second story, students can write brief essays on the characters of Holmes and Watson. Questions to consider include: Why are they such good friends? Why does Holmes value Watson as a partner? Why do the two characters continue to be so popular with readers? Which character do students admire or like more? Who seems more realistic? Why?

well, he was never so truly formidable as when, for days on end, he had been lounging in his armchair amid his improvisations and his black-letter editions. Then it was that the lust of the chase would suddenly come upon him, and that his brilliant reasoning power would rise to the level of intuition, until those who were unacquainted with his methods would look askance at him as on a man whose knowledge was not that of other mortals. When I saw him that afternoon so enwrapped in the music at St. James's Hall I felt that an evil time might be coming upon those whom he had set himself to hunt down.

"You want to go home, no doubt, Doctor," he remarked as we emerged.

"Yes, it would be as well."

"And I have some business to do which will take some hours. This business at Coburg Square is serious."

"Why serious?"

"A considerable crime is in contemplation. I have every reason to believe that we shall be in time to stop it. But today being Saturday rather complicates matters. I shall want your help tonight."

"At what time?"

"Ten will be early enough."

"I shall be at Baker Street at ten."

"Very well. And, I say, Doctor, there may be some little danger, so kindly put your army revolver in your pocket." He waved his hand, turned on his heel, and disappeared in an instant among the crowd.

I trust that I am not more dense than my neighbors, but I was always oppressed with a sense of my own stupidity in my dealings with Sherlock Holmes. Here I had heard what he had heard, I had seen what he had seen, and yet from his words it was evident that he saw clearly not only what had happened but what was about to happen, while to me the whole business was still confused and grotesque. As I drove home to my house in Kensington I thought over it all, from the extraordinary story of the red-headed copier of the Encyclopedia down to the visit to Saxe-Coburg Square, and the ominous words with which he had parted from me. What was this nocturnal expedition, and why should I go armed? Where were we going, and what were we to do? I had the hint from Holmes that this smooth-faced pawnbroker's assistant was a formidable man—a man who might play a deep game. I tried to puzzle it out, but gave it up in despair and set the matter aside until night should bring an explanation.

It was a quarter past nine when I started from home and made my way across the Park, and so through Oxford Street to Baker Street. Two hansoms♦ were standing at the door, and as I entered the passage I heard the sound of voices from above. On entering his room I

Literature 25 in context — Cultural Connection

♦ ***Hansoms***

The hansom, also known as the hansom cab, is a two-wheeled covered carriage for two passengers, pulled by one horse. The cab was named for its inventor, Joseph Hansom (1803–1882), a London architect. By the late 1850s, the hansom was popular in New York and Boston as well as in London. Customers could enjoy a scenic and romantic ride in private with an unobstructed view, since the driver sat above and behind the passengers' cab. Today, hansom cabs are still a popular feature in New York's Central Park. However, in this story, they are a common form of transportation.

26 **Reading Check**

Where do Holmes and Watson go after investigating at Saxe-Coburg Square?

25 Background

Cultural Connection

Hansoms were not the only form of transportation in Holmes's London. The London Underground is one of the world's oldest subway systems; trains began running in 1863. The Metropolitan Line, the oldest in the system, was completed in 1884. By 1900, three separate companies had constructed individual train lines, some of which connected with one another at junction stations, allowing riders to transfer. On p. 107, Holmes and Watson take a Metropolitan Line train from Baker Street station, which is across the street from Holmes's flat. In a later story, "The Bruce-Partington Plans," Holmes solves a murder set in the Underground.

26 **Reading Check**

Answer: Holmes and Watson attend an afternoon concert at St. James Hall.

㉗ Reading Strategy

Finding Key Details

- Point out to students Holmes's remark to Mr. Merryweather. What does this detail suggest about Merryweather's involvement in the mystery?
  Answer: If the crime succeeds, Merryweather will lose £30,000. He must therefore be the object of the crime.
- Point out that the next page provides the detail that Merryweather is a bank director. What did Holmes see on the trip to Saxe-Coburg Square that might connect Merryweather with the mystery?
  Answer: Holmes noticed a bank branch on the street behind the square. The criminals must have wanted Jabez Wilson out of the way so that they could make preparations for robbing the bank.

found Holmes in animated conversation with two men, one of whom I recognized as Peter Jones, the official police agent, while the other was a long, thin, sad-faced man, with a very shiny hat and oppressively respectable frock coat.

"Ha! our party is complete," said Holmes, buttoning up his pea-jacket and taking his heavy hunting crop from the rack. "Watson, I think you know Mr. Jones, of Scotland Yard? Let me introduce you to Mr. Merryweather, who is to be our companion in tonight's adventure."

"We're hunting in couples again, Doctor, you see," said Jones in his consequential way. "Our friend here is a wonderful man for starting a chase. All he wants is an old dog to help him to do the running down."

"I hope a wild goose may not prove to be the end of our chase," observed Mr. Merryweather gloomily.

"You may place considerable confidence in Mr. Holmes, sir," said the police agent loftily. "He has his own little methods, which are, if he won't mind my saying so, just a little too theoretical and fantastic, but he has the makings of a detective in him. It is not too much to say that once or twice, as in that business of the Sholto murder and the Agra treasure, he has been more nearly correct than the official force."

"Oh, if you say so, Mr. Jones, it is all right," said the stranger with deference. "Still, I confess that I miss my rubber.[11] It is the first Saturday night for seven-and-twenty years that I have not had my rubber."

㉗ "I think you will find," said Sherlock Holmes, "that you will play for a higher stake tonight than you have ever done yet, and that the play will be more exciting. For you, Mr. Merryweather, the stake will be some £30,000: and for you, Jones, it will be the man upon whom you wish to lay your hands."

"John Clay, the murderer, thief, smasher, and forger. He's a young man, Mr. Merryweather, but he is at the head of his profession, and I would rather have my bracelets on him than on any criminal in

11. **rubber** card games.

CUSTOMIZE INSTRUCTION FOR UNIVERSAL ACCESS

For Gifted/Talented Students

In the first Holmes novel, *A Study in Scarlet*, Holmes gives his opinion of the fictional detectives of Poe and Gaboriau: "Dupin was a very inferior fellow. That trick of his of breaking in on a friend's thoughts with an apropos remark after a quarter of an hour's silence is really very showy and superficial. . . . Lecoq was a miserable bungler. . . . It might be made a textbook for detectives to teach them what to avoid." Challenge students to dip into Poe's Dupin stories and Gaboriau's *Monsieur Lecoq*. Do they agree with Holmes's opinions? Is Holmes really the best detective of the three? If so, which aspects of Holmes's methods make him a better detective? If not, why are Dupin and/or Gaboriau better? Students can take on the roles of the three detectives for a round-table discussion of methods.

28 London. He's a remarkable man, is young John Clay. His grandfather was a royal duke, and he himself has been to Eton[12] and Oxford.[13] His brain is as cunning as his fingers, and though we meet signs of him at every turn, we never know where to find the man himself. He'll crack a crib[14] in Scotland one week, and be raising money to build an orphanage in Cornwall the next. I've been on his track for years and have never set eyes on him yet."

"I hope that I may have the pleasure of introducing you tonight. I've had one or two little turns also with Mr. John Clay, and I agree with you that he is at the head of his profession. It is past ten, however, and quite time that we started. If you two will take the first hansom, Watson and I will follow in the second."

Sherlock Holmes was not very communicative during the long drive and lay back in the cab humming the tunes which he had heard in the afternoon. We rattled through an endless labyrinth of gas-lit streets until we emerged into Farrington Street.

"We are close there now," my friend remarked. "This fellow Merryweather is a bank director, and personally interested in the matter. I thought it as well to have Jones with us also. He is not a bad fellow, though an absolute imbecile in his profession. He has one positive virtue. He is as brave as a bulldog and as tenacious as a lobster if he gets his claws upon anyone. Here we are, and they are waiting for us."

We had reached the same crowded thoroughfare in which we had found ourselves in the morning. Our cabs were dismissed, and, following the guidance of Mr. Merryweather, we passed down a narrow passage and through a side door, which he opened for us. Within there was a small corridor, which ended in a very massive iron gate. This also was opened, and led down a flight of winding stone steps, which terminated at another formidable gate. Mr. Merryweather stopped to light a lantern, and then conducted us down a dark, earth-smelling passage, and so, after opening a third door, into a huge vault or cellar, which was piled all round with crates and massive boxes.

"You are not very vulnerable from above," Holmes remarked as he held up the lantern and gazed about him.

"Nor from below," said Mr. Merryweather, striking his stick upon the flags which lined the floor. "Why, dear me, it sounds quite hollow!" he remarked, looking up in surprise.

"I must really ask you to be a little more quiet!" said Holmes severely. "You have already imperiled the whole success of our expedition. Might I beg that you would have the goodness to sit down upon one of those boxes, and not to interfere?"

The solemn Mr. Merryweather perched himself upon a crate, with a very injured expression upon his face, while Holmes fell upon his knees upon the floor and, with the lantern and a magnifying lens, began to

12. Eton famous British secondary school for boys.
13. Oxford oldest university in Great Britain.
14. crack a crib break into and rob a house.

Literary Analysis
The Mystery A new suspect's name is mentioned here. What evidence suggests that John Clay might really be Vincent Spaulding?

29 **Reading Check**
Who is Mr. Merryweather?

28 Literary Analysis

The Mystery and Characterization

- Ask students the Literary Analysis question on p. 111: What evidence suggests that John Clay might really be Vincent Spaulding?
  Answer: Jones says that Clay is cunning and successful. Holmes has made the same comments about Spaulding. Holmes obviously knows Spaulding, because he has described him to Wilson; Holmes says he knows Clay.
- Ask students to sum up the kind of person Clay/Spaulding seems to be, based on his actions and on Holmes and Jones's comments.
  Answer: He is imaginative, since he thought up the Red-headed League as a way to get Wilson out of the shop. He is daring enough to plan a major crime. He must be smart, since he has eluded Holmes more than once (Holmes mentions having had "one or two little turns" with him; since Clay is free he must have escaped).
- Then, have students speculate about why a person from Clay's aristocratic background, with the good qualities of courage and intelligence, would become a criminal.
  Possible answers: He might be bored with the idle social life of a rich man. He might get a thrill from outwitting the authorities.

29 Reading Check

Answer: Merryweather is the director of a bank, possibly the City and Suburban branch that Holmes noticed behind Saxe-Coburg Square on p. 108.

30 Literary Analysis

The Mystery and Characterization

- Ask the first Literary Analysis question on p. 112: What possible motive is indicated by Merryweather's revelation?
  Answer: The bank contains 30,000 napoleons in gold, and this has become public knowledge.
- Have students summarize the mystery Holmes has solved. What is the most important question Holmes had to answer? Can students answer this question yet?
  Answer: Why did Spaulding and Ross/Morris want Wilson out of his pawnshop for several hours every day? They wanted to dig a tunnel through Wilson's cellar to the bank's cellar so that they could steal the gold.

Monitor Progress Ask the second Literary Analysis question on p. 112: What do the words *they may do us some harm* reveal about the criminals?
Answer: The mention of harm prepares the reader for a violent confrontation. The criminals won't hesitate to shoot or fight their way to freedom.

31 Vocabulary Development

Latin Root *-spec-*

- Write the word *expectancy* on the chalkboard and challenge students to define it.
  Answer: *Expectancy* means "state of waiting or looking forward to a probable event."
- Explain that *ex-* is a Latin prefix meaning *out* or *out of*. When *ex-* is combined with *-spec-*, the *s* is dropped, because its sound is already taken by the letter *x*. Knowing the prefix and the root helps students understand that *ex* + *spectare* means "looking out" or "looking forward."
- Have students apply the same process to define the word *inspector*.
  Answer: Since the prefix *in-* means *in* or *into*, an inspector is a person who looks into, or investigates, things.

---

examine minutely the cracks between the stones. A few seconds sufficed to satisfy him, for he sprang to his feet again and put his glass in his pocket.

"We have at least an hour before us," he remarked, "for they can hardly take any steps until the good pawnbroker is safely in bed. Then they will not lose a minute, for the sooner they do their work the longer time they will have for their escape. We are at present, Doctor—as no doubt you have divined—in the cellar of the City branch of one of the principal London banks. Mr. Merryweather is the chairman of directors, and he will explain to you that there are reasons why the more daring criminals of London should take a considerable interest in this cellar at present."

"It is our French gold," whispered the director. "We have had several warnings that an attempt might be made upon it."

"Your French gold?"

"Yes. We had occasion some months ago to strengthen our resources and borrowed for that purpose 30,000 napoleons from the Bank of France. It has become known that we have never had occasion to unpack the money, and that it is still lying in our cellar. The crate upon
30 which I sit contains 2,000 napoleons packed between layers of lead foil. Our reserve of bullion is much larger at present than is usually kept in a single branch office, and the directors have had misgivings upon the subject."

"Which were very well justified," observed Holmes.

"And now it is time that we arranged our little plans. I expect that within an hour matters will come to a head. In the meantime, Mr. Merryweather, we must put the screen over that dark lantern."

"And sit in the dark?"

"I am afraid so. I had brought a pack of cards in my pocket, and I thought that, as we were a *partie carrée*,[15] you might have your rubber after all. But I see that the enemy's preparations have gone so far that we cannot risk the presence of a light. And, first of all, we must choose our positions. These are daring men, and though we shall take them at a disadvantage, they may do us some harm unless we are careful. I shall stand behind this crate, and do you conceal yourselves behind those. Then, when I flash a light upon them, close in swiftly. If they fire, Watson, have no compunction about shooting them down."

I placed my revolver, cocked, upon the top of the wooden case behind which I crouched. Holmes shot the slide across the front of his lantern and left us in pitch darkness—such an absolute darkness as I have never before experienced. The smell of hot metal remained to assure us that the light was still there, ready to flash out at a moment's notice. To me, with my nerves worked up to a pitch of expectancy, there was something depressing and subduing in the
31 sudden gloom, and in the cold dank air of the vault.

"They have but one retreat," whispered Holmes. "That is back

15. ***partie carrée*** (pär tē´ cä rā´) French for "group of four."

Literary Analysis
The Mystery A mystery usually includes a suspect's motive for committing a crime. What possible motive is indicated by Merryweather's revelation?

Literary Analysis
The Mystery and Characterization What do the words *they may do us some harm* reveal about the criminals?

through the house into Saxe-Coburg Square. I hope that you have done what I asked you, Jones?"

"I have an inspector and two officers waiting at the front door."

"Then we have stopped all the holes. And now we must be silent and wait."

32 What a time it seemed! From comparing notes afterwards it was but an hour and a quarter, yet it appeared to me that the night must have almost gone, and the dawn be breaking above us. My limbs were weary and stiff, for I feared to change my position; yet my nerves were worked up to the highest pitch of tension, and my hearing was so acute that I could not only hear the gentle breathing of my companions, but I could distinguish the deeper, heavier in-breath of the bulky Jones from the thin, sighing note of the bank director. From my position I could look over the case in the direction of the floor. Suddenly my eyes caught the glint of a light.

At first it was but a lurid spark upon the stone pavement. Then it lengthened out until it became a yellow line, and then, without any warning or sound, a gash seemed to open and a hand appeared; a white, almost womanly hand, which felt about in the center of the little area of light. For a minute or more the hand, with its writhing fingers, protruded out of the floor. Then it was withdrawn as suddenly as it appeared, and all was dark again save the single lurid spark which marked a chink between the stones.

Its disappearance, however, was but momentary. With a rending, tearing sound, one of the broad, white stones turned over upon its side and left a square, gaping hole, through which streamed the light of a lantern. Over the edge there peeped a clean-cut, boyish face, which looked keenly about it, and then, with a hand on either side of the aperture, drew itself shoulder-high and waist-high, until one knee rested upon the edge. In another instant he stood at the side of the hole and was hauling after him a companion, lithe and small like himself, with a pale face and a shock of very red hair.

"It's all clear," he whispered. "Have you the chisel and the bags? Great Scott! Jump, Archie, jump, and I'll swing for it."

Sherlock Holmes had sprung out and seized the intruder by the collar. The other dived down the hole, and I heard the sound of rending cloth as Jones clutched at his skirts. The light flashed upon the barrel of a revolver, but Holmes's hunting crop came down on the man's wrist, and the pistol clinked upon the stone floor.

"It's no use, John Clay," said Holmes blandly. "You have no chance at all."

"So I see," the other answered with the utmost coolness. "I fancy that my pal is all right, though I see you have got his coattails."

"There are three men waiting for him at the door," said Holmes.

"Oh, indeed! You seem to have done the thing very completely. I must compliment you."

"And I you," Holmes answered. "Your red-headed idea was very new and effective."

Literary Analysis
The Mystery Which details contribute to the suspense of the mystery at this point?

33 **Reading Check**
How long do Holmes and his party wait for the criminals to arrive?

32 Literary Analysis

The Mystery

- Go through these two paragraphs with students, helping them see how Doyle builds suspense. Instead of bringing the criminals to the scene immediately, he makes the reader and his characters wait for them. As Watson says, "my nerves were worked up to the highest pitch of tension." The men have to wait in pitch darkness and silence; they can't check the time on their watches, or pass the time by speaking. They know they may be in danger of being shot. Each detail makes the reader more anxious to find out how the story will come out.
- Ask the Literary Analysis question on p. 113: Which details contribute to the suspense of the mystery at this point?
  Answer: The cellar is pitch dark. Then men have to stay in silence and darkness, without knowing how long their wait may be.

33 Reading Check

Answer: They wait an hour and fifteen minutes.

CUSTOMIZE INSTRUCTION FOR UNIVERSAL ACCESS

For Advanced Readers

Have students form a small reading group in which to share some other Holmes stories. You may wish to refer students to the titles cited in Enrichment on ATE p. 117 or to other titles readily available in the school or local library. Students can read the same story, or read different ones and share summaries of what they have read. Students can write essays on these stories. Here are possible issues for students to explore: Are Holmes and Watson consistent personalities from one story to the next? Are the methods Holmes uses to solve crimes believable and realistic? Are the stories consistently entertaining? How good a job does Doyle do at creating a variety of plots and believable minor characters?

34 Literary Analysis

Characterization

- Point out that from here to the end of p. 115, Holmes explains the deductive process he went through to arrive at this mystery's solution. Ask students what this long speech reveals about Holmes's character.
  Possible answers: He enjoys Watson's admiration. He wants someone to understand how he has accomplished his triumph. He knows that in order for Watson to write the story, Watson has to know how Holmes solved the mystery.
- Ask students to select one word that characterizes Holmes in this extended passage.
  Possible responses: Students may cite such words as *clever, ingenious, proud, vain, smug, boastful.*

"You'll see your pal again presently," said Jones. "He's quicker at climbing down holes than I am. Just hold out while I fix the derbies."[16]

"I beg that you will not touch me with your filthy hands," remarked our prisoner as the handcuffs clattered upon his wrists. "You may not be aware that I have royal blood in my veins. Have the goodness, also, when you address me always to say 'sir' and 'please.' "

"All right," said Jones with a stare and a snigger. "Well, would you please, sir, march upstairs, where we can get a cab to carry your Highness to the police station?"

"That is better," said John Clay serenely. He made a sweeping bow to the three of us and walked quietly off in the custody of the detective.

"Really, Mr. Holmes," said Mr. Merryweather as we followed them from the cellar, "I do not know how the bank can thank you or repay you. There is no doubt that you have detected and defeated in the most complete manner one of the most determined attempts at bank robbery that have ever come within my experience."

"I have had one or two little scores of my own to settle with Mr. John Clay," said Holmes. "I have been at some small expense over this matter, which I shall expect the bank to refund, but beyond that I am amply repaid by having had an experience which is in many ways unique, and by hearing the very remarkable narrative of the Red-headed League."

34 "You see, Watson," he explained in the early hours of the morning as we sat over a glass of whisky and soda in Baker Street, "it was perfectly obvious from the first that the only possible object of this rather

16. derbies handcuffs.

CUSTOMIZE INSTRUCTION FOR UNIVERSAL ACCESS

For Less Proficient Readers

There are a number of movies based on the Sherlock Holmes stories, and a recent acclaimed television series. Basil Rathbone and Nigel Bruce starred as Holmes and Watson in more than a dozen Hollywood films in the 1930s and 1940s. (Many of these films have no connection to Doyle's plots. One film takes place during World War II and has Holmes pursuing enemy spies.) On television, Jeremy Brett starred as Holmes and Edward Hardwicke was one of his two Watsons. (This series was more faithful to Doyle's original stories.) Have students gather for a screening of one of these films or television episodes. Afterwards, students can have a group discussion on how viewing the film enriched the story for them.

fantastic business of the advertisement of the League, and the copying of the Encyclopedia, must be to get this not over-bright pawnbroker out of the way for a number of hours every day. It was a curious way of managing it, but, really, it would be difficult to suggest a better. The method was no doubt suggested to Clay's ingenious mind by the color of his accomplice's hair. The £4 a week was a lure which must draw him, and what was it to them, who were playing for thousands? They put in the advertisement, one rogue has the temporary office, the other rogue incites the man to apply for it, and together they manage to secure his absence every morning in the week. From the time that I heard of the assistant having come for half wages, it was obvious to me that he had some strong motive for securing the situation."

"But how could you guess what the motive was?"

"Had there been women in the house, I should have suspected a mere vulgar intrigue. That, however, was out of the question. The man's business was a small one, and there was nothing in his house which could account for such elaborate preparations, and such an expenditure as they were at. It must, then, be something out of the house. What could it be? I thought of the assistant's fondness for photography, and his trick of vanishing into the cellar. The cellar! There was the end of this tangled clue. Then I made inquiries as to this mysterious assistant and found that I had to deal with one of the coolest and most daring criminals in London. He was doing something in the cellar—something which took many hours a day for months on end. What could it be, once more? I could think of nothing save that he was running a tunnel to some other building.

"So far I had got when we went to visit the scene of action. I surprised you by beating upon the pavement with my stick. I was ascertaining whether the cellar stretched out in front or behind. It was not in front. Then I rang the bell, and, as I hoped, the assistant answered

35 it. We have had some skirmishes, but we had never set eyes upon each other before. I hardly looked at his face. His knees were what I wished to see. You must yourself have remarked how worn, wrinkled, and stained they were. They spoke of those hours of burrowing. The only remaining point was what they were burrowing for. I walked round the corner, saw that the City and Suburban Bank abutted on our friend's premises, and felt that I had solved my problem. When you drove home after the concert I called upon Scotland Yard and upon the chairman of the bank directors, with the result that you have seen."

"And how could you tell that they would make their attempt tonight?" I asked.

"Well, when they closed their League offices that was a sign that they cared no longer about Mr. Jabez Wilson's presence—in other words, that they had completed their tunnel. But it was essential that they should use it soon, as it might be discovered, or the bullion might be removed. Saturday would suit them better than any other day, as it would give them two days for their escape. For all these reasons I expected them to come tonight."

Reading Strategy
Finding Key Details Even after the case is solved, Watson wonders how Holmes did it. Name the key details that explain the detective's solution.

36 **✔Reading Check**
As Holmes reveals his clues, what reason does he give for striking his stick against the pavement?

35 Reading Strategy
Finding Key Details

- Ask students the Reading Strategy question on p. 115: Even after the case is solved, Watson wonders how Holmes did it. Name the key details that explain the detective's solution.
  Answer: Key details included Spaulding's willingness to work for half wages; the state of the knees of his trousers; the amount of time he spent in the cellar; the fact that there was no woman in the house; and the presence in the neighborhood of the bank branch.
- Ask students to compare Holme's account of events with the way Watson has been presenting the story. How do the two accounts differ?
  Answer: Watson is writing a story for people to read; he presents events more or less as they occurred with full details. His method increases suspense and allows readers to speculate about the evidence. Holmes gives only the bare facts because those are all that really interest him. He also doesn't have to repeat information that Watson already knows.

36 ✔Reading Check
Answer: Holmes was checking to see whether the cellar was under this part of the sidewalk. A hollow sound would tell him that it was; a solid sound, that it wasn't.

CUSTOMIZE INSTRUCTION FOR UNIVERSAL ACCESS

For Less Proficient Readers	For Special Needs Students	For Advanced Readers
Have students work with partners to answer Review and Assess questions 1 and 5 on p. 117. Students can create graphic organizers that will help them work out their answers.	Have a small group of students meet to discuss the Review and Assess questions on p. 116. Encourage them to identify details in the story that support their answers.	Have students meet in a small group to discuss their answers to question 4 on p. 117. Students can debate what makes Holmes so good at his job. Have students inferred anything about Holmes that the story does not state directly? If so, what?

ASSESS

Answers for p. 116

Review and Assess

1. **(a)** Students may find the solution clever or ingenious.
   (b) Students should find the ending satisfying; the guilty people were caught and no one was harmed.
2. **(a)** Wilson wants to know what was behind his employment by the Red-headed League and why it disappeared. **(b)** Holmes has never heard a story like it; he enjoys it because it is unique and bizarre.
3. **(a)** He is asked to copy out the Encyclopedia Britannica by hand and to remain in the League office during working hours.
   (b) Wilson's job means he will be safely out of the pawnshop for four hours a day, so the criminals can dig a tunnel.
4. **(a)** Holmes and his friends hide in the cellar and catch the criminals when they return to finish the job. **(b)** The knees of Spaulding's trousers showed that he had been digging in the cellar. The pawnshop cellar was behind the building. The bank branch bordered on Wilson's property.
5. **(a)** Holmes collects facts and makes deductions. He thinks things over, then goes out looking for physical clues to support his theories. **(b)** Yes, because the same crimes are committed today—murder, robbery, and fraud—and produce evidence that can be detected.
6. **(a)** Holmes accuses Watson of "embellishing" his cases, so Holmes's version might be a bare recitation of facts. **(b)** It might be less effective because Watson's story is more suspenseful. It might be more effective because Holmes would be able to share his thoughts.
7. Like many detective stories, this one suggests that crime doesn't pay; it will be discovered and punished.

"You reasoned it out beautifully," I exclaimed in unfeigned admiration. "It is so long a chain, and yet every link rings true."

"It saved me from ennui,"[17] he answered, yawning. "Alas! I already feel it closing in upon me. My life is spent in one long effort to escape from the commonplaces of existence. These little problems help me to do so."

"And you are a benefactor of the race," said I.

He shrugged his shoulders. "Well, perhaps, after all, it is of some little use," he remarked. " '*L'homme c'est rien—l'oeuvre c'est tout,*'[18] as Gustave Flaubert wrote to George Sand."[19]

---

17. **ennui** (än´ wē) boredom.
18. ***L'homme c'est rien—l'oeuvre c'est tout*** (lum sā rē en´ lʉvr sā to͞o) French for "Man is nothing—the work is everything."
19. **Gustave Flaubert** (go͞os täv´ flō ber´) **. . . George Sand** notable French novelists of the nineteenth century.

Review and Assess

Thinking About the Selection

1. **Respond: (a)** What did you think of the solution to the mystery? **(b)** Did you find it a satisfying ending to the story? Explain.
2. **(a) Recall:** Why does Jabez Wilson come to see Sherlock Holmes? **(b) Infer:** Why does Holmes find Jabez Wilson's story interesting?
3. **(a) Recall:** As a member of the exclusive Red-headed League, what job is Wilson given? **(b) Analyze:** How does Wilson's menial job with the Red-headed League help the criminals with their attempted burglary?
4. **(a) Recall:** What happens the night of the attempted burglary? **(b) Analyze:** Which clues found at Saxe-Coburg Square help Holmes solve the crime?
5. **(a) Summarize:** What strategies would you say Holmes uses to solve crimes? **(b) Apply:** Would a real detective in today's world be able to solve a crime using Holmes's methods? Why or why not?
6. **(a) Speculate:** How would this story be different if it were told by Holmes rather than by Watson? **(b) Evaluate:** Would it be more or less effective? Why?
7. **Generalize:** The main purpose of detective stories like this one is to entertain audiences. Is it also possible to learn lessons from detective stories that can be applied to your own life? Support your answer, using this story as an example.

Sir Arthur Conan Doyle

(1859–1930)

Sir Arthur Conan Doyle began his career as an eye doctor. Finding little success, he began to write mystery stories. He probably modeled his detective, Sherlock Holmes, after a medical school professor who could diagnose illnesses from clues other doctors missed.

After several rejections from publishers, Doyle sold his first detective novel, *A Study in Scarlet*, in 1887. Perhaps remembering his own medical background, Doyle made the narrator Dr. John Watson, Holmes's devoted companion.

Readers grew to love the odd detective who solved puzzling crimes. When Doyle killed off Holmes in a story in 1893, readers protested so strongly that he was forced to bring back the beloved detective.

ASSESSMENT PRACTICE: Reading Comprehension

Context Clues (For more practice, see Test Preparation Workbook, p. 5.)

Several assessment tests measure students' ability to use context clues to choose the correct meaning of a word with multiple meanings. Use the following example to show students how context can help them answer this type of test item.

> Altogether, look as I would, there was nothing remarkable about the man save his blazing red head, and the expression of extreme chagrin and discontent upon his features.

In this passage, the word *save* means ______.

A except
B preserve
C rescue
D keep hidden

Students can substitute each of the four choices in the sentence. *Except* is the only one that makes sense. The correct answer is *A*.

Review and Assess

Literary Analysis

The Mystery

1. Identify the elements of a **mystery** within Jabez Wilson's story.
2. Which clues point to Vincent Spaulding as the probable criminal? Use a chart like the one shown here to list at least three clues. Then, show how the clues point to Spaulding as a probable criminal.

Clues		How They Point to Spaulding
	→	
	→	
	→	

Connecting Literary Elements

3. (a) How would you **characterize** Vincent Spaulding? (b) What techniques does Doyle use to reveal Spaulding's character?
4. (a) How would you characterize Sherlock Holmes? (b) Which of his personality traits help him solve mysteries? Record your answer in a chart like this one.

Holmes's Characteristics	How They Help Solve the Mystery

Reading Strategy

Finding Key Details

5. At the mystery's outset, Wilson relates his story to Holmes and Watson. Review his story and identify four **key details** that are clues to the mystery.
6. Explain how each of the four key details in Wilson's story suggests a solution to the mystery.

Extend Understanding

7. **Career Connection:** What are three other professions in which Holmes's reasoning skills could be useful? Give reasons for your choices.

Quick Review

A **mystery** is a story of suspense that usually contains a crime, a crime-solver, a criminal, suspects, and clues to the resolution.

Characterization is the act of developing characters through such techniques as description, dialogue, and actions.

Key details in a mystery are important pieces of information that have a bearing on the crime and are often clues to solving the mystery.

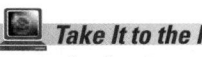

Take It to the Net

www.phschool.com

Take the interactive self-test online to check your understanding of the selection.

ENRICHMENT: Further Reading

Other Works by Sir Arthur Conan Doyle

The Hound of the Baskervilles
A Study in Scarlet
"A Scandal in Bohemia"
"The Boscombe Valley Mystery"
"The Final Problem"

Take It to the Net

Visit www.phschool.com for more information on Sir Arthur Conan Doyle.

Answers for p. 117

Review and Assess

1. Wilson has recently hired an assistant who was eager to accept half the usual salary. The assistant seems to know all about a "Red-headed League" that no one else has ever heard of, and he urges Wilson to apply for a job. The job is completely useless yet pays very well.
2.

Spaulding shows Wilson the ad.	Spaulding knows more than the ad says.
Spaulding offers to look after the shop.	He wants the shop to himself for some reason.
Spaulding's trousers are worn and stained.	Spaulding has been digging in the cellar.

3. **(a)** Spaulding is unscrupulous, clever, and dishonest.
(b) Holmes and Jones comment on how clever Spaulding is. He is unscrupulous and dishonest enough to trick Wilson.
4.

ability to observe	Holmes knows which details to look for
intelligence	Holmes is able to interpret what he sees
good listener	Holmes recalls every detail of Wilson's story
sense of humor	Holmes enjoys the stories of people like Wilson
courage	Holmes does not panic when facing criminals

5. The assistant was hired recently and works for half wages. The assistant was eager to get Wilson the job at the Red-headed League. The assistant knows all about the mysterious League. Wilson is paid well for a useless job.
6. Only someone with an ulterior motive would accept a job for half wages. Spaulding's plot is designed to keep Wilson out of the shop.
7. Holmes's abilities to listen, observe, interpret, and reason would help a lawyer, a policeman, a psychologist, or a scientist.

EXTEND

Answers for p. 118

1 Vocabulary Development

Word Analysis

1. b 2. c 3. a

Spelling Strategy

1. unclear
2. reconsider
3. misjudge

Fluency: Clarify Word Meaning

1. introspective
2. singular
3. conundrums
4. vex
5. astuteness
6. formidable
7. hoax
8. avail

2 Grammar Lesson

Sample responses:

1. heavy crystal
2. old leather-bound
3. stupid, incompetent
4. respectable, elderly
5. heavy tweed

Writing Application

Sample responses:

1. The sly, perceptive general pretended to retreat during the night.
2. The sneaky, greedy thief became stuck in the chimney.

Integrate Language Skills

1 Vocabulary Development Lesson

Word Analysis: Latin Root *-spec-*

The Latin root *-spec-* means "see" or "look." The root appears in the word *introspective*, which means "looking inward." It also appears in the words *spectator*, *inspector*, and *spectacle*. Match each word with its definition.

1. spectator a. a remarkable sight
2. inspector b. one who observes
3. spectacle c. one who looks into a matter

Spelling Strategy

When you add a prefix to a word or root, do not change the spelling of the word or root. For example, *intro-* + *spective* = *introspective*. Add a prefix such as *un-*, *re-*, *pre-*, or *mis-* to the following words to make three English words.

1. clear 2. consider 3. judge

Fluency: Context

On your paper, write the following paragraph. Using the clues you find there, fill in the blanks with words from the vocabulary list on page 95.

I'm rather shy and __?__, but my uncle has an extremely unusual and __?__ personality. He is both impatient and brilliant. When confronted with perplexing __?__, he has been known to shout wildly, "Do not __?__ me!" at no one in particular. Despite this brashness, he solves the problem. My uncle's __?__ is regarded as __?__ by those who respect him and as an elaborate __?__ by those who don't. Whenever I ask for help, however, he will __?__ himself immediately. I must say, my uncle is a very fascinating and entertaining person to know.

2 Grammar Lesson

Coordinate Adjectives

Adjectives are words that modify a noun or pronoun. **Coordinate adjectives** are adjectives of equal rank that separately modify the noun they precede. Use commas to separate coordinate adjectives.

To test whether adjectives are coordinate, switch their order. If the sentence still makes sense, the adjectives are coordinate.

Coordinate: . . . a very *stout*, *florid-faced*, *elderly* gentleman . . .
. . . an *elderly*, *florid-faced*, *stout* gentleman . . .

Not coordinate: In a *few short* hours, we'll know the outcome.

Practice On your paper, write the following sentences. Supply adjectives to complete them. Separate coordinate adjectives with a comma.

1. The __?__ __?__ goblet was stolen.
2. The __?__ __?__ book contained a clue.
3. The detective outwitted the __?__ __?__ villain.
4. People were shocked that such a __?__ __?__ citizen had committed the crime.
5. The detective wore a __?__ __?__ coat.

Writing Application Create sentences by adding nouns to each of the following pairs of coordinate adjectives.

1. sly, perceptive 2. sneaky, greedy

WG *Prentice Hall Writing and Grammar Connection: Chapter 29, Section 2*

TEACHING RESOURCES

The following resources can be used to enrich or extend the instructions for pp. 118–119.

Vocabulary

- **Selection Support:** Build Vocabulary; p. 17
- **Vocabulary and Spelling Practice Book** (Use this booklet for skills enrichment.)

Grammar

- **Selection Support,** Build Grammar Skills, p. 18
- **Writing and Grammar,** Gold Level, p. 658
- **Daily Language Practice Transparencies**

Writing

- **Writing and Grammar,** Gold Level, p. 78
- **Writing and Grammar iText CD-ROM**

BLOCK SCHEDULING: Resources marked with this symbol provide varied instruction during 90-minute blocks.

❸ Writing Lesson

Detective Story

In his story, Doyle created a detective so real that readers still write to him! Write your own detective story that will appeal to today's readers.

Prewriting Brainstorm to come up with possible crimes. Choose one of your ideas as the focus of your story. Create a diagram like the one shown, putting the crime in the center box. Elaborate with key details about the detective, the suspects, their motives, alibis, and other clues.

Computer laptop stolen from corporate office

- **Detective:** Sergeant Smith—intelligent, thin, quiet
- **Suspect:** Boris, janitor, works overnight
- **Key detail:** Company just changed its leadership.
- **Suspect:** James, office assistant, in debt

Drafting Using your diagram as a guide, write your story. Provide readers with hints to the solution of the mystery.

Revising Ask a classmate to read your story and use a highlighter to mark each clue he or she encounters. See if your classmate has noticed the hints you have provided. You may want to add hints or strengthen ones you have included.

WG *Prentice Hall Writing and Grammar Connection: Chapter 5, Section 2*

❹ Extension Activities

Listening and Speaking With a partner, **role-play an interrogation** of Spaulding by Officer Jones. When you act out the scene, focus on these kinds of body language:

- posture—the way a character stands or sits and holds his head
- gestures—how a person points or waves his hand when he talks
- eye contact—the way a person does or does not look directly at another person

After a few rehearsals, present your role play to your class. **[Group Activity]**

Research and Technology Research the science of detective work. Study fingerprinting, lie detectors, or other techniques used by detectives to arrest criminals. Refer to multiple sources, such as the Internet, journals, and criminology books, to gain more information on the subject you choose. Then, prepare a **written report.**

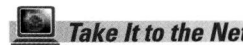

Take It to the Net www.phschool.com

Go online for an additional research activity using the Internet.

ASSESSMENT RESOURCES

The following resources can be used to assess students' knowledge and skills.

Selection Assessment

- **Formal Assessment,** pp. 13–15
- **Open Book Test,** pp. 13–15
- **Got It! Assessment Videotapes,** Tape 1
- **Test Bank Software**

Take It to the Net

Visit www.phschool.com for self-tests and additional questions on "The Red-headed League."

Writing Rubric

- **Performance Assess. and Portfolio Mgmt.,** p. 13

PRENTICE HALL ASSESSMENT SYSTEM

- **Workbook**
- **Skill Book**
- **Transparencies**
- **CD-ROM**

Lesson Support for p. 119

❸ Writing Lesson

- Remind students that before a writer begins a detective story, he or she has to know who committed the crime, and how and why it was done. A writer must determine these details in advance so that the actions of the story will be consistent with the solution.
- After students have written and revised their first drafts, have volunteers read their stories aloud. Ask them to pause in their reading to allow the class to guess possible solutions to the crimes.
- Use the Short Story rubric in **Performance Assessment and Portfolio Management,** p. 13, to evaluate students' stories.

❹ Extension Activities

Listening and Speaking

- Remind students that Jones will be taking notes during the interview. He will ask only the questions necessary to prove that Spaulding committed the crime, with help from Duncan Ross.
- Have students read over the last section of the story so that they can get an idea of how the two characters speak. For instance, Clay speaks formally, but Jones uses vivid Cockney expressions such as "derbies" for "handcuffs." Students should also note that Clay is likely to be uncooperative.

CUSTOMIZE INSTRUCTION For Universal Access

To address different learning styles, use the following activities suggested in the **Extension Activities** booklet, p. 5.

- For Verbal/Linguistic Learners, use Activities 5 and 6.
- For Visual/Spatial Learners, use Activity 6.
- For Bodily/Kinesthetic Learners, use Activity 7.

The Listeners ✦ Beware: Do Not Read This Poem ✦ Echo

Lesson Objectives and CA Correlations

1. **To analyze and respond to literary elements**
   - Literary Analysis: Imagery **R 3.7**
   - Comparing Literary Works: Diction **R 3.11**
2. **To read, comprehend, analyze, and critique poems**
   - Reading Strategy: Using Your Senses
   - Review and Assess questions
   - Assessment Practice (ATE)
3. **To develop word analysis skills, fluency, and systematic vocabulary**
   - Vocabulary Development Lesson: Poetic License and Vocabulary **R 1.2**
4. **To understand and apply written and oral language conventions**
   - Spelling Strategy
   - Grammar Lesson: Types of Adjectives **LC 1.2, 1.3**
5. **To understand and apply appropriate writing and research strategies**
   - Writing Lesson: Comparison-and-Contrast Essay **W 2.3**
   - Extension Activity: Multimedia Presentation **W 1.3**
6. **To understand and apply listening and speaking strategies**
   - Extension Activity: Dramatic Scene **LS 1.9**

STEP-BY-STEP TEACHING GUIDE	PACING GUIDE
PRETEACH	
Motivate Students and Provide Background	
Use the Motivation activity (ATE p. 120)	5 min.
Read and discuss the Preview material and Background information (SE/ATE p. 120) [A]	10 min.
Introduce the Concepts	
Introduce the Literary Analysis and Reading Strategy (SE/ATE p. 121) [A]	15 min.
Pronounce the vocabulary words and read their definitions (SE p. 121)	5 min.
TEACH	
Monitor Comprehension	
Informally monitor comprehension by circulating while students read independently or in groups [A]	15 min.
Develop vocabulary with Vocabulary notes (SE pp. 122, 124, 126)	as students read
Develop Understanding	
Develop students' understanding of imagery with Literary Analysis annotations (SE pp. 123, 124, 126; ATE pp. 123, 124, 126) [A]	10 min.
ASSESS	
Assess Mastery	
Assess students' mastery of the Reading Strategy and Literary Analysis by having them answer the Review and Assess questions (SE/ATE p. 127)	15 min.
Use one or more of the print and media Assessment Resources (ATE p. 129) [A]	up to 45 min.
EXTEND	
Apply Understanding	
Have students complete the Vocabulary Development Lesson and the Grammar Lesson (SE p. 128) [A]	20 min.
Apply students' knowledge of comparison and contrast using the Writing Lesson (SE/ATE p. 129) [A]	45 min.
Apply students' understanding using one or more of the Extension Activities (SE p. 129)	20–90 min.

[A] ACCELERATED INSTRUCTION: Use the strategies and activities identified with an [A].

UNIVERSAL ACCESS
● = Below Level Students
▲ = On-Level Students
■ = Above Level Students

Time and Resource Manager

Reading Level: Average, Easy, Easy
Average Number of Instructional Days: 3

RESOURCES		
PRINT	**TRANSPARENCIES**	**TECHNOLOGY**
• **Beyond Literature,** Cross-Curricular Connection: Science, p. 6 ▲ ■		• **Interest Grabber Video,** Tape 1 ● ▲ ■
• **Selection Support Workbook:** ● ▲ ■ Literary Analysis, p. 24 Reading Strategy, p. 23 Build Vocabulary, p. 21	• **Literary Analysis and Reading Transparencies,** pp. 11 and 12 ● ▲ ■	
		• **Listening to Literature** ● ▲ ■ Audiocassettes, Side 6 Audio CDs, CD 5
• **Literatura en español** ● ▲ • **Literary Analysis for Enrichment** ■	• **Fine Art Transparencies Volume 1,** Art Transparency 9 ● ▲ ■	
• **Formal Assessment:** Selection Test, pp. 16–18 ● ▲ ■ • **Open Book Test,** pp. 16–18 ● ▲ ■ • **Performance Assessment and Portfolio Management,** p. 16 ● ▲ ■ • Prentice Hall Assessment System ● ▲ ■	• Prentice Hall Assessment System ● ▲ ■ Skills Practice Answers and Explanations on Transparencies	• **Test Bank Software** ● ▲ ■ • **Got It! Assessment Videotapes,** Tape 1 ● ▲
• **Selection Support Workbook:** ● ▲ ■ Build Grammar Skills, p. 22 • **Writing and Grammar,** Gold Level ● ▲ ■ • **Extension Activities,** p. 6 ● ▲ ■	• **Daily Language Practice Transparencies** ● ▲	• **Writing and Grammar iText CD-ROM** ● ▲ ■ ***Take It to the Net*** www.phschool.com

BLOCK SCHEDULING: Use one 90-minute class period to preteach the selection and have students read it. Use a second 90-minute class period to assess students' mastery of skills and have them complete one of the Extension Activities.

PRETEACH

Step-by-Step Teaching Guide for pp. 120–121

Motivation

Create an eerie mood in the classroom. Dim the lights and have students close their eyes as you play some prerecorded sounds: a horse clopping, a bird call, a solo violin. Have students take a moment to imagine a story to go with each sound. Suggest that they keep the sounds and their images in mind as they read the poems.

Interest Grabber Video

As an alternative, play "Reading and Student Response" on Tape 1 to engage students' interest.

❶ Background

Art

Maurits Cornelius Escher (1898–1972) was a Dutch graphic artist famous for his black-and-white optical illusions and shifting patterns. Escher was fascinated by the contradictions of painting and drawing, which are based on representing three-dimensional scenes and objects on a two-dimensional surface. Many of his drawings play with this contradiction of dimensions: in the example on this page, the hands seem to have escaped the flat surface on which the shirt cuffs are drawn. The viewer may or may not be aware of an implied third dimension: the unseen hand of Escher drawing the *Drawing Hands.*

Prepare to Read

The Listeners ◆ Beware: Do Not Read This Poem ◆ Echo

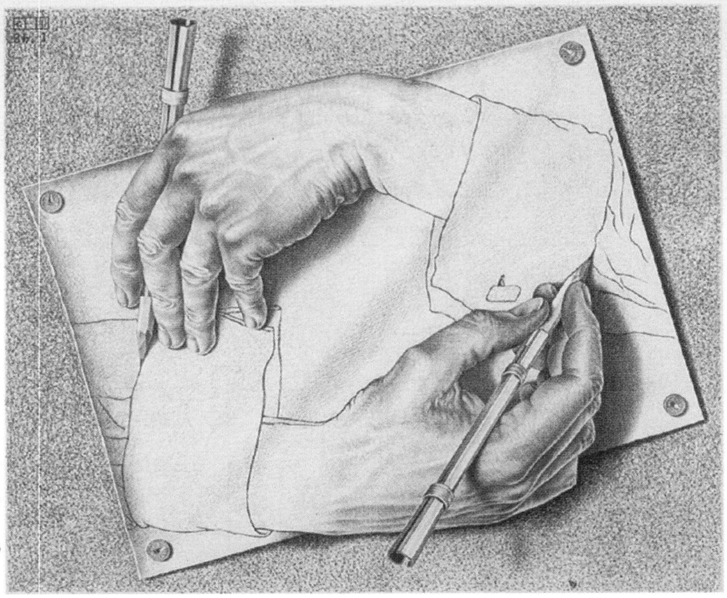

Drawing Hands, 1948, M.C. Escher/Cordon Art–Baarn–Holland

Take It to the Net

Visit www.phschool.com for interactive activities and instruction related to the selections, including

- background
- graphic organizers
- literary elements
- reading strategies

Preview

Connecting to the Literature

A man knocks on a moonlit door. A parrot screams in a jungle. A woman disappears into a mirror. Images like these are strange, and you are not sure how they connect, yet they seem to hint at an unknown story. These poems use such images to hint at mysteries and possibilities.

❶ Background

Just as poets create mystery in lines of poetry, artists create mysterious images with the lines they draw. Dutch artist M. C. Escher (1898–1972), for example, specialized in drawings that challenge the mind and delight the imagination. Look carefully at the Escher image above and consider why it is mysterious.

TEACHING RESOURCES

The following resources can be used to enrich or extend the instruction for pp. 120–121.

Motivation

Interest Grabber Video, Tape 1: Reading and Student Response

Background

Beyond Literature, p. 6 ■

Take It to the Net

Visit www.phschool.com for background and hotlinks for the poems.

Literary Analysis

Literary Analysis and Reading Transparencies, Imagery, p. 11 ■

Reading

Selection Support: Reading Strategy, p. 23; Build Vocabulary, p. 21

Literary Analysis and Reading Transparencies, Using Your Senses, p. 12

■ **BLOCK SCHEDULING:** Resources marked with this symbol provide varied instruction during 90-minute blocks.

❷ Literary Analysis

Imagery

Poets do not draw pictures with pens and brushes. However, they can use picture-painting words, called **imagery**, to help you experience their ideas with all your senses—touch, taste, smell, hearing, and sight. The poems in this section use imagery in a special way to create pictures of worlds that are haunted by mystery. Notice the vivid imagery in this passage from "Echo":

Thousands of parrots
screamed together
and rock echoed.

As you read the selections, look for images that appeal strongly to your senses and paint pictures of worlds haunted by mystery.

Comparing Literary Works

Just as individual artists have their own techniques for painting a picture, individual poets have their own ways of creating imagery. Much depends on each poet's **diction**, or word choice. The poet's choice of vocabulary and vividness of language contribute to the imagery and affect its ultimate forcefulness. As you read the selections, compare the diction in the poems. Pay particular attention to the following:

- unique or interesting words that contribute to an image
- vivid or intense language that paints a clear picture

❸ Reading Strategy

Using Your Senses

By **using your senses** when you read a poem, you let the poem's language create a picture in your mind. As you read, experience each poem through your senses by focusing on language that tells how something looks, sounds, feels, smells, or tastes. Use a diagram like the one shown to record the sensory language in each selection. Write the words and phrases you find in their appropriate boxes.

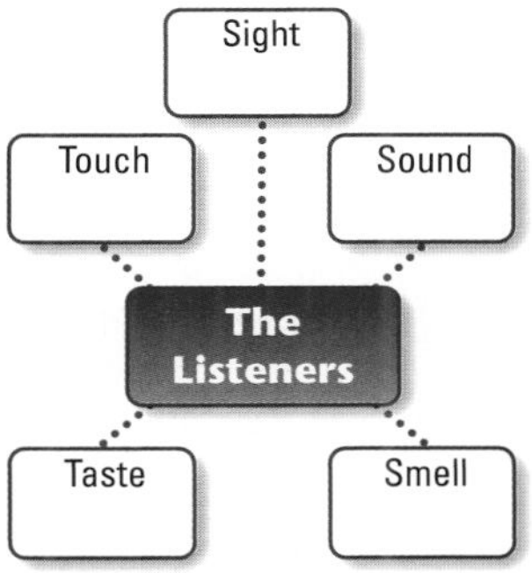

Vocabulary Development

perplexed (pər plekst′) *adj.* puzzled; full of doubt (p. 122)

thronging (thrôŋ′ iŋ) *adj.* crowding into (p. 122)

legendary (lej′ ən der′ ē) *adj.* based on legends, stories handed down from one generation to the next (p. 124)

strafing (strāf′ iŋ) *adj.* attacking with machine-gun fire (p. 126)

CUSTOMIZE INSTRUCTION FOR UNIVERSAL ACCESS

For Less Proficient Readers	For English Learners	For Advanced Readers
Have students choose partners with whom to read the poems aloud. Partners can discuss each poem, making sure that they can accurately summarize it. They should also discuss the effect of the sound images presented in each poem.	Have students read the poems aloud, or listen to them on the audiocassettes or CDs provided. Students should listen for the rhymes, rhythms, and beauty and effectiveness of the language.	Have each student choose one poem to read aloud. Students can work on their reading for a day or two, practicing at home until they are satisfied with their emphasis and expression. Volunteers can read these poems while the class listens.

❷ Literary Analysis

Imagery and Diction

- Students learned about imagery when they read "The Birds" earlier in this unit. Briefly review this literary element by having a volunteer read the first paragraph under "Imagery" on p. 121. Have students recall words and phrases from "The Birds" that appealed to one or more of the five senses. Have them recall the effects this imagery had on them.
- Ask students why writers would want to appeal to a reader's five senses. Contrast a written text with a movie. Explain that writers use words to do the work of sound effects, cinematography, musical scores, spoken dialogue, tones of actors' voices, and so on.
- Explain to students that diction not only encompasses a writer's choice of words, but how those words are arranged (syntax). As they read the following poems, encourage students to give careful attention to each poet's diction and how this diction contributes to the imagery.

❸ Reading Strategy

Using Your Senses

- Have students read the paragraph under "Using Your Senses" on p. 121. Point out that this skill is closely allied to the literary element of imagery. Students must use their senses to appreciate the three poets' use of imagery.
- Introduce the graphic organizer pictured on p. 121. Students may want to use this type of diagram, or they may find a simple two-column, five-row table easier to work with. The left column will contain one sense in each row, and the right column will include the words and phrases that appeal to this sense.

Vocabulary Development

- Pronounce each vocabulary word for students, and read the definitions as a class. Have students identify any words with which they are already familiar.

E-Teach

Visit E-Teach at www.phschool.com for teachers' essays on how to teach, with questions and answers.

TEACH

Step-by-Step Teaching Guide for pp. 122–126

CUSTOMIZE INSTRUCTION
For Visual Learners

The first two poems in this selection contain numerous striking visual images. Have students point to specific words and phrases in the poems and explain how these words and phrases helped them picture the poems' settings and characters.

❶ About the Selection

A traveler knocks on the door of a house in the forest, and calls out "Is there anybody there?" No one answers him; there are only phantoms in the house to hear his call.

❷ Background

Art

Het Blind Huis, by William Degouve de Nunques

De Nunques was a member of the Symbolist movement, which favored paintings that suggested ideas and moods rather than imitating the visible world in a realistic way.

- How does this painting help you appreciate the poem?
  Answer: It shows the loneliness of an isolated house in a forest.

❸ ▶ Critical Viewing

Possible responses: Yes, because it is a lone house in the middle of a forest. No, because there are lights in the windows, so the house must be occupied.

❹ Literary Analysis

Imagery

- Read aloud the first ten lines. Be sure to model the appropriate intonation for students.
- Ask the Literary Analysis question on p. 122: Which words convey clear images?
  Answer: *moonlit, silence, champed, ferny, flew, turret, smote, leaf-fringed*
- Ask students to describe the overall mood these images convey.
  Answer: The mood is mysterious. The silence seems threatening. The darkness makes the mood uneasy.

---

❶ The Listeners

Walter de la Mare

Het Blind Huis, William Degouve de Nunques, State Museum, Kroller-Muller, Otterlo, The Netherlands

❸ ▲ **Critical Viewing** Does this painting convey the same feeling as "The Listeners"? Why or why not? **[Explain]**

❹

'Is there anybody there?' said the Traveler,
    Knocking on the moonlit door;
And his horse in the silence champed[1] the grasses
    Of the forest's ferny floor:
And a bird flew up out of the turret,
    Above the Traveler's head:
And he smote[2] upon the door again a second time;
    'Is there anybody there?' he said.
But no one descended to the Traveler;
    No head from the leaf-fringed sill
Leaned over and looked into his gray eyes,
    Where he stood perplexed and still.
But only a host of phantom listeners
    That dwelt in the lone house then
Stood listening in the quiet of the moonlight
    To that voice from the world of men:
Stood thronging the faint moonbeams on the dark stair,
    That goes down to the empty hall,
Hearkening in an air stirred and shaken
    By the lonely Traveler's call.
And he felt in his heart their strangeness,

Literary Analysis
Imagery Which words convey clear images in the first ten lines?

perplexed (pər plekst') *adj.* puzzled; full of doubt

thronging (thrôŋ' iŋ) *adj.* crowding into

1. **champed** (champt) *v.* chewed.
2. **smote** (smōt) *v.* struck hard.

TEACHING RESOURCES

The following resources can be used to enrich or extend the instruction for pp. 122–126.

Literary Analysis

Selection Support: Literary Analysis, p. 24

Reading

Listening to Literature Audiocassettes, Side 6

Listening to Literature Audio CDs, CD 6

Extension

Fine Art Transparencies, Volume 1, Art Transparency 9

BLOCK SCHEDULING: Resources marked with this symbol provide varied instruction during 90-minute blocks.

Their stillness answering his cry,
While his horse moved, cropping the dark turf,
'Neath the starred and leafy sky;
For he suddenly smote on the door, even
Louder, and lifted his head:—
'Tell them I came, and no one answered,
That I kept my word,' he said.
Never the least stir made the listeners,
Though every word he spake[3]
Fell echoing through the shadowiness of the still house
From the one man left awake:
Ay, they heard his foot upon the stirrup,
And the sound of iron on stone,
And how the silence surged softly backward,
When the plunging hoofs were gone.

Literary Analysis
Imagery Which words paint a vivid image of a forest setting?

3. **spake** (spāk) *v.* spoke.

Review and Assess

Thinking About the Selection

1. **Respond:** Did you find this poem spooky and chilling? Why or why not?
2. **(a) Recall:** Briefly describe the time and place in which the action of the poem occurs. **(b) Analyze:** Why are the time and place important?
3. **(a) Recall:** Which words are used to describe the house? **(b) Interpret:** Which other details create the eerie, dreamlike atmosphere of the poem?
4. **(a) Recall:** What information does the poet leave out? **(b) Infer:** Why do you think there are so many unanswered questions in the poem? **(c) Speculate:** What are some possible answers to these questions?
5. **(a) Recall:** What do you learn about the traveler in the poem? **(b) Infer:** Why do you think de la Mare called the poem "The Listeners" rather than "The Traveler"?
6. **Synthesize:** Would knowing more about the Traveler's actions lessen the poem's mystery? Explain.
7. **Evaluate:** Why do you think people are compelled by mysteries like this one?

Walter de la Mare

(1873–1956)

Walter de la Mare's most famous poems, like "The Listeners," tell mysterious, incomplete stories. Perhaps de la Mare, an Englishman, used his poetry to live a more intriguing life because his daytime jobs were so unmysterious. At age seventeen, for example, he worked in the statistics department of the Anglo-American Oil Company. Poems may have been his escape from numbers!

In addition to composing poems, de la Mare wrote short stories, novels, and plays. He also edited poetry anthologies.

CUSTOMIZE INSTRUCTION FOR UNIVERSAL ACCESS

For Less Proficient Readers	For Gifted/Talented Students	For Advanced Readers
Some of the archaic vocabulary words in "The Listeners" may challenge students. Have them use the information in the footnotes to define some of these words, and encourage them to use context clues to define others.	Have students create a soundtrack for this poem. Have them begin by selecting appropriately eerie music for background, then adding sounds that occur in the poem: knocking, the flutter of a bird, the chomping of the horse, and so on. Have them play their results for the class.	Challenge students to write a prelude to "The Listeners" that tells why the Traveler originally rode away from the house and whom he left behind. Students should limit themselves to 36 lines and echo de la Mare's rhyme scheme, meter, style, and diction.

5 Literary Analysis

Imagery

- Ask the Literary Analysis question on p. 123: Which words paint a vivid image of a forest setting?
  Answer: *forest's ferny floor, leaf-fringed sill, dark turf, leafy sky*
- Have students read from line 25 to the end of the poem. Have them identify words and phrases that appeal to one or more of the five senses. Ask them to describe the effect of these images.
  Answer: Hearing: *smote, louder, spake, echoing, still, heard, sound of iron on stone, silence surged softly.* Sight: *shadowiness.* The images have an unsettling effect; the mood is mysterious.

Answers for p. 123

Review and Assess

1. Possible response: The presence of phantoms and the emptiness of the house create a spooky and chilling feeling.
2. **(a)** It's probably in the distant past since the traveler is on horseback. The setting is a forest at night. **(b)** The darkness and isolation add to the mood of mystery.
3. **(a)** *lone, still* **(b)** *silence, stillness, phantom listeners, faint moonbeams, strangeness, echoing*
4. **(a)** He doesn't say who the Traveler is, why he has come to the house, or whom he expected to find. **(b)** It makes the poem more mysterious. **(c)** Possible responses: The Traveler came to find friends or family who were depending on him. They are gone because they have died or were taken away.
5. **(a)** He has come to keep his word, but he may be very late. **(b)** Students may note that the perspective of the "phantom listeners" dominates the poem.
6. Yes, because answers diminish mystery.
7. Readers may be thrilled by the spookiness and curious about the unanswered questions.

6 About the Selection

Ishmael Reed invites readers to consider the power of a poem to draw them in and, by showing them frightening aspects of themselves, to disturb and even threaten them. Reed launches his poem by describing the plot of a television show. (*Thriller* was a weekly series that originally ran in the early 1960s. The eerie stories were introduced by Boris Karloff, an actor famous for roles in horror movies, including *Frankenstein*.)

7 Literary Analysis

Imagery and Diction

- Have students compare and contrast Reed's diction with de la Mare's. What effect does each poet achieve with his diction?
  Answer: Reed's diction includes abbreviations like those that would appear in classified ads or e-mail. He uses short, everyday words. In contrast, de la Mare uses some archaic words and many multisyllabic ones. Reed's diction gives his poem an aggressive and contemporary feel. The sound of de la Mare's is dreamy, and his vocabulary suggests a Romantic past.
- Ask students to identify the sense to which the images in lines 1–11 appeal. Why do they think Reed chose this sense?
  Answer: The images of mirrors appeal to the sense of sight. Reed appeals to this sense because reading involves looking at words on a page more than it involves any other sense.
- Ask students the Literary Analysis question on p. 124: What is most impressive about the image of the woman's house?
  Possible responses: The most memorable images are the mirrors; the woman's disappearance into a mirror.

6 BEWARE: Do Not Read This Poem

Ishmael Reed

7

tonite, *thriller* was
abt an ol woman, so vain she
surrounded her self w/
      many mirrors

It got so bad that finally she
locked herself indoors & her
whole life became the
      mirrors

one day the villagers broke
into her house, but she was too
swift for them. she disappeared
      into a mirror
each tenant who bought the house
after that lost a loved one to
      the ol woman in the mirror:
      first a little girl
      then a young woman
      then the young woman/s husband

the hunger of this poem is legendary
it has taken in many victims
back off from this poem
it has drawn in yr feet
back off from this poem
it has drawn in yr legs
back off from this poem
it is a greedy mirror
you are into this poem. from
      the waist down
nobody can hear you can they?

Literary Analysis
Imagery What is most impressive about the image of the woman's house?

legendary (lej´ ən der´ ē) *adj.* based on legends, stories handed down from one generation to the next

CUSTOMIZE INSTRUCTION FOR UNIVERSAL ACCESS

For Gifted/Talented Students

Have students compare and contrast Escher's *Drawing Hands* (p. 120) with "Beware: Do Not Read This Poem." First, have them study *Drawing Hands* and consider what it means. What message or theme does Escher convey to the viewer? How do students react to the drawing at first glance? How do they react to it after thinking about it for a while? Next, students can compare and contrast their reactions to the drawing with their reactions to the poem. Do the two works have any themes or images in common? If so, what? Make sure students explain their answers by referring to specific details from the poem and the drawing. Once students have perceived the relationship between a drawing that draws itself and a poem that pulls its readers in, challenge those with artistic ability to depict how a reader might literally be pulled into a poem.

this poem has had you up to here
belch
this poem aint got no manners
you cant call out frm this poem
relax now & go w/ this poem
move & roll on to this poem

do not resist this poem
this poem has yr eyes
this poem has his head
this poem has his arms
this poem has his fingers
this poem has his fingertips

this poem is the reader & the
reader this poem

statistic: the us bureau of missing persons reports
that in 1968 over 100,000 people disappeared
leaving no solid clues
nor trace only
a space in the lives of their friends

Review and Assess

Thinking About the Selection

1. **Respond:** What feelings did Reed's poem evoke in you? Explain.
2. **(a) Recall:** What is unique about the woman's house? **(b) Analyze:** How does the description of this house add to the mystery of the poem?
3. **(a) Recall:** What does the poem say happens to those who read it? **(b) Interpret:** What does the idea of the reader's interaction suggest about the mystery of reading?
4. **(a) Recall:** Which lines in the poem refer to the poem and the reader as one? **(b) Interpret:** What message is the speaker trying to convey when he says "this poem is the reader & the/reader is this poem"? **(c) Infer:** How would you describe the speaker's tone of voice? Support your answer.
5. **(a) Analyze:** How does the sound of the poem change in the last stanza, beginning with line 44? **(b) Evaluate:** How does such an ending extend the mystery?
6. **(a) Analyze:** What details could the poet add to clarify the poem's story? **(b) Take a Position:** Considering the ways these details might alter the poem's effectiveness, would you want to include them? Explain.

Ishmael Reed

(b. 1938)

Ishmael Reed is as mysterious, many-sided, and hilarious as his poem "Beware: Do Not Read This Poem." Born in Chattanooga, Tennessee, and raised in Buffalo, New York, Reed has worked as a hospital attendant, market researcher, newspaper manager, and unemployment-office clerk.

In addition to poetry collections like *Chattanooga* (1973), Reed has written satiric novels that make fun of American westerns, as well as slave narratives, essays, plays, songs, and even operas.

Answers for p. 125

Review and Assess

1. Students may have found it fascinating or intimidating. The rhythms and repetition may suggest rap or rock music, which may add to their enjoyment of the poem.
2. **(a)** People who move in disappear into the mirrors. **(b)** It's a mystery how the people disappear into the mirrors and uncertain what happens to them.
3. **(a)** The poem draws readers in and takes them over. **(b)** It suggests that written words are powerful, disturbing forces.
4. **(a)** lines 20, 27, 30, and 42 **(b)** He shows that the poem has a strong effect on the reader; the poem and the reader have merged because the poem has grabbed the reader's attention. **(c)** Possible answers: jeering, self-confident; The rhythm and repetition make the poem sound like rap music. The message is aggressive.
5. **(a)** Instead of cool and jazzy, the poem has become neutral and statistical. **(b)** By speaking of missing persons, the poem concludes with a new uncertainty.
6. **(a)** He could have explained more about the magic mirrors or how a reader becomes "this poem." **(b)** Additional facts would make the poem less puzzling and less challenging.

CUSTOMIZE INSTRUCTION FOR UNIVERSAL ACCESS

For English Learners

The abbreviations and lack of punctuation and capitalization in this poem may make it difficult reading for some students. Go over abbreviations such as *w/* and *abt* before students begin reading. Have them try reading the poem aloud to themselves; this will help them figure out where the complete thoughts begin and end. You may want to pass out photocopies of the poem so that students can mark them up, adding punctuation marks to help them figure out the sense of the poem on a first or second reading. Students can study these marked-up copies until they feel they understand what is happening; then, they can go back to reread the original for its effects.

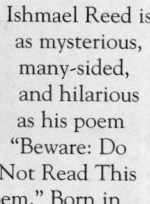

❽ About the Selection

Henriqueta Lisboa's "Echo" describes the frightening qualities of natural phenomena and implicitly evokes an even more violent human world.

❾ Literary Analysis

Imagery and Diction

- Ask students the Literary Analysis question on p. 126: What do you "hear" when you read the first stanza?
  Answer: You hear the parrot scream and the rock echo a reply.
- Have a volunteer read the third stanza. What sound is repeated? What is the effect of this repetition?
  Answer: The *s* sound is repeated. The repetition reinforces the image of echoing.

Answers for p. 126

Review and Assess

1. Shrill screams are unpleasant.
2. **(a)** A parrot screams and the sound echoes off rock, causing a violent eruption of parrot screaming. **(b)** If the parrots are in a forest, there probably aren't enough rocks around to echo their screams back at them.
3. **(a)** The rock echoes back the scream. **(b)** The rock might be demanding silence.
4. **(a)** The last line suggests a contrast between nature and the human world. **(b)** The noisy unpleasantness of nature is not as harmful as a human world of screaming bombs and strafing planes.
5. Possible responses: Some readers may feel the last line wrenches the poem in an unexpected direction. Others may feel that the line crystallizes the theme already implicit in the poem.

❽

Echo

Henriqueta Lisboa
Translated by
Hélcio Veiga Costa

Green parrot
let out a shrill scream.
Rock in sudden
anger, replied.

A great uproar
invaded the forest.
❾ Thousands of parrots
screamed together
and rock echoed.

From all sides
strafing space
steely screams rained
and rained down.

Very piercing screams!

But no one died.

Literary Analysis
Imagery and Diction
What do you "hear" when you read the first stanza?

strafing (strāf' iŋ) *adj.* attacking with machine-gun fire

Henriqueta Lisboa

(1903–1985)

A Brazilian poet, Lisboa uses a few well-chosen words to create powerful poems. By the age of twenty, she had already published her first book of poetry. Her early lyrics deal with traditional poetic themes, while her later poems tell about the history of her region. The themes she touched upon later in her life were not uncommon ones. Many of her contemporaries, such as Brazilian writer and poet Mário de Andrade, also spoke about the significance of Brazil in their works.

Review and Assess

Thinking About the Selection

1. **Respond:** What did you find pleasant or unpleasant about the sounds in the poem?
2. **(a) Recall:** What happens in the poem? **(b) Distinguish:** Which details in the poem could realistically occur, and which could not?
3. **(a) Recall:** What does the rock do when the green parrot first screams? **(b) Speculate:** What might the rock have been demanding of the parrot?
4. **(a) Analyze:** What effect does the poem's last line have on the meaning of the poem? **(b) Interpret:** What might be the message in this poem?
5. **(a) Evaluate:** Do you think the last line improves or weakens the poem? Explain.

ASSESSMENT PRACTICE: Reading Comprehension

Context Clues (For more practice, see Test Preparation Workbook, p. 6.)

Many tests require students to use context clues to determine the meaning of a word as it is used in a passage. Use the following sample to teach students to recognize antonyms as context clues.

Carlos had taken a room in spite of tales that the inn was haunted. As darkness descended, however, and the old building began to creak and groan, he felt terror rising. Now, what had seemed a trifling decision had gained a whole new significance.

In this passage, the term *trifling* means ______.

A major
B immediate
C unimportant
D necessary

Help students identify the contrast between *trifling* and *significant*. This contrast is a clue that something trifling is not significant. The correct answer is *C*.

Review and Assess

Literary Analysis

Imagery

1. Explain how the **imagery** in "The Listeners" helps you to hear "silence" and see invisible "listeners." Identify at least one sound-based image and one sight-based one.
2. In "Beware: Do Not Read This Poem," how does the image of "a greedy mirror" help you to experience the strangeness of reading?
3. Find two examples of imagery in "Echo" and show how they create a feeling of uncertainty.

Comparing Literary Works

4. For each example of **diction** below, explain the image created by the italicized words.

Title of Poem	Examples of Diction	Image Created
The Listeners	"*echoing* through the *shadowiness* of the *still* house"	
Beware: Do Not Read This Poem	"this poem has *yr* eyes"	
Echo	"parrot let out a *shrill* scream"	

5. How does the vividness of language in "The Listeners" compare to that in "Echo"?
6. In your opinion, which of the three poets creates the most powerful images? Justify your answer with details from the poem.

Reading Strategy

Using Your Senses

7. (a) Why is sound as important as sight in experiencing the world of "The Listeners"? (b) In which of the other two poems do you *hear* a mystery? Explain.
8. (a) Which of the poems asks you to picture yourself? (b) How are you invited to see yourself?

Extend Understanding

9. **Music Connection:** If you were setting these poems to music, what type of music would you choose for each? Explain.

Quick Review

Imagery is a picture that is painted, or created, with words.

Diction is a writer's word choice.

In reading a poem, **use your senses** to focus on language that tells how something looks, sounds, feels, smells, or tastes.

Take It to the Net

www.phschool.com

Take the interactive self-test online to check your understanding of the selections.

ASSESS

Answers for p. 127

Review and Assess

1. Possible response: Sound image: "Their stillness answering his cry" makes reader aware that the Traveler is listening intently but hears nothing. Visual image: "faint moonbeams on the dark stair" emphasizes the darkness and isolation of the house.
2. People bring their own experiences to everything they read, so in a sense reading reflects what the reader puts into it, like a mirror. Because so many thoughts are universal, people are often startled by finding echoes of their own thoughts in literature.
3. Possible responses: "uproar invaded the forest," "strafing space," "steely screams."These images clearly reflect war and its life-or-death uncertainty.
4. "Listeners": The moonlight creating shadows inside the empty house. "Beware": The poem has already absorbed some of the reader's identity. "Echo": The parrot called out.
5. "Echo" appeals mainly to the sense of hearing; "The Listener" appeals to the senses of hearing, sight, and touch.
6. Make sure that students defend their choices with specific details from the poems.
7. **(a)** Since "The Listeners" takes place in the dark, the Traveler relies on his sense of hearing. **(b)** In "Echo" readers hear bird cries like the sounds of war.
8. **(a)** "Beware" **(b)** Readers are invited to find something they recognize, identify with, or find fascinating.
9. Possible responses: "Listeners": eerie classical or romantic music would fit the mood. "Beware": the driving rhythms, short lines, and one- or two-syllable words suggest rap. "Echo": since the poem has no regular rhythm or rhyme scheme, contemporary music would work well.

ENRICHMENT: Further Reading

Other Works by the Authors

Works by Walter de la Mare
Best Stories of Walter de la Mare
Collected Poems

Works by Ishmael Reed
New and Collected Poems of Ishmael Reed
Conjure
Chattanooga

Works by Henriqueta Lisboa
Endearment
Godmother Moon

Take It to the Net

Visit www.phschool.com for more information on "The Listeners," "Beware: Do Not Read This Poem," and "Echoes."

EXTEND

Answers for p. 128

❶ Vocabulary Development

Word Analysis

1. smote; connotes a heavy blow
2. aint; suggests a hip, slangy attitude
3. **(a)** The line is a sentence fragment. **(b)** It emphasizes how shrill and distracting the screams were.

Fluency: Context

1. perplexed
2. legendary
3. thronging
4. strafing

Spelling Strategy

1. traveler
2. appearance
3. greenish

❷ Grammar Lesson

1. faint, dark; *adjectives*
2. plunging, *verb*
3. Her, *pronoun*; whole, *adjective* or *noun*
4. forest, *noun*; shrill, *adjective*
5. green, *adjective*; piercing, *verb*

Writing Application

Sample answers:

1. The echoing call of the migrating geese kept the baby from falling asleep.
2. When all the lights went out in the building, I knew I was in for a strange adventure.
3. Eric was the best in the office at making paper airplanes.
4. I think your attitude is very unattractive.

❶ Integrate Language Skills

Vocabulary Development Lesson

Word Analysis: Poetic License and Vocabulary in Poems

Poetic license is a poet's freedom to break rules of vocabulary, grammar, or spelling in order to create a literary effect. For example, in "The Listeners," de la Mare uses *spake* for *spoke*. The word suggests an old-fashioned feeling. Answer these questions:

1. What other unusual word does de la Mare use in lines 5–7? What does it connote, or suggest to you?
2. Find an example of poetic license in line 32 of Ishmael Reed's poem. What connotation or association does the word have?
3. (a) What poetic license does Henriqueta Lisboa take in line 14 of her poem? (b) What effect does this violation of grammar have?

Fluency: Context

Copy the following paragraph. Fill in each blank with a word from the vocabulary list on page 121.

The detective entered the deserted house and stood in front of the mirror, __?__. Deep inside the mysterious glass, he could see the __?__ parrots, a species that had never existed. Hundreds of them were __?__ a forest clearing, __?__ the trees with their steely cries.

Spelling Strategy

When you add a suffix starting with a vowel to a base word ending with a consonant, do not change the spelling of the base word: *legend* + *-ary* = *legendary*. Add each suffix indicated to form a new word.

1. travel (*-er*) 2. appear (*-ance*) 3. green (*-ish*)

❷ Grammar Lesson

Types of Adjectives

An **adjective** is a word used to describe a noun or pronoun or to give a noun or pronoun a more specific meaning. Adjectives modify nouns and pronouns by telling *what kind*, *which one*, *how many*, or *how much*. Sometimes a noun, pronoun, or verb may serve as an adjective.

Adjective: the *lone* house (modifies *house*)
Noun as Adjective: *phantom* listeners (modifies *listeners*)
Pronoun as Adjective: felt in *his* heart (modifies *heart*)
Verb as Adjective: an air *stirred* and *shaken* (modify *air*)

Practice Identify each word that serves as an adjective. Then, determine whether the word is an *adjective*, *noun*, *pronoun*, or *verb*.

1. They saw the faint moonbeams on the dark stair.
2. The silence surged backwards when the plunging hoofs disappeared.
3. Her whole life became the mirrors.
4. The forest bird let out a shrill scream.
5. Green parrots screamed piercing screams.

Writing Application Use each of the following words as an adjective in a sentence.

1. echoing
2. strange
3. paper
4. your

WG Prentice Hall Writing and Grammar Connection: Chapter 18, Section 1

TEACHING RESOURCES

The following resources can be used to enrich or extend the instructions for pp. 128–129.

Vocabulary

Selection Support: Build Vocabulary, p. 21;

Grammar

Selection Support: Build Grammar Skills, p. 22
Writing and Grammar, Gold Level, p. 380
Daily Language Practice Transparencies

Writing

Writing and Grammar, Gold Level, p. 180 ■
Writing and Grammar iText CD-ROM

■ **BLOCK SCHEDULING:** Resources marked with this symbol provide varied instruction during 90-minute blocks.

❸ Writing Lesson

Comparison-and-Contrast Essay

The poems in this section use imagery to create pictures. Write a comparison-and-contrast essay comparing the imagery found in two of the poems.

Prewriting Decide which two poems generated the strongest or clearest word pictures for you. Then, complete a Venn diagram in which you jot down the similarities and differences between these two poems.

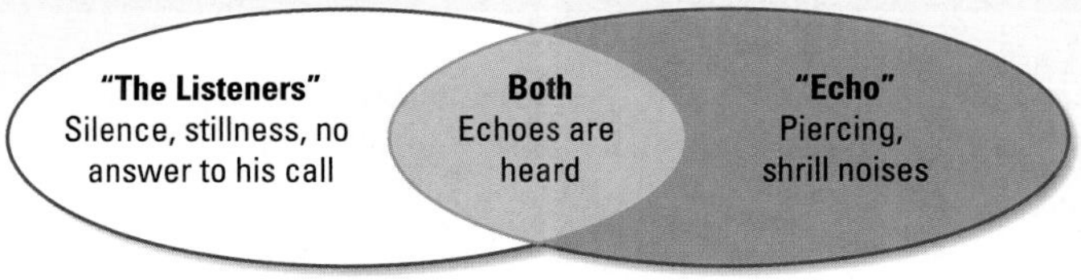

Drafting Write a sentence to identify the comparison or contrast you will address. In each body paragraph of your essay, focus on one poem, citing examples of vivid language that produces an image.

Revising Reread your essay to make sure you have used appropriate transition words. To show similarities, use words such as *all, similarly, both, in the same way,* and *equally*. To show differences, use words such as *on the other hand, in contrast,* and *however*.

WG Prentice Hall Writing and Grammar Connection: Chapter 9, Section 2

❹ Extension Activities

Listening and Speaking In a small group, write a **dramatic scene** that takes place in "the lone house" of "the listeners" after the Traveler has galloped away. Assign each group member one of the following roles: actor, director, or set designer.

- Use your scene to answer some of the questions left unanswered by the poem.
- Then, act out the scene you have created.
- You may choose to videotape your drama or produce it onstage.

After acting out your scene, ask your audience to help you analyze the production. **[Group Activity]**

Research and Technology "Echo" is set in Brazil's tropical rain forest. Give a **multimedia presentation** on this environment, taking the class on a magical mystery tour through its wonders. Use an atlas to gather information about the locations of Brazil's rain forests. Then, use the Internet to research the kinds of plants, animals, and weather found in those locations. Present your findings to the class.

Take It to the Net www.phschool.com

Go online for an additional research activity using the Internet.

ASSESSMENT RESOURCES

The following resources can be used to assess students' knowledge and skills.

Selection Assessment

- **Formal Assessment,** pp. 16–18
- **Open Book Test,** pp. 16–18
- **Got It! Assessment Videotapes,** Tape 1
- **Test Bank Software**

Take It to the Net
Visit www.phschool.com for self-tests and additional questions on the poems.

Writing Rubric

- **Performance Assess. and Portfolio Mgmt.,** p. 16

PRENTICE HALL ASSESSMENT SYSTEM

- **Workbook**
- **Skill Book**
- **Transparencies**
- **CD-ROM**

❸ Writing Lesson

- Draw a Venn diagram on the chalkboard and demonstrate its use by comparing and contrasting the characters in two of the poems (such as the woman in "Beware" and the Traveler in "Listeners".) Fill in the diagram with details suggested by the students. Then have students create their own diagrams comparing the imagery of two poems.
- After drafting is completed, have students exchange papers with partners. Each student can review the other's essay, checking for accuracy of references to the poems and for the strength of the arguments.
- Use the Comparison-and-Contrast Essay rubric in **Performance Assessment and Portfolio Management,** p. 16, to evaluate students' essays.

❹ Extension Activity

Listening and Speaking

- Meet briefly with each group of students after their first planning session to give them any guidance or advice they need.
- All group members should collaborate on planning the scene. Students can then divide up the tasks of writing the dialogue, acting out the scene, directing the rehearsals, and providing any necessary props, costumes, and music or sound effects.
- Students may want to give their scene as a radio play, a pantomime, or a shadow show with narration.

CUSTOMIZE INSTRUCTION For Universal Access

To address different learning styles, use the following activities suggested in the **Extension Activities** booklet, p. 6.

- For Musical/Rhythmic Learners, use Activity 6.
- For Verbal/Linguistic Learners, use Activities 5 and 6.
- For Visual/Kinesthetic Learners, use Activity 7.

Caucasian Mummies Mystify Chinese

Lesson Objectives and CA Correlations

1. **To analyze and respond to literary elements**
   - Literary Analysis: News Article **R 2.1**
   - Connecting Literary Elements: Objectivity **R 2.8**
2. **To read, comprehend, analyze, and critique nonfiction**
   - Reading Strategy: Finding the Main Idea
   - Reading Check questions
   - Review and Assess questions
   - Assessment Practice (ATE)
3. **To develop word analysis skills, fluency, and systematic vocabulary**
   - Vocabulary Development Lesson: Greek Suffix: *-ist* **R 1.1**
4. **To understand and apply written and oral language conventions**
   - Spelling Strategy
   - Grammar Lesson: Proper and Compound Adjectives **LC 1.2, 1.3**
5. **To understand and apply appropriate writing and research strategies**
   - Writing Lesson: News Feature **W 2.3**
   - Extension Activity: Travel Brochure
6. **To understand and apply listening and speaking strategies**
   - Extension Activity: Visual Presentation **LS 1.7**

STEP-BY-STEP TEACHING GUIDE	PACING GUIDE
PRETEACH	
Motivate Students and Provide Background	
Use the Motivation activity (ATE p. 130)	5 min.
Read and discuss the Preview material and Background information (SE/ATE p. 130) [A]	10 min.
Introduce the Concepts	
Introduce the Literary Analysis and Reading Strategy (SE/ATE p. 131) [A]	15 min.
Pronounce the vocabulary words and read their definitions (SE p. 131)	5 min.
TEACH	
Monitor Comprehension	
Informally monitor comprehension by circulating while students read independently or in groups [A]	15 min.
Monitor students' comprehension with the Reading Check notes (SE/ATE pp. 133, 135)	as students read
Develop vocabulary with Vocabulary notes (SE pp. 133, 134; ATE p. 133)	as students read
Develop Understanding	
Develop students' understanding of news features with the Literary Analysis annotations (SE pp. 133, 135; ATE pp. 133, 135) [A]	5 min.
Develop students' understanding of main idea with the Reading Strategy annotations (SE pp. 134, 135; ATE pp. 134, 135)	5 min.
ASSESS	
Assess Mastery	
Assess students' mastery of the Reading Strategy and Literary Analysis by having them answer the Review and Assess questions (SE/ATE p. 137)	15 min.
Use one or more of the print and media Assessment Resources (ATE p. 139) [A]	up to 45 min.
EXTEND	
Apply Understanding	
Have students complete the Vocabulary Development Lesson and the Grammar Lesson (SE p. 138) [A]	20 min.
Apply students' ability to grab the readers attention using the Writing Lesson (SE/ATE p. 139) [A]	45 min.
Apply students' understanding of the selection using one or more of the Extension Activities (SE p. 139)	20–90 min.

[A] ACCELERATED INSTRUCTION:
Use the strategies and activities identified with an [A].

UNIVERSAL ACCESS
● = Below Level Students
▲ = On-Level Students
■ = Above Level Students

Time and Resource Manager

Reading Level: Average
Average Number of Instructional Days: 4

RESOURCES		
PRINT	**TRANSPARENCIES**	**TECHNOLOGY**
• **Beyond Literature,** Cross-Curricular Connection: Science, p. 7 ▲ ■		• **Interest Grabber Video,** Tape 1 ● ▲ ■
• **Selection Support Workbook:** ● ▲ ■ Literary Analysis, p. 28 Reading Strategy, p. 27 Build Vocabulary, p. 25	• **Literary Analysis and Reading Transparencies,** pp. 13 and 14 ● ▲ ■	
		• **Listening to Literature** ● ▲ ■ Audiocassettes, Side 6 Audio CDs, CD 5
• **Literatura en español** ● ▲ • **Literary Analysis for Enrichment** ■		
• **Formal Assessment:** Selection Test, pp. 19–21 ● ▲ ■ • **Open Book Test,** pp. 19–21 ● ▲ ■ • **Performance Assessment and Portfolio Management,** p. 30 ● ▲ ■ • PRENTICE HALL ASSESSMENT SYSTEM ● ▲ ■	• PRENTICE HALL ASSESSMENT SYSTEM ● ▲ ■ Skills Practice Answers and Explanations on Transparencies	• **Test Bank Software** ● ▲ ■ • **Got It! Assessment Videotapes,** Tape 1 ● ▲
• **Selection Support Workbook:** ● ▲ ■ Build Grammar Skills, p. 26 • **Writing and Grammar,** Gold Level ● ▲ ■ • **Extension Activities,** p. 7 ● ▲ ■	• **Daily Language Practice Transparencies** ● ▲ • **Writing Models and Graphic Organizers on Transparencies** ● ▲ ■	• **Writing and Grammar iText CD-ROM** ● ▲ ■ *Take It to the Net* www.phschool.com

BLOCK SCHEDULING: Use one 90-minute class period to preteach the selection and have students read it. Use a second 90-minute class period to assess students' mastery of skills and have them complete one of the Extension Activities.

PRETEACH

Step-by-Step Teaching Guide for pp. 130–131

Motivation

To hook students' interest in this news article, treat it like an episode of an "unsolved mysteries" television show. Playing the part of the host, have students view the photograph on p. 132 while you read aloud the following passages:

In dim light they appeared to be sleeping, but they've been dead for up to 4000 years. . . .

Who were these people?

Where did they come from?

Have students discuss the photograph and the passage and make predictions about how the questions will be answered.

Interest Grabber Video

As an alternative, you may wish to play "The Tombs of the Pharaohs" on Tape 1 to engage students' interest.

❶ Background

Science

A mummy is a dead body preserved by embalming. Many ancient Egyptian mummies are in an excellent state of preservation because of the country's hot, dry climate.

Prepare to Read

Caucasian Mummies Mystify Chinese

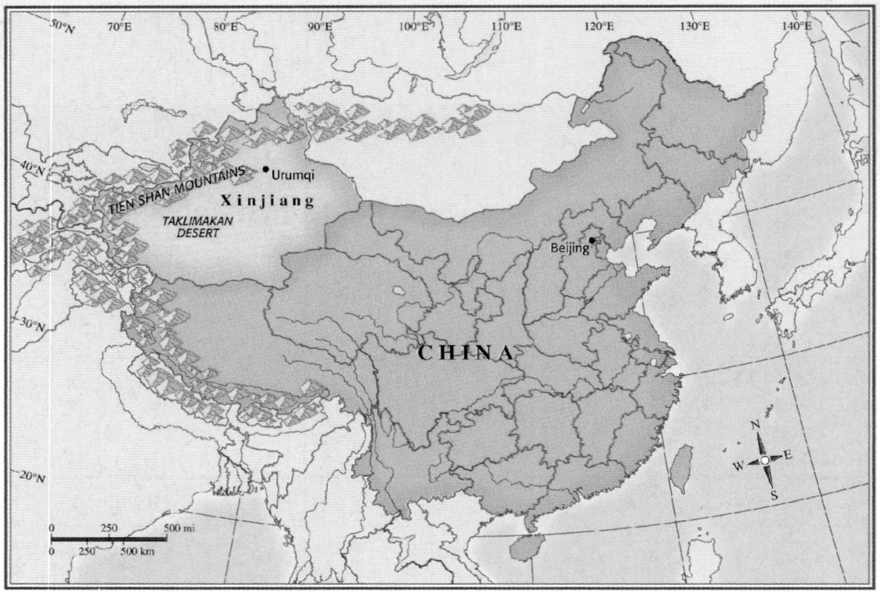

Take It to the Net

Visit www.phschool.com for interactive activities and instruction related to "Caucasian Mummies Mystify Chinese," including

- background
- graphic organizers
- literary elements
- reading strategies

Preview

Connecting to the Literature

Unsolved mysteries, such as how the Egyptian pyramids were built or why huge slabs of rock were placed in circles at Stonehenge, are popular subjects for books, articles, and television programs. This article focuses on the discovery of mysterious Caucasian mummies in what is now China.

❶ Background

While you may connect mummies with ancient Egypt, they actually have been found all over the world, including China, Europe, Peru, and Mexico. Because people often were buried with their clothes, tools, and even food, mummies can teach us much about how ancient peoples lived.

TEACHING RESOURCES

The following resources can be used to enrich or extend the instruction for pp. 130-131.

Motivation

Interest Grabber Video, Tape 1

Background

Beyond Literature, p. 7

Take It to the Net

Visit www.phschool.com for background and hotlinks for "Caucasian Mummies Mystify Chinese."

Literary Analysis

Literary Analysis and Reading Transparencies, News Article, p. 14

Reading

Selection Support: Reading Strategy, p. 28; Build Vocabulary, p. 26

Literary Analysis and Reading Transparencies, Finding the Main Idea, p. 13

BLOCK SCHEDULING: Resources marked with this symbol provide varied instruction during 90-minute blocks.

❷ Literary Analysis

News Article

The purpose of a **news article** such as "Caucasian Mummies Mystify Chinese" is to inform you—the reader—by providing facts that answer six questions: *Who? What? When? Where? Why?* and *How?* To help you answer these questions, pay close attention to the following parts of the article:

- the lead, or opening sentences
- details in the form of facts, statistics, and summaries
- opinions and quotations from experts and eyewitnesses

As you read the article, answer as many questions as you can after reading the first paragraph. Then, continue to look for additional answers in the facts and expert opinions that follow.

Connecting Literary Elements

News reporters are taught to write with **objectivity,** presenting the facts only, without opinions or judgments on the subject. By using objective language, the writer lets readers form their own opinions without influence. Pay close attention to the presentation of information in this article. Ask yourself if the writer is being objective, and notice whether certain words or details suggest an opinion or position.

❸ Reading Strategy

Finding the Main Idea

When reading a news article, **finding the main idea** is a critical skill. The main idea in a news article is its most important point. Often, the main idea is stated in the lead paragraph. You can also determine the main idea by answering the six questions addressed in the article, and then deciding on the main point based on your answers.

As you read the article, use a chart like the one shown to record answers to the six questions: *Who? What? When? Where? Why?* and *How?*

Who?	
What?	
When?	
Where?	
Why?	
How?	

Vocabulary Development

dogmas (dôg´ məz) *n.* firmly held beliefs or doctrines (p. 133)

parched (pärcht) *adj.* dried up by heat (p. 133)

archaeologist (är´ kē äl´ ə jist) *n.* person who studies the remains of ancient ways of life (p. 133)

imperialist (im pir´ ē əl ist) *adj.* here, describing a person from a country that seeks to dominate weaker countries (p. 134)

subjugation (sub´ jə gā´ shən) *n.* enslavement (p. 136)

reconcile (rek´ ən sīl´) *v.* bring into agreement (p. 136)

CUSTOMIZE INSTRUCTION FOR UNIVERSAL ACCESS

For Less Proficient Readers	For English Learners	For Advanced Readers
Have students look for the main idea of each paragraph. They can paraphrase this main idea so that the vocabulary isn't so difficult. They can then try the same technique on the supporting details.	This article is filled with sophisticated vocabulary words. Assign peer tutors to go through the article with students, helping them paraphrase the difficult words.	Have students analyze the article's use of sophisticated vocabulary. Why does Davidson use such words? What does this imply about his intended audience? What effect does his language have on readers?

❷ Literary Analysis

News Article

- Ask students whether they or their parents regularly read newspapers or news magazines. Ask why people read these items. Explain that the primary purpose of a news article is to inform readers about a discovery or an event. A secondary purpose is to entertain readers so that they will enjoy the article and get more out of it.
- Explain that readers usually approach news stories with questions. Reader want to know *when, how* and *why* certain events occurred. They want to know *who* caused these events and *who* is affected by them. Good writers will try to answer all possible questions.
- Have a volunteer read aloud the Connecting Literary Elements passage. Remind students that facts can be proven true, while opinions cannot. Encourage students to look out for opinions that are presented as objective facts.

❸ Reading Strategy

Finding the Main Idea

- Hold up the front page of a newspaper for the class. Point out that the headlines are in large, bold type; even those in the back of the room may be able to read them.
- Explain that a headline often gives an article's main idea. A headline like **TITANIC SINKS!** tells the reader the main idea in two words; the article will provide all the supporting details.

Vocabulary Development

- Pronounce each vocabulary word for students and read the definitions as a class. Have students identify any words with which they are already familiar.

E-Teach

Visit E-Teach at www.phschool.com for teachers' essays on how to teach, with questions and answers.

TEACH

Step-by-Step Teaching Guide for pp. 132–136

CUSTOMIZE INSTRUCTION
For Logical/Mathematical Learners

Encourage students to collaborate on a classroom time line that illustrates the information from this article in chronological order.

❶ About the Selection

Journalist Keay Davidson describes the discovery of more than 100 blond-haired, white-skinned mummies in China. The presence of apparently European mummies in Asia is surprising because it contradicts scientists' long-held beliefs that China evolved on its own, with little foreign input. The discovery shows that even long-held beliefs about history are subject to change. It also demonstrates that we all share the same global heritage—even societies that are far apart both geographically and culturally have traded ideas and customs from the dawn of history until the present.

❷ ▶Critical Viewing

Answer: The features of the mummy's face, the color of his hair, and the style of his clothing should help scientists deduce where he came from and when he lived.

① Caucasian Mummies Mystify Chinese

Keay Davidson
from San Francisco Examiner

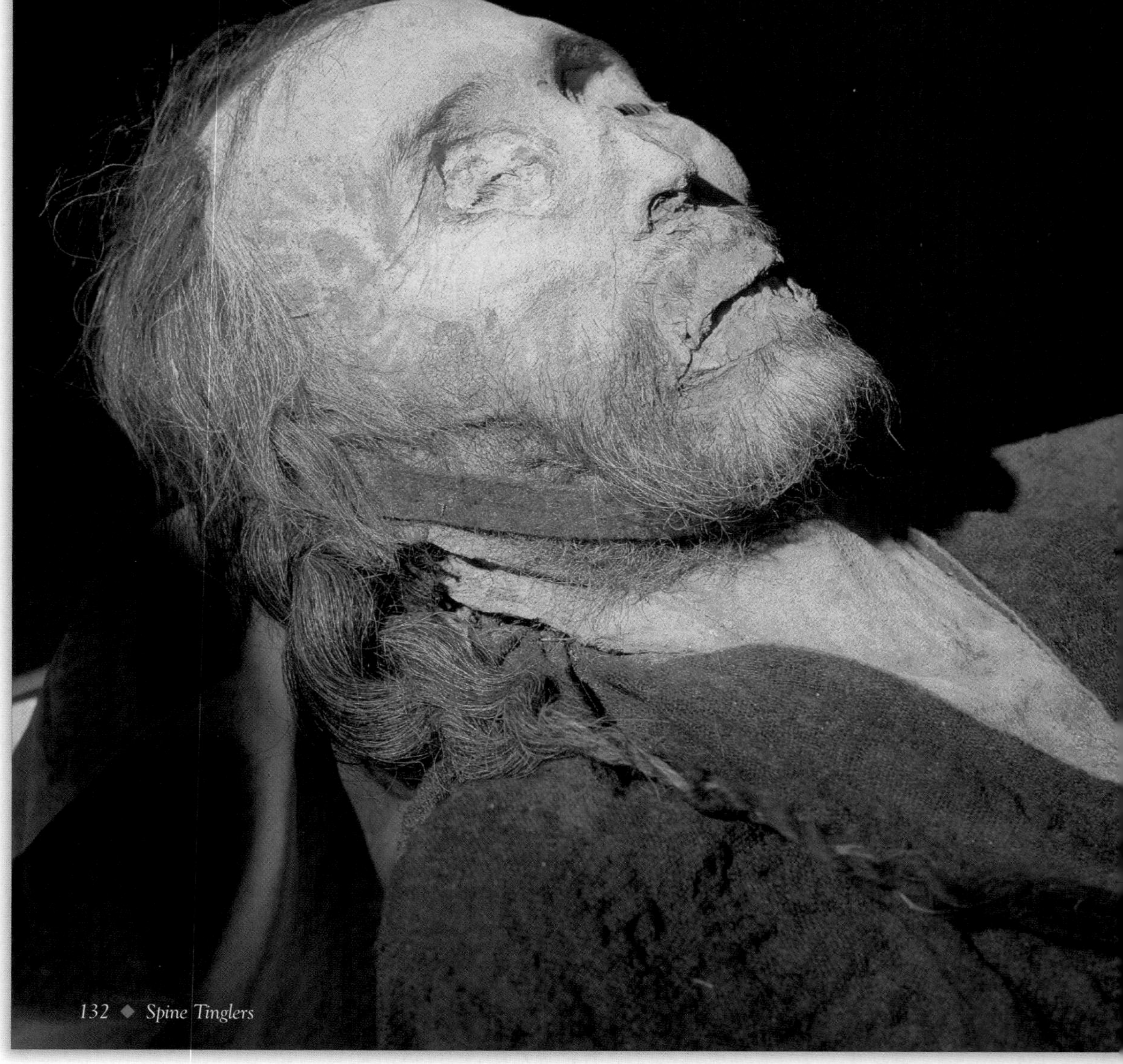

TEACHING RESOURCES

The following resources can be used to enrich or extend the instruction for pp. 132–136.

Literary Analysis

Selection Support: Literary Analysis, p. 29

Reading

Listening to Literature Audiocassettes, Side 6

Listening to Literature Audio CDs, CD 6

BLOCK SCHEDULING: Resources marked with this symbol provide varied instruction during 90-minute blocks.

3 San Francisco—In dim light they appear to be sleeping, but they've been dead up to 4,000 years: more than 100 astoundingly well-preserved mummies unearthed in a Chinese desert, whose inexplicably blond hair and white skin could topple dogmas about early human history.

A former Stanford scientist is analyzing the mummies' DNA in hopes of answering haunting questions: Who are they? Where did they come from? And what on earth were these European-looking men, women and children doing in China's parched out-back 2,000 years before Jesus, when Europe was largely a dark forest? Sixteen years after the first mummies were found, the Chinese government has granted Western researchers their first close look at these faces from prehistory: a baby in colorful swaddling clothes; a 20-year-old girl with braided hair, found buried in a curled-up position with her hands by her chest, as if dozing; a man with a pigtail, scarlet-colored clothes and red, blue, and amber leg wrappings. . . .

4 The discovery—which could have far greater impact on our understanding of societal evolution than the lone, ancient "ice man" uncovered in the Alps in 1991—is described in an article by science writer Evan Hadingham in the April 1994 issue of *Discover* magazine. Based on the *Discover* article and *San Francisco Examiner* interviews with experts on genetics and Chinese history and culture, here's how the discoveries unfolded. In 1978 and 1979, Chinese archaeologist Wang Binghua found the first of what would prove to be more than 100 mummies in Xinjiang (zin jē ang´) Province. They had white skin, blond hair, long noses and skulls, and deep-set eyes—Caucasians,[1] perhaps from Northern Europe.

dogmas (dôg´ məz) *n.* firmly held beliefs or doctrines

parched (pärcht) *adj.* dried up by heat

Literary Analysis
News Article What questions does the writer answer in this paragraph?

archaeologist (är´ kē äl´ ə jist) *n.* person who studies the remains of ancient ways of life

Little Attention in the West

Only scanty press reports have reached the West, at least partly because of the region's isolation, Chinese bureaucratic inertia and the regime's suppression of foreign contacts, particularly after the Tiananmen Square massacre[2] of 1989.

Now the cloud of mystery is lifting thanks to an investigation organized by University of Pennsylvania China scholar Victor Mair, in collaboration with researchers in China, the United States and Italy. The collaboration required delicate negotiations with Chinese officials.

It would have been "absolutely unthinkable" for Chinese authorities

1. **Caucasian** (kô kā´ zhən) *adj.* belonging to one of the major geographical groups of human beings, including the native peoples of Europe, who are loosely called the white race, though their skin colors may vary.
2. **Tiananmen** (tyen´ ə mən) **Square massacre** the murder of approximately 3,000 pro-democracy demonstrators by Chinese soldiers in Beijing, the capital of China, on June 3 and 4, 1989.

5 **Reading Check**
Where were more than 100 mummies found?

2 **Critical Viewing** What features of this mummy might help scientists to deduce facts about the man and his life? **[Deduce]**

3 Literary Analysis
News Article

- Read the article's title aloud. Ask students to volunteer questions that this title raises.
  Possible answers: Where were these mummies found? Why are the Chinese mystified about them?
- Ask the Literary Analysis question on p. 133: What questions does the writer answer in the article's third paragraph?
  Answer: Who discovered the mummies? Who first reported the discovery? Where in China were they discovered?

4 Vocabulary Development
Greek Suffix *-ist*

- Have students read the bracketed passage and identify the two words ending in the Greek suffix *-ist*. Explain that this suffix means "a person who practices or works at something." Challenge students to use this knowledge to define these two words.
  Answer: A *scientist* is someone who works in science. An *archaeologist* is someone who works in archaeology, digging up and identifying ancient objects.
- Challenge students to use a word ending in *-ist* to describe Keay Davidson's and Evan Hadingham's profession. Point out that both are writers.
  Answer: journalist

5 Reading Check

Answer: The mummies were found in Xinjiang Province, China.

CUSTOMIZE INSTRUCTION FOR UNIVERSAL ACCESS

For Special Needs Students	For Gifted/Talented Students
Have students copy the article's title and each of its subheads onto a graphic organizer. Challenge them to write one sentence that summarizes the main idea of each section. Students should then find two or three supporting details for each main idea.	Tell students that the Associated Press and United Press International are news organizations that provide information to local papers. AP and UPI articles are usually brief; papers don't leave much space for these articles. Have students pretend that they are AP or UPI reporters who have to summarize "Caucasian Mummies Mystify Chinese" in no more than a paragraph. Remind them to include all the article's main ideas.

6 ▶ **Critical Viewing**

Answer: This part of China is the closest to Europe.

7 Reading Strategy

Finding the Main Idea

- Ask students the Reading Strategy question on p. 134: How do the subheads help you to determine the article's main idea?
  Answer: Each subhead gives the main idea for its section, just as the article's title gives the main idea of the whole article.
- Have students turn back to p. 133 and read the subhead halfway down the page. Then, have them read the first sentence of the paragraph below it (beginning "Only scanty press reports"). Point out that the lead paragraph of the section begins with a sentence that rephrases the main idea of the subhead.
- Ask students why they think a news article would have subheads that stand out from the rest of the text.
  Answers: The subheads call attention to the main ideas of the article. They also show a reader which section of the article to go to for specific information.

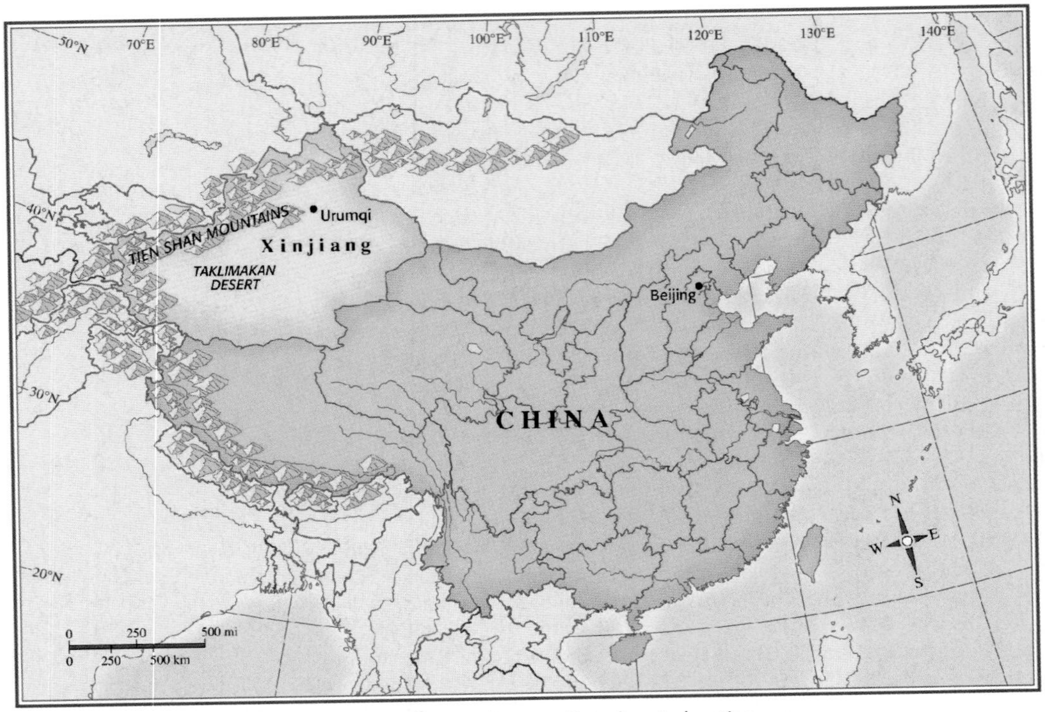

6 ▲ **Critical Viewing** Find the Xinjiang province on the map. Based on its location, explain why Europeans might have settled in that particular part of China. **[Draw Conclusions]**

to grant Westerners such access—including tissue samples from the mummies—only five years ago, Mair told *The Examiner*. "In the 1910s and 1920s, it was a game of the imperialist (Western) archaeologists to go in and take away important stuff—ancient manuscripts, artworks, paintings, statues . . . (Chinese officials are) very sensitive to that and they don't want to make the same situation recur," Mair said.

He also speculates that some Chinese officials may have initially hesitated to ballyhoo the find because they didn't know what to make of all those Caucasian faces. They date from a time when, according to regional histories and national pride, China was advancing—developing writing and metal artifacts and wheeled vehicles—without help from foreign meddlers.

7 **Bodies' Condition Excellent**

The mummies were unearthed at scattered burial sites in an approximately 500-mile-wide region of northwest China, between the so-called Celestial (Tian Shan) Mountains and the Taklimakan (täk′ li mä kän′) Desert. They range in age from 2000 B.C. to 300 B.C., based largely on radiocarbon dating.

imperialist (im pir′ ē əl ist) *adj.* here, describing a person from a country that seeks to dominate weaker countries

Reading Strategy
Finding the Main Idea
How does this subhead and others help you to determine the article's main idea?

ENRICHMENT: Science Connection

Mummification

The process of turning a corpse into a mummy is called *embalming*. First, the embalmers remove internal organs, including the brain, but not the heart and kidneys.

Once the organs were removed, the cavities left behind inside the body were filled with sawdust, wood pitch, or resin. Afterward, the body was coated in a substance called *natron*—sodium carbonate. Ancient Egyptians would then wash the body, anoint it with oil, and wrap it in linen. This process could take up to 70 days.

Nature has its own embalming methods. Archaeologists have found well-preserved remains in sites at extremely high, frigid altitudes or in extremely hot, dry environments. Some natural mummies have been found in former peat bogs, where acids from decaying vegetation acted as a preservative.

8 Where do they come from? At the University of Sassari in Italy, anthropological geneticist[3] Paolo Francalacci—who worked at Stanford until recently—hopes to determine the mummies' likely place of origin by comparing their DNA, or genetic material, with modern DNA from different societies.

"It will take time before we know anything (from the DNA analysis)," cautions Francalacci's Stanford colleague, Luigi Luca Cavalli-Sforza, a population geneticist. "It's a very tricky type of analysis. Old DNA is generally very damaged.

"What I find most surprising of all is that these mummies were in such perfect condition," Cavalli-Sforza said. Their European-looking features are "sufficient, I think, to say these people came from Northern Europe. . . . My guess is that these (people) were kind of 'scouts' (who) were, most probably, traveling east and maybe settled there (in Xinjiang)." He believes thousands of mummies may yet be found.

Why has it taken so long for the news to get Western scholars' attention? While Western news media trumpeted the 5,000-year-old "ice man" found in the Austrian and Italian Alps, they have ignored the Chinese find—almost. . . .

Poor Chinese public relations could be partly to blame. Mair suspects that in the late 1970s, Chinese scholars were so startled by the Caucasian mummies that they weren't sure what to do with them.

"I think it flummoxed them when they found these Caucasian people out there . . . it's not what they expected," he said. "They didn't know how to put it into any of their schemes for history; it just didn't make sense to them. . . ."

Nagging Questions

In 1987, Mair happened to be touring China when he entered a museum in Urumqi (ür üm´ chē) that displayed mummies of a man, woman and child—a family, as it appeared. They had died 3,000 years earlier, "yet the bodies looked as if they were buried yesterday," he said.

What left him "thunderstruck," though, was their faces: They were Caucasians, apparently of European origin. "The questions kept nagging at me: Who were these people? How did they get out here at such an early date?"

9 The April 1994 issue of *Discover* includes a gallery of color photos of the corpses. They include a man with a painted image of the sun—a religious symbol?—on the temple of his head; the baby in swaddling clothes, its eyes covered with stones—a burial ritual?; a woman in a tall, peaked hat, . . . and a woman wearing a fur-lined coat, leather mittens and a two-pointed hat that, according to Chinese archaeologists, indicates she might have had *two husbands*—a possible result of a shortage of females. They were buried in simple graves, roughly 6 feet deep, with mats at the bottom. Some graves contain artifacts

3. **anthropological geneticist** one who studies the historical development of human beings through the examination of their genes.

Reading Strategy
Finding the Main Idea
How does this question in the article help you to determine the main idea?

Literary Analysis
News Article and Objectivity Is objective writing evident in this paragraph? Why or why not?

10 **✓Reading Check**
Why does one scientist say it is difficult to analyze the DNA of the mummies?

8 Reading Strategy

Finding the Main Idea

- Have a volunteer read the first sentence on this page aloud. Point out that this sentence is a question, one that readers expect the news article to answer.
- Then read aloud the first sentence of the paragraph that begins "Why has it taken so long...." Ask students the Reading Strategy question on p. 135: How does this question help you to determine the main idea?
  Answer: This question is one that most readers would be likely to ask. It is a question that calls for some explanation.

9 Literary Analysis

News Article and Objectivity

- Ask the Literary Analysis question on p. 135: Is objective writing evident in this paragraph? Why or why not?
  Answer: Students may agree that the paragraph is objective. It states facts and, although it suggests interpretations, it phrases them as questions, indicating that these interpretations are just possibilities.

10 ✓Reading Check

Answer: Old DNA is often so damaged that results may not be conclusive.

ASSESS

Answers for p. 136

Review and Assess

1. Possible questions: Why did these ancient people travel to China? Why did they all die out?
2. **(a)** They provide the first evidence that Caucasians traveled to China 4000 years ago and that therefore some Chinese may have remote Caucasian ancestors. **(b)** They did not know what to make of the discovery and its suggestion of foreign influence on China's development. They were also concerned about Westerners stealing the mummies and taking credit for their discovery.
3. **(a)** They were from northern Europe. **(b)** Historians now believe that Chinese culture was influenced by these Europeans.
4. **(a)** 1978 **(b)** Chinese scholars and scientists could not reconcile the discovery with their views of history, and they did not trust Westerners with the knowledge.
5. **(a)** DNA tests **(b)** The tests will determine the mummies' place of origin.
6. **(a)** Students will probably say yes, because the information is repeated within the article. **(b)** Possible response: Students may cite the fact that one archaeological discovery can force a revision of history, or that it's possible to do DNA testing on bodies that are thousands of years old.
7. Possible responses: Real-life mysteries are more interesting because they deal with facts. Fictional mysteries are more interesting because there is no limit to what can happen in someone's imagination.

hinting that the living mourned the dead: For example, a baby was buried with a sort of milk bottle fashioned from a sheep's udder.

"This is my favorite story in the seven years that I've edited *Discover* . . . because we were able to publish something monumental before anyone else," said the magazine's editor, Paul Hoffman.

Traditionally, Chinese historians insist that their society evolved on its own with little foreign input. That view has played well in modern China, which resents its past subjugation to foreign imperialists.

But Mair says the traditional view is hard to reconcile with the discovery of so many Caucasians who lived in what is now the westernmost edge of China, thousands of years before Marco Polo.[4] "The archaeological, linguistic, and textual evidence forces me to conclude that China has both significantly influenced and been influenced by other civilizations throughout history and, indeed, prehistory," Mair said. . . .

subjugation (sub´ jə gā´ shən) *n.* enslavement

reconcile (rek´ ən sīl´) *v.* bring into agreement

4. **Marco Polo** (1254–1324) Italian traveler and trader considered to be the first European to cross the length of Asia.

Review and Assess

Thinking About the Selection

1. **Respond:** What else would you like to know about the Caucasian mummies and the way these ancient people lived?
2. **(a) Recall:** What is remarkable about the mummies' appearance? **(b) Analyze:** Why did Chinese officials react as they did to the discovery of the mummies?
3. **(a) Recall:** Where do experts think the people found in the Chinese desert originally lived? **(b) Infer:** How has the discovery of the mummies changed historians' views of early Chinese culture?
4. **(a) Recall:** In what year were the first mummies unearthed? **(b) Interpret:** Why was there a delay between this event and the involvement of Western scholars and scientists?
5. **(a) Recall:** What tests are scientists conducting on the mummies? **(b) Speculate:** How will the tests help unlock the mystery surrounding this discovery?
6. **(a) Evaluate:** Do you think the reporter clearly communicated why the discovery of the mummies was so important? Why or why not? **(b) Assess:** What did you find most interesting about this article? Why?
7. **Extend:** Explain whether you think that real-life mysteries, like this one, are more or less interesting than those made up by storytellers.

Keay Davidson

(b. 1953)

Keay Davidson loves to write about science and technology. As a science reporter and author of books and magazine articles, he tracks the latest information on everything from NASA to tornadoes.

Davidson began as a newspaper reporter in Georgia while still in college. He moved to Florida in 1976 and later began to write about the space program. In 1981, he became a science reporter for the *Los Angeles Times* and, later, the *San Francisco Examiner*.

As a writer, Davidson coauthored *Wrinkles in Time*, a book about new scientific theories on the origins of the universe. In 1996, when the movie *Twister* swept through theaters, Davidson explained the science behind the special effects in his book *Twister: The Science of Tornadoes*.

ASSESSMENT PRACTICE: Reading Comprehension

Greek Suffix *-ist* (For more practice, see Test Preparation Workbook, p. 7.)

Some tests require students to use knowledge of suffixes to determine the meaning of unfamiliar terms in a passage. Use the following sample to teach students to use the Greek suffix *-ist* to understand the meaning of specialized terms.

> . . . anthropological geneticist Paolo Francalacci . . . hopes to determine the mummies' likely place of origin by comparing their DNA, or genetic material, with modern DNA from different societies.

In this passage, the term *geneticist* means ______.

A someone with anthropological genes
B someone who practices genetics
C someone living in a genetic area
D someone who studies anthropology

Explain that the Greek suffix *-ist* identifies someone who does or practices something. This knowledge shows students that the correct answer is *B*.

Review and Assess

Literary Analysis

News Article

1. (a) Which details of the **news article's** lead are written to grab a reader's attention? (b) Does it make you want to read on? Why or why not?
2. (a) How do the quotations from an expert on China help you understand the news that is being reported? (b) Identify at least two quotations and explain how they extend your understanding.
3. How might this story have been different if it had been written as an encyclopedia article?

Connecting Literary Elements

4. To maintain a position of **objectivity,** the writer links positions he presents to specific authorities. Identify three opinions in the article. For each, indicate the source, or who gave the opinion.
5. How objective is Davidson's article? Support your answer.
6. How might your reaction to the article have been different if Davidson had been less objective—for example, more enthusiastic or more critical?

Reading Strategy

Finding the Main Idea

7. (a) Review the article and answer the questions in the chart shown. (b) Based on your answers to the questions, what do you think is the **main idea** of the article?

What is being tested?		**When** were the mummies found?	
Who is performing the testing?		**Why** is the discovery of these mummies important?	
Where were the mummies found?		**How** does the discovery change historians' views on early Chinese culture?	

Extend Understanding

8. **Science Connection:** In what way does the work of archaeologists have an impact on the way we live today?

Quick Review

A **news article** is written to inform you about a topic by answering six questions: *Who? What? When? Where? Why?* and *How?*

Objectivity in a news article requires the presentation of facts only, free of the writer's opinions or judgments.

The **main idea** in a news article is its most important point.

Take It to the Net

www.phschool.com

Take the interactive self-test online to check your understanding of the selection.

ENRICHMENT: Further Reading

Other Works by Keay Davidson

Twister: The Science of Tornadoes
Wrinkles in Time

Take It to the Net

Visit www.phschool.com for more information on "Caucasian Mummies Mystify Chinese."

Answers for p. 137

Review and Assess

1. **(a)** References to mummies, unexpected hair and skin color, and the potential of toppling ideas about history grab a reader's attention. **(b)** Students may agree that these details create an interest in reading further.
2. **(a)** Quotations clarify the article's subject matter because the expert has actually seen the mummies and can speak about them with firsthand knowledge. **(b)** When Mair says "the bodies looked as if they were buried yesterday," we gain a clear understanding that the mummies have been well preserved. When he says that he was "thunderstruck," because he realized the mummies were Caucasian, we understand that this discovery is truly amazing.
3. It would have lacked questions and quotations. It would have been more academic and less like a nonfiction narrative.
4. Possible response: "I think it flummoxed them," Cavalli-Sforza. "Chinese officials are very sensitive," Mair. "Old DNA is generally very damaged," Cavalli-Sforza.
5. It is fairly objective. It presents facts and does not include the writer's opinions, except where he poses these in the form of questions or uses phrases such as "indicates that" or "hinting that." The writer seems fascinated by the subject, which erodes his objectivity somewhat.
6. If the article had been slanted, readers might not have found it believable.
7. **(a)** What: The mummies' DNA. Who: University of Sassari scientists. Where: Xinjiang Province, China. When: 1978 and 1979. Why: Until this discovery, no one knew that Europeans had lived in ancient China. How: Historians now believe that Chinese culture may have been influenced by Europeans. **(b)** The discovery of Caucasian mummies in China is causing a reconsideration of established notions of Chinese history.
8. Archaeologists help us understand how people lived in the past and where our cultural, linguistic, and religious roots are.

EXTEND

Answers for p. 138

❶ Vocabulary Development

Word Analysis

1. one who practices genetics
2. one who studies languages
3. one who studies nutrition

Spelling Strategy

1. historian
2. mummify
3. reliable
4. carried

Concept Development: Synonyms

1. b
2. a
3. c
4. a
5. a
6. b

❷ Grammar Lesson

1. C: curled-up
2. P: Chinese
3. C: deep-set
4. P: Chinese, Western
5. C: fur-lined

Writing Application

Sample answers:

Proper adjectives:

1. The Caucasian mummy had blond hair and light skin.
2. The Chinese government hesitated to tell the rest of the world what had been found.

Compound adjectives:

3. I asked for deep-fried falafel in pita bread.
4. He wore a white tie, a tailcoat, and a silk-lined top hat.

Integrate Language Skills

❶ Vocabulary Development Lesson

Word Analysis: Greek Suffix *-ist*

The Greek suffix *-ist* means "one who practices." For example, the suffix appears in the word *archaeologist*, which means "one who practices archaeology." Use your knowledge of *-ist* to define each of these words:

1. geneticist 2. linguist 3. nutritionist

Spelling Strategy

When you add an ending to a word that ends in *y* preceded by a consonant, change the *y* to *i* before adding the suffix. For example, when you add *-ous* to *mystery*, you form the word *mysterious*. For each item, write the new word formed.

1. history + *-an*
2. mummy + *-fy*
3. rely + *-able*
4. carry + *-ed*

Concept Development: Synonyms

For each item below, write the word that is the best synonym, or closest match, for the first word.

1. dogmas: (a) documents, (b) beliefs, (c) rumors
2. parched: (a) dried, (b) sophisticated, (c) curved
3. archaeologist: (a) leader, (b) caretaker, (c) scientist
4. imperialist: (a) dominating, (b) wise, (c) proud
5. subjugation: (a) enslavement, (b) freedom, (c) celebration
6. reconcile: (a) interpretation, (b) settle, (c) begin

❷ Grammar Lesson

Proper and Compound Adjectives

A **proper adjective** is a proper noun used as an adjective or an adjective formed from a proper noun. A **compound adjective** is an adjective that is made up of more than one word. Compound adjectives are usually hyphenated. In a few cases, they are written as combined words.

Proper Adjective: *February* weather (a proper noun used as an adjective)

Proper Adjective: *Chinese* government (a form of a proper noun, *China*, used as an adjective)

Compound Adjective: *fur-lined* coat; *underpaid* researchers

Practice Identify the proper and compound adjectives in each sentence below.

1. The mummy of a young woman in a curled-up position was found.
2. A Chinese archaeologist found the first of the mummies.
3. The mummies had deep-set eyes.
4. The Chinese government allowed Western researchers to see the findings.
5. Some of the photos of the corpses showed a woman in a fur-lined coat.

Writing Application Write four sentences, using at least two proper adjectives and at least two compound adjectives.

WG Prentice Hall Writing and Grammar Connection: Chapter 18, Section 1

TEACHING RESOURCES

The following resources can be used to enrich or extend the instructions for pp. 138–139.

Vocabulary

Selection Support: Build Vocabulary, p. 26

Grammar

Selection Support: Build Grammar Skills, p. 27

Writing and Grammar Gold Level, p. 380

Daily Language Practice Transparencies

Writing

Writing and Grammar Gold Level, p. 256 ■

Writing and Grammar iText CD-ROM

■ **BLOCK SCHEDULING:** Resources marked with this symbol provide varied instruction during 90-minute blocks.

❸ Writing Lesson

News Feature

Though usually based at least indirectly on a news event, news features, like Davidson's article, provide information of general interest, explore the human-interest angle of a news story, or describe a personality. Write your own news feature about a subject of interest—perhaps a hobby, sports hero, or fashion trend.

Prewriting Start by planning a lead that will grab the reader's attention. If none comes to mind, think of the questions you will answer in the feature. One of your answers may spark an idea.

Model: Grabbing the Reader's Attention

It stretches. It twists. It comes in all sizes and colors. And it never needs washing. What's the latest fad to hit high schools all across America? It's rubber-band jewelry.

This lead gets the reader's attention by offering several details about the subject before identifying it.

Drafting Once you have created an attention-grabbing lead, keep readers interested with details that answer *who, what, when, where, why,* and *how* about your subject. Remember to offer facts only, without your personal opinion.

Revising Read your news feature as though you know nothing about the topic. Circle words or ideas that need more elaboration, and then add any details that will clarify the writing.

WG *Prentice Hall Writing and Grammar Connection: Chapter 12, Section 2*

❹ Extension Activities

Listening and Speaking Imagine that you were the first archaeologist to uncover the Caucasian mummies of China. Now, you have been invited by colleagues to do a **visual presentation** of your findings at an archaeology conference. Using maps and photographs, explain to your colleagues

- how you came to discover the mummies.
- what happened as a result of your discovery.
- why your discovery is so important.

Answer as many *who, what, where, when, why,* and *how* questions as possible in your presentation.

Research and Technology In a group, create a **travel brochure** promoting a tour of archaeological sites in China where mummies have been uncovered. Make sure your brochure includes maps, illustrations, and detailed explanations of the important sites. Use library resources to find photographs and information about the sites included in your brochure. **[Group Activity]**

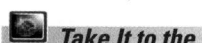

Take It to the Net www.phschool.com

Go online for an additional research activity using the Internet.

ASSESSMENT RESOURCES

The following resources can be used to assess students' knowledge and skills.

Selection Assessment

- **Formal Assessment,** pp. 19–21
- **Open Book Test,** pp. 19–21
- **Got It! Assessment Videotapes,** Tape 1
- **Test Bank Software**

Take It to the Net

Visit www.phschool.com for self-tests and additional questions on the selection.

Listening and Speaking Rubric

- **Performance Assess. and Portfolio Mgmt.,** p. 30

PRENTICE HALL ASSESSMENT SYSTEM

- **Workbook**
- **Transparencies**
- **Skill Book**
- **CD-ROM**

❸ Writing Lesson

- Have students look through newspapers and magazines to get an idea of what feature stories should include.
- Go over the instructions on the page with students. Have them clear their topics with you before they begin writing.
- Before they begin writing, students should make lists of questions they would like their article to answer. They can check this list against their first drafts to be sure that they have answered all the questions.

❹ Extension Activity

Listening and Speaking

- Remind students to base the details of their presentations on the facts in the article. Encourage interested students to do some further reading on the subject.
- Students may want to work with partners or in small groups.
- Use the rubric for Exposition Presentation with Visual Aids, p. 30 in **Performance Assessment and Portfolio Management.**

CUSTOMIZE INSTRUCTION for Universal Access

To address different learning styles, use the following activities suggested in the **Extension Activities** booklet, p. 7.

- For Visual/Spatial Learners, use Activity 5.
- For Verbal/Linguistic Learners, use Activities 6 and 7.

Lesson Objectives

1. To write an autobiographical narrative
2. To use writing strategies to generate ideas, plan, organize, evaluate, and revise the narrative

Model From Literature

In the excerpt from *Rosa Parks: My Story,* (p. 168), Rosa Parks tells a story from her life.

Prewriting

- Tell students that they should try to look at their blueprints from the perspective of someone who does not know them. Sometimes a writer may be so familiar with something that he or she does not think it would make an interesting topic. Remind students of the importance of narrowing their topics so that they can describe it effectively in their narratives.
- Explain to students that the events in their narratives do not necessarily have to be told in chronological order, but that it will help them to put these events on a timeline in order to organize their thoughts.
- Remind students of the purpose of this writing activity. An autobiographical narrative should offer their personal thoughts, feelings, and views on the events that are described. For each event listed on their timelines, encourage students to write down a sentence or two about how they personally felt about it.

Writing WORKSHOP

Narration: Autobiographical Narrative

In an **autobiographical narrative,** a writer relates an experience from his or her life. In this workshop, you will write an autobiographical narrative that tells a story from your life.

Assignment Criteria. Your autobiographical narrative should have the following characteristics:

- Yourself as the main character
- A sequence of events that suggests an insight you gained
- Action that accommodates shifts in time and mood
- Concrete details that describe sights, sounds, smells, and physical sensations
- Your personal feelings, thoughts, or views

To preview the criteria on which your autobiographical narrative may be assessed, see the Rubric on page 143.

Prewriting

Choose a topic. Write your autobiographical narrative about a topic of importance to you. Try **blueprinting** to identify an idea. First, sketch a blueprint of a place you remember well. Label each room or area. Then, jot down words or phrases you associate with these areas. Choose one of these ideas as the topic of your narrative.

Gather details. Record as many details as possible about the idea you have chosen. One idea may remind you of others. Review your notes and narrow your list to the details you will include in your narrative.

Structure the sequence. Create a detailed record of the order of events in your narrative by making a **timeline.** Write down the first event related to the subject of your narrative. Record subsequent events in the order in which they occurred.

Timeline

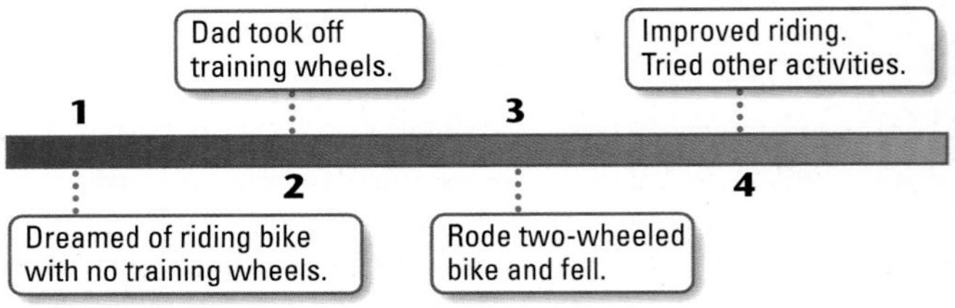

Add personal thoughts. Look at the list of events you will include in your narrative, and note what you were thinking when each event occurred. Consider adding these thoughts to your narrative to enrich the writing.

Example

Event: My mom suggested I play outside.
First Thought: I thought of riding my bike without training wheels.
Second Thought: I worried about whether I could ride a two-wheeled bike without falling.

TEACHING RESOURCES

The following resources can be used to enrich or extend the instruction for pp. 140–143.

Writing and Grammar, Gold Level, Chapter 4, pp. 48–73

Performance Assessment and Portfolio Management, pp. 8, 34

Writing Models and Graphic Organizers on Transparencies, pp. 21–28

Writing and Grammar iText CD-ROM
Students can use the following tools as they complete their autobiographical narratives:

- Timeline
- Sensory Word Bins
- Sentence Openers Variety

Student Model

Before you draft your autobiographical narrative, read this student model and review the characteristics of effective autobiographical narrative.

Albert Kim
Palos Verdes, CA

Leaving Fear Behind

It all happened one day when my mom suggested that I go outside and play, not just stay inside as I usually did. At five years old, I really enjoyed staying inside my cozy house. The only outdoor activity that I ever did up to that point was ride a rusty bicycle with training wheels on it, but I often thought of what it would be like to ride it without those wheels.

> Albert is the main character in this narrative.

One night I dreamed of riding a bike with no training wheels. The bike felt large and unsteady. I couldn't keep my balance, and I fell down. I woke up right when I hit the ground. Then I was more scared than ever.

Every day I thought about riding that bike. Then I said to myself that I needed to do whatever I could to get rid of the tension. I decided that I had to do it. I had to ride a bike without those old wheels so I could feel good again.

> Words that indicate time passing suggest a sequence of events.

Late one afternoon, my dad used all kinds of tools to take off those old, rusty training wheels. My bike was ready. I got on, trying to sit still, while my dad held the back of the seat. I was still shaking because I was scared. Pedaling as fast as I could, I didn't realize that my dad had already let go. I was riding! This was unbelievable! I felt the soft, cool breeze rushing across my face.

Suddenly, something went wrong. My joy quickly faded. I couldn't stop my bike! I was barreling toward the end of the street. There was a very sharp and narrow curve ahead. To my horror, I realized I hadn't yet learned how to make a sharp turn, not even with wheels on. When I was about two feet from the curve, I turned the front wheel as hard as I could and my feet got stuck in the pedals. WHAM! I crashed and scraped my leg. The next thing I knew, I was laughing. Even though I was hurt, I was very happy and glad that I had accomplished what I had wanted to do.

> The writer describes the action using physical sensations and shifts in mood.

Since then I have tried many new things: swimming, games, and other activities. I found out that I am really good at the things I have tried. Learning to ride without training wheels was the first time I ever took a chance on trying something new. Because I was successful, I was not afraid to try other things. I crossed a threshold in my life and left fear behind.

> The writer suggests an insight he gained as a result of the experience.

Student Model

- Explain that the Student Model is a sample, and that their essays may be longer.
- Have students identify any words in the third paragraph that signal a passing of time.
  Answer: Students may note that "every day" and "then" help to suggest a sequence of events.
- Point out that Albert uses details to describe how he thought and felt at the time, which allows readers to see the experience from his perspective.
- Remind students that an autobiographical narrative provides a personal insight gained from the particular experience described. Lead students to see how Albert's comments about taking chances and not being afraid of new experiences reveal the lesson that he learned and show how the experience changed the way he looked at life.
- For an additional model, display the Personal Narrative transparencies in **Writing Models and Graphic Organizers on Transparencies,** pp. 21–28.

Real-World Connection

Explain to students that autobiographical writing is not limited to nonfiction literary works. There are many times in their lives when students may be asked to discuss significant experiences from their lives and the insights they gained from these experiences. Many college applications, for example, require students to write an autobiographical essay detailing an important lesson they learned in their lives.

CUSTOMIZE INSTRUCTION FOR UNIVERSAL ACCESS

For Less Proficient Writers	For English Learners	For Advanced Writers
If students have difficulty choosing a topic, model the process of blueprinting to show students how they can generate a topic by exploring a place (or an event) that they remember well.	Many students can focus on their experiences as an English learner to generate a topic for their autobiographical narratives. Encourage students to explore any meaningful lessons they have learned about their lives from the experience of living in a new culture.	While students work to choose a topic, encourage them to identify a series of different experiences that taught them similar lessons. Students can then write about these different experiences and the lessons they learned from them.

Drafting

- Explain to students that their autobiographical essays should have a clearly defined main point. Students will have an easier time drafting their essays if they identify this main point and keep it in mind as they write.
- Have students review the information on their timelines. Suggest that they delete any details on their timelines that do not reinforce their main points. Remind students that their essays are not just a retelling of chronological events, but stories that highlight a central conflict and build to a climax.
- Review the elaboration tips in the chart on this page. Explain to students that elaborating their ideas will help readers understand their experiences from their own perspectives.

Revising

- Suggest that students use self-sticking notes to identify places in their drafts that require further elaboration. Students should look for places in which adding details will make their writing more vivid and engaging to readers.
- Review the model with students. Have a volunteer read the sentence to the class, first without the added detail and then with the detail. Ask students to discuss how this new detail adds to their appreciation of the experience being described.
- Students should try to achieve a balance of physical and emotional details as they revise their essays.

(continued on page 143)

Drafting

Identify your main point. As you draft your narrative, think about why the story you have chosen to tell might be meaningful to others. When you have determined what you want your audience to understand, organize your details to highlight the importance of that main point.

Organize events. The description of events adds substance to your autobiographical essay. Too much description, however, can distract a reader from your main point. Instead, choose details to accomplish these goals:

- Highlighting the central conflict that sets the events in motion.
- Creating tension that builds to a climax, or turning point.
- Offering insights related to your main point.

Basic Story Element	Elaboration Tip
Experience to narrate	Explain its main effect on you.
Time and place	Describe impressions using sensory details, including sights, smells, sounds, and tastes.
Suspense	Add details that raise the tension and heighten the story's problem.
Main events of story	Include thoughts or feelings that occurred to you at the time of the events.
Story outcome	Consider other possible outcomes of events.

Elaborate. As you draft your autobiographical narrative, remember that you can make your story even more vivid by providing detailed information. The chart shown here provides some tips to help you elaborate further on an idea.

Revising

Explode a moment. To help your readers experience the event as you did, add details that bring your thoughts and feelings to life. Read your draft and highlight moments in your narrative where you can expand your idea by telling more about what you were thinking, what it looked or felt like, or how others reacted. Then, jot down these details on a separate piece of paper and incorporate them into your revised draft.

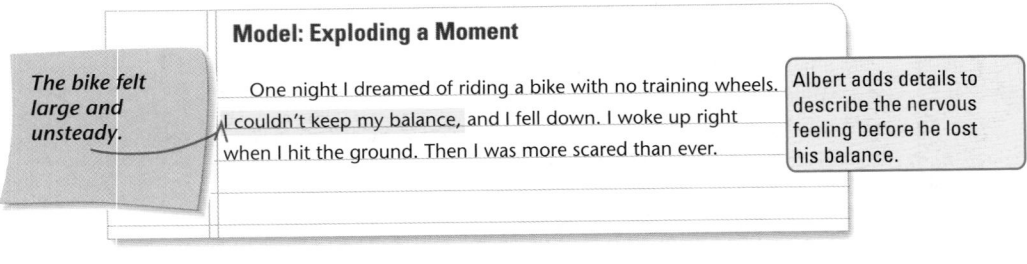

Model: Exploding a Moment

The bike felt large and unsteady.

One night I dreamed of riding a bike with no training wheels. I couldn't keep my balance, and I fell down. I woke up right when I hit the ground. Then I was more scared than ever.

Albert adds details to describe the nervous feeling before he lost his balance.

USING TECHNOLOGY IN WRITING

If students are using word processors to draft and revise their autobiographical essays, suggest that they use the comments feature when elaborating and revising their drafts. This feature allows students to insert comments in specific places in the text, which they can review later and choose to incorporate in their drafts or delete.

Students can also use the organizing tools and revision checkers on the **Writing and Grammar iText CD-ROM**.

Revise to vary your sentences. Even though your autobiographical narrative is about an event that happened to you, you should avoid beginning every sentence with *I*. Look closely at the sentences in your draft, and vary sentence beginnings to make your draft more interesting. Compare the model and the nonmodel. Why is the model more effective than the nonmodel?

Nonmodel	Model
I didn't realize that my dad had already let go. I was riding! I couldn't believe it! I felt the soft, cool breeze rushing across my face.	My dad had already let go without me realizing it. I was riding! This was unbelievable! I felt the soft, cool breeze rushing across my face.

Publishing and Presenting

Share your writing with a wider audience by presenting your story to your classmates.

Deliver an oral presentation. Practice reading your story aloud. Mark up a copy of your autobiographical narrative, underlining any dialogue, thoughts, or conversations that you believe your audience would enjoy. As you present to your classmates, emphasize those passages.

Post your essay. Create a bulletin board display of the essays written by you and your classmates. Have each writer supply a short comment about the event or idea that inspired the writing. Add photographs if they are available.

Speaking Connection

To learn more about presenting an autobiographical narrative, see the **Listening and Speaking Workshop**, p. 144.

WG *Prentice Hall Writing and Grammar Connection: Chapter 4*

Rubric for Self-Assessment

Evaluate your autobiographical narrative using the following criteria and rating scale:

Criteria	Rating Scale: Not very				Very
How central are you to the action of the story?	1	2	3	4	5
How clearly organized is the sequence of events?	1	2	3	4	5
How well does the action accommodate shifts in time and mood?	1	2	3	4	5
How powerfully are concrete and sensory details used to describe events?	1	2	3	4	5
How well do you convey your insights, thoughts, and feelings?	1	2	3	4	5

Revising (continued)

- Tell students that beginning every sentence with "I" will only make their essays sound monotonous. To keep readers' interest, students should vary sentence beginnings.
- Ask students to compare the model and nonmodel and respond to the question in their text: Why is the model more effective than the nonmodel?
  Possible response: The model avoids the monotony of beginning each sentence with "I."
- Make sure that students vary sentence beginnings in an appropriate manner. Explain that they should only vary the beginning when it makes sense to do so; students should not simply vary the beginnings for the sake of variety.

Publishing and Presenting

- Before they present their stories to the class, encourage students to practice reading them aloud. Have students make any notes that might help them orally present their stories.
- Suggest that students supplement their oral presentations with any photographs or objects that play an important role in their stories. Students may also want to enhance their presentations with music.

Assessment

- Review with students the assessment criteria.
- Have students use the rubric to score the Student Model for each of the criteria listed. Make sure students support their scores with details from the model.
- The rubric on this page, and another rubric in an alternative format, can be found on pp. 8 and 34 in **Performance Assessment and Portfolio Management.**

TEST-TAKING TIP

When students are taking a test that requires them to respond to a narrative writing prompt, they should allot a majority of their time to the drafting stage of the writing process. Tell students that the key to effective writing (and to making the most of the allotted time) is organizing their thoughts in the drafting stage. If students pay careful attention to the main points of their response and provide adequate support for these points, they will have an easier time revising their responses.

Lesson Objectives

1. To deliver a narrative presentation in an effective manner
2. To choose a compelling story that engages the audience's interest
3. To modulate one's voice and use gestures and facial expressions to enhance the presentation of the narrative

Prepare the Presentation

- In addition to choosing a story that lends itself to an oral retelling, students should also keep in mind the length of the work. You may want to establish an agreed-upon time limit so that students do not select long works. In these cases, suggest that students present an excerpt from the work.
- As students rehearse their presentations, encourage them to keep notes to help them improve their delivery. Students should first practice to familiarize themselves with the text. Then, students can focus on their delivery.

Deliver the Presentation

- Ask students why it's important for a speaker to vary his or her voice when delivering a narrative presentation. Lead students to see that the speaker must translate the drama of the story through voice inflections and modulations.
- Point out to students that an appropriate pace will assist their audience in paying attention to the presentation. Students should remember to not speak too quickly or too slowly.
- Encourage students to practice delivering their portions of their presentations with a variety of inflections and gestures. Students can then determine which inflections and gestures best suit the text.

Listening and Speaking WORKSHOP

Delivering a Narrative Presentation

Narrative presentations use storytelling to describe a sequence of events with meaning for an audience. You give a narrative presentation every time you tell friends what happened in a movie or sports event. Certain qualities make a narrative presentation effective—a clear story line, a description of place and time, a sense of mood, and an indication of importance to the audience or speaker.

Prepare the Presentation

Choose a compelling story. The best stories are so interesting they actually compel the audience to pay attention. For your presentation, choose a true or fictional story that lends itself easily to retelling and will have an impact on your audience.

Practice telling the story. Practice delivering your narrative to family members or friends first. After you learn which parts people like best, you can emphasize those. Your story will get better with every retelling.

Deliver the Presentation

The same aspects that you enjoy when watching an exciting performance are the ones that will make your presentation enjoyable for an audience. Incorporate these strategies into your presentation:

Use variation to hook your audience. Make your narrative more interesting by varying your voice and body language.

- Let your voice rise and fall according to the effect you want to create. Add dramatic pauses to create suspense.
- Quicken your pace to show excitement or slow it down to indicate the passage of time.
- Use gestures and facial expressions to enhance story events.

Indicate significance. When you tell a personal narrative, communicate how the event had an impact on your life. If you are giving a narrative about a larger event, such as the Civil War, explain its influence on other events of the time.

Control nervous energy. As you speak before a group, you may fidget or sway. Work to stand still, making only movements that enhance your words.

Narrative Presentation Self-Evaluation

- Do you think your audience understood the point of your presentation? If not, how could you have communicated this better?
- Which aspects of your story did others like best? Do you agree? Why?
- Which parts of your narrative were hard to describe?
- What changes would you make to improve your presentation?

***Activity:* Analyzing a Speech** Rehearse and deliver a short narrative presentation in front of a group. Use the feedback you get from others and the self-evaluation form above to help you critique your presentation.

CUSTOMIZE INSTRUCTION FOR UNIVERSAL ACCESS

For English Learners	For Less Proficient Readers
Students may be fearful of delivering an oral presentation of a narrative. Have students carefully review their selected narratives, making sure that they comprehend the story as well as know how to pronounce any unfamiliar words. Encourage students to make notes as necessary to help them get through any tricky passages.	Have students carefully rehearse their narratives, making note of any difficult or confusing passages. Work with students to break down these passages in order to improve comprehension. Suggest that students make notes in the margin of their narratives to help them when delivering their presentations.

Assessment WORKSHOP

Context Clues

The reading sections of some tests require you to read a passage and answer multiple-choice questions about word meanings. Frequently, you can determine the meanings of unfamiliar words by using context clues. The following strategies can help you answer test questions on word meanings:

- Skim the *context* of an unfamiliar word—words or phrases surrounding the word that might provide clues to its meaning.
- Search for explanations or descriptions that include details or examples.
- Consider the ideas presented in the sentences before and after an unfamiliar word or phrase. Determine a meaning consistent with the entire passage.

Test-Taking Strategies

- Use the context of an unfamiliar word to list potential substitute words.
- Reread the paragraph using the substitute words to see whether it makes sense.

Sample Test Item

Directions: Read the passage, and then answer the question that follows.

Fred was furious that Jonathan hadn't put any gas in his car after borrowing it for the day. Even though they had not discussed it, Fred was sure they had a tacit understanding that Jonathan would return the car with a full tank.

1. The word tacit in this passage means ___?___

   A written
   B spoken
   C legal
   D unspoken

Answer and Explanation

D is the correct answer. There is no context that supports ***A, B,*** or ***C.*** The phrase "Even though they had not discussed it" provides a clue that *tacit* means "unspoken."

Practice

Directions: Read the passage, and then answer the questions that follow.

After the entry-level position had gone unfilled for two months, Ms. Harding reviewed Carl Borden's application. He had seemed somewhat reticent at the start of his interview, but perhaps his silent manner was due to nervousness. After a few rounds of light banter, he was talking comfortably about his qualifications.

1. In this passage, the word reticent means ___?___

   A untruthful
   B relaxed
   C reserved
   D argumentative

2. The word banter means ___?___

   A analysis
   B debate
   C persuasion
   D small talk

Lesson Objective

To use context clues to determine the meanings of unfamiliar words

Applying Reading Strategies

Tell students that they can use context clues to help them figure out the meaning of any unfamiliar word they come across when they read. Remind students that *context* refers to the words, phrases, and sentences around the unfamiliar word.

Applying Test-Taking Strategies

- Have students read the Sample Test Item. Ask them to identify the word in the passage that they are being asked to define.
- Ask students to suggest the context clues they can use to determine the meaning of *tacit.* Possible response: "Even though they had not discussed it" is a context clue. If Fred thinks that he and Jonathan had an understanding that wasn't discussed, then *tacit* must mean "unspoken."

Answers

1. The correct answer is *C*. The phrase "his silent manner" provides a context clue to determine the meaning of *reticent. Reserved* is the only word that is similar in meaning to "silent manner." Answers *A* and *D* have no relation to the context clue. Answer *B,* while similar in meaning, is incorrect because the passage states that Carl may have been nervous.
2. The correct answer is *D*. The words "light" and "talking comfortably" are clues to the meaning of *banter.* Neither *A* nor *B* is associated with comfortable talk, and *C* does not fit the context of an interview.

ASSESSMENT RESOURCES

The following resources can be used to enrich or extend the instruction for p. 145.

PRENTICE HALL ASSESSMENT SYSTEM

- **Workbook**
- **Skill Book**
- **Transparencies**
- **CD-ROM**

Unit Objectives

1. To read selections in different genres that develop the theme "Challenges and Choices"
2. To apply a variety of reading strategies, particularly interactive reading strategies, appropriate for reading these selections
3. To analyze literary elements
4. To use a variety of strategies to build vocabulary
5. To learn elements of grammar, usage, and style
6. To use recursive writing processes to write in a variety of forms
7. To develop listening and speaking skills
8. To express and support responses to various types of texts
9. To prepare, organize, and present literary interpretations

Meeting the Objectives

With each selection, you will find instructional materials through which students can meet these objectives. Further, you will find additional practice pages for reading strategies, literary analysis, vocabulary, and grammar in the **Selection Support: Skills Development Workbook** in your **Teaching Resources.**

Background

Art

Human Achievement, by Tsing-Fang Chen

This artwork celebrates human achievements in science, exploration, film, literature, music, art, philosophy, and athletics. One focal point is the realistically rendered face of Albert Einstein under his famous formula, $E = mc^2$. Ask students the following question:

What achievements and achievers does this artist celebrate?
Answers: Possibilities include Shakespeare, Einstein, the moon landings, and others.

UNIT 2 Challenges and Choices

Human Achievement, Tsing-Fang Chen, Lucia Gallery, NYC

UNIT FEATURES

Connections	Reading Informational Material
Every unit contains a feature that connects literature to a related topic, such as art, science, or history. In this unit, the Literature and Music feature on p. 167 discusses a song by the Irish rock band U2 that honors Martin Luther King, Jr., and the continued impact of his message. Use the information and questions on the Connections pages to enrich students' understanding of the selections presented within the unit.	These selections will help students learn to analyze and evaluate informational texts, such as workplace documents, technical directions, and consumer materials. They will expose students to the organization and features unique to nonnarrative texts. In this unit, students learn the structure and elements of an effective business document.

▲ **Critical Viewing** What different types of human achievement are represented in this painting? **[Analyze]**

Exploring the Theme

An athlete challenges herself to be the best she can be. A powerful leader makes difficult decisions that can affect an entire nation. No matter who you are, life involves facing challenges and making choices. In these stories, poems, and essays, you will see how people in many different situations confront challenges and choices in their daily lives.

Rosa Parks did not know that her refusal to give up her seat on a Birmingham bus would spark a crucial struggle in the civil rights movement. In "My Story," Parks shows us that people approach challenges in different ways and make decisions for all kinds of reasons. Some decisions are made quietly, by ordinary people with little fanfare. But they can take as much courage, and have as much impact, as the decisions of a president.

Assessing Student Progress

Listed below are the tools that are available to measure the degree to which students meet the unit objectives.

Informal Assessment

The questions in the Review and Assess sections are a first-level response to the concepts and skills presented with the selections. Students' responses provide a brief, informal measure of their grasp of the material. These responses can indicate where further instruction and practice are needed. Follow up with the practice pages in **Selection Support: Skills Development Workbook.**

Formal Assessment

The **Formal Assessment** booklet contains the Selection Tests and Unit Tests.

- Selection Tests measure comprehension and skills acquisition for each selection or group of selections.
- Each Unit Test provides students with thirty multiple-choice questions and five essay questions designed to assess students' knowledge of the literature and skills taught in the unit.

The **Open Book Tests** ask students to demonstrate their ability to synthesize and communicate information from selections or groups of selections.

To assess student writing, you will find rubrics and scoring models in the **Performance Assessment and Portfolio Management** booklet. In this booklet, you will also find scoring rubrics for listening and speaking activities.

Alternative Assessment

The **Extension Activities** booklet contains writing activities, listening and speaking activities, and research and technology activities that are appropriate for students with different ability levels. You may also use these activities as an alternative measure of students' growth.

▶Critical Viewing

Answer: This painting features human achievement in the areas of science, exploration, film, literature, music, art, philosophy, and athletics.

ASSESSMENT RESOURCES

- **Selection Support: Skills Development Workbook**
- **Formal Assessment**
- **Open Book Tests**
- **Performance Assessment and Portfolio Management**
- **Extension Activities**

Why Read Literature?

The "Why Read Literature?" page in each unit presents a list of possible purposes for reading. Each purpose for reading is connected to one or more of the selections in the unit. Good readers set a purpose before reading to help them read actively and focus on meaningful details.

Unit 2 introduces three purposes for reading. "Read for the Love of Literature," encourages students to enjoy a poem about basketball. "Read to Be Inspired" provides background for one of the most inspiring speeches in history. "Read for Information" points out that myths are an important source of historical information.

How to Use This Page

- Tell students that before reading each selection in this unit, they should set a purpose for reading. This will help them read in a more active and focused manner.
- Explain that students can increase their love of literature by picturing the action described in Yusef Komunyakaa's poem "Slam, Dunk, and Hook," or by watching another contest unfold in ancient China in Ray Bradbury's story "The Golden Kite, the Silver Wind."
- Students may be more inspired when reading Dr. King's "I Have a Dream" speech knowing that a good part of the speech was not scripted but came from spontaneous, heartfelt emotion.
- Reading to obtain information is another valuable purpose for reading. As students read Edith Hamilton's myth "Perseus," have them watch for factual details about the values, views, and beliefs of the ancient Greeks.

Why Read Literature?

Whenever you read, you have a purpose, or reason. Perhaps you choose a literary work because you know little about its subject. Or maybe you pick up a selection because the subject is familiar and you enjoy reading about it. Preview some purposes you might set before reading the works in this unit.

Night Games, Ernie Barnes, The Company of Art, Los Angeles

1 Read for the Love of Literature

Interestingly, certain stories seem enhanced by their predictability. The fun is in watching the details unfold and finding out whether you guessed right in the end. Predict the winner of a showdown in ancient China in Ray Bradbury's **"The Golden Kite, the Silver Wind,"** page 178.

Most of us would come up short if asked to describe the complex give and take, graceful arcs, and physical battering of a good pickup game of basketball. If it takes a poem to capture the twists and turns, fakes, and sudden soaring movements of a beautiful game, you could do no better than Yusef Komunyakaa's **"Slam, Dunk, and Hook,"** page 228.

2 Read for Information

Even if a story is completely mythical, it can still be a rich source of information. Greek myths tell us much about the values, views, and beliefs of the ancient Greeks. Find out why a little help from the gods was not considered dishonest for a hero with fate on his side in Edith Hamilton's **"Perseus,"** page 214.

3 Read to Be Inspired

In his autobiography, Martin Luther King, Jr., reveals that he stopped looking at his notes halfway through his speech at the March on Washington. Knowing that he spoke from spontaneous heartfelt emotion could explain the power of a speech considered one of the most eloquent in human history. Join the millions who drew inspiration from King's words as you read **"I Have a Dream,"** page 164.

Take It to the Net

Visit the Web site for online instruction and activities related to each selection in this unit.
www.phschool.com

ENRICHMENT: Further Reading

Have students choose one or more of the works below to extend the unit theme "Challenges and Choices" or to read more by the unit authors.

I Know Why the Caged Bird Sings by Maya Angelou
In this autobiography, Maya Angelou shares the story of how a special person helps her develop self-esteem.

Magic City by Yusef Komunyakaa
A collection of poems focuses on a boy's coming of age in the rural American South and can be found in the **Prentice Hall Literature Library.**

Odyssey by Homer
This ancient Greek epic recounts the challenges faced by Odysseus on his journey from the war in Troy to his home on the Greek Island of Ithaca.

How to Read Literature

Use Interactive Reading Strategies

When you read, you are not just viewing words on a page. You are also thinking about the ideas, images, and information presented in the text. With difficult or unfamiliar topics, you might find it harder to interact with the text. Use these strategies to help you get involved.

1. Establish a purpose for reading.

- Determine the reason you wish to read a work of literature. For example, you might read for entertainment or to learn information.
- Read the selection and note the facts and details that help you achieve your original purpose.
- Use a K-W-L chart, like the one at right, to help define your purpose and evaluate the selection.

Carl Sandburg's "A Lincoln Preface"

What I **K**now	What I **W**ant to know	What I **L**earned
Lincoln was a famous U.S. President of the nineteenth century.	What did Lincoln accomplish during his presidency?	

2. Respond.

Readers bring their own set of expectations, beliefs, and experiences to the literature they read. To tap your own responses:

- Compare events in the selection with your own experiences.
- Use the author's text as a way to examine your own feelings about the subject.
- Consider the lessons of the piece and how you might use them in your own life.

3. Predict.

- Pause as you complete sections of a story to think about what might happen next.
- Base your predictions on what has already happened in the story, personal experience, or prior knowledge of the subject.

4. Generate questions.

To make sure you remain fully involved with a selection, generate questions to answer as you read.

- Use the common question words *who, what, where, when, why,* and *how* to review what you have read.
- Think about any unanswered questions you might still have as you read future passages.
- If you still have unanswered questions after finishing, discuss the work with others or do research to complete your understanding.

As you read the selections in this unit, apply these reading strategies to interact with the text.

How to Read Literature

The "How to Read Literature" page in each unit presents a set of strategies to help readers understand authors' words and ideas. Each reading strategy is taught in conjunction with one or more of the selections within the unit. Good readers develop a bank of strategies from which they can draw as needed.

Unit 2 introduces four strategies for interactive reading. It is important for students to interact with what they read in order to fully comprehend it. The strategies on this page help readers go beyond a simple scan of a text.

How to Use This Page

Introduce the strategies for interactive reading, presenting each as a tool for developing understanding when reading the selections in this unit.

- When they read the excerpt from "A Lincoln Preface" (p. 152), students will set a purpose for reading.
- As they read the excerpt from *Rosa Parks: My Story* (p. 168), students will respond to Parks's descriptions of how she felt.
- As they read "The Golden Kite, the Silver Wind" (p. 178), students will predict the daughter's actions and their consequences.
- Before they read "The Road Not Taken" (p. 188), students will generate questions about the poem and then look for answers to the questions as they read.

MODEL A READING STRATEGY: Establish a Purpose for Reading

Explain to students that setting a purpose for reading can help them focus better on the main points and details of the selection.

Show students how to establish a purpose for reading by listing types of information that they think they might learn as they read the excerpt from "A Lincoln Preface."

Students may learn information about Lincoln and his life, presidential politics, or key issues of the period.

You may want to point out to students that another purpose for reading can be to find out more about the author's opinions about Lincoln.

from A Lincoln Preface

Lesson Objectives and CA Correlations

1. **To analyze and respond to literary elements**
   - Literary Analysis: Anecdote **R 3.9**
   - Connecting Literary Elements: Narration
2. **To read, comprehend, analyze, and critique nonfiction**
   - Reading Strategy: Establishing a Purpose for Reading
   - Reading Check questions
   - Review and Assess questions
   - Assessment Practice (ATE)
3. **To develop word analysis skills, fluency, and systematic vocabulary**
   - Vocabulary Development Lesson: Anglo-Saxon Suffix *–ic* **R 1.1**
4. **To understand and apply written and oral language conventions**
   - Spelling Strategy
   - Grammar Lesson: Transitive and Intransitive Verbs **LC 1.3**
5. **To understand and apply appropriate writing and research strategies**
   - Writing Lesson: Character Profile **W 2.1**
   - Extension Activity: Timeline **W 1.8**
6. **To understand and apply listening and speaking strategies**
   - Extension Activity: Panel Discussion **LS 1.1**

STEP-BY-STEP TEACHING GUIDE	PACING GUIDE
PRETEACH	
Motivate Students and Provide Background	
Use the Motivation activity (ATE p. 150)	5 min.
Read and discuss the Preview material and Background information (SE/ATE p. 150) [A]	10 min.
Introduce the Concepts	
Introduce the Literary Analysis and Reading Strategy (SE/ATE p. 151) [A]	15 min.
Pronounce the vocabulary words and read their definitions (SE p. 151)	5 min.
TEACH	
Monitor Comprehension	
Informally monitor comprehension by circulating while students read independently or in groups [A]	20 min.
Monitor students' comprehension with the Reading Check notes (SE/ATE pp. 153,155,157)	as students read
Develop vocabulary with Vocabulary notes (SE pp.153, 155–158; ATE p. 154)	as students read
Develop Understanding	
Develop students' understanding of anecdotes with the Literary Analysis annotations (SE pp. 153, 157; ATE pp. 153, 157) [A]	10 min.
Develop students' ability to establish a purpose for reading with the Reading Strategy annotation (SE p. 155; ATE p. 155)	10 min.
ASSESS	
Assess Mastery	
Assess students' mastery of the Reading Strategy and Literary Analysis by having them answer the Review and Assess questions (SE/ATE p. 159)	20 min.
Use one or more of the print and media Assessment Resources (ATE p. 161) [A]	up to 50 min.
EXTEND	
Apply Understanding	
Have students complete the Vocabulary Development Lesson and the Grammar Lesson (SE p. 160) [A]	20 min.
Apply students' ability to gather details using the Writing Lesson (SE/ ATE, p. 161) [A]	45 min.
Apply students' understanding of the selection using one or more of the Extension Activities (SE p. 161)	20–90 min.

[A] ACCELERATED INSTRUCTION: Use the strategies and activities identified with an [A].

UNIVERSAL ACCESS
● = Below Level Students
▲ = On-Level Students
■ = Above Level Students

Time and Resource Manager

Reading Level: Challenging
Average Number of Instructional Days: 4

RESOURCES		
PRINT	**TRANSPARENCIES**	**TECHNOLOGY**
• **Beyond Literature,** Workplace Skills: Leadership, p. 8 ▲ ■		• **Interest Grabber Video,** Tape 1 ● ▲ ■
• **Selection Support Workbook:** ● ▲ ■ Literary Analysis, p. 32 Reading Strategy, p. 31 Build Vocabulary, p. 29	• **Literary Analysis and Reading Transparencies,** pp. 15 and 16 ● ▲ ■	
• **Adapted Reader's Companion** ● • **Reader's Companion** ●		• **Listening to Literature** ● ▲ ■ Audiocassettes, Side 6 Audio CDs, CD 6
• **English Learner's Companion** ● ▲ • **Literatura en español** ● ▲ • **Literary Analysis for Enrichment** ■		
• **Formal Assessment:** Selection Test, pp. 26–28 ● ▲ ■ • **Open Book Test,** pp. 22–24 ● ▲ ■ • **Performance Assessment and Portfolio Management,** pp. 18, 29 ● ▲ ■ • PRENTICE HALL ASSESSMENT SYSTEM ● ▲ ■	• PRENTICE HALL ASSESSMENT SYSTEM ● ▲ ■ Skills Practice Answers and Explanations on Transparencies	• **Test Bank Software** ● ▲ ■ • **Got It! Assessment Videotapes,** Tape 1 ● ▲
• **Selection Support Workbook:** ● ▲ ■ Build Grammar Skills, p. 31 • **Writing and Grammar,** Gold Level ● ▲ ■ • **Extension Activities,** p. 8 ● ▲ ■	• **Daily Language Practice Transparencies** ● ▲ • **Writing Models and Graphic Organizers on Transparencies,** pp. 9–15 ● ▲ ■	• **Writing and Grammar iText CD-ROM** ● ▲ ■ *Take It to the Net* www.phschool.com

BLOCK SCHEDULING: Use one 90-minute class period to preteach the selection and have students read it. Use a second 90-minute class period to assess students' mastery of skills and have them complete one of the Extension Activities.

PRETEACH

Step-by-Step Teaching Guide for pp. 150–151

Motivation

During his lifetime, Abraham Lincoln was recognized as a remarkable man. In the years since his assassination, he has been mythologized. Present movie or video clips of some of the many films about Lincoln to your class to give students a feel for how he has been portrayed. After students have read the selection, have them compare Sandburg's view of Lincoln to the views of the filmmakers.

Interest Grabber Video

As an alternative, play "Lincoln's Remarkable Life" on Tape 1 to engage student interest.

1 Background

Slavery had caused contention since the birth of the United States in 1776. Thomas Jefferson's original Declaration of Independence suggested that slavery was wrong, but southern delegates were unwilling to give up the way of life that slavery made possible, and the final Declaration did not refer to slavery. Many Americans were aware of the contradiction of fighting a war for independence and yet denying a substantial percentage of the population that independence. Each time a new state entered the Union, Congress debated fiercely over whether it would be a slaveholding or free state. In 1860, when Lincoln was elected, the southern slaveholding states knew that if they did not fight to keep new states open to slavery, they would soon be outnumbered in Congress and would be forced to submit to the North. President-elect Lincoln refused to support any congressional proposal that would allow for new slave states. This refusal on both sides to compromise led to the outbreak of war in April 1861.

Prepare to Read

from A Lincoln Preface

Lincoln Proclaiming Thanksgiving, Dean Cornwell, The Lincoln Museum, Fort Wayne, Indiana, a part of Lincoln National Corp.

Take It to the Net

Visit www.phschool.com for interactive activities and instruction related to "A Lincoln Preface," including

- background
- graphic organizers
- literary elements
- reading strategies

Preview

Connecting to the Literature

Whether we admire them for their achievements, abilities, or fine qualities, we are often inspired to pay tribute to our heroes in some way. Imagine being inspired to write a six-volume biography, as Carl Sandburg did for his hero, Abraham Lincoln.

1 Background

Abraham Lincoln is remembered as one of our greatest presidents, yet at the time of his election in 1860, less than half the country supported him. One reason is that Lincoln was opposed to slavery—and many landowners in the south still kept slaves. After seven southern states left the Union, the Civil War broke out in April 1861. By June 1861, a total of eleven states had left the Union and joined the Confederacy.

TEACHING RESOURCES

The following resources can be used to enrich or extend the instruction for pp. 150–151.

Motivation

Interest Grabber Video, Tape 1

Background

Beyond Literature, p. 8

Take It to the Net

Visit www.phschool.com for background and hotlinks for "A Lincoln Preface."

Literary Analysis

Literary Analysis and Reading Transparencies, Anecdote, p. 16

Reading

Selection Support: Reading Strategy, pp. 32–33; Build Vocabulary, p. 30

Literary Analysis and Reading Transparencies, Establishing a Purpose for Reading, p. 15

BLOCK SCHEDULING: Resources marked with this symbol provide varied instruction during 90-minute blocks.

❷ Literary Analysis

Anecdote

An **anecdote** is a brief story about an interesting, amusing, or strange event told to illustrate a point. Carl Sandburg helps readers see Lincoln's attitude and sense of humor through anecdotes like this one:

> As [Lincoln] shook hands with the correspondent of the London *Times*, he drawled, "Well, I guess the London *Times* is about the greatest power on earth—unless perhaps it is the Mississippi River."

As you read the anecdotes in "A Lincoln Preface," jot down in a word or two what each one tells about Lincoln.

Connecting Literary Elements

Anecdotes are a type of **narration**—writing that tells a story. Sometimes, anecdotes are woven into a longer story. In this selection, for example, Sandburg weaves together anecdotes to tell the larger story of Lincoln's role in the Civil War.

❸ Reading Strategy

Establishing a Purpose for Reading

Before you begin to read a selection, **establish a purpose**—decide *why* you are reading it. Sometimes, you read purely for enjoyment, but often you read to learn something new. For example, if you already know some information about Lincoln, you may be reading to learn more. Before reading the excerpt from "A Lincoln Preface," decide what else you would like to learn about Lincoln and start a K-W-L chart like the one shown here. Follow these steps:

- Use the title and introductory paragraphs to determine the topic of a selection, and write down what you know about that topic.
- Jot down what you hope to learn from the selection, and focus on these points as you read.

Continue to complete your chart as you read.

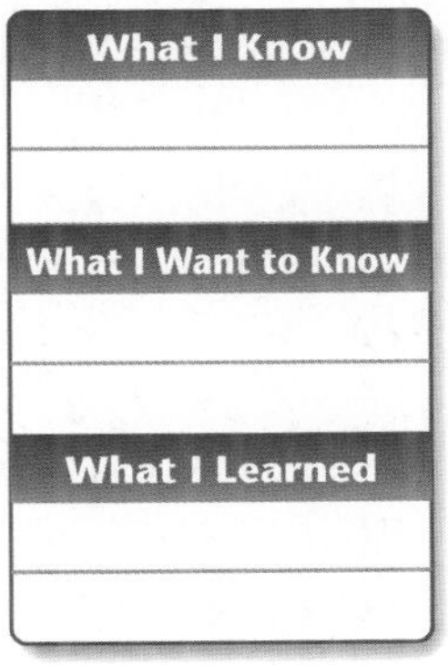

Vocabulary Development

despotic (des pät′ ik) *adj.* like an absolute ruler or tyrant (p. 153)

chattel (chat′ əl) *n.* a movable item of personal property (p. 153)

cipher (sī′ fər) *adj.* code (p. 155)

slouching (slouch′ iŋ) *adj.* drooping (p. 155)

censure (sen′ shər) *n.* strong disapproval (p. 156)

gaunt (gônt) *adj.* thin and bony (p. 157)

droll (drōl) *adj.* comic and amusing in an odd way (p. 158)

❷ Literary Analysis

Anecdote

- Tell students a brief anecdote of your own—perhaps something amusing that happened on your way to school one morning. Explain that this short, humorous story is an example of an anecdote.
- Write the term *anecdote* on the chalkboard. Tell students that it comes from a Greek word meaning "not published." The term used to connote secret or private details of a public person's career. Although this connotation has faded, anecdotes still tend to reveal a person's private side. Anecdotes are a form of narration that deal with the little things in everyday life rather than with great affairs of state.
- Have students consider what a series of brief stories of everyday moments can reveal about a person. Challenge students to think of anecdotes that illustrate the personalities of people they know well.

❸ Reading Strategy

Establishing a Purpose for Reading

- Ask students what they are reading on their own—comics, magazines, books, the sports page, and so on. Ask them why they are reading these things. Make a list of purposes for reading on the chalkboard. Point out that no one reads anything without a purpose. To pass the time, to find out who won the game last night, to be scared by a good mystery—these are all valid purposes for reading.
- Encourage students to consider what they might learn from this selection. Point out that their purpose may change as they read the selection.

Vocabulary Development

- Pronounce each vocabulary word for students, and read the definitions as a class. Have students identify any words with which they are already familiar.

CUSTOMIZE INSTRUCTION FOR UNIVERSAL ACCESS

For Special Needs Students	For Less Proficient Readers	For English Learners
Have students read the adapted version from "A Lincoln Preface" in the **Adapted Reader's Companion.** This version provides basic-level instruction in an interactive format with questions and write-on lines. Completing the adapted version will prepare students to read the selection in the Student Edition.	Have students read the selection in the **Reader's Companion.** This version provides basic-level instruction in an interactive format with questions and write-on lines. After students finish the selection in **Reader's Companion,** have them complete the questions and activities in the Student Edition.	Have students read the adapted version of the selection in the **English Learner's Companion.** This version provides basic-level instruction in an interactive format with questions and write-on lines. Completing the adapted version will prepare students to read the selection in the Student Edition.

E-Teach

Visit E-Teach at www.phschool.com for teachers' essays on how to teach, with questions and answers.

TEACH

Step-by-Step Teaching Guide for pp. 152–158

CUSTOMIZE INSTRUCTION For Verbal/Linguistic Learners

Have students study Lincoln's diction as they read this excerpt, which is filled with quotations of his actual words. How would students describe Lincoln's style of speaking? What impression does his diction give them of his personality? Does he have different ways of speaking to different people? Have students analyze Lincoln's character by means of his words. Encourage interested students to do some further reading of Lincoln's speeches and letters.

1 About the Selection

In this selection from the preface to his monumental biography of Abraham Lincoln, Carl Sandburg strings together a series of anecdotes that show Lincoln's humor, determination, and political skills.

2 Background

Art

Lincoln Proclaiming Thanksgiving by Dean Cornwell

Lincoln created the national holiday of Thanksgiving by proclamation in 1863. He declared that Thanksgiving would always be celebrated on the last Thursday in November. In 1944, Congress ruled the day would be celebrated on the fourth Thursday of November.

American illustrator Dean Cornwell (1892–1960) was born in Lincoln's native state, Kentucky. In this oil painting, Cornwell not only presents a thoughtful man at work, but also hints at the magnitude and complexity of the President's job. Use this question for dicussion:

What might Lincoln be thinking about?
Answer: He might be thinking about the proclamation he has just signed. He might be thinking about the first European immigrants who came to America in search of freedom.

3 ▶Critical Viewing

Answer: Students may say that the painting depicts Lincoln as serious, introspective, and hard-working.

1 *from* A Lincoln Preface

Carl Sandburg

2

Lincoln Proclaiming Thanksgiving, Dean Cornwell, The Lincoln Museum, Fort Wayne, Indiana, a part of Lincoln National Corp.

3 ▲ **Critical Viewing** What can you tell about Lincoln from this painting? **[Infer]**

TEACHING RESOURCES

The following resources can be used to enrich or extend the instruction for pp. 152–158.

Literary Analysis

Selection Support: Literary Analysis, p. 32

Reading

Reader's Companion

English Learner's Companion

Listening to Literature Audiocassettes, Side 6 ■

Listening to Literature Audio CDs, CD 6 ■

■ **BLOCK SCHEDULING:** Resources marked with this symbol provide varied instruction during 90-minute blocks.

4 In the time of the April lilacs in the year 1865, a man in the City of Washington, D.C., trusted a guard to watch at a door, and the guard was careless, left the door, and the man was shot, lingered a night, passed away, was laid in a box, and carried north and west a thousand miles; bells sobbed; cities wore crepe;[1] people stood with hats off as the railroad burial car came past at midnight, dawn or noon.

During the four years of time before he gave up the ghost, this man was clothed with despotic power, commanding the most powerful armies till then assembled in modern warfare, enforcing drafts of soldiers, abolishing the right of habeas corpus,[2] directing politically and spiritually the wild, massive forces loosed in civil war.

Four billion dollars' worth of property was taken from those who had been legal owners of it, confiscated, wiped out as by fire, at his instigation and executive direction; a class of chattel property recognized as lawful for two hundred years went to the scrap pile.

When the woman who wrote *Uncle Tom's Cabin*[3] came to see him in the White House, he greeted her, "So you're the little woman who wrote the book that made this great war," and as they seated themselves at a fireplace, "I do love an open fire: I always had one at home." As they were finishing their talk of the days of blood, he said, "I shan't last long after it's over."

5 An Illinois Congressman looked in on him as he had his face lathered for a shave in the White House and remarked, "If anybody had told me that in a great crisis like this the people were going out to a little one-horse town and pick out a one-horse lawyer for president, I wouldn't have believed it." The answer was, "Neither would I. But it was a time when a man with a policy would have been fatal to the country. I never had a policy. I have simply tried to do what seemed best each day, as each day came."

"I don't intend precisely to throw the Constitution overboard, but I will stick it in a

despotic (des pät′ ik) *adj.* like an absolute ruler or tyrant

chattel (chat′ 'l) *n.* a movable item of personal property

Literary Analysis
Anecdote What point does this anecdote make about Lincoln's devotion to his country?

1. **crepe** (krāp) *n.* thin, black cloth worn to show mourning.
2. **habeas corpus** (hā bē əs kôr′ pəs) right of an imprisoned person to have a court hearing.
3. **woman . . . Cabin** Harriet Beecher Stowe (1811–1896), whose novel stirred up opinion against slavery.

6 **✓Reading Check**
What did Lincoln do during the four years before he was killed?

4 Background
History
On April 14, 1865, actor and Confederate sympathizer John Wilkes Booth entered the presidential box at Ford's Theater and shot Lincoln through the head. The President was carried to a nearby house, where he died the next morning. His funeral procession traveled through several cities; thousands of mourners, some weeping, others silent, lined the streets to watch the coffin pass by.

Lee had surrendered to Grant about a week earlier, and the Civil War was nearly over. Interestingly, as related further along in this selection, Lincoln had predicted that he wouldn't last long after the war. The slaves (the chattel property referred to in paragraph three) were now free. Lincoln had spent the previous week focusing on how to heal the wounds of the nation, now that the end of the war was in sight.

5 Literary Analysis
Anecdote
- Have students read the paragraph beginning "When the woman . . ." Ask what each of Lincoln's three comments reveals about him.
  Answers: The first comment shows that he has a sense of humor; the war was a tremendous burden for him, but he can still speak in a lighthearted manner. The second shows that he is an ordinary person who loves ordinary human comforts; he is not grand or pretentious. The third shows that he is exhausted by the burden of trying to keep the country together.
- Ask the Literary Analysis question on p. 153: What point does this anecdote make about Lincoln's devotion to his country?
  Answer: It shows that Lincoln did not take office with a fixed idea of what he wanted, but that he tried to respond to each situation as it came up. He tried to do what was best for the country.

6 ✓Reading Check
Answer: Lincoln had commanded the northern armies during the Civil War. He had, among other things, drafted soldiers, abolished slavery, and exercised "despotic power."

CUSTOMIZE INSTRUCTION FOR UNIVERSAL ACCESS

For Less Proficient Readers	For Advanced Readers
Most of Sandburg's sentences are long and complex. Encourage students to break down lengthy sentences to help them determine meaning. As a class, work through the first paragraph on this page, which is one long sentence. Then, have students break down the long sentences in the next two paragraphs. You may wish to divide students into groups to discuss what is being said.	Challenge students to do some further reading of Lincoln's speeches and letters. Have them each choose a short excerpt to read to the class. Students can introduce their excerpts by giving the date on which Lincoln spoke or wrote, who the audience or recipient was, and any necessary background information. This activity will give the entire class a chance to appreciate Lincoln's superb use of language and his cogent way of expressing himself.

❼ Background

Art

Peculiarsome Abe, **by N.C. Wyeth**

Newell Convers Wyeth (1882–1945) was a native of Massachusetts. He is best remembered for the dramatic oil paintings with which he illustrated a series of children's classics such as *Robin Hood, Treasure Island,* and *Kidnapped.* Wyeth's illustrations also graced magazine covers, stories, and advertisements.

1. This painting might be considered an anecdote about Lincoln. What might the two men sitting at the left on the wagon say about him? How might he respond, based on what you have read so far?
   Answer: They might respect his interest in reading. They might tease him about his reading. Lincoln would probably respond with a good-humored joke.
2. How does this image of Lincoln contrast with the images in Sandburg's preface?
   Answer: The figure is youthful and relaxed. He is a country boy who has been working in the field. Sandburg's Lincoln is mature, powerful, and faced with bigger tasks than harvesting corn.

❽ ▶ Critical Viewing

Possible responses: It shows that he loved reading. It shows that he understood hard work. It shows that he was intellectually curious. It shows that he was solitary.

❾ Vocabulary Development

Anglo-Saxon Suffix *-ic*

- Write the word *Pacific* on the chalkboard, underlining the suffix *-ic.*
- Explain that this suffix means "like" or "pertaining to." Tell students that "pacific" is not just the name of an ocean; it is a common adjective. Challenge students to define it. If they have trouble, explain that *pac-* is from the Latin *pax,* meaning *peace. Pacific* means *peaceful.*

hole if I can," he told a Cabinet officer. The enemy was violating the Constitution to destroy the Union, he argued, and therefore, "I will violate the Constitution, if necessary, to save the Union." He instructed a messenger to the Secretary of the Treasury, "Tell him not to bother himself about the Constitution. Say that I have that sacred instrument here at the White House, and I am guarding it with great care."

❼

Peculiarsome Abe, N. C. Wyeth, The Free Library of Philadelphia

When he was renominated, it was by the device of seating delegates from Tennessee, which gave enough added votes to seat favorable delegates from Kentucky, Missouri, Louisiana, Arkansas, and from one county in Florida. Until late in that campaign of 1864, he expected to lose the November election; military victories brought the tide his way; the vote was 2,200,000 for him and 1,800,000 against him. Among those who bitterly fought him politically, and accused him of blunders or crimes, were Franklin Pierce, a former president of the United States; Horatio Seymour, the Governor of New York; Samuel F. B. Morse, inventor of the telegraph; Cyrus H. McCormick, inventor of the farm reaper; General George B. McClellan, a Democrat who had commanded the Army of the Potomac; and the *Chicago Times,* a daily newspaper. In all its essential propositions the Southern Confederacy had the moral support of powerful, respectable elements throughout the North, probably more than a million votes believing in the justice of the cause of the South as compared with the North.

❽ ▲ **Critical Viewing** What message does this painting convey about Lincoln? **[Describe]**

❾ While propagandas raged, and the war winds howled, he sat in the White House, the Stubborn Man of History, writing that the Mississippi was one river and could not belong to two countries, that the plans for railroad connection from coast to coast must be pushed through and the Union Pacific[4] realized.

His life, mind and heart ran in contrasts. When his white kid gloves broke into tatters while shaking hands at a White House reception, he remarked, "This looks like a general bustification." When he talked with an Ohio friend one day during the 1864 campaign, he

4. **Union Pacific** railroad chartered by Congress in 1862 to form part of a transcontinental system.

ENRICHMENT: Social Studies Connection

Union Pacific

Once the best route for a transcontinental railroad had been determined, Congress gave the Central Pacific Railroad the money to begin laying track eastward across the Sierra Nevada mountains. At the same time, the Union Pacific would begin laying track from the city of Omaha westward across the Great Plains.

Trying to build a railroad in wartime was not easy; supplies were difficult to get and prices were high. The Central Pacific, far west of the fighting, began construction in 1862, but the Union Pacific could not start work until the war ended. The two lines finally met in Utah on May 10, 1869. The railroad linked the two coasts of North America and greatly accelerated the settlement of the West.

mentioned one public man, and murmured, "He's a thistle! I don't see why God lets him live." Of a devious Senator, he said, "He's too crooked to lie still!" And of a New York editor, "In early life in the West, we used to make our shoes last a great while with much mending, and sometimes, when far gone, we found the leather so rotten the stitches would not hold. Greeley is so rotten that nothing can be done with him. He is not truthful; the stitches all tear out." As he sat in the telegraph office of the War Department, reading cipher dispatches, and came to the words, Hosanna and Husband, he would chuckle, "Jeffy D.,"[5] and at the words, Hunter and Happy, "Bobby Lee."[6]

cipher (sī′ fər) *adj.* code

While the luck of war wavered and broke and came again, as generals failed and campaigns were lost, he held enough forces of the Union together to raise new armies and supply them, until generals were found who made war as victorious war has always been made, with terror, frightfulness, destruction, and valor and sacrifice past words of man to tell.

11 A slouching, gray-headed poet,[7] haunting the hospitals at Washington, characterized him as "the grandest figure on the crowded canvas of the drama of the nineteenth century—a Hoosier Michael Angelo."[8]

slouching (slouch′ iŋ) *adj.* drooping

10 His own speeches, letters, telegrams and official messages during that war form the most significant and enduring document from any one man on why the war began, why it went on, and the dangers beyond its end. He mentioned "the politicians," over and again "the politicians," with scorn and blame. As the platoons filed before him at a review of an army corps, he asked, "What is to become of these boys when the war is over?"

Reading Strategy
Establishing a Purpose for Reading What two sides of Lincoln's personality do these paragraphs reveal?

He was a chosen spokesman: yet there were times he was silent; nothing but silence could at those times have fitted a chosen spokesman; in the mixed shame and blame of the immense wrongs of two crashing civilizations, with nothing to say, he said nothing, slept not at all, and wept at those times in a way that made weeping appropriate, decent, majestic.

His hat was shot off as he rode alone one night in Washington; a son he loved died as he watched at the bed; his wife was accused of betraying information to the enemy, until denials from him were necessary; his best companion was a fine-hearted and brilliant son with a deformed palate and an impediment of speech; when a Pennsylvania Congressman told him the enemy had declared they would break into the city and hang him to a lamppost, he said he had considered "the violent preliminaries" to such a scene; on his left thumb was a scar where an ax had nearly chopped the thumb off when he was a boy; over one eye was a scar where he had been hit with a club in the hands of a man trying to steal the cargo off a

12 **✓ Reading Check**
Name at least three people who fought against Lincoln politically.

5. **"Jeffy D."** Jefferson Davis (1808–1889), president of the Confederacy.
6. **"Bobby Lee"** Robert E. Lee (1807–1870), commander in chief of the Confederate army.
7. **slouching . . . poet** Walt Whitman (1819–1892).
8. **Michael Angelo** Michelangelo (mik′ əl an′ jə lō′), famous Italian artist (1475–1564).

10 Reading Strategy
Establishing a Purpose for Reading

- Remind students that establishing a purpose for reading can help them get more out of what they read.
- Point out that, when reading to learn or discover, it is sometimes necessary to determine what information is being supplied. For example, while the first paragraph in the section relates that the luck of war wavered and broke, the fact that Lincoln held the forces together shows that he was a capable leader.
- Encourage students to record any new information they discover in their K-W-L charts. Suggest that new information may also add more items to the "What I Want to Know" category.
- Ask students the Reading Strategy question on p. 155: Describe the two sides of Lincoln's personality that these paragraphs reveal.
  Answer: He was highly intellectual, articulate, and a great statesman on the one hand; he was silent and emotional on the other.

11 Background
Literature

Walt Whitman was too old to fight when the Civil War broke out. Instead, he became a nurse in the hospitals for the wounded. Whitman had no medical training, but did whatever was needed—changing bandages, washing patients, emptying bedpans, writing and reading letters, and keeping the soldiers cheerful. Whitman's mournful poem "The Wound-Dresser" from the collection *Drum-Taps* describes his time in the hospitals.

12 ✓ Reading Check

Answer: Political enemies included Franklin Pierce, Horatio Seymour, Samuel F.B. Morse, Cyrus McCormick, George McClellan, and the *Chicago Times.*

CUSTOMIZE INSTRUCTION FOR UNIVERSAL ACCESS

For Special Needs Students	For Gifted/Talented Students
Share the background information in this teachers' edition with students before they begin reading. Have students share what they already know about Lincoln. Assign peer tutors with whom students can meet to discuss the selection at intervals of one or two pages. Students should keep track of questions as they read. Tutors should help them answer the questions and make sure that they understand the information conveyed in the excerpt.	At the outbreak of World War II, American composer Aaron Copland (1900–1990) was commissioned to write *A Lincoln Portrait.* The piece blends original music with American folk tunes to accompany a script based on Lincoln's own words. Have students locate and listen to *A Lincoln Portrait.* Have them compare and contrast Copland's portrait of Lincoln to Sandburg's. Ask students to describe the similarities and differences of the two portrayals.

⓭ Background

History

Students may be very surprised to learn what the Emancipation Proclamation actually says. On September 22, 1862, President Lincoln proclaimed that as of January 1, 1863, all slaves in states or territories in rebellion against the Union would be "thenceforward, and forever, free." The proclamation went on to say that states or territories would no longer be considered in rebellion against the Union if, on that date, they were represented in Congress. In other words, any Confederate state that rejoined the Union could keep its slaves. However, no state accepted this offer. On January 1, therefore, Lincoln issued a second proclamation that all slaves in these states were freed, that they would be welcomed into the Union army, and that the military and government of the United States would protect them. Lincoln made his intentions clear in a subsequent letter:

I struggled for nearly a year and a half to get along without touching the "institution" [i.e., slavery] . . . . I gave a hundred days fair notice of my purpose, to all the States and people, within which time they could have turned it wholly aside, by simply again becoming good citizens of the United States. They chose to disregard it, and I made the peremptory proclamation on what appeared to me to be a military necessity. And being made, it must stand.

Mississippi River flatboat; he threw a cashiered[9] officer out of his room in the White House, crying, "I can bear censure, but not insult. I never wish to see your face again."

As he shook hands with the correspondent of the London *Times*, he drawled, "Well, I guess the London *Times* is about the greatest power on earth—unless perhaps it is the Mississippi River." He rebuked with anger a woman who got on her knees to thank him for a pardon that saved her son from being shot at sunrise; and when an Iowa woman said she had journeyed out of her way to Washington just for a look at him, he grinned, "Well, in the matter of looking at one another, I have altogether the advantage."

He asked his Cabinet to vote on the high military command, and after the vote, told them the appointment had already been made; one Cabinet officer, who had been governor of Ohio, came away personally baffled and frustrated from an interview, to exclaim, to a private secretary, "That man is the most cunning person I ever saw in my life"; an Illinois lawyer who had been sent on errands carrying his political secrets, said, "He is a trimmer[10] and such a trimmer as the world has never seen."

He manipulated the admission of Nevada as a state in the Union, when her votes were needed for the Emancipation Proclamation,♦ saying, "It is easier to admit Nevada than to raise another million of soldiers." At the same time he went to the office of a former New York editor, who had become Assistant Secretary of War, and said the votes of three congressmen were wanted for the required three-quarters of votes in the House of Representatives, advising, "There are three that you can deal with better than anybody else. . . . Whatever promise you make to those men, I will perform it." And in the same week, he said to a Massachusetts politician that two votes were lacking, and, "Those two votes must be procured. I leave it to you to determine how it shall be done; but remember that I am President of the United States and clothed with immense power, and I expect you to procure those votes." And while he was thus employing every last resource and device of practical politics to constitutionally abolish slavery, the abolitionist[11] Henry Ward Beecher attacked him with javelins of scorn and detestation in a series of editorials that brought from him the single comment, "Is thy servant a dog?"

When the King of Siam sent him a costly sword of exquisite

censure (sen´ shər) *n.* strong disapproval

Literature ⓭ in context — History Connection

♦ The Emancipation Proclamation

When Lincoln signed the Emancipation Proclamation, he recognized its enormous symbolic power while understanding its limitations. Some argued it was really only a partial emancipation—freeing slaves in unconquered Confederate territory—but it was an important first step. Not only did the document give Southern blacks cause to hope, rebel, and escape, it also served as a recruitment incentive for the new black regiments of the Union Army. As the army advanced, liberating slaves along the way, it was clear that the Emancipation Proclamation had done what it was designed to do: pave the way for the total abolition of slavery.

Lincoln at the Signing of the Emancipation Proclamation

9. **cashiered** (ka shird´) *v.* dishonorably discharged.
10. **trimmer** (trim´ ər) *n.* person who changes his opinion to suit the circumstances.
11. **abolitionist** (ab´ ə lish´ ən ist) *n.* person in favor of doing away with slavery in the United States.

ENRICHMENT: World History

The King of Siam

The King of Siam who sent gifts to the United States was King Mongkut, who had been crowned in 1851. Mongkut was a highly educated man who cherished the ambition to lead Siam to take its place among the modern nations of the West. During this period, Britain, France, and the United States were beginning to explore, invade, and colonize Southeast Asia; Mongkut's diplomatic and political skills kept Thailand free from any takeover.

King Mongkut died in 1868. He was immortalized in the memoirs of Anna Leonowens, the Welsh governess of his children. Margaret Landon later wrote a popular biography of Leonowens called *Anna and the King of Siam*, on which are based the Rodgers and Hammerstein musical *The King and I* and the recent film *Anna and the King.*

14 embellishment, and two elephant tusks, along with letters and a photograph of the King, he acknowledged the gifts in a manner as lavish as the Orientals. Addressing the King of Siam as "Great and Good Friend," he wrote thanks for each of the gifts, including "also two elephant's tusks of length and magnitude, such as indicate they could have belonged only to an animal which was a native of Siam." After further thanks for the tokens received, he closed the letter to the King of Siam with strange grace and humor, saying, "I appreciate most highly your Majesty's tender of good offices in forwarding to this Government a stock from which a supply of elephants might be raised on our soil. . . . our political jurisdiction, however, does not reach a latitude so low as to favor the multiplication of the elephant, and steam on land as well as water has been our best agent of transportation . . . Meantime, wishing for your Majesty a long and happy life, and, for the generous and emulous people of Siam, the highest possible prosperity, I commend both to the blessing of Almighty God."

He sent hundreds of telegrams, "Suspend death sentence" or "Suspend execution" of So-and-So, who was to be shot at sunrise. The telegrams varied oddly at times, as in one, "If Thomas Samplogh, of the First Delaware Regiment, has been sentenced to death, and is not yet executed, suspend and report the case to me." And another, "Is it Lieut. Samuel B. Davis whose death sentence is commuted? If not done, let it be done."

While the war drums beat, he liked best of all the stories told of him, one of two Quakeresses[12] heard talking in a railway car. "I think that Jefferson will succeed." "Why does thee think so?" "Because Jefferson is a praying man." "And so is Abraham a praying man." "Yes, but the Lord will think Abraham is joking."

An Indiana man at the White House heard him say, "Voorhees, don't it seem strange to you that I, who could never so much as cut off the head of a chicken, should be elected, or selected, into the midst of all this blood?"

A party of American citizens, standing in the ruins of the Forum in Rome, Italy, heard there the news of the first assassination of the first American dictator, and took it as a sign of the growing up and the aging of the civilization on the North American continent. Far out 15 in Coles County, Illinois, a beautiful, gaunt old woman in a log cabin said, "I knowed he'd never come back."

Of men taking too fat profits out of the war, he said, "Where the carcass is there will the eagles be gathered together."

An enemy general, Longstreet, after the war, declared him to have been "the one matchless man in forty millions of people," while one of his private secretaries, Hay, declared his life to have been the most perfect in its relationships and adjustments since that of Christ.

Between the days in which he crawled as a baby on the dirt floor of

12. **Quakeresses** (kwāk′ ər es əz) *n.* female members of the religious group known as the Society of Friends, or Quakers.

Literary Analysis
Anecdote What does this anecdote about gifts from Siam convey about Lincoln's personality?

gaunt (gônt) *adj.* thin and bony

16 ✓**Reading Check**
What story regarding the Quakeresses did Lincoln appreciate?

14 Literary Analysis
Anecdote

Monitor Progress Ask students the Literary Analysis question on p. 157: What does this anecdote about gifts from Siam convey about Lincoln's personality?
Answer: He is very polite and considerate. The offer of elephants must have amused him, but he treats the offer as seriously as it was made.

- Ask students their opinion of the anecdote about the death sentences. You might point out that because this was a civil war, soldiers' loyalties were often confused. Often, members of one family would end up fighting on opposite sides. Desertion was rampant because youths and men needed to look after their families and their crops. Many offenses, according to army discipline, were punishable by execution. Ask students what Lincoln's telegrams suggest about his feeling for the soldiers.
Answer: He is reluctant to have anyone shot. He probably was aware of the situation of a common man forced to leave his farm and family for months on end. He understood about divided loyalties. He wanted everyone treated fairly.

15 Background
History

The "beautiful, gaunt old woman" was Lincoln's stepmother Sarah. Lincoln's beloved mother, Nancy Hanks, had died when he was quite young. His father soon remarried. Sarah Lincoln and her stepson were extremely close. When he became President, she predicted that he would be killed.

16 ✓Reading Check

Answer: He appreciated the story of a Quakeress saying that the Lord would think Lincoln was joking when he prayed for help.

CUSTOMIZE INSTRUCTION FOR UNIVERSAL ACCESS

For Advanced Readers

Encourage students who enjoyed this selection to dip into the work from which it is taken: Sandburg's classic biography of Lincoln, *The Prairie Years* and *The War Years.* Students can establish a purpose for reading before they begin. They should choose one period in Lincoln's life about which they would like to know more—for example, his boyhood, his law practice in Illinois, or the night of his assassination. Students can look through the biography for this particular period, reading a few chapters or pages here and there as they try to find the answers to their questions. Students can give brief class presentations on what they learn about Lincoln. Encourage them to read as much of the biography as they want to, but reassure them that there is no need to try to read it cover to cover.

ASSESS

Answers for p. 158

Review and Assess

1. Choices will vary. Ask students to give reasons for their choices.
2. **(a)** Harriet Beecher Stowe **(b)** Lincoln had probably read her book and was impressed with her presentation of the evils of slavery.
3. **(a)** He felt the war would be over sooner and he might save a million soldiers' lives. **(b)** Lincoln asked Congress to vote on a military commander and then announced that he had already appointed someone.
4. **(a)** The anecdotes reveal all these aspects of Lincoln's personality; the mention of his children, for example, shows that he was a loving father. **(b)** He clearly admired him.
5. Students will probably say yes. Lincoln believed that destroying the Union was a violation of the Constitution. Because his oath of office required him to "preserve, protect, and defend the Constitution," and the Constitution and the Union were the same thing to him, he would have been justified.
6. Possible response: Like other great leaders, Lincoln stood up for what he believed and he did not give up or give in when the situation became difficult.

a Kentucky cabin, and the time when he gave his final breath in Washington, he packed a rich life with work, thought, laughter, tears, hate, love.

With vast reservoirs of the comic and the droll, and notwithstanding a mastery of mirth and nonsense, he delivered a volume of addresses and letters of terrible and serious appeal, with import beyond his own day, shot through here and there with far, thin ironics, with paragraphs having raillery[13] of the quality of the Book of Job,[14] and echoes as subtle as the whispers of wind in prairie grass.

Perhaps no human clay pot has held more laughter and tears.

The facts and myths of his life are to be an American possession, shared widely over the world, for thousands of years, as the tradition of Knute or Alfred, Lao-tse or Diogenes, Pericles or Caesar,[15] are kept. This because he was not only a genius in the science of neighborly human relationships and an artist in the personal handling of life from day to day, but a strange friend and a friendly stranger to all forms of life that he met.

He lived fifty-six years of which fifty-two were lived in the West—the prairie years.

droll (drōl) *adj.* comic and amusing in an odd way

13. **raillery** (rāl´ ər ē) *n.* good-natured teasing.
14. **Book of Job** (jōb) book of the Old Testament in which a man named Job is tested by God.
15. **Knute** (kno͞ot) **or Alfred, Lao-tse** (lou´ dzu´) **or Diogenes** (dī äj´ ə nēz), **Pericles** (per´ ə klēz) **or Caesar** (sē´ zər) well-known thinkers and leaders from different eras and places.

Carl Sandburg

(1878–1967)

At the age of thirteen, Carl Sandburg dropped out of school; for the next seven years, he worked as a porter, scene changer, truck handler, dishwasher, potter, and farm worker. Sandburg served briefly in Puerto Rico during the Spanish-American War, and that experience brought on the strong antiwar feelings that Sandburg would hold throughout his life.

After the war, Sandburg discovered literature. He read a great deal and spent eighteen years researching and writing *Abraham Lincoln: The Prairie Years* and *Abraham Lincoln: The War Years*. Sandburg received two Pulitzer Prizes—one for his Lincoln biography and one for poetry. He also gained recognition for having written what many consider the greatest historical biography of the 1900s.

Review and Assess

Thinking About the Selection

1. **Respond:** Which anecdote interested you the most?
2. **(a) Recall:** To whom did Lincoln refer as "the little woman who wrote the book that made this great war"? **(b) Infer:** Why do you think Lincoln wanted to meet with this woman?
3. **(a) Recall:** How did Lincoln justify admitting Nevada to the Union? **(b) Analyze:** What other examples can you find of Lincoln's use of "practical politics"?
4. **(a) Distinguish:** How does Sandburg show that Lincoln "packed a rich life with work, thought, laughter, tears, hate, love"? **(b) Evaluate:** What do you think Sandburg thought about his subject?
5. **Evaluate:** Do you think Lincoln was justified in violating the Constitution to save the Union? Why or why not?
6. **Extend:** How does Lincoln's life, based on Sandburg's portrait, compare to the lives of other great leaders?

ASSESSMENT PRACTICE: Reading Comprehension

Recognize Facts and Details **(For more practice, see Test Preparation Workbook, p. 8.)**

Many tests require students to recognize facts and details. Use the following sample test item to show students how to use this skill to answer a multiple-choice question correctly.

> When he [Lincoln] was renominated, it was by the device of seating delegates from Tennessee, which gave enough votes to seat favorable delegates. . . . Until late in that campaign, he expected to lose the November election.

What did Lincoln expect after he was renominated?

A to win in Tennessee
B to get favorable delegates seated
C to lose the November election
D to win the November election

Point out the key word *expect* in the question. The last line of the passage says that Lincoln expected to lose the election. The other choices all echo key words from the passage, but only choice *C* is correct.

Review and Assess

Literary Analysis

Anecdote

1. Use an organizer like the one shown to analyze **anecdotes** from the selection. For each, summarize the story and then identify the personality trait it reveals.

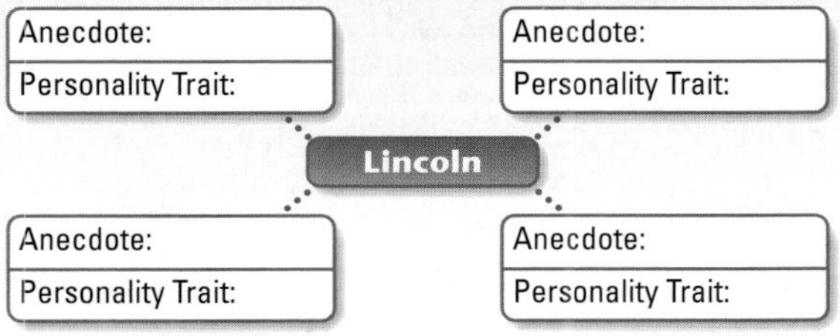

2. Why do you think Sandburg included in this work some anecdotes that portrayed Lincoln in a less-than-pleasing light?
3. Which of your previous notions about Lincoln does the narration change?

Connecting Literary Elements

4. What is the central problem that ties this **narrative** together?
5. How does Sandburg's narration paint a verbal picture of Lincoln?
6. (a) How does a biography built on anecdotes differ from other biographies you have read? (b) How do the anecdotes strengthen the narrative?

Reading Strategy

Establishing a Purpose for Reading

7. Identify two different **purposes** readers may bring to this selection.
8. Identify three pieces of information from the selection that helped you achieve the purpose of learning more about Abraham Lincoln.
9. If you were reading to learn more about the Civil War, which details in the selection would help you?

Extend Understanding

10. **Literature Connection:** Why do you think people are fascinated with political biographies that reveal the positive and negative inner workings of a politician's life?

Quick Review

An **anecdote** is a brief story about an interesting, amusing, or strange event.

Narrative is writing that tells a story.

To **establish a purpose for reading,** decide what you want to know about the content of a selection, and then read the selection to discover it.

Take It to the Net

www.phschool.com

Take the interactive self-test online to check your understanding of the selection.

ENRICHMENT: Further Reading

Other Works by Carl Sandburg

Rootabaga Stories
Rootabaga Pigeons
The Complete Poems of Carl Sandburg

Take It to the Net

Visit www.phschool.com for more information on Carl Sandburg.

Answers for p. 159

Review and Assess

1. Possible response: Anecdote: Lincoln meets Stowe and jokes about her book being responsible for the war. Personality trait: humor
2. Sandburg wanted readers to learn about the real Lincoln, who had flaws as well as admirable character traits.
3. Possible response: Students who thought that Lincoln fought a war to free the slaves will now know that he fought a war primarily to save the Union. Students who thought that Lincoln was a saint now know that he had a temper and was capable of political trickery.
4. The central problem is capturing in words the many sides of a complex man dealing with complex issues.
5. The anecdotes give glimpses of public and private sides of Lincoln's personality, such as his effort to halt the executions of soldiers and his love for his children.
6. **(a)** Students are probably familiar with biographies that presented facts about a person's life in chronological order. **(b)** The anecdotes are a breath of fresh air; they make the reader feel that he or she has actually met and spoken to Lincoln. They give a flavor of his personality.
7. Readers may want to learn facts about Lincoln. Readers may want to learn about the Civil War.
8. Sample answer: Lincoln had many political enemies. Lincoln's primary goal was to preserve the Union, not to free the slaves. Lincoln was a pragmatic politician.
9. The selection discusses soldiers under threat of execution, and mentions that the war was destructive and violent.
10. Possible answer: Politicians are faced with difficult decisions that affect people's lives, sometimes for many years afterward: for instance, all living US citizens are affected by Lincoln's decision to free the slaves. People are eager to learn how these far-reaching decisions were made.

EXTEND

Answers for p. 160

❶ Vocabulary Development

Word Analysis

1. pertaining to art or artists
2. similar to or based on reality
3. full of problems

Spelling Strategy

1. artistic
2. poetic
3. classic
4. patriotic

Concept Development: Analogies

1. chattel
2. censure
3. cipher
4. slouching
5. despotic
6. gaunt
7. droll

❷ Grammar

1. transitive
2. intransitive
3. transitive
4. intransitive
5. intransitive

Writing Application

Have students exchange papers, underline the transitive verbs, and double-underline the intransitive verbs. Partners can go over their work together.

Integrate Language Skills

❶ Vocabulary Development Lesson

Word Analysis: Anglo-Saxon Suffix *-ic*

The Anglo-Saxon suffix *-ic* means "like" or "pertaining to." It creates the adjective form of many words, such as *despotic*, which means "like a despot, or tyrant." Define each of the following words, incorporating the definition of *-ic* into each answer.

1. artistic 2. realistic 3. problematic

Spelling Strategy

To add an ending like *-ic* to a word that ends in a consonant, simply add the suffix. For example, *carbon* becomes *carbonic*. Create the adjective form of the following words by adding the suffix *-ic* to each one. Then, write a sentence using the new word.

1. artist
2. poet
3. class
4. patriot

Concept Development: Analogies

When you analyze vocabulary analogies, first study the relationship between a given word pair, and then complete a second word pair to show the same relationship.

Copy the following analogies. Complete each one with the appropriate word from the vocabulary list on page 151.

1. tradition : custom :: possession : __?__
2. war : peace :: praise : __?__
3. garbled : speech :: __?__ : message
4. standing tall : alert :: __?__ : tired
5. tolerant : democratic :: repressive : __?__
6. well-fed : plump :: undernourished : __?__
7. strange : bizarre :: funny : __?__

❷ Grammar Lesson

Transitive and Intransitive Verbs

An action verb is **transitive** if it directs action toward someone or something named in the same sentence. An action verb is **intransitive** if it does not direct action toward something or someone named in the same sentence. To determine whether a verb is transitive or intransitive, ask *Whom?* or *What?* after the verb. If you can find the answer in the sentence, the verb is transitive. If not, the verb is intransitive.

Transitive: The president read the documents.

Intransitive: The president read every day.

Practice: Identify each underlined verb as *transitive* or *intransitive*.

1. Several people bitterly fought him politically.
2. Propagandas raged and the war winds howled.
3. He asked his cabinet to vote on the issue.
4. He spoke forcefully during the war.
5. The telegrams varied at times.

Writing Application Write a brief paragraph about a modern-day leader. In your writing, use three transitive verbs and three intransitive verbs.

WG Prentice Hall Writing and Grammar Connection: Chapter 17, Section 1

TEACHING RESOURCES

The following resources can be used to enrich or extend the instructions for pp. 160–161.

Vocabulary

Selection Support: Build Vocabulary, p. 30

Vocabulary and Spelling Practice Book (Use this booklet for skills enrichment.)

Grammar

Selection Support: Build Grammar Skills, p. 31

Writing and Grammar, Gold Level, p. 363 ■

Daily Language Practice Transparencies

Writing

Writing and Grammar, Gold Level, p. 109

Writing and Grammar iText CD-ROM ■

Writing Models and Graphic Organizers on Transparencies, pp. 9–15

■ **BLOCK SCHEDULING:** Resources marked with this symbol provide varied instruction during 90-minute blocks.

❸ Writing Lesson

Character Profile

Write a short profile of Lincoln, describing the traits, talents, and special skills that helped him succeed as president. Use Sandburg's narrative and your own knowledge to create your profile.

Prewriting Use a chart like the one shown to jot down descriptions of Lincoln. Then, provide evidence for each description you list.

Model: Gathering Details About a Person

Description	Evidence
determined	He manipulated the admission of Nevada as a state into the Union to win votes for the Emancipation Proclamation.

Drafting As you draft, use a solid organization. You might begin by explaining some of Lincoln's minor personality traits and move to addressing his most impressive traits, or do the reverse.

Revising Reread your draft. Check to make sure that each description of Lincoln is backed up with evidence. Add any details needed to present a clear profile of Lincoln.

WG *Prentice Hall Writing and Grammar Connection: Chapter 5, Section 2*

❹ Extension Activities

Listening and Speaking In a group, conduct a **panel discussion** on Lincoln's use of "practical politics" to end slavery with the passage of the Emancipation Proclamation.

- Panel members should prepare their remarks in advance.
- Each speaker can present a brief opening statement.
- The panel can then debate the issue to reach a conclusion.

After the discussion, ask audience members to evaluate the event. **[Group Activity]**

Research and Technology Create a **timeline** of the most significant events in Lincoln's life and presidency as Sandburg reports them. In the appropriate places, include situations in which he made famous speeches or suffered personal tragedies. Use graphics software to create your timeline, and present it to your class.

Take It to the Net www.phschool.com

Go online for an additional research activity using the Internet.

ASSESSMENT RESOURCES

The following resources can be used to assess students' knowledge and skills.

Selection Assessment

- **Formal Assessment,** pp. 26–28
- **Open Book Test,** pp. 22–24
- **Got It! Assessment Videotapes,** Tape 1
- **Test Bank Software**

Take It to the Net
Visit www.phschool.com com for self-tests and additional questions on "A Lincoln Preface."

Writing Rubric

- **Performance Assess. and Portfolio Mgmt.,** p. 18

Listening and Speaking Rubric

- **Performance Assess. and Portfolio Mgmt.,** p. 29

PRENTICE HALL ASSESSMENT SYSTEM

- **Workbook**
- **Transparencies**
- **Skill Book**
- **CD-ROM**

Lesson Support for p. 161

❸ Writing Lesson

- Go over the prewriting chart with students, to make sure they understand how it is used. If necessary, discuss an additional descriptive term, along with evidence, in class.
- Point out that the objective of this character profile is to examine what contributed to Lincoln's success, not simply to show his personality.
- Lead students through the drafting and revising process using the Biographical Profile model on pp. 9–15 of the **Writing Models and Graphic Organizers on Transparencies.** Emphasize the need for organization and for supporting points.
- Use the Description Rubric in **Performance Assessment and Portfolio Management,** p. 18, to evaluate students' character profiles.

❹ Listening and Speaking

- Meet with interested students to discuss this activity. Have each student focus on a different aspect of Lincoln the politician so that work is not duplicated. Help students locate library and online sources for research. Ask panel members to provide bibliographies of books they consulted in their research.
- Meet with each student a second time, just before the discussion. Listen to the student's ideas for his or her statement. Give each student any necessary guidance.
- Encourage questions and comments from audience members. Have students use the rubric for Presenting an Oral Response to Literature on p. 29 in **Performance Assessment and Portfolio Management.**

CUSTOMIZE INSTRUCTION for Universal Access

To address different learning styles, use the following activities suggested in the **Extension Activities** booklet, p. 8.

- For Verbal/Linguistic and Logical/Mathematical Learners, use Activity 4.
- For Musical/Rhythmic Learners, use Activity 5.
- For Visual/Spatial Learners, use Activity 6.

I Have a Dream ✦ *from* Rosa Parks: My Story
There Is a Longing ✦ I Hear America Singing

Lesson Objectives and CA Correlations

1. **To analyze and respond to literary elements**
   - Literary Analysis: Author's Purpose **R 2.8**
   - Comparing Literary Works: Tone **R 3.9**
2. **To read, comprehend, analyze, and critique nonfiction and poetry**
   - Reading Strategy: Responding
   - Reading Check questions
   - Review and Assess questions
   - Assessment Practice (ATE)
3. **To develop word analysis skills, fluency, and systematic vocabulary**
   - Vocabulary Development Lesson: Latin Word Root: *-cred-* **R 1.1**
4. **To understand and apply written and oral language conventions**
   - Spelling Strategy
   - Grammar Lesson: Action and Linking Verbs **LC 1.2**
5. **To understand and apply appropriate writing and research strategies**
   - Writing Lesson: Proposal for a School Speaker **W 2.4**
   - Extension Activity: Multimedia Presentation **W 1.3**
6. **To understand and apply listening and speaking strategies**
   - Extension Activity: Radio News Report **LS 1.4**

STEP-BY-STEP TEACHING GUIDE	PACING GUIDE
PRETEACH	
Motivate Students and Provide Background	
Use the Motivation activity (ATE p. 162)	5 min.
Read and discuss the Preview material and Background information (SE/ATE p. 162) A	15 min.
Introduce the Concepts	
Introduce the Literary Analysis and Reading Strategy (SE/ATE p. 163) A	15 min.
Pronounce the vocabulary words and read their definitions (SE p. 163)	5 min.
TEACH	
Monitor Comprehension	
Informally monitor comprehension by circulating while students read independently or in groups A	20 min.
Monitor students' comprehension with the Reading Check note (SE/ATE p. 165)	as students read
Develop vocabulary with Vocabulary notes (SE pp. 165, 166, 168–170; ATE p. 165)	as students read
Develop Understanding	
Develop students' understanding of author's purpose with the Literary Analysis annotations (SE pp. 168, 172; ATE pp. 164, 165, 168, 170, 172) A	10 min.
Develop students' understanding of responding with the Reading Strategy annotations (SE/ATE pp. 166, 169, 170)	10 min.
ASSESS	
Assess Mastery	
Assess students' mastery of the Reading Strategy and Literary Analysis by having them answer the Review and Assess questions (SE/ATE p. 173)	20 min.
Use one or more of the print and media Assessment Resources (ATE p. 175) A	up to 50 min.
EXTEND	
Apply Understanding	
Have students complete the Vocabulary Development Lesson and the Grammar Lesson (SE p. 174) A	20 min.
Apply students' ability to make and support a proposal using the Writing Lesson (SE/ATE p. 175) A	45 min.
Apply students' understanding using one or more of the Extension Activities (SE p. 175)	20–90 min.

A **ACCELERATED INSTRUCTION:**
Use the strategies and activities identified with an A.

UNIVERSAL ACCESS
● = Below-Level Students
▲ = On-Level Students
■ = Above-Level Students

Time and Resource Manager

Reading Level: Average/Easy/Average/Average
Average Number of Instructional Days: 4

RESOURCES		
PRINT	**TRANSPARENCIES**	**TECHNOLOGY**
• **Beyond Literature,** Career Connection: Past and Present, p. 9 ▲ ■		• **Interest Grabber Video,** Tape 1 ● ▲ ■
• **Selection Support Workbook:** ● ▲ ■ Literary Analysis, p. 38 Reading Strategy, p. 35 Build Vocabulary, p. 33	• **Literary Analysis and Reading Transparencies,** pp. 17 and 18 ● ▲ ■	
• **Adapted Reader's Companion** ● • **Reader's Companion** ●		• **Listening to Literature** ● ▲ ■ Audiocassettes, Side 7 Audio CDs, CD 6
• **English Learner's Companion** ● ▲ • **Literatura en español** ● ▲ • **Literary Analysis for Enrichment** ■	• **Fine Art Transparencies, Volume 1,** Art Transparencies 3, 13 ● ▲ ■	
• **Formal Assessment:** Selection Test, pp. 29–31 ● ▲ ■ • **Open Book Test,** pp. 25–27 ● ▲ ■ • **Performance Assessment and Portfolio Management,** pp. 10, 28 ● ▲ ■ • PRENTICE HALL ASSESSMENT SYSTEM ● ▲ ■	• PRENTICE HALL ASSESSMENT SYSTEM ● ▲ ■ Skills Practice Answers and Explanations on Transparencies	• **Test Bank Software** ● ▲ ■ • **Got It! Assessment Videotapes,** Tape 1 ● ▲
• **Selection Support Workbook:** ● ▲ ■ Build Grammar Skills, p. 34 • **Writing and Grammar,** Gold Level ● ▲ ■ • **Extension Activities,** p. 9 ● ▲ ■	• **Daily Language Practice Transparencies** ● ▲ • **Writing Models and Graphic Organizers on Transparencies,** pp. 17–20 ● ▲ ■	• **Writing and Grammar iText CD-ROM** ● ▲ ■ *Take It to the Net* www.phschool.com

BLOCK SCHEDULING: Use one 90-minute class period to preteach the selection and have students read it. Use a second 90-minute class period to assess students' mastery of skills and have them complete one of the Extension Activities.

PRETEACH

Step-by-Step Teaching Guide for pp. 162–163

Motivation

Play a brief passage from Dr. King's "I Have a Dream" speech. Have students describe the ideal circumstances of which Dr. King dreams. You might list key points on the board. Compare King's vision with students' ideas of "the American dream." Suggest that students consider how "the dream" is embodied in each of the selections in this group.

Interest Grabber Video

As an alternative, play "The Civil Rights Movement" on Tape 1 to engage student interest.

❶ Background

History

Rosa Parks and Martin Luther King became famous all over the country at about the same time. When Parks was arrested for refusing to give up her seat on the bus (see *Rosa Parks: My Story,* p. 168), King was thrust into the leadership of the Montgomery Improvement Association (MIA). This was a group of mostly black citizens of Montgomery who wanted to guarantee fair treatment for blacks, who made up 75% of the city's bus passengers. The MIA sponsored a boycott of city buses. Despite their dependence on public transportation, African Americans held to the boycott with remarkable solidarity. MIA leaders arranged car pools, and black taxi drivers charged only the ten-cent bus fare to transport black passengers. The boycott lasted for a little over a year; finally, the bus company and the city agreed to desegregate the buses. By this time Dr. King had become a front-page name and was viewed as the spokesman of the civil rights movement.

Prepare to Read

I Have a Dream ◆ *from* Rosa Parks: My Story ◆ There Is a Longing ◆ I Hear America Singing

Take It to the Net

Visit www.phschool.com for interactive activities and instruction related to the selections, including
- background
- graphic organizers
- literary elements
- reading strategies

Preview

Connecting to the Literature

Think of a time when you were inspired by a speech, a work of writing, or even a conversation. Often, as you will see in these selections, we find inspiration in the words of people who challenge us to be the best we can be.

❶ Background

The freedom of speech guaranteed by the United States Constitution is a civil right, a freedom that people are entitled to as members of a society. Some Americans have not always enjoyed these rights and have had to struggle for equality. Their fight—marked by demonstrations and legal challenges—is known as the civil rights movement. It began in the 1950s and was led by figures such as Martin Luther King, Jr., and Rosa Parks.

TEACHING RESOURCES

The following resources can be used to enrich or extend the instruction for pp. 162–163.

Motivation

Interest Grabber Video, Tape 1

Background

Beyond Literature, p. 9 ■

Take It to the Net

Visit www.phschool.com for background and hotlinks for the selections.

Literary Analysis

Literary Analysis and Reading Transparencies, Author's Purpose, p. 18 ■

Reading

Selection Support: Reading Strategy, p. 37; Build Vocabulary, p. 35

Literary Analysis and Reading Transparencies, Responding, p. 17

■ **BLOCK SCHEDULING:** Resources marked with this symbol provide varied instruction during 90-minute blocks.

❷ Literary Analysis

Author's Purpose

An **author's purpose** is his or her reason for writing. For example, an author may want to entertain, inform, or persuade the reader. This example from "I Have a Dream" reveals the author's purpose: to urge all Americans, regardless of background, to accept one another as equals.

> With this faith, we will be able to transform the jangling discords of our nation into a beautiful symphony of brotherhood.

As you read, determine each author's purpose, and evaluate the author's techniques to decide how successfully he or she has conveyed that purpose.

Comparing Literary Works

An author's purpose helps shape his or her **tone**—the attitude toward the subject that an author conveys in a piece of writing. Identify the tone of each piece by looking for words that indicate how the author feels. Try to select adjectives that capture each tone. Then, look at the similarities and differences in the tones of the four selections.

❸ Reading Strategy

Responding

When you read something, you cannot help but **respond,** or react, to it.

- As you read, ask yourself how you are reacting.
- Note your feelings, such as anger or sympathy.
- Look for the words or ideas that have provoked your response.

Use a chart like this one to write down your responses as you read.

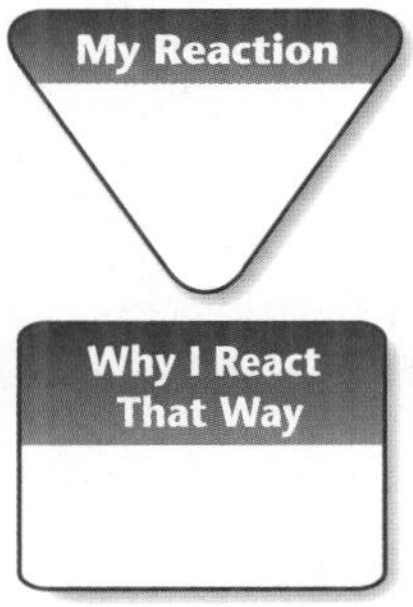

Vocabulary Development

creed (krēd) *n.* statement of belief (p. 165)

oppression (ə presh′ ən) *n.* keeping others down by the unjust use of power (p. 165)

oasis (ō ā′ sis) *n.* fertile place in the desert (p. 165)

exalted (eg zôlt′ əd) *v.* lifted up (p. 165)

prodigious (prə dij′ əs) *adj.* wonderful; of great size (p. 166)

hamlet (ham′ lit) *n.* small village (p. 166)

complied (kəm plīd′) *v.* carried out or fulfilled a request (p. 168)

manhandled (man′ han′ dəld) *v.* treated roughly (p. 169)

determination (dē tʉr′ mi nā′ shən) *n.* firm intention (p. 170)

endurance (en dŏŏr′ əns) *n.* ability to withstand hardship and continue on (p. 170)

CUSTOMIZE INSTRUCTION FOR UNIVERSAL ACCESS

For Special Needs Students	For Less Proficient Readers	For English Learners
Have students read the adapted version from "I Have a Dream" in the **Adapted Reader's Companion.** This version provides basic-level instruction in an interactive format with questions and write-on lines. Completing the adapted version will prepare students to read the selection in the Student Edition.	Have students read the selection in the **Reader's Companion.** This version provides basic-level instruction in an interactive format with questions and write-on lines. After students finish the selection in **Reader's Companion,** have them complete the questions and activities in the Student Edition.	Have students read the adapted version of the selection in the **English Learner's Companion.** This version provides basic-level instruction in an interactive format with questions and write-on lines. Completing the adapted version will prepare students to read the selection in the Student Edition.

❷ Literary Analysis

Author's Purpose

- Tell students that authors always have a reason for writing. Sometimes they write to meet readers' needs—if readers need information, the writer may write to inform. Authors may also write to entertain, to report, to explain, or to persuade.
- Point out that sometimes these purposes are used in combination. For example, information can increase the impact of writing designed to persuade. Persuasive or informative writing can be entertaining.
- Ask if students have ever heard the words "Don't use that tone of voice with me." Tone of voice indicates an attitude. Explain that *tone* in writing shows the author's attitude toward the subject. Have students select adjectives and compare tone, as directed in Comparing Literary Works.
- Ask students to think about the purposes of these selections. Have them consider whether or not they have the same opinion after reading.

❸ Reading Strategy

Responding

- Ask students to sum up in one word their reactions to some of the previous selections in this book, such as "The Cask of Amontillado" or "Casey at the Bat." Ask what aspects of these works made students react and respond the way they did.
- Read the King quotation under "Author's Purpose" aloud. Ask students what their response is. Which words and phrases in this sentence made them respond in this way?
- As students read, have them keep track of their responses to each selection in a chart like the one shown.

Vocabulary Development

- Pronounce each vocabulary word for students, and read the definitions as a class. Have students identify any words with which they are already familiar.

E-Teach

Visit E-Teach at www.phschool.com for teachers' essays on how to teach, with questions and answers.

TEACH

Step-by-Step Teaching Guide for pp. 164–172

CUSTOMIZE INSTRUCTION
For Verbal/Linguistic Learners

"I Have a Dream" makes a tremendous impression on everyone who hears King speak it. If possible, show students the television broadcast of this speech. If this is not possible, have students listen to the audiotape or CD that accompanies the selection. Have students discuss the impact of hearing the speech delivered, rather than simply reading the words on the page.

❶ About the Selection

King blended simple words and images with biblical and political references to urge his audience to strive to eliminate oppression, prejudice, segregation, and injustice.

❷ ▶Critical Viewing

Answer: A huge crowd gathered to hear King. They were willing to put up with discomfort and tiredness to show their support for his message. This suggests that the message was very important to them.

❸ Literary Analysis

Author's Purpose

- Have a volunteer read aloud this paragraph. Ask students what purpose King implies for giving this speech.
  Answer: He implies that he is speaking for the cause of freedom and equality.
- Ask students if King is trying to persuade, to inform, to entertain, or to explain. Or does he have some other purpose? Make sure students support their responses.
  Answer: Because he speaks in generalities, he isn't trying to inform his audience. He speaks about a problem everyone knows about. His subject is serious, so he isn't trying to entertain. He is trying to persuade people that his dream is the right one for the country and that they can all help to make it a reality.

❶ "I Have a Dream"

Martin Luther King, Jr.

TEACHING RESOURCES

The following resources can be used to enrich or extend the instruction for pp. 164–172.

Literary Analysis

Selection Support: Literary Analysis, p. 36

Reading

Listening to Literature Audiocassettes, Side 7 ▪

Listening to Literature Audio CDs, CD 6 ▪

Extension

Fine Art Transparencies, Volume 1, Art Transparencies 3, 13 ▪ (Have students discuss which elements of the selections are illustrated by these two paintings.)

▪ **BLOCK SCHEDULING:** Resources marked with this symbol provide varied instruction during 90-minute blocks.

This speech by Martin Luther King, Jr., was part of the March on Washington, a demonstration demanding civil rights legislation and jobs. The march drew a diverse crowd of 250,000 to Washington, D.C., on August 28, 1963. In a time of unrest, King's televised speech showed the vast potential of interracial cooperation.

. . . I say to you today, my friends, that in spite of the difficulties and frustrations of the moment I still have a dream. It is a dream deeply rooted in the American dream.

4 3 I have a dream that one day this nation will rise up and live out the true meaning of its creed: "We hold these truths to be self-evident; that all men are created equal."

I have a dream that one day on the red hills of Georgia the sons of former slaves and the sons of former slaveowners will be able to sit down together at the table of brotherhood.

I have a dream that one day even the state of Mississippi, a desert state sweltering with the heat of injustice and oppression, will be transformed into an oasis of freedom and justice.

I have a dream that my four little children will one day live in a nation where they will not be judged by the color of their skin but by the content of their character.

I have a dream today.

I have a dream that one day the state of Alabama, whose governor's lips are presently dripping with the words of interposition and nullification,[1] will be transformed into a situation where little black boys and black girls will be able to join hands with little white boys and white girls and walk together as sisters and brothers.

I have a dream today.

5 I have a dream that one day every valley shall be exalted, every hill and mountain shall be made low, the rough places will be made plains, and the crooked places will be made straight, and the glory of the Lord shall be revealed, and all flesh shall see it together.[2]

This is our hope. This is the faith with which I return to the South. With this faith we will be able to transform the jangling discords of our nation into a beautiful symphony of brotherhood. With this faith we will be able to work together, to pray together, to

creed (krēd) *n.* statement of belief

oppression (ə presh′ ən) *n.* keeping others down by the unjust use of power

oasis (ō ā′ sis) *n.* fertile place in the desert

exalted (eg zôlt′ əd) *v.* lifted up

1. **Interposition** (in′ tər pə zish′ ən) **and nullification** (nul′ ə fi kā′ shən) disputed doctrine that a state can reject federal laws considered to be violations of its rights.
2. **every valley . . . all flesh shall see it together** reference to a biblical passage (Isaiah 40:4–5).

2 ◀ **Critical Viewing** What does this photograph tell you about the importance of Dr. King's message to those who heard his speech? Explain. **[Draw Conclusions]**

6 **Reading Check**

What is King's dream for his four children?

4 Vocabulary Development

Latin Root *-cred-*

- Point out the word *creed* in this paragraph. Have a volunteer read the definition in the margin aloud.
- Explain that the Latin root *-cred-* means "belief." Challenge students to list and define other related words that contain this root. If students are having difficulty suggesting words, write on the board the words listed as answers. Then, have students discuss how "belief" contributes to the meaning of each word.
  Answers: credence, credit, credible, incredible, credibility, credo, credentials, credulous, incredulous

5 Literary Analysis

Author's Purpose

- King quotes at some length from the biblical Book of Isaiah. What do students think this suggests about the purpose of his speech? What does this biblical reference lend to King's speech?
  Answer: It shows that the cause of freedom and equality is sacred to him. It shows that he wants to persuade listeners that the cause is holy.

Monitor Progress Point out that in the speech's second paragraph, King quotes the Declaration of Independence. What is his purpose in doing this?
Answer: He makes his cause legitimate by proving that Thomas Jefferson and the other founders believed in equality. He uses the reference to the Declaration to strengthen his case.

6 Reading Check

Answer: King wants his children to be judged on their merits, not on the color of their skin.

CUSTOMIZE INSTRUCTION FOR UNIVERSAL ACCESS

For Gifted/Talented Students

The passage King quotes from the biblical Book of Isaiah appears in the *Messiah,* an oratorio by Georg Friederich Handel. Have students locate a recording of the *Messiah* and listen to "Every Valley" and "The Glory of the Lord." Have them compare Handel's setting of these words with King's use of them. Which do students find more inspirational? Why?

7 Reading Strategy

Responding

- Read aloud the bracketed passage to students.
- Ask students the Reading Strategy question on page 166: What feelings do the words "Let freedom ring" evoke in you? Why?
  Possible answers: These words may evoke feelings of nationalism, national pride, shame at the blots on American history, or exaltation at the thought of bells ringing out the sound of freedom.

Answers for p. 166

Review and Assess

1. Possible answers: Pride, elation, hope, enthusiasm for freedom and friendship
2. **(a)** Any four or more of the following: Georgia, Alabama, Mississippi, Colorado, New Hampshire, New York, Pennsylvania, and California **(b)** Dr. King wants to emphasize the idea that civil rights are the concern of all Americans, no matter where they live.
3. **(a)** King dreams of a society in which people are judged by their character, not their backgrounds. **(b)** King probably suffered from racial discrimination, and probably saw other black people suffer as well.
4. **(a)** "My country, 'tis of thee, sweet land of liberty, of thee I sing. Land where my fathers died, land of the pilgrims' pride, from every mountainside, let freedom ring." **(b)** He reminds everyone that the country was founded on a promise of liberty.
5. **(a)** Students should say it was very persuasive. **(b)** The cause for which King speaks is just, and he speaks well and forcefully.
6. **(a)** The speech has lived on because it was an important point of an important era in history. **(b)** It deserves to be remembered because the goals of freedom and brotherhood are still worthwhile goals.
7. It has not. The country still suffers from racial prejudice.

struggle together, to go to jail together, to stand up for freedom together, knowing that we will be free one day.

This will be the day when all of God's children will be able to sing with new meaning "My country 'tis of thee, sweet land of liberty, of thee I sing. Land where my fathers died, land of the pilgrim's pride, from every mountainside, let freedom ring."

And if America is to be a great nation this must become true. So let freedom ring from the <u>prodigious</u> hilltops of New Hampshire. Let freedom ring from the mighty mountains of New York. Let freedom ring from the heightening Alleghenies of Pennsylvania!

7 Let freedom ring from the snowcapped Rockies of Colorado!

Let freedom ring from the curvaceous peaks of California!

But not only that: let freedom ring from Stone Mountain of Georgia!

Let freedom ring from every hill and molehill of Mississippi. From every mountainside, let freedom ring.

When we let freedom ring, when we let it ring from every village and every <u>hamlet</u>, from every state and every city, we will be able to speed up that day when all of God's children, black men and white men, Jews and Gentiles, Protestants and Catholics, will be able to join hands and sing in the words of that old Negro spiritual, "Free at last! Free at last! Thank God almighty, we are free at last!"

prodigious (prə dij′ əs) *adj.* wonderful; of great size

Reading Strategy
Responding What feelings do the words "Let freedom ring" evoke in you? Why?

hamlet (ham′ lit) *n.* small village

Review and Assess

Thinking About the Selection

1. **Respond:** What feelings does King's speech stir in you?
2. **(a) Recall:** Name at least four states King mentions in his speech. **(b) Infer:** Why do you think he refers to so many parts of the country?
3. **(a) Recall:** In your own words, briefly state King's dream. **(b) Infer:** Based on this dream, what do you think was the reality of King's life?
4. **(a) Recall:** What words does King quote from "My Country 'Tis of Thee"? **(b) Connect:** What message does he send by quoting these lines?
5. **(a) Evaluate:** How persuasive do you think King's speech is? **(b) Support:** What specific aspects of the speech make it so?
6. **(a) Make a Judgment:** Why do you think King's speech has lived on as one of the best-known speeches of all time? **(b) Evaluate:** Does it deserve this standing? Why or why not?
7. **Connect:** Do you think the dream in King's speech has been fully realized today? Support your answer.

Martin Luther King, Jr.

(1929–1968)

Born in Atlanta, Georgia, the son of a minister, Dr. Martin Luther King, Jr., was a dynamic civil rights leader of the twentieth century. During the 1950s and 1960s, King organized nonviolent protests that helped to bring about equal rights for all Americans. His tireless efforts for civil rights inspired people of all races and earned King the 1964 Nobel Peace Prize. At thirty-five, he was the youngest man and only the third black man to be awarded this prestigious honor.

CUSTOMIZE INSTRUCTION FOR UNIVERSAL ACCESS

For English Learners	For Advanced Readers
King's speech refers to several states, such as Mississippi, and geographical features, such as the Alleghenies. Have students find all these places on a map of the United States. Partners can challenge one another until both can spell all these geographical names correctly and give their general location within the U.S.	Have students choose any two works in this group of four and compare and contrast them. What themes do the works have in common? How are the writers' points of view similar or different? What might the two writers say to one another? How might each one respond to the other's poem, speech, or story? Students can write essays answering these and similar questions.

CONNECTIONS
Literature and Music
Voices of Peace

People admire Martin Luther King, Jr., for his courage in preaching nonviolence during a violent era. In the lyrics to "Pride," the Irish rock group U2 pays tribute to King by celebrating his message. As a message that has survived despite King's violent death, it continues to inspire.

Pride
(In The Name Of Love)

Bono and The Edge

One man come in the name of love
One man come and go
One man come, he to justify
One man to overthrow

Chorus:

In the name of love
What more in the name of love
In the name of love
What more in the name of love

One man caught on a barbed wire fence
One man he resist
One man washed on an empty beach
One man betrayed with a kiss

(Chorus)

Early morning, April four
Shot rings out in the Memphis sky
Free at last
They took your life
They could not take your pride

(Chorus)

U2

U2 formed in 1978, basing its sound around the expressive vocals of lead singer Bono (Paul Hewson), the distinctive echoing style of guitarist The Edge (David Evans), and the driving rhythms of bassist Adam Clayton and drummer Larry Mullen, Jr. The band has experimented with many styles over a long career. They have used their lasting popularity to support causes ranging from famine relief to debt forgiveness for developing nations.

Connecting Literature and Music

1. What emotion does this song evoke? Explain.
2. How does the song's message relate to King's message in "I Have a Dream"?
3. (a) Why might U2 have chosen "pride" as the quality that best characterized King? (b) Which characteristic would you choose?

Lesson Objectives

1. To understand the connection between Dr. King's powerful message of nonviolence and his death, which was caused by a violent act
2. To explore pride and other emotions evoked by King's life story

Connections

King's "I Have a Dream" speech conveys one man's courageous vision. U2's "Pride" mourns the death of several courageous men who, over a span of thousands of years, gave their lives for their causes. After students read "Pride," have them reread "I Have a Dream," identifying parts of the speech that illustrate this line of the song: "They could not take your pride."

Voices of Peace

- Point out that the lyrics of the song "Pride" compare the sacrifice of King's life to that of other martyrs for causes throughout the ages.
- Explain that the betrayal by a kiss refers to the betrayal of Jesus by Judas, which set in motion events that led to Jesus' eventual death on a cross.
- Point out that both works address the qualities of pride and courage. The speech exemplifies these attributes, while the poem praises these qualities even as it expresses sadness about the outcome.

Answers

Connecting Literature and Music

1. The song evokes emotions of sadness and anger.
2. The song validates King's dream in that it states that even death cannot destroy the causes King supported in life.
3. **(a)** Students may say that U2 chose pride because of King's confidence in African Americans and their ability to succeed and be free. **(b)** Student responses might include courage or leadership.

❽ About the Selection

Rosa Parks's small act of civil disobedience became a turning point for America. Heroism isn't always a great feat or act of physical strength. A quiet act of inner strength can break new ground. Parks writes in the plain style of an ordinary person who, in retrospect, recognizes her impact, but who never meant to be a symbol. The calm way she tells what happened on a Montgomery city bus in 1955 shows how her personal experiences and values led her to act on her beliefs.

❾ Literary Analysis

Author's Purpose

- After students have read the first paragraph, ask what they think the author's purpose is in writing. Which details support students' answers?
  Answer: She wants to inform readers what happened on the evening of December 1. She tells her story matter-of-factly, including details, in chronological order. She doesn't speculate, persuade, or question, she simply narrates facts.
- Ask the Literary Analysis question on p. 168: Why do you think Rosa Parks included this background information in her story of the encounter on the bus?
  Answer: It seems likely that Parks included the information to show how segregation laws affected bus riding, and to underscore the fact the she didn't get on the bus intending to make trouble. She was even sitting in the designated black section. It also suggests that, if the mean-looking driver hadn't been there, the incident might not have happened.

❿ ▶Critical Viewing

The picture shows both a man and a woman, one white and one black, seated near one another on a bus.

❽

from Rosa Parks: My Story

Rosa Parks (with Jim Haskins)

The Beginning, Artis Lane

❾ When I got off from work that evening of December 1, I went to Court Square as usual to catch the Cleveland Avenue bus home. I didn't look to see who was driving when I got on, and by the time I recognized him, I had already paid my fare. It was the same driver who had put me off the bus back in 1943, twelve years earlier. He was still tall and heavy, with red, rough-looking skin. And he was still mean-looking. I didn't know if he had been on that route before—they switched the drivers around sometimes. I do know that most of the time if I saw him on a bus, I wouldn't get on it.

I saw a vacant seat in the middle section of the bus and took it. I didn't even question why there was a vacant seat even though there were quite a few people standing in the back. If I had thought about it at all, I would probably have figured maybe someone saw me get on and did not take the seat but left it vacant for me. There was a man sitting next to the window and two women across the aisle.

The next stop was the Empire Theater, and some whites got on. They filled up the white seats, and one man was left standing. The driver looked back and noticed the man standing. Then he looked back at us. He said, "Let me have those front seats," because they were the front seats of the black section. Didn't anybody move. We just sat right where we were, the four of us. Then he spoke a second time: "Y'all better make it light on yourselves and let me have those seats."

The man in the window seat next to me stood up, and I moved to let him pass by me, and then I looked across the aisle and saw that the two women were also standing. I moved over to the window seat. I could not see how standing up was going to "make it light" for me. The more we gave in and complied, the worse they treated us.

I thought back to the time when I used to sit up all night and didn't

❿ **▲ Critical Viewing** How does this painting reflect the ideal of equal rights for all people? **[Analyze]**

Literary Analysis
Author's Purpose Why do you think Rosa Parks included this background information in her story of the encounter on the bus?

complied (kəm plīd´) *v.* carried out or fulfilled a request

ENRICHMENT: Social Studies Connection

Jackie Robinson

In the decades before the Montgomery bus boycott, African Americans could not sit with whites on buses nor play professional baseball with them. The first African American major leaguer, catcher Moses "Fleetwood" Walker, had been forced out of the major leagues in the 1880s by prejudice. In 1947, infielder Jackie Robinson of the Negro League Kansas City Monarchs became the first modern African American to play in the major leagues. Robinson's great talents helped him surmount the racism displayed by both fans and players, even some of his own teammates. Because baseball was so popular, Robinson's success story was highly visible to everyone and constituted a clear message that African Americans were the equals of whites in merit and talent. Although it was only a game, baseball played an important role in the civil rights movement.

sleep, and my grandfather would have his gun right by the fireplace, or if he had his one-horse wagon going anywhere, he always had his gun in the back of the wagon. People always say that I didn't give up my seat because I was tired, but that isn't true. I was not tired physi-
11 cally, or no more tired than I usually was at the end of a working day. I was not old, although some people have an image of me as being old then.

I was forty-two. No, the only tired I was, was tired of giving in.

The driver of the bus saw me still sitting there, and he asked was I going to stand up.

I said, "No." He said, "Well, I'm going to have you arrested." Then I said, "You may do that." These were the only words we said to each other. I didn't even know his name, which was James Blake, until we were in court together. He got out of the bus and stayed outside for a few minutes, waiting for the police.

As I sat there, I tried not to think about what might happen. I knew that anything was possible. I could be manhandled or beaten. I could be arrested. People have asked me if it occurred to me then that I could be the test case the NAACP[1] had been looking for. I did not think about that at all. In fact if I had let myself think too deeply about what might happen to me, I might have gotten off the bus. But I chose to remain.

Reading Strategy
Responding What is your reaction to this quotation by Rosa Parks: "No, the only tired I was, was tired of giving in"? Why?

manhandled (man′ han′ dəld) *v.* treated roughly

1. **NAACP** *abbr.* National Association for the Advancement of Colored People.

Review and Assess

Thinking About the Selection

1. **Respond:** What do you think about Rosa Parks's actions? Explain.
2. **(a) Recall:** In which section did Rosa Parks sit on the bus? **(b) Interpret:** Why did the bus driver ask the people in her row to give up their seats?
3. **(a) Recall:** Summarize her memory of her grandfather. **(b) Interpret:** How does her childhood memory affect her action that day, many years later?
4. **(a) Recall:** What reason does Rosa Parks give for staying in her seat? **(b) Interpret:** How did her refusal to stand up contribute to the civil rights movement?
5. **Compare and Contrast:** Both Rev. King and Rosa Parks helped win equality for minorities. How are their actions similar and different?
6. **Speculate:** Do you think that if Rosa Parks had given up her seat, integration would have taken place anyway? Explain.

Rosa Parks

(b. 1913)

In 1955, Rosa Parks was arrested for breaking an unjust law—she refused to give up her seat on a public bus to a white man. This incident sparked a boycott that led to the end of segregation on the Montgomery bus system. Her courageous action marked the start of the civil rights movement. In 1999, she was granted the Congressional Gold Medal. This is the highest honor given to a civilian in the United States.

CUSTOMIZE INSTRUCTION FOR UNIVERSAL ACCESS

For Special Needs Students	For Gifted/Talented Students
Have students make timelines of the event Rosa Parks describes. What happens first? What happens next? How much time elapses over the course of her story? Which two events of the long past does she refer to in brief flashbacks of memory? In what order did these two events happen? Students can work with partners to put the story events in correct chronological order.	Have students work together on a classroom display of important figures of the civil rights movement. Remind them to consider white people who played major roles, too. You may want to give students a few suggestions of names to research, such as Marian Anderson, Thurgood Marshall, and W.E.B. DuBois. The display should include portraits of the people and brief descriptions of their contributions to the civil rights movement.

11 Reading Strategy

Responding

- Remind students that responding is a reaction or feeling. Suggest that an emotional response can lead to further evaluation of information. This may in turn create deeper understanding.
- Ask students the Reading Strategy question on p. 169: What is your reaction to this quotation by Rosa Parks: "No, the only tired I was, was tired of giving in"? Why?
Answer: Most students should understand and sympathize with Parks.

Answers for p. 169

Review and Assess

1. Students will probably admire her for standing up for her beliefs.
2. **(a)** She sat in the front row of the black section. **(b)** All the seats in the white section were full and a white man was standing.
3. **(a)** Parks remembers her grandfather carrying a gun to protect himself and his family. **(b)** She knew it was wrong for her grandfather to always have been afraid, and she was determined to do her part to eliminate black people's fear.
4. **(a)** She says she was tired of giving in. **(b)** It was the test case that the NAACP had been looking for, and it triggered the boycott of the Montgomery bus system.
5. Rosa Parks was a quiet hero who simply did what she thought was right for herself on one given day. King took a public leadership position and used it to persuade everyone to end segregation.
6. Integration would certainly have taken place anyway because segregation was unconstitutional and more and more people were uncomfortable with segregation.

12 About the Selection

Chief Dan George believes that Native Americans must ensure their survival and their standing in today's world by acknowledging their ancient heritage and pride in traditional values as they also work to embrace what is best of "the white man's success."

13 Literary Analysis

Author's Purpose

- Ask students what Chief Dan George hopes to inspire in his people about their future.
  Answer: He wants them to work hard to grasp the best of both worlds, to succeed and become a vital part of society, participating in business, government, and education.
- At the end of the first section, ask students to whom they think the chief is addressing these words, and why they think so.
  Possible answer: He is addressing a non-Native American audience, because he doesn't refer to his people as "you," but as "they."

14 Reading Strategy

Responding

- Ask the Reading Strategy question on p. 170: What do you think is the most persuasive part of the writer's message?
  Possible answer: His comment that, by pursuing education and other new "tools," he can build his people into the proudest segment of society.
- Ask students how they respond to the invocation to the Great Spirit in lines 20–25.
  Answer: Students may find this rather startling. It may sweep some along because it is fervent. Others may find it touching or moving.

12 There Is a Longing

Chief Dan George

13 There is a longing in the heart of my people to reach out and grasp that which is needed for our survival. There is a longing among the young of my nation to secure for themselves and their people the skills that will provide them with a sense of worth and purpose. They will be our new warriors. Their training will be much longer and more demanding than it was in olden days. The long years of study will demand more <u>determination</u>; separation from home and family will demand <u>endurance</u>. But they will emerge with their hand held forward, not to receive welfare, but to grasp the place in society that is rightly ours.

I am a chief, but my power to make war is gone, and the only weapon left to me is speech. It is only with tongue and speech that I can fight my people's war.

14 Oh, Great Spirit![1] Give me back the courage of the olden Chiefs. Let me wrestle with my surroundings. Let me once again, live in harmony with my environment. Let me humbly accept this new culture and through it rise up and go on. Like the thunderbird[2] of old, I shall rise again out of the sea; I shall grab the instruments

determination (dē tʉr´ mi nā´ shən) *n.* firm intention

endurance (en do͝or´ əns) *n.* ability to withstand hardship and continue on

Reading Strategy
Responding What do you think is the most persuasive part of the writer's message?

---

1. **Great Spirit** for many Native Americans, the greatest power or god.
2. **thunderbird** a powerful supernatural creature that was thought to produce thunder by flapping its wings and produce lightning by opening and closing its eyes. In the folklore of some Native American nations, the thunderbird is in constant warfare with the powers beneath the waters.

We the People, Kathy Morrow, Courtesy of the artist

of the white man's success—his
education, his skills. With these new tools
I shall build my race into the proudest
segment of your society. I shall see our
young braves and our chiefs sitting in
the houses of law and government, ruling
and being ruled by the knowledge and
freedoms of *our* great land.

⓰ ▲ Critical Viewing Which images in this painting reflect ideas found in the poem? **[Interpret]**

Review and Assess

Thinking About the Selection

1. **Respond:** How did you feel as you read "There Is a Longing"? Explain.
2. **(a) Recall:** What does Chief Dan George say is his community's longing? **(b) Draw Conclusions:** What is his greatest fear?
3. **(a) Recall:** What is the training the new warriors will have to endure? **(b) Analyze:** Why does Chief Dan George think this training is necessary?
4. **(a) Infer:** In what way is Chief Dan George different from his predecessors? **(b) Interpret:** What does the chief mean by fighting a war "with tongue and speech"?
5. **(a) Analyze:** In what ways does Chief Dan George believe the Great Spirit will help his people? **(b) Deduce:** What do you think the Chief himself will have to do to help them?
6. **Assess:** Do you think the Chief's goal of achieving success through education and skills is the best means for improving his people's lives? Explain.

Chief Dan George

(1899–1981)

Chief Dan George had many careers, including actor and writer. Chief of a Salish Band of Native Americans in British Columbia, Canada, he was deeply concerned about developing mutual respect between Native Americans and other North Americans. As an actor, he accepted only roles that presented Native Americans with dignity. As a writer and public speaker, he emphasized respect and understanding among people.

⓯ Background

Art

We the People, by Kathy Morrow

Kathy Morrow grew up on Apache and Sioux reservations, where her father trained Native American police forces. Her title is taken from the preamble to the United States Constitution: "We, the people of the United States of America. . . ."

1. How does this work convey a sense of longing and determination?
   Answer: Students may observe that the outstretched hands convey a sense of reaching out. The movement of the eagle seems focused, and follows the direction of the reaching.
2. Why do you think Morrow titled her painting with a quotation from the Constitution?
   Answer: She wanted to show that Native Americans are part of "we the people."

⓰ ▶Critical Viewing

Answer: The painting illustrates the blending of old and new traditions. It illustrates the chief's wish that his people be "the proudest segment of your society . . . ruling and being ruled by the knowledge and freedoms of our great land."

Answers for p. 171

Review and Assess

1. Students may have been touched, moved, or impressed by the dignity of the poem and the intelligence of the proposed solutions.
2. **(a)** His people long to take their place in society. **(b)** He fears that he may not have the courage and wisdom of chiefs from the past.
3. **(a)** They will need many years of school so that they can work as doctors, teachers, and so on. **(b)** He wants his people to have every opportunity that white people have; there is no opportunity without education.
4. **(a)** He can only fight with words while they fought with weapons. Also, he does not live in the old traditional ways. **(b)** He means that he can make speeches and use reason and logic as his weapons.

continued

Answers continued

5. **(a)** He believes that the Great Spirit will give him courage and help him lead his people and build them up. **(b)** He will have to encourage, support, and lead them.
6. If his people follow his suggestions, their lives will be improved; they will be able to find fulfilling and challenging jobs and they will be able to help their families.

(17) About the Selection

This early poem appears in the opening section of Whitman's monumental *Leaves of Grass.* The speaker celebrates the common working men and women of America.

(18) Literary Analysis

Author's Purpose

Reteach Remind students that paying careful attention to an author's choice of words can help them determine the purpose for writing.

- Ask students the Literary Analysis question on p. 172: Which word in the opening lines helps identify Whitman's purpose?
  Answer: The word "singing" explains Whitman's purpose. He wants his readers to celebrate the songs of the workers.

Answers for p. 172

Review and Assess

1. Students' responses will vary, depending on their interests. Explanations will probably connect "songs" with hobbies, acquaintances, or goals.
2. **(a)** "Singers" include mechanics, carpenter, mason, boatman, deckhand, shoemaker, hatter, wood-cutter, ploughboy, mother, wife, girl, and party of young fellows. **(b)** He means that he is aware of the pleasure they take in being alive, being busy, and having work that they like.
3. **(a)** The mason sings in the morning or evening. The ploughboy sings in the morning, at noon, or at sundown. **(b)** Whitman understood the rhythm and flow of life. It is these daily changes that create the rhythm of the "songs."
4. Whitman depicts a strong, happy, hard-working nation. He also shows that this is a land of opportunities, that all work is honorable, and that everyone contributes to making the country strong.
5. All the jobs Whitman lists still exist by the thousands; however, not so many people today work with their hands.

(17) I Hear America Singing

Walt Whitman

(18)
I hear America singing, the varied carols I hear,
Those of mechanics, each one singing his as it should be
 blithe and strong,
The carpenter singing his as he measures his plank or beam,
The mason singing his as he makes ready for work, or
 leaves off work,
The boatman singing what belongs to him in his boat, the
 deckhand singing on the steamboat deck,
The shoemaker singing as he sits on his bench, the hatter
 singing as he stands,
The wood-cutter's song, the ploughboy's on his way in the
 morning, or at noon intermission or at sundown,
The delicious singing of the mother, or of the young wife at
 work, or of the girl sewing or washing,
Each singing what belongs to him or her and to none else,
The day what belongs to the day—at night the party of
 young fellows, robust, friendly,
Singing with open mouths their strong melodious songs.

Literary Analysis
Author's Purpose Which word in the opening lines helps identify Whitman's purpose?

Walt Whitman

(1819–1892)
Walt Whitman, one of America's greatest poets, was a lover of democracy and a champion of the common individual. Part of Whitman's mission as a poet was to inspire and vitalize the United States through the ecstatic vision of democratic life. His expansive vision and spirit are reflected in "I Hear America Singing."

Review and Assess

Thinking About the Selection

1. **Respond:** Which of the "songs" speaks to you the most? Explain.
2. **(a) Recall:** Identify three singers Whitman names.
   (b) Interpret: What does Whitman mean when he says that he hears their songs?
3. **(a) Recall:** When does the mason sing? The ploughboy?
   (b) Distinguish: Why do you think Whitman pictures the American worker in various situations and times of day?
4. **Generalize:** What kind of nation does Whitman depict?
5. **Speculate:** Do you think modern-day America is similar to the world Whitman presents? Why or why not?

ASSESSMENT PRACTICE: Reading Comprehension

Chronological Order (For more practice, see Test Preparation Workbook, p. 9.)

Many tests require students to arrange events in chronological order. Use the following sample test item to give students practice at this skill. Have students read p. 168 of "Rosa Parks: My Story." Then write the question and answer choices on the board:

Which of these did Rosa Parks do first?

A wondered if the driver had been reassigned
B recognized the driver
C paid her fare
D took a seat

Since Rosa Parks says she paid her fare before recognizing the driver, the correct answer is *C*.

Review and Assess

Literary Analysis

Author's Purpose

1. Choose one of the selections you have just read. Using a chart like the one shown here, note details of content and style that help you determine the **author's purpose.**

Content	Style		Author's Purpose
		→	

2. How does King's use of repetition help to achieve his purpose?
3. Chief Dan George voices his appeal for his people's future. To whom is he speaking? Native Americans? Others? Explain.

Comparing Literary Works

4. (a) Analyze each writer's **tone** by completing a chart like the one shown here. For each selection, note words that reflect the writer's attitude toward the subject. Then, select a single adjective to identify the writer's tone. (b) In what ways does each writer use tone to emphasize the importance of his or her subject?

	Word Choice	
King		Parks
Chief Dan George		Whitman

5. Both King and Parks write about the civil rights movement in the United States. (a) How are the tones of the two pieces different? (b) What is the reason for this difference?

Reading Strategy

Responding

6. Choose one "carol" from "I Hear America Singing" and explain the **response** it generated in you.
7. Which selection provoked the strongest response in you? Explain.

Extend Understanding

8. **Social Studies Connection:** Do the ideas and issues in these selections still hold true today? Explain.

Quick Review

An **author's purpose** is his or her reason for writing.

The **tone** of a piece of writing is the author's attitude toward the subject.

When you **respond** to what you read, you acknowledge your personal reaction to the writing.

Take It to the Net

www.phschool.com

Take the interactive self-test online to check your understanding of these selections.

ENRICHMENT: Further Reading

Other Works by the Authors

Works by Walt Whitman
Leaves of Grass

Works by Chief Dan George
My Heart Soars

Works by Rosa Parks
Quiet Strength

Take It to the Net

Visit www.phschool.com for more information on the selections.

ASSESS

Answers for p. 173

Review and Assess

1. Possible response for Whitman:

Content	catalog of American workers
Style	free verse, long lines, repetition
Author's Purpose	to celebrate the common worker's joy and pride in his or her work

2. When words and phrases are repeated, it is more likely that listeners will remember them. With every repetition of a key phrase, King impresses his hopes for America more fully on his listeners.
3. Chief Dan George addresses the Great Spirit directly. The poem is an invocation or prayer to this spirit.
4. **(a)** Sample answers: King: "I have a dream," "let freedom ring." Adjective: inspirational. Parks: "I was tired of giving in." Adjective: informative. Chief Dan George: "longing," "courage," "humbly accept." Adjective: pleading. Whitman: "singing," "strong melodious songs." Adjective: celebrating. **(b)** King's tone is inspirational, encouraging listeners to pursue his dream. Parks's tone is informative, reporting facts. Chief Dan George's tone is pleading and promising because he is asking for spiritual help. Whitman's tone is celebratory, emphasizing the nobility of the workers.
5. Parks's tone is informative. She is simply describing her experience. She is modest. King's tone is inspirational. He is trying to convince his listeners to act.
6. Sample answer: The mechanics' carols lifted the readers' spirits because each one was "blithe and strong."
7. Answers will vary. Make sure students refer to specific details of their chosen selections.
8. Students will probably say yes. People in all societies hope for freedom, justice, and equal treatment.

EXTEND

Answers for p. 174

❶ Vocabulary Development

Word Analysis

Possible responses:

a. "You never give me any credit for the work I do, "she said angrily.

b. His statement that the dog had eaten his homework was incredible.

c. The officer had to show her credentials before the baker let her in.

d. Because she had not seen the events and didn't know anyone involved, her comments about the situation lacked credibility.

Spelling Strategy

1. sensory **3.** likable
2. imaginary **4.** driving

Concept Development: Synonyms and Antonyms

1. A **6.** A
2. A **7.** S
3. A **8.** S
4. S **9.** A
5. S **10.** S

❷ Grammar

1. L: am, is
2. A: hear (twice)
3. A: have, L: shall be
4. A: shall build
5. L: was; A: put

Writing Application

Have students exchange papers with partners and check one another's work. Partners can go over papers together and resolve any disagreements by referring to **Writing and Grammar** Gold Level.

Integrate Language Skills

❶ Vocabulary Development Lesson

Word Analysis: Latin Root *-cred-*

Creed comes from the Latin verb *credere*, which means "to believe." Applying the meaning of *-cred-*, use each of the following words in a sentence.

a. credit **c.** credentials
b. incredible **d.** credibility

Spelling Strategy

Before adding a suffix beginning with a vowel to a word that ends in silent *e*, you usually drop the *e*. For example, when adding the suffix *-ance* to *endure*, the silent *e* is dropped and the word becomes *endurance*. Write the correct spelling of the following words. Then, write a sentence using each new word.

1. sense + *-ory* **3.** like + *-able*
2. imagine + *-ary* **4.** drive + *-ing*

Concept Development: Synonyms and Antonyms

Synonyms are words with similar meanings, such as *happy* and *cheerful*. Antonyms are words with opposite meanings, such as *light* and *dark*. Identify the relationships of the following word pairs. Use **S** for synonyms and **A** for antonyms.

1. creed, statement of doubt
2. oppression, liberty
3. oasis, desert
4. exalted, dignified
5. prodigious, remarkable
6. hamlet, city
7. complied, obeyed
8. manhandled, shoved
9. determination, weakness
10. endurance, stamina

❷ Grammar Lesson

Action and Linking Verbs

Action verbs express physical or mental actions, like *jump* or *think*. In contrast, **linking verbs,** including forms of the verb *be*, express a state of being. They connect the subject to a word that renames or describes the subject.

Action verbs: I *saw* a seat and *took* it.

Linking verbs: I *was* tired of giving in.

Practice Copy the following sentences from the selections. Underline the action verbs and circle the linking verbs.

1. I am a chief, but my power is gone.
2. I hear America singing, the varied carols I hear.
3. I have a dream that one day every valley shall be exalted.
4. I shall build my race into the proudest segment of your society.
5. It was the same driver who had put me off the bus back in 1943, twelve years earlier.

Writing Application Write a paragraph about a person whose words or actions inspire you. Circle the verbs you have chosen, and then identify whether each is an action or a linking verb.

WG Prentice Hall Writing and Grammar Connection: Chapter 17, Sections 1 and 2

TEACHING RESOURCES

The following resources can be used to enrich or extend the instructions for pp. 174–175.

Vocabulary

Selection Support, Build Vocabulary, p. 33

Vocabulary and Spelling Practice Book (Use this booklet for skills enrichment.) ■

Grammar

Selection Support: Build Grammar Skills, p. 34

Writing and Grammar, Gold Level, p. 362

Daily Language Practice Transparencies

Writing

Writing and Grammar, Gold Level, p. 134 ■

Writing and Grammar iText CD-ROM

Writing Models and Graphic Organizers on Transparencies, pp. 17–20

■ **BLOCK SCHEDULING:** Resources marked with this symbol provide varied instruction during 90-minute blocks.

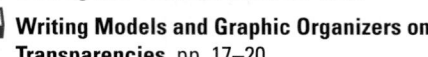

❸ Writing Lesson

Proposal for a School Speaker

Consider the benefit of having a great speaker, like Martin Luther King, Jr., speak at your school. Write a proposal to your principal, presenting a persuasive argument in favor of inviting a specific speaker to a school assembly.

Prewriting Think about problems that your classmates face daily, and consider the ways a speaker might address them. Make a list of potential speakers, and describe the benefit that each speech would provide.

Model: Gathering Evidence

Speaker	Benefit speaker will provide
Toni Morrison	Her success could inspire students to express themselves through writing.

Drafting As you draft, explain how the speaker you have chosen could help address important issues in your school. End with an appeal that will convince the principal to act on your proposal.

Revising Review your proposal to see that your examples are persuasive and simply stated. Check your final paragraph to be sure that you end with an appeal noting the benefits of the speaker's visit.

WG *Prentice Hall Writing and Grammar Connection: Chapter 7, Section 2*

❹ Extension Activities

Listening and Speaking Compose a **radio news report** in which you provide on-the-spot coverage of King's speech and explain his dream for America. Include the following in your report:

- background information about the civil rights movement
- excerpts from King's speech
- description of the effect it had on the crowd

Share your report with your class. Tape-record yourself while broadcasting so that you can evaluate your work later.

Research and Technology In a group, create a **multimedia presentation** on a single aspect of the American civil rights movement, such as laws, marches, or specific leaders. Assemble photographs for your presentation, as well as video or audio recordings of civil rights speeches and events. Present your findings to your class. **[Group Activity]**

Take It to the Net www.phschool.com

Go online for an additional research activity using the Internet.

❸ Writing Lesson

- Go around the room and have each student name the person he or she would like to invite to speak. Remind students that these people should be well-known. You may want to limit their choices to living people, but encourage them to consider people from outside the United States.
- Lead students through the drafting and revising process using the Descriptive and Observational Writing model on pp. 17–20 of the **Writing Models and Graphic Organizers on Transparencies.** Emphasize the need for organization and for supporting points.
- Use the rubric for Persuasive Composition on p. 10 in **Performance Assessment and Portfolio Management** to evaluate students' work.

❹ Extension Activity

Listening and Speaking

- Encourage students to do some further reading about the day King gave the speech. Students can consult biographies of King, such as David J. Garrow's Pulitzer Prize-winning *Bearing the Cross* (1986) for this purpose. Students can also consult encyclopedias and reference books for background about the Civil Rights movement. Encourage them to interview any family members who remember listening to or seeing a broadcast of King's speech.
- You may want to bring in examples of radio news reports to familiarize students with the end product.
- Use the rubric for Delivering a Descriptive Presentation on p. 28 in **Performance Assessment and Portfolio Management** to evaluate students' work.

CUSTOMIZE INSTRUCTION for Universal Access

To address different learning styles, use the following activities suggested in the **Extension Activities** booklet, p. 9.

- For Interpersonal and Verbal/Linguistic Learners, use Activities 4 and 5.
- For Visual/Spatial Learners, use Activity 6.

ASSESSMENT RESOURCES

The following resources can be used to assess students' knowledge and skills.

Selection Assessment

- **Formal Assessment,** pp. 29–31
- **Open Book Test,** pp. 25–27
- **Got It! Assessment Videotapes,** Tape 1
- **Test Bank Software**

Take It to the Net

Visit www.phschool.com for self-tests and additional questions on the selections.

Writing Rubric

- **Performance Assess. and Portfolio Mgmt.,** p. 10

Listening and Speaking Rubric

- **Performance Assess. and Portfolio Mgmt.,** p. 28

PRENTICE HALL ASSESSMENT SYSTEM

- **Workbook**
- **Transparencies**
- **Skill Book**
- **CD-ROM**

The Golden Kite, the Silver Wind

Lesson Objectives and CA Correlations

1. **To analyze and respond to literary elements**
   - Literary Analysis: Fable **R 3.7**
   - Connecting Literary Elements: Dialogue **R 3.4**
2. **To read, comprehend, analyze, and critique a short story**
   - Reading Strategy: Predicting Consequences of Actions
   - Reading Check questions
   - Review and Assess questions
   - Assessment Practice (ATE)
3. **To develop word analysis skills, fluency, and systematic vocabulary**
   - Vocabulary Development Lesson: Latin Word Root: *-clam-* **R 1.1**
4. **To understand and apply written and oral language conventions**
   - Spelling Strategy
   - Grammar Lesson: Compound Verbs **LC 1.3**
5. **To understand and apply appropriate writing and research strategies**
   - Writing Lesson: Persuasive Letter **W 2.4**
   - Extension Activity: Historical Report **W 1.3**
6. **To understand and apply listening and speaking strategies**
   - Extension Activity: Dramatic Interpretation **LS 1.9**

STEP-BY-STEP TEACHING GUIDE	PACING GUIDE
PRETEACH	
Motivate Students and Provide Background	
Use the Motivation activity (ATE p. 176)	5 min.
Read and discuss the Preview material and Background information (SE/ATE p. 176) [A]	10 min.
Introduce the Concepts	
Introduce the Literary Analysis and Reading Strategy (SE/ATE p. 177) [A]	15 min.
Pronounce the vocabulary words and read their definitions (SE p. 177)	5 min.
TEACH	
Monitor Comprehension	
Informally monitor comprehension by circulating while students read independently or in groups [A]	20 min.
Monitor students' comprehension with the Reading Check notes (SE/ATE pp. 179, 181)	as students read
Develop vocabulary with Vocabulary notes (SE pp. 179, 180; ATE p. 180)	as students read
Develop Understanding	
Develop students' understanding of fables with the Literary Analysis annotations (SE/ATE pp. 179, 181, 182) [A]	10 min.
Develop students' ability to predict the consequences of actions with the Reading Strategy annotation (SE/ATE p. 180)	10 min.
ASSESS	
Assess Mastery	
Assess students' mastery of the Reading Strategy and Literary Analysis by having them answer the Review and Assess questions (SE/ATE p. 183)	20 min.
Use one or more of the print and media Assessment Resources (ATE p. 185) [A]	up to 50 min.
EXTEND	
Apply Understanding	
Have students complete the Vocabulary Development Lesson and the Grammar Lesson (SE p. 184) [A]	20 min.
Apply students' knowledge of evaluating support for an argument with the Writing Lesson (SE p. 185) [A]	45 min.
Apply students' understanding using one or more of the Extension Activities (SE p. 185)	20–90 min.

[A] ACCELERATED INSTRUCTION: Use the strategies and activities identified with an [A].

UNIVERSAL ACCESS
● = Below-Level Students
▲ = On-Level Students
■ = Above-Level Students

Time and Resource Manager

Reading Level: Average
Average Number of Instructional Days: 4

RESOURCES		
PRINT	**TRANSPARENCIES**	**TECHNOLOGY**
• **Beyond Literature,** Cross-Curricular Connection: Social Studies, p. 10 ▲ ■		• **Interest Grabber Video,** Tape 1 ● ▲ ■
• **Selection Support Workbook:** ● ▲ ■ Literary Analysis, p. 40 Reading Strategy, p. 39 Build Vocabulary, p. 37	• **Literary Analysis and Reading Transparencies,** pp. 19 and 20 ● ▲ ■	
• **Authors In Depth,** Gold Level ■		• **Listening to Literature** ● ▲ ■ Audiocassettes, Side 7 Audio CDs, CD 6
• **Literatura en español** ● ▲ • **Literary Analysis for Enrichment** ■		
• **Formal Assessment:** Selection Test, pp. 32–34 ● ▲ ■ • **Open Book Test,** pp. 28–30 ● ▲ ■ • **Performance Assessment and Portfolio Management,** pp. 10, 27 ● ▲ ■ • PRENTICE HALL ASSESSMENT SYSTEM ● ▲ ■	• PRENTICE HALL ASSESSMENT SYSTEM ● ▲ ■ Skills Practice Answers and Explanations on Transparencies	• **Test Bank Software** ● ▲ ■ • **Got It! Assessment Videotapes,** Tape 1 ● ▲
• **Selection Support Workbook:** ● ▲ ■ Build Grammar Skills, p. 38 • **Writing and Grammar,** Gold Level ● ▲ ■ • **Extension Activities,** p. 10 ● ▲ ■	• **Daily Language Practice Transparencies** ● ▲ • **Writing Models and Graphic Organizers on Transparencies,** pp. 71–73 ● ▲ ■	• **Writing and Grammar iText CD-ROM** ● ▲ ■ ***Take It to the Net*** www.phschool.com

BLOCK SCHEDULING: Use one 90-minute class period to preteach the selection and have students read it. Use a second 90-minute class period to assess students' mastery of skills and have them complete one of the Extension Activities.

PRETEACH

Step-by-Step Teaching Guide for pp. 176–177

Motivation

Initiate a discussion of rivalry. Include questions like these: How do rivals behave toward one another? How far will rivals go to outdo one another? What kinds of outcomes can result from a rivalry? Students may answer these questions in terms of actual experience. Explain that they are about to read a story of the unexpected results of a rivalry.

Interest Grabber Video

As an alternative, play "The Cold War Era" on Tape 1 to engage student interest.

1 Background

The Cold War is called "cold" because no fighting was involved. The Cold War was a standoff between the U.S. and the Soviet Union, which were the only great powers in the world at the end of World War II. One of the most dramatic episodes in the Cold War was the Cuban missile crisis. When U.S. reconnaissance planes discovered Soviet nuclear missiles in Cuba in October 1962, the world waited tensely for a nuclear strike. However, President John F. Kennedy and Premier Nikita Khrushchev resolved the situation without a shot being fired or a bomb being dropped.

Prepare to Read

The Golden Kite, the Silver Wind

Rectangular Box, Avery Brundage Collection, Asian Art Museum of San Francisco

Take It to the Net

Visit www.phschool.com for interactive activities and instruction related to "The Golden Kite, The Silver Wind," including

- background
- graphic organizers
- literary elements
- reading strategies

Preview

Connecting to the Literature

Have you and a friend ever tried to outdo each other? The two of you may have become consumed by rivalry, but most likely, no one else was hurt as a result of it. In this story, a rivalry becomes so intense that it leads to widespread suffering.

1 Background

"The Golden Kite, the Silver Wind" was written during the Cold War, a period of intense rivalry between the United States and the former Soviet Union. During this time, each action by one country—the creation of a weapon, the launching of a satellite—was countered by a reaction from the other country. As you read, think about the parallels between the story events and the history of the Cold War.

TEACHING RESOURCES

The following resources can be used to enrich or extend the instruction for pp. 176–177.

Motivation

Interest Grabber Video, Tape 1 ■

Background

Beyond Literature, p. 10

Take It to the Net

Visit www.phschool.com for background and hotlinks for "The Golden Kite, the Silver Wind."

Literary Analysis

Literary Analysis and Reading Transparencies, Fable, p. 20 ■

Reading

Selection Support: Reading Strategy, p. 39; Build Vocabulary, p. 37

Literary Analysis and Reading Transparencies, Predicting Consequences of Actions, p. 19

■ **BLOCK SCHEDULING:** Resources marked with this symbol provide varied instruction during 90-minute blocks.

❷ Literary Analysis

Fable

"The Golden Kite, the Silver Wind" is a **fable,** a brief story that teaches a lesson. This lesson, or moral, may be directly stated, or it may be shown through the choices the characters make. In this fable, the actions of two rival towns teach a lesson about the value of cooperation over competition. The following example from the story highlights the unhealthy competition existing between the towns.

> "They build their wall," said the Mandarin, "in the shape of a pig! Do you see? Our own city wall is built in the shape of an orange. That pig will devour us, greedily!"

As you read, consider what lesson can be learned from this fable.

Connecting Literary Elements

A **dialogue** is a conversation between characters. As a complement to a writer's narration, dialogue is used to reveal more about a character and to advance action in a story. In this story, the dialogue quickens the action, introduces each Mandarin's tactics, and helps reveal the lesson of the fable.

❸ Reading Strategy

Predicting Consequences of Actions

Try to **predict the consequences of each action** in a story by considering events that have already occurred. Then, read on to see whether your predictions were correct. To help you, follow these suggestions:

- Write down each event as it occurs.
- Before you read further, predict the consequences of that event.
- Look for a pattern that will lead you to the moral of the story.

Use a chart like the one shown to help you predict as you read.

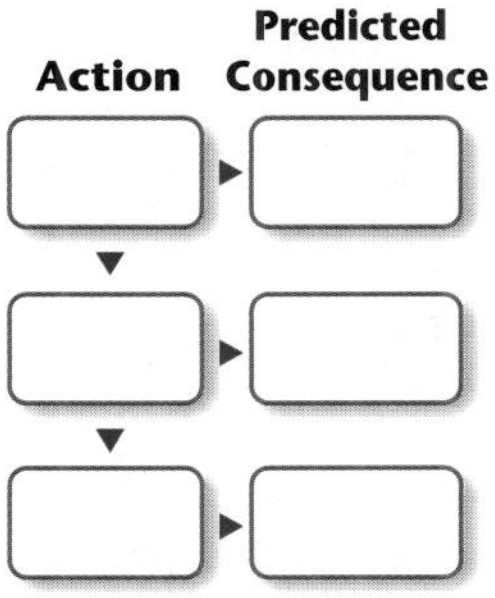

Vocabulary Development

portents (pôr′ tentz) *n.* things that are thought to be signs of events to come; omens (p. 179)

vile (vīl) *adj.* evil; wicked (p. 179)

ravenous (rav′ ə nəs) *adj.* greedily hungry (p. 179)

acclaimed (ə klāmd′) *v.* greeted with loud applause or approval (p. 180)

pandemonium (pan′ də mōn′ nē əm) *n.* wild disorder, noise, or confusion (p. 180)

spurn (spurn) *v.* reject in a scornful way (p. 180)

CUSTOMIZE INSTRUCTION FOR UNIVERSAL ACCESS

For Less Proficient Readers	For English Learners	For Advanced Readers
As they read, have students compare and contrast this story with any fable they know well. In what ways is this story a typical fable? In what ways is it unlike other fables?	Have students compare and contrast this fable with fables from their own cultures. Do any stories from their cultures teach the same lesson as this story? If so, how are the two stories different?	As students read, have them watch for characteristics of a fable. In particular, have them think about the possible symbolic meaning of the walls, the cities, the characters and their relationships, and so on.

❷ Literary Analysis

Fable

- Have students read the definition of the term *fable* in their textbooks. Ask them to give examples of fables they have read.
- Point out that many familiar fables, like "The Fox and the Crow" and "The Ant and the Grasshopper" have been retold to every new generation since ancient times. Because fables teach simple lessons about getting along, they apply to all times and places.
- Make sure students understand that the moral, or lesson, of the fable may be stated directly or shown through the choices (both good and bad) that the characters make. As they read, encourage students to pay attention to how the lesson of this fable is revealed.

❸ Reading Strategy

Predicting Consequences of Actions

- Tell students that all actions have consequences. However, people often do not think about the consequences of their actions. If they thought about what might happen, people might not be surprised by consequences—or they might change their actions.
- In a story, the reader can often predict what will happen as a result of characters' actions. Tell students that, as each new action takes place, they should consider what has already occurred, as well as what they know about the characters and their motives. This will enable them to make predictions.
- Encourage students to use a chart like the one on the student page to record events as they happen, along with their predictions.

Vocabulary Development

- Pronounce each vocabulary word for students, and read the definitions as a class. Have students identify any words with which they are already familiar.

E-Teach

Visit E-Teach at www.phschool.com for teachers' essays on how to teach, with questions and answers.

TEACH

Step-by-Step Teaching Guide for pp. 178–182

CUSTOMIZE INSTRUCTION For Verbal/Linguistic Learners

Have students note the metaphors and similes in this story, such as "Their breaths fluttered like winter winds in their mouths" (p. 181). Have students analyze Bradbury's use of figurative language. What does it contribute to the story? What would be the effect if it was replaced with plainer language? Students can write brief essays answering these questions.

1 About the Selection

This fable highlights the negative consequences of having competition be the only form of interaction. It symbolizes the behaviors of nations or groups that, from fear or arrogance, build up their defenses rather than trying to work out their differences. On a literal level, the fable is about two rival towns that construct ever more complex walls to empower and protect themselves. As the competition escalates, both communities suffer unforeseen consequences.

2 Background

Art

The Nymph of the Lo River (detail), by Ku K'ai-Chin

To the ancient Chinese, the world was full of supernatural creatures. Places often had guardian spirits; a dragon might live in a body of water, a Chinese unicorn on a mountain. In this watercolor, the guardian of the Lo River has taken human form and is advising an official. Use these questions for discussion:

1. What setting can you infer from the details of this work of art?
   Answer: The details of the figures and their clothing suggest East Asia long ago.
2. What does this work of art have in common with a fable?
   Answer: It conveys its message using only essential details.

3 ▸Critical Viewing

Answer: The mood of the painting is serene. The Mandarin's mood is agitated.

1 The Golden Kite, the Silver Wind

Ray Bradbury

"In the shape of a *pig*?" cried the Mandarin.[1]

"In the shape of a pig," said the messenger, and departed.

"Oh, what an evil day in an evil year," cried the Mandarin. "The town of Kwan-Si, beyond the hill, was very small in my childhood. Now it has grown so large that at last they are building a wall."

3 ▼Critical Viewing How does the mood of this artwork contrast with that of the Mandarin? **[Compare and Contrast]**

1. **Mandarin** (man´ de rin) a high official of China; here, the ruling leader.

2

The Nymph of the Lo River, Attributed to Ku K'ai-Chin, Freer Gallery of Art, Smithsonian Institution, Washington, D.C.

TEACHING RESOURCES

The following resources can be used to enrich or extend the instruction for pp. 178–182.

Literary Analysis

- **Selection Support:** Literary Analysis, p. 40

Reading

- **Listening to Literature Audiocassettes,** Side 7 ▪
- **Listening to Literature Audio CDs,** CD 6 ▪

Extension

- **Authors In Depth,** Gold Level (The collection includes four additional selections by Ray Bradbury for extended reading.) ▪

▪ **BLOCK SCHEDULING:** Resources marked with this symbol provide varied instruction during 90-minute blocks.

"But why should a wall two miles away make my good father sad and angry all within the hour?" asked his daughter quietly.

"They build their wall," said the Mandarin, "in the shape of a pig! Do you see? Our own city wall is built in the shape of an orange. That pig will devour us, greedily!"

"Ah."

They both sat thinking.

❹ Life was full of symbols and omens. Demons lurked everywhere, Death swam in the wetness of an eye, the turn of a gull's wing meant rain, a fan held so, the tilt of a roof, and, yes, even a city wall was of immense importance. Travelers and tourists, caravans, musicians, artists, coming upon these two towns, equally judging the portents, would say, "The city shaped like an orange? No! I will enter the city shaped like a pig and prosper, eating all, growing fat with good luck and prosperity!"

The Mandarin wept. "All is lost! These symbols and signs terrify. Our city will come on evil days."

"Then," said the daughter, "call in your stonemasons and temple builders. I will whisper from behind the silken screen and you will know the words."

The old man clapped his hands despairingly. "Ho, stonemasons!

"Ho, builders of towns and palaces!"

The men who knew marble and granite and onyx and quartz came quickly. The Mandarin faced them most uneasily, himself waiting for a whisper from the silken screen behind his throne. At last the whisper came.

"I have called you here," said the whisper.

"I have called you here," said the Mandarin aloud, "because our city is shaped like an orange, and the vile city of Kwan-Si has this day shaped theirs like a ravenous pig—"

Here the stonemasons groaned and wept. Death rattled his cane in the outer courtyard. Poverty made a sound like a wet cough in the shadows of the room.

"And so," said the whisper, said the Mandarin, "you raisers of walls must go bearing trowels and rocks and change the shape of *our* city!"

The architects and masons gasped. The Mandarin himself gasped at what he had said. The whisper whispered. The Mandarin went on: "And you will change our walls into a club which may beat the pig and drive it off!"

The stonemasons rose up, shouting. Even the Mandarin, delighted at the words from his mouth, applauded, stood down from his throne. "Quick!" he cried. "To work!"

Literary Analysis
Fable Based on the Mandarin's answer to his daughter's question, what rivalry exists between the two towns?

portents (pôr´ tentz) *n.* things that are thought to be signs of events to come; omens

vile (vīl) *adj.* evil; wicked

ravenous (rav´ ə nəs) *adj.* greedily hungry

❺ **Reading Check**
Who is whispering to the king from behind a silken screen?

❹ Literary Analysis
Fable

- After students have read the opening paragraphs, ask them which aspects of this story remind them of other fables they have read.
  Answer: The story is set in a far-away but undefined time and place. There is mention of magic and mysterious secrets.

Monitor Progress Ask the Literary Analysis question on p. 179: Based on the Mandarin's answer to his daughter's question, what rivalry exists between the two towns?
Answer: They compete for tourists and travelers. Each leader wants his city to look more attractive than the other one.

❺ Reading Check
Answer: The Mandarin's daughter is whispering from behind the screen.

CUSTOMIZE INSTRUCTION FOR UNIVERSAL ACCESS

For Less Proficient Readers	For Advanced Readers
This story is a chain of causes and effects. As students read, they can keep track of the plot by listing various effects and what caused them. For instance, the Mandarin's panic causes him to ask his daughter's advice, and her advice causes him to order his people to rebuild the wall, and so on. Students can use this chain of causes and effects to understand how the story arrives at its conclusion.	Have students analyze the character of the Mandarin's daughter. What does the Mandarin think of her? Why does he think this? Is her advice good or bad? What makes it good or bad? Do students think the advice she gives at the beginning of the story is necessary in order to bring about the happy conclusion? If not, what else might she have advised the Mandarin to do? Students can write brief essays analyzing this character.

❻ Vocabulary Development

Latin Word Root *-clam-*

- Direct students' attention to the word *acclaimed* and its definition. Tell students that the Latin word root *–clam-* (or its variation, *-claim-*) means "call out" or "shout." Point out that being *acclaimed* includes the ideas that the individual was greeted by shouts, that people would call out words of praise or the person's name.
- Have students suggest words and phrases that contain this root, and list them on the board. Possibilities include *exclaim, exclamation, proclaim, proclamation, clamor, clamorous,* and *claim.* (You may add to the list on the board any words that students do not suggest.)
- Next, have students look up these words in the dictionary. Encourage them to check the word origin, as well as the meaning. Discuss how the meaning of the original root contributes to the current meaning of the word.

❼ Critical Thinking

Infer

- Have a volunteer read aloud the bracketed passage.
- Ask what students can infer about the place of women in this society. Have them explain their answers.
Answer: Women are expected to be modest and stupid. The highest compliment the Mandarin can pay his daughter is to say that she thinks like a son.

❽ Reading Strategy

Predicting Consequences of Actions

- Point out the consequences of the Mandarin's order to rebuild the walls in the shape of a club. The people have had to neglect their crops and the whole city is impoverished.
- Ask the Reading Strategy question on p. 180: What do you think the consequence of this latest action will be?
Answer: Each city will rebuild its wall in a shape superior to the shape chosen by the other city.

When his men had gone, smiling and bustling, the Mandarin turned with great love to the silken screen. "Daughter," he whispered, "I will embrace you." There was no reply. He stepped around the screen, and she was gone.

Such modesty, he thought. She has slipped away and left me with a triumph, as if it were mine.

6 The news spread through the city; the Mandarin was acclaimed. Everyone carried stone to the walls. Fireworks were set off and the demons of death and poverty did not linger, as all worked together. At
7 the end of the month the wall had been changed. It was now a mighty bludgeon with which to drive pigs, boars, even lions, far away. The Mandarin slept like a happy fox every night.

"I would like to see the Mandarin of Kwan-Si when the news is learned. Such pandemonium and hysteria; he will likely throw himself from a mountain! A little more of that wine, oh Daughter-who-thinks-like-a-son."

But the pleasure was like a winter flower; it died swiftly. That very afternoon the messenger rushed into the courtroom. "Oh, Mandarin, disease, early sorrow, avalanches, grasshopper plagues, and poisoned well water!"

The Mandarin trembled.

"The town of Kwan-Si," said the messenger, "which was built like a pig and which animal we drove away by changing our walls to a mighty stick, has now turned triumph to winter ashes. They have built their city's walls like a great bonfire to burn our stick!"

The Mandarin's heart sickened within him, like an autumn fruit upon an ancient tree. "Oh, gods! Travelers will spurn us. Tradesmen, reading the symbols, will turn from the stick, so easily destroyed, to the fire, which conquers all!"

"No," said a whisper like a snowflake from behind the silken screen.

"No," said the startled Mandarin.

"Tell my stonemasons," said the whisper that was a falling drop of rain, "to build our walls in the shape of a shining lake."

The Mandarin said this aloud, his heart warmed.

"And with this lake of water," said the whisper and the old man, "we will quench the fire and put it out forever!"

The city turned out in joy to learn that once again they had been saved by the magnificent Emperor of ideas. They ran to the walls and built them nearer to this new vision, singing, not as loudly as before, of course, for they were tired, and not as quickly, for since it had
8 taken a month to rebuild the wall the first time, they had had to neglect business and crops and therefore were somewhat weaker and poorer.

There then followed a succession of horrible and wonderful days, one in another like a nest of frightened boxes.

"Oh, Emperor," cried the messenger, "Kwan-Si has rebuilt their walls to resemble a mouth with which to drink all our lake!"

acclaimed (ə klāmd′) *v.* greeted with loud applause or approval; hailed

pandemonium (pan′ də mōn′ nē əm) *n.* wild disorder, noise, or confusion

spurn (spʉrn) *v.* reject in a scornful way

Reading Strategy
Predicting Consequences of Actions What do you think will be the consequence of this latest action?

CUSTOMIZE INSTRUCTION FOR UNIVERSAL ACCESS

For Advanced Readers

Suggest that students read additional works by Ray Bradbury. Provide them with the titles listed in the Enrichment box, ATE p. 183. You may also wish to use **Authors In Depth,** Gold Level, which contains the following selections:

- "The Flying Machine" (fiction, p. 33)
- "The Pedestrian," (fiction, p. 37)
- "The Other Me," (poetry, p. 42)
- "January 1999: Rocket Summer" from *The Martian Chronicles* (fiction, p. 44)

"The Flying Machine" features another fearful Chinese ruler, and may be a good pairing with this selection, though the contrast with other works may interest students more. After students have read these or other works by Bradbury, have them form discussion groups in which they compare and contrast the selections they have read. To extend the activity, have volunteers present to the class brief oral reports on their favorite Bradbury selections.

"Then," said the Emperor, standing very close to his silken screen, "build our walls like a needle to sew up that mouth!"

"Emperor!" screamed the messenger. "They make their walls like a sword to break your needle!"

The Emperor held, trembling, to the silken screen. "Then shift the stones to form a scabbard to sheathe that sword!"[2]

"Mercy," wept the messenger the following morn, "they have worked all night and shaped their walls like lightning which will explode and destroy that sheath!"

9 Sickness spread in the city like a pack of evil dogs. Shops closed. The population, working now steadily for endless months upon the changing of the walls, resembled Death himself, clattering his white bones like musical instruments in the wind. Funerals began to appear in the streets, though it was the middle of summer, a time when all should be tending and harvesting. The Mandarin fell so ill that he had his bed drawn up by the silken screen and there he lay, miserably giving his architectural orders. The voice behind the screen was weak now, too, and faint, like the wind in the eaves.

"Kwan-Si is an eagle. Then our walls must be a net for that eagle. They are a sun to burn our net. Then we build a moon to eclipse their sun!"

Like a rusted machine, the city ground to a halt.

At last the whisper behind the screen cried out:

"In the name of the gods, send for Kwan-Si!"

Upon the last day of summer the Mandarin Kwan-Si, very ill and withered away, was carried into our Mandarin's courtroom by four starving footmen. The two mandarins were propped up, facing each other. Their breaths fluttered like winter winds in their mouths.

A voice said:

"Let us put an end to this."

The old men nodded.

10 "This cannot go on," said the faint voice. "Our people do nothing but rebuild our cities to a different shape every day, every hour. They have no time to hunt, to fish, to love, to be good to their ancestors and their ancestors' children."

"This I admit," said the mandarins of the towns of the Cage, the Moon, the Spear, the Fire, the Sword and this, that, and other things.

"Carry us into the sunlight," said the voice.

The old men were borne out under the sun and up a little hill. In the late summer breeze a few very thin children were flying dragon kites in all the colors of the sun, and frogs and grass, the color of the sea and the color of coins and wheat.

The first Mandarin's daughter stood by his bed.

"See," she said.

"Those are nothing but kites," said the two old men.

Literary Analysis

Fable What lesson are the mandarins beginning to learn?

11 **Reading Check**

What kind of wall was built to defeat Kwan-si's sun?

2. scabbard (skab´ ərd) **to sheathe** (shēth) **that sword!** case to hold the blade of the sword.

9 Critical Thinking

Analyze Causes and Effects

- Explain to students that the entire story is structured through cause and effect. Each action taken by one city results in an action taken in the other one.
- Read aloud the bracketed passage. Point out to students that the people have to keep on rebuilding the walls. What effect do students think this has on the city?
Answer: It stops all other work in the city. Crops are not harvested and business is ignored.
- Explain to students that the work on the walls leaves the people sick, weak, and hungry. Ask students what effect this will have on the city in the long run.
Answer: Eventually, the city will cease to exist. The people will die.

10 Literary Analysis

Fable

Reteach Remind students that there is a lesson to be learned at the heart of any fable. Have students reflect on what they have read thus far.

- Then, ask students the Literary Analysis question on p. 181: What lesson are the mandarins beginning to learn?
Answer: They are beginning to learn that their constant attempts to best one another are destroying their people.

11 Reading Check

Answer: A moon was built to defeat Kwan-si's sun.

CUSTOMIZE INSTRUCTION FOR UNIVERSAL ACCESS

For Special Needs Students	For Gifted/Talented Students
The figurative language in this story may prove difficult for students. Go over the story, discussing what the images express. If possible, illustrate some images. For example, on p. 181, it says that the population "resembled Death…clattering his white bones like musical instruments in the wind." You might discuss students' ideas of skeletons and wind chimes, and how people might sound like clattering bones, or you might bring in pictures of bones or a set of wind chimes to aid the discussion.	As students read, have them pay attention to the many striking examples of figurative language. Have them use Bradbury's metaphors, similes, and examples of personification to create posters or illustrations for the story, or to retell it in comic-strip form. Students may want to use the works of art pictured on pp. 176 and 178 for inspiration, but encourage them to concentrate mainly on the pictures Bradbury draws in words. Post their completed work in the classroom.

ASSESS

12 Literary Analysis

Fable and Dialogue

- Have two volunteers read aloud the dialogue in brackets.
- Ask the Literary Analysis question on p. 182: What do you learn from the dialogue between the daughter and the two mandarins?
  Answer: We learn that a peaceful solution to the standoff is possible.
- Ask students to identify the statement that indicates the moral of the fable.
  Answer: "One without the other is nothing. Together, all will be beauty and cooperation and a long and enduring life."

Answers for p. 182

Review and Assess

1. Students may say that the advice at the start of the story was not good because it led to so much destruction, but the advice at the end was good. Some students may think the advice at the beginning was necessary so that the two Mandarins would learn a lesson.
2. **(a)** Kwan-Si has built a new wall that the Mandarin thinks is intended as an insult to his city. **(b)** He is very superstitious.
3. **(a)** She whispers what he should do from behind a screen. **(b)** She needs to hide so that people will think the ideas are the Mandarin's. (Alternatively, students may reply that she advised him to build different walls, because she knew it would appeal to his vanity and superstition.)
4. **(a)** They are loyal and obedient. They are as superstitious as the Mandarin. They are happy to think that they are better than the people of Kwan-Si. **(b)** They might have been wise to plead with the Mandarin to be allowed to tend their crops.
5. The fable suggests that if you always try to be better than your neighbor, you won't have time for anything else—work, fun, or even sleep. This lesson applies to anyone anywhere; all rivalries are destructive.

"But what is a kite on the ground?" she said. "It is nothing. What does it need to sustain it and make it beautiful and truly spiritual?"

"The wind, of course!" said the others.

"And what do the sky and the wind need to make *them* beautiful?"

"A kite, of course—many kites, to break the monotony, the sameness of the sky. Colored kites, flying!"

12 "So," said the Mandarin's daughter. "You, Kwan-Si, will make a last rebuilding of your town to resemble nothing more nor less than the wind. And we shall build like a golden kite. The wind will beautify the kite and carry it to wondrous heights. And the kite will break the sameness of the wind's existence and give it purpose and meaning. One without the other is nothing. Together, all will be beauty and cooperation and a long and enduring life."

Whereupon the two mandarins were so overjoyed that they took their first nourishment in days, momentarily were given strength, embraced, and lavished praise upon each other, called the Mandarin's daughter a boy, a man, a stone pillar, a warrior, and a true and unforgettable son. Almost immediately they parted and hurried to their towns, calling out and singing, weakly but happily.

And so, in time, the towns became the Town of Golden Kite and the Town of the Silver Wind. And harvestings were harvested and business tended again, and the flesh returned, and disease ran off like a frightened jackal. And on every night of the year the inhabitants in the Town of the Kite could hear the good clear wind sustaining them. And those in the Town of the Wind could hear the kite singing, whispering, rising, and beautifying them.

"So be it," said the Mandarin in front of his silken screen.

Literary Analysis
Fable and Dialogue What do you learn from the dialogue between the daughter and the two mandarins?

Ray Bradbury

(b. 1920)

Born in Waukegan, Illinois, Bradbury developed a love of fantasy and suspenseful writing at an early age. In 1932, Bradbury's family moved to Tucson, Arizona, where he wrote his first stories. In 1934, they moved to Los Angeles, where he has lived ever since.

A year after he graduated from high school, Bradbury founded and edited a publication called *Futuria Fantasia*. By this time, he was already writing at least one story a week.

One of America's most celebrated science-fiction writers, Bradbury has earned the World Fantasy Award for lifetime achievement and the Grand Master Award from the Science Fiction Writers of America.

Review and Assess

Thinking About the Selection

1. **Respond:** Do you think the Mandarin's daughter gave her father good advice? Explain.
2. **(a) Recall:** Which event at the beginning of the story upsets and angers the Mandarin? **(b) Infer:** What does his reaction tell you about his beliefs?
3. **(a) Recall:** How does the Mandarin's daughter advise her father? **(b) Infer:** Why do you think she needs to advise him in such a way?
4. **(a) Infer:** What can you infer about the townspeople based on their response to the Mandarin's plans? **(b) Evaluate:** Should they have continued to follow his advice?
5. **Apply:** How can the lesson from this story be applied to everyday life situations?

ASSESSMENT PRACTICE: Reading Comprehension

Sequential Order (For more practice, see Test Preparation Workbook, p. 10.)

Many tests require students to arrange events in sequential order. Use the following sample test item to give students practice at determining the sequence of events in written texts.

The men who knew marble and granite and onyx and quartz came quickly. The Mandarin faced them most uneasily, himself waiting for a whisper from the silken screen behind his throne. At last the whisper came.

What happened after the Mandarin faced the men?

A A whisper came from behind the screen.
B The men came quickly.
C The Mandarin looked behind his throne.
D The Mandarin became uneasy.

B tells what happened before the Mandarin faced the men. *C* does not happen at all. *D* happens as the Mandarin faces the men. Choice *A* is correct.

Review and Assess

Literary Analysis

Fable

1. (a) What poor choices were made by both the Mandarin and his daughter in this **fable**? (b) What happened as a result?
2. Use a chart like this one to list key responsibilities of leaders. What lesson does this fable teach us about powerful leaders and their responsibilities to the people they represent?

Responsibilities	Mandarins' Leadership Abilities

3. In your own words, express the moral of the fable in one sentence.

Connecting Literary Elements

4. Most of the **dialogue** in the story is provided by the daughter speaking from behind a screen. What does this dialogue reveal to us about the daughter and the Mandarin?
5. (a) Note places in the story where dialogue moves the action along more quickly. (b) Why does dialogue work better than description in the story?

Reading Strategy

Predicting Consequences of Actions

6. What were the first hints that the rivalry between the two towns would be disastrous? Support your answer.
7. At what point were you able to **predict** the outcome? Explain.
8. (a) What do you predict will be the result of the actions taken at the end of the story? (b) Which details support your answer?

Extend Understanding

9. **World History Connection:** This story was written during the Cold War. (a) Why would the story have been especially appropriate for that time? (b) Which countries or cultures from today's world could the two villages represent? Explain.

Quick Review

A **fable** is a brief story that teaches a lesson, or moral. The moral may be directly stated, or indirectly shown through the choices the characters make.

Dialogue—a conversation between characters—is used to reveal more about the characters and to move the action of the story along.

To **predict consequences of actions,** guess the outcome of a story based on the events that have already occurred.

Take It to the Net

www.phschool.com

Take the interactive self-test online to check your understanding of this selection.

ENRICHMENT: Further Reading

Other Works by Ray Bradbury

Dandelion Wine
The Martian Chronicles
Fahrenheit 451
"All Summer in a Day"

Take It to the Net

Visit www.phschool.com for more information on Ray Bradbury.

Review and Assess

1. **(a)** They chose to try to build better walls than those of Kwan-Si. **(b)** Both cities were devastated because everyone had to build; no one was free to tend crops.
2. Responsibilities include working and passing laws that will benefit the people. Both Mandarins order work done on their walls because they think this will benefit their people. When they see that they were wrong, they change their course of action.
3. Cooperation is more beneficial than competition.
4. The daughter is wiser and more decisive than the Mandarin. The Mandarin wants the credit for her ideas.
5. **(a)** Students will note the reports of the messengers and the daughter's whispers. **(b)** Dialogue is more immediate and faster paced than description.
6. The first hint was the people's exhaustion after rebuilding the orange-shaped wall to look like a club.
7. When the daughter suggested sending for Kwan-Si, students should have realized that there would be an attempt to reach a peaceful solution.
8. **(a)** The cities will both prosper again. **(b)** The daughter's description of how the two cities will help one another suggests a happy future.
9. **(a)** The story was appropriate to the Cold War because it mirrors the Cold War situation of a standoff between two rival societies. **(b)** Students may suggest countries or ethnic groups whose people and leaders seem unable to reach a peaceful solution of their differences.

EXTEND

Answers for p. 184

❶ Vocabulary Development

Word Analysis

Sample sentences:

1. The sudden appearance of a caterpillar in my salad bowl caused me to exclaim, "Yikes!"
2. Lincoln read aloud a proclamation stating that from this day forward, no United States citizen could own another one as property.
3. The clamorous honking of the huge flock of migrating geese heralded the coming of winter.

Spelling Strategy

1. eccentric: Emma's friends considered her passion for baseball eccentric.
2. assign: I had to assign Gilberto an extra credit project since he finished his term paper two weeks early.

Fluency: Context

1. portents
2. pandemonium
3. ravenous
4. vile
5. Spurning
6. acclaimed

❷ Grammar

1. spoke, directed
2. worked, shaped
3. moaned, wept
4. parted, hurried
5. carry, sustain

Writing Application

Possible Answers:

1. The Mandarin worried and wept about the wall.
2. The walls rose and fell in the same week.

Integrate Language Skills

❶ Vocabulary Development Lesson

Word Analysis: Latin Root *-clam-*

In this story, the word *acclaimed*, meaning "greeted with loud applause or approval," contains *-claim-*, a variation of the Latin root *-clam-*, meaning "call out" or "shout." Applying the meaning of *-clam-*, write a sentence for each word below.

1. exclaim 2. proclamation 3. clamorous

Spelling Strategy

The final consonant of a prefix sometimes changes to match the first letter of the word to which it is attached. The result is a doubled consonant. For example, the prefix *in-* changes to *ir-* in *irregular*.

Rewrite each item below by adding the given prefix. Then, write a sentence using the new word.

1. *ex-* + centric 2. *ad-* + sign

Fluency: Context

Write each sentence below, filling in the blanks with words from the vocabulary list on page 177, or forms of those words.

The __?__ for the kingdom were not good. The crops had failed, lightning had struck the bell tower, and a dragon was causing __?__ across the countryside. Fierce and __?__, the dragon terrified the peasants and devoured their livestock, leaving the people hungry and frightened. "That __?__ dragon must be destroyed!" exclaimed the princess. __?__ offers of assistance, she rode off to fight the dragon. On her triumphant return home, the dragon-slaying princess was __?__ by her grateful people for her bravery and determination.

❷ Grammar Lesson

Compound Verbs

A **compound verb** is two or more verbs that have the same subject and are joined by a conjunction such as *and* or *or*. In the following example from "The Golden Kite, the Silver Wind," the subject is underlined and the parts of the compound verb are italicized.

Example: "<u>They</u> *ran* to the walls and *built* them nearer to this new vision. . . ." (S = They; V = ran, built)

Both *ran* and *built* have the same subject, *They*, and the verbs are connected by the conjunction *and*.

Practice Identify the compound verbs in each sentence below.

1. She spoke and directed people through the silken screen.
2. The townspeople worked all night and shaped their walls like lightning.
3. The people moaned and wept.
4. They parted and hurried back to work.
5. The wind will carry and sustain the kite.

Writing Application Use each word below as the subject in a sentence, and create compound verbs to accompany each subject.

1. Mandarin 2. walls

WG *Prentice Hall Writing and Grammar Connection: Chapter 20, Section 1*

TEACHING RESOURCES

The following resources can be used to enrich or extend the instructions for pp. 184–185.

Vocabulary

- **Selection Support,** Build Vocabulary, p. 37
- **Vocabulary and Spelling Practice Book** (Use this booklet for skills enrichment.)

Grammar

- **Selection Support:** Build Grammar Skills, p. 38
- **Writing and Grammar,** Gold Level, p. 422
- **Daily Language Practice Transparencies**

Writing

- **Writing and Grammar,** Gold Level, p. 141
- **Writing and Grammar iText CD-ROM**
- **Writing Models and Graphic Organizers on Transparencies,** pp. 71–73

BLOCK SCHEDULING: Resources marked with this symbol provide varied instruction during 90-minute blocks.

❸ Writing Lesson

Persuasive Letter

Imagine you were living in one of the cities featured in "The Golden Kite, the Silver Wind." Write a letter to the Mandarin, letting him know how concerned you are about the competition between the cities and urging him to resolve the conflict.

Prewriting Brainstorm a list of points you would like to make about the conflict. Keep your audience in mind and think about what you can say that would affect the Mandarin's thoughts about the issue.

Drafting As you draft, make sure your arguments are supported. Whenever possible, prove your point by providing examples, facts, or details.

Revising As you revise, underline all of your arguments and highlight the support. If a point needs more evidence, add details. If there is no stronger evidence, eliminate your point.

Model: Evaluating Support for Your Arguments

The people of the city will not survive the competition.

and people are dying

Everyone is working on the walls. Sickness has spread.

Added information supports the argument that the people of the city will not survive.

Prentice Hall Writing and Grammar Connection: Chapter 7, Section 4

❹ Extension Activities

Listening and Speaking In a small group, present a **dramatic interpretation** of Bradbury's story. Make these necessary decisions to organize your interpretation properly.

- Assign the roles of the two mandarins, the daughter, and a messenger.
- Assign the role of director to one person in the group who can listen objectively and give advice on pitch and tone of voice.

Present your interpretation to the class, and ask your audience to evaluate your presentation. **[Group Activity]**

Research and Technology Bradbury's fable addresses issues raised by the Cold War. Research some aspect of the Cold War. For example, you might study the alliances each side formed or the weapons buildup that took place. Use library resources like the Internet, an atlas, and history books. Then, compare the events in Bradbury's story to produce a **historical report.**

Take It to the Net www.phschool.com

Go online for an additional research activity using the Internet.

ASSESSMENT RESOURCES

The following resources can be used to assess students' knowledge and skills.

Selection Assessment

- **Formal Assessment,** pp. 32–34
- **Open Book Test,** pp. 28–30
- **Got It! Assessment Videotapes,** Tape 1
- **Test Bank Software**

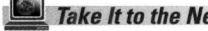

Take It to the Net

Visit www.phschool.com for self-tests and additional questions on "The Golden Kite, the Silver Wind."

Writing Rubric

- **Performance Assess. and Portfolio Mgmt.,** p. 10

Listening and Speaking Rubric

- **Performance Assess. and Portfolio Mgmt.,** p. 27

PRENTICE HALL ASSESSMENT SYSTEM

- **Workbook**
- **Skill Book**
- **Transparencies**
- **CD-ROM**

❸ Writing Lesson

- Have students go through the story and list all the points they would like to make in their letters to the Mandarin.
- You may wish to suggest that students use the Herringbone Organizer, pp. 71–73 of **Writing Models and Graphic Organizers on Transparencies,** to record main ideas and supporting details.
- Remind students that a letter to the Mandarin must be phrased tactfully. The purpose of the letter is to persuade him to do what is best for his people, not to accuse or antagonize him.
- Use the Persuasive Composition rubric in **Performance Assessment and Portfolio Management,** p. 10, to evaluate students' letters.

❹ Extension Activity

Listening and Speaking

- Have students meet to divide up the responsibilities for their presentation. Students not interested in playing a character in the story can direct rehearsals, plan and locate costumes and props, or collaborate on the script.
- Point out that students can present the story in any way they like. A puppet show, a radio play, or a shadow play are only three possibilities. Encourage students to use their creativity and imagination.
- Encourage students to perform their play for classes at a nearby elementary school.
- Have students use the rubric for Delivering a Narrative Presentation, p. 27 in **Performance Assessment and Portfolio Management.**

CUSTOMIZE INSTRUCTION for Universal Access

To address different learning styles, use the following activities suggested in the **Extension Activities** booklet, p. 10.

- For Interpersonal and Verbal/Linguistic Learners, use Activity 4.
- For Logical/Mathematical Learners, use Activity 5.
- For Bodily/Kinesthetic Learners, use Activity 6.

The Road Not Taken ✦ To be of use ✦ New Directions

Lesson Objectives and CA Correlations

1. **To analyze and respond to literary elements**
   - Literary Analysis: Figurative Language **R 3.7**
   - Comparing Literary Works
2. **To read, comprehend, analyze, and critique poetry and nonfiction**
   - Reading Strategy: Generating Questions **R 2.3**
   - Reading Check questions
   - Review and Assess questions
   - Assessment Practice (ATE)
3. **To develop word analysis skills, fluency, and systematic vocabulary**
   - Vocabulary Development Lesson: Anglo-Saxon Suffix: *-ly* **R 1.1**
4. **To understand and apply written and oral language conventions.**
   - Spelling Strategy
   - Grammar Lesson: Regular Verbs **LC 1.2**
5. **To understand and apply appropriate writing and research strategies**
   - Writing Lesson: Evaluation of Figurative Language **W 2.2**
   - Extension Activity: Videotape an Interview **W 1.3**
6. **To understand and apply listening and speaking strategies**
   - Extension Activity: Job Interview **LS 1.9**

STEP-BY-STEP TEACHING GUIDE	PACING GUIDE
PRETEACH	
Motivate Students and Provide Background	
Use the Motivation activity (ATE p.186)	5 min.
Read and discuss the Preview material and Background information (SE/ATE p. 186) [A]	10 min.
Introduce the Concepts	
Introduce the Literary Analysis and Reading Strategy (SE/ATE p. 187) [A]	15 min.
Pronounce the vocabulary words and read their definitions (SE p.187)	5 min.
TEACH	
Monitor Comprehension	
Informally monitor comprehension by circulating while students read independently or in groups [A]	15 min.
Monitor students' comprehension with the Reading Check notes (SE/ATE p. 191)	as students read
Develop vocabulary with Vocabulary notes (SE pp. 189–192; ATE p. 191)	as students read
Develop Understanding	
Develop students' understanding of the use of figurative language with Literary Analysis annotations (SE p. 189; ATE pp. 189, 190) [A]	10 min.
Develop students' ability to generate questions with the Reading Strategy annotations (SE pp. 191, 192; ATE pp. 191, 192)	10 min.
ASSESS	
Assess Mastery	
Assess students' mastery of the Reading Strategy and Literary Analysis by having them answer the Review and Assess questions (SE/ATE p. 193)	20 min.
Use one or more of the print and media Assessment Resources (ATE p. 195) [A]	up to 50 min.
EXTEND	
Apply Understanding	
Have students complete the Vocabulary Development Lesson and the Grammar Lesson (SE p. 194) [A]	20 min.
Apply students' ability to evaluate figurative language with the Writing Lesson (SE p. 195) [A]	45 min.
Apply students' understanding using one or more of the Extension Activities (SE p. 195)	20–90 min.

[A] **ACCELERATED INSTRUCTION:**
Use the strategies and activities identified with an [A].

UNIVERSAL ACCESS
● = Below Level Students
▲ = On-Level Students
■ = Above Level Students

Time and Resource Manager

Reading Level: Easy, Average, Average
Average Number of Instructional Days: 4

RESOURCES		
PRINT	**TRANSPARENCIES**	**TECHNOLOGY**
• **Beyond Literature,** Cross-Curricular Connection: Social Studies, p. 11 ▲ ■		• **Interest Grabber Video,** Tape 1 ● ▲ ■
• **Selection Support Workbook:** ● ▲ ■ Literary Analysis, p. 44 Reading Strategy, p. 43 Build Vocabulary, p. 41	• **Literary Analysis and Reading Transparencies,** pp. 21 and 22 ● ▲ ■	
		• **Listening to Literature** ● ▲ ■ Audiocassettes, Side 7 Audio CDs, CD 6
• **English Learner's Companion** ● ▲ • **Literatura en español** ● ▲ • **Literary Analysis for Enrichment** ■		
•**Formal Assessment:** Selection Test, pp. 35–37 ● ▲ ■ • **Open Book Test,** pp. 31–33 ● ▲ ■ • **Performance Assessment and Portfolio Management,** pp. 15, 26 ● ▲ ■ • PRENTICE HALL ASSESSMENT SYSTEM ● ▲ ■	• PRENTICE HALL ASSESSMENT SYSTEM ● ▲ ■ Skills Practice Answers and Explanations on Transparencies	• **Test Bank Software** ● ▲ ■ • **Got It! Assessment Videotapes,** Tape 1 ● ▲
• **Selection Support Workbook:** ● ▲ ■ Build Grammar Skills, p. 42 • **Writing and Grammar,** Gold Level ● ▲ ■ • **Extension Activities,** p. 11 ● ▲ ■	• **Daily Language Practice Transparencies** ● ▲ • **Writing Models and Graphic Organizers on Transparencies,** p. 95 ● ▲ ■	• **Writing and Grammar iText CD-ROM** ● ▲ ■ ***Take It to the Net*** www.phschool.com

BLOCK SCHEDULING: Use one 90-minute class period to preteach the selection and have students read it. Use a second 90-minute class period to assess students' mastery of skills and have them complete one of the Extension Activities.

PRETEACH

Step-by-Step Teaching Guide for pp. 186–187

Motivation

Write the first few words of Frost's poem "The Road Not Taken" on the chalkboard. Either as a class or in small groups, have students create a poem of their own that begins with Frost's famous words. Have students take turns adding lines until they feel that their poem is complete.

Interest Grabber Video

As an alternative, play "Reading and Student Response" on Tape 1 to engage student interest.

1 Background

Careers

All the works in this selection explore decisions and the impact they can have on lives and careers. Piercy writes of finding meaningful work, which Annie Johnson succeeded in doing. Annie Johnson saw a need and filled it, overcoming difficulties to create success. In this, her story is much like that of Levi Strauss. Strauss made his fortune in the 1850s, during the California Gold Rush, by selling clothes to the prospectors. As the creator of blue jeans, he has had a huge and lasting impact on American culture. Strauss was a Jewish immigrant who became a U.S. citizen only two months before he opened his business. Annie Johnson was an African American woman with little education. Hard work as well as insight played a large part in their successes. The ability to creatively match one's skills to a need one can identify is still valuable in the job market. The road "less traveled by" is often the fastest route to success, or at least to personal satisfaction.

Prepare to Read

The Road Not Taken ◆ To be of use ◆ New Directions

Take It to the Net

Visit www.phschool.com for interactive activities and instruction related to the selections, including
- background
- graphic organizers
- literary elements
- reading strategies

Preview

Connecting to the Literature

You face choices big and small every day. The questions of how to challenge yourself in a new way or which career path to pursue present decisions with major implications. The selections that follow explore these kinds of life choices—critical forks in the road of life.

1 Background

In the early 1900s, job opportunities were limited for many Americans—particularly for African Americans like Annie Johnson in Maya Angelou's "New Directions." Then, the most common jobs for African American women were cleaning, childcare, and general household labor. For women who had families, caring for someone else's household was an extra burden. No wonder Annie Johnson struck off in a "new direction."

TEACHING RESOURCES

The following resources can be used to enrich or extend the instruction for pp. 186–187.

Motivation

Interest Grabber Video, Tape 1

Background

Beyond Literature, p. 11

Take It to the Net

Visit www.phschool.com background and hotlinks for "The Road Not Taken," "To be of use," and "New Directions."

Literary Analysis

Literary Analysis and Reading Transparencies, Figurative Language, p. 22

Reading

Selection Support: Reading Strategy, p. 43; Build Vocabulary, p. 41

Literary Analysis and Reading Transparencies, Generating Questions, p. 21

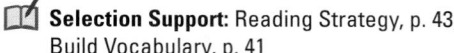

BLOCK SCHEDULING: Resources marked with this symbol provide varied instruction during 90-minute blocks.

❷ Literary Analysis

Figurative Language

Figurative language, language that means more than it says literally, is often used to create vivid impressions by introducing comparisons between dissimilar things. Look at the following example of figurative language found in Marge Piercy's "To be of use":

> The people I love the best
> jump into work head first,
> without dallying in the shallows.

Piercy is not stating that the people she loves best are deep-sea divers. Rather, she is expressing admiration for people who take on challenges courageously. As you read the selections, take note of vivid language that implies more than its literal meaning.

Comparing Literary Works

While making difficult decisions and working toward a goal, the people you will encounter in these selections have put themselves to the test. In the words of Robert Frost, "that has made all the difference." Compare and contrast the ways each writer uses figurative language to convey larger ideas about decisions and their impact.

❸ Reading Strategy

Generating Questions

To better understand what you read, **generate questions** based on the text. Begin with the common questions words *who, what, where, when, why*, and *how*. Write questions that come to mind as you read a passage, and try to answer those questions as you progress. Use a chart like the one shown to jot down your questions and answers.

Who?	
What?	
When?	
Where?	
Why?	
How?	

Vocabulary Development

diverged (dī vʉrjd´) *v.* branched out in different directions (p. 189)

dallying (dal´ ē iŋ) *v.* wasting time; loitering (p. 190)

submerged (səb mʉrjd´) *adj.* covered with something; underwater (p. 190)

harness (här´ nis) *v.* attach, as with straps for pulling or controlling (p. 190)

amicably (am´ i kə blē) *adv.* agreeably (p. 191)

meticulously (mə tik´ yo͞o ləs lē) *adv.* very carefully and precisely (p. 191)

specters (spek´ tərz) *n.* ghostly images; phantoms (p. 191)

ominous (äm´ ə nəs) *adj.* threatening; menacing (p. 192)

unpalatable (un pal´ it ə bəl) *adj.* distasteful; unpleasant (p. 192)

CUSTOMIZE INSTRUCTION FOR UNIVERSAL ACCESS

For Less Proficient Readers	For English Learners	For Advanced Readers
As students read the selections in this group, have them write down their questions. At the end of each selection, students can compare questions with partners. Partners should work together to find answers to their questions.	Assign peer tutors to go over each selection with students, helping them to answer questions related to the literal meaning of unfamiliar words and idioms. Students can then reread the selections, this time posing questions related to theme, hidden meanings, and so on.	After reading the three pieces, have each student choose one question that remained unanswered. Have students reread the piece two or three times over the course of a day or two, searching for clues to the answer. Finally, have students write essays in which they discuss this question and its possible answers.

❷ Literary Analysis

Figurative Language

- Explain to students that figurative language is used to help the reader experience what the author is describing.
- Tell students that the most common types of figurative language are *metaphor, simile,* and *personification.* A metaphor is a direct comparison: A *is* B. A simile is a less direct comparison: A is *like* B. (Similes usually use *as* or *like.*) Personification is the attribution of human characteristics to an object, animal, concept, or force of nature: "Death rattled his cane in the outer courtyard."
- Use the Figurative Language transparency in **Literary Analysis and Reading Strategy Transparencies,** p. 22, to demonstrate for students how to identify and evaluate figurative language.

❸ Reading Strategy

Generating Questions

- Ask students to think about the questions a reporter asks during an interview and why. Point out that reporters need to understand the story and want to know the person being interviewed.
- Tell students that a similar technique works on a written text. Reading is a bit like engaging in a conversation with the writer. Asking questions keeps the reader actively involved in the text, looking for answers as he or she reads on.
- Remind students that they won't find satisfactory answers to every question on a first reading. Sometimes readers go back to a text, rereading it to determine its true meaning.

Vocabulary Development

- Pronounce each vocabulary word for students, and read the definitions as a class. Have students identify any words with which they are already familiar.

E-Teach

Visit E-Teach at www.phschool.com for teachers' essays on how to teach, with questions and answers.

TEACH

Step-by-Step Teaching Guide for pp. 188–192

CUSTOMIZE INSTRUCTION
For Musical/Rhythmic Learners

Have students identify the ABAAB rhyme scheme of the poem and notice how this scheme influences the syntax Frost uses. Ask them to evaluate whether the rhythm of the language seems natural or forced.

❶ About the Selection

Frost's poem is about much more than a walk in the woods. It's about what to do when faced with a crossroads in life—a time when there's an important decision to make. The speaker must decide whether to pursue a more conventional direction in his life or to resist conformity by following his individual desires and leading a less routine life. He chooses the less conventional path, and as he reflects back years later, he feels he made the right decision.

❷ ▶Critical Viewing

After reading the poem, ask students how the road in this image compares to the road described in the poem.

Answer: The photograph has a misty, dreamlike quality, which seems to hint at the look back in time that ends the poem. The well-traveled road looks like an easier choice, but the path covered in leaves looks more interesting. The poet speaks of a yellow wood and grassy paths, which seem more springlike and brighter than the photographic image.

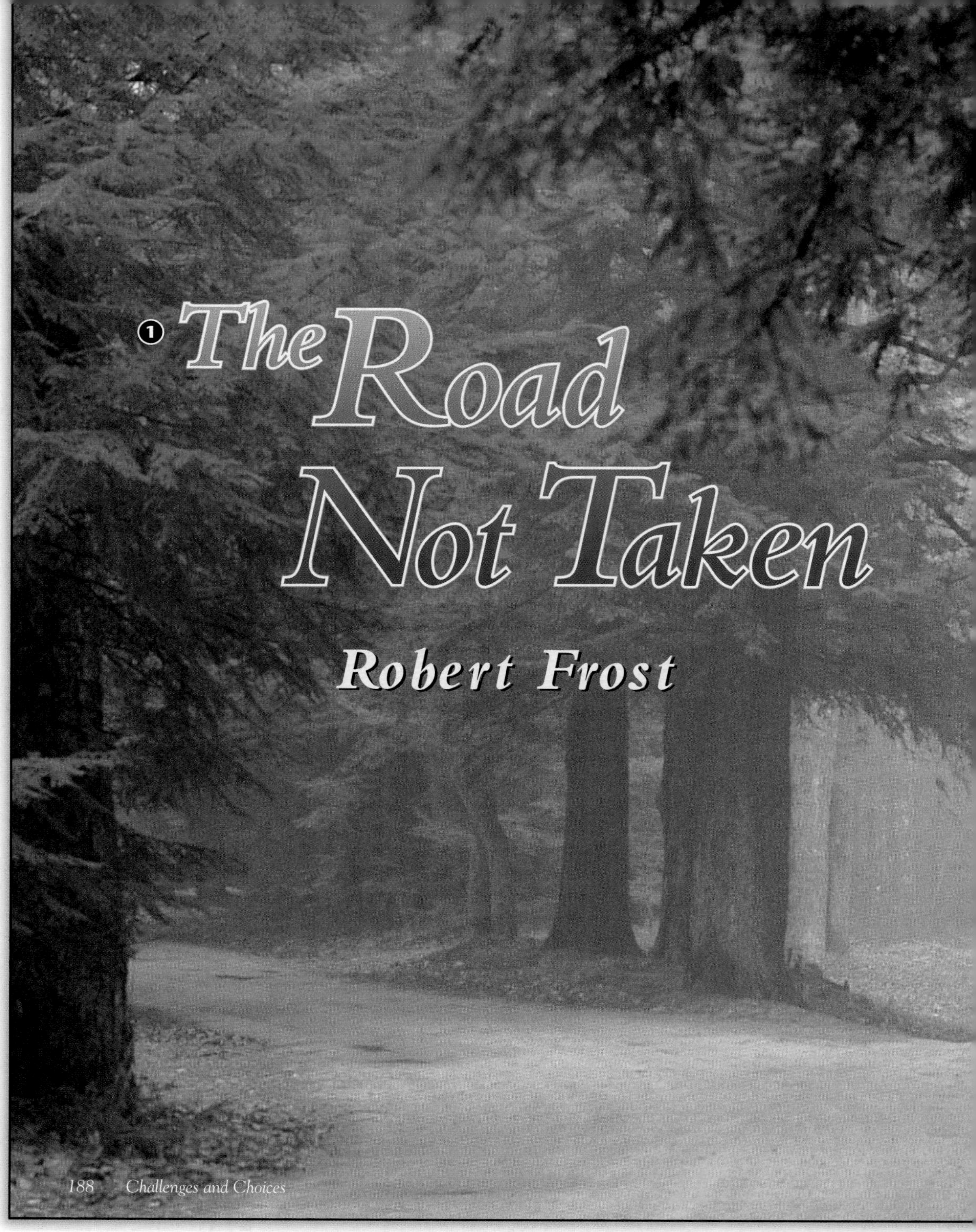

① The Road Not Taken

Robert Frost

TEACHING RESOURCES

The following resources can be used to enrich or extend the instruction for pp. 188–192.

Literary Analysis

- **Selection Support:** Literary Analysis, p. 44

Reading

- **Listening to Literature Audiocassettes,** Side 7 ■
- **Listening to Literature Audio CDs,** CD 6 ■

■ **BLOCK SCHEDULING:** Resources marked with this symbol provide varied instruction during 90-minute blocks.

Two roads diverged in a yellow wood,
And sorry I could not travel both
And be one traveler, long I stood
And looked down one as far as I could
To where it bent in the undergrowth;

Then took the other, as just as fair,
And having perhaps the better claim,
❸ Because it was grassy and wanted wear;
Though as for that, the passing there
Had worn them really about the same,

And both that morning equally lay
In leaves no step had trodden black.
Oh, I kept the first for another day!
Yet knowing how way leads on to way,
I doubted if I should ever come back.

I shall be telling this with a sigh
Somewhere ages and ages hence:
Two roads diverged in a wood, and I—
I took the one less traveled by,
And that has made all the difference.

diverged (di vʉrjd′) *v.* branched out in different directions

Literary Analysis
Figurative Language What is the figurative meaning of the two roads diverging?

Review and Assess

Thinking About the Selection

1. **Respond:** Which of the speaker's feelings or experiences seem most relevant to your own life? Why?
2. (a) **Recall:** What two options does the speaker face? (b) **Recall:** Which does he choose? (c) **Classify:** By making this choice, what sort of person does the speaker seem to be?
3. (a) **Recall:** What is the speaker sorry he could not do? (b) **Speculate:** Why do you think he was sorry?
4. (a) **Interpret:** According to the fourth stanza, how does the speaker expect he will feel about the decision? (b) **Draw Conclusions:** Why do you think the speaker expects to sigh when recalling this incident in the future?
5. **Evaluate:** Robert Frost once said that a poem "begins as a lump in the throat, a sense of wrong, a homesickness, a loneliness." Would you say that description applies in any way to this poem? Explain.
6. **Apply:** Do you think it is generally a good idea to choose a less-traveled path in life? Explain.

Robert Frost

(1874–1963)

In January 1961, when John F. Kennedy took the helm as president of the United States, he called on fellow New Englander Robert Frost—at the time, America's most famous living poet—to recite two poems at the inauguration. Earlier in his career, Frost was not so well received in his native land. In 1912, unable to earn a living as a poet, he packed up his family and moved to England. After British editions of his poetry volumes *A Boy's Will* (1913) and *North of Boston* (1914) won praise on both sides of the Atlantic, Frost returned to the United States a celebrity.

CUSTOMIZE INSTRUCTION FOR UNIVERSAL ACCESS

For Special Needs Students	For Gifted/Talented Students
Read the poem aloud while students follow along in the book. Then, have small groups of students work together to generate questions about the poem. Have them work together to answer the questions. Suggest that they consider the short Frost biography as well as the poem. Be available to help them answer questions.	Have students study the poem and the short Frost biography. Then have them create a list of questions that they would like to ask Frost, about the poem or about his life, if they had the opportunity to meet him. Encourage them to find information about Frost to answer these questions. You may wish to have them share their discoveries with the class.

❸ Literary Analysis

Figurative Language

- Ask the Literary Analysis question on p. 189: What is the figurative meaning of the two roads diverging? Point out that the poem is an implied metaphor; Frost does not directly state the answer to this question.
  Answer: The speaker has to choose between two options.
- The speaker emphasizes that the two roads are "really about the same." What does this suggest about the implied metaphor of the whole poem?
  Answer: Life does not offer just one right choice to anybody; there are many equally tempting and attractive careers that a person can choose.

Answers for p. 189

Review and Assess

1. Possible answer: Students may often face the choice of conforming or being true to themselves.
2. **(a)** traveling down either of two paths in a forest **(b)** the one that looks slightly less worn down by passing feet **(c)** The speaker seems to be solitary, unconventional, and individual.
3. **(a)** The speaker is sorry that he can't take both paths. **(b)** The speaker regrets this because both paths seem attractive.
4. **(a)** The phrase "with a sigh" in line 16 suggests that the speaker anticipates a sense of regret for the road he does not follow. **(b)** The speaker knows that choosing one path means closing off the other, which may have been just as attractive.
5. The speaker seems solitary, if not lonely; he makes this decision without consulting anyone else. The expectation of future regret in line 16 is in accordance with Frost's statement.
6. Possible answer: The most important thing is to be true to what you want. The number of other people making the same choice should never be a consideration.

4 About the Selection

This poem celebrates the nature of work and workers. The poet admires those who display determination and strength, who plunge into tasks wholeheartedly, and who work cooperatively with others.

5 Literary Analysis

Figurative Language

- Have students identify the type of figurative language used in lines 1–7. Have them explain what the speaker is saying about the people.
  Answer: Lines 1–7 are a metaphor comparing people who plunge into work to seals who plunge into the water.

Reteach Remind students that figurative language often appeals to one or more of the five senses.

- Ask students to discuss the effect of the figurative language in lines 8–11. Make sure they explain their answers.
  Answer: It makes the reader feel how hard manual labor is, but it also suggests that such work is satisfying. Words like *pull, strain, mud,* and *muck* appeal to the sense of touch and remind readers of hard physical work they have done and the pleasure they took in doing it well.

6 Literary Analysis

Figurative Language

- Point out to students the word *water* in line 25. Have students look back through the poem for other references to water or images of water.
  Answer: dallying in the shallows, swim off with sure strokes, half-submerged balls, water buffalo, mud and the muck, submerge, fire be put out, common as mud
- Lead a class discussion on this extended image of water. Ask students why Piercy chose to stress the image of water. What effect does her choice have on the overall impact of the poem?
  Possible answers: Water is necessary for life, it makes things grow. Work that is "real" is also necessary, and makes people and socities grow. Water and work can both take several forms. Both can be refreshing.

4 To be of use

Marge Piercy

5

The people I love the best
jump into work head first
without dallying in the shallows
and swim off with sure strokes almost out of sight.
They seem to become natives of that element,
the black sleek heads of seals
bouncing like half-submerged balls.

I love people who harness themselves, an ox to a heavy cart,
who pull like water buffalo, with massive patience,
who strain in the mud and the muck to move things forward,
who do what has to be done, again and again.

I want to be with people who submerge
in the task, who go into the fields to harvest
and work in a row and pass the bags along,
who are not parlor generals and field deserters
but move in a common rhythm
when the food must come in or the fire be put out.

The work of the world is common as mud.
Botched, it smears the hands, crumbles to dust.
But the thing worth doing well done
has a shape that satisfies, clean and evident.
Greek amphoras[1] for wine or oil,
Hopi[2] vases that held corn, are put in museums
but you know they were made to be used.

6

The pitcher cries for water to carry
and a person for work that is real.

dallying (dal′ ē iŋ) *v.* wasting time; loitering

submerged (səb mʉrjd′) *adj.* covered with something; underwater

harness (här′ nis) *v.* attach, as with straps for pulling or controlling

1. **amphoras** (am′ fər əz) *n.* tall jars that have a narrow neck and base and two handles, used by the ancient Greeks and Romans.
2. **Hopi** (hō′ pē) *n.* Pueblo tribe of Indians in northeastern Arizona.

Marge Piercy

(b. 1936)

The young Marge Piercy seemed an unlikely future writer. Born into economic hardship in Detroit, Michigan, Piercy was the first person in her family to attend college. It took her more than ten years to win recognition as a writer, during which time six of her novels were rejected for publication. Now even better known as a poet, Piercy's *To be of use* (1973) and many other highly praised verse collections have been published.

7 # New Directions
Maya Angelou

In 1903 the late Mrs. Annie Johnson of Arkansas found herself with two toddling sons, very little money, a slight ability to read and add simple numbers. To this picture add a disastrous marriage and the burdensome fact that Mrs. Johnson was a Negro.

When she told her husband, Mr. William Johnson, of her dissatisfaction with their marriage, he conceded that he too found it to be less than he expected, and had been secretly hoping to leave and study religion. He added that he thought God was calling him not only to preach but to do so in Enid, Oklahoma. He did not tell her that he knew a minister in Enid with whom he could study and who had a friendly, unmarried daughter. They parted amicably, Annie keeping the one-room house and William taking most of the cash to carry himself to Oklahoma.

8 Annie, over six feet tall, big-boned, decided that she would not go to work as a domestic and leave her "precious babes" to anyone else's care. There was no possibility of being hired at the town's cotton gin or lumber mill, but maybe there was a way to make the two factories work for her. In her words, "I looked up the road I was going and back the way I come, and since I wasn't satisfied, I decided to step off the road and cut me a new path." She told herself that she wasn't a fancy cook but that she could "mix groceries well enough to scare hungry away and from starving a man."

9 She made her plans meticulously and in secret. One early evening to see if she was ready, she placed stones in two five-gallon pails and carried them three miles to the cotton gin. She rested a little, and then, discarding some rocks, she walked in the darkness to the saw mill five miles farther along the dirt road. On her way back to her little house and her babies, she dumped the remaining rocks along the path.

That same night she worked into the early hours boiling chicken and frying ham. She made dough and filled the rolled-out pastry with meat. At last she went to sleep.

The next morning she left her house carrying the meat pies, lard, an iron brazier,[1] and coals for a fire. Just before lunch she appeared in an empty lot behind the cotton gin. As the dinner noon bell rang, she dropped the savors into boiling fat and the aroma rose and floated over to the workers who spilled out of the gin, covered with white lint, looking like specters.

Most workers had brought their lunches of pinto beans and biscuits or crackers, onions and cans of sardines, but they were

Reading Strategy
Generating Questions
What question might you ask about the character of Annie's husband?

amicably (am´ i kə blē) *adv.* agreeably

meticulously (mə tik´ yo͞o ləs lē) *adv.* very carefully and precisely

specters (spek´ tərz) *n.* ghostly images; phantoms

10 **Reading Check**
What did Annie's husband do when she told him she was dissatisfied with their marriage?

1. **iron brazier** (brā´ zhər) pan for holding burning charcoal or coals as a heat source for cooking; a portable barbecue.

CUSTOMIZE INSTRUCTION FOR UNIVERSAL ACCESS

For Advanced Readers

Have students compare and contrast "To be of use" with Walt Whitman's "I Hear America Singing" (p. 172). Point out that both poems celebrate ordinary working people. Ask students to look at differences between the two. Which speaker identifies more with the workers? Which poem does a better job of helping the reader identify with the workers? Which poet makes a more effective use of figurative language? Which poem did students prefer and why? Students can write comparison-contrast essays on these two poems.

7 About the Selection

This piece is more than a biographical sketch of one woman's road from adversity to success. Like "The Road Not Taken," it is about choices. Annie Johnson is temporarily the victim of circumstances. She could give up, but she doesn't. Instead, she shows us that, despite life's many obstacles, success follows those who are courageous, creative, and flexible in their decisions. With hard work and initiative, it is possible to "cut a new path."

8 Reading Strategy
Generating Questions

- Ask students the Reading Strategy question on p. 191: What questions might you ask about the character of Annie's husband?
  Possible answer: What had he expected from the marriage? Why did he really want to go to Oklahoma? What does this suggest about why the marriage was "disastrous"?

Monitor Progress What questions might students ask about Annie?
Possible answers: What are her plans? Will her plans succeed?

9 Vocabulary Development
The Anglo Saxon Suffix *-ly*

- Call students' attention to the word *meticulously* and its definition. Tell them that the Anglo-Saxon suffix *-ly* turns adjectives into adverbs. It means *how, in what manner, in what way,* or *to what degree.* So a person who is *cheerful* (adjective) might behave *cheerfully* (in a cheerful manner).
- Explain that most adjectives can easily be turned into adverbs by adding *-ly*. If an adjective ends in *-y*, the *-y* changes to *-i* before *-ly* is added. Have students suggest some adjectives along with an adverb created by adding *-ly*.
  Possible answers: happy/happily; helpful/helpfully; warm/warmly.
- Point out that sometimes this suffix appears at the end of an adjective. Examples are friendly, lonely, and lovely. Students should be aware of this, but should remember that *-ly* is more often used for creating adverbs.

10 Reading Check

Answer: Annie's husband told her he felt the same way and indicated his desire to move to Oklahoma.

ASSESS

⓫ Reading Strategy

Generating Questions

- Read aloud the bracketed passage to students.
- Ask students the Reading Strategy question on p. 192: What question does this paragraph spark in your mind?
  Possible answers: Are the workers aware that Annie is alternating the days on which they get fresh hot pies? Do they appreciate her fairness?
- Ask students what questions they would like to ask Annie if they could meet her.
  Possible answers: Do you mind working in all weathers? Are the workers good customers? Were you nervous during the first few days of slow business?

Answers for p. 192

Review and Assess

1. Students might prefer to meet Annie because she is a worker.
2. **(a)** The speaker loves people who dive right into their work. **(b)** They possess physical strength and stamina, pride and pleasure in their work, energy, and endurance.
3. **(a)** Her husband took most of their money when they got divorced. **(b)** She didn't want to leave her children in someone else's care.
4. **(a)** She sells her homemade meat pies to factory and mill workers. **(b)** It suggests that poeple can rise above circumstances, and that as long as the spirit is unbroken, it will find a way to survive.
5. Students may reply that feeling useful builds self-esteem and makes life richer.

tempted by the hot meat pies which Annie ladled out of the fat. She wrapped them in newspapers, which soaked up the grease, and offered them for sale at a nickel each. Although business was slow, those first days Annie was determined. She balanced her appearances between the two hours of activity.

⓫ So, on Monday if she offered hot fresh pies at the cotton gin and sold the remaining cooled-down pies at the lumber mill for three cents, then on Tuesday she went first to the lumber mill presenting fresh, just-cooked pies as the lumbermen covered in sawdust emerged from the mill.

For the next few years, on balmy spring days, blistering summer noons, and cold, wet, and wintry middays, Annie never disappointed her customers, who could count on seeing the tall, brown-skin woman bent over her brazier, carefully turning the meat pies. When she felt certain that the workers had become dependent on her, she built a stall between the two hives of industry and let the men run to her for their lunchtime provisions.

She had indeed stepped from the road which seemed to have been chosen for her and cut herself a brand-new path. In years that stall became a store where customers could buy cheese, meal, syrup, cookies, candy, writing tablets, pickles, canned goods, fresh fruit, soft drinks, coal, oil, and leather soles for worn-out shoes.

Each of us has the right and the responsibility to assess the roads which lie ahead, and those over which we have traveled, and if the future road looms ominous or unpromising, and the roads back uninviting, then we need to gather our resolve and, carrying only the necessary baggage, step off that road into another direction. If the new choice is also unpalatable, without embarrassment, we must be ready to change that as well.

Reading Strategy
Generating Questions What question does this paragraph spark in your mind?

ominous (äm′ ə nəs) *adj.* threatening; menacing

unpalatable (un pal′ it ə bəl) *adj.* distasteful; unpleasant

Review and Assess

Thinking About the Selections

1. **Respond:** Would you rather meet Annie Johnson or the speaker of "To be of use"? Explain.
2. **(a) Recall:** In the first stanza of "To be of use," what kind of people does the speaker say she loves best? **(b) Analyze:** What kinds of qualities or traits do these people possess?
3. **(a) Recall:** Why does Annie Johnson have to find a source of income? **(b) Infer:** Why do you think Annie Johnson chose not to pursue a factory job or a job as a domestic?
4. **(a) Recall:** How does Annie Johnson earn a living? **(b) Draw Conclusions:** What does Johnson's achievement suggest about the human spirit in general?
5. **Apply:** What are the positive consequences of feeling useful?

Maya Angelou

(b. 1928)

Three decades after Frost's appearance at the Kennedy inauguration, President-elect Bill Clinton invited fellow Arkansan Maya Angelou to read one of her poems at his inaugural ceremonies. In both her poetry and her nonfiction, Angelou draws on her own experience, frequently exploring the problems of poverty, racism, and sexism.

ASSESSMENT PRACTICE: Reading Comprehension

Recognize Supporting Details (For more practice, see Test Preparation Workbook, p.11.)

Many tests require students to recognize supporting details. Use the following sample to teach students how to recognize which details are relevant to and support a main idea.

On balmy spring days, blistering summer noons, and cold, wet, and wintry middays, Annie never disappointed her customers, who could count on seeing the tall, brown-skin woman bent over her brazier, carefully turning the meat pies.

Which detail shows that Annie is determined and dependable?

A She is tall.
B She never disappoints her customers.
C She doesn't work when it's wet.
D Her customers like her meat pies.

Choices *A* and *D* are true, but they aren't relevant to Annie's reliability. Choice *C* is false. The correct answer is *B*.

Review and Assess

Literary Analysis

Figurative Language

1. Why is the description of life as a road or path an effective use of **figurative language**?
2. Use a chart like this one to record four examples of figurative language from "To be of use." Explain the meaning of each example.

Figurative Language:	1. ________	2. ________	3. ________	4. ________
Meaning:				

Comparing Literary Works

3. (a) Compare Frost's "less traveled" road with the "new path" that Johnson carves for herself. (b) What similar approaches to life do these images convey?
4. (a) Contrast the way Frost's speaker approaches the roads and the way the people in Piercy's opening stanza approach the water. (b) What different approaches to life does the figurative language convey?

Reading Strategy

Generating Questions

5. Using a chart like the one shown, identify at least three of the **questions** and answers you **generated** while reading the selections.

	Who?	What?	When?	Where?	Why?	How?
Question:						
Answer:						

6. Which questions helped you understand the selections best?

Extend Understanding

7. **History Connection:** Annie Johnson's situation shows the struggle that many African American women faced in the early 1900s. How have situations changed for African Americans in the United States over the last century?

Quick Review

Figurative language is language that means more than it says literally. It is often used to create vivid impressions by setting up comparisons between dissimilar things.

To better understand what you read, **generate questions** based on the text. Begin with the common question words *who, what, where, when, why,* and *how* about a selection.

Take It to the Net

www.phschool.com

Take the interactive self-test online to check your understanding of the selections.

ENRICHMENT: Further Reading

Other Works by Ray Bradbury

Works by Robert Frost
"Stopping by Woods on a Snowy Evening"

Works by Maya Angelou
I Know Why the Caged Bird Sings
All God's Children Need Traveling Shoes

Works by Marge Piercy
Breaking Camp
"For the Young Who Want To"

Take It to the Net

Visit www.phschool.com for more information on the selections.

Answers for p. 193

Review and Assess

1. A road stretches out in front of a person looking at it. A road has to be traveled, just as a life has to be lived. A life has to be lived in chronological order; a road must be traveled from its beginning to its end.
2. Sample answers: "They seem to become . . . seals" describes people immersing themselves in their work; "pull like water buffalo, with massive patience" refers to people who don't give up when life is hard; "the work of the world is as common as mud" reflects the idea that, like mud or clay, work can be either sloppy or carefully crafted; "the pitcher cries for water to carry" means we all need meaningful work.
3. **(a)** Both images show the writers' choices of lives other than the ordinary. **(b)** Both chose routes that were personally satisfying and more productive, rather than an easier, more common route.
4. **(a)** Frost's speaker hesitates over the choice of roads; Piercy's workers do the opposite: They plunge into their work. **(b)** Some people may approach choices in a hesitant manner; others are very confident in themselves.
5. Questions will vary. Make sure students support their answers with details from the selections.
6. Answers will vary. Have students share some of the questions they asked and how the questions helped them understand the selections.
7. African Americans are no longer limited to manual labor. Workplaces and schools are desegregated.

EXTEND

Answers for p. 194

❶ Vocabulary Development

Word Analysis

1. amicably
2. meticulously
3. ominously

Spelling Strategy

1. dismayed
2. catching
3. flexed
4. flowing

Fluency: True or False

1. T
2. F
3. F
4. T
5. F
6. F
7. T
8. F
9. T

❷ Grammar

1. look, is looking, looked, has looked
2. diverge, is diverging, diverged, has diverged
3. observe, is observing, observed, has observed
4. harvest, is harvesting, harvested, has harvested
5. work, is working, worked, has worked
6. walk, is walking, walked, has walked
7. jump, is jumping, jumped, has jumped
8. cook, is cooking, cooked, has cooked
9. expect, is expecting, expected, has expected
10. cover, is covering, covered, has covered

Writing Application

Possible responses:

1. I travel whenever I can get a few days off. present
2. I am traveling through North Africa on a camel. present participle
3. I traveled to Vietnam to photograph orphaned children. past
4. I have traveled to all the continents except Australia and Antarctica. past participle

Integrate Language Skills

❶ Vocabulary Development Lesson

Word Analysis: Anglo-Saxon Suffix *-ly*

Words that end in *-ly* are often adjectives turned into adverbs of manner—adverbs that tell *how* or *in what manner*. Use the suffix *-ly* to turn the following adjectives into adverbs.

1. amicable (friendly)
2. meticulous (very careful or thorough)
3. ominous (menacing; threatening)

Spelling Strategy

Do not double the letters *w*, *h*, *x*, or *y* at the end of a word before adding an ending such as *-ing* or *-ed*. For example, *box* + *-ed* = *boxed*. Write the new words formed by adding the given suffixes below, and then use each word in a sentence.

1. dismay + *-ed*
2. catch + *-ing*
3. flex + *-ed*
4. flow + *-ing*

Fluency: True or False

Indicate whether each of the following statements is true or false. Explain your answer.

1. If a stream *diverged*, two parts of it probably moved in different directions.
2. If you and your friend part *amicably*, you are most likely in a bad mood.
3. If you clean your room *meticulously*, it is messy.
4. Some children dress as *specters* on Halloween.
5. A smile is usually an *ominous* expression.
6. Most chefs try to cook *unpalatable* meals.
7. Window shoppers seem to enjoy *dallying*.
8. Flowers are *submerged* in the soil.
9. In Alaska, some people *harness* dogs to a sled.

❷ Grammar Lesson

Regular Verbs

A **verb** has four principal parts: the present, the present participle, the past, and the past participle. Most of the verbs in the English language, such as the verb *talk*, are regular, and you can form these parts following a predictable pattern. Notice that the final *e* may be dropped in forming the present participle.

Present: talk; race
Present Participle: (is) talking; (is) racing
Past: talked; raced
Past Participle: (has) talked; (has) raced

Practice Write the four principal parts of each of the following verbs.

1. look
2. diverge
3. observe
4. harvest
5. work
6. walk
7. jump
8. cook
9. expect
10. cover

Writing Application Write four sentences using each of the principal parts of the regular verb *travel*. After each sentence, identify which part you used.

Prentice Hall Writing and Grammar Connection: Chapter 23, Section 1

TEACHING RESOURCES

The following resources can be used to enrich or extend the instructions for pp. 194–195.

Vocabulary

- **Selection Support:** Build Vocabulary, p. 41
- **Vocabulary and Spelling Practice Book** (Use this booklet for skills enrichment.) ■

Grammar

- **Selection Support,** Build Grammar Skills, p. 42
- **Writing and Grammar,** Gold Level, p. 526
- **Daily Language Practice Transparencies**

Writing

- **Writing and Grammar,** Gold Level, p. 291 ■
- **Writing and Grammar iText CD-ROM**
- **Writing Models and Graphic Organizers on Transparencies,** p. 95

■ **BLOCK SCHEDULING:** Resources marked with this symbol provide varied instruction during 90-minute blocks.

❸ Writing Lesson

Evaluation of Figurative Language

By using figurative language—such as the image of a road in Frost's poem to suggest a life—writers hope to add clarity and color to their writing. Choose one of the selections and write an essay evaluating the writer's use of figurative language.

Prewriting List examples of figurative language that you find in your chosen selection. Identify the basic comparisons that are stated or implied. As you make your list, decide whether the language leaves you confused or if the choice of words is logical. Also, notice whether the comparison is an overused expression or a fresh, new idea.

Model: Evaluating Figurative Language

Figurative Language	Comments
"[people] who pull like water buffalo, with massive patience"	This is original and makes a clear comparison to people who work diligently and patiently.

The comment evaluates the unique qualities of the poet's use of figurative language.

Drafting State your reaction to the figurative language, and then cite examples to support your reaction. Present the examples in order of importance or in the order in which they appear in the work.

Revising Make sure you have offered enough examples to support all general statements. Check to see that your sentences are logical.

WG Prentice Hall Writing and Grammar Connection: Chapter 13, Section 2

❹ Extension Activities

Listening and Speaking Working with another student, role-play a **job interview** that might take place between Annie Johnson and a potential employer.

- Analyze the occasion and decide what each speaker needs to say.
- Decide what the potential employer wants to hear.

During the interview, use effective, formal language to convey the character and the situation. When appropriate, use gestures and eye contact to make a point.

Research and Technology Working in a small group, **videotape an interview** with a local businessperson, a teacher, or another professional to learn about the stages of that person's career. After watching the video, compare the aspects of your subject's career to those of Annie Johnson's. **[Group Activity]**

Take It to the Net www.phschool.com

Go online for an additional research activity using the Internet.

ASSESSMENT RESOURCES

The following resources can be used to assess students' knowledge and skills.

Selection Assessment

- **Formal Assessment**, pp. 35–37
- **Open Book Test**, pp. 31–33
- **Got It! Assessment Videotapes**, Tape 1

Take It to the Net

Visit www.phschool.com for self-tests and additional questions on the selections.

Writing Rubric

- **Performance Assess. and Portfolio Mgmt.**, p. 15

Listening and Speaking Rubric

- **Performance Assess. and Portfolio Mgmt.**, p. 26

PRENTICE HALL ASSESSMENT SYSTEM

- **Workbook**
- **Transparencies**
- **Skill Book**
- **CD-ROM**

Lesson Support for p. 195

❸ Writing Lesson

- In class, discuss the example in the Model. What is a water buffalo like? What kind of work does it do? How big is it? What does the image tell readers about the writer's attitude toward those who do hard work? Encourage students to think about why images are used and what they tell the reader.
- Display the Outline transparency, p. 95 of **Writing Models and Graphic Organizers on Transparencies.** Suggest that students use a similar format to organize their essays and to make certain that each reaction is supported by examples.
- Use the Response to Literature rubric, p. 15 of **Performance Assessment and Portfolio Management** to evaluate students' essays.

❹ Extension Activity

Listening and Speaking

- Briefly review with students the kinds of questions that are asked at a job interview.
- Remind students to keep Annie Johnson's job skills in mind as they plan their interviews.
- Use the Conducting an Interview rubric, p. 26 of **Performance Assessment and Portfolio Management** to evaluate students' interviews. You may wish to review the evaluation criteria before students do their presentations, to make certain they are aware of what is expected.

CUSTOMIZE INSTRUCTION for Universal Access

To address different learning styles, use the following activities suggested in the **Extension Activities** booklet, p. 11.

- For Interpersonal Learners, use Activities 4 and 5.
- For Visual/Spatial and Logical/Mathematical Learners, use Activity 5.
- For Verbal/Linguistic Learners, use Activities 5 and 6.

Lesson Objectives

1. To understand how to analyze a document's structure and format
2. To identify the six parts of a business letter
3. To describe qualities of a well-written business document

About Business Documents

- Ask students to name different types of business documents. Answers: Answers may include business letters, reports, memos, meeting notes, agendas, and e-mail messages.
- Have students review the Types of Business Documents shown in the example on p. 196.
- Ask a student to read aloud the bulleted list of qualities of an effective business document.
- Invite students to share the types of business documents that they may have had occasion to write. Answers: Students may mention letters inquiring about scholarship opportunities, job application forms, meeting minutes for a school club, or written notes to teachers.

Reading Strategy

Analyzing Document Structure and Format

- Ask students to provide examples of business documents they have been required to compose or complete, such as health insurance applications or thank-you letters.
- Ask students to imagine that they have been accused of misconduct at school. The principal asks the students to write letters explaining their view of the incident. Why would each part of a business letter be important in such a situation? Possible answers: Writing a formal letter with all expected components shows that the writer took care to present information in a formal, proper way. The body of the letter provides an opportunity to state the case clearly. The signature validates the genuineness of the letter's content.

READING INFORMATIONAL MATERIALS

Business Documents

About Business Documents

A business document is a formal piece of writing relating to the workplace. The purpose of a business document is to communicate specific information effectively by presenting facts and other pertinent details.

This chart shows the variety and function of business documents.

Types of Business Documents

Print	Electronic
Letter: a formal, written message sent by regular mail **Agenda:** a schedule for a meeting **Memo:** a brief message with pertinent information for internal company use only **Meeting minutes:** the notes and a summary of a business meeting **Form/application:** a document filled out by an applicant	**Voice mail:** a spoken message recorded on an answering machine **E-mail:** a typed message sent by computer **Fax:** a printed copy of a handwritten or typed message transmitted via phone lines

A well-written business document meets these criteria:

- It imparts accurate information in a clear, direct, and concise way.
- It addresses specific issues and anticipates readers' questions.
- It is neatly formatted, well organized, and error-free.

Reading Strategy

Analyzing Document Structure and Format

The structure of a business document suits its purpose. Look at the structure and format of these common business documents:

A **business letter** addresses a work-related issue, such as a request for service or a clarification of company policy. The letter has six parts: the heading, inside address, salutation, body, closing, and signature. It is written in paragraph form that follows an acceptable format of indentation.

A **business agenda** outlines the schedule for a meeting. An agenda contains a title identifying the subject, a list of starting and ending times for scheduled events, and descriptions of each part of the agenda.

Letter of Welcome

In the following business letter, California senator Martha Escutia welcomes students to a college conference. Notice that the language of the letter, which uses block format, is welcoming but formal and polite.

The **heading** provides the business address of the senator.

The **salutation** identifies and greets the letter's recipients.

The **body** explains the letter writer's purpose for writing.

The **closing,** written in Spanish, means "It is possible." Typical English closings include "Sincerely" and "Yours truly."

Senator
MARTHA ESCUTIA
California State Senate 30th District
400 N. Montebello Blvd. #101
Montebello, CA 90640

Representing the communities of:

Bell
Bell Gardens
Commerce
Cudahy
East Los Angeles
Florence-Graham
Huntington Park
Maywood
Miramonte
Montebello
Norwalk
Pico Rivera
Santa Fe Springs
South El Monte
South Gate
Vernon
Walnut Park
Whittier

Dear Students:

I want to welcome you to the 8th Annual Southeast College Conference. It is my privilege to host this exciting event and to share the many educational opportunities at your disposal.

You have reached a critical time in your life, a time filled with questions. Where do you want to go in life? How will you get there? Education is definitely the vehicle to your success in any career you choose. Education will help develop you into leaders of the next generation. It will empower you intellectually and enable you to grow into valuable, contributing citizens of your community.

As a young girl I learned the importance of a college education. I armed myself with information that enabled me to pursue my dream. Believe me, my quest for higher education was not easy. I remember the financial and social obstacles my family and community had to overcome. Their sacrifices inspired me to educate myself and give back to my community.

When I was first elected to the Assembly, I was overjoyed. I finally had the opportunity to give back by passing legislation to improve the quality of life in my community. This year, as your Senator, I passed SB 1689, the Advanced Placement Challenge Grant Program. This measure allocated $16.5 million dollars to fund Advanced Placement (AP) classes in schools that lack teachers and support systems for AP students. I also passed SB 1683, which will ensure that every student at risk of not graduating will receive the extra academic help he or she needs. Its focus is to give the students the tools they need to establish a stronger educational foundation.

Please make today an opportunity of a lifetime. Ask questions, participate in the workshops, let your voice be heard and, most importantly, have fun. Today I am very proud to have the opportunity to meet the great minds of the future. I wish you the best of luck and continued success in your future educational endeavors.

SÍ, SE PUEDE

Senator Martha Escutia

Senator Martha Escutia

Letters of Welcome

- Point out that students might receive letters of welcome from a school, club, or other organization. Explain that the letter of welcome on p. 197 greets students who are attending a conference.
- Have students read the letter and the notes that identify its main elements. Point out that the letter is from a California senator.
- Explain that although this is a formal letter, it is a friendly one. Ask students to reread the body of the letter, watching for details that give the letter its friendly tone. **Answer:** The use of the first and second pronouns, "I" and "you," connects the writer with the reader. In addition, the writer's sharing of personal life experiences and feelings adds to the friendly tone.

CUSTOMIZE INSTRUCTION FOR UNIVERSAL ACCESS

For English Learners	For Gifted/Talented Students
Some students may not be familiar with the use of particular words and phrases in Senator Escutia's letter. For example, "critical time" and "vehicle to success" may need clarification. Have students write down any words or phrases they do not fully understand, and then lead a discussion that clarifies these concepts.	Point out that parts of Senator Escutia's letter sound like an inspirational speech. Have students practice reading the letter aloud as if it were a welcoming speech at the conference.

Conference Agenda

- Ask students if they have ever attended an event that had a formal agenda. Examples might include a graduation ceremony, wedding, church service, or conference. Point out that an agenda is a schedule of events.
- Have students read the agenda for the 8th Annual Southeast College Conference.
- Ask students to point out elements of the agenda that will help them predict the day's activities. **Answer:** Elements include the time, name, speaker, and brief description of each event.

Conference Agenda

In addition to the business letter welcoming them to the 8th Annual Southeast College Conference, students attending also received this agenda. The agenda outlines activities from 8 A.M. to 2 P.M.

Program Agenda

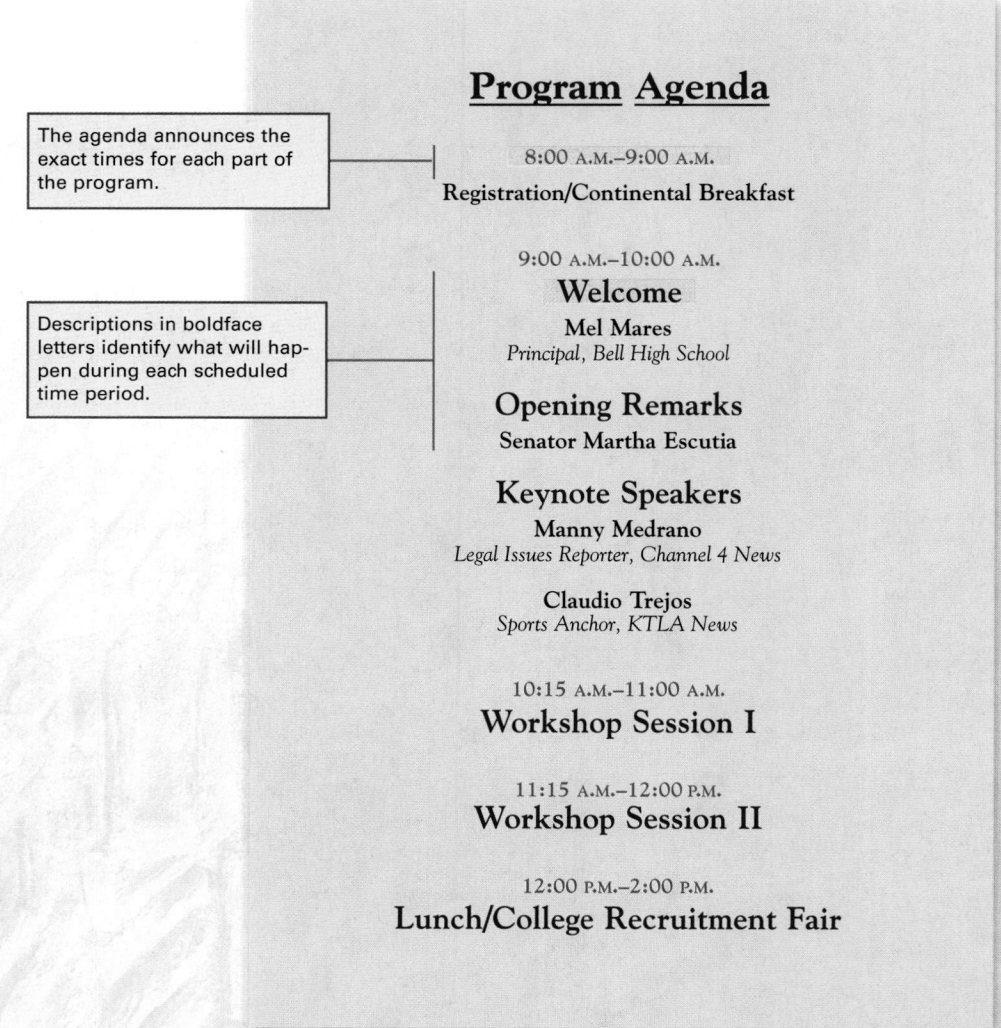

The agenda announces the exact times for each part of the program.

8:00 A.M.–9:00 A.M.
Registration/Continental Breakfast

Descriptions in boldface letters identify what will happen during each scheduled time period.

9:00 A.M.–10:00 A.M.
Welcome
Mel Mares
Principal, Bell High School

Opening Remarks
Senator Martha Escutia

Keynote Speakers
Manny Medrano
Legal Issues Reporter, Channel 4 News

Claudio Trejos
Sports Anchor, KTLA News

10:15 A.M.–11:00 A.M.
Workshop Session I

11:15 A.M.–12:00 P.M.
Workshop Session II

12:00 P.M.–2:00 P.M.
Lunch/College Recruitment Fair

Check Your Comprehension

1. What is Senator Escutia's purpose for writing her business letter?
2. What personal information does the senator share to make her letter friendly to students?
3. According to the agenda, who is delivering the opening remarks?
4. When will Workshop Session I be held?

Applying the Reading Strategy

Analyzing Document Structure and Format

5. What is the relationship between the opening and closing paragraphs of this business letter?
6. What is the purpose of the paragraph in which the author discusses her accomplishments as senator?
7. Why do you think the senator chose to write her closing in Spanish?

Activity

Writing a Letter of Welcome to Parents

Write a business letter in which you welcome parents to a school event such as a parent-teacher conference or talent show. Assume that the letter will be distributed to parents as they enter the building. In your letter, include information that tells when and where the event takes place. Also, explain the purpose of the event. Use friendly but formal language. Keep track of the parts of your business letter by using the chart at right.

Outline for Letter of Welcome to Parents

Heading: Your Address
Salutation: "Dear Parents:"
Body:
- Letter's Purpose (in opening paragraph)
- Explanation of Event
- Where and When

Polite Closing:
Signature:

Contrasting Informational Texts

Document Formats

1. For each situation below, indicate the best format to convey information. Choose voice mail, e-mail, fax, business letter, agenda, memo, meeting minutes, or application form. Explain your choice.
   (a) Formally introducing your business to a new client
   (b) Reminding a co-worker about an idea you had and asking for her input
   (c) Supplying the information needed to open a bank account
   (d) Sharing a sketch of your idea with someone in another office
   (e) Recording decisions made at a meeting
   (f) Instructing employees about a complex new policy

Answers for p. 199

Check Your Comprehension

1. The purpose of Senator Escutia's letter is to welcome students to a conference.
2. The senator shares her own experiences in college and her feelings about how important this educational opportunity is for all students.
3. Mel Mares is delivering the opening remarks.
4. The session will be held from 10:15 A.M. to 11:00 A.M.

Applying the Reading Strategy

5. The two paragraphs emphasize welcome, the importance of this opportunity for students, and the senator's good wishes for them.
6. The paragraph explains the senator's legislative achievements in promoting education.
7. By closing in Spanish, the senator acknowledges her Spanish heritage.

Activity

Suggest that students recall parent events they have participated in or helped host. Point out that a brief agenda is especially important in this case because many parents are not familiar with the school's layout and will need to know exactly when and where they should be for various activities.

Contrasting Informational Texts

Answers

a. A business letter would best cover the points you want to make in a welcoming tone.
b. Voice mail or e-mail would serve well as an informal reminder.
c. An application form would allow you to provide the information needed.
d. An informal memo would accommodate a sketch of your idea.
e. Meeting minutes would best record decisions made at a meeting.
f. A formal memo would best spell out a complex new policy.

Old Man of the Temple

Lesson Objectives and CA Correlations

1. **To analyze and respond to literary elements**
   - Literary Analysis: Fantasy **R 3.7**
   - Connecting Literary Elements: Setting
2. **To read, comprehend, analyze, and critique a short story**
   - Reading Strategy: Distinguishing Fantasy From Reality
   - Reading Check questions
   - Review and Assess questions
   - Assessment Practice (ATE)
3. **To develop word analysis skills, fluency, and systematic vocabulary**
   - Vocabulary Development Lesson: Using the Latin Suffix *-ity* **R 1.1**
4. **To understand and apply written and oral language conventions**
   - Spelling Strategy
   - Grammar Lesson: Adverbs **LC 1.3**
5. **To understand and apply appropriate writing and research strategies**
   - Writing Lesson: Travel Brochure **W 2.4**
   - Extension Activity: Research Report **W 1.5**
6. **To understand and apply listening and speaking strategies**
   - Extension Activity: Dramatic Monologue **LS 1.9**

STEP-BY-STEP TEACHING GUIDE	PACING GUIDE
PRETEACH	
Motivate Students and Provide Background	
Use the Motivation activity (ATE p. 200)	5 min.
Read and discuss the Preview material and Background information (SE/ATE p. 200) [A]	10 min.
Introduce the Concepts	
Introduce the Literary Analysis and Reading Strategy (SE/ATE p. 201) [A]	15 min.
Pronounce the vocabulary words and read their definitions (SE p. 201)	5 min.
TEACH	
Monitor Comprehension	
Informally monitor comprehension by circulating while students read independently or in groups [A]	15 min.
Monitor students' comprehension with the Reading Check notes (SE/ATE pp. 205, 207)	as students read
Develop vocabulary with Vocabulary notes (SE pp. 203, 204, 206–208; ATE p. 203)	as students read
Develop Understanding	
Develop students' understanding of fantasy with Literary Analysis annotations (SE p. 204; ATE p. 204) [A]	10 min.
Develop students' ability to distinguish fantasy from reality with Reading Strategy annotations (SE pp. 205, 206; ATE pp. 205, 206)	10 min.
ASSESS	
Assess Mastery	
Assess students' mastery of the Reading Strategy and Literary Analysis by having them answer the Review and Assess questions (SE/ATE p. 209)	20 min.
Use one or more of the print and media Assessment Resources (ATE p. 211) [A]	up to 50 min.
EXTEND	
Apply Understanding	
Have students complete the Vocabulary Development Lesson and the Grammar Lesson (SE p. 210) [A]	20 min.
Apply students' knowledge of using a persuasive tone with the Writing Lesson (SE/ATE p. 211) [A]	45 min.
Apply students' understanding using one or more of the Extension Activities (SE p. 211)	20–90 min.

A **ACCELERATED INSTRUCTION:**
Use the strategies and activities identified with an [A].

UNIVERSAL ACCESS
● = Below Level Students
▲ = On-Level Students
■ = Above Level Students

Time and Resource Manager

Reading Level: Average
Average Number of Instructional Days: 4

RESOURCES		
PRINT	**TRANSPARENCIES**	**TECHNOLOGY**
• **Beyond Literature,** Humanities Connection: Art, p. 12 ▲ ■		• **Interest Grabber Video,** Tape 1 ● ▲ ■
• **Selection Support Workbook:** ● ▲ ■ Literary Analysis, p. 48 Reading Strategy, p. 47 Build Vocabulary, p. 45	• **Literary Analysis and Reading Transparencies,** pp. 23 and 24 ● ▲ ■	
• **Adapted Reader's Companion** ● • **Reader's Companion** ●		• **Listening to Literature** ● ▲ ■ Audiocassettes, Side 8 Audio CDs, CD 6
• **English Learner's Companion** ● ▲ • **Literatura en español** ● ▲ • **Literary Analysis for Enrichment** ■		
• **Formal Assessment:** Selection Test, pp. 38–40 ● ▲ ■ • **Open Book Test,** pp. 34–36 ● ▲ ■ • PRENTICE HALL ASSESSMENT SYSTEM ● ▲ ■	• PRENTICE HALL ASSESSMENT SYSTEM ● ▲ ■ Skills Practice Answers and Explanations on Transparencies	• **Test Bank Software** ● ▲ ■ • **Got It! Assessment Videotapes,** Tape 1 ● ▲
• **Selection Support Workbook:** ● ▲ ■ Build Grammar Skills, p. 46 • **Writing and Grammar,** Gold Level ● ▲ ■ • **Extension Activities,** p. 12 ● ▲ ■	• **Daily Language Practice Transparencies** ● ▲	• **Writing and Grammar iText CD-ROM** ● ▲ ■ *Take It to the Net* www.phschool.com

BLOCK SCHEDULING: Use one 90-minute class period to preteach the selection and have students read it. Use a second 90-minute class period to assess students' mastery of skills and have them complete one of the Extension Activities.

PRETEACH

Step-by-Step Teaching Guide for pp. 200–201

Motivation

People all over the world hear, read, and tell ghost stories to entertain, instruct, or warn. They respond to ripples of fear, unexplained mystery, and gruesome detail. The nature of ghosts varies. In some cultures, ghosts are dead ancestors, angry because they've been excluded from paradise. Some are upset over unfinished work. Others return to contact relatives, friends, or enemies. Write the following passage from this story on the chalkboard, or read it aloud:

> *"Dead! Dead!" he said. "Don't talk nonsense. How can I be dead when you see me before you now? If I am dead how can I be saying this and that?"*

Have students discuss what kind of ghost this is and whom he may be addressing.

Interest Grabber Video

As an alternative, play "Celebrating Janamashtami" on Tape 1 to engage student interest.

❶ Background

Culture

Most of Narayan's stories take place in the fictional town of Malgudi. While Malgudi is a distinctly southern Indian place, the tales that Narayan tells about it are universal. If you change the backdrop of any of Narayan's tales to a modern American town, you will find that the characters' struggles, plans, hopes, and dreams still apply. There is no aspect of the human experience about which Narayan has not written. It is this universal quality that makes his writing so special.

Prepare to Read

Old Man of the Temple

Take It to the Net

Visit www.phschool.com for interactive activities and instruction related to "Old Man of the Temple," including

- background
- graphic organizers
- literary elements
- reading strategies

Preview

Connecting to the Literature

You see a shadow dart behind a tree, but when you reach the tree and look, there is nothing there—what could it be? The narrator's experience in this story is universal: He sees something and cannot believe his eyes. It is this element of mystery that can make a story so much fun to read.

❶ Background

"Old Man of the Temple" takes place near Malgudi, a fictional town in southern India. Although it is imaginary, it could be any one of thousands of rural southern Indian towns. Its roads are unpaved, and cattle roam the dirt paths as farmers till the fields. It is a place where the ruins of temples hundreds of years old decay amid the creeping tropical vines.

TEACHING RESOURCES

The following resources can be used to enrich or extend the instruction for pp. 200–201.

Motivation

Interest Grabber Video, Tape 1

Background

Beyond Literature, p. 12

Take It to the Net

Visit www.phschool.com for background and hotlinks for "Old Man of the Temple."

Literary Analysis

Literary Analysis and Reading Transparencies, Fantasy, p. 23

Reading

Selection Support: Reading Strategy, p. 47; Build Vocabulary, p. 45

Literary Analysis and Reading Transparencies, Distinguish Fantasy From Reality, p. 24

BLOCK SCHEDULING: Resources marked with this symbol provide varied instruction during 90-minute blocks.

❷ Literary Analysis

Fantasy

"Old Man of the Temple" is a **fantasy**—a work of fiction that includes characters, places, and events that could not really exist or happen. When you read fantasy, you leave the real world behind in order to enjoy the tale. Yet, fantasies always contain some realistic elements—just to give perspective to the fantastical elements. The following passage from the story presents the fantastic idea of a dead person coming back to life.

> "Don't feel hurt; I say you shouldn't be here any more because you are dead."

As you read, notice how reality combines with fantasy to create a ghostly tale.

Connecting Literary Elements

The **setting**—the time and place in which the action occurs—of this story contributes greatly to the fantasy. Because the story takes place in India, details of the action are interwoven with ideas and symbols from Indian history and legend. Notice how the setting contributes to the fantasy of the story.

❸ Reading Strategy

Distinguishing Fantasy From Reality

As this story begins, a man and his driver are driving down a lonely rural road at night. That much can be established. Very soon, however, it becomes more and more difficult to **distinguish fantasy from reality**.

- If you feel confused by something that has happened in the story, reread the section.
- Determine which details could or could not happen in real life.

Use a chart like the one on the right to distinguish those elements that are real and those that are fantastic, or impossible.

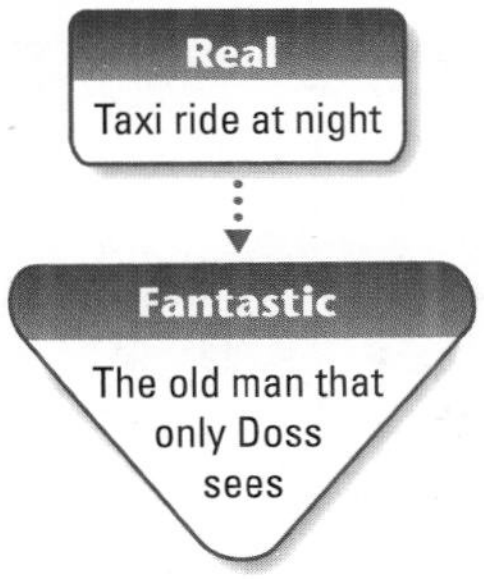

Vocabulary Development

sobriety (sə brī′ ə tē) *n.* moderation, especially in the use of alcoholic beverages (p. 203)

awry (ə rī′) *adj.* not straight (p. 204)

literally (lit′ ər əl ē) *adv.* actually; in fact (p. 206)

longevity (län jev′ ə tē) *n.* the length or duration of a life (p. 206)

imperative (im per′ ə tiv) *adj.* absolutely necessary; urgent (p. 207)

venture (ven′ chər) *n.* chance (p. 208)

❷ Literary Analysis

Fantasy

- Tell students that *fantasy* involves characters, places, and events that could not exist or happen in reality, but that also incorporate realistic elements to bring the fantasy to life.
- Tell students that *fantasy, fantastic, phantasm, phantom,* and *fancy* all come from a Greek word meaning "to show." Just as a phantom is something visible but unreal, a fantasy is something you can see or imagine but that doesn't exist. Fancy, in this sense, is a synonym for "imagine": on p. 206 of this story, when the old man says, "Fancy never knowing the king," this is what he means.

❸ Reading Strategy

Distinguishing Fantasy From Reality

- Explain that fantasy and reality are opposites. Fantasy is what a person imagines; reality is what actually exists. However, characters' imaginings can be very real to them. This is what makes it difficult to distinguish between fantasy and reality in a story.
- To tell fantasy and reality in literary works apart, students should ask themselves "Could this actually happen?" If the answer is no, they know they are reading a story with elements of fantasy.
- As they read, encourage students to use a chart like the one shown to help them distinguish between the fantastic and real elements in the story.

Vocabulary Development

- Pronounce each vocabulary word for students, and read the definitions as a class. Have students identify any words with which they are already familiar.

CUSTOMIZE INSTRUCTION FOR UNIVERSAL ACCESS

For Special Needs Students	For Less Proficient Readers	For English Learners
Have students read the adapted version of "Old Man of the Temple" in the **Adapted Reader's Companion.** This version provides basic-level instruction in an interactive format with questions and write-on lines. Completing the adapted version will prepare students to read the selection in the Student Edition.	Have students read the selection in the **Reader's Companion.** This version provides basic-level instruction in an interactive format with questions and write-on lines. After students finish the selection in **Reader's Companion,** have them complete the questions and activities in the Student Edition.	Have students read the adapted version of the selection in the **English Learner's Companion.** This version provides basic-level instruction in an interactive format with questions and write-on lines. Completing the adapted version will prepare students to read the selection in the Student Edition.

E-Teach

Visit E-Teach at www.phschool.com for teachers' essays on how to teach, with questions and answers.

TEACH

Step-by-Step Teaching Guide for pp. 202–208

CUSTOMIZE INSTRUCTION
For Interpersonal Learners

As students read, have them pay special attention to the Talkative Man's reactions to the situation in which he finds himself. Does he show any emotions? If so, what do students think he is feeling? If not, why do students think he is so calm and matter-of-fact when coming face to face with a ghost? How do students think they would have behaved in the same situation? How does the personality of the Talkative Man affect the story? Students can gather for a group analysis and discussion of the narrator's character.

❶ About the Selection

The Talkative Man describes a long-ago encounter with the ghost of an old man who has temporarily taken over the body of the Talkative Man's driver, Doss. The Talkative Man helps the ghost find its way to a permanent departure. The story explores a timeless theme: people's inability to let go of the past.

❷ Background

Architecture

The Hindu temple pictured here is located in western India. The elaborate relief carvings of gods, goddesses, and demons reflect Hindu beliefs in reincarnation and in a god of many forms and natures. In northern India, many Hindu temples have tall, tapering towers with curving sides. In southern India, temple towers rise in rectangular stone pyramids.

❷

202 ◆ Challenges and Choices

TEACHING RESOURCES

The following resources can be used to enrich or extend the instruction for pp. 202–208.

Literary Analysis

- **Selection Support:** Literary Analysis, p. 48

Reading

- **Reader's Companion**
- **English Learner's Companion**
- **Listening to Literature Audiocassettes,** Side 8 ■
- **Listening to Literature Audio CDs,** CD 7 ■

■ **BLOCK SCHEDULING:** Resources marked with this symbol provide varied instruction during 90-minute blocks.

❶ # Old Man of the Temple

R. K. Narayan

The Talkative Man said:

It was some years ago that this happened. I don't know if you can make anything of it. If you do, I shall be glad to hear what you have to say; but personally I don't understand it at all. It has always mystified me. Perhaps the driver was drunk; perhaps he wasn't.

I had engaged a taxi for going to Kumbum, which, as you may already know, is fifty miles from Malgudi.[1] I went there one morning and it was past nine in the evening when I finished my business and started back for the town. Doss [däs], the driver, was a young fellow of about twenty-five. He had often brought his car for me and I liked him. He was
❸ a well-behaved, obedient fellow, with a capacity to sit and wait at the wheel, which is really a rare quality in a taxi driver. He drove the car smoothly, seldom swore at passers-by, and exhibited perfect judgment, good sense, and sobriety; and so I preferred him to any other driver whenever I had to go out on business.

It was about eleven when we passed the village

sobriety (sə brī´ə tē) *n.* moderation, especially in the use of alcoholic beverages

1. **Malgudi** (mäl go͞o´ dē) fictional city about which Narayan often writes.

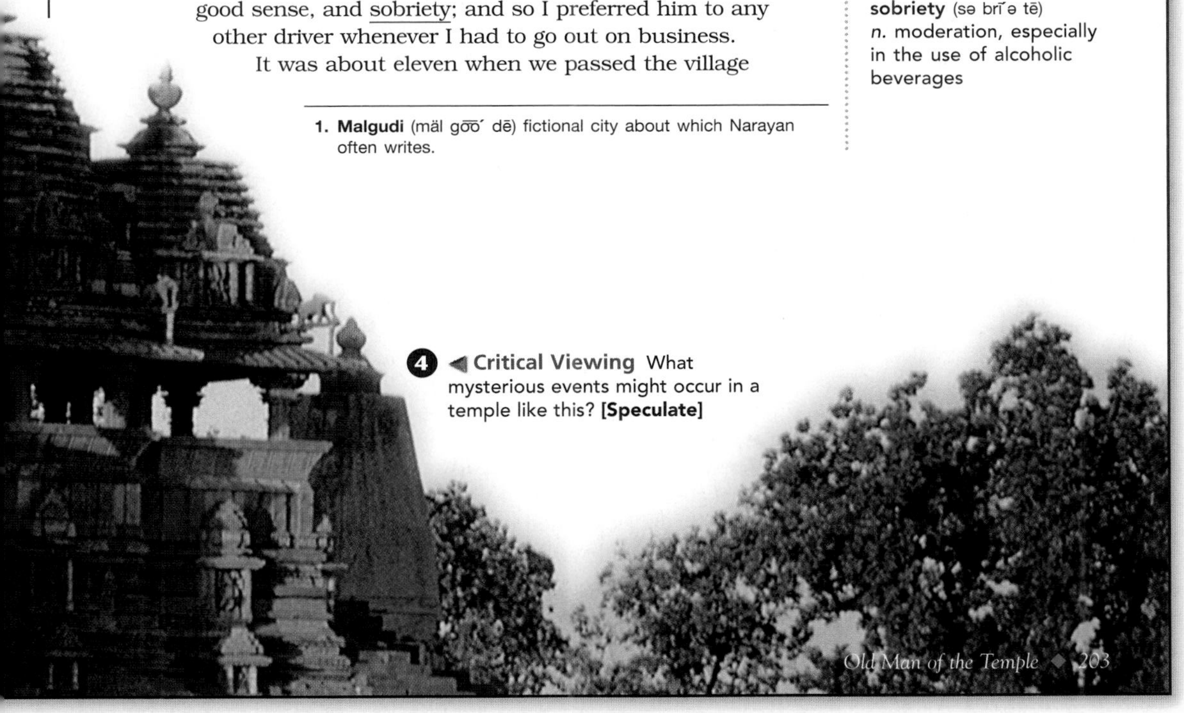

❹ ◀ **Critical Viewing** What mysterious events might occur in a temple like this? **[Speculate]**

❸ Vocabulary Development

Latin Suffix *-ity*

- Tell student that the Latin suffix *-ity* indicates a state or condition of being. *Prosperity,* for example, is a state of being prosperous or wealthy. Have students identify the two words in this paragraph formed with the suffix *-ity* and use this information to define them. Answer: *Capacity* means "state of being able to accept, take, or absorb." *Sobriety* means "state of being sober or calm."
- Challenge students to use each of these two words correctly in a sentence.
- Ask volunteers to share their sentences with the class.

❹ ▶ Critical Viewing

Answer: Students may suggest that ghosts or demons might lurk inside the temple. The architecture is so exotic that almost anything might happen.

CUSTOMIZE INSTRUCTION FOR UNIVERSAL ACCESS

For Special Needs Students	For Advanced Readers
Have a volunteer read the story's opening aloud. Point out that the phrase "some years ago" indicates that the story is a flashback. From the words "I had engaged" until the end of the story, the Talkative Man is the first-person narrator. As students continue reading, have them list each character and describe his or her relationship to the other characters. At the end of the story, students should be able to identify each character and briefly explain how each character's actions affect the others.	Have students read a few more of Narayan's stories set in Malgudi and then discuss what kind of place it is. What does Narayan say about this town? What kinds of people live there? What details do students learn about its appearance, climate, the kinds of houses, and so on? Students can pool their information and give the class a talk on Malgudi.

❺ Literary Analysis

Fantasy

- Remind students that a fantasy will often combine realistic and fantastic elements to heighten its impact. Students must pay attention to the characters, events, and other details as they read.
- Ask students the first Literary Analysis question on p. 204: Which realistic elements in these lines set the stage for a developing fantasy?
  Answer: the darkness outside; the deserted street; the passenger's drowsiness

❻ Critical Thinking

Deduce

- Have a volunteer read aloud the bracketed passage.
- Ask students to describe the narrator's demeanor in this conversation. What do they think accounts for his lack of fear or panic?
  Answer: He is perfectly calm; he doesn't seem at all surprised or shocked that his driver can see an old man who is invisible to him. Students may suggest that ghosts are common in Hindu culture, that the narrator is simply not susceptible to panic, or that he is too sleepy to fully understand what's going on.

❼ Literary Analysis

Fantasy

- Ask the second Literary Analysis question on p. 204: Which elements of fantasy arise from the description of Doss?
  Answer: He stoops over and his hands tremble as if he were suddenly aged.

Monitor Progress Ask students why they think this element is an example of fantasy.
Answer: Although a person could fall asleep in real life and then suddenly act old, Doss doesn't seem to be acting. People do not age in an instant.

---

❺ Koopal [ko͞o päl′], which is on the way down. It was the dark half of the month and the surrounding country was swallowed up in the night. The village street was deserted. Everyone had gone to sleep; hardly any light was to be seen. The stars overhead sparkled brightly. Sitting in the back seat and listening to the continuous noise of the running wheels, I was half lulled into a drowse.

All of a sudden Doss swerved the car and shouted: "You old fool! Do you want to kill yourself?"

I was shaken out of my drowse and asked: "What is the matter?"

❻ Doss stopped the car and said, "You see that old fellow, sir. He is trying to kill himself. I can't understand what he is up to."

I looked in the direction he pointed and asked, "Which old man?"

"There, there. He is coming towards us again. As soon as I saw him open that temple door and come out I had a feeling, somehow, that I must keep an eye on him."

I took out my torch, got down, and walked about, but could see no one. There was an old temple on the roadside. It was utterly in ruins; most portions of it were mere mounds of old brick; the walls were awry; the doors were shut to the main doorway, and brambles and thickets grew over and covered them. It was difficult to guess with the aid of the torch alone what temple it was and to what period it belonged.

"The doors are shut and sealed and don't look as if they had been opened for centuries now," I cried.

"No, sir," Doss said coming nearer. "I saw the old man open the doors and come out. He is standing there; shall we ask him to open them again if you want to go in and see?"

I said to Doss, "Let us be going. We are wasting our time here."

We went back to the car. Doss sat in his seat, pressed the self-starter, and asked without turning his head, "Are you permitting this fellow to come with us, sir? He says he will get down at the next milestone."

"Which fellow?" I asked.

Doss indicated the space next to him.

"What is the matter with you, Doss? Have you had a drop of drink or something?"

"I have never tasted any drink in my life, sir," he said, and added, "Get down, old boy. Master says he can't take you."

"Are you talking to yourself?"

"After all, I think we needn't care for these unknown fellows on the road," he said.

"Doss," I pleaded. "Do you feel confident you can drive? If you feel dizzy don't drive."

"Thank you, sir," said Doss. "I would rather not start the car now. I am feeling a little out of sorts." I looked at him anxiously. He closed his eyes, his breathing became heavy and noisy, and gradually his head sank.

❼ "Doss, Doss," I cried desperately. I got down, walked to the front seat, opened the door, and shook him vigorously. He opened his eyes, assumed a hunched-up position, and rubbed his eyes with his hands, which trembled like an old man's.

Literary Analysis
Fantasy Which realistic elements in these lines set the stage for a developing fantasy?

awry (ə rī′) *adj.* not straight

Literary Analysis
Fantasy Which elements of fantasy arise from the description of Doss?

"Do you feel better?" I asked.

"Better! Better! Hi! Hi!" he said in a thin, piping voice.

"What has happened to your voice? You sound like someone else," I said.

"Nothing. My voice is as good as it was. When a man is eighty he is bound to feel a few changes coming on."

"You aren't eighty, surely," I said.

"Not a day less," he said. "Is nobody going to move this vehicle? If not, there is no sense in sitting here all day. I will get down and go back to my temple."

"I don't know how to drive," I said. "And unless you do it, I don't see how it can move."

"Me!" exclaimed Doss. "These new chariots! God knows what they are drawn by, I never understand, though I could handle a pair of bullocks[2] in my time. May I ask a question?"

"Go on," I said.

"Where is everybody?"

"Who?"

"Lots of people I knew are not to be seen at all. All sorts of new fellows everywhere, and nobody seems to care. Not a soul comes near the temple. All sorts of people go about but not one who cares to stop and talk. Why doesn't the king ever come this way? He used to go this way at least once a year before."

"Which king?" I asked.

"Let me go, you idiot," said Doss, edging towards the door on which I was leaning. "You don't seem to know anything." He pushed me aside, and got down from the car. He stooped as if he had a big hump on his back, and hobbled along towards the temple. I followed him, hardly knowing what to do. He turned and snarled at me: "Go away, leave me alone. I have had enough of you."

"What has come over you, Doss?" I asked.

"Who is Doss, anyway? Doss, Doss, Doss. What an absurd name! Call me by my name or leave me alone. Don't follow me calling 'Doss, Doss.' "

"What is your name?" I asked.

9 "Krishna Battar [krish´ nə bə tar´], and if you mention my name people will know for a hundred miles around. I built a temple where there was only a cactus field before. I dug the earth, burnt every brick, and put them one upon another, all single-handed. And on the day the temple held up its tower over the surrounding country, what a crowd gathered! The king sent his chief minister . . ."

"Who was the king?"

"Where do you come from?" he asked.

"I belong to these parts certainly, but as far as I know there has been only a collector at the head of the district. I have never heard of any king."

2. **bullocks** (bo͝ol´ əks) *n.* oxen; steer.

Literature 8 in context — Cultural Connection

Hinduism and Reincarnation

Hinduism is the religion of the majority of people in India, the setting for "Old Man of the Temple." Drawing from a set of beliefs that is thousands of years old, Hinduism teaches that death is a temporary stage in an endless cycle of reincarnations, or rebirths. The actions that someone performs in one life, good and bad, will determine the conditions of future rebirths. Therefore, it is not surprising that Narayan includes aspects of reincarnation in his story.

Reading Strategy

Distinguishing Fantasy From Reality Which clues in this paragraph sound real and which sound fantastic?

10 **Reading Check**

How old does Doss say he is when he wakes up?

8 Background

Culture

The word *Hinduism* comes from a term coined by ancient Greeks to describe the inhabitants of the Indus Valley. Indians did not use the word "Hindu" until the sixteenth century, and then only to identify their origin rather than their religion. Veda, or Vedic religion, are the Indian terms for what westerners call Hinduism. In modern times, however, Indians have accepted this term to designate their religion.

Hindus believe that everyone's view of the truth is affected by his or her time, place, origins, experiences, gender, age, and other factors. This view is conducive to a broad, all-embracing view of religious truth; because of their respect for a variety of points of view, Hindus believe that the supreme religious virtue is tolerance.

9 Reading Strategy

Distinguishing Fantasy From Reality

- Make sure students understand that Doss has been taken over by a spirit.
- Ask the Reading Strategy question on p. 205: Which clues in this paragraph sound real and which sound fantastic?
  Answer: Krishna Battar's story sounds entirely realistic, but he is speaking through the body of Doss. He provides realistic details of building a temple, but the temple—as the reader knows—is now an ancient ruin. This suggests that Krishna Battar is a spirit from the distant past.

10 Reading Check

Answer: Doss says that he is eighty.

⓫ Reading Strategy

Distinguishing Fantasy From Reality

- Encourage students to focus on each statement the old man makes in this passage and determine whether it seems fantastic or real.
- Ask students the Reading Strategy question on p. 206: Does the old man's story sound fantastic or realistic to you? Explain.
  Answer: The details of the mugging sound realistic. Students might doubt that Krishna Battar survived the beating; it was probably his ghost that got up and followed the robbers.

"Hi! Hi! Hi!" he cackled, and his voice rang through the gloomy silent village. "Fancy never knowing the king! He will behead you if he hears it."

"What is his name?" I asked.

This tickled him so much that he sat down on the ground, literally unable to stand the joke any more. He laughed and coughed uncontrollably.

"I am sorry to admit," I said, "that my parents have brought me up in such utter ignorance of worldly affairs that I don't know even my king. But won't you enlighten me? What is his name?"

"Vishnu Varma [vish´ no͞o vär´ mə], the emperor of emperors . . ."

I cast my mind up and down the range of my historical knowledge but there was no one by that name. Perhaps a local chief of pre-British days, I thought.

"What a king! He often visited my temple or sent his minister for the Annual Festival of the temple. But now nobody cares."

"People are becoming less godly nowadays," I said. There was silence for a moment. An idea occurred to me, I can't say why. "Listen to me," I said. "You ought not to be here any more."

"What do you mean?" he asked, drawing himself up, proudly.

"Don't feel hurt; I say you shouldn't be here any more because you are dead."

"Dead! Dead!" he said. "Don't talk nonsense. How can I be dead when you see me before you now? If I am dead how can I be saying this and that?"

⓫ "I don't know all that," I said. I argued and pointed out that according to his own story he was more than five hundred years old, and didn't he know that man's longevity was only a hundred? He constantly interrupted me, but considered deeply what I said.

He said: "It is like this . . . I was coming through the jungle one night after visiting my sister in the next village. I had on me some money and gold ornaments. A gang of robbers set upon me. I gave them as good a fight as any man could, but they were too many for me. They beat me down and knifed me; they took away all that I had on me and left thinking they had killed me. But soon I got up and tried to follow them. They were gone. And I returned to the temple and have been here since . . ."

I told him, "Krishna Battar, you are dead, absolutely dead. You must try and go away from here."

"What is to happen to the temple?" he asked.

"Others will look after it."

"Where am I to go? Where am I to go?"

"Have you no one who cares for you?" I asked.

"None except my wife. I loved her very much."

"You can go to her."

"Oh, no. She died four years ago . . ."

Four years! It was very puzzling. "Do you say four years back from now?" I asked.

"Yes, four years ago from now." He was clearly without any sense of time.

literally (lit´ ər əl ē) *adv.* actually; in fact

longevity (län jev´ə tē) *n.* the length or duration of a life

Reading Strategy
Distinguishing Fantasy From Reality Does the old man's story sound fantastic or realistic to you? Explain.

ENRICHMENT: World History

British India

The Talkative Man refers to the "pre-British days" of India. During the 1700s, war broke out between British and French forces in India, and by 1775 British rule extended to the Upper Ganges. Britain ruled India until just after World War II, when India regained its independence and the Muslim state of Pakistan was created. The period of British rule is known as the Raj.

British rule both helped and harmed India. The British attitude toward Indians was racist, condescending, and exploitive. However, Britain was responsible for laying the nearly 40,000 miles of railroad tracks that link far-flung parts of the nation, and English became a common, unifying language for a people who spoke hundreds of different dialects.

12

So I asked, "Was she alive when you were attacked by thieves?"

"Certainly not. If she had been alive she would never have allowed me to go through the jungle after nightfall. She took very good care of me."

"See here," I said. "It is imperative you should go away from here. If she comes and calls you, will you go?"

"How can she when I tell you that she is dead?"

I thought for a moment. Presently I found myself saying, "Think of her, and only of her, for a while and see what happens. What was her name?"

"Seetha [sē´ thə], a wonderful girl . . ."

"Come on, think of her." He remained in deep thought for a while. He suddenly screamed, "Seetha is coming! Am I dreaming or what? I will go with her . . ." He stood up, very erect; he appeared to have lost all the humps and twists he had on his body. He drew himself up, made a dash forward, and fell down in a heap.

13 ◀ **Critical Viewing**
How do the details of this painting compare to the details of the story's setting? **[Support]**

imperative (im per´ ə tiv) *adj.* absolutely necessary; urgent

14 **Reading Check**
According to the old man, how many years ago did his wife die?

12 Background

Art

A Procession in a Palace Courtyard, leaf from a royal manuscript of the Shah-Jehan Nameh, Mogul, mid-seventeenth century

Manuscript books like the one shown here were made in workshops, with different artists responsible for different scenes, calligraphy, and other decorative elements. An illuminated manuscript like this one would have been possessed only by the very wealthy; it took much time and money to create. Like most Indian art of its period, this scene shows both Persian and European influences. Use the following question for discussion:

- What elements of this scene reflect old India?
  Answer: Students may mention the traditional clothing, separation of men and women, use of horses for transportation, and architecture.

13 ▶ Critical Viewing

Answer: The story is set in modern times at the side of a road near a temple. The painting shows a palace courtyard in a long-ago time. The story's setting is almost deserted; the painting's setting is crowded. In the story, people travel in cars; in the painting they travel on horses and elephants.

14 Reading Check

Answer: The old man says his wife died four years ago. However, he has no sense of time.

CUSTOMIZE INSTRUCTION FOR UNIVERSAL ACCESS

For Less Proficient Readers	For Special Needs Students	For Advanced Learners
Have students discuss their answers to Review and Assess question 8 on p. 209. Students should refer to specific points in the story and explain why they were uncertain whether these scenes were fantastical or realistic.	Have students work together to answer the Review and Assess questions on p. 208. If students come to completely different conclusions, have them refer to the text to try to come to a consensus. Remind students to respect one another's opinions.	Have students discuss their answers to questions 4 and 5 on p. 209. You might have them give the rest of the class a panel discussion on the story's setting and what they believe it contributes to the overall effect.

ASSESS

Answers for p. 208

Review and Assess

1. **Possible response:** Students may choose to explain events to the narrator ("Your driver was possessed by a ghost!") or simply to evaluate the quality of his yarn.
2. **(a)** Doss sees an old man. **(b)** The narrator doesn't believe Doss because he can't see anyone.
3. **(a)** Doss falls heavily asleep and awakens when the narrator shakes him. He then moves and speaks like an old man. **(b)** The narrator is bewildered.
4. **(a)** The narrator suggests that the old man think about his wife. **(b)** The narrator doesn't seem susceptible to emotion. He doesn't show fear or horror when he's confronted by a ghost, and he develops a solution to the ghost's predicament.
5. The family's explanation of the frequent knocking at the door shows the narrator that he (and Doss) did not imagine the encounter with the old man.
6. Students may have been frightened or intrigued. They may have questioned the ghost or run away from him.

Doss lay on the rough ground. The only sign of life in him was his faint breathing. I shook him and called him. He would not open his eyes. I walked across and knocked on the door of the first cottage. I banged on the door violently.

Someone moaned inside, "Ah, it is come!"

Someone else whispered, "You just cover your ears and sleep. It will knock for a while and go away." I banged on the door and shouted who I was and where I came from.

I walked back to the car and sounded the horn. Then the door opened, and a whole family crowded out with lamps. "We thought it was the usual knocking and we wouldn't have opened if you hadn't spoken."

"When was this knocking first heard?" I asked.

"We can't say," said one. "The first time I heard it was when my grandfather was living; he used to say he had even seen it once or twice. It doesn't harm anyone, as far as I know. The only thing it does is bother the bullock carts passing the temple and knock on the doors at night . . ."

I said as a venture, "It is unlikely you will be troubled any more."

It proved correct. When I passed that way again months later I was told that the bullocks passing the temple after dusk never shied now and no knocking on the doors was heard at nights. So I felt that the old fellow had really gone away with his good wife.

venture (ven´ chər) *n.* chance

R. K. Narayan

(b. 1906)

Within a career that has spanned more than sixty years, R. K. Narayan has written more than fifteen novels, as well as numerous collections of short stories, travel books, and essays. Born in the city of Madras in southern India, he was one of nine children of a middle-class family. He attended Maharaja's College in Mysore, and after briefly working as a teacher, he became a writer.

In his novels, legends, and short stories, Narayan skillfully combines Western plots and themes with Indian subject matter. In 1958, he won the National Prize of the Indian Literary Academy, his nation's highest literary honor.

Review and Assess

Thinking About the Selection

1. **Respond:** The narrator tells you, "I don't know if you can make anything of it. If you do, I shall be glad to hear what you have to say. . . ." How would you answer him?
2. **(a) Recall:** Early in the story, what does Doss say he sees when he swerves the car? **(b) Analyze:** Why does the narrator find Doss's words unbelievable?
3. **(a) Recall:** Describe the transformation that happens to Doss. **(b) Analyze:** How does the narrator react to the change?
4. **(a) Recall:** What does the narrator say to cause the old man to think about his own situation? **(b) Infer:** Do you think the narrator is ruled more by his feelings or by reason? Why?
5. **Connect:** What purpose does the introduction of the family serve?
6. **Assess:** How might you respond if you found yourself in the narrator's situation?

ASSESSMENT PRACTICE: Reading Comprehension

Fact and Opinion (For more practice, see Test Preparation Workbook, p. 12.)

Many tests require students to read passages and answer questions about them. Use the following sample test item to show students how to distinguish facts from opinions.

Which of the following quotations from the story is a statement of opinion?

A It was some years ago that this happened.
B "I don't know how to drive," I said.
C "My voice is as good as it was."
D "I have never tasted any drink in my life, sir," he said.

Remind students that a statement of fact can be proved but a statement of opinion cannot. Only choice *C* is not capable of proof. Therefore it is the correct answer.

Review and Assess

Literary Analysis

Fantasy

1. Why is "Old Man of the Temple" a **fantasy**?
2. How do the fantastic elements add to the story?
3. Using a chart like the one below, show how the realistic elements found in the story contribute to an atmosphere in which fantasy can develop.

Realistic Elements	→	How They Set the Stage for Fantasy

Connecting Literary Elements

4. Use a chart like the one below to help you answer the following questions. (a) How does the **setting** contribute to the fantasy in the story? (b) How does the setting contribute to the reality in the story?

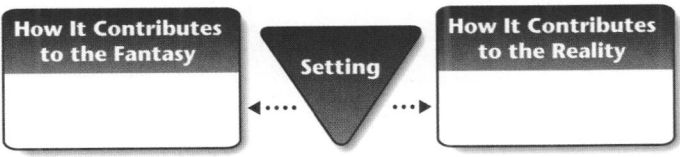

How It Contributes to the Fantasy	← Setting →	How It Contributes to the Reality

5. How might this story be different if it were set in a modern American city?

Reading Strategy

Distinguishing Fantasy From Reality

6. Name two elements of the story that are fantastic.
7. At what point in the story does the plot change from realistic to fantastic? Explain.
8. During which scenes in the story is it difficult to **distinguish fantasy from reality**? Explain.

Extend Understanding

9. **Media Connection:** Compare this story with fantasy movies. (a) Which elements are similar? (b) Which are different?

Quick Review

Fantasy is fiction that includes characters, places, and events that could not exist or happen in real life.

The **setting** of a story is the time and place in which the action occurs.

To **distinguish fantasy from reality,** determine which elements of a story could or could not happen in real life.

Take It to the Net

www.phschool.com

Take the interactive self-test online to check your understanding of the selection.

Review and Assess

1. It is the story of a meeting between a ghost and two living people, in which the ghost takes over the body of one of them.
2. Without the fantastic elements, there would be no story. One of the main characters is a ghost and his activity creates the conflict of the story.
3. **Realistic Elements:** darkness of night, deserted streets, the temple, narrator's unfamiliarity with place
   ↓
   How They Set the Stage: realistic elements create an eerie mood
4. **(a)** The ruined temple and a dark deserted street add a mystical quality to the story. **(b)** The modern times in which the story takes place, especially the presence of the car, add to the reality.
5. Possible answer: The characters might not feel safe sitting by the road talking. They might be interrupted by passers-by; a city is bound to be less deserted than a country road.
6. Elements of fantasy include the ghost and its possession of Doss's body.
7. The story becomes a fantasy when Doss first sees the ghost.
8. It is difficult to distinguish the two when the ghost is talking about what happened to him in the past.
9. **(a)** Possible answer: the presence of a ghost; haunted ruins; unexplainable events
   (b) Possible answer: the Indian setting; the narrator's nonchalance at meeting a ghost; the fact that the ghost is so ordinary and unthreatening

ENRICHMENT: Further Reading

Other Works by R. K. Narayan

"A Tiger for Malgudi"
"Swami and his Friends"
Under the Banyan Tree and Other Stories

Take It to the Net

Visit www.phschool.com for more information on R. K. Narayan.

EXTEND

Answers for p. 210

❶ Vocabulary Development

Word Analysis

1. state of being agile; liveliness
2. state of being severe; harshness
3. state of being generous; bountifulness
4. state of being individual; distinctiveness

Spelling Strategy

1. correct
2. correct
3. majesty

Concept Development: Synonyms

1. c
2. b
3. a
4. c
5. a
6. b

❷ Grammar

1. believed, verb
2. good, adjective
3. dead, adjective
4. laughed, verb
5. go, verb

Writing Application

Sample Sentences:

1. He was completely bewildered by the change in Doss; modifies *bewildered,* adjective
2. I am not entirely convinced that he didn't dream the whole thing; modifies *convinced,* verb
3. Please come in quietly so you won't wake the baby; modifies *come,* verb

Integrate Language Skills

❶ Vocabulary Development Lesson

Word Analysis: Latin Suffix *-ity*

In the word *longevity*, you find the suffix *-ity*, meaning "state of" or "condition of." One way to define *longevity* is "the condition of having a long life." Using the meaning of *-ity*, write definitions for the following words:

1. agility
2. severity
3. generosity
4. individuality

Spelling Strategy

When spelling a word that contains the *j* sound before an *e*, you usually use a *g*, as in *longevity*. There are exceptions, however, such as *subject*. For each word below, write "Correct" if the word is spelled correctly. If the spelling is incorrect, write the proper spelling.

1. suggest 2. injection 3. magesty

Concept Development: Synonyms

In each numbered item, choose the word whose meaning is closest to that of the word from the vocabulary list on page 201.

1. sobriety: (a) sadness, (b) loneliness, (c) moderation
2. awry: (a) sophisticated, (b) crooked, (c) clever
3. literally: (a) actually, (b) scholarly, (c) differently
4. longevity: (a) height, (b) endurance, (c) duration
5. imperative: (a) essential, (b) unnecessary, (c) ruler
6. venture: (a) satisfaction, (b) risk, (c) university

❷ Grammar Lesson

Adverbs

Adverbs are words that modify verbs, adjectives, and other adverbs. They answer the questions *Where? When? In what way?* and *To what extent?* about the words they modify. You can often make descriptions more meaningful by adding an adverb to a sentence. Look at the following examples:

Modifying a Verb: Doss drove the car *smoothly*. (*smoothly* modifies the verb *drove*)

Modifying an Adjective: He drove an *extremely* large car. (*extremely* modifies the adjective *large*)

Modifying an Adverb: He drove the car *very* smoothly. (*very* modifies the adverb *smoothly*)

Practice Copy each sentence. Underline the word or words modified by the adverb in italics. Then, identify whether the word modified is a verb, an adjective, or an adverb.

1. He *certainly* believed that he was right.
2. His wife took *very* good care of him.
3. Doss told him that he was *absolutely* dead.
4. He laughed *uncontrollably* at the news.
5. He needed to go *away* from there.

Writing Application Use each of the following adverbs in a sentence. At the end of the sentence, write which word each one modifies.

1. completely 2. entirely 3. quietly

WG *Prentice Hall Writing and Grammar Connection: Chapter 18, Section 2*

TEACHING RESOURCES

The following resources can be used to enrich or extend the instructions for pp. 210–211.

Vocabulary

Selection Support, Build Vocabulary, p. 45

Grammar

Selection Support: Build Grammar Skills, p. 46

Writing and Grammar, Gold Level, p. 390 ■

Daily Language Practice Transparencies

Writing

Writing and Grammar, Gold Level, p. 139 ■

Writing and Grammar iText CD-ROM ■

■ **BLOCK SCHEDULING:** Resources marked with this symbol provide varied instruction during 90-minute blocks.

❸ Writing Lesson

Travel Brochure

India, where "Old Man of the Temple" takes place, is a land of ancient cultures, colorful ceremonies, and joyous celebrations—an excellent visitor destination. Using the setting of the story and additional information about India, write a travel brochure that will entice travelers to visit.

Prewriting Decide on the features you will describe in your brochure. Review the selection and research India to gather appealing details.

Drafting Many qualities can make the tone of your brochure persuasive. For instance, vivid descriptions will appeal to readers' imaginations and dreams, and a sense of humor will spark a receptive attitude.

Model: Using a Persuasive Tone

From mysterious and historical temple ruins to breathtaking views of snow-peaked mountains soaring to incredible heights, you can experience the splendor of a culture rich in beauty and tradition.

Words like *breathtaking* and *soaring* convey the splendor of India and appeal to a tourist's desire for an unforgettable experience.

Revising Reread your draft. Make sure that your readers will be persuaded to visit. Add information that can make your tone more persuasive and your travel brochure more appealing.

WG *Prentice Hall Writing and Grammar Connection: Chapter 7, Section 3*

❹ Extension Activities

Listening and Speaking Prepare a **dramatic monologue** in which the old man relates the story from his point of view. Follow these suggestions as you write your monologue:

- Use appropriate word choice—select words that the old man would use.
- Describe experiences found in the story.
- Enhance your performance by adding new information about the old man that you did not learn in the story.

Perform your monologue for the class.

Research and Technology Southern India, where this story takes place, is overwhelmingly Hindu. In a group, do a **research report** on Hinduism and explain how Hinduism enriches your understanding of this story. Use library resources, including the Internet, to find information to strengthen your report. **[Group Activity]**

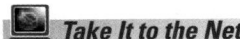

Take It to the Net www.phschool.com

Go online for an additional research activity using the Internet.

Lesson Support for p. 211

❸ Writing Lesson

- Bring in some examples of travel brochures for students to review. Remind students that a good travel brochure relies on a persuasive combination of words and images to draw the attention of potential travelers.
- Have students look through the travel brochures to see what kinds of information they should include.
- Suggest that students illustrate their brochures. They can find pictures of India in encyclopedias, travel books, or on the Internet. Students may want to use these sources to draw their own illustrations.

❹ Extension Activity

Listening and Speaking

- Since Krishna Battar dies for the final time during the course of the story, students should consider to whom he might be describing his encounter with the Talkative Man.
- Have students reread the story, inferring further details about Krishna Battar's life from the details in the story.
- As an alternative, students may want to retell the story from Doss's point of view. They will have to decide where Doss's spirit went when Krishna Battar possessed his body.
- Encourage questions and comments from audience members.

CUSTOMIZE INSTRUCTION for Universal Access

To address different learning styles, use the following activities suggested in the **Extension Activities** booklet, p. 12.

- For Visual/Spatial Learners, use Activity 4.
- For Intrapersonal Learners, use Activity 5.
- For Verbal/Linguistic Learners, use Activity 6.

ASSESSMENT RESOURCES

The following resources can be used to assess students' knowledge and skills.

Selection Assessment

- **Formal Assessment,** pp. 38–40
- **Open Book Test,** pp. 34–36
- **Got It! Assessment Videotapes,** Tape 1
- **Test Bank Software**

Take It to the Net

Visit www.phschool.com for self-tests and additional questions on "Old Man of the Temple."

PRENTICE HALL ASSESSMENT SYSTEM

- **Workbook**
- **Skill Book**
- **Transparencies**
- **CD-ROM**

Perseus

Lesson Objectives and CA Correlations

1. **To analyze and respond to literary elements**
   - Literary Analysis: Hero in a Myth **R 3.4**
   - Connecting Literary Elements: Antagonist **R 3.3**
2. **To read, comprehend, analyze, and critique a myth**
   - Reading Strategy: Predicting **R 3.6**
   - Reading Check questions
   - Review and Assess questions
   - Assessment Practice (ATE)
3. **To develop word analysis skills, fluency, and systematic vocabulary**
   - Vocabulary Development Lesson: Latin Word Root: *-mort-* **R 1.1**
4. **To understand and apply written and oral language conventions**
   - Spelling Strategy
   - Grammar Lesson: Active and Passive Voice **LC 1.2, 1.3**
5. **To understand and apply appropriate writing and research strategies**
   - Writing Lesson: Speech of Introduction **W 2.4, LS 1.4**
   - Extension Activity: Illustrated Map **W 1.8**
6. **To understand and apply listening and speaking strategies**
   - Extension Activity: Opening Argument **LS 1.4**

STEP-BY-STEP TEACHING GUIDE	PACING GUIDE
PRETEACH	
Motivate Students and Provide Background	
Use the Motivation activity (ATE p. 212)	5 min.
Read and discuss the Preview material and Background information (SE/ATE p. 212) [A]	10 min.
Introduce the Concepts	
Introduce the Literary Analysis and Reading Strategy (SE/ATE p. 213) [A]	15 min.
Pronounce the vocabulary words and read their definitions (SE p. 213)	5 min.
TEACH	
Monitor Comprehension	
Informally monitor comprehension by circulating while students read independently or in groups [A]	20 min.
Monitor students' comprehension with the Reading Check notes (SE/ATE pp. 215, 217, 219, 221)	as students read
Develop vocabulary with Vocabulary notes (SE pp. 215–217, 219–220)	as students read
Develop Understanding	
Develop students' understanding of heroes in myths with Literary Analysis annotations (SE pp. 216, 219, 220; ATE pp. 216, 218, 220) [A]	10 min.
Develop students' ability to make predictions with Reading Strategy annotations (SE/ATE pp. 215, 216, 219, 220)	10 min.
ASSESS	
Assess Mastery	
Assess students' mastery of the Reading Strategy and Literary Analysis by having them answer the Review and Assess questions (SE/ATE p. 223)	20 min.
Use one or more of the print and media Assessment Resources (ATE p. 225) [A]	up to 50 min.
EXTEND	
Apply Understanding	
Have students complete the Vocabulary Development Lesson and the Grammar Lesson (SE p. 224) [A]	20 min.
Apply students' knowledge of listing appealing details using the Writing Lesson (SE p. 225) [A]	45 min.
Apply students' understanding using one or more of the Extension Activities (SE p. 225)	20–90 min.

[A] **ACCELERATED INSTRUCTION:**
Use the strategies and activities identified with an [A].

UNIVERSAL ACCESS
● = Below-Level Students
▲ = On-Level Students
■ = Above-Level Students

Time and Resource Manager

Reading Level: Challenging
Average Number of Instructional Days: 4

RESOURCES		
PRINT	**TRANSPARENCIES**	**TECHNOLOGY**
• **Beyond Literature,** Cross-Curricular Connection: Art, p. 13 ▲ ■		• **Interest Grabber Video,** Tape 1 ● ▲ ■
• **Selection Support Workbook:** ● ▲ ■ Literary Analysis, p. 52 Reading Strategy, p. 51 Build Vocabulary, p. 49	• **Literary Analysis and Reading Transparencies,** pp. 25 and 26 ● ▲ ■	
		• **Listening to Literature** ● ▲ ■ Audiocassettes, Side 8 Audio CDs, CD 7
• **Literatura en español** ● ▲ • **Literary Analysis for Enrichment** ■		
• **Formal Assessment:** Selection Test, pp. 41–43 ● ▲ ■ • **Open Book Test,** pp. 37–38 ● ▲ ■ • **Performance Assessment and Portfolio Management,** p. 23 ● ▲ ■ • PRENTICE HALL ASSESSMENT SYSTEM ● ▲ ■	• PRENTICE HALL ASSESSMENT SYSTEM ● ▲ ■ Skills Practice Answers and Explanations on Transparencies	• **Test Bank Software** ● ▲ ■ • **Got It! Assessment Videotapes,** Tape 1 ● ▲
• **Selection Support Workbook:** ● ▲ ■ Build Grammar Skills, p. 50 • **Writing and Grammar,** Gold Level ● ▲ ■ • **Extension Activities,** p. 13 ● ▲ ■	• **Daily Language Practice Transparencies** ● ▲	• **Writing and Grammar iText CD-ROM** ● ▲ ■ *Take It to the Net* www.phschool.com

BLOCK SCHEDULING: Use one 90-minute class period to preteach the selection and have students read it. Use a second 90-minute class period to assess students' mastery of skills and have them complete one of the Extension Activities.

PRETEACH

Step-by-Step Teaching Guide for pp. 212–213

Motivation

Engage students' interest by reading this passage from "Perseus":

> *He was young and proud and keenly mortified. He stood up before them all and did exactly what the King had hoped he would do, declared that he would give him a present better than any there. He would go off and kill Medusa and bring back her head as a gift . . . No one in his senses would have made such a proposal. Medusa was one of the Gorgons.*

Urge students to imagine what type of creature Medusa might be. Do they imagine that Perseus, the subject of this passage, will succeed in bringing back her head? Tell them they will have to read the selection to find out.

Interest Grabber Video

As an alternative, play "Greek Mythology" on Tape 1 to engage student interest.

❶ Background

Zeus is the chief of all the Greek gods and rules over the earth. His two brothers, Poseidon and Hades, rule over the seas and the underworld, the resting place of the dead. Athena is Zeus' daughter; she has no mother. She sprang fully grown and armed from his head. Athena plays a major role in the *Odyssey,* Homer's famous epic of the aftermath of the Trojan War (see Unit 12). Hermes is the son of Zeus and Maia, and is a messenger of the gods. The medical insignia students can see on all doctors' diplomas depicts the staff of Hermes.

Prepare to Read

Perseus

Danaë with young Perseus arriving on the island of Seripo, Museo Archeologico, Ferrara, Italy

Take It to the Net

Visit www.phschool.com for interactive activities and instruction related to "Perseus," including

- background
- graphic organizers
- literary elements
- reading strategies

Preview

Connecting to the Literature

Some people love to rise to the challenge of difficult situations, while others prefer to keep their lives on an even keel. Perseus, the main character in this selection, is the first sort of person—the type who thrives on grappling with thorny problems. Before reading, consider which type of person you relate to more.

❶ Background

"Perseus" takes place in a mythological world populated by Greek gods and goddesses. Among them are Zeus, the chief god, who fathered a number of human children; Athena, goddess of war and wisdom; and Hermes, the messenger god. Each god plays a pivotal role in Perseus' heroic adventure.

TEACHING RESOURCES

The following resources can be used to enrich or extend the instruction for pp. 212–213.

Motivation

Interest Grabber Video, Tape 1

Background

Beyond Literature, p. 13

Take It to the Net

Visit www.phschool.com for background and hotlinks for "Perseus."

Literary Analysis

Literary Analysis and Reading Transparencies, Hero in a Myth, p. 25

Reading

Selection Support: Reading Strategy, p. 51; Build Vocabulary, p. 49

Literary Analysis and Reading Transparencies, Predicting, p. 26

BLOCK SCHEDULING: Resources marked with this symbol provide varied instruction during 90-minute blocks.

❷ Literary Analysis

Hero in a Myth

A **hero in a myth** is a character who performs amazing feats in a tale involving supernatural beings and fantastic events. The hero in a myth is often aided by sympathetic gods and magical elements. Nevertheless, the hero must exhibit admirable qualities such as courage, loyalty, and fairness. The following excerpt shows the loyalty and courage of Perseus, the hero in this myth.

> [Perseus] did exactly what the King had hoped he would do, declared that he would . . . go off and kill Medusa and bring back her head as his gift. . . . No one in his senses would have made such a proposal.

As you read, think about how Perseus' positive traits make him worthy of the supernatural help he gets.

Connecting Literary Elements

An **antagonist** is a character or force in conflict with the main character or hero in a story. In this story, Perseus is faced with conflicts between two antagonists, his grandfather Acrisius and the king Polydectes. As you read, take note of the actions and choices of these antagonists, which create great struggles and challenges for the hero, Perseus.

❸ Reading Strategy

Predicting

When you read, you can **predict** outcomes by thinking about the world presented in the literature and about the logical consequences of the characters' actions. Use these strategies to help you predict outcomes in "Perseus":

- Look for details and facts to suggest what may occur later.
- Decide what would be the likely outcome of an event.

Use a chart like the one shown here to note your predictions.

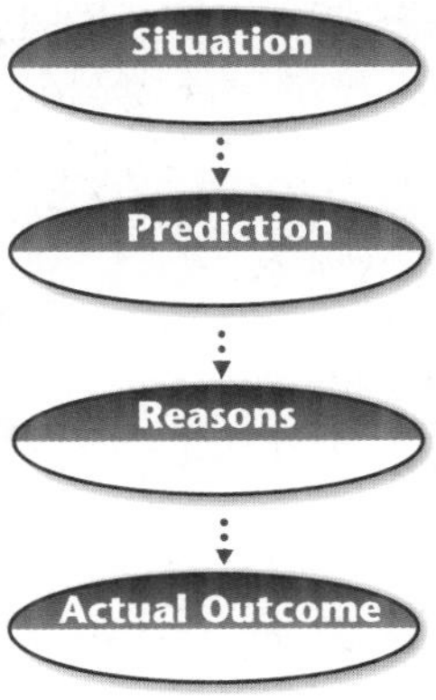

Vocabulary Development

kindred (kin´ drid) *n.* relatives (p. 215)

mortified (môrt´ ə fīd´) *adj.* embarrassed (p. 216)

despair (di sper´) *n.* hopelessness (p. 217)

wavering (wā´ vər iŋ) *adj.* flickering (p. 219)

revelry (rev´ əl rē) *n.* party (p. 219)

deity (dē´ ə tē) *n.* a god (p. 220)

reconciled (rek´ ən sīld´) *adj.* became friends again (p. 222)

❷ Literary Analysis

Hero in a Myth

- Write the word *hero* on the chalkboard. Ask students to name the characteristics they associate with that word. List their answers on the board.
- Have students review selections they have read so far this year and identify any heroes in them. Did these heroes depend on assistance to accomplish their heroic deeds? Who were their assistants, and how did these people help them?
- Have students read the paragraph under "Connecting Literary Elements" on p. 213. Explain that *antagonist* comes from two Greek words that mean "against" and "contest." Many stories derive their main conflicts from tension between the main characters and their antagonists.

❸ Reading Strategy

Predicting

- Remind students that a prediction is not a wild guess. A prediction is based on knowledge of a character's personality and on hints about what may happen next or how another character may react.
- Suggest that students create simple charts like the one on p. 213. Ask that they try to make a prediction each time they turn a page of the story.

Vocabulary Development

- Pronounce each vocabulary word for students, and read the definitions as a class. Have students identify any words with which they are already familiar.

CUSTOMIZE INSTRUCTION FOR UNIVERSAL ACCESS

For Less Proficient Readers	For English Learners	For Advanced Readers
Have students discuss their knowledge of Greek mythology. They can use their knowledge to make predictions about how the gods and goddesses will behave, whom they will help, and how they will help.	Have students discuss their knowledge of Greek mythology. Students may know some of the gods and goddesses by different names. Students can pool their knowledge and use it to help them understand the story. If students have no knowledge of Greek mythology, introduce the names and descriptions of the gods and goddesses described in the story.	Have students discuss their knowledge of the family relationships among the Greek gods and goddesses. As they read, have them think about how these relationships affect the characters' decisions and actions. Do the gods and goddesses seem human?

E-Teach

Visit E-Teach at www.phschool.com for teachers' essays on how to teach, with questions and answers.

TEACH

Step-by-Step Teaching Guide for pp. 214–222

CUSTOMIZE INSTRUCTION
For Visual/Spatial Learners

Invite students to acquire fine art images of the characters in the myth and compare them with Hamilton's descriptions. Or, have them draw their own sketches based on the written descriptions.

❶ About the Selection

When the Delphic oracle prophesies that Acrisius will die by the hand of his grandson, Acrisius shuts his daughter Danaë away to prevent her meeting men. However, Zeus transforms himself into a shower of gold and visits Danaë, and she conceives a son. Acrisius sets her and baby Perseus adrift in a wooden chest, but they are rescued. When he is grown, Perseus sets out to kill the Gorgon. Athena and Hermes help him carry out his plan. He then kills a sea monster, sets the princess Andromeda free, and marries her. Perseus uses the Gorgon's head to turn wicked King Polydectes and his courtiers to stone. Later, in an athletic contest, he accidentally throws a discus into the crowd of spectators. It hits and kills Acrisius.

❷ Background

Art

Andromeda Liberated,
by Pierre Mignard

This painting depicts the aftermath of Perseus' rescue of Andromeda (see p. 220). Baroque painter Pierre Mignard (1610–1695) is best known for his court paintings for King Louis XIV of France.

After students complete "Perseus" they may wish to analyze details of the painting. For now:

- Ask students what seems to be Perseus' reaction to the crowd. Answer: He seems unaware of the crowd; he has eyes only for Andromeda.

❶ Perseus

Edith Hamilton

❷

Andromeda Liberated, Pierre Mignard. Louvre, Paris, France

❸ ▲ **Critical Viewing** The man with the sword is Perseus as an adult. Judging from this painting, how do you think others perceive him? Cite details in the art to support your answer. **[Draw Conclusions]**

King Acrisius [a kris´ ē əs] of Argos had only one child, a daughter, Danaë [dan´ ā ē]. She was beautiful above all the other women of the land, but this was small comfort to the King for not having a son. He journeyed to Delphi to ask the god if there was any hope that some day he would be the father of a boy. The priestess told him no, and added what was far worse: that his daughter would have a son who would kill him.

TEACHING RESOURCES

The following resources can be used to enrich or extend the instruction for pp. 214–222.

Literary Analysis

Selection Support: Literary Analysis, p. 52

Reading

Listening to Literature Audiocassettes, Side 8 ▪

Listening to Literature Audio CDs, CD 7 ▪

▪ **BLOCK SCHEDULING:** Resources marked with this symbol provide varied instruction during 90-minute blocks.

The only sure way to escape that fate was for the King to have Danaë instantly put to death—taking no chances, but seeing to it himself. This Acrisius would not do. His fatherly affection was not strong, as events proved, but his fear of the gods was. They visited with terrible punishment those who shed the blood of kindred. Acrisius did not dare slay his daughter. Instead, he had a house built all of bronze and sunk underground, but with part of the roof open to the sky so that light and air could come through. Here he shut her up and guarded her.

kindred (kin´ drid) *n.* relatives

4
So Danaë endured, the beautiful,
To change the glad daylight for brass-bound walls,
And in that chamber secret as the grave
She lived a prisoner. Yet to her came
Zeus in the golden rain.

As she sat there through the long days and hours with nothing to do, nothing to see except the clouds moving by overhead, a mysterious thing happened, a shower of gold fell from the sky and filled her chamber. How it was revealed to her that it was Zeus who had visited her in this shape we are not told, but she knew that the child she bore was his son.

5
For a time she kept his birth secret from her father, but it became increasingly difficult to do so in the narrow limits of that bronze house and finally one day the little boy—his name was Perseus—was discovered by his grandfather. "Your child!" Acrisius cried in great anger. "Who is his father?" But when Danaë answered proudly, "Zeus," he would not believe her. One thing only he was sure of, that the boy's life was a terrible danger to his own. He was afraid to kill him for the same reason that had kept him from killing her, fear of Zeus and the Furies who pursue such murderers. But if he could not kill them outright, he could put them in the way of tolerably certain death. He had a great chest made, and the two placed in it. Then it was taken out to sea and cast into the water.

In that strange boat Danaë sat with her little son. The daylight faded and she was alone on the sea.

When in the carven chest the winds and waves
Struck fear into her heart she put her arms,
Not without tears, round Perseus tenderly
She said, "O son, what grief is mine.
But you sleep softly, little child,
Sunk deep in rest within your cheerless home,
Only a box, brass-bound. The night, this darkness visible,
The scudding waves so near to your soft curls,
The shrill voice of the wind, you do not heed,
Nestled in your red cloak, fair little face."

Reading Strategy
Predicting What do you think will happen to Danaë and Perseus after they are sent off in the chest?

6 **Reading Check**
What was Acrisius told would happen to him when his daughter had a son?

Through the night in the tossing chest she listened to the waters that seemed always about to wash over them. The dawn came, but with no comfort to her for she could not see it. Neither could she see

3 ▶Critical Viewing

Answer: All the people in the painting look at or touch Perseus with gratitude and admiration. He is the center of attention and the fact that the king is bowing down to him suggests that he is very important.

4 Background

Literature

Hamilton includes several translations from ancient versions of Perseus' story. Simonides of Ceos, a sixth-century poet, wrote the descriptions of Danaë on this page; Hamilton also quotes the poets Hesiod and Pindar.

5 Reading Strategy

Predicting

- Point out that Acrisius is acting on a prediction—that Perseus will kill him one day. This shows that Acrisius believes that the oracle has the power to see the future.
- Ask students the Reading Strategy question on p. 215: What do you think will happen to Danaë and Perseus after they are sent off in the chest?
  Answer: Since "Perseus" is the title of the story, Perseus will probably not drown in babyhood. Danaë does not panic, which suggests that she may have the courage to survive. They will probably be rescued.

6 Reading Check

Answer: Acrisius was told that his grandson would kill him.

CUSTOMIZE INSTRUCTION FOR UNIVERSAL ACCESS

For Special Needs Students

The formal, academic style of this version of Perseus' story may prove a barrier to some students. Have them locate and read "The Gorgon's Head" in Nathaniel Hawthorne's *A Wonder Book,* a nineteenth-century American collection of the Greek myths written for children. "The Gorgon's Head" tells the same story as "Perseus" in a somewhat lighter and more entertaining style. Have students read this story and discuss it with partners, making sure that they can identify all the characters and summarize the events of the plot. Afterward, students should be ready to read "Perseus" and answer the Review and Assess questions at the end.

7 Reading Strategy

Predicting

- Ask students to summarize the situation that Danaë and Perseus are in.
- Ask students the Reading Strategy question on p. 216: Do you think Danaë and Perseus will survive? Why?
  Answer: The oracle predicted that Perseus would eventually kill Acrisius, so he probably will survive. Zeus has the power to save them, and he may want to do this since he was in love with Danaë and Perseus is their child.

8 Literary Analysis

Hero in a Myth

- Go back to the list of heroic characteristics that students created on p. 213. Ask if anything up to this point suggests that Perseus will be the hero of this myth.
  Answer: He is the son of a god, so he may have superhuman powers. The god has helped him to survive.

Monitor Progress Ask students the Literary Analysis question on p. 216: What is heroic about Perseus' offer to the King?
Answer: The offer is one that only a brave man would make; it is an offer to do something that seems impossible.

9 Vocabulary Development

Latin Root *-mort-*

- Point out that humans are described as *mortals,* gods as *immortals.*
- Tell students that the root *-mort-* is from the Latin for death. *Mortals* are subject to death; *immortals* never die.
- Note that the word *mortified* in the preceding paragraph also shares this root. It may help students to think of *mortified* as being "embarrassed to death."

---

7 that around them there were islands rising high above the sea, many islands. All she knew was that presently a wave seemed to lift them and carry them swiftly on and then, retreating, leave them on something solid and motionless. They had made land; they were safe from the sea, but they were still in the chest with no way to get out.

Fate willed it—or perhaps Zeus, who up to now had done little for his love and his child—that they should be discovered by a good man, a fisherman named Dictys. He came upon the great box and broke it open and took the pitiful cargo home to his wife who was as kind as he. They had no children and they cared for Danaë and Perseus as if they were their own. The two lived there many years, Danaë content to let her son follow the fisherman's humble trade, out of harm's way. But in the end more trouble came. Polydectes [pol i dek′ tēz], the ruler of the little island, was the brother of Dictys, but he was a cruel and ruthless man. He seems to have taken no notice of the mother and son for a long time, but at last Danaë attracted his attention. She was still radiantly beautiful even though Perseus by now was full grown, and Polydectes fell in love with her. He wanted her, but he did not want her son, and he set himself to think out a way of getting rid of him.

8 There were some fearsome monsters called Gorgons who lived on an island and were known far and wide because of their deadly power. Polydectes evidently talked to Perseus about them; he probably told him that he would rather have the head of one of them than anything else in the world. This seems practically certain from the plan he devised for killing Perseus. He announced that he was about to be married and he called his friends together for a celebration, including Perseus in the invitation. Each guest, as was customary, brought a gift for the bride-to-be, except Perseus alone. He had nothing he could give. He was young and proud and keenly <u>mortified</u>. He stood up before them all and did exactly what the King had hoped he would do, declared that he would give him a present better than any there. He would go off and kill Medusa and bring back her head as his gift. Nothing could have suited the King better. No one in his senses would have made such a proposal. Medusa was one of the Gorgons,

9 And they are three, the Gorgons, each with wings
And snaky hair, most horrible to mortals.
Whom no man shall behold and draw again
The breath of life,

for the reason that whoever looked at them were turned instantly into stone. It seemed that Perseus had been led by his angry pride into making an empty boast. No man unaided could kill Medusa.

But Perseus was saved from his folly. Two great gods were watching over him. He took ship as soon as he left the King's hall, not daring to see his mother first and tell her what he intended, and he sailed to Greece to learn where the three monsters were to be found. He went to Delphi, but all the priestess would say was to bid him

Reading Strategy
Predicting Do you think Danaë and Perseus will survive? Why?

mortified (môrt′ ə fīd′) *adj.* embarrassed

Literary Analysis
Hero in a Myth What is heroic about Perseus' offer to the King?

Danaë with young Perseus arriving on the island of Seripo, Museo Archeologico, Ferrara, Italy

seek the land where men eat not Demeter's golden grain, but only acorns. So he went to Dodona, in the land of oak trees, where the talking oaks were which declared Zeus's will and where the Selli lived who made their bread from acorns. They could tell him, however, no more than this, that he was under the protection of the gods. They did not know where the Gorgons lived.

When and how Hermes and Athena came to his help is not told in any story, but he must have known despair before they did so. At last, however, as he wandered on, he met a strange and beautiful person. We know what he looked like from many a poem, a young man with the first down upon his cheek when youth is loveliest, carrying, as no other young man ever did, a wand of gold with wings at one end, wearing a winged hat, too, and winged sandals. At sight of him hope must have entered Perseus' heart, for he would know that this could be none other than Hermes, the guide and the giver of good.

This radiant personage told him that before he attacked Medusa he must first be properly equipped, and that what he needed was in the possession of the nymphs of the North. To find the nymphs' abode, they must go to the Gray Women who alone could tell them the way. These women dwelt in a land where all was dim and shrouded in twilight. No ray of sun looked ever on that country, nor the moon by

10 ▲ **Critical Viewing**
Which scene in the story does this art illustrate? **[Assess]**

despair (di sper′) *n.* hopelessness

11 **Reading Check**
Who is Hermes?

10 ▶ Critical Viewing

Answer: The art illustrates the scene in which Dictys finds Danaë and her baby inside the chest. The man can't be Acrisius setting them adrift, because he isn't wearing a crown.

11 Reading Check

Answer: Hermes is a young god, a guide and messenger and "giver of good," or healer.

CUSTOMIZE INSTRUCTION FOR UNIVERSAL ACCESS

For Gifted/Talented Students	For Advanced Readers
It is an ancient human custom to build monuments to honor heros, often by building statues. Ask students to design a monument for Perseus. Have students work in teams to decide what particular deed to emphasize and what physical details should be included. Students can then draw plans for their monument or create an actual model.	Challenge students to create a brief encyclopedia of mythology that informs readers about all the places and characters alluded to in this story. Students can look in reference books or collections of myths to find out who the Seli are, where Dodona is, and so on. Each page of the encyclopedia can give a verbal explanation and show an illustration of the place or the character.

⓬ Critical Thinking

Evaluate

- Point out that Perseus is being coached and equipped by the gods. Ask: Does this assistance make Perseus seem less heroic? Possible answers: Some students may feel this aid reduces Perseus' heroism. Others may note that he took on the task by himself and that his obstacles are superhuman.
- Ask students as they read further to continue to weigh Perseus' individual actions against the help and guidance he receives.

⓭ ▶Critical Viewing

Answer: Students should recognize Medusa from the snakes that wreathe her face.

night. In that gray place the three women lived, all gray themselves and withered as in extreme old age. They were strange creatures, indeed, most of all because they had but one eye for the three, which it was their custom to take turns with, each removing it from her forehead when she had had it for a time and handing it to another.

All this Hermes told Perseus and then he unfolded his plan. He would himself guide Perseus to them. Once there Perseus must keep hidden until he saw one of them take the eye out of her forehead to pass it on. At that moment, when none of the three could see, he must rush forward and seize the eye and refuse to give it back until they told him how to reach the nymphs of the North.

⓬ He himself, Hermes said, would give him a sword to attack Medusa with—which could not be bent or broken by the Gorgon's scales, no matter how hard they were. This was a wonderful gift, no doubt, and yet of what use was a sword when the creature to be struck by it could turn the swordsman into stone before he was within striking distance? But another great deity was at hand to help. Pallas Athena stood beside Perseus. She took off the shield of polished bronze which covered her breast and held it out to him. "Look into this when you attack the Gorgon,"

⓭ ▼ **Critical Viewing** Who is portrayed in this art? How do you know? **[Connect]**

CUSTOMIZE INSTRUCTION FOR UNIVERSAL ACCESS

For Advanced Readers

Challenge students to locate and read another version of this myth. Two possible choices are the version in Books IV–V of Ovid's *Metamorphoses* and that in Nathaniel Hawthorne's *A Wonder Book* (see p. 215 of this Teacher's Edition). Both these versions provide a contrast in style to Hamilton's retelling of the myth, and Ovid's version includes details of incidents not found in "Perseus." (You might explain that since Ovid was Roman, he refers to the gods by their Roman names—Zeus as Jove, Athena as Minerva, and so on.) Students can compare and contrast the content and style of the two versions of the myth. Which did they prefer? Why? Which was the most exciting? The most realistic? What are the most important differences between the two versions, and what do students think might account for these differences? Students can answer these questions in brief essays.

she said. "You will be able to see her in it as in a mirror, and so avoid her deadly power."

Now, indeed, Perseus had good reason to hope. The journey to the twilight land was long, over the stream of Ocean and on to the very border of the black country where the Cimmerians dwell, but Hermes was his guide and he could not go astray. They found the Gray Women at last, looking in the wavering light like gray birds, for they had the shape of swans. But their heads were human and beneath their wings they had arms and hands. Perseus did just as Hermes had said, he held back until he saw one of them take the eye out of her forehead. Then before she could give it to her sister, he snatched it out of her hand. It was a moment or two before the three realized they had
14 lost it. Each thought one of the others had it. But Perseus spoke out and told them he had taken it and that it would be theirs again only when they showed him how to find the nymphs of the North. They gave him full directions at once; they would have done anything to get their eye back. He returned it to them and went on the way they had pointed out to him. He was bound, although he did not know it, to the blessed country of the Hyperboreans [hī per bō´ rē anz], at the back of the North Wind, of which it is said: "Neither by ship nor yet by land shall one find the wondrous road to the gathering place of the Hyperboreans." But Perseus had Hermes with him, so that the road lay open to him, and he reached that host of happy people who are always banqueting and holding joyful revelry. They showed him great kindness: they welcomed him to their feast, and the maidens dancing to the sound of flute and lyre paused to get for him the gifts he sought. These were three: winged sandals, a magic wallet which would always become the right size for whatever was to be carried in it, and,
15 most important of all, a cap which made the wearer invisible. With these and Athena's shield and Hermes' sword Perseus was ready for the Gorgons. Hermes knew where they lived, and leaving the happy land the two flew back across Ocean and over the sea to the Terrible Sisters' island.

By great good fortune they were all asleep when Perseus found them. In the mirror of the bright shield he could see them clearly, creatures with great wings and bodies covered with golden scales and hair a mass of twisting snakes. Athena was beside him now as well as Hermes. They told him which one was Medusa and that was important, for she alone of the three could be killed; the other two were immortal. Perseus on his winged sandals hovered above them, looking, however, only at the shield. Then he aimed a stroke down at Medusa's throat and Athena guided his hand. With a single sweep of his sword he cut through her neck and, his eyes still fixed on the shield with never a glance at her, he swooped low enough to seize the head. He dropped it into the wallet which closed around it. He had nothing to fear from it now. But the two other Gorgons had awakened and, horrified at the sight of their sister slain, tried to pursue the slayer. Perseus was safe; he had on the cap of darkness and they could not find him.

wavering (wā´ vər iŋ) *adj.* flickering

Literary Analysis

Hero in a Myth Which heroic quality does Perseus reveal in his treatment of the Gray Women?

revelry (rev´ əl rē) *n.* party

Reading Strategy

Predicting How do you think Perseus will use the wallet and the cap that were gifts from the Hyperboreans?

16 ✓ **Reading Check**

What does Athena give to Perseus to help fight the Gorgon?

14 Literary Analysis

Hero in a Myth

- Have students review the information they have learned about Perseus thus far.
- Ask the Literary Analysis question on p. 219: Which heroic quality does Perseus reveal in his treatment of the Gray Women?
  Answer: He follows the directions Hermes gave him. He is brave enough to snatch the eye away and fair enough to give it back as soon as he has the information he needs.

15 Reading Strategy

Predicting

- Ask students whether Perseus will succeed in killing the Gorgon. Which details make them predict this?
  Answer: He will succeed. He has Hermes to guide him, he has the power of invisibility, and a means to keep the head hidden from his sight once he has it. He can follow directions and show courage.
- Ask the Reading Strategy question on p. 219: How will Perseus use the wallet and cap?
  Answer: The cap will make him invisible, so the Gorgon won't see him coming to kill her. The magic wallet will hold the Gorgon's head, so Perseus won't catch sight of it accidentally.

16 ✓ Reading Check

Answer: Athena gives Perseus her shield of polished bronze.

17 Reading Strategy

Predicting

- Ask students whether Andromeda's story reminds them of any folk or fairy tale. What happens to the heroine of that tale? Use this answer to predict what will happen to Andromeda and Cassiopeia.
  Answer: Students should notice a resemblance to the story of Snow White and her vain, cruel stepmother. Since Snow White lived happily ever after and her stepmother was punished, students may predict the same fate for Andromeda and Cassiopeia.

Monitor Progress Ask the Reading Strategy question on p. 220: What part do you think Andromeda will play in Perseus' journey?
Answer: Since Andromeda is a lovely maiden, Perseus will probably try to rescue her and fall in love with her. So, she will probably play the part of his romantic interest.

18 Literary Analysis

Hero in a Myth

- Ask students to compare and contrast the confrontation with the sea monster and the encounter with the Gorgon. In which situation is Perseus more of a hero? Why?
  Answer: He is more heroic in the fight with the sea monster because he is acting on his own, without help or guidance. There is no Hermes to advise him, no Athena to guide his sword arm.
- Ask the Literary Analysis question on p. 220: What new challenge does Perseus face?
  Answer: Perseus will have to try to find Danaë and Dictys. He will also have to confront King Polydectes with his success.

So over the sea rich-haired Danaë's son,
Perseus, on his winged sandals sped,
Flying swift as thought.
In a wallet of silver,
A wonder to behold,
He bore the head of the monster,
While Hermes, the son of Maia,
The messenger of Zeus,
Kept ever at his side.

On his way back he came to Ethiopia and alighted there. By this time Hermes had left him. Perseus found, as Hercules was later to find, that a lovely maiden had been given up to be devoured by a horrible sea serpent. Her name was Andromeda and she was the daughter of a silly vain woman,

17 That starred Ethiop queen who strove
To set her beauty's praise above
The sea-nymphs, and their power offended.

She had boasted that she was more beautiful than the daughters of Nereus, the Sea-god. An absolutely certain way in those days to draw down on one a wretched fate was to claim superiority in anything over any deity; nevertheless people were perpetually doing so. In this case the punishment for the arrogance the gods detested fell not on Queen Cassiopeia [kas´ ē ō pē´ ə], Andromeda's mother, but on her daughter. The Ethiopians were being devoured in numbers by the serpent; and, learning from the oracle that they could be freed from the pest only if Andromeda were offered up to it, they forced Cepheus [sē fəs], her father, to consent. When Perseus arrived the maiden was on a rocky ledge by the sea, chained there to wait for the coming of the monster. Perseus saw her and on the instant loved her. He waited beside her until the great snake came for its prey; then he cut its head off just as he had the Gorgon's. The headless body dropped back into the water; Perseus took Andromeda to her parents and asked for her hand, which they gladly gave him.

18 With her he sailed back to the island and his mother, but in the house where he had lived so long he found no one. The fisherman Dictys' wife was long since dead, and the two others, Danaë and the man who had been like a father to Perseus, had had to fly and hide themselves from Polydectes, who was furious at Danaë's refusal to marry him. They had taken refuge in a temple, Perseus was told. He learned also that the King was holding a banquet in the palace and all the men who favored him were gathered there. Perseus instantly saw his opportunity. He went straight to the palace and entered the hall. As he stood at the entrance, Athena's shining buckler on his breast, the silver wallet at his side, he drew the eyes of every man there. Then before any could look away he held up the Gorgon's head; and at the sight one and all, the cruel King and his servile courtiers, were turned into stone. There they sat, a row of statues,

Reading Strategy
Predicting What part do you think Andromeda will play in Perseus' journey? Why?

deity (dē´ ə tē) *n.* a god

Literary Analysis
Hero in a Myth What new challenge does Perseus face?

ENRICHMENT: Science

Constellations

A constellation is a specific group of stars. The ancients observed and cataloged the constellations, and mariners used them to navigate. The Greeks named the constellations after mythological characters suggested by the shapes the stars would form if connected by lines. These names are still used to identify them.

Perseus, Andromeda, Cassiopeia, Cepheus, Cetus (the sea monster), and Pegasus (born when Perseus killed Medusa) are all major constellations close together in the sky. On autumn nights, they are visible across most of the United States. Cassiopeia is a group of five stars that form a W. Cepheus looks like a child's drawing of a steep-roofed house. Andromeda gives her name to both a constellation and a whole galaxy; the galaxy is dimly visible from the Earth as a fuzzy glow. Algol, the second-brightest star of Perseus, is sometimes called "Medusa's Eye" or "the Demon Star."

each, as it were, frozen stiff in the attitude he had struck when he first saw Perseus.

When the islanders knew themselves freed from the tyrant it was easy for Perseus to find Danaë and Dictys. He made Dictys king of the island, but he and his mother decided that they would go back with Andromeda

20 ◀ Critical Viewing
Which heroic qualities does this image illustrate? **[Support]**

21 Reading Check
What does Perseus learn has happened to Dictys and Danaë?

19 Background

Art

Perseus and Andromeda (detail), by Paolo Veronese

Paolo Veronese ("Paolo of Verona") (1528–1588), Tintoretto, and Titian are three great painters of the end of the Italian Renaissance. All are known for their brilliant colors and the epic sweep of their historical, religious, and mythological scenes.

This detail from Veronese's painting shows Perseus in the act of slaying the sea monster.

1. What details of Perseus' equipment does the artist include?
   Answer: Students should recognize the sword, magic cap, winged sandals, and magic wallet.
2. How does color contribute to the drama of the scene?
   Answer: The blood-red colors of Perseus' clothing flow toward the gaping red mouth of the monster. The vivid colors highlight the two combatants.

20 ▶ Critical Viewing

Answer: Perseus proves that he can take action and perform heroic deeds on his own, without help from the gods.

21 Reading Check

Answer: Perseus learns that Dictys and Danaë have hidden in a temple to escape from King Polydectes.

CUSTOMIZE INSTRUCTION FOR UNIVERSAL ACCESS

For Special Needs Students	For Less Proficient Readers
Have students discuss their opinions of Perseus as a hero. Do they find him heroic? Why or why not? How does Perseus compare to students' personal heroes or to heroes they admire from films, television, or other stories? Does Perseus seem more heroic as the story progresses, or does he seem heroic right from the beginning? Have students defend their opinions with specific details from the myth.	Have students work together to answer Review and Assess questions 4 and 5 on p. 223. They can use their ideas about Perseus' two chief antagonists as a starting place for a group discussion of how these two kings affect the story. Remind students that Medusa and the sea monster are also antagonists that Perseus must defeat.

ASSESS

Answers for p. 222

Review and Assess

1. Possible answer: Students may choose the rescue of Andromeda, because Perseus acts alone to save a beautiful princess.
2. **(a)** She predicts that Danaë's son will kill him. **(b)** Acrisius shuts Danaë up in a buried chamber, then sets her and her son adrift in a chest. **(c)** He is arrogant enough to believe that he can defeat the prophecies of the gods and selfish enough to sacrifice his own daughter and grandson to save his own life.
3. **(a)** He is embarrassed because he has no gift for the King and rashly promises to bring the best gift of all. **(b)** They both tell him what he must do, and they give him the sword and shield he'll need to kill the Gorgon. **(c)** Like Athena and Hermes, Perseus is a child of Zeus.
4. **(a)** Watching Medusa's reflection in his shield, Perseus uses the sword Hermes gave him to cut off her head. **(b)** He might never have found Medusa. He might have wandered forever. If he had found Medusa, she and her sisters would probably have killed him.
5. Possible answers: He deserves his fate because he was brutally cruel to his child and grandchild. He doesn't deserve his fate because he was acting in self-defense: he expected Perseus to kill him.
6. The myth suggests that only the gods can affect fate. Acrisius goes to great extremes to escape his destiny, yet he is still killed as prophesied.
7. **(a)** First audiences may have learned to respect their gods and to accept their fates. **(b)** Students may suggest that people still need to accept situations that are beyond their power to change.

to Greece and try to be reconciled to Acrisius, to see if the many years that had passed since he had put them in the chest had not softened him so that he would be glad to receive his daughter and grandson. When they reached Argos, however, they found that Acrisius had been driven away from the city, and where he was no one could say. It happened that soon after their arrival Perseus heard that the King of Larissa, in the North, was holding a great athletic contest, and he journeyed there to take part. In the discus-throwing when his turn came and he hurled the heavy missile, it swerved and fell among the spectators. Acrisius was there on a visit to the King, and the discus struck him. The blow was fatal and he died at once.

So Apollo's oracle was again proved true. If Perseus felt any grief, at least he knew that his grandfather had done his best to kill him and his mother. With his death their troubles came to an end. Perseus and Andromeda lived happily ever after. Their son, Electryon, was the grandfather of Hercules.

Medusa's head was given to Athena, who bore it always upon the aegis, Zeus's shield, which she carried for him.

reconciled (rek′ ən sīld′) *adj.* became friends again

Review and Assess

Thinking About the Selection

1. **Respond:** Which of Perseus' adventures would make the best action-adventure movie? Why?
2. **(a) Recall:** What prediction does the priestess make to Acrisius? **(b) Connect:** What two actions does Acrisius take to prevent the prediction from coming true? **(c) Infer:** What is revealed about Acrisius' character through the actions he takes to escape fate?
3. **(a) Recall:** Why does Perseus set out to kill Medusa? **(b) Connect:** What help does he receive from Hermes and Athena? **(c) Infer:** What detail of Perseus' background might have led Athena and Hermes to help Perseus in his quest?
4. **(a) Recall:** How does Perseus manage to kill Medusa? **(b) Hypothesize:** What might have happened to Perseus if he had not received help from the gods?
5. **Make a Judgment:** Considering the actions he takes against Danaë and Perseus, does Acrisius deserve his fate? Why or why not?
6. **Draw Conclusions:** What does this myth suggest about one's ability to escape or control fate? Explain.
7. **Extend:** This myth from ancient Greece is thousands of years old. **(a)** What lessson do you think it taught its first audiences? **(b)** In what ways is it still relevant today?

Edith Hamilton

(1867–1963)

Edith Hamilton's long journey on Earth began soon after the Civil War and ended in the Space Age. Her heart took an even longer journey—back to the worlds of ancient Greece and Rome—to find messages that modern people could apply to their lives.

Hamilton started as a groundbreaking educator who helped found the Bryn Mawr School in Baltimore, the first college preparatory school for women. She taught a generation of young women the lesson she had learned: not to limit their goals simply because they were not men.

After leaving Bryn Mawr, Hamilton began writing articles about ancient Greece, which she later turned into a book entitled *The Greek Way*, published in 1930. Her other books include *The Roman Way* (1932), *The Prophets of Israel* (1936), and *Mythology* (1942).

ASSESSMENT PRACTICE: Reading Comprehension

Sequential Order **(For more practice, see Test Preparation Workbook, p. 13.)**

Many tests require students to understand sequential order. Use the following sample test item to show students how to arrange events into sequential order.

Before he could attack Medusa, Perseus had to receive help from Athena and Hermes. Later he delivered the Gorgon's head to the cruel Polydectes, but only after saving Andromeda on his way back.

Which of these actions happens last?

A Perseus saves Andromeda.
B Perseus attacks Medusa.
C Perseus brings Polydectes the Gorgon's head.
D Athena and Hermes help Perseus.

Using references such as *before, later,* and *after,* students should recognize that bringing the Gorgon's head, *C*, happens last.

Review and Assess

Literary Analysis

Hero in a Myth

1. Perseus accepts the help of Hermes and Athena in his pursuit of Medusa, but which **heroic qualities** of his own does he draw upon to accomplish his goals?
2. Which heroic quality does Perseus exhibit when he decides to return to Argos to see Acrisius?
3. Which of Danaë's qualities might Perseus have inherited from her? Use the following chart to analyze the connection between mother and son. In each case, provide an example of each quality you identify.

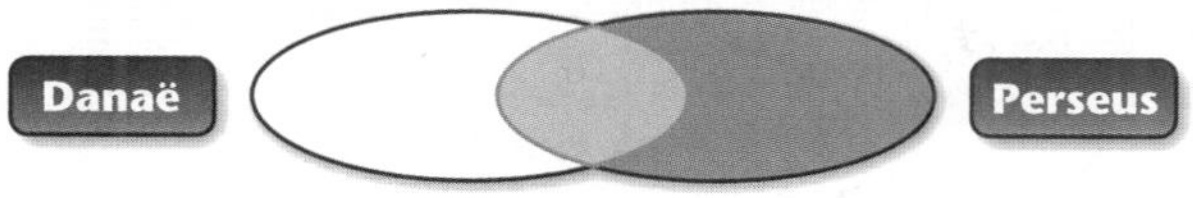

Connecting Literary Elements

4. In what ways are Acrisius and Polydectes **antagonists** of Perseus? In a chart like the following, trace their actions, the difficulties they create for Perseus, and the ways he overcomes these challenges.

Antagonist	Actions	Effect on Perseus	End Result

5. How do the actions of the two antagonists make Perseus an even stronger hero?

Reading Strategy

Predicting

6. What evidence in the story made it possible to **predict** that Perseus would be successful in killing Medusa?
7. (a) Why is Acrisius' death a logical outcome? (b) What aspects of his death could not have been predicted?

Extend Understanding

8. **Literature Connection:** (a) What situations from other works of literature, movies, or real life can you recall in which someone tried to escape or control fate? (b) What were the outcomes?

Quick Review

A **hero in a myth** is a character who performs amazing feats in a tale involving supernatural beings and fantastic events.

An **antagonist** is a character or force in conflict with the hero.

To **predict** story events, look for details and facts to suggest what may occur later.

Take It to the Net

www.phschool.com

Take the interactive self-test online to check your understanding of the selections.

Answers for p. 223

Review and Assess

1. Perseus is brave, determined, stubborn, and careful to do what he's told.
2. He exhibits courage and forgiveness.
3. Danaë's main characteristic is a refusal to give up hope, even when locked in the chest at sea. Perseus shows a similar hopefulness in seeking out his grandfather.
4. Antagonist: Acrisius; Action: sets Perseus adrift in a chest, hoping he will drown; Result: Perseus throws a discus that kills him. Antagonist: Polydectes; Action: tricks Perseus into attempting a feat everyone thinks will result in his death; Result: Perseus turns the trick against him and uses the Gorgon's head to turn him to stone.
5. The two antagonists are powerful, and they put sizable obstacles in Perseus' path. Because of them, his achievements are more remarkable.
6. Perseus has heroic qualities and is being advised and equipped by gods.
7. **(a)** The death was logical because the oracle predicted this outcome. **(b)** No one could predict that Acrisius would be struck by a discus. Perseus threw it with no intention of hitting him.
8. Possible answers: Oedipus' father tried to escape death at the hands of his son; Oedipus, not knowing the man, killed him. In Arthurian legend, Guinevere and Lancelot try to quell their love for each other; they end by destroying the Round Table, and both Lancelot and Arthur are killed. Students may suggest other examples from literature or movie plots.

ENRICHMENT: Further Reading

Other Works by Edith Hamilton

Three Greek Plays
The Great Age of Greek Literature
Echo of Greece

Take It to the Net

Visit www.phschool.com for more information on Edith Hamilton.

EXTEND

Answers for p. 224

❶ Vocabulary Development

Word Analysis

1. condition of living forever
2. one who prepares the dead for burial
3. fatally
4. to cause to live forever

Spelling Strategy

1. withering
2. transmitted
3. referred

Concept Development: Synonyms

1. b
2. c
3. a
4. a
5. b
6. c
7. a

❷ Grammar

1. was imprisoned, passive
2. were placed, passive
3. found, active
4. was helped, passive
5. rescued, active

Writing Application

Sample Sentences:

Active voice:

1. Perseus beheaded Medusa.
2. Perseus held Medusa's head aloft and turned everyone to stone.

Passive voice:

3. Andromeda was rescued by Perseus.
4. The eye of the Gray Women was taken by Perseus.

Integrate Language Skills

❶ Vocabulary Development Lesson

Word Analysis: Latin Root *-mort-*

The word *mortified*, meaning "deeply humiliated," is based on the Latin root *-mort-*, meaning "death." Use the meaning of *-mort-* to help you define the following words.

1. immortality
2. mortician
3. mortally
4. immortalize

Spelling Strategy

When you add an ending that begins with a vowel to a word of more than one syllable that ends in a consonant preceded by a vowel, you normally do not double the final consonant. Thus, *cancel* + *-ed* = *canceled*. However, if the word's stress is on the final syllable, you usually double the consonant. Thus, *compel* + *-ing* = *compelling*. Add the ending shown to each of the words below.

1. wither + *-ing* 2. transmit + *-ed* 3. refer + *-ed*

Concept Development: Synonyms

On your paper, write the word or phrase whose meaning is closest to that of the first word. If necessary, review the vocabulary word list on page 213.

1. deity: (a) goodness, (b) god, (c) generosity
2. mortified: (a) cleansed, (b) stiff, (c) humiliated
3. revelry: (a) grand party, (b) rude awakening, (c) loud disagreement
4. despair: (a) hopelessness, (b) ruin, (c) sacrifice
5. reconciled: (a) guessed again, (b) became friends again, (c) forgot again
6. wavering: (a) greeting, (b) stumbling, (c) flickering
7. kindred: (a) relatives, (b) childhood, (c) hostility

❷ Grammar Lesson

Active and Passive Voice

A verb in the **active voice** expresses an action done *by* its subject. A verb in the **passive voice** expresses an action done *to* its subject.

Active voice: Edith Hamilton *wrote* "Perseus." [The subject, *Edith Hamilton*, performs the action of the verb *wrote*.]

Passive voice: "Perseus" *was written* by Edith Hamilton. [The subject, *"Perseus,"* receives the action of the verb *was written*.]

Sentences written in the active voice are often less wordy and more direct than those written in the passive voice. Therefore, use the active voice to create more forceful and lively writing.

Practice Copy the following sentences and underline the verb or verbs in each one. Determine whether the underlined verbs are in the active or passive voice.

1. Danaë was imprisoned by Acrisius.
2. They were placed in a chest in the sea.
3. Dictys found them on the beach.
4. In his search for Medusa, Perseus was helped by Hermes and Athena.
5. Perseus rescued Andromeda.

Writing Application Write four sentences about Perseus' heroic actions, two in the active voice and two in the passive voice.

WG Prentice Hall Writing and Grammar Connection: Chapter 23, Section 2

TEACHING RESOURCES

The following resources can be used to enrich or extend the instructions for pp. 224–225.

Vocabulary

Selection Support: Build Vocabulary, p. 49

Grammar

Selection Support, Build Grammar Skills, p. 50

Writing and Grammar, Gold Level, p. 540 ■

Daily Language Practice Transparencies

Writing

Writing and Grammar Gold Level, p. 134

Writing and Grammar iText CD-ROM ■

■ **BLOCK SCHEDULING:** Resources marked with this symbol provide varied instruction during 90-minute blocks.

❸ Writing Lesson

Speech of Introduction

Imagine that you have to deliver a speech introducing Perseus at a large public gathering. Your speech should tell your audience something of Perseus' background and should go on to describe and praise his deeds before finally introducing him.

Prewriting Start by listing the important facts of Perseus' life. Then, highlight the events that will appeal to the audience in various ways—by touching people's emotions or by amusing them, for example.

Model: Listing Details That Appeal to Your Audience

1. Dictys found Perseus and his mother in a chest.
2. Perseus told Polydectes he would bring back Medusa's head.
3. He did not tell his mother, and he sailed off to Greece.
4. Perseus received help from Athena and Hermes.

The highlighted information accents Perseus' heroic qualities—qualities audiences should find compelling.

Drafting Organize your information in time order, or group the details into categories by focusing on each of Perseus' character traits. Then, cite details from his life that relate to each trait.

Revising Reread your draft and make sure you have chosen the most appealing material from Perseus' story to help win over your audience.

WG *Prentice Hall Writing and Grammar Connection: Chapter 7, Section 2*

❹ Extension Activities

Listening and Speaking Imagine that Acrisius escapes death and is brought to trial for his treatment of Danaë and Perseus. As a prosecuting attorney, present an **opening argument** to a jury of your classmates, accusing the king of intent to commit murder. Follow these tips to help you:

- Explain how Acrisius put Danaë and Perseus in a life-threatening situation.
- Point out Acrisius' motive—the reason he wanted to kill them.

Present your opening argument to the class.

Research and Technology In a group, prepare an **illustrated map** showing Perseus' travels from the time of his birth until the end of the story. Refer back to the story and list the places he goes to in his travels. Then, create your map. Illustrate the map with pictures of the various gods and monsters he meets. Use graphics software to design the map. **[Group Activity]**

Take It to the Net www.phschool.com

Go online for an additional research activity using the Internet.

ASSESSMENT RESOURCES

The following resources can be used to assess students' knowledge and skills.

Selection Assessment

- **Formal Assessment,** pp. 41–43
- **Open Book Test,** pp. 37–39
- **Got It! Assessment Videotapes,** Tape 1
- **Test Bank Software**

Take It to the Net

Visit www.phschool.com for self-tests and additional questions on "Perseus."

Listening and Speaking Rubric

- **Performance Assess. and Portfolio Mgmt.,** p. 23

PRENTICE HALL ASSESSMENT SYSTEM

- **Workbook**
- **Skill Book**
- **Transparencies**
- **CD-ROM**

Lesson Support for p. 225

❸ Writing Lesson

- Have students recall speeches of introduction made at awards shows they may have seen on television. These speeches will be good models for this exercise. Usually the main attraction at a ceremony is the prominent person being introduced, and most of his or her accomplishments are common knowledge in any case. An introductory speech should be very brief, succinct, and witty so that the audience will enjoy it without growing bored or impatient.
- You may want to allow students to write speeches of introduction for other characters if they wish; for example, Athena, Hermes, or Danaë.

❹ Extension Activity

Listening and Speaking

- Students have probably seen many examples of opening arguments on television shows. Remind them to keep their arguments brief.
- Have students choose partners on whom to try out their arguments before the class presentation. Partners should argue the opposite point of view so that students can anticipate objections and strengthen their statements.
- You may want to extend the activity by having other students argue that Acrisius is innocent on the grounds of self-defense. After hearing the arguments, the jury can debate them and reach a verdict.
- Assess students' work with Evaluating a Speech, p. 23 in **Performance Assessment and Portfolio Management.**

CUSTOMIZE INSTRUCTION for Universal Access

To address different learning styles, use the following activities suggested in the **Extension Activities** booklet, p. 13.

- For Visual/Spatial and Logical/Mathematical Learners, use Activity 5.
- For Musical/Rhythmic and Interpersonal Learners, use Activity 6.

Slam, Dunk, & Hook ✦ The Spearthrower ✦ Shoulders

Lesson Objectives and CA Correlations

1. **To analyze and respond to literary elements**
   - Literary Analysis: Theme in Poetry **R 3.5**
   - Comparing Literary Works
2. **To read, comprehend, analyze, and critique poetry**
   - Reading Strategy: Forming Mental Images
   - Review and Assess questions
   - Assessment Practice (ATE)
3. **To develop word analysis skills, fluency, and systematic vocabulary**
   - Vocabulary Development Lesson: Specialized Vocabulary: Jargon **R 1.2**
4. **To understand and apply written and oral language conventions**
   - Spelling Strategy
   - Grammar Lesson: Irregular Verbs **LC 1.2, 1.3**
5. **To understand and apply appropriate writing and research strategies**
   - Writing Lesson: Editorial **W 2.4**
   - Extension Activity: Research Report **W 1.5**
6. **To understand and apply listening and speaking strategies**
   - Extension Activity: Sportscast **LS 1.8**

STEP-BY-STEP TEACHING GUIDE	PACING GUIDE
PRETEACH	
Motivate Students and Provide Background	
Use the Motivation activity (ATE p. 226)	5 min.
Read and discuss the Preview material and Background information (SE/ATE p. 226) [A]	10 min.
Introduce the Concepts	
Introduce the Literary Analysis and Reading Strategy (SE/ATE p. 227) [A]	15 min.
Pronounce the vocabulary words and read their definitions (SE p. 227)	5 min.
TEACH	
Monitor Comprehension	
Informally monitor comprehension by circulating while students read independently or in groups [A]	10 min.
Develop vocabulary with Vocabulary notes (SE pp. 229, 231; ATE p. 229)	as students read
Develop Understanding	
Develop students' understanding of theme in poetry with Literary Analysis annotations (SE/ATE p. 232) [A]	10 min.
Develop students' ability to form mental images with Reading Strategy annotations (SE p. 231; ATE pp. 227, 231)	10 min.
ASSESS	
Assess Mastery	
Assess students' mastery of the Reading Strategy and Literary Analysis by having them answer the Review and Assess questions (SE/ATE p. 233)	20 min.
Use one or more of the print and media Assessment Resources (ATE p. 235) [A]	up to 50 min.
EXTEND	
Apply Understanding	
Have students complete the Vocabulary Development Lesson and the Grammar Lesson (SE p. 234) [A]	20 min.
Apply students' knowledge of anticipating questions using the Writing Lesson (SE/ATE p. 235) [A]	45 min.
Apply students' understanding using one or more of the Extension Activities (SE p. 235)	20–90 min.

[A] **ACCELERATED INSTRUCTION:**
Use the strategies and activities identified with an [A].

UNIVERSAL ACCESS
● = Below-Level Students
▲ = On-Level Students
■ = Above-Level Students

Time and Resource Manager

Reading Level: Average/Easy/Easy
Average Number of Instructional Days: 4

RESOURCES		
PRINT	**TRANSPARENCIES**	**TECHNOLOGY**
• **Beyond Literature,** Cross-Curricular Connection: Physical Education, p. 14 ▲ ■		• **Interest Grabber Video,** Tape 1 ● ▲ ■
• **Selection Support Workbook:** ● ▲ ■ Literary Analysis, p. 56 Reading Strategy, p. 55 Build Vocabulary, p. 53	• **Literary Analysis and Reading Transparencies,** pp. 27 and 28 ● ▲ ■	
		• **Listening to Literature** ● ▲ ■ Audiocassettes, Side 9 Audio CDs, CD 7
• **Literatura en español** ● ▲ • **Literary Analysis for Enrichment** ■	• **Fine Art Transparencies Volume 1,** Art Transparency 5 ● ▲ ■	
• **Formal Assessment:** Selection Test, pp. 44–46 ● ▲ ■ • **Open Book Test,** pp. 40–42 ● ▲ ■ • **Performance Assessment and Portfolio Management,** p. 10 ● ▲ ■ • PRENTICE HALL ASSESSMENT SYSTEM ● ▲ ■	• PRENTICE HALL ASSESSMENT SYSTEM ● ▲ ■ Skills Practice Answers and Explanations on Transparencies	• **Test Bank Software** ● ▲ ■ • **Got It! Assessment Videotapes,** Tape 1 ● ▲
• **Selection Support Workbook:** ● ▲ ■ Build Grammar Skills, p. 54 • **Writing and Grammar,** Gold Level ● ▲ ■ • **Extension Activities,** p. 14 ● ▲ ■	• **Daily Language Practice Transparencies** ● ▲	• **Writing and Grammar iText CD-ROM** ● ▲ ■ *Take It to the Net* www.phschool.com

BLOCK SCHEDULING: Use one 90-minute class period to preteach the selection and have students read it. Use a second 90-minute class period to assess students' mastery of skills and have them complete one of the Extension Activities.

PRETEACH

Step-by-Step Teaching Guide for pp. 226–227

Motivation

Write the words *poetry* and *sports* on the chalkboard. Ask students what the two have in common. Students may say that the two have little in common. Have students brainstorm for a list of images describing exciting moments from sporting events. Show them that these images make excellent starting points for poems about sports. Finally, tell students that the poems they are about to read capture the excitement of sports through vivid images like the ones they have listed.

Interest Grabber Video

As an alternative, play "Naomi Shihab Nye on Making Connections" on Tape 1 to engage student interest.

1 Background

History

The Olympic Games date back to at least 776 B.C. in Greece. The earliest Olympics involved only one footrace; later, they included wrestling and other events. The first modern Olympic Games were held in Athens in the summer of 1896 and have continued every four years to the present day, interrupted only by World Wars I and II. Winter Olympic festivals also occur every four years, featuring sports that are played on snow or ice (hockey, skiing, figure skating, and so on). Originally, the Olympic Games were intended for amateur athletes, but since the 1980s more and more professional athletes have been permitted to compete.

Prepare to Read

Slam, Dunk, & Hook ◆ The Spearthrower ◆ Shoulders

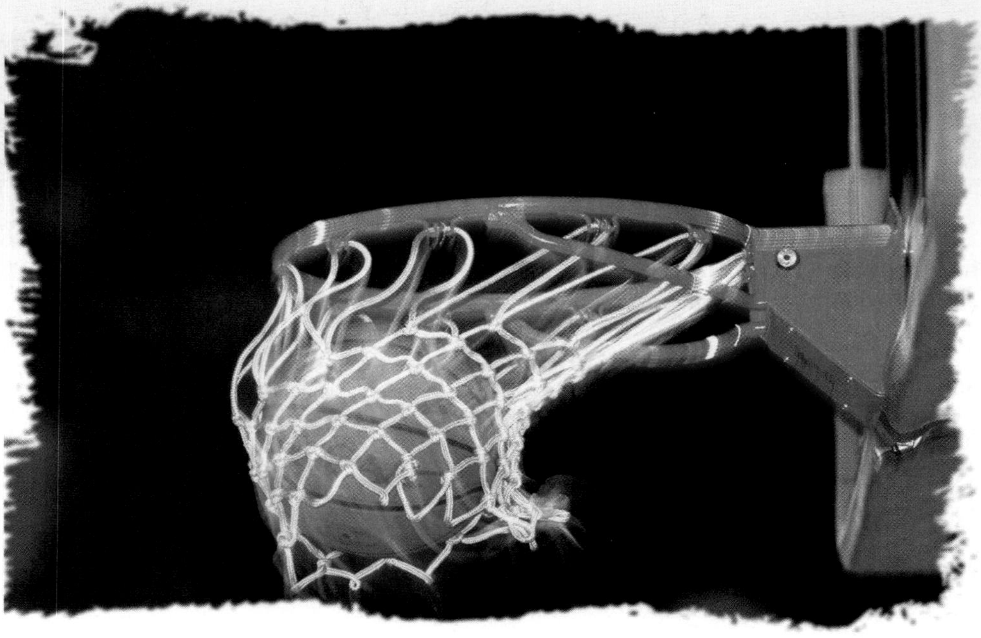

Take It to the Net

Visit www.phschool.com for interactive activities and instruction related to the selections, including

- background
- graphic organizers
- literary elements
- reading strategies

Preview

Connecting to the Literature

These poems are about the exhilaration of pure physical action that comes from a disciplined focus on an important goal. As you read, experience the sensation described and imagine what it means to spend every ounce of your strength for something you want with all your heart.

1 Background

The title "The Spearthrower" refers not only to a javelin thrower but also to a poet who sends her "signed song" of praise for women athletes into the "bullying dark" of athletic events once dominated by men. In associating the poet with the athlete, the poet Lillian Morrison follows a tradition from ancient Greece, where poets sang songs honoring Olympic athletics.

TEACHING RESOURCES

The following resources can be used to enrich or extend the instruction for pp. 226–227.

Motivation

Interest Grabber Video, Tape 1

Background

Beyond Literature, p. 14

Take It to the Net

Visit www.phschool.com for background and hotlinks for "Slam, Dunk, & Hook," "The Spearthrower," and "Shoulders."

Literary Analysis

Literary Analysis and Reading Transparencies, Theme in Poetry, p. 27

Reading

Selection Support: Reading Strategy, p. 55; Build Vocabulary, p. 53

Literary Analysis and Reading Transparencies, Forming Mental Images, p. 28

BLOCK SCHEDULING: Resources marked with this symbol provide varied instruction during 90-minute blocks.

❷ Literary Analysis

Theme in Poetry

On their surface, these poems vividly describe physical action, but underneath that surface is a **theme,** a central message or insight about life that sits at the center of each poem. The following lines from "The Spearthrower" address such a theme, suggesting that the athlete throws her javelin not only for herself but for other female athletes as well.

her quick laps
on the curving track,
that the sprinter surge
and the hurdler leap, . . .

As you read these poems, look for the insights or messages at their core.

Comparing Literary Works

In poetry, as in other literature, theme can be hinted at sideways or stated directly. In "The Spearthrower" and "Shoulders," the themes are stated directly. In contrast, in "Slam, Dunk, & Hook," the theme is implied; there seems to be much more than a game at stake. Compare and contrast the themes in each of the poems, paying close attention to the meaning that lies just beneath the words.

❸ Reading Strategy

Forming Mental Images

A poet writes words that let you see pictures in your mind's eye. To **form mental images** of a poem, turn the poet's words into pictures by applying your own experiences. These strategies will help you form mental images as you read poetry:

- Picture the scene that the poet sketches for you in words.
- If a picture does not come to mind easily, relate the words to events in your own life or to another poem or story you have read.

Use the chart shown at the right to help you form mental images as you read.

Words: ________

↓

Image Created in Your Mind: ________

Vocabulary Development

metaphysical (met´ə fiz´i kəl) *adj.* spiritual; beyond the physical (p. 229)

jibed (jībd) *v.* stopped short and turned from side to side (p. 229)

feint (fānt) *v.* deliver a pretended move to catch an opponent off guard (p. 229)

surge (surj) *v.* increase suddenly; speed up (p. 231)

CUSTOMIZE INSTRUCTION FOR UNIVERSAL ACCESS

For Less Proficient Readers	For English Learners	For Advanced Readers
The broken lines of "Slam, Dunk, & Hook" may make comprehension difficult. Remind students that the capital letters that begin each line don't necessarily begin new sentences. Students should pay attention to the punctuation to see where the complete thoughts begin and end.	Students may have trouble with the slang and jargon in which "Slam, Dunk, & Hook" is written. If any students in the class play basketball, have them answer questions about the poem's specialized language.	Have students discuss the effectiveness of the diction in "Slam, Dunk, & Hook." How do the word choices relate to the characters and setting? What do they add to the poem's overall effect? What might the effect have been if the same ideas were expressed in standard English?

❷ Literary Analysis

Theme in Poetry

- Explain that the *theme* is the central underlying message of a work—the idea the writer wants the reader to continue thinking about after closing the book. The desire to convey this message is the author's purpose for writing. It is also the work's main idea—its most important message.
- Remind students that writers rarely state a theme directly. They leave it to the reader to infer the theme. One exception to this general rule is a fable, which may conclude with a direct statement of the moral. Usually, however, readers must study the characters' thoughts and actions, the writer's use of figurative language, and other elements of the work to understand the theme.

❸ Reading Strategy

Forming Mental Images

- Explain that every time a person tells a story, listeners picture the story in their minds. An illustrated storybook comes with its own images, but most of the time readers or listeners have to develop their own mental illustrations.
- Challenge students to cover up the illustrations in their textbooks and read the three poems in this group without looking at the pictures. Have them write brief descriptions of some of the mental images they form. They can compare these with the pictures chosen for the book.

Vocabulary Development

- Pronounce each vocabulary word for students, and read the definitions as a class. Have students identify any words with which they are already familiar.

E-Teach

Visit E-Teach at www.phschool.com for teachers' essays on how to teach, with questions and answers.

TEACH

Step-by-Step Teaching Guide for pp. 228–232

CUSTOMIZE INSTRUCTION For Bodily/Kinesthetic Learners

Have students act out the physical movements described by the poets—dribbling, feinting, corkscrewing, and so on. They might also demonstrate how the man in "Shoulders," p. 232, carries his son across the street.

❶ About the Selection

A youth rhapsodizes about the neighborhood basketball games he plays with his buddies. The intensity of the games carry one player through a grievous loss.

❷ Background

Art

Night Games, Ernie Barnes

Ernie Barnes studied art history and painting before becoming a professional football player. As an artist, he puts all the "violence and power" he had felt on the field into his paintings. Ask students:

1. What can you infer about the players' lives?
   Possible answers: The skyline indicates the players live in a city. Some are barefoot, and their basket is makeshift; this suggests a lack of resources.
2. How does the painting compare to details of the poem?
   Answers: In both poem and painting players are poised in midair, lanky, and intense.

❸ ▶Critical Viewing

Answer: The two boys at the basket illustrate lines 9, 13–14, and 33. All four boys illustrate lines 16–17, 21, 27–29, and 35–40.

❶ Slam, Dunk, & Hook

Yusef Komunyakaa

Fast breaks. Lay ups. With Mercury's[1]
Insignia[2] on our sneakers,
We outmaneuvered the footwork
Of bad angels. Nothing but a hot
Swish of strings like silk
Ten feet out. In the roundhouse[3]
Labyrinth[4] our bodies
Created, we could almost
Last forever, poised in midair
Like storybook sea monsters.
A high note hung there
A long second. Off
The rim. We'd corkscrew
Up & dunk balls that exploded

1. **Mercury's** Mercury was the Roman god of travel, usually depicted with wings on his feet.
2. **insignia** (in sig´ nē ə) *n.* emblems or badges; logos.
3. **roundhouse** *n.* area on the court beneath the basket.
4. **labyrinth** (lab´ ə rinth) *n.* maze.

❷

❸ ▶**Critical Viewing** Which details in this painting relate to lines in the poem "Slam, Dunk, & Hook"? **[Connect]**

TEACHING RESOURCES

The following resources can be used to enrich or extend the instruction for pp. 228–232.

Literary Analysis

Selection Support: Literary Analysis, p. 56

Reading

Listening to Literature Audiocassettes, Side 9

Listening to Literature Audio CDs, CD 7

Extension

Fine Art Transparencies, Volume 1, Art Transparency 5 (Have students compare the scene shown in the painting with the mood and details of the poem.)

BLOCK SCHEDULING: Resources marked with this symbol provide varied instruction during 90-minute blocks.

The skullcap of hope & good
Intention. Bug-eyed, lanky,
All hands & feet . . . sprung rhythm.
We were metaphysical when girls
Cheered on the sidelines.
Tangled up in a falling,
Muscles were a bright motor
Double-flashing to the metal hoop
Nailed to our oak.
When Sonny Boy's mama died
He played nonstop all day, so hard
Our backboard splintered.
Glistening with sweat, we jibed
& rolled the ball off our
Fingertips. Trouble
Was there slapping a blackjack
Against an open palm.
4 Dribble, drive to the inside, feint,
& glide like a sparrow hawk.
Lay ups. Fast breaks.
We had moves we didn't know
We had. Our bodies spun
On swivels of bone & faith,
Through a lyric slipknot
Of joy, & we knew we were
Beautiful & dangerous.

metaphysical (met′ə fiz′i kəl) *adj.* spiritual; beyond the physical

jibed (jībd) *v.* stopped short and turned from side to side

feint (fānt) *v.* deliver a pretended move to catch an opponent off guard

Yusef Komunyakaa

(b. 1947)

Komunyakaa has said that he likes "connecting the abstract to the concrete," and that is precisely what he does in "Slam, Dunk, & Hook."

Komunyakaa won the Pulitzer Prize for poetry for his book *Neon Vernacular: New and Selected Poems* (1993). He grew up in Bogalusa, Louisiana, and earned the Bronze Star in Vietnam, serving as reporter and editor of the military newspaper *The Southern Cross.* He now teaches at Princeton University.

Review and Assess

Thinking About the Selection

1. **Respond:** Which images in this poem were clearest to you? Explain your answer.
2. **(a) Recall:** How does the speaker describe the action in lines 3–4? **(b) Infer:** Who or what do you think are the "bad angels" to which Komunyakaa refers?
3. **(a) Recall:** How does Sonny Boy play on the day his mother dies? **(b) Infer:** Why do you think he plays this way?
4. **(a) Interpret:** How does the first line of the poem convey the fast action of a game? **(b) Infer:** What might have been the purpose of starting the poem in such a way?
5. **(a) Analyze:** Why might the basketball players be both "beautiful" and "dangerous"? **(b) Infer:** What does playing basketball help the neighborhood boys to do?
6. **Apply:** Do you think sports are just for fun or do you think they help in other ways?

4 Vocabulary Development

Specialized Vocabulary: Jargon

- Point out that basketball, like other sports, has its own specialized vocabulary or *jargon*. Ask students what jargon appears in the poem's title.
  Answer: *Slam* and *dunk* are shots that are forcefully jammed through the basket. A *hook* is a one-handed shot (see the painting on p. 228 for an example).
- Have students list other examples of basketball jargon in the poem. Have students familiar with the game explain or demonstrate the meaning of such terms as *fast break, lay up,* and *dribble.*

Answers for p. 229

Review and Assess

1. Make sure students support their answers with details from the poem.
2. **(a)** The speaker describes playing a game against "bad angels." **(b)** The "bad angels" may be the temptations and pressures awaiting urban youths: drugs, crime, and family loss.
3. **(a)** He plays all day long and so intensely that he breaks the backboard. **(b)** The game provides an outlet for his grief and rage.
4. **(a)** The short sentence fragments, one-syllable words, and basketball jargon all give the line a fast pace and athletic rhythm. **(b)** The poet has recreated the feel of a game in words.
5. The players are beautiful because they are good at the game. They are dangerous because the game has given them strength, confidence, and unity. **(b)** It helps them to know their own value as athletes and human beings. Because of basketball, they make friends and avoid trouble.
6. Students may suggest that sports foster cooperation, competitiveness, and determination.

CUSTOMIZE INSTRUCTION FOR UNIVERSAL ACCESS

For Less Proficient Readers	For English Learners
Have students go through the poem, identifying all the vivid verbs they can find, such as *outmaneuvered, poised, corkscrew, dunk,* and *slapping.* Have students discuss the effect of these verbs. Why are these action verbs more effective than linking verbs? Challenge students to try writing a few sentences about basketball or another sport they enjoy, using vivid verbs like those in this poem.	Suggest that students focus on their favorite sport (other than basketball). Have students work in teams to make a list of special terms used to describe the sport. Then, have students write simple definitions of the terms to help newcomers to the sport.

❺ About the Selection

The poem describes a female athlete throwing a "javelin of light" through the darkness, encouraging athletes to run faster, soar higher, and throw farther than before while crowds cheer.

❻ ▶Critical Viewing

Answer: She is thinking of nothing but the throw of the javelin. She is straining every thought and nerve to throw it as far as possible.

❺ The Spearthrower

Lillian Morrison

❻ ▲ **Critical Viewing**
Based on the young woman's expression, what might her feelings be at this moment? **[Infer]**

CUSTOMIZE INSTRUCTION FOR UNIVERSAL ACCESS	
For Gifted/Talented Students	**For Advanced Readers**
Challenge students to write their own poems about sports. Each student can choose a sport he or she is very familiar with, either as a spectator or as a player. Remind them to use vivid verbs, specific adjectives, and concrete nouns to convey the movement and excitement of the sport to the readers.	Challenge students to choose one of the three poems in this group and write a detailed analysis of the way the poet uses action and figurative language to convey theme. Students should read their chosen poem once or twice each day for a few days, gathering ideas before they begin writing. Their essays should include specific reference to lines and phrases in the poems. You may want to ask students to read their finished essays to the class.

7

She walks alone
to the edge of the park
and throws into
the bullying dark
her javelin
of light,
her singing sign
her signed song
that the runner may run
far and long
her quick laps
on the curving track,
that the sprinter surge
and the hurdler leap,
that the vaulter soar,
clear the highest bar,
and the discus fly
as the great crowds cry
to their heroines
Come on!

Reading Strategy
Forming Mental Images Describe the picture you see in your mind as you read lines 1–6.

surge (surj) *v.* increase suddenly; speed up

Review and Assess

Thinking About the Selection

1. **Respond:** How did this poem make you feel when you read it? Why?
2. **(a) Recall:** What surroundings does Morrison describe at the beginning of the poem? **(b) Analyze:** Which words add mood to this description? **(c) Interpret:** Why do you think Morrison refers to the dark as "bullying"?
3. **(a) Recall:** Who "walks alone" in the poem? **(b) Evaluate:** What is the effect of starting the poem this way?
4. **(a) Recall:** Which athletes does Morrison mention in lines 9–16? **(b) Interpret:** Which details in the poem support the interpretation that the spearthrower is not an athlete, but a poet?
5. **Analyze:** What benefit does the spearthrower "pass on" to other female athletes?
6. **Speculate:** What do you think motivates great athletes the most?
7. **Extend:** Do you believe that the successes and failures a person experiences can greatly affect others? Explain.

Lillian Morrison

(b. 1917)

Lillian Morrison has worked as a librarian and has written and compiled many books. She has published several books of her own poetry, including *Whistling the Morning In* (1992). She has also edited several anthologies of poems about sports (including one focused on basketball and entitled, coincidentally, *Slam, Dunk*), along with collections of riddles, playground chants, and autograph sayings.

7 Reading Strategy

Forming Mental Images

- Read the bracketed passage to students. Encourage students to close their eyes and focus on the words you are reading.
- Ask students the Reading Strategy question on p. 231: Describe the picture you see in your mind as you read lines 1–6.
  Answer: Students may see the literal picture—an athletic woman hurling a javelin into the darkness. Some students may visualize a goddess throwing a "spear" of light.

Answers for p. 231

Review and Assess

1. Some students may say the poem made them feel proud or thrilled.
2. **(a)** She describes a park and a hostile, dark atmosphere. **(b)** *alone, bullying* **(c)** "Bullying" suggests that female athletes have had to overcome obstacles and prejudice to enter the sports arena.
3. **(a)** Possible responses: a goddess, the spirit of feminism or athleticism, a personification of determination, a groundbreaking athlete **(b)** It draws the reader in, creating a mysterious and intriguing atmosphere.
4. **(a)** She mentions a runner, a sprinter, a hurdler, and a gymnast. **(b)** Support for this interpretation is in lines 7–8; the image of "her singing sign/her signed song."
5. She gives them a confidence-building example.
6. Possible responses: Athletes may be motivated by their own desire to succeed or to surpass others; the support of their loved ones; the cheers of the crowd; the sheer fun of the sport; their competitive instincts.
7. Students may cite current examples of people in athletics, military service, or ordinary life who have inspired others by succeeding.

ASSESS

❽ About the Selection

A man carefully and tenderly carries his small son on his shoulders through the rain. The speaker comments that all people should take this much care with one another.

❾ Literary Analysis

Theme in Poetry

- Ask students the Literary Analysis question on p. 232: Why does the poet point out that the child is not marked "fragile"?
  Answer: The father knows how fragile the child is without having to be told.
- Ask students what theme the image of the father hearing the child's dream suggests.
  Possible answers: The bond between a father and son is very strong.

Answers for p. 232

Review and Assess

1. Possible answers: Students may cite the father hearing the son's dream; the possibility that if we don't treat each other with care, the rain will never stop falling.
2. **(a)** They are crossing a street in the rain. **(b)** The poet wanted to contrast the harshness of the weather and the risks of the street with the beauty of the father's protective love.
3. **(a)** He doesn't want to jostle or wake his child. **(b)** The son may represent all vulnerable people.
4. **(a)** The poet suggests that if people don't care for one another, the world will be a harsh place. **(b)** The warning suggests an unsafe and difficult world for all people, possibly a world where people's lives are endangered.
5. **(a)** People must care for one another as the father cares for his child. **(b)** Students may disagree. People tend to ignore strangers altogether, and they often fail in kindness toward those they know.

❽ Shoulders

Naomi Shihab Nye

A man crosses the street in rain,
stepping gently, looking two times north and south,
because his son is asleep on his shoulder.

No car must splash him.
No car drive too near to his shadow.

❾ This man carries the world's most sensitive cargo
but he's not marked.
Nowhere does his jacket say FRAGILE,
HANDLE WITH CARE.

His ear fills up with breathing.
He hears the hum of the boy's dream
deep inside him.

We're not going to be able
to live in the world
if we're not willing to do what he's doing
with one another.

The road will only be wide.
The rain will never stop falling.

Literary Analysis
Theme in Poetry Why does the poet point out that the child is not marked "fragile"?

Naomi Shihab Nye

(b. 1952)

Naomi Shihab Nye spent her teenage years in Jerusalem and has since worked as a visiting writer at several colleges and universities, including the University of Texas. Her books of poems have received such awards as the Pushcart Prize. In addition, her work has received recognition from the American Library Association. Nye says, "For me poetry has always been a way of paying attention to the world. . . ."

Review and Assess

Thinking About the Selection

1. **Respond:** Which images in the poem "spoke" to you? Why?
2. (a) **Recall:** Where are the father and child as the poem begins? (b) **Interpret:** Why might the poet have chosen this setting?
3. (a) **Recall:** Why is the father in the poem "stepping gently"? (b) **Speculate:** What does the son represent in the poem?
4. (a) **Interpret:** What warning does the poet give to the world in lines 17–18? (b) **Draw Conclusions:** What dangers does this warning seem to suggest?
5. (a) **Infer:** What does the speaker of the poem say that people must do for one another? (b) **Apply:** Do you think most people treat each other the way this man treats his son? Explain.

ASSESSMENT PRACTICE: Reading Comprehension

Supporting Details (For more practice, see Test Preparation Workbook, p. 14.)

Use the following sample to teach students how to recognize which details are relevant to and support a main idea.

The title "Spearthrower" does not refer to an athlete, but rather to a poet who sends her "signed song" of praise into the "bullying dark" of athletic events dominated by men. In associating the poet with the athlete in a contemporary poem, Morrison follows a tradition from ancient Greece.

To what or whom does the title "Spearthrower" refer?

A a female athlete
B a Greek athlete
C an ancient Greek poet
D a contemporary poet

Although all four answers include details mentioned in the text, the passage clearly states that the title refers to a contemporary poet. Choice *D* is correct.

Review and Assess

Literary Analysis

Theme in Poetry

1. (a) What does "Slam, Dunk, & Hook" say about the role of basketball in the street life of the neighborhood kids? (b) Which details of the poem suggest that **theme**?
2. How does the "spearthrower" (that is, the poet who sings of women athletes) enable the runner to run and the discus to fly?
3. Use the chart below to analyze the insights in "Shoulders."
   (a) What message does the speaker convey about the role of a parent in a child's life? (b) What message is implied about the responsibility of all human beings?

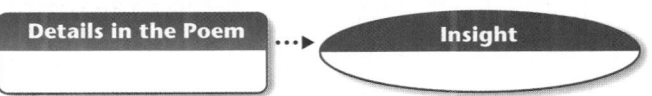

Details in the Poem	Insight

4. What idea about life is Nye expressing when she talks about the road always being wide and the rain always falling?

Comparing Literary Works

5. Using the chart below, compare the action, images, and themes of the three poems. (a) Which poem best conveys physical action? Explain. (b) Which poem best conveys emotional challenges? Explain.

Poem	Summary of Action	Images Created	Theme

Reading Strategy

Forming Mental Images

6. Which **image** in "Slam, Dunk, & Hook" creates the most vivid picture in your mind?
7. Describe what you see in the final image of "Shoulders."

Extend Understanding

8. **Sports Connection:** "The Spearthrower" shows women overcoming great obstacles in sports. Name a famous female athlete, and explain the impact she has had on sports and other athletes.

Quick Review

A **theme** is a central message or insight into life revealed through a literary work.

To **form mental images** of a poem, turn the poet's words into pictures in your mind.

Take It to the Net

www.phschool.com

Take the interactive self-test online to check your understanding of the selections.

ENRICHMENT: Further Reading

Other Works by the Authors

Works by Yusef Komunyakaa
Magic City

Works by Lillian Morrison
The Sidewalk Racer (poems)

Works by Naomi Shihab Nye
Hugging the Jukebox

Take It to the Net

Visit www.phschool.com for more information on these authors.

Answers for p. 233

Review and Assess

1. **(a)** The poem suggests that basketball gives players an outlet for their energies, a sense of accomplishment, and a source of pride. **(b)** Details include the reference to defeating "bad angels," the many images of the beauty of the game, and the conclusion "we knew we were beautiful and dangerous."
2. The spearthrower's spear of light—her poem—gives the athletes courage, hope, and determination.
3. **(a)** The speaker suggests that a parent's role is to love and protect a child. **(b)** People should care for one another.
4. She suggests that the world is a harsh place in which to live without love and protectiveness.
5. "Slam, Dunk, & Hook": Action: youths play basketball in their neighborhood. Images: players poised in midair, glistening with sweat and effort. Theme: Sports can be a powerful positive force in a person's life. "Spearthrower": Action: A female figure hurls a "javelin of light" into the darkness, encouraging female athletes. Images: javelin of light, bullying darkness, vaulter soaring. Theme: Athletes thrive on encouragement and determination. "Shoulders": Action: A father carefully carries his sleeping child across a rainy street. Images: wide street, rain falling, father stepping carefully. Theme: We must all care for one another.
6. Possible response: "Trouble slapping a blackjack against an open palm" is a vivid image of menace.
7. Students may see a wide, rainy road stretching to the horizon, or they may see a difficult future for the human race.
8. Students are likely to cite recent Olympic stars in gymnastics, soccer, skating, and track.

EXTEND

Answers for p. 234

1 Vocabulary Development

Word Analysis

1. to bounce the ball rapidly and repeatedly; impression: calmness, poise
2. to take the ball close to the basket to shoot; impression: aggressiveness
3. a drive down the court at a high speed; impression: urgency
4. sprints around a track or playing area; impression: speediness

Spelling Strategy

1. correct
2. correct
3. received
4. seize

Fluency: Words in Context

1. feint
2. jibed
3. metaphysical
4. surge

2 Grammar

1. began, have begun
2. hung, have hung
3. sprang, have sprung
4. fell, have fallen
5. drove, have driven
6. sang, have sung
7. stood, have stood
8. swung, have swung
9. led, have led
10. won, have won

Writing Application

Possible answers:

1. Try to spin the ball off the backboard.
2. The ball spun off my fingers and went out of bounds.
3. The guard had spun away from his defender and was racing downcourt.

Integrate Language Skills

1 Vocabulary Development Lesson

Specialized Vocabulary: Jargon

Some poems use **jargon,** specialized vocabulary used in a particular occupation, sport, or other well-defined activity. For example, the term *feint* in "Slam, Dunk, & Hook" refers to a pretended move meant to take an opponent off guard. For each item, write the meaning of the jargon and the impression each word or phrase suggests.

1. dribble
2. drive to the inside
3. fast breaks
4. quick laps

Spelling Strategy

Remember the following rule: Place *i* before *e* except after *c* or when sounded like *a* as in *neighbor* and *weigh.* For each word, write "Correct" if the word is spelled correctly. If the spelling is incorrect, write the correct spelling.

1. yield
2. height
3. recieved
4. sieze

Fluency: Words in Context

Rewrite the following paragraph, filling in the blanks with words from the vocabulary list on page 227.

Emotions were high as the game entered the last quarter. The score was tied. The winning team would make it to the playoffs. We saw the center ___?___ left, then pass the ball to the right, confusing the player guarding her. The player who caught the ball then ___?___, looking for a teammate on either side of her who was closer to the basket. The moment was almost ___?___ as she found an opening among the group of girls that allowed her to ___?___ past the guard and make her shot. The home team was going to the playoffs, and the visiting team was left feeling stunned.

2 Grammar Lesson

Irregular Verbs

Unlike regular verbs, the past tense and past participle of **irregular verbs** are not formed by adding *-ed* to the present form. Instead, the past tense and past participle are formed in various ways. Some change vowels or consonants within the word. Others change both vowels and consonants. Some verbs use the same form for the present, past, and past participle. Look at the various forms of the verbs *run* and *catch.*

Present: run; catch

Past: ran; caught

Past Participle: (have) run; (have) caught

Practice

Test your knowledge of irregular verbs by identifying the past and past participle of each present-tense verb below. Use a dictionary if you are not sure about a particular form.

1. began
2. hang
3. spring
4. fall
5. drive
6. sing
7. stand
8. swing
9. lead
10. won

Writing Application Write three sentences using the present, past, and past participle of *spin.*

WG *Prentice Hall Writing and Grammar Connection: Chapter 23, Section 1*

TEACHING RESOURCES

The following resources can be used to enrich or extend the instructions for pp. 234–235.

Vocabulary

Selection Support, Build Vocabulary, p. 53

Grammar

Selection Support: Build Grammar Skills, p. 54

Writing and Grammar, Gold Level, p. 526 ■

Daily Language Practice Transparencies

Writing

Writing and Grammar, Gold Level, p. 134 ■

Writing and Grammar iText CD-ROM

■ **BLOCK SCHEDULING:** Resources marked with this symbol provide varied instruction during 90-minute blocks.

❸ Writing Lesson

Editorial

Write an **editorial**—a brief piece of writing that presents one side of an issue—related to one of the selections. For example, using information you gathered from "Slam, Dunk, & Hook," you could write an editorial about the need for more funding for neighborhood sports because of the effect sports have on self-esteem.

Prewriting To persuade your readers, try to anticipate questions from those who might disagree with you. Imagine how opponents might question your opinions, and jot down questions and opposing viewpoints.

Model: Anticipating Readers' Questions

Topic: Our neighborhood needs more money for sports programs.
Questions: How much money will it cost our city?
Will funding come out of taxpayer money?

Generating questions that readers might have helps you address all of the important aspects of an issue.

Drafting Write your editorial by stating the issue clearly and expressing your opinion reasonably. Address the questions you anticipated.

Revising Show your editorial to several people. Try to find at least one reader who disagrees with you. Ask that person whether your opinion sounds fair and if you have answered all objections effectively. If you hear a point you should have raised, consider adding it to your editorial.

WG *Prentice Hall Writing and Grammar Connection: Chapter 7, Section 2*

❹ Extension Activities

Listening and Speaking A good sportscast captures the thrills of the game. Choose one of the track-and-field events in "The Spearthrower." Create a **sportscast** describing the contest from start to finish. Use these tips to guide your preparation:

- Give a play-by-play of the game.
- Focus attention on exciting or disappointing moments.
- Use vivid and lively language.

When you have written your sportscast, rehearse it and then present it to your class.

Research and Technology In a group, do a **research report** on some aspect of women's athletic competitions—for example, a biography of one outstanding athlete or an explanation of an exciting current topic. Use library resources, including the Internet and sports magazines, to help you with your research. Include photographs, recordings, and videotapes, if possible. **[Group Activity]**

Take It to the Net www.phschool.com
Go online for an additional research activity using the Internet.

ASSESSMENT RESOURCES

The following resources can be used to assess students' knowledge and skills.

Selection Assessment

- **Formal Assessment,** pp. 44–46
- **Open Book Test,** pp. 40–42
- **Got It! Assessment Videotapes,** Tape 1
- **Test Bank Software**

Take It to the Net
Visit www.phschool.com for self-tests and additional questions on the selections.

Writing Rubric

- **Performance Assess. and Portfolio Mgmt.,** p. 10

PRENTICE HALL ASSESSMENT SYSTEM

- **Workbook**
- **Transparencies**
- **Skill Book**
- **CD-ROM**

Lesson Support for p. 235

❸ Writing Lesson

- Go over the assignment with the whole class before students begin writing. Encourage them to look at the sports pages, particularly on Sundays, for models.
- If students have trouble finding topics, you might suggest the following: students can take the positions given or argue the opposite view.

  Baseball's designated-hitter position should be eliminated.

  Prize money in Grand Slam tennis tournaments should be equal for men and women.

  Pro athletes make too much money.
- Remind students to state their opinions clearly and back up their opinions with facts and details.
- Use the Persuasive Composition rubric in **Performance Assessment and Portfolio Management,** p.10, to evaluate students' work.

❹ Extension Activity

Listening and Speaking

- You may wish to allow students to write about any sport they like, since not all students will be familiar with track events.
- Encourage students to listen to radio broadcasts of sports events, so that they will have an idea of what to include.

CUSTOMIZE INSTRUCTION for Universal Access

To address different learning styles, use the following activities suggested in the **Extension Activities** booklet, p. 14.

- For Visual/Spatial Learners, use Activity 4.
- For Verbal/Linguistic and Interpersonal Learners, use Activity 5.
- For Bodily/Kinesthetic and Logical/ Mathematical Learners, use Activity 6.

Lesson Objectives

1. To write a business letter
2. To use writing strategies to generate ideas, plan, organize, evaluate, and revise the narrative

Prewriting

- Encourage students to complete a chart like the one on p. 236. Remind them that personal strengths do not have to be business strengths; instead, they are positive personality traits and skills. Allow students to work as partners to help each other complete the "Dream Jobs" section of their charts.
- Help students identify key words they can use to conduct an Internet search. When students find a professional contact in online or print resources, have them picture themselves sitting in the person's office. What questions would they ask?
- Students may have a variety of purposes for writing. Some may want the recipient to send information about a type of job; others may want to make an appointment to interview the recipient about the job.
- Have students find reference materials about careers that interest them. Knowing more about the career ahead of time will help students include pertinent information in their letters.

Writing WORKSHOP

Workplace Writing: Business Letter

The form of writing commonly used by those in the workplace is a **business letter.** Business letters may take the form of job offer letters, requests for information, or letters of introduction. In this workshop, you will write a business letter to learn more about a profession.

Assignment Criteria. Your business letter should have the following characteristics:

- a heading, inside address, greeting, body, closing, and signature
- formal, polite language that outlines a clear purpose and provides relevant background information
- standard formatting with consistent spacing and indentation

To preview the criteria on which your business letter may be assessed, see the Rubric on page 239.

Prewriting

Choose a topic. To write a business letter, **list and itemize** to identify some of your strengths. In a chart like the one shown, match your strengths with "dream jobs" that require those abilities. Choose a profession from the list that you would like to learn more about. Use this career as the subject of your business letter.

Choose a Topic

Personal Strength	Dream Jobs Requiring This Strength
artistic	painter, sculptor
avid reader	teacher, writer, journalist
fast runner	professional running back
good joke teller	comedian

Make connections. Use the Internet, the classified section in the newspaper, or your local phone book to find the address, name, and title of the person to whom you will send your letter. Then, jot down any questions you might like to ask someone in that profession.

Research. Gather some background information about the dream job you have chosen. Use your school or local library or the Internet to research salary level, employment opportunities, and other pertinent information. Jot this down for use in the draft of your business letter.

Identify your purpose. Before you write your business letter, consider why you are writing. Review your notes and come up with a sentence that expresses this information clearly. You may want to incorporate this information later into the body of your draft.

Example: I have taken guitar lessons for years, and I want to learn about the job of a studio musician.

TEACHING RESOURCES

The following resources can be used to enrich or extend the instruction for pp. 236–239.

- **Writing and Grammar,** Gold Level, Chapter 15, pp. 324–333
- **Performance Assessment and Portfolio Management,** p. 9
- **Writing Models and Graphic Organizers on Transparencies,** pp. 53–56
- **Writing and Grammar iText CD-ROM**
  Students can use the following tools as they complete their business letters:
  - Business Letter Shell
  - Topic Bin
  - Transition Words

Student Model

Before you begin drafting your business letter, read this model from Robin Weber, a student in St. Petersburg, Florida.

Intelligent Productions
220 Any Street, Suite 112
Any Town, NY 10000
December 13, 2001

> In his letter, Robin assumes the voice of a business that he created for this assignment.

G-2000 Computers
310 Infinite Loop
Any City, CA 94000

Dear Sirs:

My business is currently in the market for several high-end, reliable server computers. I would like to obtain more information about your line of server products.

> The author states his purpose clearly and concisely.

The computers we use are operating twenty-four hours a day, seven days a week, as servers hosting a high-traffic Internet Web site. Therefore, it would be unacceptable for my company to purchase computers that require periods of inactivity in order to remain in working condition. We are also concerned about technical support issues and cost.

> In this paragraph, the author provides important background information.

I would appreciate if you could send me the exact specifications on catalog items number 1444, as well as number 2314. There is no information on warranties in your product descriptions. Any information in this regard would be very helpful in making my purchasing decision. Also, would it be possible to obtain a high volume discount? How would such an order affect delivery time?

> The author uses modified block format.

> The letter includes specific questions that Robin would like answered.

Please send me any information you have on these issues. I look forward to hearing from you.

> The conclusion summarizes the request using polite language.

Sincerely,

Robin Weber

Robin Weber
Intelligent Productions

Student Model

- Explain that the Student Model is a sample, and that business letters may be longer.
- Have students identify the sentence in the first paragraph that states the writer's purpose.
- Point out that the writer provides background information that will help the reader understand why the letter has been written.
- Ask students to identify the paragraph in which the writer specifies her needs.
  Answer: The third paragraph details the writer's needs.
- Ask students to point out a sentence in the last paragraph that is similar to a sentence in the first paragraph. Explain that this echoing of information helps the writer summarize what the letter is about.
- For an additional model, display the Business Letter transparencies in **Writing Models and Graphic Organizers on Transparencies,** pp. 53–56.

Real-World Connection

Explain to students that writing a business letter may seem like a skill they will not need for a long time; in reality, they may need the skill sooner than they think. Point out that job applications often ask for a written statement, students may be called upon to take minutes for a meeting, or they may be asked to write to a local official on behalf of a club or other organization.

CUSTOMIZE INSTRUCTION FOR UNIVERSAL ACCESS

For Less Proficient Writers	For English Learners	For Advanced Writers
If students have difficulty identifying personal strengths, encourage them to brainstorm with friends for a list of good qualities that others see in them.	Encourage students to draw upon their experiences in their home cultures to write their list of possible dream jobs. They may think of some jobs that are less common in the United States, but that are highly valued in the global community.	As part of their research on jobs, have students prepare a biographical profile of an individual who has a job they would like to have someday. Information for the profile can be gathered from the Internet, magazines, books, and personal interviews.

Drafting

- Point out to students the two traditional formats for writing a business letter: block format and modified block format. Ask students to choose which of these formats they will use.
- As students write their drafts, have them check off each element in the Business Letter Standards chart as they write it. This will help them make certain they have included all essential parts of the form.

Revising

- Read the three steps under the Revising section aloud to the class.
- Point out the revisions made on the example on p. 238.
- Direct students to follow the three Revising steps as they revise their drafts.
- Have each student imagine sitting in the office of the recipient, and then read the draft letter aloud. It should sound both conversational and professional.

Drafting

Selecting a format. Select a standard format that uses traditional font and spacing. Acceptable formats for business letters include the following:

- **Block format**—each part of the letter begins at the left margin
- **Modified block format**—the heading, closing, and signature are indented to the center of the page

Adhere to standards. As you draft your business letter, be certain you have included all of the essential parts of the form. Use the checklist at right to verify that your business letter has all of the proper elements. Add any elements that are missing from your checklist.

Consider your audience. Remember that you are addressing a busy professional. Include only information that is essential; do not provide flowery elaboration that will detract from your main purpose. Make sure to provide information clearly and use formal vocabulary, style, and tone of address.

Call for action. As you draft, include information that tells your reader what you want him or her to do. For example, you may want to set up an interview, arrange a phone call, or you may want the recipient to provide you with some information. Make sure the outcome you want is clearly stated.

Business Letter Standards

- ☐ **Heading**—indicates the writer's address and affiliation (if any) and the date
- ☐ **Inside Address**—indicates where letter will be sent
- ☐ **Greeting**—always punctuated by a colon
- ☐ **Body**—states the writer's purpose
- ☐ **Closing**—an appropriate farewell
- ☐ **Signature**—a signed name

Revising

Revise to support your purpose. Your business letter must address the reasons for your writing. Verify that this reason is clearly stated early in the body of your business letter. To evaluate your letter, look over your draft to find places where you can offer detail to support your purpose.

1. Review your draft and underline your purpose for writing.
2. Highlight any other details in your business letter that reinforce your purpose for writing.
3. Cross out details that are not essential for the reader to know.

Model: Supporting Your Purpose

I would like to obtain more information about your line of server products. The computers we use are operating twenty-four hours a day, seven days a week, as servers hosting a high-traffic Internet Web site. ~~Intelligent Productions was the fastest growing privately owned company in the year 2000.~~

This information is not essential to the writer's purpose.

USING TECHNOLOGY IN WRITING

Point out that some software programs offer preformatted business letters. Have students explore this option on the software they use to prepare their business letters. If the software does provide this feature, have students check the format against the Business Letter Standards on p. 238 to make sure the software format includes all necessary elements.

Students can also use the organizing tools and revision checkers on the **Writing and Grammar iText CD-ROM.**

Revise to make language formal. Look for words in your business letter that can be replaced to create a more formal effect. In the following example, *excels* creates a more formal effect than *is good.*

Example: He *is good* at playing chess.
He *excels* at playing chess.

Compare the model and the nonmodel. Why is the model more effective than the nonmodel?

Nonmodel	Model
I want a good, reliable server. Can you get me some information on your products?	My business is currently in the market for several high-end, reliable server computers. I would like to obtain more information about your line of server products.

Publishing and Presenting

Consider sharing your writing with a wider audience in one of the following ways.

Send your letter. If your letter is written to an existing business, mail it. When you get a response, share it with classmates.

Apply your knowledge to another situation: write a letter of complaint. Pair up with a partner. Write a letter of complaint to your partner's fictional company, using formal language and following the standard format for a business letter. Ask your partner to draft a polite business letter addressing your complaint. Afterward, discuss whether you were each satisfied with the letter you received.

WG *Prentice Hall Writing and Grammar Connection: Chapter 15*

Read to Write
To learn more about writing business documents, see **Reading Informational Materials**, p. 196.

Rubric for Self-Assessment

Evaluate your business letter using the following criteria and rating scale:

Criteria	Rating Scale Not very				Very
How well does the letter incorporate all the elements of a business letter?	1	2	3	4	5
How clear and formal is the language of the letter?	1	2	3	4	5
How well does the letter follow appropriate formatting?	1	2	3	4	5
How well does the letter include appropriate background information?	1	2	3	4	5
How clearly is the purpose stated?	1	2	3	4	5

Publishing and Presenting

- Before students present their business letters to the class, encourage them to practice reading them aloud. Have students make any notes that might help them convey a friendly yet professional tone.
- Suggest that the other students imagine that they are the recipients of the letter as the student reads it. Lead a discussion on how well the class thinks the letter accomplished the writer's purpose. Focus on providing the writer with constructive criticism, the kind of commentary and feedback that helps a writer improve a draft.

Assessment

- Review with students the assessment criteria.
- Have students use the rubric to score their business letters for each of the criteria listed. Make sure students support their scores with details from their letters.
- Another rubric for a business letter can be found on p. 9 in **Performance Assessment and Portfolio Management.**

TEST-TAKING TIP

When students are taking a test that requires them to evaluate the components of a business letter, they may have difficulty remembering all six elements (heading, inside address, greeting, body, closing, and signature). Encourage students to combine their past experiences in writing business letters with common sense and then read the letter through to see if it seems as if anything is missing.

Lesson Objectives

1. To conduct an interview
2. To choose a topic and interview a candidate of interest
3. To use a question staircase in conducting an interview

Prepare for the Interview

- Help students identify an interview topic or candidate that interests them by brainstorming for a list of possibilities with the class.
- Have students identify a purpose for their interviews (beyond the fact that it is a class assignment).
- Guide students to appropriate sources of research for their interviews. They may need to locate medical journals, research a company, or make a list of what they know already and what they would like to find out from the interview.
- Help students write open-ended questions, questions that must be answered with more than one word. Help students come up with good question starters, such as "What was it like when . . ." or "What inspired you to . . ."

Conduct the Interview

- Before students conduct their interviews, point out the Question Staircase on p. 240.
- Explain that students can use this strategy spontaneously during an interview when they hear something they want to question further.

Listening and Speaking WORKSHOP

Conducting Interviews

You do not need to be a talk-show host to produce a good interview. All you need is curiosity about a subject, a willingness to put in some preparation time, and a chance to connect with someone who can provide the detailed information you need.

Prepare for the Interview

Whether you are using an interview to gather data for a research paper or to find a new job, you want to start off feeling prepared. To plan:

Identify your purpose. Determine what kind of information you need to obtain from an interview. Your purpose might be to find a few personal stories for a history paper or facts for a school newspaper article.

Do research. Perform enough preliminary research so that you can ask informed questions. For a job interview, find out more about the employer. Before interviewing an expert on the psychology of twins, look at studies on twin behavior.

Draw up questions. The best questions inspire answers in which people talk about themselves and their experiences. Everyone has a conversation "combination lock." Your challenge is to find the right combination of insightful, provocative questions that lets you open that lock.

Conduct the Interview

Once your preparation is complete, consider these tips for conducting a productive interview:

Build a question staircase. Think of the answers in your interview as the steps in a staircase you are building upward. Each *question* should build on the *answer* you just received, as well as the previous question. See the chart at right for guidance.

Building a Question Staircase

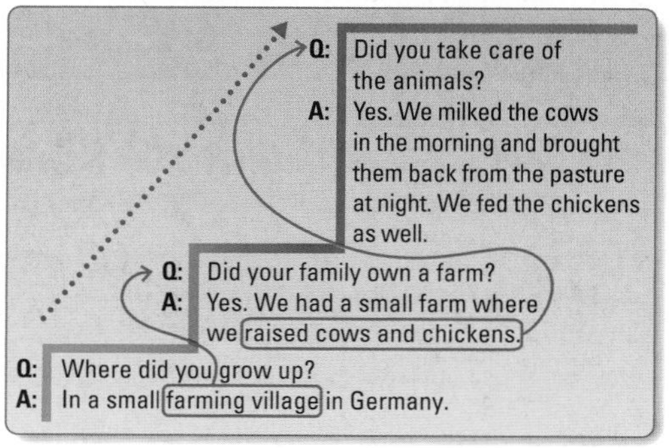

Q: Did you take care of the animals?
A: Yes. We milked the cows in the morning and brought them back from the pasture at night. We fed the chickens as well.
Q: Did your family own a farm?
A: Yes. We had a small farm where we raised cows and chickens.
Q: Where did you grow up?
A: In a small farming village in Germany.

Stick to your subject. Maintain focus by keeping your original purpose in mind. If the other person seems confused, you may have gone off-topic or asked an overly complicated question. Simplify your question, make sure it is relevant, and give examples to get back on track.

Activity: Interview and Evaluation Practice your skills by interviewing a community member with a particular expertise. Use the graphic to help you evaluate the quality of information you receive. After the interview, determine what you did well and areas you could improve.

CUSTOMIZE INSTRUCTION FOR UNIVERSAL ACCESS	
For Special Needs Students	**For English Learners**
Encourage students to interview someone they already know, such as a teacher, the principal, or a friend or family member. Help the students structure questions that will reveal more in-depth information about topics with which students are already familiar.	Encourage students to interview someone who speaks the language with which each student is most comfortable. Point out that although the interview may be conducted in another language, reports to the class must be presented in English.

Assessment WORKSHOP

Facts and Details

The reading sections of some tests require you to read a passage and answer multiple-choice questions about supporting ideas in a passage. The supporting ideas in a text are the facts and details that provide information about a main idea. Use the following strategies to help you answer test questions about supporting ideas:

- Think of a statement that summarizes the main idea of the passage.
- Look for facts or details that relate to the main idea.
- Check to see whether the test question is answered by the main idea or a supporting detail.
- Eliminate responses that supply details unrelated to the question.

Test-Taking Strategies

- Look at the test question before reading the passage to give yourself the appropriate focus.
- Even if you think you know the correct answer, read all the answer choices before choosing one.

Sample Test Item

Directions: Read the following passage, and then answer the question that follows.

As Yolanda read the application for summer camp counselor, she felt doubtful. She was interested in teaching art and sports, but the position required experience. Did she qualify? She made a list of what she had done: two terms of a child-development lab last year, babysitting for four years, one year as an art and soccer teacher for day camp.

1. Which of Yolanda's experiences is the closest match for the position?
   - **A** her experience as a babysitter
   - **B** the classes she took in child development
   - **C** her experience as an art and soccer teacher
   - **D** her certification in CPR

Answer and Explanation

The correct answer is *C,* which describes her art and sports experience. ***A*** and ***B*** are experiences that relate to the position, but neither is a close match. While Yolanda may be certified in CPR, this detail is not directly stated in the passage; ***D*** is therefore incorrect.

Practice

Directions: Read the following passage, and then answer the question that follows.

Dr. Ellen Ochoa is a woman of many talents. She was born and raised in southern California, where her primary interests as a child included reading and playing flute. Graduating as the top-ranked math student in high school, she went on to earn an undergraduate degree in physics, as well as a master's and a doctorate in electrical engineering.

In 1993, she became the first Hispanic female astronaut to travel in space, where she and her team studied the sun's radiation levels. She even played the flute in space!

1. Dr. Ochoa's childhood interests included ___?___.
   - **A** reading
   - **B** electrical engineering
   - **C** band
   - **D** physics
2. What success is not included in the passage?
   - **A** earning a doctoral degree
   - **B** becoming an astronaut
   - **C** graduating from high school
   - **D** leading a university marching band

Lesson Objective

To recognize facts and details

Applying Reading Strategies

Encourage students to first identify the author's purpose when they begin to read a selection. Then, they can look for supporting details and facts that relate to the purpose.

Applying Test-Taking Strategies

- Have students read the Sample Test Item to identify the author's purpose. In the example on p. 241, the author's purpose could be to show how Yolanda determined whether she was qualified for a job she wanted.
- Next, point out which parts of the paragraph give the details that reveal Yolanda's qualifications.
- Finally, point out that students could immediately rule out item *D* because it did not appear in the passage at all.
- Have students use these same strategies to answer the Practice questions on their own.

Answers

1. The correct answer is *A.* Answers *B* and *D* are incorrect because they were adult, not childhood, interests. Answer *C* is an interest that was not listed in the passage.
2. The correct answer is *D,* the only item not mentioned in the passage.

TEACHING RESOURCES

The following resources can be used to enrich or extend the instruction for p. 241.

PRENTICE HALL ASSESSMENT SYSTEM

- **Workbook**
- **Skill Book**
- **Transparencies**
- **CD-ROM**

Unit Objectives

1. To read selections in different genres that develop the theme "Moments of Discovery"
2. To apply a variety of reading strategies, particularly strategies for constructing meaning, appropriate for reading these selections
3. To analyze literary elements
4. To use a variety of strategies to build vocabulary
5. To learn elements of grammar, usage, and style
6. To use recursive writing processes to write in a variety of forms
7. To develop listening and speaking skills
8. To express and support responses to various types of texts
9. To prepare, organize, and present literary interpretations

Meeting the Objectives

With each selection, you will find instructional materials through which students can meet these objectives. Further, you will find additional practice pages for reading strategies, literary analysis, vocabulary, and grammar in the **Selection Support: Skills Development Workbook** in your **Teaching Resources.**

Background

Art

Waiting Girl, by Yan Hsia

This painting focuses on an island of stillness and expectation amid the urgency and bustle of a city street. Ask students the following question about the painting:

How has the artist created a quiet moment in this painting?

Answer: By contrasting the clear, still figure of the waiting woman with the blurred motions of all other figures, the artist creates a moment of calm in the center of the painting.

UNIT 3 Moments of Discovery

Waiting Girl, 1978, Yan Hsia, Asian American Arts Center

UNIT FEATURES	
Connections	**Reading Informational Material**
Every unit contains a feature that connects literature to a related topic, such as art, science, or history. In this unit, the Literature and Media feature on p. 276 describes Amy Tan's experiences as her novel *The Joy Luck Club* becomes a major motion picture. Use the information and questions on the Connections pages to enrich students' understanding of the selections presented within the unit.	These selections will help students learn to analyze and evaluate informational texts, such as workplace documents, technical directions, and consumer materials. They will expose students to the organization and features unique to nonnarrative texts. In this unit, students will learn how to find and evaluate information on Web sites.

Exploring the Theme

Any insight can be a moment of discovery—children identifying an entire animal from a fragment of jawbone or a woman suddenly recognizing a common thread that she shares with her mother and grandmother. Whether big or small, these moments of discovery teach people something about themselves, others, and the world around them.

In Amy Tan's "Rules of the Game," Waverly Jong gains sudden insights in successive waves during her childhood in San Francisco's Chinatown. Insight into the intricacies of chess allows her to succeed beyond everyone's expectations. This same success, though, alienates her from the rest of her family and a more carefree past. In just a few pages of the story, you will experience moments of discovery of every variety—exhilarating, bittersweet, and full of pain.

▲ **Critical Viewing** What emotions would you imagine this woman is experiencing? **[Analyze]**

ASSESSMENT RESOURCES

- **Selection Support: Skills Development Workbook**
- **Formal Assessment**
- **Open Book Tests**
- **Performance Assessment and Portfolio Management**
- **Extension Activities**

Assessing Student Progress

Listed below are the tools that are available to measure the degree to which students meet the unit objectives.

Informal Assessment

The questions in the Review and Assess sections are a first-level response to the concepts and skills presented with the selections. Students' responses provide a brief, informal measure of their grasp of the material. These responses can indicate where further instruction and practice are needed. Follow up with the practice pages in **Selection Support: Skills Development Workbook.**

Formal Assessment

The **Formal Assessment** booklet contains the Selection Tests and Unit Tests.

- Selection Tests measure comprehension and skills acquisition for each selection or group of selections.
- Each Unit Test provides students with thirty multiple-choice questions and five essay questions designed to assess students' knowledge of the literature and skills taught in the unit.

The **Open Book Tests** ask students to demonstrate their ability to synthesize and communicate information from selections or groups of selections.

To assess student writing, you will find rubrics and scoring models in the **Performance Assessment and Portfolio Management** booklet. In this booklet, you will also find scoring rubrics for listening and speaking activities.

Alternative Assessment

The **Extension Activities** booklet contains writing activities, listening and speaking activities, and research and technology activities that are appropriate for students with different ability levels. You may also use these activities as an alternative measure of students' growth.

▶Critical Viewing

Answer: Students may suggest that the woman is experiencing feelings of impatience, concern, or expectation.

Why Read Literature?

The "Why Read Literature?" page in each unit presents a list of possible purposes for reading. Each purpose for reading is connected to one or more of the selections in the unit. Good readers set a purpose before reading to help them read actively and focus on meaningful details.

Unit 3 introduces three purposes for reading. "Read for the Love of Literature" offers real-world and fictional turning points for young people. "Read to Appreciate an Author's Style" focuses on two quite different poetic styles. "Read for Information" explores the communication strategies of a Web site.

How to Use This Page

- Tell students that as they read each selection in this unit, they should set a purpose for reading. This will help them read in an active and focused manner.
- Explain that students can increase their love of literature by making inferences about the two teenage characters in Cynthia Rylant's story "Checkouts"; they will discover the personal courage revealed in *In My Place.*
- Students will appreciate E.E. Cummings' unique capitalization and punctuation when they see how the author's style helps achieve the desired feelings in the reader. A more conventional, conversational poetic style is evident in William Stafford's "Fifteen."
- Reading to obtain information is another valuable purpose for reading. By visiting the Audubon Society Web site, students can learn more about nature and improve their Internet skills.

Why Read Literature?

Perhaps we always read to gain insight or to learn more about the world around us. You might be interested in specific information or you might just enjoy the way an author puts words together. Preview these three purposes you might set before reading works in this unit.

1 Read for the Love of Literature

The early 1960s was an excruciating time for southern African American students attending formerly all-white schools. These students were pioneers, venturing into new territory where many angry voices were raised against them. Discover the meaning of personal courage in Charlayne Hunter-Gault's classic account "**In My Place,**" page 296.

Many readers enjoy stories that reveal inner truths about themselves. If you have ever regretted missing an opportunity to meet someone—for a reason too ridiculous to remember—then you may sympathize with the main character in Cynthia Rylant's "**Checkouts**," page 282.

2 Read to Appreciate an Author's Style

When you read any of E. E. Cummings's poems, you will quickly realize that regular rules of grammar do not apply. Capital letters are reincarnated as lower case letters and parentheses appear magically out of nowhere. Although it may seem random, Cummings's style is closely tailored to the way the poem makes you feel. To gain an appreciation for Cummings's unusual choices, read "**maggie and milly and molly and may,**" page 328.

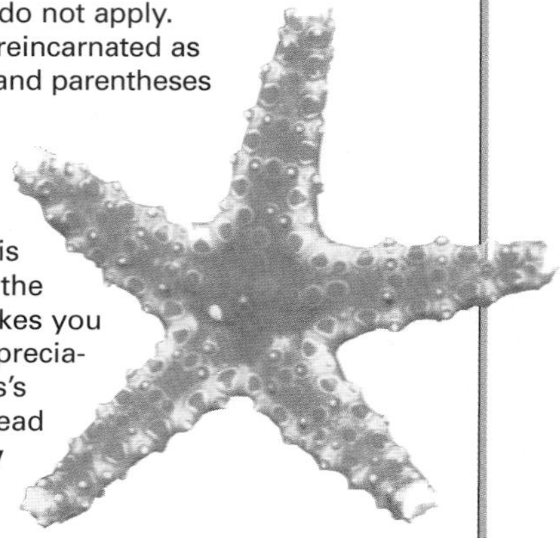

William Stafford's writing has a conversational style that can make you feel like you are listening to a friend tell a good story. See how Stafford creates this effect in "**Fifteen,**" page 286, a poem about a motorcycle and the intensity of youth.

3 Read for Information

The National Audubon Society was inspired by a group of Boston women who were horrified by the mistreatment of birds. In 1896, they banded together, boycotting products such as hats and clothing adorned with bird feathers. Their dedication, more than a century ago, has grown to include Audubon chapters nationwide. In addition to producing mailings and publications, the National Audubon Society has established a presence online to spread information and encourage action. To find out about navigating the Web to learn more about this group, see the **Audubon Society Web site,** page 257.

Take It to the Net

Visit the Web site for online instruction and activities related to each selection in this unit.
www.phschool.com

ENRICHMENT: Further Reading

Have students choose one or more of the works below to extend the unit theme "Moments of Discovery" or to read more by the unit authors.

I Know Why the Caged Bird Sings by Maya Angelou
In this first of five volumes of autobiography, Maya Angelou courageously shares the story of how she survived her early life experiences.

Sayonara by James Michener
This compelling story of love in the midst of war is a **Prentice Hall Literature Library** selection.

How to Read Literature

Use Strategies for Constructing Meaning

You have to go a step beyond the literal meaning of each word on a page to fully understand what you are reading. Next steps include putting words and ideas together, forming judgments about plot and character, reading between the lines, and relating material to past experiences. This process is called constructing meaning. Use these strategies to help you construct meaning.

1. Relate generalizations and evidence.

- To find a generalization, look for a statement that is broad and strongly worded.
- Check to see whether an author backs up his or her generalization with convincing evidence. If the evidence is weak, you might decide that you disagree with the generalization.

2. Identify causes and effects.

- Find at least one reason *(cause)* for each result *(effect)* in a story.
- Use cause and effect to understand the chain of events in fiction and nonfiction. The chart at right shows the start of a cause-and-effect analysis of "The Interlopers."

Cause and Effect

Question
Why does Ulrich hate Georg so deeply?

Cause
Georg repeatedly hunts without permission on land that legally belongs to Ulrich.

Effect
Ulrich is hunting down Georg so that he can settle this quarrel.

3. Make inferences about character.

You can use inferences—reasonable conclusions based on details in the text—to predict how characters will react to certain situations.

- Consider the details that the author includes about characters.
- Pay close attention to physical descriptions and to actions that might shed light on character traits. Look at this example:

> I assumed he had learned from the hotel manager that I was to be in Herat for five days, and it was obvious that he felt confident that within that period he could wear me down and persuade me to buy a rug.
>
> —from "**The Rug Merchant**"

From this quotation, you can infer that the author is smart enough to know that he will be the target of a sales strategy. You might also infer that he is suspicious of others' motives.

4. Relate to personal experience.

Think about events in the selection and how they might resemble events in your life. Then, use your experiences to understand a story's characters and predict what might happen next.

As you read the selections in this unit, use these strategies for constructing meaning to enrich your understanding of the literature.

How to Read Literature

The "How to Read Literature" page in each unit presents a set of strategies to help readers understand authors' words and ideas. Each reading strategy is taught in conjunction with one or more of the selections within the unit. Good readers develop a bank of strategies from which they can draw as needed.

Unit 3 introduces four strategies for constructing meaning. Students learn to relate generalizations and evidence, identify causes and effects, make inferences, and relate to personal experiences.

How to Use This Page

Introduce the strategies for constructing meaning, presenting each as a tool for developing understanding when reading the selections in this unit.

- As they read "Children in the Woods" (p. 248), students can evaluate the evidence that supports the writer's generalizations.
- As they read "The Rug Merchant" (p. 316), students will see that the author allows them to draw their own conclusions (make their own inferences) as the story unfolds.
- As they read "The Interlopers" (p. 304), students will notice causes and effects that connect each event in the story.
- When they read "Checkouts" (p. 282), students will identify with the characters because of similar personal experiences.

MODEL A READING STRATEGY: Relate Generalizations and Evidence

Help your students relate generalizations and evidence by modeling your thinking with this example from Barry Lopez's "Children in the Woods":

> The quickest door to open in the woods for a child is the one that leads to the smallest room, by knowing the name each thing is called.

Tell students:

> This generalization begins the final paragraph of Lopez's essay. Lopez has already provided several examples of his experiences walking in the woods with children. He has demonstrated several times how children can be caught by small details ("the smallest room"), so his final generalization is well supported.

Children in the Woods

Lesson Objectives and CA Correlations

1. **To analyze and respond to literary elements**
   - Literary Analysis: Reflective Essay **R 3.4**
   - Connecting Literary Elements: Sensory Language **R 3.7**
2. **To read, comprehend, analyze, and critique nonfiction**
   - Reading Strategy: Relating Generalizations and Evidence **R 2.8**
   - Reading Check questions
   - Review and Assess questions
   - Assessment Practice (ATE)
3. **To develop word analysis skills, fluency, and systematic vocabulary**
   - Vocabulary Development Lesson: Latin Prefixes: *extra-* **R 1.1**
4. **To understand and apply written and oral language conventions**
   - Spelling Strategy
   - Grammar Lesson: Prepositions **LC 1.3**
5. **To understand and apply appropriate writing and research strategies**
   - Writing Lesson: Field Guide **W 2.6**
   - Extension Activity: Rain Forest Presentation **W 1.3**
6. **To understand and apply listening and speaking strategies**
   - Extension Activity: Teaching Children **LS 1.3**

STEP-BY-STEP TEACHING GUIDE	PACING GUIDE
PRETEACH	
Motivate Students and Provide Background	
Use the Motivation activity (ATE p. 246)	5 min.
Read and discuss the Preview material and Background information (SE/ATE p. 246) [A]	5 min.
Introduce the Concepts	
Introduce the Literary Analysis and Reading Strategy (SE/ATE p. 247) [A]	15 min.
Pronounce the vocabulary words and read their definitions (SE p. 247)	5 min.
TEACH	
Monitor Comprehension	
Informally monitor comprehension by circulating while students read independently or in groups [A]	15 min.
Monitor students' comprehension with the Reading Check notes (SE/ATE pp. 249, 251)	as students read
Develop vocabulary with Vocabulary notes (SE pp. 247, 249–251)	as students read
Develop Understanding	
Develop students' understanding of reflective essays with Literary Analysis annotations (ATE pp. 249–251) [A]	10 min.
Develop students' ability to relate generalizations and evidence with Reading Strategy annotations (SE p. 249; ATE pp. 249–250)	10 min.
ASSESS	
Assess Mastery	
Assess students' mastery of the Reading Strategy and Literary Analysis by having them answer the Review and Assess questions (SE/ATE p. 253)	20 min.
Use one or more of the print and media Assessment Resources (ATE p. 255) [A]	up to 50 min.
EXTEND	
Apply Understanding	
Have students complete the Vocabulary Development Lesson and the Grammar Lesson (SE p. 254) [A]	20 min.
Apply students' knowledge of specific examples using the Writing Lesson (SE/ATE p. 255) [A]	45 min.
Apply students' understanding using one or more of the Extension Activities (SE p. 255)	20–90 min.

[A] **ACCELERATED INSTRUCTION:** Use the strategies and activities identified with an [A].

UNIVERSAL ACCESS
● = Below Level Students
▲ = On-Level Students
■ = Above Level Students

Time and Resource Manager

Reading Level: Challenging
Average Number of Instructional Days: 4

RESOURCES		
PRINT	**TRANSPARENCIES**	**TECHNOLOGY**
• **Beyond Literature,** Career Connection: Conservation Jobs, p. 15 ▲ ■		• **Interest Grabber Video,** Tape 2 ● ▲ ■
• **Selection Support Workbook:** ● ▲ ■ Literary Analysis, p. 60 Reading Strategy, p. 59 Build Vocabulary, p. 57	• **Literary Analysis and Reading Transparencies,** pp. 29 and 30 ● ▲ ■	
		• **Listening to Literature** ● ▲ ■ Audiocassettes, Side 9 Audio CDs, CD 7
• **Literatura en español** ● ▲ • **Literary Analysis for Enrichment** ■		
• **Formal Assessment:** Selection Test, pp. 51–53 ● ▲ ■ • **Open Book Test,** pp. 43–45 ● ▲ ■ • **Performance Assessment and Portfolio Management,** p. 18 ● ▲ ■ • PRENTICE HALL ASSESSMENT SYSTEM ● ▲ ■	• PRENTICE HALL ASSESSMENT SYSTEM ● ▲ ■ Skills Practice Answers and Explanations on Transparencies	• **Test Bank Software** ● ▲ ■ • **Got It! Assessment Videotapes,** Tape 2 ● ▲
• **Selection Support Workbook:** ● ▲ ■ Build Grammar Skills, p. 58 • **Writing and Grammar,** Gold Level ● ▲ ■ • **Extension Activities,** p. 15 ● ▲ ■	• **Daily Language Practice Transparencies** ● ▲	• **Writing and Grammar iText CD-ROM** ● ▲ ■ ***Take It to the Net*** www.phschool.com

BLOCK SCHEDULING: Use one 90-minute class period to preteach the selection and have students read it. Use a second 90-minute class period to assess students' mastery of skills and have them complete one of the Extension Activities.

PRETEACH

Step-by-Step Teaching Guide for pp. 246–247

Motivation

This essay chronicles Lopez's journey into the woods with children. Ask students if they enjoy taking nature hikes or walking in the woods. Have students identify reasons why they enjoy these activities. Encourage students to share their experiences of nature hikes and walks, making sure that they use as many sensory details as possible.

Interest Grabber Video

As an alternative, play "Appreciating the Natural World" on Tape 2 to engage student interest.

1 Background

Science

In addition to studying the particulars of animal and plant species, scientists today also focus on the larger picture. For example, why do certain species of birds and mammals live in an ecosystem with certain species of trees or why does an ecosystem contain many amphibians, or few, or none? Every single living thing is part of a much larger system, and the life of each creature or plant is connected in a multitude of unseen ways.

Prepare to Read

Children in the Woods

Take It to the Net

Visit www.phschool.com for interactive activities and instruction related to "Children in the Woods," including

- background
- graphic organizers
- literary elements
- reading strategies

Preview

Connecting to the Literature

Some of your ideas about how the world works may have come from observations and discoveries you made as a child. Mixing red and yellow paint to get orange, for example, might have shown you how colors are formed. In "Children in the Woods," Barry Lopez shares his thoughts on how to help children discover and understand their world.

1 Background

At one time, the emphasis in science was to describe the natural world in as much detail as possible. In the early nineteenth century, in fact, collecting and cataloging such objects as birds' eggs and orchids was a popular hobby. Today, although scientists need to know the names of living things, they focus more upon theories and explanations.

TEACHING RESOURCES

The following resources can be used to enrich or extend the instruction for pp. 246–247.

Motivation

Interest Grabber Video, Tape 2

Background

Beyond Literature, p. 15

Take It to the Net

Visit www.phschool.com for background and hotlinks for "Children in the Woods."

Literary Analysis

Literary Analysis and Reading Transparencies, Reflective Essay and Sensory Language, p. 30

Reading

Selection Support: Reading Strategy, p. 60; Build Vocabulary, p. 57

Literary Analysis and Reading Transparencies, Relating Generalizations and Evidence, p. 29

BLOCK SCHEDULING: Resources marked with this symbol provide varied instruction during 90-minute blocks.

❷ Literary Analysis

Reflective Essay

A **reflective essay** is a short nonfiction work that focuses on the writer's thoughts about a personal experience. Most reflective essays have a friendly tone and convey a sense of discovery. Consider the reflective nature of this statement from the selection.

> Whenever I walk with a child, I think how much I have seen disappear in my own life.

As you read, consider Lopez's "discoveries."

Connecting Literary Elements

In a reflective essay, sensory language can help readers share in the experience that the writer explores. **Sensory language** is writing or speech that appeals to one or more of the senses. Sensory language often helps you "see" what the writer is describing, but some words or phrases can also suggest sounds, textures, smells, and tastes.

❸ Reading Strategy

Relating Generalizations and Evidence

The key point of Lopez's reflective essay is a **generalization**—a broad principle that is supported by particulars, or **evidence**. Use these tips to relate generalizations and evidence:

- Look for broad personal opinions in the essay that might direct you toward generalizations. There may be small generalizations throughout, but somewhere there should be a large generalization that states the overall "point" of the essay.
- Find specific details to back up those generalizations.

Record your evidence and generalization on a chart like this one.

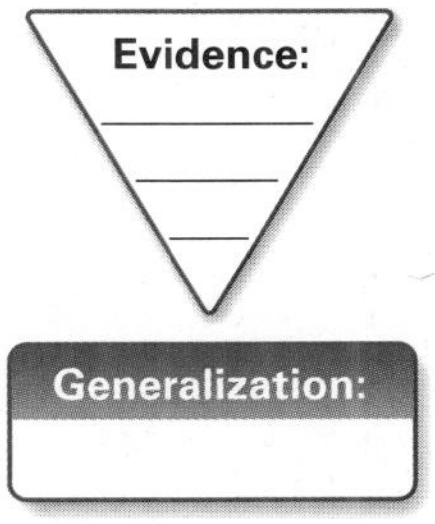

Vocabulary Development

charged (chärjd) *adj.* intense (p. 249)

acutely (ə kyo͞ot´ lē) *adv.* sharply (p. 249)

elucidate (ə lo͞o´ sə dāt´) *v.* explain (p. 249)

extrapolation (ek strap´ ə lā´ shən) *n.* conclusions drawn by speculation on the basis of facts (p. 250)

detritus (dē trīt´ əs) *n.* debris (p. 250)

effervesce (ef´ ər ves´) *v.* to be lively (p. 250)

myriad (mir´ ē əd) *adj.* countless; innumerable (p. 250)

insidious (in sid´ ē əs) *adj.* treacherous in a sly, tricky way (p. 250)

ineffable (in ef´ ə bəl) *adj.* too overwhelming to be expressed in words (p. 251)

CUSTOMIZE INSTRUCTION FOR UNIVERSAL ACCESS

For Less Proficient Readers	For English Learners	For Advanced Readers
Model for students how to use sensory language in description. For example, read the following slowly and ask students to make a list of sensory language words or phrases they hear: *Our dog Major is a brown ball of short, wiry hair. After a rain he smells musky and damp. He has a loud bark that sounds like a truck horn.*	Ask students to make lists of words that describe creatures or objects in the natural world in a sensory way. For example, write *cloud: puffy, pillowy, wispy* and *bird: screeching, twittering, chirping* on the board to illustrate sight and sound.	Encourage students to write a description of a woodland hike or other outdoor experience they have had recently. Have them describe the experience so that readers can see, hear, feel, and smell what the writer did. Have them compare their descriptions with those of Barry Lopez as they read the selection.

❷ Literary Analysis

Reflective Essay and Sensory Language

- Tell students that the selection "Children in the Woods" is a reflective essay that relates the writer's thoughts about his personal experience with children and nature.
- Read the instruction together as a class. Ask students what Lopez has learned from walking with a child in the woods.
- Use the instruction for Connecting Literary Elements to alert students to look for sensory language as they read the essay.

❸ Reading Strategy

Relating Generalizations and Evidence

- Remind students that a *generalization* is a broad statement that must be backed up by evidence or examples.
- Tell students that a series of examples that supports a generalization can create a structure for a personal essay.
- Instruct students to create their own charts to keep track of the evidence Lopez provides to support his basic generalization.

Vocabulary Development

- Pronounce each vocabulary word for students and read the definitions as a class. Have students identify any words with which they are already familiar.

E-Teach

Visit E-Teach at www.phschool.com for teachers' essays on how to teach, with questions and answers.

TEACH

Step-by-Step Teaching Guide for pp. 248–252

CUSTOMIZE INSTRUCTION
For Logical/Mathematical Learners

Have students make a timeline for the paragraph beginning "In the beginning, years ago . . ." that indicates how the author's relationship with his "students"—the children he takes for walks—has changed over the years. How many entries will they have on their timelines? What information will they include in each entry?

Answers: Students' timelines should have three entries: 1: the author says too much, naming all the plants and animals; 2: the author says less and less; 3: the author speaks little, only to answer a question or draw attention to something.

❶ About the Selection

In this personal essay, Barry Lopez asserts that the most important thing we can teach a child—and ourselves—is that everything in the natural world fits together, making an interrelated whole much larger than the sum of its parts. Lopez demonstrates that the best way to teach this concept to children is to take them walking in the woods. He believes one should refrain from lecturing or speaking too much, and set an example by expressing awe at the wonders of nature.

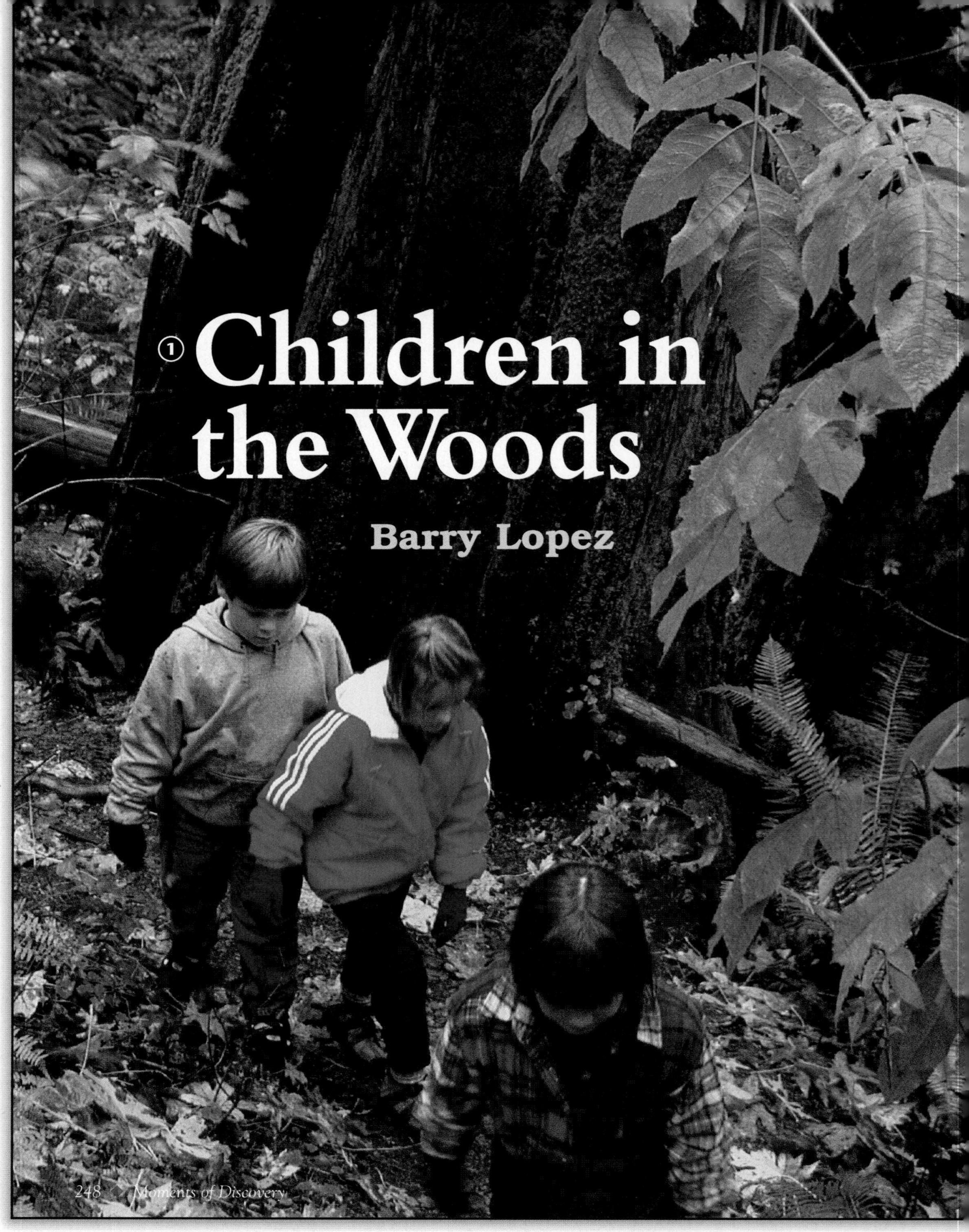

① Children in the Woods

Barry Lopez

TEACHING RESOURCES	
The following resources can be used to enrich or extend the instruction for pp. 248–252.	
Literary Analysis	**Reading**
Selection Support: Literary Analysis, p. 60	**Listening to Literature Audiocassettes,** Side 9 ■
	Listening to Literature Audio CDs, CD 7 ■

■ **BLOCK SCHEDULING:** Resources marked with this symbol provide varied instruction during 90-minute blocks.

When I was a child growing up in the San Fernando Valley in California, a trip into Los Angeles was special. The sensation of movement from a rural area into an urban one was sharp. On one of these charged occasions, walking down a sidewalk with my mother, I stopped suddenly, caught by a pattern of sunlight trapped in a spiraling imperfection in a windowpane. A stranger, an
2 elderly woman in a cloth coat and a dark hat, spoke out spontaneously, saying how remarkable it is that children notice these things.

I have never forgotten the texture of this incident. Whenever I recall it I am moved not so much by any sense of my young self but by a sense of responsibility toward children, knowing how acutely I was affected in that moment by that woman's words. The effect, for all I know, has lasted a lifetime.

Now, years later, I live in a rain forest in western Oregon, on the banks of a mountain river in relatively undisturbed country, surrounded by 150-foot-tall Douglas firs,[1] delicate deerhead orchids, and clearings
3 where wild berries grow. White-footed mice and mule deer, mink and coyote move through here. My wife and I do not have children, but children we know, or children whose parents we are close to, are often here. They always want to go into the woods. And I wonder what to tell them.

In the beginning, years ago, I think I said too much. I spoke with an encyclopedic knowledge of the names of plants or the names of birds passing through in season. Gradually I came to say less. After a while the only words I spoke, beyond answering a question or calling attention quickly to the slight difference between a sprig of red cedar and a sprig of incense cedar,[2] were to elucidate single objects.

I remember once finding a fragment of a raccoon's jaw in an alder thicket. I sat down alongside the two children with me and encouraged them to find out who this was—with only the three teeth still intact in a

1. **Douglas firs** tall evergreen trees of the pine family.
2. **sprig of red cedar . . . incense cedar** twigs from two types of trees of the pine family.

charged (chärjd) *adj.* tensely expectant; intense

acutely (ə kyo͞ot′ lē) *adv.* sharply

Reading Strategy
Relating Generalizations and Evidence What evidence supports the generalization that Lopez loves nature and is knowledgeable about plants and animals?

elucidate (ə lo͞o′ sə dāt′) *v.* explain

4 **Reading Check**
When he first started his walks in the woods with children, how does Lopez say he spoke to them?

2 Literary Analysis

Reflective Essay and Sensory Language

- Ask students to read the bracketed passage.
- Then, ask a volunteer to identify the specific memory Lopez has of the encounter with the woman.
  Answer: He had stopped suddenly to look at a pattern of sunlight. The woman said how remarkable it is that children notice things.
- Ask students how Lopez reflects on this memory as an adult—that is, how the incident caused him to think about children.
  Answer: Lopez has developed a sense of responsibility toward children and how they are affected by experiences they have when they are young.

3 Reading Strategy

Relating Generalizations and Evidence

- Read the bracketed passage aloud. Ask students what Lopez is describing.
  Answer: Lopez is describing the place where he lives; how the country looks; what kinds of animals and plants are found there; his knowledge of the names of plants and animals.

▶ **Monitor Progress** Ask students the Reading Strategy question on p. 249: What evidence supports the generalization that Lopez loves nature and is knowledgeable about plants and animals?
Answer: Lopez has chosen to live away from the city in "relatively undisturbed country," in a rain forest on the banks of a mountain river; he identifies some of the species of tree, plant, and animal in this location. He has learned many names of plants and animals during his life.

4 Reading Check

Answer: Lopez speaks too much, giving the names of everything seen in the woods.

CUSTOMIZE INSTRUCTION FOR UNIVERSAL ACCESS

For Special Needs Students	For Less Proficient Readers
To help students understand long and complex sentences, work with them through the first sentence in Paragraph 3. Encourage them to see that even though a sentence may be long, they can understand it by breaking it up into chunks separated by commas. Read each phrase and ask students what information it contains:"Now"—at this time; "years later"—long after the incident in the first paragraphs; "I live in a rain forest in western Oregon"—the location of the writer's home, and so on.	Work with students to decode the names of the plants and animals mentioned on this page. Some have uncommon or difficult letter/sound combinations, such as *orchid, coyote, and raccoon.* Review using the dictionary to find pronunciations of words, and encourage students to continue to look up words they may have difficulty decoding.

❺ Reading Strategy

Relating Generalizations and Evidence

- Remind students that a writer must support a large general statement with examples or evidence.
- Ask students to read the bracketed passage. Then, have volunteers state in their own words the generalization the author makes here.
  Possible responses: Learning the names of things is not as important as learning the relationships among things; learning names is easy; observing relationships takes a lifetime.
- Have students read the text on this spread to find examples that the author uses as evidence to support his generalization.
  Possible responses: The author shows the relationship between the raccoon and its surroundings, the relationship between humans and the places in which they live, and the relationship between those who lived thousands of years ago and those who live today.

❻ Literary Analysis

Reflective Essay and Sensory Language

- Remind students that they can recognize sensory language by noting whether the language helps them to see, hear, or feel what the writer is describing.
- Ask volunteers to identify the examples of sensory language in this passage and tell which sense each appeals to.
  Answer: Students may cite "the high note of the winter wren"—hearing; "the thick perfume of propolis"—smell; "the brightness of wood chips"—sight.

piece of the animal's maxilla[3] to guide them. The teeth told by their shape and placement what this animal ate. By a kind of visual extrapolation its size became clear. There were other clues, immediately present, which told, with what I could add of climate and terrain, how this animal lived, how its broken jaw came to be lying here. Raccoon, they surmised. And tiny tooth marks along the bone's broken edge told of a mouse's hunger for calcium.

We set the jaw back and went on.

If I had known more about raccoons, finer points of osteology,[4] we might have guessed more: say, whether it was male or female. But what we deduced was all we needed. Hours later, the maxilla, lost behind us in the detritus of the forest floor, continued to effervesce. It was tied faintly to all else we spoke of that afternoon.

In speaking with children who might one day take a permanent interest in natural history—as writers, as scientists, as filmmakers, as anthropologists[5]—I have sensed that an extrapolation from a single fragment of the whole is the most invigorating experience I can share with them. I think
❺ children know that nearly anyone can learn the names of things; the impression made on them at this level is fleeting. What takes a lifetime to learn, they comprehend, is the existence and substance of myriad relationships: it is these relationships, not the things themselves, that ultimately hold the human imagination.

The brightest children, it has often struck me, are fascinated by metaphor . . .

The brightest children, it has often struck me, are fascinated by metaphor—with what is shown in the set of relationships bearing on the raccoon, for example, to lie quite beyond the raccoon.
❻ In the end, you are trying to make clear to them that everything found at the edge of one's senses—the high note of the winter wren, the thick perfume of propolis that drifts downwind from spring willows, the brightness of wood chips scattered by beaver—that all this fits together. The indestructibility of these associations conveys a sense of permanence that nurtures the heart, that cripples one of the most insidious of

extrapolation (ek strap′ ə lā′ shən) *n.* conclusions drawn by speculation on the basis of facts

detritus (dē trīt′ əs) *n.* debris

effervesce (ef′ ər ves′) *v.* to be lively

myriad (mir′ ē əd) *adj.* countless; innumerable

insidious (in sid′ ē əs) *adj.* treacherous in a sly, tricky way

3. **maxilla** (maks il′ ə) *n.* upper jaw.
4. **osteology** (äs′ tē äl′ ə jē) *n.* study of the structure and function of bones.
5. **anthropologists** (an′ *thr*ō päl′ ə jists) *n.* specialists in the study of mankind, especially the cultures of mankind.

ENRICHMENT: Science Connection

Biologist/Zoologist/Botanist

Students who are particularly engaged by this essay may have an interest in biology (the branch of science that studies life), zoology (the branch that studies animals), or botany (the branch that studies plants).

Whether as curators for natural history museums, writers of field guides, college professors, or experts on water, air, and land pollution, people in these fields study the living world. These three sciences will be among the leading sciences for the future, since they focus on problems that all living creatures face, such as the threatened environment.

Encourage interested students to gather information about these careers and the education and preparation necessary to pursue them. Have the class discuss how taking walks in the woods with Barry Lopez could encourage a child to aspire to a career in the life sciences.

❼ ▲ **Critical Viewing** Do you agree with the author that discoveries children make in nature can help them understand the world around them? **[Assess]**

human anxieties, the one that says, you do not belong here, you are unnecessary.

Whenever I walk with a child, I think how much I have seen disappear in my own life. What will there be for this person when he is my age? If he senses something ineffable in the landscape, will I know enough to encourage it?—to somehow show him that, yes, when people talk about violent death, spiritual exhilaration, compassion, futility, final causes, they are drawing on forty thousand years of human meditation on *this*—as we embrace Douglas firs, or stand by a river across whose undulating back we skip stones, or dig out a camas bulb,[6] biting down into a taste so much wilder than last night's potatoes. ❽

The most moving look I ever saw from a child in the woods was on

ineffable (in ef´ ə bəl) *adj.* too overwhelming to be expressed in words

❾ **Reading Check**

What do the children learn from the raccoon jaw?

6. **camas** (kam´ əs) **bulbs** underground buds of a sweet and edible American plant.

❼ ▶Critical Viewing

Answer: Most students will agree with the author. Some may point out that observation is an essential part of science, and that the purpose of science is to describe and explain the world around us.

❽ Literary Analysis

Reflective Essay and Sensory Language

- Remind students that a reflective essay can use a writer's personal experience to make a point about the larger human experience.
- Have students identify what Lopez is reflecting on in the first part of this passage.
  Possible response: He remembers that he has forgotten a lot since he was a child and wonders if he, as an adult, is guiding children in a way that allows them to remember the important things about their early experiences.
- Point out to students that Lopez links an individual's childhood with his or her adulthood, and he links the early people of the Oregon forests with those of today when he refers to "drawing on forty thousand years of human meditation."

▶ **Monitor Progress** Ask students to identify the sensory language in this passage and tell which sense each appeals to.
Answer: Embracing a Douglas fir and skipping stones across a river appeal to the sense of touch; the "undulating back" of a river appeals to the sense of sight; biting into a camas bulb appeals to the sense of taste.

❾ Reading Check

Answer: The children learn by the teeth's shape and placement in the jaw what this animal ate.

CUSTOMIZE INSTRUCTION FOR UNIVERSAL ACCESS

For Less Proficient Readers	For English Learners	For Advanced Readers
Lopez's use of sophisticated language may make some of his passages difficult for students to understand. Have less proficient readers work in groups to break down difficult sentences into their parts, identify the key ideas, then restate these ideas in their own words.	Encourage students to find other contexts to use the vocabulary words. For example, the essay speaks of the *detritus* of the forest floor. Have a student define the word *detritus* and then suggest another place in which it could be found. What does *effervesce* mean and what else could *effervesce* besides the raccoon's jawbone?	Have students read other short selections by Barry Lopez and compare them with this selection. Are the styles similar? How do the settings of the selections change? Suggest titles from the ENRICHMENT: Further Reading note on p. 253.

ASSESS

Answers for p. 252

Review and Assess

1. Most students will probably say they would enjoy this experience.
2. **(a)** The woman finds it remarkable that children notice things such as a pattern of sunlight on a windowpane. **(b)** The woman's words tell Lopez something very important about his ability to learn.
3. **(a)** Activities include examining a raccoon bone, hugging a tree, skipping stones across a river, eating a camas bulb, and making handprints in mud. **(b)** Lopez thinks it is important to know about the relationships that bind all parts of nature to one another.
4. **(a)** He knows from his own experience that anything he says may leave a lasting impression. **(b)** He realizes that he was not emphasizing what was really important—the relationships among living things and their surroundings. **(c)** Children construct meaning from what they see, and also come to understand that they, too, are a part of the natural world.
5. **(a)** He has gained more knowledge and peace himself. **(b)** Students may agree, because a person can realize that he or she fits into the natural world, too.
6. **(a)** Lopez mentions what has disappeared in his lifetime; he repeatedly refers to "permanent," and "lifetime." **(b)** Interaction with children gives him hope that the feeling of life "need never be lost."
7. Possible responses: The greatest benefit is learning that we are all part of nature.
8. Instead of explaining technical details, let children experiment and make discoveries about color and design for themselves.

a mud bar by the footprints of a heron.[7] We were on our knees, making handprints beside the footprints. You could feel the creek vibrating in the silt and sand. The sun beat down heavily on our hair. Our shoes were soaking wet. The look said: I did not know until now that I needed someone much older to confirm this, the feeling I have of life here. I can now grow older, knowing it need never be lost.

The quickest door to open in the woods for a child is the one that leads to the smallest room, by knowing the name each thing is called. The door that leads to the cathedral is marked by a hesitancy to speak at all, rather to encourage by example a sharpness of the senses. If one speaks it should only be to say, as well as one can, how wonderfully all this fits together, to indicate what a long, fierce peace can derive from this knowledge.

7. **heron** (her′ ən) wading bird with a long neck, long legs, and a long, tapered bill.

Review and Assess

Thinking About the Selection

1. **Respond:** Would you like to explore the woods or parks near your home with someone like Barry Lopez? Explain.
2. **(a) Recall:** What does the elderly woman in Los Angeles say to Lopez's mother? **(b) Infer:** Why do her words affect Lopez so greatly?
3. **(a) Recall:** List three activities that take place on Lopez's walks in the woods. **(b) Infer:** Why does Lopez use the method he does to teach children about nature?
4. **(a) Interpret:** Why is the author concerned about what he tells children? **(b) Draw Conclusions:** Why does the author change his approach to teaching children about nature? **(c) Analyze:** What do children gain from an understanding of relationships in nature?
5. **(a) Infer:** How do you think Lopez himself grows and develops from the moments of discovery he shares with children? **(b) Speculate:** Do you think that a greater understanding of nature can bring more peace to a person?
6. **(a) Interpret:** Which details in the essay indicate that Lopez is concerned with the passage of time? **(b) Speculate:** Why do you think this concern is intensified by his interaction with children?
7. **Assess:** What is the greatest benefit of learning about nature?
8. **Apply:** How could you apply Barry Lopez's ideas to teaching art to children?

Barry Lopez

(b. 1945)

If you have any interest in nature, you will be moved by the poetic nonfiction of Barry Lopez. In his writing, Lopez speaks for those that cannot speak for themselves—Santa Ana winds, wolves, cottonwood trees, and more. Lopez has said, "I like to use the word *isumatug*. It's of eastern Arctic Eskimo dialect and refers to the storyteller, meaning 'the person who creates the atmosphere in which wisdom reveals itself.'"

An avid explorer, Lopez has journeyed to Alaska, the Galapagos Islands, Australia, Africa, the Antarctic, and the Arctic. In fact, he defines himself as "a writer who travels. Some writers stay at home or inside a room. I am a writer who travels."

ASSESSMENT PRACTICE: Reading Comprehension

Implied Main Idea (For more practice, see Test Preparation Workbook, p. 15.)

Use the following sample test item to demonstrate for students how to identify an implied main idea:

. . . children know that nearly anyone can learn the names of things: the impression made on them at this level is fleeting. What takes a lifetime to learn, they comprehend, is the existence and substance of myriad relationships.

What is the implied main idea of this passage?

A Children need to learn names.

B Children sense that understanding how things fit together is more important that knowing what things are called.

C The author wishes he knew more about nature as an adult than he did as a child.

D Children sense the importance of knowing what things are called.

Guide students to recognize that *B* best captures the implied main idea of the passage.

Review and Assess

Literary Analysis

Reflective Essay

1. Which elements of "Children in the Woods" make it a good example of a **reflective essay?** Use a chart like the one below to record your answer.

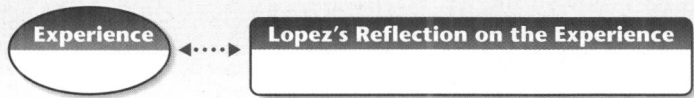

Experience	Lopez's Reflection on the Experience

2. (a) If Lopez wrote "Children in the Woods" in the third person, telling about someone else's experiences, how would it differ from the essay he wrote? (b) Do you think it would be as effective?

Connecting Literary Elements

3. When Lopez recalls making handprints next to footprints of a heron, which **sensory language** brings that personal experience to life?
4. Using a chart like the one below, list examples of sensory language in the essay and explain why the language appeals to your senses.

Example	Sight	Sound	Taste	Touch	Smell

5. How do the images help you understand Lopez's personal thoughts?

Reading Strategy

Relating Generalizations and Evidence

6. (a) What **generalization** does the author make about speaking to children? (b) What **evidence** from his childhood in Los Angeles supports this?
7. (a) What do you think is the key point, or greatest generalization, of "Children in the Woods"? (b) Name three pieces of evidence that relate to the generalization.

Extend Understanding

8. **Career Connection:** Lopez believes that seeing relationships is better than just learning the names of things. Why might this approach help a person who is studying to be a doctor?

Quick Review

A **reflective essay** is a short nonfiction work that focuses on the writer's thoughts about a personal experience.

Sensory language is writing or speech that appeals to one or more of the senses.

To relate **generalizations and evidence,** find a broad principle that is supported by particulars.

Take It to the Net

www.phschool.com

Take the interactive self-test online to check your understanding of the selections.

Answers for p. 253

1. Experiences: Lopez's encounter with the woman who said that children notice things; the children's finding of the raccoon jaw and the resulting discussion; the look given Lopez by the boy on the sandbar. Lopez's reflection on the experience: He realizes that early experiences remain with a child for a long time; he realizes that the raccoon jawbone sparked discussion long after it had been left behind; he realizes that a child needs an adult to confirm the "feeling of life" for him or her and to understand that this need never be lost.
2. The element of reflection would be lost, because Lopez would simply be narrating the events about someone else. Students may suggest that it would not be as effective because it would not contain the author's personal reflections.
3. Sensory language includes: kneeling on a mudbar, making handprints, feeling the creek vibrating, feeling the sun beating down heavily on their hair, feeling their soaking wet shoes.
4. Possible responses: Sight: raccoon teeth in the jawbone; Sound: the high note of the winter wren; Taste: the taste of a camas bulb; Touch: the feeling of sun beating down on one's hair; Smell: the thick perfume of propolis. The language helps the reader to imagine the sensory experience that the writer had.
5. The images help the reader to see what is important to Barry Lopez—the experiences he has in the natural world and the relationships he finds there.
6. **(a)** He feels a great responsibility about what he says to children because he knows that what adults say to a child stays with the child for a long time. **(b)** His memory of the woman's words in Los Angeles support this viewpoint.
7. **(a)** Children should learn about the wholeness of the natural world instead of being limited to the names of individual things. **(b)** The author changes his teaching approach from giving names to helping children discover

continued

Answers continued

relationships; the discussion about the raccoon jawbone leads the group to notice all the other things related to it; a child learns that he is not alone in the world, that he is related to all others.

8. Understanding how parts of the body work together can help a doctor understand the origin of an illness.

ENRICHMENT: Further Reading

Other Works by Barry Lopez

River Notes: The Dance of the Herons
Crossing Open Ground
Crow and Weasel
Of Wolves and Men

Take It to the Net

Visit www.phschool.com for more information on Barry Lopez.

EXTEND

Answers for p. 254

❶ Vocabulary Development

Word Analysis

1. outside the ordinary
2. outside the curriculum
3. outside the normal senses
4. outside the earth

Spelling Strategy

1. residence
2. invigorating

Fluency: Clarify Word Meaning

1. effervesce
2. elucidate
3. extrapolation
4. charged
5. detritus
6. acutely
7. insidious
8. myriad
9. ineffable

❷ Grammar

1. They saw rabbits across the stream.
2. The water flowed from the mountain and into the river.
3. The children walked along the path and looked at the roots of the tree.
4. Around the corner from the hiking trail we spotted a chipmunk.
5. The children can look at life a little differently because of the walk in the woods.

Integrate Language Skills

❶ Vocabulary Development Lesson

Word Analysis: Latin Prefix *extra-*

Extrapolate contains the Latin prefix *extra-*, which means "outside." When you extrapolate, you put facts together to reach a conclusion that is "outside" the information you had when you started. Using the meaning of *extra-*, explain the following terms. Use a dictionary to check your answers.

1. extraordinary
2. extracurricular
3. extrasensory
4. extraterrestrial

Spelling Strategy

When adding an ending that begins with a vowel to a word that ends in a silent *e*, drop the *e* before you add the ending. For example, *make* + *-ing* = *making*. Write the word formed by adding each ending.

1. reside + *-ence*
2. invigorate + *-ing*

Fluency: Clarify Word Meaning

Identify the word from the vocabulary list on page 247 that answers each question.

1. What does soda do when you open the can?
2. What is another word for "explain"?
3. What do scientists get when they use facts to help them draw conclusions?
4. What word describes a tense game?
5. What would you find scattered around a junkyard?
6. How might someone experience a bad headache?
7. How might you describe a disease that is deadly but very hard to detect?
8. How many stars are in the sky?
9. How could you describe a feeling so strong that you could not put it into words?

❷ Grammar Lesson

Prepositions

A **preposition** is a word that relates a noun or pronoun that appears with it to another word in the sentence. Although most prepositions, such as *at*, *by*, *in*, and *with*, are single words, some prepositions, such as *because of* and *in addition to*, are compound. In this example from "Children in the Woods," the prepositions are in italics:

Example: The most moving look I ever saw *from* a child *in* the woods was *on* a mud bar *by* the footprints *of* a heron. We were *on* our knees, making handprints *beside* the footprints.

Practice Write each sentence, underlining all prepositions.

1. They saw rabbits across the stream.
2. The water flowed from the mountain and into the river.
3. The children walked along the path and looked at the roots of the tree.
4. Around the corner from the hiking trail we spotted a chipmunk.
5. The children can look at life a little differently because of the walk in the woods.

Writing Application Write a paragraph about nature using the following prepositions: *over*, *outside*, and *ahead of*.

WG Prentice Hall Writing and Grammar Connection: Chapter 19, Section 1

TEACHING RESOURCES

The following resources can be used to enrich or extend the instruction for pp. 254–255.

Vocabulary

- **Selection Support:** Build Vocabulary, p. 57;
- **Vocabulary and Spelling Practice Book** (Use this booklet for skills enrichment.) ■

Grammar

- **Selection Support:** Build Grammar Skills, p. 58
- **Writing and Grammar,** Gold Level, p. 402
- **Daily Language Practice Transparencies**

Writing

- **Writing and Grammar,** Gold Level, p. 256
- **Writing and Grammar iText CD-ROM** ■

■ **BLOCK SCHEDULING:** Resources marked with this symbol provide varied instruction during 90-minute blocks.

❸ Writing Lesson

Field Guide

In "Children in the Woods," Barry Lopez vividly describes the woods around his home. A field guide provides detailed information about particular types of wildlife in a region. Write your own field guide about nature found right outside your home.

Prewriting Brainstorm for a list of animals that live near your home. For each general group, itemize by naming specific examples. From your list, select the subjects for your field guide.

Model: Listing and Itemizing

Around My House

squirrels	cardinals
chipmunks	sparrows
birds	goldfinches
rabbits	

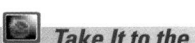

Specific examples make a field guide clearer and more useful to its readers.

Drafting As you draft, be specific, factual, and objective. Show what the animals look like and how they behave. For example, if you are describing the feeding habits of rabbits, tell exactly which plants they eat.

Revising Have classmates read your field guide and list their unanswered questions. Use these questions to guide your revisions.

WG *Prentice Hall Writing and Grammar Connection: Chapter 12, Section 2*

❹ Extension Activities

Listening and Speaking Keeping Barry Lopez's ideas in mind, devise a **lesson plan** to teach children about one aspect of nature. Use these suggestions as you plan:

- Select a topic that you know rather well.
- Use visuals to help inform your audience.
- Practice your lesson. If possible, videotape yourself to find room for improvement.

When you have finished preparing, teach your lesson to a child or a small group of children.

Research and Technology The woods described by Lopez are part of a temperate rain forest. In a group, prepare a **rain forest presentation.** Use resources at the library and on the Internet to find your facts. In your presentation, include a world map that shows where temperate rain forests are located. **[Group Activity]**

Take It to the Net www.phschool.com
Go online for an additional research activity using the Internet.

ASSESSMENT RESOURCES

The following resources can be used to assess students' knowledge and skills.

Selection Assessment

- **Formal Assessment:** Selection Test, pp. 51–53
- **Open Book Test,** pp. 43–45
- **Got It! Assessment Videotapes,** Tape 2
- **Test Bank Software**

Take It to the Net
Visit www.phschool.com for self-tests and additional questions on "Children in the Woods."

Writing Rubric

- **Performance Assess. and Portfolio Mgmt.,** p. 18

PRENTICE HALL ASSESSMENT SYSTEM

- **Workbook**
- **Transparencies**
- **Skill Book**
- **CD-ROM**

❸ Writing Lesson

- Display one or more Aubudon, Peterson, or other field guides to show students the content and organization of such books.
- Have students make a list of animals in their own community. Students who live on the same street or block may work together.
- Have students classify the species on their lists according to the following: mammals, birds, reptiles, amphibians, fish. If they need to know how a turtle, snake, or woodchuck is classified, have them use one of the field guides, or look up the animal in a dictionary.
- Use the Description rubric, p. 18 in **Performance Assessment and Portfolio Management,** to evaluate students' work.

❹ Listening and Speaking

- Have students choose their topic. Help them in narrowing their interests into a teachable topic.
- Conduct class discussion to pinpoint main teaching ideas, including those from Barry Lopez's essay. Write suggestions on the board: "Show, don't tell." "Use names as a starting point but focus on relationships among things in natural world." "Make clear statements and back them up with visuals." "Encourage children's own powers of discovery."
- Suggest places for finding visuals: magazines, newspapers, original drawings, photographs, and computer/web resources.

CUSTOMIZE INSTRUCTION for Universal Access

To address different learning styles, use the activities suggested in the **Extension Activities** booklet, p. 15.

- For Verbal/Linguistic Learners, use Activity 4.
- For Interpersonal Learners, use Activity 5.
- For Visual/Spatial Learners, use Activity 6.

Lesson Objectives

1. To learn how to evaluate credibility of sources
2. To understand basic elements of a Web site, including the home page and links
3. To understand that links provide more detailed information on a Web site

About Web Sites

- Ask students to name some of their favorite Web sites and explain what makes them especially appealing.
- If possible, use a computer to show students several Web sites that you like to visit.
- Many students have their own Web sites. You may want to invite students to show their home pages in class. (Check the Web sites ahead of time for appropriate content.)

Reading Strategy

Evaluating Credibility of Sources

- Ask students to share some definitions of *credibility*.
  Possible answers: Students may cite "believability," "reliability," "trustworthiness," or "dependability."
- Explain that when students do research on Web sites, it's important to evaluate the accuracy and reliability of the information presented there.
- Point out that students also need to be able to distinguish between fact and opinion, because they may find both types of information on any one Web site.
- Point out the Credibility organizer on p. 256. If possible, have students use computers to go to the National Audubon Society's Web site and complete a Credibility organizer for a link they find there.

READING INFORMATIONAL MATERIALS

Web Sites

About Web Sites

A Web site is a collection of information located at a specific address on the World Wide Web, a part of the Internet accessible by computer. Software known as a browser enables an Internet user to access millions of Web sites around the world. To connect to a Web site, a user can either type a specific address or click on a word or picture that is electronically linked to the address. Often, a Web site begins with a home page, which is similar to the table of contents in a book. The user clicks on a specific home page listing, or link, to access the Web site's information on that topic.

Reading Strategy

Evaluating Credibility of Sources

When you access Web sites for information, it is important to evaluate the credibility of your sources. Use these questions to determine whether or not a source can be trusted:

- Who is the sponsor of the site?
- What are their credentials and background?
- Are both sides of issues represented?
- How current is the information?

You can trust the National Audubon Society, an established group, to give accurate Web site information on the Endangered Species Act, a strictly factual topic. However, the Audubon Web page titled "New Hunting Bill Is Overkill" presents an opinion, so you must treat that information more cautiously. Use a graphic organizer like the one shown here to rate the credibility of each link on the Audubon Web site home page.

Link	Credibility
National Wildlife Refuges	**Sponsor?** National Audubon Society. **Credentials?** 100-year-old organization that runs wildlife preservation programs. **Both sides shown?** Page presents factual information, not opinion. **Information current?** Yes. **Credible or not?** Credible. An organization dedicated to conservation would keep an accurate list of national wildlife refuges.

Audubon Web Site

If you are looking for information on wildlife conservation on the Internet, you are likely to come across the Web site for the National Audubon Society. The National Audubon Society is an organization that is dedicated to wildlife conservation and habitat restoration. The home page of the organization is shown below, providing a table of contents with links to the various pages of the site.

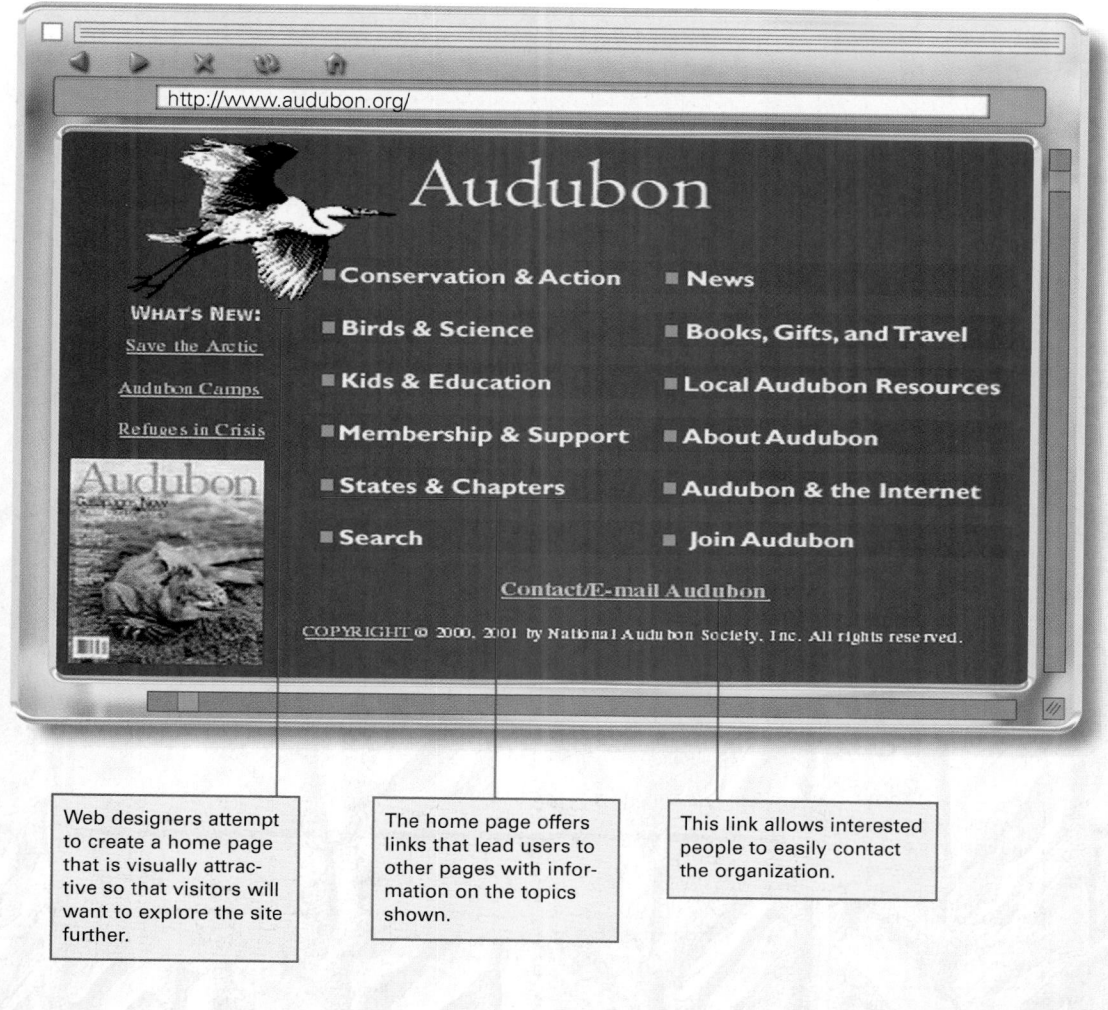

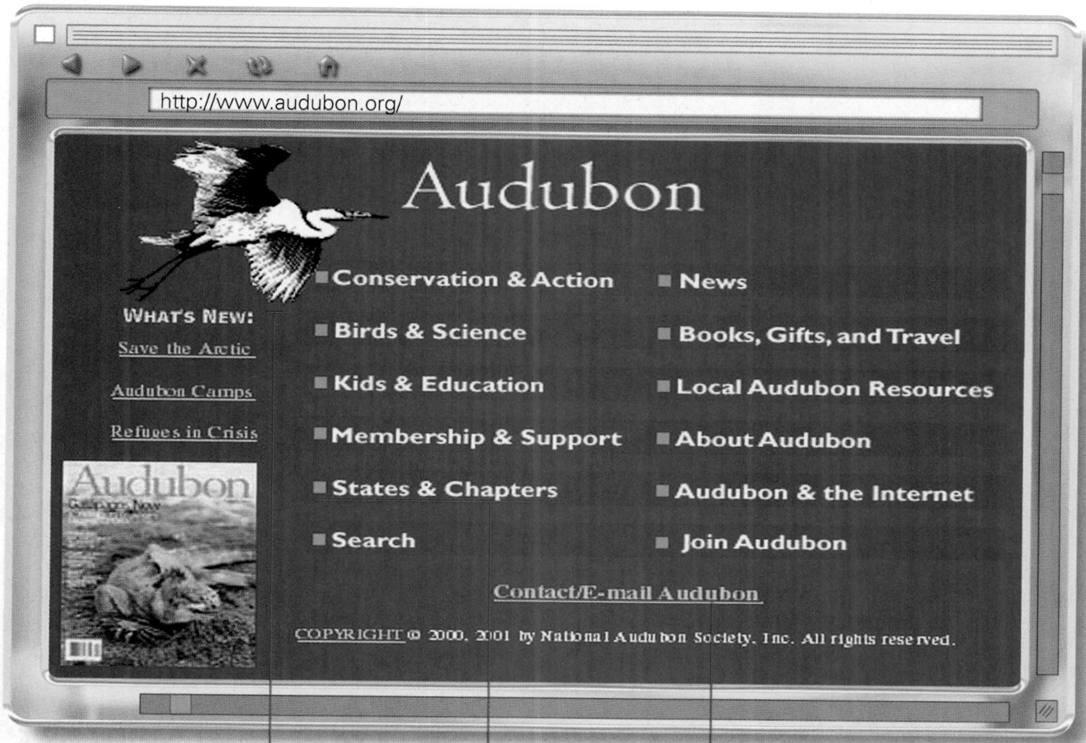

Web designers attempt to create a home page that is visually attractive so that visitors will want to explore the site further.

The home page offers links that lead users to other pages with information on the topics shown.

This link allows interested people to easily contact the organization.

Audubon Web Site

- Ask students to share circumstances in which they might visit the Audubon Web site.
  Possible answers: Students may visit the site if they are interested in birds or conservation, when they are researching a related subject, or when they wish to join the Audubon Society.
- Point out the call-out box on home page design. Ask students to critique the design they see here, pointing out what they like and dislike about it.
- Ask students how they can tell what's "clickable" on the home page.
  Answer: Underlined words and phrases are almost always clickable links. Colored type is another indicator. Photographs and images are often clickable, too.

CUSTOMIZE INSTRUCTION FOR UNIVERSAL ACCESS

For English Learners	For Advanced Readers
Ask students to explore the Audubon Web site online. Have them note any words they don't understand. Ask students to notice how graphics and photographs can help them infer meaning. Encourage students to locate a Web site that is written in a language other than English and compare it to the Audubon site.	Have students create lists of their "top five Web sites." For each Web site they list, have students describe what is good about the site, then use a graphic organizer (like the one on p. 256) to evaluate one link on each Web site.

Internal Pages

- Have students review the Web page pictured on p. 258. Point out the call-out in boxes on the page.
- Ask students what links they would click to learn more about the Endangered Species Act.
  Answer: Students would click the numbered links on the lower portion of the page.
- Ask students what action they could take if they found an error on the page.
  Answer: Students could use the e-mail address to send a notice to the organization.
- Point out that most Web pages include navigation, or clues for moving around the site. This page offers two navigational choices. What are they?
  Answer: The choices are "Back to Endangered Species" and "HOME."

Internal Pages

Since there is too much information to fit on a single page, and because the Internet is suited to the presentation of unlimited information, the Audubon site is designed with multiple levels to organize its information. Users move down a level every time they click on a link on a page. The page shown below, from the fourth level of the site, provides detailed information about the Endangered Species Act.

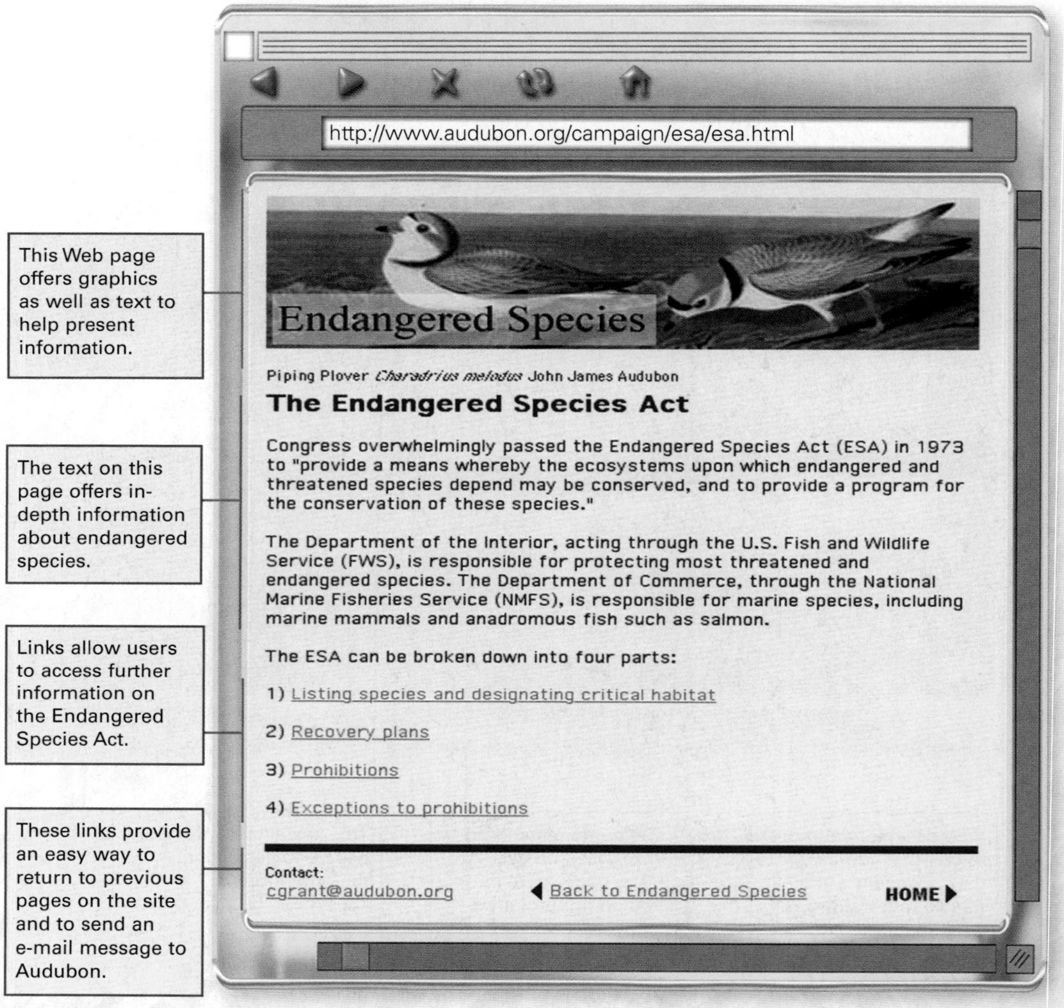

http://www.audubon.org/campaign/esa/esa.html
Endangered Species
Piping Plover *Charadrius melodus* John James Audubon
The Endangered Species Act
Congress overwhelmingly passed the Endangered Species Act (ESA) in 1973 to "provide a means whereby the ecosystems upon which endangered and threatened species depend may be conserved, and to provide a program for the conservation of these species."
The Department of the Interior, acting through the U.S. Fish and Wildlife Service (FWS), is responsible for protecting most threatened and endangered species. The Department of Commerce, through the National Marine Fisheries Service (NMFS), is responsible for marine species, including marine mammals and anadromous fish such as salmon.
The ESA can be broken down into four parts:
1) Listing species and designating critical habitat
2) Recovery plans
3) Prohibitions
4) Exceptions to prohibitions
Contact:
cgrant@audubon.org
Back to Endangered Species
HOME
This Web page offers graphics as well as text to help present information.
The text on this page offers in-depth information about endangered species.
Links allow users to access further information on the Endangered Species Act.
These links provide an easy way to return to previous pages on the site and to send an e-mail message to Audubon.

Check Your Comprehension

1. Which link or links on the home page lead to information about education and resources?
2. Where would you find contact information?
3. In what year was the Endangered Species Act passed?

Applying the Reading Strategy

Evaluating Credibility of Sources

4. Cite two links on the Audubon home page that lead to information you can easily accept, along with two links you might evaluate more cautiously. Record your answers in the chart like the one below.

Credible	Explanation
Link:	
Evaluate More Cautiously	**Explanation**
Link:	

Activity

Researching a Web Site

You can find information on virtually any topic by using the World Wide Web. Choose a topic of interest to you. Then, use one or more Web sites to find information on your topic. For each site you visit, record information on an index card like the one shown here. Rank at least three sites in order of usefulness.

Conducting a Web Search
Topic:
Web address:
Web sponsor or author:
Credibility:
_____Excellent _____Good _____Fair _____Poor
Date site was last updated:
Interesting facts:

Contrasting Informational Texts

Web Sites and Traditional Resources

1. Suppose that you wished to learn about the Endangered Species Act without logging on to the Internet. (a) How could you find information on your topic in an encyclopedia? (b) Explain how this search process differs from using a Web site.
2. List resources other than the Internet and encyclopedias that you could use to find information on the Endangered Species Act. Explain how to use each source and how using each one differs from using a Web site.

Answers for p. 259

Check Your Comprehension

1. "Kids and Education" and "Local Audubon Resources" would lead to information on education and resources.
2. Contact information is contained in the e-mail address on the home page.
3. The Endangered Species Act was passed in 1973.

Applying the Reading Strategy

Credible: Birds and Science, News; Explanation: Both of these links would be based on factual information; Evaluate More Cautiously: Conservation and Action, Join Audubon; Explanation: The conservation link could contain opinions. The Audubon link could contain promotional material.

Activity

Suggest that students brainstorm for a list of topics they're interested in. Point out that students can locate information on a topic by conducting a key word search on the Internet or by using a search engine.

Contrasting Informational Texts

1. **(a)** Students could find the topic in an encyclopedia by looking under the heading "Endangered Species." **(b)** This process is different from using a Web site because all the information is contained in one (usually long) article that may or may not have graphics and that may not provide contacts.
2. Possible answers: Using a card file or online search in a library would provide students with a variety of books, magazines, and other print sources of information. More information might be found this way, but students would have to read through more text to find specific information. Writing the Audubon Society or another organization for information would result in print information, but it would be a slow process.

Rules of the Game

Lesson Objectives and CA Correlations

1. **To analyze and respond to literary elements**
   - Literary Analysis: Generational Conflict **R 3.3**
   - Connecting Literary Elements: Motivation **R 3.4**
2. **To read, comprehend, analyze, and critique a short story**
   - Reading Strategy: Contrasting Characters **R 3.3**
   - Reading Check questions
   - Review and Assess questions
   - Assessment Practice (ATE)
3. **To develop word analysis skills, fluency, and systematic vocabulary**
   - Vocabulary Development Lesson: Word Origins: Words From French **R 1.1**
4. **To understand and apply written and oral language conventions**
   - Spelling Strategy
   - Grammar Lesson: Prepositional Phrases **LC 1.3**
5. **To understand and apply appropriate writing and research strategies**
   - Writing Lesson: Advice Column **W 1.1**
   - Extension Activity: Radio Commentary **W 2.4**
6. **To understand and apply listening and speaking strategies**
   - Extension Activity: Dialogue **LS 2.1**

STEP-BY-STEP TEACHING GUIDE	PACING GUIDE
PRETEACH	
Motivate Students and Provide Background	
Use the Motivation activity (ATE p. 260)	5 min.
Read and discuss the Preview material and Background information (SE/ATE p. 260) [A]	5 min.
Introduce the Concepts	
Introduce the Literary Analysis and Reading Strategy (SE/ATE p. 261) [A]	15 min.
Pronounce the vocabulary words and read their definitions (SE p. 261)	5 min.
TEACH	
Monitor Comprehension	
Informally monitor comprehension by circulating while students read independently or in groups [A]	30 min.
Monitor students' comprehension with the Reading Check notes (SE/ATE pp. 263, 265, 267, 269, 271)	as students read
Develop vocabulary with Vocabulary notes (SE pp. 263, 267, 269, 270)	as students read
Develop Understanding	
Develop students' understanding of generational conflict with the Literary Analysis annotations (SE pp. 263, 266, 269, 271; ATE pp. 263–266, 269, 271) [A]	10 min.
Develop students' ability to contrast characters with the Reading Strategy annotations (SE pp. 264, 265, 270; ATE pp. 264, 265, 268, 270)	10 min.
ASSESS	
Assess Mastery	
Assess students' mastery of the Reading Strategy and Literary Analysis by having them answer the Review and Assess questions (SE/ATE p. 273)	20 min.
Use one or more of the print and media Assessment Resources (ATE p. 275) [A]	up to 50 min.
EXTEND	
Apply Understanding	
Have students complete the Vocabulary Development Lesson and the Grammar Lesson (SE p. 274) [A]	20 min.
Apply students' knowledge of objective tone using the Writing Lesson (SE/ATE p. 275) [A]	45 min.
Apply students' understanding of the selection using one or more of the Extension Activities (SE p. 275)	20–90 min.

[A] ACCELERATED INSTRUCTION: Use the strategies and activities identified with an [A].

UNIVERSAL ACCESS
● = Below-Level Students
▲ = On-Level Students
■ = Above-Level Students

Time and Resource Manager

Reading Level: Average
Average Number of Instructional Days: 4

RESOURCES		
PRINT	**TRANSPARENCIES**	**TECHNOLOGY**
• **Beyond Literature,** Cross-Curricular Connection: Performing Arts, p. 16 ▲ ■		• **Interest Grabber Video,** Tape 2 ● ▲ ■
• **Selection Support Workbook:** ● ▲ ■ Literary Analysis, p. 64 Reading Strategy, p. 63 Build Vocabulary, p. 61	• **Literary Analysis and Reading Transparencies,** pp. 31 and 32 ● ▲ ■	
• **Adapted Reader's Companion** ● • **Reader's Companion** ●		
• **English Learner's Companion** ● ▲ • **Literatura en español** ● ▲ • **Literary Analysis for Enrichment** ■	• **Fine Art Transparencies, Volume 1,** Art Transparency 7 ● ▲ ■	
• **Formal Assessment:** Selection Test, pp. 54–56 ● ▲ ■ • **Open Book Test,** pp. 46–48 ● ▲ ■ • **Performance Assessment and Portfolio Management,** p. 14 ● ▲ ■ • PRENTICE HALL ASSESSMENT SYSTEM ● ▲ ■	• PRENTICE HALL ASSESSMENT SYSTEM ● ▲ ■ Skills Practice Answers and Explanations on Transparencies	• **Test Bank Software** ● ▲ ■ • **Got It! Assessment Videotapes,** Tape 2 ● ▲
• **Selection Support Workbook:** ● ▲ ■ Build Grammar Skills, p. 62 • **Writing and Grammar,** Gold Level ● ▲ ■ • **Extension Activities,** p. 16 ● ▲ ■	• **Daily Language Practice Transparencies** ● ▲	• **Writing and Grammar iText CD-ROM** ● ▲ ■ ***Take It to the Net*** www.phschool.com

BLOCK SCHEDULING: Use one 90-minute class period to preteach the selection and have students read it. Use a second 90-minute class period to assess students' mastery of skills and have them complete one of the Extension Activities.

PRETEACH

Step-by-Step Teaching Guide for pp. 260–261

Motivation

Have students look at the pictures of chess pieces that illustrate the story. Poll the class to find out how many students know the basic rules of chess and the functions of each piece. Invite volunteers to share what they know about the game, as well as mental strategies for successful play. Explain that Waverly Jong, the narrator of "Rules of the Game," must develop a special mental toughness to succeed as a chess champion. At the same time she is trying to negotiate between two worlds—the Chinese world of her heritage and the American world of her daily experience.

Interest Grabber Video

As an alternative, play "San Francisco's Chinatown" on Tape 2 to engage student interest.

❶ Background

The game of chess was originally known as *chaturanga,* a name that referred to the four divisions of the Indian army of the sixth century: elephants, horses, chariots, and foot soldiers. During the Middle Ages, games of chess became part of courtship rituals between knights and ladies.

Prepare to Read

Rules of the Game

Take It to the Net

Visit www.phschool.com for interactive activities and instruction related to "Rules of the Game," including

- background
- graphic organizers
- literary elements
- reading strategies

Preview

Connecting to the Literature

In "Rules of the Game," a generational tug of war is complicated by a conflict between Chinese and American cultures. No matter what your cultural background might be, however, the battle of wills that takes place in this selection should be familiar to you.

❶ Background

Chess, which plays a central role in this story by Amy Tan, is believed to have evolved from a game first played in India in the sixth century. The game spread to Persia (the present Iran), and the Arab invaders who conquered Persia in the seventh century later introduced chess to other lands around the Mediterranean Sea. Today, chess is played by people of all ages and cultural backgrounds around the world.

TEACHING RESOURCES

The following resources can be used to enrich or extend the instruction for pp. 260–261.

Motivation

Interest Grabber Video, Tape 2 ■

Background

Beyond Literature, p. 16

Take It to the Net

Visit www.phschool.com for background and hotlinks for "Rules of the Game."

Literary Analysis

Literary Analysis and Reading Transparencies, Generational Conflict, p. 32 ■

Reading

Selection Support: Reading Strategy, p. 63; Build Vocabulary, p. 61

Literary Analysis and Reading Transparencies, Contrasting Characters, p. 31

■ **BLOCK SCHEDULING:** Resources marked with this symbol provide varied instruction during 90-minute blocks.

❷ Literary Analysis

Generational Conflict

A **generational conflict** is a struggle that exists between characters when beliefs and values change from one generation to another. The following passage from "Rules of the Game" demonstrates the generational conflict that exists in the story.

> One day, after we left a shop I said under my breath, "I wish you wouldn't do that, telling everybody I'm your daughter." My mother stopped walking. . . . "Aiii-ya. So shame be with mother?"

As you read the story, pay attention to the conflicts, or struggles, between the characters and consider why the conflicts exist.

Connecting Literary Elements

Motivation is the reason behind a character's thoughts, feelings, and actions. The motives of characters often contribute to the conflict in a story. In "Rules of the Game," young Waverly's motivation to be a successful chess player, and her mother's motivation to become involved with Waverly's success, greatly contribute to the conflict.

❸ Reading Strategy

Contrasting Characters

Throughout the story, you will see Waverly and her mother engaged in conflict. In order to follow the story, you need to understand how the two main characters are contrasted.

- As you read, **contrast,** or notice the differences in, the way each character expresses herself.
- Consider how each character feels about the other.

Use a chart like the one shown here to keep track of the actions, words, traits, and hopes of Waverly and her mother.

Waverly	Mrs. Jong
Born in the U.S.	Born in China
Significant Actions	
Significant Statements	
Personality Traits	
Hopes	

Vocabulary Development

pungent (pun′ jənt) *adj.* producing a sharp sensation of smell (p. 263)

benevolently (bə nev′ ə lent lē) *adv.* in a kind and well-meaning way (p. 267)

retort (ri tôrt′) *n.* sharp or clever reply (p. 267)

prodigy (präd′ ə jē) *n.* person who is amazingly talented or intelligent (p. 269)

malodorous (mal ō′ dər əs) *adj.* having a bad smell (p. 269)

concessions (kən sesh′ ənz) *n.* things given or granted as privileges (p. 270)

CUSTOMIZE INSTRUCTION FOR UNIVERSAL ACCESS

For Special Needs Students	For Less Proficient Readers	For English Learners
Have students read the adapted version of "Rules of the Game" in the **Adapted Reader's Companion.** This version provides basic-level instruction in an interactive format with questions and write-on lines. Completing the adapted version will prepare students to read the selection in the Student Edition.	Have students read the selection in the **Reader's Companion.** This version provides basic-level instruction in an interactive format with questions and write-on lines. After students finish the selection in **Reader's Companion,** have them complete the questions and activities in the Student Edition.	Have students read the adapted version of the selection in the **English Learner's Companion.** This version provides basic-level instruction in an interactive format with questions and write-on lines. Completing the adapted version will prepare students to read the selection in the Student Edition.

❷ Literary Analysis

Generational Conflict and Motivation

- Remind students that *conflict* in a story is a struggle between characters or forces. An external conflict occurs between a central character and another character or outside force.
- Tell students that as they read "Rules of the Game" they will see a generational conflict being played out between Waverly and her mother. The two are of different generations and have different ideas about life.
- Point out that students can often identify conflicts between characters by figuring out what each character wants or needs.
- Use the instruction for Connecting Literary Elements to connect the generational conflict in the story to the characters' motivations.
- Use the Generational Conflict transparency in **Literary Analysis and Reading Transparencies,** p. 32 to demonstrate some of the differences between Waverly and Mrs. Jong.

❸ Reading Strategy

Contrasting Characters

- Remind students that to *contrast* is to find the differences between two people, things, ideas, or events.
- Use the chart to demonstrate to students one major difference between Waverly and her mother— their place of birth.
- Instruct students to create their own contrast chart and to keep track of the characters' differences as they read the story.

Vocabulary Development

- Pronounce each vocabulary word for students and read the definitions as a class. Have students identify any words with which they are already familiar.

E-Teach

Visit E-Teach at www.phschool.com for teachers' essays on how to teach, with questions and answers.

TEACH

Step-by-Step Teaching Guide for pp. 262–272

CUSTOMIZE INSTRUCTION
For Logical/Mathematical Learners

Encourage students to discuss different types of board games and what they have in common: rules, movable pieces, and a board on which to play. Have students distinguish complex games, such as chess, from simpler games such as checkers. Now have the group create a new board game. They will need to make up rules, and create a board and pieces. Provide art materials for this project and when students have completed their board game, have them introduce it to the rest of the class.

❶ About the Selection

"Rules of the Game" focuses on the relationship between a mother who was born and raised in China and her daughter, born in America. Against a backdrop of the daughter's success as a chess champion, the two clash over their generational and cultural differences, but behind these conflicts are their similarities. Both characters are proud, intelligent, and stubborn—personality traits that almost guarantee conflict.

❷ Critical Thinking

Interpret

- After students have read the passage, ask them to speculate on what the statement "Strongest wind cannot be seen" means. Possible response: A person who is quiet and does not challenge everything is more likely to get what he or she wants.
- Have students consider whether or not the narrator listens to her mother's advice.
- Ask students if the narrator acts like the "strongest wind" in this passage. Answer: She does act like the strongest wind by being silent about wanting the plums.

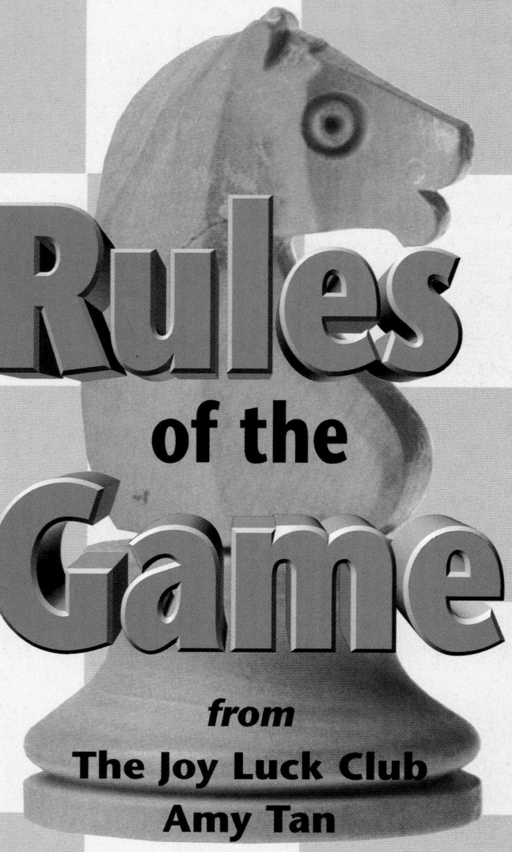

❶ Rules of the Game

from The Joy Luck Club

Amy Tan

I was six when my mother taught me the art of invisible strength. It was a strategy for winning arguments, respect from others, and eventually, though neither of us knew it at the time, chess games.

❷ "Bite back your tongue," scolded my mother when I cried loudly, yanking her hand toward the store that sold bags of salted plums. At home, she said, "Wise guy, he not go against wind. In Chinese we say, Come from South, blow with wind—poom!—North will follow. Strongest wind cannot be seen."

The next week I bit back my tongue as we entered the store with the forbidden candies. When my mother finished her shopping, she quietly plucked a small bag of plums from the rack and put it on the counter with the rest of the items.

TEACHING RESOURCES

The following resources can be used to enrich or extend the instruction for pp. 262–272.

Literary Analysis

- **Selection Support:** Literary Analysis, p. 64

Reading

- **Reader's Companion**
- **English Learner's Companion**
- **Listening to Literature Audiocassettes,** Side 9
- **Listening to Literature Audio CDs,** CD 7 ▣

Extension

- **Fine Art Transparencies, Volume 1,** Art Transparency 7 (Ask students to explain how the painting, *Cool Dragon,* reflects some of the conflicts in the story.) ▣

▣ **BLOCK SCHEDULING:** Resources marked with this symbol provide varied instruction during 90-minute blocks.

3 My mother imparted her daily truths so she could help my older brothers and me rise above our circumstances. We lived in San Francisco's Chinatown. Like most of the other Chinese children who played in the back alleys of restaurants and curio shops,[1] I didn't think we were poor. My bowl was always full, three five-course meals every day, beginning with a soup full of mysterious things I didn't want to know the names of.

We lived on Waverly Place, in a warm, clean, two-bedroom flat that sat above a small Chinese bakery specializing in steamed pastries and dim sum.[2] In the early morning, when the alley was still quiet, I could smell fragrant red beans as they were cooked down to a pasty sweetness. By daybreak, our flat was heavy with the odor of fried sesame balls and sweet curried chicken crescents. From my bed, I would listen as my father got ready for work, then locked the door behind him, one-two-three clicks.

At the end of our two-block alley was a small sandlot playground with swings and slides well-shined down the middle with use. The play area was bordered by wood-slat benches where old-country people sat cracking roasted watermelon seeds with their golden teeth and scattering the husks to an impatient gathering of gurgling pigeons. The best playground, however, was the dark alley itself. It was crammed with daily mysteries and adventures. My brothers and I would peer into the medicinal herb shop, watching old Li dole out onto a stiff sheet of white paper the right amount of insect shells, saffron-colored[3] seeds and pungent leaves for his ailing customers. It was said that he once cured a woman dying of an ancestral curse that had eluded the best of American doctors. Next to the pharmacy was a printer who specialized in gold-embossed wedding invitations and festive red banners.

Farther down the street was Ping Yuen Fish Market. The front window displayed a tank crowded with doomed fish and turtles struggling to gain footing on the slimy green-tiled sides. A hand-written sign informed tourists, "Within this store, is all for food, not for pet." Inside, the butchers with their bloodstained white smocks deftly gutted the fish while customers cried out their orders and shouted, "Give me your freshest," to which the butchers always protested, "All are freshest." On less crowded market days, we would inspect the crates of live frogs and crabs which we were warned not to poke, boxes of dried cuttlefish, and row upon row of iced prawns, squid, and slippery fish. The sanddabs made me shiver each time; their eyes lay on one flattened side and reminded me of my mother's story of a careless girl who ran into a crowded street and was crushed by a cab. "Was smash flat," reported my mother.

1. **curio** (kyo͞or´ ē ō´) **shops** shops that sell unusual or rare items.
2. **dim sum** (dim´ sum´) shells of dough filled with meat and vegetables and served as a light meal.
3. **saffron-colored** orange-yellow.

Literary Analysis
Generational Conflict
How does the mother's view of her family's situation contrast with that of the narrator?

pungent (pun´ jənt) *adj.* producing a sharp sensation of smell

4 **Reading Check**
What does the mother give to her daughter when she behaves in the candy store?

3 Literary Analysis

Generational Conflict and Motivation

- Have students think about other generational conflicts they know of as they read this passage.
- Ask students where the family lives. Why might the mother feel that she has to rise above her circumstances?
  Answer: The family lives in San Francisco's Chinatown.

  People born in other countries who emigrate to the United States often feel that they have to work very hard to "make it" and "fit in."
- Have students answer the Literary Analysis question on p. 263: How does the mother's view of family's situation contrast with that of the narrator?
  Answer: The mother feels the family has to rise above their circumstances. The narrator doesn't think the family is poor. She has enough to eat and even questions the content of some of the dishes she eats.

4 Reading Check

Answer: The mother buys her daughter some plums.

CUSTOMIZE INSTRUCTION FOR UNIVERSAL ACCESS

For Special Needs Students	For Less Proficient Readers	For Gifted/Talented Students
Students may benefit from watching the Interest Grabber Video titled "San Francisco's Chinatown" on Tape 2 and comparing what they see with what they learn about Chinatown from the author's description. Are the shops in the video similar to the ones in Waverly's neighborhood?	Encourage students to observe and write a description of a small shop or other business in their own community. Have them reread these pages to see what kinds of descriptions the author uses about her own community and to model their descriptions on these.	Have students create diagrams, charts, or other visuals to demonstrate chess moves. They might also wish to bring in the chess columns from the daily newspapers and have contests to solve the board contests that are often reproduced in the columns.

❺ Literary Analysis

Generational Conflict and Motivation

- Have students recall times when they have asked a question to get a rise out of a parent.
- After students have read the passage, have them speculate on whether or not Waverly really wants to know the definition of Chinese torture or whether she merely wants to give her mother a hard time. Have them justify their choice of answer.
  Answer: Waverly seems to be giving her mother a hard time. She thinks her mother is "without a trace of knowing how wicked I was being."

Monitor Progress Ask students what generational conflict is expressed in this passage.
Answer: Waverly criticizes her own community, like many young people, while her mother defends her community, which is characteristic of many adults.

❻ Reading Strategy

Contrasting Characters

- Ask students to recall situations in which they were joking with someone and the person did not realize this fact, but responded in all seriousness.
- After students have read the passage again, have them answer the Reading Strategy question on p. 264: What does this conversation between Waverly and her mother reveal about each character's personality?
  Answer: Waverly has a sense of humor and teases her mother about "Chinese torture." Mrs. Jong answers her seriously, even going so far as to say that Chinese people do the best torture.

At the corner of the alley was Hong Sing's, a four-table cafe with a recessed stairwell in front that led to a door marked "Tradesmen." My brothers and I believed the bad people emerged from this door at night. Tourists never went to Hong Sing's, since the menu was printed only in Chinese. A Caucasian[4] man with a big camera once posed me and my playmates in front of the restaurant. He had us move to the side of the picture window so the photo would capture the roasted duck with its head dangling from a juice-covered rope. After he took the picture, I told him he should go into Hong Sing's and eat dinner. When he smiled and asked me what they served, I shouted, "Guts and duck's feet and octopus gizzards!" Then I ran off with my friends, shrieking with laughter as we scampered across the alley and hid in the entryway grotto[5] of the China Gem Company, my heart pounding with hope that he would chase us.

My mother named me after the street that we lived on: Waverly Place Jong, my official name for important American documents. But my family called me Meimei [mā´ mā´], "Little Sister." I was the youngest, the only daughter. Each morning before school, my mother would twist and yank on my thick black hair until she had formed two tightly wound pigtails. One day, as she struggled to weave a hard-toothed comb through my disobedient hair, I had a sly thought.

I asked her, "Ma, what is Chinese torture?" My mother shook her head. A bobby pin was wedged between her lips. She wetted her palm and smoothed the hair above my ear, then pushed the pin in so that it nicked sharply against my scalp.

❺ "Who say this word?" she asked without a trace of knowing how wicked I was being. I shrugged my shoulders and said, "Some boy in my class said Chinese people do Chinese torture."

❻ "Chinese people do many things," she said simply. "Chinese people do business, do medicine, do painting. Not lazy like American people. We do torture. Best torture."

Reading Strategy
Contrasting Characters What does this conversation between Waverly and her mother reveal about each character's personality?

My older brother Vincent was the one who actually got the chess set. We had gone to the annual Christmas party held at the First Chinese Baptist Church at the end of the alley. The missionary ladies had put together a Santa bag of gifts donated by members of another church. None of the gifts had names on them. There were separate sacks for boys and girls of different ages.

❼ One of the Chinese parishioners had donned a Santa Claus costume and a stiff paper beard with cotton balls glued to it. I think the only children who thought he was the real thing were too young to

4. **Caucasian** (kô kā´ zhən) *adj.* person of European ancestry.
5. **entryway grotto** (grät´ ō) *n.* entryway resembling a cave.

know that Santa Claus was not Chinese. When my turn came up, the Santa man asked me how old I was. I thought it was a trick question; I was seven according to the American formula and eight by the
7 Chinese calendar. I said I was born on March 17, 1951. That seemed to satisfy him. He then solemnly asked if I had been a very, very good girl this year and did I believe in Jesus Christ and obey my parents. I knew the only answer to that. I nodded back with equal solemnity.

Having watched the other children opening their gifts, I already knew that the big gifts were not necessarily the nicest ones. One girl my age got a large coloring book of biblical characters, while a less greedy girl who selected a small box received a glass vial of lavender toilet water. The sound of the box was also important. A ten-year-old boy had chosen a box that jangled when he shook it. It was a tin globe of the world with a slit for inserting money. He must have thought it was full of dimes and nickels, because when he saw that it had just ten pennies, his face fell with such undisguised disappointment that his mother slapped the side of his head and led him out of the church hall, apologizing to the crowd for her son who had such bad manners he couldn't appreciate such a fine gift.

As I peered into the sack, I quickly fingered the remaining presents, testing their weight, imagining what they contained. I chose a heavy, compact one that was wrapped in shiny silver foil and a red satin ribbon. It was a twelve-pack of Life Savers and I spent the rest of the party arranging and rearranging the candy tubes in the order of my favorites. My brother Winston chose wisely as well. His present turned out to be a box of intricate plastic parts; the instructions on the box proclaimed that when they were properly assembled he would have an authentic miniature replica of a World War II submarine.

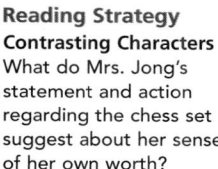

Vincent got the chess set, which would have been a very decent present to get at a church Christmas party except it was obviously used and, as we discovered later, it was missing a black pawn and a white knight. My mother graciously thanked the unknown benefactor, saying, "Too good. Cost too much." At which point, an old lady with
8 fine white, wispy hair nodded toward our family and said with a whistling whisper, "Merry, merry Christmas."

When we got home, my mother told Vincent to throw the chess set away. "She not want it. We not want it," she said, tossing her head stiffly to the side with a tight, proud smile. My brothers had deaf ears. They were already lining up the chess pieces and reading from the dog-eared instruction book.

I watched Vincent and Winston play during Christmas week. The chess board seemed to hold elaborate secrets waiting to be untangled. The chessmen were more powerful than Old Li's magic herbs that cured ancestral curses. And my brothers wore such serious faces that I was sure something was at stake that was greater than avoiding the tradesmen's door to Hong Sing's.

Literary Analysis
Generational Conflict and Motivation What motivates Waverly to produce the right answers for Santa Claus?

Reading Strategy
Contrasting Characters What do Mrs. Jong's statement and action regarding the chess set suggest about her sense of her own worth?

9 **Reading Check**
What gift does Vincent receive at the Christmas party?

CUSTOMIZE INSTRUCTION FOR UNIVERSAL ACCESS

For English Learners

Students might benefit by recasting some of the phrases spoken by Mrs. Jong and the other Chinese characters into Standard English. Point out to students that people learning a new language often start out using phrases in which the basic ideas are stated, but often they are out of context. For example, write this sign on the board: "Within this store, is all for food, not for pet." How would students communicate the meaning of this sign in Standard English? (**Possible answer:** The animals in this store are sold as food, not as pets.) Encourage students to flesh out the main ideas in the phrases "Give me your freshest," "Was smash flat," and other phrases throughout the story.

7 Literary Analysis

Generational Conflict and Motivation

- Point out to students that Santa Claus is not part of the Chinese culture, so Waverly feels offended by his presence and is on the look-out to avoid any encounter that will make her look bad or stupid.
- After students have read the passage, ask them why Waverly answers the questions the way she does.
  Answer: Waverly knows the correct answers to Santa Claus's questions, even though she does not believe in Santa Claus customs herself.
- Have students answer the Literary Analysis question on p. 265: What motivates Waverly to produce the right answers for Santa Claus?
  Answer: Waverly does not want to anger him and perhaps lose her present.

8 Reading Strategy

Contrasting Characters

- Have volunteers read aloud the passage and notice the different reactions of Mrs. Jong, Vincent, and Winston to the gift of the chess set.
- Then, have the class discuss how they would feel if they were given a used game that was missing vital pieces.
  Possible response: Students may say that being given something used is acceptable, but the action may be insulting if the item is incomplete or broken.
- Ask students the Reading Strategy question on p. 265: What do Mrs. Jong's statement and action regarding the chess set suggest about her sense of her own worth?
  Answer: Mrs. Jong is too proud to be comfortable with the incomplete, discarded set and asks Vincent to throw it out.

9 Reading Check

Answer: Vincent receives a used chess set.

10 Literary Analysis

Generational Conflict and Motivation

- Tell students that a character's motive for saying or doing something can be stated or implied in a selection. Ask them to look for stated motivations as they read this passage and the preceding paragraph on p. 265.
- Have students answer the Literary Analysis question on p. 266: What motivates Waverly's desire to play? What motivates Vincent to let her play?
  Answer: Waverly was fascinated watching her brothers play chess. She thinks the game holds important secrets and she wants to be part of the process. Vincent finally lets Waverly play because she offers him her Life Savers and he wants to use two of them for the missing chess pieces.

11 Literary Analysis

Generational Conflict and Motivation

- Have students read the passage and consider whether Waverly and Mrs. Jong are concerned with the same kind of rules.
  Possible response: Waverly is concerned about learning the rules for playing chess, but Mrs. Jong is concerned about the rules for getting through life.
- Have students answer the second Literary Analysis question on p. 266: What motivates Mrs. Jong to tell Waverly she has to figure out the rules for herself?
  Answer: She believes that if one figures out the rules for oneself, one will more likely succeed. If one accepts other people's explanations of the rules, one will probably have less power.

---

10 "Let me! Let me!" I begged between games when one brother or the other would sit back with a deep sigh of relief and victory, the other annoyed, unable to let go of the outcome. Vincent at first refused to let me play, but when I offered my Life Savers as replacements for the buttons that filled in for the missing pieces, he relented. He chose the flavors: wild cherry for the black pawn and peppermint for the white knight. Winner could eat both. As our mother sprinkled flour and rolled out small doughy circles for the steamed dumplings that would be our dinner that night, Vincent explained the rules, pointing to each piece. "You have sixteen pieces and so do I. One king and queen, two bishops, two knights, two castles, and eight pawns. The pawns can only move forward one step, except on the first move. Then they can move two. But they can only take men by moving crossways like this, except in the beginning, when you can move ahead and take another pawn."

"Why?" I asked as I moved my pawn. "Why can't they move more steps?"

"Because they're pawns," he said.

"But why do they go crossways to take other men. Why aren't there any women and children?"

"Why is the sky blue? Why must you always ask stupid questions?" asked Vincent. "This is a game. These are the rules. I didn't make them up. See. Here. In the book." He jabbed a page with a pawn in his hand. "Pawn. P-A-W-N. Pawn. Read it yourself."

My mother patted the flour off her hands. "Let me see book," she said quietly. She scanned the pages quickly, not reading the foreign English symbols, seeming to search deliberately for nothing in particular.

11 "This American rules," she concluded at last. "Every time people come out from foreign country, must know rules. You not know, judge say, Too bad, go back. They not telling you why so you can use their way go forward. They say, Don't know why, you find out yourself. But they knowing all the time. Better you take it, find out why yourself." She tossed her head back with a satisfied smile.

I found out about all the whys later. I read the rules and looked up all the big words in a dictionary. I borrowed books from the Chinatown library. I studied each chess piece, trying to absorb the power each contained.

I learned about opening moves and why it's important to control the center early on; the shortest distance between two points is straight down the middle. I learned about the middle game and why tactics between two adversaries are like clashing ideas; the one who plays better has the clearest plans for both attacking and getting out of traps. I learned why it is essential in the endgame* to have foresight, a mathematical understanding of all possible moves, and patience; all weaknesses and advantages become evident to a strong adversary and are obscured to

Literary Analysis
Generational Conflict and Motivation What motivates Waverly's desire to play? What motivates Vincent to let her play?

Literary Analysis
Generational Conflict and Motivation What motivates Mrs. Jong to tell Waverly she has to figure out the rules for herself?

ENRICHMENT: Social Studies Connection

The Art of War

The names of the many "secret" strategies for winning which Lau Po provides to Waverly, such as "The Double Attack from East and West Shores" and "Sand in the Eyes of Advancing Forces," may at first seem strangely colorful and mysterious. In fact, Lau Po is introducing Waverly to an ancient Chinese tradition, the application of military terms and metaphors to other competitive areas of life.

Point out to students that in the 1980s, a centuries-old set of precepts, *The Art of War,* by warrior-philosopher Sun-Tsu, became a popular manual for those who work in the competitive arena of the business world. Another important part of the Chinese cultural heritage is a collection of similar axioms, called *The Thirty-Six Strategems,* which can be applied to a wide range of interpersonal situations. Have interested students find these books and report on them to the class.

a tiring opponent. I discovered that for the whole game one must gather invisible strengths and see the endgame before the game begins.

12 I also found out why I should never reveal "why" to others. A little knowledge withheld is a great advantage one should store for future use. That is the power of chess. It is a game of secrets in which one must show and never tell.

I loved the secrets I found within the sixty-four black and white squares. I carefully drew a handmade chessboard and pinned it to the wall next to my bed, where at night I would stare for hours at imaginary battles. Soon I no longer lost any games or Life Savers, but I lost my adversaries. Winston and Vincent decided they were more interested in roaming the streets after school in their Hopalong Cassidy[6] cowboy hats.

On a cold spring afternoon, while walking home from school, I detoured through the playground at the end of our alley. I saw a group of old men, two seated across a folding table playing a game of chess, others smoking pipes, eating peanuts, and watching. I ran home and grabbed Vincent's chess set, which was bound in a cardboard box with rubber bands. I also carefully selected two prized rolls of Life Savers. I came back to the park and approached a man who was observing the game.

"Want to play?" I asked him. His face widened with surprise and he grinned as he looked at the box under my arm.

"Little sister, been a long time since I play with dolls," he said, smiling benevolently. I quickly put the box down next to him on the bench and displayed my retort.

Lau Po, as he allowed me to call him, turned out to be a much better player than my brothers. I lost many games and many Life Savers. But over the weeks, with each diminishing roll of candies, I added new secrets. Lau Po gave me the names. The Double Attack from the East and West Shores. Throwing Stones on the Drowning Man. The Sudden Meeting of the Clan. The Surprise from the Sleeping Guard. The Humble Servant Who Kills the King. Sand in the Eyes of Advancing Forces. A Double Killing Without Blood.

13 There were also the fine points of chess etiquette. Keep captured men in neat rows, as well-tended prisoners. Never announce "Check" with vanity, lest someone with an unseen sword slit your throat. Never hurl pieces into the sandbox after you have lost a game, because then you must find them again, by yourself, after apologizing to all around you. By the end of the summer, Lau Po had taught me all he knew, and I had become a better chess player.

6. **Hopalong Cassidy** character in cowboy movies during the 1950s.

Literature in context — Cultural Connection

◆ ***Endgame***

Endgame describes a tense period in a chess game when the end seems close at hand. With fewer pieces left, lines of attack and defense become clearer to both players. Mistakes are magnified in an endgame, when the margin between victory and defeat can be a single ill-considered move. In this story, Waverly develops a keen awareness of the strategies needed in the endgame to secure a victory.

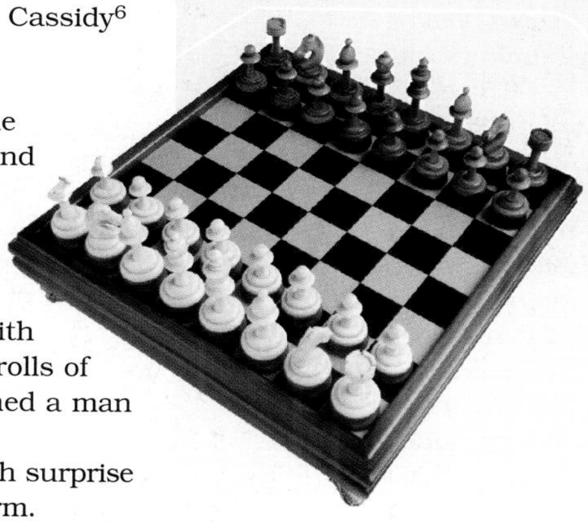

benevolently (bə nev′ ə lent lē) *adv.* in a kind and well-meaning way

retort (ri tôrt′) *n.* sharp or clever reply

14 **✓Reading Check**

How does Waverly quench her desire to understand the rules of chess?

12 Background

Cultural Connection

In a typical endgame, both players have lost their queens and have limited resources. They attempt to checkmate each other's king—trapping the king in a position where no move is possible. Note to students that the terms *endgame* and *checkmate* are frequently applied beyond the game of chess—especially in military, political, and athletic contests.

13 Critical Thinking

Interpret

- As students read the passage, have them compare the rules of chess with the rules of life. What are some rules of etiquette in the game of chess?
  Answer: Keep captured pieces orderly and in neat rows. Don't be arrogant or vain about announcing "Check." Don't lose your temper when you lose a piece or lose the game.
- Ask students what rules of life Waverly might learn from these rules of chess.
  Answer: She learns that if one behaves badly, in chess or in life, one has to repair the damage one does.

14 ✓Reading Check

Answer: Waverly reads, plots imaginary games, and studies with Lau Po.

CUSTOMIZE INSTRUCTION FOR UNIVERSAL ACCESS

For Special Needs Students	For Less Proficient Readers	For Gifted/Talented Students
Students might enjoy listening to a portion of the audiocassette recording of "Rules of the Game." After they have listened to a passage, have them replay the passage and read along with the narrator. Then, have them use the reader's delivery as a model to read aloud different sections of the story.	Have students make a chart with pictures and moves of the different chess pieces. They may draw their own pieces or make photocopies of drawings or photographs in a book. After they have completed their chart, have them reread the portions of the text that deal specifically with chess moves and see if they have a better understanding of the game.	Have students use chess terms and concepts to create different kinds of analogies. Some examples are: *part to whole*—pawn to chess; *kind*—chess to game; *lesser to greater*—rook to queen; *cause to effect*—checkmate to win; *antonyms*—win to lose. Encourage students to create as many other analogies as they can.

15 Reading Strategy

Contrasting Characters

- Have students recall Mrs. Jong's statement—"Bite back your tongue"—to Waverly at the beginning of the story. Have them state what Mrs. Jong meant by this statement.
  Possible response: Don't be too eager; don't be so open with what you want. Protect yourself by keeping many things secret.
- After students read the passage, ask them what Mrs. Jong means by "Is shame you fall down nobody push you."
  Possible response: It's too bad if you lose by not even getting into the game.

Monitor Progress Have students compare Waverly's behavior here with her mother's earlier behavior.
Answer: Waverly knows her mother would not let her play if she asked her mother directly, so she pretends she doesn't want to play with American rules. Her mother responds by trying to shame her into playing. Waverly gets what she wants by pretending the opposite, just as she did in the earlier scene.

16 Critical Viewing

Answer: The expressions of the chess players, rather than the positions of the pieces on the board (which are not clear enough to distinguish) reveal that the girl has the upper hand. The man looks a little upset and is concentrating hard; the girl looks confident and pleased with herself.

17

A small weekend crowd of Chinese people and tourists would gather as I played and defeated my opponents one by one. My mother would join the crowds during these outdoor exhibition games. She sat proudly on the bench, telling my admirers with proper Chinese humility, "Is luck."

Chess Mates, 1992, Pamela Chin Lee, Courtesy of the artist

15 A man who watched me play in the park suggested that my mother allow me to play in local chess tournaments. My mother smiled graciously, an answer that meant nothing. I desperately wanted to go, but I bit back my tongue. I knew she would not let me play among strangers. So as we walked home I said in a small voice that I didn't want to play in the local tournament. They would have American rules. If I lost, I would bring shame on my family.

"Is shame you fall down nobody push you," said my mother.

During my first tournament, my mother sat with me in the front row as I waited for my turn. I frequently bounced my legs to unstick them from the cold metal seat of the folding chair. When my name was called, I leapt up. My mother unwrapped something in her lap. It was her chang, a small tablet of red jade which held the sun's fire. "Is luck," she whispered, and tucked it into my dress pocket. I turned to my opponent, a fifteen-year-old boy from Oakland. He looked at me, wrinkling his nose.

As I began to play, the boy disappeared, the color ran out of the room, and I saw only my white pieces and his black ones waiting on the other side. A light wind began blowing past my ears. It whispered secrets only I could hear.

16 **Critical Viewing** Based on details in the painting, who do you think is winning this chess game? Why? **[Support]**

"Blow from the South," it murmured. "The wind leaves no trail." I saw a clear path, the traps to avoid. The crowd rustled. "Shhh! Shhh!" said the corners of the room. The wind blew stronger. "Throw sand from the East to distract him." The knight came forward ready for the sacrifice. The wind hissed, louder and louder. "Blow, blow, blow. He cannot see. He is blind now. Make him lean away from the wind so he is easier to knock down."

"Check," I said, as the wind roared with laughter. The wind died down to little puffs, my own breath.

My mother placed my first trophy next to a new plastic chess set that the neighborhood Tao society[7] had given to me. As she wiped
18 each piece with a soft cloth, she said, "Next time win more, lose less."

"Ma, it's not how many pieces you lose," I said. "Sometimes you need to lose pieces to get ahead."

"Better to lose less, see if you really need."

At the next tournament, I won again, but it was my mother who wore the triumphant grin.

"Lost eight piece this time. Last time was eleven. What I tell you? Better off lose less!" I was annoyed, but I couldn't say anything.

I attended more tournaments, each one farther away from home. I won all games, in all divisions. The Chinese bakery downstairs from our flat displayed my growing collection of trophies in its window, amidst the dust-covered cakes that were never picked up. The day after I won an important regional tournament, the window encased a fresh sheet cake with whipped-cream frosting and red script saying, "Congratulations, Waverly Jong, Chinatown Chess Champion." Soon after that, a flower shop, headstone engraver, and funeral parlor offered to sponsor me in national tournaments. That's when my mother decided I no longer had to do the dishes. Winston and Vincent had to do my chores.

"Why does she get to play and we do all the work," complained Vincent.

"Is new American rules," said my mother. "Meimei play, squeeze all her brains out for win chess. You play, worth squeeze towel."

By my ninth birthday, I was a national chess champion. I was still some 429 points away from grand-master status, but I was touted as the Great American Hope, a child prodigy and a girl to boot. They ran a photo of me in *Life* magazine next to a quote in which Bobby Fischer[8] said, "There will never be a woman grand master." "Your move, Bobby," said the caption.

The day they took the magazine picture I wore neatly plaited braids clipped with plastic barrettes trimmed with rhinestones. I was playing in

Literary Analysis
Generational Conflict and Motivation What motivates the mother to advise Waverly, instead of complimenting her daughter on her win?

prodigy (präd′ ə jē) *n.* person who is amazingly talented or intelligent

7. **Tao** (dou) **society** group of people who believe in Taoism, a Chinese religion that stresses simplicity and unselfishness.
8. **Bobby Fischer** born in 1943, this American chess prodigy attained the high rank of grand master in 1958.

19 **Reading Check**
Why was Waverly featured in *Life* magazine?

17 Background

Art

Chess Mates, 1992, by Pamela Chin Lee

Pamela Chin Lee draws on her Chinese heritage in this painting of a chess game. Although the two figures in the painting are playing a competitive game, their relaxed postures suggest a friendly relationship between the two. Students may wish to consider the following: Which figure in the painting is emphasized and why? How does this painting reflect what happens in "Rules of the Game"?
Answer: Though the figure of the man is larger, the painting emphasizes the move the girl is making. The story, like the painting, focuses on a young girl who learns to beat older, male opponents at chess.

18 Literary Analysis

Generational Conflict and Motivation

- After students have read the passage, ask them if they think Mrs. Jong understands the rules of chess.
  Possible responses: Some students will say she does not understand because she thinks the more pieces you lose, the worse you are playing. Others may suggest that she understands the rules, but still thinks it looks bad to lose a lot of pieces even if you win the game.
- Ask students to answer the Literary Analysis question on p. 269: What motivates the mother to advise Waverly, instead of complimenting her daughter on her win?
  Answer: Mrs. Jong finds it difficult to give compliments and may be afraid that Waverly will play more carelessly next time if she is full of pride.

19 Reading Check

Answer: There has been never a female grand master in chess, and Waverly is seen as someone who might achieve this status.

CUSTOMIZE INSTRUCTION FOR UNIVERSAL ACCESS

For Less Proficient Readers	For Advanced Readers
Students may benefit from working with the vocabulary words that appear on these pages. Have them answer questions about the words, such as "When would you speak *benevolently* to someone?" "What kind of *retort* might you offer to someone who called you an insulting name?" "What would you expect from a math *prodigy*?" and "Which would be more likely to give off a *malodorous* odor, a locker room after a game or a kitchen in which cookies are baking?"	Students may enjoy finding the words on this spread with the following etymologies: from the Old French *torneier,* meaning "to take part in a contest"; from the Middle French *trophee,* meaning "sign of victory"; from the Old French *parler,* meaning "to speak"; from the French *caillou du Rhin,* meaning "pebble of the Rhine."

20 Critical Thinking

Analyze

- After students have read the passage, ask them what picture they have of Waverly from the description.
  Possible response: She is dressed in very feminine clothing and acts dainty and childlike.
- Point out to students that both Waverly and her mother have the trait of being secretive. How is Waverly being secretive in this passage?
  Answer: She is acting like a typical young girl, and the typical young girl is not a chess champion.
- Have students consider how Waverly uses her gender and her age to her advantage in this passage.
  Answer: Waverly's opponents do not expect much competition from a young girl in frilly clothing and innocent behavior. Her clothes and behavior disarm them.

21 Reading Strategy

Contrasting Characters

- Point out to students that Mrs. Jong wants to be involved in her daughter's chess career. Is the way she is acting here the way to go about it?
  Answer: No, she is just making Waverly nervous.
- Ask students the Reading Strategy question on p. 270: What does this passage reveal about the way each character communicates?
  Answer: Waverly states her wishes outright by asking her mother not to stand over her while she is practicing. Her mother is more hidden, and makes noise with the pots and pans to express her feelings.

a large high school auditorium that echoed with phlegmy coughs and the squeaky rubber knobs of chair legs sliding across freshly waxed wooden floors. Seated across from me was an American man, about the same age as Lau Po, maybe fifty. I remember that his sweaty brow seemed to weep at my every move. He wore a dark, malodorous suit. One of his pockets was stuffed with a great white kerchief on which he wiped his palm before sweeping his hand over the chosen chess piece with great flourish.

malodorous (mal ō´ dər əs) *adj.* having a bad smell

20 In my crisp pink-and-white dress with scratchy lace at the neck, one of two my mother had sewn for these special occasions, I would clasp my hands under my chin, the delicate points of my elbows poised lightly on the table in the manner my mother had shown me for posing for the press. I would swing my patent leather shoes back and forth like an impatient child riding on a school bus. Then I would pause, suck in my lips, twirl my chosen piece in midair as if undecided, and then firmly plant it in its new threatening place, with a triumphant smile thrown back at my opponent for good measure.

I no longer played in the alley of Waverly Place. I never visited the playground where the pigeons and old men gathered. I went to school, then directly home to learn new chess secrets, cleverly concealed advantages, more escape routes.

21 But I found it difficult to concentrate at home. My mother had a habit of standing over me while I plotted out my games. I think she thought of herself as my protective ally. Her lips would be sealed tight, and after each move I made, a soft "Hmmmmph" would escape from her nose.

"Ma, I can't practice when you stand there like that," I said one day. She retreated to the kitchen and made loud noises with the pots and pans. When the crashing stopped, I could see out of the corner of my eye that she was standing in the doorway. "Hmmmmph!" Only this one came out of her tight throat.

Reading Strategy
Contrasting Characters
What does this passage reveal about the way each character communicates?

My parents made many concessions to allow me to practice. One time I complained that the bedroom I shared was so noisy that I couldn't think. Thereafter, my brothers slept in a bed in the living room facing the street. I said I couldn't finish my rice; my head didn't work right when my stomach was too full. I left the table with half-finished bowls and nobody complained. But there was one duty I couldn't avoid. I had to accompany my mother on Saturday market days when I had no tournament to play. My mother would proudly walk with me, visiting many shops, buying very little. "This my daughter Wave-ly Jong," she said to whoever looked her way.

concessions (kən sesh´ ənz) *n.* things given or granted as privileges

One day, after we left a shop I said under my breath, "I wish you wouldn't do that, telling everybody I'm your daughter." My mother stopped walking. Crowds of people with heavy bags pushed past us on the sidewalk, bumping into first one shoulder, then another.

"Aiii-ya. So shame be with mother?" She grasped my hand even tighter as she glared at me.

I looked down. "It's not that, it's just so obvious. It's just so embarrassing."

ENRICHMENT: Social Studies Connection

Chess

Young people regularly compete in chess tournaments. In April, 2000, Vinay Bhat, 15, earned the International Master title, and became the youngest person ever to do so. Eighteen-year-old Andrew Whatley of Alabama won the U.S. Junior Open in July, 1999, while Jordy Mont-Reynaud, 16, won the U.S. Cadet Championship the same year. School teams also compete. In 2000, some winning teams included Masterman High School of Philadelphia, Renaissance Junior High School of Detroit, and Phoenix Country Day School. All won championships in their respective competitions. Phoenix Country Day School won its third consecutive title.

In 2000, ground was broken on the World Chess Hall of Fame and Sidney Samole Museum in Miami, Florida. Samole invented chess games that can be played on personal computers. The entryway of the museum is a 45-foot chess piece—a rook, or castle. The museum features interactive displays and memorabilia of famous players.

"Embarrass you be my daughter?" Her voice was cracking with anger.

"That's not what I meant. That's not what I said."

"What you say?"

I knew it was a mistake to say anything more, but I heard my voice speaking. "Why do you have to use me to show off? If you want to show off, then why don't you learn to play chess." My mother's eyes turned into dangerous black slits. She had no words for me, just sharp silence.

I felt the wind rushing around my hot ears. I jerked my hand out of my mother's tight grasp and spun around, knocking into an old woman. Her bag of groceries spilled to the ground.

"Aii-ya! Stupid girl!" my mother and the woman cried. Oranges and tin cans careened down the sidewalk. As my mother stooped to help the old woman pick up the escaping food, I took off.

22 I raced down the street, dashing between people, not looking back as my mother screamed shrilly, "Meimei! Meimei!" I fled down an alley, past dark curtained shops and merchants washing the grime off their windows. I sped into the sunlight, into a large street crowded with tourists examining trinkets and souvenirs. I ducked into another dark alley, down another street, up another alley. I ran until it hurt and I realized I had nowhere to go, that I was not running from anything. The alleys contained no escape routes.

My breath came out like angry smoke. It was cold. I sat down on an upturned plastic pail next to a stack of empty boxes, cupping my chin with my hands, thinking hard. I imagined my mother, first walking briskly down one street or another looking for me, then giving up and returning home to await my arrival. After two hours, I stood up on creaking legs and slowly walked home.

The alley was quiet and I could see the yellow lights shining from our flat like two tiger's eyes in the night. I climbed the sixteen steps to the door, advancing quietly up each so as not to make any warning sounds. I turned the knob; the door was locked. I heard a chair moving, quick steps, the locks turning—click! click! click!—and then the door opened.

"About time you got home," said Vincent. "Boy, are you in trouble."

He slid back to the dinner table. On a platter were the remains of a large fish, its fleshy head still connected to bones swimming upstream in vain escape. Standing there waiting for my punishment, I heard my mother speak in a dry voice.

"We not concerning this girl. This girl not have concerning for us."

Nobody looked at me. Bone chopsticks[9] clinked against the insides of bowls being emptied into hungry mouths.

Literary Analysis
Generational Conflict
What makes Waverly upset with her mother's behavior?

23 **Reading Check**
What does Waverly say to her mother when they walk through the Saturday market?

9. **chopsticks** (chäp´ stiks´) two small sticks of wood, bone, or ivory, held together in one hand and used as utensils for eating, cooking, and serving food.

22 Literary Analysis

Generational Conflict and Motivation

- After students have read the passage, ask them to make a statement about how Waverly's mother is acting.
  Possible response: She is acting as if Waverly is a trophy herself, not Mrs. Jong's daughter.
- Ask students the Literary Analysis question on p. 271: What makes Waverly upset with her mother's behavior?
  Answer: Waverly feels her mother is using her to make herself look good and important. There is a difference between being proud of a family member and using that pride to make oneself look important.

23 Reading Check

Answer: Waverly says her mother's behavior embarrasses her, but she does not mean she is embarrassed to be her mother's daughter.

ASSESS

Answers for p. 272

Review and Assess

1. Students may make a case for any of the characters being the most realistic. For example, Waverly's brothers are realistic because they are not concerned with the finer points of Chinese culture versus American culture; they just want to learn how to play chess.
2. **(a)** Waverly begs her mother for some salted plums and her mother says "Bite back your tongue," which means keep your needs secret. Waverly does so, and the next week her mother buys some plums without being asked or begged. **(b)** She uses the art of "invisible strength" to manipulate her mother to buy her some plums.
3. **(a)** She gives the rules of behavior in the form of Chinese sayings. **(b)** She pretends to be weaker than she is. Meanwhile, she grows stronger by studying chess all the time. **(c)** She manipulates her mother by pretending not to want things she does want. She tries to keep her feelings secret.
4. Waverly will win the game of doing what she wants to do. She has the advantage of youth, a passion for the game she wishes to play, and she has learned strategy from her mother.
5. This strategy could also apply to any life situation in which one is in competition with someone else or something else.
6. The story is not only about chess; it is also about strategies in relationships.
7. **(a)** The battle of wills between parents and children is universal. **(b)** The strong family values and respect for the tradition of Chinese culture provide the special circumstances of the battle between Waverly and her mother.
8. Possible answers: Yes, because her mother is standing in the way of Waverly being a success. No, because her mother is just trying to protect her daughter in an alien culture.

I walked into my room, closed the door, and lay down on my bed. The room was dark, the ceiling filled with shadows from the dinnertime lights of neighboring flats.

In my head, I saw a chessboard with sixty-four black and white squares. Opposite me was my opponent, two angry black slits. She wore a triumphant smile. "Strongest wind cannot be seen," she said.

Her black men advanced across the plane, slowly marching to each successive level as a single unit. My white pieces screamed as they scurried and fell off the board one by one. As her men drew closer to my edge, I felt myself growing light. I rose up into the air and flew out the window. Higher and higher, above the alley, over the tops of tiled roofs, where I was gathered up by the wind and pushed up toward the night sky until everything below me disappeared and I was alone.

I closed my eyes and pondered my next move.

Amy Tan

(b. 1952)

Like Waverly, the nine-year-old chess champion in this story, Amy Tan was something of a child prodigy, displaying literary promise at the ripe age of eight. As a young woman, Tan supported herself as a technical writer, playing piano and writing fiction for relaxation. Through writing, she discovered her own ethnic identity. She has said in interviews that she had tried to minimize her ethnicity when she was younger. All that changed when she began to write about the painful but rich experiences of Chinese American women.

In 1985, Tan wrote "Rules of the Game," which she later included in *The Joy Luck Club*, set in Oakland, California, where she was born. The novel weaves together the stories of four Chinese mothers and their American-born daughters.

Review and Assess

Thinking About the Selection

1. **Respond:** Which character did you find most realistic? Explain.
2. **(a) Recall:** Explain the salted plums incident in the beginning of the story. **(b) Analyze:** Which strategy does Waverly use with her mother even before she starts playing chess?
3. **(a) Recall:** How does Mrs. Jong teach Waverly rules of behavior? **(b) Connect:** How does Waverly use these rules to win at chess? **(c) Extend:** How does she use them in her struggle with her mother?
4. **Speculate:** The story ends without a final showdown. Who do you think will eventually "win" the game? Why?
5. **Apply:** Referring to chess, Waverly says that "for the whole game one must gather invisible strengths and see the endgame before the game begins." In which more general situations does this idea apply? Explain.
6. **Interpret:** Why do you think Amy Tan called this story "Rules of the Game"?
7. **(a) Assess:** Which elements of the struggle between Waverly and her mother are universal, relating to people from all cultures? Explain. **(b) Extend:** Which elements are uniquely Chinese American? Explain.
8. **Take a Position:** Do you think that Waverly's anger toward her mother is justified? Why or why not?

ASSESSMENT PRACTICE: Reading Comprehension

Implied Main Idea (For more practice, see Test Preparation Workbook, p. 16.)

Many tests, including the SAT, require students to identify an implied main idea. Use the following sample test item to give students practice in identifying an implied main idea.

There were also fine points of chess etiquette. Keep captured men in neat rows, as well-tended prisoners. Never announce "Check" with vanity . . . Never hurl pieces into the sandbox . . . By the end of the summer . . . I had become a better chess player.

What is the main idea of this passage?

A Neatness is important in a chess game.
B The unwritten rules of chess are as important as the moves.
C Children shouldn't play chess.
D Chess players have good manners.

By saying that learning chess etiquette made her a better chess player, the narrator is implying the main idea stated in *B*.

Review and Assess

Literary Analysis

Generational Conflict

1. What does Waverly resent about her mother's behavior when they are shopping together?
2. What might Mrs. Jong feel that her child does not yet understand?
3. (a) Use a chart like the one shown below to list statements made by Waverly and her mother that suggest a conflict. (b) Based on their statements, how would you rate the **generational conflict** on a scale from 1 to 10? Explain.

Speaker	Statement

Connecting Literary Elements

4. What motivates Mrs. Jong's involvement in Waverly's chess success?
5. How does Waverly's **motivation** to be a successful chess player contribute to her conflict with her mother?

Reading Strategy

Contrasting Characters

6. In what ways are Waverly and Mrs. Jong more alike than they admit? Using a chart like the one below, analyze their similarities and differences.

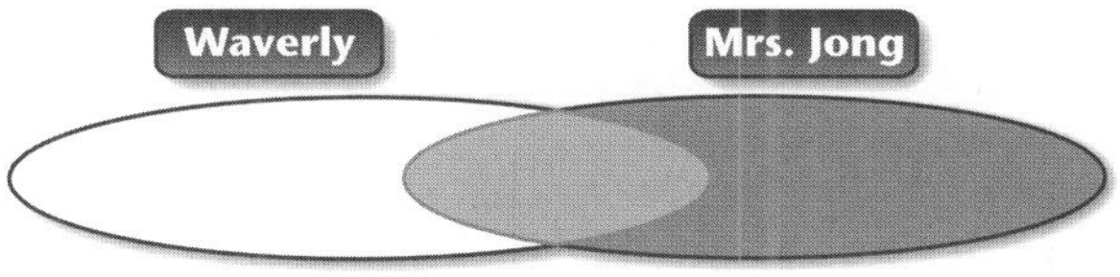

7. Why is Waverly in a better position than her mother to understand "American rules"?
8. What does Mrs. Jong want for her daughter that she does not have herself?

Extend Understanding

9. **Humanities Connection:** What other stories do you know in which a child uses success in some activity to outgrow a parent?

Quick Review

Generational conflict is the struggle between two characters that occurs when beliefs and values change from one generation to another.

Motivation is the reason that explains why a character thinks, feels, or behaves in a certain way.

To **contrast characters,** find the differences that exist between people in a story.

Take It to the Net

www.phschool.com

Take the interactive self-test online to check your understanding of the selection.

ENRICHMENT: Further Reading

Other Works by Amy Tan

The Moon Lady
The Kitchen God's Wife
The Hundred Secret Senses
The Bonesetter's Daughter

Take It to the Net

Visit www.phschool.com for more information on Amy Tan.

Answers for p. 273

Review and Assess

1. She probably feels her mother is trying to steal some of her own success. She is also embarrassed by the way her mother calls attention to both of them.
2. Mrs. Jong knows what it means to lose her birth culture and have to adapt to a new culture; she fears that Waverly will be hurt as she tries to fit into an alien society.
3. Possible answers: **(a)** Speaker: Waverly. Statement: "I wish you wouldn't do that, telling everybody I'm your daughter." Speaker: Mrs. Jong. Statement: "Aiii-ya. So shame be with mother? . . . Embarrass you be my daughter?" **(b)** Students will probably rate the conflict at 8 or higher. The gulf between the Chinese woman and her Chinese American daughter is great.
4. Mrs. Jong wants to be part of her daughter's life and also wants to share in any success Waverly achieves.
5. Waverly wants something that will involve her directly in the American culture. Her mother fears American culture, and wants to protect her daughter from any harm that may come to her.
6. Similarities: strong-willed, focused, intelligent, proud, manipulative, secretive; Differences: Mrs. Jong: Chinese born, believes in skill, lost a culture; Waverly: American born, believes in luck, has a Chinese American culture
7. Waverly was born in America; her daily life is steeped in American culture.
8. She wants Waverly to have opportunities for success, probably by "fitting into" American culture and playing by its "rules."
9. Students may cite examples from myth and legend, such as Phaëthon and Icarus. Encourage students to reference characters from contemporary stories they have read.

EXTEND

Answers for p. 274

❶ Vocabulary Development

Word Origins

1. rules
2. circumstances
3. tournament

Spelling Strategy

1. correct
2. apology
3. effigy

Concept Development: Synonyms

1. a
2. b
3. b
4. c
5. b
6. c

❷ Grammar

1. at Waverly (Waverly)
2. on them (them)
3. for inserting money (money)
4. in chess (chess)
5. After the game (game); in the case (case)

Writing Application

Possible responses:

1. Don't tell that story about me.
2. We met shortly before the game.
3. Mr. Po helped me work through a strategy for winning chess games.
4. Waverly stomped after Mrs. Jong.

Integrate Language Skills

❶ Vocabulary Development Lesson

Word Origins: Words From French

Several words found in "Rules of the Game" come from the French language, including *etiquette* (rules of behavior) and *souvenirs* (mementos).

In your notebook, write the English equivalent of these Old French words.

1. *rieules* 2. *circonstances* 3. *torneiement*

Spelling Strategy

Most English words ending in *-gy* are spelled with an *o* before the *-gy*. *Prodigy*, however, is one of only four words in common usage that do not follow this rule. Review the items below. If the spelling of a word is correct, write *Correct*. If the spelling is wrong, write the proper spelling.

1. strategy 2. apoligy 3. effegy

Concept Development: Synonyms

For each item below, identify the letter of the word or phrase whose meaning is closest to that of the first word.

1. concessions: (a) things granted, (b) large meetings, (c) secrets
2. retort: (a) foolish deed, (b) clever reply, (c) old wisdom
3. malodorous: (a) evil-minded, (b) bad-smelling, (c) beautiful-sounding
4. prodigy: (a) young child, (b) large amount, (c) talented person
5. pungent: (a) sweet-tasting, (b) sharp-smelling, (c) witty
6. benevolently: (a) wealthily, (b) attractively, (c) in a kind way

❷ Grammar Lesson

Prepositional Phrases

A **prepositional phrase** is a group of words that includes a preposition and a noun or pronoun, called the *object of the preposition*. Generally, the object of the preposition is found after the preposition. In the following examples from the story, prepositional phrases are underlined, prepositions are italicized, and objects of prepositions are boldface.

Examples: She won respect *from* **others**.

No one knew it *at* the **time**.

During the tense **game**, she showed great concentration.

Practice Find the prepositional phrases in the following sentences. For each, identify the object of the preposition.

1. Nobody looked at Waverly.
2. The gifts did not have names on them.
3. The tin globe had a slit for inserting money.
4. She loved the secrets she found in chess.
5. After the game, she put the pieces in the case.

Writing Application Write four sentences, using one of these prepositional phrases in each.

1. about me
2. before the game
3. through a strategy
4. after Mrs. Jong

WG Prentice Hall Writing and Grammar Connection: Chapter 19, Section 1

TEACHING RESOURCES

The following resources can be used to enrich or extend the instruction for pp. 274–275.

Vocabulary

- **Selection Support:** Build Vocabulary, p. 61;
- **Vocabulary and Spelling Practice Book** (Use this booklet for skills enrichment.)

Grammar

- **Selection Support:** Build Grammar Skills, p. 62
- **Writing and Grammar,** Gold Level, p. 402 ■
- **Daily Language Practice Transparencies** ■

Writing

- **Writing and Grammar,** Gold Level, p. 238
- **Writing and Grammar iText CD-ROM**

■ **BLOCK SCHEDULING:** Resources marked with this symbol provide varied instruction during 90-minute blocks.

❸ Writing Lesson

Advice Column

Imagine you are a newspaper advice columnist. Write a column that provides advice to Waverly and her mother about how they can resolve their conflict.

Prewriting Jot down all of the issues between Waverly and Mrs. Jong. Next to each issue, make a suggestion about how the conflict can be resolved.

Drafting Your column should include suggestions for both characters. Remember to keep an objective tone—do not favor one character over another, but instead show concern for both of them.

Revising Read your draft, paying attention to the tone. Highlight and rewrite any language that sounds biased, or overly supportive of one character. Make sure you have addressed every issue and provided reasonable solutions to their problems.

Model: Revising to Keep an Objective Tone

Biased:	Objective:
It's not surprising that Waverly was completely embarrassed when you put her on display at the market.	It's obvious that you are very proud of your daughter, but it will help both of you if you express your pride differently.

The objective statement shows concern for both people.

WG Prentice Hall Writing and Grammar Connection: Chapter 11, Section 4

❹ Extension Activities

Listening and Speaking With a classmate, write a **dialogue** between Waverly and her mother that takes place years after the events in this story, when Waverly is an adult.

- Consider the character traits you think Waverly will have as an adult.
- Decide whether the dialogue will reflect conflict in their relationship or a better way of communicating.

Read your dialogue aloud to the class. **[Group Activity]**

Research and Technology Imagine that you are a radio announcer. Give a **radio commentary** describing a national chess tournament in which Waverly Jong is a finalist. Start your commentary by explaining the significance of the event. Remember to use a tone of voice that captures the mood of the scene. After practicing, present the commentary to your class.

Take It to the Net www.phschool.com

Go online for an additional research activity using the Internet.

Lesson Support for p. 275

❸ Writing Lesson

- Read one or two examples from an advice column in your local newspaper to give students a sense of tone for their own responses.
- After students have jotted down the issues between Waverly and her mother, work as a class to rank them according to importance.
- Select one issue and model for students an appropriate solution to the problem.
- Remind students that they are to maintain a balance between their advice to both people in the conflict.
- Use the Problem-Solution rubric, p. 14 in **Performance Assessment and Portfolio Management** to evaluate students' results.

❹ Listening and Speaking

- Discuss with students how Waverly may have changed as an adult.
- Ask students to consider whether Mrs. Jong has adjusted to American ways in later years.

CUSTOMIZED INSTRUCTION
For Universal Access

To address different learning styles use the activities suggested in the **Extension Activities** booklet, p. 16.

- For Musical/Rhythmic Learners, use Activity 4.
- For Verbal/Linguistic Learners, use Activity 5.
- For Visual/Spatial and Intrapersonal Learners, use Activity 6.

ASSESSMENT RESOURCES

The following resources can be used to assess students' knowledge and skills.

Selection Assessment

- **Formal Assessment,** Selection Test, pp. 54–56
- **Open Book Test,** pp. 46–48
- **Got It! Assessment Videotapes,** Tape 2
- **Test Bank Software**

Take It to the Net
Visit www.phschool.com for self-tests and additional questions on "Rules of the Game."

Writing Rubric

- **Performance Assess. and Portfolio Mgmt.,** p. 14

PRENTICE HALL ASSESSMENT SYSTEM

- **Workbook**
- **Skill Book**
- **Transparencies**
- **CD-ROM**

Lesson Objectives

1. To understand the connection between an author's role in writing a book and adapting the book to a movie format
2. To explore the discoveries that Amy Tan made during the movie-making process

Connections

"Rules of the Game" is an excerpt from Amy Tan's book *The Joy Luck Club*. "Joy, Luck, and Hollywood" is Tan's autobiographical account of the process of adapting her book into a movie script. Have students read "Rules of the Game" before they read this excerpt from "Joy, Luck, and Hollywood." Then, ask students to connect Tan's experiences as a moviemaker with the experiences of the characters in "Rules of the Game."

CONNECTIONS

Literature and Media

From Printed Page to Silver Screen

Amy Tan included "Rules of the Game" in her first novel, *The Joy Luck Club*. The book sold extremely well because readers connected emotionally with its characters. After only two weeks in print, *The Joy Luck Club* had become a best-seller. Tan was then asked to consider adapting her novel as a movie. Despite the allure of such an offer, this was not an easy decision for the young novelist to make. She feared losing creative control of her story and worried that a movie made in Hollywood might end up portraying stereotypes of Asian Americans. She also was not sure that the book, with its complex structure and notable lack of car chase scenes, could be adapted to the movie screen.

Tan managed to put her initial fears aside after meeting the director and co-writer, but during the filmmaking process she encountered a new set of worries. In the following excerpt from a newspaper article, Tan discusses how the process of making a movie from her book was more difficult—and rewarding—than she ever anticipated.

from Joy, Luck, and Hollywood

Amy Tan

Los Angeles Times, September 5, 1993

I CRIED MY EYES OUT

I saw all the dailies,[1] most of them on video format at home. I cried throughout the making of the movie. I was very moved by what I was seeing. I was exhausted watching what the actors went through. At major stages, Ron and I worked with Wayne and the editor, Maysie Hoy, as the movie was being cut. That process was fascinating but tedious. I ended up thinking Maysie was a saint.

Around April, I got to see a first rough cut.[2] I was supposed to watch it and take notes of problem areas and such. But I was too mesmerized to do anything but watch it pretty much like an ordinary moviegoer. I laughed, I cried. The second time I saw it, I said to Wayne: "I want you to remember this day. We're going to get a lot of different reactions to this film later down the road. But I want us to remember that on this day, you, Ron and I were proud with what we've accomplished. We made our vision."

Ron insisted that I come to the test previews because there I'd get some of the biggest highs or lows of my life, seeing how a real audience reacted. Fortunately, it was the former. I was surprised, though, whenever people laughed during a scene I never considered funny. I suppose it was one of those ironic laughs, in which one recognizes the pain of some childhood humiliation.

I've now seen the movie about 25 times, and I am not ashamed to say I'm moved to tears each time.

By the time you read this, I will have seen the movie with my mother and my half sister, who just immigrated from China. So that'll be my version of life imitating art, or sitting in front of it. I'm nervous about what my mother will think. I'm afraid she'll be overwhelmed by

mesmerized (mez′ mər izeď) *v.* hypnotized; fascinated

ironic (ī rän′ ik) *adj.* directly opposite to what is or what might be expected

1. **dailies** (dā′ lēz) *n.* movie term to describe the photographic prints made from the previous day's filming. Directors and actors use dailies to assess the progress of the film and the quality of actors' performances.
2. **rough cut** *n.* early version of an entire film. The rough cut allows the director and writers to receive reactions and suggest additional revisions for the finished film.

Reading Check

What was Amy Tan's initial reaction to seeing the first rough cut?

From Printed Page to Silver Screen

- Point out that *The Joy Luck Club* (the source of the story "Rules of the Game") is a book based on Amy Tan's personal experiences growing up as the daughter of a woman who was born and raised in China.
- Explain that "Joy, Luck, and Hollywood" is an autobiographical account of Tan's experiences adapting her book to a movie.
- Point out that creating the movie forced the author to face her fears of losing control over the story she had crafted from her own life experiences.

Reading Check

Answer: Tan was "mesmerized" by the film and delighted that she and the filmmakers had achieved their vision.

Background

Amy Tan

Amy Tan was born in Oakland, California, on February 19, 1952. She spent her childhood in the San Francisco Bay Area, then graduated from high school in Montreux, Switzerland. Tan received her master's degree in linguistics from San Jose State University in California. Since her first book, *The Joy Luck Club,* was published, Tan has written several more books and has become one of the most acclaimed authors in the United States.

▶ Critical Viewing

Possible responses: Students may note that the photograph shows Amy Tan in a thoughtful, reflective mood.

▲ **Critical Viewing** What impression does this portrait convey about the author, Amy Tan? **[Respond]**

some of the scenes that are taken from her life, especially the one that depicts the suicide of her mother.

I hope those in the audience are moved by the film, that they connect with the emotions and feel changed at the end, that they feel closer to another person as a result. That's what I like to get out of a book, a connection with the world.

As to reviews, I've already imagined all the bad things that can be said. That way I'll be delighted by anything good that comes out. I'm aware that the success of this movie will depend on good reviews and word-of-mouth reactions. But there comes a point when you've done all you can. And then it's out of your control. Certainly I hope the movie's a success at the box office,[3] mostly for Wayne and Ron's sakes, as well as the cast and crew who worked on this. And certainly I hope Disney feels it was more than justified in taking a risk on this movie. By my score, however, the movie is already a success. We made the movie we wanted to make. It's not perfect, but we're happy with it. And I'll be standing in line, ready to plunk down $7 to see it.

In the meantime, I've got a whole mess of Chinese lucky charms that are absolutely guaranteed to bring the gods to the theater.

I'VE LEARNED MY LESSONS

At different points in the making of the movie, I vowed I'd never do this again. It's too time-consuming. It's rife with ups and downs. There's so much business. I've developed calluses and a certain sang-froid[4] attitude about some of the inherent difficulties of filmmaking.

Yet, against all my expectations, I like working collaboratively from time to time. I like fusing ideas into one vision. I like seeing that vision come to life with other people who know exactly what it took to get there.

My love of fiction is unaltered. It's my first love. But, yes, I'll make another film with Ron and Wayne. It'll probably be my second novel, "The Kitchen God's Wife." We've already started breaking the scenes out with page counts and narrative text. We started the day after we saw the first rough cut of "The Joy Luck Club."

Thematic Connection
Do you think that readers react the same way to books as audiences react to movie adaptations?

rife (rīf) *adj.* abundant

inherent (in her′ənt) *adj.* existing as a natural, inborn quality

collaboratively (kə lab′ə rə tiv lē) *adv.* together as a team

---

3. **box office** *n.* place where movie tickets are sold.
4. **sang-froid** (sän frwä′) coolness under pressure. (From the French, meaning "cold blood.")

Connecting Literature and Media

1. Which parts of "Rules of the Game" might be difficult to adapt to the movie screen?
2. Which parts of the story are especially well suited to a movie adaptation?
3. What did Tan find most rewarding about the transformation of her work to film?

Thematic Connection

Answer: Readers' reactions to books often vary from audiences' reactions to movies. Books leave much more room for the reader's imagination, while movies provide a specific visual interpretation.

Answers

Connecting Literature and Media

1. It might be difficult to express the narrator's thoughts and personal observations on screen.
2. Scenes of action and dialogue are especially well-suited to a movie adaptation.
3. Tan found it most rewarding that, in producing the movie, she was successful at expressing her "vision."

ENRICHMENT: Media Connection

Film Review

"Rules of the Game" is from Amy Tan's book *The Joy Luck Club,* which was made into a movie in 1993. A movie critic from a Chicago newspaper said the movie "comes rushing off the screen in a torrent of memories, as if its characters have been saving their stories for years, waiting for the right moment to share them. . . . [The stories] bring the past back in all of its power, and show . . . how children who think they are so very different are deeply affected by the experiences of their parents.

Checkouts ✦ Fifteen

Lesson Objectives and CA Correlations

1. **To analyze and respond to literary elements**
   - Literary Analysis: Irony **R 3.8**
   - Comparing Literary Works
2. **To read, comprehend, analyze, and critique a short story and a poem**
   - Reading Strategy: Relating to Personal Experience
   - Reading Check questions
   - Review and Assess questions
   - Assessment Practice (ATE)
3. **To develop word analysis skills, fluency, and systematic vocabulary**
   - Vocabulary Development Lesson: Latin Suffix: *-ment* **R 1.1**
4. **To understand and apply written and oral language conventions**
   - Spelling Strategy
   - Grammar Lesson: Prepositional Phrases as Modifiers **LC 1.3**
5. **To understand and apply appropriate writing and research strategies**
   - Writing Lesson: Character's Journal **W 2.2**
   - Extension Activity: Script for a Scene **W 1.1**
6. **To understand and apply listening and speaking strategies**
   - Extension Activity: Oral Story **LS 1.8**

STEP-BY-STEP TEACHING GUIDE	PACING GUIDE
PRETEACH	
Motivate Students and Provide Background	
Use the Motivation activity (ATE p. 280)	5 min.
Read and discuss the Preview material and Background information (SE/ATE p. 280) [A]	10 min.
Introduce the Concepts	
Introduce the Literary Analysis and Reading Strategy (SE/ATE p. 281) [A]	15 min.
Pronounce the vocabulary words and read their definitions (SE p. 281)	5 min.
TEACH	
Monitor Comprehension	
Informally monitor comprehension by circulating while students read independently or in groups [A]	20 min.
Monitor students' comprehension with the Reading Check note (SE/ATE p. 283)	as students read
Develop vocabulary with Vocabulary notes (SE pp. 283–285)	as students read
Develop Understanding	
Develop students' understanding of irony with the Literary Analysis annotations (SE/ATE pp. 283, 284) [A]	10 min.
Develop students' ability to relate to personal experience with the Reading Strategy annotations (SE/ATE p. 284)	10 min.
ASSESS	
Assess Mastery	
Assess students' mastery of the Reading Strategy and Literary Analysis by having them answer the Review and Assess questions (SE/ATE p. 287)	20 min.
Use one or more of the print and media Assessment Resources (ATE p. 289) [A]	up to 50 min.
EXTEND	
Apply Understanding	
Have students complete the Vocabulary Development Lesson and the Grammar Lesson (SE p. 288) [A]	20 min.
Apply students' knowledge of writing to their audience using the Writing Lesson (SE/ATE p. 289) [A]	45 min.
Apply students' understanding using one or more of the Extension Activities (SE p. 289)	20–90 min.

[A] **ACCELERATED INSTRUCTION:** Use the strategies and activities identified with an [A].

UNIVERSAL ACCESS
- ● = Below-Level Students
- ▲ = On-Level Students
- ■ = Above-Level Students

Time and Resource Manager

Reading Level: Average, Easy
Average Number of Instructional Days: 4

RESOURCES		
PRINT	**TRANSPARENCIES**	**TECHNOLOGY**
• **Beyond Literature,** Humanities Connection: Fine Art, p. 17 ▲ ■		• **Interest Grabber Video,** Tape 2 ● ▲ ■
• **Selection Support Workbook:** ● ▲ ■ Literary Analysis, p. 68 Reading Strategy, p. 67 Build Vocabulary, p. 65	• **Literary Analysis and Reading Transparencies,** pp. 33 and 34 ● ▲ ■	
• **Adapted Reader's Companion** ● • **Reader's Companion** ●		• **Listening to Literature** ● ▲ ■ Audiocassettes, Side 9 Audio CDs, CD 7
• **English Learner's Companion** ● ▲ • **Literatura en español** ● ▲ • **Literary Analysis for Enrichment** ■	• **Fine Art Transparencies, Volume 1,** Art Transparency 19 ● ▲ ■	
• **Formal Assessment:** Selection Test, pp. 57–59 ● ▲ ■ • **Open Book Test,** pp. 49–51 ● ▲ ■ • **Performance Assessment and Portfolio Management,** p. 28 ● ▲ ■ • PRENTICE HALL ASSESSMENT SYSTEM ● ▲ ■	• PRENTICE HALL ASSESSMENT SYSTEM ● ▲ ■ Skills Practice Answers and Explanations on Transparencies	• **Test Bank Software** ● ▲ ■ • **Got It! Assessment Videotapes,** Tape 2 ● ▲
• **Selection Support Workbook:** ● ▲ ■ Build Grammar Skills, p. 66 • **Writing and Grammar,** Gold Level ● ▲ ■ • **Extension Activities,** p. 17 ● ▲ ■	• **Daily Language Practice Transparencies** ● ▲	• **Writing and Grammar iText CD-ROM** ● ▲ ■ ***Take It to the Net*** www.phschool.com

BLOCK SCHEDULING: Use one 90-minute class period to preteach the selection and have students read it. Use a second 90-minute class period to assess students' mastery of skills and have them complete one of the Extension Activities.

PRETEACH

Step-by-Step Teaching Guide for pp. 280–281

Motivation

In class, have five students form a panel to discuss briefly their opinions about what can happen when people fall in love or develop a strong infatuation at first sight. Then, open up the discussion to comments and questions from the rest of the class. Wrap up the activity and explain that "Checkouts" describes one course that love at first sight can take.

Interest Grabber Video

As an alternative, play "White-Water Rafting Guides" on Tape 2 to engage student interest.

1 Background

Cultural Connection

Explain to students that in many cultures, work experiences are a way that teens learn more about their abilities, interests, strengths, and weaknesses. Rural teens may perform work that requires them to drive farm machinery and trucks. Suburban and urban teens often work in retail, in malls or supermarkets. The bag boy in this story has one of the more common jobs for teenagers.

Prepare to Read

Checkouts ◆ Fifteen

Food City, 1967, Richard Estes, Collection of the Akron Art Museum, Akron, Ohio

Take It to the Net

Visit www.phschool.com for interactive activities and instruction related to the selections, including
- background
- graphic organizers
- literary elements
- reading strategies

Preview

Connecting to the Literature

You get on the school bus and sit alone instead of taking a seat next to someone you do not know. You cannot go to a concert because you are battling the flu. Missed opportunities for new adventures occur just about every day. In these two selections, young people experience lost opportunities for different reasons.

1 Background

In "Checkouts," the main character is compared to "a Tibetan monk in solitary meditation." The Buddhist monks of Tibet live in seclusion, often meditating, or clearing the mind of all thoughts, to achieve a state of perfect calmness. In "Checkouts," the main character achieves this state by grocery shopping!

TEACHING RESOURCES

The following resources can be used to enrich or extend the instruction for pp. 280–281.

Motivation

Interest Grabber Video, Tape 2

Background

Beyond Literature, p. 17 ■

Take It to the Net

Visit www.phschool.com for background and hotlinks for the selections.

Literary Analysis

Literary Analysis and Reading Transparencies, Irony, p. 34

Reading

Selection Support: Reading Strategy, p. 67; Build Vocabulary, p. 65

Literary Analysis and Reading Transparencies, Relating to Personal Experience, p. 34 ■

■ **BLOCK SCHEDULING:** Resources marked with this symbol provide varied instruction during 90-minute blocks.

❷ Literary Analysis

Irony

Irony is the contrast between an actual outcome and what the reader or the characters expect, or what might logically be expected. Irony can add humor to some situations; it can also invite readers to stop and think. In this example from "Checkouts," notice the discrepancy in ideas and how it creates irony.

> Then one day the bag boy dropped her jar of mayonnaise and that is how she fell in love.

You would probably expect a person to be frustrated if a bag boy dropped a jar of mayonnaise. In "Checkouts," however, the action generates an unexpected outcome.

Comparing Literary Works

The following selections share a theme of self-discovery. In "Checkouts," a girl falls in love, and in "Fifteen," a boy chances upon a riderless motorcycle. These opportunities for new experiences lead the teenagers to discoveries about themselves. As you read, compare and contrast the opportunities, losses, and discoveries each character faces.

❸ Reading Strategy

Relating to Personal Experience

You can appreciate and understand a character's story by **relating it to your personal experience**. To do this, use the following strategies:

- Decide how the events in the story are like your own experiences.
- Consider how you or people you know would feel in the same situation.

Make a chart like the one shown here to keep track of your thoughts.

Story Detail
The bag boy's job

Personal Experience the Incident Recalls
My first job as a grocery store cashier

Feelings It Evokes
Nervousness, anxiety

Vocabulary Development

intuition (in´ to͞o ish´ ən) *n.* knowledge of something without reasoning (p. 283)

reverie (rev´ ər ē) *n.* dreamy thought of pleasant things (p. 283)

shards (shärdz) *n.* broken pieces (p. 283)

harried (har´ ēd) *adj.* worried (p. 283)

brazen (brā´ zən) *adj.* shamelessly bold (p. 283)

dishevelment (di shev´ əl ment) *n.* state of being untidy (p. 284)

perverse (pər vʉrs´) *adj.* contrary and willful (p. 284)

articulate (är tik´ yo͞o lāt´) *v.* express in words (p. 284)

lingered (liŋ´ gərd) *v.* stayed on, as if unwilling to leave (p. 285)

demure (di myoor´) *adj.* shy or modest (p. 286)

❷ Literary Analysis

Irony and Comparing Literary Works

- Tell students that as they read "Checkouts," they will focus on *irony*, the contrast between what is expected by the characters and the readers and what actually occurs.
- Now have the class read the instruction about irony and call their attention to the example from the story.
- Use the instruction for Comparing Literary Works to alert students to look for examples of young people making discoveries about themselves in the two selections.

❸ Reading Strategy

Relating to Personal Experience

- Remind students that reading about the experiences of others often helps people remember similar experiences in their own lives, as well as the feelings and lessons associated with those experiences.
- Assign the class to work through the Reading Transparency in **Literary Analysis and Reading Transparencies,** p. 33. Then, have them create a chart, like the one on this page, to keep track of details from the story that remind them of similar experiences in their own lives.

Vocabulary Development

- Pronounce each vocabulary word for students, and read the definitions as a class. Have students identify any words with which they are already familiar.

CUSTOMIZE INSTRUCTION FOR UNIVERSAL ACCESS

For Special Needs Students	For Less Proficient Readers	For English Learners
Have students read the adapted version of "Checkouts" in the **Adapted Reader's Companion.** This version provides basic-level instruction in an interactive format with questions and write-on lines. Completing the adapted version will prepare students to read the selection in the Student Edition.	Have students read the selection in the **Reader's Companion.** This version provides basic-level instruction in an interactive format with questions and write-on lines. After students finish the selection in **Reader's Companion,** have them complete the questions and activities in the Student Edition.	Have students read the adapted version of the selection in the **English Learner's Companion.** This version provides basic-level instruction in an interactive format with questions and write-on lines. Completing the adapted version will prepare students to read the selection in the Student Edition.

E-Teach

Visit E-Teach at www.phschool.com for teachers' essays on how to teach, with questions and answers.

TEACH

Step-by-Step Teaching Guide for pp. 282–286

CUSTOMIZE INSTRUCTION
For Visual/Spatial Learners

Encourage students to use the art on this page to help them picture the story's setting. What details are included in the art that are not included in the story?

Answer: There are numerous details, including the price listings and the stacks of food, which are shown in the art but not mentioned in the story.

❶ About the Selection

In this story, a girl and a boy fall in love at first sight, but never actually meet. Readers might expect such a missed opportunity to lead to a sad ending, but in "Checkouts," the plot takes a different turn. For both characters, the unrealized romance leads to new opportunities, not only for friendships and romance, but also for self-discovery. Students will easily relate to this story—a familiar one to many teenagers.

❷ ▶Critical Viewing

Answer: The bright signs and many displays of food in the aisles and in the windows might help distract people.

❶

Checkouts

Cynthia Rylant

Food City, 1967, Richard Estes, Akron Art Museum, Akron, Ohio, © Richard Estes / Licensed by Vaga, New York, NY / Courtesy of Marlborough Gallery, NY

Her parents had moved her to Cincinnati, to a large house with beveled glass[1] windows and several porches and the *history* her mother liked to emphasize. You'll love the house, they said. You'll be lonely at first, they admitted, but you're so nice you'll make friends fast. And as an impulse tore at her to lie on the floor, to hold to their ankles and tell them she felt she was dying, to offer anything, anything at all, so they might allow her to finish growing up in the town of her childhood, they firmed their mouths and spoke from their chests and they said, It's decided.

❷ ▲ **Critical Viewing** What distractions found in a supermarket might help people take their minds off their troubles? **[Analyze]**

1. **beveled** (bev´ əld) **glass** glass having angled or slanted edges.

TEACHING RESOURCES

The following resources can be used to enrich or extend the instruction for pp. 282–286.

Literary Analysis

- **Selection Support:** Literary Analysis, p. 68 ■

Reading

- **Reader's Companion**
- **English Learner's Companion**
- **Listening to Literature Audiocassettes,** Side 10
- **Listening to Literature Audio CDs,** CD 8

Extension

- **Fine Art Transparencies, Volume 1,** Art Transparency 19 (Have students infer what can be known about the person who owns the objects pictured in this still life.) ■

■ **BLOCK SCHEDULING:** Resources marked with this symbol provide varied instruction during 90-minute blocks.

They moved her to Cincinnati, where for a month she spent the greater part of every day in a room full of beveled glass windows, sifting through photographs of the life she'd lived and left behind. But it is difficult work, suffering, and in its own way a kind of art, and finally she didn't have the energy for it anymore, so she emerged from the beautiful house and fell in love with a bag boy at the supermarket. Of course, this didn't happen all at once, just like that, but in the sequence of things that's exactly the way it happened.

3 She liked to grocery shop. She loved it in the way some people love to drive long country roads, because doing it she could think and relax and wander. Her parents wrote up the list and handed it to her and off she went without complaint to perform what they regarded as a great sacrifice of her time and a sign that she was indeed a very nice girl. 4 She had never told them how much she loved grocery shopping, only that she was "willing" to do it. She had an intuition which told her that her parents were not safe for sharing such strong, important facts about herself. Let them think they knew her.

Once inside the supermarket, her hands firmly around the handle of the cart, she would lapse into a kind of reverie and wheel toward the produce. Like a Tibetan monk in solitary meditation, she calmed to a point of deep, deep happiness; this feeling came to her, reliably, if strangely, only in the supermarket.

Then one day the bag boy dropped her jar of mayonnaise and that is how she fell in love.

He was nervous—first day on the job—and along had come this fascinating girl, standing in the checkout line with the unfocused stare one often sees in young children, her face turned enough away that he might take several full looks at her as he packed sturdy bags full of food and the goods of modern life. She interested him because her hair was red and thick, and in it she had placed a huge orange bow, nearly the size of a small hat. That was enough to distract him, and when finally it was her groceries he was packing, she looked at him and smiled and he could respond only by busting her jar of mayonnaise on the floor, shards of glass and oozing cream decorating the area around his feet.

She loved him at exactly that moment, and if he'd known this perhaps he wouldn't have fallen into the brown depression he fell into, which lasted the rest of his shift. He believed he must have looked the fool in her eyes, and he envied the sureness of everyone around him: the cocky cashier at the register, the grim and harried store manager, the bland butcher, and the brazen bag boys who smoked in the warehouse on their breaks. He wanted a second chance. Another chance to be confident and say witty things to her as he threw tin cans into her bags, persuading her to allow him to help her to her car so he might learn just a little about her, check out the floor of the car for signs of hobbies or fetishes and the bumpers for clues as to beliefs and loyalties.

But he busted her jar of mayonnaise and nothing else worked out for the rest of the day.

Literary Analysis
Irony What is ironic about her love for grocery shopping?

intuition (in´ to͞o ish´ ən) *n.* knowledge of something without reasoning

reverie (rev´ ər ē) *n.* dreamy thought of pleasant things

shards (shärdz) *n.* broken pieces

harried (har´ ēd) *adj.* worried

brazen (brā´ zən) *adj.* shamelessly bold

5 **Reading Check**
Why does the girl fascinate the bag boy?

CUSTOMIZE INSTRUCTION FOR UNIVERSAL ACCESS

For Less Proficient Readers	For Gifted/Talented Students
Ask students to use the given definition and the context of the vocabulary words on this page to answer the following extension questions: Do you remember the last time you had a *reverie?* What it was about? What do you have in your home that would turn into *shards* if you dropped it? Which of these situations would cause you to be *harried:* studying for a difficult test or playing with the family pet? Which of these is a *brazen* act: washing the car, talking to a friend on the phone, or having a noisy outdoor party late on a school night?	Suggest that students put themselves in the character of the red-haired girl or the bag boy when the boy drops the mayonnaise jar. Have students compose a diary entry describing what happened as he or she lived through the experience. Students may describe their actions, thoughts, and feelings and conclude their diary entry by answering this question: What did this experience teach me about myself?

3 Critical Thinking

Infer

- Point out that most people keep some of their thoughts secret, even from those closest to them. Students might think about their own secrets, which they consider too personal and/or important to be shared even with family members or friends.
- Ask students what is meant by the last two sentences in this passage. **Possible response:** The girl thinks her parents are not to be trusted with certain knowledge about their daughter. If she keeps things secret, they will think they know her.
- Have students speculate on how their knowledge that the girl has secret likes and dislikes can add to their own enjoyment of the story. **Answer:** Similar personal experiences help a reader identify with a character.

4 Literary Analysis

Irony

- Remind students that irony is a literary technique in which the outcome of a situation is different from what the reader or the characters would logically expect.
- Ask students how the parents feel about their daughter when she goes shopping. **Answer:** They think she is a very nice girl to do this task, which they consider a sacrifice of time.
- Have the class answer the Literary Analysis question on p. 283: What is ironic about her love for grocery shopping? **Answer:** She loves grocery shopping, so when her parents give her credit for sacrificing her time to do what they consider to be a boring task, she is really doing a job she loves.

5 Reading Check

Answer: The bag boy is fascinated by her thick, red hair with the huge orange bow. Also, she distracts him from his boring job.

6 Literary Analysis

Irony

- Ask students to identify some of the words and phrases that describe the bag boy.
  Possible response: *clumsiness, hair falling into his eyes, tattered brown shoes, no socks, awkwardness,* and *dishevelment*
- Then, have students identify the words and phrases that describe the girl's feelings about the boy in this passage.
  Possible response: *stars in her eyes, loved* the way he worked and looked, and *wonderful contrast*

Monitor Progress Ask students to recall the meaning of irony. Then, ask them the Literary Analysis question on p. 284: What is ironic about the teenagers' response to each other?
Answer: Generally, one would not think that *awkwardness, shabbiness,* and *clumsiness* are characteristics that inspire the beginnings of love or infatuation. Ironically, these feelings are exactly what the girl experiences.

7 Reading Strategy

Relating to Personal Experience

- Have students read the passage and think of times in their lives during which the possibility of seeing someone or doing something kept them happy to be alive.
- Ask students the Reading Strategy question on p. 284: Why might it be easy for a teenage reader to appreciate what the bag boy is feeling?
  Answer: Teenagers feel emotions very strongly. They are often bored with school and after-school work and are very eager to find something that makes them feel alive.

6 Strange, how attractive clumsiness can be. She left the supermarket with stars in her eyes, for she had loved the way his long nervous fingers moved from the conveyor belt to the bags, how deftly (until the mayonnaise) they had picked up her items and placed them in her bags. She had loved the way the hair kept falling into his eyes as he leaned over to grab a box or a tin. And the tattered brown shoes he wore with no socks. And the left side of his collar turned in rather than out.

The bag boy seemed a wonderful contrast to the perfectly beautiful house she had been forced to accept as her home, to the *history* she hated, to the loneliness she had become used to, and she couldn't wait to come back for more of his awkwardness and dishevelment.

Incredibly, it was another four weeks before they saw each other again. As fate would have it, her visits to the supermarket never coincided with his schedule to bag. Each time she went to the store, her eyes scanned the checkouts at once, her heart in her mouth. And each hour he worked, the bag boy kept one eye on the door, watching for the red-haired girl with the big orange bow.

7 Yet in their disappointment these weeks there was a kind of ecstasy. It is reason enough to be alive, the hope you may see again some face which has meant something to you. The anticipation of meeting the bag boy eased the girl's painful transition into her new and jarring life in Cincinnati. It provided for her an anchor amid all that was impersonal and unfamiliar, and she spent less time on thoughts of what she had left behind as she concentrated on what might lie ahead. And for the boy, the long and often tedious hours at the supermarket which provided no challenge other than that of showing up the following workday . . . these hours became possibilities of mystery and romance for him as he watched the electric doors for the girl in the orange bow.

And when finally they did meet up again, neither offered a clue to the other that he, or she, had been the object of obsessive thought for weeks. She spotted him as soon as she came into the store, but she kept her eyes strictly in front of her as she pulled out a cart and wheeled it toward the produce. And he, too, knew the instant she came through the door—though the orange bow was gone, replaced by a small but bright yellow flower instead—and he never once turned his head in her direction but watched her from the corner of his vision as he tried to swallow back the fear in his throat.

It is odd how we sometimes deny ourselves the very pleasure we have longed for and which is finally within our reach. For some perverse reason she would not have been able to articulate, the girl did not bring her cart up to the bag boy's checkout when her shopping was done. And the bag boy let her leave the store, pretending no notice of her.

This is often the way of children, when they truly want a thing, to pretend that they don't. And then they grow angry when no one tried harder to give them this thing they so casually rejected, and they

Literary Analysis
Irony What is ironic about the teenagers' response to each other?

dishevelment (di shev´ əl ment) *n.* state of being untidy

Reading Strategy
Relating to Personal Experience Why might it be easy for a teenage reader to appreciate what the bag boy is feeling?

perverse (pər vʉrs´) *adj.* contrary and willful

articulate (är tik´ yə lāt) *v.* express in words

ENRICHMENT: Art Connection

Architecture

The only detail mentioned about the house in Cincinnati is the "beveled glass windows." Because most modern homes have plain windows, beveling suggests an older style of architecture. Students may be interested in finding out more about older styles of architecture found in American houses:

- New England or Cape Cod houses are made of wood with small rooms and sloping roofs.
- Southern Colonial houses are large with high-pitches roofs, columns in front, and porches.
- Victorian houses have elaborate designs and large rooms.

Have students choose a style of architecture to research and report on. Suggest that picturing the girl in "Checkouts" in a particular type of house might help make the story more real for them.

soon find themselves in a rage simply because they cannot say yes when they mean yes. Humans are very complicated. (And perhaps cats, who have been known to react in the same way, though the resulting rage can only be guessed at.)

The girl hated herself for not checking out at the boy's line, and the boy hated himself for not catching her eye and saying hello, and they most sincerely hated each other without having ever exchanged even two minutes of conversation.

Eventually—in fact, within the week—a kind and intelligent boy who lived very near her beautiful house asked the girl to a movie and she gave up her fancy for the bag boy at the supermarket. And the bag boy himself grew so bored with his job that he made a desperate search for something better and ended up in a bookstore where
8 scores of fascinating girls lingered like honeybees about a hive. Some months later the bag boy and the girl with the orange bow again crossed paths, standing in line with their dates at a movie theater, and, glancing toward the other, each smiled slightly, then looked away, as strangers on public buses often do, when one is moving off the bus and the other is moving on.

lingered (liŋ´ gərd) *v.* stayed on, as if unwilling to leave

Cynthia Rylant

(b. 1954)

Quiet, thoughtful characters who are isolated in some way are Cynthia Rylant's specialty. She has said, "I don't want to deal with the people who have what they want. I want to deal with people who don't have what they want, to show their lives, too."

Rylant discovered a love of good writing in college English classes. She never considered becoming a writer herself, however, until she took a job as a librarian and began reading children's books. Since publishing *When I Was Young in the Mountains* in 1982, Rylant has produced picture books, poetry, short stories, and novels. In 1993, her novel *Missing May* won the Newbery Award.

Review and Assess

Thinking About the Selection

1. **Respond:** Were you disappointed that the girl and boy did not get together? Explain.
2. **(a) Recall:** How does the girl feel about grocery shopping? **(b) Infer:** What do you learn about the girl from her attitude toward grocery shopping?
3. **(a) Recall:** What do the boy and girl think about while they are apart? **(b) Analyze:** How might their unacknowledged romance be useful to both the girl and the boy?
4. **(a) Recall:** What happens at the end of the story? **(b) Speculate:** How do you think the two characters feel when they see each other at the movie theater?
5. **(a) Compare:** How are the girl and the bag boy alike? **(b) Analyze:** What effect do their similarities have on the tension of the story?
6. **Evaluate:** One critic said that in some stories, Cynthia Rylant relies on telling rather than showing what her characters are like. Do you think this criticism applies to this story? Give examples to support your opinion.
7. **Draw Conclusions:** Does the experience described in the story seem like a missed opportunity or a necessary outcome? Explain.

ASSESS

8 Critical Thinking

Generalize

- Encourage students to suggest a moral for the story, such as "It takes many infatuations to find a true romance," or "A closed mouth is no way to make a date," and so forth.
- After students have reread the passage, ask them what each character might be thinking when they both meet again.
  Possible response: They might wish they had spoken up when they had the chance, or they might think that their relationship was not meant to be, and so on.

Answers for p. 285

Review and Assess

1. Many students will express disappointment that the two characters do not get together. Readers might say that they have been led to expect this kind of ending from a traditional story.
2. **(a)** The girl loves grocery shopping. **(b)** She likes ordinary activities rather than adventure or excitement.
3. **(a)** They think about each other. **(b)** The unspoken romance helps the girl to stop dwelling on the past and to make a transition to her new community. It gives the boy the courage to look for a new, less boring job.
4. **(a)** The boy and the girl see each other standing in a movie line, each on a date with someone else. **(b)** Each may feel that the other is much like a stranger one smiles at in passing.
5. **(a)** Both are unwilling to take risks and reach out for adventure. **(b)** Their similarities prevent them from reaching out to each other and developing a relationship.
6. Some students may agree with the criticism, pointing to several paragraphs in which the author makes general statements. For example the one that begins, "This is often the way of children. . ." Others may argue that the criticism does not apply by mentioning that the author shows a very specific reason for the girl's falling in love.

continued

Answers continued

7. Some students will say that it seems like a necessary outcome because if they had really wanted to meet, they would have made more of an effort. Others will say it was a missed opportunity because it's hard to find someone similar in disposition.

ASSESS

9 About the Selection

In this poem, a fifteen-year-old boy's discovery of a motorcycle leads him to an even more important discovery about himself. Although he fantasizes about the wonderful adventures he might have with the motorcycle, he ends up finding and helping the injured rider—allowing the mature side of his character to prevail.

10 Reading Strategy

Relating to Personal Experience

- Have students speculate why the poet repeats the line "I was fifteen" several times.
  Possible response: Students may suggest that the narrator is feeling good about making a strong moral decision at such a young age. They may also suggest that he is making a case that he is too young to be expected to give up the motorcycle in place of doing the right thing.
- Since students are already fifteen or are just about to turn fifteen, ask them to write an account of something they have learned about themselves at this age. Do they think that fifteen is too young to learn important life lessons?

Answers for p. 286

Review and Assess

1. Most students will probably say that they would have looked for the owner of the motorcycle because that would be the ethical thing to do.
2. **(a)** Words and phrases include: *flanks, demure, companion, got back a confident opinion.* **(b)** He admires its "pulsing gleam."
3. **(a)** He imagines finding the end of a road and meeting the sky. **(b)** It represents adventure.
4. **(a)** He helps the owner walk to the motorcycle. **(b)** Instead of indulging his fantasy, he looks for the owner of the motorcycle. **(c)** He has a youthful spirit of adventure, but he is developing a mature sense of responsibility.
5. Fantasy is about having whatever you wish for. Reality is about balancing such wishes with responsibility.

9 Fifteen

William Stafford

South of the bridge on Seventeenth
I found back of the willows one summer
day a motorcycle with engine running
as it lay on its side, ticking over
slowly in the high grass. I was fifteen.

I admired all that pulsing gleam, the
shiny flanks, the demure headlights
fringed where it lay; I led it gently
to the road and stood with that
companion, ready and friendly. I was fifteen.

We could find the end of a road, meet
the sky on out Seventeenth. I thought about
hills, and patting the handle got back a
confident opinion. On the bridge we indulged
a forward feeling, a tremble. I was fifteen.

10
Thinking, back farther in the grass I found
the owner, just coming to, where he had flipped
over the rail. He had blood on his hand, was pale—
I helped him walk to his machine. He ran his hand
over it, called me a good man, roared away.

I stood there, fifteen.

demure (di myoor′) *adj.* shy or modest

William Stafford

(1914–1993)

Reading a poem by William Stafford is like conversing with the poet. According to commentator Robert Bly, Stafford's poems are "spoken like a friend over coffee."

Stafford grew up in Kansas but later taught and wrote in Oregon. He did not publish his first book, *West of Your City*, until he was forty-six. From then on, he was prolific. He wrote a poem every day and published numerous collections, including *Traveling Through the Dark*, winner of the National Book Award in 1963.

Review and Assess

Thinking About the Selection

1. **Respond:** What would you have done if you had been in the speaker's place? Why?
2. **(a) Recall:** Which words in the first half of the poem make the motorcycle seem human? **(b) Infer:** On what basis is the speaker first attracted to the motorcycle?
3. **(a) Recall:** What does the boy imagine doing with the motorcycle? **(b) Infer:** What does the motorcycle represent to him?
4. **(a) Recall:** How does the speaker help the owner of the motorcycle? **(b) Compare and Contrast:** How do the speaker's actions contrast with his fantasy? **(c) Draw Conclusions:** What does this contrast tell you about the speaker?
5. **Apply:** What message does this poem convey about the contrasts between fantasy and reality? Explain.

ASSESSMENT PRACTICE: Reading Comprehension

Stated Main Idea (For more practice, see Test Preparation Workbook, p. 17.)

Write the following sample item on the board.

Reading a poem by William Stafford is like having a conversation with the poet. He uses familiar language and relates ordinary events. Through his poems, he asks and answers questions. Like a conversation, his poems leave you thinking.

Which of the following states the main idea?

A He uses familiar language and relates ordinary events.

B Through his poems he asks and answers questions.

C Reading a poem by William Stafford is like having a conversation with the poet.

D Like a conversation, his poems leave you thinking.

Only *C* states a main idea that encompasses the other details in the paragraph.

Review and Assess

Literary Analysis

Irony

1. Why is it **ironic** that the girl falls in love with the bag boy?
2. In "Fifteen," why is it ironic that the owner of the motorcycle calls the speaker "good man"?
3. (a) Using a chart like the one shown below, explain what is ironic about the endings of "Checkouts" and "Fifteen." (b) In each story, what point does the ironic ending make?

Action of Story	Expected Ending	Actual Ending

Comparing Literary Works

4. (a) Using a chart like the one below, compare the two characters in "Checkouts" to the boy in "Fifteen." (b) Who do you think learns the most about himself or herself? Why?

Character	Experiences	Feelings	Missed Opportunity	Self-discovery

Reading Strategy

Relating to Personal Experience

5. (a) Which **personal experiences** do the events in "Fifteen" call to mind? (b) How do your memories of these experiences help you to appreciate the speaker's feelings and actions?
6. What advice would you have given the girl in "Checkouts"?
7. Do you think that the unacknowledged romance in "Checkouts" is true to life? Why or why not?

Extend Understanding

8. **Cultural Connection:** Teenagers sometimes are said to have a culture all their own. Do you think that reading either selection would help adults understand "teen culture" better? Why or why not?

Quick Review

Irony is the discrepancy between what readers or characters expect and what actually happens.

Relate a story **to personal experience** by connecting characters and events to people, situations, and feelings you know.

Take It to the Net

www.phschool.com

Take the interactive self-test online to check your understanding of the selections.

ENRICHMENT: Further Reading

Other Works by the Authors

Other Works by Cynthia Rylant

A Couple of Kooks and Other Stories About Love

Every Living Thing

Other Works by William Stafford

Traveling Through the Dark

West of Your City

Take It to the Net

Visit www.phschool.com for more information on Cynthia Rylant and William Stafford.

Answers for p. 287

Review and Assess

1. It is ironic because one might reasonably expect her to fall in love with someone attractive and self-assured.
2. The speaker is only fifteen.
3. **(a)** "Checkouts": **Action of Story:** Girl and boy see each other at supermarket; **Expected Ending:** Girl and boy will meet and have a romance; **Actual Ending:** Neither character takes the risk of meeting the other. "Fifteen": **Action of Poem:** Teenager finds a motorcycle and considers an adventure; **Expected Ending:** Character will ride off; **Actual Ending:** Character helps the injured rider. **(b)** The ironic endings suggest that people's fantasies enlarge their lives but not in expected ways.
4. **(a)** **Character:** girl; **Experiences:** lonely in new home, sees boy at supermarket; **Feelings:** falls in love with the boy; **Missed Opportunity:** never says anything to the boy; **Self-discovery:** realizes she has to meet people
   Character: boy; **Experiences:** bored at bag boy job, sees girl at job; **Feelings:** falls in love with the girl; **Missed Opportunity:** never speaks to the girl; **Self-discovery:** realizes he needs a new job
   Character: boy in "Fifteen"; **Experiences:** finds a seemingly abandoned motorcycle; **Feelings:** bonds with the motorcycle; **Missed Opportunity:** does not take the motorcycle but finds the injured owner; **Self-discovery:** realizes that fifteen is not too young to think of someone else
   (b) Whatever their choices, students should note that the girl's and both boys' discoveries will affect future relationships and their views of themselves.
5. **(a)** and **(b)** Ask volunteers to describe memories evoked by the poem and how their memories help them to understand the speaker's feelings.
6. Students might suggest that she introduce herself to the boy.
7. Students may say that "Checkouts" is true to life because everyone experiences missed opportunities.

continued

Answers continued

8. Students may suggest that deep feelings expressed in both selections are true of teenagers and might have been forgotten by adults.

EXTEND

Answers for p. 288

❶ Vocabulary Development

Word Analysis

1. amusement: The dog's antic behavior gave us much amusement.
2. enlightenment: The boring television documentary did not provide much enlightenment.
3. disappointment: The team's loss filled their fans with disappointment.
4. disillusionment: When he realized his brother had lied, he was struck with disillusionment.

Spelling Strategy

1. denied
2. correct
3. variable

Fluency: Clarify Word Meaning

1. e
2. a
3. f
4. h
5. j
6. b
7. c
8. i
9. g
10. d

❷ Grammar

1. *to the road*; modifies the verb *took*; adverb phrase
2. *at the store*; modifies the verb *looked*; adverb phrase
   for the boy; modifies the verb *looked*; adverb phrase
3. *of mayonnaise*; modifies the noun *jar*; adjective phrase
   to the floor; modifies the verb *fell*; adverb phrase
4. *of the bike*; modifies the noun *color*; adjective phrase
5. *at a theater*; modifies the verb *were*; adverb phrase
   with their dates; modifies the verb *were*; adverb phrase

Writing Application

1. We had lunch after the trip. (adverb phrase)
2. The girl on the motorcycle had a protective helmet. (adjective phrase)

Integrate Language Skills

❶ Vocabulary Development Lesson

Word Analysis: Latin Suffix *-ment*

The Latin suffix *-ment* means "state or condition of." It can be added to some verbs to form nouns, changing *dishevel* to *dishevelment*. Change each verb below to a noun by adding *-ment*, and use each new word in a sentence.

1. amuse
2. enlighten
3. disappoint
4. disillusion

Spelling Strategy

When you add an ending to words ending in *y* preceded by a consonant, change the *y* to *i*, unless the ending begins with an *i*. For example, *carry* + *-ed* = *carried*, but *carry* + *-ing* = *carrying*.

If the spelling of each word is correct, write *Correct*. If it is wrong, write the correct spelling.

1. denyed 2. denying 3. varyable

Fluency: Clarify Word Meaning

For each numbered item, choose the letter of the word that is closest in meaning to the vocabulary list word.

1. intuition	a. daydream
2. reverie	b. untidiness
3. shards	c. willfully contrary
4. harried	d. shy
5. brazen	e. a feeling beyond thought
6. dishevelment	f. broken pieces
7. perverse	g. stayed on
8. articulate	h. worried
9. lingered	i. express in words
10. demure	j. bold

❷ Grammar Lesson

Prepositional Phrases as Modifiers

A **prepositional phrase** is made up of a preposition and a noun or pronoun, called the object of the preposition.

A prepositional phrase can function as either an adjective or an adverb, depending on the word it modifies. An adjective phrase modifies nouns and pronouns. An adverb phrase modifies verbs, adjectives, and adverbs. Look at the following examples:

Adjective phrase: The girl *in the grocery store* fell in love. (modifies the noun *girl*)

Adverb phrase: She smiled *at the bag boy*. (modifies the verb *smiled*)

Practice Identify the prepositional phrases in these sentences. Then, for each phrase, identify the word it modifies and indicate whether it is an adjective or adverb phrase.

1. He took the motorcycle to the road.
2. At the store, she looked for the boy.
3. The jar of mayonnaise fell to the floor.
4. He didn't mention the color of the bike.
5. They were at a theater with their dates.

Writing Application Use the following prepositional phrases in sentences. Explain whether the phrase is an adjective or adverb phrase.

1. after the trip 2. on the motorcycle

WG Prentice Hall Writing and Grammar Connection: Chapter 21, Section 1

TEACHING RESOURCES

The following resources can be used to enrich or extend the instruction for pp. 288–289.

Vocabulary

Selection Support: Build Vocabulary, p. 65

Vocabulary and Spelling Practice Book (Use this booklet for skills enrichment.)

Grammar

Selection Support: Build Grammar Skills, p. 66

Writing and Grammar, Gold Level, p. 450

Daily Language Practice Transparencies

Writing

Writing and Grammar, Gold Level, p. 286

Writing and Grammar iText CD-ROM

BLOCK SCHEDULING: Resources marked with this symbol provide varied instruction during 90-minute blocks.

❸ Writing Lesson

Character's Journal

In order to focus more on the feelings of the characters in "Checkouts," retell the events of the story by creating contrasting journals. For each date of an entry, prepare "he-said/she-said" entries.

Prewriting Review the story to list three key events. For each event, note the likely response of each character.

Model: Finding Subjects for Each Journal

Girl	Event	Boy
thought the boy was very sweet	boy drops and breaks jar	mortified and wanted to hide

Drafting Begin each paired journal entry with the date and a headline that summarizes the main idea of the entry. Then, in the voice of the character, write the ideas and emotions the event provoked.

Revising Review your draft, looking for opportunities to tighten the connection between the entries. For example, if one character includes a specific detail, consider adding that detail—and a contrasting response—to the other character's journal.

WG Prentice Hall Writing and Grammar Connection: Chapter 13, Section 2

❹ Extension Activities

Listening and Speaking Imagine you are the girl from "Checkouts," talking on the telephone to a friend in your old hometown. Tell the story of your infatuation with the bag boy.

- Start by telling your friend where you met the boy and why you like him.
- Use appropriate expressions to convey the emotions of the girl.

Write down the story you have created, practice reading it, and then present your **oral story** to your class.

Research and Technology In a group, develop a **script for a scene** from a teen soap opera based on the story from "Checkouts." In your script, make sure that you include stage directions to describe the action and the characters' emotions. Remember that you want your characters to speak and act in a way that will appeal to teenagers. **[Group Activity]**

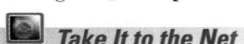

Take It to the Net www.phschool.com
Go online for an additional research activity using the Internet.

Lesson Support for p. 289

❸ Writing Lesson

- You may wish to have students work in pairs, with each student focusing on entries for one character.
- Remind students that they need to provide comparable entries for both characters for each event.
- After students have read their first drafts, have several volunteers read entries for the same key event.

❹ Research and Technology

- Give students the option of creating their oral story from the bag boy's perspective.
- Suggest that students sketch a timeline of the key events in the infatuation.
- As a class, make a list of words and phrases that teens typically use to describe people to whom they are attracted.
- Have students use the rubric for Delivering a Descriptive Presentation, p. 28 in **Performance Assessment and Portfolio Management.**

CUSTOMIZE INSTRUCTION
For Universal Access

To address different learning styles, use the activities suggested in the **Extension Activities** booklet, p. 17.

- For Verbal/Linguistic Learners, use Activity 4.
- For Bodily/Kinesthetic Learners, use Activity 5.
- For Verbal/Linguistic and Visual/Spatial Learners, use Activity 6.

ASSESSMENT RESOURCES

The following resources can be used to assess students' knowledge and skills.

Selection Assessment

- **Formal Assessment,** Selection Test, pp. 57–59
- **Open Book Test,** pp. 49–51
- **Got It! Assessment Videotapes,** Tape 2
- **Test Bank Software**

Take It to the Net
Visit www.phschool.com for self-tests and additional questions on the selections.

Listening and Speaking Rubric

- **Performance Assess. and Portfolio Mgmt.,** p. 28

PRENTICE HALL ASSESSMENT SYSTEM

- **Workbook**
- **Skill Book**
- **Transparencies**
- **CD-ROM**

Sympathy ✦ Caged Bird ✦ We never know how high we are ✦ *from* In My Place

Lesson Objectives and CA Correlations

1. **To analyze and respond to literary elements**
   - Literary Analysis: Symbol **R 3.7**
   - Comparing Literary Works
2. **To read, comprehend, analyze, and critique poetry and nonfiction**
   - Reading Strategy: Drawing Conclusions **R 3.8**
   - Reading Check questions
   - Review and Assess questions
   - Assessment Practice (ATE)
3. **To develop word analysis skills, fluency, and systematic vocabulary**
   - Vocabulary Development Lesson: Levels of Diction **R 1.2**
4. **To understand and apply written and oral language conventions**
   - Spelling Strategy
   - Grammar Lesson: Preposition or Adverb? **LC 1.1**
5. **To understand and apply appropriate writing and research strategies**
   - Writing Lesson: Editorial **W 2.4**
   - Extension Activity: Historical Report **W 1.5**
6. **To understand and apply listening and speaking strategies**
   - Extension Activity: Oral Presentation **LS 2.4**

STEP-BY-STEP TEACHING GUIDE	PACING GUIDE
PRETEACH	
Motivate Students and Provide Background	
Use the Motivation activity (ATE p. 290)	5 min.
Read and discuss the Preview material and Background information (SE/ATE p. 290) [A]	10 min.
Introduce the Concepts	
Introduce the Literary Analysis and Reading Strategy (SE/ATE p. 291) [A]	15 min.
Pronounce the vocabulary words and read their definitions (SE p. 291)	5 min.
TEACH	
Monitor Comprehension	
Informally monitor comprehension by circulating while students read independently or in groups [A]	15 min.
Monitor students' comprehension with the Reading Check notes (SE/ATE pp. 293, 297)	as students read
Develop vocabulary with Vocabulary notes (SE pp. 292, 295, 297, 298; ATE p. 291)	as students read
Develop Understanding	
Develop students' understanding of symbols with the Literary Analysis annotations (SE p. 292; ATE pp. 292, 295, 297) [A]	10 min.
Develop students' ability to draw conclusions with the Reading Strategy annotations (SE pp. 293, 297; ATE pp. 292, 293, 296)	10 min.
ASSESS	
Assess Mastery	
Assess students' mastery of the Reading Strategy and Literary Analysis by having them answer the Review and Assess questions (SE/ATE p. 299)	20 min.
Use one or more of the print and media Assessment Resources (ATE p. 301) [A]	up to 30 min.
EXTEND	
Apply Understanding	
Have students complete the Vocabulary Development Lesson and the Grammar Lesson (SE p. 300) [A]	20 min.
Apply students' knowledge of transitions using the Writing Lesson (SE p. 301) [A]	45 min.
Apply students' understanding using one or more of the Extension Activities (SE p. 301)	20–90 min.

[A] **ACCELERATED INSTRUCTION:** Use the strategies and activities identified with an [A].

UNIVERSAL ACCESS
● = Below Level Students
▲ = On-Level Students
■ = Above Level Students

Time and Resource Manager

Reading Level: Average, Easy, Average, Challenging
Average Number of Instructional Days: 4

RESOURCES		
PRINT	**TRANSPARENCIES**	**TECHNOLOGY**
• **Beyond Literature,** Workplace Skills: Setting and Achieving Short-Term Goals, p. 18 ▲ ■		• **Interest Grabber Video,** Tape 2 ● ▲ ■
• **Selection Support Workbook:** ● ▲ ■ Literary Analysis, p. 72 Reading Strategy, p. 71 Build Vocabulary, p. 69	• **Literary Analysis and Reading Transparencies,** pp. 35 and 36 ● ▲ ■	
• **Authors In Depth,** Gold Level, p. 179 ■		• **Listening to Literature** ● ▲ ■ Audiocassettes, Side 9 Audio CDs, CD 7
• **Literatura en español** ● ▲ • **Literary Analysis for Enrichment** ■		
• **Formal Assessment:** Selection Test, pp. 60–62 ● ▲ ■ • **Open Book Test,** pp. 52–54 ● ▲ ■ • **Performance Assessment and Portfolio Management,** p. 10 ● ▲ ■ • PRENTICE HALL ASSESSMENT SYSTEM ● ▲ ■	• PRENTICE HALL ASSESSMENT SYSTEM ● ▲ ■ Skills Practice Answers and Explanations on Transparencies	• **Test Bank Software** ● ▲ ■ • **Got It! Assessment Videotapes,** Tape 2 ● ▲
• **Selection Support Workbook:** ● ▲ ■ Build Grammar Skills, p. 70 • **Writing and Grammar,** Gold Level ● ▲ ■ • **Extension Activities,** p. 18 ● ▲ ■	• **Daily Language Practice Transparencies** ● ▲	• **Writing and Grammar iText CD-ROM** ● ▲ ■ *Take It to the Net* www.phschool.com

BLOCK SCHEDULING: Use one 90-minute class period to preteach the selection and have students read it. Use a second 90-minute class period to assess students' mastery of skills and have them complete one of the Extension Activities.

PRETEACH

Step-by-Step Teaching Guide for pp. 290–291

Motivation

Before students read these selections, ask them to gather information about breakthroughs in African American rights from the Civil War to the present. Using the information students collect, work as a class to create a timeline capturing important events in this progression. Then, discuss what it might have been like to be an African American during the various eras. Tell students that three of these selections vividly capture what it felt like to be an African American during the period recorded on the timeline.

Interest Grabber Video

As an alternative, play "Segregation and Desegregation" on Tape 2 to engage student interest.

❶ Background

Social Studies

Thurgood Marshall (1908–1994) was the first black justice appointed to the Supreme Court. He was named to the court by President Lyndon B. Johnson in 1967 and served until 1991. Marshall's early career included serving as the chief counsel for the *Brown* v. *Board of Education* suit in which racial segregation in education—the "separate but equal" doctrine—was declared unconstitutional. Marshall, the great-grandson of a slave, was considered a giant in the fight for civil rights for all Americans.

Prepare to Read

Sympathy ◆ Caged Bird ◆ We never know how high we are ◆ *from* In My Place

Take It to the Net

Visit www.phschool.com for interactive activities and instruction related to the selections, including

- background
- graphic organizers
- literary elements
- reading strategies

Preview

Connecting to the Literature

The writers in this group tell about the way a dream can focus our lives. If you have ever been driven by a dream, you will be able to relate to the authors' messages—even if you have had a very different experience.

❶ Background

Until the 1950s, Southern public schools and universities were segregated; African American students did not attend the same schools as white students. In the landmark *Brown* v. *Board of Education* decision of 1954, however, the Supreme Court overturned the doctrine of "separate but equal" schools and ruled that separate schools for different races could not offer equivalent education. In the early 1960s, various African American students like writer Charlayne Hunter-Gault enrolled at formerly all-white institutions.

TEACHING RESOURCES

The following resources can be used to enrich or extend the instruction for pp. 290–291.

Motivation

Interest Grabber Video, Tape 2

Background

Beyond Literature, p. 18

Take It to the Net

Visit www.phschool.com for background and hotlinks for the selections.

Literary Analysis

Literary Analysis and Reading Transparencies, Symbol, p. 36

Reading

Selection Support: Reading Strategy, p. 71; Build Vocabulary, p. 69

Literary Analysis and Reading Transparencies, Drawing Conclusions, p. 35

BLOCK SCHEDULING: Resources marked with this symbol provide varied instruction during 90-minute blocks.

❷ Literary Analysis

Symbol

A **symbol** is an object, person, or idea that represents something beyond itself. Authors may use symbols to make a point, create a mood, or reinforce a theme. For example, in literature, springtime often represents new life and hope. Notice how the bird in the following lines from "Caged Bird" symbolizes human circumstance:

> But a bird that stalks / down his narrow cage / can seldom see through / his bars of rage. . . .

In these selections, look for details that symbolize a larger meaning.

Comparing Literary Works

As these writers suggest, dreams are part of our identity. The dream may be to acquire freedom or love or success; it may come true, or it may not. As you read these selections, compare and contrast the message each author conveys about reaching for a dream.

❸ Reading Strategy

Drawing Conclusions

Whether you are reading or just observing life, you often make sense of information by **drawing conclusions.**

- When you draw conclusions, you form an opinion about something based upon evidence that you can identify.
- Pay attention to ideas about the work that occur to you but that are not actually stated.

Each of the works in this group invites you to draw a particular conclusion about the value of aspiring to something beyond your current circumstances. Use a chart like the one shown to record your conclusions and the evidence for them.

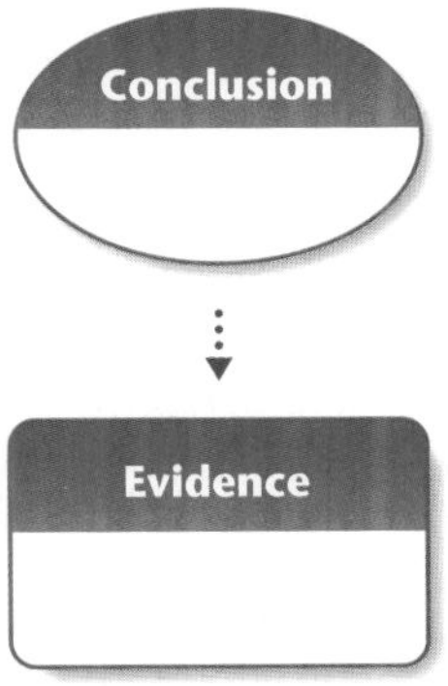

Vocabulary Development

keener (kēn´ ər) *adj.* sharper (p. 292)

warp (wôrp) *v.* twist; distort (p. 295)

epithets (ep´ ə thetz) *n.* abusive words or phrases (p. 297)

effigies (ef´ i jēz) *n.* crude figures representing hated people or groups (p. 297)

disperse (di spurs´) *v.* drive off or scatter in different directions (p. 297)

imbued (im byo͞od´) *v.* inspired (p. 298)

perpetuated (pər pech´ o͞o āt´ id) *v.* caused to continue indefinitely (p. 298)

CUSTOMIZE INSTRUCTION FOR UNIVERSAL ACCESS

For Less Proficient Readers	For English Learners	For Advanced Readers
Have students view the "Segregation and Desegregation" videotape and write a brief summary about what they learned. Interested students might also wish to take note of events that would fit onto the class timeline.	Play the **Listening to Literature Audiocassettes,** Side 9, to help students appreciate the sound of the poems. After students have listened to the poems, encourage them to read them aloud with the tape.	Ask students to imagine that they are reporters working for a newspaper at some point in African American history after the Civil War. Have them write an article for a newspaper describing one of the events on the class timeline.

❷ Literary Analysis

Symbol and Comparing Literary Works

- Tell students that as they read the selections they should look for *symbols*—objects, animals, people, or ideas that represent something beyond themselves. Make sure students are able to not only identify the symbol, but also what is being represented by the symbol.
- Have students recall the motorcycle in the poem, "Fifteen," on p. 286. Ask them what the motorcycle symbolizes for the boy. Answer: freedom, adventure, and adulthood
- Read the instruction about symbol together as a class, and call students' attention to the example from the first poem.
- Use the instruction for Comparing Literary Works to alert students to references to dreams and dreaming in the selections.
- Use the Symbols transparency in **Literary Analysis and Reading Transparencies,** p. 36, to introduce students to ways of identifying symbols and their meanings.

❸ Reading Strategy

Drawing Conclusions

- Remind students that much of what they take away from a selection is based on unstated ideas as well as identifiable evidence. Forming opinions based on stated and unstated ideas is called drawing conclusions.
- Instruct students to create a graphic organizer like the one on p. 35 of **Literary Analysis and Reading Transparencies.** Have them list the conclusions they draw as they read the selections as well as the evidence for each conclusion.

Vocabulary Development

- Pronounce each vocabulary word for students, and read the definitions as a class. Have students identify any words with which they are already familiar.

E-Teach

Visit E-Teach at www.phschool.com for teachers' essays on how to teach, with questions and answers.

TEACH

Step-by Step Teaching Guide for pp. 292–298

CUSTOMIZE INSTRUCTION For Verbal/Linguistic Learners

Ask students to imagine that they are working to secure freedom for something or someone—an unfairly convicted person in prison or a group of refugees being kept in detention. How might they communicate the importance of their goal in a poem? What would they use as symbols for their struggle? Ask volunteers to read their completed poems to the class and display them in the classroom.

❶ About the Selections

In the first poem, Dunbar draws a parallel between the feelings of African Americans during his lifetime and the irrepressible desire of a caged bird to gain its freedom.

Echoing words from Dunbar's poem written generations earlier, Maya Angelou contrasts a free bird and a caged bird in the second selection.

❷ Literary Analysis

Symbol

- Ask students what the poet is describing in lines 2–6 of the first stanza.
  Answer: The poet is describing a natural setting including a meadow and a river.
- Have students answer the Literary Analysis question on p. 292: What kind of situation do the details of the first stanza represent?
  Answer: freedom

❸ Reading Strategy

Drawing Conclusions

- Point out that Dunbar says, "I know why" the bird beats his wing on the "cruel bars." Ask students if the poet states the reason here.
  Answer: No
- Ask students why the bird beats its wing. What evidence supports their conclusion?
  Answer: The poem suggests that the bird is struggling to get free of the cage. He would rather be on a tree branch than on his perch.

❶ Sympathy

Paul Laurence Dunbar

❷
I know what the caged bird feels, alas!
When the sun is bright on the upland slopes;
When the wind stirs, soft through the springing grass,
And the river flows like a stream of glass;
When the first bird sings and the first bud opes,
And the faint perfume from its chalice[1] steals—
I know what the caged bird feels!

❸
I know why the caged bird beats his wing
Till its blood is red on the cruel bars;
For he must fly back to his perch and cling
When he fain[2] would be on the bough a-swing;
And a pain still throbs in the old, old scars
And they pulse again with a keener sting—
I know why he beats his wing!

I know why the caged bird sings, ah me,
When his wing is bruised and his bosom sore,—
When he beats his bars and he would be free;
It is not a carol of joy or glee,
But a prayer that he sends from his heart's deep core,
But a plea, that upward to Heaven he flings—
I know why the caged bird sings!

Literary Analysis
Symbol What kind of situation do the details of the first stanza represent?

keener (kēn′ ər) *adj.* sharper

Paul Laurence Dunbar

(1872–1906)
He died before reaching his thirty-fifth birthday, but Paul Laurence Dunbar produced a tremendous outpouring of poetry and fiction during his brief lifetime. Born in Dayton, Ohio, the child of former slaves, Dunbar is widely recognized as the first African American poet of national stature.

1. **chalice** (chal′ is) *v.* cup or goblet; here, the cup-shaped part of a budding flower.
2. **fain** (fān) *adv.* gladly; eagerly.

TEACHING RESOURCES

The following resources can be used to enrich or extend the instruction for pp. 292–298.

Literary Analysis
Selection Support: Literary Analysis, p. 72

Reading
Listening to Literature Audiocassettes, Side 9
Listening to Literature Audio CDs, CD 7

Extension
Authors In Depth, Gold Level, p. 179 (The collection includes fifteen additional poems by Emily Dickinson for extended reading.)

BLOCK SCHEDULING: Resources marked with this symbol provide varied instruction during 90-minute blocks.

Caged Bird

Maya Angelou

4
A free bird leaps
on the back of the wind
and floats downstream
till the current ends
and dips his wing
in the orange sun rays
and dares to claim the sky.

But a bird that stalks
down his narrow cage
can seldom see through
his bars of rage
his wings are clipped and
his feet are tied
so he opens his throat to sing.

5
The caged bird sings
with a fearful trill
of things unknown
but longed for still
and his tune is heard
on the distant hill
for the caged bird
sings of freedom.

6 **▲ Critical Viewing**
Which poem best captures the spirit conveyed by this image? Explain. **[Make a Judgment]**

Reading Strategy
Drawing Conclusions
Can the bird in the second stanza expect to be free? Why or why not?

7 **✔ Reading Check**
According to "Caged Bird," how does a free bird interact with his environment?

4 Critical Thinking

Contrast

- Ask students what basic symbol is used in both poems.
  Answer: A bird is used as a symbol in both poems.
- Have students contrast the life of the free bird in this stanza of Angelou's poem with the life of the caged bird in Dunbar's poem.
  Possible response: The free bird is happy and strong. The caged bird is miserable and longs to be free.

5 Reading Strategy

Drawing Conclusions

- Ask students to speculate on what the cage symbolizes in this poem.
  Possible response: The cage symbolizes a society that enslaves or oppresses certain groups of people.
- Have students answer the Reading Strategy question on p. 293: Can the bird in the second stanza expect to be free? Why or why not?
  Answer: No because the bird is not only caged, but has had its wings clipped and feet tied.

6 ▶Critical Viewing

Answer: "Caged Bird" best captures the spirit of this image because its first stanza describes a bird that is free.

7 ✔Reading Check

Answer: A free bird goes with the wind and "dares to claim the sky."

CUSTOMIZE INSTRUCTION FOR UNIVERSAL ACCESS

For Less Proficient Readers	For Advanced Readers
To help students grasp the symbolism in "Sympathy" and "Caged Bird," have them create a chart in which they record the characteristics and desires of the birds described in each poem. When they've finished, discuss with students how these details might relate to people.	Invite these students to restate passages from the three poems in ordinary conversational speech. Then, have students form groups and discuss why the language used by the poets has more impact than the expression of the same ideas in everyday speech.

ASSESS

Answers for p. 294

Review and Assess

1. Students may identify feelings of fear that have made them feel like a caged bird.
2. **(a)** It describes a sunny meadow with a river running through it. **(b)** The caged bird feels enraged that it cannot be free.
3. **(a)** The bird's main activity is beating his wings against the cage bars. **(b)** He is trying to get out of the cage.
4. **(a)** "I know why the caged bird. . ." appears regularly. **(b)** The speaker sympathizes with the bird because African Americans have suffered from slavery and various forms of oppression that have limited their freedom.
5. **(a)** Readers meet the caged bird in the second stanza. **(b)** The life of the free bird is described first to make the image of the caged bird more stark and outrageous.
6. **(a)** He has been crippled in his view by rage. He has also been crippled by having his wings clipped and his feet tied. **(b)** He sings because that is the only way he can express himself; this suggests that he will not be silenced.
7. **(a)** The bird in "Sympathy" sings a prayer and a plea. The bird in "Caged Bird" sings with a fearful trill. **(b)** They sing because they are unable to fly, and singing is the only way that they can express themselves.
8. Students may suggest that singing is good because it keeps the birds alive and draws attention to their plight; it keeps hope alive.

The free bird thinks of another breeze
and the trade winds soft through the sighing trees
and the fat worms waiting on a dawn-bright lawn
and he names the sky his own.

But a caged bird stands on the grave of dreams
his shadow shouts on a nightmare scream
his wings are clipped and his feet are tied
so he opens his throat to sing.

The caged bird sings
with a fearful trill
of things unknown
but longed for still
and his tune is heard
on the distant hill
for the caged bird
sings of freedom.

Review and Assess

Thinking About the Selections

1. **Respond:** What, if anything, has made you feel like the caged bird that Dunbar describes?
2. **(a) Recall:** What outdoor scene does the first stanza of "Sympathy" describe? **(b) Infer:** What does the caged bird feel at this time?
3. **(a) Recall:** In the second stanza of "Sympathy," what is the bird's main activity? **(b) Infer:** Why does the caged bird beat its wing against the bars of its cage?
4. **(a) Recall:** What expression appears repeatedly in "Sympathy"? **(b) Interpret:** Why do you think the speaker can sympathize so well with the caged bird?
5. **(a) Recall:** In "Caged Bird," in which stanza do readers meet the caged bird? **(b) Analyze:** Why do you think that the life of the free bird is described first?
6. **(a) Recall:** How has the caged bird been crippled? **(b) Infer:** If he still sings "with a fearful trill" despite this experience, what can you conclude about his character?
7. **(a) Recall:** How do the caged birds sing in each of the poems? **(b) Infer:** Why do they sing as they do?
8. **Speculate:** What good, if any, results from each caged bird's singing?

Maya Angelou

(b. 1928)

Born Marguerite Johnson in St. Louis, Missouri, Maya Angelou grew up in Arkansas and California. Her difficult childhood became the source for her extremely popular autobiography, *I Know Why the Caged Bird Sings* (1969), which takes its title from Paul Laurence Dunbar's "Sympathy."

In her adult life, she achieved success as a singer, an actress, a civil rights worker, and a writer of nonfiction, fiction, poetry, and plays. In her book *Wouldn't Take Nothin' for My Journey Now* (1993), she shares her reflections on life.

ASSESSMENT PRACTICE: Reading Comprehension

Implied Main Idea (For more practice, see Test Preparation Workbook, p. 18.)

Use this sample test item to help your students to recognize implied main ideas in poetry.

A free bird leaps
On the back of the wind
And floats downstream . . .
And dares to claim the sky.

Which of the following is the implied main idea of this text?

A Some birds are freer than others.
B Freedom is linked to optimism and courage.
C Caged birds dare to reach high.
D Only free birds can fly.

Help students to see that the poet is using the qualities of optimism and courage, which she's ascribed to a bird that can fly, to convey a main idea about freedom. This main idea is expressed in choice *B.*

(8) # We never know how high we are

Emily Dickinson

(10)

Bubbles, Watercolor, 39" x 29". Courtesy of Scott Burdick

(9)

We never know how high we are
Till we are asked to rise
And then if we are true to plan
Our statures touch the skies—
The Heroism we recite
Would be a normal thing
Did not ourselves the Cubits[1] warp
For fear to be a King—

warp (wôrp) *v.* twist; distort

1. **Cubits** (kyo͞o′ bitz) ancient measure using the length of the arm from the end of the middle finger to the elbow (about 18–22 inches).

Emily Dickinson

(1830–1886)

Emily Dickinson was born and lived most of her life in Amherst, Massachusetts. Outwardly, her life was uneventful. The range and depth of her inner life, however, are suggested by the fact that she wrote at least 1,775 poems—each one compact with emotional power. She hid these poems in a bureau drawer, where they remained until after her death.

Review and Assess

Thinking About the Selection

1. **Respond:** What personal experiences does this poem call to mind? Explain.
2. **(a) Recall:** According to the poem, what happens when we are asked to rise to an occasion? **(b) Hypothesize:** Why might this happen?
3. **(a) Recall:** What happens "if we are true to plan"? **(b) Speculate:** How might Dickinson define heroism?
4. **(a) Recall:** According to the poem, what prevents people from acting heroically all the time? **(b) Distinguish:** Does Dickinson think people do not live to their full potential or that they are too humble to accept praise? Explain.
5. **Extend:** What advice do you think Dickinson would give someone who was just offered a challenging job opportunity?

ASSESS

(8) About the Selection

Emily Dickinson's poem speaks of the human fear of achieving greatness. According to the speaker, we impose limitations on ourselves because life seems safer in a cage than outside.

(9) Literary Analysis

Symbol

- After students have read the poem, ask them what is meant by the first two lines.
  Answer: We don't know our true potential until we are asked to meet new challenges.
- Have students speculate on what the figure of King symbolizes in the last line of the poem.
  Answer: The King symbolizes greatness and importance—all the things Dickinson believes humans fear.

Answers for p. 295

Review and Assess

1. Ask volunteers to describe experiences brought to mind by the poem.
2. **(a)** We are fearful of rising too high. **(b)** The higher we rise, the farther we can fall.
3. We respond to demands that we accept new challenges but often do not take credit for our successes. **(b)** She might define heroism as being honest about oneself, even when it means acknowledging success.
4. **(a)** People fear appearing to stand out or be important. **(b)** She believes that people can and do rise to greatness, but often don't give themselves credit for their accomplishments.
5. She would probably encourage the person to do the best job he or she could.

(10) Background

Art

Bubbles, by Scott Burdick

Scott Burdick attended the American Academy of Art in Chicago and studied Life Drawing and Oil Painting under Bill Parks.

continued

Answers continued

He has received several awards for his art, including the 1996 Silver Medal of Honor from the American Watercolor Society. In this painting, a young woman is waving a bubble wand, creating a whole spectrum of dazzling colors around her. Her body position and facial expression suggest feelings of joy and freedom. Use these questions for discussion:

1. How does the picture of the girl suggest the mood of Emily Dickinson's poem?
   Possible response: The girl's pose and manner suggest that her "stature touches the sky."
2. If the girl in the painting could read the line, "We never know how high we are," how do you think she would respond?
   Possible response: She might agree with the poem; she might say that her purpose in life is to enjoy herself, not to be a hero.

⓫ About the Selection

In this brief segment from Charlayne Hunter-Gault's autobiography, the author describes the unquenchable desire for equal opportunity that drove her to become one of the first African Americans to enroll at the University of Georgia. The piece captures the ability of the human spirit to overcome tremendous obstacles and hardships in order to achieve an important goal. Encourage students to think of other situations in which people have exhibited this type of courage and determination.

⓬ Reading Strategy

Drawing Conclusions

- Ask students what was unusual about Charlayne Hunter-Gault walking onto the campus at the University of Georgia on January 9, 1961.
  Answer: Hunter-Gault is African American and no student of her race had ever been admitted before.
- Ask students to answer the Reading Strategy question on p. 297: What evidence supports the conclusion that Hunter-Gault faced a major struggle?
  Answer: Hunter-Gault had to battle in the courts for two and a half years to get into the University of Georgia.

ENRICHMENT: Art Connection

Photography

Ask students to summarize what the photograph shows: a young African American woman—apparently from some time in the past, based on people's clothing and hair styles—being photographed and observed by onlookers as she walks down a sidewalk. Tell students that the photograph shows Charlayne Hunter-Gault as a student at the University of Georgia. Use the following for discussion:

1. What might Hunter-Gault be thinking in the photograph?
   Answer: She appears determined to ignore the attention she is drawing.
2. Compare and contrast the photograph of Hunter-Gault with the experience of reading her story. In what ways can a picture show you more than a section of writing, and in what ways might it be more limited?
   Answer: A photograph can make an action seem more real and can include many small details; a photograph can only suggest people's thoughts, while a written piece can actually describe those thoughts.

from

⓫ In My Place

Charlayne Hunter-Gault

⓬ On January 9, 1961, I walked onto the campus at the University of Georgia to begin registering for classes. Ordinarily, there would not have been anything unusual about such a routine exercise, except, in this instance, the officials at the university had been fighting for two and a half years to keep me out. I was not socially, intellectually, or morally undesirable. I was Black. And no Black student had ever been admitted to the University of Georgia in its 176-year history. Until the landmark *Brown* v. *Board of Education* decision that in 1954 declared separate but equal schools unconstitutional, the university was protected by law in its exclusion of people like me. In applying to the university, Hamilton Holmes and I were making one of the first major tests of the court's ruling in Georgia, and no one was sure just how hard it would be to challenge nearly two hundred years of exclusive white privilege. It would take us two and a half years of fighting our way through the system and the courts, but finally, with the help of the NAACP[1] Legal Defense and Educational Fund, Inc., and with the support of our family and friends, we won the right that should have been ours all along. With the ink barely dry on the court order of three days before, Hamilton Holmes and I walked onto the campus and into history.

⓭ We would be greeted by mobs of white students, who within forty-eight hours would hurl epithets, burn crosses and Black effigies, and finally stage a riot outside my dormitory while, nearby, state patrolmen ignored the call from university officials to come and intervene. ⓮ Tear gas would disperse the crowd, but not before I got word in my dorm room, now strewn with glass from a rock through my window, that Hamilton and I were being suspended for our own safety. It might have been the end of the story but for the fact that the University of

1. **NAACP** *abbr.* National Association for the Advancement of Colored People.

⓯ ◀ **Critical Viewing** Which character traits does Charlayne Hunter-Gault display in this photograph? **[Analyze]**

Reading Strategy
Drawing Conclusions What evidence supports the conclusion that Hunter-Gault faced a major struggle?

epithets (ep´ ə *th*etz) *n.* abusive words or phrases

effigies (ef´ i jēz) *n.* crude figures representing hated people or groups

disperse (di spurs´) *v.* drive off or scatter in different directions

⓰ ✔ **Reading Check**
What happened when Hunter-Gault walked onto the campus?

⓭ Critical Thinking

Infer

- Ask students if the writer ever states directly why she and Hamilton Holmes were willing to risk their lives to attend the University of Georgia.
  Answer: No.
- Ask students why Hunter-Gault and Holmes were willing to endure this ugly situation.
  Possible response: They were not just attempting to graduate from a particular school. Backed up by the new law, they were making a heroic stand to give African American students nationwide equal opportunities for education.

⓮ Literary Analysis

Symbol

- Remind students of the symbols encountered in the selections they have read so far—birds, cages, and a King, for example.
- Ask students what is symbolized in this passage by the effigies, and why this is a particularly hateful and frightening symbol.
  Answer: The effigies symbolize the real persons of Hunter-Gault and Hamilton Holmes. Their use is frightening and ugly because when people burn an effigy they are suggesting that the real person symbolized by the effigy should be destroyed.

⓯ ▶ Critical Viewing

Answer: Hunter-Gault displays the traits of focus, determination, and the ability to ignore the fuss surrounding her.

⓰ ✔ Reading Check

Answer: Mobs of white students screamed things at her, burned crosses and effigies of her, and rioted outside her dormitory.

CUSTOMIZE INSTRUCTION FOR UNIVERSAL ACCESS

For Special Needs Students	For Advanced Readers
To ensure that students have the context they need to understand this selection, have them read and discuss the Background on p. 290 immediately before they begin reading. Also, explain that *Brown* v. *Board of Education* was a United States Supreme Court decision. Therefore, it had to be heeded in all states, even if some state governments and local citizens objected to it.	Have students compare the images of courage and rage in Charlayne Hunter-Gault's account here with the substance of Maya Angelou's poem, "Caged Bird." What parallels are there, and which persons might Ms. Angelou see as the caged bird? Is it possible to view the rioting students as being caged birds? In what way might they be trapped?

ASSESS

17 Reading Strategy

Drawing Conclusions

- Ask students what Hunter-Gault says would have been the case if she had had her dream to be a journalist in the South of her early years instead of the South of *Brown* v. *Board of Education.*
  Answer: Her dream might have been thinkable but not doable.
- Have students use evidence from the selection to draw a conclusion about why she would not have been able to realize her dream earlier.
  Possible response: Her dream of becoming a journalist would have been hard to accomplish because in earlier times, African American students were prevented from attending most schools and she would not have been able to get an education. Even if she had been able to teach herself how to write, it's unlikely that anyone would have given an African American woman a job on a newspaper.

Answers for p. 298

Review and Assess

1. Students may admit that they would not have been able to stand up to the threats.
2. **(a)** No African American student had been admitted in the history of the university. **(b)** In contrast to white students, Hunter-Gault spent years fighting in the courts to be allowed to attend the university and was greeted by rioting mobs.
3. **(a)** Students yelled epithets, burned effigies and crosses, and staged a riot. **(b)** Whites were used to the segregation of the races, which was sanctioned by law. They wanted the university to remain segregated.
4. **(a)** She was determined to stay. **(b)** She needed courage, determination, and moral strength.
5. **(a)** "But no one ever told me not to dream, and when the time came to act on that dream, I would not let anything stand in the way of fulfilling it." **(b)** She had the kind of courage seen in people who help to make major changes in society.

continued

Georgia was now the lead case in a series of events that would become Georgia's entry into the Civil Rights Revolution. And we—like the legions of young Black students to follow in other arenas—were now imbued with an unshakable determination to take control of our destiny and force the South to abandon the wretched Jim Crow laws[2] it had perpetuated for generations to keep us in our place.

imbued (im byo͞od′) *v.* inspired

perpetuated (pər pech′ o͞o āt′ id) *v.* caused to continue indefinitely

17 The newfound sense of mission that now motivated us evolved for me out of a natural desire to fulfill a dream I had nurtured from an early age. With a passion bordering on obsession, I wanted to be a journalist, a dream that would have been, if not unthinkable, at least undoable in the South of my early years. But no one ever told me not to dream, and when the time came to act on that dream, I would not let anything stand in the way of fulfilling it.

2. **Jim Crow laws** upholding or practicing discrimination against African Americans. Jim Crow was a derogatory name given to African Americans from the title of a nineteenth-century minstrel song.

Review and Assess

Thinking About the Selection

1. **Respond:** If you had faced the obstacles that Hunter-Gault did, how would you have handled the situation?
2. **(a) Recall:** What had been true of the University of Georgia for 176 years? **(b) Compare and Contrast:** How was Hunter-Gault's arrival on campus different from the experiences of most other students?
3. **(a) Recall:** What specific student actions met Hunter-Gault and Hamilton Holmes at the university during their first two days? **(b) Analyze:** Why was there such a violent reaction to Hunter-Gault's attempt to attend college?
4. **(a) Recall:** How did Hunter-Gault respond when she learned that she would be suspended? **(b) Deduce:** What qualities did she need in order to succeed in her mission?
5. **(a) Recall:** With which statement does Hunter-Gault conclude her essay? **(b) Draw Conclusions:** What conclusion can you draw from this idea?
6. **(a) Connect:** How does Hunter-Gault's chosen career connect with her experiences and dreams? **(b) Generalize:** How can a sense of pursuing a larger purpose, as well as one's personal goals, give someone strength?
7. **Evaluate:** Do you think Hunter-Gault is a hero? Why or why not?

Charlayne Hunter-Gault

(b. 1942)

Born into a minister's family in South Carolina, Charlayne Hunter-Gault showed writing talent early in life and was accepted into several universities. When she was encouraged by civil rights leaders to apply to the University of Georgia, however, she made history as one of the first African American students to enter an all-white institution.

As an adult, Hunter-Gault achieved her dream of becoming a journalist, working for the "MacNeil/Lehrer Report," the *New Yorker*, and the *New York Times*, among others. Her work in broadcast journalism has won her many awards, including two Emmys and a Peabody for excellence in broadcast journalism.

Answers continued

6. **(a)** She dreamed of being a journalist and she overcame many obstacles to fulfill that dream. **(b)** People draw courage from knowing that their actions can benefit others as well as themselves.
7. Students may suggest that Hunter-Gault is a hero because she displays courage and determination even in the face of great danger and overwhelming odds.

Review and Assess

Literary Analysis

Symbol

1. In Dunbar's poem, what might the cage **symbolize**?
2. In a chart like the one below, list the experiences of the birds, and then explain how their experiences symbolize those of humans.

3. In Dickinson's poem, what might *high* and *rise* symbolize?

Comparing Literary Works

4. Use a Venn diagram to compare and contrast the spirit and behavior of the caged birds in "Sympathy" and "Caged Bird."

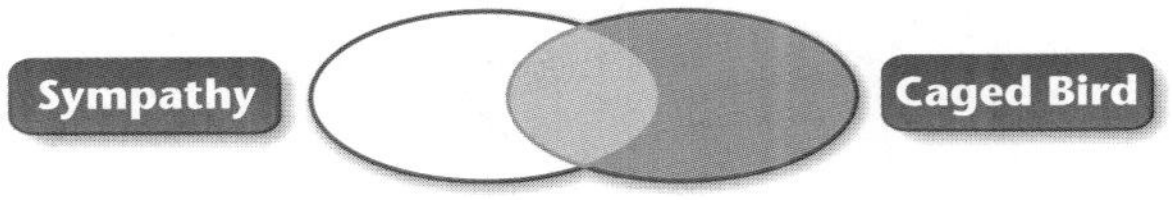

5. Based on the message of her poem, do you think Dickinson would have seen people as caged or free? Explain.
6. Would you compare Hunter-Gault's experience to that of a caged or a free bird?

Reading Strategy

Drawing Conclusions

7. What **conclusion** can you draw from Dunbar's and Angelou's poems about freedom? Why?
8. What can you conclude from Dickinson's poem about who is responsible for a life falling short of its potential?
9. What conclusion can you draw from Hunter-Gault's circumstance about her commitment to her dream?

Extend Understanding

10. **World Events Connection:** Identify and explain a situation, past or present, in a different country from your own, in which you think one or more of these selections would apply.

Quick Review

A **symbol** is an object, person, or idea that represents something beyond itself.

To **draw conclusions**, form opinions about things based upon evidence that you can identify in your reading.

Take It to the Net

www.phschool.com

Take the interactive self-test online to check your understanding of the selections.

Answers for p. 299

Review and Assess

1. The cage might represent slavery or discrimination.
2. Free Bird: flies free of a cage; Caged Bird: kept captive in a cage; Human Experience: Some humans are restricted by slavery or other forms of oppression from achieving their dreams; others live in freer societies, or rise above social oppression to reach their goals.
3. The word *high* might symbolize success or accomplishment, and the word *rise* might symbolize meeting a challenge.
4. Differences: "Sympathy": bruised, bloody wing; sore breast; sings a plea and a prayer; "Caged Bird": clipped wings; tied feet; sings with a fearful trill; Similarities: both long to be free
5. Dickinson's poem suggests that people fear greatness, and therefore may see themselves as caged birds.
6. Students may suggest that Hunter-Gault's experience is that of a caged bird that has flown to freedom.
7. Creatures continue to strive for freedom, even when the struggle is difficult and sometimes unsuccessful.
8. Each individual is responsible for not living up to his or her potential.
9. Hunter-Gault's dream was stronger than her fear of physical danger.
10. Student responses will vary. Possible response: "Sympathy" and "Caged Bird" may apply to the situation of apartheid in South Africa.

ENRICHMENT: Further Reading

Other Works by the Authors

Works by Paul Laurence Dunbar
The Paul Laurence Dunbar Reader

Works by Emily Dickinson
The Poems of Emily Dickinson

Works by Maya Angelou
I Know Why the Caged Bird Sings

Take It to the Net

Visit www.phschool.com for more information on Paul Laurence Dunbar, Maya Angelou, Emily Dickinson, and Charlayne Hunter-Gault.

EXTEND

Answers for p. 300

❶ Vocabulary Development

Diction

1. "Alas," "opes," "fain," and "a-swing" are examples of old-fashioned diction.
2. They define the speaker as literate and thoughtful.

Spelling Strategy

1. protected
2. correct
3. correct

Concept Development: Synonyms

1. b
2. a
3. b
4. c
5. a
6. c
7. b

❷ Grammar

1. <u>from</u>—preposition
2. <u>before</u>—adverb
3. <u>inside</u>—adverb
4. <u>for</u>—preposition
4. <u>after</u>—preposition

Writing Application

1. The enthusiastic fans cheered throughout. adverb
2. Ticket buyers waited outside the office. preposition
3. We were to meet at the corner before noon. preposition
4. Our neighbors put a safety fence around their pond. preposition
5. The vacationing family brought their pets along. adverb
6. She left town after graduation and hasn't been seen since. adverb

Integrate Language Skills

❶ Vocabulary Development Lesson

Levels of Diction

Diction is word choice. A writer's diction depends on his or her purpose, audience, and mood. For example, Dunbar uses elevated, or formal, diction when he refers to a song as a "carol," but Angelou uses the more down-to-earth "tune."

1. Find two more examples of old-fashioned or formal diction in "Sympathy."
2. What impression of the speaker is created?

Spelling Strategy

When adding an ending to a word that ends in more than one consonant, never double the final consonant. For example, *warp* + *-ed* = *warped.* If the spelling of each word below is correct, write *Correct*. If the spelling is incorrect, write the correct spelling.

1. protectted 2. wanting 3. deterring

Concept Development: Synonyms

For each item below, identify the letter of the word whose meaning is closest to that of the first word. If necessary, review the vocabulary words listed on page 291.

1. warp: (a) hit, (b) distort, (c) build
2. disperse: (a) scatter, (b) steal, (c) scold
3. perpetuated: (a) generated, (b) prolonged, (c) honored
4. effigies: (a) speeches, (b) insults, (c) dummies
5. keener: (a) sharper, (b) sweeter, (c) smarter
6. imbued: (a) painted, (b) placed, (c) inspired
7. epithets: (a) books, (b) slurs, (c) legends

❷ Grammar Lesson

Preposition or Adverb?

Many words that act as prepositions can also act as adverbs, depending on their usage. A **preposition** must have an object and be part of a prepositional phrase. **Adverbs** modify verbs, adjectives, and adverbs but do not have objects.

Preposition: She had to pass *through* an angry mob. (the object is *mob*)

Adverb: She walked right *through*. (no object following *through*; modifies *walked*)

Practice Identify each underlined word as a preposition or an adverb.

1. Charlayne was not accepted <u>from</u> the moment she arrived.
2. The school had never admitted a black student <u>before</u>.
3. I'm sure she didn't even feel safe <u>inside</u>.
4. She received word that she was suspended <u>for</u> her own safety.
5. <u>After</u> the news, she decided she would continue to fight for equality.

Writing Application Use each of the following words in a sentence. Then, determine whether the word functions as a preposition or as an adverb.

1. throughout
2. outside
3. at
4. around
5. along
6. since

Prentice Hall Writing and Grammar Connection: Chapter 19, Section 1

TEACHING RESOURCES

The following resources can be used to enrich or extend the instruction for pp. 300–301

Vocabulary

Selection Support: Build Vocabulary, p. 69

Vocabulary and Spelling Practice Book (Use this booklet for skills enrichment.)

Grammar

Selection Support: Build Grammar Skills, p. 70

Writing and Grammar, Gold Level, p. 402

Daily Language Practice Transparencies

Writing

Writing and Grammar, Gold Level, p. 238

Writing and Grammar iText CD-ROM

BLOCK SCHEDULING: Resources marked with this symbol provide varied instruction during 90-minute blocks.

❸ Writing Lesson

Editorial

Write an editorial, an essay that offers an opinion on an issue, for the student newspaper at the University of Georgia at the time of Charlayne Hunter-Gault's enrollment. Try to persuade the students at the university to change their behavior toward the new African American students.

Prewriting Jot down your point of view on the topic. Make a list of reasons to explain why students should change their behavior. Highlight the most important reasons.

Drafting As you draft, be sure to use a solid organization. You might choose to start with your least important reasons and build toward your most important reasons, or do the reverse.

Revising Reread your draft to make sure you have made smooth transitions between sentences. Add transition words such as *also*, *since*, and *therefore* to smooth out your writing and clarify your ideas.

Model: Adding Transitions to Smooth Writing

Although
~~They~~ they came here to seek an education, they have only dealt with
Therefore,
prejudice so far. ~~It~~ it is time for us to make a change.

Transitions like *although* and *therefore* help to connect ideas and make arguments more logical.

WG Prentice Hall Writing and Grammar Connection: Chapter 11, Section 4

❹ Extension Activities

Listening and Speaking Plan and prepare an **oral presentation** that compares Hunter-Gault's experience with the experiences of the birds found in "Sympathy" and "Caged Bird."

- Jot down Hunter-Gault's experiences and the experiences of the free and caged birds.
- Note the similarities and differences.
- Organize your notes in a way that will clearly convey your comparison.

After you have given your presentation, ask your classmates if they agree with your views.

Research and Technology In a small group, prepare a **historical report** on the *Brown* v. *Board of Education* decision of 1954. In your report, explain how the Supreme Court ruling helped Charlayne Hunter-Gault attend a previously all-white school. Use library resources, including the Internet, to find information on the subject. **[Group Activity]**

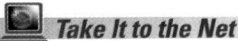

Take It to the Net www.phschool.com

Go online for an additional research activity using the Internet

Lesson Support for p. 301

❸ Writing Lesson

- Display newspaper editorials as models for students to follow.
- Tell students that when they write an editorial, they take a position and explain why readers should also take such a position.
- Use the Writing Lesson to guide students in selecting the strongest reasons in support of their positions.
- Use the rubric for Persuasion, p. 10 in **Performance Assessment and Portfolio Management** to evaluate students' editorials.

❹ Listening and Speaking

- Remind students that a dramatic monologue is a conversation or talk given by one performer or speaker to an audience.
- Have students prepare a list of people or groups of people to whom Charlayne Hunter-Gault would have wanted to speak
- Work with students to brainstorm the things Charlayne Hunter-Gault might have wanted to say to her listeners.

CUSTOMIZE INSTRUCTION
For Universal Access

To address different learning styles, use the following activities suggested in the **Extension Activities** booklet, p. 18.

- For Visual/Spatial and Intrapersonal Learners, use Activity 4.
- For Logical/Mathematical and Verbal/Linguistic Learners, use Activity 5.
- For Intrapersonal and Bodily/Kinesthetic Learners, use Activity 6.

ASSESSMENT RESOURCES

The following resources can be used to assess students' knowledge and skills.

Selection Assessment
- **Formal Assessment,** pp. 60–62
- **Open Book Test,** pp. 52–54
- **Got It! Assessment Videotapes,** Tape 2
- **Test Bank Software**

Take It to the Net
Visit www.phschool.com for self-tests and additional questions on the selections.

Writing Rubric
- **Performance Assess. and Portfolio Mgmt.,** p. 10

PRENTICE HALL ASSESSMENT SYSTEM
- **Workbook**
- **Skill Book**
- **Transparencies**
- **CD-ROM**

The Interlopers

Lesson Objectives and CA Correlations

1. **To analyze and respond to literary elements**
   - Literary Analysis: Conflict **R 3.3**
   - Connecting Literary Elements: Indirect Characterization **R 3.4**
2. **To read, comprehend, analyze, and critique a short story**
   - Reading Strategy: Identifying Causes and Effects
   - Reading Check questions
   - Review and Assess questions
   - Assessment Practice (ATE)
3. **To develop word analysis skills, fluency, and systematic vocabulary**
   - Vocabulary Development Lesson: Latin Word Root: *-dol-* **R 1.2**
4. **To understand and apply written and oral language conventions**
   - Spelling Strategy
   - Grammar Lesson: Different Kinds of Conjunctions **LC 1.2, 1.3**
5. **To understand and apply appropriate writing and research strategies**
   - Writing Lesson: News Story **W 2.3**
   - Extension Activity: Brochure **W 1.8**
6. **To understand and apply listening and speaking strategies**
   - Extension Activity: Debate **LS 1.5**

STEP-BY-STEP TEACHING GUIDE	PACING GUIDE
PRETEACH	
Motivate Students and Provide Background	
Use the Motivation activity (ATE p. 302)	5 min.
Read and discuss the Preview material and Background information (SE/ATE p. 302) [A]	10 min.
Introduce the Concepts	
Introduce the Literary Analysis and Reading Strategy (SE/ATE p. 303) [A]	15 min.
Pronounce the vocabulary words and read their definitions (SE p. 303)	5 min.
TEACH	
Monitor Comprehension	
Informally monitor comprehension by circulating while students read independently or in groups [A]	20 min.
Monitor students' comprehension with the Reading Check notes (SE/ATE pp. 305, 307, 309)	as students read
Develop vocabulary with Vocabulary notes (SE pp. 304–307, 309; ATE p. 307)	as students read
Develop Understanding	
Develop students' understanding of conflict with Literary Analysis annotations (SE pp. 305, 307, 308; ATE pp. 305, 307) [A]	10 min.
Develop students' ability to identify cause and effect with Reading Strategy annotations (SE p. 305; ATE pp. 305, 306, 309)	10 min.
ASSESS	
Assess Mastery	
Assess students' mastery of the Reading Strategy and Literary Analysis by having them answer the Review and Assess questions (SE/ATE p. 311)	20 min.
Use one or more of the print and media Assessment Resources (ATE p. 313) [A]	up to 50 min.
EXTEND	
Apply Understanding	
Have students complete the Vocabulary Development Lesson and the Grammar Lesson (SE p. 312) [A]	20 min.
Apply students' knowledge of using elaboration to create understanding with the Writing Lesson (SE/ATE p. 313) [A]	45 min.
Apply students' understanding using one or more of the Extension Activities (SE p. 313)	20–90 min.

[A] **ACCELERATED INSTRUCTION:**
Use the strategies and activities identified with an [A].

UNIVERSAL ACCESS
● = Below-Level Students
▲ = On-Level Students
■ = Above-Level Students

Time and Resource Manager

Reading Level: Challenging
Average Number of Instructional Days: 4

RESOURCES		
PRINT	**TRANSPARENCIES**	**TECHNOLOGY**
• **Beyond Literature,** Workplace Skills: Problem Solving, p. 19 ▲ ■		• **Interest Grabber Video,** Tape 2 ● ▲ ■
• **Selection Support Workbook:** ● ▲ ■ Literary Analysis, p. 76 Reading Strategy, p. 75 Build Vocabulary, p. 73	• **Literary Analysis and Reading Transparencies,** pp. 37 and 38 ● ▲ ■	
• **Adapted Reader's Companion** ● • **Reader's Companion** ●		• **Listening to Literature** ● ▲ ■ Audiocassettes, Side 9 Audio CDs, CD 7
• **English Learner's Companion** ● ▲ • **Literatura en español** ● ▲ • **Literary Analysis for Enrichment** ■		
• **Formal Assessment:** Selection Test, pp. 63–65 ● ▲ ■ • **Open Book Test,** pp. 55–57 ● ▲ ■ • PRENTICE HALL ASSESSMENT SYSTEM ● ▲ ■	• PRENTICE HALL ASSESSMENT SYSTEM ● ▲ ■ Skills Practice Answers and Explanations on Transparencies	• **Test Bank Software** ● ▲ ■ • **Got It! Assessment Videotapes** ● ▲
• **Selection Support Workbook:** ● ▲ ■ Build Grammar Skills, p. 74 • **Writing and Grammar,** Gold Level ● ▲ ■ • **Extension Activities,** p. 19 ● ▲ ■	• **Daily Language Practice Transparencies** ● ▲	• **Writing and Grammar iText CD-ROM** ● ▲ ■ ***Take It to the Net*** www.phschool.com

BLOCK SCHEDULING: Use one 90-minute class period to preteach the selection and have students read it. Use a second 90-minute class period to assess students' mastery of skills and have them complete one of the Extension Activities.

PREACH

Step-by-Step Teaching Guide for pp. 302–303

Motivation

Ask students to imagine that they are trapped alone in the classroom with someone they dislike. There seems to be no hope for escape, and they have only each other to talk to. Initiate a discussion by asking such questions as: How might being trapped together affect your feelings about each other? What would you say to each other? What might happen to your relationship?

Tell students that the story focuses on a feud between enemies and that the ending—typical of stories by Saki—really packs a punch.

Interest Grabber Video

As an alternative, you may wish to play "Saki: A Man of Many Surprises" on Tape 2 to engage student interest.

1 Background

Social Studies

The feud between the Hatfields, who lived on the West Virginia side of a stream that divides West Virginia and Kentucky, and the McCoys, who lived on the Kentucky side, has fascinated the public since the 1880s. It has passed into legend as the bloodiest disagreement among neighbors in American history.

Bad feelings had existed between the families since the Civil War, but it was a legal dispute over two hogs that led to the first shootings in 1878. Perhaps the climax of the feud came in 1888, when at least six people were killed, including one young McCoy woman and the Hatfield convicted and executed for her murder. The two family patriarchs who began the feud lived to great old age.

Prepare to Read

The Interlopers

Take It to the Net

Visit www.phschool.com for interactive activities and instruction related to "The Interlopers," including

- background
- graphic organizers
- literary elements
- reading strategies

Preview

Connecting to the Literature

All people get into arguments from time to time, but most disagreements do not last for a lifetime, as is the case with the characters in "The Interlopers." Think about how a long-standing dispute between two people can come to a disastrous end.

1 Background

A feud is a bitter, prolonged fight, typically between families or clans, that may continue for years or even generations. It may start with a single insult or injury, which provokes an act of revenge. This act in turn prompts a response, and the cycle of anger and violence is set in motion. The brutality of a feud can make for gripping drama, as it does in "The Interlopers."

TEACHING RESOURCES

The following resources can be used to enrich or extend the instruction for pp. 302–303.

Interest Grabber Video, Tape 2

Background

Beyond Literature, Workplace Skills, p. 19

Take It to the Net

Visit www.phschool.com for background and hotlinks for "The Interlopers."

Literary Analysis

Literary Analysis and Reading Transparencies, Conflict, p. 38

Reading

Selection Support: Literary Analysis, p. 76

Literary Analysis and Reading Transparencies, Identifying Causes and Effects, p. 37

BLOCK SCHEDULING: Resources marked with this symbol provide varied instruction during 90-minute blocks.

❷ Literary Analysis

Conflict

The **conflict** in a story is the struggle between opposing forces. A conflict may be internal or external. An **internal conflict** occurs within a character who experiences opposing ideas or feelings. In contrast, an **external conflict** occurs between characters or between a character and a force of nature. This passage shows a conflict between two men:

> The two enemies stood glaring at one another for a long silent moment. Each had a rifle in his hand, each had hate in his heart and murder uppermost in his mind.

As you read "The Interlopers," look for details that describe and explain the conflicts between and within the two main characters.

Connecting Literary Elements

To build the conflict of this story, the author uses **indirect characterization,** revealing only what a character does, says, and thinks. This leaves readers to draw their own conclusions about the nature of the characters and the conflict. In "The Interlopers," the writer allows the words and deeds of Ulrich and Georg to disclose what they are really like. Their actions and speech demonstrate and build the underlying conflict between them.

❸ Reading Strategy

Identifying Causes and Effects

Understanding the causes and effects in a story can help clarify a conflict between characters.

- A **cause** is the reason for an action or event. In "The Interlopers," the cause of a long-standing feud is an old land dispute.
- An **effect** is the result of an action or event. In the story, the effect of the ancient land dispute is the personal feud between the two men.

Record the causes and effects of the story in a chart like this one.

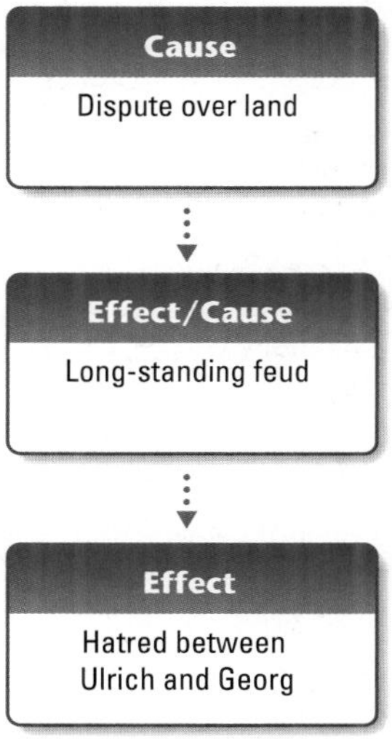

Vocabulary Development

precipitous (prē sip´ ə təs) *adj.* steep; sheer (p. 304)

marauders (mə rôd´ ərz) *n.* raiders; people who take goods by force (p. 305)

medley (med´ lē) *n.* mixture of things not usually found together (p. 306)

condolences (kən dō´ lən səz) *n.* expressions of sympathy with a grieving person's pain (p. 307)

languor (laŋ´ gər) *n.* lack of vigor; weakness; weariness (p. 307)

succor (suk´ ər) *n.* relief; aid; assistance (p. 309)

CUSTOMIZE INSTRUCTION FOR UNIVERSAL ACCESS

For Less Proficient Readers	For English Learners	For Advanced Readers
To help students understand conflicts in literature, point out that conflicts between characters in stories are no different from conflicts between people in real life. You may wish to cite other "border disputes" that have caused conflicts.	As you discuss conflict with students, draw a graphic representation on the board, such as two facing arrows, to make sure they understand the word *conflict.* Graphics can also help English learners distinguish between the words *internal* and *external.*	Encourage students to gather in small groups to talk about some recent conflicts among nations. Ask them to identify the opposing forces, describe the causes and effects, and suggest possible solutions to each of the conflicts they discuss.

❷ Literary Analysis

Conflict

- Tell students that as they read "The Interlopers," they will focus on *conflict,* the struggle between opposing internal or external forces.
- Read the instruction together as a class. Make sure students understand that the sample passage from the story shows an external conflict. Have students provide examples of internal conflict from their own lives.
- Use the instruction for Connecting Literary Elements to sensitize students to the internal and external conflicts revealed by the actions of both characters.
- Use the Conflict transparency in **Literary Analysis and Reading Transparencies,** p. 38, to trace the internal and external conflicts of the two characters.

❸ Reading Strategy

Identifying Causes and Effects

- Remind students that *causes* make things happen and *effects* are what happens. Point out that events can be both effects of previous causes and causes of subsequent effects.
- Use the Cause-and-Effect Chart in the student book to demonstrate how a chain of causes and effects advances the plot of a story.
- Instruct students to create their own cause-and-effect charts to record significant events as they read "The Interlopers."

Vocabulary Development

- Pronounce each vocabulary word for students, and read the definitions as a class. Have students identify any words with which they are already familiar.

E-Teach

Visit E-Teach at www.phschool.com for teachers' essays on how to teach, with questions and answers.

TEACH

Step-by-Step Teaching Guide for pp. 304–310

CUSTOMIZE INSTRUCTION For Interpersonal Learners

As students read "The Interlopers," have them identify points in the story at which the feuding families might have resolved their disagreement, as well as specific ways they might have gone about it. Ask students to invent the constructive dialogue Ulrich von Gradwitz and Georg Znaeym might have had that would have forestalled the destruction suggested at the ending of the story.

❶ About the Selection

This story shows that a feud not only fuels feelings of hatred and bitterness, but it has the power to destroy feuding parties. "The Interlopers" begins at the climax of a generations-long feud, as two of the antagonists find themselves face to face in the forest. As they are about to destroy each other, a tree crashes down and traps them. During the time they are trapped, they agree to reconcile. As the story ends, however, it appears that their decision has come too late. Written in the early 1900s, the story resonates today when people and nations still cannot put an end to their feuding.

❶ The Interlopers

Saki

In a forest of mixed growth somewhere on the eastern spurs of the Carpathians,[1] a man stood one winter night watching and listening, as though he waited for some beast of the woods to come within the range of his vision, and, later, of his rifle. But the game for whose presence he kept so keen an outlook was none that figured in the sportsman's calendar as lawful and proper for the chase: Ulrich von Gradwitz (o͞ol′ rik fôn gräd′ vitz) patrolled the dark forest in quest of a human enemy.

The forest lands of Gradwitz were of wide extent and well stocked with game; the narrow strip of precipitous woodland that lay on its outskirt was not remarkable for the game it harbored or the shooting it afforded, but it was the most jealously guarded of all its owner's territorial possessions. A famous lawsuit, in the days of his grandfather, had wrested it from the illegal possession of a neighboring family of petty landowners; the dispossessed party had never acquiesced in the judgment

precipitous (prē sip′ ə təs) *adj.* steep; sheer

1. **Carpathians** (kär pā′ thē ənz) mountains in central Europe.

TEACHING RESOURCES

The following resources can be used to enrich or extend the instruction for pp. 304–310.

Literary Analysis

- **Selection Support:** Literary Analysis, p. 76

Reading

- **Reader's Companion**
- **English Learner's Companion**
- **Listening to Literature Audiocassettes,** Side 9 ■
- **Listening to Literature Audio CDs,** CD 7 ■

■ **BLOCK SCHEDULING:** Resources marked with this symbol provide varied instruction during 90-minute blocks.

of the Courts, and a long series of poaching affrays[2] and similar scandals had embittered the relationships between the families for three generations. The neighbor feud had grown into a personal one since Ulrich had come to be head of his family; if there was a man in the world whom he detested and wished ill to it was Georg Znaeym (gā´ ôrg znä´ im), the inheritor of the quarrel and the tireless game-snatcher and raider of the disputed border-forest. The feud might,
2 perhaps, have died down or been compromised if the personal ill will of the two men had not stood in the way; as boys they had thirsted for one another's blood, as men each prayed that misfortune might fall on the other, and this wind-scourged winter night Ulrich had banded together his foresters to watch the dark forest, not in quest of four-footed quarry, but to keep a lookout for the prowling thieves whom he suspected of being afoot from across the land boundary. The roebuck[3] which usually kept in the sheltered hollows during a storm wind, were running like driven things tonight, and there was movement and unrest among the creatures that were wont to sleep through the dark hours. Assuredly there was a disturbing element in the forest, and Ulrich could guess the quarter from whence it came.

He strayed away by himself from the watchers whom he had placed in ambush on the crest of the hill, and wandered far down the steep slopes amid the wild tangle of undergrowth, peering through the tree trunks and listening through the whistling and skirling of the wind and the restless beating of the branches for sight or sound of the marauders. If only on this wild night, in this dark, lone spot, he might come across Georg Znaeym, man to man, with none to witness—that was the wish that was uppermost in his thoughts. And as he stepped round the trunk of a huge beech he came face to face with the man he sought.

The two enemies stood glaring at one another for a long silent moment. Each had a rifle in his hand, each had hate in his heart and murder uppermost in his mind. The chance had come to give full play to the passions of a lifetime. But a man who has been brought up under the code of a restraining civilization cannot easily nerve himself
3 to shoot down his neighbor in cold blood and without word spoken, except for an offense against his hearth and honor. And before the moment of hesitation had given way to action a deed of Nature's own violence overwhelmed them both. A fierce shriek of the storm had been answered by a splitting crash over their heads, and ere they could leap aside a mass of falling beech tree had thundered down on them. Ulrich von Gradwitz found himself stretched on the ground, one arm numb beneath him and the other held almost as helplessly in a tight tangle of forked branches, while both legs were pinned beneath the fallen mass. His heavy shooting-boots had saved his feet from being crushed to pieces, but if his fractures were not as serious

2. **poaching affrays** (pōch´ iŋ ə frāz´) disputes about hunting on someone else's property.
3. **roebuck** (rō´ buk´) *n.* male deer.

Reading Strategy
Identifying Causes and Effects What event is the cause for the feud?

marauders (mə rôd´ ərz) *n.* raiders; people who take goods by force

Literary Analysis
Conflict How is the bitterness between the two landowners evident in this passage?

4 ✓**Reading Check**
What happens to the men when they come face to face?

2 Reading Strategy
Identifying Causes and Effects
- Ask students the Reading Strategy question on p. 305: What event is the cause for the feud?
  Answer: A lawsuit over a narrow strip of land is the cause for the feud.
- Then, read aloud the bracketed passage. Ask students to identify what causes the feud to continue and what immediate effect the feud has on Ulrich.
  Answer: The personal hatred between Ulrich and Georg causes the feud to continue. The immediate effect on Ulrich is to send him into the forest where he suspects thieves are prowling.

3 Literary Analysis
Conflict
- Read aloud the bracketed passage. Then, ask a volunteer to identify the conflict and explain whether it is internal or external. Make sure the volunteer supports his or her response with details from the text.
  Answer: The conflict over the disputed piece of land is between two characters, Ulrich and Georg, so it is external.
- Ask students the Literary Analysis question on p. 305: How is the bitterness between the two landowners evident in this passage?
  Answer: The landowners' bitterness has brought their conflict to the point of deadly violence.

4 ✓Reading Check
Answer: The men glare at each other, but before they can shoot, a tree falls and pins them to the ground.

CUSTOMIZE INSTRUCTION FOR UNIVERSAL ACCESS

Special Needs Students	Less Proficient Readers	For Gifted/Talented Students
Read the first four paragraphs aloud to students or have students listen to the paragraphs on the **Listening to Literature Audiocassettes,** Side 9 or **Audio CDs,** CD 7, as they follow along in their book. Have volunteers summarize each paragraph. Define any words students cannot figure out from context.	For extra support, pair less proficient readers with students who read at grade level. Have students read the first four paragraphs of the story aloud together twice. The first time, they should read straight through. The second time, encourage students to stop as necessary to puzzle out difficult syntax and vocabulary.	Challenge students to demonstrate their understanding of the story by writing a ballad about the feud between the von Gradwitz and Znaeym families. Ask students to base their ballad on the information they gather in the first four paragraphs of "The Interlopers."

❺ Reading Strategy

Identifying Causes and Effects

- Ask students what causes Ulrich to give thanks and curse, and Georg to laugh.
  Answer: The story explains that relief and exasperation cause Ulrich's mixed reactions. Georg laughs at his enemy's predicament. In a deeper sense, both characters' fear at their situation causes them to put on a show of bravado.
- The difficult situation also causes Ulrich and Georg to boast about what their men will do when they find Ulrich and Georg. After exploring the causes of their statements, ask students what effect Georg and Ulrich hope to achieve by telling each other about how their men will find them.
  Answer: The most plausible explanation for the effect the characters wish to have is that they hope to intimidate each other and by doing so to boost their own morale.
- Have students record these causes and their effects in the charts they created at the beginning of this selection.

❻ ▶Critical Viewing

Answer: The cold and darkness intensify the danger and reduce chances of rescue by searchers.

as they might have been, at least it was evident that he could not move from his present position till someone came to release him. The descending twigs had slashed the skin of his face, and he had to wink away some drops of blood from his eyelashes before he could take in a general view of the disaster. At his side, so near that under ordinary circumstances he could almost have touched him, lay Georg Znaeym, alive and struggling, but obviously as helplessly pinioned down as himself. All round them lay a thick-strewn wreckage of splintered branches and broken twigs.

Relief at being alive and exasperation at his captive plight brought a strange medley of pious thank-offerings and sharp curses to Ulrich's lips. Georg, who was nearly blinded with the blood which trickled across his eyes, stopped his struggling for a moment to listen, and then gave a short, snarling laugh.

"So you're not killed, as you ought to be, but you're caught, anyway," he cried; "caught fast. Ho, what a jest, Ulrich von Gradwitz ❺ snared in his stolen forest. There's real justice for you!"

And he laughed again, mockingly and savagely.

"I'm caught in my own forest land," retorted Ulrich. "When my men come to release us you will wish, perhaps, that you were in a better plight than caught poaching on a neighbor's land, shame on you."

Georg was silent for a moment; then he answered quietly:

"Are you sure that your men will find much to release? I have men, too, in the forest tonight, close behind me, and *they* will be here first

medley (med′ lē) *n.* mixture of things not usually found together

❻ ▼ **Critical Viewing** Why does the setting—a snowy forest like the one shown here—intensify the danger of the conflict? **[Connect]**

Untitled, Rob Wood, Illustration by Wood Ronsaville Harlin, Inc.

ENRICHMENT: Social Studies Connection

Border Disputes

Disputes over land play large—and sometimes violent—roles in the history of individuals and nations. The continental borders of the United States were shaped in part by purchase and treaty, but also by war (the Mexican War, for example, and multiple conflicts with Native Americans). In Europe, territorial disputes over regions such as Alsace-Lorraine, the Balkan Peninsula, and the Danzig Corridor aggravated tensions that led to two world wars. Significant territorial disputes continue in eastern Europe and the Far East, and many land claims of Native American tribes are pending in federal courts.

and do the releasing. When they drag me out from under these branches it won't need much clumsiness on their part to roll this mass of trunk right over on the top of you. Your men will find you dead under a fallen beech tree. For form's sake I shall send my condolences to your family."

"It is a useful hint," said Ulrich fiercely. "My men had orders to follow in ten minutes' time, seven of which must have gone by already, and when they get me out—I will remember the hint. Only as you will have met your death poaching on my lands I don't think I can decently send any message of condolence to your family."

"Good," snarled Georg, "good. We fight this quarrel out to the death, you and I and our foresters, with no cursed interlopers to come between us. Death and damnation to you, Ulrich von Gradwitz."

"The same to you, Georg Znaeym, forest-thief, game-snatcher."

Both men spoke with the bitterness of possible defeat before them, for each knew that it might be long before his men would seek him out or find him; it was a bare matter of chance which party would arrive first on the scene.

Both had now given up the useless struggle to free themselves from the mass of wood that held them down; Ulrich limited his endeavors to an effort to bring his one partially free arm near enough to his outer coat pocket to draw out his wine flask. Even when he had accomplished that operation it was long before he could manage the unscrewing of the stopper or get any of the liquid down his throat. But what a heaven-sent draft it seemed! It was an open winter, and little snow had fallen as yet, hence the captives suffered less from the cold than might have been the case at that season of the year; nevertheless, the wine was warming and reviving to the wounded man, and he looked across with something like a throb of pity to where his enemy lay, just keeping the groans of pain and weariness from crossing his lips.

"Could you reach this flask if I threw it over to you?" asked Ulrich suddenly; "there is good wine in it, and one may as well be as comfortable as one can. Let us drink, even if tonight one of us dies."

"No, I can scarcely see anything; there is so much blood caked round my eyes," said Georg, "and in any case I don't drink wine with an enemy."

Ulrich was silent for a few minutes, and lay listening to the weary screeching of the wind. An idea was slowly forming and growing in his brain, an idea that gained strength every time that he looked across at the man who was fighting so grimly against pain and exhaustion. In the pain and languor that Ulrich himself was feeling the old fierce hatred seemed to be dying down.

"Neighbor," he said presently, "do as you please if your men come first. It was a fair compact. But as for me, I've changed my mind. If my men are the first to come you shall be the first to be helped, as though you were my guest. We have quarreled like devils all our lives over this stupid strip of forest, where the trees can't even stand

condolences (kən dō´ lən səz) *n.* expressions of sympathy with a grieving person's pain

Literary Analysis
Conflict and Indirect Characterization What can you conclude about the men's characters from their exchange of comments here?

languor (laŋ´ gər) *n.* lack of vigor; weakness; weariness

10 **Reading Check**
What happens to the two men after the tree falls?

7 Vocabulary Development

The Latin Word Root *-dol-*

- Call students' attention to the meaning of the word *condolence*. Explain that the Latin root *–dol–* means "pain." It is derived from the word *dolore*.
- Have students think of other words with this root and then define each word.
  Answer: *doldrums,* "period of stagnation or unhappy listlessness," *doleful,* "full of sadness caused by pain," and *dolorous,* "marked by sorrow or pain."
- Have a volunteer look up in a dictionary the words that no one can define confidently.

8 Literary Analysis

Conflict and Indirect Characterization

Reteach Remind students that when an author uses indirect characterization as in "The Interlopers," the author does not comment directly on the characters but lets their actions, words, and thoughts reveal them.

- Ask the Literary Analysis question on p. 307: What can you conclude about the men's characters from their exchange of comments here?
  Answer: The exchange reveals the men's intractable hatred of each other.

9 Critical Thinking

Compare and Contrast

- Remind students that comparing and contrasting are useful strategies for gaining meaning from text.
- Draw students' attention to Ulrich's offer of wine to Georg and Georg's rebuff. Then, ask students to explain why the men have different attitudes.
  Answer: Ulrich is in a better position to be magnanimous because the court decision was in his family's favor. Georg is trespassing on Ulrich's property, so he is more defensive than Ulrich is.

10 Reading Check

Answer: The men are pinned under the tree and can't free themselves.

CUSTOMIZE INSTRUCTION FOR UNIVERSAL ACCESS

For Less Proficient Readers	For English Learners	For Advanced Readers
Have students focus on the vocabulary words in the story. Ask them to read aloud each word, its definition, and the sentence in which it appears in the story. Then, ask students to use each vocabulary word in a sentence of their own to help their comprehension of these words in the selection.	Ask students to choose several words from the story they would like to make part of their spoken and written vocabularies. Have them practice saying the words. Then, ask them to make a flash card for each word by writing the word on one side of an index card and the meaning and a context sentence on the other.	Have students consider how Saki's choice of words contributes to the mood and tone of "The Interlopers." Have them write a short paper on the topic of Saki's word choice in "The Interlopers" in which they include examples of words and phrases from the story.

⓫ ▶Critical Viewing

Answer: Students may suggest that unexpected and dangerous encounters would occur in such a bleak setting. They may find the trail of footsteps ominous.

⓬ Literary Focus

Conflict

- Ask students the Literary Analysis question on p. 308: How has the nature of the conflict between the two men now changed?
  Answer: Georg's response to Ulrich's peace offering resolves both the conflict between them and Georg's internal conflict as well.
- Ask students to speculate about why trying circumstances, such as the one in "The Interlopers," can cause the characters to change dramatically. Urge students to think about causes of change in their own lives as they discuss this issue.

⓭ Critical Thinking

Analyze Character

- Note that this is the second time Georg has referred to *interlopers.* Ask students why this word is significant to him.
  Answer: Georg believes that interlopers (members of the court) caused his family to lose its land.
- Have students recall other interlopers they have encountered in stories as well as in their own lives. Ask: "Is being an interloper always wrong?"
  Answer: Students may point out that if someone observes an injustice or a danger, being an interloper, or meddling, can be the right thing to do. Sherlock Holmes and other civilian detectives of fiction could be described as interlopers.

upright in a breath of wind. Lying here tonight, thinking, I've come to think we've been rather fools; there are better things in life than getting the better of a boundary dispute. Neighbor, if you will help me to bury the old quarrel I—I will ask you to be my friend."

Georg Znaeym was silent for so long that Ulrich thought, perhaps, he had fainted with the pain of his injuries. Then he spoke slowly and in jerks.

"How the whole region would stare and gabble if we rode into the market square together. No one living can remember seeing a Znaeym ⓬ and a von Gradwitz talking to one another in friendship. And what peace there would be among the forester folk if we ended our feud tonight. ⓭ And if we choose to make peace among our people there is none other to interfere, no interlopers from outside . . . You would come and keep the Sylvester night beneath my roof, and I would come and feast on some high day at your castle . . . I would never fire a shot on your land, save when you invited me as a guest; and you should come and shoot with me down in the marshes where the wildfowl are. In all the countryside there are none that could hinder if we willed to make peace. I never thought to have wanted to do

⓫ ▲ **Critical Viewing** What kinds of encounters or incidents might occur in this setting? **[Analyze]**

Literary Analysis

Conflict How has the nature of the conflict between the two men now changed?

other than hate you all my life, but I think I have changed my mind about things too, this last half-hour. And you offered me your wine flask . . . Ulrich von Gradwitz, I will be your friend."

For a space both men were silent, turning over in their minds the wonderful changes that this dramatic reconciliation would bring about. In the cold, gloomy forest, with the wind tearing in fitful gusts through the naked branches and whistling round the tree trunks, they lay and waited for the help that would now bring release and succor to both parties. And each prayed a private prayer that his men might be the first to arrive, so that he might be the first to show honorable attention to the enemy that had become a friend.

14 15 Presently, as the wind dropped for a moment, Ulrich broke silence. "Let's shout for help," he said; "in this lull our voices may carry a little way."

"They won't carry far through the trees and undergrowth," said Georg, "but we can try. Together, then."

The two raised their voices in a prolonged hunting call.

"Together again," said Ulrich a few minutes later, after listening in vain for an answering halloo.

succor (suk´ ər) *n.* relief; aid; assistance

16 **Reading Check**

What response does Georg give when Ulrich asks him to be his friend?

14 Reading Strategy

Identifying Causes and Effects

- Ask students what effect the wind dying down has on Ulrich.
  Answer: Ulrich suggests that he and Georg call for help since the lull may let their voices carry farther.

Monitor Progress Explain to students that once they have identified an effect, they can look for a cause. Ask them to identify the cause for Ulrich to suggest that he and Georg call for help.
Answer: The lull in the wind causes Ulrich's suggestion.

15 Critical Thinking

Predict

- Have students stop their reading at this point.
- Have them consider how the story may end based on what has happened in the story so far, what they have learned about the characters, and how the characters have changed.
  Answer: Many students will predict that the two men will be saved, the feud will end forever, and the story will end happily. They will soon learn how wrong they were.

16 Reading Check

Answer: Georg is silent for a while and then gratefully accepts Ulrich's offer of friendship.

CUSTOMIZE INSTRUCTION FOR UNIVERSAL ACCESS

For Less Proficient Readers	For Gifted/Talented Students	For Advanced Readers
Point out to students that on this page they read what the characters say and what they think. They also read sentences that tell what happens and thus advance the plot. Ask volunteers to identify speech, thought, and narration on this page.	Have students discuss Ulrich and Georg's feelings as this point in the story. Then, drawing from this discussion, let them perform the page as Reader's Theater with one person reading Ulrich's words, one reading Georg's words, and a narrator reading the text that is not dialogue.	Ask volunteers to describe Ulrich and Georg's feelings at this point in the story. Then, have students discuss with each other whether they find Ulrich and Georg's changes of heart plausible. Urge them to support their opinions with evidence from the story.

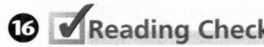

ASSESS

Answers for p. 310

Review and Assess

1. Students may sympathize with Ulrich because Georg was poaching Ulrich's land; or with Georg because his family had been dispossessed by a judgment of the Courts; or with neither man because the men were unwilling to compromise.
2. **(a)** Ulrich's family won possession of the land. **(b)** Georg doesn't accept the Court's decision, so he doesn't consider himself a poacher.
3. **(a)** The feud reached back through Ulrich and Georg's families for two generations. **(b)** As head of his family, Ulrich deeply resents Georg as a "game-snatcher" and "raider" of his family's land.
4. **(a)** Both men are pinned under the tree. **(b)** Their difficult circumstances help the men to realize how much better their lives would be if they were friends.
5. **(a)** Most students will believe that the men would have fulfilled their promises of friendship. **(b)** The men's change in attitude occurs in a life-or-death situation and seems heartfelt.
6. **(a)** Some students may believe that the men deserved their fate because of their stubbornness in holding onto their hatred. **(b)** One possible lesson is that people should resolve their differences while they have the opportunity to do so.
7. **(a)** Students may believe that people inherit their traditions, their likes and dislikes, and their beliefs from their families and that to change family traditions would be to disavow their families. **(b)** Students may believe that such feuds will never end as long as human nature remains as it is.

"I heard something that time, I think," said Ulrich.

"I heard nothing but the pestilential wind," said Georg hoarsely.

There was silence again for some minutes, and then Ulrich gave a joyful cry.

"I can see figures coming through the wood. They are following in the way I came down the hillside."

Both men raised their voices in as loud a shout as they could muster.

"They hear us! They've stopped. Now they see us. They're running down the hill toward us," cried Ulrich.

"How many of them are there?" asked Georg.

"I can't see distinctly," said Ulrich; "nine or ten."

"Then they are yours," said Georg; "I had only seven out with me."

"They are making all the speed they can, brave lads," said Ulrich gladly.

"Are they your men?" asked Georg. "Are they your men?" he repeated impatiently as Ulrich did not answer.

"No," said Ulrich with a laugh, the idiotic chattering laugh of a man unstrung with hideous fear.

"Who are they?" asked Georg quickly, straining his eyes to see what the other would gladly not have seen.

"Wolves."

Review and Assess

Thinking About the Selection

1. **Respond:** With whom did you sympathize: Ulrich, Georg, neither, or both? Why?
2. (a) **Recall:** Whose family won possession of the disputed land in the lawsuit? (b) **Interpret:** Why does Georg not consider himself a poacher?
3. (a) **Recall:** How far back does the hatred between Ulrich and Georg go? (b) **Infer:** Which factors about the feud seem to contribute the most to Ulrich's anger at Georg?
4. (a) **Recall:** In what condition does the fallen tree leave each man? (b) **Draw Conclusions:** Why do the men end their feud?
5. (a) **Speculate:** How might the story have continued if the two men had been rescued? (b) **Support:** Why do you think so?
6. (a) **Evaluate:** Considering the cause of their predicament, do you think the two men deserved their fate? Why or why not? (b) **Extend:** What lesson can be learned from the experiences of Ulrich and Georg?
7. (a) **Apply:** What is it about human nature that leads to feuds like the one in the story? (b) **Speculate:** Will it ever be possible to end such feuds? Explain.

Saki

(1870–1916)

Saki is the pen name of the British writer H. H. Munro. Born in Burma, he was sent at age two to live in England, where he was raised in a strict household by two aunts. As a young adult, he returned to Burma to serve in the police force. Two years later, however, poor health forced him to return to England, where he began working as a jounalist. After serving as a newspaper correspondent in Russia and France, Saki settled in London.

In 1904, his first collection of short stories was published. He later wrote more short stories and two novels.

Saki was killed in France during World War I. In his honor, the king of England issued a scroll that concludes, "Let those who come after see to it that his name is not forgotten."

ASSESSMENT PRACTICE: Reading Comprehension

Stated Main Idea (For more practice, see Test Preparation Workbook, p. 19.)

Many tests, including the SAT, require students to recognize main ideas. Use the following sample test item to demonstrate for students how to identify a stated main idea. Have students read the opening paragraph of "The Interlopers." Write the question and answer choices on the chalkboard.

What is the stated main idea of the passage?

A A man stood one winter night watching and listening.

B A forest of mixed growth is located on the eastern spurs of the Carpathians.

C Ulrich was in quest of a human enemy.

D The sportsman's game was not lawful and proper for the chase.

To help students identify the main idea, suggest that they try to summarize the passage. *C* is correct; it states the main idea. *B* describes the setting and *A* and *D* are supporting details.

Review and Assess

Literary Analysis

Conflict

1. What **external conflict** pits a character against another character in "The Interlopers"?
2. Identify a conflict that pits a character against a force of nature.
3. Give an example of an **internal conflict** within Ulrich or Georg.
4. Using a chart like the one shown, analyze a conflict that changes or develops as the story continues.

Developing conflict	Reason for change

Connecting Literary Elements

5. Using a character-trait diagram like this one, list the traits you detect in each man. Cite examples from the story.

Character	Traits		Examples
	______	···▸	______
	______	···▸	______

6. How does the use of **indirect characterization** illuminate the conflict between the two men? Give specific details.

Reading Strategy

Identifying Causes and Effects

7. (a) What **causes** the beech tree to fall over? (b) What is the **effect** of that event?
8. (a) Why do the men shout together at the end? (b) What is the effect of their shouting? (c) Is it the effect they expect?

Extend Understanding

9. **Social Studies Connection:** (a) Explain the options for resolving a bitter territorial dispute among nations in today's world. (b) Why are such problems so complicated?

Quick Review

Conflict in a story is the struggle between opposing forces.
An **internal conflict** occurs within a character.
An **external conflict** occurs between characters or between a character and a force of nature.

When using **indirect characterization,** an author reveals only what a character does, says, and thinks, leaving readers to draw conclusions about the nature of the character.

A **cause** is the reason for an action or event.
An **effect** is what results from that action or event.

Take It to the Net
www.phschool.com
Take the interactive self-test online to check your understanding of the selections.

ENRICHMENT: Further Reading

Other Works by Saki

The Story-teller: Thirteen Tales by Saki
"The Open Window"
"Sredni Vashtar"

Take It to the Net
Visit www.phschool.com for more information on Saki.

Answers for p. 311

Review and Assess

1. The main external conflict in the story is Ulrich and Georg's personal hatred stemming from their families' conflict over the land.
2. Possible response: The characters' struggle against the tree that has them pinned is an example of characters battling nature.
3. Possible response: Ulrich has an internal conflict between his hatred of Georg and the pity he feels as he watches Georg suffer.
4.

Developing conflict	hatred between George and Urich
Reason for change	tree traps George and Ulrich

5. Character: Ulrich; Trait: hate-filled; Example: wants to kill Georg.
Character: Georg; Trait: stubborn; Example: hunts on Ulrich's land
6. Students may cite the indirect characterization demonstrated in the blustering speeches Ulrich and Georg make to each other just after they are pinned by the tree. They make terrible threats about what will happen when their men discover them, but their talk clearly reveals just how empty their boasts are.
7. **(a)** Lightning hits the tree. **(b)** Both enemies are trapped and injured.
8. **(a)** The men begin to shout for help. **(b)** Thier cries attract a pack of wolves. **(c)** This is not the effect they had hoped for.
9. **(a)** Options range from diplomatic discussions, to summit meetings and mediation by international organizations, to war. **(b)** Such problems are complicated by long, bitter histories, conflicting though valid claims, and geopolitical alliances among nations.

EXTEND

Answers for p. 312

❶ Vocabulary Development

Word Analysis

1. full of sadness caused by pain; possible sentence: He woke up doleful about their quarrel.
2. lazy; avoiding the pain of work; Deon enjoys being indolent on Sunday afternoons.

Spelling Strategy

1. spies
2. journeyed
3. strayed
4. flies

Fluency: Words in Context

Possible sentences:

1. Masked marauders broke into Pfaff Pharmacy at 2:00 A.M.
2. The landscape featured precipitous drops into deep ravines.
3. The rescue workers threw life jackets to the flood victims and then gave them food and other succor.
4. I would like to extend my condolences to you for the loss of your beloved Aunt Bea.
5. After so much time in bed with flu, I suffered considerable languor.
6. The program will feature a medley of Sousa marches.

❷ Grammar

1. and; coordinating
2. and; coordinating
3. neither, nor; correlative
4. so that; subordinating
5. but; coordinating

Writing Application

Possible response: Because of their families' longstanding feud over land rights, Ulrich von Gradwitz and Georg Znaeym nurture their hatred of each other. Ulrich searches for thieves in his forest late at night, and the two men come face to face. Before they can shoot each other, a tree pins them both to the ground. They come to reconcile, not because they are exceptional people, but because their plight has forced them to empathize with each other. Unfortunately their reconciliation has probably come too late because a pack of wolves is approaching.

Integrate Language Skills

❶ Vocabulary Development Lesson

Word Analysis: Latin Root *-dol-*

The Latin root *-dol-* means "pain." The root appears in the word *condolence*, meaning "an expression of sympathy with a grieving person's pain." Using the meaning of *-dol-*, define *doleful* and *indolent* and use each in a sentence.

Spelling Strategy

For many verbs ending in *y*, you must change the *y* to *i* or *ie* when you add an ending such as *-s* or *-ed*. For those that end in *y* preceded by a vowel, however, the spelling remains unchanged. For example, *medley* + *-s* = *medleys*.

For each item, add the ending shown and write the new word created.

1. spy + *-s*
2. journey + *-ed*
3. stray + *-ed*
4. fly + *-s*

Fluency: Words in Context

Write sentences as described below, using one word from the vocabulary list on page 303 for each sentence.

1. Write the lead sentence of a news article describing a robbery.
2. Describe the site of a rock-climbing expedition.
3. Explain what a group of rescue workers provides for flood victims.
4. Begin a letter to a friend who has lost an elderly family member.
5. Describe your feelings after spending a week in bed with the flu.
6. Write a description of a program honoring the composer of many famous songs.

❷ Grammar Lesson

Different Kinds of Conjunctions

A main clause is a group of words with a subject and a verb that makes sense even when it stands alone. In contrast, a subordinate clause makes sense only when it is linked to a main clause. **Conjunctions** connect words, word groups, or clauses.

A **subordinating conjunction** links a subordinate clause to the main clause of a sentence.

> **Subordinating:** *Before* they moved, the tree fell on them.

A **coordinating conjunction** joins main clauses or words of equal importance.

> **Coordinating:** They waited, *but* no one arrived.

Correlative conjunctions are pairs of conjunctions that link words of equal rank.

> **Correlative:** Ulrich watched, *not* in quest of quarry *but* to wait for thieves.

Practice Identify the conjunctions and classify each as *subordinating*, *coordinating*, or *correlative*.

1. Ulrich and Georg were enemies.
2. A tree fell, and the two men were trapped.
3. Neither Ulrich nor Georg was brave.
4. They yelled so that help would come.
5. Interlopers arrived, but they were wolves.

Writing Application Summarize the story, making use of at least one of each type of conjunction.

Prentice Hall Writing and Grammar Connection: Chapter 19, Section 2

TEACHING RESOURCES

The following resources can be used to enrich or extend the instruction for pp. 312–313.

Vocabulary

- **Selection Support:** Build Vocabulary, p. 73

Grammar

- **Selection Support:** Build Grammar Skills, p. 74
- **Writing and Grammar,** Gold Level, p. 408
- **Daily Language Practice Transparencies** ■

Writing

- **Writing and Grammar,** Gold Level, p. 106
- **Writing and Grammar iText CD-ROM** ■

■ **BLOCK SCHEDULING:** Resources marked with this symbol provide varied instruction during 90-minute blocks.

❸ Writing Lesson

News Story

Nature's own violence spells doom for Ulrich and Georg. Imagine you are a news reporter. Write a story about the freak accident and its aftermath.

Prewriting Focus on the questions *who? what? when? where? why?* and *how?* Include facts, quotations, and details below each heading in a chart. Then, plan your lead, or opening paragraph, which should summarize the news story.

Model: Recording Details in an Organizer

Who?	What?	When?	Where?	Why?	How?
Ulrich and Georg	Hit by a tree limb	Night	Ulrich's land	A beech tree fell on them	Tree blown down by storm

Drafting As you write the body of your story, use elaboration—the development of ideas and details—to help readers understand the news event. Clarify as much of the event as you can.

Revising Read your story aloud to a classmate. Change any part of the story that is unclear or requires further elaboration.

WG *Prentice Hall Writing and Grammar Connection: Chapter 6, Section 2*

❹ Extension Activities

Listening and Speaking To present a **debate** about the disputed land, form groups to represent each man. Each group should

- offer reasons why its character is entitled to the land.
- use quotations and other citations from the story to support its point of view.
- present an introductory statement, a rebuttal, and a closing statement.

Allot each team the same amount of time, and then ask the audience to decide which group was more persuasive. **[Group Activity]**

Research and Technology The chilling ending of "The Interlopers" comes about because of the unexpected arrival of wolves. Create a **brochure** that presents information about wolves. Design and publish your document with software and graphics programs that make charts, maps, or other graphics. Show where wolves live and how they raise their young, form packs, and hunt.

Take It to the Net www.phschool.com

Go online for an additional research activity using the Internet.

❸ Writing Lesson

- Display, distribute photocopies, or read a well-written news report to students.
- Have volunteers locate the answers to the questions *who? what? when? where? why?* and *how?* in the news report.
- Examine the order of importance of the information in the news report. Make sure students understand that the information in the article appears in decreasing order of importance, so that the article may be cut for length without losing the essential facts.
- Explain that students can prepare to write their own news report by filling in a chart similar to the one shown on p. 313 to make sure they answer the five questions.

❹ Research and Technology

- Have students form small groups to produce their brochures. Group members should choose research and production tasks: researching various aspects of the topic, drafting, editing and proofreading, design and illustration, and publishing.
- Suggest that at least one person in each group become familiar with the software program they will use to produce the brochure. Group members who are less adept at using technology can learn from these experts.
- All group members should review the brochure at the rough draft stage and make suggestions and corrections.

CUSTOMIZE INSTRUCTION for Universal Access

To address different learning styles, use the activities suggested in the **Extension Activities** booklet, p. 19.

- For Verbal/Linguistic Learners, use Activity 4.
- For Interpersonal and Verbal/Linguistic Learners, use Activity 5.
- For Bodily/Kinesthetic and Verbal/Linguistic Learners, use Activity 6.

ASSESSMENT RESOURCES

The following resources can be used to assess students' knowledge and skills.

Selection Assessment

- **Formal Assessment,** pp. 63–65
- **Open Book Test,** pp. 55–57
- **Got It! Assessment Videotapes,** Tape 2
- **Test Bank Software**

Take It to the Net
Visit www.phschool.com for self-tests and additional questions on "The Interlopers."

PRENTICE HALL ASSESSMENT SYSTEM

- **Workbook**
- **Skill Book**
- **Transparencies**
- **CD-ROM**

The Rug Merchant

Lesson Objectives and CA Correlations

1. **To analyze and respond to literary elements**
   - Literary Analysis: Characterization in Essays **R 3.3, 3.4**
   - Connecting Literary Elements: First Person Narration **R 3.4**
2. **To read, comprehend, analyze, and critique nonfiction**
   - Reading Strategy: Making Inferences About Characters **R 3.3, 3.4**
   - Reading Check questions
   - Review and Assess questions
   - Assessment Practice (ATE)
3. **To develop word analysis skills, fluency, and systematic vocabulary**
   - Vocabulary Development Lesson: Latin Word Root: *-vis-* **R 1.1**
4. **To understand and apply written and oral language conventions**
   - Spelling Strategy
   - Grammar Lesson: Interjections **LC 1.3**
5. **To understand and apply appropriate writing and research strategies**
   - Writing Lesson: Letters of Recommendation **W 2.5**
   - Extension Activity: Oral Presentation **W 1.3, LS 1.7**
6. **To understand and apply listening and speaking strategies**
   - Extension Activity: Role Play **LS 1.9**

STEP-BY-STEP TEACHING GUIDE	PACING GUIDE
PRETEACH	
Motivate Students and Provide Background	
Use the Motivation activity (ATE p. 314)	5 min.
Read and discuss the Preview material and Background information (SE/ATE p. 314) [A]	10 min.
Introduce the Concepts	
Introduce the Literary Analysis and Reading Strategy (SE/ATE p. 315) [A]	15 min.
Pronounce the vocabulary words and read their definitions (SE p. 315)	5 min.
TEACH	
Monitor Comprehension	
Informally monitor comprehension by circulating while students read independently or in groups [A]	20 min.
Monitor students' comprehension with the Reading Check notes (SE/ATE pp. 317, 319)	as students read
Develop vocabulary with Vocabulary notes (SE pp. 317, 319, 320; ATE p. 317)	as students read
Develop Understanding	
Develop students' understanding of characterization in essays with Literary Analysis annotations (SE/ATE pp. 317, 318) [A]	10 min.
Develop students' ability to make inferences about characters with Reading Strategy annotations (SE p. 318; ATE pp. 317, 318)	10 min.
ASSESS	
Assess Mastery	
Assess students' mastery of the Reading Strategy and Literary Analysis by having them answer the Review and Assess questions (SE/ATE p. 321)	20 min.
Use one or more of the print and media Assessment Resources (ATE p. 323) [A]	up to 50 min.
EXTEND	
Apply Understanding	
Have students complete the Vocabulary Development Lesson and the Grammar Lesson (SE p. 322) [A]	20 min.
Apply students' knowledge of writing a clear explanation of a problem using the Writing Lesson (SE/ATE p. 323) [A]	45 min.
Apply students' understanding using one or more of the Extension Activities (SE p. 323)	20–90 min.

A **ACCELERATED INSTRUCTION:**
Use the strategies and activities identified with an [A].

UNIVERSAL ACCESS
● = Below-Level Students
▲ = On-Level Students
■ = Above-Level Students

Time and Resource Manager

Reading Level: Average
Average Number of Instructional Days: 4

RESOURCES		
PRINT	**TRANSPARENCIES**	**TECHNOLOGY**
• **Beyond Literature,** Cross-Curricular Connection: Social Studies, p. 20 ▲ ■		• **Interest Grabber Video,** Tape 2 ● ▲ ■
• **Selection Support Workbook:** ● ▲ ■ Literary Analysis, p. 80 Reading Strategy, p. 79 Build Vocabulary, p. 77	• **Literary Analysis and Reading Transparencies,** pp. 39 and 40 ● ▲ ■	
		• **Listening to Literature** ● ▲ ■ Audiocassettes, Side 10 Audio CDs, CD 8
• **Literatura en español** ● ▲ • **Literary Analysis for Enrichment** ■		
• **Formal Assessment:** Selection Test, pp. 66–68 ● ▲ ■ • **Open Book Test,** pp. 58–60 ● ▲ ■ • **Performance Assessment and Portfolio Management,** p. 9 ● ▲ ■ • PRENTICE HALL ASSESSMENT SYSTEM ● ▲ ■	• PRENTICE HALL ASSESSMENT SYSTEM ● ▲ ■ Skills Practice Answers and Explanations on Transparencies	• **Test Bank Software** ● ▲ ■ • **Got It! Assessment Videotapes** ● ▲
• **Selection Support Workbook:** ● ▲ ■ Build Grammar Skills, p. 78 • **Writing and Grammar,** Gold Level ● ▲ ■ • **Extension Activities,** p. 20 ● ▲ ■	• **Daily Language Practice Transparencies** ● ▲	• **Writing and Grammar iText CD-ROM** ● ▲ ■ ***Take It to the Net*** www.phschool.com

BLOCK SCHEDULING: Use one 90-minute class period to preteach the selection and have students read it. Use a second 90-minute class period to assess students' mastery of skills and have them complete one of the Extension Activities.

PRETEACH

Step-by-Step Teaching Guide for pp. 314–315

Motivation

Students may have seen television commercials in which celebrities are stunned to be asked for identification when trying to pay for something with a personal check. Have the class come up with humorous situations in which a personal check from someone famous is refused—for instance, Bill Gates trying to write a check at a computer outlet. You might even have volunteers act out a few of the situations. Then, tell students that the essay they are about to read also involves a surprising situation involving payment by personal check.

Interest Grabber Video

As an alternative, you may wish to play "Let's Make a Deal" on Tape 2 to engage student interest.

❶ Background

Art

The Persian carpet tradition began in Iran some 2,500 years ago when Persian nomads wove small rugs to cover the entrances and floors of their tents to keep out the cold and damp. The bright colors and astonishing designs undoubtedly cheered their spirits as the cotton, wool, and silk rugs warmed their homes. Persian rugs served as furniture, prayer mats, and modes of communication for illiterate tribesmen. The earliest Persian rug, which dates from about 500 B.C., was discovered in a burial mound in the mountains of Siberia. It is a beautiful deep red rug with two wide borders, one showing deer and the other depicting horsemen.

Prepare to Read

The Rug Merchant

Take It to the Net

Visit www.phschool.com for interactive activities and instruction related to "The Rug Merchant," including

- background
- graphic organizers
- literary elements
- reading strategies

Preview

Connecting to the Literature

Sometimes you make up your mind and then find yourself changing it. You think you have someone sized up and then discover that a bit more measuring tape is needed. James Michener finds himself in this position in "The Rug Merchant."

❶ Background

Persian rugs—like the ones sold by Zaqir, the rug merchant in the essay—are mostly made of wool, but the finest are made of silk. Different designs are linked with specific regions. Most designs are abstract or geometric patterns, although some depict people, plants, and animals.

TEACHING RESOURCES

The following resources can be used to enrich or extend the instruction for pp. 314–315.

Motivation

Interest Grabber Video, Tape 2

Background

Beyond Literature, Cross-Curricular Connection: Social Studies, p. 20 ■

Take It to the Net

Visit www.phschool.com for background and hotlinks for "The Rug Merchant."

Literary Analysis

Literary Analysis and Reading Transparencies, Characterization, p. 40

Reading

Selection Support: Reading Strategy, p. 79; Build Vocabulary, p. 77

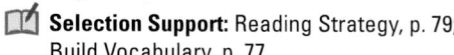

Literary Analysis and Reading Transparencies, Making Inferences About Characters, p. 39 ■

■ **BLOCK SCHEDULING:** Resources marked with this symbol provide varied instruction during 90-minute blocks.

❷ Literary Analysis

Characterization in Essays

Writers create and in essays develop their characters by means of a process called **characterization.** In an essay, a person's speech and actions, the reactions of others, and the author's comments all contribute to the person's characterization. Look at this description of Zaqir, a rug merchant in Afghanistan:

> . . . a very thin, toothy man with longish black hair and a perpetual smile entered and started throwing onto the dirt floor twenty or thirty of the most enchantingly beautiful Persian rugs I had ever seen.

Note how the author focuses on the man's appearance and behavior. While reading "The Rug Merchant," look for more details that characterize the seller.

Connecting Literary Elements

"The Rug Merchant" is a nonfiction essay that uses **first-person narration**—the author is part of the story and thus makes use of the words *I*, *me*, and *my*. Michener relates his own experiences with a rug merchant. In so doing, Michener ends up characterizing not only Zaqir but also himself. Authors using first-person narration inevitably tell readers as much about themselves as about other characters.

❸ Reading Strategy

Making Inferences About Characters

When you **make inferences about characters,** you draw conclusions about them by using details such as the following:

- Their appearance and actions
- What they say—including what they say about themselves—in narration and dialogue

Use a chart like the one shown to record details from "The Rug Merchant." For each detail you note, jot down the inference you draw.

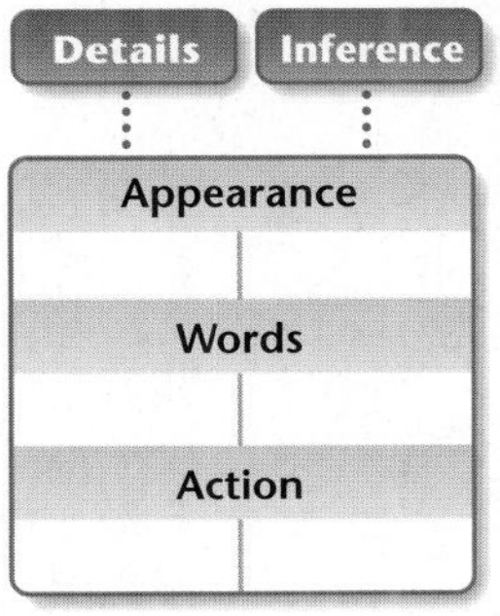

Vocabulary Development

improvised (im′ prə vīzd) *adj.* put together spontaneously (p. 317)

laden (lād′ ’n) *adj.* burdened (p. 317)

encompassed (en kum′ pəst) *v.* surrounded (p. 317)

impose (im pōz′) *v.* put to some trouble (p. 319)

ingeniously (in jēn′ yəs lē) *adv.* very cleverly (p. 320)

CUSTOMIZE INSTRUCTION FOR UNIVERSAL ACCESS

For Less Proficient Readers	For English Learners	For Advanced Readers
Have students stop after reading each page of the story to think about what the author wrote and what they already know about the subject. Ask students to list one inference they drew. Ask them to explain which details in the piece led them to draw that conclusion and what they predict might happen next.	After reading each page of the selection, have students list words they don't understand, an important fact they learned, and an inference they made. Ask a student who is proficient in English to help each English learner figure out the problematic words.	After reading each page of the selection (except the last one), have students stop to make some inferences about Zaqir's personality and ability as a salesman. Have students answer the following question: "What sales techniques Zaqir uses are described on this page, and how effective are they?"

❷ Literary Analysis

Characterization

- Urge students to pay close attention to *characterization*—the process by which author James Michener develops the character of Muhammad Zaqir and reveals aspects of his own personality—as they read "The Rug Merchant."
- Have a volunteer read aloud the excerpt. Ask students to discuss what this passage reveals about Zaqir. You may wish to use the Make Inferences About Characters transparency in **Literary Analysis and Reading Transparencies,** p. 40, to record students' impressions.
- Review the instruction for Connecting Literary Elements to help students understand that first-person narration lets Michener state his feelings and reactions directly.

❸ Reading Strategy

Making Inferences About Characters

- Remind students that authors rarely state directly everything readers need to understand a piece of writing. Readers need to make inferences, or draw conclusions, to better understand what they read.
- Refer students to the chart in their books. Ask them to suggest an inference they might draw about Zaqir from a detail of his appearance or behavior described in the excerpt.
- Instruct students to create their own charts to keep track of other inferences they draw about Zaqir and author Michener from their thoughts, words, and actions.

Vocabulary Development

- Pronounce each vocabulary word for students, and read the definitions as a class. Have students identify any words with which they are already familiar.

E-Teach

Visit E-Teach at www.phschool.com for teachers' essays on how to teach, with questions and answers.

TEACH

Step-by-Step Teaching Guide for pp. 316–320

CUSTOMIZE INSTRUCTION
For Visual/Spatial Learners

The photographs on this page and on the following pages can be invaluable aids in helping students picture the story's setting and characters. Take the time to discuss such details as the physical appearance of the man and his rugs (p. 316) and to explore what the mule (p. 318) reveals about the setting.

❶ About the Selection

This essay shows that people of different backgrounds can bridge a cultural gap. At first, Muhammad Zaqir and James Michener are at cross-purposes. Zaqir wants to sell rugs, and Michener refuses to consider buying. Over a few days, a change takes place. As the men talk, they decide to trust each other. Michener trusts Zaqir to send the rugs, and Zaqir trusts Michener to honor his promise to pay for them.

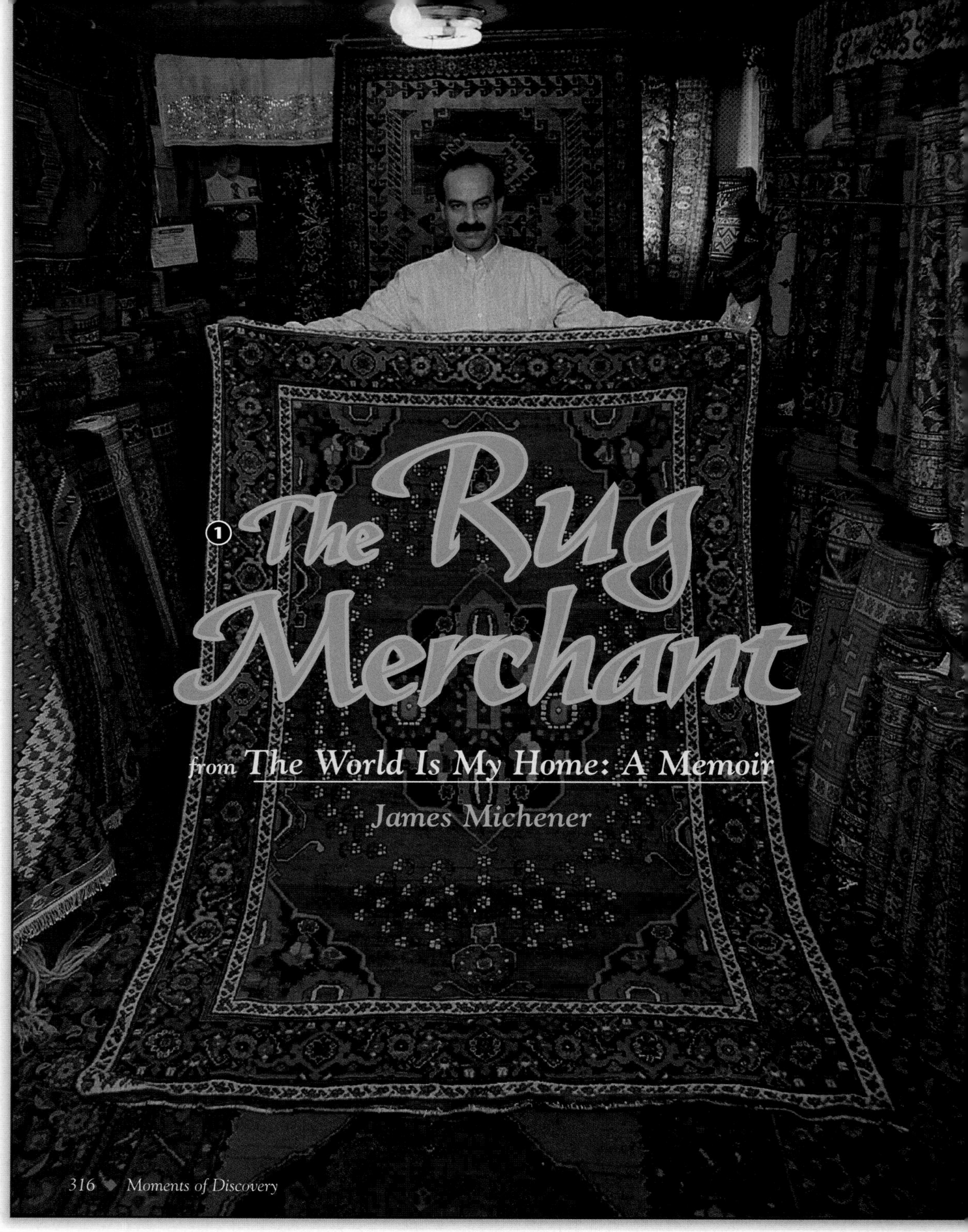

① The Rug Merchant

from *The World Is My Home: A Memoir*

James Michener

TEACHING RESOURCES

The following resources can be used to enrich or extend the instruction for pp. 316–320.

Literary Analysis

- **Selection Support:** Literary Analysis, p. 80
- **Literary Analysis and Reading Transparencies,** p. 39 ■

Reading

- **Listening to Literature Audiocassettes,** Side 10 ■
- **Listening to Literature Audio CDs,** CD 8

■ **BLOCK SCHEDULING:** Resources marked with this symbol provide varied instruction during 90-minute blocks.

I once made a long trip over the Dasht-i-Margo, the desert in Afghanistan, to the ancient city of Herat (he rät´), where I lodged in a former mosque with earthen floors. I had been in my improvised quarters only a few minutes when a very thin,
2 toothy man with longish black hair and a perpetual smile entered and started throwing onto the dirt floor twenty or thirty of the most enchantingly beautiful Persian rugs I had ever seen. Their designs were miraculous—intricate interweavings of Koranic symbols framed in geometric patterns that teased the eye—but their colors were also sheer delight: reds, yellows, greens and especially dark blues that were radiant.

They made my room a museum, one rug piled atop another, all peeking out at me, and when they were in place and the smiling man was satisfied with his handiwork—I supposed that this was a service of the so-called hotel—to my amazement he handed me a scrap of paper on which was written in pencil in English: "muhammad zaqir, rug merchant, herat."

3 Aware at last of how I had been trapped, I protested: "No! No! No rugs!" but without relaxing his smile the least bit he said in English: "No necessity to buy. I leave here. You study, you learn to like," and before I could protest further he was gone. I ran out to make him take back his rugs, for I wanted none of them, but he was already leading his laden camel away from the old mosque.

I assumed he had learned from the hotel manager that I was to be in Herat for five days, and it was obvious that he felt confident that within that period he could wear me down and persuade me to buy a rug. He started on the evening of that first day; he came back after supper to sit
4 with me in the shadowy light cast by a flickering lamp. He said: "Have you ever seen lovelier rugs? That one from my friend in Meshed. Those two from the dealer in Bukhara. This one from a place you know, maybe? Samarkand."

When I asked him how he was able to trade with such towns in the Soviet Union[1] he shrugged: "Borders? Out here we don't bother," and with a sweep of his hand that encompassed all the rugs he said: "Not one woven in Afghanistan," and I noted the compelling pronunciation he gave that name: Ahf-han-ee-stahn.

He sat for more than an hour with me that evening, and next day he was back before noon to start his serious bargaining: "Michener-sahib,[2] name German perhaps?" I told him it was more likely English, at which he laughed: "English, Afghans, many battles, English always win but next day you march back to India, nothing change." When I corrected him: "I'm not English," he said: "I know. Pennsylvania. Three, four, maybe five of your rugs look great your place Pennsylvania."

"But I don't need rugs there. I don't really want them."

"Would they not look fine Pennsylvania?" and as if the rugs were of

improvised (im´ prə vīzd) *adj.* put together spontaneously

Literary Analysis Characterization in Essays How would you describe Michener, based on where he is lodging?

laden (lād´ 'n) *adj.* burdened

encompassed (en kum´ pəst) *v.* surrounded

1. **Soviet Union** The Union of Soviet Socialist Republics consisted of fifteen republics strictly controlled by the country's central government until independence movements in 1991.
2. **Michener-sahib** (sä´ ib) Mr. Michener.

5 **✓Reading Check**

What does the visitor bring to Michener's room?

2 Vocabulary Development

The Latin Word Root *-vis-*

- Have students write the word *improvise* and its definition. Explain that *-vis-* means "see."
- Ask students to think of other words that have this root. List their suggestions on the board.
  Possible responses: *visual, visitor, supervisor, vision, visible, invisible,* and *revise.*
- Have students define the words and explain how each relates to the root *-vis-*. Let students use a dictionary if necessary.

3 Literary Analysis

Characterization

- Ask students to think of adjectives that describe Muhammad Zaqir. Jot down their responses on the board.
  Possible adjectives: *determined, pushy, cheerful, clever*
- Discuss details of the character's appearance, behavior, and speech that contribute to students' impressions of him.
- Ask students the Literary Analysis question on p. 317: How would you describe Michener, based on where he is lodging?
  Possible response: Michener must be adventurous to travel to Herat and stay in a former mosque.

4 Reading Strategy

Making Inferences About Characters

- Ask students what inferences they can make about Zaqir as a salesperson.
  Possible response: Zaqir is perceptive and persistent. He has learned how long Michener will be in Herat, and he comes back after supper to continue his sales campaign.
- Ask students to explain the inferences they make about Zaqir from his comments about the rugs and the places they come from.
  Possible response: Zaqir seems comfortable and self-confident as he talks about the rugs.

5 ✓Reading Check

Answer: The visitor brings twenty to thirty Persian rugs.

CUSTOMIZE INSTRUCTION FOR UNIVERSAL ACCESS

Special Needs Students	Gifted/Talented Students	For Advanced Readers
To help students visualize the setting, show them some pictures of a mosque in the Middle East, preferably one in Afghanistan. Remind students that Michener's hotel is a former mosque. Discuss the effect a pile of colorful Persian rugs piled up on the earthen floor of one's hotel room might have on a visitor.	Have students do quick color sketches of Michener's hotel room in the former mosque, with its earthen floor and colorful Persian rugs piled many layers deep. Students should rely on Michener's description to create their drawings.	Ask students to describe as many details of the setting as they can from the information presented on this page and inferences they draw. Then, have them use what they know about Michener's hotel room and what they imagine to write a one-paragraph description of his room.

❻ Literary Analysis

Characterization

- Read aloud the bracketed passage. Then, ask volunteers to rate Zaqir as a salesperson.
- Next, ask the Literary Analysis question on p. 318: What do Zaqir's persistence and sales technique suggest about his understanding of people?
  Possible answer: Zaqir knows that the more he talks, the more likely people are to buy.

❼ Reading Strategy

Making Inferences About Characters

- Have a volunteer summarize Zaqir and author Michener's interactions to this point.
  Answer: Zaqir has appeared in Michener's hotel room with piles of Persian rugs that he is trying to sell. He leaves the rugs and returns for several days, trying different strategies to persuade Michener to buy.
- Ask students the Reading Strategy question on p. 318: What causes Michener to conclude that Zaqir is an honest man?
  Possible answers: Zaqir is friendly and open. The testimonial letters are also persuasive.
- To explore some of the inferences readers can make about Michener, use the **Literary Analysis and Reading Transparencies,** p. 39.

little value, he kicked the top ones aside to reveal the glowing wonders of those below.

When he returned that second night he got down to even more serious business: "The big white and gold one you like, six hundred dollars." On and on he went, and when it was clear that I had no interest whatever in the big ones, he subtly covered them over with the smaller six- by four-foot ones already in the room; then he ran out to his camel to fetch seven or eight of the size that I had in some unconscious way disclosed I might consider, and by the end of that session he knew that I was at least a possible purchaser of four or five of the handsome rugs.

"Ah, Michener-sahib, you have fine eye. That one from China, silk and wool, look at those tiny knots." Then he gave me a lesson in rug making; he talked about the designs, the variation in knots, the wonderful compactness of the Chinese variety, the dazzling colors of the Samarkand. It was fascinating to hear him talk, and all the while he was wearing me down.

He was a persistent rascal, always watching till he saw me return to my mosque after work, then pouncing on me. On the third day, as he sat drinking tea with me while our chairs were perched on his treasury of rugs, four and five deep at some places and covering the entire floor, he knocked down one after another of my objections: "You can't take
❻ them with you? No traveler can. I send them to you, camel here, ship Karachi, train New York, truck to your home Pennsylvania." Pasted onto
❼ the pages of his notebook were addresses of buyers from all parts of the world to whom he had shipped his rugs, and I noticed that they had gone out from Meshed in Iran, Mazar-e-Sharif in Afghanistan and Bukhara (bü kär´ ə) in Russia; apparently he really moved about with his laden camel. But he also had, pasted close to the shipping address, letters from his customers proving that the rugs had finally reached their new owners. In our dealings he seemed to me an honest man.

On that third night, when it began to look as if I might escape without making a purchase even though I had shown an interest in six rugs, he hammered at me regarding payments: "Now, Michener-sahib, I can take American dollars, you know."

"I have no American dollars." Rapidly he ran through the currencies that he would accept, British, Indian, Iranian, Pakistani, Afghani, in that descending order, until I had to stop him with a truthful statement: "Muhammad, my friend, I have no money, none of any kind," and before the last word had been uttered he cried: "I take traveler's checks, American Express, Bank America in California," and then I had to tell him the sad news: "Muhammad, friend. I have no traveler's checks. Left them all locked up in the American embassy in Kabul. Because there are robbers on the road to Meshed."

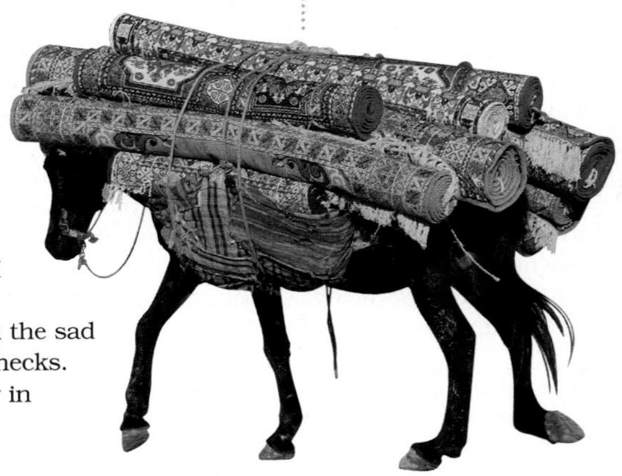

Literary Analysis
Characterization in Essays What do Zaqir's persistence and sales technique suggest about his understanding of people?

Reading Strategy
Making Inferences About Characters What causes Michener to conclude that Zaqir is an honest man?

ENRICHMENT: Economics Connection

Rugs as Wealth

Ask students to think of precious items in which people invest. Students are likely to mention such items as gold and diamonds. If no one mentions Persian carpets, tell them that Persian carpets are among the world's most sought-after treasures.

Iran produces more Persian rugs than all the other countries of the world combined. Many Iranians invest their entire wealth in Persian rugs, which some people call Iran's stocks and bonds. Vaults under Tehran's bazaar are filled with valuable Persian rugs being stored as investments. When investors are ready to sell, they can be sure museums and collectors around the world will want to buy.

"I know. I know. But you are an honest man, Michener-sahib. I take your personal check."

When I said truthfully that I had none, he asked simply: "You like those six rugs?"

"Yes, you have made me appreciate them. I do."

With a sweeping gesture he gathered the six beauties, rolled them deftly into a bundle and thrust them into my arms: "You take them. Send me a check when you get to Pennsylvania."

"You would trust me?"

"You look honest. Don't I look honest?" And he picked up one of his larger rugs, a real beauty, and showed me the fine knots: "Bukhara. I got it there, could not pay. I send the money when I sell. Man in Bukhara trusts me. I trust you."

I said I could not impose on him in that way. Something might happen to me or I might prove to be a crook, and the discussion ended, except that as he left me he asked: "Michener, if you had the money, what rugs would you take with you?" and I said "None, but if you could ship them, I'd take those four," and he said: "Those four you shall have. I'll find a way."

Next day he was back in the mosque right after breakfast with an astonishing proposal: "Michener-sahib, I can let you have those four rugs, special price, four hundred fifty dollars." Before I could repeat my inability to pay, he said: "Bargain like this you never see again. Tell you what to do. You write me a check."

9 When I said, distressed at losing such a bargain: "But I really have no blank checks," he said: "You told me yesterday. I believe you. But draw me one," and from his folder he produced a sheet of ordinary paper and a pencil. He showed me how to draw a copy of a blank check, bearing the name of the bank, address, amount, etc.—and for the first time in my life I actually drew a blank check, filled in the amount and signed it, whereupon Muhammad Zaqir placed it in his file, folded the four rugs I had bought, tied them with string and attached my name and address.

He piled the rugs onto his camel, and then mounted it to proceed on his way to Samarkand.

Back home in Pennsylvania I started to receive two different kinds of letters, perhaps fifteen of each. The following is a sample of the first category:

> I am a shipping agent in Istanbul and a freighter arrived here from Karachi bringing a large package, well wrapped, addressed to you in Pennsylvania. Upon receipt of your check for $19.50 American I will forward the package to you.

From Karachi, Istanbul, Trieste, Marseilles and heavens knows where else I received a steady flow of letters over a three-year period, and always the sum demanded was less than twenty dollars, so that I would say to myself: "Well, I've invested so much in it already, I may as well

Literature in context 8 Geography Connection

Michener and the World

"The Rug Merchant" comes from James Michener's autobiography, *The World Is My Home: A Memoir*. In fact, Michener visited countless places around the world and wrote books about many of them. His books often relate fascinating histories and describe exotic lands. *The Bridges at Toko-Ri, Hawaii, Tales of the South Pacific, Caravans, Poland, Iberia, Chesapeake, Texas, Alaska, Caribbean,* and *Space* are some of the approximately twenty novels he wrote. The practiced eye of a lifelong traveler comes in handy for someone describing Zaqir, the merchant in this story.

impose (im pōz') *v.* put to some trouble

10 **Reading Check**

What kind of payment does Michener give Zaqir for the rugs?

8 Background

Geography

Two of Michener's novels, *The Bridges at Toko-Ri* (1953) and *Sayonara* (1954), are both set in Japan. Michener has written about the Holy Land in *The Source* (1965), Spain in *Iberia* (1968), and South Africa in *The Covenant* (1980). Michener has also found inspiration closer to home. *Centennial* (1974) covers centuries of life in Colorado, while *Chesapeake* (1978) does the same for Maryland's eastern shore region. In *Texas* (1985), Michener worked in his own backyard; he resided in Austin for years.

9 Literary Analysis

First-Person Narration

Reteach Remind students that they can easily identify first-person narration in a selection by looking for the words *I, me,* and *we*. In a first-person narrative, the author takes part in the action of the story.

- Ask students to explain how they can identify this passage as an example of first-person narration.
  Answer: The author is part of the story, appearing in the story as *I*.

10 Reading Check

Answer: Michener gives Zaqir a homemade check that he draws on a sheet of paper.

CUSTOMIZE INSTRUCTION FOR UNIVERSAL ACCESS

For Less Proficient Readers	For English Learners	For Advanced Readers
Urge students to reread any parts of this page that they don't understand completely. Tell them to note words they can't figure out from context and decide whether the words seem important to understanding the gist of the passage. If so, they should ask another student what the words mean or look them up in a dictionary.	Review the conventions of dialogue with students: the use of quotation marks to mark the beginning and ending of a quotation and the starting a new paragraph to indicate a change in speaker. Then, have students figure out which character is saying each line of dialogue.	Ask students to imagine being in Michener's place. How do they think they would have reacted to Zaqir's sales tactics? Ask students to imagine themselves and Zaqir in a hotel room piled with Persian rugs and write a page or two of dialogue between themselves and the rug merchant.

ASSESS

Answers for p. 320

Review and Assess

1. Many students will say that they would have bought Zaqir's rugs because the salesman was charming and the rugs were beautiful and seemed to be a bargain.
2. **(a)** Zaqir leaves the rugs in Michener's hotel room. **(b)** Michener is curious about the rugs and about the rug merchant.
3. **(a)** On the second night, Zaqir continues serious bargaining by discussing prices and focusing on rugs of the size Michener is interested in. **(b)** Michener calls Zaqir a rascal because of the rug seller's persistence, and honest because Zaqir can prove that he actually sends the rugs customers order.
4. **(a)** He proposes that Michener draw a check on a sheet of paper. **(b)** Zaqir's culture may rely more on informal agreements and Michener's more on formal contracts.
5. Michener concludes that Zaqir is a great salesperson, and, although a bit of a rascal, an honest and honorable man.
6. Possible response: This essay might teach people to rely on their instincts when deciding whom to trust as well as being honest themselves and expecting honesty from others. Note that the mutual trust shown in this essay endured over thousands of miles and several years.

risk a little more." And off the check would go, with the rugs never getting any closer. Moreover, I was not at all sure that if they ever did reach me they would be my property, for my unusual check had never been submitted for payment, even though I had forewarned my local bank: "If it ever does arrive, pay it immediately, because it's a debt of honor."

The second group of letters explained the long delay:

> I am serving in Kabul as the Italian ambassador and was lately in Herat where a rug merchant showed me that remarkable check you gave him for something like five hundred dollars. He asked me if I thought it would be paid if he forwarded it and I assured him that since you were a man of good reputation it would be. When I asked him why he had not submitted it sooner, he said: "Michener-sahib a good name. I show his check everybody like you, sell many rugs."

These letters came from French commercial travelers, English explorers, Indian merchants, almost anyone who might be expected to reach out-of-the-way Herat and take a room in that miserable old mosque.

In time the rugs arrived, just as Muhammad Zaqir had predicted they would, accompanied by so many shipping papers they were a museum in themselves. And after my improvised check had been used as an advertisement for nearly five years, it too came home to roost and was honored. Alas, shortly thereafter the rugs were stolen, but I remember them vividly and with longing. Especially do I remember the man who spent four days ingeniously persuading me to buy.

ingeniously (in jēn´ yəs lē) *adv.* cleverly

James Michener

(1907–1997)

James Michener was raised as a Quaker by his adoptive mother in Doylestown, Pennsylvania. After graduating from college, he worked as a book editor before joining the navy during World War II.

Michener's war experiences inspired him to write *Tales of the South Pacific* (1947), which won the Pulitzer Prize—a remarkable achievement for a first-time novelist.

Michener was a tireless portrayer of other lands and peoples. Among the many places he wrote about were the Holy Land, in *The Source* (1965), and South Africa, in *The Covenant* (1980).

Review and Assess

Thinking About the Selection

1. **Respond:** Would you have bought rugs from Zaqir? Explain.
2. **(a) Recall:** What does Zaqir do after Michener first protests that he does not want the rugs? **(b) Infer:** Why does Michener keep discussing the rugs with Zaqir?
3. **(a) Recall:** When Zaqir returns on the second night, how has he altered his sales pitch? **(b) Distinguish:** Zaqir's behavior prompts Michener to describe him as both "an honest man" and "a rascal." What provokes this reaction?
4. **(a) Recall:** What business proposal does Zaqir eventually make to Michener? **(b) Generalize:** What does the proposal suggest about the differences between Zaqir's culture and Michener's?
5. **Speculate:** What do you think Michener finally concludes about Zaqir as a result of their dealings?
6. **Extend:** What could this essay teach someone about trust and honesty?

ASSESSMENT PRACTICE: Reading Comprehsnsion

Implied Main Idea **(For more practice, see Test Preparation Workbook, p. 20.)**

Many tests require students to recognize the implied main idea of a passage. Use the following sample test item to give students practice in this skill:

> Michener has traveled to most of the places he writes about. His books are filled with realistic details and fine description that reflect personal experience. His rich accounts help readers to feel as if they, too, had visited the places in his books.

What is the implied main idea of this passage?

A Michener has traveled to many places.
B Readers enjoy Michener's books.
C Michener is a good writer.
D Michener's firsthand experiences enrich his writing.

Choice *A* is a detail, not a main idea. Choices *B* and *C* do not express the main idea of this passage. The correct answer is *D* because it states the main idea.

Review and Assess

Literary Analysis

Characterization in Essays

1. As first **characterized,** does Zaqir seem believable to you? Write your response in the center of a cluster map like the one shown. Then, show which actions and words support your opinion.

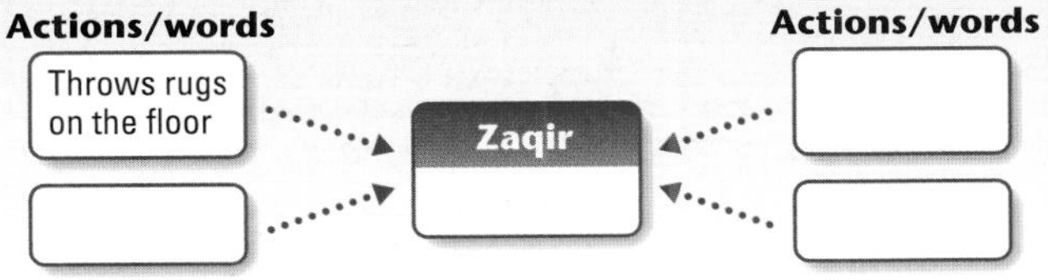

2. Does your overall impression of Zaqir change over the course of the story? Explain.
3. Describe Michener as a character. Base your answer on his actions, attitudes, and words.

Connecting Literary Elements

4. **First-person narration** reveals the ideas and opinions of the writer. In which specific ways is your opinion of Zaqir influenced by Michener's narration?
5. Cite specific ways in which your impression of Zaqir might be different if he had narrated the story.

Reading Strategy

Making Inferences About Characters

6. Michener pays shipping charges for three years while awaiting the rugs' arrival. What does this fact lead you to **infer** about him?
7. One detail and the responses it generates can reveal the traits of two characters. (a) What inferences can you draw about Michener based on the blank check he draws? (b) What can you infer about Zaqir based on his interaction with the check?

Extend Understanding

8. **Cultural Connection:** Which cultural differences influence the nature of the salesperson-customer relationship in this essay?

Quick Review

Characterization involves an author's use of speech, actions, reactions, and comments to create and develop characters.

In nonfiction, **first-person narration** allows the author to be part of the action and to use the words *I*, *me*, and *my*.

To **make inferences about characters**, draw conclusions about them from their appearance, actions, and words.

Take It to the Net

www.phschool.com

Take the interactive self-test online to check your understanding of the selections.

ENRICHMENT: Further Reading

Other Works by James Michener

Tales of the South Pacific
Hawaii
The Source
Centennial
Texas
Iberia

Take It to the Net

Visit www.phschool.com for more information on James Michener.

Answers for p. 321

Review and Assess

1. **Possible response:** Yes, Zaqir is believable. He is a sly, aggressive salesman who won't take "no" for an answer.
2. **Possible response:** Zaqir becomes more likable by the end. As the author warms up to him, so does the reader.
3. **Possible response:** Michener's matter-of-fact recounting of his travel to Herat implies that he is a veteran traveler. His fascination with Zaqir suggests that he is interested in people and their stories. Urging his bank to immediately honor the check he had written to Zaqir indicates his honesty.
4. **Possible response:** Michener's initial description of Zaqir throwing beautiful rugs on the dirt floor immediately piques reader interest. His recounting of their conversations, such as the one in which they talk about where Michener hails from, shows the rug seller's persistence and conversational ability. Zaqir's step-by-step instructions on how to make one's own check reveals his ingenuity.
5. **Possible response:** We probably wouldn't have an initial impression of him as pushy and constantly smiling. Zaqir might focus on his plans to overcome Michener's sales resistance and thus seem more manipulative and less likable.
6. He is a curious person and thinks it's worth risking losing some money to follow the story to its end.
7. **(a)** Michener is an honest person and willing to assume Zaqir is too. **(b)** Zaqir can overcome almost any barrier to making a sale.
8. Zaqir is clearly accustomed to more extended and personal interactions between seller and buyer than is typical in the United States.

EXTEND

Answers for p. 322

❶ Vocabulary

Word Analysis

1. supervisor
2. invisible
3. visitor
4. visual aid
5. envision
6. revise

Concept Development: Synonyms

1. b
2. a
3. c
4. a
5. b

Spelling Strategy

1. enthralling
2. embarrassment
3. correct

❷ Grammar

1. no; possible emotion: anger
2. ah; possible emotion: relief
3. well; possible emotion: hesitancy
4. my goodness; possible emotion: dismay
5. alas; possible emotion: sadness

Writing Application

Possible response: When I corrected him: "Alas, I'm not English," he said: "I know." "Oh, I have no American dollars." "Gosh! You would trust me?"

Integrate Language Skills

❶ Vocabulary Development Lesson

Word Analysis: Latin Root *-vis-*

The Latin root *-vis-* means "see." The root appears in the word *improvised,* which literally means "not seen before." It also appears in these words and phrases:

visitor
supervisor
invisible
revise
visual aid
envision

Identify the word or phrase above that matches each clue.

1. A person who oversees and directs you in your work
2. Not able to be seen
3. One who comes to see you
4. Something you see that helps explain an idea
5. To see in your mind
6. To "see again" and change

Concept Development: Synonyms

Identify the synonym, or word with nearly the same meaning, for the first word in each item.

1. laden: (a) spoon, (b) burdened, (c) hurt
2. improvised: (a) unplanned, (b) entertaining, (c) careful
3. encompassed: (a) directed, (b) watched, (c) surrounded
4. ingeniously: (a) cleverly, (b) dishonestly, (c) stupidly
5. impose: (a) arrange, (b) trouble, (c) stand

Spelling Strategy

For a word that ends in a double consonant, do not drop the final consonant before adding an ending: *encompass* + *-ed* = *encompassed.*

Identify the misspelled word or words below and correct the spelling.

1. enthraling **2.** embarrassment **3.** reference

❷ Grammar Lesson

Interjections

An **interjection** is a word or phrase that expresses a feeling or an emotion and functions independently of the other words in a sentence. An interjection might express pain, joy, annoyance, or surprise.

In the following example, the interjection expresses a feeling of discovery.

Example:
Oh, Michener-sahib, you have a fine eye.

Punctuate mild interjections with commas and strong ones with exclamation marks.

Practice Identify the interjections below. Then, describe the emotion that each expresses.

1. No! I want no rugs!
2. Ah, Michener-sahib, I can take American dollars.
3. Well, you make me appreciate them.
4. My goodness, I've already invested so much.
5. Alas, the rugs were stolen.

Writing Application Select three sentences from "The Rug Merchant" and rewrite them, using interjections to add emotion.

WG *Prentice Hall Writing and Grammar Connection: Chapter 19, Section 2*

TEACHING RESOURCES

The following resources can be used to enrich or extend the instruction for pp. 322–323.

Vocabulary

Selection Support: Build Vocabulary, p. 77

Grammar

Selection Support: Build Grammar Skills, p. 78
Writing and Grammar, Gold Level, p. 408
Daily Language Practice Transparencies ■

Writing

Writing and Grammar, Gold Level, p. 141
Writing and Grammar iText CD-ROM ■

■ **BLOCK SCHEDULING:** Resources marked with this symbol provide varied instruction during 90-minute blocks.

❸ Writing Lesson

Letter of Recommendation

If a problem had arisen with the rugs that Michener bought from Zaqir, he might have written a letter of complaint to the merchant. Instead, he seems to have been pleased with his purchase. As Michener, write a letter encouraging others to buy from Zaqir.

Prewriting Review the story to find examples of Zaqir's behavior and sales approach. Also, note Michener's evolving responses to Zaqir.

Drafting Write your letter, clearly stating your feelings about the rug merchant. As a testimonial, your letter should explain Michener's experiences and draw generalizations about them.

Revising Review your draft, underlining the main impression you want to convey to other consumers. Where necessary, add more examples to support this idea.

Model: Revising to Create a Main Impression

Working with Zaqir is entertainment in itself.

Personally, I received my goods years after I purchased them, but the memory of this persistent salesman—piling rug over rug—lingers.

The added text elaborates on the writer's positive memories.

WG *Prentice Hall Writing and Grammar Connection: Chapter 7, Section 4*

❹ Extension Activities

Listening and Speaking With a classmate, **role-play** a conversation between Michener and Zaqir. Combine dialogue from the essay with original dialogue. Follow these points:

- Analyze the situation the men are in before constructing your dialogue.
- Use nonverbal techniques—voice, gestures, and eye contact—to convey the characters' essence.

Rehearse your conversation together, using a tape recorder to check its effectiveness. Then, present the conversation to your class. **[Group Activity]**

Research and Technology Search the Internet for additional information about Persian rugs, like those described in "The Rug Merchant." Display what you learn in an **oral presentation.** Use graphics, such as pictures of vibrant rugs, to enhance the appeal and accuracy of your report, and prepare concise notes to help you in your delivery.

Take It to the Net www.phschool.com

Go online for an additional research activity using the Internet.

ASSESSMENT RESOURCES

The following resources can be used to assess students' knowledge and skills.

Selection Assessment

- **Formal Assessment,** Selection Test, pp. 66–68
- **Open Book Test,** pp. 58–60
- **Got It! Assessment Videotapes,** Tape 2
- **Test Bank Software**

Take It to the Net
Visit www.phschool.com for self-tests and additional questions on "The Rug Merchant."

Writing Rubric

- **Performance Assess. and Portfolio Mgmt,** p. 9

PRENTICE HALL ASSESSMENT SYSTEM

- **Workbook**
- **Skill Book**
- **Transparencies**
- **CD-ROM**

❸ Writing Lesson

- To help students understand how important a recommendation might be to a salesperson, ask students to consider how strongly personal recommendations influence their own buying decisions. Remind students that Zaqir keeps letters from customers pasted in a notebook and uses the letters to help him sell rugs to other customers.
- Explain to students that their letters of recommendation should include specific examples of Zaqir's behavior that support global statements such as "I'd never buy a Persian carpet from anyone but Zaqir."
- Have volunteers cite a few examples of Zaqir's sales abilities that they might include in their letter, such as his knowledge of how Persian rugs are made and where they come from.
- Use the Business Letter rubric in **Performance Assessment and Portfolio Management,** p. 9 to evaluate students' letters of recommendation.

❹ Research and Technology

- Remind students to evaluate the information they gather from the Internet carefully. A good rule of thumb for students to follow is to confirm any information they gather in at least two, and preferably three, sources.
- After they do some preliminary research on the Internet, urge students to make simple outlines of some of the topics they want to include in their oral presentations, such as where the rugs are made and how they are woven.
- Emphasize the importance of strong visual support to their presentations.

CUSTOMIZE INSTRUCTION for Universal Access

To address different learning styles, use the activities suggested in the **Extension Activities** booklet, p. 20.

- For Visual/Spatial and Interpersonal Learners, use Activity 4.
- For Visual/Spatial and Verbal/Linguistic Learners, use Activity 5.
- For Musical/Rhythmic and Verbal/Linguistic Learners, use Activity 6.

Combing ✦ Women ✦ maggie and milly and molly and may ✦ Astonishment

Lesson Objectives and CA Correlations

1. **To analyze and respond to literary elements**
   - Literary Analysis: Moment of Insight **R 3.5**
   - Comparing Literary Works: Theme **R 3.5**
2. **To read, comprehend, analyze, and critique poetry**
   - Reading Strategy: Interpreting Meaning **R 3.8**
   - Review and Assess questions
   - Assessment Practice (ATE)
3. **To develop word analysis skills, fluency, and systematic vocabulary**
   - Vocabulary Development Lesson: Words With Multiple Meanings **R 1.2**
4. **To understand and apply written and oral language conventions**
   - Spelling Strategy
   - Grammar Lesson: Parenthetical Expressions **LC 1.2, 1.3**
5. **To understand and apply appropriate writing and research strategies**
   - Writing Lesson: Journal Entry on a Moment of Insight **W 2.1**
   - Extension Activity: Photo Essay **W 1.3, LS 1.7**
6. **To understand and apply listening and speaking strategies**
   - Extension Activity: Oral Reading **LS 1.11**

STEP-BY-STEP TEACHING GUIDE	PACING GUIDE
PRETEACH	
Motivate Students and Provide Background	
Use the Motivation activity (ATE p. 324)	5 min.
Read and discuss the Preview material and Background information (SE/ATE p. 324) [A]	10 min.
Introduce the Concepts	
Introduce the Literary Analysis and Reading Strategy (SE/ATE p. 325) [A]	15 min.
Pronounce the vocabulary words and read their definitions (SE p. 325)	5 min.
TEACH	
Monitor Comprehension	
Informally monitor comprehension by circulating while students read independently or in groups [A]	15 min.
Develop vocabulary with Vocabulary notes (SE pp. 326, 327, 329)	as students read
Develop Understanding	
Develop students' understanding of moments of insight with Literary Analysis annotations (ATE p. 327) [A]	10 min.
Develop students' ability to interpret meaning with Reading Strategy annotations (SE pp. 326, 329, 330; ATE pp. 326, 327, 328)	10 min.
ASSESS	
Assess Mastery	
Assess students' mastery of the Reading Strategy and Literary Analysis by having them answer the Review and Assess questions (SE/ATE p. 331)	20 min.
Use one or more of the print and media Assessment Resources (ATE p. 333) [A]	up to 50 min.
EXTEND	
Apply Understanding	
Have students complete the Vocabulary Development Lesson and the Grammar Lesson (SE p. 332) [A]	20 min.
Apply students' knowledge of eliminating unnecessary information using the Writing Lesson (SE/ATE p. 333) [A]	45 min.
Apply students' understanding using one or more of the Extension Activities (SE p. 333)	20–90 min.

A **ACCELERATED INSTRUCTION:**
Use the strategies and activities identified with an [A].

UNIVERSAL ACCESS
● = Below Level Students
▲ = On-Level Students
■ = Above Level Students

Time and Resource Manager

Reading Level: Easy, Average
Average Number of Instructional Days: 4

RESOURCES		
PRINT	**TRANSPARENCIES**	**TECHNOLOGY**
• **Beyond Literature,** Humanities Connection: Fine Art, p. 21 ▲ ■		• **Interest Grabber Video,** Tape 2 ● ▲ ■
• **Selection Support Workbook:** ● ▲ ■ Literary Analysis, p. 84 Reading Strategy, p. 83 Build Vocabulary, p. 81	• **Literary Analysis and Reading Transparencies,** pp. 41 and 42 ● ▲ ■	
• **Authors In Depth,** Gold Level ■		• **Listening to Literature** ● ▲ ■ Audiocassettes, Side 10 Audio CDs, CD 8
• **Literatura en español** ● ▲ • **Literary Analysis for Enrichment** ■	• **Fine Art Transparencies Volume 1,** Art Transparency 12 ● ▲ ■	
• **Formal Assessment:** Selection Test, pp. 69–71 ● ▲ ■ • **Open Book Test,** pp. 61–63 ● ▲ ■ • PRENTICE HALL ASSESSMENT SYSTEM ● ▲ ■	• PRENTICE HALL ASSESSMENT SYSTEM ● ▲ ■ Skills Practice Answers and Explanations on Transparencies	• **Test Bank Software** ● ▲ ■ • **Got It! Assessment Videotapes,** Tape 2 ● ▲
• **Selection Support Workbook:** ● ▲ ■ Build Grammar Skills, p. 82 • **Writing and Grammar,** Gold Level ● ▲ ■ • **Extension Activities,** p. 21 ● ▲ ■	• **Daily Language Practice Transparencies** ● ▲	• **Writing and Grammar iText CD-ROM** ● ▲ ■ *Take It to the Net* www.phschool.com

BLOCK SCHEDULING: Use one 90-minute class period to preteach the selection and have students read it. Use a second 90-minute class period to assess students' mastery of skills and have them complete one of the Extension Activities.

PRETEACH

Step-by-Step Teaching Guide for pp. 324–325

Motivation

Write the question "Who are you?" on the chalkboard and tell students they have three minutes to write an answer. Suggest that they begin their answers with the phrase, "I am a person who . . ." When three minutes have elapsed, invite volunteers to share their responses, if they wish. Then, tell students they are about to read four poems in which the speaker grapples with the issue of identity.

Interest Grabber Video

As an alternative, you may wish to play "Reading and Student Response" on Tape 2 to engage student interest.

❶ Background

History

On May 17, 1954, the Supreme Court ruled on one of its landmark cases, *Brown v. the Board of Education of Topeka*. In a unanimous decision, the Court overturned the doctrine of separate but equal school systems for black and white students established by the Court in *Plessy v. Ferguson* (1896). Chief Justice Earl Warren wrote for the Court: ". . . in the field of public education the doctrine of 'separate but equal' has no place. Separate educational facilities are inherently unequal. Therefore, we hold that the plaintiffs . . . are, by reason of the segregation complained of, deprived of the equal protection of the laws guaranteed by the 14th Amendment."

Prepare to Read

Combing ◆ Women ◆ maggie and milly and molly and may ◆ Astonishment

The Quiltmaker, Paul Goodnight, Color Circle Art Publishing Inc.

Take It to the Net

Visit www.phschool.com for interactive activities and instruction related to the selections, including
- background
- graphic organizers
- literary elements
- reading strategies

Preview

Connecting to the Literature

Throughout our lives, we make discoveries that show us who we are. Each of the poems that follow presents such a discovery. You may find that the discoveries of the poems' speakers lead you to discoveries of your own.

❶ Background

In "Women," the speaker expresses admiration for African American women who fought for public school desegregation in the American South. Until the 1950s, these schools were segregated—that is, black and white students attended different schools. In 1954, the U.S. Supreme Court ruled that segregated public schooling was not permissible because it was inherently unequal. Some state governments and local school districts resisted the new ruling.

TEACHING RESOURCES

The following resources can be used to enrich or extend the instruction for pp. 324–325.

Motivation

Interest Grabber Video, Tape 2

Background

Beyond Literature, Humanities Connection: Fine Art, p. 21

Take It to the Net

Visit www.phschool.com for background and hotlinks for the selections.

Literary Analysis

Literary Analysis and Reading Transparencies, Moment of Insight, p. 42

Reading

Selection Support: Reading Strategy, p. 83; Build Vocabulary, p. 81

Literary Analysis and Reading Transparencies, Interpreting Meaning, p. 41

BLOCK SCHEDULING: Resources marked with this symbol provide varied instruction during 90-minute blocks.

❷ Literary Analysis

Moment of Insight

A **moment of insight** is a fresh, new thought that arises from a poet's musings or reflections. Specific details in a poem add up to a general insight into life. This excerpt from "Combing" offers one such insight:

> Bending, I bow my head
> And lay my hand upon
> Her hair, combing, and think
> How women do this for
> Each other.

The poet connects her own action with something all women have done. Look for other moments of insight as you read the four selections. Use a chart like the one shown to record the details and insights you find.

Details
She combs her daughter's hair.

↓

Insight
She realizes that this is something all women do.

Comparing Literary Works

A moment of insight is usually closely related to a poem's **theme,** or central message about life. The poems that follow all focus on a theme, related to the issue of identity. Each poem explores a different way of thinking about identity—through family connections, nature, and an appreciation of the surrounding world. As you read, compare and contrast the messages about identity that the poems convey. With which poet's message do you most identify? Why?

❸ Reading Strategy

Interpreting Meaning

When you **interpret the meaning** of a poem, you seek to understand the point or insight that the poet communicates. To help interpret the meaning of a poem, apply the following techniques:

- Use sensory images—things you can see, hear, taste, smell, or touch—to picture what is being described.
- Ask yourself why the poet has chosen those specific images.
- Connect what is being said to your own experience.

As you read, try to interpret the meaning of each poem.

Vocabulary Development

intent (in tent′) *adj.* firmly fixed; concentrated (p. 326)
plaiting (plāt′ iŋ) *v.* braiding (p. 326)
stout (stout) *adj.* sturdy (p. 327)
languid (laŋ′ gwid) *adj.* drooping; weak (p. 329)

CUSTOMIZE INSTRUCTION FOR UNIVERSAL ACCESS

For Less Proficient Readers	For English Learners	For Advanced Readers
Explain to students that they must read these poems—and all poems—in meaningful phrases to understand them. Stress that line breaks do not necessarily signal the end of phrases or sentences. Have students listen to this group of poems on CD or audiocassette.	Have students listen to the poems on CD or audiocassette. Explain expressions that may be unfamiliar to them including, "vinegar-rinsed," "piano wire," "head-ragged," and "booby-trapped." Then, have them listen to the poems again as they follow along in their books.	Have students listen to the poems on CD or audiocassette and then read them carefully, paying particular attention to the style of each one. Then, have them choose one of the four poems and rewrite it in the style of one of the other poems.

❷ Literary Analysis

Moment of Insight

- Encourage students to identify and appreciate the poets' *moments of insight,* or fresh new thoughts, as they read the four poems.
- Have a volunteer read the excerpt from "Combing" aloud to the class. Have students identify the insight the poet describes to readers and the action that prompted the insight as shown on the chart.
- Use the instruction for Comparing Literary Works to make students aware of the similar theme that links the four poets' insights. Ask students to compare and contrast the insights that the poets draw and the way the poems express the theme as they read the four works.
- Display the Moment of Insight transparency in **Literary Analysis and Reading Transparencies,** p. 42, and have a volunteer tell you what to write under What Led to Insight for "Combing."

❸ Reading Strategy

Interpreting Meaning

- Remind students that when readers interpret the meaning of a poem, they strive to understand the big picture—the most important message or insight the poet communicates.
- Explain that noting the sensory details in the poems can help students both become aware of the insights and interpret each poem's meaning.
- Instruct students to create their own charts to track some of the details in the poems and the insights the poets draw from them.

Vocabulary Development

- Pronounce each vocabulary word for students, and read the definitions as a class. Have students identify any words with which they are already familiar.

E-Teach

Visit E-Teach at www.phschool.com for teachers' essays on how to teach, with questions and answers.

TEACH

Step-by-Step Teaching Guide for pp. 326–329

CUSTOMIZE INSTRUCTION
For Verbal/Linguistic Learners

Encourage students to analyze and discuss the figurative language and other poetic devices in the four poems. For example, students might focus on simile and metaphor in "Combing," metaphor in "Women," alliteration in "maggie and milly and molly and may," and syntax in "Astonishment."

❶ About the Selections

In these poems, the speakers express a moment of insight in which an important aspect of personal identity is suddenly revealed. In "Combing," the speaker discovers her bond with other women in her family. In "Women," the speaker recognizes that her way has been paved by African American women of previous generations. These two poems explore clues that lead to moments of self-discovery.

❷ Reading Strategy

Interpreting Meaning

- Choose a volunteer to review the meaning of the phrase "sensory language."
  Answer: Sensory language is language that appeals to the senses.
- Read aloud the bracketed stanza.
- Ask students the Reading Strategy question on p. 326: Identify the sensory language in this stanza that help you interpret the poem's meaning.
  Answer: Touching and combing the wet, fragrant hair evokes the senses sight, touch, and smell.
- Then, ask students how this language helps them interpret the poem.
  Possible response: It helps readers picture what the speaker sees and hints at how she feels.

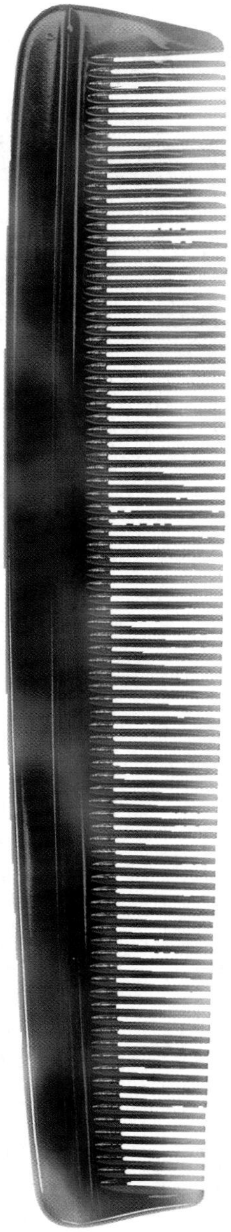

❶ Combing

Gladys Cardiff

Bending, I bow my head
And lay my hand upon
Her hair, combing, and think
How women do this for
❷ Each other. My daughter's hair
Curls against the comb,
Wet and fragrant—orange
Parings. Her face, downcast,
Is quiet for one so young.

I take her place. Beneath
My mother's hands I feel
The braids drawn up tight
As a piano wire and singing,
Vinegar-rinsed. Sitting
Before the oven I hear
The orange coils tick
The early hour before school.

She combed her grandmother
Mathilda's hair using
A comb made out of bone.
Mathilda rocked her oak wood
Chair, her face downcast,
Intent on tearing rags
In strips to braid a cotton
Rug from bits of orange
And brown. A simple act,

Preparing hair. Something
Women do for each other,
Plaiting the generations.

Reading Strategy
Interpreting Meaning
Identify the sensory language in this stanza that helps you interpret the poem's meaning.

intent (in tent′) *adj.* firmly fixed; concentrated

plaiting (plāt′ iŋ) *v.* braiding

Gladys Cardiff

(b. 1942)

Born in Montana, where her Cherokee father and Irish/Welsh mother taught school on a Blackfoot reservation, Gladys Cardiff grew up in Seattle, Washington, and received both Bachelor and Master of Arts degrees in creative writing from the University of Washington.

TEACHING RESOURCES

The following resources can be used to enrich or extend the instruction for pp. 326–329.

Literary Analysis

Selection Support: Literary Analysis, p. 84

Reading

Listening to Literature Audiocassettes, Track 10 ■

Listening to Literature Audio CDs, CD 8 ■

Extension

Authors In Depth, Gold Level (The collection includes eight additional selections by Alice Walker for extended reading.) ■

Fine Art Transparencies, Volume 1, Art Transparency 12

■ **BLOCK SCHEDULING:** Resources marked with this symbol provide varied instruction during 90-minute blocks.

The Quiltmakers, Paul Goodnight, Color Circle Art Publishing, Inc.

3 ▲**Critical Viewing** Draw conclusions about the artist's attitude toward these women. Is it similar to the one expressed by Alice Walker? **[Draw Conclusions]**

1

Women

Alice Walker

They were women then
My mama's generation
Husky of voice—Stout of
Step
With fists as well as
Hands
4 How they battered down
Doors
And ironed
Starched white
Shirts
How they led
Armies
Headragged Generals
Across mined
Fields
Booby-trapped
Ditches
To discover books
Desks
A place for us
How they knew what we
Must know
5 Without knowing a page
Of it
Themselves.

stout (stout) *adj.* sturdy

Alice Walker

(b. 1944)

Alice Walker was born in Eatonton, Georgia. From the age of eight, she kept a journal and wrote poems. Many teachers encouraged her love of reading and writing.

Walker has written poetry, short stories, nonfiction, and novels, including the highly acclaimed *The Color Purple*.

3 ▶Critical Viewing

Answer: The artist, like Alice Walker, seems to see the women as powerful and determined.

4 Reading Strategy

Interpreting Meaning

- Discuss the importance of distinguishing between literal and figurative meanings in poetry. Stress that poetic language often has both literal and figurative meanings.

▶ **Monitor Progress** Ask students to identify the underlying meaning of the phrase "battered down doors."
Possible response: The underlying meaning refers to the efforts these women made to fight limitations on African Americans' civil rights and educational and other opportunities.

5 Literary Analysis

Moment of Insight

- Ask students to read the bracketed passage.
- Then, ask a volunteer to restate the passage in his or her own words.
  Possible answer: The women knew that education was the key to their children's success even though they lacked it themselves.
- Ask students to identify the poet's insight.
  Possible answer: These women were bright, strong, and determined.

CUSTOMIZE INSTRUCTION FOR UNIVERSAL ACCESS

For Advanced Readers

Suggest that students read additional poems by Alice Walker. Provide students with titles listed in the Enrichment box, ATE p. 331. These same poems are available in **Authors In Depth,** Gold Level.

After students have read these or other poems by Alice Walker, have them form discussion groups in which they compare and contrast the selections they read. Suggest criteria for comparison, such as figurative language, speaker, images, and moments of insight. To extend the activity, have volunteers present to the class brief oral reports on their favorite Walker selections.

❻ About the Selection

In "maggie and milly and molly and may," each character makes a self-discovery as a result of contemplating nature.

❼ Reading Strategy

Interpret Meaning

- Ask students whether they have held a shell to their ear to hear a rushing sound. Was that sound actually the crashing of the sea? Could the sound be described as the singing of the shell?
- Ask students the Reading Strategy question on p. 329: What does the poet mean by "a shell that sang"? **Possible responses:** The poet probably intends both a literal and a metaphoric meaning. Maggie is so transported by her experience of the shell that she forgets her day-to-day preoccupations.

❽ Critical Thinking

Interpret

- Read aloud the passage to students.
- Ask them if it is possible for people to both lose themselves and find themselves. How? Then, have volunteers interpret the meaning of the passage.
  Answer: Losing "a you or a me" means putting aside one's ordinary preoccupations; finding "ourselves" indicates finding one's true or larger self through communing with nature.

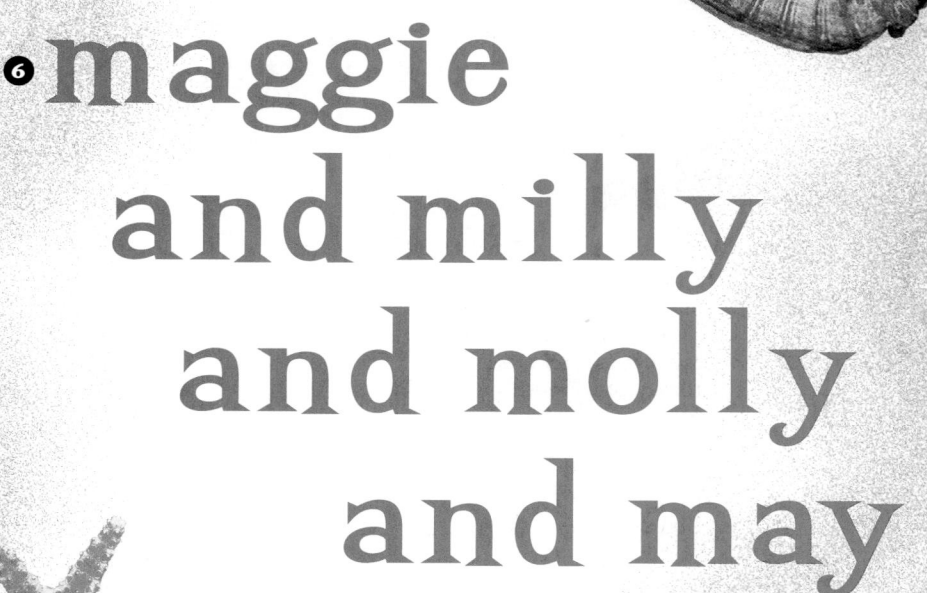

❻ maggie and milly and molly and may

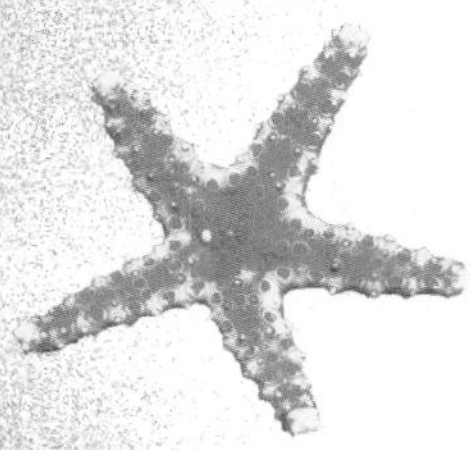

E. E. Cummings

ENRICHMENT: Science Connection

Starfish

The "stranded star" to which the poet refers is a sea star or starfish. Starfish, as any tide-pool gazer knows, are not fish, but rather marine invertebrates with rays, or arms, surrounding a sort of disk. The 1,800 species of starfish are found in all the oceans of the world and range in size from less than eight inches to about two feet across.

Most starfish have five or six hollow arms and are hard to the touch, but some starfish have many more arms and feel soft and mushy. Starfish have tube feet that often have suction disks on their ends. The tube feet are used for crawling and obtaining food.

maggie and milly and molly and may
went down to the beach (to play one day)

7 and maggie discovered a shell that sang
so sweetly she couldn't remember her troubles, and

milly befriended a stranded star
whose rays five languid fingers were;

and molly was chased by a horrible thing
which raced sideways while blowing bubbles: and

may came home with a smooth round stone
as small as a world and as large as alone.

8 For whatever we lose (like a you or a me)
it's always ourselves we find in the sea

Reading Strategy
Interpreting Meaning
What does the poet mean by "a shell that sang"?

languid (laŋ´ gwid) *adj.* drooping; weak

E. E. Cummings

(1894–1962)

Born in Cambridge, Massachusetts, E. E. Cummings graduated from Harvard University. Serving in Europe during World War I, he was briefly imprisoned because of his connection to an American who French authorities thought was critical of the war effort.

Both as poet and playwright, Cummings became notorious for his unconventional style, which reflected his individualistic outlook. Though much of his work is playful and lyrical, he often disregarded rules of grammar, spelling, and punctuation. In addition, he frequently coined his own words and ran sentences together.

Review and Assess

Thinking About the Selections

1. **Respond:** Which of these poems did you like best? Why?
2. **(a) Recall:** How many generations of her family does the speaker in "Combing" mention? **(b) Analyze:** What do you think "plaiting the generations" means to the poet?
3. **(a) Recall:** Whom does the speaker in "Women" describe as being "husky of voice" and "stout of step"? **(b) Support:** What do these words convey about the women?
4. **(a) Interpret:** What makes women who "knew . . . without knowing" remarkable? **(b) Speculate:** How might these women have described themselves?
5. **(a) Recall:** Who are the four characters in Cummings's poem? **(b) Infer:** Do they seem different from one another? Explain.
6. **Infer:** According to Cummings, what kinds of things can you find out about yourself at sea?
7. **(a) Speculate:** Would the speaker in "Combing" or "Women" be more likely to agree with the insight in Cummings's poem? **(b) Support:** Which specific details influenced your choice?
8. **Evaluate:** Do you think a person can gain a better understanding of him- or herself by reflecting on past generations or by reflecting on individual experiences? Explain.

CUSTOMIZE INSTRUCTION FOR UNIVERSAL ACCESS

For Special Needs Students	For Gifted/Talented Students	For Advanced Readers
Help students study each poem by dividing each one into stanzas or other meaningful segments. Read each segment several times and have students analyze it. Ask: What is happening in this part? What is the speaker doing? Feeling?	Have groups of students create a tableau for each poem. Allow class members to guess which poem is being depicted. Allow time for discussion of choices.	Ask students to identify a core metaphor in each poem, such as braiding hair as a metaphor for linking the generations in "Combing." Encourage students to compare the use of metaphorical language across the four poems.

ASSESS

Answers for p. 329

Review and Assess

1. Students' responses will reflect their individual interests and tastes.
2. **(a)** The speaker refers to three generations in "Combing." **(b)** "Plaiting the generations" means linking the generations through shared habits and traditions.
3. **(a)** The speaker in "Women" refers to the women of her mother's generation. **(b)** These words convey the sturdiness and determination of the women.
4. **(a)** The women were able to see beyond the limitations of their own educations to plan a better future for their children. **(b)** Possible answer: These women may have described themselves as ordinary people.
5. **(a)** The four characters are maggie, milly, molly, and may. **(b)** The characters seem similar to each other because they all celebrate the natural world at the beach.
6. Cummings says we can find our connections with our essential selves as part of nature at the seashore.
7. **(a)** The speaker in "Combing" might be more likely to agree with the insight in Cummings's poem. **(b)** The poet in "Combing" stresses the idea of continuity through the generations, which might be related to the continuity in nature expressed in Cummings's poem.
8. Possible responses: Persons might understand themselves better by reflecting on previous generations and how they fit in. Individuals might gain a better understanding of themselves by examining responses and feelings than by reflecting on their ancestors.

9 About the Selection

In this poem, the speaker ponders the nature of reality, but discovers, instead, the reality of here and now: a growling dog.

10 Reading Strategy

Interpreting Meaning

- Remind students to try to interpret the point or insight the poet is making.
- Have students read the passage and the line that precedes it. Then, ask students the Reading Strategy question on p. 330: To which "small star" does the speaker refer in line 6?
  Answer: The "small star" is the sun.

Answers for p. 330

Review and Assess

1. Some students will find the questions thought provoking. Others may find the repeated questions irritating or boring.
2. **(a)** The word *why* is used most often. **(b)** The speaker must be a curious, thoughtful person.
   (c) The questions do point in the same direction, as they all relate to existence.
3. **(a)** The speaker is astonished at being who he or she is and existing at the moment that he or she does. **(b)** The speaker remarks at the coincidence of looking over at the dog at the very moment it looks up and growls.
4. **(a)** Cummings would be likely to agree with the insight expressed in this poem. **(b)** The sense of astonishment at and connection with nature is similar in both poems. For example, the "horrible thing" in "maggie and milly and molly and may" resembles the "growling thing" in "Astonishment."
5. Many students will agree that pondering the meaning of life is worthwhile, but some students may feel that it is better to live life rather than to think about it constantly.

9 Astonishment

Wisława Szymborska

Translated by Grażyna Drabik, Austin Flint, and Sharon Olds

Why as one person, and one only?
Why this one, not another? And why here?
On Tuesday? At home, not in a nest?
Why in skin, not scales? With a face, not a leaf?
And why do I come, I myself, only once?
10 On this earth? Near a small star?
After many epochs[1] of absence?
Instead of always, and as all?
As all insects, and all horizons?
And why right now? Why bone and blood?
Myself as myself with myself? Why—
not nearby or a hundred miles away,
not yesterday or a hundred years ago—
do I sit and stare into a dark corner,
just as it looks up, suddenly raising its head,
this growling thing that is called a dog?

1. **epochs** (ep′ əks) *n.* periods or spans of time.

Reading Strategy
Interpreting Meaning To which "small star" does the speaker refer in line 6?

Review and Assess

Thinking About the Selection

1. **Respond:** How do you react to the poet's style of presenting the entire poem as a series of questions? Explain.
2. **(a) Recall:** Which questioning word is used the most?
   (b) Infer: What do the questions indicate about the speaker?
   (c) Draw Conclusions: Do they all seem to point in the same direction, or not? Explain.
3. **(a) Interpret:** What does the speaker find astonishing?
   (b) Connect: How do the final lines reinforce this idea?
4. **(a) Speculate:** Would E. E. Cummings be likely to agree with the insight expressed in this poem? **(b) Support:** Draw on images and ideas in both poems to support your answer.
5. **Evaluate:** Do you think pondering the meaning of life, as the speaker does, can enrich a person's life? Why or why not?

Wisława Szymborska

(b. 1923)

In her poem "Astonishment," Wisława Szymborska uses the word *why* eight times. "Question authority" might be the motto of this Polish poet. During World War II, when the Nazis closed Polish secondary schools and universities, Szymborska attended school illegally.

Today, Szymborska lives quietly in Poland. She prefers letting her poetry speak for her. In 1996, she was awarded the Nobel Prize for Literature.

ASSESSMENT PRACTICE: Reading Comprehension

Implied Main Idea **(For more practice, see Test Preparation Workbook, p. 21.)**

Use the following sample test item to show students how to recognize implied main ideas in poetry.

Preparing hair. Something
Women do for each other,
Plaiting the generations.

Which of the following best states the implied main idea in this, the final verse of "Combing"?

A Preparing each other's hair is central to women's lives.
B Women prepare each other's hair.
C By preparing each other's hair, women forge connections across generations.
D Women communicate through gestures.

Students should recognize that *C* is the correct answer.

Review and Assess

Literary Analysis

Moment of Insight

1. (a) Which details lead to the **moments of insight** in "Combing" and "Women"? (b) At what line in each poem is the insight revealed?
2. Which words express the moment of insight in "maggie and milly and molly and may"?
3. (a) What is the insight expressed in "Astonishment"? (b) What provokes it?

Comparing Literary Works

4. Exploring identity is the **theme** common to all four poems. How does each poet address this theme? In the center of a chart like this one, record the similarities you find. In the outer boxes, note the differences in the poems' ideas.

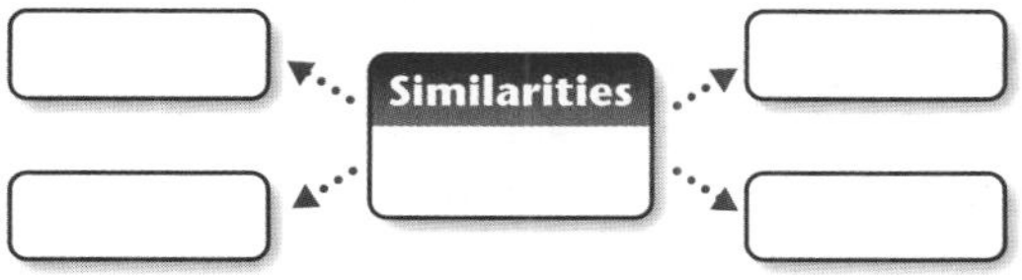

5. Of the four moments of insight, which came as the greatest surprise to you? Explain your answer.
6. Which moment of insight meant the most to you? Explain.

Reading Strategy

Interpreting Meaning

7. Which images and interpretations came to mind while you read "Combing" and "Women"?
8. In his poem, Cummings focuses on playing, while in hers, Szymborska focuses on the single question *why?* What is the effect of each poet's strategy?

Extend Understanding

9. **Career Connection:** What value might the insights in the four poems have for a teacher, a counselor, or anyone in the position of giving guidance to young people?

Quick Review

A **moment of insight** is a fresh, new thought that arises from a poet's musings.

The **theme** is the message or central insight at the heart of a work of literature.

To **interpret the meaning** of a poem, work to understand the point or insight that the poet is making.

Take It to the Net

www.phschool.com
Take the interactive self-test online to check your understanding of the selections.

ENRICHMENT: Further Reading

Other Works by Alice Walker

The Same River Twice: Alice Walker on Alice Walker
The Color Purple
In Search of Our Mothers' Gardens
"My Heart Has Reopened to You"
"How Poems Are Made: A Discredited View"
"Remember?"
"Expect Nothing"
"We Alone"
"Poem at Thirty-Nine"

Take It to the Net
Visit www.phschool.com for more information on Alice Walker.

Answers for p. 331

Review and Assess

1. **(a)** The details about the speaker combing her daughter's hair and the memories of the speaker's mother and grandmother lead to the insight in "Combing." The memories of the speaker's mother and other women of that generation lead to the insight in "Women." **(b)** The insight is revealed in the final stanza of "Combing" and the last five lines of "Women."
2. The words "For whatever we lose (like a you or a me) it's always ourselves we find in the sea" reveal the insight in Cummings's poem.
3. **(a)** The insight expressed in "Astonishment" is the speaker's astonishment at coincidences in nature that bring every being into existence. **(b)** The speaker looks into a corner just as a dog raises its head and growls.
4. Similarity: tone of celebration, moment of insight appears at end, characters are women
Differences: rhyme scheme and syntax, emphasis on nature, punctuation, use of sentence fragments
5. Students may find it surprising that the simple act of combing hair leads to a moment of insight in the poem "Combing." They might also be surprised by the dark corner turning into a growling dog in "Astonishment."
6. The moments of insight that students cite as most meaningful will depend on their backgrounds, experiences, and temperaments.
7. The image of tightly drawn braids can be interpreted as motherly love; the image of tearing rags to braid a rug can be interpreted as "weaving" together the generations; the image of headragged generals can be interpreted as strong women battling for their children.
8. Each poet takes a different approach, but both poets focus on the idea of self-discovery through an individual search.
9. Anyone in the position of giving guidance to young people can learn the importance of self-exploration for students by reading these poems.

EXTEND

Answers for p. 332

❶ Vocabulary Development

Word Analysis

1. aim or purpose; firmly fixed
2. looking down; depressed
3. hard covering on certain animals; something that has the form of a shell
4. sheet in a book; call over a loudspeaker or electronic device

Concept Development: Antonyms

1. languid
2. plaiting
3. intent
4. stout

Spelling Strategy

1. ghoulish
2. screamer
3. braided
4. appearing

❷ Grammar

1. It is, I think, a powerful poem.
2. Oh, I was amazed by what I saw.
3. Her hair was braided neatly and beautifully, I might add.
4. Yes, they certainly were determined and strong women.
5. Yours, like mine, is a smooth shell.

Writing Application

Paragraphs should include at least two parenthetical expressions. Be sure students use commas appropriately to set off the expressions.

Integrate Language Skills

❶ Vocabulary Development Lesson

Word Analysis: Words With Multiple Meanings

Some words have more than one meaning. For example, in "Women," the poet uses the word *stout* to mean "sturdy." *Stout* can also mean "courageous" or "heavyset." When a word has multiple meanings, its context determines the meaning that applies.

Write two definitions for each italicized word. Underline the definition that applies in the sentence based on the context.

1. The growling dog made its *intent* plain.
2. I was saddened to see her *downcast* expression.
3. Maggie found a *shell* on the beach that made her forget her troubles.
4. He understood the book without having read a *page* of it.

Concept Development: Antonyms

Write the word from the vocabulary list on page 325 that is an antonym for, or has the opposite meaning of, each of these words.

1. vigorous
2. unbraiding
3. distracted
4. weak

Spelling Strategy

For a word that ends in the pattern *vowel-vowel-consonant*, do not double the consonant before adding an ending.

Example: *plait* + *-ing* = *plaiting*

Think of an ending for each word shown, and use it to write a new word. Use each ending only once.

1. ghoul
2. scream
3. braid
4. appear

❷ Grammar Lesson

Parenthetical Expressions

As you have seen in Cummings's poem, parentheses are sometimes used to set off a nonessential phrase within a sentence. Commas can also set off these **parenthetical expressions,** or nonessential words or phrases that interrupt the sentence's general flow. Look at how parenthetical expressions are used below:

Direct Address: Please help me, *Milly*.
Mild Interjection: *Well,* I never saw such a beautiful shell.
Common Expression: It is, *in my opinion*, tiny.
Transition: The ocean, *however*, is huge.
Contrast: This one, *unlike mine*, is blue.

Practice Copy each sentence, inserting any commas necessary to set off the parenthetical expression.

1. It is I think a powerful poem.
2. Oh I was amazed by what I saw.
3. Her hair was braided neatly and beautifully I might add.
4. Yes they certainly were determined and strong women.
5. Yours like mine is a smooth shell.

Writing Application Write a paragraph about one or two of the poems you liked best. Use at least two parenthetical expressions.

WG *Prentice Hall Writing and Grammar Connection: Chapter 29, Section 2*

TEACHING RESOURCES

The following resources can be used to enrich or extend the instruction for pp. 332–333.

Vocabulary

Selection Support: Build Vocabulary, p. 81

Grammar

Selection Support: Build Grammar Skills, p. 82
Writing and Grammar, Gold Level, p. 658
Daily Language Practice Transparencies ■

Writing

Writing and Grammar, Gold Level, p. 2
Writing and Grammar iText CD-ROM ■

■ **BLOCK SCHEDULING:** Resources marked with this symbol provide varied instruction during 90-minute blocks.

❸ Writing Lesson

Journal Entry on a Moment of Insight

Writing poetry is one way of exploring ideas and feelings. Journal writing is another. Write a journal entry about a moment of insight that you had in the recent past as a result of something that happened either locally or nationally.

Prewriting Start by jotting down important events that have occurred over the past several years. Then, choose one of those as your topic. Gather details by noting the sensory details of the event or experience. These will add emotional depth to your entry.

Drafting Using your notes as a starting point, recount the experience or event. Include details that will help your readers *feel* what you are describing. Reveal the moment of insight at the end of your journal entry.

Revising Read over your journal entry. Delete details that do not add to your insight. Look for places where more sensory details would add to the emotional depth of your writing.

Model: Eliminating Unnecessary Information

moving through the frenzy with silent focus

The rescue workers—~~dressed in blue coveralls~~—treated the accident victims with great compassion.

Words like *frenzy* and *silent focus* add to the emotional depth of the writing.

Prentice Hall Writing and Grammar Connection: Chapter 1, Section 1

❹ Extension Activities

Listening and Speaking With three classmates, prepare an **oral reading** of "maggie and milly and molly and may."

- Plan individual speaking assignments, but read the first and last stanzas together.
- Consider your audience, and practice changing your tone of voice to improve the presentation's impact on your audience.

After you have rehearsed, perform your interpretation for your classmates and invite them to offer their reactions. **[Group Activity]**

Research and Technology Using "Combing" and "Women" as inspiration, prepare a **photo essay** about mothers and daughters. Try to include women of varying ages and backgrounds. Use the Internet to help you find photos, or take pictures of subjects you know. Then, prepare captions that reflect your response to each photo. Present a display in your classroom or school library.

Take It to the Net www.phschool.com

Go online for an additional research activity using the Internet.

ASSESSMENT RESOURCES

The following resources can be used to assess students' knowledge and skills.

Selection Assessment

- **Formal Assessment,** Selection Test, pp. 69–71
- **Open Book Test,** pp. 61–63
- **Got It! Assessment Videotapes,** Tape 2
- **Test Bank Software**

PRENTICE HALL ASSESSMENT SYSTEM

- **Workbook**
- **Skill Book**
- **Transparencies**
- **CD-ROM**

Take It to the Net

Visit www.phschool.com for self-tests and additional questions on the selections.

❸ Writing Lesson

- To prepare students to write journal entries about a moment of insight, model the process for them. First, describe an event that affected you greatly.
- Then, jot down a few of your initial reactions to the event on the board. Let the students choose one to be the focus of the journal entry.
- Write a draft of a journal entry.
- Have the students decide which details distract from the main point of the entry and suggest details that would make the entry more affecting.
- Have students use the Writing Lesson and example to guide them in writing and revising a journal entry about a moment of insight.

❹ Listening and Speaking

- Divide the class into groups of four to prepare their oral reading.
- Have the group members choose the lines they will read.
- Ask each student to practice his or her lines several times. Encourage students to try reading the lines with various emphasis and intonation and choose the reading they believe will contribute to making the moment of insight in the poem most vivid to listeners.

CUSTOMIZE INSTRUCTION for Universal Access

To address different learning styles, use the activities suggested in the **Extension Activities** booklet, p. 21.

- For Logical/Mathematical and Interpersonal Learners, use Activity 4.
- For Visual/Spatial Learners, use Activity 5.
- For Visual/Spatial and Verbal/Linguistic Learners, use Activity 6.

Lesson Objectives

1. To write a persuasive essay
2. To learn the characteristics of a persuasive essay
3. To acknowledge counter-arguments in a persuasive essay

Model From Literature

Martin Luther King, Jr.'s speech "I Have a Dream" is a persuasive expression on the subject of human rights.

Prewriting

- Encourage students to choose a topic they feel strongly about, so that they can quickly generate persuasive arguments.
- Have students answer this question to develop their thesis statements: What exactly is my position on this topic?
- Have students imagine being on the other side of their issue. What arguments can be made against their thesis? Encourage students to address these arguments in their persuasive essays.

Writing WORKSHOP

Persuasion: Persuasive Essay

A **persuasive essay** is a work in which a writer presents a case for or against a particular position. In this workshop, you will write a persuasive essay on a topic of importance to you.

Assignment Criteria. Your persuasive essay should have the following characteristics:

- A clear thesis statement—a statement of your position on an issue
- Evidence that supports your position and anticipates your readers' counterarguments
- An effective organization
- Persuasive language that builds your argument

To preview the criteria on which your persuasive essay may be assessed, see the Rubric on page 337.

Prewriting

Choose a topic. Pair up with a classmate and brainstorm for topics that are important to each of you, noting those that cause the most disagreement. Select an issue that has compelling arguments on both sides. Then, choose a position to support.

Look at both sides. A persuasive essay is always more effective if it acknowledges and addresses counterarguments. Make a chart like the one below by jotting down facts and ideas that support or contradict your position.

Evidence for school uniforms	Evidence against school uniforms
• May reduce violence and discrimination	• Take choice away from students
• Promote school image	• Can cause resentment among students

Gather evidence. Gather evidence from a wide variety of sources. Collect quotations and facts. As you investigate, keep track of any ideas or phrases that are not your own so that you can give appropriate credit.

Write a thesis statement. Review your notes and the evidence that you have gathered from additional research. Develop a thesis statement that clearly expresses your position.

TEACHING RESOURCES

The following resources can be used to enrich or extend the instruction for pp. 334–337.

Writing and Grammar, Gold Level, Chapter 7, pp. 128–155

Performance Assessment and Portfolio Management, pp. 10, 39

Writing and Grammar iText CD-ROM
Students can use the following tools as they complete their persuasive essays:

- Pros and Cons Chart
- Self-Interview
- Unity and Coherence

Student Model

Before you begin drafting your persuasive essay, read this student model and review the characteristics of powerful persuasion.

Braden Danbury
Cumming, GA

Dress Codes May Succeed Where School Uniforms Have Failed

School uniforms are becoming increasingly popular as a way to combat school violence and discrimination. Uniforms, while they may help somewhat, cause problems of their own. Students argue that it is their right to wear what they choose and uniforms violate that right. A less strict code is the answer to both of these problems, keeping appropriate attire in the schools while allowing individuals to choose what they wear.

> The author offers a clear thesis statement in the form of a proposal that addresses a key problem.

Uniforms require students to wear specific shirt and pant types, thus eliminating the element of choice. Dress codes, on the other hand, are less restrictive than school uniforms and cause less resentment among students. Students enjoy choosing what to wear to school each day, coordinating what they wear with how they feel. School uniforms may cause friction between students and school officials, which can have negative consequences.

While it might make sense to have students' safety as a leading justification for requiring uniforms, safety hits the bottom of the list in a press release from the National Association of Elementary School Principals. Safety ranks below such trivial things as school image. This calls into question why uniforms are touted as the answer to school safety issues. Dress codes make the difference where it counts. They keep students safe while forcing them to do nothing other than make sure their clothes meet acceptable standards. An added benefit of dress codes is that schools with uniform policies pay much more than schools with dress codes. Schools with uniforms have to design, order, sell, and distribute the uniforms they wish to have for their school. Dress codes are much less expensive to implement and follow.

> Braden finds a way to deal with counterarguments based on safety concerns.

> Braden offers evidence that supports his position.

With the rise in violence, students and their dress often come under suspicion and scrutiny. In addition, the wide variety of clothing in our high schools may lead students to make prejudicial judgments about each other. Dress codes address the problems of violence without causing resentment among students. They are less strict, giving the students more freedom in how they dress, while allowing school officials to set general guidelines. The amount of money it would take to implement a dress code is a fraction of the cost of school uniforms. Dress codes are not the only answer, but they are a step toward combating violence and discrimination in schools.

> The author restates his thesis and summarizes his evidence. He also offers an additional insight.

Student Model

- Explain that the Student Model is a sample, and that persuasive essays may be longer.
- Point out that the thesis statement is in the first paragraph, but not at the beginning. The writer builds up to the thesis statement by providing background information in the first three sentences. This information will help the reader better understand the writer's thesis statement.
- Explain that including information from a published press release adds credibility to Braden's arguments.
- Ask students to identify the additional insight the student offers in the concluding paragraph.
  Answer: The writer suggests that a wide variety of clothing styles may lead students to make prejudicial judgments about each other.

Real-World Connection

Ask students to consider instances in which they use persuasive writing or speaking. For example, they may persuade a friend to go hiking instead of swimming, or they might write a note requesting a teacher's permission to attend a special event instead of class. As students grow older, they may choose careers in which persuasion plays an important role. Ask students to brainstorm for a list of careers in which persuasive skills play an important role. They may list law, customer relations, and politics.

CUSTOMIZE INSTRUCTION FOR UNIVERSAL ACCESS

For Special Needs Students	For English Learners	For Advanced Readers
Encourage students to work in pairs to discuss a topic that's important to them. Have them write down each argument and counter-argument they develop.	Invite students to share examples of persuasive writing or speaking used in other cultures. For example, how is persuasion used in advertising?	Have students conduct research on the Internet to locate persuasive content in Web sites. Ask them to share their results with the class, evaluating the effectiveness of the persuasive techniques.

Drafting

- Encourage students to work in pairs to develop arguments and counterarguments they will include in their persuasive essays. Often, another student's viewpoint stimulates additional ideas.
- If students have chosen a topic that is of city, state, or national interest, the Internet is a useful resource for statistics and expert opinions. If students have chosen a topic that is more closely related to their own lives, they may need to conduct surveys or interviews on their own.
- Encourage students to consider using the first-person point of view if their essays include testimonials.

Revising

- Have students work in small groups to share their drafts with each other, jotting down questions and counterarguments that come to mind as they read. Have the writers make sure they address these questions as they make their revisions.
- As students revise, have them focus on opportunities to replace weak verbs with strong verbs and to reject general nouns and adjectives in favor of strong, specific nouns and adjectives.

Drafting

Organize your arguments. It is useful to sketch out a logical structure for your essay before you write it. Decide which arguments you will present in support of your thesis statement and the order of presentation. Be sure to include a place in your outline to address counterarguments. The organization at right demonstrates one effective way to write a persuasive essay.

Organizing Your Arguments

Present thesis statement.
↓
Present arguments to support thesis.
↓
Address counterarguments.
↓
Provide strongest argument in support of thesis.
↓
Conclude by restating thesis and presenting a memorable final thought or quotation.

Provide evidence. For each point you make, provide evidence to back up your argument. Types of effective evidence include the following:

- **Statistics:** Cite numbers that show the impact of your proposal.
- **Expert opinions:** Include the advice of those who have training and experience related to your topic.
- **Personal observations:** Tell your readers about your own experiences with the topic.
- **Testimonials:** Include statements from peers that reinforce your argument.

Write with a respectful tone. Let your ideas be the strength of your essay. Avoid insulting the opposition. Instead, use a tone that shows respect.

Revising

Revise to address readers' concerns. To convince those who may not agree with your position, show them that you understand their concerns.

1. Look over your draft to highlight controversial claims that a critic of your position would oppose.
2. For each of these claims, determine strong counterarguments that you can make with explanations and evidence.
3. Look for a place where you can insert this information and incorporate it into your draft.

Model: Addressing the Opposition

Dress codes make the difference where it counts. They keep students safe while forcing them to do nothing other than make sure their clothes meet acceptable standards.

Braden could provide evidence *and* address concerns by finding a statistic that shows that schools with dress codes are just as safe as, or safer than, schools with uniforms.

USING TECHNOLOGY IN WRITING

Encourage students to use online dictionaries and thesauruses to find vivid verbs, nouns, and adjectives to use in their persuasive essays. Point out that some software programs check for "readability." Students can use these programs to identify passive verbs that could be replaced with active verbs. Students can also use spell check and other revision tools available on the **Writing and Grammar iText CD-ROM.**

Revise to strengthen persuasive language. Look for words that can be replaced with more persuasive language. For example, in the following example, *refused* creates a stronger impression than *did not want.*

Example: She *did not want* to leave her home.
She *refused* to leave her home.

Compare the model and the nonmodel. Why is the model more effective than the nonmodel?

Nonmodel	Model
Students argue that it is their right to wear what they choose and that uniforms withdraw that right.	Students argue that it is their right to wear what they choose and that uniforms violate that right.

Publishing and Presenting

Present your writing to a wider audience. Sharing your persuasive essay might possibly achieve results—your ideas could inspire a positive change in behavior, open minds to a new perspective, or help change an unfair policy.

Deliver an oral presentation. Read your persuasive composition aloud in front of your classmates. After you have finished reading, take an unofficial poll to determine whether or not you convinced your audience of your position.

Publish in a newspaper. Send your essay as an opinion piece to your school or community newsletter, or condense it into a letter to the editor.

Speaking Connection
To learn more about analyzing persuasive arguments, see the **Listening and Speaking Workshop**, page 338.

WG Prentice Hall Writing and Grammar Connection: Chapter 7

Rubric for Self-Assessment

Evaluate your persuasive essay using the following criteria and rating scale:

Criteria	Rating Scale: Not very				Very
How clear is the thesis statement?	1	2	3	4	5
How well is the thesis supported by evidence?	1	2	3	4	5
How well are readers' concerns anticipated and addressed?	1	2	3	4	5
How effectively are arguments organized?	1	2	3	4	5
How powerful is the persuasive language?	1	2	3	4	5

Publishing and Presenting

- Before students deliver their persuasive compositions to the class, have them practice reading their writing aloud.
- Remind students that they are trying to change other people's minds, and they can use dramatic techniques to help this effort in their delivery.
- Ask students to brainstorm for delivery techniques they can use, such as emphasizing key words, planning for pauses in effective places, using a confident voice, and making eye contact.

Assessment

- Review with students the assessment criteria, pointing out that they measure the writing, not the delivery, of the persuasive essay.
- As students listen to each other's essays, have them use the rubric criteria to rate their deliveries on a five-point scale.
- The rubric on this page, and another rubric in an alternative format, can be found on pp. 10 and 39 in **Performance Assessment and Portfolio Management.**

TEST-TAKING TIP

Remind students that when they take written tests, it's important to clearly understand the writing prompt. A good strategy for this is to look for key words in the prompt. For example, seeing the word *persuasive* in the prompt gives them a clue about what to expect in the rest of the question and how to respond.

Lesson Objectives

1. To learn to analyze types of arguments
2. To recognize components of argument structure
3. To identify five different argument types

Recognize Argument Structure

- Have students read the information in this section on p. 338.
- Point out that an argument relies on premises to support it. If the premises are many and strong, the argument will stand; if the premises are few and weak, the argument will crumble.
- Explain that when students are analyzing an argument, they should examine the conclusion first. Sometimes the conclusion is stated early in the argument; sometimes it is stated last.
- Explain that after students identify the conclusion, they can then look for the premises—or building blocks—that support it.
- In analyzing the premises, students should ask if the premise supports the argument. They may find themselves discarding some premises as irrelevant.

Identify Argument Types

- Review with the class the information in this section on p. 338.
- Have the class work in small groups to complete the Analyzing Types of Argument chart. First, have each group analyze the structure of one of the arguments provided on this page. Next, have each group come up with examples for each of the argument types.

Listening and Speaking WORKSHOP

Analyzing Types of Arguments

We normally think of an argument as a shouting match or disagreement. However, an argument, as it is used to describe speeches, essays, and debates, is a series of statements that support a particular conclusion. Learning how to analyze an argument will improve your own ability to build persuasive arguments.

Recognize Argument Structure

Just as the human body is supported by its skeleton, the body of an argument is bolstered with supporting statements, or premises. Recognizing an argument's structure will help you figure out whether it is strong—supported by many powerful premises—or weak.

Identify the conclusion. The conclusion is the main idea of an argument. It should be easy to identify because it is broadly stated, general, and supported by individual pieces of evidence.

Identify premises. Premises are the basic building blocks of an argument. The best way to find individual premises is to work backward from a conclusion to find its supporting statements or evidence.

Identify Argument Types

Persuasive speakers use a variety of argument types to convince audiences. For example, if you had to prepare a persuasive speech on why solar energy is better than energy from coal, you might use the following argument types:

- **Analogy (Making a comparison):** You could argue that not using solar energy is like paying to drive your car to school when you could take a free school bus.
- **Authority (Citing expert opinion):** You might point to specific research that links the burning of coal to air pollution.
- **Emotion (Appealing to sense of right and wrong):** You could indicate the harmful effects that pollution might have on a child with asthma.
- **Logic (Using reasoning):** You could indicate that solar energy is cleaner than coal and exists in greater supply.
- **Causation (Using cause-and-effect analysis):** You could walk your audience through the coal energy process, from the burning of coal to its effect on living organisms.

Analyzing Types of Arguments

Argument Structure

Conclusion: ______

Premise: ______ Premise: ______ Premise: ______

Argument Types

Type	Example
Analogy	
Authority	
Emotion	
Logic	
Causation	

***Activity:* Observation and Analysis** Watch a video of a debate or an important speech, such as a presidential address. As you listen, complete a chart like the one shown. Note an example of each type of argument you hear in the speech. Use the flowchart to diagram one of the main arguments.

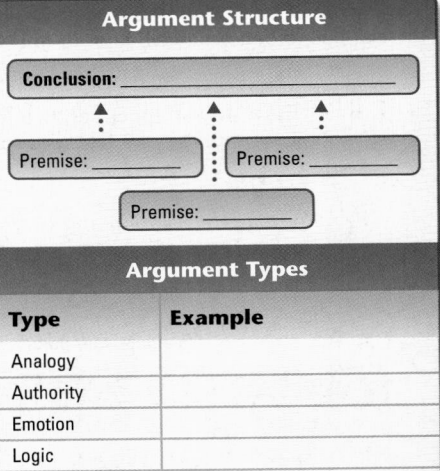

CUSTOMIZE INSTRUCTION FOR UNIVERSAL ACCESS

For Special Needs Students	For English Learners
Encourage students to focus primarily on one of the argument types, such as Analogy or Emotion. Have the students draw on their personal experiences to develop examples.	Assign students to watch an hour of television at home, jotting down a brief description of persuasive arguments they hear in television commercials.

Assessment WORKSHOP

Stated and Implied Main Idea

In the reading sections of some tests, you are required to read passages and answer multiple-choice questions about stated and implied main ideas. Use the following strategies to answer such questions:

- Look for a topic sentence that is a statement of the main idea of a passage.
- If a main idea is not stated, it may be implied or suggested.
- To identify an implied main idea, read the passage and summarize the author's message in a single statement.
- To make sure that you have identified the topic sentence correctly, check that the other sentences support the idea of the sentence you have chosen.

Test-Taking Strategies

- Check implied main ideas by making sure all of the sentences support your one-sentence summary.
- Consider the title you might assign a passage. This may reinforce the main idea.

Sample Test Item

Directions: Read the passage, and then answer the question that follows.

Despite dropping temperatures and decreased daylight, finches, sparrows, and mockingbirds are birds commonly seen in winter. These species feed primarily on seeds and berries, which are plentiful even through the coldest months.

1. What is the main idea implied in this passage?
   - **A** Birds feed on seeds and berries in winter.
   - **B** Birds that are seen in winter are finches, sparrows, and mockingbirds.
   - **C** During winter, birds look for food near trees and shrubs.
   - **D** Finches, sparrows, and mockingbirds can survive the coldest winter months.

Answer and Explanation

The correct answer is ***D,*** because both sentences support the main idea. ***A*** and ***B*** are details, but they are not the central idea of the passage. ***C*** is not stated in the passage.

Practice

Directions: Read the passage, and then answer the question that follows.

Everyone has a fever at some point. A fever is a symptom, not a disease. It is an indication that your body is fighting an infection or illness. While it causes discomfort, a fever may be a sign of recovery.

You do not need to call a doctor immediately if you develop a low-grade fever. You should drink fluids and get plenty of rest. Record your temperature every two hours, and note any change in symptoms.

1. What is the stated main idea of the first paragraph?
   - **A** Everyone gets a fever at some point.
   - **B** A fever is a symptom of a disease, not the disease itself.
   - **C** A fever indicates that your body is fighting an infection or illness.
   - **D** A fever may be a sign of your body's recovery.

Lesson Objective

To correctly answer test questions about stated and implied ideas

Applying Reading Strategies

Encourage students to look for relationships between main ideas and details in a sample passage. Identifying these relationships can help students construct the meaning of the main idea.

Applying Test-Taking Strategies

- Have students read the Sample Test Item, then identify the main idea and details.
- Point out that all the details have a supporting relationship to the main idea.
- Explain that the main idea is the most general or conclusive statement in the passage. The other statement provides individual details that help fill in the complete picture.
- Have students use these same strategies to answer the Practice question on their own.

Answer:

The correct answer is C because it expresses the most important point about fevers. Answers A, B, and D provide helpful details that support the main idea.

TEACHING RESOURCES

The following resources can be used to enrich or extend the instruction for p. 339.

PRENTICE HALL ASSESSMENT SYSTEM

- Workbook
- Skill Book
- Transparencies
- CD-ROM

Unit Objectives

1. To read selections in different genres that develop the theme "The Lighter Side"
2. To apply a variety of reading strategies, particularly interactive strategies, appropriate for reading these selections
3. To analyze literary elements
4. To use a variety of strategies to build vocabulary
5. To learn elements of grammar, usage, and style
6. To use recursive writing processes to write in a variety of forms
7. To develop listening and speaking skills
8. To express and support responses to various types of texts
9. To prepare, organize, and present literary interpretations

Meeting the Objectives

With each selection, you will find instructional materials through which students can meet these objectives. Further, you will find additional practice pages for reading strategies, literary analysis, vocabulary, and grammar in the **Selection Support: Skills Development Workbook** in your **Teaching Resources.**

Background

Art

Scientists' Hobby: Failure #18 of the Anti-Gravity Pack, by Bruce Widdows

The title of this drawing helps create the comical idea of a persistent inventor trying to defy gravity. Ask the following question about the drawing:

What makes this potentially hazardous situation so amusing?

Answer: The earnest demeanors of the men, the silly-looking device, the reference (in the title) to seventeen previous attempts, and the cartoon-like drawing all make the situation funny.

UNIT 4 The Lighter Side

Scientist's Hobby: Failure #18 of the Anti-Gravity Pack, 1992, Bruce Widdows, Courtesy of George Adams Gallery, New York

UNIT FEATURES	
Connections	**Reading Informational Material**
Every unit contains a feature that connects literature to a related topic, such as art, science, or history. In this unit, the Literature and Childhood feature on pp. 380–383 presents a bittersweet childhood memory of Gary Soto. Use the information and questions on the Connections pages to enrich students' understanding of the selections presented within the unit.	These selections will help students learn to analyze and evaluate informational texts, such as workplace documents, technical directions, and consumer materials. They will expose students to the organization and features unique to nonnarrative texts. In this unit, students will learn to analyze the text structure of newspaper articles.

Exploring the Theme

What's so funny? It might be an animal trainer teaching 5,000 flies how to "act." It might be an overstressed husband taking a mental leave of absence, or it might be an outlandish poem told in nonsense language. Check out these stories, essays, poems, and more. You are sure to find something to make you smile.

You may never have played football on a crowded street in Philadelphia, like Bill Cosby in **"Go Deep to the Sewer."** But you will probably still laugh when you recognize yourself—and the games you improvised with your friends—in Cosby's humorous reminiscence. This is only one of the many types of laughter you will find in the pieces that follow—the laughter of recognition.

▲ **Critical Viewing** Which aspects of this drawing add to its humorous impact? **[Analyze]**

ASSESSMENT RESOURCES

- **Selection Support: Skills Development Workbook**
- **Formal Assessment**
- **Open Book Tests**
- **Performance Assessment and Portfolio Management**
- **Extension Activities**

Assessing Student Progress

Listed below are tools that are available to measure the degree to which students meet the unit objectives.

Informal Assessment

The questions on the Review and Assess sections are a first-level response to the concepts and skills presented with the selections. Students' responses provide a brief, informal measure of their grasp of the material. These responses can indicate where further instruction and practice are needed. Follow up with the practice pages in **Selection Support: Skills Development Workbook.**

Formal Assessment

The **Formal Assessment** booklet contains the Selection Tests and Unit Tests.

- Selection Tests measure comprehension and skills acquisition for each selection or group of selections.
- Each Unit Test provides students with thirty multiple-choice questions and five essay questions designed to assess students' knowledge of the literature and skills taught in the unit.

The **Open Book Tests** ask students to demonstrate their ability to synthesize and communicate information from selections or groups of selections.

To assess student writing, you will find rubrics and scoring models in the **Performance Assessment and Portfolio Management** booklet. In this booklet, you will also find scoring rubrics for listening and speaking activities.

Alternative Assessment

The **Extension Activities** booklet contains writing activities, listening and speaking activities, and research and technology activities that are appropriate for students with different ability levels. You may also use these activities as an alternative measure of students' growth.

▶Critical Viewing

Answer: The serious expressions on the men's faces as they perch perilously on a rooftop to try a silly experiment add a touch of ironic humor to the drawing. The antigravity pack and the rest of the gear add humor, too.

Why Read Literature?

The "Why Read Literature?" page in each unit presents a list of possible purposes for reading. Each purpose for reading is connected to one or more of the selections in the unit. Good readers set a purpose before reading to help them read actively and focus on meaningful details.

Unit 4 introduces three purposes for reading. "Read for the Love of Literature" invites students to enjoy amusing language in a poem and amusing characters in a play. "Read for Information" provides fascinating details about insects in apartments—and in movies. "Read to Be Entertained" invites students to glimpse into a world of daydreams.

How to Use This Page

- Tell students that before reading each selection in this unit, they should get ready to develop skills in interactive reading. This will help them set a purpose for reading.
- Explain that students can increase their love of literature by enjoying the humorous play *The Inspector-General* by Anton Chekhov and the nonsense poem "Jabberwocky" by Lewis Carroll.
- Point out that students will learn some interesting facts about insects in both "An Entomological Study of Apartment 4A" by Patricia Volk and "Fly Away" by Ralph Helfer.
- In "Read to Be Entertained," students will step into someone else's daydreams in "The Secret Life of Walter Mitty" by James Thurber.

Why Read Literature?

Whenever you read, you have a purpose, or reason. You might read to find a particular type of information, to be entertained, or to further your understanding of a certain kind of literature. Preview three purposes you could set for yourself before reading works in this unit.

The Jabberwock, 1872, John Tenniel

1 Read for the Love of Literature

In Russian literature there is a tradition of poking fun at government officials that has landed some writers in trouble. The negative reaction to Nikolai Gogol's play *The Inspector-General* caused Gogol to seek exile. See how dramatist Anton Chekhov takes Gogol's play, in which townspeople mistake a local scoundrel for a government inspector, and turns it on its head in his version of ***The Inspector-General,*** page 358.

You know something is not quite right when you read a poem like "Jabberwocky." Maybe it is the fact that author Lewis Carroll invents his own language as he goes along. Maybe it is the feeling that, in spite of all the bizarre phrases, you still understand what he is saying. Test your wits and chortle along with the inspired nonsense of **"Jabberwocky,"** page 400.

2 Read for Information

You might be surprised at some of the trickery trainers use to get animals to do what movie directors want. Find out how one trainer coaxed five thousand winged extras to fly on cue as he takes you behind the scenes in **"Fly Away,"** page 373.

If you have ever wondered what insects eat or hungered to know the name of that bug you found crawling across your bathroom floor, you can find the answers in Patricia Volk's essay **"An Entomological Study of Apartment 4A,"** page 386.

3 Read to Be Entertained

We all have moments when we take a mental break and pretend to be somewhere or someone we are not. James Thurber attempts to answer the question "What would it be like to daydream all the time?" in his humorous story entitled **"The Secret Life of Walter Mitty,"** page 346.

Take It to the Net

Visit the Web site for online instruction and activities related to each selection in this unit.
www.phschool.com

ENRICHMENT: Further Reading

Have students choose one or more of the works below to extend the unit theme "The Lighter Side" or to read more by the unit authors.

Alice's Adventures in Wonderland by Lewis Carroll
This story begins with a young girl who follows the White Rabbit into Wonderland, a place where strange adventures take place.

Congratulations! Now What?: A Book for Graduates by Bill Cosby
Get some funny advice as you set your sights on college.

The Far Side Gallery Five by Gary Larson
Enjoy a collection of cartoons from this author's best-sellers.

A Midsummer Night's Dream by William Shakespeare
This comedy follows the adventures of a group of young people who spend a summer's night in the forest; it can be found in the **Prentice Hall Literature Library.**

How to Read Literature

Use Interactive Reading Strategies

To get the most out of many things in life, you have to get involved. This rule is as true in reading as it is in playing sports or visiting new places. Use these strategies to interact with what you are reading.

1. Read back or read ahead.

Even the best readers can find themselves confused when they encounter difficult passages. If you lose focus or encounter complex sentences with unfamiliar words, follow these steps:

- Pause to think about what you have just read and to look up new words. If necessary, go back to the last portion of the text you understood and reread from that point.
- Read ahead to clear up confusion—especially when reading texts in which the action is presented before explanations are given.

2. Read between the lines.

- Notice details that might provide indications of a deeper message or future plot development.
- Keep track of suspicions you might have about characters and their motives by using a chart like the one shown.

Read Between the Lines

Character	Driver in *The Inspector-General*
What I already know about the character	Driver knows many personal details about the new Inspector-General.
What the author might be suggesting	Driver might be able to recognize the Inspector-General if he were to meet him.

3. Recognize situational humor.

When you laugh because you relate to the set of circumstances an author is describing, you are recognizing situational humor. Keep in mind the following tips:

- Look for humor that involves familiar experiences.
- Notice techniques like contrast or exaggeration that play up the humor of a given situation.

4. Question characters' actions.

As you read, ask questions and offer explanations for why characters act the way they do. Base your answers on characters' past actions and your own experiences. For example, you might want to determine the main character's motive in this passage.

> Mr. Johnson . . . came forward and, touching his hat civilly, said, "Perhaps I can keep an eye on your little boy for you."
>
> —*from* "One Ordinary Day, With Peanuts"

Start by asking why a character might offer help. He might be acting out of kindness or expecting something in return. Use your answers to evaluate the character's behavior as you continue reading.

As you read, review these reading strategies and use the notes in the selection margin to interact with the text.

How to Read Literature

The "How to Read Literature" page in each unit presents a set of strategies to help readers understand authors' words and ideas. Each reading strategy is taught in conjunction with one or more of the selections within the unit. Good readers develop a bank of strategies from which they can draw as needed.

Unit 4 introduces interactive strategies that give readers an approach for comprehending text, including reading between the lines, recognizing situational humor, and questioning characters' actions.

How to Use This Page

Introduce the strategies for interactive reading, presenting each as a tool for developing understanding when reading the selections in this unit.

- Point out that in James Thurber's story "The Secret Life of Walter Mitty" (p. 346), students should read back or read ahead to keep track of Mitty's transition from daydream to real life.
- Explain that the strategy of reading between the lines will help students go beyond characters' words to see what they actually mean in *The Inspector-General* (p. 358), a play by Anton Chekhov.
- Encourage students to look for familiar experiences in their own lives as they read "Go Deep to the Sewer" (p. 368), by Bill Cosby.
- Point out that in Shirley Jackson's story "One Ordinary Day, With Peanuts" (p. 420), students should question Mr. Johnson's actions.

MODEL A READING STRATEGY: Read Back or Read Ahead

Sudden transitions in a story can disorient even good readers. Demonstrate how to read back or read ahead by modeling your thinking with this example from James Thurber's "The Secret Life of Walter Mitty:

> . . . "It's the millionaire banker, Wellington McMillan," said the pretty nurse. "Yes?" said Walter Mitty, removing his gloves slowly.

Tell students:

This is Mitty's second shift between dream and reality. By reading back to the first transition and reading forward to the next, I find that Thurber clearly signals the change by using ellipsis points (. . .). He also includes some real-life detail in each dream—gloves, for example.

The Secret Life of Walter Mitty

Lesson Objectives and CA Correlations

1. **To analyze and respond to literary elements**
   - Literary Analysis: Point of View **R 3.9**
   - Connecting Literary Elements: Round vs. Flat Characters
2. **To read, comprehend, analyze, and critique a short story**
   - Reading Strategy: Reading Back and Reading Ahead
   - Reading Check questions
   - Review and Assess questions
   - Assessment Practice (ATE)
3. **To develop word analysis skills, fluency, and systematic vocabulary**
   - Vocabulary Development Lesson: Latin Word Root: *-scrut-* **R 1.1**
4. **To understand and apply written and oral language conventions**
   - Spelling Strategy
   - Grammar Lesson: Complete Subjects and Predicates **LC 1.2**
5. **To understand and apply appropriate writing and research strategies**
   - Writing Lesson: Character Profile **W 2.1**
   - Extension Activity: Learning Log **W 1.5**
6. **To understand and apply listening and speaking strategies**
   - Extension Activity: Dramatic Skit **LS 1.9**

STEP-BY-STEP TEACHING GUIDE	PACING GUIDE
PRETEACH	
Motivate Students and Provide Background	
Use the Motivation activity (ATE p. 344)	5 min.
Read and discuss the Preview material and Background information (SE/ATE p. 344) [A]	10 min.
Introduce the Concepts	
Introduce the Literary Analysis and Reading Strategy (SE/ATE p. 345) [A]	15 min.
Pronounce the vocabulary words and read their definitions (SE p. 345)	5 min.
TEACH	
Monitor Comprehension	
Informally monitor comprehension by circulating while students read independently or in groups [A]	15 min.
Monitor students' comprehension with the Reading Check notes (SE/ATE pp. 347, 349)	as students read
Develop vocabulary with Vocabulary notes (SE pp. 347–350, 352)	as students read
Develop Understanding	
Develop students' understanding of point of view with Literary Analysis annotations (SE pp. 348, 350; ATE pp. 348, 349, 350) [A]	10 min.
Develop students' ability to read back and read ahead with the Reading Strategy annotations (SE p. 350; ATE pp. 348, 350)	10 min.
ASSESS	
Assess Mastery	
Assess students' mastery of the Reading Strategy and Literary Analysis by having them answer the Review and Assess questions (SE/ATE p. 353)	20 min.
Use one or more of the print and media Assessment Resources (ATE p. 355) [A]	up to 50 min.
EXTEND	
Apply Understanding	
Have students complete the Vocabulary Development Lesson and the Grammar Lesson (SE p. 354) [A]	20 min.
Apply students' knowledge of main impressions using the Writing Lesson (SE p. 355) [A]	45 min.
Apply students' understanding of the selection using one or more of the Extension Activities (SE p. 355)	20–90 min.

[A] ACCELERATED INSTRUCTION:
Use the strategies and activities identified with an [A].

UNIVERSAL ACCESS
● = Below Level Students
▲ = On-Level Students
■ = Above Level Students

Time and Resource Manager

Reading Level: Average
Average Number of Instructional Days: 4

RESOURCES		
PRINT	**TRANSPARENCIES**	**TECHNOLOGY**
• **Beyond Literature,** Humanities Connection: Fine Art, p. 22 ▲ ■		• **Interest Grabber Video,** Tape 2 ● ▲ ■
• **Selection Support Workbook:** ● ▲ ■ Literary Analysis, p. 88 Reading Strategy, p. 87 Build Vocabulary, p. 85	• **Literary Analysis and Reading Transparencies,** pp. 43 and 44 ● ▲ ■	
• **Adapted Reader's Companion** ● • **Reader's Companion** ●		• **Listening to Literature** ● ▲ ■ Audiocassettes, Side 10 Audio CDs, CD 8
• **English Learner's Companion** ● ▲ • **Literatura en español** ● ▲ • **Literary Analysis for Enrichment** ■		
• **Formal Assessment:** Selection Test, pp. 76–78 ● ▲ ■ • **Open Book Test,** pp. 64–66 ● ▲ ■ • **Performance Assessment and Portfolio Management,** p. 18 ● ▲ ■ • Prentice Hall ASSESSMENT SYSTEM ● ▲ ■	• Prentice Hall ASSESSMENT SYSTEM ● ▲ ■ Skills Practice Answers and Explanations on Transparencies	• **Test Bank Software** ● ▲ ■ • **Got It! Assessment Videotapes,** Tape 2 ● ▲
• **Selection Support Workbook:** ● ▲ ■ Build Grammar Skills, p. 86 • **Writing and Grammar,** Gold Level ● ▲ ■ • **Extension Activities,** p. 22 ● ▲ ■	• **Daily Language Practice Transparencies** ● ▲	• **Writing and Grammar iText CD-ROM** ● ▲ ■ ***Take It to the Net*** www.phschool.com

BLOCK SCHEDULING: Use one 90-minute class period to preteach the selection and have students read it. Use a second 90-minute class period to assess students' mastery of skills and have them complete one of the Extension Activities.

PREPEACH

PRETEACH

Step-by-Step Teaching Guide for pp. 344–345

Motivation

Write the word *dreams* on the chalkboard. Engage students in a discussion of the importance of dreams. Point out that what we dream about often tells us about our wishes and hopes, as well as our deepest fears. Tell students that they will read about a famous dreamer, Walter Mitty. Have them look for the differences between the dreams and the reality of the character as they read.

Interest Grabber Video

As an alternative, play "Turning Dreams into Reality" on Tape 2 to engage student interest.

1 Background

Scientists believe that all people dream; in fact, dreaming seems to be necessary to mental health. However, many people do not remember the dreams they have when they are sleeping, while others remember only the parts of dreams that occur just before waking. Dreams can be recorded with an *electroencephalograph* (an electronic device for graphing, or drawing, the activity of the brain). Most dreams occur during a stage of sleep called REM, which stands for rapid eye movement. A person in REM sleep moves his or her eyes quickly, as if watching a series of events. People immediately wakened from a REM sleep often remember their dreams in great detail.

Prepare to Read

The Secret Life of Walter Mitty

Portrait XIV, Donald C. Martin, Private Collection

Take It to the Net

Visit www.phschool.com for interactive activities and instruction related to "The Secret Life of Walter Mitty," including

- background
- graphic organizers
- literary elements
- reading strategies

Preview

Connecting to the Literature

There you are, a movie star, accepting an Academy Award. . . . Suddenly, a dog barks, bringing you back to the real world . . . in a bus on your way home. Perhaps you can recall daydreams that seemed sweeter than reality. "The Secret Life of Walter Mitty" is about a man whose frequent daydreams are more real to him than his workaday existence.

1 Background

Psychologists say that a person's thoughts often consist of seemingly unconnected insights, memories, and reflections, and that single incidents can prompt an unpredictable mental response. In James Thurber's story, random events cause Walter Mitty's thoughts to jump back and forth between his exciting "secret" life and his humdrum everyday life.

TEACHING RESOURCES

The following resources can be used to enrich or extend the instruction for pp. 344–345.

Interest Grabber Video, Tape 2

Background

Beyond Literature, p. 22

Take It to the Net

Visit www.phschool.com for background and hotlinks for "The Secret Life of Walter Mitty."

Literary Analysis

Literary Analysis and Reading Transparencies, Point of View, p. 44

Reading

Selection Support Workbook: Reading Strategy, p. 87; Build Vocabulary, p. 85

Literary Analysis and Reading Transparencies, Reading Back and Reading Ahead, p. 43

BLOCK SCHEDULING: Resources marked with this symbol provide varied instruction during 90-minute blocks.

❷ Literary Analysis

Point of View

In stories told in the **first-person point of view,** the narrator is one of the characters. In the **third-person point of view,** the narrator does not participate in the action. The third-person point of view can be either *omniscient*, in which the narrator sees into the minds of all the characters, or *limited*, in which the narrator sees the world through one character's eyes and reveals only that character's thoughts.

This story is written from the third-person point of view. As you read, notice that the narrator lets you see Mitty's thoughts and feelings in a way you would not experience in real life.

Connecting Literary Elements

Walter Mitty, a bumbling husband but a man of action in his dreams, is an example of a **round character**—a character who exhibits many traits, including faults as well as virtues. Mrs. Mitty, a wife who does nothing but scold Walter, is an example of a **flat character**—a character who seems to have only a single surface or aspect to her personality. As you read, notice the many traits of Walter Mitty.

❸ Reading Strategy

Reading Back and Reading Ahead

Walter Mitty's thoughts consistently shift from fantasy to reality. To understand the shifts in the story, read back and read ahead.

- **Read back** to see if you have overlooked any important facts.
- **Read ahead** to clarify an unclear situation.

Use a chart like this one to clarify insights you gain by reading back and reading ahead.

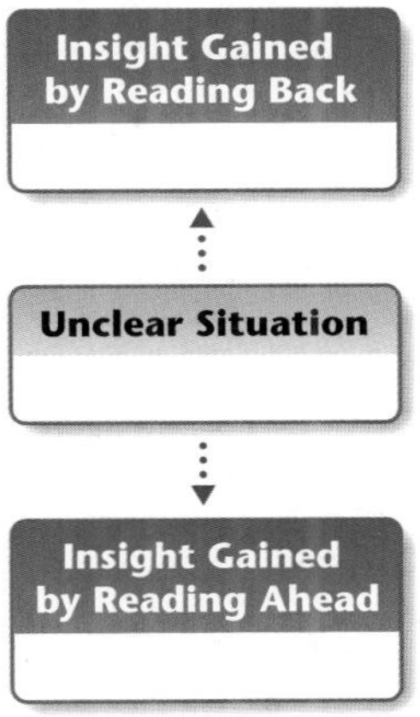

Vocabulary Development

rakishly (rāk′ ish lē) *adv.* with a trim, casual look; dashingly (p. 347)

hurtling (hurt′ liŋ) *adj.* moving swiftly and with great force (p. 347)

distraught (di strôt′) *adj.* extremely troubled; confused; distracted (p. 348)

haggard (hag′ ərd) *adj.* having a worn look, as from sleeplessness (p. 348)

insolent (in′ sə lənt) *adj.* boldly disrespectful (p. 349)

insinuatingly (in sin′ yo͞o āt′ iŋ lē) *adv.* suggesting indirectly (p. 349)

cur (kur) *n.* mean, contemptible person; mean, ugly dog (p. 349)

cannonading (kan′ ən ād′ iŋ) *n.* continuous firing of artillery (p. 350)

derisive (di rī′ siv) *adj.* showing contempt or ridicule (p. 352)

inscrutable (in skro͞ot′ ə bəl) *adj.* baffling; mysterious (p. 352)

❷ Literary Analysis

Point of View

- Remind students that they can recognize the first-person point of view in a selection by looking for the pronouns *I*, *me*, and *my* in the narration.
- Read the instruction about Point of View together as a class. Ask students which pronouns they would expect to find in a third-person narrative. (Students may suggest *he*, *she*, *him*, *her*, and so forth.)
- Be sure students understand the difference between third-person omniscient and third-person limited point of view. Ask them to be prepared to identify the character in the selection from whose point of view the story is told.
- Use the instruction for Connecting Literary Elements to alert students to watch for examples of round and flat characterization as they read.

❸ Reading Strategy

Reading Back and Reading Ahead

- Ask students what they can do if they reach a point in a narrative at which they are not sure what is going on. (Students may suggest that they can reread a passage to refresh their memories.)
- Tell students that they can read back and also read ahead. Since Walter Mitty jumps back and forth from his real life to his fantasy life, this reading technique may help students determine where Mitty "is" at any given point.
- Encourage students to use a chart like the one shown to help them make sense out of confusing situations as they read.

Vocabulary Development

- Pronounce each vocabulary word for students, and read the definitions as a class. Have students identify any words with which they are already familiar.

CUSTOMIZE INSTRUCTION FOR UNIVERSAL ACCESS

For Special Needs Students	For Less Proficient Readers	For English Learners
Have students read the adapted version of "The Secret Life of Walter Mitty" in the **Adapted Reader's Companion.** This version provides basic-level instruction in an interactive format with questions and write-on lines. Completing the adapted version will prepare students to read the selection in the Student Edition.	Have students read the selection in the **Reader's Companion.** This version provides basic-level instruction in an interactive format with questions and write-on lines. After students finish the selection in **Reader's Companion,** have them complete the questions and activities in the Student Edition.	Have students read the adapted version of the selection in the **English Learner's Companion.** This version provides basic-level instruction in an interactive format with questions and write-on lines. Completing the adapted version will prepare students to read the selection in the Student Edition.

E-Teach

Visit E-Teach at www.phschool.com for teachers' essays on how to teach, with questions and answers.

TEACH

Step-by-Step Teaching Guide for pp. 346–352

CUSTOMIZE INSTRUCTION For Bodily/Kinesthetic Learners

Walter Mitty's daydreams are full of action. Students may wish to act out some of the verbs they come across as they read. Examples from the first page, listed here in present participle form, include *pounding, twisting, switching, bending, hurtling, grinning, driving,* and *tensing*. Invite volunteers to demonstrate one or more of these actions.

1 About the Selection

In this famous story, James Thurber creates for readers a vivid image of an ineffectual person who suffers from a complete inability to cope with the world around him. Feeling powerless and picked-on by everyone—from his wife to parking-lot attendants, from police officers to anonymous passersby—Mitty retreats into a daydream world where he becomes dashing, powerful, and in control.

2 Background

Art

The Man With Three Masks, by John Rush

John Rush (b. 1948) considers the greatest single influence on his art to be Michelangelo, the highly gifted Italian Renaissance sculptor, painter, and poet. In this painting, a conservatively dressed man holds a mask up to his face. The masks in the background suggest that he will try them on as well. Use these questions for discussion:

1. What symbolic meanings might the man and the masks have in this painting?
   Answer: Students may say that the man represents the person's real self and the masks represent ways in which he would like others to see him.
2. If the man is Walter Mitty, what might the masks represent?
   Answer: The masks might represent the characters Mitty imagines himself to be.

2

The Man With Three Masks, John Rush, Courtesy of the artist

3 ▲ **Critical Viewing** Analyze the significance of the mask in this painting. Why might the man hold one mask up to his face and have other masks nearby? **[Analyze]**

TEACHING RESOURCES

The following resources can be used to enrich or extend the instruction for pp. 346–352.

Literary Analysis

- **Selection Support Workbook:** Literary Analysis, p. 88

Reading

- **Reader's Companion**
- **English Learner's Companion**
- **Listening to Literature Audiocassettes,** Side 10 ■
- **Listening to Literature Audio CDs,** CD 8 ■

■ **BLOCK SCHEDULING:** Resources marked with this symbol provide varied instruction during 90-minute blocks.

❶ The Secret Life of Walter Mitty

James Thurber

❹ We're going through!" The Commander's voice was like thin ice breaking. He wore his full-dress uniform, with the heavily braided white cap pulled down rakishly over one cold gray eye. "We can't make it, sir. It's spoiling for a hurricane, if you ask me." "I'm not asking you, Lieutenant Berg," said the Commander. "Throw on the power lights! Rev her up to 8,500! We're going through!" The pounding of the cylinders increased: ta-pocketa-pocketa-pocketa-*pocketa-pocketa*. The Commander stared at the ice forming on the pilot window. He walked over and twisted a row of complicated dials. "Switch on No. 8 auxiliary!" he shouted. "Switch on No. 8 auxiliary!" repeated Lieutenant Berg. "Full strength in No. 3 turret!" shouted the Commander. "Full strength in No. 3 turret!" The crew, bending to their various tasks in the huge, hurtling eight-engined Navy hydroplane,[1] looked at each other and grinned. "The Old Man'll get us through," they said to one another. "The Old Man ain't afraid of Hell!". . .

"Not so fast! You're driving too fast!" said Mrs. Mitty. "What are you driving so fast for?"

"Hmm?" said Walter Mitty. He looked at his wife, in the seat beside him, with shocked astonishment. She seemed grossly unfamiliar, like a strange woman who had yelled at him in a crowd. "You were up to fifty-five," she said. "You know I don't like to go more than forty. You were up to fifty-five." Walter Mitty drove on toward Waterbury in silence, the roaring of the SN202 through the worst storm in twenty years of Navy flying fading in the remote, intimate airways of his mind. "You're tensed up again," said Mrs. Mitty. "It's one of your days. I wish you'd let Dr. Renshaw look you over."

Walter Mitty stopped the car in front of the building where his wife went to have her hair done. "Remember to get those overshoes while

rakishly (rāk′ ish lē) *adv.* with a trim, casual look; dashing

hurtling (hurt′ liŋ) *adj.* moving swiftly and with great force

❺ **Reading Check**
Why is Mrs. Mitty upset?

1. **hydroplane** (hī′ drō plān′) *n.* seaplane.

❸ ▶Critical Viewing

Answer: The masks may represent different "faces" the man presents to other people. Each mask gives the man a different self.

❹ Critical Thinking

Infer

- Read aloud the bracketed passage to students. Have them focus on the details that Thurber uses to characterize the Commander.
- Ask students what kind of character the Commander is.
  Answer: He is loud, confident, and trusted by his men.
- Ask students if they think the Commander is a real character in this story? If not, who is he?
  Answer: Students may realize that they have met the first of Walter Mitty's fantasy selves.

❺ Reading Check

Answer: Mrs. Mitty is upset because she thinks Mitty is driving too fast.

❻ Reading Strategy

Reading Back and Reading Ahead

- First, ask students what kind of character Walter Mitty has become at the beginning of this passage.
  Answer: He is a famous surgeon.
- Next, invite students to read back, starting with the paragraph that begins on p. 347.
- Read aloud the bracketed passage and have students note the details of "Doctor" Mitty in the passage.
- Ask students which real life event seems to set off Walter Mitty's daydream.
  Answer: After Mitty's wife demands that he put on his gloves, he does so, but then takes them off. When the cop insults him, he puts them on again. In the daydream, the gloves become an acceptable part of his costume as a well-respected doctor.

❼ Literary Analysis

Point of View and Round Characters

- Ask students what Mitty is doing at the beginning of this passage, and if the scene takes place in his fantasy life or reality.
  Answer: As a famous surgeon, Mitty is getting ready to operate. He is having one of his daydreams.
- Have students speculate on where Mitty is in the second part of the passage, and again, whether the scene is fantasy or reality.
  Answer: Mitty is back in reality, in a parking garage.
- Ask students the Literary Analysis question on p. 348: How does this shift in scenes show that Walter Mitty is a round character?
  Answer: Mitty is able to shift back and forth between his real personality and his various daydream characters. This shows that he is a round character because he has more than one aspect to his personality.

I'm having my hair done," she said. "I don't need overshoes," said Mitty. She put her mirror back into her bag. "We've been all through that," she said, getting out of the car. "You're not a young man any longer." He raced the engine a little. "Why don't you wear your gloves? Have you lost your gloves?" Walter Mitty reached in a pocket and brought out the gloves. He put them on, but after she had turned and gone into the building and he had driven on to a red light, he took them off again. "Pick it up, brother!" snapped a cop as the light changed, and Mitty hastily pulled on his gloves and lurched ahead. He drove around the streets aimlessly for a time, and then he drove past the hospital on his way to the parking lot.

❻ . . . "It's the millionaire banker, Wellington McMillan," said the pretty nurse. "Yes?" said Walter Mitty, removing his gloves slowly. "Who has the case?" "Dr. Renshaw and Dr. Benbow, but there are two specialists here, Dr. Remington from New York and Mr. Pritchard-Mitford from London. He flew over." A door opened down a long, cool corridor and Dr. Renshaw came out. He looked distraught and haggard. "Hello, Mitty," he said. "We're having the devil's own time with McMillan, the millionaire banker and close personal friend of Roosevelt. Obstreosis of the ductal tract.[2] Tertiary. Wish you'd take a look at him." "Glad to," said Mitty.

distraught (di strôt′) *adj.* extremely troubled; confused; distracted

haggard (hag′ ərd) *adj.* having a worn look, as from sleeplessness

In the operating room there were whispered introductions: "Dr. Remington, Dr. Mitty. Mr. Pritchard-Mitford, Dr. Mitty." "I've read your book on streptothricosis," said Pritchard-Mitford, shaking hands. "A brilliant performance, sir." "Thank you," said Walter Mitty. "Didn't know you were in the States, Mitty," grumbled Remington. "Coals to Newcastle,[3] bringing Mitford and me up here for tertiary." "You are very kind," said Mitty. A huge, complicated machine, connected to the operating table, with many tubes and wires, began at this moment to go pocketa-pocketa-pocketa. "The new anesthetizer is giving way!" shouted an intern. "There is no one in the East who knows how to fix it!" "Quiet, man!" said Mitty, in a low, cool voice. He sprang to the machine, which was now going pocketa-pocketa-queep-pocketa-queep. He began fingering delicately a row of glistening dials. "Give me a fountain pen!" he snapped. Someone handed him a fountain pen. He pulled a faulty piston out of the machine and inserted the pen in its place. "That will hold for ten minutes," he said. "Get on with the operation." A nurse hurried over and whispered to Renshaw, and Mitty saw the man turn pale.

❼ "Coreopsis has set in," said Renshaw nervously. "If you would take over, Mitty?" Mitty looked at him and at the craven figure of Benbow, who drank, and at the grave, uncertain faces of the two great specialists. "If you wish," he said. They slipped a white gown on him; he adjusted a mask and drew on thin gloves; nurses handed him shining . . .

"Back it up, Mac! Look out for that Buick!" Walter Mitty jammed on

Literary Analysis
Point of View and Round Characters How does this shift in scenes show that Walter Mitty is a round character?

2. **obstreosis of the ductal tract** Thurber has invented this and other medical terms.
3. **coals to Newcastle** The proverb "bringing coals to Newcastle" means bringing things to a place unnecessarily—Newcastle, England, was a coal center and so did not need coal brought to it.

7 the brakes. "Wrong lane, Mac," said the parking-lot attendant, looking at Mitty closely. "Gee. Yeh," muttered Mitty. He began cautiously to back out of the lane marked "Exit Only." "Leave her sit there," said the attendant. "I'll put her away." Mitty got out of the car. "Hey, better leave the key." "Oh," said Mitty, handing the man the ignition key. The attendant vaulted into the car, backed it up with insolent skill, and put it where it belonged.

8 They're so cocky, thought Walter Mitty, walking along Main Street; they think they know everything. Once he had tried to take his chains off, outside New Milford, and he had got them wound around the axles. A man had had to come out in a wrecking car and unwind them, a young, grinning garageman. Since then Mrs. Mitty always made him drive to a garage to have the chains taken off. The next time, he thought, I'll wear my right arm in a sling; they won't grin at me then. I'll have my right arm in a sling and they'll see I couldn't possibly take the chains off myself. He kicked at the slush on the sidewalk. "Overshoes," he said to himself, and he began looking for a shoe store.

When he came out into the street again, with the overshoes in a box under his arm, Walter Mitty began to wonder what the other thing was his wife had told him to get. She had told him, twice, before they set out from their house for Waterbury. In a way he hated these weekly trips to town—he was always getting something wrong. Kleenex, he thought, Squibb's, razor blades? No. Toothpaste, toothbrush, bicarbonate, carborundum, initiative and referendum?[4] He gave it up. But she would remember it. "Where's the what's-its-name?" she would ask. "Don't tell me you forgot the what's-its-name." A newsboy went by shouting something about the Waterbury trial.

. . . "Perhaps this will refresh your memory." The District Attorney suddenly thrust a heavy automatic at the quiet figure on the witness stand. "Have you ever seen this before?" Walter Mitty took the gun and examined it expertly. "This is my Webley-Vickers 50.80," he said calmly. An excited buzz ran around the courtroom. The Judge rapped for order. "You are a crack shot with any sort of firearms, I believe?" said the District Attorney, insinuatingly. "Objection!" shouted Mitty's attorney. "We have shown that the defendant could not have fired the shot. We have shown that he wore his right arm in a sling on the night of the fourteenth of July." Walter Mitty raised his hand briefly and the bickering attorneys were stilled. "With any known make of gun," he said evenly, "I could have killed Gregory Fitzhurst at three hundred *feet with my left hand.*" Pandemonium broke loose in the courtroom. A woman's scream rose above the bedlam and suddenly a lovely, dark-haired girl was in Walter Mitty's arms. The District Attorney struck at her savagely. Without rising from his chair, Mitty let the man have it on the point of the chin. "You miserable cur!" . . .

4. **carborundum** (kär´ bə run´ dəm), **initiative** (i nish´ ē ə tiv) **and referendum** (ref´ ə ren´ dəm) Thurber is purposely making a nonsense list; *carborundum* is a hard substance used for scraping, *initiative* is the right of citizens to introduce ideas for laws, and *referendum* is the right of citizens to vote on laws.

insolent (in´ sə lənt) *adj.* boldly disrespectful

insinuatingly (in sin´ yo͞o āt´ iŋ lē) *adv.* suggesting indirectly

cur (kʉr) *n.* mean, contemptible person; mean, ugly dog

9 **Reading Check**

Why does Mitty say that next time he will wear his arm in a sling?

8 Literary Analysis

Point of View

- Ask students how the parking-lot attendant and the garageman are characterized by Mitty in this passage.
  Answer: The parking-lot man acts insolent and the garageman is young and grinning at Mitty. Mitty resents the fact that his wife says he's not a young man any more.

Reteach Have students refresh their memories and define the third-person limited point of view, distinguishing it from the third-person omniscient point of view.
Answer: The third-person limited point of view sees the action from the point of view of only one character in the story. The omniscient point of view sees the action from outside the story but can see into most or all of the characters' minds.

- Ask students if they can fully trust the descriptions of the parking-lot attendant and the garageman in this passage. Why or why not?
  Answer: Since the characters are seen only through the eyes of Walter Mitty, they may appear worse than they really are because of Mitty's low opinion of himself.

9 Reading Check

Answer: Mitty thinks that if he has his arm in a sling, the garageman will not expect him to be able to take off the car chains without help.

CUSTOMIZE INSTRUCTION FOR UNIVERSAL ACCESS

For Less Proficient Readers	For Special Needs Students	For Advanced Readers
Invite students to begin a list of characters that Mitty plays in his fantasies. What kind of person is the character? What can the character do that Mitty cannot? At the end of the selection have the group vote on the most interesting character—the one they think Mitty would have chosen to be if he could have made his fantasy into reality.	Check to see that students are learning to recognize the clues that distinguish a dream sequence from a scene that takes place in real life. On p. 348, emphasize the disrespectful way Mitty is treated by his wife and the police officer versus the respectful way he is treated in the hospital.	Invite students to create a chart of the various characters Mitty assumes in his daydreams, with descriptions of each. Then, have them identify the common aspect of Mitty's dreams.

⑩ Literary Analysis

Point of View

- Remind students that this selection is narrated from a third-person limited point of view.
- Ask students what picture they have of Mrs. Mitty after reading this passage.
  Answer: She tells Mr. Mitty what to do. She wants him to be at the hotel when she gets there; she doesn't want to wait for him.
- Have students describe what Mr. Mitty does, based on their understanding of his wife.
  Answer: He checks his watch to see when she will arrive and then sits in the lobby to wait for her.
- Ask students the Literary Analysis question on p. 350: Through whose eyes do you obtain this view of Mrs. Mitty?
  Answer: The characterization of Mrs. Mitty comes from Walter Mitty, the viewpoint character.

⑪ Reading Strategy

Reading Back and Reading Ahead

- Remind students that the daydream about Mitty being a bomber pilot takes place while Mitty is waiting for his wife in the hotel lobby.
- As students read the first sentence in the last paragraph that begins on p. 350, ask them if they at first imagine that Mitty has been hit with machine gun fire, or some other artillery. Why might they do so?
  Possible response: In his daydream, Mitty has been living through a battle and preparing to bomb an ammunition dump. Being hit by some kind of fire would be a logical next step.

Monitor Progress Ask students the Reading Strategy question on p. 350: To clarify Mitty's location, would you read ahead or read back at this point? Explain.
Answer: Students should say that they would read ahead to see if Mitty were still in his daydream being hit by machine gun fire or if he were back in reality being hit in the shoulder by something else.

"Puppy biscuit," said Walter Mitty. He stopped walking and the buildings of Waterbury rose up out of the misty courtroom and surrounded him again. A woman who was passing laughed. "He said 'Puppy biscuit,'" she said to her companion. "That man said 'Puppy biscuit' to himself." Walter Mitty hurried on. He went into an A. & P., not the first one he came to but a smaller one farther up the street. "I want some biscuit for small, young dogs," he said to the clerk. "Any special brand, sir?" The greatest pistol shot in the world thought a moment. "It says 'Puppies Bark for It' on the box," said Walter Mitty.

⑩ His wife would be through at the hairdresser's in fifteen minutes, Mitty saw in looking at his watch, unless they had trouble drying it; sometimes they had trouble drying it. She didn't like to get to the hotel first; she would want him to be there waiting for her as usual. He found a big leather chair in the lobby, facing a window, and he put the overshoes and the puppy biscuit on the floor beside it. He picked up an old copy of *Liberty* and sank down into the chair. "Can Germany Conquer the World Through the Air?" Walter Mitty looked at the pictures of bombing planes and of ruined streets.

. . . "The cannonading has got the wind up in young Raleigh,[5] sir," said the sergeant. Captain Mitty looked up at him through tousled hair. "Get him to bed," he said wearily. "With the others. I'll fly alone." "But you can't, sir," said the sergeant anxiously. "It takes two men to handle that bomber and the Archies[6] are pounding hell out of the air. Von Richtman's circus[7] is between here and Saulier." "Somebody's got to get that ammunition dump," said Mitty. "I'm going over. Spot of brandy?" He poured a drink for the sergeant and one for himself. War thundered and whined around the dugout and battered at the door. There was a rending of wood and splinters flew through the room. "A bit of a near thing," said Captain Mitty carelessly. "The box barrage is closing in," said the sergeant. "We only live once, Sergeant," said Mitty, with his faint, fleeting smile. "Or do we?" He poured another brandy and tossed it off. "I never see a man could hold his brandy like you, sir," said the sergeant. "Begging your pardon, sir." Captain Mitty stood up and strapped on his huge Webley-Vickers automatic. "It's forty kilometers through hell, sir," said the sergeant. Mitty finished one last brandy. "After all," he said softly, "what isn't?" The pounding of the cannon increased; there was the rat-tat-tatting of ⑪ machine guns, and from somewhere came the menacing pocketa-pocketa-pocketa of the new flame-throwers. Walter Mitty walked to the door of the dugout humming "Auprès de Ma Blonde."[8] He turned and waved to the sergeant. "Cheerio!" he said. . . .

Something struck his shoulder. "I've been looking all over this hotel

Literary Analysis
Point of View Through whose eyes do you obtain this view of Mrs. Mitty?

cannonading (kan′ ən ād′ iŋ) *n.* continuous firing of artillery

Reading Strategy
Reading Back and Reading Ahead To clarify Mitty's location, would you read ahead or read back at this point? Explain.

5. **has got the wind up in young Raleigh** has made young Raleigh nervous.
6. **Archies** slang term for antiaircraft guns.
7. **Von Richtman's circus** German airplane squadron.
8. **"Auprès de Ma Blonde"** (ō prā′ də mä blôn′ də) "Next to My Blonde," a popular French song.

ENRICHMENT: Cultural Connection

The Secret Life of Walter Mitty

Thurber's comic tale was adapted for the big screen in 1947. The film version, directed by Norman Z. McLeod, starred Danny Kaye as the daydreaming Mitty. Producer Sam Goldwyn originally had purchased the rights to Thurber's story, but Thurber, who did not want his classic short story filmed, offered Goldwyn $10,000 not to produce it. Goldwyn went ahead and sank more than $3 million into this visually-appealing showcase for Kaye.

The film version takes many liberties with Thurber's story. Kaye's Mitty is not married but is bossed by his mother and his fiancée. He actually meets the woman of his daydreams (played by Virginia Mayo) and finds himself plunged into a real adventure involving vicious Nazi spies.

12

13 ▲ **Critical Viewing** Describe a situation that might make Walter Mitty daydream about being a circus performer like the one shown. **[Hypothesize]**

12 Background

Art

New Orleans Fantasy (detail) by Max Papart

In this lithograph, a colorfully dressed acrobat swings from a trapeze. While Walter Mitty never imagines himself an acrobat in the story, the freedom and daring represented by the trapeze artist characterize Mitty's fantasies.

Max Papart (1911–1985) was a French lithographer whose fanciful style is represented in this painting. He studied art in Marseilles, but traced his greatest influence to the works of surrealist painters he encountered at an exhibit in Paris in 1938. Use the following questions for discussion:

1. What associations do you have with the words *trapeze artist,* or the picture of one in this painting?
   Answer: Students may associate words such as *daring, balance, graceful,* or *breathtaking.*
2. What introduction can you suggest for a Walter-Mitty-like fantasy about being a trapeze artist?
   Answer: Students may suggest a passage that describes the entrance of the famous artist Waltero Mitzini, or some variant.

13 ▶Critical Viewing

Answer: Walter Mitty's daydreams reflect a way to overcome any recent experience that embarrasses or humiliates him. A daydream about being a graceful trapeze artist might result after Mitty has done something clumsy, or has been made to feel clumsy by others.

CUSTOMIZE INSTRUCTION FOR UNIVERSAL ACCESS

For English Learners	For Gifted/Talented Students
Students may benefit by recognizing that some of the sound-effects terms used in Mitty's daydreams are nonsense words. Help students find the examples on this page and list the sounds and what each is supposed to represent: *(rat-tat-tatting*—machine guns; *pocketa-pocketa-pocketa*—flame throwers) and then find others throughout the story.	Ask the group how they can tell that this story is set in a much earlier time. When they have given examples such as *Liberty* Magazine, news about Germany and the war, and so on, have interested students look up some of the references on this spread and in the rest of the story, and report on their findings to the rest of the class.

ASSESS

Answers for p. 352

Review and Assess

1. Some students may say they feel sorry for Mitty because he does not get the respect he wants from people in his life. Others may say they do not feel sorry for him because he can live such an exciting life in his imagination.
2. **(a)** They are going about their ordinary weekly trip to get Mrs. Mitty's hair done: Mitty drops Mrs. Mitty at the hairdresser, buys a pair of overshoes, picks up some dog food, and waits for her at the hotel. **(b)** No, she thinks his absentmindedness is due to his aging, or perhaps illness. She does not realize he is simply bored and disappointed in his life.
3. **(a)** His wife tells him he is driving too fast. **(b)** He behaves like a bold leader in the daydream; in his real life he does what other people tell him to do.
4. **(a)** He passes a newsboy who is shouting the news about an ongoing trial. **(b)** Mitty is treated as a respected hero in his daydreams and as an incompetent fool in real life.
5. **(a)** Mrs. Mitty's patronizing treatment of her husband is so demoralizing that the firing squad daydream may represent a final escape. Or, she harasses him to the point that he finally says something in his own defense, much as a prisoner being berated by a guard might do. **(b)** By telling her what he is thinking, Mitty has stood up to his wife, and he may be anticipating what will happen to him when they get home.
6. If Mitty had more self-esteem in his real life, he could stand up to people who bully him and take charge of his own destiny.
7. Students may suggest that daydreaming can allow the imagination to work in positive ways, such as in solving a problem, but that too much daydreaming leads people to avoid real life commitments.

for you," said Mrs. Mitty. "Why do you have to hide in this old chair? How did you expect me to find you?" "Things close in," said Walter Mitty vaguely. "What?" Mrs. Mitty said. "Did you get the what's-its-name? The puppy biscuit? What's in that box?" "Overshoes," said Mitty. "Couldn't you have put them on in the store?" "I was thinking," said Walter Mitty. "Does it ever occur to you that I am sometimes thinking?" She looked at him. "I'm going to take your temperature when I get you home," she said.

They went out through the revolving doors that made a faintly derisive whistling sound when you pushed them. It was two blocks to the parking lot. At the drugstore on the corner she said, "Wait here for me. I forgot something. I won't be a minute." She was more than a minute. Walter Mitty lighted a cigarette. It began to rain, rain with sleet in it. He stood up against the wall of the drugstore, smoking. . . . He put his shoulders back and his heels together. "To hell with the handkerchief," said Walter Mitty scornfully. He took one last drag on his cigarette and snapped it away. Then, with that faint, fleeting smile playing about his lips, he faced the firing squad; erect and motionless, proud and disdainful, Walter Mitty the Undefeated, inscrutable to the last.

derisive (di rī′ siv) *adj.* showing contempt or ridicule

inscrutable (in skrōōt′ ə bəl) *adj.* baffling; mysterious

Review and Assess

Thinking About the Selection

1. **Respond:** Do you feel sorry for Walter Mitty? Why or why not?
2. **(a) Recall:** In the "real" world, what are Mitty and his wife actually doing? **(b) Deduce:** Does Mrs. Mitty understand the reasons for Walter's absentmindedness? Explain.
3. **(a) Recall:** What jars Mitty out of his first daydream? **(b) Compare and Contrast:** How does he behave in this daydream? In his real life?
4. **(a) Recall:** What event triggers Mitty's courtroom daydream? **(b) Draw Conclusions:** Explain the significant difference between the way people treat Mitty in his real life and the way they treat him in his daydreams.
5. **(a) Infer:** Which aspects of Mrs. Mitty's personality trigger Mitty's last daydream? **(b) Draw Conclusions:** In what way is this daydream a comment on his fate in real life?
6. **Hypothesize:** How might Mitty's life be altered if he could transfer the self-esteem he experiences in his daydreams into his conscious life?
7. **Take a Position:** Can daydreaming ever benefit a person? Explain.

James Thurber

(1894–1961)

Born in Columbus, Ohio, James Thurber began his writing career at the *Columbus Evening Dispatch*, where he was a reporter. He later achieved fame as a humorous writer and cartoonist during his many years at *The New Yorker* magazine.

Thurber's plays, stories, essays, fables, reminiscences, and verse fill more than twenty volumes. He lost his sight in the 1940s but continued to write until his death. In 1960, he won the Antoinette Perry award for his revue *A Thurber Carnival*.

ASSESSMENT PRACTICE: Reading Comprehension

Predict Outcomes **(For more practice, see Test Preparation Workbook, p. 22.)**

Many tests require students to predict outcomes. Use the following sample test item to lead students to make a prediction.

When he came out into the street again, with the overshoes in a box under his arm, Walter Mitty began to wonder what the other thing was his wife had told him to get. She had told him twice . . . In a way, he hated these weekly trips.

You can tell from this excerpt that Walter Mitty's wife is most likely to—

A thank him for getting the shoes.
B remind him of what he forgot.
C be annoyed that he forgot.
D suggest that they go to lunch in town.

Point out that Mitty forgot something his wife told him twice. This detail should lead students to choose *C*, predicting that Mrs. Mitty will be annoyed.

Review and Assess

Literary Analysis

Point of View

1. Is there a moment when you realize that you are seeing Walter Mitty's world through his eyes? Explain.
2. How are your feelings about Mitty influenced by seeing things from his **point of view**?
3. If the **limited third-person narration** had focused on Mrs. Mitty instead of Walter, how would the story have been different? Use a Venn diagram to gather details for a response.

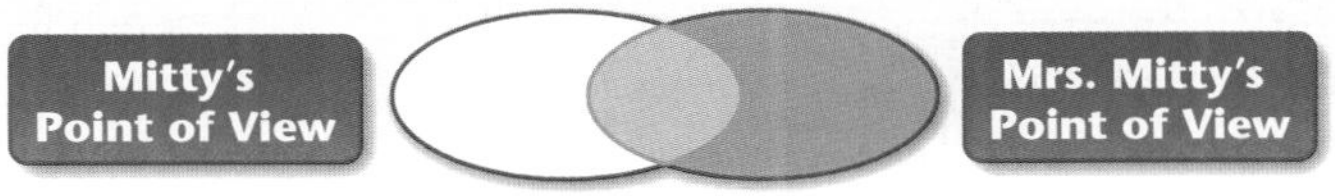

Connecting Literary Elements

4. (a) What evidence suggests that Walter Mitty is a **round character**? (b) What evidence shows Mrs. Mitty is a **flat character**?
5. Using a chart like the one shown here, analyze the characters in Walter's daydreams.

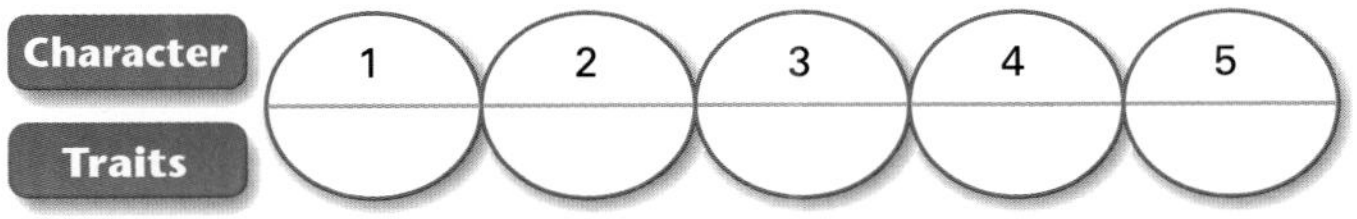

6. (a) Do the characters in Mitty's daydreams seem as flat as those in his real life? (b) How does this characterization influence the story?

Reading Strategy

Reading Back and Reading Ahead

7. Cite two places where **reading back or ahead** helped you fully understand the meaning of a scene in the story.

Extend Understanding

8. **Career Connection:** (a) In reality, could Mitty perform the work he thinks about in his daydreams? Why or why not? (b) Suggest a fulfilling career for Walter. Explain your choice.

Quick Review

Point of view is the perspective from which a story is told.

A **limited third-person narrator** reveals the thoughts of only one character, through whose eyes you see the other characters.

A **round character** exhibits many traits, including both virtues and faults.

A **flat character** exhibits only a single quality or trait.

You **read back** to see if you have overlooked any important facts.

You **read ahead** to look for an explanation of a passage you do not understand.

Take It to the Net

www.phschool.com

Take the interactive self-test online to check your understanding of the selection.

ENRICHMENT: Further Reading

Other Works by James Thurber

My Life and Hard Times
Fables for Our Time
More Fables for Our Time
My World and Welcome To It

Take It to the Net

Visit www.phschool.com for more information on James Thurber.

Answers for p. 353

Review and Assess

1. When the first daydream starring Mitty changes into the first scene in his real life, the reader realizes that Mitty is the viewpoint character.
2. The reader develops sympathy for Mitty.
3. Mitty's Point of View: Mrs. Mitty is overbearing, patronizing, demoralizing. Mrs. Mitty's Point of View: Mr. Mitty is quiet, dull, passive, and drab. Similarities: Mr. Mitty does what other tell him to do; Mrs. Mitty is always angry and frustrated. In a story told from Mrs. Mitty's point of view we might see a woman who has dreams of an interesting life, but whose husband is boring.
4. **(a)** Mitty has a personality in public that is subject to other people's demands. In his dreams he is a respected, powerful person. **(b)** Mrs. Mitty acts only in one way—to make demands on her husband and to tell him how worthless he is.
5. Character: Naval officer; Doctor; Defendant in murder trial; Bomber pilot; Prisoner about to be executed; Traits: forceful, commanding, called the "Old Man"; awes other surgeons, quick to solve medical emergencies; expert with guns, protector of beautiful women in distress; undertakes mission alone, cheerful in face of danger; scornful of being blindfolded, proud, inscrutable.
6. **(a)** Mitty's daydream characters exhibit several admirable traits. Mitty's real-life persona is flat—he is quiet and harassed by those around him. **(b)** This characterization makes the story humorous and builds sympathy for Mitty.
7. Students may cite any of the breaks between a Mitty daydream and a Mitty real-life episode.
8. **(a)** Students may doubt whether Mitty has the temperament for such challenging roles. **(b)** Mitty might make a good counselor in any kind of situation in which he helped people realize a dream or a goal.

EXTEND

Answers for p. 354

1 Vocabulary Development

1. a close search or examination
2. to examine very carefully
3. the quality of not being understandable; mysteriousness

Spelling Strategy

1. raking
2. curative
3. courageous
4. sanity

Concept Development: Synonyms

1. j
2. e
3. i
4. g
5. f
6. c
7. d
8. b
9. h
10. a

2 Grammar

1. The commander spoke seriously.
2. He looked at his wife.
3. A huge machine, connected to the operating table, was very noisy.
4. He could not remember what she asked him to buy.
5. The District Attorney spoke to the man on the witness stand.
6. War rumbled and whined at the door.

Writing Application

. . ."Cheerio," he said... The captain crawled through intense bombardment across the field. The huge machine-gun battery, sounding like ten thunderstorms, threatened to deafen him.

Integrate Language Skills

1 Vocabulary Development Lesson

Word Analysis: Latin Root *-scrut-*

The Latin root *-scrut-* means "to search carefully or examine." The word *inscrutable* literally means "not able to be searched or examined" or "not easily understood." Define each of the following words.

1. scrutiny 2. scrutinize 3. inscrutability

Spelling Strategy

When a word ends in silent *e*, you often drop the *e* before adding an ending that begins with a vowel. For example, *cannonade* + *-ing* = *cannonading*. However, there are many exceptions to this rule. For example, *manage* + *-able* = *manageable*. Write the new word that is formed when you combine these words and suffixes.

1. rake + *-ing*
2. cure + *-ative*
3. courage + *-ous*
4. sane + *-ity*

Concept Development: Synonyms

On your paper, write the letter of the word in the second column that is closest in meaning to each word in the first column. To help you, review the vocabulary list on page 345.

1. rakishly	a. baffling
2. hurtling	b. bombarding
3. distraught	c. implying
4. haggard	d. scoundrel
5. insolent	e. speeding
6. insinuatingly	f. insulting
7. cur	g. exhausted
8. cannonading	h. disrespectful
9. derisive	i. troubled
10. inscrutable	j. stylishly

2 Grammar Lesson

Complete Subjects and Predicates

The **complete subject** of a sentence consists of the simple subject and all the words associated with it. The **complete predicate** consists of the simple predicate, or verb, and all the words associated with it.

COMPLETE SUBJ — A woman's scream; COMPLETE PRED — rose above the bedlam.

A woman's scream rose above the bedlam.

Practice Copy each sentence. Underline the complete subject once and the complete predicate twice.

1. The Commander spoke seriously.
2. He looked at his wife in astonishment.
3. A huge machine, connected to the operating table, was very noisy.
4. He could not remember what she asked him to buy.
5. The District Attorney spoke to the man on the witness stand.
6. War rumbled and whined at the door.

Writing Application Write two or three sentences to add more details to one of Walter Mitty's adventures in the story. Underline each complete subject once and each complete predicate twice.

WG *Prentice Hall Writing and Grammar Connection: Chapter 20, Section 1*

TEACHING RESOURCES

The following resources can be used to enrich or extend the instruction for pp. 354–355.

Vocabulary

Selection Support Workbook: Build Vocabulary, p. 85

Vocabulary and Spelling Practice Book (Use this booklet for skills enrichment.)

Grammar

Selection Support Workbook: Build Grammar Skills, p 86

Writing and Grammar, Gold Level, p. 422

Daily Language Practice Transparencies

Writing

Writing and Grammar, Gold Level, p. 286

Writing and Grammar iText CD-ROM

BLOCK SCHEDULING: Resources marked with this symbol provide varied instruction during 90-minute blocks.

❸ Writing Lesson

Character Profile

Walter Mitty sees himself as one fearless character after another. Use one of Mitty's daydreams to inspire a character profile that vividly describes a personality he becomes in his dreams.

Prewriting Use a cluster map like the one shown to jot down details that capture the character's appearance, personality, achievements, and feelings.

Model: Creating a Character Profile

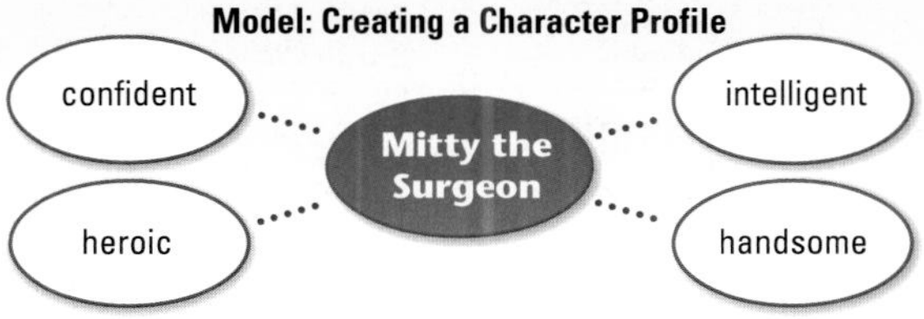

Drafting Decide on the impression you want to convey, and present details so that they all point toward it. Build toward the most important point.

Revising Review your work to be sure you have used details from each prewriting category. Ask a classmate to identify the main impression of your character description. If the response is not what you expected, revise to clarify your focus. Provide more details that support the main impression, and eliminate those that do not.

WG *Prentice Hall Writing and Grammar Connection: Chapter 13, Section 2*

❹ Extension Activities

Listening and Speaking Take these steps to adapt one of Walter Mitty's daydreams as a **dramatic skit:**

- In a group, choose the daydream you find most appealing.
- Decide who will play the various roles.

Consider incorporating the phrase *ta-pocketa-pocketa* to ensure that the scene truly captures Mitty. Perform your skit for the class. **[Group Activity]**

Research and Technology Use library resources, including the Internet, to research scientific facts and theories about daydreaming. Record the information in a **learning log,** a written record of what you discover about the topic. Compare your findings to the story. Decide whether Walter Mitty is really as different from others as he seems.

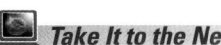

Take It to the Net www.phschool.com

Go online for an additional research activity using the Internet.

Lesson Support for page 355

❸ Writing Lesson

- Tell students that when they write about a character, either real or fictional, they need to describe the character as fully as possible. Their descriptions should include physical characteristics and character traits such as honesty, timidity, or carelessness.
- Using the Mitty Web as an example, work with students through the Writing Lesson to create a character profile.
- Use the Description rubric in **Performance Assessment and Portfolio Management,** p. 18 to evaluate students' character profiles.

❹ Listening and Speaking

- Divide the class into small groups to prepare their skits. Each group can decide on casting for the parts of Mitty, Mrs. Mitty, and additional characters.
- Have groups discuss how parts should be played and dialogue delivered. Some groups might wish to experiment with having the same student play Mitty in both his daydreams and real life, while others might wish to cast different students as the two Mittys.

CUSTOMIZE INSTRUCTION for Universal Access

To address different learning styles, use the activities suggested in the **Extension Activities** booklet, p. 22.

- For Verbal/Linguistic Learners, use Activity 5.
- For Visual/Spatial and Intrapersonal Learners, use Activity 6.
- For Logical/Mathematical Learners, use Activity 7.

ASSESSMENT RESOURCES

The following resources can be used to assess students' knowledge and skills.

Selection Assessment

- **Formal Assessment,** Selection Test, pp. 76–78
- **Open Book Test,** pp. 64–66
- **Got It! Assessment Videotapes,** Tape 2
- **Test Bank Software**

Take It to the Net

Visit www.phschool.com for self-tests and additional questions on "The Secret Life of Walter Mitty."

Writing Rubric

- **Performance Assess. and Portfolio Mgmt.,** p. 18

PRENTICE HALL ASSESSMENT SYSTEM

- **Workbook**
- **Transparencies**
- **Skill Book**
- **CD-ROM**

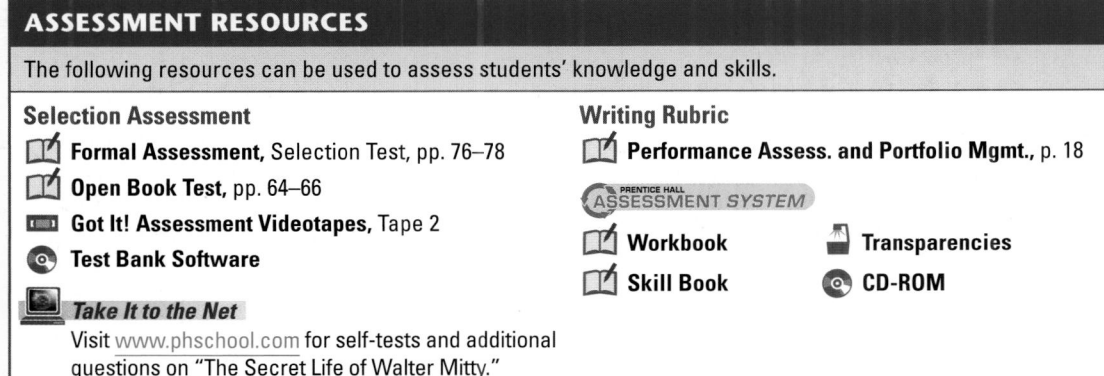

The Inspector-General

Lesson Objectives and CA Correlations

1. **To analyze and respond to literary elements**
   - Literary Analysis: Irony **R 3.8**
   - Connecting Literary Elements: Dialogue **R 3.4**
2. **To read, comprehend, analyze, and critique drama**
   - Reading Strategy: Reading Between the Lines **R 3.8**
   - Reading Check questions
   - Review and Assess questions
   - Assessment Practice (ATE)
3. **To develop word analysis skills, fluency, and systematic vocabulary**
   - Vocabulary Development Lesson: Greek Word Root: *-nym-* **R 1.1**
4. **To understand and apply written and oral language conventions**
   - Spelling Strategy
   - Grammar Lesson: Compound Subjects and Compound Predicates **LC 1.2**
5. **To understand and apply appropriate writing and research strategies**
   - Writing Lesson: Ad for a New Inspector-General **W 2.4**
   - Extension Activity: Concept Map **W 1.5, LS 1.7**
6. **To understand and apply listening and speaking strategies**
   - Extension Activity: Readers Theatre Presentation **LS 1.9**

STEP-BY-STEP TEACHING GUIDE	PACING GUIDE
PRETEACH	
Motivate Students and Provide Background	
Use the Motivation activity (ATE p. 356)	5 min.
Read and discuss the Preview material and Background information (SE/ATE p. 356) [A]	10 min.
Introduce the Concepts	
Introduce the Literary Analysis and Reading Strategy (SE/ATE p. 357) [A]	15 min.
Pronounce the vocabulary words and read their definitions (SE p. 357)	5 min.
TEACH	
Monitor Comprehension	
Informally monitor comprehension by circulating while students read independently or in groups [A]	15 min.
Monitor students' comprehension with the Reading Check notes (SE/ATE pp. 359, 361)	as students read
Develop vocabulary with Vocabulary notes (SE pp. 359, 360, 362; ATE p. 359)	as students read
Develop Understanding	
Develop students' understanding of irony with Literary Analysis annotations (SE/ATE pp. 359, 360, 361) [A]	10 min.
Develop students' ability to read between the lines with the Reading Strategy annotation (ATE p. 360)	10 min.
ASSESS	
Assess Mastery	
Assess students' mastery of the Reading Strategy and Literary Analysis by having them answer the Review and Assess questions (SE/ATE p. 363)	20 min.
Use one or more of the print and media Assessment Resources (ATE p. 365) [A]	up to 50 min.
EXTEND	
Apply Understanding	
Have students complete the Vocabulary Development Lesson and the Grammar Lesson (SE p. 364) [A]	20 min.
Apply students' knowledge of grabbing the reader's attention using the Writing Lesson (SE p. 365) [A]	45 min.
Apply students' understanding using one or more of the Extension Activities (SE p. 365)	20–90 min.

A **ACCELERATED INSTRUCTION:** Use the strategies and activities identified with an [A].

UNIVERSAL ACCESS
- ● = Below-Level Students
- ▲ = On-Level Students
- ■ = Above-Level Students

Time and Resource Manager

Reading Level: Average
Average Number of Instructional Days: 4

RESOURCES		
PRINT	**TRANSPARENCIES**	**TECHNOLOGY**
• **Beyond Literature,** Community Connection: Local Services, p. 23 ▲ ■		• **Interest Grabber Video,** Tape 2 ● ▲ ■
• **Selection Support Workbook:** ● ▲ ■ Literary Analysis, p. 92 Reading Strategy, p. 91 Build Vocabulary, p. 89	• **Literary Analysis and Reading Transparencies,** pp. 45 and 46 ● ▲ ■	
		• **Listening to Literature** ● ▲ ■ Audiocassettes, Side 11 Audio CDs, CD 8
• **Literatura en español** ● ▲ • **Literary Analysis for Enrichment** ■		
• **Formal Assessment:** Selection Test, pp. 79–81 ● ▲ ■ • **Open Book Test,** pp. 67–69 ● ▲ ■ • **Performance Assessment and Portfolio Management,** p. 19 ● ▲ ■ • PRENTICE HALL ASSESSMENT SYSTEM ● ▲ ■	• PRENTICE HALL ASSESSMENT SYSTEM ● ▲ ■ Skills Practice Answers and Explanations on Transparencies	• **Test Bank Software** ● ▲ ■ • **Got It! Assessment Videotapes,** Tape 2 ● ▲
• **Selection Support Workbook:** ● ▲ ■ Build Grammar Skills, p. 90 • **Writing and Grammar,** Gold Level ● ▲ ■ • **Extension Activities,** p. 23 ● ▲ ■	• **Daily Language Practice Transparencies** ● ▲	• **Writing and Grammar iText CD-ROM** ● ▲ ■ *Take It to the Net* www.phschool.com

BLOCK SCHEDULING: Use one 90-minute class period to preteach the selection and have students read it. Use a second 90-minute class period to assess students' mastery of skills and have them complete one of the Extension Activities.

PRETEACH

Step-by-Step Teaching Guide for pp. 356–357

Motivation

Ask students to imagine that they are writers for a television situation comedy. Invite them to continue this story idea: Kim knows that her nosy younger brother Lee likes to listen in on her phone conversations. One day, Kim decides to get back at her brother. . . .

Ask volunteers to share their ideas. Then tell students that the play they are about to read deals with a somewhat similar situation. Encourage the class to look for ways in which a "snoop" gets what he deserves.

Interest Grabber Video

As an alternative, play "Anton Chekhov: His Life and Works" on Tape 2 to engage student interest.

❶ Background

Chekhov's work had a profound influence on the literature of England. All of his major works have been translated into English, several by more than one translator. English writers who paid tribute to Chekhov include Arnold Bennett, E.M. Forster, Virginia Woolf, Katherine Mansfield, and George Bernard Shaw, who said that reading Chekhov's plays made him want to destroy his own. Shaw wrote *Heartbreak House* in honor of Chekhov.

Prepare to Read

The Inspector-General

Valmondois Sous la Neige, Maurice Vlaminck

Take It to the Net

Visit www.phschool.com for interactive activities and instruction related to "The Inspector-General," including

- background
- graphic organizers
- literary elements
- reading strategies

Preview

Connecting to the Literature

Sometimes, people hide their identities or pretend to be someone else. They may be trying to impress someone or play a practical joke. Unexpectedly, the results can be embarrassing or even funny, as the title character of this selection discovers.

❶ Background

"The Inspector-General" is set in imperial Russia, before the 1917 communist revolution, when the country was ruled by an emperor, or czar. To oversee the many minor officials in Russia's vast expanse, the czars employed people called inspectors general. They observed how local schools, courts, and hospitals were functioning. Many people resented the czar's authority, however, and inspectors general were as unpopular as other officials.

TEACHING RESOURCES

The following resources can be used to enrich or extend the instruction for pp. 356–357.

Interest Grabber Video, Tape 2

Background

Beyond Literature, p. 23

Take It to the Net

Visit www.phschool.com for background and hotlinks for "The Inspector-General."

Literary Analysis

Literary Analysis and Reading Transparencies, Irony, p. 46

Reading

Selection Support Workbook: Reading Strategy, p. 91; Build Vocabulary, p. 89

Literary Analysis and Reading Transparencies, Reading Between the Lines, p. 45

BLOCK SCHEDULING: Resources marked with this symbol provide varied instruction during 90-minute blocks.

❷ Literary Analysis

Irony

When a literary work like "The Inspector-General" takes a surprising turn, it creates **irony**—a contrast between what is expected or believed and what is actual. Following are some of the types of irony used in literature:

- **Verbal irony:** A word or phrase is used to suggest the opposite of its usual meaning.
- **Dramatic irony:** There is a contradiction between what a character thinks and what the reader knows is true.
- **Situational irony:** An event directly contradicts the expectations of readers or characters.

As you will see, irony can create humor.

Connecting Literary Elements

In this play, **dialogue**—the conversation between characters—helps to convey the irony. Through dialogue, the driver's vivid descriptions paint a picture for his traveler, and the irony of the situation is revealed. Watch for the driver's descriptions of the inspector general, as revealed through his dialogue, and decide how accurate they are.

❸ Reading Strategy

Reading Between the Lines

When you read a drama, **read between the lines,** or draw conclusions about a person or idea by using the information provided through dialogue. These tips can help you read between the lines:

- Think critically about a character based on what he or she says or does, or based on details of appearance, as revealed through dialogue.
- Pay attention to questions that one character asks another.

Use a diagram like the one shown here to record ideas that you find between the lines.

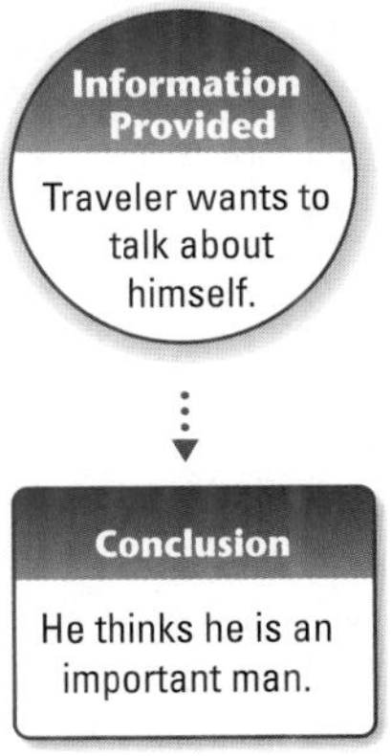

Information Provided
Traveler wants to talk about himself.
Conclusion
He thinks he is an important man.

Vocabulary Development

incognito (in käg′ ni tō′) *n.* a disguised condition (p. 359)

anonymous (ə nän′ ə məs) *adj.* without a known or acknowledged name (p. 359)

trundle (trun′ dəl) *v.* to roll along; to rotate (p. 359)

valet (val′ it) *n.* a man's personal servant who takes care of the man's clothes (p. 360)

buffet (bə′ fā′) *n.* restaurant with a counter or table where refreshments are served (p. 362)

❷ Literary Analysis

Irony and Dialogue

- Review the three kinds of irony that students will encounter in their reading. If possible, have students cite examples of each kind of irony from selections they have already read.
- Use the instruction for Connecting Literary Elements to help students see that the dialogue in a selection is a good place to identify irony because characters may say something that they don't mean.
- Use the Irony transparency in **Literary Analysis and Reading Transparencies,** p. 46, to help students prepare to identify examples of irony as they read the selection.

❸ Reading Strategy

Reading Between the Lines

- Tell students that reading between the lines is similar to drawing a conclusion. Readers use the stated events and dialogue in a selection to make a judgment about what is really going on.
- Instruct students to create a chart like the one shown on p. 357 to record information and draw conclusions about the information as they read.

Vocabulary Development

- Pronounce each vocabulary word for students, and read the definitions as a class. Have students identify any words with which they are already familiar.

CUSTOMIZE INSTRUCTION FOR UNIVERSAL ACCESS

For Less Proficient Readers	For English Learners	For Advanced Readers
Tell students that in reading a play, they need to pay attention to stage directions showing how a character speaks ("sourly") and acts. This information will help them grasp the ironies of "The Inspector-General."	In speech, verbal irony can be emphasized by tone of voice. Ask students how they would say "What beautiful weather!" to describe a rain storm. Have them try out similar ironic tones in sentences of their own. Then ask them to look for verbal ironies in the play.	Students may wish to read Chekhov's short story to see what kinds of changes have been made in the adaptation for stage. Which version do students think is more effective, and why? Is there a difference in the irony of each version?

E-Teach

Visit E-Teach at www.phschool.com for teachers' essays on how to teach, with questions and answers.

TEACH

Step-by-Step Teaching Guide for pp. 358–362

CUSTOMIZE INSTRUCTION for Bodily/Kinesthetic Learners

The stage directions in "The Inspector-General" include gestures and facial expressions that help reveal the characters' feelings and motives. Bodily/kinesthetic learners can help classmates appreciate this aspect of the comedy by performing a version that captures these important nonverbal details.

1 About the Selection

Brimming with sly ironies, this one-act play shows what happens when the tables are turned on a self-satisfied fellow who takes pride in his own craftiness. Traveling "incognito on a secret inspection," Pyotr Pavlovich Posudin soon discovers that the joke is on him.

2 Background

Art

Valmondois Sous la Neige, by Maurice de Vlaminck

Maurice de Vlaminck was born in Paris in 1876. In the early 1900s, he belonged to a group of artists dubbed the Fauves—meaning "wild beasts"—because of their bold use of color. De Vlaminck later turned to painting evocative landscapes. Use the following suggestion for discussion:

- Imagine that people are looking out the windows as the inspector-general rides by. Using details from the play, give examples of their statements or thoughts.
  Answer: Students may suggest: "There goes that sneaky inspector, thinking no one knows who he is . . ."

3 ▶Critical Viewing

Answer: Students may say that life would be dreary and uneventful.

1 # The Inspector-General

Anton Chekhov Adapted by Michael Frayn

2 

Valmondois Sous la Neige, Maurice de Vlaminck

3 ▲ Critical Viewing What might life be like in a setting such as this one? **[Speculate]**

TEACHING RESOURCES

The following resources can be used to enrich or extend the instruction for pp. 358–362.

Literary Analysis

Selection Support Workbook: Literary Analysis, p. 92

Reading

Listening to Literature Audiocassettes, Side 11 ■

Listening to Literature Audio CDs, CD 8 ■

■ **BLOCK SCHEDULING:** Resources marked with this symbol provide varied instruction during 90-minute blocks.

The curtain goes up to reveal falling snow and a cart facing away from us. Enter the STORYTELLER, *who begins to read the story. Meanwhile, the* TRAVELER *enters. He is a middle-aged man of urban appearance, wearing dark glasses and a long overcoat with its collar turned up. He is carrying a small traveling bag. He climbs into the cart and sits facing us.*

STORYTELLER. The Inspector General. In deepest incognito, first by express train, then along back roads, Pyotr Pavlovich Posudin[1] was
4 hastening toward the little town of N, to which he had been summoned by an anonymous letter. "I'll take them by surprise," he thought to himself. "I'll come down on them like a thunderbolt out of the blue. I can just imagine their faces when they hear who I am . . ." [*Enter the* DRIVER, *a peasant, who climbs onto the cart, so that he is sitting with his back to us, and the cart begins to trundle slowly away from us.*] And when he'd thought to himself for long enough, he fell into conversation with the driver of the cart. What did he talk about? About himself, of course. [*Exit the* STORYTELLER.]

TRAVELER. I gather you've got a new Inspector-General in these parts.

DRIVER. True enough.

TRAVELER. Know anything about him? [*The driver turns and looks at the* TRAVELER, *who turns his coat collar up a little higher.*]

DRIVER. Know anything about him? Of course we do! We know everything about all of them up there! Every last little clerk—we know the color of his hair and the size of his boots! [*He turns back to the front, and the* TRAVELER *permits himself a slight smile.*]

TRAVELER. So, what do you reckon? Any good, is he? [*The* DRIVER *turns around.*]

DRIVER. Oh, yes, he's a good one, this one.

TRAVELER. Really?

DRIVER. Did one good thing straight off.

TRAVELER. What was that?

DRIVER. He got rid of the last one. Holy terror he was! Hear him coming five miles off! Say he's going to this little town. Somewhere like we're going, say. He'd let all the world know about it a month
5 before. So now he's on his way, say, and it's like thunder and lightning coming down the road. And when he gets where he's going he has a good sleep, he has a good eat and drink—and then he starts. Stamps his feet, shouts his head off. Then he has another good sleep, and off he goes.

1. **Pyotr Pavlovich Posudin** (pyō´ tr pȧv lō´ vich pō syōō´ dən)

incognito (in käg´ ni tō´) *n.* a disguised condition

anonymous (ə nän´ ə məs) *adj.* without a known or acknowledged name

trundle (trun´ dəl) *v.* to roll along; to rotate

Literary Analysis
Irony What is ironic about the driver's words here?

6 **Reading Check**
What does the driver say about the last inspector general?

4 Vocabulary Development

Greek Root *-nym-*

- Point out to students *-nym-* is derived from the Greek word for "name."
- Have students examine the word *anonymous* to observe how the root contributes to the meaning "without a known or acknowledged name."
- Ask students to think of other words having this root. Write the words on the board and have the class provide brief definitions. Possible responses: *pseudonym,* "fictitious name"; *synonymous,* "having nearly the same meaning."

5 Literary Analysis

Irony

- Have students reread the Literary Analysis lesson on p. 357 and define *situational irony.* Answer: Situational irony occurs when an event contradicts the expectations of readers or characters.
- Ask students what good thing the driver says the new inspector-general has done. Answer: The cart driver says the new inspector-general has gotten rid of the old one.
- Ask students the Literary Analysis question on p. 359: What is ironic about the driver's words here? Answer: The driver says the one good thing the current official has done is get rid of the former official. This is situational irony because the traveler has expected to hear something positive about his own work.

6 Reading Check

Answer: He says the last inspector-general was a holy terror.

CUSTOMIZE INSTRUCTION FOR UNIVERSAL ACCESS

For English Learners	For Advanced Readers
Point out to students that dialogue is a basic way for writers to develop characterization. However, speakers of dialogue in plays and stories are not required to use correct grammar consistently. Have students note the driver's use of incomplete sentences, double negatives, and other examples of nonstandard grammar in the dialogue. Work as a class to create correct versions of these inconsistencies.	Have students categorize the many ironies that contribute to the play's humor. Students can create a chart with three headings: Verbal, Dramatic, and Situational. Have students find as many examples of each type of irony as they can in the selection.

7 Literary Analysis

Irony

- Have students review the definition of *dramatic irony* from the lesson on page 357.
  Answer: Dramatic irony occurs when there is a contradiction between what a character thinks and what the reader knows is true.
- Ask students the Literary Analysis question on p. 360: Why is the description of the new inspector-general ironic?
  Answer: The driver is supposedly describing someone other than the man in his cart, when he is in fact describing the traveler.

Monitor Progress Ask students why this passage is an example of dramatic irony.
Answer: The traveler thinks the driver does not know that the traveler is the inspector-general. The readers know that the driver knows very well whom he is describing.

8 Reading Strategy

Reading Between the Lines

- Ask students to identify the servants or employees mentioned in this passage.
  Answer: A valet, coachman, and housekeeper are mentioned.
- Reading between the lines, what do you conclude about the employees' attitudes toward their employer?
  Possible response: Students may conclude that the employees despise the inspector-general. The housekeeper "runs circles around him," and the valet and coachman gossip about his secret drinking. The would-be "spy" is spied upon by his own servants.

TRAVELER. But the new one's not like that?

7 **DRIVER.** Oh, no, the new one goes everywhere on the quiet, like. Creeps around like a cat. Don't want no one to see him, don't want no one to know who he is. Say he's going to this town down the road here. Someone there sent him a letter on the sly, let's say. "Things going on here you should know about." Something of that kind. Well, now, he creeps out of his office, so none of them up there see him go. He hops on a train just like anyone else, just like you or me. Then when he gets off he don't go jumping into a cab or nothing fancy. Oh, no. He wraps himself up from head to toe so you can't see his face, and he wheezes away like an old dog so no one can recognize his voice.

TRAVELER. Wheezes? That's not wheezing! That's the way he talks! So I gather.

DRIVER. Oh, is it? But the tales they tell about him. You'd laugh till you burst your tripes![2]

TRAVELER [*sourly*]. I'm sure I would.

DRIVER. He drinks, mind!

TRAVELER [*startled*]. Drinks?

DRIVER. Oh, like a hole in the ground. Famous for it.

TRAVELER. He's never touched a drop! I mean, from what I've heard.

DRIVER. Oh, not in public, no. Goes to some great ball—"No thank you, not for me." Oh, no, he puts it away at home! Wakes up in the morning, rubs his eyes, and the first thing he does, he shouts, "Vodka!" So in runs his valet with a glass. Fixed himself up a tube behind his desk, he has. Leans down, takes a pull on it, no one the wiser.

TRAVELER [*offended*]. How do you know all this, may I ask?

8 **DRIVER.** Can't hide it from the servants, can you? The valet and the coachman have got tongues in their heads. Then again, he's on the road, say, going about his business, and he keeps the bottle in his little bag. [*The* TRAVELER *discreetly pushes the traveling bag out of the* DRIVER'S *sight.*] And his housekeeper . . .

TRAVELER. What about her?

DRIVER. Runs circles around him, she does, like a fox round his tail. She's the one who wears the trousers.[3] The people aren't half so frightened of him as they are of her.

TRAVELER. But at least he's good at his job, you say?

DRIVER. Oh, he's a blessing from heaven, I'll grant him that.

TRAVELER. Very cunning—you were saying.

Literary Analysis
Irony Why is the description of the new inspector general ironic?

valet (val′ it) *n.* a man's personal servant who takes care of the man's clothes

---

2. **tripes** (trīps) *n.* parts of the stomach, usually of an ox or a sheep.
3. **wears the trousers** has the greatest authority; is really in charge.

ENRICHMENT: Literature Connection

Literary Criticism

In *Landmarks of Russian Literature,* Maurice Baring wrote the following:

> "Tolstoy is reported to have said that [Chekhov] was a photographer, a very talented photographer, it is true, but still only a photographer. But [Chekhov] has one quality which is difficult to find among photographers and that is humor. His stories are frequently deliciously droll. They are also often full of pathos . . . "

You may wish to have students write a journal entry in which they respond to Baring's statement. Ask students to explore how Chekhov's writing is like a photograph, and if they agree or disagree with Baring's assessment.

White Night, Edvard Munch, National Gallery, Oslo

9 ◀ **Critical Viewing** How well does the mood of this painting match the mood of this play? Explain. **[Connect]**

10 **DRIVER.** Oh, he creeps around all right.

TRAVELER. And then he pounces, yes? I should think some people must get the surprise of their life, mustn't they?

DRIVER. No, no—let's be fair, now. Give him his due. He don't make no trouble.

TRAVELER. No, I mean, if no one knows he's coming . . .

DRIVER. Oh, that's what *he* thinks, but *we* all know.

TRAVELER. You know?

DRIVER. Oh, some gentleman gets off the train at the station back there with his greatcoat up to his eyebrows and says, "No, I don't want a cab, thank you, just an ordinary horse and cart for me." Well, we'd put two and two together, wouldn't we! Say it was you, now, creeping along down the road here. The lads would be down there in a cab by now! By the time you got there the whole town would be as regular

Literary Analysis
Irony and Description
What makes the driver's description funny?

11 ✔ **Reading Check**
What does the driver say that the new inspector general does at night?

9 ▶ **Critical Viewing**

Answer: Students may say that the mood of the painting matches the mood of the play quite well. The painting depicts a rural scene that is quiet and calm, much like the setting of the play.

10 Literary Analysis

Irony

- Have a volunteer read aloud the bracketed passage.
- Ask students to identify what the driver appears to do in this passage.
  Possible response: The driver describes the inspector-general's dramatic effect on the townspeople, and he says that the inspector-general's visit is not a big deal.
- Now, ask students the Literary Analysis question on p. 361: What makes the driver's description funny?
  Answer: The inspector-general, and the readers, are expecting the driver to confirm the traveler's description of his pouncing on the townspeople.

11 ✔ **Reading Check**

Answer: The driver contends that the inspector-general drinks in private.

CUSTOMIZE INSTRUCTION FOR UNIVERSAL ACCESS

For Less Proficient Readers

Invite students to use the stage directions to give them more information about the characters and the action of the selection. For example, when the driver says the passenger would laugh at the tales told about the inspector-general, the passenger says "I'm sure I would." Ask students if the stage-direction word *sourly* suggests that the traveler means what he says. Encourage students to use stage directions as an aid to understanding and interpreting whenever they read a play.

For Advanced Readers

Invite students to identify the idioms in this selection, including those on this spread. Use the following to generate interest:

- What is the meaning of an idiom that says that someone drinks 'like a hole in the ground'?
- Translate the idiom 'You'd laugh till you burst your tripes!' into an American idiom.
- What does the idiom 'We'd put two and two together, wouldn't we?' mean?

ASSESS

Answers for p. 362

Review and Assess

1. Some students may feel sorry for the inspector-general because it is never pleasant to realize that those you are trying to fool are way ahead of you.
2. **(a)** Townspeople have learned that the official will try to disguise himself from them for secret inspections. **(b)** He is sneaky and dishonest.
3. **(a)** He discreetly pushes his bag out of sight of the driver. **(b)** The traveler is probably carrying a bottle of vodka in his bag.
4. **(a)** The driver says the townspeople have heard about the inspector-general's arrival by telegraph and have food and drink all prepared. **(b)** He realizes the townspeople know all about him, and he fears their contempt if he should appear among them.
5. Possible responses: In order not to have to visit this town again, the inspector-general might give a glowing report about the competence of the town's officials. Or, in order to punish them for making him feel like a fool, he might give a very negative report of the town.
6. The inspector-general will be a poor leader because once people learn that he lies and tries to trick them, they will not cooperate. No one can lead effectively without the consent of the led.
7. Students will probably say that the driver is wiser because he is intelligent enough to see through the disguise of the inspector-general and to turn the tables on him.

as clockwork! And you'd think to yourself, "Oh, look at that! As clean as a whistle! And they didn't know I was coming!" No, that's why he's such a blessing after the other one. This one believes it!

TRAVELER. Oh, I see.

DRIVER. What, you thought we wouldn't know him? Why, we've got the electric telegraph these days! Take today, now. I'm going past the station back there this morning, and the fellow who runs the buffet comes out like a bolt of lightning. Arms full of baskets and bottles. "Where are you off to?" I say. "Doing drinks and refreshments for the Inspector-General!" he says, and he jumps into a carriage and goes flying off down the road here. So there's the old Inspector-General, all muffled up like a roll of carpet, going secretly along in a cart somewhere—and when he gets there, nothing to be seen but vodka and cold salmon!

buffet (bə fā´) *n.* restaurant with a counter or table where refreshments are served

TRAVELER [*shouts*]. Right—turn around, then . . . !

DRIVER [*to the horse*]. Whoa, boy! Whoa! [*To the* TRAVELER.] Oh, so what's this, then? Don't want to go running into the Inspector-General, is that it? [*The* TRAVELER *gestures impatiently for the* DRIVER *to turn the cart around.* DRIVER *to the horse.*] Back we go, then, boy. Home we go. [*He turns the cart around, and the* TRAVELER *takes a swig from his traveling bag.*] Though if I know the old devil, he's like as not turned around and gone home again himself. [*Blackout.*]

Review and Assess

Thinking About the Selection

1. **Respond:** Did you feel any sympathy for the inspector general? Why or why not?
2. **(a) Recall:** What have townspeople learned about the inspector general's habits? **(b) Draw Conclusions:** What do these habits reveal about the official's character?
3. **(a) Recall:** What does the traveler do when the driver mentions that the inspector general keeps a flask of vodka? **(b) Infer:** What does this action tell you about the traveler?
4. **(a) Recall:** How does the driver describe the preparations for the inspector general's arrival? **(b) Interpret:** Why does this account provoke the traveler's demand to turn around?
5. **Speculate:** What kind of report might the inspector general make to the czar about his mission? Give specific details.
6. **Assess:** Based on his actions, what kind of leader do you think the inspector general will be?
7. **Evaluate:** Who do you think is the wiser man, the driver or the traveler? Explain.

Anton Chekhov

(1860–1904)

The grandson of a former serf who had purchased his freedom, Chekhov grew up in a small Russian coastal town. He later attended medical school in Moscow, where he began writing humorous sketches and short stories. Writing soon became his major focus, but he practiced medicine part-time throughout his life.

Chekhov wrote more than one thousand short stories as well as several acclaimed plays, including *The Seagull* (1896), *Uncle Vanya* (1899), and *The Three Sisters* (1901). He is considered one of the finest playwrights and short-story writers who ever lived.

ASSESSMENT PRACTICE: Reading Comprehension

Cause and Effect (For more practice, see Test Preparation Workbook, p. 23.)

Many tests require students to perceive cause-and-effect relationships. Use the following sample test item to give students practice in this skill.

From the 1500s until the Marxist revolution of 1917, Russia was ruled by czars. To keep a close eye on local officials throughout Russia's vast landscape, czars employed inspectors-general. Because people resented the czar's authority, inspectors-general were often unpopular among the public.

Why were the inspectors-general unpopular?

A The revolution was approaching.
B They kept a close eye on local officials.
C They were agents of the czar.
D Russia's landscape was vast and varied.

Guide students to notice the word *because* in the passage. The text that follows, explaining the cause for the unpopularity of the inspectors-general, is best expressed in *C*.

Review and Assess

Literary Analysis

Irony

1. The humor in "The Inspector-General" comes from the use of **irony.** In a chart like the one shown here, note the traveler's assumptions and the driver's ironic observations.

What the Traveler Thinks
What the Driver Says

2. Explain why the traveler's attempt to hide his identity presents **situational irony.**
3. Explain why the driver's remark that the inspector general is "a good one" is an example of **verbal irony.**

Connecting Literary Elements

4. (a) What image of the inspector general is revealed through the **dialogue**? (b) Explain the irony in the driver's description of the new inspector general.
5. As the dialogue between the men continues, the situation becomes ever funnier. Use a flowchart like the one shown here to record the most important details leading to the comic reversal.

Driver says, "He drinks."
Traveler turns back.

Reading Strategy

Reading Between the Lines

6. (a) When did you first realize that the traveler is the inspector general? (b) Which details led you to this conclusion?
7. As the driver goes on speaking, the traveler resorts to saying "so I gather" and "from what I've heard." **Read between the lines** to explain why he uses these expressions.

Extend Understanding

8. **Cultural Connection:** What makes a person of authority popular or unpopular in the public eye?

Quick Review

Irony is a contrast between what is expected and what is actual.

In **situational irony,** events contradict expectations.

In **verbal irony,** words are used to mean their opposite.

In **dramatic irony,** there is a contrast between what the characters and the audience know.

Dialogue is a conversation between characters.

To **read between the lines,** use information the writer provides to understand something that is not stated directly.

Take It to the Net

www.phschool.com

Take the interactive self-test online to check your understanding of the selection.

ENRICHMENT: Further Reading

Other Works by Anton Chekhov

The Cherry Orchard
The Marriage Proposal
The Seagull
"The Bet"

Take It to the Net

Visit www.phschool.com for more information on Anton Chekhov.

Answers for p. 363

Review and Assess

1.

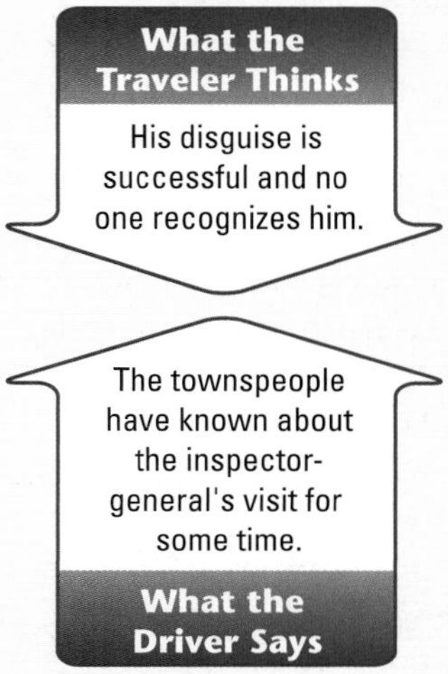

What the Traveler Thinks
His disguise is successful and no one recognizes him.
The townspeople have known about the inspector-general's visit for some time.
What the Driver Says

2. The attempts to hide his identity represent situational irony, because he is the only one who thinks he is successful.
3. The driver considers the inspector-general "good" because he is easily "found out." This actually means that the inspector-general is bad at his job.
4. **(a)** The inspector-general is revealed to be sneaky, sly, dishonest, and thoroughly untrustworthy. **(b)** The irony is situational; the driver describes the "new" inspector-general, who is really the traveler listening to a description of himself.
5. "He drinks"; his servants reveal his secrets; his housekeeper is the real power in his household; the town has been expecting him; "Turn around!"
6. **(a)** Students may have caught on when the traveler reacts to the driver's remark about "wheezes." **(b)** The traveler pulls his collar up to hide his face, just as the inspector-general is said to do. He also hides his bag when the driver says that the inspector-general carries vodka in a bag.
7. He uses these expressions to keep from seeming to know too much about the inspector-general—himself.
8. Students may cite harshness, dishonesty, or greediness as unpopular qualities and honesty, friendliness, and firmness as popular qualities.

EXTEND

Answers for p. 364

❶ Vocabulary Development

1. a name that comes from a father's name
2. a word with the same or similar meaning as that of another word
3. a word formed from the first letters or syllables of other words

Spelling Strategy

1. childish
2. traveler
3. acceptance

Fluency: Sentence Completions

1. trundled
2. anonymous
3. valet
4. buffet
5. incognito

❷ Grammar

1. Snow and ice make travel difficult.
2. The driver and the traveler took a ride.
3. As they ride, the traveler asks questions and hopes for the right response.
4. The driver's manner and his ideas reveal an interesting situation.
5. He makes a decision and chooses to leave.

Writing Application

1. Every last clerk and each peasant knows the color of his hair.
2. The traveler chatted and joked with the driver.

Integrate Language Skills

❶ Vocabulary Development Lesson

Word Analysis: Greek Root *-nym-*

The Greek root *-nym-*, meaning "name," is used in many English words, including *anonymous*, which means "without a known name." Use a dictionary to define the following words.

1. patronymic 2. synonym 3. acronym

Spelling Strategy

When you add a suffix that begins with a vowel to a word that ends in a consonant, the spelling of the original word does not change. For example, *inspect* + *-or* = *inspector*.

Add *-ance*, *-ish*, or *-er* to each word below to form three properly spelled words.

1. child 2. travel 3. accept

Fluency: Sentence Completions

In your notebook, complete each sentence with a word from the vocabulary list on page 357.

1. The heavy trucks slowly ___?___ along the bumpy road.
2. An ___?___ donor gave ten thousand dollars to the hospital fund. We're still not sure who made the donation.
3. The ___?___ cleaned and ironed the pants of the hotel guest.
4. The ___?___ featured delicious main courses and desserts. Everyone moved along, placing their favorite foods on their plates.
5. Traveling ___?___, with sunglasses, a fake mustache, and a hat, the spy checked into the motel under a false name.

❷ Grammar Lesson

Compound Subjects and Compound Predicates

A sentence may have two or more subjects with the same verb (a **compound subject**) or two or more verbs, or predicates, with the same subject (a **compound predicate**). It may even have both at once. The parts of a compound subject or predicate are joined by a conjunction, such as *and* or *or*.

Compound subject: Glasses and an overcoat were worn by the inspector general. Glasses, an overcoat, and a traveling bag were some of his belongings.

Compound predicate: They traveled and talked in the cart. The driver turns, looks, and nods at the traveler.

Practice Copy each sentence. Underline each compound subject once and each compound predicate twice.

1. Snow and ice make travel difficult.
2. The driver and the traveler took a ride.
3. As they ride, the traveler asks questions and hopes for the right response.
4. The driver's manner and his ideas reveal an interesting situation.
5. He makes a decision and chooses to leave.

Writing Application Write two sentences about "The Inspector-General," using a compound subject in one and a compound predicate in the other.

WG Prentice Hall Writing and Grammar Connection: Chapter 20, Section 1

TEACHING RESOURCES

The following resources can be used to enrich or extend the instruction for pp. 364–365.

Vocabulary

- **Selection Support Workbook:** Build Vocabulary, p. 89
- **Vocabulary and Spelling Practice Book** (Use this booklet for skills enrichment.) ■

Grammar

- **Selection Support Workbook:** Build Grammar Skills, p. 90
- **Writing and Grammar,** Gold Level, p. 422
- **Daily Language Practice Transparencies,** ■

Writing

- **Writing and Grammar,** Gold Level, p. 163 ■
- **Writing and Grammar iText CD-ROM**

■ **BLOCK SCHEDULING:** Resources marked with this symbol provide varied instruction during 90-minute blocks.

❸ Writing Lesson

Ad for a New Inspector General

Imagine that you are the czar and have just fired the old inspector general. Write a newspaper ad to find a replacement. Your ad should provide information that will appeal to potential applicants and clarify whether they are qualified for the job.

Prewriting Jot down ideas in the following categories: (a) job title and responsibilities; (b) necessary experience and background; (c) salary and benefits; (d) contact information, such as the company's phone number or address.

Drafting Begin with an attention-grabbing introduction. Then, devote a short paragraph to each of the four categories.

Model: Grabbing Your Reader's Attention

Love to travel? Ready to take on fascinating new responsibilities? Consider becoming an inspector general!

An effective ad is based on a catchy and memorable message.

Revising Compare your ad to your prewriting notes, underlining key details in your draft. If you discover information that is unclear or incomplete, revise to present a more accurate picture of the job.

WG *Prentice Hall Writing and Grammar Connection: Chapter 8, Section 3*

❹ Extension Activities

Listening and Speaking With two other students, prepare to perform a **Readers Theatre presentation** of "The Inspector-General." Do not provide props or staging; instead, focus on a well-prepared reading of the play.

- Choose roles—the traveler, the driver, and a narrator who reads the introduction and any stage directions you feel should be shared.
- Experiment to find the tone of voice and style of delivery that seem to work best.

Then, perform the play in front of a small group or the entire class. **[Group Activity]**

Research and Technology Research what life was like in Russia during the rule of the czars. Explain the responsibilities of inspectors general during this time. Use two or more Internet search engines to broaden the scope of your findings. Display your findings in a **concept map** or another graphic organizer and present it to your class. Ask your class to compare inspectors general in history to the inspector general in this story.

Take It to the Net www.phschool.com

Go online for an additional research activity using the Internet.

ASSESSMENT RESOURCES

The following resources can be used to assess students' knowledge and skills.

Selection Assessment

- **Formal Assessment,** Selection Test, pp. 79–81
- **Open Book Test,** pp. 67–69
- **Got It! Assessment Videotapes,** Tape 2
- **Test Bank Software**

Take It to the Net
Visit www.phschool.com for self-tests and additional questions on "The Inspector-General."

Writing Rubric

- **Performance Assess. and Portfolio Mgmt.,** Persuasion, p. 19

PRENTICE HALL ASSESSMENT SYSTEM

- **Workbook**
- **Transparencies**
- **Skill Book**
- **CD-ROM**

Lesson Support for p. 365

❸ Writing Lesson

- Display job ads from a local newspaper for students to use as models.
- Tell students that when writing their job ad for the inspector-general they must be specific about the qualifications they are looking for and what they are paying for the job.
- Use the Writing Lesson to guide students in developing their job ad.
- Use the Persuasion: Advertisement rubric in **Performance Assessment and Portfolio Management,** p. 19, to evaluate students' ads.

❹ Listening and Speaking

- Divide the class into groups of three. Have them assign the three roles—narrator, driver, traveler.
- Help students work not only with their voice but with their body language to convey the responses and emotions of the characters.
- When each group has had time to rehearse, ask for volunteers to perform their play for the class.

CUSTOMIZE INSTRUCTION For Universal Access

To address different learning styles, use the activities suggested in the **Extension Activities** booklet, p. 23.

- For Bodily/Kinesthetic and Verbal/Linguistic Learners, use Activity 5.
- For Verbal/Linguistic Learners, use Activity 6.
- For Logical/Mathematical Learners, use Activity 7.

Go Deep to the Sewer ✦ Fly Away

Lesson Objectives and CA Correlations

1. **To analyze and respond to literary elements**
   - Literary Analysis: Humorous Remembrance **R 3.5**
   - Comparing Literary Works **R 3.5**
2. **To read, comprehend, analyze, and critique nonfiction**
   - Reading Strategy: Recognizing Situational Humor
   - Reading Check questions
   - Review and Assess questions
   - Assessment Practice (ATE)
3. **To develop word analysis skills, fluency, and systematic vocabulary**
   - Vocabulary Development Lesson: Specialized Vocabulary: Sports Jargon **R 1.2**
4. **To understand and apply written and oral language conventions**
   - Spelling Strategy
   - Grammar Lesson: Direct Objects **LC 1.3**
5. **To understand and apply appropriate writing and research strategies**
   - Writing Lesson: Humorous Personal Narrative **W 2.1**
   - Extension Activity: Visual Report **W 1.5, LS 1.7**
6. **To understand and apply listening and speaking strategies**
   - Extension Activity: Monologue **LS 1.4**

STEP-BY-STEP TEACHING GUIDE	PACING GUIDE
PRETEACH	
Motivate Students and Provide Background	
Use the Motivation activity (ATE p. 366)	5 min.
Read and discuss the Preview material and Background information (SE/ATE p. 366) [A]	5 min.
Introduce the Concepts	
Introduce the Literary Analysis and Reading Strategy (SE/ATE p. 367) [A]	15 min.
Pronounce the vocabulary words and read their definitions (SE p. 367)	5 min.
TEACH	
Monitor Comprehension	
Informally monitor comprehension by circulating while students read independently or in groups [A]	20 min.
Monitor students' comprehension with the Reading Check notes (SE/ATE pp. 369, 371, 373, 375)	as students read
Develop vocabulary with Vocabulary notes (SE pp. 368, 370, 371)	as students read
Develop Understanding	
Develop students' understanding of humorous remembrances with Literary Analysis annotations (SE pp. 371, 375; ATE pp. 370, 371, 375) [A]	10 min.
Develop students' ability to recognize situational humor with the Reading Strategy annotations (SE pp. 368, 372–374; ATE pp. 368, 371, 373, 374)	10 min.
ASSESS	
Assess Mastery	
Assess students' mastery of the Reading Strategy and Literary Analysis by having them answer the Review and Assess questions (SE/ATE p. 377)	20 min.
Use one or more of the print and media Assessment Resources (ATE p. 379) [A]	up to 50 min.
EXTEND	
Apply Understanding	
Have students complete the Vocabulary Development Lesson and the Grammar Lesson (SE p. 378) [A]	20 min.
Apply students' knowledge of strong introductions using the Writing Lesson (SE p. 379) [A]	45 min.
Apply students' understanding using one or more of the Extension Activities (SE p. 379)	20–90 min.

[A] ACCELERATED INSTRUCTION: Use the strategies and activities identified with an [A].

UNIVERSAL ACCESS
● = Below Level Students
▲ = On-Level Students
■ = Above Level Students

Time and Resource Manager

Reading Level: Average/Easy
Average Number of Instructional Days: 4

RESOURCES		
PRINT	**TRANSPARENCIES**	**TECHNOLOGY**
• **Beyond Literature,** Workplace Skills: Acting Responsibly, p. 24 ▲ ■		• **Interest Grabber Video,** Tape 2 ● ▲ ■
• **Selection Support Workbook:** ● ▲ ■ Literary Analysis, p. 96 Reading Strategy, p. 95 Build Vocabulary, p. 93	• **Literary Analysis and Reading Transparencies,** pp. 47 and 48 ● ▲ ■	
• **Adapted Reader's Companion** ● • **Reader's Companion** ●		• **Listening to Literature** ● ▲ ■ Audiocassettes, Side 13 Audio CDs, CD 9
• **English Learner's Companion** ● ▲ • **Literatura en español** ● ▲ • **Literary Analysis for Enrichment** ■	• **Fine Art Transparencies Volume 1,** Art Transparency 5 ● ▲ ■	
• **Formal Assessment:** Selection Test, pp. 82–84 ● ▲ ■ • **Open Book Test,** pp. 70–72 ● ▲ ■ • **Performance Assessment and Portfolio Management,** p. 8 ● ▲ ■ • Prentice Hall Assessment System ● ▲ ■	• Prentice Hall Assessment System ● ▲ ■ Skills Practice Answers and Explanations on Transparencies	• **Test Bank Software** ● ▲ ■ • **Got It! Assessment Videotapes,** Tape 2 ● ▲
• **Selection Support Workbook:** ● ▲ ■ Build Grammar Skills, p. 94 • **Writing and Grammar,** Gold Level ● ▲ ■ • **Extension Activities,** p. 24 ● ▲ ■	• **Daily Language Practice Transparencies** ● ▲	• **Writing and Grammar iText CD-ROM** ● ▲ ■ ***Take It to the Net*** www.phschool.com

BLOCK SCHEDULING: Use one 90-minute class period to preteach the selection and have students read it. Use a second 90-minute class period to assess students' mastery of skills and have them complete one of the Extension Activities.

PRETEACH

Step-by-Step Teaching Guide for pp. 366–367

Motivation

Hook students' interest by asking them to describe some of the funniest moments from movies or television shows that feature Bill Cosby, or some of the most amazing moments from movies or television shows that include performances by wild animals. After students have recounted some special moments, point out that the selections will give a behind-the-scenes look at both Bill Cosby and animal performances. The first selection is written by Cosby about his boyhood, and the second is written by an animal trainer who trains wild animals to act in movies.

Interest Grabber Video

As an alternative, play "Commercial Beekeeping" on Tape 2 to engage student interest.

1 Background

Ralph Helfer says, "Instead of dealing with my animals physically, I deal with them emotionally." He argues that animals trained through fear remain dangerous to work with. In addition to *The Beauty of the Beast,* Helfer wrote *Modoc,* which tells the heartwarming story of the long life of an exceptional elephant and her devoted companion and trainer.

Prepare to Read

Go Deep to the Sewer ◆ Fly Away

Take It to the Net

Visit www.phschool.com for interactive activities and instruction related to the selections, including
- background
- graphic organizers
- literary elements
- reading strategies

Preview

Connecting to the Literature

When life hands out lemons, some people make lemonade. Other people make big lemon meringue pies to toss so that others will laugh. Maybe you are one of those people who can find something funny even in difficult situations. These selections focus on the lighter side of personal experiences.

1 Background

For years, Ralph Helfer, an animal trainer and the author of "Fly Away," used an animal-training method based on fear. After being injured several times, Helfer developed a new system, "affection training," with which the trainer wins an animal's loyalty through understanding, patience, and love. Since using this system, neither Helfer nor any of his animals have been injured.

TEACHING RESOURCES

The following resources can be used to enrich or extend the instruction for pp. 366–367.

Interest Grabber Video, Tape 2

Background

Beyond Literature, p. 24

Take It to the Net

Visit www.phschool.com for background and hotlinks for the selections.

Literary Analysis

Literary Analysis and Reading Transparencies, Humorous Remembrance, p. 48

Reading

Selection Support Workbook: Reading Strategy, p.95; Build Vocabulary, p. 93

Literary Analysis and Reading Transparencies, Recognize Situational Humor, p. 47

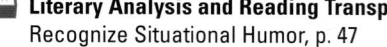

BLOCK SCHEDULING: Resources marked with this symbol provide varied instruction during 90-minute blocks.

❷ Literary Analysis

Humorous Remembrance

A **humorous remembrance** is a story that emphasizes what is funny in a writer's past experiences. The following excerpt from "Go Deep to the Sewer" relates a ten-year-old quarterback's instructions to his team, whose football field was an urban street in Philadelphia.

> ". . . Arnie, you go down to the corner of Locust an' fake takin' the bus. An' Cos, you do a zig out to the bakery. See if you can shake your man before you hit the rolls."

As you read the selections, notice how both writers find something to laugh about in experiences that may have had their painful moments as well.

Comparing Literary Works

Humorous remembrances are all amusing, whether or not the writers initially intended them to be. Humor is the most important ingredient in both of these stories, and laughter may be the reader's most frequent reaction. Compare the humorous and serious sides of the experiences these authors convey in each of their stories.

❸ Reading Strategy

Recognizing Situational Humor

Situational humor, as found in these humorous remembrances, arises from conditions that mix people, actions, and settings in funny and often improbable ways:

- In "Go Deep to the Sewer," a stickball player is tagged out at third base because the car that takes the place of the base is suddenly driven away.
- In "Fly Away," the trainer amazingly gets several thousand flies to take to the air on cue.

Use a chart like this one to capture and categorize specific examples of situational humor you find as you read.

What Is Being Done?	Who Is Doing It?
Where?	**Using What?**

Vocabulary Development

lateral (lat´ ər əl) *adj.* sideways (p. 368)
yearned (yʉrnd) *v.* longed for (p. 370)
decoy (dē´ koi´) *n.* person used to lure others into a trap (p. 370)
interpretation (in tʉr´ prə tā´ shən) *n.* explanation (p. 371)
skeptical (skep´ ti kəl) *adj.* doubting; questioning (p. 375)

❷ Literary Analysis

Humorous Remembrance

- Explain to students that a humorous remembrance is a writer's reflection on a past event told in an amusing way.
- Tell students that they will look for humorous situations as they read the two selections.
- Read the instruction about humorous remembrance together as a class. Call students' attention to the example from "Go Deep to the Sewer."
- Use the Humorous Remembrance transparency in **Literary Analysis and Reading Transparencies,** p. 48, to demonstrate to students the difference between a humorous recounting of an event and a matter-of-fact account of the same event.

❸ Reading Strategy

Recognizing Situational Humor

- Call on students to reflect on their own lives in the past week to come up with a humorous situation.
- Point out to students that situational humor often grows out of an ordinary situation that is made humorous by the addition of something unexpected or silly.
- Have students create a chart like the one shown to record the events they read about in the selections.

Vocabulary Development

- Pronounce each vocabulary word for students, and read the definitions as a class. Have students identify any words with which they are already familiar.

CUSTOMIZE INSTRUCTION FOR UNIVERSAL ACCESS

For Special Needs Students	For Less Proficient Readers	For English Learners
Have students read the adapted version of "Go Deep to the Sewer" in the **Adapted Reader's Companion.** This version provides basic-level instruction in an interactive format with questions and write-on lines. Completing the adapted version will prepare students to read the selection in the Student Edition.	Have students read the selection in the **Reader's Companion.** This version provides basic-level instruction in an interactive format with questions and write-on lines. After students finish the selection in **Reader's Companion,** have them complete the questions and activities in the Student Edition.	Have students read the adapted version of the selection in the **English Learner's Companion.** This version provides basic-level instruction in an interactive format with questions and write-on lines. Completing the adapted version will prepare students to read the selection in the Student Edition.

E-Teach

Visit E-Teach at www.phschool.com for teachers' essays on how to teach, with questions and answers.

TEACH

Step-By-Step Teaching Guide for pp. 368–376

CUSTOMIZE INSTRUCTION
For Bodily-Kinesthetic Learners

Students might gain a greater appreciation of the events Bill Cosby describes if they act out the movements of the football and stickball games. Encourage them to read the selection carefully and, if necessary, make a diagram showing the players' moves. Then, they can demonstrate the action for the class.

❶ About the Selection

This personal narrative describes the games that Bill Cosby used to play as a boy. As he looks back with a fond, self-mocking eye toward his past, Cosby paints a funny and heartwarming picture of what it was like to grow up on the streets of Philadelphia.

❷ Reading Strategy

Recognizing Situational Humor

- As students read the bracketed passage, ask them what problems Cosby and his friends might have had in playing football in the street.
  Answer: Students may agree that the boys faced the danger of being hit by cars or running into cars.
- Have students determine what is humorous about Cosby's statement about his mother having a seat a scalper would prize.
  Possible response: The best seats for watching Cosby's football games were not on the 50-yard line of a football field but an apartment window overlooking the street where the boys played.
- Ask students the Reading Strategy question on p. 368: Why did few players get to make "end runs"? What is funny about this situation?
  Answer: The "field" was narrow and lined with parked cars. End runs were only possible when cars moved and became—comically—blockers for the runner.

❶ Go Deep to the Sewer

Bill Cosby

The essence of childhood, of course, is play, which my friends and I did endlessly on streets that we reluctantly shared with traffic. As a daring receiver in touch football, I spent many happy years running up and down those asphalt fields, hoping that a football would hit me before a Chevrolet did.

My mother was often a nervous fan who watched me from her window.

"Bill, don't get run over!" she would cry in a moving concern for me.

❷ "Do you see me getting run over?" I would cleverly reply.

And if I ever *had* been run over, my mother had a seat for it that a scalper[1] would have prized.

Because the narrow fields of those football games allowed almost no lateral movement, an end run was possible only if a car pulled out and blocked for you. And so I worked on my pass-catching, for I knew I had little chance of ever living my dream: taking a handoff and sweeping to glory along the curb, dancing over the dog dung like Red Grange.

The quarterback held this position not because he was the best passer but because he knew how to drop to one knee in the huddle and diagram plays with trash.

"Okay, Shorty," Junior Barnes would say, "this is you: the orange peel."

"I don' wanna be the orange peel," Shorty replied. "The orange peel is Albert. I'm the gum."

lateral (lat´ ər əl) *adj.* sideways

Reading Strategy
Recognizing Situational Humor Why did few players get to make "end runs"? What is funny about this situation?

1. **scalper** (skalp´ ər) *n.* person who buys tickets and sells them later at higher than regular prices.

TEACHING RESOURCES

The following resources can be used to enrich or extend the instruction for pp. 368–376.

Literary Analysis
- **Selection Support Workbook:** Literary Analysis, p. 96

Reading
- **Reader's Companion**
- **English Learner's Companion**
- **Listening to Literature Audiocassettes,** Side 11 ■

- **Listening to Literature Audio CDs,** CD 8

Extension
- **Fine Art Transparencies, Volume 1,** Art Transparency 5 (Have students compare and contrast the pick-up game shown in the painting with the street games Cosby describes.) ■

■ **BLOCK SCHEDULING:** Resources marked with this symbol provide varied instruction during 90-minute blocks.

Young Brothers in the Hood, Tom McKinney

❸ ◄ **Critical Viewing** How does this painting help you picture the setting and the characters in Cosby's essay? **[Connect]**

❹

"But let's make 'em *think* he's the orange peel," I said, "an' let 'em think Albert's the manhole."

"Okay, Shorty," said Junior, "you go out ten steps an' then cut left behind the black Oldsmobile."

"I'll sorta go *in* it first to shake my man," said Shorty, "an' then, when he don' know where I am, you can hit me at the fender."

"Cool. An' Arnie, you go down to the corner of Locust an' fake takin' the bus. An' Cos, you do a zig out to the bakery. See if you can shake your man before you hit the rolls."

"Suppose I start a fly pattern to the bakery an' then do a zig out to the trash can," I said.

"No, they'll be expecting that."

❺ **Reading Check** Where do Cosby and his friends play football?

❸ ► Critical Viewing

Answer: The painting depicts two young boys, obviously friends, sitting on the stoop of a city dwelling. The painting captures the essence of an urban setting and also emphasizes the bond of friendship between youngsters like those described by Cosby.

❹ Background

Art

Young Brothers in the Hood, by Tom McKinney

This piece of art shows two young boys sitting on the stoop of a city apartment building. Discuss the following question:

- What details in the painting make it a good illustration for Cosby's personal narrative?
  Answer: The setting for the painting is urban; the boys' expressions and body positions indicate that they are friends or relations who enjoy each other's company. The boy on the left has a mischievous expression on his face, as Cosby might have had when responding to his mother's warnings about cars.

❺ Reading Check

Answer: They play in the street.

CUSTOMIZE INSTRUCTION FOR UNIVERSAL ACCESS

For English Learners

Invite students to play a quiz game using the selection vocabulary words. Ask the following questions; each is answered by one of the vocabulary words. "How would you feel if someone told you a story that you just could not believe?" "What word would you use to describe how you felt when you wanted a new CD very, very badly?" "What word would you use to describe a police officer who pretends to be a victim in order to flush out a criminal?" "If a snake were described as moving from side to side instead of straight ahead, what other word could you use to describe that movement?" "If you were reading a confusing story, what would you ask the teacher to give you?" (*skeptical, yearned, decoy, lateral, interpretation*)

PRETEACH

❻ Literary Analysis

Humorous Remembrance

- Remind students that a *humorous remembrance* is a story that emphasizes what is funny in a writer's past experience.
- Have students identify the things that prevented Cosby from being the great football player he wished to be.
  Answer: Cosby as a child was short and thin, and his hands were too small to catch a football on the run.
- Ask students what is amusing about the view of his childhood Cosby presents here.
  Answer: Cosby longed to run fast and gracefully, but instead staggered and more often than not dropped the ball when it was passed to him. He makes comparisons between catching the ball and catching a load of wet wash; he says he would have done better using a butterfly net.

❼ ▶Critical Viewing

Answer: Like Cosby and his friends, the stickball player has no real baseball bat or uniform.

---

❻ I spent most of my boyhood trying to catch passes with the easy grace of my heroes at Temple;[2] but easy grace was too hard for me. Because I was short and thin, my hands were too small to catch a football with arms extended on the run. Instead, I had to stagger backwards and smother the ball in my chest. How I yearned to grab the ball in my hands while striding smoothly ahead, rather than receiving it like someone who was catching a load of wet wash. Often, after a pass had bounced off my hands, I returned to the quarterback and glumly said, "Jeeze, Junior, I don' know what happened." He, of course, knew what had happened: he had thrown the ball to someone who should have been catching it with a butterfly net.

yearned (yurnd) *v.* longed for

Each of these street games began with a quick review of the rules: two-hand touch, either three or four downs, always goal-to-go, forward passing from anywhere, and no touchdowns called back because of traffic in motion. If a receiver caught a ball near an oncoming car while the defender was running for his life, the receiver had guts, and possibly a long excuse from school.

decoy (dē´ koi´) *n.* person used to lure others into a trap

I will never forget one particular play from those days when I was trying so hard to prove my manhood between the manholes. In the huddle, as Junior, our permanent quarterback, dropped to one knee to arrange the garbage offensively, I said, "Hey, Junior, make me a decoy on this one."

Pretending to catch the ball was what I did best.

"What's a decoy?" he said.

"Well, it's—"

"I ain't got time to learn. Okay, Eddie, you're the Dr Pepper cap an' you go deep toward New Jersey."

"An' I'll fool around short," I said.

"No, Cos, you fake goin' deep an' then buttonhook at the DeSoto. An' Harold, you do a zig out between 'em. *Somebody* get free."

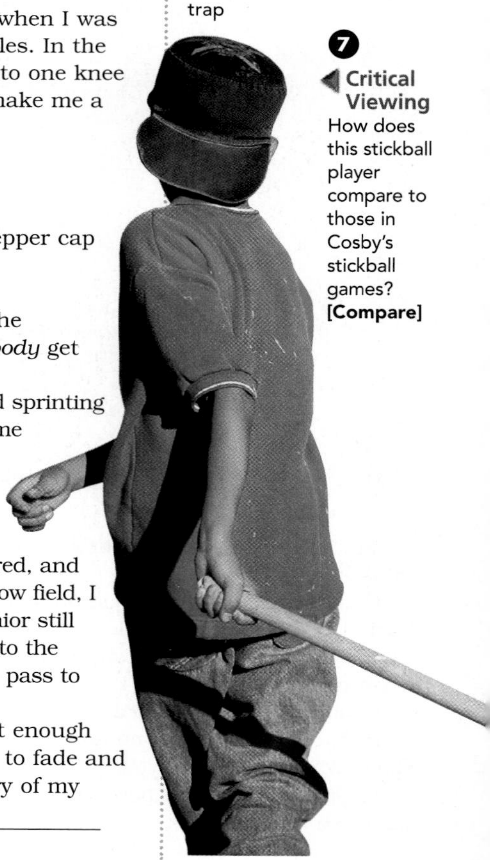

❼ ◀ **Critical Viewing** How does this stickball player compare to those in Cosby's stickball games? **[Compare]**

Moments later, the ball was snapped to him and I started sprinting down the field with my defender, Jody, who was matching me stride for stride. Wondering if I would be able to get free for a pass sometime within the next hour, I stopped at the corner and began sprinting back to Junior, whose arm had been cocked for about fifteen seconds, as if he'd been posing for a trophy. Since Eddie and Harold also were covered, and since running from scrimmage was impossible on that narrow field, I felt that this might be touch football's first eternal play: Junior still standing there long after Eddie, Harold, and I had dropped to the ground, his arm still cocked as he tried to find some way to pass to himself.

But unlimited time was what we had and it was almost enough for us. Often we played in the street until the light began to fade and the ball became a blur in the dusk. If there is one memory of my

---

2. Temple Temple University in Philadelphia, Pennsylvania.

childhood that will never disappear, it is a bunch of boys straining to find a flying football in the growing darkness of a summer night.

8 There were, of course, a couple of streetlamps on our field, but they were useful only if your pattern took you right up to one of them to make your catch. The rest of the field was lost in the night; and what an adventure it was to refuse to surrender to that night, to hear the quarterback cry "Ball!" and then stagger around in a kind of gridiron blindman's buff.

"Hey, you guys, dontcha think we should call the game?" said Harold one summer evening.

"Why do a stupid thing like that?" Junior replied.

"'Cause I can't see the ball."

"Harold, that don't make you special. Nobody can see the ball. But y' *know* it's up there."

And we continued to stagger around as night fell on Philadelphia and we kept looking for a football that could have been seen only on radar screens.

One day last year in a gym, I heard a boy say to his father, "Dad, what's a Spal*deen*?"

This shocking question left me depressed, for it is one thing not to know the location of the White House or the country that gave its name to Swiss cheese, but when a boy doesn't know what a Spal*deen* is, our educational system has failed. For those of you ignorant of basic American history, a Spal*deen* was a pink rubber ball with more bounce than can be imagined today. Baseball fans talk about the lively ball, but a lively baseball is a sinking stone compared to a Spal*deen*, which could be dropped from your eye level and bounce back there again, if you wanted to do something boring with it. And when you connected with a Spal*deen* in stickball, you put a pink rocket in orbit, perhaps even over the house at the corner and into another neighborhood, where it might gently bop somebody's mother sitting on a stoop.

9 I love to remember all the street games that we could play with a Spal*deen*. First, of course, was stickball, an organized version of which is also popular and known as baseball. The playing field was the same rectangle that we used for football: it was the first rectangular diamond. And for this game, we had outfield walls in which people happened to live and we had bases that lacked a certain uniformity: home and second were manhole covers, and first and third were the fenders of parked cars.

One summer morning, this offbeat infield caused a memorable interpretation of the official stickball rules. Junior hit a two-sewer shot and was running toward what should have been third when third suddenly drove away in first. While the bewildered Junior tried to arrive safely in what had become a twilight zone, Eddie took my throw from center field and tagged him out.

"I'm not out!" cried Junior in outrage. "I'm right here on third!"

And he did have a point, but so did Eddie, who replied, not without a certain logic of his own, "But third ain't there anymore."

Literary Analysis
Humorous Remembrance Which details about playing at night are exaggerated?

interpretation (in tʉr′ prə tā′ shən) *n.* explanation

10 **Reading Check**
What is the one memory Cosby has of his childhood that he says will never disappear?

8 Literary Analysis

Humorous Remembrance

- Remind students that when they are trying to entertain their friends with a personal story, they often exaggerate for humorous effect.
- Ask students the Literary Analysis question on p. 371: Which details about playing at night are exaggerated?
  Answer: The darkness of evening play is exaggerated, as is the staggering around of the players in the dark.

9 Reading Strategy

Recognizing Situational Humor

- Remind students that *situational humor* arises from conditions that mix people, actions, and settings in funny and often improbable ways.

Monitor Progress Ask the class: What makes this situation—the bases' lack of "a certain uniformity"—humorous?
Answer: The image of a baseball field with two manhole-cover bases and two car-fender bases is ridiculous, and therefore amusing.

10 Reading Check

Answer: Cosby says he will never forget trying to find a flying football in the dark.

CUSTOMIZE INSTRUCTION FOR UNIVERSAL ACCESS

For Special Needs Students	For Less Proficient Readers	For Gifted/Talented Students
Students might benefit by reading along with the story selection on **Listening to Literature Audiocassette,** Side 11. Others may wish to read aloud some of the scenes to show the different kinds of voices needed for the dialogue.	Suggest that students use the Humorous Remembrance transparency on p. 48 of **Literary Analysis and Reading Transparencies** to help them see the difference between the way Cosby remembers his childhood play and the way a writer who was not a humorist would remember it.	Bill Cosby says, "I love to remember all the street games that we could play with a Spaldeen." Have students invent a street game they could play with a Spaldeen or any other kind of ball. Have them construct a diagram of the playing field, describe the purpose of the game, and develop a set of rules.

11 Reading Strategy

Recognizing Situational Humor

- Point out to students that what is funny to one person is not necessarily humorous to someone else.
- Ask students the Reading Strategy question on p. 372: What do you find most humorous in this passage? Possible response: Students may cite the first base driving away, Fat Albert's struggling just to make first when he had hit at least a double, or the right field throw hitting the postman.

ASSESS

Answers for p. 372

Review and Assess

1. Some students might appreciate the adventure of playing these sports under difficult circumstances; others might prefer a more orderly setup.
2. **(a)** He regrets not being taller or stronger. **(b)** Cosby could not catch passes with the easy grace of the players at Temple University.
3. **(a)** Junior knew how to drop to one knee in the huddle and diagram plays with trash. **(b)** Yes, because even though the players often argue with Junior, he always has a reason for calling a play the way he does.
4. **(a)** Cosby exaggerates the effect of hitting a Spaldeen in order to show how much fun it was to play with such a lively ball. **(b)** No, Cosby is exaggerating to add humor.
5. **(a)** Children need more than anything else to play and pretend. **(b)** Most students will agree that children need opportunities to play.

In those games, our first base was as mobile as our third; and it was a floating first that set off another lively division of opinion on the day that Fat Albert hit a drive over the spot from which first base had just driven away, leaving us without a good part of the right field foul line.

11 The hit would have been at least a double for anyone with movable legs, but Albert's destination was first, where the play might have been close had the right fielder hit the cutoff man instead of a postman.

"Foul ball!" cried Junior, taking a guess that happened to be in his favor.

"You're out of your mind, Junior!" cried Albert, an observation that often was true, no matter what Junior was doing. "It went right over the fender!"

"What fender?"

"If that car comes back, you'll see it's got a fender," said Albert, our automotive authority.

However, no matter how many pieces of our field drove away, nothing could ever take away the sweetness of having your stick connect with a Spal*deen* in a magnificent *whoppp* and drive it so high and far that it bounced off a window with a view of New Jersey and then caromed back to the street, where Eddie would have fielded it like Carl Furillo[3] had he not backed into a coal chute.

3. **Carl Furillo** (kärl fər il′ ō) baseball player for the Brooklyn Dodgers in the 1950s.

Reading Strategy
Recognizing Situational Humor What do you find most humorous in this passage?

Review and Assess

Thinking About the Selection

1. **Respond:** Would you enjoy playing stickball or football by the rules Bill Cosby describes? Explain.
2. **(a) Recall:** What does Cosby regret about his physical size during his boyhood? **(b) Compare and Contrast:** How was Cosby like and unlike his heroes at Temple University?
3. **(a) Recall:** Why was Junior always the quarterback for the neighborhood football games? **(b) Analyze:** Was Junior's method of calling plays successful? Explain.
4. **(a) Recall:** How does Cosby describe the experience of connecting with a Spaldeen? **(b) Interpret:** Does Cosby really mean what he says about hitting a Spaldeen? Explain.
5. **(a) Speculate:** What does Cosby mean when he says "The essence of childhood . . . is play"? **(b) Evaluate:** Do you agree with this idea? Explain.

Bill Cosby

(b. 1937)

The son of a navy cook and a domestic worker, Bill Cosby grew up in the housing projects of Philadelphia. Although he left high school to join the navy, he earned a diploma through a correspondence course. During the 1960s, he performed stand-up comedy in Philadelphia and soon became nationally famous.

Cosby has won awards for his television shows and his books, which include *Fatherhood* (1986) and *Time Flies* (1987).

ENRICHMENT: Further Reading

Other Works by Bill Cosby

Fatherhood
Time Flies
Childhood

Take It to the Net

Visit www.phschool.com for more information on Bill Cosby.

12

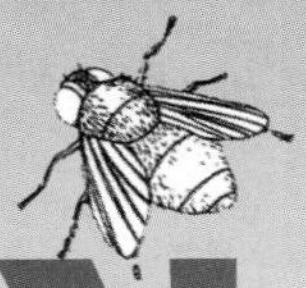

Fly Away

Ralph Helfer

"I need 5,000 trained flies. Can you do it? Yes or no!" The voice at the other end of the phone was insistent.

"Well, I . . ."

"Of course you can't, Helfer. *Nobody* can. Look, I told the director I'd make a couple of calls. So, now I have. The answer is obviously NO!"

"I *can* do it," I said, fitting my sentence neatly in between my caller's constant jabber, "but I'll need a couple of days."

13 The voice on the phone was silent a moment. Then: "You're kidding."

"No, really. Two days, and I'll be ready. What do they have to do?"

"There's this artificial, dead-looking 'thing' lying on the ground in the forest. The director wants thousands of flies to be crawling on it without flying away."

"Okay," I said. "Consider it done."

"No, wait. Then, he wants them *all* to fly away, on command—but not before."

"Okay, no problem," I said. "Two days."

"Wait. Did you hear what I said? They can't leave until he says okay. How are you going to keep them there, let alone have them fly away when he wants them to??"

"I'll stick each of their 20,000 legs in glue! Look, don't worry. Call me later, and I'll give you the figure. 'Bye."

Sometimes affection training was not the only answer. One could not "pet" a fly or earn its respect. I knew I would have to resort to the laws of nature for the answer to this one. I'd had the opportunity to

Reading Strategy
Recognizing Situational Humor How does the caller's attitude create humor?

14 **✓Reading Check**
What does the director's assistant ask Helfer to do?

12 About the Selection

This personal narrative uses humor to recall a memorable incident in the life of expert animal trainer Ralph Helfer. As Helfer tells how he managed to train 5,000 flies for a movie, he also reveals his love for and pride in his work.

13 Reading Strategy

Recognize Situational Humor

- Remind students that *situational humor* mixes people, setting, and events in funny ways.
- Ask students the Reading Strategy question on p. 373: How does the caller's attitude create humor?
  Answer: The caller's frantic intensity and pessimism is in comical contrast to the narrator's calm confidence.

Monitor Progress Ask students what is unexpected about the exchange between the caller and the trainer.
Possible response: Students may suggest that, based on what they have learned about Helfer, they expected the caller to want a trained dog, horse, or tiger, rather than 5,000 trained flies. The idea of training flies, or any insect, is humorous in itself.

14 ✓Reading Check

Answer: The director's assistant wants Helfer to provide 5,000 trained flies for a movie scene.

CUSTOMIZE INSTRUCTION FOR UNIVERSAL ACCESS

For Less Proficient Readers	For English Learners	For Advanced Readers
Have students work in pairs to read aloud the conversation between Helfer and the assistant director. Have them note the different tones of voice—the assistant director is excitable, almost hysterical, while Helfer is calm and reasonable. Help students to see that some of the situational humor comes from this contrast.	Help students figure out the antecedents for the pronoun referents on this page. Write the following on the board with the specified words underlined and ask students to identify the antecedent for each: "I can do it, . . . "They can't leave until he says okay."	Invite students to do some research into the training of animals for film work. Who are some of the trainers? What are the titles of some recent movies with animal scenes? Why might real animals be needed less and less in today's film community? Ask students to present some of their findings to the class.

15 ▶ **Critical Viewing**

Answer: Students may point out that animals can be uncooperative, unpredictable, and even dangerous when they are taken out of their natural habitat; they might grow even more anxious when confronted by the strange surroundings of a movie set.

16 Reading Strategy

Recognizing Situational Humor

- Ask students if anything about the information on this page surprised them.
  Possible response: Students may suggest that they had no idea that controlling thousands of flies, without hurting them, could be accomplished in a scientific manner.
- Ask students the Reading Strategy question on p. 374: Why are the workers on the movie set making jokes? Do they expect Helfer to be successful?
  Answer: The workers obviously think the situation is impossible and they are waiting to see Helfer make a fool of himself.

work with various insects in the past. But *5,000!* I hoped I hadn't bitten off more than I could chew.

I went to work, first converting an old box in which we'd been keeping crickets (we raised them to feed to the tarantulas). The box was about three feet high by two feet square. Patching up a few holes, I scrubbed it clean, fixed a crooked door, and set it inside the snake room.

The next day I visited a good friend of mine, Professor Jonathan Ziller, an entomologist and researcher. His work area consisted of twenty to thirty lab-type cages made of fine-mesh wire. Each contained a different species of insect. Over a cup of coffee, I told him of my needs. We walked over to a cage that was being heated by a special infrared lamp. Inside I could see massive swarms of maggots—fly larvae, ready to be hatched into their next stage. As I stood there, the professor calculated the exact time when they would become flies. As his watch struck the "birthing" time, thousands of flies left their maggot bodies and were suddenly airborne, buzzing about the cage.

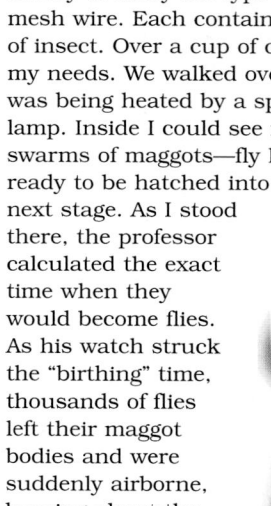

15 ▲ **Critical Viewing** What other challenges, like having flies act on cue, can you think of that might be faced by people in the film industry who work with animals? **[Speculate]**

We both agreed that these flies, an unusually large type that resembled the horsefly, would be perfect. An added plus was the fact that they were all hybrid, incapable of breeding. Hence, in releasing them I would not be running the risk of upsetting the natural balance of the environment.

The professor gave me a batch of fly larvae, which he'd calculated would hatch on the morning of the shoot, along with a vial of a special, harmless tranquilizer in a gas capsule. The gas would be released when the tip of the cigarette-sized plastic tube was broken. With the vial set inside the fly box, all the flies could be put to sleep within seconds. Once the gas had dissipated in a matter of moments, the flies would awaken. The tranquilizer was, of course, harmless to people. A handshake later, I was off, gently carrying my brood with me.

16 On the morning of the shoot, all the flies hatched right on schedule. I loaded up and headed for the studio location. When I arrived, I was greeted by a crew of disbelievers with tongue-in-cheek attitudes. Bets and jokes were being made in every direction, all in good-natured fun.

Reading Strategy
Recognizing Situational Humor Why are the workers on the movie set making jokes? Do they expect Helfer to be successful?

ENRICHMENT: Career Connection

Animal Trainers

Ralph Helfer trains animals to appear in movies. Another kind of animal training involves preparing animals to aid humans. Some trainers work with guide dogs that help people who are blind. Others teach dogs or monkeys to fetch and carry for people who are physically challenged. Trainers can also teach dogs to be "ears" for people who are deaf. These dogs alert their owners to noises, such as ringing telephones, car horns, sirens, or even a baby's cry. Animal trainers can teach animals to work in therapy programs for people who are physically or mentally challenged. Many nursing homes have instituted visitation programs in which cats, dogs, and other pets are brought in to interact with patients.

The director, a big, friendly sort, came over to me with a suspicious look in his eyes. "Is it true?"

"What?"

"That you can put 5,000 flies on something and they'll crawl around, but you can guarantee they won't fly right off?"

"It's true."

"Then when I tell you to let them go, they'll all fly away immediately?"

"Give or take a few."

"A few what?"

"Flies that won't fly away."

"If you pull this off, I'll double your fee," he said in disbelief.

"Ready whenever you are," I said, and headed for my fly house.

The camera was set. The "dead thing" turned out to be a special-effects monster baby that had supposedly died a while back and was now to be swarming with flies. Somebody was to walk by, and the flies would then have to fly away.

Everything was ready.

The skeptical assistant director yelled for the "fly man." One of my trainers and I carried the fly house over and set it near the camera. The loud buzzing of an enormous number of flies was obvious. Sheets of heavy paper prevented anyone from seeing into the box.

"Now, Ralph, I'll roll the camera whenever you say—okay?" asked the director.

17 "Sure, but everything has to be ready. I've only got 10,042 flies—just enough for two shots."

His look told me he wasn't sure whether I was putting him on or not.

"10,042—really!" he mumbled, and walked over to the camera.

With everything set, I opened the small door of the fly house. Hiding the gas capsule in the palm of my hand and reaching inside, I broke it open, closed the door, and waited for fifteen seconds. To everybody's amazement, the buzzing stopped. Next, I opened the door and scooped out three or four handfuls of flies. I shook them out as one would when counting a pound of peanuts. Putting the little sleeping flies all over the "body," I began to dramatically count the last few: "Five-thousand twenty, five-thousand twenty-one, five-thousand twenty-one . . . that makes it half!"

I told everyone to hold still, then I gave the flies a verbal cue: "Okay guys—Jack, Bill, Mary—come on, up and at 'em!"

Slowly the flies started to awaken, then move around. In a few moments the whole mass of them was swarming all over the "thing," but they were still too drowsy to fly, as my professor friend had told me they would be.

"Okay, roll!" yelled the director. The camera rolled on the fly swarm, and I shot a look at the crew. They appeared to be in shock. Then, having gotten enough footage, the director shouted, "Okay, Ralph, *now!*"

My great moment.

"Okay, group," I said to the flies. "Get ready: on the count of three, all of you take off."

skeptical (skep´ ti kəl) *adj.* doubting; questioning

Literary Analysis
Humorous Remembrance
Helfer says he has exactly 10,042 flies. What makes this statement funny?

18 **Reading Check**
What does Helfer put in the fly house before scooping out the flies?

CUSTOMIZE INSTRUCTION FOR UNIVERSAL ACCESS

For Less Proficient Readers	For Gifted/Talented Students
Students may benefit from viewing the film "Commercial Beekeeping" on Tape 2 of **Interest Grabber Video.** When they have finished watching the tape, ask them to respond in one of these ways: illustrate something of interest that they saw on the tape; write a short article based on the information they learned; speculate on how "training" bees might be different from "training" flies.	Ask students to compete in small groups to conceive a similar movie stunt involving unlikely animals. The groups should imagine a trick, devise a training method, and ensure the health and safety of all the creatures. Have the groups compare their plans.

17 Literary Analysis
Humorous Remembrance

- Ask students how Helfer uses his special knowledge to tease others.
  Answer: Helfer does something that few people know anything about, which makes it possible for him to get laughs at the expense of others' ignorance.
- Ask students to reread the exchange between Helfer and the director at the top of the page. How does Helfer use the large number of flies to tease the director?
  Answer: When the director asks if the flies will all fly away immediately on cue, Helfer says "Give or take a few." He is teasing the director, who still does not believe Helfer can pull off this stunt.

Monitor Progress Ask students the Literary Analysis question on p. 375: Helfer says he has exactly 10,042 flies. What makes the statement funny?
Answer: The number is so large, so specific, and so unconfirmable that it is funny, which is what Helfer intends.

18 Reading Check

Answer: Helfer releases a tranquilizing gas in the fly house.

ASSESS

Answers for p. 376

Review and Assess

1. Students may respond that they had not known that the hatching of flies and their activity could be so well controlled.
2. **(a)** He would take newly hatched flies to the shoot, and tranquilize them for a few minutes with a harmless gas; the flies would fly away when the gas wore off. **(b)** He is experienced and also knows an expert on flies. He is under little pressure, because no one believes the trick is possible.
3. **(a)** He has tranquilized the flies and they will not wake up immediately. **(b)** He is pretending that he has really trained the flies and that they understand his instructions.
4. **(a)** The director is amazed and amused. **(b)** He explicitly states he would work with Helfer whenever he needed anything trained.
5. Students may agree that it would not benefit Helfer to have told the director how he performed the fly trick, because his secret knowledge will make him more desirable to directors in the future.
6. Skills that are needed include knowledge of and respect for animals, kindness, resourcefulness, patience, attention to detail, and ability to analyze a situation quickly.
7. **(a)** Students may suggest that live effects are less and less needed because of the advent of computer-generated images. **(b)** Students may note that using computer effects means fewer animals would be put in danger. Some may suggest that the audience's fun in figuring out how the filmmakers create an illusion would be lost.

The crew, absolutely bug-eyed (forgive the pun), was hypnotized.

"One," I counted. They looked from the flies to me.

"Two."

"Three!" I yelled, clapping my hands and stamping my foot at the same time. Five thousand twenty-one flies flew up, up, around and around. The camera hummed until the director, rousing himself from his amazed state, said, "Cut!"

The entire crew was silent for a moment, and then they burst into applause and delighted laughter.

"You did it, you really did it!" said the director, slapping me heartily on the back. "I'm not even going to ask you how. I don't even want to know. But if I ever need a trained *anything*, you're the man I'll call!"

Straight-faced, I said, "Well, actually, I've recently trained 432 flies to form a chorus line on my arm, and on cue they all kick a leg at the same time."

The director, poker-faced, looked straight at me. "Which one?" he asked.

"Which one what?"

"Which leg?"

"The left one, of course!"

We all broke up laughing and headed home.

Review and Assess

Thinking About the Selection

1. **Respond:** What did you find most interesting about Ralph Helfer's remembrance? Explain.
2. **(a) Recall:** What plan does Helfer develop to make the flies do what is needed for the movie? **(b) Draw Conclusions:** Why do you think he feels comfortable making the deal?
3. **(a) Recall:** How does Helfer know that the flies will not fly away as soon as they are released? **(b) Infer:** Why does he speak to the flies as if they understand him?
4. **(a) Recall:** What is the director's reaction to the fly stunt? **(b) Infer:** Would he want to work with Helfer again? Why?
5. **Assess:** Would it have benefited Helfer to tell the director how he did the fly trick? Explain.
6. **Speculate:** What specific skills are needed to be a good animal trainer? Explain.
7. **(a) Evaluate:** Do you think Helfer's live effects are still needed in the computer age? **(b) Support:** What would be gained or lost by using only computers for special effects?

Ralph Helfer

(b. 1937)

Ralph Helfer, one of the world's leading animal trainers, has worked in more than 5,000 movies and television programs. In his book *The Beauty of the Beasts* (1989), Helfer describes being "clawed by lions, attacked by bears, bitten by poisonous snakes, and nearly suffocated by pythons."

Since instituting affection training, however, Helfer has been bite-free. He and his trained animals have won 18 PATSY awards for the best animal performances on screen.

ASSESSMENT PRACTICE: Reading Comprehension

Predict Outcomes (For more practice, see Test Preparation Workbook, p. 24.)

Use the following sample item to demonstrate for students how to predict an outcome based on information in a passage:

> I needed 5,000 "trained" flies by Monday. I'd have to work fast. I knew affection training was not the answer here. I'd have to resort to the laws of nature—make the flies' natural tendencies work for me. But first, I needed to find out what those natural tendencies were.

The narrator is most likely to—

A observe flies over a period of a month.
B visit a scientist who knows about the behavior of flies.
C use affection training on the flies.
D buy 5,000 trained flies from a friend.

The narrator says he is going to find out what flies' natural tendencies are, making *B* the correct choice.

Review and Assess

Literary Analysis

Humorous Remembrance

1. Use a chart like the one below to record details that identify "Go Deep to the Sewer" as a **humorous remembrance.**

2. How does Cosby give readers the sense that they are part of the action as they move through the story?
3. (a) What overall impression of his work does Helfer communicate in his remembrance? (b) Which humorous details make the writing entertaining?

Comparing Literary Works

4. (a) Review each selection and compare the serious elements or ideas in each of these humorous remembrances. (b) Which selection conveyed the more serious ideas? Explain.
5. Cosby's story strings together experiences of childhood play. Helfer's memoir focuses on one memorable job. Which piece do you find more appealing? Why?

Reading Strategy

Recognizing Situational Humor

6. How does Cosby use his **situation**—being obliged to play football and stickball in the street—to humorous advantage?
7. Helfer pretends to count the sleeping flies. Why is this funny?
8. How does the audience's reaction to Helfer's achievement add to the situation's humor?

Extend Understanding

9. **Cultural Connection:** Do you think Cosby's story could only be appreciated by people who have lived in a city? Explain.

Quick Review

A **humorous remembrance** is a story that communicates what is funny about the writer's past experiences.

Situational humor arises from conditions that mix people, actions, and settings in funny and often improbable ways.

Take It to the Net

www.phschool.com

Take the interactive self-test online to check your understanding of the selection.

Answers for p. 377

Review and Assess

1. Details: Playing in the street where they could be hit by cars; diagramming plays with orange peels and gum; running a decoy play that never ends; playing football at night when no one could see the ball.
2. Cosby makes readers feel they are part of the action by describing it through the dialogue of the characters.
3. **(a)** Helfer communicates pride and amusement at the cleverness of his work. **(b)** Students may cite Helfer's comic showmanship in "counting" the flies and issuing commands to them, as well as the amazed reactions of his audience.
4. **(a)** Serious elements in the Cosby selection include the boys' poverty, the potential danger of playing in the street, and the pain children feel when they do not measure up to their own expectations. Serious elements in the Helfer selection include his references to affection training with animals and the responsibility he has not to interfere with the natural balance of the environment. **(b)** Some students may cite the Cosby selection because it concerns people rather than insects.
5. Some students may prefer Cosby's essay because it resonate with their own experiences. Others may prefer Helfer's essay because the idea of trained flies is appealingly bizarre.
6. Cosby exploits the humor of incorporating trash cans, sewer covers, even moving cars into a ball game.
7. It is preposterous that Helfer could actually keep track of thousands of flies.
8. Because the reader knows Helfer's secret, the audience's awe and amazement seem humorously out of proportion.
9. Students may suggest that Cosby's story could be appreciated by anyone who has enjoyed playing outdoors as a child.

EXTEND

Answers for p. 378

❶ Vocabulary Development

Concept Development: Sports Jargon

1. *slam dunk*—a forceful, sure shot in basketball. Any emphatic or sure-to-succeed action could be a slam dunk.
2. *punt*—a kick that gives the football to the opposing team, a "wait until next time" tactic. Any action that gives up responsibility or initiative to someone else could be a punt.
3. *on deck*—ready; waiting to take one's turn, particularly a batter in baseball. Anyone who is "next in line" could be on deck.
4. *huddle*—a close gathering of a team's players in football to receive instructions. Any group gathered to talk or plan might form a huddle.

Spelling Strategy

1. wonderfully
2. civilly
3. correct
4. correct

Concept Development: Analogies

1. c
2. c
3. b
4. a
5. c

❷ Grammar

1. D.O.: play (forget)
2. D.O.: pattern (start)
3. D.O.: that (expecting)
4. D.O.: camera (roll)
5. D.O.: batch (gave)

Writing Application

Jan caught the high pop fly. She threw the ball to second base. Sylvia tagged the runner who was caught off-base. The team made a double play.

Integrate Language Skills

❶ Vocabulary Development Lesson

Concept Development: Sports Jargon

Jargon is special language related to a particular activity, profession, sport, or art. Use a dictionary to find the meanings of the following sports terms. Then, explain how each term might be used in everyday speech.

1. slam dunk
2. punt
3. on deck
4. huddle

Spelling Strategy

When you add *-ly* to a word ending with a short vowel followed by an *l*, keep the final *l*. For example, *lateral* + *-ly*= *laterally*.

Identify the misspelled words in the following list and correct their spelling.

1. wonderfuly
2. civily
3. thoughtfully
4. politically

Concept Development: Analogies

Complete the following analogies by analyzing the word relationship in the first pair of words. Then, create the same relationship in the second pair by choosing the most suitable word.

1. forward : ahead :: lateral : __?__
   (a) nearby (b) quickly (c) sideways (d) far
2. dislike : like :: yearn : __?__
   (a) long for (b) realize (c) reject (d) behave
3. false : wrong :: decoy : __?__
   (a) duck (b) bait (c) coach (d) invite
4. seasoning : spice :: interpretation : __?__
   (a) version (b) behavior (c) satisfaction (d) play
5. prisoner : pardon :: skeptic : __?__
   (a) remedy (b) lightly (c) convince (d) enemy

❷ Grammar Lesson

Direct Objects

A **direct object** is the noun or pronoun that receives the action of a verb. You can determine whether a word is a direct object by asking *whom?* or *what?* after an action verb.

Examples:

Junior threw the *football* to Cosby. (threw *what?*)

He told *Albert* to pass the ball. (told *whom?*)

Junior devised elaborate *plans* for the team. (devised *what?*)

The boy asked his *father*. (asked *whom?*)

Practice In each sentence, identify the direct object and the verb whose action it completes.

1. I will never forget one particular play.
2. Suppose I start a fly pattern to the bakery.
3. "No," said Junior, "they'll be expecting that."
4. "Now, Ralph, I'll roll the camera whenever you say—okay?"
5. The professor gave me a batch of fly larvae.

Writing Application Write a short paragraph about a sports experience you have had. Try to include a direct object in every sentence. Then, underline each direct object.

WG *Prentice Hall Writing and Grammar Connection: Chapter 20, Section 3*

TEACHING RESOURCES

The following resources can be used to enrich or extend the instruction for pp. 378–379.

Vocabulary

Selection Support Workbook: Build Vocabulary, p. 93

Vocabulary and Spelling Practice Book (Use this booklet for skills enrichment.) ▪

Grammar

Selection Support Workbook: Build Grammar Skills, p. 94

Writing and Grammar, Gold Level, p. 434

Daily Language Practice Transparencies ▪

Writing

Writing and Grammar, Gold Level, p. 58 ▪

Writing and Grammar iText CD-ROM

▪ **BLOCK SCHEDULING:** Resources marked with this symbol provide varied instruction during 90-minute blocks.

❸ Writing Lesson

Humorous Personal Narrative

Choose a memorable experience and write a humorous narrative about it. Catch your readers' attention and help them anticipate the comedy in your writing. Use the essays by Cosby and Helfer as inspirations for your own brand of humor.

Prewriting Jot down details that you know will make your readers laugh. Focus on details that can be exaggerated for comic effect.

Drafting The best groundwork for any kind of narrative writing—especially a humorous narrative—is a strong introduction. A striking quotation is one of a number of things that will make a good start.

Model: Writing a Strong Introduction

The voice on the phone was insistent: "I need a dozen rabbits, and I need them now!"

An interesting quotation or a surprising observation can provide a strong introduction to a narrative.

Revising Review your draft to evaluate whether your introduction will make your readers want to read further. Then, check that your narrative maintains its humorous tone throughout.

WG *Prentice Hall Writing and Grammar Connection: Chapter 4, Section 3*

❹ Extension Activities

Listening and Speaking Bill Cosby's memoir originated as part of his stand-up comedy routine. Working with a partner, use a real or imagined incident from your own life or one you have seen in a book, movie, or television show as the basis for a brief **monologue.** Your partner can help you judge whether the incident has comic potential.

- Emphasize the humor of the situation.
- End the story in a satisfying way.

Use your partner's feedback to revise your monologue before presenting it to a small group of friends or classmates. **[Group Activity]**

Research and Technology Use books, magazines, reference materials, or online resources to do research about current methods of training animals. Focus on learning about the training methods used with two or three specific kinds of animals. Organize what you learn into a **visual report** using charts, graphs, or other appropriate visual aids. Share your findings with your class.

Take It to the Net www.phschool.com

Go online for an additional research activity using the Internet.

Lesson Support for p. 379

❸ Writing Lesson

- Model an opening to a humorous personal narrative by rereading the openings to Cosby's and Helfer's selections.
- Have students choose a humorous event from their past and determine whether they will start their account with a straight third-person narrative or a dialogue.
- Use the Writing Lesson to guide students in developing the introductions to their personal narratives.
- Use the Autobiographical Narrative rubric in **Performance Assessment and Portfolio Management,** p. 8, to evaluate students' introductions.

❹ Listening and Speaking

- Divide the class into pairs. Have each pair discuss the kind of comedy routine they would like to write and present.
- Have each pair try out routines on each other to test their humor content.
- Ask volunteer pairs to present their routines to the rest of the class.

CUSTOMIZE INSTRUCTION For Universal Access

To address different learning styles, use the activities suggested in the **Extension Activities** booklet, p. 24.

- For Bodily/Kinesthetic learners, use Activity 5.
- For Visual/Spatial learners, use Activity 6.
- For Interpersonal and Logical/Mathematical learners, use Activity 7.

ASSESSMENT RESOURCES

The following resources can be used to assess students' knowledge and skills.

Selection Assessment

- **Formal Assessment,** Selection Test, pp. 82–84
- **Open Book Test,** pp. 70–72
- **Got It! Assessment Videotapes,** Tape 2
- **Test Bank Software**

Take It to the Net

Visit www.phschool.com for self-tests and additional questions on the selections.

Writing Rubric

- **Performance Assess. and Portfolio Mgmt.,** p. 8

PRENTICE HALL ASSESSMENT SYSTEM

- **Workbook**
- **Skill Book**
- **Transparencies**
- **CD-ROM**

Lesson Objectives

1. To recognize differences in mood between two childhood memories
2. To compare and contrast two author's recollections of their childhood

Connections

In "Go Deep to the Sewer," Bill Cosby looks back with humor on some of the good times of his childhood. In "The Talk," by contrast, Gary Soto recalls a more poignant experience. As students read the two selections, ask them to think of situations in their own lives that are similar to both the happy and the bittersweet stories.

CONNECTIONS

Literature and Childhood

Memories of Youth

In "Go Deep to the Sewer," Bill Cosby captures the sights and sounds of the Philadelphia neighborhood where he grew up. His childhood, spent playing with colorful characters with nicknames like Fat Albert and Weasel, provided him with a uniquely humorous way of looking at the world. Cosby's comedy rings true because he can summon up his childhood with such clarity, reminding us of similar experiences we otherwise might have forgotten.

The writer Gary Soto also draws upon the memories of his childhood to provide inspiration for his writing. Soto grew up in the Mexican American community of Fresno, California, and his memories of childhood are sometimes bittersweet. As you read Soto's account, you may be struck by the difference in mood that Cosby and Soto bring to their vivid memories of childhood.

The Talk

Gary Soto

My best friend and I knew that we were going to grow up to be ugly. On a backyard lawn—the summer light failing west of the mulberry tree where the house of the most beautiful girl on the street stood—we talked about what we could do: shake the second-base dirt from our hair, wash our hands of frog smells and canal water, and learn to smile without showing our crooked teeth. We had to stop spitting when girls were looking and learn not to pile food onto a fork and into a fat cheek already churning hot grub.

We were twelve, with lean bodies that were beginning to grow in weird ways. First, our heads got large, but our necks wavered, frail as crisp tulips. The eyes stayed small as well, receding into pencil dots on each side of an unshapely nose that cast remarkable shadows when we turned sideways. It seemed that Scott's legs sprouted muscle and renegade veins, but his arms, blue with ink markings, stayed short and hung just below his waist. My gangly arms nearly touched my kneecaps. In this way, I was built for picking up grounders[1] and doing cartwheels, my arms swaying just inches from the summery grass.

We sat on the lawn, with the porch light off, waiting for the beautiful girl to turn on her bedroom light and read on her stomach with one leg stirring the air. This stirred us, and our dream was a clean dream of holding hands and airing out our loneliness by walking up and down the block.

When Scott asked whom I was going to marry, I said a brown girl from the valley. He said that he was going to marry a strawberry blonde who would enjoy Millerton Lake, dirty as it was. I said mine would like cats and the sea and would think nothing of getting up at night from a warm, restless bed and sitting in the yard under the icy stars. Scott said his wife would work for the first year or so, because he would go to trade school[2] in refrigeration. Since our town was made with what was left over after God made hell, there was money in air conditioning, he reasoned.

I said that while my wife would clean the house and stir pots of nice grub, I would drive a truck to my job as a carpenter, which would allow me to use my long arms. I would need only a stepladder to hand a fellow worker on the roof a pinch of nails. I could hammer,

receding (ri sēd′ ing) *v.* withdrawing; diminishing

renegade (ren′ ə gād′) *adj.* disloyal; traitorous

gangly (gaŋ′ glē) *adj.* thin, tall, and awkward; of lanky build

Thematic Connection
How do the boys' dreams of the future compare with their present-day realities?

1. **picking up grounders** catching balls as they bounce along the ground.
2. **trade school** school in which students specialize in learning one set of skills for a particular profession.

Memories of Youth

- Have students read Bill Cosby's story "Go Deep to the Sewer" before they read Gary Soto's "The Talk."
- Ask students to watch for details that set the bittersweet mood as they read "The Talk."

Thematic Connection

Possible response: The boys dream of the work they will do and the women they will marry. At present, they find themselves at a particularly awkward phase of adolescence (their bodies growing in "weird ways"), yearning for a girl beyond their reach.

"The Talk"

- Remind students to use the reading strategies featured in this unit as they read "The Talk."
- Have students read back or read ahead for greater understanding when they reach a point that they find confusing.
- Ask students to read between the lines by drawing on their own childhood experiences as they read.
- Point out that the story, though bittersweet, offers some smiles through situational humor.
- Remind students to question the characters' actions as they read.

saw, lift beams into place, and see the work I got done at the end of the day. Of course, she might like to work, and that would be okay, because then we could buy two cars and wave at each other if we should see the other drive by. In the evenings, we would drink Kool-Aid and throw a slipper at our feisty dog at least a hundred times before we went inside for a Pop-Tart and hot chocolate.

Scott said he would work hard too, but now and then he would find money on the street and the two of them could buy extra things like a second TV for the bedroom and a Doughboy swimming pool for his three kids. He planned on having three kids and a ranch house on the river, where he could dip a hand in the water, drink, and say, "Ahh, tastes good."

feisty (fīs′ tē) *adj.* full of spirit; energetic

But that would be years later. Now we had to do something about our looks. We plucked at the grass and flung it into each other's faces.

"Rotten luck," Scott said. "My arms are too short. Look at 'em."

"Maybe we can lift weights. This would make up for our looks," I said.

"I don't think so," Scott said, depressed. "People like people with nice faces."

He was probably right. I turned onto my stomach, a stalk of grass in my mouth. "Even if I'm ugly, my wife's going to be good-looking," I said. "She'll have a lot of dresses and I'll have more shirts than I have now. Do you know how much carpenters make?"

Then I saw the bedroom light come on and the beautiful girl walk into the room drying her hair with a towel. I nudged Scott's short arm and he saw what I saw. We flicked the stalks of grass, stood up, and walked over to the fence to look at her scrub her hair dry. She plopped onto the bed and began to comb it, slowly at first because it was tangled. With a rubber band, she tied it back, and picked up a book that was thick as a good-sized sandwich.

Scott and I watched her read a book, now both legs in the air and twined together, her painted toenails like red petals. She turned the pages slowly, very carefully, and now and then lowered her face into the pillow. She looked sad but beautiful, and we didn't know what to do except nudge each other in the heart and creep away to the front yard.

"I can't stand it anymore. We have to talk about this," Scott said.

"If I try, I think I can make myself better looking," I said. "I read an article about a girl whitening her teeth with water and flour."

So we walked up the street, depressed. For every step I took, Scott took two, his short arms pumping to keep up. For every time Scott said, "I think we're ugly," I said two times, "Yeah, yeah, we're in big trouble."

Gary Soto

(b. 1952)

Gary Soto was not a person who could accurately predict what he would be when he grew up. Making a living as a writer did not occur to him in a house where reading was not encouraged. In college, after a brief flirtation with geography, he discovered the allure of writing. Soto went on to write several award-winning novels, short stories, and books of poetry. Much of his writing has been inspired by his childhood in the Mexican American community of Fresno, California.

Connecting Literature and Childhood

1. What does the girl in the window seem to represent for the two young boys?
2. What types of character traits can you infer from the boys' choice of future careers?
3. How does the humor differ in Cosby's and Soto's recollections of their childhoods?
4. How might their stories have been written differently if Cosby and Soto had written them as children?

Answers

Connecting Literature and Childhood

1. The girl seems to represent beauty and the kind of life that is just out of the boys' reach. Merely looking at her causes the boys to think about their futures.
2. The boys seem prepared to work hard at a physical trade to be good providers for their families. They probably drew their strong work ethic and vocational plans from observing the men of their community.
3. Cosby's humor uses broad exaggeration and makes light of or ignores the unpleasant aspects of being poor. Soto also makes abundant use of exaggeration, but includes less pleasant feelings of being young and poor: insecurity, awkward physical appearance, unreachable ideals.
4. If the authors had written their stories as children, the stories would be more factual, emphasize different details, and lack the insights and tone added by the adult perspective.

An Entomological Study of Apartment 4A

Lesson Objectives and CA Correlations

1. **To analyze and respond to literary elements**
   - Literary Analysis: Feature Article **R 3.8**
   - Connecting Literary Elements: Main Idea
2. **To read, comprehend, analyze, and critique nonfiction**
   - Reading Strategy: Establishing a Purpose for Reading
   - Reading Check questions
   - Review and Assess questions
   - Assessment Practice (ATE)
3. **To develop word analysis skills, fluency, and systematic vocabulary**
   - Vocabulary Development Lesson: Greek Prefix: *micro-* **R 1.1**
4. **To understand and apply written and oral language conventions**
   - Spelling Strategy
   - Grammar Lesson: Indirect Objects **LC 1.3**
5. **To understand and apply appropriate writing and research strategies**
   - Writing Lesson: Letter to an Expert **W 2.5**
   - Extension Activity: Entomological Study **W 1.3**
6. **To understand and apply listening and speaking strategies**
   - Extension Activity: Examining Advertisements **LS 1.8**

STEP-BY-STEP TEACHING GUIDE	PACING GUIDE
PRETEACH	
Motivate Students and Provide Background	
Use the Motivation activity (ATE p. 384)	5 min.
Read and discuss the Preview material and Background information (SE/ATE p. 384) **A**	5 min.
Introduce the Concepts	
Introduce the Literary Analysis and Reading Strategy (SE/ATE p. 385) **A**	15 min.
Pronounce the vocabulary words and read their definitions (SE p. 385)	5 min.
TEACH	
Monitor Comprehension	
Informally monitor comprehension by circulating while students read independently or in groups **A**	20 min.
Monitor students' comprehension with the Reading Check notes (SE/ATE pp. 387, 389)	as students read
Develop vocabulary with Vocabulary notes (SE pp. 386, 389, 390; ATE p. 386)	as students read
Develop Understanding	
Develop students' understanding of feature articles with Literary Analysis annotations (SE p. 388; ATE pp. 388, 389) **A**	10 min.
Develop students' ability to establish a purpose for reading with the Reading Strategy annotations (SE pp. 387, 388; ATE pp. 387, 388)	10 min.
ASSESS	
Assess Mastery	
Assess students' mastery of the Reading Strategy and Literary Analysis by having them answer the Review and Assess questions (SE/ATE p. 391)	20 min.
Use one or more of the print and media Assessment Resources (ATE p. 393) **A**	up to 50 min.
EXTEND	
Apply Understanding	
Have students complete the Vocabulary Development Lesson and the Grammar Lesson (SE p. 392) **A**	20 min.
Apply students' knowledge of levels of formality using the Writing Lesson (SE p. 393) **A**	45 min.
Apply students' understanding of the selection using one or more of the Extension Activities (SE p. 393)	20–90 min.

A **ACCELERATED INSTRUCTION:**
Use the strategies and activities identified with an **A**.

UNIVERSAL ACCESS
● = Below Level Students
▲ = On-Level Students
■ = Above Level Students

Time and Resource Manager

Reading Level: Challenging
Average Number of Instructional Days: 4

RESOURCES		
PRINT	**TRANSPARENCIES**	**TECHNOLOGY**
• **Beyond Literature,** Cross-Curricular Connection: Science, p. 25 ▲ ■		• **Interest Grabber Video,** Tape 2 ● ▲ ■
• **Selection Support Workbook:** ● ▲ ■ Literary Analysis, p. 100 Reading Strategy, p. 99 Build Vocabulary, p. 97	• **Literary Analysis and Reading Transparencies,** pp. 49 and 50 ● ▲ ■	
		• **Listening to Literature** ● ▲ ■ Audiocassettes, Side 11 Audio CDs, CD 8
• **Literatura en español** ● ▲ • **Literary Analysis for Enrichment** ■		
• **Formal Assessment:** Selection Test, pp. 85–87 ● ▲ ■ • **Open Book Test,** pp. 73–75 ● ▲ ■ • **Performance Assessment and Portfolio Management,** p. 9 ● ▲ ■ • PRENTICE HALL ASSESSMENT SYSTEM ● ▲ ■	• PRENTICE HALL ASSESSMENT SYSTEM ● ▲ ■ Skills Practice Answers and Explanations on Transparencies	• **Test Bank Software** ● ▲ ■ • **Got It! Assessment Videotapes,** Tape 2 ● ▲
• **Selection Support Workbook:** ● ▲ ■ Build Grammar Skills, p. 98 • **Writing and Grammar,** Gold Level ● ▲ ■ • **Extension Activities,** p. 25 ● ▲ ■	• **Daily Language Practice Transparencies** ● ▲ • **Writing Models and Graphic Organizers on Transparencies,** p. 53 ● ▲ ■	• **Writing and Grammar iText CD-ROM** ● ▲ ■ *Take It to the Net* www.phschool.com

BLOCK SCHEDULING: Use one 90-minute class period to preteach the selection and have students read it. Use a second 90-minute class period to assess students' mastery of skills and have them complete one of the Extension Activities.

PRETEACH

Step-by-Step Teaching Guide for pp. 384–385

Motivation

Interest students in the selection by asking, "What is the most extraordinary bug you have ever seen?" Ask what size and color the bug was, how it behaved, and what else made it fascinating, "gross," or annoying. Then ask students why they think some people fear or are disgusted by bugs, while others find them fascinating or fun.

Interest Grabber Video

As an alternative, play "All About Bugs" on Tape 2 to engage student interest.

1 Background

Science is very particular about the use of words and names. Referring to a spider as a *bug* or an *insect,* which many people do, is worse than calling a cat a dog. At least cats and dogs are both mammals. Insects are six-legged animals such as flies, ants, bees, and butterflies. Spiders, scorpions, mites, and ticks—all of which have eight legs—are not insects but arachnids. Insects also include true bugs, which, as Volk points out in her article, "have a modified beak-like mouth." True bugs have a mouth with a long feeding tube, a pair of thin, delicate back wings, and a pair of front wings that cross and overlap. Some examples are bedbugs, aphids, and water bugs.

Prepare to Read

An Entomological Study of Apartment 4A

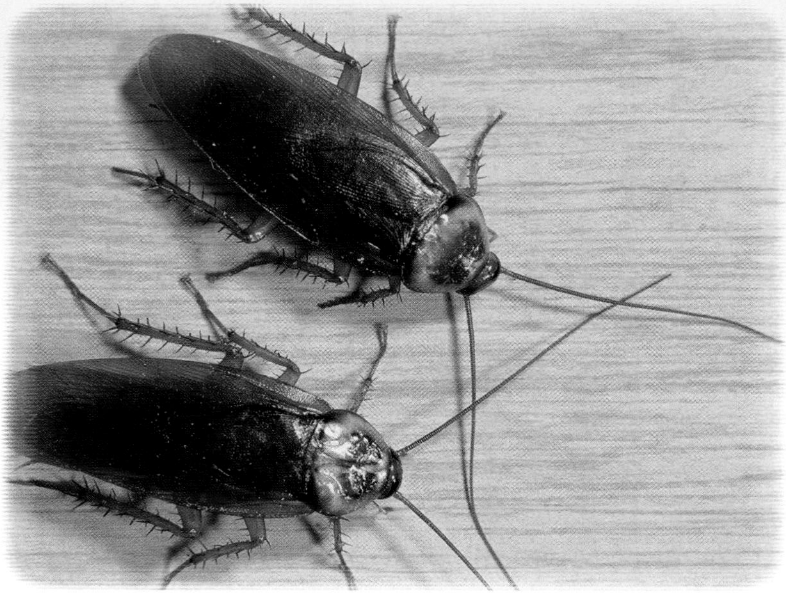

Take It to the Net

Visit www.phschool.com for interactive activities and instruction related to "An Entomological Study of Apartment 4A," including

- background
- graphic organizers
- literary elements
- reading strategies

Preview

Connecting to the Literature

Often, we are fascinated by creatures that repel us. Even if you would rather not look at that many-legged thing that just scurried under the stove, you may still want to know what it is. This natural curiosity inspired writer Patricia Volk to collect the bugs she found in her apartment and take them to an expert for identification.

1 Background

In everyday speech, the words *insect* and *bug* are used for all sorts of pests, but no entomologist, like Louis Sorkin in this article, would use these terms loosely. An entomologist studies insects—their behavior, their eating habits, and the differences among the dozens of species that are often smaller than a human fingernail.

TEACHING RESOURCES

The following resources can be used to enrich or extend the instruction for pp. 384–385.

Interest Grabber Video, Tape 2

Background

Beyond Literature, p. 25

Take It to the Net

Visit www.phschool.com for background and hotlinks for "An Entomological Study of Apartment 4A."

Literary Analysis

Literary Analysis and Reading Transparencies, Feature Article, p. 50

Reading

Selection Support: Reading Strategy, p. 100; Build Vocabulary, p. 97

Literary Analysis and Reading Transparencies, Set a Purpose for Reading, p. 49

BLOCK SCHEDULING: Resources marked with this symbol provide varied instruction during 90-minute blocks.

❷ Literary Analysis

Feature Article

A **feature article** is a newspaper or magazine story written to entertain readers or to provide information on a subject of human interest. Such an article may be designed to evoke an emotional response to its subject's achievements or problems. One way a writer can evoke a strong response from readers is by sharing a personal experience. In this excerpt, note how Patricia Volk personalizes a common problem.

> A black crawly thing with more legs than the Rockettes had staked out the north bedroom wall . . . and a bug as shiny as patent leather had moved into the water gauge of our electric coffee maker.

Notice how Volk's subject matter entertains while informing you.

Connecting Literary Elements

A well-written article holds your attention because it never wanders far from its main idea. The **main idea** is the central or underlying point of an article. The fact that every sentence in "An Entomological Study of Apartment 4A" is related to the writer's investigation of insects and bugs shapes the article and gives it impact. By the end of the article, Volk reveals the main idea and the insights it generates.

❸ Reading Strategy

Establishing a Purpose for Reading

To get the most out of what you read, **establish a purpose** for reading and then read to achieve this purpose. Your purpose may be

- to discover something new or to gather information for a report; if so, focus on obtaining useful facts.
- simply to enjoy reading; if so, look for fascinating details and descriptions.

Set a purpose for reading this selection and use a chart like this one to jot down notes that will help fulfill your purpose.

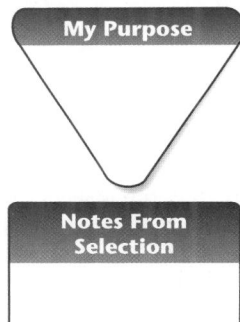

My Purpose

Notes From Selection

Vocabulary Development

microcosms (mī´ krō käz´əms) *n.* little worlds (p. 386)

metaphors (met´ə fôrz) *n.* ways of speaking of things as though they were something else (p. 386)

poignant (poin´ yənt) *adj.* drawing forth compassion; moving (p. 389)

malevolence (mə lev´ ə ləns) *n.* bad or evil feelings or intentions (p. 389)

immortalized (i môr´ tə līzd) *v.* given lasting fame (p. 390)

❷ Literary Analysis

Feature Article

- Tell students that the selection they are about to read is a feature article, written both to entertain and inform.
- Provide examples of feature articles from a daily newspaper, and help students distinguish these from news articles.
- Read the instruction about feature articles with the class and draw students' attention to the example from the selection. How can they tell that the article will be entertaining as well as informative?
- Use the instruction for Connecting Literary Elements to review the concept of main idea with students. Urge them to look for main ideas as they read the selection.
- Use the Feature Article transparency in **Literary Analysis and Reading Transparencies,** p. 50, to introduce students to the feature article format.

❸ Reading Strategy

Setting a Purpose for Reading

- Remind students that their purpose for reading changes from selection to selection.
- Tell students that setting a purpose for reading is an important reading skill, because it will help focus their attention as they read.
- Have students look through the selection, noting the title, photographs, and author information. Display the Set a Purpose for Reading transparency in **Literary Analysis and Reading Transparencies,** p. 49, to help them organize their information.

Vocabulary Development

- Pronounce each vocabulary word for students, and read the definitions as a class. Have students identify any words with which they are already familiar.

CUSTOMIZE INSTRUCTION FOR UNIVERSAL ACCESS

For Less Proficient Readers	For English Learners	For Advanced Readers
Guide students to identify the implications of Volk's question, "What is this stuff, anyway?" Point out that the question reflects Volk's purpose to explore alternative methods of controlling insects. This knowledge should help students set their own purpose for reading.	Students might enjoy comparing their home language words for common insects such as *fly, mosquito, bee, cockroach,* as well as arachnids such as a *garden spider* or *scorpion.* They might benefit by keeping a glossary throughout this selection with the English name of each creature Volk mentions.	Encourage interested students to do research on an insect that intrigues them. Ask students to research the questions: Could human beings continue to live on Earth without insects? Could insects continue to live on Earth without human beings?

E-Teach

Visit E-Teach at www.phschool.com for teachers' essays on how to teach, with questions and answers.

TEACH

Step-by-Step Teaching Guide for pp. 386–390

CUSTOMIZE INSTRUCTION For Logical/Mathematical Learners

Encourage students to find pictures of insects and make an insect display, labeling each "specimen" with its correct name. Invite students to present their displays to the class.

❶ About the Selection

This feature article takes a lighthearted, humorous approach to a problem that frustrates many: the proliferation of bugs and other insect life in city apartments. The author consults a renowned entomologist to find help in her search for a natural way to control insect life. While it doesn't solve her problem, the visit gives her a new appreciation for the diversity and mystery of the insect world. Readers will learn many fascinating facts about insects—but they may also develop a new sense of our connection to the natural world and its creatures.

❷ Vocabulary Development

Greek Prefix: *micro-*

- Point out that the Greek prefix *micro-* means "small."
- Direct students to the word *microcosms* and note how the prefix contributes to the meaning "little worlds."
- Write the words *chip, film,* and *scope* on the board. Ask students to add *micro-* to each word and provide a definition.
  Answer: *microchip,* "a small integrated circuit"; *microfilm,* "film for making very small photographs"; *microscope,* "instrument for viewing small things."

❶ An Entomological Study of Apartment 4A

Patricia Volk

Louis Sorkin has a prominent forehead, gently rounded abdomen and powerful bandy legs. During the day, he can be found in the entomology department of the American Museum of Natural History. Sorkin, a senior scientific assistant, has agreed to identify the insects that have been calling my home home since we asked Fred, the building pest control operator, to stop spraying.

"God bless you," Fred used to say at the door, as if we might be seeing each other for the last time.

"What's in this stuff, anyway?" I said to him one day. Malathion, a controversial pesticide, was on the list.

Normally I admire bugs, which happens to be the scientific name for insects that have a modified beaklike mouth. As a child, I collected them in glass cigar tubes my father brought home from his restaurant. ❷ Bugs are microcosms and microcosms are metaphors. But something was eating grooves in my favorite brown hat. A black crawly thing with more legs than the Rockettes had staked out the north bedroom wall. There was a fauna in the freezer and a bug as shiny as patent leather had moved into the water gauge of our electric coffee maker. Darkest of

microcosms (mī´ krō käz´ əms) *n.* little worlds

metaphors (met´ ə fôrz´) *n.* ways of speaking of things as though they were something else

TEACHING RESOURCES

The following resources can be used to enrich or extend the instruction for pp. 386–390.

Literary Analysis

Selection Support: Literary Analysis, p. 100 ■

Reading

Listening to Literature Audiocassettes, Side 13 ■

Listening to Literature Audio CDs, CD 9

■ **BLOCK SCHEDULING:** Resources marked with this symbol provide varied instruction during 90-minute blocks.

all, there were definite signs of wildlife in the back-room closet a former tenant had jury-rigged into a shower. Whatever it was, it was big.

What I'm hoping Louis N. Sorkin will tell me is what eats what and whether biological warfare is an apartment possibility. California used Australian ladybugs to get rid of cottony-cushion scale. The Mormons lucked out when sea gulls saved them from the locusts. Could my pests have natural enemies on the food chain, something besides the Tokay gecko that barks at night and looks like a Tokay gecko?

3 Sorkin greets me in a hall stacked six feet high with drawers of Pyraustinae, a moth. We scuttle into a room crammed with journals, papers and boxes of stoppered vials. On the wall, a sign reads, "Feeling Lousy?" Sorkin's desk is littered with dental tools, mail, baby food jars and mugs with spoons—roach heaven.

I hand him my hat. He tweezes something off the brim and puts it under his microscope.

"This is a shed skin of one of the dermestid beetles in the larval stage," he says. "I think this one is the Anthrenus species. They've been grazing along it here . . . here . . . they like wool. In New York City, they live under the parquet floor.[1] Hair is a very good food source for them."

"What do they eat on hair?"

"The hair itself. It's protein."

I empty two shopping bags filled with takeout containers and hand over the freezer specimen.

It turns out that it's an immature German cockroach, which means, Sorkin says, it could have been found anywhere. Of my 21 specimens, 11 are German cockroaches. This comes as a big surprise because some look like black dots, some are pear-shaped with pale dorsal banding and some look like greasy pecan shells. Sorkin explains that roaches have a three-stage metamorphosis, going from egg to wingless nymph to adult. During the nymph stage, they molt up to seven times.

"German cockroaches are called Belgian cockroaches in Germany," Sorkin says, scratching his arm. I scratch mine too. "They're also called steam-bugs, shiners and Yankee settlers."

He studies a bug I found in my colander under the grapes.

"Oh! Otiorhynchus ovatus! A strawberry root weevil. It's an outdoor weevil that sometimes comes into homes as it migrates."

"How would it get into a fourth-floor apartment?"

"They crawl."

"Would it eat my roaches?"

"It would starve."

I show him an arachnid that has spun a web in its container. Maybe it eats strawberry root weevils.

Reading Strategy
Establishing a Purpose for Reading What purpose have you set for reading this article?

4 Reading Check
What does Sorkin say is a very good food source for dermestid beetles?

1. **parquet** (pär kā´) **floor** wooden floor in which the pieces of wood fit together to form a pattern.

3 Reading Strategy
Establishing a Purpose for Reading

- Ask students what kind of feature article they think this will be, based on what they have read so far.
  Possible response: Students may say that the author is writing about material that informs the reader, adding her own humorous touches.
- Ask students the Reading Strategy question on p. 387: What purpose have you set for reading this article?
  Possible response: Students may say they are reading to find out what kinds of insects are in the author's apartment, or that they are reading to enjoy the author's humorous descriptions.

4 Reading Check
Answer: Sorkin says that dermestid beetles like to eat hair, which is made of protein.

❺ Literary Analysis

Feature Article and Main Idea

- Ask students the Literary Analysis question on p. 388: Which humorous lines add human interest to the article?
  Possible response: Students may cite Sorkin's mustache-twitching reaction to the house centipede or his description as "the 911 of insect emergencies" as humorous.
- Remind students that one of the author's goals for consulting Sorkin has been to find a nonpoisonous method for controlling the insect population in her apartment.

Monitor Progress Have students read to find out whether the presence of house centipedes will solve Volk's cockroach problem completely.
Answer: No, it will not, because there are too many ways for cockroaches to gain access to a building.

❻ Reading Strategy

Establishing a Purpose for Reading

- Ask students what Volk learns from Sorkin about follicle mites.
  Answer: These mites live around the human nose and forehead and feed on hair follicles.
- Is Volk able to see any of the mites that supposedly live on her face? Why or why not?
  Answer: She cannot see any of them under the microscope and wonders if the moisturizer she uses on her face kills them.

Monitor Progress Have students answer the Reading Strategy question on p. 388: What reading purpose do these odd and interesting facts support?
Answer: These facts support a strategy of reading to discover something new and fascinating.

"This is a jumping spider. Normally it would be outside."

Sorkin peers into the container with the north-wall stalker.

"A house centipede!" His mustache twitches. "This is a neat animal! Chilopoda have their front legs modified to inject venom. They're predators. They live on roaches and spiders and probably other centipedes."

❺ Bingo! A natural roach enemy. "So if I introduce more Chilopods, they'll get rid of the roaches?"

"Not completely. You'd have to isolate your apartment. If you could keep them from gaining access through cracks and wall voids and holes around pipes and the door to the hallway, yeah, you could have a really insect-free zone."

The phone rings. It rings all day. Louis Sorkin is the 911 of insect emergencies. If you open your safe and bugs fly in your face or you need to know whether New Mexican centipedes produce cyanide, Sorkin's your man.

He studies two flies I found on the bathroom windowsill. There's no masking his disgust.

"These are a little moldy or fungus-y. They look like houseflies, Musca domestica."

He checks a dust ball from under our bed for dust mites, which spend their days with their mouths open, waiting for scales to drop from our skin.

"Can't see much here."

"Is it true that there are things that live on our eyelids?"

"There are two species of certain follicle mites around the nose and forehead."

"What's the reason for us to have them?"

❻ "They're just there. Demidex folliculorum. They feed on the material in the hair follicles and usually don't cause any trouble whatsoever. Hold your skin tight like this"—Sorkin pulls his forehead to the side with four fingers—"and push it with a 3-by-5 card and look at what you pushed on a slide, you might even find them."

I try it, but even with magnification of 200, nothing shows up. Maybe moisturizer kills them.

Sorkin checks sweepings from the back-room closet shower.

"This is an American cockroach. You also have the shed skin of what looks like another Anthrenus species and an Odd beetle. The reason it has that name is because the male and female don't look alike. So you've got three different things in here."

On deck is my strangest bug. It suspends itself in liquid, like a peanut in pudding.

"Oh yeah." Sorkin recognizes it instantly. "This is a tortoise beetle. When they're alive they're sometimes gold-colored."

"How did it get in the apartment?"

"Flew."

Sorkin helps me load the containers back into the

Literary Analysis
Feature Article Which humorous lines add human interest to the article?

Reading Strategy
Establishing a Purpose for Reading What reading purpose do these odd and interesting facts support?

ENRICHMENT: Science Connection

Insects

There are more than 800,000 known species of insects, divided into a number of orders. Insects include beetles, moths, butterflies, wasps, ants, bees, flies, mosquitoes, cockroaches, grasshoppers, and true bugs. Fossil records reveal that this amazing form of animal life first appeared on earth about 400 million years ago. All insects have six legs and a segmented body composed of a head; a thorax that includes three pairs of jointed legs, and, in most insects, one or two pairs of wings; and an abdomen. Insects have a complicated relationship with humans. On one hand, they carry disease, infect food, and destroy crops. On the other hand, they pollinate plants, kill and eat pests harmful to people and other species, and make up an important part of the food chain for many species of animals. Have students identify their own questions about insects, based on the information in the feature article, and do research to find the answers.

shopping bag. I head home thinking about the high drama that goes on behind the kitchen pegboard and wondering about the strawberry root weevil. What compelled it to climb four stories to a place where it would find nothing to eat? A strawberry root weevil entering an apartment is a suicidal gesture . . . .

The next morning, while I'm getting coffee, a juvenile roach heads for the food processor. Although I can do 3.8 m.p.h. on the treadmill and the fastest roach in the world can only go 2.9, I'm no match for it. In the sink, there's a mature female that looks like she's carrying a
7 purse. She died with her egg case stuck in her. Before Sorkin, I never would have found this poignant. Sipping coffee, I gaze at the ceiling. That's when it hits me: I've neglected my prime bug habitat.

poignant (poin′ yənt) *adj.* drawing forth compassion; moving

Back at the museum, Sorkin rotates a new container with hundreds of insects and insect fragments I've retrieved from our glass ceiling fixture.

"There's . . . a hover fly . . . a spotted cucumber beetle . . . staphylinid beetles . . . a carabid stink beetle . . . ichneumon wasps . . . leaf hoppers . . . a ladybird beetle . . . a fungus beetle . . . a silverfish . . . mirid plant bugs . . . a chironomid midge . . . drugstore beetles . . . and . . . more dermestids. All these insects are attracted to light and they fly in. Then they die and the dermestids eat them."

"How do the dermestids know they're in there?"

"They smell them."

I ask Sorkin about my most surprising insect encounter:

"One night, I was making guacamole and when I put in the chili powder it started to move. How could insects live on something so hot?"

"Oh, cigarette beetles are very common in dried pepper. They do quite well. Some insects feed on insecticide."

I follow Sorkin to another room. He points to a heap of black molts from his tarantula (they would make terrific earmuffs), then lifts the lid off a plastic tray. There it is, ready to pounce, a furry ball of malevolence. Sorkin shows me a jar of preserved insects saved at the 100th anniversary dinner of the New York Entomological Society. There's a cerambycid larva as big as a parsnip, giant meal worms and a black thing the size of a small hamburger.

malevolence (mə lev′ ə ləns) *n.* bad or evil feelings or intentions

"This is a belostomadid, or true water bug, from Thailand. The body has a Gorgonzola cheese flavor."

Sorkin's personal favorite is grubs over easy.

"Tastes like bacon," he says.

"Are bugs kosher?"[2]

"Uh, well, yes and no. There are references in the Bible that say six species of locust are kosher, but there's some discussion that people were really referring to locust *beans*."

Sorkin is encyclopedic. Sorkin can answer anything. Talking to Sorkin is like playing "Stump the Stars": No, a roach cannot live on the glue of one postage stamp for a year. Even though we find them that

8 **✓Reading Check**
What happens to Volk's guacamole when she adds chili powder?

2. **kosher** (kō′ shər) *adj.* fit to eat according to Jewish dietary laws.

7 Literary Analysis

Feature Article

- Have students identify the sites in which Volk sees or finds insects in this short passage.
  Answer: She finds insects on the kitchen counter, in the kitchen sink, and in the light fixture on the ceiling.
- As students read the passage, have them think about how the information fits with a main idea of the feature article.

Monitor Progress Ask students to identify a main idea of the article that is illustrated in this passage.
Answer: Insects can be found everywhere.

8 ✓Reading Check

Answer: The guacamole starts to move (due to the presence of insects).

CUSTOMIZE INSTRUCTION FOR UNIVERSAL ACCESS

For English Learners	For Gifted/Talented Students
Encourage students to make a list of the insects described on pp. 388–389. Ask them to write one or two sentences about each one that tells something interesting about the insect. Example: "A house centipede is a predator that eats roaches and spiders. It can inject venom from its front legs." "Dust mites eat the scales that drop from human skin."	Invite students to write a story with one of the insects in this selection as a main character. They can do research to find more information on each insect. Examples might include an Odd beetle, a strawberry root weevil, a cigarette beetle, and so forth.

ASSESS

Answers for p. 390

Review and Assess

1. Students may cite the characteristics of a specific insect or the sheer variety of insect forms.
2. **(a)** Volk wants to identify the insects in her apartment and to find out whether they can be controlled by introducing natural predators rather than controversial pesticides. **(b)** Students may suggest that the stated reason is sensible, though it is not something everyone would have tried.
3. **(a)** Most of the insects in the first batch are German cockroaches. **(b)** This surprises the author because of the great diversity of sizes and shapes among the cockroaches.
4. **(a)** Volk becomes more tolerant of, and sympathetic toward, bugs. **(b)** In the second-to-last paragraph, she justifies her new live-and-let-live attitude toward bugs. In the last paragraph, she identifies with insects, equating handshaking in humans with antennating in insects.
   (c) Students may agree that Volk's attitude will last, at least until she experiences a severe insect infestation.
5. Students might say that such a casual attitude keeps people from worrying unnecessarily and enables them to see problems in their proper perspective.

way, insects don't always die on their backs. (Their legs bend in or they twitch and fall over.) There is no such thing as a *hen*-roach. It would not destroy the balance of nature if all pest species were eliminated from apartments, since that's not their natural habitat anyway. Roaches probably got into Biosphere 2 on packaging, same as we import them from the supermarket. After you've finished the bananas, fruit flies go back outside. Centipedes don't have a hundred legs. They have one pair per body segment, and 20 to 30 segments is normal. New insects are being discovered all the time. Recently Sorkin was immortalized by a parasitic moth mite, Charletonia sorkini.

"Can you look at a bite and tell what did it?"

"Sometimes," Sorkin says. "Bedbugs bite in a line. Fleas," he taps his sock, "usually bite at ground level."

I show him the back of my neck.

"None of your samples did that."

I thank Sorkin for his help. While my problem hasn't been solved, at least I know more about it. And I don't have cereal mites, black carpet beetles, termites, bedbugs, furniture carpet beetles, Trogoderma beetles, fleas and Anthrenus carpet beetles. Head lice, now that the kids are out of elementary school, are a thing of the past. If many of my insects come in with fresh air, what's the alternative? When you think about it, living close to nature, even on a tiny scale, is a privilege in a city.

When greeting, insects antennate, tapping each other with their antennae to check out who they're dealing with. Sorkin and I nod goodbye and shake hands, a Homo sapiens-specific ritual.

immortalized (i môr′ tə līzd) *v.* given lasting fame

Review and Assess

Thinking About the Selection

1. **Respond:** What was the most interesting thing you learned from this article?
2. **(a) Recall:** What reason does Patricia Volk give for visiting the entomologist? **(b) Analyze:** Does her stated reason strike you as a sensible response? Why?
3. **(a) Recall:** What do most of the bugs in the first batch turn out to be? **(b) Deduce:** Why does this surprise Volk?
4. **(a) Infer:** How is the author's attitude toward bugs changed by what she learns? **(b) Analyze:** How does she demonstrate her change in attitude? **(c) Speculate:** Do you think her new attitude will be temporary or long-term?
5. **Evaluate:** The author seems to imply that problems and annoyances are easier to cope with if you maintain a light, easygoing attitude. Do you agree or disagree? Explain.

Patricia Volk

(b. 1943)

In her youth, Volk focused on the visual arts. She worked as an art director at advertising agencies and at magazines such as *Seventeen* and *Harper's Bazaar*. A passion for writing soon emerged, and in 1988 she became a full-time writer.

Her short stories, articles, and novels—even the award-winning advertisements she has written—display her quirky sense of humor. Having spent almost all her life in New York City, she has a keen sense of the everyday humor of modern urban life.

ASSESSMENT PRACTICE: Reading Comprehension

Cause and Effect (For more practice, see Test Preparation Workbook, p. 25.)

Use the following sample test item to give your students practice in perceiving cause-and-effect relationships:

Since she always found dead insects lying on their backs, she asked the entomologist if they always die while on their backs. He told her that they do not always die that way. In fact, their legs bend in after death and the body tips over.

Why are dead insects usually found on their backs?

A They die that way.
B Their antennae curl and flip them over.
C That's how people find them.
D Their legs bend and their bodies tip.

Students should choose *D*. This cause is the only one identified in the text to explain why people find dead bugs on their backs.

Review and Assess

Literary Analysis

Feature Article

1. How well does "An Entomological Study of Apartment 4A" fit the criteria for a **feature article**?
2. What is one entertaining aspect of the article? Explain.
3. Using a chart like the one shown here, identify at least four facts you found in the article. For each, identify how it is useful or valuable.

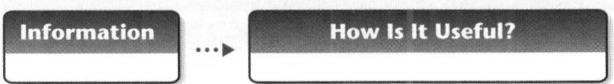

Information	How Is It Useful?

4. Do you consider Patricia Volk's article to be a genuine human-interest story? Why?

Connecting Literary Elements

5. By the end of the article, the **main idea** is revealed to the reader. (a) What is this central point? (b) Use a chart like this to explain which details from the article help to convey the main idea.

Main Idea:		
Details:	Details:	Details:

6. The author finds a dead cockroach and describes the scene as "poignant." Does a moment like this reinforce or depart from the main idea? Explain.

Reading Strategy

Establishing a Purpose for Reading

7. (a) What was your own **purpose for reading**? (b) Why did you select this particular purpose?
8. Identify at least three facts or incidents from the article that helped you achieve your purpose.

Extend Understanding

9. **Science Connection:** The use of pesticides is often a subject of debate. Do you agree with Patricia Volk's approach to pest control? Explain why or why not.

Quick Review

A **feature article** is a newspaper or magazine story written to entertain readers or to provide information on a subject of human interest.

The **main idea** is the central or underlying point of an article.

To **establish a purpose for reading,** decide what you want to learn and approach a selection with this goal in mind.

Take It to the Net

www.phschool.com

Take the interactive self-test online to check your understanding of the selection.

ENRICHMENT: Further Reading

Other Works by Patricia Volk

The Yellow Banana (short stories)
White Light (novel)
All It Takes (short stories)

Take It to the Net

Visit www.phschool.com for more information on the author.

Answers for p. 391

Review and Assess

1. The article provides interesting information in a personable and entertaining way.
2. Students may choose the descriptions of different insects, the characterization of Sorkin, or some other aspect.
3. Information: **(1)** Insects can be found everywhere; **(2)** Some insects prey on other insects; **(3)** Insects find many ways into houses and apartments; **(4)** Some insect bites can be identified.
How Is It Useful: **(1)** Insects are a part of the ecosystem everywhere; **(2)** Insects can be used to control other insects; **(3)** No one should be surprised to find insects in their living quarters; **(4)** Remedies for bites can be applied.
4. Students may note that the article focuses on two individuals whose interaction is both humorous and informative.
5. **(a)** Humans share the earth with insects, creatures of fascinating diversity and complexity.
(b) Details: Insects are found everywhere; there are eleven species of German cockroach; some insects live on the human skin; the Odd beetle gets its name because the male and female don't look alike; humans can travel faster than cockroaches; insects have social communities just as humans do; and so on.
6. This moment reinforces the main idea, demonstrating Volk's growing appreciation of the insect world.
7. **(a)** Students may suggest that their purpose was either to be informed about insects or to be entertained by a humorous account. **(b)** Ask volunteers to share their reasons.
8. Students may cite any of the multiple facts about insects.
9. Some students may agree that pesticides have harmful consequences. Others may say pesticides are sometimes the most effective solution to serious insect problems.

EXTEND

Answers for p. 392

❶ Vocabulary Development

Word Analysis

1. microcomputer
2. microorganism
3. microfilm

Spelling Strategy

1. misfire
2. hemisphere
3. illegal

Fluency: Sentence Completions

1. metaphor
2. malevolence
3. microcosms
4. immortalized
5. poignant

❷ Grammar

1. Patricia Volk
2. entomologist
3. her
4. them
5. her

Writing Application

1. I left the cockroaches some bread crumbs.
2. She gave the apartment a thorough cleaning.

Integrate Language Skills

❶ Vocabulary Development Lesson

Word Analysis: Greek Prefix *micro-*

The Greek prefix *micro-* means "small." Thus, the word *microcosm* means "small world." Using this information, match each of the following words with its definition.

a. microorganism **b.** microfilm **c.** microcomputer

1. an electronic device of reduced size
2. a tiny life form
3. a format for storing reduced-size images

Spelling Strategy

When you attach a prefix to a word, the spelling of the original word does not change. For example, *im-* + *mortal* = *immortal*.

Add *il-*, *mis-*, or *hemi-* to each word below to form three properly spelled words.

1. fire 2. sphere 3. legal

Fluency: Sentence Completions

On your paper, write the following sentences. Then, fill in the blanks with a form of the most appropriate word from the vocabulary list on page 389.

1. In poems and stories, a road is often a __?__ for life.
2. The wicked villain planned to blow up the city out of sheer __?__.
3. Philosophers have said that human beings are __?__ of nature; by understanding people, you can understand nature.
4. The hero's adventures were __?__ in song and story.
5. The __?__ plot had us all sniffling by the end of the movie.

❷ Grammar Lesson

Indirect Objects

An **indirect object** is a noun or pronoun that names the person or thing that receives the action of the verb. You can tell whether a word is the indirect object by finding the direct object and asking *to / for whom?* or *to / for what?* after the action verb. An indirect object always comes between the subject and its direct object, and it never appears in a sentence without a direct object.

Example: Patricia Volk (S) gave (V) Louis Sorkin (IO) some insects (DO). *(gave insects to whom?)*

Practice Identify the indirect object in each sentence.

1. Fred gave Patricia Volk a promise that he would stop spraying.
2. I handed the entomologist my hat with the grooves in it.
3. Sorkin offered her some information on the bugs in her house.
4. The bugs gave them an itchy feeling.
5. Later, Sorkin showed her a jar of insects.

Writing Application Use each word below as an indirect object in a sentence.

1. cockroaches 2. apartment

WG Prentice Hall Writing and Grammar Connection: Chapter 20, Section 3

TEACHING RESOURCES

The following resources can be used to enrich or extend the instruction for pp. 392–393.

Vocabulary

- **Selection Support Workbook:** Build Vocabulary, p. 97
- **Vocabulary and Spelling Practice Book** (Use this booklet for skills enrichment.) ■

Grammar

- **Selection Support Workbook:** Build Grammar Skills, p. 98
- **Writing and Grammar,** Gold Level, p. 434
- **Daily Language Practice Transparencies** ■

Writing

- **Writing and Grammar,** Gold Level, p. 326 ■
- **Writing and Grammar iText CD-ROM**
- **Writing Models and Graphic Organizers on Transparencies,** p. 53 ■

■ **BLOCK SCHEDULING:** Resources marked with this symbol provide varied instruction during 90-minute blocks.

❸ Writing Lesson

A Letter to an Expert

The entomologist Louis Sorkin played an important part in Patricia Volk's article. Write a letter asking him for information on an interesting insect you have found.

Prewriting List insects that you frequently see around your neighborhood. Choose one that interests you. Then, jot down some questions about it.

Drafting In the body of the letter, identify yourself, explain why you are interested in the insect, and ask your questions. Your letter should be straightforward and have the right level of formality: In this case, use the recipient's title and last name, be polite, and avoid slang.

Revising Make sure that your letter includes a heading, an inside address, a salutation, body, closing, and signature. Then, revise to eliminate any language that may be too informal.

Model: Revising for the Right Level of Formality

I have noticed ~~tons of~~ *several* gray fuzzy insects on the sidewalks near my house. ~~Gross!~~ They appeared one day last week.

When in doubt, use formal language. It is better to be considered too proper rather than impolite.

Prentice Hall Writing and Grammar Connection: Chapter 15, Section 1

❹ Extension Activities

Listening and Speaking Patricia Volk has grown wary of pesticides. Work with a partner or a group to conduct a **print and television ad review** for pest-control products. You should

- identify the techniques used to sell these products.
- compare advertising claims for the various pesticides.

Follow up with a small-group discussion of what you have learned. **[Group Activity]**

Research and Technology Volk's feature article is meant to entertain, yet it addresses a broad subject—the world of insects. Use the article as a springboard for your own **entomological study.** Identify the categories or criteria you will use to classify the insects you study. Then, generate a database that provides information on a variety of bugs.

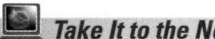

Take It to the Net www.phschool.com

Go online for an additional research activity using the Internet.

Lesson Support for p. 393

❸ Writing Lesson

- Display the Business Letter transparency, p. 53 in **Writing Models and Graphic Organizers on Transparencies.** Point out the heading, inside address, salutation, body, closing, and signature.
- Help students brainstorm a letter to Dr. Sorkin. Ask them where Sorkin's name will be found in the parts of their business letter. Where will their name appear?
- Remind students that business letters, unlike informal letters written to family or friends, are written in formal language without slang.
- Use the Business Letter rubric in **Performance Assessment and Portfolio Management,** p. 9, to assess students' letters.

❹ Listening and Speaking

- Divide the class into groups. Have each group collect ads, both from television and print sources, for pest control products.
- Invite students surveying television ads to keep a notebook of the ads, telling what each one advertises and when each is seen.
- Allow class time for the groups to make short presentations based on what they have learned.

CUSTOMIZE INSTRUCTION
For Universal Access

To address different learning styles, use the activities suggested in the **Extension Activities** booklet, p. 25.

- For Verbal/Linguistic and Logical/Mathematical Students, use Activity 5.
- For Visual/Spatial and Verbal/Linguistic Students, use Activity 6.
- For Musical/Rhythmic Students, use Activity 7.

ASSESSMENT RESOURCES

The following resources can be used to assess students' knowledge and skills.

Selection Assessment

- **Formal Assessment:** Selection Test, pp. 85–87
- **Open Book Test,** pp. 73–75
- **Got It! Assessment Videotapes,** Tape 2
- **Test Bank Software**

Take It to the Net

Visit www.phschool.com for self-tests and additional questions on the selection.

Writing Rubric

- **Performance Assess. and Portfolio Mgmt.,** p. 9

PRENTICE HALL ASSESSMENT SYSTEM

- **Workbook**
- **Skill Book**
- **Transparencies**
- **CD-ROM**

Lesson Objectives

1. To understand characteristics of newspaper articles
2. To analyze text structure as a reading strategy

About Newspapers

- If possible, provide different types of newspapers for students to review in the classroom.
- Ask students to look through the newspapers and find examples of each newspaper type listed on p. 394 (daily, weekly, and special-interest).
- Invite students to share their personal experience with newspapers, such as seeing adults read them or reading newspapers themselves. Ask students what sections of a paper they read frequently and what parts they usually ignore.

Reading Strategy

Analyzing Text Structure

- Point out that text structure is the way a piece of writing is organized and presented.
- Have students review a front-page news article, pointing out that the first paragraph contains the basic facts of the story.
- Have students review a feature article, pointing out that the structure is more relaxed.
- Direct students' attention to the graphic organizer on p. 394, pointing out that the organizer contains several categories of information that can be found in a newspaper article.
- Have students create a graphic organizer like the one on p. 394 to use as they read "Cows on Parade."

READING INFORMATIONAL MATERIALS

Newspaper Articles

About Newspaper Articles

A newspaper is a form of print media. Its main purpose is to inform the public by presenting news and commentary.

- A *daily newspaper* covers international, national, state, and local news with articles on topics such as politics, economics, education, and science. Newspapers also present feature articles that showcase trends, unusual people and events, and other topics of continuing interest.
- A *weekly newspaper* usually has a smaller readership than a daily. Its articles report more personal kinds of news, such as local weddings or fires.
- A *special-interest newspaper* runs articles of interest to one particular group of people, such as teachers, parents, or immigrants.

Reading Strategy

Analyzing Text Structure

Text structure is the way a piece of writing is organized and presented. Writers use different structures for a variety of needs. In a front-page news article, for example, the first paragraph contains the basic facts of the story. In a feature article, the structure may be more relaxed.

"Cows on Parade" is a feature article written for a special-interest business newspaper, *The Business Journal* of Milwaukee. The writer adopts a casual tone and does not present any financial information until the fourth paragraph. As you read the article, use a chart like the one below to note the kinds of information—factual details, quotations, summaries—included in the text. Indicate the location of each type of information you find.

	Vivid Scene	Summary of Central Event	Details: *who, what, when, where,* or *how*	Quotation	General Background Information
Paragraph 1			*Where:* Chicago *What:* the cow		
Paragraph 2	320 painted fiberglass cows				

'Cows on parade' find sweet home in Chicago

After success in big city, cow caravan not herded for dairy state

David Schuyler

The city of Chicago has adopted one of Wisconsin's dearest symbols—the cow.

Make that 320 of them, to be exact. They're made of fiberglass, painted, prettied up by local artists and displayed about the city's streets in what may be the country's goofiest and most well-received public art project ever.

Chicago's "Cows on Parade" public art spectacle, a project of the Public Art Program of the Department of Cultural Affairs, is being credited for a boom in the tourism trade that could add an extra $100 million or more to the city's economy. Not bad for a bunch of beautified bovines that only had to hang around—literally, for some—for four months.

"We really didn't anticipate the effect they would have on people," said Dorothy Coyle, director of tourism for the city of Chicago. "The publicity was tremendous and it did result in people traveling to Chicago just to see the cows."

Given the success of the cows in the big city, what about the idea of displaying the cows in their true home state as a tourist attraction?

Members of the Milwaukee Riverwalk District Board recently visited Chicago to view the display and consider the possibility of bringing the cows to Milwaukee, said board member Marsha Sehler.

"They were terrific, but what was more terrific was the reaction. Everybody was buying film and cameras at that Walgreens on Michigan Avenue," said Sehler.

NOT A COWTOWN

The organization, however, has since decided not to pursue the project.

Fellow Riverwalk District Board member Lisa Bailey believed that Milwaukee would not receive any benefit from hosting the cows, particularly with a number of other American cities considering a similar display.

"It didn't make sense to bring the cows here to Milwaukee," she said. "We don't want to look like a secondhand city."

If any plans to bring the cows to Wisconsin are in the works, they have yet to be made public.

The life-size cow replicas were displayed in Chicago from June 15 to Oct. 31, and received with open arms by both natives and visitors of the city with big shoulders. People crowded around cows in a variety of settings: on the sidewalks along North Michigan Avenue, outside of the Museum of Science and Industry, floating in the terminal of O'Hare International Airport, and climbing up the sides of buildings.

Cows appeared along

continued next page

A quotation by someone directly involved in the event provides important information for readers.

Background information about the event helps you understand the current situation better.

"Cows on Parade"

- Remind students to use a chart like the one on p. 394 as they read the newspaper article on this page.
- Ask students to determine what type of newspaper article this is. Answer: This is a feature article.

"Cows on Parade"

- Point out that subheads help readers predict the type of information they'll find in each section of this newspaper article.
- Point out that the subheads also reflect the light-hearted tone of the whole article.

city streets adorned as ladybugs, as waiters, as Picasso paintings and, of course, as the cow that jumped over the moon. One of three representations of Mrs. O'Leary's cow, long-blamed for starting the Chicago fire of 1871, still had monkeys on its back. In one bad pun, a cow, sponsored by Harry Caray's Restaurant, had holes drilled through it to represent the late WGN sportscaster's exclamation, "Holy cow!"

Chicago adapted the idea from the Swiss. Chicago businessman Peter Hanig saw a similar display while on vacation in Zurich, Switzerland, last year and promoted the concept for the city, said Coyle.

Zurich displayed 800 cows in its "Cow Parade" project, resulting in approximately $100 million in additional tourism dollars coming into the city, Coyle said.

Chicago tourism officials won't have any figures on the project's economic impact until December, but they are confident of its success.

"We believe that we will actually surpass that amount," Coyle said.

OUT-MOO-NEUVERING NYC

Chicago, however, wasn't the only city that had heard of the Zurich event. When the city discovered that New York City was also considering having a cow parade, Chicago officials moved quickly.

The city negotiated a licensing agreement with the Swiss government to exclusively feature a United States cow event for 1999.

The city received a $100,000 grant from the state of Illinois to help fund the project. An additional $100,000 was raised from Michigan Avenue businesses by the Cows on Parade Committee, co-chaired by Hanig.

This paragraph would be of particular interest to a business newspaper's readers.

The city purchased 320 fiberglass cows and charged local businesses and individuals $3,500 each to have an artist produce a cow with a design approved by the city. Businesses could also choose to have an artist draw up their own design, which still had to be approved by city officials, Coyle said.

Some more renowned artists demanded more, a cost which was picked up by the company buying the cow. One cow was reportedly sold for $11,000.

ALLEN-EDMONDS HAS A COW

Footwear businessman Hanig contacted Port Washington-based Allen-Edmonds Shoe Corp. about purchasing one of the cows, said Louis Ripple, director of sales and marketing.

The company became interested in its industry colleague's pitch and decided to buy a cow and have it displayed in front of its Michigan Avenue store.

"The customers really enjoyed it," he said. "We certainly had a lot of comments."

Ripple credits the cow—Shoe Horn—for bringing people into the store and even purchasing shoes. With the Chicago project now completed, the company plans to bring the cow to Wisconsin and have it displayed in its Port Washington headquarters, Ripple said.

The cows' combination of public art with something recognizably down-home may account for their popularity, said Curtis Carter, director of the Haggerty Museum of Art in Milwaukee.

"They are easily accessible to a wide range of the population," he said. "You don't need a degree in art history to appreciate these."

Juxtaposing a rural symbol with an urban setting also fits well with the socially provocative nature of public art and adds to the irony and wit of the sculptures, Carter said.

While Milwaukee takes a pass, at least 28 other cities are exploring their own cow parades, Coyle said. Variations on the theme are also being considered, such as pigs, lizards, lions, coffee cups and basketballs, she said.

As for Chicago, "we will come up with something completely different," said Coyle.

A brief subhead signals that a new main idea will follow. You can find the main idea and its supporting details in the section that follows.

CUSTOMIZE INSTRUCTION FOR UNIVERSAL ACCESS

For Special Needs Students	For Advanced Readers
Have students read the article section by section, summarizing the main idea of each section as they proceed through the article.	Ask students to locate additional feature articles, either in print or online, that are written in a different tone (for example more serious or more scientific) than the tone of "Cows on Parade."

Check Your Comprehension

1. What effect did the cows have on tourism in Chicago?
2. Why did Milwaukee officials vote against the cows?
3. Where did the idea of the cows originate?

Applying the Reading Strategy

Analyzing Text Structure

4. How does "Cows on Parade" differ in format from an article you might see on the front page of a daily newspaper?
5. How does the paragraph about cows appearing as ladybugs, waiters, and Picasso paintings help reinforce the writer's purpose?

Activity

Developing a K-W-L Chart

Having read a newspaper article about painted fiberglass cows, you now possess a certain amount of knowledge on the subject. However, you may wish to learn even more about the topic.

Create a K-W-L chart like the one shown here. In the first column, write down important details that you already **know** about the cows. In the second column, list questions indicating what you still **want** to learn about them. Consult newspapers and magazines in a library and go to Internet Web sites to find information that can answer your questions. In the third column of the chart, record what you **learned** and how you obtained the information.

What I *Know*	What I *Want* to Know	What I *Learned* and Where
Cows were a success in Chicago.	What reaction did they generate in New York City?	
One cow was sold for $11,000.	What is the most anyone paid for a cow?	

Contrasting Informational Materials

Feature Articles, Art Reviews, and Advertisements

1. "Cows on Parade" is a feature article: The author draws in readers with humor and does not present hard facts for several paragraphs. Imagine that the cow display had been the subject of an art critic's review instead of a reporter's feature story. Explain how the information and details would have been structured differently.
2. Imagine that the cow exhibit were the subject of an advertisement or brochure meant to draw tourists to Chicago. How would the writing differ in structure from the feature article?

Answers for p. 397

Check Your Comprehension

1. The cows caused a boom of up to $100 million in the tourist trade in Chicago.
2. According to Lisa Baily, Milwaukee didn't want to look like a "secondhand city."
3. The idea originated in Zurich, Switzerland.

Applying the Reading Strategy

4. "Cows on Parade" is a feature article, structured in a more casual way than a front-page article that leads with the factual information.
5. The examples of cows representing different characters supports the writer's purpose of communicating information in a humorous tone.

Activity

- Read the Activity on p. 397 aloud to the class. Point out that K-W-L stands for "what I Know, what I Want to learn, and what I Learned."
- After students complete the activity, invite them to share what they learned.

Contrasting Informational Materials

1. An art critic might have started the article with factual information about the exhibit and its artist or sponsor.
2. In an advertisement or brochure, the information would be presented in a more succinct style, with a persuasive tone, more photographs, and more details about how and where to find the cow exhibit.

Jabberwocky ✦ Macavity: The Mystery Cat ✦ Problems With Hurricanes

Lesson Objectives and CA Correlations

1. **To analyze and respond to literary elements**
   - Literary Analysis: Humorous Diction **R 3.8**
   - Comparing Literary Works: Repetition
2. **To read, comprehend, analyze, and critique poems**
   - Reading Strategy: Contrasting the Serious and the Ridiculous **R 3.8**
   - Reading Check questions
   - Review and Assess questions
   - Assessment Practice (ATE)
3. **To develop word analysis skills, fluency, and systematic vocabulary**
   - Vocabulary Development Lesson: Word Origins: Portmanteau Words **R 1.1**
4. **To understand and apply written and oral language conventions**
   - Spelling Strategy
   - Grammar Lesson: Predicate Adjectives **LC 1.3**
5. **To understand and apply appropriate writing and research strategies**
   - Writing Lesson: Fantastic Poem
   - Extension Activity: Television News Report **LS 2.1**
6. **To understand and apply listening and speaking strategies**
   - Extension Activity: News Article **LS 2.1**

STEP-BY-STEP TEACHING GUIDE	PACING GUIDE
PRETEACH	
Motivate Students and Provide Background	
Use the Motivation activity (ATE p. 398)	5 min.
Read and discuss the Preview material and Background information (SE/ATE p. 398) [A]	10 min.
Introduce the Concepts	
Introduce the Literary Analysis and Reading Strategy (SE/ATE p. 399) [A]	15 min.
Pronounce the vocabulary words and read their definitions (SE p. 399)	5 min.
TEACH	
Monitor Comprehension	
Informally monitor comprehension by circulating while students read independently or in groups [A]	15 min.
Monitor students' comprehension with the Reading Check notes (SE/ATE pp. 403, 405)	as students read
Develop vocabulary with Vocabulary notes (SE pp. 401, 403–405)	as students read
Develop Understanding	
Develop students' understanding of humorous diction with Literary Analysis annotations (ATE pp. 403, 405) [A]	10 min.
Develop students' ability to contrast the serious and the ridiculous with the Reading Strategy annotations (SE p. 404; ATE pp. 401, 403)	10 min.
ASSESS	
Assess Mastery	
Assess students' mastery of the Reading Strategy and Literary Analysis by having them answer the Review and Assess questions (SE/ATE p. 407)	20 min.
Use one or more of the print and media Assessment Resources (ATE p. 409) [A]	up to 50 min.
EXTEND	
Apply Understanding	
Have students complete the Vocabulary Development Lesson and the Grammar Lesson (SE p. 408) [A]	20 min.
Apply students' knowledge of precise details using the Writing Lesson (SE/ATE p. 409) [A]	45 min.
Apply students' understanding using one or more of the Extension Activities (SE p. 409)	20–90 min.

A **ACCELERATED INSTRUCTION:**
Use the strategies and activities identified with an [A].

UNIVERSAL ACCESS
● = Below-Level Students
▲ = On-Level Students
■ = Above-Level Students

Time and Resource Manager

Reading Level: Average/Easy/Average
Average Number of Instructional Days: 4

RESOURCES		
PRINT	**TRANSPARENCIES**	**TECHNOLOGY**
• **Beyond Literature,** Workplace Skills: Effective Communication, p. 26 ▲ ■		• **Interest Grabber Video,** Tape 2 ● ▲ ■
• **Selection Support Workbook:** ● ▲ ■ Literary Analysis, p. 104 Reading Strategy, p. 103 Build Vocabulary, p. 101	• **Literary Analysis and Reading Transparencies,** pp. 51 and 52 ● ▲ ■	
• **Authors In Depth,** Gold Level, p. 71 ■		• **Listening to Literature** ● ▲ ■ Audiocassettes, Side 12 Audio CDs, CD 8
• **Literatura en español** ● ▲ • **Literary Analysis for Enrichment** ■		
• **Formal Assessment:** Selection Test, pp. 88–90 ● ▲ ■ • **Open Book Test,** pp. 76–78 ● ▲ ■ • **Performance Assessment and Portfolio Management,** p. 30 ● ▲ ■ • PRENTICE HALL ASSESSMENT SYSTEM ● ▲ ■	• PRENTICE HALL ASSESSMENT SYSTEM ● ▲ ■ Skills Practice Answers and Explanations on Transparencies	• **Test Bank Software** ● ▲ ■ • **Got It! Assessment Videotapes,** Tape 2 ● ▲
• **Selection Support Workbook:** ● ▲ ■ Build Grammar Skills, p. 102 • **Writing and Grammar,** Gold Level ● ▲ ■ • **Extension Activities,** p. 26 ● ▲ ■	• **Daily Language Practice Transparencies** ● ▲	• **Writing and Grammar iText CD-ROM** ● ▲ ■ ***Take It to the Net*** www.phschool.com

BLOCK SCHEDULING: Use one 90-minute class period to preteach the selection and have students read it. Use a second 90-minute class period to assess students' mastery of skills and have them complete one of the Extension Activities.

PRETEACH

Step-by-Step Teaching Guide for pp. 398–399

Motivation

With students, make a list of fantastic, non-human or super-human characters that students know from movies, television, or comic books. Add "Jabberwocky" and "Macavity" to the list. Tell students that, in the poems in these selections, they are going to encounter characters who are equally as unusual as the characters they named.

Interest Grabber Video

As an alternative, play "The Devastation of Hurricane Andrew" on Tape 2 to engage student interest.

1 Background

The threat posed by storm surges is not limited to beachfront property. Hurricane winds also push ocean water up inland bays, rivers, and streams. A computer program called MEOW (Maximum Envelope of Water) pinpoints the likely storm surge effect at any point along the Gulf and Atlantic coasts from Texas to Maine. Such information is used to help local officials determine which areas should be evacuated during powerful storms.

Prepare to Read

Jabberwocky ◆ Macavity: The Mystery Cat ◆ Problems With Hurricanes

Take It to the Net

Visit www.phschool.com for interactive activities and instruction related to the selections, including

- background
- graphic organizers
- literary elements
- reading strategies

Preview

Connecting to the Literature

You can probably remember enjoying silly nursery rhymes and songs when you were young. Not all funny poems are written for children, though. As you will see, poems like the ones you are about to read can make you laugh out loud.

1 Background

The farmer, or "campesino," in "Problems With Hurricanes" says, "Don't worry about the water / Don't worry about the wind—," but that is exactly what you should worry about in such a storm. As a hurricane approaches land, strong rains form huge ocean waves, called storm surges, that can cause severe flooding. Puerto Rico, the poet's homeland, is in a hurricane region where the storm season extends from August to October.

TEACHING RESOURCES

The following resources can be used to enrich or extend the instruction for pp. 398–399.

Motivation

Interest Grabber Video, Tape 2

Background

Beyond Literature, p. 26

Take It to the Net

Visit www.phschool.com for background and hotlinks for the selections.

Literary Analysis

Literary Analysis and Reading Transparencies, Humorous Diction, p. 52

Reading

Selection Support Workbook: Reading Strategy, p. 103; Build Vocabulary, p. 101

Literary Analysis and Reading Transparencies, Contrast the Serious and the Ridiculous, p. 51

BLOCK SCHEDULING: Resources marked with this symbol provide varied instruction during 90-minute blocks.

❷ Literary Analysis

Humorous Diction

A writer's **diction**, or word choice, can help create a humorous effect. For example, writers may intentionally use the wrong word, use formal or informal English, or even invent unusual words. In the following line from "Macavity: The Mystery Cat," notice how the sophisticated words used to describe a cat contribute to the humor:

> For he's a fiend in feline shape, a monster of depravity.

As you read these three poems, think about how each writer's word choice makes you smile.

Comparing Literary Works

In each of the poems you are about to read, repetition is used to create a unique effect. **Repetition** is the use of any element of language—a sound, word, phrase, clause, or sentence—more than once. Poets use many kinds of repetition to add emphasis, drama, or musical rhythm to a poem. Compare the way lines, words, or stanzas are repeated in these poems, and consider the effect of the repetition.

❸ Reading Strategy

Contrasting the Serious and the Ridiculous

One way in which these poems achieve humor is by combining the **serious** with the **ridiculous**. Consider, for example, these lines from "Problems With Hurricanes":

> How would your family / feel if they had to tell
> The generations that you / got killed by a flying / Banana.

Death is serious indeed, but a flying banana is just plain silly, and the combination of the two details makes most readers chuckle. To help you contrast the serious and ridiculous details, use a chart like this one.

Vocabulary Development

chortled (chôrt´ 'ld) *v.* made a jolly, chuckling sound (p. 401)

bafflement (baf´ əl mənt) *n.* puzzlement; bewilderment (p. 403)

levitation (lev i tā´ shən) *n.* the illusion of keeping a heavy body in the air without visible support (p. 403)

feline (fē´ līn) *adj.* catlike (p. 403)

depravity (dē prav´ ə tē) *n.* crookedness; corruption (p. 403)

larder (lärd´ ər) *n.* place where food is kept; pantry (p. 403)

suavity (swä´ və tē) *n.* quality of being socially smooth (p. 404)

projectiles (prō jek´ təlz) *n.* objects that are hurled through the air (p. 405)

❷ Literary Analysis

Humorous Diction

- Tell students that *diction* is a writer's word choice. Through his or her diction, a writer can express humor.
- Read the instruction about humorous diction together as a class. Call students' attention to the example from the first poem. Have students discuss why this line is a good example of humorous diction. You may need to review the meanings of the unfamiliar words in the example first.
- Use the instruction for Comparing Literary Works to help students understand how the repeated use of sounds, words, and phrases creates poetic effects.
- Use the Humorous Diction transparency in **Literary Analysis and Reading Transparencies,** p. 52, to demonstrate how serious subject matter and humorous diction can be combined.

❸ Reading Strategy

Contrasting the Serious and the Ridiculous

- Point out to students that writers can combine both serious and ridiculous elements in the same selection, often for humorous effect.
- Demonstrate the combination of elements in "Problems With Hurricanes" by having students identify the serious and humorous elements.
- Have students create a chart like the one on p. 399 to help them identify the serious and ridiculous details as they read.

Vocabulary Development

- Pronounce each vocabulary word for students, and read the definitions as a class. Have students identify any words with which they are already familiar.

CUSTOMIZE INSTRUCTION FOR UNIVERSAL ACCESS

For Less Proficient Readers	For English Learners	For Advanced Readers
Display some collections of cartoonist Gary Larson's work for students. Larson is well known for choosing situations that are ordinarily serious and treating them humorously. Have students apply what they learn from analyzing these cartoons to the mixture of the serious and the ridiculous in the poems in this selection.	Explain to students that reading nonsense words, such as those they will meet in "The Jabberwocky," may seem like reading words in a foreign language. Make sure students realize that these nonsense words are intentionally unrecognizable and are often used for humorous effect.	By using context and their understanding of parts of speech, have students create definitions for Carroll's nonsense words. Have them begin by identifying the word as a noun, verb, adjective, or adverb.

E-Teach

Visit E-Teach at www.phschool.com for teachers' essays on how to teach, with questions and answers.

TEACH

Step-by-Step Teaching Guide for pp. 400–406

CUSTOMIZE INSTRUCTION For Interpersonal Learners

The infectious fun of these three poems provides an opportunity for group reading and spontaneous discussion. Interpersonal learners will welcome this activity. Involve them in choral reading and discussions of humor.

❶ About the Selection

"Jabberwocky" parodies medieval legends by using invented words. The seriousness of tone contrasted with the nonsensical words has a comical effect.

❷ Background

Art

The Jabberwock, 1872, by Sir John Tenniel.

Sir John Tenniel's original illustrations for Lewis Carroll's *Alice* books are still the best-loved illustrations for those books today. Tenniel was also a political cartoonist, working for the British humor magazine *Punch* for half a century. Use these questions for discussion:

1. What is serious about the picture and what is funny?
   Answer: Students may say that the style and subject matter are serious, as is the human figure, but the Jabberwock looks totally ridiculous.
2. If you were illustrating "Jabberwocky" for a new edition today, how would you make it different from Tenniel's original?
   Answer: Students' answers will vary, but some may suggest a style of art that flows from modern-day science fiction and fantasy works, and that uses computer graphics.

❶ Jabberwocky

Lewis Carroll

'Twas brillig, and the slithy toves
　　Did gyre and gimble in the wabe;
All mimsy were the borogoves,
　　And the mome raths outgrabe.

"Beware the Jabberwock, my son!
　　The jaws that bite, the claws that catch!
Beware the Jubjub bird, and shun
　　The frumious Bandersnatch!"

He took his vorpal sword in hand:
　　Long time the manxome foe he sought—
So rested he by the Tumtum tree,
　　And stood awhile in thought.

❷

The Jabberwock, 1872, John Tenniel

Literature in context — Language Connection

Alice encounters a creature called a Jabberwock in the first chapter of *Through the Looking-Glass*. She cannot understand it, so the character Humpty Dumpty explains some of its words, including these:

brillig: four o'clock in the afternoon, the time when you begin broiling things for dinner

toves: creatures that are something like badgers, something like lizards, and something like corkscrews

gyre: go round and round like a gyroscope

gimble: make holes like a gimlet (a hand tool that bores holes)

wabe: grass plot around a sundial

mome: having lost the way home

raths: something like green pigs

TEACHING RESOURCES

The following resources can be used to enrich or extend the instruction for pp. 400–406.

Literary Analysis

Selection Support: Literary Analysis, p. 104

Reading

Listening to Literature Audiocassettes, Side 12

Listening to Literature Audio CDs, CD 8 ■

Extension

Authors In Depth, Gold Level (The collection includes four additional selections by Lewis Carroll for extended reading.) ■

■ **BLOCK SCHEDULING:** Resources marked with this symbol provide varied instruction during 90-minute blocks.

And as in uffish thought he stood,
The Jabberwock, with eyes of flame,
Came whiffling through the tulgey wood,
And burbled as it came!

3

One, two! One, two! And through and through
The vorpal blade went snicker-snack!
He left it dead, and with its head
He went galumphing back.

"And hast thou slain the Jabberwock?
Come to my arms, my beamish boy!
O frabjous day! Callooh! Callay!"
He chortled in his joy.

'Twas brillig, and the slithy toves
Did gyre and gimble in the wabe;
All mimsy were the borogoves,
And the mome raths outgrabe.

chortled (chôrt´ 'ld) v. made a jolly, chuckling sound

Lewis Carroll

(1832–1898)

Charles Lutwidge Dodgson was a professor of mathematics, an ordained deacon in the Church of England, and a talented early photographer. Yet today, he is best remembered for two children's books he wrote under the pen name Lewis Carroll: *Alice's Adventures in Wonderland* (1865) and its sequel, *Through the Looking-Glass* (1871). Both feature a young girl named Alice whose curiosity leads her into amazing fantasy worlds. Huge bestsellers almost from the moment they appeared, the *Alice* books have been the basis of numerous stage plays, television adaptations, and live and animated movies.

Review and Assess

Thinking About the Selection

1. **Respond:** What images did this poem bring to mind?
2. **(a) Recall:** State in your own words the warning given in the second stanza of the poem. **(b) Analyze:** How would you describe the overall mood of "Jabberwocky"?
3. **(a) Recall:** What does the hero do after being warned about the Jabberwock? **(b) Evaluate:** One critic said that "Jabberwocky," despite its odd language, tells a story like many legends of knights and dragons. Do you agree? Why or why not? **(c) Assess:** Do you think the poem pokes fun at knighthood? Explain.
4. **(a) Interpret:** You can often tell the part of speech of a word even if you do not understand it. Identify the part of speech of three of the made-up words in this poem. Explain how you arrived at each answer. **(b) Apply:** How can a poem like "Jabberwocky" give readers a better understanding of language?
5. **Speculate:** Do you think it is easier or more challenging to write a poem with invented language? Explain.

3 Reading Strategy

Contrasting the Serious and the Ridiculous

- Remind students that serious and ridiculous elements can be combined in the same selection.
- Ask students what the serious tale is behind the silly words in stanza 4. Possible response: The serious tale involves a battle between the ferocious Jabberwock and a man who ultimately kills it.

Answers for p. 401

Review and Assess

1. Students may respond that they imagined strange looking creatures, trees, and humans.
2. **(a)** Be careful of the teeth and claws of the Jabberwock; Watch out for the Jubjub bird and the Bandersnatch. **(b)** Students may describe the mood as silly because of the invented words.
3. **(a)** He slays the Jabberwock. **(b)** Students may agree, citing such examples as the dragonlike Jabberwock and the "vorpal sword." **(c)** Students may agree that the poem is at least mocking stories of knighthood.
4. **(a)** Possible response: *Toves* and *wabe* are nouns because they clearly name something. *Gyre* and *gimble* are verbs because they follow the helping verb *did* and indicate actions. *Slithy* is an adjective because it describes *toves*. **(b)** "Jabberwocky" helps readers see the structure of language, apart from the meaning of words.
5. Even an invented language must somehow communicate with readers; that task may seem more difficult to some students.

❹ About the Selection

"Macavity: The Mystery Cat" describes the mischievousness of a cat as if the characteristic were evidence of a super-criminal mind. Throughout, however, the lively verse of T.S. Eliot enlivens the poem with humor.

❺ ▶Critical Viewing

Possible response: The spirit of the poem is playful, judging from the illustration. Students should relate the illustration to the repeated line, "Macavity's not there!" The three Scotland Yard investigators can't find Macavity because they are looking in all the wrong places.

❻ Background

Art

Macavity Eluding the Police, (detail, from T.S. Eliot's *Old Possum's Book of Practical Cats),* 1982, by Edward Gorey.

The picture shows London "bobbies" looking in vain for the elusive Macavity. Gorey, a Chicago-born illustrator (1925–2000), was known for his detailed black-and-white illustrations in mock-Victorian style, seen among other places in the opening of PBS's popular *Mystery* series. He also wrote and illustrated his own macabre limericks and fables. Use these questions for discussion:

1. Which aspects of the illustration are realistic, and which are ridiculous or fantastic?
   Answer: Uniforms, flashlight, and wall are realistic; the stylized depiction of three identical men and the flying cat are unrealistic.
2. In what ways is the illustration similar in style to the poem?
   Answer: The picture and the poem both use a serious, formal style to depict a ridiculous situation.

❹ *Macavity:*

❻

Illustration from *Old Possum's Book of Practical Cats,* Edward Gorey

T. S. Eliot

❺ ◀ **Critical Viewing** Judging from this illustration, what do you think is the spirit of the poem? **[Infer]**

ENRICHMENT: Drama

The Musical *Cats*

T.S. Eliot's *Old Possum's Book of Practical Cats* is the basis for the acclaimed musical *Cats.* The Broadway production of *Cats* came within a whisker of a full eighteen-year run; it closed in September 2000 as—by far—the longest-running Broadway hit in history. *Cats* has been presented in over 300 cities, 26 countries, and 10 languages.

A *USA Today* reader reacts to a drama review of *Cats* by David Patrick Stearns with these comments:

In truth, the "middlebrow entertainment" Stearns writes about in his review never could have come to life without the series of poems so exquisitely crafted for the neighborhood children by the master poet who certainly could and did "rub brows" with the highest of the highbrow set.

The Mystery Cat

Macavity's a Mystery Cat: he's called the Hidden Paw—
For he's the master criminal who can defy the Law.
He's the bafflement of Scotland Yard,[1] the Flying Squad's[2]
despair:
For when they reach the scene of crime—*Macavity's not*
there!

Macavity, Macavity, there's no one like Macavity,
He's broken every human law, he breaks the law of gravity.
His powers of levitation would make a fakir[3] stare,
❼ And when you reach the scene of crime—*Macavity's not there!*
You may seek him in the basement, you may look up in the
air—
But I tell you once and once again, *Macavity's not there!*

Macavity's a ginger cat, he's very tall and thin;
You would know him if you saw him, for his eyes are sunken in.
His brow is deeply lined with thought, his head is highly
❽ domed;
His coat is dusty from neglect, his whiskers are uncombed.
He sways his head from side to side, with movements like a
snake;
And when you think he's half asleep, he's always wide awake.

Macavity, Macavity, there's no one like Macavity,
For he's a fiend in feline shape, a monster of depravity.
You may meet him in a by-street, you may see him in the
square—
But when a crime's discovered, then *Macavity's not there!*

He's outwardly respectable. (They say he cheats at cards.)
And his footprints are not found in any file of Scotland Yard's.
And when the larder's looted, or the jewel-case is rifled,
Or when the milk is missing, or another Peke's[4] been stifled,
Or the greenhouse glass is broken, and the trellis past repair—
Ay, there's the wonder of the thing! *Macavity's not there!*

bafflement (baf′ əl mənt) *n.* puzzlement; bewilderment

levitation (lev i tā′ shən) *n.* the illusion of keeping a heavy body in the air without visible support

feline (fē′ līn) *adj.* catlike

depravity (dē prav′ ə tē) *n.* crookedness; corruption

larder (lärd′ ər) *n.* place where food is kept; pantry

❾ **Reading Check**

Which unusual detail links or separates Macavity from crime scenes?

1. **Scotland Yard** London police.
2. **Flying Squad** criminal-investigation department.
3. **fakir** (fə kir′) *n.* Muslim or Hindu beggar who claims to perform miracles.
4. **Peke** short for Pekingese, a small dog with long, silky hair and a pug nose.

❼ Literary Analysis

Humorous Diction

- Ask students to explain how a cat could break the law of gravity.
  Answer: Cats jump so high and land so lightly that they appear to ignore the law of gravity.
- Now, have students identify the play on words in the second line of this stanza.
  Possible response: Macavity is a "criminal" and breaks the law of the state; he also breaks the law of gravity, producing a clever rhyme.

❽ Reading Strategy

Contrast the Serious and the Ridiculous

- Ask students what serious matter is presented in this stanza.
  Answer: The speaker is providing a detailed physical description of a wanted criminal.

Monitor Progress Now, have students identify the ridiculous element of this stanza.
Answer: The criminal being described is a cat.

❾ Reading Check

Answer: Macavity is nowhere to be found.

CUSTOMIZE INSTRUCTION FOR UNIVERSAL ACCESS

For English Learners	For Gifted/Talented Students
Students may benefit from making lists of the rhyming words that end each couplet in "Macavity." Each pair will give them a sense of sounds in English—the same sounds are often spelled alike *(paw, law)*, but at other times are spelled differently *(there, air; square, there)*.	Have students create a "most wanted" poster for Macavity. Their poster should include a written physical description and a list of alleged crimes, as well as an "artist's rendering" of Macavity, carefully based on details provided in the poem. Students may wish to list Macavity's known associates or to invent some aliases for the criminal feline.

10 Reading Strategy

Contrasting the Serious and the Ridiculous

- Be sure students understand that the Foreign Office and the Admiralty are equivalent to the American State Department and the Navy. Ask students to respond to the Reading Strategy question on p. 404. What is funny about lines 33–34?
  Answer: The idea that a criminal cat would be involved in affairs of state and the military is funny.

Answers for p. 404

Review and Assess

1. Students should give specific examples of amusing lines and clever rhymes.
2. **(a)** Macavity is a tall, thin ginger cat with sunken eyes, deeply lined brow, highly domed head, dusty coat, and uncombed whiskers. **(b)** He is described as if he were a disheveled human being.
3. **(a)** "Macavity, Macavity, there's no one like Macavity"; "Macavity's not there!" **(b)** The repetition emphasizes Macavity's uniqueness and elusiveness. The multiple repetitions of his name have a rhythmic, amusing effect.
4. **(a)** Police cannot catch Macavity; he is never around after committing a crime. **(b)** Students may suggest that a possible reason that Macavity is never there is that he hasn't committed the crimes.
5. Cats are quiet, aloof, sometimes seem sneaky, are active at night, and are often missing when someone is trying to find them.
6. Students may cite examples of animal behavior, both positive and negative, that remind them of human characteristics.

And when the Foreign Office[5] find a Treaty's gone astray,
Or the Admiralty[6] lose some plans and drawings by the way,
There may be a scrap of paper in the hall or on the stair—
But it's useless to investigate—*Macavity's not there!*
And when the loss has been disclosed, the Secret Service say:
'It *must* have been Macavity!'—but he's a mile away.
You'll be sure to find him resting, or a-licking of his thumbs,
Or engaged in doing complicated long division sums.

Macavity, Macavity, there's no one like Macavity,
There never was a Cat of such deceitfulness and suavity.
He always has an alibi, and one or two to spare:
At whatever time the deed took place—MACAVITY WASN'T THERE!
And they say that all the Cats whose wicked deeds are widely known
(I might mention Mungojerrie, I might mention Griddlebone)
Are nothing more than agents for the Cat who all the time
Just controls their operations: the Napoleon of Crime![7]

Reading Strategy
Contrasting the Serious and the Ridiculous What is funny about lines 33–34?

suavity (swä′ və tē) *n.* quality of being socially smooth

5. **Foreign Office** British equivalent of the U.S. Department of State.
6. **Admiralty** British government department in charge of naval affairs.
7. **the Napoleon of Crime** a criminal mastermind; an emperor of crime—just as Napoleon Bonaparte (1769–1821) was a masterful military strategist who had himself crowned emperor.

Review and Assess

Thinking About the Selection

1. **Respond:** Did you find this poem amusing? Why or why not?
2. **(a) Recall:** Briefly describe Macavity's appearance.
   (b) Support: How does the description of his appearance contribute to the humor found in the poem?
3. **(a) Recall:** What words and phrases are repeated throughout the poem? **(b) Analyze:** Why do you think Eliot keeps repeating these words?
4. **(a) Recall:** Why are the police unable to charge Macavity?
   (b) Make a Judgment: Do you think Macavity is guilty? Explain.
5. **Speculate:** Which qualities of cats that you have known might have prompted Eliot to associate them with criminal activities?
6. **Extend:** In the collection of poems that includes "Macavity," Eliot associates a variety of human characteristics with cats. Do you think that animals possess any "human" characteristics, either good or bad? Explain.

T. S. Eliot

(1888–1965)

T. S. Eliot's collection of humorous poems, *Old Possum's Book of Practical Cats* (1939), was the inspiration for *Cats!*—one of the most popular musicals of all time. The work was something of a departure for Eliot, who was better known as a serious poet.

Although born in the United States, Eliot settled in England while still a young man, working as a teacher and bank clerk. He first won literary attention with his poetry collection *Prufrock, and Other Observations*, published in 1917. Eliot went on to become one of the world's leading poets, winning the Nobel Prize for Literature in 1948.

CUSTOMIZE INSTRUCTION FOR UNIVERSAL ACCESS

For Advanced Readers

Suggest that students read additional works by Lewis Carroll. Provide students with the titles listed in the Enrichment box, ATE p. 407. You may also wish to use **Authors In Depth**, Gold Level, which contains the following selections:

- "The Garden of Live Flowers" from *Through the Looking-Glass* (fiction, p. 71)
- "A Mad Tea-Party" from *Alice's Adventures in Wonderland* (fiction, p. 78)
- "How Doth the Little Crocodile" (poem, p. 84)
- "The White Knight's Song" (poem, p. 85)

After students have read these or other works by Carroll, have them form discussion groups in which they compare and contrast the selections they have read. Suggest criteria for comparison, such as language, nonsense elements, theme, and characters. To extend the activity, have volunteers present to the class brief oral reports on their favorite Carroll selections.

11 Problems With Hurricanes

Victor Hernández Cruz

12

A campesino[1] looked at the air
And told me:
With hurricanes it's not the wind
or the noise or the water.
I'll tell you he said:
it's the mangoes, avocados
Green plantains[2] and bananas
flying into town like projectiles.

How would your family
feel if they had to tell
The generations that you
got killed by a flying
Banana.

projectiles (pro jek´ təlz) *n.* objects that are hurled through the air

1. **campesino** (käm´ pe sē´ nō) *n.* Spanish term for a simple farmer or another person who lives in a rural area.
2. **plantains** (plan´ tins) *n.* starchy tropical fruits that resemble bananas.

13 **Reading Check**

What does the campesino say is the problem with hurricanes?

11 About the Selection

"Problems With Hurricanes" is comical when it warns the reader to beware of flying fruit, but the poet may be speaking symbolically when he says that the greatest danger is not from "the fury of the wind," but "mangoes / And all such beautiful / sweet things."

12 Literary Analysis

Humorous Diction

- Ask students what kind of advice the reader might be expecting from the campesino when he first begins to speak.
  Possible response: The reader might be expecting to learn something important about surviving the violence of a hurricane.
- Have students speculate on what the campesino might have said if this poem were a very serious poem.
  Possible response: The speaker might tell people to get to high ground, stay inside, or evacuate their homes.
- Ask students to respond to this question: What specific words make the campesino's advice humorous?
  Answer: The words "mangoes, avocados / Green plantains and bananas" are unexpected and, therefore, humorous.

13 Reading Check

Answer: The campesino says the real danger in hurricanes is flying fruit.

CUSTOMIZE INSTRUCTION FOR UNIVERSAL ACCESS

For Special Needs Students	For English Learners	For Advanced Readers
Suggest that students view the **Interest Grabber Video** "The Devastation of Hurricane Andrew" on Tape 2. Ask them to pay attention to the kind of damage that can be done by a hurricane. Instead of fruit, what kinds of objects become projectiles in a high wind?	Ask students familiar with the tropical fruits mentioned in the poem to describe them to the rest of the class. They might bring pictures of the fruit to class, or describe specific recipes based on mangoes and plantains.	Have students research the origins of words used to identify storms, for example, *hurricane, cyclone, tornado,* and *typhoon.* Ask students to share their findings with the class, illustrating their presentation with diagrams of each storm's characteristics.

ASSESS

Answers for p. 406

Review and Assess

1. Students may suggest that images of flying fruit, particularly when they hit human beings, can be amusing.
2. **(a)** The campesino says that being killed by a flying mango or plantain would be worse. **(b)** A noble death arises from a natural or powerful cause; a shameful death stems from a freak occurrence like flying fruit.
3. **(a)** How would a family feel if they had to tell succeeding generations that someone was killed by a flying banana? **(b)** People are affected by the stories of how their ancestors died. **(c)** Students may agree that the campesino seems a good judge of human behavior.
4. Students might suggest that the reader would be left unclear about the poet's final message, the potential danger of beautiful things.
5. **(a)** Students may find the tone of the poem humorous. **(b)** They might cite the several references to high-velocity fruit and the apparently serious remark "beware of mangoes."

Death by drowning has honor
If the wind picked you up
and slammed you
Against a mountain boulder
This would not carry shame
But
to suffer a mango smashing
Your skull
or a plantain hitting your
Temple at 70 miles per hour
is the ultimate disgrace.

The campesino takes off his hat—
As a sign of respect
toward the fury of the wind
And says:
Don't worry about the noise
Don't worry about the water
Don't worry about the wind—
If you are going out
beware of mangoes
And all such beautiful
sweet things.

Review and Assess

Thinking About the Selection

1. **Respond:** What amusing images does this poem create?
2. (a) **Recall:** According to the campesino, which causes of death would be worse than drowning or being slammed into a mountain by the wind? (b) **Distinguish:** What seems to be the difference for him between a noble and a shameful hurricane death?
3. (a) **Recall:** Which question does the campesino ask in the second stanza? (b) **Infer:** What is he suggesting about how one family member's death affects future generations? (c) **Assess:** Do you think the campesino is a reliable judge of human behavior?
4. **Modify:** How would the poem be affected if the last four lines were not included?
5. (a) **Analyze:** How would you describe the tone or mood of this poem? (b) **Support:** Which words or images create this tone?

Victor Hernández Cruz

(b. 1949)

A native of Puerto Rico, Victor Hernández Cruz moved to New York City with his family while still a boy. As a poet, Cruz pioneered a style called Nuyorican, a combination of English and Spanish dotted with slang that became popular among New York poets of Puerto Rican descent. He is also known for powerful oral readings that twice saw him crowned World Heavyweight Poetry Champion in Taos, New Mexico.

ASSESSMENT PRACTICE: Reading Comprehension

Cause and Effect **(For more practice, see Test Preparation Workbook, p. 26.)**

Use the following item to demonstrate how to link causes and effects.

Macavity's a Mystery Cat: he's called the Hidden Paw—

For he's the master criminal who can defy the Law.

He's the bafflement of Scotland Yard, the Flying Squad's despair

For when they reach the scene of crime - Macavity's not there.

Why is Scotland Yard baffled by Macavity?

A He is called the Hidden Paw.
B He creates despair in the Flying Squad.
C He is never found at the scene of the crime.
D He is a cat.

Have students reread the lines in the poem, replacing the word *for* with the word *because*. Students should then be able to recognize *C* as the correct answer to the question.

Review and Assess

Literary Analysis

Humorous Diction

1. Find at least three words or phrases in "Macavity" that seem typical of mystery or crime fiction. How do these words contribute to the poem's **humorous diction**?
2. (a) Rewrite three sentences from "Jabberwocky" using familiar words. (b) Is it still funny? Explain.

Comparing Literary Works

3. (a) Using a chart like the one below, compare the humorous diction found in each poem. (b) Does diction play an equally strong role in creating humor in each poem? Explain.

Poem	Serious Subject	Humorous Diction

4. (a) Compare the technique of **repetition** used in each of the poems. (b) In your opinion, which poem makes the best use of repetition?

Reading Strategy

Contrasting the Serious and the Ridiculous

5. Sum up what is most serious and most ridiculous in each of the three poems.
6. What point do you think each poet is making through this contrast?
7. Of the three, which poem do you think is the most serious? Explain your choice.

Extend Understanding

8. **Cultural Connection:** "Macavity: The Mystery Cat" refers to several qualities of cats. Cats have played an important role in human society for thousands of years. "Curiosity killed the cat" is a common saying in our society. Explain the meaning of this saying. Come up with two more sayings or legends about cats and explain their meanings.

Quick Review

Humorous diction is word choice used to create a humorous effect.

Repetition is the use of any language element—a sound, word, phrase, clause, or sentence—more than once to create an effect.

To **contrast the serious and the ridiculous,** separate details in a selection into two categories: absurd, unusual details and serious ones.

Take It to the Net

www.phschool.com

Take the interactive self-test online to check your understanding of these selections.

ENRICHMENT: Further Reading

Other Works by the Authors

Works by Lewis Carroll
Alice's Adventures in Wonderland
Through the Looking Glass

Works by T. S. Eliott
Old Possum's Book of Practical Cats

Works by Victor Hernández Cruz
Rhythm, Content and Flavor: New and Selected Poems

Take It to the Net

Visit www.phschool.com for more information on the authors.

Answers for p. 407

Review and Assess

1. Students may cite such words as "master criminal," "defy the Law," "Scotland Yard," "Flying Squad," "scene of crime," and "alibi." The words become amusing in a poem about a criminal cat.
2. **(a)** In rewriting, students should choose alternatives to Carroll's invented words: "*'Twas brillig*" might become "It was afternoon." **(b)** Students may find that their rewrites lack the humor of Carroll's nonsensical language.
3. **(a)** Humorous diction: "Jabberwocky": invented language; "Macavity": "a fiend in feline shape" and other extravagant references to a criminal cat; "Problems With Hurricanes": deadly, high-speed fruit
(b) Students may feel that the humor in "Jabberwocky" springs mainly from diction; in "Problems With Hurricanes" it comes primarily from situation; in "Macavity" the humor derives equally from diction and situation.
4. **(a)** "Jabberwocky" closes by repeating its first stanza. "Macavity" repeats line 5 twice (at 17 and 35); "Macavity's not there" appears six times. "Hurricanes" repeats "Don't worry" three times. **(b)** Students may agree that "Macavity" makes the best use of repetition, both in frequency and humorous effect.
5. Possible response: "Jabberwocky": a deadly battle is described in nonsensical language. "Macavity": law enforcers relentlessly seek a criminal cat. "Hurricanes": destructive storms can kill with flying fruit.
6. Carroll seems to celebrate words and language. Eliot focuses on the cleverness of cats. Cruz warns that beauty and sweetness can be dangerous.
7. Possible response: Students may find Cruz's poem, with its final warning about dangerous beauty, to be the most serious.
8. "Curiosity killed the cat" is usually invoked as a caution against prying or snoopiness. Allow time for students to explore other sayings about cats.

EXTEND

Answers for p. 408

❶ Vocabulary Development

1. *smoke + fog*
2. *breakfast + lunch*
3. *motor + hotel*

Spelling Strategy

1. decision
2. transmission
3. translation

Fluency: Sentence Completion

1. levitation
2. projectiles
3. feline
4. bafflement
5. larder
6. depravity
7. chortled
8. suavity

❷ Grammar

1. [is] deep (modifies *brow*)
2. [was] good (modifies *Macavity*)
3. [appears] respectable and smart (modifies *he*)
4. [are] uncombed (modifies *whiskers*)
5. [are] thorough (modifies *they*)

Writing Application

1. The criminal is deceitful.
2. The police were shocked and dismayed to find that Macavity had again outsmarted them.

Integrate Language Skills

❶ Vocabulary Development Lesson

Word Origins: Portmanteau Words

"Jabberwocky" contains many invented words, including some formed by blending two words into one—like *chortled,* combining *chuckle* and *snort,* or *mimsy,* combining *miserable* and *flimsy.* Such words are now known as **portmanteau words.**

Use a dictionary, if necessary, to explain the origins of these portmanteau words:

1. smog 2. brunch 3. motel

Spelling Strategy

The *shun/zhun* sound in a suffix is spelled *ssion* or *tion/sion.* The *shun* sound can be heard in *fission* and *levitation*; the *zhun* sound, in *invasion.*

Complete each word below with the correct form of the *shun/zhun* sound.

1. deci___ 2. transmi___ 3. transla___

Fluency: Sentence Completion

Complete each sentence with a vocabulary word from the list on page 399.

1. The magician seemed to perform __?__, for it looked as if a person floated in air.
2. Bullets and darts are types of __?__.
3. Lions are part of the __?__ family.
4. The poem was written in invented language, to the __?__ of many readers.
5. Store the food in the __?__.
6. The sinner had engaged in many forms of __?__.
7. Jack __?__ as he observed the outcome of his practical joke.
8. Cary Grant was an actor of great sophistication and __?__.

❷ Grammar Lesson

Predicate Adjectives

In sentences formed with linking verbs, the verb can be completed with a predicate adjective. A **predicate adjective** is an adjective that appears with a linking verb and describes the subject of the sentence. Linking verbs, including forms of the verb *be,* express a state of being.

Example: The cat (S) was (V) *tall* (PA).

A **compound predicate adjective** is two or more adjectives that appear with the linking verb and describe the subject.

Example: The cat (S) was (V) *sneaky* (PA) and *mischievous* (PA).

Practice Copy the following sentences. Circle the linking verb. Then, underline each predicate adjective and draw an arrow to the word it modifies.

1. His brow is deep.
2. Macavity was good at escaping.
3. He appears respectable and smart.
4. The whiskers are uncombed.
5. They have looked for him everywhere because they are thorough.

Writing Application Write two sentences using the following items as predicate adjectives.

1. deceitful
2. shocked and dismayed

WG *Prentice Hall Writing and Grammar Connection: Chapter 20, Section 3*

TEACHING RESOURCES

The following resources can be used to enrich or extend the instruction for pp. 408–409.

Vocabulary

Selection Support Workbook: Build Vocabulary, p. 101

Vocabulary and Spelling Practice Book (Use this booklet for skills enrichment.) ■

Grammar

Selection Support: Build Grammar Skills, p. 102

Writing and Grammar, Gold Level, p. 434

Daily Language Practice Transparencies

Writing

Writing and Grammar, Gold Level, p. 122 ■

Writing and Grammar iText CD-ROM

■ **BLOCK SCHEDULING:** Resources marked with this symbol provide varied instruction during 90-minute blocks.

❸ Writing Lesson

Fantastic Poem

The poems in this section are unusual, to say the least. Write your own unusual poem about one of the fantastic creatures or events you have just read about.

Prewriting List precise details that you might use to describe this unusual creature or event. Choose details that you think will help you achieve an overall mood—humorous, eerie, or something else.

Drafting Write either a free-verse poem—one without a regular rhythm or rhyme scheme—or one with a regular rhythm and rhyme scheme. Use descriptive details that contribute to your overall mood.

Revising Read your poem aloud. Highlight weak or vague words, and replace them with more precise language.

Model: Revising to Add Precise Details

Macavity ~~came~~ *leaped* out, ~~holding~~ *gripping* a key in one paw,

Curious, he ~~looked~~ *gazed* around and ~~liked~~ *admired* what he saw.

Words like *leaped* and *gazed* add precise details to the poem.

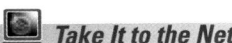

WG *Prentice Hall Writing and Grammar Connection: Chapter 6, Connected Assignment*

❹ Extension Activities

Research and Technology The poet of "Problems With Hurricanes" is a native of Puerto Rico, a hurricane region. In a group, research and present a **television news report** on weather conditions and foods grown in Puerto Rico.

- Find maps, photographs, and other visuals.
- Look for generalizations you can draw about the climate of the region.

Rehearse and then present your broadcast to the class. **[Group Activity]**

Listening and Speaking Write a **news article** reporting the events found in "Macavity: The Mystery Cat." Give a description of Macavity's appearance. Then, explain why he is considered a master criminal. Try to stay objective, reporting only the facts without including personal opinions. Present the news article to your class.

Take It to the Net www.phschool.com

Go online for an additional research activity using the Internet.

Lesson Support for p. 409

❸ Writing Lesson

- Read one or more stanzas from "Jabberwocky" as a model for students.
- Invite students to brainstorm for ideas about a fantasy creature or situation about which they might write a poem.
- Have students work in groups to make up nonsense words and phrases to fit into their poems.
- Allow time for volunteers to present their poems in class.

❹ Research and Technology

- Divide the class into groups. Each group can research one of the following characteristics of Puerto Rico: crops, weather, history, and the arts.
- Have each group research its topic, finding books, photos, videos, and creating a short presentation.
- Have each group present its findings, asking the class to listen and respond critically.
- Evaluate the broadcasts using the rubric for Delivering an Exposition Presentation with Visual Aids, p. 30 in **Performance Assessment and Portfolio Management.**

CUSTOMIZE INSTRUCTION
For Universal Access

To address different learning styles, use the activities suggested in the **Extension Activities** booklet, p. 26.

- For Verbal/Linguistic and Logical/Mathematical Learners, use Activity 5.
- For Visual/Spatial Learners, use Activity 6.

ASSESSMENT RESOURCES

The following resources can be used to assess students' knowledge and skills.

Selection Assessment

- **Formal Assessment,** Selection Test, pp. 88–90
- **Open Book Test,** pp. 76–78
- **Got It! Assessment Videotapes,** Tape 2
- **Test Bank Software**

Take It to the Net

Visit www.phschool.com for self-tests and additional questions on the selections.

Listening and Speaking Rubric

- **Performance Assess. and Portfolio Mgmt.,** p. 30

PRENTICE HALL ASSESSMENT SYSTEM

- **Workbook**
- **Skill Book**
- **Transparencies**
- **CD-ROM**

Talk

Lesson Objectives and CA Correlations

1. **To analyze and respond to literary elements**
   - Literary Analysis: Humorous Folk Tale **R 3.7**
   - Connecting Literary Elements: Personification **R 3.7**
2. **To read, comprehend, analyze, and critique a folk tale**
   - Reading Strategy: Recognizing Illogical Situations **R 3.8**
   - Reading Check questions
   - Review and Assess questions
   - Assessment Practice (ATE)
3. **To develop word analysis skills, fluency, and systematic vocabulary**
   - Vocabulary Development Lesson: Latin Prefix: *re-* **R 1.1**
4. **To understand and apply written and oral language conventions**
   - Spelling Strategy
   - Grammar Lesson: Predicate Nominatives **LC 1.3**
5. **To understand and apply appropriate writing and research strategies**
   - Writing Lesson: Humorous Folk Tale **W 2.1**
   - Extension Activity: Cultural Report **W 1.5**
6. **To understand and apply listening and speaking strategies**
   - Extension Activity: Interview **LS 1.8, 2.3**

STEP-BY-STEP TEACHING GUIDE	PACING GUIDE
PRETEACH	
Motivate Students and Provide Background	
Use the Motivation activity (ATE p. 410)	5 min.
Read and discuss the Preview material and Background information (SE/ATE p. 410) A	5 min.
Introduce the Concepts	
Introduce the Literary Analysis and Reading Strategy (SE/ATE p. 411) A	15 min.
Pronounce the vocabulary words and read their definitions (SE p. 411)	5 min.
TEACH	
Monitor Comprehension	
Informally monitor comprehension by circulating while students read independently or in groups A	10 min.
Monitor students' comprehension with the Reading Check note (SE/ATE p. 413)	as students read
Develop vocabulary with Vocabulary notes (SE pp. 413, 414)	as students read
Develop Understanding	
Develop students' understanding of humorous folk tales with Literary Analysis annotation (ATE p. 413) A	10 min.
Develop students' ability to recognize illogical situations with the Reading Strategy annotation (ATE p. 412)	10 min.
ASSESS	
Assess Mastery	
Assess students' mastery of the Reading Strategy and Literary Analysis by having them answer the Review and Assess questions (SE/ATE p. 415)	20 min.
Use one or more of the print and media Assessment Resources (ATE p. 417) A	up to 50 min.
EXTEND	
Apply Understanding	
Have students complete the Vocabulary Development Lesson and the Grammar Lesson (SE p. 416) A	20 min.
Apply students' knowledge of clear and realistic details using the Writing Lesson (SE/ATE p. 417) A	45 min.
Apply students' understanding using one or more of the Extension Activities (SE p. 417)	20–90 min.

A ACCELERATED INSTRUCTION: Use the strategies and activities identified with an A.

UNIVERSAL ACCESS
● = Below Level Students
▲ = On-Level Students
■ = Above Level Students

Time and Resource Manager

Reading Level: Easy
Average Number of Instructional Days: 3

RESOURCES		
PRINT	**TRANSPARENCIES**	**TECHNOLOGY**
• **Beyond Literature,** Cross-Curricular Connection: Social Studies, p. 27 ▲ ■		• **Interest Grabber Video,** Tape 2 ● ▲ ■
• **Selection Support Workbook:** ● ▲ ■ Literary Analysis, p. 108 Reading Strategy, p. 107 Build Vocabulary, p. 105	• **Literary Analysis and Reading Transparencies,** pp. 53 and 54 ● ▲ ■	
• **Adapted Reader's Companion** ● • **Reader's Companion** ●		• **Listening to Literature** ● ▲ ■ Audiocassettes, Side 12 Audio CDs, CD 8
• **English Learner's Companion** ● ▲ • **Literatura en español** ● ▲ • **Literary Analysis for Enrichment** ■		
• **Formal Assessment:** Selection Test, pp. 91–93 ● ▲ ■ • **Open Book Test,** pp. 79–81 ● ▲ ■ • **Performance Assessment and Portfolio Management,** p. 13 ● ▲ ■ • PRENTICE HALL ASSESSMENT SYSTEM ● ▲ ■	• PRENTICE HALL ASSESSMENT SYSTEM ● ▲ ■ Skills Practice Answers and Explanations on Transparencies	• **Test Bank Software** ● ▲ ■ • **Got It! Assessment Videotapes,** Tape 2 ● ▲
• **Selection Support Workbook:** ● ▲ ■ Build Grammar Skills, p. 106 • **Writing and Grammar,** Gold Level ● ▲ ■ • **Extension Activities,** p. 27 ● ▲ ■	• **Daily Language Practice Transparencies** ● ▲	• **Writing and Grammar iText CD-ROM** ● ▲ ■ ***Take It to the Net*** www.phschool.com

BLOCK SCHEDULING: Use one 90-minute class period to preteach the selection and have students read it. Use a second 90-minute class period to assess students' mastery of skills and have them complete one of the Extension Activities.

PRETEACH

Step-by-Step Teaching Guide for pp. 410–411

Motivation

Ask students to share any appropriate jokes that they have heard. Then, discuss what makes people laugh at jokes. In addition to their own ideas, tell students that elements such as outlandish situations, repetitions, and a character's false sense of superiority over others contribute to humor. Tell students to look for these elements in "Talk."

Interest Grabber Video

As an alternative, play "Communicating with Dolphins" on Tape 2 to engage student interest.

1 Background

Many of the details of this story reflect the everyday reality of life in the Republic of Ghana. The first character in the story is a "country man" (more than 65 percent of the population in Ghana is rural) who sets out to dig yams. A river also figures prominently in "Talk"—more than half of Ghana's landmass is occupied by the Volta River basin, which is filled with streams, marshes, and lagoons.

Prepare to Read

Talk

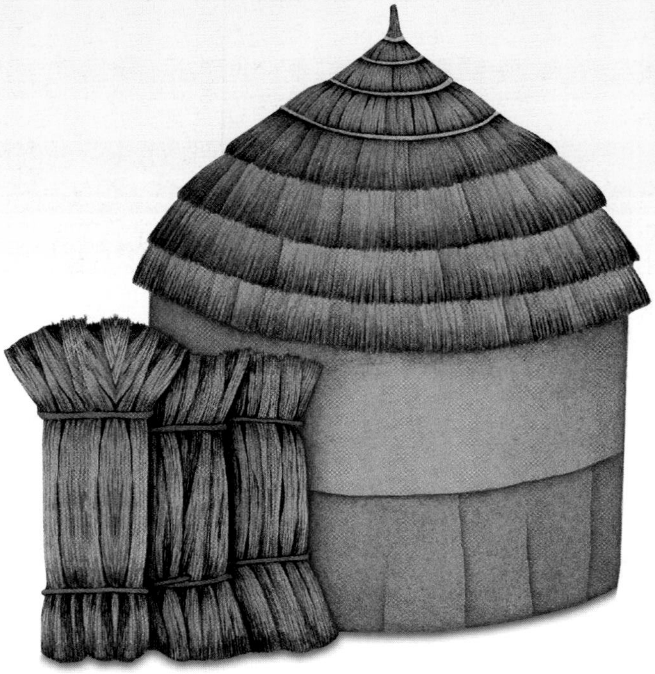

Take It to the Net

Visit www.phschool.com for interactive activities and instruction related to "Talk," including
- background
- graphic organizers
- literary elements
- reading strategies

Preview

Connecting to the Literature

Your breakfast muffin somersaults out of your hands and lands jam side down on the floor. Although the muffin may be called an "inanimate object," it seems to have a mischievous mind of its own. "Talk" is an African folk tale that whimsically nudges this idea a step further.

1 Background

"Talk" is set on the west coast of Africa, in the country now known as the Republic of Ghana. Many of the story's details reflect the everyday reality of life there. For example, yams, mentioned often in the story, are one of the staples of the diet of rural Ghanaians. In addition, the characters include a fisherman and a weaver, common occupations in Ghana, a country known for its beautiful hand-woven fabrics.

TEACHING RESOURCES

The following resources can be used to enrich or extend the instruction for pp. 410–411.

Motivation

Interest Grabber Videos, Tape 2

Background

Beyond Literature, p. 27

Take It to the Net

Visit www.phschool.com for background and hotlinks for "Talk."

Literary Analysis

Literary Analysis and Reading Transparencies, Humorous Folk Tale, p. 54

Reading

Selection Support Workbook: Reading Strategy, p. 107; Build Vocabulary, p. 105

Literary Analysis and Reading Transparencies, Recognizing Illogical Situations, p. 53

BLOCK SCHEDULING: Resources marked with this symbol provide varied instruction during 90-minute blocks.

❷ Literary Analysis

Humorous Folk Tale

A **folk tale** is an anonymous story passed down by word of mouth from one generation to the next. With everyday language, folk tales express the beliefs and values of the cultures that create them, and they typically present simple characters and far-fetched situations. A **humorous folk tale**, meant to entertain and to instruct, uses humor or exaggeration to appeal to its audiences. Look at the following example from "Talk":

> . . . a country man went out to his garden to dig up some yams to take to market. While he was digging, one of the yams said to him, "Well at last you're here . . ."

You will see that this fantastic idea of objects that suddenly speak is repeated throughout the story for humorous effect.

Connecting Literary Elements

Personification, often used in folk tales, occurs when a nonhuman subject is given human characteristics. In "Talk," personification contributes to the humor in the folk tale by giving objects the ability to speak. As you read, notice the nonhuman things that seem to come to life.

❸ Reading Strategy

Recognizing Illogical Situations

When reading a folk tale, you might come across situations that could not possibly happen in real life. Illogical situations can make a work of fantasy more fantastic and entertaining. However, these situations can distract you, so it is important to **recognize illogical situations** when you read. To prevent illogical situations from distracting you, follow these strategies:

- Jot down confusing or unusual situations.
- Decide why a situation is illogical.
- Consider what the situation adds to the story.

Use a chart like the one shown here to keep track of the illogical situations you come across in "Talk."

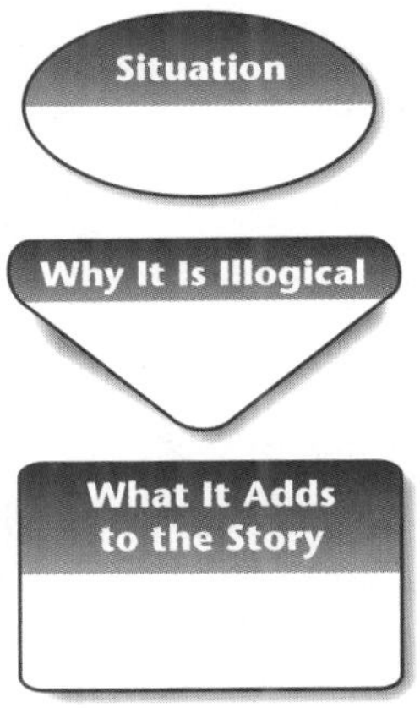

Vocabulary Development

ford (fôrd) *n.* shallow place in a river that can be crossed (p. 413)

refrain (ri frān′) *v.* hold back (p. 414)

scowling (skoul′ iŋ) *v.* contracting the eyebrows and frowning to show displeasure (p. 414)

❷ Literary Analysis

Humorous Folk Tale

- Tell students that folk tales often use humor to communicate the basic beliefs and values of a culture. Encourage students to name some folk tales with which they are familiar.
- Use the instruction for Connecting Literary Elements to provide an example of personification in literature. Explain to students that personification is a form of figurative language.
- Use the Humorous Folk Tale transparency in **Literary Analysis and Reading Transparencies,** p. 54, to show students examples of the personification of inanimate classroom objects. Ask them to add other examples to the transparency chart.

❸ Reading Strategy

Recognizing Illogical Situations

- Remind students they often will encounter fantasy elements in folk tales. These elements are humorous and add color to the tale.
- Have students recall "Jabberwocky" and "Macavity: The Mystery Cat" from their previous group of selections. Invite them to make a list of some of the illogical situations from these poems and tell what each one added to the reading experience.

Vocabulary Development

- Pronounce each vocabulary word for students, and read the definitions as a class. Have students identify any words with which they are already familiar.

CUSTOMIZE INSTRUCTION FOR UNIVERSAL ACCESS

For Special Needs Students	For Less Proficient Readers	For English Learners
Have students read the adapted version of "Talk" in the **Adapted Reader's Companion.** This version provides basic-level instruction in an interactive format with questions and write-on lines. Completing the adapted version will prepare students to read the selection in the Student Edition.	Have students read the selection in the **Reader's Companion.** This version provides basic-level instruction in an interactive format with questions and write-on lines. After students finish the selection in **Reader's Companion,** have them complete the questions and activities in the Student Edition.	Have students read the adapted version of the selection in the **English Learner's Companion.** This version provides basic-level instruction in an interactive format with questions and write-on lines. Completing the adapted version will prepare students to read the selection in the Student Edition.

E-Teach

Visit E-Teach at www.phschool.com for teachers' essays on how to teach, with questions and answers.

TEACH

Step-by-Step Teaching Guide for pp. 412–414

CUSTOMIZE INSTRUCTION
For Verbal/Linguistic Learners

Have students work in groups to read the sections in which several "characters" speak. Encourage students to take turns playing an inanimate "character" and a human character. Be sure they understand that the more quickly and frantically the dialogue is read, the more humorous the story becomes.

❶ About the Selection

Folk tales are often based on the illogical and humorous premise that objects and animals can speak. The real humor stems from everyone's enjoyment of a good put-down—a chance to make fun of someone who thinks herself or himself superior to others. In the folk tale, beginning with the farmer who digs up the talking yam, each character makes fun of the previous character's fear, then is frightened in turn. Perhaps readers love stories like this because we learn that the "chiefs" among us are no better than everyone else.

❷ Reading Strategy

Recognize Illogical Situations

- Remind students that fantasy is a main component of folk tales. Ask the class to define an illogical situation to make sure they understand the concept.
  Answer: An illogical situation is one that could never happen in real life.
- Ask students to identify the first illogical situation that occurs in this selection.
  Answer: The yam talks to the farmer.

TALK ❶

African (Ashanti) Folk Tale

Retold by Harold Courlander and George Herzog

Once, not far from the city of Accra on the Gulf of Guinea, a country man went out to his garden to dig up some yams to take to market. While he was digging, one of the yams said to him, "Well, at last you're here. You never weeded me, but now you come around with your digging stick. Go away and leave me alone!"

❷ The farmer turned around and looked at his cow in amazement. The cow was chewing her cud and looking at him.

"Did you say something?" he asked.

The cow kept on chewing and said nothing, but the man's dog spoke up. "It wasn't the cow who spoke to you," the dog said. "It was the yam. The yam says leave him alone."

The man became angry, because his dog had never talked before, and he didn't like his tone besides. So he took his knife and cut a branch from a palm tree to whip his dog. Just then the palm tree said, "Put that branch down!"

TEACHING RESOURCES

The following resources can be used to enrich or extend the instruction for pp. 412–414.

Literary Analysis

- **Selection Support Workbook:** Literary Analysis, p. 108 ▪

Reading

- **Reader's Companion**
- **English Learner's Companion**
- **Listening to Literature Audiocassettes,** Side 12 ▪
- **Listening to Literature Audio CDs,** CD 8

▪ **BLOCK SCHEDULING:** Resources marked with this symbol provide varied instruction during 90-minute blocks.

The man was getting very upset about the way things were going, and he started to throw the palm branch away, but the palm branch said, "Man, put me down softly!"

He put the branch down gently on a stone, and the stone said, "Hey, take that thing off me!"

This was enough, and the frightened farmer started to run for his village. On the way he met a fisherman going the other way with a fish trap on his head.

"What's the hurry?" the fisherman asked.

"My yam said, 'Leave me alone!' Then the dog said, 'Listen to what the yam says!' When I went to whip the dog with a palm branch the tree said, 'Put that branch down!' Then the palm branch said, 'Do it softly!' Then the stone said, 'Take that thing off me!'"

"Is that all?" the man with the fish trap asked. "Is that so frightening?"

"Well," the man's fish trap said, "did he take it off the stone?"

"Wah!" the fisherman shouted. He threw the fish trap on the ground and began to run with the farmer, and on the trail they met a weaver with a bundle of cloth on his head.

"Where are you going in such a rush?" he asked them.

3 "My yam said, 'Leave me alone!'" the farmer said. "The dog said, 'Listen to what the yam says!' The tree said, 'Put that branch down!' The branch said, 'Do it softly!' And the stone said, 'Take that thing off me!'"

"And then," the fisherman continued, "the fish trap said, 'Did he take it off?'"

"That's nothing to get excited about," the weaver said. "No reason at all."

"Oh, yes it is," his bundle of cloth said. "If it happened to you you'd run too!"

"Wah!" the weaver shouted. He threw his bundle on the trail and started running with the other men.

They came panting to the ford in the river and found a man bathing. "Are you chasing a gazelle?" he asked them.

The first man said breathlessly, "My yam talked at me, and it said, 'Leave me alone!' And my dog said, 'Listen to your yam!' And when I cut myself a branch the tree said, 'Put that branch down!' And the branch said, 'Do it softly!' And the stone said, 'Take that thing off me!'"

The fisherman panted. "And my trap said, 'Did he?'"

The weaver wheezed. "And my bundle of cloth said, 'You'd run too!'"

"Is that why you're running?" the man in the river asked.

"Well, wouldn't you run if you were in their position?" the river said.

The man jumped out of the water and began to run with the others. They ran down the main street of the village to the house of the chief. The chief's servant brought his stool out, and he came and sat on it to listen to their complaints. The men began to recite their troubles.

Literature 4 in context Cultural Connection

West African Folk Tales

Every culture has its own folk tales. In West Africa, folk tales that entertain and teach lessons are an essential part of a rich oral tradition.

A common folk-tale theme, in a part of the world teeming with plant and animal life, is the relationship between nature and people. Many cultures of this region believe that all living things possess a spirit, so it is not unusual in folk tales for plants and animals to take on human qualities. For example, Anansi, the spider, is a major figure in African folklore. This spider takes on human qualities ranging from wisdom to foolishness. Even with flawed qualities, Anansi always conveys a lesson. Therefore, it is not surprising that a yam and a dog take on human characteristics in "Talk."

ford (fôrd) *n.* shallow place in a river that can be crossed

5 **Reading Check**

What happens when the country man starts digging yams?

3 Literary Analysis

Humorous Folk Tale

- Ask students what happens each time the farmer tells about the yam.
  Answer: Each time the story is told, a different creature or thing speaks up and joins the conversation.
- Have students explain the effect the repetition in the men's stories has on the reader.
  Answer: Students may note that each repetition adds one more illogical event to the mix and intensifies the humor of the situation.

4 Background

West African Folk Tales

Many Ashanti folk tales involve a traditional trickster figure. These folk tales form a cycle in which there is no particular sequence and the different adventures are independent of each other. Trickster tales are almost always placed in the "animal tales" genre, with the trickster himself—he seems always to be male—identified with a particular animal.

5 Reading Check

Answer: One of the yams tells him to go away and leave it alone.

CUSTOMIZE INSTRUCTION FOR UNIVERSAL ACCESS

For Special Needs Students	For Gifted/Talented Students
Students may benefit by working with the Recognize Illogical Situations transparency, p. 53 in **Literary Analysis and Reading Transparencies**. Have them identify the illogical element of the first situation, using the information given on the transparency. Then, have them fill in other situations as they read, including those on the transparency. Additional examples include the talking fish trap, the talking bundle of cloth, and the talking river.	Ask students to analyze the story in terms of the values of the culture telling the story. For example, the tale is told by a culture that is highly dependent on the natural world for its food (yams, fish), work (weaving), transportation (river), and so forth. If Americans were to make up a similar folk tale, which objects in our culture might substitute for the yam, dog, tree, stone, and river?

ASSESS

Answers for p. 414

Review and Assess

1. Students may cite any of the humorous parts of the story. Perhaps the final speaker, the stool, provides the best "punch line" in the story.
2. **(a)** He reacts calmly, because he thinks the story is too incredible to be believed. **(b)** When the fish trap speaks to him, he realizes the story is true.
3. **(a)** Either an object or an animal speaks to him. **(b)** Perhaps they feel that they have been taken for granted or mistreated.
4. **(a)** He tells them that their story is wild and they should get back to work. **(b)** Students may suggest that the chief should have asked for proof of the story rather than dismissing it as nonsense.
5. **(a)** Perhaps the chief might have the same astonished reaction as the other men. **(b)** The story is funnier without the chief's response because the stool's remark punctuates the story at a peak of humor and allows the reader to imagine how the chief would react.
6. **(a)** Elements unique to the setting include the geography, yams, and weaving. Universal elements include human feelings of superiority and pride, fear of the unknown, and reliance on the natural world. **(b)** Students may say that the humor spans the cultural gap and is funny to Americans because of the easily understood situations and character traits.
7. **(a)** The "superior" character becomes fearful, too. **(b)** The story ridicules human feelings of superiority to the natural world.

"I went out to my garden to dig yams," the farmer said, waving his arms. "Then everything began to talk! My yam said, 'Leave me alone!' My dog said, 'Pay attention to your yam!' The tree said, 'Put that branch down!' The branch said, 'Do it softly!' And the stone said, 'Take it off me!'"

"And my fish trap said, 'Well, did he take it off?'" the fisherman said.

"And my cloth said, 'You'd run too!'" the weaver said.

"And the river said the same," the bather said hoarsely, his eyes bulging.

The chief listened to them patiently, but he couldn't refrain from scowling. "Now this is really a wild story," he said at last. "You'd better all go back to your work before I punish you for disturbing the peace."

So the men went away, and the chief shook his head and mumbled to himself, "Nonsense like that upsets the community."

"Fantastic, isn't it?" his stool said. "Imagine, a talking yam!"

refrain (ri frān´) *v.* hold back

scowling (skoul´ iŋ) *v.* contracting the eyebrows and frowning to show displeasure

Review and Assess

Thinking About the Selection

1. **Respond:** Which situation in "Talk" struck you as the funniest? Why?
2. **(a) Recall:** How does the fisherman react when the country man tells his crazy story? **(b) Analyze:** Why does he get so upset when his fish trap speaks to him?
3. **(a) Recall:** What upsets each man who joins the country man? **(b) Deduce:** What reason might the objects and animals have for speaking all of a sudden?
4. **(a) Recall:** What does the chief say to the men when they come rushing in to tell their stories? **(b) Modify:** What do you think the chief should have said to the men?
5. **(a) Hypothesize:** What might the chief say when his stool talks back to him? **(b) Evaluate:** Would the story have been funnier if it had included what the chief said or did after the stool spoke? Explain.
6. **(a) Compare and Contrast:** What aspects of the story are unique to its West African setting? What elements of the story are universal? **(b) Make a Judgment:** Would most Americans find "Talk" funny? Explain.
7. **(a) Recall:** What happens to every human character after he insults each man who is afraid? **(b) Draw Conclusions:** Which aspects of human nature does the story hold up to ridicule?

Harold Courlander

(b. 1908)

Harold Courlander has had a long, distinguished career as a builder of bridges between different cultures. The settings for his novels range from eighteenth-century Africa to rural Mississippi to the Hopi Nation before the arrival of the Europeans.

George Herzog

(1901–1983)

Born in Budapest, Hungary, George Herzog was a pioneer in the field of ethnomusicology, the study of music for its cultural values and social significance. He also taught courses in linguistics and cultural anthropology and published numerous books on folk music.

ASSESSMENT PRACTICE: Reading Comprehension

Predict Outcomes (For more practice, see Test Preparation Workbook, p. 27.)

Many tests require students to make predictions about future outcomes based on information in the text. Use the following item to demonstrate how this skill might be tested.

The farmer became frightened when the yam spoke to him. He ran to tell the fisherman, but the fish trap frightened them both by speaking. They ran to tell the weaver, but the weaver's cloth asked a question.

You can tell from the passage that the men are most likely to—

A leave town to get away from their talking things.
B run to tell someone else what is happening.
C sell all their belongings.
D write a story about their experiences.

Students should recognize that the story pattern makes *B* the best answer.

Review and Assess

Literary Analysis

Humorous Folk Tale

1. Use a chart like the one below to show how "Talk" fits the criteria of a **humorous folk tale.**

Characters	Simple Language	Far-fetched Situations	Point About Human Nature

2. What image of its culture does "Talk" seem to project? Why?

Connecting Literary Elements

3. Use a chart like the one below to show how the nonhuman characters are **personified** in the folk tale. Write the words that are spoken and the feelings that are conveyed by each character.

Words	◄···	Character	···►	Feelings

4. How does personification create a humorous effect in the story?

Reading Strategy

Recognizing Illogical Situations

5. What is illogical about what happens to each man in "Talk"?
6. Does the use of **illogical situations** grow funnier or less funny as the story goes on? Explain.
7. (a) Is the chief's reaction to the men logical or illogical? Explain. (b) How does his response add to the humor?

Extend Understanding

8. **Cultural Connection:** (a) If objects or animals in the United States could speak for a day, which ones might have the most to say? (b) What might they say? Explain.

Quick Review

Humorous folk tales are stories from the oral tradition that both entertain and instruct.

Personification is the attribution of human characteristics to animals or inanimate objects.

To **recognize illogical situations,** test them against your own experiences and knowledge. Then, decide how the illogical situations add to a story.

Take It to the Net

www.phschool.com

Take the interactive self-test online to check your understanding of the selection.

ENRICHMENT: Further Reading

Other Work by Harold Courlander

The African

8. **(a)** Possible response: Students might cite animals in zoos, circuses, feedlots, cages, and other exploitative situations. Encour-age students to think of inanimate things as well: cars, telephones, and computers, for example. **(b)** Students might list complaints of exploitation, lack of care, overwork.

Answers for p. 415

Review and Assess

1. Characters: farmer, weaver, fisherman; Simple Language: dialogue, statements, questions; Far-fetched Situations: talking animals and objects; Point about Human Nature: Humans think they are better than creatures and things in the natural world.
2. The folk tale seems to project an image of a culture that values community and the wisdom of its leader.
3. Possible response: **Words:** "Go away and leave me alone!" **Character:** yam **Feelings:** wants to be left alone; **Words:** "The yam says leave him alone." **Character:** dog **Feelings:** repeats yam's complaints; **Words:** "Put that branch down!" **Character:** palm tree **Feelings:** defends dog; **Words:** "Take that thing off me!" **Character:** stone **Feelings:** protests being covered by the branch; **Words:** "did he take it off the stone?" **Character:** fish trap **Feelings:** inquires about the farmer's actions; **Words:** "If it happened to you you'd run too!" **Character:** bundle of cloth **Feelings:** disagrees with the weaver; **Words:** "Well, wouldn't you run if you were in their position?" **Character:** river **Feelings:** questions the bathing man; **Words:** "Imagine, a talking yam!" **Character:** stool **Feelings:** agrees that talking objects are "fantastic."
4. Students may agree that personification—giving voice and personality to everyday things—is inherently amusing in this story.
5. It is illogical that inanimate objects, plants, and animals talk to each man.
6. Students may agree that the repetition of illogical situations increases the humor of the story.
7. **(a)** The chief's reaction is a logical response to what is for him an unbelievable story. **(b)** It sets up the "joke" (a voiceless animal or object speaking to its human user) for a fifth and final time.

EXTEND

Answers for p. 416

1 Vocabulary Development

1. c
2. b
3. d
4. a

Concept Development: Antonyms

1. b
2. c
3. c

Spelling Strategy

1. shouted; The yam shouted at the farmer to leave it alone.
2. looking; The cow was looking at the man but did not speak.
3. weeded; The farmer never weeded his crops.

2 Grammar

1. subject: story; verb: is; <u>folk tale</u>
2. subject: chief; verb: was; <u>skeptic</u>
3. subject: men; verb: were; <u>sprinters</u>
4. subject: branch and stone; verb: were; <u>talkers</u>
5. subject: object; verb: was; <u>yam</u>

Writing Application

1. In this story the yam and the tree are talking <u>objects</u>.
2. The chief will become the tribe's <u>leader</u>.

Integrate Language Skills

1 Vocabulary Development Lesson

Word Analysis: Latin Prefix *re-*

The word *refrain* uses the Latin prefix *re-*, which means "back" or "again." Thus, the word *refrain* means "to hold oneself back." Other words that use the Latin prefix *re-* include *rewrite* (to write something *again*) and *reflect* (to think *back*).

Using the meaning of *re-*, write the word from the following list that is the best match for each definition below.

a. rethink **b.** refresh **c.** regenerate **d.** redo

1. Produce or grow again
2. Make cooler than before
3. Start over; try again
4. Give something another thought

Concept Development: Antonyms

Write the letter of the word whose meaning is most nearly opposite to that of the first word.

1. scowling: (a) frowning, (b) smiling, (c) resting
2. ford: (a) icy canal, (b) shallow underwater spot, (c) deep underwater spot
3. refrain: (a) continue, (b) stop, (c) begin

Spelling Strategy

In words ending in two vowels plus a consonant, do not double the final consonant before adding an ending that starts with a vowel. For example, *refrain* + *-ed* = *refrained*. In your notebook, write the correct spelling of each word. Then, use each word in a sentence.

1. shout + *-ed* 2. look + *-ing* 3. weed + *-ed*

2 Grammar Lesson

Predicate Nominatives

A **predicate nominative** is a noun or pronoun that appears with a linking verb (commonly a form of *be*). A predicate nominative renames, identifies, or explains the subject of the sentence. The linking verb acts as an equal sign between the subject and the predicate nominative; both the subject and the predicate nominative name the same person or thing.

In the examples below, the subject is in boldface, the linking verb is in italics, and the predicate nominative is underlined.

Examples: The **yam** *was* the <u>first</u> to talk. (S, LV, PN)

Now **this** *is* really a wild <u>story</u>. (S, LV, PN)

Practice Copy the following sentences. Label the subject and verb. Then, underline the predicate nominative in each.

1. The story is a folk tale.
2. The chief was a skeptic.
3. The men were sprinters.
4. The branch and stone were talkers.
5. One object in the story was the yam.

Writing Application Use each of the following in a sentence, and then underline the predicate nominative.

1. are talking objects
2. The chief will become

WG *Prentice Hall Writing and Grammar Connection: Chapter 20, Section 3*

TEACHING RESOURCES

The following resources can be used to enrich or extend the instruction for pp. 416–417.

Vocabulary

- **Selection Support Workbook:** Build Vocabulary, p. 105
- **Vocabulary and Spelling Practice Book** (Use this booklet for skills enrichment.)

Grammar

- **Selection Support Workbook:** Build Grammar Skills, p. 106
- **Writing and Grammar,** Gold Level, p. 434
- **Daily Language Practice Transparencies**

Writing

- **Writing and Grammar,** Gold Level, p. 78
- **Writing and Grammar iText CD-ROM**

BLOCK SCHEDULING: Resources marked with this symbol provide varied instruction during 90-minute blocks.

❸ Writing Lesson

Humorous Folk Tale

Think of your school as a community, with its own culture, customs, and values. Write your own humorous folk tale set in your school. Use simple characters, simple language, and a far-fetched situation. To add humor, personify some of the objects in your school, just as nonhuman things were personified in "Talk."

Prewriting Choose an event that has happened in your school. Add unusual details to the real-life event to create a far-fetched situation. Gather details about your characters, using a chart like the one shown.

Character	Actions	Description
desk	It can walk and talk.	When it "wakes up," it has a friendly and boisterous personality.

Drafting As you draft, show, rather than tell, what is happening in the story. Use characters' actions, details of setting, and dialogue to show readers what you want them to see.

Revising Ask a partner to read your folk tale aloud. Listen closely to the language you have included in your story. Rewrite any dialogue that sounds unnatural to make your characters sound more realistic.

WG *Prentice Hall Writing and Grammar Connection: Chapter 5, Section 2*

❹ Extension Activities

Listening and Speaking Imagine that a famous television interviewer or talk-show host conducts an **interview** with one of the nonhuman characters in "Talk." With another student, role-play this situation.

- Ask questions that will inform and entertain your audience.
- Use appropriate mannerisms and gestures as you talk.

Present your interview to your class. **[Group Activity]**

Research and Technology "Talk" is set in West Africa, near the Gulf of Guinea. Prepare a **cultural report** about this region. Include as many multimedia elements as you can: a map; photographs of people, land, and art; tapes of voices and music; and actual art objects and clothes, if you can find them. Consider creating a multimedia presentation to share your findings.

Take It to the Net www.phschool.com

Go online for an additional research activity using the Internet.

❸ Writing Lesson

- Have students identify elements of the setting of "Talk" and then make a list of elements that would serve as a setting for a folk tale set in their school or community.
- Invite students to discuss community values and brainstorm ways that these values could be expressed in a humorous folk tale.
- Use the Writing Lesson to guide students in developing their folk tales.
- Use the Short Story rubric in **Performance Assessment and Portfolio Management,** p. 13, to evaluate students' folk tales.

❹ Listening and Speaking

- Divide the class into pairs and have each pair determine who will be the interviewer and who will be the guest.
- Guide each pair to make up questions for the interviewer and to develop responses for the character.
- Allow time for volunteer pairs to present their interviews to the class.

CUSTOMIZE INSTRUCTION
For Universal Access

To address different learning styles, use the activities suggested in the **Extension Activities** booklet, p. 27.

- For Logical/Mathematical and Visual/Spatial Learners, use Activity 5.
- For Verbal/Linguistic and Musical/Rhythmic Learners, use Activity 6.
- For Verbal/Linguistic and Logical/Mathematical Learners, use Activity 7.

ASSESSMENT RESOURCES

The following resources can be used to assess students' knowledge and skills.

Selection Assessment

- **Formal Assessment,** Selection Test, pp. 91–93
- **Open Book Test,** pp. 79–81
- **Got It! Assessment Videotapes,** Tape 2
- **Test Bank Software**

Take It to the Net

Visit www.phschool.com for self-tests and additional questions on "Talk."

Writing Rubric

- **Performance Assess. and Portfolio Mgmt.,** p. 13

PRENTICE HALL ASSESSMENT SYSTEM

- **Workbook**
- **Transparencies**
- **Skill Book**
- **CD-ROM**

One Ordinary Day, With Peanuts

Lesson Objectives and CA Correlations

1. **To analyze and respond to literary elements**
   - Literary Analysis: Surprise Ending **R 3.8**
   - Connecting Literary Elements: Plot
2. **To read, comprehend, analyze, and critique a short story**
   - Reading Strategy: Questioning Characters' Actions **R 3.4**
   - Reading Check questions
   - Review and Assess questions
   - Assessment Practice (ATE)
3. **To develop word analysis skills, fluency, and systematic vocabulary**
   - Vocabulary Development Lesson: Using Related Words **R 1.1**
4. **To understand and apply written and oral language conventions**
   - Spelling Strategy
   - Grammar Lesson: Direct Object or Object of a Preposition? **LC 1.3**
5. **To understand and apply appropriate writing and research strategies**
   - Writing Lesson: Summary **W 2.2**
   - Extension Activity: Research Report **W 1.4**
6. **To understand and apply listening and speaking strategies**
   - Extension Activity: Monologue **LS 1.9**

STEP-BY-STEP TEACHING GUIDE	PACING GUIDE
PRETEACH	
Motivate Students and Provide Background	
Use the Motivation activity (ATE p. 418)	5 min.
Read and discuss the Preview material and Background information (SE/ATE p. 418) [A]	10 min.
Introduce the Concepts	
Introduce the Literary Analysis and Reading Strategy (SE/ATE p. 419) [A]	15 min.
Pronounce the vocabulary words and read their definitions (SE p. 419)	5 min.
TEACH	
Monitor Comprehension	
Informally monitor comprehension by circulating while students read independently or in groups [A]	25 min.
Monitor students' comprehension with the Reading Check notes (SE/ATE pp. 421, 423, 425, 427, 429)	as students read
Develop vocabulary with Vocabulary notes (SE pp. 421, 423, 427, 428, 430; ATE p. 423)	as students read
Develop Understanding	
Develop students' understanding of surprise endings with Literary Analysis annotations (SE/ATE pp. 421, 428) [A]	10 min.
Develop students' ability to question characters' actions with the Reading Strategy annotations (SE pp. 422, 424, 429; ATE pp. 422, 424, 427)	10 min.
ASSESS	
Assess Mastery	
Assess students' mastery of the Reading Strategy and Literary Analysis by having them answer the Review and Assess questions (SE/ATE p. 431)	20 min.
Use one or more of the print and media Assessment Resources (ATE p. 433) [A]	up to 50 min.
EXTEND	
Apply Understanding	
Have students complete the Vocabulary Development Lesson and the Grammar Lesson (SE p. 432) [A]	20 min.
Apply students' understanding of transitions using the Writing Lesson (SE/ATE p. 433) [A]	45 min.
Apply students' understanding of the selection using one or more of the Extension Activities (SE p. 433)	20–90 min.

A **ACCELERATED INSTRUCTION:**
Use the strategies and activities identified with an [A].

UNIVERSAL ACCESS
● = Below-Level Students
▲ = On-Level Students
■ = Above-Level Students

Time and Resource Manager

Reading Level: Challenging
Average Number of Instructional Days: 4

RESOURCES		
PRINT	**TRANSPARENCIES**	**TECHNOLOGY**
• **Beyond Literature,** Cross-Curricular Connection: Math, p. 28 ▲ ■		• **Interest Grabber Video,** Tape 2 ● ▲ ■
• **Selection Support Workbook:** ● ▲ ■ Literary Analysis, p. 112 Reading Strategy, p. 111 Build Vocabulary, p. 109	• **Literary Analysis and Reading Transparencies,** pp. 55 and 56 ● ▲ ■	
		• **Listening to Literature** ● ▲ ■ Audiocassettes, Side 12 Audio CDs, CD 9
• **Literatura en español** ● ▲ • **Literary Analysis for Enrichment** ■		
• **Formal Assessment:** Selection Test, pp. 94–96 ● ▲ ■ • **Open Book Test,** pp. 82–84 ● ▲ ■ • **Performance Assessment and Portfolio Management,** p. 27 ● ▲ ■ • PRENTICE HALL ASSESSMENT SYSTEM ● ▲ ■	• PRENTICE HALL ASSESSMENT SYSTEM ● ▲ ■ Skills Practice Answers and Explanations on Transparencies	• **Test Bank Software** ● ▲ ■ • **Got It! Assessment Videotapes,** Tape 2 ● ▲
• **Selection Support Workbook:** ● ▲ ■ Build Grammar Skills, p. 110 • **Writing and Grammar,** Gold Level ● ▲ ■ • **Extension Activities,** p. 28 ● ▲ ■	• **Daily Language Practice Transparencies** ● ▲ • **Writing Models and Graphic Organizers on Transparencies,** p. 83 ● ▲ ■	• **Writing and Grammar iText CD-ROM** ● ▲ ■ *Take It to the Net* www.phschool.com

BLOCK SCHEDULING: Use one 90-minute class period to preteach the selection and have students read it. Use a second 90-minute class period to assess students' mastery of skills and have them complete one of the Extension Activities.

PRETEACH

Step-by-Step Teaching Guide for pp. 418–419

Motivation

"Don't talk to strangers" is one of the first lessons that young children are taught. Write these words on the chalkboard. Have students discuss why they are given this advice. Then, point out that they are about to read a story about a stranger who seems so nice that no one can resist talking to him and trusting him. What's his game? Is he for real? What is he getting out of being so nice to strangers? Is he really to be trusted? These are questions students won't be able to answer until they read the entire story.

Interest Grabber Video

As an alternative, play "A Tour of New York City" on Tape 2 to engage student interest.

❶ Background

Though Jackson never specifically names the city in which her tale is set, the details she gives in passing—Coney Island, for example, and the Bronx Zoo—all indicate a New York City setting.

Prepare to Read

One Ordinary Day, With Peanuts

Take It to the Net

Visit www.phschool.com for interactive activities and instruction related to "One Ordinary Day, With Peanuts," including

- background
- graphic organizers
- literary elements
- reading strategies

Preview

Connecting to the Literature

Sometimes it may seem as though there are not enough hours in the day. People often criticize the pace of modern life, complaining that they find it too hectic. As you will see, several of the characters in Shirley Jackson's story are experiencing one of life's frenzied days.

❶ Background

Shirley Jackson's story is set in New York City. More than 8 million people live in the five boroughs that officially make up the city. On a typical workday, a few million more travel in from the suburbs—most of them to work in the island borough of Manhattan. For many people, Manhattan defines their image of New York City.

TEACHING RESOURCES

The following resources can be used to enrich or extend the instruction for pp. 418–419.

Motivation

Interest Grabber Video, Tape 2

Background

Beyond Literature, p. 28

Take It to the Net

Visit www.phschool.com for background and hotlinks for "One Ordinary Day, With Peanuts."

Literary Analysis

Literary Analysis and Reading Transparencies, Surprise Ending, p. 56

Reading

Selection Support Workbook: Reading Strategy, p. 111; Build Vocabulary, p. 109

Literary Analysis and Reading Transparencies, Question Characters' Actions, p. 55

BLOCK SCHEDULING: Resources marked with this symbol provide varied instruction during 90-minute blocks.

❷ Literary Analysis

Surprise Ending

A **surprise ending** is an unexpected twist at the close of a story. The writer makes a surprise ending believable by hinting at it earlier in the story, without giving the surprise away. This example shows that the writer carefully conceals some ideas from the reader, hinting at a surprise ending:

> Finally, from half a block away, he saw what he wanted, and moved out into the center of the traffic to intercept a young man, who was hurrying . . .

Based on what you learn in the story, try to predict the ending.

Connecting Literary Elements

The **plot** is the sequence of events that drives the action. In "One Ordinary Day, With Peanuts," the story focuses on the actions of Mr. Johnson after he leaves his apartment early one morning. Events take a surprising twist when he returns home at the end of the day. Notice how the events of the plot lead you to anticipate the story's conclusion.

❸ Reading Strategy

Questioning Characters' Actions

The title of the story suggests that Mr. Johnson's actions are ordinary, but the reader must decide if that is really the case. One way to do so is to **question a character's actions.** For each event, ask these questions:

- What reasons might the character have for this action?
- What behavior on the part of other characters may have led to this action?
- Does the action seem consistent with the character's personality or past behavior?

Use a chart like this one to record your questions and answers.

Action
Mr. Johnson offers to watch the little boy.
Question
What are his motives?
Answer

Vocabulary Development

irradiated (ir rā´ dē āt´ id) *v.* gave out; radiated (p. 421)

loitered (loit´ ərd) *v.* hung about; lingered (p. 421)

endeavoring (en dev´ ər iŋ) *v.* trying; attempting (p. 421)

ominously (äm´ ə nəs lē) *adv.* in a threatening way (p. 423)

buffeted (buf´ it ed) *v.* jostled; knocked about (p. 427)

insatiable (in sā´ shə bəl) *adj.* unable to be satisfied (p. 427)

omen (ō´ mən) *n.* sign foretelling a future event, either good or evil (p. 428)

impertinent (im purt´ 'n ənt) *adj.* rude; impolite (p. 430)

❷ Literary Analysis

Surprise Ending

- Invite students to discuss surprise endings they have read, or seen in films or on television. Were they able to anticipate the surprise or "twist"?
- Use the instruction for Connecting Literary Elements to emphasize that students must follow a story plot in order to make predictions about its conclusion.
- Use the Surprise Ending transparency, p. 56 in **Literary Analysis and Reading Transparencies** to help students get ready to chart the story hints indicating a surprise ending.

❸ Reading Strategy

Questioning Characters' Actions

- Explain to students that by questioning characters' actions, they become more actively involved in what they read.
- Have students use the Reading Strategy transparency, p. 55, in **Literary Analysis and Reading Transparencies** to learn how to chart a character's actions, ask questions about such actions, and offer possible answers.

Vocabulary Development

- Pronounce each vocabulary word for students, and read the definitions as a class. Have students identify any words with which they are already familiar.

CUSTOMIZE INSTRUCTION FOR UNIVERSAL ACCESS

For Less Proficient Readers	For English Learners	For Advanced Readers
To prepare for reading the story and analyzing character actions, students might benefit from setting up a chart like the one shown on p. 419. Define *motive* for students as "a reason for doing something." Warn students that Mr. Johnson's reasons are never what they seem.	To provide a context for Mr. Johnson's many encounters, discuss how people usually acted and spoke when they met total strangers in their home culture. How does this compare to practices in that country today?	Ask students to chart the progression of the story "Talk" in terms of its surprise ending. What hints did readers have that there might be an ending that was surprising? What might have masked the possibility of a surprise ending?

E-Teach

Visit E-Teach at www.phschool.com for teachers' essays on how to teach, with questions and answers.

TEACH

Step-by-Step Teaching Guide for pp. 420–430

CUSTOMIZE INSTRUCTION For Logical/Mathematical Learners

This story has an unusual plot structure—the real climax doesn't come until the last few lines. There really is no rising action or falling action, nor is there a resolution. Use the Story Map on p. 83 in **Writing Models and Graphic Organizers on Transparencies** to help students analyze plot structure. Challenge students to diagram the plot of Jackson's story and to compare their diagrams to those of one or two other stories they have read. Have them discuss, in a group, how the abrupt surprise ending contributes to the subtle horror of the story.

❶ About the Selection

Shirley Jackson's stock in trade is looking for—and finding—the menacing shadows that lurk just beneath the surface of ordinary experience. In this story she chronicles what appears to be an ordinary day in the life of a character. His actions seem positive up to the last moment, when the author unleashes a final surprise. Only then will we be able to answer the question, "Just what is 'ordinary'?"

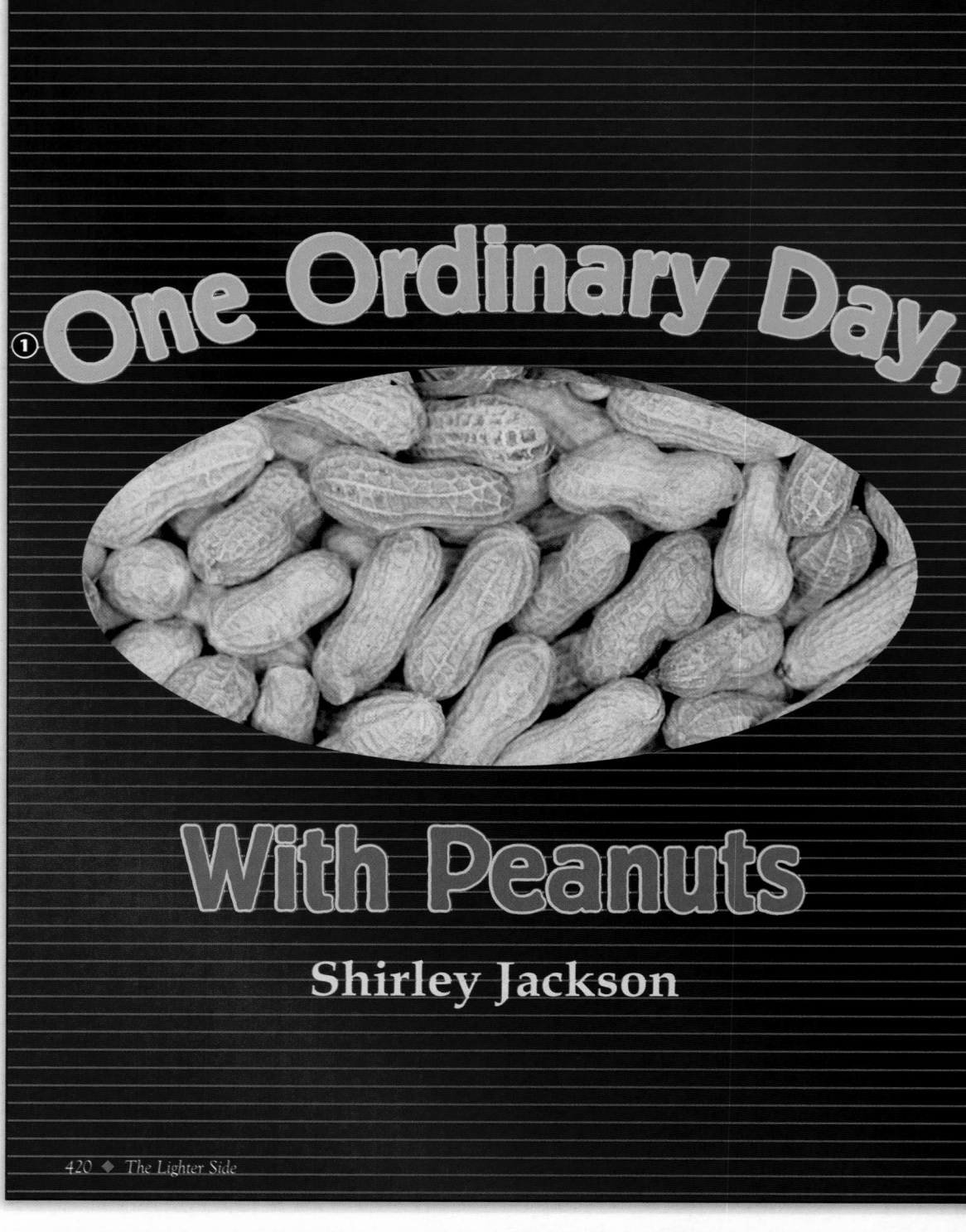

① One Ordinary Day,

With Peanuts

Shirley Jackson

TEACHING RESOURCES

The following resources can be used to enrich or extend the instruction for pp. 420–430.

Literary Analysis

- **Writing Models and Graphic Organizers on Transparencies,** p. 83
- **Selection Support,** p. 112

Reading

- **Listening to Literature Audiocassettes,** Side 12 ▪
- **Listening to Literature Audio CDs,** CD 9 ▪

▪ **BLOCK SCHEDULING:** Resources marked with this symbol provide varied instruction during 90-minute blocks.

2 Mr. John Philip Johnson shut his front door behind him and came down his front steps into the bright morning with a feeling that all was well with the world on this best of all days, and wasn't the sun warm and good, and didn't his shoes feel comfortable after the resoling, and he knew that he had undoubtedly chosen the precise very tie which belonged with the day and the sun and his comfortable feet, and, after all, wasn't the world just a wonderful place? In spite of the fact that he was a small man, and the tie was perhaps a shade vivid, Mr. Johnson irradiated this feeling of well-being as he came down the steps and onto the dirty sidewalk, and he smiled at people who passed him, and some of them even smiled back. He stopped at the newsstand on the corner and bought his paper, saying "*Good* morning" with real conviction to the man who sold him the paper and the two or three other people who were lucky enough to be buying papers when Mr. Johnson skipped up. He remembered to fill his pockets with candy and peanuts, and then he set out to get himself uptown. He stopped in a flower shop and bought a carnation for his buttonhole, and stopped almost immediately afterward to give the carnation to a small child in a carriage, who looked at him dumbly, and then smiled, and Mr. Johnson smiled, and the child's mother looked at Mr. Johnson for a minute and then smiled too.

3 When he had gone several blocks uptown, Mr. Johnson cut across the avenue and went along a side street, chosen at random; he did not follow the same route every morning, but preferred to pursue his eventful way in wide detours, more like a puppy than a man intent upon business. It happened this morning that halfway down the block a moving van was parked, and the furniture from an upstairs apartment stood half on the sidewalk, half on the steps, while an amused group of people loitered, examining the scratches on the tables and the worn spots on the chairs, and a harassed woman, trying to watch a young child and the movers and the furniture all at the same time, gave the clear impression of endeavoring to shelter her private life from the people staring at her belongings. Mr. Johnson stopped, and for a moment joined the crowd, and then he came forward and, touching his hat civilly, said, "Perhaps I can keep an eye on your little boy for you?"

The woman turned and glared at him distrustfully, and Mr. Johnson added hastily, "We'll sit right here on the steps." He beckoned to the little boy, who hesitated and then responded agreeably to Mr. Johnson's genial smile. Mr. Johnson brought out a handful of peanuts from his pocket and sat on the steps with the boy, who at first refused the peanuts on the grounds that his mother did not allow him to accept food from strangers; Mr. Johnson said that probably his mother had not intended peanuts to be included, since elephants at the circus ate them, and the boy considered, and then agreed solemnly. They sat on the steps cracking peanuts in a comradely fashion, and Mr. Johnson said, "So you're moving?"

Literary Analysis
Surprise Ending What might the words "best of all days" indicate about the way the day will end for Mr. Johnson?

irradiated (ir rā′ dē āt′ id) *v.* gave out; radiated

loitered (loit′ ərd) *v.* hung about; lingered

endeavoring (en dev′ ər iŋ) *v.* trying; attempting

4 ✓**Reading Check**
How does Mr. Johnson offer to help the woman who is moving out of her apartment?

2 Literary Analysis

Surprise Ending

- Remind students that a surprise ending in a selection is often hinted at throughout a story.
- Ask students to identify Mr. Johnson's feelings at the beginning of this day.
  Answer: Students should realize that Mr. Johnson is comfortable, the weather is lovely, and he believes the world is a wonderful place.
- Ask students to respond to the Literary Analysis question on p. 421: What might the words "best of all days" indicate about the way the day will end for Mr. Johnson?
  Possible response: Students may suggest that setting up a scene in a very positive way is a common method for leading a reader into shocking reversals of expectations.

3 Critical Thinking

Make Judgments

- Ask students whether they thought at first that Mr. Johnson was headed for a specific place.
- **Possible response:** A reader might suppose that Mr. Johnson was headed for work, or for some other place he went to regularly.
- Ask students what is odd about Mr. Johnson's behavior in this passage.
  Answer: He apparently does not have any goal in mind, but is choosing his route at random, something he does each day.

4 ✓Reading Check

Answer: Mr. Johnson offers to keep his eye on the woman's little boy for her.

CUSTOMIZE INSTRUCTION FOR UNIVERSAL ACCESS

For Special Needs Students	For Less Proficient Readers	For Gifted/Talented Students
Students may have difficulty determining the tone of the dialogue throughout the story. Have them listen to the audio recording of the selection on **Listening to Literature Audiocassettes,** Side 12, or read along as classmates read the dialogue aloud.	Encourage students to make up their own *Jeopardy!* quiz game for their classmates, based on the definitions given for the vocabulary words. Call on a student, who must ask another student a question based on a word—for example, "the way someone would describe you if you were being rude"; "What is *impertinent?*"	Invite students to imagine they are the casting director for a play based on this story. They are to find actors to portray the characters. What would they look for? Have students write descriptions for a casting agent, telling the agent what physical and personality traits they are seeking for each of the characters on this page.

5 Reading Strategy

Questioning Characters' Actions

- Point out to students that although Mr. Johnson's behavior seems friendly in this scene, could it really be called ordinary?
- Possible response: Students may note that, since parents tell children not to talk to strangers or accept treats from them, this kind of behavior is not really ordinary. It might be perceived as inappropriate or even threatening.
- Ask students to respond to the Reading Strategy question on p. 422: Why do you think Mr. Johnson watched the boy? Possible response: Students may suggest that even though they do not understand his motives, Mr. Johnson apparently watched the boy to be helpful.

"Yep," said the boy.

"Where you going?"

"Vermont."

"Nice place. Plenty of snow there. Maple sugar, too; you like maple sugar?"

"Sure."

"Plenty of maple sugar in Vermont. You going to live on a farm?"

"Going to live with Grandpa."

"Grandpa like peanuts?"

"Sure."

"Ought to take him some," said Mr. Johnson, reaching into his pocket. "Just you and Mommy going?"

"Yep."

"Tell you what," Mr. Johnson said. "You take some peanuts to eat on the train."

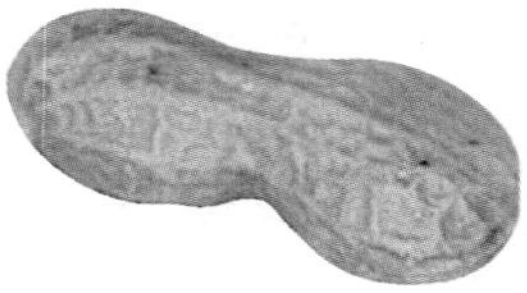

The boy's mother, after glancing at them frequently, had seemingly decided that Mr. Johnson was trustworthy, because she had devoted herself wholeheartedly to seeing that the movers did not—what movers rarely do, but every housewife believes they will—crack a leg from her good table, or set a kitchen chair down on a lamp. Most of the furniture was loaded by now, and she was deep in that nervous stage when she knew there was something she had forgotten to pack—hidden away in the back of a closet somewhere, or left at a neighbor's and forgotten, or on a clothesline—and was trying to remember under stress what it was.

"This all, lady?" the chief mover said, completing her dismay.

Uncertainly, she nodded.

"Want to go on the truck with the furniture, sonny?" the mover asked the boy, and laughed. The boy laughed too and said to Mr. Johnson, "I guess I'll have a good time at Vermont."

"Fine time," said Mr. Johnson, and stood up. "Have one more peanut before you go," he said to the boy.

5 The boy's mother said to Mr. Johnson, "Thank you so much; it was a great help to me."

"Nothing at all," said Mr. Johnson gallantly. "Where in Vermont are you going?"

The mother looked at the little boy accusingly, as though he had given away a secret of some importance, and said unwillingly, "Greenwich."

"Lovely town," said Mr. Johnson. He took out a card, and wrote a name on the back. "Very good friend of mine lives in Greenwich," he said. "Call on him for anything you need. His wife makes the best doughnuts in town," he added soberly to the little boy.

"Swell," said the little boy.

"Goodbye," said Mr. Johnson.

He went on, stepping happily with his new-shod feet, feeling the warm sun on his back and on the top of his head. Halfway down the block he met a stray dog and fed him a peanut.

Reading Strategy
Questioning Characters' Actions Why do you think Mr. Johnson watched the boy?

ENRICHMENT: Art Connection

Interpreting Photographs

Students might use the photograph on p. 423 to help them visualize the hectic surroundings within which the conversation between Mr. Johnson and the boy takes place. Tell them to imagine that this photograph depicts the street on which the family is moving from their apartment. Have the class consider such questions as "How noisy is this scene?" "How many people are in and around the family, their furniture, and the moving truck?" "How would the mother's behavior be affected by all her responsibilities plus the noise and confusion of the street?" Have them respond to the questions as they place the story characters into the photograph.

At the corner, where another wide avenue faced him, Mr. Johnson decided to go on uptown again. Moving with comparative laziness, he was passed on either side by people hurrying and frowning, and people brushed past him going the other way, clattering along to get somewhere quickly. Mr. Johnson stopped on every corner and waited patiently for the light to change, and he stepped out of the way of anyone who seemed to be in any particular hurry, but one young lady came too fast for him, and crashed wildly into him when he stooped to pat a kitten which had run out onto the sidewalk from an apartment house and was now unable to get back through the rushing feet.

"Excuse me," said the young lady, trying frantically to pick up Mr. Johnson and hurry on at the same time, "terribly sorry."

The kitten, regardless now of danger, raced back to its home. "Perfectly all right," said Mr. Johnson, adjusting himself carefully. "You seem to be in a hurry."

"Of course I'm in a hurry," said the young lady. "I'm late."

She was extremely cross and the frown between her eyes seemed well on its way to becoming permanent. She had obviously awakened late, because she had not spent any extra time in making herself look pretty, and her dress was plain and unadorned with collar or brooch, and her lipstick was noticeably crooked. She tried to brush past Mr. Johnson, but, risking her suspicious displeasure, he took her arm and said, "Please wait."

6 ▲ **Critical Viewing** This scene is filled with anonymous people moving about. What might Mr. Johnson think about these people? **[Speculate]**

7 "Look," she said ominously, "I ran into you and your lawyer can see my lawyer and I will gladly pay all damages and all inconveniences suffered therefrom but please this minute let me go because *I am late.*"

"Late for what?" said Mr. Johnson; he tried his winning smile on her but it did no more than keep her, he suspected, from knocking him down again.

ominously (äm´ ə nəs lē) *adv.* in a threatening way

8 **Reading Check**

What happens to Mr. Johnson when he stoops to pat a kitten?

6 ▶ **Critical Viewing**

Answer: Students may say that Mr. Johnson considers everyone on the street to be possible targets of his goodwill. His thinking might be: the more people, the more possibilities to do good.

7 Vocabulary Development

Using Related Words

- Point out that *omen* means "a sign, an object or event that signals good or bad fortune."
- Then, note that two words related to *omen* have distinctly negative, rather than neutral, meanings. *Ominous* means "unfavorable"; *ominously* means "in a threatening way."
- Write *omen, ominous,* and *ominously* on the board and ask students to write sentences using each.
  Sample sentences: The clear sunrise seemed the omen of a great day. The absence of other pedestrians on the gloomy street struck me as ominous. Gray, billowing clouds loomed ominously in the west.

8 **Reading Check**

Answer: A young lady crashed wildly into Mr. Johnson.

CUSTOMIZE INSTRUCTION FOR UNIVERSAL ACCESS

For Less Proficient Readers

Invite students to make two lists of action words—those that describe Mr. Johnson's movements and those that describe the movements of the people around him. Examples for Mr. Johnson: *moving with comparative laziness, waited patiently, adjusting himself carefully.* Examples for other people: *hurrying and frowning; brushed past him; clattering along.* Ask students to compare the movements of Mr. Johnson with the movement of the other characters and tell how the descriptions affect the picture they have of the characters.

❾ Reading Strategy

Questioning Characters' Actions

- Ask students why Mr. Johnson continues to delay the young woman.
  Answer: Mr. Johnson needs the woman to stay for some unrevealed purpose of his own.
- Ask students to respond to the first Reading Strategy question on p. 424: What could be Mr. Johnson's motive for offering to pay for the young woman's time?
  Answer: He wants her to stay and is willing to make it worth her while.

Monitor Progress Ask students what would have happened between Mr. Johnson and the woman in a normal story.
Answer: Mr. Johnson would have let the woman go to work, since she was obviously upset about being late. Most people would not allow themselves to be delayed by a complete stranger.

❿ Reading Strategy

Questioning Characters' Actions

- Ask students if they have figured out Mr. Johnson's general motives.
  Possible answer: Students may suggest that they are not sure of his motives, but that Mr. Johnson appears committed to doing good deeds for people, even when these deeds are not always welcome.
- Have students respond to the second Reading Strategy question on p. 424: What is unusual about Mr. Johnson's actions?
  Possible response: Mr. Johnson is apparently considering and rejecting oncoming people, and finally settles on a particular young man.

"Late for work," she said between her teeth. "Late for my employment. I have a job and if I am late I lose exactly so much an hour and I cannot really afford what your pleasant conversation is costing me, be it *ever* so pleasant."

❾ "I'll pay for it," said Mr. Johnson. Now these were magic words, not necessarily because they were true, or because she seriously expected Mr. Johnson to pay for anything, but because Mr. Johnson's flat statement, obviously innocent of irony, could not be, coming from Mr. Johnson, anything but the statement of a responsible and truthful and respectable man.

"What *do* you mean?" she asked.

"I said that since I am obviously responsible for your being late I shall certainly pay for it."

"Don't be silly," she said, and for the first time the frown disappeared. "I wouldn't expect you to pay for anything—a few minutes ago I was offering to pay *you*. Anyway," she added, almost smiling, "it *was* my fault."

"What happens if you don't go to work?"

She stared. "I don't get paid."

"Precisely," said Mr. Johnson.

"What do you mean, precisely? If I don't show up at the office exactly twenty minutes ago I lose a dollar and twenty cents an hour, or two cents a minute or . . . " She thought. ". . . Almost a dime for the time I've spent talking to you."

Mr. Johnson laughed, and finally she laughed, too. "You're late already," he pointed out. "Will you give me another four cents worth?"

"I don't understand why."

❿ "You'll see," Mr. Johnson promised. He led her over to the side of the walk, next to the buildings, and said, "Stand here," and went out into the rush of people going both ways. Selecting and considering, as one who must make a choice involving perhaps whole years of lives, he estimated the people going by. Once he almost moved, and then at the last minute thought better of it and drew back. Finally, from half a block away, he saw what he wanted, and moved out into the center of the traffic to intercept a young man, who was hurrying, and dressed as though he had awakened late, and frowning.

"Oof," said the young man, because Mr. Johnson had thought of no better way to intercept anyone than the one the young woman had unwittingly used upon him. "Where do you think you're going?" the young man demanded from the sidewalk.

"I want to speak to you," said Mr. Johnson ominously.

The young man got up nervously, dusting himself and eyeing Mr. Johnson. "What for?" he said. "What'd *I* do?"

"That's what bothers me most about people nowadays," Mr. Johnson complained broadly to the people passing. "No matter whether they've done anything or not, they always figure someone's after them. About what you're going to do," he told the young man.

"Listen," said the young man, trying to brush past him, "I'm late,

Reading Strategy
Questioning Characters' Actions What could be Mr. Johnson's motive for offering to pay for the young woman's time?

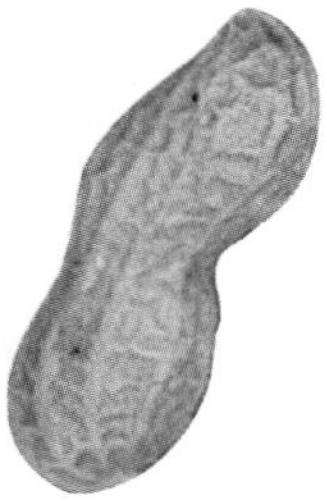

Reading Strategy
Questioning Characters' Actions What is unusual about Mr. Johnson's actions?

11 ▲ **Critical Viewing** Based upon this photograph, what can you infer about the setting of this story? **[Infer]**

and I don't have any time to listen. Here's a dime, now get going."

"Thank you," said Mr. Johnson, pocketing the dime. "Look," he said, "what happens if you stop running?"

"I'm late," said the young man, still trying to get past Mr. Johnson, who was unexpectedly clinging.

"How much you make an hour?" Mr. Johnson demanded.

"A communist, are you?" said the young man. "Now will you please let me—"

"No," said Mr. Johnson insistently, "*how* much?"

"Dollar fifty," said the young man. "And *now* will you—"

"You like adventure?"

The young man stared, and, staring, found himself caught and held by Mr. Johnson's genial smile; he almost smiled back and then

12 ✓ **Reading Check**

How does Mr. Johnson respond when the woman says she is late for work?

ENRICHMENT: Social Studies Connection

Communism

Communism is a political, economic, and social system intended to empower the working class. A central element of communism is government ownership of land, property, and enterprise. Revolutions early in the twentieth century installed communist systems in many countries (most notably, Russia). The ensuing rivalries and conflicts between communist nations and free-enterprise democracies produced a stormy era known as the Cold War.

"One Ordinary Day, With Peanuts" is set at a time when Cold-War feelings were at their height. Most Americans of the time regarded "communists" as enemies and traitors. The careers of many Americans were damaged or destroyed on the mere suspicion that they held communistic beliefs. The label "communist" still carries a problematic taint for many citizens today, long after the 1990s collapse of most communist regimes.

11 ▶ **Critical Viewing**

Answer: The photograph depicts a crowded sidewalk on a busy street lined with tall buildings; people are moving in different directions, going about their business. Students can use these clues to infer that the setting is a large city.

12 ✓ **Reading Check**

Answer: Mr. Johnson offers to pay for the time she will lose by being late.

13 Background

Coney Island

The modern roller coaster was born at Coney Island. Before 1907, roller coasters were less thrilling, with a slow ride that took wide turns and gentle hills. The terror-filled *Drop-the-Dip* debuted in 1907 with a high-speed ride broken up by steep drops and tight turns. Early coasters of this type did not yet utilize friction on the undersides of the wheels, so high side-rails were needed to keep the cars on the track.

14 Critical Thinking

Analyze

- Have students discuss Mr. Johnson's behavior in light of people's response to him. Ask them what readers might think of his actions if people responded positively to those actions?
  Answer: Students may agree that if people's responses to Mr. Johnson were positive, his actions could be seen as positive.
- Ask students what kind of vocabulary is used to describe the responses of the young man and young woman to Mr. Johnson's behavior.
  Answer: *surprised, dazedly, helplessly, stiffly, nervously,* and so forth.
- Ask students what other judgment could be made of Mr. Johnson's behavior, based on responses to it.
  Answer: His behavior, rather than consisting of good deeds, consists of interrupting people who only want to complete their own plans for the day.
- Ask students the Reading Strategy question on p. 426: Why might Mr. Johnson have "captured" the young man?
  Possible response: He wanted to introduce the young man to the girl.

repressed it and made an effort to tear away. "I got to *hurry*," he said.

"Mystery? Like surprises? Unusual and exciting events?"

"You selling something?"

"Sure," said Mr. Johnson. "You want to take a chance?"

The young man hesitated, looking longingly up the avenue toward what might have been his destination and then, when Mr. Johnson said, "I'll pay for it," with his own peculiar convincing emphasis, turned and said, "Well, okay. But I got to see it first, what I'm buying."

Mr. Johnson, breathing hard, led the young man over to the side where the girl was standing; she had been watching with interest Mr. Johnson's capture of the young man and now, smiling timidly, she looked at Mr. Johnson as though prepared to be surprised at nothing.

Mr. Johnson reached into his pocket and took out his wallet. "Here," he said, and handed a bill to the girl. "This about equals your day's pay."

"But no," she said, surprised in spite of herself. "I mean, I *couldn't*."

"Please do not interrupt," Mr. Johnson told her. "And *here*," he said to the young man, "this will take care of *you*." The young man accepted the bill dazedly, but said, "Probably counterfeit," to the young woman out of the side of his mouth. "Now," Mr. Johnson went on, disregarding the young man, "what is your name, miss?"

14 "Kent," she said helplessly. "Mildred Kent."

"Fine," said Mr. Johnson. "And you, sir?"

"Arthur Adams," said the young man stiffly.

"Splendid," said Mr. Johnson. "Now, Miss Kent, I would like you to meet Mr. Adams. Mr. Adams, Miss Kent."

Miss Kent stared, wet her lips nervously, made a gesture as though she might run, and said, "How do you do?"

Mr. Adams straightened his shoulders, scowled at Mr. Johnson, made a gesture as though he might run, and said, "How do you do?"

"Now *this*," said Mr. Johnson, taking several bills from his wallet, "should be enough for the day for both of you. I would suggest, perhaps, Coney Island◆—although I personally am not fond of the place—or perhaps a nice lunch somewhere, and dancing, or a matinee,[1] or even a movie, although take care to choose a really good one;

1. **matinee** here, an afternoon performance of an on- or off-Broadway show.

Literature in context 13 — Geography Connection

◆ ***Coney Island***

Coney Island—the place to which Mr. Johnson suggests Miss Kent and Mr. Adams might go—is a famous beach area and amusement park in Brooklyn, one of the five boroughs of New York City. During the first half of the twentieth century, it was one of the largest amusement areas in the world. Millions of New Yorkers were drawn to its rides, games, entertainment, restaurants, and swimming each year. Although attendance was down during the early 1950s because of the polio epidemic and the resulting fear of contagion, by 1955—when this story was published—attendance was back up to 1.5 million on July 4th.

The Cyclone at Coney Island

Reading Strategy
Questioning Characters' Actions Why might Mr. Johnson have "captured" the young man?

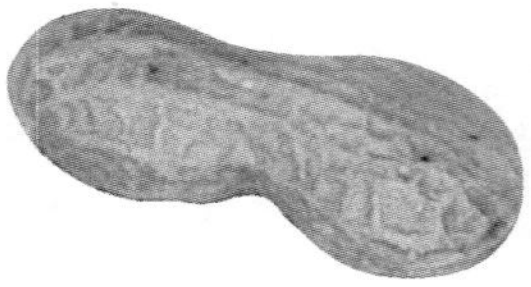

there are so many bad movies these days. "You might," he said, struck with an inspiration, "visit the Bronx Zoo, or the Planetarium.[2] Anywhere, as a matter of fact," he concluded, "that you would like to go. Have a nice time."

As he started to move away, Arthur Adams, breaking from his dumbfounded stare, said, "But see here, mister, you *can't* do this. Why—how do you know—I mean, *we* don't even know—I mean, how do you know we won't just take the money and not do what you said?"

"You've taken the money," Mr. Johnson said. "You don't have to follow any of my suggestions. You may know something you prefer to do—perhaps a museum, or something."

"But suppose I just run away with it and leave her here?"

"I know you won't," said Mr. Johnson gently, "because you remembered to ask *me* that. Goodbye," he added, and went on.

As he stepped up the street, conscious of the sun on his head and his good shoes, he heard from somewhere behind him the young man saying, "Look, you know you don't have to if you don't want to," and the girl saying, "But unless you don't want to . . ." Mr. Johnson smiled to himself and then thought that he had better hurry along; when he wanted to he could move very quickly, and before the young woman had gotten around to saying, "Well, *I* will if *you* will," Mr. Johnson was several blocks away and had already stopped twice, once to help a lady lift several large packages into a taxi and once to hand a peanut to a seagull. By this time he was in an area of large stores and many more people and he was buffeted constantly from either side by people hurrying and cross and late and sullen. Once he offered a peanut to a man who asked him for a dime, and once he offered a peanut to a bus driver who had stopped his bus at an intersection and had opened the window next to his seat and put out his head as though longing for fresh air and the comparative quiet of the traffic. 15 The man wanting a dime took the peanut because Mr. Johnson had wrapped a dollar bill around it, but the bus driver took the peanut and asked ironically, "You want a transfer, Jack?"

On a busy corner Mr. Johnson encountered two young people—for one minute he thought they might be Mildred Kent and Arthur Adams—who were eagerly scanning a newspaper, their backs pressed against a storefront to avoid the people passing, their heads bent together. Mr. Johnson, whose curiosity was insatiable, leaned onto the storefront next to them and peeked over the man's shoulder; they were scanning the "Apartments Vacant" columns.

Mr. Johnson remembered the street where the woman and her little boy were going to Vermont and he tapped the man on the shoulder and said amiably, "Try down on West Seventeen. About the middle of the block, people moved out this morning."

buffeted (buf′ it ed) *v.* jostled; knocked about

insatiable (in sā′ shə bəl) *adj.* unable to be satisfied

16 **Reading Check**

What does Mr. Johnson offer to the man who asks him for a dime?

2. **Planetarium** the Hayden Planetarium, adjoining the American Museum of Natural History in New York City.

15 Reading Strategy

Questioning Characters' Actions

- Ask students why the bus driver asks Mr. Johnson, "You want a transfer, Jack?"
  Answer: In many bus systems, a passenger who pays for a ticket gets a transfer to another bus if he or she asks for it. The bus driver is sarcastically wondering if Mr. Johnson expects something in exchange for the peanut.
- Have students identify what the bus driver may be feeling about Mr. Johnson.
  Possible response: The bus driver may be suspicious of Mr. Johnson's motives.

Monitor Progress Ask students if they think readers should be suspicious of Mr. Johnson's motives, and if so, why?
Answer: Students may suggest that even though Mr. Johnson appears to be doing good, his true motives for doing so remain unexplained.

16 Reading Check

Answer: Mr. Johnson offers the man a peanut.

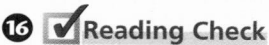

CUSTOMIZE INSTRUCTION FOR UNIVERSAL ACCESS

For English Learners	For Gifted/Talented Students
Invite students to identify capitalized proper nouns on pp. 426–427. (*Mildred Kent* - specific person; *Arthur Adams* - specific person; *Coney Island* - specific place; *Bronx Zoo* - specific place; *Jack* - nickname for Mr. Johnson; *Vermont* - specific place; *West Seventeen* - specific place.) Remind students that in English the specific names of persons, places, and things are capitalized.	Ask students to note the reference to Mr. Johnson's feeling the sun on his head near the top of p. 427. Have them reread the selection to find other references to his sense of being warmed and lighted by the sun. What do students think the writer means this image to suggest about Mr. Johnson, or at least about Mr. Johnson's perception of himself? Is this description ironic?

17 Literary Analysis

Surprise Ending

- Remind students that they have had hints throughout the story that Mr. Johnson's kindness is not what it might appear to be. What kind of acts does he perform in this passage?
  Answer: He feeds pigeons in the park, referees two checker games, and watches a small boy and girl whose mother had fallen asleep.
- Ask students why the mother described in this passage awakened in surprise and fear.
  Answer: She had been watching her boy and girl and did not mean to fall asleep. At first waking, she feared that something might have happened to her children.
- Have students respond to the Literary Analysis question on p. 428: When she awoke and saw Mr. Johnson, the mother's fear changed to amusement. What do you think the story's tone will be at the end?
  Possible response: Students may suggest that this scene is hinting that the story will end on a tone that is surprising, given what has gone on previously.

18 Reading Strategy

Questioning Characters' Actions

- Ask students what reasons Mr. Johnson gives for his race advice to the cab driver.
  Answer: His reasons seem based on superstitions about "fire signs," grain, names, and days of the week.
- Ask students to respond to the Reading Strategy question on p. 429: Is Mr. Johnson's behavior in the cab consistent with the impression you have of him up to this point?
  Possible response: Mr. Johnson continues to be helpful, but his bizarre, superstitious explanations provide a late but important clue to his strange motives.

"Say, what do you—" said the man, and then, seeing Mr. Johnson clearly, "Well thanks. Where did you say?"

"West Seventeen," said Mr. Johnson. "About the middle of the block." He smiled again and said, "Good luck."

"Thanks," said the man.

"Thanks," said the girl, as they moved off.

"Goodbye," said Mr. Johnson.

He lunched alone in a pleasant restaurant, where the food was rich, and only Mr. Johnson's excellent digestion could encompass two of their whipped-cream-and-chocolate-and-rum-cake pastries for dessert. He had three cups of coffee, tipped the waiter largely, and went out into the street again into the wonderful sunlight, his shoes still comfortable and fresh on his feet. Outside he found a beggar staring into the windows of the restaurant he had left and, carefully looking through the money in his pocket, Mr. Johnson approached the beggar and pressed some coins and a couple of bills into his hand. "It's the price of the veal cutlet lunch plus tip," said Mr. Johnson. "Goodbye."

17 After his lunch he rested; he walked into the nearest park and fed peanuts to the pigeons. It was late afternoon by the time he was ready to start back downtown, and he had refereed two checker games and watched a small boy and girl whose mother had fallen asleep and awakened with surprise and fear which turned to amusement when she saw Mr. Johnson. He had given away almost all of his candy, and had fed all the rest of his peanuts to the pigeons, and it was time to go home. Although the late afternoon sun was pleasant, and his shoes were still entirely comfortable, he decided to take a taxi downtown.

He had a difficult time catching a taxi, because he gave up the first three or four empty ones to people who seemed to need them more; finally, however, he stood alone on the corner and—almost like netting a frisky fish—he hailed desperately until he succeeded in catching a cab which had been proceeding with haste uptown and seemed to draw in towards Mr. Johnson against its own will.

"Mister," the cab driver said as Mr. Johnson climbed in, "I figured you was an omen, like. I wasn't going to pick you up at all."

18 "Kind of you," said Mr. Johnson ambiguously.

"If I'd of let you go it would of cost me ten bucks," said the driver.

"Really?" said Mr. Johnson.

"Yeah," said the driver. "Guy just got out of the cab, he turned around and give me ten bucks, said take this and bet it in a hurry on a horse named Vulcan,[3] right away."

"Vulcan?" said Mr. Johnson, horrified. "A fire sign[4] on a Wednesday?"

"What?" said the driver. "Anyway, I said to myself if I got no fare between here and there I'd bet the ten, but if anyone looked like they

Literary Analysis
Surprise Ending When she awoke and saw Mr. Johnson, the mother's fear changed to amusement. What do you think the story's tone will be at the end?

omen (ō′ mən) *n.* sign foretelling a future event, either good or evil

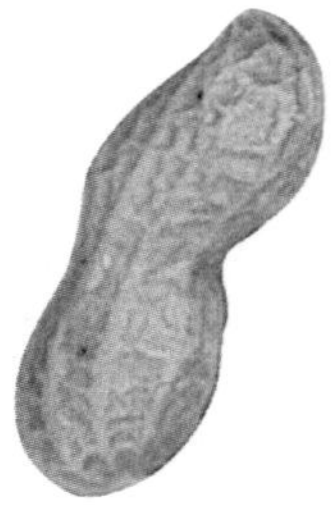

3. **Vulcan** also the name of the Roman god of fire.
4. **fire sign** term borrowed from astrology, referring here to Vulcan.

CUSTOMIZE INSTRUCTION FOR UNIVERSAL ACCESS

For Less Proficient Readers	For Gifted/Talented Students
Have students view "A Tour of New York City" on the **Interest Grabber Video,** Tape 2. Ask them to imagine that Mr. Johnson is present in the film. Which people seen in the film do they think he might have chosen for one of his good deeds? Invite interested students to write a short dialogue between Mr. Johnson and one or more of the people in the film.	What if, on this "Ordinary Day," it had been Mr. Johnson's turn to do harm? Have students review Mr. Johnson's encounters in the story and speculate how each might have turned out if Mr. Johnson had wanted to create problems for the people he meets.

needed the cab I'd take it as an omen and I'd take the ten home to the wife."

"You were very right," said Mr. Johnson heartily. "This is Wednesday, you would have lost your money. Monday, yes, or even Saturday. But never never never a fire sign on a Wednesday. Sunday would have been good, now."

"Vulcan don't run on Sunday," said the driver.

"You wait till another day," said Mr. Johnson. "Down this street, please, driver. I'll get off on the next corner."

"He *told* me Vulcan, though," said the driver.

"I'll tell you," said Mr. Johnson, hesitating with the door of the cab half open. "You take that ten dollars and I'll give you another ten dollars to go with it, and you go right ahead and bet that money on any Thursday on any horse that has a name indicating . . . let me see, Thursday . . . well, grain. Or any growing food."

"Grain?" said the driver. "You mean a horse named, like, Wheat or something?"

"Certainly," said Mr. Johnson. "Or, as a matter of fact, to make it even easier, any horse whose name includes the letters C, R, L. Perfectly simple."

"Tall corn?" said the driver, a light in his eye. "You mean a horse named, like, Tall Corn?"

"Absolutely," said Mr. Johnson. "Here's your money."

"Tall Corn," said the driver. "Thank *you*, mister."

"Goodbye," said Mr. Johnson.

He was on his own corner and went straight up to his apartment. He let himself in and called "Hello?" and Mrs. Johnson answered from the kitchen, "Hello, dear, aren't you early?"

"Took a taxi home," Mr. Johnson said. "I remembered the cheesecake, too. What's for dinner?"

Mrs. Johnson came out of the kitchen and kissed him; she was a comfortable woman, and smiling as Mr. Johnson smiled. "Hard day?" she asked.

"Not very," said Mr. Johnson, hanging his coat in the closet. "How about you?"

"So-so," she said. She stood in the kitchen doorway while he settled into his easy chair and took off his good shoes and took out the paper he had bought that morning. "Here and there," she said.

"I didn't do so badly," Mr. Johnson said. "Couple young people."

19 "Fine," she said. "I had a little nap this afternoon, took it easy most of the day. Went into a department store this morning and accused

Reading Strategy

Questioning Characters' Actions Is Mr. Johnson's behavior in the cab consistent with the impression you have of him up to this point? Why or why not?

20 Reading Check

Why does Mr. Johnson have a hard time catching a cab?

19 Literary Analysis

Surprise Ending

- Ask students what is surprising about the wife's day compared to Mr. Johnson's day.
  Answer: While Mr. Johnson was doing good deeds, Mrs. Johnson was causing harm.

Reteach Remind students that, in the plots of many stories, the climax is reached before the end of the story. The climax is usually followed by falling action and a resolution. Stories with surprise endings follow a different pattern. Use the following diagrams to visually represent these differences.

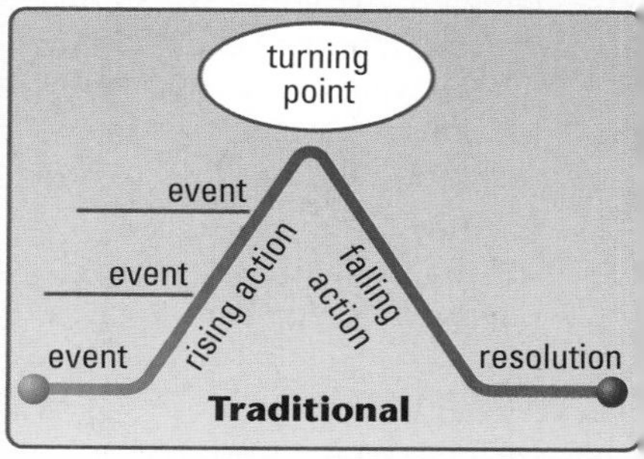

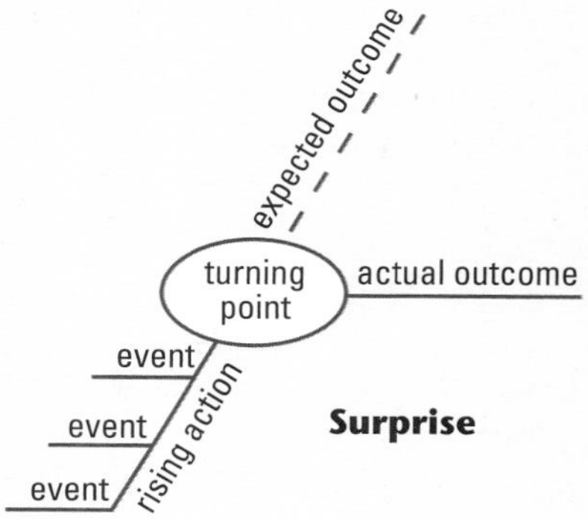

20 Reading Check

Answer: Mr. Johnson gave four empty cabs to people in need and it was late in the day when cabs are in demand.

ASSESS

Answers for p. 430

Review and Assess

1. Most students may have anticipated some unusual ending, but still may have been unprepared for the actual surprise.
2. **(a)** Mr. Johnson watches the son of the woman moving to Vermont; he introduces a young man and young woman to one another; he gives a poor man money for a meal. **(b)** He helps them appreciate life and leisure.
3. **(a)** She has spent the day causing harm to people. **(b)** Students may say that they expected to meet a woman who shared Mr. Johnson's commitment to doing good.
4. **(a)** They will change roles. **(b)** They take turns doing good deeds and doing harm to people. **(c)** He will do something to cause them pain.
5. **(a)** It is a typical workday for most of the people Mr. Johnson meets, and he and his wife seem to find his own behavior and hers completely ordinary. **(b)** Few people go around cities helping others; few people have the leisure time Mr. Johnson seems to have; his intentional benevolence is matched by his wife's malevolence, and both seem to have extraordinary powers of some sort.
6. The story pokes fun at the fast pace of modern life, lack of leisure time, overwhelming interest in making money, suspicion of strangers, and lack of goodwill.
7. **(a)** Students might suggest that they would have tried to get away from him without being rude. **(b)** Students may suggest that it is always wise to question behavior that is too good to be true.

the woman next to me of shoplifting, and had the store detective pick her up. Sent three dogs to the pound—you know, the usual thing. Oh, and listen," she added, remembering.

"What?" asked Mr. Johnson.

"Well," she said, "I got onto a bus and asked the driver for a transfer, and when he helped someone else first I said that he was impertinent, and quarreled with him. And then I said why wasn't he in the army, and I said it loud enough for everyone to hear, and I took his number and I turned in a complaint. Probably got him fired."

"Fine," said Mr. Johnson. "But you do look tired. Want to change over tomorrow?"

"I would like to," she said. "I could do with a change."

"Right," said Mr. Johnson. "What's for dinner?"

"Veal cutlet."

"Had it for lunch," said Mr. Johnson.

impertinent (im pʉrt´ ən ənt) *adj.* rude; impolite

Shirley Jackson

(1919–1965)

As a writer, Shirley Jackson seems to wear two hats. On one hand, she writes warm-hearted portraits of family life. On the other, she is a master of horror fiction. Jackson brings her comic eye to both forms, capturing the humor of family life and adding a touch of humor to her tales of horror by grounding strange happenings in everyday events.

Born in San Francisco, Jackson spent most of her adult life in the East. She first won attention with her short story "The Lottery," which appeared in 1948 in the literary magazine *The New Yorker*. This eerie tale of a bizarre and deadly small-town New England lottery provoked more reader reaction than other work the magazine had published. Her horror novels include *The Bird's Nest* (1954), *The Sundial* (1958), and *The Haunting of Hill House*, which became the basis of the popular 1963 film, *The Haunting*.

Review and Assess

Thinking About the Selection

1. **Respond:** How did you feel when you read the ending? Explain.
2. **(a) Recall:** Give at least three examples from the story that show how Mr. Johnson helped people. **(b) Infer:** Through his actions, what might Mr. Johnson teach people?
3. **(a) Recall:** According to what she tells her husband when he gets home, how did Mrs. Johnson spend her day? **(b) Make a Judgment:** Is this the sort of wife you would have imagined for Mr. Johnson, based on your impressions of his personality up to that point? Explain.
4. **(a) Recall:** What do the couple decide they will do on the next day? **(b) Infer:** What do you discover about the two of them? **(c) Hypothesize:** How do you suppose Mr. Johnson will treat each of the people he met today if he runs into them again tomorrow?
5. **(a) Compare:** In what ways is Mr. Johnson's day ordinary, as the title suggests? **(b) Contrast:** In what ways is his day out of the ordinary?
6. **Apply:** At which aspects of modern life does this story poke fun?
7. **(a) Extend:** How would you have responded to Mr. Johnson if you had been Miss Kent or Mr. Adams? **(b) Take a Position:** Do you think it is helpful or harmful to be suspicious of strangers doing good deeds? Explain.

ASSESSMENT PRACTICE: Reading Comprehension

Cause and Effect (For more practice, see Test Preparation Workbook, p. 28.)

Use the following sample test item to show students how to identify the cause of a literary effect.

Mary practiced the lines for weeks before the drama club auditions. Her friends grew tired of listening to her talk about the part she wanted. She even started wearing clothes that made her look like the character! On the day of try-outs, however, Mary did not appear.

Why is it surprising that Mary did not appear?

A Her friends didn't want to hear about the part.
B She probably didn't feel ready.
C Her clothes matched the character's.
D Her actions indicated that she really wanted to get a part.

The correct answer, *D*, is a synthesis of all the reasons in the text that cause readers to expect Mary to show up. This is the cause of the surprise.

Review and Assess

Literary Analysis

Surprise Ending

1. Considering Mr. Johnson's behavior throughout the story, why does the ending come as a **surprise**?
2. What hints point to the unexpected ending? Explain.
3. What might the ending suggest about unexpected acts of kindness or mean behavior?

Connecting Literary Elements

4. In many stories, the climax, or high point of the **plot**, occurs toward the end, leaving the reader with more information following the climax to help tie up loose ends. Using a chart like the one shown, analyze the placement of the high point of this story.

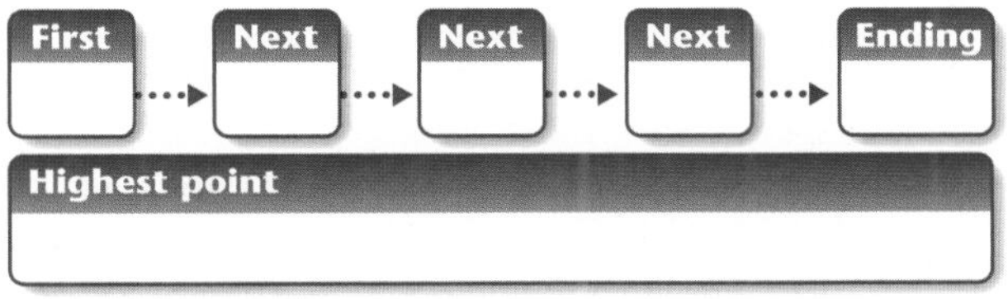

5. What is the effect of this unusual order of events?

Reading Strategy

Questioning Characters' Actions

6. What seems to motivate Mr. Johnson in his behavior toward others as he travels around New York?
7. Why do you think Mr. Johnson chose to help the particular individuals mentioned in the story?
8. What does the decision to change roles with his wife suggest about his motives?

Extend Understanding

9. **Cultural Connection:** (a) How does the setting of this story—a busy city—affect the Johnsons' work? (b) Would the story have been as successful if it had been set in a small town? Explain.

Quick Review

A **surprise ending** is an unexpected close to a story.

The **plot** is the sequence of events that drives the action.

To **question characters' actions,** look for reasons behind their words and deeds.

Take It to the Net

www.phschool.com

Take the interactive self-test online to check your understanding of the selection.

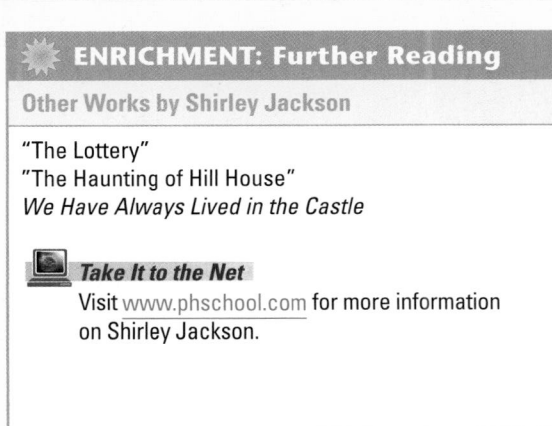

ENRICHMENT: Further Reading

Other Works by Shirley Jackson

"The Lottery"
"The Haunting of Hill House"
We Have Always Lived in the Castle

Take It to the Net

Visit www.phschool.com for more information on Shirley Jackson.

Answers for p. 431

Review and Assess

1. Mr. Johnson seems to have been motivated by benevolence, but in the end we discover he had ulterior motives.
2. Possible hints include Mr. Johnson's insistent behavior with the young couple suggests that he has an agenda that is something more than trying to be nice to people; the cab driver calling Mr. Johnson an omen; and Mr. Johnson's omen-filled advice to the cab driver.
3. Human experience, whether pleasurable or painful, is whimsical, inexplicable, and beyond human control.
4. First: scene with moving mother and son: Next: scene with young man and young woman; Next: scene with cab driver; Ending: scene with wife in apartment; Highest Point: realization that husband and wife go out each day to do good and evil.
5. The effect of this unusual order is a sense of dislocation and unease. The ending is downbeat and disturbing.
6. Goodwill and benevolence seem to motivate Mr. Johnson.
7. He saw them as needy people who would be willing to accept his offers of friendship.
8. The decision to switch roles reveals that Mr. Johnson's true motive lies in a bizarre, superstitious plan.
9. **(a)** The busyness and hectic quality of the city make it more likely that people will be willing to accept Mr. Johnson's aid. **(b)** A more leisurely pace in a small town might contribute to people's asking more questions or having more concerns about Mr. Johnson's behavior.

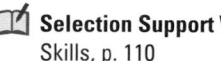

EXTEND

Answers for p. 432

❶ Vocabulary Development

1. sent out energy
2. place where one can learn about planets
3. unable to be satisfied

Spelling Strategy

1. passed
2. dumbly
3. ticking

Concept Development: Synonyms

1. b
2. c
3. a
4. a
5. c
6. a
7. b
8. c

❷ Grammar

1. S: woman; V: ran; OBJ of PREP: Mr. Johnson
2. S: Mr. Johnson; V: spoke; OBJ of PREP: people
3. S: She; V: watched; DO: Mr. Johnson; OBJ of PREP: interest
4. S:He; V: gave: DO: peanuts; OBJ of PREP: people
5. S: He; V: paid; DO: her; OBJ of PREP: hours

Writing Application

Sample response: Mr. Johnson approached a man on the sidewalk. He handed the man a peanut. The man thanked him for his generosity.

Integrate Language Skills

❶ Vocabulary Development Lesson

Related Words: *omen*

An *omen* is "a sign or event that foretells the future." Such signs can be positive or negative, but the word *ominously* focuses only on the negative: It means "in a way that seems to foretell doom." Write the meaning of each word below, using the meaning of the related word.

1. *irradiated*—related word: *radiant*
2. *planetarium*—related word: *planet*
3. *insatiable*—related word: *satisfy*

Spelling Strategy

When you add an ending to a word that ends with two or more consonants, never double the final consonant. Thus, *impertinent* becomes *impertinently*, but *final* becomes *finally*. Write the correct spelling for each item below.

1. pass + *-ed* 2. dumb + *-ly* 3. tick + *-ing*

Concept Development: Synonyms

Choose the letter of the word that is most nearly the same in meaning as the first word.

1. irradiated: (a) darkened, (b) glowed, (c) frozen
2. loitered: (a) dirtied, (b) delivered, (c) lingered
3. endeavoring: (a) trying, (b) asking, (c) preparing
4. ominously: (a) threateningly, (b) brightly, (c) loudly
5. buffeted: (a) cooked, (b) shined, (c) shoved
6. insatiable: (a) unquenchable, (b) indefinite, (c) odd
7. omen: (a) stamp, (b) signal, (c) cause
8. impertinent: (a) impatient, (b) unrelated, (c) impolite

❷ Grammar Lesson

Direct Object or Object of a Preposition?

A **direct object** is a noun or pronoun that receives the action of a transitive action verb. The **object of the preposition** is the noun or pronoun at the end of a prepositional phrase. Look at the following examples.

S V DO

Direct Object: Mr. Johnson ate *lunch*. (*lunch* receives the action of *ate*)

S V

Object of a Preposition: Mr. Johnson ate

PREP PHRASE

at a pleasant *restaurant*. (*restaurant* is the object of the preposition *at*)

Practice Copy each sentence. Label the subjects and verbs. Circle each direct object. Underline each object of a preposition.

1. The woman ran into Mr. Johnson.
2. Mr. Johnson spoke to the people.
3. She watched Mr. Johnson with interest.
4. He gave peanuts to the people he met.
5. He paid her for the hours she missed.

Writing Application Write a paragraph about "One Ordinary Day, With Peanuts" that includes at least one direct object and one prepositional phrase.

WG Prentice Hall Writing and Grammar Connection: Chapter 20, Section 3

TEACHING RESOURCES

The following resources can be used to enrich or extend the instruction for pp. 432–433.

Vocabulary

- **Selection Support:** Build Vocabulary, p. 109
- **Vocabulary and Spelling Practice Book** (Use this booklet for skills enrichment.)

Grammar

- **Selection Support Workbook:** Build Grammar Skills, p. 110
- **Writing and Grammar,** Gold Level, p. 434 ■

Daily Language Practice Transparencies

Writing

- **Writing and Grammar,** Gold Level, p. 141 ■
- **Writing and Grammar iText CD-ROM** ■

■ **BLOCK SCHEDULING:** Resources marked with this symbol provide varied instruction during 90-minute blocks.

❸ Writing Lesson

Summary

A summary provides only the most important details of a story or event. Write a summary of Mrs. Johnson's day.

Prewriting Start by imagining Mrs. Johnson's unusual day. Fill out an hour-by-hour schedule showing all her activities. Underline the most important events in your list.

Drafting Recount the events of the day in chronological order. Use transitions like *next*, *meanwhile*, and *later* to clarify the order of events.

Revising Reread your summary to make sure that you have included all of the important details of the day. Place boxes between sentences to help you evaluate whether you need to add transitions. Where necessary, add transition words to make your writing clearer.

Model: Revising to Add Transitions

☑She shut the door, ready to start her day. ☐ *First,* she bought the paper, giving everyone an angry snarl. ☐ *Then,* she looked for her first victim.

Transition words smooth out the writing and make the sequence of events clear.

WG *Prentice Hall Writing and Grammar Connection: Chapter 7, Section 4*

❹ Extension Activities

Listening and Speaking Imagine meeting both Mr. Johnson and Mrs. Johnson on this not-so-ordinary day. Prepare a **monologue** describing your feelings before and after the encounter. Review the story before you write.

- Notice how people reacted to Mr. Johnson's generosity.
- Think about how Mrs. Johnson probably treated people and how her actions would compare with Mr. Johnson's.

Rehearse your monologue, and present it to your class.

Research and Technology In a small group, put together a **research report** about the setting of the story, New York City in the 1950s. Before starting your research, generate research questions about the tourist attractions in New York City and the kinds of changes that took place in the 1950s. Use library sources, including encyclopedias on CD-ROM, to help you. **[Group Activity]**

Take It to the Net www.phschool.com

Go online for an additional research activity using the Internet.

Lesson Support for p. 433

❸ Writing Lesson

- Model a summary for students by summarizing one of the stories they have read recently.
- Tell students that when they summarize they note only the most important events and details of a story.
- Have students exchange summaries with partners to check use of transitions.

❹ Listening and Speaking

- Invite the class to work individually to create monologues about their meetings with the Johnsons.
- Ask pairs to present their monologues to one another in preparation for presentation to the whole class.
- Evaluate students' presentations using the rubric for Delivering a Narrative Presentation, p. 27 in **Performance Assessment and Portfolio Management.**

CUSTOMIZE INSTRUCTION For Universal Access

To address different learning styles, use the activities suggested in the **Extension Activities** booklet, p. 28.

- For Interpersonal and Verbal/Linguistic Learners, use Activity 5.
- For Visual/Spatial Learners, use Activity 6.
- For Verbal/Linguistic Learners, use Activity 7.

ASSESSMENT RESOURCES

The following resources can be used to assess students' knowledge and skills.

Selection Assessment

- **Formal Assessment:** Selection Test, pp. 94–96
- **Open Book Test,** pp. 82–84
- **Got It! Assessment Videotapes,** Tape 2
- **Test Bank Software**

Take It to the Net

Visit www.phschool.com for self-tests and additional questions on the selection.

Listening and Speaking Rubric

- **Performance Assess. and Portfolio Mgmt.**, p. 27

PRENTICE HALL ASSESSMENT SYSTEM

- **Workbook**
- **Skill Book**
- **Transparencies**
- **CD-ROM**

Lesson Objectives

1. To write a test essay
2. To learn the criteria included in a successful test essay
3. Use writing strategies to choose a topic, gather details, plan, organize, write, and revise a test essay

Model From Literature

Explain that in Unit 4, students will encounter various types of essays.

Writing for Assessment: Test Essay

- Have students read the text that appears in this section on p. 434.
- Point out that students will be asked to meet the Assignment Criteria (bulleted list on p. 434) as they create their responses to literature.

Prewriting

- Point out that in this assignment, students may choose the topic they will write about. This may not always be the case on tests.
- Have students create their own "essay question," based on the topic of their choice.
- Direct students' attention to the chart on p. 434. Ask students to identify key words in the essay questions they have created.
- Have students read the Example Essay Question on p. 434. Ask students to model their own essay question and main idea after the example.

Writing WORKSHOP

Writing for Assessment: Test Essay

To make sure that you are learning the information and skills you need to succeed, teachers frequently assess your knowledge. Tests, oral reports, and research papers are ways of evaluating your progress. Essay tests are the most common type of **writing for assessment.**

Assignment Criteria. Successful writing for assessment usually has the following characteristics:

- a direct response to the test question
- a thesis statement that is clearly worded and well supported
- specific information about the topic, drawn from your reading or from class discussion
- a clear organization

To preview the criteria on which your writing for assessment may be judged, see the Rubric on page 437.

Prewriting

Choose a topic. On some essay tests, a single topic is assigned. In cases in which you have the opportunity to choose a topic, use the following techniques:

- **Consider what you know.** Jot down specific details for each topic. You should choose a topic that you know well.
- **Pinpoint your strengths.** The question may ask you to *analyze*, to *predict*, or to *explain*. Choose a topic for which you can provide facts to support the type of response required.

Narrow your response. As you prepare to write your essay, circle key words in the question and take notes to help you interpret the directions. The chart on this page shows how specific verbs should direct the purpose of your writing.

Draft a single sentence. Identify in a single sentence the main idea you will develop in your essay. Once you choose your topic, jot down this sentence and refer to it to remind you of your position. Use your main idea to formulate your thesis statement when you draft.

Example Essay Question: Discuss how someone you admire overcame an obstacle in order to succeed.

Main Idea: I will discuss how Stevie Wonder and Jackie Joyner-Kersee overcame their disabilities.

Narrow Your Response

Key Words	Essay Objectives
Analyze	Examine how various elements contribute to the whole.
Describe	Give main features and examples of each
Compare and Contrast	Stress how two works or other items are alike and different.
Discuss	Support a generalization with facts and examples.
Explain	Clarify by probing reasons, causes, results, and effects.
Defend	Support your position with examples from the text.

TEACHING RESOURCES

The following resources can be used to enrich or extend the instruction for pp. 434–435.

Writing and Grammar, Gold Level, pp. 308–317

Performance Assessment and Portfolio Management, pp. 11, 44

Writing and Grammar iText CD-ROM
Students can use the following tools as they complete their responses to literature:
- KWL Chart
- Topic Bank
- Descriptive Word Bin

Student Model

Before you begin drafting your writing for assessment, read this student model and review the characteristics of effective writing for assessment.

Eddie Harris
Chicago, IL

Question: *In an essay, discuss how someone you admire overcame an obstacle in order to succeed.*

The best way to overcome a disability is to face it head-on and not let it prevent you from achieving great things. This is the lesson I draw from the lives of two people whom I admire—the musician Stevie Wonder and the track-and-field star Jackie Joyner-Kersee. I respect them for their courage and strength in overcoming obstacles. Both are African Americans with disabilities who defied obstacles in order to be successful in their fields.

> The author uses a general statement to introduce his response to the essay question.

> This author presents a thesis statement that focuses his answer to the essay question.

Stevie Wonder became blind after he was born prematurely and received too much oxygen. But that did not stop him from becoming one of the best musicians ever. He started out singing rock and roll songs outside a church in Detroit. Eventually, he found his way to Motown Studios at a time when Motown was one of the top recording studios in America. There his career skyrocketed. He became one of the best Motown singers even though he was only ten years old.

He has since been nominated for more Grammy awards than any other musician. His blindness is no disability for him. On the music charts, Stevie Wonder opened the gates for a new sound . . . not just for African Americans but for everyone else as well.

Another person that I admire for the way she overcame obstacles is Jackie Joyner-Kersee, a famous track-and-field star. She was born in East St. Louis, Illinois, and her family was very poor. Her parents thought that track and field were inappropriate for a girl. When she was nine, she entered her first track-and-field competition. Even though she lost, she didn't give up. Jackie entered another race. Her parents were shocked when she won.

In the late 1980s, she was diagnosed with asthma. This has not interfered with her performance as an athlete. Jackie is a world champion in both the long jump and heptathlon and has many Olympic medals to prove it.

> In the body of the essay, the author supports his general statement with specific factual information.

Jackie Joyner-Kersee continues to be a role model for young people with disabilities like me. I think that Jackie Joyner-Kersee and Stevie Wonder are admirable for overcoming their disabilities. Stevie Wonder overcame blindness to bring music to the world. Joyner-Kersee stunned us with her athleticism, despite her asthma. They teach me to never give up, no matter how intimidating the obstacles I face in life.

> The author concludes by restating his thesis and reinforcing it with personal insight.

Student Model

- Point out that the Student Model is a sample. Students' essays may be longer.
- Have students locate the direct response to the test question. ("The best way to overcome a disability is to face it head-on and not let it prevent you from achieving great things.")
- Have students locate specific factual information that supports the thesis statement.
- Point out that the student organizes the essay by introducing the two people he admires, then presenting facts about each person in the order in which he introduced them.

Real-World Connection

Ask students to think of instances in real life in which they may need to prepare essay responses. Answers may include state or national exams and class tests in high school or college.

Drafting

- Point out the Find Your Focus chart on p. 436. Have students use this information to help focus their ideas.
- Have students read the information about the introduction, body, and conclusion of an essay on p. 436.
- Point out that students will not have as much time to prepare their responses in a test situation as they have for this assignment. However, as they budget their more limited time they should allot adequate attention to the prewriting stage. A time limit often pressures students into rushing into the drafting phase.

Revising

- Have students read the Revising section on this page.
- Point out the Model on p. 436 and have students check Eddie's finished essay to see if he included either of the sentences shown in the Model.

(continued on p. 437)

Drafting

Find a focus. Once you choose your topic, develop a focus for your essay. Consider the type of writing you are creating, and draft a statement that directly responds to the question. Use the information at right to help you focus your ideas.

Plan a structure. When you sketch an outline for your essay, divide it into three parts: introduction, body, and conclusion.

- The **introduction** should state your thesis.
- The **body** of the essay should present at least two main points that support your thesis.
- The **conclusion** should restate the answer to the essay question and sum up the main points in the body.

Fill in the details. In a test situation, you normally have limited time. List the evidence, facts, examples, and quotations you will need to prove your point. Jot down as many details as you can remember or generate. Refer to this list as you draft.

Find Your Focus

Exposition
Develop a thesis statement to address the question, gearing your response to the expectation of problem-and-solution, cause-and-effect, or comparison-and-contrast essays.

Persuasion
Choose a position to argue, and identify the support you'll use to defend it.

Response to Literature
In a single sentence, identify your focus. You may decide to evaluate a character or analyze a setting.

Revising

Revise for coherence. When you have finished writing, compare the first paragraph of your essay with the last:

1. The first paragraph should contain your focus or thesis in response to the essay question.
2. The final paragraph should restate the thesis statement and summarize your supporting evidence.
3. If the main points in the first and final paragraphs do not match, revise either paragraph to make the writing more coherent. If necessary, revise body paragraphs or add transitional sentences to make sure that the essay flows and holds together well.

Model: Revising a Conclusion

I think that Jackie Joyner-Kersee and Stevie Wonder are admirable for overcoming their disabilities. They teach me to never give up, no matter how intimidating the obstacles I face in my life.

Stevie Wonder overcame blindness to bring music to the world. Joyner-Kersee stunned us with her athleticism, despite her asthma.

Eddie could summarize his supporting arguments to give greater weight and clarity to his thesis.

USING TECHNOLOGY IN WRITING

Encourage students to create their drafts on a computer to make revising easier and faster by using features such as Cut and Paste. Students can also use spell check and other revision tools on the **Writing and Grammar iText CD-ROM.**

Revise for formal language. Look for words in your writing that can be replaced with words that are more appropriate to your purpose. In the following example, *element* creates a more formal effect than *thing.*

Informal: The railroad was the *thing* that most contributed to the success of new businesses.
Formal: The railroad was the *element* that most contributed to the success of new businesses.

Compare the model and the nonmodel. Why is the model more effective than the nonmodel?

Nonmodel	Model
The first person I want to talk about is a great African American musician by the name of Stevie Wonder.	One person who serves as a powerful example of someone who has overcome a disability is the African American musician Stevie Wonder.

Publishing and Presenting

After you receive an essay back from your teacher with comments, keep a copy in your portfolio. Consider this suggestion to make further use of it:

Organize a study group. Compare your response with those of your classmates. Read the essays and discuss with other members of the study group the ways you could improve your essay writing. If it is helpful, list the strengths and weaknesses of each essay. Use the lists to improve your performance on your next essay test.

Rubric for Self-Assessment

Evaluate your writing for assessment using the following criteria and rating scale:

Criteria	Rating Scale Not very				Very
How directly does the essay answer the question?	1	2	3	4	5
How well is the thesis supported by evidence?	1	2	3	4	5
How specific is the supporting information?	1	2	3	4	5
How effectively is information drawn from reading or discussion incorporated?	1	2	3	4	5
How effectively are arguments organized?	1	2	3	4	5

Revising (continued)

- Have students read "Revise for formal language" on p. 437, including the model and non-model.
- Point out that language in a test essay should be formal rather than conversational.
- In real-world test-taking, students often leave inadequate time for revision. Encourage students to give themselves enough time to review and revise their work.

Publishing and Presenting

- After students receive their corrected essays, have them form small groups to discuss improvements they could make in future assignments or test situations.

Assessment

- Review with students the assessment criteria, pointing out that they evaluate the Assignment Criteria listed at the beginning of the exercise on p. 434.
- As students evaluate their own essays, have them use the rubric criteria on p. 437.
- The rubric on this page, and another rubric in an alternative format, can be found on pp. 11 and 44 of **Performance Assessment and Portfolio Management.**

TEST-TAKING TIP

Explain that in timed tests, students should consider quickly creating an outline of their essay on a piece of scrap paper. The outline can then serve as a sort of first draft.

Lesson Objectives

1. To prepare for a descriptive presentation by picturing and defining the topic
2. To deliver a descriptive presentation

Delivering a Descriptive Presentation

- Point out that an effective descriptive presentation must be well organized and contain clear details.

Prepare the Presentation

- Go over the information in this section on p. 438.
- Remind students that sensory details appeal to sight, sound, smell, taste, and touch.
- Point out the Defining Your Topic chart on p. 438. Encourage students to use such a chart when preparing their presentations.

Deliver the Presentation

- Have students come up with synonyms for the word *dynamic*. Answers: Students may cite such synonyms as *energetic, vigorous, active, alive, electric, peppy, lively, spirited, powerful, strong,* and *effective.*
- Point out that if students are extremely familiar with their presentations before delivery, they will find it easier to pick up the pace or otherwise change the presentation during delivery.

Listening and Speaking WORKSHOP

Delivering a Descriptive Presentation

In a **descriptive presentation**, you communicate an experience by describing it in detail. The ability to deliver a memorable descriptive presentation is as important for telling a good story as it is for telling someone how to operate machinery. The following techniques will help you organize and deliver a descriptive presentation.

Prepare the Presentation

Much of the creative work that goes into putting together a descriptive presentation involves gathering details and organizing them logically.

Picture the topic that you are describing. Project yourself into the situation you are describing. Think about what you see, hear, and feel around you. Make a list of these sensory details, selecting those that would best help your audience to picture the situation. For example, you might describe the feeling of terror when the person teaching you to ride your bike let go, and you suddenly forgot how to brake.

Define your topic. Too much descriptive detail can slow you down or get you sidetracked. To avoid this problem, start off with a single generalization that sums up your presentation and suits your purpose. Then, consider whether details are essential or inessential to capturing your generalization. Adjust the balance if you feel you have too much or too little detail.

Defining Your Topic

Purpose: To entertain
Audience: Fellow students

Essential Details	Inessential Details
I received a bike for my sixth birthday.	
I felt the wheel shake when I was first gaining my balance.	My bike was a three speed.
I didn't know how to brake when my dad let go.	

Deliver the Presentation

When it comes time to deliver your presentation, use the following techniques to provide greater impact.

Be dynamic. An audience will pay closer attention to a speaker who is animated and varies his or her voice. The more interested you are in your topic, the easier it will be to give a dynamic presentation.

Gauge audience reaction. Look at the audience frequently to check how people are reacting. If you feel your audience is losing interest, leave out some details and pick up your pace. If people are actively engaged, do not be afraid to elaborate on aspects that seem to play well with your audience.

Activity: Analyzing a Speech

Pair up with another student. Choose a topic that you know well but your partner does not. Take turns presenting to each other, using as much description as you feel necessary. When you have finished, ask your partner to recall as many details as possible. Use this feedback to evaluate your presentation.

Assessment WORKSHOP

Cause and Effect

The reading sections of some tests often require you to read a passage and answer multiple-choice questions about cause-and-effect relationships. Use these strategies to help you answer test questions on cause and effect:

- Remember that a *cause* is an event that makes something happen, and an *effect* is a result of that event.
- To recognize cause and effect, ask yourself, "What happened in this passage? Why did this event come about?"
- Do not limit your search to a single cause and effect. One cause may have several effects, and one effect may have several causes.

Test-Taking Strategies

- Look for words and phrases such as "factor," "because," and "as a result" that signal cause-and-effect statements.
- Keep track of multiple cause-and-effect relationships by circling and labeling causes and effects and drawing arrows between them.

Sample Test Item

Directions: Read the passage, and then answer the question that follows.

Marcus dressed quickly, gulped breakfast, and bolted out the door. As he hurried to school, he mentally reviewed his notes and realized that he felt confident. He had been unprepared for the last biology exam. This would be his last chance to improve his final grade. This time, he had made a serious effort to study for the exam.

1 Why did Marcus feel confident?

A This was his last chance to pass biology.
B He arrived at school on time.
C He had not done well on the last exam.
D He had studied hard for the exam.

Answer and Explanation

The correct answer is ***D***. ***A*** and ***C*** might make Marcus more nervous, but not confident. ***B*** is not found in the paragraph.

Practice

Directions: Read the passage, and then answer the question that follows.

Lauren looked at the car repair bill. She thought about the day that Shelly, her sister, had borrowed her car. Lauren had reluctantly given her the keys. Shelly had promised to be back in time for Lauren to go to work, so five hours later, Shelly returned and sheepishly explained how she had crushed the rear fender. Lauren had lost a day's pay. "Well, I've learned something," she thought.

1 Why did Lauren lose a day's pay?

A She had to have her car repaired.
B Shelly had an accident.
C She couldn't go to work.
D Shelly begged her for the car.

2 Why did Lauren give Shelly the keys to her car?

A She needed money to pay a bill.
B It was a rainy day.
C They were sisters.
D Shelly made a promise to be back on time.

Lesson Objective

To correctly answer test questions that require a response about cause-and-effect relationships

Applying Reading Strategies

Read aloud the bulleted list under "Cause and Effect" on p. 439. Point out that students can keep these concepts in mind when they are asked to give cause-and-effect responses in test questions.

Applying Test-Taking Strategies

- Have students read the Sample Test Item, then share their responses to the question orally with the rest of the class.
- Point out that in this example, "realized," "felt confident," and "This time" give clues to the cause-and-effect structure of the passage.
- Point out the Answers and Explanations section on p. 439. Ask students to discuss how their responses compare to the example given.
- Next, have students respond independently to the Practice question.

Answer

1. The correct answer is C. Lauren was not able to go to work. Answers *A* and *D* did not cause the loss of pay. Answer *B*, Shelly's accident, was a contributing factor but not the direct cause.
2. The correct answer is D. Lauren gave the keys as a result of Shelly's promise. Answers *A* an *B* are not mentioned in the passage. Answer *C* represents a contributing factor, but not the direct cause.

TEACHING RESOURCES

The following resources can be used to enrich or extend the instruction for p. 439.

PRENTICE HALL ASSESSMENT SYSTEM

- Workbook
- Skill Book
- Transparencies
- CD-ROM

Unit Objectives

1. To read selections in different genres that develop the theme "Visions of the Future"
2. To apply a variety of reading strategies, particularly strategies for reading critically, appropriate for reading these selections
3. To analyze literary elements
4. To use a variety of strategies to build vocabulary
5. To learn elements of grammar, usage, and style
6. To use recursive writing processes to write in a variety of forms
7. To develop listening and speaking skills
8. To express and support responses to various types of texts
9. To prepare, organize, and present literary interpretations

Meeting the Objectives

With each selection, you will find instructional materials through which students can meet these objectives. Further, you will find additional practice pages for reading strategies, literary analysis, vocabulary, and grammar in the **Selection Support: Skills Development Workbook** in your **Teaching Resources.**

Background

Art

Untitled

The art on this page depicts levels of an infinite iteration. The "big picture" represents a computer network. Each computer within that network displays another image of the network — and so on, by implication, to infinity. Ask students the following question:

In addition to the computers, how else does the painting suggest a world of technology?

Answer: Students may say the grid lines, the geometric pattern of the links, and the predominating blue color are suggestive of technology.

UNIT 5 Visions of the Future

UNIT FEATURES

Connections	Reading Informational Material
Every unit contains a feature that connects literature to a related topic, such as art, science, or history. In this unit, the Literature Past and Present feature on p. 466 presents a first-person account of technology in trouble: an airliner is struck by lightning. Use the information and questions on the Connections pages to enrich students' understanding of the selections presented within the unit.	These selections will help students learn to analyze and evaluate informational texts, such as workplace documents, technical directions, and consumer materials. They will expose students to the organization and features unique to nonnarrative texts. In this unit, students learn the features and purposes of product information.

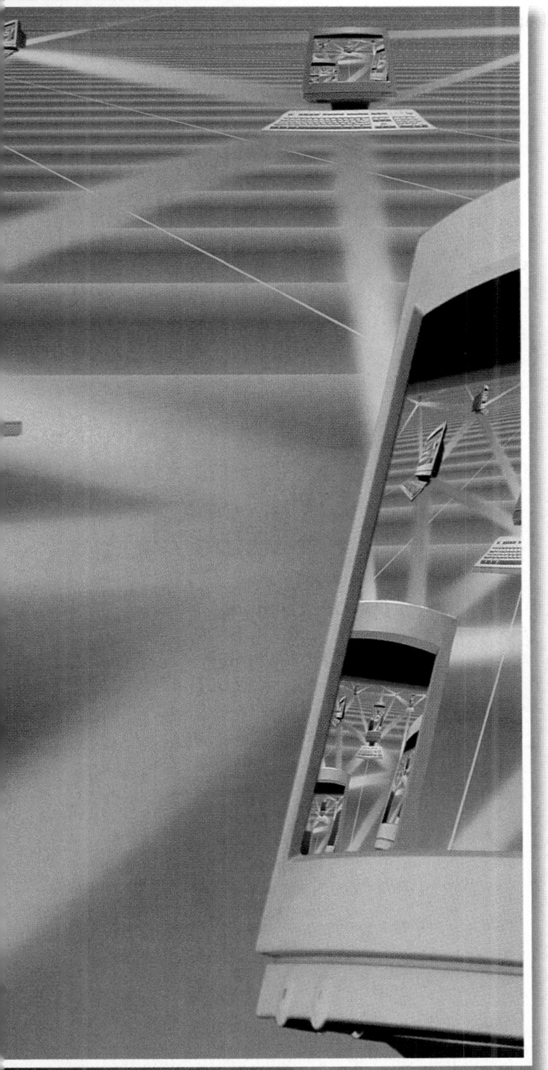

Exploring the Theme

People have always tried to imagine the future. Some have worried that today's human carelessness will produce the problems of tomorrow. Others have looked optimistically toward the future, hoping that technological progress will offer us a way to solve our current problems. Still others have predicted that each set of advancements will bring its own set of problems and solutions, in an endless cycle of human wisdom and folly.

Bryan Woolley incorporates elements of all three outlooks in his time capsule essay, "To the Residents of A.D. 2029." Addressing future citizens, Woolley acknowledges the problems of our time. Through it all, though, he manages to find perspective, humor, and a glimmer of hope.

▲ **Critical Viewing** Which elements of this picture suggest that computer technology opens infinite possibilities? **[Infer]**

ASSESSMENT RESOURCES

- **Selection Support: Skills Development Workbook**
- **Formal Assessment**
- **Open Book Tests**
- **Performance Assessment and Portfolio Management**
- **Extension Activities**

Assessing Student Progress

Listed below are the tools that are available to measure the degree to which students meet the unit objectives.

Informal Assessment

The questions on the Review and Assess sections are a first-level response to the concepts and skills presented with the selections. Students' responses provide a brief, informal measure of their grasp of the material. These responses can indicate where further instruction and practice are needed. Follow up with the practice pages in **Selection Support: Skills Development Workbook.**

Formal Assessment

The Formal Assessment booklet contains the Selection Tests and Unit Tests.

- Selection Tests measure comprehension and skills acquisition for each selection or group of selections.
- Each Unit Test provides students with thirty multiple-choice questions and five essay questions designed to assess students' knowledge of the literature and skills taught in the unit.

The **Open Book Tests** ask students to demonstrate their ability to synthesize and communicate information from selections or groups of selections.

To assess student writing, you will find rubrics and scoring models in the **Performance Assessment and Portfolio Management** booklet. In this booklet, you will also find scoring rubrics for listening and speaking activities.

Alternative Assessment

The **Extension Activities** booklet contains writing activities, listening and speaking activities, and research and technology activities that are appropriate for students with different ability levels. You may also use these activities as an alternative measure of students' growth.

▶Critical Viewing

Possible response: Students may note that the pictures-within-pictures-within-pictures on the monitors suggest infinity.

Why Read Literature?

The "Why Read Literature?" page in each unit presents a list of possible purposes for reading. Each purpose for reading is connected to one or more of the selections in the unit. Good readers set a purpose before reading to help them read actively and focus on meaningful details.

Unit 5 introduces three purposes for reading. "Read for the Love of Literature," encourages students to enjoy science fiction. "Read for Information" invites students to look into the future of technology. "Read to be inspired" prepares students to read Nelson Mandela's inspiring speech "Glory and Hope."

How to Use This Page

- Tell students that as they read each selection in this unit, they should set a purpose for reading. This will help them read in a more active and focused manner.
- Explain that students can increase their love of literature by discovering new perspectives on technology in "All Watched Over by Machines of Loving Grace" by Richard Brautigan and "The Machine That Won the War" by Isaac Asimov.
- Students can read for information as they consider two contrasting visions of the future in excerpts from *The Road Ahead* by Bill Gates and *Silent Spring* by Rachel Carson.
- Nelson Mandela's inaugural speech "Glory and Hope" offers students an opportunity to read to be inspired.

Why Read Literature?

Whenever you read science fiction, you have a purpose, or reason. You might read to appreciate a new view of the future, or because the social issues an author raises interest you. Preview the three purposes you might set before reading works in this unit.

1 Read for the Love of Literature

Science fiction is particularly compelling when a writer interweaves technological progress with great moral dilemmas. If you have ever wondered—or worried—what it might be like when humans rely completely on technology, you may find a surprising answer in Isaac Asimov's **"The Machine That Won the War,"** page 456.

Many works of science fiction are tales of wayward computers destroying the world with murderous abandon. But why not try to imagine a world where technology and nature coexist peacefully? If this concept intrigues you, read Richard Brautigan's **"All Watched Over by Machines of Loving Grace,"** page 476.

2 Read for Information

In 1993, when the first Internet browser was introduced, few could have predicted how important the Internet would become. How difficult is it for you to imagine the state of technology five years from now? Find out Bill Gates's vision for the future in video technology and see if it matches your own in **"The Road Ahead,"** page 446.

In 1962, pesticide use was widespread and companies dumped toxins into our streams. It took a biologist named Rachel Carson to draw the vital connection between technology and destruction of the environment. Read an excerpt from ***Silent Spring***—the book that helped spawn the environmental movement—on page 491.

3 Read to Be Inspired

Imprisoned for twenty-seven years for his opposition to racial segregation, Nelson Mandela served as the conscience of South Africa. After he was released and elected president, Mandela was faced with the overwhelming task of creating a just society out of poverty and inequality. See how he viewed this as an opportunity to issue a stirring call to action in **"Glory and Hope,"** page 506.

Take It to the Net

Visit the Web site for online instruction and activities related to each selection in this unit.
www.phschool.com

ENRICHMENT: Further Reading

Have students choose one or more of the works below to extend the unit theme "Visions of the Future" or to read more by the unit authors.

Foundation by Isaac Asimov
This book is set so far in the future that life on Earth is just a distant memory. But even in that distant future, all is not well in the galaxy.

Canyons by Gary Paulsen
This story of two boys facing the challenge of becoming men reaches across centuries and cultures.

How to Read Literature

Use Critical Reading Strategies

When you read a work that presents an individual's perspective, it is a good idea to read critically. Reading critically involves examining and questioning the author's ideas. Use these strategies to help you read critically:

1. Recognize bias.

No matter how impartial writers seem, they inevitably bring some of their own experiences and beliefs to their writing. The bias that results influences both their writing and your reaction. To increase your awareness of bias:

- Weigh the facts that support or contradict the author's position. Then, see if your conclusion is the same as the author's.
- Consider what the author is omitting, as well as including.
- Learn about the author's background to determine which experiences may have influenced his or her writing.

2. Identify relevant details.

To help process information as you read, it is useful to screen passages for relevant detail.

- Details that have the most relevance are those that are essential to your understanding of the story's plot, characters, and setting.
- Do not expect to know what is or is not relevant from the very beginning. As you read further, the distinction will become clearer.

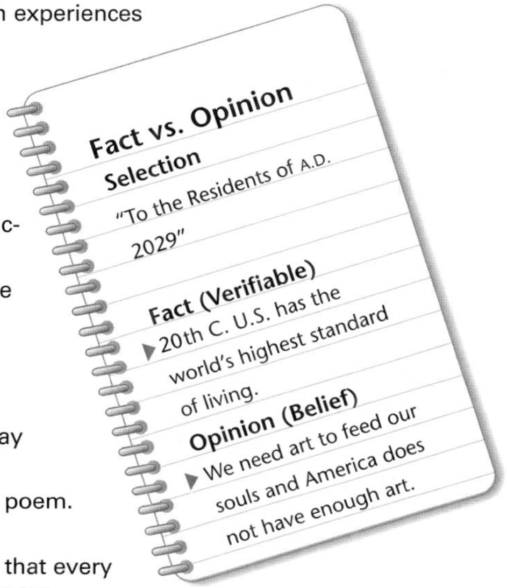
Fact vs. Opinion
Selection
"To the Residents of A.D. 2029"
Fact (Verifiable)
▶ 20th C. U.S. has the world's highest standard of living.
Opinion (Belief)
▶ We need art to feed our souls and America does not have enough art.

3. Recognize a poet's purpose.

- Look for recurring ideas and images in the poem that may provide clues to a poet's reason for writing.
- Pay close attention to the opening and closing lines of a poem. Poets will often announce their intentions in these lines.
- Remember that a poet may have multiple purposes and that every reader may bring a slightly different interpretation to a poem.

4. Distinguish fact from opinion.

- Facts can be verified for accuracy by checking a reference book; opinions cannot. Note the examples of the distinction between fact and opinion at right.
- Opinions, though often stated strongly, will always be an interpretation based on a writer's beliefs or values.

As you read the selections in this unit, review the critical reading strategies and apply them to interact with the text.

How to Read Literature

The "How to Read Literature" page in each unit presents a set of strategies to help readers understand authors' words and ideas. Each reading strategy is taught in conjunction with one or more of the selections within the unit. Good readers develop a bank of strategies from which they can draw as needed.

Unit 5 introduces four strategies for reading critically. When reading selections, it is important for students to recognize bias, identify relevant details, distinguish fact from opinion, and understand a writer's purpose. The strategies on this page will help readers examine a text with a critical eye.

How to Use This Page

Introduce the strategies for reading critically, presenting each as a tool for developing understanding when reading the selections in this unit.

- As they read the excerpt from *The Road Ahead* (p. 446), students should watch for the writer's motives and bias.
- As they read "The Machine That Won the War" (p. 456), students will have an opportunity to identify relevant details.
- When they read "The Horses" (p. 474), students will be asked to recognize the poet's purpose.
- As they read "If I Forget Thee, Oh Earth" (p. 486), students will have the opportunity to distinguish between fact and opinion.

MODEL A READING STRATEGY: Recognize Bias

Explain to students that they should be aware of a writer's bias as they read. Demonstrate how to recognize and respond to bias by modeling your thinking with this passage from Bill Gates's *The Road Ahead:*

> Television has been around for fewer than sixty years, but in that time it has become a major influence in the life of almost everyone in the developed nations. In some ways, though, television was just an enhancement of commercial radio, which had been bringing electronic entertainment to homes for twenty years.

Tell students:

"Just an enhancement of commercial radio" shows that Gates is biased against television as an "old" technology. Since I know that Gates represents a computer software company, his preference for computerized alternatives is understandable. I suspect Gates will follow this statement by promoting new technology from his company.

from The Road Ahead

Lesson Objectives and CA Correlations

1. **To analyze and respond to literary elements**
   - Literary Analysis: Expository Writing
   - Connecting Literary Elements: Author's Purpose **R 2.8**
2. **To read, comprehend, analyze, and critique nonfiction**
   - Reading Strategy: Recognizing a Writer's Bias **R 2.8**
   - Reading Check questions
   - Review and Assess questions
   - Assessment Practice (ATE)
3. **To develop word analysis skills, fluency, and systematic vocabulary**
   - Vocabulary Development Lesson: Latin Word Root: *-simul-* **R 1.1**
4. **To understand and apply written and oral language conventions**
   - Spelling Strategy
   - Grammar Lesson: Main and Subordinate Clauses **LC 1.1**
5. **To understand and apply appropriate writing and research strategies**
   - Writing Lesson: Consumer Response **W 2.5**
   - Extension Activity: Annotated List **W 1.7**
6. **To understand and apply listening and speaking strategies**
   - Extension Activity: Presentation **LS 1.7**

STEP-BY-STEP TEACHING GUIDE	PACING GUIDE
PRETEACH	
Motivate Students and Provide Background	
Use the Motivation activity (ATE p. 444)	5 min.
Read and discuss the Preview material and Background information (SE/ATE p. 444) [A]	5 min.
Introduce the Concepts	
Introduce the Literary Analysis and Reading Strategy (SE/ATE p. 445) [A]	15 min.
Pronounce the vocabulary words and read their definitions (SE p. 445)	5 min.
TEACH	
Monitor Comprehension	
Informally monitor comprehension by circulating while students read independently or in groups [A]	10 min.
Monitor students' comprehension with the Reading Check notes (SE/ATE pp. 447, 449)	as students read
Develop vocabulary with Vocabulary notes (SE pp. 447, 449, 450; ATE p. 446)	as students read
Develop Understanding	
Develop students' understanding of expository writing with Literary Analysis annotations (SE pp. 447, 449; ATE pp. 447, 449) [A]	10 min.
Develop students' ability to recognize a writer's bias with the Reading Strategy annotations (SE p. 449; ATE p. 449)	10 min.
ASSESS	
Assess Mastery	
Assess students' mastery of the Reading Strategy and Literary Analysis by having them answer the Review and Assess questions (SE/ATE p. 451)	20 min.
Use one or more of the print and media Assessment Resources (ATE p. 453) [A]	up to 50 min.
EXTEND	
Apply Understanding	
Have students complete the Vocabulary Development Lesson and the Grammar Lesson (SE p. 452) [A]	20 min.
Apply students' knowledge of brainstorming using the Writing Lesson (SE/ATE p. 453) [A]	45 min.
Apply students' understanding using one or more of the Extension Activities (SE p. 453)	20–90 min.

[A] **ACCELERATED INSTRUCTION:** Use the strategies and activities identified with an [A].

UNIVERSAL ACCESS
- ● = Below Level Students
- ▲ = On-Level Students
- ■ = Above Level Students

Time and Resource Manager

Reading Level: Challenging
Average Number of Instructional Days: 3

RESOURCES		
PRINT	**TRANSPARENCIES**	**TECHNOLOGY**
• **Beyond Literature,** Media Connection: Documentaries, p. 29 ▲ ■		• **Interest Grabber Video,** Tape 3 ● ▲ ■
• **Selection Support Workbook:** ● ▲ ■ Literary Analysis, p. 116 Reading Strategy, p. 115 Build Vocabulary, p. 113	• **Literary Analysis and Reading Transparencies,** pp. 57 and 58 ● ▲ ■	
• **Adapted Reader's Companion** ● • **Reader's Companion** ●		
• **English Learner's Companion** ● ▲ • **Literatura en español** ● ▲ • **Literary Analysis for Enrichment** ■		
• **Formal Assessment:** Selection Test, pp. 101–103 ● ▲ ■ • **Open Book Test,** pp. 85–87 ● ▲ ■ • **Performance Assessment and Portfolio Management,** p. 30 ● ▲ ■ • PRENTICE HALL ASSESSMENT SYSTEM ● ▲ ■	• PRENTICE HALL ASSESSMENT SYSTEM ● ▲ ■ Skills Practice Answers and Explanations on Transparencies	• **Test Bank Software** ● ▲ ■ • **Got It! Assessment Videotapes,** Tape 3 ● ▲
• **Selection Support Workbook:** ● ▲ ■ Build Grammar Skills, p. 114 • **Writing and Grammar,** Gold Level ● ▲ ■ • **Extension Activities,** p. 29 ● ▲ ■	• **Daily Language Practice Transparencies** ● ▲	• **Writing and Grammar iText CD-ROM** ● ▲ ■ *Take It to the Net* www.phschool.com

BLOCK SCHEDULING: Use one 90-minute class period to preteach the selection and have students read it. Use a second 90-minute class period to assess students' mastery of skills and have them complete one of the Extension Activities.

PRETEACH

Step-by-Step Teaching Guide for pp. 444–445

Motivation

Tell students to imagine that all the computers in their city or town just stopped working. Have them brainstorm a list of ways this will affect the rest of their day. Point out that computers control traffic lights, approve or deny credit card sales in stores, monitor hospital patients' vital signs, and so on. Tell students that they will be reading about additional applications for computer technology.

Interest Grabber Video

As an alternative, play "From Research to Reality" on Tape 3 to engage student interest.

1 Background

Science

In 1999, nearly 200 million people all over the world used the Internet. Experts expect that this figure will jump to 1 billion by 2005. In order to get on the Internet, a person needs a sufficiently powerful computer, a modem, and a telephone line. Today, most computers have built-in modems. People pay a monthly access fee to an Internet service provider. People without computers of their own can log on to the Internet in a library or other facility by paying a small fee per minute—just as if they were using a pay phone!

Prepare to Read

from The Road Ahead

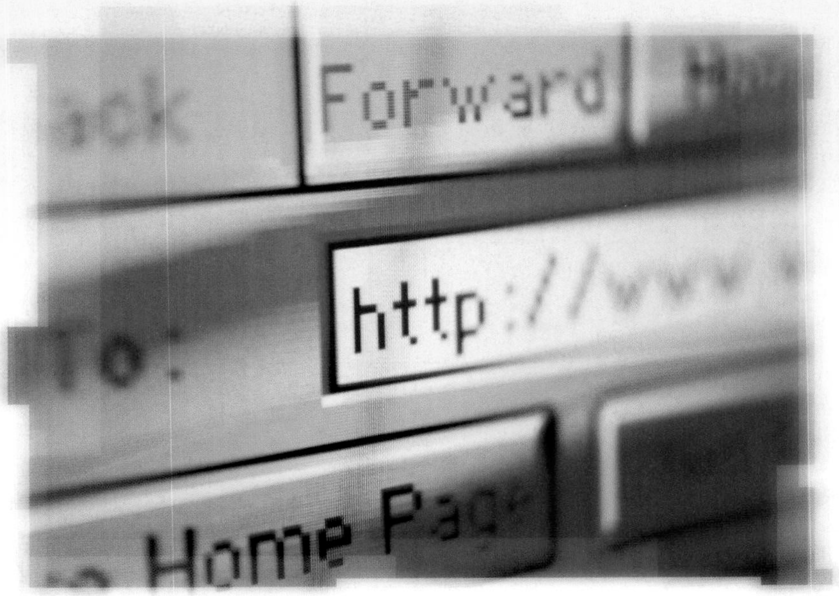

Take It to the Net

Visit www.phschool.com for interactive activities and instruction related to *The Road Ahead*, including

- background
- graphic organizers
- literary elements
- reading strategies

Preview

Connecting to the Literature

Technology changes at an astounding pace. Computers that were marvels of technology a few years ago now lack the processing power, memory, and features to complete the new tasks people take for granted. Let this essay by computer mogul Bill Gates encourage you to speculate how future innovations will replace today's cutting-edge technology and affect your life.

1 Background

The Internet consists of thousands of computer networks connected via telephone lines and cable wires. The Internet provides access to vast amounts of information, including text, graphics, and sound, with links to other sites and "pages." In *The Road Ahead*, Gates envisions a new Internet service—the delivery of high-quality video programming when customers want it.

TEACHING RESOURCES

The following resources can be used to enrich or extend the instruction for pp. 444–445.

Motivation

Interest Grabber Video, Tape 3

Background

Beyond Literature, p. 29

Take It to the Net

Visit www.phschool.com for background and hotlinks for the selection.

Literary Analysis

Literary Analysis and Reading Transparencies, Expository Writing, p. 57

Reading

Selection Support: Reading Strategy, p. 115; Build Vocabulary, p. 113

Literary Analysis and Reading Transparencies, Recognizing a Writer's Bias, p. 58

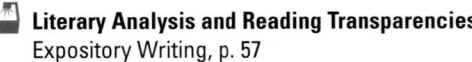

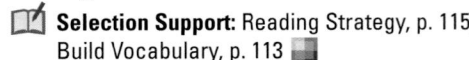

BLOCK SCHEDULING: Resources marked with this symbol provide varied instruction during 90-minute blocks.

❷ Literary Analysis

Expository Writing

Expository writing informs the reader, explaining its subject by presenting details, examples, and facts. This passage from the selection uses details to explain the concept of conventional television:

> Conventional television allows us to decide what we watch but not when we watch it. . . . Viewers have to synchronize their schedules with the time of a broadcast. . . .

Although the focus of expository writing is to present information, the writer may also express personal opinions based on experience. As you read this excerpt from *The Road Ahead*, note how the author uses facts and examples to explain his subject and support his views.

Connecting Literary Elements

In expository writing, an **author's purpose** is his or her reason for writing—to inform, to entertain, or to persuade, for example. Of course, an author may have more than one purpose: Bill Gates writes persuasively to convince you of his opinions. At the same time, he informs and entertains you. To help you organize the opinions and supporting facts in Gates's essay, use a chart like the one shown here.

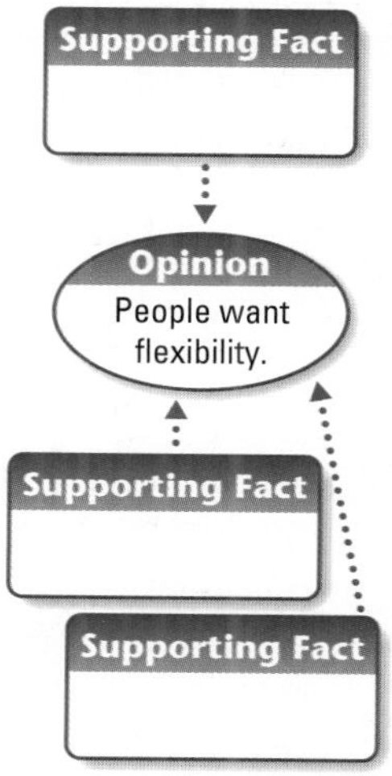

❸ Reading Strategy

Recognizing a Writer's Bias

Even within expository writing, an author may show bias—a strong feeling for or against something. To **recognize a writer's bias,** pay attention to the following:

- loaded words—words that trigger a positive or negative response
- a single viewpoint that does not address an opposing viewpoint
- an opinion or assumption that is not backed up with facts

In this selection, Gates's involvement in his software company probably influences his positive attitude toward technology.

Vocabulary Development

simultaneously (sī′ məl tā′ nē əs lē) *adv.* at the same time (p. 447)

capacious (kə pā′ shəs) *adj.* able to hold much; roomy (p. 449)

precursors (prē kʉr′ sərz) *n.* things that prepare the way for what will follow (p. 450)

infrared (in′ frə red′) *adj.* of light waves that lie just beyond the red end of the visible spectrum (p. 450)

parlance (pär′ ləns) *n.* style of speaking or writing; language (p. 450)

❷ Literary Analysis

Expository Writing

- Write the word *expose* on the chalkboard. Remind students that it means "uncover" or "reveal." Expository writing, therefore, uncovers or reveals information about a given topic.
- Review the terms *main idea* and *supporting details.* A writer must defend ideas and opinions with supporting details. If an expository piece lacks evidence, readers will not find it believable or interesting.
- Use the Expository Writing transparency in **Literary Analysis and Reading Transparencies,** p. 57, to monitor Gates's supporting facts.

❸ Reading Strategy

Recognizing a Writer's Bias

- Tell students that bias means "angle" or "slant." In writing, an author's opinions are his or her bias—prejudice, leaning—for or against an issue.
- No writer can entirely disguise or neutralize his or her bias toward a topic. Read over the bulleted list of clues on p. 445. Remind students to look for examples of these items as they read.
- Have students read the author biography on p. 450. Ask them to share any other information they know about Bill Gates. Have students think about what this information may indicate about probable biases that may show in Gates's writing.

Vocabulary Development

- Pronounce each vocabulary word for students, and read the definitions as a class. Have students identify any words with which they are already familiar.

CUSTOMIZE INSTRUCTION FOR UNIVERSAL ACCESS

For Special Needs Students	For Less Proficient Readers	For English Learners
Have students read the adapted version of *The Road Ahead* in the **Adapted Reader's Companion.** This version provides basic-level instruction in an interactive format with questions and write-on lines. Completing the adapted version will prepare students to read the selection in the Student Edition.	Have students read the selection in the **Reader's Companion.** This version provides basic-level instruction in an interactive format with questions and write-on lines. After students finish the selection in **Reader's Companion,** have them complete the questions and activities in the Student Edition.	Have students read the adapted version of the selection in the **English Learner's Companion.** This version provides basic-level instruction in an interactive format with questions and write-on lines. Completing the adapted version will prepare students to read the selection in the Student Edition.

E-Teach

Visit E-Teach at www.phschool.com for teachers' essays on how to teach, with questions and answers.

TEACH

Step-by-Step Teaching Guide for pp. 446–450

CUSTOMIZE INSTRUCTION
For Interpersonal Learners

Have students discuss their television watching habits. Do they tend to watch television or rented films alone or with friends and family members? Do they discuss their favorite weekly shows with their friends at school the morning after watching them? Next, have them consider how their viewing habits would change if they could watch any program at any time, and watch it on their computer screen. Would people still watch television together? Have students discuss whether they think the technology described in the article would have a negative or positive effect on family relationships and friendships.

1 About the Selection

The cofounder of Microsoft Corporation writes about television of the future. One day, Gates says, the Internet will enable people to watch television on their computer screens. Video-on-demand, Gates believes, will become a "killer application " required by consumers.

2 Vocabulary Development

Latin Root *-simul-*

- Explain that the Latin root *simul* means "same." Thus, *simultaneously* means "at the same time."
- Write the word *simulate* on the board and ask students to define the word based on its root. Then, have students use the word in a sentence.
  Possible response: *Simulate* means "to look or act like; pretend." Some computer screens simulate the appearance of a desktop.

TEACHING RESOURCES

The following resources can be used to enrich or extend the instruction for pp. 446–450.

Literary Analysis

Selection Support: Literary Analysis, p. 116

Reading

Reader's Companion

English Learner's Companion

BLOCK SCHEDULING: Resources marked with this symbol provide varied instruction during 90-minute blocks.

from ❶ The Road Ahead

Bill Gates

When I was a kid, *The Ed Sullivan Show* came on at eight o'clock on Sunday nights. Most Americans with television sets tried to be at home to watch it because that might be the only time and place to see the Beatles, Elvis Presley, the Temptations, or that guy who could spin ten ❷ plates simultaneously on the noses of ten dogs. But if you were driving back from your grandparents' house or on a Cub Scout camping trip, too bad. Not being at home on Sunday at eight meant that you also missed out on the Monday morning talk about Sunday night's show.

Conventional television allows us to decide what we watch but not when we watch it. The technical term for this sort of broadcasting is "synchronous."[1] Viewers have to synchronize their schedules with the time of a broadcast that's sent to everybody at the same time. That's how I watched *The Ed Sullivan Show* thirty years ago, and it's how most of us will watch the news tonight.

❸ In the early 1980's the videocassette recorder gave us more flexibility. If you cared enough about a program to fuss with timers and tapes in advance, you could watch it whenever you liked. You could claim from the broadcasters the freedom and luxury to serve as your own program scheduler—and millions of people do. When you tape a television show, or when you let your answering machine take an incoming message so that you don't have to pick up the phone, you're converting synchronous communications into a more convenient form: "asynchronous" communications.

It's human nature to find ways to convert synchronous communications into asynchronous forms. Before the invention of writing 5,000

simultaneously (sī′ məl tā′ nē əs lē) *adv.* at the same time

Literary Analysis
Expository Writing Which details support Gates's claim that the videocassette recorder offered flexibility?

❺ **✓Reading Check**
What does Gates say conventional television allows us to do?

1. **synchronous** (siŋ′ krə nəs) *adj.* happening at the same time; simultaneous.

❹ ◀ **Critical Viewing** Which details of this computer-generated art suit the double meaning of this selection's title? **[Connect]**

❸ Literary Analysis

Expository Writing

- Ask the Literary Analysis question on p. 447: What details support Gates's claim that the videocassette recorder offered flexibility?
  Answer: A videocassette recorder can record programs that viewers can watch at any time.
- Point out to students that this question includes a restatement of the main idea of the paragraph. Asking similar questions will help readers clarify a writer's main points.

❹ ▶Critical Viewing

Answer: The art expresses Gates's belief that "the road ahead" is the "information superhighway" of computer technology.

❺ ✓Reading Check

Answer: Conventional television allows people to decide what to watch but not when to watch it.

6 Critical Thinking

Analyze Causes and Effects

- Remind students that a *cause* is an action or event that makes something else happen. That result is the *effect.*
- Ask students to find one cause-and-effect relationship in this paragraph.
  Answer: Cause: People invented writing. Effect: Messages or information could be created at one time but read at any later time.

7 Background

Film

Elvis and the Beatles will probably need no introduction to students. Greta Garbo (1905–1990) was a Swedish actress who became a Hollywood star of the silent film era. When sound was introduced to motion pictures in the late 1920s. Garbo's deep and exotic-sounding speaking voice allowed her to make the transition painlessly. Throughout the 1930s, she was considered by many to be the most beautiful and glamorous woman in Hollywood. She retired from films in 1941. Many of her films were tragic love stories, two of the most popular being *Anna Karenina* (1935) and *Camille* (1937), both based on literary classics.

8 ▶Critical Viewing

Answer: Students may say that they write messages, complete assignments, play games, search for information, and retrieve sports scores via computers.

years ago, the only form of communication was the spoken word and the listener had to be in the presence of the speaker or miss his message. Once the message could be written, it could be stored and read 6 later by anybody, at his or her convenience. I'm writing these words at home on a summer evening, but I have no idea where or when you'll read them. One of the benefits the communications revolution will bring to all of us is more control over our schedules.

Once a form of communication is asynchronous, you also get an increase in the variety of selection possibilities. Even people who rarely record television programs routinely rent movies from the thousands of choices available at local video rental stores for just a few dollars each. The home viewer can spend any evening with Elvis, the 7 Beatles—or Greta Garbo.

Television has been around for fewer than sixty years, but in that time it has become a major influence in the life of almost everyone in the developed nations. In some ways, though, television was just an

8 ▼ Critical Viewing Computers and the Internet are now a part of everyday life. How do Gates's predictions about future technologies relate to your own experiences? **[Apply]**

ENRICHMENT: Cultural Connection

The Ed Sullivan Show

Called *The Toast of the Town* until 1955, *The Ed Sullivan Show* was a variety show broadcast from New York City from 1948 until 1971.

Sullivan, a newspaper columnist by trade, invited the entire spectrum of the entertainment world to appear on his program. Stars from Broadway musicals came on the show to give audiences a glimpse of what they might see in theaters. Novelty acts like the plate-spinner Gates describes were also highlights of the show. Audiences enjoyed the mix of acts, which might include everything from classical ballet to a talking mechanical mouse on one night.

Elvis Presley's first appearance on Sullivan's show was an epochal moment in American television history. The American debut of the Beatles on the show in 1964 had a similar impact.

enhancement of commercial radio, which had been bringing electronic entertainment into homes for twenty years. But no broadcast medium we have right now is comparable to the communications media we'll have once the Internet evolves to the point at which it has the
9 broadband capacity[2] necessary to carry high-quality video.

Because consumers already understand the value of movies and are used to paying to watch them, video-on-demand is an obvious development. There won't be any intermediary VCR. You'll simply select what you want from countless available programs.

No one knows when residential broadband networks capable of supporting video-on-demand will be available in the United States and other developed countries, let alone in developing countries. Many corporate networks already have enough bandwidth,[3] but . . . even in the U.S. most homes will have to make do for some time—maybe more than a decade—with narrowband and midband access. Fortunately, these lower-capacity bandwidths work fine for many Internet-based services such as games, electronic mail, and banking. For the next few years, interactivity in homes will be limited to these kinds of services, which will be delivered to personal computers and other information appliances.

Even after broadband residential networks have become common, television shows will continue to be broadcast as they are today, for synchronous consumption. But after they air, these shows—as well as thousands of movies and virtually all other kinds of video—will also be available whenever you want to view them. If a new episode of
10 *Seinfeld* is on at 9:00 P.M. on Thursday night, you'll also be able to see it at 9:13 P.M., 9:45 P.M., or 11:00 A.M. on Saturday. And there will be thousands of other choices. Your request for a specific movie or TV show episode will register, and the bits[4] will be routed to you across the network. It will feel as if there's no intermediary machinery between you and the object of your interest. You'll indicate what you want, and presto! you'll get it.

Movies, TV shows, and other kinds of digital information will be stored on "servers," which are computers with capacious disks. Servers will provide information for use anywhere on the network, just as they do for today's Internet. If you ask to see a particular movie, check a fact, or retrieve your electronic mail, your request will be routed by switches to the server or servers storing that information. You won't know whether the movie, TV show, query response, or e-mail that arrives at your house is stored on a server down the road or on the other side of the country, and it won't matter to you.

The digitized data will be retrieved from the server and routed by switches back to your television, personal computer, or telephone—your "information appliance." These digital devices will succeed for

2. **broadband capacity** *n.* ability to transmit a huge amount of electronic information quickly.
3. **bandwidth** *n.* amount of electronic information that can be transmitted in a given amount of time; capacity.
4. **bits** *n.* units of electronic information.

Literary Analysis
Expository Writing and Author's Purpose What is Gates's purpose in this part of his essay?

Reading Strategy
Recognizing a Writer's Bias How does Gates's bias toward technology affect his views and enthusiasm in this paragraph?

capacious (kə pā′ shəs) *adj.* able to hold much; roomy

11 **✓ Reading Check**
In the future, where will digital information be stored, according to the writer?

9 Literary Analysis
Expository Writing and Author's Purpose

- Ask the Literary Analysis question on p. 449: What is Gates's purpose in this part of the essay?
  Answer: Gates introduces the main idea of the selection in this paragraph: the ability to broadcast television over the Internet will revolutionize the communications media.
- Have students recall Gates's comments about videocassette recorders on p. 447 as they read this passage. Ask why he criticizes videocassette recorders.
  Answer: Gates wants to persuade readers that the ability to watch television over the Internet will improve their lives, so he criticizes the limited technology that's available today.

10 Reading Strategy
Recognizing a Writer's Bias

- Ask the Reading Strategy question on p. 449: How does Gates's bias toward technology affect his views and enthusiasm in this paragraph?
  Answer: Gates clearly thinks customized viewing is a great benefit, and he does not question the value of watching television.
- Ask students how the new technology Gates describes is an improvement on the videocassette recorder.
  Answer: The new technology would allow viewing to begin at any time (even in mid-broadcast) without fussing with a machine.

11 ✓ Reading Check

Answer: Digital information will be stored on "servers," or computers with capacious disks.

CUSTOMIZE INSTRUCTION FOR UNIVERSAL ACCESS

For Special Needs Students	For Gifted/Talented Students
Students may have trouble with the highly technical vocabulary Gates uses. Have students work with peer tutors, paraphrasing difficult paragraphs or sections. At the end of the article, tutors should make sure that students understand the article's main idea and key supporting details. Students can then discuss their opinion of the article with their tutors.	Have students imagine that they work for the publishing company to which Bill Gates has just submitted this segment of his book. Students should review the excerpt, recommending that the company either reject or accept the book, and giving their reasons. Students may also suggest changes Gates might make.

ASSESS

Answers for p. 450

Review and Assess

1. Some students will probably think it sounds like a wonderful idea. Other students may say that a videocassette recorder already allows them as much flexibility as they need.
2. **(a)** *The Ed Sullivan Show* **(b)** Gates points out that people have to schedule their activities around a conventional broadcast.
3. **(a)** Programs are broadcast everywhere at one specific time. **(b)** Programs will be stored on servers so that people can retrieve them at any time. **(c)** People will have control of video viewing without need of recording devices.
4. **(a)** He expects it to be available about a decade from the time the piece was written. **(b)** He seems to think it's unfortunate that people will have to "make do" for so long.
5. The advances might free students from having to watch any particular program at a particular time.
6. **(a)** Possible responses: People may spend too much time watching television. Families and friends will lose the common experience of watching and discussing the same broadcast. **(b)** Students may debate whether or not video-on-demand would create disruption or convenience in people's lives.

the same reason their analog precursors did—they'll make some aspect of life easier. Unlike the dedicated word processors[5] that brought the first microprocessors to many offices, most of these information appliances will be general-purpose, programmable computers connected to the network.

Even if a show is being broadcast live, you'll be able to use your infrared remote control to start it, stop it, or go to any earlier part of the program, at any time. If somebody comes to the door, you'll be able to pause the program for as long as you like. You'll be in absolute control—except, of course, you won't be able to forward past part of a live show as it's taking place.

Most viewers can appreciate the benefits of video-on-demand and will welcome the convenience it gives them. Once the costs to build a broadband network are low enough, video-on-demand has the potential to be what in computer parlance is called a "killer application," or just "killer app"—a use of technology so attractive to consumers that it fuels market forces and makes the underlying invention on which it depends all but indispensable. Killer applications change technological advances from curiosities into moneymaking essentials.

precursors (prē kʉr′ sərz) *n.* things that prepare the way for what will follow

infrared (in′ frə red′) *adj.* of light waves that lie just beyond the red end of the visible spectrum

parlance (pär′ ləns) *n.* style of speaking or writing; language

5. **dedicated word processors** *n.* machines that can be used only for word processing. Unlike personal computers, dedicated machines perform only one function.

Review and Assess

Thinking About the Selection

1. **Respond:** What do you think about an Internet video service like the one Gates describes?
2. **(a) Recall:** Which television show does Gates cite at the start of his essay? **(b) Connect:** Why is its popularity important to the point he is trying to make?
3. **(a) Recall:** How did video delivery work when Gates wrote his essay? **(b) Compare and Contrast:** In what ways does Gates think future video delivery will be different? **(c) Infer:** Why will the Internet's broadband development be significant?
4. **(a) Recall:** How long does Gates estimate Americans will have to wait for video-on-demand to be available? **(b) Infer:** How do you think Gates feels about the length of time this development will take?
5. **Speculate:** How might the advances that Gates predicts directly affect your future?
6. **(a) Extend:** What negative impacts might video-on-demand have on our society? **(b) Assess:** Do you think the benefits outweigh the negative impacts? Explain.

Bill Gates

(b. 1955)

In 1997, *Newsweek* magazine called Bill Gates "the richest man in the world, and maybe the smartest." He is chief executive officer and cofounder of Microsoft Corporation, the world's largest computer software company.

In the eighth grade, Gates taught himself the computer language BASIC and began writing programs. In 1975, he and Paul Allen wrote the first version of BASIC for a microcomputer. They soon started Microsoft, which now has over 20,000 employees. In *The Road Ahead* (1996), Gates examines the future of computer technology.

ASSESSMENT PRACTICE: Reading Comprehension

Make Generalizations (For more practice, see Test Preparation Workbook, p. 29.)

Many tests require students to make generalizations. Use this sample test item:

In the past, one had no choice but to watch a television show only when it was broadcast. With today's technology, people can control what they watch, when they watch it, and where they watch it.

Which generalization does this passage support?

A We are better off today than we were before.
B Life was simpler when we had less advanced technology.
C Changes in technology affect our lives directly.
D Technology is changing faster than ever.

All four statements are generalizations. However, choice *C* is the only one supported by the passage.

Review and Assess

Literary Analysis

Expository Writing

1. Using a chart like the one shown here, identify the main idea Gates proposes. Then, identify three facts that support this idea.

Main Idea → **Supporting Details**

2. Which details and descriptions help Gates give the essay a personal flavor?
3. Which opinions does the author introduce in his essay?

Connecting Literary Elements

4. (a) Is Gates's idea persuasive? (b) Which supporting details are most or least convincing?
5. What is the **author's** primary **purpose**? Explain.

Reading Strategy

Recognizing a Writer's Bias

6. How does Gates show a **bias** in the way he describes and explains videocassette recorders of the early 1980s?
7. (a) Use a chart like the one shown to categorize the biases in Gates's writing. Identify those details that help Gates make his case and those that do not help. (b) Do Gates's biases ultimately make his writing more or less effective for a general audience? Explain.

Helpful to Case → ← **Not Helpful to Case**

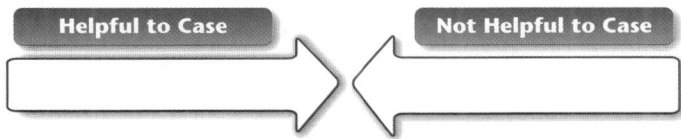

Extend Understanding

8. **Technology Connection:** In your opinion, which technological development is the most important for the present and future—the communications revolution or something else? Why?

Quick Review

Expository writing informs the reader, explaining something by presenting details, examples, and facts.

An **author's purpose** is his or her reason for writing—for example, it may be to inform, to entertain, or to persuade.

A writer's work may exhibit **bias,** a strong feeling for or against something, based on knowledge or personal experience.

Take It to the Net

www.phschool.com

Take the interactive self-test online to check your understanding of the selection.

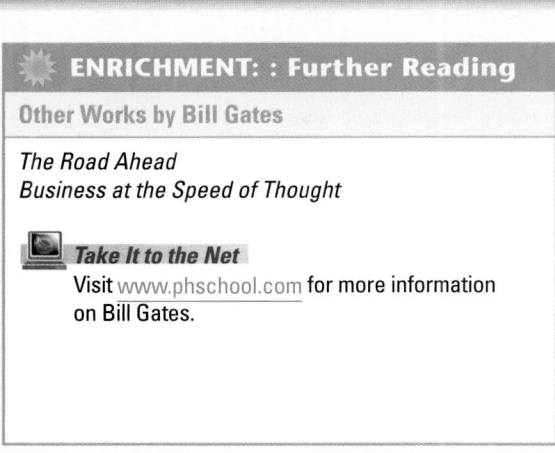

ENRICHMENT: : Further Reading

Other Works by Bill Gates

The Road Ahead
Business at the Speed of Thought

Take It to the Net

Visit www.phschool.com for more information on Bill Gates.

Answers for p. 451

Review and Assess

1. **Main Idea:** Internet technology will revolutionize television viewing
   Supporting Details: computers replace televisions; VCRs unnecessary; viewers watch what and when they want
2. Gates's recollection of watching *The Ed Sullivan Show* gives the essay a personal flavor.
3. Gates believes that television was only an "enhancement" of radio; that videocassette recorders are inconvenient; and that video-on-demand will be a "killer application."
4. **(a)** Students may find Gates persuasive. **(b)** They may find his analogy to the invention of writing most convincing and his dismissal of videocassette recorders least convincing.
5. Gates's primary purpose is to promote the value of broadband networks for video-on-demand.
6. He emphasizes their drawbacks by using phrases like "if you cared to fuss with timers and tapes in advance."
7. **(a)** Helpful: The Internet will allow people to watch programs at their convenience. Not helpful: This technology will take at least ten years to implement in every home. **(b)** Less effective because he doesn't suggest any drawbacks to the new technology.
8. Possible responses: Students may cite space travel, new energy sources, or biogenetics as vital technological developments.

EXTEND

Answers for p. 452

1 Vocabulary Development

Word Analysis

1. simulcast
2. simulate

Spelling Strategy

1. prerecord
2. misspell
3. unnecessary

Fluency: Word Choice

1. capacious
2. simultaneously
3. parlance
4. infrared
5. precursors

2 Grammar

1. M: you taped it; S: if you cared about a program
2. M: this medium will offer shows; S: that you can watch any time
3. M: the demand is growing; S: even as I write
4. M: the revolution will succeed; S: before much more time passes
5. M: viewers welcome convenience; S: which video-on-demand will give them

Writing Application

1. Since you taped that program, you cared about seeing it.
2. You can watch the shows that this medium will offer at any time.
3. I write while the demand grows.
4. Not much time will pass before the revolution succeeds.
5. Video-on-demand will give viewers convenience, which they will welcome.

Integrate Language Skills

1 Vocabulary Development Lesson

Word Analysis: Latin Root *-simul-*

The Latin root *-simul-* means "same" or "at the same time." This fact explains the meaning of *simultaneously*—"happening at the same time." This root also appears in *simulate* and *simulcast;* identify the definition that matches each word.

1. broadcast at the same time on radio and television
2. look or act like; feign

Spelling Strategy

Do not change the spelling of a base word when you add a prefix to it. For example, *infra-* + *red* = *infrared*.

Add *un-*, *mis-*, or *pre-* to each word below to form three properly spelled words.

1. record 2. spell 3. necessary

Fluency: Word Choice

In each sentence, replace the italicized words with the appropriate one from the word list on page 445. Rephrase as necessary.

1. The expert hiker could pack an amazing amount of gear in the *large and roomy* backpack.
2. The two runners reached the finish line *at the same time*.
3. In computer *language*, restarting a computer is called "rebooting."
4. Ultraviolet radiation is more dangerous than *that of light waves beyond the red end of the spectrum*.
5. Vinyl records were the *things that came before and prepared the way for* compact discs.

2 Grammar Lesson

Main and Subordinate Clauses

A **clause** is a group of words with a subject and a verb. A **main,** or **independent, clause** can stand by itself as a complete sentence. In contrast, a **subordinate clause** cannot stand by itself.

In a sentence, a subordinate clause may either follow or precede a main clause.

Main Clause:
The Internet is expanding.
Main Clause, Subordinate Clause:
It offers more *as time passes*.
Subordinate Clause, Main Clause:
If we let it, it can change our lives.

Practice Copy each sentence. Underline the main clause and circle the subordinate clause.

1. If you cared about a program, you taped it.
2. This medium will offer shows that you can watch any time.
3. The demand is growing, even as I write.
4. Before much more time passes, the revolution will succeed.
5. Viewers welcome convenience, which video-on-demand will give them.

Writing Application Rephrase each of the preceding sentences by converting main clauses to subordinate ones and subordinate clauses to main ones.

WG Prentice Hall Writing and Grammar Connection: Chapter 21, Section 2

TEACHING RESOURCES

The following resources can be used to enrich or extend the instructions for pp. 452–453.

Vocabulary

- **Selection Support:** Build Vocabulary, p. 113
- **Vocabulary and Spelling Practice Book,** (Use this booklet for skills enrichment.)

Grammar

- **Selection Support:** Build Grammar Skills, p. 114
- **Writing and Grammar,** Gold Level, p. 468 ■
- **Daily Language Practice Transparencies**

Writing

- **Writing and Grammar,** Gold Level, p. 212
- **Writing and Grammar iText CD-ROM** ■

■ **BLOCK SCHEDULING:** Resources marked with this symbol provide varied instruction during 90-minute blocks.

❸ Writing Lesson

Consumer Response

Bill Gates uses his experience as a businessman and technology specialist to offer his views about the future. In an essay that responds to his, use your experiences as a television viewer or computer user to tell technology developers which advances you would like to see.

Prewriting Review the essay, noting key advances that Gates mentions. Evaluate the worth of each one to you. Then, brainstorm to add your own ideas for innovation. For each idea, list the benefits of your proposal.

Model: Brainstorming to Identify Benefits

Idea →	Benefit
1. full-screen, real-time videophones	1. Allows people to see each other clearly, without choppiness of current technology.

This idea comes from the writer's disappointment with existing video applications.

Drafting Begin with an introduction that establishes your authority as a consumer. Then, devote a paragraph to each of your ideas, explaining both your innovation and its benefits.

Revising Evaluate the body paragraphs to decide whether you have effectively argued the effects of your proposal. If necessary, add more details about current technology's shortcomings to support the need for change.

WG Prentice Hall Writing and Grammar Connection: Chapter 10, Section 2

❹ Extension Activities

Listening and Speaking Working in a group, organize a **presentation** on important inventions of the past one hundred years.

- The group should agree on the inventions to be discussed.
- Each student should research a single invention.
- Use charts and other visuals in creating a display to support the discussion.

Conclude your presentation by inviting questions from your audience. **[Group Activity]**

Research and Technology The future is likely to see many more technological advances besides video-on-demand. Use the Internet to learn what Bill Gates and three (or more) other experts think will be the big technological breakthroughs in the coming decades. Prepare a handout with an **annotated list** of Web sites you found most helpful.

Take It to the Net www.phschool.com

Go online for an additional research activity using the Internet.

ASSESSMENT RESOURCES

The following resources can be used to assess students' knowledge and skills.

Selection Assessment

- **Formal Assessment,** pp. 101–103
- **Open Book Test,** pp. 85–87
- **Got It! Assessment Videotapes,** Tape 3
- **Test Bank Software**

Take It to the Net

Visit www.phschool.com for self-tests and additional questions on "The Road Ahead."

Listening and Speaking Rubric

- **Performance Assess. and Portfolio Mgmt.,** p. 30

PRENTICE HALL ASSESSMENT SYSTEM

- **Workbook**
- **Skill Book**
- **Transparencies**
- **CD-ROM**

Lesson Support for p. 453

❸ Writing Lesson

- Go around the room and have each student suggest some development he or she would like to see in television or computer technology. Create a list of topics from which students can choose.
- Remind students that their essays will be written from their points of view as *consumers*—the people who buy and use these services.
- Suggest that students outline their proposals before writing. Each main idea in favor of their proposal can be a main head in the outline. Each supporting detail will be a subhead below the main head to which it applies. This outline will help ensure a well-organized essay with no irrelevant details.

❹ Extension Activity

Listening and Speaking

- Group students working on related inventions. For instance, those working on home appliances can work together.
- If students are interested in specific inventions that date back further than one hundred years, you might expand the activity to allow them to research these inventions.
- Evaluate students' work using Delivering an Exposition Presentation with Visual Aids, p. 30 in **Performance Assessment and Portfolio Management.**

CUSTOMIZE INSTRUCTION For Universal Access

To address different learning styles, use the following activities suggested in the **Extension Activities** booklet, p. 29.

- For Verbal/Linguistic Learners, use Activities 5 and 6.
- For Logical/Mathematical Learners, use Activity 4.

The Machine That Won the War

Lesson Objectives and CA Correlations

1. **To analyze and respond to literary elements**
   - Literary Analysis: Science Fiction
   - Connecting Literary Elements: Setting **R 3.6**
2. **To read, comprehend, analyze, and critique a short story**
   - Reading Strategy: Identifying Relevant Details
   - Reading Check questions
   - Review and Assess questions
   - Assessment Practice (ATE)
3. **To develop word analysis skills, fluency, and systematic vocabulary**
   - Vocabulary Development Lesson: Latin Prefix: *circum-* **R 1.1**
4. **To understand and apply written and oral language conventions**
   - Spelling Strategy
   - Grammar Lesson: Adverb Clauses and Noun Clauses **LC 1.1**
5. **To understand and apply appropriate writing and research strategies**
   - Writing Lesson: Newspaper Story **W 2.3**
   - Extension Activity: Illustrated Report **W 1.8**
6. **To understand and apply listening and speaking strategies**
   - Extension Activity: Discussion **LS 1.8**

STEP-BY-STEP TEACHING GUIDE	PACING GUIDE
PRETEACH	
Motivate Students and Provide Background	
Use the Motivation activity (ATE p. 454)	5 min.
Read and discuss the Preview material and Background information (SE/ATE p. 454) **A**	5 min.
Introduce the Concepts	
Introduce the Literary Analysis and Reading Strategy (SE/ATE p. 455) **A**	15 min.
Pronounce the vocabulary words and read their definitions (SE p. 455)	5 min.
TEACH	
Monitor Comprehension	
Informally monitor comprehension by circulating while students read independently or in groups **A**	20 min.
Monitor students' comprehension with the Reading Check notes (SE/ATE pp. 457, 459, 461)	as students read
Develop vocabulary with Vocabulary notes (SE pp. 457, 459, 460; ATE p. 460)	as students read
Develop Understanding	
Develop students' understanding of science fiction with Literary Analysis annotations (ATE p. 458) **A**	10 min.
Develop students' ability to identify relevant details with Reading Strategy annotations (SE pp. 459, 460, 463; ATE pp. 457, 459, 460)	10 min.
ASSESS	
Assess Mastery	
Assess students' mastery of the Reading Strategy and Literary Analysis by having them answer the Review and Assess questions (SE/ATE p. 463)	20 min.
Use one or more of the print and media Assessment Resources (ATE p. 465) **A**	up to 50 min.
EXTEND	
Apply Understanding	
Have students complete the Vocabulary Development Lesson and the Grammar Lesson (SE p. 464) **A**	20 min.
Apply students' knowledge of attention-grabbing leads using the Writing Lesson (SE/ATE p. 465) **A**	45 min.
Apply students' understanding using one or more of the Extension Activities (SE/ATE p. 465)	20–90 min.

A **ACCELERATED INSTRUCTION:** Use the strategies and activities identified with an **A**.

UNIVERSAL ACCESS
● = Below-Level Students
▲ = On-Level Students
■ = Above-Level Students

Time and Resource Manager

Reading Level: Average
Average Number of Instructional Days: 4

RESOURCES		
PRINT	**TRANSPARENCIES**	**TECHNOLOGY**
• **Beyond Literature,** Cross-Curricular Connection: Science Fact and Fiction, p. 30 ▲ ■		• **Interest Grabber Video,** Tape 3 ● ▲ ■
• **Selection Support Workbook:** ● ▲ ■ Literary Analysis, p. 120 Reading Strategy, p. 119 Build Vocabulary, p. 117	• **Literary Analysis and Reading Transparencies,** pp. 59 and 60 ● ▲ ■	
• **Adapted Reader's Companion** ● • **Reader's Companion** ●		• **Listening to Literature** ● ▲ ■ Audiocassettes, Side 13 Audio CDs, CD 9
• **English Learner's Companion** ● ▲ • **Literatura en español** ● ▲ • **Literary Analysis for Enrichment** ■		
• **Formal Assessment:** Selection Test, pp. 104–106 ● ▲ ■ • **Open Book Test,** pp. 88–90 ● ▲ ■ • PRENTICE HALL ASSESSMENT SYSTEM ● ▲ ■	• PRENTICE HALL ASSESSMENT SYSTEM ● ▲ ■ Skills Practice Answers and Explanations on Transparencies	• **Test Bank Software** ● ▲ ■ • **Got It! Assessment Videotapes,** Tape 3 ● ▲
• **Selection Support Workbook:** ● ▲ ■ Build Grammar Skills, p. 118 • **Writing and Grammar,** Gold Level ● ▲ ■ • **Extension Activities,** p. 30 ● ▲ ■	• **Daily Language Practice Transparencies** ● ▲	• **Writing and Grammar iText CD-ROM** ● ▲ ■ ***Take It to the Net*** www.phschool.com

BLOCK SCHEDULING: Use one 90-minute class period to preteach the selection and have students read it. Use a second 90-minute class period to assess students' mastery of skills and have them complete one of the Extension Activities.

PRETEACH

Step-by-Step Teaching Guide for pp. 454–455

Motivation

Present students with the following scenario: The world's number-one-ranked chess player has two crucial matches coming up. One is against the world's number-two player. The other is against a newly unveiled chess-playing computer. Which match is the number-one player likely to be more nervous about? Why?

Interest Grabber Video

As an alternative, play "The Cray Computer" on Tape 3 to engage student interest.

❶ Background

The first electronic digital computer, ENIAC *(Electronic Numerical Integrator and Computer)* was 10 feet tall, 1,800 square feet in area, and weighed about 30 tons. It contained about 18,000 vacuum tubes, which failed at a rate of about 50 per day. Like the Multivac in Asimov's story, ENIAC was originally used during wartime for military purposes.

Prepare to Read

The Machine That Won the War

Take It to the Net

Visit www.phschool.com for interactive activities and instruction related to "The Machine That Won the War," including

- background
- graphic organizers
- literary elements
- reading strategies

Preview

Connecting to the Literature

The success of everyday life has come to depend on computers. Machines track store purchases, banking transactions, and school records. Sometimes, as you will see in "The Machine That Won the War," computers run important military applications.

❶ Background

When Isaac Asimov wrote this story, computers were big, bulky machines; small, personal computers had not yet been invented. Solving problems required the setting of thousands of cables and switches by hand. The early computers had names like UNIVAC and ENIAC. Perhaps Asimov was thinking of them when he devised the name "Multivac"—the powerful computer in this story.

TEACHING RESOURCES

The following resources can be used to enrich or extend the instruction for pp. 454–455.

Motivation

Interest Grabber Video, Tape 3

Background

Beyond Literature, p. 30

Take It to the Net

Visit www.phschool.com for background and hotlinks for "The Machine That Won the War."

Literary Analysis

Literary Analysis and Reading Transparencies, Science Fiction, p. 59

Reading

Selection Support: Reading Strategy, p. 119; Build Vocabulary, p. 117

Literary Analysis and Reading Transparencies, Identifying Relevant Details, p. 60

BLOCK SCHEDULING: Resources marked with this symbol provide varied instruction during 90-minute blocks.

❷ Literary Analysis

Science Fiction

Science fiction is a form of literature in which the writer makes free use of his or her imagination to create settings, characters, and situations not found in reality. Whatever changes the author introduces, however, are based on real science. This passage from Asimov's story describes an unreal setting and situation:

> "What do you know of the data Multivac had to use: predigested from a hundred subsidiary computers here on Earth, on the Moon, on Mars, even on Titan. . . ."

In addition to the names of actual planets and moons that Asimov cites, notice how many of the details in "The Machine That Won the War" combine imagination with scientific fact.

Connecting Literary Elements

A story's **setting** is the time and place in which the action occurs. In science fiction, the setting may be

- an alternative past.
- an altered present.
- a possible future.

Many details of Asimov's story suggest that it is set in a possible future.

❸ Reading Strategy

Identifying Relevant Details

Relevant details are those descriptions or events that are important in helping you understand the plot, characters, and setting of a story. Asimov's story mentions computers on the Moon, Mars, and Titan. These details are relevant because they make it clear that the setting is in the future.

Use a chart like the one shown to record specific details about characters, setting, technology, or the war found in the story, and explain why each is relevant.

Details	Relevance

Vocabulary Development

erratic (er rat′ ik) *adj.* irregular; random (p. 457)

grisly (griz′ lē) *adj.* horrifying; gruesome (p. 457)

imperturbable (im′ pər tʉr′ bə bəl) *adj.* unable to be excited or disturbed (p. 457)

oracle (ôr′ ə kəl) *n.* source of knowledge or wise counsel (p. 457)

surcease (sʉr′ sēs′) *n.* end (p. 459)

subsidiary (səb sid′ ē er′ ē) *adj.* secondary; supporting (p. 459)

circumvent (sʉr′ kəm vent′) *v.* avoid; go around (p. 460)

❷ Literary Analysis

Science Fiction

- Write the term *science fiction* on the chalkboard. Have students cite elements that they would include in a story or film in this genre (for example, settings in the future, alien life forms, wondrous technology).
- Explain that science fiction takes genuine scientific premises to an extent beyond reality.
- As students read "The Machine That Won the War," they can look for elements of science and see how Asimov exaggerated or extended them.

❸ Reading Strategy

Identifying Relevant Details

- Ask students whether they have ever cried out, "Get to the point!" when a friend was telling them a long story.
- Explain that what they are objecting to is hearing too many irrelevant details. Good stories focus on relevant details—information that develops plot and character, builds suspense, and supports the theme or themes.
- One good test of relevance is whether a passage can be eliminated without destroying or altering the story's impact. Have students use self-sticking notes to mark any passages in Asimov's story that seem unnecessary on a first reading. Afterward, have them go back over these passages. Could they be removed without damaging the overall story? If so, why do students think Asimov included them?

Vocabulary Development

- Pronounce each vocabulary word for students, and read the definitions as a class. Have students identify any words with which they are already familiar.

CUSTOMIZE INSTRUCTION FOR UNIVERSAL ACCESS

For Special Needs Students	For Less Proficient Readers	For English Learners
Have students read the adapted version of "The Machine That Won the War" in the **Adapted Reader's Companion.** This version provides basic-level instruction in an interactive format with questions and write-on lines. Completing the adapted version will prepare students to read the selection in the Student Edition.	Have students read the selection in the **Reader's Companion.** This version provides basic-level instruction in an interactive format with questions and write-on lines. After students finish the selection in **Reader's Companion,** have them complete the questions and activities in the Student Edition.	Have students read the adapted version of the selection in the **English Learner's Companion.** This version provides basic-level instruction in an interactive format with questions and write-on lines. Completing the adapted version will prepare students to read the selection in the Student Edition.

E-Teach

Visit E-Teach at www.phschool.com for teachers' essays on how to teach, with questions and answers.

TEACH

Step-by-Step Teaching Guide for pp. 456–462

CUSTOMIZE INSTRUCTION
For Logical/Mathematical Learners

As students read, they can note aspects of the story that clearly define it as science fiction. Ask whether students think the scenario Asimov imagines could ever actually happen. If not, why not?

❶ About the Selection

Swift, Henderson, and Jablonsky meet in a quiet corner inside the giant computer Multivac. Multivac's calculations have been directing the conduct of an interplanetary war for the past ten years, and with the victory the computer has become the hero of the hour. As the men reveal the ways in which they "corrected" and ultimately disregarded the mighty computer's data, it becomes clear that the computer is no match for the complex and unpredictable human mind.

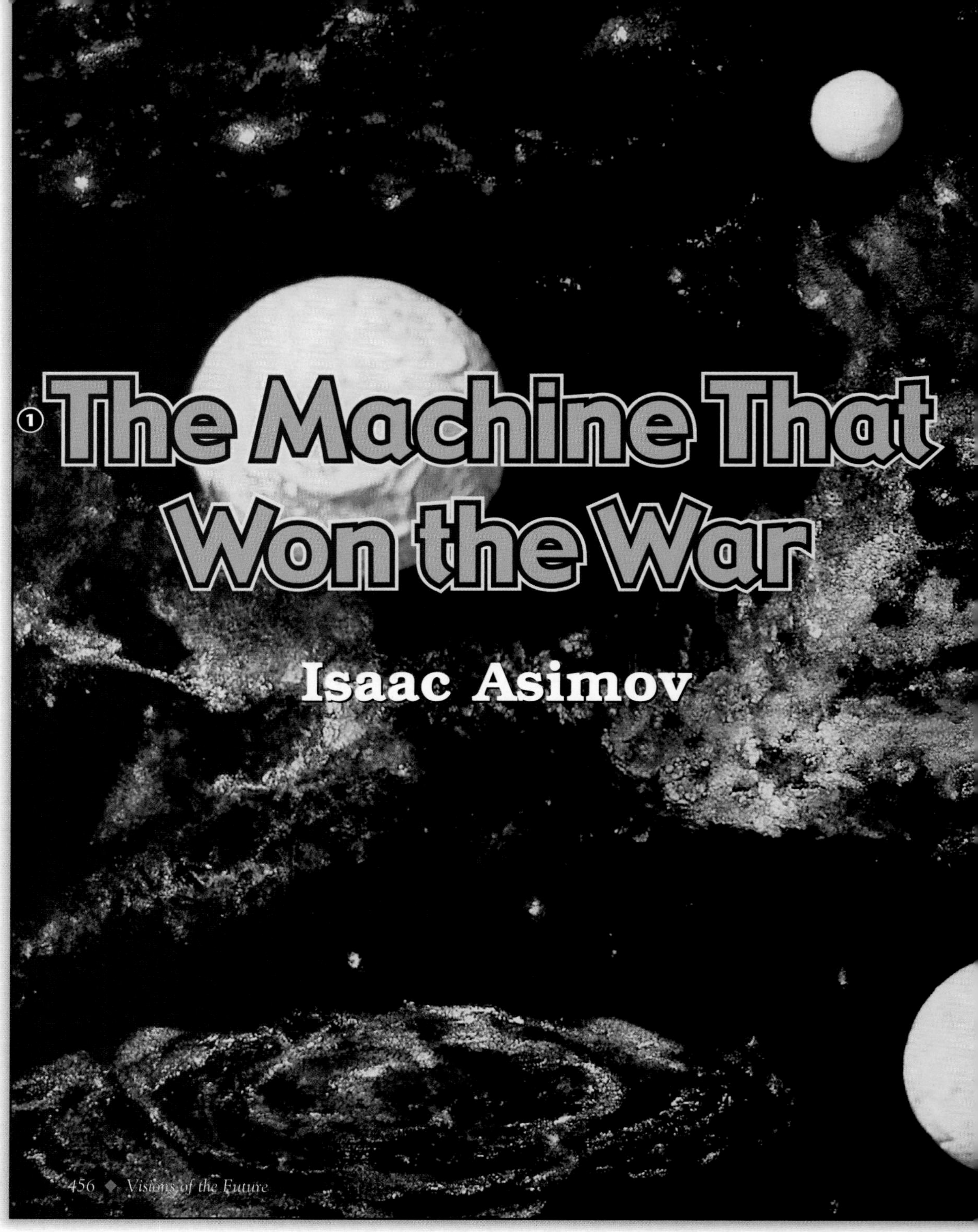

❶ The Machine That Won the War

Isaac Asimov

TEACHING RESOURCES

The following resources can be used to enrich or extend the instruction for pp. 456–462.

Literary Analysis

Selection Support: Literary Analysis, p. 120

Reading

Reader's Companion

English Learner's Companion

Listening to Literature Audiocassettes, Side 13 ■

Listening to Literature Audio CDs, CD 9 ■

■ **BLOCK SCHEDULING:** Resources marked with this symbol provide varied instruction during 90-minute blocks.

The celebration had a long way to go and even in the silent depths of Multivac's underground chambers, it hung in the air.

If nothing else, there was the mere fact of isolation and silence. For the first time in a decade, technicians were not scurrying about the vitals of the giant computer, the soft lights did not wink out their erratic patterns, the flow of information in and out had halted.

It would not be halted long, of course, for the needs of peace would be pressing. Yet now, for a day, perhaps for a week, even Multivac might celebrate the great time, and rest.

Lamar Swift took off the military cap he was wearing and looked down the long and empty main corridor of the enormous computer. He sat down rather wearily in one of the technician's swing-stools, and his uniform, in which he had never been comfortable, took on a heavy and wrinkled appearance.

He said, "I'll miss it all after a grisly fashion. It's hard to remember when we weren't at war with Deneb, and it seems against nature now to be at peace and to look at the stars without anxiety."

The two men with the Executive Director of the Solar Federation were both younger than Swift. Neither was as gray. Neither looked quite as tired.

John Henderson, thin-lipped and finding it hard to control the relief he felt in the midst of triumph, said, "They're destroyed! They're destroyed! It's what I keep saying to myself over and over and I still can't believe it. We all talked so much, over so many years, about the menace hanging over Earth and all its worlds, over every human being, and all the time it was true, every word of it. And now we're alive and it's the Denebians who are shattered and destroyed. They'll be no menace now, ever again." **2**

"Thanks to Multivac," said Swift, with a quiet glance at the imperturbable Jablonsky, who through all the war had been Chief Interpreter of science's oracle. "Right, Max?"

Jablonsky shrugged. He said, "Well, that's what *they* say." His broad thumb moved in the direction of his right shoulder, aiming upward.

"Jealous, Max?"

"Because they're shouting for Multivac? Because Multivac is the big hero of mankind in this war?" Jablonsky's craggy face took on an air of suitable contempt. "What's that to me? Let Multivac be the machine that won the war, if it pleases them." **3**

Henderson looked at the other two out of the corners of his eyes. In this short interlude that the three had instinctively sought out

erratic (er rat′ ik) *adj.* irregular; random

grisly (griz′ lē) *adj.* horrifying; gruesome

imperturbable (im′ pər tʉr′ bə bəl) *adj.* unable to be excited or disturbed

oracle (ôr′ ə kəl) *n.* source of knowledge or wise counsel

3 Reading Check

Why are the characters enjoying a brief rest as the story begins?

2 Reading Strategy

Identifying Relevant Details

- Ask students to identify specific details in this passage and state whether the details seem relevant to plot, character, setting, or theme.
  Answer: The details about the characters' appearance and their emotions are relevant to character. The information about the war is relevant to the plot.
- Ask whether students think any details on this page might be omitted as not highly relevant to the story. Why might Asimov have included these details?
  Answer: Students may cite some details of physical description. For example, Henderson and Jablonsky are younger and not as tired-looking as Swift. Students may note that these details help readers visualize the characters.

3 Reading Check

Answer: A long, hard-fought war has just come to an end, and there is a lull in work to be done.

CUSTOMIZE INSTRUCTION FOR UNIVERSAL ACCESS

For Gifted/Talented Students

Have students plan and perform a dramatic version of "The Machine That Won the War." Three students could play the roles of Jablonsky, Swift, and Henderson. Others in the group could direct rehearsals, collaborate on a script, and decide on a type of presentation (dramatic reading, radio play, video, and so on). One team of students might work on developing a set. What props or sound effects would suggest the interior of a giant computer? Allow time for rehearsals, then have students perform for the class. Afterward, have the audience compare the play with the story, comment on any differences, and discuss their effect on the overall impact of the piece.

4 ▶ Critical Viewing

Possible responses: The night sky seems mysterious, and each star represents a world of possibility—alien planets and unearthly life forms.

5 Literary Analysis

Setting and Science Fiction

- Note to students that the "peaceful corner" in which the men meet is inside a giant computer. What assumption has Asimov made about computers in the future?
  Answer: Asimov assumes that future computers will be gigantic.
- How does this setting reinforce the science fiction aspects of the story?
  Answer: The meeting place emphasizes technology. The men are sitting in Multivac in order to discuss Multivac.

4 ▲ **Critical Viewing** What attraction might the night sky, as shown here, have for science-fiction writers? **[Hypothesize]**

ENRICHMENT: Science

Y2K

Modern computers are far more reliable than Asimov's Multivac. As the year 2000 approached, however, many people feared a massive breakdown in digital technology. To save space in the first computers' memory, programming languages told computers that all years began with the two digits "19." Thus, each year took up two digits of memory instead of four: 85 stood for 1985, for example. Programmers assumed that their work would soon be replaced by newer systems, but the old systems were still in use at the twentieth century's end. When the calendars inside the computers advanced from 12/31/99 to 01/01/00, the computers would assume that 00 stood for 1900, not 2000. This meant that a computer at a bank might mark a payment as 100 years overdue, that social security checks would not be sent out because they were not due for 100 years, and so on. By working throughout 1999, programmers prevented all but a few minor glitches from occurring on New Year's Day 2000.

5 in the one peaceful corner of a metropolis gone mad; in this entr'acte[1] between the dangers of war and the difficulties of peace; when, for one moment, they might all find surcease; he was conscious only of his weight of guilt.

Suddenly, it was as though that weight were too great to be borne longer. It had to be thrown off, along with the war; now!

Henderson said, "Multivac had nothing to do with victory. It's just a machine."

"A big one," said Swift.

"Then just a big machine. No better than the data fed it." For a moment, he stopped, suddenly unnerved at what he was saying.

Jablonsky looked at him. "You should know. You supplied the data. Or is it just that you're taking the credit?"

"*No*," said Henderson angrily. "There is no credit. What do you know of the data Multivac had to use: predigested from a hundred subsidiary computers here on Earth, on the Moon, on Mars, even on Titan. With Titan always delayed and always feeling that its figures would introduce an unexpected bias."

"It would drive anyone mad," said Swift, with gentle sympathy.

6 Henderson shook his head. "It wasn't just that. I admit that eight years ago when I replaced Lepont as Chief Programmer, I was nervous. But there was an exhilaration about things in those days. The war was still long range; an adventure without real danger. We hadn't reached the point where manned vessels had had to take over and where interstellar warps could swallow up a planet clean, if aimed correctly. But then, when the real difficulties began—"

Angrily—he could finally permit anger—he said, "You know nothing about it."

"Well," said Swift. "Tell us. The war is over. We've won."

"Yes." Henderson nodded his head. He had to remember that. Earth had won, so all had been for the best. "Well, the data became meaningless."

"Meaningless? You mean that literally?" said Jablonsky.

"Literally. What would you expect? The trouble with you two was that you weren't out in the thick of it. You never left Multivac, Max, and you, Mr. Director, never left the Mansion except on state visits where you saw exactly what they wanted you to see."

"I was not as unaware of that," said Swift, "as you may have thought."

"Do you know," said Henderson, "to what extent data concerning our production capacity, our resource potential, our trained manpower—everything of importance to the war effort, in fact—had become unreliable and untrustworthy during the last half of the war? Group leaders, both civilian and military, were intent on projecting their own improved image, so to speak, so they obscured the bad and magnified the good. Whatever the machines might do, the men who programmed

1. **entr'acte** (än trakt') *n.* interval.

surcease (sur' sēs') *n.* end

subsidiary (səb sid' ē er' ē) *adj.* secondary; supporting

Reading Strategy
Identifying Relevant Details Which details in this paragraph are relevant to helping you understand the plot?

7 **Reading Check**
What does Henderson say about Multivac's role in winning the war?

6 Reading Strategy
Identifying Relevant Details

- Have students reread the bracketed passage, listing all the details in the paragraph they can.
- Then, ask students the Reading Strategy question on p. 459: Which details in this paragraph are relevant to helping you understand the plot?
  Answer: Henderson is Chief Programmer of Multivac, a very responsible position. The references to "manned vessels" and planet-swallowing "interstellar warps" hint at the dangerous scope of the war.

7 Reading Check

Answer: Henderson says "Multivac had nothing to do with victory."

CUSTOMIZE INSTRUCTION FOR UNIVERSAL ACCESS

For Special Needs Students	For Gifted/Talented Students
To help students distinguish the roles of three men, create a flow chart on the board to show how each man handled the information from Multivac. As students go through the story, make sure they know who is speaking each line of dialogue.	Have students speculate about what would happen if the three men realized that the Denebians were not totally destroyed. Tell students to write a sequel to the story. Before writing, have them consider the opinions and actions of each character and plan the direction of the plot.

8 Vocabulary Development

Latin Prefix *circum-*

- Point out that the word *circumvent* begins with the Latin prefix *circum-*, which means "around." Knowing this prefix helps a reader to understand that *circumvent* means "to go around; avoid."
- Write the words *circumscribe* and *circumnavigate*. Give students opportunity to use their knowledge of prefixes and roots to determine that *circumscribe* means "to draw a line around; confine." *Circumnavigate* means "to sail around."

9 Reading Strategy

Identifying Relevant Details

- Ask students the Reading Strategy question on p. 460: What are the most relevant details in this paragraph?
  Answer: Jablonsky's statement that he ignored unauthorized uses of Multivac because "nothing mattered" seems relevant.

Monitor Progress Have students read on to the phrase ". . . won the war" near the top of p. 461. Have them go back to this page and use the relevant details to summarize what Henderson and Jablonsky have done.
Answer: Henderson corrected and adjusted unreliable data. Jablonsky, suspecting that the data were unreliable, corrected and adjusted the computer's interpretations of the data.

them and interpreted the results had their own skins to think of and competitors to stab. There was no way of stopping that. I tried, and failed."

"Of course," said Swift, in quiet consolation. "I can see that you would."

"Yet I presume you provided Multivac with data in your programming?" Jablonsky said. "You said nothing to us about unreliability."

"How could I tell you? And if I did, how could you afford to believe me?" demanded Henderson, savagely. "Our entire war effort was geared to Multivac. It was the one great weapon on our side, for the Denebians had nothing like it. What else kept up morale in the face of doom but the assurance that Multivac would always predict and
8 circumvent any Denebian move, and would always direct and prevent the circumvention of our moves? Great Space, after our Spy-warp was blasted out of hyperspace we lacked any reliable Denebian data to feed Multivac and we didn't dare make *that* public."

"True enough," said Swift.

"Well, then," said Henderson, "if I told you the data was unreliable, what could you have done but replace me and refuse to believe me? I couldn't allow that."

"What did you do?" said Jablonsky.

"Since the war is won, I'll tell you what I did. I corrected the data."

"How?" asked Swift.

"Intuition, I presume. I juggled them till they looked right. At first, I hardly dared. I changed a bit here and there to correct what were obvious impossibilities. When the sky didn't collapse about us, I got braver. Toward the end, I scarcely cared. I just wrote out the necessary data as it was needed. I even had the Multivac Annex prepare data for me according to a private programming pattern I had devised for the purpose."

"Random figures?" said Jablonsky.

"Not at all. I introduced a number of necessary biases."

Jablonsky smiled, quite unexpectedly, his dark eyes sparkling behind the crinkling of the lower lids. "Three times a report was brought to me about unauthorized uses of the Annex, and I let it go each time. If it had mattered, I would have followed it up and spotted you, John, and found out what you were doing. But, of course, nothing about Multivac mattered in those days, so you got away with it."

"What do you mean, nothing mattered?" asked Henderson, suspiciously.

9 "Nothing did. I suppose if I had told you this at the time, it would have spared you your agony, but then if you had told me what you were doing, it would have spared me mine. What made you think Multivac was in working order, whatever the data you supplied it?"

"Not in working order?" said Swift.

"Not really. Not reliably. After all, where were my technicians in the last years of the war? I'll tell you, they were feeding computers on a thousand different space devices. They were gone! I had to make do

circumvent (sur´ kəm vent´) *v.* avoid; go around

Reading Strategy
Identifying Relevant Details What are the most relevant details in this paragraph?

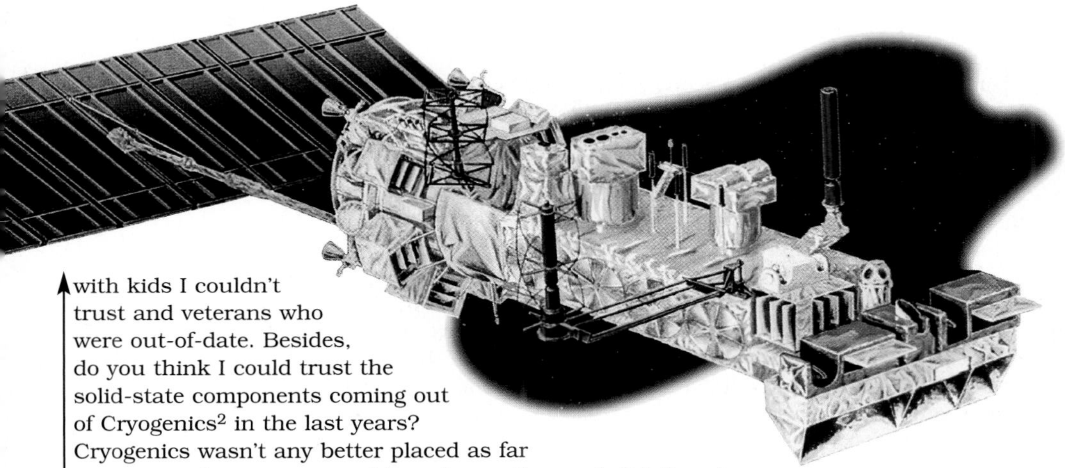

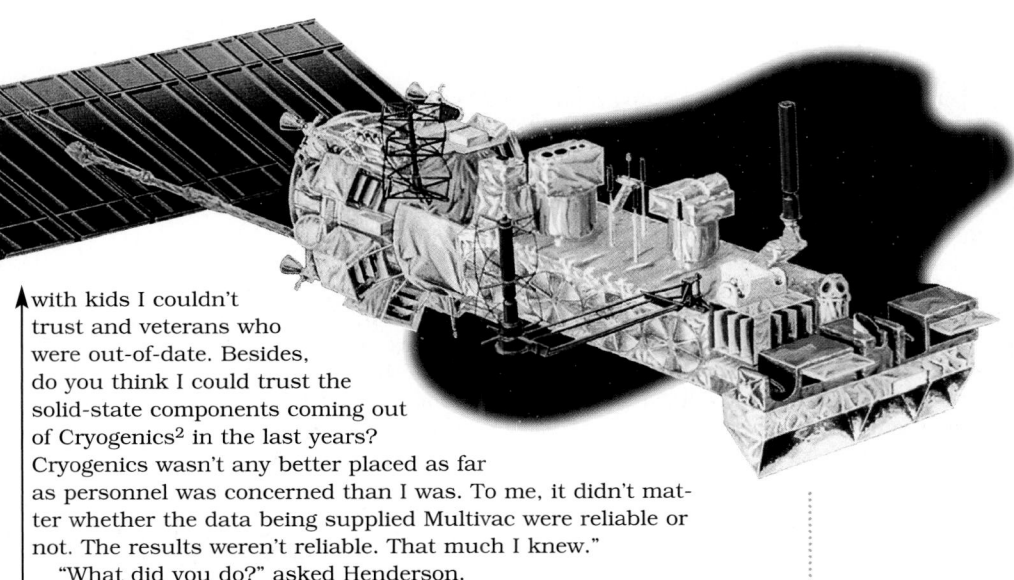

with kids I couldn't trust and veterans who were out-of-date. Besides, do you think I could trust the solid-state components coming out of Cryogenics[2] in the last years? Cryogenics wasn't any better placed as far as personnel was concerned than I was. To me, it didn't matter whether the data being supplied Multivac were reliable or not. The results weren't reliable. That much I knew."

"What did you do?" asked Henderson.

"I did what you did, John. I introduced the bugger factor. I adjusted matters in accordance with intuition—and that's how the machine won the war."

Swift leaned back in the chair and stretched his legs out before him. "Such revelations. It turns out then that the material handed me to guide me in my decision-making capacity was a man-made interpretation of man-made data. Isn't that right?"

"It looks so," said Jablonsky.

"Then I perceive I was correct in not placing too much reliance upon it," said Swift.

"You didn't?" Jablonsky, despite what he had just said, managed to look professionally insulted.

"I'm afraid I didn't. Multivac might seem to say, Strike here, not there; do this, not that; wait, don't act. But I could never be certain
10 that what Multivac seemed to say, it really did say; or what it really said, it really meant. I could never be certain."

"But the final report was always plain enough, sir," said Jablonsky.

"To those who did not have to make the decision, perhaps. Not to me. The horror of the responsibility of such decisions was unbearable and not even Multivac was sufficient to remove the weight. But the point is I was justified in doubting and there is tremendous relief in that."

Caught up in the conspiracy of mutual confession, Jablonsky put titles aside. "What was it you did then, Lamar? After all, you did make decisions. How?"

11 Reading Check

What kind of data and interpretation of data were given to Swift during the war?

2. **Cryogenics** (krī́ ō jen´ iks) here, a department concerned with the science of low-temperature phenomena.

10 Critical Thinking

Analyze Causes and Effects

- Remind students that many important events in a story are related through cause and effect.
- Have students reread the bracketed passage.
- Ask students to use relevant details to explain the chain of causes and effects that led Swift to doubt the reports and suggestions from Multivac. You may want to have them complete a graphic organizer like the one shown.

Cause

Because his sources were trying to make their departments look good rather than admit their data were unreliable . . .

Effect

Henderson altered the data.

- Ask students what might have happened if the three men had accepted the computer's information at face value.
  Possible answers: They might have lost the war.

11 Reading Check

Answer: The data and interpretations of data given to Swift were altered because Henderson knew the original data was unreliable and Jablonsky knew that Multivac might not be interpreting data correctly.

CUSTOMIZE INSTRUCTION FOR UNIVERSAL ACCESS

For Less Proficient Readers	For Advanced Readers
Have a small group of students work together to answer Review and Assess questions 5–7 on p. 463. Afterward, have them discuss the importance of the setting to the story. How would the story be different if the three men had met in the middle of the noisy celebrations, or in Swift's office in the Mansion? Have students discuss why Asimov set the story inside the computer.	Have students discuss their answers to Review and Assess questions 3 and 4 on p. 463. Have each student imagine a realistic story in which the same three characters are faced with similar conflicts—what to do when you must make a decision that will affect the lives of all your fellow citizens. Students can write their stories, working on their own or with partners. Let writers read their stories aloud to the class.

ASSESS

Answers for p. 462

Review and Assess

1. Students may report that Multivac's importance seemed to diminish as they read the story.
2. **(a)** A ten-year interstellar war has just ended. **(b)** They do not celebrate. Instead, they gather in a quiet corner.
3. **(a)** Swift is Executive Director of the Solar Federation. Jablonsky is Multivac's Chief Interpreter. Henderson is Multivac's Chief Programmer. **(b)** Henderson feeds data into the computer; Jablonsky interprets the resulting information; Swift acts on the information.
4. **(a)** Multivac was expected to direct all strategy. **(b)** It played a lesser role because its data and interpretations were bypassed at crucial points.
5. **(a)** The men altered the data. **(b)** A coin can always be counted on to give one of two responses. Multivac might give a great variety of responses.
6. Possible responses: The war might have been lost.
7. Possible responses: Computers can process information and perform calculations with far greater speed and accuracy than humans. However, as Asimov makes clear, computers are completely dependent on the quality of information they are given—by humans.

"Well, it's time to be getting back perhaps, but—I'll tell you first. Why not? I did make use of a computer, Max, but an older one than Multivac, much older."

He groped in his own pocket and brought out a scattering of small change; old-fashioned coins dating to the first years before the metal shortage had brought into being a credit system tied to a computer-complex.

Swift smiled rather sheepishly. "I still need these to make money seem substantial to me. An old man finds it hard to abandon the habits of youth." He dropped the coins, one by one, back into his pocket.

He held the last coin between his fingers, staring absently at it. "Multivac is not the first computer, friends, nor the best-known, nor the one that can most efficiently lift the load of decision from the shoulders of the executive. A machine *did* win the war, John; at least a very simple computing device did; one that I used every time I had a particularly hard decision to make."

With a faint smile of reminiscence, he flipped the coin he held. It glinted in the air as it spun and came down in Swift's outstretched palm. His hand closed over it and brought it down on the back of his left hand. His right hand remained in place, hiding the coin.

"Heads or tails, gentlemen?" said Swift.

Review and Assess

Thinking About the Selection

1. **Respond:** How did your opinion of Multivac change as you read the story?
2. **(a) Recall:** What is behind the celebration mentioned at the opening of the story? **(b) Connect:** Do the three men join in the celebratory mood? Explain.
3. **(a) Recall:** What are the job titles of the three men in the story? **(b) Compare and Contrast:** How are the men's jobs related yet different?
4. **(a) Recall:** What was Multivac's expected role in the war? **(b) Draw Conclusions:** What was its true role in the war?
5. **(a) Recall:** What did the men do to the data fed to Multivac? **(b) Deduce:** Did their actions make Multivac less reliable than Swift's "simple computing device"? Explain.
6. **Speculate:** If all three men had done their jobs properly, would the war's outcome have been different? Explain.
7. **Take a Position:** Do you think it is better to rely on information from humans or from computers? Why?

Isaac Asimov

(1920–1992)

Asimov came to the United States from Russia at the age of three. His parents spoke no English, but he taught himself to read the language before entering first grade.

Disliking the need to return library books and wanting a permanent library of his own, Asimov decided to write his own books. Overall, he wrote more than 470 books on subjects including science, history, Shakespeare, and the Bible, as well as science fiction, for which he is best known.

Some of his most famous works include *I Robot* (1950), the *Foundation* trilogy (1951–53), and *Fantastic Voyage* (1966), which was made into a movie.

ASSESSMENT PRACTICE: Reading Comprehension

Draw Inferences (For more practice, see Test Preparation Workbook, p. 30.)

Many tests require students to draw inferences. Have students read the paragraph beginning "Do you know" (pp. 459–460). Then ask:

Which of the following can you infer from Henderson's statement?

A Multivac had enough data and potential to correct for human error.

B The team that programmed Multivac was incompetent.

C The data programmed into Multivac was unreliable because the workers were self-absorbed.

D Henderson tried to stop the group leaders from being untrustworthy.

Choice *C* is the best inference because Henderson found that the workers' self-interest interfered with their objectivity.

Review and Assess

Literary Analysis

Science Fiction

1. In **science fiction,** some elements must be based on scientific ideas. Use a chart like this to classify key elements of the story.

Science-Based	◄·····►	Non-Science-Based

2. Which plot details indicate that the story is science fiction?
3. Could the characters in this story exist in real life? Why or why not?
4. Good science fiction carefully balances scientific and imaginative elements. Is this story good science fiction? Explain.

Connecting Literary Elements

5. Which details of time and place indicate that the story's **setting** is the future? Record your answers in a chart like the one below.

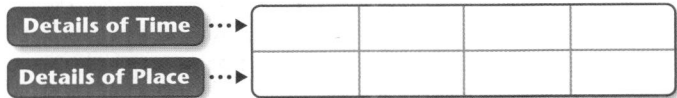

Details of Time ···►				
Details of Place ···►				

6. On the basis of what you know about the present and the past, does Asimov's future seem genuinely possible? Explain.
7. Could a story have the same setting as Asimov's and *not* be science fiction? Explain.

Reading Strategy

Identifying Relevant Details

8. In this story, the space program is both vast and advanced. (a) Find two details that support this statement. (b) Are these details **relevant** to the plot? Explain your answer.
9. (a) Which detail in the story shows how the monetary system in Asimov's future world differs from the present system? (b) Is the changed system relevant? Explain.

Extend Understanding

10. **Technology Connection:** Computers solve many—but not all—problems. Name areas where they are not useful now, and then speculate whether future computers might be useful in those areas.

Quick Review

Science fiction is a form of fiction in which the writer makes free use of imagination to create settings, characters, and situations not found in reality.

A story's **setting** is the time and place in which its action occurs.

To **identify relevant details,** find those that make the plot, characters, and setting understandable.

Take It to the Net

www.phschool.com

Take the interactive self-test online to check your understanding of the selection.

ENRICHMENT: Further Reading

Other Works by Isaac Asimov

I, Robot (short stories)
The Caves of Steel
Foundation

Take It to the Net

Visit www.phschool.com for more information on Isaac Asimov.

Answers for p. 463

Review and Assess

1. Science-based elements: Multivac; extraterrestrial worlds; interstellar warps; Spy Warp
   Non-science-based elements: human motives, actions, and emotions
2. Science-fiction details include the idea of an interstellar war, the Solar Federation, and Spy Warp weapons.
3. The characters seem realistic. They feel ordinary emotions like guilt, responsibility, and friendship.
4. Students may agree that the story balances realistic characters against the science-fiction elements of an interstellar war.
5. Details of place include the reference to other planets and to the Solar Federation. Time details include the length of the war and the replacement of "old-fashioned" coins.
6. Students may disagree about the feasibility of interstellar travel, the existence of other worlds, or the size of future computers.
7. Yes. If all interstellar elements were replaced by a war on earth, the story would work as conventional fiction.
8. **(a)** Interplanetary travel, communication, and alliances are apparently routine. **(b)** The details are relevant to the conduct of an interstellar war.
9. **(a)** Coins have been replaced by a credit system. **(b)** The changed system does not affect the plot, but Swift's use of a tossed coin reinforces the triumph of old methods over new technology.
10. Students may note that computers may never become useful in complex personal and social situations involving emotions rather than data.

EXTEND

Answers for p. 464

❶ Vocabulary Development

Word Analysis

Sample Sentences:

1. the distance around: She painted a border on the circumference of the plate.
2. to limit the area around something: This fence will circumscribe our entire property.
3. the situation around an event: Given our crowded circumstance, I volunteered to sleep on the couch.
4. to travel around: The space shuttle will circumnavigate the earth more than one hundred times on this mission.

Spelling Strategy

1. realistically: Nan has a talent for planning realistically.
2. hectically: The ants worked hectically to rebuild their nest.
3. terrifically: It was terrifically hot yesterday.

Concept Development: Synonyms

1. b
2. c
3. a
4. a
5. c
6. c
7. a

❷ Grammar

1. after the war ended, adverb clause
2. that he had changed the rules, noun clause
3. if it was used right, adverb clause
4. that it was a hero, noun clause
5. before he made a decision, adverb clause

Writing Application

Sample Sentences:

1. While Swift was Executive Director, he concealed the fact that he made decisions by chance.
2. Though they were shocked, Henderson and Jablonsky did not say what they were thinking.

Integrate Language Skills

❶ Vocabulary Development Lesson

Word Analysis: Latin Prefix *circum-*

The Latin prefix *circum-* means "around." *Circumvent*, for instance, means "go around" or "avoid." Apply the meaning of *circum-* to define each word below. Then, use each word in a sentence.

1. circumference
2. circumscribe
3. circumstance
4. circumnavigate

Spelling Strategy

To add the suffix *-ly* to a word that ends in *-ic*, spell the suffix *-ally*. For example, *erratic* becomes *erratically*. (An exception to this rule is *publicly*.) Add *-ally* to the following adjectives to make them adverbs. Then, use each adverb in a sentence.

1. realistic 2. hectic 3. terrific

Concept Development: Synonyms

Choose the letter of the word or phrase that has the same meaning as the first word.

1. erratic: (a) slow, (b) random, (c) rapid
2. grisly: (a) private, (b) oily, (c) horrifying
3. imperturbable: (a) unexcitable, (b) increasing, (c) unhappy
4. oracle: (a) wise person, (b) loyal pet, (c) generous host
5. surcease: (a) a beginning, (b) an overabundance, (c) an end
6. subsidiary: (a) foremost, (b) subsiding, (c) secondary
7. circumvent: (a) avoid, (b) encourage, (c) reward

❷ Grammar Lesson

Adverb Clauses and Noun Clauses

A **subordinate clause** is a group of words with a subject and verb that cannot stand alone as a sentence. An **adverb clause** is a subordinate clause that modifies a verb, an adjective, or an adverb. It tells *where*, *when*, *why*, *how*, or *to what extent*.

> **Adverb Clause:** Swift was surprised *when he heard the news*. (modifies the adjective *surprised* by telling *when*)

A **noun clause** is a subordinate clause that acts as a noun.

> **Noun Clause:** The decision was *whether they should trust Multivac*. (acts as predicate nominative)

Practice Identify the subordinate clause in each sentence, and tell whether it functions as an adverb clause or a noun clause.

1. The three men confessed after the war ended.
2. Each man's secret was that he had changed the rules.
3. Multivac was valuable if it was used right.
4. The computer didn't know that it was a hero.
5. Swift tossed a coin before he made a decision.

Writing Application "Since the war is won, I'll tell you what I did." Using this sentence as a model, write two original sentences that incorporate both an adverb clause and a noun clause.

WG Prentice Hall Writing and Grammar Connection: Chapter 21, Section 2

TEACHING RESOURCES

The following resources can be used to enrich or extend the instruction for pp. 464–465.

Vocabulary

- **Selection Support:** Build Vocabulary, p. 117
- **Vocabulary and Spelling Practice Book,** (Use this booklet for skills enrichment.)

Grammar

- **Selection Support:** Build Grammar Skills, p. 118
- **Writing and Grammar,** Gold Level, p. 468 ■
- **Daily Language Practice Transparencies**

Writing

- **Writing and Grammar,** Gold Level, p. 291
- **Writing and Grammar iText CD-ROM** ■

■ **BLOCK SCHEDULING:** Resources marked with this symbol provide varied instruction during 90-minute blocks.

❸ Writing Lesson

Newspaper Story

Write a newspaper story about the end of the war between Earth and Deneb. Use references from "The Machine That Won the War" and your own ideas to explain what the war was about and what the victory might mean for Earthlings.

Prewriting Start by jotting down answers to the five W's—*who, what, where, when,* and *why*. Then, plan an attention-grabbing headline.

Drafting Begin your news story with a striking lead sentence that captures the effect the war has had on both Earthlings and Denebians. As you write the body of your article, make sure that each of the questions is addressed and answered.

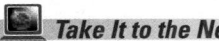

Model: Writing an Attention-Grabbing Lead

After a ten-year struggle, Earth is at peace. Denebians are no longer a threat, and Earthlings must now begin to rebuild a planet shattered by war.

Words like *struggle, peace, threat,* and *shattered* immediately grab the reader's attention.

Revising Ask a classmate to read your draft aloud to you. As you listen, consider which scenes are unclear, and then provide further elaboration.

WG *Prentice Hall Writing and Grammar Connection: Chapter 13, Section 3*

❹ Extension Activities

Listening and Speaking In Asimov's story, the three main characters relied on intuition to adjust the data fed to Multivac. In a small group, conduct a **discussion** on the role of intuition in any decision. Use these questions to guide you:

- When is it proper to ignore instructions and follow your instincts?
- When may using your intuition be the wrong thing to do?

Take notes on the points group members make. Then, use your notes to share a summary of the discussion with the class. **[Group Activity]**

Research and Technology Prepare an **illustrated report** on the history of computers, including an essay accompanied by drawings, photos, and magazine ads. Incorporate Asimov's Multivac into your writing, explaining how it compares to computers throughout history. Design and publish your illustrated report by using desktop software and graphic programs.

Take It to the Net www.phschool.com

Go online for an additional research activity using the Internet.

❸ Writing Lesson

- Identifying relevant details is a skill all journalists need, because they must keep their articles to a certain length. Remind students to eliminate irrelevant details. Outlining their stories before writing will help them organize their ideas.
- Students may want to include quotations from a statement Director Swift made to the press, illustrate their articles, or add other elements that will make them stand out.

❹ Extension Activity

Listening and Speaking

- You might begin a discussion by asking students to imagine that they are senators about to vote on a crucial bill. Their constituents want them to vote one way, but their own judgment is urging them to vote the opposite way. What should they do in this situation?
- You may want to make this activity a whole-class discussion, since all students should have opinions on this topic. Encourage students to discuss times in their lives when they have had to choose between using their judgment and following instructions.

CUSTOMIZE INSTRUCTION
For Universal Access

To address different learning styles, use the following activities suggested in the **Extension Activities** booklet, p. 30.

- For Musical/Rhythmic and Interpersonal Learners, use Activity 5.
- For Visual/Spatial Learners, use Activity 6.
- For Verbal/Linguistic and Logical/Mathematical Learners, use Activity 7.

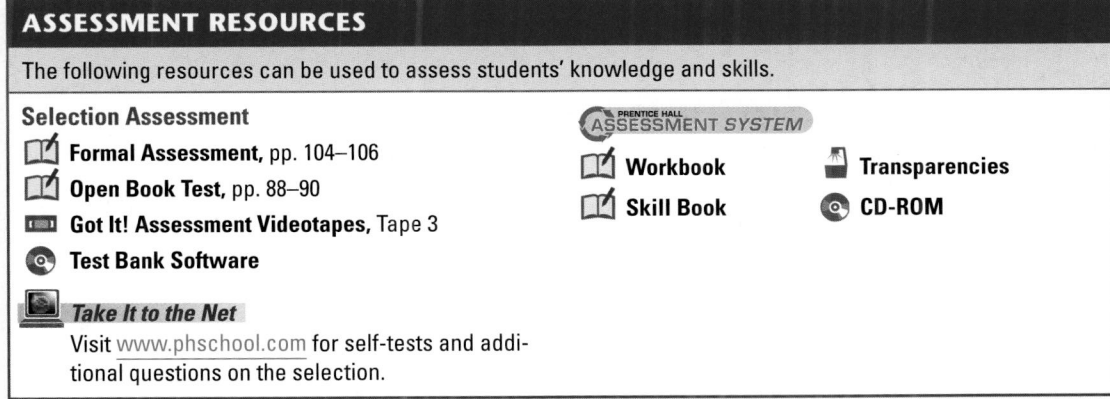

ASSESSMENT RESOURCES

The following resources can be used to assess students' knowledge and skills.

Selection Assessment

- **Formal Assessment,** pp. 104–106
- **Open Book Test,** pp. 88–90
- **Got It! Assessment Videotapes,** Tape 3
- **Test Bank Software**

PRENTICE HALL ASSESSMENT SYSTEM

- **Workbook**
- **Skill Book**
- **Transparencies**
- **CD-ROM**

Take It to the Net

Visit www.phschool.com for self-tests and additional questions on the selection.

Lesson Objectives

1. To understand the connections between technology and the past, present, and future
2. To explore fears people have about depending on technology

Connections

In "The Machine That Won the War," Isaac Asimov describes a world where powerful, unfeeling computers seem to be in control. In Julia Alverez's "Aha Moment," passengers on a jet flight experience terror when technology loses control. Have students read "Aha Moment" after they review "The Machine That Won the War." What can they conclude about the relationship between technology and humankind?

CONNECTIONS
Literature Past and Present
In Technology We Trust

In "The Machine That Won the War," Isaac Asimov depicts a world in which humans seem to have surrendered control to powerful computers. When Asimov was writing the story in 1961, popular culture was filled with conflicting impressions about the changes that technological progress would bring. In one way, it was evident from the explosion of new products and labor-saving devices that life would become easier. In contrast, there was a deep uneasiness about depending completely on new technology and losing control to automation. The deadly spiral of nuclear warfare was the most potent symbol of this fear, hanging over this Cold War period like an ominous cloud.

Fast-forward several decades to a routine flight on a commercial jet airliner transporting author Julia Alvarez. Commercial jet technology, while new in 1961, has been around long enough for most people to take their safety for granted. Those fears about depending on technology, however, are never far from the surface. An act of nature and a mechanical failure forced the writer Alvarez to rethink her relationship with technology and her fellow humans.

AHA MOMENT

Julia Alvarez

I was in the tiny bathroom in the back of the plane when I felt the slamming jolt, then the horrible swerve that threw me against the door. Oh, Lord, I thought, this is it! Somehow I managed to unbolt the door and scramble out. The flight attendants, already strapped in, waved wildly for me to sit down. As I lunged ahead toward my seat, passengers looked up at me with the stricken expression of creatures who know they are about to die.

In Technology We Trust

- Point out that "Aha Moment" is a true, personal account of the author's experience while flying in a jet that is hit by lightning.
- Explain that, rather than touting or criticizing technology, Alvarez's story points out how technological failures can suddenly create life-or-death experiences.
- Point out that Alvarez's conclusion has nothing to do with technology at all, but with human kindness.

Background

The Authors

Both Isaac Asimov and Julia Alvarez came to the United States as immigrants, Asimov from Russia and Alvarez from the Dominican Republic. As young children, both writers realized that learning English was their bridge into a new culture. Asimov began writing books at age eleven and kept writing until his death, producing more than 470 books. Just as readers treasure Asimov's exceptional talent, they look forward to reading additional new works by the gifted Alvarez.

Thematic Connection

Answer: The shock, concern, and worry expressed by the author and other passengers shows an abrupt loss of confidence in a technology—jet aircraft—they had been taking for granted.

"I think we got hit by lightning," the girl in the seat next to mine said. She was from a small town in east Texas, and this was only her second time on an airplane. She had won a trip to England by competing in a high school geography bee and was supposed to make a connecting flight when we landed in Newark.

In the next seat, at the window, sat a young businessman who had been confidently working. Now he looked worried—something that really worries me: when confident-looking businessmen look worried. The laptop was put away. "Something's not right," he said.

The pilot's voice came over the speaker. I heard vaguely through my fear, "Engine number two. . .hit. . .emergency landing. . .New Orleans." When he was done, the voice of a flight attendant came on, reminding us of the emergency procedures she had reviewed before takeoff. Of course I never paid attention to this drill, always figuring that if we ever got to the point where we needed to use life jackets, I would have already died of terror.

Now we began a roller-coaster ride through the thunderclouds. I was ready to faint, but when I saw the face of the girl next to me I pulled myself together. I reached for her hand and reassured her that we were going to make it. "What a story you're going to tell when you get home!" I said. "After this, London's going to seem like small potatoes."

"Yes, ma'am," she mumbled.

I wondered where I was getting my strength. Then I saw that my other hand was tightly held by a ringed hand. Someone was comforting *me*—a glamorous young woman across the aisle, the female equivalent of the confident businessman. She must have seen how scared I was and reached over.

"I tell you," she confided, "the problems I brought up on this plane with me sure don't seem real big right now." I loved her southern drawl, her indiscriminate use of perfume, her soulful squeezes. I was sure that even if I survived a plane crash, I'd have a couple of broken fingers from all the T.L.C.[1] "Are you okay?" she kept asking me.

Among the many feelings going through my head during those excruciating 20 minutes was pride—pride in how well everybody was behaving. No one panicked. No one screamed. As we jolted and screeched our way downward, I could hear small pockets of soothing conversation everywhere.

I thought of something I had heard a friend say about the wonderful gift his dying father had given the family: He had died peacefully, as if not to alarm any of them about an experience they would all have to go through someday.

And then—yes!—we landed safely. Outside on the ground, attendants and officials were waiting to transfer us to alternate flights. But we passengers clung together. We chatted about the lives we now felt blessed to be living, as difficult or rocky as they might be. The young

Thematic Connection
What do the descriptions of passengers and their varied reactions show us about dependence on technology?

drawl (drôl) *n.* a slow speech pattern, characterized by prolonged vowels

indiscriminate (in′di skrim′ i nit) *adj.* ignoring standards of good taste

1. **T.L.C.** abbreviation for "Tender Loving Care"

businessman lamented that he had not had a chance to buy his two little girls a present. An older woman offered him her box of expensive Lindt chocolates, still untouched, tied with a lovely bow. "I shouldn't be eating them anyhow," she said. My glamorous aisle mate took out her cell phone and passed it around to anyone who wanted to make a call to hear the reassuring voice of a loved one.

There was someone I wanted to call. Back in Vermont, my husband, Bill, was anticipating my arrival late that night. He had been complaining that he wasn't getting to see very much of me because of my book tour. That's why I had decided to take this particular flight—oh, yes, one of those stories! I had planned to surprise him by getting in a few hours early. Now I just wanted him to know I was okay and on my way.

When my name was finally called to board my new flight, I felt almost tearful to be parting from people whose lives had so intensely, if briefly, touched mine.

Even now, back on terra firma,[2] walking down a Vermont road, I sometimes hear an airplane and look up at that small, glinting piece of metal. I remember the passengers on that fateful, lucky flight and wish I could thank them for the many acts of kindness I witnessed and received. I am indebted to my fellow passengers and wish I could pay them back.

But then, remembering my aisle mate's hand clutching mine while I clutched the hand of the high school student, I feel struck by lightning all over again: The point is not to pay back kindness but to pass it on.

lamented (lə ment′ id) *v.* expressed sorrow; regretted

2. **terra firma** (ter′ə fur′mə) *n.* Latin phrase meaning "solid ground."

Julia Alvarez

(b. 1950)

Julia Alvarez immigrated to the United States from the Dominican Republic when she was ten years old. This sudden adjustment to an unfamiliar country with a strange language influenced her decision to write. ". . . I realized that language was going to be how I connected with these babbles. . . . Language was a portable homeland." Since this early realization, Alvarez has written several successful novels and volumes of poetry, in addition to teaching writing to college students, senior citizens, and bilingual students. Alvarez's work has been praised for its humor, sensitivity, and insight into the way people think and interact.

Connecting Literature Past and Present

1. How does Alvarez's story reflect the often hidden role technology plays in our lives?
2. Why do you think the passengers reacted the way they did when their plane was hit?
3. (a) How does the narrative reflect an "aha moment"? (b) In what ways might the experience change the writer's life? Explain.
4. (a) In what ways were the situations of the men in "The Machine That Won the War" and the passengers in the Alvarez story similar? (b) How did they differ?
5. What do both of these stories have to tell us about human faith in technology?

Answers

Connecting Literature Past and Present

1. People often don't notice technology until it fails; then they realize how much their lives depend on it.
2. The passengers were stunned by the jolt and then fearful of consequences as the plane flew "like a roller-coaster" through the clouds.
3. **(a)** The narrative presents a moment of truth as the passengers confront the possibility of dying, then reach out to comfort each other. **(b)** Remembering her fateful flight reminds the narrator of the need "not to pay back kindness but to pass it on."
4. **(a)** The situations are similar in that people's lives depended not on technology, as they had believed, but on human judgment, determination, and action. **(b)** The situations are different because one takes place in the context of the future, during a galactic war that affected millions. Alvarez's story describes an actual event on a jetliner, affecting a smaller number of people.
4. These stories remind readers that people are both in control of and at the mercy of technology.

Fire and Ice ✦ All Watched Over by Machines of Loving Grace ✦ There Will Come Soft Rains ✦ The Horses

Lesson Objectives and CA Correlations

1. **To analyze and respond to literary elements**
   - Literary Analysis: Alliteration **R 3.7**
   - Comparing Literary Works
2. **To read, comprehend, analyze, and critique poems**
   - Reading Strategy: Recognizing a Poet's Purpose **R 3.8, 3.11**
   - Review and Assess questions
   - Assessment Practice (ATE)
3. **To develop word analysis skills, fluency, and systematic vocabulary**
   - Vocabulary Development Lesson: Latin Suffix: *-ous* **R 1.1**
4. **To understand and apply written and oral language conventions**
   - Spelling Strategy
   - Grammar Lesson: Adjective Clauses **LC 1.1**
5. **To understand and apply appropriate writing and research strategies**
   - Writing Lesson: Poem to a Future Generation **W 1.2**
   - Extension Activity: Panel Discussion **LS 1.8**
6. **To understand and apply listening and speaking strategies**
   - Extension Activity: Dramatic Reading **LS 1.9**

STEP-BY-STEP TEACHING GUIDE	PACING GUIDE
PRETEACH	
Motivate Students and Provide Background	
Use the Motivation activity (ATE p. 470)	5 min.
Read and discuss the Preview material and Background information (SE/ATE p. 470) [A]	10 min.
Introduce the Concepts	
Introduce the Literary Analysis and Reading Strategy (SE/ATE p. 471) [A]	15 min.
Pronounce the vocabulary words and read their definitions (SE p. 471)	5 min.
TEACH	
Monitor Comprehension	
Informally monitor comprehension by circulating while students read independently or in groups [A]	15 min.
Develop vocabulary with Vocabulary notes (SE pp. 472–475)	as students read
Develop Understanding	
Develop students' understanding of alliteration with Literary Analysis annotations (SE p. 474; ATE p. 474) [A]	10 min.
Develop students' ability to recognize a poet's purpose with the Reading Strategy annotations (SE pp. 475, 476; ATE pp. 475, 476)	10 min.
ASSESS	
Assess Mastery	
Assess students' mastery of the Reading Strategy and Literary Analysis by having them answer the Review and Assess questions (SE/ATE p. 477)	20 min.
Use one or more of the print and media Assessment Resources (ATE p. 479) [A]	up to 50 min.
EXTEND	
Apply Understanding	
Have students complete the Vocabulary Development Lesson and the Grammar Lesson (SE p. 478) [A]	20 min.
Apply students' knowledge of brevity and clarity using the Writing Lesson (SE p. 479) [A]	45 min.
Apply students' understanding of the selection using one or more of the Extension Activities (SE p. 479)	20–90 min.

[A] ACCELERATED INSTRUCTION:
Use the strategies and activities identified with an [A].

UNIVERSAL ACCESS
● = Below Level Students
▲ = On-Level Students
■ = Above Level Students

Time and Resource Manager

Reading Level: Easy/Average/Easy/Challenging
Average Number of Instructional Days: 4

RESOURCES		
PRINT	**TRANSPARENCIES**	**TECHNOLOGY**
• **Beyond Literature,** Career Connection: Computers in the Workplace, p. 31 ▲ ■		• **Interest Grabber Video,** Tape 3 ● ▲ ■
• **Selection Support Workbook:** ● ▲ ■ Literary Analysis, p. 124 Reading Strategy, p. 123 Build Vocabulary, p. 121	• **Literary Analysis and Reading Transparencies,** pp. 61 and 62 ● ▲ ■	
		• **Listening to Literature** ● ▲ ■ Audiocassettes, Side 13 Audio CDs, CD 9
• **Literatura en español** ● ▲ • **Literary Analysis for Enrichment** ■		
• **Formal Assessment:** Selection Test, pp. 107–109 ● ▲ ■ • **Open Book Test,** pp. 91–93 ● ▲ ■ • PRENTICE HALL ASSESSMENT SYSTEM ● ▲ ■	• PRENTICE HALL ASSESSMENT SYSTEM ● ▲ ■ Skills Practice Answers and Explanations on Transparencies	• **Test Bank Software** ● ▲ ■ • **Got It! Assessment Videotapes,** Tape 3 ● ▲
• **Selection Support Workbook:** ● ▲ ■ Build Grammar Skills, p. 122 • **Writing and Grammar,** Gold Level ● ▲ ■ • **Extension Activities,** p. 31 ● ▲ ■	• **Daily Language Practice Transparencies** ● ▲	• **Writing and Grammar iText CD-ROM** ● ▲ ■ ***Take It to the Net*** www.phschool.com

BLOCK SCHEDULING: Use one 90-minute class period to preteach the selection and have students read it. Use a second 90-minute class period to assess students' mastery of skills and have them complete one of the Extension Activities.

PRETEACH

Step-by-Step Teaching Guide for pp. 470–471

Motivation

Ask students why so many human beings seem to be fascinated with death and destruction. What movies or books can they name that focus on threats to end the world? Tell them that in these four poems, they will read about various visions of worldly destruction.

Interest Grabber Video

As an alternative, play "The Reality of War" on Tape 3 to engage student interest.

1 Background

History

The catalyst for World War I was the assassination of Austrian Archduke Franz Ferdinand and his wife Sophie in the Bosnian city of Sarajevo in 1914. Germany invaded France in 1914, but the German march toward Paris was stopped short and four years of costly but futile trench warfare ensued. The lines of battle barely moved while hundreds of thousands were killed in the so-called no-man's land between the trenches. The British fought on the side of the French, and in late 1917 the Americans joined them, swinging the balance toward an eventual Allied victory in 1918. An estimated ten million soldiers died in the war.

Prepare to Read

Fire and Ice ◆ "There Will Come Soft Rains" ◆ The Horses ◆ All Watched Over by Machines of Loving Grace

Wild Mustang, Red Desert, Wyoming

Take It to the Net

Visit www.phschool.com for interactive activities and instruction related to the selections, including
- background
- graphic organizers
- literary elements
- reading strategies

Preview

Connecting to the Literature

Is the world heading toward a gloomy destruction or a golden age of harmony? The poets in these four works explore their individual visions of the future. As you read the poems, consider your own ideas on the subject.

1 Background

Sara Teasdale's poem mentions "the war" without specifying which one. She and her husband both opposed World War I (1914–1918), even though their position was unpopular. Called at the time the Great War, it was the first one fought with machine guns, weapons that could spit out 600 to 700 bullets a minute. Soldiers on the battlefield knew that large numbers of them would be brutally cut down by machine-gun fire. The impersonality of this type of warfare horrified many.

TEACHING RESOURCES

The following resources can be used to enrich or extend the instruction for pp. 470–471.

Motivation

Interest Grabber Video, Tape 3

Background

Beyond Literature, p. 31

Take It to the Net

Visit www.phschool.com for background and hotlinks for the selections.

Literary Analysis

Literary Analysis and Reading Transparencies, Alliteration, p. 61

Reading

Selection Support: Reading Strategy, p. 123; Build Vocabulary, p. 121

Literary Analysis and Reading Transparencies, Recognizing a Poet's Purpose, p. 62

BLOCK SCHEDULING: Resources marked with this symbol provide varied instruction during 90-minute blocks.

❷ Literary Analysis

Alliteration

Alliteration is the repetition of a consonant sound at the beginning of two or more words. Poets use this sound technique mainly to emphasize certain words but also to create musical effects and to help create a mood. In these lines from "The Horses," four words begin with *w*:

> We saw the heads
> Like a wild wave charging and were afraid.

The repetition of the sound draws attention to these words and their meaning. When read aloud, the words slow the reader's pace and suggest a sense of awe. Look for other examples of alliteration in the selections, and think about how it affects the poems' sound and meaning.

Comparing Literary Works

Each poem in this section presents a vision of the future. While one poem's vision may be more or less disturbing than another's, each poet sends a particular message or warning to people. Compare and contrast the visions presented in each poem. Decide whether a particular poem presents a hopeful, gloomy, or frightening vision of the future, and consider how effectively a message is conveyed.

❸ Reading Strategy

Recognizing a Poet's Purpose

Each poem in this group calls attention to a troubling situation or attitude. To **recognize a poet's purpose,** or reason for writing a poem, read the work closely. Follow these suggestions:

- Look for the meaning behind the words in the poem.
- Note words that seem startling or jarring.
- Consider why the poet chose those specific words.

Use a chart like the one shown to note key details. Jot down the effects of each and determine the poet's purpose.

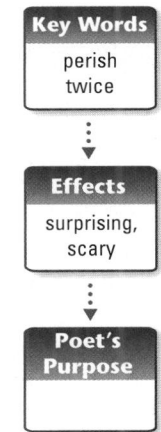

Key Words
perish
twice

↓

Effects
surprising,
scary

↓

Poet's Purpose

Vocabulary Development

perish (per´ ish) *v.* die (p. 472)
suffice (sə fīs´) *v.* be enough (p. 472)
tremulous (trem´ yo͞o ləs) *adj.* quivering (p. 473)
covenant (kuv´ ə nənt) *n.* agreement; pact (p. 474)
confounds (kən foundz´) *v.* bewilders; confuses (p. 474)
steeds (stēdz) *n.* horses (p. 475)
archaic (är kā´ ik) *adj.* seldom used; old-fashioned (p. 475)

❷ Literary Analysis

Alliteration

- Tell students that just as an artist uses color to create emphasis in a painting, a poet can use alliteration to create emphasis in a poem.
- Note that alliteration is commonly used in newspaper headlines (especially in sports stories) and in advertising. Discuss recent examples and note how alliteration attracts attention.
- Remind students that alliteration affects reading rate and often contributes to the mood or emotional effect of the poem.
- As students read the four poems in this group, they should not simply identify instances of alliteration but also consider how this device enhances each poem.

❸ Reading Strategy

Recognizing a Poet's Purpose

- Point out that, like prose writers, poets write to entertain, persuade, and even inform. The poet wants to express his or her feelings or opinions and provoke the reader to react to and think about them.
- Use the Reading Strategy transparency, p. 62 in **Literary Analysis and Reading Transparencies,** to show students how word choice can reveal a poet's purpose.

Vocabulary Development

- Pronounce each vocabulary word for students, and read the definitions as a class. Have students identify any words with which they are already familiar.

CUSTOMIZE INSTRUCTION FOR UNIVERSAL ACCESS

For Less Proficient Readers	For English Learners	For Advanced Readers
To help students hear alliteration, play recordings of the poems from **Listening to Literature,** Sides 15 and 16. Have students raise their hands when they hear alliteration, then pause to discuss the effect.	Use the Literary Analysis transparency, p. 61 in **Literary Analysis and Reading Transparencies,** to give students additional practice in recognizing alliteration.	Ask students to analyze the emotional effect of alliterative sounds in English. What sounds are hard or harsh? What sounds are soothing? What sounds are light or amusing? Have students create a "glossary" of sounds that poets might use.

E-Teach

Visit E-Teach at www.phschool.com for teachers' essays on how to teach, with questions and answers.

TEACH

Step-by-Step Teaching Guide for pp. 472–476

CUSTOMIZE INSTRUCTION
For Visual Learners

Have students preview the visuals that accompany the poems before reading. Encourage them to make predictions about each poem based on the accompanying artwork. After reading, have them discuss in what way, if any, the artwork shaped their reactions to the poems.

❶ About the Selections

The speaker in Frost's poem considers two possible ends to the world—fire and ice—and links them to two powerful, potentially destructive emotions.

The speaker of the second poem foresees the coming of spring, when the world will awaken and bloom with no awareness of a recent war. The speaker feels that nature would neither know nor care if people ceased to exist.

❷ Critical Thinking

Interpret

- Once students have read "Fire and Ice," have them focus on lines 3–8.
- Challenge students to interpret lines 3–4 and 6–8. Which emotions does the speaker identify with fire and ice?
  Answer: The speaker identifies fire with desire and ice with hate.
- Ask students what the speaker is suggesting by linking these emotions to fire and ice.
  Possible response: The world will die from either too much warm feeling—passion or desire—or too much cold feeling—hate or indifference.

❶ Fire and Ice

Robert Frost

Some say the world will end in fire,
Some say in ice.
From what I've tasted of desire
I hold with those who favor fire.
❷ But if it had to perish twice,
I think I know enough of hate
To say that for destruction ice
Is also great
And would suffice.

perish (per´ ish) *v.* die

suffice (sə fīs´) *v.* be enough

Robert Frost

(1874–1963)

Like the title of his poem "Fire and Ice," Robert Frost seemed witty and warm to some, cold and bitter to others. All agreed, however, that poetry came first in his life. Frost is known for being the poet called upon to recite two poems at the inauguration of John F. Kennedy in 1961.

Frost produced a large body of work and became the most popular American poet of his time, winning four Pulitzer Prizes.

Review and Assess

Thinking About the Selection

1. **Respond:** How does the speaker's view of the future make you feel? Explain.
2. **(a) Recall:** With which opinion of the world's end does Frost first side? **(b) Interpret:** How might desire bring an end to the world?
3. **(a) Recall:** Why does Frost think the world might end in ice? **(b) Interpret:** In what way is ice a fitting metaphor for hatred?
4. **Assess:** How do the rhyming words affect the poem's mood?
5. **Speculate:** How have desire and hatred already affected the safety of people in the world?

TEACHING RESOURCES

The following resources can be used to enrich or extend the instruction for pp. 472–476.

Literary Analysis

Selection Support: Literary Analysis, p. 124

BLOCK SCHEDULING: Resources marked with this symbol provide varied instruction during 90-minute blocks.

"There Will Come Soft Rains"

(War Time)

Sara Teasdale

There will come soft rains and the smell of the ground,
And swallows circling with their shimmering sound;

And frogs in the pools singing at night,
And wild plum-trees in tremulous white;

Robins will wear their feathery fire
Whistling their whims on a low fence-wire;

And not one will know of the war, not one
Will care at last when it is done.

Not one would mind, neither bird nor tree
If mankind perished utterly;

And Spring herself, when she woke at dawn,
Would scarcely know that we were gone.

tremulous (trem´ yo͞o ləs) *adj.* quivering

Sara Teasdale

(1884–1933)

Sara Teasdale's poetry—much of it on the subject of love—was rooted in her own difficulties with personal relationships. Teasdale had a sad life and often expressed her sadness through poetry.

She once commented that "poems are written because of a state of emotional irritation" and that the poem "free[s] the poet from an emotional burden."

Review and Assess

Thinking About the Selection

1. **Respond:** Do you think that nature "has an attitude" toward humans, as this poem suggests? Explain.
2. (a) **Recall:** According to the poet, what will animals do after the war is over? **(b) Compare and Contrast:** How will the animals' fate differ from people's?
3. **Recall:** What will be Spring's reaction to human absence after the war? **(b) Generalize:** What theme about war does Spring's reaction, in combination with other details in the poem, suggest?
4. **Speculate:** Teasdale died before an even more destructive war broke out. What might her reaction have been to World War II?

Answers for p. 472

Review and Assess

1. Possible response: Students may be surprised that the speaker adopts a casual—even flippant—attitude toward the possible destruction of the world.
2. **(a)** The speaker thinks the world will end in fire. **(b)** Desire in the sense of greed or uncontrolled passions might lead to world war.
3. **(a)** The speaker notes that ice—hatred—is highly destructive. **(b)** Hatred is often expressed as cold, icy, distant behavior.
4. Possible answer: The rhymes give the poem a light, playful tone, in sharp contrast to the dreadful subject matter.
5. Greed and hatred have already caused wars, genocide, and the stockpiling of atomic weapons.

Answers for p. 473

Review and Assess

1. Most students may doubt that nature can have thoughts and feelings.
2. **(a)** Animals will behave just as they did before the war. **(b)** People will have to recover—if the human race survives at all.
3. **(a)** Spring will never know that human beings are gone. **(b)** This reaction suggests nature's indifference to humans' destructive wars—and to human significance.
4. The horrors of World War II might have intensified Teasdale's despair.

CUSTOMIZE INSTRUCTION FOR UNIVERSAL ACCESS

For Advanced Readers

Have students locate and read Ray Bradbury's 1950 short story "There Will Come Soft Rains." Set in 2026, this story tells of an automated house that talks to the people who live in it, cleans itself, and does all the chores, all the while unaware that the people have vanished, killed by a nuclear explosion. Bradbury was inspired by Teasdale's poem, from which he took his title and which he quotes in full in the text of the story. Have students compare and contrast the poem and the story. Do they think the authors shared a common purpose? Do the two works have a common theme? What might Teasdale have thought of Bradbury's story? Students can read the story and then have a group discussion of these questions. As an extension, students can compare Bradbury's vision of cooperation between people and computers with Richard Brautigan's.

❸ About the Selection

One year after a brief but devastating war, communications systems have not yet begun to function again. People live in a silent world and farm as their ancestors did. One day, a herd of horses comes to the survivors, seeming to offer help and solace.

❹ Literary Analysis

Alliteration

- Ask students to identify the repeated consonant sound in lines 15–17. What effect does this repetition have on these lines?
  Answer: Many words begin with *s* or *sh*. This sound suggests whispering, echoing the idea of someone speaking into a silence. The alliteration helps the reader hear and feel the silence and stillness.
- Read aloud lines 48–50 and ask students the Literary Analysis question on p. 474: What examples of alliteration do you see in line 20?
  Answer: Repetition of *g* sound in the words *great gulp*. This sound is picked up in the word *again*.

❺ ▶Critical Viewing

Answer: There is a colt in the picture, as there are colts among the herd in the poem. Like the horses in the poem, these horses appear to be galloping toward someone or something.

❻ Reading Strategy

Recognizing a Poet's Purpose

- Read aloud lines 48–50 and ask students: How does the phrase "broken world" hint at the poet's purpose for writing the poem?
  Answer: The phrase hints that a broken world might recover with a return to an old relationship with nature.

Monitor Progress Do students think that Muir imagines a world that can be put back together, or one that cannot?
Possible response: Students may cite the horses as Muir's sign that a new beginning is possible.

❸ The Horses

Edwin Muir

Barely a twelvemonth after
The seven days war that put the world to sleep,
Late in the evening the strange horses came.
By then we had made our covenant with silence,
But in the first few days it was so still
We listened to our breathing and were afraid.
On the second day
The radios failed; we turned the knobs; no answer.
On the third day a warship passed us, heading north,
Dead bodies piled on the deck. On the sixth day
A plane plunged over us into the sea. Thereafter
Nothing. The radios dumb;
And still they stand in corners of our kitchens,
And stand, perhaps, turned on, in a million rooms
All over the world. But now if they should speak,
If on a sudden they should speak again,
❹ If on the stroke of noon a voice should speak,
We would not listen, we would not let it bring
That old bad world that swallowed its children quick
At one great gulp. We would not have it again.
Sometimes we think of the nations lying asleep,
Curled blindly in impenetrable sorrow,
And then the thought confounds us with its strangeness.

The tractors lie about our fields; at evening
They look like dank sea-monsters couched and waiting.
We leave them where they are and let them rust:

covenant (kuv′ ə nənt) *n.* agreement; pact

Literary Analysis
Alliteration What examples of alliteration do you see in line 20?

confounds (kən foundz′) *v.* bewilders; confuses

❺ **▼Critical Viewing** In what ways do these horses compare to those the poet describes? **[Connect]**

CUSTOMIZE INSTRUCTION FOR UNIVERSAL ACCESS	
For English Learners	**For Advanced Readers**
In "The Horses," help students understand that *barely a twelvemonth* means "no more than a year" and *put the world to sleep* indicates almost universal destruction. Point out that the short duration (*seven days*) and great destruction of the conflict suggest a nuclear war.	Have students compare and contrast the form and style of the four poems. Each is written in a different verse form; each poet uses rhyme differently; each poem has a different rhythm. Have students analyze the effect of each poem's form on its meaning and impact. They can consider how changes in form and style might have altered each poem's message. How do the poets' choices of form reveal their purposes for writing?

'They'll moulder away and be like other loam'.[1]
We make our oxen drag our rusty ploughs,
Long laid aside. We have gone back
Far past our fathers' land.
And then, that evening
Late in the summer the strange horses came.
We heard a distant tapping on the road,
A deepening drumming; it stopped, went on again
And at the corner changed to hollow thunder.
We saw the heads
Like a wild wave charging and were afraid.
We had sold our horses in our fathers' time
To buy new tractors. Now they were strange to us
As fabulous steeds set on an ancient shield
Or illustrations in a book of knights.
We did not dare go near them. Yet they waited,
Stubborn and shy, as if they had been sent
By an old command to find our whereabouts
And that long-lost archaic companionship.
In the first moment we had never a thought
That they were creatures to be owned and used.
Among them were some half-a-dozen colts
6 Dropped in some wilderness of the broken world,
Yet new as if they had come from their own Eden.[2]
Since then they have pulled our ploughs and borne our loads,
But that free servitude still can pierce our hearts.
Our life is changed; their coming our beginning.

steeds (stēdz) *n.* horses

archaic (är kā′ ik) *adj.* seldom used; old-fashioned

1. **loam** (lōm) *n.* dark, rich soil.
2. **Eden** in the Bible, the garden where life began with Adam and Eve; paradise.

Review and Assess

Thinking About the Selection

1. **Respond:** How did the arrival of the horses in the poem make you feel? Explain.
2. **(a) Recall:** What has been the result of the "seven days war"? **(b) Support:** What words led you to this opinion?
3. **(a) Recall:** What did the "old bad world" do to its children? **(b) Analyze:** Is this event a sufficient explanation for the sorrow and confusion the speaker refers to?
4. **(a) Recall:** What has happened to the tractors? **(b) Interpret:** Why are the tractors and the horses placed side by side?
5. **Speculate:** Do you see any reason to believe that the note of hope the speaker associates with the horses' arrival will survive into the future? Explain your response.

Edwin Muir

(1887–1959)

A prolific writer who produced many volumes of poetry and several novels, Muir had visions of the future that were rooted in his past. He spent his first fourteen years on a farm in the Orkney Islands north of the Scottish mainland. Much of his imagery comes from this place.

Answers for p. 475

Review and Assess

1. Possible answers: Students may report that the arrival made them feel hopeful, relieved, or glad.
2. **(a)** The war produced almost universal death and destruction. **(b)** Students may cite "covenant with silence," "the radios failed," "we would not let it bring / That old bad world that swallowed its children," and "impenetrable sorrow."
3. **(a)** It killed them, swallowing them "at one great gulp." **(b)** The death of millions is sufficient cause for people to feel that the world has fallen apart.
4. **(a)** The tractors are abandoned to rust in the fields. **(b)** The tractors represent the world of machines that produced catastrophe. The horses represent the natural world that offers hope and renewal.
5. Possible answer: Students may agree that hope will survive at least temporarily, because "life is changed," renewed by the arrival of the horses. Survivors continue to reject the technologies of their "old bad world."

CUSTOMIZE INSTRUCTION FOR UNIVERSAL ACCESS

For Special Needs Students	For Gifted/Talented Students
Have students work together to answer the questions at the end of each of the four poems. They can meet in a small group afterward to compare answers. If there is significant disagreement, have students identify words, phrases, and lines from the poems that support their interpretations.	Have each student choose one of the four poems and write a detailed analysis and interpretation of its meaning. Students can try paraphrasing lines and stanzas in their search for what the poems mean. Encourage them to do some background reading about the poets and to examine other works by them as they try to interpret these poems.

ASSESS

❼ About the Selection

The speaker imagines a world in which people and animals live in apparent peace, watched by benevolent computers.

❽ Reading Strategy

Recognizing a Poet's Purpose

- Ask students if they have ever visited an indoor "habitat" at a zoo or theme park. Ask volunteers to explain how the habitat creates sun, rain, foliage and other simulations of nature.
- Then, ask students: The poet uses *cybernetic*—a word related to computers—three times. What is striking about how he uses it?
Answer: The use of this word in connection with meadow, forest, and ecology—natural things—is startling and paradoxical, because computers are unnatural mechanisms.

Answers for p. 476

Review and Assess

1. Some students may find the peaceful vision attractive. Others may find the idea of being guarded by machines disturbing.
2. **(a)** Possible response: He sees computers as doing all the work, so that people and animals can simply live together in peace.
(b) The speaker sees a world of peace and ease—at the cost of personal freedom and responsibility.
3. **(a)** Students may find Brautigan's scene peaceful only if they find being watched over by machines a nonstressful experience.
(b) Computers are used to control many systems in buildings, but they have not been applied to large outdoor environments.

❼ All Watched Over by Machines of Loving Grace

Richard Brautigan

I like to think (and
the sooner the better!)
of a cybernetic meadow
where mammals and computers
live together in mutually
programming harmony
like pure water
touching clear sky.

I like to think
   (right now, please!)
❽ of a cybernetic forest
filled with pines and electronics
where deer stroll peacefully
past computers
as if they were flowers
with spinning blossoms.

I like to think
   (it has to be!)
of a cybernetic ecology
where we are free of our labors
and joined back to nature,
returned to our mammal
brothers and sisters,
and all watched over
by machines of loving grace.

Richard Brautigan

(1935–1984)

With his 1967 novel *Trout Fishing in America,* Brautigan became a spokesperson of the hippie generation. Ironically, though, he was at least fifteen years older than the hippies and thus a product of the beat generation that preceded them. Nevertheless, he was certainly a free spirit in his writing.

Review and Assess

Thinking About the Selection

1. **Respond:** What emotions does this poem evoke in you?
2. **(a) Recall:** Why does Brautigan describe computers as "machines of loving grace"? **(b) Draw Conclusions:** On the basis of your answer, describe Brautigan's vision of the future.
3. **(a) Assess:** Does he describe a peaceful or a stressful environment? **(b) Speculate:** Has Brautigan's vision become a reality yet?

ASSESSMENT PRACTICE: Reading Comprehension

Draw Inferences and Conclusions **(For more practice, see Test Preparation Workbook, p. 31.)**

Many tests require students to draw inferences and conclusions from a written text. Use this sample test item:

We had sold our horses in our fathers' time
To buy new tractors. Now they were strange to us
As fabulous steeds set on an ancient shield
Or illustrations in a book of knights.

Which of the following words best describes the speaker's mood?

A thoughtful
B angry
C happy
D proud

The speaker's wistful observations and fancies can help students infer that choice *A* is correct.

Review and Assess

Literary Analysis

Alliteration

1. Using a chart like the one below, record examples of **alliteration** in "There Will Come Soft Rains" and "The Horses," along with the effect they produce.

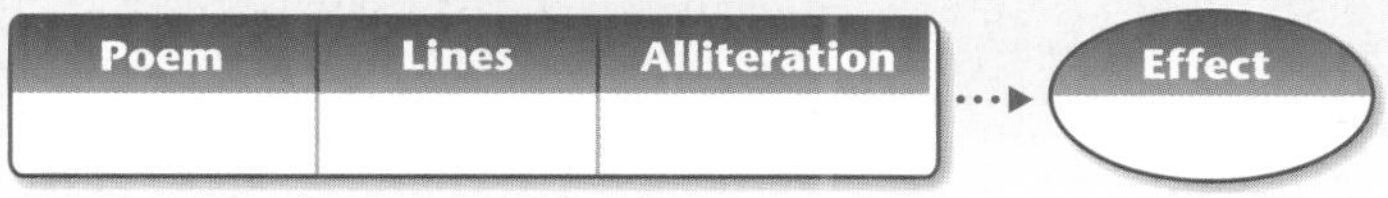

2. Find two examples of alliteration in "Fire and Ice," and explain their effect on the poem's meaning.

Comparing Literary Works

3. (a) Compare the visions of the future that Frost and Brautigan introduce in their poems. (b) Do you think the ideas in Brautigan's poem are more optimistic than those in Frost's? Explain.
4. Both Teasdale and Muir imagine the world after a devastating war. Use a Venn diagram to compare and contrast Teasdale's and Muir's visions of the future.

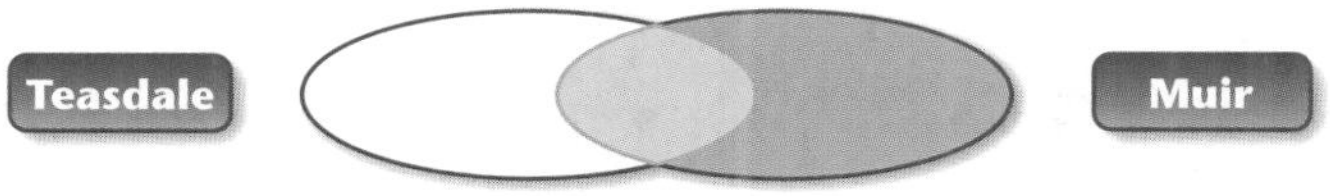

5. What similar ideas do you think Teasdale and Muir had about the war itself?

Reading Strategy

Recognizing a Poet's Purpose

6. (a) Briefly describe each poet's **purpose.** (b) What words, phrases, and ideas led you to your answer in each case?
7. In "All Watched Over by Machines of Loving Grace," how does the phrase "cybernetic meadow" help you recognize the poet's purpose?

Extend Understanding

8. **World Events Connection:** If these poets were alive today, which present-day conflicts or events might inspire their response? Explain.

Quick Review

Alliteration is the repetition of a consonant sound at the beginning of two or more words.

To **recognize a poet's purpose,** discover his or her reason for writing a poem.

Take It to the Net

www.phschool.com

Take the interactive self-test online to check your understanding of these selections.

ENRICHMENT: : Further Reading

Other Works by the Authors

Works by Robert Frost
"Mending Wall"
"The Death of the Hired Man"
A Boy's Will
North of Boston

Works by Sara Teasdale
Love Songs
Flame and Shadow

Works by Edwin Muir
The Voyage
The Labyrinth

Works by Richard Brautigan
"Xerox Candy Bar"
The Return of the Rivers

Take It to the Net
Visit www.phschool.com for more information on the authors.

Answers for p. 477

Review and Assess

1. Sample answers: "There Will Come Soft Rains": *s* sound in lines 1–2. Effect: echoes the whispering sounds of a quiet rainfall. "The Horses": "deepening drumming" in line 34. Effect: echoes the sound of hoofbeats on the road.
2. The phrases "world will" in line 1; "favor fire" in line 4 contribute to the almost playful tone of the poem.
3. **(a)** Frost calmly envisions the destruction of the world by ice or fire; Brautigan anticipates a peaceful world controlled by computers. **(b)** Some students may find Brautigan's ideas more optimistic since they include survival.
4. Teasdale: Nature ignores humans' fate. Muir: Horses help human survivors. Both: Nature continues after war.
5. Both Teasdale and Muir suggest that war is a terrible, destructive force.
6. **(a)** Frost: destructive emotions could end the world; Teasdale: nature can survive and ignore the destructive destiny of humans; Muir: only a return to nature will save humans; Brautigan: only computers can create a world of harmony. **(b)** Frost uses almost frivolous words ("nice," "suffice"). Teasdale uses sensory language ("soft," "shimmering," "feathery"). Muir uses stark images of war to contrast with the restorative naturalness of horses. Brautigan uses odd connections ("cybernetic meadow") to express his unusual vision.
7. Possible response: The absurdity of "cybernetic meadow" emphasizes the impossibility of creating a perfect world through computers.
8. Possible responses: The poets might be provoked into poetry by many current examples of terrorism, international conflict, school violence, crime, and continued destruction of the environment.

EXTEND

Answers for p. 478

❶ Vocabulary Development

Word Analysis

1. c
2. a
3. b

Spelling Strategy

1. tremulousness
2. avoidance
3. stoical

Concept Development: Synonyms

1. b
2. b
3. c
4. c
5. a
6. c
7. c

❷ Grammar

1. that put the world to sleep; modifies *war*
2. when people used tractors; modifies *time*
3. who favor fire; modifies *those*
4. which could help us with our labor; modifies *horses*
5. where robins whistle; modifies *plains*

Writing Application

Have partners exchange papers and check each other's work to ensure the presence of three adjective clauses.

Integrate Language Skills

❶ Vocabulary Development Lesson

Word Analysis: Latin Suffix *-ous*

The Latin suffix *-ous* means "full of " or "characterized by," as in the word *tremulous*, which means "characterized by trembling." Match each word below with its definition.

1. perilous **2.** courageous **3.** clamorous

a. characterized by bravery
b. noisy; loud; marked by vehemence
c. risky; full of danger

Spelling Strategy

If a word ends in a vowel-vowel-consonant combination, do not double the consonant before adding a suffix. For example, *archaic* + *-ally* = *archaically*. Add *-ness*, *-ance*, or *-al* to each word below to form a properly spelled new word.

1. tremulous **2.** avoid **3.** stoic

Concept Development: Synonyms

Identify the word that is a synonym for, or is closest in meaning to, each word from the vocabulary list on page 471.

1. perish: (a) live, (b) die, (c) decide
2. suffice: (a) help, (b) satisfy, (c) mistake
3. steeds: (a) rewards, (b) cattle, (c) horses
4. confounds: (a) irritates, (b) surprises, (c) confuses
5. tremulous: (a) quivering, (b) huge, (c) emotional
6. archaic: (a) curved, (b) simple, (c) old-fashioned
7. covenant: (a) church, (b) argument, (c) agreement

❷ Grammar Lesson

Adjective Clauses

A **subordinate clause** is a group of words with a subject and verb that cannot stand on its own in a sentence.

An **adjective clause** is a subordinate clause that modifies a noun or pronoun by answering the question *what kind?* or *which one?* It is usually introduced by a **relative pronoun,** such as *who*, *whom*, *whose*, *which*, or *that*, or by a **conjunction,** such as *where*, *when*, or *why*.

In this example, the adjective clause is underlined and the noun it modifies is in italics.

Example: I see a *meadow* where they(S) live(V) together. (which *meadow?*)

Practice Write each sentence on your paper. Underline the adjective clauses and circle the word that each one modifies.

1. It was a seven days war that put the world to sleep.
2. There was a time when people used tractors.
3. I hold with those who favor fire.
4. We saw the horses, which could help us with our labor.
5. Listen to the plains where robins whistle.

Writing Application Write a short paragraph about the poem you liked best. Use at least three adjective clauses in your paragraph.

WG Prentice Hall Writing and Grammar Connection: Chapter 21, Section 2

TEACHING RESOURCES

The following resources can be used to enrich or extend the instruction for pp. 478–479.

Vocabulary

Selection Support: Build Vocabulary, p. 121
Vocabulary and Spelling Practice Book, (Use this booklet for skills enrichment.) ■

Grammar

Selection Support: Build Grammar Skills, p. 122
Writing and Grammar, Gold Level, p. 468
Daily Language Practice Transparencies

Writing

Writing and Grammar, Gold Level, p. 112 ■
Writing and Grammar iText CD-ROM

■ **BLOCK SCHEDULING:** Resources marked with this symbol provide varied instruction during 90-minute blocks.

❸ Writing Lesson

Poem to a Future Generation

The poems in this section describe the future in order to make you think critically about the present. Write a short poem that describes the positive aspects of today's world for people of the future.

Prewriting Decide on a positive message. Then, make a list of images drawn from the present-day world that will help convey your message. Try to use words that create alliteration and convey a particular mood.

Drafting Use precise language and sensory details to present a clear picture of the present. Make sure that you present each image in as few words as possible.

Revising As you discuss your poem with a classmate, highlight any words that do not create a clear picture or do not seem necessary. Consider rephrasing for clarity or eliminating the unnecessary words.

Model: Rephrasing to Clarify an Image

The sky was ~~streaming with~~ *awash in* a ~~beautiful~~ *silvery* light,
As we sat in silence, ~~watching the birds overhead~~ *the somber ravens soared*.

Precise adjectives like *silvery* and *somber* help build and clarify the images while keeping them forceful and brief.

Prentice Hall Writing and Grammar Connection: Chapter 6, Section 4

❹ Extension Activities

Listening and Speaking Prepare and present a **dramatic reading** of "Fire and Ice," "All Watched Over by Machines of Loving Grace," or "There Will Come Soft Rains."

- Concentrate on your tone of voice and use of facial expressions to express meaning.
- Practice making eye contact with your audience.

Videotape your rehearsal for later review, or practice in front of a mirror. After presenting, invite listeners to comment on the effectiveness of your reading.

Research and Technology Watch a video or TV program set in the future. As you watch, jot down some specific futuristic elements at work. As a participant in a **panel discussion,** discuss whether the program presents a positive or negative vision of the future. Then, compare this vision to the visions of the poems in this section. **[Group Activity]**

Take It to the Net www.phschool.com

Go online for an additional research activity using the Internet.

❸ Writing Lesson

- Work as a class or in small groups to make lists of "what's right with the world." Then, ask students to express these good things in two or three words each.
- Suggest that students look through their text to find examples of different forms of poetry that seem to fit the statement they want to make.
- Allow time for volunteers to share their finished poems with the class.

❹ Extension Activity

Listening and Speaking

- Allow students time to rehearse their readings in private. Suggest that they reread the poem silently several times before reading aloud.
- Students need not memorize the poems, but they should be thoroughly familiar with them so that they can maintain eye contact with their audience.
- Encourage students to try out their interpretations on friends or family members and ask for feedback that will help improve their readings.

CUSTOMIZE INSTRUCTION
For Universal Access

To address different learning styles, use the following activities suggested in the **Extension Activities** booklet, p. 31.

- For Visual/Spatial Learners, use Activity 5.
- For Verbal/Linguistic Learners, use Activities 5 and 6.
- For Logical/Mathematical Learners, use Activity 6.

ASSESSMENT RESOURCES

The following resources can be used to assess students' knowledge and skills.

Selection Assessment

- **Formal Assessment,** pp. 107–109
- **Open Book Test,** pp. 91–93
- **Got It! Assessment Videotapes,** Tape 3
- **Test Bank Software**

Take It to the Net

Visit www.phschool.com for self-tests and additional questions on the selections.

PRENTICE HALL *ASSESSMENT SYSTEM*

- **Workbook**
- **Skill Book**
- **Transparencies**
- **CD-ROM**

Lesson Objectives

1. To analyze the purpose of product information
2. To learn how to locate various types of product information

About Product Information

- If possible, collect several examples of product directions and warranties. You may wish to have students bring samples to class.
- Ask students to think of the last time they purchased a CD player, cell phone, or other technological product that came with a warranty or instructions. Ask students what they did with these documents. (Often, students and others simply disregard them.)
- Read the first paragraph on p. 480 aloud to the students, then ask them to respond to this question: Why is it a good idea to pay attention to documentation that comes with a product?
  Possible answers: Documentation can tell you how to operate the product successfully and what to do if the product needs repair or replacement.

Reading Strategy

Analyzing the Purpose of Product Information

- Ask students to imagine that they have purchased a new computer. What type of documentation would they need to set it up and operate it?
  Possible answers: Students may cite installation and operating instructions.
- Point out that technical directions explain how to put a product together, operate it, and become familiar with its special features.
- Direct students' attention to the chart on p. 480. Point out the different types of product information and their purposes. Ask students if they know of any other features that might be added to the chart.

READING INFORMATIONAL MATERIALS

Product Information

About Product Information

Product information is printed material that comes packaged with a manufactured item. Two common types of product information are **technical directions** and **warranties.**

- Technical directions explain the safe, proper, and efficient uses of a product and may include diagrams to help convey information.
- Warranties explain the contractual obligations between a consumer and the manufacturer.

You might find these printed features after opening a new item such as a camera, computer, or calculator.

Reading Strategy

Analyzing the Purpose of Product Information

To get the most out of product information, you need to know where to locate the information you want.

Technical directions offer step-by-step instructions for using the item. They may explain procedures such as the following:

- How to assemble the item
- How to turn the item on and off
- How to operate specific features

A **warranty** explains what the manufacturer agrees to provide the consumer in terms of service and maintenance. It may tell, for example, how long the manufacturer will repair a part at no additional charge. Often, the consumer must mail in a signed warranty card to the manufacturer in order for the agreement to become effective.

As you read product information, check to see that it contains the features and purposes outlined in the chart below.

Product Information	Features	Purpose
Technical directions	• Assembling, operating, maintenance instructions • Informal language	Explains how to assemble, use, and protect the merchandise
Warranty	• Charts or graphs • Printed contract between manufacturer and user • Formal language	Details manufacturer's service obligation to user

Technical Directions

Following are technical directions for using a graphing calculator. The product manual, included with the purchase, outlines the procedures for a variety of calculating functions. The directions on this page specifically offer step-by-step instructions for displaying and tracing a graph. They assume the user has a basic knowledge of the calculator.

The heading conveniently indicates the function being explained.

DISPLAYING AND TRACING THE GRAPH

Now that you have defined the function to be graphed and the WINDOW in which to graph it, you can display and explore the graph. You can trace along a function with TRACE.

1. Press [GRAPH] to graph the selected function in the viewing WINDOW.

   The graph of Y_1=(W–2X)(L/2–X)X is shown in the display.

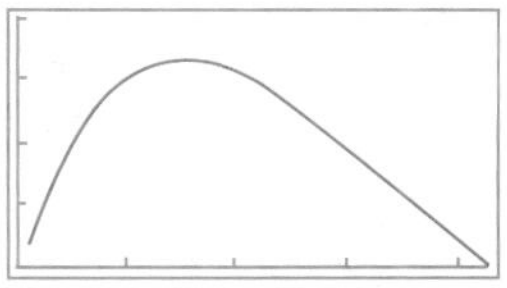

2. Press [▶] once to display the free-moving graph cursor just to the right of the center of the screen. The bottom line of the display shows the X and Y coordinate values for the position of the graph cursor.

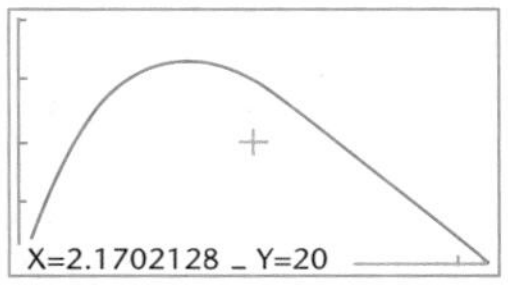

The directions provide visual aids to accompany the instructional text.

3. Use the cursor-keys ([◀], [▶], [▲] and [▼]) to position the free-moving cursor at the apparent maximum of the function.

   As you move the cursor, X and Y coordinate values are updated continually with the cursor position.

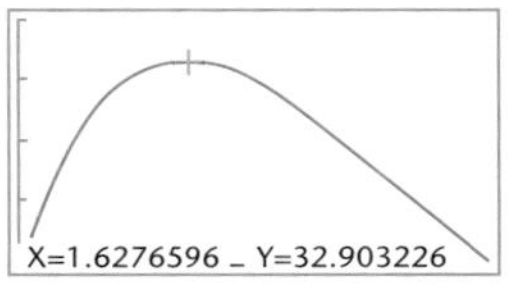

Directions are numbered to show the user the exact order of the steps.

4. Press [TRACE]. The TRACE cursor appears on the Y_1 function near the middle of the screen. 1 in the upper right corner of the display shows that the cursor is on Y_1. As you press [◀] and [▶], you TRACE along Y_1, one X dot at a time, evaluating Y_1 at each X.

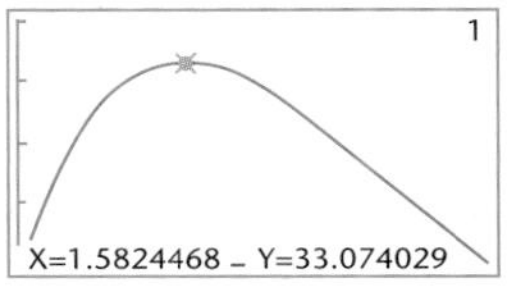

   Press [◀] and [▶] until you are on the maximum Y value. This is the maximum of Y_1(X) for the X pixels. (There may be a maximum "in between" pixels.)

These directions assume a certain level of knowledge, using vocabulary that is not defined in the instructions.

Instructions for a Graphical Calculator

- Point out how the instructions are placed in close proximity to the illustrations they relate to.
- Have students read Step 2, then locate the *X* and *Y* coordinates in the illustration.
- Point out that, as in this case, it is important to follow directions in a step-by-step order.

CUSTOMIZE INSTRUCTION FOR UNIVERSAL ACCESS

For Special Needs Students	For Gifted/Talented Students
Provide these students with an electronic product, such as a calculator, that has instructions. With the students, read a portion of the instructions that explain how to perform a function. Ask students to perform the function as you read the instructions again.	Ask these students to identify a computer function that they think is unique or interesting, such as a shortcut key or other keyboard command that isn't easily apparent to the average computer user. Have the students write a set of instructions for performing this function.

One-Year Limited Warranty

- Have students come up with synonyms for the word *warranty.* **Possible answers:** Students may cite *guarantee, agreement, promise*.
- Ask students to read the warranty on p. 482. Do their synonyms accurately describe this document?
- Review each element of the warranty.
- Point out that product warranties are important, but often seem hard to read. Explain that the language in warranties must often conform to legal requirements, so it may seem stiff and formal.

One-Year Limited Warranty

The warranty below is included in the product manual for the graphing calculator. Its language outlines the manufacturer's and the consumer's responsibilities. The warranty also explains the process a consumer should follow to get the product repaired.

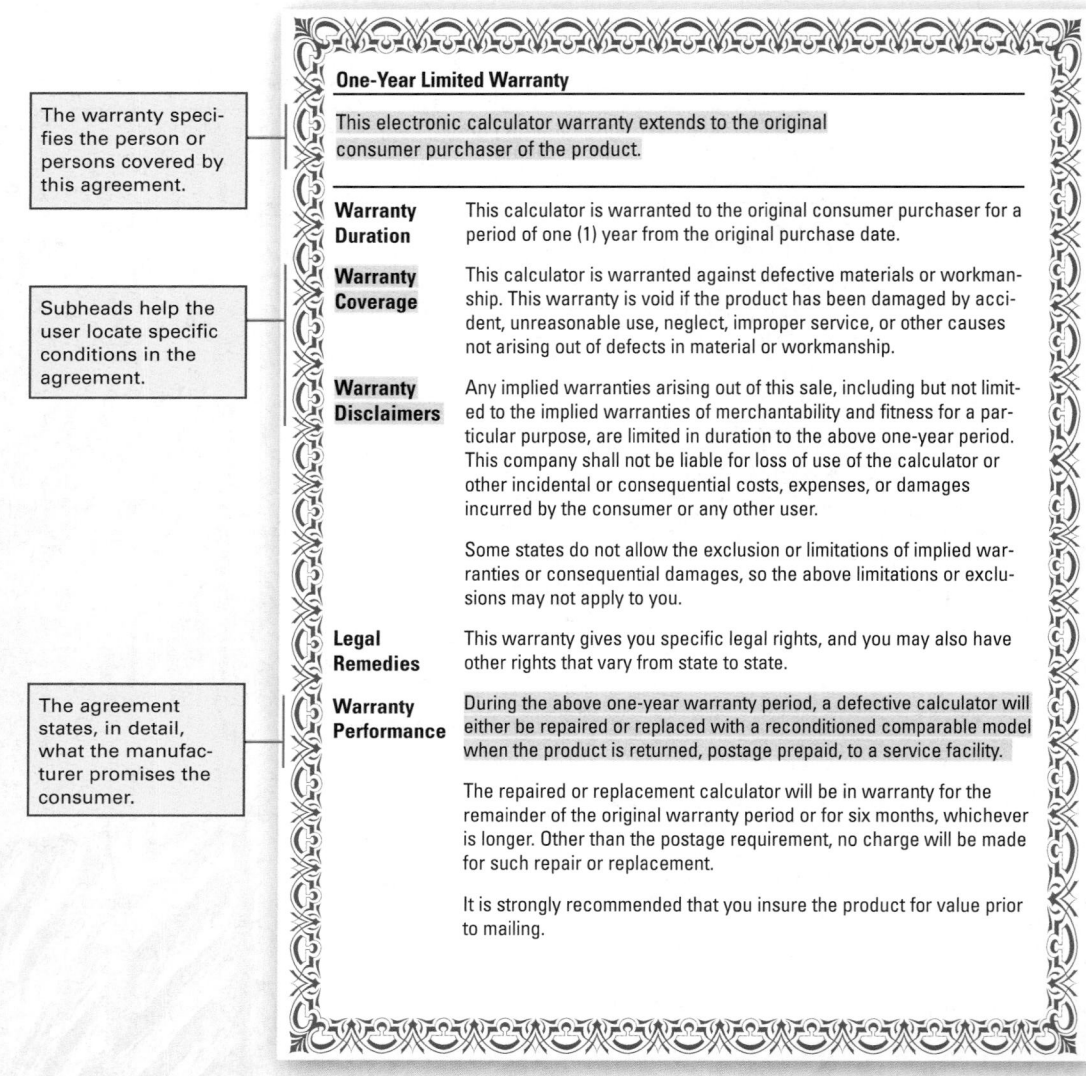

The warranty specifies the person or persons covered by this agreement.

Subheads help the user locate specific conditions in the agreement.

The agreement states, in detail, what the manufacturer promises the consumer.

One-Year Limited Warranty

This electronic calculator warranty extends to the original consumer purchaser of the product.

Warranty Duration This calculator is warranted to the original consumer purchaser for a period of one (1) year from the original purchase date.

Warranty Coverage This calculator is warranted against defective materials or workmanship. This warranty is void if the product has been damaged by accident, unreasonable use, neglect, improper service, or other causes not arising out of defects in material or workmanship.

Warranty Disclaimers Any implied warranties arising out of this sale, including but not limited to the implied warranties of merchantability and fitness for a particular purpose, are limited in duration to the above one-year period. This company shall not be liable for loss of use of the calculator or other incidental or consequential costs, expenses, or damages incurred by the consumer or any other user.

Some states do not allow the exclusion or limitations of implied warranties or consequential damages, so the above limitations or exclusions may not apply to you.

Legal Remedies This warranty gives you specific legal rights, and you may also have other rights that vary from state to state.

Warranty Performance During the above one-year warranty period, a defective calculator will either be repaired or replaced with a reconditioned comparable model when the product is returned, postage prepaid, to a service facility.

The repaired or replacement calculator will be in warranty for the remainder of the original warranty period or for six months, whichever is longer. Other than the postage requirement, no charge will be made for such repair or replacement.

It is strongly recommended that you insure the product for value prior to mailing.

Check Your Comprehension

1. What is the first thing you must do in order to graph the selected function in the viewing window?
2. How long does the warranty on this graphing calculator last?
3. Who must pay the postage when a damaged calculator is shipped to a service facility for repair?

Applying the Reading Strategy

Analyzing Purpose of Product Information

4. What purpose do the technical directions serve for the consumer?
5. Why do the technical directions include visuals?
6. Why would it be necessary for the manufacturer to have verification of the calculator's purchase date?
7. Why does the manufacturer recommend insuring the product prior to mailing?

Activity

Using Information From Consumer Documents

Find the product information that accompanies a product such as a VCR or a digital alarm clock. Read the manufacturer's technical directions and warranty. Use the chart below to record the three important pieces of information from each document. Explain their importance.

Product Information for ______________________

	Key Information	Reasons
Technical Directions		
Warranty		

Contrasting Informational Materials

Product Information, Advertisements, and Consumer Articles

1. Technical directions and warranties are two types of product information. Advertisements are also a kind of product information since they, too, offer details about a product. However, an advertisement does not share the same purpose or language as technical directions or a warranty. Explain the differences in purpose and language between **(a)** technical directions and an advertisement, and **(b)** a warranty and an advertisement.
2. Find a product review in a magazine such as *Consumer Reports*. Explain how the purpose and language of the review differ from those found in technical directions and a warranty.

Answers for p. 483

Check Your Comprehension

1. The user must press the GRAPH key.
2. The warranty lasts one year.
3. The owner must pay the postage.

Applying the Reading Strategy

4. Technical directions enable the consumer to assemble and operate a new product.
5. The visuals clarify the printed instructions, showing the user what to expect.
6. If the product is under warranty for one year, the company must know exactly when it was purchased.
7. Insuring the product would compensate the sender if the product were lost in the mail.

Activity

Sample response:

Technical Directions: Key Information: How to connect the VCR with a TV; How to turn on the VCR; How to record programs; Reasons: The information is important because without it, you might not be able to use even the basic functions of the product. **Warranty:** Key Information: Duration; Coverage; Repair; Reasons: The information tells you how long you are protected against defects in the product, what types of damages the warranty covers, and how you can get the product repaired.

Contrasting Informational Texts

1. **(a)** Technical directions use factual language and step-by-step organization. Explain how to use the product; an advertisement uses persuasive language to entice you to buy the product. **(b)** A warranty uses factual and legal language that tells you what your rights are as a consumer; an advertisement uses persuasive language to entice you to buy the product.
2. Possible answers: The purpose of a product analysis is to evaluate how well a particular product performs and whether it is a good buy. The language in a product analysis is factual (describing test outcomes) as well as persuasive (giving the reviewer's opinion of the product).

If I Forget Thee, Oh Earth ✦ *from* Silent Spring
To the Residents of A.D. 2029

Lesson Objectives and CA Correlations

1. **To analyze and respond to literary elements**
   - Literary Analysis: Persuasive Appeal **R 3.8, 3.9**
   - Comparing Literary Works: Imagery **R 3.7**
2. **To read, comprehend, analyze, and critique a short story and nonfiction**
   - Reading Strategy: Distinguishing Between Fact and Opinion **R 3.8**
   - Reading Check questions
   - Review and Assess questions
   - Assessment Practice (ATE)
3. **To develop word analysis skills, fluency, and systematic vocabulary**
   - Vocabulary Development Lesson: Latin Root: *-ann-* **R 1.1**
4. **To understand and apply written and oral language conventions**
   - Spelling Strategy
   - Grammar Lesson: Compound and Complex Sentences **LC 1.3**
5. **To understand and apply appropriate writing and research strategies**
   - Writing Lesson: Environmental Report **W 2.3**
   - Extension Activity: Memo **W 2.6**
6. **To understand and apply listening and speaking strategies**
   - Extension Activity: Speech **LS 1.5**

STEP-BY-STEP TEACHING GUIDE	PACING GUIDE
PRETEACH	
Motivate Students and Provide Background	
Use the Motivation activity (ATE p. 484)	5 min.
Read and discuss the Preview material and Background information (SE/ATE p. 484) [A]	10 min.
Introduce the Concepts	
Introduce the Literary Analysis and Reading Strategy (SE/ATE p. 485) [A]	15 min.
Pronounce the vocabulary words and read their definitions (SE p. 485)	5 min.
TEACH	
Monitor Comprehension	
Informally monitor comprehension by circulating while students read independently or in groups [A]	30 min.
Monitor students' comprehension with the Reading Check notes (SE/ATE pp. 487, 489, 497)	as students read
Develop vocabulary with Vocabulary notes (SE pp. 487, 489, 492, 493, 497, 498; ATE p. 489)	as students read
Develop Understanding	
Develop students' understanding of persuasive appeal with Literary Analysis annotations (SE/ATE p. 489) [A]	10 min.
Develop students' ability to distinguish between fact and opinion with the Reading Strategy annotations (SE/ATE p. 487)	10 min.
ASSESS	
Assess Mastery	
Assess students' mastery of the Reading Strategy and Literary Analysis by having them answer the Review and Assess questions (SE/ATE p. 499)	20 min.
Use one or more of the print and media Assessment Resources (ATE p. 501) [A]	up to 50 min.
EXTEND	
Apply Understanding	
Have students complete the Vocabulary Development Lesson and the Grammar Lesson (SE p. 500) [A]	20 min.
Apply students' knowledge of elaborating with facts and statistics using the Writing Lesson (SE/ATE p. 501) [A]	45 min.
Apply students' understanding using one or more of the Extension Activities (SE p. 501)	20–90 min.

[A] **ACCELERATED INSTRUCTION:**
Use the strategies and activities identified with an [A].

UNIVERSAL ACCESS
● = Below-Level Students
▲ = On-Level Students
■ = Above-Level Students

Time and Resource Manager

Reading Level: Average, Average, Average
Average Number of Instructional Days: 4

RESOURCES		
PRINT	**TRANSPARENCIES**	**TECHNOLOGY**
• **Beyond Literature,** Cross-Curricular Connection: Math, p. 32 ▲ ■		• **Interest Grabber Video,** Tape 3 ● ▲ ■
• **Selection Support Workbook:** ● ▲ ■ Literary Analysis, p. 128 Reading Strategy, p. 127 Build Vocabulary, p. 125	• **Literary Analysis and Reading Transparencies,** pp. 63 and 64 ● ▲ ■	
• **Adapted Reader's Companion** ● • **Reader's Companion** ● • **Authors In Depth,** Gold Level ■		• **Listening to Literature** ● ▲ ■ Audiocassettes, Side 14 Audio CDs, CD 9
• **English Learner's Companion** ● ▲ • **Literatura en español** ● ▲ • **Literary Analysis for Enrichment** ■	• **Fine Art Transparencies Volume 1,** Art Transparency 2 ● ▲ ■	
• **Formal Assessment:** Selection Test, pp. 110–112 ● ▲ ■ • **Open Book Test,** pp. 94–96 ● ▲ ■ • **Performance Assessment and Portfolio Management,** pp. 17, 23 ● ▲ ■ • PRENTICE HALL ASSESSMENT SYSTEM ● ▲ ■	• PRENTICE HALL ASSESSMENT SYSTEM ● ▲ ■ Skills Practice Answers and Explanations on Transparencies	• **Test Bank Software** ● ▲ ■ • **Got It! Assessment Videotapes,** Tape 3 ● ▲
• **Selection Support Workbook:** ● ▲ ■ Build Grammar Skills, p. 126 • **Writing and Grammar,** Gold Level ● ▲ ■ • **Extension Activities,** p. 32 ● ▲ ■	• **Daily Language Practice Transparencies** ● ▲	• **Writing and Grammar iText CD-ROM** ● ▲ ■ ***Take It to the Net*** www.phschool.com

BLOCK SCHEDULING: Use one 90-minute class period to preteach the selection and have students read it. Use a second 90-minute class period to assess students' mastery of skills and have them complete one of the Extension Activities.

PRETEACH

Step-by-Step Teaching Guide for pp. 484–485

Motivation

Write the following quotation from Arthur C. Clarke's story on the chalkboard or read it aloud:

Never again would the supply ships come flaming down through the stars with gifts from home. . . . On the shadowed globe the lights of the cities had dimmed and died, and they were alone at last, as no man had ever been alone before.

Use this quotation as a teaser to motivate students to read. Tell them that they must read the story to find out what place is being described and what has happened.

Interest Grabber Video

As an alternative, play "The Dangers of DDT" on Tape 3 to engage student interest.

❶ Background

Science

Ozone is a gaseous form of oxygen which occurs in both the lower and upper atmospheres of Earth. The nitric oxide in airplane exhaust and the chlorine in most industrially manufactured gases have reduced the ozone in the upper atmosphere. A severe ozone hole was discovered above Antarctica in the mid-1980s. Scientists believe that the depletion of ozone over North America and Europe, which continues at a rate of 0.5 percent per year, will bring serious ecological consequences, possibly in a very short time. Many nations, including the United States, are implementing regulations to reduce the production of chlorofluorocarbons (CFCs).

Prepare to Read

"If I Forget Thee, Oh Earth . . ." ◆ *from* Silent Spring ◆ To the Residents of A.D. 2029

Take It to the Net

Visit www.phschool.com for interactive activities and instruction related to the selections, including

- background
- graphic organizers
- literary elements
- reading strategies

Preview

Connecting to the Literature

Perhaps you are aware of local dangers to the environment and of individuals or groups that are seeking to correct them. In these selections, the authors encourage readers to think about environmental problems and their solutions.

❶ Background

Many environmentalists today are concerned with the ozone layer, which shields Earth from 95 to 99 percent of the sun's harmful ultraviolet rays. Since the mid-1970s, scientists have worried about a breakdown in the ozone layer caused by the use of CFCs found in aerosol sprays and refrigerants. Environmental scientists continue to monitor the situation.

TEACHING RESOURCES

The following resources can be used to enrich or extend the instruction for pp. 484–485.

Motivation

Interest Grabber Video, Tape 3

Background

Beyond Literature, p. 32

Take It to the Net

Visit www.phschool.com for background and hotlinks for the selections.

Literary Analysis

Literary Analysis and Reading Transparencies, Persuasive Appeal, p. 63

Reading

Selection Support: Reading Strategy, p. 127; Build Vocabulary, p. 125

Literary Analysis and Reading Transparencies, Distinguishing Between Fact and Opinion, p. 64

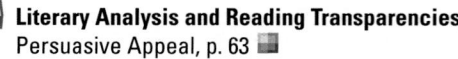

BLOCK SCHEDULING: Resources marked with this symbol provide varied instruction during 90-minute blocks.

❷ Literary Analysis

Persuasive Appeal

A **persuasive appeal** is an urgent appeal or warning that aims to convince the reader to think or act in a certain way. A persuasive appeal may exist in fiction or nonfiction, and it may be stated or implied. In this excerpt from *Silent Spring,* Rachel Carson warns how the indiscriminate use of pesticides threatens our environment:

> Then a strange blight crept over the area and everything began to change . . . mysterious maladies swept the flocks of chickens; the cattle and sheep sickened and died.

As you read, find other warnings about environmental conditions.

Comparing Literary Works

The writers of these selections use **imagery**, or descriptive language, to create pictures in the reader's mind. Imagery is intended to appeal to one or more of the senses—sight, hearing, touch, taste, or smell. Compare the imagery in each selection, and decide how it strengthens the warning.

❸ Reading Strategy

Distinguishing Between Fact and Opinion

When you read literature that makes a persuasive appeal, it is important to distinguish between fact and opinion. A **fact** is a statement that can be proved, or tested for accuracy. An **opinion** is a statement of personal preference and cannot be proved. Look at the following examples from "To the Residents of A.D. 2029."

Fact: Parts of our land are overcrowded, parts neglected, parts abused, parts destroyed.

Opinion: Our present disrespect for the natural world is our most serious stupidity to date.

Use a chart like this one to separate facts from opinions as you read.

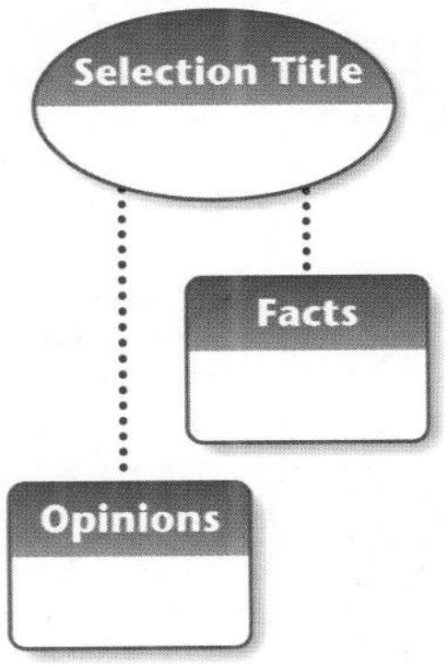

Vocabulary Development

purged (pʉrjd) *v.* cleansed (p. 487)

pyre (pīr) *n.* pile of wood on which a body is burned at a funeral (p. 489)

perennial (pər en´ ē əl) *adj.* constant (p. 489)

blight (blīt) *n.* something that destroys or prevents growth (p. 492)

moribund (môr´ i bund´) *adj.* dying (p. 493)

postulated (päs´ chə lāt´ ed) *v.* claimed (p. 497)

beleaguered (bē lē´ gərd) *adj.* worried; tormented (p. 498)

schism (siz´ əm) *n.* division (p. 498)

❷ Literary Analysis

Persuasive Appeal

- Remind students that one of the main purposes of both prose writers and poets is to persuade readers to act or to believe something.
- Point out that poems and works of fiction are effective instruments of persuasive appeal.
- As students read, have them think about the message these three selections convey to them. Have them consider which selection was most persuasive.

❸ Reading Strategy

Distinguishing Between Fact and Opinion

- Tell students that distinguishing fact from opinion is especially important in reading nonfiction. Good readers focus on statements that can be proven true and carefully evaluate the evidence that supports a writer's statements of opinion.
- Display the Reading Strategy transparency in **Literary Analysis and Reading Transparencies,** p. 64, to show students how to monitor facts and opinions as they read the selections.

Vocabulary Development

- Pronounce each vocabulary word for students, and read the definitions as a class. Have students identify any words with which they are already familiar.

CUSTOMIZE INSTRUCTION FOR UNIVERSAL ACCESS

For Special Needs Students	For Less Proficient Readers	For English Learners
Have students read the adapted version from *Silent Spring* in the **Adapted Reader's Companion.** This version provides basic-level instruction in an interactive format with questions and write-on lines. Completing the adapted version will prepare students to read the selection in the Student Edition.	Have students read the selection in the **Reader's Companion.** This version provides basic-level instruction in an interactive format with questions and write-on lines. After students finish the selection in **Reader's Companion,** have them complete the questions and activities in the Student Edition.	Have students read the adapted version of the selection in the **English Learner's Companion.** This version provides basic-level instruction in an interactive format with questions and write-on lines. Completing the adapted version will prepare students to read the selection in the Student Edition.

E-Teach

Visit E-Teach at www.phschool.com for teachers' essays on how to teach, with questions and answers.

TEACH

Step-by-Step Teaching Guide for pp. 486–498

CUSTOMIZE INSTRUCTION
For Visual/Spatial Learners

The photograph on this page, a view of Earth as seen from the Moon, can help students visualize the setting of the story. This and similar photographs were taken by NASA astronauts during the Apollo series of six lunar landings between 1969 and 1972.

1 About the Selection

The story's title is a quotation from Psalm 137:

If I forget thee, O Jerusalem, let my right hand forget her cunning.

This vow expresses the emotions of Jews who were forced into exile in Babylon in 597 B.C. The exiles in Arthur C. Clarke's story are the sole survivors of a nuclear holocaust, now living on the moon.

The story provides an alarming warning that the human race might someday be forced into exile in space and be left with only memories of life on Earth.

1 "If I Forget Thee, Oh Earth..."

Arthur C. Clarke

TEACHING RESOURCES

The following resources can be used to enrich or extend the instruction for pp. 486–498.

Literary Analysis
- **Selection Support:** Literary Analysis, p. 128

Reading
- **Reader's Companion**
- **English Learner's Companion**
- **Listening to Literature Audiocassettes,** Side 14
- **Listening to Literature Audio CDs,** CD 9

Extension
- **Authors In Depth,** Gold Level (The collection includes additional selections by Rachel Carson for extended reading.)

BLOCK SCHEDULING: Resources marked with this symbol provide varied instruction during 90-minute blocks.

When Marvin was ten years old, his father took him through the long, echoing corridors that led up through Administration and Power, until at last they came to the uppermost levels of all and were among the swiftly growing vegetation of the Farmlands. Marvin liked it here: it was fun watching the great, slender plants creeping with almost visible eagerness toward the sunlight as it filtered down through the plastic domes to meet them. The smell of life was everywhere, awakening inexpressible longings in his heart: no longer was he breathing the dry, cool air of the residential levels, purged of all smells but the faint tang of ozone.[1] He wished he could stay here for a little while, but Father would not let him. They went onward until they had reached the entrance to the Observatory, which he had never visited: but they did not stop, and Marvin knew with a sense of rising excitement that there could be only one goal left. For the first time in his life, he was going Outside.

purged (purjd) *v.* cleansed

There were a dozen of the surface vehicles, with their wide balloon tires and pressurized cabins, in the great servicing chamber. His father must have been expected, for they were led at once to the little scout car waiting by the huge circular door of the airlock. Tense with expectancy, Marvin settled himself down in the cramped cabin while his father started the motor and checked the controls. The inner door of the lock slid open and then closed behind them: he heard the roar of the great air pumps fade slowly away as the pressure dropped to zero. Then the "Vacuum" sign flashed on, the outer door parted, and before Marvin lay the land which he had never yet entered.

He had seen it in photographs, of course: he had watched it imaged on television screens a hundred times. But now it was lying all around him, burning beneath the fierce sun that crawled so slowly across the jet-black sky. He stared into the west, away from the blinding splendor of the sun—and there were the stars, as he had been told but had never quite believed. He gazed at them for a long time, marveling that anything could be so bright and yet so tiny. They were intense unscintillating points, and suddenly he remembered a rhyme he had once read in one of his father's books:

Twinkle, twinkle, little star,
How I wonder what you are.

Well, *he* knew what the stars were. Whoever asked that question must have been very stupid. And what did they mean by "twinkle"? You could see at a glance that all the stars shone with the same steady, unwavering light. He abandoned the puzzle and turned his attention to the landscape around him.

Reading Strategy
Distinguishing Between Fact and Opinion Is the statement "They were intense unscintillating points" a fact or an opinion? Explain.

4 **Reading Check**
Where is Marvin going for the first time in his life?

1. **ozone** (ō´ zōn) *n.* form of oxygen with a sharp odor.

2 Reading Strategy

Distinguishing Between Fact and Opinion

- Ask students to list some facts this first paragraph gives them about Marvin's life.
  Answers: Marvin is ten and lives in an underground residential community where he never breathes fresh air; he has never been "Outside" before.
- As students continue to read, have them pause after every few paragraphs and list some of the facts they have learned.

3 Reading Strategy

Distinguishing Between Fact and Opinion

- Ask the Reading Strategy question on p. 487: Is the statement "They were intense unscintillating points" a fact or an opinion? Explain.
  Answer: "Unscintillating" is a fact; the stars' light is constant and unblinking. "Intense" is an opinion; Marvin finds the light intense, but other people might not describe it this way.

Monitor Progress Have students go through this passage, identifying statements of fact and statements of opinion. Does Clarke give more facts, or more opinions?
Answer: Almost all the sentences in this passage are statements of fact. Marvin's judgment that the questioner in the rhyme was "stupid" is an opinion.

4 Reading Check

Answer: Marvin is going Outside—beyond the underground area in which he lives.

CUSTOMIZE INSTRUCTION FOR UNIVERSAL ACCESS

For Special Needs Students	For Advanced Readers
Tell students that certain words can be signals of a statement of opinion. In the story, words like *beautiful, strange, fun, cramped, curiously, reckless, exhilarating,* express a person's feelings, not facts. Have students look for these and similar "signals of opinion" as they read.	Have students reread the descriptive passages of this story and discuss the importance of the setting to the appeal the writer is trying to make. Have students consider the amount of detail Clarke gives about the setting, and what importance the setting has to Marvin and his father. After discussion, students can write brief essays about the setting and the effects of Clarke's use of descriptive writing.

5 Background

Science

The international space station generates its own electric power by means of giant solar panels. However, the ISS remains dependent on the "home planet" for resupply of oxygen, food, fuel, and other consumables.

The ISS is the most inclusive space project ever undertaken. The United States and Russia are providing spacecraft and transport. Canada is providing a giant robotic arm. Japan and the European Community are contributing laboratory modules and space vehicles.

6 Critical Thinking

Deduce

- Have a student read this description of the setting aloud. Ask students what they can deduce about Marvin's home location from this description and the details given on p. 487.
  Answer: The place is apparently barren and the air not safe to breathe, since all the people have to live underground and plants grow in an observatory where they are under a protective shield.
- Ask students if they can deduce the Colony's location from the details given so far. If they have no idea, explain that Clarke has not invented this description; it is an accurate description of an actual place.
  Answer: Students may associate the word "craters" with the Moon.

They were racing across a level plain at almost a hundred miles an hour, the great balloon tires sending up little spurts of dust behind them. There was no sign of the Colony: in the few minutes while he had been gazing at the stars, its domes and radio towers had fallen below the horizon. Yet there were other indications of man's presence, for about a mile ahead Marvin could see the curiously shaped structures clustering round the head of a mine. Now and then a puff of vapor would emerge from a squat smokestack and would instantly disperse.

6 They were past the mine in a moment: Father was driving with a reckless and exhilarating skill as if—it was a strange thought to come into a child's mind—he were trying to escape from something. In a few minutes they had reached the edge of the plateau on which the Colony had been built. The ground fell sharply away beneath them in a dizzying slope whose lower stretches were lost in shadow. Ahead, as far as the eye could reach, was a jumbled wasteland of craters, mountain ranges, and ravines. The crests of the mountains, catching the low sun, burned like islands of fire in a sea of darkness: and above them the stars still shone as steadfastly as ever.

There could be no way forward—yet there was. Marvin clenched his fists as the car edged over the slope and started the long descent. Then he saw the barely visible track leading down the mountainside, and relaxed a little. Other men, it seemed, had gone this way before.

Night fell with a shocking abruptness as they crossed the shadow line and the sun dropped below the crest of the plateau. The twin searchlights sprang into life, casting blue-white bands on the rocks ahead, so that there was scarcely need to check their speed. For hours they drove through valleys and past the foot of mountains whose peaks seemed to comb the stars, and sometimes they emerged for a moment into the sunlight as they climbed over higher ground.

And now on the right was a wrinkled, dusty plain, and on the left, its ramparts and terraces rising mile after mile into the sky, was a wall of mountains that marched into the distance until its peaks sank from sight below the rim of the world. There was no sign that men had ever explored this land, but once they passed the skeleton of a crashed rocket, and beside it a stone cairn[2] surmounted by a metal cross.

It seemed to Marvin that the mountains stretched on forever: but at last, many hours later, the range ended in a towering, precipitous headland[3] that rose steeply from a cluster of little hills. They drove down into a shallow valley that curved in a great arc toward the far side of the mountains: and as they did so, Marvin slowly realized that something very strange was happening in the land ahead.

The sun was now low behind the hills on the right: the valley before them should be in total darkness. Yet it was awash with a cold white

Literature in context 5 — Science Connection

International Space Station

In Arthur Clarke's story, a space colony is all that remains of the human species. If the idea of a space colony seems implausible, consider the fact that a small colony is being developed directly over your head in the form of an international space station. Fourteen nations are contributing different components to the station, which will take 44 missions to complete. When it is finished in 2005, seven crew members will be able to live for extended periods in space—by choice, one hopes, and not by necessity, as in Marvin's case.

---

2. cairn (kern) *n.* pile of stones left as a monument.
3. precipitous headland (prē sip´ ə təs hed´ land) steep cliff.

radiance that came spilling over the crags beneath which they were driving. Then, suddenly, they were out in the open plain, and the source of the light lay before them in all its glory.

It was very quiet in the little cabin now that the motors had stopped. The only sound was the faint whisper of the oxygen feed and an occasional metallic crepitation as the outer walls of the vehicle radiated away their heat. For no warmth at all came from the great silver crescent that floated low above the far horizon and flooded all this land with pearly light. It was so brilliant that minutes passed before Marvin could accept its challenge and look steadfastly into its glare, but at last he could discern the outlines of continents, the hazy border of the atmosphere, and the white islands of cloud. And even at this distance, he could see the glitter of sunlight on the polar ice.

It was beautiful, and it called to his heart across the abyss of space. There in that shining crescent were all the wonders that he had never known—the hues of sunset skies, the moaning of the sea on pebbled shores, the patter of falling rain, the unhurried benison of snow. These and a thousand others should have been his rightful heritage, but he knew them only from the books and ancient records, and the thought filled him with the anguish of exile.

Why could they not return? It seemed so peaceful beneath those
7 lines of marching cloud. Then Marvin, his eyes no longer blinded by the glare, saw that the portion of the disk that should have been in darkness was gleaming faintly with an evil phosphorescence:[4] and he remembered. He was looking upon the funeral pyre of a world—upon the radioactive aftermath of Armageddon.[5] Across a quarter of a million
8 miles of space, the glow of dying atoms was still visible, a perennial reminder of the ruinous past. It would be centuries yet before that deadly glow died from the rocks and life could return again to fill that silent, empty world.

And now Father began to speak, telling Marvin the story which until this moment had meant no more to him than the fairy tales he had once been told. There were many things he could not understand: it was impossible for him to picture the glowing, multicolored pattern of life on the planet he had never seen. Nor could he comprehend the forces that had destroyed it in the end, leaving the Colony, preserved by its isolation, as the sole survivor. Yet he could share the agony of those final days, when the Colony had learned at last that never again would the supply ships come flaming down through the stars with gifts from home. One by one the radio stations had ceased to call: on the shadowed globe the lights of the cities had dimmed and died, and they were alone at last, as no men had ever been alone before, carrying in their hands the future of the race.

Then had followed the years of despair, and the long-drawn battle

Literary Analysis
Persuasive Appeal What warning is implied in this description of Earth?

pyre (pīr) *n.* pile of wood on which a body is burned at a funeral

perennial (pə ren′ ē əl) *adj.* constant

9 **Reading Check**
What does Marvin realize he is seeing?

4. **phosphorescence** (fäs′ fə res′ əns) *n.* emission of light resulting from exposure to radiation.
5. **Armageddon** (är′ mə ged′ ən) *n.* in the Bible, the place where the final battle between good and evil is to be fought.

7 Literary Analysis

Persuasive Appeal

- Have students read the bracketed passage, paying careful attention to the description of nuclear weapons.
- Ask students the Literary Analysis question on p. 489: What warning is implied in this description of Earth?
  Answer: The description implies a warning of the dangers of nuclear weapons. Clarke describes an Earth glowing with radiation and says it will be uninhabitable for centuries to come.

Monitor Progress Have students compare and contrast the two paragraphs beginning "It was beautiful" and "Why could they not return?" How does this contrast reinforce Clarke's appeal to the reader?
Answer: Clarke describes a beautiful world and then abruptly tells the reader that all this beauty was destroyed by violence. The description of Earth's beauty makes the warning more poignant.

8 Vocabulary Development

Latin Root *-ann-*

- Draw students' attention to the word *perennial*. Point out that the Latin root *-ann-* sometimes appears as *-enn-*. It means "year."
- Ask students to think of three other words based on this root. Write them on the board and ask students to give definitions for each.
  Possible response: *annual:* "occurring once a year"; *anniversary:* "yearly observance of a special date"; *semiannual:* "occurring every half year."
- Finally, have students use each listed word in a sentence.
  Sample sentences: The annual report showed an increase in profits. We celebrated our parents' anniversary last night. We will make our semiannual trip to the cabin next week.

9 Reading Check

Answer: Marvin is seeing a planet on which life was destroyed by radiation.

CUSTOMIZE INSTRUCTION FOR UNIVERSAL ACCESS

For Advanced Readers	For Gifted/Talented Students
Have students consider why Clarke chose not to include any dialogue in this story. Although Marvin is told the story of the destruction of life on Earth, readers are not given the father's actual words. What effect does this lack of dialogue have on the reader? How does the lack of dialogue relate to the story's tone and message? Students can write brief essays analyzing these questions.	Have students write the story Marvin's father tells about the nuclear holocaust on Earth. Remind them that the father did not witness the disaster; he only knows what he has inferred or been told. Students should reread pp. 489–490 for details the father would include in the story.

Answers for p. 490

Review and Assess

1. Student responses may reflect the difficulties of sustaining hope across many generations of exile.
2. **(a)** "Twinkle, Twinkle, Little Star" **(b)** The landscape is a wasteland of craters, mountains, and ravines. There is no atmosphere. Night falls abruptly. **(c)** Human beings have actually traveled to the Moon, and there are some suggestions that human life may be sustainable there under carefully controlled conditions.
3. **(a)** Marvin determines to take this trip one day with his own son. **(b)** Marvin's father wanted to pass on his own dream of returning to Earth.
4. **(a)** Earth was destroyed by nuclear missiles. **(b)** Clarke might suggest that nuclear weapons be banned and that nations find peaceful ways to settle differences.

Reading Strategy

Distinguishing Between Fact and Opinion

Ask students the Reading Strategy question on p. 490: Is the statement about the Colony's need for a goal a fact or an opinion?

Answer: This statement is an opinion because it cannot be proved that the only way the Colony can have the will to live is with a goal.

for survival in their fierce and hostile world. That battle had been won, though barely: this little oasis of life was safe against the worst that Nature could do. But unless there was a goal, a future toward which it could work, the Colony would lose the will to live, and neither machines nor skill nor science could save it then.

So, at last, Marvin understood the purpose of this pilgrimage. He would never walk beside the rivers of that lost and legendary world, or listen to the thunder raging above its softly rounded hills. Yet one day—how far ahead?—his children's children would return to claim their heritage. The winds and the rains would scour the poisons from the burning lands and carry them to the sea, and in the depths of the sea they would waste their venom until they could harm no living things. Then the great ships that were still waiting here on the silent, dusty plains could lift once more into space, along the road that led to home.

That was the dream: and one day, Marvin knew with a sudden flash of insight, he would pass it on to his own son, here at this same spot with the mountains behind him and the silver light from the sky streaming into his face.

He did not look back as they began the homeward journey. He could not bear to see the cold glory of the crescent Earth fade from the rocks around him, as he went to rejoin his people in their long exile.

Reading Strategy
Distinguishing Between Fact and Opinion Is the statement about the Colony's need for a goal a fact or an opinion? Explain.

Review and Assess

Thinking About the Selection

1. **Respond:** Could you endure the kind of life that Marvin has with only the hope that some distant descendants could return to Earth? Explain.
2. **(a) Recall:** What rhyme does Marvin remember as he looks outside? **(b) Infer:** What evidence indicates that the story is set on the moon? **(c) Analyze:** How does the choice of setting make the story more realistic?
3. **(a) Recall:** At the end of the story, what does Marvin determine to do? **(b) Draw Conclusions:** What was the purpose of Marvin's trip with his father?
4. **(a) Infer:** How did Earth come to be destroyed? **(b) Extend:** What suggestions do you think Clark would make about how to prevent a situation like the one in the story from occurring?

Arthur C. Clarke

(b. 1917)

For more than fifty years, Arthur C. Clarke has been turning out exceptional works of fiction and nonfiction. A child of Somerset, England, he wrote his first science-fiction stories during his teens.

Of more than fifty works, Clarke's most famous is his collaboration with film director Stanley Kubrick on the screenplay for *2001: A Space Odyssey*. Equally distinguished is Clarke's nonfiction. In a 1945 essay, he predicted the development of communications satellites long before they were a reality.

from Silent Spring

(10) (11)

Rachel Carson

There was once a town in the heart of America where all life seemed to live in harmony with its surroundings. The town lay in the midst of a checkerboard of prosperous farms, with fields of grain and hillsides of orchards where, in spring, white clouds of bloom drifted above the green fields. In autumn, oak and maple and birch set up a blaze of color that flamed and flickered across a backdrop of pines. Then foxes barked in the hills and deer silently crossed the fields, half hidden in the mists of the fall mornings.

(10) About the Selection

In this passage from her landmark book, Rachel Carson sounds a warning about how the indiscriminate use of pesticides threatens our environment. At the time Carson wrote, most people had little idea about the unintended harm these chemicals produced. In the tradition of many writers who have an unpleasant lesson to teach, Carson introduces her ideas in the form of a fable. This approach allows readers to distance themselves from uncomfortable ideas and to consider them objectively. In addition, the mysterious qualities of the excerpt spark readers' interest and encourage them to read on.

(11) Literary Analysis

Persuasive Appeal

- Call on volunteers to give their reactions to the selection title. How does the title convey a warning? Is spring normally a silent season? What sounds do students associate with spring? What might it mean if these sounds were no longer heard?
  Answer: Sounds of spring include songbirds, lawn mowers or farm machinery, newborn animals, children playing outdoors, and breezes through the leaves of trees. If these sounds are absent, something must be very wrong. Some environmental disaster must have silenced the birds and animals and kept all the children indoors.
- Have students read on to note further warning signs in the text. Have them list specific words and phrases that convey a warning.

CUSTOMIZE INSTRUCTION FOR UNIVERSAL ACCESS

For Less Proficient Readers	For Gifted/Talented Students
Have students read the first sentence of the selection, and point out the similarities to the fairy-tale beginning "Once upon a time. . ." Lead students to understand that Carson isn't referring to one specific town, but instead is capturing the qualities that characterize many towns throughout the United States and the world.	Divide students into two groups. Ask one group to create a poster using art or photographs to depict life in Carson's town before the disaster; the other group can prepare an "after" poster. Suggest that they select appropriate music and sound effects to accompany a presentation of their "before" and "after" images.

⓬ Literary Analysis

Persuasive Appeal

- Point out that the first two paragraphs of this text are descriptive. Ask students whether these paragraphs convey any warning to them, and if so, how Carson does this.
  Answer: Students may find the description simply too good to be true. They may note that both paragraphs are written in the past tense, indicating that conditions have changed.
- Ask the Literary Analysis question on p. 493: What persuasive appeal does the author present in this paragraph?
  Answer: The author uses negative, emotionally charged words ("blight," "evil," "shadow of death") to warn readers about a deadly threat.

Along the roads, laurel, viburnum and alder, great ferns and wildflowers delighted the traveler's eye through much of the year. Even in winter the roadsides were places of beauty, where countless birds came to feed on the berries and on the seed heads of the dried weeds rising above the snow. The countryside was, in fact, famous for the abundance and variety of its bird life, and when the flood of migrants was pouring through in spring and fall people traveled from great distances to observe them. Others came to fish the streams, which flowed clear and cold out of the hills and contained shady pools where trout lay. So it had been from the days many years ago when the first settlers raised their houses, sank their wells, and built their barns.

⓬ Then a strange blight crept over the area and everything began to change. Some evil spell had settled on the community: mysterious maladies swept the flocks of chickens; the cattle and sheep sickened and died. Everywhere was a shadow of death. The farmers spoke of

blight (blīt) *n.* something that destroys or prevents growth

ENRICHMENT: Science Connection

Pesticides

Pesticides are chemical compounds intended to destroy crop-eating insects. Pesticides can be lethal to many species besides the insects they are intended to kill. Because they are carried by the wind and because they linger in an area up to twelve years after they are sprayed, they can do tremendous ecological damage. Another difficulty with pesticides is that in destroying an insect population, they deprive the insects' natural predators of food, thus killing them off as well.

The pesticide DDT is a chlorinated hydrocarbon compound that came into use after World War II. DDT attacks an animal's central nervous system. Partly because of the publication of *Silent Spring*, the United States began phasing out DDT in 1970 and banned it and certain other pesticides entirely in 1972. Populations of many species of birds have made strong recoveries since the DDT ban.

much illness among their families. In the town the doctors had become more and more puzzled by new kinds of sickness appearing among their patients. There had been several sudden and unexplained deaths, not only among adults but even among children, who would be stricken suddenly while at play and die within a few hours.

13 There was a strange stillness. The birds, for example—where had they gone? Many people spoke of them, puzzled and disturbed. The feeding stations in the backyards were deserted. The few birds seen anywhere were moribund; they trembled violently and could not fly. It was a spring without voices. On the mornings that had once throbbed with the dawn chorus of robins, catbirds, doves, jays, wrens, and scores of other bird voices there was now no sound; only silence lay over the fields and woods and marsh.

On the farms the hens brooded, but no chicks hatched. The farmers complained that they were unable to raise any pigs—the litters were small and the young survived only a few days. The apple trees

Literary Analysis
Persuasive Appeal What persuasive appeal does the author present in this paragraph?

moribund (môr′ i bund′) *adj.* dying

14 ▼ **Critical Viewing** What might the author think about the aerial spraying of crops to kill pests? **[Connect]**

13 Reading Strategy
Distinguishing Between Fact and Opinion

- Have students identify the one statement of opinion in this paragraph.
  Answer: The first sentence is a statement of opinion. The silence is a fact, but the adjective "strange" makes this a statement of opinion.
- Have students look back over the first few paragraphs of the text and explain whether so far it has been mostly facts or opinions. What is the effect of this balance of facts and opinions?
  Answer: Most of the statements are a mix of fact and opinion. For instance, it is a fact that countless birds come to this town in the winter, but it is an opinion that this makes the roadside a place of beauty. The effect is to give a subjective portrait of the town which the reader may or may not accept as accurate.

Monitor Progress Ask whether students agree with the writer's opinions and have them explain why.
Answer: Most students may agree that human beings respond positively to the beauties of nature.

14 ▶Critical Viewing
Answer: The author would disapprove of this. Since the sprays kill insects, they are probably harmful to other living creatures.

CUSTOMIZE INSTRUCTION FOR UNIVERSAL ACCESS
For Advanced Readers

Have students locate and read more of *Silent Spring.* Students can write reviews of the book after they have read some more of it (time may not permit reading the entire book). Remind them not to simply summarize the information and argument Carson presents, but to evaluate her argument. They should decide whether her appeal is persuasive, whether her opinions are adequately supported by facts, and whether her message is important and well-presented.

For shorter readings, you may wish to refer students to **Authors In Depth,** Gold Level, which includes the following selections by Carson:

- excerpt from *The Sea Around Us*
- excerpt from *Always, Rachel*
- "An Island I Remember"
- excerpt from *Under the Sea-Wind*

Answers for p. 494

Review and Assess

1. Some students may find the technique effective because it tends to universalize the problems Carson describes. Other students might find the use of a fictional device to be misleading in a work of nonfiction.
2. **(a)** Life is idyllic. The world is clean and beautiful. **(b)** The condition of life changes for the worse. Animals and people get sick, and vegetation is destroyed.
3. **(a)** They get sick and die. **(b)** Carson's reference to the "white granular powder" indicates that the source of the problem is chemicals.
4. **(a)** The vegetation dries out and dies. **(b)** Students may note that vegetation is a source of food, shade, and oxygen. "All living things" have deserted the lifeless branches.
5. **(a)** Carson reveals that the town is fictional. **(b)** Some students may note that had Carson used a real town, she could have proven her case. Others may suggest that by using a fictional town, Carson can create a more vivid example.
6. **(a)** Carson blames people for causing the problem. **(b)** She would probably suggest that people not spray their crops with pesticides, and that they show much more respect for the environment.
7. Most students will say it motivates them by warning them of the specific consequences of abuse of the environment.

were coming into bloom but no bees droned among the blossoms, so there was no pollination and there would be no fruit.

The roadsides, once so attractive, were now lined with browned and withered vegetation as though swept by fire. These, too, were silent, deserted by all living things. Even the streams were now lifeless. Anglers no longer visited them, for all the fish had died.

In the gutters under the eaves and between the shingles of the roofs, a white granular powder still showed a few patches; some weeks before it had fallen like snow upon the roofs and the lawns, the fields and streams.

No witchcraft, no enemy action had silenced the rebirth of new life in this stricken world. The people had done it themselves.

This town does not actually exist, but it might easily have a thousand counterparts in America or elsewhere in the world. I know of no community that has experienced all the misfortunes I describe. Yet every one of these disasters has actually happened somewhere, and many real communities have already suffered a substantial number of them. A grim specter has crept upon us almost unnoticed, and this imagined tragedy may easily become a stark reality we all shall know.

Review and Assess

Thinking About the Selection

1. **Respond:** Is Carson's technique of describing environmental problems in a fictional town effective? Explain.
2. **(a) Recall:** What is the condition of life at the beginning of Carson's story? **(b) Compare and Contrast:** How does the condition of life change as the story continues?
3. **(a) Recall:** What happens to the farm animals? **(b) Infer:** What causes this sudden change?
4. **(a) Recall:** What becomes of the vegetation in the town? **(b) Connect:** Why does the fate of the vegetation affect the fate of humans?
5. **(a) Recall:** What information about the town does Carson reveal at the end of her story? **(b) Speculate:** Would Carson's story have been more effective had the town been real? Why or why not?
6. **(a) Recall:** According to Carson, who caused the problem? **(b) Draw Conclusions:** What suggestions do you think Carson would make to humans?
7. **Apply:** Does a warning like Carson's motivate you to become more involved in environmental issues? Explain.

Rachel Carson

(1907–1964)

As a young woman, Rachel Carson studied writing at the Pennsylvania College for Women. A lifelong love of science and nature, however, caused her to change her field of study to marine biology. She was later able to pursue both fields by writing eloquently about nature.

Carson's widely praised book *The Sea Around Us* (1951), came out of her years as a biologist and editor at the United States Fish and Wildlife Service. Her most significant work was *Silent Spring* (1962), a chilling and well-documented warning about the dangers of pesticides. Before her book, few people understood the dangers of pollution or the interconnectedness of all life.

15 To the Residents of A.D. 2029

Bryan Woolley

Every writer's secret dream has been fulfilled for me. I know, as surely as anyone can know such things, that my works will be read fifty years from now. Well, one work, anyway.

16 This is because Collin County is about to dedicate a new courthouse and jail in McKinney, and somewhere in the vicinity of that structure the Collin County Historical Commission is going to bury a time capsule that will be opened in A.D. 2029, assuming that somebody's still around then, and that he can read. And I've been asked to contribute something to the capsule, probably because Mrs. Elisabeth Pink—the lady responsible for its contents—and I knew each other slightly long ago, in an era that by 2029 will be known as Prehistory.

15 About the Selection

Bryan Woolley addresses the readers of the year 2029, who will read his essay when they open the time capsule in which it is buried. He muses on the fast-disappearing resources such as petroleum, natural gas, and coal on which people have grown to depend. He closes with a short list of wishes for the people of 2029: that they learn from past mistakes, that they respect nature, that they appreciate beauty, and that they maintain a sense of humor.

16 Background

Social Studies

A time capsule is a tightly sealed container that holds documents and objects chosen to give those who open the capsule in the future an impression of how people lived at a particular time. Time capsules are often placed in the cornerstones of new buildings, or buried on public property on special occasions, such as local or national centennials. Perhaps the ultimate time capsule is riding in Voyager 1, a space probe launched in 1977 and now speeding billions of miles into deep space. The probe contains recorded sounds of nature, messages in more than fifty-five modern and ancient languages, a variety of music, and 115 images. It may be some time before this time capsule is ever opened. Voyager 1 will not approach another planetary system for 40,000 years.

⓱ Literary Analysis

Persuasive Appeal

- Ask students to pay attention to any persuasive language they encounter as they review this passage.
- Ask the Literary Analysis question on p. 496: Which words indicate that the author's persuasive appeal is beginning?
  Answer: The opening sentence shows that the writer is going to convey a warning about the state of society.

⓲ Reading Strategy

Distinguishing Between Fact and Opinion

- Ask the Reading Strategy Question on p. 496: Which facts here support the writer's opinion about a sense of decline?
  Answer: Water and air are polluted, the population is not evenly distributed, and people are using up the unrenewable fuels on which they depend.
- Ask students how these facts affect their reaction to the writer's opinion.
  Answer: Since the writer supports his opinion with facts, his opinion is more acceptable and convincing. An unsupported opinion would not be as persuasive.

⓳ ▶Critical Viewing

Answer: Some students may note that an appreciation of nature has a calming, enriching effect on people. Others may respond more practically that our respect for nature is repaid many times over in the food, shelter, and other resources that are derived from nature.

My contribution, Mrs. Pink's letter says, "could be either on our current status or what you think the future will hold."

⓱ I wish I could report to the future that our current status is hunky-dory, that we live in the Golden Age of something or other. Until recently it was possible for Americans to believe that. There's no doubt that in the twentieth century, at least, the people of the United States have enjoyed the highest standard of living that the world has known up to this point in history. We've had so much of everything, in fact, that we've thought our supplies of the essentials of life—land, food, air, water, fuel—would last forever, and we've been wasteful. Sometimes we've even been wasteful of human life itself.

⓲ Lately, though, a sense of decline has set in. We've begun to realize that we're in trouble. We've poured so much filth into our water that much of it is undrinkable, and no life can live in it. Even the life of the ocean, the great mother of us all, is threatened. Scientists say the last wisp of pure, natural air in the continental United States was absorbed into our generally polluted atmosphere over Flagstaff, Arizona, several years ago. Parts of our land are overcrowded, parts neglected, parts abused, parts destroyed. We continue to depend on unrenewable resources—petroleum; natural gas, and coal—for most of the fuel that heats and cools our homes; runs our industry, agriculture, and business; and propels our transportation. We've suddenly discovered that those resources are disappearing forever. Without usable land, air, water, and fuel, food production would be impossible, of course. In addition, the United States and the Soviet Union are at this moment trying to make treaties that we hope will keep us from destroying all life and the possibility of life if we decide to destroy each other before the fuel runs out.

Literary Analysis
Persuasive Appeal Which words indicate that the author's persuasive appeal is beginning?

Reading Strategy
Distinguishing Between Fact and Opinion Which facts here support the writer's opinion about a sense of decline?

⓳ ◀ **Critical Viewing**
How can respect for wildflowers and other parts of nature improve the quality of human life? **[Speculate]**

20 ▶ Critical Viewing

Answer: The image supports Woolley's vision that people are slowly destroying their environment.

21 Reading Check

Answer: Woolley says that these countries are trying to make treaties that will prevent humankind from destroying the world.

So I would classify the current status that Mrs. Pink mentions as shaky, which makes the outlook for the future—even so near a future as A.D. 2029—uncertain.

An uncertain future is no new thing, of course. The future has always existed only in the imagination, a realm of hope and dread with which we can do little more than play games. But the games sometimes become serious. The Europeans postulated another land across the ocean for centuries and then came and found it. Jules Verne traveled under the sea and to the moon in his mind many years before we could make the machines to catch up with him. If, as we say, Necessity is the mother of Invention, then Desire is the father of Possibility.

Because of man's amazing record of making his dreams come true, I refuse to be pessimistic about the future, despite the frightening aspects of the present. As long as we—both as a race and as a crowd of individuals—retain our capacity for dreaming, we also keep the possibility of doing. And when doing becomes necessary, we invent a means to do so. Especially when we're in danger, as we are now.

Some of our present dangers surely will be around in 2029, for they're part of being human. We're too far from solving poverty, disease, and probably even war to be done with them in another half-century. Collin County probably will still need its courts and its jail—

20 ▲ Critical Viewing How does this image relate to Woolley's vision? **[Connect]**

postulated (päs′ chə lāt′ ed) *v.* claimed

21 Reading Check

What does Woolley say the United States and the Soviet Union are doing "at this moment"?

CUSTOMIZE INSTRUCTION FOR UNIVERSAL ACCESS

For Special Needs Students	For Advanced Readers
Have students work in small groups to list items they would place in a time capsule that will be buried on school grounds and opened in A.D. 2029. What objects, pictures, and printed materials would they use to show students in the future how the present generation lives: food, clothing, shelter, work, transportation, entertainment? If feasible, students may gather the actual materials for their capsules.	Have students imagine that they have been asked to write personal essays on "our current status and what you think the future will hold" for the readers of fifty years in the future. Have them list four wishes for these future readers, modeled on the wishes at the end of Woolley's essay. What do students think these readers will need most for survival and happiness? Why do they think so? Have students share their wishes with the rest of the class.

ASSESS

Answers for p. 498

Review and Assess

1. Some students will take heart from Woolley's optimism. Others may think Woolley is unrealistically optimistic.
2. **(a)** His essay will be removed from a time capsule and read at that time. **(b)** He wants his work to be read in the future.
3. **(a)** Possible responses: Students may cite depletion of fossil fuels, air and water pollution, and overpopulation. **(b)** He thinks poverty, disease, war, and crime will continue.
4. He mentions that Europeans imagined land across the Atlantic Ocean long before it was discovered, and Jules Verne wrote of space travel and submarines long before they became facts.
5. **(a)** He means that all times and places have serious problems and that people tend to remember past times as being better than they actually were.
   (b) Woolley fears that people in the future may minimize the seriousness of problems people are undergoing today.
6. **(a)** Sample response: respect for nature, understanding of history, appreciation of beauty, sense of humor **(b)** Sample explanation: Respect for nature must come first or there will be no life. Understanding of history must come next because this will avoid repeating the mistakes of the past. Appreciation of beauty and a sense of humor are crucial as an incentive to live and keep trying to make the world a safer and better place.

maybe more courts and a newer, stronger jail.

But if my generation and my sons' generation do what we must to prolong the possibility of survival and the likelihood of this being read, most of the problems about which I'm worrying may seem quaint. If so, they'll be replaced by others that will seem as serious to those who gather to open the time capsule as mine do to me. Golden Ages exist only in retrospect, never for those who are trying to cope with them.

So for the beleaguered residents of 2029 I wish four things:

—A deeper understanding of history, to better avoid repeating the errors of the past, for if each generation keeps on inventing its own mistakes, some of the old ones will have to be thrown out.

—A healing of the schism between man and the rest of nature. Our present disrespect for the natural world is our most serious stupidity to date. We must realize that man can't long outlive the other living creatures.

—A wider and more profound appreciation of beauty. Music, poetry, pictures, and stories feed the soul as surely as wheat and meat and rice feed the body, and the soul of America is malnourished.

—A sense of humor. If man ever stops laughing at himself, he can no longer endure life, nor will he have reason to.

beleaguered (bi lē′ gərd) *adj.* worried; tormented

schism (siz′ əm) *n.* division

Review and Assess

Thinking About the Selection

1. **Respond:** Based on Woolley's ideas, do you take a pessimistic or an optimistic view of the future? Why?
2. **(a) Recall:** Why is the author guaranteed an audience in the future? **(b) Infer:** What prompted the author to accept the invitation to write this essay?
3. **(a) Recall:** Name two environmental problems mentioned by the author. **(b) Analyze:** Identify at least two pessimistic signs for the future that Woolley foresees.
4. **Support:** What specific evidence does Woolley offer to support his assertion that human beings have a record of making dreams come true?
5. **(a) Analyze:** What does Woolley mean when he says "Golden Ages exist only in retrospect, never for those who are trying to cope with them"? **(b) Connect:** What does this statement reveal about the author's fears for 2029?
6. **(a) Categorize:** Review the four wishes Woolley makes at the end of his essay, and rank them in order from most important to least important. **(b) Support:** Explain the priorities you have set.

Bryan Woolley

(b. 1937)

Born in Texas, Bryan Woolley has been a teacher, a journalist, and a novelist. His novel *November 22,* about the events in Dallas on the day President John F. Kennedy was assassinated, was praised by *Texas Monthly* as an outstanding book. In 1979, the author wrote "To the Residents of A.D. 2029," addressing his concerns for the present and his hopes for the future.

ASSESSMENT PRACTICE: Reading Comprehension

Make Generalizations (For more practice, see Test Preparation Workbook, p. 32.)

Many tests require students to make generalizations based on a passage. Use the following sample test item to give students practice at this skill.

Amelia watched a video about environmental issues with her class, but her mind was really on the hiking trip she had planned for the weekend. Her goal was to climb the highest mountain in the region. Growing up, she had climbed the hills in the state park every summer. She was ready for the challenge of the mountains.

Which generalization reflects the information in the passage?

A Amelia goes hiking every weekend.
B Amelia cares about preserving the state park.
C Amelia is interested in protecting natural resources.
D Amelia enjoys being outdoors.

Only choice *D* is supported by the text.

Review and Assess

Literary Analysis

Persuasive Appeal

1. What details does Clarke include to make his science-fiction story believable enough to be taken seriously as **persuasive appeal**?
2. Carson creates a fictional place to show many examples of the dangers of pesticides. What effect does this have on her warning?
3. (a) What argument for an optimistic outlook does Woolley use in his writing? (b) What is the effect of his positive outlook?

Comparing Literary Works

4. (a) Using a chart like the one below, compare the **imagery** used in each selection. (b) How does each author's use of imagery strengthen the persuasive appeal?

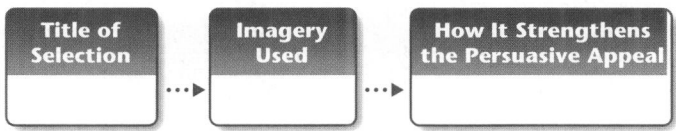

Title of Selection	Imagery Used	How It Strengthens the Persuasive Appeal

5. In your opinion, which selection is most powerful or persuasive? Explain.

Reading Strategy

Distinguishing Between Fact and Opinion

6. Identify one **fact** and one **opinion** mentioned in Clarke's story.
7. (a) What is one opinion expressed in the chapter from *Silent Spring*? (b) Which facts support this opinion?
8. Using a chart like the one below, identify at least two facts and two opinions in Woolley's essay, and explain what makes each a fact or an opinion.

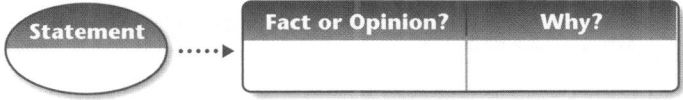

Statement	Fact or Opinion?	Why?

Extend Understanding

9. **Media Link:** Which of the three selections would be the best choice for adaptation as a science-fiction movie? Why?

Quick Review

In all forms of literature, writers may use **persuasive appeals** to warn readers and urge action. The message of such appeals may be stated or implied.

Imagery is the use of descriptive language to create pictures in the reader's mind.

A **fact** is a statement that can be proved, or tested for accuracy.

An **opinion** is a statement of personal preference and cannot be proved.

Take It to the Net

www.phschool.com

Take the interactive self-test online to check your understanding of these selections.

Answers for p. 499

Review and Assess

1. Clarke accurately describes the Moon, provides plausible details on the life-support systems of the Colony, and describes a possible way Earth can be destroyed.
2. A fictional town enables Carson to concentrate many effects of poisoning, intensifying the power of her warning.
3. **(a)** Woolley points out that human beings make their dreams come true. **(b)** Some students may think he is unrealistic; others may be encouraged.
4. Clarke uses visual imagery of the Moon and the glowing Earth to show the enduring devastation of nuclear war. Carson uses images of sight and sound to show the consequences of chemical pollution. Woolley relies less on images and more on assertions to portray contemporary problems.
5. Possible answers: Students may cite the "Silent Spring" excerpt for its serious tone and devastating images.
6. Fact: Marvin did not look back as they began the homeward journey. Opinion: Someday, human beings will return to Earth.
7. **(a)** Sample answer: All life seemed to live in harmony with its surroundings. **(b)** The air and water are clean, The animals are healthy. The plants are thriving.
8. Sample answers: Facts: Mrs. Pink is in charge of the capsule project; humans depend on unrenewable resources. These details can be verified. Opinions: The outlook for the future is uncertain. People will invent the means of preventing danger. These opinions cannot be proven.
9. Sample answer: Clarke's story would make the best movie because it has human characters and a futuristic setting.

ENRICHMENT: Further Reading

Other Works by the Authors

Works by Arthur C. Clarke
The Fountains of Paradise
"The Sentinel"

Works by Rachel Carson
The Sea Around Us

Works by Bryan Woolley
Some Sweet Day

Take It to the Net

Visit www.phschool.com for self-tests and additional questions on the authors.

EXTEND

Answers for p. 500

❶ Vocabulary Development

Word Analysis

1. once every year
2. once every two years
3. once every six months

Spelling Strategy

1. quickly; The electrician quickly identified the problem.
2. catching; At this hour, we have a good chance of catching the train.
3. expectation; His expectation that people would notice his new suit was unfulfilled.
4. warning; Our visitor arrived without warning.

Fluency: Sentence Completion

1. beleaguered, moribund
2. blight, perennial
3. pyre
4. postulated
5. schism
6. purged

❷ Grammar

1. complex; when he was ten
2. compound; but
3. complex; after pesticide was sprayed
4. compound; and
5. complex; if we care about the world

Writing Application

Have students exchange papers with partners and check one another's work. Partners can go over papers together and check for the presence of compound and complex sentences.

Integrate Language Skills

❶ Vocabulary Development Lesson

Word Analysis: Latin Root *-ann-*

The Latin root *-ann-* means "year." The root appears, in modified form, in the word *perennial*, meaning "through the years." Perennial flowers blossom year after year, whereas annual flowers blossom for only one season, then die. Use the meaning of *-ann-* to write the correct definition of each of the following words.

1. annually **2.** biannual **3.** semiannual

Spelling Strategy

When a word ends in two or more consonants, do not double the final consonant before adding a suffix. For example, *blight* + *-ed* = *blighted*. Add each suffix shown below to form a new word. Then, use each new word in a sentence.

1. quick + *-ly*
2. catch + *-ing*
3. expect + *-ation*
4. warn + *-ing*

Fluency: Sentence Completion

On your paper, rewrite the following sentences, filling in each blank with a word from the vocabulary list on page 485.

1. The __?__ politician pleaded with his colleagues to revive the __?__ bill he had proposed.
2. Brown spots on the shrubs warned of a __?__ in the __?__ garden.
3. After his death, the holy man was cremated on a __?__.
4. The police __?__ that the burglar would return.
5. There was a __?__ in the group because some people had different beliefs from the rest of the group.
6. She wished she had __?__ all negativity from her group.

❷ Grammar Lesson

Compound and Complex Sentences

A **compound sentence** consists of two or more independent clauses. The clauses can be joined by a comma and a coordinating conjunction or by a semicolon. A **complex sentence** consists of one independent clause, which can stand by itself, and at least one subordinate clause, which cannot stand by itself as a sentence. In the following examples, the independent clauses are underlined and the subordinate clause is italicized.

Compound sentence: <u>The stars shone</u>, and <u>he remembered an old nursery rhyme</u>.

Complex sentence: *When the stars shone*, <u>he remembered an old nursery rhyme</u>.

Practice Identify each sentence below as *compound* or *complex*. For compound sentences, identify the coordinating conjunction. For complex sentences, identify the subordinate clause.

1. When he was ten, Marvin went outside.
2. He saw Earth, but no one lived there.
3. Life changed after pesticide was sprayed.
4. The animals grew ill, and vegetation died.
5. We must act now if we care about the world.

Writing Application Write a paragraph about one of these selections. Use and identify two compound sentences and two complex sentences in your writing.

WG Prentice Hall Writing and Grammar Connection: Chapter 21, Section 2

TEACHING RESOURCES

The following resources can be used to enrich or extend the instruction for pp. 500–501.

Vocabulary

- **Selection Support:** Build Vocabulary, p. 125
- **Vocabulary and Spelling Practice Book** (Use this booklet for skills enrichment.) ■

Grammar

- **Selection Support,** Build Grammar Skills, p. 126
- **Writing and Grammar,** Gold Level, p. 468
- **Daily Language Practice Transparencies**

Writing

- **Writing and Grammar,** Gold Level, p. 261 ■
- **Writing and Grammar iText CD-ROM**

■ **BLOCK SCHEDULING:** Resources marked with this symbol provide varied instruction during 90-minute blocks.

❸ Writing Lesson

Environmental Report

Rachel Carson's *Silent Spring* had an enormous impact on the way people viewed pest control, due partly to its well-documented facts. Using information from the selections and additional research, prepare a factual report on an environmental issue.

Prewriting Choose an environmental issue of interest to you. Decide which facts from the selections and from your research are the most valuable. Jot these key findings on note cards. Put your cards in an order that makes sense and use your cards to make an outline.

Drafting Write a strong introduction, body, and conclusion for your report. As you write, elaborate with facts and statistics to prove your point.

Model: Elaborating to Prove a Point

In 1995, our town had 35 ducks swimming on Birch Pond. Today, only 8 ducks remain. Why? The answer comes in a single word: pollution.

The author provides an exact year and specific statistics to help prove the point that the waters are polluted.

Revising Reread your draft and add any facts that would strengthen the main point you want to convey.

WG *Prentice Hall Writing and Grammar Connection: Chapter 12, Section 3*

❹ Extension Activities

Listening and Speaking Prepare a **speech** about an environmental issue that concerns you. As you prepare and rehearse your speech, consider these tips:

- Offer strong arguments supported with facts and statistics to help you win over your audience.
- Tell listeners exactly which action you wish them to take.

After delivering the speech, invite your audience to evaluate the effectiveness of your arguments.

Research and Technology Imagine that you are a descendant of Marvin in "If I Forget Thee, Oh Earth. . . ." You and the other members of the Colony are preparing to return to Earth. In a group, research information about the ozone layer. Write a **memo** that gives suggestions to your fellow travelers about ways they can protect Earth when they return. **[Group Activity]**

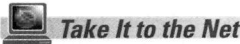

Take It to the Net www.phschool.com

Go online for an additional research activity using the Internet.

Lesson Support for p. 501

❸ Writing Lesson

- Tell students that Rachel Carson focused her book *Silent Spring* on the dangers of pesticides. Remind them to choose one issue, or one aspect of an issue, and make this the focus of their reports.
- As students gather facts and make outlines for their reports, remind them to eliminate material that does not relate to their main idea. Part of the strength of a brief report is the relevance of its details to the main idea.
- Use the Research Report rubric in **Performance Assessment and Portfolio Management,** p. 17, to evaluate students' reports.

❹ Extension Activity

Listening and Speaking

- Encourage students to link this activity to the Writing Lesson described on this page. Students can use information from their reports to write their speeches.
- Remind students to use the opportunity of a speech to urge their listeners to help change things. They should look back over the three selections in this group for models of emotional and logical appeals to an audience.
- Give students a set time limit, such as ten minutes, and require them to keep their speeches within this limit. This exercise will be useful in helping them eliminate all details except the strongest and most relevant ones.
- Have students use the Evaluating a Speech rubric in **Performance Assessment and Portfolio Management,** p. 23.

CUSTOMIZE INSTRUCTION for Universal Access

To address different learning styles, use the following activities suggested in the **Extension Activities** booklet, p. 32.

- For Intrapersonal Learners, use Activity 5.
- For Verbal/Linguistic Learners, use Activities 5–7.
- For Interpersonal Learners, use Activity 6.

ASSESSMENT RESOURCES

The following resources can be used to assess students' knowledge and skills.

Selection Assessment

- **Formal Assessment,** pp. 110–112
- **Open Book Test,** pp. 94–96
- **Got It! Assessment Videotapes,** Tape 3
- **Test Bank Software**

Take It to the Net
Visit www.phschool.com for self-tests and additional questions on the selections.

Writing Rubric

- **Performance Assess. and Portfolio Mgmt.,** p. 17

Listening and Speaking Rubric

- **Performance Assess. and Portfolio Mgmt.,** p. 23

PRENTICE HALL ASSESSMENT SYSTEM

- **Workbook**
- **Transparencies**
- **Skill Book**
- **CD-ROM**

Gifts ✦ Glory and Hope

Lesson Objectives and CA Correlations

1. **To analyze and respond to literary elements**
   - Literary Analysis: Tone **R 3.5**
   - Comparing Literary Works
2. **To read, comprehend, analyze, and critique a poem and a speech**
   - Reading Strategy: Evaluating the Writer's Message **R 3.11**
   - Reading Check questions
   - Review and Assess questions
   - Assessment Practice (ATE)
3. **To develop word analysis skills, fluency, and systematic vocabulary**
   - Vocabulary Development Lesson: Greek Suffix: *-logy* **R 1.1**
4. **To understand and apply written and oral language conventions**
   - Spelling Strategy
   - Grammar Lesson: Parallelism: Clauses **LC 1.1, 1.3**
5. **To understand and apply appropriate writing and research strategies**
   - Writing Lesson: Letter to Nelson Mandela **W 2.4**
   - Extension Activity: Research Report **W 1.5**
6. **To understand and apply listening and speaking strategies**
   - Extension Activity: Panel Discussion **LS 1.8**

STEP-BY-STEP TEACHING GUIDE	PACING GUIDE
PRETEACH	
Motivate Students and Provide Background	
Use the Motivation activity (ATE p. 502)	5 min.
Read and discuss the Preview material and Background information (SE/ATE p. 502) [A]	10 min.
Introduce the Concepts	
Introduce the Literary Analysis and Reading Strategy (SE/ATE p. 503) [A]	15 min.
Pronounce the vocabulary words and read their definitions (SE p. 503)	5 min.
TEACH	
Monitor Comprehension	
Informally monitor comprehension by circulating while students read independently or in groups [A]	15 min.
Monitor students' comprehension with the Reading Check note (SE/ATE p. 507)	as students read
Develop vocabulary with Vocabulary notes (SE pp. 505–507)	as students read
Develop Understanding	
Develop students' understanding of tone with Literary Analysis annotations (SE p. 506; ATE pp. 505, 506) [A]	10 min.
Develop students' ability to evaluate a writer's message with the Reading Strategy annotations (ATE p. 507)	10 min.
ASSESS	
Assess Mastery	
Assess students' mastery of the Reading Strategy and Literary Analysis by having them answer the Review and Assess questions (SE/ATE p. 509)	20 min.
Use one or more of the print and media Assessment Resources (ATE p. 511) [A]	up to 50 min.
EXTEND	
Apply Understanding	
Have students complete the Vocabulary Development Lesson and the Grammar Lesson (SE p. 510) [A]	20 min.
Apply students' knowledge of listing words to describe feelings using the Writing Lesson (SE/ATE p. 511) [A]	45 min.
Apply students' understanding using one or more of the Extension Activities (SE p. 511)	20–90 min.

A **ACCELERATED INSTRUCTION:**
Use the strategies and activities identified with an [A].

UNIVERSAL ACCESS
● = Below-Level Students
▲ = On-Level Students
■ = Above-Level Students

Time and Resource Manager

Reading Level: Easy/Challenging
Average Number of Instructional Days: 4

RESOURCES		
PRINT	**TRANSPARENCIES**	**TECHNOLOGY**
• **Beyond Literature,** Cross-Curricular Connection: Social Studies, p. 33 ▲ ■		• **Interest Grabber Video,** Tape 3 ● ▲ ■
• **Selection Support Workbook:** ● ▲ ■ Literary Analysis, p. 132 Reading Strategy, p. 131 Build Vocabulary, p. 129	• **Literary Analysis and Reading Transparencies,** pp. 65 and 66 ● ▲ ■	
		• **Listening to Literature** ● ▲ ■ Audiocassettes, Sides 14, 15 Audio CDs, CDs 9, 10
• **Literatura en español** ● ▲ • **Literary Analysis for Enrichment** ■		
• **Formal Assessment:** Selection Test, pp. 113–115 ● ▲ ■ • **Open Book Test,** pp. 97–99 ● ▲ ■ • **Performance Assessment and Portfolio Management,** p. 17 ● ▲ ■ • PRENTICE HALL ASSESSMENT SYSTEM ● ▲ ■	• PRENTICE HALL ASSESSMENT SYSTEM ● ▲ ■ Skills Practice Answers and Explanations on Transparencies	• **Test Bank Software** ● ▲ ■ • **Got It! Assessment Videotapes,** Tape 3 ● ▲
• **Selection Support Workbook:** ● ▲ ■ Build Grammar Skills, p. 130 • **Writing and Grammar,** Gold Level ● ▲ ■ • **Extension Activities,** p. 33 ● ▲ ■	• **Daily Language Practice Transparencies** ● ▲ • **Writing Models and Graphic Organizers on Transparencies,** p. 44 ● ▲ ■	• **Writing and Grammar iText CD-ROM** ● ▲ ■ *Take It to the Net* www.phschool.com

BLOCK SCHEDULING: Use one 90-minute class period to preteach the selection and have students read it. Use a second 90-minute class period to assess students' mastery of skills and have them complete one of the Extension Activities.

PREACH

Step-by-Step Teaching Guide for pp. 502–503

Motivation

Today's students may be too young to recall the apartheid system of South Africa or the events in Tiananmen Square in China. Organize students into two groups and assign one topic to each group for research before they read the selections. Share the Background and Enrichment information to start students off. Groups can present the results of their research to the class.

Interest Grabber Video

As an alternative, play "A New South Africa" on Tape 3 to engage student interest.

❶ Background

History

The Dutch began to settle in South Africa during the mid-1600s. A century later, the British began disputing Dutch control of the area. The Afrikaners (the Dutch Africans) and the British fought all-out war for control of the country in the 1880s and again in 1903. British victories led to the 1934 annexation of South Africa as a self-governing state within the British Empire. Afrikaners and British conspired to prevent black South Africans from acquiring any power or privileges.

Apartheid laws categorized all South Africans as either white, black, Asian, or "colored" (meaning "of mixed ancestry"). These groups were to live apart in defined areas and have their own separate political institutions. Intermarriage between races was illegal. Black South Africans were the least privileged of the four groups.

The 1991 repeal of apartheid did not solve South Africa's problems overnight, and some painful legacies remain to be overcome.

Prepare to Read

Gifts ◆ Glory and Hope

Take It to the Net

Visit www.phschool.com for interactive activities and instruction related to the selections, including

- background
- graphic organizers
- literary elements
- reading strategies

Preview

Connecting to the Literature

As you watch the newscast of a demonstration for freedom in a foreign land, you may not feel personally affected. Yet, as these selections show, freedom is a concern shared by people throughout the world.

❶ Background

Apartheid, which means "apartness" in Afrikaans (one of the languages of South Africa), is the policy of segregation and discrimination that was once practiced against nonwhites by the South African government. When apartheid became law in 1948, it affected housing, education, and transportation. In order to help end apartheid, many nations reduced trade with South Africa. Apartheid was finally abolished in 1991.

TEACHING RESOURCES

The following resources can be used to enrich or extend the instruction for pp. 502–503.

Motivation

Interest Grabber Video, Tape 3

Background

Beyond Literature, p. 33 ▪

Take It to the Net

Visit www.phschool.com for background and hotlinks for "Gifts" and "Glory and Hope."

Literary Analysis

Literary Analysis and Reading Transparencies, Tone, p. 65 ▪

Reading

Selection Support: Reading Strategy, p. 131; Build Vocabulary, p. 129

Literary Analysis and Reading Transparencies, Evaluating the Writer's Message, p. 66

▪ **BLOCK SCHEDULING:** Resources marked with this symbol provide varied instruction during 90-minute blocks.

❷ Literary Analysis

Tone

Tone is the attitude a writer takes toward an audience or subject. The tone might be formal or informal, playful or serious. Recognizing the author's word choice is key to understanding the tone of a piece. Consider the formal and hopeful tone of this passage from "Glory and Hope."

> Today, all of us do, by our presence here, and by our celebrations in other parts of our country and the world, confer glory and hope to newborn liberty.

As you read, notice the tone conveyed through the author's word choice.

Comparing Literary Works

You will discover that these selections share a common theme: hope for a peaceful future and freedom for all people. Though the authors represent different lands and people, both writers show concern for peace and freedom for all. While reading, compare the ways that each author expresses his or her hopes, and pay special attention to the tone used to express the theme.

❸ Reading Strategy

Evaluating the Writer's Message

Tone helps convey a writer's message—the idea that he or she wants to communicate. To **evaluate a writer's message,** first identify the message, and then determine whether the message meets these criteria:

- Is it logical, or clearly reasoned-out?
- Is it well-supported, or backed up with facts or personal experience?

You can evaluate a message without necessarily agreeing with it. Use a chart like the one shown to evaluate the writer's message.

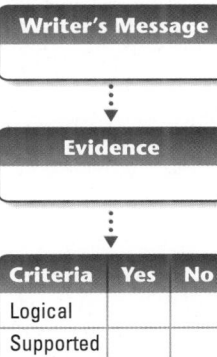

Writer's Message

↓

Evidence

↓

Criteria	Yes	No
Logical		
Supported		

Vocabulary Development

pinions (pin′ yənz) *n.* last bony sections of a bird's wings (p. 505)

hieroglyphics (hī′ ər ō′ glif′ iks) *n.* pictures that represent words or ideas (p. 505)

confer (kən fur′) *v.* to give (p. 506)

pernicious (pər nish′ əs) *adj.* destructive (p. 507)

ideology (ī′ dē äl′ ə jē) *n.* ideas on which a political, economic, or social system is based (p. 507)

chasms (kaz′ əmz) *n.* deep cracks in Earth's surface (p. 507)

covenant (kuv′ ə nənt) *n.* agreement or contract (p. 507)

inalienable (in āl′ yən ə bəl) *adj.* not able to be taken away (p. 507)

CUSTOMIZE INSTRUCTION FOR UNIVERSAL ACCESS

For Less Proficient Readers	For English Learners	For Advanced Readers
To help students hear the tone of Mandela's speech, play the tape or CD of **Listening to Literature.** Or, have a prepared student deliver the speech to the class.	Have students choose partners with whom to read each selection. Partners can help one another with unfamiliar words. Partners can then work together to state each writer's message.	Have students identify the tone of each selection and relate it to the writer's message. Have students write brief essays considering whether the writer might have delivered the same message in a text with a completely different tone.

❷ Literary Analysis

Tone

- Explain that *tone*—the author's attitude—creates *mood*—the emotion invoked in the reader. The dignified, formal tone of the quotation from "Hope and Glory" creates a solemn but joyous mood in the reader.
- Have students try to define the mood each of these selections creates in them. Their answers to this question will help them define and describe the tone of the poem and the speech.

❸ Reading Strategy

Evaluating the Writer's Message

- Explain that a writer's message is his or her main idea, the message that the writer wants readers to remember after they have closed the book. A writer's message is the overriding idea or concept around which a speech, essay, poem, or other work is written.
- Explain that a writer may state a message directly or imply one. Tell students that they will find examples of direct and implied messages in the two selections they are about to read.
- Have students use a graphic organizer like the one on p. 503 to help them evaluate the messages of the two selections.

Vocabulary Development

- Pronounce each vocabulary word for students, and read the definitions as a class. Have students identify any words with which they are already familiar.

E-Teach

Visit E-Teach at www.phschool.com for teachers' essays on how to teach, with questions and answers.

TEACH

Step-by-Step Teaching Guide for pp. 504–508

CUSTOMIZE INSTRUCTION
For Verbal/Linguistic Learners

Have students compare and contrast the effect of parallelism—repetition of grammatical structures—in the two selections. For example, Shu Ting's translator Donald Finkel opens each of the first three stanzas with a matching sentence, while Nelson Mandela begins several paragraphs of his speech with the word "We" followed by a verb. Have students write brief essays analyzing the effect of this technique on the message and tone of each selection.

❶ About the Selection

Using a pond, sunlight, and birds as metaphors, the speaker in this poem celebrates a journey from a troubled past to a bright future.

❷ ▶Critical Viewing

Answer: The photo shows a mirroring effect and displays the beauty nourished by a pond. Students' imagery should support and shed light on their dreams.

❶ Gifts

Shu Ting

Translated by Donald Finkel

❷ ▲ **Critical Viewing** Relate this photograph to the first stanza of the poem. Which image from nature could illustrate your "dream"? **[Connect]**

TEACHING RESOURCES

The following resources can be used to enrich or extend the instruction for pp. 504–508.

Literary Analysis

- **Writing Models and Graphic Organizers on Transparencies,** p. 44 ■
- **Selection Support:** Literary Analysis, p. 132

Reading

- **Listening to Literature Audiocassettes,** Sides 14, 15 ■
- **Listening to Literature Audio CDs,** CDs 9, 10 ■

■ **BLOCK SCHEDULING:** Resources marked with this symbol provide varied instruction during 90-minute blocks.

My dream is the dream of a pond
Not just to mirror the sky
But to let the willows and ferns
Suck me dry.
I'll climb from the roots to the veins,
And when leaves wither and fade
I will refuse to mourn
Because I was dying to live.

My joy is the joy of sunlight.
In a moment of creation
I will leave shining words
In the pupils of children's eyes
Igniting golden flames.
Whenever seedlings sprout
I shall sing a song of green.
I'm so simple I'm profound!

My grief is the grief of birds.
The Spring will understand:
Flying from hardship and failure
To a future of warmth and light.
There my blood-stained pinions
Will scratch hieroglyphics
On every human heart
For every year to come.

Because all that I am
Has been a gift from earth.

pinions (pin′ yənz) *n.* last bony sections of a bird's wings

hieroglyphics (hī′ ər ō′ glif′ iks) *n.* pictures that represent words or ideas

Shu Ting

(b. 1952)

Shu Ting began writing poetry in 1979. While still in her twenties, she gained nationwide fame as a poet.

During the 1980s, Shu Ting became known as one of the "Misty Poets of China." The term derives from a government literary critic's appraisal of an anticommunist poem by poet Gu Chen as "misty." The writings of the Misty Poets have fueled—and continue to inspire—a ceaseless struggle for democracy in China.

Shu Ting uses poetry to express her personal feelings—even though the Communist government of China has condemned such expression as anticommunist.

Review and Assess

Thinking About the Selection

1. **Respond:** Which image in the poem is most powerful? Explain.
2. **(a) Recall:** Which image does the speaker use to express her dream? **(b) Draw Conclusions:** Why does the speaker wish to be sucked dry by the willows and ferns? **(c) Interpret:** What are the seedlings that sprout from the poet's words?
3. **(a) Analyze:** How does the speaker use sunlight as a way of expressing hope? **(b) Interpret:** Why are birds an appropriate image to convey the speaker's grief? **(c) Speculate:** What kind of message do you think will be scratched by the blood-stained pinions?
4. **Apply:** How might the words in "Gifts" inspire people who are fighting for freedom?

❸ Literary Analysis

Tone

- Ask students what tone is projected in lines 7–8. What words convey that tone?
  Answer: The phrase "refuse to mourn" conveys defiance. The phrase "dying to live" conveys determination and endurance. The tone is one of confident dedication.
- Have students describe the mood the second stanza creates in them. Is the mood different from that of the first stanza? How would they describe the tone of this stanza?
  Answer: In contrast to the dark, sacrificial emotions of the first stanza ("dry," "wither," "fade," "dying"), the second stanza exudes joy and hope ("joy," "shining," "golden," "song," "green").

Answers for p. 505

Review and Assess

1. Possible answer: The image of the pond allowing itself to be sucked dry to be free is a powerful expression of determination. The image of the blood-stained feathers scratching messages on human hearts is also potent.
2. **(a)** The speaker dreams of being a pond nourishing willows and ferns. **(b)** The speaker will escape the pond through the plants' root systems. **(c)** The seedlings are implicitly ideas that have been passed on to children.
3. **(a)** Sunlight expresses the speaker's joy and passion, which shine in children's eyes and ignite "flames" of ideas.
   (b) Birds endure hardship in their migrations to "warmth and light"; so, too, will the speaker experience grief to win a better future. **(c)** The pinions will engrave an indelible message about the blood-stained cost of freedom.
4. Others might be inspired by the speaker's determination, passion, and sacrificial spirit.

❹ About the Selection

In the inaugural address given the day he took office, President Nelson Mandela of South Africa leads his listeners from a divided past toward a united future. He urges his listeners to face the challenges that lie ahead with hope and determination.

❺ ▶ Critical Viewing

Answer: Mandela may have felt nervous, proud, vindicated, hopeful, optimistic, or confident.

❻ Literary Analysis

Tone

- Have students evaluate the tone of the opening of Mandela's speech. Have them point to specific words and phrases that create this tone.
  Answer: The tone is formal, dignified, and inspirational. Phrases like "glory and hope," "newborn liberty," and "hopes for a glorious life for all" inspire listeners and readers.

▶ **Monitor Progress** Ask students the Literary Analysis question on p. 506: How does the speaker establish a tone of pride in this passage?
Answer: He speaks of the beauty of his own and his listeners' homeland. This arouses a feeling of patriotism in the audience and conveys Mandela's own sense of national pride.

❹

Glory and Hope

Nelson Mandela

Your majesties, your royal highnesses, distinguished guests, comrades and friends: Today, all of us do, by our presence here, and by our celebrations in other parts of our country and the world, confer glory and hope to newborn liberty.

Out of the experience of an extraordinary human disaster that lasted too long must be born a society of which all humanity will be proud.

❻ Our daily deeds as ordinary South Africans must produce an actual South African reality that will reinforce humanity's belief in justice, strengthen its confidence in the nobility of the human soul and sustain all our hopes for a glorious life for all.

All this we owe both to ourselves and to the peoples of the world who are so well represented here today.

To my compatriots, I have no hesitation in saying that each one of us is as intimately attached to the soil of this beautiful country as are the famous jacaranda trees of Pretoria and the mimosa trees of the bushveld.[1]

1. **bushveld** (bo͝osh´ velt) *n.* South African grassland with abundant shrubs and thorny vegetation.

❺ **▲ Critical Viewing** How do you think Mandela felt when this picture was taken as he presented this speech? **[Interpret]**

confer (kən fur´) *v.* to give

Literary Analysis
Tone How does the speaker establish a tone of pride in this passage?

ENRICHMENT: Social Studies Connection

Era of Freedom

Mandela gave this speech as he was inaugurated president of South Africa, a few years after apartheid ended. Mandela's leadership began a new era of freedom and equality. South African schools began to admit students of all races. Health care ceased to be provided on a racial basis. Imports and exports began to flow freely. South African athletes were allowed to participate in international sporting events.

The changes also brought problems, such as high unemployment and unequal distribution of some services. South Africans struggled though the difficulties of their newly gained freedoms. Now, many South Africans are optimistic about the future.

Each time one of us touches the soil of this land, we feel a sense of personal renewal. The national mood changes as the seasons change.

We are moved by a sense of joy and exhilaration when the grass turns green and the flowers bloom.

That spiritual and physical oneness we all share with this common homeland explains the depth of the pain we all carried in our hearts as we saw our country tear itself apart in terrible conflict, and as we saw it spurned, outlawed and isolated by the peoples of the world, precisely because it has become the universal base of the pernicious ideology and practice of racism and racial oppression.

7 We, the people of South Africa, feel fulfilled that humanity has taken us back into its bosom, that we, who were outlaws not so long ago, have today been given the rare privilege to be host to the nations of the world on our own soil.

We thank all our distinguished international guests for having come to take possession with the people of our country of what is, after all, a common victory for justice, for peace, for human dignity.

We trust that you will continue to stand by us as we tackle the challenges of building peace, prosperity, nonsexism, nonracialism and democracy.

8 We deeply appreciate the role that the masses of our people and their democratic, religious, women, youth, business, traditional and other leaders have played to bring about this conclusion. Not least among them is my Second Deputy President, the Honorable F. W. de Klerk.

We would also like to pay tribute to our security forces, in all their ranks, for the distinguished role they have played in securing our first democratic elections and the transition to democracy, from bloodthirsty forces which still refuse to see the light.

The time for the healing of the wounds has come.

The moment to bridge the chasms that divide us has come.

The time to build is upon us.

We have, at last, achieved our political emancipation. We pledge ourselves to liberate all our people from the continuing bondage of poverty, deprivation, suffering, gender and other discrimination.

We succeeded to take our last steps to freedom in conditions of relative peace. We commit ourselves to the construction of a complete, just and lasting peace.

We have triumphed in the effort to implant hope in the breasts of the millions of our people. We enter into a covenant that we shall build the society in which all South Africans, both black and white, will be able to walk tall, without any fear in their hearts, assured of their inalienable right to human dignity—a rainbow nation at peace with itself and the world.

As a token of its commitment to the renewal of our country, the new Interim Government of National Unity will, as a matter of urgency, address the issue of amnesty for various categories of our people who are currently serving terms of imprisonment.

We dedicate this day to all the heroes and heroines in this country

pernicious (pər nish′ əs) *adj.* destructive

ideology (ī′ dē äl′ ə jē) *n.* ideas on which a political, economic, or social system is based

chasms (kaz′ əmz) *n.* deep cracks in Earth's surface

covenant (kuv′ ə nənt) *n.* agreement or contract

inalienable (in āl′ yən ə bəl) *adj.* not able to be taken away

9 **✓ Reading Check**

Which challenges does South Africa face, according to Mandela?

7 Reading Strategy

Evaluating the Writer's Message

- Have students identify the message Mandela conveys in this section of his speech.
  Answer: Mandela says that all South Africans suffered under apartheid and that he hopes that in the future they will treat one another as equals and work together to build a democratic society.
- Have students evaluate this message. Do they think it is an achievable goal? Why or why not?
  Possible responses: Yes, because many other societies have done this, although sometimes it takes several generations. No, discrimination and poverty will never disappear completely because they are too deeply rooted in society.

8 Background

World History

De Klerk, a member of the formerly ruling white minority, was the president of South Africa from 1989 to 1994. Under his presidency, South Africa underwent an era of reform that culminated in the end of apartheid and the first elections in which people of all races could vote. De Klerk lost the presidency to Mandela in 1994. His participation in Mandela's government was an important contribution to national reconciliation.

9 ✓ Reading Check

Answer: Challenges include poverty, discrimination, and the "bloodthirsty forces" that resist change.

CUSTOMIZE INSTRUCTION FOR UNIVERSAL ACCESS

For Less Proficient Readers	For Gifted/Talented Students
Have students choose partners with whom to read sections of "Glory and Hope" aloud. Students can break the speech up into short sections and alternate sections as they read. They can help one another pronounce difficult words. At the end of each section, partners can summarize what they have read. When partners have fully comprehended the speech, they can work individually to answer the Review and Assess questions on p. 508.	Each student can choose one of these two selections and deliver it aloud to the class. Students should prepare in advance, inviting a small audience to hear them so that they can get some feedback and improve their delivery. Afterwards, have students discuss how hearing the selections read aloud enriched their appreciation of the message of each.

ASSESS

Answers for p. 508

Review and Assess

1. Students may admire Mandela's idealism and the eloquence with which he expresses himself.
2. **(a)** Liberty is newborn.
   (b) "Newborn" creates a sense of freshness and excitement, but it may also suggest incompleteness and vulnerability.
3. **(a)** The reference to chasms suggests that South Africa was deeply divided by racial, gender, and class conflicts. **(b)** Mandela envisions a South Africa in which all citizens will "walk tall" in dignity and without fear.
4. **(a)** The covenant is to create a "rainbow nation at peace with itself and the world."
   (b) Students may cite such ideas as equality, dignity, and peace.
5. **(a)** The title sums up the ideas in the speech. Mandela feels that the present moment is glorious and the future is hopeful.
   (b) Both are positive emotions. Glory is the triumph of actual results, while hope is optimism about future results.
6. Many South Africans may have been impressed by Mandela's ideas and inspired by his eloquence.
7. Possible answer: Perhaps Mandela's greatest challenge is overcoming the racism that had characterized the country for decades.

and the rest of the world who sacrificed in many ways and surrendered their lives so that we could be free.

Their dreams have become reality. Freedom is their reward.

We are both humbled and elevated by the honor and privilege that you, the people of South Africa, have bestowed on us, as the first President of a united, democratic, nonracial and nonsexist South Africa, to lead our country out of the valley of darkness.

We understand it still that there is no easy road to freedom.

We know it well that none of us acting alone can achieve success.

We must therefore act together as a united people, for national reconciliation, for nation building, for the birth of a new world.

Let there be justice for all.

Let there be peace for all.

Let there be work, bread, water and salt for all.

Let each know that for each the body, the mind and the soul have been freed to fulfill themselves.

Never, never and never again shall it be that this beautiful land will again experience the oppression of one by another and suffer the indignity of being the skunk of the world.

The sun shall never set on so glorious a human achievement!

Let freedom reign. God bless Africa!

Review and Assess

Thinking About the Selection

1. **Respond:** What do you admire most about the message in Mandela's speech? Why?
2. (a) **Recall:** According to Mandela, what is "newborn" in South Africa? (b) **Interpret:** Which emotion does the word "newborn" add to his remarks?
3. (a) **Recall:** Citing examples, describe what life was like in the old South Africa. (b) **Draw Conclusions:** Describe the new South Africa that Mandela envisions.
4. (a) **Recall:** What "covenant" does Mandela say the South African people are now entering? (b) **Generalize:** Which ideas in the speech are especially important for safeguarding the human rights of all people throughout today's world?
5. (a) **Connect:** How does the title of the speech connect with the ideas that Mandela conveys? (b) **Compare and Contrast:** What are the similarities and differences between "glory" and "hope"?
6. **Extend:** How do you think the people of South Africa reacted to Mandela's inaugural speech?
7. **Take a Position:** Basing your answer on Mandela's speech, what do you think was the new leader's greatest challenge? Why?

Nelson Mandela

(b. 1918)

Nelson Mandela was born in South Africa, a nation whose white government maintained a strict policy of apartheid, or legal discrimination against blacks. In 1944, Mandela began protesting apartheid. Twenty years later, after several arrests, he was sentenced to life in prison for acts of sabotage.

After twenty-seven years of imprisonment, Mandela was released in 1990. He continued to fight for equal rights for all South Africans. In 1991, apartheid was finally abolished and, in 1993, Mandela and South African president F. W. de Klerk shared the Nobel Peace Prize. The next year, Mandela became the first black man to be elected president of South Africa.

ASSESSMENT PRACTICE: Reading Comprehension

Draw Inferences (For more practice, see Test Preparation Workbook, p. 33.)

Many tests require students to draw inferences from a variety of written texts. Use the following sample test item to give students practice at this skill.

To my compatriots, I have no hesitation in saying that each one of us is as intimately attached to the soil of this beautiful country as are the famous jacaranda trees of Pretoria and the mimosa trees of the bushveld.

Which phrase best describes the feeling that the speaker hopes to create?

A national independence
B national pride
C national outrage
D national hope

Choice *A*, independence, is not a feeling. The evocation of the trees of South Africa will not evoke outrage or hope. Choice *B* is correct.

Review and Assess

Literary Analysis

Tone

1. Using a chart like the one below, analyze the **tone** of "Glory and Hope" and "Gifts."

Title	Memorable Words or Phrases	Tone	Effect of the Tone

2. Given the format of each selection, would you say the tone is appropriate in each case? Explain.

Comparing Literary Works

3. Using a chart like the one below, compare the ways that Shu Ting and Nelson Mandela express hope for a peaceful future.

4. Which selection do you feel does a better job of justifying its optimism for the future? Explain.

Reading Strategy

Evaluating the Writer's Message

5. (a) What is Nelson Mandela's **message**? (b) How does he support his message?
6. Which evidence from your own knowledge or experience would support—or challenge—the validity of Mandela's message?
7. Evaluate Shu Ting's message in "Gifts."

Extend Understanding

8. **Social Studies Connection:** What is currently being done to help oppressed people in other parts of the world attain their human rights and freedom?

Quick Review

Tone is the attitude a writer takes toward an audience or subject.

To **evaluate a writer's message,** decide whether the ideas of the writer are logical and well-supported.

Take It to the Net

www.phschool.com

Take the interactive self-test online to check your understanding of these selections.

ENRICHMENT: Further Reading

Other Works by the Authors

Other Works by Nelson Mandela

Long Walk to Freedom: The Autobiography of Nelson Mandela

Other Works by Shu Ting

Selected Poems

Take It to the Net

Visit www.phschool.com for more information on the authors.

Answers for p. 509

Review and Assess

1. Possible answers: "Gifts": "Flying from hardship and failure/To a future of warmth and light" gives the poem a tone of triumph. This creates a mood of exaltation in the reader. "Glory and Hope": Repetition and parallelism create a formal, dignified tone that ensures the speaker's ideas will be taken seriously.
2. Students may agree that it is appropriate for an inaugural address to express pride and dignity. It is appropriate for a poem to celebrate life and hope.
3. The speaker of "Gifts" hopes for a future of "shining words," "golden flames," and "warmth and light." Mandela expresses hope directly in phrases like "Let freedom reign" and "Let there be peace for all."
4. "Gifts" justifies its optimism with metaphors, which are perhaps not as convincing as Mandela's citations of actual social progress.
5. **(a)** Mandela envisions a society of peace, equality, and democracy. **(b)** He notes how much South Africa has already achieved and expects further progress as a united people.
6. Possible answers: Students may cite racial and social conflicts in this and other countries to support the possibility of change—or the elusiveness of peace and social justice.
7. The speaker's message is that people can achieve their dreams despite costly struggles. Students may find this message valid.
8. Possible answers: Students may cite the work of organizations like the United Nations.

EXTEND

Answers for p. 510

❶ Vocabulary Development

Word Analysis

1. the study of animals
2. the study of human societies
3. the study of life

Spelling Strategy

1. referred
2. inference
3. deferring

Fluency: Sentence Completion

1. confer
2. inalienable
3. pernicious ideology
4. covenant
5. pinions
6. hieroglyphics
7. chasms

❷ Grammar

1. Let there be
2. To be free is a
3. The time to [verb] has come
4. I shall [verb] to [noun]
5. is a privilege

Writing Application

1. Let there be freedom.
2. To be free is a right.
3. The time to repair has come.
4. I shall shout to happiness.
5. Equality is a privilege.

Integrate Language Skills

❶ Vocabulary Development Lesson

Word Analysis: Greek Suffix *-logy*

The Greek suffix *-logy* means "the study, science, or theory of." The suffix appears in the word *ideology,* which means "the study of ideas" or "a set of ideas." Define each of the following words.

1. zoology 2.sociology 3. biology

Spelling Strategy

If a word ends in a single consonant preceded by a single vowel and the last syllable is accented, double the final consonant before adding most endings. For example, *confer* becomes *conferred.* However, do not double the final consonant before adding *-ence,* as in *conference.* (*Occurrence* is an exception to this rule.) For each item, add the suffix shown and write the new word. Then, use each new word in a sentence.

1. refer + *-ed* 2. infer + *-ence* 3. defer + *-ing*

Fluency: Sentence Completion

Identify the word from the vocabulary list on page 503 that correctly completes each sentence below.

1. The general will ___?___ a medal upon the heroic soldier.
2. In a free society, liberty and freedom are ___?___ rights for everyone.
3. A term to describe a destructive system of ideas is a ___?___ ___?___.
4. Once you enter into a ___?___, you are not supposed to back out.
5. The ___?___ on the birds' wings were red with spots of white.
6. The scientist studied the ___?___ that had been scratched into the cave wall.
7. If you should go out walking after an earthquake, do not fall into any ___?___.

❷ Grammar Lesson

Parallelism: Clauses

Parallelism is the repetition of grammatically similar words or groups of words. The parallelism may appear in the form of related **clauses**—groups of words with subjects and verbs—if a clause is presented for the first time, and then its pattern is repeated in subsequent clauses or sentences. Parallelism gives the writing a sense of rhythm, evenness, and structure. Look at this example from "Gifts."

Example: My dream is the dream of a pond.
My joy is the joy of sunlight.
My grief is the grief of birds.

Practice Copy each pair of sentences below. Underline the words that are repeated in order to create parallelism.

1. Let there be justice. Let there be peace.
2. To be free is a gift. To be free is a treasure.
3. The time to heal has come. The time to build has come.
4. I shall sing to life. I shall dance to love.
5. Freedom is a privilege. Life is a privilege.

Writing Application Using the parallelism you have identified, add another sentence to each practice item.

WG Prentice Hall Writing and Grammar Connection: Chapter 21, Section 2

TEACHING RESOURCES

The following resources can be used to enrich or extend the instruction for pp. 510–511.

Vocabulary

- **Selection Support:** Build Vocabulary, p. 129
- **Vocabulary and Spelling Practice Book** (Use this booklet for skills enrichment.) ■

Grammar

- **Selection Support:** Build Grammar Skills, p. 130
- **Writing and Grammar,** Gold Level, p. 468
- **Daily Language Practice Transparencies**

Writing

- **Writing Models and Graphic Organizers on Transparencies,** p. 44 ■
- **Writing and Grammar,** Gold Level, p. 326 ■
- **Writing and Grammar iText CD-ROM**

■ **BLOCK SCHEDULING:** Resources marked with this symbol provide varied instruction during 90-minute blocks.

❸ Writing Lesson

Letter to Nelson Mandela

In his speech "Glory and Hope," Nelson Mandela presents a memorable message about the future of South Africa. Write a letter to Nelson Mandela in which you share the parts of his speech that you found most inspiring.

Prewriting Make a list of words that describe how Mandela's speech makes you feel. Next to each word, write the section of the speech that evoked that particular emotion.

Model: Listing Words to Describe Feelings

Feeling	Example From Speech
hope	The sun shall never set on so glorious a human achievement!

The example from the speech explains the hopeful feeling.

Drafting As you draft, use a friendly yet respectful tone. Your opening paragraph should address your reason for writing. The body of your letter should address your feelings about his speech. In your closing paragraph, sum up the way in which the speech inspired you.

Revising Read your letter to a classmate to make sure that you have maintained a respectful tone throughout your letter.

WG *Prentice Hall Writing and Grammar Connection: Chapter 15, Section 1*

❹ Extension Activities

Listening and Speaking In a group, hold a **panel discussion** on the kind of world you would like to leave to future generations. Keep in mind the human rights issues that Nelson Mandela addresses in "Glory and Hope." Consider these tips:

- Make note cards to use for extemporaneous, or unrehearsed, delivery of your ideas.
- During your discussion, show respect for everyone's opinions and speak in turn.

Afterward, analyze the process to decide how you might improve future discussions. **[Group Activity]**

Research and Technology Write a **research report** about the changes in South Africa since the end of apartheid. Use library resources, including the Internet, to gather information from at least three sources, synthesizing the details and facts you find into your writing. Then, share your report with classmates..

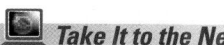

Take It to the Net www.phschool.com

Go online for an additional research activity using the Internet.

ASSESSMENT RESOURCES

The following resources can be used to assess students' knowledge and skills.

Selection Assessment

- **Formal Assessment,** pp. 113–115
- **Open Book Test,** pp. 97–99
- **Got It! Assessment Videotapes,** Tape 2
- **Test Bank Software**

Take It to the Net

Visit www.phschool.com for self-tests and additional questions on "Gifts" and "Glory and Hope."

Writing Rubric

- **Performance Assess. and Portfolio Mgmt.,** p. 17

PRENTICE HALL ASSESSMENT SYSTEM

- **Workbook**
- **Skill Book**
- **Transparencies**
- **CD-ROM**

Lesson Support for p. 511

❸ Writing Lesson

- Encourage students to keep their letters within a two-page limit. You may find it helpful to use the Letter to the Editor model in **Writing Models and Graphic Organizers on Transparencies,** p. 41, to give students a sense of scope and format for their own letters.
- Suggest that students avoid quoting long passages of the speech verbatim; Mandela is familiar with his own speech.

❹ Extension Activity

Research and Technology

- Remind students to consult recent sources. Texts published before 1994 will not contain any information about the transition from apartheid. As always when consulting the Internet, students should choose their sources with care.
- Encourage students to try to locate a variety of viewpoints about apartheid and its abolition. If possible, students should consult at least one source written by a South African who lived under the system.
- Use the rubric for Research Report in **Performance Assessment and Portfolio Management,** p. 17, to evaluate students' reports.

CUSTOMIZE INSTRUCTION for Universal Access

To address different learning styles, use the following activities suggested in the **Extension Activities** booklet, p. 33.

- For Interpersonal Learners, use Activity 5.
- For Verbal/Linguistic Learners, use Activities 5 and 7.
- For Visual/Spatial Learners, use Activity 6.

Lesson Objectives

1. To write a how-to manual
2. To use writing strategies to generate ideas, plan, organize, evaluate, and revise a manual

Prewriting

- Make sure that students choose a topic with which they are familiar. This will make explaining the process easier for students.
- Tell students that narrowing their topic will make writing the manual an easier process. If the scope of their topic is too large, students will have too much information to cover. Similarly, if the scope is too narrow, students will not have enough details to adequately describe the process.
- Tell students that identifying their target audience is an important steps in the prewriting phrase. Students should identify the audience and keep the age and educational level of their audience in mind as they write. This will help determine the language that students use in their manuals.
- Explain to students that the more details they can provide about the process they are describing, the easier it will be for their readers to follow the steps in the process. First, have students make sure they have recorded all the necessary information needed to explain the process adequately. Students may want to add new information or delete anything that is unnecessary.

Writing WORKSHOP

Exposition: How-to Essays

A how-to essay or manual provides detailed step-by-step instructions that tell you how to perform a certain task. In this workshop, you will write a how-to essay on a process you know well.

Assignment Criteria. Your how-to essay should have the following characteristics:

- Specific factual information presented logically and accurately
- Rules of behavior for each particular situation
- Examples and definitions that demonstrate key concepts
- Instructions that anticipate readers' potential mistakes

To preview the criteria on which your how-to essay may be assessed, see the Rubric on page 515.

Prewriting

Choose a topic. Make a calendar of your schedule. For each day of the week, write down your activities. Then, identify an activity from your calendar to describe in a how-to manual. Or, if you prefer, describe another activity with which you are familiar.

Use a target diagram. Once you have chosen an activity to describe in a how-to manual, use the diagram on this page to narrow your topic. In the outer circle, write your general topic. Then, consider the aspect of your topic on which you will focus in your manual; write this in the inner circle. To complete the diagram, write an even narrower topic in the center of the target.

Narrowing Your Topic With a Target Diagram

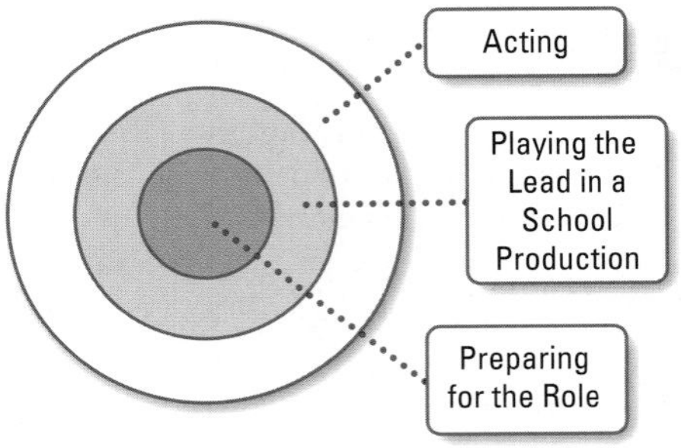

Gather information. As you prepare to draft your how-to manual, remember to provide your reader with all the tools needed to perform the activity you are describing:

- Make a list of materials needed
- Note all the steps involved, in the order in which they occur
- Collect any additional information or hints of use to the reader

TEACHING RESOURCES

The following resources can be used to enrich or extend the instruction for pp. 512–515.

Writing and Grammar, Gold Level, Chapter 4, pp. 228-242

Performance Assessment and Portfolio Management, p. 12

Writing and Grammar iText CD-ROM
Students can use the following tools as they complete their how-to manuals:

- List
- Audience Profile
- Transition

Student Model

Before you begin drafting, read this student model and review the characteristics of effective how-to essays.

numbering sys- allows Carmen ·esent informa- logically.

ffering time ɟestions, the y anticipates ers' questions concerns.

·oration about arching demon- :es the writer's ɟestions.

se ideas offer s of conduct, aining the value ach strategy.

Carmen Rose Viviano-Crafts
Syracuse, NY

Preparing for a Dramatic Role

One of the first challenges of a new dramatic role is the task of memorizing lines. Use the following guidelines to memorize lines more efficiently:

1. Read the entire play at least twice to familiarize yourself with the setting and situations. When performing, it is essential to know what is going on around you in order to provide the appropriate reactions.
2. Highlight or underline all your lines to identify when your character speaks.
3. Begin to concentrate solely on your parts. Look at the script scene by scene, memorizing one or two scenes a day, depending on how much time you have. Reading the lines out loud speeds up the process by making the lines more memorable.
4. Once you feel confident enough, begin to "run" your lines (read them aloud), with another person reading the other characters' lines. This prepares you for being onstage with other actors.
5. When you begin rehearsing with fellow cast members, you will be able to try out different ways of saying things, and you'll start to develop your character. Here are the steps to use when developing a character:
   - If your role is based on a real person, research that person or observe someone in a similar situation. Try to find out as much information as you can so that you can play the part realistically.
   - If you are playing a fictional character, study the script closely. The character's words can tell you about his or her feelings, likes, and dislikes.
   - Once you have learned some aspects of your character, begin to delve into the mind and soul of the person. Make up an entire life story for your character. The more you know about the person, the easier it is to put yourself in his or her place. Think of a past experience to relate to something your character is going through. Bring the emotions you felt in that situation to your character's situation.
   - Finally, conduct general conversations with other cast members, with each of you speaking from your own character's point of view. Ask things like "How do you feel about me?" and "How do you think I feel about you?" This lets you know how you are perceived by the other actors/characters in the play, and allows you to react more realistically.
6. After each rehearsal, consider what worked well and what felt wrong to you. Use your after-rehearsal notes as feedback to improve your performance.

Student Model

- Explain that the Student Model is a sample, and that manuals may be longer.
- Lead students to see that Carmen uses a numbering system to clearly identify the order of the steps in the process she is describing.
- Explain to students that Carmen has also kept her audience in mind as she wrote her manual. Because of this, she was able to anticipate questions and concerns her audience may have as they read the manual.
- Point out that Carmen has provided important details to elaborate specific steps in the process. She is careful to provide her readers with all the necessary information they need to understand and carry out the process described.
- Finally, draw students' attention to the way in which Carmen offers suggestions to help the reader better perform the process, as well as explanations to reinforce the importance of the information she has chosen to include in her manual.

Real-World Connection

Explain to students that there are many instances in their lives in which they will have to explain the steps in a process. At work, for example, they might be required to provide information to coworkers about how to use a particular computer program. At home, they might have to explain to a parent how to use a VCR to record a favorite program.

CUSTOMIZE INSTRUCTION FOR UNIVERSAL ACCESS

For Less Proficient Readers	For English Learners
If students have difficulty choosing a topic, suggest that they brainstorm for a list of activities the enjoy doing (and that lend themselves to a how-to manual). For example, students may want to explain the process of baking their favorite cookies or playing a favorite video game.	If students have trouble deciding on a topic for their manuals, suggest that they choose a favorite activity from their homelands. Make sure that students do not choose a topic that will prove to be overwhelming for students to adequately describe in their manuals.

Drafting

- To help students organize their information, review the four points listed on this page. Explain to students that a well-organized manual will more clearly communicate information to readers.
- As they provide elaboration for the steps in their manuals, remind students to keep their audiences in mind. This will help them decide how much elaboration to provide in order to explain each step in enough detail.
- Tell students that graphic devices, such as photographs and diagrams, can help clarify important details of the process being described. Students should think carefully about places in their manuals that would benefit from visual explanations. Caution students to use these graphics only when necessary.

Revising

- Have students carefully reread their drafts, identifying points in their manuals that require more clarification based on the traits of their audiences. Students should try to put themselves in the place of their readers to address any questions left unanswered or concerns raised in their manuals.
- Review the Student Model with students. Have students describe how the changes Carmen made improve the clarity of her writing.

(continued on page 515)

Drafting

Organize information. Now that you have gathered all the information you want to include in your draft, choose an organization that will make sense to your reader. Chronological, or step-by-step, order is usually best suited to this kind of writing. Use the chart at right to help you organize your information effectively.

Organize Information
1. State the purpose of your technical document.
2. List the materials and conditions necessary to complete the activity.
3. Provide examples to demonstrate the activity.
4. List steps to complete in consecutive order.
5. Suggest solutions to common problems when performing the activity.

Elaborate each stage in a process. Provide information to fully explain each step in the process:

- Explain why each step is important.
- Define terms.
- Include graphics where necessary.

Give thorough descriptions and explanations so your readers can complete the task you describe.

Use graphic devices. Photographs, diagrams, and drawings are a great way to help readers follow an explanation. Create or locate graphics to reinforce your instructions, and place them at the appropriate points in your essay. To work effectively, each graphic must be clear and complete. Each should illustrate a step in the process you are explaining. Finally, a graphic should include labels to make strong connections back to your essay.

Consider formatting techniques. In your how-to essay, lengthy paragraphs may not be the best way to present information. Brief paragraphs, bullets, or numbered lists will help keep your how-to essay clear and easy for readers to manage.

Revising

Revise for clarity. Look over your draft to identify instructions, steps, or information that may be unclear to your reader. Mark these sections and go back to them, rewriting any confusing passages with language that informs in a logical manner.

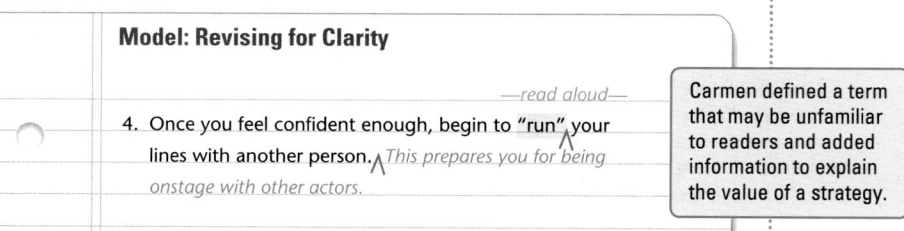

Model: Revising for Clarity

4. Once you feel confident enough, begin to "run" *—read aloud—* your lines with another person. *This prepares you for being onstage with other actors.*

Carmen defined a term that may be unfamiliar to readers and added information to explain the value of a strategy.

USING TECHNOLOGY IN WRITING

If students are using word processors to draft and revise their manuals, suggest that they use the formatting features of the program to help them create visually-appealing manuals. Students can use the automatic numbering and bulleting features to indicate each step in the process they are describing, or use the graphics features to create helpful diagrams and drawings.

Students can also use the organizing tools and revision checkers on the **Writing and Grammar iText CD-ROM.**

Revise for transitions. Look for sections in your draft that need transitional language to connect the steps in your activity. In the following example, adding the words *first* and *then* makes the instruction easier to understand.

Example: Wash the bowl and add the eggs.
First, wash the bowl, and *then* add the eggs.

Compare the model and the nonmodel. Why is the model more effective than the nonmodel?

Nonmodel	Model
Look at the script scene by scene, memorizing one or two scenes a day. Begin to "run" your lines. This prepares you for being onstage with other actors.	Begin to concentrate solely on your parts. Look at the script scene by scene, memorizing one or two scenes a day, depending on how much time you have. Once you feel confident, begin to "run" your lines. This prepares you for being onstage with other actors.

Publishing and Presenting

How-to essays or manuals are meant to be shared. Consider this option for sharing your writing with a wider audience.

Deliver an oral presentation. Prepare and distribute a handout of your draft for your classmates. Give an instructional presentation, providing elaboration if you feel something is unclear. Ask for feedback on the clarity of your how-to manual and presentation. If possible, have a classmate attempt the activity you described in order to gauge the effectiveness of your manual and presentation.

Rubric for Self-Assessment

Evaluate your how-to essay using the following criteria and rating scale:

Criteria	Rating Scale: Not very				Very
Is factual information expressed logically and correctly?	1	2	3	4	5
Are the rules of behavior or action for a specific situation clearly conveyed?	1	2	3	4	5
How well incorporated are examples and definitions that demonstrate concepts?	1	2	3	4	5
How well are readers' mistakes anticipated?	1	2	3	4	5

Revising (continued)

- Tell students that transitional words and phrases help readers follow the correct order of steps in a process.
- Have students suggest transitional words and phrases they can use as they revise their manuals. Refer students to the **Writing and Grammar iText CD-ROM** for helpful transitions.
- Have one volunteer read aloud the nonmodel and then have another volunteer read aloud the model. Ask students to compare the two. Which version do students think is more clear and easier to follow?

Publishing and Presenting

- Before students give their oral presentations, encourage them to practice reading the manuals aloud. Have students make any adjustments to their manuals or jot down notes that will help them improve their presentations.
- Encourage students to think of other options for publishing their manuals. For example, students might post their manuals on a Web site to reach a larger audience.

Assessment

- Review with students the assessment criteria.
- Have students score the Student Model based on all four criteria. Make sure students support their scores with details from the Model.
- The rubric on this page can be found on p. 12 in **Performance Assessment and Portfolio Management.**

TEST-TAKING TIP

When students are taking a test that requires them to explain the steps in a process, they can use an outline to help them organize their information in a logical manner. Each step in the process can be numbered with a Roman numeral. Students can then use capital letters to record any important details that provide elaboration for each of the steps in the process. Using an outline will help students visualize the organization of the information, allowing them to evaluate how well the steps are organized and how well each step is explained in detail.

Lesson Objectives

1. To take notes effectively
2. To learn how to listen carefully by focusing on the speaker's delivery and recognizing barriers to listening
3. To learn how to take notes by determining a speaker's main points and key details that support these points

Listen Carefully

- To help students appreciate the skill of listening, read aloud the information under Listen Carefully to students. Have them close their eyes as they listen. Be sure to add emphasis and vary the tone of your voice as you read.
- Have students identify possible barriers to listening to a speaker in different situations (an auditorium, an outdoor public space, and so on). Then, work with students to devise ways they might overcome these distractions.

Take Notes

- Explain to students that not everyone takes notes in exactly the same way. The kind of notes students will take will often depend on the speaker and the nature of the topic.
- Suggest that students practice taking notes in outline form and in summary form. In an outline, students list the speaker's main ideas and supporting details. A summary is written in paragraph form and also identifies a speaker's main points and supporting details.
- Remind students that they should not concern themselves with recording every word the speaker utters. Students should focus on important words and phrases and abbreviate as much as possible. This will help them pay more attention to what the speaker is saying.

Listening and Speaking WORKSHOP

Effective Listening and Note Taking

Even when they are presenting information to an audience, some people speak very rapidly, leaving you struggling to keep up. The good news is that you can keep up with even the fastest speakers through careful listening. Once you have perfected your listening and note-taking skills, you can use them any time you need to remember something you have heard.

Listen Carefully

Listen to how something is said. Speakers often give you clues to what they consider important. If someone adds emphasis, changes his or her tone of voice, or repeats certain aspects often, then these are points you should capture in your notes.

Recognize barriers to listening. A major barrier to effective listening is the distractions all around you. Make sure to sit in a place that is as close to the speaker as possible, away from side conversations or visual distractions. Try not to let your mind wander—stay focused on what the speaker is saying.

Take Notes

Understand what the speaker is saying. Sometimes, we are too busy with the act of taking notes to think about what the speaker is saying. Focus on the speaker's ideas to decide which points are important and what form your notes should take.

Write main points and key details. You should not try to take down in your notes every word a speaker says. Instead, determine the speaker's main points and capture a few supporting details that illustrate each main point.

Rephrase and rewrite. To save time, try to rephrase the speaker's words using minimal punctuation, partial phrases, and abbreviations wherever possible. Also, the more you can rewrite the information simply, in your own words, the better you will understand it later.

Review your notes. To reinforce what you heard, review your notes as soon as possible after writing them. While your memory is still fresh, add significant details, rewrite confusing notes, and highlight important information.

Activity: Observation and Discussion With other students, watch a video of a television interview. Take notes without stopping the video. Afterward, use your notes to present a summary of the speaker's main points. Use the chart to evaluate and compare notes to see how they differ in length and emphasis.

Note-Taking Evaluation

Rating System
+ = Excellent ✔ = Average – = Weak

Notes:
Organization:
____ Inappropriate ____ Sensible
Coherence:
____ Confusing ____ Clear
Length:
____ Too Long ____ Adequate ____ Too Short

Summaries:
How did your note taking affect your summary?
Did you feel you missed any main points that the other students found?
Did you have any main points that you now feel should be considered supporting details (or vice versa)?

CUSTOMIZE INSTRUCTION FOR UNIVERSAL ACCESS

For English Learners

Students learning English may have difficulty focusing on a speaker's words and taking notes if they encounter unfamiliar words and phrases. Encourage students to keep their attention focused by recording as much they can when listening to a speaker. If a student encounters an unfamiliar word, have them write down the word phonetically. Later, they can use a dictionary to locate the correct spellings and meanings of these words and correct their notes accordingly.

Assessment WORKSHOP

Generalizations

The reading sections of some tests require you to read a passage and answer multiple-choice questions about generalizations. Use the following strategies to help you answer these kinds of test questions:

- Remember that a generalization is a broad statement that can be applied to a variety of situations.
- Generalizations often illustrate a key theme, or lesson, of a passage.
- To make a generalization, list the main points or events in the passage. Then, devise a general principle that applies to all of the items in your list.

Test-Taking Strategies

- Generalizations can be easily recognized when they use signal words such as "in general," "most," "often," and "usually."
- Test a generalization by checking to see whether it can be applied to multiple elements of the passage.

Sample Test Item

Directions: Read the passage, and then answer the question that follows.

When you vote for class president, remember this: If you don't care about class trips or adequate funding, vote for Jessie Smith again. If you want to have more outings and more money, vote for Helen Aquino. Her plans include three fund-raising events and a class outing after each one! Make this year one to remember—vote for Helen Aquino!

1 Which of these statements is a generalization about the passage?

A Class elections are often pointless.
B Political ads try to make opponents look bad.
C A new candidate is always better.
D Most students don't vote.

Answer and Explanation

The correct answer is ***B***. The advertisement characterizes her opponent as uncaring about issues that Aquino considers important. Answers ***A, C,*** and ***D*** may be applicable in other situations, but they do not reflect ideas contained in this specific passage.

Practice

Directions: Read the passage, and then answer the question that follows.

When we moved to this city a month ago, I never expected to have to make so many adjustments. I have had to consult so many transit schedules and I have gotten lost so many times that I am no longer interested in exploring my new surroundings. I also thought I would have some new friends by now.

1 Which generalization applies to the passage?

A Getting lost is part of adjusting to a new city.
B Transit schedules are often complicated.
C It takes a long time to meet people.
D Adjusting to new situations and surroundings can be difficult.

Lesson Objective

To make valid generalizations about a passage

Applying Reading Strategies

Because they are broad statements, generalizations can be valid or invalid. It is up to the students to determine if there is sufficient evidence to support the generalization.

Applying Test-Taking Strategies

- Have students read the Sample Test Passage. Lead students to see that the main point of the passage is to persuade students to vote for Helen instead of Jessie.
- Then, ask students how the passage attempts to persuade students to vote for Helen and not Jessie.
- Have students read each of the possible choices. They should recognize that each one is a generalization, but only one is valid in relation to the passage.
- Because the passage is attempting to persuade students to vote for Helen by making Jessie look like a bad choice, the correct answer is *B*.
- Have students use these same strategies to answer the Practice question on their own.

Answer

The correct answer is *D*. While choices *A, B,* and *C* are valid statements based on the passage, they do not offer the most inclusive statement about the passage. Answer *D* covers all the information mentioned in the passage.

TEACHING RESOURCES

The following resources can be used to enrich or extend the instruction for p. 517.

PRENTICE HALL ASSESSMENT SYSTEM

Workbook | **Transparencies**
Skill Book | **CD-ROM**

Unit Objectives

1. To develop skill in reading short stories
2. To apply a variety of reading strategies appropriate for reading fiction
3. To analyze literary elements
4. To use a variety of strategies to build vocabulary
5. To learn elements of grammar, usage, and style
6. To use recursive writing processes to write in a variety of forms
7. To develop listening and speaking skills
8. To express and support responses to various types of texts
9. To prepare, organize, and present literary interpretations

Meeting the Objectives

With each selection, you will find instructional materials through which students can meet these objectives. Further, you will find additional practice pages for reading strategies, literary analysis, vocabulary, and grammar in the **Selection Support: Skills Development Workbook** in your **Teaching Resources.**

Background

Art

Reading, By Billy Morrow Jackson

Billy Morrow Jackson received his bachelor's degree in Fine Arts from Washington University and his master's from the University of Illinois, where he painted several murals and taught for many years before his retirement in 1987. Jackson paints chiefly in oils and watercolors.

Point out that the young woman reading on the steps is probably sitting in a classroom building. Explain that the painting is full of secrets. Ask students where the secrets might lie.

Answer: The secrets might lie upstairs, downstairs, behind the various doors, or in the young woman's book.

UNIT 6 Short Stories

Reading, 1973, by Billy Morrow Jackson

UNIT FEATURES

Connections	Reading Informational Material
Every unit contains a feature that connects literature to a related topic, such as art, science, or history. In this unit, the Literature and Society feature on p. 534 links a fictional shopping experience in the early 1900s with the modern experience of shopping online. Use the information and questions on the Connections pages to enrich students' understanding of the selections presented within the unit.	These selections will help students learn to analyze and evaluate informational texts, such as workplace documents, technical directions, and consumer materials. They will expose students to the organization and features unique to nonnarrative texts. In this unit, students will analyze the persuasive techniques of advertisements.

Exploring the Genre

A short story is a brief visit to an imaginary world. This world could be nineteenth-century Paris, the American Southwest, or the swamp country of South Carolina. Wherever you travel, you will meet characters who deal with problems that are surprisingly real—for example, how to win someone's love or how to treat a younger brother. As you live through these problems with the characters, you may gain a deeper understanding of the world around you.

Despite their varied content, almost all short stories have the following elements in common:

- **Plot—** the sequence of events that catches your interest and takes you through the story.
- **Characters—** the people, animals, or other beings that take part in the story's action.
- **Setting—** the time and location in which the story takes place.
- **Theme—** the message about life that the story conveys.

This unit highlights the elements of the short story while showing the power and variety of the form.

▲ **Critical Viewing** How does the mood of this painting match your notion of reading? **[Compare]**

Assessing Student Progress

Listed below are the tools that are available to measure the degree to which students meet the unit objectives.

Informal Assessment

The questions in the Review and Assess sections are a first-level response to the concepts and skills presented with the selections. Students' responses provide a brief, informal measure of their grasp of the material. These responses can indicate where further instruction and practice are needed. Follow up with the practice pages in the **Selection Support: Skills Development Workbook**.

Formal Assessment

The **Formal Assessment** booklet contains Selections Tests and Unit Tests.

- Selection Tests measure comprehension and skills acquisition for each selection or group of selections.
- Each Unit Test provides students with thirty multiple-choice questions and five essay questions designed to assess students' knowledge of the literature and skills taught in the unit.

The **Open Book Tests** ask students to demonstrate their ability to synthesize and communicate information from selections or groups of selections.

To assess student writing, you will find rubrics and scoring models in the **Performance Assessment and Portfolio Management** booklet. In this booklet, you will also find scoring rubrics for listening and speaking activities.

Alternative Assessment

The **Extension Activities** booklet contains writing activities, listening and speaking activities, and research and technology activities that are appropriate for students with different ability levels. You may also use these activities as an alternative measure of students' growth.

▶Critical Viewing

Answer: Students may reply that the mood is warm (painted in gold and brown tones), familiar (set inside a school building), and safe (the girl is relaxed and absorbed in her reading). Some students will find this mood familiar in reading situations; others may not have experienced pleasant times absorbed in books.

ASSESSMENT RESOURCES

- Selection Support: Skills Development Workbook
- Formal Assessment
- Open Book Tests
- Performance Assessment and Portfolio Management
- Extension Activities

Why Read Literature?

The "Why Read Literature?" page in each unit presents a list of possible purposes for reading. Each purpose for reading is connected to one or more of the selections in the unit. Good readers set a purpose before reading to help them read actively and focus on meaningful details.

Unit 6 introduces three purposes for reading. "Read for the Love of Literature" invites students to enjoy "The Gift of the Magi," a story that has been treasured for generations. "Read to Appreciate an Author's Style" encourages students to fall under the spell of master storyteller Mark Twain. "Read for Information" offers a unique view into two cultures as well as a look back in time.

How to Use This Page

- Tell students that before reading each selection in this unit, they should set a purpose for reading. This will help them read in an active and focused manner.
- Explain that students can increase their love of literature by discovering the ironic ending in O. Henry's "The Gift of the Magi."
- Point out that Mark Twain's "The Invalid's Story" reflects the humorous, good-natured style of the author.
- As students view "Advertisement for Automobile," encourage them to look for information about American culture in the early 1900s.

Why Read Literature?

Whenever you read fiction, you have a purpose, or reason. You might find the topic interesting or love the characters a certain author creates. Preview three purposes you might set before reading works in this unit.

1 Read for the Love of Literature

We may no longer use pocket watches or sell our hair like the main characters in "The Gift of the Magi." Nevertheless, this story of a couple in love is still widely read and admired today. Find out why generations of people have treasured this simple O. Henry tale when you read **"The Gift of the Magi,"** page 524.

A powerful story may teach a lesson yet still entertain. When a woman sacrifices the financial stability of her household to appear wealthier than she is, you might appreciate the irony of her downfall in Guy de Maupassant's story, **"The Necklace,"** page 608.

2 Read to Appreciate an Author's Style

Some may associate lying in bed with laziness, but Mark Twain found it to be the best position to inspire good writing. Propped up with pillows, Twain would write stories with an informal, humorous style that reflected the good-natured ease of his surroundings. Fall under the spell of a master storyteller as you read Twain's **"The Invalid's Story,"** page 596.

Realism blends with fantasy in Isabel Allende's stories. Enjoy her unique style in the tale of an eccentric uncle who turns his family's town upside down in **"Uncle Marcos,"** page 577.

3 Read for Information

Advertisements can convey a great deal of information about a society and culture at a specific point in time. Place yourself in the shoes of a customer looking for a good automotive deal in 1913 as you scan the **"Advertisement for Automobile,"** page 536.

Stories that examine the intersection of two cultures usually end up revealing something hidden about each one. Native American ritual combines with Catholicism in unexpected ways in Leslie Marmon Silko's **"The Man to Send Rain Clouds,"** page 590.

Take It to the Net

Visit the Web site for online instruction and activities related to each selection in this unit.
www.phschool.com

ENRICHMENT: Further Reading

Have students choose one or more of the works below to read more by the unit authors.

The Adventures of Huckleberry Finn and ***The Adventures of Tom Sawyer*** by Mark Twain

Read these famous tales by America's master storyteller in the **Prentice Hall Literature Library.**

The Best Short Stories of O. Henry by O. Henry, Bennett A. Cerf, and Van H. Cartmell

This collection offers thirty-eight of O. Henry's best short stories, selected from more than 600 written by this prolific author.

The Best Short Stories by Guy de Maupassant

Enjoy selections of one of the best-known short-story writers in the world.

How to Read Literature

Use Strategies for Reading Fiction

Fiction is literature of the imagination. Authors of fiction invent the characters and events that populate their short stories and novels. Fiction can be closely associated with real people and events or it can be entirely fabricated. The following strategies will help you get more out of the fiction you read.

1. Ask questions.

Pause occasionally when reading to jot down two types of questions:

- Basic questions about what is happening in the story.
- Deeper-level questions about characters' motivations or the author's overall message.

2. Draw conclusions.

As soon as you find answers to your questions, you are ready to draw conclusions. Put details together to arrive at an understanding of the story, as the chart at right demonstrates.

- Carefully examine the evidence before drawing a conclusion. For example, look at characters' past actions before you attribute a general habit pattern to them.
- Make sure that your conclusions fit the general theme or tone of the story.

Drawing Conclusions

Character: Madame Loisel in Guy de Maupassant's "The Necklace"	
Details	**Conclusions**
Character's Action	**Reason for the Action**
She cries when she receives invitation to an evening party.	She is afraid she will be ridiculed if she goes to the party.

3. Identify with a character.

If you have ever sympathized with a character you might never have known in real life, you have identified with a character. Here are some tips to help you relate to the characters you encounter as you read:

- Imagine yourself in the character's situation.
- Think about how you might feel or react in that situation.

4. Use your senses.

Many stories are rich with descriptions of sensory details such as sights, sounds, and smells. As you read, make these descriptions come alive.

- Match the descriptions of sights, sounds, smells, and feelings with similar situations that you have personally experienced.
- Use your imagination and the details that the author provides to picture the action in your mind.

As you read the selections in this unit, review the reading strategies and apply them to interact with the text.

How to Read Literature

The "How to Read Literature" page in each unit presents a set of strategies to help readers understand authors' words and ideas. Each reading strategy is taught in conjunction with one or more of the selections within the unit. Good readers develop a bank of strategies from which they can draw as needed.

Unit 6 introduces four strategies for reading fiction. It is important for students to understand the plot and characters in a short story in order to get meaning from it. The strategies on this page help readers go beyond a simple scan of a work of fiction.

How to Use This Page

Introduce the strategies for reading fiction, presenting each as a tool for reading the selections in this unit.

- As they read "The Gift of the Magi" (p. 524), encourage students to ask questions about how the characters' feelings for one another might affect their actions.
- After students find the answers to their questions, they can draw conclusions — conclusions that may surprise them, as in Guy de Maupassant's "The Necklace" (p. 608).
- As students read James Hurst's "The Scarlet Ibis" (p. 554), encourage them to identify with the narrator of the story.
- Students can enjoy the rich sensory details as they read for information in Leslie Marmon Silko's story "The Man to Send Rain Clouds" (p. 590).

MODEL A READING STRATEGY: Draw Conclusions

Explain to students that drawing conclusions can help them put details together to gain an understanding of a story.

Show students how to draw conclusions by asking them to watch for the point at which they suspect an unusual ending in O. Henry's "Gift of the Magi." Encourage them to pay attention to the characters' goals, and how they plan to achieve their goals.

Students may say they begin drawing conclusions about the ending when Jim sees that Della has cut her hair.

Encourage students to use a chart like the one above to record details in the story that can help them draw conclusions.

The Gift of the Magi

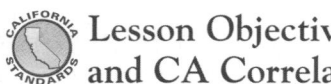

Lesson Objectives and CA Correlations

1. **To analyze and respond to literary elements**
   - Literary Analysis: Plot **R 3.9**
   - Connecting Literary Elements: Surprise Ending **R 3.7**
2. **To read, comprehend, analyze, and critique a short story**
   - Reading Strategy: Asking Questions
   - Reading Check questions
   - Review and Assess questions
   - Assessment Practice (ATE)
3. **To develop word analysis skills, fluency, and systematic vocabulary**
   - Vocabulary Development Lesson: Latin Prefix: *de-* **R 1.1**
4. **To understand and apply written and oral language conventions**
   - Spelling Strategy
   - Grammar Lesson: Adverb Phrases **LC 1.1**
5. **To understand and apply appropriate writing and research strategies**
   - Writing Lesson: Story From Jim's Point of View **W 2.2**
   - Extension Activity: Illustrated Report **W 1.8**
6. **To understand and apply listening and speaking strategies**
   - Extension Activity: Performance **LS 1.9**

STEP-BY-STEP TEACHING GUIDE	PACING GUIDE
PRETEACH	
Motivate Students and Provide Background	
Use the Motivation activity (ATE p. 522)	5 min.
Read and discuss the Preview material and Background information (SE/ATE p. 522) [A]	5 min.
Introduce the Concepts	
Introduce the Literary Analysis and Reading Strategy (SE/ATE p. 523) [A]	15 min.
Pronounce the vocabulary words and read their definitions (SE p. 523)	5 min.
TEACH	
Monitor Comprehension	
Informally monitor comprehension by circulating while students read independently or in groups [A]	20 min.
Monitor students' comprehension with the Reading Check notes (SE/ATE pp. 525, 527, 529)	as students read
Develop vocabulary with Vocabulary notes (SE pp. 526, 527, 529; ATE p. 526)	as students read
Develop Understanding	
Develop students' understanding of plot with Literary Analysis annotations (SE p. 525; ATE pp. 525, 529) [A]	10 min.
Develop students' ability to ask questions with the Reading Strategy annotations (SE p. 525; ATE pp. 525, 529)	10 min.
ASSESS	
Assess Mastery	
Assess students' mastery of the Reading Strategy and Literary Analysis by having them answer the Review and Assess questions (SE/ATE p. 531)	20 min.
Use one or more of the print and media Assessment Resources (ATE p. 533) [A]	up to 50 min.
EXTEND	
Apply Understanding	
Have students complete the Vocabulary Development Lesson and the Grammar Lesson (SE p. 532) [A]	20 min.
Apply students' knowledge of consistency of viewpoint with the Writing Lesson (SE/ATE p. 533) [A]	45 min.
Apply students' understanding using one or more of the Extension Activities (SE p. 533)	20–90 min.

[A] ACCELERATED INSTRUCTION:
Use the strategies and activities identified with an [A].

UNIVERSAL ACCESS
● = Below-Level Students
▲ = On-Level Students
■ = Above-Level Students

Time and Resource Manager

Reading Level: Average
Average Number of Instructional Days: 4

RESOURCES		
PRINT	**TRANSPARENCIES**	**TECHNOLOGY**
• **Beyond Literature,** Cross-Curricular Connection: Math, p. 34 ▲ ■		• **Interest Grabber Video,** Tape 3 ● ▲ ■
• **Selection Support Workbook:** ● ▲ ■ Literary Analysis, p. 136 Reading Strategy, p. 135 Build Vocabulary, p. 133	• **Literary Analysis and Reading Transparencies,** pp. 67 and 68 ● ▲ ■	
• **Adapted Reader's Companion** ● • **Reader's Companion** ●		• **Listening to Literature** ● ▲ ■ Audiocassettes, Side 15 Audio CDs, CD 10
• **English Learner's Companion** ● ▲ • **Literatura en español** ● ▲ • **Literary Analysis for Enrichment** ■		
• **Formal Assessment:** Selection Test, pp. 120–122 ● ▲ ■ • **Open Book Test,** pp. 100–102 ● ▲ ■ • **Performance Assessment and Portfolio Management,** p. 13 ● ▲ ■ • PRENTICE HALL ASSESSMENT SYSTEM ● ▲ ■	• PRENTICE HALL ASSESSMENT SYSTEM ● ▲ ■ Skills Practice Answers and Explanations on Transparencies	• **Test Bank Software** ● ▲ ■ • **Got It! Assessment Videotapes,** Tape 3 ● ▲
• **Selection Support Workbook:** ● ▲ ■ Build Grammar Skills, p. 134 • **Writing and Grammar,** Gold Level ● ▲ ■ • **Extension Activities,** p. 34 ● ▲ ■	• **Daily Language Practice Transparencies** ● ▲ • **Writing Models and Graphic Organizers on Transparencies,** p. 83 ● ▲ ■	• **Writing and Grammar iText CD-ROM** ● ▲ ■ *Take It to the Net* www.phschool.com

BLOCK SCHEDULING: Use one 90-minute class period to preteach the selection and have students read it. Use a second 90-minute class period to assess students' mastery of skills and have them complete one of the Extension Activities.

PRETEACH

Step-by-Step Teaching Guide for pp. 522–523

Motivation

Encourage students to describe unusual gifts they've received. Have them tell how they reacted when they received them. Then, lead a discussion about gifts that at first disappointed them but later took on a special meaning. Tell students that the story they're about to read focuses on some surprising twists relating to a young couple's efforts to find special gifts for each other.

Interest Grabber Video

As an alternative, play "Gift-Giving Traditions" on Tape 3 to engage student interest.

1 Background

History

Explain to students that in order to convert the sums of money in this story to present-day prices, they will have to multiply them by anywhere from 10 to 100. The story is set in New York City in about 1905. In that time and place, a newspaper cost from 1¢ to 3¢, and a ride on the brand-new subway cost 5¢. In 2001, the daily *New York Times* cost 75¢, and the subway fare was $1.50. The monthly rent of many one-room Manhattan apartments was close to 50 times more than the $32 Jim and Della pay.

Prepare to Read

The Gift of the Magi

Wishful Thinking, Peter Szumowski, Private Collection

Take It to the Net

Visit www.phschool.com for interactive activities and instruction related to "The Gift of the Magi," including

- background
- graphic organizers
- literary elements
- reading strategies

Preview

Connecting to the Literature

With excitement, you tear the wrapping paper off a birthday gift, only to be disappointed by the present you uncover. You hide your feelings, remembering it is the thought that counts. Gifts may be either less appropriate or more meaningful than they first appear. In "The Gift of the Magi," a husband and wife discover the problems and joys of giving gifts.

1 Background

In a story that was written years ago, any prices quoted may seem very low. Inflation, the steady increase in the prices of most things, is the reason: It reduces money's purchasing power. In this story, written around 1905, $32 is roughly a month's rent for Della and Jim. Today, for many people, that amount would not cover one week's rent.

TEACHING RESOURCES

The following resources can be used to enrich or extend the instruction for pp. 522–523.

Motivation

Interest Grabber Video, Tape 3: Gift-Giving Traditions

Background

Beyond Literature, p. 34

Take It to the Net

Visit www.phschool.com for background and hotlinks for "The Gift of the Magi."

Literary Analysis

Literary Analysis and Reading Transparencies, Plot, p. 68

Reading

Selection Support: Reading Strategy, p. 135; Build Vocabulary, p. 133

Literary Analysis and Reading Transparencies, Asking Questions, p. 67

BLOCK SCHEDULING: Resources marked with this symbol provide varied instruction during 90-minute blocks.

❷ Literary Analysis

Plot

Plot is the sequence of events that make up a story. Plot is divided into five stages:

- **Exposition**—the scene is set and background information is provided
- **Rising action**—the central conflict, or struggle, is introduced
- **Climax**—the high point of the conflict
- **Falling action**—the conflict lessens
- **Resolution**—the conflict concludes and loose ends get tied up

As you read "The Gift of the Magi," notice how its events apply to the stages of plot development.

Connecting Literary Elements

During the resolution, you learn how a story will end. In "The Gift of the Magi," the resolution reveals a **surprise ending,** a conclusion that differs from the reader's expectations, but in a way that is both logical and believable. As you read, look for clues to the surprise ending.

❸ Reading Strategy

Asking Questions

To fully understand the plot of a story, **ask questions** about characters and events. Ask yourself these kinds of questions while you read:

- Why does a character act in a certain way?
- What does an event really mean?
- Why does the narrator reveal or conceal information?

Use a chart like the one shown to help you as you look for the answers to your questions in the story.

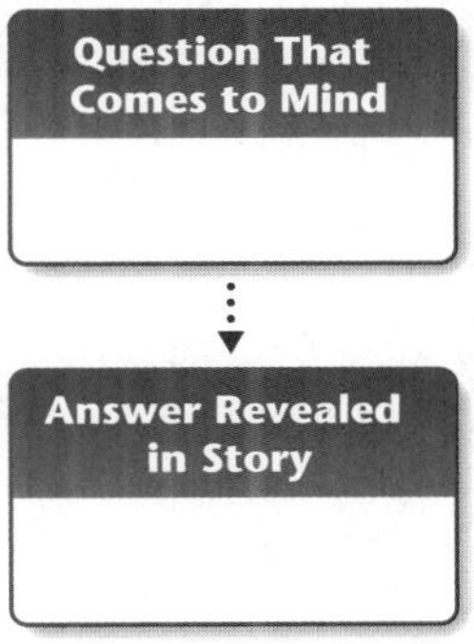

Vocabulary Development

instigates (in′ stə gāts′) *v.* urges on; stirs up (p. 525)

depreciate (dē prē′ shē āt′) *v.* reduce in value (p. 526)

cascade (kas kād′) *n.* waterfall (p. 526)

chaste (chāst) *adj.* pure or clean in style; not ornate (p. 526)

meretricious (mer′ ə trish′ əs) *adj.* attractive in a cheap, flashy way (p. 526)

ravages (rav′ ij iz) *n.* ruins (p. 527)

discreet (di skrēt′) *adj.* tactful; respectful (p. 529)

❷ Literary Analysis

Plot

- Draw this basic plot diagram on the chalkboard and label each part as shown. Discuss these terms and relate the events of the story to the shape of the diagram.

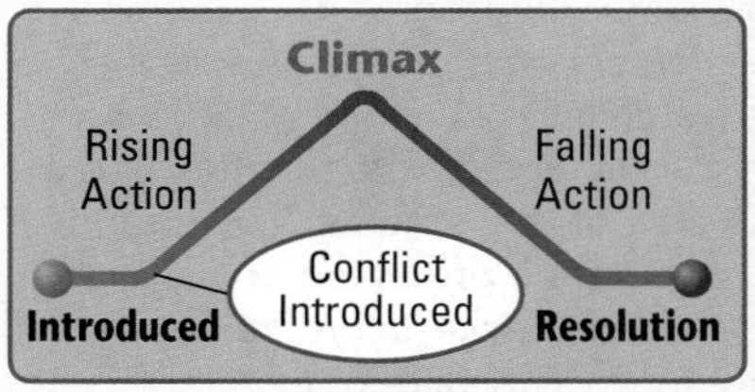

- Point out that although the diagram you just drew is symmetrical, a climax rarely occurs exactly halfway through a story. In detective stories, for example, the climax is the solution of the crime, which usually happens near the story's end.
- For another version of a plot diagram, see the Story Map of p. 83 in **Writing Models and Graphic Organizers on Transparencies.**

❸ Reading Strategy

Asking Questions

- Remind students that asking questions is the best way to find out what they want to know.
- Suggest that students take notes as they read "The Gift of the Magi." As questions occur to them, they can write them down. Then, as they come to passages in the story that answer their questions, they can cross them off the list.

Vocabulary Development

- Pronounce each vocabulary word for students, and read the definitions as a class. Have students identify any words with which they are already familiar.

CUSTOMIZE INSTRUCTION FOR UNIVERSAL ACCESS

For Special Needs Students	For Less Proficient Readers	For English Learners
Have students read the adapted version of "The Gift of the Magi" in the **Adapted Reader's Companion.** This version provides basic-level instruction in an interactive format with questions and write-on lines. Completing the adapted version will prepare students to read the selection in the Student Edition.	Have students read the story in the **Reader's Companion.** This version provides basic-level instruction in an interactive format with questions and write-on lines. After students finish the selection in **Reader's Companion,** have them complete the questions and activities in the Student Edition.	Have students read the adapted version of the story in the **English Learner's Companion.** This version provides basic-level instruction in an interactive format with questions and write-on lines. Completing the adapted version will prepared students to read the selection in the Student Edition.

E-Teach

Visit E-Teach at www.phschool.com for teachers' essays on how to teach, with questions and answers.

TEACH

Step-by-Step Teaching Guide for pp. 524–530

CUSTOMIZE INSTRUCTION for Visual/Spatial Learners

Use the photographs of the ornamental comb on p. 529 and the watch and chain on p. 527 to help students grasp the function and value of these items. The comb is not a mere grooming device but the attractive accessory of a well-coifed woman of Della's time. Similarly, the watch chain or fob is not simply an attaching device but also a significant fashion accessory for a man of Jim's time. Ask students to think of present-day personal accessories that might be as cherished by a modern young man and woman as the chain and comb were prized by Jim and Della.

❶ About the Selection

This classic story of self-sacrificing love—and its ironic consequences—has been a favorite for generations. On Christmas Eve, Della Young has only $1.87 to spend on a gift for her beloved husband Jim—not nearly enough to buy him something special. Impulsively, Della decides to sell her beautiful knee-length brown hair. She buys Jim a platinum chain for his prized gold watch, curls and combs her short hair, and nervously waits for Jim to come home. When he sees her hair, he stops dead in the doorway, then slowly gives her his Christmas gift—a set of ornamental combs for her hair. When she gives him his watch chain, he confesses that he sold the watch to pay for the combs.

The title alludes to the wise men or Magi who brought gifts to the infant Jesus.

① The Gift of the Magi

O. Henry

TEACHING RESOURCES

The following resources can be used to enrich or extend the instruction for pp. 524–530.

Literary Analysis

- **Writing Models and Graphic Organizers on Transparencies,** p. 83 ■
- **Selection Support:** Literary Analysis, p. 136

Reading

- **Reader's Companion**
- **English Learner's Companion**
- **Listening to Literature Audiocassettes,** Side 15 ■
- **Listening to Literature Audio CDs,** CD 10 ■

■ **BLOCK SCHEDULING:** Resources marked with this symbol provide varied instruction during 90-minute blocks.

One dollar and eighty-seven cents. That was all. And sixty cents of it was in pennies. Pennies saved one and two at a time by bulldozing the grocer and the vegetable man and the butcher until one's cheeks burned with the silent imputation of parsimony[1] that such close dealing implied. Three times Della counted it. One dollar and eighty-seven cents. And the next day would be Christmas.

There was clearly nothing to do but flop down on the shabby little couch and howl. So Della did it. Which instigates the moral reflection that life is made up of sobs, sniffles, and smiles, with sniffles predominating.

While the mistress of the home is gradually subsiding from the first stage to the second, take a look at the home. A furnished flat[2] at $8 per week. It did not exactly beggar description,[3] but it certainly had that word on the lookout for the mendicancy squad.[4]

In the vestibule below was a letter-box into which no letter would go, and an electric button from which no mortal finger could coax a ring. Also appertaining thereunto was a card bearing the name "Mr.
2 James Dillingham Young."

The "Dillingham" had been flung to the breeze during a former period of prosperity when its possessor was being paid $30 per week. Now, when the income was shrunk to $20, the letters of "Dillingham" looked blurred, as though they were thinking seriously of contracting to a modest and unassuming D. But whenever Mr. James Dillingham Young came home and reached his flat above he was called "Jim" and greatly hugged by Mrs. James Dillingham Young, already introduced to you as Della. Which is all very good.

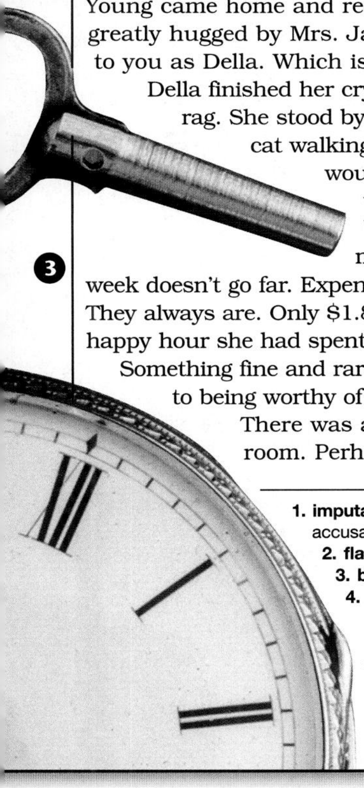

Della finished her cry and attended to her cheeks with the powder rag. She stood by the window and looked out dully at a gray cat walking a gray fence in a gray backyard. Tomorrow would be Christmas Day, and she had only $1.87 with which to buy Jim a present. She had been saving every penny she could for months, with this result. Twenty dollars a
3 week doesn't go far. Expenses had been greater than she had calculated. They always are. Only $1.87 to buy a present for Jim. Her Jim. Many a happy hour she had spent planning for something nice for him. Something fine and rare and sterling—something just a little bit near to being worthy of the honor of being owned by Jim.

There was a pier glass[5] between the windows of the room. Perhaps you have seen a pier glass in an $8 flat.

Reading Strategy
Asking Questions What question might you ask, based on this paragraph?

instigates (in´ stə gāts´) *v.* urges on; stirs up

Literary Analysis
Plot What conflict is introduced at this point?

4 **Reading Check**
How much money does Della have to buy a present for Jim?

1. **imputation** (im pyo͞o tā´ shən) **of parsimony** (pär´ sə mō´ nē) accusation of stinginess.
2. **flat** *n.* apartment.
3. **beggar description** resist description.
4. **it certainly . . . mendicancy** (men´ di kən´ sē) **squad** it would have been noticed by the police who arrested beggars.
5. **pier** (pir) **glass** tall mirror.

2 Reading Strategy
Asking Questions

- Have a volunteer read aloud the bracketed passage. Ask students to write down any questions that come to mind as they hear this passage read.
- Ask the Reading Strategy question on p. 525: What question might you ask, based on this paragraph?
  Possible questions: Why is Della so poor? What does she have to buy for Christmas? For whom does she have to buy it?

Reteach If students can't think of any questions at this point in the story, share the questions you have as a reader. You may need to model your questioning technique several times as the class continues the story.

3 Literary Analysis
Plot

- Challenge students to summarize the situation in one sentence.
  Answer: It is Christmas Eve, and Della doesn't have enough money to buy a present for her husband.
- Ask the Literary Analysis question on p. 525: What conflict is introduced at this point?
  Answer: The conflict is between Della's poverty and her desire to buy something special for Jim.

Monitor Progress Ask students to identify another conflict introduced on this page.
Answer: The first paragraph describes a conflict between Della's desire to save money and her embarrassment at seeming stingy.

4 Reading Check
Answer: Della has $1.87.

CUSTOMIZE INSTRUCTION FOR UNIVERSAL ACCESS

For Gifted/Talented Students	For Advanced Readers
Ask students to recreate this story in a present-day setting. Challenge them to use the same characters involved in the same plot. The only difference: students must substitute new alternatives for Della's cherished hair and Jim's treasured watch. Students might work in groups to think of possessions that might be treasured by a modern couple, and that might lead to the same ironic outcome as in O. Henry's story.	Remind students that plot is only one element of a short story. Have them choose one of the other three elements—character, setting, or theme—and write brief essays analyzing the importance of this element to the story and its relationship to the plot.

❺ Background

History

The wristwatch was invented at around the time of this story, but it was regarded as a woman's accessory until World War I. Since soldiers' uniforms did not provide watch pockets, men's wristwatches became popular during the war years. In O. Henry's day, all men's suits included waistcoats or vests that had watch pockets. Today, the two-piece suit (jacket and trousers only) is more popular. The rise in popularity of the wristwatch and the decline of the waistcoat combined to make the pocket watch a rarity.

❻ Vocabulary Development

Latin Prefix: *de-*

- Write the word *depreciate* on the board and point out that it is based on the Latin word for "price." The prefix *de-* here means "lower." *Depreciate* means "to lower or lessen price or value."
- Tell students that the prefix *de-* has other meanings: "away; off"; "remove"; "lower; down"; and "do the opposite of." Generally, the prefix has a "negative" effect, lowering or undoing the meaning of the root.
- Ask students to think of other words that have the *de-* prefix and write them on the board. Work as a class to provide brief definitions. Possible answers: *derail,* "to go off the track"; *depress,* "to press down"; *decentralize,* "to spread out"; *deflate,* "removed the air from."

A very thin and very agile person may, by observing his reflection in a rapid sequence of longitudinal strips, obtain a fairly accurate conception of his looks. Della, being slender, had mastered the art.

Suddenly she whirled from the window and stood before the glass. Her eyes were shining brilliantly, but her face had lost its color within twenty seconds. Rapidly she pulled down her hair and let it fall to its full length.

Now, there were two possessions of the James Dillingham Youngs in which they both took a mighty pride. One was Jim's gold watch that had been his father's and his grandfather's. The other was Della's hair. Had the Queen of Sheba[6] lived in the flat across the airshaft, Della would have let her hair hang out the window some day to dry just to depreciate Her Majesty's jewels and gifts. ❻ Had King Solomon been the janitor, with all his treasures piled up in the basement, Jim would have pulled out his watch every time he passed, just to see him pluck at his beard from envy.

So now Della's beautiful hair fell about her rippling and shining like a cascade of brown waters. It reached below her knee and made itself almost a garment for her. And then she did it up again nervously and quickly. Once she faltered for a minute and stood still while a tear or two splashed on the worn red carpet.

On went her old brown jacket; on went her old brown hat. With a whirl of skirts and with the brilliant sparkle still in her eyes, she fluttered out the door and down the stairs to the street.

Where she stopped the sign read: "Mme. Sofronie. Hair Goods of All Kinds." One flight up Della ran, and collected herself, panting. Madame, large, too white, chilly, hardly looked the "Sofronie."

"Will you buy my hair?" asked Della.

"I buy hair," said Madame. "Take yer hat off and let's have a sight at the looks of it."

Down rippled the brown cascade.

"Twenty dollars," said Madame, lifting the mass with a practiced hand.

"Give it to me quick," said Della.

Oh, and the next two hours tripped by on rosy wings. Forget the hashed metaphor. She was ransacking the stores for Jim's present.

She found it at last. It surely had been made for Jim and no one else. There was no other like it in any of the stores, and she had turned all of them inside out. It was a platinum fob chain◆ simple and chaste in design, properly proclaiming its value by substance alone and not by meretricious ornamentation—as all good things should do. It was even worthy of The Watch. As soon as she saw it she knew that

Literature in context ❺ Cultural Connection

◆ *Watch Fob Chain*

A fob chain is central to the plot of "The Gift of the Magi." The word *fob* probably entered the English language from the German dialect word *Fuppe,* meaning "pocket." During the nineteenth century, before the wristwatch became common, a man would carry a pocket watch that fit in a special vest pocket. To keep the watch from falling or becoming lost, it was fastened to the vest by means of a strap or chain (sometimes with an ornament, or fob, at the end) that was attached to a pin with a locking clasp, making it quite secure. Sometimes, as pictured at right, a chain had finely detailed metalwork, making it a work of art.

A fob chain was often handed down from father to son, as was Jim Young's in O. Henry's story. This fact alone made it very precious to its owner, despite its modest intrinsic value.

depreciate (dē prē´ shē āt´) *v.* reduce in value

cascade (kas kād´) *n.* waterfall

chaste (chāst) *adj.* pure or clean in style; not ornate

meretricious (mer´ ə trish´ əs) *adj.* attractive in a cheap, flashy way

6. **Queen of Sheba** in the Bible, the beautiful queen who visited King Solomon to test his wisdom.

ENRICHMENT: Literature Connection

A Woman's Sacrifice

Della is not the only famous literary character to sacrifice her hair for love. In Louisa May Alcott's classic *Little Women,* fifteen-year-old Jo March makes the same impulsive decision. When her father falls ill in an army hospital, they must borrow money so that her mother can go to him. Determined to contribute to the fund, Jo sells her abundant chestnut hair for $25. "I'd do it again tomorrow, if I could," she tells her sister that night. "It's only the vain, selfish part of me that goes and cries in this silly way . . . for my one beauty."

Fantine, a luckless waif in Victor Hugo's *Les Misérables,* gets only ten francs for the hair she sells to buy warm clothing for her child. Unknown to her, the child's temporary guardians give the clothing to their own daughter, so that Fantine's sacrifice is made in vain.

it must be Jim's. It was like him. Quietness and value—the description applied to both. Twenty-one dollars they took from her for it, and she hurried home with the 87 cents. With that chain on his watch Jim might be properly anxious about the time in any company. Grand as the watch was he sometimes looked at it on the sly on account of the old leather strap that he used in place of a chain.

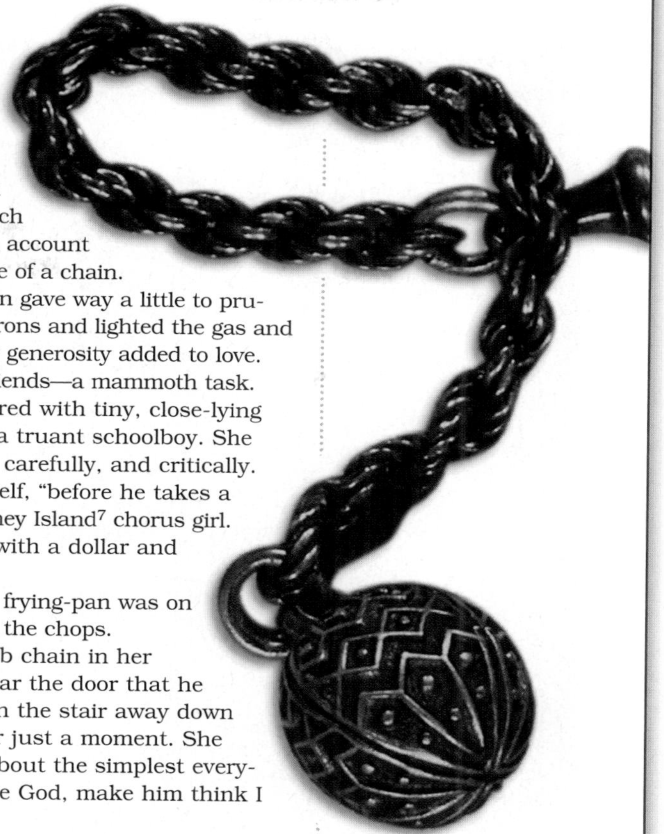

When Della reached home her intoxication gave way a little to prudence and reason. She got out her curling irons and lighted the gas and went to work repairing the ravages made by generosity added to love. Which is always a tremendous task, dear friends—a mammoth task.

Within forty minutes her head was covered with tiny, close-lying curls that made her look wonderfully like a truant schoolboy. She looked at her reflection in the mirror long, carefully, and critically.

"If Jim doesn't kill me," she said to herself, "before he takes a second look at me, he'll say I look like a Coney Island[7] chorus girl. But what could I do—oh! what could I do with a dollar and eighty-seven cents?"

At 7 o'clock the coffee was made and the frying-pan was on the back of the stove hot and ready to cook the chops.

Jim was never late. Della doubled the fob chain in her hand and sat on the corner of the table near the door that he always entered. Then she heard his step on the stair away down on the first flight, and she turned white for just a moment. She had a habit of saying little silent prayers about the simplest everyday things, and now she whispered: "Please God, make him think I am still pretty."

7 The door opened and Jim stepped in and closed it. He looked thin and very serious. Poor fellow, he was only twenty-two—and to be burdened with a family! He needed a new overcoat and he was without gloves.

Jim stopped inside the door, as immovable as a setter at the scent of quail. His eyes were fixed upon Della, and there was an expression in them that she could not read, and it terrified her. It was not anger, nor surprise, nor disapproval, nor horror, nor any of the sentiments that she had been prepared for. He simply stared at her fixedly with that peculiar expression on his face.

Della wriggled off the table and went for him.

"Jim, darling," she cried, "don't look at me that way. I had my hair cut off and sold it because I couldn't have lived through Christmas without giving you a present. It'll grow out again—you won't mind, will you? I just had to do it. My hair grows awfully fast. Say 'Merry Christmas!' Jim, and let's be happy. You don't know what a nice—what a beautiful, nice gift I've got for you."

ravages (rav´ ij iz) *n.* ruins

8 Reading Check

What does Della sell for twenty dollars?

7. **Coney Island** beach and amusement park in Brooklyn, New York.

7 Critical Thinking

Infer

- Ask why Della bought Jim a watch chain when he needs a new coat and a pair of gloves.
  Answer: A coat and gloves are everyday things. Della wanted her gift to be something special that would show Jim how much she loved him.
- What can you infer about Jim from his need of a new coat and gloves?
  Answer: Jim currently lacks money and has been unable to afford new clothing.

8 Reading Check

Answer: Della sells her hair.

CUSTOMIZE INSTRUCTION FOR UNIVERSAL ACCESS

For Special Needs Students

Have students choose any question they asked while reading the story that they were not able to answer. They can discuss their questions with a partner. Have students look back at the story to try and find the answers. Remind them that not all questions readers have are answered in a story; sometimes readers have to answer questions for themselves. After this exercise, students can gather in a group, introduce their questions, and discuss their attempts to find answers. Have students share ideas about their answers to each other's questions. Remind them to keep all answers consistent with the details given in the story.

9 Background

Art

Hairdresser's Window, by John Sloan

John Sloan (1871–1951) was one of a group of young painters known as The Eight. Most had known one another during their student days in Paris and Philadelphia. While they worked toward fame and success, they supported themselves as magazine and newspaper illustrators. Eventually, they gravitated toward New York City.

Sloan and the rest of The Eight did not sentimentalize city life, but painted what they saw in all its liveliness, vividness, and warmth. Their frequent depictions of poor neighborhoods earned them the nickname "Ashcan School."

1. This painting shows New York City at the period of this story. How does it help you understand what Della's everyday life is like?
   Answer: The city is crowded. The colors are drab. There is little privacy. People stare at one another with curiosity rather than sympathy.
2. What details in the picture teach you something about the story's setting?
   Answer: The painting shows the hairstyles and styles of hats and clothing people wore, the prevalence of advertising signs, the mix of businesses in one block, and the atmosphere of a crowded city neighborhood.

10 ▶ Critical Viewing

Possible responses: Della may have felt afraid, nervous, confused, or self-conscious.

9

Hairdresser's Window, 1907, John Sloan, Wadsworth Atheneum, Hartford, Connecticut

10 ▲ **Critical Viewing** How do you think Della felt as she approached Madame Sofronie's shop? **[Analyze]**

ENRICHMENT: History Connection

The Magi

The Magi were an educated class of priests in ancient Persia who served as counselors to the king and who studied medicine and astrology. Magi are mentioned in the Old Testament book of Jeremiah. In the New Testament Gospel of Matthew, Magi appear in Jerusalem seeking the newborn King of the Jews; they explain that they have been guided by a star. In Catholic tradition, the Magi become three kings called Caspar, Melchior, and Balthazar. The Feast of the Three Kings, also known as Epiphany or Twelfth Night, is celebrated on January 6, the day on which the Magi are said to have offered their gifts to the infant Jesus. They brought gold, frankincense (incense used for fumigation), and myrrh (essence used for perfume and embalming).

"You've cut off your hair?" asked Jim, laboriously, as if he had not arrived at that patent fact yet even after the hardest mental labor.

"Cut it off and sold it," said Della. "Don't you like me just as well, anyhow? I'm me without my hair, ain't I?"

Jim looked about the room curiously.

"You say your hair is gone?" he said, with an air almost of idiocy.

"You needn't look for it," said Della. "It's sold, I tell you—sold and gone, too. It's Christmas Eve, boy. Be good to me, for it went for you.
11 Maybe the hairs of my head were numbered," she went on with a sudden serious sweetness, "but nobody could ever count my love for you. Shall I put the chops on, Jim?"

Out of his trance Jim seemed quickly to wake. He enfolded his Della. For ten seconds let us regard with <u>discreet</u> scrutiny some inconsequential object in the other direction. Eight dollars a week or a million a year—what is the difference? A mathematician or a wit would give you the wrong answer. The Magi brought valuable gifts, but that was not among them. This dark assertion will be illuminated later on.

discreet (di skrēt′) *adj.* tactful; respectful

13 ▼ **Critical Viewing** How might Della have felt about an elaborate, expensive comb like this one? **[Connect]**

Jim drew a package from his overcoat pocket and threw it upon the table.

"Don't make any mistake, Dell," he said, "about me. I don't think there's anything in the way of a haircut or a shave or a shampoo that could make me like my girl any less. But if you'll unwrap that package you may see why you had me going a while at first."

White fingers and nimble tore at the string and paper. And then an ecstatic scream of joy; and then, alas! a quick feminine change to hysterical tears and wails, necessitating the immediate employment of all the comforting powers of the lord of the flat.

For there lay The Combs—the set of combs, side and back, that Della had worshipped for long in a Broadway window. Beautiful combs, pure tortoise shell, with jeweled rims—just the shade to wear in the
12 beautiful vanished hair. They were expensive combs, she knew, and her heart had simply craved and yearned over them without the least hope of possession. And now, they were hers, but the tresses that should have adorned the coveted adornments were gone.

But she hugged them to her bosom, and at length she was able to look up with dim eyes and a smile and say: "My hair grows so fast, Jim!"

And then Della leaped up like a little singed cat and cried, "Oh, oh!"

Jim had not yet seen his beautiful present. She held it out to him

14 ✓ **Reading Check** What gift does Jim give to Della?

11 Literary Analysis

Plot and Third-Person Point of View

- Ask students the following question: How does the use of a third-person narrator help to make this scene the story's climax?
  Answer: The narrator doesn't let the reader know what Jim thinks or why he reacts to Della's short haircut as he does. These omissions maximize suspense.

▶ **Monitor Progress** If students feel that this scene is not the climax of the story, challenge them to read on to identify the climax. Urge them to defend their answers with specific evidence from the text.
Answer: Students may feel the climax occurs when Jim gives Della the combs. For these students, this moment in the story is the highest point of interest.

12 Reading Strategy

Asking Questions

- Have students read this paragraph and generate two questions of their own.
  Possible questions: Why didn't Della save money to buy the combs for herself? How did Jim afford the combs?
- If students fail to ask "Where did Jim get the money for the combs?" suggest the question to them. Have students predict the answer to the question before they read on.
  Answer: Students may predict that, like Della, Jim sold something. Since the narrator has already said that the only valuable thing he owns is his watch, he may have sold that.

13 ▶ Critical Viewing

Answer: Della probably would have loved it because it would draw attention to her hair.

14 ✓ Reading Check

Answer: Jim gives her a set of combs for her hair.

CUSTOMIZE INSTRUCTION FOR UNIVERSAL ACCESS

For Gifted/Talented Students

Explain that people sometimes pawn valuable items for ready cash; in 1905, this was much more common than it is today. A pawnbroker would give cash for such items as jewelry, watches, and other personal property and hold them for a time. If the customer was able to raise the money, he or she could redeem the pledge. Della certainly could not have pawned her hair, but Jim might easily have pawned his watch instead of selling it. Have students consider why he did not do this. How would pawning the watch have changed the story? You might point out that Della's hair will grow back, but Jim's watch is gone for good.

O. Henry shows the sale of Della's hair but not the sale of Jim's watch. Ask students to write a short narrative depicting that event.

ASSESS

Answers for p. 530

Review and Assess

1. Possible response: Students would probably say they would feel deeply grateful but also perhaps a little guilty at the loss someone had suffered for their sake.
2. **(a)** They are in love. **(b)** Della always hugs Jim when he comes home. Each of them knows just what the other one wants for Christmas and sacrifices a treasure to purchase that gift.
3. **(a)** Della sells her hair. **(b)** She is generous and self-sacrificing.
4. **(a)** Jim is stunned. **(b)** She is afraid that Jim no longer finds her attractive.
5. **(a)** He has sold his watch. **(b)** He smiles and suggests that they should put their presents away. **(c)** He knows the chain won't be of any use since he no longer has the watch; he smiles at the irony of the situation.
6. Wisdom is understanding that some things are more important than money or coveted gifts: love, generosity, and kindness.
7. Possible responses: Yes, because material possessions are much less important than love. No, because possessions may have more value than an impermanent relationship.

eagerly upon her open palm. The dull precious metal seemed to flash with a reflection of her bright and ardent spirit.

"Isn't it a dandy, Jim? I hunted all over town to find it. You'll have to look at the time a hundred times a day now. Give me your watch. I want to see how it looks on it."

Instead of obeying, Jim tumbled down on the couch and put his hands under the back of his head and smiled.

"Dell," said he, "let's put our Christmas presents away and keep 'em a while. They're too nice to use just at present. I sold the watch to get the money to buy your combs. And now suppose you put the chops on."

The Magi, as you know, were wise men—wonderfully wise men—who brought gifts to the Babe in the manger. They invented the art of giving Christmas presents. Being wise, their gifts were no doubt wise ones, possibly bearing the privilege of exchange in case of duplication. And here I have lamely related to you the uneventful chronicle of two foolish children in a flat who most unwisely sacrificed for each other the greatest treasures of their house. But in a last word to the wise of these days let it be said that of all who give gifts these two were the wisest. Of all who give and receive gifts, such as they are wisest. Everywhere they are wisest. They are the magi.

Review and Assess

Thinking About the Selection

1. **Respond:** If you were Jim or Della, how would you feel about the gift you received?
2. (a) **Recall:** How do Jim and Della feel toward each other? (b) **Support:** What evidence from the story leads you to your opinion?
3. (a) **Recall:** What does Della do to get money for Jim's present? (b) **Infer:** What does her action suggest about her character?
4. (a) **Recall:** How does Jim react when he sees that Della has cut her hair? (b) **Analyze:** Why does Della misunderstand Jim's reaction?
5. (a) **Recall:** How did Jim get the money for Della's gift? (b) **Connect:** How does he react to the watch chain? (c) **Infer:** Why does he react in such a way?
6. **Draw Conclusions:** O. Henry says of these "two foolish children" that they were "the wisest." How do you think he would define wisdom?
7. **Take a Position:** Do you believe it is wise to give up your most treasured possessions to buy something meaningful for a loved one? Why or why not?

O. Henry

(1862–1910)

William Sydney Porter, alias O. Henry, was born in Greensboro, North Carolina, and left school at sixteen to work at his uncle's drugstore. In 1882, he moved to Texas. In Austin he worked at a ranch, a general land office, and then the First National Bank. In Houston, he became a reporter, columnist, and cartoonist for the *Houston Post*.

In 1896, Porter was indicted for embezzling bank funds. He fled to Honduras but returned to Texas when he learned his wife was dying. After her death, Porter was arrested, convicted, and sent to prison in Ohio, where he began writing short stories that made him immensely popular.

Released from prison, he changed his name to O. Henry and moved to New York City. Many of his stories, including "The Gift of the Magi," draw upon his observations of the lives of everyday New Yorkers.

ASSESSMENT PRACTICE: Reading Comprehension

Author's Point of View **(For more practice, see Test Preparation Workbook, p. 34.)**

Many tests require students to recognize an author's point of view. Use this sample test item.

> One dollar and eighty-seven cents. That was all. And sixty cents of it was in pennies. Pennies saved one or two at a time by bulldozing the grocer . . . until one's cheeks burned with the silent imputation of parsimony that such close dealing implied.

The passage suggests that the author views the person saving money with ____.

A contempt
B sympathy
C honor
D pleasure

The author shows the difficulty of saving even such small sums and describes the embarrassment of bargaining. Therefore, *B* is the correct answer.

Review and Assess

Literary Analysis

Plot

1. What is the central conflict, or struggle, in the **plot** of "The Gift of the Magi"?
2. What occurs at the climax, or high point, of the story?
3. Which events form the resolution?
4. The exposition extends to the introduction of the central conflict. Use this graphic organizer to help you describe the remaining stages in the plot of "The Gift of the Magi."

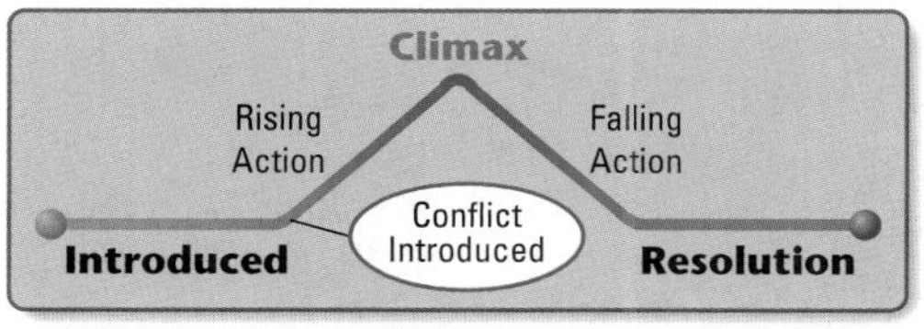

Connecting Literary Elements

5. In what ways was the ending different from what you expected?
6. Look back at the story. Which hints point to the **surprise ending**?
7. Although it was a surprise, did you find the ending logical and believable? Explain.

Reading Strategy

Asking Questions

8. Which **questions** about Della and Jim came to your mind as you read?
9. (a) List three details that the narrator reveals and three that he does not reveal. (b) What is the effect of the narrator's choice of details?

Extend Understanding

10. **History Connection:** This story takes place about a hundred years ago. How might the story—and especially Della and Jim—be different if the story took place today?

Quick Review

Plot is the sequence of events that make up a story. Plot is divided into five stages: **exposition** (the scene is set and background information is provided), **rising action** (the central conflict, or struggle, is introduced), **climax** (the high point of the conflict), **falling action** (the conflict lessens), and **resolution** (the conflict concludes and loose ends get tied up).

A **surprise ending** is a conclusion that differs from what a reader expects.

To fully understand the plot, **ask questions** about characters, events, and information the narrator reveals or conceals.

Take It to the Net

www.phschool.com

Take the interactive self-test online to check your understanding of the selection.

ENRICHMENT: Further Reading

Other Works by O. Henry

"The Last Leaf"
"After Twenty Years"
"A Retrieved Reformation"
The Best Short Stories of O. Henry

Take It to the Net

Visit www.phschool.com for more information on O. Henry.

Answers for p. 531

Review and Assess

1. The central conflict is an external conflict between Della's poverty and her wish to buy a present for her husband.
2. The climax occurs when Della opens Jim's present and sees the coveted combs.
3. The story is resolved when Jim tells Della that he sold his watch; her present is as useless as his.
4. Rising action: Della makes a decision, sells her hair, buys the chain, curls her short hair, waits for Jim, and tells him what she has done. Climax: Jim gives Della the combs. Falling action: She reacts to the combs, they embrace, she gives him the chain. Resolution: Jim reveals that he sold his watch.
5. Most students probably thought that Jim would put his watch on the new chain and that he and Della would admire it together.
6. Hints include the emphasis on Jim and Della's love for one another and Jim's shock that Della's hair has been cut.
7. Since Della sold her treasure to buy something that would help Jim enjoy his treasure more, it is logical and plausible that he did the same for her.
8. Possible questions: How will Jim react when he sees Della with short hair? Will Jim like the chain? What will Jim give Della for Christmas?
9. **(a)** The narrator reveals that Della and Jim are poor, that they are in love, and that Della sells her hair. The narrator does not reveal that Della had longed for the combs, that Jim sold his watch, or how Jim felt about selling his watch. **(b)** The revealed details make readers care about the characters. The concealed details create suspense and make the ending a surprise.
10. Given their poverty, Della would probably have a job. It's no longer possible to walk around the corner and sell one's hair, and pocket watches are rarely worn anymore. A writer using a similar plot today would have to invent two different precious possessions.

EXTEND

Answers for p. 532

❶ Vocabulary Development

Word Analysis

1. b
2. c
3. a

Concept Development: Synonyms

1. g
2. c
3. a
4. b
5. d
6. e
7. f

Spelling Strategy

1. chained
2. hourly
3. kneeling

❷ Grammar

1. in the next flat modifies *lived;* out the window modifies *hang.*
2. on rosy wings modifies *tripped*
3. within forty minutes modifies *covered*
4. at her modifies *stared;* with that peculiar expression modifies *stared*
5. to him modifies *held;* upon her open palm modifies *held*

Writing Application
In addition to underlining the adverb phrases, have students label each sentence as responding to *How? Where?* or *When?* Students can exchange their sentences with partners to check the work.

Integrate Language Skills

❶ Vocabulary Development Lesson

Word Analysis: Latin Prefix *de-*

In "The Gift of the Magi," you will encounter the word *depreciate,* meaning "to reduce in value." This word is derived from a Latin word meaning "price" and contains the Latin prefix *de-*, which in this case means "down." When something *depreciates,* its price goes down. The prefix *de-* can also mean "away from," as in *deviate,* or "undo," as in *defrost.*

Using what you know about the meaning of *de-*, match each phrase shown here with one of the words below.

a. demerit b. derail c. deform

1. run off the tracks
2. undo something's shape
3. grade for poor work

Concept Development: Synonyms

Write the word that is a synonym for, or means the same as, the vocabulary word on the right.

1. instigates	a. waterfall
2. depreciate	b. gaudy
3. cascade	c. cheapen
4. meretricious	d. pure
5. chaste	e. tactful
6. discreet	f. ruins
7. ravages	g. provokes

Spelling Strategy

If a word ends in a single consonant that is preceded by two vowels, do not double the final consonant when you add an ending. Thus, *discreet* + *-ly* = *discreetly*. Add *-ly*, *-ing*, or *-ed* to each word below to form a properly spelled new word.

1. chain 2. hour 3. kneel

❷ Grammar Lesson

Adverb Phrases

An **adverb phrase** is a prepositional phrase that modifies a verb, an adjective, or an adverb. An adverb phrase answers the question *how? in what way? where? when?* or *to what extent?*

In this example, the adverb phrase is italicized.

Example: She let her hair fall *to its full length.* (to what extent did it fall?)

Practice Copy each of these sentences from the story. Underline the adverb phrases, and write the word or words each adverb phrase modifies.

1. Had the Queen of Sheba lived in the next flat across the airshaft, Della would have let her hair hang out the window.
2. The next two hours tripped by on rosy wings.
3. Within forty minutes her head was covered with tiny, close-lying curls.
4. He simply stared at her fixedly with that peculiar expression on his face.
5. She held it out to him eagerly upon her open palm.

Writing Application Write four sentences that contain adverb phrases. Each sentence should include a response to at least one of these questions: *How? Where? When?* Underline the phrases you have included.

WG Prentice Hall Writing and Grammar Connection: Chapter 21, Section 1

532 ◆ Short Stories

TEACHING RESOURCES

The following resources can be used to enrich or extend the instruction for pp. 532–533.

Vocabulary
- **Selection Support:** Build Vocabulary, p. 133
- **Vocabulary and Spelling Practice Book** (Use this booklet for skills enrichment.) ■

Grammar
- **Selection Support:** Build Grammar Skills, p 134
- **Writing and Grammar,** Gold Level, p. 450 ■
- **Daily Language Practice Transparencies**

Writing
- **Writing and Grammar,** Gold Level, p. 78 ■
- **Writing and Grammar iText CD-ROM**

■ **BLOCK SCHEDULING:** Resources marked with this symbol provide varied instruction during 90-minute blocks.

❸ Writing Lesson

Story From Jim's Point of View

As you read "The Gift of the Magi," you learn about the experiences of Della and Jim through a narrator who stands outside the story. Rewrite the story, telling it from Jim's point of view.

Prewriting Review the story and use a chart like the one shown to jot down information that is revealed about Jim. Next to each piece of information, write a sentence from Jim's perspective.

Model: Writing From a First-Person Perspective

Information From the Story	In Jim's Words
They took great pride in Jim's gold watch, which had been passed down to him.	I always cherished this watch, not for the gold, but for the memory of my father.

Drafting Using Jim's words, draft your story. Remember that the entire narrative must be from Jim's perspective. Any information about Della that you include must be from Jim's point of view.

Revising Reread your draft, checking for any inconsistencies in viewpoint. Decide whether Jim would truly know the information you provide. Rewrite any passage that is not written from Jim's perspective.

WG *Prentice Hall Writing and Grammar Connection: Chapter 5, Section 2*

❹ Extension Activities

Listening and Speaking In a small group, prepare a **performance** of "The Gift of the Magi."

- Consider the best approach to take to show the characters and the setting.
- Work out the best way to include the information the narrator provides.
- Decide who will play each part.

If possible, tape your rehearsals for review. Perform the play for your classmates. Invite them to write a brief response. **[Group Activity]**

Research and Technology Prepare an **illustrated report** about life in New York or any other large American city around 1905, when "The Gift of the Magi" was written. Use reference books as well as an Internet search engine to find information and period illustrations. Look especially for pictures of clothing that appears very different from what people wear today.

Take It to the Net www.phschool.com

Go online for an additional research activity using the Internet.

ASSESSMENT RESOURCES

The following resources can be used to assess students' knowledge and skills.

Selection Assessment

- **Formal Assessment,** pp. 120–122
- **Open Book Test,** pp. 100–102
- **Got It! Assessment Videotapes,** Tape 3
- **Test Bank Software**

Take It to the Net

Visit www.phschool.com for self-tests and additional questions on "The Gift of the Magi."

Writing Rubric

- **Performance Assess. and Portfolio Mgmt.,** p. 13

PRENTICE HALL ASSESSMENT SYSTEM

- **Workbook**
- **Transparencies**
- **Skill Book**
- **CD-ROM**

Lesson Support for p. 533

❸ Writing Lesson

- Remind students to avoid including information that Jim cannot know. For instance, Jim may be aware that Della bargains with the grocer to save pennies, but he knows nothing about the sale of her hair or the purchase of the chain.
- Have students consider how Jim spent the day, including the sale of the watch. Remind them that he has a job and would have had to work most of the day.
- Students may want to write their stories in the first person, with Jim as the narrator, or they may want to write from a third-person limited point of view, in which the narrator reveals only Jim's thoughts and feelings.
- Use the Short Story rubric in **Performance Assessment and Portfolio Management,** p. 13, to evaluate students' stories.

❹ Research and Technology

- One good starting point for illustrations is the art of John Sloan (see p. 528). The realistic paintings of this group will give students a good feel for the look and atmosphere of the city at the turn of the nineteenth century.
- If students work on this activity in a group, suggest that they divide the research into different areas of interest. One student can research the city's architecture, another the clothing and hairstyles of the period.

CUSTOMIZE INSTRUCTION For Universal Access

To address different learning styles, use the following activities suggested in the **Extension Activities** booklet, p. 34.

- For Verbal/Linguistic Learners, use Activity 5.
- For Visual/Spatial Learners, use Activities 5 and 7.
- For Logical/Mathematical Learners, use Activity 6.

Lesson Objectives

1. To understand the connection between a fictional shopping experience from one hundred years ago and online shopping experiences today
2. To explore the process of online shopping

Connections

Online shopping is a concept that would have had no meaning in the early 1900s, when "Gift of the Magi" was written. But today, online shopping is becoming more and more popular as a way to save time and money when buying gifts. Have students read "Gift-Giving in the Technological World" after they read "Gift of the Magi." Encourage students to speculate how the story might have differed if online shopping had been available to Della and Jim.

Answers

Connecting Literature and Society

1. Students may answer that, since Della had a limited amount of money to spend, she might get the best buy at an online auction.
2. Online shopping offers a wider selection and saves time and possibly money. A disadvantage of online shopping is the difficulty of assessing the quality of an item without seeing it in person.

CONNECTIONS

Literature and Society

Gift-Giving in the Technological World

In "The Gift of the Magi," Della spends the day before Christmas frantically searching stores for Jim's present. Had she lived in modern times, she could have saved time and trouble by shopping online via the Internet.

Search Engines

Della had no idea which store carried the platinum watch chain she sought. Today, she could use the Internet to locate the store and item. After logging on to the search engine of her choice, she would simply enter the object of her search: "watch-chain store." If her search yielded 500 watch stores in 12 different countries, she might wish to narrow her search further by doing an "AND" search. In this case, she would use the search engine's advanced search screen to add "New York City" to her search terms. The results would list only New York City watch-chain stores, saving Della the cost of travel.

Store Web Sites

If Della already knew of stores that sold watch chains online, she could log on directly to each store's Web site. Sites sometimes include a "Search" box for typing in the name of a particular item. If the watch chain were in stock, Della might even be able to order it online and have it rush-delivered in time for Christmas. However, because online merchants are not likely to accept hair as payment, Della might have to apply for a credit card—another advance in the modern world.

Online Auctions

Della might have saved some money by bidding for her watch chain at an online auction. After logging on to an auction Web site, she would have identified the item she was seeking and found a list of available items. Della could then have bid against other buyers, with the item going to the highest bidder.

Connecting Literature and Society

1. Which method of online shopping do you think would have suited Della's needs best? Why?
2. What are the advantages of shopping online as opposed to shopping the way Della and Jim did? What are the disadvantages?

ENRICHMENT: Social Studies

New York City

New York City, the probable setting for the "Gift of the Magi," has long been a place where very wealthy and very poor people live in close proximity. O. Henry was part of a group of American writers, including Stephen Crane and Theodore Dreiser, who described these extremes. At that time, young women in particular had few job opportunities other than cleaning houses, sewing in sweatshops, or working as shop assistants.

Both differences and similarities exist between the New York City of O. Henry's time and the New York City of today. One difference is that countless jobs and careers are open to today's women. A similarity is that the wealthy and the poor still live and often work side by side.

READING INFORMATIONAL MATERIALS

Advertisements

About Advertisements

An **advertisement** is a message intended to promote a product, a service, or an idea. People use advertisements for many purposes:

- Manufacturers advertise to persuade consumers to buy their goods.
- Companies advertise to create a positive public image of themselves.
- Politicians advertise to win votes.
- Special-interest groups advertise to promote causes they favor.
- Individuals advertise to sell homes, cars, and other property.

You can find advertisements in many places—in newspapers and magazines, on television and radio, on billboards and posters, and in your mail and e-mail.

Reading Strategy

Analyzing Persuasive Techniques: Appeal Through Expertise

Advertisers use many techniques to persuade consumers to buy products. One technique is the **appeal through expertise,** which takes advantage of the average customer's ignorance about the product.

The automobile advertisement on the next page states that the R-C-H automobile has a "semi-floating type" of rear axle. However, there is no explanation of what a semi-floating axle is or why it should be considered a unique and valuable feature. For all you know, every car is made with such an axle. Yet, the phrase sounds impressive. The ad reads as if it were written by experts, and readers might trust it, based solely on the technical language the copywriter uses.

As you read the entire ad, list each feature that it describes. Ask yourself: Is this feature likely to be familiar to customers? If the answer is no, list it in your notebook as an appeal through expertise.

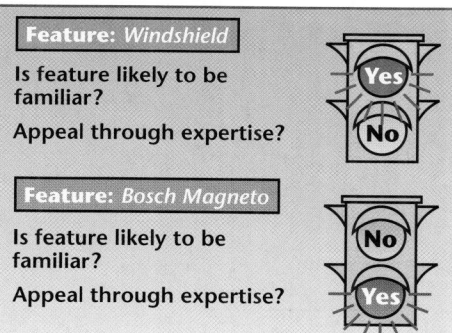

Feature: *Windshield*

Is feature likely to be familiar?

Appeal through expertise?

Feature: *Bosch Magneto*

Is feature likely to be familiar?

Appeal through expertise?

Lesson Objectives

1. To understand the purposes of advertisements.
2. To understand the concept of persuasive techniques
3. To recognize the advertising technique of appealing through expertise

About Advertisements

- Point out that an advertisement is a message and may have one or more purposes.
- Ask a student to read the list of purposes on p. 535 aloud.
- Invite the class to brainstorm for other purposes of advertisements.

Reading Strategy

Analyzing Persuasive Techniques: Appeal Through Expertise

- Ask students to explain what *expertise* means.
  Answer: *Expertise* means "the skill, knowledge, and judgment of an expert."
- Point out that the advertisement's use of the term "semi-floating type" of axle is aimed at demonstrating the company's expertise in car-making.
- Also, point out that just because a company says it has expertise in an area does not necessarily mean the statement is true, or that expertise in this area is unique to this company. Students should double check claims they read in advertisements.
- Point out the two questions students can ask about features on p. 535. Have students answer these questions as they examine the claims of the advertisement on p. 536.

Advertisement for Automobile

- Ask students to step back in time and imagine looking at this advertisement as shoppers who have $900 in the bank.
- Ask students to identify features of the car with which they are not familiar.
  Possible answers: Students might mention long-stroke motor, two-bearing crank shaft, irreversible worm gear, spark and throttle control, semi-floating axles, double parabolic lens, Bosch Magneto.
- Point out that, since students aren't familiar with several features listed, the company is using the "appeal through expertise" advertising technique.
- Explain that wise shoppers would research these features and draw their own conclusions about them.

Advertisement for Automobile

Before 1908, owning an automobile was a luxury. Henry Ford and other manufacturers changed that, producing affordable cars such as the R-C-H "Twenty-Five." The following is an advertisement for the car.

R-C-H Announcement 191
R-C-H "Twenty-Five"
We are determined to build the best all'round five-passenger touring car in the world and sell it, completely equipped, for
$900
The Car
Motor— Long-stroke; 4 cylinders cast en bloc; 3¼ inch bore, 5 inch stroke. Two-bearing crank shaft.
Drive— Left Side. Irreversible worm gear, 16 inch steering wheel. Spark and throttle control on steering column.
Axles— Front, I-beam, drop-forged; rear, semi-floating type.
The Equipment
Non-skid tires—32x3½.
12-inch Bullet electric head lights with double parabolic lens.
Bosch Magneto.
Demountable rims.
Extra rim and holders.
Tally-ho horn.
Jiffy curtains—up or down instantaneously.
R-C-H CORPORATION, 133 Lycaste Street, Detroit, Michi

Including a handsome profile of the car appeals to consumers' desire for status and pride of ownership.

The ad uses the superlative *best* to convince readers that no other car is as good as this one.

Extra suggests that buyers are getting even more than they are paying for.

The words *Jiffy* and *instantaneously* are appealing because they imply the greatest possible speed.

CUSTOMIZE INSTRUCTION FOR UNIVERSAL ACCESS

For English Learners	For Advanced Readers
Explain that the words *tally-ho* and *jiffy* are slang words commonly used one hundred years ago. Ask students to come up with some slang words that they see frequently in advertisements today. They might bring in copies of newspaper or magazine advertisements to share with the class.	Have students use the two questions on p. 535 to identify instances in which the car manufacturer is using the "appeal to expertise" technique of advertising. Then, have students research one or more of the unfamiliar features and share their newly acquired expertise with the class.

Check Your Comprehension

1. How many passengers was the car designed to carry?
2. Which appealing details describe the car's headlights?

Applying the Reading Strategy

Analyzing Persuasive Techniques: Appeal Through Expertise

3. On a separate piece of paper, list each feature described in the ad. Which of those features suggest an appeal through expertise?

Activity

Researching a Product

An appeal through expertise can be effective only if consumers are unfamiliar with the product's advertised features. The best way for consumers to protect themselves is by finding out as much about the product as possible. Then, they can better evaluate the advertisement.

Find a current advertisement for a product. In a chart like the one shown, list the advertised features that may be unfamiliar to many consumers. Then, conduct research using an encyclopedia, owner's manual, Internet Web site, or other resource to learn the function and importance of each feature.

Feature	Function	Importance
crank shaft	controls timing and motion of pistons, which fire to power the engine	significant
convertible top	allows the car's top to be raised and lowered	minor

Comparing Informational Texts

Persuasive Techniques Then and Now

1. Review current advertisements to determine persuasive techniques being used today. Identify examples of (a) slogans or catchy phrases, (b) testimonials, (c) celebrity endorsements, (d) sales or financial incentives, and (e) statistics.
2. Locate newspapers and magazines to find current car advertisements. Compare the ads you find with the one for the R-C-H "Twenty-Five." Use these points of comparison:
   - Analyze the way the ads persuade readers, noting the appealing words and phrases employed in each advertisement.
   - Notice the use of images and fonts to create an impression.

Share your findings with the class.

Answers for p. 537

Check Your Comprehension

1. The car was designed to carry five passengers.
2. The car's headlights are "12-inch Bullet electric" lights with "double parabolic lens."

Applying the Reading Strategy

3. Students should list features that would be unfamiliar to the average consumer. They might mention long-stroke motor, two-bearing crank shaft, irreversible worm gear, spark and throttle control, semi-floating axles, double parabolic lens, and Bosch Magneto.

Activity

- Encourage students to choose a product they would really like to buy. This will help provide incentive for them to learn about the product's features.
- Encourage students to use this research method when making actual purchases in the future.

Comparing Informational Texts

1. When they finish, have students share their findings in small groups and discuss the effectiveness of each.
2. Students may point out that well-positioned photographs, use of brand names, and appeals through expertise are similar. Differences in today's ads may include use of high-tech graphics, contemporary slang words, and special offers.

Sonata for Harp and Bicycle

Lesson Objectives and CA Correlations

1. **To analyze and respond to literary elements**
   - Literary Analysis: Rising Action **R 3.6**
   - Connecting Literary Elements: Climax **R 3.6**
2. **To read, comprehend, analyze, and critique a short story**
   - Reading Strategy: Predicting **R 3.6**
   - Reading Check questions
   - Review and Assess questions
   - Assessment Practice (ATE)
3. **To develop word analysis skills, fluency, and systematic vocabulary**
   - Vocabulary Development Lesson: Words From Myths **R 1.3**
4. **To understand and apply written and oral language conventions**
   - Spelling Strategy
   - Grammar Lesson: Participial Phrases **LC 1.1**
5. **To understand and apply appropriate writing and research strategies**
   - Writing Lesson: Critical Review **W 1.1**
   - Extension Activity: Mystery Timeline **W 1.5**
6. **To understand and apply listening and speaking strategies**
   - Extension Activity: Talk-Show Interview **LS 2.3**

STEP-BY-STEP TEACHING GUIDE	PACING GUIDE
PRETEACH	
Motivate Students and Provide Background	
Use the Motivation activity (ATE p. 538)	5 min.
Read and discuss the Preview material and Background information (SE/ATE p. 538) [A]	5 min.
Introduce the Concepts	
Introduce the Literary Analysis and Reading Strategy (SE/ATE p. 539) [A]	15 min.
Pronounce the vocabulary words and read their definitions (SE p. 539)	5 min.
TEACH	
Monitor Comprehension	
Informally monitor comprehension by circulating while students read independently or in groups [A]	20 min.
Monitor students' comprehension with the Reading Check notes (SE/ATE pp. 541, 543, 545, 547)	as students read
Develop vocabulary with Vocabulary notes (SE pp. 541–544, 546–548; ATE p. 542)	as students read
Develop Understanding	
Develop students' understanding of rising action with the Literary Analysis annotations (SE/ATE pp. 542–544, 546–547) [A]	10 min.
Develop students' ability to make predictions with the Reading Strategy annotations (SE pp. 542, 546; ATE pp. 542–543, 546)	10 min.
ASSESS	
Assess Mastery	
Assess students' mastery of the Reading Strategy and Literary Analysis by having them answer the Review and Assess questions (SE/ATE p. 549)	20 min.
Use one or more of the print and media Assessment Resources (ATE p. 551) [A]	up to 50 min.
EXTEND	
Apply Understanding	
Have students complete the Vocabulary Development Lesson and the Grammar Lesson (SE p. 550) [A]	20 min.
Apply students' knowledge of satisfactory endings using the Writing Lesson (SE/ATE p. 551) [A]	45 min.
Apply students' understanding using one or more of the Extension Activities (SE p. 551)	20–90 min.

[A] **ACCELERATED INSTRUCTION:** Use the strategies and activities identified with an [A].

UNIVERSAL ACCESS
● = Below-Level Students
▲ = On-Level Students
■ = Above-Level Students

Time and Resource Manager

Reading Level: Average
Average Number of Instructional Days: 4

RESOURCES		
PRINT	**TRANSPARENCIES**	**TECHNOLOGY**
• **Beyond Literature,** Cross-Curricular Connection: Music, p. 35 ▲ ■		• **Interest Grabber Video,** Tape 3 ● ▲ ■
• **Selection Support Workbook:** ● ▲ ■ Literary Analysis, p. 140 Reading Strategy, p. 139 Build Vocabulary, p. 137	• **Literary Analysis and Reading Transparencies,** pp. 69 and 70 ● ▲ ■	
		• **Listening to Literature** ● ▲ ■ Audiocassettes, Side 15 Audio CDs, CD 10
• **Literatura en español** ● ▲ • **Literary Analysis for Enrichment** ■		
• **Formal Assessment:** Selection Test, pp. 123–125 ● ▲ ■ • **Open Book Test,** pp. 103–105 ● ▲ ■ • **Performance Assessment and Portfolio Management,** p. 15 ● ▲ ■ • Prentice Hall Assessment System ● ▲ ■	• Prentice Hall Assessment System ● ▲ ■ Skills Practice Answers and Explanations on Transparencies	• **Test Bank Software** ● ▲ ■ • **Got It! Assessment Videotapes,** Tape 3 ● ▲
• **Selection Support Workbook:** ● ▲ ■ Build Grammar Skills, p. 138 • **Writing and Grammar,** Gold Level ● ▲ ■ • **Extension Activities,** p. 35 ● ▲ ■	• **Daily Language Practice Transparencies** ● ▲	• **Writing and Grammar iText CD-ROM** ● ▲ ■ ***Take It to the Net*** www.phschool.com

BLOCK SCHEDULING: Use one 90-minute class period to preteach the selection and have students read it. Use a second 90-minute class period to assess students' mastery of skills and have them complete one of the Extension Activities.

PRETEACH

Step-by-Step Teaching Guide for pp. 538–539

Motivation

Tell students that Aiken's story is about an advertising copywriter who goes to work at a company in which all of the employees are hurried out of the building each evening at five o'clock. The reason for this policy is a secret that employees don't learn until they have been with the company a long time. The copywriter is overwhelmed with curiosity. Challenge students to predict what the secret might be.

Interest Grabber Video

As an alternative, play "True Love" on Tape 3 to engage student interest.

1 Background

Music

The musical structure of a sonata can be compared to a story's plot structure. It begins with an *exposition* (conflict introduced), which introduces a main and a secondary theme. Next comes the *development* (rising action), which freely plays with and spins out the two themes of the exposition until it reaches a climax. The next stage is the *recapitulation* (falling action), which repeats the exposition, often varying it somewhat. The sonata ends with the *coda* (resolution), which is a kind of comment on or summary of the previous stages. The coda is often much shorter than the other three sections.

Prepare to Read

Sonata for Harp and Bicycle

Take It to the Net

Visit www.phschool.com for interactive activities and instruction related to "Sonata for Harp and Bicycle," including

- background
- graphic organizers
- literary elements
- reading strategies

Preview

Connecting to the Literature

Mysteries are everywhere. Some people find safety in ignoring them or simply wondering about them without trying to figure them out. Certain people, however, feel compelled to solve these mysteries—even if danger is involved. In this story, a young man stumbles into a strange situation and tries to get to the bottom of it, come what may.

1 Background

A sonata [sə nät′ ə] is a musical composition in several movements, or parts, for one or more instruments. Sonatas are frequently written for solo piano or for piano and another instrument (such as a harp). In titling her story "Sonata for Harp and Bicycle," Joan Aiken playfully suggests a musical structure that will, like a sequence of chords, be resolved at the end.

TEACHING RESOURCES

The following resources can be used to enrich or extend the instruction for pp. 538–539.

Motivation

Interest Grabber Video, Tape 3: True Love

Background

Beyond Literature, p. 35

Take It to the Net

Visit www.phschool.com for background and hotlinks for "Sonata for Harp and Bicycle."

Literary Analysis

Literary Analysis and Reading Transparencies, Rising Action, p. 70

Reading

Selection Support: Reading Strategy, p. 139; Build Vocabulary, p. 137

Literary Analysis and Reading Transparencies, Predicting, p. 69

BLOCK SCHEDULING: Resources marked with this symbol provide varied instruction during 90-minute blocks.

❷ Literary Analysis

Rising Action

The most suspenseful part of a story is the **rising action**—the part that introduces and develops the main conflict of the plot. The rising action of "Sonata for Harp and Bicycle" includes a complicated, puzzling mystery that fuels suspense as this passage from the story suggests:

> "—fire escape," he heard, as they came into the momentary hush of the carpeted entrance hall. And "—it's to do with a bicycle. A bicycle and a harp."

As you read, watch for the way in which a harp and a bicycle surprisingly converge.

Connecting Literary Elements

The rising action builds until it reaches the **climax,** or high point of interest. The climax is the emotional peak of the story—the moment toward which the plot builds. It is also the point from which the action winds down toward the resolution. As you read, use a chart like this one to record details leading to the climax and to explain the mystery.

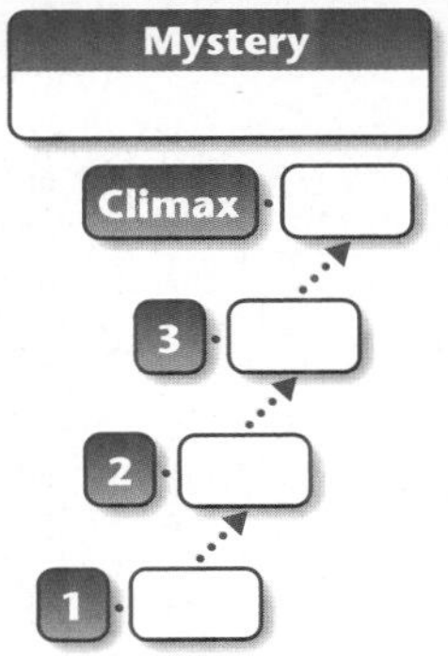

❸ Reading Strategy

Predicting

When you **predict,** you guess what will happen on the basis of what you already know. While reading the story,

- make predictions by looking for clues about future events.
- record each clue you find, along with a prediction of where it will lead.

Revise your predictions as you read, and compare them with what actually happens at the end.

Vocabulary Development

encroaching (en krōch′ iŋ) *adj.* intruding in a sneaking way (p. 541)

tantalizingly (tan′ tə līz′ iŋ lē) *adv.* in a teasing way (p. 542)

furtive (fʉr′ tiv) *adj.* sneaky (p. 543)

menacing (men′ əs iŋ) *v.* threatening (p. 544)

reciprocate (ri sip′ rə kāt) *v.* return (p. 546)

ardent (ärd′ 'nt) *adj.* passionate (p. 546)

gossamer (gäs′ ə mər) *adj.* light, thin, and filmy (p. 546)

preposterous (prē päs′ tər əs) *adj.* absurd (p. 546)

engendered (en jen′ dərd) *adj.* produced (p. 547)

improbably (im präb′ ə blē) *adv.* unlikely to happen (p. 548)

❷ Literary Analysis

Rising Action

- Remind students that rising action is the series of events that begins with the introduction of the conflict and culminates in the climax of a story.
- Tell students that in most mystery stories, the climax is the solution of the mystery, and this usually comes near the end of the story. Since "Sonata for Harp and Bicycle" is a mystery story, students can expect that its climax will be near the end.

❸ Reading Strategy

Predicting

- Remind students that a prediction is not a wild guess; it is an educated guess based on hints and clues in a story.
- Challenge students to pause at the end of every page or two of "Sonata for Harp and Bicycle" to predict what will happen next or what Jason will discover. Use the Predict transparency, p. 69 in **Literary Analysis and Reading Transparencies,** to show students a chart for recording their predictions.

Vocabulary Development

- Pronounce each vocabulary word for students, and read the definitions as a class. Have students identify any words with which they are already familiar.

CUSTOMIZE INSTRUCTION FOR UNIVERSAL ACCESS

For Less Proficient Readers	For English Learners	For Advanced Readers
Encourage students to stop at the end of each page of the story and predict what will happen to Jason on the next page. Have them jot down short notes about the details that spark their predictions. After they read, they can review and assess their predictions.	Some students may be unfamiliar with terms relating to office buildings and the advertising business. Go over such words as *intercom, switchboard, service entrance, copywriter,* and *layout* before students read.	Have students analyze Aiken's use of foreshadowing and relate it to their ability to make accurate predictions about story events.

E-Teach

Visit E-Teach at www.phschool.com for teachers' essays on how to teach, with questions and answers.

TEACH

Step-by-Step Teaching Guide for pp. 540–548

CUSTOMIZE INSTRUCTION
For Musical/Rhythmic Learners

Share the background information on sonata form on p. 538 of this teacher's edition. Have students read to see whether this story is in any sense written in sonata form. You might start them off by pointing out that the story is in three long sections followed by a final short paragraph, and have them compare this to a sonata's exposition, development, recapitulation, and coda. Remind students that *theme* is both a musical and a literary term.

❶ About the Selection

This intriguing story combines the elements of mystery, romance, and the supernatural—with a wink at Greek mythology included. A hero challenges the absurd rules of his office and the fears of his co-workers by entering the office building after dark—a forbidden act. He uses his problem-solving skills to rid the building of two ghosts and to ensure a triumph for love. Students will enjoy the skill with which Aiken uses visual and musical imagery to build suspense, as well as the touches of humor that lighten this modern-day ghost story.

TEACHING RESOURCES

The following resources can be used to enrich or extend the instruction for pp. 540–548.

Literary Analysis

- **Writing Models and Graphic Organizers on Transparencies,** p. 83 ■
- **Selection Support:** Literary Analysis, p. 140

Reading

- **Listening to Literature Audiocassettes,** Side 15 ■
- **Listening to Literature Audio CDs,** CD 10 ■

■ **BLOCK SCHEDULING:** Resources marked with this symbol provide varied instruction during 90-minute blocks.

3 "No one is allowed to remain in the building after five o'clock," Mr. Manaby told his new assistant, showing him into the little room that was like the inside of a parcel.

"Why not?"

"Directorial policy," said Mr. Manaby. But that was not the real reason.

Gaunt and sooty, Grimes Buildings lurched up the side of a hill toward Clerkenwell.[1] Every little office within its dim and crumbling exterior owned one tiny crumb of light—such was the proud boast of the architect—but toward evening the crumbs were collected as by an immense vacuum cleaner, absorbed and demolished, yielding to an uncontrollable mass of dark that came tumbling in through windows and doors to take their place. Darkness infested the building like a flight of bats returning willingly to roost.

"Wash hands, please. Wash hands, please," the intercom began to bawl in the passages at a quarter to five. Without much need of prompting, the staff hustled like lemmings along the corridors to green- and blue-tiled washrooms that mocked with an illusion of cheerfulness the encroaching dusk.

encroaching (en krōch′ iŋ) *adj.* intruding in a sneaking way

"All papers into cases, please," the voice warned, five minutes later. "Look at your desks, ladies and gentlemen. Any documents left lying about? Kindly put them away. Desks must be left clear and tidy. Drawers must be shut."

A multitudinous shuffling, a rustling as of innumerable bluebottle flies might have been heard by the attentive ear after this injunction, as the employees of Moreton Wold and Company thrust their papers into cases, hurried letters and invoices into drawers, clipped statistical abstracts together and slammed them into filing cabinets, dropped discarded copy into wastepaper baskets. Two minutes later, and not a desk throughout Grimes Buildings bore more than its customary coating of dust.

4 **Reading Check**

What is the new assistant told about being in the building after five o'clock?

1. **Clerkenwell** district of London.

2 Background

Architecture

Tower Bridge is a well-known landmark on the London skyline. It was built between 1886 and 1894 by Sir Horace Jones and Sir John Wolfe Barry. Jones and Barry's idea for a low bridge that could be raised by steam power to allow ships to pass through was revolutionary in its day. Since 1975, the bridge has been raised and lowered by electric power. The two sturdy towers were designed to complement the nearby Tower of London. They anchor the bridge and make it instantly recognizable.

3 Literary Analysis

Rising Action

- Point out that Aiken creates suspense with the very first words of her story. Ask students to explain the effect of the first sentence on the reader.
  Answer: The opening line immediately draws readers into the story by making them wonder why no one is allowed in the building after five o'clock.
- Ask students how they expect the story might develop from this opening line.
  Answer: Students might suggest that the plot will involve discoveries about what goes on in the building during the night.

4 Reading Check

Answer: The new assistant is told that no one is allowed to remain in the building after five o'clock.

CUSTOMIZE INSTRUCTION FOR UNIVERSAL ACCESS

For Gifted/Talented Students	For Advanced Readers
Directions are announced to employees as the day ends at the Grimes Building. Ask students to use these as a model for their own set of instructions for running a student government meeting, organizing a family trip, or some other group enterprise. Encourage students to imitate the officious, fussy tone evident in the Grimes announcements.	Have students analyze the mix of the elements of comedy and horror in this story. Do they think Aiken combines these two elements effectively, or is she trying to do too many things? Does the comedy negate the horror? Does the horror accentuate the comedy? Have students gather in a small group and discuss their reactions to the story's two moods.

5 Literary Analysis

Rising Action

- Tell students that conflict often arises because people do not share the same emotions or personality traits. Ask students how Jason's and Miss Golden's feelings are different in this section.
  Answer: Jason is curious and a little impatient. Miss Golden is terrified.
- Ask the Literary Analysis question on p. 542: What conflict is introduced here to begin the rising action?
  Answer: The conflict is between Jason's desire to know why the staff are urged out the door so promptly and Miss Golden's refusal to tell him.

6 Vocabulary Development

Words From Myths

- Write the vocabulary word *tantalizingly* on the chalkboard and read its definition aloud.
- Tell students that this word is derived from Greek mythology. Tantalus was a mortal who seriously misbehaved. His punishment in the underworld was to have food and drink always placed just beyond his reach. To *tantalize* means "to tempt and tease without giving satisfaction."

7 Reading Strategy

Predicting

- Tell students that they should use information from the story along with their own experiences to make predictions.
- Ask the Reading Strategy question on p. 542: Do you think the relationship between Miss Golden and Jason will develop into a romance? Which details help you decide?
  Possible answers: Yes, because she likes him, and he is tantalized by her. No, because he is only interested in the secret information that she knows.

"Hats and coats on, please. Hats and coats on, please. Did you bring an umbrella? Have you left any shopping on the floor?" At three minutes to five the homegoing throng was in the lifts[2] and on the stairs; a clattering, staccato-voiced flood darkened momentarily the great double doors of the building, and then as the first faint notes of St. Paul's[3] came echoing faintly on the frosty air, to be picked up near at hand by the louder chimes of St. Biddulph's-on-the-Wall, the entire premises of Moreton Wold stood empty.

"But why is it?" Jason Ashgrove, the new copywriter, asked his secretary one day. "Why are the staff herded out so fast? Not that I'm against it, mind you; I think it's an admirable idea in many ways, but
5 there is the liberty of the individual to be considered, don't you think?"

"Hush!" Miss Golden, the secretary, gazed at him with large and terrified eyes. "You mustn't ask that sort of question. When you are taken onto the Established Staff you'll be told. Not before."

6 "But I want to know now," Jason said in discontent. "Do you know?"

"Yes, I do," Miss Golden answered tantalizingly. "Come on, or we shan't have finished the Oat Crisp layout by a quarter to." And she stared firmly down at the copy in front of her, lips folded, candyfloss hair falling over her face, lashes hiding eyes like peridots,[4] a girl with a secret.

Jason was annoyed. He rapped out a couple of rude and witty rhymes which Miss Golden let pass in a withering silence.

"What do you want for your birthday, Miss Golden? Sherry? Fudge? Bubble bath?"

"I want to go away with a clear conscience about Oat Crisps," Miss Golden retorted. It was not true; what she chiefly wanted was Mr. Jason Ashgrove, but he had not realized this yet.

"Come on, don't tease! I'm sure you haven't been on the Established Staff all that long," he coaxed her. "What happens when one is taken on, anyway? Does the Managing Director have us up for a confidential
7 chat? Or are we given a little book called *The Awful Secret of Grimes Buildings*?"

Miss Golden wasn't telling. She opened her drawer and took out a white towel and a cake of rosy soap.

"Wash hands, please! Wash hands, please!"

Jason was frustrated. "You'll be sorry," he said. "I shall do something desperate."

"Oh no, you mustn't!" Her eyes were large with fright. She ran from the room and was back within a couple of moments, still drying her hands.

"If I took you out for a coffee, couldn't you give me just a tiny hint?"

Side by side Miss Golden and Mr. Ashgrove ran along the green-floored passages, battled down the white marble stairs among the hundred other employees from the tenth floor, the nine hundred from the floors below.

Literary Analysis
Rising Action What conflict is introduced here to begin the rising action?

tantalizingly (tan´ tə līz´ iŋ lē) *adv.* in a teasing way

Reading Strategy
Predicting Do you think the relationship between Miss Golden and Jason will develop into a romance? Which details help you decide?

---

2. **lifts** *n.* British term for elevators.
3. **St. Paul's** famous church in London.
4. **peridots** (per´ i däts´) *n.* yellowish-green gems.

He saw her lips move as she said something, but in the clatter of two thousand feet the words were lost.

"—fire escape," he heard, as they came into the momentary hush of the carpeted entrance hall. And "—it's to do with a bicycle. A bicycle and a harp."

"I don't understand."

8 Now they were in the street, chilly with the winter dusk smells of celery on carts, of swept-up leaves heaped in faraway parks, and cold layers of dew sinking among the withered evening primroses in the bombed areas. London lay about them wreathed in twilit mystery and fading against the barred and smoky sky. Like a ninth wave the sound of traffic overtook and swallowed them.

"Please tell me!"

But, shaking her head, she stepped onto a scarlet homebound bus and was borne away from him.

Jason stood undecided on the pavement, with the crowds dividing around him as around the pier of a bridge. He scratched his head, looked about him for guidance.

An ambulance clanged, a taxi hooted, a drill stuttered, a siren wailed on the river, a door slammed, a brake squealed, and close beside his ear a bicycle bell tinkled its tiny warning.

A bicycle, she had said. A bicycle and a harp.

Literary Analysis
Rising Action What effect does Miss Golden's silence have on the rising action?

Jason turned and stared at Grimes Buildings.

Somewhere, he knew, there was a back way in, a service entrance. He walked slowly past the main doors, with their tubs of snowy chrysanthemums, and up Glass Street. A tiny furtive wedge of darkness beckoned him, a snicket, a hacket, an alley carved into the

9 thickness of the building. It was so narrow that at any moment, it seemed, the overtopping walls would come together and squeeze it out of existence.

furtive (fur′ tiv) *adj.* sneaky

Walking as softly as an Indian, Jason passed through it, slid by a file of dustbins,[5] and found the foot of the fire escape. Iron treads rose into the mist, like an illustration to a Gothic[6] fairy tale.

He began to climb.

When he had mounted to the ninth story he paused for breath. It was a lonely place. The lighting consisted of a dim bulb at the foot of every flight. A well of gloom sank beneath him. The cold fingers of the wind nagged and fluttered at the tails of his jacket, and he pulled the string of the fire door and edged inside.

Grimes Buildings were triangular, with the street forming the base of the triangle, and the fire escape the point. Jason could see two long passages coming toward him, meeting at an acute angle where he stood. He started down the left-hand one, tiptoeing in the cavelike silence. Nowhere was there any sound, except for the faraway drip of a tap.

10 **Reading Check**
Which question does Jason Ashgrove want answered by Miss Golden?

5. **dustbins** British term for garbage cans.
6. **Gothic** *adj.* mysterious.

8 Literary Analysis
Rising Action
- Have students summarize the action in this passage.
- Then, ask the Literary Analysis question on p. 543: What effect does Miss Golden's silence have on the rising action?
  Answer: Her silence withholds information, increasing suspense. Jason must continue his quest, and the reader must continue to read.

Monitor Progress Ask students what the effect would have been if Miss Golden had remained completely silent instead of giving Jason a hint.
Answer: The hint is more interesting than silence would have been. The suggestion that the secret is related to a harp and a bicycle is so strange that Jason and the reader are even more eager to find out what the secret is.

9 Reading Strategy
Predicting
- Challenge students to use what they have learned so far to predict what may happen to Jason in the Grimes Building.
  Possible responses: Since other staff members know the secret, it probably isn't anything too terrible. However, Miss Golden was frightened when he asked about it, so he may run into danger. Whatever he finds should involve a bicycle and a harp.
- Ask students if they are still in the rising action part of the story. Why or why not?
  Answer: Yes, because Jason still hasn't learned what is going on. The climax would be when he discovers the reason for the secrecy, which hasn't occurred yet.

10 Reading Check
Answer: Jason wants to know why the staff is forced to leave the building so abruptly.

CUSTOMIZE INSTRUCTION FOR UNIVERSAL ACCESS

For Special Needs Students	For Advanced Readers
This is a gripping story to hear, as well as to read. You may want to play part or all of the story using the **Listening to Literature** audiocassette or CD. Play at least to the point when Jason is about to enter the Grimes Building after hours.	Challenge students to discuss the elements of characterization. Are the characters in this story realistic and believable, or are they stick figures? Do they fulfill Aiken's purpose in writing the story? How? Have students discuss why they think Aiken took the approach to characterization that she did, and how effective her approach is.

⓫ Literary Analysis

Rising Action

- Ask the Literary Analysis question on p. 544: What effect does the sound of the bell have on the plot?
  Answer: The bell signals a new complication. The ringing is a new mystery for Jason—and the reader— to investigate.
- Tell students that writers often try to appeal to the reader's senses: sight, hearing, touch, taste, smell. Ask students to identify senses other than hearing that Aiken appeals to in this section.
  Possible responses: Students may cite taste, when Jason is reminded of ice cream; touch, when Jason thinks of a flurry of snowflakes; sight, when he sees the shimmer of an invisible wheel.

⓬ ▶Critical Viewing

Answer: Students may find that the buildings shown in the picture create a serious, somber mood, but perhaps not the eerie, menacing mood of the story.

⓭ Critical Thinking

Speculate

- Have students read the story of Jason's encounter with the ghost. Challenge them to speculate on why the ghost haunts the Grimes Building and why it urges Jason to leap from the fire escape.
  Possible answers: Daisy may be the ghost's lost love. Since the ghost is waiting for an answer from Daisy, Daisy must have failed to give this answer during the ghost's lifetime.
- Have students continue reading to find out about the ghost.

No night watchman would stay in the building; none was needed. Burglars gave the place a wide berth.

Jason opened a door at random; then another. Offices lay everywhere about him, empty and forbidding. Some held lipstick-stained tissues, spilled powder, and orange peels; others were still foggy with cigarette smoke. Here was a Director's suite of rooms—a desk like half an acre of frozen lake, inch-thick carpet, roses, and the smell of cigars. Here was a conference room with scattered squares of doodled blotting paper. All equally empty.

⓫ He was not sure when he first began to notice the bell. Telephone, he thought at first, and then he remembered that all the outside lines were disconnected at five. And this bell, anyway, had not the regularity of a telephone's double ring: there was a tinkle, and then silence; a long ring, and then silence; a whole volley of rings together, and then silence.

Jason stood listening, and fear knocked against his ribs and shortened his breath. He knew that he must move or be paralyzed by it. He ran up a flight of stairs and found himself with two more endless green corridors beckoning him like a pair of dividers.

Another sound now: a waft of ice-thin notes, riffling up an arpeggio[7] like a flurry of snowflakes. Far away down the passage it echoed. Jason ran in pursuit, but as he ran the music receded. He circled the building, but it always outdistanced him, and when he came back to the stairs he heard it fading away to the story below.

He hesitated, and as he did so heard again the bell; the bicycle bell. It was approaching him fast, bearing down on him, urgent, <u>menacing</u>. He could hear the pedals, almost see the shimmer of an invisible wheel. Absurdly, he was reminded of the insistent clamor of an ice-cream vendor, summoning children on a sultry Sunday afternoon.

⓭ There was a little fireman's alcove beside him, with buckets and pumps. He hurled himself into it. The bell stopped beside him, and then there was a moment while his heart tried to shake itself loose in his chest. He was looking into two eyes carved out of expressionless air; he was held by two hands knotted together out of the width of dark.

⓮ "Daisy, Daisy?" came the whisper. "Is that you, Daisy? Have you come to give me your answer?"

Jason tried to speak, but no words came.

Literary Analysis
Rising Action What effect does the sound of the bell have on the plot?

menacing (men´ əs iŋ) *v.* threatening

⓬ **▼ Critical Viewing** How does the mood of these buildings compare to the mood of the setting of the story? **[Compare]**

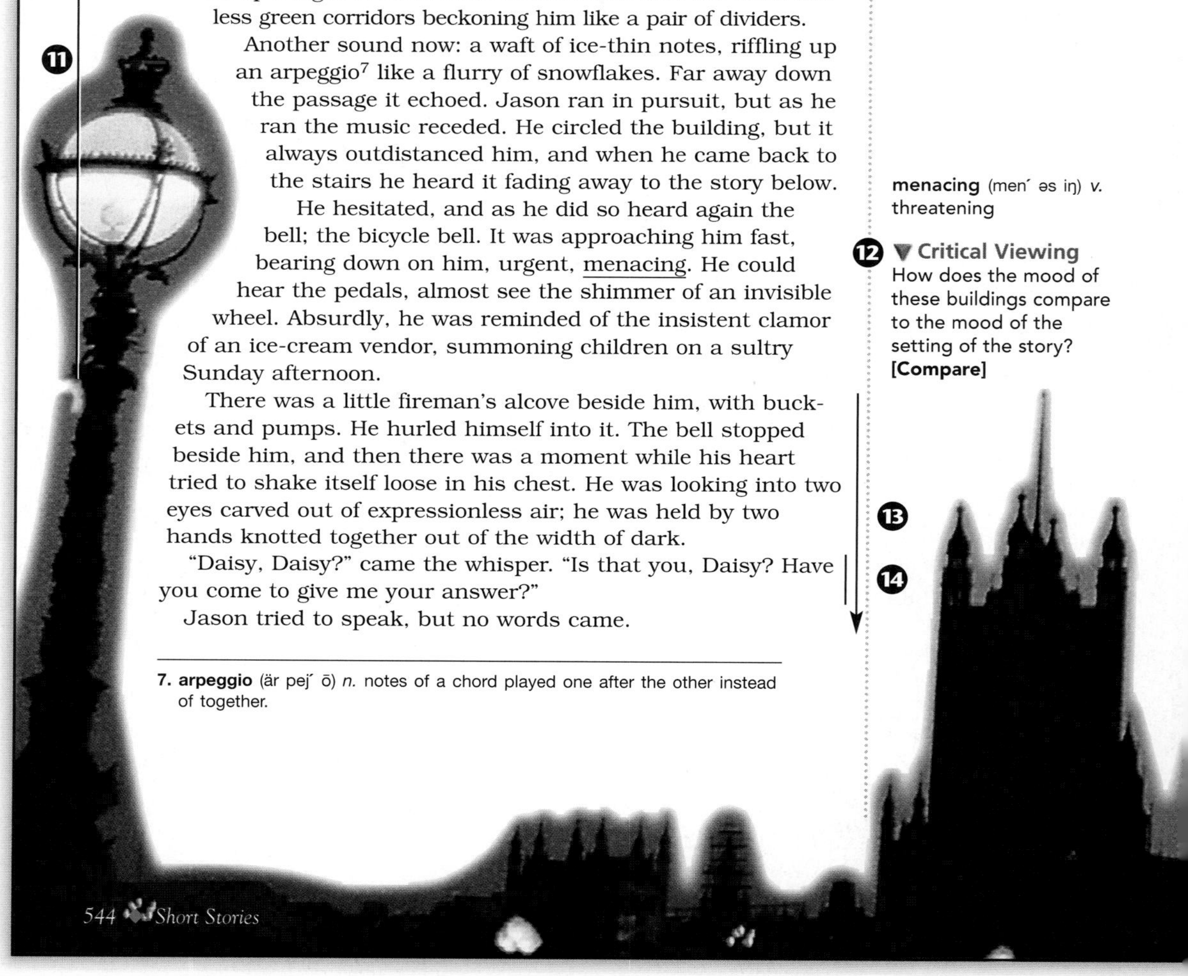

7. **arpeggio** (är pej´ ō) *n.* notes of a chord played one after the other instead of together.

ENRICHMENT: Architecture Connection

The Houses of Parliament

Shown across pp. 544–545 are the Houses of Parliament, famous London landmarks. Parliament first met on this site in the year 1275 and made its permanent home here in 1532. The original buildings burned down in 1834. The buildings shown here were completed between 1837 and 1858, badly damaged by German bombs during World War II, and rebuilt afterward. The Moorish spires that decorate them make them unique among London buildings. The clock tower at the far right houses Big Ben, one of the world's most famous bells. Big Ben chimes the hours to this day. The lamps of Westminster Bridge gleam along the bottom of the photo.

"It's not Daisy! Who are you?" The sibilants[8] were full of threat. "You can't stay here. This is private property."

He was thrust along the corridor. It was like being pushed by a whirlwind—the fire door opened ahead of him without a touch, and he was on the openwork platform, clutching the slender railing. Still the hands would not let him go.

"How about it?" the whisper mocked him. "How about jumping? It's an easy death compared with some."

Jason looked down into the smoky void. The darkness nodded to him like a familiar.[9]

"You wouldn't be much loss, would you? What have you got to live for?"

Miss Golden, Jason thought. She would miss me. And the syllables Berenice Golden lingered in the air like a chime. Drawing on some unknown deposit of courage he shook himself loose from the holding hands and ran down the fire escape without looking back.

Next morning when Miss Golden, crisp, fragrant, and punctual, shut the door of Room 492 behind her, she stopped short of the hat-pegs with a horrified gasp.

"Mr. Ashgrove, your hair!"

"It makes me look more distinguished, don't you think?" he said.

It had indeed this effect, for his impeccable dark cut had turned to a stippled silver which might have been envied by many a diplomat.

"How did it happen? You've not—" her voice sank to a whisper—"*you've not been in Grimes Buildings after dark?*"

"Miss Golden—Berenice," he said earnestly. "Who was Daisy? Plainly you know. Tell me the story."

"Did you see him?" she asked faintly.

"Him?"

"William Heron—The Wailing Watchman. Oh," she exclaimed in terror, "I can see you did. Then you are doomed—doomed!"

"If I'm doomed," said Jason, "let's have coffee, and you tell me the story quickly."

"It all happened over fifty years ago," said Berenice, as she spooned out coffee powder with distracted extravagance. "Heron was the night watchman in this building, patrolling the corridors from dusk to dawn every night on his bicycle. He fell in love with a Miss Bell who taught the harp. She rented a room—this room—

8. **sibilants** (sib´ əl əntz) *n.* hissing sounds.
9. **a familiar** a spirit.

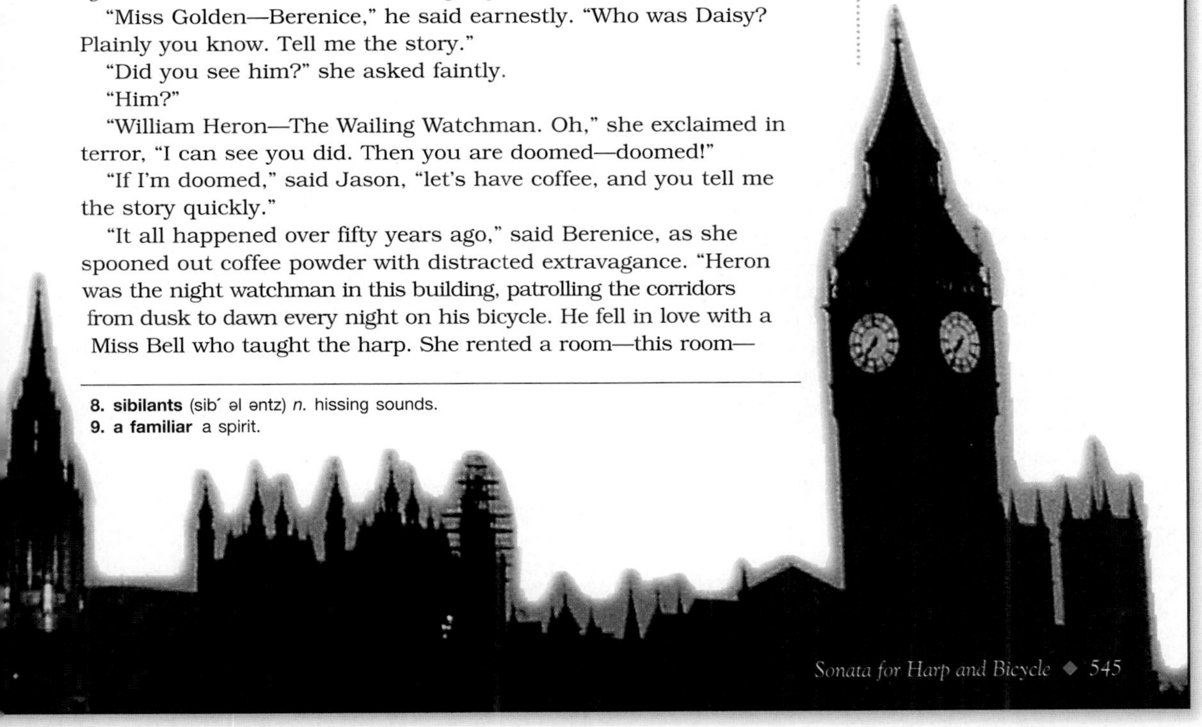

15 **Reading Check**
What happens to Jason inside the Grimes Buildings?

14 Background

Music

Aiken may be alluding to the popular music-hall song "A Bicycle Built for Two" (1892) by Harry Dacre:

Daisy, Daisy, give me your answer true,
I'm half crazy all for the love of you.
It won't be a stylish marriage,
I can't afford a carriage,
But you'll look sweet
Upon the seat
Of a bicycle built for two.

15 Reading Check

Answer: Jason encounters and is threatened by a ghostly bicyclist.

16 Literary Analysis

Rising Action

- Ask the Literary Analysis question on p. 546: How does this information change the nature of the story's conflict?
  Answer: Earlier, the conflict was between Jason's curiosity and Miss Golden's refusal to reveal the secret. Now, having met the ghost of William Heron, Jason must cope with a supernatural threat of death.

Monitor Progress Have students explain how this shift in the conflict contributes to the rising action of the story's plot.
Answer: The first conflict of the story has just been resolved; Jason has found out the secret of the building. Without a new conflict, there would be no reason to continue the story.

- Point out that in effective stories, each complication is more serious and intense than the last. Ask students if Aiken has accomplished that goal here.
  Answer: Students may agree that Aiken has increased tension by shifting from discovering a secret to surviving a fatal curse.

17 Reading Strategy

Predicting

- Have students summarize the action of the story thus far.
- Then, ask the Reading Strategy question on p. 546: How do you think Jason plans to "remedy the matter"?
  Answer: Since the central problem he faces is that the two ghosts have never met, he probably plans to arrange a meeting between them.

Monitor Progress Encourage students to predict the specifics of Jason's plan. The class can enjoy sharing speculations before students continue reading. Remind them to base their predictions on the information they have learned thus far.

---

and gave lessons in it. She began to reciprocate his love, and they used to share a picnic supper every night at eleven, and she'd stay on a while to keep him company. It was an idyll,[10] among the fire buckets and the furnace pipes.

"On Halloween he had summoned up the courage to propose to her. The day before he had told her he was going to ask her a very important question, and he came to the Buildings with a huge bunch of roses and a bottle of wine. But Miss Bell never turned up.

"The explanation was simple. Miss Bell, of course, had been losing a lot of sleep through her nocturnal romance, and so she used to take a nap in her music room between seven and ten, to save going home. In order to make sure that she would wake up, she persuaded her father, a distant relative of Graham Bell,[11] to attach an alarm-waking fixture to her telephone which called her every night at ten. She was too modest and shy to let Heron know that she spent those hours in the building, and to give him the pleasure of waking her himself.

16 "Alas! On this important evening the line failed, and she never woke up. The telephone was in its infancy at that time, you must remember.

"Heron waited and waited. At last, mad with grief and jealousy, having called her home and discovered that she was not there, he concluded that she had betrayed him; he ran to the fire escape, and cast himself off it, holding the roses and the bottle of wine.

"Daisy did not long survive him but pined away soon after. Since that day their ghosts have haunted Grimes Buildings, he vainly patrolling the corridors on his bicycle, she playing her harp in the room she rented. *But they never meet.* And anyone who meets the ghost of William Heron will himself, within five days, leap down from the same fatal fire escape."

She gazed at him with tragic eyes.

17 "In that case we must lose no time," said Jason, and he enveloped her in an embrace as prompt as it was ardent. Looking down at the gossamer hair sprayed across his pin-stripe, he added, "Just the same it is a preposterous situation. Firstly, I have no intention of jumping off the fire escape—" here, however, he repressed a shudder as he remembered the cold, clutching hands of the evening before—"and secondly, I find it quite nonsensical that those two inefficient ghosts have spent fifty years in this building without coming across each other. We must remedy the matter, Berenice. We must not begrudge our new-found happiness to others."

He gave her another kiss so impassioned that the electric typewriter against which they were leaning began chattering to itself in a frenzy of enthusiasm.

"This very evening," he went on, looking at his watch, "we will put matters right for that unhappy couple and then, if I really have only five more days to live, which I don't for one moment believe, we will

reciprocate (ri sip′ rə kāt) *v.* return

Literary Analysis
Rising Action How does this information change the nature of the story's conflict?

ardent (ärd′ 'nt) *adj.* passionate

gossamer (gäs′ ə mər) *adj.* light, thin, and filmy

preposterous (prē päs′ tər əs) *adj.* absurd

Reading Strategy
Predicting How do you think Jason plans to "remedy the matter"?

10. **idyll** (ī′ dəl) *n.* romantic scene, usually in the country.
11. **Graham Bell** Alexander Graham Bell (1847–1922), the inventor of the telephone.

proceed to spend them together, my bewitching Berenice, in the most advantageous manner possible."

She nodded, spellbound.

"Can you work a switchboard?" he added. She nodded again. "My love, you are perfection itself. Meet me in the switchboard room then, at ten this evening. I would say, have dinner with me, but I shall need to make one or two purchases and see an old R.A.F.[12] friend. You will be safe from Heron's curse in the switchboard room if he always keeps to the corridors."

"I would rather meet him and die with you," she murmured.

"My angel, I hope that won't be necessary. Now," he said, sighing, "I suppose we should get down to our day's work."

Strangely enough the copy they wrote that day, although engendered from such agitated minds, sold more packets of Oat Crisps than any other advertising matter before or since.

engendered (en jen′ dərd) *adj.* produced

18 That evening when Jason entered Grimes Buildings he was carrying two bottles of wine, two bunches of red roses, and a large canvas-covered bundle. Miss Golden, who had concealed herself in the switchboard room before the offices closed for the night, eyed these things with surprise.

"Now," said Jason, after he had greeted her, "I want you first to ring our own extension."

"No one will reply, surely?"

"I think she will reply."

Sure enough, when Berenice rang Extension 170 a faint, sleepy voice, distant and yet clear, whispered, "Hullo?"

"Is that Miss Bell?"

"Yes."

Berenice went a little pale. Her eyes sought Jason's and, prompted by him, she said formally, "Switchboard here, Miss Bell. Your ten o'clock call."

"Thank you," the faint voice said. There was a click and the line went blank.

Literary Analysis
Rising Action and Climax Which details in this paragraph suggest that the story is nearing its climax?

"Excellent," Jason remarked. He unfastened his package and slipped its straps over his shoulders. "Now plug into the intercom."

Berenice did so, and then said, loudly and clearly, "Attention. Night watchman on duty, please. Night watchman on duty. You have an urgent summons to Room 492. You have an urgent summons to Room 492." The intercom echoed and reverberated through the empty corridors, then coughed itself to silence.

"Now we must run. You take the roses, sweetheart, and I'll carry the bottles."

Together they raced up eight flights of stairs and along the passages to Room 492. As they neared the door a burst of music met them—harp music swelling out, sweet and triumphant. Jason took a bunch of roses from Berenice, opened the door a little way, and gently deposited them,

19 **Reading Check**
According to Berenice, what happens to anyone who meets the ghost of William Heron?

12. **R.A.F.** Royal Air Force.

18 Literary Analysis
Rising Action and Climax

- Ask the Literary Analysis question on p. 547: What details in the paragraph suggest the story is nearing its climax?
  Answer: Jason has brought replacements for the roses and wine that the watchman brought Miss Bell fifty years earlier. This suggests that he is going to arrange a meeting for the two ghosts.
- Ask students to explain the purpose of Berenice's telephone call to Extension 170.
  Answer: Berenice has made the wake-up call that Miss Bell did not receive 50 years earlier. Miss Bell will now be awake to meet Heron.

19 Reading Check

Answer: Anyone who encounters the ghost will jump from the fire escape within five days.

CUSTOMIZE INSTRUCTION FOR UNIVERSAL ACCESS

For Less Proficient Readers	For Advanced Readers
Have students work individually to answer the Review and Assess questions on p. 548. They can then meet in a group to discuss their answers. If students disagree, have them go back to the story and refer to specific details that support their answers. After discussion, they can move on to the Review and Assess questions on p. 549.	By naming her protagonists "Jason" and "Miss Golden," the author seems be making a joking reference to the Greek myth, "Jason and the Golden Fleece." Have students compare Jason's quest, obstacles, and dangers with those of a Greek hero they have read about. (Refer to "Perseus" on p. 214 if students have read that selection.) What effect does this allusion have on the story?

ASSESS

Answers for p. 548

Review and Assess

1. Possible answers: Yes, because curiosity would overcome any hesitation over the risks. No, because it might be dangerous, or a cause for being fired.
2. **(a)** Miss Golden drops hints about a fire escape, a bicycle, and a harp. **(b)** Jason finds the fire escape and uses it to get into the building.
3. **(a)** His hair has turned silvery. **(b)** The color change occurs immediately after his life-threatening encounter with a ghost. According to convention, severe shock can cause hair to whiten overnight.
4. **(a)** He jumps off the fire escape, but does so securely strapped in a parachute. **(b)** Berenice was more concerned because she assumed the curse could not be escaped and was not aware of Jason's plan. **(c)** She is in love with Jason.
5. If Heron hadn't killed himself, he would have seen Miss Bell the next day; she would have explained about the alarm, and they could have had a happy life together.

with a bottle, inside the door. As he closed it again Berenice said breathlessly, "Did you see anyone?"

"No," he said. "The room was too full of music." She saw that his eyes were shining.

They stood hand in hand, reluctant to move away, waiting for they hardly knew what. Suddenly the door opened again. Neither Berenice nor Jason, afterward, would speak of what they saw but each was left with a memory, bright as the picture on a Salvador Dali[13] calendar, of a bicycle bearing on its saddle a harp, a bottle of wine, and a bouquet of red roses, sweeping improbably down the corridor and far, far away.

improbably (im präb´ ə blē) *adv.* unlikely to happen

"We can go now," Jason said.

He led Berenice to the fire door, tucking the bottle of Médoc in his jacket pocket. A black wind from the north whistled beneath them as they stood on the openwork platform, looking down.

"We don't want our evening to be spoiled by the thought of a curse hanging over us," he said, "so this is the practical thing to do. Hang onto the roses." And holding his love firmly, Jason pulled the rip cord of his R.A.F. friend's parachute and leaped off the fire escape.

A bridal shower of rose petals adorned the descent of Miss Golden, who was possibly the only girl to be kissed in midair in the district of Clerkenwell at ten minutes to midnight on Halloween.

13. **Salvador Dali** (sal´ və dôr´ dä´ lē) modern artist (1904–1989) famous for his unusual pictures.

Joan Aiken

(b. 1924)

Joan Aiken, the daughter of the poet Conrad Aiken, was born in England and lived with her family in an eerie old house, an experience that helped foster her fascination with mystery and the unexplained.

Aiken began writing at five and published her first story at sixteen. After working in London for a magazine, an advertising agency, and the United Nations, she decided to pursue what she has called "the family trade." Her immense output includes novels, poems, plays, and stories.

Known for her wit, Aiken called her first short-story collection *All You Ever Wanted* and her second *More Than You Bargained For*.

Like other writers, she sometimes uses personal experiences in her work. Jason Ashgrove, the main character of "Sonata for Harp and Bicycle," writes advertising copy, as Aiken once did.

Review and Assess

Thinking About the Selection

1. **Respond:** If you were Jason, would you try to solve the mystery of the Grimes Buildings? Explain.
2. **(a) Recall:** What three things does Miss Golden mention to Jason as they leave the Grimes Buildings at five P.M.? **(b) Connect:** How does he use this information?
3. **(a) Recall:** How has Jason changed when he sees Miss Golden the next day? **(b) Analyze Cause and Effect:** What evidence is there that his encounter in the closed building causes the change?
4. **(a) Recall:** How does Jason avoid the curse that awaits anyone who sees Heron's ghost? **(b) Speculate:** Who was more concerned about the curse—Jason or Berenice? Explain. **(c) Infer:** Why do you think Berenice agrees to assist Jason?
5. **Generalize:** What lesson do the circumstances of William Heron's death teach about the danger of making rash decisions?

ASSESSMENT PRACTICE: Reading Comprehension

Author's Purpose (For more practice, see Test Preparation Workbook, p. 35.)

Many tests require students to recognize an author's purpose. Use this sample test item.

With a sharp edge of the mysterious, Joan Aiken tells a story of misguided fates. But this is no ordinary ghost story. Surpassing the stereotypes, "Sonata for Harp and Bicycle" must be read by anyone with an inclination toward love and mystery.

The author's purpose is to ___.

A persuade
B warn
C inform
D entertain

The phrase "must be read" indicates that the author's purpose is to persuade. Therefore, *A* is the correct answer.

Review and Assess

Literary Analysis

Rising Action

1. At what point in the story does the **rising action** begin? Explain.
2. Why do the sounds that Jason hears in the empty building increase the tension and suspense of the rising action?
3. What information keeps the action of the plot rising on the morning after Jason's escape from Heron?

Connecting Literary Elements

4. Using a chart like the one shown, identify two events in the rising action and determine which event marks the **climax** of the story.

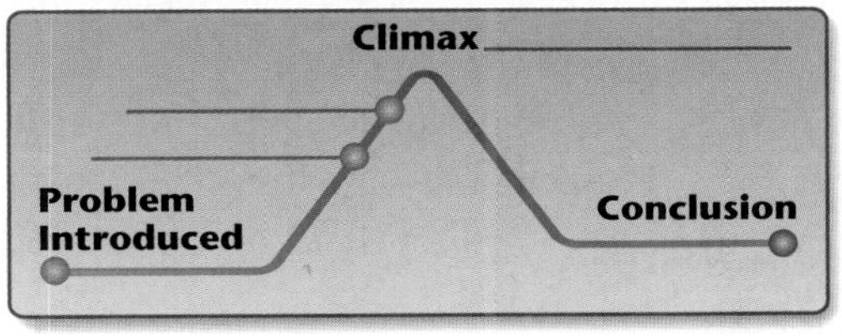

5. What makes the climax the true emotional peak?
6. Which specific events preceding the climax lead you to believe that the climax is imminent? Explain.

Reading Strategy

Predicting

7. Jason enters the Grimes Buildings after closing and hears a bicycle bell tinkling. What **predictions** did you make based on this event?
8. Using a chart like the one shown, explain which clues in the story helped you make the most accurate predictions.

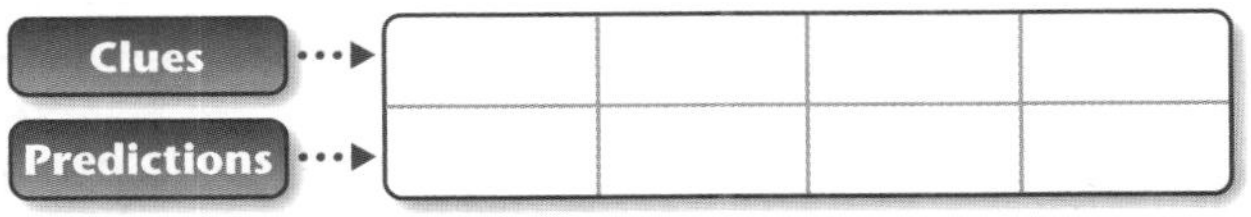

Extend Understanding

9. **Cultural Connection:** This story is set in London and refers to local landmarks. Does the effect of the story depend on its setting, or could it just as well be set in any large city? Explain.

Quick Review

The **rising action** introduces the conflict and builds to the climax of the story.

The **climax** concludes the rising action and is the point of highest interest in the story.

When you **predict**, you guess what will happen next on the basis of what you already know.

Take It to the Net

www.phschool.com

Take the interactive self-test online to check your understanding of the selection.

Answers for p. 549

Review and Assess

1. Miss Golden's refusal to reveal the secret causes Jason to reenter the building, setting off a chain of events.
2. Street noises create a sense of stress and urgency before Jason hears the nearby tinkling of a bell that warns him that he is not alone.
3. Jason learns the full story of the ghost and discovers that he himself is subject to a fatal curse.
4. Rising action: Jason encounters the ghost; he learns the tragic history from Berenice; he reenters the building with Berenice and a plan. Climax: The ghosts are reunited and leave the building.
5. Students may note that bicycle and harp are united; two pairs of lovers are united; and all danger is past.
6. Berenice's telephone call and her announcement over the intercom suggest that the climax is imminent.
7. Based on Berenice's hint about a bicycle, readers may predict that Jason will soon have a direct encounter with the source of the mystery.
8. Sample answer: Jason's curiosity was a clue that he would try to break into the Grimes Building to explain the mystery.
9. Some students may suggest that any urban setting would suffice for this plot. Others may note that historic London is the most appropriate setting for a story featuring ghosts from the past.

ENRICHMENT: Further Reading

Other Works by Joan Aiken

A Creepy Company: Ten Tales of Terror
A Fit of Shivers: Tales for Late at Night
The Wolves of Willoughby Chase
Black Hearts in Battersea

Take It to the Net

Visit www.phschool.com for more information on Joan Aiken.

EXTEND

Answers for p. 550

❶ Vocabulary Development

Word Analysis

1. a repetition of sounds
2. extraordinarily strong or heroic
3. self-love or self-obsession

Spelling Strategy

1. golden
2. helpful
3. collective

Concept Development: Synonyms

1. h
2. e
3. g
4. b
5. j
6. a
7. d
8. i
9. c
10. f

❷ Grammar

1. "Frightened by what she saw" modifies *she*
2. "patrolling from dusk to dawn" modifies *watchman*
3. "bewitching" modifies *Berenice*
4. "covered" modifies *bundle*
5. "Hanging in the air" modifies *danger,* not *Jason*. The sentence should read: Jason felt danger hanging in the air.

Writing Application

Sample sentences: Jason heard a tinkling bicycle bell. He entered the building carrying red roses. Floating through the air, the couple kissed.

Integrate Language Skills

❶ Vocabulary Development Lesson

Word Analysis: Words From Myths

Many English words derive their meaning from names in Greek mythology. *Echo* is a nymph who pined away until only her voice remained. *Hercules* is a son of Zeus known for his strength. *Narcissus* is a handsome youth in love with his reflection.

Use the clues above to write a definition for each word below.

1. echo 2. herculean 3. narcissism

Spelling Strategy

If a word ends in two consonants, do not change the consonants when you add a word ending. Thus, *encroach* + *-ing* = *encroaching*. Add *-ful*, *-ive*, or *-en* to the words below to create three properly spelled new words.

1. gold 2. help 3. collect

Concept Development: Synonyms

Correctly match each word on the left with its synonym on the right. To help you, review the vocabulary list on p. 539.

1. encroaching	a. passionate
2. tantalizingly	b. frightening
3. furtive	c. created
4. menacing	d. delicate
5. reciprocate	e. teasingly
6. ardent	f. unlikely
7. gossamer	g. secretive
8. preposterous	h. intruding
9. engendered	i. nonsensical
10. improbably	j. return

❷ Grammar Lesson

Participial Phrases

A **participle** is a verb form that acts as an adjective. A **participial phrase** is a participle with an accompanying adverb, adverb phrase, or complement. To avoid misplaced modifiers—participles or participial phrases that seem to modify the wrong words—place a participle or participial phrase as close to the word it modifies as possible.

Participle: He heard a *clattering* noise. (modifies *noise*)
Participial Phrase: He heard them *clattering down the stairs*. (modifies *them*)
Misplaced Modifier: *Converging*, Jason saw down the corridors. (modifies *Jason*)
Correct: Jason saw down the *converging* corridors. (modifies *corridors*)

Practice Identify each participle or participial phrase. Indicate the word each one modifies and correct any misplaced modifiers.

1. Frightened by what she saw, she told him the story.
2. Heron was the watchman, patrolling from dusk to dawn.
3. We will spend our time together, my bewitching Berenice.
4. He carried red roses and a covered bundle.
5. Hanging in the air, Jason felt danger.

Writing Application Rewrite three sentences from the story, using a participle or participial phrase correctly in each.

WG Prentice Hall Writing and Grammar Connection: Chapter 21, Section 1

TEACHING RESOURCES

The following resources can be used to enrich or extend the instructions for pp. 550–551.

Vocabulary

- **Selection Support:** Build Vocabulary, p. 137
- **Vocabulary and Spelling Practice Book** (Use this booklet for skills enrichment.) ■

Grammar

- **Selection Support:** Build Grammar Skills, p. 138
- **Writing and Grammar,** Gold Level, p. 450
- **Daily Language Practice Transparencies**

Writing

- **Writing and Grammar,** Gold Level, p. 286 ■
- **Writing and Grammar iText CD-ROM**

■ **BLOCK SCHEDULING:** Resources marked with this symbol provide varied instruction during 90-minute blocks.

❸ Writing Lesson

Critical Review

Joan Aiken has said, "A flat or unsatisfactory ending is the worst sin a writer can commit." Write a critical review evaluating the ending of "Sonata for Harp and Bicycle," and indicate whether Aiken has provided a satisfactory or unsatisfactory ending.

Prewriting Make a list of the qualities that you think create satisfactory and unsatisfactory endings to stories. Then, check off the qualities that relate to Aiken's story.

Model: Evaluating a Story's Ending

Satisfactory	Unsatisfactory
☑ when problems are resolved for characters	☐ when events are predictable

Drafting The first sentence of your review should state your opinion about the ending. Follow up by referring to examples from the story to provide support for your views.

Revising Reread your draft. Circle any descriptive words you use to convey positive or negative criticism. If you have used vague or overused words, consider replacing them with more precise words.

WG *Prentice Hall Writing and Grammar Connection: Chapter 13, Section 2*

❹ Extension Activities

Listening and Speaking Develop and perform a **talk-show interview** featuring Berenice, Jason, the two ghosts, and the host of the program.

- Review the story and jot down the experiences of Berenice and Jason and the two ghosts.
- Plan the interview so that the two pairs of guests tell what happened at the Grimes Buildings from their own perspectives.
- Practice your interview, providing enough time for each character to speak.

Present your interview to your class. **[Group Activity]**

Research and Technology Research a famous real-life mystery, and create a **timeline** outlining the facts and summarizing the details. Search the Internet or the library for help in locating information about your subject. Compare the elements of the real-life mystery to those of the mystery in "Sonata for Harp and Bicycle." Present the timeline and your comparison to the class.

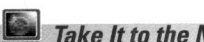

Take It to the Net www.phschool.com

Go online for an additional research activity using the Internet.

ASSESSMENT RESOURCES

The following resources can be used to assess students' knowledge and skills.

Selection Assessment

- **Formal Assessment,** pp. 123–125
- **Open Book Test,** pp. 103–105
- **Got It! Assessment Videotapes,** Tape 3
- **Test Bank Software**

Take It to the Net

Visit www.phschool.com for self-tests and additional questions on "Sonata for Harp and Bicycle."

Writing Rubric

- **Performance Assess. and Portfolio Mgmt.,** p. 15

PRENTICE HALL ASSESSMENT SYSTEM

- **Workbook**
- **Skill Book**
- **Transparencies**
- **CD-ROM**

Lesson Support for p. 551

❸ Writing Lesson

- Remind students that a review does not retell the events of the plot. Have them start off their review by asking the simple question, "Did you enjoy the story?" If the answer is yes, the review should be positive.
- Remind students to refer to specific story details in their reviews.
- Use the Response to Literature rubric in **Performance Assessment and Portfolio Management,** p. 15, to evaluate students' reviews.

❹ Listening and Speaking

- Divide the class into at least three groups to prepare separate versions of the talk-show interview.
- If possible, show a video of an actual televised interview of a celebrity or newsmaker to help students identify characteristics and tone for their own efforts.
- Students might choose to have the program-host imitate an actual on-air interviewer.
- Allow sufficient time for all groups to make their presentations in class.

CUSTOMIZE INSTRUCTION For Universal Access

To address different learning styles, use the following activities suggested in the **Extension Activities** booklet, p. 35.

- For Visual/Spatial and Logical/Mathematical Learners, use Activity 5.
- For Verbal/Linguistic Learners, use Activities 6 and 7.
- For Bodily/Kinesthetic Learners, use Activity 6.
- For Musical/Rhythmic Learners, use Activity 7.

The Scarlet Ibis

Lesson Objectives

1. **To analyze and respond to literary elements**
   - Literary Analysis: Point of View
   - Connecting Literary Elements: Dynamic Character
2. **To read, comprehend, analyze, and critique a short story**
   - Reading Strategy: Identifying With a Character
   - Reading Check questions
   - Review and Assess questions
   - Assessment Practice (ATE)
3. **To develop word analysis skills, fluency, and systematic vocabulary**
   - Vocabulary Development Lesson: Latin Prefix *in-*
4. **To understand and apply written and oral language conventions**
   - Spelling Strategy
   - Grammar Lesson: Gerund Phrases
5. **To understand and apply appropriate writing and research strategies**
   - Writing Lesson: Journal Entry
   - Extension Activity: Travel Brochure
6. **To understand and apply listening and speaking strategies**
   - Extension Activity: Presentation

STEP-BY-STEP TEACHING GUIDE	PACING GUIDE
PRETEACH	
Motivate Students and Provide Background	
Use the Motivation activity (ATE p. 552)	5 min.
Read and discuss the Preview material and Background information (SE/ATE p. 552) [A]	5 min.
Introduce the Concepts	
Introduce the Literary Analysis and Reading Strategy (SE/ATE p. 553) [A]	15 min.
Pronounce the vocabulary words and read their definitions (SE p. 553)	5 min.
TEACH	
Monitor Comprehension	
Informally monitor comprehension by circulating while students read independently or in groups [A]	30 min.
Monitor students' comprehension with the Reading Check notes (SE/ATE pp. 555, 557, 559, 561, 563)	as students read
Develop vocabulary with Vocabulary notes (SE pp. 558–561, 563; ATE p. 559)	as students read
Develop Understanding	
Develop students' understanding of point of view with Literary Analysis annotations (SE/ATE pp. 555, 557, 559, 560, 563) [A]	10 min.
Develop students' students' ability to identify with a character with the Reading Strategy annotations (SE/ATE pp. 554, 558, 562, 563)	10 min.
ASSESS	
Assess Mastery	
Assess students' mastery of the Reading Strategy and Literary Analysis by having them answer the Review and Assess questions (SE/ATE p. 565)	20 min.
Use one or more of the print and media Assessment Resources (ATE p. 567) [A]	up to 50 min.
EXTEND	
Apply Understanding	
Have students complete the Vocabulary Development Lesson and the Grammar Lesson (SE p. 566) [A]	20 min.
Apply students' knowledge of listing to elaborate using the Writing Lesson (SE p. 567) [A]	45 min.
Apply students' understanding using one or more of the Extension Activities (SE p. 567)	20–90 min.

[A] ACCELERATED INSTRUCTION: Use the strategies and activities identified with an [A].

UNIVERSAL ACCESS
● = Below Level Students
▲ = On-Level Students
■ = Above Level Students

Time and Resource Manager

Reading Level: Average
Average Number of Instructional Days: 4

RESOURCES		
PRINT	**TRANSPARENCIES**	**TECHNOLOGY**
• **Beyond Literature,** Cross-Curricular Connection: Science, p. 36 ▲ ■		• **Interest Grabber Video,** Tape 3 ● ▲ ■
• **Selection Support Workbook:** ● ▲ ■ Literary Analysis, p. 144 Reading Strategy, p. 143 Build Vocabulary, p. 141	• **Literary Analysis and Reading Transparencies,** pp. 71 and 72 ● ▲ ■	
• **Adapted Reader's Companion** ● • **Reader's Companion** ●		• **Listening to Literature** ● ▲ ■ Audiocassettes, Side 16 Audio CDs, CD 11
• **English Learner's Companion** ● ▲ • **Literatura en español** ● ▲ • **Literary Analysis for Enrichment** ■		
• **Formal Assessment:** Selection Test, pp. 126–128 ● ▲ ■ • **Open Book Test,** pp. 106–108 ● ▲ ■ • **Performance Assessment and Portfolio Management,** p. 8 ● ▲ ■ • PRENTICE HALL ASSESSMENT SYSTEM ● ▲ ■	• PRENTICE HALL ASSESSMENT SYSTEM ● ▲ ■ Skills Practice Answers and Explanations on Transparencies	• **Test Bank Software** ● ▲ ■ • **Got It! Assessment Videotapes,** Tape 3 ● ▲
• **Selection Support Workbook:** ● ▲ ■ Build Grammar Skills, p. 142 • **Writing and Grammar,** Gold Level ● ▲ ■ • **Extension Activities,** p. 36 ● ▲ ■	• **Daily Language Practice Transparencies** ● ▲ • **Writing Models and Graphic Organizers on Transparencies,** p. 83 ● ▲ ■	• **Writing and Grammar iText CD-ROM** ● ▲ ■ ***Take It to the Net*** www.phschool.com

BLOCK SCHEDULING: Use one 90-minute class period to preteach the selection and have students read it. Use a second 90-minute class period to assess students' mastery of skills and have them complete one of the Extension Activities.

PRETEACH

Step-by-Step Teaching Guide for pp. 552–553

Motivation

Draw students into this compelling story by writing the following quotation on the chalkboard:

> At times I was mean to Doodle. One day I took him up to the barn loft and showed him his casket, telling him how we all believed he would die.

Explain that the narrator is Doodle's older brother, and that Doodle is frail. Ask students to predict how the relationship between the brothers might affect the story.

Interest Grabber Video

As an alternative, play "Symbolism in Literature" on Tape 3 to engage student interest.

1 Background

Science

Altogether, there are about 20 species of Ibis. This long-legged water bird is related to the heron, crane, and stork. Ibises eat plants, small crustaceans, and mollusks. Ancient Egyptians worshiped the sacred ibis of northern Africa, a relative of the scarlet ibis of this story. Thoth, the Egyptian god of wisdom and magic, has been depicted as a man with the head of an ibis.

Prepare to Read

The Scarlet Ibis

Take It to the Net

Visit www.phschool.com for interactive activities and instruction related to "The Scarlet Ibis," including

- background
- graphic organizers
- literary elements
- reading strategies

Preview

Connecting to the Literature

Sometimes your best pal is also the biggest pain in your neck. The narrator of "The Scarlet Ibis" has these conflicting feelings toward his younger brother. Although his brother is his closest companion, the narrator is embarrassed by him and makes tremendous demands on him.

1 Background

Found mostly in the South American tropics, the strikingly beautiful scarlet ibis is a wading bird with long legs, a long, slender neck, black-tipped wings, and a wingspan of more than three feet. Since it seldom appears in the United States north of Florida, the discovery of such a bird in coastal North Carolina, the setting of this story, is unexpected and dramatic.

TEACHING RESOURCES

The following resources can be used to enrich or extend the instruction for pp. 552–553.

Motivation

Interest Grabber Video, Tape 3

Background

Beyond Literature, p. 36

Take It to the Net

Visit www.phschool.com for background and hotlinks for "The Scarlet Ibis."

Literary Analysis

Literary Analysis and Reading Transparencies, Point of View, p. 72

Reading

Selection Support: Reading Strategy, p. 143; Build Vocabulary, p. 141

Literary Analysis and Reading Transparencies, Identifying With a Character, p. 71

BLOCK SCHEDULING: Resources marked with this symbol provide varied instruction during 90-minute blocks.

❷ Literary Analysis

Point of View

Point of view is the perspective from which a story is told. In **third-person point of view,** the narrator does not participate in the story. In **first-person point of view,** the narrator is a character who refers to himself or herself as "I." Look at this passage from "The Scarlet Ibis":

> . . . one afternoon as I watched him, my head poked between the iron posts of the foot of the bed, he looked straight at me and grinned. I skipped through the room, . . . shouting, "Mama, he smiled. He's all there! He's all there!" and he was.

In using this point of view, the writer enables you to experience the narrator's feelings firsthand.

Connecting Literary Elements

A first-person point of view lets you see firsthand how a character changes. A **dynamic character** is one who develops and grows during the course of a story. In contrast, a **static character** does not change. In "The Scarlet Ibis," Doodle's brother is a dynamic character whose emotions range among love, frustration, anger, and sadness over the course of the story.

❸ Reading Strategy

Identifying With a Character

Authors who write from a first-person point of view invite you to walk through the story in the shoes of one of the characters. **Identify with the character** using these steps:

- Put yourself in his or her place.
- Consider how you would respond if you were in the same situation.

Use a chart like this one to record events from the story, the narrator's reaction to each event, and how *you* might have reacted.

Vocabulary Development

imminent (im´ ə nənt) *adj.* likely to happen soon (p. 558)

iridescent (ir´ ə des´ ənt) *adj.* having shifting, rainbowlike colors (p. 559)

vortex (vôr´ teks´) *n.* rushing whirl, drawing in all that surrounds it (p. 559)

infallibility (in fal´ ə bil´ ə tē) *n.* condition of being unable to fail (p. 559)

entrails (en´ trālz) *n.* internal organs, specifically intestines (p. 560)

precariously (prē ker´ ē əs lē) *adv.* insecurely (p. 561)

evanesced (ev´ ə nest´) *v.* faded away (p. 563)

❷ Literary Analysis

Point of View

- Emphasize to students that the narrator's use of "I" and other first-person pronouns are the clearest signal of this point of view.
- Point out that the first-person viewpoint can make a narrative seem more vivid, personal, and real; the reader seemingly encounters an actual person.
- First-person viewpoints limit the reader to a single perception of events and only one character's ideas and opinions. Ask students to consider the advantages and disadvantages of this viewpoint as they read.

❸ Reading Strategy

Identifying With a Character

- To identify with a character means to understand and sympathize with the character's feelings, or to know that one would react to certain situations in the same way as the character. Ask volunteers to name literary characters, from this text or other readings, with whom they identify. Have them explain why.
- Point out that a first-person narrator is often the easiest character to identify with, because this character shares thoughts and feelings openly with the reader.
- Display the Reading Strategy transparency on p. 71 of **Literary Analysis and Reading Transparencies** and encourage students to keep a similar reaction chart as they read.

Vocabulary Development

- Pronounce each vocabulary word for students, and read the definitions as a class. Have students identify any words with which they are already familiar.

CUSTOMIZE INSTRUCTION FOR UNIVERSAL ACCESS

For Special Needs Students	For Less Proficient Readers	For English Learners
Have students read the adapted version of "The Scarlet Ibis" in the **Adapted Reader's Companion.** This version provides basic-level instruction in an interactive format with questions and write-on lines. Completing the adapted version will prepare students to read the selection in the Student Edition.	Have students read the story in the **Reader's Companion.** This version provides basic-level instruction in an interactive format with questions and write-on lines. After students finish the selection in **Readers' Companion,** have them complete the questions and activities in the Student Edition.	Have students read the adapted version of the story in the **English Learner's Companion.** This version provides basic-level instruction in an interactive format with questions and write-on lines. Completing the adapted version will prepare students to read the selection in the Student Edition.

E-Teach

Visit E-Teach at www.phschool.com for teachers' essays on how to teach, with questions and answers.

TEACH

Step-by-Step Teaching Guide for pp. 554–564

CUSTOMIZE INSTRUCTION For Interpersonal Learners

From Genesis in the Bible to *Little Women,* literature offers endless examples of the challenges and conflicts that arise between siblings. Ask students to discuss why such conflicts are difficult to resolve, the options people have for resolving them, and how cultural expectations may affect the situation.

❶ About the Selection

This story reveals that cruelty and selfishness can be entwined with love. The narrator begins by recounting his disappointment that his brother was born with severe physical disabilities. Motivated by pride and self-interest, the narrator helps his brother, Doodle, to exceed all expectations by learning to walk. Not satisfied, the narrator pushes Doodle to learn to swim and to run so that his brother would not be "different" when he started school. Frustrated by Doodle's lack of progress, the narrator abandons Doodle during a storm. Doodle collapses and dies, his fate foreshadowed by that of a storm-tossed rare bird, the scarlet ibis of the title. Only at Doodle's death does the narrator realize the depth of his feelings for his brother.

❷ ▶Critical Viewing

Answer: Any familiar setting can spark a memory.

❸ Reading Strategy

Identifying With a Character

- Ask the Reading Strategy question on page 554: What provokes the narrator to refer to time as being "ground away"?
  Answer: The presence of a grindstone prompts the narrator's word choice.
- Ask students whether they have ever sat still and drifted into memories. Ask how this shared experience makes them feel about the narrator.
  Answer: Shared experiences usually bring readers closer to a character.

❶ The Scarlet Ibis

James Hurst

It was in the clove of seasons, summer was dead but autumn had not yet been born, that the ibis lit in the bleeding tree. The flower garden was stained with rotting brown magnolia petals and ironweeds grew rank amid the purple phlox. The five o'clocks by the chimney still marked time, but the oriole nest in the elm was untenanted and rocked back and forth like an empty cradle. The last graveyard flowers were blooming, and their smell drifted across the cotton field and through every room of our house, speaking softly the names of our dead.

❸ It's strange that all this is still so clear to me, now that the summer has long since fled and time has had its way. A grindstone stands where the bleeding tree stood, just outside the kitchen door, and now if an oriole sings in the elm, its song seems to die up in the leaves, a silvery dust. The flower garden is prim, the house a gleaming white, and the pale fence across the yard stands straight and spruce. But sometimes (like right now), as I sit in the cool, green-draped parlor, the grindstone begins to turn, and time with all its changes is ground away—and I remember Doodle.

❷ ▲ **Critical Viewing** The narrator uses a description of nature to introduce a story from the past. Why might a natural setting, like the one shown here, spark a memory? **[Hypothesize]**

Reading Strategy
Identifying With a Character What provokes the narrator to refer to time as being "ground away"?

TEACHING RESOURCES

The following resources can be used to enrich or extend the instruction for pp. 554–564.

Literary Analysis

- **Writing Models and Graphic Organizers on Transparencies,** p. 83 ■
- **Selection Support:** Literary Analysis, p. 144

Reading

- **Reader's Companion**
- **English Learner's Companion**
- **Listening to Literature Audiocassettes,** Side 16 ■
- **Listening to Literature Audio CDs,** CD 11 ■

■ **BLOCK SCHEDULING:** Resources marked with this symbol provide varied instruction during 90-minute blocks.

Doodle was just about the craziest brother a boy ever had. Of course, he wasn't a crazy crazy like old Miss Leedie, who was in love with President Wilson and wrote him a letter every day, but was a nice crazy, like someone you meet in your dreams. He was born when I was six and was, from the outset, a disappointment. He seemed all head, with a tiny body which was red and shriveled like an old man's. Everybody thought he was going to die—everybody except Aunt Nicey, who had delivered him. She said he would live because he was born in a caul[1] and cauls were made from Jesus' nightgown. Daddy had Mr. Heath, the carpenter, build a little mahogany coffin for him. But he didn't die, and when he was three months old Mama and Daddy decided they might as well name him. They named him William Armstrong, which was like tying a big tail on a small kite. Such a name sounds good only on a tombstone.

4 I thought myself pretty smart at many things, like holding my breath, running, jumping, or climbing the vines in Old Woman Swamp, and I wanted more than anything else someone to race to Horsehead Landing, someone to box with, and someone to perch with in the top fork of the great pine behind the barn, where across the fields and swamps you could see the sea. I wanted a brother. But Mama, crying, told me that even if William Armstrong lived, he would never do these things with me. He might not, she sobbed, even be "all there." He might, as long as he lived, lie on the rubber sheet in the center of the bed in the front bedroom where the white marquisette curtains billowed out in the afternoon sea breeze, rustling like palmetto fronds.[2]

It was bad enough having an invalid brother, but having one who possibly was not all there was unbearable, so I began to make plans to kill him by smothering him with a pillow. However, one afternoon as I watched him, my head poked between the iron posts of the foot of the bed, he looked straight at me and grinned. I skipped through the rooms, down the echoing halls, shouting, "Mama, he smiled. He's all there! He's all there!" and he was.

When he was two, if you laid him on his stomach, he began to try to move himself, straining terribly. The doctor said that with his weak heart this strain would probably kill him, but it didn't. Trembling, he'd push himself up, turning first red, then a soft purple, and finally collapse back onto the bed like an old worn-out doll. I can still see Mama watching him, her hand pressed tight across her mouth, her eyes wide and unblinking. But he learned to crawl (it was his third winter), and we brought him out of the front bedroom, putting him on the rug before the fireplace. For the first time he became one of us.

As long as he lay all the time in bed, we called him William Armstrong, even though it was formal and sounded as if we were referring to one of our ancestors, but with his creeping around on the deerskin rug and beginning to talk, something had to be done about

Literary Analysis
Point of View Which details indicate the point of view from which this story is written?

5 **Reading Check**
How does William Armstrong respond when the narrator pokes his head through the posts of the bed to look at him?

1. **caul** (kôl) *n.* membrane enclosing a baby at birth.
2. **palmetto fronds** palm leaves.

4 Literary Analysis

Point of View

- Ask the Literary Analysis question on p. 555: Which details indicate the point of view from which this story is written?
  Answer: The pronoun *I* shows that the story is narrated in the first person.
- How do you think this lengthy introduction of Doodle might be different if the story were told from the point of view of Aunt Nicey, Mama, or Daddy? Why do you think so?
  Answer: The narrator is concerned only about the effect of the situation on himself—he doesn't want a disabled brother, so he actually considers smothering him. If one of the adults told the story, he or she would probably express more compassionate and protective sentiments.

5 Reading Check

Answer: Doodle grins at the narrator.

CUSTOMIZE INSTRUCTION FOR UNIVERSAL ACCESS

For Less Proficient Readers	For English Learners
Long sentences like the one beginning "I thought myself pretty smart . . ." (page 555) may prove a barrier to some students' enjoyment of the story. Have students break down long sentences like these by first identifying the main subject(s) and verb(s) (in this case, the subject is *I* and the verbs are *thought* and *wanted*). The rest of the sentence's phrases and clauses give further details about this subject and verb. Once students have identified the sentence's main idea, they can look at the details.	With its references to many different plants, this story's setting provides students with an opportunity to extend their vocabularies. Have students list such words as *magnolia, bleeding tree, phlox, five o'clocks,* and so on and look them up in illustrated nature guides or encyclopedias.

❻ Literary Analysis

Point of View

- Have students describe the narrator's feelings about his brother.
  Answer: The narrator seems impatient with his brother's special needs and tends to ignore them. He is irritated that Doodle must always accompany him.
- Do you detect a change in the narrator's attitude in this passage? Explain.
  Answer: Once the narrator resigns himself to Doodle's constant presence, he decides to share the beauties of Old Woman Swamp with his brother.

❼ Background

Art

Two Boys in a Punt, by N. C. Wyeth

N. C. Wyeth studied for two years at the Howard Pyle School of Art in Wilmington, Delaware. Pyle, himself a well-known illustrator and graphic artist, emphasized realism and authenticity. Wyeth became one of the school's most successful and famous graduates. His best-known and most successful works are the brilliant oil paintings with which he illustrated *Treasure Island, Robin Hood, The Last of the Mohicans,* and others.

Use the following item for discussion:

- Compare and contrast the boys in the painting to the brothers in the story.
  Answer: Both pairs spend time together. Both pairs are in a rural setting. Neither boy in the painting appears dependent on the other one.

❽ ▶Critical Viewing

Answer: Brothers in the story and in the painting share relaxed experiences in the outdoors.

his name. It was I who renamed him. When he crawled, he crawled backwards, as if he were in reverse and couldn't change gears. If you called him, he'd turn around as if he were going in the other direction, then he'd back right up to you to be picked up. Crawling backward made him look like a doodle-bug, so I began to call him Doodle, and in time even Mama and Daddy thought it was a better name than William Armstrong. Only Aunt Nicey disagreed. She said caul babies should be treated with special respect since they might turn out to be saints. Renaming my brother was perhaps the kindest thing I ever did for him, because nobody expects much from someone called Doodle.

❻ Although Doodle learned to crawl, he showed no signs of walking, but he wasn't idle. He talked so much that we all quit listening to what he said. It was about this time that Daddy built him a go-cart and I had to pull him around. At first I just paraded him up and down the piazza, but then he started crying to be taken out into the yard and it ended up by my having to lug him wherever I went. If I so much as picked up my cap, he'd start crying to go with me and Mama would call from wherever she was, "Take Doodle with you."

He was a burden in many ways. The doctor had said that he mustn't get too excited, too hot, too cold, or too tired and that he must always be treated gently. A long list of don'ts went with him, all of which I ignored once we got out of the house. To discourage his coming with me, I'd run with him across the ends of the cotton rows and careen him around corners on two wheels. Sometimes I accidentally turned him over, but he never told Mama. His skin was very sensitive, and he had to wear a big straw hat whenever he went out. When the going got rough and he had to cling to the sides of the go-cart, the hat slipped all the way down over his ears. He was a sight. Finally, I could see I was licked. Doodle was my brother and he was going to cling to me forever, no matter what I did, so I dragged him across the burning cotton field to share with him the only beauty I knew, Old Woman Swamp. I pulled the go-cart through the saw-tooth fern, down into the green dimness where the palmetto fronds whispered by the stream. I lifted him out and set him down in the soft rubber grass beside a tall pine. His eyes were round with wonder as he gazed about him, and his little hands began to stroke the rubber grass. Then he began to cry.

"For heaven's sake, what's the matter?" I asked, annoyed.

❼

Two Boys in a Punt, N. C. Wyeth, Courtesy of Dr. and Mrs. William A. Morton, Jr.

❽ ▲ **Critical Viewing**
What can you tell about the brothers' relationship from this illustration and the details in the story? **[Infer]**

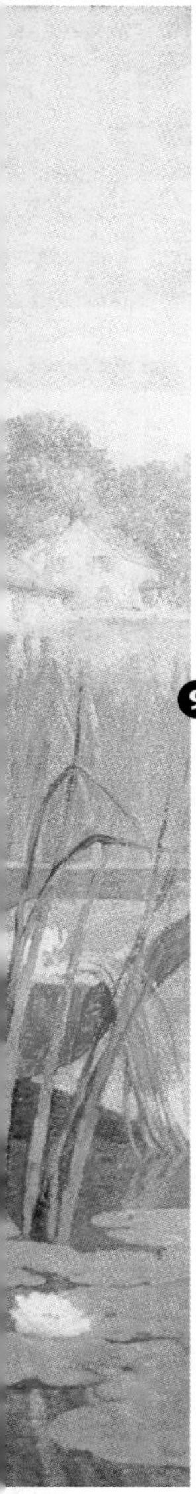

"It's so pretty," he said. "So pretty, pretty, pretty."

After that day Doodle and I often went down into Old Woman Swamp. I would gather wildflowers, wild violets, honeysuckle, yellow jasmine, snakeflowers, and water lilies, and with wire grass we'd weave them into necklaces and crowns. We'd bedeck ourselves with our handiwork and loll about thus beautified, beyond the touch of the everyday world. Then when the slanted rays of the sun burned orange in the tops of the pines, we'd drop our jewels into the stream and watch them float away toward the sea.

There is within me (and with sadness I have watched it in others) a knot of cruelty borne by the stream of love, much as our blood sometimes bears the seed of our destruction, and at times I was mean to Doodle. One day I took him up to the barn loft and showed him his casket, telling him how we all had believed he would die. It was covered with a film of Paris green[3] sprinkled to kill the
9 rats, and screech owls had built a nest inside it.

Doodle studied the mahogany box for a long time, then said, "It's not mine."

"It is," I said. "And before I'll help you down from the loft, you're going to have to touch it."

"I won't touch it," he said sullenly.

"Then I'll leave you here by yourself," I threatened, and made as if I were going down.

Doodle was frightened of being left. "Don't go leave me, Brother," he cried, and he leaned toward the coffin. His hand, trembling, reached out, and when he touched the casket he screamed. A screech owl flapped out of the box into our faces, scaring us and covering us with Paris green. Doodle was paralyzed, so I put him on my shoulder and carried him down the ladder, and even when we were outside in the bright sunshine, he clung to me, crying, "Don't leave me. Don't leave me."

When Doodle was five years old, I was embarrassed at having a brother of that age who couldn't walk, so I set out to teach him. We were down in Old Woman Swamp and it was spring and the sick-sweet smell of bay flowers hung everywhere like a mournful song. "I'm going to teach you to walk, Doodle," I said.

He was sitting comfortably on the soft grass, leaning back against the pine. "Why?" he asked.

I hadn't expected such an answer. "So I won't have to haul you around all the time."

"I can't walk, Brother," he said.

Literary Analysis
Point of View How would this part of the story be different if a third-person narrator told it?

10 **Reading Check**
What does the narrator force Doodle to touch?

3. **Paris green** poisonous green powder.

9 Literary Analysis

Point of View

- How might the description of the boys in the swamp be different if the story were narrated by an outside voice?
  Answer: An objective narrator might not convey the deep happiness and pleasure the boys feel in the swamp and its flowers.
- Ask the Literary Analysis question on p. 557: How would this part of the story be different if a third-person narrator told it?
  Answer: A third-person narrator might describe Doodle's thoughts and feelings in the loft, or explain more clearly why the narrator feels the urge to treat Doodle cruelly.
- Ask students whether a third-person narrator might judge the narrator's actions as harshly as he himself seems to do.
  Answer: Students may debate whether the narrator's self-judgment of his cruelty is warranted, or whether a more objective third-person narrator would place those actions in a more tolerant context. The narrator is a child himself and has been burdened with great responsibilities.

10 Reading Check

Answer: The narrator makes Doodle touch the coffin that was made for him when he was born.

CUSTOMIZE INSTRUCTION FOR UNIVERSAL ACCESS

For Gifted/Talented Students	For Advanced Readers
Ask students to rewrite the scene with the narrator and Doodle in the barn loft in the first person from Doodle's point of view. Their versions should be no longer than one page and should reflect his feelings about his older brother, as well as his reactions to what happens in the loft. Have volunteers share their versions with the class.	Have students discuss how they think Doodle feels about his brother. As they read, they should keep an eye out for clues about Doodle's feelings. They should also think about how they would feel if they were in Doodle's situation. Does Doodle admire his brother? Is he afraid of him? Does he love him? Make sure students support their answers with details from the story and from their own experience.

⓫ Reading Strategy

Identifying With a Character

- Ask the Reading Strategy question on p. 558: How would you feel if you were in Doodle's situation? Why?
  Possible answers: Student responses may include scared, nervous, afraid to fail, uncertain.
- Ask students why they think Doodle cooperates in the narrator's project to teach him to walk. Does Doodle want to learn to walk for his own sake or his brother's? Have students support their answers with evidence from the text.
  Answer: Some students will say that he agrees to learn to walk to please the narrator and make him proud. Evidence: Doodle always clings to the narrator, which suggests that he loves and admires him. Others will say that he wants to learn for his own sake, so that he won't be a little old man being pulled along in a go-cart.

"Who says so?" I demanded.

"Mama, the doctor—everybody."

"Oh, you can walk," I said, and I took him by the arms and stood him up. He collapsed onto the grass like a half-empty flour sack. It was as if he had no bones in his little legs.

"Don't hurt me, Brother," he warned.

"Shut up. I'm not going to hurt you. I'm going to teach you to walk." I heaved him up again, and again he collapsed.

This time he did not lift his face up out of the rubber grass. "I just can't do it. Let's make honeysuckle wreaths."

"Oh yes you can, Doodle," I said. "All you got to do is try. Now come on," and I hauled him up once more.

It seemed so hopeless from the beginning that it's a miracle I didn't give up. But all of us must have something or someone to be proud of, and Doodle had become mine. I did not know then that pride is a
⓫ wonderful, terrible thing, a seed that bears two vines, life and death. Every day that summer we went to the pine beside the stream of Old Woman Swamp, and I put him on his feet at least a hundred times each afternoon. Occasionally I too became discouraged because it didn't seem as if he was trying, and I would say, "Doodle, don't you *want* to learn to walk?"

He'd nod his head, and I'd say, "Well, if you don't keep trying, you'll never learn." Then I'd paint for him a picture of us as old men, white-haired, him with a long white beard and me still pulling him around in the go-cart. This never failed to make him try again.

Finally one day, after many weeks of practicing, he stood alone for a few seconds. When he fell, I grabbed him in my arms and hugged him, our laughter pealing through the swamp like a ringing bell. Now we knew it could be done. Hope no longer hid in the dark palmetto thicket but perched like a cardinal in the lacy toothbrush tree, brilliantly visible. "Yes, yes," I cried, and he cried it too, and the grass beneath us was soft and the smell of the swamp was sweet.

With success so imminent, we decided not to tell anyone until he could actually walk. Each day, barring rain, we sneaked into Old Woman Swamp, and by cotton-picking time Doodle was ready to show what he could do. He still wasn't able to walk far, but we could wait no longer. Keeping a nice secret is very hard to do, like holding your breath. We chose to reveal all on October eighth, Doodle's sixth birthday, and for weeks ahead we mooned around the house, promising everybody a most spectacular surprise. Aunt Nicey said that, after so much talk, if we produced anything less tremendous than the Resurrection,[4] she was going to be disappointed.

At breakfast on our chosen day, when Mama, Daddy, and Aunt Nicey were in the dining room, I brought Doodle to the door in the go-cart just as usual and had them turn their backs, making them cross

Reading Strategy
Identifying With a Character How would you feel if you were in Doodle's situation? Why?

imminent (im′ ə nənt) *adj.* likely to happen soon

4. **the Resurrection** (rez′ ə rek′ shən) the rising of Jesus Christ from the dead after his death and burial.

CUSTOMIZE INSTRUCTION FOR UNIVERSAL ACCESS

For Gifted/Talented Students	For Advanced Readers
The ibis, the screech owl, and an imaginary peacock play meaningful roles in this story. Ask students to create a poster, collage, or other artwork based on images of these birds. Challenge students to visually express the emotions and meanings these birds have for Doodle in the story.	Have students write essays analyzing the symbolic importance of birds in this story, such as the screech owl (p. 557), the peacock (p. 559), and the ibis (p. 561). At what point in the plot does each bird appear? What actions does the bird take? How do the human characters react to the bird? Does this bird already have a symbolic value?

their hearts and hope to die if they peeked. I helped Doodle up, and when he was standing alone I let them look. There wasn't a sound as Doodle walked slowly across the room and sat down at his place at the table. Then Mama began to cry and ran over to him, hugging him and kissing him. Daddy hugged him too, so I went to Aunt Nicey, who was thanks praying in the doorway, and began to waltz her around. We danced together quite well until she came down on my big toe with her brogans, hurting me so badly I thought I was crippled for life.

Doodle told them it was I who had taught him to walk, so everyone wanted to hug me, and I began to cry.

12 "What are you crying for?" asked Daddy, but I couldn't answer. They did not know that I did it for myself; that pride, whose slave I was, spoke to me louder than all their voices, and that Doodle walked only because I was ashamed of having a crippled brother.

Within a few months Doodle had learned to walk well and his go-cart was put up in the barn loft (it's still there) beside his little mahogany coffin. Now, when we roamed off together, resting often, we never turned back until our destination had been reached, and to help pass the time, we took up lying. From the beginning Doodle was a terrible liar and he got me in the habit. Had anyone stopped to listen to us, we would have been sent off to Dix Hill.

My lies were scary, involved, and usually pointless, but Doodle's were twice as crazy. People in his stories all had wings and flew wherever they wanted to go. His favorite lie was about a boy named Peter who had a pet peacock with a ten-foot tail. Peter wore a golden robe that glittered so brightly that when he walked through the sunflowers they turned away from the sun to face him. When Peter was ready to go to sleep, the peacock spread his magnificent tail, enfolding the boy gently like a closing go-to-sleep flower, burying him in the gloriously iridescent, rustling vortex. Yes, I must admit it. Doodle could beat me lying.

Doodle and I spent lots of time thinking about our future. We decided that when we were grown we'd live in Old Woman Swamp and pick dog-tongue for a living. Beside the stream, he planned, we'd build us a house of whispering leaves and the swamp birds would be our chickens. All day long (when we weren't gathering dog-tongue) we'd swing through the cypresses on the rope vines, and if it rained we'd huddle beneath an umbrella tree and play stickfrog. Mama and Daddy could come and live with us if they wanted to. He even came up with the idea that he could marry Mama and I could marry Daddy. Of course, I was old enough to know this wouldn't work out, but the picture he painted was so beautiful and serene that all I could do was whisper Yes, yes.

13 Once I had succeeded in teaching Doodle to walk, I began to believe in my own infallibility and I prepared a terrific development program for him, unknown to Mama and Daddy, of course. I would teach him to run, to swim, to climb trees, and to fight. He, too, now

Literary Analysis
Point of View What effect does the narrator's admission of his motive have on your perception of his development?

iridescent (ir′ ə des′ ənt) *adj.* having shifting, rainbowlike colors

vortex (vôr′ teks′) *n.* rushing whirl, drawing in all that surrounds it

infallibility (in fal′ ə bil′ ə tē) *n.* condition of being unable to fail

14 **✔Reading Check**
What surprise do the narrator and Doodle present to their parents?

12 Literary Analysis

Point of View and Dynamic Character

- Remind students that a dynamic character develops and changes over the course of a story.
- Ask students to identify the narrator's motive in wanting Doodle to walk.
- Then, ask the Literary Analysis question on p. 559: What effect does the narrator's admission of his motive have on your perception of his development?
  Answer: Students will probably appreciate the narrator's honesty; some of them may recognize similar feelings in their own secret thoughts; others may dislike the narrator for his pettiness.

13 Vocabulary Development

Latin Prefix *in-*

- Write the word *infallible* on the board and tell students that the prefix *in-* is a variant of *un-* and usually means "not." *Infallible* means "not fallible" or "not able to fail."
- Write the following words on the board: *secure, sufficient, elegant, direct,* and *accurate.* Ask students to add the prefix *in-* to each word, and then write brief definitions.
  Answer: *insecure:* "not safe"; *insufficient:* "not enough"; *inelegant:* "not elegant; crude"; *indirect:* "not direct; roundabout"; *inaccurate:* "not exact; containing mistakes."

14 ✔Reading Check

Answer: The narrator has helped Doodle to walk by himself.

15 Background

History

This passage refers to the summer of 1918 and mentions key World War I battles that involved American soldiers and marines. The United States entered World War I in the spring of 1917. By spring 1918, more than 300,000 American soldiers had landed in France; by that summer, the numbers had swelled to more than 1.5 million. The American forces reinforced and energized their French and British allies and helped win an end to the war on November 11, 1918.

16 Literary Analysis

Point of View

- Ask the Literary Analysis question on p. 560: Based on this passage, what do you learn about the narrator and his wishes for his brother? **Answer:** He is determined that Doodle keep up with everyone at school; he doesn't want Doodle to be different.
- Have students compare and contrast Doodle's and the narrator's feelings about the importance of being like everyone else at school. Why do they feel this way? **Answer:** The narrator thinks it's very important to be like everyone else; Doodle doesn't understand why. Doodle has never been around other children except for his brother; he is accustomed to being different from everyone else. The narrator goes to school and is aware of its social pressures.

Monitor Progress Have students discuss whether they agree or disagree with the narrator's view that it's important to fit in at school. Suggest that they write about this question in their journals.

believed in my infallibility, so we set the deadline for these accomplishments less than a year away, when, it had been decided, Doodle could start to school.

That winter we didn't make much progress, for I was in school and Doodle suffered from one bad cold after another. But when spring came, rich and warm, we raised our sights again. Success lay at the end of summer like a pot of gold, and our campaign got off to a good start. On hot days, Doodle and I went down to Horsehead Landing and I gave him swimming lessons or showed him how to row a boat. Sometimes we descended into the cool greenness of Old Woman Swamp and climbed the rope vines or boxed scientifically beneath the pine where he had learned to walk. Promise hung about us like the leaves, and wherever we looked, ferns unfurled and birds broke into song.

That summer, the summer of 1918, was blighted. In May and June there was no rain and the crops withered, curled up, then died under the thirsty sun. One morning in July a hurricane came out of the east, tipping over the oaks in the yard and splitting the limbs of the elm trees. That afternoon it roared back out of the west, blew the fallen oaks around, snapping their roots and tearing them out of the earth like a hawk at the entrails of a chicken. Cotton bolls were wrenched from the stalks and lay like green walnuts in the valleys between the rows, while the cornfield leaned over uniformly so that the tassels touched the ground. Doodle and I followed Daddy out into the cotton field, where he stood, shoulders sagging, surveying the ruin. When his chin sank down onto his chest, we were frightened, and Doodle slipped his hand into mine. Suddenly Daddy straightened his shoulders, raised a giant knuckly fist, and with a voice that seemed to rumble out of the earth itself began cursing heaven, hell, the weather, and the Republican Party. Doodle and I, prodding each other and giggling, went back to the house, knowing that everything would be all right.

entrails (en´ trālz) *n.* internal organs, specifically intestines

15 And during that summer, strange names were heard through the house: Chateau Thierry, Amiens, Soissons, and in her blessing at the supper table, Mama once said, "And bless the Pearsons, whose boy Joe was lost at Belleau Wood."[5]

16 So we came to that clove of seasons. School was only a few weeks away, and Doodle was far behind schedule. He could barely clear the ground when climbing up the rope vines and his swimming was certainly not passable. We decided to double our efforts, to make that last drive and reach our pot of gold. I made him swim until he turned blue and row until he couldn't lift an oar. Wherever we went, I purposely walked fast, and although he kept up, his face turned red and his eyes became glazed. Once, he could go no further, so he collapsed on the ground and began to cry.

Literary Analysis
Point of View Based on this passage, what do you learn about the narrator and his wishes for his brother?

5. **Château Thierry** (shá´ tō´ tē er´ ē), **Amiens** (á myan´), **Soissons** (swä sôn´), . . . **Belleau** (be lō´) **Wood** places in France where battles were fought during World War I.

17 "Aw, come on, Doodle," I urged. "You can do it. Do you want to be different from everybody else when you start school?"

"Does it make any difference?"

"It certainly does," I said. "Now, come on," and I helped him up.

As we slipped through dog days, Doodle began to look feverish, and Mama felt his forehead, asking him if he felt ill. At night he didn't sleep well, and sometimes he had nightmares, crying out until I touched him and said, "Wake up, Doodle. Wake up."

It was Saturday noon, just a few days before school was to start. I should have already admitted defeat, but my pride wouldn't let me. The excitement of our program had now been gone for weeks, but still we kept on with a tired doggedness. It was too late to turn back, for we had both wandered too far into a net of expectations and had left no crumbs behind.

Daddy, Mama, Doodle, and I were seated at the dining-room table having lunch. It was a hot day, with all the windows and doors open in case a breeze should come. In the kitchen Aunt Nicey was humming softly. After a long silence, Daddy spoke. "It's so calm, I wouldn't be surprised if we had a storm this afternoon."

"I haven't heard a rain frog," said Mama, who believed in signs, as she served the bread around the table.

"I did," declared Doodle. "Down in the swamp."

"He didn't," I said contrarily.

"You did, eh?" said Daddy, ignoring my denial.

"I certainly did," Doodle reiterated, scowling at me over the top of his iced-tea glass, and we were quiet again.

Suddenly, from out in the yard, came a strange croaking noise. Doodle stopped eating, with a piece of bread poised ready for his mouth, his eyes popped round like two blue buttons. "What's that?" he whispered.

I jumped up, knocking over my chair, and had reached the door when Mama called, "Pick up the chair, sit down again, and say excuse me."

By the time I had done this, Doodle had excused himself and had slipped out into the yard. He was looking up into the bleeding tree. "It's a great big red bird!" he called.

The bird croaked loudly again, and Mama and Daddy came out into the yard. We shaded our eyes with our hands against the hazy glare of the sun and peered up through the still leaves. On the topmost branch a bird the size of a chicken, with scarlet feathers and long legs, was perched precariously. Its wings hung down loosely, and as we watched, a feather dropped away and floated slowly down through the green leaves.

"It's not even frightened of us," Mama said.

"It looks tired," Daddy added. "Or maybe sick."

Doodle's hands were clasped at his throat, and I had never seen him stand still so long. "What is it?" he asked.

Daddy shook his head. "I don't know, maybe it's—"

Reading Strategy

Identifying With a Character How do you think Doodle feels when his brother asks him if he wants to be different from everybody else?

precariously (prē ker´ ē əs lē) *adv.* insecurely

18 **Reading Check**

What does Doodle find in the yard?

17 Reading Strategy

Identifying with a Character

- Ask students the Reading Strategy question on p. 561: How do you think Doodle feels when his brother asks him if he wants to be different from everybody else?
  Answer: Doodle does not seem concerned about being different. His anxious symptoms probably stem from his fear of failing and embarrassing his brother.
- Do students identify with Doodle's feelings? Why or why not?
  Answer: Students have probably all felt fears of the first day at a new school, especially if someone has made them worry that they won't fit in or measure up, as the narrator has made Doodle feel.

18 Reading Check

Answer: Doodle finds a big red bird.

CUSTOMIZE INSTRUCTION FOR UNIVERSAL ACCESS

For Less Proficient Readers	For Advanced Readers
Have students use this story to review the literary elements of Plot, Climax, and Rising Action that they worked on in previous selections in this unit. You may wish to display the Story Map, p. 83 in **Writing Models and Graphic Organizers on Transparencies,** to assist students in their review.	Have students identify and discuss the various conflicts that make up this story. Remind them that some conflicts, such as a war between two countries, are external. Others, like a conflict between duty and inclination, are internal. Ask students to decide what is the central conflict in "The Scarlet Ibis" and to support their answers with details from the story.

19 Background

Art

Scarlet Ibis, by John James Audubon

John James Audubon (1785–1851) was born in Haiti and lived in France as a boy. He came to the United States in 1803. Audubon spent his life on the ambitious project of producing life-sized, accurate watercolor paintings of every bird in America. His two massive works, *The Birds of America* (1827–1838) and *Ornithological Biography* (1831–1839), are classics of science and art. Use these questions for discussion:

1. How does this illustration of the ibis help you appreciate the family's reaction to seeing it in their yard?
   Answer: The bird's brilliant color and distinctive appearance make the ibis seem rare and exotic.
2. Compare and contrast the ibis to Doodle.
   Answer: Both are unusual, out of place, fragile, with their own special beauty.

20 ▶Critical Viewing

Possible response: Students might be excited, intrigued, awed.

21 Reading Strategy

Identifying With a Character

- Ask the Reading Strategy question on p. 562: With whose response to the ibis do you identify most strongly? Why?
  Answer: All family members appreciate the bird's beauty and exoticism. Students will probably identify with the father's scientific curiosity or Doodle's grief.
- Ask students whether they identify with the family's mirth at Doodle's attempt to dig the ibis a grave. Why or why not?
  Answer: Students will probably say that they wouldn't be tempted to laugh at Doodle, given the sadness of the situation.

At that moment the bird began to flutter, but the wings were uncoordinated, and amid much flapping and a spray of flying feathers, it tumbled down, bumping through the limbs of the bleeding tree and landing at our feet with a thud. Its long, graceful neck jerked twice into an S, then straightened out, and the bird was still. A white veil came over the eyes and the long white beak unhinged. Its legs were crossed and its clawlike feet were delicately curved at rest. Even death did not mar its grace, for it lay on the earth like a broken vase of red flowers, and we stood around it, awed by its exotic beauty.

"It's dead," Mama said.

"What is it?" Doodle repeated.

"Go bring me the bird book," said Daddy.

I ran into the house and brought back the bird book. As we watched, Daddy thumbed through its pages. "It's a scarlet ibis," he said, pointing to a picture. "It lives in the tropics—South America to Florida. A storm must have brought it here."

Sadly, we all looked back at the bird. A scarlet ibis! How many miles it had traveled to die like this, in our yard, beneath the bleeding tree.

"Let's finish lunch," Mama said, nudging us back toward the dining room.

"I'm not hungry," said Doodle, and he knelt down beside the ibis.

"We've got peach cobbler for dessert," Mama tempted from the doorway.

Doodle remained kneeling. "I'm going to bury him."

21 "Don't you dare touch him," Mama warned. "There's no telling what disease he might have had."

"All right," said Doodle. "I won't."

Daddy, Mama, and I went back to the dining-room table, but we watched Doodle through the open door. He took out a piece of string from his pocket and, without touching the ibis, looped one end around its neck. Slowly, while singing softly "Shall We Gather at the River," he carried the bird around to the front yard and dug a hole in the flower garden, next to the petunia bed. Now we were watching him through the front window, but he didn't know it. His awkwardness at digging the hole with a shovel whose handle was twice as long as he was made us laugh, and we covered our mouths with our hands so he wouldn't hear.

When Doodle came into the dining room, he found us seriously eating our cobbler. He was pale and lingered just inside the screen door. "Did you get the scarlet ibis buried?" asked Daddy.

Doodle didn't speak but nodded his head.

"Go wash your hands, and then you can have some peach cobbler," said Mama.

"I'm not hungry," he said.

"Dead birds is bad luck," said Aunt Nicey, poking her head from the kitchen door. "Specially *red* dead birds!"

As soon as I had finished eating, Doodle and I hurried off to

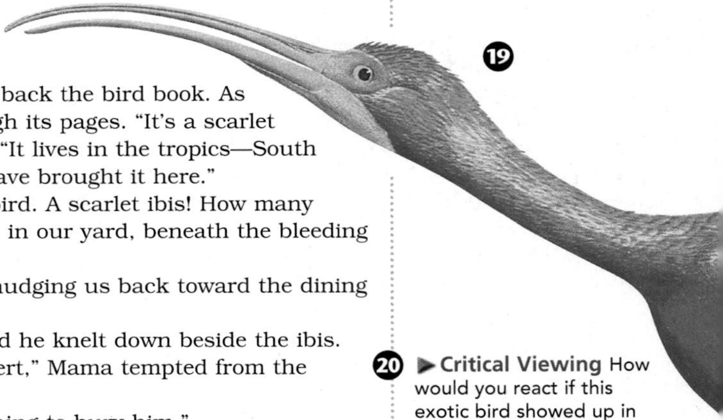

19

20 ▶**Critical Viewing** How would you react if this exotic bird showed up in your back yard? **[Relate]**

Reading Strategy
Identifying With a Character With whose response toward the ibis do you identify most strongly? Why?

Scarlet Ibis, John James Audubon, New-York Historical Society

Horsehead Landing. Time was short, and Doodle still had a long way to go if he was going to keep up with the other boys when he started school. The sun, gilded with the yellow cast of autumn, still burned fiercely, but the dark green woods through which we passed were shady and cool. When we reached the landing, Doodle said he was too tired to swim, so we got into a skiff and floated down the creek with the tide. Far off in the marsh a rail was scolding, and over on the beach locusts were singing in the myrtle trees. 22 Doodle did not speak and kept his head turned away, letting one hand trail limply in the water.

After we had drifted a long way, I put the oars in place and made Doodle row back against the tide. Black clouds began to gather in the southwest, and he kept watching them, trying to pull the oars a little faster. When we reached Horsehead Landing, lightning was playing across half the sky and thunder roared out, hiding even the sound of the sea. The sun disappeared and darkness descended, almost like night. Flocks of marsh crows flew by, heading inland to their roosting trees, and two egrets, squawking, arose from the oyster-rock shallows and careened away.

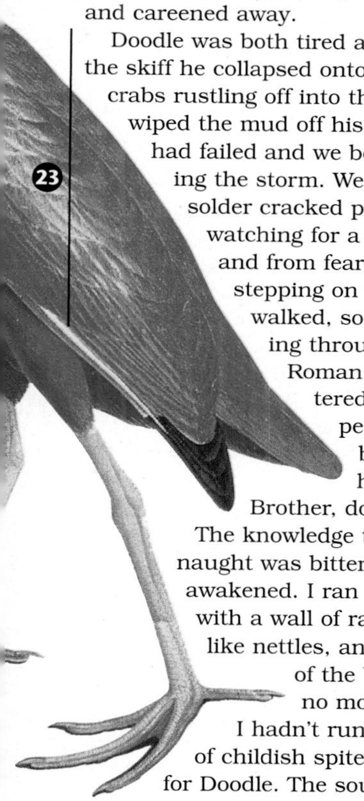

Doodle was both tired and frightened, and when he stepped from the skiff he collapsed onto the mud, sending an armada of fiddler crabs rustling off into the marsh grass. I helped him up, and as he wiped the mud off his trousers, he smiled at me ashamedly. He had failed and we both knew it, so we started back home, rac-
23 ing the storm. We never spoke (What are the words that can solder cracked pride?), but I knew he was watching me, watching for a sign of mercy. The lightning was near now, and from fear he walked so close behind me he kept stepping on my heels. The faster I walked, the faster he walked, so I began to run. The rain was coming, roaring through the pines, and then, like a bursting Roman candle, a gum tree ahead of us was shattered by a bolt of lightning. When the deafening peal of thunder had died, and in the moment before the rain arrived, I heard Doodle, who had fallen behind, cry out, "Brother, Brother, don't leave me! Don't leave me!"

The knowledge that Doodle's and my plans had come to naught was bitter, and that streak of cruelty within me awakened. I ran as fast as I could, leaving him far behind with a wall of rain dividing us. The drops stung my face like nettles, and the wind flared the wet glistening leaves of the bordering trees. Soon I could hear his voice no more.

I hadn't run too far before I became tired, and the flood of childish spite evanesced as well. I stopped and waited for Doodle. The sound of rain was everywhere, but the wind had died and it fell straight down in parallel paths like ropes

Literary Analysis
Point of View What might you learn about Doodle's silence here if the story were told from his point of view?

Reading Strategy
Identifying With a Character How do you think the narrator feels about his brother's failure?

evanesced (ev′ ə nest′) v. faded away

24 **Reading Check**
What does Doodle do with the dead ibis?

22 Literary Analysis
Point of View

- Ask the Literary Analysis question on p. 563: What might you learn about Doodle's silence here if the story were told from his point of view?
  Answer: You might learn how he feels about having seen and buried the ibis.

Monitor Progress Ask students why they think Doodle is silent about his experience. Would students also be silent in this situation?
Answer: Doodle is probably silent because the experience upset him deeply and he's afraid he will cry if he starts talking about it. He may also feel that his brother wouldn't understand, since his brother didn't help Doodle bury the ibis.

23 Reading Strategy
Identifying With a Character

- Ask the Reading Strategy question on p. 563: How do you think the narrator feels about his brother's failure?
  Answer: The narrator seems frustrated and very angry.
- How do you think Doodle feels at this moment in the story? Why do you think so?
  Answer: He watches "for a sign of mercy," which suggests that he feels guilty and ashamed about letting his brother down.

Monitor Progress Ask students why the narrator walks faster and faster and then starts to run.
Answer: He wants to distance himself from Doodle to show his displeasure.

24 Reading Check

Answer: Doodle buries the bird in the garden.

CUSTOMIZE INSTRUCTION FOR UNIVERSAL ACCESS

For Gifted/Talented Students	For Advanced Readers
Have students write an additional scene for the story, in which the narrator brings Doodle's body home. The scene should include the narrator's explanation to his parents and aunt of how and why Doodle died. Students should think about what the narrator might say, whether he would be entirely truthful about his treatment of Doodle, whether his parents had always known about his cruelty to his brother, how they felt about it, and whether they will blame him for Doodle's death.	Students can gather for a small-group discussion about motivation—the reasons characters do things. The narrator is open about his motives, but do readers believe him absolutely, or is he hiding the truth from himself? What motivates him to push Doodle so hard? What motivates Doodle to cling to him? What did he intend by attempting to run away from Doodle during the storm?

ASSESS

Answers for p. 564

Review and Assess

1. Possible responses: Yes, because he pushed Doodle too far and then abandoned him in the storm. No, because he couldn't have known that Doodle would die of fright and exhaustion; Doodle's health was always precarious.
2. **(a)** Doodle gazes at it with wonder and he cries. **(b)** He is sensitive to beauty.
3. **(a)** They reveal that Doodle can walk by himself. **(b)** The story does not suggest that the family guessed the narrator's selfish motive for teaching Doodle to walk.
4. **(a)** He wants to teach him to swim, climb, run, and fight. **(b)** Possible answers: He is encouraged by Doodle's success at walking; he wants Doodle to fit in at school so he himself won't be embarrassed.
5. **(a)** The ibis dies and Doodle buries it. **(b)** Doodle may have identified with the ibis in its strangeness and weakness.
6. Like the ibis, Doodle is different and out of place, but with vivid, unique qualities. Doodle is also vulnerable to sickness and death.
7. Students will probably say yes. An age gap of a few years can create tension; a small brother or sister can be an annoying responsibility; an older one who bosses and bullies can be intimidating. A brother or sister can also be a lifetime friend.

hanging from the sky. As I waited, I peered through the downpour, but no one came. Finally I went back and found him huddled beneath a red nightshade bush beside the road. He was sitting on the ground, his face buried in his arms, which were resting on his drawn-up knees. "Let's go, Doodle," I said.

He didn't answer, so I placed my hand on his forehead and lifted his head. Limply, he fell backwards onto the earth. He had been bleeding from the mouth, and his neck and the front of his shirt were stained a brilliant red.

"Doodle! Doodle!" I cried, shaking him, but there was no answer but the ropy rain. He lay very awkwardly, with his head thrown far back, making his vermilion neck appear unusually long and slim. His little legs, bent sharply at the knees, had never before seemed so fragile, so thin.

I began to weep, and the tear-blurred vision in red before me looked very familiar. "Doodle!" I screamed above the pounding storm and threw my body to the earth above his. For a long long time, it seemed forever, I lay there crying, sheltering my fallen scarlet ibis from the heresy[6] of rain.

6. **heresy** (her′ i sē) idea opposed to the beliefs of a religion or philosophy.

James Hurst

(b. 1922)

James Hurst grew up in coastal North Carolina, a place of quiet landscapes and violent storms. Before becoming a writer, he studied both chemical engineering and opera, served in the army during World War II, and eventually took a job in a New York bank. Hurst's career at the bank lasted for thirty-four years.

While at the bank, Hurst spent his evenings writing short stories. "The Scarlet Ibis," his most popular story, was published in 1960. One of the qualities that makes it such a powerful story is Hurst's use of symbols—objects, people, or ideas that have an underlying meaning. Hurst wrote, "I wanted [the ibis] to represent [the character of Doodle]—not Doodle's physical self, but his spirit."

Review and Assess

Thinking About the Selection

1. **Respond:** Do you blame the narrator for Doodle's death? Why or why not?
2. **(a) Recall:** How does Doodle react to Old Woman Swamp? **(b) Analyze:** What does Doodle's reaction suggest about his character?
3. **(a) Recall:** What do the brothers reveal on Doodle's sixth birthday? **(b) Deduce:** Do you think the family guessed the reason for the narrator's tears? Explain.
4. **(a) Recall:** What does the narrator want to teach Doodle to do next? **(b) Interpret:** Why do you think he sets such demanding goals for Doodle?
5. **(a) Recall:** What happens after the appearance of the scarlet ibis? **(b) Infer:** What do you think motivates Doodle to treat the ibis as he does?
6. **Compare:** How is Doodle like the scarlet ibis?
7. **Extend:** Do you think it is normal to have mixed feelings about a brother or sister? Why or why not?

ASSESSMENT PRACTICE: Reading Comprehension

Author's Point of View (For more practice, see Test Preparation Workbook, p. 36.)

Many tests require students to recognize an author's point of view. Use this sample test item.

There is within me (and with sadness I have watched it in others) a knot of cruelty borne by the stream of love, much as our blood sometimes bears the seed of our destruction, and at times I was mean to Doodle.

The author views the narrator with ________.

A admiration
B sympathy
C impatience
D disapproval

The passage suggests that the author sees cruelty as a common by-product of human love. The correct answer is *B*.

Review and Assess

Literary Analysis

Point of View

1. Does Hurst's use of the **first-person point of view** make you feel more involved in the story? Why or why not?
2. What is the effect of having the narrator look back at the events years after they occurred?
3. If it were told from another point of view, the story would be very different. In a chart like the one shown, record how various events might be seen from Daddy's and Mama's perspective.

Connecting Literary Elements

4. Is Doodle a **dynamic** or a **static character**? Using a chart like this one, cite story details that will help you answer the question.

5. Are the mother and father in the story **dynamic characters?** Explain.
6. (a) Do you think a first-person narrator must always be a dynamic character? (b) Would "The Scarlet Ibis" be an effective story if the narrator never changed? Why or why not?

Reading Strategy

Identifying With a Character

7. **Identify** with the narrator by describing how you might have treated Doodle if he had been your little brother.
8. What can you learn from the narrator's experiences that you can apply to your relationships?

Extend Understanding

9. **Cultural Connection:** The story refers briefly to World War I, then raging in Europe. What connections can be made between the horrors of war and the pain of ordinary life? Explain.

Quick Review

Point of view is the perspective from which a story is told.

In **third-person point of view,** the narrator does not participate in the story.

In **first-person point of view,** the narrator is a character within the story who refers to himself or herself as "I."

A **dynamic character** is one who develops and grows during the course of the story. A **static character** does not change.

To **identify with a character,** put yourself in his or her place by considering how you would act in similar circumstances.

Take It to the Net

www.phschool.com

Take the interactive self-test online to check your understanding of the selection.

ENRICHMENT: Further Reading

Other Works by James Hurst

"August Snow"
"Once There Came a Cobra"
"The Summer of Two Figs"

Take It to the Net

Visit www.phschool.com for more information on James Hurst.

Answers for p. 565

Review and Assess

1. Students will probably agree that they feel more involved because the narrator directly shares details of his thoughts and feelings.
2. The narrator is able to assess his motives accurately from the vantage point of adulthood.
3. Sample answer: Event: Doodle walking on his own. Perspective: Both parents would feel thrilled at his accomplishment and relieved to see this sign that he might not always be totally dependent on others.
4. Possible response: Doodle is a dynamic character. Over the course of the story, he still needs a lot of help, but he grows in ability. And his personality has changed: he has become brave, determined, and somewhat optimistic.
5. The parents are static characters. They do not change during the story.
6. **(a)** No; a narrator might simply be an observer of the dynamic characters around him or her. **(b)** No; the whole point of the story is that at the beginning the narrator resents Doodle and by the end realizes—though too late—that he loved his brother.
7. Some students would like to think that they would have been kinder to Doodle, but others may admit that they would have had as much difficulty as the narrator did.
8. Possible response: Students may cite the need to meet differences and disabilities with greater respect and empathy.
9. Students may note that ordinary life, like war, can include random cruelty, physical suffering, and sudden death.

EXTEND

Answers for p. 566

❶ Vocabulary Development

Word Analysis

1. *Incorrect* means "wrong," the opposite of *correct.*
2. *Independent* means "needing no help from others," the opposite of *dependent.*
3. *Incompatible* means "unable to get along," the opposite of *compatible.*

Spelling Strategy

1. indexes or indices
2. appendixes or appendices
3. apexes
4. matrixes or matrices

Possible answers:

1. The indexes of all of the books showed the name of the president I needed to research.
2. She looked in the appendixes of the textbooks to find the information she needed.
3. They could see the apexes of three mountains from where they were standing.
4. Melted metal was poured into the matrices to create metal candleholders.

Concept Development: Synonyms and Antonyms

1. synonyms
2. antonyms
3. antonyms
4. synonyms
5. synonyms
6. antonyms
7. synonyms

❷ Grammar

1. Crawling backward; subject
2. Renaming my brother; subject
3. walking; object of preposition
4. practicing; object of preposition
5. Keeping a secret; subject. holding your breath; subject

Writing Application

Sample sentences: Thinking about the future was a favorite pastime. I grew tired of pulling the go-cart. Walking by himself was Doodle's proudest moment.

Integrate Language Skills

❶ Vocabulary Development Lesson

Word Analysis: Latin Prefix *in-*

The Latin prefix *in-*, a variant spelling of the prefix *un-*, usually means "not." *Infallible*, then, means "not fallible" or "not able to fail." For each word below, explain how adding *in-* changes its meaning.

1. correct 2. dependent 3. compatible

Spelling Strategy

The plural of some words ending in *x* may be formed by changing the *x* to *ces*. Sometimes, you may need to change the vowel that precedes the *x*, too. One plural form of the word *vortex*, for example, is *vortices*.

Look up the plural form(s) of the following words, and use each plural form in a sentence.

1. index 2. appendix 3. apex 4. matrix

Concept Development: Synonyms and Antonyms

Review the vocabulary word list on page 553. Then, decide whether the word pairs below are synonyms, words with similar meanings, or antonyms, words with opposite meanings. Write your answer in your notebook.

1. entrails, guts
2. infallibility, unreliability
3. precariously, securely
4. vortex, whirlpool
5. imminent, proximate
6. endured, evanesced
7. shimmering, iridescent

❷ Grammar Lesson

Gerund Phrases

A **gerund** is a verb form ending in *-ing* that acts as a noun. In a sentence, a gerund can be the subject, object, or object of a preposition. A **gerund phrase** is a gerund with modifiers or a complement, all acting together as a noun. (Do not confuse a gerund with a **present participle,** which acts as an adjective and also ends in *-ing*.)

Look at the following examples.

Gerund: *Boating* was a challenge. (*subject*)

Gerund Phrase: *Boating with Doodle* was even harder. (*subject*)

He faced the challenge of *boating with Doodle.* (*object of preposition*)

Practice Write the gerund or gerund phrase in each sentence, and identify its function.

1. Crawling backward was a necessity.
2. Renaming my brother was my idea.
3. He learned to crawl, but he showed no signs of walking.
4. One day, after weeks of practicing, he stood alone for a few seconds.
5. Keeping a secret is hard to do, like holding your breath.

Writing Application Choose and rewrite three sentences from "The Scarlet Ibis," using gerund phrases in all of them.

WG Prentice Hall Writing and Grammar Connection: Chapter 21, Section 1

TEACHING RESOURCES

The following resources can be used to enrich or extend the instructions for pp. 566–567.

Vocabulary

- **Selection Support:** Build Vocabulary, p. 141
- **Vocabulary and Spelling Practice Book** (Use this booklet for skills enrichment.)

Grammar

- **Selection Support:** Build Grammar Skills, p. 142
- **Writing and Grammar,** Gold Level, p. 450
- **Daily Language Practice Transparencies**

Writing

- **Writing and Grammar,** Gold Level, p. 286
- **Writing and Grammar iText CD-ROM**

BLOCK SCHEDULING: Resources marked with this symbol provide varied instruction during 90-minute blocks.

❸ Writing Lesson

Journal Entry

Put yourself in the place of the narrator in "The Scarlet Ibis," and write a journal entry describing your feelings about Doodle's death.

Prewriting Start by making a list of the emotions you think the narrator might have felt after his brother's death, and the reasons for those emotions. Then, make a list of Doodle's qualities based on the story.

Model: Listing to Elaborate Emotions

Emotion	Reason
guilt	I ran away from him in the storm.

Providing a reason for a particular emotion conveys a clear image for the journal entry.

Drafting Using the lists you have generated, write one paragraph explaining how you feel about the loss of Doodle. Then, write another paragraph explaining what you miss most about him.

Revising Read your journal entry to a classmate. Make sure that you have conveyed all of the feelings you listed. Add additional details or insights to reveal the true emotions of the narrator.

WG *Prentice Hall Writing and Grammar Connection: Chapter 13, Section 2*

❹ Extension Activities

Research and Technology Coastal North Carolina—the setting of "The Scarlet Ibis"—is an area of striking natural beauty. In a group, gather information to prepare a **travel brochure** about the region.

- Use Internet resources to gather maps and photographs of the region.
- Include appealing information to make sure that the presentation is directed toward attracting tourists.

If possible, use desktop graphics software to publish your brochure. **[Group Activity]**

Listening and Speaking Research the role of the ibis in Egyptian myth and religion and deliver a **presentation** about it. Compare and contrast the Egyptian attitude toward the ibis with that of the characters in the story. After your presentation, ask your class for feedback.

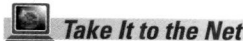

Take It to the Net www.phschool.com

Go online for an additional research activity using the Internet.

ASSESSMENT RESOURCES

The following resources can be used to assess students' knowledge and skills.

Selection Assessment

- **Formal Assessment,** pp. 126–128
- **Open Book Test,** pp. 106–108
- **Got It! Assessment Videotapes,** Tape 3
- **Test Bank Software**

Take It to the Net

Visit www.phschool.com for self-tests and additional questions on "The Scarlet Ibis."

Writing Rubric

- **Performance Assess. and Portfolio Mgmt.,** p. 8

PRENTICE HALL ASSESSMENT SYSTEM

- **Workbook**
- **Skill Book**
- **Transparencies**
- **CD-ROM**

Lesson Support for p. 567

❸ Writing Lesson

- Work with the class to generate two additional reasons in the model on p. 567.
- Remind students that in a journal, a character can be entirely honest. Journal entries are meant for the writer's eyes only.
- Use the Autobiographical Narrative rubric in **Performance Assessment and Portfolio Management,** p. 8, to evaluate students' journal entries.

❹ Research and Technology

- Provide, or have students bring to class, travel brochures to be used as models.
- Have students use the descriptions and the names of plants and birds in this story as starting points for their research.
- Remind students that a brochure is limited in scope. Students will have to be selective in their use of detail.

CUSTOMIZE INSTRUCTION For Universal Access

To address different learning styles, use the following activities suggested in the **Extension Activities** booklet, p. 36.

- For Visual/Spatial Learners, use Activities 5–7.
- For Verbal/Linguistic Learners, use Activity 5.
- For Bodily/Kinesthetic Learners, use Activity 6.

Blues Ain't No Mockin Bird ✦ Uncle Marcos

Lesson Objectives and CA Correlations

1. **To analyze and respond to literary elements**
   - Literary Analysis: Characterization **R 3.4**
   - Comparing Literary Works
2. **To read, comprehend, analyze, and critique short stories**
   - Reading Strategy: Making Inferences About Characters **R 3.3, 3.4**
   - Reading Check questions
   - Review and Assess questions
   - Assessment Practice (ATE)
3. **To develop word analysis skills, fluency, and systematic vocabulary**
   - Vocabulary Development Lesson: Latin Prefix: *dis-* **R 1.1**
4. **To understand and apply written and oral language conventions**
   - Spelling Strategy
   - Grammar Lesson: Infinitive Phrases **LC 1.1**
5. **To understand and apply appropriate writing and research strategies**
   - Writing Lesson: Magazine Feature **W 1.1**
   - Extension Activity: Comparison-and-Contrast Brochure **W 1.3**
6. **To understand and apply listening and speaking strategies**
   - Extension Activity: Monologue **LS 2.1**

STEP-BY-STEP TEACHING GUIDE	PACING GUIDE
PRETEACH	
Motivate Students and Provide Background	
Use the Motivation activity (ATE p. 568)	5 min.
Read and discuss the Preview material and Background information (SE/ATE p. 568) [A]	10 min.
Introduce the Concepts	
Introduce the Literary Analysis and Reading Strategy (SE/ATE p. 569) [A]	15 min.
Pronounce the vocabulary words and read their definitions (SE p. 569)	5 min.
TEACH	
Monitor Comprehension	
Informally monitor comprehension by circulating while students read independently or in groups [A]	40 min.
Monitor students' comprehension with the Reading Check notes (SE/ATE pp. 571, 573, 575, 577, 579, 581, 583)	as students read
Develop vocabulary with Vocabulary notes (SE pp. 570, 574, 577–578, 583; ATE p. 581)	as students read
Develop Understanding	
Develop students' understanding of characterization with Literary Analysis annotations (SE/ATE pp. 571–572, 574–575, 579–580, 582) [A]	15 min.
Develop students' ability to make inferences about a character with the Reading Strategy annotations (SE/ATE pp. 570, 574, 577–578, 580, 581, 583)	15 min.
ASSESS	
Assess Mastery	
Assess students' mastery of the Reading Strategy and Literary Analysis by having them answer the Review and Assess questions (SE/ATE p. 585)	20 min.
Use one or more of the print and media Assessment Resources (ATE p. 587) [A]	up to 50 min.
EXTEND	
Apply Understanding	
Have students complete the Vocabulary Development Lesson and the Grammar Lesson (SE p. 586) [A]	20 min.
Apply students' ability to include details that support the main impression using the Writing Lesson (SE p. 587) [A]	45 min.
Apply students' understanding using one or more of the Extension Activities (SE p. 587)	20–90 min.

[A] **ACCELERATED INSTRUCTION:** Use the strategies and activities identified with an [A].

UNIVERSAL ACCESS
● = Below-Level Students
▲ = On-Level Students
■ = Above-Level Students

Time and Resource Manager

Reading Level: Average/Challenging
Average Number of Instructional Days: 5

RESOURCES		
PRINT	**TRANSPARENCIES**	**TECHNOLOGY**
• **Beyond Literature,** Career Connection: Journalist, p. 37 ▲ ■		• **Interest Grabber Video,** Tape 3 ● ▲ ■
• **Selection Support Workbook:** ● ▲ ■ Literary Analysis, p. 148 Reading Strategy, p. 147 Build Vocabulary, p. 145	• **Literary Analysis and Reading Transparencies,** pp. 73 and 74 ● ▲ ■	
		• **Listening to Literature** ● ▲ ■ Audiocassettes, Side 16 Audio CDs, CD 11
• **Literatura en español** ● ▲ • **Literary Analysis for Enrichment** ■	• **Fine Art Transparencies Volume 1,** Art Transparencies 14, 16 ● ▲ ■	
• **Formal Assessment:** Selection Test, pp. 129–131 ● ▲ ■ • **Open Book Test,** pp. 109–111 ● ▲ ■ • PRENTICE HALL ASSESSMENT SYSTEM ● ▲ ■	• PRENTICE HALL ASSESSMENT SYSTEM ● ▲ ■ Skills Practice Answers and Explanations on Transparencies	• **Test Bank Software** ● ▲ ■ • **Got It! Assessment Videotapes,** Tape 3 ● ▲
• **Selection Support Workbook:** ● ▲ ■ Build Grammar Skills, p. 146 • **Writing and Grammar,** Gold Level ● ▲ ■ • **Extension Activities,** p. 37 ● ▲ ■	• **Daily Language Practice Transparencies** ● ▲ • **Writing Models and Graphic Organizers on Transparencies,** p. 63 ● ▲ ■	• **Writing and Grammar iText CD-ROM** ● ▲ ■ ***Take It to the Net*** www.phschool.com

BLOCK SCHEDULING: Use one 90-minute class period to preteach the selection and have students read it. Use a second 90-minute class period to assess students' mastery of skills and have them complete one of the Extension Activities.

PRETEACH

Step-by-Step Teaching Guide for pp. 568–569

Motivation

Have students create detailed character sketches based on the following rough descriptions of the central characters from the two stories they're about to read: (1) a strong-willed elderly woman who values her privacy, and (2) an eccentric inventor and world adventurer whose relatives find him peculiar and at times embarrassing. Have students read the stories to see if the characters they've come up with are as interesting as the ones the writers developed.

Interest Grabber Video

As an alternative, play "Isabel Allende on Memorable Characters" on Tape 3 to engage student interest.

1 Background

Literature

The name "magic realism" shows the contrast on which this literary style is based—it highlights and reveals magical occurrences in everyday life. An example of the style that came to be called magic realism is the opening of Franz Kafka's short novel *The Metamorphosis:* One morning, Gregor Samsa wakes up to find that he has been transformed into a gigantic insect. Every other aspect of the novel is realistic; people treat Gregor as if he had a rare and disgusting disease, but no one seems surprised at the concept of a man changing magically into a beetle.

Magic realism is a style most readers associate with modern and contemporary Latin American writers, but it is an international style. Magic realists include Salman Rushdie, Milan Kundera, and a number of other European and Eastern writers.

Prepare to Read

Blues Ain't No Mockin Bird ◆ Uncle Marcos

Take It to the Net

Visit www.phschool.com for interactive activities and instruction related to the selections, including
- background
- graphic organizers
- literary elements
- reading strategies

Preview

Connecting to the Literature

Certain people you meet in childhood may become etched in memory forever because of their unique personality traits or the lessons they teach you. In these stories, you will meet two memorable characters who leave an indelible impression on the stories' narrators.

1 Background

Imagine a world in which people can float in the air and it can rain continuously for years. These fantastic details capture the way a group of writers, including Isabel Allende, use words. The authors practice a style of writing known as "magical realism," in which fantastic details blend with realistic ones to stretch the boundaries of readers' imaginations.

TEACHING RESOURCES

The following resources can be used to enrich or extend the instruction for pp. 568–569.

Motivation

Interest Grabber Video, Tape 3

Background

Beyond Literature, p. 37

Take It to the Net

Visit www.phschool.com for background and hotlinks for the selections.

Literary Analysis

Literary Analysis and Reading Transparencies, Characterization, p. 74

Reading

Selection Support: Reading Strategy, p. 147; Build Vocabulary, p. 145

Literary Analysis and Reading Transparencies, Making Inferences About Characters, p. 73

BLOCK SCHEDULING: Resources marked with this symbol provide varied instruction during 90-minute blocks.

❷ Literary Analysis

Characterization

Characterization refers to the way a writer reveals a character's personality traits. With **direct characterization,** writers directly state a character's personality traits. In **indirect characterization,** a writer uses a character's actions, thoughts, and feelings to suggest a character's traits. In this passage from "Uncle Marcos," the writer characterizes Marcos indirectly:

> He spent the whole night making incomprehensible movements in the drawing room; later they turned out to be exercises . . .

Notice how the authors of these selections let their characters' words and actions, along with the reactions of others, reveal what they are like.

Comparing Literary Works

A character's personality traits are often revealed through the **narrator**—the person from whose perspective a story is told.

- A **third-person narrator** is not a character in the story.
- A **first-person narrator** is a character within the story.

The narrator in "Blues Ain't No Mockin Bird" is part of the story, while the narrator of "Uncle Marcos" stands outside the story. Compare the author's choice of narrator in each selection.

❸ Reading Strategy

Making Inferences About Characters

When you **make an inference about a character,** you draw a conclusion using details the author provides. For example, in "Uncle Marcos," you will learn that Marcos once serenaded a woman. From this, you can infer that he is romantic and unpredictable.

To make inferences, look beyond the words on the page, and ask yourself what the author implies about the characters. On a chart like this one, list details from the selections and the inferences you make from them.

Vocabulary Development

lassoed (las´ ōd´) *adj.* wrapped around (p. 570)

formality (fôr mal´ ə tē) *n.* established rules or customs (p. 574)

pallid (pal´ id) *adj.* pale (p. 577)

vanquished (vaŋ´ kwisht) *adj.* defeated (p. 577)

fetid (fet´ id) *adj.* smelly (p. 577)

impassive (im pas´ iv) *adj.* showing no emotion (p. 578)

disconsolately (dis kän´ sə lit lē) *adv.* unhappily (p. 581)

unrequited (un ri kwīt´ id) *adj.* not reciprocated (p. 583)

❷ Literary Analysis

Characterization

- Ask students to identify the following statements from previous selections as examples of direct characterization, indirect characterization, or both.

  "Father was driving with a reckless and exhilarating skill," p. 488—"If I Forget Thee, Oh Earth," (indirect)

  "Doodle was just about the craziest brother a boy ever had," p. 555—"The Scarlet Ibis" (direct)

  "Miss Golden, crisp, fragrant, and punctual, shut the door," p. 545—"Sonata for Harp and Bicycle" (direct)

  "Holmes chuckled and wriggled in his chair, as was his habit when in high spirits," p. 99—"The Red-headed League" (both direct and indirect)

❸ Reading Strategy

Making Inferences About Characters

- Students have practiced the skill of inferring throughout the year. Briefly review it with them.
- Display the Reading Strategy transparency, p. 73 in **Literary Analysis and Reading Transparencies,** and work as a class to make inferences about the characters in the passage.
- As students read these two stories, remind them to pay attention to what the characters do and say, and what they leave unsaid and undone. Students can record their observations in a chart like the one shown.

Vocabulary Development

- Pronounce each vocabulary word for students, and read the definitions as a class. Have students identify any words with which they are already familiar.

CUSTOMIZE INSTRUCTION FOR UNIVERSAL ACCESS

For Less Proficient Readers	For English Learners	For Advanced Readers
Have students write each main character's name in the center of a Sunburst diagram. Use the diagram on p. 63 of **Writing Models and Graphic Organizers on Transparencies** as a model. On the rays branching from the center, they can write actions the characters take and statements they make.	Make sure students understand that this story is written in dialect—the characters drop the *g* at the end of words, use double negatives, and say *ain't.* As students work at understanding the dialect, have them think about how it affects characterization.	Have students pay special attention to the minor characters in both stories. Have them gather for a group discussion of how both writers draw vivid personalities with a minimum number of words. Have students explain which are their favorite characters and why.

E-Teach

Visit E-Teach at www.phschool.com for teachers' essays on how to teach, with questions and answers.

TEACH

Step-by-Step Teaching Guide for pp. 570–584

CUSTOMIZE INSTRUCTION For Interpersonal Learners

As students read these two stories, have them think about the points of view from which they are narrated. Point out that both stories are narrated by minor characters. Ask students how the stories would have been different if they had been told from the points of view of the main characters, Granny and Uncle Marcos. Challenge students to write brief summaries of both stories, no longer than a page or two, from the points of view of Granny and Uncle Marcos.

❶ About the Selection

Bambara's story explores the issues of family dignity and the right to privacy. When photographers come to gather footage for a documentary about the county food stamp campaign, Granny Cain stares at them until they back away. When the intruders persist, their camera is opened and they are forced to leave.

❷ Reading Strategy

Making Inferences About Characters

- Ask students how they would characterize Cathy. Which of her actions indicate particular character traits? **Answer:** Cathy's comparison of the cracks in the ice to a crazy spider web suggests that she is imaginative. Her criticism of Terry suggests that she is contemptuous and scornful.
- What do the other children think of Cathy? Why do they think this? **Answer:** The phrase "Cathy grown-up" shows that the narrator thinks Cathy acts older than her age and is bossy.

❶ BLUES AIN'T NO MOCKIN BIRD

Toni Cade Bambara

The puddle had frozen over, and me and Cathy went stompin in it. The twins from next door, Tyrone and Terry, were swingin so high out of sight we forgot we were waitin our turn on the tire. Cathy jumped up and came down hard on her heels and started tap-dancin. And the frozen patch splinterin every which way underneath kinda spooky. "Looks like a plastic spider web," she said. "A sort of weird spider, I guess, with many mental problems." But really it looked like the crystal paperweight Granny kept in the parlor. She was on the back porch, Granny was, making the cakes drunk. The old ladle dripping rum into the Christmas tins, like it used to drip maple syrup into the pails when we lived in the Judson's woods, like it poured cider into the vats when we were on the Cooper place, like it used to scoop buttermilk and soft cheese when we lived at the dairy. ❷

"Go tell that man we ain't a bunch of trees."

"Ma'am?"

"I said to tell that man to get away from here with that camera." Me and Cathy look over toward the meadow where the men with the station wagon'd been roamin around all mornin. The tall man with a huge camera lassoed to his shoulder was buzzin our way.

"They're makin movie pictures," yelled Tyrone, stiffenin his legs and twistin so the tire'd come down slow so they could see.

"They're makin movie pictures," sang out Terry.

"That boy don't never have anything original to say," say Cathy grown-up.

lassoed (las´ ōd´) *adj.* wrapped around

TEACHING RESOURCES

The following resources can be used to enrich or extend the instruction for pp. 570–584.

Literary Analysis

- **Writing Models and Graphic Organizers on Transparencies,** p. 63 ■
- **Selection Support:** Literary Analysis, p. 148

Reading

- **Listening to Literature Audiocassettes,** Side 16 ■
- **Listening to Literature Audio CDs,** CD 11 ■

Extension

- **Fine Art Transparencies,** Volume 1, Art Transparencies 14, 16 (Use these paintings to discuss the dignity of the families in the two stories.)

■ **BLOCK SCHEDULING:** Resources marked with this symbol provide varied instruction during 90-minute blocks.

❸

Sharecropper, Elizabeth Catlett, Courtesy Evan Tibbs Collection

❹ ▲ **Critical Viewing** As you read, compare Granny with the woman in the illustration. **[Compare and Contrast]**

By the time the man with the camera had cut across our neighbor's yard, the twins were out of the trees swingin low and Granny was onto the steps, the screen door bammin soft and scratchy against her palms. "We thought we'd get a shot or two of the house and everything and then—"

❺ **Reading Check**

What does the man bring to Granny's property?

❸ Background

Art

Sharecropper, Elizabeth Catlett

Elizabeth Catlett (born 1919) grew up in Washington, D.C., during the era of segregation. She studied art with American regionalist Grant Wood (best known for his painting *American Gothic*). Wood urged Catlett to paint what she knew, which she believes is why so many of her subjects are black women.

"Art must be realistic for me," Catlett wrote. "I have always wanted my art to service my people—to reflect us, to relate to us, to stimulate us, to make us aware of our potential. . . ."

Use this question for discussion:

- What predictions can you make about the story by looking at this illustration?
  Answer: An African-American woman may play an important part in the story. The characters are probably poor.

❹ ▶ Critical Viewing

Answer: They are both poor; the woman in the picture holds her coat together with a safety pin. They are both old; the woman in the picture has white hair. Granny's personality is forceful and hard; the woman in the picture is portrayed in strong, angular lines.

❺ Reading Check

Answer: The man brings a camera.

CUSTOMIZE INSTRUCTION FOR UNIVERSAL ACCESS

For Special Needs Students	For Advanced Readers
Have students gather in a small group and read the story aloud as though it were a play, with each reader taking one role. You may want to take the role of the narrator yourself, since it is much more extensive than the others. Pause two or three times during the reading to ask students some questions, or to give students a chance to ask some questions.	Have students write detailed analyses of Granny's character. How would they describe her personality? Which clues in the story support their answers? What has her past life been like? What do the four children in the story think of her? What is her relationship with Granddaddy? With her neighbors? Why have she and Granddaddy moved so often? Which story details support students' speculations about Granny?

❻ Literary Analysis

Characterization

- Ask a volunteer to read this sentence aloud and identify it as either direct or indirect characterization.
  Answer: indirect
- What can students tell about the photographer from this sentence?
  Answer: He is embarrassed. He feels guilty about what he is doing. Granny intimidates him.

❼ Background

Dialects

"You don't know about me without you have read a book by the name of *The Adventures of Tom Sawyer,* but that ain't no matter." As this opening sentence of *The Adventures of Huckleberry Finn* shows, many great works of literature are written entirely or partly in dialect. The plays of August Wilson, the stories of Guy de Maupassant, and the novels of Charles Dickens are peopled with characters who speak a variety of dialects.

Dialect on a page echoes the way a character would actually speak. It adds color, liveliness, and realism to a story, play, or novel. Mark Twain showed his belief in the importance of dialect in a brief explanatory note to *Huckleberry Finn*: "The shadings [of the seven dialects in the novel] have not been done in a haphazard fashion, or by guesswork; but painstakingly. . . . I make this explanation for the reason that without it many readers would suppose that all these characters were trying to talk alike and not succeeding."

❽ Literary Analysis

Characterization and Narrator

- Ask the Literary Analysis question on p. 572: Who is the narrator?
  Answer: The man addresses Granny, Cathy, and the narrator as "ladies," so the narrator is female. She is playing with the other children. She is probably Granny's granddaughter.
- Then, ask students how the narrator characterizes Granny—directly or indirectly? **Answer:** She characterizes her both directly and indirectly. She says that Granny is always teaching (direct). She describes Granny's actions and tone of voice and tells what she says to the men and how they react to her (indirect).

"Good mornin," Granny cut him off. And smiled that smile.

❻ "Good mornin," he said, head all down the way Bingo does when you yell at him about the bones on the kitchen floor. "Nice place you got here, aunty. We thought we'd take a—"

"Did you?" said Granny with her eyebrows. Cathy pulled up her socks and giggled.

"Nice things here," said the man, buzzin his camera over the yard. The pecan barrels, the sled, me and Cathy, the flowers, the printed stones along the driveway, the trees, the twins, the toolshed.

"I don't know about the thing, the it, and the stuff," said Granny, still talkin with her eyebrows. "Just people here is what I tend to consider."

Camera man stopped buzzin. Cathy giggled into her collar.

"Mornin, ladies," a new man said. He had come up behind us when we weren't lookin. "And gents," discoverin the twins givin him a nasty look. "We're filmin for the county," he said with a smile. "Mind if we shoot a bit around here?"

"I do indeed," said Granny with no smile. Smilin man was smiling up a storm. So was Cathy. But he didn't seem to have another word to say, so he and the camera man backed on out the yard, but you could hear the camera buzzin still. "Suppose you just shut that machine off," said Granny real low through her teeth, and took a step down off the porch and then another.

"Now, aunty," Camera said, pointin the thing straight at her.

"Your mama and I are not related."

❽ Smilin man got his notebook out and a chewed-up pencil. "Listen," he said movin back into our yard, "we'd like to have a statement from you . . . for the film. We're filmin for the county, see. Part of the food stamp campaign. You know about the food stamps?"

Granny said nuthin.

"Maybe there's somethin you want to say for the film. I see you grow your own vegetables," he smiled real nice. "If more folks did that, see, there'd be no need—"

Granny wasn't sayin nuthin. So they backed on out, buzzin at our clothesline and the twins' bicycles, then back on down to the meadow. The twins were danglin in the tire, lookin at Granny. Me and Cathy were waitin, too, cause Granny always got somethin to say. She teaches steady with no let-up. "I was on this bridge one time," she started off. "Was a crowd cause this man was goin to jump, you understand. And a minister was there and the police and some other folks. His woman was there, too."

"What was they doin?" asked Tyrone.

"Tryin to talk him out of it was what they was doin. The minister talkin about how it was a mortal sin, suicide. His woman takin bites out of her own hand and not even knowin it, so nervous and cryin and talkin fast."

Literature in context ❼ Cultural Connection

Dialect

"Blues Ain't No Mockin Bird" is written in dialect—a way of speaking that is common to people in a particular region or group. Dialect affects pronunciation, word choice, and sentence structure. You will notice, for example, that the characters in Bambara's story do not pronounce the *g* on the ends of *-ing* words—a common speech pattern in the American South. Bambara's use of dialect makes her story sound informal and intimate, as if it were being related orally.

Literary Analysis
Characterization and Narrator Who is the narrator? How do you know?

ENRICHMENT: Music Connection

The Blues

The blues is more than a musical style—it is a state of mind. If a person has the blues, he or she is weary and sad. A blues song is a lament, often about sorrow in love. The famous "blue notes" (the flatted third and seventh notes of the scale) add color and expressiveness to the music. Blue notes also represent the meeting of European and African musical scales; the blues scale is not African, but African American. Much jazz music is based on the blues. Singing or playing the blues is a cathartic experience for both performer and listener, who pour out feelings of anguish and afterward feel resigned to their situation and perhaps even optimistic about it. Great blues composers include W. C. Handy and Duke Ellington; many classical pieces, such as George Gershwin's *Rhapsody in Blue,* were inspired by the blues.

"So what happened?" asked Tyrone.

"So here comes . . . this person . . . with a camera, takin pictures of the man and the minister and the woman. Takin pictures of the man in his misery about to jump, cause life so bad and people been messin with him so bad. This person takin up the whole roll of film practically. But savin a few, of course."

"Of course," said Cathy, hatin the person. Me standin there wonderin how Cathy knew it was "of course" when I didn't and it was *my* grandmother.

After a while Tyrone say, "Did he jump?"

"Yeh, did he jump?" say Terry all eager. And Granny just stared at the twins till their faces swallow up the eager and they don't even care any more about the man jumpin. Then she goes back onto the porch and lets the screen door go for itself. I'm lookin to Cathy to finish the story cause she knows Granny's whole story before me even. Like she knew how come we move so much and Cathy ain't but a third cousin we picked up on the way last Thanksgivin visitin. But she knew it was on account of people drivin Granny crazy till she'd get up in the night and start packin. Mumblin and packin and wakin everybody up sayin, "Let's get on away from here before I kill me somebody." Like people wouldn't pay her for things like they said they would. Or Mr. Judson bringin us boxes of old clothes and raggedy magazines. Or Mrs. Cooper comin in our kitchen and touchin everything and sayin how clean it all was.
9 Granny goin crazy, and Granddaddy Cain pullin her off the people, sayin, "Now, now, Cora." But next day loadin up the truck, with rocks all in his jaw, madder than Granny in the first place.

"I read a story once," said Cathy soundin like Granny teacher. "About this lady Goldilocks who barged into a house that wasn't even hers. And not invited, you understand. Messed over the people's groceries and broke up the people's furniture. Had the nerve to sleep in the folks' bed."

"Then what happened?" asked Tyrone. "What they do, the folks, when they come in to all this mess?"

"Did they make her pay for it?" asked Terry, makin a fist. "I'd've made her pay me."

I didn't even ask. I could see Cathy actress was very likely to just walk away and leave us in mystery about this story which I heard was about some bears.

"Did they throw her out?" asked Tyrone, like his father sounds when he's bein extra nasty-plus to the washin-machine man.

"Woulda," said Terry. "I woulda gone upside her head with my fist and—"

"You woulda done whatcha always do—go cry to Mama, you big baby," said Tyrone. So naturally Terry starts hittin on Tyrone, and next thing you know they tumblin out the tire and rollin on the ground. But Granny didn't say a thing or send the twins home or step out on the steps to tell us about how we can't afford to be fightin amongst ourselves. She didn't say nuthin. So I get into the tire to take my turn. And I could see her leanin up against the pantry table, staring at the cakes

Reading Strategy
Making Inferences About Characters What can you infer about the attitudes of the children toward Granny?

10 Reading Check
How does Granny respond when the camera crew ask her to make a statement?

9 Reading Strategy

Making Inferences About Characters

- Ask the Reading Strategy question on p. 573: What can you infer about the attitudes of the children toward Granny?
  Answer: Cathy imitates Granny, which suggests admiration. The twins shut up when she looks at them, which suggests fear and respect. The narrator notes that Granny is neither patient nor tolerant of stupidity, ignorance, or interference.

Monitor Progress Have students compare and contrast their own opinions of Granny with those of the children.

10 Reading Check

Answer: Granny asks the camera crew to shut their machines off.

⓫ Literary Analysis

Characterization

- How does the narrator characterize Granddaddy Cain—directly or indirectly? Explain.
  Answer: She characterizes him both ways. She says that he is "tall and quiet and like a king" (direct) and that "people just can't stand it" (indirect).

Monitor Progress Ask students why Granddaddy's manner makes people "go for him sometimes."
Answer: People resent Granddaddy's regal appearance. Their instincts tell them that he makes them look inferior, and they don't like this feeling.

⓬ Reading Strategy

Making Inferences About Characters

- Ask the Reading Strategy question on p. 574: What inferences can you make about the camera crew from their reaction to Granddaddy Cain?
  Possible responses: They probably find him an interesting subject for their camera; they lack sufficient respect to speak to him or ask permission to follow him.
- Ask students if they think the cameramen's inferences are correct.
  Answer: They are probably correct that he would look good on film—but only if he decided to cooperate.

she was puttin up for the Christmas sale, mumblin real low and grumpy and holdin her forehead like it wanted to fall off and mess up the rum cakes.

Behind me I hear before I can see Granddaddy Cain comin through the woods in his field boots. Then I twist around to see the shiny black oilskin cuttin through what little left there was of yellows, reds, and oranges. His great white head not quite round cause of this bloody thing high on his shoulder, like he was wearin a cap on sideways. He takes the shortcut through the pecan grove, and the sound of twigs snapping overhead and underfoot travels clear and cold all the way up to us. And here comes Smilin and Camera up behind him like they was goin to do somethin. Folks like to go for him sometimes. Cathy say it's because he's so tall and quiet and like a king. And people just can't stand it. But Smilin and Camera don't hit him in the head or nuthin. They just buzz on him as he stalks by with the chicken hawk slung over his shoulder, squawkin, drippin red down the back of the oilskin. He passes the porch and stops a second for Granny to see he's caught the hawk at last, but she's just starin and mumblin, and not at the hawk. So he nails the bird to the toolshed door, the hammerin crackin through the eardrums. And the bird flappin himself to death and droolin down the door to paint the gravel in the driveway red, then brown, then black. And the two men movin up on tiptoe like they was invisible or we were blind, one.

"Get them persons out of my flower bed, Mister Cain," say Granny moanin real low like at a funeral.

"How come your grandmother calls her husband 'Mister Cain' all the time?" Tyrone whispers all loud and noisy and from the city and don't know no better. Like his mama, Miss Myrtle, tell us never mind the formality as if we had no better breeding than to call her Myrtle, plain. And then this awful thing—a giant hawk—come wailin up over the meadow, flyin low and tilted and screamin, zigzaggin through the pecan grove, breakin branches and hollerin, snappin past the clothesline, flyin every which way, flyin into things reckless with crazy.

"He's come to claim his mate," say Cathy fast, and ducks down. We all fall quick and flat into the gravel driveway, stones scrapin my face. I squinch my eyes open again at the hawk on the door, tryin to fly up out of her death like it was just a sack flown into by mistake. Her body holdin her there on that nail, though. The mate beatin the air overhead and clutchin for hair, for heads, for landin space.

The camera man duckin and bendin and runnin and fallin, jigglin the

Reading Strategy
Making Inferences About Characters What inferences can you make about the camera crew from their reaction to Granddaddy Cain?

formality (fôr mal′ ə tē) *n.* established rules or customs

CUSTOMIZE INSTRUCTION FOR UNIVERSAL ACCESS

For Advanced Readers

Have students discuss the symbolism of the two hawks in the story. You might have students consider the following facts about hawks:

- Hawks are birds of prey.
- Female hawks are usually larger than male hawks.
- Hawks mate for life.

Have students consider whether the two hawks stand for Granny and Granddaddy. If so, have them explain why they think so and support their answers. Ask whether students think the hawks represent the photographers who prey on country families to make their documentary.

13 camera and scared. And Smilin jumpin up and down swipin at the huge bird, tryin to bring the hawk down with just his raggedy ole cap. Granddaddy Cain straight up and silent, watchin the circles of the hawk, then aimin the hammer off his wrist. The giant bird fallin, silent and slow. Then here comes Camera and Smilin all big and bad now that the awful screechin thing is on its back and broken, here they come. And Granddaddy Cain looks up at them like it was the first time noticin, but not payin them too much mind cause he's listenin, we all listenin, to that low groanin music comin from the porch. And we figure any minute, somethin in my back tells me any minute now, Granny gonna bust through that screen with somethin in her hand and murder on her mind. So Granddaddy say above the buzzin, but quiet, "Good day, gentlemen." Just like that. Like he'd invited them in to play cards and they'd stayed too long and all the sandwiches were gone and Reverend Webb was droppin by and it was time to go.

They didn't know what to do. But like Cathy say, folks can't stand Granddaddy tall and silent and like a king. They can't neither. The smile the men smilin is pullin the mouth back and showin the teeth. Lookin like the wolf man, both of them. Then Granddaddy holds his hand out—

14 this huge hand I used to sit in when I was a baby and he'd carry me through the house to my mother like I was a gift on a tray. Like he used to on the trains. They called the other men just waiters. But they spoke of Granddaddy separate and said, The Waiter. And said he had engines in his feet and motors in his hands and couldn't no train throw him off and couldn't nobody turn him round. They were big enough for motors, his hands were. He held that one hand out all still and it gettin to be not at all a hand but a person in itself.

"He wants you to hand him the camera," Smilin whispers to Camera, tiltin his head to talk secret like they was in the jungle or somethin and come upon a native that don't speak the language. The men start untyin the straps, and they put the camera into that great hand speckled with the hawk's blood all black and crackly now. And the hand don't even drop with the weight, just the fingers move, curl up around the machine. But Granddaddy lookin straight at the men. They lookin at each other and everywhere but at Granddaddy's face.

"We filmin for the county, see," say Smilin. "We puttin together a movie for the food stamp program . . . filmin all around these parts. Uhh, filmin for the county."

"Can I have my camera back?" say the tall man with no machine on his shoulder, but still keepin it high like the camera was still there or needed to be. "Please, sir."

Then Granddaddy's other hand flies up like a sudden and gentle bird, slaps down fast on top of the camera and lifts off half like it was a calabash[1] cut for sharing.

"Hey," Camera jumps forward. He gathers up the parts into his chest and everything unrollin and fallin all over. "Whatcha tryin to do? You'll

1. **calabash** (kal′ ə bash) *n.* large gourdlike fruit.

Literary Analysis
Characterization and Narrator How do the narrator's memories of Granddaddy influence your reaction to him?

15 **Reading Check**
What does Granddaddy do to let the camera crew know he wants their camera?

13 Critical Thinking
Compare and Contrast

- Have students compare and contrast Granddaddy's reaction to the hawk with the reactions of Smilin and Camera.
  Answer: Granddaddy remains calm and deals easily with the situation. Smilin and Camera panic; once Granddaddy kills the hawk, they pretend they were never scared.
- Ask students what this contrast tells them about the characters.
  Answer: Granddaddy is self-possessed and fearless. The other two men seem small and cowardly by comparison.

14 Literary Analysis
Characterization and Narrator

- Ask students the Literary Analysis question on p. 575: How do the narrator's memories of Granddaddy influence your reaction to him?
  Answer: She describes him as graceful, always able to keep his balance on moving trains. Her memories of being carried in one of his hands suggest his great size and gentleness.

Monitor Progress Have students relate these memories of Granddaddy to his actions in the present-day story.
Answer: Granddaddy uses his size and silence to intimidate the strangers. His huge hands take violent but measured actions: killing the remaining hawk and opening the camera to expose the film.

15 Reading Check

Answer: Granddaddy opens the camera and exposes the film.

Answers for p. 576

Review and Assess

1. Possible responses: Students may select Granddaddy because he is so imposing, or the narrator because she is perceptive.
2. **(a)** She gets angry and tells the children to send him away. **(b)** She means that they have feelings; they are not scenery to be photographed without their permission.
3. **(a)** They are making a documentary about the food-stamp program. **(b)** She is asserting her dignity and personal rights; she is expressing anger at their trespassing.
4. **(a)** Instead of showing sensitivity to the man's heartbreak, the photographer intrusively took pictures. **(b)** She insists on being treated with respect and understanding.
5. **(a)** He is tall and regal, striding noisily toward the house with a captured hawk slung across his back. **(b)** She asks him to get the photographers out of the garden. **(c)** He is a quiet but forceful man who takes direct action.
6. Possible responses: Yes, because the photographers were rude, insensitive trespassers. No, because Granddaddy destroyed expensive film instead of simply telling them to go away.

ruin the film." He looks down into his chest of metal reels and things like he's protectin a kitten from the cold.

"You standin in the misses' flower bed," say Granddaddy. "This is our own place."

The two men look at him, then at each other, then back at the mess in the camera man's chest, and they just back off. One sayin over and over all the way down to the meadow, "Watch it, Bruno. Keep ya fingers off the film." Then Granddaddy picks up the hammer and jams it into the oilskin pocket, scrapes his boots, and goes into the house. And you can hear the squish of his boots headin through the house. And you can see the funny shadow he throws from the parlor window onto the ground by the string-bean patch. The hammer draggin the pocket of the oilskin out so Granddaddy looked even wider. Granny was hummin now—high not low and grumbly. And she was doin the cakes again, you could smell the molasses from the rum.

"There's this story I'm goin to write one day," say Cathy dreamer. "About the proper use of the hammer."

"Can I be in it?" Tyrone say with his hand up like it was a matter of first come, first served.

"Perhaps," say Cathy, climbin onto the tire to pump us up. "If you there and ready."

Toni Cade Bambara

(1939–1995)

Toni Cade Bambara's interest in her African American heritage comes through clearly in her writing. Her cultural identity is evident even in her name, Bambara—the name of an African tribe known for its textiles—which she made her own after finding it on a sketchbook belonging to her great-grandmother.

Bambara wrote two collections of short stories—*Gorilla, My Love*, where "Blues Ain't No Mockin Bird" appeared, and *The Sea Birds Are Still Alive*—as well as a novel, *The Salt Eaters*.

Review and Assess

Thinking About the Selection

1. **Respond:** Which character from the story would you most like to meet? Why?
2. **(a) Recall:** How does Granny react when she notices the man with the camera? **(b) Analyze:** What does she mean when she says "we ain't a bunch of trees"?
3. **(a) Recall:** Why are the photographers filming in the area? **(b) Generalize:** What kind of message is Granny giving the men through her speech and actions?
4. **(a) Generalize:** What is the main point of Granny's story about the man who attempted suicide? **(b) Draw Conclusions:** How does the story help explain Granny's behavior?
5. **(a) Recall:** How is Granddaddy described when he first appears on the scene? **(b) Connect:** What does Granny ask Granddaddy to do when he appears? **(c) Infer:** What does the description of his actions suggest about his character?
6. **Evaluate:** Is Granddaddy's treatment of the photographers justified? Support your view with details from the story.

16 # Uncle Marcos

from *The House of the Spirits*

Isabel Allende

17 . . . It had been two years since Clara had last seen her Uncle Marcos, but she remembered him very well. His was the only perfectly clear image she retained from her whole childhood, and in order to describe him she did not need to consult the daguerreotype[1] in the drawing room that showed him dressed as an explorer leaning on an old-fashioned double-barreled rifle with his right foot on the neck of a Malaysian tiger, the same triumphant position in which she had seen the Virgin standing between plaster clouds and pallid angels at the main altar, one foot on the vanquished devil. All Clara had to do to see her uncle was close her eyes and there he was, weather-beaten and thin, with a pirate's mustache through which his strange, sharklike smile peered out at her. It seemed impossible that he could be inside that long black box that was lying in the middle of the courtyard.

Each time Uncle Marcos had visited his sister Nivea's home, he had stayed for several months, to the immense joy of his nieces and nephews, particularly Clara, causing a storm in which the sharp lines of domestic order blurred. The house became a clutter of trunks, of animals in jars of formaldehyde,[2] of Indian lances and sailor's bundles. In every part of the house people kept tripping over his equipment, and all sorts of unfamiliar animals appeared that had traveled from remote lands only to meet their death beneath Nana's irate broom in the farthest corners of the house. Uncle Marcos's manners were those of a cannibal, as Severo put it. He spent the whole night making incomprehensible movements in the drawing room; later they turned out to be exercises designed to perfect the mind's control over the body and to improve digestion. He performed alchemy[3] experiments in the kitchen, filling the house with fetid smoke and ruining pots and pans with solid substances that stuck to their bottoms and were impossible to remove. While the rest of the household tried to sleep, he dragged his suitcases up and down the halls, practiced making strange, high-pitched sounds

pallid (pal′ id) *adj.* pale

vanquished (vaŋ′ kwisht) *adj.* defeated

fetid (fet′ id) *adj.* smelly

18 **Reading Check**

How long does Uncle Marcos stay when he visits Nivea's home?

1. **daguerreotype** (də ger′ ō tīp′) *n.* early type of photograph.
2. **formaldehyde** (for mal′ də hīd′) *n.* solution used as a preservative.
3. **alchemy** (al′ kə mē) *adj.* early form of chemistry, with philosophic and magical associations.

16 About the Selection

In this excerpt from *The House of the Spirits,* Clara del Valle recalls her eccentric Uncle Marcos. Laughed at by some, but loved by many, Uncle Marcos impresses his community with his daring adventures in courtship, flight, rebirth, and clairvoyance. Through Clara's eyes Uncle Marcos earns the renown he had gained only fitfully in his lifetime. The story conveys an important message about how individuals can be misjudged or underappreciated by some people but beloved by others.

17 Reading Strategy

Making Inferences About Characters

- After students have read the opening paragraph, ask what they can infer about Marcos's character. Have them identify details that support their answers.
  Answer: The picture with the rifle and tiger suggests that he is brave and adventurous. The pirate's mustache and sharklike smile create a rascally impression.
- What does the comparison between Marcos's photograph and the statue of the Virgin suggest?
  Possible answer: It suggests that Marcos is somehow good in spirit, in spite of his adventurous nature, or that he has special powers.

18 Reading Check

Answer: Uncle Marcos stays for several months at a time.

CUSTOMIZE INSTRUCTION FOR UNIVERSAL ACCESS

For Less Proficient Readers	For English Learners
The long paragraphs and sentences of this excerpt may challenge some students. Have them find the main idea of each paragraph, then use this list of main ideas to summarize Marcos's adventures. Have students go back over the excerpt, noting how the details of each paragraph support and illuminate the main idea.	If any students are native speakers of Spanish, or are fluent in that language, encourage them to locate and read this excerpt in Spanish, the original language of *The House of the Spirits (La casa de los espíritus).* Challenge them to choose any two-paragraph section of the excerpt and translate it into English. They can then compare and contrast their versions with the one in the textbook.

⑲ Reading Strategy

Making Inferences About Characters

- Ask students what they can infer about Marcos from his method of winning Antonieta's hand in marriage.
  Answer: He is eager to please people, since he wants to entertain the public as well as win Antonieta. He is original and unusual, since the narrator says his methods are not conventional. He is self-confident, since he doesn't seem to mind that his family feels embarrassed.

Monitor Progress Ask students what they can infer about Antonieta from her actions.
Answer: She cares what other people think. She is embarrassed, not pleased, that Marcos pays such unusual attentions to her. She quickly marries in order to leave the area.

⑳ ▶Critical Viewing

Answer: Such an inventor would be creative, imaginative, persistent, clever, and determined. He or she would persevere even if other people laughed or expressed doubts.

on savage instruments, and taught Spanish to a parrot whose native language was an Amazonic dialect. During the day, he slept in a hammock that he had strung between two columns in the hall, wearing only a loincloth that put Severo in a terrible mood but that Nivea forgave because Marcos had convinced her that it was the same costume in which Jesus of Nazareth had preached. Clara remembered perfectly, even though she had been only a tiny child, the first time her Uncle Marcos came to the house after one of his voyages. He settled in as if he planned to stay forever. After a short time, bored with having to appear at ladies' gatherings where the mistress of the house played the piano, with playing cards, and with dodging all his relatives' pressures to pull himself together and take a job as a clerk in Severo del Valle's law practice, he bought a barrel organ and took to the streets with the hope of seducing his Cousin Antonieta and entertaining the public in the bargain. The machine was just a rusty box with wheels, but he painted it with seafaring designs and gave it a fake ship's smokestack. It ended up looking like a coal stove. The organ played either a military march or a waltz, and in between turns of the handle the parrot, who had managed to learn Spanish although he had not lost his foreign accent, would draw a crowd with his piercing shrieks. He also plucked slips of paper from a box with his beak, by way of selling fortunes to the curious. The little pink, green, and blue papers were so clever that they always divulged the exact secret wishes of the customers. Besides fortunes there were little balls of sawdust to amuse the children. The idea of the organ was a last desperate attempt to win the hand of Cousin Antonieta after more conventional means of courting her had failed. Marcos thought no woman in her right mind could remain impassive before a barrel-organ serenade. He stood beneath her window one evening and played his military march and his waltz just as she was taking tea with a group of female friends. Antonieta did not realize the music was meant for her
⑲ until the parrot called her by her full name, at which point she appeared in the window. Her reaction was not what her suitor had hoped for. Her friends offered to spread the news to every salon[4] in the city, and the next day people thronged the downtown streets hoping to see Severo del Valle's brother-in-law playing the organ and selling little sawdust balls with a motheaten parrot, for the sheer pleasure of proving that even in the best of families there could be good reason for embarrassment. In the face of this stain to the family reputation, Marcos was

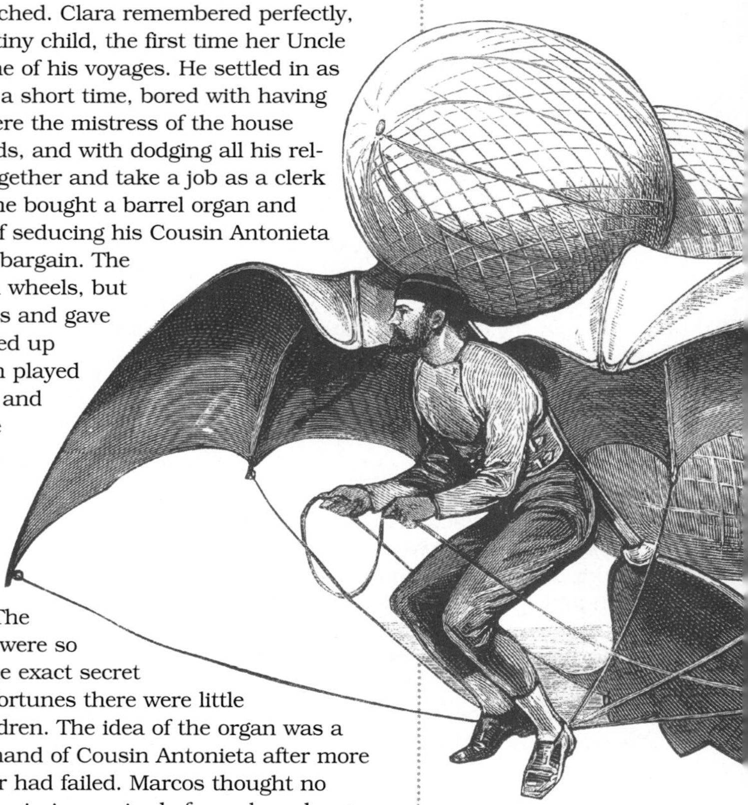

⑳ ▲ **Critical Viewing** In this story, a man tries to build a flying machine. Which character traits might you find in someone who would try to do this? **[Speculate]**

impassive (im pas′ iv) *adj.* showing no emotion

4. **salon** (sə län′) *n.* regular gathering of distinguished guests that meets in a private home.

ENRICHMENT: Literature Connection

The House of the Spirits

The House of the Spirits (1982) is Allende's first novel. Set in an unnamed South American country, it tells the story of the del Valle-Trueba family from 1900 to 1975. The central characters are four women—Rosa, Clara (who appears in this excerpt), Blanca, and Alba—and one man, Esteban Trueba. Trueba is Clara's husband, Blanca's father, and Alba's grandfather. The novel's women are strong and creative, defying and resisting the patriarchal society in which they live. Nívea, who appears in this excerpt, fights for women's suffrage; Alba joins the student movement. The novel's narrating voice is Alba's as she pieces together the details of her female relatives' lives from letters, records, and family documents.

forced to give up organ grinding and resort to less conspicuous ways of winning over his Cousin Antonieta, but he did not renounce his goal. In any case, he did not succeed, because from one day to the next the
19 young lady married a diplomat who was twenty years her senior; he took her to live in a tropical country whose name no one could recall, except that it suggested negritude,[5] bananas, and palm trees, where she managed to recover from the memory of that suitor who had ruined her seventeenth year with his military march and his waltz. Marcos sank
21 into a deep depression that lasted two or three days, at the end of which he announced that he would never marry and that he was embarking on a trip around the world. He sold his organ to a blind man and left the parrot to Clara, but Nana secretly poisoned it with an overdose of cod-liver oil, because no one could stand its lusty glance, its fleas, and its harsh, tuneless hawking of paper fortunes and sawdust balls.

That was Marcos's longest trip. He returned with a shipment of enormous boxes that were piled in the far courtyard, between the chicken coop and the woodshed, until the winter was over. At the first signs of spring he had them transferred to the parade grounds, a huge park where people would gather to watch the soldiers file by on Independence Day, with the goosestep they had learned from the Prussians. 22 When the crates were opened, they were found to contain loose bits of wood, metal, and painted cloth. Marcos spent two weeks assembling the contents according to an instruction manual written in English, which he was able to decipher thanks to his invincible imagination and a small dictionary. When the job was finished, it turned out to be a bird of prehistoric dimensions, with the face of a furious eagle, wings that moved, and a propeller on its back. It caused an uproar. The families of the oligarchy[6] forgot all about the barrel organ, and Marcos became the star attraction of the season. People took Sunday outings to see the bird; souvenir vendors and strolling photographers made a fortune. Nonetheless, the public's interest quickly waned. But then Marcos announced that as soon as the weather cleared he planned to take off in his bird and cross the mountain range. The news spread, making this the most talked-about event of the year. The contraption lay with its stomach on terra firma,[7] heavy and sluggish and looking more like a wounded duck than like one of those newfangled airplanes they were starting to produce in the United States. There was nothing in its appearance to suggest that it could move, much less take flight across the snowy peaks. Journalists and the curious flocked to see it. Marcos smiled his immutable[8] smile before the avalanche of questions and posed for photographers without offering

5. negritude (neg′ rə to͞od′) *n.* blacks and their cultural heritage.
6. oligarchy (äl′ i gär′ kē) *n.* government ruled by a few.
7. terra firma (ter′ ə fur′ ma) *n.* Latin term meaning "firm earth; solid ground."
8. immutable (im myo͞ot′ ə bəl) *adj.* never changing.

Literary Analysis
Direct and Indirect Characterization What does the fact that Uncle Marcos's deep depression lasted only a few days tell you about his character?

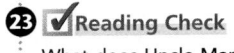

23 **Reading Check**
What does Uncle Marcos do with the barrel organ?

21 Literary Analysis
Direct and Indirect Characterization

- Ask the Literary Analysis question on p. 579: What does the fact that Uncle Marcos's deep depression lasted only a few days tell you about his character?
  Possible responses He bounces back quickly from disappointments. His temperament is naturally cheerful and optimistic. He apparently was not deeply in love with Antonieta.
- Ask students if these two sentences contain direct or indirect characterization.
  Answer: Both. The first sentence is direct; the second sentence is indirect.

22 Background
History

The goose step is a stiff-legged marching step; soldiers on parade kick each leg forward in turn without bending the knee. Students may have seen goose-stepping in documentary film of Nazi Germany. This step is used only when soldiers are on parade; it is not practical for actual combat marches.

23 Reading Check

Answer: Marcos sells it to a blind man.

24 Literary Analysis

Characterization

- Ask the Literary Analysis question on p. 580: What does the people's reaction to Marcos's plan for a plane trip tell you about him?
  Possible answers: Marcos has a reputation for improbable escapades. He can draw huge interest in his planned flight because people expect something unusual.
- Then, ask students what the people's reactions to Marcos tell you about them.
  Answer: They welcome any excuse to take a holiday. They go to watch him take off even though they doubt he will succeed.
- If students have difficulty distinguishing between direct and indirect characterization, use the following graphic organizer.

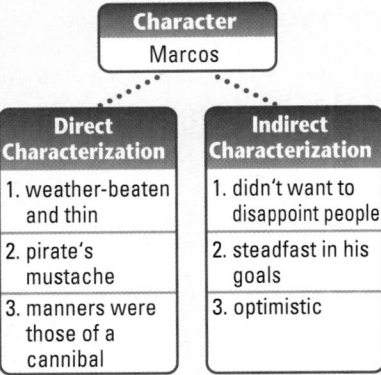

Character
Marcos

Direct Characterization	Indirect Characterization
1. weather-beaten and thin	1. didn't want to disappoint people
2. pirate's mustache	2. steadfast in his goals
3. manners were those of a cannibal	3. optimistic

25 Reading Strategy

Making Inferences About Characters

- Ask the Reading Strategy question on p. 580: What can you infer about Uncle Marcos's motives for attempting to fly in his "bird"?
  Answer: Marcos enjoys risk, the unknown, and the attention of the crowd.
- The people watching Marcos fly decided it was a miracle. Do students think Marcos thought it was a miracle too? Explain.
  Possible responses: No: People underestimated Marcos, but he knew he was more capable than people thought. Yes: Marcos wasn't an aviator; he was as surprised as everyone else that he succeeded.

the least technical or scientific explanation of how he hoped to carry out his plan. People came from the provinces to see the sight. Forty years later his great-nephew Nicolás, whom Marcos did not live to see, unearthed the desire to fly that had always existed in the men of his lineage. Nicolás was interested in doing it for commercial reasons, in a gigantic hot-air sausage on which would be printed an advertisement for carbonated drinks. But when Marcos announced his plane trip, no one believed that his contraption could be put to any practical use. The appointed day dawned full of clouds, but so many people had turned out that Marcos did not want to disappoint them. He showed up punctually at the appointed spot and did not once look up at the sky, which was growing darker and darker with thick gray clouds. The astonished crowd filled all the nearby streets, perching on rooftops and the balconies of the nearest houses and squeezing into the park. No political gathering managed to attract so many people until half a century later, when the first Marxist candidate attempted, through strictly democratic channels, to become President. Clara would remember this holiday as (24) long as she lived. People dressed in their spring best, thereby getting a step ahead of the official opening of the season, the men in white linen suits and the ladies in the Italian straw hats that were all the rage that year. Groups of elementary-school children paraded with their teachers, clutching flowers for the hero. Marcos accepted their bouquets and joked that they might as well hold on to them and wait for him to crash, so they could take them directly to his funeral. The bishop himself, accompanied by two incense bearers, appeared to bless the bird without having been asked, and the police band played happy, unpretentious music that pleased everyone. The police, on horseback and carrying lances, had trouble keeping the crowds far enough away from the center of the park, where Marcos waited dressed in mechanic's overalls, with huge racer's goggles and an explorer's helmet. He was also equipped with a compass, a telescope, and several strange maps that he had traced himself based on various theories of Leonardo da Vinci and on the polar knowledge of the Incas.[9] Against all logic, on the second try the bird lifted off without mishap and with a certain elegance, accompanied by the creaking of its skeleton and the roar of its (25) motor. It rose flapping its wings and disappeared into the clouds, to a send-off of applause, whistlings, handkerchiefs, drumrolls, and the sprinkling of holy water. All that remained on earth were the comments of the amazed crowd below and a multitude of experts, who attempted to provide a reasonable explanation of the miracle. Clara continued to stare at the sky long after her uncle had become invisible. She thought she saw him ten minutes later, but it was only a migrating sparrow. After three days the initial euphoria that had accompanied the first airplane flight in the country died down and no one gave the episode another thought, except for Clara, who continued to peer at the horizon.

Literary Analysis
Characterization What does the people's reaction to Marcos's plan for a plane trip tell you about him?

Reading Strategy
Making Inferences About Characters What can you infer about Uncle Marcos's motives for attempting to fly in his "bird"?

9. **Leonardo da Vinci** (lē′ ə när′ dō də vin′ chē) **. . . Incas** Leonardo da Vinci (1452–1519) was an Italian painter, sculptor, architect, and scientist. The Incas were Native Americans who dominated ancient Peru until the Spanish conquest.

ENRICHMENT: Art/Science Connection

Leonardo da Vinci

One of the greatest creative geniuses of history, Leonardo takes his name from his native village Vinci in the Italian region of Tuscany. He divided most of his artistic career between the cities of Florence and Milan. He produced comparatively few paintings; those that remain, including the *Mona Lisa* and the great mural *The Last Supper,* are among the greatest masterpieces of the Italian Renaissance. Leonardo was interested not only in art but also in all branches of the arts and sciences. His notebooks contain designs for submarines, helicopters, and other inventions that would not be built for centuries. Leonardo was one of the first artists to acquire an exact knowledge of human anatomical proportions by dissecting and studying cadavers. His writings show an inexhaustible curiosity about and wonder at the workings of the universe.

After a week with no word from the flying uncle, people began to speculate that he had gone so high that he had disappeared into outer space, and the ignorant suggested he would reach the moon. With a mixture of sadness and relief, Severo decided that his brother-in-law and his machine must have fallen into some hidden crevice of the
26 cordillera,[10] where they would never be found. Nivea wept disconsolately and lit candles to San Antonio, patron of lost objects. Severo opposed the idea of having masses said, because he did not believe in them as a way of getting into heaven, much less of returning to earth, and he maintained that masses and religious vows, like the selling of indulgences, images, and scapulars,[11] were a dishonest business. Because of his attitude, Nivea and Nana had the children say the rosary,[12] behind their father's back for nine days. Meanwhile, groups of volunteer explorers and mountain climbers tirelessly searched peaks and passes, combing every accessible stretch of land until they finally returned in triumph to hand the family the mortal remains of the deceased in a sealed black coffin. The intrepid traveler was laid to rest in a grandiose funeral. His death made him a hero and his name was on the front page of all the papers for several days. The same multitude that had gathered to see him off the day he flew away in his bird paraded past his coffin. The
27 entire family wept as befit the occasion, except for Clara, who continued to watch the sky with the patience of an astronomer. One week after he had been buried, Uncle Marcos, a bright smile playing behind his pirate's mustache, appeared in person in the doorway of Nivea and Severo del Valle's house. Thanks to the surreptitious[13] prayers of the women and children, as he himself admitted, he was alive and well and in full possession of his faculties, including his sense of humor. Despite the noble lineage of his aerial maps, the flight had been a failure. He had lost his airplane and had to return on foot, but he had not broken any bones and his adventurous spirit was intact. This confirmed the family's eternal devotion to San Antonio, but was not taken as a warning by future generations, who also tried to fly, although by different means. Legally, however, Marcos was a corpse. Severo del Valle was obliged to use all his legal ingenuity to bring his brother-in-law back to life and the full rights of citizenship. When the coffin was pried open in the presence of the appropriate authorities, it was found to contain a bag of sand. This discovery ruined the reputation, up till then untarnished, of the volunteer explorers and mountain climbers, who from that day on were considered little better than a pack of bandits.

Marcos's heroic resurrection made everyone forget about his barrel-organ phase. Once again he was a sought-after guest in all the city's salons and, at least for a while, his name was cleared. Marcos stayed in

disconsolately (dis kän′ sə lit lē) *adv.* unhappily

Reading Strategy
Making Inferences About Characters What inference can you make about Clara from her belief concerning her uncle and his fate?

28 **Reading Check**
What happens to Uncle Marcos after he loses his airplane?

10. **cordillera** (kôr′ dil yer′ə) *n.* system or chain of mountains.
11. **indulgences, images, and scapulars** (skap′ yə lərz) Indulgences are pardons for sins, images are pictures or sculptures of religious figures, and scapulars are garments worn by Roman Catholics as tokens of religious devotion.
12. **say the rosary** use a set of beads to say prayers.
13. **surreptitious** (sʉr′ əp tish′ əs) *adj.* secretive.

26 Vocabulary Development

Latin Prefix *dis-*

- Write the word *disconsolate* on the board. Tell students that the Latin prefix *dis-* means "not." Students may recognize *console* as meaning "comfort." Adding the prefix *dis-* creates the meaning "unable to be comforted; dejected."
- Write the words *loyal, obey,* and *prove* on the board. Ask students to add the prefix *dis-* to these words, then briefly define them. **Answer:** *disloyal,* not loyal; unfaithful; *disobey,* fail to obey; *disprove,* prove to be false or incorrect.

27 Reading Strategy

Making Inferences About Characters

- Ask the Reading Strategy question on p. 581: What inference can you make about Clara from her belief concerning her uncle and his fate? **Answer:** Clara keeps watch because she has faith that Marcos has not failed and is still alive.
- Display the Sunburst transparency, p. 63 in **Writing Models and Graphic Organizers on Transparencies.** Ask students to create a similar diagram of their own and to write *Clara* in the center. In the rays branching from the center, they can note Clara's thoughts and actions that suggest character traits. Have students compare their Sunbursts after they have completed the story.

28 Reading Check

Answer: Marcos returns home on foot to find that he's been declared legally dead.

29 Literary Analysis

Characterization and Narrator

- Ask the Literary Analysis question on p. 582: Which words does the narrator use to characterize Clara directly?
  Possible answers: *upset, closer to him, prophesying powers*
- How is Clara characterized indirectly in this section?
  Answer: We learn that she walked in her sleep and sucked her thumb. She has a "gift."

30 ▶Critical Viewing

Answer: Marcos probably would have liked and admired him. They are kindred spirits.

his sister's house for several months. One night he left without saying goodbye, leaving behind his trunks, his books, his weapons, his boots, and all his belongings. Severo, and even Nivea herself, breathed a sigh of relief. His visit had gone on too long. But Clara was so upset that she spent a week walking in her sleep and sucking her thumb. The little girl, who was only seven at the time, had learned to read from her uncle's storybooks and been closer to him than any other member of the family because of her prophesying powers. Marcos maintained that his niece's gift could be a source of income and a good opportunity for him to cultivate his own clairvoyance.[14] He believed that all human beings possessed this ability, particularly his own family, and that if it did not function well it was simply due to a lack of training. He bought a crystal ball in the Persian bazaar, insisting that it had magic powers and was from the East (although it was later found to be part of a buoy from a fishing boat), set it down on a background of black velvet, and announced that he could tell people's fortunes, cure the evil eye, and improve the quality of dreams, all for the modest sum of five centavos.[15] His first customers were the maids from around the neighborhood. One of them had been accused of stealing, because her employer had misplaced a valuable ring. The crystal ball revealed the exact location of the object in question: it had rolled beneath a wardrobe. The next day there was a line outside the front door of the house. There were coachmen, storekeepers, and milkmen; later a few municipal employees and distinguished ladies made a discreet appearance, slinking along the side walls of the house to keep from being recognized. The customers were received by Nana, who ushered them into the waiting room and collected their fees. This task kept her busy throughout the day and demanded so much of her time that the family began to complain that all there ever was for dinner was old string beans and jellied quince.[16] Marcos decorated the carriage house with some frayed curtains that had once belonged in the drawing room but that neglect and age had turned to dusty rags. There he and Clara received the customers. The two divines wore tunics "color of the men of light," as Marcos called the color yellow. Nana had dyed them with saffron powder, boiling them in pots usually reserved for rice and pasta. In addition to his tunic, Marcos wore a turban around his head and an Egyptian amulet around his neck. He had grown a beard and let his hair grow long and he was thinner than ever before. Marcos and Clara were utterly convincing, especially because the child had no need to look into the crystal ball to guess what her clients wanted to hear. She would whisper in her Uncle Marcos's ear, and he in turn would transmit the

Literary Analysis
Characterization and Narrator Which words does the narrator use here to characterize Clara directly?

30 ▼ Critical Viewing This sketch of a helicopter by Italian artist and inventor Leonardo da Vinci predates the first working helicopters by about 450 years. What do you think Uncle Marcos would have thought of Leonardo da Vinci? **[Speculate]**

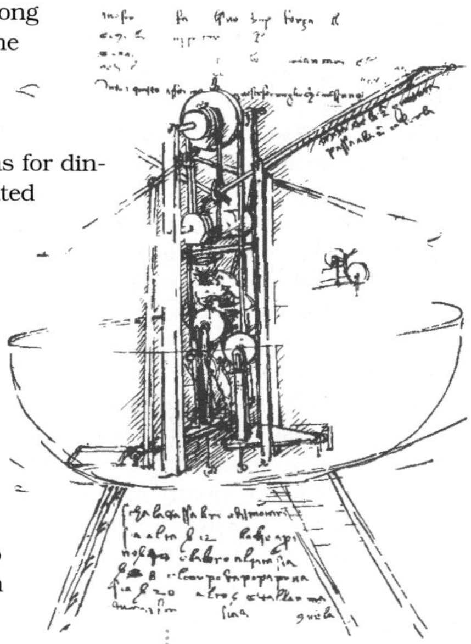

14. **clairvoyance** (kler voi´ əns) *n.* supposed ability to perceive unseen things.
15. **centavos** (sen tä´ vōs) *n.* coins equal to 1/100 of a cruzeiro, the basic monetary unit of Brazil.
16. **quince** (kwins) golden or greenish-yellow, hard, apple-shaped fruit.

message to the client, along with any improvisations of his own that he thought pertinent. Thus their fame spread, because all those who arrived sad and bedraggled at the consulting room left filled with hope.

31 Unrequited lovers were told how to win over indifferent hearts, and the poor left with foolproof tips on how to place their money at the dog tracks. Business grew so prosperous that the waiting room was always packed with people, and Nana began to suffer dizzy spells from being on her feet so many hours a day. This time Severo had no need to intervene to put a stop to his brother-in-law's venture, for both Marcos and Clara, realizing that their unerring guesses could alter the fate of their clients, who always followed their advice to the letter, became frightened and decided that this was a job for swindlers. They abandoned theircarriage-house oracle and split the profits, even though the only one who had cared about the material side of things had been Nana.

unrequited (un ri kwīt′ id) *adj.* not reciprocated

Of all the del Valle children, Clara was the one with the greatest interest in and stamina for her uncle's stories. She could repeat each and every one of them. She knew by heart words from several dialects of the Indians, was acquainted with their customs, and could describe the exact way in which they pierced their lips and earlobes with wooden shafts, their initiation rites, the names of the most poisonous snakes, and the appropriate antidotes for each. Her uncle was so eloquent that the child could feel in her own skin the burning sting of snakebites, see reptiles slide across the carpet between the legs of the jacaranda[17] room divider, and hear the shrieks of macaws behind the drawing-room drapes. She did not hesitate as she recalled Lope de Aguirre's search for El Dorado,[18] or the unpronounceable names of the flora and fauna her extraordinary uncle had seen; she knew about the lamas who take salt tea with yak lard and she could give detailed descriptions of the opulent women of Tahiti, the rice fields of China, or the white prairies of the North, where the eternal ice kills animals and men who lose their way, turning them to stone in seconds. Marcos had various travel journals in which he recorded his excursions and impressions, as well as a collection of maps and books of stories and fairy tales that he kept in the trunks he stored in the junk room at the far end of the third courtyard. From there they were hauled out to inhabit the dreams of his descendants, until they were mistakenly burned half a century later on an infamous pyre.

Now Marcos had returned from his last journey in a coffin. He had died of a mysterious African plague that had turned him as yellow and wrinkled as a piece of parchment. When he realized he was ill, he set out for home with the hope that his sister's ministrations and Dr. Cuevas's knowledge would restore his health and youth, but he was unable to withstand the sixty days on ship and died at the latitude of

17. **jacaranda** (jak′ ə ran′ də) type of tropical American tree.
18. **Lope de Aguirre's** (lō′ pā dā ä gēr′ rās) . . . **El Dorado** Lope de Aguirre was a Spanish adventurer (1510–1561) in colonial South America who searched for a legendary country called El Dorado, which was supposedly rich in gold.

32 **Reading Check**

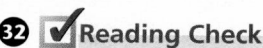

What power does Marcos believe Clara holds?

31 Reading Strategy

Making Inferences About Characters

- Ask students why Marcos and Clara decide to give up their business.
  Answer: They realize that they have too much power over people and that they might be responsible for a person's doing something foolish in order to change a prediction that Marcos and Clara made.
- Ask students what they can infer about Marcos and Clara from this decision.
  Possible responses: They don't care about money. They have integrity.

32 Reading Check

Answer: Marcos believes that Clara can predict the future.

CUSTOMIZE INSTRUCTION FOR UNIVERSAL ACCESS

For Advanced Readers

Have students discuss the element of magic in this excerpt. Share the information about magic realism on p. 568 of this teacher's edition. Have students discuss what the magical elements add to (or detract from) the story. Encourage them to refer to other magic realist works they have read, if applicable. Specifically, students should consider what the element of magic contributes to their impressions of the characters of Marcos and Clara.

ASSESS

Answers for p. 584

Review and Assess

1. Possible response: Students may cite the flight over the mountains because of the pleasure of flying.
2. **(a)** He serenades her with a barrel organ. **(b)** No, his efforts produce the opposite of what he intended. **(c)** Marcos swears he will never marry, then goes on a trip around the world. Antonieta marries and leaves for a faraway place.
3. **(a)** He makes a flying machine. **(b)** Students may say that Marcos seeks risk and adventure in front of a huge audience.
4. **(a)** Severo feels sad but relieved; Nívea feels sad; Clara never doubts that Marcos will return alive; the people search for him and declare him dead. **(b)** Though there is no indication that Marcos deliberately faked his death, he clearly relishes the sensation his "death" and reappearance caused.
5. Some strangers might react to Marcos simply as a crazy attention-seeker. Others might have respected him as an adventurer who would settle for nothing less than an exciting life.

Guayaquil,[19] ravaged by fever and hallucinating about musky women and hidden treasure. The captain of the ship, an Englishman by the name of Longfellow, was about to throw him overboard wrapped in a flag, but Marcos, despite his savage appearance and his delirium, had made so many friends on board and seduced so many women that the passengers prevented him from doing so, and Longfellow was obliged to store the body side by side with the vegetables of the Chinese cook, to preserve it from the heat and mosquitoes of the tropics until the ship's carpenter had time to improvise a coffin. At El Callao[20] they obtained a more appropriate container, and several days later the captain, furious at all the troubles this passenger had caused the shipping company and himself personally, unloaded him without a backward glance, surprised that not a soul was there to receive the body or cover the expenses he had incurred. Later he learned that the post office in these latitudes was not as reliable as that of far-off England, and that all his telegrams had vaporized en route. Fortunately for Longfellow, a customs lawyer who was a friend of the del Valle family appeared and offered to take charge, placing Marcos and all his paraphernalia in a freight car, which he shipped to the capital to the only known address of the deceased: his sister's house. . . .

---

19. **Guayaquil** (gwī ä kēl′) seaport in western Ecuador.
20. **El Callao** (kə yä′ ō) seaport in western Peru.

Review and Assess

Thinking About the Selection

1. **Respond:** Which of Uncle Marcos's adventures would you most like to share with him? Why?
2. (a) **Recall:** What does Uncle Marcos do to try to win the hand of Cousin Antonieta? (b) **Connect:** Is her reaction what Uncle Marcos expects? (c) **Compare and Contrast:** What subsequent actions does each take in the wake of his courtship?
3. (a) **Recall:** What does Uncle Marcos make from the materials in the "enormous boxes"? (b) **Infer:** What do you think motivates Uncle Marcos to undertake this project?
4. (a) **Recall:** How do various people in the family and community react to Uncle Marcos's disappearance? (b) **Deduce:** Do you think Marcos wanted to fool everyone about his fate? Explain.
5. **Speculate:** In the story, you see the reactions of people who knew Uncle Marcos. How do you think people who did not know him might have reacted to him? Explain.

Isabel Allende

(b. 1942)

Isabel Allende has said, "I had a very lonely life when I was a child but very interesting—only adults around me . . . a very extravagant family." She grew up in Chile, where she lived with her grandparents. Her uncle was the former Chilean president Salvador Allende.

Allende's first novel, *The House of the Spirits* (1985), from which "Uncle Marcos" is excerpted, was inspired by her family. Her other books include *Of Love and Shadows* (1987), *Eva Luna* (1988), *The Stories of Eva Luna* (1991), *The Infinite Plan* (1993), and *Paula* (1995).

ASSESSMENT PRACTICE: Reading Comprehension

Author's Point of View (For more practice, see Test Preparation Workbook, p. 37.)

Many tests require students to recognize an author's point of view. Use this sample test item.

Of all the del Valle children, Clara was the one with the greatest interest in and stamina for her uncle's stories. She could repeat each and every one of them.

The author views Clara with ___.

A pity
B admiration
C disgust
D uncertainty

The words *greatest* and *stamina* suggest that Clara's interest requires skill and energy. The correct answer is *B*.

Review and Assess

Literary Analysis

Characterization

1. Using a chart like this one, find examples of **indirect characterization** for two people in each story. Rewrite each example to **directly characterize** the person.

2. Which character does Isabel Allende indirectly characterize in the most detail? Support your answer.
3. Which form of characterization does each writer seem to prefer? Explain and support your answer.

Comparing Literary Works

4. Using the Venn diagram below, compare the information revealed about the characters through the **narration** in each story. Consider each character's appearance, traits, actions, and thoughts.

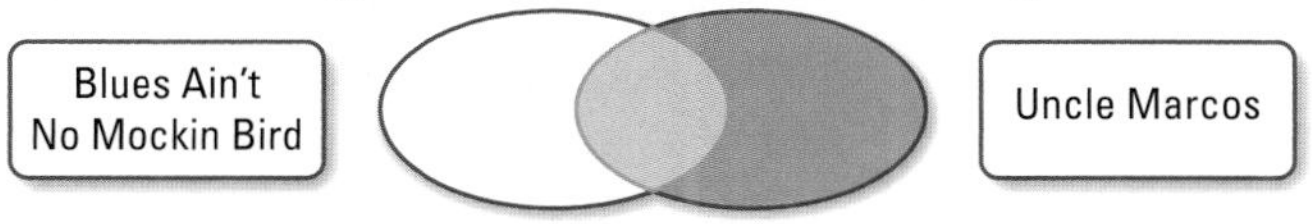

5. How would these stories be different if their narration styles were switched? Provide specific examples.

Reading Strategy

Making Inferences About Characters

6. **Make an inference** to explain how the photographer in "Blues Ain't No Mockin Bird" feels about the people he is filming.
7. In "Uncle Marcos," which details might lead you to infer that Clara is an unusual child?

Extend Understanding

8. **Media Connection:** (a) What insights might journalists gain from reading Bambara's story? (b) Are there any times when the public's right to know outweighs individual privacy? Explain.

Quick Review

Characterization is the set of techniques writers use to reveal the personalities of characters in fiction.

With **direct characterization,** a writer simply states a fact about a character.

With **indirect characterization,** a writer implies facts about a character through the character's words and actions and the reactions of others.

A **first-person narrator** relates events from the perspective of a character in the story.

A **third-person narrator** relates a story's events, but he or she is not a character in the story.

To make inferences about characters, draw conclusions using details the author provides.

Take It to the Net

www.phschool.com

Take the interactive self-test online to check your understanding of the selections.

ENRICHMENT: Further Reading

Other Works by the Authors

Works by Toni Cade Bambara
Gorilla, My Love
The Sea Birds Are Still Alive

Works by Isabel Allende
Eva Luna
The House of the Spirits

Take It to the Net

Visit www.phschool.com for more information on the authors.

Answers for p. 585

Review and Assess

1. Sample answers: Indirect: Granny cut him off and smiled that smile. Direct: Granny was annoyed. Indirect: Marcos smiled after returning from his "death." Direct: Marcos enjoyed shocking people with his return.
2. Marcos is the story's central character, and every paragraph characterizes him indirectly by describing his adventures and people's reactions to them.
3. Both authors seem to rely more on indirect characterization.
4. **(a)** In both stories, the narrating voice describes the characters' actions. A few details are provided about characters' physical appearance. Characters' thoughts and feelings are implied rather than stated.
(b) Students probably found the characters in "Blues Ain't No Mockin Bird" easier to understand because the narration is more straightforward and the characters less exotic.
5. "Uncle Marcos" might include more dialogue, in which the narrator would be a participant. "Blues" would be more descriptive, and perhaps Granddaddy would become even more mythically imposing.
6. The photographer views the people only as images for his film; he shows no concern for their plight and never asks permission to take pictures.
7. Clara is the only one who feels a sort of kinship with Uncle Marcos. She may have the gift of clairvoyance, and despite her youth she is able to absorb all the information Marcos brings her from around the world.
8. **(a)** Journalists might learn to be sensitive to the people they interview and photograph.
(b) Refer students to recent local or national events in which private individuals are placed under media scrutiny.

EXTEND

Answers for p. 586

❶ Vocabulary Development

Word Analysis

1. c
2. a
3. b

Spelling Strategy

1. informality
2. uncover
3. impassive
4. nonsense

Concept Development: Analogies

1. a
2. c
3. d
4. b
5. d
6. a
7. c
8. a

❷ Grammar

1. (to get) a statement; noun
2. (to chase); adjective
3. (to throw) him overboard; noun
4. (to soar) over the mountains; adverb [Note: *to a new life* is a prepositional phrase]
5. (to win) the hand of Cousin Antonieta; adjective

Writing Application

Sample sentences: To film a poor family was the crew's only goal. They never thought to ask permission. Uncle Marcos hoped to fly away. Volunteers set out to find the missing flyer.

Integrate Language Skills

❶ Vocabulary Development Lesson

Word Analysis: Latin Prefix *dis-*

The Latin prefix *dis-* means "opposite." Thus, *disconsolate* means "the opposite of consolable," or "dejected; cheerless."

Match each word on the left with its definition on the right.

1. dishonest	a. take apart
2. disassemble	b. doubt
3. distrust	c. not truthful

Spelling Strategy

When you add a prefix to a word, do not change the spelling of the original word. For example, *un-* + *requited* = *unrequited.* Add *in-*, *im-*, *non-*, or *un-* to each word below to form four properly spelled new words.

1. formality	3. passive
2. cover	4. sense

Concept Development: Analogies

For each item, complete the analogy.

1. disconsolately : joyously :: rain : ___?___
   a. sunshine b. leaf c. spring d. grass
2. fetid : smelly :: pond : ___?___
   a. rain b. duck c. pool d. egg
3. formality : tuxedo :: relaxation : ___?___
   a. chair b. snow c. red d. swimsuit
4. impassive : calm :: search : ___?___
   a. find b. explore c. begin d. reason
5. lassoed : released :: day : ___?___
   a. sad b. week c. pocket d. night
6. pallid : ruddy :: bend : ___?___
   a. straighten b. swirl c. trade d. fry
7. unrequited : shared :: calm : ___?___
   a. dry b. windy c. excited d. cold
8. vanquished : beaten :: survived : ___?___
   a. persevered b. horse c. hunter d. peril

❷ Grammar Lesson

Infinitive Phrases

An **infinitive** is a verb form preceded by the word *to* that acts as a noun, adjective, or adverb. An **infinitive phrase** is an infinitive with its modifiers or complements. Like infinitives, infinitive phrases can function as nouns, adjectives, or adverbs. Unlike a **prepositional phrase** that begins with *to* and ends with a noun, an infinitive phrase always ends with a verb.

Infinitive: Granny decided *to stare*. (noun)

Infinitive Phrase: Clara was afraid *to speak her mind*. (acts as an adverb by modifying *afraid*)

Prepositional Phrase: Antonieta did not speak *to Marcos*.

Practice Copy the sentences below. Circle the infinitives and underline the infinitive phrases. Identify the part of speech of each phrase.

1. The men wanted to get a statement from Granny.
2. Soon there were no more hawks to chase.
3. He wanted to throw him overboard.
4. The machine was made to soar over the mountains to a new life.
5. The organ was a last attempt to win the hand of Cousin Antonieta.

Writing Application Write two sentences about each selection, using infinitives and infinitive phrases in each.

WG Prentice Hall Writing and Grammar Connection: Chapter 21, Section 1

TEACHING RESOURCES

The following resources can be used to enrich or extend the instruction for pp. 586–587.

Vocabulary

- **Selection Support:** Build Vocabulary, p. 145
- **Vocabulary and Spelling Practice Book** (Use this booklet for skills enrichment.) ■

Grammar

- **Selection Support:** Build Grammar Skills, p. 146
- **Writing and Grammar,** Gold Level, p. 450
- **Daily Language Practice Transparencies**

Writing

- **Writing and Grammar,** Gold Level, p. 286 ■
- **Writing and Grammar iText CD-ROM**

■ **BLOCK SCHEDULING:** Resources marked with this symbol provide varied instruction during 90-minute blocks.

❸ Writing Lesson

Magazine Feature

These selections feature amazing characters, brought to life with vivid details. Use one of the characters in this section as the basis for a magazine feature—an article that is meant to entertain or provide information on a subject of interest.

Prewriting As you prepare, decide what makes the character truly remarkable. To help you gather relevant ideas, list specific details concerning the person's appearance, personality, and achievements.

Model: Organizing Details

Talents	Goals
adventurous	to fly
eccentric	to travel the world

These specific details, under the general ideas *Talents* and *Goals,* will support the main impression and make a feature article believable.

Drafting Use your notes to focus your writing on the main impression: the amazing qualities of your character. As you write, provide examples illustrating each characteristic you mention.

Revising Review your work to ensure that you communicate your main impression. Add more details if necessary, and discard any details that are not relevant or that detract from your focus.

WG *Prentice Hall Writing and Grammar Connection: Chapter 13, Section 2*

❹ Extension Activities

Research and Technology Sometimes, a person like Uncle Marcos is seen as irresponsible. However, imaginative and adventurous people like him are responsible for making some of the most important discoveries in history.

- In a group, research people in history who, through their adventures, made great discoveries.
- Show how these people compare to Marcos.

Compile your notes to create a **comparison-and-contrast brochure.**

Listening and Speaking Assume that you are the cameraman in "Blues Ain't No Mockin Bird," and prepare a **monologue** explaining to your boss what happened to your camera. Do not omit anything important, and do not exaggerate. Be polite, and use language appropriate to your situation. Read or perform the monologue for a friend or a small group.

Take It to the Net www.phschool.com

Go online for an additional research activity using the Internet.

ASSESSMENT RESOURCES

The following resources can be used to assess students' knowledge and skills.

Selection Assessment

- **Formal Assessment,** pp. 129–131
- **Open Book Test,** pp. 109–111
- **Got It! Assessment Videotapes,** Tape 3
- **Test Bank Software**

Take It to the Net

Visit www.phschool.com for self-tests and additional questions on the selections.

PRENTICE HALL ASSESSMENT SYSTEM

- **Workbook**
- **Skill Book**
- **Transparencies**
- **CD-ROM**

Lesson Support for p. 587

❸ Writing Lesson

- Bring in issues of contemporary magazines so that students can get an idea of what to include in a feature article.
- Suggest that students illustrate their features with photographs or drawings.
- If students want to include invented quotations from their subjects, remind them to keep the details consistent with the characterizations and events in the story.

❹ Research and Technology

- You might suggest that students look in an almanac if they have trouble finding subjects.
- Encourage students to discuss this assignment with their history or social studies teachers, who may be able to suggest subjects for research and sources of information.
- Students may want to use Venn diagrams to organize their notes before they start writing.

CUSTOMIZE INSTRUCTION For Universal Access

To address different learning styles, use the following activities suggested in the **Extension Activities** booklet, p. 37.

- For Visual/Spatial Learners, use Activity 5.
- For Verbal/Linguistic Learners, use Activities 5–7.
- For Intrapersonal Learners, use Activity 6.

The Man to Send Rain Clouds ✦ The Invalid's Story

Lesson Objectives and CA Correlations

1. **To analyze and respond to literary elements**
   - Literary Analysis: Setting **R 3.7**
   - Comparing Literary Works
2. **To read, comprehend, analyze, and critique short stories**
   - Reading Strategy: Using Your Senses **R 3.7**
   - Reading Check questions
   - Review and Assess questions
   - Assessment Practice (ATE)
3. **To develop word analysis skills, fluency, and systematic vocabulary**
   - Vocabulary Development Lesson: Latin Suffix: *-ous* **R 1.1**
4. **To understand and apply written and oral language conventions**
   - Spelling Strategy
   - Grammar Lesson: Prepositional Phrase or Infinitive? **LC 1.1**
5. **To understand and apply appropriate writing and research strategies**
   - Writing Lesson: Letter **W 2.4**
   - Extension Activity: Research Report **W 1.5**
6. **To understand and apply listening and speaking strategies**
   - Extension Activity: Monologue **LS 2.1**

STEP-BY-STEP TEACHING GUIDE	PACING GUIDE
PRETEACH	
Motivate Students and Provide Background	
Use the Motivation activity (ATE p. 588)	5 min.
Read and discuss the Preview material and Background information (SE/ATE p. 588) [A]	10 min.
Introduce the Concepts	
Introduce the Literary Analysis and Reading Strategy (SE/ATE p. 589) [A]	15 min.
Pronounce the vocabulary words and read their definitions (SE p. 589)	5 min.
TEACH	
Monitor Comprehension	
Informally monitor comprehension by circulating while students read independently or in groups [A]	25 min.
Monitor students' comprehension with the Reading Check notes (SE/ATE pp. 591, 593, 597, 599, 601)	as students read
Develop vocabulary with Vocabulary notes (SE pp. 594, 597–600; ATE p. 597)	as students read
Develop Understanding	
Develop students' understanding of setting with Literary Analysis annotations (SE/ATE pp. 591, 592, 594, 595, 597, 600) [A]	10 min.
Develop students' ability to use their senses with the Reading Strategy annotations (SE/ATE pp. 594, 598, 599, 601)	10 min.
ASSESS	
Assess Mastery	
Assess students' mastery of the Reading Strategy and Literary Analysis by having them answer the Review and Assess questions (SE/ATE p. 603)	20 min.
Use one or more of the print and media Assessment Resources (ATE p. 605) [A]	up to 50 min.
EXTEND	
Apply Understanding	
Have students complete the Vocabulary Development Lesson and the Grammar Lesson (SE p. 604) [A]	20 min.
Apply students' knowledge of strong openings using the Writing Lesson (SE p. 605) [A]	45 min.
Apply students' understanding of the selections using one or more of the Extension Activities (SE p. 605)	20–90 min.

[A] **ACCELERATED INSTRUCTION:** Use the strategies and activities identified with an [A].

UNIVERSAL ACCESS
● = Below Level Students
▲ = On-Level Students
■ = Above Level Students

Time and Resource Manager

Reading Level: Easy/Average
Average Number of Instructional Days: 4

RESOURCES		
PRINT	**TRANSPARENCIES**	**TECHNOLOGY**
• **Beyond Literature,** Cross-Curricular Connection: Social Studies, p. 38 ▲ ■		• **Interest Grabber Video,** Tape 3 ● ▲ ■
• **Selection Support Workbook:** ● ▲ ■ Literary Analysis, p. 152 Reading Strategy, p. 151 Build Vocabulary, p. 149	• **Literary Analysis and Reading Transparencies,** pp. 75, 76 ● ▲ ■	
• **Authors In Depth,** Gold Level, p. 113 ■		• **Listening to Literature** ● ▲ ■ Audiocassettes, Side 22 Audio CDs, CD 12
• **Literatura en español** ● ▲ • **Literary Analysis for Enrichment** ■	• **Fine Art Transparencies Volume 1,** Transparencies 10, 15 ● ▲ ■	
• **Formal Assessment:** Selection Test, pp. 132–134 ● ▲ ■ • **Open Book Test,** pp. 112–114 ● ▲ ■ • PRENTICE HALL ASSESSMENT SYSTEM ● ▲ ■	• PRENTICE HALL ASSESSMENT SYSTEM ● ▲ ■ Skills Practice Answers and Explanations on Transparencies	• **Test Bank Software** ● ▲ ■ • **Got It! Assessment Videotapes,** Tape 3 ● ▲
• **Selection Support Workbook:** ● ▲ ■ Build Grammar Skills, p. 150 • **Writing and Grammar,** Gold Level ● ▲ ■ • **Extension Activities,** p. 38 ● ▲ ■	• **Daily Language Practice Transparencies** ● ▲	• **Writing and Grammar iText CD-ROM** ● ▲ ■ ***Take It to the Net*** www.phschool.com

BLOCK SCHEDULING: Use one 90-minute class period to preteach the selection and have students read it. Use a second 90-minute class period to assess students' mastery of skills and have them complete one of the Extension Activities.

PREETEACH

Step-by-Step Teaching Guide for pp. 588–589

Motivation

Have students name any movie they've seen that involves either the honor and respect arising from death or the humorous treatment of the events surrounding death. Discuss the ways in which death can provoke such different responses. Tell students that these contrasting views of death in their examples parallel the views of death in these two stories.

Interest Grabber Video

As an alternative, play "The Web of Life" on Tape 3 to engage student interest.

1 Background

The Pueblos have lived in the southwestern United States for nearly 2,000 years. They first came into contact with Europeans when the Spanish arrived in the 1500s. In modern times, the Pueblos have incorporated many aspects of the industrial world into their traditional lives. There are many Pueblo peoples, including the Hopi, Zuni, Taos, Tiwa, Laguna, Pecos, Jemez, and San Ildefonso, who speak different languages yet share a common heritage. Leslie Marmon Silko is a member of the Laguna people.

Prepare to Read

The Man to Send Rain Clouds ◆ The Invalid's Story

Feast Day, San Juan Pueblo, 1921, William Penhallow Henderson, National Museum of American Art, Smithsonian Institution

Take It to the Net

Visit www.phschool.com for interactive activities and instruction related to the selections, including

- background
- graphic organizers
- literary elements
- reading strategies

Preview

Connecting to the Literature

People cope with the loss of a loved one in different ways. Some try to preserve their memories of the deceased; others try to fulfill the loved one's last wishes. These stories offer two sets of circumstances surrounding death and others' responses to it.

1 Background

"The Man to Send Rain Clouds" explores the traditions of the Pueblo people of the southwestern United States. Over time, the Pueblo people have tried to maintain their ancient belief that if they live in harmony with the natural world, nature will give them what they need. The Pueblos' balancing of traditional and modern ways provides the central conflict in Leslie Marmon Silko's story.

TEACHING RESOURCES

The following resources can be used to enrich or extend the instruction for pp. 588–589.

Motivation

Interest Grabber Video, Tape 3

Background

Beyond Literature, p. 38

Take It to the Net

Visit www.phschool.com for background and hotlinks for the selections.

Literary Analysis

Literary Analysis and Reading Transparencies, Setting, p. 76

Reading

Selection Support Workbook: Reading Strategy, p. 151; Build Vocabulary, p. 149

Literary Analysis and Reading Transparencies, Use Your Senses, p. 75

BLOCK SCHEDULING: Resources marked with this symbol provide varied instruction during 90-minute blocks.

❷ Literary Analysis

Setting

In each of these stories, **setting**—the time and place in which the story unfolds—strongly influences the action. Time may include not only the historical period but also a specific year, season, or time of day. Place may involve not only the geographical place but also the social, economic, and cultural environment. The following excerpt reveals the cultural environment of "The Man to Send Rain Clouds":

> Leon stared at the new moccasins that Teofilo had made for the ceremonial dances in the summer. They were nearly hidden by the red blanket.

In some stories, the setting simply provides a backdrop for the action; in other stories, including these, setting shapes the character's actions.

Comparing Literary Works

Although both stories deal with death, the settings of the stories are very different. One is the high desert of New Mexico; the other is a train on its way to Wisconsin. While reading, compare and contrast the brief journey of the aged Pueblo with the somewhat longer one of John B. Hackett. Note the way story events seem to emerge from each distinctive setting.

❸ Reading Strategy

Using Your Senses

The setting of each story, like a stifling boxcar with a smelly package, gives your **senses** a virtual workout. Draw from your own experiences to see, hear, smell, taste, or feel what each author describes. Then, try to re-create senses in your mind. Use a chart like the one shown to record key details appealing to each sense.

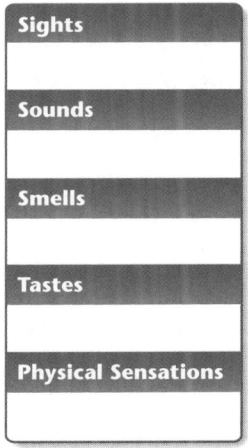

Sights
Sounds
Smells
Tastes
Physical Sensations

Vocabulary Development

cloister (klois´ tər) *n.* place devoted to religious seclusion (p. 594)

pagans (pā´ gənz) *n.* people who are not Christians, Muslims, or Jews (p. 594)

perverse (pər vʉrs´) *adj.* continuing in a stubborn way to do what is wrong or harmful (p. 594)

prodigious (pro dij es) *adj.* enormous (p. 597)

deleterious (del´ ə tir´ ē əs) *adj.* harmful to health or well-being (p. 598)

ominous (äm´ ə nəs) *adj.* threatening (p. 599)

judicious (jo͞o dish´ əs) *adj.* showing good judgment (p. 599)

placidly (plas´ id lē) *adv.* calmly; quietly (p. 599)

desultory (des´ əl tôr´ ē) *adj.* random (p. 600)

CUSTOMIZE INSTRUCTION FOR UNIVERSAL ACCESS

For Less Proficient Readers	For English Learners	For Advanced Readers
Ask students to list several sensory experiences they can identify in their classroom or in the school as a whole. For example, are the sounds of games or practices in the gym high-pitched, roaring, sharp? Encourage students to use particular words that capture a specific sense.	To prepare students to read a selection with sensory imagery, have them create a chart like the one shown on this page. Provide students with a sample setting, such as a beach or flower garden, and have them complete the chart by identifying sensory details that can be used to describe this setting.	Have students skim the two selections and identify the setting in each. Then, encourage them to identify sensory details that they think they will encounter as they read the stories.

❷ Literary Analysis

Setting

- Tell students that as they read these two selections they will focus on *setting*, the time and place in which the story occurs.
- Read the instruction about setting as a class. Have students identify elements of setting in their own community—for example, historic period, year, season, and culture.
- Call students' attention to the example from the story, and ask them to identify details of the setting.
  Answer: Mention of *moccasins* and *pueblo road* indicates Native American culture. Cold temperatures suggest that it is not yet summer; *gray dust* suggests an arid environment.
- Use the Setting transparency in **Literary Analysis and Readings Transparencies,** p. 76, to demonstrate how students might organize details about setting.

❸ Reading Strategy

Using Your Senses

- Remind students that sensory imagery is language that appeals to the reader's five senses.
- Tell students that being able to identify and appreciate sensory imagery is one important way for readers to connect with characters' experiences.
- Display the Use Your Senses transparency in **Literary Analysis and Reading Transparencies,** p. 75, to show students how to record sensory language as they read the selections.

Vocabulary Development

- Pronounce each vocabulary word for students, and read the definitions as a class. Have students identify any words with which they are already familiar.

E-Teach

Visit E-Teach at www.phschool.com for teachers' essays on how to teach, with questions and answers.

TEACH

Step-by-Step Teaching Guide for pp. 590–602

CUSTOMIZE INSTRUCTION
For Verbal/Linguistic Learners

To help students understand the cross-cultural aspects of this story, have them keep a journal as they read the story, jotting down details that reveal the customs and beliefs that are of Native American origin and those of Catholic origin. For example, from the first few paragraphs of the story, readers might enter the details about the Pueblo rituals to prepare a newly deceased person for burial.

1 About the Selection

In Leslie Marmon Silko's story, the death of an elderly Native American, Teofilo, serves as a backdrop to illuminate the actions, reactions, and interactions of the living. Although characters lead their lives according to centuries-old cultural rules and beliefs, these customs have been modified by outside influences. The funeral rites for Teofilo provide just such an enriching and redefining moment, as Native American and Christian traditions are combined.

2 ▸Critical Viewing

Answer: The physical features include the dryness of the desert landscape; the desert plants that grow in this environment, such as cacti; and the brightness of the sun.

1 The Man To Send Rain Clouds

LESLIE MARMON SILKO

They found him under a big cottonwood tree. His Levi jacket and pants were faded light blue so that he had been easy to find. The big cottonwood tree stood apart from a small grove of winterbare cottonwoods which grew in the wide, sandy arroyo. He had been dead for a day or more, and the sheep had wandered and scattered up and down the arroyo. Leon and his brother-in-law, Ken, gathered the sheep
3 and left them in the pen at the sheep camp before they returned to the cottonwood tree. Leon waited under the tree while Ken drove the truck through the deep sand to the edge of the arroyo. He squinted up at the sun and unzipped his jacket—it sure was hot for this time of year. But high and northwest the blue mountains were still in snow. Ken came sliding down the low, crumbling bank about fifty yards down, and he was bringing the red blanket.

Before they wrapped the old man, Leon took a piece of string out of his pocket and tied a small gray feather in the old man's long white hair. Ken gave him the paint. Across the brown wrinkled forehead he drew a

2 ▲Critical Viewing Which physical features of the New Mexico landscape are revealed in this photograph? **[Analyze]**

4 streak of white and along the high cheekbones he drew a strip of blue paint. He paused and watched Ken throw pinches of corn meal and pollen into the wind that fluttered the small gray feather. Then Leon painted with yellow under the old man's broad nose, and finally, when he had painted green across the chin, he smiled.

"Send us rain clouds, Grandfather." They laid the bundle in the back of the pickup and covered it with a heavy tarp before they started back to the pueblo.

They turned off the highway onto the sandy pueblo road. Not long after they passed the store and post office they saw Father Paul's car coming toward them. When he recognized their faces he slowed his car and waved for them to stop. The young priest rolled down the car window.

"Did you find old Teofilo?" he asked loudly.

Leon stopped the truck. "Good morning, Father. We were just out to the sheep camp. Everything is O.K. now."

5 ✓Reading Check

How do Leon and Ken prepare the old man's body before they move it?

3 Literary Analysis

Setting

- Ask students to visualize what the scene looks like at the beginning of this selection. Which images appeal to the sense of sight? Which appeal to the sense of touch?
  Answer: Students may cite a variety of sensory images. For sight: the cottonwood tree, faded light blue pants, the sheep, deep sand, the blue mountains covered in snow, the red blanket; for touch: the heat of the sun and sliding down a bank.
- Remind students that the setting of a story indicates its time and place. What details about time and place can they identify?
  Answer: The place is someplace in the Southwest or someplace with a desert environment. The time is probably late winter or early spring.

4 Critical Thinking

Make Inferences

- Have students reread the bracketed passage.
- Ask students to think about the actions that are taken when someone in their family or community dies. Then, ask them why Leon and Ken might be performing these actions.
  Answer: They are performing a funeral ritual of their culture.

5 ✓Reading Check

Answer: Leon and Ken tie a feather into Teofilo's hair and mark his face with strips of paint.

TEACHING RESOURCES

The following resources can be used to enrich or extend the instruction for pp. 590–591.

Literary Analysis

Selection Support Workbook: Literary Analysis, p. 152

Reading

Listening to Literature Audiocassettes, Side 17

Listening to Literature Audio CDs, CDs 11 and 12

Extension

Authors In Depth, Gold Level, p. 113 (The collection includes three additional selections by Mark Twain for extended reading.) ■

Fine Art Transparencies, Volume 1, Transparencies 10, 15 (Use these two paintings to help students grasp the cultural contexts of the people of the Southwest.) ■

■ **BLOCK SCHEDULING:** Resources marked with this symbol provide varied instruction during 90-minute blocks.

❻ Literary Analysis

Setting

▶ **Reteach** Remind students that the setting of a selection includes the time and place of the action but might also include the time of year or time of day.

- Recall with students that they have identified the time of year as late winter or early spring, but not because it was stated directly. The story stated that "it sure was hot for this time of year" and referred to the mountains still covered with snow.
- Ask students what time of day they can identify from stated information in this passage.
  Answer: It is almost noon at the beginning and reaches noon at the end.
- Finally, have students infer the time Leon and Ken found Teofilo from the information given.
  Answer: They found him early in the morning, because Louise and Teresa have lunch ready when the two men return with Teofilo's body.

❼ Literary Analysis

Setting

- Tell students that an important part of any setting is the cultural environment in which a story takes place. Have them cite the two basic cultural elements they have been able to identify so far.
  Answer: The two cultural elements are Catholicism and the religion and culture of the Pueblo Indians.
- Have students respond to the Literary Analysis question on p. 592: Which cultural elements are represented in Louise's request to the priest?
  Possible response: Students may identify the blending of Native American and Catholic traditions. The Catholics use holy water as a symbol of purification; the Native Americans' interpretation has a more literal and practical link to the afterlife.

"Thank God for that. Teofilo is a very old man. You really shouldn't allow him to stay at the sheep camp alone."

"No, he won't do that any more now."

"Well, I'm glad you understand. I hope I'll be seeing you at Mass[1] this week—we missed you last Sunday. See if you can get old Teofilo to come with you." The priest smiled and waved at them as they drove away.

❻ Louise and Teresa were waiting. The table was set for lunch, and the coffee was boiling on the black iron stove. Leon looked at Louise and then at Teresa.

"We found him under a cottonwood tree in the big arroyo near sheep camp. I guess he sat down to rest in the shade and never got up again." Leon walked toward the old man's bed. The red plaid shawl had been shaken and spread carefully over the bed, and a new brown flannel shirt and pair of stiff new Levi's were arranged neatly beside the pillow. Louise held the screen door open while Leon and Ken carried in the red blanket. He looked small and shriveled, and after they dressed him in the new shirt and pants he seemed more shrunken.

It was noontime now because the church bells rang the Angelus.[2] They ate the beans with hot bread, and nobody said anything until after Teresa poured the coffee.

Ken stood up and put on his jacket. "I'll see about the gravediggers. Only the top layer of soil is frozen. I think it can be ready before dark."

Leon nodded his head and finished his coffee. After Ken had been gone for a while, the neighbors and clanspeople came quietly to embrace Teofilo's family and to leave food on the table because the gravediggers would come to eat when they were finished.

The sky in the west was full of pale yellow light. Louise stood outside with her hands in the pockets of Leon's green army jacket that was too big for her. The funeral was over, and the old men had taken their candles and medicine bags[3] and were gone. She waited until the body was laid into the pickup before she said anything to Leon. She touched his arm, and he noticed that her hands were still dusty from the corn meal that she had sprinkled around the old man. When she spoke, Leon could not hear her.

❼ "What did you say? I didn't hear you."

"I said that I had been thinking about something."

"About what?"

"About the priest sprinkling holy water for Grandpa. So he won't be thirsty."

Leon stared at the new moccasins that Teofilo had made for the ceremonial dances in the summer. They were nearly hidden by the red blanket. It was getting colder, and the wind pushed gray dust down the

Literary Analysis
Setting Which cultural elements are represented in Louise's request to the priest?

1. **Mass** (mas) church service celebrated by Roman Catholics.
2. **Angelus** (an´ jə ləs) bell rung at morning, noon, and evening to announce a prayer.
3. **medicine bags** bags containing objects that were thought to have special powers.

ENRICHMENT: : Social Studies Connection

Pueblo Customs

The new clothing that Louise and Teresa lay out for Teofilo is a traditional Pueblo activity in preparing the dead for burial. Besides painting the face and tying a feather into the hair of the dead person, Pueblo ancestors also washed the body of the dead person and dressed him or her in the best clothing available. When Louise sprinkles corn meal around Teofilo, she is paying tribute to the importance of corn in the daily life of the Pueblo people. Scattering corn meal and corn pollen was traditionally accompanied by asking a favor of the supernatural elements that ruled the world; in this case, Louise is probably asking that Teofilo be granted a good life in the next world.

narrow pueblo road. The sun was approaching the long mesa where it disappeared during the winter. Louise stood there shivering and watching his face. Then he zipped up his jacket and opened the truck door. "I'll see if he's there."

Ken stopped the pickup at the church, and Leon got out: and then Ken drove down the hill to the graveyard where people were waiting. Leon knocked at the old carved door with its symbols of the Lamb.[4] While he waited he looked up at the twin bells from the king of Spain with the last sunlight pouring around them in their tower.

The priest opened the door and smiled when he saw who it was.

4. the Lamb Jesus Christ, as the sacrificial Lamb of God.

8 ▲ Critical Viewing How do the images in this painting compare to images created by the story? **[Compare]**

10 ✔ Reading Check What do the old men take with them when the funeral is over?

8 ▶ Critical Viewing

Answer: Red rock formations, adobe homes, desert roads, and a Catholic church are all part of the New Mexico landscape.

9 Background

Art

Feast Day, San Juan Pueblo, 1921, by William Penhallow Henderson.

Henderson's painting illustrates the presence of Catholicism in a Native American community. The looming church evokes an air of mystery and secrecy. In contrast, the villagers are gathering for their feast day in a circle of warmth and light. Use the following questions for discussion:

1. How does the painting evoke the Catholic influence on and the Catholic ties to the community?
   Answer: The church has a strong presence in the village scene, although it is separated from the main square by trees and buildings.
2. How does the artist use composition, light, and shadow to express the gulf between the two cultures?
   Answer: The church is hidden in shadow, but the village square is bathed in light; all pathways to the church appear to be physically blocked; the figure by the door to the building at the lower right may be a priest left out of the festivities.

10 ✔ Reading Check

Answer: The old men take their candles and medicine bags with them.

CUSTOMIZE INSTRUCTION FOR UNIVERSAL ACCESS

For Special Needs Students	For Gifted/Talented Students
Point out the text breaks in Silko's story, and explain that these indicate a change in time, place, or situation. Suggest that students work in pairs to identify how the setting changes at each of the text breaks. For example, the paragraph at the top of p. 592—before the first story break—takes place on the highway. Where are the characters on the other side of the story break?	Have students draw or paint one of the scenes in "The Man to Send Rain Clouds." They might draw the general setting: sheep, a large cottonwood tree, a sandy arroyo, or Teofilo's face as painted by Leon and Ken. Have students identify the details they used from the story to create their illustrations. You may wish to display Transparency 10 in **Fine Art Transparencies** to show students how a modern artist has incorporated traditional Southwestern motifs in his work.

⓫ Literary Analysis

Setting

- Ask students what elements of setting are the primary focus in this passage.
  Answer: The cultural and environmental context is important here.
- Have students summarize the difference of opinion expressed by the priest and by Leon.
  Answer: The priest believes that the Last Rites were necessary for Teofilo to have a Christian burial. Leon believes that all Teofilo needs from the priest is a sprinkling of holy water so that he will not be thirsty.
- Ask students to read the entire passage and to determine which cultural element becomes dominant. How can they tell?
  Possible answer: The Native American beliefs are dominant, because Leon is willing to leave the priest rather than be persuaded that Teofilo should have a Catholic burial.

⓬ Reading Strategy

Using Your Senses

- As students read this passage, ask them to note which sense is appealed to more than any other.
  Answer: The sense of touch, or feeling, is very strong in this passage.
- Have students identify one or two of the sensory images that appeal to the sense of touch.
  Answer: Images include: "frozen ground," "cold loose sand," "little clouds of steam puffing from their faces," "cold dry wind," "last warmth of the sun on their backs."
- Ask students how the sense of touch is used to let the reader "feel" the weather.
  Answer: Students can identify the author's use of images suggesting cold—such as "little clouds of steam puffing from their faces"—to make the reader feel the chill of the late winter afternoon.

"Come in! What brings you here this evening?"

The priest walked toward the kitchen, and Leon stood with his cap in his hand, playing with the earflaps and examining the living room—the brown sofa, the green armchair, and the brass lamp that hung down from the ceiling by links of chain. The priest dragged a chair out of the kitchen and offered it to Leon.

"No thank you, Father. I only came to ask you if you would bring your holy water to the graveyard."

The priest turned away from Leon and looked out the window at the patio full of shadows and the dining-room windows of the nuns' cloister across the patio. The curtains were heavy, and the light from within faintly penetrated; it was impossible to see the nuns inside eating supper. "Why didn't you tell me he was dead? I could have brought the Last Rites[5] anyway."

cloister (klois′ tər) *n.* place devoted to religious seclusion

Leon smiled. "It wasn't necessary, Father."

The priest stared down at his scuffed brown loafers and the worn hem of his cassock. "For a Christian burial it was necessary."

His voice was distant, and Leon thought that his blue eyes looked tired.

⓫ "It's O.K. Father, we just want him to have plenty of water."

The priest sank down into the green chair and picked up a glossy missionary magazine. He turned the colored pages full of lepers and pagans without looking at them.

pagans (pā′ gənz) *n.* people who are not Christians, Muslims, or Jews

"You know I can't do that, Leon. There should have been the Last Rites and a funeral Mass at the very least."

Leon put on his green cap and pulled the flaps down over his ears. "It's getting late, Father. I've got to go."

When Leon opened the door Father Paul stood up and said, "Wait." He left the room and came back wearing a long brown overcoat. He followed Leon out the door and across the dim churchyard to the adobe steps in front of the church. They both stooped to fit through the low adobe entrance. And when they started down the hill to the graveyard only half of the sun was visible above the mesa.

The priest approached the grave slowly, wondering how they had managed to dig into the frozen ground; and then he remembered that this was New Mexico, and saw the pile of cold loose sand beside the hole. The people stood close to each other with little clouds of steam puffing from their faces. The priest looked at them and saw a pile of jackets, gloves, and scarves in the yellow, dry tumbleweeds that grew in
⓬ the graveyard. He looked at the red blanket, not sure that Teofilo was so small, wondering if it wasn't some perverse Indian trick—something they did in March to ensure a good harvest—wondering if maybe old Teofilo was actually at sheep camp corraling the sheep for the night. But there he was, facing into a cold dry wind and squinting at the last sunlight, ready to bury a red wool blanket while the faces of his parishioners were in shadow with the last warmth of the sun on their backs.

perverse (pər vʉrs′) *adj.* continuing in a stubborn way to do what is wrong or harmful

5. **the Last Rites** religious ceremony for a dying person or for someone who has just died.

ENRICHMENT: Social Studies Connection

Irrigation Systems

The sprinkling of holy water on Teofilo and the wish for him to bring rain clouds are not just symbolic. The Pueblo people live in a land of little rain. Their ancestors were engineering geniuses in terms of irrigating their land with what rain did fall. They built stone dams to store water from running streams. They also constructed dikes made of earth to slow down the runoff from rain and snowmelt that rushed down from the mountains in early spring. Floodwaters were funneled into fields through a system of dams and dikes. Sadly, these systems mostly disappeared when the ancient ones—the Anasazi—disappeared several centuries ago.

His fingers were stiff, and it took him a long time to twist the lid off the holy water. Drops of water fell on the red blanket and soaked into dark icy spots. He sprinkled the grave and the water disappeared almost before it touched the dim, cold sand; it reminded him of something—he tried to remember what it was, because he thought if he could remember he might understand this. He sprinkled more water; he shook the container until it was empty, and the water fell through the light from sundown like August rain that fell while the sun was still shining, almost evaporating before it touched the wilted squash flowers.

The wind pulled at the priest's brown Franciscan robe[6] and swirled away the corn meal and pollen that had been sprinkled on the blanket. They lowered the bundle into the ground, and they didn't bother to untie the stiff pieces of new rope that were tied around the ends of the blanket. The sun was gone, and over on the highway the eastbound lane
13 was full of headlights. The priest walked away slowly. Leon watched him climb the hill, and when he had disappeared within the tall, thick walls, Leon turned to look up at the high blue mountains in the deep snow that reflected a faint red light from the west. He felt good because it was finished, and he was happy about the sprinkling of the holy water; now the old man could send them big thunderclouds for sure.

Literary Analysis
Setting In what ways does the setting described in the last paragraph contribute to the action in the story?

6. **Franciscan** (fran sis´ kən) **robe** robe worn by a member of the Franciscan religious order, founded in 1209 by Saint Francis of Assisi.

Review and Assess

Thinking About the Selection

1. **Respond:** What did you think about the way in which the tribespeople buried Teofilo's body? Why?
2. **(a) Recall:** What do Leon and Ken find at the opening of the story? **(b) Analyze:** Why doesn't Leon tell Father Paul about Teofilo's death at first?
3. **(a) Recall:** Why does Louise ask Leon to bring the priest to Teofilo's grave? **(b) Compare and Contrast:** What does this story reveal about the contrasts between Pueblo and Christian beliefs?
4. **(b) Analyze:** Why is Father Paul upset about the burial ceremony? **(b) Infer:** What insight into the Pueblo people do you think Father Paul gained during the ceremony?
5. **(a) Recall:** How are Leon's feelings described at the end of the story? **(b) Draw Conclusions:** What do Leon's thoughts after Teofilo's burial suggest about his views of death?
6. **Extend:** What lesson can be taken from this story about working out differences in cultural beliefs?

Leslie Marmon Silko

(b. 1948)

Storytelling has always been an important part of Leslie Marmon Silko's life. Raised on the Laguna Pueblo reservation in New Mexico, she grew up listening to tribal stories told by her great-grandmother and great-aunts.

In her stories, novels, and poems, Silko explores what life is like for Native Americans in today's world. Many of her works capture the contrast between traditional values and beliefs and the elements of modern-day life.

13 Literary Analysis

Setting

- Ask students to summarize the action occurring in the last paragraph of the story.
  Answer: Teofilo is lowered into the ground; the priest walks away; Leon watches him climb the hill, and then Leon looks at the mountain and feels happy because it is finished.
- Have students respond to the Literary Analysis question on p. 595: In what ways does the setting described in this last paragraph contribute to the action in the story?
  Answer: The last paragraph suggests that the Native American beliefs are stronger than the Catholic beliefs. After the funeral, the priest disappears into the church, while Leon stays immersed in the natural setting, which is sacred to the Native American.

Answers for p. 595

Review and Assess

1. Students may agree that the burial was moving and appropriate because it reflected Teofilo's Native American heritage.
2. **(a)** Leon and Ken find Teofilo's body. **(b)** Leon wants to give Teofilo a Native American funeral.
3. **(a)** Louise wants the priest to sprinkle holy water on Teofilo so he will not be thirsty. **(b)** Pueblo beliefs about death include providing physical necessities, such as clothes, for the deceased to use in the afterlife. In contrast, Christians provide spiritual rites for the deceased.
4. **(a)** Father Paul is upset because the ceremony does not include the rites of the Catholic Church. **(b)** Father Paul learns that the Pueblo people honor those who die and believe that the deceased can help the living.
5. **(a)** Leon gazes at the mountain and feels happy about the ritual that has just been completed. **(b)** He believes that life continues after death; death is a transition.
6. People can compromise by combining elements of different cultures.

⓮ About the Selection

It may be said that death permeates Mark Twain's comic story in a very physical way. The narrator tells the story of the train trip he takes to bring the body of his newly deceased friend to his final resting place. The narrator and railway expressman suffer intolerably from what they believe is the odor of the decomposing corpse. They struggle in a foul-smelling railway express car to maintain an unbearable and, as it happens, unnecessary vigil over a dead body, according to the parameters and conventions of civilized society. The vigil is unnecessary because the coffin has been mistakenly replaced by a box of guns, and the foul smell is coming from a block of Limburger cheese.

⓯ Background

Burial Customs

As students read the story, they may wonder why the narrator and Thompson, the expressman, don't just move to another car to escape the smell. Thompson was probably obliged by his job to stay with the cargo. But the narrator had a responsibility to accompany his dead friend to his final resting-place, and that meant just that—staying with the body. Moreover, in Twain's time it was not as easy to determine a person's death as it is today. Often, people would appear to be dead for a period of time and then, quite shockingly, "wake up." The possibility of being buried alive haunted most people in a way that we cannot conceive of today. Therefore, it was important that someone stay with a coffin for as long as necessary to be certain that the person thought to be deceased was really dead.

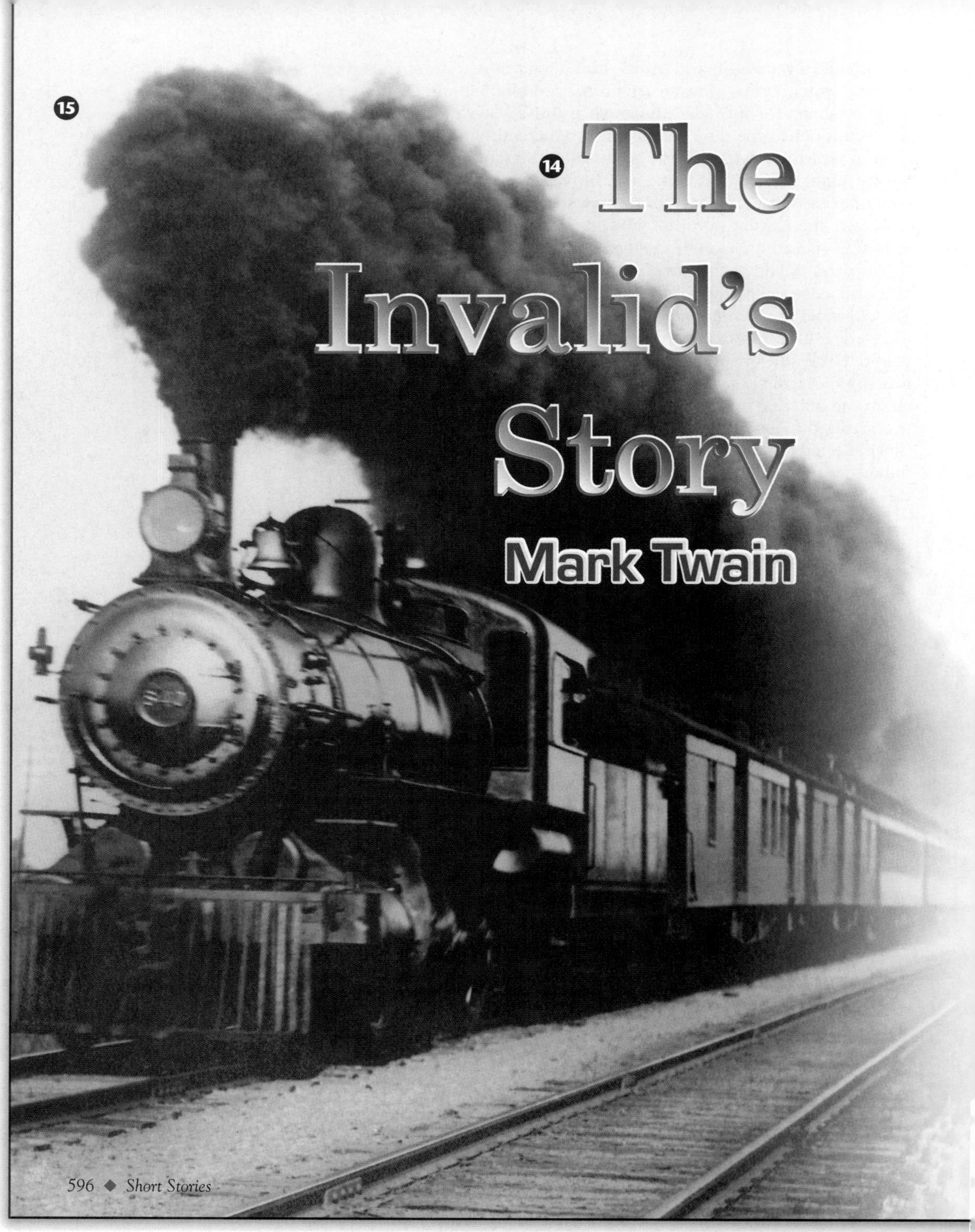

ENRICHMENT: Science Connection

Cheese

The cheese students probably encounter most often, although they may not even know its name, is mozzarella—the cheese used by pizza makers everywhere. However, there are more than 400 kinds of cheese. Most cheese—like mozzarella— is made from cow's milk. Some cheese in Europe and Asia is also made from the milk of buffalo, goats, or sheep. Laplanders make reindeer cheese and Tibetans make yak cheese.

Limburger, a German cheese, is known for its strong, pungent smell and is said to "be able to fell trees." To many people, the name reminds them of anything that smells potent enough to be detected for many miles. One source cites a man named Limburger who had changed his name because people avoided him as if he were the cheese itself! Still, many people in various countries eat and enjoy Limburger.

I seem sixty and married, but these effects are due to my condition and sufferings, for I am a bachelor, and only forty-one. It will be hard for you to believe that I, who am now but a shadow, was a hale, hearty man two short years ago—a man of iron, a very athlete!—yet such is the simple truth. But stranger still than this fact is the way in which I lost my health. I lost it through helping to take care of a box of guns on a two-hundred-mile railway journey one winter's night. It is the actual truth, and I will tell you about it.

16 I belong in Cleveland, Ohio. One winter's night, two years ago, I reached home just after dark, in a driving snowstorm, and the first thing I heard when I entered the house was that my dearest boyhood friend and schoolmate, John B. Hackett, had died the day before, and that his last utterance had been a desire that I would take his remains home to his poor old father and mother in Wisconsin. I was greatly shocked and grieved, but there was no time to waste in emotions; I must start at once. I took the card, marked "Deacon Levi Hackett, Bethlehem, Wisconsin," and hurried off through the whistling storm to the railway station. Arrived there I found the long white-pine box which had been described to me; I fastened the card to it with some tacks, saw it put safely aboard the express car, and then ran into the eating room to provide myself with a sandwich and some cigars. When I returned, presently, there was my coffin-box *back again,* apparently, and a young fellow examining around it, with a card in his hands, and some tacks and a hammer! I was astonished and puzzled. He began to nail on his card, and I rushed out to the express car, in a good deal of a state of mind, to ask for an explanation. But no—there was my box, all right, in the express car; it hadn't been disturbed. [The fact is that without my
17 suspecting it a prodigious mistake had been made. I was carrying off a box of *guns* which that young fellow had come to the station to ship to a rifle company in Peoria, Illinois, and *he* had got my corpse.] Just then the conductor sang out "All aboard," and I jumped into the express car and got a comfortable seat on a bale of buckets. The expressman was there, hard at work—a plain man of fifty, with a simple, honest, good-natured face, and a breezy, practical heartiness in his general style. As the train moved off a stranger skipped into the car and set a package of peculiarly mature and capable Limburger cheese[1] on one end of my coffin-box—I mean my box of guns. That is to say, I know now that it was Limburger cheese, but at that time I never had heard of the article in my life, and of course was wholly ignorant of its character. Well, we sped through the wild night, the bitter storm raged on, a cheerless misery stole over me, my heart went down, down, down! The old expressman made a brisk remark or two about the tempest and the arctic weather, slammed his sliding doors to, and bolted them, closed his window down tight, and then went bustling around, here and there and yonder, setting things to rights, and all the time contentedly humming "Sweet By and By" in a low tone, and flatting a good deal. Presently I

Literary Analysis
Setting Describe the setting at the beginning of this paragraph.

prodigious (prō dij′ əs) *adj.* enormous

18 **Reading Check**
What is the first thing the narrator hears when he enters his house during a snowstorm?

1. **Limburger cheese** cheese with a strong odor.

Critical Viewing How do the sensory details in this image compare to the sensory details in the story? **[Compare]**

16 Literary Analysis
Setting

Monitor Progress Have students name some of the general elements that make up the setting of a story.
Answer: Setting elements include basic time and place, specific geographical place, time of year and/or day, and cultural beliefs and customs.

- Ask students the Literary Analysis question on p. 597: Describe the setting at the beginning of this paragraph.
Answer: The time is two years before the conversation that is now occurring. The place is Cleveland, Ohio, on a winter night during a driving snowstorm.

17 Vocabulary Development
Latin Suffix: *-ous*

- Write the word *prodigious.* Tell students that it means "enormous" or "wonderful."
- Point out that the Latin suffix *-ous* usually means "full of" or "characterized by." The Latin root *prodigium* or *prodigy* originally meant "omen; sign," leading to a meaning of "full of signs or wonders; marvelous."
- Write the words *beauty, joy, glory, nerve,* and *thunder.* Ask students to add the *-ous* suffix to these words and briefly define them. (They will need to alter spellings in some cases.)
Answer: *beauteous:* "full of beauty"; *joyous:* "full of joy"; *glorious:* "full of glory"; *nervous:* "characterized by nerves; anxious"; *thunderous:* "full of thunder; loud."

18 Reading Check

Answer: The narrator hears that his dearest boyhood friend and schoolmate has died and has requested that the narrator take his body home to his parents in Wisconsin.

CUSTOMIZE INSTRUCTION FOR UNIVERSAL ACCESS

For Special Needs Students	For Less Proficient Readers	For Advanced Readers
Students may be confused by the fact that readers know early on that the coffin has been replaced with a box of guns, and may wonder why the narrator and the expressman don't know it. Point out to students the bracketed passage in the middle of this page, beginning, "The fact is that without my suspecting it . . ."	Provide context teaching for some of the words on this page. For example, ask students whether the word *shadow* means that the narrator is literally a shadow. Help them to see that the writer is contrasting his former self—*a hale, hearty man*—with his current very thin self.	Alert students to Twain's use of understatement in this selection. Point out as an example the narrator's statement about the Limburger cheese: he "of course was wholly ignorant of its character." Ask students what Twain means to imply by using this understatement.

19 Reading Strategy

Using Your Senses

Monitor Progress Have students cite the senses to which a writer can appeal with sensory language.
Answer: Sensory imagery can appeal to a reader's sense of sight, hearing, taste, smell, or touch.

- Invite students to respond to the Reading Strategy question on p. 598: Which senses can you use to experience this description? How can an "odor" be "searching"?
Answer: The passage appeals to the senses of smell (the odor) and touch (the frozen air). Students may suggest that a bad odor seems to fill a space as if trying to "search out" every corner.

20 Critical Viewing

Answer: Students will probably say that getting from one place to another was very difficult in 1874. The painting shows that people had to rely on horse-drawn carriages to get to the train station. Moreover, people walking toward their train at the station had to avoid horses crossing their path. The trunk in the foreground clearly shows that most nineteenth-century luggage wasn't easy to handle.

21 Background

Art

Sacramento Railroad Station, 1874, by William Hahn.

William Hahn's painting gives a dynamic and detailed glimpse of the rigors of transportation and the ordeal of travel in the late 1800s. Use the following for discussion:

1. How does the depiction of the station help to show how the boxes in the Twain story could have been switched?
Answer: Students may say that the confusion and disorganization depicted make it easy to see how the mix-up occurred.
2. What would this station scene be like in winter?
Answer: Have students list details that might be added to a winter scene, such as slush, snow, ice, and sleighs.

19 began to detect a most evil and searching odor stealing about on the frozen air. This depressed my spirits still more, because of course I attributed it to my poor departed friend. There was something infinitely saddening about his calling himself to my remembrance in this dumb, pathetic way, so it was hard to keep the tears back. Moreover, it distressed me on account of the old expressman, who, I was afraid, might notice it. However, he went humming tranquilly on, and gave no sign; and for this I was grateful. Grateful, yes, but still uneasy; and soon I began to feel more and more uneasy every minute, for every minute that went by that odor thickened up the more, and got to be more and more gamy and hard to stand. Presently, having got things arranged to his satisfaction, the expressman got some wood and made up a tremendous fire in his stove. This distressed me more than I can tell, for I could not but feel that it was a mistake. I was sure that the effect would be deleterious upon my poor departed friend. Thompson—the expressman's name was Thompson, as I found out in the course of the night—now went poking around his car, stopping up whatever stray cracks he could find, remarking that it didn't make any difference what kind of a night it was outside, he calculated to make us comfortable, anyway. I said nothing, but I believed he was not choosing the right way. Meantime he was humming to himself just as before; and meantime, too, the stove was getting hotter and hotter, and the place closer and closer. I felt myself growing pale and qualmish,[2] but grieved

Reading Strategy
Using Your Senses Which senses can you use to experience this description? How can an "odor" be "searching"?

deleterious (del′ ə tir′ ē əs) *adj.* injurious; harmful to health or well-being

20 **▼ Critical Viewing**
Examine this painting of a railway station in 1874. How difficult do you think it was to get from one place to another at this time in history? Which details in the painting support your ideas? **[Support]**

2. **qualmish** (kwäm′ ish) *adj.* slightly ill.

21

Sacramento Railroad Station, 1874, William Hahn, The Fine Arts Museum of San Francisco

ENRICHMENT: History Connection

Trains Across the Nation

In 1828, the Baltimore and Ohio railroad—America's first—began operating, running horse-drawn carts along the established route. In 1830, a steam-powered locomotive, the *Tom Thumb,* made its first successful run and the era of engine-powered rail travel was born. One advantage of rail travel over canal travel was the reliability of the railroad in all kinds of weather, as Twain's story can attest. The Atlantic rail network was connected to the Great Lakes in 1850, to Chicago in 1853, and west of the Mississippi in 1856. In May 1869, the last spike was driven into the rails at Promontory Point, Utah, to complete the transcontinental railroad.

Students might wish to discuss how the dynamics of arranging for the transport of Hackett's body and the ensuing confusion depend on the chosen method of transportation and the limitations of the historical setting.

in silence and said nothing. Soon I noticed that the "Sweet By and By" was gradually fading out; next it ceased altogether, and there was an ominous stillness. After a few moments Thompson said—

"Pfew! I reckon it ain't no cinnamon't I've loaded up thish-year stove with!"

He gasped once or twice, then moved toward the cof—gun-box, stood over that Limburger cheese part of a moment, then came back and sat down near me, looking a good deal impressed. After a contemplative pause, he said, indicating the box with a gesture—

"Friend of yourn?"

"Yes," I said with a sigh.

"He's pretty ripe, ain't he!"

Nothing further was said for perhaps a couple of minutes, each being busy with his own thoughts; then Thompson said, in a low awed voice—

"Sometimes it's uncertain whether they're really gone or not—*seem* gone, you know—body warm, joints limber—and so, although you *think* they're gone, you don't really know. I've had cases in my car. It's perfectly awful, becuz *you* don't know what minute they'll rise up and look at you!" Then, after a pause, and slightly lifting his elbow toward the box,—"But *he* ain't in no trance! No, sir, I go bail for *him*!"

22 We sat some time, in meditative silence, listening to the wind and the roar of the train; then Thompson said, with a good deal of feeling:

"Well-a-well, we've all got to go, they ain't no getting around it. Man that is born of woman is of few days and far between, as Scriptur'[3] says. Yes, you look at it any way you want to, it's awful solemn and cur'us: they ain't *nobody* can get around it; *all's* got to go—just *everybody*, as you may say. One day you're hearty and strong"—here he scrambled to his feet and broke a pane and stretched his nose out at it a moment or two, then sat down again while I struggled up and thrust my nose out at the same place, and this we kept on doing every now and then—"and next day he's cut down like the grass, and the places which knowed him then knows him no more forever, as Scriptur' says. Yes'ndeedy, it's awful solemn and cur'us; but we've all got to go, one time or another; they ain't no getting around it."

There was another long pause; then—

"What did he die of?"

I said I didn't know.

"How long has he ben dead?"

It seemed judicious to enlarge the facts to fit the probabilities; so I said:

"Two or three days."

But it did no good: for Thompson received it with an injured look which plainly said. "Two or three *years*, you mean." Then he went right along, placidly ignoring my statement, and gave his views at considerable length upon the unwisdom of putting off burials too long. Then he lounged off toward the box, stood a moment, then came back on a

3. **Scriptur'** scripture; the Bible.

ominous (äm′ ə nəs) *adj.* threatening

Reading Strategy
Using Your Senses How does Twain rely on sound to set the mood for the following scene?

judicious (jo͞o dish′ əs) *adj.* showing good judgment

placidly (plas′ id lē) *adv.* calmly; quietly

23 **Reading Check**
What does the narrator say depressed his spirits?

22 Reading Strategy

Using Your Senses

- Ask students what Thompson is describing in the first paragraph of this passage.
  Answer: Thompson is describing situations in which people believed to be dead were in fact alive and sat up in their coffins to look at the mourners.
- Ask students why the expressman is sure that the narrator's friend is not likely to revive.
  Answer: The awful smell in the car is proof to Thompson that the corpse is decomposing.
- Ask students the Reading Strategy question on p. 599: How does Twain rely on sound to set the mood for the following scene?
  Answer: The sound of the storm's wind and the roar of the train set up a reflective, although uncanny atmosphere for Thompson to state his thoughts on the nature of death and dying.

23 Reading Check

Answer: An "evil" odor depressed the narrator's spirits because he thought it was the smell of his dead friend.

CUSTOMIZE INSTRUCTION FOR UNIVERSAL ACCESS

For Less Proficient Readers	For English Learners	For Gifted/Talented Students
Help students see the humor in the actions of Thompson, the expressman. First, he tries to make the car as airtight and warm as possible, to protect him and his passenger from the winter storm. Then, when the cheese starts to smell, he tries to undo everything he's done in order to get some air into the car.	Tell students that they can sometimes figure out the meaning of an unfamiliar word by thinking of a related word. Refer them to the words *contemplative* (line 8) and *meditative* (line 21). Ask students if they are familiar with any of these words: *contemplate, contemplation, meditate, meditation.*	Invite students to create a painting of the two men in the railroad car. Invite them to review the details of time period, setting, mood, and characters to decide how they will depict the scene. Remind them to consider the personalities of the characters as well as conditions inside and outside the car.

24 Literary Analysis

Setting

- Ask students what is gradually happening to the two men in the railroad car.
  Answer: They are suffocating from the smell of the cheese and the lack of air.
- Invite students to describe how Twain uses color to show the effects of the smell on the men.
  Possible response: Twain contrasts Thompson's red handkerchief with the gray and colorless faces of the two men.
- Have students answer the Literary Analysis question on p. 600: What kind of atmosphere do the details in these paragraphs create?
  Answer: The details create an atmosphere of extreme discomfort for the men. Thompson rocks himself back and forth to try to get some relief. The narrator's face has lost all its color.

25 Critical Thinking

Infer

- What have the two men tried that has failed to affect the smell in the railroad car?
  Answer: They have tried smoking cigars.
- When Thompson asks what they should do next, how does the narrator respond?
  Answer: He does not respond; he cannot talk.
- Ask students what they think the narrator is implying here about his physical state.
  Answer: He is swallowing repeatedly to try to keep from vomiting.

sharp trot and visited the broken pane, observing:

"'Twould 'a' ben a durn sight better, all around, if they'd started him along last summer."

24 Thompson sat down and buried his face in his red silk handkerchief, and began to slowly sway and rock his body like one who is doing his best to endure the almost unendurable. By this time the fragrance—if you may call it fragrance—was just about suffocating, as near as you can come at it. Thompson's face was turning gray: I knew mine hadn't any color left in it. By and by Thompson rested his forehead in his left hand, with his elbow on his knee, and sort of waved his red handkerchief toward the box with his other hand, and said:

Literary Analysis
Setting What kind of atmosphere do the details in these paragraphs create?

"I've carried a many a one of 'em—some of 'em considerable overdue, too—but, lordy, he just lays over 'em all!—and does it *easy*. Cap, they was heliotrope[4] to *him*!"

This recognition of my poor friend gratified me, in spite of the sad circumstances, because it had so much the sound of a compliment.

Pretty soon it was plain that something had got to be done. I suggested cigars. Thompson thought it was a good idea. He said:

"Likely it'll modify him some."

We puffed gingerly along for a while, and tried hard to imagine that things were improved. But it wasn't any use. Before very long, and without any consultation, both cigars were quietly dropped from our nerveless fingers at the same moment. Thompson said, with a sigh:

"No, Cap, it don't modify him worth a cent. Fact is, it makes him worse, becuz it appears to stir up his ambition. What do you reckon we better do, now?"

25 I was not able to suggest anything: indeed, I had to be swallowing and swallowing all the time, and did not like to trust myself to speak. Thompson fell to maundering,[5] in a desultory and low-spirited way, about the miserable experiences of this night: and he got to referring to my poor friend by various titles—sometimes military ones, sometimes civil ones; and I noticed that as fast as my poor friend's effectiveness grew, Thompson promoted him accordingly—gave him a bigger title. Finally he said:

desultory (des´ əl tôr´ ē) *adj.* random

"I've got an idea. Suppos'n' we buckle down to it and give the Colonel a bit of a shove toward t'other end of the car?—about ten foot, say. He wouldn't have so much influence, then, don't you reckon?"

I said it was a good scheme. So we took in a good fresh breath at the broken pane, calculating to hold it till we got through: then we went there and bent over that deadly cheese and took a grip on the box. Thompson nodded "All ready," and then we threw ourselves forward with all our might: but Thompson slipped, and slumped down with his nose on the cheese, and his breath got loose. He gagged and gasped, and floundered up and made a break for the door, pawing the air and saying hoarsely, "Don't hender me!—gimme the road! I'm a-dying;

4. **heliotrope** (hē´ lē ə trōp´) *n.* sweet-smelling plant.
5. **maundering** (môn´ dər iŋ) *v.* talking in an unconnected way.

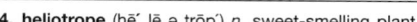

CUSTOMIZE INSTRUCTION FOR UNIVERSAL ACCESS

For Advanced Readers

Suggest that students read additional works by Mark Twain. Provide students with the titles listed in the Enrichment box, ATE, p. 603. You may also wish to use **Authors In Depth,** Gold level, which contains the following selections:

- from *A Connecticut Yankee In King Arthur's Court* (fiction, p. 113)
- "A Fable" (fiction, p. 124)
- from *Roughing It* (nonfiction, p. 127)

After students have read these or other works by Twain, have them form discussion groups in which they compare and contrast the selections. Suggest criteria for comparison, such as setting, theme, characters, dialect, and humor. To extend the activity, have volunteers present to the class brief oral reports on their favorite Twain selections.

26 gimme the road!" Out on the cold platform I sat down and held his head awhile, and he revived. Presently he said:

"Do you reckon we started the Gen'rul any?"

I said no: we hadn't budged him.

"Well, then, *that* idea's up the flume. We got to think up something else. He's suited wher' he is, I reckon; and if that's the way he feels about it, and has made up his mind that he don't wish to be disturbed, you bet he's a-going to have his own way in the business. Yes, better leave him right wher' he is, long as he wants it so; becuz he holds all the trumps, don't you know, and so it stands to reason that the man that lays out to alter his plans for him is going to get left."

But we couldn't stay out there in that mad storm; we should have frozen to death. So we went in again and shut the door, and began to suffer once more and take turns at the break in the window. By and by, as we were starting away from a station where we had stopped a moment Thompson pranced in cheerily, and exclaimed:

"We're all right, now! I reckon we've got the Commodore this time. I judge I've got the stuff here that'll take the tuck out of him."

It was carbolic acid. He had a carboy[6] of it. He sprinkled it all around everywhere; in fact he drenched everything with it, rifle-box, cheese and all. Then we sat down, feeling pretty hopeful. But it wasn't for long. You see the two perfumes began to mix, and then—well, pretty soon we made a break for the door; and out there Thompson swabbed his face with his bandanna and said in a kind of disheartened way:

27 "It ain't no use. We can't buck agin *him*. He just utilizes everything we put up to modify him with, and gives it his own flavor and plays it back on us. Why, Cap, don't you know, it's as much as a hundred times worse in there now than it was when he first got a-going. I never *did* see one of 'em warm up to his work so, and take such a dumnation interest in it. No, sir, I never did, as long as I've ben on the road: and I've carried a many a one of 'em, as I was telling you."

28 We went in again after we were frozen pretty stiff; but my, we couldn't stay in, now. So we just waltzed back and forth, freezing, and thawing, and stifling, by turns. In about an hour we stopped at another station; and as we left it Thompson came in with a bag, and said—

"Cap, I'm a-going to chance him once more—just this once; and if we don't fetch him this time, the thing for us to do, is to just throw up the sponge and withdraw from the canvass.[7] That's the way *I* put it up."

He had brought a lot of chicken feathers, and dried apples, and leaf tobacco, and rags, and old shoes, and sulphur, and asafetida,[8]

6. **carboy** (kär′ boi′) *n.* large glass bottle enclosed in basketwork to prevent it from breaking.
7. **withdraw from the canvass** (kan′ vəs) give up the attempt.
8. **asafetida** (as′ ə fet′ ə də) *n.* bad-smelling substance from certain plants, used as medicine.

Reading Strategy
Using Your Senses Which sense do you use when you envision the narrator and Thompson out on the platform?

27 **▼ Critical Viewing**
Imagine yourself on a train like the one in "The Invalid's Story." What might you see, hear, feel, and smell on such a journey? **[Connect]**

29 **Reading Check**
What does Thompson do with the carbolic acid?

CUSTOMIZE INSTRUCTION FOR UNIVERSAL ACCESS

For Special Needs Students	For Advanced Readers
Thompson's dialogue may be confusing for some students. Invite them to listen to the story on either the audiocassette or the CD in **Listening to Literature.** Have them stop the recording when they come to parts of the story they do not understand and discuss what might be happening, or what one of the characters is saying.	Invite students to list some of Thompson's idioms and other examples of dialect and see if they can figure out what each one means. Examples are "Likely it'll modify him some," "Well then, *that* idea's up the flume," ". . . better leave him right wher' he is . . . becuz he holds all the trumps . . . ." "He just utilizes everything we put up to modify him with, and gives it his own flavor and plays it back on us."

26 Reading Strategy
Using Your Senses

- Ask students to contrast the atmosphere in the railroad car with the weather outside. Which senses do they use to create a contrasting image?
  Possible response: The car is hot, stuffy, and smelly. Outside it is cold, windy, and fresh. The senses used are touch and smell.
- Have students identify the main problem the men would face if they go outside and stay outside.
  Answer: They would freeze.
- Ask students the Reading Strategy question on page 601: Which sense do you use when you envision the narrator and Thompson out on the platform?
  Answer: The sense of touch or feeling helps one envision the men on the freezing platform.

27 ▶Critical Viewing

Answer: Students should mention elements of nineteenth-century rail travel, such as the sight of the countryside passing by, the sound of the steam locomotive whistle, the feel of the seat upholstery and the rhythms of the train, and the smell of coal smoke.

28 Background
Art

American Express Train, by Currier and Ives.

Currier and Ives were New York lithographers whose prints chronicled and glorified history, technology, and customs of nineteenth-century American life. Have students look at the print and discuss the following question:

- How does the print enhance appreciation for the setting and circumstances of the story?
  Answer: Seeing the old-fashioned train may help students focus on other details of the period during which the story takes place—an element of the setting.

29 Reading Check

Answer: Thompson drenches everything in the railroad car with the carbolic acid.

ASSESS

Answers for p. 602

Review and Assess

1. Many students may find the story entertaining or amusing.
2. **(a)** The narrator must accompany the body of his friend back to the home of the friend's parents. **(b)** Students may suggest that the contrast between the stifling interior and the clean but freezing exterior would be difficult to replicate on another mode of transportation.
3. **(a)** The men believe the smell is coming from the dead body of the narrator's friend. **(b)** It's coming from warm Limburger cheese. **(c)** If the characters knew that the smell came from the cheese, they could simply dispose of the cheese. There is also a huge difference in the psychological effect of a bad food smell and the odor of death. Because the reader has all the facts, the character's predicament seems humorous.
4. **(a)** Examples of exaggeration include suggesting that the corpse has been dead for two or three days, saying the odor is a hundred times worse, and saying typhoid fever will result. **(b)** Exaggeration magnifies humorous elements.
5. The attitude that the corpse is trying to smell bad adds to the humor through irony. It is ironic that a dead person is seen as making conscious decisions.
6. Students may suggest that many successful comedies are made with gross and exaggerated content. Some students may note that it might be difficult to film a story so dependent on the nonvisual element of odor.

and one thing or another: and he piled them on a breadth of sheet iron in the middle of the floor, and set fire to them.

When they got well started, I couldn't see, myself, how even the corpse could stand it. All that went before was just simply poetry to that smell—but mind you, the original smell stood up out of it just as sublime as ever—fact is, these other smells just seemed to give it a better hold: and my, how rich it was! I didn't make these reflections there—there wasn't time—made them on the platform. And breaking for the platform, Thompson got suffocated and fell: and before I got him dragged out, which I did by the collar, I was mighty near gone myself. When we revived, Thompson said dejectedly:

"We got to stay out here, Cap. We got to do it. They ain't no other way. The Governor wants to travel alone, and he's fixed so he can outvote us."

And presently he added:

"And don't you know, we're *pisoned.* It's our last trip, you can make up your mind to it. Typhoid fever is what's going to come of this. I feel it a-coming right now. Yes, sir, we're elected, just as sure as you're born."

We were taken from the platform an hour later, frozen and insensible, at the next station, and I went straight off into a virulent fever, and never knew anything again for three weeks. I found out, then, that I had spent that awful night with a harmless box of rifles and a lot of innocent cheese; but the news was too late to save me; imagination had done its work, and my health was permanently shattered; neither Bermuda nor any other land can ever bring it back to me. This is my last trip; I am on my way home to die.

Mark Twain

(1835–1910)

Born Samuel Langhorne Clemens, this great American humorist grew up in the river town of Hannibal, Missouri. Even though Twain traveled and lived all over the United States, it is the great Mississippi River that courses through the heart of his life and work.

As a young man, Twain learned the trade of the riverboat pilot and took his name from a sounding cry used on steamboats on the Mississippi: 'By the mark—twain,' which means the water is two fathoms deep. Although Twain worked as a printer, prospector, reporter, editor, and lecturer, writing was his true calling. Some of his most popular works include *Tom Sawyer, The Adventures of Huckleberry Finn*, and *Life on the Mississippi*.

Review and Assess

Thinking About the Selection

1. **Respond:** Did you find this story entertaining? Why or why not?
2. **(a) Recall:** What is the purpose of the narrator's journey? **(b) Speculate:** Would the story be as effective if it were not set on a train? Why or why not?
3. **(a) Recall:** What do the men believe is creating the awful smell? **(b) Recall:** What is actually creating the smell? **(c) Compare and Contrast:** How does the contrast between what they think is true and what is really true contribute to the humor?
4. **(a) Recall:** Find at least three places in the story where the narrator exaggerates details. **(b) Analyze:** How does the use of exaggeration contribute to the story's humor?
5. **Analyze:** How does Thompson's description of the corpse as deliberately trying to smell bad add to the story's humor?
6. **Extend:** Would this story make a good movie? Why or why not?

ASSESSMENT PRACTICE: Reading Comprehension

Recognize Author's Point of View (For more practice, see Test Preparation Workbook, p. 38.)

Many tests require students to recognize an author's point of view. Use the following sample test item to practice recognizing author's point of view.

Leon nodded his head and finished his coffee. After Ken had been gone for a while, the neighbors and clanspeople came quietly to embrace Teofilo's family and to leave food on the table, because the gravediggers would come to eat when they were finished.

You can tell from the passage that the author views these events as if they were ____.

A sad
B chaotic
C conflicted
D somber

The writer offers few words revealing bias. Instead, the events are described with respect. The correct response is *D*.

Review and Assess

Literary Analysis

Setting

1. (a) In "The Man to Send Rain Clouds," which aspects of the Native American culture affect the action, and how? (b) Why is the desert important to the action? Use a chart like the one below to analyze the story's **setting.**

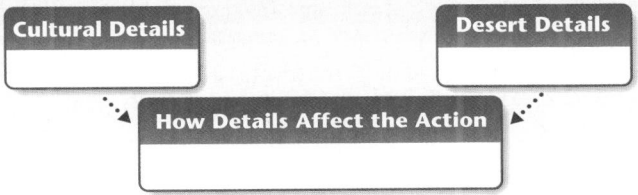

Cultural Details | **Desert Details** → **How Details Affect the Action**

2. (a) In "The Invalid's Story," describe the physical environment in which the narrator and Thompson sit. (b) Which factors in this setting drive the action of the story?

Comparing Literary Works

3. (a) Compare both stories to evaluate how the setting influences the action in each. (b) In which story is the setting more critical to the action? Explain.
4. (a) Compare the details of the winter settings found in each story. (b) How would each story be affected if it were set during a different season? Explain.

Reading Strategy

Using Your Senses

5. In "The Man to Send Rain Clouds," to which two **senses** would you say Silko appeals the most? Support your answer.
6. "The Invalid's Story" is one of the few stories to play almost exclusively to the sense of smell. Find two images in the story that most vividly capture the smell of the cheese. Explain your choice.

Extend Understanding

7. **Cultural Connection:** Silko's story illustrates conflict between cultures. (a) Describe another situation in which two cultures have clashed. (b) What can be done to resolve such conflicts?

Quick Review

The **setting** of a story is the time and place in which the story unfolds. In some stories, it can greatly influence the action.

To **use your senses,** draw from your own experiences to see, hear, smell, taste, or feel what each author describes.

Take It to the Net

www.phschool.com

Take the interactive self-test online to check your understanding of the selections.

ENRICHMENT: Further Reading

Other Works by the Authors

Works by Leslie Marmon Silko

Ceremony

Yellow Woman and a Beauty of the Spirit

Works by Mark Twain

The Celebrated Jumping Frog of Calaveras County and Other Sketches

Great Short Works of Mark Twain

The Adventures of Huckleberry Finn

Answers for p. 603

Review and Assess

1. **(a)** Possible response: The details concerning Native American religious practices and rituals helps to set up a conflict with the Catholic practices and rituals.
   (b) Possible response:

   Cultural Details: tying the feather to Teofilo's hair and painting his face

   Desert Details: desert gets very little rain

   How Details Affect the Action: Cultural details set up conflict with Father Paul; desert details set up the need for rain clouds

2. **(a)** They sit in a small, hot, airless railroad car with a stinking box believed to contain a corpse.
   (b) The close confinement of the railway car and the overpowering smell force the men to try various remedies.
3. **(a)** "The Man to Send Rain Clouds"; desert setting. "The Invalid's Story"; confined railroad car in freezing weather.
   (b) Students may suggest that the setting in "The Invalid's Story" is more critical to the action because the cold forces the men to stay in the railway car.
4. **(a)** The winter setting in "The Man to Send Rain Clouds" is benign. The winter setting in "The Invalid's Story" intensifies the men's predicament. **(b)** "The Man to Send Rain Clouds" would not be affected by a change of season. "The Invalid's Story" would be affected, because it is the deadly cold that traps the men in the stuffy railway car.
5. Silko appeals most to the senses of sight and touch. She describes rugged details of the landscape, including the changing colors of mountains and sky. She also describes the textures of soil, structures, and clothing.
6. Students might choose the image of Thompson burying his face in his handkerchief and rocking his body or the image of

continued

Answers continued

the burning materials whose smells seem to give the original smell "a better hold."

7. **(a)** Students' responses will range from personal disagreements to wars. **(b)** Students may suggest that conflicts, whether local or global, can be solved through compromise.

EXTEND

Answers for p. 604

❶ Vocabulary Development

Word Analysis

1. melodious; sweet-sounding
2. prestigious; important
3. riotous; disorderly

Spelling Strategy

1. loneliest
2. unnecessarily
3. flying

Concept Development: Synonyms

1. c
2. a
3. b
4. c
5. a
6. c
7. a
8. b
9. b

❷ Grammar

1. *to embrace*: infinitive
2. *to help*: infinitive
3. *to the railway station*: prepositional phrase
4. *to the smell*; prepositional phrase
5. *to suffer*; infinitive

Writing Application

Paragraphs should focus on a reaction to one of the stories. Have students exchange paragraphs with partners to check for the presence of two infinitives and two prepositional phrases.

Integrate Language Skills

❶ Vocabulary Development Lesson

Word Analysis: Latin Suffix *-ous*

Several words in "The Invalid's Story" end in *-ous*. The Latin suffix *-ous* generally means "full of" or "characterized by," as in *courageous*, meaning "full of courage." Add *-ous* to each word to form a new word. Then, define each new word.

1. melody 2. prestige 3. riot

Spelling Strategy

When adding a suffix to words ending in *y* preceded by a consonant, change the *y* to *i* unless the suffix itself starts with *i*. For example, *desultory* + *-ly* = *desultorily*. However, *try* + *-ing* = *trying*.

Write the new word formed by adding each suffix.

1. lonely + *-est*
2. unnecessary + *-ly*
3. fly + *-ing*

Concept Development: Synonyms

Choose the word that is closest in meaning to the first word.

1. deleterious: (a) delaying, (b) tasty, (c) harmful
2. cloister: (a) retreat, (b) group, (c) injury
3. judicious: (a) legal, (b) prudent, (c) rash
4. desultory: (a) kind, (b) evil, (c) random
5. placidly: (a) quietly, (b) coldly, (c) politely
6. pagans: (a) aliens, (b) villains, (c) nonbelievers
7. ominous: (a) threatening, (b) dishonest, (c) dark
8. prodigious: (a) inventive, (b) enormous, (c) joyous
9. perverse: (a) untidy, (b) improper, (c) clean

❷ Grammar Lesson

Prepositional Phrase or Infinitive?

An **infinitive** is a verbal consisting of the word *to* and a verb. A **prepositional phrase**, however, consists of a preposition and a noun or pronoun, as well as any modifiers.

It is important not to confuse a prepositional phrase beginning with *to* with an infinitive. A prepositional phrase always ends with a noun or pronoun, while an infinitive always ends with a verb.

Examples: **Infinitive:** He needed *to bring* the coffin on a train.

Prepositional Phrase: Leon carried Teofilo *to the truck*.

Practice Copy each sentence in your notebook, circling each phrase beginning with *to*. Then, label each a *prepositional phrase* or an *infinitive*.

1. Neighbors came to embrace Teofilo's family.
2. They asked the priest to help them by sprinkling holy water.
3. He walked to the railway station.
4. Thompson reacted strongly to the smell.
5. The cheese was causing them to suffer.

Writing Application Write a short paragraph about your reaction to either story, including at least two infinitives and two prepositional phrases in your writing.

WG Prentice Hall Writing and Grammar Connection: Chapter 21, Section 1

TEACHING RESOURCES

The following resources can be used to enrich or extend the instruction for pp. 604–605.

Vocabulary

Selection Support Workbook: Build Vocabulary, p. 149

Vocabulary and Spelling Practice Book (Use this booklet for skills enrichment.) ■

Grammar

Selection Support Workbook: Build Grammar Skills, p. 150

Writing and Grammar, Gold Level, p. 450 ■

Daily Language Practice Transparencies

Writing

Writing and Grammar, Gold Level, p. 236 ■

Writing and Grammar iText CD-ROM

■ **BLOCK SCHEDULING:** Resources marked with this symbol provide varied instruction during 90-minute blocks.

❸ Writing Lesson

Letter From Father Paul

Imagine that you are Father Paul in "The Man to Send Rain Clouds." Write a letter to a friend addressing the cultural differences you have encountered and how you would like to deal with them.

Prewriting Review the story. Jot down the ways Father Paul deals with the differences in the cultures. Then, note additional ways you think the two cultures can work together.

Drafting In your opening paragraph, express the feelings of Father Paul. Next, explain the differences in the cultures from his point of view. Finally, explain the way he intends to work with the Native American culture in the future.

Model: Drafting a Strong Opening Sentence

I am very fortunate to be working in this community, but I feel a conflict within myself and I struggle to know the best way to handle our differences.

Words like *fortunate* and *struggle* convey the varied feelings of Father Paul.

Revising Reread your letter. Make sure that you have addressed and explained each of the ways you think the two cultures can work together.

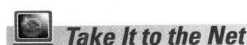

WG *Prentice Hall Writing and Grammar Connection: Chapter 11, Section 3*

❹ Extension Activities

Listening and Speaking Prepare a **monologue** in which Thompson from "The Invalid's Story" explains the experience on the train from his perspective.

- Review the story to gain a better understanding of Thompson.
- Use the tone of voice and gestures you think Thompson would use.
- Maintain a humorous tone.

Present your monologue to the class, and ask classmates if they agree with your interpretation of Thompson.

Research and Technology In a small group, prepare a **research report** about the Pueblo people. Use library resources, including the Internet and books about Native Americans, to gather information about their traditions and beliefs. In your report, explain which elements of Silko's story reflect the Pueblo culture best. **[Group Activity]**

Take It to the Net www.phschool.com

Go online for an additional research activity using the Internet.

❸ Writing Lesson

- Have students work as a class to list the cultural differences between Father Paul and Teofilo's family.
- Encourage students to think of a strong way to open a letter from Father Paul to a friend.
- Use the Writing Lesson to guide students in developing their letter.

❹ Listening and Speaking

- Have students list some of the things Thompson said and did during "The Invalid's Story."
- Ask students to write a monologue describing the train trip from Thompson's point of view. Remind students that he might have seen things differently from the narrator.
- Ask volunteers to perform their monologues for the class.

CUSTOMIZE INSTRUCTION For Universal Access

To address different learning styles, use the activities suggested in the **Extension Activities** booklet, p. 38.

- For Verbal/Linguistic and Bodily/Kinesthetic Learners, use Activity 5.
- For Visual/Spatial Learners, use Activity 6.
- For Verbal/Linguistic and Bodily/Kinesthetic Learners, use Activity 7.

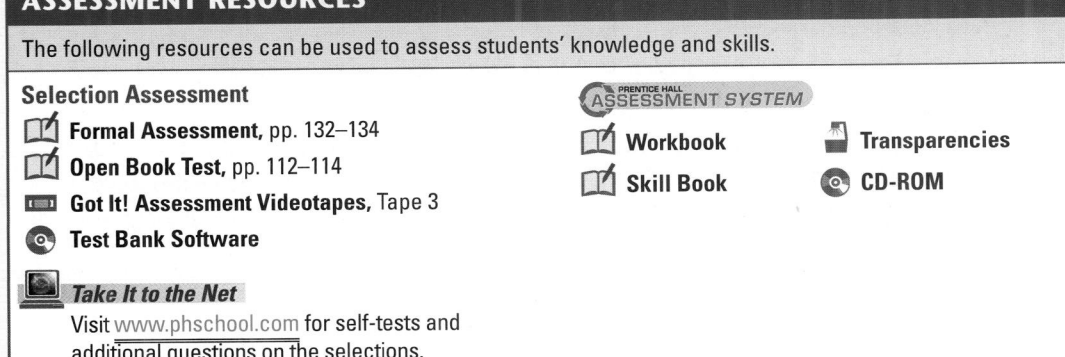

ASSESSMENT RESOURCES

The following resources can be used to assess students' knowledge and skills.

Selection Assessment

- **Formal Assessment,** pp. 132–134
- **Open Book Test,** pp. 112–114
- **Got It! Assessment Videotapes,** Tape 3
- **Test Bank Software**

PRENTICE HALL ASSESSMENT SYSTEM

- **Workbook**
- **Skill Book**
- **Transparencies**
- **CD-ROM**

Take It to the Net

Visit www.phschool.com for self-tests and additional questions on the selections.

The Necklace ✦ The Harvest

Lesson Objectives and CA Correlations

1. **To analyze and respond to literary elements**
   - Literary Analysis: Theme **R 3.2**
   - Comparing Literary Works
2. **To read, comprehend, analyze, and critique short stories**
   - Reading Strategy: Drawing Conclusions **R 3.8**
   - Reading Check questions
   - Review and Assess questions
   - Assessment Practice (ATE)
3. **To develop word analysis skills, fluency, and systematic vocabulary**
   - Vocabulary Development Lesson: Latin Root: *-ject-* **R 1.1**
4. **To understand and apply written and oral language conventions**
   - Spelling Strategy
   - Grammar Lesson: Appositive Phrases **LC 1.3**
5. **To understand and apply appropriate writing and research strategies**
   - Writing Lesson: Scene for a Television Drama **W 1.9**
   - Extension Activity: Flowchart **W 1.8**
6. **To understand and apply listening and speaking strategies**
   - Extension Activity: Improvisation **LS 1.9**

STEP-BY-STEP TEACHING GUIDE	PACING GUIDE
PRETEACH	
Motivate Students and Provide Background	
Use the Motivation activity (ATE p. 606)	5 min.
Read and discuss the Preview material and Background information (SE/ATE p. 606) [A]	10 min.
Introduce the Concepts	
Introduce the Literary Analysis and Reading Strategy (SE/ATE p. 607) [A]	15 min.
Pronounce the vocabulary words and read their definitions (SE p. 607)	5 min.
TEACH	
Monitor Comprehension	
Informally monitor comprehension by circulating while students read independently or in groups [A]	30 min.
Monitor students' comprehension with the Reading Check notes (SE/ATE pp. 609, 611, 613, 617, 619)	as students read
Develop vocabulary with Vocabulary notes (SE pp. 609, 611, 614, 619)	as students read
Develop Understanding	
Develop students' understanding of theme with Literary Analysis annotations (SE/ATE pp. 609, 610, 612, 614, 617) [A]	10 min.
Develop students' ability to draw conclusions with the Reading Strategy annotations (SE pp. 611, 613, 619; ATE pp. 609, 611, 613, 614, 619)	10 min.
ASSESS	
Assess Mastery	
Assess students' mastery of the Reading Strategy and Literary Analysis by having them answer the Review and Assess questions (SE/ATE p. 621)	20 min.
Use one or more of the print and media Assessment Resources (ATE p. 623) [A]	up to 50 min.
EXTEND	
Apply Understanding	
Have students complete the Vocabulary Development Lesson and the Grammar Lesson (SE p. 622) [A]	20 min.
Apply students' understanding of stage directions using the Writing Lesson (SE p. 623) [A]	45 min.
Apply students' understanding of the selection using one or more of the Extension Activities (SE p. 623)	20–90 min.

[A] **ACCELERATED INSTRUCTION:**
Use the strategies and activities identified with an [A].

UNIVERSAL ACCESS
● = Below-Level Students
▲ = On-Level Students
■ = Above-Level Students

Time and Resource Manager

Reading Level: Easy/Easy
Average Number of Instructional Days: 4

RESOURCES		
PRINT	**TRANSPARENCIES**	**TECHNOLOGY**
• **Beyond Literature,** Humanities Connection: Defining Values, p. 39 ▲ ■		• **Interest Grabber Video,** Tape 3 ● ▲ ■
• **Selection Support Workbook:** ● ▲ ■ Literary Analysis, p. 156 Reading Strategy, p. 155 Build Vocabulary, p. 153	• **Literary Analysis and Reading Transparencies,** pp. 77 and 78 ● ▲ ■	
• **Adapted Reader's Companion** ● • **Reader's Companion** ●		• **Listening to Literature** ● ▲ ■ Audiocassettes, Side 18 Audio CDs, CD 12
• **English Learner's Companion** ● ▲ • **Literatura en español** ● ▲ • **Literary Analysis for Enrichment** ■	• **Fine Art Transparencies Volume 1,** Transparency 3 ● ▲ ■	
• **Formal Assessment:** Selection Test, pp. 135–137 ● ▲ ■ • **Open Book Test,** pp. 115–117 ● ▲ ■ • PRENTICE HALL ASSESSMENT SYSTEM ● ▲ ■	• PRENTICE HALL ASSESSMENT SYSTEM ● ▲ ■ Skills Practice Answers and Explanations on Transparencies	• **Test Bank Software** ● ▲ ■ • **Got It! Assessment Videotapes,** Tape 3 ● ▲
• **Selection Support Workbook:** ● ▲ ■ Build Grammar Skills, p. 154 • **Writing and Grammar,** Gold Level ● ▲ ■ • **Extension Activities,** p. 39 ● ▲ ■	• **Daily Language Practice Transparencies** ● ▲	• **Writing and Grammar iText CD-ROM** ● ▲ ■ ***Take It to the Net*** www.phschool.com

BLOCK SCHEDULING: Use one 90-minute class period to preteach the selection and have students read it. Use a second 90-minute class period to assess students' mastery of skills and have them complete one of the Extension Activities.

PRETEACH

Step-by-Step Teaching Guide for pp. 606–607

Motivation

Engage students' interest in these stories by asking the following question: About how many times a day do you look in the mirror? Discuss with the class why we care so much about our physical appearance. Ask students the following questions: Can a beautiful or handsome person be dishonest or mean? Can an ordinary looking person be intelligent, generous, and kind? Suggest that while we do care about appearances, we are often fooled by them, as are some of the characters in both stories students are about to read.

Interest Grabber Video

As an alternative, play "Cesar Chavez" on Tape 3 to engage student interest.

1 Background

Tomás Rivera and the characters in "The Harvest" share an identity with close to one million migrant workers throughout the United States. Many migrant workers are themselves children, unprotected by the child labor laws that forbid exploitation in all other industries. Migrant workers as young as sixteen years are allowed to work with scissors, machetes, and pruning shears. They and their parents are often exposed to harmful agricultural chemicals and pesticides. Most American migrant workers live in California, Texas, or Florida, where the long growing seasons give them regular, although low-paying, winter work. Then, in the spring, they migrate north to work on farms.

Prepare to Read

The Necklace ◆ The Harvest

Campesino, 1976, Daniel DeSiga, Wright Gallery, University of California, Los Angeles

Take It to the Net

Visit www.phschool.com for interactive activities and instruction related to the selections, including
- background
- graphic organizers
- literary elements
- reading strategies

Preview

Connecting to the Literature

You may remember a time when a simple or surprising discovery made a strong impression on your life. Both of these stories capture the lasting impact of a character's discovery. Watch for the moment of discovery, and think about how it changes each character's world.

1 Background

Moving from place to place, harvesting and processing crops for low pay, migrant workers face many obstacles in the United States, such as difficulty in obtaining unemployment compensation, disability insurance, and sufficient education for their children. A former migrant worker himself, Tomás Rivera's concern is reflected in both "The Harvest" and his work as an educator.

TEACHING RESOURCES

The following resources can be used to enrich or extend the instruction for pp. 606–607.

Motivation

Interest Grabber Video, Tape 3

Background

Beyond Literature, p. 39

Take It to the Net

Visit www.phschool.com for background and hotlinks for the selections.

Literary Analysis

Literary Analysis and Reading Transparencies, Theme, p. 78

Reading

Selection Support Workbook: Literary Analysis, p. 156

Literary Analysis and Reading Transparencies, Draw Conclusions, p. 77

BLOCK SCHEDULING: Resources marked with this symbol provide varied instruction during 90-minute blocks.

❷ Literary Analysis

Theme

The **theme** of a literary work is the insight about life that it communicates. Sometimes, the theme of a work is stated directly. More often, however, the theme is expressed indirectly through the experiences of the characters, through the events and the setting of the work, or through the use of devices such as irony or symbols. The following excerpt from "The Necklace" raises questions about the importance of money and attention:

> She had no dowry, no hopes, not the slightest chance of being appreciated, understood, loved, and married by a rich and distinguished man; so she slipped into marriage with a minor civil servant at the Ministry of Education.

As you read these stories, pay attention to insights into life that are indirectly expressed.

Comparing Literary Works

Although the cultures and settings presented in the following stories are very different, both stories include a moment of discovery that greatly affects a character's life and indirectly expresses each story's theme. Compare the moments of insight the characters experience in the following stories.

❸ Reading Strategy

Drawing Conclusions

In determining a theme, you usually need to **draw conclusions** about characters and events. Follow these steps:

- Gather details about characters and events in the story.
- Make decisions about the underlying meaning of the details.

Using a chart like the one shown here, note details and draw conclusions about each character's actions. Then, decide how these actions might relate to each theme.

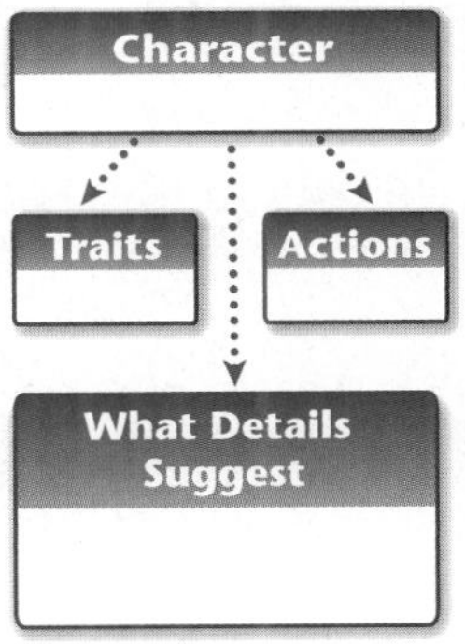

Vocabulary Development

déclassée (dā′ klä sā′) *French fem. adj.* lowered in social status (p. 609)

rueful (ro͞o′ fəl) *adj.* feeling sorrow or regret (p. 609)

resplendent (ri splen′ dənt) *adj.* shining brightly (p. 611)

disheveled (di shev′ əld) *adj.* disarranged and untidy (p. 614)

profoundly (prō found′ lē) *adv.* deeply and intensely (p. 615)

harrowed (har′ ōd) *v.* broken up by a harrow, a frame with spikes drawn by a horse or tractor (p. 619)

astutely (ə sto͞ot′ lē) *adv.* cleverly or cunningly (p. 619)

❷ Literary Analysis

Theme

- Tell students that as they read the two selections, they will be looking for an important message about life or human nature in each. This main message is called the *theme.*
- Read the instruction about theme together as a class, and call students' attention to the example from "The Necklace."
- Use the instruction for Comparing Literary Works to alert students to look for a moment of discovery on the part of the major characters in the selections that helps communicate the theme of each work.
- Use the Theme transparency in **Literary Analysis and Reading Transparencies,** p. 78, to show students how to set up a theme organizer for the selections.

❸ Reading Strategy

Drawing Conclusions

- Remind students that not all the important information about characters, events, or meaning is directly stated in a selection.
- Tell students they can learn to *draw conclusions* about people and events by paying attention to what people say and do throughout a selection and how their actions affect events in the story.
- Instruct students to create a Draw Conclusions chart like the one in their book or the one on p. 77 of **Literary Analysis and Reading Transparencies**.

Vocabulary Development

- Pronounce each vocabulary word for students, and read the definitions as a class. Have students identify any words with which they are already familiar.

CUSTOMIZE INSTRUCTION FOR UNIVERSAL ACCESS

For Special Needs Students	For Less Proficient Readers	For English Learners
Have students read the adapted version of "The Necklace" in the **Adapted Reader's Companion**. This version provides basic-level instruction in an interactive format with questions and write-on lines. Completing the adapted version will prepare students to read the selection in the Student Edition.	Have students read the story in the **Reader's Companion**. This version provides basic-level instruction in an interactive format with questions and write-on lines. After students finish the selection in **Reader's Companion**, have them complete the questions and activities in the Student Edition.	Have students read the adapted version of the story in the **English Learner's Companion**. This version provides basic-level instruction in an interactive format with questions and write-on lines. Completing the adapted version will prepared students to read the selection in the Student Edition.

E-Teach

Visit E-Teach at www.phschool.com for teachers' essays on how to teach, with questions and answers.

TEACH

CUSTOMIZE INSTRUCTION
For Visual/Spatial Learners

Encourage students to use the photograph on p. 608 and the painting on p. 612 to gain a clearer sense of the clothing and jewelry worn by the characters and the type of world in which they lived.

❶ About the Selection

In "The Necklace," Madame Loisel loses a borrowed diamond necklace that takes her and her husband ten years of hard labor to replace—only to discover that the original was a fake. Madame Loisel's real discovery is that she has wasted her life for the sake of appearing wealthy—her reason for borrowing the necklace in the first place.

❷ Critical Thinking

Interpret

- Ask students to summarize the information in this passage.
  Answer: A beautiful and charming woman with little money is unable to marry a rich man. She settles for a marriage to a minor civil servant.
- Invite students to infer what the narrator means by describing the woman as being born, "as if by an error of Fate, into a petty official's family."
  Possible response: The narrator is suggesting that a beautiful and charming woman should be born into a family with wealth and that her beauty and charm are wasted on the class into which she was born.

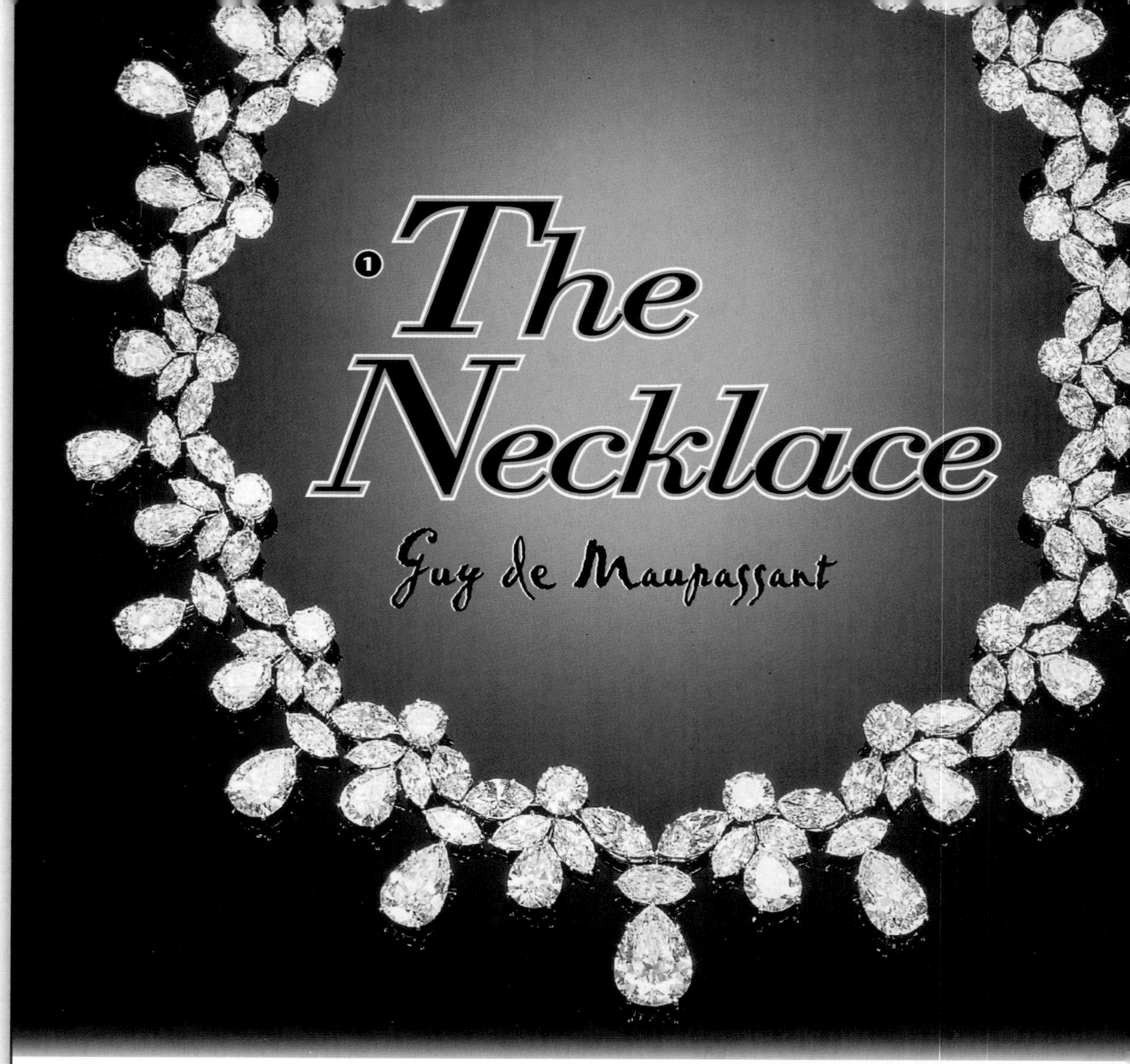

❶ The Necklace

Guy de Maupassant

❷ She was one of those pretty, charming young women who are born, as if by an error of Fate, into a petty official's family. She had no dowry,[1] no hopes, not the slightest chance of being appreciated, understood, loved, and married by a rich and distinguished man; so she slipped into marriage with a minor civil servant at the Ministry of Education.

1. **dowry** (dou´ rē) *n.* property that a woman brought to her husband at marriage.

TEACHING RESOURCES

The following resources can be used to enrich or extend the instruction for pp. 608–620.

Literary Analysis

- **Selection Support Workbook:** Reading Strategy, p. 155; Build Vocabulary, p. 153

Reading

- **Reader's Companion**
- **English Learner's Companion**
- **Listening to Literature Audiocassettes,** Side 18 ■
- **Listening to Literature Audio CDs,** CD 12 ■

Extension

- **Fine Art Transparencies, Volume 1,** Transparency 3 (Use this painting to help students' understanding the working conditions of migrant laborers in "The Harvest.")

■ **BLOCK SCHEDULING:** Resources marked with this symbol provide varied instruction during 90-minute blocks.

Unable to afford jewelry, she dressed simply: but she was as wretched as a *déclassée*, for women have neither caste nor breeding—in them beauty, grace, and charm replace pride of birth. Innate refinement, instinctive elegance, and suppleness of wit give them their place on the only scale that counts, and these qualities make humble girls the peers of the grandest ladies.

déclassée (dā′ klä sā′) *French fem. adj.* lowered in social status

3 She suffered constantly, feeling that all the attributes of a gracious life, every luxury, should rightly have been hers. The poverty of her rooms—the shabby walls, the worn furniture, the ugly upholstery—caused her pain. All these things that another woman of her class would not even have noticed, tormented her and made her angry. The very sight of the little Breton girl who cleaned for her awoke rueful thoughts and the wildest dreams in her mind. She dreamt of thick-carpeted reception rooms with Oriental hangings, lighted by tall, bronze torches, and with two huge footmen in knee breeches, made drowsy by the heat from the stove, asleep in the wide armchairs. She dreamt of great drawing rooms upholstered in old silks, with fragile little tables holding priceless knickknacks, and of enchanting little sitting rooms redolent of perfume, designed for tea-time chats with intimate friends—famous, sought-after men whose attentions all women longed for.

rueful (ro͞o′ fəl) *adj.* feeling sorrow or regret

Literary Analysis
Theme What theme might be hinted at in the description of Madame Loisel's longings?

When she sat down to dinner at her round table with its three-day-old cloth, and watched her husband opposite her lift the lid of the soup tureen and exclaim, delighted: "Ah, a good homemade beef stew! There's nothing better . . ." she would visualize elegant dinners with gleaming silver amid tapestried walls peopled by knights and ladies and exotic birds in a fairy forest; she would think of exquisite dishes served on gorgeous china, and of gallantries whispered and received with sphinx-like smiles[2] while eating the pink flesh of trout or wings of grouse.

She had no proper wardrobe, no jewels, nothing. And those were the only things that she loved—she felt she was made for them. She would have so loved to charm, to be envied, to be admired and sought after.

She had a rich friend, a schoolmate from the convent she had attended, but she didn't like to visit her because it always made her so miserable when she got home again. She would weep for whole days at a time from sorrow, regret, despair, and distress.

Then one evening her husband arrived home looking triumphant and waving a large envelope.

4 "There," he said, "there's something for you."

She tore it open eagerly and took out a printed card which said:

"The Minister of Education and Madame Georges Ramponneau [ma dam′ zhôrzh ram pə nō′] request the pleasure of the company of M. and Mme. Loisel [lwa zel′] at an evening reception at the Ministry on Monday, January 18th."

Instead of being delighted, as her husband had hoped, she tossed the invitation on the table and muttered, annoyed:

5 **Reading Check**
Which word best describes Mme. Loisel's life?

2. **gallantries whispered and received with sphinx** (sfiŋks)**-like smiles** flirtatious compliments whispered and received with mysterious smiles.

3 Literary Analysis
Theme

- Have students determine why Madame Loisel is aware of her poverty in a way that another woman of her class would not be aware of it.
- **Answer:** Because Madame Loisel is beautiful, she thinks this characteristic entitles her to the same status as women born to wealth.
- Remind students that the theme of a selection is the insight about life or human nature the writer wishes to communicate.
- Ask students to respond to the Literary Analysis question on p. 609: What theme might be hinted at in the description of Madame Loisel's longings?
Possible response: Students may suggest that unhappiness with one's economic place in life can lead to bad choices.

4 Reading Strategy
Drawing Conclusions

- Ask students to read the passage through "Monday, January 18th." Ask them how they would expect Madame Loisel to respond to the invitation.
Answer: Students will probably say that they expected Madame Loisel to be overjoyed by the invitation.
- Have students recall Madame Loisel's fantasies about the life she would like to live and think about what kinds of conclusions they can draw about her character.
Possible response: Madame Loisel's lavish dreams suggest that she is ambitious, vain, and self-centered.
- Ask students to answer the Reading Strategy question on p. 610: What conclusions can you draw about the feelings of Madame Loisel on the basis of her reaction to this invitation?
Answer: Although Madame Loisel wishes for a grand social life, she is too vain to want to attend the reception in her poor clothes.

5 Reading Check

Possible answer: Students may say *boring, empty, dreary, sad* and so on.

CUSTOMIZE INSTRUCTION FOR UNIVERSAL ACCESS

For Less Proficient Readers	For Gifted/Talented Students
The vocabulary in this selection may be daunting for some students. Help the group look for context clues to understand some of the words. For example, the phrase "The poverty of her rooms" is following by three examples that help readers see that *poverty* means "being poor," or "having little money." Other passages offer series of synonyms, such as *sorry, regret, despair,* and *distress,* which follow a description of Madame Loisel weeping for days at a time, suggesting that the four words are all different ways to say *unhappiness.*	Encourage students to look for examples of irony in this selection. For example, ask them what is ironic about Madame Loisel's response to the homemade beef stew in the middle of p. 609? Answer: Her husband loves the simple fare she serves for dinner; it is Madame Loisel who is disenchanted. Have students keep a list of other examples of irony as they read.

6 Literary Analysis

Theme

- Ask students to characterize Madame Loisel's husband from what they have read so far.
  Answer: Loisel appears to love his wife very much and wants to give her whatever she desires.
- Have students summarize what occurs in this passage.
  Possible response: Madame Loisel is upset about having nothing to wear to the reception. Her husband asks her how much a new evening dress would cost and when she tells him, he agrees to let her buy one.
- Ask students to answer the Literary Analysis question on p. 610: Which details do you learn in these paragraphs that might suggest the story's ending and theme?
  Possible response: Students may suggest that the husband will overextend himself in helping his wife and that the theme might be one cautioning against living beyond one's means.

7 Background

Economics

The franc is the official currency of France. Madame Loisel is asking for an amount equivalent to the cost of a hunting rifle—perhaps a few hundred dollars in today's money.

"What do you expect me to do with that?"

"Why, I thought you'd be pleased, dear. You never go out and this would be an occasion for you, a great one! I had a lot of trouble getting it. Everyone wants an invitation; they're in great demand and there are only a few reserved for the employees. All the officials will be there."

She looked at him, irritated, and said impatiently:

"I haven't a thing to wear. How could I go?"

It had never even occurred to him. He stammered:

"But what about the dress you wear to the theater? I think it's lovely. . . ."

He fell silent, amazed and bewildered to see that his wife was crying. Two big tears escaped from the corners of her eyes and rolled slowly toward the corners of her mouth. He mumbled:

6 "What is it? What is it?"

But, with great effort, she had overcome her misery; and now she answered him calmly, wiping her tear-damp cheeks:

"It's nothing. It's just that I have no evening dress and so I can't go to the party. Give the invitation to one of your colleagues whose wife will be better dressed than I would be."

He was overcome. He said:

"Listen, Mathilde [ma tēld′], how much would an evening dress cost—a suitable one that you could wear again on other occasions, something very simple?"

She thought for several seconds, making her calculations and at the same time estimating how much she could ask for without eliciting an immediate refusal and an exclamation of horror from this economical government clerk.

At last, not too sure of herself, she said:

7 "It's hard to say exactly but I think I could manage with four hundred francs."

He went a little pale, for that was exactly the amount he had put aside to buy a rifle so that he could go hunting the following summer near Nanterre, with a few friends who went shooting larks around there on Sundays.

However, he said:

"Well, all right, then. I'll give you four hundred francs. But try to get something really nice."

As the day of the ball drew closer, Madame Loisel seemed depressed, disturbed, worried—despite the fact that her dress was ready. One evening her husband said:

"What's the matter? You've really been very strange these last few days."

And she answered:

"I hate not having a single jewel, not one stone, to wear. I shall look so dowdy.[3] I'd almost rather not go to the party."

Reading Strategy
Drawing Conclusions What conclusions can you draw about the feelings of Madame Loisel on the basis of her reaction to this invitation?

Literary Analysis
Theme Which details do you learn in these paragraphs that might suggest the story's ending and theme?

3. **dowdy** (dou′dē) *adj.* shabby.

ENRICHMENT: Music Connection

The Waltz

Madame Loisel dances merrily to a waltz, a dance in three-quarter time. Despite the fact that it was considered scandalous, because the man and woman maintained close physical contact throughout the dance, the waltz became very popular in Europe during the eighteenth century. By the nineteenth century, the time of the story, the waltz was well established. The most famous waltzes of the time were those by Johann Strauss (1804–1849) and his son Johann the Younger (1825–1899).

If possible, play samples of Strauss waltzes—*Blue Danube* or *Tales from the Vienna Woods*—for the class as they imagine the elegantly dressed guests dancing at the party with Madame Loisel among them.

8 He suggested:

"You can wear some fresh flowers. It's considered very chic[4] at this time of year. For ten francs you can get two or three beautiful roses."

That didn't satisfy her at all.

"No . . . there's nothing more humiliating than to look poverty-stricken among a lot of rich women."

Then her husband exclaimed:

"Wait—you silly thing! Why don't you go and see Madame Forestier [fôr əs tyā'] and ask her to lend you some jewelry. You certainly know her well enough for that, don't you think?"

She let out a joyful cry.

"You're right. It never occurred to me."

The next day she went to see her friend and related her tale of woe.

Madame Forestier went to her mirrored wardrobe, took out a big jewel case, brought it to Madame Loisel, opened it, and said:

"Take your pick, my dear."

9 Her eyes wandered from some bracelets to a pearl necklace, then to a gold Venetian cross set with stones, of very fine workmanship. She tried on the jewelry before the mirror, hesitating, unable to bring herself to take them off, to give them back. And she kept asking:

"Do you have anything else, by chance?"

"Why yes. Here, look for yourself. I don't know which ones you'll like."

All at once, in a box lined with black satin, she came upon a superb diamond necklace, and her heart started beating with overwhelming desire. Her hands trembled as she picked it up. She fastened it around her neck over her high-necked dress and stood there gazing at herself ecstatically.

Hesitantly, filled with terrible anguish, she asked:

"Could you lend me this one—just this and nothing else?"

"Yes, of course."

She threw her arms around her friend's neck, kissed her ardently, and fled with her treasure.

The day of the party arrived. Madame Loisel was a great success. She was the prettiest woman there—resplendent, graceful, beaming, and deliriously happy. All the men looked at her, asked who she was, tried to get themselves introduced to her. All the minister's aides wanted to waltz with her. The minister himself noticed her.

She danced enraptured—carried away, intoxicated with pleasure, forgetting everything in this triumph of her beauty and the glory of her success, floating in a cloud of happiness formed by all this homage, all this admiration, all the desires she had stirred up—by this victory so complete and so sweet to the heart of a woman.

When she left the party, it was almost four in the morning. Her husband had been sleeping since midnight in a small, deserted sitting room, with three other gentlemen whose wives were having a wonderful time.

4. **chic** (shēk) *adj.* fashionable.

Reading Strategy
Drawing Conclusions
What conclusions can you draw about Madame Loisel's feelings toward her husband?

resplendent (ri splen' dənt) *adj.* shining brightly

10 **Reading Check**
Why does Madame Loisel visit Madame Forestier?

8 Reading Strategy

Drawing Conclusions

- Ask students what they might have expected Madame Loisel to feel once she bought her new dress.
  Answer: Students will probably say they expected her to be happy and looking forward to the reception.
- Have students describe Madame Loisel's actions in this passage.
  Answer: She complains about not having any jewelry to wear and says she would rather not go. When her husband suggests that she wear fresh flowers, she says that would identify her as being poverty-stricken and would humiliate her.

Monitor Progress Ask students to respond to the Reading Strategy question on p. 611: What conclusions can you draw about Madame Loisel's feelings toward her husband?
Answer: Madame Loisel seems unconcerned about her husband's feelings. She complains about her lack of jewelry after he has sacrificed his own pleasure to buy her a new dress.

9 Critical Thinking

Analyze

- Ask students to identify the kinds of jewels Madame Loisel examines in this passage.
  Answer: She examines pearls, gold, and diamonds.
- Have students analyze what Madame Loisel is really after as she looks at the jewelry.
  Possible response: She is only satisfied when she reaches the diamond necklace. She wants the life of comfort and beauty that diamonds represent.

10 Reading Check

Answer: Madame Loisel wishes to borrow some jewelry from her wealthy friend.

⓫ Literary Analysis

Theme

- Ask students what brings Madame Loisel down from her intoxicated delight in dancing and being admired by all.
  Answer: Her husband brings her wraps and she realizes that they are shabby compared to her evening dress.
- Ask students to answer the Literary Analysis question on page 612: What insight about Madame Loisel's life is suggested by the contrast between her beautiful dress and the "plain wraps of her everyday life"?
  Answer: Despite Madame Loisel's appearance at the party, her underlying reality has more to do with the shabby wraps than with the beautiful gown and jewels.

⓬ ▶Critical Viewing

Answer: Students may say that Madame Loisel is vain and desperately wants the kind of lifestyle that is represented by the jewels.

⓭ Background

Art

The New Necklace, 1910, by William McGregor Paxton.

William McGregor Paxton (1869–1941) was an American artist best known for his portraits of upper-class life. Use these questions for discussion:

1. If these women were Madame Loisel and Madame Forestier, which would you identify as Madame Loisel?
   Answer: The contrasting clothing and attitudes of the two women and the artist's use of light and shadow suggest that the figure standing on the right is Madame Loisel.
2. What does the painting suggest about the two women's attitudes toward the necklace?
   Answer: The seated woman seems to be holding the necklace carelessly, whereas the standing woman is reaching for it with great care. This suggests that the seated woman is accustomed to wealth, but the other woman is in awe of it.

⓫ He brought her wraps so that they could leave and put them around her shoulders—the plain wraps from her everyday life whose shabbiness jarred with the elegance of her evening dress. She felt this and wanted to escape quickly so that the other women, who were enveloping themselves in their rich furs, wouldn't see her.

Loisel held her back.

"Wait a minute. You'll catch cold out there. I'm going to call a cab."

But she wouldn't listen to him and went hastily downstairs. Outside in the street, there was no cab to be found; they set out to look for one, calling to the drivers they saw passing in the distance.

They walked toward the Seine,[5] shivering and miserable. Finally, on the embankment, they found one of those ancient nocturnal broughams[6] which are only to be seen in Paris at night, as if they were ashamed to show their shabbiness in daylight.

It took them to their door in the Rue des Martyrs, and they went sadly upstairs to their apartment. For her, it was all over. And he was thinking that he had to be at the Ministry by ten.

She took off her wraps before the mirror so that she could see herself in all her glory once more. Then she cried out. The necklace was gone; there was nothing around her neck.

Her husband, already half undressed, asked:

"What's the matter?"

She turned toward him in a frenzy:

"The . . . the . . . necklace—it's gone."

He got up, thunderstruck.

"What did you say? . . . What! . . . Impossible!"

And they searched the folds of her dress, the folds of her wrap, the pockets, everywhere. They didn't find it.

He asked:

"Are you sure you still had it when we left the ball?"

"Yes. I remember touching it in the hallway of the Ministry."

"But if you had lost it in the street, we would have heard it fall. It must be in the cab."

"Yes, most likely. Do you remember the number?"

"No. What about you—did you notice it?"

"No."

They looked at each other in utter dejection. Finally Loisel got dressed again.

"I'm going to retrace the whole distance we covered on foot," he said, "and see if I can't find it."

And he left the house. She remained in her evening dress, too weak to go to bed, sitting crushed on a chair, lifeless and blank.

Literary Analysis
Theme What insight about Madame Loisel's life is suggested by the contrast between her beautiful dress and the "plain wraps of her everyday life"?

⓬ **▼ Critical Viewing** Imagine Mathilde trying on piece after piece of her wealthy friend's jewelry. What can you tell about her personality from this behavior? **[Infer]**

⓭

5. **Seine** (sān) river flowing through Paris.
6. **broughams** (bro͞oms) *n.* horse-drawn carriages.

ENRICHMENT: History Connection

Usury

Loisel fears the worst when he cannot find the necklace because he is forced to borrow money from moneylenders and *usurers,* people who lend money at enormously high interest rates, often illegally. For a simple civil servant who has always lived within his means, this is a terrible, frightening, and humiliating situation.

14 Her husband returned at about seven o'clock. He had found nothing.

He went to the police station, to the newspapers to offer a reward, to the offices of the cab companies—in a word, wherever there seemed to be the slightest hope of tracing it.

She spent the whole day waiting, in a state of utter hopelessness before such an appalling catastrophe.

Loisel returned in the evening, his face lined and pale; he had learned nothing.

"You must write to your friend," he said, "and tell her that you've broken the clasp of the necklace and that you're getting it mended. That'll give us time to decide what to do."

She wrote the letter at his dictation.

By the end of the week, they had lost all hope.

Loisel, who had aged five years, declared:

"We'll have to replace the necklace."

The next day they took the case in which it had been kept and went to the jeweler whose name appeared inside it. He looked through his ledgers:

"I didn't sell this necklace, madame. I only supplied the case."

Then they went from one jeweler to the next, trying to find a necklace like the other, racking their memories, both of them sick with worry and distress.

In a fashionable shop near the Palais Royal, they found a diamond necklace which they decided was exactly like the other. It was worth 40,000 francs. They could have it for 36,000 francs.

They asked the jeweler to hold it for them for three days, and they stipulated that he should take it back for 34,000 francs if the other necklace was found before the end of February.

Loisel possessed 18,000 francs left him by his father. He would borrow the rest.

He borrowed, asking a thousand francs from one man, five hundred from another, a hundred here, fifty there. He signed promissory notes,[7] borrowed at exorbitant rates, dealt with usurers and the entire race of moneylenders. He compromised his whole career, gave his signature even when he wasn't sure he would be able to honor it, and horrified by the anxieties with which his future would be filled, by the black misery about to descend upon him, by the prospect of physical privation and moral suffering, went to get the new necklace, placing on the jeweler's counter 36,000 francs.

When Madame Loisel went to return the necklace, Madame Forestier said in a faintly waspish tone:

"You could have brought it back a little sooner! I might have needed it."

She didn't open the case as her friend had feared she might. If she had noticed the substitution, what would she have thought? What would she have said? Mightn't she have taken Madame Loisel for a thief? 15

7. **promissory** (präm´ i sôr´ē) **notes** written promises to pay back borrowed money.

Reading Strategy
Drawing Conclusions
What conclusions can you draw about the personalities of M. and Mme. Loisel from their actions after the necklace is lost?

15 ✓ Reading Check
What do the Loisels do to replace the necklace?

14 Reading Strategy

Drawing Conclusions

- Ask students what actions the husband and wife take when the necklace is discovered missing.
  Answer: Loisel retraces their steps over the evening, and the next day goes to the police station, to the newspapers to offer a reward, and to the cab companies. Madame Loisel remains seated in a chair overnight, lifeless and blank, and the next day waits hopelessly.
- Ask students to respond to the Reading Strategy question on p. 613: What conclusions can you draw about the personalities of M. and Mme. Loisel from their actions after the necklace is lost?
  Answer: Loisel is practical and decisive in response to disaster. Madame Loisel is overcome by her emotions and becomes passive under stress.

15 ✓ Reading Check

Answer: The Loisels borrow enough money from several sources to buy a necklace to replace the missing one.

CUSTOMIZE INSTRUCTION FOR UNIVERSAL ACCESS

For English Learners	For Advanced Readers
Direct students to words using prefixes on this spread, including *undressed, impossible, dejection, retrace, remained, returned, replace*. Help students to combine the meaning of each prefix with the rest of the word so as to comprehend the meaning of the whole word. Ask them which prefix means "again," which means "down," and which two mean "not" or "the opposite of."	Have students do research to find out how much 36,000 francs represents in today's American money. Then have them imagine borrowing this sum at an extortionate interest rate, such as thirty percent for a ten-year period. What monthly amount would they have to pay on such a loan?

⑯ Literary Analysis

Theme

- Have students recall Madame Loisel's feelings about being poor from the beginning of the story.
  Answer: She hated being poor and having possessions that made her appear poverty-stricken.
- Ask students to identify Madame Loisel's actions in this passage. What discovery does she makes about herself?
  Answer: She determines to pay the debt, resigns herself to being poor, dismisses her maid, and finds she has the strength to do all three.

Monitor Progress Have students respond to the Literary Analysis question on p. 614: What insight into hardship does this description of Madame Loisel suggest?
Answer: When faced with the worst that can happen, many people respond with unexpected courage and conviction.

⑰ Reading Strategy

Drawing Conclusions

- Have students describe the two women at the time of their meeting.
  Answer: Madame Loisel is disheveled, plainly dressed, thin, and with reddened hands. Madame Forestier is still young, still beautiful, still charming.
- Ask students what they can conclude about the fact that Madame Loisel appears haggard while Madame Forestier still appears young.
  Answer: People who are poor and perform physical work age faster than people who live a life of ease.

⑯ Madame Loisel came to know the awful life of the poverty-stricken. However, she resigned herself to it with unexpected fortitude. The crushing debt had to be paid. She would pay it. They dismissed the maid; they moved into an attic under the roof.

She came to know all the heavy household chores, the loathsome work of the kitchen. She washed the dishes, wearing down her pink nails on greasy casseroles and the bottoms of saucepans. She did the laundry, washing shirts and dishcloths which she hung on a line to dry; she took the garbage down to the street every morning, and carried water upstairs, stopping at every floor to get her breath. Dressed like a working-class woman, she went to the fruit store, the grocer, and the butcher with her basket on her arm, bargaining, outraged, contesting each sou[8] of her pitiful funds.

Every month some notes had to be honored and more time requested on others.

Her husband worked in the evenings, putting a shopkeeper's ledgers in order, and often at night as well, doing copying at twenty-five centimes a page.

And it went on like that for ten years.

After ten years, they had made good on everything, including the usurious rates and the compound interest.

⑰ Madame Loisel looked old now. She had become the sort of strong woman, hard and coarse, that one finds in poor families. Disheveled, her skirts askew, with reddened hands, she spoke in a loud voice, slopping water over the floors as she washed them. But sometimes, when her husband was at the office, she would sit down by the window and muse over that party long ago when she had been so beautiful, the belle of the ball.

How would things have turned out if she hadn't lost that necklace? Who could tell? How strange and fickle life is! How little it takes to make or break you!

Then one Sunday when she was strolling along the Champs Elysées[9] to forget the week's chores for a while, she suddenly caught sight of a woman taking a child for a walk. It was Madame Forestier, still young, still beautiful, still charming.

Madame Loisel started to tremble. Should she speak to her? Yes, certainly she should. And now that she had paid everything back, why shouldn't she tell her the whole story?

She went up to her.

"Hello, Jeanne."

The other didn't recognize her and was surprised that this plainly dressed woman should speak to her so familiarly. She murmured:

"But . . . madame! . . . I'm sure . . . You must be mistaken."

"No, I'm not. I am Mathilde Loisel."

Literary Analysis
Theme What insight into hardship does this description of Madame Loisel suggest?

disheveled (di shev´ əld) *adj.* disarranged and untidy

8. **sou** (so͞o) *n.* former French coin, worth very little; the centime (sän´ tēm´), mentioned later, was also of little value.
9. **Champs Elysées** (shän zā lē zā´) fashionable street in Paris.

CUSTOMIZE INSTRUCTION FOR UNIVERSAL ACCESS

For Gifted/Talented Students	For Advanced Readers
Ask students to create "before" and "after" portraits of Madame Loisel. Suggest that they include elements of clothing, accessories, and background details that show her glamorous image in the time before the necklace was lost and other details that convey the drabness and difficulty of her life afterwards. Challenge students to try to express a change in Madame Loisel's character in the two portraits.	Ask students to consider what obligations Jeanne Forestier is under at the end of the story. She now knows that she possesses a necklace of enormous value, though she had loaned only paste jewelry to her friend. Have students work in groups to decide whether or not Jeanne Forestier needs to take any action in light of what Madame Loisel tells her. Have the groups compare their conclusions.

Her friend gave a little cry.

"Oh! Oh, my poor Mathilde, how you've changed!"

"Yes, I've been through some pretty hard times since I last saw you and I've had plenty of trouble—and all because of you!"

"Because of me? What do you mean?"

"You remember the diamond necklace you lent me to wear to the party at the Ministry?"

"Yes. What about it?"

"Well, I lost it."

"What are you talking about? You returned it to me."

"What I gave back to you was another one just like it. And it took us ten years to pay for it. You can imagine it wasn't easy for us, since we were quite poor. . . . Anyway, I'm glad it's over and done with."

Madame Forestier stopped short.

"You say you bought a diamond necklace to replace that other one?"

"Yes. You didn't even notice then? They really were exactly alike."

And she smiled, full of a proud, simple joy.

Madame Forestier, profoundly moved, took Mathilde's hands in her own.

"Oh, my poor, poor Mathilde! Mine was false. It was worth five hundred francs at the most!"

profoundly (prō found′ lē) *adv.* deeply and intensely

Guy de Maupassant

(1850–1893)

Perhaps the best-known short-story writer in the world, Guy de Maupassant is known for his realistic stories that capture the surprising twists and turns of life. Maupassant was raised in northern France. As a young man, he served in the Franco-Prussian War, gathering experiences that would later appear in some of his stories. Later, he became a government clerk and devoted his spare time to writing. Eventually, Maupassant became the literary apprentice of well-known writer Gustave Flaubert, who introduced him to other illustrious writers of the day.

Despite the wealth he accumulated, Maupassant's later years were shadowed by ill health and depression.

Review and Assess

Thinking About the Selection

1. **Respond:** Do you feel sorry for Mathilde? Why or why not?
2. **(a) Recall:** As the story begins, why is Madame Loisel so unhappy with her life? **(b) Infer:** Do you think the author wants readers to sympathize with her unhappiness at this time? Why or why not?
3. **(a) Recall:** How does Madame Loisel's husband respond to her disappointment over the invitation? **(b) Compare and Contrast:** How is Madame Loisel different from her husband?
4. **(a) Recall:** Why is Madame Loisel so happy when her husband suggests that she go to see her wealthy friend, Madame Forestier? **(b) Interpret:** What symbolic meaning does the necklace have for Madame Loisel when she wears it?
5. **(a) Recall:** How does Madame Loisel change over the ten years she works to pay off the cost of the necklace? **(b) Analyze:** What actually causes her to change?
6. **Interpret:** How is the ending of the story ironic or surprising?
7. **Speculate:** Do you think people who value material possessions too much are likely to face hardship in life? Why or why not?

Answers for p. 615

Review and Assess

1. Students may feel sorry for Madame Loisel because she loses so much of her life to impoverished living conditions based on a mistaken assumption. Some may say that she is responsible for her own misfortune.
2. **(a)** Madame Loisel is beautiful and charming yet was born into the lower class, so she cannot expect to marry into money. **(b)** The author shows some sympathy for the fact that Madame Loisel is trapped in a boring, hopeless life. On the other hand, he shows her petulance and self-centeredness.
3. **(a)** Loisel responds by saying he will buy her a new dress. **(b)** Madame Loisel values the outward appearance of being wealthy and desirable. Her husband values the fundamental elements of life, such as a hearty meal or a good job.
4. **(a)** Madame Loisel realizes she will be able to wear some good jewelry to the reception. **(b)** The necklace symbolizes the "good," or upper-class life to Madame Loisel.
5. **(a)** She changes from pretty but weak to coarse but strong. **(b)** Working to pay off the necklace causes the change.
6. The ending is ironic because Madame Loisel gives up everything of true value for something that has no value.
7. Students may suggest that people who focus on material possessions can achieve financial well-being. Others may note that such people can face hardship if their circumstances change.

ENRICHMENT: Social Studies

Women and Economics

Students may judge Madame Loisel harshly in this selection, but they should be aware that at the time and place in which this story is set, women had no standing in society other than that bestowed on them by marriage. Being beautiful and charming rarely compensated for not being born into the upper class. Moreover, a beautiful but economically deprived woman often was not able to improve her lot by marrying a rich man. In this selection, Madame Loisel, who is both beautiful and charming, longs for the upper-class life to which she believe her looks entitle her; she feels she deserves a "better" marriage. You may find it interesting to see if students' judgments about Madame Loisel change between the beginning of the selection and the end, when they see to what straits her unrealistic expectations have brought her.

⓲ About the Selection

Focusing on the lives of migrant farm workers and their families, "The Harvest" describes the curiosity of a group of young men who notice that an old man, Don Trine, who seems peculiar to them, goes on mysterious walks. Convinced that following Don Trine will lead them to buried treasure, the boys follow him and later return to the place where he ended his walk. Only one boy discoveries what Don Trine's treasure is—a connection to the earth and a love of the land.

⓳ ▶Critical Viewing

Answer: The painting suggests that migrant work involves difficult, stooped postures that bring people close to the earth.

⓴ Background

Art

Campesino, **1976, by Daniel DeSiga.**

In this painting, a *campesino,* or farm worker, bends down toward the earth to harvest a crop. Daniel DeSiga is a Chicano artist who uses art to address compelling issues in Chicano culture, such as the plight of farm workers. Use these questions for discussion:

1. Compare and contrast the figure in the painting with the character Don Trine in the story.
   Answer: The figure in the painting is a farm worker, and he is stooping close to the earth. Although he is hard at work, he does not seem to be "communicating" with the earth as Don Trine does.
2. Do you think the man in the painting is enjoying his work or not?
   Answer: Answers may vary, but students should note that there is something about the downward slope of his massive shoulders that suggests both strength and fatigue.

Campesino, 1976, Daniel DeSiga, Wright Art Gallery, University of California, Los Angeles

⓴

⓲ The Harvest

Tomás Rivera

ENRICHMENT: Social Studies Connection

Harvest Festivals

Agriculture, the raising of crops and livestock, began about 8,000 to 10,000 years ago. By allowing for stable settlement, agriculture eventually led to the growth of cities and civilizations. It is no wonder that the land was considered sacred then and to a large degree still is today by many people. This reverence is reflected in the many harvest festivals that exist around the world.

Students might wish to research different celebrations of harvest. Possibilities include Thanksgiving, the Nigerian New Yam festival, the Czech Posviceni festival, the Zulu festival of first fruits, or the Jewish festival of Sukkot. Students might also explore the attitudes of different cultures toward the land, such as the widespread Native American belief that no one can own the land or the European notion of inherited property.

21 The end of September and the beginning of October. That was the best time of the year. First, because it was a sign that the work was coming to an end and that the return to Texas would start. Also, because there was something in the air that the folks created, an aura of peace and death. The earth also shared that feeling. The cold came more frequently, the frosts that killed by night, in the morning covered the earth in whiteness. It seemed that all was coming to an end. The folks felt that all was coming to rest. Everyone took to thinking more. And they talked more about the trip back to Texas, about the harvests, if it had gone well or bad for them, if they would return or not to the same place next year. Some began to take long walks around the grove. It seemed like in these last days of work there was a wake over the earth. It made you think.

That's why it wasn't very surprising to see Don Trine take a walk by himself through the grove and to walk along the fields every afternoon. This was at the beginning, but when some youngsters asked him if they could tag along, he even got angry. He told them he didn't want anybody sticking behind him.

"Why would he want to be all by hisself, anyway?"
"To heck with him: it's his business."
"But, you notice, it never fails. Every time, why, sometimes I don't even think he eats supper, he takes his walk. Don't you think that's a bit strange?"
"Well, I reckon. But you saw how he got real mad when we told him we'd go along with him. It wasn't anything to make a fuss over. This ain't his land. We can go wherever we take a liking to. He can't tell us what to do."
"That's why I wonder, why'd he want to walk by hisself?"

22 And that's how all the rumors about Don Trine's walks got started. The folks couldn't figure out why or what he got out of taking off by himself every afternoon. When he would leave, and somebody would spy on him, somehow or other he would catch on, then take a little walk, turn around and head right back to his chicken coop. The fact of the matter is that everybody began to say he was hiding the money he had earned that year or that he had found some buried treasure and every day, little by little, he was bringing it back to his coop. Then they began to say that when he was young he had run around with a gang in Mexico and that he always carried around a lot of money with him. They said, too, that even if it was real hot, he carried a belt full of money beneath his undershirt. Practically all the speculation centered on the idea that he had money.

19 ◀**Critical Viewing** What does this painting suggest about the lives of the migrant workers in this story? **[Infer]**

Literary Analysis
Theme What insights about life might be provided in this paragraph?

23 ✓**Reading Check**
What does everyone see Don Trine do every afternoon?

21 Literary Analysis

Theme

- Remind students that the *theme* of a selection is the insight it offers about life and human nature.
- After students read the passage, ask them why this time of year is important.
  Answer: Students may note that the end of the growing season is the end of the work cycle and a time for rest. It is also the time when migrant workers can return to their homes.
- Have students answer the Literary Analysis question on p. 617: What insights about life might be provided in this paragraph?
  Possible response: The rhythms of the earth affect the rhythms of farm workers' lives. When the earth "rests," people can rest.

22 Critical Thinking

Interpret

- Ask students what they might fantasize about if they were very hungry and without funds to buy a meal.
  Answer: Students may say that when you are hungry and without food, all you can think about is food.
- Have students read the passage and determine why the boys' fantasies about Don Trine all seem to center on money.
  Answer: As farm workers, they make very little money, so they probably dream of having more. They incorporate their desire to possess money into their fantasies about Don Trine's past.

23 ✓Reading Check

Answer: They see Don Trine walk off by himself each afternoon.

CUSTOMIZE INSTRUCTION FOR UNIVERSAL ACCESS

For Special Needs Students	For Less Proficient Readers
Have students view "Cesar Chavez" on Tape 3 in **Interest Grabber Video.** When they have completed the tape, ask them some basic questions about Cesar Chavez and his work with the United Farm Workers. Have students work as a group to make a list of characteristics of farm workers' lives to compare to the information they learn in this story.	Because the dialogue passage is indented, students may have difficulty with it. After you inform students that the passage shows people talking about Don Trine, help them find the different statements. Remind them that each separate passage of dialogue—that is, each different speaker—is enclosed in quotation marks. If a new pair of quotation marks appears, a different person is talking. Divide the group into pairs and have them practice reading the dialogue.

24 ▶**Critical Viewing**

Answer: Students may find that the setting in the painting gives the impression of late harvest, just as the story does.

25 Background

Art

Farmworker de Califas, by Tony Ortega.

Working under a burning sun, the subject of this painting typifies the struggle of farm laborers everywhere. Use the following for discussion:

1. How does Ortega's use of color help you sense how the farm worker feels?
   Answer: Ortega paints ribbons of color like fire that let you know how hot the field must be.
2. Does the author fully describe the setting in the story? How does this painting add to your experience of the story?
   Answer: Students may say that there is little description in the story; therefore, the painting provides a visual image of the setting.

"Let's see, who's he got to take care of? He's an old bachelor. He ain't never married or had a family. So, with him working so many years . . . Don't you think he's bound to have money? And then, what's that man spend his money on? The only thing he buys is his bit of food every Saturday. Once in a while, a beer, but that's all."

"Yeah, he's gotta have a pile of money, for sure. But, you think he's going to bury it around here?"

"Who said he's burying anything? Look, he always goes for his food on Saturday. Let's check close where he goes this week, and on Saturday, when he's on his errand, we'll see what he's hiding. Whadda you say?"

"Good'nuff. Let's hope he doesn't catch on to us."

24 ▼**Critical Viewing** Does this image capture the setting of the story as you imagine it? Why or why not? **[Evaluate]**

25

Farmworker de Califas, Tony Ortega, Courtesy of the artist

ENRICHMENT: Social Studies Connection

Cesar Chavez

One person who fought for the rights of migrant workers was California labor leader Cesar Chavez (1927–1993). In 1962, Chavez, a Mexican American farm worker, established the National Farm Workers Association to organize California grape pickers. In 1966, his union merged with another union to become the United Farm Workers Organizing Committee, which later became the United Farm Workers of America—the first successful union of farm workers in the United States.

Chavez organized national boycotts against fruit and vegetable growers who refused to accept the unions. In all of his actions on behalf of farm workers, Chavez, like Dr. Martin Luther King, Jr., supported a position of nonviolence.

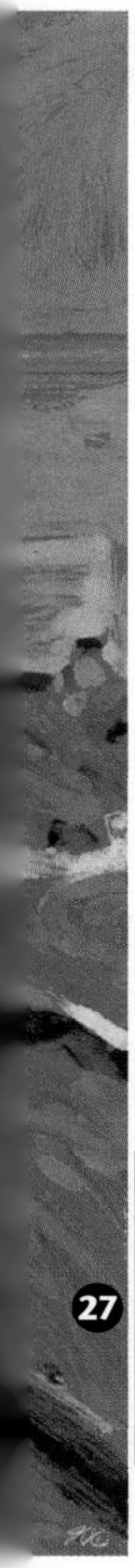

26 That week the youngsters closely watched Don Trine's walks. They noticed that he would disappear into the grove, then come out on the north side, cross the road then cross the field until he got to the irrigation ditch. There he dropped from sight for a while, then he reappeared in the west field. It was there where he would disappear and linger the most. They noticed also that, so as to throw people off his track, he would take a different route, but he always spent more time around the ditch that crossed the west field. They decided to investigate the ditch and that field the following Saturday.

When that day arrived, the boys were filled with anticipation. The truck had scarcely left and they were on their way to the west field. The truck had not yet disappeared and they had already crossed the grove. What they found they almost expected. There was nothing in the ditch, but in the field that had been harrowed after pulling the potatoes they found a number of holes.

"You notice all the holes here? The harrow didn't make these. Look, here's some foot prints, and notice that the holes are at least a foot deep. You can stick your arm in them up to your elbow. No animal makes these kind of holes. Whadda you think?"

"Well, it's bound to be Don Trine. But, what's he hiding? Why's he making so many holes? You think the landowner knows what he's up to?"

"Naw, man. Why, look, you can't see them from the road. You gotta come in a ways to notice they're here. What's he making them for? What's he using them for? And, look, they're all about the same width. Whadda you think?"

"Well, you got me. Maybe we'll know if we hide in the ditch and see what he does when he comes here."

"Look, here's a coffee can. I bet you this is what he digs with."

"I think you're right."

The boys had to wait until late the following Monday to discover the reason for the holes. But the word had spread around so that everybody already knew that Don Trine had a bunch of holes in that field. They tried not to let on but the allusions they made to the holes while they were out in the fields during the day were very obvious. Everybody thought there had to be a big explanation. So, the youngsters spied more carefully and astutely.

27 That afternoon they managed to fool Don Trine and saw what he was doing. They saw, and as they had suspected, Don Trine used the coffee can to dig a hole. Every so often, he would measure with his arm the depth of the hole. When it went up to his elbow, he stuck in his left arm, then filled dirt in around it with his right hand, all the way up to the elbow. Then he stayed like that for some time. He seemed very satisfied and even tried to light a cigarette with one hand. Not being able to, he just let it hang from his lips. Then he dug another hole and repeated the process. The boys could not understand why

Reading Strategy
Drawing Conclusions
What conclusion would you draw about Don Trine from his mysterious behavior?

harrowed (har′ ōd) *v.* broken up by a harrow, a frame with spikes drawn by a horse or tractor

Reading Strategy
Drawing Conclusions
What conclusion can you draw, so far, about Don Trine based on his actions?

astutely (ə stoot′ lē) *adv.* cleverly or cunningly

28 **✓ Reading Check**
What do the youngsters witness Don Trine doing with the dirt?

CUSTOMIZE INSTRUCTION FOR UNIVERSAL ACCESS

For English Learners	For Advanced Readers
The dialect in "The Harvest" may prove unfamiliar to students. Preview these idiomatic expressions and slang before students read the story: *It never fails, I reckon, this ain't, by hisself, catch on, I bet you.*	Suggest that students read from the book *Voices from the Fields: Children of Migrant Farmworkers Tell Their Stories,* edited by interviewer S. Beth Atkin. The selections include both poetry and biography. Students might wish to compare these young people's lives with those of the characters in "The Harvest." They may also read aloud some of the selections to the rest of the class.

26 Reading Strategy
Drawing Conclusions

- Have students recall that Don Trine has already discouraged the boys from accompanying him. What else does he do here in order to keep his activities to himself?
  Answer: He sometimes takes a different route to trick his followers.
- Ask students if the passage describes Don Trine's character directly.
  Answer: The passage does not describe Don Trine's character but only his actions.
- Have students respond to the first Reading Strategy question on p. 619: What conclusion would you draw about Don Trine from his mysterious behavior?
  Answer: Don Trine's movements indicate a desire to be secretive about whatever he is doing.

27 Reading Strategy
Drawing Conclusions

- Have students use a chart like the one shown to record the details about Don Trine in this passage.

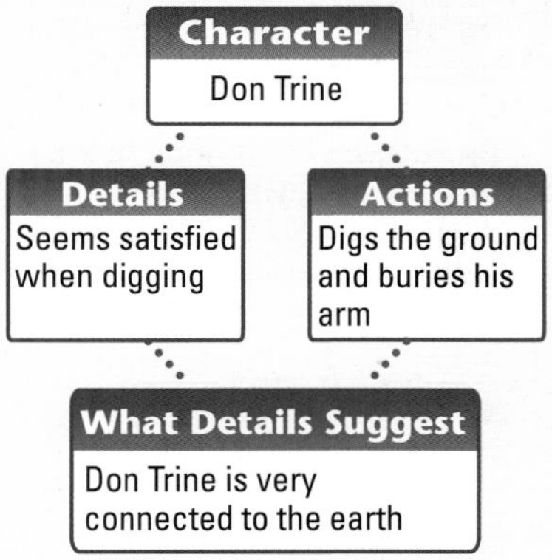

Character
Don Trine
Details
Seems satisfied when digging
Actions
Digs the ground and buries his arm
What Details Suggest
Don Trine is very connected to the earth

Monitor Progress Have students answer the second Reading Strategy question on p. 619: What conclusion can you draw, so far, about Don Trine based on his actions?
Answer: Don Trine is a person with a very close relationship with the earth.

28 ✓ Reading Check

Answer: When Don Trine can put his arm into the hole up to his elbow, he puts the dirt back into the hole around his arm.

ASSESS

Answers for p. 620

Review and Assess

1. Students may say that they respect Don Trine as a person who truly loves nature.
2. **(a)** The story takes place at the end of the harvest season. **(b)** The "aura of peace and death" spoken of in the opening paragraph foreshadows the earth falling "fast asleep" at the end of the story.
3. **(a)** The boys think he is checking on money that he has buried. **(b)** The boys' speculations reveal that they are materialistic and not very imaginative.
4. **(a)** The boy discovers that Don Trine is simply appreciating the feel of the harvested earth. **(b)** The boy sensed the movement of the earth, grasping and caressing his fingers. **(c)** The boy's ability to empathize suggests that he is as sensitive to the earth as Don Trine is.
5. **(a)** Suggestions include: outdoor sports and activities such as hiking, camping, canoeing and bird-watching; protecting endangered plant and animal species; working with environmental groups, and so forth. **(b)** Students may say that people would benefit both emotionally and spiritually from communing with nature.

he did this. That was what puzzled them the most. They had believed that, with finding out what it was he did, they would understand everything. But it didn't turn out that way at all. The boys brought the news to the rest of the folks in the grove and nobody there understood either. In reality, when they found out that the holes didn't have anything to do with money, they thought Don Trine was crazy and even lost interest in the whole matter. But not everybody.

The next day one of the boys who discovered what Don Trine had been up to went by himself to a field. There he went through the same procedure that he had witnessed the day before. What he experienced and what he never forgot was feeling the earth move, feeling the earth grasp his fingers and even caressing them. He also felt the warmth of the earth. He sensed he was inside someone. Then he understood what Don Trine was doing. He was not crazy, he simply liked to feel the earth when it was sleeping.

That's why the boy kept going to the field every afternoon, until one night a hard freeze came on so that he could no longer dig any holes in the ground. The earth was fast asleep. Then he thought of next year, in October at harvest time, when once again he could repeat what Don Trine did. It was like when someone died. You always blamed yourself for not loving him more before he died.

Review and Assess

Thinking About the Selection

1. **Respond:** What do you think of Don Trine at the end of the story? Why?
2. **(a) Recall:** At what time of year does this story take place? **(b) Apply:** How does the opening paragraph foreshadow, or hint at, the ending of the story?
3. **(a) Recall:** What do the boys think Don Trine is doing every afternoon? **(b) Infer:** What do the boys' speculations about Don Trine reveal about them?
4. **(a) Recall:** When the one boy goes into the field later, what does he learn about Don Trine? **(b) Recall:** What does he realize when he imitates Don Trine's actions? **(c) Infer:** What does this ability to understand Don Trine suggest about the boy?
5. **(a) Extend:** Don Trine finds a way to make a connection with nature. In what other ways do people connect with nature? **(b) Speculate:** Do you think most people would benefit from taking time to appreciate nature? Why or why not?

Tomás Rivera

(1935–1984)

Born in Crystal City, Texas, Tomás Rivera soon joined what he called the "migrant labor stream" that traveled throughout the farmlands of the United States. Faced with the challenge of alternating schooling with work in the fields, Rivera pursued his education tirelessly. His persistence paid off, as he eventually earned a Ph.D. in Spanish Literature.

Rivera's concern for the education of minorities led him to a career as an educator, limiting the time he could devote to his writing. Nevertheless, he has become one of the most renowned Mexican American authors in the United States. His work most often focuses on the experiences of migrant farm workers.

ASSESSMENT PRACTICE: Reading Comprehension

Recognize Author's Purpose (For more practice, see Test Preparation Workbook, p. 39.)

Use the following sample test item to provide practice for recognizing an author's purpose.

Chavez organized national boycotts against fruit and vegetable growers who refused to accept unions. In all of his actions on behalf of farm workers, Chavez firmly supported a position of nonviolence.

In this passage, the author's purpose is ____

A to persuade readers to boycott nonunion produce.
B to entertain readers with interesting information.
C to inform readers about Cesar Chavez's life.
D to inspire readers to support farm workers.

While the author's tone is positive, it is not persuasive or inspirational, nor is the information meant to be entertaining. Thus, the correct answer is *C*.

Review and Assess

Literary Analysis

Theme

1. Toward the end of "The Necklace," Madame Loisel thinks, "How strange and fickle life is! How little it takes to make or break you!" What does this statement suggest about the complexity of life?
2. Considering the course of events for Madame Loisel, what would you say is the **theme** of "The Necklace"? Explain.
3. Using a chart like the one below, analyze the last two paragraphs of "The Harvest" and explain the theme of the story.

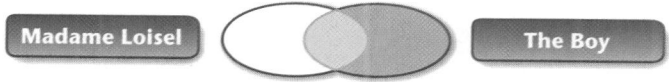

Words From the Text	Insights
Theme:	

Comparing Literary Works

4. (a) Summarize the moment of insight for Madame Loisel in "The Necklace" and for the boy at the end of the "The Harvest."
(b) Using a Venn diagram like the one below, explain how their discoveries are similar and different.

Madame Loisel

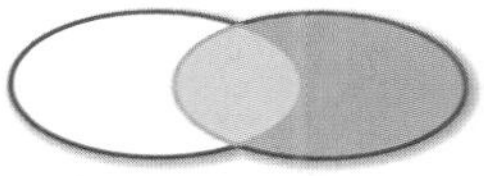

The Boy

5. Who do you think will be affected more by their insight? Explain.

Reading Strategy

Drawing Conclusions

6. Madame Loisel places a high value on material goods. On the basis of the story, what **conclusion** can you draw about such values?
7. Based on the ending of "The Harvest," what conclusion can you draw about the importance of nature to the human spirit?

Extend Understanding

8. **Cultural Connection:** (a) What does "The Necklace" show you about life in middle-class French society in the late nineteenth century? (b) Do you think there are parallels in modern American society? Explain.

Quick Review

The **theme** of a literary work is the insight about life that it communicates.

To **draw conclusions,** gather details and make decisions about the underlying meaning of these details.

Take It to the Net

www.phschool.com

Take the interactive self-test online to check your understanding of the selections.

ENRICHMENT: Further Reading

Other Works by the Authors

Works by Guy de Maupassant
"Two Friends"

Works by Tomás Rivera
The Searchers: Collected Poetry
The Migrant Earth

Take It to the Net

Visit www.phschool.com for more information on the authors.

Answers for p. 621

Review and Assess

1. This statement suggests that life is too complex for most people, including Madame Loisel, to understand. Her own values have undermined her, putting her in a position to be devastated by a bit of bad luck.
2. Suggested response: Living wholly for material values shrinks your spirit and leaves you open to the fickleness of fortune.
3. Words from the Text: "He was not crazy, he simply liked to feel the earth when it was sleeping." Insight: Don Trine liked to feel what it must be like to grow in the earth. Words from the Text: "You always blamed yourself for not loving him more before he died." Insight: Take advantage of experiences that enrich your life before it is too late. Theme: Human beings need to acknowledge their deep connection to the natural world.
4. **(a)** When Madame Loisel hears that the necklace is fake, she realizes that she has wasted much of her life. The boy discovers his connection to the earth, a connection that can be renewed season to season. **(b)** Similaritites: Both Madame Loisel and the boy make a discovery that changes their view of life and of their place in it. Differences: Madame Loisel: Her discovery tells her she has wasted much of her life. The boy: His discovery tells him what is important about life and he commits to being a different kind of person.
5. Students may suggest that the boy will be affected more because he has many years ahead of him.
6. The story makes such values seem hollow and ultimately unsatisfying, and the people who live by them shallow.
7. Possible response: Human beings are deeply connected to the cycles of nature and need to recognize that tie.
8. **(a)** The story shows that the type of life a person led depended greatly upon wealth and social status. **(b)** Some students may say that the same is largely true today.

EXTEND

Answers for p. 622

❶ Vocabulary Development

Word Analysis

1. a path something takes when it is thrown
2. to throw out or away
3. to throw something into the middle of; to interrupt

Spelling Strategy

1. entirely: I am entirely full of pizza.
2. hopeful: We are hopeful that they will get here before the storm.
3. awesome: That was an awesome concert!

Concept Development: Synonyms

1. a
2. a
3. b
4. b
5. c
6. c
7. b

❷ Grammar

1. a woman from a middle-class background: Mathilde
2. a kind and generous man: husband
3. a wealthy woman with an upper-class background: Madame Forestier
4. a strand of fake jewels: necklace
5. a meager and simple apartment: home

Writing Application

Sample sentences: Madame Loisel, worn by hard work, looked older than her age. The boys, curious about the old man, followed him. One boy, wiser than the rest, understood Don Trine.

Integrate Language Skills

❶ Vocabulary Development Lesson

Word Analysis: Latin Root *-ject-*

The word *dejection*, meaning "a state of sadness," is formed from the Latin word root *-ject-*, which means "to throw." Considering the meaning of *-ject-*, write a definition for each word below.

1. trajectory 2. eject 3. interject

Spelling Strategy

For words that end in silent *e*, keep the *e* before adding an ending that begins with a consonant. For example, when you add *-ful* to the word *rue*, you form the word *rueful*. Add the given suffixes to the words below. Then, write a sentence for each new word.

1. entire + *-ly* 2. hope + *-ful* 3. awe + *-some*

Concept Development: Synonyms

Choose the word or phrase that is closest in meaning to the first word.

1. astutely: (a) cleverly, (b) grandly, (c) thriftily
2. resplendent: (a) radiant, (b) wealthy, (c) sturdy
3. profoundly: (a) slowly, (b) deeply, (c) quietly
4. déclassée: (a) decorated, (b) lowered in social status, (c) tardy
5. harrowed: (a) mad, (b) frightened, (c) plowed
6. rueful: (a) angry, (b) sweet, (c) sorry
7. disheveled: (a) old, (b) messy, (c) rusty

❷ Grammar Lesson

Appositive Phrases

An **appositive phrase** is a noun or pronoun with modifiers that is placed next to a noun or pronoun to provide more information. The modifiers added to make an appositive phrase can be adjectives, adjective phrases, or other groups of words acting as adjectives. Look at the following example from "The Necklace."

Example: She had a rich friend, *a schoolmate from the convent she had attended*, but she didn't like to visit her because it always made her so miserable when she got home again.

(The appositive phrase in italics renames *friend*.)

Practice Write the appositive phrase in each sentence and the word or words it renames.

1. Mathilde, a woman from a middle-class background, was unhappy with her life.
2. Her husband, a kind and generous man, could not provide the life she desired.
3. She spoke to Madame Forestier, a wealthy woman with an upper-class background.
4. The necklace, a strand of fake jewels, was lost.
5. She went back to her home, a meager and simple apartment, to speak to her husband.

Writing Application Write three sentences about a character in one of the stories you have just read, including an appositive phrase in each.

WG Prentice Hall Writing and Grammar Connection: Chapter 21, Section 1

TEACHING RESOURCES

The following resources can be used to enrich or extend the instruction for pp. 622–623.

Vocabulary

- **Selection Support Workbook:** Build Vocabulary, p. 153
- **Vocabulary and Spelling Practice Book** (Use this booklet for skills enrichment.)
- **Writing and Grammar,** Gold Level, p. 450
- **Daily Language Practice Transparencies**

Grammar

- **Selection Support Workbook:** Build Grammar Skills, p. 154

Writing

- **Writing and Grammar,** Gold Level, p. 94
- **Writing and Grammar iText CD-ROM**

BLOCK SCHEDULING: Resources marked with this symbol provide varied instruction during 90-minute blocks.

❸ Writing Lesson

Scene for a Television Drama

Imagine that one of the stories you have just read will be adapted for presentation as a television drama. Choose either "The Necklace" or "The Harvest" and write the final, dramatic scene for this production.

Prewriting Make a list of the events you would like to include in the scene. Note the actions that make up the climax, or highest point of the story, and plan the events that will happen after the climax.

Drafting As you draft your television drama, try to hear your characters speak. Create dialogue that fits each character's personality, age, and background. Use stage directions to describe each scene.

Model: Using Script Format

[Madame Loisel enters the room and looks in the mirror, reaches for her neck, and lets out a scream.]

M. Loisel: What's the matter?

Mme. Loisel: The . . . the . . . necklace—is gone.

The stage directions in brackets and the dialogue create a dramatic interpretation.

Revising Reread your scene to determine whether the events can be clearly understood. Rewrite any dialogue that does not sound realistic.

WG *Prentice Hall Writing and Grammar Connection: Chapter 5, Connected Assignment*

❹ Extension Activities

Listening and Speaking With another student, improvise a conversation between Madame Loisel and her husband after she returns from meeting her old friend ten years later. Jot some notes before you start your **improvisation**.

- Think about how you would feel if you were Madame Loisel.
- Consider the reaction her husband would have after hearing the news.

Since you will be working without a script, work to integrate your comments and ideas with those of your partner. **[Group Activity]**

Research and Technology Farmers, like those featured in "The Harvest," make up only a small part of the population today, but just a few decades ago farmers were the bulk of the population. Research your family or community history back far enough to find farmers. Then, create a **flow chart** that shows the results of your research.

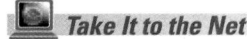

Take It to the Net www.phschool.com

Go online for an additional research activity using the Internet.

ASSESSMENT RESOURCES

The following resources can be used to assess students' knowledge and skills.

Selection Assessment

- **Formal Assessment,** pp. 135–137
- **Open Book Test,** pp. 115–117
- **Got It! Assessment Videotapes,** Tape 3
- **Test Bank Software**

PRENTICE HALL ASSESSMENT SYSTEM

- **Workbook**
- **Skill Book**
- **Transparencies**
- **CD-ROM**

Take It to the Net

Visit www.phschool.com for self-tests and additional questions on the selections.

❸ Writing Lesson

- Have students discuss the differences between a short story and a dramatized presentation of a short story.
- Tell students that when they transpose the story to dramatic form, they must rely on dialogue and actions as the only means of expressing the thoughts and emotions of the characters.
- If time and equipment permit, have students use a videocamera to produce their scenes for viewing by the class.

❹ Listening and Speaking

- Have students work in pairs to brainstorm some of the exchanges that might take place between Madame Loisel and her husband.
- Encourage students to focus on the emotional makeup of each character as they talk to one another.
- Have each pair practice their presentation. Then, ask for volunteers to present their improvisations to the class.

CUSTOMIZE INSTRUCTION
For Universal Access

To address different learning styles, use the activities suggested in the **Extension Activities** booklet, p. 39.

- For Verbal/Linguistic, Logical/Mathematical, and Visual/Spatial Learners, use Activity 5.
- For Verbal/Linguistic, Interpersonal, and Logical/Mathematical Learners, use Activity 6.
- For Verbal/Linguistic and Bodily/Kinesthetic Learners, use Activity 7.

Lesson Objectives

1. To write a short story
2. To use writing strategies to generate ideas, plan, organize, evaluate, and revise the short story

Model From Literature

"Uncle Marcos" by Isabel Allende is a short story with a vivid and memorable main character.

Prewriting

- Lead students in brainstorming for additonal sentence starters for their short stories.
- Remind students that a short story is usually only a few pages long, so the plots they create should not be extremely involved.
- Point out that students can model one or more of their characters after real people.

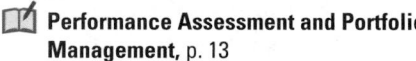

Writing WORKSHOP

Narration: Short Story

A **short story** is a work of fiction that combines plot, setting, and characters to present a brief narrative. In this workshop, you will write and revise a short story.

Assignment Criteria. Your short story should have the following characteristics:

- A main character who takes part in the action
- Details that describe a particular time and place
- A conflict, or problem, to be introduced, developed, and resolved
- A succession of events that make up the plot, incorporating changes in time and mood
- A central theme or generalization about life

To preview the criteria on which your short story may be assessed, see the Rubric on page 627.

Prewriting

Choose a topic. Use **sentence starters** to spark your creativity when brainstorming for a topic. Use one sentence starter to write freely for five minutes without worrying about grammar or sentence structure. Draw from your memories or imagination to develop interesting situations. Then, circle intriguing conflicts or themes and choose one to build into a story. Consider these sentence starters or make up your own:

- *What would happen if . . .*
- *One person I will never forget is . . .*

Based on your work, choose an idea as the basis for a story.

Summarize the plot. Briefly describe the incidents that make up the plot of your story. If you need more than a few sentences to do this, you may be trying to do too much in your writing.

Develop characters. Bring the characters and conflict of your story to life by providing enough detail for readers to imagine the world you create. Establish details about each of your characters to incorporate into your draft later.

Character	Details
Grandfather Clock	• Lonely, because everyone grows up and moves away • Wants to be loved and cared for • Is winding down from lack of human care

TEACHING RESOURCES

The following resources can be used to enrich or extend the instruction for pp. 624–625.

Writing and Grammar, Gold Level, Chapter 5, pp. 74–90

Performance Assessment and Portfolio Management, p. 13

Writing Models and Graphic Organizers on Transparencies, p. 83

Writing and Grammar iText CD-ROM
Students can use the following tools as they complete their persuasive essays:

- Story Map
- Topic Bank
- Character Trait Word Bin
- Unity and Coherence

Student Model

Before you begin drafting your short story, read this abridged student model and its side notes. The full text of the story can be found at www.phschool.com

Katie Hartwell
Newberry, Florida

> The main character in this first-person story is the grandfather clock.

Grandfather Clock

Tick, tock, tick, tock. I'm sitting here, watching the moments of my existence pass slowly away. My house has been empty for such a long time, and I'm lonely and forgotten. As I sit here, by myself, all that I can do is look back and reminisce. I could tell you stories that only walls would know. But walls can't speak.

> In the opening paragraph, the author describes setting and mood.

I came to this place many years ago, tugged along behind an old man. . . . Sadly, he was with me for only three short years before he passed on. . . .

For a time, I was left alone, while people came and looked at the house. . . . Then, one day a nice couple moved in with a young son. From the beginning, their son Danny was fascinated by me, and I was completely taken with him. He always looked as if he loved the stories I told, most of which began with, "Back in my day . . ." and "When I was younger. . . ." I sometimes thought that he didn't really understand what I was saying, but it felt good to be loved. . . . When Danny went off to college, I was crushed. Soon afterward, his parents sold the house. . . .

> The mood changes as time passes and new events occur.

New owners came and went. Then, one day I heard a new family was moving into the house. You can't even imagine my surprise when, out of the blue, Danny walked through the front door. He had a wife and kids now. I was so overjoyed when I saw him that I put all my energy into my daily activities. . . . I spent the next twenty years watching Danny's kids grow up, with a mixture of pride and anxiety about what would happen next.

The kids finally grew up and Danny sold the house. That was about five years ago. . . . Some of the local kids have started the rumor that the house is haunted—and, in a fashion, it is. It is haunted by the memories of all the people who have lived in it. Every second has left its mark on me. I have been counting them down and they are almost up for me. . . . I hope that someday somebody will remember me, and come to wind me again. Maybe then I'll get a new home and a chance for a whole new set of memories.

> The author restates the problem and central theme in the closing lines of the story.

Student Model

- Explain that the Student Model is a sample, and that students' short stories may be longer.
- Point out details that help establish the setting and mood, such as the rhythm of the first sentence and the perspective of looking back in time.
- Point out that the mood swings up and down, depending on what portion of the story the main character is telling.
- Ask students what they see next in the grandfather clock's future.

Real-World Connection

Ask students to think of times they had a story to tell, and they couldn't wait to tell it. Point out that short-story writers sometimes feel that way about the stories they write. Explain also that at other times, short story writers must sit down and plan out the details of their stories, just as the students are doing in this writing exercise.

CUSTOMIZE INSTRUCTION FOR UNIVERSAL ACCESS

For Special Needs Students	For English Learners	For Gifted/Talented Students
Ask students to think of a story about something that has happened to them. Encourage them to elaborate on the story, creating a fictional story in which they may "star" as the main character.	Review with students the main parts of a plot: exposition, rising action, climax, falling action, and resolution. Ask them to identify these elements in one of the short stories in this unit.	Ask these students to include an element of surprise or mystery as they create their stories. Suggest that they reread "The Gift of the Magi" or "The Necklace" as models.

Drafting

- Have students make four columns on a piece of paper, labeling them *Characters, Setting, Conflict,* and *Action.* Ask students to list the details they plan to include to satisfy these story components.
- After students write a portion of their first draft, have them look at the "Elaborate" chart on p. 626.
- Encourage students to evaluate the sentences they've written so far, to make sure that the sentences tell, not show.

Revising

- Have students read their drafts, highlighting instances in their stories where events occur that might cause a change in mood.
- Have students make sure they include characters' emotional reactions after the highlighted sentences.
- Ask students to look for forms of the verb *to be* in their stories, and replace these passive constructions with active ones wherever possible.

Drafting

Organize details. As you draft your short story, check that you have included the following story components:

- **Characters**—actors in the story with unique characteristics, attitudes, and relationships to one another
- **Setting**—the specific time and place of the action of your story
- **Conflict**—a struggle between opposing forces or characters
- **Action**—specific events in the plot that show how the conflict intensifies and how it is resolved

Elaborate. If you find yourself writing sentences that tell readers what you want them to think, challenge yourself to be a better storyteller. Provide details that will make the writing speak for itself. Follow up "telling" sentences with "showing" ones. Use the chart at right as a guide for drafting more revealing sentences.

Elaborate: Show, Don't Tell

Telling	Showing
Danny seemed to like me.	He would spend hours in front of me, staring up at my face, and raptly listening to everything I said. When I spoke, the little boy would stare up at me, smiling.

Revising

Revise to emphasize changes in mood. The power of a story depends on its ability to appeal to a reader's emotions. One dramatic technique that writers use is an abrupt shift in mood to keep the reader emotionally involved. Review your story and note instances where events occur that would fit naturally with a change in mood. Then, add descriptions to show how the characters might react emotionally to the new event.

Model: Stressing a Change in Mood

For a time I was left alone, while people came and looked at the house. ^*I lost hope that the house would ever be occupied again.* Then, one day a nice couple moved in with a young son. ^*Naturally, I was ecstatic.* From the beginning, their son Danny was fascinated by me, and I was completely taken with him.

Katie adds description and insight to show the clock's shifting emotions.

USING TECHNOLOGY IN WRITING

Encourage students to use the "Save As" feature on their computers to save different versions of their drafts in case they want to refer to earlier versions as they write. Students might find that they can use sentences or descriptions from earlier drafts, even if they cannot reuse entire paragraphs.

Students that students also use the character trait word bin on the **Writing and Grammar iText CD-ROM** to develop vivid and believable characters.

Revise to use the active voice. In sentences whose verbs take the active voice, the subject performs the action of a sentence. To create dynamic sentences in which characters are acting instead of being acted upon, choose the active voice instead of the passive voice. In the following example, the active voice makes the writing stronger.

Passive Voice: The bus was caught by Daniel.

Active Voice: Daniel caught the bus.

Compare the model and the nonmodel. Why is the model more effective than the nonmodel?

Nonmodel	Model
I hope that someday I will be remembered by somebody and that I will be wound again.	I hope that someday someone will remember me, and come to wind me again.

Publishing and Presenting

When you are satisfied with your short story, share your writing with a wider audience.

Deliver an oral presentation. Read your short story aloud to your classmates. As you read passages with dialogue, alter your voice to convey the different personalities of your characters. Ask for feedback from your classmates and consider revisions based on their comments. Then, compile your work with that of your classmates to publish an anthology or collection of your short stories in book form.

Speaking Connection

To learn more about analyzing presentations, see the **Listening and Speaking Workshop,** p. 628.

WG Prentice Hall Writing and Grammar Connection: Chapter 5

Rubric for Self-Assessment

Evaluate your short story using the following criteria and rating scale:

Criteria	Rating Scale: Not very 1	2	3	4	Very 5
How well do you establish your setting?	1	2	3	4	5
Is the main character well developed?	1	2	3	4	5
How well do you develop, introduce, and resolve your central conflict?	1	2	3	4	5
How well developed is your plot?	1	2	3	4	5
How effectively does the story convey a theme or generalization about life?	1	2	3	4	5

Publishing and Presenting

- Before students read their short stories to the class, have them practice reading their stories aloud.
- Encourage students to use highlighters to mark mood changes in their stories, so they will be aware of when to match their voices with the changes in mood as they read aloud.
- Students whose stories contain a lot of dialogue might ask a classmate to take the part of one of the characters.

Assessment

- Review with students the assessment criteria, pointing out that they measure specific characteristics of a short story.
- To get acquainted with the rubric, have students choose two or three of the elements on the rubric and use them to score the Student Model.
- The rubric on this page, and another rubric in an alternative format, can be found on pp. 13 and 49 of **Performance Assessment and Portfolio Management.**

TEST-TAKING TIP

Remind students that memory aids can be helpful in timed writing situations. Encourage students to memorize the components of a short story (exposition, rising action, climax, falling action, resolution), and then jot them down when asked to write a sample of fiction on a test. Students can use this memory aid to make sure they've included all the components of a short story.

Lesson Objectives

1. To analyze a media presentation
2. To establish categories of media presentations
3. To note personal responses to media presentations
4. To note the presentations' strengths and weaknesses

Analyze the Media Presentation

- Have students read the information on p. 628, noting the types of presentations that are usually classified as fiction and nonfiction.
- Ask students to create a chart like the one shown on p. 628. Make sure they understand why different criteria are needed when evaluating fiction and nonfiction presentations.

Evaluate the Media Presentation

- Make sure students understand that they will be completing the chart they've created as they watch the presentation.
- Encourage students to use a numerical rating system as well as descriptive adjectives to indicate their opinions about the presentation's strengths and weaknesses.

Listening and Speaking WORKSHOP

Analyzing a Media Presentation

People enjoy watching a movie review and then agreeing—or vehemently disagreeing—with the critic's opinions. In order to explain your own reaction to a movie or television show, it is useful to know how to **analyze a media presentation**. As with any type of analysis, interpreting involves breaking different elements of a program apart and examining them.

Analyze the Media Presentation

Establish categories. Since they cannot address every aspect of a production, critics use established categories to analyze and evaluate media presentations.

- For *fiction,* including movies and television programs, critics use categories such as plot, setting, dialogue, and believability.
- For *nonfiction,* including news programs, documentaries, and infomercials, critics use categories such as clarity of presentation, credibility of sources, and appropriateness of special effects.

Note your responses. As you watch the presentation, use a chart like the one shown to record your impressions. For each category, make brief notes about aspects that struck you favorably or unfavorably. Compare the presentation to movies or shows you have seen in the past.

Rating a Media Presentation

	Category	Opinion	Evidence
FICTION	Plot Setting Dialogue Realistic Portrayal		
NONFICTION	Clarity of Presentation Credibility of Sources Organization Added Effects		

Evaluate the Media Presentation

When you have finished viewing, review your notes to find a central idea.

Indicate strengths and weaknesses. Describe your overall impression of the media presentation, and then assess the movie's individual aspects. You can do this by assigning numerical ratings or by choosing adjectives to convey your impressions of various aspects of the program—for example, identify a *weak* plot, *shallow* characters, *clever* dialogue, *brilliant* special effects, or *inventive* camera work.

Cite examples to support your view. Since others may not share your opinion, use your analysis as an opportunity for persuasion. Cite examples from the movie or show to justify your opinions. For example, if you criticized the dialogue as unrealistic, you might cite a ridiculous conversation between two characters to support this view.

Activity: Analysis and Discussion In a small group, watch a movie, a news report, or another type of media presentation. Using the chart shown, analyze the program. Share your reviews with the other members of the group to discuss differences in opinion.

CUSTOMIZE INSTRUCTION FOR UNIVERSAL ACCESS

For Special Needs Students	For English Learners	For Advanced Readers
Provide time for these students to watch the media presentation more than once. Give them plenty of time to record and discuss their opinions after each viewing.	Have these students keep a list of unfamiliar words they hear while listening to the presentation. After it ends, they can use a dictionary to define the words.	Ask students to watch several examples of one type of presentation outside class, rating each example as they watch. Then, have students compare the results, choosing the presentation they believe was most effective. Have students report the results of this process in class.

Assessment WORKSHOP

Author's Point of View

The reading sections of some tests require you to read a passage and answer multiple-choice questions about the author's point of view. Use these strategies to help you answer test questions about the author's point of view:

- Look for language to help you understand the author's perspective or thoughts on a subject.
- Use the author's tone and choice of details as clues to his or her point of view.
- Remember that the author's point of view is often implied, not directly stated.

Test-Taking Strategies

- Look for strong language that seems calculated to sway readers' emotions. Then, infer the author's approval or disapproval.
- Examine the opening and closing statements carefully as an indication of an author's attitude.

Sample Test Item

Directions: Read the passage, and then answer the question that follows.

Jane Addams founded a settlement house in Chicago, Illinois, in 1889. Hull House offered hot lunches, child care, and tutoring in English and other subjects. Most important, Hull House developed a neighborhood spirit among recent immigrants. Addams said that she was just "a simple person," but her ideas and actions had far-reaching consequences.

1. The author views Jane Addams with ___?___.

A suspicion
B affection
C admiration
D fear

Answer and Explanation

The correct answer is ***C***. The author selects facts that highlight Addams's positive qualities. The passage mentions no negative characteristics, which might justify ***A*** or ***D***. The author does not discuss Addams in an openly personal way, so ***B*** is not the best answer.

Practice

Directions: Read the passage, and then answer the question that follows.

Jonah Hart, a student, was in-line skating when he fell and hit his head. He was unconscious for several days. Jonah probably would have walked away with only scrapes and bruises if he had been wearing a helmet. The National Safe Kids Campaign says that wearing helmets lowers the risk of head injury by 85 percent. Kids should always wear helmets when they skate. A helmet could save your life!

1. The author's point of view is that ___?___.

A helmets are not expensive
B everyone should join the National Safe Kids Campaign
C Jonah Hart could have avoided injury if he had been a better skater
D kids risk injury if they skate without helmets

Lesson Objective

To use an author's word choice, tone, and details to identify his or her point of view

Applying Reading Strategies

Encourage students to analyze an author's perspective by looking for clues in the author's tone, details, and language. Remind students that a point of view may be implied, rather than stated.

Applying Test-Taking Strategies

- Have students read the sample test item, and then identify the author's point of view.
- Remind students to look for clues in tone, details, and language.
- Point out that the author's point of view is implied, not stated directly.
- After students have selected their answers, point out that the correct answer is C, based on details the author uses to highlight Addams' positive qualities and accomplishments.

Answer

The correct answer to the Practice question is D because the author believes helmets can save lives. The author does not mention the cost of helmets, so A is incorrect. Answer B is wrong because the author encourages skaters to wear helmets, not to join the National Safe Kids Campaign. Answer C is incorrect because the author advises all skaters, regardless of their ability level, to wear helmets.

TEACHING RESOURCES

The following resources can be used to enrich or extend the instruction for p. 629.

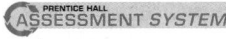

PRENTICE HALL ASSESSMENT SYSTEM

- Workbook
- Skill Book
- Transparencies
- CD-ROM

Unit Objectives

1. To develop skill in reading nonfiction
2. To apply a variety of reading strategies appropriate for reading nonfiction
3. To analyze literary elements
4. To use a variety of strategies to build vocabulary
5. To learn elements of grammar, usage, and style
6. To use recursive writing processes to write in a variety of forms
7. To develop listening and speaking skills
8. To express and support responses to various types of texts
9. To prepare, organize, and present literary interpretations

Meeting the Objectives

With each selection, you will find instructional materials through which students can meet these objectives. Further, you will find additional practice pages for reading strategies, literary analysis, vocabulary, and grammar in the **Selection Support: Skills Development Workbook** in your **Teaching Resources.**

Background

Art

Mural on PAL center

This mural expresses the diversity of Santa Monica, California. Ask students the following question:

What different aspects of diversity are displayed in the mural?

Possible response: The mural shows people of various ages and cultural backgrounds wearing a variety of different clothing while engaged in a multiplicity of different activities in several different areas of a city.

UNIT 7 Nonfiction

Mural on PAL center depicts the diverse community in Santa Monica, CA

UNIT FEATURES

Connections	Reading Informational Material
Every unit contains a feature that connects literature to a related topic, such as art, science, or history. In this unit, the Literature and Social Studies feature on pp. 680–681 compares the role of Lady Bird Johnson with the roles of other influential first ladies of the United States. Use the information and questions on the Connections pages to enrich students' understanding of the selections presented within the unit.	These selections will help students learn to analyze and evaluate informational texts, such as workplace documents, technical directions, and consumer materials. They will expose students to the organization and features unique to nonnarrative texts. In this unit, students learn to evaluate the author's purpose when listening to a persuasive speech.

Exploring the Genre

If fiction takes you on imaginative flights of fancy, nonfiction grounds you in reality. This does not make nonfiction any less fascinating or diverse. When you want to encounter real people with interesting experiences, learn a new skill, or read viewpoints on a controversial issue, you can turn to nonfiction.

The nonfiction in this unit falls into several categories:

- An **autobiography** is the writer's own story, describing notable events of his or her life.
- A **biography** is the story of a life from another person's perspective.
- An **essay** is a short nonfiction work that addresses a specific subject. A **reflective essay** shares the writer's inner thoughts and feelings. A **narrative essay** tells a story about an actual event or person. An **expository essay** explains certain aspects of a subject. A **persuasive essay** attempts to convince the reader to think or act in a certain way.
- A **speech** is a talk or an address presented to an audience.

▲ **Critical Viewing** Which nonfiction subjects could this image effectively illustrate? **[Hypothesize]**

ASSESSMENT RESOURCES

- Selection Support: Skills Development Workbook
- Formal Assessment
- Open Book Tests
- Performance Assessment and Portfolio Management
- Extension Activities

Assessing Student Progress

Listed below are the tools that are available to measure the degree to which students meet the unit objectives.

Informal Assessment

The questions in the Review and Assess sections are a first-level response to the concepts and skills presented with the selections. Students' responses provide a brief, informal measure of their grasp of the material. These responses can indicate where further instruction and practice are needed. Follow up with the practice pages in the **Selection Support: Skills Development Workbook.**

Formal Assessment

The **Formal Assessment** booklet contains Selections Tests and Unit Tests.

- Selection Tests measure comprehension and skills acquisition for a selection or group of selections.
- Each Unit Test provides students with thirty multiple-choice questions and five essay questions designed to assess students' knowledge of the literature and skills taught in the unit.

The **Open Book Tests** ask students to demonstrate their ability to synthesize and communicate information from selections or groups of selections.

To assess student writing, you will find rubrics and scoring models in the **Performance Assessment and Portfolio Management** booklet. In this booklet, you will also find scoring rubrics for listening and speaking activities.

Alternative Assessment

The **Extension Activities** booklet contains writing activities, listening and speaking activities, and research and technology activities that are appropriate for students with different ability levels. You may also use these activities as an alternative measure of students' growth.

▶Critical Viewing

Answer: Students might mention basketball, martial arts, boxing, photography, writing, swimming, and spending time with family and friends.

Why Read Literature?

The "Why Read Literature?" page in each unit presents a list of possible purposes for reading. Each purpose for reading is connected to one or more of the selections in the unit. Good readers set a purpose before reading to help them read actively and focus on meaningful details.

Unit 7 introduces three purposes for reading. "Read for the Love of Literature" invites students to meet author Isaac Bashevis Singer's personal hero in "The Washwoman." "Read for Information" encourages students to enjoy an astronaut's eye view in "Single Room, Earth View" by Sally Ride. "Read to Be Inspired" highlights two insightful stories about sports.

How to Use This Page

- Tell students that before reading each selection in this unit, they should set a purpose for reading. This will help them read in an active and focused manner.
- Explain that students can increase their love of literature by witnessing an author's change of mind in Lorraine Hansberry's essay "On Summer."
- Point out that students will learn some new information about the circumstances surrounding the assassination of President John F. Kennedy when they read the excerpt from Lady Bird Johnson's memoir, *A White House Diary.*
- Sports stars often inspire young people, as exemplified in a book review, "In These Girls, Hope Is a Muscle" by Steve Geitschier.

Why Read Literature?

Whenever you read nonfiction, you have a purpose, or reason. You might be curious about a topic or fascinated by an author's memory of an important event. Preview three purposes you might set before reading works in this unit.

1 Read for the Love of Literature

Even your longest-held opinions can change, if you keep an open mind. As a child, Lorraine Hansberry strongly disliked summer. Learn how her initial feelings turned into an enthusiastic embrace of the season in her eloquent essay **"On Summer,"** page 656.

Powerful literature can make unlikely heroes out of ordinary people. Some people might not think twice about an old woman walking in the snow, bent under the weight of several bags of laundry. For Isaac Bachevis Singer, though, this woman presents an opportunity to memorialize a personal hero in **"The Washwoman,"** page 650.

2 Read for Information

Lady Bird Johnson became First Lady as a result of one of the most traumatic episodes in American history: the assassination of President John F. Kennedy in 1963. Observe Johnson's impressions as momentous events swirled around her when you read **from *A White House Diary,*** page 674.

Not many people have viewed Earth from a vantage point two hundred miles away. Discover the complex answer to the question "What was it like?" when you read astronaut Sally Ride's essay **"Single Room, Earth View,"** page 636.

3 Read to Be Inspired

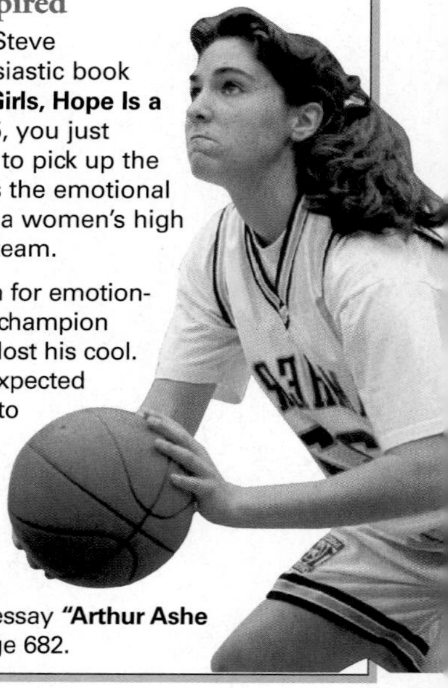

After you read Steve Gietschier's enthusiastic book review **"In These Girls, Hope Is a Muscle,"** page 715, you just might be tempted to pick up the book, which traces the emotional highs and lows of a women's high school basketball team.

In a sport known for emotional behavior, tennis champion Arthur Ashe never lost his cool. Yet, when others expected such a cool player to play cautiously, he attacked the ball with a fierce intensity. Learn more about this remarkable athlete in John McPhee's essay **"Arthur Ashe Remembered,"** page 682.

Take It to the Net

Visit the Web site for online instruction and activities related to each selection in this unit.
www.phschool.com

ENRICHMENT: Further Reading

Have students choose one or more of the works below to read more by the unit authors.

To Space and Back by Sally Ride

This is a factual and fascinating account of a trip to space by astronaut Sally Ride.

Of Time and Change: A Memoir by Frank Waters and Rudolfo A. Anaya

Through notes and letters, the authors trace Waters's lifelong quest to find the "thread of my inner life."

How to Read Literature

Use Strategies for Reading Nonfiction

Although works of nonfiction vary in topic, type, and purpose, they all share one common characteristic: They all claim to be true. This does not mean that you should accept everything an author writes without question. Use these strategies to help you judge the facts and form your own opinions.

1. Identify the author's attitude.

To identify an author's attitude, examine the selection of language and evidence presented in the text.

- If the text includes language with strong positive or negative connotations, this can provide you with valuable clues to the author's attitude.
- When an author uses neutral language, he or she may wish to be perceived as even-handed and objective.
- If the author highlights certain facts or details and omits others, note it as possible evidence of personal bias.

2. Find the writer's main points and support.

Taking apart a writer's argument for analysis is the first step to forming your own opinion on the subject. Use the model at right to guide you.

- To determine the main points of a selection, ask yourself what the author wants you to learn or think as a result of reading the text.
- Summarize the ideas of individual paragraphs or chapters to determine how an author is supporting the main points.

Finding Main Points and Support:

"Arthur Ashe Remembered"

Ashe was a great tennis player.

- Maintained control, even in tight spots
- Played with energy, grace, and power
- Willing to take risks to win games

Ashe was difficult to read.

- Didn't react emotionally, kept cool
- Would attempt unpredictable shots

3. Vary your reading rate.

- To find specific information, skim the text quickly, looking for key words and phrases.
- To absorb a complex argument or appreciate descriptive passages, slow your reading pace.

4. Use visuals as a key to meaning.

Nonfiction authors frequently use drawings, charts, and graphs to supplement their written text. To get the most out of visuals, first summarize the main point that the visual attempts to convey. Then, determine how the illustration, chart, or graph complements the main points that the author is trying to make.

As you read the selections in this unit, review the reading strategies and apply them to interact with the text.

How to Read Literature

The "How to Read Literature" page in each unit presents a set of strategies to help readers understand authors' words and ideas. Each reading strategy is taught in conjunction with one or more of the selections within the unit. Good readers develop a bank of strategies from which they can draw as needed.

Unit 7 introduces four strategies for reading nonfiction. It is important to recognize that reading nonfiction often requires an approach different from that used to read fiction.

How to Use This Page

Introduce the strategies for reading nonfiction, presenting each as a tool for developing understanding when reading the selections in this unit.

- Point out that in Isaac Bashevis Singer's story "The Washwoman" (p. 650), students should watch for language and details that reveal the author's attitude.
- Before students read Joan Didion's "Georgia O'Keeffe" (p. 685), have them ask themselves this question to find the writer's main points and support: What does the author want me to learn or think after reading this selection?
- Encourage students to vary their reading rate as they read "Single Room, Earth View" (p. 636) by Sally Ride.
- Have students use the visuals as a key to meaning as they read from *Understanding Comics* (p. 696) by Scott McCloud.

MODEL A READING STRATEGY: Find the writer's main points and support

Explain to students that finding the writer's main points and support will help students understand a writer's argument and form their own opinions.

Draw students' attention to the note paper on p. 633. Ask them to add to this list as they read "Arthur Ashe Remembered."

Students may add details about Ashe's medical history and untimely death.

Ask students to watch for details in the story that can help them find the writer's main points and support.

Single Room, Earth View

Lesson Objectives and CA Correlations

1. **To analyze and respond to literary elements**
   - Literary Analysis: Observation **R 3.7, 3.8**
   - Connecting Literary Elements: Description **R 3.7**
2. **To read, comprehend, analyze, and critique an observation**
   - Reading Strategy: Varying Your Reading Rate
   - Reading Check questions
   - Review and Assess questions
   - Assessment Practice (ATE)
3. **To develop word analysis skills, fluency, and systematic vocabulary**
   - Vocabulary Development Lesson: Latin Root: *-nov-* **R 1.1**
4. **To understand and apply written and oral language conventions**
   - Spelling Strategy
   - Grammar Lesson: Subject-Verb Agreement **LC 1.2, 1.3**
5. **To understand and apply appropriate writing and research strategies**
   - Writing Lesson: Observation From Space **W 2.6**
   - Extension Activity: Space Exploration Report **W 1.5**
6. **To understand and apply listening and speaking strategies**
   - Extension Activity: Presentation **LS 1.7**

STEP-BY-STEP TEACHING GUIDE	PACING GUIDE
PRETEACH	
Motivate Students and Provide Background	
Use the Motivation activity (ATE p. 634)	5 min.
Read and discuss the Preview material and Background information (SE/ATE p. 634) [A]	5 min.
Introduce the Concepts	
Introduce the Literary Analysis and Reading Strategy (SE/ATE p. 635) [A]	15 min.
Pronounce the vocabulary words and read their definitions (SE p. 635)	5 min.
TEACH	
Monitor Comprehension	
Informally monitor comprehension by circulating while students read independently or in groups [A]	15 min.
Monitor students' comprehension with the Reading Check notes (SE/ATE pp. 637, 639)	as students read
Develop vocabulary with Vocabulary notes (SE pp.637–640; ATE p. 637)	as students read
Develop Understanding	
Develop students' understanding of observations with Literary Analysis annotations (SE p. 637; ATE p. 637) [A]	10 min.
Develop students' ability to vary their reading rate with the Reading Strategy annotations (SE p. 639; ATE p. 639)	10 min.
ASSESS	
Assess Mastery	
Assess students' mastery of the Reading Strategy and Literary Analysis by having them answer the Review and Assess questions (SE/ATE p. 641)	20 min.
Use one or more of the print and media Assessment Resources (ATE p. 643) [A]	up to 50 min.
EXTEND	
Apply Understanding	
Have students complete the Vocabulary Development Lesson and the Grammar Lesson (SE p. 642) [A]	20 min.
Apply students' knowledge of vivid adjectives using the Writing Lesson (SE/ATE p. 643) [A]	45 min.
Apply students' understanding using one or more of the Extension Activities (SE p. 643)	20–90 min.

[A] **ACCELERATED INSTRUCTION:**
Use the strategies and activities identified with an [A].

UNIVERSAL ACCESS
● = Below Level Students
▲ = On-Level Students
■ = Above Level Students

Time and Resource Manager

Reading Level: Challenging
Average Number of Instructional Days: 4

RESOURCES		
PRINT	**TRANSPARENCIES**	**TECHNOLOGY**
• **Beyond Literature,** Cross-Curricular Connection: Science, p. 40 ▲ ■		• **Interest Grabber Video,** Tape 4 ● ▲ ■
• **Selection Support Workbook:** ● ▲ ■ Literary Analysis, p. 160 Reading Strategy, p. 159 Build Vocabulary, p. 157	• **Literary Analysis and Reading Transparencies,** pp. 79 and 80 ● ▲ ■	
• **Adapted Reader's Companion** ● • **Reader's Companion** ●		• **Listening to Literature** ● ▲ ■ Audiocassettes, Side 19 Audio CDs, CD 12
• **English Learner's Companion** ● ▲ • **Literatura en español** ● ▲ • **Literary Analysis for Enrichment** ■	• **Fine Art Transparencies Volume 1,** Art Transparency 11 ● ▲ ■	
• **Formal Assessment:** Selection Test, pp. 142–144 ● ▲ ■ • **Open Book Test,** pp. 118–120 ● ▲ ■ • PRENTICE HALL ASSESSMENT SYSTEM ● ▲ ■	• PRENTICE HALL ASSESSMENT SYSTEM ● ▲ ■ Skills Practice Answers and Explanations on Transparencies	• **Test Bank Software** ● ▲ ■ • **Got It! Assessment Videotapes,** Tape 4 ● ▲
• **Selection Support Workbook:** ● ▲ ■ Build Grammar Skills, p. 158 • **Writing and Grammar,** Gold Level ● ▲ ■ • **Extension Activities,** p. 40 ● ▲ ■	• **Daily Language Practice Transparencies** ● ▲ • **Writing Models and Graphic Organizers on Transparencies,** p. 87 ● ▲ ■	• **Writing and Grammar iText CD-ROM** ● ▲ ■ ***Take It to the Net*** www.phschool.com

BLOCK SCHEDULING: Use one 90-minute class period to preteach the selection and have students read it. Use a second 90-minute class period to assess students' mastery of skills and have them complete one of the Extension Activities.

PRETEACH

Step-by-Step Teaching Guide for pp. 634–635

Motivation

Have students share anything they know about astronaut Sally Ride. Then write the following quotation from "Single Room, Earth View" on the chalkboard:

> We could see smoke rising from fires that dotted the entire east coast of Africa, and . . . only moments later, ice floes jostling for position in the Antarctic.

Ask students where Ride must have been to see this view. Explain that in the essay they are about to read, Ride describes the experience of looking at Earth from the windows of the space shuttle.

Interest Grabber Video

As an alternative, play "The View from Space" on Tape 4 to engage student interest.

❶ Background

Science

On January 28, 1986, *Challenger* lifted off at Cape Canaveral, Florida, and thundered into space. Less than one second into the flight, *Challenger* burst into flames, and everyone on board was killed. A faulty rubber ring that sealed the joints between sections of the shuttle's rocket boosters caused the accident. The rings were redesigned, and the next shuttle, *Discovery*, launched successfully on September 29, 1988.

Prepare to Read

Single Room, Earth View

Take It to the Net

Visit www.phschool.com for interactive activities and instruction related to "Single Room, Earth View," including

- background
- graphic organizers
- literary elements
- reading strategies

Preview

Connecting to the Literature

At street level, a city can be a confusing place. When you look at that city from a high floor of a tall building, however, its layout becomes apparent. In this essay, you will see what it is like to look down on Earth, as the astronaut Sally Ride describes her view from space.

❶ Background

On June 18, 1983, when she soared aloft as flight engineer and mission specialist aboard the shuttle *Challenger*—the same shuttle that would explode shortly after liftoff three years later—Sally Ride became the first American woman in space. Her historic mission allowed her to experience what she recounts in "Single Room, Earth View."

TEACHING RESOURCES

The following resources can be used to enrich or extend the instruction for pp. 634–635.

Motivation

Interest Grabber Video, Tape 4

Background

Beyond Literature, p. 40 ■

Take It to the Net

Visit www.phschool.com for background and hotlinks for "Single Room, Earth View."

Literary Analysis

Literary Analysis and Reading Transparencies, Observation, p. 80 ■

Reading

Selection Support: Reading Strategy, p. 159; Build Vocabulary, p. 157

Literary Analysis and Reading Transparencies, Varying Your Reading Rate, p. 79

■ **BLOCK SCHEDULING:** Resources marked with this symbol provide varied instruction during 90-minute blocks.

Everyone I've met has a glittering, if vague, mental image of space travel. And naturally enough, people want to hear about it from an astronaut: "How did it feel . . . ?" "What did it look like . . . ?" "Were you scared?" Sometimes, the questions come from reporters, their pens poised and their tape recorders silently reeling in the words; sometimes, it's wide-eyed, ten-year-old girls who want answers. I find a way to answer all of them, but it's not easy.

Imagine trying to describe an airplane ride to someone who has never flown. An articulate traveler could describe the sights but would find it much harder to explain the difference in perspective provided by the new view from a greater distance, along with the feelings, impressions, and insights that go with that new perspective. And the difference is enormous: Spaceflight moves the traveler another giant step farther away. Eight and one-half thunderous minutes after launch, an astronaut is orbiting high above the Earth, suddenly able to watch typhoons form, volcanoes smolder, and meteors streak through the atmosphere below.

articulate (är tik´ yoo lit) *adj.* expressing oneself clearly and easily

While flying over the Hawaiian Islands, several astronauts have marveled that the islands look just like they do on a map. When people first hear that, they wonder what should be so surprising about Hawaii looking the way it does in the atlas. Yet, to the astronauts it is an absolutely startling sensation: The islands really *do* look as if that part of the world has been carpeted with a big page torn out of Rand-McNally,[1] and all we can do is try to convey the surreal quality of that scene.

surreal (sər rē´ əl) *adj.* strange

2 In orbit, racing along at five miles per second, the space shuttle circles the Earth once every 90 minutes. I found that at this speed, unless I kept my nose pressed to the window, it was almost impossible to keep track of where we were at any given moment—the world below simply changes too fast. If I turned my concentration away for too long, even just to change film in a camera, I could miss an entire land mass. It's embarrassing to float up to a window, glance outside, and then have to ask a crewmate, "What continent is this?"

Literary Analysis
Observation Which details does Ride use to focus her observation in this paragraph?

We could see smoke rising from fires that dotted the entire east coast of Africa, and in the same orbit only moments later, ice floes jostling for position in the Antarctic. We could see the Ganges River dumping its murky, sediment-laden water into the Indian Ocean and watch ominous hurricane clouds expanding and rising like biscuits in the oven of the Caribbean.

ominous (äm´ ə nəs) *adj.* threatening

Mountain ranges, volcanoes, and river deltas appeared in salt-and-flour relief, all leading me to assume the role of a novice geologist. In such moments, it was easy to imagine the dynamic upheavals that created jutting mountain ranges and the internal wrenchings that created

3 **novice** (näv´ is) *adj.* beginner

5 **Reading Check**
According to Ride, how have astronauts described the Hawaiian Islands?

1. **Rand-McNally** publisher of atlases.

4 **Critical Viewing** Based on this photograph, do you think you would enjoy a trip on the space shuttle? Why or why not? **[Connect]**

2 Literary Analysis

Observation

- Have students identify the central observation in the paragraph beginning "While flying . . ." Ask students how Ride supports this main idea.
  Answer: From the shuttle, Hawaii looks just like it does on a map. Each sentence amplifies or restates this observation.
- Ask the Literary Analysis question on p. 525: Which details does Ride use to focus her observation in this paragraph?
  Answer: Ride focuses on the speed at which the shuttle travels. She explains that this speed makes it easy to miss a lot of sights.

3 Vocabulary Development

Latin Root: *-nov-*

- Write the word *novice* on the board. Point out the root, *nov-*, and explain that it means "new." Ask students how they would describe a *novice* geologist.
  Answer: Students may define the term as an "inexperienced or beginner geologist."
- Write the words *novel* and *novelty* on the board and ask students to write brief definitions based on their knowledge of the root.
  Answer: *Novel:* "new; unfamiliar." *Novelty:* "newness; a new thing."

4 Critical Viewing

Answer: Most students will say that a trip on the space shuttle would be an exciting adventure.

5 Reading Check

Answer: Astronauts say that the islands look just like their images on a map.

CUSTOMIZE INSTRUCTION FOR UNIVERSAL ACCESS

For Gifted/Talented Students	For Advanced Readers
Sally Ride was able to see the "entire boot of Italy" from the space shuttle. Ask students to characterize a single geographic feature of their own region in a similar way. First, have students develop a simile or metaphor that verbally describes the feature. Then, ask students to create a painting or a sketch that shows how the feature might appear when viewed from an orbiting space shuttle.	Ask students to think back to plane flights they have taken. Have them write essays comparing and contrasting their view from the plane's window to Sally Ride's description of the view from the shuttle. Could they see things from the plane that Ride was too far away to see? What could she see that wasn't visible to them? Have students share their observations with the class.

❻ Background

Plate Tectonics

Many scientists have long believed that all the continents were once joined in a super continent, Pangaea, that drifted apart millions of years ago. This theory of "continental drift" is a forerunner of the concept of plate tectonics.

Plate tectonics has revolutionized the study of Earth by positing a dynamic, active, shifting surface. Earth's outer shell, or crust, is broken into a dozen or more moving plates. Continents grow in a process called *accretion*, when sea plates collide with continental plates. When two sea plates collide, they create a chain of islands. When plates squeeze Earth's surface, they create folds or bends in layers of rock. When they grind or slide past each other, they create cracks known as *fault lines*. Sudden, violent movements along the fault lines are called *earthquakes*.

❼ Reading Strategy

Varying Your Reading Rate

- Remind students that the rate at which they read a text or part of a text depends on their purpose for reading.
- Ask the Reading Strategy question on p. 638: How quickly would you read this paragraph if you wanted to learn about effects on the environment viewed from space?
Answer: Students may say they would read slowly and carefully because environmental effects are the topic of this entire paragraph.

rifts and seas. I also became an instant believer in plate tectonics;* India really *is* crashing into Asia, and Saudi Arabia and Egypt really *are* pulling apart, making the Red Sea wider. Even though their respective motion is really no more than mere inches a year, the view from overhead makes theory come alive.

Spectacular as the view is from 200 miles up, the Earth is not the awe-inspiring "blue marble" made famous by the photos from the moon. From space shuttle height, we can't see the entire globe at a glance, but we can look down the entire boot of Italy, or up the East Coast of the United States from Cape Hatteras to Cape Cod. The panoramic view inspires an appreciation for the scale of some of nature's phenomena. One day, as I scanned the sandy expanse of Northern Africa, I couldn't find any of the familiar landmarks—colorful outcroppings of rock in Chad, irrigated patches of the Sahara. Then I realized they were obscured by a huge dust storm, a cloud of sand that enveloped the continent from Morocco to the Sudan.

Since the space shuttle flies fairly low (at least by orbital standards; it's more than 22,000 miles lower than a typical TV satellite), we can make out both natural and manmade features in surprising detail. Familiar geographical features like San Francisco Bay, Long Island, and Lake Michigan are easy to recognize, as are many cities, bridges, and airports. The Great Wall of China is *not* the only man-made object visible from space.

The signatures of civilization are usually seen in straight lines (bridges or runways) or sharp delineations (abrupt transitions from desert to irrigated land, as in California's Imperial Valley). A modern city like New York doesn't leap from the canvas of its surroundings, but its straight piers and concrete runways catch the eye—and around them, the city materializes. I found Salina, Kansas (and pleased my in-laws, who live there) by spotting its long runway amid the wheat fields near the city. Over Florida, I could see the launch pad where we had begun our trip, and the landing strip, where we would eventually land.

❼ Some of civilization's more unfortunate effects on the environment are also evident from orbit. Oil slicks glisten on the surface of the Persian Gulf, patches of pollution-damaged trees dot the forests of central Europe. Some cities look out of focus, and their colors muted, when viewed through a pollutant haze. Not surprisingly, the effects are more noticeable now than they were a decade ago. An astronaut who has flown in both Skylab and the space shuttle reported that the horizon didn't seem quite as sharp, or the colors quite as bright, in 1983 as they had in 1973.

Of course, informal observations by individual astronauts are one thing, but more precise measurements are continually being made from space: The space shuttle has carried infrared film to document

Literature in context ❻ Science Connection

♦ *Plate Tectonics*

In the 1960s, scientists proposed a theory that Earth's outer shell consists of a number of rigid segments, or "plates." The shell, called the lithosphere, is about 45 to 95 miles thick and seems to be in constant motion. The plates slowly slide on a soft, flexible layer of rock and move from 0.5 to 4 inches a year.

If one plate pushes against another, the collision can form mountains. Major earthquakes occur when two plates slide past each other. Not all scientists, however, are as convinced as Sally Ride was, circling the planet 22 miles up, that the plate tectonic theory is valid.

Reading Strategy
Varying Your Reading Rate How quickly would you read this paragraph if you wanted to learn about effects on the environment viewed from space?

muted (myoot´ əd) *adj.* weaker; less intense

ENRICHMENT: Science Connection

Ocean Currents

Space shuttles and satellites have provided new information to oceanographers, particularly those who study currents. In both the Northern and Southern hemispheres of the Earth, winds blow primarily from the west far from the equator and from the east as one nears the equator. These winds determine the oceans' currents. They cause the waters of Earth to move in a twisting pattern, moving clockwise north of the equator and counterclockwise south of the equator.

The rotation of Earth also contributes to ocean currents, making them stronger toward the west coasts of oceans than they are toward the east coasts. This actions can be visualized by rotating a tennis ball in a bowl of water and watching the movement of the water against different areas of the ball.

damage to citrus trees in Florida and in rain forests along the Amazon. It has carried even more sophisticated sensors in the payload bay. Here is one example: sensors used to measure atmospheric carbon monoxide levels, allowing scientists to study the environmental effects of city emissions and land-clearing fires.

Most of the Earth's surface is covered with water, and at first glance it all looks the same: blue. But with the right lighting conditions and a couple of orbits of practice, it's possible to make out the intricate patterns in the oceans—eddies and spirals become visible because of the subtle differences in water color or reflectivity.

Observations and photographs by astronauts have contributed significantly to the understanding of ocean dynamics, and some of the more intriguing discoveries prompted the National Aeronautics and Space Administration to fly an oceanographic observer for the express purpose of studying the ocean from orbit. Scientists' understanding of the energy balance in the oceans has increased significantly as a result of the discoveries of circular and spiral eddies tens of kilometers in diameter, of standing waves hundreds of kilometers long, and of spiral eddies that sometimes trail into one another for thousands of kilometers. If a scientist wants to study features on this scale, it's much easier from an orbiting vehicle than from the vantage point of a boat.

Believe it or not, an astronaut can also see the wakes of large ships and the contrails[2] of airplanes. The sun angle has to be just right, but when the lighting conditions are perfect, you can follow otherwise invisible oil tankers on the Persian Gulf and trace major shipping lanes through the Mediterranean Sea. Similarly, when atmospheric conditions allow contrail formation, the thousand-mile-long condensation trails let astronauts trace the major air routes across the northern Pacific Ocean.

8 Part of every orbit takes us to the dark side of the planet. In space, night is very, very black—but that doesn't mean there's nothing to look at. The lights of cities sparkle; on nights when there was no moon, it was difficult for me to tell the Earth from the sky—the twinkling lights could be stars or they could be small cities. On one nighttime pass from Cuba to Nova Scotia, the entire East Coast of the United States appeared in twinkling outline.

When the moon is full, it casts an eerie light on the Earth. In its light, we see ghostly clouds and bright reflections on the water. One night, the Mississippi River flashed into view, and because of our viewing angle and orbital path, the reflected moonlight seemed to flow downstream—as if Huck Finn[3] had tied a candle to his raft.

Of all the sights from orbit, the most spectacular may be the

eddies (ed′ ēz) *n.* circular currents

subtle (sut′ ′l) *adj.* not obvious

eerie (ir′ ē) *adj.* mysterious

9 **Reading Check**

What is the infrared film carried in a space shuttle used to document?

2. **contrails** (kän′ trāls′) *n.* white trails of condensed water vapor that sometimes form in the wake of aircraft.
3. **Huck Finn** hero of Mark Twain's novel *The Adventures of Huckleberry Finn.*

8 Critical Thinking

Compare and Contrast

- Have students turn back to the story "'If I Forget Thee, Oh Earth'" and compare Marvin's description of the night sky from space (p. 487) to Sally Ride's.
  Answer: Both agree that the sky is completely black except for the stars. She can see electric lights on Earth; he can't. She says the stars twinkle; he says they don't.
- Ask why electric lights on Earth might appear to twinkle.
  Answer: Students may suggest that atmospheric conditions may cause the twinkling effect.

9 Reading Check

Answer: The film documents damage to trees on Earth.

ASSESS

Answers for p. 640

Review and Assess

1. Some students may say they would like to be an astronaut because they are interested in technology and space exploration. Others may say that it seems too dangerous a profession.
2. **(a)** *Challenger* **(b)** The shuttle travels at a far greater distance from Earth at a far greater speed than an airplane.
3. **(a)** Ride observed ice floes, continents, mountain ranges, volcanoes, deltas, islands, and oceans. **(b)** Ride felt that she could almost see geological forces working the way the theories say they work.
4. **(a)** Ride saw damage to the environment and the haze that obscures most big cities. **(b)** The dimming of colors reflects an additional ten years of pollution.
5. **(a)** Yes; a literal bird's-eye view allows astronauts to see air pollution, environmental damage, weather, ocean currents, and other ongoing processes. The shuttle can photograph and document these phenomena for scientists. **(b)** Ride describes several examples of scientifc observations from the shuttle, including infrared photography, carbon monoxide sensors, and oceanographic studies.
6. Students may say that the essay has given them a new sense of the unity and fragility of the planet Earth.

magnificent displays of lightning that ignite the clouds at night. On Earth, we see lightning from below the clouds; in orbit, we see it from above. Bolts of lightning are diffused by the clouds into bursting balls of light. Sometimes, when a storm extends hundreds of miles, it looks like a transcontinental brigade is tossing fireworks from cloud to cloud.

As the shuttle races the sun around the Earth, we pass from day to night and back again during a single orbit—hurtling into darkness, then bursting into daylight. The sun's appearance unleashes spectacular blue and orange bands along the horizon, a clockwork miracle that astronauts witness every 90 minutes. But I really can't describe a sunrise in orbit. The drama set against the black backdrop of space and the magic of the materializing colors can't be captured in an astronomer's equations or an astronaut's photographs.

I once heard someone (not an astronaut) suggest that it's possible to imagine what spaceflight is like by simply extrapolating from the sensations you experience on an airplane. All you have to do, he said, is mentally raise the airplane 200 miles, mentally eliminate the air noise and the turbulence, and you get an accurate mental picture of a trip in the space shuttle.

Not true. And while it's natural to try to liken spaceflight to familiar experiences, it can't be brought "down to Earth"—not in the final sense. The environment is different, the perspective is different. Part of the fascination with space travel is the element of the unknown—the conviction that it's different from earthbound experiences. And it is.

diffused (di fyo͞ozd′) *v.* spread out

extrapolating (ek strap′ ə lāt′ iŋ) *v.* arriving at a conclusion by making inferences based on known facts

Sally Ride

(b. 1951)

Although best known as an astronaut, Sally Ride was also a talented athlete in her youth. She received both undergraduate and graduate degrees from Stanford University.

In 1978, she read about NASA's search for astronauts and ultimately was chosen as one of the six women and twenty-five men accepted from among 8,000 applicants. In 1983, Sally Ride became the first American woman in space. She played a key role in the investigation of the *Challenger* tragedy in 1986.

Ride retired from NASA in 1987. She currently teaches physics at the University of California and is the author of several books on space.

Review and Assess

Thinking About the Selection

1. **Respond:** Would you like to be an astronaut? Why or why not?
2. **(a) Recall:** On which space shuttle did Ride travel? **(b) Compare and Contrast:** According to Ride, how is travel on the space shuttle different from travel on an airplane?
3. **(a) Recall:** Which geological features did Ride observe from orbit? **(b) Interpret:** Why did Ride find it easier to imagine geological forces from space?
4. **(a) Recall:** Which "unfortunate effects" did Ride see from orbit? **(b) Infer:** Why would these effects make colors seen in 1983 seem not as bright as those seen in 1973?
5. **(a) Draw Conclusions:** Does space travel aid in understanding conditions on Earth? **(b) Support:** Cite evidence from Ride's essay to explain your point of view.
6. **Connect:** How have Ride's descriptions of Earth changed the way you think about our planet?

ASSESSMENT PRACTICE: Reading Comprehension

Connotation and Denotation (For more practice, see Test Preparation Workbook, p. 40.)

Many tests ask students to distinguish between connotations and denotations of words. Use this sample test item.

The signatures of civilization are usually seen in straight lines (bridges and runways) or sharp delineations (abrupt transitions from desert to irrigated land).

In this passage, the word *signatures* connotes ____.

A something visible
B a characteristic mark or sign
C something that looks like writing
D something odd or uncharacteristic

Since *signatures* clearly means "something that identifies civilization," *B* is the correct answer.

Review and Assess

Literary Analysis

Observation

1. Which details in the essay show Ride's talent for **observation** in finding civilization's "signatures"?
2. How does Ride prove herself to be a careful observer of Earth's oceans?
3. Choose a particularly powerful observation of Ride's, and explain what makes it memorable. Use a chart like the following to record facts, events, and vivid details.

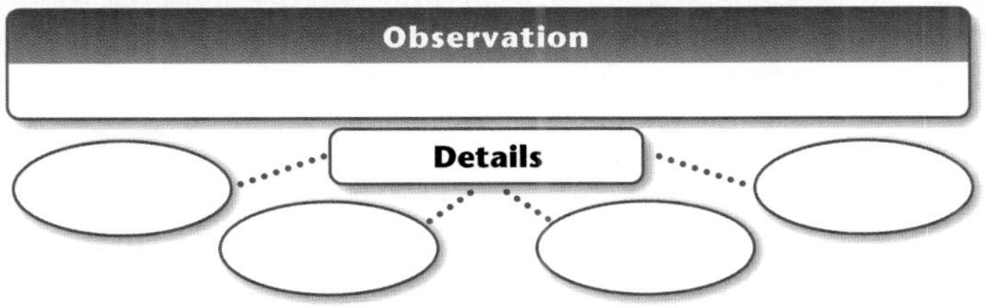

Connecting Literary Elements

4. Find an example from Ride's selection of **descriptive** language that appeals to the sense of touch.
5. How does Ride use comparisons to everyday phenomena to help readers follow her observations?
6. Does Ride's attention to descriptive details compromise her ability to be objective or strengthen her ability to convey her ideas?

Reading Strategy

Varying Your Reading Rate

7. (a) If you were reading to learn about Ride's description of cities in the United States, which paragraphs could you skim through quickly? (b) Which paragraphs would you read more carefully?
8. Why might you recommend that someone else read the entire essay slowly? Refer to the selection as you answer.

Extend Understanding

9. **Science Connection:** How has Sally Ride's essay affected what you think about the space program? Explain.

Quick Review

An **observation** describes an event that a writer saw firsthand, and it includes many details and vivid, precise words.

A **description** is a portrait in words of a person, place, or object.

To **vary your reading rate**, adjust your reading speed according to your purpose for reading.

Take It to the Net

www.phschool.com

Take the interactive self-test online to check your understanding of the selection.

ENRICHMENT: Further Reading

Other Works by Sally Ride

The Third Planet: Exploring Earth From Space (with Tam O'Shaughnessy)
To Space and Back (with Susan Oakie)

Take It to the Net

Visit www.phschool.com for more information on Sally Ride.

Answers for p. 641

Review and Assess

1. Ride is able to see that civilizations' signatures are usually straight lines or sharp delineations—bridges, runways, and piers, for example.
2. Ride describes ocean colors and the patterns made by the ebb and flow of water and by the wakes of ships.
3.

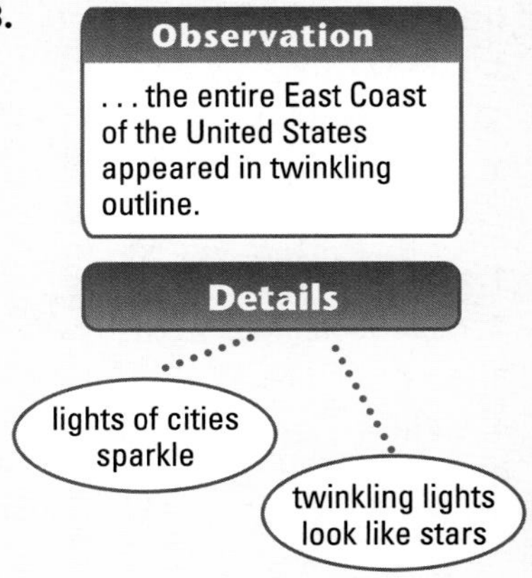

Observation
. . . the entire East Coast of the United States appeared in twinkling outline.
Details
lights of cities sparkle
twinkling lights look like stars

4. Possible response: "nose pressed to the window," p. 637
5. Ride sees similarities between everyday things that her readers have seen, like biscuits in the oven, to the things she can see in space, like hurricane clouds.
6. The descriptive details make the view from the shuttle come alive for readers and help them appreciate and share Ride's experience.
7. **(a)** Students may say they would skim most of the essay. **(b)** Students may say that they would read carefully the paragraph beginning "Since the space shuttle flies fairly low . . ." on p. 638; also the paragraph beginning "Part of every orbit . . ." on p. 639.
8. Readers who want to know details of space travel should read the essay slowly. Readers who are curious about the oceans or about pollution effects should read with care.
9. Students may appreciate that the space program can affect one's perception of the planet Earth.

EXTEND

Answers for p. 642

❶ Vocabulary Development

Word Analysis

1. new
2. to make new again
3. to make changes; try something new

Spelling Strategy

1. rarest
2. using; usable
3. articulating

Fluency: Context

1. articulate; novice
2. muted; ominous
3. subtle; diffused
4. surreal
5. extrapolate
6. eerie; eddies

❷ Grammar

1. circles
2. capture
3. come
4. flash
5. describes

Writing Application

Possible responses:

1. The islands really do look as if that part of the world has been carpeted . . . / The island really does look as if that part of the world has been carpeted . . .
2. Oil slicks glisten on the surface of the Persian Gulf . . . / An oil slick glistens on the surface of the Persian Gulf . . .
3. Not surprisingly, the effects are more noticeable now than they were a decade ago. / Not surprisingly, the effect is more noticeable than it was a decade ago.

Integrate Language Skills

❶ Vocabulary Development Lesson

Word Analysis: Latin Root *-nov-*

The Latin root *-nov-* means "new." The root appears in the word *novice*, which means "someone new to an activity; a beginner."

Use your knowledge of the root *-nov-* to define each of the following words, incorporating *new* into each definition.

1. novel (*adj.*) **2.** renovate **3.** innovate

Spelling Strategy

If a word ends in silent *e*, drop the *e* before adding a suffix that starts with a vowel. Thus, *extrapolate* + *-ing* = *extrapolating* and *diffuse* + *-ion* = *diffusion*.

Add *-able*, *-ing*, or *-est* to each word below to form three properly spelled new words.

1. rare **2.** use **3.** articulate

Fluency: Context

Fill in each blank with a word (or a form of the word) from the vocabulary list on page 635.

1. Normally __?__, the veteran scientist felt like a tongue-tied __?__ speaker.
2. The low, __?__ murmuring of her audience was frightening and __?__, giving her a bad feeling.
3. She turned on the projector, and the smell of burning dust, __?__ but unmistakable, __?__ through the air.
4. "This will seem weird, even __?__," she said, putting on the strange first slide.
5. "However, what we can __?__ from the facts and evidence is clear."
6. "The odd, __?__ patterns of __?__ and whirlpools on Planet X are mysterious signs of intelligent life."

❷ Grammar Lesson

Subject-Verb Agreement

The **subject** is the word or group of words in a sentence that tells whom or what the sentence is about. The **verb,** or *predicate*, is the word or group of words in a sentence that expresses an action, condition, or state of being.

Subjects and verbs must agree in number. A singular subject requires a singular verb. A plural subject requires a plural verb.

	S V
Singular:	The astronaut *orbits* Earth.
Plural:	The astronauts *orbit* Earth.

Practice In each sentence, choose the form of the verb that agrees with the subject.

1. The shuttle (circle, circles) the planet.
2. Cameras (capture, captures) the experience.
3. A mountain and a river (come, comes) into view.
4. Bolts of lightning (flash, flashes) quickly.
5. Sally Ride (describe, describes) her trip.

Writing Application Find three sentences in "Single Room, Earth View" that have a plural subject and verb, and rewrite each with a singular subject and verb.

WG Prentice Hall Writing and Grammar Connection: Chapter 25, Section 1

TEACHING RESOURCES

The following resources can be used to enrich or extend the instruction for pp. 642–643.

Vocabulary

- **Selection Support:** Build Vocabulary, p. 157
- **Vocabulary and Spelling Practice Book,** (Use this booklet for skills enrichment.) ▪

Grammar

- **Selection Support:** Build Grammar Skills, p 158
- **Writing and Grammar,** Gold Level, p. 572
- **Daily Language Practice Transparencies**

Writing

- **Writing and Grammar,** Gold Level, p. 112 ▪
- **Writing and Grammar iText CD-ROM**
- **Writing Models and Graphic Organizers on Transparencies,** p. 87

▪ **BLOCK SCHEDULING:** Resources marked with this symbol provide varied instruction during 90-minute blocks.

❸ Writing Lesson

Observation From Space

Imagine that you are an astronaut in space, like Sally Ride. Perhaps you are orbiting this planet in a space shuttle or planting a flag on the surface of Mars. Write an observation that describes the event for readers back home on Earth.

Prewriting Consult actual photographs taken from space to gain a sense of what you might see as an astronaut. Make a list of the features on Earth that you want to include in your observation.

Drafting To ensure that you get all your ideas on paper, write a first draft without stopping to change what you have written. Concentrate on getting across what you perceive through your senses.

Revising Look for places where you can add vivid adjectives to enliven your description. Replace vague words with more exact ones.

Model: Revising to Incorporate Vivid Adjectives

I stepped onto the ^*gray, rocky, and desolate* surface of the moon. Seeing the great bulk of Earth overhead was an ^*awesome* ~~interesting~~ experience.

Vivid adjectives such as *gray, rocky, desolate,* and *awesome* make the description come to life.

Prentice Hall Writing and Grammar Connection: Chapter 6, Section 4

❹ Extension Activities

Listening and Speaking In a group, study detailed photographs of Earth taken from space. Design a **presentation** to share one of the images you choose.

- Conduct research to learn about the features you want to highlight.
- Let your viewers know exactly what they see in the photograph.
- Describe each important feature.

Encourage your classmates to ask questions about the information in your presentation. **[Group Activity]**

Research and Technology Prepare a **report** on one aspect of space exploration, such as women astronauts or the space shuttle. Access NASA's Web site and related sites to obtain information and illustrations for your report. Where needed, identify and explain any discrepancies you find among the various Web sites.

Take It to the Net www.phschool.com

Go online for an additional research activity using the Internet.

Lesson Support for p. 643

❸ Writing Lesson

- Students may be able to find photographs for this activity at the NASA Web site or other related sites on the Internet. They should also consult reference books on outer space.
- Remind students that their observations should include as many descriptive details as possible. They may find it helpful to use the Cubing Organizer, p. 87 in **Writing Models and Graphic Organizers on Transparencies** to develop descriptive details.

❹ Research and Technology

- Encourage students to discuss this activity with science teachers, who may be able to suggest additional sources of information.
- Remind students to limit the scope of their research topics so that they can cover all the necessary details within the scope of their reports.
- Students may want to make a bulletin board display that illustrates their research.

CUSTOMIZE INSTRUCTION
For Universal Access

To address different learning styles, use the following activities suggested in the **Extension Activities** booklet, p. 40.

- For Visual/Spatial Learners, use Activity 5.
- For Logical/Mathematical Learners, use Activities 6 and 7.
- For Verbal/Linguistic Learners, use Activity 7.

ASSESSMENT RESOURCES

The following resources can be used to assess students' knowledge and skills.

Selection Assessment

- **Formal Assessment,** pp. 142–144
- **Open Book Test,** pp. 118–120
- **Got It! Assessment Videotapes,** Tape 4
- **Test Bank Software**

PRENTICE HALL ASSESSMENT SYSTEM

- **Workbook**
- **Skill Book**
- **Transparencies**
- **CD-ROM**

Take It to the Net

Visit www.phschool.com for self-tests and additional questions on "Single Room, Earth View."

Lesson Objectives

1. To understand the purpose of persuasive speeches
2. To understand what makes a convincing argument
3. To evaluate a speaker's purpose

About Persuasive Speeches

- Point out that a persuasive speech has one purpose: to convince listeners to accept a particular point of view or take a specific action.
- Explain that persuasive speeches rely on convincing arguments to be successful.
- Invite students to think of speakers they've heard who have used facts, statistics, examples, or anecdotes to make their points.

Reading Strategy

Evaluating Author's Purpose

- Point out that after students identify a speaker's purpose, they will more fully understand what the speaker is saying.
- Explain that locating the main ideas and details in a speech is the best way to figure out the speaker's purpose.
- Direct students' attention to the chart on p. 644. Ask them to complete this chart as they read John F. Kennedy's speech "The New Frontier."

READING INFORMATIONAL MATERIALS

Persuasive Speeches

About Persuasive Speeches

A **persuasive speech** is an oral presentation whose purpose is to convince listeners to accept a particular opinion or to take a specific action. For example, a speaker might deliver a speech that explains why democracy is the best form of government, or that urges audience members to vote for a particular political candidate.

Persuasive speeches are only as good as the arguments they set forth. Speakers, therefore, must support their opinions with strong arguments in order to be convincing. Speakers may appeal to logic or emotion and may use facts, statistics, examples, or anecdotes to reinforce their arguments.

Reading Strategy

Evaluating the Author's Purpose

Evaluating the speaker's purpose helps you put the overall argument into a framework that is easier to understand. Once you have identified the purpose, you can then determine which details the speaker uses to achieve that purpose.

Evaluate John F. Kennedy's purpose for giving the following speech by locating the main ideas he uses to support his argument. Then, determine if the purpose is reasonable and whether Kennedy achieves his purpose through the speech.

Evaluating Purpose					
Purpose: To convince Americans of the need to continue the peaceful exploration of space in the name of progress and national pride.					
➢ Detail:					
➢ Detail:					
➢ Detail:					
Evaluation:	**Not Very**				**Very**
Is Kennedy's purpose reasonable?	1	2	3	4	5
How effectively does Kennedy achieve his purpose?	1	2	3	4	5

The New Frontier

John F. Kennedy

Speech at Rice University, Houston, Texas, 1962

. . . No man can fully grasp how far and how fast [humanity has] come, but condense, if you will, the 50,000 years of man's recorded history in a time span of but a half-century. Stated in these terms, we know very little about the first forty years, except at the end of them advanced man had learned to use the skins of animals to cover him. Then about ten years ago, under this standard, man emerged from his caves to construct other kinds of shelter. Only five years ago man learned to write and use a cart with wheels. Christianity began less than two years ago. The printing press came this year, and then less than two months ago, during this whole fifty-year span of human history, the steam engine provided a new source of power.

Newton[1] explored the meaning of gravity. Last month electric lights and telephones and automobiles and airplanes became available. Only last week did we develop penicillin and television and nuclear power, and now if America's new space craft succeeds in reaching Venus, we will have literally reached the stars before midnight tonight.

The listing of past milestones is intended to persuade readers that the space program is equally as important.

This is a breathtaking pace, and such a pace cannot help but create new ills as it dispels old, new ignorance, new problems, new dangers. Surely the opening vistas of space promise high costs and hardships, as well as high reward.

So it is not surprising that some would have us stay where we are a little longer to rest, to wait. But this city of Houston, this State of Texas, this country of the United States was not built by those who waited and rested and wished to look behind them. This country was conquered by those who moved forward—and so will space.

William Bradford, speaking in 1630 of the founding of the Plymouth Bay Colony,[2] said that all great and honorable actions are accompanied with great difficulties,

1. **Newton** Sir Isaac Newton (1642–1727), English scientist and mathematician who formulated the idea of gravity.
2. **William Bradford . . . Plymouth Bay Colony** Bradford (1590–1657), a Pilgrim leader, was the second governor of Plymouth Colony, an early English colony in America, established by the Pilgrims in 1620.

The New Frontier

- Remind students to complete a chart like the one on p. 644 as they read this speech by John F. Kennedy.
- Ask students why they think Kennedy compressed a history of 50,000 years into fifty.
  Possible answer: Kennedy wanted to dramatize the rate at which change has occurred.
- Ask students how Kennedy connects the past with the state of Texas and of future space travel.
  Possible answer: Kennedy points out that Texas was once a frontier in our fast-paced history, and that the next frontier is space.

CUSTOMIZE INSTRUCTION FOR UNIVERSAL ACCESS

For Special Needs Students	For Advanced Readers
Have students read along in the text as you read Kennedy's speech aloud. Stop at the end of each paragraph to summarize Kennedy's main points. Then, have students point out the details that support each main point.	Ask students to identify the strongest argument they think Kennedy makes for the space program. Have them write a paragraph explaining why they believe this argument is so convincing. What persuasive strategies did Kennedy use?

Background

History

In the 1960s, the United States and the Soviet Union raced each other to see who could first land a person on the moon. Space pilots in both countries lost their lives in accidents during this time period. On July 20, 1969, the contest ended in victory for the United States when astronauts Neil Armstrong and Edward Aldrin stepped onto the surface of the moon.

and both must be enterprised and overcome with answerable courage.

If this capsule history of our progress teaches us anything, it is that man, in his quest for knowledge and progress, is determined and cannot be deterred. The exploration of space will go ahead, whether we join in it or not, and it is one of the great adventures of all time, and no nation which expects to be the leader of other nations can expect to stay behind in the race for space.[3]

> By praising the accomplishments of previous generations, Kennedy appeals to the emotion of pride.

Those who came before us made certain that this country rode the first waves of the industrial revolutions, the first waves of modern invention, and the first wave of nuclear power, and this generation does not intend to founder in the backwash of the coming age of space. We mean to be a part of it—we mean to lead it. For the eyes of the world now look into space, to the moon and to the planets beyond, and we have vowed that we shall not see it governed by a hostile flag of conquest, but by a banner of freedom and peace. We have vowed that we shall not see space filled with weapons of mass destruction, but with instruments of knowledge and understanding.

Yet the vows of this Nation can only be fulfilled if we in this Nation are first, and, therefore, we intend to be first. In short, our leadership in science and in industry, our hopes for peace and security, our obligations to ourselves as well as others, all require us to make this effort, to solve these mysteries, to solve them for the good of all men, and to become the world's leading space-faring nation.

> The opening sentence of this paragraph offers three reasons why space travel is important.

We set sail on this new sea because there is new knowledge to be gained, and new rights to be won, and they must be won and used for the progress of all people. For space science, like nuclear science and all technology, has no conscience of its own. Whether it will become a force for good or ill depends on man, and only if the United States occupies a position of pre-eminence can we help decide whether this new ocean will be a sea of peace or a new terrifying theater of war. I do not say that we should or will go unprotected against the hostile misuse of space any more than we go unprotected against the hostile use of land or sea, but I do say that space can be explored and mastered without feeding the fires of war, without repeating the mistakes that man has made in extending his writ[4] around this globe of ours.

There is no strife, no prejudice, no national conflict in outer space as yet. Its hazards are hostile to us all. Its conquest deserves the best of all mankind, and its opportunity for peaceful cooperation may never come again. But why, some say, the moon? Why choose this as our goal? And they may well ask why climb the highest mountain? Why, 35 years ago, fly the Atlantic? Why does Rice play Texas?[5]

We choose to go to the moon. We choose to go to the moon in this decade and do the other things, not because they are easy, but because they are hard, because that goal will serve to organize and measure the best of our energies and skills, because that challenge is one that we are willing to accept, one we are unwilling to postpone, and one which we intend to win, and the others, too. . . .

3. **race for space** Starting in the 1950s, the United States and the Soviet Union competed for mastery of space. In 1961, the Soviets sent the first man into orbit.
4. **writ** (rit) *n.* here, "claims or laws."
5. **Why does Rice play Texas?** Rice, typically low-ranked in football, played games against the powerhouse University of Texas team.

Check Your Comprehension

1. What idea does Kennedy express by quoting William Bradford?
2. What reasons does Kennedy offer for going to the moon?

Applying the Reading Strategy

Evaluating the Author's Purpose

3. How does Kennedy support his purpose by using a historical analogy about human development at the beginning of his speech?
4. Kennedy assumes that the United States will use space exploration peacefully and responsibly. (a) Explain why he makes this assumption. (b) How is it linked with the purpose of his speech?

Activity

Preparing a Bibliography

One way to evaluate the arguments in a persuasive speech is by researching the topic yourself to confirm that the speaker's facts, details, and examples are valid.

Research America's involvement in the space program during the past 30 years to determine whether Kennedy's arguments would still have merit today. Use a variety of resources to ensure accuracy, including government reports, magazine and newspaper articles, and encyclopedia articles. Then, prepare a bibliography, or a reference list of the sources you have consulted. See pages R30–R32 for bibliographical format.

Comparing Informational Materials

Persuasive Techniques in Nonfiction

1. Read or review Sally Ride's essay "Single Room, Earth View" on page 636. Compare the techniques that Ride uses to persuade readers about the virtues of the space program with the techniques that Kennedy employs. Use these questions to guide your comparison:

	Kennedy's Speech	Ride's Essay
Persuasive reasons offered		
Effectiveness of persuasion		

   - How are their arguments and reasons similar or different?
   - How does the format affect the writer's choice of words or details?
   - Is the essay or the speech more persuasive? Why?

2. Locate and analyze NASA's Web site. (a) What techniques does the site use to persuade readers about the value of the space program? (b) How do these techniques compare to the ways Kennedy tries to persuade his audience?

Answers for p. 647

Check Your Comprehension

1. Kennedy expresses the notion that all things worth doing are difficult to do.
2. Kennedy says that the United States must go to the moon because the nation must hold its place as a leader in the quest for knowledge, progress, and peace.

Applying the Reading Strategy

3. Kennedy draws a parallel between great achievements of the past and great achievements of the future.
4. **(a)** Kennedy makes the assumption because the United States was recognized as the world leader in peace. **(b)** He links this assumption with the purpose of his speech by saying that we must get to the moon first to assure peace in space as well as on Earth.

Activity

- Encourage students to use both print and online resources.
- Point out that by exploring the nation's leading libraries online, students may be able to locate primary source material—information recorded by eyewitnesses to historical events.

Comparing Informational Materials

1. Both writers argue that space travel "is the right thing to do." Kennedy emphasizes the importance of world leadership, while Ride emphasizes the scientific importance as well as the incomparable experience.

   Ride's written format offers her more time to include dramatic details and first-person accounts. Kennedy's spoken format demands that he make his arguments both dramatically and quickly.

   Some students may find the essay more persuasive because of the first-person point of view. Other students may find the inspiring words of the speech more persuasive.

continued

continued Answers

2. **(a)** NASA's Web site uses pictures and specific Web pages to answer questions, provide information, and stress the value of the space program. **(b)** Both Kennedy's speech and NASA's Web site offer inspiration as a way to persuade their audiences to support the space program.

The Washwoman ✦ On Summer ✦ A Celebration of Grandfathers

Lesson Objectives and CA Correlations

1. **To analyze and respond to literary elements**
   - Literary Analysis: Essay **R 3.2**
   - Comparing Literary Works
2. **To read, comprehend, analyze, and critique essays**
   - Reading Strategy: Identifying the Author's Attitude
   - Reading Check questions
   - Review and Assess questions
   - Assessment Practice (ATE)
3. **To develop word analysis skills, fluency, and systematic vocabulary**
   - Vocabulary Development Lesson: Anglo-Saxon Prefix: *fore-* **R 1.1**
4. **To understand and apply written and oral language conventions**
   - Spelling Strategy
   - Grammar Lesson: Consistency of Verb Tense **LC 1.2, 1.3**
5. **To understand and apply appropriate writing and research strategies**
   - Writing Lesson: Essay on Summer **W 1.1**
   - Extension Activity: Interview **W 1.3**
6. **To understand and apply listening and speaking strategies**
   - Extension Activity: Movie Review **LS 1.8**

STEP-BY-STEP TEACHING GUIDE	PACING GUIDE
PRETEACH	
Motivate Students and Provide Background	
Use the Motivation activity (ATE p. 648)	5 min.
Read and discuss the Preview material and Background information (SE/ATE p. 648) [A]	5 min.
Introduce the Concepts	
Introduce the Literary Analysis and Reading Strategy (SE/ATE p. 649) [A]	15 min.
Pronounce the vocabulary words and read their definitions (SE p. 649)	5 min.
TEACH	
Monitor Comprehension	
Informally monitor comprehension by circulating while students read independently or in groups [A]	35 min.
Monitor students' comprehension with the Reading Check notes (SE / pp. 651. 653, 657, 659, 663, 665, 667)	as students read
Develop vocabulary with Vocabulary notes (SE pp. 650–651, 653–654, 656, 662–664)	as students read
Develop Understanding	
Develop students' understanding of essays with Literary Analysis annotations (SE/ATE pp. 651, 653–654, 656, 659–660, 664, 666–667) [A]	10 min.
Develop students' ability to identify the author's attitude with the Reading Strategy annotations (SE/ATE pp. 651, 653–654, 660, 662, 664, 666)	10 min.
ASSESS	
Assess Mastery	
Assess students' mastery of the Reading Strategy and Literary Analysis by having them answer the Review and Assess questions (SE/ATE p. 669)	20 min.
Use one or more of the print and media Assessment Resources (ATE p. 671) [A]	up to 50 min.
EXTEND	
Apply Understanding	
Have students complete the Vocabulary Development Lesson and the Grammar Lesson (SE p. 670) [A]	20 min.
Apply students' knowledge of connecting to an author's experience using the Writing Lesson (SE/ATE p. 671) [A]	45 min.
Apply students' understanding using one or more of the Extension Activities (SE p. 671)	20–90 min.

[A] **ACCELERATED INSTRUCTION:**
Use the strategies and activities identified with an [A].

UNIVERSAL ACCESS
● = Below Level Students
▲ = On-Level Students
■ = Above Level Students

Time and Resource Manager

Reading Level: Easy/Average/Average
Average Number of Instructional Days: 4

RESOURCES		
PRINT	**TRANSPARENCIES**	**TECHNOLOGY**
• **Beyond Literature,** Community Connection: Learning From Our Elders, p. 41 ▲ ■		• **Interest Grabber Video,** Tape 4 ● ▲ ■
• **Selection Support Workbook:** ● ▲ ■ Literary Analysis, p. 164 Reading Strategy, p. 163 Build Vocabulary, p. 161	• **Literary Analysis and Reading Transparencies,** pp. 81 and 82 ● ▲ ■	
• **Adapted Reader's Companion** ● • **Reader's Companion** ● • **Authors In Depth,** Gold Level, p. 135 ■		• **Listening to Literature** ● ▲ ■ Audiocassettes, Sides 19, 20 Audio CDs, CD 13
• **English Learner's Companion** ● ▲ • **Literatura en español** ● ▲ • **Literary Analysis for Enrichment** ■		
• **Formal Assessment:** Selection Test, pp. 145–147 ● ▲ ■ • **Open Book Test,** pp. 121–123 ● ▲ ■ • **Performance Assessment and Portfolio Management,** p. 26 ● ▲ ■ • PRENTICE HALL ASSESSMENT SYSTEM ● ▲ ■	• PRENTICE HALL ASSESSMENT SYSTEM ● ▲ ■ Skills Practice Answers and Explanations on Transparencies	• **Test Bank Software** ● ▲ ■ • **Got It! Assessment Videotapes,** Tape 4 ● ▲
• **Selection Support Workbook:** ● ▲ ■ Build Grammar Skills, p. 162 • **Writing and Grammar,** Gold Level ● ▲ ■ • **Extension Activities,** p. 41 ● ▲ ■	• **Daily Language Practice Transparencies** ● ▲ • **Writing Models and Graphic Organizers on Transparencies,** p. 83 ● ▲ ■	• **Writing and Grammar iText CD-ROM** ● ▲ ■ *Take It to the Net* www.phschool.com

BLOCK SCHEDULING: Use one 90-minute class period to preteach the selection and have students read it. Use a second 90-minute class period to assess students' mastery of skills and have them complete one of the Extension Activities.

PRETEACH

Step-by-Step Teaching Guide for pp. 648–649

Motivation

The media often portray older people unrealistically or in unflattering ways. Ask students to think of examples of older characters in movies or on television. Then, encourage them to think of positive contributions older people make to society.

Interest Grabber Video

As an alternative, play "Rudolfo Anaya on Using Personal Experiences" on Tape 4 to engage student interest.

1 Background

History

From 1830 until recently, Russia (and then the Soviet Union) repeatedly tried to absorb or dominate Poland, both culturally and politically. In 1921, Poland fought the Bolshevik government and emerged independent and with nearly its original boundaries, but these gains were lost during World War II. With Germany attacking on one side and the Soviet Union on the other, Poland was overcome and its Jewish population was almost entirely exterminated. At the war's end, the Soviets installed a Communist government in Poland. In the late 1980s, a democratic movement based in trade and labor unions achieved a largely peaceful political revolution. Today Poland is an independent republic with a fast-growing economy and free elections.

Prepare to Read

The Washwoman ◆ On Summer ◆ A Celebration of Grandfathers

Don Nemesio, 1977, Esperanza Martinez

Take It to the Net

Visit www.phschool.com for interactive activities and instruction related to the selections, including

- background
- graphic organizers
- literary elements
- reading strategies

Preview

Connecting to the Literature

The authors of these selections journey deep into their past to find people who gave them gifts that were not boxed or tied with bows. Think about similar special gifts in your life, about the people who gave them to you, and about what these gifts have meant to you.

1 Background

In the early 1900s, Russia, Austria-Hungary, and Germany ruled the territories that make up modern Poland, the scene of "The Washwoman." In this area, few people were well off—most worked long hours merely to earn enough to survive. The area had a sizable Jewish population, most of whom spoke Yiddish and maintained their own cultural traditions. These conditions form the backdrop for Isaac Bashevis Singer's narrative essay.

TEACHING RESOURCES

The following resources can be used to enrich or extend the instruction for pp. 648–649.

Motivation

Interest Grabber Video, Tape 4

Background

Beyond Literature, p.41

Take It to the Net

Visit www.phschool.com for background and hotlinks for the selections.

Literary Analysis

Literary Analysis and Reading Transparencies, Essay, p. 82

Reading

Selection Support: Reading Strategy, p. 163; Build Vocabulary, p. 161

Literary Analysis and Reading Transparencies, Identifying the Author's Attitude, p. 81

BLOCK SCHEDULING: Resources marked with this symbol provide varied instruction during 90-minute blocks.

❷ Literary Analysis

Essay

An **essay** is a short piece of nonfiction in which a writer expresses a personal view on a topic. In this example, Rudolfo Anaya tells why he thinks his dying grandfather acted with uncharacteristic impatience:

> It was because he could not care for himself, because he was returning to that state of childhood, and all those wishes and desires were now wrapped in a crumbling body.

As you read, look for details that express each writer's point of view.

Comparing Literary Works

Within the broad range of essays, there are specific types, each with a different purpose.

- **Narrative essays** tell a story.
- **Persuasive essays** present an opinion in order to convince readers to accept a position or take a course of action.
- **Reflective essays** reveal a writer's feelings about a topic of personal importance.

Compare these essays by considering which category each one represents. Then, compare the specific effects each essay has on the reader.

❸ Reading Strategy

Identifying the Author's Attitude

In an essay, the **author's attitude** toward the subject colors the presentation of information. For example, a writer describing someone he or she respects will use descriptive words and details that convey that respect.

Use a diagram like the one shown to help you identify the author's attitude. Note words or details that hint at the author's feelings. Then, indicate what these hints suggest about the author's attitude.

Vocabulary Development

forebears (fôr′ bərz′) *n.* ancestors (p. 650)

rancor (raŋ′ kər) *n.* deep spite or bitter hate (p. 651)

obstinacy (äb′ stə nə sē) *n.* stubbornness (p. 653)

pious (pī′ əs) *adj.* showing religious devotion (p. 654)

aloofness (ə lo͞of′ nəs) *n.* state of being distant or removed (p. 656)

perplexes (pər pleks′ iz) *v.* confuses or makes hard to understand (p. 662)

permeate (pur′ mē āt′) *v.* spread or flow throughout (p. 663)

epiphany (ē pif′ ə nē) *n.* moment of sudden understanding (p. 664)

❷ Literary Analysis

Essay

- Tell students that an *essay* is a writer's attempt to describe something or someone, to persuade readers to believe or do something, to tell a story, or simply to share reflections and emotions.
- As students read the three essays in this group, have them think about what makes each one an essay.

❸ Reading Strategy

Identifying the Author's Attitude

- Explain that an author's attitude toward a subject usually informs his or her purpose. For example, an attitude of fury over segregationist laws might make a writer produce a persuasive essay that would get readers to help change the laws.
- Explain that an author's attitude toward his or her subject sets the tone of a piece of writing. If a writer loves baseball and writes about his feelings of joyous anticipation as opening day of the season approaches, his tone may be warm, nostalgic, and happy.
- As students read, they should analyze the tone of each essay by using a chart like the one shown. This will help them identify the writers' attitudes.

Vocabulary Development

- Pronounce each vocabulary word for students, and read the definitions as a class. Have students identify any words with which they are already familiar.

CUSTOMIZE INSTRUCTION FOR UNIVERSAL ACCESS

For Special Needs Students	For Less Proficient Readers	For English Learners
Have students read the adapted versions of "On Summer" and "A Celebration of Grandfathers" in the **Adapted Reader's Companion.** These versions provide basic-level instruction in an interactive format. Completing the adapted versions will prepare students to read the selections in the Student Edition.	Have students read the selections in the **Reader's Companion.** These versions provide basic-level instruction in an interactive format with questions and write-on lines. After students finish the selections in **Reader's Companion,** have them complete the questions and activities in the Student Edition.	Have students read the adapted versions of the selections in the **English Learner's Companion.** These versions provide basic-level instruction in an interactive format with questions and write-on lines. Completing the adapted versions will prepare students to read the selections in the Student Edition.

E-Teach

Visit E-Teach at www.phschool.com for teachers' essays on how to teach, with questions and answers.

TEACH

Step-by-Step Teaching Guide for pp. 650–668

CUSTOMIZE INSTRUCTION
For Musical/Rhythmic Learners

In all three essays, the old people are either silent or taciturn; they say little. As students read, have them "listen" to the silence of the old people. What effect does this silence have on them? Do they agree with Rudolfo Anaya's opinion of the silence? Why is silence sometimes more effective and impressive than speech? Have students discuss their impressions of these quiet or silent characters as they finish reading each essay.

❶ About the Selection

Singer recalls the woman who did his family's laundry when he was a child in Poland. On a bitterly cold day in an unusually cold winter, she takes a large bundle of laundry and fails to return with it. More than two months later, she reappears with the clean laundry, explaining that she was desperately ill in the cold. The writer never sees her again and never forgets her courage and endurance.

❷ Vocabulary Development

Anglo-Saxon Prefix: *fore-*

- Draw students' attention to the word *forebears* and tell students that its Anglo-Saxon prefix, *fore-*, means "before." Students should readily see how the prefix contributes to the word's meaning: "those who came before" or "ancestors."
- Ask students to think of other words containing *fore-* and list them on the board. Work as a class to write brief definitions for each.
  Sample responses: *Foretell:* "to say before; predict"; *forewarn:* "to warn before"; *forenoon:* "before noon"; *forecast:* "to estimate or plan ahead; predict."

❶

The Washwoman

Isaac Bashevis Singer

Our home had little contact with Gentiles.[1] The only Gentile in the building was the janitor. Fridays he would come for a tip, his "Friday money." He remained standing at the door, took off his hat, and my mother gave him six groschen.[2]

Besides the janitor there were also the Gentile washwomen who came to the house to fetch our laundry. My story is about one of these.

She was a small woman, old and wrinkled. When she started washing for us, she was already past seventy. Most Jewish women of her age were sickly, weak, broken in body. All the old women in our street had bent backs and leaned on sticks when they walked. But this wash-
❸ woman, small and thin as she was, possessed a strength that came from genera-
❷ tions of peasant forebears. Mother would count out to her a bundle of laundry that had accumulated over several weeks. She would lift the unwieldy pack, load it on her narrow shoulders, and carry it the long way home. She lived on Krochmalna Street too, but at the other end, near the

1. **Gentiles** any persons not Jewish; here, specifically Christians.
2. **groschen** (grō´ shən) Austrian cent or penny.

forebears (fôr´ bərs´) *n.* ancestors

TEACHING RESOURCES

The following resources can be used to enrich or extend the instruction for pp. 650–668.

Literary Analysis
- **Writing Models and Graphic Organizers on Transparencies,** p. 83 ▪
- **Selection Support:** Literary Analysis, p. 164

Reading
- **Reader's Companion**
- **English Learner's Companion**

- **Listening to Literature Audiocassettes,** Sides 19, 20 ▪
- **Listening to Literature Audio CDs,** CD 13 ▪

Extension
- **Authors In Depth,** Gold Level (The collection includes three additional selections by Rudolfo Anaya for extended reading.)

▪ **BLOCK SCHEDULING:** Resources marked with this symbol provide varied instruction during 90-minute blocks.

Wola section. It must have been a walk of an hour and a half.

She would bring the laundry back about two weeks later. My mother had never been so pleased with any washwoman. Every piece of linen sparkled like polished silver. Every piece was neatly ironed. Yet she charged no more than the others. She was a real find. Mother always had her money ready, because it was too far for the old woman to come a second time.

Laundering was not easy in those days. The old woman had no faucet where she lived but had to bring in the water from a pump. For the linens to come out so clean, they had to be scrubbed thoroughly in a washtub, rinsed with washing soda, soaked, boiled in an enormous pot, starched, then ironed. Every piece was handled ten times or more. And the drying! It could not be done outside because thieves would steal the laundry. The wrung-out wash had to be carried up to the attic and hung on clotheslines. In the winter it would become as brittle as glass and almost break when touched. And there was always a to-do with other housewives and washwomen who wanted the attic clothesline for their own use. Only God knows all the old woman had to endure each time she did a wash!

She could have begged at the church door or entered a home for the penniless and aged. But there was in her a certain pride and love of labor with which many Gentiles have been blessed. The old woman did not want to become a burden, and so she bore her burden.

My mother spoke a little Polish, and the old woman would talk with her about many things. She was especially fond of me and used to say I looked like Jesus. She repeated this every time she came, and Mother would frown and whisper to herself, her lips barely moving, "May her words be scattered in the wilderness."

The woman had a son who was rich. I no longer remember what sort of business he had. He was ashamed of his mother, the washwoman, and never came to see her. Nor did he ever give her a groschen. The old woman told this without rancor. One day the son was married. It seemed that he had made a good match. The wedding took place in a church. The son had not invited the old mother to his wedding, but she went to the church and waited at the steps to see her son lead the "young lady" to the altar.

The story of the faithless son left a deep impression on my mother. She talked about it for weeks and months. It was an affront not only to the old woman but to the entire institution of motherhood. Mother would argue, "Nu, does it pay to make sacrifices for children? The mother uses up her last strength, and he does not even know the meaning of loyalty."

And she would drop dark hints to the effect that she was not certain of her own children: Who knows what they would do some day? This, however, did not prevent her from dedicating her life to us. If there was any delicacy in the house, she would put it aside for the children and invent all sorts of excuses and reasons why she herself did not want to taste it. She knew charms that went back to ancient times, and she

Literary Analysis
Essay Which type of essay do you think Singer is writing? Why?

Reading Strategy
Identifying the Author's Attitude Which words and phrases indicate the author's admiration for the washwoman?

rancor (raŋ´ kər) *n.* deep spite or bitter hate

5 **Reading Check**
Why does the washwoman's son never come to see her?

3 Literary Analysis
Essay

- Have students identify the three types of essays they read about on p. 649.
- Ask students the Literary Analysis question on p. 651: Which type of essay do you think Singer is writing? Why?
  Answer: The sentence "My story is about one of these" on p. 650 suggests that he is writing a narrative essay.

Monitor Progress Ask students to identify the narrative elements of the essay up to this point.
Answer: Singer has established his setting—two apartment buildings on Krochmalna Street in a Polish city. He has introduced his major character—the washwoman—and has described her in detail.

4 Reading Strategy
Identifying the Author's Attitude

- Have students describe the tone of Singer's comments about the washwoman. Make sure students support their responses with details from the text.
  Answer: His tone is respectful and admiring. He is amazed that the washwoman can do such hard work at her age and impressed that she does it so well.
- Ask the Reading Strategy question on p. 651: Which words and phrases indicate the author's admiration for the washwoman?
  Answer: Students may cite: "Only God knows all the old woman had to endure," "a certain pride and love of labor," "did not want to become a burden."

Monitor Progress Ask students why they think Singer chose to write about the washwoman. Challenge them to link his attitude to his purpose.
Answer: Singer deeply admired the washwoman and wants her character to be known and remembered.

5 Reading Check
Answer: Her son is ashamed of her.

❻ Background

Art

The Oldest Inhabitant, by Julian Alden Weir

American painter Julian Alden Weir (1852–1919) was one of a family of artists and teachers. His father, Robert Weir, was a self-taught painter who spent most of his career teaching art at the U.S. Military Academy in West Point, New York. His two sons, John and Julian, became painters and teachers.

Julian Weir studied art first with his father and later at the École des Beaux-Arts in Paris. *The Oldest Inhabitant* was painted during a summer trip to the French villages of Portrieux and Pont-Aven. Use these questions for discussion:

1. How would you describe the painter's attitude toward his subject?
   Answer: The dignity of her pose and the soft lighting suggest that the painter respected and admired her and believed that she was beautiful.
2. Compare and contrast the woman in the painting to the washwoman in the essay.
   Answer: Both are old and poor. Both seem to have qualities of endurance, patience, and determination.

❼ ▶Critical Viewing

Answer: The woman is probably poor, because her garments are simple and plain. Her expression is cheerful and patient. Her cane suggests that she is physically frail but still determined to walk under her own power.

❻

The Oldest Inhabitant, 1876, Julian Alden Weir, Butler Institute of American Art, Youngstown, Ohio

◀Critical Viewing ❼
Based on her clothing and her expression, what do you imagine this woman is like? Why? **[Infer]**

ENRICHMENT: Cultural Connection

Special Clothing

People wear special kinds of clothing or jewelry as a mark of their religious beliefs and to celebrate important occasions. For example, the Orthodox Jewish men in "The Washwoman" wear a special fringed garment beneath their regular clothes. They also undoubtedly wear a skullcap (in Hebrew, *kipah*; in Yiddish *yarmulke*) during their waking hours. These two articles of clothing represent their obedience to God. Other religions have special clothing, especially for religious leaders. For example, Buddhist monks and nuns may wear saffron robes, and Catholic cardinals wear scarlet robes.

Special clothing is also worn for significant occasions. For example, a Chinese bride might wear a red silk robe, a Norwegian bride might wear an elaborately embroidered white-on-white apron, and an American bride might wear a long white gown.

8 used expressions she had inherited from generations of devoted mothers and grandmothers. If one of the children complained of a pain, she would say, "May I be your ransom and may you outlive my bones!" Or she would say, "May I be the atonement for the least of your fingernails." When we ate she used to say, "Health and marrow in your bones!" The day before the new moon she gave us a kind of candy that was said to prevent parasitic worms. If one of us had something in his eye, Mother would lick the eye clean with her tongue. She also fed us rock candy against coughs, and from time to time she would take us to be blessed against the evil eye. This did not prevent her from studying *The Duties of the Heart, The Book of the Covenant*, and other serious philosophic works.

But to return to the washwoman. That winter was a harsh one. The streets were in the grip of a bitter cold. No matter how much we heated our stove, the windows were covered with frostwork and decorated with icicles. The newspapers reported that people were dying of the cold. Coal became dear. The winter had become so severe that parents stopped sending children to cheder,[3] and even the Polish schools were closed.

On one such day the washwoman, now nearly eighty years old, came to our house. A good deal of laundry had accumulated during the past weeks. Mother gave her a pot of tea to warm herself, as well as some bread. The old woman sat on a kitchen chair trembling and shaking, and warmed her hands against the teapot. Her fingers were gnarled from work, and perhaps from arthritis too. Her fingernails were strangely white. These hands spoke of the stubbornness of mankind, of the will to work not only as one's strength permits but beyond the limits of one's power. Mother counted and wrote down the list: men's undershirts, women's vests, long-legged drawers, bloomers, petticoats, shifts, featherbed covers, pillowcases, sheets, and the men's fringed garments. Yes,
9 the Gentile woman washed these holy garments as well.

The bundle was big, bigger than usual. When the woman placed it on her shoulders, it covered her completely. At first she swayed, as though she were about to fall under the load. But an inner obstinacy seemed to call out: No, you may not fall. A donkey may permit himself to fall under his burden, but not a human being, the crown of creation.

It was fearful to watch the old woman staggering out with the enormous pack, out into the frost, where the snow was dry as salt and the air was filled with dusty white whirlwinds, like goblins dancing in the cold. Would the old woman ever reach Wola?

She disappeared, and Mother sighed and prayed for her.

Usually the woman brought back the wash after two or, at the most, three weeks. But three weeks passed, then four and five, and nothing was heard of the old woman. We remained without linens. The cold had become even more intense. The telephone wires were now as thick as ropes. The branches of the trees looked like glass. So much snow had fallen that the streets had become uneven, and sleds were able to glide

3. **cheder** (khā´ dər) *n.* religious school.

Reading Strategy
Identifying the Author's Attitude Based on this paragraph, what do you think the author's attitude is toward his mother?

Literary Analysis
Essay Which personal view does the author express here?

obstinacy (äb´ stə nə sē) *n.* stubbornness

10 **Reading Check**
How does the washwoman handle the unusually large bundle of laundry?

CUSTOMIZE INSTRUCTION FOR UNIVERSAL ACCESS

For Special Needs Students	For Advanced Readers
Have students treat this narrative essay as if it were a short story. Use the Story Map transparency in **Writing Models and Graphic Organizers on Transparencies,** p. 83, to help students identify the setting, list the characters, summarize the events of the plot, and state the theme. Filling out such an organizer will help ensure that students comprehend the story that the essay tells.	Have students consider which narrative element—plot, character, setting, or theme—is most important to this narrative essay. Have them write brief essays in which they identify the most important element, support their answers with evidence from the text, and explain how their answers are linked to Singer's purpose in writing the essay.

8 Reading Strategy
Identifying the Author's Attitude

- Read aloud the bracketed passage to students. As you read, have students use a chart like the one shown on p. 649 to record details that Singer provides about his mother. Students' charts may look similar to the following:

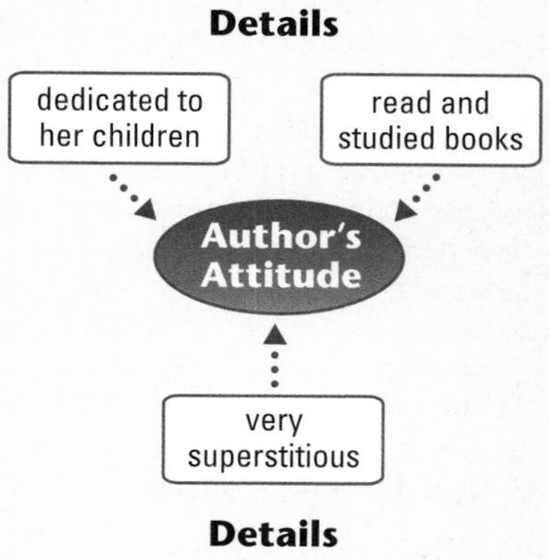

- Then, ask students the Reading Strategy question on p. 653: Based on this paragraph, what do you think the author's attitude is toward his mother?
Answer: Singer thinks she is fussy and overprotective, but devoted to her children. He thinks her love for her children makes her superstitious in spite of her intelligence.

9 Literary Analysis
Essay

- Call students' attention to the sentence that begins "These hands spoke of the stubbornness of mankind..." Ask students to paraphrase this sentence.
- Ask students the Literary Analysis question on p. 653: Which personal view does the author express here?
Answer: Singer believes that it is human nature to strive to overcome obstacles. He admires stubbornness.

10 Reading Check

Answer: The washwoman shoulders it and staggers away.

⓫ Literary Analysis

Essay

- Ask students to identify narrative elements in these two paragraphs.
  Answer: The first paragraph discusses a conflict: the family's need for laundry and concern for the washwoman versus the washwoman's unexplained absence. The second paragraph contains the climax of the story: The washwoman reappears with the laundry.
- Then, ask students the Literary Analysis question on p. 654: Which words convey strong personal feelings about the washwoman's absence?
  Answer: "mourned," "toil-worn," "grown close to us," "served us so faithfully"

⓬ Reading Strategy

Identifying the Author's Attitude

- Have students identify the details that Singer includes about the washwoman's illness in this passage.
  Answer: The washwoman's illness was so severe that the doctor summoned a priest and her son made funeral plans.
- Ask the Reading Strategy question on p. 654: How would you describe the author's attitude toward the washwoman, based on this information about her illness?
  Answer: Singer feels sorrow and pity for her because the illness has worn her out and her son remains indifferent.

Monitor Progress Ask why the author includes the old woman's words, "The wash would not let me die." What does including this quotation suggest about his attitude?
Answer: Singer admires her for her refusal to quit until her work was done. He admires her for her determination to honor her contract.

---

down many streets as on the slopes of a hill. Kindhearted people lit fires in the streets for vagrants[4] to warm themselves and roast potatoes in, if they had any to roast.

⓫ For us the washwoman's absence was a catastrophe. We needed the laundry. We did not even know the woman's address. It seemed certain that she had collapsed, died. Mother declared she had had a premonition, as the old woman left our house that last time, that we would never see our things again. She found some old torn shirts and washed and mended them. We mourned, both for the laundry and for the old, toil-worn woman who had grown close to us through the years she had served us so faithfully.

More than two months passed. The frost had subsided, and then a new frost had come, a new wave of cold. One evening, while Mother was sitting near the kerosene lamp mending a shirt, the door opened and a small puff of steam, followed by a gigantic bundle, entered. Under the bundle tottered the old woman, her face as white as a linen sheet. A few wisps of white hair straggled out from beneath her shawl. Mother uttered a half-choked cry. It was as though a corpse had entered the room. I ran toward the old woman and helped her unload her pack. She was even thinner now, more bent. Her face had become more gaunt, and her head shook from side to side as though she were saying no. She could not utter a clear word, but mumbled something with her sunken mouth and pale lips.

⓬ After the old woman had recovered somewhat, she told us that she had been ill, very ill. Just what her illness was, I cannot remember. She had been so sick that someone had called a doctor, and the doctor had sent for a priest. Someone had informed the son, and he had contributed money for a coffin and for the funeral. But the Almighty had not yet wanted to take this pain-racked soul to Himself. She began to feel better, she became well, and as soon as she was able to stand on her feet once more, she resumed her washing. Not just ours, but the wash of several other families too.

"I could not rest easy in my bed because of the wash," the old woman explained. "The wash would not let me die."

"With the help of God you will live to be a hundred and twenty," said my mother, as a benediction.

"God forbid! What good would such a long life be? The work becomes harder and harder . . . my strength is leaving me . . . I do not want to be a burden on anyone!" The old woman muttered and crossed herself, and raised her eyes toward heaven.

Fortunately there was some money in the house and Mother counted out what she owed. I had a strange feeling: the coins in the old woman's washed-out hands seemed to become as worn and clean and pious as she herself was. She blew on the coins and tied them in a kerchief. Then she left, promising to return in a few weeks for a new load of wash.

Literary Analysis
Essay Which words convey strong personal feelings about the washwoman's absence?

Reading Strategy
Identifying the Author's Attitude How would you describe the author's attitude toward the washwoman, based on this information about her illness?

pious (pī´ əs) *adj.* showing religious devotion

4. **vagrants** (vā´ grəntz) *n.* people who wander from place to place, especially those without regular jobs.

But she never came back. The wash she had returned was her last effort on this earth. She had been driven by an indomitable will to return the property to its rightful owners, to fulfill the task she had undertaken.

13 And now at last her body, which had long been no more than a shard[5] supported only by the force of honesty and duty, had fallen. Her soul passed into those spheres where all holy souls meet, regardless of the roles they played on this earth, in whatever tongue, of whatever creed. I cannot imagine paradise without this Gentile washwoman. I cannot even conceive of a world where there is no recompense for such effort.

---

5. **shard** (shärd) *n.* fragment or broken piece.

Reading Strategy
Identifying the Author's Attitude Which attitude toward the washwoman does Singer express here?

Review and Assess

Thinking About the Selection

1. **Respond:** Why do you think the washwoman gives so much and asks so little in return?
2. **(a) Recall:** Which job does the washwoman perform for Singer's family? **(b) Connect:** Which laborious obstacles to doing the job well does Singer describe?
3. **(a) Recall:** How does Singer's mother feel about the washwoman? **(b) Compare and Contrast:** In what ways is the washwoman like and unlike the author's mother?
4. **(a) Recall:** What prevents the washwoman from returning to the family for several months? **(b) Draw Conclusions:** What does the washwoman's eventual return tell you about her character?
5. **(a) Interpret:** What significance, beyond her work alone, does the washwoman have for Singer? **(b) Speculate:** In light of his own words, how might Singer's life have been different if he had never known her?
6. **(a) Interpret:** What difficulties does Singer imply about the washwoman? **(b) Assess:** Which details of her life are omitted from the essay? **(c) Evaluate:** What effect do these omissions have on the effectiveness of the selection?
7. **(a) Assess:** Do you think the washwoman had a fulfilling life? Explain. **(b) Apply:** What lessons can we learn from the washwoman?
8. **(a) Evaluate:** What are the benefits of a life of service? **(b) Extend:** What are the costs?

Isaac Bashevis Singer

(1904–1991)

I. B. Singer once said that he believed that "life itself is a story." This belief is reflected in his many short stories, novels, and essays that capture the lessons of everyday life.

Born in Poland, Singer moved to New York City in 1935 and later took American citizenship. Writing in Yiddish, the language of some Eastern European Jews and their descendants, Singer became a widely popular and respected writer. He won the Nobel Prize for Literature in 1978.

13 Reading Strategy

Identifying the Author's Attitude

- Ask the Reading Strategy question on p. 655: Which attitude toward the washwoman does Singer express here?
  Answer: Singer expresses reverence for a woman who seems holy to him for her honesty and duty.
- Ask students what this final paragraph suggests about Singer's purpose in writing this essay.
  Answer: He wants to celebrate the life of a person he believed was truly good and holy. He wants to show that an ordinary, humble, insignificant person can be a hero simply by refusing to give up.

Answers for p. 655

Review and Assess

1. The washwoman believes in doing her duty at a fair price.
2. **(a)** She does the laundry. **(b)** Singer cites the need to haul water and compete for drying space in the attic.
3. **(a)** She appreciates her hard work but is uncomfortable with her religion. **(b)** The mother tries to make her children feel guilty; the washwoman doesn't complain about her son. Both seem devoted to their children.
4. **(a)** The washwoman is ill. **(b)** She is dedicated to her work.
5. **(a)** The washwoman stands for the human determination to strive. **(b)** He might not have so much respect for humanity.
6. **(a)** The woman has become impoverished in some way and is oddly abandoned by her wealthy son. **(b)** Singer says nothing about her family history or what she does in the present besides laundry. **(c)** The omissions make the reader focus on the washwoman's working life.
7. **(a)** Students may say yes because she took pride in her work and carried it out faithfully, and she never had to depend on others. **(b)** Students may say that the washwoman teaches the virtues of duty, honesty, work, and endurance.
8. **(a)** The washwoman can take pride in her work and is a burden on no one. **(b)** Her work takes a terrible physical toll on her.

⓮ About the Selection

Hansberry recalls her childhood dislike of summers. She remembers playing games with friends in the streets of Chicago and sleeping in the park when the nights made the house too hot. During her eighth summer, she meets her grandmother in Tennessee. On a summer trip to Maine as an adult, she meets an elderly woman dying of cancer. Through conversations with this woman, Hansberry learns to respect and value summer as "the noblest of the seasons."

⓯ Literary Analysis

Essay

- Ask the Literary Analysis question on p. 656: What personal view does Hansberry express? Have students point to details that support their answers.
  Answer: She doesn't like summer. Words and phrases such as "acutely disliked," "displeasure," "too-grainy," "icky-perspirey," "maddeningly excessive," and "light too blinding" all make summer seem uncomfortable.

▶ **Monitor Progress** Ask students whether they think Hansberry's essay is narrative, persuasive, or reflective, and have them defend their answers.
Answer: It has narrative elements because it tells brief stories, but it is not one connected narrative like "The Washwoman." It has persuasive elements because she shares strong feelings about summer and supports them with details that might sway readers. It has reflective elements because she is exploring personal memories.

⓮ On Summer

Lorraine Hansberry

It has taken me a good number of years to come to any measure of respect for summer. I was, being May-born, literally an "infant of the spring" and, during the later childhood years, tended, for some reason or other, to rather worship the cold aloofness of winter. The adolescence, admittedly lingering still, brought the traditional passionate commitment to melancholy autumn—and all that. For the longest kind of time I simply thought that *summer* was a mistake.

In fact, my earliest memory of anything at all is of waking up in a darkened room where I had been put to bed for a nap on a summer's afternoon, and feeling very, very hot. I acutely disliked the feeling then and retained the bias for years. It had originally been a matter of the heat but, over the years, I came actively to associate displeasure with most of the usually celebrated natural features and social by-products of the season: the too-grainy texture of sand; the too-cold coldness of the various waters we constantly try to escape into, and the icky-perspiry feeling of bathing caps.

⓯ It also seemed to me, esthetically[1] speaking, that nature had got inexcusably carried away on the summer question and let the whole thing get to be rather much. By duration alone, for instance, a summer's day seemed maddeningly excessive; an utter overstatement. Except for those few hours at either end of it, objects always appeared in too sharp a relief against backgrounds; shadows too pronounced and light too blinding. It always gave me the feeling of walking around in a motion picture which had been too artsily-craftsily exposed. Sound also had a way of coming to the ear without that muting influence, marvelously common to winter, across patios or beaches or through the woods. I suppose I found it too stark and yet too intimate a season.

aloofness (ə lo͞of′ nəs) *n.* state of being distant or removed

Literary Analysis
Essay What personal view does Hansberry express?

1. **esthetically** (es thet′ ik lē) *adv.* artistically.

CUSTOMIZE INSTRUCTION FOR UNIVERSAL ACCESS		
For Less Proficient Readers	**For Special Needs Students**	**For English Learners**
To help them learn about characterization, have students compare and contrast the old woman in Maine with the washwoman from Singer's essay. Students can use Venn diagrams to note similarities and differences between the two women.	Have students approach this essay as a series of short narratives. Students can design graphic organizers with main heads *City, Tennessee,* and *Maine*. Under these heads they can list the main characters, the settings, and brief summaries of the events described.	Have students read the rhyme on this page aloud, clapping along with the rhythm. Explain that the purpose of the rhyme is to help the rope jumpers and turners keep a rhythm by which to play their game.

My childhood Southside[2] summers were the ordinary city kind, full of the street games which other rememberers have turned into fine ballets these days and rhymes that anticipated what some people insist on calling modern poetry:

Oh, Mary Mack, Mack, Mack
With the silver buttons, buttons, buttons
All down her back, back, back
She asked her mother, mother, mother
For fifteen cents, cents, cents
To see the elephant, elephant, elephant
Jump the fence, fence, fence
Well, he jumped so high, high, high
'Til he touched the sky, sky, sky
And he didn't come back, back, back
'Til the Fourth of Ju-ly, ly, ly!

16 ▲ **Critical Viewing**
How well does this photograph fit the essay? Explain. **[Evaluate]**

17 ✓ **Reading Check**
What is Hansberry's earliest memory?

2. **Southside** section of Chicago, Illinois.

16 ▶ **Critical Viewing**

Answer: Students may find the photograph appropriate because it shows one of the images from the essay — city children playing street games.

17 ✓ **Reading Check**

Answer: Hansberry remembers feeling too hot when she wakes up from a summer afternoon nap.

ENRICHMENT: Music Connection

Street Songs

Point out that Hansberry has vivid memories of the street songs that children in her neighborhood sang. These songs vary from neighborhood to neighborhood and are used in games such as jump rope and ring games. Students who are interested in finding out more about street songs and poems can look in books such as *Shake It to the One that You Love Best: Play Songs and Lullabies From Black Musical Traditions* and *Anna Banana: 101 Jump-Rope Rhymes* by Joanna Cole.

18 Reading Strategy

Identifying the Author's Attitude

- Ask students to describe Hansberry's attitude toward summer in this paragraph.
  Answer: She has pleasant memories of summer nights in the park.
- Have students compare and contrast the attitude of this paragraph with the attitude they identified on the previous two pages.
  Answer: Hansberry stated that she didn't like summer and explained why, but in this paragraph she shows that there were some summer occasions that she loved.

Monitor Progress As students continue reading, have them look for further shifts in the author's attitude toward summer. Have them think about why her attitude seems to change from one paragraph to the next.

19 Critical Viewing

Answer: After students have read the description of Hansberry's trip to Maine on pp. 660–661, they will say that this photograph illustrates the area Hansberry describes and helps them understand why the old woman was determined to live long enough to see another summer.

18 Evenings were spent mainly on the back porches where screen doors slammed in the darkness with those really very special summertime sounds. And, sometimes, when Chicago nights got too steamy, the whole family got into the car and went to the park and slept out in the open on blankets. Those were, of course, the best times of all because the grownups were invariably reminded of having been children in rural parts of the country and told the best stories then. And it was also cool and sweet to be on the grass and there was usually the scent of freshly cut lemons or melons in the air. And Daddy would lie on his back, as fathers must, and explain about how men thought the stars above us came to be and how far away they were. I never did learn to believe that anything could be as far away as *that*. Especially the stars.

19 **Critical Viewing** How does this photograph of the Maine coast add to the descriptions in the essay? **[Connect]**

20 My mother first took us south to visit her Tennessee birthplace one summer when I was seven or eight, I think. I woke up on the back seat of the car while we were still driving through some place called Kentucky and my mother was pointing out to the beautiful hills on both sides of the highway and telling my brothers and my sister about how her father had run away and hidden from his master in those very hills when he was a little boy. She said that his mother had wandered among the wooded slopes in the moonlight and left food for him in secret places. They were very beautiful hills and I looked out at them for miles and miles after that wondering who and what a *master* might be.

I remember being startled when I first saw my grandmother rocking away on her porch. All my life I had heard that she was a great

Literary Analysis
Essay Which details suggest that Hansberry is trying to convince you to accept her opinion about summer?

21 **Reading Check**
Whom does Hansberry visit in Tennessee?

CUSTOMIZE INSTRUCTION FOR UNIVERSAL ACCESS

For Gifted/Talanted Students	For Advanced Readers
Ask students to create to create posters or collages that visually suggest characteristics of their own favorite season of the year. You may wish to have students form groups based on the seasons they prefer. Suggest that students create images or collect photographs from magazines that express both pleasant and unpleasant aspects of the season that they enjoy most. Exhibit the posters in the classroom.	Have students read to appreciate Hansberry's use of figurative language. Have them identify details that appeal to each of the five senses. Student can gather in a group and discuss their reactions to the essay's sensory details. How does figurative language enhance their ability to understand and share Hansberry's experiences?

20 Literary Analysis
Essay

- Go back over the previous three pages of the essay with students. Challenge them to identify Hansberry's purpose in writing this essay. Have them indicate words and phrases that support their answers.
  Possible response: She wants to share her personal feelings about summer; she uses strong language to describe its bad qualities and discomforts and vivid language to describe its charms.
- Ask the Literary Analysis question on p. 659: Which details suggest that Hansberry is trying to convince you to accept her opinion about summer?
  Answer: In her description on p. 658, Hansberry uses inviting sensory language to describe the "best times": "cool and sweet," "the scent of freshly cut lemons or melons."

21 Reading Check

Answer: Hansberry visits her maternal grandmother.

22 Reading Strategy
Identifying the Author's Attitude

- Ask students the Reading Strategy question on p. 660: How would you describe the author's attitude toward her grandmother?
  Answer: Hansberry's tone is affectionate. She remembers the wonderful cupcakes and her grandmother's fascination with cars. Her attitude is loving and protective.
- Have students compare and contrast Hansberry's attitude toward her grandmother and her attitude toward the woman in Maine. Have them list specific words and phrases that describe each
  Answer: Grandmother: "wonderful cupcakes," "sweet," "captivated by automobiles," "a little afraid," "loved driving." Woman in Maine: "purposeful and courageous," "radical viewpoint," "energetically believe," "absolutely refused." She loves her grandmother; she admires and respects the other woman.

23 Literary Analysis
Essay

- As students read this section about the grandmother and the old woman in Maine, ask them why they think Hansberry wrote about these two women.
  Possible responses: Hansberry wanted to describe the different kinds of strength she finds in old women. She wants each character to serve as a contrast to the other.
- Ask the Literary Analysis question on p. 660: Which words convey the reflective nature of Hansberry's essay?
  Answer: The phrase "I do not think that I will forget" shows that she is writing about memories.

beauty and no one had ever remarked that they meant a half century before. The woman that I met was as wrinkled as a prune and could hardly hear and barely see and always seemed to be thinking of other times. But she could still rock and talk and even make wonderful cupcakes which were like cornbread, only sweet. She was captivated by automobiles and, even though it was well into the Thirties,[3] I don't think she had ever been in one before we came down and took her driving. She was a little afraid of them and could not seem to negotiate the windows, but she loved driving. She died the next summer **22** and that is all that I remember about her, except that she was born in slavery and had memories of it and they didn't sound anything like *Gone With the Wind*.[4]

Like everyone else, I have spent whole or bits of summers in many different kinds of places since then: camps and resorts in the Middle West and New York State; on an island; in a tiny Mexican village; Cape Cod, perched atop the Truro bluffs at Longnook Beach that Millay[5] wrote about; or simply strolling the streets of Provincetown[6] before the hours when the parties begin.

And, lastly, I do not think that I will forget days spent, a few summers ago, at a beautiful lodge built right into the rocky cliffs of a bay on the Maine coast. We met a woman there who had lived a purposeful and courageous life and who was then dying of cancer. She had, characteristically, just written a book and taken up painting. She had also been of radical viewpoint all her life; one of those people who **23** energetically believe that the world *can* be changed for the better and spend their lives trying to do just that. And that was the way she thought of cancer; she absolutely refused to award it the stature of tragedy, a devastating instance of the brooding doom and inexplicability[7] of the absurdity of human destiny, etc., etc. The kind of characterization given, lately, as we all know, to far less formidable foes in life than cancer.

But for this remarkable woman it was a matter of nature in imperfection, implying, as always, work for man to do. It was an *enemy*, but a palpable one with shape and effect and source; and if it existed, it could be destroyed. She saluted it accordingly, without despondency, but with a lively, beautiful and delightfully ribald anger. There was one thing, she felt, which would prove equal to its relentless ravages and that was the genius of man. Not his mysticism, but man with tubes and slides and the stubborn human notion that the stars are very much within our reach.

The last time I saw her she was sitting surrounded by her paintings with her manuscript laid out for me to read, because, she said,

Reading Strategy
Identifying the Author's Attitude How would you describe the author's attitude toward her grandmother?

Literary Analysis
Essay Which words convey the reflective nature of Hansberry's essay?

3. **Thirties** the 1930s.
4. ***Gone With the Wind*** novel set in the South during the Civil War period.
5. **Millay** Edna St. Vincent Millay (1892–1950), American poet.
6. **Provincetown** resort town at the northern tip of Cape Cod, Massachusetts.
7. **inexplicability** (in eks′ pli kə bil′ ə tē) *n.* condition that cannot be explained.

CUSTOMIZE INSTRUCTION FOR UNIVERSAL ACCESS

For Less Proficient Readers	For Advanced Readers
Ask students to identify their own favorite season of the year and then to list special events, activities, and feelings that they think of in relation to that time of year. You may wish to have students form small groups based on their seasonal preference. Conclude by having each group create a poster that completes the statement "[Season] is the best because . . ." by combining favorite items of group members.	Have students write essays on any season of their choice. Their essays need not be as long as Hansberry's but should describe similar memories they associate with the season they choose. Encourage students to use figurative language that will appeal to the reader's five senses and draw him or her into the memories described. Let volunteers read their essays aloud.

she wanted to know what a *young person* would think of her thinking; one must always keep up with what *young people* thought about things because, after all, they were *change*.

Every now and then her jaw set in anger as we spoke of things people should be angry about. And then, for relief, she would look out at the lovely bay at a mellow sunset settling on the water. Her face softened with love of all that beauty and, watching her, I wished with all my power what I knew that she was wishing: that she might live to see at least one more *summer*. Through her eyes I finally gained the
24 sense of what it might mean; more than the coming autumn with its pretentious melancholy; more than an austere and silent winter which must shut dying people in for precious months; more even than the frivolous spring, too full of too many false promises, would be the gift of another summer with its stark and intimate assertion of neither birth nor death but life at the apex; with the gentlest nights and, above all, the longest days.

I heard later that she did live to see another summer. And I have retained my respect for the noblest of the seasons.

Review and Assess

Thinking About the Selection

1. **Respond:** How do Hansberry's ideas about summer compare with your own?
2. **(a) Recall:** What are some of Hansberry's memories of childhood summers? **(b) Compare and Contrast:** Do her memories seem to support or contradict the opinion of summer she stated earlier? Explain.
3. **(a) Recall:** When does Hansberry first visit her grandmother? **(b) Infer:** Why do you think she includes the section about her grandmother in her essay?
4. **(a) Recall:** When does Hansberry's attitude toward summer change? **(b) Connect:** At the end, she calls summer "the noblest of the seasons." What do you think she means by this phrase?
5. **(a) Analyze:** What point of view does Hansberry try to persuade you to accept in her essay? **(b) Support:** What emotional appeals does she use to reach this goal?
6. **(a) Extend:** What experience have you had to cause your attitude about a season to change? **(b) Synthesize:** Is such a transformation of childhood opinions an important part of growing up? Why?
7. **Take a Position:** Which do you think affects a person's opinions more—personal experience or some other kind of learning? Explain.

Lorraine Hansberry

(1930–1965)

Lorraine Hansberry was born and raised in Chicago, Illinois. After high school, she studied art for two years before moving to New York City, where she worked for an African American newspaper called *Freedom*. While in New York, she wrote *A Raisin in the Sun*, which takes its name from a Langston Hughes poem, and in 1959 it became the first play by an African American woman to be produced on Broadway.

The essay "On Summer" comes from *To Be Young, Gifted, and Black*, a collection of Hansberry's writings that was published after her death.

24 Reading Strategy

Identifying the Author's Attitude

- Have students compare and contrast the final paragraph of Hansberry's essay with its opening paragraph. Ask students how Hansberry's attitude toward summer has changed.
  Answer: She disliked summer during her childhood; she now respects it as "the noblest of seasons."
- Ask why her attitude has changed.
  Answer: Hansberry's deepening understanding of life and a host of positive summer experiences cause her attitude to change.

Answers for p. 661

Review and Assess

1. Students probably enjoy summer for its freedom from school, vacations, and outdoor activities
2. **(a)** She remembers playing street games with her friends and spending hot nights in the park with her family. **(b)** They seem to contradict it; the memories she describes are pleasant.
3. **(a)** Hansberry is eight at her first visit. **(b)** It is a memory of a specific summer; it provides a contrast to her description of the woman in Maine.
4. **(a)** Hansberry's attitude changes during her time in Maine with the old woman. **(b)** She considers summer noble because it represents life "at the apex," in its most complete form.
5. **(a)** Hansberry wants the reader to share her deepening appreciation of summer — and of life. **(b)** Emotional appeals include the sympathetic characterization of the old woman and the figurative language used to describe summer experiences.
6. **(a)** Encourage students to share their stories of seasons. **(b)** Students may agree that adjusting childhood views is a part of maturation.
7. Students may say that personal experience has more influence because it is direct, vivid, and memorable.

25 About the Selection

Rudolfo Anaya celebrates the culture of his native New Mexico, where old people were respected and honored. He describes his own grandfather, a man who set a tremendous example of strength and endurance. After the grandfather's death at age 94, the narrator wonders whether the values of the old man's generation are gone for good.

26 Reading Strategy

Identifying the Author's Attitude

- Ask students the Reading Strategy question on p. 662: Which facts about the author's past help you understand his attitude toward his subject?
  Answer: The narrator supports his original point that old people deserve respect with specific examples from his childhood. The old people he lived with daily deserved respect because they were wiser and more experienced than the young.

Monitor Progress Have students identify specific details that show why the writer respects the elders.
Answer: He describes their cooperation and collaboration with one another. He respects their belief that individual interests are less important than the welfare of a community. He says that they share what they have in both good and bad times.

25 A Celebration of Grandfathers

Rudolfo A. Anaya

"Buenos días le de Dios, abuelo."[1] God give you a good day, grandfather. This is how I was taught as a child to greet my grandfather, or any grown person. It was a greeting of respect, a cultural value to be passed on from generation to generation, this respect for the old ones.

The old people I remember from my childhood were strong in their beliefs, and as we lived daily with them we learned a wise path of life to follow. They had something important to share with the young, and when they spoke the young listened. These old abuelos and abuelitas[2] had worked the earth all their lives, and so they knew the value of nurturing, they knew the sensitivity of the earth. The daily struggle called for cooperation, and so every person contributed to the social fabric, and each person was respected for his contribution.

26 The old ones had looked deep into the web that connects all animate and inanimate forms of life, and they recognized the great design of the creation.

These *ancianos*[3] from the cultures of the Río Grande, living side by side, sharing, growing together, they knew the rhythms and cycles of time, from the preparation of the earth in the spring to the digging of the acequias[4] that brought the water to the dance of harvest in the fall. They shared good times and hard times. They helped each other through the epidemics and the personal tragedies, and they shared what little they had when the hot winds burned the land and no rain came. They learned that to survive one had to share in the process of life.

Hard workers all, they tilled the earth and farmed, ran the herds and spun wool, and carved their saints and their kachinas[5] from cottonwood late in the winter nights. All worked with a deep faith which perplexes the modern mind.

Their faith shone in their eyes; it was in the strength of their grip, in the creases time wove into their faces. When they spoke, they spoke plainly and with few words, and they meant what they said.

Reading Strategy
Identifying the Author's Attitude Which facts about the author's past help you understand his attitude toward his subject?

perplexes (pər pleks´ iz) *v.* confuses or makes hard to understand

1. **Buenos días le de Dios, abuelo** (bwā´ nəs dē´ äs lā dā dē´ ōs ä bwā´ lō)
2. **abuelitas** (a bwā lē´ täs) grandmothers.
3. ***ancianos*** (än cē ä´ nōs) old people; ancestors.
4. **acequias** (ä sā kē´ əs) irrigation ditches.
5. **kachinas** (kə chē´ nəz) small wooden dolls, representing the spirit of an ancestor or a god.

CUSTOMIZE INSTRUCTION FOR UNIVERSAL ACCESS

For Advanced Readers

Suggest that students read additional works by Rudolfo Anaya. You may wish to use **Authors In Depth**, Gold Level, which contains the following selections:

- "A New Mexico Christmas"
- "At a Crossroads"
- from *A Chicano in China* (two excerpts)

After students have read these or other works by Anaya, have them form discussion groups in which they compare and contrast the selections they have read. Suggest criteria for comparison, such as theme, characters, and viewpoints. To extend the activity, have volunteers present to the class brief oral reports on their favorite Anaya selections.

27

When they prayed, they went straight to the source of life. When there were good times, they knew how to dance in celebration and how to prepare the foods of the fiestas.[6] All this they passed on to the young, so that a new generation would know what they had known, so the string of life would not be broken.

Today we would say that the old abuelitos lived authentic lives.

Newcomers to New Mexico often say that time seems to move slowly here. I think they mean they have come in contact with the inner strength of the people, a strength so solid it causes time itself to pause. Think of it. Think of the high, northern New Mexico villages, or the lonely ranches on the open llano.[7] Think of the Indian pueblo[8] which lies as solid as rock in the face of time. Remember the old people whose eyes seem like windows that peer into a distant past that makes absurdity of our contemporary world. That is what one feels when one encounters the old ones and their land, a pausing of time.

We have all felt time stand still. We have all been in the presence of power, the knowledge of the old ones, the majestic peace of a mountain stream or an aspen grove or red buttes rising into blue sky. We have all felt the light of dusk permeate the earth and cause time to pause in its flow.

6. **fiestas** (fē es´ təz) celebrations; feasts.
7. **llano** (yä´ nō) plain.
8. **pueblo** (pweb´ lō) village or town.

28 **▲ Critical Viewing** Which aspects of the man in this painting are similar to the description of the elders in the essay? **[Compare and Contrast]**

permeate (pur´ mē āt´) *v.* spread or flow throughout

29 **Reading Check** Why was Anaya taught as a child to give his grandfather a proper greeting?

27 Background

Art

Don Nemesio, by Esperanza Martinez

An elderly man rests his head on his hand as he either looks intently at something out of the bounds of the painting, or perhaps simply thinks to himself. Use these questions for discussion:

1. What can you tell about the man in the painting from the objects the artist chose to depict?
   Answer: He is Latino, probably of Mexican heritage, because he sits beside a stack of tortillas. The bowl on the table has a design that could be Mexican.
2. How does the man in the painting compare to your mental picture of Anaya's grandfather?
   Possible response: They are both old and thoughtful.

28 ▶Critical Viewing

Answer: The old people in the essay lead "authentic lives" and are close to the earth. The old man's spare surroundings and expression suggest that he shares these qualities.

29 Reading Check

Answer: Everyone in Anaya's culture respected elders and looked up to them.

CUSTOMIZE INSTRUCTION FOR UNIVERSAL ACCESS

For English Learners	For Advanced Readers
If any students speak Spanish fluently, ask them to pronounce the Spanish words and phrases in this essay so that classmates can learn and appreciate them. Encourage students to amplify the translations of Spanish words in the footnotes, explaining their specific denotations and connotations.	Point out the phrase "the old abuelitos lived authentic lives" on p. 663. Have students explain what Anaya means by this. Encourage them to look up the word *authentic* in the dictionary. Why does Anaya say "authentic" instead of "real," "genuine," or some other synonym?

30 Literary Analysis

Essay

- Ask students to explain the connection Anaya feels between natural features like mountains and the power of the old ones.
  Answer: The natural features he looks at are old; they have endured through the years, and they are still majestic and strong. He sees the same kind of strength and endurance in old people.
- Ask the Literary Analysis question on p. 664: Which of Anaya's personal experiences help him reflect on his feelings about the strength and power of the old ones?
  Answer: Anaya uses his experiences with the strength and beauty of nature to compare with his experiences of the strength and wisdom of his elders, drawing an analogy that emphasizes his deep feelings for the old ones.

31 Reading Strategy

Identifying the Author's Attitude

- Why does the writer find his grandfather's silence memorable?
  Answer: His grandfather's silence may contrast with other people's talkativeness.
- Anaya remembers not only his grandfather's silence but also his words. What is memorable about what the grandfather says?
  Answer: The grandfather speaks in brief, simple phrases that convey larger meanings. For example, his advice to "know where you stand" means not only to avoid anthills, but to be sure of your place in the world.
- Ask the Reading Strategy question on p. 664: What attitude toward his grandfather is the author communicating?
  Answer: Anaya is expressing his respect for his grandfather's wisdom and authority.

I felt this when first touched by the spirit of Ultima, the old *curandera*[9] who appears in my first novel, *Bless Me, Ultima*. This is how the young Antonio describes what he feels:

> When she came the beauty of the llano unfolded before my eyes, and the gurgling waters of the river sang to the hum of the turning earth. The magical time of childhood stood still, and the pulse of the living earth pressed its mystery into my living blood. She took my hand, and the silent, magic powers she possessed made beauty from the raw, sun-baked llano, the green river valley, and the blue bowl which was the white sun's home. My bare feet felt the throbbing earth, and my body trembled with excitement. Time stood still . . .

30

At other times, in other places, when I have been privileged to be with the old ones, to learn, I have felt this inner reserve of strength upon which they draw. I have been held motionless and speechless by the power of curanderas. I have felt the same power when I hunted with Cruz, high on the Taos [tä´ ōs] mountain, where it was more than the incredible beauty of the mountain bathed in morning light, more than the shining of the quivering aspen, but a connection with life, as if a shining strand of light connected the particular and the cosmic. That feeling is an epiphany of time, a standing still of time.

But not all of our old ones are curanderos or hunters on the mountain. My grandfather was a plain man, a farmer from Puerto de Luna[10] on the Pecos River. He was probably a descendent of those people who spilled over the mountain from Taos, following the Pecos River in search of farmland. There in that river valley he settled and raised a large family.

Bearded and walrus-mustached, he stood five feet tall, but to me as a child he was a giant. I remember him most for his silence. In the summers my parents sent me to live with him on his farm, for I was to learn the ways of a farmer. My uncles also lived in that valley, the valley called Puerto de Luna, there where only the flow of the river and the whispering of the wind marked time. For me it was a magical place.

31

I remember once, while out hoeing the fields, I came upon an anthill, and before I knew it I was badly bitten. After he had covered my welts with the cool mud from the irrigation ditch, my grandfather calmly said: "Know where you stand." That is the way he spoke, in short phrases, to the point.

One very dry summer, the river dried to a trickle, there was no water for the fields. The young plants withered and died. In my sadness and with the impulses of youth I said, "I wish it would rain!" My grandfather touched me, looked up into the sky and whispered, "Pray for rain." In his language there was a difference. He felt connected to the cycles that brought the rain or kept it from us. His prayer was a

Literary Analysis
Essay Which of Anaya's personal experiences help him reflect on his feelings about the strength and power of the old ones?

epiphany (ē pif´ ə nē) *n.* moment of sudden understanding

Reading Strategy
Identifying the Author's Attitude What attitude toward his grandfather is the author communicating?

9. **curandera** (ko͞o rän dā´ rä) medicine woman.
10. **Puerto de Luna** (pwer´ tō dā lo͞o´ nə) Port of the Moon, the name of a town.

ENRICHMENT: Career Connection

Farmers

Point out to students that farming is one of the most important jobs a person can do. Everyone needs food, and most of the food the world eats comes from crops and livestock on farms. Farming is a business, and farmers must concentrate not only on the best way to raise crops or livestock but on accounting, marketing, and the science of farming. Interested students can find out information such as the number of farmers in the United States, reasons why that number has dropped so precipitously, the average size of farms, and the average gross income of a farm.

Encourage students to think about how today's farms differ from the farm that Anaya's grandfather worked.

32

El Lenador, 1934, Tom Lea, Museum of Fine Arts, Museum of New Mexico

33 ◀Critical Viewing
How does the elderly farmer in this painting compare with the image you have of the author's grandfather? **[Compare and Contrast]**

meaningful action, because he was a participant with the forces that filled our world, he was not a bystander.

A young man died at the village one summer. A very tragic death. He was dragged by his horse. When he was found I cried, for the boy was my friend. I did not understand why death had come to one so young. My grandfather took me aside and said: "Think of the death of the trees and the fields in the fall. The leaves fall, and everything rests, as if dead. But they bloom again in the spring. Death is only this small transformation in life."

These are the things I remember, these fleeting images, few words.

I remember him driving his horse-drawn wagon into Santa Rosa in the fall when he brought his harvest produce to sell in the town. What a tower of strength seemed to come in that small man huddled on the seat of the giant wagon. One click of his tongue and the horses obeyed, stopped or turned as he wished. He never raised his

34 ✓Reading Check
What does Anaya's grandfather tell him to do when there is no water for the fields?

32 Background

Art

El Leñador, by Tom Lea

A *leñador* is a woodcutter. This painting shows the woodcutter and his donkey with a load of wood. He is probably using the stick to steer the animal on the uphill path. Use the following questions for discussion:

1. What can you infer about the life of the *leñador* in the painting?
   Answer: He probably works hard because he is all alone and has chopped a lot of wood. He does manual labor and has only one donkey. His expression is tough and determined, suggesting that his tasks are difficult and strenuous.
2. What can you infer about the man's relationship with the donkey?
   Answer: They seem to be partners; the donkey wears no halter and is being directed only by a light stick. They apparently work well together and trust each other.

33 ▶Critical Viewing

Answer: The man in the painting looks strong and vigorous, not old. Some students may think his face is stern. Anaya's grandfather is also tough and determined; he probably appears older.

34 ✓Reading Check

Answer: Anaya's grandfather tells him to pray for rain.

35 Reading Strategy

Identifying the Author's Attitude

- Have students describe the tone of this paragraph. Ask them to link this tone to the author's purpose.
  Answer: The tone is one of serious concern. The author's purpose is to warn readers not to bury the old ways when the old people die.
- Ask the Reading Strategy question on p. 666: How would you describe the author's attitude toward the potential loss of old values?
  Answer: He is very concerned that his generation will abandon the old ways. He feels that if this happens, people will lose some of their humanity.

36 Literary Analysis

Essay

- Ask students to identify the tone of this paragraph. Point out the repetition of "we" or "We need." Ask students what effect it has on the reader.
  Answer: The tone is urgent. The repetition of "we" includes readers and the author as one group that he feels must take certain actions.
- Ask the Literary Analysis question on p. 666: Which words in this paragraph signify that the purpose of Anaya's essay moves from reflection to persuasion?
  Answer: The repeated "We need" shows that Anaya is urging his reader to take a series of actions.

▶ **Monitor Progress** As students continue reading, have them think about what Anaya is trying to persuade them to do and/or believe.

whip. How unlike today when so much teaching is done with loud words and threatening hands.

I would run to greet the wagon, and the wagon would stop. "Buenos días le de Dios, abuelo," I would say. This was the prescribed greeting of esteem and respect. Only after the greeting was given could we approach these venerable old people. "Buenos días te de Dios, mi hijo,"[11] he would answer and smile, and then I could jump up on the wagon and sit at his side. Then I, too, became a king as I rode next to the old man who smelled of earth and sweat and the other deep aromas from the orchards and fields of Puerto de Luna.

35 We were all sons and daughters to him. But today the sons and daughters are breaking with the past, putting aside los abuelitos. The old values are threatened, and threatened most where it comes to these relationships with the old people. If we don't take the time to watch and feel the years of their final transformation, a part of our humanity will be lessened.

I grew up speaking Spanish, and oh! how difficult it was to learn English. Sometimes I would give up and cry out that I couldn't learn. Then he would say, "Ten paciencia."[12] Have patience. *Paciencia*, a word with the strength of centuries, a word that said that someday we would overcome. *Paciencia*, how soothing a word coming from this old man who could still sling hundred-pound bags over his shoulder, chop wood for hours on end, and hitch up his own horses and ride to town and back in one day.

"You have to learn the language of the Americanos,"[13] he said. "Me, I will live my last days in my valley. You will live in a new time, the time of the gringos."[14]

36 A new time did come, a new time is here. How will we form it so it is fruitful? We need to know where we stand. We need to speak softly and respect others, and to share what we have. We need to pray not for material gain, but for rain for the fields, for the sun to nurture growth, for nights in which we can sleep in peace, and for a harvest in which everyone can share. Simple lessons from a simple man. These lessons he learned from his past which was as deep and strong as the currents of the river of life, a life which could be stronger than death.

He was a man; he died. Not in his valley, but nevertheless cared for by his sons and daughters and flocks of grandchildren. At the end, I would enter his room which carried the smell of medications and Vicks, the faint pungent odor of urine, and cigarette smoke. Gone were the aroma of the fields, the strength of his young manhood. Gone also was his patience in the face of crippling old age. Small things bothered him; he shouted or turned sour when his expectations were not met. It was because he could not care for himself, because he was returning to that state of childhood, and all those

Reading Strategy
Identifying the Author's Attitude How would you describe the author's attitude toward the potential loss of old values?

Literary Analysis
Essay Which words in this paragraph signify that the purpose of Anaya's essay has shifted from reflection to persuasion?

---

11. **mi hijo** (mē ē´ hō) my son.
12. **Ten paciencia** (ten pä sē en´ sē ä)
13. **Americanos** (ä mer´ ē kä´ nōs) Americans.
14. **gringos** (griŋ´ gōs) foreigners; North Americans.

wishes and desires were now wrapped in a crumbling old body.

"Ten paciencia," I once said to him, and he smiled. "I didn't know I would grow this old," he said. "Now, I can't even roll my own cigarettes." I rolled a cigarette for him, placed it in his mouth and lit it. I asked him why he smoked, the doctor had said it was bad for him. "I like to see the smoke rise," he said. He would smoke and doze, and his quilt was spotted with little burns where the cigarettes dropped. One of us had to sit and watch to make sure a fire didn't start.

I would sit and look at him and remember what was said of him when he was a young man. He could mount a wild horse and break it, and he could ride as far as any man. He could dance all night at a dance, then work the acequia the following day. He helped neighbors, they helped him. He married, raised children. Small legends, the kind that make up everyman's life.

He was 94 when he died. Family, neighbors, and friends gathered;
37 they all agreed he had led a rich life. I remembered the last years, the years he spent in bed. And as I remember now, I am reminded that it is too easy to romanticize old age. Sometimes we forget the pain of the transformation into old age, we forget the natural breaking down
38 of the body. Not all go gentle into the last years, some go crying and cursing, forgetting the names of those they loved the most, withdrawing into an internal anguish few of us can know. May we be granted the patience and care to deal with our ancianos.

For some time we haven't looked at these changes and needs of the old ones. The American image created by the mass media is an image of youth, not of old age. It is the beautiful and the young who are praised in this society. If analyzed carefully, we see that same damaging thought has crept into the way society views the old. In response to the old, the mass media have just created old people who act like the young. It is only the healthy, pink-cheeked, outgoing, older persons we are shown in the media. And they are always selling something, as if an entire generation of old people were salesmen in their lives. Commercials show very lively old men, who must always be in excellent health according to the new myth, selling insurance policies or real estate as they are out golfing; older women selling coffee or toilet paper to those just married. That image does not illustrate the real life of the old ones.

Real life takes into account the natural cycle of growth and change. My grandfather pointed to the leaves falling from the tree. So time brings with its transformation the often painful, wearing-down process. Vision blurs, health wanes; even the act of walking carries with it the painful reminder of the autumn of life. But this process is something to be faced, not something to be hidden away by false images. Yes, the old can be young at heart, but in their own way, with their own dignity. They do not have to copy the always-young image of the Hollywood star.

My grandfather wanted to return to his valley to die. But by then the families of the valley had left in search of a better future. It is only now that there seems to be a return to the valley, a revival. The

Literary Analysis
Essay What reflections does Anaya convey in this part of his essay?

39 **Reading Check**
What does Anaya's grandfather say to him as the writer struggles to learn English?

37 Literary Analysis

Essay

- Ask students to define the purpose of Anaya's essay. Remind them that it may have more than one purpose.
  Answer: It has narrative elements because it tells the story of Anaya's grandfather's life. It is persuasive because it tries to convince readers that the ways of the old people were valuable and that readers should try to live this way too. It is reflective because the writer shares his thoughts and memories, wanting only that the reader should understand and connect with them.
- Then, ask the Literary Analysis question on p. 667: What reflections does Anaya convey in this part of his essay?
  Answer: He reflects on his grandfather's youth, the ordinary work and play that filled his days, and the great physical struggle that comes with death.

38 Background

Literature

Anaya alludes to a famous poem by Welsh poet Dylan Thomas (1914–1953), "Do Not Go Gentle into That Good Night." The speaker urges his father to "rage, rage against the dying of the light"—to die with rage and passion rather than passively accept death.

39 Reading Check

Answer: His grandfather tells him to "have patience," because Anaya will live in a new time and must know the language of the Americanos.

CUSTOMIZE INSTRUCTION FOR UNIVERSAL ACCESS

For Special Needs Students	For Advanced Readers
Encourage students to describe "small legends" that occur in their own family experiences. Point out that to be legendary, one doesn't need to be famous, wealthy, or a speaker of English. Anaya celebrates the generations that preceded him but resists glamorizing old age. Ask students to think of older members of their family, how age has changed them, and how these older people dealt with that transformation.	Have students write essays about grandparents or other older relatives they admire and respect. Their essays can be narrative, reflective, persuasive, or a combination. Students may want to outline their ideas before they begin writing. Encourage them not to interpret the old people for readers but rather describe their actions and let this speak for them. Students may want to share their essays in class.

ASSESS

Answers for p. 668

Review and Assess

1. The author respects and venerates the "old ones."
2. **(a)** Anaya remembers their wisdom, knowledge, readiness to help one another, and generosity. **(b)** The old ones in the essay are self-sufficient, strong, wise, and independent. Modern mass media, according to Anaya, create misleading images of "youthful" old people—lively, healthy, pink-cheeked.
3. **(a)** His grandfather was a farmer. **(b)** The author is a writer who has had to assimilate into modern culture. He no longer lives on the land, but he respects the values he learned from his grandfather.
4. **(a)** Anaya's grandfather refers to the present day, when time moves faster and does not allow for patience. **(b)** Anaya implies that the new time will cause people to lose sight of the natural cycles of change.
5. Possible response: **(a)** By ending as the essay began, the essay echoes the natural cycle of life, death, and rebirth. **(b)** Anaya speaks of the cycles of nature, of generations, of his grandfather's life throughout the essay.
6. **(a)** Old people should be treated with great patience and care, because the transformations of age can be painful and damaging. **(b)** Students will probably agree. They may offer their own experiences of seeing or caring for grandparents or other older relatives shortly before their death.

new generation seeks its roots, that value of love for the land moves us to return to the place where our ancianos formed the culture.

I returned to Puerto de Luna last summer, to join the community in a celebration of the founding of the church. I drove by my grandfather's home, my uncles' ranches, the neglected adobe[15] washing down into the earth from whence it came. And I wondered, how might the values of my grandfather's generation live in our own? What can we retain to see us through these hard times? I was to become a farmer, and I became a writer. As I plow and plant my words, do I nurture as my grandfather did in his fields and orchards? The answers are not simple.

"They don't make men like that anymore," is a phrase we hear when one does honor to a man. I am glad I knew my grandfather. I am glad there are still times when I can see him in my dreams, hear him in my reverie. Sometimes I think I catch a whiff of that earthy aroma that was his smell, just as in lonely times sometimes I catch the fragrance of Ultima's herbs. Then I smile. How strong these people were to leave such a lasting impression.

So, as I would greet my abuelo long ago, it would help us all to greet the old ones we know with this kind and respectful greeting: "Buenos días le de Dios."

---

15. **adobe** (ə dō´ bē) *n.* sun-dried clay brick.

Review and Assess

Thinking About the Selection

1. **Respond:** How would you describe the author's attitude toward the "old ones"?
2. **(a) Recall:** What qualities of old people does Anaya remember from his childhood? **(b) Distinguish:** How are these qualities different from the images created by American mass media?
3. **(a) Recall:** What kind of work did Anaya's grandfather do? **(b) Compare and Contrast:** How do the author's work and values differ from those of his grandfather?
4. **(a) Recall:** What is the "new time" that Anaya's grandfather mentions? **(b) Infer:** What does the author imply about this "new time"?
5. **(a) Analyze:** Why do you think the essay ends with the very same words with which it begins? **(b) Support:** Use evidence from the essay to support your view.
6. **(a) Generalize:** What perspective does Anaya offer on the way old people should be treated as they age and die? **(b) Take a Position:** Do you agree with him? Explain.

Rudolfo Anaya

(b. 1937)

Rudolfo Anaya was born in Pastura, New Mexico, and his writing reflects his Mexican American heritage.

Many of his novels, stories, and articles concern the past. His first novel, *Bless Me, Ultima* (1972), was acclaimed for its depiction of the culture and history of New Mexico. Anaya has also published *Heart of Aztlan* (1976) and *Tortuga* (1979).

His essay "A Celebration of Grandfathers" reflects on the "old ones" he remembers from his childhood.

ASSESSMENT PRACTICE: Reading Comprehension

Literary Elements **(For more practice, see Test Preparation Workbook, p. 41.)**

Many tests measure students' ability to describe and analyze literary elements. Use this sample test item.

> She was a small woman, old and wrinkled. When she started washing for us, she was already past seventy. . . . All the old women in our street had bent backs and leaned on sticks when they walked. But this washwoman, small and thin as she was, possessed a strength that came from generations of peasant forebears.

Which literary element is most important to this passage?

A plot
B character
C setting
D theme

The passage only hints at plot, theme, and setting. It describes a character in detail. Therefore, choice *B* is correct.

Review and Assess

Literary Analysis

Essay

1. Using a chart like the one shown, analyze the ideas presented in each of these **essays.**

2. What personal views about life does Singer express in his essay?
3. What are some of the facts and reasons Hansberry presents to persuade you to accept her opinion about summer?
4. Rudolfo Anaya celebrates his grandfather and other "old ones." Which people or things seem, in his view, less worthy of praise?

Comparing Literary Works

5. Which essay is the most **persuasive**?
6. Which essay includes the most **reflections** by the author?
7. Which essay has the strongest emotional effect on the reader? Why?
8. How are the three authors' attitudes toward elderly people similar and different? Cite specific details.

Reading Strategy

Identifying the Author's Attitude

9. Which three adjectives might Singer use to describe his attitude toward the washwoman? Explain your answer.
10. Do you think Anaya could convince others who do not share his background to adopt his attitude? Explain.

Extend Understanding

11. **Cultural Connection:** Are today's elderly treated with what the three authors would consider appropriate respect? Explain.

Quick Review

An **essay** is a short piece of nonfiction in which a writer expresses a personal point of view.

A **narrative essay** tells a story.

A **persuasive essay** tries to convince readers to accept a position or take a course of action.

A **reflective essay** presents a writer's feelings about a topic of personal importance.

The **author's attitude** toward his or her subject colors the presentation of information.

Take It to the Net

www.phschool.com

Take the interactive self-test online to check your understanding of these selections.

Answers for p. 669

Review and Assess

1. "The Washwoman": **Main Idea:** Human pride can resist age and illness. **Key Details:** The aged washwoman is determined to do her job. "On Summer": **Main Idea:** Hansberry comes to see summer as "the noblest of seasons." **Key Details:** As Hansberry grows older, she associates summer with cool nights in the park, her beloved grandmother, and an indomitable old woman in Maine. "A Celebration of Grandfathers": **Main Idea:** Old people deserve respect. **Key Details:** Old people are wise and experienced and have much to teach.
2. He believes that human pride and determination can overcome despair.
3. Hansberry describes happy family times on summer nights and the summer beauty of Tennessee hills and the coast of Maine.
4. People who do not respect one another, people who ignore their elders and their elders' customs, and people who concentrate on material gain do not deserve respect in Anaya's view.
5. **Possible responses:** Students may find Singer's essay to be most persuasive because the washwoman is a focused example that illustrates his point about human dignity and pride.
6. Students may agree Anaya's essay includes the most reflections.
7. Students may connect emotionally with any or all of the essays, depending on events from their own lives.
8. **Similar:** All three describe old people whom they admire and respect. All three describe old people who battle with serious illness. **Different:** Hansberry shows a protective attitude toward her grandmother. Anaya believes that all old people are wise, patient, and enduring, while Singer focuses on just one extraordinary woman.
9. **Sample adjectives:** *enduring, proud, hard-working, patient, determined, courageous.* The washwoman defies age, cold, even deadly illness to do her work.

continued

continued Answers

10. Students may agree that Anaya is convincing because he provides specific examples and relevant anecdotes.
11. Students may agree that the American mass media do not stress respect for the elderly, but this doesn't necessarily reflect how elderly persons may be treated within particular families.

ENRICHMENT: Further Reading

Other Works by the Authors

Works by Isaac Bashevis Singer
Gimpel the Fool and Other Stories

Works by Lorraine Hansberry
A Raisin in the Sun

Works by Rudolfo Anaya
Heart of Aztlan

Take It to the Net

Visit www.phschool.com for more information on the authors.

EXTEND

Answers for p. 670

❶ Vocabulary Development

Word Analysis

1. the front section of a picture
2. to predict
3. planning or thinking ahead

Spelling Strategy

1. boxes
2. fizzes
3. clashes

Sample words from selections: *churches, matches, addresses, beaches.*

Fluency: Word Choice

1. perplexes
2. aloofness
3. forebears
4. rancor
5. epiphany
6. obstinacy
7. pious
8. permeates

❷ Grammar

1. Yesterday I worked, then rested.
2. The woman came early and left late.
3. When Grandmother sings to me I record her.
4. Tomorrow we will travel and visit friends.
5. I ran to greet the wagon, and it stopped.

Writing Application

Possible responses:

1. Yesterday I was working, then resting.
2. The woman comes early and leaves late.
3. When Grandmother sang to me, I recorded her.
4. Tomorrow we will be traveling and visiting friends.
5. I run to greet the wagon and it stops.

Integrate Language Skills

❶ Vocabulary Development Lesson

Word Analysis: Anglo-Saxon Prefix *fore-*

The Anglo-Saxon prefix *fore-* means "before." The prefix appears in the word *forebears,* which means "ancestors" or "those who came before us."

Use the meaning of *fore-* to define each word below.

1. foreground **2.** foresee **3.** forethought

Spelling Strategy

To form the plural (or some verb forms) of words ending in *z, x, sh, ch,* or *s,* add *-es* instead of *-s*. Thus, *perplex* + *-es* = *perplexes*.

Add *-es* to each word below. Then, find four other words in the selections that would follow this rule.

1. box **2.** fizz **3.** clash

Fluency: Word Choice

For each item below, write the word from the vocabulary list on page 649 that best matches each clue.

1. creates confusion
2. the condition of showing disinterest, distance, or uninvolvement
3. one's relatives who lived long ago
4. the opposite of peaceful agreement and harmony
5. a sudden feeling of discovery
6. a quality of donkeys
7. deeply religious
8. what a heavy rain does when it falls on dry soil

❷ Grammar Lesson

Consistency of Verb Tense

A **verb** is a word that expresses an action or a state of being. A verb has various **tenses,** such as past, present, and future. These forms of the verb are used to show the time of the action or condition.

To maintain a **consistency of verb tense,** analyze the verbs in your writing. If you begin a passage in the past tense, for instance, do not suddenly switch to present tense to talk about the past.

Unnecessary Tense Shift: We *paid* the washwoman. She *thanks* us.

Correct: We *paid* the washwoman. She *thanked* us.

Practice Rewrite each pair of sentences to maintain consistency of verb tense.

1. Yesterday I worked. Then, I will rest.
2. The woman comes early. She left late.
3. When Grandmother sings to me, I recorded her.
4. Tomorrow, we will travel and visited friends.
5. I ran to greet the wagon, and the wagon stops.

Writing Application Change the tense of the first verb in each of the practice sentences above, and then adjust the tense of the second verb to match the first.

WG Prentice Hall Writing and Grammar Connection: Chapter 23, Section 1

TEACHING RESOURCES

The following resources can be used to enrich or extend the instruction for pp. 670–671.

Vocabulary

- **Selection Support,** Build Vocabulary, p. 161
- **Vocabulary and Spelling Practice Book** (Use this booklet for skills enrichment.) ■

Grammar

- **Selection Support,** Build Grammar Skills, p 162
- **Writing and Grammar,** Gold Level, p. 526
- **Daily Language Practice Transparencies**

Writing

- **Writing and Grammar,** Gold Level, p. 286 ■
- **Writing and Grammar iText CD-ROM**

■ **BLOCK SCHEDULING:** Resources marked with this symbol provide varied instruction during 90-minute blocks.

❸ Writing Lesson

Essay on Summer

Write an essay that summarizes the ideas Hansberry presents in her essay "On Summer." Provide your own personal connections to agree or disagree with her views.

Prewriting List Hansberry's reflections on summer, and then list personal experiences that connect to the reflection. If you find that you do not connect with her experience, explain why.

Model: Connecting to the Author's Experience

Hansberry's Reflection	My Connection
Sleeping outside on hot summer nights	It reminds me of my camping trips to Vermont.

Drafting As you draft, make sure to support each opinion with a specific example. In the closing paragraph of your essay, state your final views on summer.

Revising Read your draft to a classmate. Ask your classmate if your views on summer are clear. Add any necessary details to strengthen your description of your experiences and to improve your analysis.

WG Prentice Hall Writing and Grammar Connection: Chapter 13, Section 2

❹ Extension Activities

Listening and Speaking To learn more about the authors, watch the movie version of either Lorraine Hansberry's *A Raisin in the Sun* or Isaac B. Singer's *Yentl*. Then, prepare a **movie review** for your classmates.

- Determine what you liked and disliked about the film's acting, directing, and costuming.
- Find any connection between the movie and the author's essay in this book.
- Prepare concise notes to use in an oral presentation of your review.

Later, invite your audience to evaluate the effectiveness of your review. **[Group Activity]**

Research and Technology Conduct an **interview** with an older person whom you know and admire. Find out key details about the person's life and important lessons that he or she has learned. Videotape the interview and share it with your class. After you present the video, compare the elderly person in your interview with the grandfather in "A Celebration of Grandfathers."

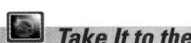

Take It to the Net www.phschool.com

Go online for an additional research activity using the Internet.

ASSESSMENT RESOURCES

The following resources can be used to assess students' knowledge and skills.

Selection Assessment

- **Formal Assessment,** pp. 145–147
- **Open Book Test,** pp. 121–123
- **Got It! Assessment Videotapes,** Tape 4
- **Test Bank Software**

Take It to the Net

Visit www.phschool.com for self-tests and additional questions on the selections.

Listening and Speaking Rubric

- **Performance Assess. and Portfolio Mgmt.,** p. 26

PRENTICE HALL ASSESSMENT SYSTEM

- **Workbook**
- **Skill Book**
- **Transparencies**
- **CD-ROM**

❸ Writing Lesson

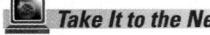

- Explain to students that they are to compare and contrast their own feelings about summer with Hansberry's. The point is not to see whether they have had experiences identical to Hansberry's, but whether they have felt the same way about summer that she feels.
- Remind students to use figurative language appealing to the five senses. Have them look at Hansberry's imagery for ideas.

❹ Research and Technology

- Have students go over the three essays in this group for ideas about the kinds of questions they want to ask.
- Point out that "The Washwoman" and "A Celebration of Grandfathers" both prove that ordinary people can be heroic and fascinating.
- Give students a set time limit, such as half an hour, so that their interviews maintain focus.
- If subjects are unwilling to be interviewed on camera, allow students to tape-record conversations instead.
- Use the Conducting an Interview rubric in **Performance Assessment and Portfolio Management,** p. 26, to evaluate students' interviews.

CUSTOMIZE INSTRUCTION For Universal Access

To address different learning styles, use the following activities suggested in the **Extension Activities** booklet, p. 41.

- For Logical/Mathematical Learners, use Activity 5.
- For Verbal/Linguistic Learners, use Activity 5.
- For Visual/Spatial Learners, use Activity 6.
- For Interpersonal Learners, use Activities 6 and 7.

from A White House Diary ✦ Arthur Ashe Remembered ✦ Georgia O'Keeffe

Lesson Objectives and CA Correlations

1. **To analyze and respond to literary elements**
   - Literary Analysis: Biographical and Autobiographical Writing **R 3.2**
   - Comparing Literary Works
2. **To read, comprehend, analyze, and critique nonfiction**
   - Reading Strategy: Finding the Writer's Main Points and Support
   - Reading Check questions
   - Review and Assess questions
   - Assessment Practice (ATE)
3. **To develop word analysis skills, fluency, and systematic vocabulary**
   - Vocabulary Development Lesson: Latin Root: *-sent-/-sens-* **R 1.1**
4. **To understand and apply written and oral language conventions**
   - Spelling Strategy
   - Grammar Lesson: Subject-Verb Agreement: Confusing Subjects **LC 1.2, 1.3**
5. **To understand and apply appropriate writing and research strategies**
   - Writing Lesson: Awards Speech **W 1.1**
   - Extension Activity: Visual Presentation **W 1.3**
6. **To understand and apply listening and speaking strategies**
   - Extension Activity: Radio News Report **LS 1.4**

STEP-BY-STEP TEACHING GUIDE	PACING GUIDE
PRETEACH	
Motivate Students and Provide Background	
Use the Motivation activity (ATE p. 672)	5 min.
Read and discuss the Preview material and Background information (SE/ATE p. 672) [A]	5 min.
Introduce the Concepts	
Introduce the Literary Analysis and Reading Strategy (SE/ATE p. 673) [A]	15 min.
Pronounce the vocabulary words and read their definitions (SE p. 673)	5 min.
TEACH	
Monitor Comprehension	
Informally monitor comprehension by circulating while students read independently or in groups [A]	25 min.
Monitor students' comprehension with the Reading Check notes (SE/ATE pp. 675, 677, 683, 689)	as students read
Develop vocabulary with Vocabulary notes (SE pp. 676–678, 683, 685–686, 689; ATE p. 687)	as students read
Develop Understanding	
Develop students' understanding of biographical and autobiographical writing with Literary Analysis annotations (SE pp. 675, 686, 689; ATE pp. 676, 678) [A]	10 min.
Develop students' ability to find the writer's main points and support with the Reading Strategy annotations (SE pp. 684, 686; ATE pp. 675, 683, 684, 686)	10 min.
ASSESS	
Assess Mastery	
Assess students' mastery of the Reading Strategy and Literary Analysis by having them answer the Review and Assess questions (SE/ATE p. 691)	20 min.
Use one or more of the print and media Assessment Resources (ATE p. 693) [A]	up to 50 min.
EXTEND	
Apply Understanding	
Have students complete the Vocabulary Development Lesson and the Grammar Lesson (SE p. 692) [A]	20 min.
Apply students' knowledge of smooth transitions using the Writing Lesson (SE/ATE p. 693) [A]	45 min.
Apply students' understanding using one or more of the Extension Activities (SE p. 693)	20–90 min.

A **ACCELERATED INSTRUCTION:** Use the strategies and activities identified with an [A].

UNIVERSAL ACCESS
● = Below-Level Students
▲ = On-Level Students
■ = Above-Level Students

Time and Resource Manager

Reading Level: Easy/Average/Challenging
Average Number of Instructional Days: 4

RESOURCES		
PRINT	**TRANSPARENCIES**	**TECHNOLOGY**
• **Beyond Literature,** Humanities Connection: Personal Courage, p. 42 ▲ ■		• **Interest Grabber Video,** Tape 4 ● ▲ ■
• **Selection Support Workbook:** ● ▲ ■ Literary Analysis, p. 164 Reading Strategy, p. 163 Build Vocabulary, p. 161	• **Literary Analysis and Reading Transparencies,** pp. 83 and 84 ● ▲ ■	
		• **Listening to Literature** ● ▲ ■ Audiocassettes, Sides 25, 26 Audio CDs, CDs 13, 14
• **Literatura en español** ● ▲ • **Literary Analysis for Enrichment** ■		
• **Formal Assessment:** Selection Test, pp. 148–150 ● ▲ ■ • **Open Book Test,** pp. 124–126 ● ▲ ■ • PRENTICE HALL ASSESSMENT SYSTEM ● ▲ ■	• PRENTICE HALL ASSESSMENT SYSTEM ● ▲ ■ Skills Practice Answers and Explanations on Transparencies	• **Test Bank Software** ● ▲ ■ • **Got It! Assessment Videotapes,** Tape 4 ● ▲
• **Selection Support Workbook:** ● ▲ ■ Build Grammar Skills, p.162 • **Writing and Grammar,** Gold Level ● ▲ ■ • **Extension Activities,** p. 42 ● ▲ ■	• **Daily Language Practice Transparencies** ● ▲	• **Writing and Grammar iText CD-ROM** ● ▲ ■ ***Take It to the Net*** www.phschool.com

BLOCK SCHEDULING: Use one 90-minute class period to preteach the selection and have students read it. Use a second 90-minute class period to assess students' mastery of skills and have them complete one of the Extension Activities.

PREACH

Step-by-Step Teaching Guide for pp. 672–673

Motivation

Read this quotation to students: "Suddenly there was a sharp, loud report. It sounded like a shot." Ask students if they have relatives or friends who recall where they were on November 22, 1963, when they heard that the president had been shot. Have them think about how Vice President Lyndon B. Johnson and his wife Lady Bird must have felt that day. Then, have them read the first essay of this selection.

Interest Grabber Video

As an alternative, play "President Kennedy's Assassination" on Tape 4 to engage students' interest.

1 Background

History

Shortly after President Kennedy's assassination, Lee Harvey Oswald, a supporter of Communist Cuba, was arrested for the crime. Two days later, during a transfer between jails, Oswald was fatally shot by a nightclub owner named Jack Ruby, who soon thereafter died of cancer. Neither man lived to stand trial.

Newly sworn-in President Johnson immediately ordered a special investigation into the assassination. The investigating committee was headed by Supreme Court Chief Justice Earl Warren and included future president Gerald Ford among its members. In September 1964, the committee reported to Johnson that it had found no evidence of a conspiracy to assassinate the Kennedy, nor any evidence to connect Oswald to Ruby.

Perhaps because Oswald was never put on trial, some people have refused to accept the conclusions in the report. Conspiracy theories continue to be advanced. However, no person has ever confessed to involvement in such a conspiracy, nor has any other hard evidence contradicted the Warren Commission's conclusions.

Prepare to Read

from A White House Diary ◆ Arthur Ashe Remembered ◆ Georgia O'Keeffe

The White Trumpet Flower, Georgia O'Keeffe, San Diego Museum of Art

Take It to the Net

Visit www.phschool.com for interactive activities and instruction related to the selections, including

- background
- graphic organizers
- literary elements
- reading strategies

Preview

Connecting to the Literature

In the following selections, you will have a rare chance to see the private sides of three famous Americans. As you read, think about how the triumphs and tragedies in your own life have led you to discover what really matters.

1 Background

The assassination of President John F. Kennedy on November 22, 1963, was a stunning and unforgettable event. As the news media reported the tragedy, the United States came to a halt. People wept openly in their homes and in the streets. Kennedy had been a young, vibrant, and popular leader. A mournful nation agreed with his successor, Lyndon Johnson, who said of the assassination, "We have suffered a loss that cannot be weighed."

TEACHING RESOURCES

The following resources can be used to enrich or extend the instruction for pp. 672–673.

Motivation

Interest Grabber Video, Tape 4: President Kennedy's Assassination

Background

Beyond Literature, p. 42

Take It to the Net

Visit www.phschool.com for background and hotlinks for the selections.

Literary Analysis

Literary Analysis and Reading Transparencies, Biographical and Autobiographical Writing, p. 84

Reading

Selection Support: Reading Strategy, p. 163; Build Vocabulary, p. 161

Literary Analysis and Reading Transparencies, Finding the Writer's Main Points and Support, p. 83

BLOCK SCHEDULING: Resources marked with this symbol provide varied instruction during 90-minute blocks.

❷ Literary Analysis

Biographical and Autobiographical Writing

Biographical writing is nonfiction in which a writer tells the story of another person's life. **Autobiographical writing** is nonfiction in which a writer tells the story of his or her own life. This excerpt from *A White House Diary* lets you share Lady Bird Johnson's thoughts and feelings:

> One last happy moment I had was looking up and seeing Mary Griffith leaning out of a window waving at me.

As you read, notice the emotions conveyed through each piece.

Comparing Literary Works

Biographical and autobiographical writing offer readers two distinctly different experiences. The differences in the presentation of views and experiences in each type of writing can influence the way readers interpret the events. Compare the selections and consider how each type of writing influences your attitude toward the person at the center of the work.

❸ Reading Strategy

Finding the Writer's Main Points and Support

A key to understanding biographies and autobiographies is the ability to **find the writer's main points** and the details that **support** those points.

- Read each paragraph to determine the main idea it conveys.
- Locate the facts, events, details, or quotations that elaborate, develop, or support the main idea.
- Once you have finished reading a selection, try to determine the main points of the work as a whole.

Use a chart like the one shown here to help you as you read.

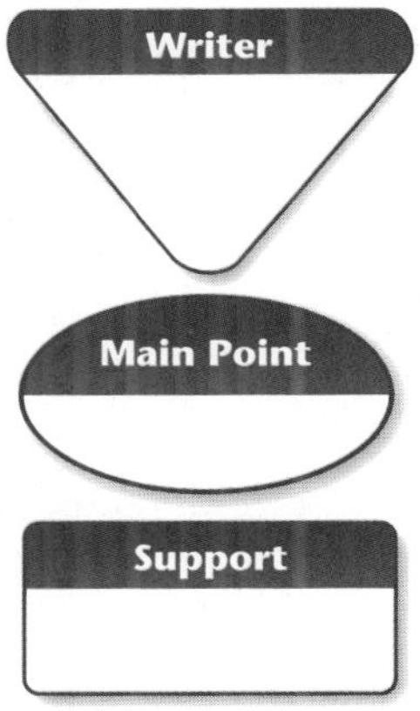

Vocabulary Development

tumultuous (to͞o mul′ cho͞o əs) *adj.* greatly disturbed (p. 676)

implications (im′ pli kā′ shənz) *n.* indirect indications (p. 677)

poignant (poin′ yənt) *adj.* drawing forth pity or compassion (p. 678)

legacy (leg′ ə sē) *n.* anything handed down from an ancestor (p. 683)

enigma (i nig′ mə) *n.* puzzling or baffling matter; riddle (p. 683)

condescending (kän′ di sen′ diŋ) *adj.* characterized by looking down on someone (p. 685)

sentimental (sen′ tə ment′ ′l) *adj.* excessively emotional (p. 686)

genesis (jen′ ə sis) *n.* origin (p. 686)

rancor (raŋ′ kər) *n.* hatred (p. 689)

immutable (im myo͞ot′ ə bəl) *adj.* never changing (p. 689)

CUSTOMIZE INSTRUCTION FOR UNIVERSAL ACCESS

For Less Proficient Readers	For English Learners	For Advanced Readers
Have students identify the main characters of each selection and note what they learn about each character. Have them use this information in a group discussion to identify each essay as the story of the writer, the story of some other character, or the story of both the writer and others.	Share some background information about the people described in these essays before students begin reading; students from other countries may not know any of the names. Help them understand the historical importance of the people about whom they will read.	As students read, have them look for both biographical and autobiographical elements in all three essays. Have them think about and discuss how all biographical writing is also autobiographical and all autobiographical writing is also biographical.

❷ Literary Analysis

Biographical and Autobiographical Writing

- Remind students that an autobiography is the story of the writer's life, and a biography is the story of some other person's life.
- All autobiographies contain biographical elements if they include characters besides the writer. For example, "The Washwoman," p. 650, is autobiographical because it tells about events the writer lived through. It is biographical because its central character is another person, the washwoman.
- Challenge students to brainstorm for a list of various forms of autobiographical writing.
  Answers: Students may cite diaries, personal essays, poems in which the writer is the speaker, and letters telling about oneself.

❸ Reading Strategy

Finding the Writer's Main Points and Support

- Remind students that the *main idea* is the concept that the writer most wants the reader to remember and consider. Writers support their main ideas with facts and details so that readers will find their arguments convincing.
- As students read, they should ask questions. What is the most important point in this paragraph? Which statements support this main idea? How do the main ideas of the individual paragraphs constitute supporting details for the main idea of the entire essay?
- Encourage students to use a chart like the one shown to help them find the writer's main point and support as they read.

Vocabulary Development

- Pronounce each vocabulary word for students, and read the definitions as a class. Have students identify any words with which they are already familiar.

E-Teach

Visit E-Teach at www.phschool.com for teachers' essays on how to teach, with questions and answers.

TEACH

Step-by-Step Teaching Guide for pp. 674–690

CUSTOMIZE INSTRUCTION
For Visual/Spatial Learners

Have students take particular note of the photographs and the reproductions of O'Keeffe's paintings as they read the third essay. Students can discuss the visual impact of the illustrations. How are O'Keeffe's paintings also her autobiography? Have students discuss the information and emotions conveyed by the illustrations.

❶ About the Selection

Lady Bird Johnson recalls the day President John F. Kennedy was shot in Dallas, Texas. Johnson, wife of the vice president, was in Kennedy's motorcade when the shots rang out. She describes the feelings of shock, horror, and helplessness at the event and recalls details of the somber plane flight back to Washington.

❷ ▶Critical Viewing

Answer: The president and first lady are beaming at the crowd. Most people in the crowd are either attentive or smiling. The mood seems cheerful and happy.

from

❶ A White House Diary

Lady Bird Johnson

❷ ▲ **Critical Viewing** What does this photograph reveal about the mood in the moments leading up to the assassination? **[Infer]**

TEACHING RESOURCES

The following resources can be used to enrich or extend the instruction for pp. 674–690.

Literary Analysis

Selection Support: Literary Analysis, p. 164

Reading

Listening to Literature Audiocassettes, Sides 25, 26 ■

Listening to Literature Audio CDs, CDs 13, 14 ■

■ **BLOCK SCHEDULING:** Resources marked with this symbol provide varied instruction during 90-minute blocks.

DALLAS, FRIDAY, NOVEMBER 22, 1963

3 It all began so beautifully. After a drizzle in the morning, the sun came out bright and clear. We were driving into Dallas. In the lead car were President and Mrs. Kennedy, John and Nellie Connally,[1] a Secret Service[2] car full of men, and then our car with Lyndon and me and Senator Ralph Yarborough.

The streets were lined with people—lots and lots of people—the children all smiling, placards, confetti, people waving from windows. One last happy moment I had was looking up and seeing Mary Griffith leaning out of a window waving at me. (Mary for many years had been in charge of altering the clothes which I purchased at Neiman-Marcus.)

Then, almost at the edge of town, on our way to the Trade Mart for the Presidential luncheon, we were rounding a curve, going down a hill, and suddenly there was a sharp, loud report. It sounded like a shot. The sound seemed to me to come from a building on the right above my shoulder. A moment passed, and then two more shots rang out in rapid succession. There had been such a gala air about the day that I thought the noise must come from firecrackers—part of the celebration. Then the Secret Service men were suddenly down in the lead car. Over the car radio system, I heard "Let's get out of here!" and our Secret Service man, Rufus Youngblood, vaulted over the front seat on top of Lyndon, threw him to the floor, and said, "Get down."

4 Senator Yarborough and I ducked our heads. The car accelerated terrifically—faster and faster. Then, suddenly, the brakes were put on so hard that I wondered if we were going to make it as we wheeled left and went around the corner. We pulled up to a building. I looked up and saw a sign, "HOSPITAL." Only then did I believe that this might be what it was. Senator Yarborough kept saying in an excited voice, "Have they shot the President? Have they shot the President?" I said something like, "No, it can't be."

As we ground to a halt—we were still the third car—Secret Service men began to pull, lead, guide, and hustle us out. I cast one last look over my shoulder and saw in the President's car a bundle of pink, just like a drift of blossoms, lying on the back seat. It was Mrs. Kennedy lying over the President's body.

The Secret Service men rushed us to the right, then to the left, and then onward into a quiet room in the hospital—a very small room. It was lined with white sheets, I believe.

People came and went—Kenny O'Donnell, the President's top aide, Congressman Homer Thornberry, Congressman Jack Brooks. Always there was Rufe right there and other Secret Service agents—Emory Roberts, Jerry Kivett, Lem Johns, and Woody Taylor. People spoke of how widespread this might be. There was talk about where we would go—to the plane, to our house, back to Washington.

1. **John and Nellie Connally** John Connally, then Governor of Texas, and his wife, Nellie.
2. **Secret Service** division of the U.S. Treasury Department, responsible for protecting the president.

Literary Analysis
Biographical and Autobiographical Writing Which words in this passage tell you that Johnson's writing is autobiographical?

Literary Analysis
Finding the Writer's Main Points and Support Which details does the writer use to support her main point that she was in disbelief about the shooting?

5 **✓Reading Check**
Where are the Johnsons taken after a shot is heard?

3 Literary Analysis
Biographical and Autobiographical Writing

- Have students read the opening paragraphs of this diary entry. Ask them to identify biographical elements.
  Answer: References to the president and Mrs. Kennedy show that the writer is describing events in the lives of two prominent people. This is biographical writing.
- Ask the Literary Analysis question on p. 675: What words in this passage tell you that Johnson's writing is autobiographical?
  Answer: The sentence "We were driving into Dallas" shows that the writer is describing events in which she participated.

4 Reading Strategy
Finding the Writer's Main Points and Support

- Have students identify the main idea of the essay's opening paragraphs. Have them identify details that support this main idea.
  Answer: The main idea is that the day was a happy occasion. The crowds were cheering, people were waving from windows, the weather was sunny, and Johnson was pleased to see a friend waving to her.
- Ask the Reading Strategy question on p. 675: What details does the writer use to support her main point that she was in disbelief about the shooting?
  Answer: Johnson mentions her thought that it must be fireworks. She also says that only when they drove to the hospital did she believe that the president had been shot, and that even then she says "No, it can't be."

5 ✓Reading Check
Answer: The Johnsons are rushed to the hospital.

CUSTOMIZE INSTRUCTION FOR UNIVERSAL ACCESS

For Special Needs Students	For Gifted/Talented Students
As students read this diary entry, have them identify its characters and setting and note the major events of the narrative. After reading, partners can check that each can accurately summarize the sequence of events. Students can use this exercise as a springboard to a group discussion of why Johnson wrote this diary entry and what makes her perspective historically valuable.	Challenge students to write diary entries discussing the events of the assassination from the point of view of one of the other people—Lyndon Johnson, Mrs. Kennedy, or a Secret Service agent. Students may want to do some further research. Remind them to keep their version of events consistent with what Johnson describes.

6 Background

Social Studies

Make sure students understand that "John" in this paragraph and below refers to Texas Governor John Connally, not President John F. Kennedy. The Johnsons and Connallys were close friends, so the use of the first name is appropriate. No one but a family member, however, would refer to the president of the United States by his first name.

7 Literary Analysis

Biographical and Autobiographical Writing

- Ask students whether the paragraph beginning "I asked the Secret Service . . ." is biographical, autobiographical, or both. Have them explain their answers.
  Answer: It is biographical because it conveys an impression of Mrs. Kennedy at a great crisis of her life. It is autobiographical because Johnson describes her own actions and feelings.
- Have students compare and contrast Johnson's encounter with Mrs. Kennedy and her encounter with Mrs. Connally. Ask what Johnson reveals about herself in these two paragraphs.
  Answer: Johnson doesn't know what to say to Mrs. Kennedy, but she knows just what to say to Mrs. Connally. This suggests that she and Mrs. Kennedy are not close, in contrast to her intimacy with Mrs. Connally.

8 ▶Critical Viewing

You may want to identify the people in the photograph for students. Mrs. Johnson is on the left, Vice President Johnson is in the center with his hand raised, taking the oath of office. Judge Sarah Hughes is facing him with her back to the camera. Mrs. Kennedy is on the right.
Answer: They look solemn and serious. Mrs. Kennedy looks shocked, stunned, and on the verge of tears.

Through it all Lyndon was remarkably calm and quiet. He suggested that the Presidential plane ought to be moved to another part of the field. He spoke of going back out to the plane in unmarked black cars. Every face that came in, you searched for the answer. I think the face I kept seeing the answer on was the face of Kenny O'Donnell, who loved President Kennedy so much.

It was Lyndon who spoke of it first, although I knew I would not leave without doing it. He said, "You had better try to see Jackie and
6 Nellie." We didn't know what had happened to John.

7 I asked the Secret Service if I could be taken to them. They began to lead me up one corridor and down another. Suddenly I found myself face to face with Jackie in a small hallway. I believe it was right outside the operating room. You always think of someone like her as being insulated, protected. She was quite alone. I don't think I ever saw anyone so much alone in my life. I went up to her, put my arms around her, and said something to her. I'm sure it was something like "God, help us all," because my feelings for her were too <u>tumultuous</u> to put into words.

And then I went to see Nellie. There it was different, because Nellie and I have gone through so many things together since 1938. I hugged her tight and we both cried and I said, "Nellie, John's going to be all right." And Nellie said, "Yes, John's going to be all right." Among her many other fine qualities, she is also strong.

I turned and went back to the small white room where Lyndon was. Mac Kilduff, the President's press man on this trip, and Kenny O'Donnell were coming and going. I think it was from Kenny's face that I first knew the truth and from Kenny's voice that I first heard the words "The President is dead." Mr. Kilduff entered and said to Lyndon, "Mr. President."

It was decided that we would go immediately to the airport. Hurried plans were made about how we should get to the cars and who was to ride in which car. Our departure from the hospital and approach to the cars was one of the swiftest walks I have ever made.

We got in. Lyndon told the agents to stop the sirens. We drove along as fast as we could. I looked up at a building and there, already, was a flag at half-mast. I think that was when the enormity of what had happened first struck me.

When we got to the field, we entered *Air Force One*[3] for the first time. There was a TV set on and the commentator was saying, "Lyndon B. Johnson, now President of the United States." The news commentator was saying the President had been shot with a 30-30 rifle. The police had a suspect. They were not sure he was the assassin.

On the plane, all the shades were lowered. We heard that we were going to wait for Mrs. Kennedy and the coffin. There was a telephone

8 ▲ **Critical Viewing**
What do the group's facial expressions reveal about their feelings following President Kennedy's assassination? **[Infer]**

tumultuous (to͞o mul′ cho͞o əs) *adj.* greatly disturbed

3. ***Air Force One*** name of the airplane officially assigned to transport the president of the United States.

ENRICHMENT: History Connection

The Johnson Administration

Lady Bird Johnson begins her diary of the Johnson administration with the November 22, 1963 entry. Her purpose, she explained in her introduction, was to share with the world the point of view of the nation's first lady about important events. The diary ends on January 20, 1969, the inauguration day of Richard Nixon and the day the Johnsons left Washington. Johnson originally recorded the entire diary on cassette tapes, sometimes a week after the events described. She used memoranda, schedules, and newspaper headlines to refresh her memory of events. "The diary is throughout completely personal and subjective," she wrote. "It is the way I saw and lived these events and knew these people."

9 call to Washington—I believe to the Attorney General.[4] It was decided that Lyndon should be sworn in here as quickly as possible, because of national and world implications, and because we did not know how widespread this was as to intended victims. Judge Sarah Hughes, a Federal Judge in Dallas—and I am glad it was she—was called and asked to come in a hurry to administer the oath.

4. **Attorney General** chief law officer of the nation, head of the U.S. Department of Justice; at the time, the position was held by Robert Kennedy, the president's brother.

implications (im′ pli kā′ shənz) *n.* indirect indications

10 **Reading Check**

Why is it decided that Lyndon Johnson needs to be sworn in as soon as possible?

9 Background

History

The attorney general was Robert F. Kennedy, President Kennedy's younger brother. This was the first time in history that a president's sibling held a Cabinet office. Robert Kennedy was his brother's most trusted adviser. He was largely responsible for the peaceful conclusion of the Cuban Missile Crisis of October 1962. Robert Kennedy served as President Johnson's attorney general until the end of 1964.

In 1968, Robert F. Kennedy ran for president of the United States. He was shot and killed by Sirhan Sirhan in Los Angeles during a June campaign appearance.

10 Reading Check

Answer: Johnson must be sworn in quickly because the country has to have a president and the extent of the threat to the country was not known.

⓫ Literary Analysis

Biographical and Autobiographical Writing

- Ask students to identify the biographical and autobiographical elements in this passage.
  Answer: Biographical elements include the report of Mrs. Kennedy's words and actions, the description of her clothing, and the writer's interpretation of her state of mind. Autobiographical elements include Mrs. Johnson's description of her own actions and thoughts.
- Tell students that Mrs. Kennedy was famous for her style and her elegant clothing and appearance. Ask them to give their impressions of this biographical detail of her refusal to change her bloodstained clothes.
  Answer: The image is powerful, showing the depth of Mrs. Kennedy's shock, grief, and anger. The anecdote tells the reader that Mrs. Kennedy must have had tremendous strength of will and determination.

⓬ ▶ Critical Viewing

Answer: Johnson may be concerned about the various problems he will now have to solve.

Mrs. Kennedy had arrived by this time, as had the coffin. There, in the very narrow confines of the plane—with Jackie standing by Lyndon, her hair falling in her face but very composed, with me beside him, Judge Hughes in front of him, and a cluster of Secret Service people, staff, and Congressmen we had known for a long time around him—Lyndon took the oath of office.

It's odd the little things that come to your mind at times of utmost stress, the flashes of deep compassion you feel for people who are really not at the center of the tragedy. I heard a Secret Service man say in the most desolate voice—and I hurt for him: "We never lost a President in the Service." Then, Police Chief Curry of Dallas came on the plane and said, "Mrs. Kennedy, believe me, we did everything we possibly could." That must have been an agonizing moment for him.

⓫ We all sat around the plane. The casket was in the corridor. I went in the small private room to see Mrs. Kennedy, and though it was a very hard thing to do, she made it as easy as possible. She said things like, "Oh, Lady Bird, we've liked you two so much. . . . Oh, what if I had not been there. I'm so glad I was there."

I looked at her. Mrs. Kennedy's dress was stained with blood. One leg was almost entirely covered with it and her right glove was caked, it was caked with blood—her husband's blood. Somehow that was one of the most poignant sights—that immaculate woman exquisitely dressed, and caked in blood.

I asked her if I couldn't get someone in to help her change and she said, "Oh, no. Perhaps later I'll ask Mary Gallagher but not right now." And then with almost an element of fierceness—if a person that

⓬ ▲ **Critical Viewing** This photograph shows Lyndon Johnson beginning to assume his duties as president. Based on the details in the photo, how do you think he felt at that time? Why? **[Analyze]**

poignant (poin´ yənt) *adj.* drawing forth pity or compassion

ENRICHMENT: History Connection

The Kennedy Funeral

President Kennedy is buried at Arlington National Cemetery. This cemetery for the war dead is on the former Custis-Lee estate in Arlington, Virginia. On the day he was buried, a great funeral procession wound its way through the streets of Washington, D.C. Mourners lined the sidewalks, watching in silence as a riderless black horse brought up the rear of the procession. Mrs. Kennedy had set her personal grief aside to plan every aspect of the procession. Dressed in black with a heavy veil over her face, she held her two children by the hand and watched the procession pass. Prompted by a whisper from his mother, two-year-old John F. Kennedy, Jr. stepped forward and saluted as his father's coffin passed.

gentle, that dignified, can be said to have such a quality—she said, "I want them to see what they have done to Jack."

I tried to express how we felt. I said, "Oh, Mrs. Kennedy, you know we never even wanted to be Vice President and now, dear God, it's come to this." I would have done anything to help her, but there was nothing I could do, so rather quickly I left and went back to the main part of the airplane where everyone was seated.

The flight to Washington was silent, each sitting with his own thoughts. One of mine was a recollection of what I had said about Lyndon a long time ago—he's a good man in a tight spot. I remembered one little thing he had said in that hospital room—"Tell the children to get a Secret Service man with them."

Finally we got to Washington, with a cluster of people waiting and many bright lights. The casket went off first, then Mrs. Kennedy, and then we followed. The family had come to join her. Lyndon made a very simple, very brief, and, I think, strong statement to the people there. Only about four sentences. We got in helicopters, dropped him off at the White House, and I came home in a car with Liz Carpenter.[5]

5. Liz Carpenter Mrs. Johnson's press secretary.

Lady Bird Johnson

(b. 1912)

Texas-born Claudia Alta Taylor received her nickname at age two, when a nurse said she was as pretty as a lady bird. In 1934, she married Lyndon Johnson, then a congressional secretary. Throughout her husband's political career, Lady Bird was a most valued advisor and campaigner.

On November 22, 1963, after President John F. Kennedy was killed by an assassin in Dallas, Texas, Lady Bird Johnson became First Lady of the United States. Aboard *Air Force One*, the president's airplane, Vice President Johnson took the oath of office to become the thirty-sixth president of the United States. On his left stood Kennedy's widow, Jackie, her clothing still spattered with her husband's blood. On his right stood his wife, Lady Bird.

Review and Assess

Thinking About the Selection

1. **Respond:** What do you admire most about Lady Bird Johnson? Why?
2. **(a) Recall:** What are the writer's thoughts about Mrs. Kennedy at the hospital? **(b) Deduce:** In what ways is Mrs. Kennedy alone?
3. **(a) Recall:** What is the most noticeable aspect of Mrs. Kennedy's appearance when Mrs. Johnson speaks with her on *Air Force One*? **(b) Interpret:** In what way is wearing the clothing a tribute to her husband?
4. **(a) Recall:** Where does Lyndon Johnson take the oath of office? **(b) Support:** Which details from the text indicate that the Johnsons are up to the tasks before them?
5. **(a) Recall:** How does Mrs. Kennedy behave after the death of her husband? **(b) Compare and Contrast:** What similarities do you find between Mrs. Kennedy and Mrs. Johnson? Explain your answer.
6. **Assess:** Why might a diary entry be an effective way for a person to grieve and cope with a tragic event?

Answers for p. 679

Review and Assess

1. Possible response: Her great sympathy for other people's feelings is her best quality. She is aware of the grief of everyone around her and tries to help them all.
2. **(a)** Johnson thinks she has never seen anyone so alone. **(b)** She is physically alone in the hallway; she has lost her husband; none of her family is present; the people around her are not personal friends.
3. **(a)** She is spattered with blood from the shooting; she has not changed her clothes. **(b)** She wants the nation to see the stark evidence of the brutality of the assassination.
4. **(a)** Lyndon Johnson takes the oath on *Air Force One*. **(b)** Mrs. Johnson says that her husband is "a good man in a tight spot." Even in the emergency he remembers to ensure Secret Service protection for his children. Johnson herself is calm and helpful throughout the ordeal.
5. **(a)** She remains outwardly calm, composed, and gracious to others. **(b)** Both are capable of great self-control; both think of other people first.
6. Students may say that a diary entry is an effective, private place to express powerful emotions and personal thoughts.

Lesson Objectives

1. To understand the connection between Lady Bird Johnson, Eleanor Roosevelt, and Mamie Eisenhower
2. To explore the different roles of first ladies

Connections

Each first lady has played a unique role in the history of the United States. Some first ladies preferred to stay behind the scenes, while others stepped to the forefront of social action. Have students reread the excerpt from Lady Bird Johnson's *A White House Diary* after they read about Eleanor Roosevelt and Mamie Eisenhower. What similarities and differences can students see among the three first ladies?

The Role of the First Lady

- Tell students that the role of the First Lady of the United States changes with each administration.
- Ask students to name three ways in which Eleanor Roosevelt was socially active.
  Possible answers: Mrs. Roosevelt went on fact-finding tours for her husband, gave speeches to the poor during the Great Depression, and traveled around the world working for young people and minority groups.
- Then, ask students to describe Mamie Eisenhower's role as first lady.
  Answer: Mrs. Eisenhower rarely spoke out on social issues. Instead, she worked hard to make visitors from the United States and abroad feel welcome in the White House.

CONNECTIONS
Literature and Social Studies
The Role of the First Lady

The excerpt from *A White House Diary* by Lady Bird Johnson offers a keen insight into the kinds of pressures and responsibilities that a president's spouse can face. Despite these pressures, first ladies often carve out their own niches by advancing special causes. Johnson went on to become a respected advocate for natural resource conservation. Throughout our nation's history, first ladies have applied their own style and personalities to the ways in which they defined and carried out their duties as the wife of the president.

Eleanor Roosevelt: Social Activist

Eleanor Roosevelt was married to Franklin D. Roosevelt, president of the United States from 1933 to 1945. During her years in the White House, Mrs. Roosevelt became the most socially active first lady in American history. Because of her husband's physical restrictions due to polio, Mrs. Roosevelt often went on fact-finding tours on his behalf. During the Depression, she spoke in cities across America to bring hope to the poor and desperate. She also traveled to Europe, Latin America, and many other parts of the world, working for young people and minority groups. Privately, Mrs. Roosevelt urged her husband to take stronger actions on social problems like racial inequality. She raised money for humanitarian causes by writing magazine articles and a daily newspaper column. During World War II, she visited American troops overseas.

©White House Collection, Courtesy White House Historical Association

Roosevelt's Legacy

Roosevelt's activism inspired a more recent first lady, Hillary Clinton. When Mrs. Clinton worked on issues ranging from health care to children's welfare, she explicitly mentioned her debt to Mrs. Roosevelt in redefining the role of first lady. Like Mrs. Roosevelt, who went on to become a United Nations delegate, Mrs. Clinton also took on a high visibility, post-White House career—as a United States senator representing New York.

ENRICHMENT: History

The Assassination of John F. Kennedy

Many Americans remember vividly November 22, 1963, the day President John F. Kennedy was assassinated. Even later generations have read stories and seen movies and television coverage of this tragic event. The stunned nation shared the feelings of newly sworn-in President Lyndon Johnson when he said, "This is a sad time for all people. We have suffered a loss that cannot be weighed. For me, it is a deep personal tragedy."

Mamie Eisenhower: Hostess and Housewife

Mamie Eisenhower was married to Dwight D. Eisenhower, president of the United States from 1953 to 1961. Mrs. Eisenhower defined her role in the White House primarily as a popular hostess. As a result of increased air travel in the 1950s, the Eisenhowers entertained more state and foreign leaders than any previous presidential couple. Beloved for her unpretentious yet dignified style, Mrs. Eisenhower personally greeted thousands of tourists at the White House. The American public regarded her as the ideal American woman of the 1950s. She described herself as "perfectly satisfied as a housewife," and served as an inspiration to homemakers across the country who felt she reflected their own values.

Eisenhower's Legacy

When emotional issues, such as school desegregation, were on people's minds, Mrs. Eisenhower largely refrained from taking public positions. On the rare occasions when she did speak out, she did so with gracious impartiality. In the 1952 election, for instance, she urged Americans to vote, even if they chose to vote for her husband's opponent, Adlai Stevenson. Her legacy can be seen in the highly visible roles that subsequent first ladies have assumed in serving as coordinators of White House social and diplomatic events.

Connecting Literature and Social Studies

1. Based on these descriptions, how did Eleanor Roosevelt and Mamie Eisenhower view their role as first lady?
2. Which first lady defined her role similarly to Lady Bird Johnson? Why?
3. What type of first lady would appeal to most Americans today? Explain your opinion.

Answers

Connecting Literature and Social Studies

1. Eleanor Roosevelt viewed her role as an outspoken ambassador, while Mamie Eisenhower saw herself primarily as a hostess and housewife.
2. Eleanor Roosevelt and Lady Bird Johnson defined similar roles for themselves—as representatives of social causes.
3. Students may answer that a first lady who thinks for herself and has courage to fulfill her role in the way she sees best would appeal to most Americans today.

⓭ About the Selection

John McPhee recalls American tennis champion Arthur Ashe as a cool, self-controlled player who always took risks on the court.

⓮ Background

Sports

Arthur Ashe began playing tennis in a neighborhood park at the age of seven. As the first African American man to achieve greatness in the sport of tennis, Ashe created history with virtually every championship he won (including the 1968 U.S. Open that John McPhee celebrated in his book *Levels of the Game*). The crowning achievement of his tennis career was winning the Wimbledon singles championship in 1975. Throughout his life, Ashe used his prominence as an athlete in the service of many causes—including campaigns against racial prejudice, apartheid in South Africa, and AIDS. Ashe's career was cut short by heart problems. He later contracted AIDS from a transfusion during by-pass surgery.

⓮

ENRICHMENT: Literature Connection

Literary Criticism

In his introduction to *The John McPhee Reader,* William L. Howarth comments, "A reviewer once suggested that some of McPhee's early books made too much of their 'heroes,' or main characters. The charge oversimplifies his idea of character; it also ignores some of his fundamental values. . . . If he really worshipped heroes they would seem identical, a mere series of stereotypes. But McPhee has actually described many types of 'heroes,' and the types have grown more complex with each new book." Read Howarth's comment to students. Then, have students discuss how his remarks might be applied to McPhee's description of Arthur Ashe. Have students write a journal entry in which they answer the following question: Do you agree with the reviewer or with Howarth? Support your answer with details from the text.

Arthur Ashe Remembered

13

John McPhee

He once described his life as "a succession of fortunate circumstances." He was in his twenties then. More than half of his life was behind him. His memory of his mother was confined to a single image: in a blue corduroy bathrobe she stood in a doorway looking out on the courts and playing fields surrounding their house, which stood in the center of a Richmond playground. Weakened by illness, she was taken to a hospital that day, and died at the age of twenty-seven. He was six.

It was to be his tragedy, as the world knows, that he would leave his own child when she was six, that his life would be trapped in a medical irony as a result of early heart disease, and death would come to him prematurely, as it had to his mother.

His mother was tall, with long soft hair and a face that was gentle and thin. She read a lot. She read a lot to him. His father said of her, "She was just like Arthur Junior. She never argued. She was quiet, easygoing, kindhearted."

15 If by legacy her son never argued, he was also schooled, instructed, coached not to argue, and as he moved alone into alien country he fashioned not-arguing into an enigma and turned the enigma into a weapon. When things got tough (as I noted in these pages twenty-four years ago[1]), he had control. Even in very tight moments, other players thought he was toying with them. They rarely knew what he was thinking. They could not tell if he was angry. It was maddening, sometimes, to play against him. Never less than candid, he said that what he liked best about himself on a tennis court was his demeanor: "What it is is controlled cool, in a way. Always have the situation under control, even if losing. Never betray an inward sense of defeat."

legacy (leg´ ə sē) *n.* anything handed down from an ancestor

enigma (i nig´ mə) *n.* puzzling or baffling matter; riddle

1. **twenty-four years ago** McPhee refers to an article published in 1969.

16 ◀ **Critical Viewing** In 1975, Arthur Ashe won the men's singles championship at Wimbledon. What do you think is going through his mind as he displays his trophy? **[Speculate]**

17 **✓Reading Check**

What happens to Ashe's mother at the age of twenty-seven?

15 Reading Strategy

Finding the Writer's Main Points and Support

- Have students identify the main point McPhee makes about Arthur Ashe in this passage.
  Answer: Ashe was strong because he was self-controlled.
- Then, have students identify details that support this argument.
  Answer: Ashe was brought up not to argue. Other tennis players never knew what he was thinking because he would not lose his temper.

16 ▶Critical Viewing

Answer: Ashe is probably excited, proud, and happy.

17 ✓Reading Check

Answer: Ashe's mother dies.

CUSTOMIZE INSTRUCTION FOR UNIVERSAL ACCESS

For English Learners	For Advanced Readers
Encourage students who play tennis or who follow the sport to explain the meaning of the tennis terms in the second half of the essay. These students can demonstrate various strokes (such as lob and volley) and help others understand how McPhee uses the way Ashe played tennis as a metaphor for the way he lived.	Throughout the second half of his essay, McPhee uses an extended metaphor as he compares Ashe's tennis game to the way he lived. Have students analyze this metaphor in detail. They can consult reference books on tennis or friends who play the game if they don't understand all the tennis vocabulary. Have students discuss whether they think this is an appropriate metaphor for Ashe, and whether they think McPhee's use of it is successful.

18 Reading Strategy

Finding the Writer's Main Points and Support

- Have students summarize this long paragraph in one sentence. Possible answer: Ashe always had the confidence to attempt the impossible.
- Ask the Reading Strategy question on p. 684: What is the writer's main point in this paragraph? Answer: He argues that Ashe was courageous and daring and that his impassive, "unreadable" behavior made him a more effective player.

Answers for p. 684

Review and Assess

1. Students may report feelings of respect, interest, admiration, and curiosity.
2. **(a)** Ashe called his life a succession of fortunate circumstances. **(b)** He died young under tragic circumstances.
3. **(a)** Ashe used "controlled cool," refusing to argue or show any temper or emotion. **(b)** Opponents thought he didn't take them seriously; they thought he didn't care about the game because he showed no feelings.
4. **(a)** LIke his mother, Ashe was quiet, easygoing, and kind-hearted; he never argued. **(b)** Ashe likes the fact that he keeps control and never betrays "an inward sense of defeat." **(c)** Ashe was self-controlled, dignified, enigmatic, and unpredictable.
5. **(a)** Ashe's shots on the court were unpredictable and daring; his demeanor was always controlled. In life, too, Ashe was daring, and he never gave way to that "sense of defeat." **(b)** People should do what is necessary in difficult life situations, even if risk or hardship is involved.

And of course he never did—not in the height of his athletic power, not in the statesmanship of the years that followed, and not in the endgame of his existence. If you wished to choose a single image, you would see him standing there in his twenties, his lithe body a braid of cables, his energy without apparent limit, in a court situation indescribably bad, and all he does is put his index finger on the bridge of his glasses and push them back up the bridge of his nose. In the shadow of disaster, he hits out. Faced with a choice between a conservative, percentage return or a one-in-ten flat-out blast, he chooses the blast. In a signature manner, he extends his left arm to point upward at lobs as they fall toward him. His overheads, in fire bursts, put them away. 18 His backhand is, if anything, stronger than his forehand, and his shots from either side for the most part are explosions. In motions graceful and decisive, though, and with reactions as fast as the imagination, he is a master of drop shots, of cat-and-mouse, of miscellaneous dinks and chips and (riskiest of all) the crosscourt half-volley. Other tennis players might be wondering who in his right mind would attempt something like that, but that is how Ashe plays the game: at the tensest moment, he goes for the all but impossible. He is predictably unpredictable. He is unreadable. His ballistic serves move in odd patterns and come off the court in unexpected ways. Behind his impassive face—behind the enigmatic glasses, the lifted chin, the first-mate-on-the-bridge look—there seems to be, even from this distance, a smile.

Reading Strategy
Finding the Writer's Main Points and Support What is the writer's main point in this paragraph?

Review and Assess

Thinking About the Selection

1. **Respond:** After reading this selection, what are your feelings about Arthur Ashe? Why?
2. **(a) Recall:** How did Ashe once describe his life? **(b) Connect:** What later proved to be tragically ironic about this statement?
3. **(a) Recall:** Which "weapon" did Ashe use against opponents on the court? **(b) Interpret:** Why did Ashe's opponents often think he was toying with them?
4. **(a) Recall:** According to his father, how was Ashe like his mother? **(b) Recall:** What does Ashe say he likes best about himself on the court? **(c) Draw Conclusions:** Based on this article, how would you describe Ashe's character?
5. **(a) Connect:** Use examples to show how the writer uses the way Arthur Ashe played tennis to illustrate how Ashe lived life. **(b) Apply:** How can one aspect of Ashe's approach to tennis—going for the difficult shot when in trouble—be applied as an approach to life?

John McPhee

(b. 1931)

After graduating from Princeton University, John McPhee worked at *Time* magazine and then at *The New Yorker*. McPhee has written many nonfiction books and essays.

McPhee has found success in writing about topics that fascinate him. One such subject is sports. In his book *Levels of the Game* (1969), an account of the 1968 U.S. Open Tennis Championship, McPhee reveals his admiration for Arthur Ashe.

20

The White Trumpet Flower, Georgia O'Keeffe, San Diego Museum of Art

19

Georgia O'Keeffe

Joan Didion

"Where I was born and where and how I have lived is unimportant," Georgia O'Keeffe told us in the book of paintings and words published in her ninetieth year on earth. She seemed to be advising us to forget the beautiful face in the Stieglitz[1] photographs. She appeared to be dismissing the rather condescending romance that had attached to her by then, the romance of extreme good looks and advanced age and deliberate isolation. "It is what I have done with where I have been that should be

21 ▲ **Critical Viewing**
What can you guess about the personality of the artist from her work? **[Deduce]**

condescending (kän′ di sen′ diŋ) *adj.* characterized by looking down on someone

1. **Stieglitz** (stēg′ lits) Alfred Stieglitz (1864–1946); U.S. photographer and husband of Georgia O'Keeffe.

19 About the Selection

This biographical essay on Georgia O'Keeffe analyzes her character and her work. O'Keeffe is portrayed as a hard person and a "straight shooter" who is determined to paint her own vision in spite of art-world criticism.

20 Background

Art

The White Trumpet Flower, by Georgia O'Keeffe

Georgia O'Keeffe's many paintings of flowers were heavily influenced by the motifs of the Art Nouveau design that prevailed throughout the 1910s and early 1920s. Curves, swirls, spirals, and arabesques are the hallmarks of Art Nouveau design, and O'Keeffe's flowers reflect these patterns. Use these questions for discussion:

1. What do you notice about this flower that you might not notice in a real flower in nature?
   Possible responses: Details, such as various flower parts, are noticeable in this large painting. These details may be too small to notice in a real flower, unless one looked at it very closely.
2. Describe the mood of this painting. What gives it that mood?
   Possible response: The mood seems triumphant. The flower almost seems to blare open like a trumpet.

21 ▶Critical Viewing

Possible responses: Students might deduce that O'Keeffe is bold, assertive, confident, and energetic.

CUSTOMIZE INSTRUCTION FOR UNIVERSAL ACCESS

For Gifted/Talented Students

Have students study and interpret O'Keeffe's paintings in light of this essay. They can begin with the three paintings used to illustrate these pages, then look for further reproductions in the library, in a local museum, or on the Internet. Have students read the many O'Keeffe quotations in the essay and write brief essays comparing their impressions of her painting with her own statements about her work. Suggest to them that O'Keeffe's paintings are an autobiography. Have them think about and react to your suggestion.

22 Literary Analysis

Biographical and Autobiographical Writing

- Point out that biographical writing can have autobiographical elements. Ask the Literary Analysis question on p. 686: How does the author personalize her biographical writing about O'Keeffe?
  Answer: She describes the impact O'Keeffe's work had on her own daughter.
- Ask students what the writer reveals about herself in the paragraph beginning "My daughter . . ."
  Answer: Didion reveals that she admires O'Keeffe and that she believes that all artists put their own personal stamp on the paintings, books, or poems they create.
- As students continue reading, have them think about what this essay reveals not only about the subject but also about the writer. Remind them of Didion's point in this paragraph: "Style is character."

23 Reading Strategy

Finding the Writer's Main Points and Support

- Ask the Reading Strategy question on p. 686: What is the writer's main point in this paragraph?
  Answer: Her main point is that Georgia O'Keeffe is "hard"—that she doesn't make artistic compromises.
- Ask students to categorize the details that support the writer's point.
  Answer: Almost all the details in the passage are quotations of O'Keeffe's own words. O'Keeffe says that creators must show courage, and she criticizes a contemporary as "dreamy." She paints what she wants without worrying whether it will "touch everyone's heart."

of interest." I recall an August afternoon in Chicago in 1973 when I took my daughter, then seven, to see what Georgia O'Keeffe had done with where she had been. One of the vast O'Keeffe "Sky Above Clouds" canvases floated over the back stairs in the Chicago Art Institute that day, dominating what seemed to be several stories of empty light, and my daughter looked at it once, ran to the landing, and kept on looking. "Who drew it," she whispered after a while. I told her. "I need to talk to her," she said finally.

22 My daughter was making, that day in Chicago, an entirely unconscious but quite basic assumption about people and the work they do. She was assuming that the glory she saw in the work reflected a glory in its maker, that the painting was the painter as the poem is the poet, that every choice one made alone—every word chosen or rejected, every brush stroke laid or not laid down—betrayed one's character. *Style is character.* It seemed to me that afternoon that I had rarely seen so instinctive an application of this familiar principle, and I recall being pleased not only that my daughter responded to style as character but that it was Georgia O'Keeffe's particular style to which she responded: this was a hard woman who had imposed her 192 square feet of clouds on Chicago.

23 "Hardness" has not been in our century a quality much admired in women, nor in the past twenty years has it even been in official favor for men. When hardness surfaces in the very old we tend to transform it into "crustiness" or eccentricity, some tonic pepperiness to be indulged at a distance. On the evidence of her work and what she has said about it, Georgia O'Keeffe is neither "crusty" nor eccentric. She is simply hard, a straight shooter, a woman clean of received wisdom and open to what she sees. This is a woman who could early on dismiss most of her contemporaries as "dreamy," and would later single out one she liked as "a very poor painter." (And then add, apparently by way of softening the judgment: "I guess he wasn't a painter at all. He had no courage and I believe that to create one's own world in any of the arts takes courage.") This is a woman who in 1939 could
24 advise her admirers that they were missing her point, that their appreciation of her famous flowers was merely sentimental. "When I paint a red hill," she observed coolly in the catalogue for an exhibition that year, "you say it is too bad that I don't always paint flowers. A flower touches almost everyone's heart. A red hill doesn't touch everyone's heart." This is a woman who could describe the genesis of one of her most well-known paintings—the "Cow's Skull: Red, White and Blue" owned by the Metropolitan[2]—as an act of quite deliberate and derisive orneriness. "I thought of the city men I had been seeing in the East," she wrote. "They talked so often of writing the Great American Novel—the Great American Play—the Great American Poetry. . . . So as I was painting my cow's head on blue I thought to

Literary Analysis
Biographical and Autobiographical Writing How does the author personalize her biographical writing about O'Keeffe?

Reading Strategy
Finding the Writer's Main Points and Support What is the writer's main point in this paragraph?

sentimental (sen´ tə ment´ 'l) *adj.* excessively emotional

genesis (jen´ ə sis) *n.* origin

2. **Metropolitan** Metropolitan Museum of Art in New York City.

ENRICHMENT: Fine Arts Connection

Alfred Stieglitz

"The Stieglitz photographs" to which Didion refers on p. 685 are the result of a famous collaboration between an artist and his model. Over the course of twenty years, Stieglitz took hundreds of photographs of O'Keeffe, who became his wife in 1924. This series of portraits, now in the collections of America's major museums, is perhaps his most famous and finest work and forms a unique biography of O'Keeffe. Stieglitz and O'Keeffe met in 1916 when he first saw some of her paintings. From 1918 until his death in 1946, he exhibited her work regularly in his New York gallery, thus ensuring that it would be seen and noticed by both art lovers and critics.

25

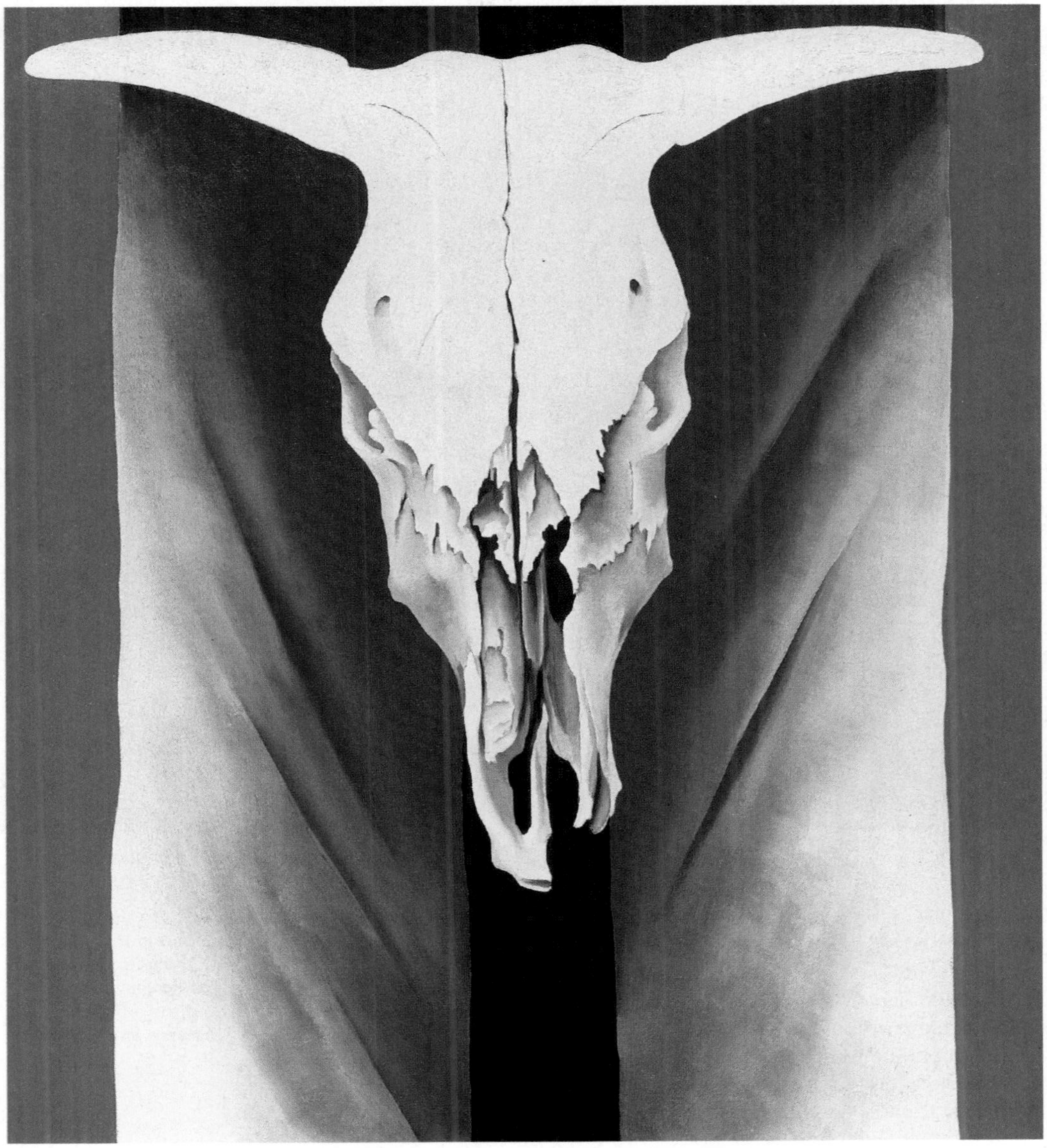

Cow's Skull: Red, White, and Blue, Georgia O'Keeffe, The Metropolitan Museum of Art

26 ▲ **Critical Viewing** What information in the text helps you understand this painting better? **[Connect]**

24 Vocabulary Development

Latin Root *-sent-*

- Write the word *sentimental* on the board. Tell students that the Latin root *-sent-* means "feeling." *Sentimental* means "excessively emotional." *Sentimentalizing* (on p. 688) means "being emotional about" or "indulging in feelings."
- Have students identify other words containing this Latin root and provide definitions for them.
  Possible responses: *sensitive:* "keen capacity for feeling"; *senseless:* "unconscious; unable to feel"; *sensational:* "extremely exciting."

25 Background

Art

Cow's Skull: Red, White, and Blue, by Georgia O'Keeffe

Explain that the Southwestern deserts, where O'Keeffe spent much of her career, are dotted here and there with the skulls and bones of cattle. Such an object is a familiar sight to any Southwesterner. O'Keeffe often painted these skulls, bleached white by the sun. Draw attention to the place in the text (bottom of p. 686) where Didion discusses O'Keeffe's explanation of this painting. Use the following question for discussion:

- Which elements in this painting might symbolize America?
  Answer: Students may cite the red, white, and blue colors and the cow's skull that is a common sight in the Southwest.

26 ▶Critical Viewing

Answer: In the text, O'Keeffe is quoted saying, "I'll make it an American painting," in response to "city men" who boasted of creating American novels, plays, and poetry. Didion says that O'Keeffe painted it to be "ornery."

CUSTOMIZE INSTRUCTION FOR UNIVERSAL ACCESS

For Advanced Readers

Have students read the sentence from O'Keeffe's writing quoted on this page: "I made you take time to look at what I saw and when you took time to really notice my flower you hung all your associations with flowers on my flower and you write about my flower as if I think and see what you think and see—and I don't." Have students analyze the style of this sentence and discuss what they think O'Keeffe's writing style says about her character. First, have students come to a consensus on what O'Keeffe is saying. Then, have them discuss the style and tone of her language. Have them consider word choice, punctuation (and lack of it), repetition, tone, and so on.

27 Background

Art

The Lawrence Tree, by Georgia O'Keeffe

O'Keeffe reveals her very personal experience through this painting. She says: "I spent several weeks up at the Lawrence ranch. There was a long weathered carpenter's bench under the tall tree in front of the little old house that Lawrence had lived in there. I often lay on that bench looking up into that tree—past the trunk and up into the branches. It was particularly fine at night with the stars above the trees." Use the following question for discussion:

- What is O'Keeffe saying about nature in this work?
  Possible response: Her message seems to be that nature is lofty and that its grandness and majesty dwarf people on Earth.

28 ▶ Critical Viewing

Possible response: The painting of the flower is realistic—almost superrealistic. It is larger than life and almost "in your face." The painting of the tree is less detailed—it shows a trunk and branches and solid dark green, not individual leaves. This painting creates a feeling of the vastness of nature and the universe, perhaps also a sense of awe.

27

The Lawrence Tree, 1929, Georgia O'Keeffe, Wadsworth Atheneum, Hartford

myself, 'I'll make it an American painting. They will not think it great with the red stripes down the sides—Red, White and Blue—but they will notice it.'"

The city men. The men. They. The words crop up again and again as this astonishingly aggressive woman tells us what was on her mind when she was making her astonishingly aggressive paintings. It was those city men who stood accused of sentimentalizing her flowers: "I made you take time to look at what I saw and when you took time to really notice my flower you hung all your associations with flowers on my flower and you write about my flower as if I

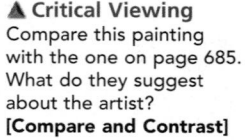

28 ▲ **Critical Viewing**
Compare this painting with the one on page 685. What do they suggest about the artist?
[Compare and Contrast]

think and see what you think and see—and I don't." *And I don't.* Imagine those words spoken, and the sound you hear is *don't tread on me.*[3] "The men" believed it impossible to paint New York, so Georgia O'Keeffe painted New York. "The men" didn't think much of her bright color, so she made it brighter. The men yearned toward Europe so she went to Texas, and then New Mexico. The men talked about Cézanne,[4] "long involved remarks about the 'plastic quality' of his form and color," and took one another's long involved remarks, in the view of this angelic rattlesnake in their midst, altogether too seri-
29 ously. "I can paint one of those dismal-colored paintings like the men," the woman who regarded herself always as an outsider remembers thinking one day in 1922, and she did: a painting of a shed "all low-toned and dreary with the tree beside the door." She called this act of rancor "The Shanty" and hung it in her next show. "The men seemed to approve of it," she reported fifty-four years later, her contempt undimmed. "They seemed to think that maybe I was beginning to paint. That was my only low-toned dismal-colored painting."

Some women fight and others do not. Like so many successful guerrillas in the war between the sexes, Georgia O'Keeffe seems to have been equipped early with an immutable sense of who she was and a fairly clear understanding that she would be required to prove it. On the surface her upbringing was conventional. She was a child on the Wisconsin prairie who played with china dolls and painted watercolors with cloudy skies because sunlight was too hard to paint and, with her brother and sisters, listened every night to her mother read stories of the Wild West, of Texas, of Kit Carson and Billy the Kid. She told adults that she wanted to be an artist and was embarrassed when they asked what kind of artist she wanted to be: she had no idea "what kind." She had no idea what artists did. She had never seen a picture that interested her, other than a pen-and-ink Maid of Athens in one of her mother's books, some Mother Goose illustrations printed on cloth, a tablet cover that showed a little girl with pink roses, and the painting of Arabs on horseback that hung in her grandmother's parlor. At thirteen, in a Dominican convent, she was mortified when the sister corrected her drawing. At Chatham Episcopal Institute in Virginia she painted lilacs and sneaked time alone to walk out to where she could see the line of the Blue Ridge Mountains on the horizon. At the Art Institute in Chicago she was shocked by the presence of live models and wanted to abandon anatomy lessons. At the Art Students League in New York one of her fellow students advised her that, since he would be a great painter and she would end up teaching painting in a girls' school, any work of hers was less important than modeling for him. Another painted over her work to show her how the Impressionists did trees. She had

Literary Analysis
Biographical and Autobiographical Writing
What does this paragraph reveal about O'Keeffe?

rancor (raŋ′ kər) *n.* hatred

immutable (im myo͞ot′ ə bəl) *adj.* never changing

30 **Reading Check**
What made O'Keeffe's childhood "conventional"?

---

3. ***Don't tread on me*** motto of the first official American flag to be flown by a naval vessel, on December 3, 1775.
4. **Cézanne** (sā zän) Paul Cézanne (1839–1906), French Impressionist and Post-Impressionist painter.

29 Literary Analysis

Biographical and Autobiographical Writing

- Ask the Literary Analysis question on p. 689: What does this paragraph reveal about O'Keeffe?
  Answer: O'Keeffe has little respect for her male critics, and she deliberately defies their standards and expectations.
- Ask what this paragraph and the ones preceding it reveal about the writer of this essay. In what way is the essay autobiographical?
  Answer: Didion apparently admires O'Keeffe for standing up to the male establishment and scorning its opinions. This suggests that Didion also has struggled to be accepted by male writers and critics.

30 Reading Check

Answer: O'Keeffe played with dolls and watercolor paints and listened to her mother's stories.

CUSTOMIZE INSTRUCTION FOR UNIVERSAL ACCESS

For Less Proficient Readers

Have students complete the following organizer for this selection. Discuss with students the main idea. Have students look for supporting details and write them in the spaces provided. Have students then discuss how well Didion supports her main idea.

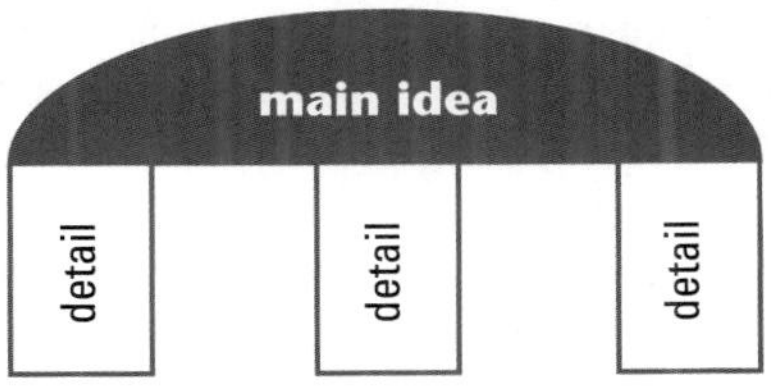

ASSESS

Answers for p. 690

Review and Assess

1. Students will probably admire O'Keeffe's refusal to compromise and her determination to create the art she wanted.
2. **(a)** Didion attributes "hardness" to O'Keeffe. **(b)** She means that O'Keeffe refused to compromise, that she knew her own mind and did not allow herself to be persuaded to paint to other people's expectations.
3. **(a)** She paints one canvas in drab colors — "The Shanty." **(b)** She is energetic, quick-tempered, sarcastic, and scornful. She likes being able to sneer at people she considers foolish.
4. **(a)** She moves to Texas. **(b)** She loved the night sky and the horizon; she finds the flat, open landscape attractive.
5. Didion means that O'Keeffe's sense of self was strong and that her views could not easily be changed by outside opinions or pressures.
6. **(a)** An artist's character is responsible for his or her artistic choices. **(b)** O'Keeffe shows repeatedly that she has her own way of looking at things and that her character and tastes are responsible for her paintings looking the way they do. She paints the way she is.
7. **(a)** It probably contributed greatly, because her individuality is what made her famous. If she had painted like everyone else she may never have been noticed. **(b)** Students may agree that boldness and individualism are essential for any artist.

not before heard how the Impressionists did trees and she did not much care.

At twenty-four she left all these opinions behind and went for the first time to live in Texas, where there were no trees to paint and no one to tell her how not to paint them. In Texas there was only the horizon she craved. In Texas she had her sister Claudia with her for a while, and in the late afternoons they would walk away from town and toward the horizon and watch the evening star come out. "That evening star fascinated me," she wrote. "It was in some way very exciting to me. My sister had a gun, and as we walked she would throw bottles into the air and shoot as many as she could before they hit the ground. I had nothing but to walk into nowhere and the wide sunset space with the star. Ten watercolors were made from that star." In a way one's interest is compelled as much by the sister Claudia with the gun as by the painter Georgia with the star, but only the painter left us this shining record. Ten watercolors were made from that star.

Review and Assess

Thinking About the Selection

1. **Respond:** Which of O'Keeffe's qualities do you admire most? Why?
2. **(a) Recall:** Which primary character trait does the writer attribute to O'Keeffe? **(b) Interpret:** What does the writer mean by "hardness"? Give examples.
3. **(a) Recall:** How does O'Keeffe respond when " 'the men' didn't think much of her bright color"? **(b) Draw Conclusions:** What does her response tell you about her character?
4. **(a) Recall:** Where does O'Keeffe move and find what she craves? **(b) Infer:** What do you think she found attractive about this place?
5. **Interpret:** What does Didion mean when she says O'Keeffe had "an immutable sense of who she was"?
6. **(a) Analyze:** What do the words "style is character" mean? **(b) Draw Conclusions:** Explain how the statement is appropriate for Georgia O'Keeffe. Cite evidence from the text to support your answer.
7. **(a) Speculate:** To what extent do you think O'Keeffe's disregard for the opinions of others contributed to her success? **(b) Assess:** Do you think an artist needs to be bold and individualistic to be successful?

Joan Didion

(b. 1934)

Joan Didion is descended from a long line of pioneers. Her great-great-grandmother went west in a covered wagon in 1846.

As a young woman, Didion won a writing contest sponsored by *Vogue* magazine. Eventually, she became an editor there. Her reputation in the literary world, however, is based on her novels and essays. Didion has said, "I write entirely to find out what I'm thinking, what I'm looking at, what I see and what it means."

The essay "Georgia O'Keeffe" pays tribute to an artist who herself displayed a strong pioneer spirit.

ASSESSMENT PRACTICE: Reading Comprehension

Connotation and Denotation (For more practice, see Test Preparation Workbook, p. 42.)

Many tests require students to discriminate between connotative and denotative meanings of words. Use this sample test item.

A moment passed, and then two more shots rang out in rapid succession. . . . Our Secret Service man, Rufus Youngblood, ______ over the front seat.

Which word best completes this sentence?

A vaulted
B hopped
C moved
D pounced

Although each word is a verb that would get a person over an obstacle, their connotations are all different. *Hopped* is playful, *moved* is neutral, *pounced* suggests an attack. Choice *A*, *vaulted*, is the correct answer.

Review and Assess

Literary Analysis

Biographical and Autobiographical Writing

1. Using a chart like this one, provide evidence to show whether each selection is a **biography** or an **autobiography.**

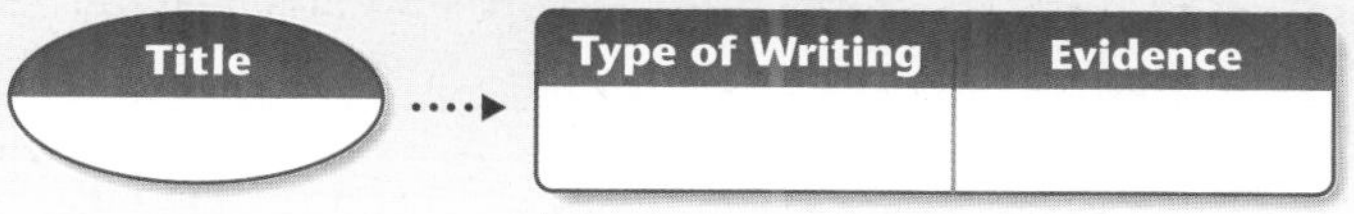

2. What are two details from *A White House Diary* that reveal the compassion of Lady Bird Johnson?
3. What does McPhee reveal about Ashe's personal nature?
4. In what ways was Georgia O'Keeffe portrayed as a "loner"?

Comparing Literary Works

5. (a) Which of the three selections reveals the most to you about the qualities of the person portrayed? (b) Which of the three selections evokes the most emotion in you? Why?
6. (a) How would *A White House Diary* be different if it were written as a biography? (b) Use a Venn diagram like this one to compare the ways each type of writing would present Lady Bird Johnson.

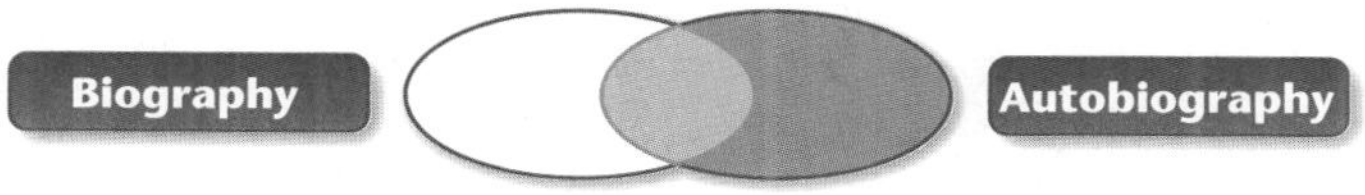

Reading Strategy

Finding the Writer's Main Points and Support

7. For each main point below, explain which details the writer provides to support the main point:
   (a) Mrs. Kennedy made Lady Bird's visit with her as easy as possible.
   (b) Remaining cool on the court was a potent weapon for Ashe.
   (c) Georgia O'Keeffe was a hard, straight shooter.

Extend Understanding

8. **Social Studies Connection:** Why are biographical and autobiographical writings valuable sources for historians and teachers?

Quick Review

Biographical writing is nonfiction in which a writer tells the story of another person's life.

Autobiographical writing is nonfiction in which a writer tells the story of his or her own life.

A writer's **main points** are the main ideas expressed in a selection. **Support** for these points can include facts, events, quotations, and other details that prove or elaborate each main idea.

Take It to the Net

www.phschool.com

Take the interactive self-test online to check your understanding of these selections.

ENRICHMENT: Further Reading

Other Works by the Authors

Works by Joan Didion
Play It as It Lays
Democracy
Slouching Towards Bethlehem

Works by John McPhee
Coming Into the Country
Assembling California
Levels of the Game

Take It to the Net

Visit www.phschool.com for more information on the authors.

Answers for p. 691

Review and Assess

1. "White House Diary" is an autobiography because it is told from the writer's point of view and describes events in which the writer participated. "Arthur Ashe Remembered" and "Georgia O'Keeffe" are biographies because they center on the lives of people other than the writers.
2. Possible responses: Students may cite Johnson's attempts to comfort the first lady and her awareness of the distress of the Secret Service.
3. McPhee reveals that Ashe was quiet and reserved, but a bold risk-taker in moments of pressure.
4. O'Keeffe did not follow anyone's advice or listen to any of her critics but developed her own style.
5. **(a)** Students may say "Georgia O'Keeffe" because she is quoted so extensively. **(b)** Students may say "White House Diary" because it deals with violent death and its effects.
6. **(a)** A biography of Lady Bird Johnson would probably center more on her and less on the people around her, such as Mrs. Kennedy. **(b)** An autobiography would provide a fuller record of Johnson's thoughts and feelings. A biography might give more details about Johnson's accomplishments.
7. **(a)** Mrs. Kennedy didn't cry or ask for help. She remained poised and gracious. **(b)** Ashe's opponents never knew what he was thinking or which shot he might try. **(c)** O'Keeffe heaped scorn on her critics.
8. These writings focus on people's lives, including details about their thoughts and feelings, not just their words and actions.

EXTEND

Answers for p. 692

❶ Vocabulary Development

Word Analysis

1. make able to feel
2. with awareness of the feelings of others
3. excessive emotion; overdependence on feeling

Spelling Strategy

1. preeminent
2. disservice
3. unnatural
4. improper

Fluency: Definitions

1. e
2. d
3. b
4. a
5. c

❷ Grammar

1. were
2. was
3. were
4. were
5. was

Writing Application

Sample answers:

1. The tennis players practice every day.
2. The painter uses bold colors and large shapes.

Integrate Language Skills

❶ Vocabulary Development Lesson

Word Analysis: Latin Root *-sent-/-sens-*

The Latin root *-sent-/-sens-* means "feeling." The root appears in the word *sentimental*, which means "having excessive feelings." Using the meaning of *-sent-/-sens-*, define each word below.

1. sensitize 2. sensitively 3. sentimentality

Spelling Strategy

Do not change the spelling of a base word when adding a prefix to it. For example, *im-* + *mutable* = *immutable.*

Add the prefix shown to form the new word. Then, use each word in a sentence.

1. *pre-* + eminent
2. *dis-* + service
3. *un-* + natural
4. *im-* + proper

Fluency: Definitions

Review the vocabulary list on page 673. Then, match each of the following phrases on the left with its correct definition on the right.

1. poignant genesis	a. emotional riddle
2. tumultuous implications	b. unchangeable inheritance
3. immutable legacy	c. patronizing hatred
4. sentimental enigma	d. turbulent indications
5. condescending rancor	e. moving beginning

❷ Grammar Lesson

Subject-Verb Agreement: Confusing Subjects

The **subject** and **verb** in a sentence must agree in number. A singular subject takes the singular form of the verb. A plural subject takes the plural form of the verb. If a subject follows a verb in a sentence, the subject and verb must still agree.

In the following examples, the verbs are italicized and the subjects are underlined.

Singular:	There *was* a sharp, loud <u>report</u>.
Plural:	There *were* sharp, loud <u>reports</u>.

If the subject is *any* or *all*, the verb agrees with the noun to which the pronoun refers.

Singular:	<u>All</u> the danger *was* over.
Plural:	<u>All</u> the shades *were* lowered.

Practice Identify the subject in each sentence. Then, choose the correct verb to complete each sentence.

1. There (was, were) Secret Service men all over.
2. His entire life (was, were) a series of victories.
3. Some of his opponents (was, were) baffled.
4. There on the wall (was, were) her paintings.
5. Each painting in the group (was, were) a masterpiece.

Writing Application Use each item as the subject in a sentence. Make sure you use a verb that agrees in number with the subject.

1. tennis players 2. painter

WG *Prentice Hall Writing and Grammar Connection: Chapter 25, Section 1*

TEACHING RESOURCES

The following resources can be used to enrich or extend the instruction for pp. 692–693.

Vocabulary

- **Selection Support:** Build Vocabulary, p. 165
- **Vocabulary and Spelling Practice Book** (Use this booklet for skills enrichment.)

Grammar

- **Selection Support:** Build Grammar Skills, p. 166
- **Writing and Grammar,** Gold Level, p. 572
- **Daily Language Practice Transparencies**

Writing

- **Writing and Grammar,** Gold Level, p. 141
- **Writing and Grammar iText CD-ROM**

BLOCK SCHEDULING: Resources marked with this symbol provide varied instruction during 90-minute blocks.

❸ Writing Lesson

Awards Speech

Imagine that you are an official at an awards ceremony for Lady Bird Johnson, Arthur Ashe, or Georgia O'Keeffe. Using the selections you have just read, write a speech that introduces the award winner.

Prewriting Select the person from these selections whom you admire most. Jot down the points you would like to make about that person.

Drafting Begin your speech with an attention-grabbing opening. In the body of your speech, present your main points in a logical order.

Revising Read your speech and ask a classmate to suggest places where you can add details to make your ideas more coherent. Add transition words, such as *then* and *as a result*, to clarify your speech.

Model: Adding Smooth Transitions

Tonight we are honoring an admirable woman.
But even more importantly,
^We are honoring a great American. She has worked tirelessly
As a result,
for our country.^ She has brought all of us closer together.

The inserted words create smoother transitions between sentences.

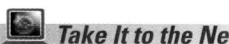

Prentice Hall Writing and Grammar Connection: Chapter 7, Section 4

❹ Extension Activities

Listening and Speaking In a small group, develop and present a **radio news report** on the assassination of President Kennedy.

- Use library resources to find relevant information on the subject.
- Use details such as quotations and anecdotes in your report.
- Organize the information in the best possible order, using transition words where helpful.

Present your radio news report to the class. **[Group Activity]**

Research and Technology Prepare a **visual presentation** on the paintings of Georgia O'Keeffe. Find reproductions of her paintings and use them as your primary source of information. Then, use the Internet to find more information about her and her paintings. Write informational captions for each painting. Present your findings to your class.

Take It to the Net www.phschool.com

Go online for an additional research activity using the Internet.

ASSESSMENT RESOURCES

The following resources can be used to assess students' knowledge and skills.

Selection Assessment

- **Formal Assessment,** pp. 148–150
- **Open Book Test,** pp. 124–126
- **Got It! Assessment Videotapes,** Tape 4
- **Test Bank Software**

Take It to the Net

Visit www.phschool.com for self-tests and additional questions on the selections.

PRENTICE HALL ASSESSMENT SYSTEM

- **Workbook**
- **Skill Book**
- **Transparencies**
- **CD-ROM**

❸ Writing Lesson

- Remind students that an introductory speech should be brief; the audience has come to honor the person being introduced, not the one who does the introducing.
- Introductory speeches should be complimentary; they should never criticize, even though the speaker may not admire everything about the person.
- Students may want to do a little further reading about Johnson, Ashe, or O'Keeffe to find more details for their speeches.

❹ Listening and Speaking

- If your library has a good video collection, encourage students to make use of it. On the day of Kennedy's death, many special news broadcasts aired; students can get ideas from these broadcasts.
- Encourage students to interview older relatives or friends. People who lived through Kennedy's assassination have never forgotten where they were or what they were doing when they heard the news.
- Students can present their reports live, as if they are happening on the day of the assassination, or they can tape-record their broadcasts.

CUSTOMIZE INSTRUCTION
For Universal Access

To address different learning styles, use the following activities suggested in the **Extension Activities** booklet, p. 42.

- For Visual/Spatial and Intrapersonal Learners, use Activity 5.
- For Logical/Mathematical Learners, use Activity 6.
- For Musical/Rhythmic and Verbal/Linguistic Learners, use Activity 7.

from Understanding Comics

Lesson Objectives and CA Correlations

1. **To analyze and respond to literary elements**
   - Literary Analysis: Visual Essay
   - Connecting Literary Elements: Tone **R 3.9**
2. **To read, comprehend, analyze, and critique an illustrated essay**
   - Reading Strategy: Using Visuals as a Key to Meaning
   - Review and Assess questions
   - Assessment Practice (ATE)
3. **To develop word analysis skills, fluency, and systematic vocabulary**
   - Vocabulary Development Lesson: Latin Root: *-stat-* **R 1.1**
4. **To understand and apply written and oral language conventions**
   - Spelling Strategy
   - Grammar Lesson: Varieties of English: Standard and Nonstandard **LC 1.3**
5. **To understand and apply appropriate writing and research strategies**
   - Writing Lesson: Essay on Humor **W 2.2**
   - Extension Activity: Comic Strip **W 1.8**
6. **To understand and apply listening and speaking strategies**
   - Extension Activity: Visual Presentation **LS 1.7**

STEP-BY-STEP TEACHING GUIDE	PACING GUIDE
PRETEACH	
Motivate Students and Provide Background	
Use the Motivation activity (ATE p. 694)	5 min.
Read and discuss the Preview material and Background information (SE/ATE p. 694) [A]	5 min.
Introduce the Concepts	
Introduce the Literary Analysis and Reading Strategy (SE/ATE p. 695) [A]	15 min.
Pronounce the vocabulary words and read their definitions (SE p. 695)	5 min.
TEACH	
Monitor Comprehension	
Informally monitor comprehension by circulating while students read independently or in groups [A]	15 min.
Develop vocabulary with Vocabulary note (ATE p. 703)	as students read
Develop Understanding	
Develop students' understanding of visual essays with Literary Analysis annotations (ATE pp. 697–698, 700) [A]	10 min.
Develop students' ability to use visuals as a key to meaning with the Reading Strategy annotations (ATE pp. 697–699, 703)	10 min.
ASSESS	
Assess Mastery	
Assess students' mastery of the Reading Strategy and Literary Analysis by having them answer the Review and Assess questions (SE/ATE p. 705)	20 min.
Use one or more of the print and media Assessment Resources (ATE p. 707) [A]	up to 50 min.
EXTEND	
Apply Understanding	
Have students complete the Vocabulary Development Lesson and the Grammar Lesson (SE p. 706) [A]	20 min.
Apply students' understanding of gathering relevant details using the Writing Lesson (SE p. 707) [A]	45 min.
Apply students' understanding using one or more of the Extension Activities (SE p. 707)	20–90 min.

[A] ACCELERATED INSTRUCTION: Use the strategies and activities identified with an [A].

UNIVERSAL ACCESS
● = Below Level Students
▲ = On-Level Students
■ = Above Level Students

Time and Resource Manager

Reading Level: Challenging
Average Number of Instructional Days: 4

RESOURCES		
PRINT	**TRANSPARENCIES**	**TECHNOLOGY**
• **Beyond Literature,** Humanities Connection: Comic Art, p. 43 ▲ ■		• **Interest Grabber Video,** Tape 4 ● ▲ ■
• **Selection Support Workbook:** ● ▲ ■ Literary Analysis, p. 172 Reading Strategy, p. 171 Build Vocabulary, p. 169	• **Literary Analysis and Reading Transparencies,** pp. 85 and 86 ● ▲ ■	
		• **Listening to Literature** ● ▲ ■ Audiocassettes, Side 26 Audio CDs, CD 14
• **Literatura en español** ● ▲ • **Literary Analysis for Enrichment** ■		
• **Formal Assessment:** Selection Test, pp. 151–153 ● ▲ ■ • **Open Book Test,** pp. 127–129 ● ▲ ■ • PRENTICE HALL ASSESSMENT SYSTEM ● ▲ ■	• PRENTICE HALL ASSESSMENT SYSTEM ● ▲ ■ Skills Practice Answers and Explanations on Transparencies	• **Test Bank Software** ● ▲ ■ • **Got It! Assessment Videotapes,** Tape 4 ● ▲
• **Selection Support Workbook:** ● ▲ ■ Build Grammar Skills, p. 170 • **Writing and Grammar,** Gold Level ● ▲ ■ • **Extension Activities,** p. 43 ● ▲ ■	• **Daily Language Practice Transparencies** ● ▲ • **Writing Models and Graphic Organizers on Transparencies,** p. 71 ● ▲ ■	• **Writing and Grammar iText CD-ROM** ● ▲ ■ ***Take It to the Net*** www.phschool.com

BLOCK SCHEDULING: Use one 90-minute class period to preteach the selection and have students read it. Use a second 90-minute class period to assess students' mastery of skills and have them complete one of the Extension Activities.

PRETEACH

Step-by-Step Teaching Guide for pp. 694–695

Motivation

Ask students how they would respond to the statement that comics are "bright, colorful magazines filled with bad art, stupid stories, and guys in tights." Ask students to name comics that fit this description and comics that don't. Have students suggest characteristics shared by all comics. Then, tell them they are about to read an essay by someone who once despised comics but who now writes and draws them himself.

Interest Grabber Video

As an alternative, play "Every Picture Tells a Story" on Tape 4 to engage student interest.

1 Background

History

Comics are so popular that many have been adapted into other formats—movies, television shows, even stage musicals! Movies based on comic-strip characters include *Popeye*, which starred Robin Williams. The beloved *Little Orphan Annie* strip of the 1930s became the Broadway musical *Annie*, in which Annie escapes from the wicked Miss Hannigan's orphanage to be adopted by the wealthy Daddy Warbucks. *Peanuts* became a Broadway musical called *You're a Good Man, Charlie Brown*; it also inspired a series of animated cartoon holiday specials, including *It's the Great Pumpkin, Charlie Brown!* and *A Charlie Brown Christmas*. Superhero Batman was the source for a television show and a series of action movies.

Prepare to Read

excerpt from Understanding Comics

Take It to the Net

Visit www.phschool.com for interactive activities and instruction related to *Understanding Comics*, including

- background
- graphic organizers
- literary elements
- reading strategies

Preview

Connecting to the Literature

Most people associate comics with superheroes, humorous animals, and amusing people with exaggerated facial features. As you read this excerpt from *Understanding Comics*, consider how much the writer/illustrator changes your impressions and ideas about a typical comic strip.

1 Background

Comics first appeared in American newspapers in the late 1800s. One early strip featuring a character called the Yellow Kid was so popular that it boosted sales for its newspaper. Soon, other newspapers were running their own comics, too. Comic books first appeared in the 1930s. The *Superman* comic began in 1938 and is still popular today. In recent years, the popularity of comic books has increased dramatically among adults.

TEACHING RESOURCES

The following resources can be used to enrich or extend the instruction for pp. 694–695.

Motivation

Interest Grabber Video, Tape 4

Background

Beyond Literature, p. 43

Take It to the Net

Visit www.phschool.com for background and hotlinks for "Understanding Comics."

Literary Analysis

Literary Analysis and Reading Transparencies, Visual Essay, p. 86

Reading

Selection Support: Reading Strategy, p. 171; Build Vocabulary, p. 169

Literary Analysis and Reading Transparencies, Using Visuals as a Key to Meaning, p. 85

BLOCK SCHEDULING: Resources marked with this symbol provide varied instruction during 90-minute blocks.

❷ Literary Analysis

Visual Essay

A **visual essay** is an exploration of a topic that conveys its ideas through visual elements as well as language. Like a standard essay, a visual essay presents an author's views of a topic. Unlike other essays, however, much of the meaning in a visual essay is conveyed through illustrations or photographs. For example, the following excerpt from *Understanding Comics* will take on new meaning when you read it along with a visual element in the comic:

> The artform—the *medium*—known as comics is a *vessel* which can hold any *number* of *ideas* and *images*.

Note how the visual elements of *Understanding Comics* heighten your understanding and appreciation of the text.

Connecting Literary Elements

The **tone** of a visual essay is the writer's attitude toward his or her audience and subject, and it can be conveyed through both words and images. Often, the tone can be described in a single adjective, such as *formal* or *informal*, *serious* or *playful*, *bitter* or *ironic*. As you read a comic, consider how the pictures and the letters—for example, the size of the letters and the repetition of words—contribute to the author's overall tone.

❸ Reading Strategy

Using Visuals as a Key to Meaning

You can **use visuals as a key to meaning** by looking carefully at each illustration or photograph and deciding how it adds to the ideas presented in the written text. Pictures can reinforce and extend words in the following ways:

- They add humor to apparently straightforward statements.
- They add details, without having to use additional words.
- They signal flashbacks in time or the element of fantasy.

Use a chart like the one shown to record details about the text and the illustrations. Then, explain how the visual extends meaning.

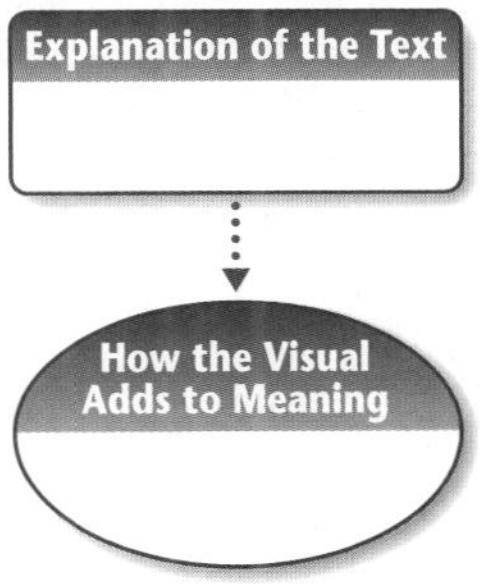

Vocabulary Development

obsessed (əb sest′) *adj.* greatly occupied with

aesthetic (es thet′ ik) *adj.* relating to the appreciation of beauty

arbitrary (är′ bə trer′ ē) *adj.* not fixed by rules, but left to one's judgment

CUSTOMIZE INSTRUCTION FOR UNIVERSAL ACCESS

For Less Proficient Readers	For English Learners	For Advanced Readers
Have students read each panel in three steps: read the words, look at the details in the picture, then put picture and words together.	The essay contains some difficult vocabulary. Ask students to use the pictures to help them understand any unfamiliar words. Encourage them to use context clues to figure out definitions before using a dictionary.	Have students think about the connection between McCloud's format, the visual essay, and his subject, comics. Have them consider how a different format would have changed the essay's impact.

❷ Literary Analysis

Visual Essay

- Explain that a *visual essay* relies on pictures to help tell the story. If Lady Bird Johnson, p. 674, had written a visual essay, it might have consisted of photographs with captions. If Joan Didion, p. 65, had written a visual essay, it might have combined Georgia O'Keeffe's words with reproductions of her paintings.
- As students read "Understanding Comics," have them think about the reason McCloud wrote his essay in this visual format. What is the relationship between the message and the presentation?

❸ Reading Strategy

Using Visuals as a Key to Meaning

- Have students discuss their general feelings about illustrations in texts. What can illustrations add to the experience of reading? What effect do they have on readers?
- Use the Reading Strategy transparency on p. 85 in **Literary Analysis and Reading Transparencies** to help students experience the difference between text only and text-with-visuals.
- As students read, have them think about the effect this essay would have if it had been written like a "regular" essay without illustrations. This will help them articulate the value that the visual elements add to the essay. Encourage them to use a chart like the one shown to help them explore how the visuals add meaning.

Vocabulary Development

- Pronounce each vocabulary word for students, and read the definitions as a class. Have students identify any words with which they are already familiar.

E-Teach

Visit E-Teach at www.phschool.com for teachers' essays on how to teach, with questions and answers.

TEACH

Step-by-Step Teaching Guide for pp. *696–704*

CUSTOMIZE INSTRUCTION
For Visual/Spatial Learners

Have students discuss how the visual style of this essay added to its effect. Challenge them to think about what the essay would have been like if McCloud had made his arguments in words only, with no pictures. Would they have enjoyed it less? Would it have been less effective? Have students explain their answers to these questions.

❶ About the Selection

A comic strip that defines comics represents an ideal match between form and content: Scott McCloud's visual essay uses both words and pictures to explain an art that uses both words and pictures. Students will acquire a deeper understanding of this medium by paying close attention not only to what McCloud says, but to how he says it. His pictures add humor, graphically illustrate concepts, and heighten the interest of the essay.

TEACHING RESOURCES

The following resources can be used to enrich or extend the instruction for pp. 696–704.

Literary Analysis	Reading
Selection Support: Literary Analysis, p. 172	**Listening to Literature Audiocassettes,** Side 21 ▪
	Listening to Literature Audio CDs, CD 14 ▪

▪ **BLOCK SCHEDULING:** Resources marked with this symbol provide varied instruction during 90-minute blocks.

❷ Reading Strategy

Using Visuals as a Key to Meaning

- Most students are probably familiar with comic strips and comic books. For those who are not, explain that a comic is read the same way as any other text: left to right, top to bottom.
- Ask students what they can infer about Scott McCloud from the details in the first frame on p. 697. Point out that while the picture contains many details, the text says only, "Hi, I'm Scott McCloud."
  Answer: McCloud is apparently an artist, since he's working at a drafting table. He is apparently a comic-book artist, since the page he's working on has frames like those of a comic book. The room shown is probably his office or workroom. His casual clothing suggests that he isn't a formal person.

❸ Literary Analysis

Visual Essay

- Point out the large type of the word *exactly* and the italicized *little kid*. Ask students what effect these changes in type size and style have on the reader.
  Answer: The differences in size and style make these words stand out.
- Ask a volunteer to read aloud the entire sentence in the balloon as he or she thinks McCloud means it to sound. Have students relate the appearance of the letters to the sound of the sentence.
  Answer: The word *exactly* is the strongest and loudest in the sentence. *Little kid* should also be stressed.

▶ **Monitor Progress** Ask students why a comic book often uses different sizes and typefaces while a standard verbal text usually does not.
Answer: These are the only indications of how to read the sentences. A comic book writer can't include indications like "said McCloud angrily" or "she whispered." Comics are dialogue only.

❹ Reading Strategy

Using Visuals as a Key to Meaning

- Point out the rays around the faces of the people in the various frames. Ask students what these rays mean.
  Answer: These lines have the effect of emphasizing the person's emotions: agitation, hilarity, anger, and so on. They serve as visual intensifiers.
- Ask students why the artist thinks these rays are needed.
  Answer: An artist can make the characters' facial expressions show various emotions, but he can't make them move. The lines give the flat drawings a little more life and make them more active.

Monitor Progress Ask students to interpret the heavy black marks around McCloud's head in the frame that begins, "Sure, I realized . . ."
Answer: They indicate confusion, frustration, and irritation. They are a visual representation of how McCloud feels when he can't get people to understand his love of comics.

❺ Literary Analysis

Visual Essay

- Ask students how the first two pictures in the bottom row reflect the sense of the words in their dialogue balloons.
  Answer: When McCloud says that people try to define comics too narrowly, he shows himself squeezed into a narrow space. When he talks about the limitless potential of comics, he shows himself against the background of the limitless universe.
- Have students consider why McCloud tries to connect the images with the words.
  Answer: The connections add humor and emphasize the ideas that he has conveyed in words.

ENRICHMENT: Social Studies Connection

The Funny Papers

Comics in the United States span the history of the twentieth century, and from the beginning they have alluded to current or historical events. The comic strip *Little Orphan Annie* was set during the Great Depression of the 1930s and often commented on it. During World War II, action heroes such as Captain America and Wonder Woman went into battle on behalf of the Allies. Walt Kelly's *Pogo* is famous for its subtle commentary on the Cold War. More recently, Garry Trudeau began drawing *Doonesbury*, which features a sarcastic group of liberal characters discussing current political topics. To this day, *The Washington Post* honors *Doonesbury* by running it in the news section instead of on the comic page with the other comic strips.

6

6 Reading Strategy

Using Visuals as a Key to Meaning

- Ask students to discuss the relationship between the image of the globe and the text in the dialogue balloon below it. You may want to have students use the chart on p. 695 to record their ideas. Students' charts should look similar to the following:

Explanation of the Text

the world of comics is a huge and varied one

How the Visual Adds to Meaning

the globe represents the world that McCloud refers to; the size of the globe and the faces on it emphasize the phrase "huge and varied"

- Ask students what the size of the globe suggests about McCloud's view of the importance of comics to modern culture.
  Answer: The size of the globe suggests that McCloud thinks comics are very important.

CUSTOMIZE INSTRUCTION FOR UNIVERSAL ACCESS

For Special Needs Students	For Gifted/Talented Students
Have students make up a game about the comic characters pictured on the globe above. Have students identify as many as they can, copy the faces onto index cards, and write each character's name on the other side of the card. Students can use the game to learn about comic characters. Encourage students who enjoy comics to add more information to the game.	After students finish reading this essay, have them review it, writing their reviews in comic-book format. Remind them that a review is a response to the writer's ideas and his way of expressing them. A good review does not simply praise a work or find fault with it; it gives specific details for its reactions. If students prefer, they may want to work in pairs, one to draw the pictures and the other to write the dialogue balloons.

❼ Literary Analysis

Visual Essay

- Guide students through this page. Point out the arrows in the frame in the upper left-hand corner. These arrows show the directions in which students should read: from the first dialogue balloon down the left column, then from the second balloon down the middle column, then down the right column.
- Ask a student to explain the relationship between the left column and the middle column.
  Answer: The left column shows individual pictures. The center column uses each of those pictures as the first frame of a comic strip, giving a second frame that shows what happens next.
- Have students describe what happens to each picture in the left column.
  Answer: The man tips his hat, the sun sets, someone screams when she hears the shot fired, the clock advances five minutes, the eye winks.

❼

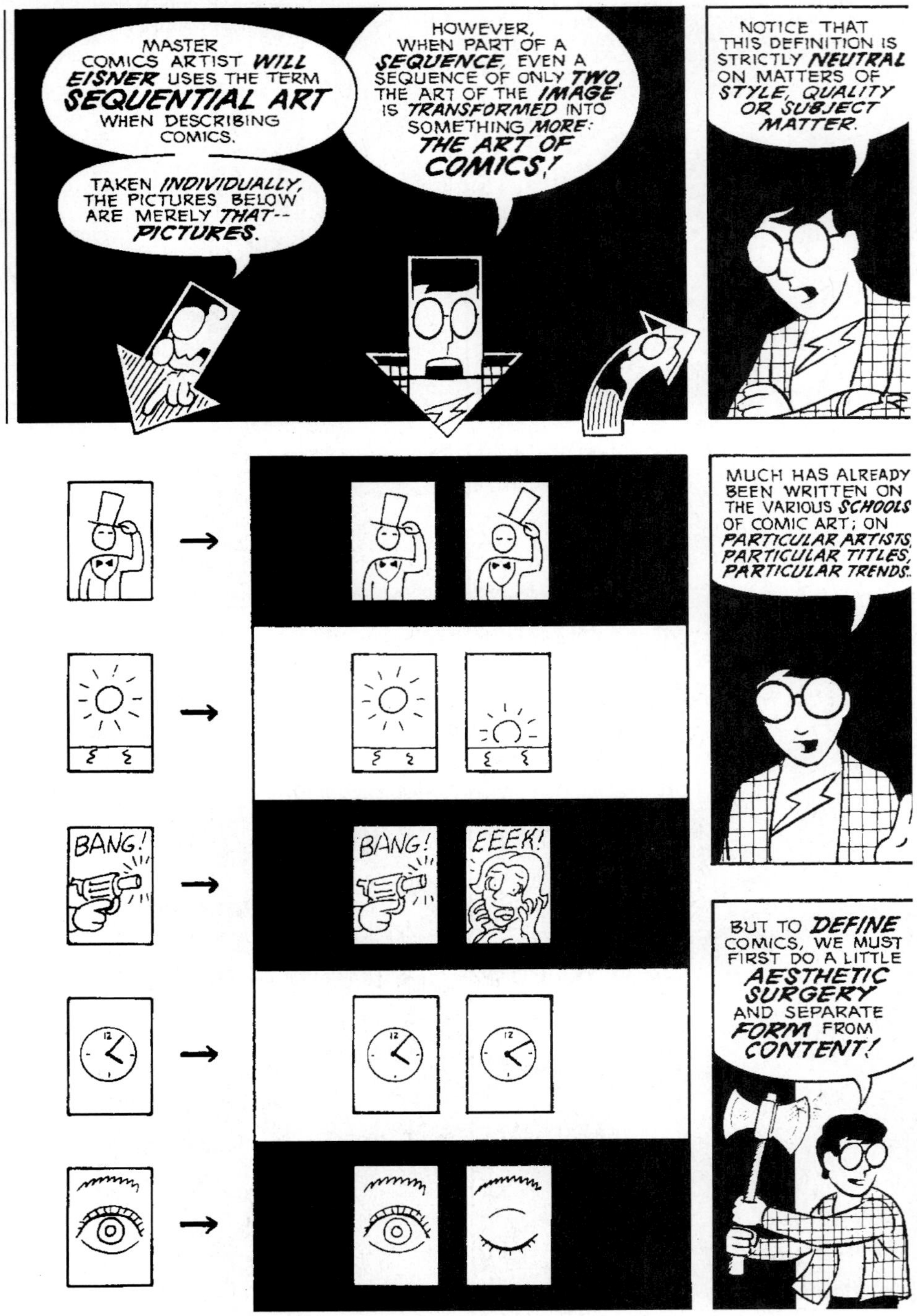

ENRICHMENT: Art Connection

Pop Art

Are comics art? Decades ago, the immediate answer might have been a resounding "No!" However, in the 1960s, Pop artists began to use the subjects and materials of mass culture in artworks that were collected in museums and galleries. Some of them, especially American painter Roy Lichtenstein (1923–1997), created prints of greatly enlarged comic strip images. Narrowing the gap between the popular and the serious from the other direction, museums and galleries in recent years have sometimes exhibited cells (original drawings of single frames) from animated films.

Invite students to search for comic-style Pop Art images in books and on the Internet. Ask them to discuss the similarities and differences they find between these paintings and "real" comics.

8

8 Critical Thinking

Interpret

- Ask students to interpret the symbol of the pitcher, the liquid inside it, and the act of drinking from it. **Answer:** The pitcher symbolizes form, the particular medium of expression—in this case, comics. The liquid symbolizes content, the many possible messages that can be expressed through the art form.
- Ask why McCloud chokes on the drink he takes from the pitcher. **Answer:** First, McCloud wants an amusing break in his discussion of form and content, and choking on a drink is a classic "sight gag" of comedians. More seriously, he may be implying that comics' messages may not appeal to everyone.

CUSTOMIZE INSTRUCTION FOR UNIVERSAL ACCESS

For English Learners	For Advanced Readers
Explain that words like *gaak* and *glug* are in a category called *onomatopoeia.* Onomatopoeic words sound like what they mean. This page features several such words. Comics often feature words like these for their value as sound effects. Action comics often use words such as *bam! pow! crash!* Have students try to define each onomatopoeic word on this page without using the word itself in the definition.	McCloud uses a pitcher and liquid as an analogy for form (type of medium: film, novels, nonfiction, and so on) and content (the particular meaning or message conveyed). Ask students to work in small groups to develop at least one analogy of their own to use in explaining the difference between form and content to younger students. To give students another analogy, try technology: Form is hardware, content is software.

❾ Critical Thinking

Evaluate

- Ask students to identify the characters in McCloud's audience in the central frame on this page. Why did McCloud put these characters in his audience?
  Answer: The speaker is Bugs Bunny; seated on his right is Mickey Mouse. It makes perfect sense for Bugs, a famous animated character, to speak up about animation.
- Ask students to describe the effect of Bugs and Mickey's appearance on them.
  Answer: Students should say this is an enjoyable joke for the reader; it adds humor to the essay and shows McCloud's wit. Point out to students that this is a purely visual joke created without a single word of text.

❾

ENRICHMENT: Career Connection

Comics

Scott McCloud has made a career as an independent comic artist. But creating comics is often a cooperative task: One person may develop a story idea, another might write the dialogue, another might ink the drawings, and a fourth might add color. Publishers of comics employ story editors, copy editors, art directors, and people in various business positions. Invite students to look at the mastheads of their favorite comics to learn what occupations exist in this field.

10

11

10 Reading Strategy

Using Visuals as a Key to Meaning

- Ask students to identify the image suggested by the border of the left-hand column of frames.
  Answer: The border looks like a strip of film, which is punched on both sides with small sprocket holes.
- Have students relate the verbal contents of the column with the visual allusion to film.
  Answer: The column illustrates the point made in the text. It shows how film looks when it isn't being run through a projector—simply a series of frames, just like a very long comic strip in which characters move only slightly from one frame to the next.

Monitor Progress Have students evaluate the effectiveness of McCloud's visual allusion.
Answer: Students may agree that the allusion is very effective because McCloud doesn't just explain his point in words; the visual element of the filmstrip also makes his point.

11 Vocabulary Development

Latin Root *-stat-*

- Point out the word *static* in this frame. Explain to students that the Latin word root *-stat-* means "to stand."
- Have students look up this word in a dictionary to find its meaning and derivation. Ask students to explain how the definition of *static* is related to the meaning of the root word.
  Possible response: Students may say that the root suggests a meaning of "standing still" or "standing unchanging."
- Encourage students to identify other words that contain this same root word. Have students provide definitions for each of these words.

The complete *Understanding Comics* is 215 pages in 9 chapters and examines all aspects of comics. The above excerpt is from Chapter One.

Review and Assess

Thinking About the Selection

1. **Respond:** Did you enjoy this selection? Why or why not?
2. **(a) Recall:** How does McCloud's view of comics change from his early childhood view to his present view? **(b) Make a Judgment:** Do you accept McCloud's final definition of comics, which says nothing about their entertainment value? Explain.
3. **Evaluate:** Do you think McCloud is justified in comparing comics to art forms such as film, music, and theater? Explain.

Scott McCloud

(b. 1960)

Scott McCloud started drawing comics at the age of twelve. After graduating from Syracuse University in 1982, he began his career as a cartoonist. He has since published an award-winning comic book series called *Zot!* as well as *Destroy!*, a parody of superhero comics.

ASSESS

Answers for p. 704

Review and Assess

1. Some students will say that they liked the pictures, the marriage of form to content, and the subject itself. Other students may report little interest in comics or say that they found the graphic format distracting.
2. **(a)** At first McCloud thought comics were stupid; today he is deeply interested in them and is a comic artist himself.
   (b) Sample responses: Yes, McCloud has shown that comics can convey serious ideas to the viewer. No, comics, by the very term *comics,* exist to amuse. McCloud's own comic essay is funny and entertaining even as it informs.
3. Possible answers: Students who agree with McCloud may note that comics, like other art forms, demand great skill, imagination, and effort. Other students may contend that the content of comics seldom reaches the heights, depths, and humanity of film, literature, music, and theater.

ASSESSMENT PRACTICE: Reading Comprehension

Connotation **(For more practice, see Test Preparation Workbook, p. 43.)**

Many tests require students to understand the connotative meanings of words. Use this sample test item.

Scott McCloud at first defines comics as juxtaposed sequential visual art.

Which word conveys a connotation of beauty or worth?

A juxtaposed **C** visual
B sequential **D** art

Explain that the first three words are neutral. Only choice *D* has connotations of beauty and/or worth.

Review and Assess

Literary Analysis

Visual Essay

1. Using a chart like this one, identify the main idea of this selection. Show how both the visuals and the text convey this idea.

2. Would the selection lose its impact if either the words or the visuals were eliminated? Explain.
3. How does McCloud's selection fit Will Eisner's description of comics as "sequential art"?

Connecting Literary Elements

4. Using a chart like this, analyze the varying **tone** of the selection.

5. Which word best describes the overall tone of the essay? Explain.

Reading Strategy

Using Visuals as a Key to Meaning

6. Find three places in which visuals add humor to text that is straightforward and serious. Explain each example.
7. Identify two illustrations that add meaning to McCloud's definition of a comic. Explain.
8. Find two illustrations that help explain the meaning of the term "sequential art." Explain how the visuals illustrate the meaning.

Extend Understanding

9. **Media Connection:** McCloud briefly addresses the difference between comics and animation. (a) What are some additional differences between comics and animation? (b) Which medium do you think is more effective in conveying a message? Why?

Quick Review

A **visual essay** is a piece of nonfiction that conveys its ideas through visual elements as well as language.

The **tone** in a literary work is the writer's attitude toward his or her audience and subject.

To **use visuals as a key to meaning,** rely on illustrations or photographs to help you understand and appreciate the meaning of accompanying text.

Take It to the Net

www.phschool.com

Take the interactive self-test online to check your understanding of the selection.

ENRICHMENT: Further Reading

Other Works by Scott McCloud

Zot!
Destroy!

Take It to the Net

Visit www.phschool.com for more information on Scott McCloud.

Answers for p. 705

Review and Assess

1. Main idea: Readers should be open to a wider definition of comics. Conveyed Through Text: He says "The world of comics is a huge and varied one. Our definition must encompass all these types," to stress his main idea; Conveyed Through Visuals: He uses an image of a globe to convey the broad "world" of comics.
2. Possible response: Most of the images would be meaningless and boring without words. The words would be harder to understand and less amusing without the images.
3. McCloud notes that each image follows the next in a certain order. The images must be read in that order for the essay to make sense.
4. The tone varies between humor and seriousness. The appearance of Bugs Bunny in the audience on p. 702 shows that McCloud enjoys comics and wants to share the fun; the sophisticated vocabulary of his final definition shows that he is serious about his art form.
5. Despite his medium and an abundance of visual jokes, McCloud's overall tone is serious. He presents his key points with great conviction.
6. Possible responses: Students may cite the squeezed image about "narrow definition"; the pitcher/liquid gag that explains form and content; Bugs Bunny posing a serious question.
7. Possible responses: The limitless universe on p. 698; the filmstrip on p. 703. Each image gives a picture of what McCloud discusses in words, thus reinforcing his point.
8. Possible response: The pairs of pictures on p. 700 and the filmstrip on p. 703 both illustrate that comics must be read in a certain order and that each frame sets up the following one.
9. **(a)** Animation includes sound. **(b)** Either message can be equally effective; they simply achieve their effects by different means.

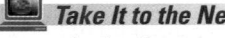

EXTEND

Answers for p. 706

❶ Vocabulary Development

Word Analysis

1. a free-standing sculpture
2. standing still, not moving
3. facts, unchanging details

Spelling Strategy

Sample sentences are given.

1. lurking; Sometimes the actor found fans lurking outside the stage door when he left the theater.
2. harshly; She harshly scolded her child for not wearing a bicycle helmet.
3. contentment; Rocking gently in the hammock brought her great contentment.
4. vastness; The vastness of the Grand Canyon took her by surprise in spite of the many photographs she had seen.

Concept Development: Analogies

1. c; *Ecstatic* is an intense form of happiness; *obsessed* is an intense form of interest.
2. a; *Stationary* and *fixed* are synonyms; so are *arbitrary* and *random*.
3. b; Sports are a physical activity; art is an aesthetic activity.

❷ Grammar

1. formal
2. nonstandard
3. informal
4. formal
5. nonstandard

Writing Application

Have partners check each other's paragraphs to see that sentences have been correctly labeled.

Integrate Language Skills

❶ Vocabulary Development Lesson

Word Analysis: Latin Root *-stat-*

The Latin root *-stat-* means "to stand." The root appears in the word *static*, which describes something that stands unchanging. Write a definition of each word below, incorporating the meaning of *-stat-* in your definition.

1. statue 2. stationary 3. statistics

Spelling Strategy

If a base word ends in two consonants, retain both consonants when adding a suffix. For example, *obsess* + *-ed* = *obsessed.*

Add the suffix shown and write each new word. Then, use each new word in a sentence.

1. lurk + *-ing*
2. harsh + *-ly*
3. content + *-ment*
4. vast + *-ness*

Concept Development: Analogies

On your paper, write the word that best completes each analogy. Then, write a sentence or two that explains the relationship between the words in each pair.

1. ecstatic : happy :: obsessed : __?__
   a. overwhelmed
   b. unconcerned
   c. interested
2. stationary : fixed :: arbitrary : __?__
   a. random
   b. specific
   c. cruel
3. physical : sports :: aesthetic : __?__
   a. people
   b. art
   c. running

❷ Grammar Lesson

Varieties of English: Standard and Nonstandard

Standard English can be either formal or informal. Formal English is used to address subjects in a serious way. Informal English is used when you want to achieve a conversational tone for casual writing. **Nonstandard English** is language that does not follow the rules of proper English usage.

Formal: Each successive frame of a movie is projected on exactly the same space.

Informal: Hi, I'm Scott McCloud. When I was a little kid I knew . . .

Nonstandard: Don't gimme that comic book talk!

Practice Identify each sentence as *formal*, *informal*, or *Nonstandard* English.

1. Comics are a visual and sequential art.
2. They're kinda like cartoons on paper.
3. Reading comics is really lots of fun.
4. To define comics, one must separate form from content.
5. I usta think comics were sorta uncool.

Writing Application Write a five-sentence paragraph about your reaction to McCloud's comics. Include both Standard and Nonstandard English, and then label each sentence *formal*, *informal*, or *Nonstandard*.

WG Prentice Hall Writing and Grammar Connection: Chapter 3, Section 3

TEACHING RESOURCES

The following resources can be used to enrich or extend the instructions for pp. 706–707.

Vocabulary

- **Selection Support:** Build Vocabulary, p. 169
- **Vocabulary and Spelling Practice Book** (Use this booklet for skills enrichment.) ■

Grammar

- **Selection Support:** Build Grammar Skills, p. 170
- **Writing and Grammar,** Gold Level, p. 42
- **Daily Language Practice Transparencies**

Writing

- **Writing Models and Graphic Organizers on Transparencies,** p. 71
- **Writing and Grammar,** Gold Level, p. 286 ■
- **Writing and Grammar iText CD-ROM**

■ **BLOCK SCHEDULING:** Resources marked with this symbol provide varied instruction during 90-minute blocks.

❸ Writing Lesson

Essay on Humor

Write a short essay about McCloud's use of humor in this excerpt from *Understanding Comics*. Discuss his use of visuals and other techniques, and explain how he uses humor both to entertain and to inform.

Prewriting Review the selection to determine the ways McCloud uses humor. On separate note cards, write each main point and the details that support the main point.

Model: Gathering Relevant Details

Main point I want to prove:
McCloud's humor is original.
Examples of original humor:
The image of the globe to convey the world of comics
The images he uses to explain sequential art

Specific details provide support for one main point.

Drafting Use your note cards to include references from the text that support your points. Include quotations or descriptions of images.

Revising Reread your draft, making sure you have used modifiers that clearly convey your thoughts and feelings. For example, the word *brilliant* conveys high praise, while *adequate* conveys mild praise.

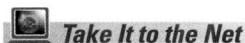

WG Prentice Hall Writing and Grammar Connection: Chapter 13, Section 2

❹ Extension Activities

Listening and Speaking In a group, research the subject of comics in all their variety and prepare a **visual presentation.** Follow these steps:

- Divide comics into five or fewer categories, such as superhero comic books, newspaper comic strips, and comic book adaptations of classic novels.
- Show an example of each type of comic.
- Discuss how each category began and how it has developed over the years.

Share your presentation with your class. **[Group Activity]**

Research and Technology Choose an activity that interests you and create a **comic strip** of your own based on the activity. Locate comics from the newspaper and consider using them as models. Use publishing software and graphic programs to publish your strip. Your tone can be serious or humorous, depending on your message.

Take It to the Net www.phschool.com

Go online for an additional research activity using the Internet.

ASSESSMENT RESOURCES

The following resources can be used to assess students' knowledge and skills.

Selection Assessment

- **Formal Assessment,** pp. 151–153
- **Open Book Test,** pp. 127–129
- **Got It! Assessment Videotapes,** Tape 4
- **Test Bank Software**

Take It to the Net

Visit www.phschool.com for self-tests and additional questions on "Understanding Comics."

PRENTICE HALL ASSESSMENT SYSTEM

- **Workbook**
- **Skill Book**
- **Transparencies**
- **CD-ROM**

Lesson Support for p. 707

❸ Writing Lesson

- You might suggest that students organize their ideas in outline form before they begin writing.
- Display the Herringbone Organizer, p. 71 in **Writing Models and Graphic Organizers on Transparencies,** to give students another means of organizing their details.
- Students may enjoy responding to McCloud's essay in the same form in which he wrote it, by writing a comic-strip essay. Students can use the Gifted/Talented activity on p. 699 of this teacher's edition as a springboard or alternative to this writing lesson.

❹ Research and Technology

- Tell students that the comic strips and cartoons that appear in newspapers are hand-drawn and hand-lettered. Encourage them to use the old-fashioned methods most comic artists use to draw and write their comic strips.
- Challenge students to come up with a week's worth of comic strips. You might have them follow the method most cartoonists use: black-and-white strips for six days and a color strip on Sunday. Have all students combine their strips into a funny paper that can be distributed to the whole class.
- Remind students that the tone of their comics is entirely up to them; comics need not be funny.

CUSTOMIZE INSTRUCTION For Universal Access

To address different learning styles, use the following activities suggested in the **Extension Activities** booklet, p. 43.

- For Intrapersonal Learners, use Activity 5.
- For Verbal/Linguistic Learners, use Activities 5 and 7.
- For Visual/Spatial Learners, use Activities 6 and 7.

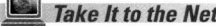

Earhart Redux ✦ In These Girls, Hope Is a Muscle

Lesson Objectives and CA Correlations

1. **To analyze and respond to literary elements**
   - Literary Analysis: Career Writing
   - Comparing Literary Works
2. **To read, comprehend, analyze, and critique nonfiction**
   - Reading Strategy: Determining the Author's Purpose
   - Reading Check questions
   - Review and Assess questions
   - Assessment Practice (ATE)
3. **To develop word analysis skills, fluency, and systematic vocabulary**
   - Vocabulary Development Lesson: Greek Root: *-dyna-* **R 1.1**
4. **To understand and apply written and oral language conventions**
   - Spelling Strategy
   - Grammar Lesson: Usage: *There, Their, They're* **LC 1.3**
5. **To understand and apply appropriate writing and research strategies**
   - Writing Lesson: Letter to Linda Finch **W 1.2**
   - Extension Activity: Research Project **W 1.4**
6. **To understand and apply listening and speaking strategies**
   - Extension Activity: Book Chat **LS 1.8**

STEP-BY-STEP TEACHING GUIDE	PACING GUIDE
PRETEACH	
Motivate Students and Provide Background	
Use the Motivation activity (ATE p. 708)	5 min.
Read and discuss the Preview material and Background information (SE/ATE p. 708) [A]	5 min.
Introduce the Concepts	
Introduce the Literary Analysis and Reading Strategy (SE/ATE p. 709) [A]	15 min.
Pronounce the vocabulary words and read their definitions (SE p. 709)	5 min.
TEACH	
Monitor Comprehension	
Informally monitor comprehension by circulating while students read independently or in groups [A]	20 min.
Monitor students' comprehension with the Reading Check notes (SE/ATE pp. 711, 713)	as students read
Develop vocabulary with Vocabulary notes (SE pp. 711, 713, 715, 717–718; ATE p. 711)	as students read
Develop Understanding	
Develop students' understanding of career writing with Literary Analysis annotations (SE p. 712; ATE pp. 712, 717) [A]	10 min.
Develop students' ability to determine the author's purpose with the Reading Strategy annotations (SE pp. 711, 715, 717; ATE pp. 711, 714–717)	10 min.
ASSESS	
Assess Mastery	
Assess students' mastery of the Reading Strategy and Literary Analysis by having them answer the Review and Assess questions (SE/ATE p. 719)	20 min.
Use one or more of the print and media Assessment Resources (ATE p. 721) [A]	up to 50 min.
EXTEND	
Apply Understanding	
Have students complete the Vocabulary Development Lesson and the Grammar Lesson (SE p. 720) [A]	20 min.
Apply students' knowledge of highlighting support with the Writing Lesson (SE p. 721) [A]	45 min.
Apply students' understanding of the selection using one or more of the Extension Activities (SE p. 721)	20–90 min.

[A] **ACCELERATED INSTRUCTION:** Use the strategies and activities identified with an [A].

UNIVERSAL ACCESS
● = Below Level Students
▲ = On-Level Students
■ = Above Level Students

Time and Resource Manager

Reading Level: Average/Easy
Average Number of Instructional Days: 4

RESOURCES		
PRINT	**TRANSPARENCIES**	**TECHNOLOGY**
• **Beyond Literature,** Career Connection: Aviation, p. 44 ▲ ■		• **Interest Grabber Video,** Tape 4 ● ▲ ■
• **Selection Support Workbook:** ● ▲ ■ Literary Analysis, p. 176 Reading Strategy, p. 175 Build Vocabulary, p. 173	• **Literary Analysis and Reading Transparencies,** pp. 87 and 88 ● ▲ ■	
		• **Listening to Literature** ● ▲ ■ Audiocassettes, Side 26 Audio CDs, CD 14
• **Literatura en español** ● ▲ • **Literary Analysis for Enrichment** ■		
• **Formal Assessment:** Selection Test, pp. 154–156 ● ▲ ■ • **Open Book Test,** pp. 130–132 ● ▲ ■ • **Performance Assessment and Portfolio Management,** p. 9 ● ▲ ■ • PRENTICE HALL ASSESSMENT SYSTEM ● ▲ ■	• PRENTICE HALL ASSESSMENT SYSTEM ● ▲ ■ Skills Practice Answers and Explanations on Transparencies	• **Test Bank Software** ● ▲ ■ • **Got It! Assessment Videotapes,** Tape 4 ● ▲
• **Selection Support Workbook:** ● ▲ ■ Build Grammar Skills, p. 174 • **Writing and Grammar,** Gold Level ● ▲ ■ • **Extension Activities,** p. 44 ● ▲ ■	• **Daily Language Practice Transparencies** ● ▲ • **Writing Models and Graphic Organizers on Transparencies,** p. 91 ● ▲ ■	• **Writing and Grammar iText CD-ROM** ● ▲ ■ *Take It to the Net* www.phschool.com

BLOCK SCHEDULING: Use one 90-minute class period to preteach the selection and have students read it. Use a second 90-minute class period to assess students' mastery of skills and have them complete one of the Extension Activities.

PRETEACH

Step-by-Step Teaching Guide for pp. 708–709

Motivation

Ask students whether they enjoy puzzling over unsolved mysteries of the past, such as how the pyramids were built or what Stonehenge was used for. Have them read the Background on p. 708 of their textbooks to learn about another unsolved mystery—the disappearance of pilot Amelia Earhart. Tell students that in this essay, they will read about a woman who attempts the same flight on which Earhart disappeared.

Interest Grabber Video

As an alternative, play "WNBA: A Dream Come True" on Tape 4 to engage student interest.

1 Background

History

Earhart's final destination was Howland Island, southwest of Hawaii in the South Pacific. The search for her plane has never abated. A 1930s woman's shoe in Earhart's size and style, along with some human remains, food cans, and other small signs of human occupation were found years later on the island of Nikumaroro, about 400 miles southeast of Howland. This island was uninhabited in 1932, but a flier reported signs of human habitation in 1937. The only known missing persons of European origin in this area were Earhart and Noonan.

Airplane components found in Nikumaroro's village (the island is now inhabited) match the plane Earhart flew. Investigators believe that she landed her plane on the reef at the island's edge, the plane was washed out to sea, and she and Noonan got to shore but did not survive long. Though the evidence they have found is highly suggestive, Earhart and Noonan's fate remains a mystery.

Prepare to Read

Earhart Redux ◆ In These Girls, Hope Is a Muscle

Take It to the Net

Visit www.phschool.com for interactive activities and instruction related to the selections, including
- background
- graphic organizers
- literary elements
- reading strategies

Preview

Connecting to the Literature

Sometimes a failure can be the most powerful incentive for a new victory. If you have ever wanted something, lost it, and then wanted it even more, you will know the truth at the heart of these true stories.

1 Background

In 1932, at age thirty-five, Amelia Earhart became the first woman to fly solo across the Atlantic Ocean. Five years later, she attempted to fly around the world, accompanied only by a navigator. After circling three quarters of the globe, the pair disappeared on July 1, 1937, near New Guinea. Earhart's final message reported empty fuel tanks. Her plane was never found. In 1997, Linda Finch successfully re-created and completed Earhart's flight around the world in a similar aircraft.

TEACHING RESOURCES

The following resources can be used to enrich or extend the instruction for pp. 708–709.

Motivation

Interest Grabber Video, Tape 3

Background

Beyond Literature, p. 44

Take It to the Net

Visit www.phschool.com for background and hotlinks for "Earhart Redux" and "In These Girls, Hope Is a Muscle."

Literary Analysis

Literary Analysis and Reading Transparencies, Career Writing, p. 88

Reading

Selection Support: Reading Strategy, p. 175; Build Vocabulary, p. 173

Literary Analysis and Reading Transparencies, Determining the Author's Purpose, p. 87

BLOCK SCHEDULING: Resources marked with this symbol provide varied instruction during 90-minute blocks.

❷ Literary Analysis

Career Writing

Writing is an important part of a wide range of occupations—for example, television reporting, advertising, even police work. **Career writing** is any writing that is done as part of a person's job responsibilities. In this example, writer Tracy Kidder presents his review of a fellow reporter's work:

> This book is the product of a perfect marriage. The subject is timely and fascinating, and Madeleine Blais is a first-rate reporter and writer.

As you read the selections, note the type of career writing that each represents. Then, consider the qualities that the pieces share.

Comparing Literary Works

Each of the following selections tells about real women who are defined by the challenges they take on. As you read, compare the different experiences and challenges of the women in each piece, as well as the ways these writers address their subjects' struggles.

❸ Reading Strategy

Determining the Author's Purpose

Career writing is shaped most of all by its purpose—the goal the writer sets out to achieve. When you **determine the author's purpose,** you seek to understand the writer's goal, which may be to inform, to entertain, or to persuade. You can determine the writer's purpose by paying close attention to details in the writing. Use a chart like the one shown to record details and identify each writer's purpose.

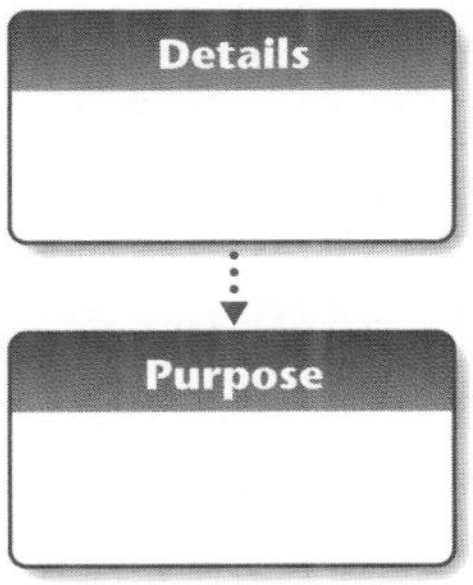

Vocabulary Development

aerodynamics (er´ ō dī nam´ iks) *n.* branch of mechanics dealing with the forces exerted by air or other gases in motion (p. 711)

hydraulic (hī drô´ lik) *adj.* operated by the movement and pressure of liquid (p. 713)

pursue (pər so͞o´) *v.* seek (p. 715)

improbable (im präb´ ə bəl) *adj.* unlikely to happen (p. 715)

derides (di rīdz´) *v.* ridicules (p. 715)

legacy (leg´ ə sē) *n.* anything handed down from an ancestor (p. 715)

riveting (riv´ it iŋ) *adj.* firmly holding attention (p. 717)

ruminative (ro͞o´ mə nə təv) *adj.* meditative (p. 717)

adept (ə dept´) *adj.* highly skilled; expert (p. 717)

compelling (kəm pel´ iŋ) *adj.* forceful (p. 718)

❷ Literary Analysis

Career Writing

- Have students brainstorm a list of jobs in which writing is an important part of the day's work. In addition to obvious answers, such as publishing, journalism, law, politics, broadcasting, and teaching, a chef has to write recipes and shopping lists, a police officer has to write "incident reports," and so on.
- As students read, have them think about the different kinds of writing required in different fields of endeavor.
- Display the Career Writing transparency, p. 88 in **Literary Analysis and Reading Strategy Transparencies,** to help guide students as they read.

❸ Reading Strategy

Determining the Author's Purpose

- Students have worked on determining the author's purpose throughout the year. You might have them turn back to p. 163 in Unit 2 and p. 471 in Unit 5 to review this strategy on their own.
- Remind students that no author writes without a purpose.
- As students read these selections, have them think about each writer's purpose. Encourage students to use a chart like the one shown to help them record details that suggest purpose.

Vocabulary Development

- Pronounce each vocabulary word for students, and read the definitions as a class. Have students identify any words with which they are already familiar.

CUSTOMIZE INSTRUCTION FOR UNIVERSAL ACCESS

For Less Proficient Readers	For English Learners	For Advanced Readers
Challenge students to make a four-column Author's Purpose table headed *Inform, Persuade, Entertain,* and *Express an Opinion.* As they read each selection, students can note details in the appropriate columns and discuss the author's purposes after reading.	Have partners read and discuss each selection together. Partners should help each other summarize the details of each selection. They can then identify the author's purposes, citing details that support their answers.	Have students think about the link between career writing and an author's purpose. Which careers require informative writing? Persuasive writing? Writing for entertainment? Have students apply these questions to the two selections. Can career writing have more than one purpose?

E-Teach

Visit E-Teach at www.phschool.com for teachers' essays on how to teach, with questions and answers.

TEACH

Step-by-Step Teaching Guide for pp. 710–718

CUSTOMIZE INSTRUCTION
For Interpersonal Learners

Have students think about what these selections suggest regarding interdependence. Have them think about whether Finch or the Lady Hurricanes could possibly achieve their goals without the help and cooperation of other people. Have students discuss the importance of working with others, as well as what can be learned from team sports beyond the sports themselves.

❶ About the Selection

Alex Chadwick interviews pilot Linda Finch on his radio show just before she attempts to duplicate Amelia Earhart's round-the-world flight. Finch describes the differences between her plane and Earhart's, answers questions about her reasons for undertaking the flight, and discusses her feelings about Earhart.

❶ Earhart Redux

Alex Chadwick

TEACHING RESOURCES

The following resources can be used to enrich or extend the instruction for pp. 710–718.

Literary Analysis

- **Writing Models and Graphic Organizers on Transparencies,** p. 91 ■
- **Selection Support:** Literary Analysis, p. 176

Reading

- **Listening to Literature Audiocassettes,** Side 21 ■
- **Listening to Literature Audio CDs,** CD 14 ■

■ **BLOCK SCHEDULING:** Resources marked with this symbol provide varied instruction during 90-minute blocks.

On March 17, 1997, national interest was piqued as Linda Finch set off to complete the flight that Amelia Earhart had attempted sixty years earlier. Alex Chadwick, a radio reporter for National Public Radio, conducted a radio interview with Linda Finch before her flight. The following is the script of Chadwick's interview.

BOB EDWARDS, HOST: This is *Morning Edition.* I'm Bob Edwards.

In Oakland, California, this morning, pilot Linda Finch takes off on an adventure that actually started 60 years ago. On this day in 1937, Amelia Earhart began her attempt to become the first person to fly around the world at the equator. She failed.

Her plane disappeared over the Pacific Ocean, but in that, she achieved a measure of immortality.

In the latest National Geographic Radio Expedition, NPR's[1] Alex Chadwick reports Linda Finch hopes to finish what Amelia Earhart began.

SOUNDS OF MACHINERY

ALEX CHADWICK, NPR REPORTER: The door to the hangar is bigger than any big theater movie screen. And it's opening slowly and improbably, folding outward on a horizontal midline and upward from the bottom. ❸ And there is Linda Finch's amazing airplane: 1930s aerodynamics, like an artifact from an old movie, or a dream.

❷ **LINDA FINCH, PILOT:** The aircraft is very rare. There were only fifteen manufactured initially in the twenties and thirties, and there are only two left in the world.

CHADWICK: Ms. Finch is pretty rare herself. A 46-year-old grandmother who owns several nursing homes in Texas, and a pilot who restores and flies vintage fighters. Even so, replicating Amelia Earhart's flight is difficult. And though she doesn't like to say so, a little risky.

SOUNDS OF DOORS OPENING AND CLOSING

FINCH: We'll be flying in an aircraft that is the exact same model Amelia flew. And we'll be following the same route that she flew around the world.

CHADWICK: Well, I'm sure some people hearing about this flight would say, what is the point of setting off in an aircraft that's already failed in this once? I mean, it's dangerous. Maybe recklessly dangerous.

FINCH: Well, I have a lot of advantages that Amelia didn't have. We will have modern navigation, communication, and flight instruments that she just didn't have available at the time. The flight, I believe, needs to be done in the right airplane, to be historically correct, to generate the excitement in order to communicate our message.

I started learning about Amelia and really feel like I came to know her. And although I think that flying was definitely a part of her being,

1. **NPR's** National Public Radio's.

aerodynamics (er´ ō dī nam´ iks) *n.* branch of mechanics dealing with the forces exerted by air or other gases in motion

Reading Strategy
Determining the Author's Purpose
What is the author's goal in this passage?

❹ **Reading Check**
What does Linda Finch hope to accomplish?

❷ Reading Strategy

Determining the Author's Purpose

- Ask students how Chadwick describes the hangar door.
  Answer: The hangar door is larger than a theater movie screen and opens in an unusual way, folding in the middle and rising.
- Then, ask students why they think Chadwick includes this description of the airplane hangar.
  Answer: Since this is a radio interview, his listeners can't see the hangar opening. He wants to tell them how this looks, and the dramatic opening of the hangar is an adroit "opening" for his interview.
- Ask the Reading Strategy question on p. 711: What is the author's goal in this passage?
  Answer: The author wants his readers to get to know some unusual qualities of his guest.

❸ Vocabulary Development

The Greek root *-dyna-*

- Point out the word *aerodynamics* in the bracketed passage. Explain to students that the Greek root *-dyna-* means "power" or "strength."
- Have students suggest other words that contain this Greek root. Then, ask students to look up the definitions of these words in a dictionary. Make sure students can explain how this root word in used in each of the words they identify.

❹ Reading Check

Answer: Finch wants to fly around the world following Amelia Earhart's route and return safely.

CUSTOMIZE INSTRUCTION FOR UNIVERSAL ACCESS

For Special Needs Students	For Gifted/Talented Students
Have students gather in a small group and read aloud "Earhart Redux" as though they were participating in the actual radio broadcast, with each student taking one role. Pause whenever necessary during the reading to ask comprehension questions, or to allow students to ask questions of their own.	Have students do some research into the transatlantic flights of Charles Lindbergh and Amelia Earhart. Students may want to compare and contrast the newspaper and radio coverage of the flights, the airplanes flown by the two pilots, their backgrounds, or other aspects. Show the Comparison-and-Contrast Organizer in **Writing Models and Graphic Organizers on Transparencies,** p. 91, to help students arrange their details.

5 Literary Analysis

Career Writing

- Ask students the Literary Analysis question on p. 712: What information did Chadwick need to research in order to prepare this writing assignment?

Answer: Chadwick needed to learn about the early history of aviation and about the first transatlantic flight. He needed to research information about Amelia Earhart's plane.

Monitor Progress Ask students how the absence of this information would affect the radio broadcast.

Answer: Many listeners might not know this information, so they wouldn't understand why Finch is making this flight or what risks she is taking.

that she really flew to get the recognition to convince people that they could do what they wanted. Especially women in the 1930s. That people weren't limited to small lives. That they could have their dreams.

CHADWICK: Amelia Earhart was an aviation pioneer, daring and determined. The second flyer after Lindbergh[2] to solo across the Atlantic. Fourteen others had died trying to repeat his flight, and Amelia nearly did when a crucial instrument failed in bad weather.

Here's that earlier flyer after her Atlantic flight, when President Hoover presented her with a gold medal from the National Geographic Society.

AMELIA EARHART, PILOT: I came down until I could see the flight path blinking in the darkness. If it had been a smooth sea, I might have come too far. Whether I was 50 feet off the water or 150, I do not know, without my altimeter. I was too close, however.

5 **CHADWICK:** The plane that Amelia used on her round-the-world attempt, the Lockheed Electra 10-E, is 38.5 feet long, with a 55-foot wingspan. The tail angles back on a small, solid rubber rear wheel. The nose tilts upwards toward the sky. She glows like a polished aluminum athlete, broad-shouldered. Beautiful as a swan dive.

SOUND OF AIRPLANE ENGINE

She carries two nine-cylinder radial Pratt and Whitney Wasp engines. These are the first air-cooled engines developed. At 650 pounds, they produced more than 400 horsepower when they were introduced in 1926, and that was an extraordinary weight-power ratio for the time.

Linda Finch's plane has later, more powerful versions of that engine, as did Amelia Earhart's. Except for new navigation and communication gear, their planes are identical.

FINCH: The aircraft was in boxes and pieces and parts. And one of the things that I discovered was that prior to World War II, there were no parts manuals. You get just a big box of pieces, and it's like a jigsaw puzzle, you have to figure out how to put it together.

CHADWICK: She describes the Electra as graceful and slow in flight. Almost peaceful. Amelia did all her flying, but carried a navigator copilot. And so will Linda. The cockpit is a narrow, confined space, barely enough room for twin controls. And the enormous, banquet-sized steering wheels.

SOUND OF WHEELS TURNING

What do these wheels feel like? They look like they came out of

Literary Analysis
Career Writing
What information did Chadwick need to research in order to prepare this writing assignment?

2. **Lindbergh** Charles Lindbergh (1902–1974) made the first solo nonstop flight across the Atlantic Ocean on May 20–21, 1927.

ENRICHMENT: Career Connection

Communications

Alex Chadwick is an electronic journalist who works as a researcher, writer, and performer. Many who work in radio and television never go in front of the microphone or on camera. Behind-the-scenes jobs in electronic journalism include work in camera operation, lighting sound, film and tape editing, and engineering.

Have interested students pick any of these careers and learn what skills and educational requirements would be needed to pursue them.

1940s British sports cars or something.

FINCH: Exactly, and the wood is so worn. We actually had some new ones we could have put in. But I like these because they're worn and they've been in the airplane, obviously, since it was new.

CHADWICK: So, this is all human-powered controls for turning things and making the airplane fly?

FINCH: Absolutely. People are very surprised that there is just a thin cable and actually you move the cable. Everyone always says, does it have hydraulic controls? Absolutely not.

hydraulic (hī drô′ lik) *adj.* operated by the movement and pressure of liquid

CHADWICK: These things here, these switches and hand controls. Those are original on the plane. This is what Amelia Earhart flew.

FINCH: Exactly. There are many things, the controls, throttle, and the propeller and mixture controls, the fuel selector gauges, the magneto switches, the gear indicator. All of the things that have to do with the airplane mechanically are in fact the same as Amelia's.

CHADWICK: The plane was in the airport in Memphis, en route for
6 tests elsewhere. Linda, and navigator Bob Fodge, had refilled the main battery the evening before, and something had gone wrong. Overnight it leaked acid, eating away at a small panel of the undercarriage. They had to remove it.

The technology is 60 and 70 years old. Linda Finch knows how it works. Why it works. Why it's reliable. But she is attempting to fly around the world in an airplane where the rivets all show. And the cockpit windows slide open, and little accidents cause the flawless aluminum skin to weaken and decay.

The navigation electronics are as good as you could get. She has an on-board satellite link to the Internet. Schools can check her progress hourly. But the actual airplane is decades older than Linda Finch herself. And on many portions of this flight, she's going to have to overload that plane with fuel in order to cross open water.

What does your daughter think? What does your family think, when you are setting off to re-create a flight that Amelia Earhart did not survive?

FINCH: Well, my daughter is very supportive and excited and pleased. And is real involved in the project. On the other hand, she's a worrier. So, she always worries.

And she's most happy that we'll actually be sending the airplane's position back on the Internet every hour. So, I think she'll be watching that quite closely to see where we are.

CHADWICK: Oakland; across the country to Miami; then San Juan, Puerto Rico; Cumana, Venezuela; Paramari, Vos Serena; down to Natale in Brazil, and across to Africa. Dakkar, Injamana, Khartoum. It'll be hot over the desert. Karachi, Calcutta, Rangoon. In a couple of

7 **Reading Check**

How does Finch say her family has responded to her adventure?

6 Critical Thinking

Evaluate

- Have students focus on the questions Chadwick asks in this section of the interview. Ask students whether these are good questions that elicit useful and interesting information. If not, why?
  Answer: The first three questions get Finch to describe her plane and help listeners understand what it looks like and how different it is from the planes they see at modern airports. The question about Finch's family is interesting because it helps listeners identify with her; she is an ordinary person, a family member whose relatives are worried about her safety.
- Ask students how these questions help listeners understand Earhart's experience.
  Answer: Like Finch, Earhart had loving relatives who were concerned about her. The questions also elicit details about the kind of plane Earhart flew.

7 Reading Check

Answer: Family members are supportive and excited but worried about her safety.

ENRICHMENT: History Connection

Finch Succeeds

Students may be relieved to learn that Linda Finch successfully completed her round-the-world flight retracing Amelia Earhart's historic but incomplete venture. On May 28, 1997, Finch landed in Oakland, California, having taken off from the same airport on March 17th, the sixtieth anniversary of Earhart's fateful departure. In the intervening weeks, Finch flew 26,004 miles, touched down on six continents, and made 34 stops in 18 countries.

Like Earhart, Finch was accompanied by a navigator (Denny Ghiringhelli), but she did all the flying. Though her Lockheed Electra 10E aircraft was virtually identical to Earhart's, Finch enjoyed a significant edge in safety with her modern navigational equipment. Many experts believe navigational problems caused the Earhart flight to miss its Howland Island destination in the Pacific.

8 Reading Strategy

Determining the Author's Purpose

- Remind students that they can determine an author's purpose by paying careful attention to the details in the writing.
- Draw students' attention to Earhart's statement which begins "I hope that this flight…." Ask students why they think Chadwick quotes Earhart's statement after her transatlantic flight.
  Answer: He wants to reinforce the connection between Earhart and Finch. He may wish to inspire listeners with this reference to a heroine.

Answers for p. 714

Review and Assess

1. Most students will say yes, because she is taking a risk and honoring the memory of a heroic woman.
2. **(a)** He describes her as a 46-year-old grandmother, an owner of nursing homes, and a pilot. **(b)** He seems to be excited about the mission, interested in the details of the aircraft, and aware of the risk Finch is taking.
3. **(a)** She and her navigator disappeared over the South Pacific, an enduring mystery. **(b)** Details about the plane's age suggest that the flight is risky.
4. **(a)** Earhart's voice is heard twice. **(b)** Chadwick emphasizes a connection between Earhart and Finch and creates the eerie illusion that Earhart is part of the interview.
5. **(a)** Students may cite sounds of machinery, doors opening and closing, airplane engines running, wheels turning, and a propeller spinning. **(b)** Sound effects help listeners feel as if they were present at the takeoff.
6. The flight might be proof that women can succeed at whatever they try.
7. The public might realize that they, too, can strive beyond the ordinary.

months, she'll get to Lahe, New Guinea, the last place that Amelia Earhart was ever seen.

Here's Amelia, after flying the Atlantic.

8 **EARHART:** I hope that the flight has meant something to women in aviation. If it has, I shall feel it justified. But I can't claim anything else.

CHADWICK: And here is Linda Finch. In a tan wool gabardine flight suit, strains showing in her face a little from the work and the stress, but mostly looking eager to go finish that great adventure.

FINCH: Well, I don't know what happened to Amelia Earhart, and neither does anyone else, certainly. When I'm reading a book about Amelia and I get to the last communications that they heard from her, that's really where I stop reading. Because I just think it doesn't matter. What does matter is what Amelia did with her life, and that's really the focus of our project.

SOUND OF AN AIRPLANE PROPELLER

CHADWICK: Pilot Linda Finch, who sets out today to fly around the world in a Lockheed Electra 10-E, the plane Amelia Earhart flew.

For Radio Expeditions, this is Alex Chadwick reporting.

Review and Assess

Thinking About the Selection

1. **Respond:** Do you admire Linda Finch for undertaking her adventure? Explain.
2. **(a) Recall:** As the interview begins, what words does Alex Chadwick use to describe Finch? **(b) Analyze:** How does Chadwick seem to feel about Finch and her mission?
3. **(a) Recall:** What happened to Amelia Earhart when she attempted to fly around the world at the equator? **(b) Evaluate:** What details of the report add to the suspense about the outcome of Finch's endeavor?
4. **(a) Recall:** How often is Amelia Earhart's voice heard in the interview? **(b) Speculate:** What effect does Chadwick create by including the voice of Earhart?
5. **(a) Recall:** What sound effects does Chadwick use in his interview? **(b) Draw a Conclusion:** Why does Chadwick use the sound effects in his work?
6. **Evaluate:** In the interview, Earhart says, "I hope that the flight has meant something to women in aviation." What do you think Finch's flight might mean to these women?
7. **Assess:** How might Finch inspire the general public?

Alex Chadwick

(b. 1947)

As you read "Earhart Redux," you may have noticed the references to sound effects. Alex Chadwick's work as a correspondent for National Public Radio for more than twenty years has been marked by his use of such sounds to anchor his stories in reality.

Before becoming a radio correspondent, Chadwick earned a degree in communications from American University in Washington, D.C., and worked in Maine as both a radio reporter and a commercial fisherman.

Chadwick's accomplishments in radio include his essays and features on the critically acclaimed radio programs *Morning Edition* and *All Things Considered*. He also co-hosted the Public Broadcasting Service television series *Childhood* in 1991.

❾ In These Girls, Hope Is a Muscle

Book Review by *Steve Gietschier*

If you have not yet had the opportunity to give your heart to a women's high school basketball team or to feel the passion of women's athletics in general, reading this book may be the start of something big. Although its poetic title alone could win an award, the text is even better: beautifully written, heartfelt, gently humorous but most important, forthright in its insistence that women as well as men should be able to pursue genuine excellence through sports.

Blais explains how improbable it is to find a championship basketball team of either gender, John Calipari's Massachusetts' squad[1] excluded, in Amherst, Mass., a town she derides as "probably the only place in the United States where men can wear berets and not get beaten up." Amherst, she says, "is, for the most part, smoke free, nuclear free and eager to free Tibet."[2] It is the proud home of Bread & Circus, the self-proclaimed world's largest health food store. More significantly, Amherst is, in Blais' view, "an achingly democratic sort of
❿ place in which tryouts for Little League, with their inevitable rejections, have caused people to suggest that more teams should be created so that no one is left out."

Far from an athlete herself, Blais nevertheless was still able to find unfolding within Amherst's "self-absorbed loftiness" the glistening struggle of superb competitors, the Lady Hurricanes of Amherst Regional High School. Picking up their story with the final game of the 1991–92 season, Blais followed their efforts throughout 1992–93, an epic campaign dedicated to overcoming a long legacy of being good, but just not good enough.

On the surface, then, this book is a simple tale of a singular basketball season. . . . Readers looking for no more than a good story

pursue (pər sōō´) *v.* seek

improbable (im präb´ ə bəl) *adj.* unlikely to happen

derides (di rīdz´) *v.* ridicules

Reading Strategy Determining the Author's Purpose Why does Gietschier include Blais's quote about the qualities of Amherst?

legacy (leg´ ə sē) *n.* anything handed down from an ancestor

1. **John Calipari's Massachusetts' squad** coach of an excellent basketball team at University of Massachusetts.
2. **to free Tibet** Once a semi-independent state, Tibet has been part of China since the 1950s.

❾ About the Selection

The review of *In These Girls, Hope Is a Muscle* entices readers to experience the complete book by providing snippets of information that will make them eager for more. The reader discovers that the book not only chronicles the championship season of a woman's high-school basketball team, but also provides insight into the extraordinary courage of each young woman on the team.

❿ Reading Strategy

Determining the Author's Purpose

- Ask the Reading Strategy question on p. 715: Why does Gietschier include Blais's quote about the qualities of Amherst?
  Answer: It gives an example of her humor and wit, showing that the book will be entertaining. It helps readers understand why Amherst is the last place one would expect to find a competitive woman's basketball team.
- Ask students what impression of Amherst is created by this quote.
  Answer: Amherst appears to be an idealistic and tolerant community that is a bit uneasy about competition.

CUSTOMIZE INSTRUCTION FOR UNIVERSAL ACCESS

For Gifted/Talented Students	For Advanced Readers
Ask students to create front and back covers for a paperback edition of *In These Girls, Hope Is a Muscle.* Bring several nonfiction sports books to class as examples, then suggest students work in groups to develop an eye-catching, dramatic cover that reflects the content of the book. Students may find useful quotes about the book from the jacket copy on p. 717 to use on their back covers.	Encourage interested students to locate and read Blais's book. Have them write reviews of their own, modeled on Gietschier's review. Students may want to glance at copies of other book reviews for models. Remind them to give their reactions to the book and to explain their reasons, not simply summarize the book's contents.

⓫ Reading Strategy

Determining the Author's Purpose

- Ask students to summarize these two paragraphs. Challenge them to state the main idea of the passage in a sentence.
  Answer: A basketball season is not only about games, but about individual journeys through hardship to discovery and achievement.
- Ask why the reviewer includes this passage. What does he want his readers to get from it?
  Answer: He wants to persuade readers to read Blais's book by showing that, even if they aren't interested in basketball, people might enjoy the book for its deep human interest.

⓬ ▶Critical Viewing

Answer: The player's face shows determination and concentration.

can chart the season game by game and turn one page after another in anticipation of the next victory.

But there is so much more here to savor and absorb. The young women who give themselves so completely to their team's quest are extraordinary each in her own way. Burdened with the pains of adolescence, the duties that high school imposes and, in some cases, the tough circumstances of families rent asunder,[3] they learn from one another how to dig deep ⓫ to find the resources they need to reach their goal.

In the process, they journey in so many ways to places Amherst women have never gone before, proving to themselves, their families, their town and all who will look with open eyes that women's sports can be an astoundingly fulfilling and moving experience.

3. **rent asunder** (ə sun´ dər) torn apart.

⓬ **▶ Critical Viewing** How might this player's facial expression reflect the experiences of the Lady Hurricanes? **[Infer]**

ENRICHMENT: Workplace Connection

Athletics

Point out that students need not be star athletes to find jobs that are connected to physical education. Encourage interested students to learn about opportunities in their area. Public swimming pools need lifeguards and maintenance personnel. Summer sports programs need coaches and assistants. Once students have learned what jobs are available, suggest that they learn how to apply for these positions, and what qualifications are needed. Parks or recreation departments might be a good place to start. Invite interested students to share the information they gather on jobs related to physical education. They might want to create a chart indicating the job openings, the job requirements, and whom to contact for further information.

As part of the marketing of a book, many publishers include brief reviews by well-known writers or public figures. Following are some of the comments that appeared on the book jacket of Madeleine Blais's book.

Book Jacket Copy for

In These Girls, Hope Is a Muscle Madeleine Blais

Advance praise for *In These Girls, Hope Is a Muscle*:

This book is the product of a perfect marriage. The subject is timely and fascinating, and Madeleine Blais is a first-rate reporter and writer.

—*Tracy Kidder*

13 Blais's narrative gift has produced a touching, exciting book about a subject largely ignored until now, namely women athletes. Her story of a year in the life of a high school basketball team and its hometown goes far beyond the obvious to illuminate how people really feel, how things really work.

—*Anne Bernays*

Begun as an article that appeared in the *New York Times Magazine*, *In These Girls, Hope Is a Muscle* offers a riveting close-up of the girls on a high school basketball team whose passion for the sport is rivaled only by their loyalty to one another. Reminiscent of John McPhee's *A Sense of Where You Are* and H. G. Bissinger's *Friday Night Lights*, Pulitzer Prize–winning journalist Madeleine Blais's book takes the reader through a singular season in the history of the Lady Hurricanes of Amherst, Massachusetts.

For years they had been known as a finesse team, talented and hard-working players who in the end lacked that final hardscrabble ingredient that would take them over the top to the state championship. They seemed doomed to mirror the college town they represented: kindly, ruminative, at times ineffectual; more adept at quoting Emily Dickinson[1] and singing nature songs than going to the basket.

14 One season, all that changed. Madeleine Blais takes us from try-outs to practices during the regular season, up through the final championship game against the mighty Hillies from Haverhill. The result is an astoundingly moving narrative that captures the complexities of girls' experiences in high school, in sports, and in our society.

riveting (riv′ it iŋ) *adj.* firmly holding attention

ruminative (ro͞o′ mə nə təv) *adj.* meditative

adept (ə dept′) *adj.* highly skilled; expert

Reading Strategy
Determining the Author's Purpose What are two goals the writer exhibits in this passage?

1. **Emily Dickinson** (1830–1886), poet who was born and lived most of her life in Amherst, Massachusetts.

13 Literary Analysis

Career Writing

- Ask students which of these quotations is more intriguing or persuasive to them.
  Answer: Students may cite the second quotation because it provides more detail on the book.
- Why would publishers want to print quotations like these on a book jacket?
  Answer: Favorable reviews like these might convince people to buy the book.

Monitor Progress Offer students several types of books—spy novel, book on baseball, history of broadcast news, a cookbook—and have them suggest names or categories of people whose comments would be persuasive on the book's jacket.
Answer: Students' suggestions should reflect two criteria for quoters: (1) they should be well known to readers; (2) they should have some expertise or authority on the book's subject area.

14 Reading Strategy

Determining the Author's Purpose

- Have students explain the purpose of book-jacket copy beyond just the title and author's name.
  Answer: The copy can inform readers about the contents of a book and can persuade them that the book is worth reading.
- Ask the Reading Strategy question on p. 717: What are two goals the writer exhibits in this passage?
  Answer: The writer provides a basic summary of the scope of the book and emphasizes distinctive qualities to pull in prospective readers.

ASSESS

Answers for p. 718

Review and Assess

1. Many students may make an affirmative response because the blurb and review describe the book as a gripping story of courage and determination.
2. **(a)** Gietschier describes the book as "beautifully written, heartfelt, gently humorous, forthright." **(b)** He apparently admires the persistence and determination of the characters in the story she tells.
3. **(a)** The book tells the story of an Amherst high-school girls' basketball team's championship season. **(b)** She admired the girls' achievements as a team, but was also intrigued by their dramatic personal stories.
4. **(a)** They prove that playing sports can be a fulfilling and moving experience. **(b)** Probable readers include athletes, especially women and girls; sports fans, especially basketball fans; and anyone who supports equality and opportunity for women and girls.
5. **(a)** Tracy Kidder and Anne Bernays **(b)** They both recommend the book. **(c)** Her main idea is that team sports are not just about playing or winning, but also about courage and determination. She obviously cares about the subject since she followed the team for a whole season and developed her observations into a book.
6. Students may describe the blurb as more informative, the review as more persuasive.

14 As their coach says, unlike training boys—whose arrogance and confidence often have to be eroded before a team can pull together—working with girls is all constructive. The way to build a girls' team is to build each player's self-confidence. During the course of this season we see the Amherst Lady Hurricanes in their fierce, funny, sisterhood-is-powerful quest for excellence.

As Blais reports, "This is just one team in one season. It alone cannot change the discrimination against girls and their bodies throughout history." But it is a compelling, funny, and touching literary exploration of one group of girls' fight for success and, perhaps most of all, respect. *In These Girls, Hope Is a Muscle* is both a dramatization of the success of the women's movement and a testimony to all the changes that have yet to come.

compelling (kəm pel′ iŋ) *adj.* forceful

Madeleine Blais worked at the *Miami Herald* for eight years. A collection of her work, *The Heart Is an Instrument: Portraits in Journalism*, was published by the University of Massachusetts Press in 1992. Now a resident of Amherst, she has been on the faculty at the University of Massachusetts for six years.

Steve Gietschier

(b. 1948)

Steve Gietschier holds the game of basketball dear to his heart: His experiences coaching his daughter's team led him to seek out the assignment of reviewing *In These Girls, Hope Is a Muscle*, Madeleine Blais's gripping account of a high-school girls' basketball team's championship season.

Born in New York City, Gietschier earned his bachelor's degree from Georgetown University in Washington, D.C., and his doctorate from Ohio State University.

Since 1986, Gietschier has been the Director of Historical Records at *The Sporting News* in St. Louis, Missouri, the newspaper that originally published his review of Blais's book.

Review and Assess

Thinking About the Selection

1. **Respond:** Does reading the review and the book-jacket blurb of *In These Girls, Hope Is a Muscle* make you want to read the book itself? Explain.
2. **(a) Recall:** In the opening of his review, which words does Gietschier use to describe Blais's book? **(b) Analyze:** Why do you think Gietschier likes Blais's book?
3. **(a) Recall:** What is the subject of the book *In These Girls, Hope Is a Muscle*? **(b) Infer:** Based on Gietschier's review, why do you think Blais chose to write the book?
4. **(a) Recall:** According to the book review, what do the girls prove about women's sports? **(b) Speculate:** Who do you think would be most persuaded to buy this book after reading the review?
5. **(a) Recall:** What two people are quoted in the book-jacket copy? **(b) Compare:** What do their comments have in common? **(c) Summarize:** Since the information following the quotes closely echoes the author's writing in the book, what would you say is Blais's main idea and attitude toward the subject?
6. **Compare and Contrast:** How is the format of the book-jacket blurb different from that of Gietschier's review?

ASSESSMENT PRACTICE: Reading Comprehension

Literary Elements **(For more practice, see Test Preparation Workbook, p. 44.)**

Many tests require students to describe literary elements. Use this following sample test item.

The tail of the airplane angles back on a small, solid rubber rear wheel. The nose tilts upwards toward the sky. She glows like a polished aluminum athlete, broad-shouldered. Beautiful as a swan dive.

This passage is an example of ___.

A alliteration
B personification
C hyperbole
D irony

Personification is giving human qualities to a nonhuman object. The correct answer is *B*.

Review and Assess

Literary Analysis

Career Writing

1. Why is it important for a radio journalist to be a good writer?
2. Using a chart like the one below, list the characteristics of good radio journalism, as well as the characteristics of a well-written book review and book-jacket blurb.

Radio Journalism	Book Review	Book-Jacket Blurb

3. Based on your chart, how effective is each selection that you read?

Comparing Literary Works

4. Using a chart like the one below, compare the challenges faced by Linda Finch and the Lady Hurricanes.

Person/Group	→	Challenges	Strengths

5. How is a challenge to a team different from a challenge to an individual?
6. In your opinion, which selection is more successful at conveying the challenge its subject faces?

Reading Strategy

Determining the Author's Purpose

7. What do you think is Chadwick's **purpose** in conducting his interview with Linda Finch?
8. (a) Explain the different purposes of the book-jacket copy and the review. (b) Do you think the book review or the book-jacket copy is more effective in persuading people to read the book? Why?

Extend Understanding

9. **Career Link:** What other occupations can you think of in which writing is particularly important?

Quick Review

Career writing is writing that is done as part of a person's job.

To **determine the author's purpose,** seek to understand the writer's goal—to inform, to entertain, or to persuade, for example.

Take It to the Net

www.phschool.com

Take the interactive self-test online to check your understanding of these selections.

Answers for p. 719

Review and Assess

1. The journalist must be able to express ideas concisely; prepare questions that will elicit interesting answers; and describe people and events vividly for a listening audience.
2.

Radio Journalism	concise, entertaining, and informative
Book Review	critical and objective
Book-Jacket Blurb	persuasive, informative, and concise

3. Students may say that all three are effective. The interview is descriptive and interesting, the review is fair and thorough, and the blurb makes the book sound interesting without giving away the conclusion.
4. Finch faces the challenge of flying around the world. This requires skill, courage, a sense of adventure, and the ability to cope with potential emergencies. The team faces the challenge of winning games repeatedly. This requires cooperation with other players, strength, stamina, the will to win, and the ability to cope with defeat.
5. An individual does not have to rely on others to achieve victories. Team members must work together to achieve anything.
6. Students may say that the interview gives more specific details about Finch's venture than the review gives about the team's challenges.
7. He wants to inform listeners about a notable event and its historic context. He wants listeners to become acquainted not only with Linda Finch, but with Amelia Earhart.
8. **(a)** The review is intended to evaluate the book objectively. The book-jacket copy is intended to persuade readers to buy the book. **(b)** Students may find the review more effective, because the critic has no ulterior motive for praising the book.
9. Students may cite a variety of professions that require effective writing.

EXTEND

Answers for p. 720

❶ Vocabulary Development

Word Analysis

1. ruling or most powerful family
2. having to do with the force or motion of fluids

Spelling Strategy

1. nobly
2. capably
3. legibly

Concept Development: Synonyms

1. b
2. a
3. a
4. b
5. a
6. b
7. b
8. a
9. b
10. a

❷ Grammar

1. contraction meaning "they are"
2. possessive pronoun modifying *coach*
3. adverb indicating place
4. expletive at start of sentence
5. possessive pronoun modifying *arrival*

Writing Application

Have partners review each other's paragraphs for correct usage of *there, their,* and *they're.*

Integrate Language Skills

❶ Vocabulary Development Lesson

Word Analysis: Greek Root *-dyna-*

The Greek root *-dyna-* means "power" or "strength." The root appears in the word *aerodynamics*, which means "the branch of mechanics dealing with the power exerted by air or other gases in motion." Write the definition for each word below. Use a dictionary if you need help.

1. dynasty
2. hydrodynamic

Spelling Strategy

To create the adverbial form of an adjective of more than one syllable that ends in *-le*, change the *e* to *y*. Do not double the *l*. For example, *improbable* becomes *improbably*. In one-syllable words ending in *-le*, the final consonant may double, as in *whole* and *wholly*. Write the adverbial form of each word below.

1. noble
2. capable
3. legible

Concept Development: Synonyms

Write the word or phrase that means the same as the first word in each item. To help you, review the list of vocabulary words on page 709.

1. hydraulic: (a) strong, (b) liquid-powered
2. pursue: (a) chase, (b) quarrel
3. aerodynamics: (a) air movement, (b) flight
4. riveting: (a) pretty, (b) gripping
5. improbable: (a) unlikely, (b) impossible
6. compelling: (a) noisy, (b) fascinating
7. adept: (a) clumsy, (b) skillful
8. ruminative: (a) meditative, (b) wealthy
9. legacy: (a) victory, (b) heritage
10. derides: (a) ridicules, (b) ignores

❷ Grammar Lesson

Usage: *there, their, they're*

Because the words *there*, *their*, and *they're* sound alike, they are often misused in sentences. ***There*** can be used either as an adverb meaning "at that place" or as an expletive at the start of a sentence. ***Their,*** a possessive pronoun, always modifies a noun. ***They're*** is a contraction for *they are*. Look at the following examples:

There:	Linda's airplane is over *there*. (used to mean "at that place")
There:	*There* were only fifteen manufactured. (used as an expletive)
Their:	Some players got *their* rejections. (used to modify *players*)
They're:	*They're* brave to fly in that plane. (used as a contraction)

Practice For each item below, indicate how the underlined word is used.

1. They're playing in a championship game.
2. Their coach is very nervous.
3. The flight manual is over there.
4. There are few differences between them.
5. Have you heard news of their arrival?

Writing Application Use *there*, *their*, and *they're* in a paragraph about these two selections.

WG Prentice Hall Writing and Grammar Connection: Chapter 27, Section 2

TEACHING RESOURCES

The following resources can be used to enrich or extend the instruction for pp. 720–721.

Vocabulary

- **Selection Support,** Build Vocabulary, p. 173
- **Vocabulary and Spelling Practice Book** (Use this booklet for skills enrichment.) ■

Grammar

- **Selection Support,** Build Grammar Skills, p. 174
- **Writing and Grammar,** Gold Level, p. 620
- **Daily Language Practice Transparencies**

Writing

- **Writing and Grammar,** Gold Level, p. 238
- **Writing and Grammar iText CD-ROM** ■

■ **BLOCK SCHEDULING:** Resources marked with this symbol provide varied instruction during 90-minute blocks.

❸ Writing Lesson

Letter to Linda Finch

Write a letter to Linda Finch explaining how you feel about her adventure. Whether you admire her or think she is taking too much of a risk, let her know in a respectful and friendly manner.

Prewriting Make a list of your feelings about Finch's endeavor. Then, provide a reason for each feeling.

Drafting In your introductory paragraph, explain why you are writing to her. In the next two paragraphs, explain how you feel about her adventure. Your final paragraph should explain what you have learned.

Revising Review your draft, underlining each point you have made. Then, highlight the support you have provided. Add any details needed to support your feelings on the subject.

Model: Highlighting to Find Support

I am impressed with your devotion and determination. You understand the risk involved, but your desire to live out a dream is stronger than your fear.

The highlighted information shows that the point has been effectively supported.

WG *Prentice Hall Writing and Grammar Connection: Chapter 13, Section 2*

❹ Extension Activities

Listening and Speaking In a group, stage a **book chat** in which you review a book that the entire group has recently read. Ask each group member to prepare note cards about the following aspects of the book:

- Characters
- The writer's style
- The theme, or message, of the book

During the discussion, express what you liked or disliked about each aspect of the book, using your note cards. Give examples from the book.

Research and Technology In a small group, do a **research project** about one aspect of the role of women in aviation—for example, women who have flown in space or who have piloted planes in wartime. Develop your main idea through descriptions of the women and their experiences. Present your information as an oral report with visual displays. **[Group Activity]**

Take It to the Net www.phschool.com

Go online for an additional research activity using the Internet.

Lesson Support for p. 721

❸ Writing Lesson

- Suggest that students keep their letters to one page in length. Explain that letters from fans or people the recipient doesn't know are more likely to be read if they are concise.
- Remind students to use appropriate formality. They should not address Finch by her first name. They should use standard English rather than colloquial language.
- Use the Business Letter rubric in **Performance Assessment and Portfolio Management,** p. 9, to evaluate students' letters.

❹ Research and Technology

- To avoid duplication, each group member can research a different aspect of the topic.
- Have students mount their display in the classroom.
- Encourage students to discuss this assignment with their history teacher, who may be able to suggest subjects for research and sources of information.

CUSTOMIZE INSTRUCTION For Universal Access

To address different learning styles, use the following activities suggested in the **Extension Activities** booklet, p. 44.

- For Interpersonal Learners, use Activity 5.
- For Visual/Spatial Learners, use Activities 5 and 7.
- For Intrapersonal and Verbal/Linguistic Learners, use Activity 6.

ASSESSMENT RESOURCES

The following resources can be used to assess students' knowledge and skills.

Selection Assessment

- **Formal Assessment,** pp. 154–156
- **Open Book Test,** pp. 130–132
- **Got It! Assessment Videotapes,** Tape 4
- **Test Bank Software**

Take It to the Net

Visit www.phschool.com for self-tests and additional questions on the selections.

Writing Rubric

- **Performance Assess. and Portfolio Mgmt.,** p. 9

PRENTICE HALL ASSESSMENT SYSTEM

- **Workbook**
- **Skill Book**
- **Transparencies**
- **CD-ROM**

Lesson Objectives

1. To write a problem-and-solution essay
2. To learn the characteristics of a problem-and-solution essay
3. To create a problem profile

Model From Literature

In "The Interlopers" by Saki, the writer uses emotional language to help readers "feel" the problem that has occurred.

Prewriting

- Encourage students to bring in newspapers and scan newsworthy Web sites to find topics of interest.
- Point out the chart on p. 722. Have students complete a chart like this one as they research their problem and potential solutions.
- Have students think of a person they know who fits their target audience. Point out that it will help students to imagine writing their essays directly to that person.

Writing WORKSHOP

Exposition: Problem-and-Solution Essay

A **problem-and-solution essay** identifies and explains a problem and then proposes a practical solution. In this workshop, you will write a problem-and-solution essay.

Assignment Criteria. Your problem-and-solution essay should have the following characteristics:

- A statement of the problem and a suggested solution
- Facts, statistics, and details that show the problem's scope and indicate how it can be solved
- Language appropriate to the level of knowledge of your audience
- A logical organization

To preview the criteria on which your problem-and-solution essay may be assessed, see the Rubric on page 725.

Prewriting

Choose a topic. Write your problem-and-solution essay about an issue of interest to you. One strategy is to conduct a **media scan,** reviewing local newspapers and television news programs for items about community issues and problems. List problems for which you can imagine practical solutions. Choose one as your essay topic.

Create a problem profile. Once you have chosen a topic, create a profile to help you determine which aspect of the problem you will address in your essay. Answer the following questions about the problem:

- Who or what is affected by the problem?
- What causes the problem to occur?
- What are some possible solutions to the problem?

Gather information. Collect the information you will need to start your draft. Assess all the possible solutions and weed out the less practical ones to narrow your list.

Identify your audience. Keep a specific audience in mind while you write: readers who have the ability to implement your suggestions. As you narrow your list of solutions, identify the aspects of each idea that will most likely appeal to your target audience.

Problem Profile

Problem: Litter is creating an unsafe environment.

Who is affected? *Everyone on Earth.*

What causes the problem?

Lack of:

- *responsibility*
- *environmental education*
- *sense of ownership*

What are possible solutions? *Stiffer fines, more policing, more environmental education, volunteer trash pickup*

TEACHING RESOURCES

The following resources can be used to enrich or extend the instruction for pp. 722–725.

- **Writing and Grammar,** Gold Level, Chapter 11, pp. 228–249
- **Performance Assessment and Portfolio Management,** pp. 14, 53
- **Writing Models and Graphic Organizers on Transparencies,** pp. 63–65

Writing and Grammar iText CD-ROM
Students can use the following tools as they complete their problem-solving essays:

- Topic Bin
- Pros and Cons Chart
- Language Variety

Student Model

Before you begin drafting your problem-and-solution essay, read this student model and review the characteristics of effective problem-and-solution essays.

Naomi Barrowclough
Maplewood, NJ

Environmental Un-Consciousness

During a recent Earth Day cleanup, I became disgusted by the amount of trash I picked up within a two-hour period. People had thrown little papers, bits of plastic, and candy wrappers until the mess formed a multicolored carpet over the green grass. What people who litter may not realize is that litter creates serious environmental problems, in addition to prompting concerns over appearance.

> In the opening paragraph, the author provides a general statement of the problem.

We've all been told not to litter, but it does not seem to sink in. One person may think his or her contribution is only a microscopic addition when viewed against the whole. But if every person shared this sense of irresponsibility, Earth would soon be overwhelmed by pollution.

Litter is harmful for many reasons. For one, roadside litter is eventually washed into our waterways and oceans—water we use for drinking and recreation. Also, animals might entangle themselves or mistake trash for food and swallow it. In our public spaces, children spend a great deal of time in areas where they could be physically harmed by the pollution caused by litter.

> Here, the author provides greater detail to explain the problem more fully.

There is no simple solution to the problem of litter, only an array of possible solutions with one strategy in common: Create a feeling of ownership over public spaces. Some of the most popular sites for litter are beaches and parks because people feel no sense of ownership over these places. These same people might think twice about littering in their own homes.

> The author introduces a general solution here.

To create a feeling of ownership, it is necessary to educate children early about the environmental consequences of littering. Schools could lead field trips to local beaches or parks where students pick up trash and test water quality. If kids have to fish two shopping carts from the side of a stream, as I did, they might think twice about throwing something else on the ground. If they see that contaminated water is harmful to humans and wildlife, they might stop someone they see littering.

> In this paragraph, specific strategies for achieving the solution are introduced.

There is no easy way to stop littering. Fines and policing alone will not do the trick because people will just look before they litter. Until people understand that littering is irresponsible and has devastating environmental consequences, there will continue to be litterbugs. The solution lies in education and creating a sense of ownership about our public spaces.

> In the final paragraph, the author addresses a potential concern and then restates her solution.

Student Model

- Explain that the Student Model is a sample, and that students' essays may be longer.
- Ask students to paraphrase the author's general statement of the problem.
- Ask students to identify the paragraph in which the author gives more details about the problem. Answer: The author gives more details in the third paragraph.
- Have students identify the proposed solution to the problem. Answer: The proposed solution is to create a feeling of ownership of public spaces.
- Ask students to share their opinions on the effectiveness of the author's proposed solution. Answer: The proposed solution is to create a feeling of ownership of public spaces.

Real-World Connection

Ask students to think of instances in which they may need to offer problem-and-solution arguments. Point out that such arguments don't have to be delivered as written works, but can be delivered in speeches or in everyday conversations.

CUSTOMIZE INSTRUCTION FOR UNIVERSAL ACCESS

For Special Needs Students	For English Learners	For Gifted and Talented Students
Encourage these students to find a problem that is important to them. This will offer incentive for them to look for possible solutions.	Provide these students with additional examples of problem-and-solution essays. Have them identify the problem and the proposed solutions in each.	Encourage students to take on an issue that they can really do something about. If the issue is newsworthy, encourage students to submit their essays to the opinions section of a local newspaper.

Drafting

- Point out the four types of evidence listed on p. 724.
- Encourage students to work in pairs to decide which types of evidence best fit their topic.
- Ask students to include at least two of the four types of evidence in their essay.

Revising

- Have students read the Revising section on this page, and then complete the three steps suggested for making sure they have supported their ideas with facts and details.
- Have students exchange drafts and role-play a member of the target audience, answering this question: Does the essay address your concerns as a reader? Have students revise their drafts according to the responses they receive.

continued

Drafting

Organize your ideas. An effective organization for your essay breaks your ideas into clear categories. After an introduction that raises your audience's interest, develop the problem with detailed examples. Next, offer a solution. Use your conclusion to drive home the soundness of your ideas.

Elaborate. In order to persuade your readers, consider these types of evidence:

- **Statistics:** Provide numbers to show how many people would be affected by your solution.
- **Expert opinions:** Include the advice of those who have training and experience related to your topic.
- **Personal anecdotes:** Tell your readers about your own experiences with the problem or solution.
- **Testimonials:** Include comments from others on the effectiveness of your proposed solution.

Elaborate to Provide Evidence

Subject: Problem-and-solution essay on litter

Statistics to include:

Number of tons of litter deposited in local park/year

Water quality studies related to pollution from litter

Experts to cite:

Environmental organizations

Park and beach sanitation officials

Local police

Anecdote to include:

Earth Day trash pickup experience

Testimonials to provide:

Educators involved with environmental issues

Park officials

Address readers' concerns. To convince those who may not approve of your solution, show them that you understand their concerns. Address their objections with explanations and evidence that suggest your solution is the best course of action.

Revising

Revise to support generalizations. Look at each paragraph to be sure that the details support or explain the main idea of its topic sentence. Use the following strategies:

1. Highlight your topic sentence, the general statement from which the rest of the paragraph flows.
2. Underline the supporting sentences that develop this main idea.
3. Eliminate any sentences that do not support the main idea and cut those that simply restate it.

Model: Supporting Generalizations

Litter is harmful for many reasons. For one, roadside litter is eventually washed into our waterways and oceans— water we use for drinking and recreation. ~~It is also unpleasant to see trash floating in the water.~~ Also, animals might entangle themselves or mistake trash for food and swallow it.

Naomi chose to eliminate the third sentence since it did not relate directly to her topic sentence.

USING TECHNOLOGY IN WRITING

Encourage students to collect their online evidence in a word-processing document, making sure to note the source of each fact or opinion. Students may find it useful to print out this document and highlight evidence they will use in their essays.

Students can also use spell check and other revision tools on the **Writing and Grammar iText CD-ROM** as they write and revise.

Revise to evaluate and refine word choice.

Review your draft as if you were a member of your target audience. Find terms that need to be defined, or vocabulary that seems too difficult or easy for your readers. Then, make changes accordingly.

General Audience: Another way to fight fatigue is to exercise regularly.

Target Audience of Experts: Another way to raise low levels of blood sugar is to get more exercise.

Compare the two sentences below. Why would the model be more appropriate than the nonmodel if you were presenting an essay to third graders?

Nonmodel	Model
But if every person shared this sense of irresponsibility, Earth would soon be overwhelmed by pollution.	If no one cared about how much pollution he or she caused, Earth would be completely polluted.

Publishing and Presenting

To make the best use of your problem-and-solution essay, share it with the people who can help you make a difference.

Send a letter. Send your essay to the appropriate government official, agency, or group. Share any responses you receive with classmates.

Read to Write
To see another example of problem-and-solution writing, see "To the Residents of A.D. 2029" on page 495.

WG Prentice Hall Writing and Grammar Connection: Chapter 11

Rubric for Self-Assessment

Evaluate your problem-and-solution essay using the following criteria and rating scale:

Criteria	Rating Scale: Not very				Very
Is the problem explored adequately in the essay?	1	2	3	4	5
How effective is the suggested solution?	1	2	3	4	5
Do facts, statistics, and details effectively illustrate the problem and solution?	1	2	3	4	5
How appropriate is the language for the audience's knowledge level?	1	2	3	4	5
Was the information logically organized and presented?	1	2	3	4	5

continued from p. 724

- Have students examine the model and the nonmodel. Ask students why the model would be more appropriate than the nonmodel if they were presenting an essay to third graders.
Answer: Students might say that the word choice in the model is more appropriate for young readers because it is simpler.

Publishing and Presenting

- Before students read their essays to the class, have them explain the audience they have written for. Ask students to imagine being a member of this audience as they listen to the essay.
- Have students brainstorm for a list of publications or public officials to whom they might send their essays.
- Encourage students to write cover letters to accompany their work. In these letters, they should introduce themselves and explain the purpose of their essays.

Assessment

- Review with students the assessment criteria. Have them score the Student Model based on the criteria in the rubric.
- The rubric on this page, and another rubric in an alternative format, can be found on pp. 14 and 53 of **Performance Assessment and Portfolio Management.**

TEST-TAKING TIP

Point out that students may be asked to identify a problem and solution in a reading passage on a test. Explain that students can ask themselves one question to identify the problem (What's wrong?) and another question to identify the solution (How does the writer propose to fix what's wrong?).

Lesson Objectives

1. To evaluate a speech
2. To assess arguments for quality
3. To observe the speaker's choice of language
4. To listen to the speaker's voice

Evaluate Content

- Direct students' attention to the chart on p. 726.
- Make sure students understand both the types of arguments and their potential flaws.
- Point out the organizational structure of a good speech: the main argument, supporting evidence, and a strong conclusion.

Evaluate Delivery

- Remind students to listen for powerful language when they hear speeches.
- Point out that when they hear powerful language, students should ask themselves whether the speaker is using it only to advance arguments, or if the language is based on sound ideas.
- Encourage students to notice how a speaker uses his or her voice to hold an audience's attention.

Listening and Speaking WORKSHOP

Evaluating a Speech

Public speaking can be daunting for someone who is not used to presenting ideas in front of an audience. It may be easier to be evaluating the speech as an audience member. The two skills are closely related. In this workshop, you will learn how to **evaluate a speech**, which will give you a solid basis for preparing your own oral presentation.

Evaluate Content

Assess arguments for quality. A convincing speech should present arguments that are easily understood. While evaluating speeches, you may catch flaws or "holes" in poorly presented arguments. To find errors in arguments, use the following tips:

- Determine the type of argument the speaker uses.
- Decide whether you can identify a potential flaw, or consider whether you know of specific information that contradicts the argument.

Use the chart at right to anticipate common weaknesses in these types of arguments.

Type of Argument	Potential Flaw
Analogy: Compares one situation to another	Are the two situations really alike?
Authority: Cites the opinion of an expert	Is the expert knowledgeable and unbiased?
Emotion: Appeals to audience's feelings	Is the full argument balanced between logic and emotion?
Logic: Appeals to sense of rationalism	
Causation: Shows cause-and-effect relationship	Does the argument oversimplify?

Evaluate development of arguments. A good speech has a logical development and organization. Main points are introduced and developed with supporting evidence in the form of facts, statistics, anecdotes, charts, or graphs. In a conclusion, the speaker summarizes the main argument. The speaker might vary this organization slightly, but the structure should always be apparent to the audience.

Evaluate Delivery

Observe the speaker's choice of language. Speakers often include powerful language to make their speech more memorable and persuasive. As you listen, note instances where the speaker uses words or phrases with strong positive or negative *connotations,* or associations. Think about how the use of this language influences your own attitude toward the topic. Be alert to the fact that some speakers may rely on powerful or emotional language instead of reasoned arguments to advance their ideas.

Listen to the speaker's voice. Determine whether the speaker's voice is varied enough to hold an audience's attention and whether key points are emphasized. Also, think about whether the speaker's delivery creates a mood and tone that are appropriate to the subject.

Activity: **Analyzing a Speech** Evaluate a famous speech, such as Martin Luther King's "I Have a Dream" speech, with your classmates. As a group, assess the argument for quality and generate a list of positive and negative qualities of that speech.

CUSTOMIZE INSTRUCTION FOR UNIVERSAL ACCESS

For Special Needs Students	For English Learners	For Gifted and Talented Students
Provide these students with a video of a powerfully delivered speech. Help them to identify reasons, such as word choice and the speaker's tone, that the speech is so effective.	While they listen to a speech, encourage students to jot down unfamiliar words. They can look up these words when the speech ends, rather than being distracted by them during the delivery.	Have students do research to find examples of powerful speeches. Ask the students to each choose one speech to practice and deliver for the class.

Assessment WORKSHOP

Connotation and Denotation

The reading sections of some tests require you to read a passage and answer multiple-choice questions about the meaning of a word or phrase. Use these strategies to help you distinguish between two different types of meaning:

- *Denotation* refers to the literal, or exact, meaning of a word. Denotations are characterized by a neutral, objective tone. For example, *thin* and *skinny* have similar denotations. They each describe a quality of depth or size.
- *Connotation* is the implied, or suggested, meaning of a word or phrase. A connotation can be positive or negative, depending on its context and each reader's past experience. For example, many people would say *thin* has a positive connotation but *skinny* has a negative one.

Test-Taking Strategies

- To determine a word's connotation, notice the reaction a word or phrase elicits from you.
- When searching for a denotation, look for a synonym that defines the word exactly, without placing it in a positive or negative light.

Sample Test Item

Directions: Read the passage, and then answer the question that follows.

Arlene Johnson's 1956 Cadillac convertible was a battleship. With its long silver body and huge chrome tail fins, this well-cared-for antique cruised through the streets of Coberton every morning with Arlene sitting proudly at the wheel. She was a petite woman, and even with the top down, the car swallowed her up.

1. What is the connotation of battleship in this passage?
   A large warship with guns and armor
   B large, powerful vehicle
   C compact, new vehicle
   D dilapidated, unsafe vehicle

Answer and Explanation

The correct answer is ***B,*** the implied meaning of *battleship*. ***A*** is a literal definition of battleship and is therefore a denotation that does not make sense in the context of the passage. ***C*** and ***D*** are incorrect because the passage indicates an older, larger vehicle that is well maintained.

Practice

Directions: Read the passage, and then answer the questions that follow.

The Elmont High School Blazers struggled through their worst football season ever. Each week, they walked onto Elmont Field with the hope of victory and walked off with another loss. After four losses, with the stands nearly empty, the team still strode onto the field with pride.

1. What is the denotation of worst in this passage?
   A most embarrassing
   B most stunning
   C most difficult
   D most bad
2. What is the connotation of strode in this passage?
   A walked slowly and dejectedly
   B walked purposefully
   C raced at a quick pace
   D moved hesitantly

Lesson Objective

To correctly answer test questions about connotation and denotation

Applying Reading Strategies

Have students read the definitions of denotation and connotation on p. 727. Point out that connotation brings up ideas and emotions associated with a word, but denotation brings up only the word's dictionary definition.

Applying Test-Taking Strategies

- Have students read the sample test item, and then determine the connotation of *battleship* in the passage.
- Point out that the author uses the word *battleship* in creating a metaphor, or a comparison between two things.
- Point out that the correct answer is *B*. The writer does not mean a literal battleship, as indicated in *A*. Both *C* and *D* provide inaccurate details about the vehicle the writer describes.

Answers

1. The correct answer is *D*. The athletes remained proud, rather than embarassed, so *A* is incorrect. *B* and *C* are wrong because the writer does not say that the athletes were surprised by the season or that they found it difficult to deal with.
2. The correct answer is *B*. Choices *A* and *D* are wrong because they do not convey the athletes' sense of pride. *C* is incorrect because the writer mentions nothing about the athletes' speed.

TEACHING RESOURCES

The following resources can be used to enrich or extend the instruction for p. 727.

PRENTICE HALL ASSESSMENT SYSTEM

- **Workbook**
- **Skill Book**
- **Transparencies**
- **CD-ROM**

Unit Objectives

1. To develop skills in reading drama
2. To apply a variety of reading strategies appropriate for reading drama
3. To analyze literary elements
4. To use a variety of strategies to build vocabulary
5. To learn elements of grammar, usage, and style
6. To use recursive writing processes to write in a variety of forms
7. To develop listening and speaking skills
8. To express and support responses to various types of texts
9. To prepare, organize, and present literary interpretations

Meeting the Objectives

With each selection, you will find instructional materials through which students can meet these objectives. Further, you will find additional practice pages for reading strategies, literary analysis, vocabulary, and grammar in the **Selection Support: Skills Development Workbook** in your **Teaching Resources.**

Background

Art

The Sheridan Theater, by Edward Hopper

Edward Hopper was an American artist who painted ordinary scenes from American life, particularly New York City. His realistic works are recognizable by the striking arrangement of light and shade and a sense of loneliness and isolation. Ask students the following question about the painting:

In what way does this painting suggest more than one drama?
Possible response: By focusing on solitary figures at the back of a theater, the painting suggests the drama of individual lives. Even during a night of performance, Hopper finds the lonely moment.

UNIT 8 Drama

The Sheridan Theatre, 1937, Edward Hopper, Collection of the Newark Museum

UNIT FEATURES

Connections	Reading Informational Material
Every unit contains a feature that connects literature to a related topic, such as art, science, or history. In this unit, the Literature and Media feature on p. 878 explores the vitality of Shakespeare's dramas on the modern stage and in films, musicals, and television productions. Use the information and questions on the Connections pages to enrich students' understanding of the selections presented within the unit.	These selections will help students learn to analyze and evaluate informational texts, such as workplace documents, technical directions, and consumer materials. They will expose students to the organization and features unique to nonnarrative texts. In this unit, students will learn how to read atlas entries as they practice the reading strategies of skimming and scanning.

Exploring the Genre

When you read a play, *you* are the director; *you* breathe life into the characters. As you read the works in this unit, notice the following elements, which can help bring the dramas to life in your mind:

- **Dialogue** In drama, much of what you learn about the characters, setting, and events is revealed through dialogue—conversations among the characters.
- **Stage Directions** These notes convey information to the cast, crew, and readers of the drama about sound effects, actions, sets, and line readings.
- **Characters** Dramatic characters are brought to life by their dialogue and actions onstage.
- **Plot** Most dramas contain a plot in which events unfold, develop to a climax, and are resolved.
- **Theme** A theme is the central message the playwright conveys to the audience.

▲ **Critical Viewing** Why do you think the painter chose to show a portion of this theater without showing the stage or actors? **[Infer]**

Assessment Resources

- Selection Support: Skills Development Workbook
- Formal Assessment
- Open Book Tests
- Performance Assessment and Portfolio Management
- Extension Activities

Assessing Student Progress

Listed below are tools that are available to measure the degree to which students meet the unit objectives.

Informal Assessment

The questions in the Review and Assess sections are a first-level response to the concepts and skills presented with the selections. Students' responses provide a brief, informal measure of their grasp of the material. These responses can indicate where further instruction and practice are needed. Follow up with the practice pages in **Selection Support: Skills Development Workbook.**

Formal Assessment

The **Formal Assessment** booklet contains the Selection Tests and Unit Tests.

- Selection Tests measure comprehension and skills acquisition for each selection or group of selections.
- Each Unit Test provides students with thirty multiple-choice questions and five essay questions designed to assess students' knowledge of the literature and skills taught in the unit.

The **Open Book Tests** ask students to demonstrate their ability to synthesize and communicate information from selections or groups of selections.

To assess student writing, you will find rubrics and scoring models in the **Performance Assessment and Portfolio Management** booklet. In this booklet, you will also find scoring rubrics for listening and speaking activities.

Alternative Assessment

The **Extension Activities** booklet contains writing activities, listening and speaking activities, and research and technology activities that are appropriate for students with different ability levels. You may also use these activities as an alternative measure of students' growth.

▶Critical Viewing

Answer: The painter might be making the point that ordinary people, including the theater usher and a woman standing alone at the back of the theater, experience drama in their lives. He may be trying to show that, in William Shakespeare's words, "All the world's a stage."

Why Read Literature?

The "Why Read Literature?" page in each unit presents a list of possible purposes for reading. Each purpose for reading is connected to one or more of the selections in the unit. Good readers set a purpose before reading to help them read actively and focus on meaningful details.

Unit 8 introduces three purposes for reading. "Read for the Love of Literature" invites students to read *Romeo and Juliet,* William Shakespeare's drama about two teenagers in love. "Read for Information" provides some interesting behind-the-scenes information about dramatic performance in Shakespeare's day. "Read to Be Inspired" demonstrates that Shakespeare's dramas connect powerfully with people today.

How to Use This Page

- Tell students that as they read each selection in this unit, they should set a purpose for reading. This will help them read in an active and focused manner.
- Explain that students can increase their love of literature by learning of ill-fated love in William Shakespeare's *Romeo and Juliet.*
- Point out that students will learn some interesting facts about drama performances in the seventeenth century—and the twenty-first.
- In "Read to Be Inspired," students will learn that Shakespeare's themes still echo in the streets of modern life.

Why Read Literature?

A dramatic work can have multiple dimensions. You might explore one dimension while reading and then find something completely new after learning more about its history. Preview these examples that show how you can explore many sides of a single work of literature.

1 Read for the Love of Literature

No other author has been as widely read and admired as William Shakespeare. Discover Shakespeare for yourself as you read ***Romeo and Juliet,*** page 770.

2 Read for Information

It is one thing to imagine the action as you read *Romeo and Juliet,* but quite another to picture a performance in Shakespeare's time. Find out why the role of Juliet was always played by a young boy—along with other interesting facts—when you travel back to the stage of seventeenth-century England in **"The Shakespearean Theater,"** page 764.

One reason Shakespeare's plays have gained worldwide popularity is that they touch on so many aspects of the human experience. You may be amazed at just how adaptable his plays are when you read this unit's *Connections* feature, **"Shakespeare in Today's World,"** page 878.

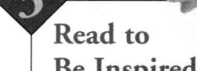

3 Read to Be Inspired

Shakespeare's story of two young lovers kept apart by a senseless feud still retains its power today. In 1993, when a young Serb man and his Muslim lover died in each other's arms during bitter ethnic warfare in Bosnia, they were instantly dubbed "Romeo and Juliet." As you read *Romeo and Juliet,* you will understand why this story continues to inspire comparison today.

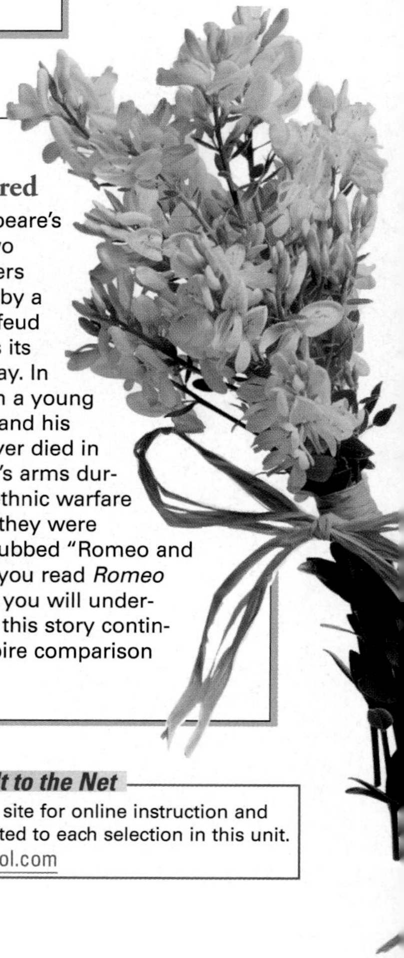

Take It to the Net

Visit the Web site for online instruction and activities related to each selection in this unit. www.phschool.com

ENRICHMENT: Further Reading

Have students choose one or more of the works below to extend their undersanding of drama or to read more works of Shakespeare.

William Shakespeare: The Complete Works by Arden General Editors
This book includes all Shakespeare's plays, complete with introductions and an extensive glossary.

A Midsummer Night's Dream by William Shakespeare
This comedy, following the adventures of a group of young people who spend a summer's night in the forest, can be found in the **Prentice Hall Literature Library.**

How to Read Literature

Use Strategies for Reading Drama

While drama shares many elements with prose, fiction, and poetry, the greatest difference is that dramas are designed to be performed on a stage before an audience. Since you will not have the benefit of a performance to help you interpret the text, use the following strategies when reading drama.

1. Picture the action.

- Use stage directions to form a mental image of the way characters move around on stage and interact with one another.
- Pay close attention to stage directions related to setting. For example, if the action takes place in a 1950s drugstore, it will have a much different feel than if it is set in a character's living room.

2. Use text aids.

Text aids are notes outside the main text that clarify the meaning of a word or phrase or add detailed information.

- Try not to let text aids interrupt the flow of your reading. If you come to an unfamiliar phrase, first try to figure it out from context.
- If you need to use a text aid, substitute the footnoted language directly into the original sentence, and then reread the new sentence with the surrounding text.

3. Read blank verse.

Blank verse is a poetic form that uses a regular meter to create a certain mood and rhythm. The author often uses blank verse to create a more formal atmosphere. To get used to the feel of blank verse, read passages aloud, stressing every second syllable. Read at a steady pace, and pause only when you see punctuation, as the model at right suggests.

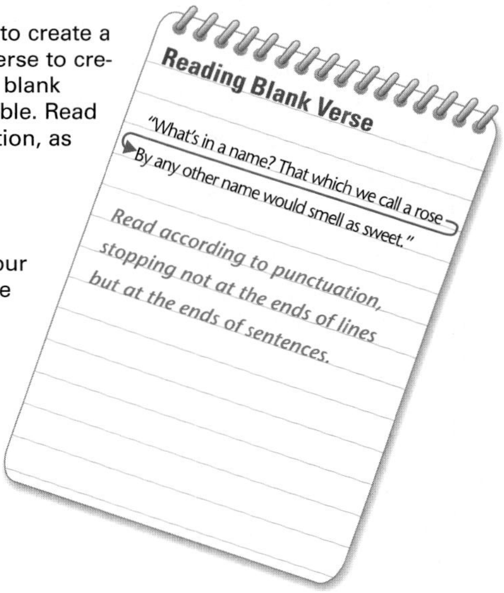

Reading Blank Verse
"What's in a name? That which we call a rose
By any other name would smell as sweet."
Read according to punctuation, stopping not at the ends of lines but at the ends of sentences.

4. Paraphrase.

Paraphrase, or summarize, a key idea or passage in your own words to ensure that you understand what you have read.

- Replace formal language with words that are more commonly used.
- When summarizing, eliminate ideas that are not essential to the meaning of the passage.

As you read the selections in this unit, review the reading strategies and apply them to strengthen your understanding of the text.

How to Read Literature

The "How to Read Literature" page in each unit presents a set of strategies to help readers understand authors' words and ideas. Each reading strategy is taught in conjunction with one or more of the selections within the unit. Good readers develop a bank of strategies from which they can draw as needed.

Unit 8 introduces four strategies for reading drama. It is important for students to visualize the action as well to understand character's speeches in a play.

How to Use This Page

Introduce the strategies for reading drama, presenting each as a tool for developing understanding and appreciation.

- Tell students that as they read each selection in this unit, they should apply strategies for reading drama. These strategies will help students construct meaning as they read.
- Point out that in Horton Foote's drama *The Dancers* (p. 734), students should pay close attention to stage directions to picture the action as the play unfolds.
- Explain that the strategy of using text aids will help students understand some of the unfamiliar words in Shakespeare's play *Romeo and Juliet*, (p. 770).
- Encourage students to read portions of *Romeo and Juliet* aloud to become familiar with the sound and rhythm of blank verse.
- Suggest that students gain deeper understanding of *Romeo and Juliet* by paraphrasing key passages.

MODEL A READING STRATEGY: Paraphrase

Help our students paraphrase by modeling your process with this example from the opening scene of *Romeo and Juliet:*

Chorus: Two households, both alike in dignity,
In fair Verona, where we lay our scene,
From ancient grudge break to new mutiny . . .

Tell students:

This passage mentions two "households," or families, that are "both alike in dignity." In other words, they are both highly regarded. They live in the city of Verona, where the story will take place. These two families have held an "ancient grudge," or long standing hostility, which now "break[s] to new mutiny," or starts up again.

The Dancers

Lesson Objectives and CA Correlations

1. **To analyze and respond to literary elements**
   - Literary Analysis: Staging **R 3.10**
   - Connecting Literary Elements: Dialogue **R 3.4, 3.10**
2. **To read, comprehend, analyze, and critique a play**
   - Reading Strategy: Picturing the Action
   - Reading Check questions
   - Review and Assess questions
   - Assessment Practice (ATE)
3. **To develop word analysis skills, fluency, and systematic vocabulary**
   - Vocabulary Development Lesson: Homographs **R 1.2**
4. **To understand and apply written and oral language conventions**
   - Spelling Strategy
   - Grammar Lesson: Pronoun Case **LC 1.2, 1.3**
5. **To understand and apply appropriate writing and research strategies**
   - Writing Lesson: Diary Entry **R 3.4**
   - Extension Activity: Movie Proposal **W 1.8**
6. **To understand and apply listening and speaking strategies**
   - Extension Activity: Soundtrack **LS 1.7**

STEP-BY-STEP TEACHING GUIDE	PACING GUIDE
PRETEACH	
Motivate Students and Provide Background	
Use the Motivation activity (ATE p. 732)	5 min.
Read and discuss the Preview material and Background information (SE/ATE p. 732) [A]	10 min.
Introduce the Concepts	
Introduce the Literary Analysis and Reading Strategy (SE/ATE p. 733) [A]	15 min.
Pronounce the vocabulary words and read their definitions (SE p. 733)	5 min.
TEACH	
Monitor Comprehension	
Informally monitor comprehension by circulating while students read independently or in groups [A]	50 min.
Monitor students' comprehension with the Reading Check notes (SE/ATE pp. 735, 737, 739, 741, 743, 745, 747, 749, 751, 753, 757, 759)	as students read
Develop vocabulary with Vocabulary notes (SE pp. 741–743, 751; ATE p. 751)	as students read
Develop Understanding	
Develop students' understanding of staging with the Literary Analysis annotations (SE/ATE pp. 735, 737, 741, 743–746, 748, 751–752, 754, 756–757) [A]	10 min.
Develop students' ability to picture the action with the Reading Strategy annotations (SE/ATE pp. 736–737, 739–742, 744, 746, 748, 752, 756, 758)	10 min.
ASSESS	
Assess Mastery	
Assess students' mastery of the Reading Strategy and Literary Analysis by having them answer the Review and Assess questions (SE/ATE p. 761)	20 min.
Use one or more of the print and media Assessment Resources (ATE p. 763) [A]	up to 50 min.
EXTEND	
Apply Understanding	
Have students complete the Vocabulary Development Lesson and the Grammar Lesson (SE p. 762) [A]	20 min.
Apply students' knowledge of precise language using the Writing Lesson (SE/ATE p. 763) [A]	45 min.
Apply students' understanding using one or more of the Extension Activities (SE p. 763)	20–90 min.

[A] ACCELERATED INSTRUCTION: Use the strategies and activities identified with an [A].

UNIVERSAL ACCESS
● = Below Level Students
▲ = On-Level Students
■ = Above Level Students

Time and Resource Manager

Reading Level: Average
Average Number of Instructional Days: 5

	RESOURCES		
	PRINT	**TRANSPARENCIES**	**TECHNOLOGY**
	• **Beyond Literature,** Career Connection: Performing Arts, p. 45 ▲ ■		• **Interest Grabber Video,** Tape 4 ● ▲ ■
	• **Selection Support Workbook:** ● ▲ ■ Literary Analysis, p. 180 Reading Strategy, p. 179 Build Vocabulary, p. 177	• **Literary Analysis and Reading Transparencies,** pp. 89 and 90 ● ▲ ■	
			• **Listening to Literature** ● ▲ ■ Audiocassettes, Side 22 Audio CDs, CD 14
	• **Literatura en español** ● ▲ • **Literary Analysis for Enrichment** ■	• **Fine Art Transparencies, Volume 1,** Art Transparency 6 ● ▲ ■	
	• **Formal Assessment:** Selection Test, pp. 161–163 ● ▲ ■ • **Open Book Test,** pp. 133–135 ● ▲ ■ • **Performance Assessment and Portfolio Management,** p. 8 ● ▲ ■ • PRENTICE HALL ASSESSMENT SYSTEM ● ▲ ■	• PRENTICE HALL ASSESSMENT SYSTEM ● ▲ ■ Skills Practice Answers and Explanations on Transparencies	• **Test Bank Software** ● ▲ ■ • **Got It! Assessment Videotapes,** Tape 4 ● ▲
	• **Selection Support Workbook:** ● ▲ ■ Build Grammar Skills, p. 178 • **Writing and Grammar,** Gold Level ● ▲ ■ • **Extension Activities,** p. 45 ● ▲ ■	• **Daily Language Practice Transparencies** ● ▲	• **Writing and Grammar iText CD-ROM** ● ▲ ■ ***Take It to the Net*** www.phschool.com

BLOCK SCHEDULING: Use one 90-minute class period to preteach the selection and have students read it. Use a second 90-minute class period to assess students' mastery of skills and have them complete one of the Extension Activities.

PREVIEW

PRETEACH

Step-by-Step Teaching Guide for pp. 732–733

Motivation

Although styles of dress and dancing have changed a lot since the 1950s, when this play is set, many of the conflicts of teenage social life remain the same. Capture students' interest in the play by having them discuss a recent dance or other social event at your school. Ask them to list some of the concerns they had and the decisions they made in the weeks before the dance. What tensions and conflicts did students have with friends and family? Ask students to look for similar conflicts as they read the play.

Interest Grabber Video

As an alternative, play "Life in the 50s" on Tape 4 to engage student interest.

❶ Background

The foxtrot was exactly that—a fast trotting dance first performed by Harry Fox, a vaudeville performer. He performed the jerky frantic steps in a vaudeville show and the dance was later adapted into a smoother dance for couples. The fox trot was initially danced to very fast music called ragtime, but became much slower over time. It was popular in the 1920s and influenced the development of the popular Charleston.

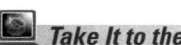

Prepare to Read

The Dancers

Take It to the Net

Visit www.phschool.com for interactive activities and instruction related to "The Dancers," including

- background
- graphic organizers
- literary elements
- reading strategies

Preview

Connecting to the Literature

Like most people, you probably experience times when your social life does not go smoothly. You might go to a party and find that you do not know anyone, or mistakenly make plans with two different people for the same evening. As you read this play, notice how the characters respond to such awkward situations.

❶ Background

In the 1950s, the setting for "The Dancers," people danced differently from the way they do now. Partners held each other, and their movements were synchronized and determined by the type of dance they were doing. It was not uncommon for children to take dance lessons in which they learned ballroom dances such as the waltz, the fox trot, and the cha-cha.

TEACHING RESOURCES

The following resources can be used to enrich or extend the instruction for pp. 732–733.

Motivation

Interest Grabber Video, Tape 4

Background

Beyond Literature, p. 45

Take It to the Net

Visit www.phschool.com for background and hotlinks for *The Dancers.*

Literary Analysis

Literary Analysis and Reading Transparencies, Staging, p. 90

Reading

Selection Support: Reading Strategy, p. 179; Build Vocabulary, p. 177

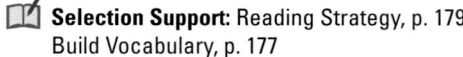

Literary Analysis and Reading Transparencies, Picturing the Action, p. 89

BLOCK SCHEDULING: Resources marked with this symbol provide varied instruction during 90-minute blocks.

❷ Literary Analysis

Staging

Staging is one of the ways in which a script is brought to life. It includes the sets, lighting, sound effects, costumes, and the way the actors move and deliver their lines. Staging is based on the stage directions, which are often bracketed and italicized. The staging excerpt below provides a brief description of the appearance and actions of one character, Emily, as she arrives on stage. In addition, it gives the time of day in which the scene takes place:

> [ELIZABETH CREWS *and her daughter* EMILY *come into the drugstore.* EMILY *is about seventeen and very pretty. This afternoon, however, it is evident that she is unhappy.*]

As you read the play, use the dialogue, stage directions, and your imagination to stage the play in your mind's eye.

Connecting Literary Elements

A drama relies completely on staging and dialogue to tell a story. **Dialogue** is a conversation between characters. It is used to reveal the qualities and situations of the characters and to advance the action of the play. As you read, notice how the staging and dialogue work together to reveal the events of the play.

❸ Reading Strategy

Picturing the Action

Plays are meant to be performed, so it is important to **picture the action** as you read. To picture the action, you should use these strategies:

- Read stage directions carefully and draw from your own experience to connect to the scene being set.
- Notice subtleties about characters' emotions, insecurities, or hopes.

Using a chart like the one on the right, note descriptions of characters and details of setting to help you picture the action.

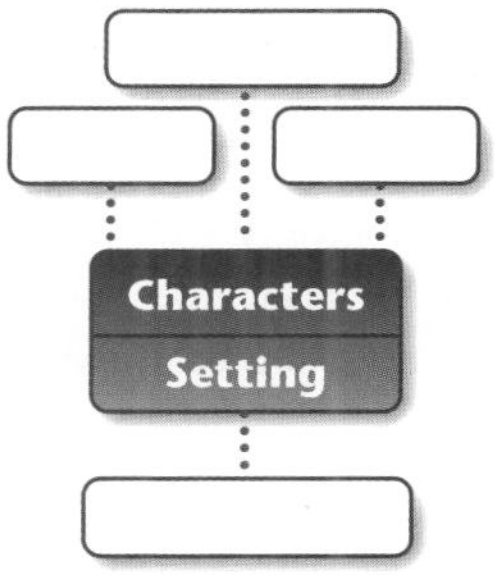

Vocabulary Development

genteel (jen tēl′) *adj.* polite (p. 741)

mortified (môrt′ ə fīd′) *v.* humiliated (p. 742)

defiance (dē fī′ əns) *n.* open resistance (p. 743)

console (kən sōl′) *v.* comfort (p. 751)

❷ Literary Analysis

Staging

- Tell students that some of the things that help bring a written script to life are costumes, lighting, sets, the actors—the way they move and speak—and sound effects.
- Read the instruction about how a director learns about all these elements and call students' attention to the example. Ask them to name the two characters that are named in the *stage directions.*
- Use the instruction for Connecting Literary Elements to alert students to the primary importance of the characters' dialogue in telling the story and giving other important information in a play.
- Use the Staging transparency in **Literary Analysis and Reading Transparencies,** p. 90, to show students how they might set up a director's chart to keep track of each scene of a play.

❸ Reading Strategy

Picturing the Action

- Tell students that unlike viewing a play, reading a play requires that they picture the action themselves.
- *Picturing the action* involves paying attention to both the stage directions and to what the characters say and how they say it.
- Instruct students to create Picturing the Action charts like the one on this page or the one on p. 89 of **Literary Analysis and Reading Transparencies** to help them keep track of specific scenes in the play.

Vocabulary Development

- Pronounce each vocabulary word for students, and read the definitions as a class. Have students identify any words with which they are already familiar.

CUSTOMIZE INSTRUCTION FOR UNIVERSAL ACCESS

For Less Proficient Students	For English Learners	For Advanced Readers
Help students decipher the stage directions shown on this page. Ask them basic questions, such as, What information is given to the reader in capital letters? What other kinds of information are given to the reader in the italic type? Based on the information given, how might an actress make it evident that Emily is unhappy?	Invite students to watch the **Interest Grabber Video** "Life in the 50s" and compare the cultural values and activities of the time with those of today, both in the United States and in their native country. Have them make a list of unfamiliar words they hear in the video, and help them look up the words in a dictionary.	Have students do research on the dances cited in the Background section on p. 732. How was each one danced? How did these dances differ from those that students do today? Ask volunteers who may be familiar with one or more of the dances to demonstrate the moves.

E-Teach

Visit E-Teach at www.phschool.com for teachers' essays on how to teach, with questions and answers.

TEACH

Step-by-Step Teaching Guide for pp. 734–760

CUSTOMIZE INSTRUCTION
For Verbal/Linguistic Learners

Assign roles to different students and have them read the first few pages of the play aloud. Encourage students to use the stage directions and dialogue to help them determine the emotional content of each speech, as well as the speaker's tone of voice. Stop the reading occasionally to explain the stage directions and to make sure students can picture the action in their minds.

❶ About the Selection

Horton Foote's one-act play is a poignant, timeless portrait of the conflicts teenagers face as they begin the process of becoming adults—dating, gaining social confidence, becoming more independent of controlling family members, and discovering and affirming their true selves. Students may recognize some of their own struggles reflected in the conflicts of Horace, Emily, and Mary Catherine that center upon who is taking whom to a dance.

❶ *The*

CHARACTERS

A WAITRESS in the local drugstore

INEZ STANLEY, Horace's older sister

ELIZABETH CREWS, Emily's mother

EMILY CREWS, a popular seventeen year old

HERMAN STANLEY, Inez's husband

HORACE, a sensitive eighteen year old

MARY CATHERINE DAVIS, a plainer girl of Emily's age

VELMA MORRISON, another young girl

TOM DAVIS, Mary Catherine's father

MRS. DAVIS, Mary Catherine's mother

SETTING

Harrison, Texas

TEACHING RESOURCES

The following resources can be used to enrich or extend the instruction for pp. 734–760.

Literary Analysis

Selection Support: Literary Analysis, p. 180

Reading

Listening to Literature Audiocassettes, Sides 27 and 28

Listening to Literature Audio CDs, CD 14 ■

Extension

Fine Arts Transparencies, Volume 1, Art Transparency 6 (Use this painting of a Native American dancer to discuss with students the significance of dances in various cultures.) ■

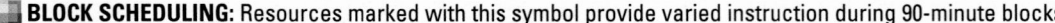

■ **BLOCK SCHEDULING:** Resources marked with this symbol provide varied instruction during 90-minute blocks.

Dancers

Horton Foote

2 3 [*Scene: The stage is divided into four acting areas: downstage left is the living room of* INEZ *and* HERMAN STANLEY. *Downstage right is part of a small-town drugstore. Upstage right is the living room of* ELIZABETH CREWS. *Upstage left, the yard and living room of* MARY CATHERINE DAVIS. *Since the action should flow continuously from one area to the other, only the barest amount of furnishings should be used to suggest what each area represents. The lights are brought up on the drugstore, downstage right.* WAITRESS *is there.* INEZ STANLEY *comes into the drugstore. She stands for a moment thinking. The* WAITRESS *goes over to her.*]

WAITRESS. Can I help you?

INEZ. Yes, you can if I can think of what I came in here for. Just gone completely out of my mind. I've been running around all day. You see, I'm expecting some company tonight. My brother Horace. He's coming on a visit.

[ELIZABETH CREWS *and her daughter* EMILY *come into the drugstore.* EMILY *is about seventeen and very pretty. This afternoon, however, it is evident that she is unhappy.*]

Hey . . .

ELIZABETH. We've just been by your house.

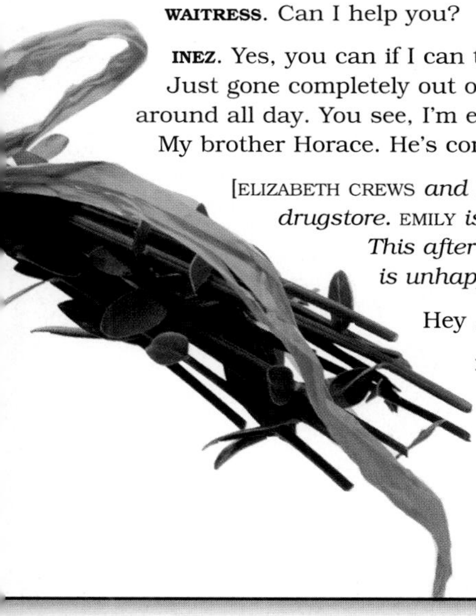

Literary Analysis
Staging What images do these stage directions create for you?

4 **Reading Check**
How does Emily look when she comes into the drugstore?

2 Literary Analysis

Staging

- Remind students that one important element of staging is the layout of the stage. Sometimes the layout changes from act to act, and sometimes it does not.
- Ask students what the four main acting areas here represent in terms of the characters in the play. Answer: The areas represent parts of the Stanley, Crews, and Davis homes, as well as the drugstore.
- Ask students to answer the Literary Analysis question on p. 735: What images do these stage directions create for you? Possible response: Students may say that the stage directions suggest that the action will move among the three houses and the drugstore.

3 Background

Stage Terms

Tell students that an important theater term for actors and director is the verb *block*. It means "to plan or sketch the movement of actors on stage in a play." It is almost a synonym of the verb *stage*. To help students visualize the action of the play, explain that *downstage* refers to the front of the stage, the part closer to the audience. *Upstage* refers to the back of the stage, opposite *downstage*. The directions *left* and *right* are determined from the viewpoint of the actors facing the audience.

Draw a sketch of the four acting areas on the board and label them STANLEY LIVING ROOM, DRUGSTORE, CREWS LIVING ROOM, and DAVIS YARD AND LIVING ROOM.

4 Reading Check

Answer: Emily looks pretty, but unhappy.

CUSTOMIZE INSTRUCTION FOR UNIVERSAL ACCESS

For Special Needs Students	For English Learners	For Gifted/Talented Students
These students will be able to visualize the action of the play more clearly if they are given the opportunity to act out one or more scenes. Have them work together to block out their motions for each scene.	Explain to students that the play takes place about fifty years ago in a small American town. Review the photos in the text to help students imagine how American teenagers of that time looked and acted.	Have students read the stage directions that say, "only the barest amount of furnishings should be used to suggest what each area represents." Then, have students make a drawing of the stage area, the four areas and what each one represents, determining what furniture and props they would use in each space.

❺ Critical Thinking

Analyze

- Ask students to describe the exchange of dialogue that goes on in this passage.
  Possible response: Students may note that Inez and Elizabeth talk "over" Emily as if she weren't there.
- Ask students to analyze the relationship between Elizabeth and her daughter, Emily, based on the fact that Elizabeth answers a question that was directed at Emily.
  Possible response: Students may say that Elizabeth is pushy and insensitive to her daughter's feelings. In addition, she is more excited about the dance than Emily is.

❻ Reading Strategy

Picturing the Action

- Ask students what they can use to picture the action while reading a play.
  Answer: The reader can use the stage directions, sound effects, costumes, and dialogue.
- Have students identify the main way readers can picture the action on this page.
  Answer: Dialogue is the basic element for picturing the action here.
- Ask students to respond to the Reading Strategy question on p. 736: What kind of expression do you think Emily has on her face when she responds to her mother? Why?
  Possible response: Emily probably has a depressed, sullen, or exasperated look on her face. Based on the dialogue, she is very quiet.

INEZ. You have? Hello, Emily.

EMILY. Hello.

ELIZABETH. We made some divinity[1] and took it over for Horace.

INEZ. Well, that's so sweet of you.

ELIZABETH. What time is he coming in?

INEZ. Six-thirty.

ELIZABETH. Are you meeting him?

INEZ. No—Herman. I've got to cook supper. Can I buy you all a drink?

ELIZABETH. No, we have to get Emily over to the beauty parlor.

INEZ. What are you wearing tonight, Emily?

5 ELIZABETH. She's wearing that sweet little net[2] I got her the end of last summer. She's never worn it to a dance here.

INEZ. I don't think I've ever seen it. I'll bet it looks beautiful on her. I'm gonna make Horace bring you by the house so I can see you before the dance.

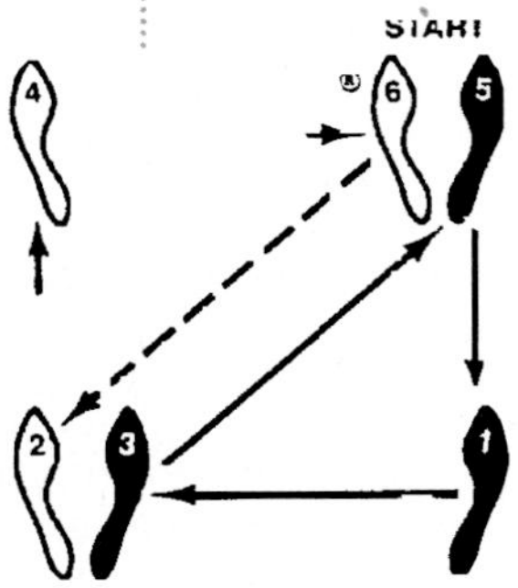

WAITRESS. Excuse me. . . .

INEZ. Yes?

WAITRESS. Have you thought of what you wanted yet? I thought I could be getting it for you.

INEZ. That's sweet, honey . . . but I haven't thought of what I wanted yet. [*To* ELIZABETH *and* EMILY.] I feel so foolish, I came in here for something, and I can't remember what.

WAITRESS. Cosmetics?

INEZ. No . . . you go on. I'll think and call you.

WAITRESS. All right. [*She goes.*]

INEZ. Emily, I think it's so sweet of you to go to the dance with Horace. I know he's going to be thrilled when I tell him.

ELIZABETH. Well, you're thrilled too, aren't you, Emily?

6 EMILY. Yes, ma'am.

ELIZABETH. I told Emily she'd thank me some day for not permitting her to sit home and miss all the fun.

EMILY. Mama, it's five to four. My appointment is at four o'clock.

Reading Strategy
Picturing the Action
What kind of expression do you think Emily has on her face when she responds to her mother? Why?

1. **divinity** soft, creamy candy made of sugar, egg whites, corn syrup, flavoring, and nuts.
2. **sweet little net** dress made of delicate, lacy fabric.

ENRICHMENT: Social Studies Connection

Teenagers and Cars

Horace may not have a car of his own yet, but many of his peers do. In the 1950s, teenagers became a consumer class for the first time in history. By the middle of the decade, they bought 43 percent of all phonograph records, 44 percent of all cameras, 39 percent of all new radios, 9 percent of all new cars, and just over half of all tickets to the movies. The scarcity and save-for-the-future values of the Depression and World War II years were a thing of the past, except to the generation that had lived through both events. However, 1950s teens had not lived through the Depression, and most were not old enough to remember the war.

7 **ELIZABETH.** Well, you go on in the car.

EMILY. How are you gonna get home?

ELIZABETH. I'll get home. Don't worry about me.

EMILY. OK. [*She starts out.*]

INEZ. 'Bye, Emily.

EMILY. 'Bye. [*She goes on out.*]

ELIZABETH. Does Horace have a car for tonight?

INEZ. Oh, yes. He's taking Herman's.

ELIZABETH. I just wondered. I wanted to offer ours if he didn't have one.

INEZ. That's very sweet—but we're giving him our car every night for the two weeks of his visit. Oh—I know what I'm after. Flowers. I have to order Emily's corsage for Horace. I came in here to use the telephone to call you to find out what color Emily's dress was going to be.

ELIZABETH. Blue.

INEZ. My favorite color. Walk me over to the florist.

ELIZABETH. All right.

[*They go out as the lights fade. The lights are brought up downstage left on the living room of* INEZ STANLEY. HERMAN STANLEY *and his brother-in-law,* HORACE, *come in.* HERMAN *is carrying* HORACE*'s suitcase.* HERMAN *is in his middle thirties.* HORACE *is eighteen, thin, sensitive, but a likable boy.*]

HERMAN. Inez. Inez. We're here.

[*He puts the bag down in the living room.* INEZ *comes running in from stage right.*]

INEZ. You're early.

HERMAN. The bus was five minutes ahead of time.

8 **INEZ.** Is that so? Why, I never heard of that. [*She kisses her brother.*] Hello, honey.

HORACE. Hello, sis.

INEZ. You look fine.

HORACE. Thank you.

INEZ. You haven't put on a bit of weight though.

HORACE. Haven't I?

INEZ. Not a bit. I'm just going to stuff food down you and put some weight on you while you're here. How's your appetite?

HORACE. Oh, it's real good. I eat all the time.

Reading Strategy
Picturing the Action Picture in your mind how Emily looks as she starts to leave the drugstore. Is she in a hurry?

Literary Analysis
Staging What kind of staging do you think could be added to this dialogue between Horace and Inez?

9 ✓ **Reading Check**
Why is Inez buying a corsage?

7 Reading Strategy
Picturing the Action

- Ask students to draw a conclusion about why Emily is so silent.
  Possible response: Students may recognize that Emily, for whatever reason, doesn't want to go to the dance with Horace and cannot join in the anticipation of the event with her mother and Inez.
- Ask students to picture the action up to this point. Then, have them answer the Reading Strategy question on p. 737: Picture in your mind how Emily looks as she starts to leave the drugstore. Is she in a hurry?
  Possible response: Students may suggest that Emily is not in a hurry because she doesn't want to go to the dance. They may also realize that she wants to get away from her mother and Inez. Students may say she leaves the drugstore uncertainly.

8 Literary Analysis
Staging

- Remind students that the content of the dialogue helps tell a director about the staging of a scene when there are no stage directions.
- Ask the Literary Analysis Question on p. 737: What kind of staging do you think could be added to this dialogue between Horace and Inez?
  Possible response: Staging might include physical movements for Inez such as gesturing at Horace when referring to his weight. Directions might also specify Inez's excited tone of voice, or Horace's discomfort at his sister's inspection.

9 ✓ Reading Check

Answer: Inez is buying a corsage for Horace to give to Emily when he takes her to the dance.

CUSTOMIZE INSTRUCTION FOR UNIVERSAL ACCESS

For Special Needs Students	For Less Proficient Readers
Remind students that they can check the character list at the beginning of the play if they are unsure of character relationships. For example, the stage directions on this page identify Inez Stanley, Herman Stanley and his brother-in-law Horace. By checking the cast list, students can confirm that Inez and Horace are brother and sister and that Herman Stanley is Inez's husband.	To confirm that students understand the function of lighting different areas of the stage, ask them where the scene just before the mid-page stage directions takes place. Then, ask students where the scene on the second half of the page takes place. What alerts the audience to the change of location? Lead students to see that the second scene on this page takes place in the living room of the Stanleys' home. The audience is alerted to the change of scene location by the lighting directions.

10 ▶ **Critical Viewing**

Answer: Students may say that the boy is skinny like Horace, but that the girl looks much too happy to be Emily.

11 Critical Thinking

Compare

- Ask students whether they think going to the dance with Emily is Horace's idea.
  Answer: No, it is not Horace's idea; it is Elizabeth and Inez's idea.
- Have students determine how the dance arrangements came about.
  Answer: Inez and Elizabeth set up the dance plans for their respective brother and daughter.
- Invite students to make a comparison about the two women in this play so far.
  Answer: Inez and Elizabeth seem to want to run their relatives' lives and to make decisions for them.

INEZ. Then why don't you put on some weight?

HORACE. I don't know. I guess I'm just the skinny type.

INEZ. How are the folks?

HORACE. Fine.

INEZ. Mother over her cold?

HORACE. Yes, she is.

INEZ. Dad's fine?

HORACE. Just fine.

INEZ. Oh, Herman, did you ask him?

HERMAN. Ask him what?

INEZ. Ask him what? About his tux.

HERMAN. No, I didn't. . . .

INEZ. Honestly, Herman. Here we have him a date with the prettiest and most popular girl in Harrison and Herman says ask him what. You did bring it, didn't you, Bubber?

HORACE. Bring what?

INEZ. Your tux.

HORACE. Oh, sure.

INEZ. Well, guess who I've got you a date with. Aren't you curious?

HORACE. Uh. Huh.

INEZ. Well, guess. . . .

[*A pause. He thinks.*]

11 HORACE. I don't know.

INEZ. Well, just try guessing. . . .

HORACE. Well . . . uh . . . [*He is a little embarrassed. He stands trying to think. No names come to him.*] I don't know.

INEZ. Emily Crews. Now isn't she a pretty girl?

HORACE. Yes. She is.

INEZ. And the most popular girl in this town. You know her mother is a very close friend of mine and she called me day before yesterday and she said I hear Horace is coming to town and I said yes you were and she said that the boy Emily is going with is in summer school and couldn't get

10 ▼ **Critical Viewing**
How do the details in this photo compare to your image of the characters in the play? **[Compare and Contrast]**

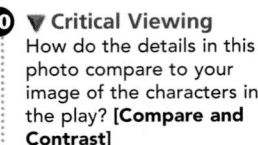

ENRICHMENT: Social Studies Connection

Matchmaking

When Inez tries to arrange the dance date between Horace and Emily, she is engaging in the common activity sometimes known as matchmaking. In this country, matchmaking is usually informal, as it is in this story; but in other cultures, the matchmaking process has been seen as something almost like a profession. In Jewish communities of Eastern Europe, for instance, the marriage broker—known as a *shadkhan*—provided a vital service for the often isolated Jewish families.

Matchmaking has developed some modern twists. Americans have long been familiar with computerized dating services. Now some culturally specific marriage-referral services use computer technology to find compatible mates for prospective brides or grooms. People who are living away from their homeland, without family members to arrange marriages in the traditional way, can find spouses with the aid of a digital matchmaker.

away this week-end and Emily said she wouldn't go to the dance at all but her mother said that she had insisted and wondered if you'd take her. . . .

HORACE. Her mother said. Does Emily want me to take her?

INEZ. That isn't the point, Bubber. The point is that her mother doesn't approve of the boy Emily is in love with and she likes you . . .

HORACE. Who likes me?

INEZ. Emily's mother. And she thinks you would make a very nice couple.

12 **HORACE.** Oh. [*A pause.*] But what does Emily think?

INEZ. Emily doesn't know what to think, honey. I'm trying to explain that to you. She's in love.

HORACE. Where am I supposed to take her to?

INEZ. The dance.

HORACE. But, Inez, I don't dance well enough. . . . I don't like to go to dances . . . yet . . .

INEZ. Oh, Horace. Mother wrote me you were learning.

HORACE. Well . . . I am learning. But I don't dance well enough yet.

INEZ. Horace, you just make me sick. The trouble with you is that you have no confidence in yourself. I bet you can dance.

HORACE. No, I can't. . . .

INEZ. Now let's see. [INEZ *goes to the radio and turns it on. She comes back to him.*] Now, come on. Show me what you've learned. . . .

HORACE. Aw, Sis . . .

HERMAN. Inez. Why don't you let the boy alone?

INEZ. Now you keep out of this, Herman Stanley. He's my brother and he's a stick. He's missing all the fun in life and I'm not going to have him a stick. I've sat up nights thinking of social engagements to keep him busy every minute of these next two weeks—I've got three dances scheduled for him. So he cannot dance. Now come on, dance with me. . . . [*He takes her by the arm awkwardly. He begins to lead her around the room.*] Now, that's fine. That's just fine. Isn't that fine, Herman?

HERMAN. Uh. Huh.

INEZ. You see all you need is confidence. And I want you to promise me you'll talk plenty when you're with the girl, not just sit there in silence and only answer when you're asked a question. . . . Now promise me.

HORACE. I promise.

Reading Strategy
Picturing the Action How do you picture Horace's reaction to the news about Emily?

13 **Reading Check**
Why does Horace say he does not like to go to dances?

12 Reading Strategy
Picturing the Action

- Ask students what they learn in this passage about Emily's mother and her desire for Emily to attend the dance with Horace.
  Answer: Readers learn that Emily has been dating a boy that Elizabeth does not like, and Elizabeth would rather that Emily date Horace.
- Ask the class to imagine Horace standing in his living room listening to his sister talk. Then, have students answer the Reading Strategy question on p. 739: How do you picture Horace's reaction to the news about Emily?
  Possible response: Horace may harbor his own feelings for Emily; however, those feelings are not yet clear. He is clearly aware that she has been forced to go out with him against her will. He is a sensitive person and considerate of Emily's feelings. Moreover, he has a certain amount of self-respect, and doesn't want to go out with someone who doesn't really like him.

13 Reading Check

Answer: Horace is just learning to dance and doesn't feel competent enough yet to do it in public.

CUSTOMIZE INSTRUCTION FOR UNIVERSAL ACCESS

For Less Proficient Readers	For English Learners	For Gifted/Talented Students
Remind students that when people talk with one another, they use informal language. In fact, they may use incomplete sentences, as seen in the dialogue throughout this play. Invite students to find examples of incomplete sentences in the dialogue and identify what the speaker means in each line.	Point out to students that the word *engagement* can mean "a promise to be married," but also can mean "an appointment to meet someone," as for a social event. Ask them which meaning of the word is used on p. 739.	Students might enjoy doing research on the teenage fashion values of the 1950s, starting with the photograph on this spread. Ask them what the shoes worn by the girl in the photograph are called, as well as her hairstyle. When students have gathered some materials on 50s fashions, invite them to make a graphic display for the class.

⓮ Reading Strategy

Picturing the Action

- Ask students what change is made to the stage directions within this passage of the text.
  Answer: Students should recognize that the scene in Horace's home ends and a scene in Emily Crews' home begins.
- Have students picture what takes place on the stage in this passage, and contrast the emotional state of Horace and Emily.
  Answer: Horace is smiling and dancing. Emily is crying.

⓯ Critical Thinking

Make Judgments

- Ask students what two excuses Emily uses in this passage in her attempt to forego the dance.
  Answer: First, she claims she doesn't feel good, and when that doesn't work, she says that Horace is a goon.
- Then, ask students whether they think Emily really thinks Horace is a goon. If not, why does she say so?
  Possible response: She is seeing another boy and does not want to date anyone else. She probably does not really think Horace is a goon, but hopes that her mother will not want her to be seen with someone who might be characterized as a "goon."

INEZ. Fine. Why, I think he dances real well. Don't you, Herman?

HERMAN. Yes, I do. Just fine, Inez.

INEZ. Just a lovely dancer, all he needs is confidence. He is very light on his feet. And he has a fine sense of rhythm—why, brother, you're a born dancer—

⓮ [HORACE *is smiling over the compliments, half wanting to believe what they say, but then not so sure. He is dancing with her around the room as the lights fade. They are brought up on the area upstage right.* EMILY CREWS *is in her living room. She has on her dressing gown.*[3] *She is crying.* ELIZABETH, *her mother, comes in from upstage right.*]

ELIZABETH. Emily.

EMILY. Yes, ma'm.

ELIZABETH. Do you know what time it is?

EMILY. Yes, ma'm.

ELIZABETH. Then why in the world aren't you dressed?

EMILY. Because I don't feel good.

ELIZABETH. Emily . . .

EMILY. I don't feel good . . . [*She begins to cry.*] Oh, Mother. I don't want to go to the dance tonight. Please, ma'm, don't make me. I'll do anything in this world for you if you promise me . . .

ELIZABETH. Emily. This is all settled. You are going to that dance. Do you understand me. You are going to that dance. That sweet, nice brother of Inez Stanley's will be here any minute. . . .

⓯ **EMILY.** Sweet, nice brother. He's a goon. That's what he is. A regular goon. A bore and a goon. . . .

ELIZABETH. Emily . . .

EMILY. That's all he is. Just sits and doesn't talk. Can't dance. I'm not going to any dance or any place else with him and that's final.

[*She runs out stage right.*]

ELIZABETH. Emily . . . Emily . . . You get ready this minute . . . [*The doorbell rings. Yelling.*] Emily . . . Emily . . . Horace is here. I want you down those stairs in five minutes . . . dressed.

[*She goes out stage left and comes back in followed by* HORACE, *all dressed up. He has a corsage box in his hand.*]

Hello, Horace.

3. **dressing gown** loose robe.

ENRICHMENT: Drama Connection

Sound Effects

There are three kinds of sound effects available for use in a stage play. Live sound might include a band or orchestra that plays for a musical production. Sound effects that are unrecorded might include a ringing telephone, a slamming door, or the groan of a murder victim offstage. Many sound effects, including everything from a windstorm to a traffic jam, are prerecorded and simply played from a recorded cassette backstage or from the light booth.

In the past, the sound of thunder was created by shaking and banging a tall flexible sheet of tin. Walking in a tray of small pebbles or gravel sounded just like what it was—someone walking on a gravel path. Empty cellophane bags that once contained potato or cheese chips could be rustled between one's fingers in front of a microphone to simulate the sound of fire burning.

HORACE. Good evening.

ELIZABETH. Sit down, won't you, Horace? Emily is a little late getting dressed. You know how girls are.

HORACE. Yes, ma'm.

[*He sits down. He seems a little awkward and shy.*]

ELIZABETH. Can I get you something to drink, Horace?

HORACE. No, ma'm.

[*A pause.* ELIZABETH *is obviously very nervous about whether* EMILY *will behave or not.*]

ELIZABETH. Are you sure I can't get you a coca-cola or something?

HORACE. No. Thank you.

16 **ELIZABETH.** How's your family?

HORACE. Just fine, thank you.

ELIZABETH. I bet your sister was glad to see you.

HORACE. Yes, she was.

ELIZABETH. How's your family? Oh, I guess I asked you that, didn't I?

HORACE. Yes, you did.

[ELIZABETH *keeps glancing off stage right, praying that* EMILY *will put in an appearance.*]

ELIZABETH. I understand you've become quite an accomplished dancer. . . .

HORACE. Oh . . . well . . . I . . .

ELIZABETH. Inez tells me you do all the new steps.

HORACE. Well—I . . .

ELIZABETH. Excuse me. Let me see what is keeping that girl.

17 [*She goes running off stage right.* HORACE *gets up. He seems very nervous. He begins to practice his dancing. He seems more unsure of himself and awkward. . . . We can hear* ELIZABETH *offstage knocking on* EMILY'S *door. At first* HORACE *isn't conscious of the knocking or the ensuing conversation and goes on practicing his dancing. When he first becomes conscious of what's to follow he tries to pay no attention. Then gradually he moves over to the far left side of the stage. The first thing we hear is* ELIZABETH'S *genteel tapping at* EMILY'S *door. Then she begins to call, softly at first, then louder and louder.*]

Emily. Emily. Emily Crews. Emily Carter Crews. . . . [*The pounding offstage is getting louder and louder.*] Emily. I can hear you in there. Now open that door.

Literary Analysis
Staging and Dialogue
Does the dialogue effectively convey Elizabeth's nervousness mentioned in the stage directions? Explain.

Reading Strategy
Picturing the Action
Describe how you picture Horace's body language as he overhears the conversation going on offstage.

genteel (jen tēl′) *adj.* polite

18 **✔Reading Check**
Why is Emily still in her dressing gown and crying when Horace arrives?

CUSTOMIZE INSTRUCTION FOR UNIVERSAL ACCESS

For Less Proficient Readers	For Gifted/Talented Students
Have students recall a time when they were greeting someone new or were nervous in the presence of company. Do they think Elizabeth's behavior is realistic for such a situation? What other questions do they think she might ask Horace in order to keep the conversation going while they both await Emily?	Have students think of a particular dance they know and enjoy, or a general kind of dancing. Then, have them compose instructions that would show Horace how to perform the dance. Allow students to choose the form the instructions take, for example, sketches, diagrams, written lists, or other modes of instruction.

16 Literary Analysis
Staging and Dialogue

- Ask students how Elizabeth and Horace's exchange of dialogue in this passage is similar to the exchange between Inez and Horace in the scene at the Stanleys' house.
  Answer: Elizabeth tries to keep the conversation going by asking questions, which Horace answers in brief.
- Based on the stage directions at the beginning of this passage, have students identify the emotional state Elizabeth is in.
  Answer: Elizabeth is very nervous.

Monitor Progress Have students answer the Literary Analysis question on p. 741: Does the dialogue effectively convey Elizabeth's nervousness mentioned in the stage directions? Explain.
Answer: The dialogue does show Elizabeth's nervousness by illustrating her attempt to keep Horace talking. She even asks the same question twice.

17 Reading Strategy
Picturing the Action

- Ask students to read the stage directions in this passage and determine who is the only character seen on stage during this period.
  Answer: Elizabeth goes offstage to knock on Emily's door. Although the audience can hear her words to Emily, they cannot see the two characters. Therefore, Horace is the only character left on stage.
- Have students respond to the Reading Strategy statement on p. 741: Describe how you picture Horace's body language as he overhears the conversation going on offstage.
  Possible response: Students may suggest that as Horace becomes aware of the conversation, he gradually moves stage left to avoid hearing what is being said. Perhaps he continues to move in his dance formation as he sidles across the stage.

18 ✔Reading Check

Answer: Emily does not want to get dressed, because she does not want to go to the dance with Horace.

⓳ Critical Thinking

Draw Conclusions

- Have students read the last sentence of the stage directions and identify what Elizabeth has decided to do.
  Answer: Elizabeth has decided to tell a fib.
- Have students read the dialogue following the stage directions. What "fibs" can they identify in Elizabeth's words to Horace?
  Possible response: Elizabeth tells Horace Emily is sick; she tells him she has called the doctor; she says Emily will be heartbroken if Horace doesn't call her tomorrow; and she tells Emily she has called Emily's father.

⓴ Reading Strategy

Picturing the Action

- Ask students what occurs when Elizabeth returns to the living room.
  Answer: She tells Horace that Emily is ill and cannot go to the dance with him.
- Have students pretend to be Horace as you read aloud Elizabeth's dialogue to the class. Then, have them respond to the Reading Strategy question on p. 742: How do you picture the facial expressions of Horace and Elizabeth as she apologizes to him?
  Possible responses: Students may say that Elizabeth probably has a frown or a look of deep sympathy on her face, while Horace is probably trying to keep from looking relieved, and so maintains an expressionless face as he pretends to believe her story.

EMILY. [*Screaming back.*] I won't. I told you I won't.

ELIZABETH. Emily Carter Crews. You open that door immediately.

EMILY. I won't.

ELIZABETH. I'm calling your father from downtown if you don't open that door right this very minute.

EMILY. I don't care. I won't come out.

ELIZABETH. Then I'll call him. [*She comes running in from stage right.* HORACE *quickly gets back to his chair and sits.*] Excuse me, Horace.

[*She crosses through the room and goes out upstage right.* HORACE *seems very ill at ease. He looks at the box of flowers. He is very warm. He begins to fan himself.* ELIZABETH *comes back in the room from upstage right. She is very nervous. But she tries to hide her nervousness in an overly social manner.* ELIZABETH *has decided to tell a fib.*]

⓴ Horace, I am so sorry to have to ruin your evening, but my little girl isn't feeling well. She has a headache and a slight temperature and I've just called the doctor and he says he thinks it's very advisable that she stay in this evening. She's upstairs insisting she go, but I do feel under the circumstances I had just better keep her in. I hope you understand.

HORACE. Oh, yes ma'm. I do understand.

ELIZABETH. How long do you plan to visit us, Horace?

HORACE. Two weeks.

⓳ **ELIZABETH.** That's nice. [*They start walking offstage left.*] Please call Emily tomorrow and ask her out again. She'll just be heartbroken if you don't.

HORACE. Yes, ma'm. Good night.

ELIZABETH. Good night, Horace. [HORACE *goes out.* ELIZABETH *calls out after him.*] Can you see, Horace? [*In the distance we hear* HORACE *answer.*]

HORACE. Yes, ma'm.

ELIZABETH. Now you be sure and call us tomorrow. You hear? [*She stands waiting for a moment. Then she walks back across stage to upstage right, screaming at the top of her voice.*] Emily Carter Crews. You have mortified me. You have mortified me to death. I have, for your information, called your father and he is interrupting his work and is coming home this very minute and he says to tell you that you are not to be allowed to leave this house again for two solid weeks. Is that perfectly clear?

[*She is screaming as she goes out upstage right. The lights are brought down. They are brought up immediately downstage right on*

Reading Strategy
Picturing the Action
How do you picture the facial expressions of Horace and Elizabeth as she apologizes to him?

mortified (môrt′ ə fīd) *v.* humiliated

ENRICHMENT: History Connection

Generation Gap

In the early 1950s, the "generation gap" between teenagers and their parents was just beginning. The "youth culture" of rock 'n' roll and rebellion took hold after the movie *Rebel Without a Cause* came out. Later in the 1950s, things changed in a way that has had a lasting effect on adult-teenager relationships. Have students compare and contrast their tastes in clothing, language, music, and movies with those of their parents. Then, ask how the "generation gap" has narrowed or widened since the early 1950s.

the drugstore. It is half an hour later. HORACE *comes in. He seats himself at the counter. He still has the box of flowers. The drugstore is deserted. A* WAITRESS *is up near the front with her arms on the counter. She keeps glancing at a clock.* HORACE *is examining a menu . . .*]

HORACE. Can I have a chicken salad sandwich?

WAITRESS. We're all out of that.

HORACE. Oh.

[*He goes back to reading the menu.*]

22 **WAITRESS.** If it's all the same to you, I'd rather not make a sandwich. I'm closing my doors in ten minutes.

HORACE. Oh. Well, what would you like to make?

WAITRESS. Any kind of ice cream or soft drinks. [*She looks up at the ice cream menu.*] Coffee is all gone.

HORACE. How about a chocolate ice cream soda?

WAITRESS. O.K. Coming up. [*She starts to mix the soda. She talks as she works.*] Going to the dance?

HORACE. No.

WAITRESS. The way you're all dressed up I thought for sure you were going.

HORACE. No. I was, but I changed my mind.

[MARY CATHERINE DAVIS *comes in the drugstore from downstage right. Somehow in her young head she has gotten the idea that she is a plain girl and in defiance for the pain of that fact she does everything she can to make herself look plainer.*]

WAITRESS. Hello, Mary Catherine. Been to the movies?

MARY CATHERINE. Yes, I have.

[*The* WAITRESS *puts the drink down in front of* HORACE. *He begins to drink.*]

WAITRESS. What'll you have, Mary Catherine?

MARY CATHERINE. Vanilla ice cream.

21 ▲ Critical Viewing What does this photograph reveal about life in the 1950s, the setting for "The Dancers"? **[Infer]**

defiance (dē fī′ əns) *n.* open resistance

23 Reading Check What excuse does Elizabeth give for Emily's refusal to go to the dance?

21 ▶ Critical Viewing

Answer: Students may say that young people in the 1950s dressed more formally on dates and liked going to "soda fountains" to enjoy each other's company over an ice-cream sundae or a soda.

22 Literary Analysis

Staging and Dialogue

- Ask students to describe what generally happens when they go into a restaurant and a waiter or waitress comes to their table.
  Possible response: Students will probably say that the server brings a menu, they order, and the server eventually brings them their food and drinks.
- Have students identify the incidents in this passage that contrast with the process they have just described.
  Answer: The waitress is waiting impatiently to get off work. Horace gets his own menu. When he asks for a sandwich, she says they're out. She says she'd rather make a dessert. Horace then orders a chocolate ice cream soda.
- Have students determine what this exchange of dialogue shows about Horace's personality.
  Answer: Horace is sensitive to other people's feelings, but he also does not stand up for himself. He is the customer, and he should have asserted his preferences more strongly to the waitress.

23 Reading Check

Answer: Elizabeth says Emily is ill.

CUSTOMIZE INSTRUCTION FOR UNIVERSAL ACCESS

For Less Proficient Readers	For Advanced Readers
Invite students to use the Staging transparency on p. 90 of **Literary Analysis and Reading Transparencies** to suggest what they would do to stage the scene that takes place on pp. 741–742. Have them work as a group to determine which part of the stage should be lighted based on the layout on p. 735, which dialogue should come from offstage, which sound effects should be used, and so forth.	Encourage students to imagine that they are directing a production of the play. As they read, have them consider how they would stage each scene and what advice they would give the actors. Have students prepare detailed director's notes for each scene.

❷❹ Literary Analysis

Staging

- Ask students why the waitress and Mary Catherine speak so openly in front of Horace about Emily and her boyfriend.
  Answer: Mary Catherine and the waitress have no idea that Horace is the "out-of-town boy."
- Have students discuss whether this conversation makes Horace feel better about his situation or worse. Why?
  Possible response: Students may suggest that hearing about Emily and her boyfriend probably makes Horace feel better about his situation, because now he knows that Emily is not just rejecting him out of hand, but has another boyfriend.
- Have students answer the Literary Analysis question on p. 744: What do you think Horace is doing in this scene to get the waitress's attention?
  Answer: He is clearing his throat, trying to make eye contact, standing up, or waving his hand.

❷❺ Reading Strategy

Picturing the Action

- Ask students how Horace finally gets the attention of the waitress. Ask them why they think he didn't do this earlier?
  Answer: He calls to her. Horace didn't do this earlier because he is too polite to interrupt the girls' conversation.
- Have students respond to the Reading Strategy question on p. 744: How do you picture Horace, based on the waitress's description?
  Answer: Horace is dressed up in a tuxedo and carrying a corsage.

WAITRESS. O.K. [*She gets the ice cream. She talks as she does so.*] There weren't many at the picture show tonight, I bet. I can always tell by whether we have a crowd in here or not after the first show. I guess everybody is at the dance.

❷❹ **MARY CATHERINE.** I could have gone, but I didn't want to. I didn't want to miss the picture show. Emily Crews didn't go. Leo couldn't get home from summer school and she said she was refusing to go. Her mother made a date for her with some bore from out of town without consulting her and she was furious about it. I talked to her this afternoon. She said she didn't know yet how she would get out of it, but she would. She said she had some rights. Her mother doesn't approve of Leo and that's a shame because they are practically engaged.

WAITRESS. I think Emily is a very cute girl, don't you?

MARY CATHERINE. Oh, yes. I think she's darling.

[HORACE *has finished his drink and is embarrassed by their talk. He is trying to get the* WAITRESS*'s attention but doesn't quite know how. He finally calls to the* WAITRESS.]

HORACE. Miss . . .

WAITRESS. Yes?

HORACE. How much do I owe you?

WAITRESS. Twenty cents.

HORACE. Thank you.

[*He reaches in his pocket for the money.*]

WAITRESS. Emily has beautiful clothes, doesn't she?

MARY CATHERINE. Oh, yes. She does.

WAITRESS. Her folks are rich?

MARY CATHERINE. She has the prettiest things. But she's not a bit stuck up. . . .

[*He holds the money out to the* WAITRESS.]

HORACE. Here you are.

❷❺ **WAITRESS.** Thank you. [*She takes the money and rings it up in the cash register.* HORACE *goes on out.* WAITRESS *shakes her head as he goes.*] There's a goofy nut if I ever saw one. He's got flowers under his arm. He's wearing a tux and yet he's not going to the dance. Who is he?

MARY CATHERINE. I don't know. I never saw him before.

[*The* WAITRESS *walks to the edge of the area and looks out. She comes back shaking her head. She sits on the stool beside* MARY CATHERINE.]

Literary Analysis
Staging What do you think Horace is doing in this scene to get the waitress's attention?

Reading Strategy
Picturing the Action How do you picture Horace, based on the waitress's description?

ENRICHMENT: History Connection

Cost of Living

Students may be surprised to read that Horace's chocolate ice cream soda only costs him 20 cents. The cost of living has risen considerably since the 1950s. In the early part of that decade, a family could buy a three-bedroom home for under $12,000, a new car for under $3,000, and a pound of hamburger for 39 cents. A boy could get a haircut for $1.50 and buy a gallon of gas for 30 cents. Of course, the cost of living matched a worker's monthly salary, which was much less than what workers earn today.

WAITRESS. [*While laughing and shaking her head.*] I ought to call the Sheriff and have him locked up. Do you know what he's doing?

26 **MARY CATHERINE.** No. What?

WAITRESS. Standing on the corner. Dancing back and forth. He's holding his arm up like he's got a girl and everything. Wouldn't it kill you? [*Goes to the front and looks out.*] See him?

MARY CATHERINE. No. He's stopped.

WAITRESS. What's he doing?

MARY CATHERINE. Just standing there. Looking kind of lost.

[MARY CATHERINE *comes back to the counter. She starts eating her ice cream again.*]

WAITRESS. Well—it takes all kinds.

MARY CATHERINE. I guess so.

[*She goes back to eating her ice cream. The lights are brought down. The lights are brought up on the area downstage left. The living room of the* STANLEYS. INEZ *is there reading a book.* HERMAN *comes in.*]

HERMAN. Hi, hon.

INEZ. Hello. . . .

HERMAN. What's the matter with you? You look down in the dumps.

INEZ. No, I'm just disgusted.

HERMAN. What are you disgusted about?

INEZ. Horace. I had everything planned so beautifully for him and then that silly Emily has to go and hurt his feelings.

HERMAN. Well, honey, that was pretty raw, the trick she pulled.

INEZ. I know. But he's a fool to let that get him down. He should have just gone to the dance by himself and proved her wrong. . . . Why like I told him. Show her up. Rush a different girl every night. Be charming. Make yourself popular. But it's like trying to talk to a stone wall. He refused to go out any more. He says he's going home tomorrow.

HERMAN. Where is he now?

INEZ. Gone to the movies.

HERMAN. Well, honey. I hate to say it, but in a way it serves you right. I've told you a thousand times if I've told you once. Leave the boy alone. He'll be all right. Only don't push him. You and your mother have pushed the boy and pushed him and pushed him.

INEZ. And I'm going to keep on pushing him. I let him off tonight

Literary Analysis
Staging Would additional stage directions convey a clearer image of Horace, or is the dialogue sufficient? Explain.

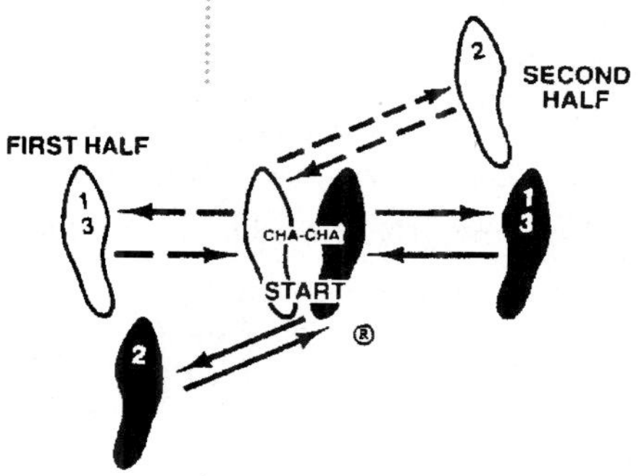

27 **Reading Check**
Why is Inez disgusted?

26 Literary Analysis

Staging and Dialogue

- Ask students what Horace does after he leaves the drugstore.
  Answer: He stands on the corner, still practicing his dancing.
- Have students consider that the waitress's words could easily have been used in slightly different form as stage directions. How would such stage directions read?
  Possible response: HORACE *stands on the corner, holding his arm up as if he is dancing with a girl. He dances back and forth.*
- Invite students to answer the Literary Analysis question on p. 745: Would additional stage directions convey a clearer image of Horace, or is the dialogue sufficient? Explain.
  Possible response: The dialogue is sufficient because the audience can see what Horace is doing while the waitress is relating what she is seeing. Moreover, the audience has already seen Horace practicing his dancing earlier in the play.

27 Reading Check

Answer: Inez is disgusted because Horace won't go to the dance and find other girls to date after Emily turned him down.

CUSTOMIZE INSTRUCTION FOR UNIVERSAL ACCESS

For Special Needs Students	For Gifted/Talented Students
Students might enjoy acting out this scene between the waitress, Mary Catherine, and Horace, up to the change of scene. Help students use the Reading Strategy transparency, p. 89 in **Literary Analysis and Reading Transparencies,** to list where the characters are placed on stage and what they say. Students may then take turns playing the different characters and presenting the scene.	Ask students to determine the current idioms for the old-fashioned usage found on this spread. Examples are "stuck up," "goofy nut," "Wouldn't it kill you?", "down in the dumps," and "pretty raw."

28 Literary Analysis

Staging and Dialogue

- Ask students to compare and contrast Inez and Herman in this scene in terms of their opinion of what should be done with Horace.
  Answer: Herman thinks Horace should be left alone to make his own way, and Inez believes Horace needs constant pushing if he is going to get anywhere in life.
- Have students note that Inez is sitting and reading a book as the scene opens on p. 745. At the end of the scene on p. 746, she is walking up and down. Ask them to imagine they are blocking this scene and must decide when they would have Inez get up from the chair.
  Possible response: Students might suggest that a good time for Inez to rise in anger is as she says, "I won't leave him alone," or, "Now you just let me handle this, Herman." Students might also suggest that as Inez rises, Herman might sit down so that she is in a lecturing position over him.
- Invite students to respond to the Literary Analysis question on p. 746: Which traits of Inez are revealed through the dialogue?
  Answer: She is overbearing and likes to run everyone else's life.

29 Reading Strategy

Picturing the Action

- Ask students why Mary Catherine is embarrassed as she enters this scene.
  Answer: Mary Catherine is embarrassed because she has learned that Horace was sitting next to her the night before as she was relating the story about Emily's refusal to attend the dance with him.
- Ask students to answer the Reading Strategy question on p. 746: How do you picture Mary Catherine as she explains the situation with Emily's date to the waitress?
  Possible answer: She is acting embarrassed, perhaps moving her arms and hands around and hanging her head.

because his feelings were hurt, but tomorrow I'm going to have a long talk with him.

HERMAN. Inez. Leave the boy alone.

INEZ. I won't leave him alone. He is my brother and I'm going to see that he learns to have a good time.

HERMAN. Inez . . .

28 **INEZ.** Now you just let me handle this, Herman. He's starting to college next year and it's a most important time in his life. He had no fun in high school . . .

HERMAN. Now. He must have had some fun. . . .

INEZ. Not like other people. And he's not going through four years of college like a hermit with his nose stuck in some old book . . . [*She jumps up.*] I'll never forgive Elizabeth for letting Emily behave this way. And I told her so. I said Elizabeth Crews. I am very upset . . .

[*She is angrily walking up and down as the lights fade. They are brought up downstage right on the drugstore area. The* WAITRESS *is there alone.* MARY CATHERINE *comes in from downstage right.*]

WAITRESS. Did you go to the movies again tonight?

MARY CATHERINE. Uh-huh. Lila, do you remember when I was telling you about Emily's date and how she wouldn't go out with him because he was such a bore?

WAITRESS. Uh . . .

MARY CATHERINE. Oh, I just feel awful. That was the boy sitting in here . . .

WAITRESS. Last night . . . ?

29 **MARY CATHERINE.** Yes. I went riding with Emily and some of the girls this afternoon and we passed by his sister's house and there sat the boy.

WAITRESS. Sh . . . sh . . . [*She has seen* HORACE *come in to the area from downstage right. He comes to the counter. He seems very silent. He picks up a menu.*] Back again tonight?

HORACE. Uh-huh.

WAITRESS. What'll you have?

HORACE. A cup of coffee. . . .

WAITRESS. All out. We don't serve coffee after eight unless we happen to have some left over from supper time. . . .

HORACE. Thanks. [*He gets up.*]

WAITRESS. Nothing else?

Literary Analysis
Staging and Dialogue Which traits of Inez are revealed through the dialogue?

Reading Strategy
Picturing the Action How do you picture Mary Catherine as she explains the situation with Emily's date to the waitress?

ENRICHMENT: Social Studies Connection

The Movies

Neither Mary Catherine nor Horace identifies the movies they have seen, but the 1950s were a time of great films in a variety of genres, many of which have since become classics. Films such as *Marty* (1955), *A Streetcar Named Desire* (1951), *Rebel Without a Cause* and *East of Eden* (both 1955) were popular because they reflected realistic situations that teenagers could identify with. There were superb science fiction classics such as *The Day the Earth Stood Still* (1951) and *The Invasion of the Body Snatchers* (1956), the latter film having been remade twice since its release. Musicals, such as *An American in Paris* (1951) and *The King and I* (1956), were popular among both teens and adults alike. The great western *High Noon* swept the Academy Awards for 1952.

31

30 ◀ **Critical Viewing**
Why do you think several scenes in "The Dancers" take place in the drugstore? **[Hypothesize]**

HORACE. No, thanks.

[*He goes over to the magazine rack. He picks up a magazine and starts looking through it.* EMILY CREWS *comes in from downstage right. She doesn't see* HORACE. *She goes right over to* MARY CATHERINE.]

EMILY. Leora and I were riding around the square and we saw you sitting here . . .

[MARY CATHERINE *points to* HORACE. *She turns around and sees him.* EMILY *looks a little embarrassed. He happens to glance up and sees her.*]

HORACE. Hello, Emily.

32 ✔ **Reading Check**
What does Mary Catherine realize about Horace?

30 ▶ Critical Viewing

Answer: Students might suggest that the drugstore is a logical place for characters to run into each other accidentally; it is believable that characters might meet there or overhear gossip, or even be talking about someone whom they don't realize is sitting next to them.

31 Background

Art

The photos with this selection illustrate scenes from small-town teenage life in the 1950s, the setting for Horton Foote's play. As students read the play, have them imagine how life was different for teenagers of that time and place. Use the following for discussion:

1. What differences can you see between teenage life in the 1950s and teenage life today?
   Answer: Students may notice differences in clothing and hairstyles, dance styles, music technology, choice of hangouts, and attitudes—as revealed by facial expressions and body language.
2. What do you find most surprising about the images of 1950s teenage life shown in the photos?
   Answer: Responses will depend upon students' knowledge of the time period and their familiarity with contrasting images of the time, such as those portrayed in the musical *Grease*.

32 ✔ Reading Check

Answer: Mary Catherine realizes Horace is the boy who was sitting next to her as she told the waitress about Emily's refusal to go to the dance with her neighbor's brother.

CUSTOMIZE INSTRUCTION FOR UNIVERSAL ACCESS

For Special Needs Students	For Gifted/Talented Students
Have students use the photo on this page to make comparisons between today and the 1950s. Ask questions such as: What kinds of items are hanging up at the back of the drugstore to be sold? Are they the same kinds of items you would find on sale in a pharmacy today? Where would you go today, in place of a drugstore, to buy ice cream sundaes and other ice cream dishes?	Students might wish to compare the jobs teenagers have today with those that 1950s teenagers held. Have students do research to see how teens in the 50s earned money after school and what kind of jobs they held after they graduated from high school.

33 Literary Analysis

Staging and Dialogue

- Ask students what they learn about Emily from this dialogue.
- Elicit from students that Emily takes responsibility for her own behavior, albeit late. She was willing to have her mother lie for her the night before, but now wants to be considerate of Horace's feelings by telling him that her behavior had nothing to do with him.
- Ask students to think about how they would block this scene, and then answer the Literary Analysis question on p. 748: Would staging enhance the dialogue in this scene? Explain.
  Possible answer: Students might suggest that stage directions could direct Emily to deliver her dialogue face-to-face with Horace, as one equal to another, rather than having one character seated and one standing.

34 Reading Strategy

Picturing the Action

- Ask students how they imagine Horace feels when confronted with Emily.
  Answer: He probably feels embarrassed but also glad that she is addressing the incident directly.
- Invite students to respond to the Reading Strategy question on p. 748: How do you picture Horace as Emily apologizes to him?
  Possible response: He is probably still acting shy, but also looking her in the eye because she is being honest with him.

EMILY. Hello, Horace. . . . Do you know Mary Catherine Davis?

HORACE. No. How do you do.

MARY CATHERINE. How do you do.

33 EMILY. I feel awfully bad about last night, Horace. My mother says that you know I wasn't really sick. I just wanted to tell you that it had nothing to do with you, Horace. It was a battle between me and my mother. Mary Catherine can tell you. I promised the boy I go with not to go with any other boys . . .

HORACE. Oh, that's all right, I understand.

EMILY. You see, we've gone steady for two years. All the other boys in town understand it and their feelings are not a bit hurt if I turn them down. Are they, Mary Catherine?

MARY CATHERINE. No.

EMILY. Mary Catherine is my best friend and she can tell you I'm not stuck up. And I would have gone, anyway, except I was so mad at my mother . . .

MARY CATHERINE. Emily is not stuck up a bit. Emily used to date all the boys before she began going with Leo steadily. . . . Didn't you, Emily?

EMILY. Uh-huh. How long are you going to be here, Horace?

HORACE. Well, I haven't decided, Emily.

34 EMILY. Well, I hope you're not still hurt with me.

HORACE. No, I'm not, Emily.

EMILY. Well, I'm glad for that. Mary Catherine, can you come with us?

MARY CATHERINE. No, I can't, Emily. Velma came in after the first show started and I promised to wait here for her and we'd walk home together.

EMILY. Come on. We can ride around and watch for her.

MARY CATHERINE. No. I don't dare. You know how sensitive Velma is. If she looked in here and saw I wasn't sitting at this counter she'd go right home and not speak to me again for two or three months.

EMILY. Velma's too sensitive. You shouldn't indulge her in it.

MARY CATHERINE. I'm willing to grant you that. But you all are going off to college next year and Velma and I are the only ones that are going to be left here and I can't afford to get her mad at me.

EMILY. O.K. I'll watch out for you and if we're still riding around when Velma gets out, we'll pick you up.

MARY CATHERINE. Fine. . . .

EMILY. 'Bye. . . .

Literary Analysis
Staging and Dialogue Would staging enhance the dialogue in this scene? Explain.

Reading Strategy
Picturing the Action How do you picture Horace as Emily apologizes to him?

MARY CATHERINE. 'Bye. . . .

EMILY. 'Bye, Horace.

HORACE. Good-bye, Emily.

[*She goes out downstage right.*]

MARY CATHERINE. She's a lovely girl. She was my closest friend until this year. Now we're still good friends, but we're not as close as we were. We had a long talk about it last week. I told her I understood. She and Eloise Dayton just naturally have a little more in common now. They're both going steady and they're going to the same college. [*A pause.*] They're going to Sophie Newcomb.[4] Are you going to college?

HORACE. Uh-huh.

MARY CATHERINE. You are? What college?

HORACE. The University. . . .

MARY CATHERINE. Oh. I know lots of people there. [*A pause.*] I had a long talk with Emily about my not getting to go. She said she thought it was wonderful that I wasn't showing any bitterness about it. [*A pause.*] I'm getting a job next week so I can save up enough money to go into Houston to Business School. I'll probably work in Houston some day. If I don't get too lonely. Velma Morrison's oldest sister went into Houston and got herself a job but she almost died from loneliness. She's back here now working at the Court House. Oh, well . . . I don't think I'll get lonely. I think a change of scenery would be good for me.

[VELMA MORRISON *comes in downstage right. She is about the same age as* MARY CATHERINE. *She is filled with excitement.*]

VELMA. Mary Catherine, you're going to be furious with me. But Stanley Sewell came in right after you left and he said he'd never forgive me if I didn't go riding with him. . . . I said I had to ask you first. As I had asked you to wait particularly for me and that I knew you were very sensitive.

MARY CATHERINE. I'm very sensitive. You're very sensitive. . . . I have never in my life stopped speaking to you over anything.

4. Sophie Newcomb H. Sophie Newcomb College for Women in New Orleans, Louisiana.

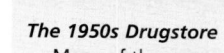

Literature in context — Cultural Connection (35)

The 1950s Drugstore

Many of the scenes in "The Dancers" are set in a drugstore. In addition to selling medicine, soap, and other necessities, the drugstore of the 1950s offered people a place to hear local gossip and get something to eat at the soda fountain. Few drugstores today have soda fountains that sell ice cream cones and sundaes.

Back in the 1950s, you could sit at the counter and have a small sandwich and a soda while you listened to the jukebox. Many owners expanded their stores by adding booths and tables and by extending the menu to include hot dogs, hamburgers, and French fries. Many booths had their own "private" jukeboxes, on which couples could play their favorite songs. Horton Foote's play captures just this type of shop.

(36) **Reading Check**

Why does Mary Catherine want to wait for Velma?

(35) Background

Music on the Jukebox

Teens playing jukebox records in a 1950s drugstore could hear some of popular music's most famous sounds. Bill Haley and the Comets' "Shake, Rattle, and Roll" might be on one record, while another held Elvis Presley's "Heartbreak Hotel." Chuck Berry, Fats Domino, the Platters, and the Drifters all contributed to the new music called rock 'n' roll that teenagers loved and their parents feared. Students might enjoy viewing the film made of the stage play that captures 50s teenage life—*Grease,* starring Olivia Newton-John and John Travolta.

(36) **Reading Check**

Answer: Mary Catherine had promised Velma she would wait for her, and if she left, Velma would be very upset.

CUSTOMIZE INSTRUCTION FOR UNIVERSAL ACCESS

For Less Proficient Readers	For English Learners
To help students analyze the behavior and personalities of Emily, Horace, and Mary Catherine, have three of them act out the scene on pp. 748–749, in which all three characters are together for the first time. Have students practice the scene until they feel they can use each character's tone of voice and body language to express his or her personality.	Have students note Mary Catherine's statement in the middle of p. 749: "I think a change of scenery would be good for me." Tell students that the word *scenery* has two meanings: the sets and other furnishings used on a stage, and the natural features of a landscape, such as mountains, rivers, cities, and so forth. Ask them which meaning of the word *scenery* Mary Catherine is using.

37 ▶ Critical Viewing

Answer: Students may suggest that modern-day CD players do not resemble record players. Moreover, the modern compact disc is much smaller than the vinyl records played on a phonograph.

38 Critical Thinking

Make Judgments

- Have two volunteers read aloud this scene to the rest of the class. Then, ask students why Elizabeth is not reassured when Emily tells her she has talked with Horace and that he now understands why Emily could not go to the dance with him.
  Answer: Elizabeth isn't really concerned about Horace and his feelings. She is concerned because her relationship with Inez is in jeopardy.
- Ask students what conclusions they can draw from the fact that Emily has to console and appease her mother over such a small social embarrassment.
  Possible response: Students may say that Elizabeth is being childish and unfairly manipulates her daughter. In many ways, Emily has learned how to behave more maturely than her own mother.

[*A car horn is heard off stage.*]

VELMA. Will you forgive me if I go?

MARY CATHERINE. Oh, sure.

[VELMA *goes running out.*]

VELMA. Thank you.

[*She disappears out the door.*]

MARY CATHERINE. I'm not nearly as close to Velma as I am to Emily. I think Emily's beautiful, don't you?

HORACE. Yes. She's very pretty.

MARY CATHERINE. Well, Lila's going to kill us if we don't stop holding her up. Which way do you go?

HORACE. Home.

MARY CATHERINE. I go that way, too. We can walk together.

HORACE. O.K. [*They go out of the area.*]

MARY CATHERINE. Good night, Lila.

WAITRESS. Good night.

[*They continue walking out downstage left as the lights fade. The lights are brought up on the living room of the* CREWS' *house.* ELIZABETH CREWS *is there, crying.* EMILY *comes in.*]

EMILY. Mother, what is it? Has something happened to Daddy?

ELIZABETH. No. He's in bed asleep.

EMILY. Then what is it?

38 **ELIZABETH.** Inez blessed me out and stopped speaking to me over last night. She says we've ruined the boy's whole vacation. You've broken his heart, given him all kinds of complexes and he's going home tomorrow. . . .

37 ▼ **Critical Viewing** The characters in "The Dancers" probably danced to music played on a record player like the one in this picture. How does this equipment compare to modern-day music players? **[Compare and Contrast]**

ENRICHMENT: Science Connection

History of Recording Technology

The photograph here shows a radio-phonograph of the early 1950s. Recording technology traces its beginnings to the invention of the phonograph in 1877 by Thomas Edison. That first phonograph played back sound recorded as squiggles in a continuous groove etched on a tin-wrapped cylinder. In the 1890s, flat, one-sided records were invented. By the 1920s, two-sided records had replaced the one-sided discs.

Two important advances in recording technology occurred during the 1940s: (1) recording tape was invented, and (2) the long-playing (LP) record was introduced. The 1950s and 1960s witnessed the development of stereo records and recorded tapes. Digital recording of sound began in the 1970s, producing recordings with virtually no background noise or distortion. In 1983, the digitally-recorded compact disc was introduced, providing superior, distortion-free sound recordings to the public.

EMILY. But I saw him at the drugstore tonight and I had a long talk with him and he said he understood . . .

ELIZABETH. But Inez doesn't understand. She says she'll never forgive either of us again.

[*She starts to cry.*]

EMILY. Oh, Mother. I'm sorry . . .

39 **ELIZABETH.** Emily, if you'll do me one favor. I promise you I'll never ask another thing of you again as long as I live. And I will never nag you about going out with Leo again as long as I live. . . .

EMILY. What is the favor, Mother?

ELIZABETH. Let that boy take you to the dance day after tomorrow. . . .

EMILY. Now, Mother . . .

40 **ELIZABETH.** Emily. I get down on my knees to you. Do me this one favor . . . [*A pause.*] Emily . . . Emily . . . [*She is crying again.*]

EMILY. Now, Mother, please. Don't cry. I'll think about it. I'll call Leo and see what he says. But please don't cry like this. . . . Mother . . . Mother.

[*She is trying to console her as the lights fade. The lights are brought up on upstage left. It is* MARY CATHERINE'*s yard and living room. Music can be heard in the distance.* HORACE *and* MARY CATHERINE *come walking in downstage left, go up the center of the stage until they reach the upstage area.*]

MARY CATHERINE. Well, this is where I live.

HORACE. In that house there?

MARY CATHERINE. Uh-huh. [*A pause.*]

HORACE. Where is that music coming from?

MARY CATHERINE. The Flats. . . .

HORACE. What's the Flats?

MARY CATHERINE. I don't know what it is. That's just what they call it. It's nothing but a bunch of barbecue restaurants and beer joints down there and they call it the Flats. There used to be a creek running down there that they called Willow Creek but it's all dry now. My father says when he was a boy, every time the river flooded, Willow Creek would fill up. The river doesn't overflow any more since they took the raft[5] out of it. I like to come out here at night and listen to the music. Do you like to dance . . . ?

HORACE. Well . . . I . . .

---

5. **raft** natural dam formed by debris, leaves, and trees.

Literary Analysis
Staging What role do sound effects play in these staging directions?

console (kən sōl′) *v.* comfort

41 **Reading Check**
What favor does Elizabeth ask of Emily?

39 Vocabulary Development
Homographs

- Write the word *nag* on the board and point out that Elizabeth uses the word as a verb, meaning "to scold or complain about." As a noun, *nag* means "one who scolds." Ask students if they know another meaning of *nag*.
  Answer: *Nag* is an uncomplimentary term for "horse."
- Explain that *nag* is a *homograph*. *Homographs* are words that are spelled the same (from the Greek for "same writing"), but have different meanings and origins; often they are pronounced differently.
- Ask students to find at least two other homographs on this page and explain their meanings.
  Answer: *Console* can mean "to comfort" or "a television cabinet" (note change in pronunciation). *Joints* can be "a place where two parts are joined" or "a cheap restaurant or other place." A *raft* can be "a floating platform of logs" or "a large number; abundance."

40 Literary Analysis
Staging

- Ask students what new stage area appears for the first time on this page.
  Answer: Following the scene at Emily's house, Mary Catherine's yard appears.
- Have students answer the Literary Analysis question on p. 751: What role do sound effects play in these staging directions?
  Answer: The music "heard in the distance" serves as a transition between scenes. In the new scene, the music sets up the right scenario for Horace to ask about it and to start a conversation with Mary Catherine.

41 Reading Check

Answer: Elizabeth asks Emily to go to a dance with Horace.

42 Reading Strategy

Picturing the Action

- Ask students what new character is introduced in the scene in this passage.
  Answer: Tom Davis, Mary Catherine's father, is introduced.
- Have students read the dialogue and the stage directions and answer the Reading Strategy question on p. 752: Do the stage directions or the dialogue provide a clearer image of Mary Catherine's dad? Explain.
  Answer: The stage directions describe how Mr. Davis is dressed and state that he works in a garage. This description is not revealed in the terse dialogue.

43 Literary Analysis

Staging

- Ask students to look back at p. 735 to see where on the stage the Davis home is set. Have them draw the four areas on a sheet of paper.
- Ask students what the stage directions on p. 735 say is included in the Davis part of the set.
  Answer: The Davis set includes a yard and a living room.
- Have students imagine the Davis' yard. Then, have them answer the Literary Analysis question on p. 752: If you could add a description of the set at this point, what would it be?
  Possible response: Students may mention the evening sky, or a tree, or porch swing, or a car in the driveway up on blocks that looks like it is being worked on.

MARY CATHERINE. I love to dance.

HORACE. Well . . . I don't dance too well.

MARY CATHERINE. There's nothing to it but confidence.

HORACE. That's what my sister says . . .

MARY CATHERINE. I didn't learn for the longest kind of time for lack of confidence and then Emily gave me a long lecture about it and I got confidence and went ahead and learned. Would you like to come in for a while?

HORACE. Well . . . if it's all right with you. . . .

MARY CATHERINE. I'd be glad to have you.

HORACE. Thank you.

[*They go into the area.* MARY CATHERINE'S *father,* TOM DAVIS, *is seated there in his undershirt. He works in a garage.*]

MARY CATHERINE. Hello, Daddy.

42 **TOM.** Hello, baby.

MARY CATHERINE. Daddy, this is Horace.

TOM. Hello, son.

HORACE. Howdy do, sir.

[*They shake hands.*]

MARY CATHERINE. Horace is Mrs. Inez Stanley's brother. He's here on a visit.

TOM. That's nice. Where's your home, son?

HORACE. Flatonia.

TOM. Oh, I see. Well, are you young people going to visit for a while?

MARY CATHERINE. Yes, sir.

TOM. Well, I'll leave you then. Good night.

MARY CATHERINE. Good night, Daddy.

43 **HORACE.** Good night, sir. [*He goes out upstage left.*] What does your father do?

MARY CATHERINE. He works in a garage. He's a mechanic. What does your father do?

HORACE. He's a judge.

MARY CATHERINE. My father worries so because he can't afford to send me to college. My mother told him that was all foolishness. That I'd rather go to business school anyway.

HORACE. Had you rather go to business school?

Reading Strategy
Picturing the Action Do the staging directions or the dialogue provide a clearer image of Mary Catherine's dad? Explain.

Literary Analysis
Staging If you could add a description of the set at this point, what would it be?

ENRICHMENT: Social Studies Connection

Foote's Texas

"The Dancers" is set in a small town in Texas, on the Gulf of Mexico, much like Horton Foote's own hometown of Wharton, Texas. Foote has said in an interview that ". . . it seems to me a more unlikely subject could not be found . . . than this attempt of mine to recreate a small Southern town and its people. But I did not choose this task, this place, or these people to write about so much as they chose me, and I try to write about them with honesty." Before World War I, the area was rich with cotton plantations, and the plantation owners were the local aristocracy. Later, the same land created more wealth through the discovery of oil. Thus, even in a small town like Harrison, the presence of valuable natural resources could generate large amounts of wealth.

MARY CATHERINE. I don't know. [*A pause.*] Not really. But I'd never tell him that. When I was in the seventh grade I thought I would die if I couldn't get there, but then when I was in the ninth, Mother talked to me one day and told me Daddy wasn't sleeping at nights for fear I'd be disappointed if he couldn't send me, so I told him the next night I decided I'd rather go to business school. He seemed relieved. [*A pause.*]

HORACE. Mary Catherine. I . . . uh . . . heard you say a while ago that you didn't dance because you lacked confidence and uh . . . then I heard you say you talked it over with Emily and she told you what was wrong and you got the confidence and you went ahead . . .

MARY CATHERINE. That's right. . . .

HORACE. Well . . . It may sound silly and all to you . . . seeing I'm about to start my first year at college . . . but I'd like to ask you a question. . . .

MARY CATHERINE. What is it, Horace?

HORACE. How do you get confidence?

MARY CATHERINE. Well, you just get it. Someone points it out to you that you lack it and then you get it. . . .

HORACE. Oh, is that how it's done?

MARY CATHERINE. That's how I did it.

HORACE. You see I lack confidence. And I . . . sure would like to get it. . . .

MARY CATHERINE. In what way do you lack confidence, Horace? . . .

44 **HORACE.** Oh, in all kinds of ways. [*A pause.*] I'm not much of a mixer[6]. . .

MARY CATHERINE. I think you're just mixing fine tonight.

HORACE. I know. That's what's giving me a little encouragement. You're the first girl I've ever really been able to talk to. I mean this way. . . .

MARY CATHERINE. Am I, Horace . . . ?

HORACE. Yes.

MARY CATHERINE. Well, I feel in some ways that's quite a compliment.

HORACE. Well, you should feel that way. [*A pause.*] Mary Catherine . . .

MARY CATHERINE. Yes, Horace?

HORACE. I had about decided to go back home tomorrow or the next day, but I understand there's another dance at the end of the week . . .

MARY CATHERINE. Uh-huh. Day after tomorrow.

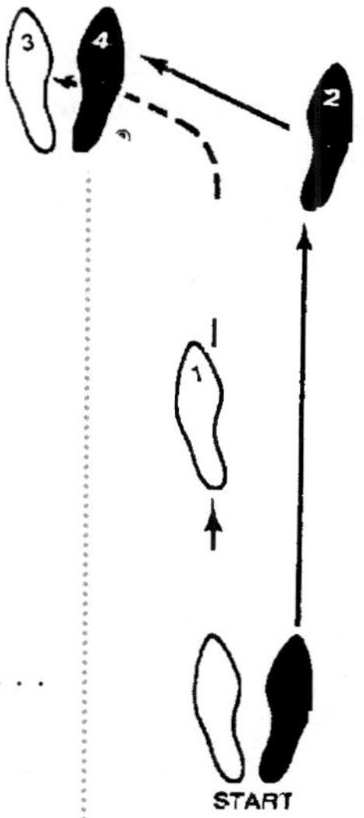

45 Reading Check

What does Horace say he lacks?

6. **a mixer** someone who socializes easily.

44 Background

Social Class

Although Horace and Mary Catherine's personalities are similar, their family backgrounds are different. Horace comes from an educated family with professional careers, status in the community, and enough money to buy him a tuxedo and send him to college. Mary Catherine's father has a working-class job; her family lives in a neighborhood near "beer joints," and they don't have enough money to send her to college.

45 Reading Check

Answer: Horace says he lacks confidence.

CUSTOMIZE INSTRUCTION FOR UNIVERSAL ACCESS

For Less Proficient Readers	For Gifted/Talented Students
The word *mixer* on p. 753 may be confusing to students. Tell them that mixer is a noun that can be used to identify a person, a device, and an event. Have students use a dictionary to find the three meanings: "someone who socializes easily," "a machine that combines elements, such as a cement mixer," and "a kind of dance." Ask them which meaning is used here.	Have students discuss Mary Catherine's decision to go to business school because her father cannot afford to send her to college. Do they think she did the right thing? Are there other alternatives she has not considered?

46 Literary Analysis

Staging

- Ask students how the stage directions describe Horace's dancing here.
  Answer: The stage directions say he is still dancing awkwardly.
- Have students speculate on why Horace is pleased with himself even though he is still dancing awkwardly.
- Lead students to see that Horace's newly found confidence, based on Mary Catherine's encouragement, causes him to be more pleased with himself, even though his dance steps are still not in any way perfect.
- Have students answer the Literary Analysis question on p. 754: What role does lighting play in these stage directions?
  Answer: Students may suggest that lighting creates a transition between scenes, from evening until morning. The fading of the light closes the dance sequence in one area of the stage; brightening light creates a morning scene at the Stanley residence.

HORACE. Well . . . I . . . don't know if you have a date or not . . . but if you don't have . . . I feel if I could take you . . . I would gain the confidence to go . . . I mean . . .

MARY CATHERINE. Well, Horace . . . You see . . .

HORACE. I know I'd gain the confidence. My sister is a swell dancer and she'll let me practice with her every living minute until it's time for the dance. Of course I don't know if I could learn to jitterbug by then or rumba or do anything fancy, you understand, but I know I could learn the fox trot and I can waltz a little now . . .

MARY CATHERINE. I'm sure you could.

HORACE. Well, will you go with me?

MARY CATHERINE. Yes, Horace. I'd love to. . . .

HORACE. Oh, thank you, Mary Catherine. I'll just practice night and day. I can't tell you how grateful Inez is going to be to you. . . . Mary Catherine, if we played the radio softly could we dance now?

MARY CATHERINE. Why certainly, Horace.

HORACE. You understand I'll make mistakes. . . .

MARY CATHERINE. I understand. . . .

[*She turns the radio on very softly.*]

HORACE. All right.

MARY CATHERINE. Yes. . . .

[*He approaches her very cautiously and takes her in his arms. He begins awkwardly to dance.* MARY CATHERINE *is very pleased and happy.*]

Why, you're doing fine, Horace. Just fine.

HORACE. Thank you, Mary Catherine. Thank you.

46 [*They continue dancing.* HORACE *is very pleased with himself although he is still dancing quite awkwardly. The lights fade. The lights are brought up on the area downstage left. It is early next morning.* INEZ *is there reading.* HORACE *comes in whistling. He seems brimming over with happiness.*]

INEZ. What are you so happy about?

HORACE. I'm just happy.

INEZ. Wait until you hear my news and you'll be happier.

HORACE. Is that so?

INEZ. Miss Emily has seen the light.

HORACE. What?

INEZ. She has succumbed.

47 ▶ **Critical Viewing** Do you think Horace would have a better time at a dance like the one shown here if he were with Mary Catherine or with Emily? Why? **[Speculate]**

Literary Analysis
Staging What role does lighting play in these stage directions?

ENRICHMENT: Art Connection

Feather Dancer

Display Transparency 6, *Feather Dancer* from **Fine Art Transparencies,** Volume 1. Have students compare and contrast Horace with the dancer in the transparency. Guide students toward character analysis, or focus on how each character represents confidence. You can broaden the discussion by asking how the cultures from which Horace and the dancer in the transparency come affect their attitude toward dancing and dancers.

47 ▶ Critical Viewing

Answer: Horace would probably have a better time at the dance with Mary Catherine because Horace and Mary Catherine enjoy each other's company. In addition, Horace feels comfortable enough with Mary Catherine to tell her about his lack of confidence and his poor dancing skills.

48 Background

Dancing and Society

The photograph on this page shows young people at a high-school prom in the 1950s. Formal dances, such as the prom pictured, are an annual event at most high schools and they may also mark important occasions like the inauguration of a president.

These dances are known as social dances, as opposed to theatrical dances such as ballet or musical theater, because their primary function is not to entertain but to foster recreation and companionship. Social dancing also includes less formal dancing, such as that done at parties and some restaurants or clubs.

In high school and college, social dancing serves as a means for people to get to know each other better. For the same reason, dancing is often a part of courtship.

Ask students to discuss dances they have participated in, such as at school functions or weddings.

49 Literary Analysis

Staging and Dialogue

- Ask students to read Inez's four descriptions of Emily in this passage and determine what the reader can conclude that Emily has done.
  Answer: Inez's words imply that Emily has given in.
- Ask students to imagine staging this scene and decide how they would have Inez behave. Then, have them respond to the Literary Analysis question on p. 756: What image of Emily is conveyed through Inez's words?
  Answer: The reader gets an image of Emily crawling on the ground in abject apology. Inez might mimic this behavior.

50 Reading Strategy

Picturing the Action

- Ask students how they imagine Horace feels when he hears about Emily.
- Lead students to see that Horace is probably experiencing anxiety because he has made plans with Mary Catherine, and he knows Inez is not going to be pleased.
- Ask students to respond to the Reading Strategy question on p. 756: What expression do you imagine Horace wears now?
  Possible response: Some students may say that Horace has a fake smile on his face while he tries to figure out what to say; others may suggest that he has a look of shock on his face.

49

HORACE. What do you mean?

INEZ. She has crawled on her knees.

HORACE. She's crawled on her knees? I don't get it. . . .

INEZ. She has eaten dirt.

HORACE. Sister, what's this all about?

INEZ. Last night around ten o'clock she called in the meekest kind of voice possible and said, Inez, I've called up to apologize to you. I have apologized to Horace in the drugstore. Did she?

HORACE. Uh. Huh.

INEZ. And now I want to apologize to you and to tell you how sorry I am I behaved so badly. . . .

HORACE. Well. Isn't that nice of her, Inez?

INEZ. Wait a minute. You haven't heard the whole thing. And then her highness added, tell Horace if he would like to invite me to the dance to call me and I'd be glad to accept. And furthermore, Elizabeth called this morning and said they were leaving for Houston to buy her the most expensive evening dress in sight. Just to impress you with.

50

HORACE. Oh . . . [*He sits down on a chair.*]

INEZ. Brother. What is the matter with you? Now are you gonna start worrying about this dancin' business all over again? You are the biggest fool sometimes. We've got today and tomorrow to practice.

HORACE. Inez . . .

INEZ. Yes?

HORACE. I already have a date with someone tomorrow. . . .

INEZ. You do?

HORACE. Yes. I met a girl last night at the drugstore and I asked her.

INEZ. What girl did you ask?

HORACE. Mary Catherine Davis. . . .

INEZ. Well, you've got to get right out of it. You've got to call her up and explain just what happened.

HORACE. But, Inez . . .

INEZ. You've got to do it, Horace. They told me they are spending all kinds of money for that dress. I practically had to threaten Elizabeth with never speaking to her again to bring this all about. Why, she will never forgive me now if I turn around and tell her you can't go. . . . Horace. Don't look that way. I can't help it. For my sake, for your sister's sake you've got to get out of this date with Mary Catherine Davis . . . tell her . . . tell her . . . anything . . .

Literary Analysis
Staging and Dialogue
What image of Emily is conveyed through Inez's words?

Reading Strategy
Picturing the Action
What expression do you imagine Horace wears now?

ENRICHMENT: Art Connection

Music and Musicians

Music played a role in another Horton Foote production—a major film event. In the early 1980s, Foote was asked by his friend, actor Robert Duvall, to write a screenplay for Duvall. The film, *Tender Mercies,* chronicled the life of a country singer who, having achieved fame, lost it and his marriage to alcoholism, and is subsequently rescued through his relationship with a widow and her son. The film won Duvall a best actor Oscar and Foote an Oscar for best screenplay at the 1983 Academy Awards. Foote had previously won a 1962 best screenplay Oscar for his adaptation of Harper Lee's *To Kill a Mockingbird,* and would be nominated again for best screenplay for *The Trip to Bountiful* (1985).

51 **HORACE.** O.K. [*A pause. He starts out.*] What can I say?

INEZ. I don't know, Horace. [*A pause.*] Say . . . well just tell her the truth. That's the best thing. Tell her that Emily's mother is your sister's best friend and that Emily's mother has taken her into Houston to buy her a very expensive dress . . .

HORACE. What if Mary Catherine has bought a dress . . .

INEZ. Well, she can't have bought an expensive dress. . . .

HORACE. Why not?

INEZ. Because her people can't afford it. Honey, you'll be the envy of every young man in Harrison, bringing Emily Crews to the dance. . . . Why, everybody will wonder just what it is you have . . .

HORACE. I'm not going to do it.

INEZ. Horace . . .

HORACE. I don't want to take Emily, I want to take Mary Catherine and that's just what I'm going to do.

INEZ. Horace . . .

HORACE. My mind is made up. Once and for all. . . .

52 **INEZ.** Then what am I gonna do? [*She starts to cry.*] Who's gonna speak to Elizabeth? She'll bless me out putting her to all this trouble. Making her spend all this money and time . . . [*She is crying loudly now.*] Horace. You just can't do this to me. You just simply can't. . . .

HORACE. I can't help it. I'm not taking Emily Crews—

INEZ. Horace . . .

HORACE. I am not taking Emily Crews.

[*He is firm. She is crying as the lights fade. The lights are brought up on the upstage left area.* MARY CATHERINE'*s father is seated there. He is in his undershirt. In the distance dance music can be heard.* MRS. DAVIS *comes in from stage left.*]

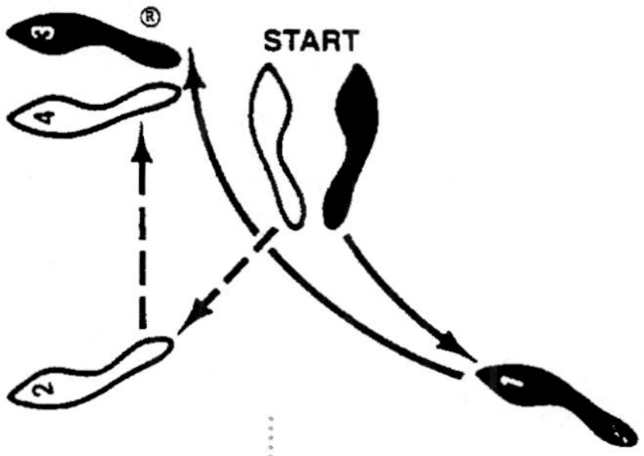

MRS. DAVIS. Don't you think you'd better put your shirt on, Tom? Mary Catherine's date will be here any minute.

TOM. What time is it?

MRS. DAVIS. Nine o'clock.

TOM. The dance has already started. I can hear the music from here.

MRS. DAVIS. I know. But you know young people, they'd die before they'd be the first to a dance. Put your shirt on, Tom.

TOM. O.K.

Literary Analysis
Staging What does "a pause" convey about Horace's feelings?

53 **Reading Check**
What does Inez tell Horace about Emily?

51 Literary Analysis

Staging

- Ask students if Inez's character has changed at all from the beginning of the play. Have them explain their answer.
  Answer: Inez is still trying to run Horace's life.
- Have students identify the arguments Inez uses to persuade Horace to get out of his date with Mary Catherine.
  Answer: Inez's arguments are that Emily's family is going to buy her a new expensive dress, and Elizabeth, Emily's mother, will never forgive Inez if Horace doesn't go to the dance with Emily.
- Ask students to answer the Reading Strategy question on p. 757: What does "a pause" convey about Horace's feelings?
  Possible response: Students may suggest that Horace's pause indicates that Horace is trying to muster the courage to stand firm and tell Inez that he will not take Emily to the dance.

52 Background

Idioms

The idiom *blessed me out* or *bless me out* has been used twice in the play. Elizabeth used it the first time on p. 750 in regards to Inez and now Inez is saying that Elizabeth will do the same to her. The idiom is a euphemism for swearing. In a far more genteel time, people hid their profane language by saying things like *darn, goldarned,* and other euphemisms. In other instances, instead of saying that one wished someone ill, people would "bless" the person.

53 Reading Check

Answer: Inez tells Horace that Emily has apologized for her previous behavior and has begged to go to the next dance with Horace.

CUSTOMIZE INSTRUCTION FOR UNIVERSAL ACCESS

For Special Needs Students	For Less Proficient Readers
Tell students that all four descriptions of Emily on pp. 755 and 756 imply that Emily has changed her mind and humbled herself before Inez. Explain that "crawled on her knees" has a similar meaning to Elizabeth's phrase "get down on my knees" on p. 751. "To eat dirt" also means to humble or humiliate oneself in front of a person whom one has previously hurt.	Help students understand that Inez thinks she is persuading Horace to accept her point of view by saying that Mary Catherine's family can't afford to buy her a dress for the dance. However, this information probably helps convince Horace to stick to his decision. Because Horace is so concerned about other people's feelings, the fact that Mary Catherine may have gone out and bought a dress she really can't afford is another reason he can't let her down.

54 Reading Strategy

Picturing the Action

- Based on this passage, ask students what kind of relationship they think Mary Catherine has with her parents.
  Answer: Davis family is probably very close and both parents are proud of their daughter.
- Ask students if there is any information in either the stage directions or the dialogue to say whether Mary Catherine is wearing a new dress.
  Answer: There is no information either way at this point.

Monitor Progress Have students answer the Reading Strategy question on p. 758: How do you picture the expressions on both characters' faces at this point? Why?
Possible response: Students may say that they both look slightly embarrassed because the mother and father are present, and they're dressed up and are going on a date; however, they also appear excited because they are fond of each other and are thrilled to go to the dance.

MRS. DAVIS. As soon as her date arrives we'll go.

TOM. O.K.

[MARY CATHERINE *comes in from stage left. She has on an evening dress and she looks very pretty.*]

MRS. DAVIS. Why, Mary Catherine. You look lovely. Doesn't she look lovely, Tom?

TOM. Yes, she does.

MRS. DAVIS. Turn around, honey, and let me see you from the back. [*She does so.*] Just as pretty as you can be, Mary Catherine.

MARY CATHERINE. Thank you.

54 [HORACE *comes in downstage left in his tux with a corsage box. He walks up the center of the stage to the upstage left area.*]

That's Horace. [*She goes to the corner of the area.*] Hello, Horace.

HORACE. Hello, Mary Catherine.

MARY CATHERINE. You've met my mother and father.

HORACE. Yes. I have. I met your father the other night and your mother yesterday afternoon.

MRS. DAVIS. Hello, Horace.

TOM. Hello, son.

MRS. DAVIS. Well, we were just going. You all have a good time tonight.

HORACE. Thank you.

MRS. DAVIS. Come on, Tom.

TOM. All right. Good night and have a nice time.

MARY CATHERINE. Thank you, Daddy. [*They go out stage left.* HORACE *hands her the corsage box. She takes it and opens it.*] Oh, thank you, Horace. Thank you so much. [*She takes the flowers out.*] They're just lovely. Will you pin them on for me?

HORACE. I'll try. [*He takes the corsage and the pin. He begins to pin it on.*] Will about here be all right?

MARY CATHERINE. Just fine. [*He pins the corsage on.*] Emily told me about the mix-up between your sister and her mother. I appreciate your going ahead and taking me anyway. If you had wanted to get out of it I would have understood. Emily and I are very good friends . . . and . . .

Reading Strategy
Picturing the Action
How do you picture the expressions on both characters' faces at this point? Why?

55

HORACE. I didn't want to get out of it, Mary Catherine. I wanted to take you.

MARY CATHERINE. I'm glad you didn't want to get out of it. Emily offered to let me wear her new dress. But I had already bought one of my own.

HORACE. It's very pretty, Mary Catherine.

MARY CATHERINE. Thank you. [*A pause.*] Well, the dance has started. I can hear the music. Can't you?

HORACE. Yes.

MARY CATHERINE. Well, we'd better get going. . . .

HORACE. All right. [*They start out.*] Mary Catherine. I hope you don't think this is silly, but could we practice just once more . . .

MARY CATHERINE. Certainly we could. . . .

[*They start to dance.* HORACE *has improved although he is no Fred Astaire. They are dancing around and suddenly* HORACE *breaks away.*]

HORACE. Mary Catherine. I'm not good enough yet. I can't go. I'm sorry. Please let's just stay here.

MARY CATHERINE. No, Horace. We have to go.

HORACE. Please, Mary Catherine . . .

MARY CATHERINE. I know just how you feel, Horace, but we have to go. [*A pause.*] I haven't told you the whole truth, Horace. This is my first dance, too. . . .

HORACE. It is?

MARY CATHERINE. Yes. I've been afraid to go. Afraid I wouldn't be popular. The last two dances I was asked to go and I said no.

HORACE. Then why did you accept when I asked you?

MARY CATHERINE. I don't know. I asked myself that afterwards. I guess

56 **Reading Check**

What does Horace want to do once more before the dance?

55 Critical Thinking

Infer

- Ask students what Mary Catherine says to Horace about the possibility of his wanting to take Emily to the dance.
  Answer: Mary Catherine tells Horace that she would have understood if he had wanted to take Emily to the dance because she and Emily are very good friends.
- Have students infer why Mary Catherine is pleased by Horace's response.
  Answer: Elicit from students that Mary Catherine is offering Horace a way out, but is delighted when he admits that he doesn't want to go to the dance with anyone but her.

56 Reading Check

Answer: Horace wants to practice his steps once more before they go to the dance.

CUSTOMIZE INSTRUCTION FOR UNIVERSAL ACCESS	
For Gifted/Talented Students	**For Advanced Readers**
Invite a group of students to stage the final scene of the play and present it to the class. Have them choose actors, lighting, costumes, and music for the scene. They should also choose a director to coach the actors on how to say their lines and how to use facial expressions and body language to communicate the feelings of the characters.	Call students' attention to the use of ellipses on this spread. Have volunteers read the exchange between Mary Catherine and Horace at the end of this page. Ask students how the ellipses affect their understanding of the characters' feelings and actions. Then, have students locate other lines of dialogue in which ellipses are used. Point out that when students write their own dialogue and wish to indicate an unfinished thought or hesitation, they can use ellipses.

ASSESS

Answers for p. 760

Review and Assess

1. Students might say they admire Horace's kindness and consideration for the feelings of others. Some might wish him to be more assertive.
2. **(a)** Inez wants Horace to date Emily because Emily is popular, pretty, and the daughter of her friend. **(b)** Elizabeth wants Emily to date Horace because Elizabeth does not like the boy Emily is dating. **(c)** The two women have in common their desire to arrange other people's lives for them.
3. **(a)** Emily says she thinks Horace is a person who rarely talks and doesn't know how to dance. She also promised the boy she's going steady with that she won't go out with anyone else. **(b)** Emily is trying to be loyal to her steady, which is honorable, but she is being rude and disrespectful to Horace.
4. **(a)** Emily tells Horace the truth. **(b)** Emily has the instinct to be honest, as long as her mother isn't in the picture.
5. **(a)** Horace meets Mary Catherine at the drugstore. **(b)** Horace and Mary Catherine are well suited to be friends because both are friendly, sensitive, and not as popular and confident as the other young people in the play. **(c)** Horace demonstrates his sensitivity by not letting Inez bully him into taking Emily to the dance instead of Mary Catherine.
6. Students will probably say that the teenagers seem more mature than Inez and Elizabeth.
7. Possible response: **(a)** People should not meddle in other people's relationships, and people should have the right, in most cases, to decide for themselves whom they want as friends. **(b)** Students may say that outsiders should not interfere with their relationships.

because you gave me a kind of confidence. [*A pause. They dance again.*] You gave me confidence and I gave you confidence. What's the sense of getting confidence, Horace, if you're not going to use it?

[*A pause. They continue dancing.*]

HORACE. That's a pretty piece.

MARY CATHERINE. Yes, it is.

[*A pause. They dance again.* HORACE *stops.*]

HORACE. I'm ready to go if you are, Mary Catherine.

MARY CATHERINE. I'm ready. [*They start out.*] Scared?

HORACE. A little.

MARY CATHERINE. So am I. But let's go.

HORACE. O.K.

[*They continue out the area down the center of the stage and off downstage right as the music from the dance is heard.*]

Horton Foote

(b. 1916)

Born in Wharton, Texas, Horton Foote left his hometown after high school to attend acting school. While studying in New York, he formed friendships with several fellow actors; together, they formed an off-Broadway theater company. He began writing plays, and since then, writing has been the focus of his career.

During the 1950s and early 1960s, television's "golden age," Foote wrote scripts for live television. One of his first teleplays, *The Trip to Bountiful*, was later made into an award-winning film. Many of Foote's plays are set in the fictional town of Harrison, Texas, based on his hometown and the people he has known.

He says that his plays are often concerned "with defining what home is and where home is and how we get to home." Recurring themes include human shortcomings, family issues, and relationships between generations.

Review and Assess

Thinking About the Selection

1. **Respond:** Do you admire Horace? Why or why not?
2. **(a) Recall:** Why is Inez determined to set up Horace with Emily? **(b) Recall:** Why is Elizabeth determined to set up Emily with Horace? **(c) Compare and Contrast:** Which qualities do Elizabeth and Inez seem to have in common?
3. **(a) Recall:** Why does Emily refuse to go to the dance with Horace? **(b) Make a Judgment:** Do you think Emily's behavior is justified? Explain.
4. **(a) Recall:** What does Emily tell Horace the next day about why she did not go to the dance? **(b) Analyze:** What does this action tell you about Emily's character?
5. **(a) Recall:** How does Horace meet Mary Catherine? **(b) Infer:** In what ways are Horace and Mary Catherine well suited to be friends? **(c) Analyze:** After asking Mary Catherine to the dance, how does Horace demonstrate that he is a sensitive and considerate person?
6. **Speculate:** Do you think the adults or the teenagers acted more maturely in this play?
7. **(a) Extend:** Identify one insight about human relationships that you gained from this play. **(b) Apply:** How can this insight be applied to your own life?

ASSESSMENT PRACTICE: Reading Comprehension

Literary Response: Defending Responses (For more practice, see Test Preparation Workbook, p. 45.)

Many tests require students to discriminate between connotation and denotation, and to analyze literary elements. Use the following sample test item to show students how to discriminate between the connotative and denotative aspects of words.

Discussing Horace early in the play, Emily says: "Sweet, nice brother. He's a goon. That's what he is. A regular goon. A bore and a goon . . ." Is Emily's characterization of Horace fair to him?

Point out to students that as they read literary works, they will respond to elements of the text in emotional ways. For example, they may dislike a character, or find the author's sense of humor appealing. Although such responses are emotional, they should be based directly on the text, and students should be able to articulate a defense of their responses using elements of the text.

Review and Assess

Literary Analysis

Staging

1. (a) Using a chart like the one below, select two examples of stage directions in "The Dancers" that leave most of the specifics up to the imagination. (b) How might you add to the **staging** you have listed to better explain the place, action, or event described in your examples? (c) Why might the author have left staging vague?

Existing Stage Directions	→	Expanded Stage Directions

2. (a) What kind of lighting would be most effective in the drugstore scenes? (b) What kind of lighting would be most effective when Horace is dancing with Mary Catherine? Why?

Connecting Literary Elements

3. Using a chart like the one below, explain which **dialogue** in the play reveals the most about each character.

Character	Dialogue	→	Reveals

4. Give two examples of staging directions that enhance the dialogue and provide a clearer image of a character or situation. Explain your answer.

Reading Strategy

Picturing the Action

5. In the opening scene, you learn that Emily is unhappy. How might Emily's face, posture, and actions show this?
6. **Picture** the scene in which Mary Catherine tells the waitress about the date Emily Crews wanted to break. (a) How do you think Horace might act as he sits at the counter? (b) What do you think the waitress might do as she listens?

Extend Understanding

7. **Drama Connection:** The characters spend most of their time in a drugstore. If you were to update this play, where might you set it to reflect today's trends? Why?

Quick Review

Staging is one of the ways a script is brought to life. It includes descriptions of the sets, lighting, sound effects, costumes, and directions about the way the actors should move and deliver their lines.

Dialogue is a conversation between characters that reveals the qualities and situations of the characters and advances the action of the play.

To **picture the action** in a play, read descriptions carefully, and draw from your own experience to see characters and actions in your mind's eye.

Take It to the Net

www.phschool.com

Take the interactive self-test online to check your understanding of the selection.

Answers for p. 761

Review and Assess

1. **(a)** Existing Stage Directions: (p. 737, top of page) **EMILY.** OK. [*She starts out.*] **(b)** Expanded Stage Directions: [*She starts out, frowning and uncertain. If she goes to the beauty parlor, she will have even less excuse not to go to the dance. She turns back, as if to say something to her mother.*]
   (a) Existing Stage Directions: p. 738, bottom: **INEZ.** Well, guess . . . [*A pause. He thinks.*]
   (b) Expanded Stage Directions: [*A pause. He thinks, looks at his Uncle Stanley for help, shoves his hands in his pockets, and clears his throat.*] **(c)** The playwright knows that the director and the actors will have their own ideas about how to construct the action and develop the characters.
2. **(a)** The drugstore lighting should represent overhead lighting, as in most drugstores. **(b)** The scene when Mary Catherine and Horace dance should be dimly lit to project the intimacy of the dance floor, as well as their feelings for each other.
3. p. 738, bottom: Character: **INEZ.** Dialogue: And the most popular girl in this town . . . she had insisted and wondered if you'd take her . . . Reveals: She just barrels ahead taking charge of Horace's life without thinking about what he might want.
   p. 753: Character: **HORACE.** Dialogue: "You see, I lack confidence. And I . . . sure would like to get it . . ." Reveals: Horace is unsure of himself and needs to have a friend who can encourage him to believe in himself more.
4. Student responses should reflect a careful reading of the play. Many students may cite the direction that Horace is firm when he states that he is not taking Emily to the dance, p. 757.
5. Possible response: She might be frowning, slouching, or making faces, or she may just be very quiet and uninvolved.
6. Possible response: **(a)** Horace might be sipping his soda and looking embarrassed.
   (b) The waitress might be

continued

Answers continued

scooping out Mary Catherine's ice cream, serving it, and making eye contact with her.

7. Students may suggest that they would set the play in a mall or at an outdoor restaurant because these are popular places where teens hang out.

ENRICHMENT: Further Reading

Other Works by Horton Foote

Selected One-Act Plays of Horton Foote, edited by Gerald C. Wood

Horton Foote: Four New Plays, introduction by Jerry Tallmer

Take It to the Net

Visit www.phschool.com for more information on Horton Foote.

EXTEND

Answers for p. 762

❶ Vocabulary Development

Homographs

1. b **2.** a

Antonyms

1. c **3.** c
2. a **4.** a

Spelling Strategy

1. tried: I tried to learn to dance.
2. emptiness: He was filled with emptiness when he learned of her death.
3. cleanliness: Personal cleanliness is one key to good health.

❷ Grammar

1. nominative
2. nominative; possessive
3. nominative; objective
4. nominative; possessive
5. possessive; objective

Writing Application

Make sure student sentences reflect an understanding of the three cases. Example: Horace hoped <u>he</u> would not have to listen to Inez telling <u>him</u> about <u>her</u> plans for the dance. nominative, objective, possessive

Integrate Language Skills

❶ Vocabulary Development Lesson

Concept Development: Homographs

In "The Dancers," Emily tries to console her mother, who has been crying. *Console* is a homograph—a word that has two or more meanings but is always spelled the same. *Console* can be a verb meaning "to comfort"; it is also a noun meaning "a television cabinet that is made to stand on the floor." The only way to determine the proper meaning and pronunciation of a homograph is to look at the context in which it appears. Choose the letter of the correct homograph for each use of *contract*.

a. contract (kən trakt′) to get, as a disease
b. contract (kän′ trakt) a binding agreement

1. The partners signed a *contract*.
2. Did Paul *contract* pneumonia?

Concept Development: Antonyms

Write the letter of the word that means the opposite of the first word.

1. genteel: (a) gentle, (b) refined, (c) impolite
2. mortified: (a) honored, (b) humiliated, (c) loved
3. defiance: (a) resistance, (b) anger, (c) cooperation
4. console: (a) cause grief, (b) ease grief, (c) table

Spelling Strategy

When you add a suffix to a word that ends in *y* preceded by a consonant, change the *y* to *i* and then add the suffix: *mortify* + *-ed* = *mortified*. Write the word formed by adding the ending to each word below. Then, use the new word in a sentence.

1. try + *-ed* **2.** empty + *-ness* **3.** cleanly + *-ness*

❷ Grammar Lesson

Pronoun Case

Case is the form of a noun or a pronoun that indicates its use in a sentence. The three **pronoun cases** are the **nominative,** in which a pronoun is used as a subject or predicate nominative; the **possessive,** in which a pronoun is used to show ownership; and the **objective,** in which a pronoun is used as a direct object, an indirect object, the object of a preposition, or the object of a verb.

Nominative:	*He* danced very well with Mary Catherine.
Possessive:	*His* sister was responsible for the disappointing outcome.
Objective:	She gave *him* dancing lessons.

Practice Identify the case of each underlined pronoun.

1. Horace thought <u>they</u> were going to the dance together.
2. <u>She</u> was tired of <u>her</u> mother's intrusive behavior.
3. Horace understood the explanation <u>she</u> gave <u>him.</u>
4. <u>He</u> ignored Inez and <u>her</u> demands.
5. <u>Their</u> conversation helped <u>him</u> gain more confidence.

Writing Application Use three pronouns in a sentence about "The Dancers." Then, identify the case of each pronoun.

WG *Prentice Hall Writing and Grammar Connection: Chapter 24, Section 1*

TEACHING RESOURCES

The following resources can be used to enrich or extend the instruction for pp. 762–763.

Vocabulary

- **Selection Support:** Build Vocabulary, p. 177
- **Vocabulary and Spelling Practice Book** (Use this booklet for skills enrichment.) ■

Grammar

- **Selection Support:** Build Grammar Skills, p. 178
- **Writing and Grammar,** Gold Level, p. 552 ■
- **Daily Language Practice Transparencies**

Writing

- **Writing and Grammar,** Gold Level, p. 112
- **Writing and Grammar iText CD-ROM**

■ **BLOCK SCHEDULING:** Resources marked with this symbol provide varied instruction during 90-minute blocks.

❸ Writing Lesson

Diary Entry

Write a diary entry that Horace might have written after Emily refused to go with him to the dance.

Prewriting Review the play to make a list of the emotions you think Horace might have felt. Think about how he felt when Inez first told him about her plans for him and Emily, and think about his confidence level at the beginning of the play.

Drafting As you draft, use a tone you think Horace would use. Show the range of emotions he felt from first hearing about his date to being rejected by Emily. Then, express Horace's feelings about Inez and Elizabeth.

Revising Reread your draft, circling any vague words and replacing them with more precise language.

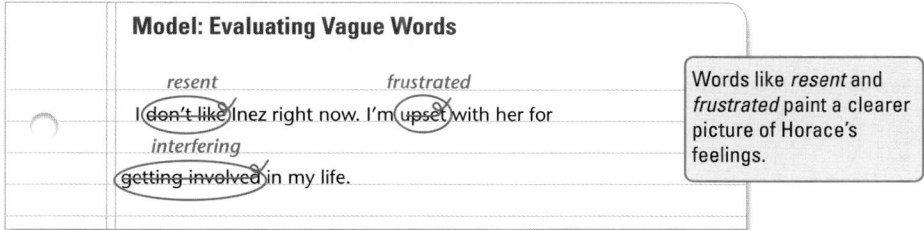

Model: Evaluating Vague Words

I ~~don't like~~ *resent* Inez right now. I'm ~~upset~~ *frustrated* with her for ~~getting involved~~ *interfering* in my life.

Words like *resent* and *frustrated* paint a clearer picture of Horace's feelings.

Prentice Hall Writing and Grammar Connection: Chapter 6, Section 4

❹ Extension Activities

Listening and Speaking In a small group, compile a **soundtrack** for a film version of "The Dancers." Consider the following points as you plan your music:

- Since the play is set in the 1950s, select some popular music from that era.
- Include music that relates to the particular mood of a scene.

When you present your soundtrack to your class, explain why you chose each piece and how it connects to the play. **[Group Activity]**

Research and Technology Write a **movie proposal** in which you explain how you would turn "The Dancers" into a movie. Start by researching clothing from the 1950s, and create a costume design catalog with the designs you think are best. Then, decide which actor you would cast in the role of each character. Share your proposal with your class.

Take It to the Net www.phschool.com

Go online for an additional research activity using the Internet.

ASSESSMENT RESOURCES

The following resources can be used to assess students' knowledge and skills.

Selection Assessment

- **Formal Assessment:** Selection Test, pp. 161–163
- **Open Book Test,** pp. 133–135
- **Got It! Assessment Videotapes,** Tape 4
- **Test Bank Software**

Take It to the Net

Visit www.phschool.com for self-tests and additional questions on "The Dancers."

Writing Rubric

- **Performance Assess. and Portfolio Mgmt.,** p. 8

PRENTICE HALL ASSESSMENT SYSTEM

- **Workbook**
- **Skill Book**
- **Transparencies**
- **CD-ROM**

❸ Writing Lesson

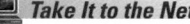

- Ask students to recall diary or journal entries they have made after a particularly bad day or embarrassing experience.
- Tell students that as they write their diary entry, in addition to the basic facts of the event, they should concentrate on the feelings Horace probably had about the event.
- When students have completed their diary entries, ask volunteers to read his or her entry to the class.
- Use the Autobiographical Narrative rubric in **Performance Assessment and Portfolio Management,** p. 8, to assess students' work.

❹ Research and Technology

- In order to get four movie proposals for consideration, divide the class into four groups.
- Encourage each group to reread parts of the play in order to have the characters alive in their minds as they cast the movie.
- When each group has completed its movie proposal, ask for a volunteer from each group to present their group's work to the class.
- When all proposals have been presented, have the class vote on the best one.

CUSTOMIZE INSTRUCTION for Universal Access

To address different learning styles, use the activities suggested in the **Extension Activities** booklet, p. 45.

- For Musical/Rhythmic and Interpersonal Learners, use Activity 5.
- For Visual/Spatial Learners, use Activity 6.
- For Verbal/Linguistic and Logical/Mathematical Learners, use Activity 7.

The Tragedy of Romeo and Juliet, Act I

Lesson Objectives and CA Correlations

1. **To analyze and respond to literary elements**
   - Literary Analysis: Character **R 3.4**
   - Connecting Literary Elements: Dramatic Foil **R 3.10**
2. **To read, comprehend, analyze, and critique drama**
   - Reading Strategy: Using Text Aids
   - Reading Check questions
   - Review and Assess questions
   - Assessment Practice (ATE)
3. **To develop word analysis skills, fluency, and systematic vocabulary**
   - Vocabulary Development Lesson: Latin Prefix: *trans-* **R 1.1**
4. **To understand and apply written and oral language conventions**
   - Spelling Strategy
   - Grammar Lesson: Pronoun Case in Elliptical Clauses **LC 1.3**
5. **To understand and apply appropriate writing and research strategies**
   - Writing Lesson: Persuasive Letter (after Act V) **W 2.4**
   - Extension Activity: Letter to an Advice Columnist **W 2.5**
6. **To understand and apply listening and speaking strategies**
   - Extension Activity: Oral Reading **LS 1.11**

STEP-BY-STEP TEACHING GUIDE	PACING GUIDE
PRETEACH	
Motivate Students and Provide Background	
Use the Motivation activity (ATE p. 768)	5 min.
Read and discuss the Preview material and Background information (SE/ATE pp. 764–768) **A**	15 min.
Introduce the Concepts	
Introduce the Literary Analysis and Reading Strategy (SE/ATE p. 769) **A**	15 min.
Pronounce the vocabulary words and read their definitions (SE p. 769)	5 min.
TEACH	
Monitor Comprehension	
Informally monitor comprehension by circulating while students read independently or in groups **A**	40 min.
Monitor students' comprehension with the Reading Check notes (SE/ATE pp. 773, 775, 777, 779, 781, 783, 785, 787, 789)	as students read
Develop vocabulary with Vocabulary notes (SE pp. 774–777, 780; ATE p. 777)	as students read
Develop Understanding	
Develop students' understanding of character with the Literary Analysis annotations (SE/ATE pp. 772–774, 776–778, 780, 782–783, 785–787, 789–790) **A**	10 min.
Develop students' ability to use text aids with the Reading Strategy annotations (SE/ATE pp. 772, 777, 779–784, 787–788, 790)	10 min.
ASSESS	
Assess Mastery	
Assess students' mastery of the Reading Strategy and Literary Analysis by having them answer the Review and Assess questions (SE/ATE p. 792)	20 min.
Use one or more of the print and media Assessment Resources (ATE p. 793) **A**	up to 45 min.
EXTEND	
Apply Understanding	
Have students complete the Vocabulary Development Lesson and the Grammar Lesson (SE p. 793) **A**	20 min.
Apply students' knowledge of persuasive appeals using the Writing Lesson (SE p. 877) **A**	45 min.
Apply students' understanding of the selection using one or more of the Extension Activities (SE p. 793)	20–90 min.

A **ACCELERATED INSTRUCTION:** Use the strategies and activities identified with an **A**.

UNIVERSAL ACCESS
● = Below Level Students
▲ = On-Level Students
■ = Above Level Students

Time and Resource Manager

Reading Level: Challenging
Average Number of Instructional Days: 4

RESOURCES		
PRINT	**TRANSPARENCIES**	**TECHNOLOGY**
• **Beyond Literature,** Cross-Curricular Connection: Social Studies, p. 46 ▲ ■		• **Interest Grabber Video,** Tape 4 ● ▲ ■
• **Selection Support Workbook:** ● ▲ ■ Literary Analysis, p. 184 Reading Strategy, p. 183 Build Vocabulary, p. 181	• **Literary Analysis and Reading Transparencies,** pp. 91 and 92 ● ▲ ■	
• **Authors In Depth,** Gold Level, p. 155 ■		• **Listening to Literature** ● ▲ ■ Audiocassettes, Side 23 Audio CDs, CD 15
• **Literatura en español** ● ▲ • **Literary Analysis for Enrichment** ■		
• **Formal Assessment:** Selection Test, pp. 164–166 ● ▲ ■ • **Open Book Test,** pp. 136–138 ● ▲ ■ • PRENTICE HALL ASSESSMENT SYSTEM ● ▲ ■	• PRENTICE HALL ASSESSMENT SYSTEM ● ▲ ■ Skills Practice Answers and Explanations on Transparencies	• **Test Bank Software** ● ▲ ■ • **Got It! Assessment Videotapes,** Tape 4 ● ▲
• **Selection Support Workbook:** ● ▲ ■ Build Grammar Skills, p. 182 • **Writing and Grammar,** Gold Level ● ▲ ■ • **Extension Activities,** p. 46 ● ▲ ■	• **Daily Language Practice Transparencies** ● ▲	• **Writing and Grammar iText CD-ROM** ● ▲ ■ ***Take It to the Net*** www.phschool.com

BLOCK SCHEDULING: Use one 90-minute class period to preteach the selection and have students read it. Use a second 90-minute class period to assess students' mastery of skills and have them complete one of the Extension Activities.

The Shakespearean Theater

Romeo and Juliet

Of all the love stories ever written, that of Romeo and Juliet is the most famous. To many people, Shakespeare's tragic lovers represent the essence of romantic love. When Shakespeare wrote *The Tragedy of Romeo and Juliet,* he was a young man, and the play is a young man's play about young love.

▼ Critical Viewing
Which attribute of the Globe theater is emphasized in this painting? **[Analyze]**

The Theater in Shakespeare's Day

Romeo and Juliet, like most of Shakespeare's plays, was produced in a public theater. Public theaters were built around roofless courtyards without artificial light. Performances, therefore, were given only during daylight hours. Surrounding the courtyard were three levels of galleries with benches on which wealthier playgoers sat. Less wealthy spectators, called groundlings, stood and watched a play from the courtyard, which was called the pit.

Most of Shakespeare's plays were performed in the Globe theater. No one is certain exactly what the Globe looked like, though Shakespeare tells us it was round or octagonal. We know that it was open to the sky and held between 2,500 and 3,000 people. Scholars disagree about its actual dimensions and size. The discovery of its foundation in 1990 was exciting because the eventual excavation will reveal clues about the plays, the actors, and the audience. The tiny

The Globe Theatre, London

Background

Literary Sources

The plot of *Romeo and Juliet,* like the plots of many of Shakespeare's plays, was borrowed from other sources. The theme appears as early as the fourth century in a Greek tale, and stories of ill-fated lovers were also popular among Italian writers in the fifteenth and sixteenth centuries. Shakespeare's most direct source, however, was a long English narrative poem written in 1562 by Arthur Brooke, called the *Tragicall Historye of Romeus and Juliet.* Shakespeare borrowed freely from Brooke's story, eliminating certain events and building up others. Although Shakespeare used the characters in Brooke's poem, he developed them in much greater depth and detail.

Background

Shakespeare's Globe Theater

Although Shakespeare did not have the advantages of the modern theater to draw on, the theaters of his day must be considered highly sophisticated. The greatest dramas in the English language were produced on the sixteenth-century English stage. This fact alone suggests how advanced the theater arts were when Shakespeare was writing his masterpieces.

The Globe theater was the site in which Shakespeare's plays were performed after 1599. The theater was built by two brothers, Richard and Cuthbert Burbage, who had owned a theater—built by their father, James Burbage—which had closed down two years previously. Richard was a leading member of the company of players who acted in Shakespeare's plays. The Burbages eventually dismantled the old theater and moved it to Bankside, a district of London's Southwark on the south bank of the River Thames, about a half mile west of London Bridge.

In 1613, during a performance of Shakespeare's *Henry VIII,* the Globe's roof was ignited by a cannon, and the entire structure was razed within an hour. By June of the following year it was completely rebuilt, this time with a tiled gallery roof and a circular shape. In 1644 it was pulled down, two years after the Puritans had closed all theaters, to build tenement housing.

ENRICHMENT: History

Moving the Globe

The Burbages had a clause in their lease of the land on which the Globe theater stood. If the lease were not renewed, they were to be allowed to move the building itself. When the lease did expire in 1597, there was some question about whether it was still legal to remove the theater from its original site after the fact. James Burbage had died, but Richard and his brother Cuthbert waited until the owner of the land was out of town and moved the theater, board by board, in the dead of winter. It was so cold that the Thames was frozen and some say the Burbages (accompanied by their mother), may have slid the boards across the frozen river. When the owner returned, he complained to the authorities, but the suit was dismissed and the theater rebuilt.

part of the foundation initially uncovered yielded a great number of hazelnut shells. Hazelnuts were Elizabethan popcorn; people munched on them all during the performance.

The stage was a platform that extended into the pit. Actors entered and left the stage from doors located behind the platform. The portion of the galleries behind and above the stage was used primarily as dressing and storage rooms. The second-level gallery right above the stage, however, was used as an upper stage. It would have been here that the famous balcony scene in *Romeo and Juliet* was enacted.

▲ Critical Viewing
Which part of the replica of the Globe theater do you think is being built in this picture? **[Speculate]**

There was no scenery in the theaters of Shakespeare's day. Settings were indicated by references in the dialogue. As a result, one scene could follow another in rapid succession. The actors wore elaborate clothing. It was, in fact, typical Elizabethan clothing, not costuming. Thus, the plays produced in Shakespeare's day were fast-paced, colorful productions. Usually, a play lasted two hours.

One other difference between Shakespeare's theater and today's is that acting companies in the sixteenth century were made up only of men and boys. Women did not perform on the stage. This was not considered proper for a woman. As a general rule, boys of eleven, twelve, or thirteen—before their voices changed—performed the female roles.

The Globe Today

Building a replica of Shakespeare's Globe was the dream of American actor Sam Wanamaker. After long years of fund-raising and construction, the theater opened in London to its first full season on June 8, 1997, with a production of *Henry V.* Like the earlier Globe, this one is made of wood, with a thatched roof and lime plaster covering the walls. The stage and the galleries are covered, but the "bear pit," where the modern-day groundlings stand, is open to the skies, exposing the spectators to the weather.

Background

The Globe Theater Today

London's new Globe theater is considered a remarkable replica of Shakespeare's original. Located on the Thames, a short distance from the site of the original, it retains the characteristics of the original—including its circular shape, open center, and thatched roof. Since few details of the original remain, the builders relied on the building contracts, which are extant, for the rival theaters, the Rose and the Fortune, which were built by the same master carpenter who built the Globe.

The new Globe seats 1,000. Because the seats curve around the stage, everyone has a different view of the action. For some, the view is blocked by pillars, but no audience member is more than fifty feet from the stage. The yard, or pit, has room for 450 groundlings, some of whom rest their arms on the edge of the stage. As in Elizabethan times, the audience tends to join in the proceedings, commenting on the action.

Plays are performed as they would have been in Shakespeare's time, with little or no scenery, people moving around in the yard, and vendors circulating to sell refreshments. The experience is a contrast to performances in modern theaters—even performances of Shakespeare's plays—which take place in a quiet, darkened theater with an attentive and respectful audience.

Background

Spelling Shakespeare

The writer whose name is on thousands of volumes of plays and other works never signed his name *Shakespeare.* There were no spelling standards in Elizabethan times and people spelled their own names however they wished to, changing them from day to day if it pleased them. *Shakespeare's* name has been spelled in over eighty different ways, including *Skakspere, Shagspeare, Shaxpere,* and *Shakestaffe*. Six documents are extant with the playwright's signature, and his name is spelled differently in each one. The current spelling of *Shakespeare* has been agreed upon by writers and historians over time.

Prepare to Read

The Tragedy of Romeo and Juliet

William Shakespeare (1564–1616)

Almost 400 years after Shakespeare's death, his 37 plays continue to be read widely and produced frequently throughout the world. They have as powerful an impact on audiences today as when they were first staged.

Starting in Stratford Not much is known about Shakespeare's early life. One reason for this lack of information is that playwrights during Shakespeare's time were not considered very important people socially. Therefore, no biographies were written about him until many years after his death. Church and town records in his hometown of Stratford-on-Avon—a busy market town about seventy-five miles northwest of London—provide some clues about Shakespeare's beginnings, however. His mother, whose maiden name was Mary Arden, was the daughter of his father's landlord. His father, John, was a prosperous merchant in Stratford and even served a term as the town's mayor. John Shakespeare's social standing made it possible for William to attend Stratford Grammar School free of charge until the age of fourteen. There, he studied Latin and Greek, as well as British and world history. Shakespeare would later put all of these lessons to use in his plays about historic figures such as Julius Caesar, Pericles, Macbeth, Richard III, and Henry IV.

Building a Love of Theater Because Stratford was a commercial center, traveling companies of professional actors visited several times a year. Young William probably attended many of these performances, inspiring his interest in the stage. In 1582, at the age of eighteen, Shakespeare married and was soon the father of three children. It is uncertain how Shakespeare spent the next few years, but he did not settle down in Stratford. His heart was set on London and the theater, so he followed his heart there sometime before 1592, leaving his patient

Elizabethan Language

As you read *Romeo and Juliet*, most of the unfamiliar words from Elizabethan English that you encounter will be explained in footnotes. The following, however, appear so frequently that learning them now will make your reading of the play easier.

against for; in preparation for
alack alas (an exclamation of sorrow)
an, and if
anon soon
aye yes
but only; except
e'en even
e'er ever
haply perhaps
happy fortunate
hence away; from here
hie hurry
hither here
marry indeed
whence where
wilt will
withal in addition; notwithstanding
would wish

family behind. Stratford nevertheless remained an important part of Shakespeare's life, and he visited often. Once he had achieved success in London, Shakespeare purchased one of Stratford's nicest homes for his family, and he retired there after his playwriting career ended.

Stage Celebrity By 1594, William Shakespeare, now a Londoner, had developed a reputation as an actor, had written several plays, and had become the principal playwright of the Lord Chamberlain's Men, a successful London theater company. He was also a part owner of the company, which meant that he earned money in three ways—from fees for his plays, from his acting salary, and from his share of the profits of the company. In 1599, the company built the famous Globe theater, where most of Shakespeare's plays were performed. When James I became king in 1603, Shakespeare and his partners renamed the company The King's Men. Shakespeare stayed with the company until 1610, when he retired to Stratford-on-Avon.

When Were They Written? Because Shakespeare wrote his plays to be performed, not published, no one knows exactly when each play was written. However, scholars have charted several distinct periods in Shakespeare's development as a playwright. During his early years, he wrote a number of comedies, several histories, and two tragedies. *Romeo and Juliet*—inspiration for the musical *West Side Story* as well as ballets, songs, stories, and movies—was written around 1595. Between that date and the turn of the seventeenth century, Shakespeare wrote several of his finest romantic comedies (*As You Like It*, *Twelfth Night*, and *Much Ado About Nothing*). During the first decade of the seventeenth century, Shakespeare created his greatest tragedies (*Hamlet*, *Othello*, *King Lear*, *Macbeth*, *Antony and Cleopatra*, and *Coriolanus*). Finally, toward the end of his career, Shakespeare wrote several plays referred to as romances or tragicomedies. Shakespeare's plays were finally published in a one-volume edition in 1623, seven years after his death. More than 1,000 copies of the first printing were sold for the considerable sum of one pound each—equivalent to more than $50 in today's currency.

Shakespeare's Impact on English

No other individual has played a more significant role in shaping the English language than William Shakespeare. In addition to introducing many new words into the language, Shakespeare penned hundreds of memorable lines that are familiar to millions of people throughout the world—even people who have never read one of Shakespeare's plays. Following are just a few of his most famous lines. See how many you recognize.

From *Hamlet:*

To be, or not to be: that is the question:
Whether 'tis nobler in the mind to suffer
The slings and arrows of outrageous fortune,
Or take arms against a sea of troubles, . . .

From *Romeo and Juliet:*

What's in a name? That which we call a rose
By any other name would smell as sweet.

. . . parting is such sweet sorrow, . . .

From *Macbeth:*

Fair is foul, and foul is fair.

From *Julius Caesar:*

Friends, Romans, countrymen, lend me your ears;
I come to bury Caesar, not to praise him.

From *As You Like It:*

All the world's a stage,
And all the men and women merely players . . .

From *Richard the Third:*

A horse, a horse! My kingdom for a horse!

From *Twelfth Night:*

If music be the food of love, play on . . .

Background

More About the Author

Shakespeare's plays have not only had a powerful impact on audiences over the centuries, but they have also affected contemporary English in a major way. Dozens of familiar words and phrases were invented by Shakespeare. Individual words of his creation include *leapfrog, majestic, hint, lonely, excellent,* and *gloomy*. Phrases include "catch cold," "laugh it off," "fair play," "disgraceful conduct," and "foregone conclusion," to name just a few. As critic Christopher Morley has written, "Everyone is a Shakespeare scholar unconsciously. You yourself have probably quoted him today . . ."

In addition to coining new words and phrases, Shakespeare is believed to have had the largest vocabulary of any writer in history.

CUSTOMIZE INSTRUCTION FOR UNIVERSAL ACCESS

For Less Proficient Readers	For English Learners	For Advanced Readers
Tell students that Shakespeare became known for many kinds of figures of speech. Point out to them the two that consist of opposites in the famous lines list: "...parting is such sweet sorrow,..." and "Fair is foul, and foul is fair." Ask them to be on the lookout for this figurative format as they read the play.	Students may wish to make a glossary for use while they read the play. They may start with the words on p. 766 and add to their glossary as they meet unfamiliar words in the text. Encourage them to use the footnotes to find the meanings of some unfamiliar words and context to find the meanings of the rest.	In addition to the famous lines on this page, students may wish to make a list of those they recognize as they read the play. In each case, have them write the phrase, line, or full speech and then write its meaning in their own words.

PRETEACH

Step-by-Step Teaching Guide for pp. 764–767

Motivation

Romeo and Juliet is probably Shakespeare's most famous play, and possibly the most famous play in all of English literature. Everyone has heard of these star-crossed lovers, even if they have never read *Romeo and Juliet*. Build students' interest in reading the play by inviting them to share what they know —or think they know—about Romeo and Juliet. List their ideas, impressions, and predictions. After they have read Act I, they can ask themselves: In what ways does the play match my expectations? In what ways does it surprise me?

Interest Grabber Video

As an alternative, play "Monday Night Shakespeare" on Tape 4 to engage student interest.

1 Background

Romeo and Juliet has been made into a film many times, but the two young lovers are not often played by teenagers. The famous actress Ellen Terry said, "As soon as a woman is old enough to understand Juliet, she's too old to play her." In the 1936 movie version, Juliet was played by the thirty-five-year-old Norma Shearer, with Leslie Howard, forty-four, as Romeo. Franco Zefferelli's 1968 film version, which starred Olivia Hussey and Leonard Whiting—fifteen and seventeen years old respectively—is said by critics to come closest to the characters as Shakespeare envisioned them.

Prepare to Read

The Tragedy of Romeo and Juliet, Act I

Take It to the Net

Visit www.phschool.com for interactive activities and instruction related to *The Tragedy of Romeo and Juliet*, including

- background
- graphic organizers
- literary elements
- reading strategies

Preview

Connecting to the Literature

The world is filled with rivalries—among countries, families, schools, even groups of friends. Occasionally, rivalries become so fierce that the members of one group refuse to associate with their rivals. In extreme cases, as you will see in this play, rivalries can even erupt into violence.

1 Background

Shakespeare based his play about star-crossed lovers from feuding Italian families on a poem published in 1562 by Arthur Brooke. Brooke's 3,000-line poem has a highly moral tone: Disobedience, as well as fate, leads to the deaths of the two lovers. Brooke's poem, in turn, was based on a French version of the story, written in 1559.

768 ◆ Drama

TEACHING RESOURCES

The following resources can be used to enrich or extend the instruction for pp. 768–769.

Motivation

Interest Grabber Video, Tape 4

Background

Beyond Literature, p. 46

Take It to the Net

Visit www.phschool.com for background and hotlinks for *The Tragedy of Romeo and Juliet.*

Literary Analysis

Literary Analysis and Reading Transparencies, Character, p. 92

Reading

Selection Support: Reading Strategy, p. 183; Build Vocabulary, p. 181

Literary Analysis and Reading Transparencies, Use Text Aids, p. 91

BLOCK SCHEDULING: Resources marked with this symbol provide varied instruction during 90-minute blocks.

❷ Literary Analysis

Character

Characters are the people or animals who take part in a literary work. Some characters are fully developed, while others are not as complex.

- A **round character** has many personality traits, like a real person.
- A **flat character** is one-dimensional, embodying only a single trait. Shakespeare's plays often include flat characters who provide comic relief.

As you read the play, use a chart like the one shown to note round and flat characters and their personality traits.

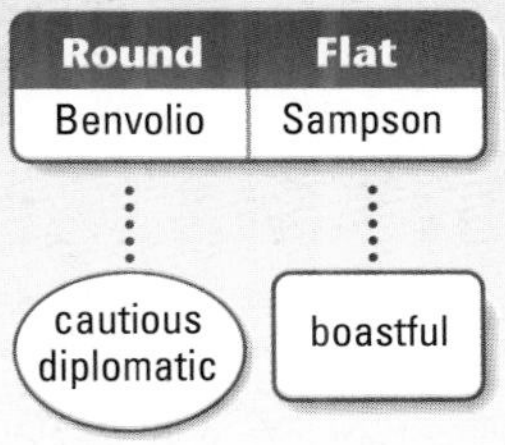

Connecting Literary Elements

A **dramatic foil** is a character who highlights the traits of another character through contrast. For example, in Act I, Benvolio, who tries to quiet a group of brawling servants, is a foil to Tybalt, who has a fiery hot temper. As you read, look for foils by identifying characters who possess contrasting personality traits. This will help you determine key differences among characters.

❸ Reading Strategy

Using Text Aids

The way the characters speak in Shakespeare's play, which was written over 400 years ago, will probably be unfamiliar to you. To make sure that you understand the dialogue, it is crucial that you use the **text aids**—the numbered explanations of Shakespeare's language that appear alongside the text.

- If you are confused by a passage, check to see if there is a footnote and read the corresponding explanation.
- Reread the passage, using your new knowledge from the footnote, to be sure that you grasp the meaning of the passage.

The footnotes should add to your enjoyment of the play by clarifying confusing language.

Vocabulary Development

pernicious (pər nish′ əs) *adj.* causing great injury or ruin (p. 774)

augmenting (ôg ment′ iŋ) *v.* increasing; enlarging (p. 775)

grievance (grēv′ əns) *n.* injustice; complaint (p. 776)

transgression (trans gresh′ ən) *n.* wrongdoing; sin (p. 777)

heretics (her′ ə tiks) *n.* those who hold to a belief opposed to the established teachings of a church (p. 780)

❷ Literary Analysis

Character

- Tell students that they will meet many characters in this play. Alert them to notice which characters have many traits and are fully *rounded*, and which are one-dimensional, or *flat*.
- Read the instruction about Character together as a class. Students may wish to practice filling out their Round/Flat character graphic organizer with one or more characters from "The Dancers," to familiarize themselves with the process.
- Use the instruction for Connecting Literary Elements to help students recognize that sometimes a character is set up to contrast with another, to act as *a dramatic foil*.
- Use the Character transparency in **Literary Analysis and Reading Transparencies**, p. 92, to demonstrate for students how to set up a character description chart.

❸ Reading Strategy

Using Text Aids

- Point out to students that the slang and idioms they use today would be unfamiliar to people in an earlier era, as they will probably be to those in a later time.
- Instruct students to read Using Text Aids in **Literary Analysis and Literary Transparencies**, p. 91, to see how they can "translate" the language of Shakespeare using the footnotes on each page.

Vocabulary Development

- Pronounce each vocabulary word for students, and read the definitions as a class. Have students identify any words with which they are already familiar.

CUSTOMIZE INSTRUCTION FOR UNIVERSAL ACCESS

For Less Proficient Readers	For English Learners	For Advanced Readers
Students may benefit from using the Character transparency in **Literary Analysis and Reading Transparencies**, p. 92, to enter personality traits about a character they have met recently in another selection, in a film, or on television. Help them determine whether the characters they choose are round or flat.	Ask students to share stories from their home culture that focus on young lovers. Have them describe what happens to the two young people; that is, does their relationship last, do the lovers separate of their own accord, or are they separated by circumstances they do not control?	Invite students to find the play on words in the Using Text Aids transparency, p. 91 in **Literary Analysis and Reading Transparencies**. Have interested students use a dictionary to find the relationship between the words *choler, cholera,* and *choleric.*

E-Teach

Visit E-Teach at www.phschool.com for teachers' essays on how to teach, with questions and answers.

TEACH

Step-by-Step Teaching Guide for pp. 770–791

CUSTOMIZE INSTRUCTION For Gifted/Talented Students

Invite students to analyze the prologue and the conflict that it foreshadows. Then, have them use their imaginations to put together a news broadcast about the conflict. Tell them to include the time, place, and reason for the conflict; then, evaluate the crisis and speculate on a peaceful resolution.

❶ About the Selection

"A pair of star-crossed lovers . . . Doth with their death bury their parents' strife." The Prologue that opens this act tells briefly of the terrible events that mark a tender but tragic love, while the five scenes that follow set these events in motion. We first meet Romeo just after a bitter and long-standing feud between members of his family, the Montagues, and their foes the Capulets, has erupted into a street brawl. Romeo's kinsman, Benvolio, suggests that they secretly attend a feast being given that night by the Capulets. There, Romeo and Juliet meet for the first time. Only after they have exchanged kisses and words of love do they learn each other's names and discover their misfortune at being the son and daughter of bitter enemies.

❷ Background

Film

The photos that illustrate this play are stills from Franco Zeffirelli's film *Romeo and Juliet*, which was released in 1968. Zeffirelli has filmed several other works of Shakespeare, including *The Taming of the Shrew* and *Hamlet*, with Mel Gibson in the title role. Zeffirelli's films display affectionate attention to period detail and capture the zest and vitality of the Age of Shakespeare.

❶ The Tragedy of ROMEO AND JULIET

William Shakespeare

❷

TEACHING RESOURCES

The following resources can be used to enrich or extend the instruction for pp. 770–791.

Literary Analysis

Selection Support: Literary Analysis, p. 184

Reading

Listening to Literature Audiocassettes, Side 23

Listening to Literature Audio CDs, CD 15 ■

Extension

Authors In Depth, Gold Level (The collection includes additional selections by William Shakespeare for extended reading. See p. 870 for further information.) ■

■ **BLOCK SCHEDULING:** Resources marked with this symbol provide varied instruction during 90-minute blocks.

CHARACTERS

CHORUS
ESCALUS, Prince of Verona
PARIS, a young count, kinsman to the Prince
MONTAGUE
CAPULET
AN OLD MAN, of the Capulet family
ROMEO, son to Montague
MERCUTIO, kinsman to the Prince and friend to Romeo
BENVOLIO, nephew to Montague and friend to Romeo
TYBALT, nephew to Lady Capulet
FRIAR LAWRENCE, Franciscan
FRIAR JOHN, Franciscan
BALTHASAR, servant to Romeo
SAMPSON, servant to Capulet
GREGORY, servant to Capulet
PETER, servant to Juliet's nurse
ABRAM, servant to Montague
AN APOTHECARY
THREE MUSICIANS
AN OFFICER
LADY MONTAGUE, wife to Montague
LADY CAPULET, wife to Capulet
JULIET, daughter to Capulet
NURSE TO JULIET
CITIZENS OF VERONA, Gentlemen and Gentlewomen of both houses, Maskers, Torchbearers, Pages, Guards, Watchmen, Servants, and Attendants

Prologue

Scene: *Verona; Mantua*

[*Enter* CHORUS.]

❸

CHORUS. Two households, both alike in dignity.[1]
In fair Verona, where we lay our scene,
From ancient grudge break to new mutiny.[2]
Where civil blood makes civil hands unclean.[3]
From forth the fatal loins of these two foes
A pair of star-crossed[4] lovers take their life;
Whose misadventured piteous overthrows[5]
Doth with their death bury their parents' strife.
The fearful passage of their death-marked love,
And the continuance of their parents' rage,
Which, but[6] their children's end, naught could remove,
Is now the two hours' traffic[7] of our stage;
The which if you with patient ears attend,
What here shall miss, our toil shall strive to mend.[8] [*Exit.*]

1. **dignity** high social rank.
2. **mutiny** violence.
3. **Where . . . unclean** in which the blood of citizens stains citizens' hands.
4. **star-crossed** ill-fated by the unfavorable positions of the stars.
5. **Whose . . . overthrows** whose unfortunate, sorrowful destruction.
6. **but** except.
7. **two hours' traffic** two hours' business.
8. **What . . . mend** What is not clear in this prologue we actors shall try to clarify in the course of the play.

Act I

Scene i. *Verona. A public place.*

[*Enter* SAMPSON *and* GREGORY, *with swords and bucklers,*[1] *of the house of Capulet.*]

❹

SAMPSON. Gregory, on my word, we'll not carry coals.[2]

GREGORY. No, for then we should be colliers.[3]

SAMPSON. I mean, an we be in choler, we'll draw.[4]

GREGORY. Ay, while you live, draw your neck out of collar.[5]

SAMPSON. I strike quickly, being moved.

1. **bucklers** small shields.
2. **carry coals** endure insults.
3. **colliers** sellers of coal.
4. **an . . . draw** If we are angered, we'll draw our swords.
5. **collar** the hangman's noose.

❸ Background

Greek Chorus

The use of a *chorus*—a figure or group of figures who comment on a play's action— goes back to ancient Greek and Roman drama. In Shakespeare's time, it was common for a chorus to deliver a *prologue*—an opening speech that introduces the play's main characters, plot, and setting.

❹ Critical Thinking

- Have students use the notes at the side to look up the meanings of footnoted terms.
- Ask students what two meanings of the phrase "to carry coals" are used in the exchange between Sampson and Gregory. As a hint, tell them that one usage is literal and one is idiomatic, or figurative.
  Answer: Literally, the phrase "carry coals" means "to sell coal," while figuratively the phrase means "to endure insults."
- Ask students what effect this wordplay has on the scene.
  Answer: Students may describe the effect as playful and humorous.

CUSTOMIZE INSTRUCTION FOR UNIVERSAL ACCESS

For Less Proficient Readers	For Advanced Readers
Advise students of the usefulness of the Characters list on p. 771. They may check it whenever they are unsure of a character's identity. As an example, ask them to use the list to find Sampson, Gregory, Juliet, and Capulet. Then, ask how Gregory and Sampson are connected to Juliet. **Answer:** Sampson and Gregory are Capulet's servants, and Juliet is Capulet's daughter. The two men work for Juliet's father.	Identify the Chorus' opening lines for students as an English sonnet, or Shakespearean sonnet. Have students scan the sonnet and mark down the rhyme scheme to compare with other examples throughout the play. **Answer:** The rhyme scheme of the Chorus' lines on p. 771 is ABAB CDCD EFEF GG.

❺ Literary Analysis

Character

- Have students identify some character traits of both Sampson and Gregory in this scene.
  Possible Response: Sampson and Gregory are boastful, flippant, insulting, and apparently eager to do battle with Montague's men.
- Have students answer the Literary Analysis question on p. 772: What does this conversation reveal about the Capulets and the Montagues?
  Answer: It reveals that there is great hostility between the two houses.

❻ Reading Strategy

Using Text Aids

- Ask students to identify the play on words used in the first two lines of this exchange.
  Possible Response: *Back* is used to mean "back you up," or "support you," as well as the back of a person who is running away in cowardice.
- Remind students to check the side of the page to see if there is any footnote information to help them understand the language of the play.
- Ask students to answer the Reading Strategy question on p. 772: How does footnote 8 help you understand Sampson's logic in line 34?
  Answer: The footnote says that the phrase "take the law of our sides" means "make sure the law is on our side." Sampson's logic is to let the other side begin the fight because that will keep the law on Sampson and Gregory's side. When officials come to break up the fight, they will be harsher on those who actually started it.

GREGORY. But thou art not quickly moved to strike.

SAMPSON. A dog of the house of Montague moves me.

GREGORY. To move is to stir, and to be valiant is to stand. Therefore, if thou art moved, thou run'st away.

SAMPSON. A dog of that house shall move me to stand. I will take the wall[6] of any man or maid of Montague's.

❺ **GREGORY.** That shows thee a weak slave; for the weakest goes to the wall.

SAMPSON. 'Tis true; and therefore women, being the weaker vessels, are ever thrust to the wall. Therefore I will push Montague's men from the wall and thrust his maids to the wall.

GREGORY. The quarrel is between our masters and us their men.

SAMPSON. 'Tis all one. I will show myself a tyrant. When I have fought with the men, I will be civil with the maids—I will cut off their heads.

GREGORY. The heads of the maids?

SAMPSON. Ay, the heads of the maids or their maidenheads. Take it in what sense thou wilt.

GREGORY. They must take it in sense that feel it.

SAMPSON. Me they shall feel while I am able to stand; and 'tis known I am a pretty piece of flesh.

GREGORY. 'Tis well thou art not fish; if thou hadst, thou hadst been Poor John. Draw thy tool![7] Here comes two of the house of Montagues.

[*Enter two other Servingmen,* ABRAM *and* BALTHASAR.]

SAMPSON. My naked weapon is out. Quarrel! I will back thee.

GREGORY. How? Turn thy back and run?

❻ **SAMPSON.** Fear me not.

GREGORY. No, marry. I fear thee!

SAMPSON. Let us take the law of our sides;[8] let them begin.

GREGORY. I will frown as I pass by, and let them take it as they list.[9]

SAMPSON. Nay, as they dare. I will bite my thumb[10] at them, which is disgrace to them if they bear it.

ABRAM. Do you bite your thumb at us, sir?

SAMPSON. I do bite my thumb, sir.

ABRAM. Do you bite your thumb at us, sir?

SAMPSON. [*Aside to* GREGORY] Is the law of our side if I say ay?

6. take the wall assert superiority by walking nearer the houses and therefore farther from the gutter

Literary Analysis
Character What does this conversation reveal about the Capulets and the Montagues?

7. tool weapon.

8. take . . . sides make sure the law is on our side.

9. list please.

10. bite . . . thumb make an insulting gesture.

Reading Strategy
Using Text Aids How does footnote 8 help you understand Sampson's logic in line 34?

GREGORY. [*Aside to* SAMPSON] No.

SAMPSON. No, sir, I do not bite my thumb at you, sir; but I bite
my thumb, sir.

GREGORY. Do you quarrel, sir?

7 ABRAM. Quarrel, sir? No, sir.

SAMPSON. But if you do, sir, I am for you. I serve as good a
man as you.

ABRAM. No better.

SAMPSON. Well, sir.

[*Enter* BENVOLIO.]

GREGORY. Say "better." Here comes one of my master's kinsmen.

SAMPSON. Yes, better, sir.

ABRAM. You lie.

SAMPSON. Draw, if you be men. Gregory, remember thy
swashing[11] blow. [*They fight.*]

BENVOLIO. Part, fools!
Put up your swords. You know not what you do.

[*Enter* TYBALT.]

8 TYBALT. What art thou drawn among these heartless hinds?[12]
Turn thee, Benvolio; look upon thy death.

BENVOLIO. I do but keep the peace. Put up thy sword,
Or manage it to part these men with me.

TYBALT. What, drawn, and talk of peace? I hate the word
As I hate hell, all Montagues, and thee.
Have at thee, coward! [*They fight.*]

[*Enter an* OFFICER, *and three or four* CITIZENS *with clubs or partisans.*[13]]

OFFICER. Clubs, bills,[14] and partisans! Strike! Beat them down!
Down with the Capulets! Down with the Montagues!

[*Enter old* CAPULET *in his gown, and his* WIFE.]

CAPULET. What noise is this? Give me my long sword, ho!

LADY CAPULET. A crutch, a crutch! Why call you for a sword?

CAPULET. My sword, I say! Old Montague is come
And flourishes his blade in spite[15] of me.

[*Enter old* MONTAGUE *and his* WIFE.]

MONTAGUE. Thou villain Capulet!—Hold me not; let me go.

LADY MONTAGUE. Thou shalt not stir one foot to seek a foe.

Literary Analysis
Character How would you describe Gregory and Sampson in this scene?

11. swashing hard downward swordstroke.

12. heartless hinds cowardly servants. *Hind* also meant "a female deer."

Literary Analysis
Character and Dramatic Foil Which contrasting personality traits do Benvolio and Tybalt reveal in their brief conversation?

13. partisans spearlike weapons with broad blades.

14. bills weapons consisting of hook-shaped blades with long handles.

15. spite defiance.

9 **Reading Check**
Whom does Tybalt fight?

7 Literary Analysis

Character

- Ask students what legal question Sampson asks Gregory in this exchange, and why does he ask it?
  Possible response: Sampson asks if the law is on their side if he admits he has insulted Abram. He asks because he wants to know what to say in reply to Abram's question.
- Invite students to respond to the first Literary Analysis question on p. 773: How would you describe Gregory and Sampson in this scene?
  Possible response: Gregroy and Sampson are playing with Montague's men, trying to insult them without having to take legal responsibility for starting a fight.

8 Literary Analysis

Character and Dramatic Foil

- Ask students what Benvolio tries to do as he enters the action.
  Answer: He tries to stop the fight between the Montague servants and Capulet servants.
- Have students interpret Tybalt's words as he enters the scene.
  Possible response: Tybalt wants to know why Benvolio has drawn his sword in the face of cowardly servants, when he could turn and face Tybalt, who wishes to kill him.
- Remind students that a *dramatic foil* is a character who highlights another character's traits by providing a contrast. Have students answer the second Literary Analysis question on p. 773: Which contrasting personality traits do Benvolio and Tybalt reveal in their brief conversation?
  Answer: Benvolio shows restraint and a sense of reason, while Tybalt is hotheaded and vindictive.

9 Reading Check

Answer: Tybalt fights Benvolio.

CUSTOMIZE INSTRUCTION FOR UNIVERSAL ACCESS

For Special Needs Students	For Less Proficient Students	For Advanced Readers
Alert students to some of the unfamiliar words they will meet often in this play, such as *wilt* for "will," and *marry* for "indeed." Tell students that the word *marry* is similar to *right*, *sure*, or *surely*, words used in contemporary English.	Have students make a list to show the different quarreling sides as the stage fills up during this scene. Starting with Sampson and Gregory on the Capulet side, where would they place Abram and Balthazar, Benvolio, Tybalt, and finally Lord and Lady Capulet and Lord and Lady Montague?	Have students speculate on whether or not the use of *Sir* among the four servants is respectful or insulting. Also, have them note the use of direct address here and throughout the play.

10 Critical Thinking

Generalize

- Ask students whom the Prince is addressing in his first few lines.
  Answer: The Prince is talking to the people doing the fighting—the family and servants of the Montagues and Capulets, as well as the two lords.
- Have students reread the scene from the entrances of the Montagues and Capulets (p. 773, starting at line 66), and then distinguish the behavior of the men from that of their wives.
  Answer: Lady Capulet tells her husband that he should be calling for a crutch rather than a sword. Lady Montague forbids her husband to take a single step in the direction of the fight.
- Ask students if they can generalize about who is doing the quarreling and fighting in this play.
  Possible response: Students may suggest that the feud is powered by the men of the two families, not the women.

11 Critical Thinking

Interpret

- Ask students what the Prince accuses the families of doing to the citizens of Verona in lines 80–86.
  Possible response: Students may say that the Prince accuses the families of having three public brawls that have forced the citizens of the city to take up arms to defend themselves.
- Ask students to identify the threat the Prince makes to the warring families.
  Answer: The prince says that the next brawl will mean the death of the participants.

[*Enter* PRINCE ESCALUS, *with his Train.*[16]]

PRINCE. Rebellious subjects, enemies to peace,
Profaners[17] of this neighbor-stainèd steel—
Will they not hear? What, ho! You men, you beasts,
That quench the fire of your pernicious rage
With purple fountains issuing from your veins!
On pain of torture, from those bloody hands
Throw your mistempered[18] weapons to the ground
And hear the sentence of your movèd prince.
Three civil brawls, bred of an airy word
By thee, old Capulet, and Montague,
10 Have thrice disturbed the quiet of our streets
And made Verona's ancient citizens
11 Cast by their grave beseeming ornaments[19]
To wield old partisans, in hands as old,
Cank'red with peace, to part your cank'red hate.[20]
If ever you disturb our streets again,
Your lives shall pay the forfeit of the peace.
For this time all the rest depart away.
You, Capulet, shall go along with me;
And, Montague, come you this afternoon,
To know our farther pleasure in this case,
To old Freetown, our common judgment place.
Once more, on pain of death, all men depart.

[*Exit all but* MONTAGUE, *his* WIFE, *and* BENVOLIO.]

MONTAGUE. Who set this ancient quarrel new abroach?[21]
Speak, nephew, were you by when it began?

BENVOLIO. Here were the servants of your adversary
And yours, close fighting ere I did approach.
I drew to part them. In the instant came
The fiery Tybalt, with his sword prepared;
Which, as he breathed defiance to my ears,
He swung about his head and cut the winds,
Who, nothing hurt withal, hissed him in scorn.
While we were interchanging thrusts and blows,
Came more and more, and fought on part and part,[22]
Till the Prince came, who parted either part.

LADY MONTAGUE. O, where is Romeo? Saw you him today?
Right glad I am he was not at this fray.

BENVOLIO. Madam, an hour before the worshiped sun
Peered forth the golden window of the East,
A troubled mind drave me to walk abroad:
Where, underneath the grove of sycamore
That westward rooteth from this city side,
So early walking did I see your son.

16. **Train** attendants.

17. **Profaners** those who show disrespect or contempt.

pernicious (pər nish′ əs) *adj.* causing great injury or ruin

18. **mistempered** hardened for a wrong purpose; bad-tempered.

19. **Cast . . . ornaments** put aside their dignified and appropriate clothing.

20. **Cank'red . . . hate** rusted from lack of use, to put an end to your malignant feuding.

21. **Who . . . abroach?** Who reopened this old fight?

22. **on . . . part** on one side and the other.

Literary Analysis
Character What can you infer about Benvolio based on his interaction with Romeo's parents?

ENRICHMENT: History Connection

Officials Throughout History

Some of Shakespeare's plays, including the tragedies *Julius Caesar* and *Anthony and Cleopatra*, and the histories *Henry IV* and *Henry V*, tell the stories of famous and powerful rulers. Other Shakespeare plays feature characters who govern on a smaller, more local level. Point out that the Prince in *Romeo and Juliet* is one such character; his civic duties include maintaining the peace and dispensing justice in the city of Verona.

Ask students to imagine an updated version of *Romeo and Juliet*, to be set in their community. Have them offer ideas on which local official or officials would take the place of the Prince. Follow up by having groups of students work together to learn more about the functions and duties of local officials in your community as well as the conditions of their terms—are they appointed or elected? For how long? What administrative region or area do they serve?

Towards him I made, but he was ware[23] of me
And stole into the covert[24] of the wood.
I, measuring his affections[25] by my own,
Which then most sought where most might not be found,[26]
Being one too many by my weary self,
Pursued my humor not pursuing his,[27]
And gladly shunned who gladly fled from me.

MONTAGUE. Many a morning hath he there been seen,
With tears augmenting the fresh morning's dew,
Adding to clouds more clouds with his deep sighs; ⓬
But all so soon as the all-cheering sun
Should in the farthest East begin to draw
The shady curtains from Aurora's* bed,
Away from light steals home my heavy[28] son
And private in his chamber pens himself,
Shuts up his windows, locks fair daylight out,
And makes himself an artificial night.
Black and portentous[29] must this humor prove
Unless good counsel may the cause remove.

BENVOLIO. My noble uncle, do you know the cause?

MONTAGUE. I neither know it nor can learn of him.

BENVOLIO. Have you importuned[30] him by any means?

MONTAGUE. Both by myself and many other friends;
But he, his own affections' counselor,
Is to himself—I will not say how true—
But to himself so secret and so close,
So far from sounding[31] and discovery,
As is the bud bit with an envious worm
Ere he can spread his sweet leaves to the air
Or dedicate his beauty to the sun.
Could we but learn from whence his sorrows grow,
We would as willingly give cure as know.

23. ware aware; wary.

24. covert hidden place.

25. measuring . . . affections judging his feelings.

26. Which . . . found which wanted to be where there was no one else.

27. Pursued . . . his followed my own mind by not following after Romeo.

augmenting (ôg ment′ iŋ) *v.* increasing; enlarging

28. heavy sad, moody.

29. portentous promising bad fortune.

30. importuned questioned deeply.

31. sounding understanding.

⓮ **Reading Check**

How does the Prince respond to the fight between Benvolio and Tybalt?

Literature ⓭ in context Humanities Connection

◆ ***Aurora***

Aurora was the Latin goddess of the dawn who began each day riding a chariot from the River Oceanus to heaven to announce the coming of the sun. She was said to dip her rosy fingers into a cup filled with dew and sprinkle drops on flowers and trees. Aurora had special feelings for young people like Romeo, whose lives were just dawning. Unlike Aurora, the moody Romeo roams at night and shuts himself in his room at dawn (I, i, 127).

⓬ Literary Analysis

Character

- Ask students what basic information is exchanged between Benvolio and Lady Montague in this scene.
  Answer: Lady Montague asks after Romeo; Benvolio says he saw Romeo earlier, but that Romeo did not want any company.
- Have students answer the Literary Analysis question on p. 774: What can you infer about Benvolio based on his interaction with Romeo's mother?
  Possible response: Benvolio is polite; he calls Lady Montague "Madam." He is sensitive; when he saw Romeo, he did not intrude but left Romeo to himself.

⓭ Literature in Context

Aurora

Romeo's father recognizes that his son is hurting, or else why would he deprive himself of the new day offered each sunrise by the goddess Aurora? Shakespeare also gives Montague an extended simile in these lines on p. 775: "But to himself so secret and so close/So far from sounding and discovery,/As is the bud bit with an envious worm/Ere he can spread his sweet leaves to the air/Or dedicate his beauty to the sun." This simile compares Romeo's melancholy state to a bud that's been eaten by a worm before it can flower.

⓮ Reading Check

Answer: The Prince says that if quarreling disturbs the peace again, participants will be put to death.

CUSTOMIZE INSTRUCTION FOR UNIVERSAL ACCESS

For Special Needs Students	For English Learners
Point out to students that Shakespearean language often inverts the subject and the verb, or puts the objects before the subject and verb. Point out examples in line 77 ("from those bloody hands/Throw your mistempered weapons to the ground"); line 91 ("And, Montague, come you this afternoon"); lines 99–100 ("In the instant came/the fiery Tybalt"); line 107 ("O, where is Romeo? Saw you him today?"); and line 108 ("Right glad I am he was not at this fray").	Have students reread Benvolio's speech to Lady Montague about Romeo on pp. 744–745. Help them work through individual phrases to understand their meaning, using the footnotes and their own common sense. For example, lines 109–110 mean simply, "Madam, an hour before sunrise,..." while the final line, 121, means "I was happy to avoid him since he wanted to be alone." Then, ask students to write Benvolio's description in contemporary English.

15 Literary Analysis

Character

- Ask students what generalization both characters make here about the effect of sadness on one's life. **Answer:** They both suggest that when one is sad time moves very slowly.
- Remind students that even a few words spoken by a character can reveal his or her traits.
- Have students respond to the Literary Analysis question on p. 776: What personality traits are revealed by Benvolio's concern for Romeo?
  Possible response: Students may say that Benvolio is sensitive and a loving cousin because he asks Romeo what is wrong, listens to the answer, and then sympathizes with Romeo's state.

16 Literary Analysis

Character

- How does Romeo's language show his confusion in the speech on pp. 776–777?
  Possible response: Romeo makes many statements that contain opposites, such as "O brawling love," "O loving hate," "O heavy lightness," to show that he is in terrible conflict about his feelings.
- Invite students to answer the first Literary Analysis question on p. 777: What do Romeo's words in lines 171–174 reveal about his personality?
  Answer: Romeo's words show Romeo to be a sensitive person with emotions that are very close to the surface.

17 ▶Critical Viewing

Answer: Both characters appear to be depressed or out of sorts—Romeo because he is in love and Benvolio because he is concerned about Romeo.

[*Enter* ROMEO.]

BENVOLIO. See, where he comes. So please you step aside;
I'll know his grievance, or be much denied.

MONTAGUE. I would thou wert so happy by thy stay
To hear true shrift.[32] Come, madam, let's away.

[*Exit* MONTAGUE *and* WIFE.]

BENVOLIO. Good morrow, cousin.

ROMEO. Is the day so young?

BENVOLIO. But new struck nine.

ROMEO. Ay me! Sad hours seem long.
Was that my father that went hence so fast?

15

BENVOLIO. It was. What sadness lengthens Romeo's hours?

ROMEO. Not having that which having makes them short.

BENVOLIO. In love?

ROMEO. Out—

BENVOLIO. Of love?

ROMEO. Out of her favor where I am in love.

BENVOLIO. Alas that love, so gentle in his view,[33]
Should be so tyrannous and rough in proof![34]

16

ROMEO. Alas that love, whose view is muffled still,[35]
Should without eyes see pathways to his will!
Where shall we dine? O me! What fray was here?
Yet tell me not, for I have heard it all.
Here's much to do with hate, but more with love.[36]
Why then, O brawling love, O loving hate,
O anything, of nothing first created!
O heavy lightness, serious vanity,
Misshapen chaos of well-seeming forms,

grievance (grēv′ əns) *n.* injustice; complaint

32. I . . . shrift I hope you are lucky enough to hear him confess the truth.

Literary Analysis
Character Which personality traits are revealed by Benvolio's concern for Romeo?

33. view appearance.

34. in proof when experienced.

35. whose . . . still Cupid is traditionally represented as blindfolded.

36. but . . . love loyalty to family and love of fighting. In the following lines, Romeo speaks of love as a series of contradictions—a union of opposites.

17 ▶ **Critical Viewing** How would you describe the feelings of each character, based on this photograph? **[Analyze]**

ENRICHMENT: Literature Connection

Oxymorons

This play contains numerous examples of a literary figure of speech called an *oxymoron*, from the Greek *oxys*, meaning "sharp," and *moros*, meaning "stupid." These paired opposites are used abundantly on these two pages, starting with Romeo's speech at the bottom of p. 776. Students may find such oxymorons as "brawling love," "loving hate," "heavy lightness," "serious vanity," and "cold fire," among others. When used by a master writer such as Shakespeare, an oxymoron can show the contradictory elements of life, the degree to which each element of a pair can generate its own opposite—love and hate, pleasure and pain. The overarching oxymoron for this particular play is, of course, youth and death.

Feather of lead, bright smoke, cold fire, sick health,
Still-waking sleep, that is not what it is!
This love feel I, that feel no love in this.
Dost thou not laugh?

BENVOLIO. No, coz,[37] I rather weep.

ROMEO. Good heart, at what?

BENVOLIO. At thy good heart's oppression.

18 **ROMEO.** Why, such is love's transgression.
Griefs of mine own lie heavy in my breast,
Which thou wilt propagate, to have it prest
With more of thine.[38] This love that thou hast shown
Doth add more grief to too much of mine own.
Love is a smoke made with the fume of sighs;
Being purged, a fire sparkling in lovers' eyes;
Being vexed, a sea nourished with loving tears.
What is it else? A madness most discreet,[39]
A choking gall,[40] and a preserving sweet.
Farewell, my coz.

19 **BENVOLIO.** Soft![41] I will go along.
And if you leave me so, you do me wrong.

ROMEO. Tut! I have lost myself; I am not here;
This is not Romeo, he's some other where.

BENVOLIO. Tell me in sadness,[42] who is that you love?

ROMEO. What, shall I groan and tell thee?

BENVOLIO. Groan? Why, no;
But sadly tell me who.

20 **ROMEO.** Bid a sick man in sadness make his will.
Ah, word ill urged to one that is so ill!
In sadness, cousin, I do love a woman.

BENVOLIO. I aimed so near when I supposed you loved.

ROMEO. A right good markman. And she's fair I love.

BENVOLIO. A right fair mark, fair coz, is soonest hit.

ROMEO. Well, in that hit you miss. She'll not be hit
With Cupid's arrow. She hath Dian's wit,[43]
And, in strong proof[44] of chastity well armed,
From Love's weak childish bow she lives uncharmed.
She will not stay[45] the siege of loving terms,
Nor bide th' encounter of assailing eyes,
Nor ope her lap to saint-seducing gold.
O, she is rich in beauty; only poor
That, when she dies, with beauty dies her store.[46]

BENVOLIO. Then she hath sworn that she will still live chaste?

Literary Analysis
Character What do Romeo's words in lines 171–174 reveal about his personality?

37. coz cousin.

transgression (trans gresh′ ən) *n.* wrongdoing; sin

38. Which . . . thine Which griefs you will increase by adding your own sorrow to them.

39. discreet intelligently sensitive.

40. gall a bitter liquid.

41. Soft! Hold on a minute.

Reading Strategy
Using Text Aids Why is footnote 41 helpful here?

42. in sadness seriously.

Literary Analysis
Character Which details in line 195 indicate that Romeo is a round character?

43. Dian's wit the mind of Diana, goddess of chastity.

44. proof armor.

45. stay endure; put up with.

46. That . . . store In that her beauty will die with her if she does not marry and have children.

21 **✓Reading Check**
What reason for his sadness does Romeo give to Benvolio?

18 Vocabulary Development

Latin Prefix *trans-*

- Call students' attention to the word *transgression* on p. 777. Tell students that the prefix *trans-* means "across, beyond, or through."
- Point out that the prefix can be followed by other word parts or elements to form common words, such as *transmit, transparent, and transplant.*
- Have students look up the meanings of these words in a dictionary, and add three new words of their own.
  Possible response: Students may suggest such words as *translate, transform, transgress,* and *transfuse.*

19 Reading Strategy

Using Text Aids

- Ask students what Romeo plans to do at the end of his speech in line 186.
  Answer: He says "Farewell, my coz," so he plans to leave and be alone again.
- Have students answer the Reading Strategy question on p. 777: Why is footnote 41 helpful here?
  Possible response: Students may say that knowing that *soft* means "Hold on a minute" helps readers to see that Benvolio is not going to let Romeo evade him again.

20 Literary Analysis

Character

- Ask students to what Romeo compares himself in this short speech.
  Answer: He compares himself—someone in love—with a sick and dying man.
- Ask students the second Literary Analysis question on p. 777: Which details in line 195 indicate that Romeo is a round character?
  Answer: Romeo is aware of feeling conflicting emotions; he is in love and it makes him sad.

21 ✓Reading Check

Answer: Romeo is sad because he is in love but is not loved in return.

CUSTOMIZE INSTRUCTION FOR UNIVERSAL ACCESS

For Special Needs Students	For English Learners	For Gifted/Talented Students
To help students understand the meaning of the images Romeo uses to describe love in lines 181 through 185, have them draw some of the actual items in Romeo's metaphors. For example, students might draw billowing smoke, a fire, a body of water, and a piece of candy.	Some students might not be familiar with the mythological beings Romeo alludes to in his speech beginning on line 199. Tell students that Cupid is the Roman god of love and Diana is the Roman goddess of chastity, and explain that according to ancient mythology, whoever is struck by one of Cupid's arrows falls in love.	Have students list the contradictory, or oxymoronic expressions found in Romeo's speech on pp. 776 and 777, showing how conflicted he is over his feelings of love. When students have completed their list, have them create some more contradictory phrases of their own to express a feeling of conflict.

❷❷ Literary Analysis

Character and Dramatic Foil

- Remind students that a *dramatic foil* is a character that contrasts with another character in a way that highlights the traits of both.
- Ask students to respond to the first Literary Analysis question on p. 778: What contrasting attitudes are revealed in this exchange between Romeo and Benvolio?
  Answer: Benvolio is more realistic and believes that if one loves someone who does not reciprocate, that person should find someone else. Romeo believes the opposite: Once having committed to love, he can see no alternative.

❷❸ Literary Analysis

Character

- Ask students what Count Paris is trying to get Capulet to agree to in this exchange.
  Answer: Count Paris wants to marry Juliet and is trying to get Capulet's consent.
- Have students summarize Capulet's objections to the marriage.
  Answer: Capulet's objections include: Juliet is only fourteen; early marriage and motherhood can hurt women; Paris has yet to woo Juliet; Capulet's consent is only part of the agreement; Juliet would have to consent, too.
- Ask students to answer the second Literary Analysis question on p. 778: What can you tell about Lord Capulet's character traits based on his talk with Paris?
  Possible response: Students may describe Capulet as reasonable, understanding, or wise. These traits are indicated by his stated intention "to keep the peace" and his decision not to rush his daughter into marriage.

ROMEO. She hath, and in that sparing make huge waste;
For beauty, starved with her severity,
Cuts beauty off from all posterity.[47]
She is too fair, too wise, wisely too fair
To merit bliss by making me despair.[48]
She hath forsworn to[49] love, and in that vow
Do I live dead that live to tell it now.

BENVOLIO. Be ruled by me; forget to think of her.

ROMEO. O, teach me how I should forget to think!

BENVOLIO. By giving liberty unto thine eyes.
Examine other beauties.

ROMEO. 'Tis the way
To call hers, exquisite, in question more.[50]
These happy masks that kiss fair ladies' brows,
Being black puts us in mind they hide the fair.
He that is strucken blind cannot forget
The precious treasure of his eyesight lost.
Show me a mistress that is passing fair:
What doth her beauty serve but as a note
Where I may read who passed that passing fair?[51]
Farewell. Thou canst not teach me to forget.

BENVOLIO. I'll pay that doctrine, or else die in debt.[52] [*Exit all.*]

Scene ii. *A street.*

[*Enter* CAPULET, COUNTY PARIS, *and the* CLOWN, *his servant.*]

CAPULET. But Montague is bound as well as I,
In penalty alike; and 'tis not hard, I think,
For men so old as we to keep the peace.

PARIS. Of honorable reckoning[1] are you both,
And pity 'tis you lived at odds so long.
But now, my lord, what say you to my suit?

CAPULET. But saying o'er what I have said before:
My child is yet a stranger in the world,
She hath not seen the change of fourteen years;
Let two more summers wither in their pride
Ere we may think her ripe to be a bride.

PARIS. Younger than she are happy mothers made.

CAPULET. And too soon marred are those so early made.
Earth hath swallowed all my hopes[2] but she;
She is the hopeful lady of my earth.[3]
But woo her, gentle Paris, get her heart;
My will to her consent is but a part.

47. in . . . posterity By denying herself love and marriage, she wastes her beauty, which will not live on in future generations.

48. She . . . despair She is being too good—she'll earn happiness in heaven by dooming me to live without her love.

49. forsworn to sworn not to.

50. 'Tis . . . more That way will only make her beauty more strongly present in my mind.

Literary Analysis
Character and Dramatic Foil What contrasting attitudes are revealed in this exchange between Romeo and Benvolio?

51. who . . . fair who surpassed in beauty that very beautiful woman.

52. I'll. . . debt I'll teach you to forget, or else die trying.

1. reckoning reputation.

Literary Analysis
Character What can you tell about Lord Capulet's character traits based on his talk with Paris?

2. hopes children.

3. She . . . earth My hopes for the future rest in her; she will inherit all that is mine.

An she agree, within her scope of choice
Lies my consent and fair according voice,[4]
This night I hold an old accustomed feast,
Whereto I have invited many a guest,
Such as I love; and you among the store,
One more, most welcome, makes my number more.
At my poor house look to behold this night
24 Earth-treading stars[5] that make dark heaven light.
Such comfort as do lusty young men feel
When well-appareled April on the heel
Of limping Winter treads, even such delight
Among fresh fennel buds shall you this night
Inherit at my house. Hear all, all see,
And like her most whose merit most shall be;
Which, on more view of many, mine, being one,
May stand in number, though in reck'ning none.[6]
Come, go with me. [*To* SERVANT, *giving him a paper*]
    Go, sirrah, trudge about
Through fair Verona; find those persons out
Whose names are written there, and to them say
My house and welcome on their pleasure stay.[7] [*Exit with* PARIS.]

SERVANT. Find them out whose names are written here? It is written that the shoemaker should meddle with his yard and the tailor with his last, the fisher with his pencil and the painter with his nets;[8] but I am sent to find those persons whose names are here writ, and can never find what names the writing person hath here writ. I must to the learned. In good time![9]

[*Enter* BENVOLIO *and* ROMEO.]

BENVOLIO. Tut, man, one fire burns out another's burning;
    One pain is less'ned by another's anguish;
Turn giddy, and be holp by backward turning;[10]
    One desperate grief cures with another's languish.
Take thou some new infection to thy eye,
And the rank poison of the old will die.

ROMEO. Your plantain leaf[11] is excellent for that.

BENVOLIO. For what, I pray thee?

ROMEO. For your broken shin.

BENVOLIO. Why, Romeo, art thou mad?

ROMEO. Not mad, but bound more than a madman is;
Shut up in prison, kept without my food,
Whipped and tormented and—God-den,[12] good fellow.

SERVANT. God gi' go-den. I pray, sir, can you read?

ROMEO. Ay, mine own fortune in my misery.

4. **and . . . voice** If she agrees, I will consent to and agree with her choice.

5. **Earth-treading stars** young ladies.

6. **Which . . . none** If you look at all the young girls, you may see her as merely one among many, and not worth special admiration.

Reading Strategy
Using Text Aids Using footnote 6, explain the main idea of Capulet's proposal to Paris.

7. **stay** await.

8. **shoemaker . . . nets** The servant is confusing workers and their tools. He intends to say that people should stick with what they know.

9. **In good time!** Just in time! The servant has seen Benvolio and Romeo, who can read.

10. **Turn . . . turning** If you are dizzy from turning one way, turn the other way.

11. **plantain leaf** leaf used to stop bleeding.

12. **God-den** good afternoon; good evening.

25 **Reading Check**
What does Capulet tell Paris he wishes for his daughter?

24 Reading Strategy
Using Text Aids

- Ask students to recall Romeo's response to Benvolio's suggestion that Romeo look at other beautiful women. What does he say in reply?
  Answer: Romeo responds that if he saw other beautiful women, he would only compare them with the woman he loves, which would not help him at all.

Monitor Progress Have students compare Capulet's advice to Paris with Benvolio's advice to Romeo as they answer the Reading Strategy question on p. 779: Using footnote 6, explain the main idea of Capulet's proposal to Paris.
Answer: Capulet proposes that Paris come to his feast, meet many of the eligible women, and see that Juliet is only one of many possibilities to be his wife.

25 Reading Check

Answer: Capulet wishes for Juliet to make her own decision about whom to marry and he will consent to her choice.

CUSTOMIZE INSTRUCTION FOR UNIVERSAL ACCESS

For Special Needs Students	For Less Proficient Readers	For English Learners
Help students to see that many unfamiliar words in the text are similar to forms students already know, and context clues can help determine their meaning. For example, in line 223, "He that is strucken blind cannot forget/...", the word *strucken* is simply an old-fashioned usage for *struck*, which makes sense in the sentence.	Have students make a list of the rhyming words in Capulet's speech starting on line 16. Have them note the "cheating" rhyme of *feast* and *guest* in lines 20–21. Rhyming words include: *heart/ part; choice/voice; feast/guest; store/more; night/light,* and so forth.	Have students use the dictionary to look up the multiple-meaning words *yard* and *last*, used in the Servant's speech on p. 779. Help them see that *last* refers to a device that shoemakers use. One definition for *yard* is a unit of measurement; a tailor measures material by the yard.

26 Literary Analysis

Character

- Ask students why a servant enters the action at this point.
  Answer: The servant has been sent into the city by Capulet to invite a list of people to a feast. Since the servant cannot read the list, he does not know whom to invite. When he sees Romeo and Benvolio, he knows by their bearing that they are able to read.
- Ask students to answer the Literary Analysis question on p. 780: Is the servant a round or flat character? Why?
  Answer: The servant is a flat character because he is in the scene solely to provide information that sets up Romeo's fateful meeting with Juliet.

27 Reading Strategy

Using Text Aids

- Have students identify the new information that Benvolio gives to the reader and audience in this speech.
  Answer: Benvolio identifies the object of Romeo's love as Rosaline, who will be at the feast.
- Ask students what Benvolio suggests Romeo do.
  Answer: Benvolio suggests that if Romeo goes to the feast and compares Rosaline with the other beautiful women, he will see that Rosaline is plain as a crow.
- Finally, have students respond to the Reading Strategy question on p. 780: How does footnote 16 convey Romeo's feelings for Rosaline?
  Answer: The footnote clarifies Romeo's devotion to Rosaline as a religious intensity; disloyalty to her would merit the fiery penalties of heresy.

26

SERVANT. Perhaps you have learned it without book.
But, I pray, can you read anything you see?

ROMEO. Ay, if I know the letters and the language.

SERVANT. Ye say honestly. Rest you merry.[13]

ROMEO. Stay, fellow; I can read. [*He reads the letter.*]
"Signior Martino and his wife and daughters;
County Anselm and his beauteous sisters;
The lady widow of Vitruvio;
Signior Placentio and his lovely nieces;
Mercutio and his brother Valentine;
Mine uncle Capulet, his wife and daughters;
My fair niece Rosaline; Livia;
Signior Valentio and his cousin Tybalt;
Lucio and the lively Helena."
A fair assembly. Whither should they come?

SERVANT. Up.

ROMEO. Whither? To supper?

SERVANT. To our house.

ROMEO. Whose house?

SERVANT. My master's.

ROMEO. Indeed I should have asked you that before.

SERVANT. Now I'll tell you without asking. My master is the great rich Capulet; and if you be not of the house of Montagues, I pray come and crush a cup of wine. Rest you merry. [*Exit.*]

27

BENVOLIO. At this same ancient[14] feast of Capulet's
Sups the fair Rosaline whom thou so loves;
With all the admirèd beauties of Verona.
Go thither, and with unattainted[15] eye
Compare her face with some that I shall show,
And I will make thee think thy swan a crow.

ROMEO. When the devout religion of mine eye
Maintains such falsehood, then turn tears to fires;
And these, who, often drowned, could never die,
Transparent heretics, be burnt for liars![16]
One fairer than my love? The all-seeing sun
Ne'er saw her match since first the world begun.

BENVOLIO. Tut! you saw her fair, none else being by,
Herself poised with herself in either eye;[17]
But in that crystal scales[18] let there be weighed
Your lady's love against some other maid
That I will show you shining at this feast,
And she shall scant show well that now seems best.

13. Rest you merry May God keep you happy—a way of saying farewell.

Literary Analysis
Character Is the servant a round or flat character? Why?

14. ancient long-established; traditional.

15. unattainted unprejudiced.

heretics (her´ ə tiks) *n.* those who hold to a belief opposed to the established teachings of a church

16. When . . . liars! When I see Rosaline as just a plain-looking girl, may my tears turn to fire and burn my eyes out!

Reading Strategy
Using Text Aids How does footnote 16 convey Romeo's feelings for Rosaline?

17. Herself . . . eye Rosaline compared with no one else.

18. crystal scales your eyes.

ENRICHMENT: Social Studies Connection

Social Classes

Like all of Shakespeare's dramas, *Romeo and Juliet* features characters from all social classes and all walks of life. The diversity of characters on the stage reflects the diversity found within the original audiences at the performances of the plays.

Shakespeare's London was a bustling, rapidly growing city. The age of overseas exploration and colonization had recently begun; people poured into the city and scores of new businesses were springing up.

Against this backdrop, London's first large theaters were built. Known as *public theaters*, they offered a range of accommodations and ticket prices to attract both wealthy patrons and those of more modest means. The performances themselves were noisy and bustling—refreshments were sold, and audience members cheered, jeered, and talked among themselves.

ROMEO. I'll go along, no such sight to be shown,
But to rejoice in splendor of mine own.[19] [*Exit all.*]

19. **mine own** my own love, Rosaline.

Scene iii. *A room in* CAPULET*'s house.*

[*Enter* CAPULET'S WIFE, *and* NURSE.]

LADY CAPULET. Nurse, where's my daughter? Call her forth to me.

NURSE. Now, by my maidenhead at twelve year old,
I bade her come. What, lamb! What, ladybird!
God forbid, where's this girl? What, Juliet!

[*Enter* JULIET.]

28

JULIET. How now? Who calls?

NURSE. Your mother.

JULIET. Madam, I am here
What is your will?

LADY CAPULET. This is the matter—Nurse, give leave[1] awhile;
We must talk in secret. Nurse, come back again.
I have rememb'red me; thou's hear our counsel.[2]
Thou knowest my daughter's of a pretty age.

NURSE. Faith, I can tell her age unto an hour.

LADY CAPULET. She's not fourteen.

NURSE. I'll lay fourteen of my teeth—
And yet, to my teen[3] be it spoken, I have but four—
She's not fourteen. How long is it now
To Lammastide?[4]

LADY CAPULET. A fortnight and odd days.[5]

NURSE. Even or odd, of all days in the year,
Come Lammas Eve at night shall she be fourteen.
Susan and she (God rest all Christian souls!)

1. **give leave** Leave us alone.

2. **thou's . . . counsel** You shall hear our conference.

Reading Strategy
Using Text Aids Based on footnotes 1 and 2, what facial expression might the Nurse have during Lady Capulet's speech?

3. **teen** sorrow.

4. **Lammastide** August 1, a holiday celebrating the summer harvest.

5. **A fortnight and odd days** two weeks plus a few days.

29 ◀ **Critical Viewing**
What do this picture and the conversation among Juliet, Lady Capulet, and the Nurse tell you about their relationship? **[Infer]**

30 ✔ **Reading Check**
What does Romeo agree to do with Benvolio?

28 Reading Strategy
Using Text Aids

- Have students read the first speech by the Nurse and speculate on what is meant by the repetition of the word *What*.
  Possible response: Students may recognize that the word is not used here as a question. The Nurse is calling to Juliet, using *What* as a word of address, meaning something like the modern-day *Hey* or *Look*.
- Have students respond to the Reading Strategy question on p. 781: Based on footnotes 1 and 2, what facial expression might the Nurse have during Lady Capulet's speech?
  Possible response: Students may suggest that the Nurse would have a look of exasperation, meaning "Make up your mind," as Lady Capulet changes her mind.

29 ▶ Critical Viewing

Answer: Students may infer that the women share a close relationship. Lady Capulet is kind but firm; the Nurse is a humorous character; and Juliet is an obedient daughter.

30 ✔ Reading Check

Answer: Romeo agrees to go the Capulets' feast with Benvolio.

CUSTOMIZE INSTRUCTION FOR UNIVERSAL ACCESS

For Gifted Students	For Advanced Readers
Ask students to pair up to read the exchange between Romeo and the servant aloud, bringing out the comic nature of the exchange. Ask if this dialogue reminds students of any comic routines they have seen in movies or television shows.	To help students understand the metaphor about heretics and how they were treated in the Middle Ages (Romeo's speech in lines 87–92), suggest that they research print and non-print resources, such as encyclopedias and the Internet. Have them use key words, such as *Catholic Church, heresy, Middle Ages,* or *Inquisition.* After students have compiled their information, hold a class discussion to interpret Shakespeare's metaphor.

31 Reading Strategy

Using Text Aids

- Have students reread the first few lines of the Nurse's speech from the beginning on p. 781 and speculate on who Susan is.
  Answer: Students should realize that Susan was the Nurse's daughter.
- Ask students to answer the Reading Strategy question on p. 782: How does the information in footnote 6 help you understand the Nurse's devotion to Juliet?
  Answer: The Nurse's daughter Susan and Juliet were the same age. When her own daughter died, the Nurse became even more devoted to Juliet.

32 Literary Analysis

Character

- Ask students to read the Nurse's dialogue, lines 34–44, and summarize what she is describing.
  Answer: The Nurse is describing a time eleven years before when Juliet fell down and the Nurse's husband picked her up.
- Have students respond to the first Literary Analysis question on p. 782: Which character traits does Nurse reveal in her speech?
  Answer: The Nurse is devoted to Juliet, but she is also long-winded and easily gets off the subject when she is talking.

33 Literary Analysis

Character and Dramatic Foil

Monitor Progress Have students recall the definition of *dramatic foil.*
Answer: A dramatic foil is a character that is contrasted to another character in order to highlight particular traits.

- Ask students the second Literary Analysis question on p. 783: In what ways does the Nurse's character contrast with the characters of Lady Capulet and Juliet?
  Answer: The Nurse talks at great length and repeats herself. Juliet and Lady Capulet speak little in this scene and when they do, they stay on the subject.

31
Were of an age.[6] Well, Susan is with God;
She was too good for me. But, as I said,
On Lammas Eve at night shall she be fourteen;
That shall she, marry; I remember it well.
'Tis since the earthquake now eleven years.
And she was weaned (I never shall forget it),
Of all the days of the year, upon that day;
For I had then laid wormwood to my dug,
Sitting in the sun under the dove house wall.
My lord and you were then at Mantua.
Nay, I do bear a brain. But, as I said,
When it did taste the wormwood on the nipple
Of my dug and felt it bitter, pretty fool,
To see it tetchy and fall out with the dug!
Shake, quoth the dovehouse! 'Twas no need, I trow,
To bid me trudge.
And since that time it is eleven years,
For then she could stand high-lone; nay, by th' rood,
She could have run and waddled all about;
For even the day before, she broke her brow;
And then my husband (God be with his soul!
32
'A was a merry man) took up the child.
"Yea," quoth he, "dost thou fall upon thy face?
Thou wilt fall backward when thou hast more wit;
Wilt thou not, Jule?" and, by my holidam,
The pretty wretch left crying and said, "Ay."
To see now how a jest shall come about!
I warrant, and I should live a thousand years,
I never should forget it. "Wilt thou not, Jule?" quoth he,
And, pretty fool, it stinted and said, "Ay."

LADY CAPULET. Enough of this. I pray thee hold thy peace.

NURSE. Yes, madam. Yet I cannot choose but laugh
To think it should leave crying and say, "Ay."
And yet, I warrant, it had upon it brow
A bump as big as a young cock'rel's stone;
A perilous knock; and it cried bitterly.
"Yea," quoth my husband, "fall'st upon thy face?
Thou wilt fall backward when thou comest to age,
33
Wilt thou not, Jule?" It stinted and said, "Ay."

JULIET. And stint thou too, I pray thee, nurse, say I.

NURSE. Peace, I have done. God mark thee to His grace!
Thou wast the prettiest babe that e'er I nursed.
And I might live to see thee married once,
I have my wish.

LADY CAPULET. Marry, that "marry" is the very theme
I came to talk of. Tell me, daughter Juliet,

6. **Susan . . . age** Susan, the Nurse's child, and Juliet were the same age.

Reading Strategy
Using Text Aids How does the information in footnote 6 help you understand the Nurse's devotion to Juliet?

Literary Analysis
Character Which character traits does the Nurse reveal in her speech?

Literary Analysis
Character and Dramatic Foil In what ways does the Nurse's character contrast with those of Lady Capulet and Juliet?

ENRICHMENT: History

Lammas Eve

The date of Juliet's birthday, Lammas Eve, marked a time of celebration for Elizabethans. Lammas (loaf mass) Day, an annual August celebration of the summer harvest, usually began with a prayer thanking God for a good harvest and blessing the grains and breads; this ritual was followed by a feast.

The Lammas feast featured breads and pastries of all types that were paraded through the feast hall. The highlight of the day was the bread making. Bakers baked bread in all sizes and in geometric, animal, and celestial shapes. They also sculpted bread into castles and multi-decked warships. The main meal was served on bread, and some of the courses themselves consisted of breads—such as currant buns, shortbread, gingerbread, and cucumber bread.

The last event of the day was a candlelight procession around the feast hall. Everyone carried a loaf of bread in which a candle was placed.

How stands your dispositions to be married?

JULIET. It is an honor that I dream not of.

NURSE. An honor? Were not I thine only nurse,
I would say thou hadst sucked wisdom from thy teat.

34

LADY CAPULET. Well, think of marriage now. Younger than you,
Here in Verona, ladies of esteem,
Are made already mothers. By my count,
I was your mother much upon these years
That you are now a maid.[7] Thus then in brief;
The valiant Paris seeks you for his love.

NURSE. A man, young lady! Lady, such a man
As all the world— Why, he's a man of wax.[8]

LADY CAPULET. Verona's summer hath not such a flower.

NURSE. Nay, he's a flower, in faith—a very flower.

LADY CAPULET. What say you? Can you love the gentleman?
This night you shall behold him at our feast.
Read o'er the volume of young Paris' face,
And find delight writ there with beauty's pen;
Examine every married lineament,
And see how one another lends content;[9]
And what obscured in this fair volume lies
Find written in the margent[10] of his eyes.
This precious book of love, this unbound lover,
To beautify him only lacks a cover.[11]
The fish lives in the sea, and 'tis much pride
For fair without the fair within to hide.
That book in many's eyes doth share the glory,
That in gold clasps locks in the golden story;
So shall you share all that he doth possess,
By having him making yourself no less.

NURSE. No less? Nay, bigger! Women grow by men.

LADY CAPULET. Speak briefly, can you like of Paris' love?

JULIET. I'll look to like, if looking liking move;[12]
But no more deep will I endart mine eye
Than your consent gives strength to make it fly.[13]

[*Enter* SERVINGMAN.]

SERVINGMAN. Madam, the guests are come, supper served up, you called, my young lady asked for, the nurse cursed in the pantry, and everything in extremity. I must hence to wait. I beseech you follow straight. [*Exit.*]

LADY CAPULET. We follow thee. Juliet, the County stays.[14]

NURSE. Go, girl, seek happy nights to happy days. [*Exit all.*]

7. I . . . maid I was your mother when I was as old as you are now.

8. he's . . . wax He's a model of a man.

Reading Strategy

Using Text Aids Why is footnote 8 essential for your understanding?

9. Examine . . . content: Examine every harmonious feature of his face, and see how each one enhances every other. Throughout this speech, Lady Capulet compares Paris to a book.

10. margent margin. Paris's eyes are compared to the margin of a book, where whatever is not clear in the text (the rest of his face) can be explained by notes.

11. cover metaphor for *wife*.

12. I'll . . . move If looking favorably at someone leads to liking him, I'll look at Paris in a way that will lead to liking him.

13. But . . . fly But I won't look harder than you want me to.

14. the County stays The Count, Paris, is waiting.

35 **Reading Check**

Why has Lady Capulet come to talk to Juliet?

34 Reading Strategy

Using Text Aids

- Have students read the exchange between Juliet and her mother. What information do they learn?
  Answer: Lady Capulet asks Juliet if she has given any thought to marriage, and Juliet responds that she hasn't.
- Have students recall Lord Capulet's dialogue with Paris on pp. 778–779, and compare his views of Juliet and marriage with Lady Capulet's views.
  Answer: Lord Capulet thinks Juliet—fourteen—is too young to be married. Lady Capulet, who was already married and a mother when she was fourteen, apparently does not think Juliet is too young.
- Ask students the Reading Strategy question on p. 783: Why is footnote 8 essential for your understanding?
  Answer: Without the footnote, the reader might think the Nurse is describing Paris in negative terms— as pliable, soft, or boring. With the footnote, readers can see that she means the reference as a compliment.

35 Reading Check

Answer: Lady Capulet wants to determine Juliet's reaction to the news that Paris wants to marry her.

CUSTOMIZE INSTRUCTION FOR UNIVERSAL ACCESS

For Special Needs Students	For English Learners
Work with students to recognize that Lady Capulet's long speech about Paris in the middle of p. 783 is an extended metaphor in which she compares Paris to a book. Have students find the references that remind them of books. You might wish to remind students that the word *volume* is another word for *book*. When they have found the comparisons, read the full speech aloud to them so they can appreciate the entire metaphor.	Have students relate Juliet's words in lines 97–99 to their own lives. First, have them put her speech into their own words. Then, have them recall times when they were asked to do something by a parent that they didn't really want to do, but they wanted to be a dutiful son or daughter.

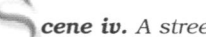

36 Reading Strategy
Using Text Aids

- Ask students to interpret what is going on here based on the stage directions and the Characters list on p. 771. For example, who is Mercutio, what do they think Maskers are, and why are there torchbearers in the scene?
  Answer: Mercutio belongs to the Prince's family and is also Romeo's friend. Maskers are people dressed in costumes and masks, and torchbearers are necessary because it is after dark.
- Ask students to infer where the group is as Scene iv opens.
  Answer: The group is in the vicinity of the Montague home.
- Finally, have students answer the Reading Strategy question on p. 784: How would you restate Romeo's questions to Benvolio using contemporary English?
  Possible response: "Should we tell people who we are when we get there, or should we go in without explaining ourselves?"

37 ▶Critical Viewing

Answer: They are dressed as rustic characters, at least two of them have musical instruments, and the character at the left appears to have a mask on his head that he will be able to pull down over his face.

Scene iv. *A street*

[*Enter* ROMEO, MERCUTIO, BENVOLIO, *with five or six other* MASKERS; TORCHBEARERS.]

ROMEO. What, shall this speech[1] be spoke for our excuse?
Or shall we on without apology?

BENVOLIO. The date is out of such prolixity.[2]
We'll have no Cupid hoodwinked with a scarf,
Bearing a Tartar's painted bow of lath,
36 Scaring the ladies like a crowkeeper,
Nor no without-book prologue, faintly spoke
After the prompter, for our entrance;
But, let them measure us by what they will,
We'll measure them a measure and be gone.

ROMEO. Give me a torch. I am not for this ambling.
Being but heavy,[3] I will bear the light.

MERCUTIO. Nay, gentle Romeo, we must have you dance.

ROMEO. Not I, believe me. You have dancing shoes
With nimble soles; I have a soul of lead
So stakes me to the ground I cannot move.

MERCUTIO. You are a lover. Borrow Cupid's wings
And soar with them above a common bound

ROMEO. I am too sore enpiercèd with his shaft
To soar with his light feathers; and so bound

Reading Strategy
Using Text Aids How would you restate Romeo's questions in lines 1–2 in contemporary English?

1. this speech Romeo asks whether he and his companions, being uninvited guests, should follow custom by announcing their arrival in a speech.

2. The . . . prolixity Such wordiness is outdated. In the following lines, Benvolio says, in sum: "Let's forget about announcing our entrance with a show. The other guests can look over as they see fit. We'll dance a while, then leave."

3. heavy weighed down with sadness.

37 ▼ Critical Viewing Which details in this photograph show how Romeo and his friends prepare to attend the feast? **[Infer]**

784 *Drama*

ENRICHMENT: Performing Arts Connection

Danger Backstage

The use of lighted torches and other incendiary props is always a danger in the theater and was even more so in the days when buildings were largely made of wood and had thatched roofs.

On June 29, 1613, the audience at the Globe Theater was watching a performance of Shakespeare's *Henry VIII*. Richard Burbage, the son of the founder of the theater, was playing the title role. When his character arrived at the home of another major character, the royal arrival was announced by the firing of a cannon. A spark from the cannon landed on the thatched roof, where it began to burn slowly, unnoticed until it was too late.

Within the hour the theater had burned to the ground. Fortunately, everyone in the audience got out safely. One man was wearing pants that caught fire, but he quickly doused the blaze with a bottle of ale. Supporters of the Globe rebuilt it by the following summer.

I cannot bound a pitch above dull woe.
Under love's heavy burden do I sink.

MERCUTIO. And, to sink in it, should you burden love—
Too great oppression for a tender thing.

ROMEO. Is love a tender thing? It is too rough,
Too rude, too boist'rous, and it pricks like thorn.

MERCUTIO. If love be rough with you, be rough with love.
Prick love for pricking, and you beat love down.
Give me a case to put my visage[4] in.
A visor for a visor![5] What care I
What curious eye doth quote deformities?[6]
Here are the beetle brows shall blush for me.

38 **BENVOLIO.** Come, knock and enter; and no sooner in
But every man betake him to his legs.[7]

ROMEO. A torch for me! Let wantons light of heart
Tickle the senseless rushes[8] with their heels;
For I am proverbed with a grandsire phrase,[9]
I'll be a candleholder and look on;
The game was ne'er so fair, and I am done.[10]

MERCUTIO. Tut! Dun's the mouse, the constable's own word![11]
If thou art Dun,[12] we'll draw thee from the mire
Of this sir-reverence love, wherein thou stickest
Up to the ears. Come, we burn daylight, ho!

ROMEO. Nay, that's not so.

MERCUTIO. I mean, sir, in delay
We waste our lights in vain, like lights by day.
Take our good meaning, for our judgment sits
Five times in that ere once in our five wits.[13]

ROMEO. And we mean well in going to this masque,
But 'tis no wit to go.

MERCUTIO. Why, may one ask?

ROMEO. I dreamt a dream tonight.

MERCUTIO. And so did I.

ROMEO. Well, what was yours?

MERCUTIO. That dreamers often lie.

ROMEO. In bed asleep, while they do dream things true.

MERCUTIO. O, then I see Queen Mab[14] hath been with you.
She is the fairies' midwife, and she comes
In shape no bigger than an agate stone
On the forefinger of an alderman,
Drawn with a team of little atomies[15]

4. visage mask.

5. A visor . . . visor! A mask for a mask—which is what my real face is like!

6. quote deformities notice my ugly features.

7. betake . . . legs start dancing.

8. Let . . . rushes Let fun-loving people dance on the floor coverings.

9. proverbed . . . phrase directed by an old saying.

10. The game . . . done No matter how much enjoyment may be had, I won't have any.

11. Dun's . . . word!: Lie low like a mouse—that's what a constable waiting to make an arrest might say.

12. Dun proverbial name for a horse.

13. Take . . . wits Understand my intended meaning. That shows more intelligence than merely following what your senses perceive.

14. Queen Mab the queen of fairyland.

Literary Analysis
Character and Dramatic Foil In what way is Mercutio a foil for the sulky Romeo?

15. atomies creatures.

39 **Reading Check**
What advice about love does Mercutio give Romeo?

38 Literary Analysis

Character and Dramatic Foil

- In his dialogue with Mercutio on pp. 784–785, what reason does Romeo give for not wanting to go to the feast?
  Answer: He is too sad and heavy-hearted to enjoy himself.
- Ask the Literary Analysis question on p. 785: In what way is Mercutio a foil for the sulky Romeo?
  Answer: Mercutio is fun-loving, good-natured, and outgoing. He is a foil for the moody, too-serious Romeo in that he is able to enjoy life and poke fun at himself and others.

39 Reading Check

Answer: Mercutio advises Romeo not to be burdened by love, which is too tender a thing to be weighted down by oppressive thoughts and feelings.

CUSTOMIZE INSTRUCTION FOR UNIVERSAL ACCESS

For Gifted/Talented Students	For Advanced Readers
Point out that Romeo continues to express his pain and sorrow while Mercutio remains determined to draw him out of his state of dejection. Encourage students to discuss which character they identify with more and why. Some students may say that Romeo is being too dramatic and gloomy about his situation, and they identify more with Mercutio. Others may identify with Romeo and say that Mercutio should be more sensitive and sympathetic to his friend.	Have students note the play on words in Shakespeare's use of the word *bound* in lines 20 and 21, first to mean "tied down" and then to mean "leap." Ask them how he uses the word *lie* in line 785 in a similar way. Students will have to read lines 49–53 to see the two ways in which Shakespeare means the word *lie* to be understood.

40 Literary Analysis

Character

- Ask students why Mercutio talks about Queen Mab in his speech on this page. They will need to reread the last few lines on p. 785.
  Possible response: Romeo has said he doesn't want to go to the dance because he had a dream. Mercutio says Romeo has been visited by Queen Mab, who brings dreams to sleeping humans.
- Have students read lines 71–73 and identify what lovers and lawyers dream about after Queen Mab has galloped through their brains.
  Answer: Lovers dream of love and lawyers dream of fees.
- Ask the first Literary Analysis question on p. 786: Which character traits does Mercutio reveal in his Queen Mab speech?
  Answer: Mercutio reveals that he has a fanciful imagination and an excellent command of the language.

41 Literary Analysis

Character and Dramatic Foil

- Ask students to speculate on the different meanings in Romeo's words to Mercutio—"Thou talk'st of nothing."
  Possible answer: Students may suggest the following: Romeo thinks Mercutio is talking nonsense; or, Romeo means that by talking about dreams, which are not real, Mercutio is literally talking about nothing.
- Have students respond to the second Literary Analysis question on p. 786: How do lines 95–96 emphasize the contrast between Romeo and Mercutio?
  Answer: Mercutio likes to indulge his sense of poetry and hear the sound of his own voice. Romeo would rather they proceed with whatever they are going to do.

Over men's noses as they lie asleep;
Her wagon spokes made of long spinners'[16] legs,
The cover, of the wings of grasshoppers;
Her traces, of the smallest spider web;
Her collars, of the moonshine's wat'ry beams;
Her whip, of cricket's bone; the lash, of film;[17]
Her wagoner, a small gray-coated gnat,
Not half so big as a round little worm
Pricked from the lazy finger of a maid;
Her chariot is an empty hazelnut,
Made by the joiner squirrel or old grub,[18]
Time out o' mind the fairies' coachmakers.
And in this state she gallops night by night
Through lovers' brains, and then they dream of love;
On courtiers' knees, that dream on curtsies straight;
O'er lawyers' fingers, who straight dream on fees;
O'er ladies' lips, who straight on kisses dream,
Which oft the angry Mab with blisters plagues,
(40) Because their breath with sweetmeats[19] tainted are.
Sometimes she gallops o'er a courtier's nose,
And then dreams he of smelling out a suit;[20]
And sometime comes she with a tithe pig's[21] tail
Tickling a parson's nose as 'a lies asleep,
Then he dreams of another benefice.[22]
Sometime she driveth o'er a soldier's neck,
And then dream he of cutting foreign throats,
Of breaches, ambuscadoes,[23] Spanish blades,
Of healths[24] five fathom deep; and then anon
Drums in his ear, at which he starts and wakes,
And being thus frighted, swears a prayer or two
And sleeps again. This is that very Mab
That plats[25] the manes of horses in the night
And bakes the elflocks[26] in foul sluttish hairs,
Which once untangled much misfortune bodes.
This is the hag, when maids lie on their backs,
That presses them and learns them first to bear,
Making them women of good carriage.[27]
This is she—

(41) **ROMEO.** Peace, peace, Mercutio, peace!
Thou talk'st of nothing.

MERCUTIO. True, I talk of dreams;
Which are the children of an idle brain,
Begot of nothing but vain fantasy;
Which is as thin of substance as the air,
And more inconstant than the wind, who woos
Even now the frozen bosom of the North
And, being angered, puffs away from thence,
Turning his side to the dew-dropping South.

16. spinners spiders.

17. film spider's thread.

18. old grub an insect that bores holes in nuts.

Literary Analysis
Character Which character traits does Mercutio reveal in his Queen Mab speech?

19. sweetmeats candy.

20. smelling . . . suit finding someone who has a petition (suit) for the king and who will pay the courtier to gain the king's favor for the petition.

21. tithe pig a pig donated to a parson.

22. benefice a church appointment that included a guaranteed income.

23. ambuscadoes ambushes.

24. healths toasts ("To your health!").

25. plats tangles.

26. elflocks tangled hair.

27. carriage posture.

Literary Analysis
Character and Dramatic Foil How do lines 95–96 emphasize the contrast between Romeo and Mercutio?

ENRICHMENT: Social Studies Connection

Astrology and the Elizabethans

At the end of Scene iv, Romeo says that he is fearful that his life will be cut short as determined by the stars. Many Elizabethans believed that the positions of the moon, sun, and planets were responsible for humans' general dispositions. For example, they believed that the Zodiac sign under which a person was born and the position of the planets at that time determined the person's general character.

Elizabethans also believed that the stars determine a person's fate. For example, it was the stars that determined if a person would live a long and happy life or a short life filled with unhappiness. It is this belief that causes Romeo to be fearful that he will die young.

BENVOLIO. This wind you talk of blows us from ourselves.
Supper is done, and we shall come too late.

42 **ROMEO.** I fear, too early; for my mind misgives
Some consequence yet hanging in the stars
Shall bitterly begin his fearful date
With this night's revels and expire the term
Of a despisèd life, closed in my breast,
By some vile forfeit of untimely death.[28]
But he that hath the steerage of my course
Direct my sail! On, lusty gentlemen!

BENVOLIO. Strike, drum.
[They march about the stage, and retire to one side.]

Scene v. *A hall in* CAPULET'S *house.*

[SERVINGMEN *come forth with napkins.*]

43 **FIRST SERVINGMAN.** Where's Potpan, that he helps not to take away? He shift a trencher![1] He scrape a trencher!

SECOND SERVINGMAN. When good manners shall lie all in one or two men's hands, and they unwashed too, 'tis a foul thing.

FIRST SERVINGMAN. Away with the join-stools, remove the court cupboard, look to the plate. Good thou, save me a piece of marchpane,[2] and, as thou loves me, let the porter let in Susan Grindstone and Nell. Anthony, and Potpan!

SECOND SERVINGMAN. Ay, boy, ready.

FIRST SERVINGMAN. You are looked for and called for, asked for and sought for, in the great chamber.

THIRD SERVINGMAN. We cannot be here and there too. Cheerly, boys! Be brisk awhile, and the longer liver take all. *[Exit.]*

[*Enter* CAPULET, *his* WIFE, JULIET, TYBALT, NURSE, *and all the* GUESTS *and* GENTLEWOMEN *to the* MASKERS.]

CAPULET. Welcome, gentlemen! Ladies that have their toes
Unplagued with corns will walk a bout[3] with you.
Ah, my mistresses, which of you all
Will now deny to dance? She that makes dainty,[4]
She I'll swear hath corns. Am I come near ye now?
Welcome, gentlemen! I have seen the day
That I have worn a visor and could tell
A whispering tale in a fair lady's ear,
Such as would please. 'Tis gone, 'tis gone, 'tis gone.
You are welcome, gentlemen! Come, musicians, play.
[Music plays, and they dance.]
A hall,[5] a hall! Give room! And foot it, girls.

28. my mind . . . death My mind is fearful that some future event, fated by the stars, shall start to run its course tonight and cut my life short.

Reading Strategy
Using Text Aids Using note 28 as a text aid, restate Romeo's words in lines 109–111 in modern English.

1. trencher wooden platter.

2. marchpane marzipan, a confection made of sugar and almonds.

Literary Analysis
Character How do flat characters like the servingmen add to the play?

3. walk a bout dance a turn.

4. makes dainty hesitates, acts shy.

5. A hall clear the floor, make room for dancing.

44 **✓ Reading Check**
What does Romeo fear might happen in the near future?

42 Reading Strategy
Using Text Aids

- Ask students what Benvolio means in line 105.
  Answer: Benvolio worries that everyone has finished eating by now and that they will all arrive late.
- Ask the Reading Strategy question on p. 787: Using note 28 as a text aid, restate Romeo's words in lines 106–111 in modern English.
  Possible response: "I'm afraid that something I can't control will start operating tonight, and the result will be my early death."

43 Literary Analysis
Character

- Ask students what is meant to be humorous about the words of the second servingman in lines 7–8.
  Possible response: Griping about Potpan, the servingman says it's a foul thing when everything is left to those whose hands are dirty. The play on words is "'tis a foul thing," meaning both "It's too bad" and that dirty hands are foul.
- Ask students to respond to the Literary Analysis question on p. 787: How do flat characters like the servingmen add to the play?
  Answer: They add humor and help set up new scenes.

44 ✓ Reading Check

Answer: Romeo fears he will die young.

CUSTOMIZE INSTRUCTION FOR UNIVERSAL ACCESS

For Special Needs Students	For Gifted/Talented Students	For Advanced Readers
Students may enjoy illustrating some of the images in the Queen Mab speech on pp. 785–786. Based on the descriptions, what do they think Queen Mab looks like—"no bigger than an agate stone . . ." and pulled by a team of small creatures over men's noses as they lie asleep, and so forth. Display students' work in the classroom.	Mercutio's Queen Mab speech is one of the finest and most famous passages of poetry in Shakespeare's early works. Have students practice the speech and perform it for the class. Encourage them to bring out the musical rhythms as well as the vivid imagery of Shakespeare's lines.	Point out to students that even though Romeo has misgivings about going to the feast, at the end of his speech on p. 787, he says, "But he that hath the steerage of my course/Direct my sail! On, lusty gentlemen!" Have students speculate on why he decides to go to the feast anyway, given his fears.

45 ▶Critical Viewing

Possible response: Some students may say that Romeo is romantic; others may say that Romeo is compulsive and naïve.

46 Critical Thinking

Infer

- Ask students to identify Romeo's meaning in lines 51–52.
  Answer: Romeo's rhetorical questions suggest that only now is he experiencing true love and true beauty.
- Ask students if they think Romeo is describing Rosaline or someone else in these lines.
  Answer: Romeo could not be describing Rosaline since he knows who she is. Therefore, he must be referring to someone else, quite probably Juliet.

47 Reading Strategy

Using Text Aids

- Have students recall Tybalt's first appearance in the play (p. 773) and compare it with his statement here. Are the two scenes similar or different?
  Answer: Tybalt here, as earlier, is instantly ready to fight and kill anyone he sees as a threat to the Capulets. He is hotheaded and dangerous.
- Ask students what Tybalt means by his first line of dialogue.
  Answer: He means that he can tell who Romeo is by his voice. Since Romeo and his friends have put on masks, they cannot be recognized by sight.
- Ask the Reading Strategy question on p. 788: What does Tybalt mean by saying that Romeo has come with an "antic face,/to fleer and scorn at our solemnity"?
  Answer: He means that Romeo has come wearing a mask to mock the Capulets in their important celebration.

More light, you knaves, and turn the tables up,
And quench the fire; the room is grown too hot.
Ah, sirrah, this unlooked-for sport comes well.
Nay, sit; nay, sit, good cousin Capulet;
For you and I are past our dancing days.
How long is't now since last yourself and I
Were in a mask?

SECOND CAPULET. By'r Lady, thirty years.

CAPULET. What, man? 'Tis not so much, 'tis not so much;
'Tis since the nuptial of Lucentio,
Come Pentecost as quickly as it will,
Some five-and-twenty years, and then we masked.

SECOND CAPULET. 'Tis more, 'tis more. His son is elder, sir;
His son is thirty.

CAPULET. Will you tell me that?
His son was but a ward[6] two years ago.

ROMEO. [*To a* SERVINGMAN] What lady's that which doth enrich the hand
Of yonder knight?

SERVINGMAN. I know not, sir.

ROMEO. O, she doth teach the torches to burn bright!
It seems she hangs upon the cheek of night
As a rich jewel in an Ethiop's ear—
Beauty too rich for use, for earth too dear!
So shows a snowy dove trooping with crows
As yonder lady o'er her fellows shows.
The measure done, I'll watch her place of stand
And, touching hers, make blessèd my rude hand.
46 Did my heart love till now? Forswear[7] it, sight!
For I ne'er saw true beauty till this night.

TYBALT. This, by his voice, should be a Montague.
Fetch me my rapier, boy. What! Dares the slave
47 Come hither, covered with an antic face,[8]
To fleer[9] and scorn at our solemnity?
Now, by the stock and honor of my kin,
To strike him dead I hold it not a sin.

CAPULET. Why, how now, kinsman? Wherefore storm you so?

TYBALT. Uncle, this is a Montague, our foe,
A villain, that is hither come in spite
To scorn at our solemnity this night.

CAPULET. Young Romeo is it?

TYBALT. 'Tis he, that villain Romeo.

45 ▲ **Critical Viewing** What can you tell about Romeo's personality from the fact that he has taken off his mask? **[Draw Conclusions]**

6. **ward** minor.

7. **Forswear** deny.

8. **antic face** strange, fantastic mask.

9. **fleer** mock.

Reading Strategy
Using Text Aids What does Tybalt mean by saying that Romeo has come to the party with an "antic face, / To fleer and scorn at our solemnity"?

ENRICHMENT: Performing Arts Connection

Music and Dance During the Renaissance

The Renaissance saw a flowering of music and dance. Shakespeare's plays often contained both songs and dances.

In Italy, a new form of composition, the *madrigal*, appeared. Composers wrote lyrics in their own language rather than in Latin, or set poetry of the time to music. Madrigals, written by composers such as John Dowland and William Byrd, were popular in England in Shakespeare's time.

During the Renaissance, especially in Italy, it was the custom for the nobility of one city to compete with the nobles of another in staging elaborate musical spectacles. Professional dancing masters were hired to create original *balli* or *balletti*. Leading composers wrote the music and talented artists, including Leonardo da Vinci, designed costumes.

CAPULET. Content thee, gentle coz,[10] let him alone.
'A bears him like a portly gentleman,[11]
And, to say truth, Verona brags of him
To be a virtuous and well-governed youth.
I would not for the wealth of all this town
Here in my house do him disparagement.[12]
Therefore be patient; take no note of him.
It is my will, the which if thou respect,
Show a fair presence and put off these frowns,
An ill-beseeming semblance[13] for a feast.

TYBALT. It fits when such a villain is a guest.
I'll not endure him.

CAPULET. He shall be endured.
What, goodman[14] boy! I say he shall. Go to![15]
Am I the master here, or you? Go to!
You'll not endure him, God shall mend my soul![16]
You'll make a mutiny among my guests!
You will set cock-a-hoop.[17] You'll be the man!

TYBALT. Why, uncle, 'tis a shame.

CAPULET. Go to, go to!
You are a saucy boy. Is't so, indeed?
This trick may chance to scathe you.[18] I know what.
You must contrary me! Marry, 'tis time–
Well said, my hearts!—You are a princox[19]—go!
Be quiet, or—more light, more light!—For shame!
I'll make you quiet. What!—Cheerly, my hearts!

TYBALT. Patience perforce with willful choler meeting[20]
Makes my flesh tremble in their different greeting.
I will withdraw; but this intrusion shall,
Now seeming sweet, convert to bitt'rest gall. *[Exit.]*

ROMEO. If I profane with my unworthiest hand
This holy shrine,[21] the gentle sin is this:
My lips, two blushing pilgrims, ready stand
To smooth that rough touch with a tender kiss.

JULIET. Good pilgrim, you do wrong your hand too much,
Which mannerly devotion shows in this;
(48) For saints have hands that pilgrims' hands do touch
(49) And palm to palm is holy palmers'[22] kiss.

ROMEO. Have not saints lips, and holy palmers too?

JULIET. Ay, pilgrim, lips that they must use in prayer.

ROMEO. O, then, dear saint, let lips do what hands do!
They pray; grant thou, lest faith turn to despair.

JULIET. Saints do not move,[23] though grant for prayers' sake.

10. **coz** Here coz is used as a term of address for a relative.

11. **'A . . . gentleman** He behaves like a dignified gentleman.

12. **disparagement** insult.

13. **ill-beseeming semblance** inappropriate appearance.

14. **goodman** term of address for someone below the rank of gentleman.

15. **Go to!** expression of angry impatience.

16. **God . . . soul!** expression of impatience, equivalent to, "God save me!"

17. **You will set cock-a-hoop** You want to swagger like a barnyard rooster.

18. **This . . . you** This trait of yours may turn to hurt you.

19. **princox** rude youngster; wise guy.

20. **Patience . . . meeting** enforced self-control mixing with strong anger.

Literary Analysis
Character Which character traits do Romeo and Juliet reveal in their words to each other?

21. **shrine** Juliet's hand.

22. **palmers** pilgrims who at one time carried palm branches from the Holy Land.

23. **move** initiate involvement in earthly affairs.

(50) **✔Reading Check**
How does Capulet respond when Tybalt says he will not tolerate Romeo's presence at the party?

(48) Literary Analysis

Character

- Ask students why Romeo apologizes in lines 92–93.
  Answer: He has taken Juliet's hand in his without asking her permission.
- Ask students what Romeo means when he asks Juliet if saints have lips. What is Juliet's answer?
  Answer: Romeo suggests that saints, if they have lips, can kiss with lips rather than touch hands. Juliet deftly responds that saints' lips are used for prayer.
- Ask the Literary Analysis question on p. 789: Which character traits do Romeo and Juliet reveal in their words to each other?
  Answer: Romeo and Juliet are both clever and playful; they also show a mixture of modesty and frankness.

(49) Background

Sonnet

Point out that lines 92–105 form a Shakespearean sonnet. Explain that during the 1590s, England experienced a sonnet craze. Almost anyone with literary aspirations experimented with this form and Shakespeare, acknowledged master of the form, demonstrated his talent by working sonnets into *Romeo and Juliet*.

The original form of the sonnet, known as the Italian or Petrarchan sonnet, was created by the Italian poet Petrarch in the fourteenth century, and consists of two stanzas: an octave with the rhyme scheme *abba abba* and a sestet with the rhyme scheme *cdecde* or *cdcdcd*. Shakespeare adapted this form for rhyme-poor English. His variant, known as the English or Shakespearean sonnet, consists of three quatrains and a terminal couplet, and has the rhyme scheme *abba cdcd efef gg*.

(50) ✔Reading Check

Answer: Capulet rebukes Tybalt's contrariness and tells him to leave Romeo alone.

CUSTOMIZE INSTRUCTION FOR UNIVERSAL ACCESS

For Special Needs Students	For Less Proficient Readers
Work with students to interpret Tybalt's words in lines 89–91. Help them to see that Tybalt fears Romeo's intrusion will lead to trouble, such as a brawl or Tybalt's revenge on Romeo. Ask students why these two responses would be bad for everyone involved, not just those who might be injured in a brawl. If they need a hint, recall with them the Prince's threat on p. 744.	Have students find the metaphor in line 94. Ask them which two things are compared in this metaphor. (Romeo compares his lips with two blushing pilgrims.) Then, have students identify the metaphor the two lovers use through line 101. Which two things are being compared and why are they objects of comparison? (Lips and hands, or palms, are being compared. They are compared because they can both be used to show affection, or to kiss.)

51 ▶ **Critical Viewing**

Answer: The photograph suggests that Romeo and Juliet are drawn to each other but are also very shy.

52 Reading Strategy

Using Text Aids

- Ask students why the Nurse's entrance and speech is so disturbing to Romeo.
  Answer: When the Nurse says Juliet's mother craves a word with her, Romeo suddenly realizes that she must be the lady of the house where the masque is being held, which would make Juliet a Capulet— enemies of his family.
- Ask the Reading Strategy question on p. 790: What do you learn from the text aid that helps you understand Romeo's conflict?
  Answer: Romeo has fallen in love with Juliet without knowing her family background. Now he realizes that the Capulets might kill him for appearing in their home.

53 Literary Analysis

Character

- Ask students what Juliet wants to know about Romeo after he leaves the masque.
  Answer: Juliet asks the Nurse who Romeo is and if he is married.
- After students have read Juliet's dialogue in lines 137–140, ask them in what ways are Juliet's thoughts shown to be similar to Romeo's?
  Answer: Juliet is appalled that she has fallen in love with the enemy of her family; she too makes an ominous reference to death.

ROMEO. Then move not while my prayer's effect I take.
Thus from my lips, by thine my sin is purged. *[Kisses her.]*

JULIET. Then have my lips the sin that they have took.

ROMEO. Sin from my lips? O trespass sweetly urged![24]
Give me my sin again. *[Kisses her.]*

JULIET. You kiss by th' book.[25]

52

NURSE. Madam, your mother craves a word with you.

ROMEO. What is her mother?

NURSE. Marry, bachelor,
Her mother is the lady of the house,
And a good lady, and a wise and virtuous.
I nursed her daughter that you talked withal.
I tell you, he that can lay hold of her
Shall have the chinks.[26]

ROMEO. Is she a Capulet?
O dear account! My life is my foe's debt.[27]

BENVOLIO. Away, be gone; the sport is at the best.

ROMEO. Ay, so I fear; the more is my unrest.

CAPULET. Nay, gentlemen, prepare not to be gone;
We have a trifling foolish banquet towards.[28]
Is it e'en so?[29] Why then, I thank you all.
I thank you, honest gentlemen. Good night.
More torches here! Come on then; let's to bed.
Ah, sirrah, by my fay,[30] it waxes late;
I'll to my rest. *[Exit all but* JULIET *and* NURSE.*]*

51 ▲ **Critical Viewing** What does this picture suggest about Romeo and Juliet's feelings for each other? **[Infer]**

24. O . . . urged! Romeo is saying, in substance, that he is happy. Juliet calls his kiss a sin, for now he can take it back—by another kiss.

25. by th' book as if you were following a manual of courtly love.

26. chinks cash.

27. My life . . . debt Since Juliet is a Capulet, Romeo's life is at the mercy of the enemies of his family.

Reading Strategy
Using Text Aids What do you learn from the text aid that helps you understand Romeo's conflict?

28. towards being prepared.

29. Is . . . so? Is it the case that you really must leave?

30. fay faith.

JULIET. Come hither, nurse. What is yond gentleman?

NURSE. The son and heir of old Tiberio.

JULIET. What's he that now is going out of door?

NURSE. Marry, that, I think, be young Petruchio.

JULIET. What's he that follows here, that would not dance?

NURSE. I know not.

JULIET. Go ask his name—If he is married,
My grave is like to be my wedding bed.

NURSE. His name is Romeo, and a Montague,
The only son of your great enemy.

JULIET. My only love, sprung from my only hate!
53 Too early seen unknown, and known too late!
Prodigious[31] birth of love it is to me
That I must love a loathèd enemy.

NURSE. What's this? What's this?

JULIET. A rhyme I learnt even now.
Of one I danced withal. [*One calls within,* "Juliet."]

NURSE. Anon, anon!
Come, let's away; the strangers all are gone. [*Exit all.*]

31. **Prodigious** monstrous; foretelling misfortune.

Review and Assess

Thinking About Act I

1. **Respond:** If you were Romeo or Juliet, would you pursue a relationship? Explain.
2. **(a) Recall:** Based on Act I, what facts do you know about Romeo's and Juliet's lives? **(b) Compare and Contrast:** How are these characters' personalities alike and different?
3. **(a) Recall:** What information about the two households is presented in the Prologue? **(b) Connect:** How does Juliet's comment in Act I, Scene v, lines 137–138, echo the Prologue?
4. **Analyze:** How do the comments of Montague and Benvolio in Act I help you understand the character of Romeo?
5. **(a) Analyze:** What threats to Romeo and Juliet's love already exist in Act I? **(b) Support:** How does Shakespeare use these threats to generate suspense in the first act?
6. **Evaluate:** Based on Romeo's behavior in Act I, do you think Shakespeare accurately portrays a teenager in love? Explain.

ASSESSMENT PRACTICE: Literary Response

Defending Interpretations **(For more practice, see Test Preparation Workbook, p. 47.)**

Many tests require students to defend their interpretation of a written passage. Use the following sample test item:

My child is yet a stranger in the world,
She hath not seen the change of fourteen years;
Let two more summers wither in their pride
Ere we may think her ripe to be a bride...
Earth hath swallowed all my hopes but she;
She is the hopeful lady of my earth
But woo her, gentle Paris, get her heart;
My will to her consent is but a part.
An she agree, within her scope of choice
Lies my consent and fair according voice...

In this passage, how would you interpret Capulet's character?

Possible answers: Capulet is a loving and protective father who will consider Juliet's wishes as well as her bests interest in a marriage.

ASSESS

Answers for p. 791

Review and Assess

1. Some students may say they would follow their hearts and continue with the relationship. Others may say that they would avoid a relationship that might conflict with family loyalty.
2. **(a)** Both Romeo and Juliet are privileged members of the society of their time. **(b)** Romeo is moody, impulsive, and romantic. Juliet, by contrast, is a dutiful young girl who, before meeting Romeo, does not seem to have given much thought to love. When they meet, they are so in tune with each other that their words create a sonnet.
3. **(a)** Both families are of high social rank in Verona, Italy. An ancient grudge between them has recently broken out again, and will engulf the young son and daughter of the respective families. **(b)** Juliet realizes that before she knew what she was doing, she fell in love with someone she should hate.
4. Both the practical Benvolio and the joking, carefree Mercutio create a sharp contrast to their extravagantly moody and romantic friend Romeo.
5. **(a)** The families are feuding, Tybalt has sworn to retaliate against Romeo for attending the party, and Juliet's parents are considering marrying her to Paris. **(b)** Students may say that these layers of complication create a suspenseful dilemma. The audience is hooked by the young lovers' predicament, despite knowing the final outcome.
6. Students may say that Romeo's single-minded passion for Rosaline, which he very quickly drops in his single-minded passion for Juliet, represents the deep feelings teenagers have, but also shows teens' ability to change the objects of their devotions quickly.

Review and Assess

1. Gregory and Sampson embody antagonism. As well as providing some off-color comic relief, they show the enmity between the two houses.
2. **Character:** Mercutio; **Personality Traits:** carefree, outgoing, joking, playful, talkative; **Character Type:** Round; **Character:** Benvolio: **Personality Traits:** cautious, loyal, diplomatic, practical, talkative: **Character Type:** Round
3. Romeo is a round character because he exhibits many personality traits; he is moody, romantic, impulsive, and pessimistic.
4. **Romeo:** impulsive, pessimistic, moody, romantic; **Benvolio:** cautious, optimistic, emotionally balanced, cynical
5. Mercutio's carefree antics serve to underscore Romeo's basically bleak outlook.
6. Neither the Nurse nor Lady Capulet is a meaningful foil to Juliet. Students may cite Rosaline, but she never appears in the play and no reliable details are known about her.
7. **(a)** Students should substitute definitions from the text aids into Capulet's speech.
   (b) Sample response: "Leave him alone. Who's in charge here, me or you? If you don't leave him alone, my guests will riot. But you want to act macho. Someday that's going to hurt you."
8. Juliet compares touching palms, or holding hands, with kissing.
9. Students may cite several areas of the world where religion, culture, race, or nationalism could be obstacles to a couple's love: Northern Ireland, Eastern Europe, the Middle East, among many others.

Review and Assess

Literary Analysis

Character

1. Which single personality trait makes Gregory and Sampson **flat characters**?
2. Which personality traits make Mercutio and Benvolio **round characters**? Use a chart like the one shown to list their character traits.

Character	Personality Traits	Character Type

3. Is Romeo a round or flat character? Explain.

Connecting Literary Elements

4. How is Benvolio a **dramatic foil** for Romeo? Using a chart like the one shown, record their contrasting personality traits.

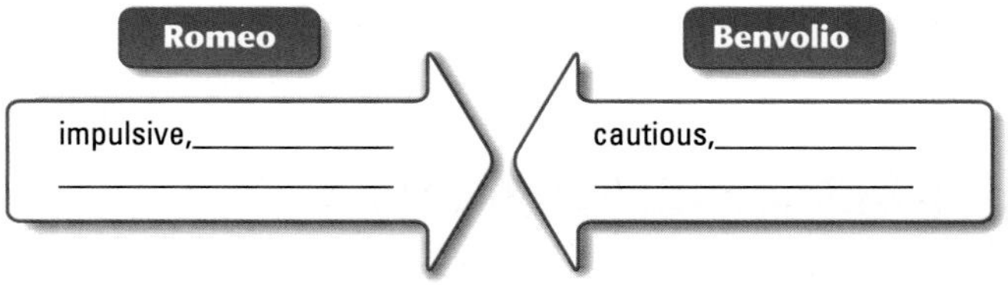

5. How is Mercutio a dramatic foil for Romeo?
6. Does Juliet have a foil? Explain.

Reading Strategy

Using Text Aids

7. (a) Use the **text aids** to restate Capulet's scolding of Tybalt in Act I, Scene v, lines 77–87. (b) Express his meaning in your own words.
8. Using text aids, explain the play on words in Juliet's speech in Act I, Scene v, lines 96–99.

Extend Understanding

9. **Social Studies Connection:** Identify a city or region in the world today where a couple from rival groups might have great difficulty establishing a relationship. Explain your choices.

Quick Review

Characters are the people or animals who take part in a literary work.
A **round character** has many personality traits.
A **flat character** embodies only a single trait.

A **dramatic foil** is a character who highlights the traits of another character through contrast.

Using text aids—footnotes or numbered explanations of word meaning—helps you to understand the language in a literary work.

Take It to the Net

www.phschool.com

Take the interactive self-test online to check your understanding of Act I.

TEACHING RESOURCES

The following resources can be used to enrich or extend the instruction for p. 792–793.

Vocabulary

- **Selection Support:** Build Vocabulary, p. 181
- **Vocabulary and Spelling Practice Book** (Use this booklet for skills enrichment.)

Grammar

- **Selection Support:** Build Grammar Skills, p 182
- **Writing and Grammar,** Gold Level, p. 559
- **Daily Language Practice Transparencies**

Writing

- **Writing and Grammar iText CD-ROM**

BLOCK SCHEDULING: Resources marked with this symbol provide varied instruction during 90-minute blocks.

Integrate Language Skills

1 Vocabulary Development Lesson

Word Analysis: Latin Prefix *trans-*

The Latin prefix *trans-* means "through" or "across," as in *transgression*, "the act of going across the boundary of appropriate behavior." Using the meaning of *trans-*, write a definition for each word below.

1. transport **2.** translate **3.** transform

Spelling Strategy

If a word ends in two consonants, do not double the final consonant when adding a suffix: *augment* + *-ing* = *augmenting*. Add *-ful*, *-al*, or *-or* to each word below to form three correct words.

1. respect **2.** ornament **3.** instruct

Concept Development: Analogies

In your notebook, write the word that best completes each analogy, or comparison.

1. thoughtful : kind :: pernicious : __?__
   (a) useful, (b) helpful, (c) harmful
2. decreasing : less :: augmenting : __?__
   (a) fewer, (b) more, (c) several
3. problem : solution :: grievance : __?__
   (a) satisfaction, (b) complaint, (c) sadness
4. habitation : home :: transgression : __?__
   (a) blessing, (b) crime, (c) illness
5. believers : agree :: heretics : __?__
   (a) heresy, (b) dissent, (c) outcasts

2 Grammar Lesson

Pronoun Case in Elliptical Clauses

In an **elliptical clause,** one or more words are unstated because they are understood. To determine the correct case of a pronoun in an elliptical clause, determine the placement of the unstated words. If the unstated words come after the pronoun, use a **nominative case pronoun.** If the unstated words come before the pronoun, use an **objective case pronoun.** In these examples, the unstated word or words are shown in brackets.

Nominative:	Juliet is younger than *he* [is].
Objective:	They gave Juliet the same warning as [they gave] *him*.

Practice Choose the correct pronoun to complete each item. State the word or phrase missing from the elliptical clause.

1. Romeo was as love-struck as (she, her).
2. He listens to him more than to (she, her).
3. No one else felt as upset as (he, him).
4. Capulet was friendlier than (he, him).
5. Nurse felt closer to Juliet than to (he, him).

Writing Application Write two sentences about Act I, using elliptical clauses in each.

WG *Prentice Hall Writing and Grammar Connection: Chapter 24, Section 2*

3 Extension Activities

Writing As Romeo or Juliet, write a letter requesting help with the problem of falling in love with the wrong person. In a **letter to an advice columnist,** explain your dilemma. Then, write the columnist's response.

Listening and Speaking Select a scene from Act I to perform with classmates. Practice reading your lines aloud and perform your **oral reading** for the class. Then, discuss how delivery of the lines affects the mood of the scene. **[Group Activity]**

ASSESSMENT RESOURCES

The following resources can be used to assess students' knowledge and skills.

Selection Assessment

- **Formal Assessment,** Selection Test, pp. 164–166
- **Open Book Test,** pp. 136–138
- **Got It! Assessment Videotapes,** Tape 4
- **Test Bank Software**

PRENTICE HALL ASSESSMENT SYSTEM

- **Workbook**
- **Skill Book**
- **Transparencies**
- **CD-ROM**

Take It to the Net

Visit www.phschool.com for self-tests and additional questions on *Romeo and Juliet.*

EXTEND

Answers for p. 793

1 Vocabulary Development

Word Analysis

1. transport: to carry something from one place to another
2. translate: to move from one place or condition to another
3. transform: to change from one form to another.

Spelling Strategy

1. respectful **2.** ornamental **3.** instructor

Concept Development: Analogies

1. c **2.** b **3.** a **4.** b **5.** b

2 Grammar

1. she (was) **2.** her (he listens) **3.** he (did) **4.** he (was) **5.** (she felt) him

Writing Application

Sample Sentences:

Romeo thought he would never love anyone as much as her.

Juliet felt as doomed by her love as he.

3 Extension Activities

Listening and Speaking

- Divide the class into groups with the appropriate numbers of students for a chosen scene.
- After each scene, discuss: Did the actors capture the right mood? Did they deliver their lines smoothly and with feeling? What did the actors and the audience learn about Shakespeare's language and characters as a result of the performance?

CUSTOMIZE INSTRUCTION
For Universal Access

To address different learning styles, use the activities suggested in the **Extension Activities** booklet, p. 46.

- For Verbal/Linguistic and Logical/Mathematical Learners, use Activity 5.
- For Musical/Rhythmic and Verbal/Linguistic Learners, use Activity 7.

The Tragedy of Romeo and Juliet, Act II

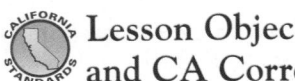

Lesson Objectives and CA Correlations

1. **To analyze and respond to literary elements**
   - Literary Analysis: Blank Verse **R 3.1, 3.7**
   - Connecting Literary Elements: Character Rank **R 3.3, 3.4**
2. **To read, comprehend, analyze, and critique drama**
   - Reading Strategy: Reading Blank Verse **R 3.1, 3.7**
   - Reading Check questions
   - Review and Assess questions
   - Assessment Practice (ATE)
3. **To develop word analysis skills, fluency, and systematic vocabulary**
   - Vocabulary Development Lesson: Latin Prefix: *inter-* **R 1.1**
4. **To understand and apply written and oral language conventions**
   - Spelling Strategy
   - Grammar Lesson: Possessive Case of Personal Pronouns **LC 1.2**
5. **To understand and apply appropriate writing and research strategies**
   - Writing Lesson: Persuasive Letter (after Act V) **W 2.4**
   - Extension Activity: Adaptation **W 1.1**
6. **To understand and apply listening and speaking strategies**
   - Extension Activity: Role Play **LS 1.11**

STEP-BY-STEP TEACHING GUIDE	PACING GUIDE
PRETEACH	
Motivate Students and Provide Background	
Read and discuss the Review and Anticipate information (SE/ATE p. 795) [A]	10 min.
Introduce the Concepts	
Introduce the Literary Analysis and Reading Strategy (SE/ATE p. 794) [A]	15 min.
Pronounce the vocabulary words and read their definitions (SE p. 794)	10 min.
TEACH	
Monitor Comprehension	
Informally monitor comprehension by circulating while students read independently or in groups [A]	40 min.
Monitor students' comprehension with the Reading Check notes (SE/ATE pp. 797, 799, 801, 803, 805, 807, 809, 811, 813)	as students read
Develop vocabulary with Vocabulary notes (SE pp. 799, 801, 803–806, 811; ATE p. 804)	as students read
Develop Understanding	
Develop students' understanding of blank verse with the Literary Analysis annotations (SE/ATE pp. 796–799, 801–802, 804, 806, 808, 810–811, 813–814) [A]	10 min.
Develop students' ability to read blank verse with the Reading Strategy annotations (SE pp. 796, 800, 802, 810, 812, 815; ATE pp. 796–800, 802, 805, 810, 812, 814)	10 min.
ASSESS	
Assess Mastery	
Assess students' mastery of the Reading Strategy and Literary Analysis by having them answer the Review and Assess questions (SE/ATE p. 816)	20 min.
Use one or more of the print and media Assessment Resources (ATE p. 817) [A]	up to 50 min.
EXTEND	
Apply Understanding	
Have students complete the Vocabulary Development Lesson and the Grammar Lesson (SE p. 817) [A]	20 min.
Apply students' knowledge of persuasive appeals using the Writing Lesson (SE p. 877) [A]	45 min.
Apply students' understanding of the selection using one or more of the Extension Activities (SE p. 817)	20–90 min.

[A] **ACCELERATED INSTRUCTION:** Use the strategies and activities identified with an [A].

UNIVERSAL ACCESS
● = Below-Level Students
▲ = On-Level Students
■ = Above-Level Students

Time and Resource Manager

Reading Level: Challenging
Average Number of Instructional Days: 4

RESOURCES		
PRINT	**TRANSPARENCIES**	**TECHNOLOGY**
• **Beyond Literature,** Media Connection: Film Adaptations, p. 47 ▲ ■		• **Interest Grabber Video,** Tape 4 ● ▲ ■
• **Selection Support Workbook:** ● ▲ ■ Literary Analysis, p. 188 Reading Strategy, p. 187 Build Vocabulary, p. 185	• **Literary Analysis and Reading Transparencies,** pp. 93 and 94 ● ▲ ■	
• **Adapted Reader's Companion** ● • **Reader's Companion** ●		• **Listening to Literature** ● ▲ ■ Audiocassettes, Side 24 Audio CDs, CD 16
• **English Learner's Companion** ● ▲ • **Literatura en español** ● ▲ • **Literary Analysis for Enrichment** ■		
• **Formal Assessment:** Selection Test, pp.167–169 ● ▲ ■ • **Open Book Test,** pp. 139–141 ● ▲ ■ • PRENTICE HALL ASSESSMENT SYSTEM ● ▲ ■	• PRENTICE HALL ASSESSMENT SYSTEM ● ▲ ■ Skills Practice Answers and Explanations on Transparencies	• **Test Bank Software** ● ▲ ■ • **Got It! Assessment Videotapes**, Tape 4 ● ▲
• **Selection Support Workbook:** ● ▲ ■ Build Grammar Skills, p. 186 • **Writing and Grammar,** Gold Level ● ▲ ■ • **Extension Activities,** p. 46 ● ▲ ■	• **Daily Language Practice Transparencies** ● ▲	• **Writing and Grammar iText CD-ROM** ● ▲ ■ *Take It to the Net* www.phschool.com

BLOCK SCHEDULING: Use one 90-minute class period to preteach the selection and have students read it. Use a second 90-minute class period to assess students' mastery of skills and have them complete one of the Extension Activities.

PRETEACH

Step-by-Step Teaching Guide for p. 794

❶ Literary Analysis

Blank Verse

- Tell students that *blank verse* is unrhymed iambic pentameter. Each line contains five metrical feet.
- Explain to students that an *iamb* is a metrical foot with two syllables, the first unstressed and the second stressed. The words *create* and *amaze* are iambic, for example.
- Use the Blank Verse transparency in **Literary Analysis and Reading Transparencies,** p. 94, to help students learn how to scan and mark a line of blank verse.
- Use the instruction for Connecting Literary Elements to connect the element of *character rank* with the kind of language a character uses.

❷ Reading Strategy

Reading Blank Verse

- Remind students that when they read a play, they must always read for the sense of a line, speech, or scene. The end of a line does not always represent the end of a thought pattern.
- Use the Reading Blank Verse transparency in **Literary Analysis and Reading Transparencies**, p. 93, to show students how to interpret lines of blank verse in terms of meaning.

Vocabulary Development

- Pronounce each vocabulary word for students, and read the definitions as a class. Have students identify any words with which they are already familiar.

Prepare to Read

The Tragedy of Romeo and Juliet, Act II

❶ Literary Analysis

Blank Verse

Blank verse is unrhymed poetry written in iambic pentameter, or lines of five stressed beats in which every second syllable is stressed. For example, when Romeo sees Juliet appear at her window, he exclaims,

> Bŭt sóft! Whăt líght thrŏugh yóndĕr wíndŏw bréaks?
> Ĭt ís thĕ éast, ănd Júlĭet ís thĕ sún!

Much of *Romeo and Juliet* is written in blank verse. This formal meter is well suited to serious subjects. As you read, say some of the lines aloud and note the effect of the stressed syllables and words spoken in blank verse.

Connecting Literary Elements

In a play, you generally learn about characters from the things they say and do and the way they speak. In Shakespeare's plays, blank verse helps reinforce **character rank:** Important or aristocratic characters typically speak in blank verse. Minor or comic characters often do not speak in verse. Use a chart like the one shown to identify a character's rank in this play.

❷ Reading Strategy

Reading Blank Verse

When **reading blank verse,** remember that thoughts or phrases often run past the end of a line. To determine its full meaning, read blank verse in sentences, pausing according to the punctuation and not necessarily at the end of each line.

Vocabulary Development

cunning (kun′ iŋ) *n.* cleverness; slyness (p. 799)

procure (prō kyoor′) *v.* get (p. 801)

vile (vīl) *adj.* worthless (p. 803)

predominant (prē däm′ ə nənt) *adj.* having dominating influence over others (p. 803)

intercession (in′ tər sesh′ ən) *n.* the act of pleading on behalf of another (p. 804)

sallow (sal′ ō) *adj.* of a sickly, pale-yellowish complexion (p. 804)

waverer (wā′ vər ər) *n.* one who changes or is unsteady (p. 805)

lamentable (lə men′ tə bəl) *adj.* distressing; sad (p. 806)

unwieldy (un wēl′ dē) *adj.* awkward; clumsy (p. 811)

TEACHING RESOURCES

The following resources can be used to enrich or extend the instruction for p. 794.

Motivation

Interest Grabber Video, Tape 4 ■

Background

Beyond Literature, p. 47

Take It to the Net

Visit www.phschool.com for background and hotlinks for *The Tragedy of Romeo and Juliet.*

Literary Analysis

Selection Support: Literary Analysis, p. 188

Literary Analysis and Reading Transparencies, Blank Verse, p. 94

Reading

Literary Analysis and Reading Transparencies, Read Blank Verse, p. 93

E-Teach

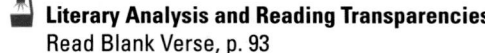

Visit E-Teach at www.phschool.com for teachers' essays on how to teach, with questions and answers.

■ **BLOCK SCHEDULING:** Resources marked with this symbol provide varied instruction during 90-minute blocks.

❶

Act II

Review and Anticipate

Act I reveals a bitter, long-standing feud between the Montagues and the Capulets. It also introduces the play's title characters, who meet at a feast and immediately fall in love, only to discover that they come from opposing sides of the feud.

Based on what you have learned about the personalities of Romeo and Juliet, how do you expect them to respond to their love for each other and to the problems it poses? How do you think their families will react?

Prologue

[*Enter* CHORUS.]

CHORUS. Now old desire[1] doth in his deathbed lie,
And young affection gapes to be his heir;[2]
That fair[3] for which love groaned for and would die,
With tender Juliet matched, is now not fair.
❷ Now Romeo is beloved and loves again,
Alike bewitchèd[4] by the charm of looks;
But to his foe supposed he must complain,[5]
And she steal love's sweet bait from fearful hooks.
Being held a foe, he may not have access
To breathe such vows as lovers use to swear,

1. old desire Romeo's love for Rosaline.

2. young . . . heir Romeo's new love for Juliet is eager to replace his love for Rosaline.

3. fair beautiful woman (Rosaline).

4. Alike bewitched Both Romeo and Juliet are enchanted.

5. complain address his words of love.

TEACH

Step-by-Step Teaching Guide for pp. 795–815

CUSTOMIZE INSTRUCTION
For Less Proficient Students

Tell students that some critics say that Juliet is more mature than Romeo and teaches him the meaning of true love. Invite students to compare the two as they read this act and the rest of the play, to see whether they agree or disagree with this assessment. Have them cite evidence for their viewpoint.

❶ About the Selection

You may wish to have students summarize the main plot points of Act I before they begin to read Act II. The main action of *Romeo and Juliet,* Act II, is the young couple's betrothal, which occurs the night they meet, and their marriage, which occurs the day after. The act invites the audience to speculate about Romeo and Juliet's love for each other. On the one hand, they are the archetypal teenage lovers—reckless, impulsive, passionate, head over heels in love. On the other hand, they are growing toward an adult version of love—marriage, devotion, and a willingness to make sacrifices and take risks. As the play progresses, their love will continue to be tested.

❷ Reading Strategy

Reading Blank Verse

- Ask students to read the first four lines of the prologue, paying attention to the meter of the *blank verse.*
- Ask students how the word *Juliet* must be pronounced in order to fit the meter.
  Answer: *Juliet* must be pronounced in two syllables; *-liet* must be spoken as one syllable.
- Then, have students read lines 5–8 to determine how the word *bewitched* is pronounced to fit the meter.
  Answer: *Bewitched* should be pronounced in three syllables—*be WITCH ed.* Point out the grave accent that indicates that *ed* is to be pronounced separately.

TEACHING RESOURCES

The following resources can be used to enrich or extend the instruction for pp. 795–815.

Reading
- **Selection Support:** Reading Strategy, p. 187; Build Vocabulary, p. 185
- **Reader's Companion**
- **English Learner's Companion**
- **Listening to Literature Audiocassettes,** Side 24
- **Listening to Literature Audio CDs,** CD 16

Extension
- **Authors In Depth,** Gold Level

BLOCK SCHEDULING: Resources marked with this symbol provide varied instruction during 90-minute blocks.

3 Background

Rhymed Couplets

Tell students that lines in iambic pentameter can also be rhymed. The rhyming of two successive lines creates a rhymed couplet. This form gives extra emphasis to the words a character speaks and creates a sense of completeness or finality. The exits of major characters and the ends of scenes are often marked by a rhymed couplet. Have students compare the rhyme scheme in the first twelve lines of the Chorus with the rhyme scheme in the final two lines.

4 Literary Analysis

Blank Verse

- Ask students why they think Romeo is alone in this first scene.
  Answer: Romeo has been struck by his sudden love for Juliet. He needs time alone to think.
- Ask the Literary Analysis question on p. 796: Line 3 breaks the pattern of blank verse. Why is this break suited to the emotion of the line?
  Possible response: Benvolio is merely calling Romeo, so ordinary speech is appropriate. Also, in breaking the iambic pattern, he is also breaking the mood.

5 Reading Strategy

Reading Blank Verse

- Ask students how Mercutio makes fun of Romeo in this speech.
  Possible response: Mercutio calls Romeo "Madman" and "Lover" and suggests that Romeo is acting lovesick and sighing over his love.
- Have students answer the Reading Strategy question on p. 796: When reading Mercutio's speech on lines 6–21, where should you pause and where should you come to a complete stop?
  Answer: Readers should pause at the commas and come to a complete stop at sentences that end in periods and exclamation points. They should stop only for a short time at the end of short addresses, such as *Romeo!* or *Ay me!*, even though these addresses are punctuated by exclamation points.

And she as much in love, her means much less
  To meet her new belovèd anywhere;
3 But passion lends them power, time means to meet,
Temp'ring extremities with extreme sweet.[6] *[Exit.]*

Scene i. *Near* CAPULET'S *orchard.*

[Enter ROMEO *alone.]*

4 **ROMEO.** Can I go forward when my heart is here?
Turn back, dull earth,[1] and find thy center[2] out.

[Enter BENVOLIO *with* MERCUTIO. ROMEO *retires.]*

BENVOLIO. Romeo! My cousin Romeo! Romeo!

MERCUTIO. He is wise.
And, on my life, hath stol'n him home to bed.

BENVOLIO. He ran this way and leapt this orchard wall.
Call, good Mercutio.

MERCUTIO. Nay, I'll conjure[3] too.
Romeo! Humors! Madman! Passion! Lover!
Appear thou in the likeness of a sigh;
Speak but one rhyme, and I am satisfied!
Cry but "Ay me!" pronounce but "love" and "dove";
Speak to my gossip[4] Venus one fair word,
One nickname for her purblind son and heir,
Young Abraham Cupid, he that shot so true
5 When King Cophetua loved the beggar maid!
He heareth not, he stirreth not, he moveth not;
The ape is dead,[5] and I must conjure him.
I conjure thee by Rosaline's bright eyes,
By her high forehead and her scarlet lip,
By her fine foot, straight leg, and quivering thigh,
And the demesnes that there adjacent lie,
That in thy likeness thou appear to us!

BENVOLIO. And if he hear thee, thou wilt anger him.

MERCUTIO. This cannot anger him. 'Twould anger him
To raise a spirit in his mistress' circle
Of some strange nature, letting it there stand
Till she had laid it and conjured it down.
That were some spite; my invocation
Is fair and honest; in his mistress' name,
I conjure only but to raise up him.

BENVOLIO. Come, he hath hid himself among these trees
To be consorted[6] with the humorous[7] night.
Blind is his love and best befits the dark.

MERCUTIO. If love be blind, love cannot hit the mark.

6. Temp'ring . . . sweet easing their difficulties with great delights.

1. dull earth lifeless body.

2. center heart, or possibly soul (Juliet).

Literary Analysis
Blank Verse Line 3 breaks the pattern of blank verse. Why is this break suited to the emotion of the line?

3. conjure recite a spell to make Romeo appear.

4. gossip merry old lady.

Reading Strategy
Reading Blank Verse When reading Mercutio's speech (lines 6–21), where should you pause and where should you come to a complete stop?

5. The ape is dead Romeo, like a trained monkey, seems to be playing.

6. consorted associated.

7. humorous humid; moody, like a lover.

ENRICHMENT: Literature Connection

The Balcony Scene

Point out to students that this is the beginning of the famous "balcony scene" in *Romeo and Juliet*—one of the most famous scenes in all of Shakespeare's plays. Help students understand that Romeo is making an extended comparison here that reveals his strong feelings for Juliet. First, he says that Juliet's beauty is so great that she lights up the world, as the sun does when it rises. Then, he says that even the moon is envious of her, the way the moon might be envious of the brighter, "more fair" sun. You may want to point out that the moon symbolizes Romeo's love for Rosaline, who is likened to Diana, goddess of the moon, in Act I.

Now will he sit under a medlar tree
And wish his mistress were that kind of fruit
As maids call medlars[8] when they laugh alone.
O, Romeo, that she were, O that she were
An open *et cetera*, thou a pop'rin pear!
Romeo, good night. I'll to my truckle bed;[9]
This field bed is too cold for me to sleep.
Come, shall we go?

BENVOLIO. Go then, for 'tis in vain
To seek him here that means not to be found.
[*Exit with others.*]

6

Scene ii. CAPULET'S *orchard.*

ROMEO. [*Coming forward*] He jests at scars that never felt a wound.

[*Enters* JULIET *at a window.*]

But soft! What light through yonder window breaks?
It is the East, and Juliet is the sun!
Arise, fair sun, and kill the envious moon,
Who is already sick and pale with grief
That thou her maid art far more fair than she.
Be not her maid, since she is envious.
Her vestal livery[1] is but sick and green,
And none but fools do wear it. Cast it off.
It is my lady! O, it is my love!
O, that she knew she were!
She speaks, yet she says nothing. What of that?
Her eye discourses; I will answer it.
7
I am too bold; 'tis not to me she speaks.
Two of the fairest stars in all the heaven,
Having some business, do entreat her eyes
To twinkle in their spheres[2] till they return.
What if her eyes were there, they in her head?
The brightness of her cheek would shame those stars
As daylight doth a lamp; her eyes in heaven
Would through the airy region stream so bright
That birds would sing and think it were not night.
See how she leans her cheek upon that hand,
O, that I were a glove upon that hand,
That I might touch that cheek!

JULIET. Ay me!

ROMEO. She speaks.
O, speak again, bright angel, for thou art
As glorious to this night, being o'er my head,
As is a wingèd messenger of heaven
Unto the white-upturnèd wond'ring eyes

8. medlars applelike fruits.

9. truckle bed trundlebed, placed under a larger bed when not in use.

Literary Analysis
Blank Verse What effect does Shakespeare achieve by breaking up a rhymed couplet—a pair of rhyming lines—into two separate scenes?

1. livery clothing or costume worn by a servant.

2. spheres orbits.

Reading Strategy
Reading Blank Verse Why does reading Romeo's speech in complete sentences instead of line by line help you grasp its meaning?

8 **✔ Reading Check**
Whom does Romeo see at the window?

6 Literary Analysis
Blank Verse

- Remind students that poets occasionally use "off rhymes"— words that are similar but not identical in sound. The words *again* and *complain* at the end of lines 5 and 7 on p. 795 are examples of off rhyme.
- Have students note the off rhyme, or near rhyme of *found* and *wound* in the couplet that makes up lines 42 and 1 on this page.
- Now, have students respond to the Literary Analysis question on p. 797: What effect does Shakespeare achieve by breaking a rhymed couplet into two separate scenes?
  Answer: By breaking up the rhymed couplet, Shakespeare causes one scene to flow smoothly and quickly to the next.

7 Reading Strategy
Reading Blank Verse

- Ask students to identify the metaphors Shakespeare uses in this speech. To what objects does Romeo compare Juliet?
  Answer: Romeo compares Juliet to the sun and her eyes to the stars.
- Have students describe how Romeo imagines he might touch Juliet's cheek, since he is too far away to do it himself.
  Answer: He wishes he were a glove upon Juliet's hand, so that when she touched her cheek with her hand, he would be touching her, too.
- Have students answer the Reading Strategy question on p. 797: Why does reading Romeo's speech in complete sentences instead of line by line help you grasp its meaning?
  Answer: The ideas in the speech are contained in sentences, not in individual lines.

8 ✔ Reading Check

Answer: Romeo sees Juliet at the window.

CUSTOMIZE INSTRUCTION FOR UNIVERSAL ACCESS

For Special Needs Students	For Less Proficient Readers	For English Learners
Have students read the adapted version of Act II, Scene ii in the **Adapted Reader's Companion.** This version provides basic-level instruction in an interactive format with questions and write-on lines. Completing the adapted version will prepare students to read the selection in the Student Edition.	Have students read the scene in the **Reader's Companion.** This version provides basic-level instruction in an interactive format with questions and write-on lines. After students finish the selection in **Reader's Companion,** have them complete the questions and activities in the Student Edition.	Have students read the adapted version of the scene in the **English Learner's Companion.** This version provides basic-level instruction in an interactive format with questions and write-on lines. Completing the adapted version will prepare students to read the selection in the Student Edition.

9 Reading Strategy

Reading Blank Verse

- Ask students to read the four lines of blank verse in Juliet's speech to see if they have any problem with the stressed and unstressed syllables. Which lines give them problems?
  Possible response: Students may note that line 33 seems to have too many syllables in it, and line 36 forces a strange pronunciation of the word *Capulet*.
- Ask students what they might do with the names *Romeo* and *Capulet* in order to have their pronunciation fit the meter.
  Answer: Students may say that the name *Romeo* would have to be pronounced *RO myo* the first two times, while *Capulet* would have to be pronounced *CAP u LET* instead of *CAP u let*.

10 Literary Analysis

Blank Verse

- Ask students who speaks line 49 on this page.
  Answer: Juliet speaks the first part of the line and Romeo speaks the second part.
- Ask students to scan line 49 to see how many beats each character speaks.
  Answer: Juliet speaks two beats of text, and Romeo speaks the remaining three beats.
- Now, ask the Literary Analysis question on p. 798: As in some other lines in this scene, the five beats of line 53 are split between two speakers. How is this suited to the fact that the two speakers are in love?
  Possible response: Students may suggest that two lovers who were talking would likely be finishing each other's sentences. They also may say that people in love "speak with one voice."

Of mortals that fall back to gaze on him
When he bestrides the lazy puffing clouds
And sails upon the bosom of the air.

9

JULIET. O Romeo, Romeo! Wherefore art thou Romeo?[3]
Deny thy father and refuse thy name;
Or, if thou wilt not, be but sworn my love,
And I'll no longer be a Capulet.

ROMEO. [*Aside*] Shall I hear more, or shall I speak at this?

JULIET. Tis but thy name that is my enemy.
Thou art thyself, though not[4] a Montague.
What's Montague? It is nor hand, nor foot,
Nor arm, nor face, nor any other part
Belonging to a man. O, be some other name!
What's in a name? That which we call a rose
By any other name would smell as sweet.
So Romeo would, were he not Romeo called,
Retain that dear perfection which he owes[5]
Without that title. Romeo, doff[6] thy name;
And for thy name, which is no part of thee,
Take all myself.

10

ROMEO. I take thee at thy word.
Call me but love, and I'll be new baptized;
Henceforth I never will be Romeo.

JULIET. What man art thou, thus bescreened in night,
So stumblest on my counsel?[7]

ROMEO. By a name
I know not how to tell thee who I am.
My name, dear saint, is hateful to myself
Because it is an enemy to thee.
Had I it written, I would tear the word.

JULIET. My ears have yet not drunk a hundred words
Of thy tongue's uttering, yet I know the sound.
Art thou not Romeo, and a Montague?

ROMEO. Neither, fair maid, if either thee dislike.

JULIET. How camest thou hither, tell me, and wherefore?
The orchard walls are high and hard to climb,
And the place death, considering who thou art,
If any of my kinsmen find thee here.

ROMEO. With love's light wings did I o'erperch[8] these walls;
For stony limits cannot hold love out,
And what love can do, that dares love attempt.
Therefore thy kinsmen are no stop to me.

JULIET. If they do see thee, they will murder thee.

3. Wherefore . . . Romeo? Why are you Romeo—a Montague?

4. though not even if you were not.

5. owes owns; possesses.

6. doff remove.

7. counsel secret thoughts.

Literary Analysis
Blank Verse As in some other lines in this scene, the five beats of line 53 are split between two speakers. How is this suited to the fact that the two speakers are in love?

8. o'erperch fly over.

ENRICHMENT: Social Studies Connection

Period Clothing

The costumes in the movie stills that illustrate this play reflect fashions that were popular during the Italian Renaissance. Men wore a shirt beneath a short, close-fitting jacket called a doublet. They also wore fitted tights, or hose, that reached from waist to toe. Sleeves were fastened to the body of the garment with laces tipped with metal aglets, as can be seen in Romeo's costume in the photograph on p. 770.

Women wore a nightgown-like chemise beneath a high-waisted gown with a tight-fitting bodice. The gown of a noble lady was made of rich fabrics such as velvet, satin, cloth-of-gold, or brocade, and was usually elaborately embroidered. Throughout the Renaissance, pearls were extremely popular gems and were used in embellishing clothing. In the photograph on p. 861, Juliet's gown and cap are studded with pearls.

(11)

ROMEO. Alack, there lies more peril in thine eye
Than twenty of their swords! Look thou but sweet,
And I am proof[9] against their enmity.

JULIET. I would not for the world they saw thee here.

ROMEO. I have night's cloak to hide me from their eyes;
And but[10] thou love me, let them find me here.
My life were better ended by their hate
Than death proroguèd,[11] wanting of thy love.

JULIET. By whose direction found'st thou out this place?

ROMEO. By love, that first did prompt me to inquire.
He lent me counsel, and I lent him eyes.
I am no pilot; yet, wert thou as far
As that vast shore washed with the farthest sea,
I should adventure[12] for such merchandise.

(12)

JULIET. Thou knowest the mask of night is on my face;
Else would a maiden blush bepaint my cheek
For that which thou hast heard me speak tonight.
Fain would I dwell on form[13]—fain, fain deny
What I have spoke; but farewell compliment![14]
Dost thou love me? I know thou wilt say "Ay";
And I will take thy word. Yet, if thou swear'st,
Thou mayst prove false. At lovers' perjuries,
They say Jove laughs. O gentle Romeo,
If thou dost love, pronounce it faithfully.
Or if thou thinkest I am too quickly won,
I'll frown and be perverse[15] and say thee nay,
So thou wilt woo; but else, not for the world.
In truth, fair Montague, I am too fond,[16]
And therefore thou mayst think my havior light;[17]
But trust me, gentleman, I'll prove more true
Than those that have more <u>cunning</u> to be strange.[18]
I should have been more strange, I must confess,
But that thou overheard'st, ere I was ware,
My truelove passion. Therefore pardon me,
And not impute this yielding to light love,
Which the dark night hath so discoverèd.[19]

ROMEO. Lady, by yonder blessèd moon I vow,
That tips with silver all these fruit-tree tops—

JULIET. O, swear not by the moon, th' inconstant moon,
That monthly changes in her circle orb,
Lest that thy love prove likewise variable.

ROMEO. What shall I swear by?

JULIET. Do not swear at all;
Or if thou wilt, swear by thy gracious self,

Literary Analysis
Blank Verse In line 72, what is the effect of the stressed syllable *swords*? Explain.

9. **proof** protected, as by armor.

10. **And but** unless.

11. **proroguèd** postponed.

12. **adventure** risk a long journey, like a sea adventurer.

13. **Fain . . . form** eagerly would I follow convention (by acting reserved).

14. **compliment** conventional behavior.

15. **be perverse** act contrary to my true feelings.

16. **fond** affectionate.

17. **my havior light** my behavior immodest or unserious.

cunning (kun′ iŋ) *n.* cleverness; slyness

18. **strange** distant and cold.

19. **discoverèd** revealed.

(13) **Reading Check**
Why does Romeo say his name is hateful to him?

CUSTOMIZE INSTRUCTION FOR UNIVERSAL ACCESS

For Special Needs Students	For Gifted/Talented Students	For Advanced Readers
Point out to students that Shakespeare added syllables to some words in the text to make them fit the meter of blank verse. Point out the word *discovered* in line 106, and *blessed* in line 107. The grave accents over these words mean that they are to be pronounced *dis COV er ED* and *BLESS ed* rather than *dis COV erd* and *blest.*	Have students look for sections of dialogue between Romeo and Juliet that they would use as the basis for a song in a musical version of the play. Have students establish criteria and then explain how their choices meet the criteria.	Point out to students that both Romeo and Juliet offer to deny their names in order to be together. Do students think they are compromising themselves in some important way just to be acceptable to someone else?

(11) Literary Analysis
Blank Verse

- Have students read Juliet's line, 70, on p. 798 and then Romeo's response, lines 71–73 on p. 799.

Monitor Progress Ask them what the speakers mean to say in these lines.
Answer: Juliet says that if the Montagues see Romeo they will kill him. Romeo replies that he would be more afraid of a look of disapproval in Juliet's eyes than the actual weapons of her family.

- Ask the Literary Analysis question on p. 799: In line 72, what is the effect of the stressed syllable *swords?* Explain.
Answer: The emphasis on *swords* leads the reader to see how serious Romeo is about loving Juliet; not even the threat of death will keep him away from her.

(12) Reading Strategy
Reading Blank Verse

- Ask students to use footnote 13 to determine what Juliet is saying in lines 87–89.
Answer: Juliet feels that she should eagerly deny what she has said to Romeo, and if she were behaving in a conventional way, she would do so. She rejects conventional behavior.
- Have students note the three uses of the word *fain,* meaning "eagerly," in line 88. Which are stressed and which not?
Answer: The first two uses of the word are unstressed, third is stressed.
- Ask students to speculate on how the same word can be used as both a stressed and unstressed syllable.
Answer: Speakers sometimes repeat a word for emphasis. For example, if someone asks if you want to see a new movie, you might say "Yes, YES, let's go." Juliet is saying in effect, "Eagerly would I [act conventionally]—eagerly, EAGERLY deny what I have spoke."

(13) Reading Check

Answer: Romeo's name is hateful to him because it is an enemy to Juliet, whose family is quarreling with Romeo's family.

14 Reading Strategy

Reading Blank Verse

- Ask students why Juliet says she has no joy in being betrothed to Romeo tonight.
  Answer: Juliet thinks that it is too soon to make vows to one another.
- Ask the Reading Strategy question on p. 800: How would you rephrase in standard English what Romeo and Juliet are saying to each other?
  Possible response: JULIET: Don't make promises; I believe you. I'm happy with you, but I'm not happy with how fast we're rushing into things. Goodnight. ROMEO: Wait. Aren't you going to promise you love me, too? JULIET: I promised to love you even before you asked me to, but I want to take back my promise. ROMEO: Why? JULIET: So I could make it again.

15 Background

Film

The picture on p. 800 shows the actress Olivia Hussey, who was fifteen when she played Juliet. Use the following for discussion:

1. Based on this image, how do you think the director envisioned Juliet?
   Answer: The director seemed to see Juliet as young, naive, passionate, and intense.
2. In this particular still, the actress playing Juliet stares out of the screen directly into the eyes of the audience. What is the effect of that stare?
   Answer: Having Juliet make direct eye contact with them draws the audience in, makes them sympathize with her, and puts them on her side.

16 ▶ Critical Viewing

Answer: The picture shows a serious character, maybe even cautious. Juliet exhibits both of these characteristics.

Which is the god of my idolatry,
And I'll believe thee.

ROMEO. If my heart's dear love—

JULIET. Well, do not swear. Although I joy in thee,
I have no joy of this contract[20] tonight.
It is too rash, too unadvised, too sudden;
Too like the lightning, which doth cease to be
Ere one can say it lightens. Sweet, good night!
This bud of love, by summer's ripening breath,
May prove a beauteous flow'r when next we meet.
Good night, good night! As sweet repose and rest
Come to thy heart as that within my breast!

14

ROMEO. O, wilt thou leave me so unsatisfied?

JULIET. What satisfaction canst thou have tonight?

ROMEO. Th' exchange of thy love's faithful vow for mine.

JULIET. I gave thee mine before thou didst request it;
And yet I would it were to give again.

ROMEO. Wouldst thou withdraw it? For what purpose, love?

JULIET. But to be frank[21] and give it thee again.
And yet I wish but for the thing I have.
My bounty[22] is as boundless as the sea,
My love as deep; the more I give to thee,

20. contract betrothal.

21. frank generous.

22. bounty what I have to give.

Reading Strategy
Reading Blank Verse
How would you rephrase in Standard English what Romeo and Juliet are saying to each other?

15

16 ◀ **Critical Viewing**
How does Juliet's expression in this picture match the feelings she has conveyed in the play so far? **[Connect]**

ENRICHMENT: Social Studies Connection

School in Shakespeare's Time

When Romeo compares love with schoolboys leaving school and the absence of love with boys going to school, he is expressing the common dislike of men of Shakespeare's time with their formal schooling.

In Stratford, boys—and only boys—were expected to start school as soon as they could read and write. Most of their learning was in Latin grammar, not English, because the school system in Renaissance England was still based on that of Medieval England, when schools basically turned out men who could work in Church positions.

Schoolboys were also expected to be able to memorize and recite Latin, and this might have provided relevant skills to the young lad who would become an actor and playwright.

(17) The more I have, for both are infinite,
I hear some noise within. Dear love, adieu!

[NURSE *calls within.*]

Anon, good nurse! Sweet Montague, be true.
Stay but a little, I will come again. [*Exit.*]

ROMEO. O blessèd, blessèd night! I am afeard,
Being in night, all this is but a dream,
Too flattering-sweet to be substantial.[23]

[*Enter* JULIET *again.*]

JULIET. Three words, dear Romeo, and good night indeed.
If that thy bent[24] of love be honorable,
Thy purpose marriage, send me word tomorrow,
By one that I'll procure to come to thee,
Where and what time thou wilt perform the rite;
And all my fortunes at thy foot I'll lay
And follow thee my lord throughout the world.

(18) **NURSE.** [*Within*] Madam!

JULIET. I come anon.—But if thou meanest not well,
I do beseech thee—

NURSE. [*Within*] Madam!

JULIET. By and by[25] I come.—
To cease thy strife[26] and leave me to my grief.
Tomorrow will I send.

ROMEO. So thrive my soul—

JULIET. A thousand times good night! [*Exit.*]

ROMEO. A thousand times the worse, to want thy light!
Love goes toward love as schoolboys from their books;
But love from love, toward school with heavy looks.

[*Enter* JULIET *again.*]

JULIET. Hist! Romeo, hist! O for a falc'ner's voice
To lure this tassel gentle[27] back again!
Bondage is hoarse[28] and may not speak aloud,
Else would I tear the cave where Echo[29] lies
And make her airy tongue more hoarse than mine
With repetition of "My Romeo!"

ROMEO. It is my soul that calls upon my name.
How silver-sweet sound lovers' tongues by night,
Like softest music to attending ears!

JULIET. Romeo!

ROMEO. My sweet?

Literary Analysis
Blank Verse Analyze lines 135–136. Do they meet the criteria of blank verse? Explain.

23. substantial real.

24. bent purpose; intention.

procure (prō kyoor′) *v.* get

Literary Analysis
Blank Verse Three speakers share the rhythm of line 151. Does the Nurse's interruption complete or break the blank verse?

25. By and by at once.

26. strife efforts.

27. tassel gentle male falcon.

28. Bondage is hoarse Being bound in by my family restricts my speech.

29. Echo In classical mythology, the nymph Echo, unable to win the love of Narcissus, wasted away in a cave until nothing was left of her but her voice.

(19) **Reading Check**
What plan do Romeo and Juliet make for the following day?

(17) Literary Analysis
Blank Verse

- Ask a student volunteer to read lines 135–136 aloud, taking care to emphasize the way the words are stressed.
- Then, ask students the first Literary Analysis question on p. 801: Analyze lines 135–136. Do they meet the criteria of blank verse?
  Answer: Yes; both lines are iambic pentameter—ten-syllable lines, with the second syllable stressed.

(18) Literary Analysis
Blank Verse

- Ask students what Juliet says to Romeo in lines 142–148.
  Answer: Juliet tells Romeo that if he really wants to marry her, he should send her word the next day. She will meet him for the marriage and give up everything to follow him.
- Have students identify the person who interrupts Juliet as she speaks to Romeo.
  Answer: The Nurse interrupts Juliet.
- Now, ask the second Literary Analysis question on p. 801: Two speakers share the rhythm of line 151. Does the Nurse's interruption complete or break the blank verse?
  Answer: The Nurse's interruption breaks the blank verse. Without the Nurse's interruption, Juliet's words would complete a full line of blank verse.

(19) Reading Check

Answer: Romeo will send word to Juliet about where to meet him, and she will go to him so they may be married.

⓴ Literary Analysis

Blank Verse and Character Rank

- Ask students what Romeo and Juliet are doing in lines 169–175.
  Answer: The two are trying to find reasons to keep from having to say good night.
- Ask the Literary Analysis question on p. 802: What can you conclude about character rank, based on the fact that Romeo and Juliet speak in blank verse?
  Answer: In Shakespeare's plays, characters who speak in blank verse are important or aristocratic. Romeo and Juliet are both.

㉑ Reading Strategy

Reading Blank Verse

- Ask students to use the footnotes to determine where Romeo is going after he leaves Juliet.
  Answer: Romeo is going to see a friar, his spiritual father, who lives in a small room somewhere in Verona.
- Then, ask the Reading Strategy question on p. 802: How do the punctuation marks in Romeo's parting comment help you understand the meaning of his words?
  Possible response: Romeo tells Juliet that he hopes that sleep will dwell in her eyes and peace in her breast. He then says that if he were that sleep and peace, he would be resting in Juliet's eyes and on her breast, a thought worthy of exclamation.

JULIET. What o'clock tomorrow
Shall I send to thee?

ROMEO. By the hour of nine.

⓴

JULIET. I will not fail. 'Tis twenty year till then.
I have forgot why I did call thee back.

ROMEO. Let me stand here till thou remember it.

JULIET. I shall forget, to have thee still stand there,
Rememb'ring how I love thy company.

ROMEO. And I'll stay, to have thee still forget,
Forgetting any other home but this.

JULIET. 'Tis almost morning. I would have thee gone—
And yet no farther than a wanton's[30] bird,
That lets it hop a little from his hand,
Like a poor prisoner in his twisted gyves,[31]
And with a silken thread plucks it back again,
So loving-jealous of his liberty.

ROMEO. I would I were thy bird.

JULIET. Sweet, so would I.
Yet I should kill thee with much cherishing.
Good night, good night! Parting is such sweet sorrow
That I shall say good night till it be morrow. [*Exit.*]

㉑

ROMEO. Sleep dwell upon thine eyes, peace in thy breast!
Would I were sleep and peace, so sweet to rest!
Hence will I to my ghostly friar's[32] close cell,[33]
His help to crave and my dear hap[34] to tell. [*Exit.*]

Scene iii. FRIAR LAWRENCE'S *cell.*

[*Enter* FRIAR LAWRENCE *alone, with a basket.*]

FRIAR. The gray-eyed morn smiles on the frowning night,

Literary Analysis
Blank Verse and Character Rank Based on the fact that Romeo and Juliet speak in blank verse, what can you conclude about their character rank?

30. wanton's spoiled, playful child's.

31. gyves (jīvz) chains.

32. ghostly friar's spiritual father's.

33. close cell small room.

34. dear hap good fortune.

Reading Strategy
Reading Blank Verse How do the punctuation marks in Romeo's parting comment help you understand the meaning of his words?

Literature in context ㉒ Literature Connection

Hyperbole

Hyperbole is deliberate exaggeration in writing or speech. For example, in lines 71–72, when Romeo says the look in Juliet's eyes is more dangerous than twenty of her kinsmen's swords, he uses hyperbole to express the power in the beauty of her eyes. Several times in this scene, as in line 169, both young lovers use hyperbole to emphasize their love.

ENRICHMENT: Social Studies Connection

The Good Friar

Friar, which comes from the Latin word for *brother*, is a general term for a member of a religious order. Friars had no worldly possessions or fixed place to live, which allowed them to devote themselves exclusively to preaching, missionary work, or other charitable undertakings. Friars wore robes or *habits* that were gray, black, or white.

Students should understand the difference between a friar, like Friar Lawrence, and a monk. A monk is a man who has taken religious vows of poverty, chastity, and obedience, and has retired from worldly life to live with other monks, studying the Scriptures, praying, and meditating. A friar lives among ordinary people and helps them, as Friar Lawrence tries, unsuccessfully, to help the two star-crossed lovers.

Check'ring the eastern clouds with streaks of light;
And fleckèd[1] darkness like a drunkard reels
From forth day's path and Titan's burning wheels.[2]
Now, ere the sun advance his burning eye
The day to cheer and night's dank dew to dry,
I must upfill this osier cage[3] of ours
With baleful[4] weeds and precious-juicèd flowers.
The earth that's nature's mother is her tomb.
What is her burying grave, that is her womb;
And from her womb children of divers kind[5]
We sucking on her natural bosom find,
Many for many virtues excellent,
None but for some, and yet all different.
O, mickle[6] is the powerful grace[7] that lies
In plants, herbs, stones, and their true qualities;
For naught so vile that on the earth doth live
But to the earth some special good doth give;
Nor aught so good but, strained[8] from that fair use,
Revolts from true birth,[9] stumbling on abuse.
Virtue itself turns vice, being misapplied,
And vice sometime by action dignified.

23

[*Enter* ROMEO.]

Within the infant rind[10] of this weak flower
Poison hath residence and medicine power;[11]
For this, being smelt, with that part cheers each part;[12]
Being tasted, stays all senses with the heart.[13]
Two such opposèd kings encamp them still[14]
In man as well as herbs—grace and rude will;
And where the worser is predominant,
Full soon the canker[15] death eats up that plant.

ROMEO. Good morrow, father.

FRIAR. *Benedicite!*[16]
What early tongue so sweet saluteth me?
Young son, it argues a distemperèd head[17]
So soon to bid good morrow to thy bed.
Care keeps his watch in every old man's eye,
And where care lodges, sleep will never lie;
But where unbruisèd youth with unstuffed[18] brain
Doth couch his limbs, there golden sleep doth reign.
Therefore thy earliness doth me assure
Thou art uproused with some distemp'rature;[19]
Or if not so, then here I hit it right—
Our Romeo hath not been in bed tonight.

ROMEO. That last is true. The sweeter rest was mine.

FRIAR. God pardon sin! Wast thou with Rosaline?

1. **fleckèd** spotted.
2. **Titan's burning wheels** wheels of the sun god's chariot.
3. **osier cage** willow basket.
4. **baleful** poisonous.
5. **divers kind** different kinds.
6. **mickle** great.
7. **grace** divine power.
8. **strained** turned away.

vile (vīl) *adj.* worthless

9. **Revolts . . . birth** conflicts with its real purpose.
10. **infant rind** tender skin.
11. **and medicine power** and medicinal quality has power.
12. **with . . . part** with that quality—odor—revives each part of the body.
13. **stays . . . heart** kills (stops the working of the five senses along with the heart).

predominant (prē däm´ ə nənt) *adj.* having dominating influence over others

14. **still** always.
15. **canker** a destructive caterpillar.
16. ***Benedicite!*** God bless you!
17. **distemperèd head** troubled mind.
18. **unstuffed** not filled with cares.
19. **distemp'rature** illness.

24 **✓Reading Check**

When Romeo leaves Juliet, what reason does he give for visiting the Friar?

22 Literature in Context

Hyperbole

Students have already encountered many examples of hyperbole in the play without necessarily knowing it. Many examples take the form of metaphors or similes. Point out these examples: on p. 798, line 64, Juliet uses a metaphor to compare the Capulet home with death because people within it would kill Romeo if they knew he was nearby. Then, on pp. 800–801, Juliet uses similes in lines 131–134 to describe her bounty as boundless as the sea, and her love as deep as the sea. Not all hyperbole takes the form of simile or metaphor, however. Juliet exaggerates again on p. 802 in line 169, when she says that it will be twenty years until nine o'clock the next day when she will see Romeo again.

Students may enjoy finding other example of hyperbole, either in the text they have already read, or in the upcoming scenes.

23 Critical Thinking

Infer

- Ask students to use the footnotes and context clues to determine what the Friar is doing in lines 7 and 8.
  Answer: The Friar is collecting plants of different kinds, both poisonous and beneficial.
- Ask students to read lines 15–22 to learn what the Friar believes about the natural world.
  Possible response: The Friar believes that things found in the natural world can be used for either good or evil.

24 ✓Reading Check

Answer: Romeo is going to visit the Friar to enlist his help in arranging a marriage for Romeo and Juliet.

CUSTOMIZE INSTRUCTION FOR UNIVERSAL ACCESS

For Less Proficient Readers	For Advanced Students
Encourage students to make a list of the end rhymes in Romeo's final speech on p. 802 and the Friar's dialogue on p. 803. In each pair of rhyming words, have them note whether the rhyming sound is spelled the same or differently. What example of off rhyme, or near rhyme, do they find? **Answer:** The following pairs are spelled differently: *rest/breast; eye/dry; ours/flowers.* The words *lies* and *qualities* are near rhymes.	Recall with students the opposites they met in Act I: "O brawling love, O loving hate . . . O heavy lightness," and so forth. Call students' attention to the Friar, who as a member of the Christian community in the Middle Ages, would have exhibited a way of thinking based upon opposites. For Christians of this period, there were two sides to everything—life and death, faith and heresy, good and evil. Ask students to find examples of the Friar's two-sided thinking in his speech on this page.

25 Vocabulary Development

Latin prefix *inter-*

- Call students' attention to the word *intercession* and its definition. Tell students that the prefix *inter-* means "between or among." The root word is based on the Latin for "go."
- Ask students to explain the word's meaning.
  Answer: An *intercession* is the "act of going between two people or groups in an effort to resolve a dispute or obtain a favor."
- Have students suggest other words with the prefix *inter-*.
  Possible responses: Students may cite *interact, intercept, interchange, international*, and many others.

26 Literary Analysis

Blank Verse

- Remind students that the emphasized words and syllables in blank verse can reveal the meaning in a speech. Ask students what they can tell about the meaning of the first four lines of Friar Lawrence's speech based on the emphasized words and/or syllables.
  Answer: The stressed words in lines 65–68 give readers the sense that Friar Lawrence is concerned about the change in Romeo's feelings, about Rosaline, whom Romeo apparently did love so dear, and who is now forsaken.
- Ask the Literary Analysis question on p. 804: What important words are stressed in the last six lines of the Friar's speech?
  Answer: Stressed words include *cheek, stain, tear, washed, woes, woes, Rosaline*, and *changed*.

ROMEO. With Rosaline, my ghostly father? No.
I have forgot that name and that name's woe.

FRIAR. That's my good son! But where hast thou been then?

ROMEO. I'll tell thee ere thou ask it me again.
I have been feasting with mine enemy,
Where on a sudden one hath wounded me
That's by me wounded. Both our remedies
Within thy help and holy physic[20] lies.
I bear no hatred, blessèd man, for, lo,
25 My intercession likewise steads my foe.[21]

FRIAR. Be plain, good son, and homely in thy drift.[22]
Riddling confession finds but riddling shrift.[23]

ROMEO. Then plainly know my heart's dear love is set
On the fair daughter of rich Capulet;
As mine on hers, so hers is set on mine,
And all combined, save[24] what thou must combine
By holy marriage. When and where and how
We met, we wooed, and made exchange of vow,
I'll tell thee as we pass; but this I pray,
That thou consent to marry us today.

FRIAR. Holy Saint Francis! What a change is here!
Is Rosaline, that thou didst love so dear,
So soon forsaken? Young men's love then lies
Not truly in their hearts, but in their eyes.
Jesu Maria! What a deal of brine[25]
Hath washed thy sallow cheeks for Rosaline!
How much salt water thrown away in waste
To season love, that of it doth not taste!
The sun not yet thy sighs from heaven clears,
Thy old groans ring yet in mine ancient ears.
Lo, here upon thy cheek the stain doth sit
Of an old tear that is not washed off yet.
26 If e'er thou wast thyself, and these woes thine,
Thou and these woes were all for Rosaline.
And art thou changed? Pronounce this sentence then:
Women may fall[26] when there's no strength[27] in men.

ROMEO. Thou chidst me oft for loving Rosaline.

FRIAR. For doting,[28] not for loving, pupil mine.

ROMEO. And badst[29] me bury love.

FRIAR. Not in a grave
To lay one in, another out to have.

ROMEO. I pray thee chide me not. Her I love now
Doth grace[30] for grace and love for love allow.[31]
The other did not so.

20. physic (fiz′ ik) medicine.

21. My . . . foe my plea also helps my enemy (Juliet, a Capulet).

intercession (in′ tər sesh′ ən) *n.* the act of pleading on behalf of another

22. and . . . drift and simple in your speech.

23. Riddling . . . shrift A confusing confession will get you uncertain forgiveness. The Friar means that unless Romeo speaks clearly, he will not get clear and direct advice.

24. And . . . save and we are united in every way, except for (save).

25. brine salt water (tears).

sallow (sal′ ō) *adj.* of a sickly, pale-yellowish complexion

26. fall be weak or inconstant.

Literary Analysis
Blank Verse Which important words are stressed in the last six lines of the Friar's speech?

27. strength constancy; stability.

28. doting being infatuated.

29. badst urged.

30. grace favor.

31. allow give.

ENRICHMENT: Literature

Foreshadowing

Despite the fact that readers and audience members know that both Romeo and Juliet will die from the early lines of the play, Shakespeare still implanted examples of foreshadowing into his text. Point out the Friar's words in line 94 "Wisely and slow. They stumble that run fast." Then tell students that Mercutio's meant-to-be funny words in lines 13–16 also foreshadow Romeo's death, even though Mercutio jokes that Romeo is already killed by Cupid's arrow.

FRIAR. O, she knew well
Thy love did read by rote, that could not spell.[32]
But come, young waverer, come go with me.
In one respect I'll thy assistant be;
For this alliance may so happy prove
To turn your households' rancor[33] to pure love.

ROMEO. O, let us hence! I stand on[34] sudden haste.

FRIAR. Wisely and slow. They stumble that run fast. [*Exit all.*]

Scene iv. *A street.*

[*Enter* BENVOLIO *and* MERCUTIO.]

MERCUTIO. Where the devil should this Romeo be?
Came he not home tonight?

BENVOLIO. Not to his father's. I spoke with his man.

MERCUTIO. Why, that same pale hardhearted wench, that Rosaline,
Torments him so that he will sure run mad.

BENVOLIO. Tybalt, the kinsman to old Capulet,
Hath sent a letter to his father's house.

MERCUTIO. A challenge, on my life.

BENVOLIO. Romeo will answer it.

MERCUTIO. Any man that can write may answer a letter.

(27) **BENVOLIO.** Nay, he will answer the letter's master, how he dares, being dared.

MERCUTIO. Alas, poor Romeo, he is already dead: stabbed with a white wench's black eye; run through the ear with a love song; the very pin of his heart cleft with the blind bow-boy's butt-shaft;[1] and is he a man to encounter Tybalt?

BENVOLIO. Why, what is Tybalt?

MERCUTIO. More than Prince of Cats.[2] O, he's the courageous captain of compliments.[3] He fights as you sing pricksong[4]—keeps time, distance, and proportion; he rests his minim rests,[5] one, two, and the third in your bosom! The very butcher of a silk button,[6] a duelist, a duelist! A gentleman of the very first house,[7] of the first and second cause.[8] Ah, the immortal *passado!* The *punto reverso!* The hay![9]

BENVOLIO. The what?

MERCUTIO. The pox of such antic, lisping, affecting fantasticoes—these new tuners of accent![10] "By Jesu, a very good blade! A very tall man! A very good whore!" Why,

32. Thy . . . spell your love recited words from memory with no understanding of them.

waverer (wā′ vər ər) *n.* one who changes or is unsteady

33. rancor hatred.

34. stand on insist on.

1. blind bow-boy's butt-shaft Cupid's blunt arrow.

2. Prince of Cats Tybalt, or a variation of it, is the name of the cat in medieval stories of Reynard the Fox.

3. captain of compliments master of formal behavior.

4. as you sing prick-song with attention to precision.

5. rests . . . rests observes all formalities.

6. button an exact spot on his opponent's shirt.

7. first house finest school of fencing.

8. the first and second cause reasons that would cause a gentleman to challenge another to a duel.

9. *passado! . . . punto reverso! . . .* hay! lunge . . . backhanded stroke . . . home thrust.

10. The pox . . . accent May the plague strike these absurd characters with their phony manners—these men who speak in weird, newfangled ways!

(28) ✔Reading Check

What does the Friar think Romeo and Juliet's love will do for the Capulets and Montagues?

(27) Reading Strategy

Reading Blank Verse

- Ask students what they learn in this exchange between Benvolio and Mercutio.
  Answer: Benvolio says that Tybalt has sent a letter to Romeo at the Montague's house, and Mercutio says it probably challenges Romeo to a duel.
- Then, ask students how they can tell that Mercutio's speech is not in blank verse.
  Answer: It does not have five beats per line.

(28) ✔Reading Check

Answer: The Friar believes the alliance between Romeo and Juliet will end the feud between the Montagues and the Capulets.

29 Literary Analysis

Blank Verse

- Ask students where Mercutio thinks Romeo has been during the night.
  Answer: Mercutio thinks Romeo has been with Rosaline.
- Then, ask the Literary Analysis question on p. 806: Why do you think the conversation between Romeo and his friends is not in blank verse?
  Possible response: Students may say that Shakespeare chose prose for this conversation because he wanted to capture the kinds of rude remarks and jokes that teenage boys might use to mock a lovesick friend.

30 Background

Film

This picture—along with the other images in the selection—is from the movie *Romeo and Juliet*, directed by Franco Zeffirelli. Use the following for discussion:

1. Based on this image from the movie, what idea about these boys do you think the director is trying to communicate?
   Answer: The director shows the boys as joking and arrogant. He uses facial expressions and body language to communicate these ideas.
2. What elements of this image help you better understand the events of the play?
   Answer: The mocking faces of the boys show how easy it can be to get into fights and feuds. The boys also look like close friends, so it is easy to imagine them defending each other.

31 ▶ Critical Viewing

Answer: Students may say that many teenage friends like to tease and joke, and that they especially like to make fun of friends who are in love (like Romeo), or adults with humorous habits (like the talkative Nurse).

is not this a lamentable thing, grandsir, that we should be thus afflicted with these strange flies, these fashionmongers, these pardon-me's,[11] who stand so much on the new form that they cannot sit at ease on the old bench? O, their bones, their bones!

[*Enter* ROMEO.]

BENVOLIO. Here comes Romeo! Here comes Romeo!

MERCUTIO. Without his roe, like a dried herring.[12] O flesh, flesh, how art thou fishified! Now is he for the numbers[13] that Petrarch flowed in. Laura,[14] to his lady, was a kitchen wench (marry, she had a better love to berhyme her), Dido a dowdy, Cleopatra a gypsy, Helen and Hero hildings and harlots, Thisbe a gray eye or so, but not to the purpose. Signior Romeo, *bon jour!* There's a French salutation to your French slop. You gave us the counterfeit fairly last night.

ROMEO. Good morrow to you both. What counterfeit did I give you?

MERCUTIO. The slip,[15] sir, the slip. Can you not conceive?

ROMEO. Pardon, good Mercutio. My business was great, and in such a case as mine a man may strain courtesy.

30

lamentable (lə men′ tə bəl) *adj.* distressing; sad

11. these pardon-me's these men who are always saying "Pardon me" (adopting ridiculous manners).

12. Without . . . herring worn out.

13. numbers verses of love poems.

14. Laura Laura and the other ladies mentioned are all notable figures of European love literature. Mercutio is saying that Romeo thinks that none of them compare with Rosaline.

15. slip escape. *Slip* is also a term for counterfeit coin.

Literary Analysis
Blank Verse Why do you think the conversation between Romeo and his friends is not in blank verse?

31 ◀ **Critical Viewing** How is the rowdy behavior of the young Montagues, as shown in this picture, typical of a group of teenaged friends? **[Generalize]**

ENRICHMENT: Performing Arts Connection

The Lovely, but Never Seen, Rosaline

From the beginning, many audiences have been uncomfortable with the presence of Rosaline in *Romeo and Juliet*, feeling that Romeo's sudden transference of supposedly undying love from Rosaline to Juliet makes him unsympathetic and untrustworthy. Other critics point out that Shakespeare knew what he was doing in showing that strong passions may shift their concentration in people who are young. Besides, say these critics, Rosaline has, according to the text, rejected Romeo.

David Garrick, the eighteenth-century Shakespearean theater manager and actor, generally cut Rosaline's part in his productions of the play. Romeo's lovesick speeches at the beginning of the play refer to Juliet, and at the Capulet ball, it is Benvolio, not Romeo, who asks the Nurse to identify Juliet.

33

32 ◀ **Critical Viewing**
How do the men in this picture compare with your image of the three men in this scene? **[Generalize]**

MERCUTIO. That's as much as to say, such a case as yours constrains a man to bow in the hams.[16]

ROMEO. Meaning, to curtsy.

MERCUTIO. Thou hast most kindly hit it.

ROMEO. A most courteous exposition.

MERCUTIO. Nay, I am the very pink of courtesy.

ROMEO. Pink for flower.

MERCUTIO. Right.

ROMEO. Why, then is my pump[17] well-flowered.

MERCUTIO. Sure wit, follow me this jest now till thou hast worn out thy pump, that, when the single sole of it is worn, the jest may remain, after the wearing, solely singular.[18]

ROMEO. O single-soled jest, solely singular for the singleness![19]

MERCUTIO. Come between us, good Benvolio! My wits faints.

ROMEO. Swits and spurs, swits and spurs; or I'll cry a match.[20]

MERCUTIO. Nay, if our wits run the wild-goose chase, I am done; for thou hast more of the wild goose in one of

16. hams hips.

17. pump shoe.

18. when . . . singular the jest will outwear the shoe and will then be all alone.

19. O . . . singleness! O thin joke, unique for only one thing—weakness!

20. Swits . . . match Drive your wit harder to beat me or else I'll claim victory in this match of word play.

34 **Reading Check**
How does Romeo respond when Mercutio says Romeo gave them "the slip" the night before?

32 ▶ **Critical Viewing**

Answer: Students may suggest that all three are boisterous and challenging, characteristics that would be exhibited by a group of young men who were having fun and hurling insults at one another.

33 Background

The Dozens

Help students understand that this conversation between Romeo and Mercutio is one long battle of wits, in which each man is making puns out of the other man's words. Understanding the exact logic of the puns is less important than understanding the spirit of the game, which you might compare to "the dozens," or to other ways that teenage boys playfully trade insults.

34 **Reading Check**

Answer: Romeo says he had important business, which took precedence over being courteous to his friends.

CUSTOMIZE INSTRUCTION FOR UNIVERSAL ACCESS

For English Learners	For Gifted/Talented Students
Students might enjoy determining if the meaning of a character's name reflects his or her personality. Tell students that the name *Benvolio* comes from the Latin words *bene*, meaning "well," and *volo*, meaning "I wish." Mercutio's name comes from the Latin name for Mercury, the messenger of the gods, who was known for his quickness, skill, wit, and eloquence. Ask students if they think the characters are well named.	After discussing the appropriateness of such names as *Benvolio* and *Mercutio,* have students work in small groups to invent similarly apt new names for the Nurse and for Friar Lawrence. Have groups present these names to the class and explain how they fit the roles the characters play in the drama.

35 Critical Thinking

Interpret

- Ask students to identify the line in which Mercutio stops joking with Romeo and says something serious.
  Answer: Mercutio gets serious in line 82, when he asks Romeo if having fun isn't better than being depressed all the time.
- Have students interpret Mercutio's words in line 83. How do they reflect his wish that Romeo rejoin the group?
  Possible answer: Students may say that Mercutio characterizes Romeo as being himself when he is sociable with his friends. This is what Mercutio has been trying to get Romeo to do from the beginning of the play.

36 Literary Analysis

Blank Verse and Character Rank

- Ask students what kind of language they would expect Mercutio to use, given that he is a member of the upper class.
  Possible response: Mercutio might be expected to speak in blank verse, the language of the upper class.
- Ask the Literary Analysis question on p. 808: How does Shakespeare reveal Mercutio's intelligence despite the fact that the character does not speak in blank verse?
  Answer: Shakespeare reveals Mercutio's intelligence through his quick and imaginative wit.

thy wits than, I am sure, I have in my whole five. Was I with you there for the goose?

ROMEO. Thou wast never with me for anything when thou wast not there for the goose.

MERCUTIO. I will bite thee by the ear for that jest.

ROMEO. Nay, good goose, bite not!

MERCUTIO. Thy wit is a very bitter sweeting;[21] it is a most sharp sauce.

ROMEO. And is it not, then, well served in to a sweet goose?

MERCUTIO. O, here's a wit of cheveril,[22] that stretches from an inch narrow to an ell broad!

ROMEO. I stretch it out for that word "broad," which added to the goose, proves thee far and wide a broad goose.

35 **MERCUTIO.** Why, is not this better now than groaning for love? Now art thou sociable, now art thou Romeo; now art thou what thou art, by art as well as by nature. For this driveling love is like a great natural[23] that runs lolling[24] up and down to hide his bauble[25] in a hole.

BENVOLIO. Stop there, stop there!

MERCUTIO. Thou desirest me to stop in my tale against the hair.[26]

BENVOLIO. Thou wouldst else have made thy tale large.

36 **MERCUTIO.** O, thou art deceived! I would have made it short; for I was come to the whole depth of my tale, and meant indeed to occupy the argument[27] no longer.

ROMEO. Here's goodly gear![28]

[*Enter* NURSE *and her Man,* PETER.]

A sail, a sail!

MERCUTIO. Two, two! A shirt and a smock.[29]

NURSE. Peter!

PETER. Anon.

NURSE. My fan, Peter.

MERCUTIO. Good Peter, to hide her face; for her fan's the fairer face.

NURSE. God ye good morrow, gentlemen.

MERCUTIO. God ye good-den, fair gentlewoman.

NURSE. Is it good-den?

MERCUTIO. 'Tis no less, I tell ye; for the bawdy hand of the

21. **sweeting** a kind of apple.

22. **cheveril** easily stretched kid leather.

23. **natural** idiot.

24. **lolling** with tongue hanging out.

25. **bauble** toy.

Literary Analysis
Blank Verse and Character Rank How does Shakespeare reveal Mercutio's intelligence despite the fact that the character does not speak in blank verse?

26. **the hair** natural inclination.

27. **occupy the argument** talk about the matter.

28. **goodly gear** good stuff for joking (Romeo sees Nurse approaching).

29. **A shirt and a smock** a man and a woman.

ENRICHMENT: History Connection

Costumes

Students may have noticed that unlike modern plays, the stage directions in this play give virtually no indication of how the set should look. The reason for this is simple: scenery and set design had not been invented in the theater of Shakespeare's time.

Costumes, however, were an important element in any production. Elizabethan audiences demanded spectacle. They were used to seeing members of the royal family and other officials parading down local streets in fine clothing, and they expected to see the same kinds of color and pageant on similar characters in a play.

Such spectacle was costly, however. Costumes were the single most expensive item in Elizabethan theater. Philip Henslowe, the owner of a rival theater to the Globe, once spent as much on costumes for a production as he spent on fourteen employees for a six-year period.

dial is now upon the prick of noon.

NURSE. Out upon you! What a man are you!

ROMEO. One, gentlewoman, that God hath made, himself to mar.

37

NURSE. By my troth, it is well said. "For himself to mar," quoth 'a? Gentlemen, can any of you tell me where I may find the young Romeo?

ROMEO. I can tell you; but young Romeo will be older when you have found him than he was when you sought him. I am the youngest of that name, for fault[30] of a worse.

NURSE. You say well.

MERCUTIO. Yea, is the worst well? Very well took,[31] i' faith! Wisely, wisely.

NURSE. If you be he, sir, I desire some confidence[32] with you.

BENVOLIO. She will endite him to some supper.

MERCUTIO. A bawd, a bawd, a bawd! So ho!

ROMEO. What hast thou found?

MERCUTIO. No hare, sir; unless a hare, sir, in a lenten pie, that is something stale and hoar ere it be spent.

[*He walks by them and sings.*]

An old hare hoar,
And an old hare hoar,
Is very good meat in Lent;
But a hare that is hoar
Is too much for a score
When it hoars ere it be spent.

Romeo, will you come to your father's? We'll to dinner thither.

ROMEO. I will follow you.

MERCUTIO. Farewell, ancient lady. Farewell, [*singing*] "Lady, lady, lady."[33] [*Exit* MERCUTIO, BENVOLIO.]

NURSE. I pray you, sir, what saucy merchant was this that was so full of his ropery?[34]

ROMEO. A gentleman, nurse, that loves to hear himself talk and will speak more in a minute than he will stand to in a month.

NURSE. And 'a[35] speak anything against me, I'll take him down, and 'a were lustier than he is, and twenty such Jacks; and if I cannot, I'll find those that shall. Scurvy knave! I am none of his flirt-gills;[36] I am none of his

30. **fault** lack.

31. **took** understood.

32. **confidence** Nurse means *conference*.

33. **"Lady . . . lady"** line from an old ballad, "Chaste Susanna."

34. **ropery** Nurse means *roguery*, the talk and conduct of a rascal.

35. **'a** he.

36. **flirt-gills** common girls.

38 **Reading Check**

Who interrupts Romeo and his friends to ask about Romeo?

37 Critical Thinking

Predict

- Apart from providing more humor, ask students what else the Nurse is doing on stage in this scene. **Answer:** She is looking for Romeo.
- Have students predict what the Nurse will talk to Romeo about when she is alone with him. **Possible response:** Students may say that the Nurse will give a message to Romeo from Juliet, or she will try to find out his intentions toward Juliet.

38 Reading Check

Answer: The Nurse interrupts Romeo and his friends.

CUSTOMIZE INSTRUCTION FOR UNIVERSAL ACCESS

For English Learners

Point out to students that first Romeo makes fun of the Nurse for her large billowing smock, then he mocks her for talking too much. He is saying that she is talking so long that "young" Romeo will be "older" by the time she finishes talking. Encourage students to compare Romeo's joke with the contemporary expression, ". . . before the next century, please."

For Advanced Readers

Recommend that students watch the video of the musical *West Side Story,* which is modeled on *Romeo and Juliet.* Set in New York City, the musical concerns Tony, a founding member of a street gang, and Maria, the sister of the leader of a rival gang. Have students note the similarities and differences in the two works, and write a brief report to present to the class.

39 Literary Analysis

Blank Verse and Character Rank

- Ask volunteers to read aloud the Nurse's speech in lines 150–159, trying to communicate both the emotion and the meaning clearly.
- Ask students to paraphrase what the Nurse is saying in these lines. **Possible response:** "I am shaking with anger. My mistress asked me to talk to you. I won't tell you what she said, but I will say that if you deceive her you will be behaving badly. She is very young, and if you betray her, it would be a terrible thing to do to any woman, and not worthy of a man."
- Have students answer the Literary Analysis question on p. 810: Why do you think Shakespeare chose to write the Nurse's lines without attention to blank verse? **Possible response:** The Nurse is a comic, lower-class character who generally speaks in a more informal manner. Shakespeare usually limited his blank verse to the upper-class characters who, according to the class bias of the time, would speak in such a poetic manner.

40 Reading Strategy

Reading Blank Verse

- Ask students what Romeo says in response to the Nurse's critical words to him. **Answer:** He protests the Nurse's opinion of him and asks her to convey his respect and best wishes to Juliet.
- Ask students to describe how the Nurse and Friar Lawrence have similar roles in the play, given what students know about the two characters so far. **Answer:** The Nurse and Friar Lawrence are both willing—perhaps too willing—to help Romeo and Juliet be together.
- Have students respond to the Reading Strategy question on p. 810: How would you rephrase Romeo's words in lines 170–171? **Possible response:** "Juliet will go to confession and then we will be married in Friar Lawrence's room."

skainsmates.[37] And thou must stand by too, and suffer
every knave to use me at his pleasure!

PETER. I saw no man use you at his pleasure. If I had, my weapon should quickly have been out, I warrant you. I dare draw as soon as another man, if I see occasion in a good quarrel, and the law on my side.

39

NURSE. Now, afore God, I am so vexed that every part about me quivers. Scurvy knave! Pray you, sir, a word; and, as I told you, my young lady bid me inquire you out. What she bid me say, I will keep to myself; but first let me tell ye, if ye should lead her in a fool's paradise, as they say, it were a very gross kind of behavior, as they say; for the gentlewoman is young; and therefore, if you should deal double with her, truly it were an ill thing to be off'red to any gentlewoman, and very weak[38] dealing.

40

ROMEO. Nurse, commend[39] me to thy lady and mistress.
I protest unto thee—

NURSE. Good heart, and i' faith I will tell her as much. Lord, Lord, she will be a joyful woman.

ROMEO. What wilt thou tell her, nurse? Thou dost not mark me.

NURSE. I will tell her, sir, that you do protest, which, as I take it, is a gentlemanlike offer.

ROMEO. Bid her devise
Some means to come to shrift[40] this afternoon;
And there she shall at Friar Lawrence' cell
Be shrived and married. Here is for thy pains.

NURSE. No, truly, sir; not a penny.

ROMEO. Go to! I say you shall.

NURSE. This afternoon, sir? Well, she shall be there.

ROMEO. And stay, good nurse, behind the abbey wall.
Within this hour my man shall be with thee
And bring thee cords made like a tackled stair.[41]
Which to the high topgallant[42] of my joy
Must be my convoy[43] in the secret night.
Farewell. Be trusty, and I'll quit[44] thy pains.
Farewell. Commend me to thy mistress.

NURSE. Now God in heaven bless thee! Hark you, sir.

ROMEO. What say'st thou, my dear nurse?

NURSE. Is your man secret? Did you ne'er hear say,
Two may keep counsel, putting one away?[45]

37. **skainsmates** criminals; cutthroats.

Literary Analysis
Blank Verse and Character Rank Why do you think Shakespeare chose to write the Nurse's lines without attention to blank verse?

38. **weak** unmanly.

39. **commend** convey my respect and best wishes.

40. **shrift** confession.

Reading Strategy
Reading Blank Verse How would you rephrase Romeo's words in lines 170–171?

41. **tackled stair** rope ladder.

42. **topgallant** summit.

43. **convoy** conveyance.

44. **quit** reward; pay you back for.

45. **Two . . . away** Two can keep a secret if one is ignorant, or out of the way.

ENRICHMENT: Social Studies Connection

Early Marriage

In Shakespeare's day it would not be unusual for parents to choose husbands or wives for their children. Nor would it be unusual for a girl as young as thirteen or fourteen to be married, as Juliet is. Women were seen as the property of the family, and they might easily be forced to marry—or prevented from marrying. Indeed, later in the play, Juliet's father offers her a choice between marrying the man of his choice or becoming a nun.

Women who married were expected to bring their husbands a *dowry*—a certain amount of goods, property, or money to compensate the husband and his family for the expense of caring for the wife for the rest of her life. Women without property were naturally at a disadvantage in the marriage market.

Invite students to discuss how the conditions surrounding marriage help to shape the plot of *Romeo and Juliet.*

ROMEO. Warrant thee my man's as true as steel.

NURSE. Well, sir, my mistress is the sweetest lady. Lord, Lord! When 'twas a little prating[46] thing— O, there is a nobleman in town, one Paris, that would fain lay knife aboard;[47] but she, good soul, had as lieve[48] see a toad, a very toad, as see him. I anger her sometimes, and tell her that Paris is the properer man; but I'll warrant you, when I say so, she looks as pale as any clout[49] in the versal world.[50] Doth not rosemary and Romeo begin both with a letter?

ROMEO. Ay, nurse; what of that? Both with an *R*.

NURSE. Ah, mocker! That's the dog's name.[51] *R* is for the— No; I know it begins with some other letter; and she hath the prettiest sententious[52] of it, of you and rosemary, that it would do you good to hear it.

ROMEO. Commend me to thy lady.

NURSE. Ay, a thousand times. [*Exit* ROMEO.] Peter!

PETER. Anon.

NURSE. Before, and apace.[53] [*Exit, after* PETER.]

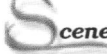

Scene v. CAPULET's *orchard.*

[*Enter* JULIET.]

41

JULIET. The clock struck nine when I did send the nurse;
In half an hour she promised to return.
Perchance she cannot meet him. That's not so.
O, she is lame! Love's heralds should be thoughts,
Which ten times faster glides than the sun's beams
Driving back shadows over low'ring[1] hills.
Therefore do nimble-pinioned doves draw Love,[2]
And therefore hath the wind-swift Cupid wings.
Now is the sun upon the highmost hill
Of this day's journey, and from nine till twelve
Is three long hours; yet she is not come.
Had she affections and warm youthful blood,
She would be as swift in motion as a ball;
My words would bandy her[3] to my sweet love,
And his to me.
But old folks, many feign[4] as they were dead—
Unwieldy, slow, heavy and pale as lead.

[*Enter* NURSE *and* PETER.]

O God, she comes! O honey nurse, what news?
Hast thou met with him? Send thy man away.

46. **prating** babbling.

47. **fain . . . aboard** eagerly seize Juliet for himself.

48. **had as lieve** would as willingly.

49. **clout** cloth.

50. **versal world** universe.

51. **dog's name** *R* sounds like a growl.

52. **sententious** Nurse means *sentences*—clever, wise sayings.

53. **Before, and apace** Go ahead of me, and quickly.

1. **low'ring** darkening.

2. **Therefore . . . Love** therefore, doves with quick wings pull the chariot of Venus, goddess of love.

Literary Analysis
Blank Verse What is the effect of hearing Juliet's blank verse right after the Nurse's prose speeches?

3. **bandy her** send her rapidly.

4. **feign** act.

unwieldy (un wēl′ dē) *adj.* awkward; clumsy

42 **Reading Check**
What does Romeo ask the Nurse to tell Juliet?

41 Literary Analysis

Blank Verse

- Ask students what basic problem Juliet has with her Nurse in this long speech. Who else has already commented on this problem with the Nurse?
  Answer: Juliet is complaining that her Nurse is late and slow; Juliet thought she would be back by now. Romeo also had trouble getting the Nurse to tell him her news without delay.
- Ask students why Juliet is so impatient.
  Answer: Juliet knows the Nurse will have word of Romeo and his plans for their marriage.
- Ask the Literary Analysis question on p. 811: What is the effect of hearing Juliet's blank verse right after the Nurse's prose speeches?
  Possible response: Students may suggest that the change in the means of expression emphasizes several other shifts: in scene, character, and emotional state.

42 Reading Check

Answer: Romeo asks the Nurse to tell Juliet to meet him at Friar Lawrence's that afternoon, after saying to her family that she is going to confession.

CUSTOMIZE INSTRUCTION FOR UNIVERSAL ACCESS

For Special Needs Students	For Less Proficient Students
Students may enjoy thinking of ways to describe their own feelings when they are waiting impatiently for something they dearly want—a phone call from a friend, the results of a test, the news from someone about a sick relative, and so forth. Have them read Juliet's speech and write images of their own. How might they use the following in descriptions of their own about time passing slowly: a striking clock, the sun, shadows, birds on the wing, day and night, hours, and so forth.	Help students to see that though she cares for Juliet dearly, the Nurse knows whom she has to please to keep her position. Have them recall how she described Paris to Juliet in Act I, as a "man of wax" (a model of a man), and a flower. Ask students to read the Nurse's words here in lines 187–195 to see what she says to Romeo about Paris and infer why she might say such a thing.

43 Reading Strategy
Reading Blank Verse

- Remind students that blank verse is unrhymed verse written in iambic pentameter, or lines of five stressed beats in which every second syllable is stressed.
- Have students respond to the Reading Strategy question on p. 812: How might an actress pronounce *lookest* to keep the meter of the blank verse?
  Answer: The actress playing Juliet might pronounce *lookest* as *lookst*— one syllable—to keep the meter of the line intact.

44 Reading Strategy
Reading Blank Verse

- Ask students to paraphrase what Juliet says to the Nurse in lines 31–34.
  Possible response: Juliet says that the Nurse is taking longer in her delay than it would take her to tell Juliet the news of Romeo.

Monitor Progress Have students describe what Juliet finally does to get an answer.
Answer: Juliet asks the Nurse to tell her simply whether the news is good or bad; she can get the details later.

- Have students read aloud lines 30–31 and notice the four uses of the word *breath*. Ask them whether *breath* is stressed or unstressed in its use, and what the effect of the repetition is.
  Answer: The word is stressed each time it is used. The effect is to emphasize the breath that the Nurse says is in short supply.

NURSE. Peter, stay at the gate. [*Exit* PETER.]

(43)
JULIET. Now, good sweet nurse—O Lord, why lookest thou sad?
Though news be sad, yet tell them merrily;
If good, thou shamest the music of sweet news
By playing it to me with so sour a face.

NURSE. I am aweary, give me leave[5] awhile.
Fie, how my bones ache! What a jaunce[6] have I!

JULIET. I would thou hadst my bones, and I thy news.
Nay, come, I pray thee speak. Good, good nurse, speak.

NURSE. Jesu, what haste? Can you not stay a while?
Do you not see that I am out of breath?

(44)
JULIET. How art thou out of breath when thou hast breath
To say to me that thou art out of breath?
The excuse that thou dost make in this delay
Is longer than the tale thou dost excuse.
Is thy news good or bad? Answer to that.
Say either, and I'll stay the circumstance.[7]
Let me be satisfied, is't good or bad?

(45)
NURSE. Well, you have made a simple[8] choice; you know not how to choose a man. Romeo? No, not he. Though his face be better than any man's, yet his leg excels all men's; and for a hand and a foot, and a body, though they be not to be talked on, yet they are past compare. He is not the flower of courtesy, but, I'll warrant him, as gentle as a lamb. Go thy ways, wench; serve God. What, have you dined at home?

JULIET. No, no. But all this I did know before.
What says he of our marriage? What of that?

NURSE. Lord, how my head aches! What a head have I!
It beats as it would fall in twenty pieces.
My back a[9] t'other side—ah, my back, my back!
Beshrew[10] your heart for sending me about
To catch my death with jauncing up and down!

JULIET. I' faith, I am sorry that thou art not well.
Sweet, sweet, sweet nurse, tell me, what says my love?

NURSE. Your love says, like an honest gentleman, and a courteous, and a kind, and a handsome, and, I warrant, a virtuous— Where is your mother?

JULIET. Where is my mother? Why, she is within.
Where should she be? How oddly thou repliest!
"Your love says, like an honest gentleman,
'Where is your mother?'"

Reading Strategy
Reading Blank Verse How might an actress pronounce *lookest* to keep the meter of blank verse?

5. give me leave excuse me; give me a moment's rest.

6. jaunce rough trip.

7. stay the circumstance wait for the details.

8. simple foolish; simple-minded.

Literary Analysis
Blank Verse and Character Rank What might Shakespeare be indicating about the Nurse's character by having her switch between prose and blank verse?

9. a on.

10. Beshrew shame on.

(46) **Critical Viewing** Which details of this picture reflect the feelings Romeo and Juliet have for each other? **[Interpret]**

(47) **Reading Check**
How does the Nurse describe Romeo?

ENRICHMENT: Performing Arts Connection
Sarah Siddons as Juliet

Tell students that various actresses who have played Juliet have brought their own interpretation of the character to the role. One famous actress was Sarah Siddons (1755–1831), who critics claimed was the greatest Shakespearean actress of her time.

Although her greatest achievement was her role as Lady Macbeth, Siddons's portrayal of Juliet was also beautiful and convincing.

The following diary entry written by Mrs. Thrale, a long-standing follower and admirer of Siddons, gives a critique of Siddons's portrayal of Juliet:

"Mrs. Siddons acted Juliet last night. She does it so naturally says someone, so artificially rather said I; but she is a great Performer . . . the pouting Scene with the old Nurse was the cleverest thing I ever saw—so pretty, so Babyish, so charming . . .

45 Literary Analysis (p. 812)

Blank Verse and Character Rank

- Ask students to read the Nurse's speech in lines 37–44 aloud. How would they identify the form of writing?
  Possible answer: Students may say that some of the lines are blank verse and others are not.
- Have students respond to the Literary Analysis question on p. 812: What might Shakespeare be indicating about the Nurse's character by having her switch between prose and blank verse?
  Answer: Shakespeare might be indicating the Nurse is trying to match Juliet's method of speech in this emotionally charged scene, but because it is not her normal way of speaking, she does not quite carry it off.

46 ▶Critical Viewing

Answer: Romeo and Juliet are holding each other, showing their affection. They are also looking upward, as if they were listening to someone like the Friar.

47 Reading Check

Answer: He is handsome and gentle but does not have good manners.

CUSTOMIZE INSTRUCTION FOR UNIVERSAL ACCESS

For Less Proficient Readers	For English Learners
Ask students if they think Juliet's treatment of the Nurse is justified. What do they think about her words and her behavior? Why is Juliet likely to get away with such behavior? Answer: Some students will say that Juliet is being rude and unsympathetic to her poor old nurse, whose tiredness and aching bones are the direct result of doing Juliet a favor. Other students will say that Juliet is justified because the Nurse is exaggerating her ailments to tease Juliet and keep her in suspense.	Remind students that words in a blank verse text must sometimes be tweaked in order to fit the meter. In addition to the word *lookest,* which they have already considered, have students find the following words on this page: *shamest,* line 23, *is't,* line 36; *I am,* line 52. Ask students how each word or phrase should be pronounced in order to fit the meter.

48 Literary Analysis

Blank Verse

- Ask students why they think the Nurse asks Juliet where her mother is.
  Answer: Nurse does not want Lady Capulet to overhear what she has to say to Juliet.
- Invite students to answer the first Literary Analysis question on p. 814: Why do you think Shakespeare broke the pattern of blank verse in line 67?
  Possible response: Students may say that the Nurse, at last, has gotten to the point. When the Nurse asks if Juliet has permission to go to confession, Juliet knows that this is how she will meet Romeo. Her response is short and to the point because she wants to discontinue the Nurse's talk.

49 Literary Analysis

Blank Verse

- Ask students to interpret the phrase "hie you hence" in line 68.
  Possible response: Students should see that the phrase means something like, "Go you then," or "You will go then."
- Have students answer the second Literary Analysis question on p. 814: What effect is created by making Juliet's last line rhyme with the Nurse's last line?
  Answer: The lines create a rhyming couplet, which Shakespeare often uses to close a scene. It also shows that the Nurse and Juliet are in agreement about Juliet's wedding plans.

50 Reading Strategy

Reading Blank Verse

- Have students review Romeo's speech in lines 24–29.
- Ask the Reading Strategy question on p. 815: How can you read Romeo's lines most effectively to grasp their meaning as well as their poetry?
  Possible response: Students may say that readers should pause at the commas because each phrase separated by two commas communicates a different idea.

NURSE. O God's Lady dear!
Are you so hot?[11] Marry come up, I trow.[12]
Is this the poultice[13] for my aching bones?
Henceforward do your messages yourself.

48

JULIET. Here's such a coil![14] Come, what says Romeo?

NURSE. Have you got leave to go to shrift today?

JULIET. I have.

NURSE. Then hie you hence to Friar Lawrence' cell;
There stays a husband to make you a wife.
Now comes the wanton[15] blood up in your cheeks:
They'll be in scarlet straight at any news.
Hie you to church: I must another way,
To fetch a ladder, by the which your love
Must climb a bird's nest soon when it is dark.
I am the drudge, and toil in your delight:
But you shall bear the burden soon at night.
Go; I'll to dinner; hie you to the cell.

49

JULIET. Hie to high fortune! Honest nurse, farewell. *[Exit all.]*

Scene vi. FRIAR LAWRENCE's *cell.*

[*Enter* FRIAR LAWRENCE *and* ROMEO.]

FRIAR. So smile the heavens upon this holy act
That afterhours with sorrow chide us not![1]

ROMEO. Amen, amen! But come what sorrow can,
It cannot countervail[2] the exchange of joy
That one short minute gives me in her sight.
Do thou but close our hands with holy words,
Then love-devouring death do what he dare—
It is enough I may but call her mine.

FRIAR. These violent delights have violent ends
And in their triumph die, like fire and powder,[3]
Which, as they kiss, consume. The sweetest honey
Is loathsome in his own deliciousness
And in the taste confounds[4] the appetite.
Therefore love moderately: long love doth so;
Too swift arrives as tardy as too slow.

[*Enter* JULIET.]

Here comes the lady. O, so light a foot
Will ne'er wear out the everlasting flint.[5]
A lover may bestride the gossamers[6]
That idles in the wanton summer air,
And yet not fall; so light is vanity.[7]

11. hot impatient; hot-tempered.
12. Marry . . . trow Indeed, cool down, I say.
13. poultice remedy.
14. coil disturbance.

Literary Analysis
Blank Verse Why do you think Shakespeare broke the pattern of blank verse in line 67?

15. wanton excited.

Literary Analysis
Blank Verse What effect is created by making Juliet's last line rhyme with the Nurse's last line?

1. That . . . not! that the future does not punish us with sorrow.
2. countervail equal.
3. powder gunpowder.
4. confounds destroys.
5. flint stone.
6. gossamers spider webs.
7. vanity foolish things that cannot last.

ENRICHMENT: Social Studies Connection

Weddings

Tell students that in many cultures, weddings are still celebrated in much the same way that Elizabethan weddings were enjoyed. For example, in some towns and villages in Greece, Italy, and in other cultures, everyone is invited to a wedding. People in the town join the bride on her way to the church. Often, the wedding is celebrated for two or three days, even after the bride and groom have left the party. There is always an abundance of food, and people dance and play games.

All cultures have their own rituals and customs for weddings. These are passed down through generations, changing very little.

Have students compare and contrast the wedding customs of cultures in the Far East, Africa, South America, and the United States. Ask students of various cultural backgrounds to describe wedding customs unique to their cultures. What wedding customs are common to all cultures? Which ones are unique?

JULIET. Good even to my ghostly confessor.

FRIAR. Romeo shall thank thee, daughter, for us both.

JULIET. As much to him,[8] else is his thanks too much.

ROMEO. Ah, Juliet, if the measure of thy joy
Be heaped like mine, and that thy skill be more
50 To blazon it,[9] then sweeten with thy breath
This neighbor air, and let rich music's tongue
Unfold the imagined happiness that both
Receive in either by this dear encounter.

JULIET. Conceit, more rich in matter than in words,
Brags of his substance, not of ornament.[10]
They are but beggars that can count their worth;
But my true love is grown to such excess
I cannot sum up sum of half my wealth.

FRIAR. Come, come with me, and we will make short work;
For, by your leaves, you shall not stay alone
Till Holy Church incorporate two in one. [*Exit all.*]

8. As . . . him the same greeting to him.

Reading Strategy
Reading Blank Verse
How can you read Romeo's lines most effectively to grasp their meaning as well as their poetry?

9. and . . . it and if you are better able to proclaim it.

10. Conceit . . . ornament Understanding does not need to be dressed up in words.

Review and Assess

Thinking About Act II

1. **Respond:** Do you think Friar Lawrence is wise to agree to marry Romeo and Juliet? Explain.
2. **(a) Recall:** Where do Romeo and Juliet first mutually declare their love for each other? **(b) Interpret:** What role does darkness play in the scene?
3. **(a) Recall:** What doubts and fears does Juliet express even as she realizes that Romeo loves her? **(b) Make a Judgment:** Do you think the couple will be able to overcome these problems? Explain.
4. **(a) Recall:** What weakness in Romeo does the Friar point out before agreeing to help? **(b) Compare and Contrast:** How do the Friar's motives differ from the couple's own motives?
5. **(a) Recall:** For whom does Juliet wait in Act II, Scene v? **(b) Interpret:** What are Juliet's feelings as she waits to hear the message Romeo has sent?
6. **Analyze:** What tragic events to come are foreshadowed in Act II?
7. **Evaluate:** Why do you think the love scene in Capulet's garden is one of the most famous in all of literature?

ASSESSMENT PRACTICE: Literary Response

Defending Responses (For more practice, see Test Preparation Workbook, p. 46.)

Many tests require students to write short, essay-type answers that respond to a written text. Use the following sample item to show students how to defend their responses to the text in an essay-type question.

Have students read Juliet, lines 38–48, p. 798. Write the following on the board:

How does Juliet feel about Romeo's name?

Remind students that their answers should be based on the text and should include supporting evidence. After students have time to write a brief response, discuss the text and the question-answer. All answers should include references to the text.

Possible answer: Juliet says a rose by any other name would smell as sweet. She doesn't care what he is called, Romeo is still a man who possesses the charm and perfection he would with any other name.

ASSESS

Answers for p. 815

Review and Assess

1. Some students may say that Friar Lawrence is wise because Romeo and Juliet seem sincere in their love for each other and because their marriage would unify the warring families. Others may characterize the Friar as well-intentioned but unwise.
2. **(a)** Romeo and Juliet mutually declare their love for each other in the balcony scene. **(b)** The darkness conceals Romeo from Juliet's relatives. It also provides an illusion of privacy so that Juliet feels she can speak her thoughts aloud. Her words of love for Romeo prompt him to come out of hiding and declare his love.
3. **(a)** Juliet fears for Romeo's life at the hands of her relatives. She fears that his love is shallow. She questions whether he can truly be in love when they barely know each other. **(b)** The answer is "no" because the Prologue to Act I says that the lovers will die.
4. **(a)** The Friar says that Romeo is fickle. Romeo argues that the situation with Rosaline was a different matter because Rosaline did not return his love and Juliet does. **(b)** The Friar's motives are to help end the feud between the families, while the couple's motives are to be together because they are in love.
5. **(a)** Juliet awaits the Nurse. **(b)** Juliet is highly impatient and her exasperation increases as she tries to extract news from the breathless Nurse.
6. Students may point out Scene ii, lines 75–78 and 116–120; Scene iii, lines 23–30; Scene iv, lines 6–8 and 13–16; and Scene vi, lines 1–2 and 9–11.
7. Students may say that the romantic words and images, the vivid descriptions, and the expressions of devotion are extremely effective.

Answers for p. 816

Review and Assess

1. Use an overhead projector to mark the unaccented and accented syllables in these passages as a class.
2. **Blank Verse Pattern:**

   ROMEO: Căn Í gŏ fórwărd whén

   mŷ héart ĭs hére?

   JULIET: Bŭt mŷ trŭe lóve ĭs

   grówn tŏ súch ĕxcéss.

   Key Words: I, forward, heart, here, my, love, grown, such, excess Significance: The words help communicate key ideas about the mutual love of Romeo and Juliet.
3. The Capulets and the Montagues, their friends, the Prince, and the Friar speak in blank verse. The servants and the Nurse are common people.
4. **(a)** Blank verse signals seriousness and status. **(b)** Shifts from verse to prose emphasize changes in mood and tone.
5. There are six sentences in these lines.
6. Suggested response: "The clock struck nine when I did send the nurse; in half an hour she promised to return. [pause] Perchance she cannot meet him. [pause] That's not so. [pause] O, she is lame! [pause] Love's heralds should be thoughts, which ten times faster glides than the sun's beams driving back shadows over low'ring hills. [pause] Therefore do nimble-pinioned doves draw Love, and therefore hath the wind-swift Cupid wings."
7. Suggested response: "It was nine o'clock when I sent the nurse, and she promised to return in half an hour. Maybe she can't meet him. Oh, she is so slow! Love's messengers should be like thoughts, which move ten times faster than sunbeams chase back shadows. Speed is the reason Love is drawn by flying doves and Cupid has wings."
8. Possible response: Students may say that Romeo and Juliet's attitude toward marriage is more traditional than contemporary teenagers' attitudes.

Review and Assess

Literary Analysis

Blank Verse

1. Copy the following passages of **blank verse.** Then, indicate the pattern of accented (´) and unaccented (˘) syllables in each line.
   (a) Act II, Scene ii, lines 43–51
   (b) Act II, Scene vi, lines 3–8
2. Using a chart like the one shown, rewrite the lines below, marking stressed and unstressed syllables. Then, indicate which key words are stressed in each line and explain why those words are important to the drama.
   (a) ROMEO. Can I go forward when my heart is here?
   (b) JULIET. But my true love is grown to such excess.

Blank Verse Pattern	Key Words	Significance

Connecting Literary Elements

3. Identify the aristocratic and common people in Acts I and II, based on whether or not they speak in blank verse.
4. (a) Why do you think Shakespeare chose to have aristocratic characters speak in blank verse instead of ordinary prose? (b) What is the effect of such a choice?

Reading Strategy

Reading Blank Verse

5. How many sentences are in lines 1–8 in Act II, Scene v?
6. Copy Act II, Scene v, lines 1–8 as a paragraph. Read your paragraph aloud, and mark it to indicate where it is natural to take a breath or pause.
7. Rewrite the paragraph in your own words.

Extend Understanding

8. **Cultural Connection:** How does the attitude that Romeo and Juliet appear to have toward marriage compare with the attitudes of teenagers in our time?

Quick Review

Blank verse is unrhymed verse written in iambic pentameter, or lines of five stressed beats in which every second syllable is stressed.

Shakespeare often uses blank verse to indicate **character rank** or importance.

When **reading blank verse,** pause according to the punctuation, not necessarily at the end of each line.

Take It to the Net
www.phschool.com
Take the interactive self-test online to check your understanding of Act II.

TEACHING RESOURCES

The following resources can be used to enrich or extend the instruction for pp. 816–817.

Vocabulary
- **Selection Support**: Build Vocabulary, p. 185
- **Vocabulary and Spelling Practice Book** (Use this booklet for skills enrichment.)

Grammar
- **Selection Support:** Build Grammar Skills, p. 186
- **Writing and Grammar,** Gold Level, p. 552

Daily Language Practice Transparencies

Writing
- **Writing and Grammar iText CD-ROM**

BLOCK SCHEDULING: Resources marked with this symbol provide varied instruction during 90-minute blocks.

Integrate Language Skills

1 Vocabulary Development Lesson

Word Analysis: Latin Prefix *inter-*

The Latin prefix *inter-*, which means "between" or "among," appears in *intercession*, meaning "the act of going between." Use the meaning of *inter-* to define each word below.

1. international **2.** interpersonal **3.** interstate

Spelling Strategy

If a word ends in one consonant preceded by one vowel and the final syllable is not accented, do not double the final consonant when adding a suffix. For example, *waver* + *-er* = *waverer*. Add the suffix shown and write the new word.

1. peril (*-ous*) **2.** gather (*-ed*) **3.** travel (*-ing*)

Fluency: Clarify Word Meaning

Review the vocabulary words on page 794. In your notebook, match each expression on the left with its meaning on the right.

1. lamentable intercession	a. low slyness
2. procure quickly	b. dominating hue
3. vile cunning	c. sickly skin tone
4. predominant color	d. awkward tool
5. sallow complexion	e. sad pleading
6. unwieldy implement	f. cowardly fluctuator
7. spineless waverer	g. obtain fast

2 Grammar Lesson

Possessive Case of Personal Pronouns

The **possessive case of personal pronouns** shows possession before nouns and gerunds. Possessive pronouns can also be used alone.

Before Noun: By *her* high forehead and *her* scarlet lip . . .
Before Gerund: Romeo did not mind *their* joking.
Alone: In such a case as *mine* a man may strain courtesy.

Practice Copy the following sentences, and underline the personal pronouns in the possessive case. Identify the function each serves.

1. Is the money yours?
2. He seems to have lost his reason.
3. Her ramblings frustrated them.
4. Our families will never understand.
5. The choice to act is ours.

Writing Application In three sentences, demonstrate all three ways to use possessive pronouns.

W G Prentice Hall Writing and Grammar Connection: Chapter 24, Section 1

3 Extension Activities

Writing In an **adaptation,** place Shakespeare's famous balcony scene in another time and place, such as medieval Japan, the United States during the Civil War, or your hometown today. Change the language and setting, but retain the underlying meaning of the original dialogue.

Listening and Speaking Romeo persuades the Friar to perform his marriage. Practice your powers of persuasion by conducting a **role play** of the situation of your choice with a partner. After your experience, ask for feedback from your partner. **[Group Activity]**

ASSESSMENT RESOURCES

The following resources can be used to assess students' knowledge and skills.

Selection Assessment

- **Formal Assessment,** Selection Test, pp. 167–169
- **Open Book Test,** pp. 139–141
- **Got It! Assessment Videotapes,** Tape 4
- **Test Bank Software**

PRENTICE HALL ASSESSMENT SYSTEM

- **Workbook**
- **Skill Book**
- **Transparencies**
- **CD-ROM**

Take It to the Net

Visit www.phschool.com for self-tests and additional questions on *Romeo and Juliet.*

EXTEND

Answers for p. 817

1 Vocabulary Development

Word Analysis

1. international: between or among nations
2. interpersonal: between or among persons
3. interstate: between or among states

Spelling Strategy

1. perilous
2. gathered
3. traveling

Fluency: Clarify Word Meaning

1. e
2. g
3. a
4. b
5. c
6. d
7. f

2 Grammar

1. yours (alone)
2. his (noun)
3. her (gerund)
4. Our (noun)
5. ours (alone)

Writing Application

Sample sentences:

The prince objected to their quarreling.

The hated names were theirs.

Juliet pledged her heart to Romeo.

3 Extension Activities

Writing Lesson

- Help students determine specific logistics for their scenes. For example, what could replace a balcony? They also need to consider other elements that would make their scene period specific, such as costume, idiomatic and colloquial language, and so forth.
- Encourage students to think of the things that could keep young lovers apart today.
- Ask volunteers to present their completed scenes to the class.

CUSTOMIZE INSTRUCTION
For Universal Access

To address different learning styles, use the activities suggested in the **Extension Activities** booklet, p. 47.

- For Verbal/Linguistic and Bodily/Kinesthetic Learners, use Activity 6.

The Tragedy of Romeo and Juliet, Act III

Lesson Objectives and CA Correlations

1. **To analyze and respond to literary elements**
   - Literary Analysis: Soliloquy, Aside, and Monologue **R 3.1**
   - Connecting Literary Elements: Allusion **R 3.7**
2. **To read, comprehend, analyze, and critique drama**
   - Reading Strategy: Paraphrasing **R 1.2**
   - Reading Check questions
   - Review and Assess questions
   - Assessment Practice (ATE)
3. **To develop word analysis skills, fluency, and systematic vocabulary**
   - Vocabulary Development Lesson: Words From Myths **R 1.3**
4. **To understand and apply written and oral language conventions**
   - Spelling Strategy
   - Grammar Lesson: Pronoun Case: *who* and *whom* **LC 1.3**
5. **To understand and apply appropriate writing and research strategies**
   - Writing Lesson: Persuasive Letter (after Act V) **W 2.4**
   - Extension Activity: Editorial **W 2.3**
6. **To understand and apply listening and speaking strategies**
   - Extension Activity: Film Review **LS 1.8**

STEP-BY-STEP TEACHING GUIDE	PACING GUIDE
PRETEACH	
Motivate Students and Provide Background	
Read and discuss the Review and Anticipate information (SE/ATE p. 819) [A]	5 min.
Introduce the Concepts	
Introduce the Literary Analysis and Reading Strategy (SE/ATE p. 818) [A]	15 min.
Pronounce the vocabulary words and read their definitions (SE p. 818)	5 min.
TEACH	
Monitor Comprehension	
Informally monitor comprehension by circulating while students read independently or in groups [A]	50 min.
Monitor students' comprehension with the Reading Check notes (SE/ATE pp. 819, 821, 823, 825, 827, 829, 831, 833, 835, 837, 839)	as students read
Develop vocabulary with Vocabulary notes (SE pp. 822–825, 836)	as students read
Develop Understanding	
Develop students' understanding of soliloquies, asides, and monologues with the Literary Analysis annotations (SE/ATE pp. 820, 824–826, 828, 830, 833, 834–835, 837, 840) [A]	10 min.
Develop students' ability to paraphrase with the Reading Strategy annotations (SE/ATE pp. 819–820, 822–824, 827–831, 834–836, 838, 840)	10 min.
ASSESS	
Assess Mastery	
Assess students' mastery of the Reading Strategy and Literary Analysis by having them answer the Review and Assess questions (SE/ATE p. 842)	20 min.
Use one or more of the print and media Assessment Resources (ATE p. 843) [A]	up to 50 min.
EXTEND	
Apply Understanding	
Have students complete the Vocabulary Development Lesson and the Grammar Lesson (SE p. 843) [A]	20 min.
Apply students' knowledge of persuasive appeals using the Writing Lesson (SE/ATE p. 877) [A]	45 min.
Apply students' understanding using one or more of the Extension Activities (SE p. 843)	20–90 min.

[A] ACCELERATED INSTRUCTION:
Use the strategies and activities identified with an [A].

UNIVERSAL ACCESS
● = Below Level Students
▲ = On-Level Students
■ = Above Level Students

Time and Resource Manager

Reading Level: Challenging
Average Number of Instructional Days: 4

RESOURCES		
PRINT	**TRANSPARENCIES**	**TECHNOLOGY**
• **Beyond Literature,** Humanities Connection: The Globe Theater, p. 48 ▲ ■		• **Interest Grabber Video,** Tape 4 ● ▲ ■
• **Selection Support Workbook:** ● ▲ ■ Literary Analysis, p. 192 Reading Strategy, p. 191 Build Vocabulary, p. 189	• **Literary Analysis and Reading Transparencies,** pp. 95 and 96 ● ▲ ■	
		• **Listening to Literature** ● ▲ ■ Audiocassettes, Side 25 Audio CDs, CD 17
• **Literatura en español** ● ▲ • **Literary Analysis for Enrichment** ■		
• **Formal Assessment:** Selection Test, pp. 170–172 ● ▲ ■ • **Open Book Test,** pp. 142–144 ● ▲ ■ • PRENTICE HALL ASSESSMENT SYSTEM ● ▲ ■	• PRENTICE HALL ASSESSMENT SYSTEM ● ▲ ■ Skills Practice Answers and Explanations on Transparencies	• **Test Bank Software** ● ▲ ■ • **Got It! Assessment Videotapes,** Tape 4 ● ▲
• **Selection Support Workbook:** ● ▲ ■ Build Grammar Skills, p. 190 • **Writing and Grammar,** Gold Level ● ▲ ■ • **Extension Activities,** p. 47 ● ▲ ■	• **Daily Language Practice Transparencies** ● ▲	• **Writing and Grammar iText CD-ROM** ● ▲ ■ ***Take It to the Net*** www.phschool.com

BLOCK SCHEDULING: Use one 90-minute class period to preteach the selection and have students read it. Use a second 90-minute class period to assess students' mastery of skills and have them complete one of the Extension Activities.

PRETEACH

Step-by-Step Teaching Guide for p. 818

❶ Literary Analysis

Soliloquy, Aside, and Monologue

- Define the three kinds of speeches for students and give an example of each from Acts I and II. Juliet delivers a soliloquy while waiting for the Nurse to return in Act II, Scene v, lines 1–18, as does the Friar in Scene iii, lines 1–22. Romeo is given an aside in Scene ii, line 37, in the balcony scene, and Mercutio's Queen Mab speech in Act I, Scene iv, is a monologue.
- Read the instruction together as a class, and use the instruction for Connecting Literary Elements to explain the use of allusions in literature.
- Use the Literary Focus transparency in **Literary Analysis and Reading Transparencies**, p. 96, to allow students to read and identify an example of soliloquy, aside, and monologue.

❷ Reading Strategy

Paraphrasing

- Remind students that they have been paraphrasing, or restating, passages in the play as they have read the first two acts.
- Use the Paraphrase transparency in **Literary Analysis and Reading Transparencies**, p. 95, to refresh students' memories about how to paraphrase.

Vocabulary Development

- Pronounce each vocabulary word for students, and read the definitions as a class. Have students identify any words with which they are already familiar.

E-Teach

Visit E-Teach at www.phschool.com for teachers' essays on how to teach, with questions and answers.

Prepare to Read

The Tragedy of Romeo and Juliet, Act III

❶ Literary Analysis

Soliloquy, Aside, and Monologue

Shakespeare's characters often deliver these types of dramatic speeches:

- A **soliloquy** is a lengthy speech in which a character—usually alone on stage—expresses his or her thoughts to the audience.
- An **aside** is a brief remark by a character revealing thoughts or feelings to the audience, unheard by other characters.
- A **monologue,** like a soliloquy, is a lengthy speech. However, a monologue is addressed to other characters on stage, not to the audience.

As you read, notice the effect created by each type of speech.

Connecting Literary Elements

Within their dramatic speeches, characters often make **allusions**—references to well-known people, places, or events from myths or literature. Shakespeare's characters often allude to figures in myths or popular stories to add meaning to their speeches. In Act II, Mercutio insultingly calls Tybalt "Prince of Cats," alluding to a cat named Tybalt in French fables. As you read Act III, record allusions you find in a chart like the one shown.

Allusion
Tybalt, Prince of Cats

Refers to
Cats in French fables

Purpose
Insults Tybalt by making fun of his name

❷ Reading Strategy

Paraphrasing

Shakespearean language and style can be difficult to understand today. One way to make sense of difficult passages is to paraphrase them. To **paraphrase,** restate text in your own words.

Shakespeare's version: This gentleman, the prince's near ally / My very friend hath got his mortal hurt / In my behalf. . . .

Paraphrase: My good friend, a close relative of the prince, has been fatally wounded defending me.

As you read Act III, paraphrase passages to help you clarify meaning.

Vocabulary Development

gallant (gal′ ənt) *adj.* brave and noble (p. 822)

fray (frā) *n.* noisy fight (p. 823)

martial (mär′ shəl) *adj.* military (p. 824)

exile (eks′ īl′) *v.* banish (p. 824)

eloquence (el′ ə kwəns) *n.* speech that is vivid, forceful, graceful, and persuasive (p. 825)

fickle (fik′ əl) *adj.* changeable (p. 836)

TEACHING RESOURCES

The following resources can be used to enrich or extend the instruction for p. 818.

Motivation

Interest Grabber Videotapes, Tape 4

Background

Beyond Literature, p. 48

Take It to the Net

Visit www.phschool.com for background and hotlinks for *The Tragedy of Romeo and Juliet.*

Literary Analysis

Literary Analysis and Reading Transparencies, Soliloquy, Aside, and Monologue, p. 96

Reading

Selection Support: Reading Strategy, p. 191; Build Vocabulary, p. 189

Literary Analysis and Reading Transparencies, Paraphrase, p. 95

BLOCK SCHEDULING: Resources marked with this symbol provide varied instruction during 90-minute blocks.

Act III ❶

Review and Anticipate

In Act II, Romeo and Juliet express their mutual love and enlist the aid of Juliet's nurse and Friar Lawrence to arrange a secret marriage ceremony. As the act closes, the young couple are about to be married. Before performing the ceremony, the Friar warns, "These violent delights have violent ends. . . ." How might this statement hint at events that will occur in Act III or later in the play?

Scene i. *A public place.*

[*Enter* MERCUTIO, BENVOLIO, *and* MEN.]

❷
BENVOLIO. I pray thee, good Mercutio, let's retire.
The day is hot, the Capels are abroad,
And, if we meet, we shall not 'scape a brawl,
For now, these hot days, is the mad blood stirring.

MERCUTIO. Thou art like one of these fellows that, when he enters the confines of a tavern, claps me his sword upon the table and says, "God send me no need of thee!" and by the operation of the second cup draws him on the drawer,[1] when indeed there is no need.

BENVOLIO. Am I like such a fellow?

1. and . . . drawer and by the effect of the second drink, draws his sword against the waiter.

❸ **✔ Reading Check**

Why does Benvolio want to get off the street?

TEACH

Step-by-Step Teaching Guide for pp. 819–841

❶ About the Selection

Circumstances and Romeo's impulsive, passionate nature conspire to wreck Romeo and Juliet's happiness in the wake of their secret wedding. Events move toward the tragic outcome that follows from Romeo's killing of Tybalt and banishment from Verona, and the Capulets' plan to marry Juliet to Paris.

❷ Reading Strategy

Paraphrasing

- Review with students what they have learned about blank verse. Ask them why the Capulets are referred to as the Capels in line 2 and why the word *escape* is spoken as *'scape* in line 3. Have students read the lines aloud.
  Answer: *Capulet* does not fit the meter of blank verse, so it has been replaced by a form that will fit. The same is true of the word *escape*, which would add an extra syllable to the line.
- Ask students to recall from earlier acts the kind of character Benvolio exhibits.
  Answer: Benvolio is reasonable and tries to keep the others from fighting.
- After students have read Benvolio's first speech, have them paraphrase it.
  Possible response: "Let's go home, Mercutio. It's a hot day, and the Capulets are out. If we meet, there's bound to be a fight, because everyone has such a nasty temper."

❸ ✔ Reading Check

Answer: Benvolio wants to avoid the street because conditions are ripe for a violent encounter with the Capulets.

TEACHING RESOURCES

The following resources can be used to enrich or extend the instruction for pp. 819–841.

Literary Analysis

Selection Support: Literary Analysis, p. 192

Reading

Listening to Literature Audiocassettes, Side 25 ■

Listening to Literature Audio CDs, CD 17 ■

Extension

Authors In Depth, Gold Level, p. 155 ■

■ **BLOCK SCHEDULING:** Resources marked with this symbol provide varied instruction during 90-minute blocks.

4 Literary Analysis

Soliloquy, Aside, and Monologue

- Have students list some of the things that Mercutio says would provoke Benvolio to get into a fight with someone.
  Possible responses: Benvolio would fight with a man who had a heavier beard than he did; with a man with hazel eyes who was cracking nuts; with someone coughing in the street or waking up a sleeping dog.
- Remind students a *soliloquy* is delivered to the audience by a character who is alone on stage, while a *monologue* is a long speech delivered to other characters in a scene. Now, ask students the Literary Analysis question on p. 820: Which details of Mercutio's speech indicate that it is a monologue and not a soliloquy?
  Answer: Mercutio is not alone when he gives the speech. He speaks directly to Benvolio, and other characters are listening.

5 Reading Strategy

Paraphrasing

- Ask students what they expect to happen when Tybalt comes on stage.
  Possible response: Students may say that because Tybalt and Mercutio are always looking for a fight, they will probably get one.
- Ask the Reading Strategy question on p. 820: How would you paraphrase the exchange between Tybalt and Mercutio to make its tone and meaning understandable to a reader today?
  Possible response: TYBALT: Hello gentlemen. I'd like a word with one of you. MERCUTIO: Just a word? You can do better. Make it a word and a punch. TYBALT: I might just do that if you give me a reason. MERCUTIO: Can't you find a reason of your own? TYBALT: Mercutio, you consort with Romeo. MERCUTIO: Consort? What do you think we are—musicians? If you're going to call us musicians, you'll be hearing some sour notes. Here's my sword—this will make you dance. Consort, my foot!

MERCUTIO. Come, come, thou art as hot a Jack in thy mood as any in Italy; and as soon moved to be moody, and as soon moody to be moved.[2]

BENVOLIO. And what to?

MERCUTIO. Nay, and there were two such, we should have none shortly, for one would kill the other. Thou! Why, thou wilt quarrel with a man that hath a hair more or a hair less in his beard than thou hast. Thou wilt quarrel with a man for cracking nuts, having no other reason but because thou hast hazel eyes. What eye but such an eye would spy out such a quarrel? Thy head is as full of
4 quarrels as an egg is full of meat; and yet thy head hath been beaten as addle[3] as an egg for quarreling. Thou hast quarreled with a man for coughing in the street, because he hath wakened thy dog that hath lain asleep in the sun. Didst thou not fall out with a tailor for wearing his new doublet[4] before Easter? With another for tying his new shoes with old riband?[5] And yet thou wilt tutor me from quarreling![6]

BENVOLIO. And I were so apt to quarrel as thou art, any man should buy the fee simple[7] of my life for an hour and a quarter.[8]

MERCUTIO. The fee simple? O simple![9]

[*Enter* TYBALT, PETRUCHIO, *and* OTHERS.]

BENVOLIO. By my head, here comes the Capulets.

MERCUTIO. By my heel, I care not.

TYBALT. Follow me close, for I will speak to them.
Gentlemen, good-den. A word with one of you.

MERCUTIO. And but one word with one of us? Couple it with something; make it a word and a blow.

TYBALT. You shall find me apt enough to that, sir, and you will give me occasion.[10]

MERCUTIO. Could you not take some occasion without giving?

5 **TYBALT.** Mercutio, thou consortest[11] with Romeo.

MERCUTIO. Consort?[12] What, dost thou make us minstrels? And thou make minstrels of us, look to hear nothing but discords.[13] Here's my fiddlestick; here's that shall make you dance. Zounds,[14] consort!

BENVOLIO. We talk here in the public haunt of men.
Either withdraw unto some private place,
Or reason coldly of your grievances,
Or else depart. Here all eyes gaze on us.

MERCUTIO. Men's eyes were made to look, and let them gaze.
I will not budge for no man's pleasure, I.

2. and . . . moved and as quickly stirred to anger as you are eager to be so stirred.

Literary Analysis
Soliloquy, Aside, and Monologue Which details of Mercutio's speech indicate that it is a monologue and not a soliloquy?

3. addle scrambled; crazy.

4. doublet jacket.

5. riband ribbon.

6. tutor . . . quarreling instruct me not to quarrel.

7. fee simple complete possession.

8. an hour and a quarter length of time that a man with Mercutio's fondness for quarreling may be expected to live.

9. O simple! O stupid!

Reading Strategy
Paraphrasing How would you paraphrase the exchange between Tybalt and Mercutio to make its tone and meaning understandable to a reader today?

10. occasion cause; reason.

11. consortest associate with.

12. Consort associate with; *consort* also meant a group of musicians.

13. discords harsh sounds.

14. Zounds exclamation of surprise or anger ("By God's wounds").

ENRICHMENT: Performing Arts Connection

Backstage at the Globe

The backstage area of any theater is a storehouse of sets, props, and actors awaiting their cues to go onstage; the audience sees but a limited number of any of these at one time.

In Elizabethan times, the props table contained the actors' parts, written on long narrow rolls of paper so the players could study them while awaiting their cues. On other tables rested such character aides as false beards, wigs, and makeup. Brick dust was used to redden the skin, and flour to whiten it. Actors aged themselves with wrinkles put on with a pen and ink.

When Mercutio and Tybalt die in this scene, blood would have had to flow. Actors slated to be stabbed or otherwise wounded carried a vinegar-soaked sponge under their armpit, giving it a hard squeeze at the appropriate time.

[*Enter* ROMEO.]

TYBALT. Well, peace be with you, sir. Here comes my man.[15]

MERCUTIO. But I'll be hanged, sir, if he wear your livery.[16]
Marry, go before to field,[17] he'll be your follower!
Your worship in that sense may call him man.

TYBALT. Romeo, the love I bear thee can afford
No better term than this: thou art a villain.[18]

6 **ROMEO.** Tybalt, the reason that I have to love thee
Doth much excuse the appertaining[19] rage
To such a greeting. Villain am I none.
Therefore farewell. I see thou knowest me not.

TYBALT. Boy, this shall not excuse the injuries
That thou hast done me; therefore turn and draw.

ROMEO. I do protest I never injured thee,
But love thee better than thou canst devise[20]
Till thou shalt know the reason of my love;
And so, good Capulet, which name I tender[21]
As dearly as mine own, be satisfied.

MERCUTIO. O calm, dishonorable, vile submission!
Alla stoccata[22] carries it away. [*Draws.*]
Tybalt, you ratcatcher, will you walk?

TYBALT. What wouldst thou have with me?

MERCUTIO. Good King of Cats, nothing but one of your nine lives. That I mean to make bold withal,[23] and, as you shall use me here-after, dry-beat[24] the rest of the eight. Will you pluck your sword out of his pilcher[25] by the ears? Make haste, lest mine be about your ears ere it be out.

TYBALT. I am for you. [*Draws.*]

ROMEO. Gentle Mercutio, put thy rapier up.

MERCUTIO. Come, sir, your *passado!* [*They fight.*]

ROMEO. Draw, Benvolio; beat down their weapons.
Gentlemen, for shame! Forbear this outrage!
Tybalt, Mercutio, the Prince expressly hath
Forbid this bandying in Verona streets.
Hold, Tybalt! Good Mercutio!

[TYBALT *under* ROMEO'S *arm thrusts* MERCUTIO *in, and flies.*]

MERCUTIO. I am hurt.
A plague a[26] both houses! I am sped.[27]
Is he gone and hath nothing?

BENVOLIO. What, art thou hurt?

15. man the man I'm looking for; "man" also meant "manservant."

16. livery servant's uniform.

17. field dueling place.

18. villain low, vulgar person.

19. appertaining appropriate.

20. devise understand; imagine.

21. tender value.

22. *Alla stoccata* at the thrust—an Italian fencing term that Mercutio uses as a nickname for Tybalt.

23. make bold withal make bold with; take.

24. dry-beat thrash.

25. pilcher scabbard.

26. a on.

27. sped wounded; done for.

7 **✓Reading Check**

What is the outcome of the duel between Tybalt and Mercutio?

6 Critical Thinking

Infer Cause and Effect

- Point out to students that the confrontation involving Tybalt, Romeo, and Mercutio is made worse because all three characters are acting on incomplete knowledge and false assumptions. Ask students what Tybalt thinks Romeo's motive was for coming to the Capulet's party, and what Romeo's real motive was.
  Answer: Tybalt thinks Romeo came to the party to mock the Capulets, but Romeo came only to see Rosaline.
- Now, point out to students that both Tybalt and Mercutio believe that Romeo is a foe of the Capulets, as he was just recently. Ask students if this is still true.
  Answer: Romeo is now married to Juliet; Tybalt is his wife's cousin. Romeo wants no more quarreling with the Capulets.

7 ✓Reading Check

Answer: Tybalt stabs Mercutio as Romeo tries to intervene.

CUSTOMIZE INSTRUCTION FOR UNIVERSAL ACCESS

For Special Needs Students	For Less Proficient Readers	For English Learners
The terms *monologue* and *soliloquy* may be difficult for students. Tell them the word monologue comes from the Latin words *monos* and *logos*, meaning "single" or "one" and "speech," while *soliloquy* comes from the Latin *solus*, meaning "alone" and *loqui*, meaning "speak."	Ask students to paraphrase Romeo's speech in lines 59–62. Have them recall what has happened to Romeo, and to use footnote 19 for guidance. **Possible response:** "Tybalt, I really should be angry at your insult, but I'll forget it because I have more reason to love you. So, good-bye; I see that you don't know me at all."	As students paraphrase sections of this act, have them compare their paraphrased lines with those of classmates. Ask them to explain, referring to the text of the play, why the paraphrases might be different.

8 Reading Strategy

Paraphrasing

- Ask students to summarize what has happened since Tybalt injured Mercutio.
  Answer: Tybalt flees; Mercutio says he is dying and blames Romeo for coming between him and Tybalt; Romeo says he was just trying to help; Mercutio curses both the Montagues and Capulets several times; Benvolio carries Mercutio offstage.

Monitor Progress Have students read Romeo's speech in lines 104–110. Ask if they think Romeo feels guilty about what has happened. Why or why not?
Possible response: Students may say that Romeo feels that Mercutio was injured by defending Romeo, who would not fight himself. If this is the case, then Romeo probably feels guilty.

- Have students answer the first Reading Strategy question on p. 822: How does Romeo say Juliet has changed him? What does he mean?
  Answer: Romeo says that his love for Juliet has made him less of a man, or less willing to fight.

9 Reading Strategy

Paraphrasing

- Ask students what news Benvolio brings to Romeo in this scene.
  Answer: Mercutio has died of his wounds.
- Have students respond to the second Reading Strategy question on p. 822: How would you paraphrase Romeo's words to Tybalt?
  Possible response: "How dare you be alive when Mercutio is dead? Forget mercy, fury will guide me now. Tybalt, take back your insult because Mercutio's soul is waiting for yours to join him. You or I, or perhaps both of us, will be with him soon."

MERCUTIO. Ay, ay, a scratch, a scratch. Marry, 'tis enough.
Where is my page? Go, villain, fetch a surgeon. [*Exit* PAGE.]

ROMEO. Courage, man. The hurt cannot be much.

MERCUTIO. No, 'tis not so deep as a well, nor so wide as a church door; but 'tis enough, 'twill serve. Ask for me tomorrow, and you shall find me a grave man. I am peppered,[28] I warrant, for this world. A plague a both your houses! Zounds, a dog, a rat, a mouse, a cat, to scratch a man to death! A braggart, a rogue, a villain, that fights by the book of arithmetic![29] Why the devil came you between us? I was hurt under your arm.

ROMEO. I thought all for the best.

MERCUTIO. Help me into some house, Benvolio,
Or I shall faint. A plague a both your houses!
They have made worms' meat of me. I have it,[30]
And soundly too. Your houses! [*Exit* MERCUTIO *and* BENVOLIO.]

ROMEO. This gentleman, the Prince's near ally,[31]
My very friend, hath got his mortal hurt
In my behalf—my reputation stained
With Tybalt's slander—Tybalt, that an hour
Hath been my cousin. O sweet Juliet,
Thy beauty hath made me effeminate
And in my temper soft'ned valor's steel!

[*Enter* BENVOLIO.]

BENVOLIO. O Romeo, Romeo, brave Mercutio is dead!
That gallant spirit hath aspired[32] the clouds,
Which too untimely here did scorn the earth.

ROMEO. This day's black fate on moe[33] days doth depend;[34]
This but begins the woe others must end.

[*Enter* TYBALT.]

BENVOLIO. Here comes the furious Tybalt back again.

ROMEO. Alive in triumph, and Mercutio slain?
Away to heaven respective lenity,[35]
And fire-eyed fury be my conduct[36] now!
Now, Tybalt, take the "villain" back again
That late thou gavest me; for Mercutio's soul
Is but a little way above our heads,
Staying for thine to keep him company.
Either thou or I, or both, must go with him.

TYBALT. Thou, wretched boy, that didst consort him here,
Shalt with him hence.

ROMEO. This shall determine that.
[*They fight.* TYBALT *falls.*]

28. peppered finished off.

29. by . . . arithmetic by formal rules.

30. I have it I've got my deathblow.

31. ally relative.

Reading Strategy
Paraphrasing How does Romeo say Juliet has changed him? What does he mean?

gallant (gal′ ənt) *adj.* brave and noble

32. aspired climbed to.

33. moe more.

34. depend hang over.

Reading Strategy
Paraphrasing How would you paraphrase Romeo's words to Tybalt?

35. respective lenity thoughtful mercy.

36. conduct guide.

ENRICHMENT: Social Studies Connection

Fencing

When Tybalt, Mercutio, and Romeo fence, they fight to kill. Fencing became a sport only in the late 1700s; today fencers compete at the Olympic Games.

The object in fencing is to touch the opponent with a sword and to avoid being touched. Three different weapons may be used: the *foil*, the *epee*, and the *saber*. These differ in size, weight, and appearance, but all include devices to blunt their points for safety.

Fencers wear a strong wire-mesh mask and protective clothing to avoid injury. They must develop precision, speed, timing, and tactical judgment. Many professional actors study and practice fencing for use on the stage.

Have students discuss what a dueling scene adds to a performance. Have them compare and contrast the dueling scenes in *Romeo and Juliet* with action scenes in contemporary movies, including fist fights, car chases, shoot-outs, and martial arts sequences.

(10)

BENVOLIO. Romeo, away, be gone!
The citizens are up, and Tybalt slain.
Stand not amazed. The Prince will doom thee death
If thou art taken. Hence, be gone, away!

ROMEO. O, I am fortune's fool![37]

BENVOLIO. Why dost thou stay? [*Exit* ROMEO.]

[*Enter* CITIZENS.]

CITIZEN. Which way ran he that killed Mercutio?
Tybalt, that murderer, which way ran he?

BENVOLIO. There lies that Tybalt.

CITIZEN. Up, sir, go with me.
I charge thee in the Prince's name obey.

[*Enter* PRINCE, OLD MONTAGUE, CAPULET, *their* WIVES, *and all.*]

PRINCE. Where are the vile beginners of this fray?

(11)

BENVOLIO. O noble Prince, I can discover[38] all
The unlucky manage[39] of this fatal brawl.
There lies the man, slain by young Romeo,
That slew thy kinsman, brave Mercutio.

LADY CAPULET. Tybalt, my cousin! O my brother's child!
O Prince! O cousin! Husband! O, the blood is spilled
Of my dear kinsman! Prince, as thou art true,

Reading Strategy
Paraphrasing What urgent warning is Benvolio giving Romeo?

37. fool plaything.

fray (frā) *n.* noisy fight

38. discover reveal.

Reading Strategy
Paraphrasing Has Benvolio reported the facts accurately?

39. manage course.

(12) ◀ **Critical Viewing**
Using this picture, explain the emotions on the street after Romeo kills Tybalt. **[Make a Judgment]**

(13) ✓ **Reading Check**
What does Romeo do to Tybalt?

(10) Reading Strategy
Paraphrasing

- Ask students what the outcome is of Romeo and Tybalt's fight.
  Answer: Romeo kills Tybalt.
- Ask the first Reading Strategy question on p. 823: What urgent warning is Benvolio giving to Romeo?
  Possible response: "Romeo, get out of here. People are coming and Tybalt is dead. Don't stand there like an idiot. The Prince will have you killed if he can capture you. Get out, go!"

(11) Reading Strategy
Paraphrasing

- Ask students what the Prince finds when he enters.
  Answer: Tybalt lies dead. Romeo and Mercutio are nowhere to be seen. A citizen has detained Benvolio in the Prince's name.
- Have students respond to the second Reading Strategy question on p. 823: Has Benvolio reported the facts accurately?
  Possible response: Yes, Benvolio accurately reports that Tybalt, who has been killed by Romeo, himself killed the Prince's kinsman, Mercutio.

(12) ▶ Critical Viewing

Answer: Romeo and his friends are shocked and terrified. Romeo seems rooted in place, not knowing what to do.

(13) ✓ Reading Check

Answer: Romeo kills Tybalt.

CUSTOMIZE INSTRUCTION FOR UNIVERSAL ACCESS

For English Learners	For Gifted/Talented Students	For Advanced Readers
Like many lines and phrases from Shakespeare's works, Mercutio's exclamation, "A plague [on] both your houses," has become famous, even among people who have never read Shakespeare. Ask students whether they have ever heard this expression before. What was the context?	Students may enjoy blocking the fight scene. Point out to them that within a sixty-line period, two fights have occurred, two main characters are dead—one having cursed the two families for their feud—Romeo has fled, and many other characters have come on stage to hear Benvolio's description of what has occurred.	Point out to students that even as he is dying, Mercutio cannot resist making a linguistic production out of the event. He creates figurative language out of his deadly wound ("not so deep as a well, nor so wide as a church door"), makes jokes ("Ask for me tomorrow and you will find me a grave man"), and curses the two warring families.

14 Reading Strategy

Paraphrasing

- Ask students why Lady Capulet shows special concern for Tybalt.
  Answer: Tybalt is her nephew, her brother's son.
- Then, ask the first Reading Strategy question on p. 824: What does Lady Capulet ask the Prince to do?
  Answer: She asks him to "shed blood of Montage."

15 Literary Analysis

Soliloquy, Aside, and Monologue

- Ask students if Benvolio's speech on p. 824 is a soliloquy or a monologue. Why?
  Answer: Benvolio's speech is a monologue. He delivers it to the Prince, and other characters listen.
- Ask the Literary Analysis question on p. 824: Is Benvolio's monologue describing the fight factual or biased? How do you know?
  Answer: His description is basically factual, though his adjectives slyly favor Mercutio, the Prince's relative.

16 Reading Strategy

Paraphrasing

- Remind students that the Prince has a personal interest in this fight: Mercutio was his kinsman.
- Then, ask the second Reading Strategy assignment on p. 824: Restate Montague's remarks in your own words.
  Possible response: "Romeo should not die, Prince. He was Mercutio's friend and he was only doing what the justice system would have done eventually—put Tybalt to death."

For blood of ours shed blood of Montague.
O cousin, cousin!

PRINCE. Benvolio, who began this bloody fray?

BENVOLIO. Tybalt, here slain, whom Romeo's hand did slay.
Romeo, that spoke him fair, bid him bethink
How nice[40] the quarrel was, and urged withal
Your high displeasure. All this—utterèd
With gentle breath, calm look, knees humbly bowed—
Could not take truce with the unruly spleen[41]
Of Tybalt deaf to peace, but that he tilts[42]
With piercing steel at bold Mercutio's breast;
Who, all as hot, turns deadly point to point,
And, with a martial scorn, with one hand beats
Cold death aside and with the other sends
It back to Tybalt, whose dexterity
Retorts it. Romeo he cries aloud,
"Hold, friends! Friends, part!" and swifter than his tongue,
His agile arm beats down their fatal points,
And 'twixt them rushes; underneath whose arm
An envious[43] thrust from Tybalt hit the life
Of stout Mercutio, and then Tybalt fled;
But by and by comes back to Romeo,
Who had but newly entertained[44] revenge,
And to't they go like lightning; for, ere I
Could draw to part them, was stout Tybalt slain;
And, as he fell, did Romeo turn and fly.
This is the truth, or let Benvolio die.

LADY CAPULET. He is a kinsman to the Montague;
Affection makes him false, he speaks not true.
Some twenty of them fought in this black strife,
And all those twenty could but kill one life.
I beg for justice, which thou, Prince, must give.
Romeo slew Tybalt; Romeo must not live.

PRINCE. Romeo slew him; he slew Mercutio.
Who now the price of his dear blood doth owe?

MONTAGUE. Not Romeo, Prince; he was Mercutio's friend;
His fault concludes but what the law should end,
The life of Tybalt.[45]

PRINCE. And for that offense
Immediately we do exile him hence.
I have an interest in your hate's proceeding.
My blood[46] for your rude brawls doth lie a-bleeding;
But I'll amerce[47] you with so strong a fine
That you shall all repent the loss of mine.
I will be deaf to pleading and excuses;

Reading Strategy
Paraphrasing What does Lady Capulet ask the Prince to do?

40. nice trivial.

41. spleen angry nature.

42. tilts thrusts.

martial (mär′ shəl) *adj.* military

Literary Analysis
Soliloquy, Aside, and Monologue Is Benvolio's monologue describing the fight factual or biased? How do you know?

43. envious full of hatred.

44. entertained considered.

45. His fault . . . Tybalt by killing Tybalt, he did what the law would have done.

Reading Strategy
Paraphrasing Restate Montague's remarks in your own words.

exile (eks′ īl′) *v.* banish

46. My blood Mercutio was related to the Prince.

47. amerce punish.

ENRICHMENT: Literature Connection

Analyzing Literary Criticism

Harold Bloom, a contemporary literary scholar, states that *Romeo and Juliet* is one of the first examples of Shakespeare's genius in creating characters. In discussing the play, he says, "Age-old directorial wisdom is that Shakespeare killed off Mercutio so quickly, because Romeo is a mere stick in contrast to his exuberant friend. But Mercutio becomes irrelevant once Juliet and Romeo fall profoundly in love with one another. What place has Mercutio in the play once it becomes dominated by Juliet's magnificent avowal of her love's infinitude:

And yet I wish but for the thing I have.
My bounty is as boundless as the sea,
My love as deep; the more I give to thee,
The more I have, for both are infinite."

Read and discuss this comparison of Shakespeare's characters with students, asking if they agree or disagree.

Nor tears nor prayers shall purchase out abuses.
Therefore use none. Let Romeo hence in haste,
Else, when he is found, that hour is his last.
Bear hence this body and attend our will.[48]
Mercy but murders, pardoning those that kill.
[*Exit with others.*]

48. **attend our will** await my decision.

Scene ii. CAPULET'S *orchard.*

[*Enter* JULIET *alone.*]

JULIET. Gallop apace, you fiery-footed steeds,[1]
Towards Phoebus' lodging![2] Such a wagoner
17 As Phaëton[3] would whip you to the west
And bring in cloudy night immediately.
Spread thy close curtain, love-performing night,
That runaways' eyes may wink,[4] and Romeo
Leap to these arms untalked of and unseen.
Lovers can see to do their amorous rites,
And by their own beauties; or, if love be blind,
It best agrees with night. Come, civil night,
Thou sober-suited matron all in black,
And learn me how to lose a winning match,
Played for a pair of stainless maidenhoods.
Hood my unmanned blood, bating in my cheeks,[5]
With thy black mantle till strange[6] love grow bold,
18 Think true love acted simple modesty,
Come, night; come, Romeo; come, thou day in night;
For thou wilt lie upon the wings of night
Whiter than new snow upon a raven's back.
Come, gentle night; come, loving, black-browed night;
Give me my Romeo; and when I shall die,
Take him and cut him out in little stars,
And he will make the face of heaven so fine
That all the world will be in love with night
And pay no worship to the garish sun
O, I have bought the mansion of a love,
But not possessed it; and though I am sold,
Not yet enjoyed. So tedious is this day
As is the night before some festival
To an impatient child that hath new robes
And may not wear them. O, here comes my nurse,

[*Enter* NURSE, *with cords.*]

And she brings news; and every tongue that speaks
But Romeo's name speaks heavenly eloquence.
Now, nurse, what news? What hast thou there, the cords
That Romeo bid thee fetch?

NURSE. Ay, ay, the cords.

1. **fiery-footed steeds** horses of the sun god, Phoebus.

2. **Phoebus' lodging** below the horizon.

3. **Phaëton** Phoebus' son, who tried to drive his father's horses but was unable to control them.

4. **That runaways' eyes may wink** so that the eyes of busybodies may not see.

5. **Hood . . . cheeks** hide the untamed blood that makes me blush.

6. **strange** unfamiliar.

Literary Analysis
Soliloquy, Aside, and Monologue Should Juliet's speech be classified as a monologue, a soliloquy, or an aside? Why?

eloquence (el′ ə kwəns) *n.* speech that is vivid, forceful, graceful, and persuasive

19 **Reading Check**
What punishment does the Prince order for Romeo?

17 Literary Analysis

Allusions

- Ask students to read lines 1–4 in Juliet's speech, concentrating on line 4. What does Juliet want to happen?
  Answer: Juliet wants night to come immediately.
- Have students read the first four lines again, with footnotes 1–3, and determine why Juliet uses *allusions* to Phoebus and Phaeton in her speech. Who are these characters?
  Possible answer: Phoebus is the mythical sun god, whose horses pull the sun across the sky from east to west. When the horses reach Phoebus's lodging, or the horizon, the sun disappears and night comes. Juliet wishes Phoebus's son, Phaeton, was driving because he would be driving fast and wildly and the sun would set sooner.

18 Literary Analysis

Soliloquy, Aside, and Monologue

- Ask students what information the stage directions provide for Scene ii.
  Answer: Scene ii is set in Capulet's orchard. Juliet enters alone.
- Have students answer the Literary Analysis question on p. 825: Should Juliet's speech be classified as a monologue, a soliloquy, or an aside? Why?
  Possible response: The speech is a soliloquy because Juliet is alone on stage and expresses her thoughts in a lengthy speech to the audience. Moreover, even though an aside is also spoken directly to the audience, it is very short.

19 Reading Check

Answer: The Prince banishes Romeo; if he returns to Verona he will be put to death.

CUSTOMIZE INSTRUCTION FOR UNIVERSAL ACCESS

For Special Needs Students	For English Learners	For Advanced Readers
Students may enjoy working with Juliet's comparison in lines 28–31 of her soliloquy. Have them determine how Juliet compares her waiting for Romeo with a child waiting for a party. Then, have them write one or two comparisons to suggest their own impatience when they are waiting for something important or exciting.	Have students work in pairs to make up sentences using the vocabulary words for this act. Encourage them to use sentences that put the words in the context of the action of the play, as in "Benvolio is Romeo's gallant friend."	Students may recall Romeo's first long speech about Juliet in Act II, in which he compares her eyes to the stars, which would burn so brightly as to turn the night to day. Ask students to read lines 20–25 of Juliet's soliloquy and determine how Shakespeare contrasts Romeo's words about Juliet with Juliet's words about Romeo here.

20 Literary Analysis

Allusions

- Ask students what news the Nurse brings to Juliet.
  Answer: The Nurse tells Juliet someone is dead, but she does not say whom.
- Have students identify the person Juliet thinks has been killed.
  Answer: Juliet thinks Romeo has been killed.
- Ask students to respond to the Literary Analysis question on p. 826: What is the effect of Juliet's allusions to hell in lines 43–44? Explain.
  Answer: Juliet thinks Romeo has been killed. This news is so devastating to her that she thinks she must be in hell and her Nurse must be a devil because only in hell could she feel as terrible as she does.

21 Literature in Context

Cockatrice

According to legend, the cockatrice is hatched from the egg of a rooster brooded by a toad or a serpent. A similar creature is the basilisk, which also possessed a lethal glance—and therefore also had a deadly fear of mirrors. Both creatures appear as literary allusions in Shakespeare's plays and other classic literature.

JULIET. Ay me! What news? Why dost thou wring thy hands?

NURSE. Ah, weraday![7] He's dead, he's dead, he's dead!
We are undone, lady, we are undone!
Alack the day! He's gone, he's killed, he's dead!

JULIET. Can heaven be so envious?

NURSE. Romeo can,
Though heaven cannot. O Romeo, Romeo!
Who ever would have thought it? Romeo!

20 **JULIET.** What devil art thou that dost torment me thus?
This torture should be roared in dismal hell.
Hath Romeo slain himself? Say thou but "Ay,"
And that bare vowel "I" shall poison more
Than the death-darting eye of cockatrice.◆
I am not I, if there be such an "Ay,"[8]
Or those eyes' shot[9] that makes thee answer "Ay."
If he be slain, say "Ay"; or if not, "No."
Brief sounds determine of my weal or woe.

NURSE. I saw the wound, I saw it with mine eyes,
(God save the mark![10]) here on his manly breast.
A piteous corse,[11] a bloody piteous corse;
Pale, pale as ashes, all bedaubed in blood,
All in gore-blood. I sounded[12] at the sight.

JULIET. O, break, my heart! Poor bankrout,[13] break at once!
To prison, eyes; ne'er look on liberty!
Vile earth, to earth resign;[14] end motion here,
And thou and Romeo press one heavy bier![15]

NURSE. O Tybalt, Tybalt, the best friend I had!
O courteous Tybalt! Honest gentleman!
That ever I should live to see thee dead!

7. **Ah, weraday!** alas!

Literary Analysis
Allusions What is the effect of Juliet's allusions to hell in lines 43–44? Explain.

8. **"Ay"** yes.

9. **eyes' shot** the Nurse's glance.

10. **God save the mark!** may God save us from evil!

11. **corse** corpse.

12. **sounded** swooned; fainted.

13. **bankrout** bankrupt.

14. **Vile . . . resign** let my body return to the earth.

15. **bier** platform on which a corpse is displayed before burial.

Literature 21 in context Humanities Connection

◆ ***Cockatrice***

In a play on words, Juliet links "Ay" with the dangerous "eye" of a cockatrice (III, ii, 47). The cockatrice is a serpent that, according to myth, could kill with a look or transform people into stone. The creature resembled a snake with the head and yellow feathers of a rooster. It feared the song of the rooster as well as its own reflection in the mirror. Juliet alludes to a cockatrice to reinforce the tormenting nature of her conversation with the Nurse.

ENRICHMENT: Music Connection

The Death of Tybalt

Sergei Prokofiev (1891–1953) was a Soviet composer whose best known work is probably the symphonic fairy tale *Peter and the Wolf.* Prokofiev also wrote symphonies, ballets, concertos, cantatas, and music for films. One of the composer's ballets is *Romeo and Juliet,* a passionate musical accounting of the story students are reading now. If you can find a CD of this work in your local library, students might enjoy comparing the musical version of the events with those in the play. The ballet is divided into scenes that identify what is happening in the story as the music plays. "Tybalt's Death" is one of the scenes. As students listen to this section, ask them to consider the following:

1. Does the music cause you to feel grief or loss? How?
2. Which instruments can you hear in this section?
3. What kinds of beats or rhythms are used in this section? Is the music high or low, or a combination?

JULIET. What storm is this that blows so contrary?[16]
Is Romeo slaught'red, and is Tybalt dead?
My dearest cousin, and my dearer lord?
Then, dreadful trumpet, sound the general doom![17]
For who is living, if those two are gone?

NURSE. Tybalt is gone, and Romeo banishèd;
Romeo that killed him, he is banishèd.

JULIET. O God! Did Romeo's hand shed Tybalt's blood?

NURSE. It did, it did! Alas the day, it did!

JULIET. O serpent heart, hid with a flow'ring face!
Did ever dragon keep so fair a cave?
Beautiful tyrant! Fiend angelical!
Dove-feathered raven! Wolvish-ravening lamb!
Despisèd substance of divinest show!
Just opposite to what thou justly seem'st—
A damnèd saint, an honorable villain!
O nature, what hadst thou to do in hell
When thou didst bower the spirit of a fiend
In mortal paradise of such sweet flesh?
Was ever book containing such vile matter
So fairly bound? O, that deceit should dwell
In such a gorgeous palace!

NURSE. There's no trust,
No faith, no honesty in men; all perjured,
All forsworn,[18] all naught, all dissemblers.[19]
Ah, where's my man? Give me some *aqua vitae*.[20]
These griefs, these woes, these sorrows make me old.
Shame come to Romeo!

JULIET. Blistered be thy tongue
For such a wish! He was not born to shame.
Upon his brow shame is ashamed to sit;
For 'tis a throne where honor may be crowned
Sole monarch of the universal earth.
O, what a beast was I to chide at him!

NURSE. Will you speak well of him that killed your cousin?

JULIET. Shall I speak ill of him that is my husband?
Ah, poor my lord, what tongue shall smooth thy name
When I, thy three-hours wife, have mangled it?
But wherefore, villain, didst thou kill my cousin?
That villain cousin would have killed my husband.
Back, foolish tears, back to your native spring!
Your tributary[21] drops belong to woe,
Which you, mistaking, offer up to joy.
My husband lives, that Tybalt would have slain;

16. contrary in opposite directions.

17. dreadful . . . doom let the trumpet that announces doomsday be sounded.

Reading Strategy
Paraphrasing Restate lines 78–79 in your own words.

18. forsworn are liars.

19. dissemblers hypocrites.

20. *aqua vitae* brandy.

21. tributary in tribute.

23 Reading Check
Initially, who does Juliet think is dead?

22 Reading Strategy

Paraphrasing

- Have students read Juliet's speech and identify some of the opposites she uses to demonstrate her conflicted feelings about Romeo.
  Possible responses: Opposites include: "Beautiful tyrant!" "Fiend angelical!" "Dove-feathered raven!" "Wolvish-ravening lamb!"
- Ask students to respond to the Reading Strategy assignment on p. 827: Restate lines 78–79 in your own words.
  Possible response: "You are the opposite of what you appeared to be, an evil saint, a villain with honor."

23 Reading Check

Answer: Juliet thinks Romeo is dead.

CUSTOMIZE INSTRUCTION FOR UNIVERSAL ACCESS

For Special Needs Students	For Less Proficient Readers
Point out to students that repetition is common in Shakespeare's work. Sometimes the repetition of a word or phrase is used to fit the meter of a line, and sometimes it is used to emphasize meaning or emotional content. Ask students to find the repetitions in the Nurse's speeches, lines 36–38 and 41–42; in Juliet's speech, line 57; in the Nurse's speech, 61–62.	Students may more readily grasp some of Juliet's comparisons in her speech in lines 73–85 if you tell them to look for descriptions of things that are beautiful on the outside and dangerous or evil on the inside. As an example, point out, "Did ever dragon keep so fair a cave?" in line 74. Ask students to find others.

E-Teach

Visit E-Teach at www.phschool.com for teachers' essays on how to teach, with questions and answers.

24 Literary Analysis

Soliloquy, Aside, and Monologue

- Ask students why they think Juliet first condemns Romeo for killing Tybalt and then changes her mind.
  Possible response: Juliet responds to the news first in terms of thinking about her family. Tybalt is her cousin and she condemns Romeo for killing him. Then, she realizes that she is Romeo's family now, and that Tybalt would have killed Romeo if he had had the chance.
- Ask the Literary Analysis question on p. 828: Is Juliet's lengthy speech a soliloquy? Why or why not?
  Answer: Juliet's speech is not a soliloquy, because she is not alone and does not deliver her words to the audience, but to her Nurse.

25 Reading Strategy

Paraphrasing

- Ask students what Juliet asks the Nurse at the end of her speech.
  Answer: Juliet asks the Nurse where her mother and father are.
- Ask the first Reading Strategy question on p. 828: How would you paraphrase the Nurse's reply to Juliet?
  Possible response: "Your parents are crying over Tybalt's body. Do you want to see them? I will take you there."

26 Reading Strategy

Paraphrasing

- Ask students to review footnote 1. It gives one meaning for the phrase in line 2 of Friar Lawrence's speech.
- Now, have students respond to the second Reading Strategy on p. 828: Paraphrase in modern English the Friar's opening lines to Romeo.
  Possible response: "Come on out, Romeo, even if you are afraid. Misfortune seems drawn to you, despite your privileged background. You and evil events seem to be a pair."

And Tybalt's dead, that would have slain my husband.
All this is comfort; wherefore weep I then?
Some word there was, worser than Tybalt's death,
That murd'red me. I would forget it fain;
But O, it presses to my memory
Like damnèd guilty deeds to sinners' minds!
"Tybalt is dead, and Romeo—banishèd."
That "banishèd," that one word "banishèd,"
Hath slain ten thousand Tybalts. Tybalt's death
Was woe enough, if it had ended there;
Or, if sour woe delights in fellowship
24 And needly will be ranked with[22] other griefs,
Why followed not, when she said "Tybalt's dead,"
Thy father, or thy mother, nay, or both,
Which modern[23] lamentation might have moved?
But with a rearward[24] following Tybalt's death,
"Romeo is banishèd"—to speak that word
Is father, mother, Tybalt, Romeo, Juliet,
All slain, all dead. "Romeo is banishèd"—
There is no end, no limit, measure, bound,
In that word's death; no words can that woe sound.
Where is my father and my mother, nurse?

25 **NURSE.** Weeping and wailing over Tybalt's corse.
Will you go to them? I will bring you thither.

JULIET. Wash they his wounds with tears? Mine shall be spent,
When theirs are dry, for Romeo's banishment.
Take up those cords. Poor ropes, you are beguiled,
Both you and I, for Romeo is exiled.
He made you for a highway to my bed;
But I, a maid, die maiden-widowèd.
Come, cords; come, nurse. I'll to my wedding bed;
And death, not Romeo, take my maidenhead!

NURSE. Hie to your chamber. I'll find Romeo
To comfort you. I wot[25] well where he is.
Hark ye, your Romeo will be here at night.
I'll to him; he is hid at Lawrence' cell.

JULIET. O, find him! Give this ring to my true knight
And bid him come to take his last farewell. [*Exit* with NURSE]

Scene iii. FRIAR LAWRENCE'S *cell.*

[*Enter* FRIAR LAWRENCE.]

26 **FRIAR.** Romeo, come forth; come forth, thou fearful man.
Affliction is enamored of thy parts,[1]
And thou art wedded to calamity.

Literary Analysis
Soliloquy, Aside, and Monologue Is Juliet's lengthy speech a soliloquy? Why or why not?

22. needly . . . with must be accompanied by.

23. modern ordinary.

24. rearward follow up; literally, a rear guard.

Reading Strategy
Paraphrasing How would you paraphrase the Nurse's reply to Juliet?

25. wot know.

Reading Strategy
Paraphrasing Paraphrase in modern English the Friar's opening lines to Romeo.

1. Affliction . . . parts misery is in love with your attractive qualities.

ENRICHMENT: Social Studies Connection

Geography

Tell students about the following points of interest related to Shakespeare and *Romeo and Juliet*:

- Stratford-on-Avon: This small English town is famous as Shakespeare's birthplace. Shakespeare's father was elected its bailiff, or mayor, in 1568.
- London: In Shakespeare's time, this English capital was thriving with commerce and entertainment. It was here that Shakespeare found work as an actor and success as a playwright and, with his company, the Lord Chamberlain's men, built the Globe theater.
- Verona (Italy): The play's main setting, this small city was a Roman colony in ancient times and a center of Italian art and culture in medieval times.
- Mantua (Italy): Like Verona, the city where Romeo seeks refuge during his banishment is rich in ancient and medieval history and culture.

[*Enter* ROMEO.]

ROMEO. Father, what news? What is the Prince's doom?[2]
What sorrow craves acquaintance at my hand
That I yet know not?

FRIAR. Too familiar
Is my dear son with such sour company.
I bring thee tidings of the Prince's doom.

ROMEO. What less than doomsday[3] is the Prince's doom?

FRIAR. A gentler judgment vanished[4] from his lips—
Not body's death, but body's banishment.

ROMEO. Ha, banishment? Be merciful, say "death";
For exile hath more terror in his look,
Much more than death. Do not say "banishment."

FRIAR. Here from Verona art thou banishèd.
Be patient, for the world is broad and wide.

ROMEO. There is no world without[5] Verona walls,
But purgatory, torture, hell itself.
Hence banishèd is banished from the world,
And world's exile is death. Then "banishèd"
Is death mistermed. Calling death "banishèd,"
Thou cut'st my head off with a golden ax
And smilest upon the stroke that murders me.

FRIAR. O deadly sin! O rude unthankfulness!
Thy fault our law calls death;[6] but the kind Prince,
Taking thy part, hath rushed[7] aside the law,
And turned that black word "death" to "banishment."
This is dear mercy, and thou seest it not.

ROMEO. 'Tis torture, and not mercy. Heaven is here,
Where Juliet lives; and every cat and dog
And little mouse, every unworthy thing,
Live here in heaven and may look on her;
But Romeo may not. More validity,[8]
More honorable state, more courtship lives
In carrion flies than Romeo. They may seize
On the white wonder of dear Juliet's hand
And steal immortal blessing from her lips,
Who, even in pure and vestal modesty,
Still blush, as thinking their own kisses sin;
But Romeo may not, he is banishèd.
Flies may do this but I from this must fly;
They are freemen, but I am banishèd.
And sayest thou yet that exile is not death?
Hadst thou no poison mixed, no sharp-ground knife,

2. doom final decision.

3. doomsday my death.

4. vanished escaped; came forth.

5. without outside.

6. Thy fault . . . death for what you did our law demands the death penalty.

7. rushed pushed.

Reading Strategy
Paraphrasing Restate Romeo's complaint in lines 29–33.

8. validity value.

29 **Reading Check**
What punishment does the Friar say Romeo could have received for his crime?

27 Reading Strategy
Paraphrasing

- Ask students how Romeo describes banishment to the Friar.
  Answer: Romeo compares banishment to death.
- Have students explain how the Friar attempts in lines 10–11, 15–16, and 27–28, to comfort Romeo in the face of his banishment.
  Possible response: The friar tells Romeo that he is not being put to death but only banished from Verona. He tells Romeo that the Prince has shown mercy, though Romeo cannot see this.
- Ask students to respond to the Reading Strategy assignment on p. 829: Restate Romeo's complaint in lines 29–33.
  Possible response: "It is not merciful to send me away. My only heaven is here with Juliet. Here everything that lives and moves can be in Juliet's presence, whether it is worthy or not. But I cannot see her."

28 Background
Foreshadowing

Remind students of earlier passages in the play in which readers are given suggestions as to what will ultimately happen—for example, Romeo and Juliet mutually sense that something will doom their love. Then, point out the foreshadowing in Romeo's monologue on this page in which he asks the Friar to give him some way to kill himself rather than leave Juliet.

Ask students to keep this scene in mind as they complete the play. The references to *poison* and to *knife* in line 44 are significant.

29 Reading Check

Answer: The Friar reminds Romeo that the Prince could have put Romeo to death.

CUSTOMIZE INSTRUCTION FOR UNIVERSAL ACCESS

For Special Needs Students	For English Learners	For Advanced Readers
Point out that instead of using the grammatically correct *who* or *whom* in lines 105 and 106, Shakespeare uses *that,* which was acceptable in his day. Ask students to reword the two lines using the grammatically correct forms.	Point out to students that Shakespeare has both Juliet and Romeo use the word *banished* numerous times in this scene. Have them speculate on why Juliet speaks the word with three syllables in lines 112, 113, 122 and 124 on p. 828, while Romeo uses it once with three syllables and once with two in line 19 on p. 829.	Have students define *alliteration* and then find examples on p. 828 in the Nurse's first speech and then Juliet's first line of reply to her, as well as Romeo's line 17 on p. 829.

30 Literary Analysis

Soliloquy, Aside, and Monologue

- In Romeo's speech, have students identify what Romeo would rather endure instead of being banished.
  Answer: Romeo asks the Friar if he has any poison, knife, or other means of death. Romeo would rather die than be banished from Juliet's presence.
- Have students answer the Literary Analysis question on p. 830: Which characteristics of a monologue are present in Romeo's lament?
  Answer: Romeo's speech is a lengthy one and is delivered to the Friar, another character.

31 Reading Strategy

Paraphrasing

- Ask students what the Friar has suggested to Romeo on p. 830 as a possible comfort to the young man.
  Answer: The Friar suggests that an armor for Romeo to use against the hated idea of banishment is philosophy.
- Have students answer the Reading Strategy question on p. 831: Summarize Romeo's ideas in lines 57–60. What do they suggest about his state of mind?
  Answer: Romeo says that philosophy is useless unless it can make a Juliet, move a town, and reverse a Prince's order. It is no help, and he doesn't want to hear any more about it. These words suggest that Romeo is overcome by emotion and cannot listen to reason.

No sudden mean[9] of death, though ne'er so mean,[10]
But "banishèd" to kill me—"banishèd"?
O friar, the damnèd use that word in hell;
Howling attends it! How hast thou the heart,
Being a divine, a ghostly confessor,
A sin-absolver, and my friend professed,
30 To mangle me with that word "banishèd"?

FRIAR. Thou fond mad man, hear me a little speak.

ROMEO. O, thou wilt speak again of banishment.

FRIAR. I'll give thee armor to keep off that word;
Adversity's sweet milk, philosophy,
To comfort thee, though thou art banishèd.

ROMEO. Yet "banishèd"? Hang up philosophy!
Unless philosophy can make a Juliet,
31 Displant a town, reverse a prince's doom,
It helps not, it prevails not. Talk no more.

FRIAR. O, then I see that madmen have no ears.

Literary Analysis
Soliloquy, Aside, and Monologue Which characteristics of a monologue are present in Romeo's lament?

9. mean method.

10. mean humiliating.

Reading Strategy
Paraphrasing Summarize Romeo's ideas in lines 57–60. What do they suggest about his state of mind?

ENRICHMENT: Performing Arts Connection

Film Editing

Surprisingly, certain stage conventions in Shakespeare's time produced effects much like those we see in movies. Elizabethan stages had no scenery; therefore a play's scenes and changes of setting could flow swiftly and smoothly, just as they do in a modern motion picture.

In movies, television shows, and all other kinds of films, the pace and rhythm of the action are achieved through film editing. Editors may work with hundreds of hours of shots to put together a film that is two hours long. One brief scene of Zeffirelli's *Romeo and Juliet,* for example, would have been shot by several different cameras from a variety of angles and points of view, including close-ups, mid-range shots, and long shots. Conferring with the director, the film's editor would have chosen and assembled the shots that produce the dramatic and visual effects that work best for the scene.

32 ◀ Critical Viewing How does Romeo's expression in this picture compare to your impression of him as you read? **[Analyze]**

ROMEO. How should they, when that wise men have no eyes?

FRIAR. Let me dispute[11] with thee of thy estate.[12]

ROMEO. Thou canst not speak of that thou dost not feel.
Wert thou as young as I, Juliet thy love,
An hour but married, Tybalt murderèd,
Doting like me, and like me banishèd,
Then mightst thou speak, then mightst thou tear thy hair,
And fall upon the ground, as I do now,
Taking the measure of an unmade grave.

[*Enter* NURSE *and knock.*]

FRIAR. Arise, one knocks. Good Romeo, hide thyself.

ROMEO. Not I; unless the breath of heartsick groans
Mistlike infold me from the search of eyes. [*Knock.*]

FRIAR. Hark, how they knock! Who's there? Romeo, arise;
33 Thou wilt be taken.—Stay awhile!—Stand up; [*Knock.*]
Run to my study.—By and by![13]—God's will,

11. **dispute** discuss.

12. **estate** condition; situation.

Reading Strategy
Paraphrasing How would you paraphrase Friar Lawrence's words in lines 74–78?

13. **By and by!** In a minute! (said to the person knocking).

34 Reading Check
What word does Romeo use repeatedly while speaking to the Friar?

CUSTOMIZE INSTRUCTION FOR UNIVERSAL ACCESS

For Gifted/Talented Students	For Advanced Readers
Point out to students that Romeo has a better relationship with the Friar than he does with his own father, whom he, and the audience, rarely see. The contrast between the Friar's older, wiser counsel and Romeo's young, impulsive actions are a difference that is often found in a parent and a child. Ask students to suggest other well-known works—novels, plays, or movies—in which the father/son relationship is given expression.	Ask students to find out more about exile as a form of punishment in other cultures, or in earlier cultures. Is Romeo's despair at being exiled solely based on his having to leave Juliet, or was banishment a humiliating punishment in other ways? When was banishment used in place of death? Have students share their findings with the rest of the class.

32 ▶ Critical Viewing

Answer: Students may suggest that Romeo's expression shows him to be distressed and in pain. Some students may also note that the way in which his hands clutch the table also communicates his deep despair.

33 Reading Strategy

Paraphrasing

- Have students contrast the behavior of the Friar and Romeo when they hear the knocking at the door. How does their respective behavior reflect their emotional state at this point?
- Lead students to see that when he hears the knocking, the Friar immediately tells Romeo to hide. He does not want Romeo to be put to death. When Romeo hears the knocking, he does not move because he does not care what happens to him. The different responses show that the Friar believes that Romeo has a life and a future, and Romeo does not.
- Have students respond to the Reading Strategy question on p. 831: How would you paraphrase Friar Lawrence's words in lines 74–78?
  Possible response: "Someone's knocking! Who's there? Get up, Romeo, or they'll find you.—Hold on!—Stand up. Run to my study.—Just a minute!—I can't believe you're acting like this.—Coming! Who's there? What do you want?"

34 Reading Check

Answer: Romeo uses the word *banished* repeatedly.

35 Reading Strategy
Paraphrasing

- Ask students to paraphrase Romeo's questions to the Nurse.
  Possible response: "Are you talking about Juliet? How is she? Does she think I am a murderer now that I have spoiled our happiness by killing her cousin? Where is she? How is she? What does my secret bride say about our shattered love?"
- Point out Romeo's remarks about his name. How do these words echo Juliet's comments about his name in Act II, Scene ii?
  Answer: Juliet had said, "Tis but thy name that is my enemy." Now Romeo imagines his name as a bullet "shot from the deadly level of a gun" that kills his beloved.

What simpleness[14] is this.—I come, I come! [*Knock.*]
Who knocks so hard? Whence come you? What's your will?

[*Enter* NURSE.]

NURSE. Let me come in, and you shall know my errand.
I come from Lady Juliet.

FRIAR. Welcome then.

NURSE. O holy friar, O, tell me, holy friar,
Where is my lady's lord, where's Romeo?

FRIAR. There on the ground, with his own tears made drunk.

NURSE. O, he is even in my mistress' case,
Just in her case! O woeful sympathy!
Piteous predicament! Even so lies she,
Blubb'ring and weeping, weeping and blubb'ring.
Stand up, stand up! Stand, and you be a man.
For Juliet's sake, for her sake, rise and stand!
Why should you fall into so deep an O?[15]

ROMEO. [*Rises.*] Nurse—

NURSE. Ah sir, ah sir! Death's the end of all.

ROMEO. Spakest thou of Juliet? How is it with her?
Doth not she think me an old murderer,
Now I have stained the childhood of our joy
With blood removed but little from her own?
Where is she? And how doth she? And what says
My concealed lady[16] to our canceled love?

NURSE. O, she says nothing, sir, but weeps and weeps;
And now falls on her bed, and then starts up,
And Tybalt calls; and then on Romeo cries,
And then down falls again.

ROMEO. As if that name,
Shot from the deadly level[17] of a gun,
Did murder her; as that name's cursèd hand
Murdered her kinsman. O, tell me, friar, tell me,
In what vile part of this anatomy
Doth my name lodge? Tell me, that I may sack[18]
The hateful mansion.

[*He offers to stab himself, and* NURSE *snatches the dagger away.*]

FRIAR. Hold thy desperate hand.
Art thou a man? Thy form cries out thou art;
Thy tears are womanish, thy wild acts denote
The unreasonable fury of a beast.
Unseemly[19] woman in a seeming man!
And ill-beseeming beast in seeming both![20]

14. simpleness silly behavior (Romeo does not move).

15. O cry of grief.

16. concealed lady secret bride.

17. level aim.

18. sack plunder.

19. Unseemly inappropriate (because unnatural).

20. And . . . both! Romeo has inappropriately lost his human nature because he seems like a man and woman combined.

ENRICHMENT: Social Studies Connection
The Renaissance in England

The Renaissance was an age of culture and learning that began in Italy around 1300. In the Middle Ages, art and philosophy had centered on the Church, but Renaissance thinkers took the ancient Greeks and Romans as models and made the individual their focus. Great artists and thinkers associated with the Italian Renaissance are Petrarch, Michelangelo, Leonardo da Vinci, and Raphael.

During the early Renaissance in Italy, England was involved in the Hundred Years' War with France, and then the War of the Roses—a struggle for the throne between two royal families. When the wars ended in 1485, the Renaissance spread to England. Under the reign of Queen Elizabeth I (1558–1603), English literature flowered with the works of such great writers as Francis Bacon, Ben Jonson, Christopher Marlowe, Edmund Spenser, and above all, William Shakespeare.

Thou hast amazed me. By my holy order,
I thought thy disposition better tempered.
Hast thou slain Tybalt? Wilt thou slay thyself?
And slay thy lady that in thy life lives,
By doing damnèd hate upon thyself?
Why railest thou on thy birth, the heaven, and earth?
Since birth and heaven and earth, all three do meet
In thee at once; which thou at once wouldst lose.
Fie, fie, thou shamest thy shape, thy love, thy wit,[21]
Which, like a usurer,[22] abound'st in all,
And usest none in that true use indeed
Which should bedeck[23] thy shape, thy love, thy wit.
Thy noble shape is but a form of wax,
Digressing from the valor of a man;
Thy dear love sworn but hollow prejury,
Killing that love which thou hast vowed to cherish;
Thy wit, that ornament to shape and love,
Misshapen in the conduct[24] of them both,
Like powder in a skilless soldier's flask,[25]
Is set afire by thine own ignorance,
And thou dismemb'red with thine own defense.[26]
What, rouse thee, man! Thy Juliet is alive,
For whose dear sake thou wast but lately dead.[27]
There art thou happy.[28] Tybalt would kill thee,
But thou slewest Tybalt. There art thou happy.
36 The law, that threat'ned death, becomes thy friend
And turns it to exile. There art thou happy.
A pack of blessings light upon thy back;
Happiness courts thee in her best array;
But, like a misbehaved and sullen wench,[29]
Thou puts up[30] thy fortune and thy love.
Take heed, take heed, for such die miserable.
Go get thee to thy love, as was decreed,
Ascend her chamber, hence and comfort her.
But look thou stay not till the watch be set,[31]
For then thou canst not pass to Mantua,
Where thou shalt live till we can find a time
To blaze[32] your marriage, reconcile your friends,
Beg pardon of the Prince, and call thee back
With twenty hundred thousand times more joy
Than thou went'st forth in lamentation.
Go before, nurse. Commend me to thy lady,
And bid her hasten all the house to bed,
Which heavy sorrow makes them apt unto.[33]
Romeo is coming.

NURSE. O Lord, I could have stayed here all the night
To hear good counsel. O, what learning is!
My lord, I'll tell my lady you will come.

21. wit mind; intellect.

22. Which, like a usurer who, like a rich money-lender.

23. bedeck do honor to.

Literary Analysis
Soliloquy, Aside, and Monologue Is the Friar's long speech addressed to another character? Is it a monologue or a soliloquy?

24. conduct management.

25. flask powder flask.

26. And thou . . . defense the friar is saying that Romeo's mind, which is now irrational, is destroying rather than aiding him.

27. but lately dead only recently declaring yourself dead.

28. happy fortunate.

29. wench low, common girl.

30. puts up pouts over.

31. watch be set watchmen go on duty.

32. blaze announce publicly.

33. apt unto likely to do.

37 **Reading Check**
What three reasons does the Friar give to persuade Romeo to change his attitude?

36 Literary Analysis
Soliloquy, Aside, and Monologue

- Ask students what Romeo has tried to do just before the Friar's speech begins.
  Answer: Romeo has tried to kill himself.

Monitor Progress Have students answer the Literary Analysis question on p. 833: Is the Friar's long speech addressed to another character? Is it a monologue or a soliloquy?
Answer: The Friar's speech is delivered to Romeo, with the Nurse listening. It is a monologue.

37 Reading Check
Answer: The Friar gives these reasons: Juliet is alive; Romeo killed Tybalt before Tybalt could kill him; Romeo has been exiled instead of being sentenced to death.

38 Reading Strategy

Paraphrasing

- Ask students if they think the Friar's plan is a good one.
  Possible response: Some students may contend that seeing Juliet will give Romeo reason to go on living. Others may say that in going to the Capulets, Romeo risks death.
- Have students answer the first Reading Strategy question on p. 834: What does Romeo mean when he says, "Bid my sweet prepare to chide"?
  Possible response: "Tell Juliet she should be ready to give me a hard time for killing Tybalt."

39 Reading Strategy

Paraphrasing

- How does the Friar say he will keep in touch with Romeo in exile?
  Answer: The Friar says he will get messages to Romeo though Romeo's servant.
- Invite students to respond to the second Reading Strategy question on p. 834: Is Romeo's parting with the Friar angry, sad, or something else? Explain.
  Answer: Romeo says that if he were not going to see Juliet, which gives him joy, he would be sad to leave the Friar. He is not angry, but somewhat sad.

40 Literary Analysis

Soliloquy, Aside, and Monologue

- Have students summarize the exchange between Lord Capulet and Paris in this scene.
  Answer: Lord Capulet says that Tybalt's death has made it impossible to discuss Paris's proposal of marriage with Juliet. Paris responds that sad times are not good for wooing and asks Lady Capulet to remember him to Juliet.
- Have students answer the Literary Analysis question on p. 834: Is Lady Capulet's brief remark in lines 10–11 an aside? Why or why not?
  Answer: An aside is delivered to the audience; Lady Capulet's remark is directed to Paris.

38

ROMEO. Do so, and bid my sweet prepare to chide.[34]
[NURSE *offers to go in and turns again.*]

NURSE. Here, sir, a ring she bid me give you, sir.
Hie you, make haste, for it grows very late. [*Exit.*]

ROMEO. How well my comfort is revived by this!

FRIAR. Go hence; good night; and here stands all your state:[35]
Either be gone before the watch be set,
Or by the break of day disguised from hence.
Sojourn[36] in Mantua. I'll find out your man,
And he shall signify[37] from time to time
Every good hap to you that chances here.
Give me thy hand. 'Tis late. Farewell; good night.

39

ROMEO. But that a joy past joy calls out on me,
It were a grief so brief to part with thee.
Farewell. [*Exit all.*]

Scene iv. *A room in* CAPULET'S *house.*

[*Enter old* CAPULET, *his* WIFE, *and* PARIS.]

CAPULET. Things have fall'n out, sir, so unluckily
That we have had no time to move[1] our daughter.
Look you, she loved her kinsman Tybalt dearly,
And so did I. Well, we were born to die.
'Tis very late; she'll not come down tonight.
I promise you, but for your company,
I would have been abed an hour ago.

PARIS. These times of woe afford no times to woo.
Madam, good night. Commend me to your daughter.

40

LADY. I will, and know her mind early tomorrow;
Tonight she's mewed up to her heaviness.[2]

CAPULET. Sir, Paris, I will make a desperate tender[3]
Of my child's love. I think she will be ruled
In all respects by me; nay more, I doubt it not.
Wife, go you to her ere you go to bed;
Acquaint her here of my son[4] Paris' love
And bid her (mark you me?) on Wednesday next—
But soft! What day is this?

PARIS. Monday, my lord.

CAPULET. Monday! Ha, ha! Well, Wednesday is too soon.
A[5] Thursday let it be—a Thursday, tell her,
She shall be married to this noble earl.
Will you be ready? Do you like this haste?
We'll keep no great ado[6]—a friend or two;
For hark you, Tybalt being slain so late,

---

34. **chide** rebuke me (for slaying Tybalt).

Reading Strategy
Paraphrasing What does Romeo mean when he says, "Bid my sweet prepare to chide"?

35. **here . . . state** this is your situation.

36. **Sojourn** remain.

37. **signify** let you know.

Reading Strategy
Paraphrasing Is Romeo's parting with the Friar angry, sad, or something else? Explain.

1. **move** discuss your proposal with.

Literary Analysis
Soliloquy, Aside, and Monologue Is Lady Capulet's brief remark in lines 10–11 an aside? Why or why not?

2. **mewed . . . heaviness** locked up with her sorrow.

3. **desperate tender** risky offer.

4. **son** son-in-law.

5. **A** on.

6. **We'll . . . ado** We won't make a great fuss.

41

It may be thought we held him carelessly,[7]
Being our kinsman, if we revel much.
Therefore we'll have some half a dozen friends,
And there an end. But what say you to Thursday?

PARIS. My lord, I would that Thursday were tomorrow.

CAPULET. Well, get you gone. A Thursday be it then.
Go you to Juliet ere you go to bed;
Prepare her, wife, against[8] this wedding day.
Farewell, my lord.—Light to my chamber, ho!
Afore me,[9] it is so very late
That we may call it early by and by.
Good night. *[Exit all.]*

7. **held him carelessly** did not respect him enough.

Reading Strategy
Paraphrasing Paraphrase lines 25–26 to explain why Capulet wants to hold a small wedding.

8. **against** for.

9. **Afore me** indeed (a mild oath).

Scene v. CAPULET'S *orchard.*

[Enter ROMEO *and* JULIET *aloft.]*

JULIET. Wilt thou be gone? It is not yet near day.
It was the nightingale, and not the lark,[1]
That pierced the fearful hollow of thine ear.
Nightly she sings on yond pomegranate tree.
Believe me, love, it was the nightingale.

ROMEO. It was the lark, the herald of the morn;
No nightingale. Look, love, what envious streaks
Do lace the severing[2] clouds in yonder East.
Night's candles[3] are burnt out, and jocund day
Stands tiptoe on the misty mountaintops.
I must be gone and live, or stay and die.

JULIET. Yond light is not daylight; I know it, I.
It is some meteor that the sun exhales[4]
To be to thee this night a torchbearer
And light thee on thy way to Mantua.
Therefore stay yet; thou need'st not to be gone.

42

ROMEO. Let me be ta'en, let me be put to death.
I am content, so thou wilt have it so.
I'll say yon gray is not the morning's eye,
'Tis but the pale reflex of Cynthia's brow;[5]
Nor that is not the lark whose notes do beat
The vaulty heaven so high above our heads.
I have more care to stay than will to go.
Come, death, and welcome! Juliet wills it so.
How is't, my soul? Let's talk; it is not day.

JULIET. It is, it is! Hie hence, be gone, away!
It is the lark that sings so out of tune,
Straining harsh discords and unpleasing sharps.[6]
Some say the lark makes sweet division;[7]

1. **nightingale . . . lark** The nightingale was associated with the night; the lark, with dawn.

2. **severing** parting.

3. **Night's candles** stars.

4. **exhales** sends out.

5. **reflex . . . brow** reflection of the moon (Cynthia was a name for the moon goddess).

6. **sharps** shrill high notes.

7. **division** melody.

43 **Reading Check**
What do the Capulets plan for Juliet on Thursday?

ENRICHMENT: Natural History Connection

Birds in Shakespeare

Over fifty different species of birds appear in Shakespeare's plays. When the young playwright lived in Stratford he was surrounded by a well-wooded valley and probably learned much about the natural history of his area and the creatures that inhabited it. Although Shakespeare was not a trained naturalist, he lived in a time when serious naturalists were beginning to identify and name animals, birds, and plants. Students may recall Benvolio, earlier in the play, telling Romeo that there are more attractive women than Rosaline:

> "Compare her face with some that I shall show,
> And I will make thee think thy swan a crow."

Shakespeare was particularly fond of the skylark and used it in fifteen of his plays, including *Richard III, Love's Labor's Lost, A Midsummer Night's Dream, Titus Andronicus, Cymbeline,* and *King Lear*, as well as in two poems. But the most famous of the lark imagery occurs in *Romeo and Juliet*, in Act III, scene v.

41 Reading Strategy

Paraphrasing

- Ask: What is ironic about this scene involving Lord and Lady Capulet and Paris? What do readers and the audience know that the Capulets and Paris do not know?
  Answer: The three are discussing the marriage of Juliet to Paris; the reader knows that Juliet is already married to Romeo.
- Have students contrast Capulet's words in this scene with his previous talk with Paris, in which he said that Juliet's consent to marriage was important to him.
  Answer: In this scene, Capulet thinks Juliet will do as he asks.
- Have students respond to the Reading Strategy assignment on p. 835: Paraphrase lines 22–26 to explain why Capulet wants to hold a small wedding.
  Answer: "It won't be a big event, just a few friends. For, I think you'll agree, since Tybalt was just killed, we may look as if we are insensitive and didn't value him as a member of the family if we hold a big, flashy event so soon."

42 Literary Analysis

Allusions

- Ask students what the two references to birds mean in this exchange between Romeo and Juliet?
  Answer: The two lovers argue about whether they hear the lark or the nightingale. Juliet says it was the nightingale, which means it is still night and Romeo can stay awhile. Romeo says it was the lark, which means it is daybreak and he must leave.
- Ask students how an allusion in line 20 is used to show that Romeo accepts Juliet's judgment about whether it is daybreak or night.
  Answer: Romeo says that what he thought was the light of morning is just a reflection of Cynthia's brow, meaning the moon. He is willing to take Juliet's word for the time of day if it means he can stay with her.

43 Reading Check

Answer: The Capulets plan to marry Juliet to Paris on the following Thursday.

44 Reading Strategy

Paraphrasing

- Have students speculate on whether or not Juliet really thinks the lark sings so out of tune. What might she really mean?
  Possible response: Juliet hates the sound of the lark because it means that daylight has come and that Romeo must leave her.
- Ask students to respond to the first Reading Strategy assignment on p. 836: Restate Romeo's complaint in line 36 to explain the contrast he makes between light and dark.
  Possible response: "As the light grows brighter and brighter, our situation grows darker and darker."

45 Reading Strategy

Paraphrasing

- Ask students how Juliet uses figurative language to show Romeo how she will age while he is absent.
  Answer: Juliet says that when Romeo is away from her, every minute will appear to be many days long, so that she will be much older when she sees him again.
- Now, ask students to respond to the second Reading Strategy assignment on p. 836: Translate Romeo and Juliet's conversation in lines 48–53 into modern English.
  Possible response: ROMEO: Good-bye! I won't miss any chance to be in touch with you, Juliet.
  JULIET: Do you think we'll ever see each other again?
  ROMEO: I'm sure of it. And later on we'll laugh about all of the problems we're having right now.

44

This doth not so, for she divideth us.
Some say the lark and loathèd toad change eyes;[8]
O, now I would they had changed voices too,
Since arm from arm that voice doth us affray,[9]
Hunting thee hence with hunt's-up[10] to the day.
O, now be gone! More light and light it grows.

ROMEO. More light and light—more dark and dark our woes.

[*Enter* NURSE.]

NURSE. Madam!

JULIET. Nurse?

NURSE. Your lady mother is coming to your chamber.
The day is broke; be wary, look about. [*Exit.*]

JULIET. Then, window, let day in, and let life out.

ROMEO. Farewell, farewell! One kiss, and I'll descend.
[*He goeth down.*]

JULIET. Art thou gone so, love-lord, ay husband-friend?
I must hear from thee every day in the hour,
For in a minute there are many days.
O, by this count I shall be much in years[11]
Ere I again behold my Romeo!

45

ROMEO. Farewell!
I will omit no opportunity
That may convey my greetings, love, to thee.

JULIET. O, think'st thou we shall ever meet again?

ROMEO. I doubt it not; and all these woes shall serve
For sweet discourses[12] in our times to come.

JULIET. O God, I have an ill-divining[13] soul!
Methinks I see thee, now thou art so low,
As one dead in the bottom of a tomb.
Either my eyesight fails, or thou lookest pale.

ROMEO. And trust me, love, in my eye so do you.
Dry sorrow drinks our blood.[14] Adieu, adieu! [*Exit.*]

JULIET. O Fortune, Fortune! All men call thee fickle.
If thou art fickle, what dost thou[15] with him
46
That is renowned for faith? Be fickle, Fortune,
For then I hope thou wilt not keep him long
But send him back.

[*Enter* MOTHER.]

LADY CAPULET. Ho, daughter! Are you up?

JULIET. Who is't that calls? It is my lady mother.

---

8. change eyes exchange eyes (because the lark has a beautiful body with ugly eyes and the toad has an ugly body with beautiful eyes).

9. affray frighten.

10. hunt's-up morning song for hunters.

Reading Strategy
Paraphrasing Restate Romeo's complaint in line 36 to explain the contrast he makes between light and dark.

11. much in years much older.

Reading Strategy
Paraphrasing Translate Romeo and Juliet's conversation in lines 48–53 into modern English.

12. discourses conversations.

13. ill-divining predicting evil.

14. Dry sorrow . . . blood it was once believed that sorrow drained away the blood.

fickle (fik′əl) *adj.* changeable

15. dost thou do you have to do.

Literary Analysis
Allusion To which quality of Fortune, the Greek goddess of chance, does Juliet allude?

Is she not down so late,[16] or up so early?
What unaccustomed cause procures her hither?[17]

LADY CAPULET. Why, how now, Juliet?

JULIET. Madam, I am not well.

LADY CAPULET. Evermore weeping for your cousin's death?
What, wilt thou wash him from his grave with tears?
And if thou couldst, thou couldst not make him live.
Therefore have done. Some grief shows much of love;
But much of grief shows still some want of wit.

JULIET. Yet let me weep for such a feeling[18] loss.

LADY CAPULET. So shall you feel the loss, but not the friend
Which you weep for.

JULIET. Feeling so the loss,
I cannot choose but ever weep the friend.

LADY CAPULET. Well, girl, thou weep'st not so much for his death
As that the villain lives which slaughtered him.

JULIET. What villain, madam?

LADY CAPULET. That same villain Romeo.

47 **JULIET.** [*Aside*] Villain and he be many miles asunder.[19]—
God pardon him! I do, with all my heart;
And yet no man like he doth grieve my heart.

LADY CAPULET. That is because the traitor murderer lives.

JULIET. Ay, madam, from the reach of these my hands.
Would none but I might venge my cousin's death!

LADY CAPULET. We will have vengeance for it, fear thou not.
Then weep no more. I'll send to one in Mantua,
Where that same banished runagate[20] doth live,
Shall give him such an unaccustomed dram[21]
That he shall soon keep Tybalt company;
And then I hope thou wilt be satisfied.

JULIET. Indeed I never shall be satisfied
With Romeo till I behold him—dead[22]—
Is my poor heart so for a kinsman vexed.
Madam, if you could find out but a man
To bear a poison, I would temper[23] it;
That Romeo should, upon receipt thereof,
Soon sleep in quiet. O, how my heart abhors
To hear him named and cannot come to him,
To wreak[24] the love I bore my cousin
Upon his body that hath slaughtered him!

LADY CAPULET. Find thou the means, and I'll find such a man.

16. Is she . . . late Has she stayed up so late?

17. What . . . hither? What unusual reason brings her here?

18. feeling deeply felt.

Literary Analysis
Soliloquy, Aside, and Monologue Which characteristics of an aside do you find in Juliet's words in lines 82–84?

19. asunder apart.

20. runagate renegade; runaway.

21. unaccustomed dram unexpected dose of poison.

22. dead Juliet is deliberately ambiguous here. Her mother thinks *dead* refers to Romeo. But Juliet is using the word with the following line, in reference to her heart.

23. temper mix; weaken.

24. wreak (reek) avenge; express.

48 **Reading Check**
Who leaves Juliet's chambers just before Lady Capulet arrives?

46 Literary Analysis (p. 836)
Allusions

- Have students identify the explanation Romeo gives for why he and Juliet both look so pale.
Answer: He says that they are both sad, and that sadness drains their blood.
- Ask students to respond to the Literary Analysis question on p. 836: To which quality of Fortune, the Greek goddess of chance, does Juliet allude?
Answer: Juliet alludes to the quality of fickleness, or changeability.

47 Literary Analysis
Soliloquy, Aside, and Monologue

- Ask students what is ironic about Lady Capulet's words to Juliet in lines 70–74.
Answer: Lady Capulet thinks Juliet is mourning Tybalt's death, but Juliet is sad because of Romeo's absence and their situation in general.
- Invite students to answer the Literary Analysis question on p. 837: Which characteristics of an aside do you find in Juliet's words in lines 82–84?
Answer: Juliet speaks her words about Romeo to the audience because she does not want her mother to hear them.

48 Reading Check
Answer: Romeo leaves Juliet's chambers just before Lady Capulet arrives.

CUSTOMIZE INSTRUCTION FOR UNIVERSAL ACCESS

For Special Needs Students	For Gifted/Talented Students	For Advanced Readers
Be sure that students understand that while Lady Capulet thinks that Juliet is weeping over Tybalt's death, Juliet is actually weeping over Romeo.	Have students identify the example of foreshadowing in lines 54–57. What do they think these lines predict? **Answer:** Juliet thinks she sees Romeo in a tomb. The lines probably predict the death of Romeo.	Students may be interested to learn that people in Elizabethan times believed that sorrow was a condition that drained the blood. Have them consider why this might have been so. Then, ask them to do research to find other medical practices and beliefs from this time period. Students may present some of their findings to the class.

49 Reading Strategy

Paraphrasing

- Have students determine whether Lady Capulet's words about telling Juliet joyful tidings are ironic. Why or why not?
  Possible response: Her words are ironic because readers and audience members know that her news will be a dreadful shock to Juliet.
- Have students respond to the Reading Strategy assignment on p. 838: Restate Lady Capulet's remarks in lines 108–111 in your own words.
  Possible response: "Well, my dear, your father is so considerate that he found a way to get your mind off your sorrow. He has chosen to give you a day of joy that will be as much a surprise to you as it was to me."

50 ▶ Critical Viewing

Answer: Students may say that the picture conveys Juliet's desperation as she pleads to her mother not to make her go through with a marriage to Paris.

But now I'll tell thee joyful tidings, girl.

JULIET. And joy comes well in such a needy time.
What are they, beseech your ladyship?

49

LADY CAPULET. Well, well, thou hast a careful[25] father, child;
One who, to put thee from thy heaviness,
Hath sorted out[26] a sudden day of joy
That thou expects not nor I looked not for.

JULIET. Madam, in happy time![27] What day is that?

LADY CAPULET. Marry, my child, early next Thursday morn
The gallant, young, and noble gentleman,
The County Paris, at Saint Peter's Church,
Shall happily make thee there a joyful bride.

JULIET. Now by Saint Peter's Church, and Peter too,
He shall not make me there a joyful bride!
I wonder at this haste, that I must wed
Ere he that should be husband comes to woo.
I pray you tell my lord and father, madam,
I will not marry yet; and when I do, I swear
It shall be Romeo, whom you know I hate,
Rather than Paris. These are news indeed!

LADY CAPULET. Here comes your father. Tell him so yourself,
And see how he will take it at your hands.

[*Enter* CAPULET *and* NURSE.]

CAPULET. When the sun sets the earth doth drizzle dew,
But for the sunset of my brother's son
It rains downright.
How now? A conduit,[28] girl? What, still in tears?
Evermore show'ring? In one little body
Thou counterfeits a bark,[29] a sea, a wind:
For still thy eyes, which I may call the sea,
Do ebb and flow with tears; the bark thy body is,
Sailing in this salt flood; the winds, thy sighs,
Who, raging with thy tears and they with them,
Without a sudden calm will overset
Thy tempest-tossèd body. How now, wife?
Have you delivered to her our decree?

51

LADY CAPULET. Ay, sir; but she will none, she gives you
thanks.[30]
I would the fool were married to her grave!

CAPULET. Soft! Take me with you,[31] take me with you, wife.
How? Will she none? Doth she not give us thanks?
Is she not proud?[32] Doth she not count her blest,
Unworthy as she is, that we have wrought[33]

25. careful considerate.

26. sorted out selected.

Reading Strategy
Paraphrasing Restate Lady Capulet's remarks in lines 108–111 in your own words.

27. in happy time just in time.

28. conduit water pipe.

29. bark boat.

30. she will none . . . thanks she'll have nothing to do with it, thank you.

31. Soft! Take . . . you Wait a minute. Let me understand you.

32. proud pleased.

33. wrought arranged.

50 ▼ **Critical Viewing** Do you think this picture accurately conveys Juliet's response to her parents' plan for her marriage? **[Analyze]**

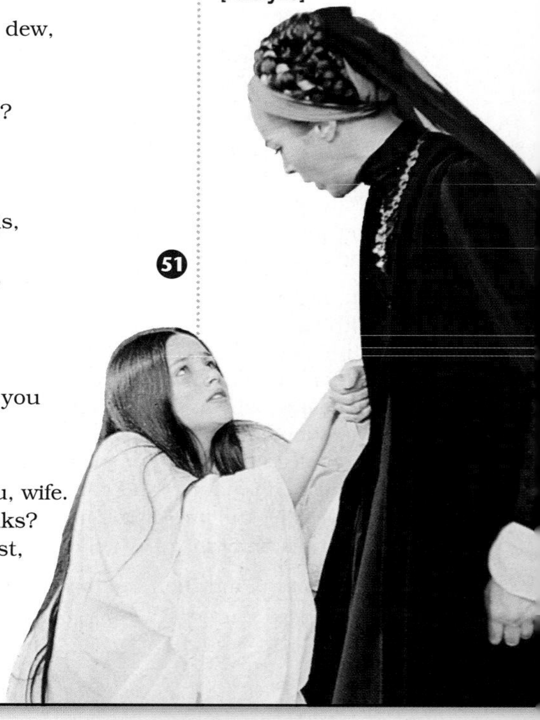

So worthy a gentleman to be her bride?

JULIET. Not proud you have, but thankful that you have.
Proud can I never be of what I hate,
But thankful even for hate that is meant love.

CAPULET. How, how, how, how, chopped-logic?[34] What is this?
"Proud"—and "I thank you"—and "I thank you not"—
And yet "not proud"? Mistress minion[35] you,
Thank me no thankings, nor proud me no prouds,
But fettle[36] your fine joints 'gainst Thursday next
To go with Paris to Saint Peter's Church,
Or I will drag thee on a hurdle[37] thither.
Out, you greensickness carrion![38] Out, you baggage![39]
You tallow-face![40]

LADY CAPULET. Fie, fie! What, are you mad?

JULIET. Good father, I beseech you on my knees,
Hear me with patience but to speak a word.

CAPULET. Hang thee, young baggage! Disobedient wretch!
I tell thee what—get thee to church a Thursday
Or never after look me in the face.
Speak not, reply not, do not answer me!
My fingers itch. Wife, we scarce thought us blest
That God had lent us but this only child;
But now I see this one is one too much,
And that we have a curse in having her.
Out on her, hilding![41]

NURSE. God in heaven bless her!
You are to blame, my lord, to rate[42] her so.

CAPULET. And why, my Lady Wisdom? Hold your tongue,
Good Prudence. Smatter with your gossips, go![43]

NURSE. I speak no treason.

CAPULET. O, God-i-god-en!

NURSE. May not one speak?

CAPULET. Peace, you mumbling fool!
Utter your gravity[44] o'er a gossip's bowl,
For here we need it not.

LADY CAPULET. You are too hot.

CAPULET. God's bread![45] It makes me mad.
Day, night; hour, tide, time; work, play;
Alone, in company; still my care hath been
To have her matched; and having now provided
A gentleman of noble parentage,
Of fair demesnes,[46] youthful, and nobly trained,

34. chopped-logic contradictory, unsound thought and speech.

35. Mistress minion Miss Uppity.

36. fettle prepare.

37. hurdle sled on which prisoners were taken to their execution.

38. greensickness carrion anemic lump of flesh.

39. baggage naughty girl.

40. tallow-face wax-pale face.

41. hilding worthless person.

42. rate scold; berate.

43. Smatter . . . go! Go chatter with the other old women.

44. gravity wisdom.

45. God's bread! By the holy Eucharist!

46. demesnes property.

52 **Reading Check**

What does Capulet say will happen if Juliet does not get married at the church on Thursday?

51 Background

Film

Many film makers have tried their hands at Shakespeare's timeless romance. In 1916, Gordon Edwards and Maxwell Karger directed a silent version with the text in subtitles. Twenty years later, George Cukor directed a talking version starring Leslie Howard and Norma Shearer in the title roles, with John Barrymore and Basil Rathbone as Mercutio and Tybalt.

In 1968, Zeffirelli's version was released. Filmed in Italy, the movie featured exquisite period costumes and settings—as can be seen in the stills accompanying the play in this text.

In 1996, Baz Luhrmann directed a movie version of *Romeo and Juliet* with an abridged text, filmed in Italy. The movie has a contemporary setting with Latin and punk-rock music on the soundtrack. Use the following for discussion:

1. If you were filming *Romeo and Juliet*, which time period would you choose for a setting? Why?
   Answer: Answers should include details about the period that would support the plot of the play.
2. Why do some directors change the period and setting of Shakespeare's play?
   Answer: Students may say that the directors want to show the audience that the play has universal meaning.

52 Reading Check

Answer: Capulet says that if Juliet does not get married on Thursday, he does not want to see her again.

CUSTOMIZE INSTRUCTION FOR UNIVERSAL ACCESS

For Less Proficient Readers	For Gifted/Talented Students
Students may not understand what Juliet means to say in lines 147–149, as her father does not. He calls her words "chopped-logic." Help students understand that Juliet is saying that she is not proud (or pleased) at what he has done, but she is thankful that he has done something that he intended for her benefit. In other words, she is saying that even though she hates what he has done, she knows that he meant to show her love.	Point out the word *marry*, the first word in line 113 of Lady Capulet's speech on p. 838. Ask students if the word is a pun as it is used here and suggest that they use the glossary of Elizabethan words on p. 766 for assistance. **Answer:** The word is used to mean "indeed," as in "Indeed, my child, early next Thursday morn." It is also used in the conventional way, meaning "to wed," in which case Lady Capulet's words mean, "You will be married, my child, early next Thursday morn."

53 Reading Strategy

Paraphrasing

- Ask students what Lord Capulet's main criticism of Juliet seems to be in lines 177–197.
  Answer: Lord Capulet says in different ways that Juliet is ungrateful for the wonderful marriage contract he has arranged for her.
- Ask students what Juliet does when she cannot convince her father to change his mind.
  Answer: Juliet turns her attention to her mother.
- Have students answer the Reading Strategy question on p. 840: In lines 200–204 what options does Juliet offer her mother?
  Answer: Juliet asks her mother not to turn her back on her, but to delay the marriage for a month, or even a week. Juliet says that if her mother won't help her, Juliet will end up dead, like Tybalt.

54 Literary Analysis (p. 841)

Soliloquy, Aside, and Monologue

- Ask students whom Juliet is calling a "wicked fiend" in line 237.
  Answer: Juliet refers to her Nurse, who has betrayed her.
- Ask students if Juliet's final speech in Act III is a monologue or a soliloquy, and why.
  Answer: Juliet's final speech is a soliloquy. Both her mother and the nurse have left the scene.

Stuffed, as they say, with honorable parts,[47]
Proportioned as one's thought would wish a man—
And then to have a wretched puling[48] fool,
A whining mammet,[49] in her fortune's tender,[50]
To answer "I'll not wed, I cannot love;
I am too young, I pray you pardon me"!
But, and you will not wed, I'll pardon you!
Graze where you will, you shall not house with me.
Look to't, think on't; I do not use to jest.
Thursday is near; lay hand on heart, advise:[51]
And you be mine, I'll give you to my friend;
And you be not, hang, beg, starve, die in the streets,
For, by my soul, I'll ne'er acknowledge thee,
Nor what is mine shall never do thee good.
Trust to't. Bethink you. I'll not be forsworn.[52] [*Exit.*]

JULIET. Is there no pity sitting in the clouds
That sees into the bottom of my grief?
O sweet my mother, cast me not away!
Delay this marriage for a month, a week;
Or if you do not, make the bridal bed
In that dim monument where Tybalt lies.

LADY CAPULET. Talk not to me, for I'll not speak a word.
Do as thou wilt, for I have done with thee. [*Exit.*]

JULIET. O God!—O nurse, how shall this be prevented?
My husband is on earth, my faith in heaven.[53]
How shall that faith return again to earth
Unless that husband send it me from heaven
By leaving earth?[54] Comfort me, counsel me.
Alack, alack, that heaven should practice stratagems[55]
Upon so soft a subject as myself!
What say'st thou? Hast thou not a word of joy?
Some comfort, nurse.

NURSE. Faith, here it is.
Romeo is banished; and all the world to nothing[56]
That he dares ne'er come back to challenge[57] you;
Or if he do, it needs must be by stealth.
Then, since the case so stands as now it doth,
I think it best you married with the County.
O, he's a lovely gentleman!
Romeo's a dishclout to him.[58] An eagle, madam,
Hath not so green, so quick, so fair an eye
As Paris hath. Beshrew my very heart,
I think you are happy in this second match,
For it excels your first; or if it did not,
Your first is dead—or 'twere as good he were
As living here and you no use of him.

47. **parts** qualities.

48. **puling** whining.

49. **mammet** doll.

50. **in . . . tender** when good fortune is offered her.

51. **advise** consider.

52. **forsworn** made to violate my promise.

Reading Strategy
Paraphrasing In lines 200–204, what options does Juliet offer her mother?

53. **my faith in heaven** my marriage vow is recorded in heaven.

54. **leaving earth** dying.

55. **stratagems** tricks; plots.

56. **all . . . nothing** the odds are overwhelming.

57. **challenge** claim.

58. **a dishclout to him** a dishcloth compared with him.

ENRICHMENT: Performing Arts Connection

Women's Roles in Elizabethan Theater

Remind students as they read this scene that in Shakespeare's time, the audience would have been watching a scene with two adult men playing Lady Capulet and the Nurse, and a young boy playing Juliet. What's more, no one at that time found anything strange about this situation. Women did not act on stage until after Charles II's ascension to the throne in 1660.

Boys went into training for the Elizabethan theater as young as age ten. They would play children, pages, and other young people until they were tall enough to play women, such as Juliet. They would play those roles until their voices changed. The boys often lived with the adult actors and their families during these years. The training they would have through this arrangement was priceless, since they could watch an experienced actor at work and learn how to stand, move, and speak in a way that was both natural and effective for the stage.

JULIET. Speak'st thou from thy heart?

NURSE. And from my soul too; else beshrew them both.

JULIET. Amen!

NURSE. What?

JULIET. Well, thou hast comforted me marvelous much.
Go in; and tell my lady I am gone,
Having displeased my father, to Lawrence' cell,
To make confession and to be absolved.[59]

NURSE. Marry, I will; and this is wisely done. *[Exit.]*

JULIET. Ancient damnation![60] O most wicked fiend!
Is it more sin to wish me thus forsworn,
Or to dispraise my lord with that same tongue
54 Which she hath praised him with above compare
So many thousand times? Go, counselor!
Thou and my bosom henceforth shall be twain.[61]
I'll to the friar to know his remedy.
If all else fail, myself have power to die. *[Exit.]*

59. absolved receive forgiveness for my sins.

60. Ancient damnation! Old devil!

61. Thou . . . twain You will from now on be separated from my trust.

Review and Assess

Thinking About Act III

1. **Respond:** What would you do if you were in Romeo or Juliet's situation?
2. **(a) Recall:** Why do Mercutio and Tybalt fight in Act III, Scene i? **(b) Interpret:** What does Mercutio mean by his dying exclamation, "A plague on both your houses!"? **(c) Connect:** How do these lines echo the ideas set forth in the play's prologue?
3. **(a) Recall:** How and why does Romeo kill Tybalt? **(b) Interpret:** What does Romeo mean when he says, after killing Tybalt, "I am fortune's fool!"?
4. **(a) Recall:** What punishment does the prince order for Romeo? **(b) Draw Conclusions:** Why does the Prince decide not to sentence Romeo to death, despite his threat in Act I?
5. **(a) Recall:** Describe the clashing emotions Juliet feels when Nurse reports Tybalt's death and Romeo's punishment. **(b) Compare and Contrast:** What reactions—both similar and different—do Juliet and Romeo have to Romeo's punishment?
6. **Speculate:** Do you think Romeo's punishment is fair? Support your answer.

ASSESS

Answers for p. 841

Review and Assess

1. Students may say that they would reveal their marriage to their families.
2. **(a)** Mercutio and Tybalt fight because Romeo refuses to fight with Tybalt, who has challenged him. Mercutio acts to defend Romeo's honor. **(b)** Mercutio means the statement as a curse, blaming both sides for the quarrel. **(c)** The lines echo the Prologue because the Prologue briefly explains the terrible events that happen to the two "star-crossed lovers" who are from the rival households.
3. **(a)** Romeo kills Tybalt in a sword fight to avenge Mercutio's death. **(b)** Romeo feels he is a victim of fate.
4. **(a)** Romeo is banished. **(b)** The Prince is lenient because Romeo killed a person whose life was already forfeit for killing Mercutio.
5. **(a)** Juliet's vascillation between rage and love is expressed in a series of oxymorons ("Fiend angelical"). Her tumultuous emotions subside into grief at Romeo's banishment. **(b)** Both Romeo and Juliet react drastically to his banishment. Juliet alludes to suicide in Scene ii, and Romeo asserts that separation from Juliet will be a torture far worse than death.
6. Some students may say that exile is far better than death. Others may say that Romeo should not be punished at all, since he was avenging Mercutio's death and did not start the fight.

ASSESSMENT PRACTICE: Literary Response

Defending Interpretations (For more practice, see Test Preparation Workbook, p. 48.)

Many tests require students to defend interpretations of a literary text. Use the following sample item to demonstrate for students how to defend an interpretation.

ROMEO: There is no world without Verona walls,
But purgatory, torture, hell itself.
Hence banished is banished from the world,
And world's exile is death. Then "banished,"
Is death mistermed. Calling death "banished,"
Thou cut'st my head off with a golden ax
And smilest upon the stroke that murders me.

How does this passage give insight into Romeo's character? Support your answer with evidence.

Possible Answer: Romeo is melodramatic and exaggerates his misery. He thinks of banishment as "purgatory, torture, hell itself." He sees it only as death, when really it is life by the Prince's mercy.

Answers for p. 842

Review and Assess

1. Juliet is impatient for the night to arrive so she can be with her new husband.
2. The Friar thinks Romeo is acting irrationally and self-destructively.
3. **(a)** Juliet means that there is a vast difference between Romeo and a villain. **(b)** It is important that Lady Capulet not hear how Juliet feels, but also that the audience knows Juliet's true feelings.
4. Mercutio calls Tybalt "rat-catcher" and "king of cats" and asks for one of his nine lives.
5. Juliet is hoping that nightfall will come soon.
6. Juliet's allusions reveal that she is educated.
7. Students may agree that allusions enhance understanding but are not always essential to a character's ideas.
8. My Words: Banishment is torture, not mercy, for heaven is where Juliet lives. While every little creature may look upon Juliet, I cannot. I must go. Even flies have it better than I, for they can hear Juliet speak. But I cannot hear Juliet's voice because I am banished. You say that exile is not death, but it is. The damned howl the word *banished* in hell. How can you torture me with the word *banished*?
9. Possible answer: Here is some comfort. Romeo is gone and unlikely to return. If he does, it will have to be done secretly. So, I think you should marry Paris. He's handsome. Romeo's nothing compared to him. I think you should be happy in this second marriage; it is much better than your first. And even if it is not, your first marriage is dead anyway.
10. Have volunteers share their sentences with the class.
11. Students may say that a homeland gives a person a history, a culture, and an identity.

Review and Assess

Literary Analysis

Soliloquy, Aside, and Monologue

1. Analyze the thoughts and feelings Juliet reveals in the **soliloquy** that opens Scene ii of Act III.
2. Which criticisms of Romeo does the Friar address in his Scene iii **monologue** beginning "Hold thy desperate hand"?
3. (a) In Act III, Scene v, when her mother refers to Romeo as a villain, Juliet utters the **aside,** "Villain and he be many miles asunder." What does Juliet mean? (b) Why is it important that the audience, but not Lady Capulet, hear this remark?

Connecting Literary Elements

4. How does Mercutio use an **allusion** to incite Tybalt to fight him in Act III, Scene i?
5. When Juliet alludes to Phoebus and Phaëton in her soliloquy opening Act III, Scene ii, what is she hoping will happen soon?
6. What do Juliet's allusions to mythology in her speeches reveal about her character?
7. Do you need to understand an allusion to understand a character's ideas? Why or why not?

Reading Strategy

Paraphrasing

8. Using a chart like the one shown, paraphrase lines 29–51 in Act III, Scene iii.

Shakespeare's Words	My Words

9. Paraphrase lines 215–227 in Act III, Scene v.
10. To reverse the process, write two sentences about Romeo and Juliet. Then, restate them in Shakespearean language.

Extend Understanding

11. **Cultural Connection:** For Romeo, being exiled from his homeland is a very harsh punishment. What important role does a person's homeland play in modern life?

Quick Review

A **soliloquy** is a lengthy speech in which a character, alone on stage, expresses his or her thoughts to the audience.

An **aside** is a character's brief remark made to the audience, unheard by other characters on stage.

A **monologue** is a lengthy speech addressed to other characters on stage.

Within their dramatic speeches, characters often make **allusions**—references to well-known people, places, or events from myths or literature.

Paraphrasing is restating text in your own words.

Take It to the Net

www.phschool.com

Take the interactive self-test online to check your understanding of Act III.

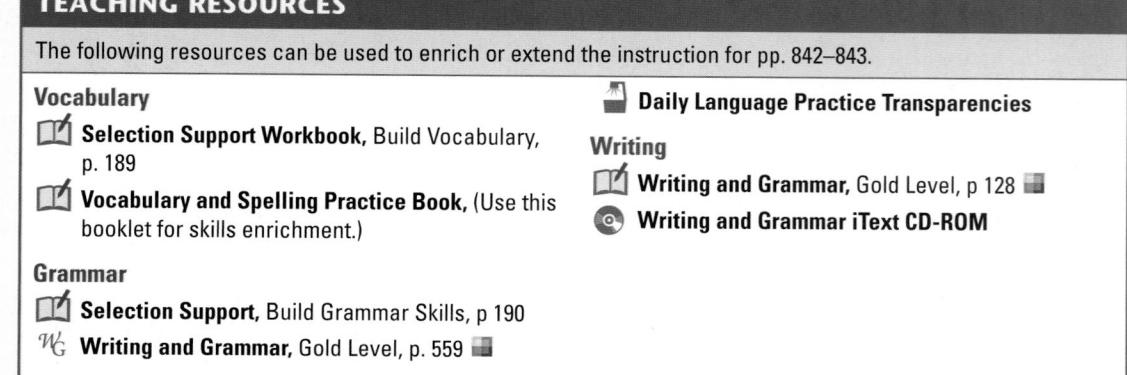

TEACHING RESOURCES

The following resources can be used to enrich or extend the instruction for pp. 842–843.

Vocabulary

Selection Support Workbook, Build Vocabulary, p. 189

Vocabulary and Spelling Practice Book, (Use this booklet for skills enrichment.)

Grammar

Selection Support, Build Grammar Skills, p 190

Writing and Grammar, Gold Level, p. 559

Daily Language Practice Transparencies

Writing

Writing and Grammar, Gold Level, p 128

Writing and Grammar iText CD-ROM

BLOCK SCHEDULING: Resources marked with this symbol provide varied instruction during 90-minute blocks.

Integrate Language Skills

❶ Vocabulary Development Lesson

Word Analysis: Words From Myths

Nemesis is the Greek goddess of vengeance. *Mercury* is the swift Roman messenger to the gods. *Odysseus* is the Greek hero who wanders for years. Using these mythological clues, write a definition for each word below.

1. nemesis 2. mercurial 3. odyssey

Spelling Strategy

To make a present-tense verb agree with a third-person singular subject, add *-s* to the verb. (*He visits her.*) If the verb ends in *ss, sh,* or *ch*, add *-es*. (*She touches his hand.*) Choose the correctly spelled word in each item below.

1. tauntes, taunts 2. reaches, reachs

Concept Development: Synonyms

Write the word that is the best synonym for the first word in each item. To help you, review vocabulary words on page 818.

1. gallant: (a) enchanting, (b) courageous, (c) cowardly
2. fray: (a) brawl, (b) condition, (c) truce
3. martial: (a) financial, (b) deputy, (c) warlike
4. exile: (a) expel, (b) discourage, (c) arrive
5. eloquence: (a) beauty, (b) expressiveness, (c) value
6. fickle: (a) fruitful, (b) constant, (c) erratic

❷ Grammar Lesson

Pronoun Case: *who* and *whom*

Use the pronoun ***who*** when it is the subject of the verb or is a predicate nominative. Use the pronoun ***whom*** when it receives the action of the verb or is the object of a preposition.

Subject:	*Who* knocks so hard?
Direct Object:	It shall be Romeo, *whom* you know I hate?

Practice In your notebook, complete each sentence with *who* or *whom*.

1. __?__ began the tragic argument?
2. Romeo, __?__ wanted peace, intervened.
3. He is someone to __?__ bad things happen.
4. Romeo is the man __?__ Juliet loves.
5. Tybalt was the man __?__ Romeo killed.

Writing Application Write two additional sentences about Act III, using *who* in one sentence and *whom* in the other.

WG Prentice Hall Writing and Grammar Connection: Chapter 24, Section 2

❸ Extension Activities

Writing Imagine that you are the editor of the Verona newspaper. Write an **editorial** addressing the Prince's response to Tybalt's death. Decide whether the ruling was appropriate, and support your arguments with details from Acts I through III.

Listening and Speaking View a film of the ballet *Romeo and Juliet*. Take notes on how the dance communicates the play's ideas. Then, use your notes to present a **film review** for your classmates. **[Group Activity]**

ASSESSMENT RESOURCES

The following resources can be used to assess students' knowledge and skills.

Selection Assessment

- **Formal Assessment,** Selection Test, pp. 170–172
- **Open Book Test,** pp. 142–144
- **Got It! Assessment Videotapes,** Tape 4
- **Test Bank Software**

PRENTICE HALL ASSESSMENT SYSTEM

- **Workbook**
- **Skill Book**
- **Transparencies**
- **CD-ROM**

Take It to the Net

Visit www.phschool.com for self-tests and additional questions on *Romeo and Juliet.*

EXTEND

Answers for p. 843

❶ Vocabulary Development

Words from Myths

1. nemesis: a person who punishes
2. mercurial: changing quickly
3. odyssey: a very long journey

Spelling Strategy

1. taunts 2. reaches

Synonyms

1. b 4. a
2. a 5. b
3. c 6. c

❷ Grammar

1. Who 4. whom
2. who 5. whom
3. whom

Writing Application

Sample sentences:

Juliet began to wonder whom she could trust.

Her Nurse, who gave her advice, told Juliet to marry Paris.

❸ Extension Activities

Writing Lesson

- Remind students that an editorial is a type of persuasion—it aims to convince readers to accept a position taken.
- Have students reread the Prince's words in Act II, scene i, taking time to clarify aspects that they do not understand.
- Remind students to use details from the first three Acts of the play to support their arguments.
- Invite volunteers to read their editorials to the class.

CUSTOMIZE INSTRUCTION
For Universal Access

To address different learning styles, use the activities suggested in the **Extension Activities** booklet, p.48.

- For Visual/Spatial and Verbal/Linguistic Learners, use Activity 5.
- For Verbal/Linguistic Learners, use Activity 6.

The Tragedy of Romeo and Juliet, Act IV

Lesson Objectives and CA Correlations

1. **To analyze and respond to literary elements**
   - Literary Analysis: Dramatic Irony **R 3.8**
   - Connecting Literary Elements: Suspense **R 3.6**
2. **To read, comprehend, analyze, and critique drama**
   - Reading Strategy: Predicting **R 3.8**
   - Reading Check questions
   - Review and Assess questions
   - Assessment Practice (ATE)
3. **To develop word analysis skills, fluency, and systematic vocabulary**
   - Vocabulary Development Lesson: Anglo-Saxon Suffix: *-ward* **R 1.1**
4. **To understand and apply written and oral language conventions**
   - Spelling Strategy
   - Grammar Lesson: Degrees of Comparison **LC 1.3**
5. **To understand and apply appropriate writing and research strategies**
   - Writing Lesson: Persuasive Letter (after Act V) **W 2.4**
   - Extension Activity: Ending **W 1.2**
6. **To understand and apply listening and speaking strategies**
   - Extension Activity: Presentation **LS 1.7**

STEP-BY-STEP TEACHING GUIDE	PACING GUIDE
PRETEACH	
Motivate Students and Provide Background	
Read and discuss the Review and Anticipate information (SE/ATE p. 845) A	10 min.
Introduce the Concepts	
Introduce the Literary Analysis and Reading Strategy (SE/ATE p. 844) A	15 min.
Pronounce the vocabulary words and read their definitions (SE p. 844)	5 min.
TEACH	
Monitor Comprehension	
Informally monitor comprehension by circulating while students read independently or in groups A	30 min.
Monitor students' comprehension with the Reading Check notes (SE/ATE pp. 845, 847, 849, 851, 853, 855)	as students read
Develop vocabulary with Vocabulary notes (SE pp. 846, 848–851, 855)	as students read
Develop Understanding	
Develop students' understanding of dramatic irony with the Literary Analysis annotations (SE/ATE pp. 846, 849–851, 853–855) A	10 min.
Develop students' ability to make predictions with the Reading Strategy annotations (SE pp. 846, 851, 854, 855, 857; ATE pp. 846–848, 851, 854–856)	10 min.
ASSESS	
Assess Mastery	
Assess students' mastery of the Reading Strategy and Literary Analysis by having them answer the Review and Assess questions (SE/ATE p. 858)	20 min.
Use one or more of the print and media Assessment Resources (ATE p.859) A	up to 50 min.
EXTEND	
Apply Understanding	
Have students complete the Vocabulary Development Lesson and the Grammar Lesson (SE p. 859) A	20 min.
Apply students' knowledge of persuasive appeals using the Writing Lesson (SE p. 877) A	45 min.
Apply students' understanding of the selection using one or more of the Extension Activities (SE p. 859)	20–90 min.

A ACCELERATED INSTRUCTION: Use the strategies and activities identified with an A.

UNIVERSAL ACCESS
● = Below-Level Students
▲ = On-Level Students
■ = Above-Level Students

Time and Resource Manager

Reading Level: Challenging
Average Number of Instructional Days: 4

RESOURCES		
PRINT	**TRANSPARENCIES**	**TECHNOLOGY**
• **Beyond Literature,** Career Connection: Medicine, p. 49 ▲ ■		• **Interest Grabber Video,** Tape 4 ● ▲ ■
• **Selection Support Workbook:** ● ▲ ■ Literary Analysis, p. 196 Reading Strategy, p. 195 Build Vocabulary, p. 193	• **Literary Analysis and Reading Transparencies,** pp. 97 and 98 ● ▲ ■	
• **Authors In Depth,** Gold Level ■		• **Listening to Literature** ● ▲ ■ Audiocassettes, Side 26 Audio CDs, CD 18
• **Literatura en español** ● ▲ • **Literary Analysis for Enrichment** ■		
• **Formal Assessment:** Selection Test, pp. 173–175 ● ▲ ■ • **Open Book Test,** pp. 145–147 ● ▲ ■ • Prentice Hall Assessment System ● ▲ ■	• Prentice Hall Assessment System ● ▲ ■ Skills Practice Answers and Explanations on Transparencies	• **Test Bank Software** ● ▲ ■ • **Got It! Assessment Videotapes,** Tape 4 ● ▲
• **Selection Support Workbook:** ● ▲ ■ Build Grammar Skills, p. 194 • **Writing and Grammar,** Gold Level ● ▲ ■ • **Extension Activities,** p. 47 ● ▲ ■	• **Daily Language Practice Transparencies** ● ▲	• **Writing and Grammar iText CD-ROM** ● ▲ ■ ***Take It to the Net*** www.phschool.com

BLOCK SCHEDULING: Use one 90-minute class period to preteach the selection and have students read it. Use a second 90-minute class period to assess students' mastery of skills and have them complete one of the Extension Activities.

PRETEACH

Step-by-Step Teaching Guide for p. 844

❶ Literary Analysis

- Remind students that as they have read the play, they have encountered scenes in which the characters do not know as much as they, the readers, do.
- Read the instruction about *dramatic irony* together as a class.
- Use the Instruction for Connecting Literary Elements to help students link *suspense* with dramatic irony.
- Use the Dramatic Irony transparency in **Literary Analysis and Reading Transparencies**, p. 98, to demonstrate how to interpret dramatic irony.

❷ Reading Strategy

Predicting

- Remind students that they *make predictions* when they read each time they guess what will happen next based on what they already know.
- Instruct students to use the Predict transparency in **Literary Analysis and Reading Transparencies**, p. 87, to learn how to set up prediction sequences as they read.

Vocabulary Development

- Pronounce each vocabulary word for students, and read the definitions as a class. Have students identify any words with which they are already familiar.

E-Teach

Visit E-Teach at www.phschool.com for teachers' essays on how to teach, with questions and answers.

Prepare to Read

The Tragedy of Romeo and Juliet, Act IV

❶ Literary Analysis

Dramatic Irony

Dramatic irony is a contradiction between what a character thinks or says and what the audience or reader knows to be true. For example, in Act III, Lord Capulet decides that the way to ensure Juliet's future happiness is to have her wed Paris. He does not know what you know—that Juliet is already married. Dramatic irony involves you emotionally in the story. You may even feel the urge to step into the play to help the characters see a situation correctly.

Connecting Literary Elements

Suspense is a feeling of curiosity or uncertainty about the outcome of events in a literary work. Suspense often results from the use of dramatic irony, as the audience anxiously wonders whether characters will discover the truth before it is too late. As you read the events of Act IV, notice how Shakespeare builds suspense through Juliet's words and actions.

❷ Reading Strategy

Predicting

When you **predict,** you make educated guesses about what may happen next in a literary work. To predict, consider each character's personality and what information he or she knows. Also, look for places where the author hints at future events. In this passage, Juliet's remark hints at deadly consequences:

> If in thy wisdom thou canst give no help,
> Do thou but call my resolution wise
> And with this knife I'll help it presently.

Use a chart like this one to make and assess predictions as you read.

What I Predict
Juliet will not marry Paris.

Why?
She says she will kill herself instead.

Actual Outcome

Vocabulary Development

pensive (pen′ siv) *adj.* thinking deeply or seriously (p. 846)

vial (vī′ əl) *n.* small bottle containing medicine or other liquids (p. 848)

enjoined (en joind′) *v.* ordered (p. 849)

wayward (wā′ wərd) *adj.* headstrong; willful (p. 850)

dismal (diz′ məl) *adj.* causing gloom or misery (p. 850)

loathsome (lōth′ səm) *adj.* disgusting (p. 851)

pilgrimage (pil′ grim ij) *n.* long journey, often for religious purposes (p. 855)

TEACHING RESOURCES

The following resources can be used to enrich or extend the instruction for p. 844.

Motivation

Interest Grabber Video, Tape 4

Background

Beyond Literature, p. 49 ▪

Take It to the Net

Visit www.phschool.com for background and hotlinks for *The Tragedy of Romeo and Juliet.*

Literary Analysis

Literary Analysis and Reading Transparencies, Dramatic Irony, p. 98

Reading

Selection Support: Reading Strategy, p. 195; Build Vocabulary, p. 193

Literary Analysis and Reading Transparencies, Predict, p. 97

▪ **BLOCK SCHEDULING:** Resources marked with this symbol provide varied instruction during 90-minute blocks.

❶

Review and Anticipate

Romeo and Juliet are married for only a few hours when disaster strikes. In Act III, Juliet's cousin Tybalt kills Mercutio, and then Romeo kills Tybalt. This leads to Romeo's banishment from Verona. To make matters worse, Juliet's parents are determined to marry her to Paris. Will Romeo and Juliet ever be able to live together as husband and wife? What, if anything, can the lovers now do to preserve their relationship?

Scene i. FRIAR LAWRENCE'S *cell.*

[*Enter* FRIAR LAWRENCE *and* COUNTY PARIS.]

❷

FRIAR. On Thursday, sir? The time is very short.

PARIS. My father[1] Capulet will have it so,
And I am nothing slow to slack his haste.[2]

FRIAR. You say you do not know the lady's mind.
Uneven is the course;[3] I like it not.

PARIS. Immoderately she weeps for Tybalt's death,
And therefore have I little talked of love;
For Venus smiles not in a house of tears.
Now, sir, her father counts it dangerous

1. **father** future father-in-law.

2. **I . . . haste** I won't slow him down by being slow myself.

3. **Uneven . . . course** irregular is the plan.

❸ **✓Reading Check**

What is the Friar's complaint to Paris about the impending wedding?

TEACH

Step-by-Step Teaching Guide for pp. 845–857

❶ About the Selection

Act IV belongs to Juliet as she interacts with the Friar, Paris, her parents, and the Nurse. Using witty wordplay and misleading statements, Juliet avoids suspicion about her true intent. Her unwillingness to confront her parents, along with her trust in the Friar, lead her further along the road to tragedy. Act IV illustrates a paradox at work within Juliet: She is brave enough to take the Friar's potion, but she is at the same time afraid to tell her parents the truth.

❷ Critical Thinking

Infer

- Ask students why Thursday is important in the Friar's words to Paris.
  Answer: Thursday is the day that has been set for Juliet's marriage to Paris.
- Ask students to interpret the Friar's words, "You say you do not know the lady's mind."
  Answer: The Friar is suggesting to Paris that he does not know whether this hasty plan for marriage is acceptable to Juliet. What the Friar really means is that Paris has no idea what is going on with Juliet.
- Ask students what they think the Friar is trying to do by asking Paris questions and referring to hastiness of the marriage plans.
  Answer: The Friar is trying to buy time for Romeo, Juliet, and the Friar to figure out a plan to reunite the married couple.

❸ ✓Reading Check

Answer: The Friar complains about the hastiness of the planned wedding.

TEACHING RESOURCES

The following resources can be used to enrich or extend the instruction for pp. 845–857.

Literary Analysis

Selection Support: Literary Analysis, p. 196

Reading

Listening to Literature Audiocassettes, Side 32

Listening to Literature Audio CDs, CD 18 ■

Extension

Authors In Depth, Gold Level ■

■ **BLOCK SCHEDULING:** Resources marked with this symbol provide varied instruction during 90-minute blocks.

4 Literary Analysis

Dramatic Irony

- Ask students what Paris is trying to explain to the Friar in his speech here.
  Answer: Paris is explaining why his marriage to Juliet must occur as quickly as possible.
- Remind students that *dramatic irony* is a contradiction between what a character thinks is true and what the reader or audience knows is true.
- Ask students what the reader and the audience know about why Juliet is crying.
  Answer: Juliet is crying because her parents are trying to marry her to Paris when she and Romeo are already married.
- Now, ask the Literary Analysis question on p. 846: In what way does Paris's comment show that he does not understand the real reason that Juliet is crying?
  Answer: Paris says that Juliet is crying over Tybalt's death.

5 Reading Strategy

Predicting

- Ask students whether Juliet actually lies to Paris at any time in this exchange. What does she do?
  Answer: Juliet does not lie to Paris but keeps him off balance with her clever wordplay.
- Have students interpret the exchange in lines 35–36.
  Answer: Paris says that Juliet's face belongs to him. Juliet seems to agree with him, but readers know that Juliet means that her face belongs to Romeo.
- Ask the Reading Strategy question on p. 846: Based on this dialogue, do you think Juliet will consider Paris an ally? Why or why not?
  Answer: Juliet will not consider Paris an ally because he wants to marry her himself. Also, she plays words games with him instead of answering him truthfully.

That she do give her sorrow so much sway,
And in his wisdom hastes our marriage
To stop the inundation[4] of her tears,
Which, too much minded[5] by herself alone,
May be put from her by society.
Now do you know the reason of this haste.

FRIAR. [*Aside*] I would I knew not why it should be slowed.—
Look, sir, here comes the lady toward my cell.

[*Enter* JULIET.]

PARIS. Happily met, my lady and my wife!

JULIET. That may be, sir, when I may be a wife.

PARIS. That "may be" must be, love, on Thursday next.

JULIET. What must be shall be.

FRIAR. That's a certain text.[6]

PARIS. Come you to make confession to this father?

JULIET. To answer that, I should confess to you.

PARIS. Do not deny to him that you love me.

JULIET. I will confess to you that I love him.

PARIS. So will ye, I am sure, that you love me.

JULIET. If I do so, it will be of more price,[7]
Being spoke behind your back, than to your face.

PARIS. Poor soul, thy face is much abused with tears.

JULIET. The tears have got small victory by that,
For it was bad enough before their spite.[8]

PARIS. Thou wrong'st it more than tears with that report.

JULIET. That is no slander, sir, which is a truth;
And what I spake, I spake it to my face.

PARIS. Thy face is mine, and thou hast sland'red it.

JULIET. It may be so, for it is not mine own.
Are you at leisure, holy father, now,
Or shall I come to you at evening mass?

FRIAR. My leisure serves me, pensive daughter, now.
My lord, we must entreat the time alone.[9]

PARIS. God shield[10] I should disturb devotion!
Juliet, on Thursday early will I rouse ye.
Till then, adieu, and keep this holy kiss. [*Exit.*]

JULIET. O, shut the door, and when thou hast done so,
Come weep with me—past hope, past care, past help!

---

4. inundation flood.

5. minded thought about.

Literary Analysis
Dramatic Irony In what way does Paris' comment show that he does not understand the real reason that Juliet is crying?

6. That's . . . text That's a certain truth.

7. price value.

8. before their spite before the harm that the tears did.

Reading Strategy
Predicting Based on this dialogue, do you think Juliet will consider Paris an ally? Why or why not?

pensive (pen´ siv) *adj.* thinking deeply or seriously

9. entreat . . . alone ask to have this time to ourselves.

10. shield forbid.

6

FRIAR. O Juliet, I already know thy grief;
It strains me past the compass of my wits.[11]
I hear thou must, and nothing may prorogue[12] it,
On Thursday next be married to this County.

JULIET. Tell me not, friar, that thou hearest of this,
Unless thou tell me how I may prevent it.
If in thy wisdom thou canst give no help,
Do thou but call my resolution wise
And with this knife I'll help it presently.[13]
God joined my heart and Romeo's, thou our hands;
And ere this hand, by thee to Romeo's sealed,
Shall be the label to another deed,[14]
Or my true heart with treacherous revolt
Turn to another, this shall slay them both.
Therefore, out of thy long-experienced time,
Give me some present counsel; or, behold,
'Twixt my extremes and me[15] this bloody knife
Shall play the umpire, arbitrating[16] that
Which the commission of thy years and art
Could to no issue of true honor bring.[17]
Be not so long to speak. I long to die
If what thou speak'st speak not of remedy.

FRIAR. Hold, daughter. I do spy a kind of hope,
Which craves[18] as desperate an execution
As that is desperate which we would prevent.
If, rather than to marry County Paris,
Thou hast the strength of will to slay thyself,
Then is it likely thou wilt undertake
A thing like death to chide away this shame,
That cop'st with death himself to scape from it;[19]
And, if thou darest, I'll give thee remedy.

JULIET. O, bid me leap, rather than marry Paris,
From off the battlements of any tower,
Or walk in thievish ways,[20] or bid me lurk
Where serpents are; chain me with roaring bears,
Or hide me nightly in a charnel house,[21]
O'ercovered quite with dead men's rattling bones,
With reeky[22] shanks and yellow chapless[23] skulls;
Or bid me go into a new-made grave
And hide me with a dead man in his shroud—
Things that, to hear them told, have made me tremble—
And I will do it without fear or doubt,
To live an unstained wife to my sweet love.

FRIAR. Hold, then. Go home, be merry, give consent
To marry Paris. Wednesday is tomorrow.
Tomorrow night look that thou lie alone;

11. past . . . wits beyond the ability of my mind to find a remedy.

12. prorogue delay.

Reading Strategy
Predicting What do you predict Juliet will do if there is no way to prevent her marriage to Paris?

13. presently at once.

14. Shall . . . deed shall give the seal of approval to another marriage contract.

15. 'Twixt . . . me between my misfortunes and me.

16. arbitrating deciding.

17. Which . . . bring which the authority that derives from your age and ability could not solve honorably.

18. craves requires.

19. That cop'st . . . it that bargains with death itself to escape from it.

20. thievish ways roads where criminals lurk.

21. charnel house vault for bones removed from graves to be reused.

22. reeky foul-smelling.

23. chapless jawless.

7 **Reading Check**
What does the Friar tell Juliet she should do when she goes home?

6 Reading Strategy
Predicting

- Ask students to identify the Friar's basic message to Juliet in lines 46–49.
  Answer: The Friar has no more ideas about what to do for the two lovers. He says that nothing will delay the marriage and Juliet should accept the inevitable.
- Ask students the Reading Strategy question on p. 847: What do you predict Juliet will do if there is no way to prevent her marriage to Paris?
  Answer: Juliet will kill herself.

7 Reading Check

Answer: The Friar tells Juliet to go home and happily pretend to give consent to her marriage to Paris.

CUSTOMIZE INSTRUCTION FOR UNIVERSAL ACCESS

For Special Needs Students	For Advanced Readers
Discuss with students the different ways they might use the glosses on each page of the play. Some students may choose to skim the definitions and explanations before reading the page; others may interrupt their reading to read only the glosses they need. Other students may pause occasionally to review all the glosses in a set of pages to see if their understanding of certain words and phrases is accurate.	Point out to students Juliet's use of hyperbole in lines 77–88. Have them first determine what message she is trying to communicate, then summarize the things she would have the Friar bid her do. Summary: She would rather leap from a tower, walk in the worst part of town, step on snakes, be chained to bears, be put in a vault with human bones, or be lowered into a grave with a dead man.

8 Reading Strategy

Predicting

- Have students read lines 92–101 and guess what the Friar's complete plan will turn out to be.
  Answer: The Friar plans to put Juliet into a deep sleep so that she appears to be dead.
- As students read lines 102–112, have them compare modern burial arrangements with those of the Capulets'.
  Answer: In Juliet's time, people were wrapped in robes and put into a large vault, or tomb. Modern funeral practices include embalming and burial; cremation is a common alternative. These practices would preclude using the Friar's plan in the present day.
- When students have completed line 112, ask them to predict what the Friar plans to have happen next, and then read the rest of his soliloquy to check their predictions.
  Possible response: The Friar will make arrangements to find Romeo and reunite him with Juliet when she awakens from her sleep in the tomb.

9 ▶Critical Viewing

Answer: The vial contains a liquid that creates a state of simulated death.

Let not the nurse lie with thee in thy chamber.
Take thou this vial, being then in bed,
And this distilling liquor drink thou off;
When presently through all thy veins shall run
A cold and drowsy humor;[24] for no pulse
Shall keep his native[25] progress, but surcease;[26]
No warmth, no breath, shall testify thou livest;
The roses in thy lips and cheeks shall fade
To wanny ashes,[27] thy eyes' windows[28] fall
Like death when he shuts up the day of life;
Each part, deprived of supple government,[29]
Shall, stiff and stark and cold, appear like death;
And in this borrowed likeness of shrunk death
Thou shalt continue two-and-forty hours,
And then awake as from a pleasant sleep.
Now, when the bridegroom in the morning comes
To rouse thee from thy bed, there art thou dead.
Then, as the manner of our country is,
In thy best robes uncovered on the bier[30]
Thou shalt be borne to that same ancient vault
Where all the kindred of the Capulets lie.
In the meantime, against[31] thou shalt awake,
Shall Romeo by my letters know our drift;[32]
And hither shall he come; and he and I
Will watch thy waking, and that very night
Shall Romeo bear thee hence to Mantua.
And this shall free thee from this present shame,
If no inconstant toy[33] nor womanish fear
Abate thy valor[34] in the acting it.

JULIET. Give me, give me! O, tell not me of fear!

vial (vī′ əl) *n.* small bottle containing medicine or other liquids

24. **humor** fluid; liquid.
25. **native** natural.
26. **surcease** stop.
27. **wanny ashes** to the color of pale ashes.
28. **eyes' windows** eyelids.
29. **supple government** ability for maintaining motion.
30. **uncovered on the bier** displayed on the funeral platform.
31. **against** before.
32. **drift** purpose; plan.
33. **inconstant toy** passing whim.
34. **Abate thy valor** lessen your courage.

9 ◀ Critical Viewing According to the play, what power does the vial hold? **[Connect]**

ENRICHMENT: Science Connection

Medicine

Students may find it difficult to believe that someone could be thought dead when he or she was not. However, tell them that the technology for determining death was very primitive in the times in which these events took place. Medieval doctors did not even have the stethoscope, which was not invented until 1816. They determined death by putting their ear next to the patient's body to hear the sounds of the organs.

People's fear of being buried alive was a legitimate one, as comas and other physiological states could mimic death for a time. Although the play never says what the Friar's potion is, it is likely to have been a very strong tranquilizer made from a local plant. Taking such a drug would be an enormous risk, and Juliet is right to be fearful. Modern-day readers are likely to be insulted for her when the Friar charges her with "womanish fear."

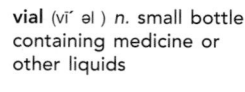

10 **FRIAR.** Hold! Get you gone, be strong and prosperous
In this resolve. I'll send a friar with speed
To Mantua, with my letters to thy lord.

JULIET. Love give me strength, and strength shall help afford.
Farewell, dear father. [*Exit with* FRIAR.]

Scene ii. *Hall in* CAPULET*'s house.*

[*Enter* FATHER CAPULET, MOTHER, NURSE, *and* SERVINGMEN, *two or three.*]

CAPULET. So many guests invite as here are writ. [*Exit a* SERVINGMAN.]
Sirrah, go hire me twenty cunning[1] cooks.

SERVINGMAN. You shall have none ill, sir; for I'll try[2] if they can lick their fingers.

CAPULET. How canst thou try them so?

SERVINGMAN. Marry, sir, 'tis an ill cook that cannot lick his own fingers.[3] Therefore he that cannot lick his fingers goes not with me.

CAPULET. Go, begone. [*Exit* SERVINGMAN.]
We shall be much unfurnished[4] for this time.
What, is my daughter gone to Friar Lawrence?

NURSE. Ay, forsooth.[5]

CAPULET. Well, he may chance to do some good on her.
A peevish self-willed harlotry it is.[6]

[*Enter* JULIET.]

NURSE. See where she comes from shrift with merry look.

CAPULET. How now, my headstrong? Where have you been gadding?

JULIET. Where I have learnt me to repent the sin
Of disobedient opposition
To you and your behests,[7] and am enjoined
By holy Lawrence to fall prostrate[8] here
To beg your pardon. Pardon, I beseech you!
Henceforward I am ever ruled by you.

11 **CAPULET.** Send for the County. Go tell him of this.
I'll have this knot knit up tomorrow morning.

JULIET. I met the youthful lord at Lawrence' cell
And gave him what becomèd[9] love I might,
Not stepping o'er the bounds of modesty.

CAPULET. Why, I am glad on't. This is well. Stand up.
This is as't should be. Let me see the County.
Ay, marry, go, I say, and fetch him hither.
Now, afore God, this reverend holy friar,
All our whole city is much bound[10] to him.

Literary Analysis
Dramatic Irony What information does Juliet now know that Romeo does not?

1. **cunning** skillful.
2. **try** test.
3. **'tis . . . fingers** It's a bad cook that won't taste his own cooking.
4. **unfurnished** unprepared.
5. **forsooth** in truth.
6. **A peevish . . . it is** It is the ill-tempered, selfish behavior of a woman without good breeding.
7. **behests** requests.

enjoined (en joind′) *v.* ordered

8. **fall prostrate** lie face down in humble submission.
9. **becomèd** suitable; proper.
10. **bound** indebted.

12 **Reading Check**
What does the Friar say will happen when Juliet drinks the contents of the vial?

10 Literary Analysis
Dramatic Irony

- Ask students what Juliet says to the Friar when he says that the plan will only work if she has courage.
  Answer: She says she doesn't want to hear from him about fear and that her love gives her strength.
- Have students reveal how the Friar intends to let Romeo know of the Friar's plan.
  Answer: The Friar says he will send another friar to Mantua with letters for Romeo.
- Ask the Literary Analysis question on p. 849: What information does Juliet now know that Romeo does not?
  Answer: Juliet now has a plan for escaping marriage to Paris by feigning death. Romeo's lack of knowledge about this plan will have fateful consequences.

11 Background
Names

Students may find the word *County* a strange one as a title for Paris. The word was an English form for the Italian *conte*, meaning "count," or "earl."

12 Reading Check

Answer: When Juliet drinks the vial, she will fall into a deep sleep for forty-two hours; she will appear to be dead.

CUSTOMIZE INSTRUCTION FOR UNIVERSAL ACCESS

For Gifted/Talented Students	For Advanced Readers
Have students work in small groups to develop a "Plan B"—a better strategy to prevent Juliet's marriage to Paris and to safely reunite her with Romeo. Tell the groups they must use only the resources of the time (no helicopter rescues, for example) and must preserve the secret of Juliet's marriage to Romeo.	Ask students to write a formal analysis of the virtues and the potential flaws in the Friar's plan. Tell students that their critiques should discuss at least three problems that could spell disaster for Romeo and Juliet.

13 Literary Analysis

Dramatic Irony

- Ask students what change in schedule is revealed in this exchange.
  Answer: Lord Capulet says they will not wait until Thursday; the wedding will occur "tomorrow."
- Ask students how this change of the wedding date might affect the outcome of the Friar's plan.
  Answer: The Friar has less time to notify Romeo, so Romeo might not be at the tomb when Juliet awakens.
- Have students read Capulet's speech to his wife and answer the first Literary Analysis question on p. 850: What is ironic about Lord Capulet's relief and joy?
  Answer: Capulet is relieved because he believes Juliet and Paris will be married tomorrow according to his wishes. In fact, the change of the date and haste of the marriage will bring tragedy to his family.

14 Literary Analysis

Dramatic Irony and Suspense

- Ask students how Juliet gets rid of her mother and the Nurse so she can be alone.
  Answer: Juliet says that her mother and the Nurse must have preparations to make for the ceremony.
- Ask students what is ironic about Lady Capulet's words to Juliet in lines 12–13.
  Possible response: Lady Capulet wishes Juliet a good night and hopes she will rest well. In fact, it is not a good night: Juliet is terrified, and her "rest" will be a deep, drug-induced sleep.
- Invite students to answer the second Literary Analysis question on p. 850: In what ways does Juliet's statement—"I have a faint cold fear thrills through my veins"—add suspense to the drama?
  Possible response: Juliet feels a cold fear about what she is going to do. This is ironic because when she drinks the vial, she will feel a literal cold through her veins as she slips into a death-like sleep.

JULIET. Nurse, will you go with me into my closet[11]
To help me sort such needful ornaments[12]
As you think fit to furnish me tomorrow?

LADY CAPULET. No, not till Thursday. There is time enough.

CAPULET. Go, nurse, go with her. We'll to church tomorrow.
[Exit JULIET *and* NURSE.*]*

LADY CAPULET. We shall be short in our provision.[13]
'Tis now near night.

CAPULET. Tush, I will stir about,
And all things shall be well, I warrant thee, wife.
Go thou to Juliet, help to deck up her.[14]
I'll not to bed tonight; let me alone.
13 I'll play the housewife for this once. What, ho![15]
They are all forth; well, I will walk myself
To County Paris, to prepare up him
Against tomorrow. My heart is wondrous light,
Since this same wayward girl is so reclaimed. *[Exit with* MOTHER.*]*

Scene iii. JULIET*'s chamber.*

[Enter JULIET *and* NURSE.*]*

JULIET. Ay, those attires are best; but, gentle nurse,
I pray thee leave me to myself tonight;
For I have need of many orisons[1]
To move the heavens to smile upon my state,[2]
Which, well thou knowest, is cross[3] and full of sin.

[Enter MOTHER.*]*

LADY CAPULET. What, are you busy, ho? Need you my help?

JULIET. No, madam; we have culled[4] such necessaries
As are behoveful[5] for our state tomorrow.
So please you, let me now be left alone,
And let the nurse this night sit up with you:
For I am sure you have your hands full all
In this so sudden business.

14 LADY CAPULET. Good night.
Get thee to bed, and rest: for thou hast need.
[Exit MOTHER *and* NURSE.*]*

JULIET. Farewell! God knows when we shall meet again.
I have a faint cold fear thrills through my veins
That almost freezes up the heat of life.
I'll call them back again to comfort me.
Nurse!—What should she do here?
My dismal scene I needs must act alone.

11. closet private room.
12. ornaments clothes.
13. short . . . provision lacking time for preparation.
14. deck up her dress her; get her ready.
15. What, ho! Capulet is calling for his servants.
wayward (wā´ wərd) *adj.* headstrong; willful

Literary Analysis
Dramatic Irony What is ironic about Lord Capulet's relief and joy?

1. orisons prayers.
2. state condition.
3. cross selfish; disobedient.
4. culled chosen.
5. behoveful desirable; appropriate.

Literary Analysis
Dramatic Irony and Suspense In what ways does Juliet's statement—"I have a faint cold fear thrills through my veins"—add suspense to the drama?

dismal (diz´ məl) *adj.* causing gloom or misery

Come, vial.
What if this mixture do not work at all?
Shall I be married then tomorrow morning?
No, no! This shall forbid it. Lie thou there. [*Lays down a dagger.*]
What if it be a poison which the friar
Subtly hath minist'red[6] to have me dead,
Lest in this marriage he should be dishonored
Because he married me before to Romeo?
I fear it is; and yet methinks it should not,
For he hath still been tried[7] a holy man.
How if, when I am laid into the tomb,
I wake before the time that Romeo
Come to redeem me? There's a fearful point!
Shall I not then be stifled in the vault,
To whose foul mouth no healthsome air breathes in,
And there die strangled ere my Romeo comes?
Or, if I live, is it not very like
The horrible conceit[8] of death and night,
Together with the terror of the place—
As in a vault, an ancient receptacle
Where for this many hundred years the bones
Of all my buried ancestors are packed;
15 Where bloody Tybalt, yet but green in earth,[9]
Lies fest'ring in his shroud; where, as they say,
At some hours in the night spirits resort—
Alack, alack, is it not like[10] that I,
So early waking—what with loathsome smells,
And shrieks like mandrakes[11] torn out of the earth,
That living mortals, hearing them, run mad—
O, if I wake, shall I not be distraught,[12]
Environèd[13] with all these hideous fears,
And madly play with my forefathers' joints,
And pluck the mangled Tybalt from his shroud,
And, in this rage, with some great kinsman's bone
As with a club dash out my desp'rate brains?
O, look! Methinks I see my cousin's ghost
16 Seeking out Romeo, that did spit his body
Upon a rapier's point. Stay, Tybalt, stay!
Romeo, Romeo, Romeo, I drink to thee.
[*She falls upon her bed within the curtains.*]

Scene iv. Hall in CAPULET*'s house.*

[*Enter* LADY OF THE HOUSE *and* NURSE.]

LADY CAPULET. Hold, take these keys and fetch more spices, nurse.

NURSE. They call for dates and quinces[1] in the pastry.[2]

6. **minist'red** given me.

7. **tried** proved.

Literary Analysis
Dramatic Irony and Suspense How do Juliet's anxieties add to the suspense for readers or audiences?

8. **conceit** idea; thought.

9. **green in earth** newly entombed.

10. **like** likely.

loathsome (lōth′ səm) *adj.* disgusting

11. **mandrakes** plants with forked roots that resemble human legs. The mandrake was believed to shriek when uprooted and cause the hearer to go mad.

12. **distraught** insane.

13. **Environèd** surrounded.

Reading Strategy
Predicting What do you think will happen when Juliet's "lifeless" body is found on her bed?

1. **quinces** golden apple-shaped fruit.
2. **pastry** baking room.

17 ✔ **Reading Check**
What does Juliet do after her mother and the Nurse leave her chambers?

15 Literary Analysis

Dramatic Irony and Suspense

- Ask students why Juliet might wonder if the Friar has given her a drink that really will kill her.
  Answer: Juliet recognizes that the Friar has put himself in a difficult position. He has married Romeo and Juliet secretly, and he has encouraged Juliet to go along with the plans for marriage to Paris. If the marriage takes place, the Friar has made Juliet a bigamist. However, if Juliet really dies, his scheme will not be revealed.
- Have students respond to the Literary Analysis question on p. 851: How do Juliet's anxieties add to the suspense for readers or audiences?
  Answer: As Juliet thinks of all the things that could go wrong, readers and audiences imagine all of them and wonder which one will actually happen.

16 Reading Strategy

Predicting

- Have students interpret Juliet's words in lines 55–57.
  Possible response: Juliet imagines she is in the Capulet tomb and sees Tybalt rising up to find Romeo. She says, "Stay," meaning "Stay away," or "Halt."
- Ask students to answer the Reading Strategy question on p. 851: What do you think will happen when Juliet's "lifeless" body is found on her bed?
  Answer: She will be placed in the Capulet tomb, and, of course, the wedding will not take place.

17 ✔ Reading Check

Answer: Juliet considers all the things that could go wrong, and then she drinks the potion.

CUSTOMIZE INSTRUCTION FOR UNIVERSAL ACCESS

For Special Needs Students	For English Learners
Juliet's soliloquy, lines 14–58, is one of the high points of the play. Therefore, this is a good time to play the recording from **Listening to Literature** Audiocassettes or Audio CDs. Students can hear Juliet's uncertainty as she weighs her decision and then her resolve as she takes action.	Have students work with Act IV vocabulary (p. 844), three examples of which are found on pp. 850–851. After they have read the definition of the three words, ask them questions such as "Who is *wayward*, and who thinks *so*?" "What scene is *dismal*?" "What are the *loathsome* smells to which Juliet refers?"

⑱ Background

Film

Juliet kneels as she drinks the fateful potion in this scene from Zeffirelli's *Romeo and Juliet*. Juliet's closed eyes and supplicating posture suggest an attitude of prayer. Use the following questions for discussion:

1. Look at Juliet's expression. What emotion or emotions is she experiencing?
   Answer: Students may say that Juliet's expression reflects her desperation or fear, her love for Romeo, or her determination to act.
2. What elements of the setting help to reinforce these emotions?
   Answer: Students may say the dimly lit background emphasizes the impending tragedy, and that Juliet's white robes emphasize her youth and purity.

ENRICHMENT: Social Studies Connection

Renaissance Wedding

Act IV involves preparations for Juliet's wedding. Since the Capulets were an upper-class family, the wedding would have been quite elaborate. Have interested students research Renaissance wedding celebrations. Some questions they might like to consider include:

- Where would the actual ceremony take place?
- Who would perform the ceremony?
- What kind of clothing would the bridal party and guests wear?
- What kind of food would be served and what kind of entertainment would occur?
- How long would the celebration last?

After students have done their research, have them share their findings with the class. In addition, encourage students of various cultural backgrounds to share and compare their wedding customs with the class.

[*Enter old* CAPULET.]

CAPULET. Come, stir, stir, stir! The second cock hath crowed,
The curfew bell hath rung, 'tis three o'clock.
Look to the baked meats, good Angelica;[3]
Spare not for cost.

NURSE. Go, you cotquean,[4] go,
Get you to bed! Faith, you'll be sick tomorrow
For this night's watching.[5]

CAPULET. No, not a whit. What, I have watched ere now
All night for lesser cause, and ne'er been sick.

LADY CAPULET. Ay, you have been a mouse hunt[6] in your time;
But I will watch you from such watching now.
[*Exit* LADY *and* NURSE.]

CAPULET. A jealous hood,[7] a jealous hood!

[*Enter three or four* FELLOWS *with spits and logs and baskets.*]

Now, fellow,
What is there?

19 **FIRST FELLOW.** Things for the cook, sir; but I know not what.

CAPULET. Make haste, make haste. [*Exit* FIRST FELLOW.] Sirrah, fetch
drier logs.
Call Peter; he will show thee where they are.

SECOND FELLOW. I have a head, sir, that will find out logs
And never trouble Peter for the matter.

CAPULET. Mass,[8] and well said; a merry whoreson, ha!
Thou shalt be loggerhead.[9] [*Exit* SECOND FELLOW, *with the others.*]
Good faith, 'tis day.
The County will be here with music straight,
For so he said he would. [*Play music.*]
I hear him near.
Nurse! Wife! What, ho! What, nurse, I say!

[*Enter* NURSE.]

Go waken Juliet; go and trim her up.
I'll go and chat with Paris. Hie, make haste,
Make haste! The bridegroom he is come already:
Make haste, I say. [*Exit.*]

Scene v. *JULIET's chamber.*

NURSE. Mistress! What, mistress! Juliet! Fast,[1] I warrant her, she.
Why, lamb! Why, lady! Fie, you slugabed.[2]
Why, love, I say! Madam; Sweetheart! Why, bride!
What, not a word? You take your pennyworths now;
Sleep for a week; for the next night, I warrant,

---

20 ◀ **Critical Viewing** Do you think Juliet's decision to take the potion is courageous? Why or why not? **[Evaluate]**

3. **Angelica** This is probably the Nurse's name.

4. **cotquean** (kat' kwēn') man who does housework.

5. **watching** staying awake.

6. **mouse hunt** woman chaser.

7. **jealous hood** jealousy.

Literary Analysis
Dramatic Irony In what way is the bustle in the Capulet household during Scene iv an example of dramatic irony?

8. **Mass** by the Mass (an oath).

9. **loggerhead** blockhead.

1. **Fast** fast asleep.

2. **slugabed** sleepy head.

21 **Reading Check**
What does Lady Capulet ask the Nurse to do?

---

19 Literary Analysis

Dramatic Irony

- Ask students what kinds of activities are taking place in this scene.
  Answer: The Capulets are making food preparations for the wedding; servants who have been on watch are now ordered to bed; Lady and Lord Capulet are insulting each other; Capulet calls to the Nurse to wake Juliet.
- Have students respond to the Literary Analysis question on p. 853: In what way is the bustle in the Capulet household during Scene iv an example of dramatic irony?
  Answer: The family is busily preparing for a wedding and celebration, when in fact Juliet is lying as if dead in her bed.

20 ▶Critical Viewing

Answer: Some students may say Juliet's decision is courageous because she believes that this is her only chance for happiness with Romeo. Others may say that her decision is foolish because she is not certain that the Friar is trustworthy, and there are too many ways the plan can go wrong.

21 Reading Check

Answer: Lady Capulet asks the Nurse to awaken Juliet.

CUSTOMIZE INSTRUCTION FOR UNIVERSAL ACCESS

For Less Proficient Readers	For English Learners	For Advanced Readers
Students unfamiliar with Shakespeare's tragedies might wonder at the silliness of the conversation between Capulet and the Fellows. Explain that the exchanges offer comic relief. The audience needs time to recover from the heightened emotions of the previous scene and time to feel the buildup of suspense.	Point out the Nurse's use of the word *Why*, at the bottom of the page. This usage will continue onto the next page. Tell students that the repetition of the word emphasizes the number of times the Nurse struggles to wake Juliet, and the word itself suggests the meaning, "Why won't you wake up, girl!" or words to that effect.	Encourage students to find the irony in the stage directions, "Play music" that interrupts line 23. Why is the playing of music a logical thing for the Capulets to be doing here? Why is it ironic, based on what the reader and the audience know?

22 Literary Analysis

Dramatic Irony

- Ask students why the Nurse is not immediately concerned when she cannot wake Juliet.
  Answer: The Nurse thinks Juliet is too deeply asleep to awaken readily.
- Ask students the first Literary Analysis question on p. 854: How does the Nurse's carefree chatter add to the irony of the scene?
  Answer: The audience knows that Juliet is not going to wake up, and that the Nurse's teasing banter will soon turn to shock and grief.

23 Reading Strategy

Predicting

- Ask students what the Nurse thinks is going on when she sees Juliet in her clothing.
  Answer: The Nurse thinks Juliet has wakened, gotten dressed, and then gone back to bed.
- Have students respond to the Reading Strategy question on p. 854: Predict what Lord and Lady Capulet will say when they see their daughter's body.
  Possible response: The Capulets will probably express shock and grief at so untimely a death.

24 Literary Analysis

Dramatic Irony

- Ask students to describe how Lady Capulet reacts when she first sees Juliet.
  Answer: She calls for help to revive Juliet.
- Have students answer the second Literary Analysis question on p. 854: What is ironic about the Capulets' behavior in lines 24–30?
  Answer: Readers and audience know that Juliet is not actually dead.

22

The County Paris hath set up his rest
That you shall rest but little. God forgive me!
Marry, and amen. How sound is she asleep!
I needs must wake her. Madam, madam, madam!
Ay, let the County take you in your bed;
He'll fright you up, i' faith. Will it not be?
[*Draws aside the curtains.*]

23

What, dressed, and in your clothes, and down again?[3]
I must needs wake you. Lady! Lady! Lady!
Alas, alas! Help, help! My lady's dead!
O weraday that ever I was born!
Some *aqua vitae*, ho! My lord! My lady!

[*Enter* MOTHER.]

LADY CAPULET. What noise is here?

NURSE. O lamentable day!

LADY CAPULET. What is the matter?

NURSE. Look, look! O heavy day!

LADY CAPULET. O me, O me! My child, my only life!
Revive, look up, or I will die with thee!
Help, help! Call help.

[*Enter* FATHER.]

CAPULET. For shame, bring Juliet forth; her lord is come.

NURSE. She's dead, deceased; she's dead, alack the day!

24

LADY CAPULET. Alack the day, she's dead, she's dead, she's dead!

CAPULET. Ha! Let me see her. Out alas! She's cold,
Her blood is settled, and her joints are stiff;
Life and these lips have long been separated.
Death lies on her like an untimely frost
Upon the sweetest flower of all the field.

NURSE. O lamentable day!

LADY CAPULET. O woeful time!

CAPULET. Death, that hath ta'en her hence to make me wail,
Ties up my tongue and will not let me speak.

[*Enter* FRIAR LAWRENCE *and the* COUNTY PARIS, *with* MUSICIANS.]

FRIAR. Come, is the bride ready to go to church?

CAPULET. Ready to go, but never to return.
O son, the night before thy wedding day
Hath Death lain with thy wife. There she lies,
Flower as she was, deflowerèd by him.
Death is my son-in-law, Death is my heir;

Literary Analysis
Dramatic Irony How does the Nurse's carefree chatter add to the irony of the scene?

3. down again back in bed.

Reading Strategy
Predicting Predict what Lord and Lady Capulet will say when they see their daughter's body.

Literary Analysis
Dramatic Irony What is ironic about the Capulets' behavior in lines 24–30?

ENRICHMENT: Literature Connection

The Role of Friar Lawrence

Discuss with students Friar Lawrence's role in *Romeo and Juliet.* Point out that literary critics see Friar Lawrence in basically two opposing ways. In one view, the Friar is a surrogate father figure to Romeo who aids and counsels him—he is Romeo's confidant. In the other view, the Friar is a well-meaning but incompetent counselor who leads Romeo and Juliet to their deaths.

Critic Edward Dowden is one who regards Friar Lawrence as an interfering, middle-aged busybody. He states in the introduction of the Arden edition of *Romeo and Juliet* that "the amiable critic of life as seen from the cloister does not understand life or hate or love . . . [he is] an actor whose wisdom is of a kind which may easily lead himself and others astray."

Ask students which view of Friar Lawrence they share. Is he a middle-aged busybody who knows nothing about life or love, or does he give Romeo good advice?

25

My daughter he hath wedded. I will die
And leave him all. Life, living, all is Death's.

PARIS. Have I thought, love, to see this morning's face,
And doth it give me such a sight as this?

LADY CAPULET. Accursed, unhappy, wretched, hateful day!
Most miserable hour that e'er time saw
In lasting labor of his pilgrimage!
But one, poor one, one poor and loving child,
But one thing to rejoice and solace[4] in,
And cruel Death hath catched it from my sight.

NURSE. O woe! O woeful, woeful, woeful day!
Most lamentable day, most woeful day
That ever ever I did yet behold!
O day, O day, O day! O hateful day!
Never was seen so black a day as this.
O woeful day! O woeful day!

26

PARIS. Beguiled,[5] divorcèd, wrongèd, spited, slain!
Most detestable Death, by thee beguiled,
By cruel, cruel thee quite overthrown.
O love! O life!—not life, but love in death!

CAPULET. Despised, distressèd, hated, martyred, killed!
Uncomfortable[6] time, why cam'st thou now
To murder, murder our solemnity?[7]
O child, O child! My soul, and not my child!
Dead art thou—alack, my child is dead,
And with my child my joys are burièd!

FRIAR. Peace, ho, for shame! Confusion's cure lives not
In these confusions.[8] Heaven and yourself
Had part in this fair maid—now heaven hath all,
And all the better is it for the maid.
Your part in her you could not keep from death,
But heaven keeps his part in eternal life.
The most you sought was her promotion,
For 'twas your heaven she should be advanced;
And weep ye now, seeing she is advanced
Above the clouds, as high as heaven itself?
O, in this love, you love your child so ill
That you run mad, seeing that she is well.[9]
She's not well married that lives married long,
But she's best married that dies married young.
Dry up your tears and stick your rosemary[10]
On this fair corse, and, as the custom is,
And in her best array bear her to church:
For though fond nature[11] bids us all lament,
Yet nature's tears are reason's merriment.[12]

Literary Analysis
Dramatic Irony How do Paris' words contribute to the dramatic irony?

pilgrimage (pil′ grim ij) *n.* long journey, often for religious purposes

4. solace find comfort.

5. Beguiled cheated.

6. Uncomfortable painful, upsetting.

7. solemnity solemn rites.

Reading Strategy
Predicting What might Capulet's remarks in lines 63–64 foreshadow about the future?

8. Confusion's . . . confusions The remedy for this calamity is not to be found in these outcries.

9. well blessed in heaven.

10. rosemary an evergreen herb signifying love and remembrance.

11. fond nature mistake-prone human nature.

12. Yet . . . merriment while human nature causes us to weep for Juliet, reason should cause us to be happy (since she is in heaven).

27 **✔Reading Check**
What does the Nurse find when she draws aside the curtains in Juliet's chamber?

25 Literary Analysis

Dramatic Irony

- Ask students to what Lord Capulet compares Death in his speech on this page.
  Answer: Capulet compares Death to Juliet's bridegroom, Capulet's son-in-law, and Capulet's heir. He says that Death will be left with everything when Capulet dies.
- Ask students the Literary Analysis question on p. 855: How do Paris's words contribute to the dramatic irony?
  Answer: Paris has come to the Capulets looking forward to seeing Juliet on their wedding day. Now he sees her dead, or so he thinks.

26 Reading Strategy

Predicting

- Ask students how Paris reacts to Juliet's death. Is it similar to or different from the responses of the Capulets?
  Possible response: Paris feels he has been cheated, rather than feeling sorrow for Juliet. All three characters focus on their own loss rather than on the fact that Juliet has been deprived of her life at a very young age.
- Have students answer the Reading Strategy question on p. 855: What might Capulet's remarks in lines 63–64 foreshadow about the future?
  Answer: Capulet's lines foreshadow Juliet's real death.

27 ✔Reading Check

Answer: The Nurse finds Juliet dressed for daytime activities but in bed, and apparently asleep. Soon after, the Nurse discovers that something is deeply wrong.

28 Critical Thinking

Make Judgments

- Ask students who is left on stage when the Capulets, the Friar, and Paris exit.
  Answer: The Nurse, Peter, and the two musicians remain, but the Nurse departs almost immediately.
- Ask students why Shakespeare chose to end Scene v with the bantering of the musicians.
  Possible responses: The banter of the musicians provides comic relief from the high drama of Juliet's actions and her family's grief. Their talk demonstrates how normal life proceeds even when some are afflicted with pain. Shakespeare may even be suggesting that the travails of the high and mighty are of little importance to ordinary people.

29 Background (p. 857)

Names

Shakespeare is having fun with names again on p. 857. The three musicians' names are based on musical terms. A *catling* is a lute string, *rebeck* is a kind of violin, and *soundpost* is a part of a violin.

30 Reading Strategy (p. 857)

Predicting

- Ask the reading strategy question on p. 857: Do you predict that the Frair's plan will succeed? Why or why not?
  Possible response: Students may note that the plan depends heavily on perfect timing and communication—and the timing has already been upset.

CAPULET. All things that we ordainèd festival[13]
Turn from their office to black funeral—
Our instruments to melancholy bells,
Our wedding cheer to a sad burial feast;
Our solemn hymns to sullen dirges[14] change;
Our bridal flowers serve for a buried corse;
And all things change them to the contrary.

FRIAR. Sir, go you in; and, madam, go with him;
And go, Sir Paris. Everyone prepare
To follow this fair corse unto her grave.
The heavens do low'r[15] upon you for some ill;
Move them no more by crossing their high will.

[Exit, casting rosemary on her and shutting the curtains. The NURSE *and* MUSICIANS *remain.]*

FIRST MUSICIAN. Faith, we may put up our pipes and be gone.

NURSE. Honest good fellows, ah, put up, put up!
For well you know this is a pitiful case.[16] *[Exit.]*

FIRST MUSICIAN. Ay, by my troth, the case may be amended.

[Enter PETER.*]*

PETER. Musicians, O, musicians, "Heart's ease," "Heart's ease"! O, and you will have me live, play "Heart's ease."

FIRST MUSICIAN. Why "Heart's ease"?

28 **PETER.** O, musicians, because my heart itself plays "My heart is full."
O, play me some merry dump[17] to comfort me.

FIRST MUSICIAN. Not a dump we! 'Tis no time to play now.

PETER. You will not then?

FIRST MUSICIAN. No.

PETER. I will then give it you soundly.

FIRST MUSICIAN. What will you give us?

PETER. No money, on my faith, but the gleek.[18] I will give you[19] the minstrel.[20]

FIRST MUSICIAN. Then will I give you the serving-creature.

PETER. Then will I lay the serving-creature's dagger on your pate.
I will carry no crotchets.[21] I'll *re* you, I'll *fa* you. Do you note me?

FIRST MUSICIAN. And you *re* us and *fa* us, you note us.

SECOND MUSICIAN. Pray you put up your dagger, and put out your wit.
Then have at you with my wit!

PETER. I will dry-beat you with an iron wit, and put up my iron

13. ordainèd festival planned to be part of a celebration.

14. dirges funeral hymns.

15. low'r frown.

16. case situation; instrument case.

17. dump sad tune.

18. gleek scornful speech.

19. give you call you.

20. minstrel a contemptuous term (as opposed to *musician*).

21. crotchets whim; quarter notes.

ENRICHMENT: Language Connection

Parallel Construction and Puns

A final example of parallel construction graces the last page of Act IV. Lord Capulet agonizes over what might have been by contrasting it with what will be. In lines 85–91, each symbol of happiness turns into its opposite, a symbol of sadness. Musical instruments change to tolling bells; a celebratory meal to a meal of mourning; wedding hymns to burial dirges; and bridal bouquets to funeral flowers.

However, as soon as Capulet and company have exited, the rapidly punning musicians enter, trading verbal jousts with the quickness of a fiddler. Students may enjoy finding the various plays on words, after which they can take turns reading the scene aloud with as much liveliness as possible.

dagger. Answer me like men.

"When griping grief the heart doth wound,
And doleful dumps the mind oppress,
Then music with her silver sound"—

Why "silver sound"? Why "music with her silver sound"? What say you, Simon Catling?

29

FIRST MUSICIAN. Marry, sir, because silver hath a sweet sound.

PETER. Pretty! What say you, Hugh Rebeck?

SECOND MUSICIAN. I say "silver sound" because musicians sound for silver.

PETER. Pretty too! What say you, James Soundpost?

THIRD MUSICIAN. Faith, I know not what to say.

PETER. O, I cry you mercy,[22] you are the singer. I will say for you. It is "music with her silver sound" because musicians have no gold for sounding.
"Then music with her silver sound
With speedy help doth lend redress." [*Exit.*]

FIRST MUSICIAN. What a pestilent knave is this same!

SECOND MUSICIAN. Hang him, Jack! Come, we'll in here, tarry for the mourners, and stay dinner. [*Exit with others.*]

22. cry you mercy beg your pardon.

30 Reading Strategy

Predicting Do you predict that the Friar's plan will succeed? Why or why not?

Review and Assess

Thinking About Act IV

1. **Respond:** Should Romeo and Juliet have followed Friar Lawrence's advice? Why or why not?
2. **(a) Recall:** What event are Paris and Juliet discussing at the beginning of Act IV? **(b) Compare and Contrast:** How do their feelings about the event differ?
3. **(a) Recall:** What is Friar Lawrence's plan for Juliet? **(b) Analyze:** Why do you think Juliet trusts the Friar?
4. **(a) Recall:** What three fears does Juliet reveal in her soliloquy in Scene iii? **(b) Interpret:** What does the soliloquy reveal about her personality?
5. **(a) Evaluate:** Do you think drinking the potion is a courageous or a foolish act? Explain. **(b) Draw Conclusions:** How has Juliet changed during the play? Explain.
6. **Evaluate:** Do you think it is appropriate for a religious person like the Friar to deceive people with the hope of positive outcomes?

ASSESS

Answers for p. 857

Review and Assess

1. Encourage students to consider the possibilities as well as the probabilities. Ask students what could unexpectedly happen to ruin Friar Lawrence's plan.
2. **(a)** They are discussing their scheduled marriage. **(b)** Paris is filled with happiness; Juliet, with dread.
3. **(a)** Friar Lawrence will give Juliet a potion to make her comatose. She will be placed in the tomb. Friar Lawrence will bring Romeo to the tomb, and they will be there when Juliet wakes. Romeo will then take Juliet to Mantua. **(b)** Possible response: Juliet trusts the Friar because he is older and a clergyman; she also has no other resources.
4. **(a)** The potion may not work; it may kill her; she may wake up before Romeo comes. **(b)** The soliloquy reveals that Juliet is fully aware of the grave risks she is undertaking and is brave enough to proceed.
5. **(a)** Possible responses: It is a courageous act because it is her only way to be with Romeo again. It is a foolish act because she is relying on an unknown potion and the actions of others to save her. **(b)** Juliet has developed a more mature and serious outlook. She is no longer a girl, but a woman willing to brave any danger for her love.
6. Students may say that the Friar is not deliberately trying to deceive anyone; he is sincere in his expectations of a positive outcome.

ASSESSMENT PRACTICE: Literary Response

Defending Responses (For more practice, see Test Preparation Workbook, p. 49.)

Use the following sample test item to give students practice in defending their responses to drama.

When Friar Lawrence hears that Juliet appears to have died, he chides her grieving father:

"And weep ye now, seeing she is advanced
Above the clouds, as high as heaven itself?
O, in this love, you love your child so ill
That you run mad, seeing that she is well."

Ask students whether the Friar's response is appropriate for the situation.

In answering, students may point out that the Friar is encouraging Juliet's family not to grieve too deeply, knowing that Juliet is still alive. Some students may say that the Friar is wrong to continue the ruse, knowing the grief it is causing. Whatever their answer, students should defend their response.

Answers for p. 858

Review and Assess

1. When Juliet goes to Friar Lawrence for help in avoiding a marriage with Paris, she unexpectedly finds Paris there arranging for that very ceremony.
2. The entire household is busy and in a good humor, getting ready for the wedding. They do not know, as the audience does, that Juliet is already still as death; the wedding will become a funeral.
3. What Character Thinks: At the beginning of Act II, Mercutio teases Romeo by talking about Rosaline. What Audience Knows: Romeo has come to the orchard to be near Juliet.
4. Suspense is created by the fact that the plan is risky: the potion may not work, or may be lethal; Romeo may receive the message too late or not at all; or Romeo may not arrive at the tomb in time.
5. Suspense builds because the audience does not know whether Juliet will take the potion or stab herself to death.
6. Suspense builds because the Nurse expects to waken Juliet for her wedding; the audience already knows the shocking discovery she is about to make.
7. Juliet never answers Paris directly; her avowels of love actually refer to Romeo.
8. The plan is complicated and risky. The potion may not work or may work too well and kill Juliet. Something may keep Romeo from learning what is going on.
9. **(a)** Romeo and Juliet threaten to kill themselves if they cannot be together. The Friar's plan involves a faked death. The Capulet's grief at Juliet's "death" foreshadows what will happen when Juliet really dies. **(b)** The focus on death foreshadows that Act V will contain real tragedy.
10. Students may suggest that both modern and Renaissance events require ceremonial preparations.

Review and Assess

Literary Analysis

Dramatic Irony

1. What **dramatic irony** results when Juliet encounters Paris in Friar Lawrence's cell?
2. What makes Act IV, Scene iv, in which Capulet prepares for Juliet's wedding, an example of dramatic irony?
3. Find at least one other example of dramatic irony in the first four acts. Use a diagram like the one shown to indicate how a character's thoughts or actions contradict what the audience knows is true.

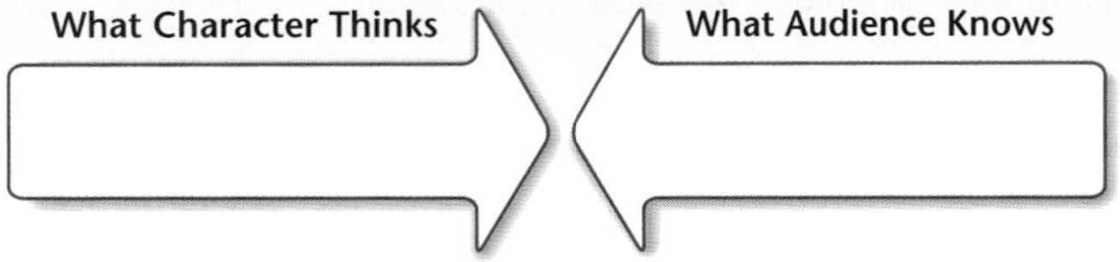

Connecting Literary Elements

4. What possible outcomes generate the feeling of **suspense** in Act IV, Scene i, when the Friar proposes his secret plan to Juliet?
5. Why does suspense build when Juliet holds the dagger and the potion in Act IV, Scene iii?
6. Why does the audience feel suspense in Act IV, Scene iv, as the Nurse prepares to waken Juliet?

Reading Strategy

Predicting

7. How do Juliet's comments to Paris in Act IV, Scene i, lead you to **predict** that she will never marry him?
8. What parts of the Friar's plan do you predict could lead to potential problems? Explain.
9. (a) In what ways is death a main focus throughout Act IV? (b) How might this focus foreshadow real tragedy in Act V?

Extend Understanding

10. **Cultural Connection:** How are the customs related to marriage and death in the play similar to or different from those generally followed in the United States today?

Quick Review

Dramatic irony is a contradiction between what a character thinks or says and what the audience or reader knows to be true.

Suspense is a feeling of curiosity or uncertainty about the outcome of events in a literary work.

To **predict**, make educated guesses about what may happen next in a literary work.

Take It to the Net

www.phschool.com

Take the interactive self-test online to check your understanding of Act IV.

TEACHING RESOURCES

The following resources can be used to enrich or extend the instruction for pp. 858–859.

Vocabulary

- **Selection Support,** Build Vocabulary, p. 193
- **Vocabulary and Spelling Practice Book** (Use this booklet for skills enrichment.) ■

Grammar

- **Selection Support,** Build Grammar Skills, p 194
- **Writing and Grammar,** Gold Level, p. 598
- **Daily Language Practice Transparencies**

Writing

- **Writing and Grammar iText CD-ROM**

■ **BLOCK SCHEDULING:** Resources marked with this symbol provide varied instruction during 90-minute blocks.

Integrate Language Skills

1 Vocabulary Development Lesson

Word Analysis: Anglo-Saxon suffix *-ward*

The Anglo-Saxon suffix *-ward* means "in a direction." The suffix appears in the word *wayward*, meaning "insistent upon going in one's own direction." Using the meaning of *-ward*, define each word below.

1. forward 2. skyward 3. outward

Spelling Strategy

The *ij* sound at the end of a word is usually spelled *age*, as in *pilgrimage*. Write each of these words, filling in the missing ending.

1. wreck__?__ 2. post__?__ 3. voy__?__

Concept Development: Analogies

Complete each analogy, or comparison, with a word from the vocabulary list on page 844.

1. *Bright* is to *glistening* as *gloomy* is to __?__.
2. *Requested* is to *asked* as *commanded* is to __?__.
3. *Exhausted* is to *rested* as *pleasant* is to __?__.
4. *Wet* is to *rain* as *long* is to __?__.
5. *Car* is to *sedan* as *container* is to __?__.
6. *Dark* is to *light* as *obedient* is to __?__.
7. *Nervous* is to *edgy* as *thoughtful* is to __?__.

2 Grammar Lesson

Degrees of Comparison

Use the **comparative** degree of an adjective to compare two things. Use *-er* or *more* to form the comparative degree of most adjectives.

Use the **superlative** form of an adjective to compare three or more things. Generally use *-est* or *most* to form the superlative degree.

Comparative:	Juliet has *greater* love for Romeo than for Paris.
Superlative:	Romeo considers Juliet the *sweetest* and *most* beautiful woman he has known.

Practice Complete each sentence with the correct degree of the adjective.

1. Romeo is (older, oldest) than Juliet.
2. Juliet is the (kinder, kindest) Capulet.
3. Act IV is the (shorter, shortest) act.
4. Romeo is the (more, most) impulsive of the two lovers.
5. Act II is the (more, most) memorable act.

Writing Application Use both degrees of comparison in two sentences comparing characters in the play.

WG *Prentice Hall Writing and Grammar Connection: Chapter 26, Section 1*

3 Extension Activities

Writing Use your prediction skills to write your own **ending** for the play. Create a narrative of events that will occur in your version of Act V. Make sure that your ending develops naturally out of the events in Acts I through IV.

Listening and Speaking With a partner, prepare an informal **presentation** on Renaissance music. Collect examples of music that would have been played by musicians in Act IV, Scene v. Present your findings to your class. **[Group Activity]**

ASSESSMENT RESOURCES

The following resources can be used to assess students' knowledge and skills.

Selection Assessment

- **Formal Assessment,** Selection Test, pp. 173–175
- **Open Book Test,** pp. 145–147
- **Got It! Assessment Videotapes,** Tape 4
- **Test Bank Software**

PRENTICE HALL ASSESSMENT SYSTEM

- **Workbook**
- **Skill Book**
- **Transparencies**
- **CD-ROM**

Take It to the Net

Visit www.phschool.com for self-tests and additional questions on *Romeo and Juliet.*

EXTEND

Answers for p. 859

1 Vocabulary Development

Word Analysis

1. forward: in the direction of the front or head
2. skyward: in the direction of the sky
3. outward: in the direction of going out

Spelling Strategy

a. wreckage
b. postage
c. voyage

Concept Development: Analogies

1. dismal
2. enjoined
3. loathsome
4. pilgrimage
5. vial
6. wayward
7. pensive

2 Grammar

1. older
2. kindest
3. shortest
4. more
5. most

Writing Application

Sample sentences:

1. Tybalt is more hotheaded than Mercutio.
2. Romeo is the most lovesick of all the Montague men.

3 Extension Activities

Writing Lesson

- Have students make a list of different ways in which the play could have ended.
- When they have chosen an ending, use the Writing Lesson to guide students in developing their Act V.
- Make sure students use the details from the previous acts to aid them in their writing.

CUSTOMIZE INSTRUCTION For Universal Access

To address different learning styles, use the activities suggested in the **Extension Activities** booklet, p. 49.

- For Verbal/Linguistic Learners, Use Activity 6
- For Visual/Spatial and Logical/Mathematical Learners, use Activity 7.

The Tragedy of Romeo and Juliet, Act V

Lesson Objectives and CA Correlations

1. **To analyze and respond to literary elements**
   - Literary Analysis: Tragedy **R 3.1**
   - Connecting Literary Elements: Character's Motive **R 3.4**
2. **To read, comprehend, analyze, and critique drama**
   - Reading Strategy: Identifying Causes and Effects
   - Reading Check questions
   - Review and Assess questions
   - Assessment Practice (ATE)
3. **To develop word analysis skills, fluency, and systematic vocabulary**
   - Vocabulary Development Lesson: Latin Prefix: *ambi-* **R 1.1**
4. **To understand and apply written and oral language conventions**
   - Spelling Strategy
   - Grammar Lesson: Agreement With Indefinite Pronouns **LC 1.2**
5. **To understand and apply appropriate writing and research strategies**
   - Writing Lesson: Persuasive Letter **W 2.4**
   - Extension Activity: Set Design **W 1.8**
6. **To understand and apply listening and speaking strategies**
   - Extension Activity: Mock Trial **LS 2.5**

STEP-BY-STEP TEACHING GUIDE	PACING GUIDE
PRETEACH	
Motivate Students and Provide Background	
Read and discuss the Review and Anticipate information (SE/ATE p. 861) [A]	10 min.
Introduce the Concepts	
Introduce the Literary Analysis and Reading Strategy (SE/ATE p. 860) [A]	15 min.
Pronounce the vocabulary words and read their definitions (SE p. 860)	5 min.
TEACH	
Monitor Comprehension	
Informally monitor comprehension by circulating while students read independently or in groups [A]	30 min.
Monitor students' comprehension with the Reading Check notes (SE/ATE pp. 861, 863, 865, 867, 869, 871, 873)	as students read
Develop vocabulary with Vocabulary notes (SE pp. 862, 869, 872–873)	as students read
Develop Understanding	
Develop students' understanding of tragedy with the Literary Analysis annotations (SE /ATE pp. 862–866, 868–869, 871–873) [A]	10 min.
Develop students' ability to identify causes and effects with the Reading Strategy annotations (SE/ATE pp. 863–864, 867–869, 871–873)	10 min.
ASSESS	
Assess Mastery	
Assess students' mastery of the Reading Strategy and Literary Analysis by having them answer the Review and Assess questions (SE/ATE p. 875)	20 min.
Use one or more of the print and media Assessment Resources (ATE p. 877) [A]	up to 50 min.
EXTEND	
Apply Understanding	
Have students complete the Vocabulary Development Lesson and the Grammar Lesson (SE p. 876) [A]	20 min.
Apply students' knowledge of persuasive appeals using the Writing Lesson (SE p. 877) [A]	45 min.
Apply students' understanding of the selection using one or more of the Extension Activities (SE p. 877)	20–90 min.

A **ACCELERATED INSTRUCTION:**
Use the strategies and activities identified with an [A].

UNIVERSAL ACCESS
● = Below Level Students
▲ = On-Level Students
■ = Above Level Students

Time and Resource Manager

Reading Level: Challenging
Average Number of Instructional Days: 4

	RESOURCES		
	PRINT	**TRANSPARENCIES**	**TECHNOLOGY**
	• **Beyond Literature,** Community Connection: Communication, p. 50 ▲ ■		• **Interest Grabber Video,** Tape 4 ● ▲ ■
	• **Selection Support Workbook:** ● ▲ ■ Literary Analysis, p. 200 Reading Strategy, p. 199 Build Vocabulary, p. 197	• **Literary Analysis and Reading Transparencies,** pp. 99 and 100 ● ▲ ■	
	• **Authors In Depth,** Gold Level, p. 155 ■		• **Listening to Literature** ● ▲ ■ Audiocassettes, Side 26 Audio CDs, CD 18
	• **Literatura en español** ● ▲ • **Literary Analysis for Enrichment** ■		
	• **Formal Assessment:** Selection Test, pp. 176–178 ● ▲ ■ • **Open Book Test,** pp. 148–150 ● ▲ ■ • PRENTICE HALL ASSESSMENT SYSTEM ● ▲ ■	• PRENTICE HALL ASSESSMENT SYSTEM ● ▲ ■ Skills Practice Answers and Explanations on Transparencies	• **Test Bank Software** ● ▲ ■ • **Got It! Assessment Videotapes,** Tape 4 ● ▲
	• **Selection Support Workbook:** ● ▲ ■ Build Grammar Skills, p.198 • **Writing and Grammar,** Gold Level ● ▲ ■ • **Extension Activities,** p. 48 ● ▲ ■	• **Daily Language Practice Transparencies** ● ▲ • **Writing Models and Graphic Organizers on Transparencies,** pp. 56, 71 ● ▲ ■	• **Writing and Grammar iText CD-ROM** ● ▲ ■ ***Take It to the Net*** www.phschool.com

BLOCK SCHEDULING: Use one 90-minute class period to preteach the selection and have students read it. Use a second 90-minute class period to assess students' mastery of skills and have them complete one of the Extension Activities.

PRETEACH

Step-by-Step Teaching Guide for p. 860

Background

Scholars are not sure when *Romeo and Juliet* was first performed, but some think the first production might have occurred in the summer of 1595 at James Burbage's Theater. When the play premiered, it was an instant success. Publications of that time period say that the play "hath been often (with great applause) played publicly," and that "it hath been sundry times publicly acted."

❶ Literary Analysis

Tragedy

- Read the instruction about *tragedy* together as a class and discuss the quotation.
- Use the instruction for Connecting Literary Elements to connect the main characters' tragedy with their *motives*.
- Use the Tragedy transparency in **Literary Analysis and Reading Transparencies**, p. 100, to demonstrate for students how to record the various elements that make up a tragedy.

❷ Reading Strategy

Cause and Effect

- Remind students that a cause is an event that leads to another event—an effect.
- Display the Identify Causes and Effects transparency in **Literary Analysis and Reading Transparencies**, p. 99, and then have students create similar charts of their own.

Vocabulary Development

- Pronounce each vocabulary word for students, and read the definitions as a class. Have students identify any words with which they are already familiar.

E-Teach

Visit E-Teach at www.phschool.com for teachers' essays on how to teach, with questions and answers.

Prepare to Read

The Tragedy of Romeo and Juliet, Act V

❶ Literary Analysis

Tragedy

A **tragedy** is a drama in which the central character, who is usually of noble stature, meets with disaster or great misfortune. The tragic hero's downfall is usually the result of fate, a serious character flaw, or a combination of both. A great tragedy is not necessarily depressing, however. It uplifts the audience by showing the greatness of spirit of which people are capable. This spirit is reflected in these lines near the end of the play:

For I will raise her statue in pure gold,
That whiles Verona by that name is known,
There shall no figure at such rate be set
As that of true and faithful Juliet.

As you read Act V of *Romeo and Juliet*, consider the reasons for the tragic events and analyze how the events make you feel about the human spirit.

Connecting Literary Elements

A **character's motive** is the reason behind an individual's thoughts or actions. In Shakespeare's tragedies, the hero's motives are basically good, although sometimes misguided. The character's fate, therefore, often seems worse than what he or she deserves.

❷ Reading Strategy

Identifying Causes and Effects

Tragedies often involve a chain of causes and effects that advances the plot and leads to the final tragic outcome.

- A **cause** is an action, an event, or a situation that produces a result.
- An **effect** is the result produced by a cause.

Use a chart like this one to record the causes and effects in Act V.

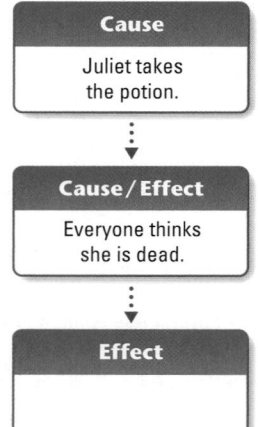

Cause
Juliet takes the potion.

Cause / Effect
Everyone thinks she is dead.

Effect

Vocabulary Development

remnants (rem′ nənts) *n.* remaining persons or things (p. 862)

penury (pen′ yo͞o rē) *n.* extreme poverty (p. 862)

haughty (hôt′ ē) *adj.* arrogant (p. 866)

sepulcher (sep′ əl kər) *n.* tomb (p. 869)

ambiguities (am′ bə gyo͞o′ ə tēz) *n.* statements or events whose meanings are unclear (p. 872)

scourge (skʉrj) *n.* whip or other instrument for inflicting punishment (p. 873)

TEACHING RESOURCES

The following resources can be used to enrich or extend the instruction for p. 860.

Motivation

Interest Grabber Video, Tape 4

Background

Beyond Literature, p. 50 ■

Take It to the Net

Visit www.phschool.com for background and hotlinks for *The Tragedy of Romeo and Juliet.*

Literary Analysis

Literary Analysis and Reading Transparencies, Tragedy, p. 100

Reading

Selection Support: Reading Strategy, p. 199; Build Vocabulary, p. 197

Literary Analysis and Reading Transparencies, Identify Causes and Effects, p. 99

■ **BLOCK SCHEDULING:** Resources marked with this symbol provide varied instruction during 90-minute blocks.

❶

Review and Anticipate

To prevent her marriage to Paris, Juliet has taken the Friar's potion and, as Act V begins, is in a temporary deathlike sleep. Her unsuspecting family plans her funeral. Meanwhile, the Friar has sent a messenger to Mantua to tell Romeo of the ruse, so that he may return and rescue Juliet from her family tomb. What do you think might go wrong with the Friar's plan?

❷

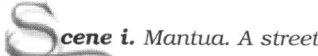

Scene i. *Mantua. A street.*

[*Enter* ROMEO.]

ROMEO. If I may trust the flattering truth of sleep,[1]
My dreams presage[2] some joyful news at hand.
My bosom's lord[3] sits lightly in his throne,
And all this day an unaccustomed spirit
Lifts me above the ground with cheerful thoughts.
I dreamt my lady came and found me dead
(Strange dream that gives a dead man leave to think!)
And breathed such life with kisses in my lips
That I revived and was an emperor.
Ah me! How sweet is love itself possessed,
When but love's shadows[4] are so rich in joy!

1. **flattering . . . sleep** pleasing illusions of dreams.
2. **presage** foretell.
3. **bosom's lord** heart.
4. **shadows** dreams; unreal images.

❸ ✔ **Reading Check**

Why is Romeo in a good mood?

TEACH

❶ About the Selection

As *Romeo and Juliet* draws to a close, circumstances conspire to exact a terrible penalty from the two lovers as the price for their families' feud. Others pay as well—Tybalt and Mercutio, earlier in the play, and now Lady Montague and Paris. Although Friar Lawrence had hoped to reconcile the Capulets and the Montagues through the marriage of their children, that reconciliation is brought about instead by the young people's deaths.

❷ Background

Greek Tragedy

Tell students that according to the ancient Greek philosopher Aristotle's definition of tragedy, the tragic hero or heroine must be of noble stature, and the action must take place within a twenty-four hour period. In addition, the audience should feel such pity and fear at the end of the play that they experience a "catharsis," or cleansing of their emotions. When students have completed Act V, you may wish to discuss how Aristotle's definition applies to *Romeo and Juliet.*

❸ ✔ Reading Check

Answer: Romeo has had a wonderfully propitious dream: Juliet had found him dead and had awakened him with kisses. Though Romeo finds this dream exhilarating, readers and audience may see an ominous foreshadowing.

TEACHING RESOURCES

The following resources can be used to enrich or extend the instruction for pp. 861–874.

Literary Analysis
- **Writing Models and Graphic Organizers,** p. 71 ▪
- **Selection Support:** Literary Analysis, p. 200

Reading
- **Listening to Literature Audiocassettes,** Side 26 ▪
- **Listening to Literature Audio CD,** CD 18

Extension
- **Authors In Depth,** Gold Level ▪

▪ **BLOCK SCHEDULING:** Resources marked with this symbol provide varied instruction during 90-minute blocks.

4 Literary Analysis

Tragedy and Character's Motive

- Have students determine the reason for Romeo's first question to Balthasar.
  Answer: Romeo has been expecting to hear from the Friar and wonders why Balthasar does not have letters for him.
- Which person is Romeo most concerned about in his questions to Balthasar?
  Answer: Romeo asks about Juliet three times and his father once.
- Have students answer the first Literary Analysis question on p. 862: What motivates Romeo's questions?
  Answer: Romeo has been away from Juliet, not by choice, and is eager to know how she is.

5 Literary Analysis

Tragedy

- Have students speculate on Balthasar's meaning in line 17.
  Answer: Balthasar means that although she is dead, Juliet is well because she is in heaven.
- Ask the second Literary Analysis question on p. 862: Which words in the exchange between Romeo and the man suggest that fate plays a role in the tragedy?
  Answer: Romeo says, "Then I defy you, stars!" He means that if the stars (representing fate) have been responsible for Juliet's death, Romeo is now their enemy. He will now defy fate, setting in motion a series of events that will culminate in tragedy.

[*Enter* ROMEO'S MAN, BALTHASAR, *booted.*]

News from Verona! How now, Balthasar?
Dost thou not bring me letters from the friar?
How doth my lady? Is my father well?
How fares my Juliet? That I ask again,
For nothing can be ill if she be well.

MAN. Then she is well, and nothing can be ill.
Her body sleeps in Capels' monument,[5]
And her immortal part with angels lives.
I saw her laid low in her kindred's vault
And presently took post[6] to tell it you.
O, pardon me for bringing these ill news,
Since you did leave it for my office,[7] sir.

ROMEO. Is it e'en so? Then I defy you, stars!
Thou knowest my lodging. Get me ink and paper
And hire post horses. I will hence tonight.

MAN. I do beseech you, sir, have patience.
Your looks are pale and wild and do import
Some misadventure.[8]

ROMEO. Tush, thou art deceived.
Leave me and do the thing I bid thee do.
Hast thou no letters to me from the friar?

MAN. No, my good lord.

ROMEO. No matter. Get thee gone.
And hire those horses. I'll be with thee straight. [*Exit* BALTHASAR.]
Well, Juliet, I will lie with thee tonight.
Let's see for means. O mischief, thou art swift
To enter in the thoughts of desperate men!
I do remember an apothecary,[9]
And hereabouts 'a dwells, which late I noted
In tatt'red weeds, with overwhelming brows,
Culling of simples.[10] Meager were his looks,
Sharp misery had worn him to the bones;
And in his needy shop a tortoise hung,
An alligator stuffed, and other skins
Of ill-shaped fishes; and about his shelves
A beggarly account[11] of empty boxes,
Green earthen pots, bladders, and musty seeds,
Remnants of packthread, and old cakes of roses[12]
Were thinly scatterèd, to make up a show.
Noting this penury, to myself I said,
"And if a man did need a poison now
Whose sale is present death in Mantua,
Here lives a caitiff[13] wretch would sell it him."
O, this same thought did but forerun my need,

Literary Analysis
Tragedy and Character's Motive What motivates Romeo's questions?

5. Capels' monument the Capulets' burial vault.

6. presently took post immediately set out on horseback.

7. office duty.

Literary Analysis
Tragedy Which words in the exchange between Romeo and the man suggest that fate plays a role in the tragedy?

8. import / Some misadventure suggest some misfortune.

9. apothecary one who prepares and sells drugs and medicines.

10. In tatt'red . . . simples in torn clothing, with overhanging eyebrows, sorting out herbs.

11. beggarly account small number.

12. cakes of roses pressed rose petals (used for perfume).

remnants (rem′ nənts) *n.* remaining persons or things

penury (pen′ yo͞o rē) *n.* extreme poverty

13. caitiff miserable.

6

And this same needy man must sell it me.
As I remember, this should be the house.
Being holiday, the beggar's shop is shut.
What, ho! Apothecary!

[*Enter* APOTHECARY.]

APOTHECARY. Who calls so loud?

ROMEO. Come hither, man. I see that thou art poor.
Hold, there is forty ducats.[14] Let me have
A dram of poison, such soon-speeding gear[15]
As will disperse itself through all the veins
That the life-weary taker may fall dead,
And that the trunk[16] may be discharged of breath
As violently as hasty powder fired
Doth hurry from the fatal cannon's womb.

APOTHECARY. Such mortal drugs I have; but Mantua's law
Is death to any he that utters[17] them.

7

ROMEO. Art thou so bare and full of wretchedness
And fearest to die? Famine is in thy cheeks,
Need and oppression starveth in thy eyes,
Contempt and beggary hangs upon thy back:
The world is not thy friend, nor the world's law;
The world affords no law to make thee rich;
Then be not poor, but break it and take this.

APOTHECARY. My poverty but not my will consents.

ROMEO. I pay thy poverty and not thy will.

APOTHECARY. Put this in any liquid thing you will
And drink it off, and if you had the strength
Of twenty men, it would dispatch you straight.

ROMEO. There is thy gold—worse poison to men's souls,
Doing more murder in this loathsome world,
Than these poor compounds[18] that thou mayst not sell.
I sell thee poison; thou hast sold me none.
Farewell. Buy food and get thyself in flesh.
Come, cordial[19] and not poison, go with me
To Juliet's grave; for there must I use thee. [*Exit all.*]

Scene ii. FRIAR LAWRENCE'S *cell.*

[*Enter* FRIAR JOHN *to* FRIAR LAWRENCE.]

JOHN. Holy Franciscan friar, brother, ho!

[*Enter* FRIAR LAWRENCE.]

LAWRENCE. This same should be the voice of Friar John.

Reading Strategy
Identifying Causes and Effects What causes Romeo to buy poison from the apothecary?

14. **ducats** (duk' əts) gold coins.

15. **soon-speeding gear** fast-working stuff.

16. **trunk** body.

17. **utters** sells.

18. **compounds** mixtures.

19. **cordial** health-giving drink.

Literary Analysis
Tragedy and Character's Motive What motivates the apothecary to sell Romeo poison?

8 **✓ Reading Check**

What does Romeo learn from Balthasar?

6 Reading Strategy

Identifying Causes and Effects

- Ask students to read Romeo's soliloquy and to infer what kind of reputation an apothecary had in these times.
  Possible response: Judging from Romeo's descriptions of the apothecary and his shop, the apothecary was not a highly respected person.
- Have students answer the Reading Strategy question on p. 863: What causes Romeo to buy poison from the apothecary?
  Answer: Romeo intends to kill himself because Juliet is dead.

7 Literary Analysis

Tragedy and Character's Motive

- Remind students that in a *tragedy*, the main character is partially brought down by a character flaw. Ask them what character flaw they see in Romeo in this scene so far.
  Answer: Romeo acts without thinking. He does not pause to verify Balthasar's news or to consider waiting until he could speak with the Friar.
- Ask students what Romeo says about the law when the apothecary tells him that it is illegal to sell poison.
  Answer: Romeo says that the law of the world is not the apothecary's friend because there is no law that will make the apothecary rich.
- Have students answer the Literary Analysis question on p. 863: What motivates the apothecary to sell Romeo poison?
  Answer: The apothecary is poor and starving; this situation will cause him to sell Romeo the poison, even though the law forbids it.

8 ✓ Reading Check

Answer: Romeo learns from Balthasar that Juliet is dead.

CUSTOMIZE INSTRUCTION FOR UNIVERSAL ACCESS

For Special Needs Students	For Less Proficient Learners	For English Learners
To help explain Romeo's rash decision to seek poision, have students recall other episodes in the play in which Romeo acts impulsively, almost without thinking at all.	Have students use a dictionary or thesaurus to find synonyms for the word *penury*, used in line 49. Then, have them try out several synonyms in the line to decide which seems closest in connotation to *penury*.	Encourage students to read aloud the exchange between Romeo and the apothecary and then to act it out. Give several pairs of students a chance to present this dramatic scene.

9 Reading Strategy

Identifying Causes and Effects

- Ask students to summarize the reason that Friar John could not deliver his news to Romeo.
  Possible response: Friar John went to look for another brother to go with him. He found the brother helping townspeople who were sick with the plague. The health officials would not let either friar leave the area, for fear they would spread the infection, so Friar John was not able to go to Mantua.
- Ask student to answer the Reading Strategy question on p. 864: What do you predict will be the effect of Friar John's failure to deliver the letter to Romeo?
  Answer: Without knowing that Juliet is actually alive, Romeo will kill himself.

10 Literary Analysis

Tragedy and Character's Motive

- After they have read the exchange between the Friars, ask students why they think Friar Lawrence asks Friar John to get him a crow.
  Answer: Students should infer that a crow is a crowbar and that Friar Lawrence will need the tool to force his way into the Capulet tomb where Juliet is lying.
- Have students answer the Literary Analysis question on p. 864: What motivates Friar Lawrence's decision to go to the monument?
  Possible response: The Friar wants to be at the monument in order to ease Juliet's shock at awakening in a tomb and to explain why Romeo is not yet there.

Welcome from Mantua. What says Romeo?
Or, if his mind be writ, give me his letter.

JOHN. Going to find a barefoot brother out,
One of our order, to associate[1] me
Here in this city visiting the sick,
And finding him, the searchers[2] of the town,
Suspecting that we both were in a house
Where the infectious pestilence did reign,
(9) Sealed up the doors, and would not let us forth,
So that my speed to Mantua there was stayed.

LAWRENCE. Who bare my letter, then, to Romeo?

JOHN. I could not send it—here it is again—
Nor get a messenger to bring it thee,
So fearful were they of infection.

LAWRENCE. Unhappy fortune! By my brotherhood,
The letter was not nice,[3] but full of charge,
Of dear import;[4] and the neglecting it
May do much danger. Friar John, go hence,
Get me an iron crow and bring it straight
Unto my cell.

JOHN. Brother, I'll go and bring it thee. [*Exit.*]

LAWRENCE. Now must I to the monument alone.
Within this three hours will fair Juliet wake.
She will beshrew[5] me much that Romeo
(10) Hath had no notice of these accidents;[6]
But I will write again to Mantua,
And keep her at my cell till Romeo come—
Poor living corse, closed in a dead man's tomb! [*Exit.*]

1. **associate** accompany.

2. **searchers** health officers who search for victims of the plague.

Reading Strategy
Identifying Causes and Effects What do you predict will be the effect of Friar John's failure to deliver the letter to Romeo?

3. **nice** trivial.

4. **full of charge, / Of dear import** urgent and important.

5. **beshrew** blame.

6. **accidents** happenings.

Literary Analysis
Tragedy and Character's Motive What motivates Friar Lawrence's decision to go to the monument?

Scene iii. *A churchyard; in it a monument belonging to the* CAPULETS.

[*Enter* PARIS *and his* PAGE *with flowers and sweet water.*]

PARIS. Give me thy torch, boy. Hence, and stand aloof.[1]
Yet put it out, for I would not be seen.
Under yond yew trees lay thee all along,[2]
Holding thy ear close to the hollow ground.
So shall no foot upon the churchyard tread
(Being loose, unfirm, with digging up of graves)
But thou shalt hear it. Whistle then to me,
As signal that thou hearest something approach.
Give me those flowers. Do as I bid thee, go.

PAGE. [*Aside*] I am almost afraid to stand alone
Here in the churchyard; yet I will adventure.[3] [*Retires.*]

PARIS. Sweet flower, with flowers thy bridal bed I strew

1. **aloof** apart.

2. **lay . . . along** lie down flat.

3. **adventure** chance it.

ENRICHMENT: Science Connection

The Bubonic Plague

The plague referred to on p. 864 is the bubonic plague, which visited Europe regularly during the Middle Ages and later. The plague bacterium was transmitted by fleas, as they themselves were carried from place to place by rats. People of the time had no knowledge of bacteria, but they knew that the plague was more common in the hot summer months and that it seemed to spread quickly in crowds. Infected houses or areas were quarantined, people had to wash their street twice a day, and only certain members of each district could shop for those who were quarantined.

In London during Shakespeare's day, the theaters and other public places were closed during plague months. In fact, many religious Londoners equated the theater with illness and other evils. In the words of one preacher, "The cause of plagues is sin, if you look to it well; and the cause of sin are plays; therefore the cause of plagues are plays."

(O woe! thy canopy is dust and stones)
Which with sweet[4] water nightly I will dew;
Or, wanting that, with tears distilled by moans.
The obsequies[5] that I for thee will keep
Nightly shall be to strew thy grave and weep. [*Whistle* BOY.]
The boy gives warning something doth approach.
What cursèd foot wanders this way tonight
To cross[6] my obsequies and true love's rite?
What, with a torch? Muffle me, night, awhile. [*Retires.*]

[*Enter* ROMEO, *and* BALTHASAR *with a torch, a mattock, and a crow of iron.*]

11

ROMEO. Give me that mattock and the wrenching iron.
Hold, take this letter. Early in the morning
See thou deliver it to my lord and father.
Give me the light. Upon thy life I charge thee,
Whate'er thou hearest or seest, stand all aloof
And do not interrupt me in my course.
Why I descend into this bed of death
Is partly to behold my lady's face,
But chiefly to take thence from her dead finger
A precious ring—a ring that I must use
In dear employment.[7] Therefore hence, be gone.
But if thou, jealous,[8] dost return to pry
In what I farther shall intend to do,

4. **sweet** perfumed.

5. **obsequies** memorial ceremonies.

6. **cross** interrupt.

Literary Analysis
Tragedy and Character's Motive What different motives do Paris and Romeo have for visiting Juliet's tomb?

7. **dear employment** important business.

8. **jealous** curious.

12 **✓Reading Check**
Why was Friar John unable to get the letter delivered?

13 **◄ Critical Viewing** Do you think this image of Romeo accurately conveys his feelings as he enters the Capulets' tomb? Why or why not? **[Interpret]**

11 Literary Analysis

Tragedy and Character's Motive

- Ask students what Paris and Romeo each bring to Juliet's tomb with them.
  Answer: Paris brings flowers and perfume, and Romeo brings tools to help him get into the tomb.
- Have students determine what Paris asks his page to do while Paris is at the tomb.
  Answer: Paris asks the page to stand in the shadows and whistle if anyone comes.
- Ask students what the page reveals in his aside.
  Answer: The page is afraid of being in a graveyard at night.
- Have students answer the Literary Analysis question on p. 865: What different motives do Paris and Romeo have for visiting Juliet's tomb?
  Answer: Paris visits the tomb to bring Juliet flowers; Romeo visits the tomb to kill himself.

12 ✓Reading Check

Answer: Friar John and his companion were forbidden to leave the plague-ridden city by health officials.

13 ► Critical Viewing

Answer: Students may say that Romeo's upright stance and facial expression suggest that he is determined to follow through on his plan to die.

CUSTOMIZE INSTRUCTION FOR UNIVERSAL ACCESS

For Special Needs Students	For Less Proficient Readers
Have students imagine they are Friar Lawrence and write, in their own words, a letter to Romeo telling him what is going on. What basic information would they include? What would they tell Romeo to do? What would they promise to do themselves, as Friar Lawrence has? Have students compare their completed letters.	Have students use the events they read about on pp. 864–865, or on previous pages, to ask questions about cause and effect. Students can work in pairs to ask and answer questions, or as a group with a quizmaster. Suggested questions for pp. 864–865: 1. Why do the health officers seal up the doors of some houses? 2. What is the effect of the Friar's letter not reaching Romeo? 3. Why does the Friar think that Juliet will blame him when she wakes up?

⓮ Literary Analysis

Tragedy and Character's Motive

- Ask students if they think Romeo really intends to kill Balthasar if the servant disobeys him.
  Possible response: Students may say that Romeo is exaggerating in order to show Balthasar how serious he is about not wanting to be disturbed.
- Ask students to read Balthasar's aside and determine whether or not he believes that Romeo has come to get a ring from Juliet's finger.
  Answer: Balthasar says he doubts Romeo's intents, or reasons. He believes Romeo has other reasons for coming to the tomb.
- Have students answer the Literary Analysis question on p. 866: Why is Romeo's intention to feed himself to the tomb especially tragic?
  Answer: Romeo's intention is especially tragic because his death will be so unnecessary. Students may add that his dead body will be discovered by Juliet when she wakes up.

⓯ ▶ Critical Viewing

Answer: Juliet does not look as if she has been dead for two days. According to lines 94–95, her lips and cheeks are rosy, rather than pale.

By heaven, I will tear thee joint by joint
And strew this hungry churchyard with thy limbs.
The time and my intents are savage-wild,
More fierce and more inexorable[9] far
Than empty[10] tigers or the roaring sea.

BALTHASAR. I will be gone, sir, and not trouble ye.

⓮ **ROMEO.** So shalt thou show me friendship. Take thou that.
Live, and be prosperous; and farewell, good fellow.

BALTHASAR. [*Aside*] For all this same, I'll hide me hereabout.
His looks I fear, and his intents I doubt. [*Retires.*]

ROMEO. Thou detestable maw,[11] thou womb of death,
Gorged with the dearest morsel of the earth,
Thus I enforce thy rotten jaws to open,
And in despite[12] I'll cram thee with more food.
[ROMEO *opens the tomb.*]

PARIS. This is that banished haughty Montague
That murd'red my love's cousin—with which grief
It is supposed the fair creature died—
And here is come to do some villainous shame
To the dead bodies. I will apprehend[13] him.
Stop thy unhallowèd toil, vile Montague!

9. **inexorable** uncontrollable.
10. **empty** hungry.
11. **maw** stomach.
12. **despite** scorn.

Literary Analysis
Tragedy and Character's Motive Why is Romeo's intention to feed himself to the tomb especially tragic?

haughty (hôt´ ē) *adj.* arrogant

13. **apprehend** seize; arrest.

⓯ **▼ Critical Viewing** In the tomb, Romeo pulls back the shroud to reveal what he thinks is Juliet's dead body. What clues about her appearance, as it is shown here, should have led him to realize she was still alive? **[Support]**

ENRICHMENT: Social Studies Connection

Queen Elizabeth I

Queen Elizabeth I loved the theater and is said to have enjoyed the plays of Shakespeare in particular. She generally demanded to see a new play. Elizabeth did not attend the theater—the theater came to her. The Chamberlain's Men, of which Shakespeare was a member, performed for the queen on at least thirty-two occasions.

Elizabeth I had high artistic expectations and was an enthusiastic audience member. If she could not hear, she would call out to the actors to speak louder, or move her chair closer to the stage. She was highly critical if she did not like something, but equally appreciative when she did.

Can vengeance be pursued further than death?
Condemnèd villain, I do apprehend thee.
Obey, and go with me; for thou must die.

ROMEO. I must indeed; and therefore came I hither.
Good gentle youth, tempt not a desp'rate man.
Fly hence and leave me. Think upon these gone;
Let them affright thee. I beseech thee, youth,
16 Put not another sin upon my head
By urging me to fury. O, be gone!
By heaven, I love thee better than myself,
For I come hither armed against myself.
Stay not, be gone. Live, and hereafter say
A madman's mercy bid thee run away.

PARIS. I do defy thy conjurations.[14]
And apprehend thee for a felon[15] here.

ROMEO. Wilt thou provoke me? Then have at thee, boy! [*They fight.*]

PAGE. O Lord, they fight! I will go call the watch. [*Exit.* PARIS *falls.*]

PARIS. O, I am slain! If thou be merciful,
Open the tomb, lay me with Juliet. [*Dies.*]

ROMEO. In faith, I will. Let me peruse[16] this face.
Mercutio's kinsman, noble County Paris!
What said my man when my betossèd[17] soul
Did not attend[18] him as we rode? I think
He told me Paris should have married Juliet.
Said he not so, or did I dream it so?
Or am I mad, hearing him talk of Juliet,
To think it was so? O, give me thy hand,
One writ with me in sour misfortune's book!
I'll bury thee in a triumphant grave.
A grave? O, no, a lanthorn,[19] slaught'red youth,
For here lies Juliet, and her beauty makes
This vault a feasting presence[20] full of light.
Death, lie thou there, by a dead man interred.
[*Lays him in the tomb.*]
How oft when men are at the point of death
Have they been merry! Which their keepers[21] call
A lightning before death. O, how may I
Call this a lightning? O my love, my wife!
Death, that hath sucked the honey of thy breath,
Hath had no power yet upon thy beauty.
Thou art not conquered. Beauty's ensign[22] yet
Is crimson in thy lips and in thy cheeks,
17 And death's pale flag is not advancèd there.
Tybalt, liest thou there in thy bloody sheet?
O, what more favor can I do to thee

Reading Strategy
Identifying Causes and Effects What do you think will be the effect of Paris' condemnation of Romeo? Why?

14. conjurations solemn appeals.

15. felon criminal.

16. peruse look over.

17. betossèd upset.

18. attend give attention to.

19. lanthorn windowed structure on top of a room to admit light; also, a lantern.

20. feasting presence chamber fit for a celebration.

21. keepers jailers.

22. ensign banner.

Reading Strategy
Identifying Causes and Effects What is the real cause for Romeo's observation that "death's pale flag is not yet advanced" in Juliet's face?

18 **✓ Reading Check**
What happens to Paris at the tomb?

16 Reading Strategy
Identifying Causes and Effects

- Remind students that other events in the play have resulted from the characters having inaccurate or incomplete information. Ask students what inaccurate information Paris has that makes him so angry at Romeo.
  Answer: Paris knows nothing of the love and marriage of Romeo and Juliet. He thinks that Juliet has died because of her grief over Tybalt, making Romeo the ultimate cause of both deaths.
- Invite students to answer the first Reading Strategy question on p. 867: What do you think will be the effect of Paris's condemnation of Romeo? Why?
  Answer: The two will probably fight, because Paris is determined to arrest Romeo for the murder of Tybalt, and Romeo is determined to resist anyone who tries to keep him away from Juliet.

17 Reading Strategy
Identifying Causes and Effects

- Have students recall another important scene in the play in which someone wanted to fight Romeo and Romeo tried to keep from doing so.
  Answer: In Act III, Scene I, Romeo tried to avoid dueling with Tybalt.
- Ask students to answer the Reading Strategy question on p. 867: What is the real cause for Romeo's observation that "death's pale flag is not yet advanced" in Juliet's face?

Answer: Juliet is not dead.

18 ✓ Reading Check
Answer: Paris is killed by Romeo.

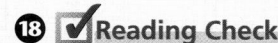

CUSTOMIZE INSTRUCTION FOR UNIVERSAL ACCESS

For English Learners	For Gifted/Talented Students	For Advanced Readers
Invite students to write sentences about Romeo and Juliet using each of the act's vocabulary words on p. 860. Ask them which word they find on this page. To whom is it applied?	Have students work in pairs to practice the exchange between Romeo and Paris and then present the scene to the class.	Have students note the extended metaphor in lines 45–48. Ask them what two things are being compared and what details of the comparison are made in Romeo's words.

19 Reading Strategy

Identifying Causes and Effects

- Ask students what Romeo suggests in lines 109–112 will be accomplished by his death.
  Possible response: Romeo believes that when he dies, the fate that has plagued him ("yoke of inauspicious stars") will come to an end.
- Ask students to answer the Reading Strategy question on p. 868: How is Friar Lawrence's late arrival another example of chance contributing to this tragedy?
  Answer: If Friar Lawrence had arrived minutes earlier, he could have prevented the deaths of Paris and Romeo.

20 Literary Analysis

Tragedy

- Ask students if they think Balthasar is a tragic figure in this play. Why or why not?
  Answer: Balthasar is not a member of the upper class, nor is he a major character, two requirements for a tragic character.
- Ask students to answer the Literary Analysis question on p. 868: Do you think Balthasar could have prevented the tragedy?
  Possible response: Students may say that Balthasar was ordered by Romeo to stay out of the tomb, so he could not have prevented the tragedy.

Than with that hand that cut thy youth in twain
To sunder[23] his that was thine enemy?
Forgive me, cousin! Ah, dear Juliet,
Why art thou yet so fair? Shall I believe
That unsubstantial Death is amorous,[24]
And that the lean abhorrèd monster keeps
Thee here in dark to be his paramour?
For fear of that I still will stay with thee
And never from this pallet[25] of dim night
Depart again. Here, here will I remain
With worms that are thy chambermaids. O, here
Will I set up my everlasting rest
And shake the yoke of inauspicious[26] stars
From this world-wearied flesh. Eyes, look your last!
Arms, take your last embrace! And, lips, O you
The doors of breath, seal with a righteous kiss
A dateless[27] bargain to engrossing[28] death!
Come, bitter conduct;[29] come, unsavory guide!
Thou desperate pilot,[30] now at once run on
The dashing rocks thy seasick weary bark!
Here's to my love! [*Drinks.*] O true apothecary!
Thy drugs are quick. Thus with a kiss I die. [*Falls.*]

[*Enter* FRIAR LAWRENCE, *with lanthorn, crow, and spade.*]

FRIAR. Saint Francis be my speed![31] How oft tonight
Have my old feet stumbled[32] at graves! Who's there?

BALTHASAR. Here's one, a friend, and one that knows you well.

19 **FRIAR.** Bliss be upon you! Tell me, good my friend,
What torch is yond that vainly lends his light
To grubs[33] and eyeless skulls? As I discern,
It burneth in the Capels' monument.

BALTHASAR. It doth so, holy sir; and there's my master,
One that you love.

FRIAR. Who is it?

BALTHASAR. Romeo.

FRIAR. How long hath he been there?

20 **BALTHASAR.** Full half an hour.

FRIAR. Go with me to the vault.

BALTHASAR. I dare not, sir.
My master knows not but I am gone hence,
And fearfully did menace me with death
If I did stay to look on his intents.

FRIAR. Stay then; I'll go alone. Fear comes upon me.
O, much I fear some ill unthrifty[34] thing.

23. **sunder** cut off.

24. **amorous** full of love.

25. **pallet** bed.

26. **inauspicious** promising misfortune.

27. **dateless** eternal.

28. **engrossing** all-encompassing.

29. **conduct** guide (poison).

30. **pilot** captain (Romeo himself).

31. **speed** help.

32. **stumbled** stumbling was thought to be a bad omen.

Reading Strategy
Identifying Causes and Effects How is Friar Lawrence's late arrival another example of chance contributing to this tragedy?

33. **grubs** worms.

Literary Analysis
Tragedy Do you think Balthasar could have prevented this tragedy?

34. **unthrifty** unlucky.

ENRICHMENT: Performing Arts Connection

David Garrick

Actor, director, and writer David Garrick (1717–1779) is credited with reviving the popularity of Shakespeare's plays. In so doing, he also set the precedent for adapting the material to suit himself. Following is Garrick's rewrite of the "death scene" of Romeo and Juliet:

ROMEO: . . . Arms take your last embrace; and lips do you/the doors of breath seal with a righteous kiss./ Soft! soft! She breathes and stirs! (*Juliet wakes.*)

JULIET: Where am I? Defend me, powers!

ROMEO: She speaks, she lives! And we shall still be blessed!/My kind propitious stars o'erpay me now/For all my sorrows past. Rise, rise, my Juliet,/And from this cave of death, this house of horror,/Quick let me snatch thee to Romeo's arms./ There breathe a vital spirit in the lips,/And call thee back to life and love! (*Takes her hand.*)

BALTHASAR. As I did sleep under this yew tree here,
I dreamt my master and another fought,
And that my master slew him.

FRIAR. Romeo!
Alack, alack, what blood is this which stains
The stony entrance of this sepulcher?
What mean these masterless[35] and gory swords
To lie discolored by this place of peace? [*Enters the tomb.*]
Romeo! O, pale! Who else? What, Paris too?
And steeped in blood? Ah, what an unkind[36] hour
Is guilty of this lamentable chance!
The lady stirs. [JULIET *rises.*]

JULIET. O comfortable[37] friar! Where is my lord?
I do remember well where I should be,
And there I am. Where is my Romeo?

FRIAR. I hear some noise. Lady, come from that nest
Of death, contagion, and unnatural sleep.
A greater power than we can contradict
Hath thwarted our intents. Come, come away.
Thy husband in thy bosom there lies dead;
And Paris too. Come, I'll dispose of thee
Among a sisterhood of holy nuns.
Stay not to question, for the watch is coming.
Come, go, good Juliet. I dare no longer stay.

JULIET. Go, get thee hence, for I will not away. [*Exit* FRIAR.]
What's here? A cup, closed in my truelove's hand?
Poison, I see, hath been his timeless[38] end.
O churl![39] Drunk all, and left no friendly drop
To help me after? I will kiss thy lips.
Haply some poison yet doth hang on them
To make me die with a restorative.[40] [*Kisses him.*]
Thy lips are warm!

CHIEF WATCHMAN. [*Within*] Lead, boy. Which way?

JULIET. Yea, noise? Then I'll be brief. O happy[41] dagger!
[*Snatches* ROMEO'S *dagger.*]
This is thy sheath; there rust, and let me die.
[*She stabs herself and falls.*]

[*Enter* PARIS' BOY *and* WATCH.]

BOY. This is the place. There, where the torch doth burn.

CHIEF WATCHMAN. The ground is bloody. Search about the churchyard.
Go, some of you; whoe'er you find attach.[42]
[*Exit some of the* WATCH.]
Pitiful sight! Here lies the County slain;
And Juliet bleeding, warm, and newly dead,

sepulcher (sep′ əl kər) *n.* tomb

35. **masterless** discarded (without masters).

36. **unkind** unnatural.

37. **comfortable** comforting.

Reading Strategy
Identifying Causes and Effects What do you think will be the effect once Juliet discovers that Romeo is dead?

Literary Analysis
Tragedy and Character's Motive Why do you think Friar Lawrence wants to "dispose of Juliet" in a sisterhood of nuns?

38. **timeless** untimely; too soon.

39. **churl** rude fellow.

40. **restorative** medicine.

41. **happy** convenient; opportune.

42. **attach** arrest.

23 **Reading Check**
What does the Friar find when he enters the vault?

21 Reading Strategy
Identifying Causes and Effects

- Ask students what is ironic about Balthasar's description of his dream.
  Answer: The events in his "dream" actually took place.
- Ask students what Juliet's first thought might be as she awakens and sees the Friar.
  Possible response: Students may surmise that Juliet will remember why she is in a tomb and be relieved that the plan is working out.
- Have students answer the Reading Strategy question on p. 869: What do you think will be the effect once Juliet discovers that Romeo is dead?
  Answer: Juliet will kill herself, too.

22 Literary Analysis
Tragedy and Character's Motive

- What explanation does the Friar give to Juliet for what has happened?
  Answer: The Friar lays the blame for the events at the feet of a greater power, which might be the gods, chance, or fate.
- Ask students the Literary Analysis question on p. 869: Why do you think Friar Lawrence wants to "dispose" of Juliet in a sisterhood of nuns?
  Possible response: The Friar may feel that a convent would be the best place for Juliet to recover from her grief and live out her ruined life. A less charitable interpretation is that the Friar hopes to prevent Juliet from revealing the full scope of the tragedy, exposing his own culpability.

23 Reading Check
Answer: The Friar finds both Paris and Romeo dead in the vault.

CUSTOMIZE INSTRUCTION FOR UNIVERSAL ACCESS

For Special Needs Students	For Gifted/Talented Students
Have students take turns reading Romeo's speech on pp. 867–868 aloud. Then, have them discuss whether the speech is a monologue or a soliloquy. Ask them to recall the definitions of both and make a judgment. **Answer:** Romeo's speech is a soliloquy, because even though he delivers it to two characters—as in a monologue—Paris is dead and Juliet cannot hear him. The speech becomes a soliloquy by default.	Ask interested students to prepare a silent performance of the events in the tomb, beginning with Romeo's confrontation with Paris and ending with Juliet's death. All dialogue and emotion will have to be expressed solely by gestures and facial expressions. Have students present their silent performance to the class.

㉔ Background

Film

This scene from Zeffirelli's *Romeo and Juliet* marks the culmination of the tragedy. Have students discuss the movie still, using the following questions:

1. What is so tragic about Juliet's death?
   Answer: Juliet is young and innocent; she had nothing to do with the blood feud between the two families. She wakes only minutes too late. Expecting her husband, she discovers his corpse.
2. Discuss the lighting for this still. What makes it effective?
   Answer: Students may say that the shadows surrounding Juliet suggest the tragic circumstances that have enveloped her, or that death is closing in on her. The lighting focuses attention on Juliet's face and also highlights a column that points visually to Romeo.

㉕ ▶Critical Viewing (p. 871)

Answer: Juliet appears sorrowful, rather than fearful, as she stabs herself.

㉔

CUSTOMIZE INSTRUCTION FOR UNIVERSAL ACCESS

For Advanced Readers

Suggest that students read additional works by William Shakespeare. Provide students with the titles listed in the Enrichment box, ATE p. 872. You may also wish to use **Authors in Depth**, Gold level, which contains the following selections:

- from The *Tragedy of King Lear*, Act I, Scene i (drama, p. 155)
- from *A Midsummer Night's Dream*, Act III, Scene i (drama, p. 161)
- Sonnet 23 (poem, p. 170)
- Sonnet 27 (poem, p. 171
- Sonnet 60 (poem, p. 172
- Sonnet 98 (poem, p. 173)

After students have read these or other works by Shakespeare, have them form discussion groups in which they compare and contrast the selections they have read.

Who here hath lain this two days buriѐd.
Go, tell the Prince; run to the Capulets;
Raise up the Montagues; some others search.
[*Exit others of the* WATCH.]
We see the ground whereon these woes do lie,
But the true ground[43] of all these piteous woes
We cannot without circumstance descry.[44]

26 [*Enter some of the* WATCH, *with* ROMEO'S MAN, BALTHASAR.]

SECOND WATCHMAN. Here's Romeo's man. We found him in
the churchyard.

CHIEF WATCHMAN. Hold him in safety till the Prince come hither.

[*Enter* FRIAR LAWRENCE *and another* WATCHMAN.]

THIRD WATCHMAN. Here is a friar that trembles, sighs and weeps.
We took this mattock and this spade from him
As he was coming from this churchyard's side.

CHIEF WATCHMAN. A great suspicion! Stay the friar too.

[*Enter the* PRINCE *and* ATTENDANTS.]

PRINCE. What misadventure is so early up,
That calls our person from our morning rest?

[*Enter* CAPULET *and his* WIFE *with others.*]

27 **CAPULET.** What should it be, that is so shrieked abroad?

LADY CAPULET. O, the people in the street cry "Romeo,"
Some "Juliet," and some "Paris"; and all run
With open outcry toward our monument.

PRINCE. What fear is this which startles in your ears?

CHIEF WATCHMAN. Sovereign, here lies the County Paris slain;
And Romeo dead; and Juliet, dead before,
Warm and new killed.

28 **PRINCE.** Search, seek, and know how this foul murder comes.

CHIEF WATCHMAN. Here is a friar, and slaughtered Romeo's man,
With instruments upon them fit to open
These dead men's tombs.

CAPULET. O heavens! O wife, look how our daughter bleeds!
This dagger hath mista'en, for, lo, his house[45]
Is empty on the back of Montague,
And it missheathѐd in my daughter's bosom!

LADY CAPULET. O me, this sight of death is as a bell
That warns my old age to a sepulcher.

[*Enter* MONTAGUE *and others.*]

25 ◄ **Critical Viewing**
Does Juliet appear more sorrowful or fearful in this picture? **[Analyze]**

43. ground cause.

44. without circumstance descry see clearly without details.

Literary Analysis
Tragedy How might the tragic ending have been averted if the characters had come to the churchyard in a different order?

Reading Strategy
Identifying Causes and Effects What effect on the local people has the tragedy caused?

Literary Analysis
Tragedy and Character's Motive What motives might the Prince have for directing others to investigate the murder?

45. house sheath.

29 **✓ Reading Check**
Why do the Watchmen search the churchyard?

26 Literary Analysis

- Ask students why the Chief Watchman is demanding that everyone in the vicinity be held, or arrested.
  Answer: The Chief Watchman is acting as a modern police officer would; he is securing the scene of the crime and rounding up suspects.
- Ask students the first Literary Analysis question on p. 871: How might the tragic ending have been averted if the characters had come to the churchyard in a different order?
  Answer: If the Friar had arrived first, he could have explained the circumstances to Romeo; if Paris had arrived after Romeo, Romeo and Juliet might have already fled to Mantua, and so forth.

27 Reading Strategy

Identifying Causes and Effects

- Ask students the Reading Strategy question on p. 871: What effect on the local people has the tragedy caused?
  Answer: All the local people are running to the churchyard, some calling for "Romeo," some for "Juliet," and some for "Paris."

28 Literary Analysis

Tragedy and Character's Motive

- Ask students if they think the Prince contributes to the tragedy in this play, and if so, how?
  Possible response: Students may suggest that the Prince could have intervened in the feuding sooner.
- Ask students the second Literary Analysis question on p. 871: What motives might the Prince have for directing others to investigate the murder?
  Answer: The Prince is related to Mercutio and Paris, so he may think he should not be part of the investigation.

29 ✓ Reading Check

Answer: The Watchmen are searching for people who can explain what has happened in the tomb.

30 Reading Strategy
Identifying Causes and Effects

- Ask students what the Prince means by telling Montague that his son is "early down."
  Answer: The Prince means that Romeo has met an untimely death.
- Have students answer the Reading Strategy question on p. 872: How did Romeo's exile affect his mother?
  Possible response: She died of grief.

31 Literary Analysis
Tragedy

- Ask students to interpret the Friar's words in lines 226–227.
  Possible response: The Friar is admitting that his actions played a part in the deaths of Romeo, Juliet, and Paris, but that he did not actually kill anyone.
- Ask students the Literary Analysis question on p. 872: What examples of fate or character flaws contribute to the tragedy the Friar recounts?
  Answer: Examples of character flaws include: Romeo and Juliet's haste in falling in love and secretly marrying; Romeo's vengeful response to Mercutio's slaying in killing Tybalt; the Capulets' haste in arranging for a marriage that Juliet did not consent to; and Romeo's rash intention to die on learning of Juliet's supposed death. Examples of fate involve messages—the true message that Romeo never receives; the false report he does receive. Multiple instances of "bad timing" on the fatal night are also fateful.

PRINCE. Come, Montague; for thou art early up
To see thy son and heir more early down.

30

MONTAGUE. Alas, my liege,[46] my wife is dead tonight!
Grief of my son's exile hath stopped her breath.
What further woe conspires against mine age?

PRINCE. Look, and thou shalt see.

MONTAGUE. O thou untaught! What manners is in this,
To press before thy father to a grave?

PRINCE. Seal up the mouth of outrage[47] for a while,
Till we can clear these ambiguities
And know their spring, their head, their true descent;
And then will I be general of your woes[48]
And lead you even to death. Meantime forbear,
And let mischance be slave to patience.[49]
Bring forth the parties of suspicion.

FRIAR. I am the greatest, able to do least,
Yet most suspected, as the time and place
Doth make against me, of this direful[50] murder;
And here I stand, both to impeach and purge[51]
Myself condemnèd and myself excused.

PRINCE. Then say at once what thou dost know in this.

31

FRIAR. I will be brief, for my short date of breath[52]
Is not so long as is a tedious tale.
Romeo, there dead, was husband to that Juliet;
And she, there dead, that's Romeo's faithful wife.
I married them; and their stol'n marriage day
Was Tybalt's doomsday, whose untimely death
Banished the new-made bridegroom from this city;
For whom, and not for Tybalt, Juliet pined.
You, to remove that siege of grief from her,
Betrothed and would have married her perforce
To County Paris. Then comes she to me
And with wild looks bid me devise some mean
To rid her from this second marriage,
Or in my cell there would she kill herself.
Then gave I her (so tutored by my art)
A sleeping potion; which so took effect
As I intended, for it wrought on her
The form of death. Meantime I writ to Romeo
That he should hither come as[53] this dire night
To help to take her from her borrowed grave,
Being the time the potion's force should cease,
But he which bore my letter, Friar John,
Was stayed by accident, and yesternight
Returned my letter back. Then all alone

46. **liege** (lēj) Lord.

Reading Strategy
Identifying Causes and Effects How did Romeo's exile affect his mother?

47. **mouth of outrage** violent cries.

ambiguities (am′ bə gyo͞o′ ə tēz) *n.* statements or events whose meanings are unclear

48. **general . . . woes** leader in your sorrow.

49. **let . . . patience** be patient in the face of misfortune.

50. **direful** terrible.

51. **impeach and purge** accuse and declare blameless.

52. **date of breath** term of life.

Literary Analysis
Tragedy What examples of fate or character flaws contribute to the tragedy the Friar recounts?

53. **as** on.

ENRICHMENT: Literature Connection
Four Hundred Years Later

If William Shakespeare were alive today, he would be making a fortune collecting residuals for *The Tragedy of Romeo and Juliet.* Residuals are fees collected by performers and writers for each rerun of filmed or taped material. Since the dawning of the motion-picture industry, many of Shakespeare's plays have been made into movies. Hollywood producers and directors realize that Shakespeare's plays combine dramatic situations with universal themes, a combination that translates into success at the box office. Movies based upon Shakespearean plays include *Romeo and Juliet, Macbeth, Othello, Hamlet, Henry V, Richard II, Julius Caesar, King Lear, Antony and Cleopatra, Titus Andronicus*, and *Kiss Me Kate* (based upon *The Taming of the Shrew*).

For more information about modern adaptations of Shakespeare's plays, see "Shakespeare in Today's World" on pp. 878–879.

At the prefixèd hour of her waking
Came I to take her from her kindred's vault;
Meaning to keep her closely[54] at my cell
Till I conveniently could send to Romeo.
But when I came, some minute ere the time
Of her awakening, here untimely lay
The noble Paris and true Romeo dead.
She wakes; and I entreated her come forth
And bear this work of heaven with patience;
But then a noise did scare me from the tomb,
And she, too desperate, would not go with me,
But, as it seems, did violence on herself.
All this I know, and to the marriage
Her nurse is privy;[55] and if aught in this
Miscarried by my fault, let my old life
Be sacrificed some hour before his time
Unto the rigor[56] of severest law.

PRINCE. We still have known thee for a holy man.
Where's Romeo's man? What can he say to this?

BALTHASAR. I brought my master news of Juliet's death;
And then in post he came from Mantua
To this same place, to this same monument.
This letter he early bid me give his father,
And threat'ned me with death, going in the vault,
If I departed not and left him there.

PRINCE. Give me the letter. I will look on it.
Where is the County's page that raised the watch?
Sirrah, what made your master[57] in this place?

BOY. He came with flowers to strew his lady's grave;
And bid me stand aloof, and so I did.
Anon comes one with light to ope the tomb;
And by and by my master drew on him;
And then I ran away to call the watch.

PRINCE. This letter doth make good the friar's words,
Their course of love, the tidings of her death;
And here he writes that he did buy a poison
Of a poor pothecary and therewithal
Came to this vault to die and lie with Juliet.
Where be these enemies? Capulet, Montague,
See what a scourge is laid upon your hate,
That heaven finds means to kill your joys with love.
And I, for winking at[58] your discords too,
Have lost a brace[59] of kinsmen. All are punished.

CAPULET. O brother Montague, give me thy hand.
This is my daughter's jointure,[60] for no more

54. closely hidden; secretly.

55. privy secretly informed about.

56. rigor strictness.

Reading Strategy
Identifying Causes and Effects What could the Friar have done differently that might have prevented the tragedy from happening?

57. made your master was your master doing.

Literary Analysis
Tragedy Explain the tragedy of Paris' circumstances.

58. winking at closing my eyes to.

59. brace pair (Mercutio and Paris).

60. jointure wedding gift; marriage settlement.

scourge (skurj) *n.* whip or other instrument for inflicting punishment

34 **Reading Check**
How do the details of the letter compare with the Friar's story?

32 Reading Strategy
Identifying Causes and Effects

- Ask students to read lines 266–269. What punishment does the Friar suggest if he is deemed responsible?
  Answer: The Friar says that if the tragedy is his fault, by law he should be executed.
- Ask students the Reading Strategy question on p. 873: What could the Friar have done differently that might have prevented the tragedy from happening?
  Answer: Students may suggest that Friar Lawrence could have avoided the feigned death and instead, arranged for Juliet to run away to join Romeo in Mantua. He could have gotten word to Romeo by more reliable means; he could have gone more quickly to the tomb; he could have prevented Juliet's suicide by insisting that she leave with him, or by staying with her to face the watch.

33 Literary Analysis
Tragedy

- Ask students to recall why Paris has come to the Capulet tomb.
  Answer: Paris has come to mourn Juliet and bring her flowers.
- Have students respond to the Literary Analysis statement on p. 873: Explain the tragedy of Paris's circumstances.
  Possible response: Students may say that Paris's tragedy is that he is always in the dark, never knowing what is going on. Even as he dies, he thinks he is trying to arrest Romeo for the death of Tybalt; he does not know Romeo and Juliet have married.

34 Reading Check

Answer: The Prince says Romeo's letter "doth make good the friar's words"; that is, the letter confirms the Friar's story.

CUSTOMIZE INSTRUCTION FOR UNIVERSAL ACCESS

For Special Needs Students	For Less Proficient Readers
Explain that in the action on these pages, everyone is being brought on stage for the *denouement,* the outcome or solution of a complex sequence of events. In the denouement, all the pieces come together and, for the first time, everyone knows the whole story. Have students relate the action in the play to the conclusions of film and television mysteries, in which the detective calls together the various characters and explains the solution to the mystery.	Students can use the information in Friar Lawrence's speech to create a graphic organizer that displays the misunderstandings that led to the tragedy. You may wish to demonstrate the Herringbone Organizer, p. 71 in **Writing Models and Graphic Organizers on Transparencies.**

ASSESS

Answers for p. 874

Review and Assess

1. Students may be surprised that Romeo kills Paris, or that Lady Montague dies of grief.
2. **(a)** Romeo is challenging fate, asserting that nothing can keep him from Juliet. **(b)** This is consistent with his rash, impulsive, dramatic character.
3. **(a)** The events include: Friar John does not deliver the plan to Romeo; the Capulets push up the date for Juliet's wedding; Romeo arrives at the tomb before the Friar; Juliet wakes up too late. **(b)** The Friar's plan relies too much on perfect communication and timing.
4. **(a)** Believing Juliet dead, Romeo takes poison. Juliet, finding Romeo dead, stabs herself with his dagger. **(b)** Students' answers may balance the rashness and impulsiveness of the lovers, the stubbornness of their families, and incompetence of the Friar against a host of bad luck: unlucky encounters, missed messages, and a too-late awakening.
5. **(a)** Students may suggest that if the apothecary had not sold the poison to Romeo, he would have found another way to kill himself. **(b)** Students may cite Friar John's failure to deliver the plan, Paris's visit to the tomb, Friar Lawrence's tardiness, and so on.
6. **(a)** The fathers shake hands and each promises to build a monument in memory of the other man's child. **(b)** Some students may say the deaths were necessary to sober the two sides. Other students may say that the marriage might have been sufficient to end the feud. **(c)** Students may say that tragedies often lead only to more tragedies.
7. The play shows that hate can lead to misunderstandings and unnecessary violence.

Can I demand.

MONTAGUE. But I can give thee more;
For I will raise her statue in pure gold,
That whiles Verona by that name is known,
There shall no figure at such rate[61] be set
As that of true and faithful Juliet.

CAPULET. As rich shall Romeo's by his lady's lie—
Poor sacrifices of our enmity![62]

PRINCE. A glooming[63] peace this morning with it brings.
The sun for sorrow will not show his head.
Go hence, to have more talk of these sad things;
Some shall be pardoned, and some punishèd;
For never was a story of more woe
Than this of Juliet and her Romeo. *[Exit all.]*

61. **rate** value.

62. **enmity** hostility.

63. **glooming** cloudy; gloomy.

Review and Assess

Thinking About Act V

1. **Respond:** Were you in any way surprised by the way in which this play ends? Why or why not?
2. **(a) Recall:** In Act V, Scene i, what news causes Romeo to exclaim, "Then I defy you, stars"? **(b) Connect:** How are Romeo's words consistent with what you know of his character?
3. **(a) Recall:** Identify at least three events that cause the Friar's scheme to fail. **(b) Analyze:** Why is it not surprising that the scheme fails?
4. **(a) Recall:** How do Romeo and Juliet die? **(b) Make a Judgment:** Which is most to blame for the lovers' deaths—chance, the lovers themselves, or their families? Explain.
5. **(a) Speculate:** How do you think events would have turned out if the apothecary had refused to sell poison to Romeo? **(b) Hypothesize:** What other unique actions in the chain of events, if avoided, could have changed the play's outcome?
6. **(a) Recall:** How does the relationship of the feuding families change at the end of the play? **(b) Draw Conclusions:** Were Romeo and Juliet's deaths necessary for the feud to end? Explain. **(c) Assess:** Do you think tragedies always lead to peace?
7. **Evaluate:** In what ways does Shakespeare's play provide a valuable lesson about the destructive effects of hatred?

ASSESSMENT PRACTICE: Literary Response

Defending Interpretations (For more practice, see Test Preparation Workbook, p. 50.)

Some tests require students to defend their interpretations of literature. Use the following excerpt to provide practice in defending interpretations.

ROMEO: Stay not, be gone. Live, and hereafter say/ A madman's mercy bid thee run away.

PARIS: I do defy thy conjurations./ And apprehend thee for a felon here.

ROMEO: Wilt thou provoke me? Then have at thee, boy! (They fight.)

What is Romeo's state of mind at this point? Support your answer with evidence from the play.

Possible answer: Romeo is distraught, as evidenced by the fact that he calls himself a madman, yet he is still at the mercy of his volatile temper, for when Paris defies him, Romeo is quick to draw his sword. Point out to students that they do not have to have the same interpretation as the sample answer, but they do have to give evidence from the text to support their interpretations.

Review and Assess

Literary Analysis

Tragedy

1. Use a chart like the one shown to list the elements that contribute to the **tragedy.**

Romeo's and Juliet's Personalities	Fate or Chance	Other Causes

2. What theme or message does Shakespeare attempt to convey through the tragic events in the play? Explain.
3. What positive message about the human spirit does Shakespeare convey through the play? Explain.

Connecting Literary Elements

4. (a) What is the Friar's **motive** for helping Romeo and Juliet? (b) Why does his plan ultimately fail?
5. What is the Nurse's motive for defying the wishes of the Capulets?
6. What are the fathers' motives for building monuments to their children at the end of the play?
7. Who is most guilty for the tragedy? Explain your choice.

Reading Strategy

Identifying Causes and Effects

8. Use a chart like this one to summarize the chain of **causes and effects** outlined by the Friar in his monologue in Act V, Scene iii.

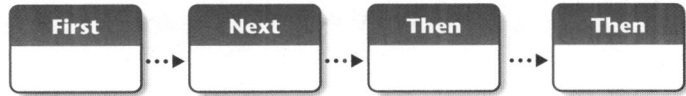

First	→ Next	→ Then	→ Then

9. What chain of events leads to the death of Paris?

Extend Understanding

10. **World Events Connection:** How might the lesson that the play teaches be applied to a specific situation in today's world?

Quick Review

A **tragedy** is a drama in which a central character of noble rank meets with disaster or overwhelming misfortune.

A **character's motive** is the reason an individual thinks and acts in a certain way.

A **cause** is an action, an event, or a situation that produces a result.

An **effect** is the result produced by a cause.

Take It to the Net

www.phschool.com

Take the interactive self-test online to check your understanding of Act V.

ENRICHMENT: Further Reading

Other Works by William Shakespeare

A Midsummer Night's Dream

The Taming of the Shrew

Antony and Cleopatra

Take It to the Net

Visit www.phschool.com for additional information on William Shakespeare.

Answers for p. 875

1. Romeo's and Juliet's Personalities: Romeo - impulsive, hotheaded, melodramatic; Juliet: strong-willed, disobedient; Fate or Chance: the accidental meeting of the two lovers; Tybalt's misunderstanding of Romeo's presence at the Capulets; the things that go wrong with the Friar's plan; the Friar's late arrival at the tomb; Other Causes: The feud between the Montagues and the Capulets
2. Shakespeare appears to be making a statement about the loyalty of the lovers in contrast to the ill-advised feud between their families. He is saying that old anger can destroy new love.
3. Shakespeare appears to be saying that young and true lovers will risk pain and danger to keep their love.
4. The Friar wants to end the feud between the families. **(b)** His plan is too elaborate and time-sensitive.
5. Some students may say that she is moved by Juliet's grief; others may say that she is fickle and impulsive in nature.
6. The fathers want to people to know that Romeo and Juliet were true and faithful to one another.
7. Students may lay the blame at the feet of Romeo and Juliet, or the Friar, or the feuding families. Some students may say that since fate is mentioned in the Prologue and elsewhere, that fate pulled all the strings.
8. First: Friar married Romeo and Juliet; Next: Romeo killed Tybalt; Then: The Capulets planned Juliet's marriage to Paris; Then: Juliet came to the Friar for help; Then: The Friar conceived the potion plan; Then: The Friar wrote to Romeo but the letters did not get to him; Then: The Friar went to Juliet's tomb and found Romeo and Paris dead: Then: Juliet awoke and, finding Romeo dead, killed herself.

continued

Answers continued

9. Paris comes to the tomb to bring flowers for Juliet; he meets Romeo there and tries to arrest him for the death of Tybalt; Paris fights Romeo and dies.
10. Students may cite specific examples of national and civil conflicts that should be set aside so that the individuals within the group do not suffer tragedy.

EXTEND

Answers for p. 876

❶ Vocabulary Development

Word Analysis

1. ambidextrous
2. ambilateral

Spelling Strategy

1. tragedies
2. furies
3. enmities

Concept Development: Synonyms

1. b
2. a
3. c
4. b
5. c
6. b

❷ Grammar

1. Both/their
2. Each/his
3. Many/their
4. One/his
5. Neither/its

Writing Application

Sample sentences:

Both fathers regretted their useless feud.

One of the servants was too frightened to stay with his master.

Integrate Language Skills

❶ Vocabulary Development Lesson

Word Analysis: Latin Prefix *ambi-*

The Latin prefix *ambi-* means "both." It appears in *ambiguities*, which means "statements or events having two or more possible meanings." In your notebook, complete each sentence below with one of the following words.

a. ambidextrous **b.** ambilateral

1. The __?__ man used both hands with equal skill.
2. The __?__ pain hurt both sides of my body.

Spelling Strategy

If a noun ends in *y* preceded by a consonant, change the *y* to *i* and add *-es* to form the plural. For example, *ambiguities* is the plural of *ambiguity*. Write the plural of each of these nouns.

1. tragedy 2. fury 3. enmity

Concept Development: Synonyms

In your notebook, write the word that is the best synonym for the first word. To help you, review the vocabulary list on page 860.

1. remnants: (a) cloths, (b) remains, (c) factors
2. penury: (a) poverty, (b) currency, (c) disease
3. haughty: (a) timid, (b) friendly, (c) arrogant
4. sepulcher: (a) monument, (b) tomb, (c) cemetery
5. ambiguities: (a) vows, (b) details, (c) uncertainties
6. scourge: (a) sorrow, (b) punishment, (c) hatred

❷ Grammar Lesson

Agreement With Indefinite Pronouns

Indefinite pronouns refer to people, places, or things, often without specifying which ones. Indefinite pronouns may be singular (such as *each*, *neither*, or *one*) or plural (such as *both* or *many*).

When you write a sentence with a personal pronoun that has an indefinite pronoun as its antecedent, you must make sure the pronouns agree in number. In the examples below, the indefinite pronoun is underlined and the personal pronoun is in italics.

Singular: One of the friars stayed in *his* quarters.
Plural: Both of the friars were quarantined in *their* house.

Practice Write each sentence, circling the indefinite pronoun and choosing the personal pronoun that completes the sentence correctly.

1. Both of the lovers lost (his, their) lives.
2. Each of the fathers mourned (his, their) child.
3. Many were shocked by (its, their) discovery.
4. One of the lovers poisoned (his, their) lips.
5. Neither of the families was happy with (its, their) loss.

Writing Application Write two sentences about Act V, using a singular indefinite pronoun and personal pronoun in one and a plural indefinite pronoun and personal pronoun in the other.

WG Prentice Hall Writing and Grammar Connection: Chapter 25, Section 2

TEACHING RESOURCES

The following resources can be used to enrich or extend the instruction for pp. 876–877.

Vocabulary

- **Selection Support:** Build Vocabulary, p. 197
- **Vocabulary and Spelling Practice Book** (Use this booklet for skills enrichment.)

Grammar

- **Selection Support:** Build Grammar Skills, p. 198 ■
- **Writing and Grammar,** Gold Level, p. 584 ■

- **Daily Language Practice Transparencies**

Writing

- **Writing and Grammar,** Gold Level, p. 141 ■
- **Writing and Grammar iText CD-ROM**
- **Writing Models and Graphic Organizers on Transparencies,** p. 56

■ **BLOCK SCHEDULING:** Resources marked with this symbol provide varied instruction during 90-minute blocks.

❸ Writing Lesson

Persuasive Letter

A letter from Friar Lawrence to both families, urging them to end their feud, might have saved Romeo and Juliet's lives. As the Friar, develop a persuasive letter to send to both families right after you have married their children.

Prewriting Your letter should appeal both to reason and to emotion. Make a list of factual evidence and emotional pleas that might convince the families to end their feud.

Drafting Begin your draft by announcing the marriage ceremony you have just performed. Then, arrange your persuasive appeals in a logical order.

Revising Read your draft as if you were Montague or Capulet. Determine whether the letter appeals equally to both your mind and heart. If not, revise it so that the appeals are both strong and balanced.

Model: Revising to Balance Persuasive Appeals

The hatred between your families is forcing your children to be apart and is threatening their happiness. *They each live behind gated walls and have to sneak into each other's homes to be together.* They are even afraid that something bad might happen if they attempt to tell their families of their marriage. Do you want your children to be miserable?

Adding factual information makes the letter more persuasive by balancing appeals to reason and emotion.

WG Prentice Hall Writing and Grammar Connection: Chapter 7, Section 4

❹ Extension Activities

Listening and Speaking Hold a **mock trial** to investigate the causes of the tragedy. Follow these steps:

- Assign roles—the main characters, the lawyer, the judge, and the jury.
- Take depositions in which each character tells the story from his or her perspective.

When the court is in session, lawyers should question and cross-examine witnesses before the jury reaches a verdict. **[Group Activity]**

Research and Technology Imagine that you and a group of classmates have been hired to create a **set design** for a modern-day version of *Romeo and Juliet*. Decide on an appropriate setting for the adaptation, such as in a large modern city. Then, use computer software or posterboard to create diagrams for your set design.

Take It to the Net www.phschool.com

Go online for an additional research activity using the Internet.

ASSESSMENT RESOURCES

The following resources can be used to assess students' knowledge and skills.

Selection Assessment

- **Formal Assessment,** Selection Test, pp. 176–178
- **Open Book Test,** pp. 148–150
- **Got It! Assessment Videotapes,** Tape 4
- **Test Bank Software**

Take It to the Net

Visit www.phschool.com for self-tests and additional questions on *Romeo and Juliet.*

PRENTICE HALL ASSESSMENT SYSTEM

- **Workbook**
- **Skill Book**
- **Transparencies**
- **CD-ROM**

❸ Writing Lesson

- Have students work in pairs to brainstorm for a list of reasons defending the secret marriage.
- After students have drafted the content of their letters, you may wish to display the Business Letter Transparency in **Writing Models and Graphic Organizers on Transparencies,** p. 56, to show students the appropriate form for their letters.
- As an extension of this activity, ask students to exchange letters with partners and write responses to the Friar as Capulet or Montague.

❹ Listening and Speaking

- Help the class to assign roles to the characters for the mock trial.
- Students giving depositions may speak into a tape recorder, or another student may write his or her testimony in writing.
- Hold the mock trial in class and determine who is to be held responsible for the deaths of Romeo and Juliet.

CUSTOMIZE INSTRUCTION For Universal Access

To address different learning styles, use the activities suggested in the **Extension Activities** booklet, p. 48.

- For Bodily/Kinesthetic and Interpersonal Learners, use Activity 5.
- For Interpersonal and Verbal/Linguistic Learners, use Activity 6.
- For Interpersonal and Verbal/Linguistic Learners, use Activity 7.

Lesson Objectives

1. To understand the connection between Shakespeare's plays and their modern adaptations
2. To become familiar with examples of modern adaptations of Shakespeare's work

Connections

Theater has been a part of civilization for thousands of years. Archaeologists have uncovered ruins of the outdoor theaters used by the ancient Greeks. The Globe theater, in which Shakespeare's plays were staged, was typical of performing spaces in the sixteenth century. Later on, theaters became grand interior spaces with seating for more than a thousand spectators. Today, theaters come in all shapes and sizes, and dramatic presentations are performed not just on stages, but in movies, television dramas, musicals, operas, and ballets.

Shakespeare in Today's World

- Take an informal survey of students to see if any have heard of —or seen—the musical *West Side Story,* or the movie *Shakespeare in Love*.
- Point out that these works are based on plays written by William Shakespeare—about four hundred years ago.
- Ask students to discuss which of these performances they have most enjoyed and why.

CONNECTIONS

Literature and Media

Shakespeare in Today's World

After reading *Romeo and Juliet*, you may be inspired to view a production of the play. You have plenty of options. Shakespeare's plays, though 400 years old, are still performed on stages throughout the world. In addition, his works have been adapted successfully as movies, television dramas, musicals, operas, and ballets.

Adaptations of *Romeo and Juliet*

If you care to watch a video of *Romeo and Juliet,* one choice is the 1968 film directed by Franco Zeffirelli. Another is the 1996 movie starring Leonardo DiCaprio. Both films remain faithful to Shakespeare's language and plot. In the 1996 version, however, the actors wear modern clothing and even drive around in cars!

To see *Romeo and Juliet* as a ballet, you could watch the 1966 film starring Rudolph Nureyev and Margot Fonteyn. This adaptation tells the story entirely through dance and contains no words.

In 1957, *Romeo and Juliet* served as the basis for a successful Broadway musical, *West Side Story*. The show's creators borrowed the basic Shakespearean plot but modernized the characters and events. The feuding Montagues and Capulets were replaced by rival New York City street gangs, the Jets and Sharks. The famous balcony scene with Juliet and Romeo became a fire-escape scene with Maria and Tony. The musical was made into a popular movie in 1961.

In 1998, the Academy Award for Best Movie went to *Shakespeare in Love*. Its story surmises the circumstances under which Shakespeare wrote *Romeo and Juliet*. You will find parallels between the characters in the story and the characters in Shakespeare's play, and knowledge of the play will enhance your understanding of the film starring Gwyneth Paltrow.

More Shakespeare at the Movies

Most of Shakespeare's plays have been adapted as movies. The first Shakespearean movie ever made was *King John,* in 1899. It was directed by Sir Herbert Beerbohm Tree, who also played the title role.

ENRICHMENT: Literature

Shakespeare's Source

Just as the movie *West Side Story* was based on Shakespeare's play *Romeo and Juliet, Romeo and Juliet* was based on a poem written in 1562 by Arthur Brooke. Shakespeare used the characters in Brooke's poem, but developed them in much greater depth and detail.

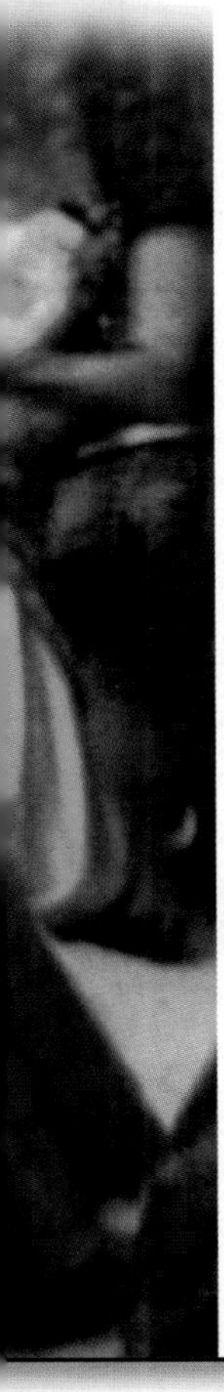

Today, popular film adaptations of Shakespeare's plays include the following:

- *Love's Labour's Lost* (2000), with Nathan Lane and Alicia Silverstone
- *Othello* (1995), with Lawrence Fishburne and Kenneth Branagh
- *Hamlet* (1990), with Mel Gibson and Glenn Close
- *Julius Caesar* (1970), with Jason Robards, Charlton Heston, and Diana Rigg; there is also a 1953 version, with Marlon Brando and John Gielgud
- *10 Things I Hate About You* (1999), a modern-day teenage comedy based on *The Taming of the Shrew*

Shakespeare on Stage

Stage directors all over the world have experimented with unusual techniques and interpretations of Shakespeare's works. For example, in 1970, Peter Brook staged *A Midsummer Night's Dream* using a large white box for the set, while two of the main characters swung on trapezes above the other actors.

Titus Andronicus is one of Shakespeare's most violent plays. In 1955, when Peter Brook staged it quite vividly at Stratford, England, with Laurence Olivier and Vivien Leigh, audience members had to be carried away in ambulances every night!

Many playwrights have created original plays based on Shakespeare's works. One noted example is Tom Stoppard's comedy *Rosencrantz and Guildenstern Are Dead*, which highlights two minor characters from *Hamlet*.

Shakespeare in Musicals

West Side Story is not the only popular Broadway musical based on a Shakespearean play. Another famous example is Cole Porter's *Kiss Me, Kate*, which presents backstage bickering among actors during their out-of-town tryout of *The Taming of the Shrew*. As the musical unfolds, the lives of the actors parallel the lives of the Shakespearean characters they portray.

Television Productions

All of Shakespeare's plays have been adapted as television dramas. Notable productions include the following:

- *Othello* (BBC, 1983), with Anthony Hopkins
- *Love's Labour's Lost* (BBC, 1984), set in the 1700s

Connecting Literature and Media

1. Why do you think Shakespeare's plays have such popular appeal as modern movies and musicals?
2. Some people object to any modernization of Shakespeare's plays, claiming that such productions cheapen the original. What is your opinion?

CUSTOMIZE INSTRUCTION FOR UNIVERSAL ACCESS

For Less Proficient Readers	For English Learners
To aid student comprehension, have students create timelines based on the information in this selection. Students can then refer to the information in their timelines to help them keep track of the events described.	Students may have difficulty with the technical language in this selection. Review with students the vocabulary words and footnotes before they read, making sure they can properly pronounce each word and understand its definition.

Answers

Connecting Literature and Media

1. Shakespeare's plays are based on timeless themes, including ill-fated love and the struggle for power. The vividness of his characters and the rich beauty of his language also sustain the appeal of his work in modern times.
2. Students will likely respond that modern adaptations of Shakespeare's plays make them seem more relevant to today's viewers. Some students may note that Shakespeare himself constantly adapted and recycled the works of other writers in his plays.

Lesson Objectives

1. To learn how to use an atlas to find information
2. To learn to skim and scan reference materials

About Atlas Entries

- If possible, have several examples of atlases available for students to review in the classroom.
- Ask students to look through the atlases and identify the types of information they contain.
  Possible answers: Many atlases contain information on population, climate, government, transportation, tourism, crops, industries, imports, and exports.
- Ask students to identify the types of information they can find in the legend of a map.
  Answers: Most legends provide information that explains the symbols used on a map to show features such as capital cities, land height, and distance.

Reading Strategy

Skimming and Scanning

- Point out that when students skim or scan informational material, they should let their eyes slip over the page, taking in titles, subheads, and other text in large or bold print.
- Explain that these key points serve as markers for more detailed information. If students see the topic they want to know about in bold letters, for example, they can stop and read that section in more detail.
- Have students use the graphic organizer on p. 880 to gain practical experience with the concepts of skimming and scanning.

READING INFORMATIONAL MATERIALS

Atlas Entries

About Atlas Entries

An atlas is a book of maps showing physical features of the world, such as cities, mountains, rivers, and roads. Some atlases include facts and statistics about the places depicted. Many modern atlases, like the Dorling Kindersley atlas (whose pages are shown here), provide brief articles on topics such as these:

- Population
- Climate
- Government
- Transportation
- Tourism

The maps in an atlas usually are accompanied by a *legend,* a key that explains the symbols and colors used in the map. For example, symbols might represent features such as national or state capitals. Color codes might be used to indicate land height or density of population. The legend also indicates to what mileage the map is scaled.

Reading Strategy

Skimming and Scanning

Atlases and other reference materials provide a broad range of information. To find what you need, adjust your reading rate by skimming or scanning.

- By **skimming,** you can get an idea of the organization and scope of a work before reading it. To skim, read quickly, taking in words in groups. Stop for headings and other text that is set off, such as bold text.
- By **scanning,** you can locate specific information fast. Move your eyes quickly over the page. Look for words related to the information you are seeking. Stop and read the paragraphs that contain the words you are seeking.

Skim the atlas entry on the following pages. Use a graphic organizer like the one at right to record each kind of information you can find on the page.

Subjects Covered	How I Know
Climate of Italy	Listed as a heading on the page
Transportation in Italy	Listed as a heading on the page, shown with icons of a ship and a plane

ITALY

Adapted from *Dorling Kindersley World Reference Atlas*

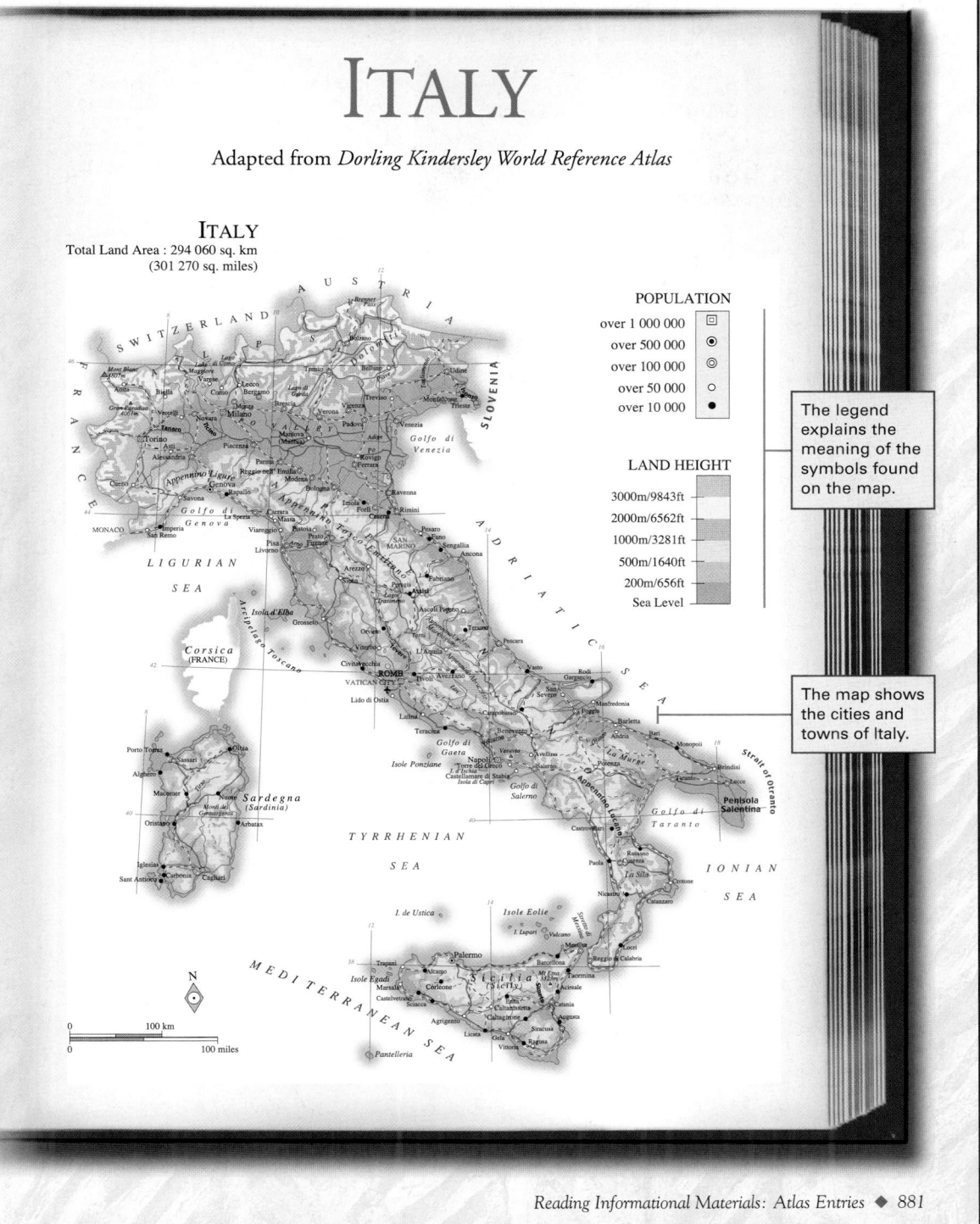

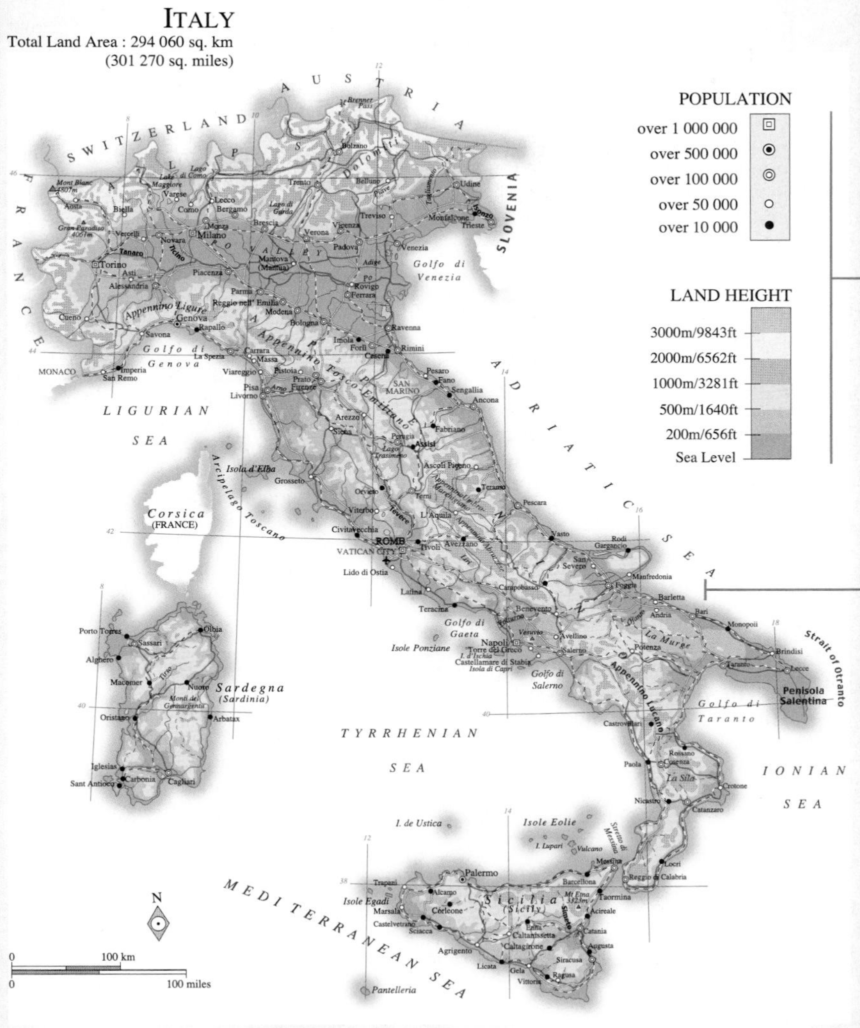

The legend explains the meaning of the symbols found on the map.

The map shows the cities and towns of Italy.

Italy

- Remind students to use a chart like the one on p. 880 as they skim and scan the map of Italy on this page.
- Ask students which features on the page most catch their eye. **Possible answers:** Students may have noticed the shape of the landmass, the main titles on the page (Italy, Population, and Land Height).

Italy

- Encourage students to use the reading strategies of skimming and scanning to catch the highlights of text on this page.
- Remind students that titles, subheads, and icons are positioned to draw the reader's eye and direct the reader to more detailed information.
- Ask students which four main subheads appear on this page. Answer: The four subheads include Climate, Transportation, Tourism, and People.

The atlas article begins with a list of basic information about the country depicted in the map.

ITALY

Official Name: *Italian Republic*
Capital: *Rome*
Population: *57.2 million*
Currency: *Italian lira*
Official Language: *Italian*

Lying in southern Europe, Italy comprises the famous boot-shaped peninsula stretching 500 miles into the Mediterranean and a number of islands—Sicily and Sardinia being the largest. The Alps form a natural boundary to the north, while the Apennine Mountains run the length of the peninsula. The south is an area of seismic activity, epitomized by the volcanoes of Mounts Etna and Vesuvius. United under ancient Roman rule, Italy subsequently developed into a series of competing kingdoms and states, not fully reunited until 1870. Italian politics was dominated by the Christian Democrats (CD) from 1945 to 1992 under a system of political patronage and a succession of short-lived governments. Investigations into corruption from 1992 on led to the demise of this system in the elections of 1994.

Subheads break the information into the same specific categories for each country.

Symbols highlight key information in each category.

CLIMATE

Southern Italy has a Mediterranean climate; the north is more temperate. Summers are hot and dry, especially in the south. Temperatures range from 75°F to over 81°F in Sardinia and Sicily. Southern winters are mild; northern ones are cooler and wetter. The mountains usually experience heavy snow. The Adriatic coast suffers from cold winds such as the bora.

TRANSPORTATION

Leonardo da Vinci (Fiumicino), Rome 15.55m passengers

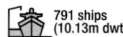

791 ships (10.13m dwt)

Many of Italy's key routes are congested. The trans-Apennine *autostrada* (expressway) from Bologna to Florence is being doubled in size. A high-speed train program (*treno ad alta velocità*—TAV) is planned to link Turin, Milan, Venice, Bologna, Florence and Naples to Rome. Most of Italy's exports travel by road, via Switzerland and Austria. Only 16% goes by sea.

TOURISM

27.5m visitors

Up 4% in 1994

Italy has been a tourist destination since the 16th century and probably invented the concept. Roman Popes consciously aimed to make their city the most beautiful in the world to attract travelers. In the 18th century, Italy was the focus of any Grand Tour. Today, its many unspoilt centers of Renaissance culture continue to make Italy one of the world's major tourism destinations. The industry accounts for 3% of Italy's GDP, and hotels and restaurants employ one million out of a working population of 21 million.

Most visitors travel to the northern half of the country, to cities such as Rome, Florence, Venice and Padova. Many are increasingly traveling to the northern lakes. Beach resorts such as Rimini attract a large, youthful crowd in summer. Italy is also growing in popularity as a skiing destination.

PEOPLE

Italian, German, French, Rhaeto-Romanic, Sardinian

505 people per sq. mile

Italy is a remarkably homogenous society. Most Italians are Roman Catholics, and Italy has far fewer ethnic minorities than its EU neighbors. Most are fairly recent immigrants from Ethiopia, the Philippines and Egypt. A sharp rise in illegal immigration in the 1980's and 1990's, from North and West Africa, Turkey and Albania, generated a right-wing backlash and tighter controls. It became a major election issue in 1993 and a factor in the rise of the federalist Northern League.

CUSTOMIZE INSTRUCTION FOR UNIVERSAL ACCESS

For Special Needs Students	For Advanced Readers
Explain to students that they don't need to read each word on p. 882. Instead, they should look for key words that show the location of more detailed information. Then, when they need to read in greater depth, they can use the key words as a road map to find the information they're looking for.	Ask students to locate two information pages on the Internet, one that is well suited to skimming and scanning, and one that is not. After students locate the pages, have them analyze why one works well for skimming and scanning and the other doesn't. Point out that the page that works well will probably use titles, subheads, and icons to catch the eye—similar to atlas entries.

Check Your Comprehension

1. Which four seas border Italy?
2. What is the approximate population of Napoli?
3. What percentage of Italy's exports travel by sea?

Applying the Reading Strategy

Skimming and Scanning

4. (a) By skimming and scanning, find and list the languages of Italy. (b) Where did you find the information?
5. Why is *Rome* printed in bold, capital letters on the map?
6. Which symbol indicates a city with more than 50,000 people?

Activity

Asking Questions About an Atlas Entry

An atlas entry presents a large amount of information. Some details are found in the map itself, and other details are found in the accompanying text.

Help your classmates assess how well they understand the atlas entry about Italy. Write several questions based on information located in the map and in the accompanying articles. Challenge your classmates to supply the answers, using the atlas entry.

Contrasting Informational Texts

Atlases and Guidebooks

1. The atlas entry you read is one place to find information about Italy. However, if you were touring Italy, you would probably use a guidebook instead of an atlas to learn about the country. Find a tourist guidebook for Italy or any other country. Skim and scan it to determine the kinds of information it offers. Completing a chart like the one shown, note key differences between the sources.

Contrasting Sources

	Tourist Guidebook	Atlas Entry
Maps		
Articles		

2. Using the information in your chart, explain how the purpose of informational materials determines their content.
3. Read several sections in your tourist guidebook. Choose one section that you find particularly interesting and helpful. Offer a brief summary of the information to classmates.

Answers for p. 883

Check Your Comprehension

1. The Adriatic, Ligurian, Tyrrhenian, and Ionian seas border Italy.
2. Napoli has a population of over one million.
3. Only 16% of Italy's exports travel by sea.

Applying the Reading Strategy

4. (a) The official language of Italy is Italian. (b) This information is given in the list of basic information at the beginning of the article.
5. Rome is the capital of Italy.
6. An empty circle indicates a city of more than 50,000.

Activity

- Read the Activity on p. 883 aloud to the class.
- Consider having students turn in their questions to you, then stage a contest to see which student(s) can most quickly locate the correct answers.

Contrasting Informational Texts

1. Students may report that guidebooks include information such as tourist attractions and more detailed accounts of history, customs, and culture.
2. Students may respond that some types of informational materials, such as atlases, are intended to provide an overview of a subject. Therefore, such materials include a small amount of information on a large number of subjects. Other informational materials are intended to provide comprehensive information on a subject. Therefore, such materials focus on a single subject, and go into greater depth with both text and illustrations.
3. Students may choose articles that focus on especially interesting land features, sights to see, or other topics of interest.

Lesson Objectives

1. To write a response to literature
2. To learn the characteristics of a response to literature
3. To use writing strategies to choose a topic, gather details, plan, organize, write, and revise a response to literature

Model From Literature

Explain that the boxed text aids that appear throughout *Romeo and Juliet* help students clarify their ideas as they respond to literature.

Response to Literature

- Have students read this section on p. 884.
- Point out that students will be asked to meet the Assignment Criteria given in the bulleted list on p. 884 as they create their responses to literature.

Prewriting

- Have students brainstorm a list of novels, short stories, and poems that they especially enjoy. Write the titles on the board to offer students a wide selection of topics.
- If students have difficulty identifying a work of literature to use, tell them that they can review the selections in *Timeless Voices, Timeless Themes,* and choose one that they especially enjoyed.
- Point out the Gathering Details chart on p. 884. After students have selected their topics, have them complete index cards that answer the two questions posed in the chart.
- Read aloud the bullet points under "Clarify your purpose" on p. 884. Point out that students can use these ideas to identify the type of response they would like to make to the work they've chosen.

Writing WORKSHOP

Response to Literature

When you write a **response to literature,** you explore *how, what,* and *why* a piece of writing communicates to you. In this workshop, you will write a response to a piece of literature that engages you as a reader.

Assignment Criteria. Your response to literature should have the following characteristics:

- An analysis of the work's content, its related ideas, or its effect on the reader
- A thesis statement that characterizes your response
- A focus on a single aspect or an overall view of the work
- Evidence from the literary work or other texts to support the opinions you present

To preview the criteria on which your response to literature may be assessed, see the Rubric on page 887.

Prewriting

Choose a topic. Think of novels, poems, and other works of literature that you consider memorable. Create a top-ten list by writing down the titles and authors of these works. Next to each, note any ideas you would like to share about the literature. Review your list and choose a topic.

Gather details. Return to the piece of literature you have selected to find examples, excerpts, and direct quotations that relate directly to your topic. You will use this evidence to help frame your main idea and supporting ideas.

> **Gathering Details**
>
> **What I want to prove:**
> General Zaroff's civilized exterior conceals a ruthless, cunning, heartless murderer.
>
> **How I can prove it:**
> - Describe the wealth of his castle
> - Include quote: "The weak were created to please the strong."

Clarify your purpose. Whether you are sharing your enthusiasm for a new writer, interpreting a well-known poem, or responding to a short story, include details that support your writing goal. Consider these tips:

- **To praise,** include concrete details about what you liked.
- **To analyze,** back up your ideas with evidence from the text.
- **To explain a personal response,** show how the work connects to your own experience or ideas.

TEACHING RESOURCES

The following resources can be used to enrich or extend the instruction for pp. 884-885.

Writing and Grammar, Gold Level, Chapter 13,
pp. 280–307

Performance Assessment and Portfolio Management, pp. 15, 57

Writing Models and Graphic Organizers on Transparencies, pp. 45–52

Writing and Grammar iText CD-ROM
Students can use the following tools as they complete their responses to literature:

- Hexagonal
- Note Cards
- Comparatives

Student Model

Before you begin drafting your response to literature, read this student model and review the characteristics of effective responses to literature.

Jeff Rutherford
Broken Arrow, OK

Characterization of General Zaroff

What lies at the heart of a refined man? In Richard Connell's short story "The Most Dangerous Game," the deranged, yet cunning and elegant, General Zaroff shares his taste for hunting with an unsuspecting visitor. Although he is civilized in his choice of lifestyle, Zaroff's beliefs reveal the murderous mind behind the illusion of a charming, charismatic man.

When we first encounter General Zaroff, our initial reaction is one of delight and admiration for his wealth and charm. Zaroff lives in a massive castle, feasts on the finest delicacies, and wears expensive clothes. His luxurious surroundings and lifestyle reflect a highly civilized, eloquent, and proper gentleman. As readers soon learn, however, there is more to Zaroff than food and elegance.

Beneath Zaroff's fine qualities, though, lies an overwhelming attitude of arrogance. This attitude comes from his firm belief that his way of thinking is superior to that of the average person. Zaroff also fancies himself a phenomenal hunter: "My hand was made for the trigger," he claims. It is this deadly mixture of arrogance, superior hunting skills, and belief that it is natural for the strong to prevail over the weak that makes him disregard the value of human life.

Zaroff's extreme beliefs lead him to conclude that only the intelligent mind of a human being can provide him with the dangerous game he desires. Rationalizing that "the weak were created to please the strong," he chooses to hunt humans instead of animals. Unfortunately, Rainsford steps into this situation. The major conflicts in "The Most Dangerous Game" demonstrate what happens during such an inhumane hunt.

However, the general's arrogance and disregard for human life blind him to the fear and desperation of his prey. His attitude leads to his own demise at the hands of Rainsford, his prey. The characterization of Zaroff as a murderer hiding behind a mask of civility shows that beneath even the most beautiful rose can lie a sharp and deadly thorn.

The title indicates that the essay is limited to a single character.

Jeff uses strong language to clearly state his thesis.

Direct quotations provide evidence for this characterization of Zaroff.

Jeff concludes his response with an analogy that neatly summarizes his analysis.

Student Model

- Point out that the title of the student model does not refer to the literature itself, but to the type of response the student has chosen to write.
- Ask students to locate the thesis statement.
  Answer: The thesis statement is the last sentence in the first paragraph.
- Show students that in the second paragraph, the writer supplies necessary background about the character and story.
- As students continue to read the model, ask them what kinds of evidence the writer uses to support his opinions.
  Answer: Evidence includes both details and quotes from the story.
- Explain that the student has woven his opinions closely with the evidence, thus creating a convincing essay. For an additional model, display the Responding to Literature transparencies in **Writing Models and Graphic Organizers on Transparencies,** pp. 45–52.

Real-World Connection

Responses to Literature in the Real World: Ask students to think of instances in real life in which they may need to prepare detailed, convincing arguments. Answers may include defending a political decision or setting forth a personal opinion on an important topic.

CUSTOMIZE INSTRUCTION FOR UNIVERSAL ACCESS

For Special Needs Students	For English Learners	For Gifted and Talented Students
Encourage students to choose to write about selections that are fairly short in length and that they truly enjoyed reading. The brevity will allow them to more comfortably reread the selections as they look for evidence to support their ideas. If they enjoyed the selection, the task will be less onerous.	Have students work in small groups to help each other clarify the meaning of the Assignment Criteria. Invite them to look up any unfamiliar words or concepts.	Encourage students to add a creative touch to their written responses. They might consider including an analogy such as the one at the end of the Student Model. They also might consider incorporating a visual response, such as a drawing.

Drafting

- Review the organizational chart on p. 886 with the students.
- Point out the individual aspects of the introduction, details, and conclusion given in the bulleted list.
- Encourage students to use this chart as a guide as they write their first drafts.
- As students choose details to include in their draft, remind them to consider quotations, examples, and paraphrases, For more details, see the bulleted list on p. 886.

Revising

- Read aloud the Revising section on p. 886.
- Invite students to work in pairs to eliminate unnecessary information from their essays.
- Have each pair of students read each other's work, looking carefully for sentences that do not support the main idea.
- Provide highlighters for the students to indicate any unneeded sentences.
- After students have returned each other's papers, invite them to discuss their findings and make changes to their essays accordingly.

Drafting

Identify your thesis. Your draft should have a clear thesis statement that you will develop throughout the essay. Review your notes to draft a single statement that brings together the ideas and evidence you have accumulated. Use this sentence, your thesis statement, to direct your essay writing.

Organize your ideas. Use the organizational chart at right to help you present your ideas in a logical way as you draft your essay.

Elaborate to prove your interpretation. Include citations from the literary work to support the points you are making. Consider these specific suggestions:

- **Quotations** can illustrate a character's attitude, a writer's word choice, or an essay's argument.
- **Examples** of a character's actions or of a specific literary element can enhance your analysis of literature.
- **Paraphrases** can help you interpret a writer's theme, discuss the conflict, analyze the character, or restate key ideas from the literature.

Organize Your Ideas

Introduction
- Grab attention with opening
- Identify author and title
- Offer brief summary of the work
- Present thesis

Details
- Present supporting ideas
- Introduce each new idea in a new paragraph
- Use details to support each idea

Conclusion
- Restate thesis
- Make a final point or present a final question or insight

Revising

Revise to eliminate unnecessary information. Read your draft to identify instances in which the information you provide may distract from your main idea.

1. Highlight sentences that do not support your thesis.
2. Consider revising details to make a tighter connection to your main idea.
3. Eliminate any paragraphs or details that do not clearly contribute to your analysis.

Model: Cutting Unnecessary Details

When we first encounter General Zaroff, our initial reaction is one of delight and admiration for his wealth and charm. Zaroff lives in a massive castle, feasts on the finest delicacies, and wears expensive clothes. ~~He had previously been in the army, and his strong personality has a frightening quality.~~

Jeff eliminates this sentence because it does not support his main point effectively.

USING TECHNOLOGY IN WRITING

Encourage students to create their first or second drafts on a computer. Explain that seeing their work as they write it will help them better evaluate its content. Point out that by using the edit tools such as Cut and Paste, students can save time as they work. Students can also use spell check and other revision tools on the **Writing and Grammar iText CD-ROM.**

Revise to indicate precise evaluation. In order to clarify your position, the words you use to convey praise or criticism in your response must be precise. In the following example, note how the word *honest* is more precise than *factual*.

Vague: Her *factual* portrayal of her family's experiences captured the audience's attention.

Precise: Her *honest* portrayal of her family's experiences captured the audience's attention.

Compare the model and the nonmodel. Why is the model more effective than the nonmodel?

Nonmodel	Model
However, the general's harsh attitude blinds him to the fear and desperation of his prey.	However, the general's arrogance and disregard for human life blind him to the fear and desperation of his prey.

Publishing and Presenting

Share your writing with a wider audience by presenting your views to your classmates.

Deliver an oral presentation. Read your response to literature aloud. You may want to have a copy of the literary work to which you are responding on hand in the event that your classmates want to review it.

Publish a collection of reviews. Gather the essays of several of your classmates. Organize them in a binder and make your ideas available in the school library.

Speaking Connection
To learn more about presenting an oral response to literature, see the **Listening and Speaking Workshop**, p. 888.

WG *Prentice Hall Writing and Grammar Connection: Chapter 13*

Rubric for Self-Assessment

Evaluate your response to literature using the following criteria and rating scale:

Criteria	Rating Scale Not very				Very
How well does the the response analyze the work's content, its related ideas, or its effect on the reader?	1	2	3	4	5
How well does the thesis statement communicate the nature of the response?	1	2	3	4	5
Is the response well focused?	1	2	3	4	5
How effectively does the work use evidence to support the writer's opinion?	1	2	3	4	5

Revising (continued)

- Have students read "Revise to indicate precise evaluation" on p. 887, including the model and non-model.
- Ask students to review their drafts for words that convey praise or criticism, revising them for precision as needed.

Publishing and Presenting

- Before students read their responses to literature aloud, have them write the name of the selection on the board as a visual reminder for the audience.
- Students may want to begin their presentations by asking how many classmates have read the selection before. After the presentation, ask those classmates if they agree or disagree with the presenter's position and invite further discussion.

Assessment

- Review with students the assessment criteria, pointing out the Assignment Criteria listed at the beginning of the exercise on p. 884.
- As students listen to each other's essays, have them use the rubric criteria to rate their work.
- The rubric on this page, and another rubric in an alternative format, can be found on pp. 15 and 57 of **Performance Assessment and Portfolio Management.**

TEST-TAKING TIP

Point out that students may be asked to respond to literature on many tests. Explain that this is an opportunity for students to draw upon their prior knowledge and personal experience. For instance, students can use events out of their own lives, stories they have already read, even family ancedotes to connect personal responses to almost any literary work.

Lesson Objectives

1. To present an oral response to literature
2. To summarize main ideas, characterize responses, and find evidence to support a response
3. To offer a response that includes a thesis statement, evidence, and a summary

Presenting an Oral Response to Literature

- Have students read the information in this section on p. 888.
- Point out that it's usually easier to create effective oral responses to literature when the piece of literature provokes a strong emotional response in the reader.
- Explain that students can identify the types of literature to which they naturally respond strongly by noting their own reactions as they read. When a literary work makes a student smile, say "Aha!," or experience a gut-wrenching feeling, students can be sure that they "have something to say" about the work.

Define Your Response

- Have students read this section on p. 888.
- On the chalkboard, write the three subheads in this section: Summarize the main ideas, Characterize your responses, and Find evidence to support your response.
- Explain that students may refer to the visual reminders on the board as they prepare their responses.

Offer Your Response

- Review with the class the bulleted points in this section on p. 888.
- Explain that students may make brief notes (e.g., on an index card) to which they can refer as they deliver their oral responses.

Listening and Speaking WORKSHOP

Presenting an Oral Response to Literature

Certain works of literature provoke a strong emotional response. Capturing those feelings in words can be a challenging task. When you present an **oral response to literature,** you articulate your response and support it with evidence from the text.

Define Your Response

Before you present a response to others, you must first determine how you feel about a selection. Review the Writing Workshop on pages 884–887. Use these steps to help you focus and define your feelings:

Summarize the main ideas. Finding the main idea gives you a basic skeleton around which to organize your response. In nonfiction, the main idea is generally found in the introduction or conclusion. For a fictional work, limit yourself to the most important ideas. Then, gather details from the work that are especially important or memorable to you.

Characterize your response. Decide whether you agree or disagree with the main ideas you have selected and determine why. Turn these reactions into a single thesis statement that captures the way you feel, and jot down at least three reasons for your reaction. These reasons will be your supporting arguments.

Find evidence to support your response. Use examples from the literature as evidence to support your arguments. Direct quotations or paraphrases give greater depth and power to the arguments you develop in your oral response.

Offer Your Response

Organize your thoughts. If possible, keep your organization clear and simple, and include these elements:

- A brief introduction outlining your thesis
- A body presenting supporting arguments along with key evidence
- A summary of your main argument

Use evocative language. To make your presentation more memorable, choose words and phrases that will have powerful associations for your audience and generate a reaction.

Activity: Book Club Forming a book club can enhance your enjoyment of reading by exchanging views with others. Discuss a work of literature in a small group. Take turns presenting and evaluating all of the group's presentations, using the chart shown. Discuss interesting variations in interpretation or response.

Feedback Form for Oral Response to Literature

Rating System
+ = Excellent ✔ = Average – = Weak

Content
_____ Clarity of thesis
_____ Support of ideas with evidence
_____ Validity of interpretation

Delivery
_____ Presentation clearly organized and presented
_____ Use of appropriate language to describe response

Answer the following questions:

Do you agree with the interpretation of the work?

What would have made the presentation more effective?

CUSTOMIZE INSTRUCTION FOR UNIVERSAL ACCESS

For Special Needs Students	For Gifted/Talented Students
Work with these students before they give their oral presentations to make sure they've chosen a topic that they feel strongly about. Encourage the students to practice in small groups before delivering their responses to the entire class.	Encourage students to use appropriate performance techniques as they deliver their oral responses. For instance, remind them to look around the room as they speak, making eye contact with various classmates. Suggest that they use facial expressions, body language, and voice intonation to give added character to their responses. If students have included quotes from the literature under discussion, make sure they deliver these passages with suitable drama and emotion.

Assessment WORKSHOP

Responses and Interpretations

The reading sections of some tests require you to read a passage and write short, essay-type answers that respond to and interpret the written text. Use the following strategies to help you defend your responses and interpretations:

- To determine your reaction, think about how the text makes you feel and how it might influence your opinions.
- When you interpret a text, give your own ideas about what the text means.
- Base your response and interpretation on information contained in the text, supporting your opinions with references.

Test-Taking Strategies

- To defend your ideas about a fictional work, use the language, plot details, and character descriptions as support.
- Search for facts, quotations, and statistics to support your interpretation of nonfiction.

Sample Test Item

Directions: Read the passage, and then answer the question that follows.

Geographers use globes and maps to represent Earth. A globe is more accurate than a map. Shaped like Earth, a globe gives a true picture of the size and shape of landmasses and of distance across oceans. Globes are awkward to carry around, however, so most people use maps instead. Even so, maps have a major drawback. Because Earth's surface is curved and maps are flat, all maps distort Earth's image in some way.

1. For what reason would you use a map? For what reason would you use a globe? Support your answers.

Answers and Explanations

Possible Answers:

You might use a map to find out how to drive to a new place. You might use a globe to see how far the United States is from China.

A successful answer should incorporate the different attributes of globes and maps.

Practice

Directions: Read the passage, and then answer the questions that follow.

Hoover Dam was built in the 1930s during the Great Depression to control the Colorado River and irrigate the farmlands of the southwestern United States. It has also provided electric power and formed a giant reservoir, Lake Mead, for drinking water, swimming, boating, and fishing. However, Hoover Dam has also changed the river's ecology, hurting some native fish and other species and flooding some parts of the Grand Canyon.

1. In what ways have technology and human intervention served the needs of the United States?
2. Do you think the advantages outweighed the disadvantages in the construction of Hoover Dam? Support your answer with evidence from the text.

Lesson Objective

To correctly answer test questions that require a response to or interpretation of written text

Applying Reading Strategies

Read aloud the bulleted list under "Responses and Interpretations" on p. 889. Point out that students should keep these concepts in mind when they are asked to respond to written text in test questions.

Applying Test-Taking Strategies

- Have students read the Sample Test Item, then share their responses to the question orally with the rest of the class.
- Point out that in this example, students are asked to respond in a specific way—by offering factual support for their responses.
- Review with the class the Answers and Explanations section on p. 889. Ask students to discuss how their responses compare to the example given.

Answers:

Possible Responses:

1. Technology, in the form of Hoover Dam, has reduced flood damage, improved farming, enhanced supplies of electric power, and increased recreational opportunities.
2. The slight damage to fish populations and minor flooding of the Grand Canyon are a small price to pay for the multiple benefits of the dam.

TEACHING RESOURCES

The following resources can be used to enrich or extend the instruction for p. 889.

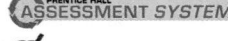

PRENTICE HALL ASSESSMENT SYSTEM

- Workbook
- Skill Book
- Transparencies
- CD-ROM

Unit Objectives

1. To develop skills in reading poetry
2. To apply a variety of reading strategies appropriate for reading poetry
3. To analyze literary elements
4. To use a variety of strategies to build vocabulary
5. To learn elements of grammar, usage, and style
6. To use recursive writing processes to write in a variety of forms
7. To develop listening and speaking skills
8. To express and support responses to various types of texts
9. To prepare, organize, and present literary interpretations

Meeting the Objectives

With each selection, you will find instructional materials through which students can meet these objectives. Further, you will find additional practice pages for reading strategies, literary analysis, vocabulary, and grammar in the **Selection Support: Skills Development Workbook** in your **Teaching Resources.**

Background

Art

Garden of Delights, by Sandy Novak

The garden of earthly delights is a traditional subject in art. Perhaps the most famous painting on this theme is by the 16th century artist Hieronymus Bosch. Here, Sandy Novak, a contemporary artist who lives in California, creates a modern version of a garden overflowing with life's pleasures.

How has the artist conveyed a sense of a garden full of richness and variety?

Answer: Like a garden in full bloom, the painting presents a variety of forms that echo both human figures and plant life. The exuberant use of color adds to the sense of abundant, overflowing life.

UNIT 9 Poetry

Garden of Delights, watercolor, 11" x 17", Sandy Novak, Omni-Photo Communications, Inc.

UNIT FEATURES	
Connections	**Reading Informational Material**
Every unit contains a feature that connects literature to a related topic, such as art, science, or history. In this unit, the Literature Past and Present feature on p. 950 offers perspectives on aging that may deepen students' understanding of Shakespeare's "Seven Ages of Man." Use the information and questions on the Connections pages to enrich students' understanding of the selections presented within the unit.	These selections will help students learn to analyze and evaluate informational texts, such as workplace documents, technical directions, and consumer materials. They will expose students to the organization and features unique to nonnarrative texts. In this unit, students will learn how to read professional journals as they practice the reading strategy of identifying a target audience's purpose.

Exploring the Genre

The poet T. S. Eliot said that poetry can be enjoyed before it is understood. A powerful poem uses language to draw you in, invite you to reread, and inspire you to find a new layer of meaning each time. A poet carefully chooses words to capture a unique and personal vision. Poetry combines meaning with sound to add music and rhythm to ideas. Each reader brings a different set of associations to a poem based on the people, places, and experiences that he or she has known.

These terms will help you discuss the variety of poems in this unit:

- **Lyric poetry** expresses vivid thoughts and feelings.
- **Narrative poetry** tells a story.
- **Dramatic poetry** uses techniques of drama, such as speaker and conflict, to tell a story.
- **Musical devices** such as alliteration, onomatopoeia, assonance, consonance, meter, repetition, and rhyme give poems a melodious quality.
- **Figurative language** uses simile, lyrical metaphor, and personification in creative, unexpected comparisons and descriptions.

▲ **Critical Viewing** Which details of this picture suggest poetry to you? **[Connect]**

ASSESSMENT RESOURCES

- **Selection Support: Skills Development Workbook**
- **Formal Assessment**
- **Open Book Tests**
- **Performance Assessment and Portfolio Management**
- **Extension Activities**

Assessing Student Progress

Listed below are tools that are available to measure the degree to which students meet the unit objectives.

Informal Assessment

The questions in the Review and Assess sections are a first-level response to the concepts and skills presented with the selections. Students' responses provide a brief, informal measure of their grasp of the material. These responses can indicate where further instruction and practice are needed. Follow up with the practice pages in **Selection Support: Skills Development Workbook.**

Formal Assessment

The **Formal Assessment** booklet contains the Selection Tests and Unit Tests.

- Selection Tests measure comprehension and skills acquisition for each selection or group of selections.
- Each Unit Test provides students with thirty multiple-choice questions and five essay questions designed to assess students' knowledge of the literature and skills taught in the unit.

The **Open Book Tests** ask students to demonstrate their ability to synthesize and communicate information from selections or groups of selections.

To assess student writing, you will find rubrics and scoring models in the **Performance Assessment and Portfolio Management** booklet. In this booklet, you will also find scoring rubrics for listening and speaking activities.

Alternative Assessment

The **Extension Activities** booklet contains writing activities, listening and speaking activities, and research and technology activities that are appropriate for students with different ability levels. You may also use these activities as an alternative measure of students' growth.

▶Critical Viewing

Answer: The artist's use of size, shape, color, and placement conveys symbolic meaning, just as a poem's structure, words, and sounds convey symbols and meanings.

Why Read Literature?

The "Why Read Literature?" page in each unit presents a list of possible purposes for reading. Each purpose for reading is connected to one or more of the selections in the unit. Good readers set a purpose before reading to help them read actively and focus on meaningful details.

Unit 9 introduces three purposes for reading. "Read for the Love of Literature" invites students to relate to the personal discoveries that poets express in their work. "Read for Information" helps students comprehend the world of professional journals. "Read to Appreciate an Author's Style" helps students explore the power of poetic language.

How to Use This Page

- Tell students that as they read each selection in this unit, they should set a purpose for reading. This will help them read in an active and focused manner.
- Explain that students can increase their love of poetry by comparing the writing process to eating overripe blackberries, as Galway Kinnell does in his poem "Blackberry Eating." Students can also discover the hidden meanings in ordinary activities when they read Julia Alvarez's "Women's Work."
- Point out the importance of learning to read professional journals as students prepare to do research during high school and college.
- Predict that as they read "The Eagle" and "Dream Deferred," students will discover the inspirational power of poetry.

Why Read Literature?

There are many different reasons to read a poem. You might read poetry because you like the way certain poets put words together or because you find their perspectives unique and intriguing. Preview three purposes you might set before reading the poems in this unit.

1 Read for the Love of Literature

A poem can provide a window into the writing process. Find out how choosing the right words for a poem is a little like eating overripe blackberries in Galway Kinnell's **"Blackberry Eating,"** page 914.

Good literature makes connections and illustrates universal themes. If you ever have been forced to stay inside and clean while others played, you can appreciate the way Julia Alvarez transforms household drudgery into personal discovery in **"Woman's Work,"** page 920.

2 Read for Information

With the rapid advances in science and technology in the last century, you might wonder how doctors, scientists, and librarians keep up with recent developments in their fields. Explore the world of professional journals in this unit's **Reading Informational Materials,** page 964.

3 Read to Appreciate an Author's Style

The eagle, subject of Alfred, Lord Tennyson's poem, has long been one of the most recognizable symbols of grace, power, and authority. See how Tennyson adds majesty to the list when you read **"The Eagle,"** page 906.

When the playwright Lorraine Hansberry read one of Langston Hughes's poems, she was so moved by his insights that she used a line from one of his works to name her play *A Raisin in the Sun.* Read Hughes's powerful poem **"Dream Deferred,"** page 904.

Take It to the Net

Visit the Web site for online instruction and activities related to each selection in this unit.
www.phschool.com

ENRICHMENT: Further Reading

Have students choose one or more of the works below to extend their understanding of poetry or to read more by the unit authors.

The Complete Tales and Poems of Edgar Allan Poe
by Edgar Allan Poe
This collection offers fifty-three of Poe's best-known poems.

Selected Poems of Langston Hughes **(Vintage Classics)** by Langston Hughes
Hughes himself selected the poems in this collection shortly before his death in 1967.

How to Read Literature

Use Strategies for Reading Poetry

If you are used to reading prose, getting accustomed to poetry may take a slight adjustment. The payoff comes when you suddenly gain insight into a poet's ideas. Here are some strategies to help make the shift from prose to poetry:

1. Use your senses.

One way to appreciate a poem more fully is to use all of your senses to place yourself in the situation the poet describes.

- Determine the poem's setting before you try to imagine individual sensations.
- Look for descriptive words that convey a specific physical sensation.
- Be aware of words that appeal to sight, sound, taste, touch, and smell.

2. Paraphrase.

Since the language of a poem can be abstract, it is helpful to rephrase lines to make sure that you understand their meaning.

- Choose words you commonly use when rephrasing what the author is saying.
- Use simple sentences and change the word order if it helps you understand the meaning better.

Paraphrasing

Original Phrasing: *"Eagerly I wished the morrow—vainly I had tried to borrow / From my books surcease of sorrow"*

Paraphrase: *Books were no help in forgetting my present troubles. I wish it were tomorrow.*

—from "The Raven," Edgar Allan Poe

3. Draw inferences about the speaker.

When you read a poem, you hear the voice of the poem's speaker, or the imaginary voice assumed by the poet. As you read, think about how you might describe the person voicing those particular lines of poetry. Use this knowledge to achieve a deeper understanding of the poem's meaning.

4. Read in sentences.

- Use punctuation, not the ends of lines, as the indication of where to pause when reading a poem.
- Periods, commas, colons, semicolons, and dashes signal where to pause or to stop reading.

As you read the selections in this unit, review the reading strategies and look at the notes in the side columns. Use the suggestions to apply the strategies and interact with the text.

How to Read Literature

The "How to Read Literature" page in each unit presents a set of strategies to help readers understand authors' words and ideas. Each reading strategy is taught in conjunction with one or more of the selections within the unit. Good readers develop a bank of strategies from which they can draw as needed.

Unit 9 introduces four strategies for reading poetry. Students learn to use their senses, paraphrase, draw inferences, and read in sentences rather than lines. The strategies on this page help readers go beyond a simple scan of a text.

How to Use This Page

Introduce the strategies for reading poetry, presenting each as a tool for developing understanding when reading the selections in this unit.

- Tell students that as they read each selection in this unit, they should apply strategies for reading poetry. These strategies will help students construct meaning as they read.
- As they read "I Wandered Lonely as a Cloud" (p. 896), students will learn to use their senses to engage with a poem.
- As they read Emily Dickinson's poem "'Hope' is the thing with feathers" (p. 908), students will learn to paraphrase to clarify meaning.
- As they read Edgar Allan Poe's spooky poem "The Raven" (p. 940), students will learn the skill of drawing inferences to gain greater insight about the speaker.
- When they encounter three haiku poems by Chiyojo, students will practice reading poetry in sentences.

MODEL A READING STRATEGY: Use Your Senses

Perhaps more than most prose writers, poets rely on sensory language both to convey meaning and help readers engage with a poem. Sensory language is that which appeals to the five senses—sight, sound, taste, touch, and smell. Demonstrate how to read and interpret sensory language by modeling your thinking with this passage from "Blackberry Eating" by Galway Kinnell:

I love to go out in late September
among the fat, overripe, icy black blackberries
to eat blackberries for breakfast,

Tell students:

The poet engages nearly all my senses in his description of the blackberries. For example, the words *fat* and *black* appeal to sight, *overripe* appeals to smell and taste, and *icy* appeals to touch. Because the poet dwells on these berries, creating such vivid imagery through his use of sensory language, I expect that they hold an important meaning for him. That proves true, as the poet goes on to create a comparison between the eating of these berries and the writing of a poem.

I Wandered Lonely as a Cloud

Lesson Objectives and CA Correlations

1. **To analyze and respond to literary elements**
   - Literary Analysis: Rhyme Scheme **R 3.7**
   - Connecting Literary Elements: Simile **R 3.8**
2. **To read, comprehend, analyze, and critique a poem**
   - Reading Strategy: Using Your Senses **R 3.7**
   - Reading Check questions
   - Review and Assess questions
   - Assessment Practice (ATE)
3. **To develop word analysis skills, fluency, and systematic vocabulary**
   - Vocabulary Development Lesson: Poetic Contractions **R 1.1, 1.2**
4. **To understand and apply written and oral language conventions**
   - Spelling Strategy
   - Grammar Lesson: Semicolons and Colons **LC 1.1**
5. **To understand and apply appropriate writing and research strategies**
   - Writing Lesson: Description of a Natural Scene **W 1.2**
   - Extension Activity: Anthology **W1.3**
6. **To understand and apply listening and speaking strategies**
   - Extension Activity: Visual Presentation **LS 1.7**

STEP-BY-STEP TEACHING GUIDE	PACING GUIDE
PRETEACH	
Motivate Students and Provide Background	
Use the Motivation activity (ATE p. 894)	5 min.
Read and discuss the Preview material and Background information (SE/ATE p. 894) [A]	5 min.
Introduce the Concepts	
Introduce the Literary Analysis and Reading Strategy (SE/ATE p. 895) [A]	15 min.
Pronounce the vocabulary words and read their definitions (SE p. 895)	5 min.
TEACH	
Monitor Comprehension	
Informally monitor comprehension by circulating while students read independently or in groups [A]	5 min.
Monitor students' comprehension with the Reading Check note (SE/ATE p. 897)	as students read
Develop vocabulary with Vocabulary notes (SE pp. 897–898; ATE p. 897)	as students read
Develop Understanding	
Develop students' understanding of rhyme scheme with the Literary Analysis annotation (ATE p. 896) [A]	10 min.
Develop students' ability to use their senses with the Reading Strategy annotation (ATE p. 897)	10 min.
ASSESS	
Assess Mastery	
Assess students' mastery of the Reading Strategy and Literary Analysis by having them answer the Review and Assess questions (SE/ATE p. 899)	20 min.
Use one or more of the print and media Assessment Resources (ATE p. 901) [A]	up to 50 min.
EXTEND	
Apply Understanding	
Have students complete the Vocabulary Development Lesson and the Grammar Lesson (SE p. 900) [A]	20 min.
Apply students' knowledge of avoiding unnecessary details using the Writing Lesson (SE/ATE p. 901) [A]	45 min.
Apply students' understanding using one or more of the Extension Activities (SE p. 901)	20–90 min.

[A] **ACCELERATED INSTRUCTION:**
Use the strategies and activities identified with an [A].

UNIVERSAL ACCESS
● = Below-Level Students
▲ = On-Level Students
■ = Above-Level Students

Time and Resource Manager

Reading Level: Average
Average Number of Instructional Days: 3

RESOURCES		
PRINT	**TRANSPARENCIES**	**TECHNOLOGY**
• **Beyond Literature,** Cross-Curricular Connection: Art, p. 51 ▲ ■		• **Interest Grabber Video,** Tape 5 ● ▲ ■
• **Selection Support Workbook:** ● ▲ ■ Literary Analysis, p. 204 Reading Strategy, p. 203 Build Vocabulary, p. 201	• **Literary Analysis and Reading Transparencies,** pp. 101 and 102 ● ▲ ■	
		• **Listening to Literature** ● ▲ ■ Audiocassettes, Side 27 Audio CDs, CD 18
• **Literatura en español** ● ▲ • **Literary Analysis for Enrichment** ■		
• **Formal Assessment:** Selection Test, pp. 183–185 ● ▲ ■ • **Open Book Test,** pp. 151–153 ● ▲ ■ • **Performance Assessment and Portfolio Management,** p. 18 ● ▲ ■ • Prentice Hall Assessment System ● ▲ ■	• Prentice Hall Assessment System ● ▲ ■ Skills Practice Answers and Explanations on Transparencies	• **Test Bank Software** ● ▲ ■ • **Got It! Assessment Videotapes,** Tape 5 ● ▲
• **Selection Support Workbook:** ● ▲ ■ Build Grammar Skills, p. 202 • **Writing and Grammar,** Gold Level ● ▲ ■ • **Extension Activities,** p. 49 ● ▲ ■	• **Daily Language Practice Transparencies** ● ▲ • **Writing Models and Graphic Organizers on Transparencies,** pp. 17–20 ● ▲ ■	• **Writing and Grammar iText CD-ROM** ● ▲ ■ ***Take It to the Net*** www.phschool.com

BLOCK SCHEDULING: Use one 90-minute class period to preteach the selection and have students read it. Use a second 90-minute class period to assess students' mastery of skills and have them complete one of the Extension Activities.

PREACH

Step-by-Step Teaching Guide for pp. 894–895

Motivation

Pique students' interest in the poem by showing them a Peanuts cartoon of Linus clutching his security blanket, a video of the song "My Favorite Things" from the musical *The Sound of Music,* or another image conveying the idea of a comforting object or memory. Ask volunteers to share their ideas about things that people think about to cheer themselves up. Tell them to close their eyes for a moment and think of something that makes them happy. Point out that special memories like these are often a person's secret treasures. Then, explain that in this poem, a poet reveals one of his special, treasured memories.

Interest Grabber Video

As an alternative, play "Reading and Student Response" on Tape 5 to engage student interest.

1 Background

Science

There are at least twenty-five species of those well-loved harbingers of spring, daffodils, all of which multiply two ways: by cloning (bulb division), or from seeds.

Narcissus and *daffodil* are synonymous terms. *Narcissus* is the Latin or botanical name of the flower; *daffodil* is the common name. Jonquils are a particular kind of narcissus, with bright yellow flowers, a strong scent, and rounded leaves.

Prepare to Read

I Wandered Lonely as a Cloud

Take It to the Net

Visit www.phschool.com for interactive activities and instruction related to "I Wandered Lonely as a Cloud," including
- background
- graphic organizers
- literary elements
- reading strategies

Preview

Connecting to the Literature

You probably have moments in your life that you replay in your memory—images to which photographs or videos cannot do justice because they cannot capture your feelings. In this poem, William Wordsworth captures both the images and the feelings connected to a special moment in his life.

1 Background

Dorothy Wordsworth was William's friend as well as his sister. She kept a journal of their activities, including what they saw as they took walks through England's Lake District. On April 15, 1802, she recorded her impressions after they suddenly saw a field crowded with daffodils. Wordsworth used his sister's comments as inspiration for this poem.

TEACHING RESOURCES

The following resources can be used to enrich or extend the instruction for pp. 894–895.

Motivation

Interest Grabber Video, Tape 5

Background

Beyond Literature, p. 51

Take It to the Net

Visit www.phschool.com for background and hotlinks for the poem.

Literary Analysis

Literary Analysis and Reading Transparencies, Rhyme Scheme, p. 102

Reading

Selection Support: Reading Strategy, p. 203; Build Vocabulary, p. 201

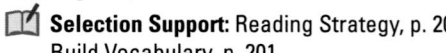

Literary Analysis and Reading Transparencies, Strategies for Reading Poetry, p. 101

BLOCK SCHEDULING: Resources marked with this symbol provide varied instruction during 90-minute blocks.

❷ Literary Analysis

Rhyme Scheme

A **rhyme scheme** is a regular pattern of rhyming words that appear at the ends of lines in a poem. You indicate the pattern of a poem's rhymes by using letters of the alphabet, assigning a new letter to each rhyme. The first stanza of "I Wandered Lonely as a Cloud" follows a rhyme scheme of *ababcc*. Look at the first three lines of the stanza:

I wandered lonely as a cloud (a)
That floats on high o'er vales and hills, (b)
When all at once I saw a crowd, (a)

Since *cloud* and *crowd* are rhyming words, lines 1 and 3 are assigned the letter *a*. *Hills* does not rhyme with *cloud*, so line 2 is assigned the letter *b*. As you read the other stanzas, determine whether Wordsworth keeps to his rhyme scheme or if he breaks the pattern he has established.

Connecting Literary Elements

A **simile** is a figure of speech in which *like* or *as* is used to make a comparison between ideas that are basically dissimilar. The title of Wordsworth's poem contains a simile in which the speaker compares himself to a cloud. As with the rhyme scheme in a poem, similes require writers to carefully consider their use of language—assessing both the words that they choose and the impressions that those words make.

❸ Reading Strategy

Using Your Senses

Once you have a basic idea of what is happening in a poem, **using your senses** can give you a greater appreciation of the ideas the poem conveys.

- Pay attention to images that appeal to your senses of sight, smell, sound, taste, and touch.
- Consider the impression each image conveys.

As you read, use a chart like the one shown to note the images that appeal to your senses, and then record how they make you feel.

Detail
waves that dance and sparkle
Sensory Appeal
sight
My Impressions
seems full of life and joy

Vocabulary Development

host (hōst) *n.* great number (p. 897)
glee (glē) *n.* joy (p. 898)
pensive (pen′ siv) *adj.* thinking deeply (p. 898)
bliss (blis) *n.* great joy or happiness (p. 898)

❷ Literary Analysis

Rhyme Scheme

- Explain to students that as they read "I Wandered Lonely as a Cloud," they will focus on *rhyme scheme,* the pattern of rhyme in the poem. The rhyme scheme is usually coded to represent the same final sounds in lines of verse, as shown on this page.
- Have a volunteer read aloud the excerpt from "I Wandered Lonely as a Cloud" to the class. Then, have another student explain why the first and last lines have the letter *a* after them and the second line has the letter *b*.
- Use the instruction for Connecting Literary Elements to make students aware of the importance of the metaphorical meanings of words in poetry.
- Display the Rhyme Scheme transparency in **Literary Analysis and Reading Transparencies,** p. 102, and show where the rhyme scheme for the first three lines of the first stanza of the poem is listed in the second column, Rhyme Scheme. Ask students whether they think the fourth line will rhyme with the first or the second line (the second).

❸ Reading Strategy

Using Your Senses

- Remind students that poems may include words that appeal to the five senses—sight, smell, touch, taste, and sound.
- Ask students to create graphic organizers similar to the one on this page on which to record words from the poem, the senses to which the words appeal, and their reactions to the words.

Vocabulary Development

- Pronounce each vocabulary word for students, and read the definitions as a class. Have students identify any words with which they are already familiar.

CUSTOMIZE INSTRUCTION FOR UNIVERSAL ACCESS

For Less Proficient Readers	For English Learners	For Advanced Readers
Have students close their eyes and listen to "I Wandered Lonely as a Cloud" on CD or audiocassette. Then, write the first stanza on the board and read it aloud. From the second line on, ask students to decide together whether the ending sound is different from the line before or the same. Show students how to code the lines *a, b,* and *c.*	Let students enjoy "I Wandered Lonely as a Cloud" on CD or audiocassette. Tell them not to worry about meaning. Then, write *cloud, hills, crowd, daffodils, trees,* and *breeze* on the board. Slowly pronounce the words together. Have students decide which words rhyme, or have the same ending sounds.	Have students listen to "I Wandered Lonely as a Cloud" on CD or audiocassette and then read it carefully, paying particular attention to both the rhyme scheme and Wordsworth's use of similes. Have them consider as they listen and then read the poem whether the sound or the meaning of the poem is more important and why.

E-Teach

Visit E-Teach at www.phschool.com for teachers' essays on how to teach, with questions and answers.

TEACH

Step-by-Step Teaching Guide for pp. 896–898

CUSTOMIZE INSTRUCTION
For Musical/Rhythmic Learners

This poem can be read chorally by two groups of students, one group reading lines 1–4 of each stanza and the other group responding with lines 5–6. Encourage students to vary the pace and emphasis of the lines as they practice their choral readings.

❶ About the Selection

Looking back on a moment when he was inspired by the beauty of nature, Wordsworth evokes a scene of golden daffodils lining a bay in the Lake District of England. That glimpse of loveliness eased his loneliness at the time and gives him pleasure each time he remembers it.

❷ Literary Analysis

Rhyme Scheme

- Ask students to explain the term *rhyme scheme.*
  Answer: A rhyme scheme is the pattern of rhyming words at the ends of lines in poems.
- Have a volunteer code the rhyme scheme in the first stanza.
  Answer: The rhyme scheme is *ababcc.*

▷ **Monitor Progress** Ask students whether the rhyme scheme of the second stanza is the same as or different from the first stanza.
Answer: The rhyme scheme of the second stanza is the same as the first stanza.

❶ I Wandered Lonely

TEACHING RESOURCES

The following resources can be used to enrich or extend the instruction for pp. 896–898.

Literary Analysis

Selection Support: Literary Analysis, p. 204

Reading

Listening to Literature Audiocassettes, Side 27 ■

Listening to Literature Audio CDs, CD 18 ■

■ **BLOCK SCHEDULING:** Resources marked with this symbol provide varied instruction during 90-minute blocks.

as a Cloud

William Wordsworth

I wandered lonely as a cloud
4 That floats on high o'er vales[1] and hills,
When all at once I saw a crowd,
A host, of golden daffodils;
2 Beside the lake, beneath the trees,
Fluttering and dancing in the breeze.

Continuous as the stars that shine
3 And twinkle on the milky way,
They stretched in never-ending line
Along the margin of a bay:
Ten thousand saw I at a glance,
Tossing their heads in sprightly dance.

host (hōst) *n.* great number

5 **Reading Check**

What was most remarkable about the flowers that the speaker saw?

1. **o'er vales** over valleys.

3 Reading Strategy

Using Your Senses

- Ask students which sense is appealed to most in this passage.
  Answer: The sense of sight is appealed to most.
- Then, ask students which words and phrases evoke the sense of sight.
  Answer: Words include *saw, fluttering, dancing, shine, twinkle, glance, tossing their heads.*
- Have students explain how and why the daffodils might toss their heads.
  Answer: "Tossing their heads" is a metaphor. The speaker sees daffodil blossoms moving in the wind.

4 Vocabulary Development

Poetic Contractions

- Call students' attention to the contraction *o'er*. Ask which letter or letters are left out.
  Answer: The letter *v* has been replaced by an apostrophe.
- Explain that *o'er* is a poetic contraction. Can students think of any other?
  Answer: Examples include *'tween, 'twill, 'twas, fore'er,* and *ne'er.*
- Ask students why poets might use this type of contraction.
  Answer: To maintain a regular rhythm or meter in a line, poets sometimes combine two syllables or words into one.

5 Reading Check

Answer: The most remarkable thing about the daffodils is their vast number.

CUSTOMIZE INSTRUCTION FOR UNIVERSAL ACCESS

For Gifted/Talented Students	For Advanced Readers
Have small groups of students interpret these stanzas of the poem in another medium of their choice. For instance, they might invent a dance that expresses the movement of the daffodils, a song about the effect the masses of daffodils had on the speaker, or an abstract painting that has blocks of yellow.	Ask students to analyze the figurative language in the stanzas. They should list the similes, metaphors, and examples of personification and explain their effect on the reader. Then, have students discuss the importance of metaphorical language to poetry.

ASSESS

6 Reading Strategy

Using Your Senses

- Ask students to identify words that appeal to the senses in the last two stanzas of the poem.
  Answer: *waves . . . danced, gazed, inward eye, dances*
- Urge volunteers to share their reactions to these sensory words.

Answers for p. 898

Review and Assess

1. Many students may feel that seeing such a huge number of daffodils at once was a rare and moving occurrence.
2. **(a)** The daffodils are beside a lake and are bobbing in the breeze. **(b)** The daffodils are compared to stars. **(c)** The comparison suggests the great number of the daffodils and their brightness.
3. **(a)** "Outdid the sparkling waves with glee," "jocund company" **(b)** The sight of the daffodils makes the speaker joyously happy.
4. **(a)** The speaker remembers the daffodils he saw. **(b)** The "wealth" is a store of happy emotions that the speaker can call upon in later times of need.
5. Students may say that natural scenes provide comfort by reminding people of their connection with something larger than themselves.
6. Observations that students recall will differ, but each student should explain why a particular scene was so moving.

The waves beside them danced; but they
Outdid the sparkling waves in glee;
A poet could not but be gay,
In such a jocund[2] company;
I gazed—and gazed—but little thought
What wealth the show to me had brought:

6

For oft, when on my couch I lie
In vacant or in pensive mood,
They flash upon that inward eye
Which is the bliss of solitude;
And then my heart with pleasure fills,
And dances with the daffodils.

glee (glē) *n.* joy

pensive (pen′ siv) *adj.* thinking deeply

bliss (blis) *n.* great joy or happiness

2. **jocund** (jak′ ənd) *adj.* cheerful.

William Wordsworth

(1770–1850)

Wordsworth was born in England's rural Lake District. As a young man, he spent time in France and became a supporter of the French Revolution's ideals of freedom, equality, and brotherhood. Although Wordsworth abandoned his desire for political change as the French Revolution turned bloody, he was able to bring about revolutionary changes in British literature.

In 1798, Wordsworth and fellow poet Samuel Taylor Coleridge published a book of poetry entitled *Lyrical Ballads*. Unlike the formal, highly intellectual poems that were popular at the time, the poems in the book used simple language to exalt the remarkable moments of everyday life.

Review and Assess

Thinking About the Selection

1. **Respond:** Why do you think this experience created such a strong impression in Wordsworth's memory?
2. **(a) Recall:** Where are the daffodils, and what are they doing? **(b) Analyze:** To what are the daffodils compared in stanza 2? **(c) Interpret:** What does the comparison suggest about the daffodils?
3. **(a) Recall:** In stanza 3, which words does the speaker use to describe the daffodils? **(b) Interpret:** How does the sight of the daffodils affect the speaker?
4. **(a) Recall:** What does the speaker say happens when he is alone in a "pensive mood"? **(b) Connect:** What "wealth" do memories of the scene give him?
5. **Assess:** How are natural scenes like the one presented in this poem valuable?
6. **Apply:** Have you ever made an observation that caused you to feel the type of connection to nature that the speaker feels? Explain.

ASSESSMENT PRACTICE: Reading Comprehension

Vocabulary: Complete Analogies (For more practice, see Test Preparation Workbook, p. 51.)

Many tests require students to answer multiple-choice questions about analogies. Use the following sample test item for student practice in determining the meaning of figurative analogies.

After reading the poem "I Wandered Lonely as a Cloud," have students complete the following analogy:

HOST: CROWD::

A joyful : happy **C** stars : shine
B vales : hills **D** daffodils : dancing

Help students see that in the poem, host is synonymous with crowd. Among the answer options, the only pair of words that could be considered synonymous is joyful and happy. The words in the other pairs do not relate as synonyms. Thus the correct answer is *A*.

Review and Assess

Literary Analysis

Rhyme Scheme

1. Complete the following chart to show the **rhyme scheme** of "I Wandered Lonely as a Cloud."

Stanza #	Rhyme Scheme

2. What happens in the rhyme scheme to set off the final two lines of each stanza?
3. How does setting off the final two lines of each stanza reinforce the meaning?

Connecting Literary Elements

4. (a) In the first stanza, what words does the speaker use to describe the clouds? (b) When the speaker compares himself to a cloud, what is he saying about himself?
5. (a) What mood or "feeling" is set by the title? (b) Is the **simile** found in the title of the poem an effective one? Explain.
6. Find and analyze another simile in the poem. Explain which two objects are being compared and what the comparison suggests.

Reading Strategy

Using Your Senses

7. (a) Which details help express the great numbers of daffodils? (b) Which of these details appeal to you most? Explain.
8. Using a chart like the one shown, explain which **senses** you engaged in reading this poem.

Detail	Sight	Sound	Smell	Touch	Taste

Extend Understanding

9. **Art Connection:** Wordsworth's poem paints a vivid portrait of the daffodils. (a) Compare and contrast his poem with a photograph or painting of the same type of scene. (b) What could not be conveyed in a photograph or painting?

Quick Review

A **rhyme scheme** is a regular pattern of rhyming words that appear at the ends of lines in a poem.

A **simile** is a figure of speech in which *like* or *as* is used to make a comparison between two ideas that are basically dissimilar.

To use your **senses** while reading poetry, pay attention to images that appeal to your senses of sight, smell, sound, taste, and touch.

Take It to the Net

www.phschool.com

Take the interactive self-test online to check your understanding of the selection.

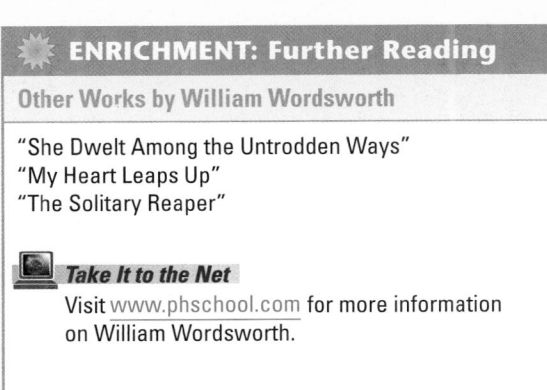

ENRICHMENT: Further Reading

Other Works by William Wordsworth

"She Dwelt Among the Untrodden Ways"
"My Heart Leaps Up"
"The Solitary Reaper"

Take It to the Net

Visit www.phschool.com for more information on William Wordsworth.

Answers for p. 899

Review and Assess

1. The rhyme scheme is *ababcc; dedeff; ghghii; jkjkll.*
2. The final words in the last two lines of each stanza rhyme with each other.
3. The final two lines of each stanza highlight the main idea or image of the stanza.
4. **(a)** Words include "lonely," "floats on high." **(b)** The speaker is isolated and lonely.
5. **(a)** The mood set by the title is one of aloneness. **(b)** Most students will believe that the simile in the title is effective because it makes them think of a cloud in a new way and evokes a feeling of airy solitude.
6. The daffodils are compared with the stars in the Milky Way. The comparison suggests the countless number of flowers.
7. **(a)** The word *host*, the comparison with stars, the never-ending line, and the number word *ten thousand* are all details that express the great numbers of daffodils **(b)** Students may identify the "tossing" of the blossoms or some other detail.
8. Possible responses: Students may cite: *saw a crowd* (sight); *fluttering and dancing* (sight, sound); *tossing their heads* (sight); *waves dance* (sight, sound); *flashed upon that inward eye* (sight). Students will find sight to be most engaged by this poem.
9. **(a)** A photograph or painting would show masses of flowers as described in the poem. In the artwork, however, the flowers would not be personified. **(b)** The emotional effect on the viewer could not be conveyed in the painting or photograph.

EXTEND

Answers for p. 900

❶ Vocabulary Development

Specialized Vocabulary: Poetic Contractions

1. it will
2. it was not
3. forever

Spelling Strategy

1. graceful
2. lovely
3. placement

Concept Development: Antonyms

1. c
2. b
3. b
4. c

❷ Grammar

1. Dorothy Wordsworth was many things: a sister, a friend, and an inspiration.
2. She wrote often in her journal; her comments are fascinating.
3. She described the field of daffodils vividly; many of her details appear in this poem.
4. According to her journal, the daffodils did the following things: tossed, reeled, danced, and laughed.
5. He used her journal entries to create his poem; it was written just as beautifully.

Writing Application

Sample sentences:

1. Three things strike me in this poem: color, movement, and mood.
2. The daffodils alone do not create the poem's effect; the "sparkling waves" of the lake are also vital.

Integrate Language Skills

❶ Vocabulary Development Lesson

Specialized Vocabulary: Poetic Contractions

Poets sometimes use **poetic contractions**—words in which one or more letters are left out—to sustain a rhythm or rhyme scheme. For example, Wordsworth uses the contraction *o'er*—short for *over*—to maintain the rhythm of line 2.

Identify the meanings of these contractions.

1. 'twill **2.** 'twasn't **3.** fore'er

Spelling Strategy

When adding a suffix that begins with a consonant to a word that ends in silent *e*, do not drop the *e*. For example, *pensive* + *-ly* = *pensively*. Add the suffix to each word below.

1. grace + *-ful* **2.** love + *-ly* **3.** place + *-ment*

Concept Development: Antonyms

Review the vocabulary list on page 895 and notice Wordsworth's use of the words in the poem. Then, in your notebook, write the word that is the antonym, or the opposite in meaning, of the first word.

1. glee: (a) intelligence, (b) happiness, (c) sorrow
2. pensive: (a) careless, (b) cheerful, (c) thoughtful
3. host: (a) army, (b) small number, (c) innkeeper
4. bliss: (a) intelligence, (b) happiness, (c) misery

❷ Grammar Lesson

Semicolons and Colons

A **semicolon** is used to join independent clauses that are closely related. It is also used to separate independent clauses or items in a series that already contain a number of commas.

A **colon** is used mainly to list items following an independent clause. Look at how the semicolon and the colon are used in the following sentences:

Semicolon:	The field of daffodils appeared unexpectedly; the sight greatly impressed Wordsworth.
Colon:	The flowers moved in ways that seemed almost human: fluttering, nodding, and dancing.

Practice Write these sentences on your paper, adding semicolons or colons wherever necessary.

1. Dorothy Wordsworth was many things a sister, a friend, and an inspiration.
2. She wrote often in her journal her comments are fascinating.
3. She described the field of daffodils vividly many of her details appear in this poem.
4. According to her journal, the daffodils did the following things tossed, reeled, danced, and laughed.
5. He used her journal entries to create his poem it was written just as beautifully.

Writing Application Write two sentences about Wordsworth's poem. Use a semicolon in one sentence and a colon in the other.

WG Prentice Hall Writing and Grammar Connection: Chapter 29, Section 3

TEACHING RESOURCES

The following resources can be used to enrich or extend the instruction for pp. 900–901.

Vocabulary

- **Selection Support:** Build Vocabulary, p. 201
- **Vocabulary and Spelling Practice Book** (Use this booklet for skills enrichment.) ■

Grammar

- **Selection Support:** Build Grammar Skills, p. 202
- **Writing and Grammar,** Gold Level, p. 674
- **Daily Language Practice Transparencies** ■

Writing

- **Writing and Grammar,** Gold Level, p. 112
- **Writing and Grammar iText CD-ROM** ■
- **Writing Models and Graphic Organizers on Transparencies,** pp. 17–20

■ **BLOCK SCHEDULING:** Resources marked with this symbol provide varied instruction during 90-minute blocks.

❸ Writing Lesson

Description of a Natural Scene

Wordsworth uses words to create a vivid portrait of a natural scene. Create your own descriptive word picture in the form of either a few paragraphs or a brief poem. Describe a beautiful natural scene that you have witnessed or seen in photographs.

Prewriting Jot down details that are related to the scene you have chosen. Next, decide on the purpose for your description. Eliminate details that do not fit your purpose and replace them with more precise details.

Drafting Decide whether your description will be a poem or a set of paragraphs. Use your notes to write your first draft.

Revising As you evaluate your writing, circle vague words and replace them with words that are more appealing to the senses. Also, eliminate details that confuse the purpose.

Model: Avoiding Unnecessary Details

Breathless,
I stood on the side of the crater. ~~I wondered what time it was.~~

massive
The sun threw shadows across the crater's ~~large~~ bowl.

Taking out unnecessary details and adding more precise words adds to the appeal of the word picture.

Prentice Hall Writing and Grammar Connection: Chapter 6, Section 4

❹ Extension Activities

Listening and Speaking Prepare a **visual presentation** about England's Lake District, where Wordsworth grew up. Follow this plan:

- Look for pictures of the region.
- Find connections between the landscape and the imagery that Wordsworth used.
- Practice giving the presentation so that you will feel comfortable speaking and displaying the visuals.

In your presentation, read Wordsworth's poem aloud to the class, and then explain your findings.

Research and Technology Wordsworth is one of the most famous British Romantic poets. With a few classmates, find out about the other Romantic poets, such as John Keats or Samuel Taylor Coleridge. Collect examples of their poetry. Using word-processing software, create an **anthology** of the poems and include an explanation of each choice. **[Group Activity]**

Take It to the Net www.phschool.com

Go online for an additional research activity using the Internet.

ASSESSMENT RESOURCES

The following resources can be used to assess students' knowledge and skills.

Selection Assessment

- **Formal Assessment,** Selection Test, pp. 183–185
- **Open Book Test,** pp. 151–153
- **Got It! Assessment Videotapes,** Tape 5
- **Test Bank Software**

Take It to the Net

Visit www.phschool.com for self-tests and additional questions on "I Wandered Lonely as a Cloud."

Writing Rubric

- **Performance Assess. and Portfolio Mgmt.,** p. 18

PRENTICE HALL ASSESSMENT SYSTEM

- **Workbook**
- **Transparencies**
- **Skill Book**
- **CD-ROM**

❸ Writing Lesson

- Stress that whether they choose to write a poem or a descriptive paragraph, students should eliminate details that do not fit the topic of their description.
- For step-by-step guidance in the writing process, use the writing process model for Descriptive and Observational Writing in **Writing Models and Graphic Organizers on Transparencies,** pp. 17–20.
- Use the Description rubric in **Performance Assessment and Portfolio Management,** p. 18, to evaluate students' descriptions.

❹ Research and Technology

- Ask groups of students to begin this project by consulting a print or online reference source to locate British Romantic poets.
- Urge students to read and discuss their favorite poems before choosing representative poems from a maximum of five poets for their anthology.
- Have students divide among themselves the tasks of writing the introductions for the poems, using a word-processing program to input the poems, and proofreading the poems meticulously to make sure that their anthology is error-free.

CUSTOMIZE INSTRUCTION for Universal Access

To address different learning styles, use the following activities suggested in the **Extension Activities** booklet, p. 49.

- For Verbal/Linguistic and Interpersonal Learners, use Activity 5.
- For Verbal/Linguistic and Rhythmic/Musical Learners, use Activity 6.

Dream Deferred ✦ Dreams ✦ The Eagle ✦ "Hope" is the thing with feathers—

Lesson Objectives and CA Correlations

1. **To analyze and respond to literary elements**
   - Literary Analysis: Figurative Language **R 3.7**
   - Comparing Literary Works: Connotation **R 3.8**
2. **To read, comprehend, analyze, and critique poems**
   - Reading Strategy: Paraphrasing
   - Review and Assess questions
   - Assessment Practice (ATE)
3. **To develop word analysis skills, fluency, and systematic vocabulary**
   - Vocabulary Development Lesson: Color Words **R 1.2**
4. **To understand and apply written and oral language conventions**
   - Spelling Strategy
   - Grammar Lesson: Dashes **LC 1.1**
5. **To understand and apply appropriate writing and research strategies**
   - Writing Lesson: Analytical Essay **W 2.2**
   - Extension Activity: Biographical Report **W 1.6**
6. **To understand and apply listening and speaking strategies**
   - Extension Activity: Inspirational Speech **LS 1.3**

STEP-BY-STEP TEACHING GUIDE	PACING GUIDE
PRETEACH	
Motivate Students and Provide Background	
Use the Motivation activity (ATE p. 902)	5 min.
Read and discuss the Preview material and Background information (SE/ATE p. 902) [A]	10 min.
Introduce the Concepts	
Introduce the Literary Analysis and Reading Strategy (SE/ATE p. 903) [A]	15 min.
Pronounce the vocabulary words and read their definitions (SE p. 903)	5 min.
TEACH	
Monitor Comprehension	
Informally monitor comprehension by circulating while students read independently or in groups [A]	15 min.
Develop vocabulary with Vocabulary notes (SE pp. 904–906, 908; ATE p. 906)	as students read
Develop Understanding	
Develop students' understanding of figurative language with the Literary Analysis annotations (ATE pp. 904, 906, 908) [A]	10 min.
Develop students' understanding of paraphrasing with the Reading Strategy annotation (ATE p. 905)	5 min.
ASSESS	
Assess Mastery	
Assess students' mastery of the Reading Strategy and Literary Analysis by having them answer the Review and Assess questions (SE/ATE p. 909)	20 min.
Use one or more of the print and media Assessment Resources (ATE p. 911) [A]	up to 50 min.
EXTEND	
Apply Understanding	
Have students complete the Vocabulary Development Lesson and the Grammar Lesson (SE p. 910) [A]	20 min.
Apply students' students' knowledge of replacing vague language using the Writing Lesson (SE/ATE p. 911) [A]	45 min.
Apply students' understanding using one or more of the Extension Activities (SE p. 911)	20–90 min.

[A] **ACCELERATED INSTRUCTION:** Use the strategies and activities identified with an [A].

UNIVERSAL ACCESS
● = Below-Level Students
▲ = On-Level Students
■ = Above-Level Students

Time and Resource Manager

Reading Level: Easy, Average, Average, Easy
Average Number of Instructional Days: 4

RESOURCES		
PRINT	**TRANSPARENCIES**	**TECHNOLOGY**
• **Beyond Literature,** Community Connection: Leadership Roles, p. 52 ▲ ■		• **Interest Grabber Video,** Tape 5 ● ▲ ■
• **Selection Support Workbook:** ● ▲ ■ Literary Analysis, p. 208 Reading Strategy, p. 207 Build Vocabulary, p. 205	• **Literary Analysis and Reading Transparencies,** pp. 103 and 104 ● ▲ ■	
• **Authors In Depth,** Gold Level, p. 179 ■		• **Listening to Literature** ● ▲ ■ Audiocassettes, Side 27 Audio CDs, CD 18
• **Literatura en español** ● ▲ • **Literary Analysis for Enrichment** ■		
• **Formal Assessment:** Selection Test, pp. 186–188 ● ▲ ■ • **Open Book Test,** pp. 154–156 ● ▲ ■ • **Performance Assessment and Portfolio Management,** p. 23 ● ▲ ■ • PRENTICE HALL ASSESSMENT SYSTEM ● ▲ ■	• PRENTICE HALL ASSESSMENT SYSTEM ● ▲ ■ Skills Practice Answers and Explanations on Transparencies	• **Test Bank Software** ● ▲ ■ • **Got It! Assessment Videotapes,** Tape 5 ● ▲
• **Selection Support Workbook:** ● ▲ ■ Build Grammar Skills, p. 206 • **Writing and Grammar,** Gold Level ● ▲ ■ • **Extension Activities,** p. 50 ● ▲ ■	• **Daily Language Practice Transparencies** ● ▲	• **Writing and Grammar iText CD-ROM** ● ▲ ■ *Take It to the Net* www.phschool.com

BLOCK SCHEDULING: Use one 90-minute class period to preteach the selection and have students read it. Use a second 90-minute class period to assess students' mastery of skills and have them complete one of the Extension Activities.

PRETEACH

Step-by-Step Teaching Guide for pp. 902–903

Motivation

Television programs about wild animals are extremely popular. These programs often show predators such as lions, cheetahs, bears, and birds of prey making their kills. Ask students whether they have ever seen such programs showing wild animals stalking and killing their prey. Then, discuss with the class why such scenes are popular with many viewers. Possible response: People admire animals' freedom and strength. Tell students that in Tennyson's poem "The Eagle" they will read about the nineteenth-century equivalent of a video sequence showing a bird of prey. Also remark that two of the other three poems in this section make use of bird imagery.

Interest Grabber Video

As an alternative, play "Resurgence of the Bald Eagle" on Tape 5 to engage student interest.

❶ Background

The Arts

The Harlem Renaissance of the 1920s and 1930s, which resulted from African American migration to cities, an international trend toward experimentation in art, and the rise of black intellectuals, was characterized by black pride and optimism about the future. The Harlem Renaissance stretched beyond the Harlem section of Manhattan to other black communities around the world and embraced many art forms: painting and sculpture, blues and jazz music, dance, film, and theater. African American painters associated with the Harlem Renaissance include Aaron Douglas, Archibald J. Motley, Jr., Jacob Lawrence, and Palmer Hayden. Blues and jazz had a strong influence on these painters, many of whose works are distinguished by hot, strong colors, seemingly improvised compositions, and syncopated rhythms.

Prepare to Read

Dream Deferred ◆ Dreams ◆ The Eagle ◆ "Hope" is the thing with feathers—

Bernard's Daddy, Raymond Lark, Edward Smith and Company

Take It to the Net

Visit www.phschool.com for interactive activities and instruction related to the selections, including
- background
- graphic organizers
- literary elements
- reading strategies

Preview

Connecting to the Literature

In your dreams, you can accomplish anything. Your hopes and dreams can provide you with the motivation you need to keep reaching for a goal. These poems explore the significance of hopes—and some of them look at what happens when dreams are shattered.

❶ Background

Harlem is a center for New York City's African American population. During the 1920s, Harlem blossomed with hope; writers and artists living there took part in a literary and cultural movement know as the Harlem Renaissance. When Langston Hughes wrote "Dream Deferred" in 1951, much of Harlem was marked by extreme poverty. As a result, many of those who lived in Harlem at the time felt a sense of hopelessness.

TEACHING RESOURCES

The following resources can be used to enrich or extend the instruction for pp. 902–903.

Motivation

Interest Grabber Videotapes, Tape 5

Background

Beyond Literature, p. 52

Take It to the Net

Visit www.phschool.com for background and hotlinks for the selections.

Literary Analysis

Literary Analysis and Reading Transparencies, Figurative Language, p. 104

Reading

Selection Support: Reading Strategy, p. 207; Build Vocabulary, p. 205

Literary Analysis and Reading Transparencies, Paraphrasing, p. 103

BLOCK SCHEDULING: Resources marked with this symbol provide varied instruction during 90-minute blocks.

❷ Literary Analysis

Figurative Language

Figurative language is writing or speech that is not meant to be taken literally. Instead, it is used to create vivid impressions by setting up comparisons between dissimilar things. Three common uses of figurative language are simile, metaphor, and personification.

- A **simile** compares one thing to another using *like* or *as*. Hughes uses a simile when he asks whether a dream deferred "stinks like rotten meat."
- A **metaphor** compares one thing to another without using *like* or *as*. Hughes uses a metaphor when he writes, "Life is a barren field."
- **Personification** gives human characteristics to an animal, object, or idea. Tennyson personifies an eagle by giving it "hands."

As you read, take note of language that creates an impression through unusual comparisons.

Comparing Literary Works

The power of figurative language is in the connotations of the words poets choose to compare. The **connotation** of a word is the idea, subtle meaning, or feeling associated with it. Hughes compares a dream deferred to a festering sore. Because the connotations of these words are powerfully negative, he conveys a feeling of sickness and despair. Compare the connotations conveyed through figurative language in these four selections.

❸ Reading Strategy

Paraphrasing

When you **paraphrase,** you use your own words to express what someone else has written. For example, Hughes's line "Hold fast to dreams" can be paraphrased as "Do not let go of dreams."

- Work through the poem one line at a time.
- Find a simpler way of expressing confusing lines.

Record your paraphrases in a chart like the one shown.

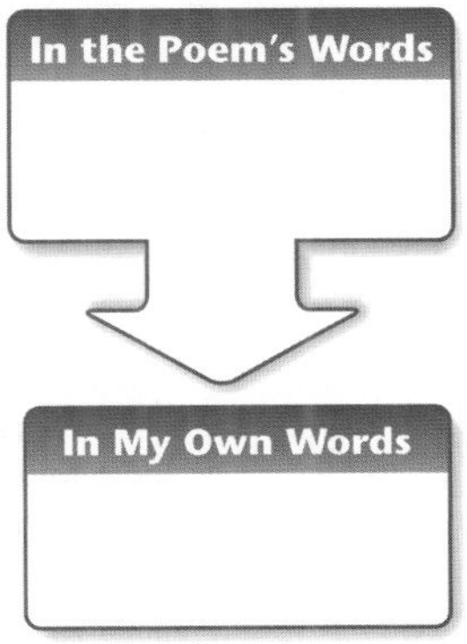

Vocabulary Development

deferred (di furd′) *adj.* put off until a future time (p. 904)

fester (fes′ tər) *v.* form pus (p. 904)

barren (bar′ ən) *adj.* empty (p. 905)

azure (azh′ ər) *adj.* blue (p. 906)

sore (sôr) *adj.* fierce; cruel (p. 908)

abash (ə bash′) *v.* embarrass (p. 908)

❷ Literary Analysis

Figurative Language

- Encourage students to pay close attention to *figurative language*—expressive language enriched by imagery and figures of speech—as they read the poems. Stress that understanding figurative language will help them to better understand and appreciate poetry.
- Review the instruction on *simile, metaphor,* and *personification.* Make sure students understand how the figurative language in the examples differs.
- Be sure students understand *connotation* as an additional association, often emotional, that adds to the literal definition of a word. *Steed, horse,* and *nag* all refer to the same animal, but each word carries a different connotation.
- Review the Figurative Language transparency in **Literary Analysis and Reading Transparencies,** p. 104, with students. With the students' help, add the examples from this page to the correct columns.

❸ Reading Strategy

Paraphrasing

- Remind students that *paraphrasing* difficult passages, by restating those parts in their own words, is a valuable method for checking comprehension.
- Refer students to the chart in their books. Explain to students that they will make a similar chart on which they will record difficult passages from the four poems and their paraphrases of those passages.

Vocabulary Development

- Pronounce each vocabulary word for students, and read the definitions as a class. Have students identify any words with which they are already familiar.

CUSTOMIZE INSTRUCTION FOR UNIVERSAL ACCESS

For Less Proficient Readers	For English Learners	For Advanced Readers
Have students read each poem silently as they listen to the audiotape or CD and then read each one aloud together. Make sure students understand that the end of a line of poetry is not necessarily the end of a thought.	Have students listen to the poems on audiotape or CD without worrying about meaning. Then, ask students to follow along in their books as they listen to each poem again for meaning. They should note each word or phrase they don't understand. Define the difficult words for students or have them look up the words in a dictionary.	Have the students read the poems independently. Then, have pairs of students discuss each poem. Ask them to figure out the rhyme scheme for each poem. Then have them consider the effect of the figurative language. In their opinion, why were or weren't the images powerful?

E-Teach

Visit E-Teach at www.phschool.com for teachers' essays on how to teach, with questions and answers.

TEACH

Step-by-Step Teaching Guide for pp. 904–908

CUSTOMIZE INSTRUCTION
For Musical/Rhythmic Learners

Have students read the poems aloud to themselves as smoothly and rhythmically as they can. If they like, they can "sing" the poems. As they read, they should tap on their desks lightly with a finger or pencil to indicate stressed words.

❶ About the Selections

What happens when dreams are dashed by frustration? "Dream Deferred" by Langston Hughes uses powerful images to depict the despair of shattered dreams. Is life worth living without hopes and dreams? In "Dreams," Hughes uses two vivid metaphors to communicate the fundamental importance of a dream to a person's life.

❷ Literary Analysis

Figurative Language

- Have a volunteer read lines 2–11 of "Dream Deferred" aloud.
- Ask students what kind of figurative language is used in this poem.
  Answer: simile
- Have students tell you what is being compared in each simile.
  Answer: A dream is compared to a raisin, a sore, rotten meat, a sweet, and a heavy load.

❸ Background

Art

Bernard's Daddy by Raymond Lark

This graphite drawing shows a young African American in a posture of tiredness or discouragement. Use these questions for discussion:

1. In what ways does the picture show the effects of a dream deferred?
   Answer: The figure looks sad and hopeless.
2. Which simile from Hughes's poem best fits this picture, and why?
   Answer: "Like a heavy load" fits the figure's weary posture.

❸

Bernard's Daddy, Raymond Lark, Edward Smith and Company

❹ ▲ **Critical Viewing** Explain why you do or do not think this piece of art is an effective illustration for the two poems. **[Evaluate]**

❶ Dream Deferred

Langston Hughes

Harlem

What happens to a dream deferred?

Does it dry up
like a raisin in the sun?
Or fester like a sore——
And then run?
❷ Does it stink like rotten meat?
Or crust and sugar over——
like a syrupy sweet?

Maybe it just sags
like a heavy load.

Or does it explode?

deferred (di fʉrd´) *adj.* put off until a future time

fester (fes´ tər) *v.* form pus

TEACHING RESOURCES

The following resources can be used to enrich or extend the instruction for pp. 904–908.

Literary Analysis

- **Selection Support:** Literary Analysis, p. 208

Reading

- **Listening to Literature Audiocassettes,** Side 27 ▪
- **Listening to Literature Audio CDs,** CD 18 ▪
- **Authors In Depth,** Gold Level (The collection includes fourteen additional poems and a letter by Emily Dickinson for extended reading.)

▪ **BLOCK SCHEDULING:** Resources marked with this symbol provide varied instruction during 90-minute blocks.

1 # Dreams

Langston Hughes

5 Hold fast to dreams
For if dreams die
Life is a broken-winged bird
That cannot fly.

Hold fast to dreams
For when dreams go
Life is a barren field
Frozen with snow.

barren (bar′ən) *adj.* empty

Langston Hughes

(1902–1967)

Langston Hughes, born in Joplin, Missouri, was the first African American to have a strictly literary career. As a young man, he held a variety of jobs—teacher, ranch hand, farmer, seaman, and night-club cook, among others. He drew on all of these experiences, but even more so on his experience as an African American man, to create his great body of work. "Dream Deferred" and "Dreams" illustrate his ability to express the spirit of black America.

Review and Assess

Thinking About the Selections

1. **Respond:** Which poem affected you more? Why?
2. **(a) Recall:** What is the first question asked in "Dream Deferred"? **(b) Infer:** How is the question answered? **(c) Speculate:** Why does Hughes use six questions and only one statement in the poem?
3. **(a) Compare and Contrast:** How does the last line of "Dream Deferred" contrast with the rest of the poem? **(b) Draw Conclusions:** What is the effect of this contrast?
4. **(a) Recall:** To what two things does the speaker in "Dreams" compare life? **(b) Interpret:** Restate in your own words the advice that "Dreams" offers.
5. **Apply:** How might you apply the advice Hughes gives in "Dreams" to your own life?
6. **(a) Assess:** What might your life be like if you were prevented from pursuing your dreams or goals? **(b) Extend:** Which personal qualities are needed to hold on to dreams in adversity?

CUSTOMIZE INSTRUCTION FOR UNIVERSAL ACCESS

For Special Needs Students	For Gifted/Talented Students
Copy both poems on the chalkboard. Circle the questions and statements in the poems and discuss each one. Note the indentation in "Dream Deferred" and explain that the possible answers to this question form the topic of the poem. In "Dreams," make sure that students notice that the first and second stanzas begin with the same line. The three other lines in each stanza describe in metaphors what happens when people's dreams are frustrated.	Ask students to choose a simile from "Dream Deferred" or a metaphor from "Dreams" and illustrate it using art materials of their choice. Encourage them to use techniques and colors that express what the figurative language brings to their minds and how the figurative language affects them emotionally.

4 ▶Critical Viewing

Possible response: The art is effective because it shows a man dreaming or in despair, which fits the moods of the two poems.

5 Reading Strategy

Paraphrasing

- Ask students to identify the line or lines in "Dreams" that sum up the poem.
  Answer: Students may cite lines one and five, "Hold fast to dreams."
- Have volunteers paraphrase this line.
  Possible response: Hold onto your dreams; don't give up your hopes.

Answers for p. 905

Review and Assess

1. Students may be affected more by "Dream Deferred" because of the power of the similes and the pattern of questions.
2. **(a)** "What happens to a dream deferred?" **(b)** The question is "answered" by five additional questions and one speculation. **(c)** Possible answer: The repetition of questions underscores the many possible tragedies of not being allowed to follow one's dreams. The single statement near the end of the poem breaks the pattern of questions, giving the final question even greater impact.
3. **(a)** The last line is set off in italic type and is a metaphor, not a simile as the other comparisons are. **(b)** The reader pays particular attention to the last line and the way it intensifies Hughes's message.
4. **(a)** The speaker compares life to an injured bird and a barren, frozen field. **(b)** Possible response: Without dreams, life is meaningless.
5. Students might apply the advice to their own dreams for future careers.
6. **(a)** Many students may say that they would be frustrated and depressed. **(b)** Students may believe that it takes determination and stubbornness to hold onto dreams.

6 About the Selection

In "The Eagle," Tennyson expresses awe and admiration for the bird's strength and majesty.

7 Critical Thinking

Analyze

- Ask students why lands might be considered lonely.
  Answer: A land that is nearly uninhabited by people or wildlife might be considered lonely.
- Then, ask students what the word *lonely* contributes to their impression of the eagle.
  Answer: The eagle's solitude makes it more majestic and awe-inspiring.

8 Vocabulary Development

Specialized Vocabulary: Color Words

- Have a volunteer read line 3.
- Ask students to identify the color word.
  Answer: The color word is *azure*.
- Have students speculate about why the poet didn't simply use the word *blue*.
  Possible answer: The word *azure* is more unusual or "poetic," has an interesting sound, and describes a clear, light shade of blue.

9 Literary Analysis

Figurative Language

- Have a volunteer read aloud line 4. Ask students to find examples of figurative language in the poem.
  Answer: "He clasps . . . with crooked hands" and "stands" are examples of personification. The poet has assigned human characteristics to the eagle. "The wrinkled sea . . . crawls" is a metaphor.
- Ask a volunteer to read aloud line 6. Ask students to identify the figurative language in this line.
  Answer: "Like a thunderbolt" is an example of simile. The eagle is compared to lightning.

6

The Eagle

Alfred, Lord Tennyson

He clasps the crag[1] with crooked hands;
7 Close to the sun in lonely lands,
8 Ring'd with the <u>azure</u> world, he stands.

9 The wrinkled sea beneath him crawls;
He watches from his mountain walls,
And like a thunderbolt he falls.

azure (azh´ ər) *adj.* blue

1. **crag** (krag) *n.* steep, rugged rock that juts out from a rock mass.

ENRICHMENT: Science Connection

Bald Eagle

The bald eagle, which has been the national bird of the United States since 1782, is the only eagle unique to North America. Eighty percent of the approximately 50,000 bald eagles in the United States are found in Alaska.

The bald eagle's scientific name, *Haliaeetus leucocephalus*, indicates that the bird is a sea eagle with a white head. (At one time, the word *bald* meant "white.")

The Bald Eagle Protection Act makes it illegal for anyone (except members of certain tribes of Native Americans) to collect or possess eagles or their feathers, eggs, or nests without a permit.

Review and Assess

Thinking About the Selection

1. **Respond:** How did you feel as you read "The Eagle"? Why?
2. **(a) Recall:** When the poem opens, where is the eagle? **(b) Interpret:** Why does Tennyson place the eagle in that setting?
3. **(a) Interpret:** What is meant by the words "close to the sun"? **(b) Assess:** What effect does this phrase have on your response to the eagle?
4. **(a) Recall:** What is the eagle doing? **(b) Make a Judgment:** Is "falls" the right word for the action of the eagle in line 6? Explain.
5. **(a) Compare and Contrast:** How is the first stanza different from the second? **(b) Evaluate:** Why do you think Tennyson breaks such a short poem into two stanzas?
6. **(a) Assess:** Which words would you use to describe an eagle? **(b) Extend:** Why do you think an eagle is the national emblem of the United States?

Alfred, Lord Tennyson

(1809–1892)

The most popular of British poets during his lifetime, Alfred, Lord Tennyson rose from the quiet of humble beginnings to the glory of the position of poet laureate of England. Although he was enthralled by the technological advances of the Victorian era, Tennyson remained a poet of nature, bringing both imagination and feeling to the landscape and its inhabitants.

Answers for p. 907

Review and Assess

1. Students may say that they felt exhilarated and impressed by the eagle and his rapid descent.
2. **(a)** The eagle is on a rocky cliff. **(b)** The setting is suited to the majestic spirit of the eagle.
3. **(a)** The eagle is at a great height. **(b)** It makes the reader even more awed by the power of the eagle.
4. **(a)** The eagle is looking down from a mountain and then descending rapidly. He is probably hunting. **(b)** If students say *falls* is the wrong word, they may mention that the eagle's action is deliberate and aimed. If students say *falls* is appropriate, they might say that it accurately conveys the steepness and speed of the eagle's descent.
5. **(a)** The two stanzas provide two different visions of the eagle. In the first stanza, the eagle is waiting. At the end of the second stanza, he descends. The key distinguishing words are the last in each stanza: *stands* and *falls.* **(b)** Tennyson is emphasizing the contrast between the eagle waiting and watching and the bird falling.
6. **(a)** Possible words include *majestic, fierce, focused, independent, proud,* and *solitary.* **(b)** Most students will believe that the impressive fierceness and independence of the eagle make it an appropriate symbol for the United States.

CUSTOMIZE INSTRUCTION FOR UNIVERSAL ACCESS

For Less Proficient Readers	For English Learners	For Advanced Readers
Focus on some of the ways "The Eagle" differs from a prose treatment of the same topic. Read the poem aloud once and then have the group read it in unison. Urge students to picture in their minds what the poet describes. Then, code the rhyme scheme (*aaa, bbb*).	Read the poem aloud and have students follow along in their books. Then, have the students read it aloud in unison. Can students hear the rhyming words? Review the less common and "poetic" words with students: *crag, ring'd, azure, thunderbolt* to make sure students understand the meaning of each word.	Have students form small groups and discuss "The Eagle," with particular emphasis on Tennyson's choice of words and rhyme scheme. Then, have students work together to write a parody of the poem, substituting a different bird in place of the eagle.

ASSESS

⑩ About the Selection

In "'Hope' is the thing with feathers—," Dickinson compares hope to a bird—small and delicate, yet constant and indomitable.

⑪ Literary Analysis

Figurative Language

- Ask a volunteer to read the first two lines of the poem.
- Point out that "perches in the soul" contains an implied metaphor for "soul."

Monitor Progress Ask students if something perches in the soul, with what is the poet comparing the soul?

Answer: Students may answer that the soul is being compared to a tree limb or a birdcage.

Answers for p. 908

Review and Assess

1. Some students will agree with Dickinson that hope is universal. Others may think that people can live without hope and that many people do.
2. **(a)** Hope is compared to a bird. **(b)** Many students will believe that the way hope causes the heart to lift can be compared to the song of a bird.
3. **(a)** Hope sings a continuous, wordless song. **(b)** Hope is a feeling, not a set of instructions; in the same way, a bird's song is a tune without words.
4. **(a)** Hope sings "sweetest" in times of extremity—in storm, "chillest land," or on "the strangest Sea." **(b)** Hope is most needed at the worst moments of people's lives.
5. In dangerous, difficult, or unhappy times, hope can keep people "warm."

⑩ "Hope" is the thing with feathers—

Emily Dickinson

⑪ "Hope" is the thing with feathers—
That perches in the soul—
And sings the tune without the words—
And never stops—at all—

And sweetest—in the Gale[1]—is heard—
And <u>sore</u> must be the storm—
That could <u>abash</u> the little Bird
That kept so many warm—

I've heard it in the chillest land—
And on the strangest Sea—
Yet, never, in Extremity,
It asked a crumb—of Me.

sore (sôr) *adj.* fierce; cruel

abash (ə bash′) *v.* embarrass

1. **gale** (gāl) *n.* strong wind.

Emily Dickinson

(1830–1886)

Shy, solitary, and brilliant, Emily Dickinson led a life filled with loneliness in Amherst, Massachusetts. Yet, despite her quiet exterior, an inner life continually raged, enabling her to produce at least 1,775 poems.

Dickinson is known for her deceptively simple subjects from nature—flies buzzing at the moment of human death, birds coming down a walk. She wrote most frequently about death, love, and some of her religious beliefs. Whatever her subject, however, Dickinson's treatment was imaginative, complex, and thought-provoking.

Review and Assess

Thinking About the Selection

1. **Respond:** How do your views about hope compare with those expressed in Dickinson's poem?
2. **(a) Recall:** What is hope compared to in the poem? **(b) Analyze:** What do the two items have in common?
3. **(a) Recall:** According to the speaker, what does hope do? **(b) Interpret:** Why is it significant that hope sings a tune without words?
4. **(a) Infer:** When does hope sing the "sweetest" tune? **(b) Interpret:** Why would it sing so well at this time?
5. **Extend:** In what kinds of situations might hope keep people "warm"?

ASSESSMENT PRACTICE: Reading Comprehension

Vocabulary: Complete Analogies (For more practice, see Test Preparation Workbook, p. 52.)

Use the following sample test items to give students practice in completing word analogies.

CRIMSON : RED : :

A pink : violet
B turquoise : blue
C orange : scarlet
D white : gray

Guide students to understand that the correct answer is *B*, because the relationship between *turquoise* (a shade of blue) and *blue* (a primary color) is parallel to that between *crimson* and *red*.

SPEED : COLLISION : :

A storm : tornado
B running : exercise
C misunderstanding : argument
D highway : travel

Students should recognize that the relationship between the first pair of words is one of cause and effect; therefore, the correct answer is *C*.

Review and Assess

Literary Analysis

Figurative Language

1. List the similes found in "Dream Deferred." Which similes are the most effective? Why?
2. (a) Change the two metaphors in "Dreams" into similes by adding *like*. (b) Does this alter the effect or meaning of the poem? Explain.
3. Using a chart like the one shown, list the **figurative language** in "'Hope' is the thing with feathers—" and "The Eagle." Then, write the comparison being made for each.

Poem	→	Simile	Metaphor	Personification

Comparing Literary Works

4. Using a chart like the one shown, compare the **connotations** of the figurative language found in each of the poems.

Poem	Figurative Language	→	Connotation

5. (a) Which poem connotes, or suggests, a feeling of despair? How? (b) Which poem connotes optimism and perseverance? How?

Reading Strategy

Paraphrasing

6. (a) **Paraphrase** the last stanza of "Dreams." (b) According to the poem, how would your life feel if it were empty of dreams?
7. Paraphrase the last stanza of "'Hope' is the thing with feathers—". Be sure to supply a noun to take the place of the pronoun *it*.

Extend Understanding

8. **Social Studies Connection:** How might civil rights leaders have used any of these poems in support of their cause?

Quick Review

Figurative language is language that says one thing and means another.

A **simile** compares one thing to another using *like* or *as*.

A **metaphor** compares one thing to another without using *like* or *as*.

Personification gives human characteristics to an animal, object, or idea.

The **connotation** of a word is the idea, or subtle meaning, associated with it.

To **paraphrase,** use your own words to express what someone else has written.

Take It to the Net

www.phschool.com

Take the interactive self-test online to check your understanding of the selections.

ENRICHMENT: Further Reading

Other Works by the Poets

Works by Langston Hughes
"Mother to Son"
The Big Sea
Works by Alfred, Lord Tennyson
"The Lady of Shalott"
"Break, Break, Break"
Works by Emily Dickinson
"I heard a fly buzz when I died"
"I'm nobody! Who are you?"

Answers for p. 909

Review and Assess

1. Similes to which a dream is compared include a "raisin," "a sore," "rotten meat," "syrupy sweet," and "heavy load." Students will cite the similes that seem most vivid to them.
2. **(a)** "Life is like a broken-winged bird"; "Life is like a barren field." **(b)** Possible response: The similes are less effective than the metaphors because they are less direct.
3. "The Eagle": Personification: "crooked hands" and "stands" liken the eagle to a human. Metaphor: the sea "crawls" in a comparison to a creature. Simile: "like a thunderbolt" compares the eagle with lightning. Metaphor: "'Hope' is the thing with feathers"; Hope is identified as a songbird.
4. "Dream Deferred": Figurative Language: "like a raisin in the sun," "like a sore," "like rotten meat," "like a syrupy sweet," and "like a heavy load." Connotation: Deferred dreams are unpleasant. "Dreams": Figurative Language: "Life is a broken-winged bird," "Life is a barren field." Connotation: Ruined dreams make life bleak. "The Eagle": Figurative Language: "wrinkled sea beneath him crawls," "like a thunderbolt he falls"; Connotation: The sea moves slowly, the eagle, rapidly. "'Hope' is the thing with feathers—": Figurative Language: "'Hope' is the thing with feathers—" Connotation: Hope is comfort and solace.
5. **(a)** Possible response: "Dream Deferred" connotes a feeling of despair by describing damaging effects; **(b)** "'Hope' is the thing with feathers—" connotes optimism and perseverance by suggesting that people never lose hope.
6. **(a)** Possible response: If you abandon your dreams, life will become meaningless. **(b)** Life would feel like an injured bird or a barren, frozen field.

continued

Answers continued

7. Possible response: No matter where you go or what you do, hope is always present.
8. Possible response: Civil rights leaders might have used "Dreams Deferred" to show the damaging effects of segregation. They might have used "Dreams" to inspire their people.

EXTEND

Answers for p. 910

❶ Vocabulary Development

Specialized Vocabulary

1. vermilion—a brilliant, scarlet red
2. emerald—a clear, deep green
3. ivory—a creamy or yellowish white
4. ebony—a deep, lustrous black

Spelling Strategy

1. planned
2. controller
3. regretted

Concept Development: Context

1. The donation helped greatly after the sore hurricane struck the family's home.
2. Changes in the work calendar resulted in deferred vacations, which upset the students.
3. The clouds were bright white against the azure sky, creating an unforgettable view.
4. Kim was feeling so confident that nothing could abash her.
5. Matt's cut began to fester.
6. The field behind the farmhouse seemed curiously barren.

❷ Grammar

1. She is an amazing writer—to think that she was never acknowledged in her lifetime.
2. Her poem—so beautifully crafted—is just one of thousands she wrote.
3. Only a handful of poems—seven, in fact—appeared in print before Dickinson's death.
4. Intensely personal, simple in language, rather free in form—Dickinson's poetry ran contrary to literary tastes of that time.
5. Perhaps if she had published more—but I suppose we will never know.

Writing Application

Paragraphs about hope should include each of the three functions of the dash; to interrupt an idea, as a summary statement, and to signal abrupt changes.

Integrate Language Skills

❶ Vocabulary Development Lesson

Specialized Vocabulary: Color Words

Azure, a shade of blue, is just one of the many words that poets use to convey meaning with more exactness and feeling.

Use a dictionary to find the meanings of these color words: *vermilion, emerald, ivory*, and *ebony*.

Spelling Strategy

If a word of more than one syllable ends in a single consonant following a single vowel, and the accent falls on the last syllable, the final consonant is usually doubled when a suffix starting with a vowel is added. For example, *defer* + *-ed* = *deferred*. Write the word formed by adding each ending. Use a dictionary to check your spelling.

1. plan + *-ed* 2. control + *-er* 3. regret + *-ed*

Concept Development: Context

Review the vocabulary list on page 903. Then, substitute a vocabulary word for the word or phrase in italics below.

1. The donation helped greatly after the *fierce* hurricane struck the family's home.
2. Changes in the work calendar resulted in *delayed* vacations, which upset the students.
3. The clouds were bright white against the *blue* sky, creating an unforgettable view.
4. Kim was feeling so confident that nothing could *embarrass* her.
5. Matt's cut began to *run with pus*.
6. The field behind the farmhouse seemed curiously *empty of life*.

❷ Grammar Lesson

Dashes

Dashes are part of Emily Dickinson's poetic style. In everyday use, the **dash** functions in three basic ways: to dramatically set off an interrupting idea, to set off a summary statement, or to indicate an abrupt change of thought.

Interrupting Idea: Dickinson—one of the greatest American poets—did not achieve fame during her lifetime.

Summary Statement: Thomas Higginson and Helen Jackson—these are two of the few friends who recognized her talent.

Abrupt Change: Let me read you this example of—now, where did I put that book of poems?

Practice Copy these sentences, adding dashes where appropriate.

1. She is an amazing writer to think that she was never acknowledged in her lifetime.
2. Her poem so beautifully crafted is just one of thousands she wrote.
3. Only a handful of poems seven, in fact appeared in print before Dickinson's death.
4. Intensely personal, simple in language rather free in form Dickinson's poetry ran contrary to literary tastes of that time.
5. Perhaps if she had published more but I suppose we will never know.

Writing Application Write a paragraph about hope that uses each function of the dash.

WG *Prentice Hall Writing and Grammar Connection: Chapter 29, Section 5*

TEACHING RESOURCES

The following resources can be used to enrich or extend the instruction for pp. 910–911.

Vocabulary

- **Selection Support:** Build Vocabulary, p. 205
- **Vocabulary and Spelling Practice Book** (Use this booklet for skills enrichment.)

Grammar

- **Selection Support:** Build Grammar Skills, p. 206
- **Writing and Grammar,** Gold Level, p. 698
- **Daily Language Practice Transparencies** ■

Writing

- **Writing and Grammar,** Gold Level, p. 286
- **Writing and Grammar iText CD-ROM** ■

■ **BLOCK SCHEDULING:** Resources marked with this symbol provide varied instruction during 90-minute blocks.

❸ Writing Lesson

Analytical Essay

Review the poems in this section, and write an essay in which you interpret the message that the poet conveys in one of the poems.

Prewriting Decide which poem you would like to interpret. Consider the message you think it conveys, and then make a list of words or lines from the poem that support your interpretation.

Drafting In the first paragraph, make sure you identify the title and author of the poem and provide a brief overview of your interpretation. In the body of your essay, develop your ideas and provide examples from the poem. Your last paragraph should restate your main point.

Revising Review your draft to determine whether you have conveyed your ideas clearly. Replace any vague language with more precise words.

Model: Replacing Vague Language

desperate
It conveys the power of hope, for even in ~~bad~~
provide comfort and strength
times, hope can ~~help~~.

The inserted words provide more precise language and clarify the interpretation.

Prentice Hall Writing and Grammar Connection: Chapter 13, Section 3

❹ Extension Activities

Listening and Speaking Use the poems of Dickinson and Hughes as the basis for an **inspirational speech** about the importance of hopes and dreams.

- Make sure that your speech includes a main idea that conveys hope.
- Prepare a conclusion that restates your main idea in a powerful way.
- Practice your speech in front of a friend.

As you present your speech, use body language and eye contact to convey your sincerity. Ask your audience to give you feedback about your performance.

Research and Technology In a small group, prepare a **biographical report** about Tennyson, Dickinson, or Hughes. In your writing, provide information about the writer's life, and use quotations from his or her work to show the writer's character. Use library resources, including the Internet, to gather information, and be sure to include citations of your materials where appropriate. **[Group Activity]**

Take It to the Net www.phschool.com

Go online for an additional research activity using the Internet.

ASSESSMENT RESOURCES

The following resources can be used to assess students' knowledge and skills.

Selection Assessment

- **Formal Assessment,** Selection Test, pp. 186–188
- **Open Book Test,** pp. 154–156
- **Got It! Assessment Videotapes,** Tape 5
- **Test Bank Software**

Take It to the Net

Visit www.phschool.com for self-tests and additional questions on the poems.

Listening and Speaking Rubric

- **Performance Assess. and Portfolio Mgmt.,** p. 23

PRENTICE HALL ASSESSMENT SYSTEM

- **Workbook**
- **Skill Book**
- **Transparencies**
- **CD-ROM**

Lesson Support for p. 911

❸ Writing Lesson

- Use a short poem the class has already read to model a prewriting analysis.
- Read the poem and share your thinking with students as you jot down the message of the poem.
- Follow the Writing Lesson to guide students through the prewriting, drafting, and revising stages of their essays.

❹ Listening and Speaking

- Read or play excerpts from an inspirational speech to students, such as Martin Luther King's "I Have a Dream," Abraham Lincoln's "Gettysburg Address," or Nelson Mandela's "Glory and Hope," p. 506.
- Discuss with the class the reasons the speech is effective. Focus on the conclusion.
- Have students work in pairs so they can test out their main ideas on partners.
- Allow class time for students to present their speeches.
- Use the Evaluating a Speech rubric in **Performance Assessment and Portfolio Management,** p. 23, to assess the speeches.

CUSTOMIZE INSTRUCTION for Universal Access

To address different learning styles, use the activities suggested in the **Extension Activities** booklet, p. 52.

- For Bodily/Kinesthetic and Verbal/Linguistic Learners, use Activity 5.
- For Logical/Mathematical and Intrapersonal Learners, use Activity 6.
- For Interpersonal and Verbal/Linguistic Learners, use Activity 7.

Blackberry Eating ✦ Memory ✦ Eulogy for a Hermit Crab ✦ Meciendo ✦ Woman's Work

Lesson Objectives and CA Correlations

1. **To analyze and respond to literary elements**
   - Literary Analysis: Imagery **R 3.7**
   - Comparing Literary Works
2. **To read, comprehend, analyze, and critique poems**
   - Reading Strategy: Picturing the Imagery **R 3.7**
   - Review and Assess questions
   - Assessment Practice (ATE)
3. **To develop word analysis skills, fluency, and systematic vocabulary**
   - Vocabulary Development Lesson: Latin Root: *-prim-* **R 1.1**
4. **To understand and apply written and oral language conventions**
   - Spelling Strategy
   - Grammar Lesson: Ellipsis Points **LC 1.1**
5. **To understand and apply appropriate writing and research strategies**
   - Writing Lesson: Letter About a Memorable Moment **W 2.1**
   - Extension Activity: Research Report **W 1.3**
6. **To understand and apply listening and speaking strategies**
   - Extension Activity: Presentation of Artwork **LS 1.7**

STEP-BY-STEP TEACHING GUIDE	PACING GUIDE
PRETEACH	
Motivate Students and Provide Background	
Use the Motivation activity (ATE p. 912)	5 min.
Read and discuss the Preview material and Background information (SE/ATE p. 912) [A]	10 min.
Introduce the Concepts	
Introduce the Literary Analysis and Reading Strategy (SE/ATE p. 913) [A]	15 min.
Pronounce the vocabulary words and read their definitions (SE p. 913)	5 min.
TEACH	
Monitor Comprehension	
Informally monitor comprehension by circulating while students read independently or in groups [A]	15 min.
Develop vocabulary with Vocabulary notes (SE pp. 914–916, 919, 920)	as students read
Develop Understanding	
Develop students' understanding of imagery with the Literary Analysis annotations (SE p. 920; ATE pp. 914, 916, 920) [A]	10 min.
Develop students' ability to picture the imagery with the Reading Strategy annotations (SE pp. 916, 919; ATE pp. 915–916, 918–919)	10 min.
ASSESS	
Assess Mastery	
Assess students' mastery of the Reading Strategy and Literary Analysis by having them answer the Review and Assess questions (SE/ATE p. 921)	20 min.
Use one or more of the print and media Assessment Resources (ATE p. 923) [A]	up to 50 min.
EXTEND	
Apply Understanding	
Have students complete the Vocabulary Development Lesson and the Grammar Lesson (SE p. 922) [A]	20 min.
Apply students' knowledge of main impressions using the Writing Lesson (SE/ATE p. 923) [A]	45 min.
Apply students' understanding using one or more of the Extension Activities (SE p. 923)	20–90 min.

[A] ACCELERATED INSTRUCTION: Use the strategies and activities identified with an [A].

UNIVERSAL ACCESS
● = Below-Level Students
▲ = On-Level Students
■ = Above-Level Students

Time and Resource Manager

Reading Level: Easy/Easy/Average/Average/Average
Average Number of Instructional Days: 4

RESOURCES		
PRINT	**TRANSPARENCIES**	**TECHNOLOGY**
• **Beyond Literature,** Cross-Curricular Connection: Science, p. 53 ▲ ■		• **Interest Grabber Video,** Tape 5 ● ▲ ■
• **Selection Support Workbook:** ● ▲ ■ Literary Analysis, p. 212 Reading Strategy, p. 211 Build Vocabulary, p. 209	• **Literary Analysis and Reading Transparencies,** pp. 105 and 106 ● ▲ ■	
• **Adapted Reader's Companion** ● • **Reader's Companion** ●		• **Listening to Literature** ● ▲ ■ Audiocassettes, Side 27 Audio CDs, CD 18
• **English Learner's Companion** ● ▲ • **Literatura en español** ● ▲ • **Literary Analysis for Enrichment** ■		
• **Formal Assessment:** Selection Test, pp. 189–191 ● ▲ ■ • **Open Book Test,** pp. 157–159 ● ▲ ■ • **Performance Assessment and Portfolio Management,** p. 30 ● ▲ ■ • PRENTICE HALL ASSESSMENT SYSTEM ● ▲ ■	• PRENTICE HALL ASSESSMENT SYSTEM ● ▲ ■ Skills Practice Answers and Explanations on Transparencies	• **Test Bank Software** ● ▲ ■ • **Got It! Assessment Videotapes,** Tape 5 ● ▲
• **Selection Support Workbook:** ● ▲ ■ Build Grammar Skills, p. 210 • **Writing and Grammar,** Gold Level ● ▲ ■ • **Extension Activities,** p. 51 ● ▲ ■	• **Daily Language Practice Transparencies** ● ▲	• **Writing and Grammar iText CD-ROM** ● ▲ ■ ***Take It to the Net*** www.phschool.com

BLOCK SCHEDULING: Use one 90-minute class period to preteach the selection and have students read it. Use a second 90-minute class period to assess students' mastery of skills and have them complete one of the Extension Activities.

PRETEACH

Step-by-Step Teaching Guide for pp. 912–913

Motivation

On the chalkboard, write the words *woman's work.* Ask students what kinds of work they would list under this heading and record their responses. The lively discussion that this exercise will spark can be harnessed in a brief, informal debate. Have the students on one side of the classroom take the affirmative position and the other side the negative position on the following statement: "There is no kind of work that should be considered exclusively 'man's work' or 'woman's work.'" Give the members of each side a chance to make several points and to respond to their opponents' points. Then, tell the class that one poem in the group of poems they will read is about the subject of their debate.

Interest Grabber Video

As an alternative, play "Woman's Work" on Tape 5 to engage student interest.

1 Background

Science

The hermit crab belongs to the hermit crab family *Paguridae.* Each hermit crab lives alone in its adopted shell, hence its name. However, large groups of these crabs often congregate in areas of the ocean floor where shells are abundant. Hermit crabs have been known to pull other crabs from their shells if empty shells are scarce.

Prepare to Read

Blackberry Eating ◆ Memory ◆ Eulogy for a Hermit Crab ◆ Meciendo ◆ Woman's Work

Take It to the Net

Visit www.phschool.com for interactive activities and instruction related to the selections, including
- background
- graphic organizers
- literary elements
- reading strategies

Preview

Connecting to the Literature

With a little thought, you can often find deeper meaning in routine events and observations. For example, gazing upon the ocean might make you think of the immensity and timelessness of nature. As these poems illustrate, one of the great qualities of poetry is that it can lead you toward such insights.

1 Background

One of the poems in this group is about a hermit crab, an animal that carries around an abandoned shell to cover its soft, unprotected abdomen. As a hermit crab grows, it must continually find larger shells—a dilemma that causes much competition among hermit crabs.

TEACHING RESOURCES

The following resources can be used to enrich or extend the instruction for pp. 912–913.

Motivation

Interest Grabber Video, Tape 5

Background

Beyond Literature, p. 53

Take It to the Net

Visit www.phschool.com for background and hotlinks for the poems.

Literary Analysis

Selection Support: Literary Analysis, p. 212 ■

Literary Analysis and Reading Transparencies, Imagery, p. 106

Reading

Literary Analysis and Reading Transparencies, Picturing the Imagery, p. 105

■ **BLOCK SCHEDULING:** Resources marked with this symbol provide varied instruction during 90-minute blocks.

❷ Literary Analysis

Imagery

Imagery is the descriptive language that paints pictures in readers' minds. An image may appeal to any of the five senses: sight, sound, taste, smell, or touch. The following example from Margaret Walker's "Memory" uses imagery that appeals to the senses of touch and sight:

> I can remember wind-swept streets of cities
> on cold and blustery nights, on rainy days;

As you read, use a chart like this one to note memorable images and to analyze the senses to which each image appeals.

Image: fat, overripe, icy, black blackberries	
Sight	✓
Sound	
Taste	✓
Smell	
Touch	✓

Comparing Literary Works

Two poets can use the same word to create different images, or they can describe similar images in different ways. For example, one poet uses *icy* to describe juicy blackberries, but another uses *icy* to describe the painful, sharp wind. Similarly, one poet describes the movement of the sea as *spinning*, whereas another describes it as *rocking*. Compare the imagery in each of the following poems and determine the effect each has on you as a reader.

❸ Reading Strategy

Picturing the Imagery

To appreciate the ideas that are being presented in a poem, form a mental **picture** of **each image.**

- Pay attention to descriptive words in the poem, and consider each word's descriptive meaning.
- Using your imagination, try to place yourself in the poem and experience what the speaker experiences at that moment.
- If possible, relate the image in the poem to something that you yourself have experienced.

As you relate to each image, remember to not only *see* but also *hear*, *feel*, *taste*, and *smell* what the poet describes.

Vocabulary Development

unbidden (un bid′ 'n) *adj.* without being asked; uninvited (p. 914)

sinister (sin′ is tər) *adj.* threatening harm; ominous (p. 915)

meticulously (mə tik′ yo͞o ləs lē) *adv.* very carefully; scrupulously (p. 916)

divine (də vīn′) *adj.* holy; sacred (p. 919)

primed (prīmd) *v.* prepared (p. 920)

CUSTOMIZE INSTRUCTION FOR UNIVERSAL ACCESS

For Special Needs Students	For Less Proficient Readers	For English Learners
Have students read the adapted versions of "Memory" and "Woman's Work" in the **Adapted Reader's Companion.** These versions provide basic-level instruction in an interactive format with questions and write-on lines. Completing the adapted versions will prepare students to read the selections in the Student Edition.	Have students read the poems in the **Reader's Companion.** These versions provide basic-level instruction in an interactive format with questions and write-on lines. After students finish the selections in **Reader's Companion,** have them complete the questions and activities in the Student Edition.	Have students read the adapted versions of the poems in the **English Learner's Companion.** These versions provide basic-level instruction in an interactive format with questions and write-on lines. Completing the adapted versions will prepare students to read the selection in the Student Edition.

❷ Literary Analysis

Imagery

- Write the words *sight, sound, taste, smell,* and *touch* on the chalkboard and have students tell you what these five words describe (the five senses).
- Ask students to think of words they associate with each sense. Write some of the students' suggestions on the chalkboard after the appropriate sense.
- Have a volunteer read the excerpt from "Memory." Discuss the senses to which the images appeal.
- Use the instruction in Comparing Literary Works to alert students to some of the various ways the poets use words and images.

❸ Reading Strategy

Picturing the Imagery

- Encourage students to read poetry as actively as possible, forming sensory images in their mind each time they read. They should ask themselves what the descriptions in a poem look, sound, taste, smell, and feel like.
- Ask students to use a chart like the one shown to record the sensory images in the poems and the senses to which they appeal.
- Ask students which columns they would check for the images in the excerpt from "Memory."

Image: wind-swept city streets on cold and blustery nights	
Sight	X
Sound	X
Taste	
Smell	
Touch	X

Vocabulary Development

- Pronounce each vocabulary word for students, and read the definitions as a class. Have students identify any words with which they are already familiar.

E-Teach

Visit E-Teach at www.phschool.com for teachers' essays on how to teach, with questions and answers.

TEACH

Step-by-Step Teaching Guide for pp. 914–920

CUSTOMIZE INSTRUCTION
For Visual/Spatial Learners

Encourage students who learn best by drawing or diagraming to sketch images that come to their minds as they read the poems. They might draw pictures to represent particular sensory images or their overall impressions.

❶ About the Selections

"Blackberry Eating" compares the sensuous experience of eating ripe fruit with the process of writing poetry—words are likened to blackberries. "Memory" describes a cold, rainy urban street that reflects the bleak outlook of the people.

❷ Literary Analysis

Images

- Have a volunteer read aloud lines 1–3. Ask students to identify the sensory image.
  Answer: The central sensory image is "fat, overripe, icy, black blackberries."
- Ask students which senses the image appeals to, and remind them to add the image and the senses to which it appeals to their charts.
  Answer: Senses include sight, taste, and smell.

Answers to p. 914

Review and Assess

1. Students may cite the "icy" blackberries or the "peculiar words" *strengths* or *squinched.*
2. **(a)** The speaker compares *strengths* and *squinched* to blackberries. **(b)** The words come to his mind unbidden as berries come to the tongue. **(c)** Eating blackberries reminds the speaker of writing poetry.
3. The poem captures the mysterious aspect of inspiration in writing poetry.
4. The speaker clearly relishes writing as much as he enjoys blackberries.

❶ BLACKBERRY EATING

Galway Kinnell

I love to go out in late September
❷ among the fat, overripe, icy, black blackberries
to eat blackberries for breakfast,
the stalks very prickly, a penalty
they earn for knowing the black art
of blackberry-making; and as I stand among them
lifting the stalks to my mouth, the ripest berries
fall almost unbidden to my tongue,
as words sometimes do, certain peculiar words
like *strengths* or *squinched,*
many-lettered, one-syllabled lumps,
which I squeeze, squinch open, and splurge well
in the silent, startled, icy, black language
of blackberry-eating in late September.

unbidden (un bid´ 'n) *adj.* without being asked; uninvited

Review and Assess

Thinking About the Selection

1. **Respond:** Which description in this poem is most appealing?
2. **(a) Recall:** Identify two words that the speaker compares to blackberries. **(b) Compare and Contrast:** What do these words have in common with blackberries?
   c) Analyze: What special meaning does eating blackberries have for the speaker?
3. **Make a Judgment:** Which aspect of writing does "Blackberry Eating" capture in lines 9–13? Explain.
4. **Speculate:** Do you think the speaker of this poem enjoys writing poetry? Why or why not?

Galway Kinnell

(b. 1927)

Galway Kinnell is an American poet whose writing addresses the themes of the inevitability of death, selfhood, and the power of nature. He has taught at various universities and has been active in the civil rights movement.

TEACHING RESOURCES

The following resources can be used to enrich or extend the instruction for pp. 914–920.

Literary Analysis

Selection Support: Literary Analysis, p. 212

Reading

Selection Support: Reading Strategy, p. 211; Build Vocabulary, p. 209

Listening to Literature Audiocassettes, Side 27

Listening to Literature Audio CDs, CD 18

BLOCK SCHEDULING: Resources marked with this symbol provide varied instruction during 90-minute blocks.

❶ Memory

Margaret Walker

I can remember wind-swept streets of cities
on cold and blustery nights, on rainy days;
heads under shabby felts[1] and parasols
and shoulders hunched against a sharp concern;
seeing hurt bewilderment on poor faces,
smelling a deep and sinister unrest
❸ these brooding people cautiously caress;
hearing ghostly marching on pavement stones
and closing fast around their squares of hate.
I can remember seeing them alone,
at work, and in their tenements at home.
I can remember hearing all they said:
their muttering protests, their whispered oaths,
and all that spells their living in distress.

sinister (sin´ is tər) *adj.* threatening harm; ominous

1. **felts** felt hats.

Margaret Walker

(1915–1998)

A poet and novelist, Margaret Walker is considered one of the legends of African American literature. She is best known for *Jubilee* (1966), her narrative on the life of the daughter of a slave and a slave owner. As a writer, Walker focused on the experiences and hardships of African Americans.

Review and Assess

Thinking About the Selection

1. **Respond:** What thoughts and feelings did "Memory" evoke in you? Explain.
2. **(a) Recall:** Describe the setting and weather in Walker's poem. **(b) Interpret:** What effect does the weather have on your understanding of the lives of the people in "Memory"?
3. **Interpret:** Explain how "Memory" can be seen as a criticism of an injustice in society.
4. **Speculate:** What do you think is a possible result of a life lived in distress? Explain.

CUSTOMIZE INSTRUCTION FOR UNIVERSAL ACCESS

For Special Needs Students	For Gifted/Talented Students
Divide the students into pairs. Give each pair a photocopy of "Blackberry Eating" and "Memory" and help the students divide each poem into four meaningful sections. Have them highlight each section with a different color marker. Then, ask the pairs to reread and compare the poems, section by section. Have students consider the following questions: What is the difference in the ways the two poems make you feel? Which poem means the most to you?	Ask students to compare the tone and images in "Blackberry Eating" and "Memory." Have them express through movement or song the differences in the images and the ways the poems make them feel.

❸ Reading Strategy

Picturing the Imagery

- Ask students to identify the sensory images in lines 5–9. Write an example on a chart similar to the one on p. 913 of the student book.
  Answer: Sensory images include seeing "hurt bewilderment"; smelling "unrest"; feeling "cold," "sharp concern," caresses; and hearing "marching."
- Ask students how literally the reader is intended to take such images as "smelling a deep and sinister unrest"?
  Answer: Students should realize that unlike "Blackberry Eating," the images in "Memory" speak more to the subjects' states of mind.
- Have the class discuss the overall tone these sensory images bring to mind.
  Answer: Most students will believe the overall tone created by these images is dark and bleak.

Answers to p. 915

Review and Assess

1. Students' thoughts and feelings may be sad or empathetic.
2. **(a)** The setting is city streets in cold, wet, blustery weather. **(b)** The rainy weather mirrors people's misery.
3. "Memory" criticizes the injustice of poverty.
4. Most students will say that lives of distress will lead people to either give up entirely or cause some kind of social unrest. References in the poem to "hate," "protests," and "oaths" point toward unrest.

E-Teach

Visit E-Teach at www.phschool.com for teachers' essays on how to teach, with questions and answers.

❹ About the Selection

"Eulogy for a Hermit Crab" describes and praises a hermit crab. The awe and appreciation the speaker expresses for this humble animal is indirect praise for nature and for universal virtues such as persistence, constancy, and being true to oneself.

❺ Reading Strategy

Picturing the Imagery

- Read aloud the bracketed passage to students. Encourage students to write down any words or details they hear about the seashore.
- Ask students the Reading Strategy question on p. 916: Which words in this description help you imagine being at the seashore?
  Answer: Words include the following: "surf-drenched rocks," "salty slough holes," "glinting grey sea," "single spotlight of the sun," "blinding spume and spray."

❻ Literary Analysis

Imagery

- Have a volunteer read from line 11 through the word *meticulously* in line 16.
- Ask students to decide which sense or senses the images in these lines appeal.
  Answer: The images "gritty orange curve" and "soft, wormlike grip" evoke the senses of sight and touch.
- Have students discuss the following images: "unrelieved wonder of your black-pea eyes" and "mystified swing . . . of your touching antennae." Ask students to consider whether the hermit crab can express wonder or be mystified and whether the speaker is personifying the crab.
  Answer: Most students will believe that the crab is unable to express emotions such as wonder and mystification and that the speaker is using personification.

❹ Eulogy for a Hermit Crab

Pattiann Rogers

You were consistently brave
On these surf-drenched rocks, in and out of their salty
Slough holes around which the entire expanse
❺ Of the glinting grey sea and the single spotlight
Of the sun went spinning and spinning and spinning
In a tangle of blinding spume and spray
And pistol-shot collisions your whole life long.
You stayed. Even with the wet icy wind of the moon
Circling your silver case night after night after night
You were here.

And by the gritty orange curve of your claws,
By the soft, wormlike grip
❻ Of your hinter body, by the unrelieved wonder
Of your black-pea eyes, by the mystified swing
And swing and swing of your touching antennae,
You maintained your name meticulously, you kept
Your name intact exactly, day after day after day.
No one could say you were less than perfect
In the hermitage of your crabness.

Now, beside the racing, incomprehensible racket
Of the sea stretching its great girth forever
Back and forth between this direction and another,
Please let the words of this proper praise I speak
Become the identical and proper sound
Of my mourning.

Reading Strategy
Picturing the Imagery Which words in this description help you imagine being at the seashore?

meticulously (mə tikʹ yo͞o ləs lē) *adj.* very carefully; scrupulously

CUSTOMIZE INSTRUCTION FOR UNIVERSAL ACCESS

For Advanced Readers

Have students read other poems by Pattiann Rogers. They can look for the following collections of her work: *A Covenant of Seasons, Eating Bread and Honey, Firekeeper: New and Selected Poems, Geocentric,* and *Splitting and Bending.* The following issues of poetry magazines also include her poems: *Orion,* Winter 2001; *The Georgia Review,* Winter 2001; *The Paris Review,* Winter 2001, *River Styx,* Fall & Winter 2001; *Poetry,* April 2001.

Ask students to assemble an anthology of Pattiann Rogers's work. They should choose a selection of five to ten poems from various sources that they particularly like and that seem to them to be related in some way. Have them use a computer word processing program or desktop publishing program to input the poems. Each poem should be preceded by a short introduction that the student writes.

7 ▲ Critical Viewing
What can you learn about hermit crabs from this photograph? **[Infer]**

Review and Assess

Thinking About the Selection

1. **Respond:** Which image in this poem do you like best? Why?
2. **(a) Recall:** Identify two details from the first stanza that describe the hermit crab's environment. **(b) Infer:** How was that environment a constant challenge? **(c) Interpret:** What evidence proves that the crab was "consistently brave"?
3. **(a) Recall:** What does the speaker say about the crab in lines 18–19? **(b) Infer:** Why might the speaker feel the need to speak on the crab's behalf?
4. **(a) Recall:** In the final line of the poem, what is the speaker's main thought about the dead hermit crab? **(b) Connect:** What do lines 23–24 suggest about the speaker's feelings of helplessness?
5. **(a) Extend:** Did your view of hermit crabs change after reading this poem? Why or why not? **(b) Apply:** Based on this poem, what lesson can people learn from hermit crabs?
6. **Take a Position:** Are funerals or memorials for pets important? Why or why not?

Pattiann Rogers

(b. 1940)

Known for the scientifically exact language of her writing, Pattiann Rogers says that the natural world has always provided a way for her to consider the important questions of why we are here.

CUSTOMIZE INSTRUCTION FOR UNIVERSAL ACCESS

For Gifted/Talented Students

Have students combine movement with choral readings of "Eulogy for a Hermit Crab." Provide each group of students several photocopies of the poem. Students should begin by analyzing the poem and deciding how they wish to perform the choral reading. Some possibilities include alternating lines or sections between single readers and groups of readers or between boy's and girl's voices. Students should also consider dynamics, how loudly or softly they wish to read certain words or lines, and emphasis. Students should devise a way of marking the photocopies, such as color coding them, to indicate who is reading when and how they are reading. Stress to students that every group's readings will vary, but that everyone's goal is to make the meaning and feeling of the poem clear. After students have developed their choral readings, they can come up with some simple movements that fit the words of the poem. Encourage groups of students to perform their pieces for an audience.

7 ▶Critical Viewing

Answer: Students may say that hermit crabs live in shells, have a spiny body covering, walk on two pairs of legs, and sense their environment with their antennae and beady eyes. Students may also infer that hermit crabs use their large front claws to manipulate food, examine new shells, attack enemies, and block the opening of their shell.

Answers for p. 917

Review and Assess

1. Some students will prefer certain images of the sea and beach; others may like the descriptions of the crab.
2. **(a)** Details include "surf-drenched rocks," "salty slough holes," "glinting grey sea," "spotlight of the sun," "tangle of blinding spume and spray, and "wet icy wind of the moon." **(b)** The crab was battered by wind and sea, sprayed by salt water, and blinded by the sun. **(c)** The crab endured its difficult environment.
3. **(a)** The speaker suggests that the crab was perfect in its "crabness." The crab fulfilled its destiny. **(b)** The crab has died.
4. **(a)** The speaker is mourning the dead crab. **(b)** The words suggest that all the speaker can do about the dead crab is praise it. Words of admiration must also serve as eulogy.
5. **(a)** Students may have known little about the crab, so the information in the poem probably changed their vague impressions. Even students who knew about hermit crabs may not have considered them "brave." **(b)** People can learn to endure and overcome difficult circumstances.
6. Many students may note that people love their pets and want and need to mark their passing.

8 About the Selection

"Meciendo" ("Rocking") uses images of the sea, the wind, and the stars to express a mother's love. The alternation of long and short lines captures the rhythmic back-and-forth motion of waves or a rocking chair.

9 Critical Thinking

Compare and Contrast

- Explain to students that they can learn something about a poem just by looking at it in its original language—even if they don't know that language.
- Have students listen to the poem in Spanish and English on the audiocassette or CD as they follow along in their books. If possible, have a volunteer fluent in Spanish read the original to the class.
- Ask students to compare the uses of rhyme and repetition in the two versions. What do they notice?
  Answer: The Spanish version rhymes, but the English translation does not. The Spanish version has slightly more repetition, since the second line in each stanza begins with the word *mece*.

10 Reading Strategy

Picturing the Imagery

- Have students identify some of the images in "Meciendo" ("Rocking") that appeal to the senses.
  Answer: Some of the sensory images include the sea rocking waves, the wind wandering and rocking the wheat, and God rocking his worlds.
- Have students decide to which sense or senses these images appeal.
  Answer: These images appeal mainly to the senses of sight, sound, and touch.

Meciendo 8

Gabriela Mistral

El mar sus millares de olas
mece, divino.
Oyendo a los mares amantes,
mezo a mi niño.

El viento errabundo en la noche
9 mece a los trigos.
Oyendo a los vientos amantes,
mezo a mi niño.

Dios Padre sus miles de mundos
mece sin ruido.
Sintiendo su mano en la sombra,
mezo a mi niño.

ENRICHMENT: Social Studies

The Nobel Prize in Literature

The Nobel Prize in Literature, which poet Gabriela Mistral won in 1945, is one of six Nobel prizes—the others are physics, chemistry, physiology or medicine, peace, and economics—awarded annually from a fund left by Swedish inventor and industrialist Alfred Nobel. Nobel, who lived from 1833 to 1896, made his fortune through his invention of dynamite and other explosives.

The first Nobel Prize in Literature was first awarded in 1901 to French poet Sully Prudhomme. Since then recipients have ranged from Albert Camus to John Steinbeck to Pablo Neruda. Recent winners of this prestigious award have included American novelist Toni Morrison, South African novelist Nadine Gordimer, Mexican poet and essayist Octavio Paz, Soviet-born American poet and essayist Joseph Brodsky, and Nigerian poet, novelist, dramatist, essayist, and critic Wole Soyinka.

Rocking

(Meciendo)

Gabriela Mistral *Translated by Doris Dana*

The sea rocks her thousands of waves.
The sea is divine.
Hearing the loving sea,
I rock my son.

(10)

The wind wandering by night
rocks the wheat.
Hearing the loving wind,
I rock my son.

(11)

God, the Father, soundlessly rocks
His thousands of worlds.
Feeling His hand in the shadow,
I rock my son.

Reading Strategy
Picturing the Imagery When you try to picture this scene in your mind, what do you see?

divine (də vīn′) *adj.* holy; sacred

Gabriela Mistral

(1889–1957)

Born in Chile and given the name Lucila Godoy y Alcayaga, this writer formed her pen name from the names of two of her favorite writers, Gabriele D'Annunzio and Frederic Mistral. The 1945 recipient of the Nobel Prize for Literature, Mistral wrote many poems about children and motherhood.

Review and Assess

Thinking About the Selection

1. **Respond:** What emotion does the poem evoke in you? Explain.
2. **(a) Recall:** Which forces of nature does the speaker name in the first two stanzas? **(b) Compare and Contrast:** What do these forces have in common with what the speaker is doing?
3. **(a) Recall:** Describe the scene in the third stanza. **(b) Interpret:** Why do you think that the speaker concludes the poem with a reference to God? **(c) Infer:** What do references to nature and God reveal about the speaker's feelings about motherhood?
4. **Generalize:** Does the sea always convey a sense of peace? Explain.

(11) Reading Strategy

Picturing the Imagery

- Have students close their eyes and make a picture in their minds as you read the poem to them. Have students draw or sketch the image that appears in their minds.
- Ask students the Reading Strategy question on p. 919: When you try to picture this scene in your mind, what do you see?
  Answer: Most students will picture a mother rocking her son in a cradle or on her lap.

Answers for p. 919

Review and Assess

1. The poem may evoke feelings of happiness, peace, or comfort for many students.
2. **(a)** The speaker names the sea and the wind. **(b)** The sea is rocking the waves, the wind is rocking the wheat, and the speaker is rocking her son.
3. **(a)** God is animating and guarding his world as the speaker rocks her son. **(b)** Students may say that the speaker sees God as a parent ("Father") rocking his creation. **(c)** The speaker feels that, as a mother rocking her son, she is participating in a divine pattern.
4. Though it conveys a sense of peace in this poem, the sea can be turbulent and deadly.

CUSTOMIZE INSTRUCTION FOR UNIVERSAL ACCESS

For Less Proficient Readers	For English Learners
Students should not need much guidance to establish what the poem is about and to notice the repeated refrain "I rock my son" in the last line of each of the three stanzas. Point out that the third lines in the first and second stanzas are also similar. Ask students how the line "Hearing the loving wind" differs from the third line in the last stanza, "Feeling His hand in the shadow." (The first image appeals to the sense of hearing; the second appeals to the sense of touch.)	Encourage students fluent in Spanish to find other poems by Gabriela Mistral that are available in both Spanish and English. Have students work in small groups to prepare readings of the works in both languages for the entire class. They might also be prepared to discuss how the two versions of each work differ in terms of rhyme scheme and other factors.

ASSESS

12 About the Selection

"Woman's Work" recalls how as a young girl the speaker resented having to help her mother with the housework. As an adult, the speaker realizes that she is still very similar to her mother.

13 Literary Analysis

Imagery

- Have students discuss how the mother in the poem treats the daughter. Ask students why the mother treats her daughter this way.
  Answer: The mother drives her daughter hard as she tries to teach her that women's work is art.
- Ask students the Literary Analysis question on p. 920: Compare the image of the way the mother treats her daughter to the image of the way she treats her house.
  Answer: Many students may say that the mother works to improve her daughter as thoroughly as she cleans her house.

Answers for p. 920

Review and Assess

1. Some students may feel that the mother was too hard on her daughter; others may believe that her quest for excellence is what helped the speaker become a poet.
2. **(a)** The mother wants her daughter to become a good housekeeper. **(b)** The daughter does not want to become like her mother. **(c)** The speaker resents being a "prisoner" of her mother's obsession, but she admires her mother's "art."
3. The daughter is similar to her mother because she works at home on her art with the same intensity as her mother had.
4. Many students may believe that housekeeping, as any other work, can be treated as an art if the person does it with dedication and energy.

12 Woman's Work

Julia Alvarez

Who says a woman's work isn't high art?
She'd challenge as she scrubbed the bathroom tiles.
Keep house as if the address were your heart.

We'd clean the whole upstairs before we'd start
downstairs. I'd sigh, hearing my friends outside.
Doing her woman's work was a hard art

to practice when the summer sun would bar
the floor I swept till she was satisfied.
She kept me prisoner in her housebound heart.

She'd shine the tines of forks, the wheels of carts,
cut lacy lattices[1] for all her pies.
Her woman's work was nothing less than art.

13

And, I, her masterpiece since I was smart,
was primed, praised, polished, scolded and advised
to keep a house much better than my heart.

I did not want to be her counterpart!
I struck out . . . but became my mother's child:
a woman working at home on her art,
housekeeping paper as if it were her heart.

Literary Analysis
Imagery Compare the image of the way the mother treats her daughter to the image of the way she treats her house.

primed (prīmd) *v.* prepared

1. **lattices** (lat´ is əz) narrow strips of pastry laid on the pie in a crisscross pattern.

Review and Assess

Thinking About the Selection

1. **Respond:** How do you feel about the mother in this poem? Why?
2. **(a) Recall:** What ambition does the mother have for her daughter? **(b) Analyze:** Why does the speaker reject that ambition? **(c) Infer:** How can you tell that the daughter both admires and resents her mother?
3. **Compare and Contrast:** How does the final stanza suggest that the daughter is similar to her mother, after all?
4. **Assess:** Do you think housekeeping can be considered an art? Explain.

Julia Alvarez

(b. 1950)

Julia Alvarez moved from the Dominican Republic to New York City with her family when she was ten years old. She says that the complexity of the many cultures in the United States is "part of what makes us rich and makes us strong."

ASSESSMENT PRACTICE: Reading Comprehension

Vocabulary: Part/Whole Analogies (For more practice, see Test Preparation Workbook, p. 53.)

Many tests require students to answer multiple-choice questions about analogies. Use the following sample test item for student practice in determining the meaning of analogies.

Have students read "Woman's Work" by Julia Alvarez carefully, then complete the analogy below.

TINES : FORK ::

A floor : house
B friends : outside
C prisoner : art
D housebound : heart

Point out to students that the relation between tines and fork is that of part to whole. Completing the analogy means finding a pair among the answers that repeats the part-to-whole relationship. Since a floor is part of a house, *A* is the correct answer. The other pairs do not include an example of the part-to-whole relationship.

Review and Assess

Literary Analysis

Imagery

1. Which **images** in "Memory" appeal to your sense of hearing?
2. Which images in "Eulogy for a Hermit Crab" reveal the most about the crab's world?
3. An image that appeals to the sense of touch or movement runs throughout "Meciendo." Name that image and explain its appeal.

Comparing Literary Works

4. (a) Use a chart like the one shown to identify words in "Blackberry Eating" and "Memory" that convey emotion.
(b) Which poem conveys a feeling of contentment?

Blackberry Eating	Emotion		Memory

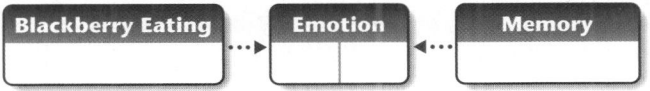

5. How do the images of the ocean in "Meciendo" and "Eulogy for a Hermit Crab" differ?

Reading Strategy

Picturing the Imagery

6. "Blackberry Eating" contains the adjectives *icy* and *prickly*, which seem unpleasant. Why, then, is picturing the images in this poem a pleasant experience?
7. Using a chart like the one below, name three images from the poems in this section that appeal to your senses, and explain how you picture the imagery.

Image	Sense Used	How I Picture It

Extend Understanding

8. **Science Connection:** (a) What can you learn about marine biology by reading "Eulogy for a Hermit Crab"? (b) What does the poem achieve that a biology book could not?

Quick Review

Imagery is the descriptive language used to create mental pictures by appealing to sight, sound, taste, touch, or smell.

To **picture the imagery,** imagine experiencing what the speaker experiences at that moment, or relate the image in the poem to something that you yourself have experienced.

Take It to the Net

www.phschool.com

Take the interactive self-test online to check your understanding of the selections.

ENRICHMENT: Further Reading

Other Works by the Poets

Works by Galway Kinnell
Imperfect Thirst
Works by Margaret Walker
For My People
Works by Gabriela Mistral
Lagar
Works by Pattiann Rogers
The Family Is All There Is

Answers for p. 921

Review and Assess

1. Images that appeal to the sense of hearing include "marching on pavement stones" and "their muttering protests, their whispered oaths."
2. The images in "Eulogy for a Hermit Crab" that reveal the most about the crab's world include "surf-drenched rocks," "slough holes," "blinding spume and spray," "pistol-shot collisions," and "racing, incomprehensible racket of the sea."
3. The image of rocking runs throughout "Meciendo." It is appealing because of its associations with mothers rocking their children.
4. **(a)** "Blackberry Eating": "love," "startled." Emotion: happiness, surprise. "Memory": "concern," "hurt bewilderment," "sinister," "brooding," "cautiously," "hate," "distress"; Emotion: worry, confusion, threat, fear, dislike, upset. **(b)** "Blackberry Eating" conveys a feeling of contentment.
5. Ocean images in "Meciendo" are benign and comforting; In "Eulogy," ocean images are harsh and threatening.
6. Possible response: The speaker explains that he loves to search for and eat blackberries; the overwhelming feeling of the poem is one of celebration and enjoyment. The sharpness of "icy" and "prickly" only add tang to the experience.
7. Possible response: Image: fat, overripe, icy, black blackberries; Sense Used: sight, smell, taste; How I Picture It: I see the blackberries waiting to be eaten. Image: hearing ghostly marching; Sense Used: hearing; How I Picture It: I see sad people walking quietly. Image: wind wandering by night; Sense Used: touch, sound; How I Picture It: I see a moonlit sky with leaves blowing.
8. **(a)** You can learn about the appearance and behavior of the hermit crab. **(b)** The poem gives the reader sympathy for the difficulties of the hermit crab's life and admiration for its bravery.

EXTEND

Answers for p. 922

❶ Vocabulary Development

Word Analysis

1. important witness
2. basic
3. preliminary election to select candidates
4. color belonging to one of the main color groups

Spelling Strategy

1. diving; While diving, I noticed several crabs.
2. revising; I spent last night revising my first draft.
3. confidence; Sylvia had confidence she would pass the driver's test.

Concept Development: Synonyms

1. a
2. b
3. b
4. a
5. a

❷ Grammar

1. Her memories of the city are clear, vivid . . . and poignant memories.
2. The speaker in "Memory" refers to "wind-swept steets of cities . . . on rainy days."
3. The people who live in "Memory" face conditions that are windy, cold, . . . and generally unpleasant.
4. The speaker in "Memory" remembers seeing them "alone, at work, and . . . at home."
5. They keep their discontent to themselves . . . but will they do so forever?

Writing Application

Have students exchange their work with partners to check for appropriate use of ellipsis points.

Integrate Language Skills

❶ Vocabulary Development Lesson

Word Analysis: Latin Root *-prim-*

The word *prime* comes from the Latin root *-prim-*, which means "first in time or in importance." In "Woman's Work," *primed* means "coached beforehand." Using your knowledge of *-prim-*, define each of these words or phrases:

1. prime witness
2. primitive
3. primary election
4. primary color

Spelling Strategy

Before adding an ending that begins with a vowel to a word that ends in silent *e*, drop the *e*: *prime* + *-ed* = *primed*. Write the new word formed by adding the suffix to each word below. Then, use each new word in a sentence.

1. dive + *-ing* **2.** revise + *-ing* **3.** confide + *-ence*

Concept Development: Synonyms

In your notebook, write the letter of the word that means about the same as the first word. To help you, review the vocabulary list on page 913.

1. unbidden: (a) uninvited, (b) unusual, (c) ordered
2. sinister: (a) innocent, (b) evil, (c) sisterly
3. primed: (a) allowed, (b) coached, (c) followed
4. meticulously: (a) carefully, (b) quickly, (c) sloppily
5. divine: (a) godlike, (b) congested, (c) divided

❷ Grammar Lesson

Ellipsis Points

Ellipsis points (. . .) are punctuation marks that are used to show that something has not been expressed. Usually, ellipsis points indicate one of the following situations:

- Words have been left out of a quotation
- A series continues beyond the items mentioned
- Time passes or action occurs in a narrative

This example, from the final stanza of "Woman's Work," indicates the passage of time or action:

Example: I struck out . . . but became my mother's child.

Practice Choose the blank that marks the most reasonable place to insert ellipsis points.

1. Her memories of the city ___ are clear, vivid ___ and poignant.
2. Walker refers to ___ "wind-swept streets of cities ___ on rainy days."
3. The people ___ who live in "Memory" face ___ conditions that are windy, cold, ___ and generally unpleasant.
4. The speaker remembers ___ seeing them "alone, at work, and ___ at home."
5. They keep their discontent to ___ themselves ___ but will they ___ do so forever?

Writing Application Write about one of the poems in this group, and illustrate at least two of the ellipsis rules in your sentences.

WG Prentice Hall Writing and Grammar Connection: Chapter 29

TEACHING RESOURCES

The following resources can be used to enrich or extend the instruction for pp. 922–923.

Vocabulary

Vocabulary and Spelling Practice Book (Use this booklet for skills enrichment.)

Grammar

Selection Support: Build Grammar Skills, p. 210

Writing and Grammar, Gold Level, p. 652

Daily Language Practice Transparencies

Writing

Writing and Grammar, Gold Level, p. 112

Writing and Grammar iText CD-ROM

BLOCK SCHEDULING: Resources marked with this symbol provide varied instruction during 90-minute blocks.

❸ Writing Lesson

Letter About a Memorable Moment

These five poems use imagery to describe memorable moments. Choose a moment that was memorable for you, whether it occurred in real life or in a picture or a movie. Write a letter about that remarkable time and place, using imagery to capture your experience.

Prewriting Once you have chosen an important moment, list sensory details that convey the main impression, such as joy, fear, pride, or awe. Gather details to show how the place or event appealed to your senses of sight, sound, taste, touch, and smell.

Drafting Use your prewriting notes to draft your letter, focusing on the main impression you want to convey. Organize your details in order of time, space, or importance.

Revising As you reread your letter, ask yourself whether each sensory detail contributes to the main impression. Add or change details to strengthen the main impression.

Model: Revising to Strengthen the Main Impression

teemed with life
Every inch of the rain forest ~~was alive~~. Trees, brushes, and
jostled for position
vines ~~were everywhere~~.

These revisions build the image of a vibrant and living landscape.

WG Prentice Hall Writing and Grammar Connection: Chapter 6, Section 4

❹ Extension Activities

Listening and Speaking In her poem, Rogers offers a description of the hermit crab that is both beautiful and highly accurate. Plan a visual **presentation of artwork** that combines the same qualities.

- Look for art that you consider to be both beautiful and true to life.
- Make brief notes about each picture.
- Practice making your presentation while displaying your pictures.

Present your findings to your class and ask them for feedback on your art choices.

Research and Technology In a small group, prepare a **research report** about how women's roles have changed over the past several decades. You might use "Woman's Work" to help you generate questions for research. Use library resources, including the Internet, and personal interviews to help you gather facts and information. **[Group Activity]**

Take It to the Net www.phschool.com
Go online for an additional research activity using the Internet.

ASSESSMENT RESOURCES

The following resources can be used to assess students' knowledge and skills.

Selection Assessment

- **Formal Assessment,** Selection Test, pp. 189–191
- **Open Book Test,** pp. 157–159
- **Got It! Assessment Videotapes,** Tape 5
- **Test Bank Software**

Take It to the Net

Visit www.phschool.com for self-tests and additional questions on the poems.

Listening and Speaking Rubric

- **Performance Assess. and Portfolio Mgmt.,** p. 30

PRENTICE HALL ASSESSMENT SYSTEM

- **Workbook**
- **Skill Book**
- **Transparencies**
- **CD-ROM**

Lesson Support for p. 923

❸ Writing Lesson

- Using your own experiences, model the selection of a memorable moment and the listing of sensory details about it.
- After describing the memorable moment you have chosen, list the five senses as headings on the chalkboard. Then, write sensory details under the appropriate headings.
- Use the Writing Lesson to guide students in writing a letter about a memorable moment.

❹ Listening and Speaking

- Guide students in their choice of artwork. Suggest that they choose a landscape, a still life, or a picture of an animal. Caution them to choose a very detailed artwork so that they will have plenty to say about it.
- Model note taking by displaying a picture you have chosen and writing notes on the board.
- When you feel confident students know how to proceed, give them access to art books or magazines from which to choose their subjects.
- Encourage students to practice their presentations.
- To assess presentations, use the rubric for Delivering an Exposition Presentation With Visual Aids, p. 30 in **Performance Assessment and Portfolio Management.**

CUSTOMIZE INSTRUCTION for Universal Access

To address different learning styles, use the activities suggested in the **Extension Activities** booklet, p. 53.

- For Visual/Spatial and Interpersonal Learners, use Activity 5.
- For Logical/Mathematical Learners, use Activity 7.

Uphill ✦ Summer ✦ Ecclesiastes 3:1–8 ✦ The Bells

Lesson Objectives and CA Correlations

1. **To analyze and respond to literary elements**
   - Literary Analysis: Lyric Poetry and Sound Devices **R 3.7**
   - Comparing Literary Works
2. **To read, comprehend, analyze, and critique poems**
   - Reading Strategy: Listening to Poetic Sounds **R 3.7**
   - Reading Check questions
   - Review and Assess questions
   - Assessment Practice (ATE)
3. **To develop word analysis skills, fluency, and systematic vocabulary**
   - Vocabulary Development Lesson: Greek Prefix: *mono-* **R 1.1**
4. **To understand and apply written and oral language conventions**
   - Spelling Strategy
   - Grammar Lesson: End Punctuation **LC 1.1**
5. **To understand and apply appropriate writing and research strategies**
   - Writing Lesson: Rap Song **W 1.9**
   - Extension Activity: Illustrated Version **W 1.3**
6. **To understand and apply listening and speaking strategies**
   - Extension Activity: Dramatic Reading **LS 1.9**

STEP-BY-STEP TEACHING GUIDE	PACING GUIDE
PRETEACH	
Motivate Students and Provide Background	
Use the Motivation activity (ATE p. 924)	5 min.
Read and discuss the Preview material and Background information (SE/ATE p. 924) [A]	5 min.
Introduce the Concepts	
Introduce the Literary Analysis and Reading Strategy (SE/ATE p. 925) [A]	15 min.
Pronounce the vocabulary words and read their definitions (SE p. 925)	5 min.
TEACH	
Monitor Comprehension	
Informally monitor comprehension by circulating while students read independently or in groups [A]	15 min.
Monitor students' comprehension with the Reading Check note (SE/ATE p. 933)	as students read
Develop vocabulary with Vocabulary notes (SE pp. 926, 932–933; ATE p. 933)	as students read
Develop Understanding	
Develop students' understanding of lyric poetry and sound devices with the Literary Analysis annotations (SE p. 933; ATE pp. 926, 932–933) [A]	10 min.
Develop students' ability to listen with the Reading Strategy annotations (SE pp. 929, 932; ATE pp. 928, 931–932)	10 min.
ASSESS	
Assess Mastery	
Assess students' mastery of the Reading Strategy and Literary Analysis by having them answer the Review and Assess questions (SE/ATE p. 935)	20 min.
Use one or more of the print and media Assessment Resources (ATE p. 937) [A]	up to 50 min.
EXTEND	
Apply Understanding	
Have students complete the Vocabulary Development Lesson and the Grammar Lesson (SE p. 936) [A]	20 min.
Apply students' knowledge of repetition using the Writing Lesson (SE/ATE p. 937) [A]	45 min.
Apply students' understanding of the selection using one or more of the Extension Activities (SE p. 937)	20–90 min.

[A] **ACCELERATED INSTRUCTION:** Use the strategies and activities identified with an [A].

UNIVERSAL ACCESS
● = Below-Level Students
▲ = On-Level Students
■ = Above-Level Students

Time and Resource Manager

Reading Level: Average/Easy/Challenging/Challenging
Average Number of Instructional Days: 4

RESOURCES		
PRINT	**TRANSPARENCIES**	**TECHNOLOGY**
• **Beyond Literature,** Humanities Connection: Seasons in Literature, p. 54 ▲ ■		• **Interest Grabber Video,** Tape 5 ● ▲ ■
• **Selection Support Workbook:** ● ▲ ■ Literary Analysis, p. 216 Reading Strategy, p. 215 Build Vocabulary, p. 213	• **Literary Analysis and Reading Transparencies,** pp. 107 and 108 ● ▲ ■	
		• **Listening to Literature** ● ▲ ■ Audiocassettes, Side 28 Audio CDs, CD 18
• **Literatura en español** ● ▲ • **Literary Analysis for Enrichment** ■		
• **Formal Assessment:** Selection Test, pp. 192–194 ● ▲ ■ • **Open Book Test,** pp. 160–162 ● ▲ ■ • Prentice Hall Assessment System ● ▲ ■	• Prentice Hall Assessment System ● ▲ ■ Skills Practice Answers and Explanations on Transparencies	• **Test Bank Software** ● ▲ ■ • **Got It! Assessment Videotapes,** Tape 5 ● ▲
• **Selection Support Workbook:** ● ▲ ■ Build Grammar Skills, p. 214 • **Writing and Grammar,** Gold Level ● ▲ ■ • **Extension Activities,** p. 52 ● ▲ ■	• **Daily Language Practice Transparencies** ● ▲	• **Writing and Grammar iText CD-ROM** ● ▲ ■ ***Take It to the Net*** www.phschool.com

BLOCK SCHEDULING: Use one 90-minute class period to preteach the selection and have students read it. Use a second 90-minute class period to assess students' mastery of skills and have them complete one of the Extension Activities.

PRETEACH

Step-by-Step Teaching Guide for pp. 924–925

Motivation

To introduce "Uphill," act out for students the role of someone who is weary of life's struggles. Ask students if they ever feel that life seems constantly uphill. Encourage them to think of specific difficulties from their lives. Explain that "Uphill" is a poem that expresses similar struggles.

Interest Grabber Video

As an alternative, play "Summer" on Tape 5 to engage student interest.

1 Background

Social Studies

In 1965, the rock-and-roll group The Byrds released a song called "Turn, Turn, Turn." With the addition of just six words to the end of Ecclesiastes 3:1-8, The Byrds were able to transform these verses into a rock 'n' roll classic. Following the last line "a time of war, and a time of peace," The Byrds added the phrase, "I swear it's not too late." Thus did Ecclesiastes enter popular culture as an antiwar song.

Prepare to Read

Uphill ◆ Summer ◆ Ecclesiastes 3:1–8 ◆ The Bells

Take It to the Net

Visit www.phschool.com for interactive activities and instruction related to the selections, including
- background
- graphic organizers
- literary elements
- reading strategies

Preview

Connecting to the Literature

Sweating through an August afternoon, you realize that the summer heat will soon change to the chill of autumn. You see parents and children enjoying the outdoors and realize that toddlers grow to adulthood. Nature and life have predictable cycles and stages. The following poems explore these cycles.

1 Background

Throughout the ages, poets have explored the stages and patterns of life. Scientists, too, describe life as comprising cycles and seasons, stages and patterns. Advances in medicine may extend life expectancy, but medicine has not been able to alter the basic cycle of life in which we are born, grow, and inevitably die.

TEACHING RESOURCES

The following resources can be used to enrich or extend the instruction for pp. 924–925.

Motivation

Interest Grabber Video, Tape 5

Background

Beyond Literature, p. 54

Take It to the Net

Visit www.phschool.com for background and hotlinks for the poems.

Literary Analysis

Literary Analysis and Reading Transparencies, Lyric Poetry and Sound Devices, p. 108

Reading

Selection Support: Reading Strategy, p. 215; Build Vocabulary, p. 213

Literary Analysis and Reading Transparencies, Listening, p. 107

BLOCK SCHEDULING: Resources marked with this symbol provide varied instruction during 90-minute blocks.

❷ Literary Analysis

Lyric Poetry and Sound Devices

These poems are examples of **lyric poetry**—verse that expresses the observations and feelings of a single speaker through a highly musical style. That style comes from various **sound devices,** including the following:

- **Rhythm:** the pattern of beats or stresses in language
- **Alliteration:** the repetition of initial consonant sounds
- **Rhyme:** the repetition of sounds at the ends of words
- **Onomatopoeia:** the use of words, like *buzz* and *whirr,* that imitate the sounds that they name

As you read, notice the musical sounds in each poem.

Comparing Literary Works

As these poems suggest, life is filled with cycles and stages. Whether addressing life milestones, the journey from birth to death, or the natural progression of seasons, each poem reveals patterns that apply to life. As you move from one poem to the next, compare and contrast the patterns and cycles presented in each to determine whether each presents a hopeful or a despairing message.

❸ Reading Strategy

Listening to Poetic Sounds

To appreciate the musical quality of lyric poems, read them aloud and **listen to the sound** of the lines. Follow these points to help you:

- Read the poem aloud to yourself or to a partner. If you wish, record your reading.
- Listen for the musical sounds created by the words.
- Consider the mood or feeling created by the sounds.

Use a chart like the one shown to help you analyze how the sound reinforces the poem's meaning.

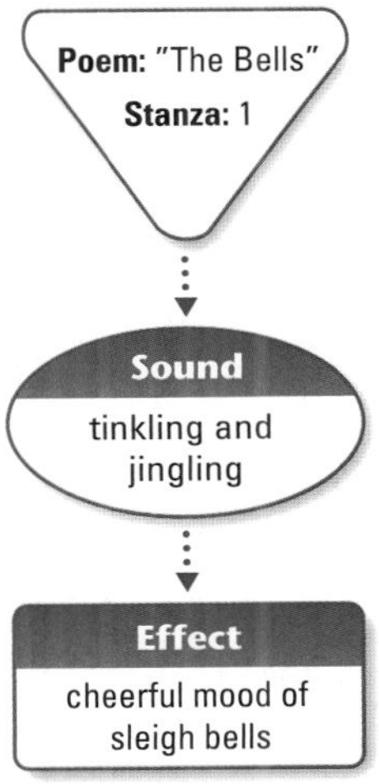

Vocabulary Development

wayfarers (wā′ fer′ ərz) *n.* travelers (p. 926)

voluminously (və lo͞om′ ə nəs lē) *adv.* fully; in great volume (p. 932)

palpitating (pal′ pə tāt′ iŋ) *adj.* beating rapidly; throbbing (p. 933)

monotone (män′ ə tōn′) *n.* uninterrupted repetition of the same tone (p. 933)

pæan (pē′ ən) *n.* song of joy or triumph (p. 933)

CUSTOMIZE INSTRUCTION FOR UNIVERSAL ACCESS

For Less Proficient Readers	For English Learners	For Advanced Readers
Have students follow along in their books as they listen to the poems on audiotape or CD. Briefly discuss the sounds in the poems: the rhyme scheme, the rhythm, and any alliteration or onomatopoeia. Then, have students do paired readings of the poems. Tell students to emphasize the rhyme and rhythm in the poems.	Have students listen to the poems on audiotape or CD. Then, have them listen a second time and tap out the rhythm with pencils on their desktops and clap when they hear rhymes. Point out several onomatopoetic words in the poems, such as *buzzin* and *ripping* in "Summer" and *tinkle, twinkle,* and *jingling* in "The Bells."	Have the students read the poems and list the sounds and effects on their charts independently. Then, ask students to compare the use of sound devices in the poems. Do all of the poems include examples of all four devices? Which device or devices seem most important in each poem?

❷ Literary Analysis

Lyric Poetry and Sound Devices

- On the chalkboard, write the four sound devices students will be studying. Discuss each one. During the discussion, be sure to mention that another word for the beats in language is *cadence*, that *alliteration* occurs at the beginning of words or syllables, and that *rhyme* usually occurs at the ends of lines in poems.
- Have students brainstorm for onomatopoetic words. Write their suggestions on the board. Here are some examples: *thump, slurp, splat, beep, buzz, murmur, crunch, hiss.*
- Go over the Lyric Poetry and Sound Devices transparency in **Literary Analysis and Reading Transparencies,** p. 108, with students to give them practice identifying the four sound devices.
- Finally, use the instruction in Comparing Literary Works to give students a focus for comparing the poems.

❸ Reading Strategy

Listening to Poetic Sounds

- Stress the importance of reading lyric poetry aloud to appreciate its sounds.
- Draw a chart like the one in the student book on the board and go over the information included on it: the poem, the stanza, the sound, and the effect.
- Ask students to use a chart like this one to record some of the sounds and effects they encounter as they read the four poems.

Vocabulary Development

- Pronounce each vocabulary word for students, and read the definitions as a class. Have students identify any words with which they are already familiar.

E-Teach

Visit E-Teach at www.phschool.com for teachers' essays on how to teach, with questions and answers.

TEACH

Step-by-Step Teaching Guide for pp. 926–934

CUSTOMIZE INSTRUCTION For Musical/Rhythmic Learners

Have students prepare dramatic readings of one or more of the four poems accompanied by prerecorded music or music they perform live. Before they prepare their readings and choose the music, students should spend some time discussing the feeling that each work expresses. What is the message of each? How do the sound devices in each poem contribute to the message?

❶ About the Selections

"Uphill," seemingly a conversation between a traveler seeking directions and a helpful expert, has serious overtones. The uphill road is life's journey, and the beds at journey's end are graves. The traveler is thus asking about the difficulty of life and whether there is hope for peace in the end.

In "Summer," internal and terminal rhymes and a strong, irregular rhythm are as important as the literal meaning of the poet's words in creating a picture of summer.

❷ Literary Analysis

Lyric Poetry and Sound Devices

- Review with students the reasons why "Uphill" and "Summer" are classified as lyric poems.
  Answer: They are short poems that express personal feelings through a musical style and are intended to make a single impression on the reader.
- Have a volunteer read aloud each poem. Then, discuss the rhyme scheme in the two poems. What is one major difference between the poems?
  Answer: "Uphill" has the same rhyme scheme in each verse (*abab*). The rhyme scheme in "Summer" is different in the first and second verses.

① Uphill

Christina Rossetti

Does the road wind uphill all the way?
    Yes, to the very end.
Will the day's journey take the whole long day?
    From morn to night, my friend.

But is there for the night a resting place?
    A roof for when the slow dark hours begin.
May not the darkness hide it from my face?
    You cannot miss that inn.

❷
Shall I meet other <u>wayfarers</u> at night?
    Those who have gone before.
Then must I knock, or call when just in sight?
    They will not keep you standing at that door.

Shall I find comfort, travel-sore and weak?
    Of labor you shall find the sum.
Will there be beds for me and all who seek?
    Yea,[1] beds for all who come.

wayfarers (wā′ fer′ ərz) *n.* travelers

Christina Rossetti

(1830–1894)

Christina Rossetti is considered by some critics to be the best female poet in English literature. Her father had come from Italy to live in England, and the famous poet and painter Dante Gabriel Rossetti was her brother. Her best-known work is the long poem "Goblin Market," a kind of supernatural fairy tale.

1. **yea** (yā) indeed; truly.

TEACHING RESOURCES

The following resources can be used to enrich or extend the instruction for pp. 926–934.

Literary Analysis

Selection Support: Literary Analysis, p. 216 ■

Reading

Listening to Literature Audiocassettes, Side 28 ■
Listening to Literature Audio CDs, CD 18 ■

■ **BLOCK SCHEDULING:** Resources marked with this symbol provide varied instruction during 90-minute blocks.

❶ # Summer

Walter Dean Myers

I like hot days, hot days
Sweat is what you got days
Bugs buzzin from cousin to cousin
❷ Juices dripping
Running and ripping
Catch the one you love days

Birds peeping
Old men sleeping
❸ Lazy days, daisies lay
Beaming and dreaming
Of hot days, hot days,
Sweat is what you got days

Walter Dean Myers

(b. 1937)

As a child, acclaimed author Walter Dean Myers never imagined himself becoming a writer. He was born into poverty in West Virginia and was writing poems and stories by his early teens, but he believed that his dream of being a writer would never be realized. Myers's dream was fulfilled, however, when he won a writing contest sponsored by the Council on Interracial Books for Children for his book *Where Does a Day Go?*

Review and Assess

Thinking About the Selections

1. **Respond:** How do you feel about the journey described in "Uphill"? Why?
2. **(a) Recall:** According to the final stanza of "Uphill," how will the traveler feel at journey's end? **(b) Interpret:** What might the uphill winding of the road represent? Explain.
3. **(a) Recall:** According to the final stanza, what is waiting for all travelers at the end of the journey? **(b) Interpret:** What is the final destination of the journey?
4. **(a) Recall:** In lines 1–2 of "Summer," how does Myers describe summer? **(b) Infer:** What kinds of juices might be dripping?
5. **(a) Recall:** What do birds do in summer? **(b) Contrast:** How does their activity contrast with that of old men?
6. **Take a Position:** Which poet more effectively conveys a particular feeling to you? Explain.

CUSTOMIZE INSTRUCTION FOR UNIVERSAL ACCESS

For Special Needs Students	For Gifted/Talented Students
Analyze "Uphill" and "Summer" verse by verse. Have volunteers read each verse, and then have students picture what the poet is describing. After each verse, have students write down some words that describe how that verse makes them feel. Then, have students use their word lists to write a few sentences that describe the feeling they got from the verse.	Ask students to jot down words that describe how "Uphill" and "Summer" make them feel. Have them use their word lists to give them ideas for collages inspired by the tone and message of the two poems. Students should use images from magazines and write or cut out words to add to the collages. They can use any other materials they like, such as newspaper, wrapping paper, leaves and twigs, to try to transmit their feelings about the poems.

❸ Reading Strategy

Listening to Poetic Sounds

- Ask students to identify examples of alliteration in "Summer."
  Answer: Students may cite "Bugs buzzin" and "cousin to cousin" in line 3; "running and ripping" in line 5; "lazy . . . lay" and "days . . . daisies" in line 9.
- Ask students what examples of internal and end rhymes they find in the poem.
  Answer: Students may cite such internal rhymes as "hot/got," "buzzin/cousin," "days/daisies," and "Beaming/Dreaming." End rhymes include "dripping/ripping" and "peeping/sleeping."
- Ask students to list any examples of onomatopoeia they find in the poem.
  Answer: Students will cite "buzzin" and "peeping."

Answers for p. 927

Review and Assess

1. Some students may feel discouraged because the uphill journey comes to a somber end; others may be cheered by the hope of comfort and rest.
2. **(a)** The exhausted traveler will find an end to effort and a place of rest. **(b)** The uphill journey represents the trials and difficulties of life. It lasts all day, all one's life.
3. **(a)** An end to labor and a bed awaits each traveler. **(b)** The final destination is death.
4. **(a)** Myers describes summer as so hot that people sweat. **(b)** Perspiration and nectar may be dripping.
5. **(a)** Birds peep in summer. **(b)** In contrast to active, peeping birds, old men sleep.
6. Some students may say that Rossetti moves them more because she writes of serious issues, literally, life and death. Other students may prefer the lighthearted tone Myers adopts in "Summer."

❹ About the Selection

Ecclesiastes 3:1–8 says that every event, good or bad, has its place and purpose in the grand scheme of things and implies that people should accept life's ups and downs as part of nature's cycles or as divine pattern. The stately rhythms and repeated phrases reinforce the passage's message.

❺ Reading Strategy

Listening to Poetic Sounds

- Have two volunteers alternate reading aloud every two lines of the passage. Ask students to focus on the rhythm and repeated words and phrases in the passage.
- Then, ask students what they notice about the rhythm and alliteration.
  Answer: The voice rises and falls in a repeated rhythm throughout the entire passage. The phrase "a time to" is repeated 29 times, so the alliteration is pronounced—the sound of *t* repeated 58 times.

❻ Reading Strategy

Listening to Poetic Sounds

- Read the poem to the class. Encourage students to pay careful attention to the rhythm of the poem as you read.
- Once you have read through the entire poem, ask students to identify the main idea of the poem.
  Answer: The main idea is expressed in the first line: there is a time and purpose for all experiences of life.
- Then, ask students the Reading Strategy question on p. 929: How does the rhythm of these lines illustrate the main idea of the passage?
  Answer: The repeated pattern of sounds echoes and reinforces the main idea about the repeating patterns of life.

ENRICHMENT: Social Studies Connection

Confucius

Every culture has its own collections of wise sayings and religious teachings, such as those in Ecclesiastes. One of the great philosophers, scholars, and teachers in Eastern culture was Confucius, who was born in 551 B.C. at a tumultuous period in Chinese history.

Confucius believed that it was the responsibility of rulers to be virtuous and to lead by moral example. His teachings were directed at establishing a moral community that cultivated a sense of humanity in politics and in society. He believed that love of learning broadened a person's knowledge and deepened self-awareness. In his teachings he said, "A man of humanity, wishing to establish himself, also establishes others, and wishing to enlarge himself, also enlarges others." A well-known teaching of Confucius says, "Do not do unto others what you would not want others to do unto you." After his death, the students of Confucius wrote down his words of wisdom in a collection called *The Analects.*

4 # ECCLESIASTES 3:1–8

(King James Version)

To every thing there is a season, and a time to
    every purpose under the heaven:
A time to be born, and a time to die; a time to
    plant, and a time to pluck up that which is planted;
A time to kill, and a time to heal; a time to break
    down, and a time to build up;
5 A time to weep, and a time to laugh; a time to
    mourn, and a time to dance;
A time to cast away stones, and a time to gather
6   stones together; a time to embrace, and a time to
    refrain from embracing;
A time to get, and a time to lose; a time to keep,
    and a time to cast away;
A time to rend,[1] and a time to sew; a time to keep
    silence, and a time to speak;
A time to love, and a time to hate; a time of war,
    and a time of peace.

1. **rend** (rend) *v.* tear.

Reading Strategy
Listening to Poetic Sounds How does the rhythm of these lines illustrate the main idea of the passage?

7 **◀ Critical Viewing**
How do the contrasts in these pictures reflect the poem? **[Connect]**

Review and Assess

Thinking About the Selection

1. **Respond:** Do you find this passage comforting? Explain why or why not.
2. **(a) Recall:** Which verse begins differently from the other verses? **(b) Analyze:** What is the relationship between that verse and the rest of the passage?
3. **(a) Recall:** Which words are repeated throughout the poem? **(b) Analyze:** Why do you think these words are repeated?
4. **(a) Recall:** Identify four pairs of actions mentioned in the passage. **(b) Infer:** What activity is suggested by the words "A time to cast away stones, and a time to gather stones together"? **(c) Analyze:** How does the pairing of opposite ideas help to communicate the message of the passage?
5. **Apply:** What comfort or guidance can a person of today find in these verses written thousands of years ago?

The King James Bible

The King James Version of the Bible was published in 1611. It was the work of a committee of English churchmen led by Lancelot Andrews. The language of the King James Version is considered by many to be so beautiful that the Bible is often ranked in English literature with the works of William Shakespeare.

According to tradition, Ecclesiastes, the section from which this selection is taken, was written by Solomon, the wise Hebrew king, who died around 932 B.C.

7 **▶ Critical Viewing**

Answer: This series of pictures effectively illustrates the poem because the series represents the four seasons, the repeating cycles of nature. Similarly, the poem represents the repeating cycles of life.

Answers to p. 929

Review and Assess

1. Students may find the passage comforting because it suggests a balance between happiness and unhappiness.
2. **(a)** The first verse begins differently from the other verses.
   (b) The first verse sets out the main idea of the passage, that everything has its time and place. The other verses give examples.
3. **(a)** The words "a time to" are repeated throughout the passage. **(b)** The words are repeated to set up a rhythm that exemplifies the message.
4. **(a)** Possible response: Four pairs of actions include: a time to be born and die, plant and harvest, kill and heal, cry and laugh.
   (b) Students may say that casting away stones suggests destruction or demolition, whereas gathering stones suggests constructive work, such as building a wall.
   (c) Suggested response: By naming opposite events, the passage also includes events in the middle; this emphasizes that all events have their time.
5. Possible response: Life today still includes extremes of good and bad, and this passage may help people prepare for and accept inevitable change.

CUSTOMIZE INSTRUCTION FOR UNIVERSAL ACCESS

For English Learners	For Advanced Readers
Make sure that students understand that the pairs of activities cited in Ecclesiastes are opposites. Explain the pairs of antonyms that will be difficult for students to understand because they include less common or archaic words or phrases, such as "pluck up," "cast away," "refrain," and "rend."	Have students locate Ecclesiastes 3:1–8 in two or three other versions of the Bible, such as the *American Standard* of 1901, *Today's English Version* (Good News for Modern Man) published in 1966, or the *New International,* which came out in 1972. Have students read the other versions and discuss them with each other. Ask students to focus their discussions on these questions: Which version is clearest and most understandable? Which version sounds the best? Which version moves you the most? Why?

❽ About the Selection

"The Bells" uses repetition and onomatopoeia to capture the sound and symbolism of four sets of bells.

❾ Background

Art

The Bells by Edmund Dulac

Edmund Dulac (1882–1953) was a French illustrator known for the color and imagination of his work. This painting, with its somber overall mood, illustrates Part IV of "The Bells."

Use these questions for discussion:

1. Using this painting as an example, what are some of the advantages of illustrating a literary work with paintings rather than photographs?
   Possible response: One advantage is a painter's ability to stray far from reality in order to create a certain impression or mood. Another is the ability to use light and composition as desired for emphasis or effect.
2. How else could this poem be illustrated?
   Possible response: Students might suggest that paintings or photographs of sleighs, weddings, or fires might be used to illustrate the other parts of the poem.

❿ ▶Critical Viewing

Answer: Some students might describe the mood of the painting as somber because of the predominantly dark scene with only an eerie source of light. Others might say the mood is bizarre because of the oddly rendered faces to the right of the steeple. The painting matches the mood of Part IV of the poem, which speaks of the iron bells and their melancholy tone.

❾

The Bells, Edmund Dulac, New York Public Library

❿ ▲ **Critical Viewing** How would you describe the mood of this painting? What do you predict the mood of the poem might be? **[Interpret]**

930 ◆ Poetry

ENRICHMENT: Literature Connection

Literary Criticism

A literary device that Poe used frequently was the refrain, a repeated line or group of lines. In this poem, the refrain is "from the bells, bells, bells, bells…"

Literary critics differ in their evaluation of the effectiveness of the refrain. Here is the opinion of critic Anthony Caputi:

"The poem which represents Poe's most ambitious effort with the refrain and at the same time his most colossal failure is 'The Bells.' Poe's purpose in the poem was apparently to synthesize the ambivalence of experience by underscoring heavily the multifaceted complexity of a single object.…Each repetition of the 'Bells, bells, bells' refrain theoretically folds in another area of experience…Poe's versatility was never more in evidence than there, and never more ineffectual."

8

The Bells

Edgar Allan Poe

I

12

Hear the sledges[1] with the bells—
Silver bells!
What a world of merriment their melody foretells!
How they tinkle, tinkle, tinkle,
In the icy air of night!
While the stars, that oversprinkle
All the heavens, seem to twinkle
With a crystalline delight;
Keeping time, time, time,
In a sort of Runic[2] rhyme,
To the tintinnabulation[3] that so musically wells
From the bells, bells, bells, bells,
Bells, bells, bells—
From the jingling and the tinkling of the bells.

11

1. **sledges** (slej´ əz) *n.* sleighs.
2. **Runic** (ro͞o´ nik) *adj.* songlike; poetical.
3. **tintinnabulation** (tin´ ti nab´ yo͞o la´ shən) *n.* ringing of bells.

11 Reading Strategy

Listening to Poetic Sounds

- Choose a volunteer to read aloud lines 11–14.
- Ask students to identify the examples of onomatopoeia in these lines.
  Answer: The examples of onomatopoeia include the words *tintinnabulation, jingling,* and *tinkling.*

▶ **Monitor Progress** Have students explain why these words are examples of onomatopoeia.
Answer: The words suggest the sound of bells ringing.

12 Critical Thinking

Analyze

- Ask students to identify the mood of the verse.
  Answer: The mood is cheerful and merry.
- Have students point out the words that establish this mood.
  Answer: The words include *merriment, tinkle, delight, musically,* and *jingling.*

⓭ Literary Analysis

Lyric Poetry and Sound Devices

- Draw students' attention to lines 32–34. Have a volunteer read these lines aloud.
- Ask students what effect is created by the repeated use of the word *bells*.
  Possible answer: Students may say that the repeated word begins to lose its meaning and become sheer sound, a result most likely intended by the poet.

⓮ Reading Strategy

Listening to Poetic Sounds

- Have students read Part III silently. Ask them what directions they would give to someone reading this passage aloud.
  Possible response: Students may suggest that the passage be read loudly, rapidly, with a breathless, frantic tone.
- Next, read the passage aloud in the manner suggested by the class. Encourage students to close their eyes and pay careful attention to the sounds created by the words.
- Ask students the Reading Strategy question on p. 932: What do the sounds in these lines suggest?
  Answer: Students may notice the sharp consonant sounds of *d* and *t* and the hissing sounds of *s* and *sh*. Students may say that these sounds suggest something sinister, perhaps the hissing and ticking sounds of fire.

II

Hear the mellow wedding bells,
Golden bells!
What a world of happiness their harmony foretells!
Through the balmy air of night
How they ring out their delight!
From the molten golden-notes,
And all in tune,
What a liquid ditty[4] floats
To the turtle-dove[5] that listens, while she gloats
On the moon!
Oh, from out the sounding cells,
What a gush of euphony[6] voluminously wells!
How it swells!
How it dwells
On the future! how it tells
Of the rapture that impels
To the swinging and the ringing
Of the bells, bells, bells,
⓭ Of the bells, bells, bells, bells
Bells, bells, bells—
To the rhyming and the chiming of the bells!

III

Hear the loud alarum[7] bells!
Brazen[8] bells!
What a tale of terror now their turbulency tells!
In the startled ear of night
How they scream out their affright!
Too much horrified to speak,
They can only shriek, shriek,
Out of tune,
In a clamorous appealing to the mercy of the fire,
In a mad expostulation[9] with the deaf and frantic fire
Leaping higher, higher, higher,
⓮ With a desperate desire,
And a resolute endeavor
Now—now to sit or never,
By the side of the pale-faced moon.
Oh, the bells, bells, bells!
What a tale their terror tells

voluminously (və lo͞om′ ə nəs lē) *adv.* fully; in great volume

Reading Strategy
Listening to Poetic Sounds What do the sounds in these lines suggest? Explain.

4. **ditty** (dit′ ē) *n.* song.
5. **turtle-dove** The turtle-dove is traditionally associated with love.
6. **euphony** (yo͞o′ fə nē) *n.* pleasing sound.
7. **alarum** (ə ler′ əm) *adj.* sudden call to arms; alarm.
8. **brazen** (brā′ zən) *adj.* made of brass; having the sound of brass.
9. **expostulation** (eks päs′ chə lā′ shən) *n.* objection; complaint.

Of Despair!
How they clang, and clash, and roar!
What a horror they outpour
On the bosom of the palpitating air!
Yet the ear it fully knows,
By the twanging
And the clanging,
How the danger ebbs and flows;
Yet the ear distinctly tells,
In the jangling,
And the wrangling,
How the danger sinks and swells,
By the sinking or the swelling in the anger of the bells—
Of the bells—
Of the bells, bells, bells, bells,
Bells, bells, bells—
In the clamor and the clangor of the bells!

IV

Hear the tolling of the bells—
Iron bells!
What a world of solemn thought their monody[10] compels!
In the silence of the night,
How we shiver with affright
15 At the melancholy menace of their tone!
For every sound that floats
From the rust within their throats
Is a groan.
And the people—ah, the people—
They that dwell up in the steeple,
All alone,
And who tolling, tolling, tolling,
16 In that muffled monotone,
Feel a glory in so rolling
On the human heart a stone—
They are neither man nor woman—
They are neither brute nor human—
They are Ghouls:[11]
And their king it is who tolls;
And he rolls, rolls, rolls,
Rolls
A pæan from the bells!
And his merry bosom swells
With the pæan of the bells!

palpitating (pal′ pə tāt′ iŋ) *adj.* beating rapidly; throbbing

Literary Analysis
Lyric Poetry and Sound Devices What effect is created by the sound devices in lines 73–78?

monotone (män′ ə tōn′) *n.* uninterrupted repetition of the same tone

pæan (pē′ ən) *n.* song of joy or triumph

10. **monody** (män′ ə dē) *n.* poem of mourning; a steady sound; music in which one instrument or voice is dominant.
11. **Ghouls** (go͞olz) *n.* evil spirits that rob graves.

17 **Reading Check**

What kind of story do the wedding bells tell?

15 Literary Analysis

Lyric Poetry and Sound Devices

- Have students read lines 73–78 to themselves.
- Then, ask students the Literary Analysis question on p. 933: What effect is created by the sound devices in lines 73–78?
  Answer: The sound devices of onomatopoeia and alliteration create an effect of threat, fear, and dread.

16 Vocabulary Development

Greek Prefix *mono-*

- Call students' attention to the word *monotone* in line 83.
- Explain that the Greek prefix *mono-* means "one," so *monotone* means "one tone."
- Have students read the formal definition of the word *monotone,* which appears in the margin: "uninterrupted repetition of the same tone."
- Challenge students to think of other words with the prefix *mono-*.
  Answer: Words with the prefix *mono-* include *monotonous, monotony, monarch, monogamy, monolith, monologue, monopoly,* and *monorail.*

17 Reading Check

Answer: The wedding bells tell the story of future happiness and harmony.

CUSTOMIZE INSTRUCTION FOR UNIVERSAL ACCESS

For Special Needs Students	For English Learners
Have students read the section of the poem that appears on p. 932 aloud together several times. After the first reading, discuss the difference in tone between Parts II and III. Focus on the first five lines of both verses. Make sure that students realize that both verses have exactly the same structure, but that the bells and their effects are completely different. Then, have the students reread using their tone of voice to express the difference in mood.	Make sure that students understand all potentially puzzling words in these verses aside from the ones defined on the page. Write some of the troublesome phrases on the board and "translate" them. For example, you might write "harmony foretells"—sound predicts, "liquid ditty"—smooth sound, "gush of euphony voluminously wells"—pleasing sound grows very loud, and so on. After students grasp the meaning of the verses, ask them to read the verses aloud together.

ASSESS

Answers for p. 934

Review and Assess

1. Possible response: The first section evokes feelings of gaiety and delight; the second section, happiness and harmony; the third, panic and fear; and the fourth, solemnity, and dread.
2. **(a)** The four sections of the poem describe silver sleigh bells, golden wedding bells, brazen alarum bells, and iron funeral bells, respectively. **(b)** The parts suggest, respectively, a sleigh ride, a wedding, a fire, and a celebration of ghouls.
3. **(a)** Possible answer: Words that refer to the sounds the bells make include *tinkle, jingling, chiming, shriek, twanging, clanging, wrangling, throbbing, moaning,* and *groaning.* **(b)** Many students may believe that Poe was successful because he captured the variety of sounds evoked by the bells.
4. **(a)** The length of the lines varies. **(b)** Students may say that Poe chose to vary line lengths to add interest.
5. **(a)** Students may note that the first line in each part begins with an exhortation to hear the bells. The second line consists of two words, an adjective and the word *bells*, followed by an exclamation mark. All stanzas contain the word *bells* repeated many times. **(b)** The mood varies dramatically from stanza to stanza, from delight to joy to panic, then to dread.
6. Students may agree with Eliot, noting that the sounds and rhythms of "The Bells" are highly interesting in themselves.
7. Students may note that bells are not as commonly used today as Poe describes. Some students may cite their reactions to class or emergency bells at school.

And he dances and he yells;
Keeping time, time, time,
In a sort of Runic rhyme,
To the pæan of the bells—
Of the bells:
Keeping time, time, time,
In a sort of Runic rhyme,
To the throbbing of the bells—
Of the bells, bells, bells—
To the sobbing of the bells;
Keeping time, time, time,
As he knells, knells, knells,
In a happy Runic rhyme,
To the rolling of the bells—
Of the bells, bells, bells—
To the tolling of the bells,
Of the bells, bells, bells, bells,
Bells, bells, bells—
To the moaning and the groaning of the bells.

Review and Assess

Thinking About the Selection

1. **Respond:** What feelings did each section of "The Bells" evoke in you?
2. **(a) Recall:** What kinds of bells are described in each of the four sections of "The Bells"? **(b) Infer:** What scenes or situations does each of the sections suggest?
3. **(a) Recall:** Identify five words in the poem that refer to the sounds that bells make. **(b) Evaluate:** How successful is Poe in capturing the sounds of bells in words? Explain.
4. **(a) Recall:** Are the lines in "The Bells" of a consistent length? Explain. **(b) Speculate:** Why do you think Poe chose to present the lines in this way?
5. **(a) Analyze:** What similarities among the four sections do you see? **(b) Compare and Contrast:** Does the mood or spirit of the poem vary from one section to another, or is it basically the same throughout? Explain.
6. **Assess:** The poet T. S. Eliot once said that poetry can be enjoyed before it is understood. Could "The Bells" be used as evidence in support of this idea? Explain.
7. **Apply:** Do you associate various feelings with different bell sounds in your own life? Explain.

Edgar Allan Poe

(1809–1849)

Edgar Allan Poe may be best known for chilling tales like "The Cask of Amontillado," but he was also a talented poet. As poems like "The Bells" illustrate, Poe was a master at using rhythm and sound effects to emphasize meaning and create a powerful musical effect.

Many scholars believe that the idea for "The Bells" was suggested to Poe by Marie Louise Shew, a woman with medical training who treated Poe when his health began to fail during his final years.

ASSESSMENT PRACTICE: Reading Comprehension

Vocabulary: Completing Analogies (For more practice, see Test Preparation Workbook, p. 54.)

Many tests require students to recognize and complete analogies. To help students, use the following sample test item:

Complete the following analogy.

DAISY : FLOWER ::

A car : transportation
B dog : retriever
C woodpecker : bird
D dream : nightmare

Have students look at the answer choices. Guide them to understand that the relationship between the first pair of words—a daisy is a part of a group of flowers—should be similar to the relationship between the second pair of words. *C* is the correct answer because a woodpecker is a part of a group of birds. *B* and *D* are incorrect because the order is reversed. *A* is incorrect because a car is a kind of transportation.

Review and Assess

Literary Analysis

Lyric Poetry and Sound Devices

1. (a) Using a chart like the one shown, check off the **sound devices** used in each poem. (b) Based on your chart, which poem has the strongest musical qualities? Explain.

Poem	Line #	Rhythm	Alliteration	Rhyme	Onomatopoeia
"Summer"	3	✓	✓ *b* and *c* sound	✓ buzzin/ cousin	✓ buzzin

2. (a) List at least four examples of onomatopoeia in "The Bells." (b) How does the use of onomatopoeia add to the poem?
3. In the **lyric poem** "Uphill," how does the speaker feel about life's journey and its ultimate destination? Support your answer.
4. (a) What emotion does "Summer" convey? (b) If you were to retitle the poem, what would you call it? Why?

Comparing Literary Works

5. (a) Compare the views of the nature of human life that are expressed in these poems. (b) Which poem most strongly conveys the theme of life's cycles? Explain.
6. (a) Which three poems deal with death? (b) How do the poems' perspectives on death differ?

Reading Strategy

Listening to Poetic Sounds

7. (a) How does reading the poems aloud help you appreciate the use of rhyme in the poems? (b) Which other sound devices are revealed by reading aloud?
8. Which poem's meaning became clearer to you when you read it aloud? Explain.

Extend Understanding

9. **Cultural Connection:** Which poem, "Uphill" or Ecclesiastes 3:1–8, might be more comforting to people who are mourning a loss? Explain your answer.

Quick Review

Lyric poetry is verse that expresses the observations and feelings of a single speaker through a highly musical style. That style comes from **sound devices** such as these:

Rhythm: the pattern of beats or stresses in language

Alliteration: the repetition of initial consonant sounds

Rhyme: the repetition of sounds at the ends of words

Onomatopoeia: the use of words that imitate the sounds that they name

To **listen to poetic sounds,** read the poem aloud, listen to the musical sound created, and consider the mood or feeling the sound suggests.

Take It to the Net

www.phschool.com

Take the interactive self-test online to check your understanding of the selections.

FURTHER READING

Other Works by the Poets

Works by Christina Rossetti
"Goblin Market"
Sing-Song
Works by Walter Dean Myers
Fallen Angels
The Young Landlords
Works by Edgar Allan Poe
Edgar Allan Poe: The Complete Tales and Poems of Edgar Allan Poe

Answers for p. 921

Review and Assess

1. **(a)** Student charts may show that "Summer" and "The Bells" use all four sound devices; that "Uphill" uses rhythm and rhyme; and that Ecclesiastes 3: 1–8 uses rhythm and alliteration. **(b)** Students may agree that "The Bells" has the strongest musical qualities due to its extensive use of alliteration and onomatopoeia.
2. **(a)** Possible examples include *tinkle, tintinnabulation, jingling, shriek*. **(b)** Onomatopoeia adds a musical quality to the poem.
3. The speaker feels that life's journey is difficult ("uphill") until it ends in a final rest. Students may cite lines 3, 5, 13, 15 and 16.
4. **(a)** "Summer" conveys a feeling of lazy contentment. **(b)** A possible title is "Hot Days."
5. **(a)** "Uphill" views life as a struggle. "Summer" views life (at least during the summer) as a pleasure. Ecclesiastes 3:1–8 views life as an inevitable cycle of experience. "The Bells" also views life as a range of varied experiences. **(b)** Ecclesiastes 3:1–8 most strongly conveys the theme of life's cycles with multiple examples.
6. **(a)** "Uphill," Ecclesiastes 3:1–8, and "The Bells" all deal with death. **(b)** "Uphill" concentrates on human solace, Ecclesiastes 3:1–8 on life cycles, and "The Bells" on the emotions connected to life events.
7. **(a)** Reading the poems aloud makes the rhymes more emphatic and effective. **(b)** Alliteration, rhythm, and onomatopoeia all become more evident when a poem is read aloud.
8. Possible response: Partly because of the extensive use of alliteration and onomatopoeia, the contrast between happiness and horror in "The Bells" becomes much clearer in reading the poem aloud.
9. Ecclesiastes 3:1–8 might be more consoling to people mourning a loss because it points to times of birth, growth, laughter, dance, and peace. "Uphill" offers only the "rest" of death.

EXTEND

Answers for p. 936

❶ Vocabulary Development

Word Analysis

1. c
2. a
3. d
4. b

Fluency

wayfarers
voluminously
palpitating
monotone
paean

Spelling Strategy

1. unnecessary; Steve wasted time by giving unnecessary explanations.
2. dissatisfied; Not one of us was dissatisfied with his plan.
3. reconstruct; With his advice we were able to reconstruct the old picnic table.
4. predetermine; We cannot predetermine who will win the tournament.

❷ Grammar

1. I will meet other wayfarers at night.
2. You like hot days?
3. Please, listen to the bells!
4. The time has come to dig up what we've planted.
5. I hear the sound of the bells!

Writing Application
Have students exchange work with partners to check that all three types of end marks were used.

Integrate Language Skills

❶ Vocabulary Development Lesson

Word Analysis: Greek Prefix *mono-*

The word *monotone* contains the Greek prefix *mono-*, which means "one." You might guess, therefore, that *monotone* means "one tone," which is close to the actual meaning, "uninterrupted repetition of the same tone."

Match each word containing the prefix *mono-* with its definition on the right.

1. monorail	a. exclusive control of the selling of something
2. monopoly	b. single large block of stone
3. monochromatic	c. railway with a single rail as a track
4. monolith	d. having or being of one color

Fluency: Clarify Word Meaning

Copy the paragraph below, completing it with words from the vocabulary list on page 925.

Commuters, __?__ heading home from work, __?__ packed the railroad platform. With their hearts __?__, they listened to an announcement delivered in a __?__. When the voice proclaimed that their train was about to arrive, they sang a __?__ as one!

Spelling Strategy

A prefix attached to a word does not affect the spelling of the original word. For example, *mono-* + *tone* = *monotone*. Rewrite each word below by adding the given prefix. Then, use each new word in a sentence.

1. *un-* + necessary
2. *dis-* + satisfied
3. *re-* + construct
4. *pre* + determine

❷ Grammar Lesson

End Punctuation

End punctuation is the period, question mark, or exclamation mark at the end of a sentence. A **period** indicates the end of a sentence or an abbreviation. A **question mark** follows a word, phrase, or sentence that asks a question. An **exclamation mark** indicates strong feeling or emotion, including surprise. In the following examples, notice how the end punctuation affects the meaning of these sentences:

Statement:	The road winds uphill.
Question:	The road winds uphill?
Exclamation:	The road winds uphill!

Practice Write each item below, using the appropriate end punctuation for the emotion indicated in parentheses.

1. I will meet other wayfarers at night (anxiety)
2. You like hot days (disbelief)
3. Please, listen to the bells (anger)
4. The time has come to dig up what we have planted (informative)
5. I hear the sound of the bells (excitement)

Writing Application Write five sentences that reflect on one of the poems you have just read. Use each type of end punctuation at least once.

WG Prentice Hall Writing and Grammar Connection: Chapter 29, Section 1

TEACHING RESOURCES

The following resources can be used to enrich or extend the instruction for pp. 936–937.

Vocabulary

Vocabulary and Spelling Practice Book (Use this booklet for skills enrichment.) ■

Grammar

Selection Support: Build Grammar Skills, p. 214
Writing and Grammar, Gold Level, p. 654 ■
Daily Language Practice Transparencies ■

Writing

Writing and Grammar, Gold Level, p. 122
Writing and Grammar iText CD-ROM

■ **BLOCK SCHEDULING:** Resources marked with this symbol provide varied instruction during 90-minute blocks.

❸ Writing Lesson

Rap Song

Like lyric poems, rap songs are musical expressions of a speaker's thoughts and feelings. Write a rap song that conveys your feelings about a season, a stage of life, or another topic that interests you.

Prewriting Choose your topic and make preliminary notes about it. Decide on your message and your key ideas. Then, think about which words or lines you could repeat to help drive home your points.

Drafting As you draft your rap song, focus on establishing a strong rhythm. Use rhymes at the ends of lines to create a musical effect. Also, consider including a refrain, a line or group of lines that is repeated throughout the song.

Revising Read your rap song aloud to check its rhythm. Make sure that your use of repetition highlights your main ideas. Make any revisions needed to improve the sound of the song.

Model: Analyzing Word Choice for Use of Repetition

Fall—everywhere I look I find leaves ~~all over~~ *abound*!

Yellow, red, orange, brown are ~~going~~ *falling* to the ground.

The rhyming words *abound* and *ground* and the repeated use of *fall* improve the sound of the song.

Prentice Hall Writing and Grammar Connection: Chapter 6, Connected Assignment

❹ Extension Activities

Listening and Speaking Prepare and present a **dramatic reading** of "The Bells" to capture the poem's musical quality.

- Read the poem aloud to yourself.
- Make notes about which words to emphasize and when to change your reading pace.
- Practice your reading, recording yourself, if possible, so that you can hear and fix problem spots.

After you present your dramatic reading, ask your listeners what they liked best about it.

Research and Technology In a group, create an **illustrated version** of the poem "Summer." Look on the Internet for images, or use photographs and original artwork that you prepare. As you conduct your visual research, try to capture the mood of the poem. Combine the poem with the art and share it with classmates. **[Group Activity]**

Take It to the Net www.phschool.com

Go online for an additional research activity using the Internet.

ASSESSMENT RESOURCES

The following resources can be used to assess students' knowledge and skills.

Selection Assessment

- **Formal Assessment,** Selection Test, pp. 192–194
- **Open Book Test,** pp. 160–162
- **Got It! Assessment Videotapes,** Tape 5
- **Test Bank Software**

PRENTICE HALL ASSESSMENT SYSTEM

- **Workbook**
- **Skill Book**
- **Transparencies**
- **CD-ROM**

Take It to the Net

Visit www.phschool.com for self-tests and additional questions on the poems.

Lesson Support for p. 937

❸ Writing Lesson

- Play a rap song for students or have volunteers sing parts of one they know.
- Discuss the rap songs. In what ways are rap songs similar to lyric poems? What is unique about rap? What feelings are conveyed in this song?
- Brainstorm with students for some possible topics for their rap songs. Emphasize that students' raps should be about topics that are important to them.

❹ Listening and Speaking

- Suggest that students make photocopies of the poem so that they can mark it up for their dramatic reading. They might use highlighting markers of various colors to code dynamics and pace. In the margins, check marks, arrows, and notes such as the word *LOUD* may be helpful.
- Before they determine how to interpret the poem and mark their photocopy, students should reread the poem several times and take notes on the feeling expressed in each part.
- Suggest that students rehearse their dramatic reading with a partner. They should ask that the partner provide constructive criticism and modify their reading accordingly.

CUSTOMIZE INSTRUCTION for Universal Access

To address different learning styles, use the activities suggested in the **Extension Activities** booklet, p. 54.

- For Rhythmic/Musical and Bodily/Kinesthetic Learners, use Activity 5.
- For Logical/Mathematical and Intrapersonal Learners, use Activity 6.
- For Interpersonal Learners, use Activity 7.

The Raven ✦ The Seven Ages of Man

Lesson Objectives and CA Correlations

1. **To analyze and respond to literary elements**
   - Literary Analysis: Narrative and Dramatic Poetry **R 3.5**
   - Comparing Literary Works
2. **To read, comprehend, analyze, and critique poems**
   - Reading Strategy: Drawing Inferences About the Speaker
   - Reading Check questions
   - Review and Assess questions
   - Assessment Practice (ATE)
3. **To develop word analysis skills, fluency, and systematic vocabulary**
   - Vocabulary Development Lesson: Latin Root: *-sol-* **R 1.1**
4. **To understand and apply written and oral language conventions.**
   - Spelling Strategy
   - Grammar Lesson: Punctuation With Quotation Marks **LC 1.1**
5. **To understand and apply appropriate writing and research strategies**
   - Writing Lesson: Scene for a Movie **W 1.2**
   - Extension Activity: Fact Sheet **W 1.5**
6. **To understand and apply listening and speaking strategies**
   - Extension Activity: Debate **LS 1.8**

STEP-BY-STEP TEACHING GUIDE	PACING GUIDE
PRETEACH	
Motivate Students and Provide Background	
Use the Motivation activity (ATE p. 938)	5 min.
Read and discuss the Preview material and Background information (SE/ATE p. 938) [A]	10 min.
Introduce the Concepts	
Introduce the Literary Analysis and Reading Strategy (SE/ATE p. 939) [A]	15 min.
Pronounce the vocabulary words and read their definitions (SE p. 939)	5 min.
TEACH	
Monitor Comprehension	
Informally monitor comprehension by circulating while students read independently or in groups [A]	15 min.
Monitor students' comprehension with the Reading Check note (SE/ATE p. 941)	as students read
Develop vocabulary with Vocabulary notes (SE pp. 940, 942–943, 945–946; ATE p. 942)	as students read
Develop Understanding	
Develop students' understanding of narrative and dramatic poetry with the Literary Analysis annotations (SE pp. 940–941, 945; ATE pp. 940–941, 945) [A]	10 min.
Develop students' ability to draw inferences about the speaker with the Reading Strategy annotations (SE pp. 940, 942; ATE pp. 940, 942)	10 min.
ASSESS	
Assess Mastery	
Assess students' mastery of the Reading Strategy and Literary Analysis by having them answer the Review and Assess questions (SE/ATE p. 947)	20 min.
Use one or more of the print and media Assessment Resources (ATE p. 949) [A]	up to 50 min.
EXTEND	
Apply Understanding	
Have students complete the Vocabulary Development Lesson and the Grammar Lesson (SE p. 948) [A]	20 min.
Apply students' knowledge of using descriptive details to set a mood using the Writing Lesson (SE/ATE p. 949) [A]	45 min.
Apply students' understanding using one or more of the Extension Activities (SE p. 949)	20–90 min.

A **ACCELERATED INSTRUCTION:**
Use the strategies and activities identified with an [A].

UNIVERSAL ACCESS
● = Below Level Students
▲ = On-Level Students
■ = Above Level Students

Time and Resource Manager

Reading Level: Challenging/Challenging
Average Number of Instructional Days: 4

RESOURCES		
PRINT	**TRANSPARENCIES**	**TECHNOLOGY**
• **Beyond Literature,** Cross-Curricular Connection: Music, p. 55 ▲ ■		• **Interest Grabber Video,** Tape 5 ● ▲ ■
• **Selection Support Workbook:** ● ▲ ■ Literary Analysis, p. 220 Reading Strategy, p. 219 Build Vocabulary, p. 217	• **Literary Analysis and Reading Transparencies,** pp. 109 and 110 ● ▲ ■	
• **Adapted Reader's Companion** ● • **Reader's Companion** ● • **Authors In Depth,** Gold Level, p. 155 ■		• **Listening to Literature** ● ▲ ■ Audiocassettes, Side 28 Audio CDs, CD 19
• **English Learner's Companion** ● ▲ • **Literatura en español** ● ▲ • **Literary Analysis for Enrichment** ■		
• **Formal Assessment:** Selection Test, pp. 195–197 ● ▲ ■ • **Open Book Test,** pp. 163–165 ● ▲ ■ • PRENTICE HALL ASSESSMENT SYSTEM ● ▲ ■	• PRENTICE HALL ASSESSMENT SYSTEM ● ▲ ■ Skills Practice Answers and Explanations on Transparencies	• **Test Bank Software** ● ▲ ■ • **Got It! Assessment Videotapes,** Tape 5 ● ▲
• **Selection Support Workbook:** ● ▲ ■ Build Grammar Skills, p. 218 • **Writing and Grammar,** Gold Level ● ▲ ■ • **Extension Activities,** p. 53 ● ▲ ■	• **Daily Language Practice Transparencies** ● ▲ • **Writing Models and Graphic Organizers on Transparencies,** p. 83 ● ▲ ■	• **Writing and Grammar iText CD-ROM** ● ▲ ■ ***Take It to the Net*** www.phschool.com

BLOCK SCHEDULING: Use one 90-minute class period to preteach the selection and have students read it. Use a second 90-minute class period to assess students' mastery of skills and have them complete one of the Extension Activities.

PRETEACH

Step-by-Step Teaching Guide for pp. 938–939

Motivation

Before you read the following paragraph to the class, tell them that it's the beginning of a horror story.

> It was midnight. I was just dozing off when I heard a faint tapping on my bedroom door. I opened the door, but there was nothing but darkness. Then the curtains began to rustle. I threw open the window and suddenly . . .

Have students speculate about what might happen next. Then, tell them they will find out when they read the poem by Edgar Allan Poe.

Interest Grabber Video

As an alternative, play "Humor in Shakespeare" on Tape 5 to engage student interest.

❶ Background

Cultural Perspectives

Have a student look up the meaning of *perspective* and share it with the class. Explain that Poe and Shakespeare had different perspectives on life as seen in their works. As they read, students might think about how the authors' perspectives are revealed in their writing. Have students consider how writers in any culture reflect their perspectives through their writing.

Prepare to Read

The Raven ◆ The Seven Ages of Man

Take It to the Net

Visit www.phschool.com for interactive activities and instruction related to the selections, including

- background
- graphic organizers
- literary elements
- reading strategies

Preview

Connecting to the Literature

Why do people act the way they do? Adults often explain the behavior of young people by saying, "It's just a phase. . . ." Do you think people go through "phases" all their lives, or do specific events in an individual's life shape his or her behavior? These two selections present different answers to the question.

❶ Background

"The Seven Ages of Man" is a speech from William Shakespeare's comedy *As You Like It*. The play is about a duke who has been deprived of his rights and exiled to the forest by his own brother. The duke's attendant, Jacques, delivers the speech to his master and reveals a cold and bitter outlook on life.

TEACHING RESOURCES

The following resources can be used to enrich or extend the instruction for pp. 938–939.

Motivation

Interest Grabber Video, Tape 5

Background

Beyond Literature, p. 55

Take It to the Net

Visit www.phschool.com for background and hotlinks for the selections.

Literary Analysis

Literary Analysis and Reading Transparencies, Narrative and Dramatic Poetry, p. 110

Reading

Selection Support: Reading Strategy, p. 219; Build Vocabulary, p. 217

Literary Analysis and Reading Transparencies, Drawing Inferences, p. 109

BLOCK SCHEDULING: Resources marked with this symbol provide varied instruction during 90-minute blocks.

❷ Literary Analysis

Narrative and Dramatic Poetry

"The Raven" is a poem that has characters, a setting, and a plot. These elements make it **narrative poetry**—poetry that tells a story. The first line of "The Raven" opens in storytelling style:

Once upon a midnight dreary, while I pondered, weak and weary,

"The Seven Ages of Man," in contrast, is a **dramatic poem**—a poem in which the lines are spoken by one or more characters to express their thoughts and feelings. The poem is spoken by a character named Jacques:

All the world's a stage,
And all the men and women merely players:

Comparing Literary Works

These two poems present different perspectives on human life. As you read, compare the speakers' views on love, hope, aging, loss, and suffering. Also, consider how the style and language of each speaker help express his feelings about life. For example, you may notice that the narrative speaker is sad and intense as he presents his story, while the dramatic speaker is direct and sarcastic in his monologue.

❸ Reading Strategy

Drawing Inferences About the Speaker

Readers sometimes mistakenly assume that a poem's speaker is always the poet. Actually, the speaker is often an imaginary voice assumed by the poet. To understand a poem, it is helpful to identify who the speaker is and then to **draw inferences**—educated guesses based on evidence—about the speaker's situation, attitudes, and personality traits. Use a chart like the one shown to record words and details that reveal information about each speaker.

Vocabulary Development

quaint (kwānt) *adj.* strange; unusual (p. 940)

beguiling (bi gīl′ iŋ) *adj.* tricking; charming (p. 942)

respite (res′ pit) *n.* rest; relief (p. 942)

desolate (des′ ə lit) *adj.* deserted (p. 942)

pallid (pal′ id) *adj.* pale (p. 943)

woeful (wō′ fəl) *adj.* full of sorrow (p. 945)

treble (treb′ əl) *n.* high-pitched voice (p. 946)

❷ Literary Analysis

Narrative and Dramatic Poetry

- Read aloud the instruction about narrative poetry, then read the first line of "The Raven."
- Ask students: What aspects of the first line let you know you're going to hear a story?
  Answer: Aspects include the use of "once upon," which is often used to start stories ("once upon a time") and the establishing of the setting and mood.
- For contrast, read aloud the first two lines of "The Seven Ages of Man." Explain that this is a dramatic poem, and that it is easy to picture a character delivering these lines.

❸ Reading Strategy

Drawing Inferences About the Speaker

- Remind students that when they draw inferences about a poem's speaker, they draw conclusions about this speaker based on his or her actions and words.
- Call students' attention to the chart on this page. Based on the beginning of "The Raven," students can infer that the speaker is in a gloomy, depressed mood. Ask students to consider what this knowledge of the speaker's situation leads them to expect in the rest of the poem.
- Encourage students to use a chart like one shown to help them record details about the speakers of the poems that they can use to draw inferences.

Vocabulary Development

- Pronounce each vocabulary word for students, and read the definitions as a class. Have students identify any words with which they are already familiar.

CUSTOMIZE INSTRUCTION FOR UNIVERSAL ACCESS

For Special Needs Students	For Less Proficient Readers	For English Learners
Have students read the adapted versions of the selections in the **Adapted Reader's Companion.** These versions provide basic-level instruction in an interactive format with questions and write-on lines. Completing the adapted versions will prepare students to read the selections in the Student Edition.	Have students read the selections in the **Reader's Companion.** These versions provide basic-level instruction in an interactive format with questions and write-on lines. After students finish the selections in **Reader's Companion,** have them complete the questions and activities in the Student Edition.	Have students read the adapted versions of the selections in the **English Learner's Companion.** These versions provide basic-level instruction in an interactive format with questions and write-on lines. Completing the adapted versions will prepare students to read the selections in the Student Edition.

E-Teach

Visit E-Teach at www.phschool.com for teachers' essays on how to teach, with questions and answers.

TEACH

Step-by-Step Teaching Guide for pp. 940–946

CUSTOMIZE INSTRUCTION
For Visual/Spatial Learners

Ask these students to imagine a performer reciting "The Raven" in a dramatic presentation. How would the performer be dressed? What props might be nearby? Have students describe, draw, or create the set.

❶ About the Selection

In "The Raven," the speaker and main character is a man whose life has been shattered by a single experience—the death of the woman he loved. Therefore, "The Raven" paints a picture of gloom.

❷ Literary Analysis

Narrative and Dramatic Poetry

- Have a student read aloud the first two stanzas of the poem. (Choose a student who can read dramatically and encourage the student to do so.) As the student reads, ask the other students to jot down background details they notice.
- Ask students the Literary Analysis question on p. 940: Which background details does the speaker provide in the first two stanzas to set the scene for the story?
  Possible answers: It was midnight; the speaker was tired and trying to stay awake; there was a tapping at the door; it was dark and bleak December; the fire was burning down; the speaker was reading to escape the pain of losing his love, Lenore.

❸ Reading Strategy

Drawing Inferences About the Speaker

- Read aloud lines 25–30 and ask students to note the speaker's increasing state of nervousness.
- Ask the Reading Strategy question on p. 940: Which words or actions by the speaker show that he is getting more and more nervous?
  Answers: Students may cite "peering into the darkness"; "fearing, doubting"; dreaming frightening dreams.

❶ The Raven

Edgar Allan Poe

❷

Once upon a midnight dreary, while I pondered, weak and weary,
Over many a quaint and curious volume of forgotten lore,[1]
While I nodded, nearly napping, suddenly there came a tapping,
As of someone gently rapping, rapping at my chamber door.
"'Tis some visitor," I muttered, "tapping at my chamber door—
Only this, and nothing more."

Ah, distinctly I remember it was in the bleak December,
And each separate dying ember wrought its ghost upon the floor.
Eagerly I wished the morrow—vainly I had tried to borrow
From my books surcease[2] of sorrow—sorrow for the lost Lenore—
For the rare and radiant maiden whom the angels name Lenore—
Nameless here for evermore.

And the silken, sad, uncertain rustling of each purple curtain
Thrilled me—filled me with fantastic terrors never felt before;
So that now, to still the beating of my heart, I stood repeating
"'Tis some visitor entreating entrance at my chamber door—
Some late visitor entreating entrance at my chamber door—
This it is and nothing more."

Presently my soul grew stronger; hesitating then no longer,
"Sir," said I, "or Madam, truly your forgiveness I implore;
But the fact is I was napping, and so gently you came rapping,
And so faintly you came tapping, tapping at my chamber door,
That I scarce was sure I heard you"—here I opened wide the door—
Darkness there, and nothing more.

❸

Deep into that darkness peering, long I stood there wondering, fearing,
Doubting, dreaming dreams no mortal ever dared to dream before;
But the silence was unbroken, and the darkness gave no token,[3]
And the only word there spoken was the whispered word, "Lenore!"
This *I* whispered, and an echo murmured back the word, "Lenore!"
Merely this, and nothing more.

1. **quaint . . . lore** strange book of ancient learning.
2. **surcease** (sʉr sēsʹ) *n.* end.
3. **token** (tōʹ kən) *n.* sign.

quaint (kwānt) *adj.* strange; unusual

Literary Analysis
Narrative and Dramatic Poetry Which background details does the speaker provide in the first two stanzas to set the scene for the story?

Reading Strategy
Drawing Inferences About the Speaker Which words or actions by the speaker show that he is getting more and more nervous?

TEACHING RESOURCES

The following resources can be used to enrich or extend the instruction for pp. 940–946.

Literary Analysis
- **Selection Support:** Literary Analysis, p. 220
- **Writing Models and Graphic Organizers on Transparencies,** p. 83 ■

Reading
- **Adapted Reader's Companion**
- **English Learner's Companion**
- **Listening to Literature Audiocassettes,** Side 28 ■
- **Listening to Literature Audio CDs,** CD 19 ■

■ **BLOCK SCHEDULING:** Resources marked with this symbol provide varied instruction during 90-minute blocks.

Then into the chamber turning, all my soul within me burning,
Soon I heard again a tapping somewhat louder than before.
"Surely," said I, "surely that is something at my window lattice;[4]
Let me see, then, what thereat[5] is, and this mystery explore—
Let my heart be still a moment and this mystery explore—
'Tis the wind, and nothing more!"

Open here I flung the shutter, when, with many a flirt[6] and flutter,
In there stepped a stately raven of the saintly days of yore;
Not the least obeisance[7] made he; not an instant stopped or
stayed he;
❹ But, with mien[8] of lord or lady, perched above my chamber door—
Perched upon a bust of Pallas[9] just above my chamber door—
Perched, and sat, and nothing more.

Then this ebony bird beguiling my sad fancy[10] into smiling,
By the grave and stern decorum of the countenance[11] it wore,
"Though thy crest be shorn and shaven, thou," I said, "art sure
no craven,[12]
Ghastly grim and ancient raven wandering from the Nightly shore—
Tell me what thy lordly name is on the Night's Plutonian[13] shore!"
Quoth[14] the raven, "Nevermore."

Much I marveled this ungainly fowl to hear discourse so plainly,
Though its answer little meaning—little relevancy bore;
For we cannot help agreeing that no sublunary[15] being
Ever yet was blessed with seeing bird above his chamber door—
Bird or beast upon the sculptured bust above his chamber door,
With such name as "Nevermore."

But the raven, sitting lonely on the placid bust, spoke only
That one word, as if his soul in that one word he did outpour.
Nothing farther then he uttered—not a feather then he fluttered—
Till I scarcely more than muttered, "Other friends have flown before—
On the morrow *he* will leave me, as my hopes have flown before."
Quoth the raven, "Nevermore."

4. **lattice** (lat′ is) *n.* framework of wood or metal.
5. **thereat** (*th*er at′) *adv.* there.
6. **flirt** (flurt) *n.* quick, uneven movement.
7. **obeisance** (ō bā′ səns) *n.* bow or another sign of respect.
8. **mien** (mēn) *n.* manner.
9. **bust of Pallas** (pal′ əs) sculpture of the head and shoulders of Pallas Athena (ə thē′ nə), the ancient Greek goddess of wisdom.
10. **fancy** (fan′ sē) *n.* imagination.
11. **countenance** (koun′ tə nəns) *n.* facial appearance.
12. **craven** (krā′ vən) *n.* coward (usually an adjective).
13. **Plutonian** (plōō tō′ nē ən) *adj.* like the underworld, ruled over by the ancient Roman god Pluto.
14. **quoth** (kwōth) *v.* said.
15. **sublunary** (sub lōōn′ ər ē) *adj.* earthly.

Literary Analysis
Narrative and Dramatic Poetry Which elements of a story plot are evident in the first eight stanzas of the poem?

❺ **Reading Check**
What is tapping at the speaker's chamber door?

❹ Literary Analysis

Narrative and Dramatic Poetry

- Remind students that narrative poems contain all the elements of a plot: exposition, rising action, climax, falling action, and resolution. Write the following diagram on the board or display the story map from **Writing Models and Graphic Organizers on Transparencies,** p. 83.

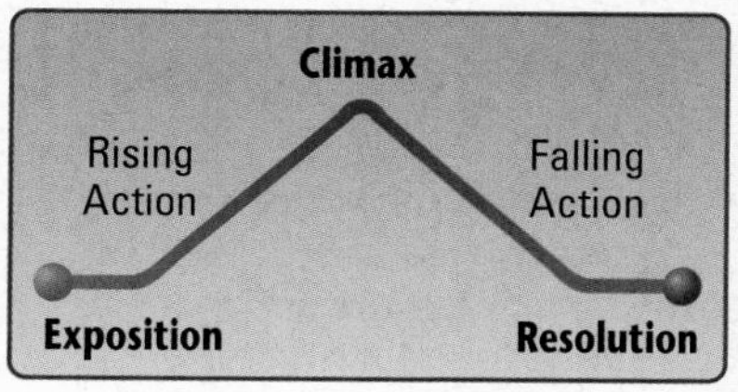

- Ask students the Literary Analysis question on p. 941: Which elements of a story plot are evident in the first eight stanzas of the poem?
Answers: Students may note exposition (stanzas 1 and 2), rising action (stanzas 3–8).

❺ Reading Check

Answer: A raven is tapping at the door.

CUSTOMIZE INSTRUCTION FOR UNIVERSAL ACCESS

For Special Needs Students	For English Learners
Play the recording of "The Raven," using the **Listening to Literature** Audiocassettes, Side 28, or Audio CDs, CD 19. Next, have the students read along as they listen to the poem again. Ask these students to explain their feelings about the poem.	Encourage these students to jot down words and phrases that are hard to understand as they read. Writing notes on notepads might suffice for some students; others may benefit by placing self-sticking notes near the hard-to-understand words and phrases. Ask students not to stop reading to look up unfamiliar words, but to use their notes for later research.

❻ Reading Strategy

Drawing Inferences About the Speaker

- Have students summarize the action of the poem up to this point. Ask them to offer their opinions about the speaker's state of mind, supporting their responses with details from the poem.
- Read aloud lines 68–69 to students. Have students discuss why they think the speaker moves his chair closer to the raven.
- Then, ask students the Reading Strategy question on p. 942: What does the speaker's action in line 68 suggest about his state of mind?
  Possible answer: By moving his chair closer to the raven, the narrator shows that he is giving serious attention to his visitor. This could suggest that the speaker is becoming more desperate to know what the raven's appearance means.

❼ Vocabulary Development

Latin Root *-sol-*

- Point out the word *desolate* in line 87. Explain to students that this word contains the Latin word root *-sol-*, which means "alone."
- Discuss with students how this word root contributes to the definition of *desolate* as "deserted; left alone."
- Then, have students identify other words they know that contain the root word *-sol-*.
  Possible answers: *Solitary*: "alone; single"; *solitude*: "state of being alone; aloneness"; *isolate*: "set apart; keep alone."

Wondering at the stillness broken by reply so aptly spoken,
"Doubtless," said I, "what it utters is its only stock and store,
Caught from some unhappy master whom unmerciful Disaster
Followed fast and followed faster—so, when Hope he would adjure,[16]
Stern Despair returned, instead of the sweet Hope he dared adjure—
    That sad answer, 'Nevermore.'"

But the raven still beguiling all my sad soul into smiling,
Straight I wheeled a cushioned seat in front of bird, and bust, and door;
Then upon the velvet sinking, I betook myself to linking
Fancy unto fancy, thinking what this ominous bird of yore—
What this grim, ungainly, ghastly, gaunt, and ominous bird of yore
    Meant in croaking "Nevermore."

This I sat engaged in guessing, but no syllable expressing
To the fowl whose fiery eyes now burned into my bosom's core;
This and more I sat divining,[17] with my head at ease reclining
On the cushion's velvet lining that the lamplight gloated o'er,
But whose velvet violet lining with the lamplight gloating o'er,
    She shall press, ah, nevermore!

Then, methought, the air grew denser, perfumed from an unseen censer[18]
Swung by angels whose faint footfalls tinkled on the tufted floor.
"Wretch," I cried, "thy God hath lent thee—by these angels he hath sent thee
Respite—respite and Nepenthe[19] from thy memories of Lenore!
Let me quaff[20] this kind Nepenthe and forget this lost Lenore!"
    Quoth the raven, "Nevermore."

"Prophet!" said I, "thing of evil!—prophet still, if bird or devil!—
Whether Tempter[21] sent, or whether tempest tossed thee here ashore,
Desolate, yet all undaunted, on this desert land enchanted—
On this home by Horror haunted—tell me truly, I implore—
Is there—is there balm in Gilead?[22]—tell me—tell me, I implore!"
    Quoth the raven, "Nevermore."

"Prophet!" said I, "thing of evil!—prophet still, if bird or devil!
By that Heaven that bends above us—by that God we both adore—

Reading Strategy Drawing Inferences About the Speaker What does the speaker's action in line 68 suggest about his state of mind?

beguiling (bi gīl′ iŋ) *adj.* tricking; charming

respite (res′ pit) *n.* rest; relief

desolate (des′ ə lit) *adj.* deserted

16. **adjure** (ə joor′) *v.* appeal to.
17. **divining** (də vīn′ iŋ) *v.* guessing.
18. **censer** (sen′ sər) *n.* container for burning incense.
19. **Nepenthe** (ni pen′ thē) *n.* drug used in ancient times to cause forgetfulness of sorrow.
20. **quaff** (kwäf) *v.* drink.
21. **Tempter** devil.
22. **balm** (bäm) **in Gilead** (gil′ ē əd) cure for suffering; the Bible refers to a medicinal ointment, or balm, made in a region called Gilead.

ENRICHMENT: Cultural Connection

The Raven as a Symbol

Poe chooses a raven to represent the supernatural in this poem. Through the ages, the raven has often been seen as a symbol of evil or negativity. For example, in Greek mythology, a raven indiscreetly reveals secrets, and the god Apollo blackens the raven's white feathers as punishment.

In contrast, some Native American myths depict the raven in a more positive light—as a creator of the natural world. Poe's raven seems more mysterious and fearful, however, and his one-word replies add to the scary mood.

Tell this soul with sorrow laden if, within the distant Aidenn,[23]
It shall clasp a sainted maiden whom the angels name Lenore—
Clasp a rare and radiant maiden whom the angels name Lenore."
Quoth the raven, "Nevermore."

"Be that word our sign of parting, bird or fiend!" I shrieked, upstarting—
"Get thee back into the tempest and the Night's Plutonian shore!
Leave no black plume as a token of that lie thy soul hath spoken!
Leave my loneliness unbroken!—quit the bust above my door!
Take thy beak from out my heart, and take thy form from off my door!"
Quoth the raven, "Nevermore."

And the raven, never flitting, still is sitting, still is sitting
On the pallid bust of Pallas just above my chamber door;
And his eyes have all the seeming of a demon that is dreaming,
And the lamplight o'er him streaming throws his shadow on the floor;
And my soul from out that shadow that lies floating on the floor
Shall be lifted—nevermore!

pallid (pal′ id) *adj.* pale

23. **Aidenn** name meant to suggest Eden or paradise.

Edgar Allan Poe

(1809–1849)

Although he is remembered mostly for his eerie short stories, Edgar Allan Poe was also a gifted poet. The haunting mood of "The Raven," his best-known poem, reflects the impact of the many misfortunes that Poe experienced during his brief, tragic life. As a young boy, Poe lost both of his parents and was taken in by a wealthy Virginia merchant, John Allan, but their relationship was often stormy.

During his literary career, Poe published numerous short stories and poems but never achieved financial success as a writer. Despite his financial struggles, Poe experienced a period of happiness following his marriage to Virginia Clemm in 1835. This happiness was shattered, however, by his wife's death in 1847. (For more on Edgar Allan Poe, see pp. 12 and 934.)

Review and Assess

Thinking About the Selection

1. **Respond:** How do you feel about the poem's speaker? Why?
2. **(a) Recall:** Who is Lenore and what has happened to her? **(b) Infer:** What can you infer about the speaker's relationship with Lenore? Explain.
3. **(a) Recall:** Which two adjectives does the speaker use to describe his mood at the beginning of the poem? **(b) Draw Conclusions:** Which adjectives would you use to describe the speaker's mood at the end of the poem? Explain. **(c) Analyze Cause and Effect:** What has caused the speaker's mood to change?
4. **(a) Recall:** What one word does the Raven speak? **(b) Draw Conclusions:** Do you think the raven is merely repeating a sound, or is it responding to each of the narrator's questions?
5. **(a) Connect:** Describe how your impression of the raven changes as the poem progresses. **(b) Analyzing Cause and Effect:** What causes your impression to change?
6. **Evaluate:** Poe considered having a parrot repeat the word "Nevermore." Would the poem have been as effective if Poe had used a parrot instead of a raven? Explain.

Answers for p. 943

Review and Assess

1. Students may feel pity for the speaker because of his deep sadness.
2. **(a)** Lenore is the speaker's beloved one; she has died. **(b)** The speaker was deeply in love with Lenore and is inconsolable after her death.
3. **(a)** He uses the adjectives *weak* and *weary*. **(b)** Students may suggest adjectives such as *hopeless* or *despairing*. Students may cite lines 100, 101, 107, and 108 to support their response. **(c)** The raven's repeated negative causes the speaker to become more and more depressed.
4. **(a)** The raven speaks the word *nevermore*. **(b)** Students may answer that the raven is actually responding to the narrator (because that is what the narrator believes).
5. **(a)** The raven is at first amusing, but it later becomes a symbol of despair. **(b)** The reader's impression changes because the speaker's questions grow ever more personal and desperate.
6. Students may recognize that use of a parrot would drastically alter the mood and other elements of the poem. Parrots are known for mindless repetition, so the repeated "nevermore" would have little significance. Students may note that a squawking parrot would not convey the sinister sense of menace and despair that the raven does.

ENRICHMENT: Further Reading

Other Works by Edgar Allan Poe

"The Cask of Amontillado"
"The Bells"
"Annabel Lee"
"The Black Cat"

Take It to the Net

Visit www.phschool.com for more information on Edgar Allan Poe.

8 Background

Art

The Seven Ages of Man, stained-glass window, Folger Shakespeare Library, Washington, D.C.

Stained glass is a term used for windows or other display pieces composed of small pieces of dyed and painted glass joined with pieces of lead and mounted in a metal framework. The art achieved its greatest expression in the Gothic cathedrals of the twelfth through the fourteenth centuries. Use these questions for discussion:

1. The window represents the seven ages of man described by Shakespeare. Why do you think the panels are arranged as they are?
   Answer: They were meant to rise to the fourth age, which was considered the age when a man is "in his prime," and then fall to the seventh age when, a man is back on the same level with the first.
2. Do you agree that the fourth age (the soldier) is man's prime? If not, which would you place in that position?
   Answer: Accept all responses that are supported with logical reasons.

9 ▶ Critical Viewing

Answer: The images represent the seven stages described in the poem. Their relative heights in the window might represent the rising and falling of physical and mental powers throughout life.

8

The Seven Ages of Man, Folger Shakespeare Library, Washington, D.C.

9 ▲ **Critical Viewing** How do the images in this stained glass window add to your understanding of the poem? **[Relate]**

10

The Seven Ages of Man

William Shakespeare

All the world's a stage,
And all the men and women merely players:[1]
They have their exits and their entrances;
And one man in his time plays many parts,
His acts being seven ages.[2] At first the infant,
Mewling[3] and puking in the nurse's arms.
And then the whining schoolboy, with his satchel,
And shining morning face, creeping like snail
11 Unwillingly to school. And then the lover,
Sighing like furnace, with a woeful ballad
Made to his mistress' eyebrow. Then a soldier,
Full of strange oaths, and bearded like the pard,[4]
Jealous in honor,[5] sudden and quick in quarrel,
Seeking the bubble reputation
Even in the cannon's mouth. And then the justice,[6]
In fair round belly with good capon[7] lined,
With eyes severe and beard of formal cut,

Literary Analysis
Narrative and Dramatic Poetry Which qualities of both poetry and drama does the selection embody?

woeful (wō′ fəl) *adj.* full of sorrow

1. **players** actors.
2. **ages** periods of life.
3. **mewling** (myo͞ol′ iŋ) *adj.* whimpering; crying weakly.
4. **pard** (pärd) *n.* leopard or panther.
5. **Jealous in honor** very concerned about his honor.
6. **justice** judge.
7. **capon** (kā′ pän) *n.* roasted chicken.

10 About the Selection

In "The Seven Ages of Man," the speaker traces the journey of all people from the cradle to the grave—a journey he sees as being meaningless. The speaker seems to provide a humorous but cynical view of life. The speech is from the play *As You Like it,* Act II, Scene vii, and is delivered by the cynical Jacques.

11 Literary Analysis

Narrative and Dramatic Poetry

- Point out that "The Seven Ages of Man" is an example of dramatic poetry. Explain that this poem is actually a speech delivered by a character in a play and is called a "dramatic monologue."
- Ask students if they think this selection is more like a poem or more like a drama. (Students will likely reply that it is a little of both.) You may wish to have students create a two-column chart and list the poetic elements in one column and the dramatic elements in the other.

Monitor Progress Ask students the Literary Analysis question on p. 945: Which qualities of both poetry and drama does the selection embody?
Possible answers: Qualities of poetry include structure of the poem, meter, and poetic language. Qualities of drama include the use of a fictional character directly expressing his thoughts.

CUSTOMIZE INSTRUCTION FOR UNIVERSAL ACCESS

For Advanced Readers

Suggest that students read additional poetry by William Shakespeare. Among other available sources, you may wish to use **Authors In Depth,** Gold Level, which contains the following selections:

- Sonnet 23
- Sonnet 27
- Sonnet 60
- Sonnet 98

After students have read other poems by Shakespeare, have them form discussion groups in which they compare and contrast the poems. Criteria for comparison can include topic, meaning, and construction. To extend the activity, students can read aloud other Shakespeare sonnets, then point out similarities and differences.

ASSESS

Answers for p. 946

Review and Assess

1. Students may suggest that today other age divisions or occupations may be more appropriate than the ones Shakespeare presented hundreds of years ago.
2. **(a)** The speaker mentions an infant, a schoolboy, a lover, a soldier, a judge, an old man, then a man near death. **(b)** The people represent infancy, childhood, young adulthood, adulthood, middle age, old age, and the very elderly.
3. **(a)** The soldier is a bearded man, very proud and quarrelsome, who acts bravely to gain fame. The judge is a fat man with a trim beard who likes to display his wisdom. **(b)** The speaker's sarcasm leads the reader to believe that the speaker sees them in a negative way.
4. **(a)** People in the final stage lack teeth, eyes, taste, everything. **(b)** During the last age, the very elderly resemble children again.
5. **(a)** The speaker seems to be expressing a detached, somewhat cynical and ironical view of life. **(b)** The speaker of "The Raven" expresses a sad but not cynical view of life.
6. Encourage students to back up their answers with examples from both the poems and their personal experience.
7. Most students may agree that people do pass through phases similar to the ones that Shakespeare describes, though they may not share the speaker's cynical attitude.
8. Students may say they would like to explore what age the speaker himself is in, or what life experiences have shaped his cynical attitude.

Full of wise saws and modern instances;[8]
And so he plays his part. The sixth age shifts
Into the lean and slippered pantaloon,[9]
With spectacles on nose and pouch on side,
His youthful hose[10] well saved, a world too wide
For his shrunk shank;[11] and his big manly voice,
Turning again toward childish treble, pipes
And whistles in his sound. Last scene of all,
That ends this strange eventful history,
Is second childishness, and mere oblivion,
Sans[12] teeth, sans eyes, sans taste, sans everything.

treble (treb′ əl) *n.* high-pitched voice

8. **wise saws and modern instances** wise sayings and modern examples that show the truth of the sayings.
9. **pantaloon** (pan′ təl o͞on′) *n.* thin, foolish old man—originally a character in old comedies.
10. **hose** (hōz) *n.* stockings.
11. **shank** (shank) *n.* leg.
12. **sans** (sanz) *prep.* without; lacking.

Review and Assess

Thinking About the Selection

1. **Respond:** Do you agree with the speaker's view of the seven stages of life? Explain.
2. **(a) Recall:** List the seven different people mentioned by the speaker. **(b) Interpret:** Which stage of life does each of these people represent?
3. **(a) Recall:** How does the speaker describe the soldier and the judge? **(b) Infer:** Are they characterized in a positive or negative way? Explain.
4. **(a) Recall:** According to the speaker, which items do the people in the final stage lack? **(b) Interpret:** How does the last age bring people back full circle to the start?
5. **(a) Draw Conclusions:** What attitude toward life does the speaker seem to be expressing? **(b) Compare and Contrast:** Do you think the speaker of "The Raven" would express the same attitude? Explain.
6. **Take a Position:** Which speaker better represents your opinion? Explain.
7. **Assess:** Does this poem in any way change your perspective about the stages of life? Why or why not?
8. **Extend:** If you could meet the speaker, which of his insights about life would you like to discuss?

William Shakespeare

(1564–1616)

Theatergoers of Shakespeare's time expected to see action, humor, and passion played out on the stage, and to hear impressive dramatic speeches like those in classical drama. Shakespeare was able to forge a perfect blend of high drama and exalted language that met his audience's twin expectations.

Altogether, Shakespeare wrote more than three dozen plays, most of which continue to be read and performed today. Because of the beauty of his language and the timelessness of his themes, speeches in his plays are quoted more often than those of any other writer. "The Seven Ages of Man" is considered one of his best speeches. (For more on William Shakespeare, see p. 766.)

ASSESSMENT PRACTICE: Vocabulary

Complete Analogies **(For more practice, see Test Preparation Workbook, p. 55.)**

Many tests require students to complete analogies. Use the following sample item for practice.

FURNACE : HEAT ::

A lamp : bulb
B stem : flower
C fire : smoke
D fan : cool

Remind students to use the strategy of creating a sentence to identify the relationship in the first pair of words in order to complete the analogy. In this test question, the sentence might be *A furnace makes heat.* Help students see that the relationship is product and function. Ask students to read each answer choice in the sentence to see which pair of words has the same relationship. Students should conclude that the correct answer is *C, Fire makes smoke.*

Review and Assess

Literary Analysis

Narrative and Dramatic Poetry

1. Summarize the story told in the **narrative poem** "The Raven."
2. How do the rhythm and rhyme scheme of "The Raven" enhance its story?
3. "The Seven Ages of Man" is from Shakespeare's play *As You Like It.* Do you think the **dramatic poem** is clear and complete by itself? Why or why not?

Comparing Literary Works

4. Briefly compare and contrast the two speakers' attitudes toward life and death, using a chart like the one shown.

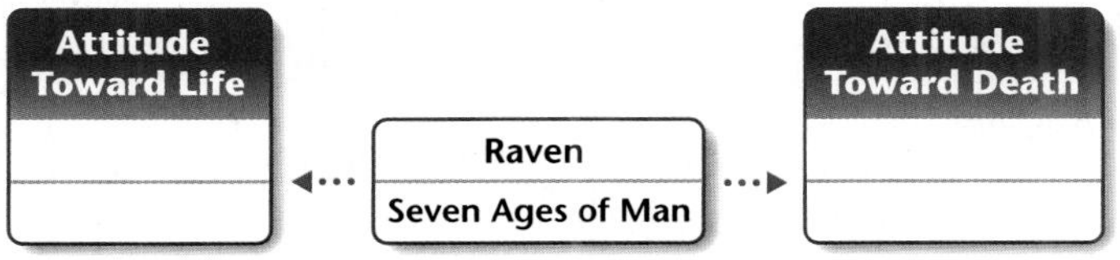

5. (a) How does the tone or attitude of Poe's narrative poem differ from that of Shakespeare's dramatic poem? (b) Which words or techniques used by the poets help to create the tone of each poem?
6. If the speakers of each poem were to meet, what advice would Shakespeare's speaker give Poe's speaker?

Reading Strategy

Drawing Inferences About the Speaker

7. In "The Raven," what can you infer about the speaker's level of education and social class from his style of speaking? Provide examples to support your answer.
8. What else can you infer about the speaker of "The Raven" from other details in the poem? Explain.
9. In lines 9–15 of "The Seven Ages of Man," what do the speaker's words reveal about his attitude toward lovers and soldiers?

Extend Understanding

10. **Cultural Connection:** Would you describe the final two stages of modern life differently from the way Jacques does? Explain.

Quick Review

Narrative poetry tells a story.

The lines of **dramatic poetry** are spoken by one or more characters to express their thoughts and feelings.

You can **draw inferences** (make educated guesses) about the speaker of a poem by noting the speaker's words, actions, and emotions.

Take It to the Net

www.phschool.com

Take the interactive self-test online to check your understanding of these selections.

ENRICHMENT: Further Reading

Other Works by William Shakespeare

"The Tragedy of Macbeth"
"The Tragedy of Julius Caesar"

Take It to the Net

Visit www.phschool.com for more information on William Shakespeare.

Answers for p. 947

Review and Assess

1. A man grieving the loss of his love, Lenore, is visited by a raven that responds to his increasingly desperate questions by repeating the same despairing answer, "Nevermore."
2. The rhythm and rhyme scheme of "The Raven" makes the poem sound a bit like a funeral dirge, echoing the cycle of sadness from stanza to stanza.
3. Students may agree that the poem is whole in meaning and complete in itself—even apart from knowledge of the speaker and context of the speech.
4. Possible responses: "The Raven": Attitude Toward Life: despairing; Attitude Toward Death: hopeless; "The Seven Ages of Man": Attitude Toward Life: cynical; Attitude Toward Death: detached acceptance.
5. **(a)** The tone in Poe's poem shifts from alarm to despair. The tone in Shakespeare's poem is consistantly sarcastic and scoffing. **(b)** In "The Raven," words such as *dreary, muttered, sad, tempest, sorrow, fiend, loneliness,* and *shadow* carry a despairing tone. The repetition of *nevermore* adds to the bleak finality. In "The Seven Ages of Man," the sarcastic word pictures reveal the speaker's cynical view.
6. Shakespeare's speaker would probably tell Poe's speaker to "lighten up," "get over it," and accept the inevitable phases of life.
7. References to books and the bust of Pallas suggest that the speaker is well-educated. The cushioned, velvet furnishing of the room and the speaker's level of diction suggest an upper-level social status.
8. The speaker is emotional, unhappy, imaginative, and highly suggestible.
9. He thinks that lovers are foolish and soldiers are foolhardy, thus devaluing love and courage.
10. Students may respond that modern medicine and better health care have prolonged and eased these last two stages.

EXTEND

Answers for p. 948

1 Vocabulary Development

1. lone; single
2. aloneness; privacy
3. remote; out of the way

Spelling Strategy

1. rustling
2. forgivable
3. donation

Concept Development: Analogies

1. desolate
2. treble
3. quaint
4. pallid
5. woeful
6. beguiling
7. respite

2 Grammar

1. The only word spoken was the word "Lenore!"
2. "Surely," said I, "something's at my window."
3. "That's the last word I'll hear from you!" I shrieked.
4. The lover declares, "She is lovely!"
5. "The soldier," he said, "is quick to exclaim, 'Let's fight!'"

Writing Application

1. "The schoolboy whined," she said.
2. "I remember," said the old man, "the night of the great storm."

Integrate Language Skills

1 Vocabulary Development Lesson

Word Analysis: Latin Root *-sol-*

The Latin root *-sol-* means "alone." This root contributes to the definition of *desolate*, meaning "deserted" or "abandoned." Use the meaning of *-sol-* to write a definition of each italicized word.

1. A *solitary* tree remains where a forest once stood.
2. Maria enjoyed the *solitude* of the morning.
3. The *isolated* cottage is surrounded by fields.

Spelling Strategy

When a word ends in silent *e*, drop the *e* when adding a suffix that begins with a vowel. For example, *beguile* + *-ing* = *beguiling*.

Add the suffix in italics to each item below, and write the new word in your notebook.

1. rustle (*-ing*) **2.** forgive (*-able*) **3.** donate (*-tion*)

Concept Development: Analogies

For each sentence below, write the word from the vocabulary list on page 939 that best completes each comparison. Then, explain your reasoning.

1. *Tired* is to *energetic* as ___?___ is to *crowded*.
2. *Baritone* is to *man* as ___?___ is to *child*.
3. *Amusing* is to *entertaining* as ___?___ is to *strange*.
4. *Faded* is to *fabric* as ___?___ is to *skin*.
5. *Tiny* is to *enormous* as ___?___ is to *joyful*.
6. *Teasing* is to *tormenting* as ___?___ is to *tricking*.
7. *Work* is to *exert* as ___?___ is to *relax*.

2 Grammar Lesson

Punctuation With Quotation Marks

In direct quotations, quotation marks enclose the exact words a person speaks. Interrupting expressions, such as *he said* or *she asked*, are set off with commas. A comma or period is placed inside the final quotation mark, but a question mark or exclamation mark is set inside the final quotation mark only if the end mark is part of the quotation.

Example:

"There is a visitor," he remarked, "knocking on my door." (interrupter set off with commas)

I yelled, "There's someone at my door!" (exclamation mark is part of quote)

Practice Copy the following sentences, adding the proper punctuation.

1. The only word spoken was the word *Lenore!*
2. Surely said I, something's at my window
3. That's the last word I'll hear from you! I shrieked.
4. The lover declares She is lovely!
5. The soldier, he said, is quick to exclaim Let's fight!

Writing Application Expand each sentence to include a direct quotation. Punctuate correctly.

1. The school boy whined.
2. I remember said the old man.

WG *Prentice Hall Writing and Grammar Connection: Chapter 29, Section 4*

TEACHING RESOURCES

The following resources can be used to enrich or extend the instruction for pp. 948–949.

Vocabulary

Vocabulary and Spelling Practice Book (Use this booklet for skills enrichment.)

Grammar

Selection Support, Build Grammar Skills, p. 218

Writing and Grammar, Gold Level, p. 684 ■

Daily Language Practice Transparencies ■

Writing

Writing and Grammar, Gold Level, p. 112 ■

Writing and Grammar iText CD-ROM ■

■ **BLOCK SCHEDULING:** Resources marked with this symbol provide varied instruction during 90-minute blocks.

❸ Writing Lesson

Scene for a Movie

Imagine that you have been hired by a film studio to create a movie based on "The Raven." Write a detailed description of the scene that a scriptwriter could use to develop a script. In your description, provide detailed instructions about the mood, setting, characters, and events of the scene.

Prewriting Start by thinking about how the poem could be expanded into a movie. Review the poem to jot down details about people, events, and setting that might appear in the opening scene.

Drafting Using the ideas you have gathered, draft your description. Start with a paragraph describing the mood you want to establish. Then, follow with paragraphs about the plot, characters, and setting.

Revising Look for places where you can add precise details to set a gloomy mood. Have one of your classmates assume the role of a scriptwriter to read your description and tell you if you have conveyed the feeling of the poem. Add further details if they are needed.

Model: Revising to Add Descriptive Details

lit by a single lamp that casts soft, eerie shadows on the wall,
In a darkened room ^ a man sits reading a heavy book.

Words such as *single lamp* and *eerie* help develop the scene.

WG *Prentice Hall Writing and Grammar Connection: Chapter 6, Section 4*

❹ Extension Activities

Listening and Speaking Stage a **debate** based on "The Seven Ages of Man."

- Form two teams of two to four speakers.
- One team should support the views expressed in "The Seven Ages of Man," while the second team should support a more optimistic view.
- Speakers for each group should present their side to the class, backing up points with examples from real life.

Afterward, have the class decide which side presented the stronger argument. **[Group Activity]**

Research and Technology Gather information for a **fact sheet** on ravens. Include details on what the birds look like, where they are found, what they eat, and other key facts. If possible, include information from Internet or encyclopedia sources that provide photos or film footage of ravens. Compare the details in your fact sheet to details about the raven found in Poe's poem.

Take It to the Net www.phschool.com

Go online for an additional research activity using the Internet.

Lesson Support for p. 949

❸ Writing Lesson

- Review the Prewriting Model, pointing out how words from the poem can lead to visual images, sounds, and other components of a movie scene.
- Have students go back through the poem, jotting down words that might prompt ideas for people, costumes, setting, sounds, and events. Next to these words (as shown in the model), have students write the ideas they come up with.
- Have each student complete the activity by incorporating the ideas into a vivid description of the opening scene.

❹ Listening and Speaking

- Point out that a debate is an organized discussion of two sides of an issue. Have students discuss debates, such as political debates, that they have witnesssed.
- In preparing for their debates, tell students to first clarify the point of view their team should support. Have students research the points they want to make by reviewing the poems and thinking of real-life examples that support their point of view.

CUSTOMIZE INSTRUCTION for Universal Access

To address different learning styles, use the following activities suggested in the **Extension Activities** booklet, p. 53.

- For Visual/Spatial Learners, use Activity 5.
- For Logical/Mathematical and Verbal/Linguistic Learners, use Activity 6.
- For Bodily/Kinesthetic and Interpersonal Learners, use Activity 7.

ASSESSMENT RESOURCES

The following resources can be used to assess students' knowledge and skills.

Selection Assessment

- **Formal Assessment,** Selection Test, pp. 195–197
- **Open Book Test,** pp. 163–165
- **Got It! Assessment Videotapes,** Tape 5
- **Test Bank Software**

Take It to the Net
Visit www.phschool.com for self-tests and additional questions on the selections.

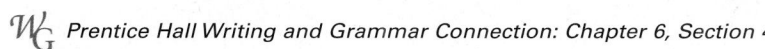

PRENTICE HALL ASSESSMENT SYSTEM

- **Workbook**
- **Skill Book**
- **Transparencies**
- **CD-ROM**

Lesson Objectives

1. To understand the connection between Shakespeare's poem "The Seven Ages of Man" and a seventy-eight-year-old man's thoughts on life and aging as told in the excerpt from *Tuesdays with Morrie*
2. To respond personally to the concept of aging

Connections

Shakespeare's poem "The Seven Ages of Man" offers a humorous if somewhat cynical view of life and its various stages. The speaker views life as a series of parts to be played in which a person gains nothing of real value. According to Shakespeare's speaker, at the end of life, one is merely returned to childhood, having lost everything. By contrast, *Tuesdays with Morrie* offers comforting insights from a man who is seventy-eight and facing death. He looks back fondly on a life well-lived, grateful for all he has experienced.

CONNECTIONS

Literature Past and Present

Perspectives on Aging

Perspectives on Aging

- Read aloud the boxed text on p. 951.
- If students haven't yet read "The Seven Ages of Man," have them read it now.
- Ask students how they feel about getting older. What do they think is an ideal age?
- Explain that, although it's almost impossible to imagine, these students will very likely be seventy-eight years old (Morrie's age) someday. Ask students to try to assume this perspective as they read the selection.

Although aging and dying are natural parts of the life cycle, we often try to put thoughts about such subjects out of our minds. Shakespeare's poem "The Seven Ages of Man" makes it clear why most people prefer not to think about their own mortality. The poem traces a gloomy pathway through life. Growing old gracefully does not seem to enter into the equation. With such a hopeless view of the end of the road, who would want to be reminded of aging and death?

Sometimes, certain events—a birthday we do not wish to acknowledge or the death of a friend or relative—make aging and dying harder to ignore. When Detroit sportswriter Mitch Albom read an interview that revealed a favorite college professor was dying, Albom made the difficult decision to visit his former teacher, Morrie. Teacher and student quickly rekindled their friendship, despite years of separation. In the remaining weeks of his life, Morrie again assumed the role of teacher. The subject was savoring life and old age, even in the face of death.

from *Tuesdays with Morrie*

Mitch Albom

Later that day, we talked about aging. Or maybe I should say the fear of aging—another of the issues on my what's-bugging-my-generation list. On my ride from the Boston airport, I had counted the billboards that featured young and beautiful people. There was a handsome young man in a cowboy hat, . . . two beautiful young women smiling over a shampoo bottle, a sultry-looking teenager . . . and a sexy woman in a black velvet dress, next to a man in a tuxedo. . . .

Not once did I see anyone who would pass for over thirty-five. I told Morrie I was already feeling over the hill, much as I tried desperately

ENRICHMENT: Literature

Morrie and Mitch

Mitch Albom, the author of *Tuesdays with Morrie,* was once a student in Professor Morrie Schwartz's sociology class at Brandeis University. When Albom learned that his former teacher was suffering from a terminal illness (known as amyotrophic lateral sclerosis, or Lou Gehrig's disease), he began paying his former professor weekly visits. Albom called these visits his "last class" and the resulting book his "term paper."

Thematic Connection

- Encourage students to read the entire selection, as well as Shakespeare's poem "The Seven Ages of Man" before they answer the question: How does Morrie's view of aging contrast with that of Jacques, the speaker of "The Seven Ages of Man"?
- Then, have students write two subheads next to each other on a sheet of paper: Jacques' View and Morrie's View.
- Tell students to list relevant information from each selection under the subheads, then use these lists to answer the question posed above.
  Possible answer: In Morrie's view of aging, one gains knowledge and wisdom as one grows older. In Jacques's view, one loses both physical and intellectual ability as one ages.

to stay on top of it. I worked out constantly. Watched what I ate. Checked my hairline in the mirror. I had gone from being proud to say my age—because of all I had done so young—to not bringing it up, for fear I was getting too close to forty and, therefore, professional oblivion.

oblivion (ə bliv´ ē ən) *n.* condition of being forgotten

Morrie had aging in better perspective.

"All this emphasis on youth—I don't buy it," he said. "Listen, I know what a misery being young can be, so don't tell me it's so great. All these kids who came to me with their struggles, their strife, their feelings of inadequacy, their sense that life was miserable. . . .

"And, in addition to all the miseries, the young are not wise. They have very little understanding about life. Who wants to live every day when you don't know what's going on? When people are manipulating you, telling you to buy this perfume and you'll be beautiful, or this pair of jeans and you'll be sexy—and you believe them! It's such nonsense."

Thematic Connection
How does Morrie's view of aging contrast with that of Jacques, the speaker of "The Seven Ages of Man"?

Weren't you *ever* afraid to grow old, I asked?

"Mitch, I *embrace* aging."

Embrace it?

"It's very simple. As you grow, you learn more. If you stayed at twenty-two, you'd always be as ignorant as you were at twenty-two. Aging is not just decay, you know. It's growth. It's more than the negative that you're going to die, it's also the positive that you *understand* you're going to die, and that you live a better life because of it."

Yes, I said, but if aging were so valuable, why do people always say, "Oh, if I were young again." You never hear people say, "I wish I were sixty-five."

He smiled. "You know what that reflects? Unsatisfied lives. Unfulfilled lives. Lives that haven't found meaning. Because if you've found meaning in your life, you don't want to go back. You want to go forward. You want to see more, do more. You can't wait until sixty-five.

"Listen. You should know something. All younger people should know something. If you're always battling against getting older, you're always going to be unhappy, because it will happen anyhow.

"And Mitch?"

He lowered his voice.

"The fact is, *you* are going to die eventually."

I nodded.

"It won't matter what you tell yourself."

I know.

"But hopefully," he said, "not for a long, long time."

He closed his eyes with a peaceful look, then asked me to adjust the pillows behind his head. His body needed constant adjustment to stay comfortable. It was propped up in the chair with white pillows, yellow foam, and blue towels. At a quick glance, it seemed as if Morrie were being packed for shipping.

"Thank you," he whispered as I moved the pillows.

No problem, I said.

"Mitch. What are you thinking?"

I paused before answering. Okay, I said, I'm wondering how you don't envy younger, healthy people.

"Oh, I guess I do." He closed his eyes. "I envy them being able to go to the health club, or go for a swim. Or dance. Mostly for dancing. But envy comes to me, I feel it, and then I let it go. Remember what I said about detachment? Let it go. Tell yourself, 'That's envy, I'm going to separate from it now.' And walk away."

He coughed—a long, scratchy cough—and he pushed a tissue to his mouth and spit weakly into it. Sitting there, I felt so much stronger than he, ridiculously so, as if I could lift him and toss him over my shoulder like a sack of flour. I was embarrassed by this superiority, because I did not feel superior to him in any other way.

How do you keep from envying . . .

"What?"

Me?

He smiled.

"Mitch, it is impossible for the old not to envy the young. But the issue is to accept who you are and revel in that. This is your time to be in your thirties. I had my time to be in my thirties, and now is my time to be seventy-eight.

"You have to find what's good and true and beautiful in your life as it is now. Looking back makes you competitive. And, age is not a competitive issue."

He exhaled and lowered his eyes, as if to watch his breath scatter into the air.

"The truth is, part of me is every age. I'm a three-year-old, I'm a five-year-old, I'm a thirty-seven-year-old, I'm a fifty-year-old. I've been through all of them, and I know what it's like. I delight in being a child when it's appropriate to be a child. I delight in being a wise old man when it's appropriate to be a wise old man. Think of all I can be! I am every age, up to my own. Do you understand?"

I nodded.

"How can I be envious of where you are—when I've been there myself?"

revel (rev′əl) *v.* take delight or pleasure

Mitch Albom

(b. 1958)

Building a career in newspaper journalism, nonfiction writing, and television commentary, Mitch Albom accomplished a great deal at an early age. He has been voted America's best sportswriter thirteen times by the Associated Press Sports Editors for his columns in the *Detroit Free Press*. He appears regularly on television and has his own radio show. Still, the impending death of his former professor made him take a step back to reevaluate his own life. *Tuesdays with Morrie* (1997) was the result of this soul-searching. More than 5 million copies of the book have been sold, securing its place on bestseller lists since its publication.

Connecting Literature Past and Present

1. How might you apply Morrie's advice on growing older to your own life?
2. How might the author's perspective have changed after hearing Morrie's views on aging and death?
3. Assess the different views on aging presented by "The Seven Ages of Man" and by Morrie. With which do you agree more?

Answers

Connecting Literature Past and Present

1. Students may apply Morrie's advice by appreciating their lives at each stage, and embracing the changes the future brings.
2. The author's perspective might have changed from a negative view on aging to a more positive view.
3. Students will probably assess Jacques's view as more cynical and negative, and Morrie's view as more positive and realistic. Students will likely agree with the speaker who reflects their own views most closely.

Three Haiku ✦ Hokku Poems ✦ On the Grasshopper and the Cricket ✦ Sonnet 30

Lesson Objectives and CA Correlations

1. **To analyze and respond to literary elements**
   - Literary Analysis: Haiku and Sonnets **R 3.5**
   - Comparing Literary Works
2. **To read, comprehend, analyze, and critique poems**
   - Reading Strategy: Reading in Sentences
   - Review and Assess questions
   - Assessment Practice (ATE)
3. **To develop word analysis skills, fluency, and systematic vocabulary**
   - Vocabulary Development Lesson: Anglo-Saxon Suffix: *-ness* **R 1.1**
4. **To understand and apply written and oral language conventions**
   - Spelling Strategy
   - Grammar Lesson: Hyphens **LC 1.1**
5. **To understand and apply appropriate writing and research strategies**
   - Writing Lesson: Haiku Series **W 1.2**
   - Extension Activity: Research Paper **W 1.6**
6. **To understand and apply listening and speaking strategies**
   - Extension Activity: Oral Presentation **LS 1.7**

STEP-BY-STEP TEACHING GUIDE	PACING GUIDE
PRETEACH	
Motivate Students and Provide Background	
Use the Motivation activity (ATE p. 954)	5 min.
Read and discuss the Preview material and Background information (SE/ATE p. 954) [A]	10 min.
Introduce the Concepts	
Introduce the Literary Analysis and Reading Strategy (SE/ATE p. 955) [A]	15 min.
Pronounce the vocabulary words and read their definitions (SE p. 955)	5 min.
TEACH	
Monitor Comprehension	
Informally monitor comprehension by circulating while students read independently or in groups [A]	10 min.
Develop vocabulary with Vocabulary notes (SE pp. 959–960)	as students read
Develop Understanding	
Develop students' understanding of haiku and sonnets with the Literary Analysis annotation (ATE p. 956) [A]	10 min.
Develop students' ability to read in sentences with the Reading Strategy annotation (ATE p. 958)	10 min.
ASSESS	
Assess Mastery	
Assess students' mastery of the Reading Strategy and Literary Analysis by having them answer the Review and Assess questions (SE/ATE p. 961)	20 min.
Use one or more of the print and media Assessment Resources (ATE p. 963) [A]	up to 50 min.
EXTEND	
Apply Understanding	
Have students complete the Vocabulary Development Lesson and the Grammar Lesson (SE p. 962) [A]	20 min.
Apply students' knowledge of listing and itemizing using the Writing Lesson (SE p. 963) [A]	45 min.
Apply students' understanding of the selection using one or more of the Extension Activities (SE p. 963)	20–90 min.

[A] **ACCELERATED INSTRUCTION:**
Use the strategies and activities identified with an [A].

UNIVERSAL ACCESS
● = Below-Level Students
▲ = On-Level Students
■ = Above-Level Students

Time and Resource Manager

Reading Level: Average/Average/Easy/Easy
Average Number of Instructional Days: 4

RESOURCES		
PRINT	**TRANSPARENCIES**	**TECHNOLOGY**
• **Beyond Literature,** Humanities Connection: Poetry Reading, p. 56 ▲ ■		• **Interest Grabber Video,** Tape 5 ● ▲ ■
• **Selection Support Workbook:** ● ▲ ■ Literary Analysis, p. 224 Reading Strategy, p. 223 Build Vocabulary, p. 221	• **Literary Analysis and Reading Transparencies,** pp. 111 and 112 ● ▲ ■	
• **Authors In Depth,** Gold Level ■		• **Listening to Literature** ● ▲ ■ Audiocassettes, Side 28 Audio CDs, CD 19
• **Literatura en español** ● ▲ • **Literary Analysis for Enrichment** ■		
• **Formal Assessment:** Selection Test, pp.198–200 ● ▲ ■ • **Open Book Test,** pp. 166–168 ● ▲ ■ • PRENTICE HALL ASSESSMENT SYSTEM ● ▲ ■	• PRENTICE HALL ASSESSMENT SYSTEM ● ▲ ■ Skills Practice Answers and Explanations on Transparencies	• **Test Bank Software** ● ▲ ■ • **Got It! Assessment Videotapes,** Tape 5 ● ▲
• **Selection Support Workbook:** ● ▲ ■ Build Grammar Skills, p. 222 • **Writing and Grammar,** Gold Level ● ▲ ■ • **Extension Activities,** p. 54 ● ▲ ■	• **Daily Language Practice Transparencies** ● ▲	• **Writing and Grammar iText CD-ROM** ● ▲ ■ *Take It to the Net* www.phschool.com

BLOCK SCHEDULING: Use one 90-minute class period to preteach the selection and have students read it. Use a second 90-minute class period to assess students' mastery of skills and have them complete one of the Extension Activities.

PRETEACH

Step-by-Step Teaching Guide for pp. 954–955

Motivation

Provide students with the following template, which represents the syllables of a haiku:

— — — — —

— — — — — — —

— — — — —

Explain that students will fill the blanks with syllables of words about a subject of their choice. (In other words, the first line can consist of multiple words, but the total syllables must not exceed five.) Create your own example and put it on the board. Point out that the completed set of words must make sense. After students finish writing, ask them to share what they've written. Tell them that the *haiku*—a form of Japanese poetry—follows this same form.

Interest Grabber Video

As an alternative, play "Timeless Shakespeare" on Tape 5 to engage student interest.

❶ Background

Science

Crickets differ from grasshoppers in a number of ways. They have prominent feelers located at the tips of their abdomens and their wings lie flat over each other on their backs. Crickets produce their "songs" using a specialized sound-producing organ located on their wings. Each wing has a "file" (a thickened vein) and a "scraper" (a hard, sharp-edged portion of the wing). The scraper of either wing can be rubbed against the file of the opposite wing to produce the sound.

Prepare to Read

Three Haiku ◆ Hokku Poems ◆ On the Grasshopper and the Cricket ◆ Sonnet 30

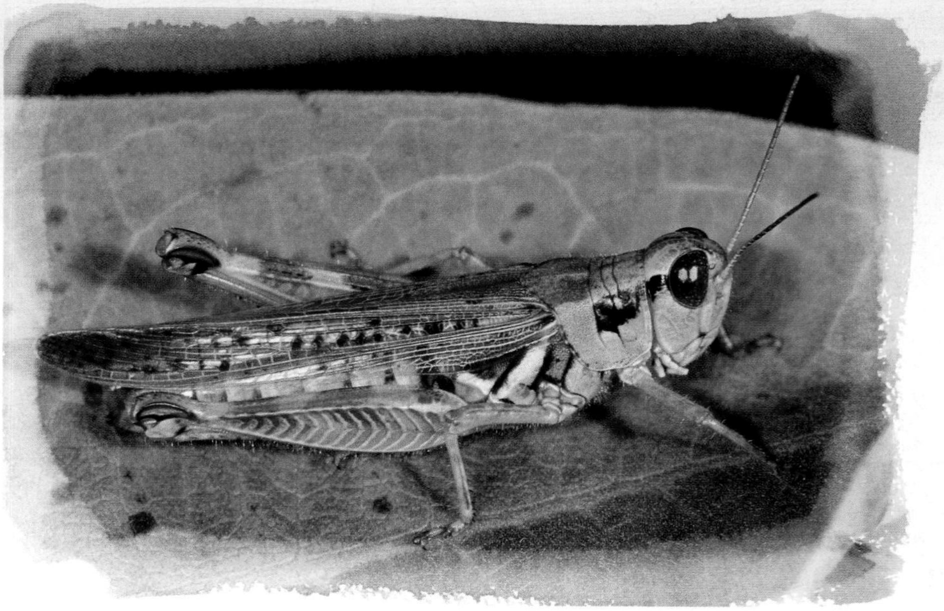

Take It to the Net

Visit www.phschool.com for interactive activities and instruction related to the selections, including

- background
- graphic organizers
- literary elements
- reading strategies

Preview

Connecting to the Literature

Almost everyone has regrets—memories of losses, disappointments, and mistakes—that can ruin the enjoyment of the present. In Sonnet 30, Shakespeare offers a way to put aside regrets about the past. The other poems in this section present a way to keep focused on the present through careful observation of nature.

❶ Background

It is not surprising that the poet Keats chose the cricket and the grasshopper when he wanted to write about the poetry of nature. These two "musical" insects produce sounds by rubbing one part of the body against another. Male crickets rub the rough surfaces of their wing covers together. Male grasshoppers usually rub a leg against a wing with a sawing motion.

TEACHING RESOURCES

The following resources can be used to enrich or extend the instruction for pp. 954–955.

Motivation

Interest Grabber Video, Tape 5 ▪

Background

Beyond Literature, p. 56

Take It to the Net

Visit www.phschool.com for background and hotlinks for the selections.

Literary Analysis

Literary Analysis and Reading Transparencies, Haiku and Sonnets, p. 112 ▪

Reading

Selection Support: Reading Strategy, p. 223; Build Vocabulary, p. 221

Literary Analysis and Reading Transparencies, Reading in Sentences, p. 111 ▪

▪ **BLOCK SCHEDULING:** Resources marked with this symbol provide varied instruction during 90-minute blocks.

❷ Literary Analysis

Haiku and Sonnets

The poems in this section represent two poetic forms with strict rules. The first seven poems in this section are **haiku,** a form of poetry developed in Japan that consists of three unrhymed lines of verse. The first and third lines have five syllables each. The second line has seven syllables. With very few words, haiku presents one or two striking images.

The other two poems are **sonnets**—lyric poems of fourteen lines, usually written in rhymed iambic pentameter (ten-syllable lines in which every second syllable is accented). Symbols for stressed syllables (´) and unstressed syllables (˘) show the meter in the first line of Keats's poem:

The pŏétry ŏf eárth ĭs névĕr deád . . .

Comparing Literary Works

These poems present contrasting observations of the natural world. As you read, compare the natural images in each poem. Decide which element of nature each poet addresses. Consider these typical points of emphasis:

- Nature's beauty
- Nature's power
- The freedom nature embodies

Record your analysis in a diagram like the one shown. Then, consider the way each poet's thoughts of nature reflect his or her thoughts about how people live.

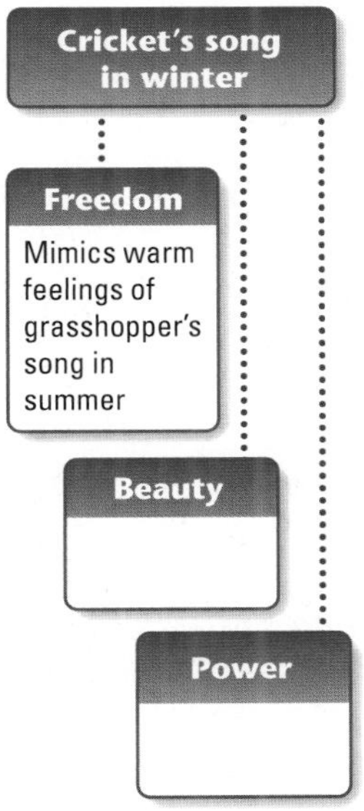

❸ Reading Strategy

Reading in Sentences

In a poem, a sentence may extend for several lines and end in the middle of a line so that the poet can keep to a rhythm and rhyme scheme. To understand the literal meaning of a poem, **read in sentences**, letting the punctuation tell you when to pause or when to come to a complete stop. Notice that the comma in this haiku indicates the poem's single internal pause:

Dragonfly catcher,
How far have you gone today
In your wandering?

Vocabulary Development

ceasing (sēs´ iŋ) *v.* stopping (p. 959)

wrought (rôt) *v.* formed; fashioned (p. 959)

drowsiness (drou´ zē nes) *n.* sleepiness (p. 959)

woes (wōz) *n.* great sorrows (p. 960)

❷ Literary Analysis

Haiku and Sonnets

- Tell students that they will be reading examples of poetry known as *haiku* and *sonnets.*
- Explain to students that haiku create fleeting but striking images with astonishingly few words. Call students' attention to the haiku at the bottom of this page. Demonstrate how the haiku conforms to the 5–7–5 syllable form.
- Explain to students that a sonnet also follows strict rules—fourteen lines of rhymed iambic pentameter. Students should be familiar with iambic pentameter from the previous unit.
- Display the Literary Analysis Transparency in **Literary Analysis and Reading Strategy Transparencies,** p. 112, to review the main elements of each type of poem.

❸ Reading Strategy

Reading in Sentences

- Point out that in poetry sentences don't necessarily begin and end at line breaks. Sentences may extend for several lines, then end in the middle of one.
- Explain that when students read poetry, they should follow punctuation clues (commas, semicolons, periods) to know where to pause in the reading—as opposed to pausing at the end of every line.
- Read aloud the haiku on this page to model for students how to read a poem in sentences.

Vocabulary Development

- Pronounce each vocabulary word for students, and read the definitions as a class. Have students identify any words with which they are already familiar.

CUSTOMIZE INSTRUCTION FOR UNIVERSAL ACCESS

For Less Proficient Readers	For English Learners	For Advanced Readers
Have students begin this selection by fully exploring the haiku poems, which offer more chance of success and enjoyment than the more complicated sonnet. After students have gained understanding of haiku, they can move on to sonnets with more confidence.	As students read through the haiku poems, ask them to write down words that are not familiar to them. Have students work together to write definitions for the words. In addition, have students write next to each definition a word or words from their native languages that mean the same thing.	Explain that each student will read one haiku poem aloud to the entire class. Provide practice time during class. Have students critique each other's readings before they give the classroom presentations.

E-Teach

Visit E-Teach at www.phschool.com for teachers' essays on how to teach, with questions and answers.

TEACH

Step-by-Step Teaching Guide for pp. 956–960

CUSTOMIZE INSTRUCTION For Intrapersonal and Verbal/Linguistic Learners

Ask these students to think of aspects of nature that bring them feelings of joy, surprise, or wonder. Have each student write a haiku about one of these nature topics. Invite students to either read their poems aloud or post them on a bulletin board.

❶ About the Selections

Although the haiku by Bashō, Chiyojo, and Richard Wright differ in subject matter, they share one quality—each one creates a dominant impression in the reader's mind with one or two striking images from nature.

❷ Literary Analysis

Haiku

- Explain to students that the word *hokku* is not precisely equivalent to *haiku*. The first refers to the "opening stanza" in a series of related verse; while the second translates as "amusing sentence." The terms are, nevertheless, often used interchangeably.
- Ask students if Wright's poems are genuine haiku.
  Answer: They are, although the first one has only four syllables in the third line.

❶ Three Haiku

Temple bells die out.
The fragrant blossoms remain.
A perfect evening!

—Bashō

Dragonfly catcher,
How far have you gone today
In your wandering?

—Chiyojo

Bearing no flowers,
I am free to toss madly
Like the willow tree.

—Chiyojo

Haiku Poets

Bashō (1644–1694)

Bashō [bash´ ō] is regarded as one of the greatest Japanese poets. In his youth, he lived in luxury as the companion to the son of a lord. Later, however, he lived apart and devoted himself to writing haiku.

Chiyojo (1887–1959)

Chiyojo [chē yō jō] was the wife of a samurai's servant. When her husband died, she became a nun and began studying poetry with a well-known teacher of haiku. Scholars celebrate the lightness of spirit in her poems.

TEACHING RESOURCES

The following resources can be used to enrich or extend the instruction for pp. 956–960.

Literary Analysis

Selection Support: Literary Analysis, p. 224

Reading

Listening to Literature Audiocassettes, Side 28

Listening to Literature Audio CDs, CD 19

BLOCK SCHEDULING: Resources marked with this symbol provide varied instruction during 90-minute blocks.

❶ Hokku Poems

Richard Wright

Make up your mind snail!
You are half inside your house
And halfway out!

In the falling snow
A laughing boy holds out his palms
Until they are white

❷

Keep straight down this block
Then turn right where you will find
A peach tree blooming

Whose town did you leave
O wild and drowning spring rain
And where do you go?

Review and Assess

Thinking About the Selections

1. **Respond:** Which of the seven haiku do you like best? Why?
2. **(a) Recall:** To which senses does Bashō's haiku appeal? **(b) Analyze Cause and Effect:** In what ways do the two things that are sensed help to make the evening perfect?
3. **(a) Recall:** In what two ways does Chiyojo say she is like a willow tree? **(b) Interpret:** What impression is she trying to convey by the comparison?
4. **(a) Recall:** Which two weather events does Richard Wright describe in his haiku? **(b) Interpret:** What different feelings does he convey about these two weather events? **(c) Analyze:** Which words in each poem help to convey the feelings?
5. **(a) Distinguish:** Which of the haiku convey humor, and which seem serious? **(b) Make a Judgment:** Do you think that the haiku form works better with a more solemn or a more humorous content? Explain.

Richard Wright

(1908–1960)

Richard Wright is best known for his acclaimed novel *Native Son* (1940), which chronicles the life of an African American boy raised in poverty in Chicago. However, Wright also produced a wide range of other types of works, including essays and poems. As a poet, Wright experimented with different forms, including the traditional Japanese haiku.

Answers for p. 957

Review and Assess

1. Encourage students to share the experiences, places, and emotions that their favorite haiku brings to mind.
2. **(a)** Bashō's haiku appeals to the senses of hearing (bells) and smell (fragrant blossoms). **(b)** As the bells die out and the blossoms' fragrance fills the air, the evening gains a sense of tranquility and quiet joy.
3. **(a)** Chiyojo "bears no flowers" and can "toss madly in the wind." **(b)** The poet may want to give the impression that she has no responsibilities or burdens that she must treat carefully. She also expresses her freedom to follow her impulses, no matter how wild they are.
4. **(a)** He refers to "falling snow" and "drowning spring rain." **(b)** He expresses feelings of joy about the snow and feelings of surprise and awe about the spring rain. **(c)** "A laughing boy" conveys joy, and "wild and drowning" conveys awe and surprise.
5. **(a)** All the haiku except "Whose town did you leave" have an element of humor or joy. **(b)** Possible response: The form works equally well with humorous and solemn content. The humorous content brings a smile, and the solemn content provides a chance to pause and reflect.

❸ About the Selection

"On the Grasshopper and the Cricket" is an expression of delight in the world of nature. Keats writes of how the cricket's song from the hearth in winter brings to mind the song of the grasshopper, and with it, summer.

❹ Reading Strategy

Reading in Sentences

- Have students read lines 5–8 to themselves. Ask students to identify all the punctuation in these lines and explain whether they would come to a full stop or simply pause.
- Then, ask students to identify how many complete sentences are contained within these 4 lines of the poem.
  Answer: There are three complete sentences.

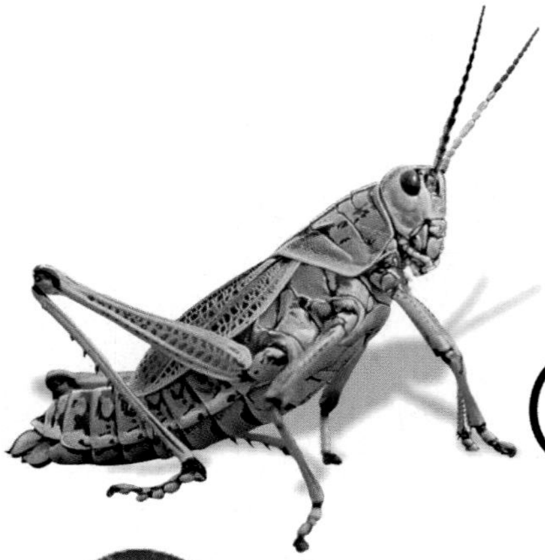

On the ❸ Grasshopper and the Cricket

John Keats

ENRICHMENT: Career Connection

Entomology

Explain that entomology is the scientific study of insects. Point out that, as environmental scientists, entomologists may conduct research on insects for any number of purposes or types of employers. For example, researchers might travel great distances to study insects in a rain forest, cataloging numbers of species. Or they might collect specimens of local species, and draw conclusions, based on their findings, about the health of a nearby ecosystem. They might conduct research in the hope of discovering an insect species that provides a cure for a human disease. They might focus on finding insects that can help control other insects in agriculture, as an alternative to pesticides. Or an entomologist might work as a teacher or as a natural history consultant. Point out that the career options of entomologists are varied and numerous.

Have interested students use the Internet, encyclopedias, and other resources to find out more about the work of entomologists.

The poetry of earth is never dead:
When all the birds are faint with the hot sun,
And hide in cooling trees, a voice will run
From hedge to hedge about the new-mown mead;[1]
That is the Grasshopper's—he takes the lead
4 In summer luxury,—he has never done
With his delights; for when tired out with fun
He rests at ease beneath some pleasant weed.
The poetry of earth is ceasing never:
On a lone winter evening, when the frost
Has wrought a silence, from the stove there shrills
The Cricket's song, in warmth increasing ever,
And seems to one in drowsiness half lost,
The Grasshopper's among some grassy hills.

ceasing (sēs′ iŋ) *v.* stopping

wrought (rôt) *v.* formed; fashioned

drowsiness (drou′ zē nes) *n.* sleepiness

1. **mead** (mēd) *n.* meadow.

Review and Assess

Thinking About the Selection

1. **Respond:** Which scene painted by the poet appeals more to you? Why?
2. **(a) Compare and Contrast:** In what ways are the two insects alike and different? **(b) Associate:** How are the two insects connected in the speaker's mind?
3. **(a) Interpret:** What does the speaker mean by saying "The poetry of earth is never dead"? **(b) Analyze:** In which other line of the poem do you find this line closely echoed? **(c) Interpret:** Do you think there is a difference in meaning between these related lines? Explain.
4. **Generalize:** What one word would you use to describe this poem? Explain your choices.
5. **Make a Judgment:** Does the sonnet form help or hinder Keats in getting across his meaning? Explain.
6. **Apply:** In your environment, what "poetry of nature" do you experience at different times of the year? Explain, citing examples from at least two seasons.

John Keats

(1795–1821)

The poems of John Keats are among the most admired in the English language. Remarkably, Keats accomplished this distinction in spite of his premature death at the age of twenty-five.

Keats is considered one of the main poets of the Romantic Movement, a group of writers who stressed the importance of individual experience and the spiritual connection between people and nature.

Answers for p. 959

Review and Assess

1. Accept all answers supported by logical reasons.
2. **(a)** Both the grasshopper and the cricket make music, but the grasshopper's song is noticed in summer, while the cricket's song is noticed in winter. **(b)** They both produce the poetry, or music, of nature.
3. **(a)** Nature is always alive with the music of its creatures and the poetry of its landscape. **(b)** "The poetry of earth is ceasing never." **(c)** The related lines carry the same meaning, but each introduces a different season that serves to illustrate the meaning.
4. Possible responses: Students may cite *continuity, endurance, never-ending* or *delight*.
5. Possible answer: The sonnet helps Keats get across his meaning by letting him use long, musical sentences that mimic the ongoing voice of the earth's poetry.
6. Students should suggest seasonal elements of nature and their respective poetic attributes.

ASSESS

5 About the Selection

In Sonnet 30, Shakespeare describes the world of memories and the world of friendship. He writes of regret and sorrow and the way in which the thought of a friend eases both.

6 Critical Thinking

Evaluate

- Ask students to read the entire sonnet. Ask them what the last two lines in this poem are called.
  Answer: They are called a rhymed couplet.
- Then, ask students how the meaning of this rhymed couplet differs from the first twelve lines.
  Answer: In the first twelve lines, the speaker laments all the losses and sorrows in his past; in the last two lines, the speaker celebrates friendship.

Answers for p. 960

Review and Assess

1. Students should support their answers with their ideas about friendship.
2. **(a)** He refers to his memories as "old woes." **(b)** The speaker feels sad about things that have happened in the past, such as failed love and friends who have died.
3. **(a)** It means "to cry." **(b)** Thinking of sad times in the past causes the speaker to cry.
4. The speaker is reviewing the "costs" of past woes.
5. Without the last two lines, the poem would convey a sense of hopelessness. The entire poem pivots on the word "But" in line 13.
6. Students should share their opinions on the ability of friendship to compensate for sorrows and losses.

5 Sonnet 30

William Shakespeare

When to the sessions of sweet silent thought
I summon up remembrance of things past,
I sigh the lack of many a thing I sought,
And with old woes' new wail my dear times waste:[1]
Then can I drown an eye, unused to flow,
For precious friends hid in death's dateless[2] night,
And weep afresh love's long since cancelled woe,
And moan the expense[3] of many a vanished sight:
Then can I grieve at grievances foregone,[4]
And heavily from woe to woe tell o'er[5]
The sad account of fore-bemoanèd moan,[6]
Which I new pay as if not paid before.
6 But if the while I think on thee, dear friend,
All losses are restored and sorrows end.

woes (wōz) *n.* great sorrows

1. **And . . . waste** and by grieving anew for past sorrows, ruin the precious present.
2. **dateless** endless.
3. **expense** loss.
4. **foregone** past and done with.
5. **tell o'er** count up.
6. **fore-bemoanèd moan** sorrows suffered in the past.

William Shakespeare

(1564–1616)

William Shakespeare was as much a poet as a playwright. He not only wrote his 37 plays in verse, but also composed 154 sonnets. Taken together, the sonnets seem to tell a story. The "plot" is not always clear, but it seems obvious that the main characters are a young nobleman, a lady, a poet (probably Shakespeare himself), and a rival poet. Some of the best sonnets, like Sonnet 30, are addressed to the nobleman. (For more on William Shakespeare, see p. 766.)

Review and Assess

Thinking About the Selection

1. **Respond:** Would you want the speaker of the poem as a friend? Explain?
2. **(a) Recall:** In the opening lines of Sonnet 30, how does the speaker refer to his memories? **(b) Infer:** In general, how does the speaker feel when he remembers the past? Explain.
3. **(a) Infer:** In line 5, what does "drown an eye" mean? **(b) Analyze Cause and Effect:** Which thoughts cause the speaker to "drown an eye"? Why?
4. **Clarify:** What is the speaker describing in lines 10–12?
5. **Hypothesize:** How would the effect of this poem be different without the final two lines?
6. **Evaluate:** Do you agree with the assessment of the value of friendship? Why or why not?

ASSESSMENT PRACTICE: Vocabulary

Complete Analogies (For more practice, see Test Preparation Workbook, p. 56.)

The verbal sections of some tests require students to complete analogies. Use the following sample test items to give students practice in completing word analogies.

LETHARGIC : ENERGETIC ::

A sleepy : drowsy
B lazy : inactive
C active : ambitious
D boring : interesting

Guide students to understand that the correct answer is *D*, because *boring* and *interesting*, like the first pair of words, are antonyms.

TARANTULA : ARACHNID ::

A water : ocean
B ocean : sea
C bicycle : motorcycle
D birch : tree

The relationship between the first pair of words is one of example to group (or species to genus); therefore, the correct answer is *D*.

Review and Assess

Literary Analysis

Haiku and Sonnets

1. (a) What are the two main images in Wright's second **haiku**? (b) What is the connection between these images?
2. A Shakespearean **sonnet** usually presents an idea or question in the first quatrain (four lines), explores the idea in the next two quatrains, and reaches a conclusion in the couplet (two lines) at the end. Use a chart like this to analyze the content of Sonnet 30.

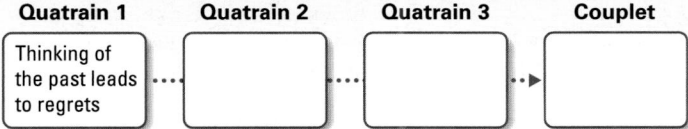

Quatrain 1	Quatrain 2	Quatrain 3	Couplet
Thinking of the past leads to regrets			

3. Keats's **sonnet** is Petrarchan, a form consisting of an octave (eight lines) and a sestet (six lines). In his poem, how is the content of the octave and the sestet related?

Comparing Literary Works

4. (a) Which of these poets use images from the natural world to explain something about human nature? (b) Which of these poets seem to focus primarily on the natural world rather than on people?
5. Do you think the haiku writers would agree with Keats that "the poetry of earth is never dead"? Explain your answer.

Reading Strategy

Reading in Sentences

6. In Sonnet 30, why do lines 1 and 10 lack punctuation marks?
7. In "On the Grasshopper and the Cricket," why do lines 1 and 9 end in colons rather than in periods?
8. How do the haiku writers use or omit punctuation to convey a dominant impression in their poems?

Extend Understanding

9. **Science Connection:** In what ways can scientists develop a different understanding of nature by reading poems that focus on natural images?

Quick Review

A **haiku** is a poem in three unrhymed lines (of five, seven, and five syllables each) that conveys a single, dominant impression by means of images from nature.

A **sonnet** is a lyric poem of fourteen lines, usually written in rhymed iambic pentameter.

To understand the literal meaning of a poem, **read in sentences** rather than lines, using punctuation to determine when to pause or stop.

Take It to the Net

www.phschool.com

Take the interactive self-test online to check your understanding of these selections.

Review and Assess

1. **(a)** The two main images are snow and a little boy. **(b)** Snow is falling; a little boy delights in the snow.
2. In quatrain 2, the regrets lead to weeping; in quatrain 3, the weeping leads to mourning; in the couplet, thinking about a friend sets all the regrets and sorrows aright.
3. The octave describes the role of the grasshopper in the "poetry of earth"; the sestet describes the role of the cricket.
4. **(a)** Chiyojo and Keats use images from the natural world to explain something about human nature. **(b)** Bashō and Wright seem to focus primarily on the natural world.
5. The haiku writers would agree because they see "the poetry of earth" in everything they notice in the natural world.
6. They are sentences that continue into the next lines for completion.
7. Lines 1 and 9 point to direct examples of the thoughts expressed in them.
8. The poets' use of punctuation helps convey their feelings. For example, an exclamation mark can indicate joy; a question mark can indicate curiosity; no punctuation can convey a fleeting thought or tentative reflection.
9. Reading a poem that focuses on a natural image can help scientists appreciate aspects of nature that go beyond functionality, such as beauty, awe, and humor.

ENRICHMENT: Further Reading

Other Works by the Authors

Works by Bashō
"Seven Poems"

Works by Keats
"Ode on a Grecian Urn"
"To Autumn"
"Ode to a Nightingale"

Works by Shakespeare
Sonnets 1–154
As You Like It

Take It to the Net

Visit www.phschool.com for more information on the authors.

EXTEND

Answers for p. 962

❶ Vocabulary Development

Word Analysis: Anglo-Saxon Suffix *-ness*

1. happiness
2. friendliness
3. thoughtfulness
4. shrillness
5. weariness

Concept Development: Antonyms

1. c
2. c
3. b
4. c

Spelling Strategy

1. grassier
   Possible answer: The damp hillside was grassier than the dry valley.
2. heavily
   Possible answer: The snow weighed heavily on the tree branches.
3. married
   Possible answer: The bride and groom got married today.

❷ Grammar

1. never-ending
2. pleasure-seeking
3. weed-ridden
4. [no hyphen required]
5. ever-increasing

Writing Application

Sample responses:

1. I'm so glad to find my long-lost friend.
2. Her tear-stained letter is evidence of her grief.

Integrate Language Skills

❶ Vocabulary Development Lesson

Word Analysis: Anglo-Saxon Suffix *-ness*

In his sonnet "On the Grasshopper and the Cricket," Keats describes a person half lost in drowsiness. *Drowsiness* ends in the Anglo-Saxon suffix *-ness*, meaning "in the state or condition of." When added to the adjective *drowsy*, the suffix *-ness* forms the noun *drowsiness*, meaning "in the state of being drowsy or sleepy."

For each definition below, add *-ness* to the adjective in italics to create a noun.

1. state of being *happy*
2. state of acting *friendly*
3. state of being *thoughtful*
4. state of being *shrill* in tone
5. state of being *weary*

Concept Development: Antonyms

In your notebook, write the lettered word that is most nearly opposite to the first word.

1. wrought: (a) created, (b) seen, (c) destroyed
2. ceasing: (a) escaping, (b) rewarding, (c) beginning
3. drowsiness: (a) frankness, (b) alertness, (c) quietness
4. woe: (a) terror, (b) ease, (c) joy

Spelling Strategy

When adding a suffix to a word ending in *y* preceded by a consonant, change the *y* to *i* and then add the suffix: *drowsy* + *-ness* = *drowsiness*

Add the suffix in italics to each word below, and then use the new word in a sentence.

1. grassy + *-er* **2.** heavy + *-ly* **3.** marry + *-ed*

❷ Grammar Lesson

Hyphens

A **hyphen** (-) is often used to connect two or more modifiers that are used together. You should use a hyphen to connect a compound modifier that comes *before* a noun. If the compound modifier comes *after* the noun, however, the hyphen is dropped.

In these examples, the compound modifier is in italics and the noun is underlined.

> **Before noun:** The grasshopper jumped from hedge to hedge in the *new-mown* <u>meadow</u>.
>
> **After noun:** The grasshopper's <u>song</u> was *well rehearsed.*

Practice Copy the following sentences in your notebook. Insert hyphens where they are needed.

1. We revel in the never ending poetry of earth.
2. The pleasure seeking grasshopper rests under a plant.
3. The weed ridden meadow is full of insects.
4. The hills are frost covered and silent.
5. The cricket's song has an ever increasing tempo.

Writing Application Write sentences that contain these hyphenated compound modifiers.

1. long-lost
2. tear-stained

Prentice Hall Writing and Grammar Connection: Chapter 29, Section 5

TEACHING RESOURCES

The following resources can be used to enrich or extend the instruction for pp. 962–963.

Vocabulary

Vocabulary and Spelling Practice Book (Use this booklet for skills enrichment.)

Grammar

Selection Support: Build Grammar Skills, p. 222

Writing and Grammar, Gold Level, p. 698 ■

Daily Language Practice Transparencies

Writing

Writing and Grammar, Gold Level, p. 106 ■

Writing and Grammar iText CD-ROM ■

■ **BLOCK SCHEDULING:** Resources marked with this symbol provide varied instruction during 90-minute blocks.

❸ Writing Lesson

Haiku Series

Write three related haiku, either about the same subject or on the same theme. Remember that a haiku captures a feeling with one or two concrete images and follows a strict format: three unrhymed lines of five, seven, and five syllables each.

Prewriting List several possible topics for the three haiku. Then, jot down several concrete images that each topic suggests.

Model: Listing and Itemizing Haiku Images

Topics	Images
Birds	Flying freely
Basketball	Singing brightly
Autumn	Fleeing winter

The images for the chosen topic are concise, yet descriptive.

Drafting As you draft, do not worry about getting exactly the right number of syllables—you can perfect the form as you revise.

Revising Count the syllables in each line. If you do not have the correct number, decide which words you can change, leave out, or add to achieve the desired number of syllables. In addition, make sure that each of your haiku conveys the impression you intended.

WG Prentice Hall Writing and Grammar Connection: Chapter 6, Section 2

❹ Extension Activities

Listening and Speaking Images from the natural world are fundamental to most haiku, particularly those created by Japanese poets. Prepare a brief **oral presentation** connecting the Japanese landscape and haiku.

- Research the geography and art of Japan.
- Print out or copy several pieces of Japanese art to accompany your presentation.

After your presentation, explain how the Japanese haiku you have read relate to the country's landscape and art.

Research and Technology Shakespeare penned 154 sonnets. Write a **research paper** about the information that is known about his sonnets. Explain the stories they tell, as well as their characters. In addition to Sonnet 30, read at least three more of his sonnets. In your report, incorporate quotations from the sonnets to support your ideas.

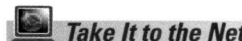

Take It to the Net www.phschool.com

Go online for an additional research activity using the Internet.

Lesson Support for p. 963

❸ Writing Lesson

- Lead students in brainstorming for topic ideas for their haiku poems. Write the topics on the board.
- Have students select a topic, then jot down several concrete images, as shown in the model. Have students repeat this process for each of the three haikus they will write.
- Invite students to share their haikus by either reading them aloud or posting them on a bulletin board.

❹ Research and Technology

- Have students use the Internet as well as print resources to collect information about Shakespeare's sonnets. Also point out the reference *Sonnets* listed in the Enrichment box on p. 961, as well as the four sonnets in **Authors In Depth,** Gold Level.
- Encourage students to form their own ideas about Shakespeare's sonnets, choosing quotations that support both experts' ideas and the student's ideas about the poet's work.
- Let students choose how to present their information—either in a written or oral report.

CUSTOMIZE INSTRUCTION for Universal Access

To address different learning styles, use the following activities suggested in the **Extension Activities** booklet, p. 54.

- For Visual/Spatial Learners, use Activity 5.
- For Logical/Mathematical Learners, use Activity 6.
- For Intrapersonal and Verbal/Linguistic Learners, use Activity 7.
- For Visual/ Spatial and Verbal/Linguistic Learners, use Activity 8.
- For Intrapersonal and Verbal/Linguistic Learners, use Activity 9.

ASSESSMENT RESOURCES

The following resources can be used to assess students' knowledge and skills.

Selection Assessment

- **Formal Assessment,** Selection Test, pp. 198–200
- **Open Book Test,** pp. 166–168
- **Got It! Assessment Videotapes,** Tape 5
- **Test Bank Software**

Take It to the Net

Visit www.phschool.com for self-tests and additional questions on the selections.

PRENTICE HALL ASSESSMENT SYSTEM

- **Workbook**
- **Skill Book**
- **Transparencies**
- **CD-ROM**

Lesson Objectives

1. To learn to interpret the information contained in professional journals
2. To identify a target audience's purpose for reading professional journals

About Professional Journals

- If possible, gather some examples of professional journals for students to look at in the classroom.
- Have students read "About Professional Journals" on p. 964.
- Ask students to look through some professional journals and describe the topics and types of articles they see.

Reading Strategy

Identifying a Target Audience's Purpose

- Have students read "Identifying a Target Audience's Purpose" on p. 964.
- Ask students to point out some differences between themselves as a target audience and the target audience for a professional journal.
  Possible answers: Students may note differences in age, education, and life experiences.
- Explain that a writer's job is to meet the needs of the intended audience, not every reader who might discover a piece of writing.

READING INFORMATIONAL MATERIALS

Professional Journals

About Professional Journals

A professional journal is a magazine or newspaper published for people who work in a specific field or industry, such as computer technology, agriculture, or finance. The articles in a professional journal inform readers about new products, techniques, and trends. "Passing Time in Times Past," excerpted here, is from *Book Links*, a professional journal for teachers and librarians.

Professional journals often present a complex, in-depth view of a subject that can be understood only by specialists in that field. For instance, different medical journals might present research on cell biology or cardiology or pediatric medicine. The editors of each journal assume that readers already possess basic knowledge of their subject, so the article can focus on presenting specific research results and analysis.

Reading Strategy

Identifying a Target Audience's Purpose

When authors write a magazine article, they do so with a specific purpose in mind, such as to entertain, to inform, or to persuade. Likewise, when you read a magazine article, you also have a specific purpose in mind. You may be reading purely for amusement, to learn about a subject, or to help you make a decision.

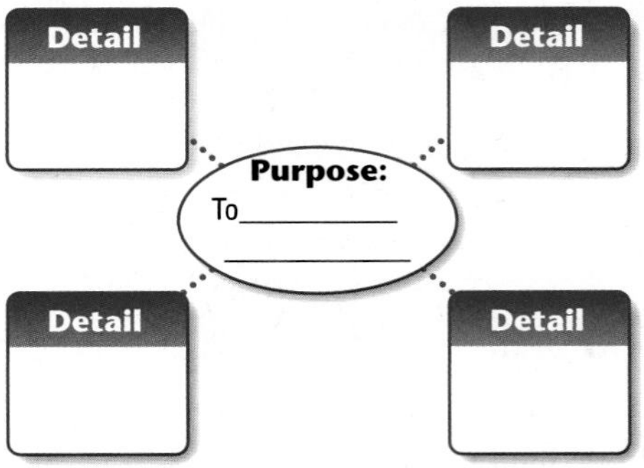

Readers of a professional journal like *Book Links* also have specific purposes for reading. They may read to achieve goals such as the following:

- To recommend new books to students
- To order books for the library
- To keep up with the latest trends and issues

As you read this excerpt from "Passing Time in Times Past," put yourself in the place of a teacher or librarian. Identify your purpose for reading, and then write down details you find that help you achieve that purpose.

Passing Time in Times Past

Virginia A. Walter

Both pundits and parents like to complain about the lack of historical knowledge displayed by today's young people. Test scores and anecdotes alike document the failure of teenagers to recognize the names of historical figures such as Lenin (frequently mistaken for a dead rock star) or Joan of Arc (sometimes confused with a biblical character who was swallowed by a whale).

This article starts with humorous examples that capture readers' interest in the topic.

On the other hand, we observe the popularity of the historical series Dear America . . . and note how enthusiastically middle-school girls read the historical novels of Karen Cushman. Certainly, some children have found reading and learning about past times to be a favorite pastime, not just a dull chunk of the social studies curriculum; and there are many skilled, creative teachers who know how to make history come alive for children whose preoccupation with the present and fascination with the future sometimes seem to leave little time for the past.

This article provides readers with an annotated list of resources.

CD-ROMs and the Internet have proven to be excellent vehicles for putting some of the raw materials of history, the primary sources used by scholars to re-create the past, in the hands of young historians. The interactive nature of CD-ROMs has also made them natural vehicles for edutainment ventures, creating game-like environments and simulations in which children can explore historical themes and events and learn while they play. The best of these CD-ROMs can support classroom learning, provide information for school reports, or provide independent, informal learning opportunities at home and in the library.

Here are some CD-ROMs and a few tantalizing books, grouped under broad topics that lend themselves to further exploration, to help more children find the delights of traveling into the past.

Castles

CD-ROMs

Castle Explorer. 1996. $29.95.

Ages 9–12. Children act as spies to the king, playing the role of maid or page boy, learning a great deal about daily life in a medieval castle while they search for answers to four questions and pieces of a map. Six books in a chained library and pop-up text provide explanatory text in this cleverly designed history game, based on Steven Biesty's book *Castle.*

Books

Macaulay, David. *Castle.* 1977. 74p. $16 (0-395-25784-0); paper, $7.95 (0-395-32920-5).

Ages 9–12. This Caldecott Honor Book for 1978 tells the story of the construction of a thirteenth-century castle with a refreshing combination of humor and authority.

Each entry includes the author, title, and price of a recommended item, as well as a brief description.

Winthrop, Elizabeth. *The Castle in the Attic.* 1985. 179p. $15.95 (0-8234-0579-6); paper, $4.99 (0-440-40941-1)

Ages 9–12. The adventures begin when William shrinks to fit into the realistic toy castle in the attic.

"Passing Time in Times Past"

- Have students read the article on p. 965.
- Ask students what audience this article is intended to reach. **Possible answers:** Teachers, parents, librarians
- Ask students if the article contains any material of interest to them, even though they are not members of the target audience. **Possible answers:** Some students may respond that the CD-ROMs and books listed sound interesting.

"Passing Time in Times Past" cont.

- As students continue to read this article from a professional journal, encourage them to notice the writer's use of formatting.
- Ask students how the formatting helps the audience understand the article.
  Answer: The use of titles, subheads, and boldfaced type helps readers follow the flow of information. It also allows readers to scan the content to find items of particular interest to them.

Journalism

CD-ROMs

Chronicle of the 20th Century. 1996. $39.95.

Ages 9–up. A charmingly anachronistic newspaper editor's office, complete with a manual typewriter and a ticker tape machine, is the starting point for this exploration of twentieth-century history up to the early days of 1996. There are multiple access points for young people searching for specific events, dates, or names, as well as some intriguing opportunities for browsing and for more in-depth research on eight major focus areas, such as the Russian Revolution, the two world wars, space exploration, and the fall of Communism. All entries contain visual materials as well as text, and many also include sound or video clips, such as Orson Welles' famous "War of the Worlds" broadcast and Yasir Arafat addressing the United Nations in Arabic. With newspapers and headlines making up the framework for this CD-ROM, it also makes a good springboard to books about journalism.

Books

Fleischman, Paul. *Dateline: Troy.* 1996. 79p. $15.99 (1-56402-469-5).

Ages 11–up. The author juxtaposes the history of the Trojan War with newspaper clippings of contemporary events, making the parallels between Homer's world and our own unmistakably clear.

Granfield, Linda. *Extra! Extra! The Who, What, Where, When, and Why of Newspapers.* Illus. by Bill Slavin. 1994. 72p. $16.99 (0-531-98683-6); paper, $7.95 (0-531-07049-2).

Ages 9–12. This book contains everything kids ever wanted to know about how a newspaper is published—including information on how to publish their own.

The Gold Rush

CD-ROMs

Klondike Gold. 1996. $39.95.

Ages 11–up. American children more familiar with the California gold rush will find some interesting differences and similarities in the Klondike gold rush that took place in the far north of Canada in 1896. A pan of gold nuggets serves as the main menu on this CD-ROM, leading to information about this rip-roaring episode in Yukon history, an interactive exploration of the placer mining process, and a rich segment on "The Cremation of Sam McGee" by Robert Service, the bard of the Yukon. Historical photographs form the foundation for multiple hypertext links to related topics, and honky-tonk music sets the tone.

Books

Fleischman, Sid. *Bandit's Moon.* Illus. by Jos. A. Smith. 1998. 136p. $15 (0-688-15830-7).

Ages 9–12. Twelve-year-old orphan Annyrose tells what happened when she was taken in by Joaquin Murieta and his band of outlaws during the California gold rush.

Service, Robert W. *The Cremation of Sam McGee.* Illus. by Ted Harrison. 1987. 32p. $18 (0-688-06903-7).

Ages 9–up. An illustrated edition of the poetic tall tale about a frozen gold miner that is featured in the *Klondike Gold* CD-ROM.

Yee, Paul. *Tales from Gold Mountain.* Illus. by Simon Ng. 1999. 64p. $18.95 (0-88899-098-7).

Ages 9–12. Yee blends folklore, fact, and fiction in these eight haunting stories about Chinese immigrants in North America.

Information is presented in three categories: *Castles, Journalism,* and *The Gold Rush.*

Teachers and librarians may find the inclusion of books and CD-ROMS especially useful.

Formatting, such as the use of titles and subheads, helps readers locate the content they wish to find.

966 ◆ *Poetry*

CUSTOMIZE INSTRUCTION FOR UNIVERSAL ACCESS

For Special Needs Students	For Advanced Readers
Invite students to choose a book or CD-ROM described in the article that has captured their interest. Have them list details in the product descriptions that they found most intriguing.	Ask students to use the Internet to find another book or CD-ROM that could also be featured in this article. Have students write up the product description in the style and tone used by the writer in "Passing Time in Times Past."

Check Your Comprehension

1. What is the advantage to children in learning from a CD-ROM, according to Virginia A. Walter?
2. What is the subject of Paul Fleischman's book *Dateline: Troy*?
3. How does Walter organize the materials that she recommends?

Applying the Reading Strategy

Identifying a Target Audience's Purpose

4. Use a chart like the one shown to identify three purposes that either a librarian or a teacher might have for reading the article in *Book Links*. For each, indicate which details in the article meet that purpose.

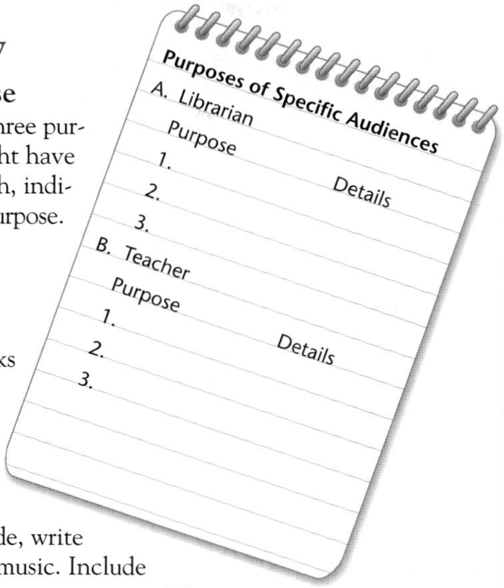

Activity

Writing an Annotated Discography

The article presented here offers reviews of books and CD-ROMs devoted to certain subjects. When the subject of a review is music, it often takes the form of an annotated discography. An annotated discography lists songs or CDs by a particular artist or in a specific genre and offers opinions about their quality. Using the chart below as a guide, write an annotated discography reviewing a category of music. Include your evaluation of each item and provide details to support our opinions.

Music Title	Your Reaction	Supporting Detail

Contrasting Informational Materials

Professional Journals and General Newspapers

1. Imagine that the books presented by Walter were reviewed in a daily newspaper with a general adult readership. (a) What book information does the professional journal article contain that a newspaper might omit? (b) What details might be expanded in a newspaper review? (c) What other information might a newspaper include that was omitted in this article?
2. Suppose that the same books in this article were reviewed in a magazine or newspaper written for young people. (a) How would the content of such a review differ from the content in the article presented here? (b) How would the style of the two kinds of reviews be different?

Answers for p. 967

Check Your Comprehension

1. CD-ROMs often feature primary sources, provide interactive experiences, and combine fun with learning.
2. The subject of the book is the Trojan War.
3. She organizes the materials by topic, then by type (book or CD-ROM).

Applying the Reading Strategy

4. Possible answers: Purpose: To find good books to buy for a school library; Details: The author meets this reader's need by pre-selecting books that students will enjoy. Purpose: To find CD-ROMs to give as personal gifts; Details: The descriptions of the CD-ROMs help readers match product features with the gift recipient they have in mind. Purpose: To prepare a budget for a school library. Details: The article provides cost information for each product described.

Activity

- Read the Activity on p. 967 aloud to the class.
- Suggest that students create a list that fits a particular musical category, such as jazz or rock music.
- Point out that students may vist music suppliers' Web sites to obtain information about the songs they include in their discography.

Contrasting Informational Materials

1. **(a)** The newspaper might omit or shorten the introductory paragraphs of the article. **(b)** Background information on the product or author might be expanded. **(c)** A newspaper article might include quotes from students, teachers, or librarians who have read the books or used the products.
2. **(a)** The content would highlight particularly interesting features in depth, stressing the interactivity and "fun" aspect of the book or CD-ROM. **(b)** The article in a young person's magazine would be easier to read, with more paragraph breaks and simpler words and sentences.

Lesson Objectives

1. To write a comparison-and-contrast essay
2. To learn the characteristics of a comparison-and-contrast essay
3. To use writing strategies to plan, organize, draft, and revise a comparison-and-contrast essay

Model From Literature

Explain that the Connections feature in this unit invites students to compare and contrast two different views on aging.

Comparison-and-Contrast Essay

- Have students read this section on p. 968.
- Point out that students will be asked to meet the Assignment Criteria given in the bulleted list on p. 968 as they create their comparison-and-contrast essays.
- Encourage students to refer to this list as they write their drafts.

Prewriting

- Help students select their topics by writing the following general subject categories on the chalkboard: sports, movies, music. Invite students to suggest two other general topic areas, and add those to the list.
- Ask students to brainstorm for specific examples related to each category.
- To each example, have students add a basic, brief description.
- Then, invite students to brainstorm for other examples that demonstrate notable differences from or similarities to the first examples.
- As students select their topics, encourage them to identify a specific audience and a primary purpose—to persuade, to explain, or to describe—for their essays.

Writing WORKSHOP

Exposition: Comparison-and-Contrast Essay

A **comparison-and-contrast essay** addresses two or more subjects to show their similarities and differences. It may describe or explain, reveal strengths and weaknesses, or persuade readers to value one subject over another. In this workshop, you will write a comparison-and-contrast essay on subjects that are suitable to this type of exposition.

Assignment Criteria. Your comparison-and-contrast essay should have the following characteristics:

- Analysis and discussion of similarities and differences between two or more things, people, places, or ideas
- Factual details about each subject
- A purpose for comparison and contrast
- Equal presentation of each subject using one of two organizations: subject-by-subject or point-by-point

To preview the criteria on which your comparison-and-contrast essay may be assessed, see the Rubric on page 971.

Prewriting

Choose a topic. Explore topics in terms of clear opposites (winter/summer), clear similarities (baseball/cricket), or close relationships (book/movie). **Brainstorm** for topics by starting with names of people, places, objects, or ideas. Then, note related subjects that come to mind. Notice relationships that interest you, and then choose one to develop.

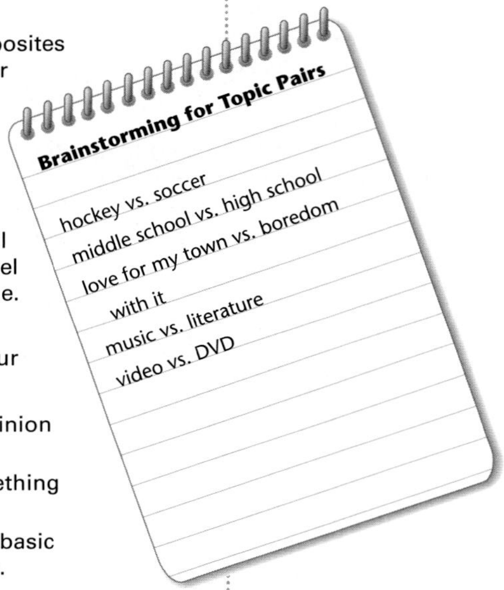
Brainstorming for Topic Pairs
hockey vs. soccer
middle school vs. high school
love for my town vs. boredom
with it
music vs. literature
video vs. DVD

Identify your audience. Your intended audience will direct the type of information you include—from the level of vocabulary you use to the level of analysis you pursue. Consider your audience as you gather information.

Specify your purpose. To identify a purpose for your essay, consider the following possibilities:

- *To persuade*—You want readers to accept your opinion that one subject is preferable to another.
- *To explain*—You want readers to understand something special about the subjects.
- *To describe*—You want readers to understand the basic similarities and differences between your subjects.

Gather details. As you generate the details to use in your comparison-and-contrast essay, look at the ideas you have collected and consider the main elements you will discuss.

TEACHING RESOURCES

The following resources can be used to enrich or extend the instruction for pp. 968-969.

Writing and Grammar, Gold Level, Chapter 9, pp. 176–201

Performance Assessment and Portfolio Management, pp. 16, 61

Writing Models and Graphic Organizers on Transparencies, pp. 33–36

Writing and Grammar iText CD-ROM
Students can use the following tools as they complete their responses to literature:

- Pros and Cons Chart
- Topic Bank
- Descriptive Word Bin

Student Model

Before you begin drafting your comparison-and-contrast essay, read this student model and review the characteristics of an effective comparison-and-contrast essay.

Lauren DeLoach
Bernice, Louisiana

Ambivalence

When I consider my conflicting feelings about my hometown, I see that there are things that I love and hate about living in Bernice, Louisiana, a nineties version of Mayberry. I love the security of a small town, and I hate it. I love the way that my town is not clouded by the smog of a city, and I hate it too. I love it and I hate that I love it.

> Lauren's essay will compare two feelings: what she loves and what she hates about her hometown.

I love and hate the security in my town for a number of reasons. I love it because I know that it is my dogs scratching at my door at 5:30 in the morning and not some dangerous stranger. In my town, a fifteen-car traffic jam is front-page news. On the other hand, I hate that it gets a little boring sometimes. I don't want criminals at my door, but a little excitement would be nice.

> Using a point-by-point organization, Lauren addresses the first contrast in her attitudes about her town: She feels ambivalence about its security.

I am fond of the size of Bernice and I detest it, too. I'm glad that only fifteen cars is a major traffic jam. But I hate that I have to drive sixteen miles to the nearest major store. I love and hate that my town is so small that I know everybody's first, middle, and last names. I like it because I have a "tab" at the grocery story and the drug store, so that eliminates the necessity of money. I hate that everybody knows me because that means that everybody finds out about whom I'm dating, whom I once dated, my height, weight, and age. I also hate that we all know each other so well that the most entertaining news we can come up with to put in the Bernice Banner is that Peggy Jane and her brother JC visited their Aunt Goosey Lou in the nursing home. But by knowing everyone so well, I've made friends who are trustworthy because we know all of each other's deepest secrets.

> These facts support the writer's ideas and opinions.

Even though I say that I detest some things, home wouldn't be home without these silly quirks. I love that my parents and their friends are known as the "elite group" because they have traveled beyond Texas, Arkansas, and Mississippi. I love saying that I have read the *Iliad* to people who think I would not read such a book. I know that it sounds like I love the provincialism that small towns can impose, but the smells of fresh-cut grass and the gardenia bush outside my door are what make my home my home.

This is what I love and what I say I hate, but I don't really. The overall feeling I get from living in Bernice is ambivalence. I love it and I hate that I love such goofy things. But the parts of home that seem so trivial are the ones that make you who you are. That makes a place your home.

> Lauren's comparison allows her to be funny, but also helps her reflect on her ideas.

Student Model

- Explain that the Student Model is a sample, and that essays may be longer.
- Have students refer to the Assignment Criteria list on p. 968, then identify details or examples in the student model that meet each criterion.

Real-World Connection

Comparison-and-contrast writing in the real world: Explain that the type of reasoning that goes into creating a comparison-and-contrast essay will be useful to students throughout their lives, as they make decisions, from choosing a restaurant to buying a car to deciding which college to attend.

CUSTOMIZE INSTRUCTION FOR UNIVERSAL ACCESS

For Special Needs Students	For English Learners	For Advanced Readers
Encourage students to choose a topic for their essays from their own lives. Then, have them brainstorm for a long list of details, including facts, opinions, sensory images, and dialogue related to the topic. Inform students that while they may not use every detail in their essays, these lists demonstrate their mastery of the topic.	Students may need help finding descriptive words to capture their meaning. Invite students to work in partnership with a student proficient in English to find language that is appropriate. Encourage students to use the **Writing and Grammar iText CD-ROM** descriptive word bin.	Invite students to write two versions of their comparison-and-contrast essays. For the first version, have students select an audience of their peers and the purpose to persuade. For the second version, have students select another audience and purpose.

Drafting

- Review the organizational charts on p. 970 and compare them.
- Inform students that with point-by-point organization, they must pay very careful attention to their transitions between subjects.
- Remind students that in both types of organization, they must support generalizations with specifics.

Revising

- Read aloud the instruction about revising to make comparisons and contrasts clear on p. 970.
- Provide highlighters or pens of different colors that students can use to complete the revising strategy on p. 970.
- After students have clarified their drafts, ask them to review their work to make sure they've included enough detail, especially factual evidence.
- Have students review the model and the nonmodel. Ask students to identify why the model is more effective.
  Possible answer: The model provides specific language that appeals to the senses and engages the reader.

Drafting

Choose an organization. Choose an organization that suits your topic. Point-by-point and subject-by-subject plans are the most common types of comparison-and-contrast writing:

- **Point-by-point organization:** This organization allows you to move between your subjects, sharpening your points of comparison and contrast and addressing each feature for both subjects.
- **Subject-by-subject organization:** This organization allows you to compare your subjects as complete units. First, address all aspects of one subject, and then devote full attention to the other. Be careful to address the same features and devote equal time to each subject.

Point-by-Point Plan
Point 1
- Subject A
- Subject B

Point 2
- Subject A
- Subject B

Subject-by-Subject Plan
Subject A
- Point 1
- Point 2

Subject B
- Point 1
- Point 2

Support generalizations with specifics. As you point out similarities and differences, include facts or information to back up your assertions. For example, if you compare and contrast the climates of Antarctica and Australia, you should provide statistics of their annual temperatures, rainfall records, and other specific evidence to demonstrate your points.

Revising

Revise to make comparisons and contrasts clear. Review each paragraph to be sure that you lead the reader to see the comparisons and contrasts you draw. Using two different colors, mark your draft to distinguish between the two subjects you discuss. Then, evaluate the places where the two subjects meet. Add transitional words or phrases to make the shift clear.

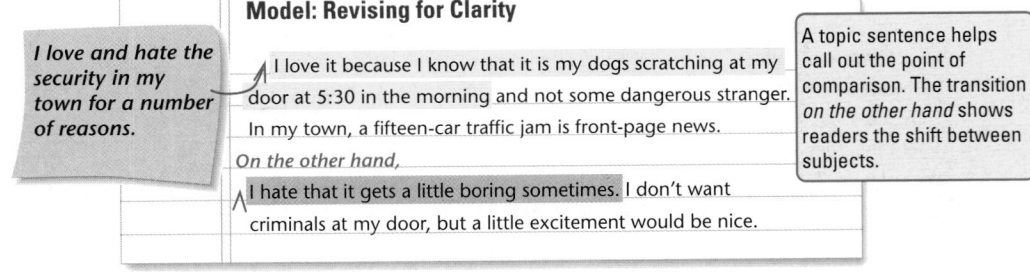

Model: Revising for Clarity

I love and hate the security in my town for a number of reasons.

I love it because I know that it is my dogs scratching at my door at 5:30 in the morning and not some dangerous stranger. In my town, a fifteen-car traffic jam is front-page news. *On the other hand,* I hate that it gets a little boring sometimes. I don't want criminals at my door, but a little excitement would be nice.

A topic sentence helps call out the point of comparison. The transition *on the other hand* shows readers the shift between subjects.

USING TECHNOLOGY IN WRITING

If students are using a word processing program, they can highlight their points in different colors on the computer (rather than with markers or pens on paper), either by using a highlighter tool or selecting different type colors.

Suggest that students also use the spell check and other revision tools on the **Writing and Grammar iText CD-ROM.**

Revise to add detail. To help your readers understand the comparison you make, add enough detail to explain the differences and similarities you see. Review your draft to find vague language. Wherever you can, add information that strengthens your description or analysis.

Vague: In contrast to literature, popular music forms a soundtrack in our lives.

Specific: In contrast to literature that we must read to enjoy, popular music, like the top 40 tunes we hear on the radio, forms a soundtrack for our lives. We can hear it as we drive, shop, or even fall asleep at night.

Compare the model and the nonmodel. Why is the model more effective than the nonmodel?

Nonmodel	Model
I know that it sounds like I love the things that small towns include, but the smells outside my door are what make my home a home.	I know that it sounds like I love the provincialism that small towns can impose, but the smells of fresh-cut grass and the gardenia bush outside my door are what make my home a home.

Publishing and Presenting

When you are satisfied with your draft, share your ideas and your writing with a wider audience.

Deliver an oral presentation. Read your comparison-and-contrast essay aloud to an audience of your classmates. If you attempted in your essay to persuade your audience to see the benefits of one subject over another, consider asking classmates whether or not they agree with your position after hearing your evidence.

WG *Prentice Hall Writing and Grammar Connection: Chapter 9*

Rubric for Self-Assessment

Evaluate your comparison-and-contrast essay using the following criteria and rating scale:

Criteria	Rating Scale: Not very				Very
How well does the essay identify similarities and differences?	1	2	3	4	5
How well does the essay provide factual details about each subject?	1	2	3	4	5
How well defined is the purpose of the essay?	1	2	3	4	5
How effective is the organization of the essay?	1	2	3	4	5

Publishing and Presenting

- Before presenting their essays, ask students to state their target audience and purpose.
- Invite the class to keep audience and purpose in mind as they listen to each essay.
- For an additional model, display the Comparison-and-Contrast transparencies in **Writing Models and Graphic Organizers on Transparencies,** pp. 33–36.
- Remind students that a confident delivery will add credibility to their work.

Assessment

- Review with students the criteria for a comparison-and-contrast essay, provided in the Assignment Criteria on p. 968.
- As students listen to each other's essays, have them ask: Which type of organization (point-by-point or subject-by-subject) did the writer use? Discuss students' choices after each presentation.
- The rubric on this page, and another rubric in an alternative format, can be found on pp. 16 and 61 of **Performance Assessment** and **Portfolio Management.**

TEST-TAKING TIP

Remind students of the distinction between *compare* (show the similarities) and *contrast* (show the differences). Point out that keeping these meanings in mind when a standardized test question focuses on comparison and contrast will help them select or organize their answers.

Lesson Objectives

1. To analyze and compare media coverage
2. To define a purpose for viewing media coverage
3. To recognize the differences between media coverages on the same subject

Comparing Media Coverage

- Have students read the information in this section on p. 972.
- Invite students to brainstorm for a list of information sources.
- Briefly, lead a discussion on the varying ways in which these sources convey information.

Prepare to View

- Have students read this section on p. 972.
- Point out that it's important to be able to compare media coverage because each media source filters information in a unique way. Comparing coverage can help students make independent judgments about a news story.
- Ask students how they usually learn about local, state, national, or international news. Note these sources on the board.
- Have students re-read the paragraph "Recognize differences." Ask them to keep this information in mind as they explore sources of media coverage.

View and Compare

- Direct students' attention to the chart on p. 972.
- Ask them to use a chart like this to note differences in media coverage on the same topic.

Listening and Speaking WORKSHOP

Comparing Media Coverage

Whether information comes from the Internet or a 24-hour cable network, it is useful to know how to analyze and compare media coverage.

Prepare to View

Every news format and news source has strengths and weaknesses. As you follow news stories, consider the way they are filtered and presented to you.

Consider your sources. Certain types of news media are designed to cover specific types of news events. Consider these sources and the variety and quality of reporting they represent:

- nightly network news or local television news
- Internet Web pages of news organizations
- public radio
- national magazines or daily newspapers
- cable news channels

Recognize differences. Before you compare media coverage, think about the differences you are likely to find among sources. A good general news source might present news coverage of a variety of topics—science, politics, and entertainment. However, if you are looking for coverage of one issue, you might be concerned with the depth of coverage rather than variety.

Identify bias. Bias occurs when an organization has a special interest in reporting the news in a particular way. If you anticipate bias, you will have a heightened awareness when you view the news source. Find out which organization sponsors the coverage, and think about how that might influence reporting of a particular issue or group of issues.

Using Criteria to Compare Coverage

Accuracy
- Are there any mistakes in the facts presented?
- Are the news reports misleading viewers by leaving out essential information?

Comprehensiveness
- Do the news reports support their assertions with evidence?
- Do the reports present an adequate level of detail and complexity?

Credibility
- How close were the reporters to the events they are reporting?
- Do the reports cite well-known authorities or published studies?

Objectivity
- Do news sources present more than one side of an issue?
- Does any source have a vested interest in presenting facts in a particular way?

View and Compare

Use consistent criteria. When you watch or listen to coverage of a news story reported by several sources, you are likely to notice differences. Consider the questions in the chart shown on this page.

Make comparisons. Once you have evaluated each news source, a side-by-side comparison, using the same criteria, should be straightforward. Notice the similarities and differences among the reports you find to determine the news sources you can trust.

Activity: Research and Discussion — Choose a current issue to research as a group. Find three sources from television, radio, or the Internet. Compare coverage of that issue and discuss your findings.

CUSTOMIZE INSTRUCTION FOR UNIVERSAL ACCESS

For Special Needs Students	For Gifted/Talented Students
Provide students with an example of media coverage from two sources on the same topic. Ask the students to locate a third example on the Internet or in newspapers. Lead students in a discussion about the way each media source presents information somewhat differently.	Have students survey several sources of media coverage, looking for bias. Invite the students to report to the class about any bias they observed.

Assessment WORKSHOP

Analogies

The reading sections of some tests often require you to answer multiple-choice questions to complete analogies. Use the following strategies to help you:

- An *analogy* establishes a relationship between one pair of words so that a similar relationship can be established between a second pair.
- To complete an analogy, identify the relationship between the initial pair of words, and then look for a second pair with a similar relationship.
- Common relationships to look for are synonyms, antonyms, cause and effect, part and whole, example and group, and product and function.

Test-Taking Strategies

- Say the relationship of the first word pair aloud to yourself in a test sentence. For example, "joy/smile" would be "When you feel joy, you smile."
- Use the same relationship when putting the second pair of words into a sentence. Discard pairs that do not make sense in your test sentence.

Sample Test Item

Directions: Read the word pair, and then choose the letter of the word pair that is most similar to the example.

1. MINT : HERB ::

A garage : car
B score : game
C snow : precipitation
D sow : harvest

Answer and Explanation

C is the correct answer. To arrive at the correct answer, identify the relationship first: "Mint is a type of herb." Then, look for a word pair that has a similar relationship. Since garage is *not* a type of car, score is *not* a type of game, and sow is *not* a type of harvest, the answer cannot be ***A, B,*** or ***D.*** Snow is a type of precipitation, therefore ***C*** is the correct choice.

Practice

Directions: Read each word pair, and then choose the letter of the word pair that is most similar to the example.

1. SUNSCREEN : PROTECT ::

A shampoo : rinse
B sand : bucket
C curtains : drapes
D label : inform

2. STATEMENT : CONFIDENCE ::

A excitement : happiness
B proposal : intuition
C question : confusion
D interruption : disappointment

3. CONDUCTOR : SYMPHONY ::

A orchestra : violin
B driver : bus
C tour guide : argument
D official : relaxation

Lesson Objective

To correctly answer test questions about analogies

Applying Reading Strategies

Read aloud out the bulleted list under "Analogies" on p. 973. Point out that students can keep these concepts in mind when they are asked to complete analogies in test questions.

Applying Test-Taking Strategies

- Point out the unique construction of an analogy in test questions (a colon follows the first word in a pair; double colons follow the second word in a pair).
- Have students read the Sample Test Item, then share their responses to the question orally with the rest of the class.
- Point out that making a sentence from the first word pair (in this case, "Mint is a type of herb") can help students locate the matching word pair.

Answers:

1. The correct answer is *D*. The purpose of sunscreen is to protect; the purpose of a label is to inform. Word pairs *A*, *B*, and *C* do not have a purpose relationship.
2. The correct answer is *C*. A statement can express confidence; a question can express confusion.
3. The correct answer is *B*. A conductor directs a symphony; a driver steers a bus.

TEACHING RESOURCES

The following resources can be used to enrich or extend the instruction for p. 973.

PRENTICE HALL ASSESSMENT SYSTEM

- Workbook
- Skill Book
- Transparencies
- CD-ROM

Unit Objectives

1. To develop skills in reading epics
2. To apply a variety of reading strategies appropriate for reading an epic
3. To analyze literary elements
4. To use a variety of strategies to build vocabulary
5. To learn elements of grammar, usage, and style
6. To use recursive writing processes to write in a variety of forms
7. To develop listening and speaking skills
8. To express and support responses to various types of texts
9. To prepare, organize, and present literary interpretations

Meeting the Objectives

With each selection, you will find instructional materials through which students can meet these objectives. Further, you will find additional practice pages for reading strategies, literary analysis, vocabulary, and grammar in the **Selection Support: Skills Development Workbook** in your **Teaching Resources.**

Background

Art

Ulysses Deriding Polyphemus, by J.M.W. Turner

Born in London, Turner (1775-1851) had a traditional training at the Royal Academy of Arts. This painting portrays one of the adventures of Odysseus, the hero of Homer's epic the *Odyssey*. Use the following question for discussion:

What effects are created by the play of light and dark in the painting?

Possible response: The characters are difficult to see in the painting's swirling mist and half-light. These techniques lend a mood of otherworldliness, mystery, and danger to the painting.

UNIT 10 The Epic

Ulysses Deriding Polyphemus, 1819, J.M.W. Turner, The National Gallery, London

UNIT FEATURES

Connections	Reading Informational Material
Every unit contains a feature that connects literature to a related topic, such as art, science, or history. In this unit, the Literature Past and Present feature on p. 1064 recounts a modern-day Odyssey, the perilous voyage to the moon by Apollo 13 astronauts. Use the information and questions on the Connections pages to enrich students' understanding of the selections presented within the unit.	These selections will help students learn to analyze and evaluate informational texts, such as workplace documents, technical directions, and consumer materials. They will expose students to the organization and features unique to nonnarrative texts. In this unit, students will learn how to read newspaper editorials as they practice the reading strategy of analyzing bias.

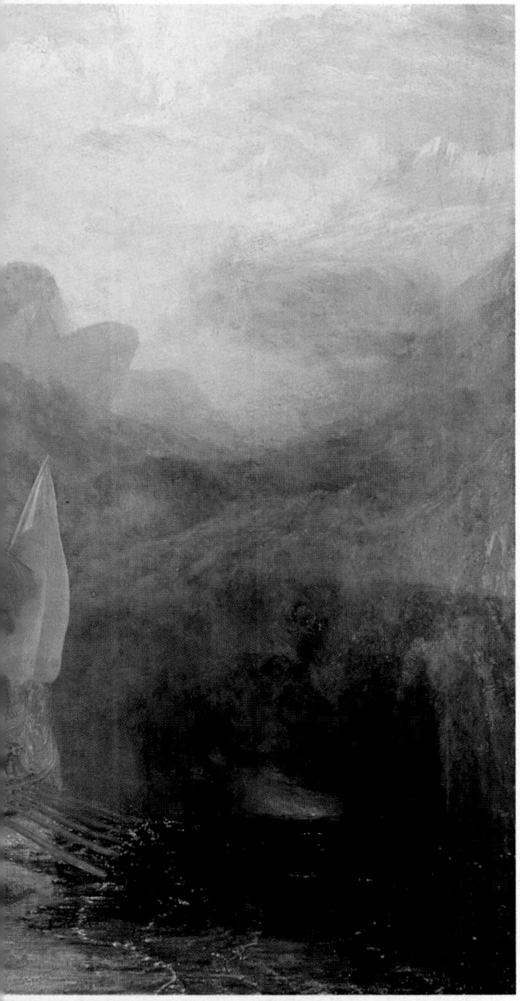

Exploring the Genre

Turn the page to enter a world of heroes, gods, and sweeping adventures. Tradition tells us that the blind poet Homer wrote the *Odyssey* after it had been passed down by generations of Greek singers. If it had not been for this ancient scribe, many generations of readers would never have learned about the heroic exploits of Odysseus and his companions.

An **epic** is a long narrative poem about the deeds of gods or heroes. Early in the *Odyssey*, Homer presents an epic question. Odysseus asks:

> "Where shall a man find sweetness to surpass his own home and his parents? In far lands he shall not, though he find a house of gold. What of my sailing, then, from Troy?"

The *Odyssey* itself is the answer.

▲ **Critical Viewing** In this painting, inspired by the *Odyssey*, which dangers seem to present themselves? **[Interpret]**

ASSESSMENT RESOURCES

- Selection Support: Skills Development Workbook
- Formal Assessment
- Open Book Tests
- Performance Assessment and Portfolio Management
- Extension Activities

Assessing Student Progress

Listed below are tools that are available to measure the degree to which students meet the unit objectives.

Informal Assessment

The questions in the Review and Assess sections are a first-level response to the concepts and skills presented with the selections. Students' responses provide a brief, informal measure of their grasp of the material. These responses can indicate where further instruction and practice are needed. Follow up with the practice pages in **Selection Support: Skills Development Workbook.**

Formal Assessment

The **Formal Assessment** booklet contains the Selection Tests and Unit Tests.

- Selection Tests measure comprehension and skills acquisition for each selection or group of selections.
- Each Unit Test provides students with thirty multiple-choice questions and five essay questions designed to assess students' knowledge of the literature and skills taught in the unit.

The **Open Book Tests** ask students to demonstrate their ability to synthesize and communicate information from selections or groups of selections.

To assess student writing, you will find rubrics and scoring models in the **Performance Assessment and Portfolio Management** booklet. In this booklet, you will also find scoring rubrics for listening and speaking activities.

Alternative Assessment

The **Extension Activities** booklet contains writing activities, listening and speaking activities, and research and technology activities that are appropriate for students with different ability levels. You may also use these activities as an alternative measure of students' growth.

▶Critical Viewing

Answer: The dangers seem to include darkness and looming rocks as well as the flung boulders of Polyphemus.

Why Read Literature?

The "Why Read Literature?" page in each unit presents a list of possible purposes for reading. Each purpose for reading is connected to one or more of the selections in the unit. Good readers set a purpose before reading to help them read actively and focus on meaningful details.

Unit 10 introduces three purposes for reading. "Read for the Love of Literature" points out that the *Odyssey* began as a tale told by "singers." "Read to Be Entertained" invites students to experience the drama of a modern-day Odyssey as they read the excerpt about Apollo 13. "Read for Information" highlights the controversy over a space flight.

How to Use This Page

- Tell students that as they read each selection in this unit, they should set a purpose for reading. This will help them read in an active and focused manner.
- Explain that students can increase their love of literature by seeing how the poet Constantine Cavafy learned a lesson from the *Odyssey*.
- Point out that the thrill of reading a gripping adventure story awaits students in the excerpt from *Lost Moon*.
- In "Read for Information," students will see different sides of an argument expressed in newspaper editorials about John Glenn's 1998 space flight.

Why Read Literature?

As you read an ancient work of literature, it is interesting to think about its influence on subsequent generations of authors and readers. The *Odyssey* is a powerful tale that has been read for many different reasons since it was first written down. Here is a sampling of reasons to read this epic and the works that follow:

1 Read for the Love of Literature

The singers who spread the tale of the *Odyssey* before it was written down were highly skilled poets. Each would change the tale slightly, embellishing certain parts to create his own dramatic effects and style. Enjoy the final product of many skillful poets as you read an excerpt from the ***Odyssey***, page 980.

A powerful story can take on new life when it is read by authors who are inspired to create works of their own. See which lesson Constantine Cavafy took from Odysseus' long absence from home when you read his poem **"Ithaca,"** page 1058.

2 Read to Be Entertained

Great adventures are not limited to the pages of ancient epics. Find the connection between ancient Greek adventure and a heart-pounding modern-day odyssey through space as you read the excerpt from ***Lost Moon***, page 1064.

3 Read for Information

In 1962, John Glenn was the first American to orbit Earth. Thirty-six years later, at the age of 77, he joined the crew of the space shuttle to go into orbit again, eliciting both admiration and controversy. Read both sides of the debate over Glenn's 1998 space flight in **Reading Informational Materials: Newspaper Editorials**, page 1066.

Take It to the Net

Visit the Web site for online instruction and activities related to each selection in this unit.
www.phschool.com

ENRICHMENT: Further Reading

Have students choose one or more of the works below to extend the unit theme of reading poetry or to read more by the unit authors.

Apollo 13 by Jim Lovell and Jeffrey Kluger
This book tells a harrowing tale of danger and courage during a spaceflight to the moon in 1970.

The Old Man and the Sea by Ernest Hemingway
This classic tale about an aging Cuban fisherman who tangles with a magnificent marlin can be found in the **Prentice Hall Literature Library.**

When the Legends Die by Hal Borland
When his father and mother both die, a young Ute Indian finds himself caught between two cultures.

How to Read Literature

Use Strategies for Reading an Epic

In ancient societies, wandering storytellers told stories of gods and heroes that would sometimes take days to complete. To help the storytellers remember such lengthy pieces, epic tales were composed in poetry and recited to musical accompaniment. Their language and sentence structure may present some difficulty for you as you read. Apply the following strategies to help you.

1. Summarize.

You can be certain that you have understood a passage when you are able to offer a clear, concise summary of the action. Stop to summarize what has happened at each pause in the action. Eliminate any aspects or events that are not directly related to the basic plot.

2. Read in sentences.

You may become confused if you stop at the end of every line of verse in an epic because sentences frequently flow to the next line.

- Be guided by the punctuation, not simply the ends of lines, in determining where to pause.
- Use periods and the ends of paragraphs to maintain the natural flow of words.

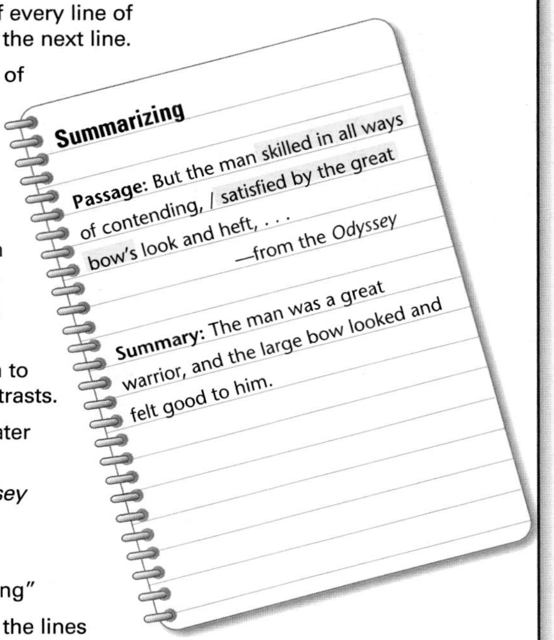

Summarizing
Passage: But the man skilled in all ways of contending, / satisfied by the great bow's look and heft, . . .
—from the Odyssey
Summary: The man was a great warrior, and the large bow looked and felt good to him.

3. Compare and contrast.

Finding similarities and recognizing differences can help you understand your reactions to different texts.

- Choose basic categories such as style, subject, and viewpoint to compare and contrast.
- Compare specific passages that are similar enough to enable you to draw effective comparisons and contrasts.

> The lovely voices in ardor appealing over the water
> made me crave to listen, . . .
>
> —from the *Odyssey*

> I don't enjoy singing
> this trio, fatal and valuable.
>
> —from "Siren Song"

The subject of these two passages is the same, but the lines express different viewpoints. The *Odyssey* uses formal, elevated language, whereas "Siren Song" uses informal language. The *Odyssey* passage simply tells the story, but "Siren Song" hints at a deeper meaning.

As you read the selections in this unit, review the reading strategies and look at the notes in the side column. Use the suggestions to apply the strategies and interact with the text.

How to Read Literature

The "How to Read Literature" page in each unit presents a set of strategies to help readers understand authors' words and ideas. Each reading strategy is taught in conjunction with one or more of the selections within the unit. Good readers develop a bank of strategies from which they can draw as needed.

Unit 10 introduces three strategies for reading epics. Students learn to summarize, to read in sentences rather than in lines, and to compare and contrast to clarify meaning.

How to Use This Page

Introduce the strategies for reading epics, presenting each as a tool for developing understanding when reading the selections in this unit.

- As they read the *Odyssey* (p. 980), students will learn to pause periodically and summarize what they've read.
- Explain that students should read epics as they read poems: stopping or pausing where punctuation indicates instead of at the ends of lines.
- Point out that making comparisons and contrasts both within an epic and between epics and other works can help students clarify their reactions to the texts.

MODEL A READING STRATEGY: Summarize

Help your students summarize by modeling your process with this passage from the *Odyssey*:

> "And now, as matters stand at last,/ I have no strength left to evade a marriage,/ cannot find any further way; my parents/ urge it upon me, and my son/ will not stand by while they eat up his property."

Tell students:

The speaker of this passage is Penelope, the wife of Odysseus, who has awaited her husband's return with legendary patience. Here, she is saying she can no longer avoid remarrying. She is tired, and her parents and son are pressuring her. Note how my summary omits all but the most essential ideas expressed in the passage.

from the Odyssey, Part 1

Lesson Objectives and CA Correlations

1. **To analyze and respond to literary elements**
   - Literary Analysis: The Epic Hero **R 3.3**
   - Connecting Literary Elements: Conflict **R 3.6, 3.7**
2. **To read, comprehend, analyze, and critique an epic**
   - Reading Strategy: Reading in Sentences
   - Reading Check questions
   - Review and Assess questions
3. **To develop word analysis skills, fluency, and systematic vocabulary**
   - Vocabulary Development Lesson: Word Origins: Words From Myths **R 1.3**
4. **To understand and apply written and oral language conventions**
   - Spelling Strategy
   - Grammar Lesson: Usage: *like, as,* and *as if* **LC 1.3**
   - Assessment Practice (ATE)
5. **To understand and apply appropriate writing and research strategies**
   - Writing Lesson: Character Study (after Part 2) **W 2.2**
   - Extension Activity: Comparison-and-Contrast Essay **1.4**
6. **To understand and apply listening and speaking strategies**
   - Extension Activity: Play-by-Play Broadcast **LS 1.11**

STEP-BY-STEP TEACHING GUIDE	PACING GUIDE
PRETEACH	
Motivate Students and Provide Background	
Use the Motivation activity (ATE p. 978)	5 min.
Read and discuss the Preview material and Background information (SE/ATE p. 978) [A]	10 min.
Introduce the Concepts	
Introduce the Literary Analysis and Reading Strategy (SE/ATE p. 979) [A]	15 min.
Pronounce the vocabulary words and read their definitions (SE p. 979)	5 min.
TEACH	
Monitor Comprehension	
Informally monitor comprehension by circulating while students read independently or in groups [A]	50 min.
Monitor students' comprehension with the Reading Check notes (SE/ATE pp. 981, 983, 987, 989, 991, 993, 994, 997, 999, 1001, 1003, 1005, 1007, 1009, 1011, 1013, 1015)	as students read
Develop vocabulary with Vocabulary notes (SE pp. 981, 984, 990, 997, 1000, 1003, 1007, 1011)	as students read
Develop Understanding	
Develop students' understanding with Literary Analysis notes (SE/ATE pp. 985, 986, 989–991, 993, 996, 999, 1000, 1001, 1005–1006, 1010–1012, 1015) [A]	10 min.
Develop students' understanding with Reading Strategy notes (SE/ATE pp. 983–984, 986, 990, 991–992, 996–997, 1000–1002, 1006–1007, 1009, 1010–1012, 1014)	10 min.
ASSESS	
Assess Mastery	
Assess students' mastery of the Reading Strategy and Literary Analysis by having them answer the Review and Assess questions (SE/ATE p. 1018)	20 min.
Use one or more of the print and media Assessment Resources (ATE p. 1019) [A]	up to 50 min.
EXTEND	
Apply Understanding	
Have students complete the Vocabulary Development Lesson and the Grammar Lesson (SE p. 1019) [A]	20 min.
Apply students' knowledge of including quotations using the Writing Lesson (SE/ATE p. 1049) [A]	45 min.
Apply students' understanding using one or more of the Extension Activities (SE p. 1019)	20–90 min.

[A] **ACCELERATED INSTRUCTION:** Use the strategies and activities identified with an [A].

UNIVERSAL ACCESS
● = Below Level Students
▲ = On-Level Students
■ = Above Level Students

Time and Resource Manager

Reading Level: Challenging
Average Number of Instructional Days: 5

RESOURCES		
PRINT	**TRANSPARENCIES**	**TECHNOLOGY**
• **Beyond Literature,** Cross-Curricular Connection: Geography, p. 57 ▲ ■		• **Interest Grabber Video,** Tape 5 ● ▲ ■
• **Selection Support Workbook:** ● ▲ ■ Literary Analysis, p. 228 Reading Strategy, p. 227 Build Vocabulary, p. 225	• **Literary Analysis and Reading Transparencies,** pp. 113 and 114 ● ▲ ■	
• **Adapted Reader's Companion** ● • **Reader's Companion** ●		• **Listening to Literature** ● ▲ ■ Audiocassettes, Side 29 Audio CDs, CD 20
• **English Learner's Companion** ● ▲ • **Literatura en español** ● ▲ • **Literary Analysis for Enrichment** ■	• **Fine Art Transparencies Volume 1,** Art Transparency 17 ● ▲ ■	
• **Formal Assessment:** Selection Test, pp. 205–207 ● ▲ ■ • **Open Book Test,** pp. 169–171 ● ▲ ■ • PRENTICE HALL ASSESSMENT SYSTEM ● ▲ ■	• PRENTICE HALL ASSESSMENT SYSTEM ● ▲ ■ Skills Practice Answers and Explanations on Transparencies	• **Test Bank Software** ● ▲ ■ • **Got It! Assessment Videotapes,** Tape 5 ● ▲
• **Selection Support Workbook:** ● ▲ ■ Build Grammar Skills, p. 226 • **Writing and Grammar,** Gold Level ● ▲ ■ • **Extension Activities,** p. 55 ● ▲ ■	• **Daily Language Practice Transparencies** ● ▲	• **Writing and Grammar iText CD-ROM** ● ▲ ■ ***Take It to the Net*** www.phschool.com

BLOCK SCHEDULING: Use one 90-minute class period to preteach the selection and have students read it. Use a second 90-minute class period to assess students' mastery of skills and have them complete one of the Extension Activities.

PRETEACH

Step-by-Step Teaching Guide for pp. 978–979

Motivation

Invite students to describe action or adventure stories they have seen in movies or on television in which a hero has to outwit monsters, villains, and other opponents far more powerful than he or she. Encourage students to tell what qualities help these heroes come out on top. Then, tell students that they will be reading one of the earliest and most enduring adventure stories of all time: Homer's *Odyssey.*

Interest Grabber Video

As an alternative, play "The Voyage of Odysseus" on tape 5 to engage student interest.

1 Background

History

The siege of Troy finally ended when the Greeks pretended to depart, leaving a giant wooden horse behind. Thinking that they had won the war, the Trojans dragged the horse inside the walls of their city. That night, Greek warriors who had hidden within the hollow horse crept out and opened the city gates to their waiting comrades, who then conquered the city.

Prepare to Read

from the Odyssey, Part 1

"Circe Meanwhile had gone her Ways . . . ," 1924, William Russell Flint, New York Public Library

Take It to the Net

Visit www.phschool.com for interactive activities and instruction related to the *Odyssey*, including

- background
- graphic organizers
- literary elements
- reading strategies

Preview

Connecting to the Literature

Whether you are journeying across town or to another country, it sometimes seems to take forever to reach your destination. Just getting there can be quite an adventure! In the *Odyssey*, you will follow a journey that took far longer than expected and experience the amazing adventures that took place along the way.

1 Background

The *Odyssey* describes what happened to the Greek hero Odysseus on his way home after the Trojan War. According to legend, the Trojan War was sparked when Paris, son of the king of Troy, ran off with Helen, the most beautiful woman in the world and the wife of Menelaus of Sparta. A Greek force attacked Troy (in modern-day Turkey) to recapture her and was finally victorious after ten years of fighting.

TEACHING RESOURCES

The following resources can be used to enrich or extend the instruction for pp. 978–979.

Motivation

Interest Grabber Videotape, Tape 5

Background

Beyond Literature, p. 57

Take It to the Net

Visit www.phschool.com background and hotlinks for the *Odyssey.*

Literary Analysis

Literary Analysis and Reading Transparencies, pp. 113–114

Reading

Selection Support: Literary Analysis, p. 228; Reading Strategy, p. 227

BLOCK SCHEDULING: Resources marked with this symbol provide varied instruction during 90-minute blocks.

❷ Literary Analysis

The Epic Hero

An epic is a long poem about the adventures of gods or heroes. The epic's central character, its **epic hero,** is a larger-than-life figure from history or legend. The hero undertakes a dangerous voyage, demonstrating traits—such as courage, loyalty, and honor—that are valued by the society in which the epic originates. In this passage, Odysseus shows his bravery and leadership:

> Now, by the gods, I drove my big hand spike
> deep in the embers, charring it again,
> and cheered my men along with battle talk
> to keep their courage up; no quitting now.

As you read, use a chart like the one shown to record traits or actions that prove Odysseus to be an epic hero.

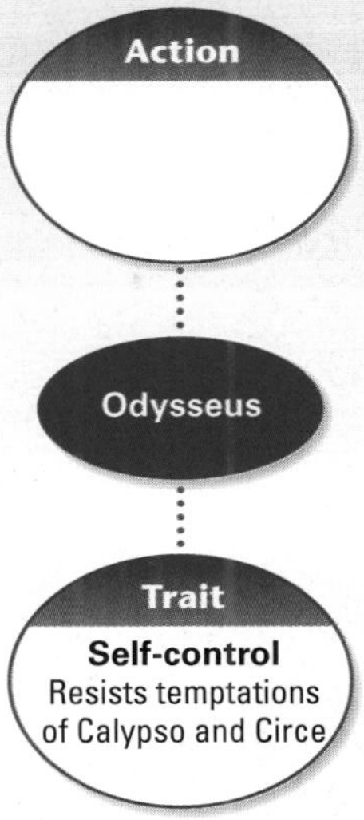

Connecting Literary Elements

At the center of every epic is a **conflict**—a struggle between opposing forces. Conflicts may occur between characters, between a character and nature, or within a character's mind. In an epic, conflicts often put the traits of the epic hero on display. In the *Odyssey,* notice that conflicts arise as the hero confronts his enemies and as he wrestles with his own thoughts.

❸ Reading Strategy

Reading in Sentences

To get the most out of a story told in verse, ignore the line breaks and **read in sentences.** Although the line breaks reveal the structure of the verse, they may make it harder for you to follow the meaning. Read the *Odyssey* the same way you might read a magazine article or a novel: Let the words flow to you in complete sentences. In some cases, you may need to rephrase the sentences in your own words to make the meaning clearer.

Vocabulary Development

plundered (plun´ dərd) *v.* took goods by force; looted (p. 981)

squall (skwôl) *n.* brief, violent storm (p. 984)

dispatched (di spacht´) *v.* finished quickly (p. 990)

mammoth (mam´ əth) *adj.* enormous (p. 993)

titanic (tī tan´ ik) *adj.* of great size or strength (p. 997)

assuage (ə swāj´) *v.* calm; pacify (p. 1000)

bereft (bi reft´) *adj.* deprived (p. 1003)

ardor (är´ dər) *n.* passion; enthusiasm (p. 1007)

insidious (in sid´ ē əs) *adj.* characterized by craftiness and betrayal (p. 1011)

❷ Literary Analysis

The Epic Hero

- Explain that the notion of hero, and the traits associated with heroism, can change across time and across cultures.
- Before reading the selection, ask students what words and phrases they associate with the word *hero.* You may wish to display the Epic Hero transparency in **Literary Analysis and Reading Transparencies,** p. 114, to show students how to complete a cluster diagram.
- Ask students to use the cluster diagram while reading the selection to record the traits that make Odysseus an epic hero.

❸ Reading Strategy

Reading in Sentences

- In epic poetry, there is a dynamic tension between meaning and structure. Rereading sections of the poem with different goals in mind can help students grasp both aspects.
- Ask students to read a short section of the poem, instructing them to read in sentences. Then, ask them to paraphrase in writing the narrative action in their own words.
- When the meaning of the passage is clear, have a volunteer read the passage aloud to the class. Point out how, now that meaning is clear, students can focus on how the language and structure underscore the drama of the narrative.

Vocabulary Development

- Pronounce each vocabulary word for students, and read the definitions as a class. Have students identify any words with which they are already familiar.

CUSTOMIZE INSTRUCTION FOR UNIVERSAL ACCESS

For Special Needs Students	For Less Proficient Readers	For English Learners
Have students read the adapted version of the Cyclops episode in the **Adapted Reader's Companion.** This version provides basic-level instruction in an interactive format with questions and write-on lines. Completing the adapted version will prepare students to read the selection in the Student Edition.	Have students read the episode in the **Reader's Companion.** This version provides basic-level instruction in an interactive format with questions and write-on lines. After students finish the selection in **Reader's Companion,** have them complete the questions and activities in the Student Edition.	Have students read the adapted version of the episode in the **English Learner's Companion.** This version provides basic-level instruction in an interactive format with questions and write-on lines. Completing the adapted version will prepare students to read the selection in the Student Edition.

E-Teach

Visit E-Teach at www.phschool.com for teachers' essays on how to teach, with questions and answers.

TEACH

Step-by-Step Teaching Guide for pp. 981–1017

CUSTOMIZE INSTRUCTION
For Visual Learners

The *Odyssey* is an epic journey, told in a language that might sometimes seem distant or difficult for modern readers. Some sense of geography and landscape can help students make better sense of the descriptive language and keep track of the action. Students can follow the story's progress with the help of the map on page 1013, which shows both real and imaginary settings for events in the *Odyssey.*

1 About the Selection

The *Odyssey* is a classic adventure story. It combines realistic elements of historical events with wildly imagined scenes of fantastic places and creatures. The epic also includes skillful characterizations. Odysseus, for example, represents the model epic hero: A leader of courage, daring and wit, he pursues his goal—to return home after many years of war—in the face of many setbacks. However, he has human traits and failings that make him seem like a real person: He enjoys life, is too curious for his own good, is foolishly cocky at times, and is clever to the point of being tricky. Some critics have interpreted the *Odyssey* as representing an individual's journey through life and the search for self-knowledge.

2 Background

Art

Ulysses Deriding Polyphemus, by J. M. W. Turner

Turner began as a watercolor painter, influenced by the baroque landscape paintings of the seventeenth century. Use this question for discussion:

In this painting, the characters are difficult to see in the swirling mist and half-light. What mood does the play of light and dark in the painting lend to the story?

Answer: The variation of light and darkness creates a mood of otherworldliness, mystery, and danger.

1

Ulysses Deriding Polyphemus, 1819, J.M.W. Turner, The National Gallery, London

3 ▲ **Critical Viewing** Do the images in this painting evoke feelings of hope or doom? **[Analyze]**

2 *from the* Odyssey

Homer Translated by Robert Fitzgerald

TEACHING RESOURCES

The following resources can be used to enrich or extend the instruction for pp. 981–1017.

Literary Analysis

- **Selection Support:** Literary Analysis, p. 228

Reading

- **Reader's Companion**
- **English Learner's Companion**
- **Listening to Literature Audiocassettes,** Side 29 ■
- **Listening to Literature Audio CDs,** CD 20 ■

Extension

- **Fine Art Transparencies,** Volume 1, Art Transparency 17 (Display this transparency to more closely analyze the painting shown on p. 980.)

■ **BLOCK SCHEDULING:** Resources marked with this symbol provide varied instruction during 90-minute blocks.

PART 1

The Adventures of Odysseus

In the opening verses, Homer addresses the muse of epic poetry. He asks her help in telling the tale of Odysseus.

Sing in me, Muse,[1] and through me tell the story
of that man skilled in all ways of contending,
the wanderer, harried for years on end,
after he plundered the stronghold
on the proud height of Troy.[2]
He saw the townlands
and learned the minds of many distant men,
and weathered many bitter nights and days
in his deep heart at sea, while he fought only
to save his life, to bring his shipmates home.
But not by will nor valor could he save them,
for their own recklessness destroyed them all—
children and fools, they killed and feasted on
the cattle of Lord Helios,[3] the Sun,
and he who moves all day through heaven
took from their eyes the dawn of their return.
Of these adventures, Muse, daughter of Zeus,[4]
tell us in our time, lift the great song again.

1. **Muse** (myo͞oz) any one of the nine goddesses of the arts, literature, and the sciences; the spirit that is thought to inspire a poet or other artist.

plundered (plun′ dərd) *v.* took goods by force; looted

2. **Troy** (troi) city in northwest Asia Minor; site of the Trojan War.

3. **Helios** (hē′ lē äs′) sun god.

4. **Zeus** (zo͞os) king of the gods.

Note: In translating the *Odyssey*, Fitzgerald spelled Greek names to suggest the sound of the original Greek. In these excerpts, more familiar spellings have been used. For example, Fitzgerald's "Kirkê," "Kyklops," and "Seirênês" are spelled here as "Circe," "Cyclops," and "Sirens."

5 **Reading Check**

Which act led to an epic journey?

3 ▶Critical Viewing

Possible answer: The rising sun suggests a sense of hope after a narrow escape from the Cyclops.

4 Literary Analysis

The Epic Hero

- Ask students what qualities of Odysseus mark him as a hero. Possible responses: Odysseus is determined (he "weathered many bitter days and nights . . . at sea"), has a "deep heart," and fought only for the noble purposes of saving his own life and bringing "his shipmates home."
- Discuss the phrase "skilled in all ways of contending." This means, in essence, "versatile"—another heroic trait, one that will be tested all through the Odyssey.

5 Reading Check

Answer: The journey begins after Odysseus leads the plunder of Troy.

CUSTOMIZE INSTRUCTION FOR UNIVERSAL ACCESS

For Less Proficient Readers	For Advanced Readers
Point out that this page describes events that will be recounted during the telling of the epic. Ask students to summarize the page, then tell what they can infer from it.	Point out to students that reading the legends, epics, myths, and folk literature of a culture will help them understand a culture. The *Odyssey* provides historical background as well as cultural insights. Encourage students to keep a log of such cultural insights. Discuss students' responses at the end of each day's reading.

❻ Literary Analysis

The Epic Hero

- Ask students which qualities cited in this passage suggest that Odysseus is a hero.
  Answer: Odysseus is famous for his guile, which makes him effective in both peace and war.
- You may wish to tell students that the plan for the Trojan horse—the tactic that ended the long war—was devised by Odysseus.

CHARACTERS

Alcinous (al sin′ ō əs)—king of the Phaeacians, to whom Odysseus tells his story

Odysseus (ō dis′ ē əs)—king of Ithaca

Calypso (kə lip′ sō)—sea goddess who loved Odysseus

Circe (sʉr′ sē)—enchantress who helped Odysseus

Zeus (zo͞os)—king of the gods

Apollo (ə päl′ ō)—god of music, poetry, prophecy, and medicine

Agamemnon (ag′ ə mem′ nän′)—king and leader of Greek forces

Poseidon (pō sī′ dən)—god of sea, earthquakes, horses, and storms at sea

Athena (ə thē′ nə)—goddess of wisdom, skills, and warfare

Polyphemus (päl′ i fē′ məs)—the Cyclops who imprisoned Odysseus

Laertes (lā ʉr′ tēz′)—Odysseus' father

Cronus (krō′ nəs)—Titan ruler of the universe; father of Zeus

Perimedes (per′ ə mē′ dēz)—member of Odysseus' crew

Eurylochus (yo͞o ril′ ə kəs)—another member of the crew

Tiresias (tī rē′ sē əs)—blind prophet who advised Odysseus

Persephone (pər sef′ ə nē)—wife of Hades

Telemachus (tə lem′ ə kəs)—Odysseus and Penelope's son

Sirens (sī′ rənz)—creatures whose songs lure sailors to their deaths

Scylla (sil′ ə)—sea monster of gray rock

Charybdis (kə rib′ dis)—enormous and dangerous whirlpool

Lampetia (lam pē′ shə)—nymph

Hermes (hʉr′ mēz′)—herald and messenger of the gods

Eumaeus (yo͞o me′ əs)—old swineherd and friend of Odysseus

Antinous (an tin′ ō əs)—leader among the suitors

Eurynome (yo͞o rin′ ə mē)—housekeeper for Penelope

Penelope (pə nel′ ə pē)—Odysseus' wife

Eurymachus (yo͞o ri′ mə kəs)—suitor

Amphinomus (am fin′ ə məs)—suitor

Sailing from Troy

Ten years after the Trojan War, Odysseus departs from the goddess Calypso's island. He arrives in Phaeacia, ruled by Alcinous. Alcinous offers a ship to Odysseus and asks him to tell of his adventures.

"I am Laertes'[5] son, Odysseus.
Men hold me
6 formidable for guile[6] in peace and war:
this fame has gone abroad to the sky's rim.
7 My home is on the peaked sea-mark of Ithaca[7]
under Mount Neion's wind-blown robe of leaves,
in sight of other islands—Dulichium,
Same, wooded Zacynthus—Ithaca
being most lofty in that coastal sea,
and northwest, while the rest lie east and south.
A rocky isle, but good for a boy's training;
I shall not see on earth a place more dear,
though I have been detained long by Calypso,[8]
loveliest among goddesses, who held me
in her smooth caves, to be her heart's delight,
as Circe of Aeaea,[9] the enchantress,
desired me, and detained me in her hall.
But in my heart I never gave consent.
8 Where shall a man find sweetness to surpass
his own home and his parents? In far lands
he shall not, though he find a house of gold.

What of my sailing, then, from Troy?
What of those years
of rough adventure, weathered under Zeus?
The wind that carried west from Ilium[10]
brought me to Ismarus, on the far shore,
a strongpoint on the coast of Cicones.[11]
I stormed that place and killed the men who fought.
Plunder we took, and we enslaved the women,
to make division, equal shares to all—
but on the spot I told them: 'Back, and quickly!
Out to sea again!' My men were mutinous,[12]
fools, on stores of wine. Sheep after sheep
they butchered by the surf, and shambling cattle,

5. Laertes (lā ur´ tēz´)

6. guile (gīl) *n.* craftiness; cunning.

7. Ithaca (ith´ ə kə) island off the west coast of Greece.

Reading Strategy
Reading in Sentences
Why do these opening lines sound more natural when you ignore the line breaks?

8. Calypso (kə lip´ sō)

9. Circe (sur´ sē) **of Aeaea** (ē´ ē ə)

10. Ilium (il ē əm) Troy.

11. Cicones (si kō´ nēz)

12. mutinous (myōōt´ ən əs) *adj.* rebellious.

9 **✓Reading Check**
Who has asked Odysseus to tell his tale?

7 Reading Strategy

Reading in Sentences

- Point out that line breaks can interrupt the flow of meaning, as when sentences end in the middle of a line or flow from one line to the next.
- Ask students the Reading Strategy question on p. 983: Why do these opening lines sound more natural when you ignore the line breaks?
  Answer: The lines sound more natural without the artificial breaks forced by the poetic structure: "Men hold me formidable for guile in peace and war. This fame has gone abroad to the sky's rim."

8 Critical Thinking

Interpret

- Point out that the desire to return home drives all of the action in the *Odyssey.*
- Explain that Calypso and Circe are two enchantresses. Calypso is a sea nymph who holds Odysseus in her spell for seven years. Circe turns Odysseus' men into pigs.
- Ask students how Odysseus feels about his home on Ithaca. Why did he stay with Calypso and Circe, if he was so eager to return to Ithaca?
  Answer: Odysseus is eager to return to his home. He says that he "never gave consent" to stay with Calypso or Circe, indicating that he was under a spell and not in control of his own actions.

9 ✓Reading Check

Answer: Alcinous, king of the Phaeacians, asks Odysseus to tell his story.

10 Critical Thinking

Draw Conclusions

- Ask students what mistakes Odysseus and his men made on Ismarus.
  Possible answers: Odysseus' men were greedy and mutinous, which exposed them to the army of the Cicones. Students may also say that Odysseus should have been more authoritative with his men.
- Ask students what price the men pay for this mistake.
  Answer: They had to fight their way back to the ships, losing many men.

11 Reading Strategy

Reading in Sentences

- Ask students periodically to read sentences aloud, pausing only at the commas, periods, and other punctuation. They can break long, difficult sentences into two by treating a dash or semicolon as the start of a new sentence.
- Ask students the Reading Strategy question on p. 985: Read lines 94–98 as a complete sentence. How does doing so help your understanding of the passage?
  Answer: Ignoring the line breaks helps make the action clearer by making it more conversational and less formal.

12 Literary Analysis

The Epic Hero

- Odysseus displays several admirable qualities in the encounter with the Lotus-Eaters. Episodes like this one can illustrate which traits the ancient Greeks valued.
- Ask students the Literary Analysis question on p. 985: Which characteristics of a hero and leader does Odysseus show in the episode with the Lotus-Eaters?
  Possible responses: Odysseus displays wisdom when he sends out a scouting party, rather than putting all of his men at risk. When Odysseus realizes the danger of the Lotus, he acts decisively, ordering his ships to sail immediately. He also shows leadership in explaining to his men why they must leave.

feasting,—while fugitives went inland, running
to call to arms the main force of Cicones.
This was an army, trained to fight on horseback
or, where the ground required, on foot. They came
with dawn over that terrain like the leaves
and blades of spring. So doom appeared to us,
dark word of Zeus for us, our evil days.
My men stood up and made a fight of it—
backed on the ships, with lances kept in play,
from bright morning through the blaze of noon
holding our beach, although so far outnumbered;
but when the sun passed toward unyoking time,
then the Achaeans,[13] one by one, gave way.
Six benches were left empty in every ship
that evening when we pulled away from death.
10
And this new grief we bore with us to sea:
our precious lives we had, but not our friends.
No ship made sail next day until some shipmate
had raised a cry, three times, for each poor ghost
unfleshed by the Cicones on that field.

The Lotus-Eaters

Now Zeus the lord of cloud roused in the north
a storm against the ships, and driving veils
of squall moved down like night on land and sea.
The bows went plunging at the gust; sails
cracked and lashed out strips in the big wind.
We saw death in that fury, dropped the yards,
unshipped the oars, and pulled for the nearest lee:[14]
then two long days and nights we lay offshore
worn out and sick at heart, tasting our grief,
until a third Dawn came with ringlets shining.
Then we put up our masts, hauled sail, and rested,
letting the steersmen and the breeze take over.

I might have made it safely home, that time,
but as I came round Malea the current
took me out to sea, and from the north
a fresh gale drove me on, past Cythera.
Nine days I drifted on the teeming sea
before dangerous high winds. Upon the tenth
we came to the coastline of the Lotus-Eaters,
who live upon that flower. We landed there

13. Achaeans (ə kē´ ənz) Greeks; here, Odysseus' men.

squall (skwôl) *n.* brief, violent storm

14. lee (lē) *n.* area sheltered from the wind.

ENRICHMENT: Science Connection

Navigation

In this epic poem, Odysseus captains a ship that travels throughout the Mediterranean. In his time, the navigators who guided ships relied on astronomical features, such as the position of the sun, moon, and stars and constellations, as well as on their detailed knowledge of the coasts along which they sailed.

Today, navigators make use of sophisticated technology to guide ships and aircraft. Global Positioning System (GPS) equipment uses links to multiple satellites to establish a position on Earth with almost pinpoint accuracy. Some commercial GPS units are small enough to fit in a shirt pocket.

Encourage students who are interested in navigation to find out more about GPS and other modern navigational equipment. Some students may wish to report on the history of navigation, focusing on the development of sextants, chronometers, and other essential devices.

to take on water. All ships' companies
mustered alongside for the mid-day meal.
Then I sent out two picked men and a runner
to learn what race of men that land sustained.
They fell in, soon enough, with Lotus-Eaters,
who showed no will to do us harm, only
11 offering the sweet Lotus to our friends—
but those who ate this honeyed plant, the Lotus,
never cared to report, nor to return:
they longed to stay forever, browsing on
that native bloom, forgetful of their homeland.
I drove them, all three wailing, to the ships,
tied them down under their rowing benches,
12 and called the rest: 'All hands aboard;
come, clear the beach and no one taste
the Lotus, or you lose your hope of home.'
Filing in to their places by the rowlocks
my oarsmen dipped their long oars in the surf,
and we moved out again on our sea faring.

Reading Strategy

Reading in Sentences Read lines 94–98 as a complete sentence. How does doing so help your understanding of the passage?

Literary Analysis

The Epic Hero Which characteristics of a hero and leader does Odysseus show in the episode with the Lotus-Eaters?

Review and Assess

Thinking About the Selection

1. **Respond:** What is your first impression of Odysseus? Which of his qualities do you admire?
2. **(a) Recall:** Describe the events on Ismarus.
   (b) Interpret: What lessons can be learned from the defeat of Odysseus and his men at Ismarus?
3. **(a) Recall:** Where is Odysseus' home? **(b) Interpret:** What significant role does his home play in Odysseus' epic journey?
4. **(a) Recall:** How do Calypso and Circe keep Odysseus from reaching home? **(b) Interpret:** What were Odysseus' feelings when he was with Calypso and Circe?
5. **(a) Recall:** What happens to the men who eat the Lotus?
   (b) Infer: What does this episode suggest about the main problem that Odysseus has with his men? **(c) Speculate:** What do you think about the way Odysseus responds to the three men who long to stay with the Lotus-Eaters?
6. **Compare and Contrast:** In what ways is the world of the *Odyssey* similar to today's world? In what ways is it different?
7. **Take a Position:** Do you admire Odysseus? Why or why not?

Answers for p. 985

Review and Assess

1. Possible response: Students might admire the determination that Odysseus maintained over his years-long voyage home and the values that motivate him to return.
2. **(a)** After an initial military success against a limited force, the Greeks become distracted by their loot. They are attacked by a large force of Cicones and must fight desperately to return to the ships, losing many men along the way. **(b)** The greediness, gluttony, and intoxication of his men lead many of them to their doom. Odysseus learns the need for complete authority over his men.
3. **(a)** Ithaca **(b)** Odysseus' entire journey is motivated by his desire to return to Ithaca.
4. **(a)** Calypso and Circe keep Odysseus from leaving through enchantment. **(b)** Though Odysseus does acknowledge the pleasant aspects of his captivity, he emphasizes that these periods were a poor substitute for his beloved homeland and wife and family.
5. **(a)** The men are lulled into a state of calm forgetfulness in which they no longer want to return home. **(b)** Odysseus apparently has trouble instilling his own sense of self-control and discipline into his men.
   (c) Possible response: Odysseus had no choice but to force the men back on the ship; their skills were needed on board to help everyone get home safely.
6. Both worlds have many temptations that distract people from doing what they should. The supernatural temptations faced by Odysseus are different from those people encounter today.

continued

Answers continued

7. Odysseus has shortcomings as a leader (as at Ismarus), but on the whole students will probably admire his courage, his dedication and determination, his leadership qualities (as in the episode with the Lotus-Eaters), and the strong value he places on his home and family.

⓭ Literary Analysis

The Epic Hero and Conflict

- Often, the conflicts in the *Odyssey* are signaled before they actually occur. Suggest that students list these warnings as they read.
- Ask students the Literary Analysis question on p. 986: Based on Odysseus' description of Cyclopes, what conflicts might arise for Odysseus and his men?
Possible responses: The Cyclopes are "giants" and "louts" "without a law to bless them," and deal out "rough justice." They are uncivilized, as illustrated by their lack of agriculture or group decision making. It seems that Odysseus and his men may have to fight if they encounter a Cyclops.

⓮ Reading Strategy

Reading in Sentences

- Tell students that they may find it helpful to paraphrase a passage where meaning is otherwise difficult to decipher.
- Have students respond to the Reading Strategy task on p. 986: Rephrase the description of the Cyclops in lines 130–133 using your own words.
Possible response: "The Cyclops was huge and uncivilized. In size and attitude, he was like a wild, solitary mountain."

The Cyclops

In the next land we found were Cyclopes,[15]
giants, louts, without a law to bless them.
In ignorance leaving the fruitage of the earth in mystery
to the immortal gods, they neither plow
nor sow by hand, nor till the ground, though grain—
⓭ wild wheat and barley—grows untended, and
wine-grapes, in clusters, ripen in heaven's rains.
Cyclopes have no muster and no meeting,
no consultation or old tribal ways,
but each one dwells in his own mountain cave
dealing out rough justice to wife and child,
indifferent to what the others do. . . .

As we rowed on, and nearer to the mainland,
at one end of the bay, we saw a cavern
yawning above the water, screened with laurel,
and many rams and goats about the place
inside a sheepfold—made from slabs of stone
earthfast between tall trunks of pine and rugged
towering oak trees.
A prodigious[16] man
slept in this cave alone, and took his flocks
to graze afield—remote from all companions,
knowing none but savage ways, a brute
⓮ so huge, he seemed no man at all of those
who eat good wheaten bread; but he seemed rather
a shaggy mountain reared in solitude.
We beached there, and I told the crew
to stand by and keep watch over the ship:
as for myself I took my twelve best fighters
and went ahead. I had a goatskin full
of that sweet liquor that Euanthes' son,
Maron, had given me. He kept Apollo's[17]
holy grove at Ismarus; for kindness
we showed him there, and showed his wife and child,
he gave me seven shining golden talents[18]
perfectly formed, a solid silver winebowl,
and then this liquor—twelve two-handled jars
of brandy, pure and fiery. Not a slave
in Maron's household knew this drink; only
he, his wife and the storeroom mistress knew;
and they would put one cupful—ruby-colored,
honey-smooth—in twenty more of water,

15. **Cyclopes** (sī klō′ pēz′) *n.* plural form of **Cyclops** (sī′ kläps′), a race of giants with one eye in the middle of the forehead.

Literary Analysis
The Epic Hero and Conflict Based on Odysseus' description of Cyclopes, what conflicts might arise for Odysseus and his men?

16. **prodigious** (prō dij′ əs) *adj.* enormous.

Reading Strategy
Reading in Sentences Rephrase the description of the Cyclops in lines 130–133, using your own words.

17. **Apollo** (ə päl′ ō) god of music, poetry, prophecy, and medicine.

18. **talents** units of money in ancient Greece.

ENRICHMENT: Art Connection

Ulysses Deriding Polyphemus

After reading "The Cyclops" episode of the *Odyssey,* display Transparency 17, a detail from *Ulysses Deriding Polyphemus* (the full painting is on p. 980). Ask students to point out how the picture is described by its title. In what way is the picture an accurate representation of the encounter between Odysseus (called Ulysses in some versions of the epic) and Polyphemus? What in the picture suggests ridicule? What adds to the dramatic tone? How does Turner's style (including his use of color and his rendering of motion and perspective) support this effect? Then, ask students to give specific examples from the text to support or refute the opinion that this work of art is an appropriate representation of the story. Encourage students to go beyond fact and plot by showing where Homer evokes ridicule and drama.

but still the sweet scent hovered like a fume
over the winebowl. No man turned away
when cups of this came round.

A wineskin full
I brought along, and victuals[19] in a bag,
for in my bones I knew some towering brute
would be upon us soon—all outward power,
a wild man, ignorant of civility.

We climbed, then, briskly to the cave. But Cyclops
had gone afield, to pasture his fat sheep,
so we looked round at everything inside:
a drying rack that sagged with cheeses, pens
crowded with lambs and kids,[20] each in its class:
firstlings apart from middlings, and the 'dewdrops,'

19. victuals (vit′ əls) *n.* food or other provisions.

20. kids *n.* young goats.

15 Reading Check
What does Odysseus bring along when he goes to inspect the Cyclops' cave?

16 ◀ Critical Viewing How does this image of Apollo compare with your impressions of the other gods Odysseus has encountered? **[Compare and Contrast]**

15 Reading Check
Answer: Odysseus brings a bag of food and a wineskin to the cave.

16 ▶ Critical Viewing
Answer: The calm dignity of this image of Apollo contrasts with the seductiveness of Calypso and the stormy wrath of Zeus, gods who have been mentioned earlier.

⓱ Literary Analysis

The Epic Hero

- In this passage, Odysseus shows one of the qualities that gets him into trouble. Have students identify that flaw.
  Answer: Odysseus' curiosity leads him to disregard good advice. He knows it would be wise to seize the food and leave, but he is too curious to see the "cave man."
- Ask students if Odysseus is aware of this character trait in himself.
  Possible response: Odysseus seems to be aware of his overactive curiosity because he explains that he knew his men's idea was sound.

⓲ Literary Analysis

The Epic Hero

- Point out to students that at several points in this tale, Odysseus overcomes his fear to act in a coolheaded fashion.
- Ask students the first Literary Analysis question on p. 989: What quality of an epic hero does Odysseus demonstrate by addressing the mighty man?
  Answer: Despite the dread he and his men feel, Odysseus finds the courage to address the Cyclops in a strong voice and ask for his assistance.

or newborn lambkins, penned apart from both.
And vessels full of whey[21] were brimming there—
bowls of earthenware and pails for milking.
My men came pressing round me, pleading:

'Why not
take these cheeses, get them stowed, come back,
throw open all the pens, and make a run for it?
We'll drive the kids and lambs aboard. We say
put out again on good salt water!'

⓱

Ah,
how sound that was! Yet I refused. I wished
to see the cave man, what he had to offer—
no pretty sight, it turned out, for my friends.
We lit a fire, burnt an offering,
and took some cheese to eat; then sat in silence
around the embers, waiting. When he came
he had a load of dry boughs[22] on his shoulder
to stoke his fire at suppertime. He dumped it
with a great crash into that hollow cave,
and we all scattered fast to the far wall.
Then over the broad cavern floor he ushered
the ewes he meant to milk. He left his rams
and he-goats in the yard outside, and swung
high overhead a slab of solid rock
to close the cave. Two dozen four-wheeled wagons,
with heaving wagon teams, could not have stirred
the tonnage of that rock from where he wedged it
over the doorsill. Next he took his seat
and milked his bleating ewes. A practiced job
he made of it, giving each ewe her suckling;
thickened his milk, then, into curds and whey,
sieved out the curds to drip in withy[23] baskets,
and poured the whey to stand in bowls
cooling until he drank it for his supper.
When all these chores were done, he poked the fire,
heaping on brushwood. In the glare he saw us.

'Strangers,' he said, 'who are you? And where from?
What brings you here by seaways—a fair traffic?
Or are you wandering rogues, who cast your lives
like dice, and ravage other folk by sea?'

21. **whey** (hwā) *n.* thin, watery part of milk separated from the thicker curds.

22. **boughs** (bouz) *n.* tree branches.

23. **withy** (with´ ē) *adj.* made from tough, flexible twigs.

ENRICHMENT: Social Studies Connection

The Seeds of Democracy

The *Odyssey* takes place during the years immediately following the Trojan War. According to tradition, the Helladic people of southern Greece, whom Homer called the Achaeans and whom historians consider to be the earliest Greeks, fought against Troy in Asia Minor. Mycenae was the Achaeans' largest city, and Agamemnon, the legendary king of Mycenae, was the richest and most powerful ruler on the mainland of Greece. It was he who is said to have led the Achaeans against the Trojans.

By 750 B.C., Greece had become overpopulated and many people emigrated to form Greek colonies in the Black Sea, Sicily and southern Italy, France, and Spain. The Greek colonies traded with their home cities, sending great wealth to Greece. However, it was the aristocrats who became rich, while the poor became discontented. It may have been this imbalance that first led to the idea of democratic government, which took form much later in Greek history.

18

We felt a pressure on our hearts, in dread
of that deep rumble and that mighty man.
But all the same I spoke up in reply:

'We are from Troy, Achaeans, blown off course
by shifting gales on the Great South Sea;
homeward bound, but taking routes and ways
uncommon; so the will of Zeus would have it.
We served under Agamemnon,[24] son of Atreus—
the whole world knows what city

19

he laid waste, what armies he destroyed.
It was our luck to come here; here we stand,
beholden for your help, or any gifts
you give—as custom is to honor strangers.
We would entreat you, great Sir, have a care
for the gods' courtesy; Zeus will avenge
the unoffending guest.'

He answered this
from his brute chest, unmoved:

'You are a ninny,
or else you come from the other end of nowhere,
telling me, mind the gods! We Cyclopes
care not a whistle for your thundering Zeus

20

or all the gods in bliss; we have more force by far.
I would not let you go for fear of Zeus—
you or your friends—unless I had a whim[25] to.
Tell me, where was it, now, you left your ship—
around the point, or down the shore, I wonder?'

He thought he'd find out, but I saw through this,
and answered with a ready lie:

'My ship?
Poseidon[26] Lord, who sets the earth a-tremble,
broke it up on the rocks at your land's end.
A wind from seaward served him, drove us there.
We are survivors, these good men and I.'

Neither reply nor pity came from him,
but in one stride he clutched at my companions
and caught two in his hands like squirming puppies
to beat their brains out, spattering the floor.
Then he dismembered them and made his meal,
gaping and crunching like a mountain lion—
everything: innards, flesh, and marrow bones.

Literary Analysis
The Epic Hero Which quality of an epic hero does Odysseus demonstrate by addressing the mighty man?

24. Agamemnon (ag′ ə mem′ nän′) king who led the Greek army during the Trojan War.

Literary Analysis
The Epic Hero and Conflict What conflict is revealed in lines 217–223?

25. whim (hwim) *n.* sudden thought or wish to do something.

26. Poseidon (pō sī′ dən) god of the sea, earthquakes, horses, and storms at sea.

21 **Reading Check**
What does Odysseus tell Cyclops happened to their ship?

19 Literary Analysis
The Epic Hero

- Ask students what can be learned from Odysseus' speech about conduct and respect for the gods.
  Answer: Odysseus asserts that his journey's wayward path has been willed by Zeus; he then asks for the Cyclops' hospitality both as a matter of custom and out of observance of the "gods' courtesy."
- Explain to students that it was customary in ancient Greece to offer hospitality to any guest—stranger or friend—who came to your door. Because the gods could assume human form, you never knew if the visitor was a mortal or a god. The safest course was to assume that any visitor was a god in disguise, so lavish generosity and hospitality were appropriate.

20 Literary Analysis
The Epic Hero and Conflict

- Ask students the second Literary Analysis question on p. 989: What conflict is revealed in lines 217–223?
  Answer: Odysseus and his men respect and fear the gods. The Cyclops makes fun of this, saying that the Cyclopes are stronger and more powerful even than Zeus, the supreme Greek god.
- Point out to students the element of foreshadowing here. Odysseus can expect that the Cyclopes will not "play fair," that is, they will not behave in any familiar or expected ways. This will lead to conflict.

21 Reading Check

Answer: Odysseus says that his ship has broken up on the rocks. He lies because he thinks that Cyclops may want to destroy his ship.

22 Reading Strategy

Reading in Sentences

- Tell students that ignoring line breaks and reading in sentences improves their understanding in action scenes.
- Have students respond to the Reading Strategy task on p. 990: Reread lines 244–250 in complete sentences, ignoring the line breaks, to help you understand the passage.
  Answer: "My heart beat high now at the chance of action, and drawing the sharp sword from my hip I went along his flank to stab him where the midriff holds the liver. I had touched the spot when sudden fear stayed me. If I killed him we perished there as well, for we could never move his ponderous doorway slab aside."

23 Literary Analysis

The Epic Hero

- After students have reread lines 244–250, ask them what heroic quality Odysseus shows in this passage.
  Answer: Odysseus is farsighted. On the brink of killing the Cyclops, he is able to stop himself and think of the consequences: With the Cyclops dead, they would be trapped permanently by the heavy doorway slab.
- Then, ask students the Literary Analysis question on p. 990: What heroic qualities does Odysseus reveal as he plots against the Cyclops?
  Answer: Odysseus is resourceful, creative, and brave. He also joins his men in the most dangerous tasks and is apparently a good judge of his men's abilities and characters.

We cried aloud, lifting our hands to Zeus,
powerless, looking on at this, appalled;
but Cyclops went on filling up his belly
with manflesh and great gulps of whey,
then lay down like a mast among his sheep.
22 My heart beat high now at the chance of action,
and drawing the sharp sword from my hip I went
along his flank to stab him where the midriff
holds the liver. I had touched the spot
when sudden fear stayed me: if I killed him
we perished there as well, for we could never
move his ponderous doorway slab aside.
So we were left to groan and wait for morning.

When the young Dawn with fingertips of rose
lit up the world, the Cyclops built a fire
and milked his handsome ewes, all in due order,
putting the sucklings to the mothers. Then,
his chores being all dispatched, he caught
another brace[27] of men to make his breakfast,
and whisked away his great door slab
to let his sheep go through—but he, behind,
reset the stone as one would cap a quiver.[28]
There was a din[29] of whistling as the Cyclops
rounded his flock to higher ground, then stillness.
And now I pondered how to hurt him worst,
if but Athena[30] granted what I prayed for.
23 Here are the means I thought would serve my turn:

a club, or staff, lay there along the fold—
an olive tree, felled green and left to season[31]
for Cyclops' hand. And it was like a mast
a lugger[32] of twenty oars, broad in the beam—
a deep-sea-going craft—might carry:
so long, so big around, it seemed. Now I
chopped out a six foot section of this pole
and set it down before my men, who scraped it;
and when they had it smooth, I hewed again
to make a stake with pointed end. I held this
in the fire's heart and turned it, toughening it,
then hid it, well back in the cavern, under
one of the dung piles in profusion there.
Now came the time to toss for it: who ventured
along with me? whose hand could bear to thrust
and grind that spike in Cyclops' eye, when mild

Reading Strategy
Reading in Sentences Reread lines 244–250 in complete sentences, ignoring the line breaks, to help you understand the passage.

dispatched (di spacht´) *v.* finished quickly

27. brace (brās) *n.* pair.

28. cap a quiver (kwiv´ ər) close a case holding arrows.

29. din *n.* loud, continuous noise; uproar.

30. Athena (ə thē´ nə) goddess of wisdom, skills, and warfare.

31. felled green and left to season chopped down and exposed to the weather to age the wood.

32. lugger (lug´ ər) *n.* small sailing vessel.

Literary Analysis
The Epic Hero Which heroic qualities does Odysseus reveal as he plots against Cyclops?

ENRICHMENT: Culture Connection

What Makes a Monster?

Ask students to describe what makes the Cyclops such a dreadful monster. Discuss the feelings evoked by his gigantic size and his single eye. Ask whether these traits would be considered monstrous by people of any time and culture, or whether they were horrible only to the ancient Greeks, who esteemed symmetry and good proportion. Have students give reasons for their opinions.

Assign students to do research about the portrayal of monsters in different cultures. Ask them to do a multicultural literature search for examples of giants, one-eyed monsters, and other kinds of monsters. Discuss their findings, comparing their examples with the original Cyclops of Homer's *Odyssey*.

sleep had mastered him? As luck would have it,
the men I would have chosen won the toss—
four strong men, and I made five as captain.

At evening came the shepherd with his flock,
his woolly flock. The rams as well, this time,
entered the cave: by some sheepherding whim—
or a god's bidding—none were left outside.
He hefted his great boulder into place
and sat him down to milk the bleating ewes
in proper order, put the lambs to suck,
and swiftly ran through all his evening chores.
Then he caught two more men and feasted on them.
My moment was at hand, and I went forward
holding an ivy bowl of my dark drink,
looking up, saying:

'Cyclops, try some wine.
Here's liquor to wash down your scraps of men.
Taste it, and see the kind of drink we carried
under our planks. I meant it for an offering
if you would help us home. But you are mad,
unbearable, a bloody monster! After this,
will any other traveler come to see you?'

24

He seized and drained the bowl, and it went down
so fiery and smooth he called for more:

'Give me another, thank you kindly. Tell me,
how are you called? I'll make a gift will please you.
Even Cyclopes know the wine grapes grow
out of grassland and loam in heaven's rain,
but here's a bit of nectar and ambrosia!'[33]

Three bowls I brought him, and he poured them down.
I saw the fuddle and flush come over him,
then I sang out in cordial tones:

'Cyclops,
you ask my honorable name? Remember
the gift you promised me, and I shall tell you.
My name is Nohbdy: mother, father, and friends,
everyone calls me Nohbdy.'

25

And he said:

Literary Analysis
The Epic Hero What plan do you think Odysseus has in mind by offering the drink?

33. nectar (nek´ tər) **and ambrosia** (am brō´ zhə) drink and food of the gods.

Reading Strategy
Reading in Sentences How would you write Odysseus' sly lie in ordinary prose?

26 **✓Reading Check**
What does Odysseus give to Cyclops to drink?

24 Literary Analysis
The Epic Hero
- Ask students the Literary Analysis question on p. 991: What plan do you think Odysseus has in mind by offering the drink?
  Answer: Odysseus plans to get the Cyclops drunk to the point of unconsciousness, so that he might drive a giant stake into his single eye, blinding him.
- Ask students if they think the plan is a good one. How might it lead to escape?
  Answer: Students may say that disabling the Cyclops may help them elude his grasp, but won't necessarily get them out of the cave.

25 Reading Strategy
Reading in Sentences
- Ask students the Reading Strategy question on p. 991: How would you write Odysseus' sly lie in regular prose?
  Possible response: "Do you want to know my name, Cyclops? If you remember that you promised to give me a gift, I'll tell you my name. It is Nohbdy [Nobody.] My mother, father, friends, and everyone else call me Nobody."
- Ask students if they think Odysseus' lie about his name is part of his plan, or simply a joke.
  Possible answer: Students may recognize that Odysseus is only flaunting his own cleverness.

26 ✓Reading Check
Answer: Odysseus gives the Cyclops three bowls of wine.

27 Reading Strategy

Reading in Sentences

- Ask students the Reading Strategy question on p. 992: What is the main idea of lines 323–326?
  Answer: Odysseus invokes the help of the gods as he heartens his men with battle talk.
- Explain to students that heating the spike as Odysseus does will harden the wood and cause maximum damage to the Cyclops.

'Nohbdy's my meat, then, after I eat his friends.
Others come first. There's a noble gift, now.'

Even as he spoke, he reeled and tumbled backward,
his great head lolling to one side; and sleep
took him like any creature. Drunk, hiccuping,
he dribbled streams of liquor and bits of men.

Now, by the gods, I drove my big hand spike
27 deep in the embers, charring it again,
and cheered my men along with battle talk
to keep their courage up: no quitting now.
The pike of olive, green though it had been,
reddened and glowed as if about to catch.
I drew it from the coals and my four fellows
gave me a hand, lugging it near the Cyclops
as more than natural force nerved them; straight
forward they sprinted, lifted it, and rammed it
deep in his crater eye, and leaned on it
turning it as a shipwright turns a drill
in planking, having men below to swing
the two-handled strap that spins it in the groove.
So with our brand we bored[34] that great eye socket
while blood ran out around the red-hot bar.
Eyelid and lash were seared; the pierced ball
hissed broiling, and the roots popped.

In a smithy
one sees a white-hot axehead or an adze
plunged and wrung in a cold tub, screeching steam—
the way they make soft iron hale and hard—:
just so that eyeball hissed around the spike.
The Cyclops bellowed and the rock roared round him,
and we fell back in fear. Clawing his face
he tugged the bloody spike out of his eye,
threw it away, and his wild hands went groping;
then he set up a howl for Cyclopes
who lived in caves on windy peaks nearby.
Some heard him; and they came by divers[35] ways
to clump around outside and call:

'What ails you,
Polyphemus?[36] Why do you cry so sore
in the starry night? You will not let us sleep.
28 Sure no man's driving off your flock? No man
has tricked you, ruined you?'

Reading Strategy
Reading in Sentences What is the main idea of lines 323–326?

34. bored (bôrd) *v.* made a hole in.

35. divers (dī´ vərz) *adj.* several; various.

36. Polyphemus (päl´ i fē´ məs)

Out of the cave
the mammoth Polyphemus roared in answer:

'Nohbdy, Nohbdy's tricked me, Nohbdy's ruined me!'

To this rough shout they made a sage[37] reply:

'Ah well, if nobody has played you foul
there in your lonely bed, we are no use in pain
given by great Zeus. Let it be your father,
Poseidon Lord, to whom you pray.'

So saying
they trailed away. And I was filled with laughter
to see how like a charm the name deceived them.
Now Cyclops, wheezing as the pain came on him,
fumbled to wrench away the great doorstone
and squatted in the breach with arms thrown wide
for any silly beast or man who bolted—
hoping somehow I might be such a fool.
But I kept thinking how to win the game:
death sat there huge; how could we slip away?
I drew on all my wits, and ran through tactics,
reasoning as a man will for dear life,
until a trick came—and it pleased me well.
The Cyclops' rams were handsome, fat, with heavy
fleeces, a dark violet.

Three abreast
I tied them silently together, twining
cords of willow from the ogre's bed;
then slung a man under each middle one
to ride there safely, shielded left and right.
So three sheep could convey each man. I took
the woolliest ram, the choicest of the flock,
and hung myself under his kinky belly,
pulled up tight, with fingers twisted deep
in sheepskin ringlets for an iron grip.
So, breathing hard, we waited until morning.

When Dawn spread out her fingertips of rose
the rams began to stir, moving for pasture,
and peals of bleating echoed round the pens
where dams with udders full called for a milking.
Blinded, and sick with pain from his head wound,
the master stroked each ram, then let it pass,

mammoth (mam´ əth) *adj.* enormous

37. sage (sāj) *adj.* wise.

Reading Strategy
Reading in Sentences How many questions do the other Cyclopes ask Polyphemus? What two basic things do they want to know?

Literary Analysis
The Epic Hero Which heroic quality does Odysseus demonstrate in lines 371–375?

30 **Reading Check**
What do the other Cyclopes think Polyphemus is saying when he says, "Nohbdy's tricked me"?

28 Reading Strategy
Reading in Sentences

- Invite students to read this passage aloud for sense, pausing at the punctuation rather than the ends of lines.
- Encourage them to read the passage aloud more than once, until they can make it sound natural and meaningful. Ask them what this process tells them about how to read this type of verse.
- Ask students the Reading Strategy question on p. 993: How many questions do the other Cyclopes ask Polyphemus? What two basic things do they want to know?
Answer: The Cyclopes ask Polyphemus three questions. They want to know two basic things: Has a man tricked him or ruined him?

29 Literary Analysis
The Epic Hero

- Ask a volunteer to read lines 371–375 aloud.
- Then, ask the Literary Analysis question on p. 993: What heroic quality does Odysseus demonstrate in lines 371–375?
Answer: Even though he and his men appeared likely to die, Odysseus was able to keep a clear mind and devise a strategy for escape, one that involved a clever trick.

30 Reading Check

Answer: When Polyphemus is saying "Nohbdy's tricked me," the other Cyclopes think he is saying "Nobody's tricked me." That is, he is saying that there is no one there; he has not been tricked.

31 ✔ Reading Check

Answer: Odysseus smuggles his men out by tying the Cyclops' sheep together in sets of three and binding one man under the middle sheep of each set. The men escape when the Cyclops releases his sheep to graze.

but my men riding on the pectoral[38] fleece
the giant's blind hands blundering never found.
Last of them all my ram, the leader, came,
weighted by wool and me with my meditations.
The Cyclops patted him, and then he said:

'Sweet cousin ram, why lag behind the rest
in the night cave? You never linger so,
but graze before them all, and go afar
to crop sweet grass, and take your stately way
leading along the streams, until at evening
you run to be the first one in the fold.
Why, now, so far behind? Can you be grieving
over your Master's eye? That carrion rogue[39]
and his accurst companions burnt it out
when he had conquered all my wits with wine.
Nohbdy will not get out alive, I swear.
Oh, had you brain and voice to tell
where he may be now, dodging all my fury!
Bashed by this hand and bashed on this rock wall
his brains would strew the floor, and I should have
rest from the outrage Nohbdy worked upon me.'

He sent us into the open, then. Close by,
I dropped and rolled clear of the ram's belly,
going this way and that to untie the men.
With many glances back, we rounded up
his fat, stiff-legged sheep to take aboard,
and drove them down to where the good ship lay.
We saw, as we came near, our fellows' faces
shining; then we saw them turn to grief
tallying those who had not fled from death.
I hushed them, jerking head and eyebrows up,
and in a low voice told them: 'Load this herd;
move fast, and put the ship's head toward the breakers.'
They all pitched in at loading, then embarked
and struck their oars into the sea. Far out,
as far off shore as shouted words would carry,
I sent a few back to the adversary:

'O Cyclops! Would you feast on my companions?
Puny, am I, in a cave man's hands?
How do you like the beating that we gave you,

38. pectoral (pek′ tə rəl) *adj.* located in or on the chest.

39. carrion (kar′ ē ən) **rogue** (rōg) repulsive scoundrel.

31 ✔ Reading Check

How do the men escape from the Cyclops' cave?

CUSTOMIZE INSTRUCTION FOR UNIVERSAL ACCESS

For Special Needs Students	For Advanced Readers
Have students imagine that they are trapped in a cave by the Cyclops. Assign students to work in small groups to develop their own plan of escape (without copying from Odysseus). Have groups present and compare their plans, then work as a class to use the best ideas to create a final strategy.	From David and Goliath to Jack and the Bean Stalk, literature is filled with stories of giants. Have students analyze at least three such stories. How do the giants compare? What type of challenge or threat do they represent? How does the hero overcome or escape the giant? Have students discuss their findings in an essay.

32

Polyphemus, The Cyclops, N. C. Wyeth, Delaware Art Museum

33 ▲ **Critical Viewing** Odysseus and his surviving men escape in their ship as the blinded Cyclops hurls boulders and curses. How does this illustration compare to your mental image of the scene? **[Analyze]**

32 Background

Art

Polyphemus, The Cyclops, by N. C. Wyeth

N. C. Wyeth (1882–1945) was an American artist whose enchanting illustrations of children's classics made him popular and successful. He illustrated several novels by Robert Louis Stevenson and James Fenimore Cooper.

This painting illustrates the moment at which Polyphemus tries to smash Odysseus' ship. The illustration was commissioned for a luxury edition of the *Odyssey* published in 1929. The illustration demonstrates the skill with which Wyeth was able to depict fantastic creatures. Use the following questions for discussion:

1. Which lines in the *Odyssey* match the moment portrayed by Wyeth in this painting? Why do you think the artist chose this particular moment to illustrate?
   Answer: The picture illustrates the lines "The blind thing in his doubled fury broke / a hilltop in his hands and heaved it after us," lines 436–437. Students should note that the artist actually chose the moment just before Polyphemus hurled the "hilltop" into the sea. Perhaps he thought that portraying the moment at which something is about to happen would be more suspenseful than the moment after.
2. How does the mood of the illustration reflect that of the story?
   Answer: The gloomy, stormy skies and seas suggest the danger and tension surrounding the event.

33 ▶Critical Viewing

Answer: The illustration depicts the moment after Odysseus taunts the Cyclops while his men sail furiously away from the island. In the image, the giant has broken off the top of a hill and is preparing to hurl it at Odysseus' ship. The artist has added some details not evident in the poem, including the swirling steam around the giant. Also, for emphasis, he adds a glow around the ship.

34 Literary Analysis

The Epic Hero

- Remind students that an epic hero is larger than life, but he or she also has some human failings.
- Ask students the Literary Analysis question on page 996: Despite his heroism, which human weaknesses does Odysseus reveal as he sails away?
  Answer: Odysseus allows his anger and relief to get the best of him; it would have been much wiser to be quiet. He is acting in a boastful and vindictive manner.

35 Reading Strategy

Reading in Sentences

- Tell students that even though Fitzgerald has translated the *Odyssey* into English, the exact meaning of the words and phrases he uses may sometimes be difficult on a first read.
- Have students respond to the Reading Strategy task on p. 996: Rephrase the sentence in lines 450–451.
  Possible Answer: "The huge wave he made on the first throw nearly grounded the boat on the shore."
- Point out that "tidal wave" in the original sentence is not meant literally; the term is used to convey a sense of the wave's size. The phrase "all but," not commonly used in today's speech, means "nearly" or "almost."

34
you damned cannibal? Eater of guests
under your roof! Zeus and the gods have paid you!'

The blind thing in his doubled fury broke
a hilltop in his hands and heaved it after us.
Ahead of our black prow it struck and sank
whelmed in a spuming geyser, a giant wave
that washed the ship stern foremost back to shore.
I got the longest boathook out and stood
fending us off, with furious nods to all
to put their backs into a racing stroke—
row, row, or perish. So the long oars bent
kicking the foam sternward, making head
until we drew away, and twice as far.
Now when I cupped my hands I heard the crew
in low voices protesting:

'Godsake, Captain!
Why bait the beast again? Let him alone!'

35
'That tidal wave he made on the first throw
all but beached us.'

'All but stove us in!'
'Give him our bearing with your trumpeting,
he'll get the range and lob a boulder.'

'Aye
He'll smash our timbers and our heads together!'
I would not heed them in my glorying spirit,
but let my anger flare and yelled:

'Cyclops,
if ever mortal man inquire
how you were put to shame and blinded, tell him
Odysseus, raider of cities, took your eye:
Laertes' son, whose home's on Ithaca!'

At this he gave a mighty sob and rumbled:
'Now comes the weird[40] upon me, spoken of old.
A wizard, grand and wondrous, lived here—Telemus,[41]
a son of Eurymus;[42] great length of days
he had in wizardry among the Cyclopes,
and these things he foretold for time to come:
my great eye lost, and at Odysseus' hands.

Literary Analysis
The Epic Hero Despite his heroism, which human weaknesses does Odysseus reveal as he sails away?

Reading Strategy
Reading in Sentences Rephrase the sentence in lines 450–451.

40. **weird** *n.* fate or destiny.
41. **Telemus** (tel e´ məs)
42. **Eurymus** (yo͞o rim´ əs)

Always I had in mind some giant, armed
in giant force, would come against me here.
But this, but you—small, pitiful and twiggy—
you put me down with wine, you blinded me.
Come back, Odysseus, and I'll treat you well,
praying the god of earthquake[43] to befriend you—
his son I am, for he by his avowal
fathered me, and, if he will, he may
heal me of this black wound—he and no other
of all the happy gods or mortal men.'

Few words I shouted in reply to him:

'If I could take your life I would and take
your time away, and hurl you down to hell!
The god of earthquake could not heal you there!'

At this he stretched his hands out in his darkness
toward the sky of stars, and prayed Poseidon:

36

'O hear me, lord, blue girdler of the islands,
if I am thine indeed, and thou art father:
grant that Odysseus, raider of cities, never
see his home: Laertes' son, I mean,
who kept his hall on Ithaca. Should destiny
intend that he shall see his roof again
among his family in his father land,
far be that day, and dark the years between.
Let him lose all companions, and return
under strange sail to bitter days at home.'

In these words he prayed, and the god heard him.
Now he laid hands upon a bigger stone
and wheeled around, titanic for the cast,
to let it fly in the black-prowed vessel's track.
But it fell short, just aft the steering oar,
and whelming seas rose giant above the stone
to bear us onward toward the island.
There
as we ran in we saw the squadron waiting,
the trim ships drawn up side by side, and all
our troubled friends who waited, looking seaward.
We beached her, grinding keel in the soft sand,
and waded in, ourselves, on the sandy beach.
Then we unloaded all the Cyclops' flock

43. god of earthquake Poseidon.

Reading Strategy
Reading in Sentences
Rephrase the second sentence of Cyclops' prayer to Poseidon.

titanic (tī tan′ ik) *adj.* of great size or strength

37 **✓Reading Check**
What does Cyclops ask for in his prayer to Poseidon?

36 Reading Strategy

Reading in Sentences

- Have students pay special attention to the Cyclops' prayer to his father Poseidon. It foretells much of what will happen to Odysseus in the coming episodes of the poem.
- One strategy to use to make certain that a passage is clear is to have students rewrite or paraphrase it in their own words.
- Have students respond to the Reading Strategy task on p. 997: Rephrase the second sentence of the Cyclops' prayer to Poseidon. **Possible Answer:** "If Odysseus ever sees his home again, let that day be far in the future, and let the years until then be dark ones."

37 ✓Reading Check

Answer: The Cyclops prays that Odysseus would lose all his men and, if he returns at all, that he would arrive home only after many "dark" years of hardship. The Cyclops' prayer amounts to an extremely precise prophecy.

38 Background

Art

Odysseus in the Land of the Dead, by N. C. Wyeth

This painting illustrates the scene in the *Odyssey* in which Odysseus visits the underworld. The painting was commissioned for a 1929 limited edition of the *Odyssey*. The 500 copies of this edition included sixteen full-color illustrations by N. C. Wyeth and were signed by the artist. Use these questions for discussion:

1. Which lines in Homer's *Odyssey* are illustrated by this picture?
   Answer: The painting illustrates lines 564–578.
2. Do you think the artist portrayed Odysseus as Homer pictured him at this moment?
   Possible response: The artist has successfully captured Homer's image of Odysseus crouching by the "bloody pit" with his drawn sword, sick with fear but determined to achieve his goal of consulting Tiresias.
3. Do you think that Wyeth has accurately portrayed the dead?
   Possible responses: Yes, because Homer says that the dead appear in "their bloody gear," or as they were when they died. No, because the dead look skeletal and long dead, rather than recently deceased.

39 ▶Critical Viewing

Answer: From the illustration, we can infer that the Greeks believed that a person's spirit continued to exist after death. The spirit had to make a long journey to the underworld and could not complete its journey unless the proper rites were observed. The spirits that had not yet reached the underworld were frightening, restless, and hungry.

38

Odysseus in the Land of the Dead, N. C. Wyeth, Delaware Art Museum

39 ▲ **Critical Viewing** What can you infer about ancient Greek beliefs concerning death and the afterlife from the text and this illustration? **[Infer]**

to make division, share and share alike,
only my fighters voted that my ram,
the prize of all, should go to me. I slew him
by the seaside and burnt his long thighbones
to Zeus beyond the stormcloud, Cronus'[44] son,
who rules the world. But Zeus disdained my offering:
destruction for my ships he had in store
and death for those who sailed them, my companions.
Now all day long until the sun went down
we made our feast on mutton and sweet wine,
till after sunset in the gathering dark
we went to sleep above the wash of ripples.

When the young Dawn with fingertips of rose
touched the world, I roused the men, gave orders
to man the ships, cast off the mooring lines;
and filing in to sit beside the rowlocks
oarsmen in line dipped oars in the gray sea.
So we moved out, sad in the vast offing,[45]
having our precious lives, but not our friends.

The Land of the Dead

Odysseus and his men sail to Aeolia,[46] where Aeolus, king of the winds, sends Odysseus on his way with a gift: a sack containing all the winds except the favorable west wind. When they are near home, Odysseus' men open the sack, letting loose a storm that drives them back to Aeolia. Aeolus casts them out, having decided that they are detested by the gods. They sail for seven days and arrive in the land of the Laestrygonians,[47] a race of cannibals. These creatures destroy all of Odysseus' ships except the one he is sailing in. Odysseus and his reduced crew escape and reach Aeaea, the island ruled by the sorceress-goddess Circe. She transforms half of the men into swine. Protected by a magic herb, Odysseus demands that Circe change his men back into human form. Before Odysseus departs from the island a year later, Circe informs him that in order to reach home he must journey to the land of the dead, Hades, and consult the blind prophet Tiresias.

Literary Analysis
The Epic Hero Which admirable quality does Odysseus show in his actions with the stolen sheep?

44. Cronus (krō´ nəs) Titan who was ruler of the universe until he was overthrown by his son Zeus.

45. offing *n.* distant part of the sea visible from the shore.

46. Aeolia (ē ō´ lē ə)

47. Laestrygonians (les tri gō´ ni anz)

41 **Reading Check**
What does Circe say Odysseus must do in order to reach home?

40 Literary Analysis

The Epic Hero

- Tell students that some leaders can be cruel, but one mark of an effective leader is fairness to those he leads.
- Ask students the Literary Analysis question on p. 999: Which admirable quality does Odysseus show in what he does with the stolen sheep?
  Answer: Odysseus shows a sense of fairness by dividing the sheep equally among his men—"share and share alike."
- His men vote the prize ram to Odysseus, and he sacrifices it to the god Zeus. Explain that sacrifices to the gods were common in ancient Greek society. This was done out of respect as well as fear. Failing to offer sacrifices could lead to the gods' anger and retribution.

41 Reading Check

Answer: Circe tells him that in order to reach home, Odysseus must travel to the land of the dead, Hades, and consult the blind prophet Tiresias.

CUSTOMIZE INSTRUCTION FOR UNIVERSAL ACCESS

For English Learners	For Advanced Readers
Students may be confused by homophones, words that sound the same but have a different meaning and spelling—such as *bourn, born,* and *borne.* In this context (line 539), *bourn* means "boundary." *Bourn* can also mean "stream," "goal," or "domain." Point out that the word *bourn* is rarely used, but its homophones *born* and *borne* often are. *Born* means "brought into life or being," and *borne* means "carried."	Because improper burial was a disgrace to the Greeks, it was customary to deny funeral rites and burial to traitors or enemies. Challenge interested students to find out how burial customs play an important part in Sophocles' tragedy *Antigone.* (In *Antigone,* Creon, the king, denies burial rites for Polynices, Antigone's brother, the leader of a rebellion. Antigone defies Creon, her uncle, by performing the ceremony anyway.)

42 Reading Strategy

Reading in Sentences

- Point out that as Odysseus and his men sail on toward the edge of the known ocean, the setting becomes more and more fantastical, and the language becomes more dramatic.
- Have students respond to the Reading Strategy task on p. 1000: Reread the sentence in lines 539–541 to explain what happens to their ship by night.
  Possible response: In this context, bourn means "boundary." At night, Odysseus' ship sailed toward the edge of the ocean, where the land of dead souls—the "Men of Winter"—lies hidden in mist.

We bore down on the ship at the sea's edge
and launched her on the salt immortal sea,
stepping our mast and spar in the black ship;
embarked the ram and ewe and went aboard
in tears, with bitter and sore dread upon us.
But now a breeze came up for us astern—
a canvas-bellying landbreeze, hale shipmate
sent by the singing nymph with sunbright hair;[48]
so we made fast the braces, took our thwarts,
and let the wind and steersman work the ship
with full sail spread all day above our coursing,
till the sun dipped, and all the ways grew dark
upon the fathomless unresting sea.

By night

42 our ship ran onward toward the Ocean's bourne,
the realm and region of the Men of Winter,
hidden in mist and cloud. Never the flaming
eye of Helios lights on those men
at morning, when he climbs the sky of stars,
nor in descending earthward out of heaven;
ruinous night being rove over those wretches.
We made the land, put ram and ewe ashore,
and took our way along the Ocean stream
to find the place foretold for us by Circe.
There Perimedes and Eulylochus[49]
pinioned[50] the sacred beasts. With my drawn blade
I spaded up the votive[51] pit, and poured
libations[52] round it to the unnumbered dead:
sweet milk and honey, then sweet wine, and last
clear water; and I scattered barley down.
Then I addressed the blurred and breathless dead,
vowing to slaughter my best heifer for them
before she calved, at home in Ithaca,
and burn the choice bits on the altar fire;
as for Tiresias, I swore to sacrifice
a black lamb, handsomest of all our flock.
Thus to assuage the nations of the dead
I pledged these rites, then slashed the lamb and ewe,
letting their black blood stream into the wellpit.
Now the souls gathered, stirring out of Erebus,[53]
brides and young men, and men grown old in pain,
and tender girls whose hearts were new to grief;
many were there, too, torn by brazen lanceheads,
battle-slain, bearing still their bloody gear.

48. singing nymph . . . hair Circe.

Reading Strategy
Reading in Sentences
Reread the sentences in lines 539–541 to explain what happens to their ship by night.

49. Perimedes (per′ ə mē′ dēz) **and Eurylochus** (yo͞o ril′ ə kəs)

50. pinioned (pin′ yənd) *v.* confined or shackled.

51. votive (vōt′ iv) *adj.* done in fulfillment of a vow or pledge.

52. libations (lī bā′ shənz) *n.* wine or other liquids poured upon the ground as a sacrifice to a god.

assuage (ə swāj′) *v.* calm; pacify

53. Erebus (er′ ə bəs) dark region under the earth through which the dead pass before entering the realm of Hades.

ENRICHMENT: Cultural Connection

Death Customs and Rituals

Begin a discussion about the many different customs and rituals surrounding death by asking students what kind of ritual they would want when they die. Would they want to have a funeral, to be buried in a cemetery, to be cremated, to have their ashes strewn in a special place? Discuss the similarities among students' ideas. Point out that the rites surrounding death have always been important in every culture, but they vary widely. Cite, for example, the funeral pyre of the Hindus, the Jewish custom of sitting shiva, and the Mandan Indian tradition of leaving the dead body outside on an elevated platform to decay naturally.

Ask students to choose a religion or culture other than their own and research the customs surrounding death in that culture. Have them share their findings with the class.

43

From every side they came and sought the pit
with rustling cries; and I grew sick with fear.
But presently I gave command to my officers
to flay those sheep the bronze cut down, and make
burnt offerings of flesh to the gods below—
to sovereign Death, to pale Persephone.[54]
Meanwhile I crouched with my drawn sword to keep
the surging phantoms from the bloody pit
till I should know the presence of Tiresias.[55]

One shade came first—Elpenor, of our company,
who lay unburied still on the wide earth
as we had left him—dead in Circe's hall,
untouched, unmourned, when other cares compelled us.
Now when I saw him there I wept for pity
and called out to him:

'How is this, Elpenor,
how could you journey to the western gloom
swifter afoot than I in the black lugger?'
He sighed, and answered:

'Son of great Laertes,
Odysseus, master mariner and soldier,
bad luck shadowed me, and no kindly power;
ignoble death I drank with so much wine.
I slept on Circe's roof, then could not see
the long steep backward ladder, coming down,
and fell that height. My neckbone, buckled under,
snapped, and my spirit found this well of dark.
Now hear the grace I pray for, in the name
of those back in the world, not here—your wife
and father, he who gave you bread in childhood,
and your own child, your only son, Telemachus,[56]
long ago left at home.

44

When you make sail
and put these lodgings of dim Death behind,
you will moor ship, I know, upon Aeaea Island;
there, O my lord, remember me, I pray,
do not abandon me unwept, unburied,
to tempt the gods' wrath, while you sail for home;
but fire my corpse, and all the gear I had,
and build a cairn[57] for me above the breakers—
an unknown sailor's mark for men to come.

Literary Analysis
The Epic Hero and Conflict Which outside forces and inner feelings does Odysseus confront as he faces the spirits of the dead?

54. Persephone (pər sef′ ə nē) wife of Hades.

55. Tiresias (tī rē′ sē əs)

Reading Strategy
Reading in Sentences As you read Elpenor's words, where do you pause if you read in sentences?

56. Telemachus (tə lem′ ə kəs)

57. cairn (kern) *n.* conical heap of stones built as a monument.

45 **Reading Check**
What does Elpenor say happened to him on Circe's roof?

43 Literary Analysis
The Epic Hero and Conflict

- Remind students that Odysseus has long since proved his hero status as both a warrior and a leader of men, but as the *Odyssey* progresses his heroic qualities are tested against a number of otherworldly elements.
- Ask the Literary Analysis question on p. 1001: Which outside forces and inner feelings does Odysseus confront as he faces the spirits of the dead?
  Possible response: Odysseus must face the phantoms themselves, who are surging toward the pit where he is trying to summon Tiresias. Inside, he feels "sick with fear." Despite these fears, he persists in facing the frightening spirits of the dead. Having the courage to overcome fear is a heroic trait.

44 Reading Strategy
Reading in Sentences

- Remind students that the characters in the *Odyssey* often address each other formally. One way to make these passages more comprehensible is to read them as sentences.
- Ask students the Reading Strategy question on p. 1001: As you read Elpenor's words, where do you pause if you read in sentences?
  Answer: Pause only at the punctuation, not at the line breaks. Example: "Now hear the grace I pray for, in the name of those back in the world, not here—your wife and father, he who gave you bread in childhood, and your own child, your only son, Telemachus, long ago left at home."

45 Reading Check

Answer: Elpenor says he drank too much wine and slept on Circe's roof. He fell off and broke his neck while attempting to climb down.

46 Reading Strategy

Reading in Sentences

- Tell students that paraphrasing passages can be one tool for understanding their meaning.
- Have students respond to the Reading Strategy task on p. 1002: In ordinary language, rephrase the lines in which Odysseus puts away his sword.
  Possible response: "I let my sword slide into the scabbard, all the way up to its silver handle."

Heap up the mound there, and implant upon it
the oar I pulled in life with my companions.'

He ceased, and I replied:

'Unhappy spirit,
I promise you the barrow and the burial.'

So we conversed, and grimly, at a distance,
with my long sword between, guarding the blood,
while the faint image of the lad spoke on.
Now came the soul of Anticlea, dead,
my mother, daughter of Autolycus,[58]
dead now, though living still when I took ship
for holy Troy. Seeing this ghost I grieved,
but held her off, through pang on pang of tears,
till I should know the presence of Tiresias.
Soon from the dark that prince of Thebes[59] came forward
bearing a golden staff; and he addressed me:

'Son of Laertes and the gods of old,
Odysseus, master of landways and seaways,
why leave the blazing sun, O man of woe,
to see the cold dead and the joyless region?
Stand clear, put up your sword;
let me but taste of blood, I shall speak true.'

46 At this I stepped aside, and in the scabbard
let my long sword ring home to the pommel silver,
as he bent down to the somber blood. Then spoke
the prince of those with gift of speech:

'Great captain,
a fair wind and the honey lights of home
are all you seek. But anguish lies ahead;
the god who thunders on the land prepares it,
not to be shaken from your track, implacable,
in rancor for the son whose eye you blinded.
One narrow strait may take you through his blows:
denial of yourself, restraint of shipmates.
When you make landfall on Thrinacia first
and quit the violet sea, dark on the land
you'll find the grazing herds of Helios
by whom all things are seen, all speech is known.

58. Autolycus (ô tăl′ i kəs)

59. Thebes (thēbz)

Reading Strategy
Reading in Sentences
In ordinary language, rephrase the lines in which Odysseus puts away his sword.

Avoid those kine,[60] hold fast to your intent,
and hard seafaring brings you all to Ithaca.
But if you raid the beeves, I see destruction
for ship and crew. Though you survive alone,
bereft of all companions, lost for years,
under strange sail shall you come home, to find
your own house filled with trouble: insolent men
eating your livestock as they court your lady.
Aye, you shall make those men atone in blood!
But after you have dealt out death—in open
combat or by stealth—to all the suitors,
go overland on foot, and take an oar,
until one day you come where men have lived
with meat unsalted, never known the sea,
nor seen seagoing ships, with crimson bows

60. **kine** (kin) *n.* cattle.

bereft (bi reft′) *adj.* deprived

47 **Reading Check**
What does Odysseus learn has happened to his mother?

48

49 ▲ **Critical Viewing** How does the description of the characters in this art compare to your image of the characters in the *Odyssey*?

47 **Reading Check**

Answer: Odysseus learns that his mother has died since he set sail for Troy.

48 Background

Art

This photograph shows an example of a Greek amphora, a pottery jar with two handles used to store wine, oil, and dry goods. It was characteristic of the Greeks to combine beauty and utility by elaborately decorating these vessels. In doing so, they gave an incalculable gift to posterity: These durable containers have transported Greek art and culture across a sea of time.

49 ▶**Critical Viewing**

Answer: Students may note that the art helps them visualize the appearance, clothing, and equipment of the characters in the *Odyssey.*

CUSTOMIZE INSTRUCTION FOR UNIVERSAL ACCESS

For Less Proficient Readers	For Gifted/Talented Students
Have students prepare a two-column chart. In one column, they should write the events Tiresias foretells. As they read on, have them fill in the adventures to which the prophecies refer. (Students will discover that line 637 refers to Scylla and Charybdis; line 638 refers to The Sirens; lines 639–646 refer to The Cattle of the Sun God; lines 649–650 refer to ". . . Twenty years gone, and I am home again" [Part 2]; and line 651 refers to Odysseus' Revenge [Part 2].)	Suggest that students draw or paint a scene from the *Odyssey* in the same style as shown on the amphora on p. 1003. Encourage them to research other examples of Greek art to gather specific details they might include, such as the patterns and borders used to frame the images.

Answers for p. 1004

Review and Assess

1. Students may say that Odysseus' plan was well thought out; for example, he did not act on his first impulse, which was to attack the Cyclops immediately.
2. **(a)** From Maron, Odysseus received gold, a silver winebowl and twelve jars of brandy. **(b)** Possible response: Hospitality is highly valued; a host is judged by his courteousness and the richness of the gifts he presents to his guests.
3. **(a)** Odysseus and his men have trepidation about the Cyclops but believe an appeal to the custom of honoring strangers will be respected. **(b)** Possible response: He violates the laws of hospitality, of honoring the gods—and the taboo against cannibalism.
4. **(a)** They attach themselves to the underside of the Cyclops' sheep. Thus camouflaged from the Cyclops' groping hands, they escape when Polyphemus lets his flocks out to graze. **(b)** Among the negative traits that Odysseus displays in the episode with the Cyclops are an overeager curiosity that leads him into danger and a vindictive boastfulness that comes back to haunt him after his escape. He also displays positive qualities, such as cleverness in devising an escape plan, leadership in inspiring his men, and bravery in attacking the Cyclops.
5. **(a)** Answer: Odysseus encounters Elpenor, a member of his company; his mother, Autolycus; and the prophet Tiresias. **(b)** Possible responses: Odysseus shows compassion for his mother and for Elpenor; he reveals determination to achieve his goal even when he is afraid.
6. **(a)** Tiresias foretells the many ordeals that Poseidon has arranged for Odysseus and what Odysseus will do when he returns home. He advises Odysseus in cryptic terms on how to get past the Sirens, why the cattle should be left alone, and how to make peace with the gods. **(b)** Students might say that Odysseus would continue because he wants to see his family and his home again, and that he really has no choice but to continue.
7. Students may say that the chief qualities Odysseus will need as he continues are an ability to resist temptation—the temptation of the Sirens and of stealing the cattle—and a steadfast commitment to his goal of reaching home.

and oars that fledge light hulls for dipping flight.
The spot will soon be plain to you, and I
can tell you how: some passerby will say,
"What winnowing fan is that upon your shoulder?"
Halt, and implant your smooth oar in the turf
and make fair sacrifice to Lord Poseidon:
a ram, a bull, a great buck boar; turn back,
and carry out pure hecatombs[61] at home
to all wide heaven's lords, the undying gods,
to each in order. Then a seaborne death
soft as this hand of mist will come upon you
when you are wearied out with rich old age,
your country folk in blessed peace around you.
And all this shall be just as I foretell.'

61. hecatombs (hek´ ə tōmz´) *n.* large-scale sacrifices in ancient Greece; often, the slaughter of 100 cattle at one time.

Review and Assess

Thinking About the Selection

1. **Respond:** What do you think of Odysseus' plan for escaping from Polyphemus?
2. **(a) Recall:** Before the meeting with the Cyclops, what had Odysseus received from Maron at Ismarus?
   (b) Generalize: What does the encounter with Maron reveal about ancient Greek attitudes regarding hospitality?
3. **(a) Recall:** How do Odysseus and his companions expect to be treated by the Cyclops? **(b) Infer:** What "laws" of behavior and attitude does Polyphemus violate in his treatment of the Greeks?
4. **(a) Recall:** How do Odysseus and his crew ultimately escape from the Cyclops? **(b) Evaluate:** Which positive and negative character traits does Odysseus demonstrate in his adventure with the Cyclops?
5. **(a) Recall:** Whom does Odysseus encounter in the Land of the Dead? **(b) Interpret:** Which character trait does Odysseus display in the Land of the Dead that he did not reveal earlier?
6. **(a) Recall:** What difficulties does Tiresias predict for the journey to come? **(b) Speculate:** Why would Odysseus continue, despite the grim prophecies?
7. **(a) Assess:** Based on Tiresias' prediction, which heroic qualities will Odysseus need to rely upon as he continues his journey? Explain.

The Sirens

Odysseus returns to Circe's island. The goddess reveals his course to him and gives advice on how to avoid the dangers he will face: the Sirens, who lure sailors to their destruction; the Wandering Rocks, sea rocks that destroy even birds in flight; the perils of the sea monster Scylla and, nearby, the whirlpool Charybdis;[62] *and the cattle of the sun god, which Tiresias has warned Odysseus not to harm.*

As Circe spoke, Dawn mounted her golden throne,
and on the first rays Circe left me, taking
her way like a great goddess up the island.
I made straight for the ship, roused up the men
to get aboard and cast off at the stern.
They scrambled to their places by the rowlocks
and all in line dipped oars in the gray sea.
But soon an offshore breeze blew to our liking—
a canvas-bellying breeze, a lusty shipmate
sent by the singing nymph with sunbright hair.
So we made fast the braces, and we rested,
letting the wind and steersman work the ship.
The crew being now silent before me, I
addressed them, sore at heart:

'Dear friends,
more than one man, or two, should know those things
Circe foresaw for us and shared with me,
so let me tell her forecast: then we die
with our eyes open, if we are going to die,
or know what death we baffle if we can. Sirens
weaving a haunting song over the sea
we are to shun, she said, and their green shore
all sweet with clover; yet she urged that I
alone should listen to their song. Therefore
you are to tie me up, tight as a splint,
erect along the mast, lashed to the mast,
and if I shout and beg to be untied,
take more turns of the rope to muffle me.'

I rather dwelt on this part of the forecast,
while our good ship made time, bound outward down
the wind for the strange island of Sirens.

62. **Charybdis** (kə rib′ dis)

Literary Analysis
The Epic Hero What does Odysseus reveal about his character by sharing information with his men?

51 **Reading Check**
What has Odysseus asked his shipmates to do in order to deal with the Sirens?

50 Literary Analysis
The Epic Hero

- Point out that Odysseus will continue to reveal new facets of his personality and new qualities as his journey progresses.
- Ask students the Literary Analysis question on p. 1005: What does Odysseus reveal about his character by sharing information with his men?
  Possible response: Odysseus is a caring leader. He also understands that by sharing information with his men, he wins their trust and is better able to get them to do what he wants.

51 Reading Check
Answer: Odysseus has asked his men to tie him to the mast.

52 Reading Strategy

Reading in Sentences

- Tell students that passages depicting action can be hard to follow because of line breaks. Students can benefit by rereading these lines as sentences.
- Ask students the Reading Strategy question on p. 1006: Reread lines 704–715 as sentences, ignoring the line breaks. What happens in each of the four sentences?
  Possible response: Odysseus' crew rolled up the sail and secured it in place, and then each of them rowed with the oars, moving the white foam in the ocean with their strokes. Odysseus rolled pieces of wax until they became soft. This didn't take long because heat came down from Helios, lord of high noon, and helped melt the wax. Odysseus put wax in the ears of each man. His crew tied him to the mast and continued rowing.

53 Literary Analysis

The Epic Hero and Conflict

- Ask students the Literary Analysis question on p. 1006: Which details in the Sirens' song are calculated to tempt a hero and bring him down?
  Possible responses: The Sirens offer a chance to be "merry" and to find companionship and an end to homesickness ("a-pining") with them. The Sirens are also flattering, singing that they admire those who fought at Troy.

Monitor Progress Ask students what the Sirens might sing to lure a real or fictional person they know or know about.

Then all at once the wind fell, and a calm
came over all the sea, as though some power
lulled the swell.

The crew were on their feet
briskly, to furl the sail, and stow it; then,
each in place, they poised the smooth oar blades
and sent the white foam scudding by. I carved
a massive cake of beeswax into bits
and rolled them in my hands until they softened—
52 no long task, for a burning heat came down
from Helios, lord of high noon. Going forward
I carried wax along the line, and laid it
thick on their ears. They tied me up, then, plumb
amidships, back to the mast, lashed to the mast,
and took themselves again to rowing. Soon,
as we came smartly within hailing distance,
the two Sirens, noting our fast ship
off their point, made ready, and they sang:

This way, oh turn your bows,
Achaea's glory,
As all the world allows—
Moor and be merry.

Sweet coupled airs we sing.
No lonely seafarer
Holds clear of entering
Our green mirror.

Pleased by each purling note
Like honey twining
53 *From her throat and my throat,*
Who lies a-pining?

Sea rovers here take joy
Voyaging onward,
As from our song of Troy
Graybeard and rower-boy
Goeth more learnèd.

All feats on that great field
In the long warfare,
Dark days the bright gods willed,
Wounds you bore there,

Reading Strategy
Reading in Sentences Reread lines 704–715 as sentences, ignoring the line breaks. What happens in each of the four sentences?

Literary Analysis
The Epic Hero and Conflict Which details in the Sirens' song are calculated to tempt a hero and bring him down?

CUSTOMIZE INSTRUCTION FOR UNIVERSAL ACCESS

For Less Proficient Readers	For Gifted/Talented Students	For Advanced Readers
Tell students that the Sirens were half bird, half woman. Discuss with students what kind of bird would be appropriate for a tempting Siren. Ask students to sketch a Siren based on their discussions.	Ask students to set the Sirens' song to music. They can select existing instrumental music or compose their own accompaniment. Offer opportunities for students to perform the song for the class.	Challenge students to update the Sirens' song for the present day. What new temptations or needs would they insert in the song? Suggest that they rewrite the song or compose a new version of their own.

Argos' old soldiery[63]
On Troy beach teeming,
Charmed out of time we see.
No life on earth can be
Hid from our dreaming.

The lovely voices in ardor appealing over the water
made me crave to listen, and I tried to say
'Untie me!' to the crew, jerking my brows;
but they bent steady to the oars. Then Perimedes
got to his feet, he and Eurylochus,
and passed more line about, to hold me still.
So all rowed on, until the Sirens
dropped under the sea rim, and their singing
dwindled away.

My faithful company
rested on their oars now, peeling off
the wax that I had laid thick on their ears;
then set me free.

54

63. Argos' old soldiery soldiers from Argos, a city in ancient Greece.

ardor (är′ dər) *n.* passion; enthusiasm

Reading Strategy
Reading in Sentences
Explain what happens in the sentence in lines 753–756.

Scylla and Charybdis

But scarcely had that island
faded in blue air than I saw smoke
and white water, with sound of waves in tumult—
a sound the men heard, and it terrified them.
Oars flew from their hands; the blades went knocking
wild alongside till the ship lost way,
with no oar blades to drive her through the water.

Well, I walked up and down from bow to stern,
trying to put heart into them, standing over
every oarsman, saying gently,

'Friends,
have we never been in danger before this?
More fearsome, is it now, than when the Cyclops
penned us in his cave? What power he had!
Did I not keep my nerve, and use my wits
to find a way out for us?

Now I say
by hook or crook this peril too shall be
something that we remember.

55 **Reading Check**
What does Odysseus put in his shipmates' ears before they hear the Sirens sing?

54 Reading Strategy

Reading in Sentences

- Point out that it wasn't essential for anyone to listen to the Sirens' song. Ask students why Odysseus decided to do so.
  Possible response: Students may agree that this is another example of Odysseus' eager curiosity. Once again he takes a risk in order to explore a new experience.
- Ask students the Reading Strategy question on p. 1007: Explain what happens in the sentence in lines 753–756.
  Answer: Odysseus' men stop rowing, take the wax from their ears, then untie him from the mast.

55 Reading Check

Answer: Odysseus puts beeswax in his shipmates' ears.

56 Background

Art

Circe Meanwhile Had Gone Her Ways . . . , by William Russell Flint

The Scottish painter and illustrator William Russell Flint (1880–1969) became interested in watercolor at a young age. For many years, this was his favorite medium, and his works were exhibited in England and Europe to much acclaim. He added another dimension to his work when he began to create illustrations for various literary works.

The watercolor *Circe Meanwhile Had Gone Her Ways . . .* was painted in 1924 for an edition of the *Odyssey.* Flint created a beautiful Circe, who looks as if she has stepped from a Grecian urn. In keeping with this stylized effect, the perspective of the painting is basically flat. Use the following questions for discussion:

1. What special abilities does Circe seem to have?
   Answer: She seems to command the attention and obedience of animals, such as the two sheep.
2. What elements in the painting give a sense of the setting of the *Odyssey*?
   Possible responses: The time and place are suggested in Circe's clothes and pose; the carved marble pedestal; the sensuous, stylized spirals of the rams' horns and wool and of the blue-and-purple decorations on the ship; and the form of the ship in the background.

57 ▶Critical Viewing

Possible response: Circe looks seductive, confident of her power, mysterious, and a bit mischievous.

56

Circe Meanwhile Had Gone Her Ways. . ., 1924, William Russell Flint Collection of the New York Public Library; Astor, Lenox, and Tilden Foundations

57 ▲ **Critical Viewing** The beautiful sorceress Circe both helps and hinders Odysseus on his journey home. What can you tell about Circe from this illustration? **[Deduce]**

Heads up, lads!
We must obey the orders as I give them.
Get the oar shafts in your hands, and lay back
hard on your benches; hit these breaking seas.
Zeus help us pull away before we founder.
You at the tiller, listen, and take in
all that I say—the rudders are your duty;
keep her out of the combers and the smoke;[64]
steer for that headland; watch the drift, or we
fetch up in the smother, and you drown us.'

That was all, and it brought them round to action.
But as I sent them on toward Scylla,[65] I
told them nothing, as they could do nothing.
They would have dropped their oars again, in panic,
to roll for cover under the decking. Circe's
bidding against arms had slipped my mind,
so I tied on my cuirass[66] and took up
two heavy spears, then made my way along
to the foredeck—thinking to see her first from there,
the monster of the gray rock, harboring
torment for my friends. I strained my eyes
upon the cliffside veiled in cloud, but nowhere
could I catch sight of her.
And all this time,
in travail,[67] sobbing, gaining on the current,
we rowed into the strait—Scylla to port
and on our starboard beam Charybdis,[68] dire
gorge[69] of the salt seatide. By heaven! when she
vomited, all the sea was like a cauldron
seething over intense fire, when the mixture
suddenly heaves and rises.
The shot spume
soared to the landside heights, and fell like rain.
But when she swallowed the sea water down
we saw the funnel of the maelstrom,[70] heard
the rock bellowing all around, and dark
sand raged on the bottom far below.
My men all blanched against the gloom, our eyes

58 **Reading Strategy**
Reading in Sentences
How would you rewrite Odysseus' pep talk in paragraph form without poetic line breaks?

64. the combers (kōm´ ərs) **and the smoke** the large waves that break on the beach and the ocean spray.

65. Scylla (sil´ ə)

66. cuirass (kwi ras´) *n.* armor for the upper body.

67. travail (trə vāl´) *n.* very hard work.

68. Charybdis (kə rib´ dis)

69. gorge (gôrj) *n.* hungry, consuming mouth.

70. maelstrom (māl´ strəm) *n.* large, violent whirlpool.

59 **Reading Check**
What orders does Odysseus give his shipmates?

58 Reading Strategy
Reading in Sentences

- Tell students that Odysseus' speech is written for the rhythm and meter of the poetic form, but its meaning can become clearer when it is read without the line breaks.
- Ask students the Reading Strategy question on p. 1009: How would you rewrite Odysseus' pep talk in paragraph form without poetic line breaks?
  Possible response: "Heads up, lads! We must obey the orders as I give them. Get the oar shafts in your hands and lay back hard on your benches. Hit these breaking seas. Zeus, help us pull away before we founder. You at the tiller, listen and take in all that I say. The rudders are your duty: keep her out of the combers and the smoke; steer for that headland; watch the drift, or we fetch up in the smother, and you drown us."

59 Reading Check

Answer: Odysseus orders his shipmates to row hard and set a course.

ENRICHMENT: Cultural Connection
Geography and the *Odyssey*

Display a map of the Mediterranean Sea and ask students how geography might relate to the selection "Scylla and Charybdis." Point out that the monster Scylla is thought to have been located at what is today known as the Strait of Messina, the passage between Sicily and the toe of the boot of Italy. Suggest that, with such an abundance of islands in the Aegean and Mediterranean seas, treacherous sea straits probably inspired the notion of a ship passing between two deadly dangers.

Then, display a map of the world. Ask students to use their knowledge of geography to pinpoint other possibly dangerous sea passages, such as the Strait of Magellan, the Strait of Gibraltar, or the Bering Strait. Suggest that students find out more about the places mentioned. Ask them to search fiction and nonfiction, historical accounts, and explorers' diaries to find descriptions of these places. Have them share their findings with the class.

60 Reading Strategy

Reading in Sentences

- Have students respond to the Reading Strategy task on p. 1010: By reading in sentences rather than line breaks, explain what happens in lines 810–814.
  Possible responses: Reading in sentences makes the action clearer and also helps strengthen the impact of the verbal images. Instead of, "Voices came down to me / in anguish . . . ," the result is, "Voices came down to me in anguish . . ."
- Suggest that students continue to apply this strategy as they read on.

61 Literary Analysis

The Epic Hero

- Remind students that genuine feeling for the men he leads is one of the traits that marks Odysseus as a hero.
- Ask students the Literary Analysis question on p. 1010: How does Odysseus show the heroic quality of loyalty in lines 823–825?
  Answer: As Odysseus witnesses the terrible death of his men, he suffers "deathly pity" and calls the sight "far the worst" he has ever suffered.

were fixed upon that yawning mouth in fear
of being devoured.

Then Scylla made her strike,
whisking six of my best men from the ship.
I happened to glance aft at ship and oarsmen
60 and caught sight of their arms and legs, dangling
high overhead. Voices came down to me
in anguish, calling my name for the last time.

A man surfcasting on a point of rock
for bass or mackerel, whipping his long rod
to drop the sinker and the bait far out,
will hook a fish and rip it from the surface
to dangle wriggling through the air:

so these
were borne aloft in spasms toward the cliff.

She ate them as they shrieked there, in her den,
in the dire grapple, reaching still for me—
and deathly pity ran me through
61 at that sight—far the worst I ever suffered,
questing the passes of the strange sea.

We rowed on.
The Rocks were now behind; Charybdis, too,
and Scylla dropped astern.

The Cattle of the Sun God

In the small hours of the third watch, when stars
that shone out in the first dusk of evening
had gone down to their setting, a giant wind
blew from heaven, and clouds driven by Zeus
shrouded land and sea in a night of storm;
so, just as Dawn with fingertips of rose
touched the windy world, we dragged our ship
to cover in a grotto, a sea cave
where nymphs had chairs of rock and sanded floors.
I mustered all the crew and said:

Reading Strategy
Reading in Sentences By reading in sentences rather than line breaks, explain what happens in lines 810–814.

Literary Analysis
The Epic Hero How does Odysseus show the heroic quality of loyalty in lines 823–825?

'Old shipmates,
our stores are in the ship's hold, food and drink;
the cattle here are not for our provision,
or we pay dearly for it.
Fierce the god is
who cherishes these heifers and these sheep:
Helios; and no man avoids his eye.'

To this my fighters nodded. Yes. But now
we had a month of onshore gales, blowing
day in, day out—south winds, or south by east.
As long as bread and good red wine remained
to keep the men up, and appease their craving,
they would not touch the cattle. But in the end,
when all the barley in the ship was gone,
hunger drove them to scour the wild shore
with angling hooks, for fishes and seafowl,
whatever fell into their hands; and lean days
wore their bellies thin.
The storms continued.
So one day I withdrew to the interior
to pray the gods in solitude, for hope
that one might show me some way of salvation.
Slipping away, I struck across the island
to a sheltered spot, out of the driving gale.
I washed my hands there, and made supplication
to the gods who own Olympus,[71] all the gods—
but they, for answer, only closed my eyes
under slow drops of sleep.
Now on the shore Eurylochus
made his insidious plea:
'Comrades,' he said,
'You've gone through everything; listen to what I say.
All deaths are hateful to us, mortal wretches,
but famine is the most pitiful, the worst
end that a man can come to.
Will you fight it?
Come, we'll cut out the noblest of these cattle
for sacrifice to the gods who own the sky;
and once at home, in the old country of Ithaca,

Reading Strategy
Reading in Sentences Explain the instructions that Odysseus gives his crew in lines 838–840.

Literary Analysis
The Epic Hero and Conflict What conflict is likely to arise from the crew's hunger?

71. Olympus (ō lim′ pəs) Mount Olympus, home of the gods.

insidious (in sid′ ē əs) *adj.* characterized by craftiness and betrayal

64 **Reading Check**
What does Scylla do to the six men she takes from the ship?

62 Reading Strategy
Reading in Sentences
- Tell students that in this translation of the *Odyssey,* thoughts are often joined by semicolons. When reading for meaning, it is often best to treat these as periods and the clauses as separate sentences.
- Have students respond to the Reading Strategy task on p. 1011: Explain the instructions that Odysseus gives his crew in lines 838–840.
  Answer: Odysseus explains that there is food and drink in the ship's hold. He warns his men not to eat the cattle they find, or there will be serious consequences.

63 Literary Analysis
The Epic Hero and Conflict
- Point out that Odysseus was warned earlier in the tale not to eat the cattle of the sun god, and in lines 838–840 he passes the warning on to his men. This can be seen as foreshadowing of a future conflict.
- Ask students the Literary Analysis question on p. 1011: What conflict is likely to arise from the crew's hunger?
  Possible response: A conflict between Odysseus and his men will likely arise. When bread and wine are plentiful, the men heed Odysseus' warning not to harm the cattle. But as the crew grows hungrier, the temptation to ignore the warning is likely to grow stronger.

64 Reading Check
Answer: Scylla eats the six men.

65 Literary Analysis

The Epic Hero and Conflict

- Tell students that even when famine appears imminent, Odysseus resists the temptation to harm the cattle. But while he is away on the other side of the island, his men falter.
- Ask students the first Literary Analysis question on p. 1012: Do you think Eurylochus' beliefs are in conflict with Odysseus' beliefs?
  Possible response: The beliefs of the two men are in conflict. Eurylochus believes it is better to tempt the wrath of the gods and sacrifice the cattle than to risk starvation on the island, while Odysseus believes that the warning to avoid eating the cattle must be observed at all costs.

66 Reading Strategy

Reading in Sentences

- When the realization dawns on Odysseus that his men have sacrificed cattle in his absence, he feels grief and anger. Remind students that reading the passage without line breaks can make the meaning clearer.
- Have students respond to the Reading Strategy task on p. 1012: Read in complete sentences to rephrase lines 894–900.
  Possible response: "I awoke suddenly and walked toward the sea. At the same time, I saw our ship and smelled cooking fat, and I realized what had happened. I was seized with grief and cried to the gods, who had caused me to sleep while my men did this mischief."

67 Literary Analysis

The Epic Hero

- Ask students the second Literary Analysis question on p. 1012: Which important ancient Greek value does Odysseus reveal through his actions concerning the sacrifice?
  Answer: By immediately confronting the gods for making him sleep, Odysseus is demonstrating the Greek belief that the gods had a hand in everything that happened.

if ever that day comes—
we'll build a costly temple and adorn it
with every beauty for the Lord of Noon.[72]
But if he flares up over his heifers lost,
wishing our ship destroyed, and if the gods
make cause with him, why, then I say: Better
open your lungs to a big sea once for all
than waste to skin and bones on a lonely island!'

65 Thus Eurylochus; and they murmured 'Aye!'
trooping away at once to round up heifers.
Now, that day tranquil cattle with broad brows
were gazing near, and soon the men drew up
around their chosen beasts in ceremony.
They plucked the leaves that shone on a tall oak—
having no barley meal—to strew the victims,
performed the prayers and ritual, knifed the kine
and flayed each carcass, cutting thighbones free
to wrap in double folds of fat. These offerings,
with strips of meat, were laid upon the fire.
Then, as they had no wine, they made libation
with clear spring water, broiling the entrails first;
and when the bones were burnt and tripes shared,
they spitted the carved meat.
                                        Just then my slumber
left me in a rush, my eyes opened,
and I went down the seaward path. No sooner
had I caught sight of our black hull, than savory
odors of burnt fat eddied around me;
66 grief took hold of me, and I cried aloud:

67 'O Father Zeus and gods in bliss forever,
you made me sleep away this day of mischief!
O cruel drowsing, in the evil hour!
Here they sat, and a great work they contrived.'[73]

Lampetia[74] in her long gown meanwhile
had borne swift word to the Overlord of Noon:

'They have killed your kine.'
                                        And the Lord Helios
burst into angry speech amid the immortals:

'O Father Zeus and gods in bliss forever,

72. Lord of Noon Helios.

Literary Analysis
The Epic Hero and Conflict Do you think Eurylochus' beliefs are in conflict with Odysseus' beliefs?

Reading Strategy
Reading in Sentences Read in complete sentences to rephrase lines 894–900.

73. contrived (kən trīvd´) *v.* thought up; devised.

74. Lampetia (lam pē´ shə) a nymph.

Literary Analysis
The Epic Hero Which important ancient Greek value does Odysseus reveal through his actions concerning the sacrifice?

ENRICHMENT: Art Connection

Early Greek Art and Architecture

Greek art and architecture are generally associated with stately temples, ideally proportioned marble statues, and elegantly painted vases—relics of the Golden Age of Athens, which started in 461 B.C., when Pericles came to power, and lasted for thirty years.

The Trojan War, however, predates this period by 700 years or more. Greeks at that time built fortresslike citadels fortified by massive walls. Their palaces had a rectangular main room called the *megaron,* built around a central hearth, with four columns supporting the roof. The walls were decorated with colorful frescoes. Odysseus' palace was built on this plan.

Typical art objects from Homer's time are clay vases decorated with intricate patterns and geometric figures of animals and humans. They look primitive and rugged compared to art of the classical period.

Literature in context Geography Connection

Tracing Odysseus' Route

(68) Odysseus' journey carries him to real places, like Troy and Sparta, and fictitious places, like Aeolia and Aeaea. Modern historians have tried to determine Odysseus' actual route. Here is one theory:

- From Troy (in present-day Turkey), Odysseus proceeded across the Aegean Sea, passing between Sparta and Crete.
- He then sailed westward on the Mediterranean Sea to Sicily, where he confronted the Cyclops. Nearby islands were home to the Lotus-Eaters, the Sirens, and Aeolus.
- After circling Sicily, Odysseus sailed north-eastward until he finally reached the island of Ithaca, his home.

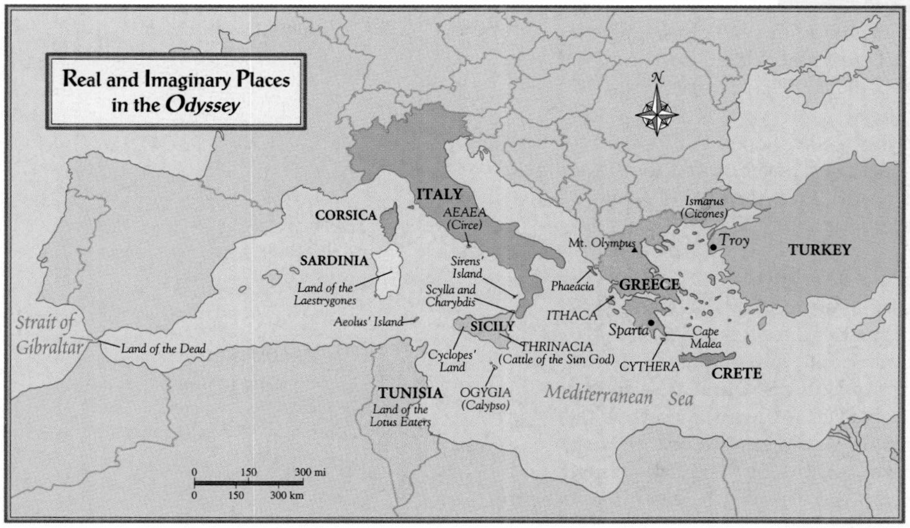

(69) ▲ **Critical Viewing** The entrance to the Land of the Dead is believed to have been the Strait of Gibraltar. Why might the ancient Greeks have considered this location frightening? **[Analyze]**

punish Odysseus' men! So overweening,
now they have killed my peaceful kine, my joy
at morning when I climbed the sky of stars,
and evening, when I bore westward from heaven.
Restitution or penalty they shall pay—
and pay in full—or I go down forever
to light the dead men in the underworld.'

Then Zeus who drives the stormcloud made reply:

'Peace, Helios: shine on among the gods,
shine over mortals in the fields of grain.
Let me throw down one white-hot bolt, and make
splinters of their ship in the winedark sea.'

(70) **Reading Check**

What do the shipmates do while Odysseus is sleeping?

(68) Literature in Context

Geography Connection

You may wish to supplement the map on p. 1013 by presenting a modern map of the Mediterranean. Be sure students understand the location of Ithaca.

(69) ▶Critical Viewing

Possible response: The Strait of Gibraltar is far from the center of Greek civilization and leads to the vast, open water of the Atlantic Ocean. At the time, the Greeks would not have known what lay beyond the strait—for all they knew the world ended there.

(70) Reading Check

Answer: While Odysseus is sleeping, his men sacrifice some of the cattle belonging to Helios.

CUSTOMIZE INSTRUCTION FOR UNIVERSAL ACCESS

For Gifted/Talented Students	For Advanced Readers
Ask students to create their own map tracing Odysseus' route. Encourage them to add photographs or their own illustrations to depict the Mediterranean setting and specific episodes and figures from the *Odyssey*.	Most sea captains keep a log, a record of events and sailing data for each day of a voyage. Ask students to write three to five entries in a ship's log that Odysseus might have kept on his journey. Entries should be based on events from Part 1 of the *Odyssey*.

71 Reading Strategy

Reading in Sentences

- The scene in which Odysseus' ship is hit with a violent storm, starting with line 940, is full of furious action. Point out how dramatic this section would be to an audience in Homer's time, hearing it told by a storyteller.
- Have students read this passage aloud, the way they imagine Odysseus would say it as he told the story. To help keep meaning clear, emphasize to students that they should read in sentences, ignoring the line breaks.
- Have students respond to the Reading Strategy task on p. 1014: By reading in sentences, explain what happens to the ship.
Possible response: "After the ship leaves the island, Zeus sends a violent storm. It immediately breaks both forestays and the mast, killing the steersman. A thunderbolt then hits the ship, flinging all the men into the sea."

—Calypso later told me of this exchange,
as she declared that Hermes[75] had told her.
Well, when I reached the sea cave and the ship,
I faced each man, and had it out; but where
could any remedy be found? There was none.
The silken beeves[76] of Helios were dead.
The gods, moreover, made queer signs appear:
cowhides began to crawl, and beef, both raw
and roasted, lowed like kine upon the spits.

Now six full days my gallant crew could feast
upon the prime beef they had marked for slaughter
from Helios' herd; and Zeus, the son of Cronus,
added one fine morning.
All the gales
had ceased, blown out, and with an offshore breeze
we launched again, stepping the mast and sail,
to make for the open sea. Astern of us
the island coastline faded, and no land
showed anywhere, but only sea and heaven,
when Zeus Cronion piled a thunderhead
above the ship, while gloom spread on the ocean.
We held our course, but briefly. Then the squall
struck whining from the west, with gale force, breaking
both forestays, and the mast came toppling aft
along the ship's length, so the running rigging
showered into the bilge.
On the afterdeck
(71) the mast had hit the steersman a slant blow
bashing the skull in, knocking him overside,
as the brave soul fled the body, like a diver.
With crack on crack of thunder, Zeus let fly
a bolt against the ship, a direct hit,
so that she bucked, in reeking fumes of sulphur,
and all the men were flung into the sea.
They came up 'round the wreck, bobbing awhile
like petrels[77] on the waves.
No more seafaring
homeward for these, no sweet day of return;
the god had turned his face from them.
I clambered

75. **Hermes** (hʉr´ mēz) herald and messenger of the gods.

76. **beeves** (bēvz) *n.* plural of *beef.*

Reading Strategy
Reading in Sentences By reading in sentences, explain what happens to the ship.

77. **petrels** (pe´ trəlz) small, dark sea birds.

fore and aft my hulk until a comber
split her, keel from ribs, and the big timber
floated free; the mast, too, broke away.
A backstay floated dangling from it, stout
rawhide rope, and I used this for lashing
mast and keel together. These I straddled,
riding the frightful storm.

Nor had I yet
seen the worst of it: for now the west wind
dropped, and a southeast gale came on—one more
twist of the knife—taking me north again,
straight for Charybdis. All that night I drifted,
and in the sunrise, sure enough, I lay
off Scylla mountain and Charybdis deep.
There, as the whirlpool drank the tide, a billow
tossed me, and I sprang for the great fig tree,
catching on like a bat under a bough.
Nowhere had I to stand, no way of climbing,
the root and bole[78] being far below, and far
above my head the branches and their leaves,
massed, overshadowing Charybdis pool.
But I clung grimly, thinking my mast and keel
would come back to the surface when she spouted.
And ah! how long, with what desire, I waited!
till, at the twilight hour, when one who hears
and judges pleas in the marketplace all day
between contentious men, goes home to supper,
the long poles at last reared from the sea.

Now I let go with hands and feet, plunging
straight into the foam beside the timbers,
pulled astride, and rowed hard with my hands
to pass by Scylla. Never could I have passed her
had not the Father of gods and men,[79] this time,
kept me from her eyes. Once through the strait,
nine days I drifted in the open sea
before I made shore, buoyed up by the gods,
upon Ogygia[80] Isle. The dangerous nymph
Calypso lives and sings there, in her beauty,
and she received me, loved me.

Literary Analysis
The Epic Hero Which of Odysseus' heroic qualities are revealed in lines 959–962?

78. bole (bōl) *n.* tree trunk.

79. Father . . . men Zeus.

80. Ogygia (o jij´ ī a).

Reading Check
How long does Odysseus drift in the open sea?

Literary Analysis

The Epic Hero

- Point out that even as the storm kills his entire crew, Odysseus struggles to survive.

Monitor Progress Ask students the Literary Analysis question on p. 1015: Which of Odysseus' heroic qualities are revealed in lines 959–962?
Possible response: Odysseus is brave, resourceful, and skillful at seafaring. He is also determined: Even though it would seem that he is destined for certain death, he refuses to give up.

Reading Check

Answer: Odysseus drifts for nine days.

74 Background

Art

La Nef De Telemachus (The Ship of Telemachus)

This is an illustration for the *Odyssey*. It was inspired by statues, pottery, and frescoes from ancient Greece. The rich blue of the ocean, echoed in the duller blue of the cloudy sky, forms a striking frame for the massive black ship. Powered by sail and oar, this craft is the kind on which Odysseus and his men would have sailed to and from Troy. Use the following questions for discussion:

1. How do you think this ship compares in size with Columbus's vessels or with a modern ocean liner?
   Answer: This ship is smaller than a fifteenth-century wooden ship, and is much smaller than a hotel-sized ocean liner.
2. How do you think this ship would fare in a storm?
   Answer: As a relatively small ship, this craft would be buffeted by a storm and might be damaged or even sunk.

75 ▶Critical Viewing

Answer: Most ships today are powered by engines and propellers rather than by the wind and oars. Today's ships make use of highly advanced technology both to navigate and to communicate with other ships.

74

La Nef de Telemachus (The Ship of Telemachus), New York Public Library Picture Collection

75 ▲**Critical Viewing** In the *Odyssey*, Telemachus searches for his father in a ship like this one. From what you observe in the painting, how does this ship compare with modern ships? **[Compare and Contrast]**

But why tell
the same tale that I told last night in hall
to you and to your lady? Those adventures
made a long evening, and I do not hold
with tiresome repetition of a story."

Review and Assess

Thinking About the Selection

1. **Respond:** In which adventure in this section does Odysseus act most heroically? Explain.
2. **(a) Recall:** How do the Sirens lure travelers to their destruction? **(b) Compare and Contrast:** How does the danger posed by the Sirens compare to that posed by the Lotus-Eaters?
3. **(a) Recall:** What are Scylla and Charybdis, and why do they pose dangers for travelers? **(b) Analyze:** Why does Odysseus choose to sail toward Scylla rather than Charybdis?
4. **(a) Make a Judgment:** Was Odysseus right not to tell his men about his decision to sail toward Scylla? **(b) Hypothesize:** What would have happened if Odysseus had told them everything?
5. **(a) Recall:** What does Eurylochus say to persuade Odysseus' men to slaughter and eat the cattle of Helios, the sun god? **(b) Analyze:** Why is Odysseus unable to keep his men from killing the cattle? **(c) Apply:** If you had been in their situation, do you think you would have eaten the cattle? Why or why not?
6. **Make a Judgment:** Do the members of the crew deserve the punishment they receive for killing the cattle?

ASSESSMENT PRACTICE: Usage and Mechanics

Punctuation **(For more practice, see Test Preparation Workbook, p. 57.)**

Many tests ask students to punctuate appositives. Use this sample test item.

Grant that Odysseus raider of cities never see his home.

Where in this sentence should a comma or commas be added?

A after *that*
B after *that* and after *Odysseus*
C after *Odysseus* and after *cities*
D no commas are needed

Students should note that "raider of cities" is an appositive that describes Odysseus. Therefore commas are needed before and after that phrase, choice *C*.

Answers for Page 1017

Review and Assess

1. Students might admire Odysseus' skill and bravery when faced with the lose-lose choice between Scylla and Charybdis.
2. **(a)** They sing an irresistible song that lures travelers to destruction. **(b)** Both involve the perils of giving in to temptation. The Sirens lure sailors by singing a seductive song. The Lotus-Eaters cause men to forget their homes and their journey by feeding them the Lotus. The Sirens seem to be aware that they are doing something wrong, whereas the Lotus-Eaters do not.
3. **(a)** Scylla is a sea monster; Charybdis is a whirlpool. **(b)** Possible response: Charybdis endangers the entire ship, whereas Scylla can cause only partial losses.
4. **(a)** Some students may reply that Odysseus was wise to keep the information from his men in order to minimize their panic. Others might think that the men have a right to know what danger lies in store for them. **(b)** Possible response: Had they known what awaited them, Odysseus' men might have panicked or refused to sail through the strait.
5. **(a)** Eurylochus claims that there is no fate worse than starvation. He also claims that Helios might be appeased later on. **(b)** The gods have put him into a deep sleep. **(c)** Some students may say they would avoid eating the cattle because of the warnings, or because it would be wrong. Others may sympathize with the plight of the hungry crew and say they would have been tempted to eat the cattle.
6. Most students will find the punishment of death harsh for the crime of killing the cattle. Some will point out, however, that the men were repeatedly warned of the dire consequences.

ASSESS

Answers for p. 1018

Review and Assess

1. Odysseus' heroic qualities: He is able to remain true to himself and his goals under seemingly impossible circumstances; he is exceptionally clever and daring. He is more like mortal men when he is homesick, curious, boastful, or afraid.
2. In lines 18–37, Odysseus reveals his cunning in peace and war, and his dedication to his home and family.
3. Based on the Cyclops' episode, students might conclude that the Greeks valued bravery and cool-headedness. Based on the episode of Scylla and Charybdis, the Greeks valued decisiveness. Based on Odysseus' dedication to returning home, students might conclude that the Greeks valued determination and loyalty.
4. Internal conflicts: the pleasure with Calypso and Circe versus his desire to go home. External conflicts: Cyclops, Scylla and Charybdis.
5. Odysseus contends with a terrible storm following the sacrifice of the cattle of Helios. A whirlpool (Charybdis) is also a force of nature.
6. Possible responses: Bravery, coolness, cleverness, tenacity, and a strong will help Odysseus succeed.
7. Students may cite five complete stops: after *cave?, fold., behind?, eye?,* and *wine.*
8. Possible response: "The crew stood up quickly to take down the sail and put it away. Then, they rowed quickly. I cut a big piece of beeswax into small pieces and rolled them in my hands until they got soft. This didn't take long, because it was noon and the sun was warm. Going past the men one by one, I stuck some in their ears. Then, they tied me to the mast in the middle of the ship and went back to their rowing."
9. Students may cite any leader who refused to give up.

Review and Assess

Literary Analysis

The Epic Hero

1. As an **epic hero,** Odysseus has both heroic and mortal qualities. Identify some of his qualities in both categories.
2. When Odysseus introduces himself in lines 18–37, which heroic traits does he reveal?
3. Based on Odysseus' actions in these episodes, which values did the ancient Greeks admire?

Connecting Literary Elements

4. Some of Odysseus' **conflicts** involve battles with enemies, and some involve clashes with thoughts and feelings within himself. On a chart like the one shown, list Odysseus' external and internal conflicts.

5. In which of the adventures does Odysseus come into conflict with forces of nature?
6. Which character traits help Odysseus to be victorious in most of his conflicts?

Reading Strategy

Reading in Sentences

7. (a) How many complete stops should you make in reading lines 398–408? (b) Where are they?
8. Rewrite lines 704–715 as a paragraph, using your own words.

Extend Understanding

9. **History Connection:** Which political or military leader whom you have read or heard about seems similar to Odysseus? Explain.

Quick Review

The **epic hero**—the central character in a long poetic tale of adventure—undertakes a dangerous voyage, demonstrating traits that are valued by the society in which the epic originates.

A **conflict** is a struggle between opposing forces. It may occur between characters, between a character and nature, or within a character's mind.

To get the most out of a story told in verse, **read in sentences**, using punctuation and ignoring the line breaks.

Take It to the Net

www.phschool.com

Take the interactive self-test online to check your understanding of the selection.

TEACHING RESOURCES

The following resources can be used to enrich or extend the instruction for pp. 1018–1019.

Vocabulary

Selection Support Workbook: Build Vocabulary, p. 225

Vocabulary and Spelling Practice Book (Use this booklet for skills enrichment.)

Grammar

Selection Support Workbook: Build Grammar Skills, p. 226

Writing and Grammar, Gold Level, p. 620

Daily Language Practice Transparencies

BLOCK SCHEDULING: Resources marked with this symbol provide varied instruction during 90-minute blocks.

Integrate Language Skills

❶ Vocabulary Development Lesson

Word Origins: Words From Myths

Titanic, meaning "huge or powerful," comes from *Titans*, giant Greek gods who once ruled the world. Define each word and explain its link to mythology.

1. helium **2.** odyssey **3.** museum **4.** siren

Spelling Strategy

If a word of more than one syllable has a vowel-consonant ending and the accent is not on the last syllable, do not double the final consonant before adding a suffix beginning with a vowel: *plunder* + *-ed* = *plundered*. Correct any misspellings below.

1. mentorring **2.** flowerred **3.** travelers

Concept Development: Antonyms

After reviewing the vocabulary on page 979, match each word below with its opposite.

1. dispatched	**a.** restored to its owner
2. bereft	**b.** begun
3. plundered	**c.** joyfully acquired
4. squall	**d.** tiny
5. mammoth	**e.** small and weak
6. assuage	**f.** calm, sunny weather
7. insidious	**g.** honest
8. titanic	**h.** aggravate
9. ardor	**i.** indifference

❷ Grammar Lesson

Usage: *like, as,* and *as if*

The words *like, as,* and *as if* all suggest comparisons, but they are often used incorrectly. **Like** is a preposition and should not be used instead of the conjunctions ***as*** or ***as if*** to introduce a clause.

Incorrect: *Like* he had boasted, he was mighty.
Correct: *As* he had boasted, he was mighty.

Incorrect: He held the men *like* they were squirming puppies.
Correct: He held the men *as if* they were squirming puppies.
Correct: He held the men *like* squirming puppies.

Practice Write these sentences on your paper, using the correct word(s) in parentheses.

1. He ate (as if, like) he had been starving.
2. The men wept (as if, like) children.
3. (Like, As) a dead man, he slept unmoving.
4. The men felt (like, as if) they were doomed.
5. Odysseus' bragging sounded (like, as) a donkey's bray to the Cyclops.

Writing Application Write three sentences about Odysseus, using *like, as,* or *as if* in one sentence each.

WG Prentice Hall Writing and Grammar Connection: Chapter 27, Section 2

❸ Extension Activities

Listening and Speaking Pick one episode from Part 1 of the *Odyssey*, and describe the action as a **play-by-play broadcast**. Reread the episode and jot down the key actions. Draft a script. Practice your broadcast and record it to play for the class.

Writing In a **comparison-and-contrast essay,** explore the concept of the hero. In your essay, show similarities and differences between Odysseus and other heroes, real or imaginary. Include several different points of comparison.

ASSESSMENT RESOURCES

The following resources can be used to assess students' knowledge and skills.

Selection Assessment

- **Formal Assessment,** pp. 205–207
- **Open Book Test,** pp. 169–171
- **Got It! Assessment Videotapes,** Tape 5
- **Test Bank Software**

Take It to the Net

Visit www.phschool.com for self-tests and additional questions on the *Odyssey.*

PRENTICE HALL ASSESSMENT SYSTEM

- **Workbook**
- **Skill Book**
- **Transparencies**
- **CD-ROM**

Answers for p. 1019

❶ Vocabulary Development

Word Origins: Words From Myths

1. *Helium* comes from Helios, the Greek god of the sun.
2. *Odyssey*, meaning "a long trip," comes from the title of Homer's epic of Odysseus' journey.
3. *Museum*, a place containing art, comes from the Greek Muses, the goddesses of the arts.
4. *Siren* comes from the Greek Sirens, who sang tempting songs. *Siren* has two English meanings—a temptress and a loud noise used as an alarm.

Spelling Strategy

1. mentoring
2. flowered
3. correct

Concept Development: Antonyms

1. b	**4.** f	**7.** g
2. c	**5.** d	**8.** e
3. a	**6.** h	**9.** i

❷ Grammar

1. as if
2. like
3. Like
4. as if
5. like

Writing Application

Possible responses: Odysseus held on to the mast as if his life depended on it. As he had hoped for so many years, he finally saw the coast of Ithaca. Old Argus thumped his tail like a puppy when he finally saw his master.

❸ Listening and Speaking

- Suggest that students choose an episode that has action and suspense, and where there is a clear competition, such as Odysseus versus the Cyclops.
- If possible, students should listen to some old radio broadcasts or sporting events to get the flavor of a good broadcast.
- Students do not have to memorize their broadcasts, but they should be familiar with them so they can read without stumbling.

from the Odyssey, Part 2

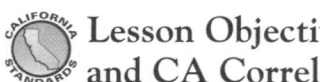

Lesson Objectives and CA Correlations

1. **To analyze and respond to literary elements**
   - Literary Analysis: Epic Simile **R 3.7**
   - Connecting Literary Elements: Imagery **R 3.7**
2. **To read, comprehend, analyze, and critique an epic**
   - Reading Strategy: Summarizing **R 3.8**
   - Reading Check questions
   - Review and Assess questions
3. **To develop word analysis skills, fluency, and systematic vocabulary**
   - Vocabulary Development Lesson: Latin Root: *-equi-* **R 1.1**
4. **To understand and apply written and oral language conventions**
   - Spelling Strategy
   - Grammar Lesson: Usage: *among* and *between* **LC 1.3**
   - Assessment Practice (ATE)
5. **To understand and apply appropriate writing and research strategies**
   - Writing Lesson: Character Study **W 2.2**
   - Extension Activity: *Odyssey* Map **W 1.3**
6. **To understand and apply listening and speaking strategies**
   - Extension Activity: Debate **LS 1.8**

STEP-BY-STEP TEACHING GUIDE	PACING GUIDE
PRETEACH	
Motivate Students and Provide Background	
Use the Motivation activity (ATE p. 1020)	5 min.
Read and discuss the Review material and Background information (SE/ATE p. 1020) [A]	5 min.
Introduce the Concepts	
Introduce the Literary Analysis and Reading Strategy (SE/ATE p. 1020) [A]	15 min.
Pronounce the vocabulary words and read their definitions (SE p. 1020)	5 min.
TEACH	
Monitor Comprehension	
Informally monitor comprehension by circulating while students read independently or in groups [A]	40 min.
Monitor students' comprehension with the Reading Check notes (SE/ATE pp. 1022, 1025, 1027, 1029, 1031, 1033, 1035, 1039, 1041, 1043, 1045)	as students read
Develop vocabulary with Vocabulary notes (SE pp. 1022, 1024, 1027, 1029, 1032, 1040)	as students read
Develop Understanding	
Develop students' understanding of epic similes with the Literary Analysis annotations (SE/ATE pp. 1022, 1025, 1031, 1032, 1039, 1041, 1042) [A]	10 min.
Develop students' ability to summarize with the Reading Strategy annotations (SE/ATE pp. 1025–1029, 1031, 1033, 1039–1041, 1045)	10 min.
ASSESS	
Assess Mastery	
Assess students' comprehension of the selection and mastery of the Reading Strategy and Literary Analysis by having them answer the Review and Assess questions (SE/ATE p. 1047)	20 min.
Use one or more of the print and media Assessment Resources (ATE p. 1049) [A]	up to 50 min.
EXTEND	
Apply Understanding	
Have students complete the Vocabulary Development Lesson and the Grammar Lesson (SE p. 1048) [A]	20 min.
Apply students' knowledge of including quotations using the Writing Lesson (SE/ATE p. 1049) [A]	45 min.
Apply students' understanding using one or more of the Extension Activities (SE p. 1049)	20–90 min.

[A] **ACCELERATED INSTRUCTION:**
Use the strategies and activities identified with an [A].

UNIVERSAL ACCESS
● = Below-Level Students
▲ = On-Level Students
■ = Above-Level Students

Time and Resource Manager

Reading Level: Challenging
Average Number of Instructional Days: 5

RESOURCES		
PRINT	**TRANSPARENCIES**	**TECHNOLOGY**
• **Beyond Literature,** Humanities Connection: Greek Gods, p. 58 ▲ ■		• **Interest Grabber Video,** Tape 5 ● ▲ ■
• **Selection Support Workbook:** ● ▲ ■ Literary Analysis, p. 232 Reading Strategy, p. 231 Build Vocabulary, p. 229	• **Literary Analysis and Reading Transparencies,** pp. 115 and 116 ● ▲ ■	
		• **Listening to Literature** ● ▲ ■ Audiocassettes, Side 31 Audio CDs, CD 20
• **Literatura en español** ● ▲ • **Literary Analysis for Enrichment** ■	• **Fine Art Transparencies Volume 1,** Transparency 18 ● ▲ ■	
• **Formal Assessment:** Selection Test, pp. 208–210 ● ▲ ■ • **Open Book Test,** pp. 172–174 ● ▲ ■ • PRENTICE HALL ASSESSMENT SYSTEM ● ▲ ■	• PRENTICE HALL ASSESSMENT SYSTEM ● ▲ ■ Skills Practice Answers and Explanations on Transparencies	• **Test Bank Software** ● ▲ ■ • **Got It! Assessment Videotapes,** Tape 5 ● ▲
• **Selection Support Workbook:** ● ▲ ■ Build Grammar Skills, p. 230 • **Writing and Grammar,** Gold Level ● ▲ ■ • **Extension Activities,** p. 56 ● ▲ ■	• **Daily Language Practice Transparencies** ● ▲	• **Writing and Grammar iText CD-ROM** ● ▲ ■ ***Take It to the Net*** www.phschool.com

BLOCK SCHEDULING: Use one 90-minute class period to preteach the selection and have students read it. Use a second 90-minute class period to assess students' mastery of skills and have them complete one of the Extension Activities.

PREteach

Step-by-Step Teaching Guide for pp. 1020–1021

Motivation

Remind students of the action heroes they talked about before reading the first part of the *Odyssey.* Now, how do they think the heroes compare with Odysseus? Has Odysseus been more or less successful than they would have been? In what ways? Tell students that Odysseus—in true epic hero fashion—does succeed in returning home. But his troubles do not end when he reaches the shores of Ithaca.

❶ Background

Social Studies

Of the two great epic poems attributed to Homer, the *Iliad* has been called a war poem, and the *Odyssey* has been called a postwar poem. The wanderings of Odysseus after his victory at Troy and the difficulties of readjusting to a civil society upon his eventual return home have helped make the themes of the *Odyssey* relevant to generation after generation. The theme of the returning veteran, with the struggles to reestablish relationships with spouses and friends (and perhaps with a child for the first time) add a human poignancy to this epic adventure. Discuss with students the difficulties and emotions that Odysseus is likely to face after twenty years away.

❶ Prepare to Read

from the Odyssey, Part 2

❷ Literary Analysis

Epic Simile

An **epic simile**, sometimes called a Homeric simile, is an elaborate comparison that may extend for several lines. Epic similes may use the words *like, as, just as,* or *so* to make the comparison. In Part 1, lines 268–271, Odysseus uses an epic simile to describe the fallen tree from which he creates the weapon used to blind the Cyclops.

> And it was like a mast / a lugger of twenty oars, broad in the beam— / a deep-sea-going craft—might carry: / so long, so big around, it seemed.

As you read, notice Homer's use of epic similes to bring descriptions to life.

Connecting Literary Elements

Similes are one example of **imagery**—descriptive language that creates word pictures. These pictures, or images, are created with details of sight, sound, taste, touch, smell, or movement. An epic simile contains imagery that shows how something looks or acts by comparing it to something else. For example, comparing a fallen tree to a broad mast stresses the size of the tree.

❸ Reading Strategy

Summarizing

You can better understand the events in an epic like the *Odyssey*—or in any other work of literature with a complicated plot—by **summarizing** the events as you read. Retell the plot briefly in your own words, jotting down details about what events occurred and why.

Use a chart like the one shown to summarize episodes in the *Odyssey*.

What Happens
As a beggar, Odysseus meets Telemachus. He is changed by Athena. He reveals his identity.

Why?
His disguise helps him find out what has changed in Ithaca. He needs his son's help.

Summary

Vocabulary Development

dissemble (di sem′ bəl) *v.* conceal under a false appearance; disguise (p. 1022)

lithe (līth) *adj.* supple; limber (p. 1024)

incredulity (in′ krə do͞o′ lə tē) *n.* inability to believe (p. 1024)

bemusing (bi myo͞oz′ iŋ) *adj.* stupefying or muddling (p. 1027)

glowering (glou′ ər iŋ) *adj.* staring with sullen anger; scowling (p. 1029)

equity (ek′ wit ē) *n.* fairness; impartiality; justice (p. 1032)

maudlin (môd′ lin) *adj.* tearfully or foolishly sentimental (p. 1032)

contempt (kən tempt′) *n.* disdain or scorn; scornful feelings or actions (p. 1040)

TEACHING RESOURCES

The following resources can be used to enrich or extend the instruction for pp. 1020–1021.

Motivation

Interest Grabber Videotape, Tape 5

Background

Beyond Literature, p. 58

Take It to the Net
Visit www.phschool.com for background and hotlinks for the *Odyssey.*

Literary Analysis

Literary Analysis and Reading Transparencies, pp. 115–116

Reading

Selection Support: Reading Strategy, p. 231; Build Vocabulary, p. 229

BLOCK SCHEDULING: Resources marked with this symbol provide varied instruction during 90-minute blocks.

from the

Odyssey

Homer Translated by Robert Fitzgerald

PART 2

The Return of Odysseus

Review and Anticipate

In Part 1 of the *Odyssey,* Odysseus and his companions face many perils on their voyage from Troy to Ithaca. At some moments, they are tempted by others to forsake their voyage; at others, their lives are endangered by powerful enemies. Ultimately, Odysseus' men bring about their own destruction at the hand of Zeus when they kill the cattle belonging to Helios.

As Part 2 begins, Odysseus is alone when he reaches Ithaca after a twenty-year absence. What do you predict will happen when Odysseus arrives home?

2 Literary Analysis

Epic Simile

- Tell students that the *epic simile* is an effective storytelling device that translated well from the oral tradition to written works. It helps the author paint a vivid and dramatic picture with words. The *Odyssey* is a natural place to find such comparisons, because so much of the poem's actions center on fantastical beings and situations that are outside the reader's (or listener's) daily experience.
- Ask students to describe an action by a modern-day "hero" (real or fictional), using an epic simile to make the action easy for their audience to understand. Example: With just seconds to go in the game, Kobe Bryant took flight, soaring like an eagle over his defenders and swooping down to put the ball through for the game-winning basket.

3 Reading Strategy

Summarizing

- Explain to students that summarizing events helps readers in two ways. The action of condensing events and retelling them in their own words is a test of how well they understand the poem. Also, the action of writing down these events can be a very effective tool for remembering events in the poem.
- To assist in summarizing Part 2 of the *Odyssey,* tell students they may find it helpful to jot down notes about important events and their causes as they read.

Vocabulary Development

- Pronounce each vocabulary word for students, and read the definitions as a class. Have students identify any words with which they are already familiar.

CUSTOMIZE INSTRUCTION FOR UNIVERSAL ACCESS

For Less Proficient Readers	For English Learners	For Advanced Readers
Have partners paraphrase the opening passage. (Possible paraphrase: "The goddess Athena, looking like a beautiful, intelligent woman, appeared to Odysseus, though she remained invisible to Telemachus, for gods appear only to certain special people. . . .")	The selection includes a large number of words or phrases that are unfamiliar. In addition to giving the literal definitions, use each vocabulary word in a sentence to create more context for students.	The *Odyssey* was written in verse, as is Fitzgerald's translation. Whereas the translation is irregular in rhythm, the original was written in dactylic hexameter—lines of six feet or "beats," usually of three syllables each, with the stress on the first syllable. Challenge students to rewrite one or two lines in this rhythm.

E-Teach

Visit E-Teach at www.phschool.com for teachers' essays on how to teach, with questions and answers.

TEACH

Step-by-Step Teaching Guide for pp. 1022–1046

CUSTOMIZE INSTRUCTION
For Musical/Rhythmic Learners

Although Odysseus has returned safely to Ithaca, the action of the *Odyssey* is far from over. Explain to students that the rhythm of writing (even prose) is more important and more noticeable when the words are describing physical actions of some kind. Encourage students to rewrite the action scenes in a poetic meter (either Homer's or one of their choosing) to make them come alive.

❶ About the Selection

With its heroes, monsters, magic, and suspense, the *Odyssey* has always appealed strongly to readers' imaginations. Another reason for its enduring popularity is its "time machine" quality; reading it is like looking through a window at a world that is very different from ours. Despite this, the *Odyssey* is timeless. As a quest narrative, it conveys a universal lesson about determination and overcoming obstacles.

❷ Literary Analysis

Epic Simile and Imagery

- Remind students that a *simile* is a figure of speech that invites comparison between two seemingly unlike ideas or objects.
- Ask students the Literary Analysis question on p. 1022: Is the description of the goddess in lines 997–1007 written as an epic simile? Why or why not?
  Answer: No. Homer does not say that Athena is *like* a "tall woman, handsome and clever at her craft"; he says that the goddess has physically taken that form in order to appear to Odysseus. Thus, no comparison is made.

❸ ✓Reading Check

Answer: Athena tells Odysseus that there are many suitors at the palace trying to persuade Penelope that Odysseus is surely dead after all this time, and so she must marry again. Each wants to be her new husband. She tells Odysseus that it is time he put an end to all this.

"Twenty years gone, and I am back again . . ."

❶ *Odysseus has finished telling his story to the Phaeacians. The next day, young Phaeacian noblemen conduct him home by ship. He arrives in Ithaca after an absence of twenty years. The goddess Athena appears and informs him of the situation at home. Numerous suitors, believing Odysseus to be dead, have been continually seeking the hand of his wife, Penelope, in marriage, while overrunning Odysseus' palace and enjoying themselves at Penelope's expense. Moreover, they are plotting to murder Odysseus' son, Telemachus, before he can inherit his father's lands. Telemachus, who, like Penelope, still hopes for his father's return, has journeyed to Pylos and Sparta to learn what he can about his father's fate. Athena disguises Odysseus as a beggar and directs him to the hut of Eumaeus,[1] his old and faithful swineherd. While Odysseus and Eumaeus are eating breakfast, Telemachus arrives. Athena then appears to Odysseus.*

. . . From the air
she walked, taking the form of a tall woman,
handsome and clever at her craft, and stood
beyond the gate in plain sight of Odysseus,
❷ unseen, though, by Telemachus, unguessed,
for not to everyone will gods appear.
Odysseus noticed her; so did the dogs,
who cowered whimpering away from her. She only
nodded, signing to him with her brows,
a sign he recognized. Crossing the yard,
he passed out through the gate in the stockade
to face the goddess. There she said to him:

"Son of Laertes and the gods of old,
Odysseus, master of landways and seaways,
dissemble to your son no longer now.
The time has come: tell him how you together
will bring doom on the suitors in the town.
I shall not be far distant then, for I
myself desire battle."

1. **Eumaeus** (yo͞o mē´ əs)

Literary Analysis
Epic Simile and Imagery Is the description of the goddess in lines 997–1007 written as an epic simile? Why or why not?

dissemble (di sem´ bəl) *v.* conceal under a false appearance; disguise

❸ **✓Reading Check**
What does Athena reveal to Odysseus about his situation at home?

TEACHING RESOURCES

The following resources can be used to enrich or extend the instruction for pp. 1022–1046.

Literary Analysis
Selection Support: Literary Analysis, p. 232

Reading
Listening to Literature Audiocassettes, Side 31
Listening to Literature Audio CDs, CD 20

Extension
Fine Art Transparencies, Volume 1, Art Transparency 18 (This collage by Romare Bearden depicts scenes from the fall of Troy.)

BLOCK SCHEDULING: Resources marked with this symbol provide varied instruction during 90-minute blocks.

❹

Eumaeus, the Swineherd, N. C. Wyeth, Delaware Art Museum

❺ ▲ **Critical Viewing** What can you tell about Eumaeus from this illustration? **[Infer]**

❹ Background

Art

Eumaeus, the Swineherd, by N. C. Wyeth

The central figure in this painting is the faithful swineherd who stands and fights beside Odysseus in his battle with the suitors.

This illustration, like many of the others in this selection, was among the sixteen paintings N. C. Wyeth, America's foremost illustrator of children's books and the classics, painted for a 1929 edition of the *Odyssey.* Use the following questions for discussion:

1. In the *Odyssey,* Eumaeus is characterized as being loyal and noble. How does Wyeth's painting convey these traits?
   Possible response: Eumaeus is pictured as tall, straight, and sturdy, leaning firmly on his staff. He looks like a man who will not be easily moved. This firmness of his stance makes him look trustworthy.
2. Which dog in the illustration might be Argus?
   Possible response: Argus is described in lines 1163–1168 as "an old dog lying near." Argus would be the dog on the left, lying down.

❺ ▶Critical Viewing

Possible response: Eumaeus appears to be patient, loyal, and practical. The pigs in the sty behind him are a clue to his profession.

6 Reading Strategy

Summarizing

- Remind students that in Part 1 of the *Odyssey,* they learned to read in sentences and also paraphrased some passages. In summarizing, students should describe the action in their own words while also shortening the description, focusing on key elements.
- Have students summarize Odysseus' response to his son in lines 1031–1033.
  Possible response: Odysseus tells his son he is not a god, but the father he lacked in childhood.

Saying no more,
she tipped her golden wand upon the man,
making his cloak pure white, and the knit tunic
fresh around him. Lithe and young she made him,
ruddy with sun, his jawline clean, the beard
no longer gray upon his chin. And she
withdrew when she had done.
Then Lord Odysseus
reappeared—and his son was thunderstruck.
Fear in his eyes, he looked down and away
as though it were a god, and whispered:
"Stranger,
you are no longer what you were just now!
Your cloak is new; even your skin! You are
one of the gods who rule the sweep of heaven!
Be kind to us, we'll make you fair oblation[2]
and gifts of hammered gold. Have mercy on us!"

The noble and enduring man replied:

6
"No god. Why take me for a god? No, no.
I am that father whom your boyhood lacked
and suffered pain for lack of. I am he."

Held back too long, the tears ran down his cheeks
as he embraced his son.
Only Telemachus,
uncomprehending, wild
with incredulity, cried out:
"You cannot
be my father Odysseus! Meddling spirits
conceived this trick to twist the knife in me!
No man of woman born could work these wonders
by his own craft, unless a god came into it
with ease to turn him young or old at will.
I swear you were in rags and old,
and here you stand like one of the immortals!"

Odysseus brought his ranging mind to bear
and said:
"This is not princely, to be swept
away by wonder at your father's presence.
No other Odysseus will ever come,
for he and I are one, the same; his bitter
fortune and his wanderings are mine.

lithe (līth) *adj.* supple; limber

2. oblation (äb lā´ shən) *n.* offering to a god.

incredulity (in´ krə do͞o´ lə tē) *n.* inability to believe

ENRICHMENT: Cultural Connection

The Welcome Home

Discuss the reception received by troops returning from war. Discuss the various ways people welcome them, such as parades, ceremonies, speeches, yellow ribbons, and so forth. Ask students if they think people of other cultures honor and welcome their soldiers in much the same way, or whether there might be different customs in other cultures.

Ask students to find out more about how different cultures, past and present, welcome home their soldiers or warriors. Have each student choose a different culture or country and do library research on the topic. Be sure to include both non-Western and Western cultures. Have students share their findings with the class.

Twenty years gone, and I am back again
on my own island.
As for my change of skin,
that is a charm Athena, Hope of Soldiers,
uses as she will; she has the knack
7 to make me seem a beggar man sometimes
and sometimes young, with finer clothes about me.
It is no hard thing for the gods of heaven
to glorify a man or bring him low."

When he had spoken, down he sat.
Then, throwing
his arms around this marvel of a father
Telemachus began to weep. Salt tears
rose from the wells of longing in both men,
and cries burst from both as keen and fluttering
8 as those of the great taloned hawk,
whose nestlings farmers take before they fly.
So helplessly they cried, pouring out tears,
and might have gone on weeping so till sundown,
had not Telemachus said:
"Dear father! Tell me
what kind of vessel put you here ashore
on Ithaca? Your sailors, who were they?
I doubt you made it, walking on the sea!"

Then said Odysseus, who had borne the barren sea:

"Only plain truth shall I tell you, child.
Great seafarers, the Phaeacians, gave me passage
as they give other wanderers. By night
over the open ocean, while I slept,
they brought me in their cutter,[3] set me down
on Ithaca, with gifts of bronze and gold
and stores of woven things. By the gods' will
these lie all hidden in a cave. I came
to this wild place, directed by Athena,
so that we might lay plans to kill our enemies.
Count up the suitors for me, let me know
what men at arms are there, how many men.
I must put all my mind to it, to see
if we two by ourselves can take them on
or if we should look round for help."
Telemachus
replied:

Reading Strategy
Summarizing How does Odysseus explain the change in his appearance?

Literary Analysis
Epic Simile In this epic simile, what is being compared?

3. cutter (kut′ər) *n.* small, swift ship or boat carried aboard a large ship to transport personnel or supplies.

9 **✔Reading Check**
Why is Telemachus initially doubtful of Odysseus' words?

7 Reading Strategy
Summarizing
- Explain to students that simplifying and summarizing the action in a scene can help them in finding the meaning in the lines.
- Ask students the Reading Strategy question on p. 1025: How does Odysseus explain the change in his appearance?
Answer: Odysseus explains that the goddess Athena has changed his appearance with a charm.

8 Literary Analysis
Epic Simile
- Remind students that an epic simile is a device to help describe what is happening in the *Odyssey.* Beyond that, however, it also serves to underscore the drama of the action and to paint vivid images in the reader's mind.
- Ask students the Literary Analysis question on p. 1025: In this epic simile, what is being compared?
Answer: The cries of Odysseus and Telemachus are compared to those of a hawk that has lost its nestlings to a farmer.

9 ✔Reading Check
Answer: Telemachus is initially doubtful because of the change in Odysseus' appearance, which leads Telemachus to assume he is a god.

⑩ Reading Strategy

Summarizing

- To explain Telemachus' response, remind students that he has just met his father for the first time and is suddenly being asked to join in a dangerous plot with him.
- Ask students the Reading Strategy question on p. 1026: Summarize Telemachus' response to his father in lines 1089–1092. What is his concern?
  Answer: Telemachus has heard of his father's fighting skill but is skeptical of taking on an entire household of men in battle.

⑪ ▶Critical Viewing

Possible response: Students may say that the scenes both decorate the pottery and honor, celebrate, or commemorate significant people and events in Greek history and mythology.

"O Father, all my life your fame
as a fighting man has echoed in my ears—
⑩ your skill with weapons and the tricks of war—
but what you speak of is a staggering thing,
beyond imagining, for me. How can two men
do battle with a houseful in their prime?[4]
For I must tell you this is no affair
of ten or even twice ten men, but scores,
throngs of them. You shall see, here and now.
The number from Dulichium alone
is fifty-two picked men, with armorers,
a half dozen; twenty-four came from Same,
twenty from Zacynthus; our own island
accounts for twelve, high-ranked, and their retainers,
Medon the crier, and the Master Harper,
besides a pair of handymen at feasts.
If we go in against all these
I fear we pay in salt blood for your vengeance.
You must think hard if you would conjure up
the fighting strength to take us through."
Odysseus
who had endured the long war and the sea
answered:
"I'll tell you now.
Suppose Athena's arm is over us, and Zeus
her father's, must I rack my brains for more?"

Clearheaded Telemachus looked hard and said:

"Those two are great defenders, no one doubts it,
but throned in the serene clouds overhead;
other affairs of men and gods they have
to rule over."

And the hero answered:

"Before long they will stand to right and left of us
in combat, in the shouting, when the test comes—
our nerve against the suitors' in my hall.
Here is your part: at break of day tomorrow
home with you, go mingle with our princes.
The swineherd later on will take me down
the port-side trail—a beggar, by my looks,
hangdog and old. If they make fun of me
in my own courtyard, let your ribs cage up

Reading Strategy
Summarizing Summarize Telemachus' response to his father in lines 1089–1092. What is his concern?

4. in their prime in the best or most vigorous stage of their lives.

⑪ **▼ Critical Viewing**
Why do you think scenes such as this were depicted on Greek pottery? **[Speculate]**

your springing heart, no matter what I suffer,
no matter if they pull me by the heels
or practice shots at me, to drive me out.
Look on, hold down your anger. You may even
plead with them, by heaven! in gentle terms
to quit their horseplay—not that they will heed you,
rash as they are, facing their day of wrath.
Now fix the next step in your mind.
                                                            Athena,
(12) counseling me, will give me word, and I
shall signal to you, nodding: at that point
round up all armor, lances, gear of war
left in our hall, and stow the lot away
back in the vaulted storeroom. When the suitors
miss those arms and question you, be soft
in what you say: answer:
                                        'I thought I'd move them
out of the smoke. They seemed no longer those
bright arms Odysseus left us years ago
when he went off to Troy. Here where the fire's
hot breath came, they had grown black and drear.
One better reason, too, I had from Zeus:
suppose a brawl starts up when you are drunk,
you might be crazed and bloody one another,
and that would stain your feast, your courtship. Tempered
iron can magnetize a man.'
                                                            Say that.
But put aside two broadswords and two spears
for our own use, two oxhide shields nearby
when we go into action. Pallas Athena
and Zeus All-Provident will see you through,
bemusing our young friends.
                                            Now one thing more.
If son of mine you are and blood of mine,
let no one hear Odysseus is about.
Neither Laertes, nor the swineherd here,
nor any slave, nor even Penelope.
But you and I alone must learn how far
the women are corrupted; we should know
how to locate good men among our hands,
the loyal and respectful, and the shirkers[5]
who take you lightly, as alone and young."

Reading Strategy
Summarizing Summarize Athena's role in Odysseus' plan.

Reading Strategy
Summarizing Summarize the events of Odysseus' reunion with Telemachus.

bemusing (bi myo͞oz′ iŋ) *adj.* stupefying or muddling

5. shirkers (shʉrk′ ərz) *n.* people who get out of doing (or leave undone) something that needs to be done.

(13) **Reading Check**
How does Odysseus tell his son to respond if the suitors "practice shots" on Odysseus?

(12) Reading Strategy

Summarizing

- Tell students that rereading the passage in which Odysseus outlines his strategy to Telemachus, then summarizing it, will aid in understanding.
- Have students respond to the first Reading Strategy task on p. 1027: Summarize Athena's role in Odysseus' plan.
  Answer: Athena will counsel Odysseus during the event, letting him know when to signal Telemachus to lock up the suitors' weapons.

Reading Strategy

Summarizing

- Read the second Reading Strategy task on p. 1027: Summarize the events of Odysseus' reunion with Telemachus.
  Possible response: Odysseus reveals himself to Telemachus. At first, Telemachus is skeptical, but then believes him and throws his arms around his father. Then, Odysseus tells Telemachus about a plan he has to fight the suitors.

(13) Reading Check

Answer: If the suitors "practice shots" on Odysseus, who is pretending to be a beggar, Telemachus is to hold his anger and refrain from acknowledging his father.

14 Reading Strategy

Summarizing

- Ask students to note the noble qualities that Homer gives to Argus, even as an "old hound."
- Have students respond to the Reading Strategy task on p. 1028: Summarize Argus' situation since Odysseus' departure.
  Possible response: Odysseus trained Argus as a puppy before he left for war. The dog had hunted with the young men of the town, but in his old age he is abandoned and treated as rubbish, lying on a heap of dung before the gates.

Argus

Odysseus heads for town with Eumaeus. Outside the palace, Odysseus' old dog, Argus, is lying at rest as his long-absent master approaches.

While he spoke
an old hound, lying near, pricked up his ears
and lifted up his muzzle. This was Argus,
trained as a puppy by Odysseus,
but never taken on a hunt before
his master sailed for Troy. The young men, afterward,
hunted wild goats with him, and hare, and deer,
but he had grown old in his master's absence.
Treated as rubbish now, he lay at last
upon a mass of dung before the gates—
manure of mules and cows, piled there until
fieldhands could spread it on the king's estate.
Abandoned there, and half destroyed with flies,
old Argus lay.
But when he knew he heard
14 Odysseus' voice nearby, he did his best
to wag his tail, nose down, with flattened ears,
having no strength to move nearer his master.
And the man looked away,
wiping a salt tear from his cheek; but he
hid this from Eumaeus. Then he said:

"I marvel that they leave this hound to lie
here on the dung pile;
he would have been a fine dog, from the look of him,
though I can't say as to his power and speed
when he was young. You find the same good build
in house dogs, table dogs landowners keep
all for style."

And you replied, Eumaeus:

"A hunter owned him—but the man is dead
in some far place. If this old hound could show
the form he had when Lord Odysseus left him,
going to Troy, you'd see him swift and strong.
He never shrank from any savage thing
he'd brought to bay in the deep woods; on the scent
no other dog kept up with him. Now misery

Reading Strategy
Summarizing Summarize Argus' situation since Odysseus' departure.

ENRICHMENT: Cultural Connection

Dogs in Different Cultures

Ask students what other famous dogs they can think of. Responses might include Lassie, Rin Tin Tin, Benji, and White Fang. Ask students why they think dogs are often called "man's best friend" and discuss their ideas. Point out that the bond between dogs and people may go back as far as 25,000 years, as shown by Paleolithic cave drawings of dogs.

Have students find out more about how dogs are viewed in different cultures. Since the dog has been portrayed in art from the Stone Age through all phases of Eastern and Western art, assign some students to find and bring in a variety of pictures of dogs in art and photography books. Assign other students to research the roles dogs have played in diverse societies, such as the hunting dog, farm dog, lap dog, sled dog, and even, in ancient Egypt, dog god. Assign other students to do a multicultural literature search to find portrayals of dogs. Have students share their findings with the class.

has him in leash. His owner died abroad,
and here the women slaves will take no care of him.
You know how servants are: without a master
they have no will to labor, or excel.
For Zeus who views the wide world takes away
half the manhood of a man, that day
he goes into captivity and slavery."

Eumaeus crossed the court and went straight forward
into the megaron[6] among the suitors:
but death and darkness in that instant closed
the eyes of Argus, who had seen his master,
Odysseus, after twenty years.

The Suitors

Still disguised as a beggar, Odysseus enters his home. He is confronted by the haughty[7] suitor Antinous.[8]

But here Antinous broke in, shouting:

"God!
What evil wind blew in this pest?
Get over,
stand in the passage! Nudge my table, will you?
Egyptian whips are sweet
to what you'll come to here, you nosing rat,
making your pitch to everyone!
These men have bread to throw away on you
because it is not theirs. Who cares? Who spares
another's food, when he has more than plenty?"

With guile Odysseus drew away, then said:

"A pity that you have more looks than heart.
You'd grudge a pinch of salt from your own larder
to your own handyman. You sit here, fat
on others' meat, and cannot bring yourself
to rummage out a crust of bread for me!"

Then anger made Antinous' heart beat hard,
and, glowering under his brows, he answered:

Reading Strategy
Summarizing Summarize the account of Argus in your own words.

6. megaron (meg´ ə rön) *n.* great, central hall of the house, usually containing a center hearth.

7. haughty (hôt´ ē) *adj.* arrogant.

8. Antinous (an tin´ ō əs)

glowering (glou´ ər iŋ) *adj.* staring with sullen anger; scowling

17 **Reading Check**
What is Argus' relationship to Odysseus?

15 Reading Strategy
Summarizing

- Because many students can relate to having a pet, this passage may provide good material for discussion. Ask them if they think their pets would behave like Argus under similar circumstances—would they recognize their owner after all this time?
- Have students respond to the Reading Strategy task on p. 1029: Summarize the account of Argus in your own words.
  Possible response: "Argus recognizes Odysseus' voice, but is too old and feeble to move. Odysseus remarks on the dog's excellent build and says he must have been a fine dog when young. Eumaeus tells Odysseus that he belonged to a hunter who has left and died, and that he was indeed a fine dog, but now is uncared for. Argus, after seeing his master for the first time in twenty years, wags his tail, then closes his eyes and dies."

16 Critical Thinking
Analyze

- Ask students how Antinous' words must have made Odysseus feel. What would Odysseus want to do at this moment? Why are his actions described as guileful?
  Possible response: Odysseus would want to hit or kill Antinous, but he has too much guile. Instead, he restrains his emotions until the time is right to reveal his identity.
- Remind students that all visitors are supposed to be well treated. How does Antinous know that this beggar is not a god in disguise? Indeed, it turns out to be worse for Antinous' fate that he insulted not a god, but Odysseus.

17 Reading Check

Answer: Odysseus owned Argus and trained him as a puppy before he left for Troy.

⓲ Background

Art

This vessel, one of several being used to illustrate this edition of the *Odyssey*, was originally used to store or transport liquids such as oil or wine. Greek artists used several methods to decorate these vessels. In the "black figure" technique, color is applied to the figures, with the background taking the natural color of the clay. The amphorae on pp. 1026 and 1030 are examples of this style. In the "red figure" technique, the process is reversed; the background is painted black. The krater, or bowl, on p. 1036 is an example of the "red figure" process.

These artifacts have survived for thousands of years—a durable art form that is not only intrinsically beautiful but that presents a detailed picture of the life and culture of the ancient Greeks.

"Now!
You think you'll shuffle off and get away
after that impudence?[9] Oh, no you don't!"

The stool he let fly hit the man's right shoulder
on the packed muscle under the shoulder blade—
like solid rock, for all the effect one saw.
Odysseus only shook his head, containing
thoughts of bloody work, as he walked on,
then sat, and dropped his loaded bag again
upon the door sill. Facing the whole crowd
he said, and eyed them all:
"One word only,
my lords, and suitors of the famous queen.
One thing I have to say.
There is no pain, no burden for the heart
when blows come to a man, and he defending
his own cattle—his own cows and lambs.
Here it was otherwise. Antinous
hit me for being driven on by hunger—
how many bitter seas men cross for hunger!
If beggars interest the gods, if there are Furies[10]
pent in the dark to avenge a poor man's wrong, then may
Antinous meet his death before his wedding day!"

Then said Eupeithes' son, Antinous:
"Enough.
Eat and be quiet where you are, or shamble elsewhere,
unless you want these lads to stop your mouth
pulling you by the heels, or hands and feet,
over the whole floor, till your back is peeled!"

But now the rest were mortified, and someone
spoke from the crowd of young bucks to rebuke him:

"A poor show, that—hitting this famished tramp—
bad business, if he happened to be a god.
You know they go in foreign guise, the gods do,
looking like strangers, turning up
in towns and settlements to keep an eye
on manners, good or bad."
But at this notion
Antinous only shrugged.

9. impudence (im´ pyo͞o dəns) *n.* quality of being shamelessly bold; disrespectful.

10. Furies (fyo͝or´ ēz) three terrible spirits who punish those whose crimes have not been avenged.

⓲

19

Telemachus,
after the blow his father bore, sat still
without a tear, though his heart felt the blow.
Slowly he shook his head from side to side,
containing murderous thoughts.

Penelope
on the higher level of her room had heard
the blow, and knew who gave it. Now she murmured:

"Would god you could be hit yourself, Antinous—
hit by Apollo's bowshot!"

And Eurynome[11]
her housekeeper, put in:

"He and no other?
If all we pray for came to pass, not one
would live till dawn!"

Her gentle mistress said:

20

"Oh, Nan, they are a bad lot; they intend
ruin for all of us; but Antinous
appears a blacker-hearted hound than any.
Here is a poor man come, a wanderer,
driven by want to beg his bread, and everyone
in hall gave bits, to cram his bag—only
Antinous threw a stool, and banged his shoulder!"

So she described it, sitting in her chamber
among her maids—while her true lord was eating.
Then she called in the forester and said:

"Go to that man on my behalf, Eumaeus,
and send him here, so I can greet and question him.
Abroad in the great world, he may have heard
rumors about Odysseus—may have known him!"

Penelope

In the evening, Penelope interrogates the old beggar.

"Friend, let me ask you first of all:
who are you, where do you come from, of what nation
and parents were you born?"

Reading Strategy
Summarizing Summarize lines 1261–1264. How is Telemachus feeling?

11. Eurynome (yo͞o rin′ əm ē)

Literary Analysis
Epic Simile Is the comparison made between Antinous and a hound in line 1274 an epic simile? How do you know?

21 **Reading Check**
How does Antinous respond to Odysseus, who is disguised as a beggar?

19 Reading Strategy

Summarizing

- Ask students the Reading Strategy question on p. 1031: Summarize lines 1261–1264. How is Telemachus feeling?
  Answer: After watching the blow his father withstands, Telemachus thinks "murderous thoughts" but restrains himself from any response.
- Ask students what Telemachus' reaction suggests about his character.
  Possible response: Telemachus' controlled response indicates that he may have inherited some of his father's cool judgment and self-restraint.

20 Literary Analysis

Epic Simile

- Tell students that Penelope witnesses Antinous' attack on Odysseus (disguised as a beggar). This passage provides the first clue we have of Penelope's opinion of her suitors.
- Ask students the Literary Analysis question on p. 1031: Is the comparison made between Antinous and a hound in line 1274 an epic simile? How do you know?
  Answer: It is not an epic simile. Although Penelope says Antinous is like ("appears") a "blacker-hearted hound than any," constituting a comparison between unlike things, it would need to be a more elaborate comparison to be considered an epic simile.

21 Reading Check

Answer: Antinous berates Odysseus, who is disguised as a beggar, and throws a stool at him.

CUSTOMIZE INSTRUCTION FOR UNIVERSAL ACCESS

For Gifted/Talented Students	For Advanced Readers
Challenge students to create a portrait of Odysseus in his disguise as a beggar. Tell students that their image should reflect not only his humble appearance, but also should suggest his hidden qualities as a hero.	In his first moments home, Odysseus is greeted with insults: "pest," "nosing rat," and "famished tramp." Have students make a list of insults given and received throughout the *Odyssey* by Odysseus and others. Ask students to write an essay analyzing the insults, showing how they reveal what Greeks despised—and, by implication, what they valued and esteemed.

(22) Literary Analysis

Epic Simile

- Point out that Odysseus finally reunites with Penelope but must maintain his disguise and talk to her as if they were strangers.
- Ask students the Literary Analysis question on p. 1032: To what does Odysseus compare his wife in the epic simile in lines 1290–1297?
  Answer: Odysseus compares her name, that is, her reputation, to the "sweet honor of some god-fearing king" who rules fairly over a prosperous kingdom.

(23) Vocabulary

Latin Root: *-equi-*

- Call students' attention to the word *equity* and its definition.
- Tell students that the Latin root *-equi-* means "same" or "equal."
- Have students suggest words that contain this root. List them on the chalkboard. Possibilities include *equidistant, equilateral,* and *equivalent.*
- Have students look up the listed words in a dictionary.
- Finally, have students use each word in a sentence that illustrates its meaning.

And he replied:
"My lady, never a man in the wide world
should have a fault to find with you. Your name
(22) has gone out under heaven like the sweet
honor of some god-fearing king, who rules
(23) in equity over the strong: his black lands bear
both wheat and barley, fruit trees laden bright,
new lambs at lambing time—and the deep sea
gives great hauls of fish by his good strategy,
so that his folk fare well.
O my dear lady,
this being so, let it suffice to ask me
of other matters—not my blood, my homeland.
Do not enforce me to recall my pain.
My heart is sore; but I must not be found
sitting in tears here, in another's house:
it is not well forever to be grieving.
One of the maids might say—or you might think—
I had got maudlin over cups of wine."

And Penelope replied:

"Stranger, my looks,
my face, my carriage,[12] were soon lost or faded
when the Achaeans crossed the sea to Troy,
Odysseus my lord among the rest.
If he returned, if he were here to care for me,
I might be happily renowned!
But grief instead heaven sent me—years of pain.
Sons of the noblest families on the islands,
Dulichium, Same, wooded Zacynthus,[13]
with native Ithacans, are here to court me,
against my wish; and they consume this house.
Can I give proper heed to guest or suppliant
or herald on the realm's affairs?
How could I?
wasted with longing for Odysseus, while here
they press for marriage.
Ruses[14] served my turn
to draw the time out—first a close-grained web
I had the happy thought to set up weaving
on my big loom in hall. I said, that day:
'Young men—my suitors, now my lord is dead,
let me finish my weaving before I marry,

equity (ek´ wit ē) *n.* fairness; impartiality; justice

Literary Analysis
Epic Simile To what does Odysseus compare his wife in the epic simile in lines 1290–1297?

maudlin (môd´ lin) *adj.* tearfully or foolishly sentimental

12. carriage (kar´ ij) *n.* posture.

13. Zacynthus (za sin´ thus)

14. ruses (ro͞oz´ əz) *n.* tricks.

or else my thread will have been spun in vain.
It is a shroud I weave for Lord Laertes
when cold Death comes to lay him on his bier.
The country wives would hold me in dishonor
if he, with all his fortune, lay unshrouded.'
I reached their hearts that way, and they agreed.
So every day I wove on the great loom,
but every night by torchlight I unwove it;
and so for three years I deceived the Achaeans.
But when the seasons brought a fourth year on,
as long months waned, and the long days were spent,
through impudent folly in the slinking maids
(24) they caught me—clamored up to me at night;
I had no choice then but to finish it.
And now, as matters stand at last,
I have no strength left to evade a marriage,
cannot find any further way; my parents
urge it upon me, and my son
will not stand by while they eat up his property.
He comprehends it, being a man full-grown,
able to oversee the kind of house
Zeus would endow with honor.
But you too
confide in me, tell me your ancestry.
You were not born of mythic oak or stone."

Penelope again asks the beggar to tell about himself. He makes up a tale in which Odysseus is mentioned and declares that Penelope's husband will soon be home.

"You see, then, he is alive and well, and headed
homeward now, no more to be abroad
far from his island, his dear wife and son.
Here is my sworn word for it. Witness this,
god of the zenith, noblest of the gods,[15]
and Lord Odysseus' hearthfire, now before me:
I swear these things shall turn out as I say.
Between this present dark and one day's ebb,
after the wane, before the crescent moon,
Odysseus will come."

Reading Strategy
Summarizing Summarize what Penelope tells the disguised Odysseus. How has she demonstrated her loyalty to her husband?

15. god of the zenith, noblest of the gods Zeus.

(25) **✓Reading Check**
How does Odysseus initially respond to Penelope's questions about his past?

(24) Reading Strategy
Summarizing

- Note to students that it is during this passage that Odysseus will learn whether his wife has been faithful during his absence. (Certainly Odysseus must have been wondering about this. After all, he has not been faithful to Penelope—though his love for her has never waned.) The ruse that Penelope has employed to keep her suitors at bay is a complicated one, and for clarity it can benefit from summarizing and paraphrasing.
- Ask students the Reading Strategy question on p. 1033: Summarize what Penelope tells the disguised Odysseus. How has she demonstrated her loyalty to her husband?
  Possible response: Penelope's fame has not given her pleasure, only grief. It has drawn an army of unwanted suitors, who freeload off her wealth and demand that she choose one for a husband. She has held them off by saying that she first had to weave a burial shroud for her father-in-law, but then, at night, undoing all the work she had completed each day. Now, however, they have found out her trick and she cannot see how to hold them off any longer. In addition, her parents are urging her to remarry, and Telemachus is angry at having to host the suitors and wants to fight them.

(25) ✓Reading Check

Answer: Odysseus says the story is too sad and painful for him to remember, so he would rather not tell her.

ENRICHMENT: Cultural Connection
Penelope's Web

Point out that the idea underlying Penelope's web—a work that is always in progress but never finished—occurs, with variations, in the stories, fables, and folktales of many cultures. Ask students if they know of any, and discuss their ideas. Responses might include the Greek myth of Sisyphus, a greedy king who is doomed forever to roll uphill a huge boulder that always rolls back down; or the Grimm's fairy tale "Rumplestiltskin," in which the king's bride, who has to spin flax endlessly, makes a bargain with Rumplestiltskin. Discuss how the tasks in the stories differ from culture to culture.

Ask students to search the literature and folktales of other cultures to find more stories with this theme. Suggest that students choose from among Native American, African American, Asian, Scandinavian, Latin American, European, Arab, and Jewish folktales. Have them share the stories they find with the class.

26 Background

Art

The Trial of the Bow, by N. C. Wyeth

Penelope promises that she will marry the man who can string Odysseus' bow and shoot an arrow through twelve ax handle sockets. In this painting, Odysseus, disguised as a beggar, has succeeded in the first part of this challenge. Use these questions for discussion:

1. Why do you think Wyeth chose this particular moment in the story to illustrate?
   Answer: This is an especially dramatic moment because Odysseus is about to win the contest, reveal his true identity to the suitors, and then take his revenge.
2. Why didn't the artist illustrate the scene a few moments later, when the arrow goes through the ax handles?
   Answer: At that point, Odysseus would no longer be focusing on the target, but would be giving instructions to Telemachus. This moment shows Odysseus at his best—muscles flexed and all his attention fixed on his target.

27 ▶ Critical Viewing

Possible responses: The emotional tension is captured in the physical tension of Odysseus' arm and leg muscles and the taut bowstring. In addition, everyone else is focused on the targets. Additional suspense comes from the point in time the picture shows: The arrow has not been released, and the viewers, like the people in the painting, wait in expectation.

26

The Trial of the Bow, N. C. Wyeth, Delaware Art Museum

27 ▲ **Critical Viewing** The winner of the archery contest will win Penelope's hand in marriage. How does the artist capture the tension in this scene? **[Interpret]**

The Challenge

Pressed by the suitors to choose a husband from among them, Penelope says she will marry the man who can string Odysseus' bow and shoot an arrow through twelve axhandle sockets. The suitors try and fail. Still in disguise, Odysseus asks for a turn and gets it.

And Odysseus took his time,
turning the bow, tapping it, every inch,
for borings that termites might have made
while the master of the weapon was abroad.
The suitors were now watching him, and some
jested among themselves:
"A bow lover!"
"Dealer in old bows!"
"Maybe he has one like it
at home!"
"Or has an itch to make one for himself."
"See how he handles it, the sly old buzzard!"

And one disdainful suitor added this:

"May his fortune grow an inch for every inch he bends it!"

But the man skilled in all ways of contending,
satisfied by the great bow's look and heft,
like a musician, like a harper, when
with quiet hand upon his instrument
he draws between his thumb and forefinger
a sweet new string upon a peg: so effortlessly
Odysseus in one motion strung the bow.
Then slid his right hand down the cord and plucked it,
so the taut gut vibrating hummed and sang
a swallow's note.

29 **Reading Check**

How does Penelope decide she will choose a suitor?

28 Literary Analysis

Epic Simile and Imagery

- Point out that Odysseus' mastery of his bow is rendered with great care, in sharp contrast to the efforts of the suitors.
- Ask students to what Odysseus' handling of the bow is compared. To which senses does the imagery appeal?
  Answer: Odysseus' handling of his bow in lines 1370–1379 is compared to that of a skilled harp player handling his instrument. The imagery appeals to the senses of touch and sight, and finally to the sense of sound.

29 Reading Check

Answer: Penelope says she will marry whoever can string Odysseus' bow and shoot an arrow through twelve ax handle sockets.

30 ▶ Critical Viewing

Possible response: Students may find the hunter's posture on the pottery to be somewhat stylized and artificial in contrast to the easy grace that Wyeth depicts in the painting on p. 1034.

In the hushed hall it smote the suitors
and all their faces changed. Then Zeus thundered
overhead, one loud crack for a sign.
And Odysseus laughed within him that the son
of crooked-minded Cronus had flung that omen down.
He picked one ready arrow from his table
where it lay bare: the rest were waiting still
in the quiver for the young men's turn to come.
He nocked[16] it, let it rest across the handgrip,
and drew the string and grooved butt of the arrow,
aiming from where he sat upon the stool.
Now flashed
arrow from twanging bow clean as a whistle
through every socket ring, and grazed not one,
to thud with heavy brazen head beyond.
Then quietly
Odysseus said:

"Telemachus, the stranger
you welcomed in your hall has not disgraced you.

30 ▲ Critical Viewing Compare Odysseus' grace, described in line 1375, with the grace of the hunter pictured here. **[Compare and Contrast]**

16. nocked set an arrow against the bowstring.

ENRICHMENT: Career Connection

Archaeology

Because there are no written records of the Trojan War, which dates back about 3,200 years, there are many unanswered questions. However, archaeologists have found pieces of buildings, objects, and works of art that Odysseus might have entered, used, or admired. Tell students that archaeology is the study of past cultures. These cultures may be thousands of years old, such as ancient Greece, or fairly recent, such as colonial America.

As well as having extensive knowledge on many subjects, an archaeologist must make careful observations and keep accurate records and have the strength to use a pick and shovel, the patience to uncover an artifact with a needle probe and small paintbrush, and the ability to cope with primitive and uncomfortable field conditions.

I did not miss, neither did I take all day
stringing the bow. My hand and eye are sound,
not so contemptible as the young men say.
The hour has come to cook their lordships' mutton—
supper by daylight. Other amusements later,
with song and harping that adorn a feast."

He dropped his eyes and nodded, and the prince
Telemachus, true son of King Odysseus,
belted his sword on, clapped hand to his spear,
and with a clink and glitter of keen bronze
stood by his chair, in the forefront near his father.

Review and Assess

Thinking About the Selection

1. **Respond:** If you were Telemachus or Penelope, how would you react to the stranger's arrival?
2. **(a) Recall:** Who does Telemachus think Odysseus is when they first reunite? **(b) Compare and Contrast:** Compare Odysseus' emotions with those of Telemachus at their reunion.
3. **(a) Recall:** Who is Argus? **(b) Recall:** How does Argus react to Odysseus' return? **(c) Analyze:** Is it a coincidence that Argus dies just when Odysseus returns? Explain.
4. **(a) Recall:** Describe Antinous' treatment of Odysseus. **(b) Analyze Causes and Effects:** Why do you think Antinous treats Odysseus so badly?
5. **(a) Analyze:** How does Penelope feel about the suitors in her house? **(b) Compare and Contrast:** How might Odysseus' feelings about the suitors differ from Penelope's?
6. **(a) Recall:** What does Odysseus tell Penelope about himself? **(b) Infer:** Why do you think Odysseus chooses not to reveal his identity to his wife?
7. **Take a Position:** Is it wrong for Odysseus to deceive his wife? Explain.

Answers for p. 1037

Review and Assess

1. Students may respond that even though Odysseus arrives disguised as a beggar, they would be more intrigued and curious than Telemachus and Penelope seem to be.
2. **(a)** Telemachus first thinks Odysseus is a beggar. Then, after Odysseus confers with Athena and changes his appearance, Telemachus thinks he is a god. **(b)** Telemachus is at first confused and skeptical, then throws his arms around his father and begins to cry. Tears run down Odysseus' face as he reveals himself to his son.
3. **(a)** Argus is Odysseus' dog, left behind when he went to war. **(b)** Argus recognizes his master's voice and raises his head, but is too feeble to move from where he lies. **(c)** Students may suggest that the dog's death is not a coincidence. With his master's return, Argus's duties are at an end and he can die.
4. **(a)** Antinous berates Odysseus, who is dressed as a beggar, and throws a stool at him. **(b)** Possible response: Antinous is described as "black-hearted" and later as leader of the suitors. His treatment of Odysseus could be seen as a display of his power, or as simple contempt for humanity.
5. **(a)** Penelope does not want to marry any of the suitors and resents their presence, though she considers Antinous worse than the others. **(b)** Possible response: Penelope may know the suitors well enough to admire or respect qualities in some of them. Odysseus sees them as an undifferentiated mob that is invading his home and threatening his marriage.
6. **(a)** Odysseus initially tells Penelope that he is a wanderer with a past too painful to reveal. **(b)** Students may suggest that Odysseus feels that he is not yet ready to trust that his wife has been loyal to him. Or, he may not want to reveal too much until he has executed his plan.

continued

Answers continued

7. Some students may say that it is always wrong to deceive a loved one. Others may say that he is acting in their mutual best interest—that to successfully execute his planned revenge, it is best not to involve his wife.

31 Background

Art

The Slaughter of the Suitors, by N. C. Wyeth

In this painting of Odysseus' revenge, Wyeth adds drama and animation to an already exciting story. Use the following questions for discussion:

1. Which lines from the Odyssey does this painting illustrate?
   Answer: It illustrates lines 1521–1530, plus the lines that are covered by the synopsis on p. 1042.
2. Who are the four figures on the right-hand side of the painting? How do you know?
   Answer: They are Odysseus, Telemachus, Eumaeus, and the cowherd. They are wearing armor, have weapons, and are obviously winning the battle.
3. What details make the painting exciting?
   Possible responses: The flung spear, the spears about to be thrown, the position of the men's bodies, or the dust of battle. The giant columns in the background create a heroic mood for the scene.

32 ▶Critical Viewing

Possible responses: Some students may agree that the suitors have deeply offended Odysseus, and he is justified in seeking to attack them. Others may feel that Odysseus' grievances do not justify an indiscriminate slaughter.

31

The Slaughter of the Suitors, N. C. Wyeth, Delaware Art Museum

32 ▲ **Critical Viewing** Do you think Odysseus' desire to fight the suitors is justified? Explain. **[Make a Judgment]**

Odysseus' Revenge

Now shrugging off his rags the wiliest[17] fighter of the islands
leapt and stood on the broad doorsill, his own bow in his hand.
He poured out at his feet a rain of arrows from the quiver
and spoke to the crowd:

"So much for that. Your clean-cut game is over.
Now watch me hit a target that no man has hit before,
if I can make this shot. Help me, Apollo."

He drew to his fist the cruel head of an arrow for Antinous
just as the young man leaned to lift his beautiful drinking cup,
embossed, two-handled, golden: the cup was in his fingers:
the wine was even at his lips: and did he dream of death?
How could he? In that revelry[18] amid his throng of friends
who would imagine a single foe—though a strong foe indeed—
could dare to bring death's pain on him and darkness on his eyes?
Odysseus' arrow hit him under the chin
and punched up to the feathers through his throat.

Backward and down he went, letting the winecup fall
from his shocked hand. Like pipes his nostrils jetted
crimson runnels, a river of mortal red,
(33) and one last kick upset his table
knocking the bread and meat to soak in dusty blood.
Now as they craned to see their champion where he lay
the suitors jostled in uproar down the hall,
everyone on his feet. Wildly they turned and scanned
(34) the walls in the long room for arms; but not a shield,
not a good ashen spear was there for a man to take and throw.
All they could do was yell in outrage at Odysseus:

"Foul! to shoot at a man! That was your last shot!"

"Your own throat will be slit for this!"

"Our finest lad is down!
You killed the best on Ithaca."

"Buzzards will tear your eyes out!"

For they imagined as they wished—that it was a wild shot,
an unintended killing—fools, not to comprehend
they were already in the grip of death.
But glaring under his brows Odysseus answered:

"You yellow dogs, you thought I'd never make it
home from the land of Troy. You took my house to plunder. . . .
You dared bid for my wife while I was still alive.

17. **wiliest** (wil´ ē əst) *adj.* craftiest; slyest.

18. **revelry** (rev´ əl rē) *n.* boisterous festivity.

Literary Analysis
Epic Simile and Imagery What color images appear in the epic simile about Antinous' wounds?

Reading Strategy
Summarizing Summarize Odysseus' interactions with Antinous and the other suitors to this point. What do you think will happen next?

(35) ✓**Reading Check**
What happens to Antinous?

(33) Literary Analysis
Epic Simile and Imagery

- Ask students why Odysseus selected Antinous as his first target.
  Possible response: Antinous was the most obnoxious suitor and the first to insult Odysseus. Odysseus may also have considered Antinous his most dangerous foe.
- Ask students the Literary Analysis question on p. 1039: What color images appear in the epic simile about Antinous' wounds?
  Answer: Antinous' nostrils are "like pipes" that jet "crimson runnels, a river of mortal red."

(34) Reading Strategy
Summarizing

- Remind students that Odysseus is able to keep restraint in his early dealings with the suitors because this is a necessary part of his plan for revenge.
- Ask students the Reading Strategy question on p. 1039: Summarize Odysseus' interactions with Antinous and the other suitors to this point. What do you think will happen next?
  Possible response: First, Antinous speaks rudely to Odysseus, then hits him with a stool. Other suitors rebuke Antinous, but they do not help the supposed beggar. During "The Challenge," the suitors mock Odysseus. When Odysseus shoots Antinous, the other suitors are appalled and frightened. They look for weapons, but find none, since Telemachus has removed them from the hall.

(35) ✓Reading Check

Answer: Antinous is the first of the suitors to die. Odysseus shoots him through the throat with an arrow.

36 Reading Strategy

Summarizing

- Have students respond to the Reading Strategy task on p. 1040: Summarize the plea made by the suitors to Odysseus.
  Answer: Eurymachus, speaking for the suitors, acknowledges "rash actions" but says that Antinous was the "cause of them all," minimizing the blame of the rest of the suitors. He asks Odysseus to spare them and offers to make restitution of all the meat and wine consumed, plus gifts of oxen, bronze, and gold.
- Ask students if they think the suitor's arguments are reasonable. Would restitution satisfy them, if they were in Odysseus' place?
  Possible response: Some students may say they would be satisfied by the replacement of supplies. Nothing, of course, will stop Odysseus from his revenge.

Contempt was all you had for the gods who rule wide heaven,
contempt for what men say of you hereafter.
Your last hour has come. You die in blood."

As they all took this in, sickly green fear
pulled at their entrails, and their eyes flickered
looking for some hatch or hideaway from death.
Eurymachus[19] alone could speak. He said:

"If you are Odysseus of Ithaca come back,
all that you say these men have done is true.
Rash actions, many here, more in the countryside.
But here he lies, the man who caused them all.
Antinous was the ringleader, he whipped us on
to do these things. He cared less for a marriage
than for the power Cronion has denied him
as king of Ithaca. For that
he tried to trap your son and would have killed him.
He is dead now and has his portion. Spare
your own people. As for ourselves, we'll make
36 restitution of wine and meat consumed,
and add, each one, a tithe of twenty oxen
with gifts of bronze and gold to warm your heart.
Meanwhile we cannot blame you for your anger."

Odysseus glowered under his black brows
and said:
"Not for the whole treasure of your fathers,
all you enjoy, lands, flocks, or any gold
put up by others, would I hold my hand.
There will be killing till the score is paid.
You forced yourselves upon this house. Fight your way out,
or run for it, if you think you'll escape death.
I doubt one man of you skins by."

They felt their knees fail, and their hearts—but heard
Eurymachus for the last time rallying them.

"Friends," he said, "the man is implacable.
Now that he's got his hands on bow and quiver
he'll shoot from the big doorstone there
until he kills us to the last man.
Fight, I say,
let's remember the joy of it. Swords out!
Hold up your tables to deflect his arrows.
After me, everyone: rush him where he stands.

contempt (kən tempt′) *n.* disdain or scorn; scornful feelings or actions

19. **Eurymachus** (yo͞o ri′ mə kəs)

Reading Strategy
Summarizing Summarize the plea made by Eurymachus to Odysseus.

If we can budge him from the door, if we can pass
into the town, we'll call out men to chase him.
This fellow with his bow will shoot no more."

37 He drew his own sword as he spoke, a broadsword of fine
bronze,
honed like a razor on either edge. Then crying hoarse and loud
he hurled himself at Odysseus. But the kingly man let fly
an arrow at that instant, and the quivering feathered butt
sprang to the nipple of his breast as the barb stuck in his liver.
The bright broadsword clanged down. He lurched and fell aside,
pitching across his table. His cup, his bread and meat,
were spilt and scattered far and wide, and his head slammed
on the ground.
Revulsion, anguish in his heart, with both feet kicking out,
he downed his chair, while the shrouding wave of mist closed on
his eyes.

Amphinomus now came running at Odysseus,
broadsword naked in his hand. He thought to make
the great soldier give way at the door.
But with a spear throw from behind Telemachus hit him
between the shoulders, and the lancehead drove
clear through his chest. He left his feet and fell
forward, thudding, forehead against the ground.
Telemachus swerved around him, leaving the long dark spear
planted in Amphinomus. If he paused to yank it out
38 someone might jump him from behind or cut him down with a
sword
at the moment he bent over. So he ran—ran from the tables
to his father's side and halted, panting, saying:

"Father let me bring you a shield and spear,
a pair of spears, a helmet.
I can arm on the run myself; I'll give
outfits to Eumaeus and this cowherd.
Better to have equipment."

Said Odysseus:

"Run then, while I hold them off with arrows
as long as the arrows last. When all are gone
if I'm alone they can dislodge me."

Quick
upon his father's word Telemachus

Literary Analysis
Epic Simile Why is the comparison of Eurymachus' sharp sword to a razor a simile but not an epic simile?

Reading Strategy
Summarizing In your own words, briefly describe the events of the battle of Odysseus and Telemachus with the suitors thus far.

39 **✔ Reading Check**
What does Telemachus want to bring to his father to help him fight the suitors?

37 Literary Analysis

Epic Simile

- Stress to students that not all similes, even those in the *Odyssey*, are epic similes.
- Ask students the Literary Analysis question on p. 1040: Why is the comparison of Eurymachus' sharp sword to a razor a simile but not an epic simile?
  Answer: This is a simile because it compares a sword to a razor. An epic simile, however, is an elaborate comparison that can run across several lines. This simile is mentioned once and is not sustained.

38 Reading Strategy

Summarizing

- The battle with the suitors is one of the most action-packed in the entire *Odyssey,* with a great deal of detail. Tell students that summarizing the action can help keep the focus on the big picture.
- Have students respond to the Reading Strategy task on p. 1041: In your own words, briefly describe the events of the battle of Odysseus and Telemachus with the suitors thus far.
  Possible response: "After Antinous and Eurymachus are killed, Telemachus runs to get spears and armor for Odysseus, Eumaeus, and the cowherd. They arm themselves in order to help Odysseus kill the suitors. Odysseus uses all his arrows, killing a suitor with every shot. He then puts on a helmet and shield and picks up his spears to finish the job."

39 ✔ Reading Check

Answer: Telemachus wants to bring his father a shield, spears, and a helmet.

40 Literary Analysis

Imagery and Epic Simile

- Tell students that epic similes help to paint an image in the mind that can heighten a scene's dramatic effect.
- Ask students the first Literary Analysis question on p. 1042: What do you picture in the epic simile in lines 1535–1539?
  Possible response: The simile suggests an image familiar from seeing pictures of modern fishing boats hauling up nets and then dumping the catch onto the deck. Students may say that they can apply this familiar image to see the aftermath of the battle, with the dead and dying suitors flopping on the floor.

41 Literary Analysis

Epic Simile

- Ask students the second Literary Analysis question on p. 1042: To what is Odysseus' hair compared? Is this comparison an epic simile?
  Answer: Odysseus' hair is compared first to petals of wild hyacinth, then to "gold infused on silver." This elaborate comparison qualifies as an epic simile.
- Ask students why Homer emphasizes Odysseus' physical attractiveness at this point.
  Possible response: Homer is creating a sharp contrast to Odysseus' previous guise as a beggar. Odysseus is being prepared almost as a new bridegroom, an appropriate comparison as he approaches Penelope to renew their marriage.

ran to the room where spears and armor lay.
He caught up four light shields, four pairs of spears,
four helms of war high-plumed with flowing manes,
and ran back, loaded down, to his father's side.
He was the first to pull a helmet on
and slide his bare arm in a buckler strap.
The servants armed themselves, and all three took their stand
beside the master of battle.
While he had arrows
he aimed and shot, and every shot brought down
one of his huddling enemies.
But when all barbs had flown from the bowman's fist,
he leaned his bow in the bright entryway
beside the door, and armed: a four-ply shield
hard on his shoulder, and a crested helm,
horsetailed, nodding stormy upon his head,
then took his tough and bronze-shod spears. . . .

Aided by Athena, Odysseus, Telemachus, Eumaeus, and other faithful herdsmen kill all the suitors.

And Odysseus looked around him, narrow-eyed,
for any others who had lain hidden
while death's black fury passed.
In blood and dust
he saw that crowd all fallen, many and many slain.

40 Think of a catch that fishermen haul in to a half-moon bay
in a fine-meshed net from the whitecaps of the sea:
how all are poured out on the sand, in throes for the salt sea,
twitching their cold lives away in Helios' fiery air:
so lay the suitors heaped on one another.

Literary Analysis
Imagery and Epic Simile In reading the epic simile in lines 1535–1539, what do you picture?

Penelope's Test

Penelope tests Odysseus to prove he really is her husband.

Greathearted Odysseus, home at last,
was being bathed now by Eurynome
and rubbed with golden oil, and clothed again
in a fresh tunic and a cloak. Athena
lent him beauty, head to foot. She made him
41 taller, and massive, too, with crisping hair

Literary Analysis
Epic Simile To what is Odysseus' hair compared? Is this comparison an epic simile?

in curls like petals of wild hyacinth
but all red-golden. Think of gold infused
on silver by a craftsman, whose fine art
Hephaestus♦ taught him, or Athena: one
whose work moves to delight: just so she lavished
beauty over Odysseus' head and shoulders.
He sat then in the same chair by the pillar,
facing his silent wife, and said:

"Strange woman,
the immortals of Olympus made you hard,
harder than any. Who else in the world
would keep aloof as you do from her husband
if he returned to her from years of trouble,
cast on his own land in the twentieth year?

Nurse, make up a bed for me to sleep on.
Her heart is iron in her breast."

Penelope
spoke to Odysseus now. She said:

"Strange man,
if man you are . . . This is no pride on my part
nor scorn for you—not even wonder, merely.
I know so well how you—how he—appeared
boarding the ship for Troy. But all the same . . .

Make up his bed for him, Eurycleia.
Place it outside the bedchamber my lord
built with his own hands. Pile the big bed
with fleeces, rugs, and sheets of purest linen."

With this she tried him to the breaking point,
and he turned on her in a flash raging:

"Woman, by heaven you've stung me now!
Who dared to move my bed?
No builder had the skill for that—unless
a god came down to turn the trick. No mortal
in his best days could budge it with a crowbar.
There is our pact and pledge, our secret sign,
built into that bed—my handiwork
and no one else's!

An old trunk of olive
grew like a pillar on the building plot,

Literature in context 42
Mythology Connection

♦ ***Hephaestus***
Any craftsman taught by Hephaestus, the Greek god of fire and metalworking, would be worth his weight in gold. His counterpart in Roman mythology was the mighty fire god Vulcan. Hephaestus was renowned for his work at the forge, crafting such items as Athena's spear, Achilles' shield, and Zeus' thunderbolts. Hephaestus was the only god with a physical deformity, caused when his father Zeus hurled him from Olympus. During his recovery, he learned how to craft beautiful objects from underwater coral and metals.

Statue of Vulcan, Hephaestus' Roman counterpart

43 **Reading Check**
How does Odysseus describe Penelope's attitude toward him?

42 Literature in Context
Mythology

There are two explanations for Hephaestus' lameness, both from Homer's *Iliad*. In one story, Zeus and Hera were arguing. Hephaestus took his mother's side, and an angry Zeus grabbed him by a foot and threw him down from Olympus. He hit the ground and became lame. In another story, Hephaestus was born lame. Hera was ashamed and so she was the one who threw him down from Olympus. He fell into the ocean, where he was saved by two ocean goddesses who took care of him in their cave for nine years. To show his gratitude, he spent those years forging jewelry for them.

43 Reading Check

Answer: Odysseus describes Penelope as hard and aloof.

44 Background

Art

The Fall of Troy, from The Odysseus Suite by Romare Bearden

Born in North Carolina, African American artist Romare Bearden grew up in New York. His work is most remarkable for its sophisticated use of the idiom of Cubism to portray the everyday realities of African American life. *The Fall of Troy* is a collage from a series done by Bearden on the adventures of Odysseus. The large white horse to the right is the Trojan horse; the boats in the harbor are waiting to carry Odysseus and his men from Troy to numerous adventures. Ask the following questions:

Which aspects of the collage recall what you have read from the *Odyssey?* Which aspects of the collage reflect a modern mind at work?

Answer: Students should recognize epic references such as the Trojan Horse, the burning towers of Troy, the sea and ships. Modern references include the collage technique; the flat, childlike style of the cutouts; and the whimsical inclusion of dolphins and other sea creatures.

45 ▶Critical Viewing

Answer: Students should compare their impressions of such specific details as the Trojan Horse, the burning towers, and the waiting ships.

44

The Fall of Troy from ***The Odysseus Suite,*** 1979, Romare Bearden, serigraph 18 x 24 © Romare Bearden Foundation / Licensed VAGA, New York NY

45 ▲ **Critical Viewing** How does your image of the events in the *Odyssey* compare to this artist's interpretation of the events? **[Compare]**

and I laid out our bedroom round that tree,
lined up the stone walls, built the walls and roof,
gave it a doorway and smooth-fitting doors.
Then I lopped off the silvery leaves and branches,
hewed and shaped that stump from the roots up
into a bedpost, drilled it, let it serve
as model for the rest. I planed them all,
inlaid them all with silver, gold and ivory,
and stretched a bed between—a pliant web
of oxhide thongs dyed crimson.
There's our sign!
I know no more. Could someone else's hand
have sawn that trunk and dragged the frame away?"

Their secret! as she heard it told, her knees
grew tremulous and weak, her heart failed her.
(46) With eyes brimming tears she ran to him,
throwing her arms around his neck, and kissed him,
murmuring:
"Do not rage at me, Odysseus!
No one ever matched your caution! Think
what difficulty the gods gave: they denied us
life together in our prime and flowering years,
kept us from crossing into age together.
Forgive me, don't be angry. I could not
welcome you with love on sight! I armed myself
long ago against the frauds of men,
(47) impostors who might come—and all those many
whose underhanded ways bring evil on! . . .
But here and now, what sign could be so clear
as this of our own bed?
No other man has ever laid eyes on it—
only my own slave, Actoris, that my father
sent with me as a gift—she kept our door.
You make my stiff heart know that I am yours."

Now from his breast into his eyes the ache
of longing mounted, and he wept at last,
his dear wife, clear and faithful, in his arms,

Reading Strategy
Summarizing How would you describe Penelope's feelings in lines 1593–1596?

(48) **✓ Reading Check**
What difficulty does Penelope say the gods gave to her and Odysseus?

(46) Reading Strategy
Summarizing

- Tell students that when summarizing scenes in their own words, they can take the opportunity to place the sometimes larger-than-life emotions into a context to which they can more easily relate.
- Ask students the Reading Strategy question on p. 1045: How would you describe Penelope's feelings in lines 1593–1596?
  Answer: When Odysseus (unwittingly) passes Penelope's test, she at first grows weak with excitement. Then, with tears in her eyes, she runs to embrace and kiss him.

(47) Critical Thinking
Analyze

- Ask students to examine Penelope's explanation of her test. What techniques does she use to persuade Odysseus not to be angry?
  Answer: Penelope reminds Odysseus that he, too, is a cautious person, implying that he shouldn't fault her for a trait that he also possesses. She then justifies her test by explaining that, over the years, experience has taught her not to be too trusting.
- Ask students if they believe Penelope's explanation is reasonable.
  Answer: Students may agree that Penelope's caution is understandable given her long separation from Odysseus and her experiences with the suitors.

(48) ✓ Reading Check

Answer: The gods kept them apart for many years, preventing them from enjoying life together.

ASSESS

Answers to p. 1046

Review and Assess

1. Students may believe that some sort of revenge was justified, but that Odysseus perhaps overreacted to the situation.
2. **(a)** After successfully completing the archery challenge, Odysseus turns and shoots Antinous through the throat. **(b)** Not knowing Odysseus' identity, the suitors are shocked by the killing and consider it murder, or perhaps a horrific accident.
3. **(a)** Odysseus plots with Telemachus to have all the suitors' weapons locked away before taking his revenge. Also, disguising his true identity helps him surprise the suitors. **(b)** Although Odysseus and his comrades are outnumbered, his planning has given him an advantage in weapons along with the element of surprise.
4. **(a)** Odysseus kills all the suitors. **(b)** He believes they are all guilty of defiling his house and family.
5. **(a)** She tests to see if he knows the secret of their bed. He describes how he constructed the bed. **(b)** After all these years, she has grown cautious and feels she must be absolutely sure. **(c)** The happiness of the reunited couple is shadowed by the difficult trials of the past.
6. **(a)** Possible response: Odysseus' planning of his revenge is consistent with the cunning and guile he has shown elsewhere in the *Odyssey.* His success in battle is not surprising. The harshness of his revenge recalls his treatment of Cyclops. **(b)** Students with a modern sense of justice may find his actions in the end at odds with their idea of a hero. Others may say his actions are in keeping with his personal sense of honor, and with the culture of his time.
7. Students may say that Odysseus should have simply forced them to leave, rather than wage war on them.

longed for as the sunwarmed earth is longed for by a swimmer
spent in rough water where his ship went down
under Poseidon's blows, gale winds and tons of sea.
Few men can keep alive through a big surf
to crawl, clotted with brine, on kindly beaches
in joy, in joy, knowing the abyss[20] behind:
and so she too rejoiced, her gaze upon her husband,
her white arms round him pressed as though forever.

20. **abyss** (ə bis´) *n.* ocean depths.

The Ending

Odysseus is reunited with his father. Athena commands that peace prevail between Odysseus and the relatives of the slain suitors. Odysseus has regained his family and his kingdom.

Review and Assess

Thinking About the Selection

1. **Respond:** Do you think that Odysseus' revenge is justified? Why or why not?
2. **(a) Recall:** Which act begins Odysseus' revenge on the suitors? **(b) Analyze:** Why does this act catch the suitors by surprise?
3. **(a) Recall:** What planning does Odysseus do before battling the suitors? **(b) Analyze:** How does his planning help him defeat his opponents?
4. **(a) Recall:** How does the fight turn out? **(b) Analyze:** Even though some suitors have been crueler than others, why does Odysseus take equal revenge on all of them?
5. **(a) Recall:** What is Penelope's test, and how does Odysseus pass it? **(b) Infer:** Why does Penelope feel the need to test Odysseus, even though he has abandoned his disguise? **(c) Interpret:** Is the mood after the test altogether happy? Explain.
6. **(a) Connect:** Are Odysseus' actions in dealing with the suitors consistent with his actions in earlier episodes of the epic? Explain. **(b) Assess:** Do you consider him heroic?
7. **Evaluate:** How do you think the problem of the suitors should have been handled? Why?

Homer

(circa 800 B.C.)

A legendary poet and historian, Homer is credited with two of the most famous and enduring epics of all time: the *Iliad* and the *Odyssey*. Their impressive length and scope have resulted in the coining of an adjective from the author's name: *homeric,* meaning "large-scale, massive, or enormous."

Facts about Homer's life have been lost over time. Scholars even disagree about whether the *Iliad* and the *Odyssey* were written by the same person—and whether Homer existed at all! According to tradition, however, Homer was born in western Asia Minor, and he was blind.

In later centuries, the *Iliad* and the *Odyssey* were the basis of Greek and Roman education.

ASSESSMENT PRACTICE: Reading Comprehension

Combining Sentences (For more practice, see Test Preparation Workbook, p. 63.)

Many tests require students to combine sentences. Use this sample test item.

The old dog Argus raised his head. Argus thumped his tail.

What is the best way to combine these sentences?

A The old dog Argus raised his head, and Argus thumped his tail.
B The old dog Argus raised his head and thumped his tail.
C The old dog Argus raised his head, and thumped his tail.
D The old dog Argus raised his head; he thumped his tail.

The question asks for the best combination. Choice *D* is grammatically correct, but it is not the best choice. Choice *B* gives all the information in the original sentences, but without awkwardness or repetition.

Review and Assess

Literary Analysis

Epic Simile

1. Identify at least three **epic similes** in Part 2 of the *Odyssey*.
2. Using a chart like the one shown, note what is being compared in each of the epic similes you identified and the purpose of the comparison.

Lines	Comparison	Purpose

Connecting Literary Elements

3. What **imagery** involving sight, sound, and movement does Homer include in the epic simile in lines 1061–1065?
4. In lines 1412–1425, to which senses do the images used in describing Antinous' death appeal?
5. (a) What is the epic simile in lines 1613–1624? (b) Why is this simile a powerful image for the conclusion of the epic?

Reading Strategy

Summarizing

6. To **summarize** Part 2, use a timeline like this to list, in order, the main events.

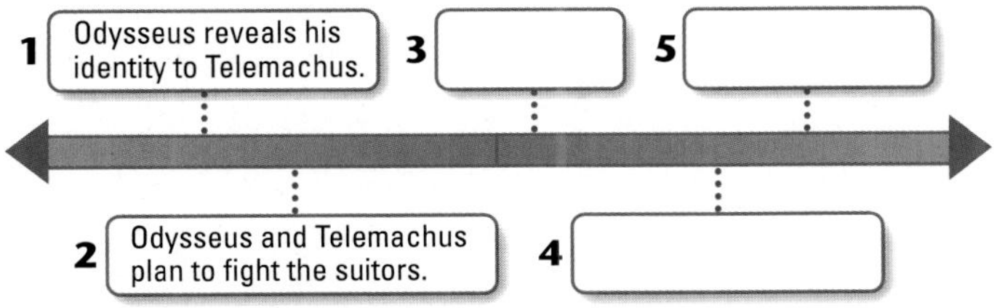

7. Explain the cause and effect of each event that you listed.

Extend Understanding

8. **Cultural Connection:** Why do you think contemporary readers still relate to the characters and the events in the *Odyssey*?

Quick Review

An **epic simile** is an elaborate comparison that may extend for several lines.

Imagery is descriptive language that writers use to create word pictures for the reader by appealing to different senses.

To **summarize** the events in a story, retell the plot briefly in your own words.

Take It to the Net

www.phschool.com

Take the interactive self-test online to check your understanding of the selection.

ENRICHMENT: Further Reading

Other Works by Homer

The Iliad

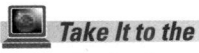

Take It to the Net

Visit www.phschool.com for more information on Homer.

Answers for p. 1047

Review and Assess

1. Possible response: Epic similes can be found in lines 1063–1065, 1290–1297, 1372–1378, 1535–1539, and 1616–1618.
2. Lines: 1372–1378; Comparison: Odysseus' handling of his bow, a harpist's handling of his instrument; Purpose: to give a sense of Odysseus' skill
3. The image of cries "as keen and fluttering as those of the great taloned hawk" that have lost their nestlings appeals to the senses of both sight and hearing.
4. The imagery in the scene of Antinous' death appeals to the sense of sight, in all of the descriptive detail; the sense of touch, in the lifting of the drinking cup; the sense of taste, in the wine; and the sense of hearing, in the sound of the arrow being released and the wine cup falling.
5. **(a)** Odysseus compares himself, in his longing for Penelope, to a shipwrecked sailor who is swimming in rough water, longing for land. **(b)** This is a moving end, because Odysseus—lost for twenty years—has found his "sunwarmed earth."
6. Possible responses: 3: Odysseus enters the hall disguised as a beggar and wins the archery challenge. 4: Odysseus reveals himself to the suitors and kills them all. 5: Odysseus and Penelope are reunited.
7. Possible responses: 3: Odysseus' disguise is part of his plan to surprise the suitors and take his revenge. 4: Odysseus takes his revenge because the suitors have defiled his home and family. 5: Husband and wife embrace, the culmination of all of Odysseus' struggles and trials.
8. Possible responses: Readers can relate to lovers who struggle to be reunited.

EXTEND

Answers for p. 1048

❶ Vocabulary Development

Word Analysis

1. equivalent
2. equidistant
3. equinox

Spelling Strategy

1. believable
2. sensible
3. security

Concept Development: Synonyms

1. c
2. c
3. a
4. b
5. b
6. a
7. c
8. a

❷ Grammar

1. among
2. between
3. among
4. between
5. among

Writing Application

Possible responses: Odysseus and his men sailed between Scylla and Charybdis. The reunion between Odysseus and Telemachus was emotional. The Cyclops slept in his cave among his sheep. Penelope was asked to choose among dozens of suitors.

Integrate Language Skills

❶ Vocabulary Development Lesson

Word Analysis: Latin Root *-equi-*

The Latin root *-equi-*, meaning "same" or "equal," appears in the word *equity*, which means "fairness" or "justice." Complete each sentence below with one of the following *-equi-* words.

a. equinox **b.** equivalent **c.** equidistant

1. Two nickels are __?__ to a dime.
2. Since the two restaurants are __?__, we could reach either one in the same time.
3. At the vernal __?__, day and night are of the same duration.

Spelling Strategy

When adding a suffix beginning with a vowel to a word that ends in silent *e*, drop the *e* and add the suffix: *bemuse* + *-ing* = *bemusing*.

Add the suffix in italics to each word below, and write the new word in your notebook.

1. believe + *-able* **2.** sense + *-ible* **3.** secure + *-ity*

Concept Development: Synonyms

Review the words in the vocabulary list on page 1020. Then, choose the word or phrase whose meaning is closest to that of the first word.

1. dissemble: (a) resemble, (b) take apart, (c) disguise
2. lithe: (a) alert, (b) young, (c) limber
3. incredulity: (a) disbelief, (b) anger, (c) naiveté
4. bemusing: (a) allowing, (b) muddling, (c) entertaining
5. glowering: (a) shining, (b) scowling, (c) laughing
6. equity: (a) fairness, (b) horses, (c) calmness
7. maudlin: (a) boring, (b) tired, (c) sentimental
8. contempt: (a) scorn, (b) pity, (c) doubt

❷ Grammar Lesson

Usage: *among* and *between*

The prepositions *among* and *between* are sometimes used incorrectly. ***Among*** always implies a relationship involving three or more items, while ***between*** generally is used with only two.

Among: Eumaeus went into the megaron *among* the suitors. (many suitors)

Between: Odysseus will come *between* this present dark and one day's ebb. (two times)

Practice Copy these sentences, using *among* or *between* to complete each one.

1. Suddenly a beggar stood __?__ all of the suitors.
2. A clash __?__ him and Antinous quickly developed.
3. Sounds of protest spread __?__ the onlookers, but Antinous paid them no heed.
4. Odysseus' deadly arrow struck __?__ Antinous' neck and shoulder.
5. Odysseus' skill as an archer is well known __?__ the Greeks.

Writing Application Write four sentences about events in the *Odyssey*. Use *among* correctly in two of the sentences and *between* correctly in the other two.

WG Prentice Hall Writing and Grammar Connection: Chapter 27, Section 2

TEACHING RESOURCES

The following resources can be used to enrich or extend the instruction for pp. 1048–1049.

Vocabulary

- **Selection Support:** Build Vocabulary, p. 229
- **Vocabulary and Spelling Practice Book,** (Use this booklet for skills enrichment.) ■

Grammar

- **Selection Support:** Build Grammar Skills, p. 230
- **Writing and Grammar,** Gold Level, p. 620
- **Daily Language Practice Transparencies**

Writing

- **Writing and Grammar,** Gold Level, p. 291
- **Writing and Grammar iText CD-ROM**

■ **BLOCK SCHEDULING:** Resources marked with this symbol provide varied instruction during 90-minute blocks.

❸ Writing Lesson

Character Study

Odysseus is an epic hero, but he may not be a good role model. In a character study, evaluate Odysseus' status as a hero by analyzing his actions and motives. Support your analysis with examples and quotations from the epic.

Prewriting Decide what you want to prove about Odysseus. To get started, write several different completions to this statement: *What I want to prove is* . . . Then, for each statement, list lines from the poem that can help you prove your point.

Drafting Develop a thesis statement that expresses your main idea. Then, organize your points in a logical order. As you draft, be sure to include quotations from the text to illustrate your ideas.

Model: Using Quotations to Illustrate Points

When the men are escaping from the Cyclops, Odysseus taunts Polyphemus against his crew's wishes. He notes, "I would not heed them in my glorying spirit, but let my anger flare and yelled" (lines 455–456).

Quotations from the text and line citations help readers see a strong connection between an argument and the text.

Revising Review your draft to determine whether your ideas come across clearly and are well supported with quotations.

WG Prentice Hall Writing and Grammar Connection: Chapter 13, Section 3

❹ Extension Activities

Listening and Speaking With several classmates, prepare a **debate** to determine whether Odysseus should be prosecuted for murder in the slaying of Penelope's suitors.

- Divide into two opposing teams.
- Prepare an argument expressing your team's position, and support it with details from the *Odyssey* or from actual legal cases found in library or Internet sources.
- Present arguments before the class.

Ask class members to decide which side presented its argument most successfully. **[Group Activity]**

Research and Technology Create an ***Odyssey* map** that traces Odysseus' voyage. Conduct library and Internet research to help you determine locations and distances between them. You might also refer to the map on page 1013. When you have completed your map, calculate the actual straight-line distance from Troy to Ithaca. Then, based on your map, approximate how far Odysseus traveled.

Take It to the Net www.phschool.com

Go online for an additional research activity using the Internet.

Lesson Support for p. 1049

❸ Writing Lesson

- With the class, generate a list of heroic character traits and write them on the board.
- Use the Writing Lesson to guide students in developing the character studies.

❹ Listening and Speaking

- Explain to students that under the law there are different kinds of "murder." There is premeditated murder, when someone plans the act in advance. That is more serious than a murder that "just happens." There are also extenuating circumstances, such as being in the grip of unmanageable emotions or self-defense.
- Students also should consider that Odysseus was not alone in killing the suitors. Other people "aided and abetted" him.
- Instead of a debate, students might like to enact a trial, with judge, jury, prosecutor and defense attorney, defendant(s), witnesses, and so on.

CUSTOMIZE INSTRUCTION
For Universal Access

To address different learning styles, use the activities suggested in the **Extension Activities** booklet, p. 58.

- For Visual/Spatial and Verbal/Linguistic Learners, use Activity 5.
- For Musical/Rhythmic Learners, use Activity 7.
- For Visual/Spatial Learners, use Activity 8.

ASSESSMENT RESOURCES

The following resources can be used to assess students' knowledge and skills.

Selection Assessment

- **Formal Assessment,** pp. 208–210
- **Open Book Test,** pp. 172–174
- **Got It! Assessment Videotapes,** Tape 5
- **Test Bank Software**

Take It to the Net

Visit www.phschool.com for self-tests and additional questions on the *Odyssey*.

PRENTICE HALL ASSESSMENT SYSTEM

- **Workbook**
- **Skill Book**
- **Transparencies**
- **CD-ROM**

An Ancient Gesture ✦ Siren Song ✦ "Prologue" and "Epilogue" *from the* Odyssey ✦ Ithaca

Lesson Objectives and CA Correlations

1. **To analyze and respond to literary elements**
   - Literary Analysis: Contemporary Interpretations **R 3.2**
   - Comparing Literary Works
2. **To read, comprehend, analyze, and critique poems, drama, and nonfiction**
   - Reading Strategy: Comparing and Contrasting **R 3.2**
   - Reading Check questions
   - Review and Assess questions
3. **To develop word analysis skills, fluency, and systematic vocabulary**
   - Vocabulary Development Lesson: Suffix: *-esque* **R 1.1**
4. **To understand and apply written and oral language conventions**
   - Spelling Strategy
   - Grammar Lesson: Sentence Variety: Sentence Lengths **LC 1.3**
   - Assessment Practice (ATE)
5. **To understand and apply appropriate writing and research strategies**
   - Writing Lesson: Comparison-and-Contrast Essay **W 2.3**
   - Extension Activity: Collection **W 1.8**
6. **To understand and apply listening and speaking strategies**
   - Extension Activity: Movie Review **LS 1.1**

STEP-BY-STEP TEACHING GUIDE	PACING GUIDE
PRETEACH	
Motivate Students and Provide Background	
Use the Motivation activity (ATE p. 1050)	5 min.
Read and discuss the Preview material and Background information (SE/ATE p. 1050) [A]	10 min.
Introduce the Concepts	
Introduce the Literary Analysis and Reading Strategy (SE/ATE p. 1051) [A]	15 min.
Pronounce the vocabulary words and read their definitions (SE p. 1051)	5 min.
TEACH	
Monitor Comprehension	
Informally monitor comprehension by circulating while students read independently or in groups [A]	15 min.
Monitor students' comprehension with the Reading Check note (SE/ATE p. 1059)	as students read
Develop vocabulary with Vocabulary notes (SE pp. 1054–1056)	as students read
Develop Understanding	
Develop students' understanding of contemporary interpretations with the Literary Analysis annotations (SE p. 1056; ATE p. 1059) [A]	10 min.
Develop students' ability to compare and contrast with the Reading Strategy annotations (SE p. 1053; ATE p. 1053–1054)	10 min.
ASSESS	
Assess Mastery	
Assess students' mastery of the Reading Strategy and Literary Analysis by having them answer the Review and Assess questions (SE/ATE p. 1061)	20 min.
Use one or more of the print and media Assessment Resources (ATE p. 1063) [A]	up to 50 min.
EXTEND	
Apply Understanding	
Have students complete the Vocabulary Development Lesson and the Grammar Lesson (SE p. 1062) [A]	20 min.
Apply students' knowledge of comparison charts using the Writing Lesson (SE/ATE p. 1063) [A]	45 min.
Apply students' understanding using one or more of the Extension Activities (SE p. 1063)	20–90 min.

[A] ACCELERATED INSTRUCTION: Use the strategies and activities identified with an [A].

UNIVERSAL ACCESS
● = Below-Level Students
▲ = On-Level Students
■ = Above-Level Students

Time and Resource Manager

Reading Levels: Easy/Average/Average/Easy
Average Number of Instructional Days: 4

RESOURCES		
PRINT	**TRANSPARENCIES**	**TECHNOLOGY**
• **Beyond Literature,** Career Connection: Travel and Tourism, p. 59 ▲ ■		• **Interest Grabber Video,** Tape 5 ● ▲ ■
• **Selection Support Workbook:** ● ▲ ■ Literary Analysis, p. 236 Reading Strategy, p. 235 Build Vocabulary, p. 233	• **Literary Analysis and Reading Transparencies,** pp. 117 and 118 ● ▲ ■	
• **Authors In Depth,** Gold Level ■		• **Listening to Literature** ● ▲ ■ Audiocassettes, Side 32 Audio CDs, CD 20
• **Literatura en español** ● ▲ • **Literary Analysis for Enrichment** ■		
• **Formal Assessment:** Selection Test, pp. 211–213 ● ▲ ■ • **Open Book Test,** pp. 175–177 ● ▲ ■ • **Performance Assessment and Portfolio Management,** p. 16 ● ▲ ■ • PRENTICE HALL ASSESSMENT SYSTEM ● ▲ ■	• PRENTICE HALL ASSESSMENT SYSTEM ● ▲ ■ Skills Practice Answers and Explanations on Transparencies	• **Test Bank Software** ● ▲ ■ • **Got It! Assessment Videotapes,** Tape 5 ● ▲
• **Selection Support Workbook:** ● ▲ ■ Build Grammar Skills, p. 234 • **Writing and Grammar,** Gold Level ● ▲ ■ • **Extension Activities,** p. 57 ● ▲ ■	• **Daily Language Practice Transparencies** ● ▲ • **Writing Models and Graphic Organizers on Transparencies,** pp. 33–36, 91 ● ▲ ■	• **Writing and Grammar iText CD-ROM** ● ▲ ■ *Take It to the Net* www.phschool.com

BLOCK SCHEDULING: Use one 90-minute class period to preteach the selection and have students read it. Use a second 90-minute class period to assess students' mastery of skills and have them complete one of the Extension Activities.

PREVIEW

PRETEACH

Step-by-Step Teaching Guide for pp. 1050–1051

Motivation

Draw a cluster diagram on the board and in the center write Penelope. Ask students what they associate with her character. Then ask what today's woman would have done in her place. (She probably would not have waited faithfully at home for twenty years for a husband who is presumed dead to return from wars or adventures.) Tell students that the poems they are going to read look at characters and events from the *Odyssey* in a fresh, new light—the perspective of the twentieth century.

Interest Grabber Video

As an alternative, play "The Epic" on Tape 5 to engage student interest.

1 Background

Social Studies

Women's roles have changed significantly since Homer's time—almost 3,000 years ago. Just as the character of Odysseus can be studied today to learn the qualities that the ancient Greeks valued in a man, so too can Penelope's character be studied for the qualities valued in a woman. Odysseus' courage, adventurous spirit, and guile are celebrated in the *Odyssey*, while Penelope is most notable for her loyalty and patience. She does, however, share some of her husband's celebrated gift for cleverness in the way that she holds off the suitors and in how she tests Odysseus' identity. Twentieth-century poet Margaret Atwood, by contrast, leaves Penelope aside and celebrates the Sirens' song—one of the terrors of the *Odyssey*.

Prepare to Read

An Ancient Gesture ◆ Siren Song ◆ Prologue and Epilogue *from the* Odyssey ◆ Ithaca

Penelope and the Suitors, 1912, J.M. Waterhouse, Aberdeen Art Gallery and Museum, Scotland

Take It to the Net

Visit www.phschool.com for interactive activities and instruction related to the selections, including
- background
- graphic organizers
- literary elements
- reading strategies

Preview

Connecting to the Literature

Two or more people looking at the same event are likely to describe it in distinctly different ways. In these selections, four writers bring their own perspectives to the events in the *Odyssey*.

1 Background

The authors of these four poems are twentieth-century men and women. Thus, their views of society and of men's and women's roles in society are very different from Homer's. For much of history in most cultures, women have had fewer legal rights and fewer opportunities than men. In fact, women in the United States did not even have the right to vote until 1920. Further progress for women was slow; they did not gain career and educational opportunities until the last few decades of the twentieth century.

TEACHING RESOURCES

The following resources can be used to enrich or extend the instruction for pp. 1050–1051.

Interest Grabber Video, Tape 5

Background

Beyond Literature, p. 59

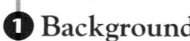

Take It to the Net

Visit www.phschool.com for background and hotlinks for the *Odyssey*.

Literary Analysis

Literary Analysis and Reading Transparencies, p. 118

Reading

Selection Support: Reading Strategy, p. 235; Build Vocabulary, p. 233

Literary Analysis and Reading Transparencies, p. 117

BLOCK SCHEDULING: Resources marked with this symbol provide varied instruction during 90-minute blocks.

❷ Literary Analysis

Contemporary Interpretations

The characters and events of the *Odyssey* are timeless and universal in their interest and significance. They are so rich in meaning that every generation sees in them ideas and values that ring true. **Contemporary interpretations** of the epic—present-day conceptions or understandings—have produced poems, plays, novels, and essays by countless writers. For instance, in "Ithaca," Constantine Cavafy transforms Ithaca from a physical place to a spiritual ideal:

> Ithaca has given you the beautiful voyage.
> Without her you would never have taken the road.

Notice how the poets use ideas from Homer's work to convey contemporary thoughts, values, beliefs, and feelings.

Comparing Literary Works

Contemporary interpretations of an epic like the *Odyssey* can differ widely in purpose, theme, and artistic method. Consider the impact the backgrounds, ideas, and feelings of these writers may have had on their interpretations of the *Odyssey*. Then, compare the ways each poet reflects and adapts ideas from Homer's epic.

❸ Reading Strategy

Comparing and Contrasting

In reading a piece of literature based on an earlier work, look for the similarities and differences between the original and the updated work.

- **Compare** an updated work with its original to discover how elements in the works are alike.
- **Contrast** an updated work with its original to decide how elements in the works are different.

As you read, use a Venn diagram like the one shown to identify similarities and differences between each poem and Homer's *Odyssey*.

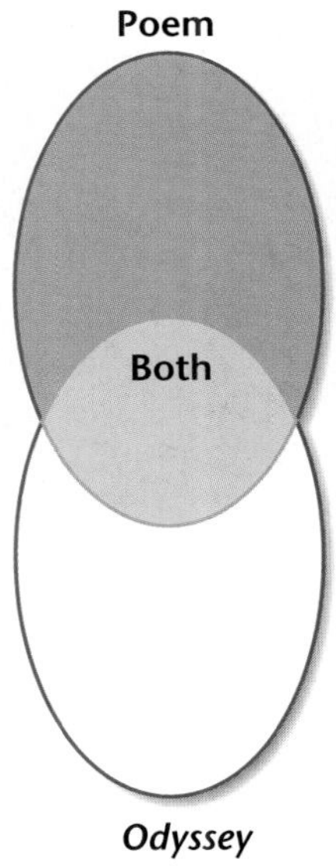

Vocabulary Development

beached (bēcht) *adj.* washed up and lying on a beach (p. 1054)

picturesque (pik´ chər esk´) *adj.* like or suggesting a picture (p. 1055)

tempests (tem´ pists) *n.* violent storms with strong winds (p. 1056)

amber (am´ bər) *n.* yellowish resin used in jewelry (p. 1059)

ebony (eb´ ə nē) *n.* hard, dark wood used for furniture (p. 1059)

defrauded (dē frôd´ id) *v.* cheated (p. 1060)

CUSTOMIZE INSTRUCTION FOR UNIVERSAL ACCESS

For Less Proficient Readers	For English Learners	For Advanced Readers
Play the **Listening to Literature** Audiocassette or CD recordings of the poems as students read in the text. Ask students to summarize each poem, then have them read again, independently.	The poetic forms in these selections are less straightforward in narrative structure than is the *Odyssey* itself, so students may need assistance recognizing allusions to the original epic.	Explain to students the concept of literary allusion—a reference in a work of literature to a character, place, or event in another literary work. Suggest that students examine the literary allusions in these poems and research those that are unfamiliar.

❷ Literary Analysis

Contemporary Interpretations

- Tell students that when modern writers interpret the *Odyssey* or some part of it creatively, they frequently use it to express their own feelings, beliefs, and experiences. Atwood, for example, uses the Sirens to say something about women. Cavafy uses a basic plot thread of the *Odyssey* —the journey home of Odysseus—to say something about life and living.
- Encourage students as they read the poems to focus on how Homer's subject matter takes on new meanings according to the special purpose of each writer.

❸ Reading Strategy

Comparing and Contrasting

- Explain that elements in a work of literature that can be compared and contrasted include details, characters and events. For example, when students read Margaret Atwood's poem "Siren Song," ask them to think about the way Atwood's portrayal of a Siren is similar to and different from Homer's portrayal.
- Once students have identified the similarities and differences, have them try to determine the reasons behind these similarities and differences. Consider what the writer is trying to accomplish with a contrasting portrayal of a character, for instance.
- As an alternative, you may wish to display the Comparison-and-Contrast Organizer in **Writing Models and Graphic Organizers on Transparencies,** p. 91, for students to use as they read the poems.

Vocabulary Development

- Pronounce each vocabulary word for students, and read the definitions as a class. Have students identify any words with which they are already familiar.

E-Teach

Visit E-Teach at www.phschool.com for teachers' essays on how to teach, with questions and answers.

TEACH

Step-by-Step Teaching Guide for pp. 1052-1060

CUSTOMIZE INSTRUCTION
For Musical/Rhythmic Learners

Have students prepare oral readings of their favorite poems from this section to perform for the class.

❶ About the Selection

In "An Ancient Gesture," Penelope's actions are viewed from a modern perspective.

❷ Background

Art

Penelope and the Suitors, by J. W. Waterhouse.

This painting illustrates Penelope working at her loom in an attempt to stave off her suitors.

Born in Rome in 1849, J. W. Waterhouse was deeply influenced by Italy's classical heritage. This sparked his interest in ancient stories such as the *Odyssey*. Use the following questions for discussion:

1. Waterhouse was a master storyteller in art, celebrated for his ability to capture the most dramatic point in a story. How is this skill apparent in *Penelope and the Suitors*?
   Possible response: The artist captures Penelope at the height of her struggle against the suitors. She is shown intent on her weaving, but the viewer knows she must be aware of the suitors close behind her with their offers of gifts and music.
2. What details in the painting can you find in the *Odyssey*? Which ones do you think came from the artist's imagination?
   Answer: The characters in the painting can be found in the *Odyssey*. The lyre, the flowers and other gifts, the clothing, and the furniture are from the artist's imagination.

❸ ▶ Critical Viewing

Answer: Penelope wants the suitors to go away, so she is pointedly ignoring them. Even though she is aware of the proffered gifts and lyre playing, she refuses to look at them and focuses on her weaving.

❶ AN ANCIENT GESTURE

Edna St. Vincent Millay

❷

Penelope and The Suitors, 1912, J. M. Waterhouse, Aberdeen Art Gallery and Museum, Scotland

❸ ▲ **Critical Viewing** What is Penelope's attitude toward the suitors? How can you tell? **[Infer; Support]**

TEACHING RESOURCES

The following resources can be used to enrich or extend the instruction for pp. 1050–1060.

Literary Analysis

Selection Support: Literary Analysis, p. 236

Reading

Listening to Literature Audiocassettes, Side 38

Listening to Literature Audio CDs, CD 21

Extension

Authors In Depth, Gold Level (The collection includes eight additional poems by Derek Walcott for extended reading.)

BLOCK SCHEDULING: Resources marked with this symbol provide varied instruction during 90-minute blocks.

I thought, as I wiped my eyes on the corner of my apron:
Penelope did this too.
And more than once: you can't keep weaving all day
And undoing it all through the night;
Your arms get tired, and the back of your neck gets tight;
And along towards morning, when you think it will never be light,
And your husband has been gone, and you don't know where,
    for years,
Suddenly you burst into tears;
There is simply nothing else to do.

And I thought, as I wiped my eyes on the corner of my apron:
This is an ancient gesture, authentic, antique,
In the very best tradition, classic, Greek;
Ulysses did this too.
But only as a gesture,—a gesture which implied
To the assembled throng that he was much too moved to speak.
He learned it from Penelope . . .
Penelope, who really cried.

Reading Strategy
Comparing and Contrasting How are the reasons for the speaker's tears similar to the reasons for Penelope's tears?

Review and Assess

Thinking About the Selection

1. **Respond:** Does this poem make you feel more or less sympathetic to Penelope than the *Odyssey* did? Explain.
2. **(a) Recall:** What similarity does the speaker of "An Ancient Gesture" see between herself and Penelope?
   (b) Analyze: What has caused the speaker to employ this "ancient gesture"?
3. **(a) Recall:** Which characters from the *Odyssey* does Millay incorporate in her poem? **(b) Distinguish:** What differences between these characters does the speaker point out?
4. **(a) Assess:** What questions about the speaker and her husband are left unanswered? **(b) Extend:** What effect is created by these unanswered questions?
5. **Speculate:** What advice do you think Penelope would give to the speaker of this poem? Explain.

Edna St. Vincent Millay

(1892–1950)

Like many other American writers of her time, Edna St. Vincent Millay is remembered for her artistic experimentation and her rebelliousness. She published several successful poetry collections, including *The Harp Weaver and Other Poems* (1923), which earned her a Pulitzer Prize.

❹ Reading Strategy

Comparing and Contrasting

- Tell students that one of the remarkable things about the *Odyssey* is not how much has changed in 2,700 years, but how powerfully the emotions and actions of the epic can still speak to modern readers.
- Ask students the Reading Strategy question on p. 1053: How are the reasons for the speaker's tears similar to the reasons for Penelope's tears?
  Answer: Like Penelope, the speaker is crying because her husband has been gone for years.

Answers for p. 1053

Review and Assess

1. Students may say that the poem makes them feel more sympathetic because it describes personal feelings in a way that feels more intimate.
2. **(a)** The speaker cries and wipes away tears, as she believes Penelope must have done.
   (b) She cries because her husband has been gone for years, and she doesn't know where he is.
3. **(a)** She mentions Penelope and Ulysses (Odysseus). **(b)** The speaker points out that Penelope "really cried," whereas Odysseus feigned tears to manipulate the crowd.
4. **(a)** We don't know why her husband has gone, or where, or whether he is still alive.
   (b) Possible responses: The unanswered questions create a sense of mystery and sadness; the lack of specific detail allows the reader to focus on emotions.
5. Possible response: Penelope might tell the speaker to keep faith, because her husband might return.

❺ About the Selection

In "Siren Song," one of the Sirens says that she is unhappy in her role of singing a song that is irresistible to men. She says that her song is actually a cry for help. However, the last stanza holds the ironic key to this poem: It is precisely the woman's cry for help that men find irresistible.

❻ Reading Strategy

Comparing and Contrasting

- After students have read "Siren Song," ask them to compare its tone with that of "An Ancient Gesture."
  Possible response: Students may note that the tone of "An Ancient Gesture" is sincere and empathetic; the speaker in "Siren Song" has a brash, ironic, almost cynical tone.
- Have students compare this Siren's song to the one in the *Odyssey*.
  Possible response: Both songs flatter the listener and tell him what he wants to hear. Homer's Sirens promise an end to loneliness, whereas Atwood's siren offers to share a secret and begs for rescue.

❺ SIREN SONG

Margaret Atwood

This is the one song everyone
would like to learn: the song
that is irresistible:

the song that forces men
to leap overboard in squadrons
even though they see the beached skulls

the song nobody knows
because anyone who has heard it
is dead, and the others can't remember.

Shall I tell you the secret
and if I do, will you get me
out of this bird suit?[1]

beached (bēcht) *adj.* washed up and lying on a beach

1. **bird suit** Sirens are usually represented as half bird and half woman.

I don't enjoy it here
squatting on this island
looking <u>picturesque</u> and mythical

with these two feathery maniacs,
I don't enjoy singing
this trio, fatal and valuable.

I will tell the secret to you,
to you, only to you.
Come closer. This song

is a cry for help: Help me!
Only you, only you can,
you are unique

at last. Alas
it is a boring song
but it works every time.

picturesque (pik′ chər esk′) *adj.* like or suggesting a picture

Review and Assess

Thinking About the Selection

1. **Respond:** How do you feel about the experience of the speaker of the poem?
2. **(a) Recall:** What does the Siren reveal about the song? **(b) Analyze:** The Siren describes the song as "fatal and valuable." Why might it be valuable?
3. **(a) Recall:** How does the speaker of "Siren Song" say she feels about being a Siren? **(b) Infer:** To whom might the Siren be speaking as she describes her feelings?
4. **Assess:** How much of "Siren Song" is based on Homer's *Odyssey* and how much is Atwood's original creation?
5. **Speculate:** What relationship between men and women does she portray in this poem?
6. **Extend:** Do you think most women would appreciate or dislike this poem?

Margaret Atwood

(b. 1939)

Since the 1960s, this Canadian author has been writing about what it means to be a woman in a period of social change. For example, her novel *The Handmaid's Tale* (1985) explores a futuristic society in which women's roles are strictly defined.

Another of Atwood's central themes is the role of mythology in people's lives. These two concerns come together in "Siren Song," an ironic look at Homer's Sirens.

Answers for p. 1053

Review and Assess

1. Students may respond that the speaker of this poem sounds bored and trapped by her role as a Siren.
2. **(a)** The song is a cry for help. **(b)** Possible response: The song is valuable because, even though it is a ploy, it succeeds in drawing people together.
3. **(a)** She claims she does not like being a Siren. **(b)** She might be speaking to a man she is trying to entice.
4. The character of the Siren is from the *Odyssey*, but Homer's poem does not put us in her mind as "Siren Song" does. Her thoughts are a creation by Atwood.
5. Atwood suggests that some relationships between men and women are based on a pretense of need.
6. Some students may feel that women would enjoy the poem's honesty and irony; others might suggest that women would find the view of relationships too cynical.

CUSTOMIZE INSTRUCTION FOR UNIVERSAL ACCESS

For Gifted/Talented Students	For Advanced Readers
Suggest that students create a picture or a sculpture of a Siren. They may research a Siren's appearance in existing works of art or rely purely on their own imaginations. Challenge some students to create an image of Margaret Atwood's modern Siren.	Margaret Atwood uses an allusion from literature to create a comment about the relationship between men and women. Ask students to write a brief essay in which they use characters from literature they have read (*Romeo and Juliet,* for example) to make their own generalizations about the relationship between men and women.

7 About the Selection

"Prologue and Epilogue from the *Odyssey*" presents a modern version of the epic's beginning and ending. This piece shows the relevance of the *Odyssey* in the modern world.

8 Literary Analysis

Contemporary Interpretations

- Point out that in line 5 the narrator is repeating a line from the *Odyssey* as it would sound in Greek, the original language of the epic.
- Ask students the Literary Analysis question on p. 1056: Which details in the Prologue give a modern twist to the *Odyssey*?
  Possible response: The narrator's name in this version is Blind Billy Blue, a name with a modern connotation, and the language is more contemporary, with a West Indian lilt to the poetry.

9 Background

Achilles and Hector

Achilles was the greatest of the Greek warriors involved in the siege of Troy. Hector was the son of the king of Troy and the greatest of the Trojan warriors. Achilles "put the hex" on Hector by killing him in combat. He himself was killed shortly thereafter, a devastating loss to the Greeks that increased their reliance on Odysseus.

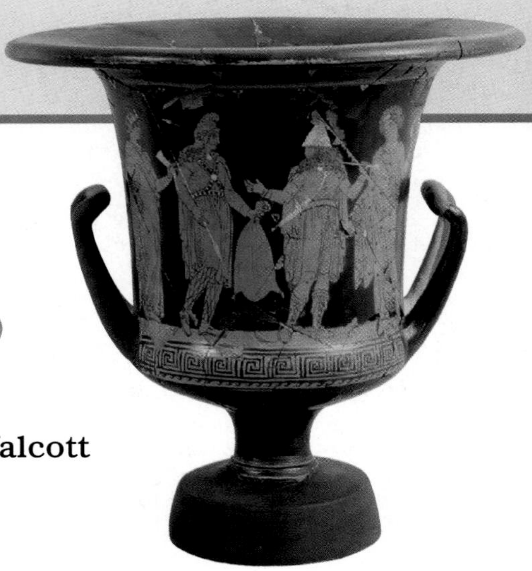

7 Prologue and Epilogue from the Odyssey

Derek Walcott

PROLOGUE

Sound of surf.

BILLY BLUE (*Sings*)
Gone sing 'bout that man because his stories please us,
Who saw trials and tempests for ten years after Troy.

8
I'm Blind Billy Blue, my main man's sea-smart Odysseus,
Who the God of the Sea drove crazy and tried to destroy.

Andra moi ennepe mousa polutropon hos mala polla . . .
The shuttle of the sea moves back and forth on this line,

All night, like the surf, she shuttles and doesn't fall
Asleep, then her rosy fingers at dawn unstitch the design.

When you hear this chord
(Chord)
Look for a swallow's wings,
A swallow arrowing seaward like a messenger

Passing smoke-blue islands, happy that the kings
Of Troy are going home and its ten years' siege is over.

So my blues drifts like smoke from the fire of that war,
Cause once Achilles was ashes, things sure fell apart.

9
Slow-striding Achilles, who put the hex on Hector
A swallow twitters in Troy. That's where we start.
(Exit.)

tempests (tem′ pists) *n.* violent storms with strong winds

Literary Analysis
Contemporary Interpretations Which details in the prologue give a modern twist to the *Odyssey*?

EPILOGUE

BILLY BLUE (*Sings*)

I sang of that man against whom the sea still rages,
Who escaped its terrors, that despair could not destroy,

Since that first blind singer, others will sing down the ages
Of the heart in its harbour, then long years after Troy, after Troy.

And a house, happy for good, from a swallow's omen,
Let the trees clap their hands, and the surf whisper amen.

For a rock, a rock, a rock, a rock-steady woman
Let the waves clap their hands and the surf whisper amen.

For that peace which, in their mercy, the gods allow men.
(*Fade. Sound of surf.*)

Review and Assess

Thinking About the Selection

1. **Respond:** Do you think the narrator is someone you would like to know? Explain.
2. **(a) Recall:** Who is the narrator? **(b) Interpret:** Which qualities of the narrator's character do the words in these passages convey?
3. **(a) Recall:** Which characters from the *Odyssey* does the narrator mention by name in the Prologue? **(b) Recall:** How does he describe Penelope in the Epilogue? **(c) Infer:** What seems to be his attitude toward her? Explain your answer.
4. **(a) Recall:** Who is the "first blind singer" referred to in the Epilogue? **(b) Analyze:** Does this reference explain why Billy Blue *sings* the Epilogue? Explain.
5. **(a) Generalize:** Overall, which elements from the *Odyssey* seem most interesting to Walcott? **(b) Assess:** How faithful is this interpretation of Homer's *Odyssey*?
6. **Evaluate:** Do you think the poet treats the original text with respect? Explain.

Derek Walcott

(b. 1930)

Born on the Caribbean island of St. Lucia, Walcott writes poems that reflect the influence of his background. His work has won worldwide acclaim, and in 1992 he won the Nobel Prize for Literature for his book *Omeros* (1990), which draws on Homer's epic. While granting the award, the Swedish Academy said, "West Indian culture has found its great poet."

In addition to being a poet, Walcott is a successful playwright and director. "Prologue" and "Epilogue" are from his stage version of the *Odyssey*.

CUSTOMIZE INSTRUCTION FOR UNIVERSAL ACCESS

For Gifted/Talented Students	For Advanced Readers
Billy Blue sings the blues in these passages. Suggest that students prepare a performance of the Prologue and Epilogue as a blues song. Ask students to find instrumental music or recordings to accompany the text. The performer might read or sing the passages to the blues rhythms.	Suggest that students read additional works by Derek Walcott. Suggest that they read *The Odyssey: A Stage Version* (from which the Prologue and Epilogue are taken). You may also wish to use **Authors In Depth,** Gold Level, which includes such poems as "Endings," "The Morning Moon," "Midsummer," and "Tobago."

Answers for p. 1057

Review and Assess

1. Students may say they would like to know the narrator because he speaks in the idiom of popular culture.
2. **(a)** Blind Billy Blue **(b)** Possible response: The character seems to be relaxed and friendly, and a natural storyteller.
3. **(a)** Odysseus is mentioned. The narrator also names Hector and Achilles, two major figures who died in the Trojan War that preceded the *Odyssey*. **(b)** He calls her a "rock-steady woman." **(c)** Possible response: The speaker admires Penelope for remaining true to Odysseus during all the time he was away.
4. **(a)** Homer is the first blind singer. **(b)** Calling Homer a singer, rather than a poet, may help explain why Billy Blue sings the Epilogue. Walcott presents Billy as a blues singer; he may be alluding as well to the first line of the *Odyssey*: "Sing in me, Muse."
5. **(a)** Possible response: Walcott seems most interested in the personal elements of the tale about a man whom "despair could not destroy." He is particularly interested in his relationship with Penelope. **(b)** Possible response: The poem is faithful in its interpretation of Penelope as a devoted wife of Odysseus.
6. Possible response: Walcott takes the language into more contemporary and less formal realms, but he is true to the action and theme of the original.

10 ▶Critical Viewing

Possible response: Students might say that "Phoenician markets" correspond to opportunities for new experiences, and that allusions to fearful creatures, such as the Lestrygonians, might represent difficult challenges or obstacles in life.

Amphora with Grapes, Loran Speck, Loran Speck Art Gallery, Carmel, CA

10 ▲ Critical Viewing The poet uses classical images from the *Odyssey*, like those pictured here, to make a connection to modern life. Which experiences in your life could correspond to some of the classical images mentioned in the poem? **[Connect]**

11

Ithaca

Constantine Cavafy

When you start on your journey to Ithaca,
then pray that the road is long,
full of adventure, full of knowledge.
Do not fear the Lestrygonians[1]
12 and the Cyclopes and the angry Poseidon.
You will never meet such as these on your path,
if your thoughts remain lofty, if a fine
emotion touches your body and your spirit.
You will never meet the Lestrygonians,
the Cyclopes and the fierce Poseidon,
if you do not carry them within your soul,
if your soul does not raise them up before you.

Then pray that the road is long.
That the summer mornings are many,
that you will enter ports seen for the first time
with such pleasure, with such joy!
Stop at Phoenician markets,
and purchase fine merchandise,
mother-of-pearl and corals, amber and ebony,

1. **Lestrygonians** (les tri gō´ nē ənz) cannibals who destroy all of Odysseus' ships except his own and kill the crews.

amber (am´ bər) *n.* yellowish resin used in jewelry

ebony (eb´ ə nē) *n.* hard, dark wood used for furniture

13 **Reading Check**

What advice does the speaker give listeners or readers about meeting the Lestrygonians?

11 About the Selection

To Cavafy, the journey to Ithaca means more than the voyage of one epic hero, Odysseus, to his home. The trip is symbolic of anyone's life journey.

12 Literary Analysis

Contemporary Interpretations

- Tell students that "Ithaca" offers another perspective on the *Odyssey*, one that places the emphasis on the value of the journey over that of the destination.
- Ask students which characters from Homer are mentioned in this poem. How does the poet use them in an original way?
  Answer: The characters from Homer are the Lestrygonians, the Cyclopes, and the angry Poseidon. In Homer, they are actual characters; in the poem, they are thoughts or ideas. Cavafy uses them to express his own thoughts and values.

13 Reading Check

Answer: If your "thoughts remain lofty," you will never meet the Lestrygonians.

CUSTOMIZE INSTRUCTION FOR UNIVERSAL ACCESS

For Special Needs Students	For Advanced Readers
This poem will become more comprehensible once students understand the meaning of Ithaca. Point out that in the *Odyssey*, Ithaca represents home, an end to struggles and effort, and a reunion with loved ones. Have students read the poem to learn how Cavafy uses those meanings of Ithaca and creates new meanings.	Have students compare "Ithaca" with Christina Rosetti's "Uphill," p. 926, another poem that explores the symbolism of a journey and a final destination. Ask students to describe each speaker's attitude toward the journey and the consequences of journey's end in a comparison-and-contrast essay.

Answers for p. 1060

Review and Assess

1. Most students may say that a journey of discovery appeals to them.
2. **(a)** People can avoid them by maintaining lofty thoughts and fine emotions, and by not carrying the Lestrygonians and the Cyclopes within their souls. **(b)** Possible response: People create their own opportunities or difficulties, depending on how they respond to life.
3. **(a)** People should pray that the road is long, that the summer mornings are many, and that they will enter ports seen for the first time. **(b)** Activities connected with these prayers include stopping at markets, buying things, and learning from those who have knowledge.
4. **(a)** Ithaca marks the end of the journey. Because the journey does eventually end, it is important to get as much out of it as possible. **(b)** Ithaca might be a metaphor for old age or death.
5. **(a)** Possible response: Even if the destination is disappointing, it is the experience gained on the journey that matters. **(b)** Most students may agree with the emphasis on the importance of the journey.
6. **(a)** Possible response: The speaker might have advised Odysseus to travel slowly and, if possible, to learn all he could from each encounter—both friendly and dangerous—he had along the way. **(b)** Encourage students to give reasons for their agreement or disagreement.

and pleasurable perfumes of all kinds,
buy as many pleasurable perfumes as you can;
visit hosts of Egyptian cities,
to learn and learn from those who have knowledge.

Always keep Ithaca fixed in your mind.
To arrive there is your ultimate goal.
But do not hurry the voyage at all.
It is better to let it last for long years;
and even to anchor at the isle when you are old,
rich with all that you have gained on the way,
not expecting that Ithaca will offer you riches.

Ithaca has given you the beautiful voyage.
Without her you would never have taken the road.
But she has nothing more to give you.

And if you find her poor, Ithaca has not defrauded you.
With the great wisdom you have gained, with so much experience,
You must surely have understood by then what Ithaca means.

defrauded (dē frôd′ id) *v.* cheated

Review and Assess

Thinking About the Selection

1. **Respond:** Does the journey to Ithaca as described in this poem appeal to you? Explain.
2. **(a) Recall:** According to the speaker, how can you avoid meeting the Lestrygonians, the Cyclopes, and Poseidon on the road to Ithaca? **(b) Infer:** Why might a person carry such terrors as these in his or her own soul?
3. **(a) Recall:** What three things does the speaker say you should pray for on the journey to Ithaca? **(b) Connect:** What activities and pleasures are linked to these prayers?
4. **(a) Recall:** Why is Ithaca important? **(b) Interpret:** What might Ithaca symbolize to the poet?
5. **(a) Infer:** What message is conveyed in the last three lines of the poem? **(b) Apply:** Do you agree with this message?
6. **(a) Speculate:** What do you think the speaker might have said to Odysseus if he could have advised him during his journey? **(b) Take a Position:** Do you agree with this advice? Explain.

Constantine Cavafy

(1863–1933)

Considered the most important Greek poet of the first half of the twentieth century, Cavafy was born to Greek parents in Alexandria, Egypt.

"Ithaca" showcases his basic creative method: using the world of Greek mythology to write poems that speak to today's reader.

ASSESSMENT PRACTICE: Grammar and Usage

Grammar and Usage **(For more practice, see Test Preparation Workbook, p. 75.)**

Many tests ask students to use verb tenses correctly. Use this sample test item.

The characters and events in the *Odyssey* are universal in their significance. They are so rich in meaning that every generation ___ in them relevant ideas and values.

Choose the word or group of words that belongs in the space.

A found

B finded

C would have found

D finds

The first sentence is in the present tense. To create parallel structure, a present-tense verb is needed in the second sentence. Therefore, *D* is the correct choice.

Review and Assess

Literary Analysis

Contemporary Interpretations

1. What timeless theme does Edna St. Vincent Millay express in her **contemporary interpretation** of the *Odyssey*?
2. Use a chart like the one shown to explain how Atwood uses similarities and differences between her Siren and Homer's to make a point about modern women.

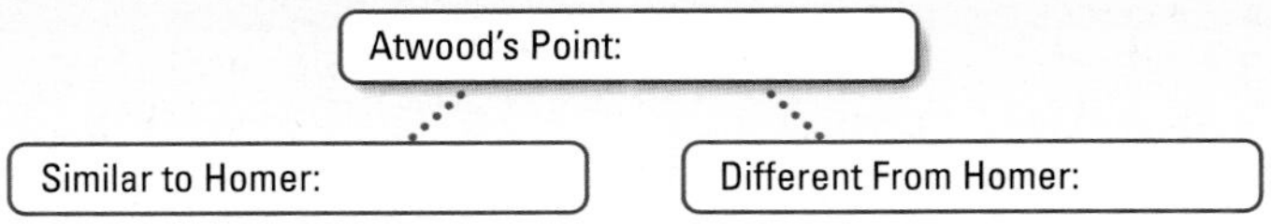

3. How does Walcott make the *Odyssey* seem contemporary?
4. Why is Odysseus' journey home good material for a poem that, like Constantine Cavafy's, concerns the course of human life?

Comparing Literary Works

5. Use a Venn diagram to identify the ways in which the attitudes toward men and women expressed in Atwood's and Millay's poems are similar or different.

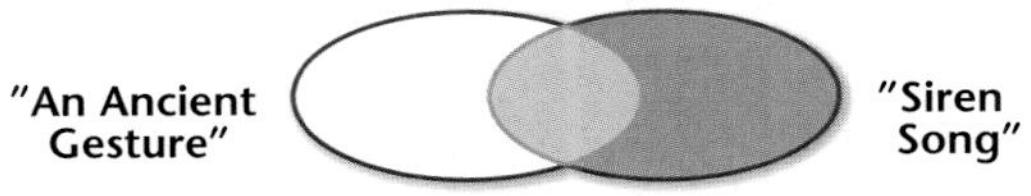

6. How is Cavafy's poem different in tone from one or more of the other poems? Explain your answer.
7. Which of the other three poets might enjoy Walcott's treatment of the *Odyssey*? Cite details from their poems that support your answer.

Reading Strategy

Comparing and Contrasting

8. How is the journey that Cavafy describes essentially different from the one that Homer describes?

Extend Understanding

9. **Fine Arts Connection:** What other classical literary works can you think of that are especially well suited for modern interpretations? Explain your answer.

Quick Review

Contemporary interpretations are present-day conceptions or understandings of a classical work whose ideas and values are relevant to the present.

To **compare** an updated work with its original, determine how the two works are alike.

To **contrast** an updated work with its original, decide how the two works are different.

Take It to the Net
www.phschool.com
Take the interactive self-test online to check your understanding of these selections.

ENRICHMENT: Further Reading

Other Works by the Poets

Works by Edna St. Vincent Millay
A Few Figs From Thistles

Works by Margaret Atwood
The Animals in That Country

Works by Derek Walcott
Collected Poems 1948–1984

Works by Constantine Cavafy
Walls

Take It to the Net
Visit www.phschool.com for more information on the poets.

Answers for p. 1061

Review and Assess

1. She sees the theme of separation from a loved one.
2. Similar to Homer: Siren is irresistible to men. Different From Homer: Atwood's Siren does not enjoy her role as a singer. Atwood's Point: Modern women don't want the attracting of men to be their chief role in life.
3. Walcott uses contemporary language, with expressions such as "my main man's sea-smart Odysseus," to bring the *Odyssey* into modern times.
4. Possible response: On his journey, Odysseus encountered a wide range of experiences—physical, emotional, and psychological. This journey therefore reflects the variety of experiences one encounters during a lifetime.
5. "An Ancient Gesture": The woman truly cries; the man does it as a gesture to a crowd. "Siren Song": The woman feigns helplessness to attract a man; the man is helpless to resist. Both: The women feel the absence of a man.
6. Possible response: Cavafy's poem is hopeful and inspirational in a broad way. Atwood's is ironic. Walcott's is buoyant and playful, yet respectful of the original. "An Ancient Gesture" is poignant, focusing on a small, private moment.
7. Possible response: Atwood might enjoy Walcott's treatment, because the poets share a playfulness with language and with a modern point of view.
8. Homer's journey is filled with danger, while Cavafy's journey is filled with opportunities to gain new experiences and wisdom.
9. Answers will vary based on what works students have read. Tell students to give specific reasons for their choices.

EXTEND

❶ Vocabulary Development

Word Analysis

1. picturesque
2. arabesque
3. statuesque

Concept Development: Analogies

1. picturesque
2. amber
3. beached
4. tempests
5. ebony
6. defrauded

Spelling Strategy

1. sweetest
2. breakage
3. veiled

❷ Grammar

Varying Sentence Length

1. Penelope cries for her husband, Odysseus. He has been away for years.
2. The Sirens' song lures men to their deaths. Sailors cannot resist it.
3. Walcott introduces Billy Blue. He substitutes for Homer, narrator of the *Odyssey.*
4. Ithaca may symbolize the end of life. It is the goal to focus on.
5. Each poet offers an interpretation of the *Odyssey.* The epic is by Homer, who lived long ago.

Writing Application

Have students exchange their paragraphs with partners to evaluate sentence lengths.

Integrate Language Skills

❶ Vocabulary Development Lesson

Word Analysis: French Suffix *-esque*

The French suffix *-esque* means "like" or "having the quality of." In "Siren Song," one of the Sirens complains of having to look too *picturesque*, which means "like or suggesting a picture." The suffix also appears in *statuesque* and *arabesque*.

Complete each sentence with one of the *-esque* words below:

a. picturesque **b.** statuesque **c.** arabesque

1. The __?__ mountain view lingered in my mind for several days.
2. The carpet was covered with __?__ designs resembling Moorish calligraphy.
3. The __?__ actress commanded the attention of the audience with her regal bearing and stunning diamonds.

Concept Development: Analogies

Complete each analogy below with a word from the vocabulary list on page 1051.

1. *Melodious* is to *voice* as __?__ is to *appearance.*
2. *Marble* is to *statue* as __?__ is to *necklace.*
3. *Fallen* is to *leaves* as __?__ is to *shells.*
4. *Floods* are to *water* as __?__ are to *wind.*
5. *Aluminum* is to *can* as __?__ is to *table.*
6. *Spoke* is to *conversed* as __?__ is to *cheated.*

Spelling Strategy

If a word ends in a vowel-vowel-consonant combination, do not double the final consonant before adding a suffix. Thus, *defraud* + *-ed* = *defrauded.* Add the suffix to each word below and then use the new word in a sentence.

1. sweet + *-est* **2.** break + *-age* **3.** veil + *-ed*

❷ Grammar Lesson

Varying Sentence Length

When you **vary sentence length,** you alternate between long and short sentences in order to make your sentences more interesting and readable. The varied rhythm of the passage below helps emphasize its meaning.

Example: Cavafy uses the journey to Ithaca as a metaphor for one's own life journey. Enjoy life, says the poet. (*Long sentence followed by short sentence*)

If you write many long sentences, it will help the flow of your writing if you break some into shorter sentences.

Practice Rewrite each sentence as two shorter sentences. Simplify where possible.

1. Penelope cries for Odysseus, who is her husband, who has been away for years.
2. Sailors cannot resist the call of the Sirens' song, which lures men to their deaths.
3. Walcott introduces Billy Blue, who substitutes for Homer, narrator of the *Odyssey*.
4. Ithaca, which may symbolize the end of life, is the goal to focus on.
5. Each poet offers an interpretation of the *Odyssey*, the epic by Homer, who lived long ago.

Writing Application Write a paragraph describing your reaction to one of the poems. Work to vary your sentence lengths.

WG Prentice Hall Writing and Grammar Connection: Chapter 22, Section 3

TEACHING RESOURCES

The following resources can be used to enrich or extend the instruction for pp. 1062–1063.

Vocabulary

- **Selection Support:** Build Vocabulary, p. 233
- **Vocabulary and Spelling Practice Book** (Use this booklet for skills enrichment.) ■

Grammar

- **Selection Support:** Build Grammar Skills, p. 234 ■
- **Writing and Grammar,** Gold Level, p. 500
- **Daily Language Practice Transparencies**

Writing

- **Writing and Grammar,** Gold Level, p. 180
- **Writing and Grammar iText CD-ROM** ■
- **Writing Models and Graphic Organizers on Transparencies,** pp. 33–36

■ **BLOCK SCHEDULING:** Resources marked with this symbol provide varied instruction during 90-minute blocks.

3 Writing Lesson

Comparison-and-Contrast Essay

All four of the poems in this section draw their inspiration from Homer's *Odyssey*. Write an essay in which you compare and contrast one of the selections with the appropriate portion of Homer's original work.

Prewriting After choosing the selection you wish to compare and contrast, list the ways that the poem and the *Odyssey* are similar and different. Prepare a comparison chart to organize the information.

Model: Finding Points of Comparison

Cavafy's "Ithaca"	Homer's *Odyssey*
1. Hopes the journey is long.	1. Hopes the journey will end.
2.	2.
3.	3.

A comparison chart is a useful tool for organizing the information to be used in an essay.

Drafting Use the notes in your chart as the starting point from which to write your draft. Use words such as *like*, *unlike*, *similarly*, and *in contrast* to show points of difference and resemblance.

Revising When you revise your essay, make sure that it is clearly organized by points of comparison and contrast. In addition to checking for accuracy, be sure you have clarified the meaning of the passages to which you draw your readers' attention.

WG *Prentice Hall Writing and Grammar Connection: Chapter 9, Section 2*

4 Extension Activities

Listening and Speaking Watch a film version of the *Odyssey*. Then, prepare a **movie review** for your classmates. In writing your review, consider these key elements of the task:

- Focus on the movie's themes and imagery.
- Formulate your own judgments about the film.
- Support those judgments with evidence.

Read your review aloud to your classmates and invite them to ask questions. **[Group Activity]**

Research and Technology Organize a **collection of literary works** inspired by the *Odyssey*. Use the Internet to help you search. Find enough information so that you can include a summary of each work you choose. If possible, use software to design your collection.

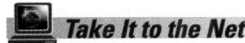

Take It to the Net www.phschool.com

Go online for an additional research activity using the Internet.

Writing Lesson

- On the board, use the comparison chart on p. 1063 to write down points of comparison between the two poems generated by class discussion.
- Use the Comparison-and-Contrast Essay transparencies in **Writing Models and Graphic Organizers on Transparencies,** pp. 33–36, to demonstrate the drafting and revising stages of the lesson.
- Use the Comparison-and-Contrast Essay rubric in **Performance Assessment and Portfolio Management,** p. 16, to evaluate students' essays.

4 Listening and Speaking

- In preparation for this assignment, bring in movie reviews from newspapers or magazines to share with the class.
- With students, outline the review. Ask questions about how the review is structured: What is the reviewer's opinion and how does he or she support it? How much plot summary is there? How much of the review focuses on acting and how much on the story or message?

CUSTOMIZE INSTRUCTION For Universal Access

To address different learning styles, use the following activities suggested in the **Extension Activities** booklet, p. 57.

For Visual/Spatial and Interpersonal Learners, use Activity 5.

For Logical/Mathematical Learners, use Activity 7.

ASSESSMENT RESOURCES

The following resources can be used to assess students' knowledge and skills.

Selection Assessment

- **Formal Assessment,** Selection Test, pp. 211–213
- **Open Book Test,** pp. 175–177
- **Got It! Assessment Videotapes,** Tape 5
- **Test Bank Software**

Take It to the Net

Visit www.phschool.com for self-tests and additional questions on the selections.

Writing Rubric

- **Performance Assess. and Portfolio Mgmt.,** p. 16

PRENTICE HALL ASSESSMENT SYSTEM

- **Workbook**
- **Skill Book**
- **Transparencies**
- **CD-ROM**

Lesson Objectives

1. To understand the connection between Homer's *Odyssey* and the real-life space adventure recorded in *Lost Moon*
2. To appreciate the qualities of a good adventure story

Connections

Homer's *Odyssey* is a written version of an ancient story that was first passed along from village to village by word of mouth. As storytellers "sang" the ancient tale, their audiences thrilled to the action and adventures. Centuries later, when the Apollo 13 space crew rocketed to the moon, people all over the world learned about the story at the same time because of media coverage provided by radio and television sources. Which do students imagine was more thrilling to audiences—the dramatic tales of the *Odyssey* or the real-life adventure of Apollo 13?

CONNECTIONS

Literature Past and Present

Modern-day Odyssey

The *Odyssey* recounts the trials and adventures of Odysseus. Two decades is a long time to be away from home, dependent on the whims of the gods and facing dangers in battle with men and monsters. Still, risk has its rewards, and ultimately the story has a happy ending.

In April 1970, the three-man crew of the *Apollo 13* spacecraft embarked on a modern-day odyssey to the moon. Like Odysseus, they set out with a spirit of anticipation and adventure. But the exploration of space has its own perils. On the third day of their mission, just as they were getting ready to sleep in the command module nicknamed Odyssey, an onboard oxygen tank ruptured. After several nerve-wracking days, the crew finally managed to return safely to Earth. In this case, survival was the ultimate reward. The following excerpt from one astronaut's narrative describes the moment when the gas leak was first discovered.

Lost Moon
The Perilous Voyage of Apollo 13

Jim Lovell and Jeffrey Kluger

ENRICHMENT: History Connection

The Trojan War

Two epics, the *Iliad* and the *Odyssey,* have their roots in the events of the Trojan War, which occurred about 1200 B.C. Until the 19th century it was widely believed that Troy and the Trojan War were imaginary. Then, in 1871, an American named Heinrich Schliemann began excavating an ancient city in Turkey. To the amazement of many, this retired businessman had discovered the lost city of Troy (also called Ilion or Ilium in Latin). Since Schliemann's initial discovery, nine cities have been found at the site, one on top of the other.

The seventh city, which was destroyed around 1250 B.C., appears to be the Troy of the ancient epics. While legend credits the abduction of Helen, the wife of a Greek king, as the reason for the Trojan war, economic conflict over control of trade in the Aegean Sea was the more likely cause.

"It looks to me," Lovell told the ground uninflectedly, "that we are venting something." Then, for impact, and perhaps to persuade himself, he repeated: "We are venting something into space."

"Roger," Lousma responded in the mandatory matter-of-factness of the Capcom, "we copy your venting."

"It's a gas of some sort," Lovell said.

"Can you tell us anything about it? Where is it coming from?"

"It's coming out of window one right now, Jack," Lovell answered, offering only as much detail as his limited vantage point provided.

The understated report from the spacecraft tore through the control room like a bullet.

"Crew thinks they're venting something," Lousma said to the loop at large.

"I heard that," Kranz said.

"Copy that, Flight?" Lousma asked, just to be sure.

"Rog," Kranz assured him. "O.K. everybody, let's think of the kinds of things we'd be venting. GNC, you got anything that looks abnormal on your system?"

"Negative, Flight."

"How about you, EECOM? You see anything with the instrumentation you've got that could be venting?"

"That's affirmed, Flight," Liebergot said, thinking, of course, of oxygen tank two. If a tank of gas is suddenly reading empty and a cloud of gas is surrounding the spacecraft, it's a good bet the two are connected, especially if the whole mess had been preceded by a suspicious, ship-shaking bang. "Let me look at the system as far as venting is concerned," Liebergot said to Flight.

"O.K., let's start scanning," Kranz agreed. "I assume you've called in your backup EECOM to see if we can get some more brain power on this thing."

"We got one here."

"Rog."

The change on the loop and in the room was palpable. No one said anything out loud, no one declared anything officially, but the controllers began to recognize that Apollo 13, which had been launched in triumph just over two days earlier, might have just metamorphosed from a brilliant mission of exploration to one of simple survival.

Connecting Literature Past and Present

1. How would you have reacted to the discovery of the oxygen leak?
2. Did the astronauts deal with adversity in a manner similar to Odysseus'? If not, how did they differ?
3. Do the roles played by the gods have any type of counterpart in the account of the flight of *Apollo 13*? Explain

Jim Lovell

(b. 1928)

Jim Lovell was a test pilot for U.S. Navy fighter aircraft before joining the space program as an astronaut. Lovell was the first man to rendezvous two spacecraft and to journey twice to the moon. He coauthored this account of the harrowing journey of *Apollo 13*'s three-man crew.

Jeffrey Kluger

(b. 1954)

Jeffrey Kluger, a senior writer for *Time* magazine, frequently writes on science and space issues. With *Apollo 13* astronaut Jim Lovell, he coauthored the book *Lost Moon*, which served as the basis for the Ron Howard film about the mission.

Modern-day Odyssey

- Have students read the boxed introductory text on p. 1064.
- Point out that in both the ancient tale of the *Odyssey*, and the modern story of Apollo 13, men cast out into the unknown, encounter terrible dangers, and struggle against all odds to return home.

Answers

Connecting Literature Past and Present

1. Students may say that they would have been extremely frightened; some may say they would have panicked; others may say they would have remained calm.
2. Odysseus responded to adversity by keeping his head and developing strategies to outwit his foes. In a similar way, the astronauts maintained their calm, and focused on finding solutions to their problems.
3. The role of the flight crew on the ground is somewhat comparable to the role of the gods.

Lesson Objectives

1. To learn how to understand the information contained in newspaper editorials
2. To analyze bias in newspaper editorials

About Newspaper Editorials

- If possible, collect some examples of newspaper editorials for students to look at in print or online.
- Have students read "About Newspaper Editorials" on p. 1066.
- Ask students to examine some newspaper editorials and summarize their contents. Invite students to note if the contents are critical, supportive, informative, or persuasive.

Reading Strategy

Analyzing Bias

- Explain that students will read two newspaper editorials about the same topic: John Glenn's second trip into space. One editorial is supportive of Glenn's voyage, and the other is critical.
- Draw students' attention to the chart on p. 1066. Have students read the text contained in the chart. Then, ask volunteers to explain any unclear terms or concepts, such as "loaded words," "opposing points not considered," or "facts not considered."
- As they read the two editorials, encourage students to complete a similar chart.

READING INFORMATIONAL MATERIALS

Newspaper Editorials

About Newspaper Editorials

A newspaper editorial is an article in which the newspaper's publisher or editor expresses his or her opinion on a current event or issue, such as criticizing or praising the actions of a public official or group. In some cases, an editorial might also attempt to persuade readers to take a particular action. For example, an editorial may promote certain political candidates and urge readers to vote for them in an upcoming election. Like a persuasive essay, an editorial can be effective only if strong arguments support the writer's opinion.

Reading Strategy

Analyzing Bias

Bias is a writer's tendency to favor one side of an issue. Writers show bias when they present unfavorable facts, use language intended to provoke an emotional response, or do not examine opposing points of view.

Both editorials that follow use loaded language—words intended to trigger a positive or negative response without reasoned support.

- The *Minneapolis Star and Tribune* refers to Senator John Glenn's decision to go into space as "volunteering." The word is meant to elicit a positive response from readers.
- *The Kansas City Star* calls Glenn's flight a "junket," a word suggesting that it is a pleasure trip. The word is intended to elicit a negative response.

As you read both editorials, use a chart like the one shown to record each instance of bias you find.

	"Veteran"	"Wrong Orbit"
Main idea		
Support		
Loaded words		
Opposing point not considered		There is symbolic value to Glenn's flight.
Facts not considered		

Veteran Returns, Becomes Symbol

Editorial in the
Minneapolis Star and Tribune,
January 19, 1998

> An editorial usually states the writer's opinion in the opening paragraph. The headline reflects the same opinion.

John Glenn went into orbit in 1962 and took America's hearts soaring with him. Who better to fire the nation's imagination again about the promise of space exploration?

NASA has done itself and its cause great good by announcing that Glenn, the astronaut-turned-U.S. senator, will fly into space once more. Though Glenn has represented Ohio in the Senate for five terms and run for president once, many Americans still consider his name synonymous with the nation's manned space program.

At a time when all astronauts were esteemed as America's best and brightest, Glenn stood out. Though not the first American in space, nor the one to seize the space-race prize—a moon landing—Glenn possessed an appeal that surpassed that of his peers.

> The editorial offers arguments that support the writer's opinion. In this paragraph, the writer offers three positive effects of Glenn's orbit.

Just as Glenn's orbital heroics inspired America when he was a young man, by joining the shuttle crew in October at age 77, he can inspire the nation again. He can reignite curiosity about the benefits and challenges for humankind that lie beyond Earth. He can let a watchful public share vicariously his delight at leaving Earth's bounds once more.

And he can again be an exemplar for his generation—a generation already setting new standards for vigor and productivity past age 70. Glenn's flight should dramatically demonstrate that age is no limit to derring-do, nor to service to one's country.

Volunteering for a space ride isn't an option for most septuagenarians. But many of Glenn's contemporaries are also volu teering, lending a hand to the young, old, sick and needy in their own communities. As America honors Glenn's past and future career in space, let the nation also take grateful note of the good works senior citizens are doing here on the ground.

Veteran Returns, Becomes Symbol

- Have students read the editorial on p. 1067.
- Ask students to summarize the main idea expressed in the first paragraph.
  Possible response: John Glenn was a great choice for a second trip into space.
- Ask students if this writer considers opposing points of view.
  Answer: The writer does not consider any opposing viewpoints.

The Wrong Orbit

- Have the students read the editorial on p. 1068.
- Ask students to point out the location of the main message in this editorial.
  Answer: The main message is given in the title and subhead.
- Ask students if this writer considers opposing points of view.
  Answer: Yes. The writer considers opposing viewpoints in the next-to-last paragraph.

The Wrong Orbit

Senator Has No Legitimate Business Blasting Into Space

Editorial in *The Kansas City Star*, January 20, 1998

Most Americans think of political lobbying as something done by special interest groups trying to curry favor with lawmakers to affect some legislation. Not so in the case of Sen. John Glenn and his former employer, the National Aeronautics and Space Administration.

Glenn, a Democratic senator from Ohio, has lobbied NASA for some time in hope of returning to space. Glenn, who will turn 77 in July, was the first American to orbit the Earth.

He plans to retire from the Senate, but for his next engagement he wants to strap on a space suit under the pretense of scientific merit. Glenn says his space jaunt would help the space program understand the effects of weightlessness on the aging human form. (C'mon, Senator, it's doubtful even you believe that, so don't expect anyone else to.)

There are much better uses for the taxpayers' money than Glenn's planned junket in space via the Discovery mission in October. Besides, as the senator ought to know, workers in the space program are being laid off around the country due to downsizing at NASA. And there's something questionable, if not downright indecent, about a U.S. senator who has been a NASA ally in Congress, calling on the space agency for a favor. Whether on this planet or another, a quid pro quo is the same.

. . .

John Glenn became a hero after his pioneering space flight, and he parlayed that status into what was said to be a successful political career. His political career was jeopardized by his involvement in the Keating Five scandal, and he became excessively shrill this year during committee hearings as the Senate defender of the Democratic presidential fund-raising debacle.

Certainly, there are times when good science and good politics mix, as happened with the launch of the U.S. space program as part of the space race with former Soviet Union.

But Glenn's proposed junket in space is neither good science nor good politics.

The writer uses the loaded word "pretense" in this paragraph.

Here, the writer acknowledges an opposing point of view. Later, the writer will argue that the position is wrong.

The editorial concludes with a restatement of the writer's opinion.

CUSTOMIZE INSTRUCTION FOR UNIVERSAL ACCESS

For Special Needs Students	For Advanced Readers
Write the following question on the board: "Does the writer think it is a good or bad idea for John Glenn to travel into space for a second time?" Then, write two columns of words from the editorials that indicate judgment: **positive:** *hero, great good, inspire, delight, vigor, honors;* **negative:** *questionable, indecent, scandal.* As you read each editorial aloud, have students listen for these words from the two lists. Then, invite them to answer the question posed above.	Have students search online archives of other newspapers to locate additional editorials about John Glenn's second trip into space. Encourage students to read several of these editorials closely, organizing arguments both for and against into specific categories. Ask students to summarize the range of arguments they find, and to report their findings to the class.

Check Your Comprehension

1. What were John Glenn's two careers?
2. What is unusual about Glenn's proposed ride in space?
3. Which editorial opposes Glenn's planned space ride?

Applying the Reading Strategy

Analyzing Bias

4. Cite two uses of loaded words in each editorial.
5. Identify two issues raised by the Kansas City editorial that are ignored by the Minneapolis editorial.

Activity

Writing an Editorial Analysis

These two editorials offer opposing points of view about John Glenn's proposed space trip. Create an outline like the one shown, listing the arguments in each editorial. Then, explain which editorial you find more convincing and why.

I. *Minneapolis Star and Tribune*
A. Main idea ____________
B. Supporting arguments
1. ____________
2. ____________
3. ____________
C. My conclusion ____________

II. *The Kansas City Star*
A. Main idea ____________
B. Supporting arguments
1. ____________
2. ____________
3. ____________
C. My conclusion ____________

Contrasting Informational Texts

Editorials and News Reports

Editorials serve a different purpose from news reports. You read an editorial to discover a different perspective, or opinion, of an event. You watch a news report to collect information that is largely free of opinion.

1. Consider the differences between the two types of writing and answer the following questions:
   (a) How would a news article presenting John Glenn's proposed space voyage differ in tone and content from an editorial on the subject?
   (b) What is the benefit of each kind of writing?
2. In a current newspaper, find two letters to the editor that present opposing views on the same topic. Summarize the arguments that each writer presents.

Contrasting Informational Texts

1. **(a)** A news article would be more factual and less opinionated. **(b)** News articles offer readers the facts about an event, so they can form their own opinions; an editorial offers opinions that readers can react to.
2. Students may look for editorials in newspapers or online.

Answers for p. 1069

Check Your Comprehension

1. John Glenn was an astronaut and a senator.
2. Glenn is much older than the other astronauts, and this is his second trip into space.
3. "The Wrong Orbit" opposes Glenn's planned space ride.

Applying the Reading Strategy

4. "Veteran Returns": "Glenn's orbital heroics inspired" and "best and brightest"; "Wrong Orbit": "pretense of scientific merit" and "downright indecent"
5. The *Kansas City Star* editorial mentions the Keating Five controversy, the downsizing of NASA, and Glenn's plans to retire from the Senate.

Activity

- Read the Activity on p. 1069 aloud to the class, and have them complete the outlines.
  Possible Answers:

Minneapolis Star and Tribune

A. Main idea: John Glenn should go into space a second time.
B. Supporting arguments
1. John Glenn has a history of inspiring Americans
2. Glenn's name is still synonymous with the nation's manned space program
3. This trip enables Glenn to be an exemplar for his generation.

C. My conclusion: If increasing our knowledge about science is the goal of space missions, another astronaut with particular expertise in an ongoing research project might be a better choice. But then, it's nice that Glenn got to go.

The Kansas City Star

A. Main idea: John Glenn should not go into space a second time.
B. Supporting arguments
1. Glenn's reason for going has little scientific merit.
2. Taxpayers' money could be used better in other ways.
3. Glenn has had a questionable political career.

C. My conclusion: There is a conflict of interest in Glenn's request to NASA as a senator, since Glenn has been an ally for NASA in Congress.

Lesson Objectives

1. To write a research report
2. To learn the characteristics of research writing
3. To use writing strategies to plan, organize, write, and revise a research report

Model From Literature

Explain that the writers who wrote the editorial opinions in the Reading Informational Materials section of this unit had to conduct research to collect the facts on which they based their opinions.

Research Writing: Research Report

- Have students read this section on p. 1070.
- Point out that students will be asked to meet the Assignment Criteria given in the bulleted list on p. 1070 as they create their research reports.
- Encourage students to refer to this list as they write their drafts.

Prewriting

- Conduct a brainstorming session as a class. Invite a volunteer to write the ideas on the board as the class calls them out.
- Draw students' attention to the question under "Identify your purpose" on p. 1070. Explain that students should develop similar questions that they can answer in their reports.
- Point out the "Organize Information" note card on p. 1070, mentioning each aspect of the information included there. Encourage students to create similar note cards or to use software that serves the same purpose as they gather information for their research reports.

Writing WORKSHOP

Research Writing: Research Report

A **research report** interprets and presents information gathered through the extensive study of a subject. In this workshop, you will write a research report that presents your findings on a subject.

Assignment Criteria. Your research report should have the following characteristics of research writing:

- A thesis statement that is clearly expressed
- Factual support from a variety of credited sources
- A clear organization that includes an introduction, body, and conclusion
- A bibliography or works-cited list that provides a complete listing of research sources

To preview the criteria on which your research report may be assessed, see the Rubric on page 1075.

Prewriting

Choose a topic. Identify an area of general interest, and **brainstorm** for a list of more specific categories. For example, from the general area of art, you might choose the following categories: sculpture, Impressionism, and Pop Art. Using these categories, find a topic you would like to research.

Identify your purpose. Before you begin your report, consider a question that you would like to answer through your research. Review your notes and jot down a question that expresses this idea clearly. You may want to incorporate this information in a slightly different form into your draft when you start writing.

Question: How did the school of painting called Impressionism begin?

Gather and organize information. As you locate information, take notes to aid you in drafting your paper and creating a reference list.

- **Source cards:** Create a separate card to note the author, title, publisher, city, date of publication, and page number of each source you consult.
- **Note cards:** For each item of information, create a separate note card to record facts accurately, as in the chart shown.

If you choose to keep an electronic log of information, be sure to include all source details. Electronic logs offer you the advantage of using key word searches to locate source details.

Organize Information with Note Cards

Marsh, Peter, M.D. *Eye to Eye: How People Interact.* Topsfield, MA: Salem House Publishers, 1988. (p. 54)

Gestures vary from culture to culture. The American "OK" symbol (thumb and forefinger) is considered insulting in Greece and Turkey.

TEACHING RESOURCES

The following resources can be used to enrich or extend the instruction for pp. 1070–1071.

- **Writing and Grammar,** Gold Level, Chapter 12, pp. 250–279
- **Performance Assessment and Portfolio Management,** pp. 17, 65
- **Writing and Grammar iText CD-ROM**
  Students can use the following tools as they complete their responses to literature:
  - Note Cards
  - Topic Bank
  - Sentence Openers Variety

Student Model

Before you begin your research report, read this student model and review the characteristics of an effective research report.

Lyndsey Regan
Canyon Country, CA

Body Language

When we speak to other people, they are not only listening to our actual words, but sensing our facial expression, tone of voice, gestures, level of eye contact, posture, and movements as well. Nonverbal communication, or body language, makes up approximately 65 percent of human communication (Aylesworth 3). Body language has a major impact on how others perceive what we say. It can also be a tool for miscommunication when the speaker and listener are from different cultures or are communicating through technology that deprives them of visual cues. In fact, we often realize the importance of body language only when we cannot interpret someone else's body language correctly.

The opening line is meant to capture the reader's attention by presenting a surprising perspective.

The author expresses her thesis statement clearly and concisely.

In *Eye to Eye: How People Interact*, Dr. Peter Marsh explains that before we speak, our gestures, posture and facial expressions are already broadcasting messages to those around us. While we are speaking, these gestures continue to communicate messages—usually clarifying what we are saying, but sometimes contradicting us in telltale ways (Marsh 116–119).

Often, body language is an unconscious act that triggers the most developed senses in other people—hearing and sight (Aylesworth 18). That is why body language is such a great way to emphasize words and ideas. Many people take advantage of this. Advertisers, for example, hire actors in their commercials who use body language that appeals to viewers.

Studies have shown that people's body language changes when they are not telling the truth (Vrij, Edward, Roberts, and Bull 239–263). If someone's body language is inconsistent with what he or she is saying, people tend to believe what the body is telling them. A good way for people to convey a positive message is to avoid certain movements, like fidgeting or letting your eyes wander. Instead, good communicators maintain steady eye contact, nod in agreement, and smile. You may notice that people on television, like hosts of infomercials and talk-show hosts, generally display this positive body language when speaking.

Student Model

- Point out that the Student Model is a sample, and that students' research reports may be longer.
- Have students refer to the Assignment Criteria list on p. 1070, then identify aspects of the student model that meet each criterion.
- Point out that Lyndsey's report uses both first- and second-person perspectives. Ask students why they think she chose to use these two different points of view. Possible answer: She could have written in second-person only, but the mixture flows well together and offers variety for the reader.

Real-World Connection

Research writing in the real world: Explain that students will use the skill of writing research reports in high school and college. They may be surprised to know that many careers also require research writing, including attorney, business manager, Web site writer, and graphic designer.

CUSTOMIZE INSTRUCTION FOR UNIVERSAL ACCESS

For Special Needs Students	For English Learners	For Gifted and Talented Students
Encourage students to choose a fairly narrow topic for their research reports so they don't become overwhelmed with facts to include. Work with students to help them create very specific, focused questions to address through their writing.	Have students work in pairs to read through the Student Model, noting any words or phrases they need to look up for better understanding.	Encourage students to choose a topic that relates to a subject they are studying in one of their other classes, such as science, foreign language, or history. Encourage these students to share their work in both classes.

Body Language

- Point out the internal citations Lyndsey uses in her report. Remind students to refer to their note cards when making citations in their reports.
- Explain that Lyndsey addresses many different topics under the main subject of body language. Ask students to identify some of the specific topics she explores. **Answer:** Under the overall subject of body language, Lyndsey addresses cultural differences and the effects of technology.

Body language is usually learned, but it can also be inherited. It is affected by age, gender, background, and situation. The meaning of body language can change depending on cultural context. According to Dr. Marsh, each culture has developed its own repertoire of symbolic gestures, many with original associations that have now been long forgotten (Marsh 53–54). This causes people to be alarmed by foreign visitors or nervous around people when they visit new countries.

In the United States, people have a wide variety of regional influences because the country is a melting pot of diverse cultures. A gesture that means the same thing throughout the United States is the "OK" sign made with the thumb and the forefinger. This gesture is interpreted similarly in some European countries, but if you were to perform this sign in Greece or Turkey, it would be considered very insulting (Marsh 54).

Whenever Lyndsey presents a specific piece of evidence that is not her own idea or common knowledge, she cites it using the appropriate format.

There are other cultural differences in body language within Europe. In Germany, body language often reflects social status, and Germans often use body language for emphasis. Italian gestures are usually passionate, emotional expressions communicated with the face, arms, and shoulders. Italians often use body language to clarify themselves or to express urgency. In France, people tend to use more formal gestures. They are generally not as expressive or insistent as Italians. The body language of the French is not nearly as casual as we are used to in America (Ruesch and Kees 23–25). As you can see by exploring a few examples from different cultures, there are many differences in body language. Therefore, when you communicate with people from other countries, take special care in your use of body language.

Technological advancements in our society affect the way we communicate. For example, when we speak on the telephone, we are unable to see the person on the other end of the line. The message that a person may be trying to convey may be misinterpreted without the additional visual information provided by his or her body language. With electronic mail, there is no visual or verbal communication whatsoever. As a result, people cannot completely understand the meaning of what is being communicated. Therefore, people using e-mail should be careful about what they write. To avoid miscommunication, communicating the old-fashioned way—in person—may be the best approach.

The author's organizational structure is logical and clear. First, she discusses how body language is used in a variety of cultures. Next, she gives examples of what happens when we do not have body language to guide us.

In conclusion, body language is a significant component of communication, even though we are often not aware of it. Body language, like facial expressions and gestures, frequently enables people to clearly understand one another, but we must remember that people cannot always be read like a book. With cultural differences, body language can take on different meanings, and this allows for potential miscommunication. Changes in technology present a different kind of problem but with a similar result. When body language cannot be seen, people may misinterpret the meaning of the communicator, making them angry or confused. As you can see, the additional information we provide with our body language plays a major role in how we communicate our thoughts and ideas.

After her conclusion, Lyndsey presents the complete information for the works cited in her report using MLA, a common style for citation.

Works-Cited List

Aylesworth, Thomas G. *Understanding Body Talk.* New York : F. Watts, 1979.

Marsh, Peter, M.D. *Eye to Eye: How People Interact.* Topsfield, MA: Salem House Publishers, 1988.

Ruesch, Jurgen, and Weldon Kees. *Nonverbal Communication: Notes on the Visual Perception of Human Relations.* Berkeley, CA: University of California Press, 1969.

Vrij, Aldert, Katherine Edward, Kim P. Roberts, and Ray Bull. "Detecting Deceit via Analysis of Verbal and Nonverbal Behavior." *Journal of Nonverbal Behavior,* Winter 2000: 239–263.

Body Language

- Point out how Lyndsey uses her conclusion to summarize and tie together all the topics she covered in her report.
- Ask students what other purposes a conclusion can serve. **Possible answer:** A conclusion can end a paper with a memorable feature, like a quote, or it can provide a strong restatement of the paper's main ideas.
- Remind students of the importance of obtaining complete information on their note cards as they conduct research, so they can easily build a bibliography at the end of their reports.

Drafting

- Remind students that a thesis statement clearly communicates the main idea or purpose of an essay.
- Point out the sample thesis statement on p. 1074, as well as the thesis statement that appears on the note card.
- Invite volunteers to share their thesis statements with the class. Ask the class if each thesis statement clearly conveys a focused idea. Possible answer: Students' responses should express whether or not each thesis statement expresses a main idea or purpose.
- Remind students to refer to their research note cards to cite sources within parentheses as they create their drafts.

Revising

- Students may have difficulty deciding if their sources are reliable. Have students work in pairs to evaluate each other's work and find additional sources to confirm information.
- Encourage students to continue working in pairs to review each other's papers for varied word choice.

Drafting

Propose a thesis statement. An effective thesis statement expresses an idea that can be supported by research. Review your notes and take a focused position that can be supported by most of the data you have gathered. Incorporate this position into your draft in the form of a statement.

Sample Thesis Statement
Claude Monet's handling of light in his water lily paintings is typical of Impressionist techniques.

Create an outline. To expand your ideas before writing the draft, use an outline. Organize your outline by using headings, as modeled in the chart shown. To construct a sentence outline, identify a topic sentence in each section. You can use these sentences to develop your draft.

Outline Using Headings

Thesis Statement: Body language has a major impact on how others perceive what we say.

I. Introduction—Body language definition and thesis
II. Importance of body language
  A. To emphasize key points
  B. To recognize falsehoods
III. Poorly understood body language
  A. Cultural differences
  B. Text or voice technology
IV. Summary and conclusion

Prepare to credit sources. When you include a direct quotation, present an original idea that is not your own, or report a fact that is available in only one source, you must include documentation. As you draft, circle ideas or words that are not your own. Use parentheses to note the author's last name and the page numbers of the material used. Later, you can use this record to create formal citation.

Revising

Revise to consider your sources. When presenting material as *fact*—information that is true and can be proven—you must confirm that the source of your information is reliable.

Underline any fact in your draft that may not have a trustworthy source. For example, you may have found an idea on another student's Web site or in a newspaper known for exaggerating ideas or events. Check to see if the fact you have marked is repeated in another, more reliable source, such as an established encyclopedia, a scholarly Web site, or a more trustworthy newspaper or magazine. If the fact is essential to your argument, you *must* find the fact in another source. If this fact is not essential to your argument, consider removing it from your draft.

Model: Evaluating Sources

A good way to convey a positive message is to avoid certain movements. ~~When people cross their arms it is always a sign of defensiveness.~~

Lyndsey found that this was a controversial claim that was supported by only one source. Since it was inessential to her basic argument, she chose to eliminate it.

USING TECHNOLOGY IN WRITING

Explain that if students collect their research information electronically, they can use the Cut and Paste feature of their word-processing software to quickly create in-text documentation as well as their works-cited lists. Students can also use spell check and other revision tools on the **Writing and Grammar iText CD-ROM.**

Revise to examine word choice. Except for the specific terminology associated with your topic, avoid using the same word over and over. Identify words that are key to your topic, and review your writing to find words that you have repeated. Circle them as you read. Using a thesaurus, generate a list of possible synonyms, and substitute them as appropriate. Look at these examples:

Example Synonym Banks

technology: innovation, invention, product, brainchild

theory: belief, policy, system, position, idea

Ronald Reagan: president, government official, leader

Finalize your research report. Before you publish your research report, you should document your sources of information. A works-cited page provides readers with complete information on each source you cite in your paper. A bibliography lists every work you used when researching, even if you did not cite it in the body of the report.

Standards for documentation are set by several organizations. Identify the format your teacher prefers. Following that format, check that each entry is complete and properly punctuated. (For more information, see Writing Criticism and Citing Sources, pages R30 and R31.)

Publishing and Presenting

Share your writing with a wider audience.

Deliver an oral presentation. Read your research report aloud in front of your classmates. You may want to provide classmates with a copy of your bibliography or works-cited page if they care to learn more about your topic.

WG *Prentice Hall Writing and Grammar Connection: Chapter 12*

Rubric for Self-Assessment

Evaluate your research report using the following criteria and rating scale:

Criteria	Rating Scale: Not very				Very
How clearly is the thesis statement expressed?	1	2	3	4	5
How sufficient is factual support from a variety of sources?	1	2	3	4	5
Is the research report well organized?	1	2	3	4	5
How comprehensive is the bibliography or works-cited list?	1	2	3	4	5

Finalize Your Research Report

- Read the first paragraph of this section aloud, drawing students' attention to the difference between a works-cited page and a bibliography.
- Direct students to use the format you prefer.

Publishing and Presenting

- Remind students to practice pronouncing difficult or unfamiliar words in their reports before they read them orally.

Assessment

- Review with students the assessment criteria, pointing out that they evaluate the report's thesis statement, factual evidence, organization, and references.
- Have students complete the self-assessment after they give their presentations.
- The rubric on this page, and another rubric in an alternative format, can be found on pp. 17 and 65 of **Performance Assessment and Portfolio Management.**

TEST-TAKING TIP

On some tests, students may be asked to evaluate a text to make judgments about the writer's bias. Remind students to look for loaded words, opposing points not considered, and facts not considered.

Lesson Objectives

1. To deliver an expository presentation
2. To prepare visuals and incorporate them into the presentation

Delivering an Expository Presentation

- Have students read the information in this section on p. 1076.
- Point out that in an expository presentation, a speaker explains a subject to the audience.
- Ask students how an expository presentation might differ from a persuasive one.
  Answer: In a persuasive presentation, the speaker will try to convince the audience of an argument. In an expository presentation, the speaker must present reliable facts and ideas, but does not need to convey an opinion.

Prepare the Presentation

- Have students read this section on p. 1076.
- Explain that it is essential for the speaker to understand the audience, so the presentation can be tailored to their particular needs and expectations.
- Add that visuals help keep an audience's attention and provide another vehicle for communicating information.

Deliver the Presentation

- Read this section on p. 1076 aloud.
- Remind students to match their tone to the subject of their presentation, using humor carefully and only when appropriate.
- Have students review their written presentations to make sure they've included direct quotes and sound references.

Listening and Speaking WORKSHOP

Delivering an Expository Presentation

In an **expository presentation,** a speaker explains a topic for an audience. Expository presentations are common in the business, scientific, and academic worlds. As with any public speech, the success of an expository presentation depends on thoughtful preparation and enthusiastic delivery.

Prepare the Presentation

Chose a topic. Decide what information you will present. You may decide to introduce your audience to your favorite hobby, to explain an interesting development in current events, or to discuss a musician whose work you admire. Narrow your topic so that you can address it in a brief presentation.

Consider your audience. The content of your presentation depends on the level of knowledge your audience already possesses. If they know little to nothing about your topic, do not present high-level material with complex detail. Conversely, do not expect an audience that is already familiar with a topic to be interested in basic-level description.

Prepare visuals. Plan to incorporate visuals to add interest to your presentation. These enhancements may include charts, graphs, bulleted outlines, illustrations, and fine art. Visuals should meet these criteria:

- They should be concise but clear.
- They should support your main thesis.
- They should present material in a new and interesting way.

Deliver the Presentation

Choose an appropriate tone. Develop a tone appropriate to the subject. If you are delivering a presentation on a serious subject, such as a bloody battle of the Civil War, adopt a serious tone. Use dramatic language and graphic visuals. Consider adding humor only when you want to put your audience at ease and inject some appropriate variety into your presentation.

Make use of source material. Direct references and quotations from source material can bring a presentation to life. Whenever appropriate, cite your sources or quote experts.

Offer varying interpretations. If a topic is controversial, address the varying interpretations of the subject. Stay on the subject when doing this, and offer your own conclusions to clarify ideas for your audience. Visual aids can help to eliminate confusion when you discuss complex topics.

Activity: Presentation and Feedback Choose a historical topic to present. Research your topic, and then deliver an expository presentation that incorporates visual aids as well as material culled from a variety of sources. Critique your presentation with the feedback form at right, and ask other students to offer their feedback.

Feedback Form for Expository Presentation

Rating System
+ = excellent ✔ = average – = weak

Preparation
Scope of Topic ________
Level of Detail ________
Use of Visuals ________

Delivery
Tone ________
Reference to Source Materials ________
Introduction of Varying Interpretations ________

Answer the following questions:
What did you learn that you did not know before?
What questions do you have about the content?
What improvements to the presentation would you recommend? Why?

CUSTOMIZE INSTRUCTION FOR UNIVERSAL ACCESS

For Special Needs Students	For Gifted/Talented Students
Ask these students to choose a topic that deals with something tangible (e.g., a hobby or favorite animal) rather than a concept or idea. Consider suggesting that students explain a process with which they are familiar, and that they incorporate the tools needed to complete that process into their presentations.	Suggest that these students rehearse their presentations so they can use dramatic techniques and visuals effectively during delivery.

Assessment WORKSHOP

Grammar, Usage, and Mechanics

The reading portions of some standardized tests require you to read a sentence or passage and answer multiple-choice questions about grammar, usage, and mechanics. Use the following information to help you:

- Grammar and usage questions test your knowledge of the parts of speech and the rules of sentence structure.
- To answer grammar and usage questions, check to see if all the parts of the sentence agree in number (singular or plural) and gender (masculine or feminine). Then, look to see whether every sentence expresses a complete thought.
- *Mechanics* refers to correct punctuation and capitalization. As you read each passage, determine whether the text makes correct use of these elements of writing.

Test-Taking Strategies

- Try to "hear" each sentence. If it sounds incorrect, check to see if all the parts of the sentence agree. If it is so long that you run out of breath, check for missing punctuation.
- If a word looks wrong, examine its spelling and capitalization.

Sample Test Item

Directions: Read the sentence and choose the best correction for the underlined word or words. If no correction is required, choose "Correct as is."

1. The use of sundials for telling time span many centuries.
   A are spanning
   B is spanning
   C spans
   D Correct as is

Answer and Explanation

The correct answer is ***C***. *Use* is the subject and is singular. Therefore, the verb with which it agrees should be in its singular form, *spans*. ***A*** is plural and is therefore incorrect. ***B*** is incorrect because it describes an action in the present progressive tense, which does not make sense in the context of this sentence. ***D*** is incorrect because the verb does not agree in number with the subject.

Practice

Directions: Read each sentence and choose the best correction for the underlined word or words. If no correction is required, choose "Correct as is."

1. Harold went to the barber shop he also went to the store.
   A shop. He
   B shop, he
   C shop—he
   D Correct as is
2. Although we want more information. We don't know where to look.
   A information: we
   B information, we
   C information—we
   D Correct as is
3. The pile of books on the table are heavy.
   A is
   B were
   C are not
   D Correct as is

Lesson Objective

To correctly answer test questions about grammar, usage, and mechanics

Applying Reading Strategies

Read aloud the bulleted list on p. 1077. Tell students to keep these points in mind when they are asked test questions about grammar, usage, and mechanics.

Applying Test-Taking Strategies

- Read the directions for the Sample Test Item aloud.
- Read the sentence in the test question aloud. Point out that reading aloud, or silent whispering can help students identify possible errors more easily.
- Ask students to select an answer choice and share their responses with the class.
- Point out the explanation for the correct answer on p. 1077. Ask students if they have any questions before they move on to the Practice test question.

Answers

1. The correct answer is *A*. *B* is wrong because a comma cannot join two independent clauses; nor can a dash, *C*.
2. The correct answer is *B*. *A* and *C* are incorrect punctuation for linking a dependent clause to a main clause.
3. The correct answer is *A*. *Pile* is a singular subject and requires a singular verb. Both *B* and *C* are plural and are therefore incorrect.

TEACHING RESOURCES

The following resources can be used to enrich or extend the instruction for p.1077.

PRENTICE HALL ASSESSMENT SYSTEM

- Workbook
- Skill Book
- Transparencies
- CD-ROM

RESOURCES

Handbooks

Indexes

SUGGESTIONS FOR SUSTAINED READING

Following are some suggestions for longer works that will give you the opportunity to experience the fun of sustained reading. Each of the suggestions further explores one of the themes in this book. Many of the titles are included in the **Prentice Hall Literature Library**.

Unit One

A Tale of Two Cities
Charles Dickens

This historical novel, set in London and Paris during the French Revolution, is filled with suspenseful plot twists such as false accusations, look-alike characters, and bitter people thirsting for revenge. At the center of it all is beautiful Lucy Manette—whose father wavers between sanity and madness after spending eighteen years in a French prison, and whose husband is later unjustly imprisoned and sentenced to die by the guillotine.

To Kill a Mockingbird
Harper Lee

This novel, set in the South in the early 1930s, is narrated by a strong-willed girl named Scout. Through Scout's narration, readers meet her older brother, Jem, and her beloved father, Atticus, a respected lawyer who defends an African American accused of attacking a white woman. Scout also recounts the chilling legend of Boo Radley, a neighborhood recluse, feared by all the children, who seems to be following Scout and her brother.

The Strange Case of Dr. Jekyll and Mr. Hyde
Robert Louis Stevenson

This is the story of a mild-mannered doctor who explores his dark side—with terrifying results. Fascinated with the idea of evil, the story's main character, Dr. Jekyll, develops a potion that changes him into the violent Mr. Hyde. Before long, however, Jekyll finds himself transforming into Hyde without the aid of the potion, leaving him, along with terrified readers, to wonder which personality will finally win out.

Unit Two

The Old Man and the Sea
Ernest Hemingway

This novel tells of a man's heroic struggle with nature. The battle begins when the old fisherman Santiago hooks a giant marlin after months without a catch. The old man puts up a fierce effort to conquer the huge and powerful fish, fighting exhaustion, hunger, injury, and even a pack of sharks. This story, told in Hemingway's lean, straightforward style, is a timeless tale of courage and adventure.

The Miracle Worker
William Gibson

This moving play is based on the true story of Helen Keller, who was left blind, deaf, and unable to speak following an illness when she was an infant. The title refers to Helen's teacher, Annie Sullivan, a young woman determined to meet the challenge of helping Helen to communicate. This play, Gibson's most famous, inspired an Academy Award-winning movie.

Rosa Parks: My Story
Rosa Parks with Jim Haskins

One of the pivotal moments of the American civil rights movement occurred on December 1, 1955, when Rosa Parks, an African American, chose not to give up her seat to a white rider on a bus in Montgomery, Alabama. Through this memoir, readers get a firsthand account of that dramatic event and its aftermath, as well as biographical information about one of the leaders of the civil rights movement.

Unit Three

Great Expectations
Charles Dickens

Set in nineteenth-century England, this classic novel traces the passage of a boy called Pip into adulthood. Along the way, he encounters many memorable characters, including a pair of escaped convicts, a wealthy old woman who hasn't left her house since being jilted on her wedding day, and a beautiful young girl who captures his heart. Through a series of adventures, Pip makes many discoveries about himself, the people close to him, and the society in which he lives.

When the Legends Die
Hal Borland

This is the story of a young man who discovers his identity and cultural heritage as he struggles with the challenges of nature. After his father kills another brave, Thomas Black Bull and his parents flee the Ute reservation in southwestern Colorado to live in the wilderness. There, they follow the old ways of Native Americans—hunting, fishing, and fighting for survival. Life is good until Thomas's parents die and he is left on his own.

The House on Mango Street
Sandra Cisneros

This book, a mixture of poetry and prose, tells the story of Esperanza Cordero, a young girl living in Chicago. Through her neighbors on Mango Street, Esperanza makes many discoveries about life as she explores questions such as these: Should a girl get married or pursue her education? How does writing help people express their ideas and solve their problems? Why is growing up so confusing?

Unit Four

The Prince and the Pauper
Mark Twain

In this social satire, set in sixteenth-century England, a young prince and a London street beggar exchange identities. Twain uses both understatement and exaggeration to describe the confusing events that follow. The amusing twists and turns of the plot ultimately reveal a deeper message—that it is wrong to judge people by their outward appearances and that anyone can be a king.

Alice's Adventures in Wonderland
Lewis Carroll

In this fanciful story, a young girl falls down a rabbit hole and finds herself in a strange country where nothing seems to make sense. At times, she grows huge as a giant; at other times, she shrinks to the size of a mouse. Along the way, Alice meets an assortment of extraordinary characters, including a talking rabbit, a sleepy dormouse, and a grinning Cheshire cat. More than just a children's story, this book uses satire and symbolism to poke fun at society.

Childhood
Bill Cosby

In this entertaining book, funnyman Bill Cosby shares humorous reminiscences of his childhood. He recalls getting scolded for his bad manners, acting up in school, suffering through crushes on girls, and playing sports on the streets of Philadelphia. Each tale is told in the sidesplitting style that has secured for Cosby his place as one of the country's best-loved comedians.

Unit Five

Fahrenheit 451
Ray Bradbury

This book is set in a time when firemen start fires—fires that burn books. Guy Montag is a fireman who enjoys his job and never thinks of questioning the system. Then, he meets a teenage girl who tells him of a time when people were not afraid to think for themselves. Suddenly Montag realizes that he can no longer blindly accept the laws of his society.

The Time Machine
H. G. Wells

In this classic science-fiction tale, written more than one hundred years ago, H. G. Wells provides a grim view of the future. The story focuses on an inventor who travels into the future in a time machine he has built. During his travels, he views the progressive destruction of society and even life itself, eventually witnessing a time when giant crabs are the only surviving life form and the sun and Earth are dying.

Dragonsong
Anne McCaffrey

Set in the imaginary world of Pern, *Dragonsong* tells the story of Menolly, a young musician. When the laws of her society prevent Menolly from developing her musical talents, she wanders away from her home and discovers a group of rare and enchanting fire lizards. Menolly's relationship with the fire lizards and her unshakeable love for her music are the basis of this fantasy story.

GLOSSARY

abash (ə bash´) *v.*: Embarrass
acclaimed (ə klāmd´) *v.*: Greeted with loud applause or approval; hailed
acutely (ə kyo͞ot´ lē) *adv.*: Sharply
adept (ə dept´) *adj.*: Highly skilled; expert
aerodynamics (er´ ō dī nam´ iks) *n.*: Branch of mechanics dealing with the forces exerted by air or other gases in motion
aloofness (ə lo͞of´ nəs) *n.*: State of being distant, removed, or uninvolved
amber (am´ bər) *n.*: Yellowish resin used in jewelry
ambiguities (am´ bə gyo͞o´ ə tēz) *n.*: Statements or events whose meanings are unclear
amicably (am´ i kə blē) *adv.*: Agreeably
anonymous (ə nän´ ə məs) *adj.*: Without a known or acknowledged name
archaeologist (är´ kē äl´ ə jist) *n.*: Person who practices the scientific study of the remains of ancient ways of life
archaic (är kā´ ik) *adj.*: Seldom used; old-fashioned
ardent (ärd´ 'nt) *adj.*: Passionate
ardor (är´ dər) *n.*: Passion; enthusiasm
articulate (är tik´ yo͞o lāt) *v.*: Express in words
articulate (är tik´ yo͞o lit) *adj.*: Expressing oneself clearly and easily
assuage (ə swāj´) *v.*: Calm; pacify
astutely (ə sto͞ot´ lē) *adv.*: Cleverly or cunningly
astuteness (ə sto͞ot´ nis) *n.*: Shrewdness
augmenting (ôg ment´ iŋ) *v.*: Increasing; enlarging
avail (ə vāl´) *v.*: Be of help
awry (ə rī´) *adj.*: Not straight
azure (azh´ ər) *adj.*: Blue
bafflement (baf´ əl mənt) *n.*: Puzzlement; bewilderment
barren (bar´ən) *adj.*: Empty
beached (bēcht) *adj.*: Washed up and lying on a beach
beguiling (bi gīl´ iŋ) *adj.*: Tricking; charming
beleaguered (bi lē´ gərd) *adj.*: Worried; tormented
bemusing (bi myo͞oz´ iŋ) *adj.*: Stupefying or muddling
benevolently (bə nev´ ə lənt lē) *adv.*: In a kind and well-meaning way
bereft (bi reft´) *adj.*: Deprived
bizarre (bi zär´) *adj.*: Odd in appearance
blandly (bland´ lē) *adv.*: In a mild and soothing way
blight (blīt) *n.*: Something that destroys or prevents growth
bliss (blis) *n.*: Great joy or happiness
brazen (brā´ zən) *adj.*: Shamelessly bold
buffet (bə fā´) *n.*: Counter or table where refreshments are served
buffeted (buf´ it ed) *v.*: Jostled; knocked about
cannonading (kan´ ən ād´ iŋ) *n.*: Continuous firing of artillery
capacious (kə pā´ shəs) *adj.*: Able to hold much; roomy
ceasing (sēs´ iŋ) *v.*: Stopping
censure (sen´ shər) *n.*: Strong disapproval
charged (chärjd) *adj.*: Tensely expectant; intense
chasms (kaz´ əmz) *n.*: Deep cracks in Earth's surface; narrow gorges
chaste (chāst) *adj.*: Pure or clean in style; not ornate
chattel (chat´ əl) *n.*: Movable item of personal property
chortled (chôrt´ əld) *v.*: Made a jolly, chuckling sound
cipher (sī´ fər) *adj.*: Code
circumvent (sʉr´ kəm vent´) *v.*: Avoid; go around
cloister (klois´ tər) *n.*: Place devoted to religious seclusion
compelling (kəm pel´ iŋ) *adj.*: Forceful
complied (kəm plīd´) *v.*: Carried out or fulfilled a request
concessions (kən sesh´ ənz) *n.*: Things given or granted as privileges
condescending (kän´ di sen´ diŋ) *adj.*: Characterized by looking down on someone
condolence (kən dō´ ləns) *n.*: Expression of sympathy for a grieving person
confer (kən fʉr´) *v.*: To give
confounds (kən foundz´) *v.*: Bewilders; confuses
console (kən sōl´) *v.*: Comfort
contempt (kən tempt´) *n.*: Actions or attitude of a person toward someone or something he or she considers low or worthless
conundrums (kə nun´ drəmz) *n.*: Puzzling questions or problems
covenant (kuv´ ə nənt) *n.*: Agreement; pact
creed (krēd) *n.*: Statement of belief
cunning (kun´ iŋ) *n.*: Clever; sly
cur (kʉr) *n.*: Mean, contemptible person; mean, ugly dog
dallying (dal´ ē iŋ) *v.*: Wasting time; loitering
déclassée (dā´ klä sā´) *French fem. adj.*: Lowered in social status
decoy (dē´ koi) *n.*: Person or thing used to lure others into a trap
deferred (di fʉrd´) *adj.*: Put off until a future time
defiance (di fī´ əns) *n.*: Open resistance
defrauded (di frôd´ əd) *v.*: Cheated
deity (dē´ ə tē) *n.*: A god
deleterious (del´ ə tir´ ē əs) *adj.*: Injurious; harmful to health or well-being
demure (di myo͝or´) *adj.*: Shy or modest
depravity (dē prav´ ə tē) *n.*: Wickedness; corruption
derides (di rīdz´) *v.*: Ridicules
derisive (di rī´ siv) *adj.*: Showing contempt or ridicule
desolate (des´ ə lit) *adj.*: Deserted; abandoned
despair (di sper´) *n.*: Hopelessness
despotic (des pät´ ik) *adj.*: Like or in the manner of an absolute ruler or tyrant
desultory (des´ əl tôr´ ē) *adj.*: Random
determination (dē tʉr´ mi nā´ shən) *n.*: Firm intention
detritus (di trīt´ əs) *n.*: Debris
diffused (di fyo͞ozd´) *v.*: Spread out
discreet (dis krēt´) *adj.*: Tactful; respectful
disheveled (di shev´ əld) *adj.*: Disarranged and untidy
dishevelment (di shev´ əl ment) *n.*: A state of being untidy
dismal (diz´ məl) *adj.*: Causing gloom or misery
dispatched (dis pacht´) *v.*: Finished quickly
disperse (di spʉrs´) *v.*: Drive off or scatter in different directions
dissemble (di sem´ bəl) *v.*: Conceal with false appearances; disguise
distraught (di strôt´) *adj.*: Extremely troubled; confused; distracted
diverged (dī vʉrjd´) *v.*: Branched out in different directions
divine (də vīn´) *adj.*: Holy; sacred
dogmas (dôg´ məz) *n.*: Firmly held beliefs or doctrines
droll (drōl) *adj.*: Comic and amusing in an odd way
drowsiness (drou´ zē nes) *n.*: Sleepiness
ebony (eb´ ə nē) *n.*: Hard, dark wood used for furniture
eddies (ed´ ēz) *n.*: Circular currents
eerie (ir´ ē) *adj.*: Mysterious
effervesce (ef´ ər ves´) *v.*: To be lively
effigies (ef´ i jēz) *n.*: Crude figures or dummies representing hated people or a group
eloquence (el´ ə kwəns) *n.*: Speech that is vivid, forceful, graceful, and persuasive
elucidate (i lo͞o´ sə dāt´) *v.*: Explain
encompassed (en kum´ pəst) *v.*: Surrounded
encroaching (en krōch´ iŋ) *adj.*: Intruding in a gradual or sneaking way
endeavoring (en dev´ ər iŋ) *n.*: Trying; attempting
endurance (en do͝or´ əns) *n.*: Ability to withstand hardship and stress and to carry on
engendered (en jen´ dərd) *v.*: Produced
enigma (i nig´ mə) *n.*: Puzzling or baffling matter; riddle
enjoined (en joind´) *v.*: Ordered
entrails (en´ trālz) *n.*: Internal organs, specifically intestines
epiphany (ē pif´ ə nē) *n.*: Moment of sudden understanding
epithets (ep´ ə thetz) *n.*: Abusive words or phrases; slurs
equity (ek´ wit ē) *n.*: Fairness; impartiality; justice
erratic (er rat´ ik) *adj.*: Irregular; random
evanesced (ev ə nest´) *v.*: Faded away
exalted (eg zôlt´ əd) *v.*: Lifted up
exile (eks´ īl´) *v.*: Banish
extrapolating (ek strap´ ə lāt´ iŋ) *v.*: Arriving at a conclusion by making inferences based on known facts

extrapolation (ek strap′ ə lā′ shən) *n.*: Conclusions drawn by speculation on the basis of facts
feint (fānt) *v.*: Pretended move to catch an opponent off guard
feline (fē′ līn) *adj.*: Catlike
fester (fes′ tər) *v.*: Form pus
fickle (fik′əl) *adj.*: Changeable
ford (fôrd) *n.*: Shallow place in a river that can be crossed
forebears (fôr′ bərs′) *n.*: Ancestors
formality (fôr mal′ ə tē) *n.*: Established rules or customs
formidable (fôr′ mə də bəl) *adj.*: Awe-inspiring
fray (frā) *n.*: Noisy fight
fretful (fret′ fəl) *adj.*: Irritable and discontented
furtive (fʉr′ tiv) *adj.*: Preventing observation; sneaky
furtively (fʉr′ tiv lē) *adv.*: Stealthily, so as to avoid being heard
futile (fyo͞ot′ əl) *adj.*: Useless; hopeless
gallant (gal′ ənt) *adj.*: Brave and noble
garish (gar′ ish) *adj.*: Too bright or gaudy
gaunt (gônt) *adj.*: Thin and bony
genesis (jen′ ə sis) *n.*: Birth; origin; beginning
genteel (jen tēl′) *adj.*: Refined; polite
glee (glē) *n.*: Joy
glowering (glou′ ər iŋ) *adj.*: Staring with sullen anger; scowling
gossamer (gäs′ ə mər) *adj.*: Light, thin, and filmy
grievance (grēv′ əns) *n.*: Injustice; complaint
grisly (griz′ lē) *adj.*: Horrifying; gruesome
grotesque (grō tesk′) *adj.*: Having a strange, bizarre design
haggard (hag′ ərd) *adj.*: Having a wild, worn look, as from sleeplessness
hamlet (ham′ lit) *n.*: Very small village
harness (här′ nis) *v.*: Attach, as with straps for pulling or controlling
harried (har′ ēd) *adj.*: Worried
harrowed (har′ ōd) *v.*: Broken up and leveled by a harrow, a frame with spikes or disks, drawn by a horse or tractor
haughty (hôt′ ē) *adj.*: Arrogant
heretics (her′ ə tiks) *n.*: Those who hold to a belief opposed to the established teachings of a church
hieroglyphics (hī′ ər ō′ glif′ iks) *n.*: Pictures or symbols that represent words or ideas
hoax (hōks) *n.*: Deceitful trick
host (hōst) *n.*: A great number
hurtling (hʉrt′ liŋ) *adj.*: Moving swiftly and with great force
hydraulic (hī drô′ lik) *adj.*: Operated by the movement and pressure of liquid
ideology (ī′ dē äl′ ə jē) *n.*: Ideas on which a political, economic, or social system is based
imbued (im byo͞od′) *v.*: Inspired
imminent (im′ ə nənt) *adj.*: Likely to happen soon
immortalized (im môrt′ ′l īzd′) *v.*: Given lasting fame
immutable (im′ myo͞ot′ ə bəl) *adj.*: Never changing
imperative (im per′ ə tiv) *adj.*: Absolutely necessary; urgent
imperialist (im pir′ ē əl ist) *adj.*: Here, describing a person from a country that seeks to dominate weaker countries
impertinent (im pʉrt′ ən ənt) *adj.*: Rude; impolite
imperturbable (im′ pər tʉr′ bə bəl) *adj.*: Unable to be excited or disturbed
implications (im′ pli kā′ shənz) *n.*: Suggestions or indirect indications
impose (im pōz′) *v.*: Put to some trouble
improbable (im präb′ ə bəl) *adj.*: Unlikely to happen
improvised (im′ prə vīzd) *adj.*: Put together on the spur of the moment
inalienable (in āl′ yən ə bəl) *adj.*: Not able to be taken away or transferred
incognito (in käg′ ni tō′) *n.*: A disguised condition
incredulity (in′ krə do͞o′ lə tē) *n.*: Inability to believe
indolently (in′ də lənt lē) *adv.*: Lazily; idly
ineffable (in ef′ ə bəl) *adj.*: Too overwhelming to be expressed in words
infallibility (in fal′ ə bil′ ə tē) *n.*: Condition of being unable to fail
infrared (in′ frə red′) *adj.*: Of light waves that lie just beyond the red end of the visible spectrum
ingeniously (in jēn′ yəs lē) *adv.*: Cleverly
insatiable (in sā′ shə bəl) *adj.*: Unable to be satisfied
inscrutable (in skro͞ot′ ə bəl) *adj.*: That which cannot be easily understood; baffling; mysterious
insidious (in sid′ ē əs) *adj.*: Treacherous in a sly, tricky way
insinuatingly (in sin′ yo͞o āt′ iŋ lē) *adv.*: Hinting or suggesting indirectly; implying
insolent (in′ sə lənt) *adj.*: Boldly disrespectful in speech or behavior
instigates (in′ stə gāts′) *v.*: Urges on; stirs up
intent (in tent′) *adj.*: Firmly fixed; concentrated
intercession (in′ tər sesh′ ən) *n.*: The act of pleading on behalf of another
interpretation (in tʉr′ prə tā′ shən) *n.*: Explanation
introspective (in′ trō spek′ tiv) *adj.*: Causing one to look into one's own thoughts and feelings
intuition (in′ to͞o ish′ ən) *n.*: Knowledge of something without reasoning
iridescent (ir′ i des′ ənt) *adj.*: Having shifting, rainbowlike colors
irradiated (ir rā′ dē āt′ id) *v.*: Gave out; radiated
jibed (jībd) *v.*: Stopped short and turned from side to side
judicious (jo͞o dish′ əs) *adj.*: Showing good judgment
keener (kēn′ ər) *adj.*: More clear; sharper
kindred (kin′ drid) *n.*: Relatives
laden (lād′ ən) *adj.*: Burdened
lamentable (lam′ ən tə bəl) *adj.*: Distressing; sad
languid (laŋ′ gwid) *adj.*: Drooping; weak
languor (laŋ′ gər) *n.*: Lack of vigor; weakness
larder (lärd′ ər) *n.*: Place where food is kept; pantry
lassoed (las′ ōd) *adj.*: Wrapped around
lateral (lat′ ər əl) *adj.*: Sideways
legacy (leg′ ə sē) *n.*: Anything handed down from an ancestor
legendary (lej′ ən der′ ē) *adj.*: Based on legends, or stories handed down for generations
levitation (lev ə tā′ shən) *n.*: The illusion of keeping a heavy body in the air without visible support
lingered (liŋ′ gərd) *v.*: Stayed on, as if unwilling to leave
literally (lit′ ər əl ē) *adv.*: Actually; in fact
lithe (līth) *adj.*: Supple; limber
loathsome (lōth′ səm) *adj.*: Disgusting
loitered (loit′ ərd) *v.*: Hung about; lingered
longevity (län jev′ə tē) *n.*: The length or duration of a life
malevolence (mə lev′ ə ləns) *n.*: Bad or evil feelings or intentions
malodorous (mal ō′ dər əs) *adj.*: Having a bad smell
mammoth (mam′ əth) *adj.*: Enormous
manhandled (man′ han′ dəld) *v.*: Treated roughly
marauders (mə rôd′ ərz) *n.*: Raiders; people who take goods by force
martial (mär′ shəl) *adj.*: Military
maudlin (môd′ lin) *adj.*: Tearfully or foolishly sentimental
medley (med′ lē) *n.*: Mixture of things not usually found together
menacing (men′ əs iŋ) *v.*: Threatening
meretricious (mer′ ə trish′ əs) *adj.*: Attractive in a cheap, flashy way
metaphors (met′ə fôrz′) *n.*: Figures of speech in which things are spoken of as if they were something else
metaphysical (met′ ə fiz′ i kəl) *adj.*: Spiritual; beyond the physical
meticulously (mə tik′ yo͞o ləs lē) *adv.*: Very carefully; scrupulously
microcosms (mī′ krō kä′ zəmz) *n.*: Little worlds
monotone (män′ ə tōn′) *n.*: Uninterrupted repetition of the same tone
moribund (môr′ i bund′) *adj.*: Dying
mortified (môrt′ ə fīd′) *v.*: Embarrassed
muted (myo͞ot′ əd) *adj.*: Weaker; less intense
myriad (mir′ ē əd) *adj.*: Countless; innumerable
naive (nä ēv′) *adj.*: Unsophisticated
novice (näv′ is) *adj.*: Beginner
oasis (ō ā′ sis) *n.*: Fertile place in the desert
obstinacy (äb′ stə nə sē) *n.*: Stubbornness
omen (ō′ mən) *n.*: Sign foretelling a future event, either good or evil
ominous (äm′ ə nəs) *adj.*: Threatening; menacing
ominously (äm′ ə nəs lē) *adv.*: In a threatening way
oppression (ə presh′ ən) *n.*: Keeping others down by the unjust use of power
oracle (ō′ rə kəl) *n.*: Source of knowledge or wise counsel
paean (pē′ ən) *n.*: Song of joy or triumph
pagans (pā′ gənz) *n.*: People who are not Christians, Muslims, or Jews
pallid (pal′ id) *adj.*: Pale

pallor (pal′ ər) *n.*: Paleness
palpable (pal′ pə bəl) *adj.*: Able to be touched or felt
palpitating (pal′ pə tāt′ iŋ) *adj.*: Beating rapidly; throbbing
pandemonium (pan′ də mō′ nē əm) *n.*: Wild disorder, noise, or confusion
parched (pärcht) *adj.*: Dried up by heat
parlance (pär′ ləns) *n.*: Style of speaking or writing; language
pensive (pen′ siv) *adj.* Thinking deeply or seriously
penury (pen′ yo͞o rē) *n.*: Extreme poverty
perennial (pə ren′ ē əl) *adj.*: Lasting through the year or for a long time
perish (per′ ish) *v.*: Die
permeate (pur′ mē āt) *v.*: Spread or flow throughout
pernicious (pər nish′ əs) *adj.*: Causing great injury or ruin; destructive
perpetuated (pər pech′ o͞o āt id) *v.*: Caused to continue indefinitely; prolonged
perplexed (pər plekst′) *adj.*: Puzzled; full of doubt
perplexes (pər′ pleks′ iz) *v.*: Confuses or makes hard to understand
perverse (pər vurs′) *adj.*: Continuing in a stubborn way to do what is wrong or harmful; improper; willful
picturesque (pik′ chər esk′) *adj.*: Like or suggesting a picture
pilgrimage (pil′ grim ij) *n.*: Long journey
pinions (pin′ yənz) *n.*: The last bony sections of a bird's wings
pious (pī′ əs) *adj.*: Showing religious devotion
placid (plas′ id) *adj.*: Tranquil; calm
placidly (plas′ id lē) *adv.*: Calmly; quietly
plaiting (plāt′ iŋ) *v.*: Braiding
plundered (plun′ dərd) *v.*: Took goods by force; looted
poignant (poin′ yənt) *adj.*: Drawing forth pity or compassion; moving
portents (pôr′ tentz) *n.*: Things that are thought to be signs of events to come; omens
postulated (päs′ chə lāt′ ed) *v.*: Claimed
precariously (prē ker′ ē əs lē) *adv.*: Insecurely
precipitous (prē sip′ ə təs) *adj.*: Steep; sheer
precluded (prē klo͞od′ id) *v.*: Prevented; made impossible in advance
precursors (prē kur′ sərz) *n.*: Things that prepare the way for what will follow
predominant (prē däm′ ə nənt) *adj.*: Having dominating influence over others
preposterous (pri päs′ tər əs) *adj.*: Absurd
primed (prīmd) *v.*: Made ready; prepared
procure (prō kyo͞or′) *v.*: Get; obtain
prodigious (prō dij′ əs) *adj.*: Wonderful; of great size
prodigy (präd′ ə jē) *n.*: Person who is amazingly talented or intelligent
profoundly (prō found′ lē) *adj.*: Deeply and intensely
projectiles (prō jek′ təlz) *n.*: Objects that are hurled through the air
pungent (pun′ jənt) *adj.*: Producing a sharp sensation of smell
purged (purjd) *v.*: Cleansed; emptied
pursue (pər so͞o′) *v.*: Seek
pyre (pīr) *n.*: Pile of wood on which a body is burned at a funeral
quaint (kwānt) *adj.*: Strange; unusual
rakishly (rāk′ ish lē) *adv.*: With a careless, casual look; dashing
rancor (raŋ′ kər) *n.*: Deep spite or bitter hate
ravages (rav′ ij iz) *n.*: Ruins; devastating damages
ravenous (rav′ ə nəs) *adj.*: Greedily hungry
reciprocate (ri sip′ rə kāt) *v.*: Return
reconcile (rek′ ən sīl′) *v.*: Bring into agreement
reconciled (rek′ ən sīld) *adj.*: Became friends again
reconnaissance (ri kän′ ə səns) *adj.*: Exploratory in nature, as when examining or observing to seek information
recounted (ri kount′ ed) *v.*: Told in detail; narrated
refrain (ri frān′) *v.*: To hold back
remnants (rem′ nənts) *n.*: Remaining persons or things
respite (res′ pit) *n.*: Rest; relief
resplendent (ri splen′ dənt) *adj.*: Shining brightly
retort (ri tôrt′) *n.*: Sharp or clever reply
retribution (re trə byo͞o′ shən) *n.*: Payback; punishment for a misdeed or reward for a good deed
revelry (rev′ əl rē) *n.*: Party
reverie (rev′ ər ē) *n.*: Dreamy thought of pleasant things
riveting (riv′ it iŋ) *adj.*: Firmly holding attention
rueful (ro͞o′ fəl) *adj.*: Feeling sorrow or regret
ruminative (ro͞o′ mə nə təv) *adj.*: Meditative
sallow (sal′ ō) *adj.*: Of a sickly, pale-yellowish complexion
schism (siz′ əm) *n.*: Split or division
scourge (skurj) *n.*: Whip or other instrument for inflicting punishment
scowling (skoul′ iŋ) *v.*: Contracting the eyebrows and frowning to show displeasure
scruples (skro͞o′ pəlz) *n.*: Misgivings about something one feels is wrong
sentimental (sen′ tə ment′ əl) *adj.*: Excessively or foolishly emotional
sepulcher (sep′ əl kər) *n.*: Tomb
shards (shärdz) *n.*: Broken pieces
simultaneously (sī′ məl tā′ nē əs lē) *adv.*: At the same time
singular (siŋ′ gyə lər) *adj.*: Extraordinary; rare
sinister (sin′ is tər) *adj.*: Threatening harm; ominous
skeptical (skep′ ti kəl) *adj.*: Doubting; questioning
slouching (slouch′ iŋ) *adj.*: Drooping
sobriety (sə brī′ ə tē) *n.*: Moderation, especially in the use of alcoholic beverages
sore (sôr) *adj.*: Fierce; cruel
specters (spek′ tərz) *n.*: Ghostly images; phantoms
spurn (spurn) *v.*: Reject in a scornful way
squall (skwôl) *n.*: Brief, violent storm
steeds (stēdz) *n.*: Horses
stout (stout) *adj.*: Sturdy; forceful
strafing (strāf′ ing) *adj.*: Attacking with machine-gun fire
suavity (swäv′ ə tē) *n.*: Quality of being socially smooth
subjugation (sub′ jə gā′ shən) *n.*: Enslavement
submerged (səb murjd′) *adj.*: Covered with something; underwater
subsidiary (səb sid′ ē er′ ē) *adj.*: Secondary; supporting
subtle (sut′ ′l) *adj.*: Not obvious
succor (suk′ ər) *n.*: Aid; help; relief
suffice (sə fīs′) *v.*: To be enough
sullen (sul′ ən) *adj.*: Gloomy; dismal
surcease (sur sēs′) *n.*: An end
surge (surj) *v.*: Increase suddenly; speed up
surreal (sə rē′ əl) *adj.*: Strange
tantalizingly (tan′ tə līz′ iŋ glē) *adv.*: In a teasing or tormenting way
tempests (tem′ pists) *n.*: Violent storms with strong winds
thronging (throŋ′ iŋ) *adj.*: Crowding into
titanic (tī tan′ ik) *adj.*: Of great size or strength
transgression (trans gresh′ ən) *n.*: Wrongdoing; sin
treble (treb′ əl) *n.*: High-pitched voice
tremulous (trem′ yo͞o ləs) *adj.*: Quivering
trundle (trun′ dəl) *v.*: To roll along; to rotate
tumult (to͞o′ məlt) *n.*: Noisy commotion
tumultuous (to͞o mul′ cho͞o əs) *adj.*: Greatly disturbed
unbidden (un bid′ ən) *adj.*: Without being asked; uninvited
unpalatable (un pal′ ət ə bəl) *adj.*: Distasteful; unpleasant
unwieldy (un wēl′ dē) *adj.*: Awkward; clumsy
valet (val′ it) *n.*: A man's personal servant who takes care of the man's clothes
vanquished (vaŋ′ kwisht) *adj.*: Defeated
venture (ven′ chər) *n.*: Chance
vex (veks) *v.*: Annoy
vial (vī′ əl) *n.*: Small bottle containing medicine or other liquids
vile (vīl) *adj.*: Evil; wicked; worthless; cheap; low
voluminously (və lo͞om′ ə nəs lē) *adv.*: Fully; in great volume
vortex (vôr′ teks) *n.*: Center of a situation, which draws in all that surrounds it
warp (wôrp) *v.*: Bend or twist out of shape; distort
waverer (wā′ vər ər) *n.*: One who changes or is unsteady
wavering (wā′ vər iŋ) *adj.*: Flickering
wayfarers (wā′ fer ərz) *n.*: Travelers
wayward (wā′ wərd) *adj.*: Insistent upon having one's own way; headstrong
woeful (wō′ fəl) *adj.*: Full of sorrow
woes (wōz) *n.*: Great sorrows
wreathed (rē*th*d) *v.*: Curled around
writhing (rī*th*′ iŋ) *v.*: Twisting; turning
wrought (rôt) *v.*: Formed; fashioned
yearned (yurnd) *v.*: Longed for; desired

LITERARY TERMS HANDBOOK

ACT *See* Drama.

ALLEGORY An *allegory* is a story or tale with two or more levels of meaning—a literal level and one or more symbolic levels. The events, setting, and characters in an allegory are symbols for ideas and qualities.

ALLITERATION *Alliteration* is the repetition of initial consonant sounds. Writers use alliteration to give emphasis to words, to imitate sounds, and to create musical effects. In the following lines from Walter de la Mare's "The Listeners," notice how the *s* sound imitates a whisper:

> Ay, they heard his foot upon the stirrup,
> And the sound of iron on stone,
> And how the silence surged softly backward. . .

ALLUSION An *allusion* is a reference to a well-known person, place, event, literary work, or work of art. In "The Gift of the Magi" (p. 524), O. Henry writes about a young couple and the Christmas gifts they give to each other. At the end of the story, the narrator explains the biblical allusion in the title: "The Magi, as you know, were wise men—wonderfully wise men—who brought gifts to the Babe in the manger. They invented the art of giving Christmas presents. Being wise, their gifts were no doubt wise ones. . . ."

ANALOGY An *analogy* makes a comparison between two or more things that are similar in some ways but otherwise unalike.

ANECDOTE An *anecdote* is a brief story about an interesting, amusing, or strange event told to entertain or to make a point. In "A Lincoln Preface" (p. 152), Carl Sandburg tells anecdotes about Abraham Lincoln.
See also Narrative.

ANTAGONIST An *antagonist* is a character or force in conflict with a main character, or protagonist.

ANTICLIMAX Like a climax, an *anticlimax* is the turning point in a story. However, an anticlimax is always a letdown. It's the point at which you learn that the story will not turn out the way you had expected. In Thayer's "Casey at the Bat," the anticlimax occurs when Casey strikes out instead of hitting a game-winning run as everyone had expected.

ASIDE An *aside* is a short speech delivered by an actor in a play. Traditionally, the aside is directed to the audience and is presumed to be inaudible to the other actors.

ASSONANCE *Assonance* is the repetition of vowel sounds followed by different consonants in two or more stressed syllables. Assonance is found in the phrase "weak and weary" in Edgar Allan Poe's "The Raven" (p. 940).

ATMOSPHERE *See* Mood.

AUTOBIOGRAPHY An *autobiography* is a form of nonfiction in which a writer tells his or her own life story. An autobiography may tell about the person's whole life or only a part of it.
See also Biography *and* Nonfiction.

BALLAD A *ballad* is a songlike poem that tells a story, often one dealing with adventure and romance. Most ballads are written in four- to six-line stanzas and have regular rhythms and rhyme schemes. A ballad often features a refrain—a regularly repeated line or group of lines.
See also Oral Tradition.

BIOGRAPHY A *biography* is a form of nonfiction in which a writer tells the life story of another person. Biographies have been written about many famous people, historical and contemporary, but they can also be written about "ordinary" people.
See also Autobiography *and* Nonfiction.

BLANK VERSE *Blank verse* is poetry written in unrhymed iambic pentameter lines. This verse form was widely used by William Shakespeare.
See also Meter.

CHARACTER A *character* is a person or an animal who takes part in the action of a literary work. The main character, or protagonist, is the most important character in a story. This character often changes in some important way as a result of the story's events. In Richard Connell's "The Most Dangerous Game" (p. 18), Rainsford is the main character and General Zaroff is the antagonist, or character who opposes the main character.

Characters are sometimes classified as round or flat, dynamic or static. A *round character* shows many different traits—faults as well as virtues. A *flat character* shows only one trait. A *dynamic character* develops and grows during the course of the story; a *static character* does not change.
See also Characterization and Motivation.

CHARACTERIZATION *Characterization* is the act of creating and developing a character. In *direct characterization*, the author directly states a character's traits. In

"Uncle Marcos," for example, a character states that "Uncle Marcos's manners were those of a cannibal."

In *indirect characterization*, an author tells what a character looks like, does, and says, as well as how other characters react to him or her. It is up to the reader to draw conclusions about the character based on this indirect information.

The most effective indirect characterizations usually result from showing characters acting or speaking.

See also Character.

CLIMAX The *climax* of a story, novel, or play is the high point of interest or suspense. The events that make up the rising action lead up to the climax. The events that make up the falling action follow the climax.

See also Conflict, Plot, *and* Anticlimax.

COMEDY A *comedy* is a literary work, especially a play, that has a happy ending. Comedies often show ordinary characters in conflict with society. These conflicts are resolved through misunderstandings, deceptions, and concealed identities, which result in the correction of moral faults or social wrongs. Types of comedy include *romantic comedy*, which involves problems among lovers, and the *comedy of manners*, which satirically challenges the social customs of a sophisticated society. Comedy is often contrasted with tragedy, in which the protagonist meets an unfortunate end.

COMIC RELIEF *Comic relief* is a technique that is used to interrupt a serious part of a literary work by introducing a humorous character or situation.

CONFLICT A *conflict* is a struggle between opposing forces. Characters in conflict form the basis of stories, novels, and plays.

There are two kinds of conflict: external and internal. In an external conflict, the main character struggles against an outside force. This force may be another character, as in Richard Connell's "The Most Dangerous Game" (p. 18), in which Rainsford struggles with General Zaroff. The outside force could also be the standards or expectations of a group, such as the family prejudices that Romeo and Juliet struggle against. Their story (p. 770) shows them in conflict with society. The outside force may be nature itself, a person-against-nature conflict. The two men who are trapped by a fallen tree in Saki's "The Interlopers" (p. 304) face such a conflict.

An *internal conflict* involves a character in conflict with himself or herself. In "Checkouts" (p. 282), two young people who meet by chance in a supermarket agonize over whether they should speak to each other.

See also Plot.

CONNOTATION The *connotation* of a word is the set of ideas associated with it in addition to its explicit meaning. In his poem "Sympathy" (p. 292), Paul Laurence Dunbar speaks of a "caged bird," which connotes a sad, trapped creature.

See also Denotation.

COUPLET A *couplet* is a pair of rhyming lines, usually of the same length and meter. In the following couplet from a poem by William Shakespeare, the speaker comforts himself with the thought of his love:

> For thy sweet love remember'd such wealth brings
> That then I scorn to change my state with kings.

See also Stanza.

DENOTATION The *denotation* of a word is its dictionary meaning, independent of other associations that the word may have. The denotation of the word *lake*, for example, is an inland body of water. "Vacation spot" and "place where the fishing is good" are connotations of the word *lake*.

See also Connotation.

DENOUEMENT *See* Plot.

DESCRIPTION A *description* is a portrait in words of a person, place, or object. Descriptive writing uses sensory details, those that appeal to the senses: sight, hearing, taste, smell, and touch. Description can be found in all types of writing. Rudolfo Anaya's essay "A Celebration of Grandfathers" (p. 662) contains descriptive passages.

DEVELOPMENT *See* Plot.

DIALECT *Dialect* is the form of language spoken by people in a particular region or group. Pronunciation, vocabulary, and sentence structure are affected by dialect. In "The Invalid's Story" (p. 596), Mark Twain uses dialect:

> "Friends of *yourn*?"
> "Yes," I said with a sigh.
> "He's pretty ripe, *ain't* he!"

DIALOGUE A *dialogue* is a conversation between characters. It is used to reveal character and to advance action. In a story or novel, quotation marks are generally used to indicate a speaker's exact words. A new paragraph usually indicates a change of speaker. Look at an example from "The Scarlet Ibis" (p. 554). The narrator is a boy who is urging his frail younger brother, Doodle, to stand up and walk fast:

> "Aw, come on Doodle," I urged. "You can do it. Do you want to be different from everybody else when you start school?"
>
> "Does it make any difference?"
>
> "It certainly does," I said. "Now come on," and I helped him up.

A drama depends entirely on dialogue and actions. Quotation marks are not used in the *script,* which is the printed version of a play. Instead, the dialogue follows the name of the speaker. Here is an example from *The Dancers* (p. 734):

> HORACE. Miss . . .
>
> WAITRESS. Yes?
>
> HORACE. How much do I owe you?

DICTION *Diction* is word choice, including the vocabulary used, the appropriateness of the words, and the vividness of the language. Diction can be formal, as in this excerpt from O. Henry's "The Gift of the Magi" (p. 524):

> In the vestibule below was a letter-box into which no letter would go, and an electric button from which no mortal finger could coax a ring.

Diction can also be informal and conversational, as in these lines from Ernest Lawrence Thayer's "Casey at the Bat" (p. 42):

> It looked extremely rocky for the Mudville nine
> that day;
> The score stood two to four; with but an inning
> left to play.
> So, when Cooney died at second, and Burrows
> did the same,
> A pallor wreathed the features of the patrons of
> the game.

See also Connotation *and* Denotation.

DIRECT CHARACTERIZATION *See* Characterization.

DRAMA A *drama* is a story written to be performed by actors. The script of a drama is made up of *dialogue*—the words the actors say—and *stage directions,* which are comments on how and where action happens.

The drama's *setting* is the time and place in which the action occurs. It is indicated by one or more sets that suggest interior or exterior scenes. *Props* are objects, such as a sword or a cup of tea, that are used onstage.

At the beginning of most plays, a brief exposition gives the audience some background information about the characters and the situation. Just as in a story or novel, the plot of a drama is built around characters in conflict.

Dramas are divided into large units called *acts,* which are divided into smaller units called *scenes.* A long play may include many sets that change with the scenes, or it may indicate a change of scene with lighting.

See also Dialogue, Genre, Stage Directions, *and* Tragedy.

DRAMATIC IRONY *See* Irony.

DRAMATIC MONOLOGUE A *dramatic monologue* is a poem or speech in which a fictional character addresses the listener.

DRAMATIC POETRY *Dramatic poetry* is poetry that utilizes the techniques of drama. The dialogue used in Edgar Allan Poe's "The Raven" (p. 940) makes it dramatic dialogue. A *dramatic monologue* is a poem spoken by one person, addressing a silent listener.

END RHYME *See* Rhyme.

EPIC An *epic* is a long narrative poem about the deeds of gods or heroes. Homer's *Odyssey* (p. 980) is an example of epic poetry. It tells the story of the Greek hero Odysseus, the king of Ithaca.

An epic is elevated in style and usually follows certain patterns. The poet begins by announcing the subject and asking a Muse—one of the nine goddesses of the arts, literature, and sciences—to help.

See also Epic Simile *and* Narrative Poem.

EPIC SIMILE An *epic simile,* also called *Homeric simile,* is an elaborate comparison of unlike subjects. In this example from the *Odyssey* (p. 980), Homer compares the bodies of men killed by Odysseus to a fisherman's catch heaped up on the shore:

> Think of a catch that fishermen haul in to a
> half-moon bay
> in a fine-meshed net from the whitecaps of the sea:
> how all are poured out on the sand, in throes
> for the salt sea,
> twitching their cold lives away in Helios' fiery air:
> so lay the suitors heaped on one another.

See also Figurative Language *and* Simile.

ESSAY An *essay* is a short nonfiction work about a particular subject. While classification is difficult, five types of essays are sometimes identified.

A *descriptive essay* seeks to convey an impression about a person, place, or object. In "A Celebration of Grandfathers" (p. 662), Rudolfo Anaya describes the cultural values that his grandfather and other "old ones" from his childhood passed down.

A *narrative essay* tells a true story. In "The Washwoman," Isaac Bashevis Singer tells of his childhood in Poland.

An *expository essay* gives information, discusses ideas, or explains a process. In "Single Room, Earth View" (p. 636), Sally Ride describes what it is like to be in outer space.

A *persuasive essay* tries to convince readers to do something or to accept the writer's point of view. In the essay, "To the Residents of A.D. 2029" (p. 495), Bryan Woolley advises future generations how to avoid calamities.

A *visual essay* is an exploration of a topic that conveys its ideas through visual elements as well as language. Like a standard essay, a visual essay presents an author's views of a single topic. Unlike other essays, however, much of the meaning in a visual essay is conveyed through illustrations or photographs.

See also Description, Exposition, Genre, Narration, Nonfiction, *and* Persuasion.

EXPOSITION *Exposition* is writing or speech that explains a process or presents information. In the plot of a story or drama, the exposition is the part of the work that introduces the characters, the setting, and the basic situation.

EXTENDED METAPHOR In an *extended metaphor*, as in regular metaphor, a writer speaks or writes of a subject as though it were something else. An extended metaphor sustains the comparison for several lines or for an entire poem. The "caged bird" of Paul Laurence Dunbar's "Sympathy" (p. 292) is an extended metaphor for a person who is not free.

See also Figurative Language *and* Metaphor.

FALLING ACTION *See* Plot.

FANTASY A *fantasy* is highly imaginative writing that contains elements not found in real life. Examples of fantasy include stories that involve supernatural elements, stories that resemble fairy tales, and stories that deal with imaginary places and creatures.

See also Science Fiction.

FICTION *Fiction* is prose writing that tells about imaginary characters and events. The term is usually used for novels and short stories, but it also applies to dramas and narrative poetry. Some writers rely on their imaginations alone to create their works of fiction. Others base their fiction on actual events and people, to which they add invented characters, dialogue, and plot situations.

See also Genre, Narrative, *and* Nonfiction.

FIGURATIVE LANGUAGE *Figurative language* is writing or speech not meant to be interpreted literally. It is often used to create vivid impressions by setting up comparisons between dissimilar things.

Some frequently used figures of speech are *metaphors, similes*, and *personifications*.

See also Literal Language.

FOIL A *foil* is a character who provides a contrast to another character. In *Romeo and Juliet* (p. 770), the fiery temper of Tybalt serves as a foil to the good nature of Benvolio.

FOOT *See* Meter.

FORESHADOWING *Foreshadowing* is the use in a literary work of clues that suggest events that have yet to occur. This technique helps to create suspense, keeping readers wondering about what will happen next.

See also Suspense.

FREE VERSE *Free verse* is poetry not written in a regular rhythmical pattern, or meter. Free verse seeks to capture the rhythms of speech.

See also Meter.

GENRE A *genre* is a category or type of literature. Literature is commonly divided into three major genres: poetry, prose, and drama. Each major genre is in turn divided into smaller genres, as follows:

1. Poetry: Lyric Poetry, Concrete Poetry, Dramatic Poetry, Narrative Poetry, and Epic Poetry
2. Prose: Fiction (Novels and Short Stories) and Nonfiction (Biography, Autobiography, Letters, Essays, and Reports)
3. Drama: Serious Drama and Tragedy, Comic Drama, Melodrama, and Farce

See also Drama, Poetry, *and* Prose.

HAIKU The *haiku* is a three-line verse form. The first and third lines of a haiku each have five syllables. The second line has seven syllables. A haiku seeks to convey a single vivid emotion by means of images from nature.

HOMERIC SIMILE *See* Epic Simile.

HYPERBOLE A *hyperbole* is a deliberate exaggeration or overstatement. In Mark Twain's "The Notorious Jumping Frog of Calaveras County," the claim that Jim Smiley would follow a bug as far as Mexico to win a bet is a hyperbole. As this example shows, hyperboles are often used for comic effect.

IAMB *See* Meter.

IMAGE An *image* is a word or phrase that appeals to one or more of the five senses—sight, hearing, touch, taste, or smell. Writers use images to re-create sensory experiences in words.
See also Description.

IMAGERY *Imagery* is the descriptive or figurative language used in literature to create word pictures for the reader. These pictures, or images, are created by details of sight, sound, taste, touch, smell, or movement.

INDIRECT CHARACTERIZATION *See* Characterization.

INTERNAL RHYME *See* Rhyme.

IRONY *Irony* is the general term for literary techniques that portray differences between appearance and reality, or expectation and result. In *verbal irony,* words are used to suggest the opposite of what is meant. In *dramatic irony,* there is a contradiction between what a character thinks and what the reader or audience knows to be true. In *irony of situation,* an event occurs that directly contradicts the expectations of the characters, the reader, or the audience.

LITERAL LANGUAGE *Literal language* uses words in their ordinary senses. It is the opposite of *figurative language.* If you tell someone standing on a diving board to jump in, you speak literally. If you tell someone on the street to jump in a lake, you are speaking figuratively.
See also Figurative Language.

LYRIC POEM A *lyric poem* is a highly musical verse that expresses the observations and feelings of a single speaker. In ancient times, lyric poems were sung to the accompaniment of the lyre, a type of stringed instrument. Modern lyric poems are not usually sung. However, they still have a musical quality that is achieved through rhythm and other devices such as alliteration and rhyme.

MAIN CHARACTER *See* Character.

METAPHOR A *metaphor* is a figure of speech in which one thing is spoken of as though it were something else. Unlike a simile, which compares two things using *like* or *as,* a metaphor implies a comparison between them. In "Dreams" (p. 905), Langston Hughes uses a metaphor to show what happens to a life without dreams:

. . . if dreams die
Life is a broken-winged bird
That cannot fly.

See also Extended Metaphor *and* Figurative Language.

METER The *meter* of a poem is its rhythmical pattern. This pattern is determined by the number and types of stresses, or beats, in each line. To describe the meter of a poem, you must scan its lines. Scanning involves marking the stressed and unstressed syllables, as shown with the following two lines from "I Wandered Lonely as a Cloud" by William Wordsworth (p. 896):

I wan|dered lone|ly as| a cloud
That floats |on high| o'er vales| and hills.

As you can see, each strong stress is marked with a slanted line (´) and each unstressed syllable with a horseshoe symbol (˘). The stressed and unstressed syllables are then divided by vertical lines (|) into groups called *feet.* The following types of feet are common in English poetry:

1. *Iamb:* a foot with one unstressed syllable followed by a stressed syllable, as in the word "again"
2. *Trochee:* a foot with one stressed syllable followed by an unstressed syllable, as in the word "wonder"
3. *Anapest:* a foot with two unstressed syllables followed by one strong stress, as in the phrase "on the beach"
4. *Dactyl:* a foot with one strong stress followed by two unstressed syllables, as in the word "wonderful"
5. *Spondee:* a foot with two strong stresses, as in the word "spacewalk"

Depending on the type of foot that is most common in them, lines of poetry are described as *iambic, trochaic, anapestic,* and so forth.

Lines are also described in terms of the number of feet that occur in them, as follows:

1. *Monometer:* verse written in one-foot lines
   All things
   Must pass
   Away.

2. *Dimeter:* verse written in two-foot lines
   Thomas | Jefferson
   What do | you say
   Under the | gravestone
   Hidden | away?
   —Rosemary and Stephen Vincent Benét,
   "Thomas Jefferson, 1743–1826"

3. *Trimeter:* verse written in three-foot lines
   I know | not whom | I meet
   I know | not where | I go.

4. *Tetrameter:* verse written in four-foot lines

5. *Pentameter:* verse written in five-foot lines

6. *Hexameter:* verse written in six-foot lines

7. *Heptameter:* verse written in seven-foot lines

Blank verse is poetry written in unrhymed iambic pentameter. Poetry that does not have a regular meter is called *free verse.*

MONOLOGUE A *monologue* is a speech by one character in a play, story, or poem. An example from Shakespeare's *Romeo and Juliet* (p. 770) is the speech in which the Prince of Verona commands the Capulets and Montagues to cease feuding (Act 1, Scene i, lines 62–84).
See also Dramatic Poetry *and* Soliloquy.

MONOMETER *See* Meter.

MOOD *Mood,* or *atmosphere,* is the feeling created in the reader by a literary work or passage. The mood is often suggested by descriptive details. Often the mood can be described in a single word, such as lighthearted, frightening, or despairing. Notice how this passage from Edgar Allan Poe's "The Cask of Amontillado" (p. 6) contributes to an eerie, fearful mood:

> "The niter!" I said; "see, it increases. It hangs like moss upon the vaults. We are below the river's bed. The drops of moisture trickle among the bones. Come, we will go back ere it is too late."

See also Tone.

MORAL A *moral* is a lesson taught by a literary work. A fable usually ends with a moral that is directly stated.

MOTIVATION *Motivation* is a reason that explains or partially explains why a character thinks, feels, acts, or behaves in a certain way. Motivation results from a combination of the character's personality and the situation he or she must deal with. Nat Hocken in "The Birds" (p. 50) is motivated by his fear of being killed by birds to board up windows and stay inside.
See also Character *and* Characterization.

MYTH A *myth* is a fictional tale that explains the actions of gods or the causes of natural phenomena. Unlike legends, myths have little historical truth and involve supernatural elements. Every culture has its collections of myths. Among the most familiar are the myths of the ancient Greeks and Romans. The *Odyssey* (p. 980) is a mythical story attributed to the ancient poet Homer.
See also Oral Tradition.

NARRATION *Narration* is writing that tells a story. The act of telling a story in speech is also called narration. Novels and short stories are fictional narratives. Nonfiction works—such as news stories, biographies, and autobiographies—are also narratives. A narrative poem tells a story in verse.
See also Anecdote, Essay, Narrative Poem, Nonfiction, Novel, *and* Short Story.

NARRATIVE A *narrative* is a story told in fiction, nonfiction, poetry, or drama.
See also Narration.

NARRATIVE POEM A *narrative poem* is one that tells a story. "Casey at the Bat" (p. 42) is a humorous narrative poem about the last inning of a baseball game. Edgar Allan Poe's "The Raven" (p. 940) is a serious narrative poem about a man's grief over the loss of a loved one.
See also Dramatic Poetry, Epic, *and* Narration.

NARRATOR A *narrator* is a speaker or character who tells a story. The writer's choice of narrator determines the story's *point of view,* which directs the type and amount of information the writer reveals.

When a character in the story tells the story, that character is a *first-person narrator.* This narrator may be a major character, a minor character, or just a witness. Readers see only what this character sees, hear only what he or she hears, and so on. The first-person narrator may or may not be reliable. We have reason, for example, to be suspicious of the first-person narrator of Edgar Allan Poe's "The Cask of Amontillado" (p. 6).

When a voice outside the story narrates, the story has a *third-person narrator.* An omniscient, or all-knowing, third-person narrator can tell readers what any character thinks and feels. For example, in Guy de Maupassant's "The Necklace" (p. 608), we know the feelings of both Monsieur and Madame Loisel. A limited third-person narrator sees the world through one character's eyes and reveals only that character's thoughts. In James Thurber's "The Secret Life of Walter Mitty" (p. 346), the narrator reveals only Mitty's experiences and feelings.
See also Speaker.

NONFICTION *Nonfiction* is prose writing that presents and explains ideas or that tells about real people, places, ideas, or events. To be classified as nonfiction, a work must be true. "Single Room, Earth View" (p. 636) is a nonfictional account of the view of Earth from space.
See also Autobiography, Biography, *and* Essay.

NOVEL A *novel* is a long work of fiction. It has a plot that explores characters in conflict. A novel may also have one or more subplots, or minor stories, and several themes.

OCTAVE *See* Stanza.

ONOMATOPOEIA *Onomatopoeia* is the use of words that imitate sounds. *Whirr, thud, sizzle*, and *hiss* are typical examples. Writers can deliberately choose words that contribute to a desired sound effect.

ORAL TRADITION The *oral tradition* is the passing of songs, stories, and poems from generation to generation by word of mouth. Many folk songs, ballads, fairy tales, legends, and myths originated in the oral tradition.
See also Myth.

PARADOX A *paradox* is a statement that seems contradictory but that actually may be true. Because a paradox is surprising, it catches the reader's attention.

PENTAMETER *See* Meter.

PERSONIFICATION *Personification* is a type of figurative language in which a nonhuman subject is given human characteristics. William Wordsworth personifies daffodils when he describes them as "Tossing their heads in sprightly dance" (p. 896).
See also Figurative Language.

PERSUASION *Persuasion* is writing or speech that attempts to convince the reader to adopt a particular opinion or course of action.

PLOT *Plot* is the sequence of events in a literary work. In most novels, dramas, short stories, and narrative poems, the plot involves both characters and a central conflict. The plot usually begins with an *exposition* that introduces the setting, the characters, and the basic situation. This is followed by the *inciting incident*, which introduces the central conflict. The conflict then increases during the *development* until it reaches a high point of interest or suspense, the *climax*. All the events leading up to the climax make up the *rising action*. The climax is followed by the *falling action*, which leads to the *denouement*, or *resolution*, in which a general insight or change is conveyed.

POETRY *Poetry* is one of the three major types of literature, the others being prose and drama. Most poems make use of highly concise, musical, and emotionally charged language. Many also make use of imagery, figurative language, and special devices of sound such as rhyme. Poems are often divided into lines and stanzas and often employ regular rhythmical patterns, or meters. However, some poems are written out just like prose, while others are written in free verse.
See also Genre.

POINT OF VIEW *See* Narrator.

PROSE *Prose* is the ordinary form of written language. Most writing that is not poetry, drama, or song is considered prose. Prose is one of the major genres of literature and occurs in two forms: fiction and nonfiction.
See also Fiction, Genre, *and* Nonfiction.

PROTAGONIST The *protagonist* is the main character in a literary work.
See also Antagonist *and* Character.

QUATRAIN A *quatrain* is a stanza or poem made up of four lines, usually with a definite rhythm and rhyme scheme.

REPETITION *Repetition* is the use of any element of language—a sound, a word, a phrase, a clause, or a sentence—more than once.

Poets use many kinds of repetition. Alliteration, assonance, rhyme, and rhythm are repetitions of certain sounds and sound patterns. A refrain is a repeated line or group of lines. In both prose and poetry, repetition is used for musical effects and for emphasis.
See also Alliteration, Assonance, Rhyme, *and* Rhythm.

RESOLUTION *See* Plot.

RHYME *Rhyme* is the repetition of sounds at the ends of words. *End rhyme* occurs when the rhyming words come at the ends of lines, as in "The Desired Swan Song" by Samuel Taylor Coleridge:

> Swans sing before they die—'twere no bad *thing*
> Should certain persons die before they *sing*.

Internal rhyme occurs when the rhyming words appear in the same line, as in the first line of Edgar Allan Poe's "The Raven" (p. 940):

> Once upon a midnight *dreary*, while I pondered, weak and *weary*,

See also Repetition *and* Rhyme Scheme.

RHYME SCHEME A *rhyme scheme* is a regular pattern of rhyming words in a poem. The rhyme scheme of a poem is indicated by using different letters of the alphabet for each new rhyme. In an *aabb* stanza, for example, line 1 rhymes with line 2 and line 3 rhymes with line 4. William Wordsworth's poem "I Wandered Lonely as a Cloud" (p. 896) uses an *ababcc* rhyme pattern:

I wandered lonely as a cloud a
That floats on high o'er vales and hills, b
When all at once I saw a crowd, a
A host, of golden daffodils; b
Beside the lake, beneath the trees, c
Fluttering and dancing in the breeze. c

Many poems use the same pattern of rhymes, though not the same rhymes, in each stanza.

See also Rhyme.

RHYTHM *Rhythm* is the pattern of *beats*, or *stresses*, in spoken or written language. Some poems have a very specific pattern, or meter, whereas prose and free verse use the natural rhythms of everyday speech.

See also Meter.

RISING ACTION *See* Plot.

ROUND CHARACTER *See* Character.

SCENE *See* Drama.

SCIENCE FICTION *Science fiction* is writing that tells about imaginary events involving science or technology. Many science-fiction stories are set in the future. Arthur C. Clarke's "If I Forget Thee, Oh Earth . . ." (p. 486) is set on the moon after a nuclear disaster on Earth.

See also Fantasy.

SENSORY LANGUAGE *Sensory language* is writing or speech that appeals to one or more of the senses.

See also Image.

SESTET *See* Stanza.

SETTING The *setting* of a literary work is the time and place of the action. Time can include not only the historical period—past, present, or future—but also a specific year, season, or time of day. Place may involve not only the geographical place—a region, country, state, or town—but also the social, economic, or cultural environment.

In some stories, setting serves merely as a backdrop for action, a context in which the characters move and speak. In others, however, setting is a crucial element.

See also Mood.

SHORT STORY A *short story* is a brief work of fiction. In most short stories, one main character faces a conflict that is resolved in the plot of the story. Great craftsmanship must go into the writing of a good story, for it has to accomplish its purpose in relatively few words.

See also Fiction *and* Genre.

SIMILE A *simile* is a figure of speech in which *like* or *as* is used to make a comparison between two basically unlike ideas. "Claire is as flighty as Roger" is a comparison, not a simile. "Claire is as flighty as a sparrow" is a simile.

See also Figurative Language.

SOLILOQUY A *soliloquy* is a long speech expressing the thoughts of a character alone on stage. In William Shakespeare's *Romeo and Juliet* (p. 861), Romeo gives a soliloquy after the servant has fled and Paris has died (Act V, Scene iii, lines 74–120).

See also Monologue.

SONNET A *sonnet* is a fourteen-line lyric poem, usually written in rhymed iambic pentameter. The *English*, or *Shakespearean*, sonnet consists of three quatrains (four-line stanzas) and a couplet (two lines), usually rhyming *abab cdcd efef gg*. The couplet usually comments on the ideas contained in the preceding twelve lines. The sonnet is usually not printed with the stanzas divided, but a reader can see distinct ideas in each. See the English sonnet by William Shakespeare on page 960.

The *Italian*, or *Petrarchan*, sonnet consists of an octave (eight-line stanza) and a sestet (six-line stanza). Often, the octave rhymes *abbaabba* and the sestet rhymes *cdecde*. The octave states a theme or asks a question. The sestet comments on or answers the question.

See also Lyric Poem, Meter, *and* Stanza.

SPEAKER The *speaker* is the imaginary voice assumed by the writer of a poem. In many poems, the speaker is not identified by name. When reading a poem, remember that the speaker within the poem may be a person, an animal, a thing, or an abstraction. The speaker in the following stanza by Emily Dickinson is a person who has died:

Because I could not stop for Death—
He kindly stopped for me—
The Carriage held but just Ourselves—
And Immortality.

STAGE DIRECTIONS *Stage directions* are notes included in a drama to describe how the work is to be performed or staged. These instructions are printed in italics and are not spoken aloud. They are used to

describe sets, lighting, sound effects, and the appearance, personalities, and movements of characters.
See also Drama.

STANZA A *stanza* is a formal division of lines in a poem, considered as a unit. Often, the stanzas in a poem are separated by spaces.

Stanzas are sometimes named according to the number of lines found in them. A *couplet*, for example, is a two-line stanza. A *tercet* is a stanza with three lines. Other types of stanzas include the following:

1. *Quatrain:* a four-line stanza
2. *Cinquain:* a five-line stanza
3. *Sestet:* a six-line stanza
4. *Heptastich:* a seven-line stanza
5. *Octave:* an eight-line stanza

See also Haiku *and* Sonnet.

STATIC CHARACTER *See* Character.

SURPRISE ENDING A *surprise ending* is a conclusion that violates the expectations of the reader but in a way that is both logical and believable.

O. Henry's "The Gift of the Magi" (p. 524) and Guy de Maupassant's "The Necklace" (p. 608) have surprise endings. Both authors were masters of this form.

SUSPENSE *Suspense* is a feeling of uncertainty about the outcome of events in a literary work. Writers create suspense by raising questions in the minds of their readers.

SYMBOL A *symbol* is anything that stands for or represents something else. An object that serves as a symbol has its own meaning, but it also represents abstract ideas. Marks on paper can symbolize spoken words. A flag symbolizes a country. A flashy car may symbolize wealth. Writers sometimes use such conventional symbols in their work, but they may also create symbols of their own through emphasis or repetition.

In James Hurst's "The Scarlet Ibis" (p. 554), the ibis symbolizes the character named Doodle. Doodle and the ibis have many traits in common. Both are beautiful and otherworldly. Both struggle against great odds. Both meet an unfortunate fate. Since a story says something about life or people in general, the ibis, in a larger sense, becomes a symbol for those who struggle.

TETRAMETER *See* Meter.

THEME A *theme* is a central message or insight into life revealed through a literary work.

The theme of a literary work may be stated directly or implied. When the theme of a work is implied, readers think about what the work suggests about people or life.

TONE The *tone* of a literary work is the writer's attitude toward his or her audience and subject. The tone can often be described by a single adjective, such as *formal* or *informal, serious* or *playful, bitter* or *ironic*. When O. Henry discusses the young couple in "The Gift of the Magi" (p. 524), he uses a sympathetic tone. By contrast, Margaret Walker uses a grieving tone in her poem "Memory" (p. 915).
See also Mood.

TRAGEDY A *tragedy* is a work of literature, especially a play, that results in a catastrophe for the main character. In ancient Greek drama, the main character was always a significant person—a king or a hero—and the cause of the tragedy was a tragic flaw, or weakness, in his or her character. In modern drama, the main character can be an ordinary person, and the cause of the tragedy can be some evil in society itself. Tragedy not only arouses fear and pity in the audience, but also, in some cases, conveys a sense of the grandeur and nobility of the human spirit.

Shakespeare's *Romeo and Juliet* (p. 770) is a tragedy. Romeo and Juliet both suffer from the tragic flaw of impulsiveness. This flaw ultimately leads to their deaths.
See also Drama.

TRIMETER *See* Meter.

UNIVERSAL THEME A *universal theme* is a message about life that can be understood by most cultures. Many folk tales and examples of classic literature address universal themes such as the importance of courage, the effects of honesty, or the danger of greed.

VERBAL IRONY *See* Irony.

VILLANELLE A *villanelle* is a lyric poem written in three-line stanzas, ending with a four-line stanza. It has two refrain lines that appear initially in the first and third lines of the first stanza; they then appear alternately as the third line of subsequent stanzas and finally as the last two lines of the poem.

VISUAL ESSAY A *visual essay* is an exploration of a topic that conveys its ideas through visual elements as well as language. Like a standard essay, a visual essay presents an author's views of a single topic. Unlike other essays, however, much of the meaning in a visual essay is conveyed through illustrations or photographs.

The Writing Process

A polished piece of writing can seem to have been effortlessly created, but most good writing is the result of a process of writing, rethinking, and rewriting. The process can roughly be divided into stages: prewriting, drafting, revising, editing, proofreading, and publishing.

It is important to remember that the writing process is one that moves backward as well as forward. Even while you are moving forward in the creation of your composition, you may still return to a previous stage—to rethink or rewrite.

Following are stages of the writing process, with key points to address during each stage.

Prewriting

In this stage, you plan out the work to be done. You prepare to write by exploring ideas, gathering information, and working out an organization plan. Following are the key steps to take at this stage.

Step 1: Analyze the writing situation. Start by clarifying your assignment, so that you know exactly what you are supposed to do.

- ***Focus your topic.*** If necessary, narrow the topic—the subject you are writing about—so that you can write about it fully in the space you have.
- ***Know your purpose.*** What is your goal for this paper? What do you want to accomplish? Your purpose will determine what you include in the paper.
- ***Know your audience.*** Who will read your paper influences what you say and how you say it.

Step 2: Gather ideas and information. You can do this in a number of ways:

- ***Brainstorm.*** When you brainstorm, either alone or with others, you come up with possible ideas to use in your paper. Not all of your ideas will be useful or suitable. You will need to evaluate them later.
- ***Consult other people about your subject.*** Speaking informally with others may suggest an idea or an approach you did not see at first.
- ***Make a list of questions about your topic.*** When your list is complete, find the answers to your questions.
- ***Do research.*** Your topic may require information that you do not have, so you will need to go to other sources to find information. There are numerous ways to find information on a topic.

The ideas and information you gather will become the content of your paper. Not all of the information you gather will be needed. As you develop and revise your paper, you will make further decisions about what to include and what to leave out.

Drafting

When you draft, you put down your ideas on paper in rough form. Working from your prewriting notes and your outline or plan, you develop and present your ideas in sentences and paragraphs.

Organize. First, make a rough plan for the way you want to present your information. Sort your ideas and notes. Decide what goes with what and which points are the most important. You can make an outline to show the order of ideas, or you can use some other organizing plan that works for you.

There are many ways in which you can organize and develop your material. Use a method that works for your topic. Following are common methods of organizing information in the development of a paper:

- ***Chronological Order*** In this method, events are presented in the order in which they occurred. This organization works best for presenting narrative material or explaining in a "how-to" format.
- ***Spatial Order*** In spatial order, details are presented as seen in space; for example, from left to right, top to bottom, or from foreground to background. This order is good for descriptive writing.
- ***Order of Importance*** This order helps readers see the relative importance of ideas. You present ideas from the most to least important or from the least to most important.
- ***Main Idea and Details*** This logical organization works well to support an idea or opinion. Present each main idea, and back it up with appropriate support.

Once you have chosen an organization, begin writing your draft. Do not worry about getting everything perfect at the drafting stage. Concentrate on getting your ideas down.

Write your draft in a way that works for you. Some writers work best by writing a quick draft—putting down all their ideas without stopping to evaluate them. Other writers prefer to develop each paragraph carefully and thoughtfully, making sure that each main idea is supported by details.

As you are developing your draft, keep in mind your purpose and your audience. These determine what you say and how you say it.

Do not be afraid to change your original plans during drafting. Some of the best ideas are those that were not planned at the beginning. Write as many drafts as you like, until you are happy with the results.

Develop an Essay Most papers, regardless of the topic, are developed with an introduction, a body, and a conclusion. Here are tips for developing these parts:

Introduction In the introduction to a paper, you want to engage your readers' attention and let them know the purpose of your paper. You may use the following strategies in your introduction:

- Startle your readers.
- Take a stand.
- Use an anecdote.
- Quote someone.

Body of the Paper In the body of your paper, you present your information and make your points. Your organization is an important factor in leading readers through your ideas. Elaborating on your main ideas is also important. Elaboration is the development of ideas to make your written work precise and complete. You can use the following kinds of details to elaborate your main ideas:

- Facts and statistics
- Anecdotes
- Sensory details
- Examples
- Explanations and definitions
- Quotations

Conclusion The ending of your paper is the final impression you leave with your readers. Your conclusion should give readers the sense that you have pulled everything together. Following are some effective ways to end your paper:

- Summarize and restate.
- Ask a question.
- State an opinion.
- Tell an anecdote.
- Call for action.
- Provide an insight.

Revising

Once you have a draft, you can look at it critically or have others review it. This is the time to make changes—on many levels. Revising is the process of reworking what you have written to make it as good as it can be.

Revising Your Overall Structure Start by examining the soundness of your structure, or overall organization. Your ideas should flow logically from beginning to end. You may strengthen the structure by reordering paragraphs or by adding information to fill in gaps.

Revising Your Paragraphs Next, examine each paragraph in your writing. Consider the way each sentence contributes to the point of the paragraph. As you evaluate your draft, rewrite or eliminate any sentences that are not effective.

Revising Your Sentences When you study the sentences in your draft, check to see that they flow smoothly from one to the next. Look to see that you have avoided the pattern of beginning most of your sentences in the same way, and vary your sentence length.

Revising Your Word Choice The final step in the process of revising your work is to analyze your choice of words. Consider the connotations, or associations each word suggests, and make sure that each word conveys the exact meaning you intended. Also, look for the repetition of words, and make revisions to polish your writing.

Peer Review After you have finished revising your draft, work with one or more classmates to get a fresh perspective on your writing. First, have your reviewer look at one element of your writing, and ask your reviewer a specific question to get the most focused feedback possible. Weigh the responses you receive, and determine which suggestions you want to incorporate in your draft.

Editing

When you edit, you look more closely at the language you have used to ensure that the way you expressed your ideas is the most effective.

- Replace dull language with vivid, precise words.
- Cut or change unnecessary repetition.
- Cut empty words and phrases—those that do not add anything to the writing.
- Check passive voice. Usually, active voice is more effective.
- Replace wordy expressions with shorter, more precise ones.

Proofreading

After you finish your final draft, proofread it, either on your own or with the help of a partner.

It is useful to have both a dictionary and a usage handbook available to help you check that your work is correct. Here are the tasks in proofreading:

- Correct errors in grammar and usage.
- Correct errors in punctuation and capitalization.
- Correct errors in spelling.

Publishing

Now your paper is ready to be shared with others. Consider sharing your writing with classmates, family, or a wider audience.

THE MODES OF WRITING

Writing is a process that begins with the exploration of ideas and ends with the presentation of a final draft. Often, the types of writing are grouped into modes according to form and purpose.

The modes addressed in this handbook are

- Narration
- Description
- Persuasion
- Exposition
- Research Writing
- Response to Literature
- Writing for Assessment
- Workplace Writing

NARRATION

Whenever writers tell any type of story, they are using **narration.** Although there are many kinds of narration, most narratives share certain elements, such as characters, a setting, a sequence of events, and, often, a theme. Following are some types of narration:

Autobiographical Writing Autobiographical writing tells a true story about an important period, experience, or relationship in the writer's life. An autobiographical narrative can be as simple as a description of a recent car trip or as complex as the entire story of a person's life. Effective autobiographical writing includes

- A series of events that involve the writer as the main character
- Details, thoughts, feelings, and insights from the writer's perspective
- A conflict or an event that affects the writer
- A logical organization that tells the story clearly
- Insights that the writer gained from the experience

A few types of autobiographical writing are autobiographical incidents, personal narratives, autobiographical narratives or sketches, reflective essays, eyewitness accounts, anecdotes, and memoirs.

Short Story A short story is a brief, creative narrative—a retelling of events arranged to hold a reader's attention. Most short stories include

- Details that establish the setting in time and place
- A main character who undergoes a change or learns something during the course of the story
- A conflict or a problem to be introduced, developed, and resolved
- A plot, the series of events that make up the action of the story
- A theme or generalization about life

A few types of short stories are realistic stories, fantasies, historical narratives, mysteries, thrillers, science-fiction stories, and adventure stories.

DESCRIPTION

Descriptive writing is writing that creates a vivid picture of a person, place, thing, or event. Descriptive writing can stand on its own or be part of a longer work, such as a short story. Most descriptive writing includes

- Sensory details—sights, sounds, smells, tastes, and physical sensations
- Vivid, precise language
- Figurative language or comparisons
- Adjectives and adverbs that paint a word picture
- An organization suited to the subject

Some examples of descriptive writing include description of ideas, observations, travel brochures, physical descriptions, functional descriptions, remembrances, and character sketches.

PERSUASION

Persuasion is writing or speaking that attempts to convince people to accept a position or take a desired action. When used effectively, persuasive writing has the power to change people's lives. As a reader and a writer, you will find yourself engaged in many forms of persuasion. Here are a few of them:

Persuasive Essay A persuasive essay presents your position on an issue, urges your readers to accept that position, and may encourage them to take an action. An effective persuasive essay

- Explores an issue of importance to the writer
- Addresses an issue that is arguable
- Uses facts, examples, statistics, or personal experiences to support a position
- Tries to influence the audience through appeals to the readers' knowledge, experiences, or emotions
- Uses clear organization to present a logical argument

Persuasion can take many forms. A few forms of persuasion include editorials, position papers, persuasive speeches, grant proposals, advertisements, and debates.

Advertisements An advertisement is a planned communication meant to be seen, heard, or read. It attempts to persuade an audience to buy a product or service, accept an idea, or support a cause. Advertisements may appear in printed form—in newspapers and magazines, on billboards, or as posters or flyers. They may appear on radio or television, as commercials or public-service announcements. An effective advertisement includes

- A memorable slogan to grab the audience's attention
- A call to action, which tries to rally the audience to do something
- Persuasive and/or informative text
- Striking visual or aural images
- Details that provide such information as price, location, date, and time

Several common types of advertisements are public-service announcements, billboards, merchandise ads, service ads, online ads, product packaging, and political campaign literature.

EXPOSITION

Exposition is writing that informs or explains. The information you include in expository writing is factual or based on fact. Effective expository writing reflects a well-thought-out organization—one that includes a clear introduction, body, and conclusion. The organization should be appropriate for the type of exposition you are writing. Here are some types of exposition:

Comparison-and-Contrast Essay A comparison-and-contrast essay analyzes the similarities and differences between two or more things. You may organize your essay either point by point or subject by subject. An effective comparison-and-contrast essay

- Identifies a purpose for comparison and contrast
- Identifies similarities and differences between two or more things, people, places, or ideas
- Gives factual details about the subjects being compared
- Uses an organizational plan suited to its topic and purpose

Types of comparison-and-contrast essays are product comparisons, essays on economic or historical developments, comparison and contrast of literary works, and plan evaluations.

Cause-and-Effect Essay A cause-and-effect essay examines the relationship between events, explaining how one event or situation causes another. A successful cause-and-effect essay includes

- A discussion of a cause, event, or condition that produces a specific result
- An explanation of an effect, outcome, or result
- Evidence and examples to support the relationship between cause and effect
- A logical organization that makes the explanation clear

Some appropriate subjects for cause-and-effect essays are science reports, current-events articles, health studies, historical accounts, and cause-and-effect investigations.

Problem-and-Solution Essay A problem-and-solution essay describes a problem and offers one or more solutions to it. It describes a clear set of steps to achieve a result. An effective problem-and-solution essay includes

- A clear statement of the problem, with its causes and effects summarized for the reader
- The most important aspects of the problem
- A proposal of at least one realistic solution
- Facts, statistics, data, or expert testimony to support the solution
- Language appropriate to the audience's knowledge and ability levels
- A clear organization that makes the relationship between problem and solution obvious

Some types of issues that might be addressed in a problem-and-solution essay include consumer issues, business issues, time-management issues, and local issues.

RESEARCH WRITING

Research writing is based on information gathered from outside sources, and it gives a writer the power to become an expert on any subject. A research paper—a focused study of a topic—helps writers explore and connect ideas, make discoveries, and share their findings with an audience. Effective research writing

- Focuses on a specific, narrow topic, which is usually summarized in a thesis statement
- Presents relevant information from a wide variety of sources
- Structures the information logically and effectively
- Identifies the sources from which the information was drawn

Besides the formal research report, there are many other specialized types of writing that depend on accurate and insightful research, including multimedia presentations, statistical reports, annotated bibliographies, and experiment journals.

Documented Essay A documented essay uses research gathered from outside sources to support an idea. What distinguishes this essay from other categories of research is the level and intensity of the research. In a documented essay, the writer consults a limited number of sources to elaborate an idea. In contrast, a formal research paper may include many more research sources. An effective documented essay includes

- A well-defined thesis that can be fully discussed in a brief essay
- Facts and details to support each main point
- Expert or informed ideas gathered from interviews and other sources
- A clear, coherent method of organization
- Full internal documentation to show sources of information

Subjects especially suited to the documented essay format include health issues, current events, and cultural trends.

Research Paper A research paper presents and interprets information gathered through an extensive study of a subject. An effective research paper has

- A clearly stated thesis statement
- Convincing factual support from a variety of outside sources, including direct quotations whose sources are credited
- A clear organization that includes an introduction, body, and conclusion
- A bibliography, or works-cited list, that provides a complete listing of research sources

Some research formats you may encounter include lab reports, annotated bibliographies, and multigenre research papers.

RESPONSE TO LITERATURE

When you write a **response-to-literature essay,** you give yourself the opportunity to discover *what, how,* and *why* a piece of writing communicated to you. An effective response

- Contains a reaction to a poem, story, essay, or other work of literature
- Analyzes the content of a literary work, its related ideas, or the work's effect on the reader
- Presents a thesis statement to identify the nature of the response
- Focuses on a single aspect of the work or gives a general overview
- Supports opinion with evidence from the work addressed

The following are just a few of the ways you might respond in writing to a literary work: reader's response journals, character analyses, literary letters, and literary analyses.

WRITING FOR ASSESSMENT

One of the most common types of school **assessment** is the written test. Most often, a written test is announced in advance, allowing you time to study and prepare. When a test includes an essay, you are expected to write a response that includes

- A clearly stated and well-supported thesis or main idea
- Specific information about the topic derived from your reading or from class discussion
- A clear organization

In your school career, you will probably encounter questions that ask you to address each of the following types of writing: explain a process; defend a position; compare, contrast, or categorize; and show cause and effect.

WORKPLACE WRITING

Workplace writing is probably the format you will use most after you finish school. It is used in offices, factories, and by workers on the road. Workplace writing includes a variety of formats that share common features. In general, workplace writing is fact-based writing that communicates specific information to readers in a structured format. Effective workplace writing

- Communicates information concisely to make the best use of both the writer's and the reader's time
- Includes a level of detail that provides necessary information and anticipates potential questions
- Reflects the writer's care if it is error-free and neatly presented

Some common types of workplace writing include business letters, memorandums, résumés, forms, and applications.

SUMMARY OF GRAMMAR

Nouns A **noun** names a person, place, or thing. **Common nouns** name any one of a class of people, places, or things. **Proper nouns** name specific people, places, or things.

Common Noun	*Proper Noun*
city	Washington, D.C.

Pronouns A **pronoun** is a word that stands for a noun or for a word that takes the place of a noun.

A **personal pronoun** refers to (1) the person speaking, (2) the person spoken to, or (3) the person, place, or thing spoken about.

	Singular	*Plural*
First Person	I, me, my, mine	we, us, our, ours
Second Person	you, your, yours	you, your, yours
Third Person	he, him, his, she, her, hers, it, its	they, them, their, theirs

A **reflexive pronoun** ends in *-self* or *-selves* and adds information to a sentence by pointing back to a noun or pronoun earlier in the sentence.

As I said these words I busied *myself* among the pile of bones of which I have before spoken.

—"The Cask of Amontillado," p. 6

An **intensive pronoun** ends in *-self* or *-selves* and simply adds emphasis to a noun or a pronoun in the same sentence.

And Spring *herself*, when she woke at dawn,
Would scarcely know that we were gone.

—"There Will Come Soft Rains," p. 473

Demonstrative pronouns (*this, these, that,* and *those*) direct attention to a specific person, place, or thing.

These are the juiciest pears I have ever tasted.

A **relative pronoun** begins a subordinate (relative) clause and connects it to another idea in the sentence.

The poet *who* wrote "Fire and Ice" is Robert Frost.

The poet *whom* I admire is Frost.

An **indefinite pronoun** refers to a person, place, or thing, often without specifying which one.

Some of the flowers were in bloom.

Everybody chose something.

Verbs A **verb** is a word that expresses time while showing an action, a condition, or the fact that something exists.

An **action verb** indicates the action of someone or something.

An action verb is **transitive** if it directs action toward someone or something named in the same sentence.

Henderson *shook* his head.

—"The Machine That Won the War," p. 456

An action verb is **intransitive** if it does not direct action toward something or someone named in the same sentence.

Earth *had won* so all *had been* for the best.

—"The Machine That Won the War," p. 456

A **linking verb** is a verb that connects the subject of a sentence with a noun or pronoun that renames or describes the subject. All linking verbs are intransitive.

Life *is* a broken-winged bird . . .

—"Dreams," p. 905

A **helping verb** is a verb that can be added to another verb to make a verb phrase.

Nor *did* I suspect that these experiences could be part of a novel's meaning.

Adjectives An **adjective** describes a noun or a pronoun or gives a noun or a pronoun a more specific meaning. Adjectives answer these questions:

What kind?	*blue* lamp, *large* tree
Which one?	*this* table, *those* books
How many?	*five* stars, *several* buses
How much?	*less* money, *enough* votes

The articles *the, a,* and *an* are adjectives. *An* is used before a word beginning with a vowel sound.

A noun may sometimes be used as an adjective.

diamond necklace   *summer* vacation

Adverbs An **adverb** modifies a verb, an adjective, or another adverb. Adverbs answer the questions *where, when, in what way,* or *to what extent.*

He could stand *there.* (modifies verb *stand*)

He was *blissfully* happy. (modifies adjective *happy*)

It ended *too* soon. (modifies adverb *soon*)

Prepositions

A **preposition** relates a noun or a pronoun that appears with it to another word in the sentence.

before the end   *near* me   *inside* our fence

Conjunctions

A **conjunction** connects other words or groups of words.

A **coordinating conjunction** connects similar kinds or groups of words.

mother *and* father   simple *yet* stylish

Correlative conjunctions are used in pairs to connect similar words or groups of words.

both Sue *and* Meg   *neither* he *nor* I

A **subordinating conjunction** connects two complete ideas by placing one idea below the other in rank or importance.

You would know him *if* you saw him.

Interjections

An **interjection** expresses feeling or emotion and functions independently of a sentence.

"*Oh*, my poor, poor, Mathilde!"

—"The Necklace," p. 608

Sentences

A **sentence** is a group of words with a subject and a predicate. Together, these parts express a complete thought.

I closed my eyes and pondered my next move.

—"Rules of the Game," p. 262

A **fragment** is a group of words that does not express a complete thought.

The Swan Theater in London

Subject and Verb Agreement

A singular verb must be used with a singular subject; a plural verb must be used with a plural subject.

Raegan is going home now.

Many *storms are* the cause of beach erosion.

In a sentence with combined singular and plural subjects, the verb should agree with the subject closest to it.

Either the *cats* or the *dog is* hungry.

Neither *Angie* nor her *sisters were* present.

Phrase

A **phrase** is a group of words, without a subject and a verb, that functions in a sentence as one part of speech.

A **prepositional phrase** is a group of words that includes a preposition and a noun or a pronoun that is the object of the preposition.

outside my window   below the counter

An **adjective phrase** is a prepositional phrase that modifies a noun or a pronoun by telling *what kind* or *which one.*

The wooden gates *of that lane* stood open.

An **adverb phrase** is a prepositional phrase that modifies a verb, an adjective, or an adverb by pointing out *where, when, in what way,* or *to what extent.*

On December *the third*, the wind changed overnight, and it was winter.

—"The Birds," p. 50

An **appositive phrase** is a noun or pronoun with modifiers, placed next to a noun or a pronoun to add information and details.

"It is a very great pleasure and honor to welcome Mr. Sanger Rainsford, *the celebrated hunter*, to my home."

—"The Most Dangerous Game," p. 18

A **participial phrase** is a participle with its modifiers or complements. The entire phrase acts as an adjective.

"Try the settee," said Holmes, *relapsing into his armchair . . .*

—"The Red-headed League," p. 96

A **gerund phrase** is a gerund with modifiers or a complement, all acting together as a noun.

The baying of the hounds drew nearer, . . .

—"The Most Dangerous Game," p. 18

An **infinitive phrase** is an infinitive (*to* and a verb) with modifiers, complements, or a subject, all acting together as a single part of speech.

I continued, as was my wont, *to smile in his face*, . . .

—"The Cask of Amontillado," p. 6

Clauses A **clause** is a group of words with a subject and a verb.

An **independent clause** has a subject and a verb and can stand by itself as a complete sentence.

A **subordinate clause** has a subject and a verb but cannot stand by itself as a complete sentence; it can only be part of a sentence.

An **adjective clause** is a subordinate clause that modifies a noun or a pronoun by telling *what kind* or *which one.*

> Walter Mitty stopped the car in front of the building *where his wife went to have her hair done.*
>
> —"The Secret Life of Walter Mitty," p. 346

An **adverb clause** modifies a verb, an adjective, an adverb, or a verbal by telling *where, when, in what way, to what extent, under what condition*, or *why.*

> The hunter shook his head several times, *as if he was puzzled.*
>
> —"The Most Dangerous Game," p. 18

A **noun clause** is a subordinate clause that acts as a noun.

> . . . I discovered *that the intoxication had worn off* . . .
>
> —"The Cask of Amontillado," p. 6

SUMMARY OF CAPITALIZATION AND PUNCTUATION

Capitalization

Capitalize the first word of a sentence and also the first word in a quotation if the quotation is a complete sentence.

> I said to him, "My dear Fortunato, you are luckily met." —"The Cask of Amontillado," p. 6

Capitalize all proper nouns and adjectives.

> O. Henry Ganges River Great Wall of China

Capitalize a person's title when it is followed by the person's name or when it is used in direct address.

> Madame Dr. Mitty General Zaroff

Capitalize titles showing family relationships when they refer to a specific person, unless they are preceded by a possessive noun or pronoun.

> Uncle Marcos Granddaddy Cain

Capitalize the first word and all other key words in the titles of books, periodicals, poems, stories, plays, paintings, and other works of art.

> *Odyssey* "I Wandered Lonely as a Cloud"

Punctuation

End Marks Use a **period** to end a declarative sentence, an imperative sentence, an indirect question, and most abbreviations.

> Mr. Jabez Wilson laughed heavily.
>
> —"The Red-headed League," p. 96

Use a **question mark** to end a direct question, an incomplete question, or a statement that is intended as a question.

> Shall I meet other wayfarers at night?
>
> —"Uphill," p. 926

Use an **exclamation mark** after a statement showing strong emotion, an urgent imperative sentence, or an interjection expressing strong emotion.

> Free at last! Free at last!
> Thank God almighty, we are Free at last!
>
> —"I Have a Dream," p. 164

Commas Use a **comma** before the coordinating conjunction to separate two independent clauses in a compound sentence.

> All at once . . . she came upon a superb diamond necklace, and her heart started beating with overwhelming desire. —"The Necklace," p. 608

Use commas to separate three or more words, phrases, or clauses in a series.

> My brothers and I would peer into the medicinal herb shop, watching old Li dole out onto a stiff sheet of white paper the right amount of insect shells, saffron-colored seeds, and pungent leaves for his ailing customers.
>
> —"Rules of the Game," p. 262

Use commas to separate adjectives of equal rank. Do not use commas to separate adjectives that must stay in a specific order.

> The big cottonwood tree stood apart from a small group of winterbare cottonwoods which grew in the wide, sandy arroyo.
>
> —"The Man to Send Rain Clouds," p. 590

> In autumn those that had not migrated overseas . . . were caught up in the same driving urge . . .
>
> —"The Birds," p. 50

Use a comma after an introductory word, phrase, or clause.

> When Marvin was ten years old, his father took him through the long, echoing corridors . . .
>
> —"If I Forget Thee, Oh Earth . . . ," p. 486

Use commas to set off parenthetical and nonessential expressions.

> An evil place can, so to speak, broadcast vibrations of evil.
>
> —"The Most Dangerous Game," p. 18

Use commas with places, dates, and titles.

> Poe was raised in Richmond, Virginia.
>
> On September 1, 1939, World War II began.
>
> Dr. Martin Luther King, Jr., was born in 1929.

Use a comma to set off a direct quotation, to prevent a sentence from being misunderstood, and to indicate the omission of a common verb in a sentence with two or more clauses.

> Michele said, "I'm going to the game tonight."
>
> *Faulty:* She stifled the sob that rose to her lips and lay motionless.
>
> *Revised:* She stifled the sob that rose to her lips, and lay motionless.
>
> In the *Odyssey,* the Cyclops may symbolize brutishness; the Sirens, knowledge.

Semicolons Use a **semicolon** to join independent clauses that are not already joined by a conjunction.

> The lights of cities sparkle; on nights when there was no moon, it was difficult for me to tell the Earth from the sky. . . .
>
> —"Single Room, Earth View," p. 636

Use a semicolon to join independent clauses separated by either a conjunctive adverb or a transitional expression.

> Edward Way Teale wrote nearly thirty books; moreover, he was also an artist and a naturalist.

Use semicolons to avoid confusion when independent clauses or items in a series already contain commas.

> Unable to afford jewelry, she dressed simply; but she was as wretched as a *déclassée,* for women have neither caste nor breeding—in them beauty, grace, and charm replace pride of birth.
>
> —"The Necklace," p. 608

Colons Use a **colon** in order to introduce a list of items following an independent clause.

> The authors we are reading include a number of poets: Robert Frost, Lewis Carroll, and Emily Dickinson.

Use a colon to introduce a formal quotation.

> I have a dream that one day this nation will rise up and live out the true meaning of its creed: "We hold these truths to be self-evident; . . ."
>
> —"I Have a Dream," p. 164

Quotation Marks A **direct quotation** represents a person's exact speech or thoughts and is enclosed in quotation marks.

> "Where I was born and where and how I have lived is unimportant," Georgia O'Keeffe told us in the book of paintings and words published in her ninetieth year on earth.
>
> —"Georgia O'Keeffe," p. 685

An **indirect quotation** reports only the general meaning of what a person said or thought and does not require quotation marks.

> The driver of the bus saw me still sitting there, and he asked was I going to stand up . . .
>
> —from *Rosa Parks: My Story,* p. 168

Always place a comma or a period inside the final quotation mark.

> "I don't know," he said slowly. "It says here the birds are hungry." —"The Birds," p. 50

Place a question mark or an exclamation mark inside the final quotation mark if the end mark is part of the quotation; if it is not part of the quotation, place it outside the final quotation mark.

> "That pig will devour us, greedily!"
>
> —"The Golden Kite, the Silver Wind," p. 178
>
> Have you ever read the poem "Dreams"?

Use single quotation marks for a quotation within a quotation.

> "'But,' said I, 'there would be millions of red-headed men who would apply.'"
>
> —"The Red-headed League," p. 96

Use quotation marks around the titles of short written works, episodes in a series, songs, and titles of works mentioned as parts of a collection.

> "I Hear America Singing" "Both Sides Now"

Dashes Use **dashes** to indicate an abrupt change of thought, a dramatic interrupting idea, or a summary statement.

> The streets were lined with people—lots and lots of people—the children all smiling, placards, confetti, people waving from windows.
>
> —from *A White House Diary,* p. 674

Parentheses Use **parentheses** to set off asides and explanations only when the material is not essential or when it consists of one or more sentences.

> One last happy moment I had was looking up and seeing Mary Griffith . . . (Mary for many years had been in charge of altering the clothes which I purchased) . . .
>
> —from *A White House Diary,* p. 674

Hyphens Use a **hyphen** with certain numbers, after certain prefixes, with two or more words used as one word, and with a compound modifier coming before a noun.

seventy-six   Post-Modernist

Apostrophes Add an **apostrophe** and *-s* to show the possessive case of most singular nouns.

Thurmond's wife   the playwright's craft

Add an apostrophe to show the possessive case of plural nouns ending in *-s* and *-es.*

the sailors' ships   the Wattses' daughter

Add an apostrophe and *-s* to show the possessive case of plural nouns that do not end in *-s* or *-es.*

the children's games   the people's friend

Use an apostrophe in a contraction to indicate the position of the missing letter or letters.

> You'll be lonely at first, they admitted, but you're so nice you'll make friends fast.
>
> —"Checkouts," p. 282

GLOSSARY OF COMMON USAGE

among, between

Among is usually used with three or more items. *Between* is generally used with only two items.

> *Among* the poems we read this year, Margaret Walker's "Memory" was my favorite.
>
> Mark Twain's "The Invalid's Story" includes a humorous encounter *between* the narrator and a character named Thompson.

amount, number

Amount refers to a mass or a unit, whereas *number* refers to individual items that can be counted. Therefore, *amount* generally appears with a singular noun, and *number* appears with a plural noun.

> Annie Sullivan's work with Helen Keller must have required a huge *amount* of patience.
>
> In her poem, "Uphill," Christina Rossetti uses a *number* of intriguing symbols.

any, all

Any should not be used in place of *any other* or *all.*

> Rajika liked Amy Tan's "Rules of the Game" better than *any other* short story.
>
> Of *all* O. Henry's short stories, "The Gift of the Magi" is one of the most famous.

around

In formal writing, *around* should not be used to mean *approximately* or *about.* These usages are allowable, however, in informal writing or in colloquial dialogue.

> Shakespeare's *Romeo and Juliet* had its first performance in *approximately* 1595.
>
> Shakespeare was *about* thirty when he wrote this play.

as, because, like, as to

The word *as* has several meanings and can function as several parts of speech. To avoid confusion, use *because* rather than *as* when you want to indicate cause and effect.

> *Because* Cyril was interested in the history of African American poetry, he decided to write his report on Paul Laurence Dunbar.

Do not use the preposition *like* to introduce a clause that requires the conjunction *as.*

> Dorothy Parker conversed *as* she wrote—wittily.

The use of *as to* for *about* is awkward and should be avoided.

> Rosa has an interesting theory *about* E. E. Cummings's unusual typography in his poems.

bad, badly

Use the predicate adjective *bad* after linking verbs such as *feel, look,* and *seem.* Use *badly* whenever an adverb is required.

> Sara Teasdale's poem "There Will Come Soft Rains" shows clearly that the author felt *bad* about the destruction of war.
>
> In O. Henry's "The Gift of the Magi," Della *badly* wants to buy a wonderful Christmas present for her husband, Jim.

because of, due to

Use *due to* if it can logically replace the phrase *caused by.* In introductory phrases, however, *because of* is better usage than *due to.*

> The popularity of Frank Stockton's "The Lady or the Tiger?" is largely *due to* the story's open ending.
>
> *Because of* her feeling that Bennie's mother had enough to worry about already, Bennie's grandmother keeps the doctor's conclusions to herself.

being as, being that

Avoid these expressions. Use *because* or *since* instead.

> *Because* the protagonist of James Hurst's "The Scarlet Ibis" is a dynamic character, he changes significantly in the course of the story.
>
> *Since* Romeo and Juliet were from feuding families, their relationship involved secrecy and risk.

beside, besides

Beside is a preposition meaning "at the side of" or "close to." Do not confuse *beside* with *besides,* which means "in addition to." *Besides* can be a preposition or an adverb.

> When our group discussed William Least Heat Moon's "Nameless, Tennessee," Luis sat *beside* Eileen.
>
> *Besides* "The Bells," can you think of any other poems by Edgar Allan Poe?

can, may

The verb *can* generally refers to the ability to act. The verb *may* generally refers to permission to act.

> The mysterious listeners in Walter de la Mare's poem *can* hear the words of the lonely traveler.
>
> *May* I tell you why I admire Edgar Lee Masters's "George Gray"?

compare, contrast

The verb *compare* can involve both similarities and differences. The verb *contrast* always involves differences. Use *to* or *with* after *compare.* Use *with* after *contrast.*

> Theo's paper *compared* James Weldon Johnson's style in "The Creation" *with* the style of African American sermons of the same period.
>
> In the opening lines of the famous speech in Shakespeare's *As You Like It,* the world is *compared to* a stage and men and women to actors or players.
>
> The speaker's tone of hysteria in the closing stanzas of Poe's "The Raven" *contrasts with* the quiet opening of the poem.

different from, different than

The preferred usage is *different from.*

> The structure of "The Meadow Mouse" is quite *different from* that of "I Wandered Lonely as a Cloud."

farther, further

Use *farther* when you refer to distance. Use *further* when you mean "to a greater degree" or "additional."

> The *farther* Rainsford traveled in the jungle in "The Most Dangerous Game," the nearer the baying of the hounds sounded.
>
> Despite his men's advice, Odysseus *further* insults the Cyclops and provokes the monster's curse.

fewer, less

Use *fewer* for things that can be counted. Use *less* for amounts or quantities that cannot be counted.

> Poetry often uses *fewer* words than prose to convey ideas and images.
>
> T. S. Eliot's humorous poems have received *less* critical attention than his serious verse has.

good, well

Use the adjective *good* after linking verbs such as *feel, look, smell, taste,* and *seem.* Use *well* whenever you need an adverb.

> In Walt Whitman's "I Hear America Singing," the "varied carols" sound *good* to the speaker.
>
> Dickens wrote especially *well* when he described eccentric characters.

hopefully

You should not loosely attach this adverb to a sentence, as in "*Hopefully*, the rain will stop by noon." Rewrite the sentence so that *hopefully* modifies a specific verb. Other possible ways of revising such sentences include using the adjective *hopeful* or a phrase such as "everyone *hopes* that."

> Dr. Martin Luther King, Jr., wrote and spoke *hopefully* about his dream of racial harmony.
>
> Akko was *hopeful* that he could find some of the unusual words from Lewis Carroll's "Jabberwocky" in an unabridged dictionary.
>
> Everyone *hopes* that the class production of *Romeo and Juliet* will be a big success.

its, it's

Do not confuse the possessive pronoun *its* with the contraction *it's*, used in place of "it is" or "it has."

> Ancient Greek society must have recognized many of *its* ideal values in the *Odyssey*.
>
> In Walter de la Mare's "The Listeners," the traveler thinks *it's* strange that no one replies to his call.

just, only

When you use *just* as an adverb meaning "no more than," be sure you place it directly before the word it logically modifies. Likewise, be sure you place *only* before the word it logically modifies.

> Shakespeare's Sonnet 30 offers *just* one remedy for the speaker's grief and depression: the thought of a dear friend.
>
> A stereotyped character exhibits *only* those traits or behavior patterns that are assumed to be typical.

kind of, sort of

In formal writing, you should not use these colloquial expressions. Instead, use a word such as *rather* or *somewhat*.

> Alfred is *rather* irresponsible in Morley Callaghan's story "All the Years of Her Life."
>
> In "The Secret Life of Walter Mitty," James Thurber characterizes Mitty as *somewhat* absent-minded.

lay, lie

Do not confuse these verbs. *Lay* is a transitive verb meaning "to set or put something down." Its principal parts are *lay, laying, laid, laid. Lie* is an intransitive verb meaning "to recline." Its principal parts are *lie, lying, lay, lain.*

> In Heyerdahl's *Kon-Tiki,* the narrator says that after the ship hit the reef, Herman *lay* pressed flat across the ridge of the cabin roof.
>
> Homer describes the slaughtered suitors *lying* dead in a heap on the floor of Odysseus' hall.

leave, let

Be careful not to confuse these verbs. *Leave* means "to go away" or "to allow to remain." *Let* means "to permit."

> In Tennyson's "The Eagle," the bird *leaves* the crag and plunges like a thunderbolt toward the sea.
>
> The lovesick Romeo asks his friends to *leave* him alone while they go to Capulet's party.
>
> "*Let* wantons light of heart / Tickle the senseless rushes with their heels," he says.

literally, figuratively

Literally means "word for word" or "in fact." The opposite of *literally* is *figuratively*, meaning "metaphorically." Be careful not to use *literally* as a synonym for *nearly*, as in informal expressions like this: "He was *literally* beside himself with rage."

> Certain specific details in "I Hear an Army" show that James Joyce does not intend us to interpret the army *literally*. Instead, the army and the speaker's nightmare are meant *figuratively* to suggest his despair at his abandonment by his love.

of, have

Do not use *of* in place of *have* after auxiliary verbs like *would, could, should, may*, or *might*.

> Sir Arthur Conan Doyle might *have* continued to practice medicine, but soon after the publication *of* his first Sherlock Holmes stories, he decided to write full time.

raise, rise

Raise is a transitive verb that usually takes a direct object. *Rise* is an intransitive verb and never takes a direct object.

In "Casey at the Bat," Ernest Lawrence Thayer suspensefully *raises* the reader's expectations throughout the poem, only to end the narrative with a mighty anticlimax.

Jorge *rose* to the challenge of interpreting Gabriel García Márquez's story "A Very Old Man With Enormous Wings."

set, sit

Do not confuse these verbs. *Set* is a transitive verb meaning "to put (something) in a certain place." Its principal parts are *set, setting, set, set.* *Sit* is an intransitive verb meaning "to be seated." Its principal parts are *sit, sitting, sat, sat.*

The opening sentence of Saki's "The Interlopers" *sets* a tone of tension and conflict for the story.

While Walter Mitty *sat* in a big leather chair in the hotel lobby, he picked up a copy of a magazine.

so, so that

Be careful not to use the coordinating conjunction *so* when your context requires *so that.* *So* means "accordingly" or "therefore" and expresses a cause-and-effect relationship. *So that* expresses purpose.

He wanted to check the clues, *so* he read "The Red-headed League" again.

The priest wanted to locate Teofilo's body *so that* he could give him the Last Rites.

than, then

The conjunction *than* is used to connect the two parts of a comparison. Do not confuse *than* with the adverb *then,* which usually refers to time.

I enjoyed reading "Jacob Lawrence: American Painter" more *than* "Autumn Gardening."

Sally Ride earned a doctorate in physics and *then* became the first American woman in space.

that, which, who

Use the relative pronoun *that* to refer to things or people. Use *which* only for things and *who* only for people.

The phrase *that* James Thurber dislikes is "you know."

Donald Justice wrote "Incident in a Rose Garden," *which* is a dramatic poem.

The sea goddess *who* loved Odysseus was Calypso.

unique

Because *unique* means "one of a kind," you should not use it carelessly to mean "interesting" or "unusual." Avoid such illogical expressions as "most unique," "very unique," and "extremely unique."

Homer occupies a *unique* position in the history of Western literature.

when, where

Do not directly follow a linking verb with *when* or *where.* Also, be careful not to use *where* when your context requires *that.*

Faulty: Foreshadowing is *when* an author uses clues to suggest future events.

Revised: In foreshadowing, an author uses clues to suggest future events.

Faulty: Ithaca was *where* Penelope awaited Odysseus.

Revised: Penelope awaited Odysseus on Ithaca.

who, whom

In formal writing, remember to use *who* only as a subject in clauses and sentences and *whom* only as an object.

Richard Wright, *who* is widely admired for his novel *Native Son,* also wrote haiku verse.

Leslie Marmon Silko, *whom* Mark quoted in his oral report, was raised on the Laguna Pueblo reservation in New Mexico.

Introduction to the Internet

The Internet is a series of networks that are interconnected all over the world. The Internet allows users to have almost unlimited access to information stored on the networks. Dr. Berners-Lee, a physicist, created the Internet in the 1980s by writing a small computer program that allowed pages to be linked together using key words. The Internet was mostly text-based until 1992, when a computer program called the NCSA Mosaic (National Center for Supercomputing Applications) was created at the University of Illinois. This program was the first Web browser. The development of Web browsers greatly eased the ability of the user to navigate through all the pages stored on the Web. Very soon, the appearance of the Web was altered as well. More appealing visuals were added, and sound, too, was implemented. This change made the Web more user-friendly and more appealing to the general public.

Using the Internet for Research

Key Word Search

Before you begin a search, you should identify your specific topic. To make searching easier, narrow your subject to a key word or a group of key words. These are your search terms, and they should be as specific as possible. For example, if you are looking for the latest concert dates for your favorite musical group, you might use the band's name as a key word. However, if you were to enter the name of the group in the query box of the search engine, you might be presented with thousands of links to information about the group that is unrelated to what you want to know. You might locate such information as band member biographies, the group's history, fan reviews of concerts, and hundreds of sites with related names containing information that is irrelevant to your search. Because you used such a broad key word, you might need to navigate through all that information before you could find a link or subheading for concert dates. In contrast, if you were to type in "Duplex Arena and [band name]," you would have a better chance of locating pages that contain this information.

How to Narrow Your Search

If you have a large group of key words and still do not know which ones to use, write out a list of all the words you are considering. Once you have completed the list, scrutinize it. Then, delete the words that are least important to your search, and highlight those that are most important.

These **key search connectors** can help you fine-tune your search:

AND: Narrows a search by retrieving documents that include both terms. For example: *baseball* AND *playoffs*

OR: Broadens a search by retrieving documents including any of the terms. For example: *playoffs* OR *championships*

NOT: Narrows a search by excluding documents containing certain words. For example: *baseball* NOT *history of*

Tips for an Effective Search

1. Remember that search engines can be case-sensitive. If your first attempt at searching fails, check your search terms for misspellings and try again.
2. If you are entering a group of key words, present them in order from the most important to the least important key word.
3. Avoid opening the link to every single page in your results list. Search engines present pages in descending order of relevancy. The most useful pages will be located at the top of the list. However, read the description of each link before you open the page.
4. Some search engines provide helpful tips for specializing your search. Take the opportunity to learn more about effective searching.

Other Ways to Search

Using Online Reference Sites How you search should be tailored to what you are hoping to find. If you are looking for data and facts, use reference sites before you jump onto a simple search engine. For example, you can find reference sites to provide definitions of words, statistics about almost any subject, biographies, maps, and concise information on many topics. Here are some useful online reference sites:

Online libraries

Online periodicals

Almanacs

Encyclopedias

You can find these sources using subject searches.

Conducting Subject Searches As you prepare to go online, consider your subject and the best way to find information to suit your needs. If you are looking for general information on a topic and you want your search results to be extensive, consider the subject search indexes on most search engines. These indexes, in the form of category and subject lists, often appear on the first page of a search engine. When you click on a specific highlighted word, you will be presented with a new screen containing subcategories of the topic you chose.

Evaluating the Reliability of Internet Resources

Just as you would evaluate the quality, bias, and validity of any other research material you locate, check the source of information you find online. Compare these two sites containing information about the poet and writer Langston Hughes:

Site A is a personal Web site constructed by a college student. It contains no bibliographic information or links to sites that he used. Included on the site are several poems by Langston Hughes and a student essay about the poet's use of symbolism. It has not been updated in more than six months.

Site B is a Web site constructed and maintained by the English Department of a major university. Information on Hughes is presented in a scholarly format, with a bibliography and credits for the writer. The site includes links to other sites and indicates new features that are added weekly.

For your own research, consider the information you find on Site B to be more reliable and accurate than that on Site A. Because it is maintained by experts in their field who are held accountable for their work, the university site will be a better research tool than the student-generated one.

Tips for Evaluating Internet Sources

1. Consider who constructed and who now maintains the Web page. Determine whether this author is a reputable source. Often, the URL endings indicate a source.
   - Sites ending in *.edu* are maintained by educational institutions.
   - Sites ending in *.gov* are maintained by government agencies (federal, state, or local).
   - Sites ending in *.org* are normally maintained by nonprofit organizations and agencies.
   - Sites ending in *.com* are commercially or personally maintained.
2. Skim the official and trademarked Web pages first. It is safe to assume that the information you draw from Web pages of reputable institutions, online encyclopedias, online versions of major daily newspapers, or government-owned sites produce information as reliable as the material you would find in print. In contrast, unbranded sites or those generated by individuals tend to borrow information from other sources without providing documentation. As information travels from one source to another, it could have been muddled, misinterpreted, edited, or revised.
3. You can still find valuable information in the less "official" sites. Check for the writer's credentials, and then consider these factors:
   - Do not be misled by official-looking graphics or presentations.
   - Make sure that the information is updated enough to suit your needs. Many Web pages will indicate how recently they have been updated.
   - If the information is borrowed, notice whether you can trace it back to its original source.

Respecting Copyrighted Material

Because the Internet is a relatively new and quickly growing medium, issues of copyright and ownership arise almost daily. As laws begin to govern the use and reuse of material posted online, they may change the way that people can access or reprint material.

Text, photographs, music, and fine art printed online may not be reproduced without acknowledged permission of the copyright owner.

Writing Criticism

Literary criticism involves studying, analyzing, interpreting, and evaluating works of literature. It can be as brief as an answer to a question or as lengthy as an essay or a book. Following are examples of three types of criticism.

Analysis

You are frequently asked to analyze, or break down into parts and examine, a passage or a work. Often you must support your analysis with specific references to the text. In this brief analysis, the writer uses words from the question to write a topic sentence and embeds quotations from the text as support.

Question In "Heat" by H.D., how does the speaker create the impression that heat is almost a solid substance?

Answer The speaker in "Heat" uses repetition and imagery to convey the impression that heat is almost a solid substance. By repeating the word *heat* in each of the three stanzas, the speaker emphasizes its physical presence. Further, the speaker uses images that appeal to the sense of touch in describing heat as if it were a substance. In the first stanza, the speaker asks the wind to "cut apart the heat," and in the third stanza, to "plow through it."

Biographical Criticism Critics who take a biographical approach use information about a writer's life to explain his or her work. In this passage of biographical criticism, Kenneth Silverman explains Edgar Allan Poe's preoccupation with death as Poe's response to the early death of his mother, Eliza.

"Much of his later writing, despite its variety of forms and styles, places and characters, is driven by the question of whether the dead remain dead. . . . The most persuasive and coherent explanation, . . . comes from the modern understanding of childhood bereavement. . . . [C]hildren who lose a parent at an early age, as Edgar lost Eliza Poe, . . . invest more feeling in and magnify the parent's image. . . . The young child . . . cannot comprehend the finality of death. . . ."

Historical Criticism Using this approach, a critic explains how an author's work responds to the events, circumstances, or ideas of the author's historical era. In the following passage of historical criticism, Jean H. Hagstrum shows how William Blake's character Urizen symbolizes the Enlightenment ideas of Newton, Locke, and Bacon that Blake detested.

"Urizen is also an active force. Dividing, partitioning, dropping the plummet line, applying Newton's compasses to the world, he creates abstract mathematical forms. Like Locke, he shrinks the senses, narrows the perceptions, binds man to natural fact. Like Bacon, he creates the laws of prudence and crucifies passion."

Using Ideas From Research

Below are three common methods of incorporating the ideas of other writers into your work. Choose the most appropriate style by analyzing your needs in each case. In all cases, you must credit your source.

- **Direct Quotation:** Use quotation marks to indicate the exact words.
- **Paraphrase:** To share ideas without a direct quotation, state the ideas in your own words.
- **Summary:** To provide information about a large body of work, identify the writer's main idea.

Avoiding Plagiarism

Whether you are presenting a formal research paper or an opinion paper on a current event, be careful to give credit for any ideas or opinions that are not your own. Presenting someone else's ideas, research, or opinion as your own—even if you have rephrased it in different words—is plagiarism, the equivalent of academic stealing, or fraud.

You can avoid plagiarism by synthesizing what you learn: Read from several sources, and let the ideas of experts help you draw your own conclusions and form your own opinions. When you choose to use someone else's ideas or work to support your view, credit the source of the material.

Preparing a Manuscript

The presentation of your written work is important. Your work should be neat, clean, and easy to read. Follow your teacher's directions for placing your name and class, along with the title and date of your work, on the paper.

Research Papers

Most formal research papers have these features:

- Title Page
- Table of Contents or Outline
- Works-Cited List or Bibliography

Citing Sources

In research writing, cite your sources. In the body of your paper, provide a footnote, an endnote, or an internal citation, identifying the sources of facts, opinions, or quotations. At the end of your paper, provide a bibliography or a works-cited list, a list of all the sources you cite. Follow an established format, such as Modern Library Association (MLA) Style.

Works-Cited List (MLA Style)

A works-cited list must contain accurate information sufficient to enable a reader to locate each source you cite. The basic components of an entry are as follows:

- Name of the author, editor, translator, or group responsible for the work
- Title
- Place and date of publication
- Publisher

For print materials, the information required for a citation generally appears on the copyright and title pages of a work. For the format of works-cited list entries, consult the examples at right and in the chart on page R32.

Internal Citations (MLA Style)

An internal citation briefly identifies the source from which you have taken a specific quotation, factual claim, or opinion. It refers the reader to one of the entries on your works-cited list. An internal citation has the following features:

- It appears in parentheses.
- It identifies the source by the last name of the author, editor, or translator.
- It gives a page reference, identifying the page of the source on which the information cited can be found.

Punctuation An internal citation generally falls outside a closing quotation mark but within the final punctuation of a clause or sentence. For a long quotation set off from the rest of your text, place the citation at the end of the excerpt without any punctuation following.

Special Cases

- If the author is an organization, use the organization's name, in a shortened version if necessary.
- If you cite more than one work by the same author, add the title or a shortened version of the title.

Sample Works-Cited Lists

Carwardine, Mark, Erich Hoyt, R. Ewan Fordyce, and Peter Gill. *The Nature Company Guides: Whales, Dolphins, and Porpoises.* New York: Time-Life Books, 1998.

Whales in Danger. "Discovering Whales." 18 Oct. 1999. <http://whales.magna.com.au/DISCOVER>

Neruda, Pablo. "Ode to Spring." *Odes to Opposites.* Trans. Ken Krabbenhoft. Ed. and illus. Ferris Cook. Boston: Little, Brown and Company, 1995.

The Saga of the Volsungs. Trans. Jesse L. Byock. London: Penguin Books, 1990.

An anonymous work is listed by title.

Both the title of the work and of the collection in which it is found are listed.

Sample Internal Citations

It makes sense that baleen whales such as the blue whale, the bowhead whale, the humpback whale, and the sei whale (to name just a few) grow to immense sizes (Carwardine, Hoyt, and Fordyce 19–21). The blue whale has grooves running from under its chin to partway along the length of its underbelly. As in some other whales, these grooves expand and allow even more food and water to be taken in (Ellis 18–21).

Author's last name

Page numbers where information can be found

MLA Style for Listing Sources

Book with one author	Pyles, Thomas. *The Origins and Development of the English Language*. 2nd ed. New York: Harcourt Brace Jovanovich, Inc., 1971.
Book with two or three authors	McCrum, Robert, William Cran, and Robert MacNeil. *The Story of English*. New York: Penguin Books, 1987.
Book with an editor	Truth, Sojourner. *Narrative of Sojourner Truth*. Ed. Margaret Washington. New York: Vintage Books, 1993.
Book with more than three authors or editors	Donald, Robert B., et al. *Writing Clear Essays*. Upper Saddle River, NJ: Prentice-Hall, Inc., 1996.
Single work from an anthology	Hawthorne, Nathaniel. "Young Goodman Brown." *Literature: An Introduction to Reading and Writing*. Ed. Edgar V. Roberts and Henry E. Jacobs. Upper Saddle River, NJ: Prentice-Hall, Inc., 1998. 376–385. [Indicate pages for the entire selection.]
Introduction in a published edition	Washington, Margaret. Introduction. *Narrative of Sojourner Truth*. By Sojourner Truth. New York: Vintage Books, 1993, pp. v–xi.
Signed article in a weekly magazine	Wallace, Charles. "A Vodacious Deal." *Time*, 14 Feb. 2000: 63.
Signed article in a monthly magazine	Gustaitis, Joseph. "The Sticky History of Chewing Gum." *American History*, Oct. 1998: 30–38.
Unsigned editorial or story	"Selective Silence." Editorial. *Wall Street Journal*, 11 Feb. 2000: A14. [If the editorial or story is signed, begin with the author's name.]
Signed pamphlet	[Treat the pamphlet as though it were a book.]
Pamphlet with no author, publisher, or date	*Are You at Risk of Heart Attack?* n.p. n.d. [n.p. n.d. indicates that there is no known publisher or date]
Filmstrips, slide programs, and videotape	*The Diary of Anne Frank*. Dir. George Stevens. Perf. Millie Perkins, Shelley Winters, Joseph Schildkraut, Lou Jacobi, and Richard Beymer. Twentieth Century Fox, 1959.
Radio or television program transcript	"The First Immortal Generation." *Ockham's Razor*. Host Robyn Williams. Guest Damien Broderick. National Public Radio. 23 May 1999. Transcript.
Internet	*National Association of Chewing Gum Manufacturers*. 19 Dec. 1999 <http://www.nacgm.org/consumer/funfacts.html> [Indicate the date you accessed the information. Content and addresses at Web sites change frequently.]
Newspaper	Thurow, Roger. "South Africans Who Fought for Sanctions Now Scrap for Investors." *Wall Street Journal*, 11 Feb. 2000: A1+ [For a multipage article, write only the first page number on which it appears, followed by a plus sign.]
Personal interview	Smith, Jane. Personal interview. 10 Feb. 2000.
CD (with multiple publishers)	Simms, James, ed. *Romeo and Juliet*. By William Shakespeare. CD-ROM. Oxford: Attica Cybernetics Ltd.; London: BBC Education; London: HarperCollins Publishers, 1995.
Signed article from an encyclopedia	Askeland, Donald R. (1991). "Welding." *World Book Encyclopedia*. 1991 ed.

Index of Authors and Titles

Page numbers in *italics* refer to biographical information.

Index of Skills

LITERARY ANALYSIS

READING STRATEGIES

GRAMMAR, USAGE, MECHANICS

VOCABULARY

CRITICAL THINKING AND VIEWING

WRITING

Writing Applications

Writing Strategies

LISTENING AND SPEAKING

RESEARCH AND TECHNOLOGY

Index of Features

HOW TO READ LITERATURE

LITERATURE IN CONTEXT

READING INFORMATIONAL MATERIALS

CONNECTIONS

WRITING WORKSHOPS

LISTENING AND SPEAKING WORKSHOPS

ASSESSMENT WORKSHOPS

The Business Journal Serving Greater Milwaukee "'Cows on parade' find sweet home in Chicago" by David Schuyler. "This article appeared in the Volume 17, No. 7 of *The Business Journal* Serving Greater Milwaukee on November 12, 1999. It has been reprinted by *The Business Journal* serving Greater Milwaukee and further reproduction by any other party is prohibited. Copyright © 1999 by *The Business Journal* serving greater Milwaukee, 600 W Virginia Street, Suite 500, Milwaukee, WI 53204, 414-278-7788." Used by permission.

Curtis Brown, Ltd., London "The Birds," copyright 1952 by Daphne du Maurier, from *Kiss Me Again Stranger* by Daphne du Maurier.

Jonathan Clowes Ltd., on behalf of Andrea Plunket "The Red-headed League," from *The Adventures of Sherlock Holmes* by Sir Arthur Conan Doyle. Copyright © 1996 Sir Arthur Conan Doyle Copyright Holders. Reprinted by kind permission of Jonathan Clowes Ltd., London, on behalf of Andrea Plunket, the Administrator of the Sir Arthur Conan Doyle Copyrights.

Coffee House Press "Problems With Hurricanes" by Victor Hernandez Cruz, from *Red Beans*. Copyright © 1991 by Victor Hernandez Cruz. Reprinted by permission of Coffee House Press.

Don Congdon Associates, Inc. "The Golden Kite, the Silver Wind" by Ray Bradbury. Copyright © 1953 by Epoch Associates; renewed 1981 by Ray Bradbury. Reprinted by permission of Don Congdon Associates, Inc.

Joan Daves Agency "Meciendo" by Gabriela Mistral ("Rocking"), translated by Doris Dana from *Selected Poems of Gabriela Mistral*, translated and edited by Doris Dana. Copyright © 1961, 1964, 1970, 1971 by Doris Dana. Reprinted by permission of the Joan Daves Agency on behalf of the estate of the author.

Dial Books for Young Readers, a division of Penguin From *Rosa Parks: My Story* by Rosa Parks with Jim Haskins. Copyright © 1992 by Rosa Parks. Used by permission of Dial Books for Young Readers, an imprint of Penguin Putnam Books for Young Readers, a division of Penguin, Putnam Inc.

Sandra Dijkstra Literary Agency From "Joy, Luck, and Hollywood" by Amy Tan from *Los Angeles Times*, Sunday, September 5, 1993. Copyright © 1993 Los Angeles Times.

Doubleday, a division of Random House, Inc. "The Machine That Won the War," copyright © 1961 by Mercury Press, Inc., from *Isaac Asimov: The Complete Stories, Vol. I* by Isaac Asimov. "The Birds," copyright 1952 by Daphne du Maurier, from *Kiss Me Again Stranger* by Daphne du Maurier. From *Tuesdays with Morrie* by Mitch Albom, copyright © 1997 by Mitch Albom. Used by permission of Doubleday, a division of Random House, Inc. "The Gift of the Magi" from *The Complete Works of O. Henry* by O. Henry. Published by Press Publications Company.

Martha Escutia Business Letter and Agenda for the 8th Annual Southeast College Conference by Martha Escutia. Used by permission.

Farrar, Straus & Giroux, Inc. "Georgia O'Keeffe" from *The White Album* by Joan Didion. Copyright © 1979 by Joan Didion. "The Washwoman" from *A Day of Pleasure* by Isaac Bashevis Singer. Copyright © 1969 by Isaac Bashevis Singer. Excerpts from *The Odyssey: A Stage Version* by Derek Walcott. Copyright © 1993 by Derek Walcott. From *In My Place* by Charlayne Hunter-Gault. Copyright © 1992 by Charlayne Hunter-Gault. Excerpts from the *Odyssey* by Homer, translated by R. Fitzgerald. Copyright © 1961, 1963 by Robert Fitzgerald and renewed 1989 by Benedict R. C. Fitzgerald.

Graywolf Press and Kim Stafford for the Estate of William Stafford "Fifteen," copyright 1966, 1998 by the Estate of William Stafford. Reprinted from *The Way It Is: New & Selected Poems* with the permission of Graywolf Press, Saint Paul, Minnesota, and Kim Stafford for the Estate of William Stafford.

Edith Hamilton c/o Alice R. Abbott "Perseus" by Edith Hamilton from *Mythology*. Copyright © 1940, 1942, by Edith Hamilton, renewed 1969.

Harcourt, Inc. "Women" from *Revolutionary Petunias & Other Poems*, copyright © 1972, 2000 by Alice Walker. "Macavity: The Mystery Cat" from *Old Possum's Book of Practical Cats*, copyright 1939 by T. S. Eliot and renewed 1967 by Esme Valerie Eliot. "A Lincoln Preface," copyright 1953 by Carl Sandburg and renewed 1981 by Margaret Sandburg, Janet Sandburg, and Helga Sandburg Crile. "Ithaca" from *The Complete Poems of Cavafy*, copyright © 1961 and renewed 1989 by Rae Dalven. Reprinted by permission of Harcourt, Inc.

HarperCollins Publishers, Inc. "Summer" from *Brown Angels: An Album of Pictures and Verse* by Walter Dean Myers. Copyright © 1993 by Walter Dean Myers. Used by permission of HarperCollins Publishers.

Helmut Hirnschall "There is a Longing..." from *My Heart Soars* by Chief Dan George and Helmut Hirnschall. Copyright © 1974 by Clarke Irwin. Used by permission.

Henry Holt and Company, Inc. "Talk" from *The Cow-Tail Switch and Other West African Stories* by Harold Courlander and George Herzog, © 1947, 1974 by Harold Courlander. "Fire and Ice" from *The Poetry of Robert Frost*, edited by Edward Connery Lathem. Copyright © 1951 by Robert Frost, Copyright © 1923, 1969 by Henry Holt and Company, Inc. Reprinted by permission of Henry Holt and Company, LLC. "The Road Not Taken" from *The Poetry of Robert Frost*, edited by Edward Connery Lathem. Published by Henry Holt and Company, Inc.

The Barbara Hogenson Agency, Inc. and Horton Foote *The Dancers* by Horton Foote. Copyright © 1955, 1983 by Horton Foote. Reprinted by arrangement with Horton Foote and the Barbara Hogenson Agency, Inc.

Rosemary Thurber and The Barbara Hogenson Agency, Inc. "The Secret Life of Walter Mitty" from *My World—And Welcome To It* copyright © 1942 by James Thurber; copyright renewed © 1971 by James Thurber. Reprinted by arrangement with Rosemary Thurber and the Barbara Hogenson Agency. All rights reserved.

Houghton Mifflin Company "Blackberry Eating" from *Mortal Acts, Mortal Words* by Galway Kinnell. Copyright © 1980 by Galway Kinnell. Excerpt from *Lost Moon: The Perilous Voyage of Apollo 13*. Copyright © 1994 by Jim Lovell and Jeffrey Kluger. "All Watched Over by Machines of Loving Grace" by Richard Brautigan, from *Trout Fishing in America, The Pill versus the*

Springhill Mine Disaster, and *In Watermelon Sugar.* Copyright © 1968, by Richard Brautigan. Reprinted by permission of Houghton Mifflin Co. All rights reserved. "Siren Song" from *You Are Happy* by Margaret Atwood. Copyright © 1974 by Margaret Atwood. Reprinted by permission of Houghton Mifflin Company.

Houghton Mifflin Company and Frances Collin, Literary Agent Excerpt from *Silent Spring* (pp. 1–3) by Rachel Carson. Copyright © 1962 by Rachel L. Carson, renewed 1990 by Roger Christie. Reprinted by permission of Houghton Mifflin Co. and Frances Collin, Literary Agent. All rights reserved.

James R. Hurst "The Scarlet Ibis" by James Hurst, published in *The Atlantic Monthly,* July 1960. Copyright © 1988 by James Hurst. Reprinted by permission of the author.

International Creative Management, Inc. "Single Room, Earth View" by Sally Ride, published in the April/May 1986 issue of *Air & Space/Smithsonian Magazine*, published by The Smithsonian Institution. Reprinted by permission of International Creative Management, Inc.

Japan Publications "Three Haiku" (originally titled "Temple bells die out" by Basho; and "Dragonfly catcher" and "Bearing no flowers" by Chiyojo) from *One Hundred Famous Haiku* by Daniel C. Buchanan, Copyright © 1973 by Japan Publications. Used by permission.

Lyndon B. Johnson Library From *A White House Diary* by Lady Bird Johnson. Reprinted by permission of the L.B.J. Library c/o Betty Tilson, assistant to Mrs. Lyndon B. Johnson.

Junior League of Seattle "Combing" by Gladys Cardiff from *Puget Soundings,* March 1971. Reprinted by permission of the Junior League of Seattle.

The Heirs to the Estate of Martin Luther King, Jr. c/o Writer's House "I Have a Dream" from *The Words of Martin Luther King, Jr.* Copyright 1963 by Martin Luther King, Jr., copyright renewed 1991 by Coretta Scott King.

Alfred A. Knopf, a division of Random House, Inc. "Uncle Marcos" from *The House of the Spirits* by Isabel Allende, translated by Magda Bogin, copyright © 1985 by Alfred A. Knopf, A Division of Random House, Inc. "Dream Deferred" and "Dreams" from *The Collected Poems of Langston Hughes* by Langston Hughes. Copyright © 1994 by The Estate of Langston Hughes. "To be of use" from *Circles on the Water* by Marge Piercy, copyright © 1982 by Marge Piercy. Used by permission of Alfred A. Knopf, a division of Random House, Inc.

Little, Brown and Company Publishers "Perseus" from *Mythology* by Edith Hamilton. Copyright © 1942 by Edith Hamilton; Copyright © renewed 1969 by Dorian Fielding Reid and Doris Fielding Reid. By permission of Little, Brown and Company Inc.

Liveright Publishing Company, an imprint of W. W. Norton & Company "maggie and milly and molly and may," copyright © 1956, 1984, 1991 by The Trustees for the E. E. Cummings Trust, from *Complete Poems: 1904–1962* by E. E. Cummings. Edited by George J. Firmage. Used by permission of Liveright Publishing Corporation.

Andrew MacAndrew "The Necklace" from *Boule de Suif and Selected Stories* by Guy de Maupassant, translated by Andrew MacAndrew. Translation copyright © 1964 by Andrew MacAndrew. Reprinted by permission of Marie-Christine MacAndrew.

Macmillan, a division of Simon & Schuster, Inc. "Jabberwocky" from *The Collected Verse of Lewis Carroll* (New York: Macmillan, 1933). "There Will Come Soft Rains" by Sara Teasdale. Reprinted from *The Collected Poems of Sara Teasdale*. Published by Macmillan, a division of Simon & Schuster, Inc.

Scott Meredith Literary Agency LP "If I Forget Thee, Oh Earth..." from *Expedition to Earth* by Arthur C. Clarke. Copyright © 1953, 1970 by Arthur C. Clarke; Copyright 1951 by Columbia Publications, Inc.

Methuen Publishing, Ltd. "The Inspector-General" from *The Sneeze: Plays and Stories* by Anton Chekhov, translated and adapted by Michael Frayn, published by Methuen Drama. Originally from *An Awl in a Sack* by Anton Chekhov, 1885. Random House, UK, Ltd. Used by permission of Methuen Publishing, Limited.

Milkweed Editions "Eulogy for a Hermit Crab" by Pattiann Rogers from *Song of the World Becoming: New and Collected Poems 1981–2001* (Minneapolis: Milkweed Editions, 2001). Copyright © 1994, 2001 by Pattiann Rogers. Reprinted with permission from Milkweed Editions.

Edna St. Vincent Millay Society "An Ancient Gesture" by Edna St. Vincent Millay. From *Collected Poems*, HarperCollins. Copyright © 1954, 1982 by Norma Millay Ellis. All rights reserved. Reprinted by permission of Elizabeth Barnett, literary executor.

National Audubon Society web page from www.audubon.org.

National Public Radio "Earhart Redux" by Alex Chadwick. Copyright © National Public Radio 1997. The news report by NPR's Alex Chadwick was originally broadcast on National Public Radio's and National Geographic Society's "Radio Expeditions" on March 17, 1997, and is used with the permission of National Public Radio, Inc. and the National Geographic Society. Any unauthorized duplication is strictly prohibited.

New American Library, a division of Penguin Putnam, Inc. From *The Tragedy of Romeo and Juliet* by William Shakespeare, edited by J. A. Bryant, Jr. Published by New American Library, a division of Penguin Putnam, Inc.

North Point Press, a division of Farrar Straus & Giroux, Inc. "Gifts" by Shu Ting from *A Splintered Mirror: Chinese Poetry from the Democracy Movement*, translated by Donald Finkel. Translation copyright © 1991 by Donald Finkel.

W. W. Norton & Company, Inc. From *The Perfect Storm* by Sebastian Junger. Copyright © 1997 by Sebastian Junger. Used by permission of W.W. Norton and Company, Inc.

Orchard Books, an imprint of Scholastic, Inc. "Checkouts" from *A Couple of Kooks and Other Stories About Love* by Cynthia Rylant. Copyright © 1990 by Cynthia Rylant. Reprinted by permission.

Oxford University Press, Inc. and Faber and Faber Limited "The Horses" from *Collected Poems* by Edwin Muir, copyright © 1960 by Willa Muir. Used by permission of Oxford University Press, Inc.

Oxford University Press, Canada "Siren Song" by Margaret Atwood from *Selected Poems 1966–1984*. Copyright © Margaret

Atwood 1990. Reprinted by permission of Oxford University Press, Canada.

G.P. Putnam's Sons, a division of Penguin Putnam, Inc. "Rules of the Game" from *The Joy Luck Club* by Amy Tan, copyright © 1989 by Amy Tan. Used by permission of G.P. Putnam's Sons, a division of Penguin Putnam, Inc.

Quarterly Review of Literature "Astonishment" by Wislawa Szymborska, translated by Grazyna Drabik, Austin Flint, and Sharon Olds. Copyright *Quarterly Review of Literature Poetry Series*, Volume XXIII, edited by T. and R. Weiss. Used by permission.

Random House, Inc. "Caged Bird," copyright © 1983 by Maya Angelou, from *Shaker, Why Don't You Sing?* by Maya Angelou. "New Directions" from *Wouldn't Take Nothin for My Journey Now* by Maya Angelou, copyright © 1993 by Maya Angelou. "Blues Ain't No Mockin Bird" by Toni Cade Bambara, copyright © 1971 by Toni Cade Bambara, from *Gorilla, My Love* by Toni Cade Bambara. "The Rug Merchant" from *The World Is My Home: A Memoir* by James Michener, copyright © 1992 by James Michener. Used by permission of Random House, Inc.

Marian Reiner, Literary Agent for Lillian Morrison "The Spear-thrower" from *The Sidewalk Racer and Other Poems of Sports and Motion* by Lillian Morrison. Copyright 1965, 1967, 1968, 1977 by Lillian Morrison. © Renewed Lillian Morrison. Reprinted by permission of Marian Reiner for the author.

The Society of Authors "The Listeners" from *The Complete Poems of Walter de la Mare* by Walter de la Mare. Used by permission of the Literary Trustees of Walter de la Mare and the Society of Authors as their representative.

Sterling Lord Literistic, Inc. "Children in the Woods" from *Crossing Open Grounds* by Barry Lopez. Copyright © 1988 by Barry Holstun Lopez. Reprinted by permission of Sterling Lord Literistic, Inc.

Texas Instruments From *TI-82 Graphing Calculator Guidebook*. "Graphing Calculator and Warranty" by Texas Instruments. Copyright © 1993 by Texas Instruments, Incorporated. Used by kind permission of Texas Instruments.

University Press of New England Gary Soto, "The Talk" from *A Summer Life*. © 1990 by University Press of New England. Used by permission.

Viking Penguin, A division of Penguin Putnam, Inc. "Go Deep to the Sewer" from *Childhood* by Bill Cosby. Copyright © 1991 by William H. Cosby, Jr. Used by permission of Viking Penguin, a division of Penguin Putnam, Inc. From *The Road Ahead* by Bill Gates. Copyright © 1995 by William H. Gates III. "Old Man of the Temple" from *Under the Banyan Tree* by R. K. Narayan, copyright © 1985 by R. K. Narayan. Used by permission of Viking Penguin, a division of Penguin Putnam, Inc. "The Interlopers" from *The Complete Short Stories of Saki* by Saki (H.H. Munro). Published by The Viking Press.

Watkins/Loomis Agency "An Entomological Study of Apartment 4A" by Patricia Volk, from *The New York Times Magazine*, March 5, 1995. Reprinted by permission of Patricia Volk and the Watkins/Loomis Agency.

The Wylie Agency, Inc. "The Man to Send Rain Clouds" from *Storyteller* by Leslie Marmon Silko. Copyright © 1981 by Leslie Marmon Silko, reprinted by permission of The Wylie Agency, Inc.

Note: Every effort has been made to locate the copyright owner of material reprinted in this book. Omissions brought to our attention will be corrected in subsequent printings.

Art Credits

Cover and Title Page *The Fog Warning,* 1885, oil on canvas, 30 1/4 x 48 1/2", Winslow Homer, Courtesy, Museum of Fine Arts, Boston. Reproduced with permission. ©2000 Museum of Fine Arts, Boston. All Rights Reserved. Otis Norcross Fund, 94.72; **xxv** ©The Stock Market/John Henley; **vii** Corel Professional Photos CD-ROM™; **viii** *Peculiarsome Abe,* N.C. Wyeth, Children's Special Collections, The Free Library of Philadelphia; **ix** Corel Professional Photos CD-ROM™; **x** Murray Wilson/Omni-Photo Communications, Inc.; **xi** Corel Professional Photos CD-ROM™; **xii** ©Alon Reininger/Contact Press/The Stock Market; **xiii** *The Oldest Inhabitant,* 1876, Julian Alden Weir, oil on canvas, 65 1/2 x 32" Signed, upper left. Butler Institute of American Art, Youngstown, Ohio; **xiv** Culver Pictures, Inc.; **xv** White/Pite/International Stock Photography, Ltd.; **xvi** ©Wolfgang Kaehler/CORBIS; **xvii** ©Araldo de Luca/CORBIS; **xviii** *Keying Up—The Court Jester* (detail), 1875, William Merritt Chase, Courtesy of the Pennsylvania Academy of the Fine Arts, Philadelphia, Gift of the Chapellier Galleries; **xx** ©The Stock Market/Pete Saloutos; **xxi** *The Quiltmakers,* Paul Goodnight, 22 11/16" x 24", Color Circle Art Publishing Inc.; **xi** Corel Professional Photos CD-ROM™; **xvi–xvii** Hulton Getty/Liaison Agency; **1** *The Storm,* 1893, Edvard Munch, Oil on canvas, 36 1/8 x 51 1/2" (91.8 x 130.8cm). The Museum of Modern Art, New York, Gift of Mr. and Mrs. H. Irgens Larsen and acquired through the Lillie P. Bliss and Abby Aldrich Rockefeller Funds. ©1997 The Museum of Modern Art, New York; **2** (t) *Baseball Players Practicing,* 1875, Thomas Eakins, Museum of Art, Rhode Island School of Design, Jesse Metcalf Fund and Walter H. Kimball Fund, (b) CORBIS; **4** ©Photo Researchers, Inc.; **6** *Keying Up—The Court Jester* (detail), 1875, William Merritt Chase, Courtesy of the Pennsylvania Academy of the Fine Arts, Philadelphia, Gift of the Chapellier Galleries; **9** ©Photo Researchers, Inc.; **11** SuperStock; **12** CORBIS-Bettmann; **16** Dr. E.R. Degginger; **18–19** *Peering Through the Jungle,* Larry Noble, Sal Barracca & Associates; **21** *Hat, Knife, and Gun in Woods,* David Mann, Sal Barracca & Associates; **22** Corel Professional Photos CD-ROM™; **26** Sovfoto/Eastfoto; **28** Grace Davies/Omni-Photo Communications, Inc.; **30** CORBIS; **31** Ann Shamel/Graphicstock; **33** CORBIS; **34** ©The Stock Market/John Dominis; **36** NYT Pictures; **40** *Baseball Players Practicing,* 1875, Thomas Eakins, Museum of Art, Rhode Island School of Design, Jesse Metcalf Fund and Walter H. Kimball Fund; **42** *Baseball Players Practicing,*1875, Thomas Eakins, Museum of Art, Rhode Island School of Design, Jesse Metcalf Fund and Walter H. Kimball Fund; **48** ©The Stock Market/Zefa Germany; **50** *Attack of the Birds,* 1994, Lev Tabenkin, Oil on canvas, 59" x 78", Maya Polsky Gallery; **52–53** Corel Professional Photos CD-ROM™; **56–57** *Landscape from a Dream,* 1936–38, Paul Nash, Tate Gallery, London/Art Resource, NY; **58** Art Hudson/American Red Cross; **60–61** Corel Professional Photos CD-ROM™; **65** ©The Stock Market/Zefa Germany; **68–69** *Wheatfield with Crows,* 1890, Vincent van Gogh, Van Gogh Museum, Amsterdam, The Netherlands, Art Resource, NY; **72–73** Corel Professional Photos CD-ROM™; **76** *Over and Above #13,* 1964, Clarence Holbrook Carter, oil on canvas, Courtesy of the Artist; **80–81** Corel Professional Photos CD-ROM™; **82** AP/Wide World Photos; **86** © Stone; **88** © John Darling/Stone; **89** Sonia Moskowitz/Globe Photos, Inc.; **91** Photofest; **94** Tony Cordoza/Liaison Agency; **96** The Granger Collection, New York; **99** © Simon Jauncey/Stone; **100–106** The Granger Collection, New York; **109** Historical Picture Archive/CORBIS; **110, 114** The Granger Collection, New York; **116** *Sir Arthur Conan Doyle* (detail), H. L. Gates, The National Portrait Gallery, London; **120** *Drawing Hands,* 1948, 1995 M.C. Escher/Cordon Art - Baarn - Holland. All rights reserved.; **122** *Het Blinde Huis,* William Degouve de Nunques, State Museum, Kröller-Müller, Otterlo, The Netherlands; **123** ©Faber & Faber Ltd; **132** Jeffery Newbury/Discover Magazine; **136** Courtesy of the author; **140** ©Tony Freeman/PhotoEdit; **146–147** *Human Achievement,* Tsing-Fang Chen, Lucia Gallery, New York City/SuperStock; **148** (b.l.) CORBIS; **148** (t) *Night Games,* Ernie Barnes, Oil on canvas, 48 x 24, Courtesy of The Company of Art, Los Angeles; **148** (b.r.) *Perseus and Andromeda* (detail), ca.1580, Paolo Veronese, Musee des Beaux-Arts, Rennes, France, Erich Lessing/Art Resource, NY; **150, 152–153** *Lincoln Proclaiming Thanksgiving,* Dean Cornwell, The Lincoln Museum, Fort Wayne, Indiana, (#1153); **154** *Peculiarsome Abe,* N.C. Wyeth, Children's Special Collections, The Free Library of Philadelphia; **156** Courtesy of the Library of Congress; **158** *Carl Sandburg,* Miriam Svet, The National Portrait Gallery, Smithsonian Institution, Washington, D.C./Art Resource, New York; **162** AP/Wide World Photos; **164** CORBIS; **166** AP/Wide World Photos; **167** Neal Preston/CORBIS; **168** *The Beginning,* Artis Lane, Courtesy of the artist; **169** AP/Wide World Photos; **170–171** *We the People,* Kathy Morrow, Original scratchboard painting with hand-loomed beadwork, Courtesy of the artist; **171** Alan Markfield/Globe Photos; **172** The Granger Collection, New York; **176** Rectangular box, detail, Woven bamboo and painted lacquer, Late Ming Dynasty, early 17th century, H. 12.1 cm x W. 34.3 cm x L. 48.3 cm, H. 4 3/4" x W. 13 1/2" x L. 19", China, Avery Brundage Collection, #B60 M427, Asian Art Museum of San Francisco; **178** *The Nymph of the Lo River,* section of a handscroll. (H.9 1/2") Attributed to Ku K'ai-chih, Courtesy of the Freer Gallery of Art, Smithsonian Institution, Washington, D.C. #14.53; **182** Thomas Victor; **186** ©The Stock Market/Alan Goldsmith; **188** ©The Stock Market/Alan Goldsmith; **189** Dimitri Kessel/Life Magazine; **190** AP/Wide World Photos; **192** Henry McGee/Globe Photos; **200** Charles Weckler/The Image Bank; **202–203** Charles Weckler/The Image Bank; **205** Historical Picture Archive/CORBIS; **207** Indian, Mughal, Leaf from a royal manuscript of the Shah-Jehan Nameh: A procession in a palace courtyard, gouache on paper, mid 17th century, 28.9 x19.7 cm. Kate S. Buckingham Endowment Fund, 1975.555. Photograph © 1996, The Art Institute of Chicago. All Rights Reserved.; **208** AP/Wide World Photos; **212** *Danae with young Perseus arriving on the island of Seripo,* Museo Archeologico, Ferrara, Italy. Scala/Art Resource, NY; **214** *Andromeda Liberated,* Pierre Mignard, Louvre, Paris, France, Erich Lessing/Art Resource, NY; **217** *Danae with young Perseus arriving on the island of Seripo,* Museo Archeologico, Ferrara, Italy. Scala/Art Resource, NY; **218** Terre del Greco Ascione Collections/Superstock; **221** *Perseus and Andromeda* (detail), ca.1580, Paolo Veronese, Musée des Beaux-Arts, Rennes, France, Erich Lessing/Art Resource, NY; **222** UPI/CORBIS–Bettmann; **226** © David Madison/Stone; **228** *Night Games,* Ernie Barnes, Oil on canvas, 48 x 24, Courtesy of The Company of Art, Los Angeles; **229** Photo by Mandy Sayer; **230** ©Allsport/Tony Duffy; **231** Photo by Isidro Rodriquez; **232** Photo by Michael Nye; **236** Corel Professional Photos CD-ROM™; **242–243** *Waiting Girl,* 1978, Yan Hsia, Asian American Arts Center; **244** (b) Corel Professional Photos CD-ROM™; **246** ©Jack Hollingsworth/Index Stock Imagery/PictureQuest; **248** ©The Stock Market/Mark Gamba; **249** Corel Professional Photos CD-ROM™; **251** ©The Stock Market/Mark Gamba; **252** Thomas Victor; **260** CORBIS; **262–267** Digital Imagery ©Copyright 2001 PhotoDisc, Inc.; **268** *Chess Mates,* 1992, Pamela Chin Lee, Courtesy of the artist, Photo by John Lei/Omni-Photo Communications, Inc.; **269, 271** Digital Imagery ©Copyright 2001 Photo-Disc, Inc.; **272** Robert Foothorap; **276** Photofest; **278** ©Robert Foothorap/Black Star Publishing/PictureQuest; **280, 282**

Food City, 1967, Richard Estes, Oil acrylic and graphite on fiberboard, 48" x 68", Collection of the Akron Art Museum, Akron, Ohio, Museum Acquisition Fund, Photo by Richman Haire, ©Richard Estes/Licensed by VAGA, New York, NY/Courtesy Marlborough Gallery, NY; **286** Kit Stafford; **290** Horrillo Iriola/A.G.E. FotoStock; **292** The Granger Collection, New York; **293** Horrillo Iriola/A.G.E. FotoStock; **294** Henry McGee/Globe Photos; **295** (t) *Bubbles,* watercolor, 39" x 29", Courtesy of Scott Burdick, (b) The Granger Collection, New York; **296** UPI/CORBIS-Bettmann; **298** AP/Wide World Photos; **302** David De Lossy/The Image Bank; **304** R. Ashenbrenner/Stock Boston; **306** David De Lossy/The Image Bank; **308–309** Kenneth Redding/The Image Bank; **310** The Granger Collection, New York; **314** Tina Buckman/Index Stock Photography, Inc.; **316** Patrick Ward/Stock Boston; **318** Tina Buckman/Index Stock Photography, Inc.; **319** Digital Imagery ©Copyright 2001 PhotoDisc, Inc.; **320** Adam Scull/Globe Photos; **324** *The Quiltmakers,* Paul Goodnight, 22 11/16" x 24", Color Circle Art Publishing Inc.; **326** Digital Imagery ©Copyright 2001 PhotoDisc, Inc.; **327** (t) *The Quiltmakers,* Paul Goodnight, 22 11/16" x 24" Color Circle Art Publishing Inc., (b) Thomas Victor; **328** (t), (m), (b) Corel Professional Photos CD-ROM™; **329** *E. E. Cummings* (detail), 1958, Self-Portrait, The National Portrait Gallery, Smithsonian Institution, Washington, D.C./Art Resource, New York; **330** AP/Wide World Photos; **334** Laima Druskis/Pearson Education; **340–341** *Scientist's Hobby: Failure #18 of the Anti-Gravity Pack,* 1992, Bruce Widdows, acrylic on canvas, 84 x 132 inches, Courtesy of George Adams Gallery, New York; **342** (t) *The Jabberwock,* 1873, John Tenniel, The Granger Collection, New York, (b), ©Danny Brass/Photo Researchers, Inc.; **344** *Portrait XIV,* Private Collection/Donald C. Martin/SuperStock; **346** *The Man With Three Masks,* John Rush, Courtesy of the artist; **351** *New Orleans Fantasy* (detail), 1985, Max Papart, Lithograph, Courtesy of Nahan Galleries, New York; **352** CORBIS-Bettmann; **356, 358** *Valmondois Sous La Neige,* Maurice de Vlaminck, Superstock; **361** *White Night,* 1901, Edvard Munch, oil on canvas, 45 1/2 x 43 1/2 in. (115.5 x 111 cm) Photo: J. Lathion ©Nasjonalgalleriet 1997; **362** CORBIS-Bettmann; **366** Chromosohm/Sohm/Stock Boston; **369** *Young Brothers in the Hood,* 17x22, Tom McKinney, Courtesy of the artist; **370** Henry Horenstein/StockBoston; **372** Globe Photos; **374** Chromosohm/Sohm/Stock Boston; **376** Courtesy of the author; **380** Michael Newman/PhotoEdit; **382** ©David Muench/CORBIS; **383** Dianne Trejo; **384** © Anthony Banniste; Gallo Images/CORBIS; **386** (t) ©Stephen Dalton/Photo Researchers, Inc., (b) ©Sturgis McKeever/Photo Researchers, Inc.; **387** ©Pat Lynch/Photo Researchers, Inc.; **388** ©R.J. Erwin/Photo Researchers, Inc.; **389** ©Louis Quitt/Photo Researchers, Inc.; **390** (t) ©John M. Burnley/Photo Researchers, Inc., (b) Photo by Larry Sillen; **395** "Hey Diddle, Diddle" by WIlliam McBride and Michael Stack, Courtesy of McBride & Kelley Architects; **398** © Churchill Kheler/Stone; **400** *The Jabberwock,* 1873, John Tenniel, The Granger Collection, New York; **401** Gernsheim Collection, Harry Ransom Humanities Research Center, The University of Texas at Austin; **402** From *Old Possum's Book of Practical Cats,* Copyright 1939 by T. S. Eliot: renewed 1967 by Esme Valerie Eliot, Reproduced by permission of Harcourt Brace Jovanovich, Inc., Illustration by Edward Gorey; **404** *T. S. Eliot* (detail), 1888–1965, Sir Gerald Kelly, National Portrait Gallery, Smithsonian Institution, Art Resource, New York; **405** (l) Corel Professional Photos CD-ROM™, (r) Corel Professional Photos CD-ROM™; **406** (t.l.), (t.r) Corel Professional Photos CD-ROM™, (b) Photo by William Lewis; **414** © 1966 by Michael Courlander; **418** ©R. Gates/Archive Photos; **420** Murray Wilson/Omni-Photo Communications, Inc.; **423** UPI/CORBIS-Bettmann; **425** ©R. Gates/Archive Photos; **426** Eugene Gordon/Pearson Education/PH College; **429** Murray Wilson/Omni-Photo Communications, Inc.; **430** AP/Wide World Photos; **434** Tony Freeman/PhotoEdit; **440** Michael Agliolo/International Stock Photography, Ltd.; **442** (r) Index Stock Photography, Inc., (l) Gideon Mendel/Magnum Photos, Inc.; **444** Digital Imagery ©Copyright 2001 PhotoDisc, Inc.; **446** Sanford/Agliolo/International Stock Photography, Ltd.; **448** Index Stock Photography, Inc.; **450** Andrea Renault/Globe Photos; **454** NASA; **456–457** Corel Professional Photos CD-ROM™; **458** Corel Professional Photos CD-ROM™; **461** NASA; **462** Thomas Victor; **466** Digital Imagery ©Copyright 2001 PhotoDisc, Inc.; **466** (inset) Corel Professional Photos CD-ROM™; **469** Prentice Hall; **470** © Eastcott/Momatiuk/Stone; **472** Dimitri Kessel/Life Magazine, (l) (r) Corel Professional Photos CD-ROM™; **473** (t) Corel Professional Photos CD-ROM™, (b) CORBIS-Bettmann; **474** Corel Professional Photos CD-ROM™; **475** Mark Gerson Photography; **476** © Vernon Merritt/Time Inc.; **484** ©Alan L. Detrick/Photo Researchers, Inc.; **486–487** NASA; **490** UPI/CORBIS-Bettmann; **491** Corel Professional Photos CD-ROM™; **492–493** Frank Whitney/The Image Bank; **494** UPI/CORBIS-Bettmann; **495** ML Sinibaldi/©The Stock Market; **496** Digital Imagery ©Copyright 2001 PhotoDisc, Inc.; **497** Ryan Williams/International Stock Photography, Ltd.; **498** Photo by Judy Walgreen; **502** Gideon Mendel/Magnum Photos, Inc.; **504** Corel Professional Photos CD-ROM™; **505** Dorothy Alexander; **506** Gideon Mendel/Magnum Photos, Inc.; **508** AP/Wide World Photos; **512** © Myrleen Cate/Stone; **518–519** *Reading,* 1973, oil on masonite, Billy Morrow Jackson, Wichita Art Museum, purchased with funds donated by Mr. and Mrs. Donald C. Slawson; **520** ©Hulton Getty/Archive Photos; **522** *Wishful Thinking,* Peter Szumowski, Private Collection/Bridgeman Art Library, London/New York; **524** Jeff Spielman/The Image Bank; **527** Corel Professional Photos CD-ROM™; **528** *Hairdresser's Window,* 1907, John Sloan, oil on canvas, 1947.240, Wadsworth Atheneum, Hartford. The Ella Gallup Sumner and Mary Catlin Sumner Collection Fund; **529** Carved Tortoiseshell Comb, mid 19th century, England or France, Cooper-Hewitt National Design Museum, Smithsonian Institution/Art Resource, NY, Bequest of Mrs. John Innes Kane, 1926-22-545, photo by Richard Goodbody; **530** CORBIS-Bettmann; **534** Amazon.Com Books, Inc.; **536** CORBIS; **538** Carl Purcell/Photo Researchers, Inc.; **540–541** ©The Stock Market/ZEFA; **544–545** ©Alon Reininger/Contact Press/The Stock Market; **552** John Kaprielian/Photo Researchers, Inc.; **556** *Two Boys in a Punt,* N. C. Wyeth, Courtesy of Dr. and Mrs. William A. Morton, Jr., Photograph from Brandywine River Museum; **562–563** *Scarlet Ibis,* John James Audubon, ©Collection of The New-York Historical Society; **568** CORBIS-Bettmann; **571** *Sharecropper,* Elizabeth Catlett, Courtesy The Estate of Thurlow E. Tibbs, Jr., ©Elizabeth Catlett/Licensed by VAGA, New York, NY; **574** Digital Imagery ©Copyright 2001 PhotoDisc, Inc.; **576** Nikky Finney; **578, 582** CORBIS-Bettmann; **584** Inge Morath/Magnum Photos; **588** *Feast Day,* San Juan Pueblo, 1921, William Penhallow Henderson, National Museum of American Art, Smithsonian Institution; Given in Memory of Joshua C. Taylor/Art Resource, New York; **590–591** Corel Professional Photos CD-ROM™; **593** *Feast Day,* San Juan Pueblo, 1921, William Penhallow Henderson, National Museum of American Art, Smithsonian Institution; Given in Memory of Joshua C. Taylor/Art Resource, New York; **595** Thomas Victor; **596** ©Hulton Getty/Archive Photos; **598** *Sacramento Railroad Station,* 1874, William Hahn, Fine Arts Museum of San Francisco; **601** The Granger Collection, New York; **602** *Samuel Langhorne Clemens (Mark Twain)* (detail), 1935, Frank Edwin Larson, National Portrait Gallery, Smithsonian Institution, Washington, D.C./Art Resource, New York; **606** *Campesino,* 1976, Oil on canvas, 50 1/2 x 59 1/2 inches, Daniel DeSiga, Wight Art Gallery, University of California, Los Angeles, Collection of Alfredo Aragon, Photo by Grey Crawford; **608** Christie's Images; **612** *The New Necklace,* 1910, William McGregor Paxton, Courtesy, Museum of Fine Arts, Boston. Reproduced with permission. Zoe Oliver Sherman Collection, 22.644 ©2000 Museum of Fine Arts, Boston. All Rights Reserved.; **615** CORBIS-Bettmann; **616** *Campesino,* 1976, Oil on canvas, 50 1/2 x 59 1/2 inches, Daniel DeSiga, Wight Art Gallery, University of California, Los Angeles, Collection of Alfredo Aragon, Photo by Grey Crawford; **618** *Farmworker de Califas,* Tony Ortega, Monotype, Courtesy of the artist; **620** Arte Público Press; **624** Tony Freeman/PhotoEdit; **630–631** David Young-Wolfe/PhotoEdit; **632** (r) Monica Almeida/NYT Permissions, (l) UPI/CORBIS-Bettmann; **634, 636, 639, 640** NASA; **645** AP/Wide World Photos; **648** *Don Nemesio,* 1977, Esperanza Martinez, Courtesy of the artist; **650** Lee Snider/CORBIS; **652** *The Oldest Inhabitant,* 1876, Julian Alden Weir, oil on canvas, 65 1/2 x 32" Signed, upper left. Butler Institute of American Art, Youngstown, Ohio; **655** Thomas Victor; **657** Enrico Ferorelli; **658–659** Robert Frerck/Woodfin Camp & Associates; **661** CORBIS-Bettmann; **663** *Don Nemesio,* 1977, Esperanza Martinez, Courtesy of the artist; **665** *El Leñador,* 1934, Tom Lea, oil on canvas, 36 x 30, Collection of the Museum of New Mexico, Museum of Fine Arts, Gift of P.E.R.A.; **668** Prentice Hall; **672** *The White Trumpet Flower,* 1932, Georgia O'Keeffe, San Diego Museum of Art, Gift of Inez Grant Parker in memory of Earle W. Grant, ©1998 The Georgia O'Keeffe Foundation/Artists Rights Society (ARS), New York; **674** CORBIS-Bettmann; **676, 677, 678** UPI/CORBIS-Bettmann; **679** ©Archive Photos; **680–681** ©White House Collection, Courtesy White House Historical Association; **682** ©Allsport/Hulton Deutsch; **684** Thomas Victor; **685** *The White Trumpet Flower,* 1932, Georgia O'Keeffe, San Diego Museum of Art, Gift of Inez Grant Parker in memory of Earle W. Grant, ©1998 The Georgia O'Keeffe Foundation/Artists Rights Society (ARS), New York; **687** *Cow's Skull: Red, White and Blue,* 1931, Georgia O'Keeffe, The Metropolitan Museum of Art, The Alfred Stieglitz Collection, 1949, Copyright © 1984 by The Metropolitan Museum of Art, Photograph by Malcolm Varon, ©1998 The Georgia O'Keeffe Foundation/Artists Rights Society (ARS), New York; **688** *The Lawrence Tree,* 1929, Georgia O'Keeffe, Wadsworth Atheneum, Hartford, The Ella Gallup Sumner and Mary Catlin Sumner Collection, ©1998 The Georgia O'Keeffe Foundation/Artists Rights Society (ARS), New York; **690** Thomas Victor; **694** *Understanding Comics* by Scott McCloud, a 215-page analysis of comics in comics form © and ™ 1994 Scott McCloud; **697–704** (t) Pages 2–9 from *Understanding Comics* by Scott McCloud, a 215-page analysis of comics in comics form. © and ™ 1994 Scott McCloud; **704** (b) Scott McCloud; **708** Monica Almeida/NYT Permissions; **710** P. DaSilva/Sygma; **712** CORBIS; **713** San Diego Aerospace Museum; **714** Photo by Max Hirshfeld; **716** Monica Almeida/NYT Permissions; **718** The Sporting News; **722** David Young-Wolff/Tony Stone Images; **728–729** *The Sheridan Theatre,* 1937, Edward Hopper, Collection of the Newark Museum, 1940, Felix Fuld Bequest Fund/Art Resource, NY; **730** (l) Culver Pictures, Inc., (r) Digital Imagery ©Copyright 2001 PhotoDisc, Inc.; **732** ©1996 Robert Brooks/FPG International Corp.; **734–735** Digital Imagery ©Copyright 2001 PhotoDisc, Inc.; **736** Footprints provided by The Arthur Murray Dance Studios; **738** FPG International Corp.; **740** Footprints provided by The Arthur Murray Dance Studios; **743** FPG International Corp.; **745** Footprints provided by The Arthur Murray Dance Studios; **747** FPG International Corp.; **749** Bettmann Archive/CORBIS; **750** FPG International Corp.; **753** Footprints provided by The Arthur Murray Dance Studio; **755** ©1996 Robert Brooks/FPG International Corp.; **757** Footprints provided by The Arthur Murray Dance Studios; **758** Digital Imagery ©Copyright 2001 PhotoDisc, Inc.; **759** ©1996 Robert Brooks/FPG International Corp.; **760** Photo by Eric H. Antoniou; **764** The Globe Theatre, London, The Granger Collection, New York; **765** Robert Harding Picture Library; **766** *William Shakespeare* (detail), Artist Unknown, by courtesy of the National Portrait Gallery, London; **768, 770** Photofest; **775** ©Araldo de Luca/CORBIS; **776** Photofest; **781** Culver Pictures, Inc.; **784** Photofest; **788** Movie Still Archives; **790, 795** Photofest; **800** Culver Pictures, Inc.; **802** Digital Imagery ©Copyright 2001 PhotoDisc, Inc.; **806, 807, 813** Photofest; **819, 823** Memory Shop; **826** Private Collection/Bridgeman Art Library, London/New York; **830–831** Culver Pictures, Inc.; **838, 845** Memory Shop; **848** Culver Pictures, Inc.; **852** Memory Shop; **861, 865, 866, 870, 878** Photofest; **881** © Dorling Kindersley; **884** © Axel Hoedt/Stone; **890–891** *Garden of Delights,* Sandy Novak/Omni-Photo Communications, Inc.; **892** (b) *Bernard's Daddy,* Raymond Lark, Master Drawing, graphite, 20 x 30 inches, Collection of Mary Moran, New Jersey. Photo courtesy of Edward Smith and Company, (t) ©The Stock Market/Pete Saloutos; **894** Corel Professional Photos CD-ROM™; **896–897** ©Wolfgang Kaehler/CORBIS; **898** The Granger Collection, New York; **902, 904** *Bernard's Daddy,* Raymond Lark, Master Drawing, graphite, 20 x 30 inches, Collection of Mary Moran, New Jersey. Photo courtesy of Edward Smith and Company; **905** *Langston Hughes* (detail), c.1925, Winold Reiss, The National Portrait Gallery, Smithsonian Institution, Washington, D.C./Art Resource, New York; **906–907** Corel Professional Photos CD-ROM™; **907** (b) *Alfred Lord Tennyson,* c.1840, S. Laurence, by courtesy of the National Portrait Gallery, London; (t) ©The Stock Market/Pete Saloutos; **908** (b) The Granger Collection, New York, (t) Digital Imagery ©Copyright 2001 Photo-Disc, Inc.; **912** ©The Stock Market/Roy Morsch; **914** Andrea Renault/Globe Photos; **915** (t) Barry Pribula/International Stock Photography, Ltd.; **917** (t) Carolina Biological/Phototake, (b) Photo by Yvonne Mozee; **918–919** (t) White/Pite/International Stock Photography, Ltd., (b) UPI/CORBIS-Bettmann; **920** Prentice Hall; **924** David De Lossy/The Image Bank; **926** (t) Index Stock Photography, Inc., (b) CORBIS-Bettmann; **927** (b) John Craig Photo, (t) Digital Imagery ©Copyright 2001 PhotoDisc, Inc.; **928** ©The Stock Market/Zefa Germany; **930** *The Bells,* Edmund Dulac, New York Public Library; Astor, Lenox and Tilden Foundations; **934** CORBIS-Bettmann; **938** Esbin/Anderson/Omni-Photo Communications, Inc.; **943** CORBIS-Bettmann; **944** By permission of the Folger Shakespeare Library, Washington,D.C.; **946** *William Shakespeare* (detail), Artist unknown, by courtesy of the National Portrait Gallery, London; **950** ©Terry Vine/CORBIS; **953** Courtesy of Detroit Free Press; **954** Digital Imagery ©Copyright 2001 PhotoDisc, Inc.; **956** The Granger Collection, New York; **957** *Richard Wright* (detail), 1949, Miriam Troop, The National Portrait Gallery, Smithsonian Institution, Washington, D.C./Art Resource, New York; **958** (b) Stephen Frisch/Stock, Boston, (b) Luis Castaneda/The Image Bank; **959** The Granger Collection, New York; **960** *William Shakespeare* (detail), Artist unknown, by courtesy of the National Portrait Gallery, London; **965** Digital Imagery ©Copyright 2001 PhotoDisc, Inc.; **966** Seaver Center for Western History Research, Natural History Museum of Los Angeles County; **968** Esbin/Anderson/Omni-Photo Communications, Inc.; **974–975** *Ulysses Deriding Polyphemus,* 1819, J.M.W. Turner, The National Gallery, London; **976** (tr) *Ulysses receives the wine with which he will make Polyphemus drunk,* Italiotic crater. Museo Eoliano, Lipari, Italy/Scala/Art Resource, NY, (tl) CORBIS-Bettmann, (b) ©Bettmann/CORBIS; **978** *Circe Meanwhile Had Gone Her Ways...,* 1924, William Russell Flint, Collection of the New York Public Library; Astor, Lenox and Tilden Foundations; **980** *Ulysses Deriding Polyphemus,* 1819, J.M.W. Turner, The National Gallery, London; **987, 990** ©Araldo de Luca/CORBIS; **995** *Polyphemus, the Cyclops* from Homer's *Odyssey,* N.C. Wyeth, Delaware Art Museum, Photo by Jon MacDowell; **998** *Odysseus in the Land of the Dead* from Homer's *Odyssey,* N.C. Wyeth, Delaware Art Museum, Photo by Jon MacDowell; **1003** ©Araldo de Luca/CORBIS;**1008** *Circe*

Meanwhile Had Gone Her Ways..., 1924, William Russell Flint, Collection of the New York Public Library; Astor, Lenox and Tilden Foundations; **1016** *La Nef De Telemachus (The Ship of Telemachus)*, New York Public Library Picture Collection; **1023** *Eumaeus, the Swineherd* from Homer's *Odyssey,* N.C. Wyeth, Delaware Art Museum, Photo by Jon MacDowell; **1026, 1030** ©Araldo de Luca/CORBIS; **1034** *The Trial of the Bow* from Homer's *Odyssey,* N.C. Wyeth, Delaware Art Museum, Photo by Jon MacDowell; **1036** Bridgeman Art Library, London/New York; **1038** *The Slaughter of the Suitors* from Homer's *Odyssey,* N.C. Wyeth, Delaware Art Museum, photo by Jon MacDowell; **1043** ©Andrew Cowin;Travel Ink/CORBIS; **1044** *The Fall of Troy* from *The Odysseus Suite,* 1979, Romare Bearden, serigraph 18x24, © Romare Bearden Foundation/Licensed by VAGA, New York, NY; **1046** CORBIS-Bettmann; **1050** *Penelope and the Suitors,* 1912, J.M. Waterhouse, 51 1/2 x 75 in. (131 x 191 cm) City of Aberdeen Art Gallery and Museums Collections, Scotland; **1053** *Edna St. Vincent Millay* (detail), Charles Ellis, The National Portrait Gallery, Smithsonian Institution, Washington, D.C./Art Resource, New York; **1054** Werner Forman/Art Resource, NY; **1055** Thomas Victor; **1056** *Ulysses receives the wine with which he will make Polyphemus drunk,* Italiotic crater. Museo Eoliano, Lipari, Italy/Scala/Art Resource, NY; **1057** Eugene Richards/Magnum/Photos, Inc.; **1058** Amphora with Grapes, oil, 15" by 19", Loran Speck, Loran Speck Art Gallery, Carmel, CA; **1060** The Granger Collection, New York; **1064** Tsado/NASA/Tom Stack & Associates; **1065** ©Bettmann/CORBIS; **1067** AP/Wide World Photos

Staff Credits

The people who made up the ***Prentice Hall Literature: Timeless Voices, Timeless Themes*** team—representing design services, editorial, editorial services, market research, marketing services, media resources, online services & multimedia development, production services, project office, and publishing processes—are listed below. Bold type denotes the core team members.

Susan Andariese, Rosalyn Arcilla, Laura Jane Bird, Betsy Bostwick, **Anne M. Bray,** Evonne Burgess, **Louise B. Capuano, Pam Cardiff,** Megan Chill, Ed Cordero, Laura Dershewitz, Philip Fried, **Elaine Goldman,** Barbara Goodchild, Barbara Grant, **Rebecca Z. Graziano, Doreen Graizzaro,** Dennis Higbee, **Leanne Korszoloski,** Ellen Lees, David Liston, **Mary Luthi, George Lychock,** Gregory Lynch, Sue Lyons, **William McAllister,** Frances Medico, Gail Meyer, Jessica S. Paladini, Wendy Perri, Carolyn Carty Sapontzis, **Melissa Shustyk, Annette Simmons, Alicia Solis,** Robin Sullivan, Cynthia Sosland Summers, Lois Teesdale, **Elizabeth Torjussen, Doug Utigard,** Bernadette Walsh, Helen Young

The following persons provided invaluable assistance and support during the production of this program.

Gregory Abrom, Robert Aleman, Diane Alimena, Michele Angelucci, Gabriella Apolito, Penny Baker, Sharyn Banks, Anthony Barone, Barbara Blecher, Helen Byers, Rui Camarinha, Lorelee J. Campbell, John Carle, Cynthia Clampitt, Jaime L. Cohen, Martha Conway, Dina Curro, Nancy Dredge, Johanna Ehrmann, Josie K. Fixler, Steve Frankel, Kathy Gavilanes, Allen Gold, Michael E. Goodman, Diana Hahn, Kerry L. Harrigan, Jacki Hasko, Evan Holstrom, Beth Hyslip, Helen Issackedes, Cathy Johnson, Susan Karpin, Raegan Keida, Stephanie Kota, Mary Sue Langan, Elizabeth Letizia, Christine Mann, Vickie Menanteaux, Kathleen Mercandetti, Art Mkrtchyan, Karyl Murray, Kenneth Myett, Stefano Nese, Kim Ortell, Lissette Quinones, Erin Rehill-Seker, Patricia Rodriguez, Mildred Schulte, Adam Sherman, Mary Siener, Jan K. Singh, Diane Smith, Barbara Stufflebeem, Louis Suffredini, Lois Tatarian, Tom Thompkins, Lisa Valente, Ryan Vaarsi, Linda Westerhoff, Jeff Zoda

Prentice Hall gratefully acknowledges the following teachers who provided student models for consideration in the program.

Kate Anders, Suzanne Arkfeld, Elizabeth Bailey, Bill Brown, Diane Cappillo, Mary Chapman, Deedee Chumley, Terry Day, Cheryl Devoe, Dan Diercks, Ellen Eberly, Nancy Fahner, Terri Fields, Patty Foster, Joanne Giardino, Julie Gold, Christopher Guarraia, Dianne Hammond, Jo Higgins, Pauline Hodges, Gaye Ingram, Charlotte Jefferies, Bill Jones, Ken Kaiser, Linda Kramer, Karen Lopez, Catherine Lynn, Ashley MacDonald, Kathleen Marshall, LouAnn McCarty, Peggy Moore, Ann Okamura, Will Parker, Maureen Rippee, Tucky Roger, Terrie Saunders, Marilyn Shaw, Ken Spurlock, Mary Stevens, Sandra Sullivan, Wanda Thomas, Jennifer Watson, Amanda Wolf